CHAMBERS

CONCISE CROSSWORD DICTIONARY

Editors

Elaine Higgleton
Catherine Schwarz

With the assistance of

Una McGovern

D1494985

CHAMBERS

CHAMBERS

An imprint of Chambers Harrap Publishers Ltd
7 Hopetoun Crescent
Edinburgh EH7 4AY

www.chambers.co.uk

First published by Chambers 2001
© Chambers Harrap Publishers Ltd 2001

A CIP catalogue record for this book is available from the British Library.

ISBN 0550 10152 7

Designed and typeset by Chambers Harrap Publishers Ltd, Edinburgh
Printed and bound in Great Britain by Mackays of Chatham Ltd

Contents

Contributors

Managing Editor	Elaine Higgleton
Consultant Editor	Catherine Schwarz
Crossword Consultants	Jonathan Crowther Don Manley
Editor	Una McGovern
Reference Editor	Gary Dexter
Contributors	Sandra Anderson Kay Cullen
Prepress	Marina Karapanovic

Chambers Crossword Consultants

Jonathan Crowther is better-known to many cryptic crossword solvers as *Azed* of *The Observer*. He has also set puzzles under the pseudonyms *Gong* and *Ozymandias*.

Don Manley sets crosswords under a variety of pseudonyms (*Duck*, *Quixote*, *Pasquale*, *Giovanni*) for many national newspapers (including *The Times*, *The Guardian*, *The Independent on Sunday* and *The Sunday Telegraph*). He is also editor of *The Church Times* Crossword and the author of *Chambers Crossword Manual*.

Preface

Chambers Concise Crossword Dictionary is for lovers of crosswords of all kinds, including 'quick' and cryptic crosswords. It contains an enormous range of words and phrases, derived from both *The Chambers Dictionary* and Chambers reference databases, to provide the user with over 230,000 possible solutions to crossword clues. As well as including synonyms for thousands of words, it includes wide-ranging reference lists that group together words usually only found in encyclopedias. The user will find, for example, lists of people (such as actors, politicians, doctors and poets), geographical lists (such as rivers, cities, mountains and lakes), lists of technical terms (such as printing terms, musical terms and scientific terms), lists from natural history (such as flowers and trees), lists from art and culture (such as singers, novels, operas, paintings), lists from belief and religion (such as biblical characters, gods and goddesses) and lists from sport (such as footballers, football teams, racehorses, stadiums). All of the words in this dictionary have been carefully categorized by topic or meaning to be presented in over 15,000 one-stop entries that combine both synonym lists and reference lists.

The dictionary also contains information on solving cryptic-crossword clues, with introductions on *The art of the crossword setter* by Jonathan Crowther (*Azed* of *The Observer*) and *Crossword English* by Don Manley (crossword setter and author of *Chambers Crossword Manual*). There is also a handy list of those words which indicate that the solution to a crossword clue is an anagram of one or more of the words in the clue.

Many people have been involved in the preparation of this dictionary, and we would like to thank everyone who worked on this project. Particular thanks are due to our external crossword consultants, Jonathan Crowther and Don Manley. As well as providing the essays on cryptic crosswords which are included in the front matter, they have given generous advice on all aspects of this project, helping shape this book and our thinking. However, any errors, infelicities or omissions are the sole responsibility of the publishers.

Chambers Concise Crossword Dictionary can be used on its own, or alongside a standard dictionary, and is an ideal and complementary companion to *The Chambers Dictionary*. We hope that it contributes to our users' enjoyment of crossword puzzles, that it helps them find solutions that are evading them, and that it helps them meet the intellectual challenges set by the cruciverbalists in our daily and Sunday newspapers.

The Editors

Introduction

Chambers Concise Crossword Dictionary does not contain definitions (for which the user is referred to *The Chambers Dictionary*) but contains an enormous range of words and phrases, derived from both *The Chambers Dictionary* and Chambers reference databases, to provide the user with over 230,000 possible solutions to crossword clues.

Word length

The words and phrases given in this dictionary contain 15 letters or fewer, reflecting the most commonly used crossword grids. However, the additional information given in many lists (see below) means that the dictionary will also be of use to people attempting crosswords that use larger or 'jumbo' grids. Also, where a list represents a closed set, that is, where a list is clearly defined and limited, then all relevant terms have been included regardless of length. For example, all of the US states and all of the plays of Shakespeare have been included even though some of these are longer than 15 letters in length:

> ► *Names of Canadian*
> *provinces and territories*:
> 05 Yukon
> 06 Quebec
> 07 Alberta, Nunavut, Ontario
> 08 Labrador, Manitoba
> 10 Nova Scotia
> 12 New Brunswick,
>   Newfoundland,
>   Saskatchewan
> 14 Yukon Territory
> 15 British Columbia
> 18 Prince Edward Island
> 20 Northwest Territories
> 23 Newfoundland and
>   Labrador

Organization of entries

1. Within the dictionary, words have been sorted into over 15,000 one-stop alphabetical entries by meaning or subject category. Thus entries present a range of words that are relevant to the headword; in many cases these words have been broadly grouped into two types of list:

- Synonym lists, which present words with similar meanings to the headword;
- Reference lists, which present a diverse variety of words derived from a range of Chambers encyclopedic and reference databases, such as proper names and place names.

Thus the entry for **administrative** presents both synonyms and a list of the different types of administrative area:

administrative

09 executive
10 management, managerial,
   regulatory
11 directorial, legislative,
   supervisory
12 governmental
13 authoritative, gubernatorial
14 organizational

▶ *Types of administrative area*:
04 area, city, town, ward
05 shire, state
06 county, parish, region, sector
07 borough, enclave, village
08 district, division, precinct,
   province
09 territory
12 constituency

2. Within entries, words are grouped firstly by length, that is by the total number of letters in each word or phrase, and then ordered alphabetically within these word-length sections:

abate

04 ease, fade, sink, slow, wane
05 allay, let up, quell, remit
06 lessen, pacify, reduce,
   soothe, weaken
07 decline, dwindle, subside
08 decrease, diminish, mitigate,
   moderate, taper off
09 alleviate, attenuate

3. The synonym lists are not constrained by conventional dictionary or thesaurus rules. Thus no distinctions are made between parts of speech, or between homonyms (words spelt the same but with different meanings), as crossword setters often play on multiple meanings and possible ambiguity in their clues. For example, the entry for **frequent** lists synonyms for both the verb (meaning *visit*) and the adjective (meaning *regular* or *recurring*):

frequent

05 haunt, usual, visit
06 attend, common, normal
08 everyday, familiar, habitual,
   numerous, repeated
09 countless, customary, hang
   out at, patronize, prevalent,
   recurring
11 commonplace
13 go to regularly

14 go to frequently, happening
    often

and the entry for **fawn** presents synonyms for what are in fact two separate words, one meaning *the colour beige* and the other *to flatter*:

fawn

04 buff
05 beige, court, crawl, creep,
    khaki, sandy, smarm, toady
06 cringe, grovel, kowtow
07 flatter
08 bootlick, butter up, pay
    court, soft-soap, suck up to
11 curry favour
12 bow and scrape
14 yellowish-brown
15 dance attendance

4. We have also included synonym lists for idioms and phrasal verbs derived from many of the headwords. Sections for idioms and phrasal verbs are marked by ▫:

behest

▫ **at the behest of**

12 at the order of
13 on the wishes of
14 at the bidding of, at the command of, at the request of

Reference lists

1. The reference lists have all been derived from the authoritative Chambers reference databases that contribute towards such prestigious titles as *Chambers Biographical Dictionary* and *Chambers Book of Facts*. Material in the reference lists is extremely wide-ranging, and includes, for example, the names of people from a variety of professions (including the arts, science, politics and history), literary, fictional, Biblical and mythological characters, place names, scientific terms, and works of art, music and literature. These reference lists are entered in the dictionary at the appropriate headword to make information easy to find. Thus users will find the names of actors and actresses at the entry for **actor, actress**; a list of parts of the brain at **brain**; lists of ancient cities, capital cities and other major towns and cities at **city**; a list of collective nouns at **collective**; names of novelists, and a list of novels and fictional works, at the entry for **novel**.

2. The reference lists in *Chambers Crossword Dictionary* include both historical and current information. For example, in the list of novelists users will find not only *Jane Austen* and *DH Lawrence*, but also contemporary writers such as *Iain Banks* and *JK Rowling*. And in the list of films, classics such as *Brief Encounter* can be found alongside modern blockbusters such as *American Beauty.*

3. The reference lists are not intended to be all-inclusive, but to focus on terms that are reasonably common and that are likely to occur in crossword solutions.

Organization of reference material

Words and phrases from Chambers encyclopedic databases have been categorized to make finding information easier. For example, there is not one list of cities, but separate lists of *ancient cities*, *capital cities*, and other *important towns and cities*; there is not one list of singers, but separate lists of *classical*, *folk*, *jazz* and *pop* singers; there is not one list of scientists, but separate lists of, for example, *anthropologists*, *astronomers*, *physicists*, *chemists* and *computer scientists*.

Additional information

Many of the reference lists contain additional information in brackets following core information. For example, first names or nicknames are given in brackets following a surname. In such lists, the core term (the unbracketed term) is presented in bold type to make these lists easier to browse through:

> ► *Names of astronauts*:
> 04 **Bean** (Alan), **Ride** (Sally)
> 05 **Foale** (Michael), **Glenn** (John), **Titov** (Gherman), **White** (Edward)
> 06 **Aldrin** (Edwin Eugene 'Buzz'), **Conrad** (Charles 'Pete'), **Lovell** (James 'Jim')
> 07 **Chaffee** (Roger), **Collins** (Michael), **Gagarin** (Yuri), **Grissom** (Gus), **Sharman** (Helen), **Shepard** (Alan)
> 09 **Armstrong** (Neil)
> 10 **Tereshkova** (Valentina)

Additional bracketed information is not included in the word-length count although it may form part of the solution to some crossword clues.

Generic terms

Common generic terms have been omitted from many of the names and terms presented in some lists, to avoid unwieldy and unnecessary repetition. For example, the word disease has not been included in names in the list of diseases at **disease**, and the word saint has been omitted from the list of saints at **saint**. Users should be aware that terms such as these may form part of the solution to crossword clues and key instances of this have been clearly marked:

> ► *Names of mountains and mountain ranges. We have omitted the words* **mount**, **mountain** *and* **mountains** *from names given in the following list but you may need to include one of these words as part of the solution to some crossword clues.*

Cross references

Chambers Crossword Dictionary is extensively cross-referenced to make finding solutions easy. There are a number of 'key' entries within the dictionary that contain banks of cross references listing all of the reference entries by subject or category. For example, at the entry for **music** there is a cross reference listing all of the other entries in the dictionary which include reference lists that fall within the broad category of *music*:

> ➤ See also **composer**;
> **conductor**; **instrument**;
> **jazz**; **libretto**; **musical**;
> **musician**; **opera**;
> **oratorio**; **singer**; **song**;
> **songwriter**

At each of the headwords listed in the cross reference at **music**, users will find a cross reference back to the entry for **music**. Thus if a user does not find the solution needed at the entry for **singer**, he or she is directed back to **music** to identify alternative lists to search:

> **singer**
> ➤ See also **music**

Key entries that contain cross-reference banks are:

animal	**music**	**scientist**
art	**mythology**	**sport**
drink	**plant**	**writer**
food	**politics**	
military	**religion**	

The art of the crossword setter
Jonathan Crowther (Azed of The Observer)

I am regularly asked – as often by people who habitually solve crosswords as by those who never do – how I set about compiling a puzzle, and especially what order I do things in. (The other commonly-asked question is how long each puzzle takes me, but I usually hedge when answering this one. A puzzle is best constructed over several sittings, and I have never bothered to calculate accurately the total time involved.) For most normal crosswords there are three distinct stages, each more time-consuming than the last: (i) constructing the grid pattern, (ii) filling this with words, and (iii) writing the clues. The three stages demand different skills, and for this reason I often compartmentalize the first two, constructing several grid patterns at a sitting and then filling all of these with words before returning to the first grid to start the lengthier and more creative process of writing the clues. Let us now look at each stage in turn.

There is no absolute rule that crosswords should be symmetrical in design, ie with their blocked squares or bars arranged so that they look the same if the grid is turned upside down or if it is given a quarter-turn. The fact is that most are, and this is the widely-accepted norm. It is also aesthetically pleasing, by no means a negligible consideration. Most importantly, the grid design should ensure a range of entries of varying lengths and a fair distribution of unchecked letters (those which belong to only one word, across or down, and are not 'checked' by a word entered in the other direction). In general the number of unchecked letters is greater in a blocked grid than in a barred one. As a rule of thumb (though one that is regularly infringed by puzzles in a number of our national dailies), no more than half the letters of a solution should be unchecked in a blocked grid. In barred grids, like mine in The Observer, the solver can expect a more generous quota of cross-checked letters because such puzzles tend to use more rare and unusual words. In both types of puzzle the inclusion of consecutive unchecked letters in answers is considered bad practice and generally frowned on. It is all a question of fairness to the solver.

There is a fundamental difference in standard grid design between British-style and American-style crosswords. British crosswords, with their tradition of cryptic clues and unchecked letters, normally require the solver to solve every clue in order to complete the puzzle. In most American crosswords, whose clues are not cryptic in the British sense, there are proportionally far fewer blocked squares and they are arranged in such a way that every letter is cross-checked, so that, in theory at least, it is possible to complete a puzzle by solving only about half its clues.

In practice, setters of most normal blocked grids in daily or Sunday newspapers in both Britain and the US do not have to concern themselves with grid construction. Each paper uses a limited number of basic patterned grids to which the setter is restricted. In an age of ever-greater standardization this is perhaps inevitable, and it reduces the risk of error, but I still regard it as regrettable and am pleased that no such restriction is placed on me. I derive much satisfaction from exploring the many different grid designs possible within the established parameters: grid size (normally 12 x 12 in my case), number of entries (usually 36), a good spread of entry lengths, and a fair number of unchecked letters. My predecessor Derrick Macnutt (the legendary Ximenes) preferred to let his patterns grow, organically as it were, around the words he wanted to include in his puzzles, effectively merging my first two stages of crossword construction into a single process. My own routine is as I have described, since I start with no preconceptions as to the words I want to use, and this only goes to show that there is no universally prescribed method. There are also no Mosaic laws governing the *size* of crosswords. Blocked grids in daily papers are usually 15 x 15, with about 32 answers (16 across and 16 down), but recent years have seen a growth in the number of 'jumbo' puzzles (typically 27 x 27, with 76 answers), presenting new challenges to solvers and setters alike by the inclusion of longer words and multi-word phrases. In a more modest way, the Azed crossword is now sometimes 13 x 11, enabling me to include 13-letter words on a regular basis. More specialized crosswords explore other designs, including circular diagrams with entries arranged circularly and radially, but these will probably remain the exception and the domain of the seriously dedicated solver.

Having completed the grid, or having chosen it from the available range, the setter moves on to fill it with words. There are computer programs which can do this in the twinkling of an eye, though they are limited to the word-lists in the program's memory. The human brain takes much longer but it can select or reject words according to their suitability for cluing and its own real-world knowledge, a crucial factor in the writing of clues. Which words does one choose, and where does one start? I personally start from what seems the natural place, the top left-hand corner of the grid, extending down and across more or less at the same time while keeping a weather eye open for potential problem areas. Anything in the dictionary is fair game, and for me this means *The Chambers Dictionary*. My task is made easier by *Chambers Words* and *Chambers Back-Words for Crosswords*, books which present the *Chambers* word-list alphabetically (or reverse-alphabetically) by length, so that I can see at a glance, say, all the 7-letter words beginning or ending with L. These aids are available to the solver as well as the setter, of course, but I like to think that whereas they are an invaluable tool for the hard-pressed setter, the solver will turn to them only as a last resort. Solving clues should be a contest of minds between setter and solver, not a series of conundrums to be resolved by reference to a published word-list. I also think the setter should be free to include non-dictionary words and phrases, especially topical ones, if these are sufficiently well known. Assessing what is and is not familiar enough to include here is of course a matter of fine judgement. Some newspapers have a policy of not allowing certain taboo words to be used as answers in their crosswords. In these liberated days such bowdlerization strikes me as rather old-fashioned. Crossword setters, like journalists and other writers, should be trusted to know where to draw the line.

The task of filling a grid with words is naturally easier in blocked diagrams than in barred ones, since the number of unchecked letters is significantly greater in blocked diagrams. In both types the setter develops with experience a feel for the 'shape' of words: common letter-clusters, the distribution of consonants and vowels, 'danger' letters (especially at the ends of words), helpful affixes and inflections, and so on. He or she must think ahead to avoid getting boxed into an awkward corner which will involve undoing part of the grid construction, an agonizing waste of time when deadlines are tight. The *Chambers Crossword Completer* is another valuable tool in this context, especially when setting blocked puzzles. It takes *The Chambers Dictionary* word-list again, this time arranging it alphabetically by word length according to the alternate letters of each word, first the odd letters (first, third, fifth, etc) and then the even ones (second, fourth, sixth, etc). Special care needs to be taken with shorter words, especially those of four or five letters. There are comparatively few of these in the language (and of these far fewer begin with vowels than with consonants), so most will have been clued many times already. Good setters try to avoid reusing old clues, however proud of them they may be, and they should also not reuse *words* too often. Guarding against this is not easy, and inevitably, there being no copyright in good ideas, similar or identical clues to the same word will recur, but I do make a conscious effort not to repeat myself and think others setters should do likewise. (As a matter of passing interest, there are more different words in the language of eight letters than of any other word length.)

I have already mentioned fair play between setter and solver. This is an important principle in grid construction, just as much as in the writing of clues. Consonants, especially the less common ones, are generally more helpful to the solver as cross-checking letters than vowels are (with obvious exceptions like I or U in final position), and the setter should recognize this. I know that as a solver I feel hard done by if faced by -A-E, one of the most frequent four-letter-word patterns, especially if the setter has made matters worse by giving the word an extra-difficult clue!

The writing of the clues for a crossword is the last and much the most important task for the setter, for it is here that one stamps one's character and personal style on the puzzle. Seasoned solvers develop clear preferences for the style of this or that setter, and satisfied solvers usually remain loyal to a particular puzzle (even, sometimes, if they are less than happy with other aspects of the paper in which it appears). I firmly believe that an impersonal style of cluing can be boring, and there is no harm at all in letting one's own interests, sense of humour, even prejudices, emerge through one's clues, provided always that these are fair and accurate. Don Manley in his introduction to this dictionary describes in detail the range of different clue types regularly used by setters. As a setter myself, I follow a method which has not changed greatly over the years. I always write clues in the order in which they appear in the puzzle. Taking the more colourful words first means leaving a 'sump' of less interesting ones till last, an encouragement to treat the latter as second-class citizens and produce second-class clues as a result. I write no more than nine or ten clues at a sitting, having found that if I try to do more staleness sets in and pedestrian clues result. The restorative effects of even quite a short break doing other things can be truly remarkable! At the same time it is important to see the puzzle as a whole and to present a reasonable variety of clue types (not too many anagrams, for example) to ensure a balanced fare for the solver. This can be tricky when a word cries out for one particular treatment but that treatment has already been used for other words in the puzzle (or for the same word in an earlier puzzle), but the principle is sound. The aim must be to divert the solver, not to massage the setter's ego, so variety is important.

Some words are much more difficult to clue interestingly than others. Scientific terms come high on my list of unfavourite words, mainly because their meaning is very specific and does not lend itself to the sort of wordplay that is at the heart of cryptic clue-writing. A word with many meanings offers far greater scope for punning and similar red herrings to strew in the solver's path. But whichever word I am cluing I always strive (with varying success, I'm sure) for three key ingredients in a clue: accuracy, economy and wit. Every clue should lead accurately and unmistakably to its solution, saying precisely and grammatically what it means (though it may not always mean what it appears to say – taking advantage of the manifold ambiguities of our language is an essential part of cryptic clue-writing). It should do this in as few words as are consistent with fair play, avoiding all superfluous verbiage or mere padding. And it should if at all possible be enjoyable to solve, leaving successful solvers feeling both satisfied at their success and pleasurably diverted by the experience.

Crossword English
Don Manley (crossword setter and author of *Chambers Crossword Manual*)

I am a monoglot, more or less. Although I studied French at school, I can't say I use it much – except when I have to on holiday, and even then it's a sort of pidgin French. But at least I feel I know English, and since (as Bernard Shaw put it) England and America are two countries separated by the same language, maybe one can be a polyglot just by watching television. Or maybe I can be a polyglot just by coming from Devon, where 'thistles' used to be called 'dashels'.

So what has this to do with crosswords? Well, in a sense Crossword English is rather like a foreign language – and it is a language that must be learnt. What may seem odd (if the cross-section of crossword setters I know is anything to go by) is that the polyglots who can speak French and English are not necessarily polyglots in the sense of knowing English and Crossword English. You're more likely to find that a crossword setter is a computer scientist, a physicist or a mathematician than a French teacher these days.

The irritating thing – to anyone who has not yet learnt Crossword English – is that it looks so like Everyday English. For the crossword which offers definitions only, this is perfectly obvious. So if the clue reads 'Cry of an ass (4)' you can write in BRAY straight away. You might have a few alternative answers for 'River (5)', and if you are living in Nottinghamshire you may be disposed to write in TRENT, but when faced with 'River in Paris (5)' you'll know that anything other than SEINE just isn't sane. So for the definition puzzle we're looking at a test of our ability to recognize synonyms or at a quiz with questions that would crop up early on in 'Who Wants to be a Millionaire?'. This is as far as most people get with solving crosswords – the verbal quiz solved with a little help from reference books: a dictionary, an atlas, and possibly an encyclopedia. They know English but not Crossword English.

So what is Crossword English? It is the language of the cryptic crossword, a language which looks like ordinary English but which has its own strange rules of grammar and construction and which has its own vocabulary. Crossword English is a series of mini-statements, mini-pictures, and mini-stories even, but the statements, the pictures, and the stories are each designed to hide a sort of riddle. So a riddle isn't a bad place to start with as an example of a cryptic clue:

> My first is in Cornwall but isn't in Devon
> For my second shun Hell and start looking in Heaven
> My third you may find in this or in that
> My whole is a creature that sits on the mat

Thus in a woeful verse of 39 words we have written a cryptic clue for CAT, and at each stage along the way we are spoon-fed with a letter at a time. It's obviously a puzzle, even if it's a pretty heavy-handed one.

Now look at these little riddles and see what you make of them:

1. Lady I rather fancy (7)
2. There's nothing in Basildon I like (3)
3. Delightful tea with the best china (8)

4. It's best to have cold sheets (5)
5. Delicate proposal (6)
6. The clock's put back? Relax! (5)
7. Company car? (3-6)
8. It could deflect battle spear (11)
9. Writer gathers wood as something that'll burn quickly (8)
10. Marsh plant enthrals artist (6)
11. Defeat brought by bowling gaining wicket – something captain controls? (9)
12. Amuse the French after a short time (6)
13. Did he have spelling lessons? (3, 9, 10)
14. Who you'd expect to find at gay weddings in the Isles?! (8)
15. Female beheaded in the sultanate (4)
16. Lab in, Tory out would suit him (4, 5)
17. Boyfriend tied ribbon from what we hear (4)
18. Rejected young troublemaker longed to be free (8)
19. Fool about fifty, one not altogether bright (6)
20. 014? (6, 5)

Here are twenty 'portrayals' – perfectly sensible 'portrayals' in generally understandable English – though 20 looks a bit odd. All of these were written by myself at some stage over the past ten years or so, and as I look at them I see not only Crossword English but a certain kind of Englishness. There is romance in 1 and 17 (and perhaps 5); there is an austere and rather snooty middle-Englishness about 2, 3 and 4; a concern with cricket in 11; hints of a threatening world outside modern England in 8 and 15; and so on. There may even be a touch of humour here and there. This is English language and English culture.

There are twenty puzzles to solve, so how are these clues different from those for BRAY and SEINE? The answer is (fairly) simple, though the implications of the answer may be complicated. It is this. In each cryptic clue there will still be a definition but the clue writer will have done one of two things. He (sometimes she – and, to be honest, we could do with more 'shes') will have either wrapped up the definition in 'cryptic language' or will have provided a definition plus some indication of the letters in the answer. Sometimes the crossword setter will have done both. In most cryptic clues there will be what we call a 'definition' followed by what we call a 'subsidiary indication', or a subsidiary indication followed by a definition, or even an indication and a definition rolled into one. The secret in decoding a clue lies in trying to solve the answer from either or both of these components while using any letters that are already filled in.

If that all sounds horrible, it's because I've tried to give you a grammar lesson, and (as we all know) it's really much better to start learning a language by speaking it or writing it. No one ever really taught me 'all that grammar stuff' when I was a fledgling **cruciverbalist** (someone who 'does' crosswords). I was lucky enough to have a father who taught me how to solve clues when I was barely out of short trousers, and the best way I can explain Crossword English is to take you through the clues one by one.

1. Lady I rather fancy (7)
   The word 'fancy' is one of a huge set of **anagram indicators**. It tells us that the letters next to it are to be made 'fancy' or jumbled up. If you jumble up 'I rather' you get

HARRIET, a lady. This clue, then is an **anagram**, perhaps the one form of cryptic clue everyone knows.

2.   There's nothing in Basildon I like (3)
     If you look carefully, you'll see that there is indeed a word meaning nothing in the sequence of letters 'Basildon I like' and it's NIL. This is a **hidden word**.

3.   Delightful tea with the best china (8)
     If you put a word for 'tea' and add it to a word for 'the best china', you will add 'char' to 'Ming' to form CHARMING, meaning 'delightful'. This is a **charade clue.**

4.   It's best to have cold sheets (5)
     As it happens, this is another charade, but this time we join an **abbreviation** 'c' to the sheets (= ream) to form CREAM (the best). Abbreviations are common in subsidiary indications.

5.   Delicate proposal (6)
     This is a **double-definition** clue, so you can look upon one definition as the official 'definition' and the other one as the 'subsidiary indication' – or vice versa. What word means both 'delicate' and 'proposal'? Answer: TENDER.

6.   The clock's put back? Relax! (5)
     This suggests (quite rightly) that you'll get an extra hour in bed when the clocks go back. But if you put back a 'timer' you will get REMIT, which means 'relax'. This is a **reversal** clue. In down clues you may see the word 'up' suggesting a reversal. And here the definition is at the end.

7.   Company car? (3-6)
     You may be tempted to think of this as another double-definition clue and look for a word that means both 'company' and 'car'. In fact the setter is inviting you to think of 'two's company, three's none', and so the answer is TWO-SEATER. There is no indication of letters in this clue, but we have noticed that it has a **cryptic definition**.

8.   It could deflect battle spear (11)
     We're looking for an anagram of battle spear and find it in BREASTPLATE, but we notice that the clue as a whole is a definition. Every word in the clue is serving as a definition and as part of the subsidiary indication. We call this an **&lit.** clue. This particular type is **anag. &lit.**

9.   Writer gathers wood as something that'll burn quickly (8)
     The word 'gathers' suggests that a word for 'wood' might be inside a writer. Put 'fir' inside 'Wilde' and you'll find WILDFIRE. This is known as a **container-and-contents** clue.

10. Marsh plant enthrals artist (6)
     This is another container-and contents clue. This time we have an abbreviation for artist (RA) inside a plant (moss) to give MORASS.

11. Defeat brought by bowling gaining wicket – something captain controls? (9)
     If you solve crosswords you'll need to get used to **cricket vocabulary**. In this charade bowling is 'over', wicket is 'w', and something the captain controls is 'helm'. Put the three together to get OVERWHELM (defeat).

12. Amuse the French after a short time (6)

Although we're talking about Crossword English, we do allow a few **foreign words** to creep in, especially definite and indefinite articles of common European languages. In this charade a short time is 'tick' added to the French, which in this case is 'le', giving the answer TICKLE (amuse).

13. Did he take spelling lessons? (3, 9, 10)

The setter is tempting you to think about spelling in the sense of getting the right letters in sequence. In fact you should think about spelling in the sense of magic. The answer is THE SORCERER'S APPRENTICE, another cryptic definition, this one being set in what we call a **misleading context** occasioned by the **double-meaning** of 'spelling'. You'll find many other double meanings including 'flower' which can mean river. One of the delights of learning Crossword English is to work these out for yourself!

14. Who you'd expect to find at gay weddings in the Isles?! (8)

This is an outrageous charade, the answer being 'he brides' (i.e. HEBRIDES). No one ever seems to have taken offence. Every crossword should have at least one clue with an element of **humour**.

15. Female beheaded in the sultanate (4)

This is a particular type of **subtractive** clue. Take the head letter off 'woman' to give the sultanate OMAN. If you take up cryptic crosswords you will also learn about 'endless' and 'heartless'.

16. Lab in, Tory out would suit him (4, 5)

This is another **anag. &lit.** Note that 'out' is a very common anagram indicator. You should be able to see TONY BLAIR quite easily.

17. Boyfriend tied ribbon from what we hear (4)

When you see words like 'we hear' or 'they say' you almost certainly have a **homophone** clue. Here 'tied ribbon' is 'bow' and BEAU is bow 'from what we hear', ie 'beau' and 'bow' are homophones.

18. Rejected young troublemaker longed to be free (8)

This is a **complex** clue in that it consists of the reverse of one word in a charade with another. A rejected troublemaker is 'Ted' backwards ('det') and longed is 'ached', which when attached makes DETACHED. Who ever calls unruly troublemakers 'teddy-boys' or 'teds' these days? Well, we do in crosswords. This is one example of **preserved obsolescence** in an area of language where we still have an extended-play record (EP) and sex-appeal is still 'it'.

19. Fool about fifty, one not altogether bright (6)

In this container-and-contents clue we make use of our knowledge of **Roman numerals**. Fifty is 'L' and 'twit' about 'L, I' is TWILIT. And there's a slightly misleading context here, isn't there?

20. 014? (6, 5)

This last clue is what one might call a **zany** or **improvised** clue – a sort of one-off cryptic definition. It depends on the solver seeing that 014 = 2 x 007. Since 007 is the agent James Bond, the answer must be DOUBLE AGENT.

With these twenty clues we have touched on all of the most important aspects of Crossword English, and maybe I have already been rather too 'English English' for some. What about other Englishes? Well, I'm writing this introduction for a Scottish publisher with a very special dictionary, *The Chambers Dictionary*. This is of course an excellent 'English English' dictionary but it also contains some excellent English words from the past and some highly unusual Scottish words. *Chambers* should be in every self-respecting crossworder's library, but its greatest treasures tend to come into play in the more difficult puzzles where Edmund (Spenser) and Jock (the archetypal Scot) make frequent appearances.

Across the Atlantic, in the USA and Canada, 'American Crossword English' is developing as cryptic puzzles, based on British puzzles, become more popular. British solvers will find one or two unfamiliar abbreviations, maybe, and the contexts will be more American – but the similarities tend to contradict Shaw's assertion mentioned earlier.

It has often been pointed out that English is ideal for the crossword because words split up so agreeably. How convenient that 'astronomer' is an anagram of 'moon-starer' and how nicely 'bestride' splits into 'best ride'. Clearly it would be difficult to imagine Crossword Urdu, and yet cryptic crosswords do exist in Hebrew, Bengali, Welsh and Dutch – and other languages too, I dare say.

It's time for a final word about the 'custodians' of Crossword English and what they are trying to do. The word 'custodian' may suggest conservatism and a grammar rule-book. There's more to it than that, of course, but there is a necessary element of grammar in crosswords which needs to be preserved. There are, after all, limits to what is acceptable in Everyday English, and it is the same in Crossword English.

In our language the strict grammarians call themselves **Ximeneans** after the crossword setter Ximenes, *The Observer* crossword setter who died in 1971. There is no space here for a digression into the grammar over which crossword setters and their editors argue, but there is an ongoing debate about what is acceptable and what is not. Today the tradition of Ximenes is upheld by his successor Azed, who tells us about his approach to crossword setting elsewhere in this introduction. Many of today's crossword setters have been competitors in Azed's clue-writing competitions, and so it is no surprise that many of the crossword setters in our national dailies are Ximenean – as are their crossword editors. Puzzles will inevitably vary in style and in level of difficulty. Crossword setters are turning Crossword English Language into Crossword English Literature and different 'readers' (solvers) will inevitably have their own favourite 'authors' (setters). But there are rules within which the custodians make sure that Crossword English operates – rules not just of grammar, but rules of taste. Practitioners of this language don't have to be absolutely politically correct, but their language is still that of the polite drawing-room, not that of the gutter. We can gently poke fun at pompous bishops and politicians (though not by name specifically!), and we can make wry comments about modern society, but we aim to entertain and not to give offence.

We want to give pleasure and intellectual challenge. Crossword English is a sort of twentieth-century poetry for all to enjoy. Long may it continue into the 21st century and beyond.

Summary of common anagram indicators

The following list includes words regularly used to indicate an anagram in cryptic crossword clues. No such list could be comprehensive. Almost any word or phrase meaning or suggesting disturbance or an abnormal state may be used as or as part of an anagram indicator in a cryptic clue. The list shows base forms of common anagram indicators; full inflected forms are not shown. Verbs in the list may appear in clues in any of their inflected forms; derivative nouns may be used; and adjectives may be found in their adverbial forms. For example, the list includes **annoy**, **arrange**, **awkward** and **random**, but omits **annoys**, **arrangement**, **awkwardly** and **at random**.

about	careless	detour
abroad	change	develop
adjust	chaotic	dicky
adrift	chip	different
afresh	chop	disconcert
all over the place	circulate	discord
alter	clumsy	discordant
amend	cocktail	diseased
amiss	collapse	disfigure
annoy	complicate	disgruntled
another: in another way	compose	disguise
anyhow	confound	dishevel
anyway	confuse	disorder
appal	construe	dispose
around	contrive	disrupt
arrange	conversion	dissipate
awful	convert	dissolute
awkward	cook	distort
bad	correct	distract
baffle	could be	distress
bastard	crack	distribute
bats	crash	disturb
batting	crazy	divert
beat up	criminal	do
become	cripple	doctor
bedevil	crooked	dreadful
bend	cruel	dress
bewilder	cuckoo	drunk
blend	curious	dubious
boil	cut	eccentric
bottle	damage	edit
break	dance	effervescent
brew	deform	embarrass
buckle	deploy	enigmatic
bust	derange	entangle
camouflage	desecrate	erratic
capriccioso	destroy	erroneous

error
erupt
evolve
explode
explosive
false
fancy
flap: in a flap
flash
flexible
flighty
flounder
fluid
form of
foul
free
fresh
frilly
fuddle
garble
gauche
ground
hammer
hammy
haphazard
hash
havoc
hit
ill
ill-
ill-composed
improper
injure
inordinate
involve
irregular
irritate
jockey
jolt
jumble
kink
knock out
labyrinthine
lax
light
loose
lost
lunatic
mad
malleable
mangle
manipulate
manoeuvre
maybe

medley
mend
mess
metamorphose
mis-
misdeliver
misguided
mislead
misshape
mistake
misuse
mix
mixture
model
mongrel
move
muddle
mutate
mutilate
mysterious
neglect
nervous
new
nobble
nonconformist
novel
nuts
oblique
obscure
obtainable
odd
off
off-
off-colour
on
order
order: out of order
organize
out
outlandish
out of
outrageous
part
peculiar
perhaps
pervert
phony
pickled
pie
place: all over the place
place: out of place
plastic
play
ply

poorly
pop
possible
potential
prepare
process
produce
pummel
punish
put off
queer
ragged
random
rearrange
recast
reckless
recollect
redevelop
rediscover
reel
reform
refurbish
relay
repair
represent
reproduce
resolve
resort
restless
restraint: without restraint
review
revise
revolt: in revolt
revolution
rewrite
rickety
rig
riotous
ripple
rocky
rollicking
rotten
rough
ruin
run
runny
sad
scramble
scratch
scuffle
sea: at sea
seethe
set off
set out

shake
shell
shift
shimmer
shiver
shock
shower
shuffle
silly: look silly
slipshod
sloppy
solution: in solution
solve
somehow
sorry
sorts: out of sorts
soup
spasmodic
spill
spray
spread
spurious
stagger
stew
stir
storm
strange
struggle
supple
suspect
swill
swim

swirl
switch
tangle
terrible
throb
throw
tipsy
tortuous
torture
train
trammel
transfer
transform
translate
transpose
treat
trip
trouble
tumble
turbulent
turnover
twirl
twist
un-
unconventional
undulate
unfit
unhappy
unnatural
unordered
unorthodox
unruly

unsettled
unsound
unstuck
untidy
unusual
unwind
upset
vague
vary
variety
version
vigorous
wander
warp
waste
wave
way: in another way
whirl: in a whirl
whisk
wicked
wild
work
worry
worsted
wreck
wrestle
wretched
writhe
wrong
wry
yank

abandon

04 drop, dump, jilt, quit
05 abort, cease, chuck, ditch, leave, scrap, waive, yield
06 desert, escape, forego, get out, give up, jack in, maroon, resign, strand, vacate
07 bail out, forsake, yield to
08 abdicate, evacuate, forswear, renounce, run out on, wildness
09 walk out on
10 break loose, depart from, relinquish
11 discontinue, impetuosity, leave behind, unrestraint
12 carelessness, recklessness
15 leave high and dry, leave in the lurch, thoughtlessness

abandoned

03 mad
04 wild
05 crazy, empty
06 unused, vacant, wanton, wicked
07 corrupt, forlorn, immoral
08 derelict, deserted, forsaken
09 debauched, dissolute, neglected, reprobate
10 profligate, unoccupied
11 uninhibited

abandonment

07 cession, jilting, leaving, neglect, waiving
08 ditching, dropping, giving-up, stopping
09 cessation, desertion, forsaking, marooning, scrapping, stranding
10 abdication, decampment
11 dereliction, resignation
12 renunciation, running out on

abase

06 debase, demean, humble, malign
07 mortify
08 belittle
09 disparage, humiliate

abashed

07 ashamed, floored, humbled
08 confused
09 affronted, mortified
10 bewildered, confounded, humiliated, shamefaced
11 discomfited, discomposed, embarrassed
12 disconcerted
15 discountenanced

abate

04 ease, fade, sink, slow, wane
05 allay, let up, quell, remit
06 lessen, pacify, reduce, soothe, weaken
07 decline, dwindle, subside
08 decrease, diminish, mitigate, moderate, taper off
09 alleviate, attenuate

abatement

04 wane
06 easing, relief
07 decline
08 decrease, lowering
09 dwindling, lessening, reduction, remission
10 diminution, mitigation, moderation, palliation, slackening, subsidence
11 alleviation, assuagement, attenuation

abbey

06 friary, priory
07 convent, minster, nunnery
08 cloister, seminary
09 cathedral, monastery

abbreviate

03 cut
04 clip, trim
06 digest, précis
07 abridge, curtail, shorten
08 condense, contract, truncate
09 constrict, summarize

abbreviation

06 digest, précis, résumé
07 acronym, summary
08 abstract, clipping, synopsis
09 reduction, short form
10 shortening, truncation

11 abridgement, compression, contraction, curtailment
13 summarization

abdicate

04 cede, quit
06 abjure, forego, give up, resign, retire
07 abandon
08 abnegate, renounce
09 repudiate, stand down

abdication

07 refusal
08 giving-up
10 abjuration, abnegation, retirement
11 abandonment, repudiation, resignation
12 renunciation, standing-down
14 relinquishment

abdomen

03 tum
04 guts
05 belly, tummy
06 paunch, venter
07 midriff, stomach
08 pot belly
11 corporation

abdominal

05 colic
07 coeliac, gastric, ventral
08 visceral
10 intestinal
11 ventricular

abduct

05 seize
06 kidnap, seduce, snatch
08 carry off, shanghai
11 appropriate, make off with
12 hold to ransom

aberrant

03 odd
05 rogue
06 quirky
07 corrupt, deviant
08 abnormal, atypical
09 anomalous, different, divergent, irregular
11 incongruous

aberration
05 lapse
06 oddity
07 anomaly, mistake
08 delusion, straying
09 deviation, oversight, variation, wandering
10 divergence
11 abnormality, peculiarity
12 eccentricity, irregularity

abet
03 aid
04 back, help, spur
05 egg on
06 assist
07 condone, endorse, promote, succour, support
09 encourage

abeyance
□ **in abeyance**
05 on ice
07 dormant, pending, shelved
09 suspended

abhor
04 hate, shun
05 spurn
06 detest, loathe
07 despise
08 execrate
09 abominate

abhorrence
04 hate
05 odium
06 enmity, hatred, malice
07 disgust
08 aversion, contempt, distaste, loathing
09 animosity, revulsion
10 execration, repugnance
11 abomination, detestation

abhorrent
05 hated
06 horrid, odious
07 hateful, heinous
08 horrible
09 execrable, loathsome, obnoxious, offensive, repellent, repugnant, repulsive, revolting
10 abominable, detestable, disgusting, nauseating

abide
04 bear, last, take
05 brook, stand
06 accept, endure, remain
07 persist, stomach
08 continue, tolerate

□ **abide by**
04 obey

06 accept, follow, fulfil, hold to, keep to, uphold
07 agree to, observe, respect
08 adhere to
09 conform to, discharge
10 comply with, toe the line

abiding
04 firm
07 eternal, lasting
08 constant, enduring, immortal, lifelong, long-term, unending
09 continual, immutable, permanent
10 continuous, persistent, unchanging
11 everlasting, long-lasting, long-running

ability
04 gift
05 flair, forte, knack, power, savvy, skill, touch
06 genius, powers, talent
07 calibre, faculty, know-how, prowess, the hang
08 aptitude, capacity, deftness, facility, strength, the knack
09 adeptness, expertise
10 adroitness, capability
11 proficiency, savoir-faire
13 qualification

abject
03 low
04 base, mean, vile
06 sordid
07 debased, forlorn, ignoble, outcast, servile
08 degraded, hopeless, pathetic, wretched
09 miserable, worthless
10 degenerate, grovelling, submissive
11 humiliating, ignominious
12 contemptible

abjure
04 deny
06 disown, eschew, reject
07 abandon, disavow, retract
08 abnegate, forswear, renege on, renounce

ablaze
05 afire, aglow, angry
06 aflame, alight, ardent, fuming, on fire, raging
07 aroused, burning, excited, fervent, flaming, furious, glowing, lighted, radiant
08 flashing, frenzied, gleaming
10 passionate, stimulated

able
03 fit
05 adept
06 adroit, clever, expert, fitted, gifted, strong, up to it
07 capable, skilful, skilled
09 competent, dexterous, effective, efficient, practised, qualified
10 proficient
11 experienced, intelligent
12 accomplished

able-bodied
03 fit
04 fine, hale
05 hardy, lusty, sound
06 hearty, robust, rugged, strong, sturdy
07 healthy, staunch
08 powerful, stalwart, vigorous
09 strapping
12 in good health
13 hale and hearty

abnegation
08 eschewal, giving-up
09 surrender
10 abjuration, abstinence, self-denial, temperance
12 renunciation
13 self-sacrifice
14 relinquishment

abnormal
03 odd
05 outré, queer, weird
07 deviant, erratic, oddball, strange, uncanny, unusual
08 aberrant, atypical, peculiar, singular, uncommon
09 anomalous, different, divergent, eccentric, irregular, unnatural
10 paranormal, unexpected
11 exceptional
13 extraordinary, preternatural

abnormality
04 flaw
06 oddity
07 anomaly
09 deformity, deviation
10 aberration, difference, divergence
11 peculiarity, singularity, strangeness, unusualness
12 eccentricity, irregularity, malformation
13 unnaturalness

abode
03 pad
04 home

07 habitat
08 domicile, dwelling, lodgings
09 residence
10 habitation
13 dwelling-place

abolish

03 axe, ban, end
04 stop
05 annul, quash
06 cancel, repeal, revoke
07 blot out, destroy, expunge, nullify, rescind, subvert, vitiate, wipe out
08 abrogate, overturn, stamp out, suppress
09 eliminate, eradicate, overthrow, terminate
10 annihilate, do away with, obliterate, put an end to

abolition

06 ending, repeal
09 annulment, overthrow
10 abrogation, extinction, rescission, revocation
11 destruction, dissolution, elimination, eradication, extirpation, rescindment
12 annihilation, obliteration
13 nullification

abominable

04 base, foul, vile
06 cursed, horrid, odious
07 hateful, heinous
08 damnable, horrible, wretched
09 abhorrent, appalling, atrocious, execrable, loathsome, obnoxious, offensive, repellent, repugnant, repulsive, revolting
10 despicable, detestable, disgusting, nauseating
12 contemptible

abominate

04 hate
05 abhor
06 detest, loathe
07 condemn, despise
08 execrate

abomination

04 evil, hate
05 curse, odium
06 hatred, horror, plague
07 offence, outrage, torment
08 anathema, atrocity, aversion, disgrace, distaste, loathing
09 hostility, revulsion

10 abhorrence, execration, repugnance
11 detestation

aboriginal

05 first, local
06 native, primal
07 ancient
08 earliest, original, primeval
09 primitive
10 indigenous
13 autochthonous

abort

03 axe, end
04 fail, halt, stop
05 check
06 thwart
07 call off, nullify, suspend
08 cut short, miscarry
09 frustrate, terminate
13 pull the plug on

abortion

11 miscarriage, termination

abortive

04 idle, vain
06 barren, failed, futile
07 sterile, useless
10 unavailing
11 ineffective, ineffectual
12 unproductive, unsuccessful

abound

04 teem
05 crowd, swarm, swell
06 be full, thrive
08 brim over, flourish, overflow
09 exuberate, luxuriate
11 be plentiful, proliferate

about

02 on, re
04 near
05 circa, round
06 almost, around, beside, nearby, nearly
07 roughly
09 apropos of, regarding
10 adjacent to, concerning, encircling, more or less, relating to, throughout
11 referring to, surrounding
12 encompassing, here and there, with regard to
13 approximately, in the region of, with respect to

▫ about to

06 all but, soon to
07 going to, ready to
12 on the point of, on the verge of

about-turn

05 U-turn

08 reversal
09 about-face, turnabout, volte-face
13 enantiodromia

above

04 atop, over, owre
05 aloft, prior
06 before, beyond, high up, higher, on high
07 earlier, on top of
08 overhead, senior to
09 aforesaid, exceeding, foregoing, preceding
10 superior to, surpassing
14 aforementioned

above-board

04 open, true
05 frank
06 candid, honest, square
07 upright
08 straight, truthful
09 reputable, veracious
10 legitimate, on the level
11 trustworthy
13 fair and square

abrade

03 rub
05 chafe, erode, grate, graze, grind, scour
06 scrape
07 scratch
08 wear away, wear down

abrasion

03 cut
05 chafe, graze
06 scrape
07 chafing, erosion, grating, rubbing, scratch
08 abrading, friction, grinding, scouring, scraping
10 scratching

abrasive

05 harsh, nasty, rough, sharp
06 biting
07 brusque, caustic, chafing, erodent, erosive, grating, hurtful
08 annoying, scraping
09 corrosive
10 frictional, irritating, scratching, unpleasant

abreast

05 level
06 au fait, well up
07 in touch
08 familiar, informed, up to date
09 au courant, on the ball
10 acquainted, side by side
12 in the picture

abridge
03 cut, lop
04 clip
05 prune
06 digest, lessen, précis, reduce
07 curtail, cut down, shorten
08 abstract, compress, condense, contract
09 summarize, synopsize
10 abbreviate

abridgement
06 abrégé, digest, précis, résumé
07 cutting, epitome, outline, summary
08 abstract, synopsis
09 reduction
10 conspectus, diminution, shortening, truncation
11 contraction

abroad
05 about
06 around, widely
07 at large, current
08 overseas, publicly
10 far and wide
14 in foreign parts, to foreign parts

abrogate
03 axe, end
05 annul, scrap
06 cancel, repeal, revoke
07 abolish, rescind, retract
08 disenact, dissolve
09 repudiate
10 do away with, invalidate
11 countermand

abrupt
04 curt, rude
05 blunt, brisk, gruff, hasty, quick, rapid, sharp, sheer, short, steep, swift, terse
06 direct, snappy, sudden
07 brusque, hurried, instant, offhand, uncivil
08 dramatic, impolite, snappish
10 surprising, unexpected

abscond
03 fly
04 bolt, flee, quit
05 scram
06 beat it, decamp, escape, run off, vanish
07 do a bunk, make off, run away, vamoose
09 disappear, do a runner, skedaddle
12 absquatulate
15 take French leave

absence
04 lack, need, want
06 dearth
07 default, paucity, truancy, vacancy, vacuity
08 omission, scarcity
09 privation
10 deficiency

absent
03 off, out
04 away, gone
05 blank
06 dreamy, truant, vacant
07 faraway, lacking, missing
09 elsewhere, oblivious
10 distracted, in absentia
11 daydreaming, inattentive, preoccupied

absent-minded
06 dreamy, musing, scatty
07 faraway, pensive, unaware
08 absorbed, distrait, dreaming, heedless
09 distraite, engrossed, forgetful, miles away, oblivious, unheeding
10 abstracted, distracted, unthinking
11 inattentive, not all there, preoccupied
13 wool-gathering
14 scatterbrained

absolute
04 full, pure, rank, sure
05 final, sheer, total, utter
06 entire
07 certain, decided, genuine, plenary, supreme
08 almighty, complete, decisive, definite, despotic, outright, positive, thorough
09 downright, out-and-out
10 autocratic, conclusive, consummate, definitive, exhaustive, omnipotent
11 autarchical, dictatorial, indubitable, unequivocal, unmitigated, unqualified
12 totalitarian, unrestrained, unrestricted
13 authoritarian, unadulterated, unconditional
14 unquestionable

absolutely
04 dead
05 fully, truly
06 purely, surely, wholly
07 exactly, finally, totally, utterly
08 entirely
09 certainly, decidedly, genuinely, perfectly, precisely, supremely
10 completely, decisively, definitely, infallibly, positively, thoroughly
12 conclusively, exhaustively
13 categorically, unequivocally
14 unquestionably, wholeheartedly
15 unconditionally

absolution
05 mercy
06 pardon, shrift
07 amnesty, freedom, release
09 acquittal, discharge, purgation, remission
10 liberation, redemption
11 deliverance, exculpation, exoneration, forgiveness, vindication
12 emancipation

absolve
04 free
05 clear, loose, remit
06 acquit, excuse, let off, pardon
07 deliver, forgive, justify, release, set free
08 liberate
09 discharge, exculpate, exonerate, vindicate
10 emancipate

absorb
04 fill, hold
06 devour, digest, draw in, engage, engulf, fill up, imbibe, ingest, occupy, retain, soak up, take in
07 consume, drink in, engross, enthral, involve, receive
09 captivate, fascinate, integrate, preoccupy, swallow up
10 assimilate, understand
11 incorporate

absorbed
07 riveted
08 involved, occupied
09 engrossed
10 captivated, enthralled, fascinated, interested
11 preoccupied, taken up with

absorbent
06 porous
07 soaking
08 blotting, pervious
09 permeable, receptive, resorbent, retentive

10 absorptive
12 assimilative, sorbefacient

absorbing

07 amusing
08 gripping, riveting
09 diverting, enjoyable
10 compelling, compulsive,
   engrossing, intriguing
11 captivating, enthralling,
   fascinating, interesting
12 entertaining, spellbinding
13 unputdownable

absorption

07 holding, osmosis
08 monopoly, riveting
09 devouring, drawing-in,
   ingestion, soaking-up
10 engagement, engrossing,
   intentness, occupation
11 captivating, consumption,
   involvement
13 concentration,
   preoccupation

abstain

04 shun, stop
05 avoid
06 desist, eschew, forego, give
   up, refuse, reject, resist
07 decline, forbear, refrain
08 keep from, renounce
09 do without, go without

abstemious

05 sober
06 frugal
07 ascetic, austere, sparing
08 moderate, teetotal
09 abstinent, temperate
11 disciplined, self-denying

abstention

09 not voting
13 refusal to vote

abstinence

07 refusal
08 eschewal, sobriety
09 avoidance, frugality,
   nephalism, restraint
10 asceticism, continence,
   declension, desistance,
   moderation, temperance
11 forbearance, self-control,
   teetotalism
12 going-without, renunciation
14 abstemiousness

abstract

03 cut
04 deep
06 arcane, detach, digest,
   précis, remove, résumé

07 abridge, complex, cut down,
   epitome, extract, general,
   isolate, outline, shorten,
   summary, take out
08 abstruse, compress,
   condense, notional,
   separate, synopsis,
   take away, withdraw
09 contrived, recondite,
   summarize
10 abbreviate, conceptual,
   conspectus, indefinite
11 abridgement, compression,
   theoretical
12 hypothetical, intellectual,
   metaphysical
14 recapitulation

abstracted

06 absent, dreamy, musing,
   scatty
07 bemused, pensive, unaware
08 absorbed, dreaming
09 engrossed, forgetful,
   oblivious, unheeding
10 distracted, unthinking
11 inattentive, preoccupied
12 absent-minded
13 wool-gathering
14 scatterbrained

abstraction

04 idea
05 dream
06 notion, theory
07 concept, theorem, thought
10 absorption, conception,
   dreaminess, extraction,
   hypothesis, separation
11 inattention, pensiveness
13 preoccupation
14 generalization

abstruse

04 deep
06 arcane
07 complex, cryptic, obscure
08 esoteric, profound, puzzling
09 enigmatic, recondite
10 mysterious, perplexing
11 inscrutable
12 unfathomable

absurd

04 daft
05 crazy, funny, inane, silly
06 stupid
07 asinine, comical, foolish,
   idiotic, risible
08 derisory, farcical, humorous
09 fantastic, illogical,
   laughable, ludicrous,
   senseless, untenable
10 irrational, ridiculous

11 harebrained, implausible,
   nonsensical, paradoxical
12 preposterous, unreasonable

absurdity

04 joke
05 farce, folly
06 drivel, humour, idiocy
07 charade, inanity, paradox,
   rubbish, twaddle
08 claptrap, daftness,
   nonsense, travesty
09 craziness, gibberish,
   silliness, stupidity
10 balderdash
11 incongruity

abundance

04 bags, glut, lots
05 heaps, loads, piles, scads
06 bounty, excess, masses,
   oodles, plenty, riches,
   stacks, wealth
07 bonanza, fortune
08 fullness, lashings, opulence,
   overflow, plethora, richness
09 affluence, amplitude,
   plenitude, profusion
10 exuberance, generosity
11 copiousness, great supply,
   munificence, prodigality

abundant

04 full, rich
05 ample
06 filled, galore, lavish
07 copious, opulent, profuse
08 affluent, generous, in plenty
09 bounteous, bountiful,
   exuberant, plentiful
11 overflowing
14 more than enough

abuse

03 hit
04 beat, harm, hurt, rail
05 bully, curse, libel, scold,
   slate, smear, wrong
06 batter, damage, defame,
   injure, injury, insult, malign,
   misuse, molest, oppugn,
   pick on, revile, tirade
07 affront, beating, calumny,
   censure, cruelty, cursing,
   exploit, insults, offence,
   oppress, slander, swear at,
   torture, upbraid, vitriol
08 derision, diatribe, ill-treat,
   maltreat, reproach,
   scolding, swearing
09 castigate, contumely,
   denigrate, disparage,
   invective, victimize
10 calumniate, defamation,
   oppression, upbraiding

abusive

11 castigation, denigration, malediction, molestation
12 calumniation, exploitation, ill-treatment, maltreatment, mistreatment, vilification, vituperation

abusive

04 rude
05 cruel
06 brutal
07 harmful, hurtful, railing
08 reviling, scathing, scolding
09 injurious, insulting, libellous, maligning, vilifying
10 censorious, defamatory, derogatory, pejorative, slanderous, upbraiding
11 castigating, denigrating, destructive, disparaging, opprobrious, reproachful
12 calumniating, contumelious, vituperative

abut

04 join
05 touch
06 adjoin, border

abysmal

05 awful, utter
06 dismal
08 complete, dreadful, shocking
09 appalling
11 disgraceful

abyss

03 pit
04 gulf, void
05 chasm, depth, gorge
06 canyon, crater, depths
07 fissure
08 crevasse
09 barathrum

academic

03 don
05 smart, tutor
06 brainy, fellow, master, pedant
07 bookish, donnish, erudite, learned, scholar, educated, highbrow, lecturer, literary, notional, well-read
09 professor, scholarly
10 irrelevant, ivory-tower, scholastic
11 conjectural, educational, impractical, pedagogical, speculative, theoretical
12 hypothetical, intellectual

accede

05 admit, bow to
06 accept, assume, attain, come to, concur, give in

07 agree to, inherit, succeed
08 assent to, back down
09 acquiesce, consent to, succeed to

accelerate

05 hurry, speed
06 hasten, step up
07 advance, forward, further, promote, quicken, speed up
08 expedite, go faster, step on it
09 festinate, stimulate
10 facilitate
11 gather speed, pick up speed, precipitate
15 put your foot down

acceleration

08 momentum
09 hastening, promotion
10 expedition, forwarding, speeding-up, stepping-up
11 advancement, furtherance

accent

04 beat, tone
05 force, pitch, pulse, twang
06 brogue, rhythm, stress
07 cadence, diction
08 emphasis, priority
09 intensity, pulsation
10 inflection, intonation, modulation, prominence
11 enunciation, underlining
12 accentuation, articulation, highlighting
13 pronunciation

accentuate

06 accent, show up, stress
08 heighten
09 emphasize, highlight, intensify, underline
10 strengthen, underscore

accept

03 buy, get
04 bear, gain, take
05 abide, admit, adopt, allow, bow to, stand, trust
06 endure, give in, obtain, secure, take on, take up
07 abide by, agree to, believe, embrace, receive, stomach, swallow
08 accede to, tolerate
09 believe in, consent to, put up with, undertake
10 comply with, concur with
11 acknowledge, go along with, take on board
12 be resigned to
13 make the best of
15 come to terms with

acceptable

02 OK
04 so-so
08 adequate, moderate, passable
09 agreeable, allowable, desirable, tolerable
10 admissible, delightful, gratifying, reasonable
11 appropriate, permissible
12 satisfactory, the done thing

acceptance

02 OK
05 faith, trust
06 assent, belief, taking
07 bearing, consent, gaining, getting, receipt
08 adoption, approval
09 accepting, accession, acquiring, admission, agreement, embracing, endurance, obtaining, receiving, tolerance
10 assumption, facing up to
11 affirmation, concurrence, endorsement, undertaking
12 acquiescence, ratification
15 acknowledgement

accepted

05 usual
06 agreed, common, normal
07 correct, regular
08 admitted, approved, orthodox, ratified, received, standard
09 customary, universal
10 authorized, recognized, sanctioned
11 appropriate, established, traditional
12 acknowledged, conventional, time-honoured

access

03 key
04 door, path, road
05 drive, entry, way in
06 course, entrée
07 gateway, ingress, passage
08 approach, driveway, entering, entrance
09 admission
10 admittance

accessible

04 near
05 handy, ready
06 nearby, on hand
09 available, reachable
10 attainable, convenient, obtainable, procurable

12 intelligible, user-friendly
14 understandable

accession
04 gift
08 addition, increase, purchase
10 assumption, possession, succession
11 acquisition, inheritance

accessory
03 aid, hat
04 belt, help
05 extra, frill, shoes
06 gloves, helper
07 abettor, adjunct, fitting, handbag, partner
08 addition, conniver, ornament, trimming
09 ancillary, appendage, assistant, associate, auxiliary, colleague, component, jewellery, secondary
10 accomplice, additional, attachment, complement, decoration, incidental, subsidiary, supplement
11 confederate, subordinate
12 contributory, supplemental
13 embellishment

accident
04 blow, fate, luck
05 crash, fluke, prang, shunt, wreck
06 chance, hazard, mishap, pile-up
07 fortune, smash-up, tragedy
08 calamity, casualty, disaster, fatality, fortuity, good luck
09 collision, mischance
10 misfortune
11 coincidence, contretemps, good fortune, serendipity
12 happenstance, misadventure

accidental
05 fluky
06 casual, chance, random
08 aleatory
09 haphazard, uncertain, unplanned, unwitting
10 fortuitous, incidental, unexpected
11 inadvertent, unlooked-for
12 adventitious, uncalculated
13 serendipitous, unintentional

accidentally
08 bechance, by chance, randomly
09 by mistake
11 haphazardly, unwittingly

12 fortuitously, incidentally, unexpectedly
13 inadvertently
14 adventitiously
15 serendipitously, unintentionally

acclaim
04 clap, hail, laud
05 cheer, exalt, extol, toast
06 cheers, eulogy, homage, honour, praise, salute
07 applaud, commend, fanfare, ovation, tribute, welcome
08 applause, approval, eulogize, plaudits
09 extolment, laudation
10 exaltation
11 acclamation, approbation, celebration
12 commendation

acclamation
05 paean
06 bravos, eulogy, homage, honour, praise
07 ovation, tribute, welcome
08 applause, approval, cheering, clapping, shouting
09 panegyric
10 enthusiasm, exaltation
11 approbation, celebration
12 commendation
13 felicitations
15 congratulations

acclimatize
05 adapt, inure
06 adjust, attune
08 accustom
09 get used to, habituate
10 naturalize
11 accommodate, acculturate, familiarize
12 find your feet
15 get your bearings

accolade
05 award
06 honour, praise
07 tribute

accommodate
03 aid, fit
04 help, hold, take
05 adapt, board, house, lodge, put up, serve
06 adjust, assist, billet, modify, oblige, settle, supply, take in
07 provide, shelter
08 accustom, cater for, domicile
09 harmonize, reconcile

11 acclimatize, be helpful to, give a hand to, have room for, lend a hand to
12 have space for

accommodating
04 kind
07 helpful, pliable, willing
08 friendly, obliging
09 agreeable, unselfish
10 hospitable
11 co-operative, complaisant, considerate, sympathetic

accommodation
05 board
07 harmony, housing, lodging, quarter, shelter
08 quarters
09 agreement
10 compromise, settlement
11 negotiation
12 negotiations
14 reconciliation

➤ *Types of accommodation*:
03 inn, pad
04 digs, flat, gite
05 b and b, hotel, motel, rooms, squat, villa
06 bedsit, billet, hostel
07 pension, shelter
08 dwelling, lodgings, quarters
09 apartment, bedsitter, residence, timeshare
10 guest house
11 youth hostel
13 boarding-house
15 bed and breakfast
➤ See also **house**

accompaniment
04 vamp
06 backup
07 adjunct, backing, support
08 addition
09 accessory, obbligato
10 background, complement, supplement
11 coexistence, concomitant

accompany
05 usher
06 attend, convoy, escort, follow, go with, squire
07 coexist, consort, partner
08 come with, play with
09 chaperone
10 complement, supplement
13 associate with
14 hang around with

accomplice
04 aide, ally, mate
06 helper
07 abettor, partner

08 henchman, sidekick
09 accessory, assistant, associate, colleague
11 confederate, conspirator
12 collaborator

accomplish
02 do
06 attain, effect, finish, fulfil
07 achieve, execute, perform, produce, realize
08 bring off, carry out, complete
09 discharge, pull it off
10 bring about, effectuate
15 deliver the goods

accomplished
05 adept
06 adroit, expert, gifted
07 skilful, skilled
08 masterly, polished, talented
09 practised
10 consummate, proficient
11 experienced
12 professional

accomplishment
03 art
04 deed, feat, gift
05 forte, skill
06 stroke, talent
07 ability, faculty, triumph
08 aptitude, fruition
09 execution, finishing
10 attainment, completion, conclusion, fulfilment, futurition, production
11 achievement, performance, proficiency, realization
12 consummation

accord
04 give, suit
05 agree, allow, endow, grant, match, unity
06 assent, bestow, concur, confer, tender
07 concert, conform
08 sympathy
09 agreement, congruity, harmonize, unanimity, vouchsafe
10 accordance, conformity, congruence, correspond
11 concurrence
14 correspondence

□**of your own accord**
06 freely
09 willingly
11 voluntarily

□**with one accord**
09 of one mind
11 unanimously

accordance
□**in accordance with**
05 after
10 in line with, obedient to
12 in relation to, in the light of
13 in concert with

according
□**according to**
05 after, as per
10 in line with, obedient to
11 as claimed by, depending on
12 in relation to, in the light of
13 in keeping with
14 in proportion to

accordingly
02 so
04 ergo, thus
05 hence
08 properly, suitably
09 as a result, therefore
12 consequently, consistently

accost
04 halt, stop
06 attack, detain, molest, waylay
07 solicit
08 approach, confront
09 importune
10 buttonhole

account
03 tab
04 bill, deem, hold, tale
05 story
06 detail, esteem, import, ledger, memoir, record, regard, report, sketch
07 adjudge, details, history, invoice, version, write-up
08 appraise, consider
09 chronicle, inventory, narration, narrative, portrayal, statement
10 commentary, communiqué, importance
11 consequence, description, distinction, explanation

□**account for**
06 make up, supply
07 clear up, explain, justify, provide
09 answer for, elucidate, represent, vindicate
10 constitute, illuminate
11 rationalize

accountability
09 liability
10 obligation
13 answerability
14 responsibility

accountable
05 bound
06 liable
07 obliged
09 obligated
10 answerable, chargeable
11 responsible

accoutrements
03 kit
04 gear
06 outfit
08 fittings, fixtures
09 caparison, equipment, trimmings
10 adornments
11 decorations, furnishings, odds and ends
13 appurtenances, bits and pieces, paraphernalia

accredited
08 approved, endorsed, licensed, official
09 appointed, certified, qualified
10 authorized, recognized
12 certificated, commissioned

accrue
05 amass, mount
07 augment, build up, collect
08 increase
10 accumulate

accumulate
04 gain, grow
05 amass, hoard, stash, store
06 accrue, gather, pile up
07 acquire, augment, collect
08 assemble, increase, multiply, snowball
09 aggregate, stockpile

accumulation
04 gain, mass, pile
05 hoard, stack, stock, store
06 growth
07 accrual, build-up, reserve
08 assembly, increase
09 aggregate, gathering, stockpile
10 collection, cumulation
11 acquisition
12 augmentation
14 conglomeration

accuracy
05 truth
06 verity
08 fidelity, veracity
09 closeness, exactness, precision
10 exactitude
11 carefulness, correctness

12 authenticity, faithfulness, scrupulosity, truthfulness, veridicality

accurate
04 fair, true
05 exact, right, sound, valid
06 bang on, spot on, strict
07 correct, perfect, precise
08 faithful, rigorous, truthful, unerring
09 authentic, veracious, veridical, well-aimed
10 meticulous
11 word-for-word, word-perfect

accursed
06 damned, doomed
07 hateful
08 wretched
09 bewitched, execrable
10 abominable, bedevilled, despicable

accusation
05 blame
06 charge
08 citation, delation, gravamen
09 complaint
10 allegation, imputation, indictment
11 arraignment, crimination, impeachment, inculpation
12 denunciation
13 incrimination, recrimination

accuse
04 book, cite
05 blame, frame
06 allege, impugn, impute, indict
07 arraign, censure, impeach
08 confront, denounce
09 attribute, criminate, implicate, prosecute
11 incriminate, recriminate
12 bring charges, press charges

accustom
05 adapt, inure
06 adjust, attune
07 conform
09 get used to, habituate
11 accommodate, familiarize

accustomed
04 used, wont
05 fixed, given, usual
06 at home, inured, normal, wonted
07 general, regular, routine
08 everyday, familiar, habitual, ordinary
09 customary

10 acquainted, habituated, prevailing
11 established, traditional
12 acclimatized, conventional
14 consuetudinary

ace
05 great, whizz
06 expert, genius, master, superb, winner
07 dab hand, hotshot, maestro, perfect
08 champion, virtuoso
09 brilliant, excellent
10 first-class
11 outstanding

acerbic
05 harsh, sharp
06 biting
07 caustic, mordant
08 abrasive, stinging
09 rancorous, trenchant, vitriolic
10 astringent
11 acrimonious

ache
04 hurt, itch, kill, long, pain, pang, pine
05 agony, crave, pound, smart, sting, throb, yearn
06 desire, hanker, hunger, suffer, thirst, twinge
07 craving, longing
08 pounding, smarting, soreness, stinging, yearning
09 hankering, suffering, throbbing

achieve
02 do
03 get, win
04 earn, gain
05 reach
06 attain, effect, finish, fulfil, manage, obtain
07 acquire, execute, perform, realize, succeed
08 carry out, complete
10 accomplish, bring about, consummate, effectuate

achievement
03 act
04 deed, feat
06 action, effort
07 exploit, success
08 activity, fruition
09 execution
10 attainment, completion, fulfilment
11 acquirement, performance, procurement, realization

12 consummation
14 accomplishment

achiever
04 doer
08 go-getter
09 high flyer, performer
12 success story

acid
04 sour, tart
05 harsh, sharp
06 acetic, acidic, biting, bitter, morose, unkind
07 acerbic, acetous, caustic, cutting, hurtful, mordant
08 critical, incisive, stinging, vinegary
09 acidulous, corrosive, sarcastic, trenchant, vitriolic
10 astringent

➤ *Types of acid. We have omitted the word* **acid** *from names given in the following list but you may need to include this word as part of the solution to some crossword clues.*
03 DNA, RNA
04 uric
05 amino, boric, folic
06 acetic, citric, formic, lactic, nitric, oxalic, phenol, tannic
07 benzoic, boracic, chloric, nitrous, nucleic, prussic, pyruvic, silicic
08 ascorbic, carbolic, carbonic, ethanoic, lysergic, tartaric
09 salicylic, sulphonic, sulphuric
10 aqua fortis, barbituric, carboxylic, phosphoric, sulphurous
11 hydrocyanic, ribonucleic
12 hydrochloric, hydrofluoric
➤ See also **amino acid**

acknowledge
04 hail
05 admit, allow, grant, greet, thank
06 accede, accept, answer, avouch, notice, salute
07 address, agree to, concede, confess, confirm, declare, own up to, react to, reply to
09 acquiesce, recognize, respond to, write back

acknowledged
06 avowed
08 accepted, approved, attested, declared
09 confirmed, professed
10 accredited, recognized

acknowledgement
03 nod
04 wave
05 reply, smile
06 answer, credit, notice
07 tribute
08 greeting, reaction, response
09 admission
10 acceptance, confession, profession, salutation
11 affirmation, recognition

acme
04 apex, peak
05 crown
06 apogee, climax, height, summit, zenith
08 pinnacle
09 high point
11 culmination

acolyte
06 helper
08 adherent, follower
09 assistant, attendant

acoustic
05 aural, sound
06 audile
07 hearing
08 auditory

acquaint
04 tell
05 brief
06 advise, inform, notify, reveal
07 apprise, divulge, let know
08 accustom, announce, disclose
09 enlighten
11 familiarize

acquaintance
06 friend
07 contact
08 confrère, intimacy
09 associate, colleague, companion, knowledge
10 cognizance, fellowship
11 association, familiarity
12 relationship
13 companionship

acquainted
05 aware
06 au fait
07 abreast
08 apprised, familiar, friendly
09 cognizant, in the know
10 conversant, well-versed
13 knowledgeable

acquiesce
05 agree, allow, defer

06 accede, accept, concur, give in, submit
07 approve, consent

acquiescence
06 assent
07 consent
08 approval, yielding
09 agreement, deference
10 acceptance, compliance
11 concurrence

acquiescent
07 servile
08 acceding, agreeing, amenable, obedient, yielding
09 accepting, agreeable, approving, compliant
10 concurrent, consenting
11 complaisant, deferential

acquire
03 bag, buy, cop, get, net, win
04 earn, gain
05 amass
06 attain, come by, gather, obtain, secure
07 achieve, collect, procure, realize, receive
08 purchase
10 accumulate

acquisition
04 gain
08 property, purchase, securing, takeover
09 accession, obtaining
10 attainment, possession
11 achievement, procurement

acquisitive
04 avid
06 greedy
08 covetous, grasping
09 predatory, rapacious, voracious
10 avaricious

acquisitiveness
05 greed
07 avarice, avidity
08 rapacity, voracity
12 covetousness, graspingness

acquit
03 act
04 bear, free
05 clear, repay
06 behave, excuse, let off, settle
07 absolve, comport, conduct, deliver, dismiss, perform, release, relieve, satisfy
08 liberate, reprieve

09 discharge, exculpate, exonerate, vindicate
13 let off the hook

acquittal
06 relief
07 freeing, release
08 excusing, reprieve
09 discharge, dismissal
10 absolution, liberation
11 deliverance, exculpation, exoneration, vindication
12 compurgation

acrid
04 acid, sour, tart
05 harsh, nasty, sharp
06 biting, bitter
07 acerbic, burning, caustic, cutting, mordant, pungent
08 incisive, sardonic, stinging, venomous, virulent
09 malicious, sarcastic, trenchant, vitriolic
10 astringent
11 acrimonious

acrimonious
05 sharp
06 biting, bitter, severe
07 abusive, acerbic, caustic, crabbed, cutting, waspish
08 petulant, spiteful, venomous, virulent
09 irascible, rancorous, splenetic, trenchant, vitriolic
10 astringent, censorious
11 ill-tempered

acrimony
04 gall
05 spite, venom
06 spleen
07 rancour, sarcasm, vitriol
08 acerbity, acridity, asperity, mordancy
09 harshness, ill temper, petulance, virulence
10 bitterness, causticity, resentment, trenchancy
11 astringency
12 irascibility

acrobat
07 gymnast, tumbler
09 aerialist
11 equilibrist, funambulist
12 somersaulter
13 contortionist, trapeze artist

act
02 be, do
03 gig, law
04 bill, deed, fake, feat, item, mime, move, play, sham, show, skit, step, turn, work

05 edict, enact, feign, front, mimic, put on, react, serve
06 affect, assume, behave, decree, ruling, sketch, stroke
07 exploit, imitate, measure, operate, perform, portray, pretend, routine, statute
08 function, pretence
09 execution, ordinance, represent, take steps
10 enterprise, take effect
11 achievement, affectation, counterfeit, dissimulate, impersonate, make-believe, performance, undertaking
12 characterize, dissemblance

❑**act on**
04 heed, obey, take
05 alter
06 affect, change, follow, fulfil
08 carry out
09 influence, transform
10 comply with

❑**act up**
06 play up
09 mess about, misbehave
10 muck around
12 cause trouble

acting
05 drama
06 deputy, pro tem, relief, supply
07 interim, reserve, stand-by, stand-in, stopgap, theatre
08 artistry, covering
09 dramatics, imitating, portrayal, temporary
10 footlights, performing, play-acting, stagecraft, substitute
11 histrionics, performance, provisional, theatricals
13 impersonation
14 performing arts

action
04 case, deed, feat, fray, move, step, suit, work
05 clash, fight, force, power
06 affray, battle, combat, effect, effort, energy, motion
07 exploit, lawsuit, measure, process, warfare
08 activity, conflict, exercise, exertion, movement, practice, skirmish, vitality
09 encounter, influence, mechanism, operation
10 engagement, enterprise, get-up-and-go, litigation, liveliness, proceeding
11 achievement, performance, prosecution, undertaking
14 accomplishment

activate
04 fire, move, stir, trip
05 impel, put on, rouse, start
06 arouse, bestir, excite, prompt, propel, turn on
07 actuate, animate, trigger
08 energize, initiate, mobilize, motivate, switch on
09 galvanize, stimulate
10 trigger off
11 set in motion

active
04 busy, spry
05 agile, alert, astir, manic, quick, vital
06 lively, nimble
07 devoted, engaged, in force, on the go, vibrant, working
08 animated, forceful, frenetic, involved, militant, occupied, spirited, vigorous
09 committed, energetic, sprightly
11 functioning, hard-working, industrious, light-footed
12 contributing, enterprising, enthusiastic
13 indefatigable

activity
03 job
04 deed, life, task, work
05 hobby
06 bustle, labour, motion
07 pastime, project, pursuit, venture
08 business, exercise, exertion, industry, interest, movement
09 avocation, commotion, diversion, endeavour
10 enterprise, hurly-burly, liveliness, occupation
11 distraction, undertaking
14 toing and froing

actor, actress
03 ham
04 mime
05 extra
06 artist, mummer, player, walk-on
07 Roscius, trouper
08 film star, Thespian
09 movie star, performer, tragedian
10 leading man, understudy
11 leading lady, tritagonist
12 impersonator
➢ See also **comedian**

▶ *Names of actors*:
03 Fox (James), Fox (Michael J), **Lee** (Christopher), **Lom** (Herbert), **Sim** (Alastair)

04 **Cage** (Nicholas), **Dean** (James), **Depp** (Johnny), **Ford** (Harrison), **Gere** (Richard), **Hope** (Bob), **Hurt** (John), **Kaye** (Danny), **Kean** (Edmund), **Peck** (Gregory), **Pitt** (Brad), **Reed** (Oliver), **Tree** (Sir Herbert Beerbohm)

05 **Bates** (Alan), **Caine** (Michael), **Clift** (Montgomery), **Flynn** (Errol), **Fonda** (Henry), **Fonda** (Peter), **Gable** (Clark), **Grant** (Cary), **Grant** (Hugh), **Hanks** (Tom), **Irons** (Jeremy), **Jason** (David), **Kelly** (Gene), **Kempe** (Will), **Lanza** (Mario), **Lorre** (Peter), **Mason** (James), **Mills** (Sir John), **Moore** (Dudley), **Moore** (Roger), **Nimoy** (Leonard), **Niven** (David), **Price** (Vincent), **Reeve** (Christopher), **Robey** (Sir George), **Scott** (George Campbell), **Sheen** (Martin), **Tracy** (Spencer), **Wayne** (John)

06 **Alleyn** (Edward), **Beatty** (Warren), **Bogart** (Humphrey), **Brando** (Marlon), **Burton** (Richard), **Cagney** (James), **Chaney** (Lon), **Coburn** (James), **Cooper** (Gary), **Cruise** (Tom), **Culkin** (Macaulay), **Curtis** (Tony), **De Niro** (Robert), **DeVito** (Danny), **Dillon** (Matt), **Finney** (Albert), **Gibson** (Mel), **Heston** (Charlton), **Hopper** (Dennis), **Howard** (Trevor), **Hudson** (Rock), **Irving** (Sir Henry), **Jacobi** (Derek), **Jouvet** (Louis), **Kemble** (John Philip), **Lemmon** (Jack), **Lugosi** (Bela), **Neeson** (Liam), **Newman** (Paul), **O'Toole** (Peter), **Pacino** (Al), **Phelps** (Samuel), **Quayle** (Sir Anthony), **Reeves** (Keanu), **Rooney** (Mickey), **Sharif** (Omar), **Sinden** (Sir Donald), **Swayze** (Patrick), **Welles** (Orson), **Wilder** (Gene), **Willis** (Bruce), **Wolfit** (Sir Donald)

07 **Bogarde** (Dirk), **Branagh** (Kenneth), **Bridges** (Jeff),

Bridges (Lloyd), **Bronson** (Charles), **Brynner** (Yul), **Burbage** (Richard), **Connery** (Sean), **Costner** (Kevin), **Cushing** (Peter), **Douglas** (Kirk), **Douglas** (Michael), **Fiennes** (Ralph), **Forrest** (Edwin), **Garrick** (David), **Gielgud** (Sir John), **Hoffman** (Dustin), **Hopkins** (Anthony), **Hordern** (Sir Michael), **Karloff** (Boris), **Marceau** (Marcel), **Matthau** (Walter), **McQueen** (Steve), **Mitchum** (Robert), **Olivier** (Sir Laurence), **Perkins** (Anthony), **Phoenix** (River), **Poitier** (Sidney), **Redford** (Robert), **Robeson** (Paul), **Roscius**, **Russell** (Kurt), **Savalas** (Telly), **Shatner** (William), **Steiger** (Rod), **Stewart** (James), **Ustinov** (Sir Peter)

08 **Barrault** (Jean-Louis), **Day-Lewis** (Daniel), **Dreyfuss** (Richard), **Eastwood** (Clint), **Guinness** (Sir Alec), **Harrison** (Sir Rex), **Kingsley** (Ben), **Laughton** (Charles), **Macready** (William Charles), **McGregor** (Ewan), **Redgrave** (Sir Michael), **Reynolds** (Burt), **Robinson** (Edward G), **Scofield** (Paul), **Stallone** (Sylvester), **Travolta** (John), **Van Cleef** (Lee), **Van Damme** (Jean-Claude), **Williams** (Robin)

09 **Barrymore** (Lionel), **Chevalier** (Maurice), **Depardieu** (Gérard), **Fairbanks** (Douglas), **Fernandel**, **Lancaster** (Burt), **Nicholson** (Jack), **Pleasence** (Donald), **Strasberg** (Lee), **Valentino** (Rudolph)

10 **Richardson** (Sir Ralph), **Sutherland** (Donald), **Sutherland** (Kiefer), **Washington** (Denzel)

11 **Mastroianni** (Marcello)

12 **Attenborough** (Sir Richard), **Stanislavsky**

14 **Schwarzenegger** (Arnold)

➤ *Names of actresses*:

04 **Ball** (Lucille), **Dern**

(Laura), **Dors** (Diana), **Duse** (Eleonora), **Gish** (Lilian), **Gwyn** (Eleanor), **Hawn** (Goldie), **Rigg** (Diana), **Ryan** (Meg), **West** (Mae)

05 **Bloom** (Clare), **Close** (Glenn), **Davis** (Bette), **Dench** (Dame Judi), **Evans** (Dame Edith), **Fonda** (Jane), **Gabor** (Zsa Zsa), **Garbo** (Greta), **Lange** (Jessica), **Leigh** (Janet), **Leigh** (Vivien), **Loren** (Sophia), **Moore** (Demi), **Ryder** (Winona), **Smith** (Dame Maggie), **Stone** (Sharon), **Terry** (Dame Ellen), **Welch** (Raquel)

06 **Adjani** (Isabelle), **Bacall** (Lauren), **Bardot** (Brigitte), **Bisset** (Jacqueline), **Farrow** (Mia), **Foster** (Jodie), **Keaton** (Diane), **Kemble** (Fanny), **Kidman** (Nicole), **Lumley** (Joanna), **Mirren** (Helen), **Monroe** (Marilyn), **Moreau** (Jeanne), **Robson** (Dame Flora), **Streep** (Meryl), **Taylor** (Elizabeth), **Temple** (Shirley), **Weaver** (Sigourney)

07 **Andress** (Ursula), **Andrews** (Julie), **Bergman** (Ingrid), **Colbert** (Claudette), **Deneuve** (Catherine), **Gardner** (Ava), **Hepburn** (Audrey), **Hepburn** (Katharine), **Huppert** (Isabelle), **Jackson** (Glenda), **Johnson** (Dame Celia), **Langtry** (Lillie), **Roberts** (Julia), **Russell** (Jane), **Seymour** (Jane), **Siddons** (Sarah), **Ullmann** (Liv)

08 **Ashcroft** (Dame Peggy), **Bancroft** (Anne), **Bankhead** (Tallulah), **Basinger** (Kim), **Campbell** (Mrs Patrick), **Crawford** (Joan), **Dietrich** (Marlene), **Goldberg** (Whoopi), **Hayworth** (Rita), **MacLaine** (Shirley), **Minnelli** (Liza), **Pickford** (Mary), **Rampling** (Charlotte), **Redgrave** (Vanessa), **Thompson** (Emma)

09 **Barrymore** (Drew), **Bernhardt** (Sarah),

Mansfield (Jayne), **Streisand** (Barbra), **Thorndike** (Dame Sybil)

10 **Rutherford** (Dame Margaret)

11 **Bracegirdle** (Anne), **Mistinguett**

12 **Bonham-Carter** (Helena), **Lollobrigida** (Gina)

actual
04 real, true
07 certain, de facto, genuine
08 absolute, bona fide, concrete, definite, material, physical, positive, tangible, truthful, verified
09 authentic, realistic
10 legitimate

actuality
04 fact
05 truth
07 reality
09 substance
10 factuality
11 historicity, materiality

actually
04 even
05 truly
06 in fact, indeed, really
07 de facto, in truth
09 in reality
10 absolutely

actuate
04 move, stir
05 rouse, start
06 arouse, prompt, set off
07 trigger
08 activate, motivate
09 instigate, stimulate
10 trigger off
11 set in motion

acumen
03 wit
05 sense
06 wisdom
07 insight
08 gumption, keenness, sagacity, sapience
09 ingenuity, intuition, judgement
10 astuteness, cleverness, perception, shrewdness
11 discernment, penetration, percipience, perspicuity
12 intelligence, perspicacity
13 judiciousness

acute
04 keen
05 grave, sharp, smart, vital

06 astute, clever, severe, shrewd, urgent
07 crucial, extreme, intense, sapient, serious, violent
08 critical, decisive, incisive
09 dangerous, judicious, observant, sensitive
10 discerning, insightful, perceptive, percipient
11 distressing, penetrating
13 perspicacious

acutely
06 keenly
07 gravely, sharply
08 strongly
09 extremely, intensely

adage
03 saw
05 axiom, maxim
06 byword, saying
07 precept, proverb
08 aphorism, paroemia
10 apophthegm

adamant
03 set
04 firm, hard
05 fixed, rigid, stiff, tough
08 obdurate, resolute, stubborn
09 immovable, insistent, unbending
10 determined, inflexible, unshakable, unyielding
12 intransigent

adapt
03 fit
04 suit
05 alter, match, shape
06 adjust, change, comply, modify, tailor
07 conform, convert, prepare, qualify, remodel
09 customize, harmonize

adaptable
07 plastic
08 amenable, flexible, variable
09 alterable, compliant, easy-going, malleable, versatile
10 adjustable, changeable
11 conformable, convertible

adaptation
05 shift
06 change
07 fitting, shaping
08 matching, revision
09 refitting, reshaping, reworking, variation
10 adjustment, alteration, conversion
11 habituation, remodelling
12 modification, refashioning

13 accommodation
15 acclimatization

add
05 affix, annex, count, put in, put on, tot up, total
06 adjoin, append, attach, tack on
07 augment, build on, combine, count up, include
08 increase
10 supplement

❑**add up**
03 add, fit
04 mean
05 count, spell, tally, total
06 amount, come to, reckon
07 compute, include, signify
08 indicate, ring true
09 calculate, make sense
10 constitute
11 add together
12 hang together
13 stand to reason

added
03 new
04 more
05 extra, fresh, spare
07 adjunct, another, further
10 additional
13 supplementary

addendum
07 adjunct, allonge, codicil
08 addition, appendix
09 appendage
10 attachment, postscript, supplement
11 endorsement
12 augmentation

addict
03 fan
04 buff, head, user
05 fiend, freak
06 junkie
07 devotee, tripper
08 adherent, follower
09 dope-fiend, drug taker, mainliner
10 enthusiast

addicted
04 fond
06 hooked
07 devoted
08 obsessed
09 dependent

addiction
05 habit, mania
06 monkey
07 craving
09 obsession
10 dependence

addition
04 gain
05 extra, rider
06 adding, annexe
07 adjunct
08 addendum, additive, appendix, increase
09 accession, accretion, appendage, extension, increment, reckoning, totalling
10 annexation, attachment, increasing, postscript, supplement
11 computation, enlargement
12 afterthought, appurtenance

❑**in addition**
03 too
04 also
06 as well
07 besides, further
08 moreover
11 furthermore
12 not to mention, over and above
14 into the bargain

additional
03 new
04 more
05 extra, fresh, other, spare
07 another, further
09 increased
10 excrescent
12 adscititious, adventitious, supervenient
13 supplementary

additionally
03 too
04 also
06 as well
07 besides, further
08 moreover
10 in addition
11 furthermore
12 over and above
14 for good measure, into the bargain

additive
05 extra
10 supplement
12 preservative

addled
07 mixed-up, muddled
08 confused
09 befuddled, flustered, perplexed
10 bewildered

address
04 call, flat, home, send, talk
05 abode, house, orate

06 sermon, speech
07 lecture, lodging, oration, speak to, welcome, write to
08 diatribe, greeting, location
09 discourse, monologue, philippic, sermonize, situation, soliloquy
10 apostrophe, directions, invocation, salutation
11 communicate
12 disquisition, dissertation
13 poste restante

□ address (yourself) to
07 focus on
08 deal with, engage in
09 undertake
10 take care of
13 concentrate on

adduce
04 cite
07 mention, present, proffer, refer to
08 allude to, evidence, point out
10 put forward

adept
04 able, deft, good
05 handy, sharp
06 adroit, clever, expert, nimble, versed, wizard
07 capable, dab hand, maestro, skilled
08 hot stuff, masterly, polished
09 competent, practised
10 proficient
11 experienced, nobody's fool
12 accomplished

adequacy
07 ability, fitness
08 fairness
10 capability, competence, mediocrity
11 passability, sufficiency, suitability
12 tolerability
13 acceptability

adequate
02 OK
03 fit
06 enough, patchy, will do
07 average, capable
08 all right, passable, suitable
09 competent, tolerable
10 acceptable, reasonable, sufficient
12 commensurate, run of the mill, satisfactory
13 unexceptional

adhere
03 fix

04 glue, grip, heed, hold, join, keep, link, obey
05 cling, paste, stick
06 attach, cement, cohere, defend, fasten, follow, fulfil
07 abide by, espouse, observe, respect, stand by, support
08 cleave to, coalesce
10 comply with

adherent
03 fan, nut
04 buff
05 freak
06 votary
07 admirer, devotee, sectary
08 advocate, disciple, follower, hanger-on, partisan
09 satellite, supporter
10 aficionado, enthusiast

adhesion
04 bond, grip
08 cohesion
10 attachment

adhesive
03 gum
04 glue, tape
05 gluey, gummy, paste, tacky
06 cement, gummed, sticky
07 Blue-tak®, holding
08 clinging, cohesive, fixative, mucilage, sticking
09 attaching, glutinous, Sellotape®, Superglue®
10 sticky tape
12 mucilaginous

adieu
06 cheers
07 cheerio, goodbye
08 au revoir, farewell
11 leave-taking, valediction, valedictory

adjacent
04 near, next, nigh
05 close
06 beside
07 closest, nearest, vicinal
08 abutting, next-door
09 adjoining, alongside, bordering, proximate
10 contiguous, juxtaposed
12 conterminous, neighbouring

adjoin
03 add
04 abut, join, link, meet
05 annex, unite, verge
06 append, attach, border
07 combine, connect
09 juxtapose, neighbour
12 interconnect

adjoining
04 near, next
07 joining, linking, uniting, verging, vicinal
08 abutting, adjacent, next door
09 bordering, combining, impinging, proximate
10 conjoining, connecting, contiguous, juxtaposed
12 neighbouring

adjourn
04 stay
05 defer, delay, pause
06 put off, repair, retire
07 suspend
08 break off, postpone, prorogue, withdraw
09 interrupt
11 discontinue

adjournment
04 stay
05 break, delay, pause
06 recess
08 deferral, interval
09 deferment
10 putting-off, suspension
11 dissolution, prorogation
12 intermission, interruption, postponement
15 discontinuation

adjudicate
05 judge
06 decide, settle, umpire
07 adjudge, referee
09 arbitrate

adjust
03 fit, fix, set
04 suit, tune
05 adapt, align, alter, amend, coapt, shape, tweak
06 change, modify, repair, revise, settle, square, temper
07 arrange, compose, convert, rectify, remodel, reshape
08 fine-tune, regulate
09 harmonize, refashion
11 accommodate

adjustable
07 movable
08 flexible
09 adaptable
11 convertible

adjustment
06 change, fixing, tuning
07 fitting, setting, shaping
08 ordering, revision
09 amendment, arranging
10 adaptation, alteration, conversion, regulation

11 arrangement, habituation, orientation, rearranging, remodelling
12 modification
13 accommodation, rearrangement
15 acclimatization

ad-lib
06 invent, made-up, make up
09 extempore, impromptu, improvise
10 improvised, off the cuff, unprepared
11 extemporize, unrehearsed

administer
03 run
04 give, head, lead, rule
05 anele, apply
06 direct, govern, impose, manage, supply
07 adhibit, conduct, control, dole out, execute, give out, mete out, oversee, provide
08 disburse, dispense, organize, regulate
09 officiate, supervise
10 distribute, measure out
11 preside over, superintend

administration
06 regime, ruling
07 control, red tape, running
08 ministry
09 direction, execution, executive, governing, paperwork
10 government, leadership, management, overseeing
11 supervision
12 term of office
13 governing body
15 superintendence

administrative
09 executive
10 management, managerial, regulatory
11 directorial, legislative, supervisory
12 governmental
13 authoritative, gubernatorial
14 organizational

► *Types of administrative area*:
04 area, city, town, ward
05 shire, state
06 county, parish, region, sector
07 borough, enclave, village
08 district, division, precinct, province
09 territory
12 constituency

administrator
04 boss, head
05 chief, ruler
06 leader
07 manager, trustee
08 chairman, director, governor, guardian, overseer
09 custodian, executive, organizer, president
10 controller, supervisor
14 chief executive, superintendent

admirable
04 fine, rare
06 choice, worthy
08 laudable, masterly, superior
09 deserving, estimable, excellent, exquisite
10 creditable
11 commendable, meritorious
12 praiseworthy

admiration
03 yen
05 kudos
06 esteem, fureur, praise, regard, wonder
07 delight, idolism, respect, worship
08 approval, pleasure, surprise
09 adulation, affection, amazement, reverence
10 veneration
11 approbation
12 appreciation, astonishment

admire
04 laud, like
05 adore, prize, value
06 esteem, praise, revere
07 applaud, approve, iconize, idolize, respect, worship
08 look up to, venerate
09 approve of
11 hero-worship
14 put on a pedestal
15 think the world of

admirer
03 fan
04 beau, buff
05 fiend, freak, lover, wooer
06 suitor
07 devotee, gallant
08 adherent, disciple, follower, idolater, idolizer
09 boyfriend, supporter
10 aficionado, enthusiast, girlfriend, sweetheart

admissible
05 licit
06 lawful
07 allowed

08 passable
09 allowable, permitted, tolerable, tolerated
10 acceptable, legitimate
11 justifiable, permissible

admission
06 access, avowal, exposé
07 ingress, peccavi
08 entrance, mea culpa
09 allowance
10 acceptance, concession, confession, disclosure, divulgence, revelation
11 affirmation, declaration, entrance fee, recognition
15 acknowledgement

admit
05 agree, allow, grant, let in, own up
06 accept, affirm, reveal, take in
07 concede, confess, declare, divulge, profess, receive
08 disclose, initiate, intromit
09 come clean, recognize
11 acknowledge

admittance
05 entry
06 access
07 ingress
08 entrance
09 letting in, reception
10 acceptance, initiation
12 introduction, right of entry
13 right of access

admixture
03 mix
05 alloy, blend
06 fusion
07 amalgam
08 compound, tincture
11 combination
12 amalgamation

admonish
04 warn
05 chide, scold
06 berate, exhort, rebuke
07 censure, correct, counsel, reprove, tell off, upbraid
09 reprimand
10 discipline

admonition
06 rebuke
07 censure, counsel, reproof, warning
08 berating, scolding
09 reprimand
10 correction, telling-off
11 exhortation
12 reprehension

adolescence

05 teens, youth
07 boyhood, puberty
08 girlhood, minority
10 boyishness, immaturity, juvenility, pubescence
11 development, girlishness
12 juvenescence, teenage years, youthfulness

adolescent

05 minor, young, youth
06 boyish, neanic
07 girlish, puerile, teenage
08 childish, immature, juvenile, teenager, youthful
09 pubescent
10 developing, young adult
11 juvenescent, young person

adopt

04 back
06 accept, assume, choose, follow, foster, ratify, select, take in, take on, take up
07 approve, embrace, endorse, espouse, support
08 maintain, nominate

adoption

06 choice
07 backing, support
08 approval, espousal, taking-in, taking-on, taking-up
09 embracing, fostering
10 acceptance
11 approbation, embracement, endorsement
12 ratification

adorable

04 dear
05 sweet
07 darling, lovable, winsome
08 charming, fetching, pleasing, precious
09 appealing, wonderful
10 attractive, bewitching, delightful, enchanting
11 captivating

adoration

04 love
06 esteem, homage, praise, regard
07 worship
08 devotion, doting on
09 reverence
10 admiration, exaltation, idolizaton, veneration
13 glorification, magnification

adore

04 love
06 admire, dote on, esteem, honour, relish, revere

07 cherish, worship
08 hold dear, venerate
11 be devoted to, be partial to
15 think the world of

adorn

04 deck, gild, trim
05 array, begem, crown, grace
06 bedeck, doll up, tart up
07 adonize, apparel, bedight, bedizen, bejewel, bestick, enhance, festoon, furbish, garnish, impearl, miniate
08 beautify, decorate, emblazon, ornament
09 embellish

adornment

05 frill
06 fallal
07 falbala, figgery, flounce, garnish, gilding
08 frippery, furbelow, ornament
09 accessory, fallalery, jewellery, trappings, trimmings
10 decoration, enrichment
11 bedizenment
13 embellishment, ornamentation

adrift

05 at sea
07 aimless
08 goalless, insecure
09 off course, unsettled
10 anchorless
13 directionless

adroit

04 able, deft
05 adept
06 clever, expert
07 skilful
09 dexterous, masterful
10 proficient

adroitness

05 skill
07 ability, finesse, mastery
08 deftness, facility
09 adeptness, dexterity, expertise
10 cleverness, competence
11 proficiency, skilfulness

adulation

06 praise
07 fawning
08 flattery
10 sycophancy
11 hero worship, idolization
12 blandishment

adulatory

07 fawning, fulsome, servile
08 praising, unctuous
10 flattering, obsequious
11 blandishing, bootlicking, sycophantic

adult

04 ripe
05 of age
06 mature
07 ephebic, grown-up, obscene, ripened
09 developed, full-grown
12 pornographic

adulterate

05 taint
06 debase, defile, dilute, weaken
07 corrupt, degrade, devalue, pollute, vitiate
09 attenuate, water down
10 bastardize, make impure
11 contaminate, deteriorate

adultery

06 affair
08 cheating
10 infidelity, unchastity
13 a bit on the side, playing around
14 unfaithfulness
15 playing the field

advance

03 pay
04 cite, give, grow, help, lend, loan, step
05 offer, speed
06 adduce, allege, assist, credit, foster, growth, hasten, move on, submit, supply
07 benefit, deposit, forward, furnish, further, go ahead, headway, present, proceed, proffer, promote, provide, suggest, support, upgrade
08 expedite, increase, progress
10 accelerate, betterment, facilitate, prepayment
11 advancement, development, down payment, furtherance, improvement, progression
12 amelioration, breakthrough, make progress

◻in advance

05 ahead, early
06 sooner
07 earlier, up front
09 in the lead
10 beforehand, previously

advanced
05 ahead
06 hi-tech, higher
07 complex, forward, leading
08 foremost, up-to-date
10 avant-garde, precocious
11 progressive, ultra-modern
13 sophisticated,
state-of-the-art
15 ahead of the times

advancement
04 gain, rise
06 growth
07 advance, headway
08 progress
09 promotion
10 betterment, preferment
11 development, furtherance,
improvement

advances
05 moves
09 addresses, overtures
10 approaches, attentions
11 proposition

advantage
03 aid, pro, use
04 boon, edge, gain, good,
help, lead, plus, sway
05 asset, avail, fruit
06 beauty, pay-off, profit, virtue
07 benefit, service
08 blessing, interest, leverage
09 dominance, head start, plus
point, upper hand
10 assistance, precedence
11 convenience,
pre-eminence, superiority

advantageous
06 useful
07 gainful, helpful
08 valuable
09 of service, opportune,
rewarding
10 beneficial, convenient,
favourable, profitable,
propitious, worthwhile
11 furthersome
12 of assistance, remunerative

advent
04 dawn
05 birth, onset
06 coming
07 arrival
08 approach, entrance
09 beginning, inception
10 appearance, occurrence
12 introduction

adventure
04 risk
05 peril
06 chance, danger, hazard
07 exploit, romance, venture
08 incident
10 enterprise, excitement,
experience, occurrence
11 speculation, undertaking

adventurer
04 hero
07 heroine, voyager
08 venturer, wanderer
09 traveller

adventurous
04 bold, rash
05 gutsy, risky
06 daring, spunky
08 exciting, intrepid, perilous,
reckless, romantic
09 audacious, dangerous,
hazardous, impetuous
10 headstrong
11 venturesome

adversary
03 foe
05 enemy, rival
07 opposer
08 attacker, opponent
09 assailant
10 antagonist, competitor

adverse
07 counter, harmful, hostile,
hurtful, unlucky
08 contrary, negative,
opposing, untoward
09 injurious
10 unfriendly
11 conflicting, detrimental,
inexpedient, inopportune,
uncongenial, unfortunate
12 antagonistic, inauspicious,
unfavourable, unpropitious
15 disadvantageous

adversity
03 woe
05 trial
06 misery, sorrow
07 bad luck, ill luck, trouble
08 calamity, disaster, distress,
hardship
09 hard times, suffering
10 affliction, misfortune
11 catastrophe, tribulation
12 wretchedness

advertise
04 hype, plug, push, sell, tout
06 inform, market, notify,
praise
07 display, promote, publish
08 announce, proclaim
09 broadcast, make known,
publicize
10 make public, promulgate
11 merchandise

advertisement
02 ad
04 bill, hype, plug
05 blurb
06 advert, jingle, notice, poster
07 display, handout, leaflet,
placard, trailer
08 circular, handbill
09 marketing, promotion,
publicity
10 commercial, propaganda

advice
03 tip
04 help, view, word
06 notice, wisdom
07 caution, counsel, warning
08 guidance
09 direction
10 injunction, suggestion
11 counselling, dos and don'ts,
information, instruction
14 recommendation

advisability
06 wisdom
07 aptness
08 prudence
09 soundness
10 expediency
11 suitability
12 desirability
13 judiciousness
15 appropriateness

advisable
03 apt, fit
04 best, wise
05 sound
06 proper, wisest
07 correct, fitting, politic,
prudent
08 sensible, suitable
09 desirable, judicious
10 beneficial, profitable
11 appropriate, recommended

advise
04 tell, urge, warn
05 guide, teach, tutor
06 enjoin, inform, notify, report
07 apprise, caution, commend,
counsel, suggest
08 acquaint, forewarn, instruct
09 make known, recommend

adviser
04 aide, guru
05 coach, guide, tutor
06 helper, lawyer, mentor
07 counsel, teacher
09 authority, confidant

10 confidante, consultant, counsellor, instructor

advisory
07 helping
08 advising
10 consulting
11 counselling
12 recommending

advocacy
07 backing, defence, support
08 adoption, espousal, proposal
09 patronage, promotion, upholding
11 advancement, campaigning, championing, propagation
12 promulgation
13 encouragement, justification
14 recommendation

advocate
04 back, urge
05 adopt, be pro, lobby
06 advise, back up, defend, favour, lawyer, uphold
07 counsel, endorse, espouse, justify, pleader, promote, propose, speaker, support
08 argue for, attorney, be behind, champion, defender, exponent, plead for, promoter, upholder
09 barrister, believe in, encourage, proponent, recommend, supporter
10 campaigner, vindicator
11 countenance
12 spokesperson

aegis
04 wing
06 favour
07 backing, support
08 advocacy, auspices
09 patronage
11 sponsorship
12 championship, guardianship

affability
06 warmth
08 courtesy, mildness
09 benignity, geniality
10 amiability, cordiality, good humour, kindliness
11 amicability, benevolence, sociability
12 congeniality, friendliness, obligingness, pleasantness
15 approachability

affable
04 mild, open, warm

06 genial, kindly
07 amiable, cordial
08 amicable, friendly, gracious, obliging, pleasant, sociable
09 agreeable, congenial
10 benevolent
12 approachable, good-humoured

affair
05 amour, event, fling, topic
06 matter
07 concern, episode, liaison, project, romance, subject
08 activity, business, incident, interest, intrigue, question
09 happening, operation
11 transaction, undertaking
12 circumstance, relationship
14 responsibility

affect
04 fake, move, sham, sway
05 act on, adopt, alter, feign, put on, touch, upset
06 assume, attack, change, impact, modify, strike
07 concern, disturb, imitate, involve, perturb, pretend, profess, trouble
08 bear upon, interest, overcome, relate to, simulate
09 influence, transform
11 counterfeit, impinge upon

affectation
03 act
04 airs, pose, sham, show
06 façade
08 pretence
09 imitation, mannerism
10 appearance, simulation
11 insincerity, theatricism
13 airs and graces, artificiality
15 pretentiousness

affected
04 fake, sham, twee
05 put-on, stiff
06 la-di-da, phoney
07 assumed, feigned, minikin, pompous, studied
08 literose, mannered, precious
09 contrived, insincere, simulated, unnatural
10 artificial
11 counterfeit, pretentious

affecting
03 sad
06 moving
07 piteous, pitiful
08 pathetic, pitiable, poignant, stirring, touching

affection
04 care, love
05 amity
06 desire, favour, warmth
07 feeling, passion
08 devotion, fondness, kindness, penchant
10 attachment, partiality, proclivity, propensity, tenderness
11 inclination
12 friendliness, predilection
14 predisposition

affectionate
04 fond, kind, warm
06 caring, loving, tender
07 amiable, cordial, devoted
08 attached, friendly
11 warm-hearted

affiliate
04 ally, join
05 annex, merge, unite
07 combine, conjoin, connect
09 associate, syndicate
10 amalgamate
11 confederate, incorporate

affiliation
03 tie
04 bond, link
05 union
06 league, merger
07 joining
08 alliance
09 coalition
10 connection, federation, membership
11 association, combination
12 amalgamation, relationship

affinity
04 bond
06 liking
07 analogy, rapport
08 fondness, likeness
09 chemistry, good terms
10 attraction, partiality, propensity, similarity
11 resemblance
13 comparability, compatibility

affirm
04 aver, avow
05 state, swear
06 assert, attest, avouch, ratify
07 certify, confirm, declare, endorse, testify, witness
10 asseverate
11 corroborate

affirmation
04 oath
06 avowal
07 witness

08 averment
09 assertion, statement, testimony
10 affirmance, avouchment, deposition
11 attestation, declaration, endorsement
12 asseveration, confirmation, ratification
13 certification, corroboration

affirmative
08 agreeing, emphatic, positive
09 approving, assenting
10 concurring, confirming
13 corroborative

affix
03 add, tag
04 bind, glue, join, tack
05 annex, paste, pin on, stick
06 append, attach, fasten
07 connect

afflict
03 try
04 harm, hurt, pain
05 beset, smite, visit, wound
06 burden, grieve, harass, plague, strike
07 oppress, torment, trouble
08 distress

affliction
03 woe
04 pain
05 cross, curse, grief, trial
06 ordeal, plague, sorrow
07 disease, illness, trouble
08 calamity, disaster, distress, hardship, sickness
09 adversity, suffering
10 depression, misfortune
11 tribulation

affluence
06 plenty, riches, wealth
07 fortune, tidy sum
08 opulence, property
09 abundance, profusion
10 prosperity

affluent
04 rich
05 flush
06 loaded
07 moneyed, opulent, wealthy, well-off
08 well-to-do
10 in the money, prosperous, well-heeled
11 comfortable, rolling in it

afford
04 bear, give
05 allow, grant, offer, spare

06 impart, manage, pay for
07 furnish, produce, provide

affray
05 brawl, brush, fight, melee, scrap, set-to
06 fracas, tussle
07 quarrel, scuffle, wrangle
08 skirmish, squabble
10 fisticuffs, free-for-all

affront
03 vex
04 slur, snub
05 anger, annoy, pique, wrong
06 injury, insult, offend, slight
07 incense, outrage, provoke
08 irritate, rudeness, vexation
09 aspersion, indignity
10 disrespect
11 discourtesy, provocation
13 slap in the face
14 kick in the teeth

afoot
05 about, astir
06 abroad, around
07 brewing, current
08 in the air
13 in the pipeline

afraid
05 sorry
06 aghast , scared, yellow
09 concerned, regretful, tremulous
10 frightened

afresh
04 anew
05 again, newly

after
07 owing to
09 because of, following
10 in honour of
11 as a result of

aftermath
04 wake
06 upshot
07 effects, outcome, results
12 after-effects, consequences
13 repercussions

afterwards
04 next, then
05 later
12 subsequently

again
04 anew
06 afresh, encore
08 once more
11 one more time

❏**again and again**
10 constantly, repeatedly

11 continually
12 time and again

against
02 on
04 anti
06 facing, versus
08 abutting, fronting, opposing, touching
09 close up to, hostile to, opposed to, resisting
10 adjacent to, opposite to

age
03 day, era
04 aeon, date, days, span, time
05 epoch, ripen, years
06 dotage, grow up, mature, mellow, old age, period, season, wither
07 decline, grow old
08 duration, maturity, senility
09 seniority
10 generation, senescence
11 decrepitude, elderliness

aged
03 old
04 grey
05 hoary
06 ageing, past it
07 ancient, doddery, elderly
08 advanced
09 geriatric, senescent
11 over the hill, patriarchal
13 superannuated
15 no spring chicken

agency
04 firm, work
05 force, means, power
06 action, bureau, effect, medium, office
07 company
08 activity, business, workings
09 influence, operation
12 intervention, organization

agenda
04 list, menu, plan
05 diary
08 calendar, schedule
09 programme, timetable

agent
03 rep, spy
04 doer, mole
05 cause, envoy, force, means, mover, proxy
06 agency, broker, deputy, factor, worker
07 channel, trustee, vehicle
08 assignee, delegate, emissary, minister, operator
09 go-between, middleman, operative, performer

10 instrument, negotiator
12 intermediary
14 representative

agglomeration
05 store
07 build-up
08 increase
09 aggregate, gathering
11 aggregation
12 accumulation

aggrandize
05 exalt, widen
06 enrich
07 amplify, elevate, enhance, enlarge, ennoble, glorify, inflate, magnify, promote
09 glamorize
10 exaggerate, make richer

aggravate
03 irk, try, vex
05 annoy, tease
06 harass, needle, pester, worsen
07 inflame, magnify, provoke
08 compound, heighten, increase, irritate
09 intensify, make worse
10 exacerbate, exasperate

aggravation
06 hassle
08 vexation
09 annoyance
10 irritation
11 irksomeness, provocation
15 thorn in the flesh

aggregate
03 sum
05 total, whole
08 entirety, sum total, totality
10 collection, grand total
11 combination
12 accumulation

aggression
06 attack, injury, strike
07 assault, offence
08 invasion
09 hostility, incursion, intrusion, militancy, offensive, onslaught, pugnacity
10 antagonism
11 bellicosity, provocation
12 belligerence
13 combativeness

aggressive
04 bold
05 pushy
06 brutal, savage
07 go-ahead, hostile, zealous
08 forceful, vigorous

09 assertive, cut-throat, ferocious, offensive
10 in-your-face, pugnacious
11 belligerent, provocative, quarrelsome
13 argumentative

aggressor
07 invader
08 attacker, intruder, offender
09 assailant, assaulter

aggrieved
04 hurt
05 upset
06 bitter, pained
07 ill-used, unhappy, wronged
08 offended, saddened
09 resentful
10 distressed, maltreated

aghast
06 amazed
07 shocked, stunned
08 appalled, dismayed, startled
09 astounded, stupefied
10 astonished, confounded

agile
04 spry
05 acute, alert, brisk, fleet, lithe, quick, sharp, swift
06 active, astute, clever, limber, lisson, mobile, nimble
07 lissome
08 athletic, flexible
09 sprightly

agility
08 mobility
09 alertness, quickness, sharpness, swiftness
10 astuteness, nimbleness
11 flexibility

agitate
04 beat, rock, stir, toss
05 argue, churn, fight, rouse, shake, upset, whisk, worry
06 arouse, excite, flurry, incite, rattle, ruffle, stir up, work up
07 disturb, ferment, fluster, perturb, trouble, unnerve
08 campaign, disquiet, unsettle
10 discompose, disconcert

agitated
05 upset
07 anxious, nervous, worried
08 troubled, unnerved
09 disturbed, flustered, in a lather, unsettled
10 distraught
12 disconcerted

agitator
07 inciter, stirrer

08 activist, fomenter
09 firebrand
10 instigator, subversive
12 rabble-rouser, troublemaker

agnostic
07 doubter, sceptic
10 unbeliever

ago
04 gone, past
05 since
07 earlier
10 previously

agog
04 avid, keen
05 eager
07 curious, excited
09 impatient
10 enthralled, in suspense
13 on tenterhooks

agonize
05 worry
06 labour, strain, strive
07 trouble, wrestle
08 struggle

agonizing
07 painful, racking
08 worrying
09 harrowing, torturous
10 tormenting
11 distressing
12 excruciating

agony
03 woe
04 hurt, pain
05 spasm
06 misery, throes
07 anguish, torment, torture
08 distress
09 suffering
10 affliction

agree
04 suit
05 admit, allow, get on, grant, match, tally, yield
06 accede, accept, accord, assent, comply, concur, go with, permit, settle
07 be at one, concede, conform, consent
08 say yes to
10 compromise, correspond
11 be of one mind, go along with, rubber-stamp, see eye to eye

agreeable
04 fine, nice
07 likable, willing
08 amenable, amicable, charming, friendly, pleasant

09 compliant, congenial,
   enjoyable
10 acceptable, attractive
11 good-natured, sympathetic

agreement
04 deal, deed, pact
05 tally, union
06 accord, assent, treaty
07 bargain, compact, concord,
   fitting, harmony
08 affinity, contract, covenant,
   matching, sympathy
09 concordat, consensus,
   indenture, unanimity
10 conformity, consonance,
   settlement, similarity
11 arrangement, concurrence,
   consistency
12 complaisance
13 compatibility, understanding
➤ See also **treaty**

agricultural
05 rural
07 bucolic, farming, georgic
08 agrarian, geoponic, pastoral,
   praedial

▬ *Types of agricultural
equipment*:
03 ATV, axe, hoe, saw
04 fork, rake
05 baler, drill, mower, spade
06 harrow, plough, scythe,
   shovel, sickle
07 hayfork, tractor, trailer
08 chainsaw
09 harvester, pitchfork,
   Rotovator®, seed drill,
   whetstone
10 cultivator
11 hedgecutter, reaping hook,
   wheelbarrow
12 muckspreader, slurry tanker
13 fork-lift truck
14 milking machine

agriculture
07 farming, tillage
08 agronomy
09 geoponics, husbandry

▬ *Names of agriculturists*:
04 **Coke** (Thomas William),
   Tull (Jethro)
05 **Lawes** (Sir John Bennet),
   Young (Arthur)
06 **Carver** (George
   Washington)
07 **Burbank** (Luther)
08 **Bakewell** (Robert)

aground
05 stuck
06 ashore

07 beached, wrecked
08 grounded, stranded
09 foundered
10 high and dry, on the rocks

ahead
06 before, onward
07 forward, in front, leading
08 advanced, superior
09 earlier on, in advance, in the
   lead, to the fore

aid
04 ease, gift, hand, help, prop
05 boost, grant, serve
06 a leg up, assist, backup,
   oblige, relief, second
07 benefit, funding, promote,
   service, speed up, subsidy,
   succour, support, sustain
08 donation, expedite
09 encourage, patronage,
   subsidize
10 assistance, facilitate, rally
   round, subvention
11 accommodate, helping
   hand, sponsorship
12 contribution
13 a shot in the arm

aide
07 adviser, attaché
08 adjutant, advocate
09 assistant, confidant
12 right-hand man

ail
04 fail, pain
05 upset, worry
06 bother, sicken, weaken
07 afflict, trouble
08 distress, irritate

ailing
03 ill
04 sick, weak
05 frail, unfit
06 feeble, infirm, poorly, sickly,
   unwell
07 failing, invalid, unsound
09 off-colour, suffering
10 indisposed, out of sorts
15 under the weather

ailment
06 malady
07 disease, illness
08 disorder, sickness, weakness
09 complaint, infirmity
10 affliction, disability
13 indisposition

aim
03 end, try
04 goal, hope, mark, mean,
   plan, seek, want, wish

05 level, point, sight, train
06 aspire, course, design,
   desire, direct, intend,
   motive, strive, target
07 attempt, mission, propose,
   purpose, resolve, shoot at
08 ambition, zero in on
09 direction, endeavour,
   intention, objective
10 aspiration

aimless
05 stray
06 chance, futile, random
07 erratic, wayward
08 drifting, goalless, rambling
09 haphazard, pointless,
   unsettled, wandering
10 irresolute, undirected
11 purposeless, unmotivated
13 directionless, unpredictable

air
03 sky
04 aura, look, waft, wind
05 blast, ether, state, utter, voice
06 aerate, aerial, breath,
   breeze, effect, manner,
   oxygen, zephyr
07 bearing, declare, draught,
   express, freshen, heavens
08 ambience, carriage
09 demeanour, make known,
   publicize, ventilate
10 appearance, atmosphere,
   impression, make public
11 communicate, disseminate

aircraft
▬ *Types of aircraft*:
03 jet, mig
04 kite, STOL, VTOL
05 blimp, jumbo, plane
06 Airbus®, Boeing, bomber,
   Fokker, glider
07 airship, balloon, biplane,
   Chinook, chopper, fighter,
   jump-jet, Tornado
08 airliner, Concorde, jumbo
   jet, sea-plane, Spitfire, spy
   plane, warplane, zeppelin
09 aeroplane, delta-wing,
   dirigible, Hurricane,
   Lancaster, monoplane
10 dive-bomber, hang-glider,
   helicopter, microlight
12 Sopwith Camel
13 Messerschmitt,
   hot-air balloon
➤ See also **vehicle**

▬ *Parts of an aircraft include*:
04 hood, wing
06 canopy, rudder

07 aileron, ammeter, cockpit,
  tail fin
08 fuselage
09 altimeter, propeller,
  tailplane
11 landing flap, landing gear,
  vertical fin
12 control stick, radio compass,
  rudder pedals
13 control column
15 magnetic compass

airing

07 voicing
08 aeration, exposure, uttering
09 broadcast, statement
10 disclosure, divulgence,
  expression, freshening
11 circulation, declaration,
  publication, ventilation

airless

05 close, heavy, muggy
06 stuffy, sultry
08 stifling
10 oppressive
11 suffocating

airport

➤ *Names of international*
airports:
03 JFK, Zia
05 McCoy, O'Hare
06 Changi, Dulles, Midway
07 Ataturk, Bradley, Entebbe,
  Gatwick, Hopkins, Lincoln,
  Lubbock, Roberts, Schipol
08 Ciampino, El Dorado, G
  Marconi, Heathrow, Jan
  Smuts, Sangster
09 Ben Gurion, Charleroi,
  Fiumicino, J F Kennedy,
  Jose Marti, Lindbergh,
  Marco Polo
10 Golden Rock, Hellenikon,
  King Khaled, Louis Botha,
  Sky Harbour
11 Capodichino, Jorge Chavez,
  Las Americas, Ninoy
  Aquino, Pointe Noire, Tito
  Menniti
12 Benito Juarez, Berline-Tegel,
  Hancock Field, Indira
  Gandhi, Jomo Kenyatta,
  Norman Manley, Queen
  Beatrix, Simon Bolivar
13 Château Bougon, Chiang
  Kai Shek
15 Charles de Gaulle, Galileo
  Galilei, Leonardo da Vinci

airs

05 swank
06 posing

07 hauteur
09 arrogance, pomposity
11 affectation, pretensions
12 affectedness

airtight

06 closed, sealed
11 impermeable
12 impenetrable, tight-fitting

airy

04 open
05 blowy, gusty, happy, roomy
06 breezy, casual, jaunty, lively
07 offhand
08 cheerful, draughty, spacious
10 nonchalant
12 high-spirited, light-hearted
14 well-ventilated

aisle

04 lane, path
07 gangway, passage, walkway
08 alleyway, corridor
10 passageway

alarm

04 bell, fear
05 alert, daunt, panic, scare,
  shock, siren
06 dismay, fright, horror, rattle,
  terror, tocsin
07 agitate, anxiety, perturb,
  startle, terrify, unnerve,
  warning
08 affright, distress, frighten
09 alarm-bell
10 make afraid, uneasiness
11 nervousness, trepidation
12 apprehension, perturbation,
  put the wind up
13 consternation
14 distress signal

alarming

05 scary
07 ominous
08 daunting, dreadful,
  shocking, worrying
09 dismaying, startling,
  unnerving
10 disturbing, perturbing,
  terrifying
11 distressing, frightening,
  threatening

alarmist

09 pessimist
11 doomwatcher, scaremonger

alcohol

05 booze, drink
06 liquor
07 spirits
09 fire-water, hard stuff, the
  bottle

10 intoxicant, stiff drink
12 Dutch courage
➤ See also **drink**

alcoholic

04 hard, lush, soak, wino
05 alkie, dipso, drunk, toper
06 ardent, boozer, strong
07 drinker, tippler
08 drunkard
09 distilled, inebriate
11 dipsomaniac, inebriating
12 heavy drinker, intoxicating

alcove

03 bay
04 nook
05 booth, niche
06 carrel, corner, recess
07 cubicle
09 cubbyhole

alert

04 warn, wary
05 agile, alarm, awake, brisk,
  quick, ready
06 active, inform, lively, nimble,
  notify, signal, tip off
07 careful, heedful, qui vive
08 forewarn, prepared, spirited,
  vigilant, watchful
09 attentive, observant, on the
  ball, wide-awake
10 on your toes, perceptive
11 circumspect, sharp-witted
12 on the lookout

algae

➤ *Types of algae and lichen*:
04 kelp
05 dulse, fucus, laver, wrack
06 desmid, diatom, nostoc
07 oak moss, oarweed,
  redware, sea lace, seaware
08 bull kelp, conferva,
  gulfweed, lecanora,
  rockweed, sea wrack
09 chlorella, Irish moss, rock
  tripe, sargassum, sea tangle,
  spirogyra, stonewort
10 Ceylon moss, sea lettuce
12 bladderwrack
➤ See also **plant**

alias

03 aka
06 anonym
07 allonym, pen name
08 formerly, nickname
09 pseudonym, sobriquet,
  stage name
10 also called, nom de plume
11 also known as, assumed
  name, nom de guerre

alibi
05 story
06 excuse, reason
07 cover-up, defence, pretext
11 explanation
13 justification

alien
06 exotic, remote
07 foreign, opposed, strange
08 newcomer, outsider,
    stranger
09 foreigner, immigrant
10 outlandish, unfamiliar
11 conflicting, incongruous

alienate
08 estrange, separate, turn
    away
09 disaffect
10 antagonize, set against

alienation
08 disunion
09 isolation, severance
10 remoteness, separation
11 turning away
12 disaffection, estrangement
14 antagonization

alight
03 lit
04 land
05 alive, fiery, lit up, perch
06 ablaze, bright, debark, get
    off, lively, on fire, settle
07 blazing, burning, descend,
    flaming, get down, ignited,
    lighted, radiant, shining
08 come down, dismount
09 disembark, touch down
10 come to rest
11 illuminated

align
04 ally, even, join, side
05 agree, order, range, unite
06 adjust, even up, line up
07 arrange, combine
08 regulate
09 affiliate, associate
10 co-ordinate, join forces,
    regularize, straighten

alignment
04 line
05 order
06 siding
07 ranging
08 alliance, lining up, sympathy
09 agreement
11 affiliation, arrangement,
    association, co-operation

alike
04 akin, even

05 equal
07 cognate, equally, similar,
    the same, uniform
08 in common, parallel
09 analogous, duplicate,
    identical, similarly
10 comparable, equivalent,
    resembling
11 analogously, much the same

alive
05 alert, awake, brisk, vital
06 active, extant, lively, living
07 alert to, animate, aware of,
    vibrant, zestful
08 animated, spirited, vigorous
09 breathing, energetic,
    heedful of, vivacious
10 full of life, having life
11 abounding in, going strong,
    in existence, teeming with
12 crawling with
15 overflowing with

all
03 sum
04 each, full
05 every, fully, total, utter, whole
06 entire, the lot, utmost,
    wholly
07 perfect, totally, utterly
08 complete, entirely, entirety,
    everyone, greatest, outright
09 aggregate, everybody
10 altogether, completely,
    every bit of, everything
12 each and every, universality
13 in its entirety

allay
04 calm, ease
05 blunt, check, quell, quiet
06 lessen, pacify, reduce,
    smooth, soften, soothe
07 compose, mollify, relieve
08 diminish, moderate
09 alleviate

allegation
05 claim
06 avowal, charge
09 assertion, statement,
    testimony
10 accusation, deposition
11 affirmation, declaration
12 asseveration

allege
04 hold
05 claim, state
06 affirm, assert, attest, insist
07 contend, declare, profess
08 maintain
10 put forward

alleged
06 stated
07 claimed, reputed, suspect
08 declared, doubtful, inferred,
    putative, so-called,
    supposed
09 described, professed
10 designated, ostensible

allegiance
04 duty
06 fealty
07 loyalty, support
08 devotion, fidelity
09 adherence, constancy,
    obedience
10 friendship, solidarity
12 faithfulness

allegorical
08 symbolic
09 parabolic
10 emblematic, figurative
11 symbolizing
12 metaphorical
13 significative
14 representative

allegory
04 myth, tale
05 fable, story
06 emblem, legend, symbol
07 analogy, parable
08 apologue, metaphor
09 symbolism

allergic
06 averse
07 hostile, opposed
08 affected
09 sensitive
11 dyspathetic, susceptible
12 antagonistic
14 hypersensitive

allergy
08 aversion, dyspathy
09 antipathy, hostility
10 antagonism, opposition
11 sensitivity
14 susceptibility

alleviate
04 dull, ease
05 abate, allay, check
06 deaden, lessen, reduce,
    soften, soothe, subdue,
    temper
07 assuage, mollify, relieve
08 diminish, mitigate,
    moderate, palliate

alleviation
06 easing, relief
07 dulling
08 soothing

09 abatement, deadening,
   lessening, reduction
10 diminution, mitigation,
   moderation, palliation
11 assuagement
13 mollification

alley
04 gate, lane, mall, road, walk
05 close
06 street
07 passage, pathway
10 back street, passageway

alliance
04 bloc, bond, pact
05 guild, union
06 cartel, league, treaty
07 compact
08 marriage
09 agreement, coalition,
   syndicate
10 connection, consortium,
   federation
11 affiliation, association,
   combination, partnership
12 conglomerate
13 confederation

allied
03 wed
05 bound, joint
06 joined, linked, united
07 coupled, kindred, married,
   related, unified
08 combined, in league
09 connected, in cahoots
10 affiliated, associated
11 amalgamated, hand in glove

allocate
04 mete
05 allot, allow
06 assign, budget, divide, ration
07 earmark, mete out
08 dispense, set aside,
   share out
09 admeasure, apportion,
   designate, parcel out
10 distribute

allocation
03 cut, lot
05 grant, quota, share, stint
06 budget, ration
07 measure, portion
09 allotment, allowance
12 distribution
13 apportionment
14 slice of the cake

allot
04 mete
05 allow, grant
06 assign, budget, divide, ration
07 dole out, earmark

08 allocate, dispense, set aside,
   share out
09 admeasure, apportion,
   designate
10 distribute

allotment
03 lot
04 land
05 grant, quota, share, stint
06 ration
07 measure, portion
08 division
09 allowance, partition
10 allocation, percentage
13 apportionment

all-out
04 full
05 total
06 utmost
07 maximum
08 complete, powerful,
   resolute, thorough, vigorous
09 full-scale, intensive,
   undivided, wholesale
10 determined, exhaustive
13 comprehensive, no-holds-
   barred, thoroughgoing

allow
02 OK
03 let, own
04 give, okay
05 admit, agree, allot, grant
06 afford, assign, enable,
   endure, permit, suffer
07 agree to, approve, concede,
   consent, provide, warrant
08 allocate, sanction, say yes to,
   tolerate
09 apportion, authorize,
   consent to, put up with
11 acknowledge
14 give the go-ahead

□**allow for**
07 foresee, include
08 consider
10 bear in mind
15 take into account

allowable
05 legal, legit, licit
06 lawful
08 all right, approved
10 acceptable, admissible,
   legitimate
11 justifiable, permissible
12 sanctionable

allowance
03 lot
05 grant, quota, share
06 amount, income, ration,
   rebate

07 annuity, benefit, payment,
   pension, portion, stipend
08 discount, expenses
09 deduction, reduction,
   weighting
10 allocation, remittance
11 maintenance,
   pocket money
12 contribution

□**make allowances**
06 excuse, pardon
07 forgive
08 consider
10 bear in mind, keep in mind

alloy
05 blend
06 fusion
07 amalgam, mixture
08 compound
09 admixture, composite
11 coalescence, combination

all right
02 OK
04 fair, safe, well
05 sound, whole
06 secure, unhurt
07 average, healthy
08 adequate, passable,
   passably, suitably, unharmed
09 allowable, uninjured
10 acceptable, acceptably,
   adequately, reasonable,
   reasonably, unimpaired
12 satisfactory
13 appropriately
14 satisfactorily

allude
04 hint
05 imply, infer, refer
06 remark
07 mention, speak of, suggest
08 intimate
09 adumbrate, insinuate,
   touch upon

allure
04 coax, lure
05 charm, tempt
06 appeal, cajole, disarm,
   entice, lead on, seduce
07 attract, beguile, enchant,
   glamour, win over
08 entrance, interest, persuade
09 captivate, fascinate,
   magnetism, seduction
10 attraction, temptation
11 captivation, enchantment,
   fascination

alluring
04 sexy
07 winning

08 arousing, engaging,
   enticing, fetching,
   sensuous, tempting
09 beguiling, desirable,
   seductive
10 attractive, bewitching,
   come-hither, enchanting
11 captivating

allusion
04 hint
06 remark
07 mention
08 citation
09 quotation, reference
10 intimation, suggestion
11 implication, insinuation

ally
04 join, link, side
05 marry, unify, unite
06 friend, helper, team up
07 combine, connect, partner
08 co-worker, sidekick
09 affiliate, associate,
   colleague, supporter
10 accomplice, amalgamate,
   fraternize, join forces
11 collaborate, confederate
12 band together, collaborator

almanac
06 annual
08 calendar, register, yearbook

almighty
05 awful, great
06 severe
07 intense, supreme
08 absolute, enormous,
   terrible
09 desperate
10 invincible, omnipotent
11 all-powerful, plenipotent

almost
05 about, quasi-
06 all but, nearly
07 close on, close to, nearing
08 as good as, well-nigh
09 just about, virtually
10 more or less, not far from,
   pretty much, pretty well
11 approaching, practically
13 approximately

alone
04 only, sole, solo
05 apart
06 lonely, single, unique
07 forlorn, unaided
08 deserted, detached,
   forsaken, isolated,
   separate, solitary
09 abandoned, Jack Jones,
   on your own, on your tod

12 single-handed
13 unaccompanied

aloof
04 cold, cool
06 chilly, formal, offish, remote
07 distant, haughty
08 detached, reserved
10 antisocial, forbidding,
   unfriendly, unsociable
11 indifferent, standoffish
12 inaccessible, supercilious,
   uninterested, unresponsive

aloud
07 audibly, clearly, noisily
10 distinctly, sonorously
12 intelligibly, resoundingly

alphabet

► *Alphabets include*:
03 IPA, i.t.a.
04 kana, ogam
05 Greek, kanji, Kufic, Roman,
   runic
06 Arabic, Glagol, Hebrew,
   nagari, naskhi, romaji   •
07 futhark, Glossic
08 Cyrillic, Georgian,
   Gurmukhi, hiragana,
   katakana
09 Byzantine, cuneiform
10 devanagari, estrangelo,
   pictograph
11 hieroglyphs

► *Letters of the Arabic
alphabet*:
02 ba, fa, ha, ra, ta, ya, za
03 ayn, dad, dai, jim, kaf, kha,
   lam, mim, nun, qaf, sad, sin,
   tha, waw, zay
04 alif, dhai, shin
05 ghayn

► *Letters of the Greek
alphabet*:
02 mu, nu, pi, xi
03 chi, eta, phi, psi, rho, tau
04 beta, iota, zeta
05 alpha, delta, gamma, kappa,
   omega, sigma, theta
06 lambda
07 epsilon, omicron, upsilon

► *Letters of the Hebrew
alphabet*:
02 he, pe
03 mem, nun, sin, tav, taw, vaw,
   waw, yod
04 alef, ayin, heth, kaph, koph,
   qoph, resh, sade, shin, teth,
   yodh
05 aleph, gimel, sadhe, zayin
06 daleth, lamedh, samekh

► *Letters of the NATO
phonetic alphabet*:
04 Echo, Golf, Kilo, Lima,
   Mike, Papa, X-ray, Zulu
05 Alpha, Bravo, Delta, Hotel,
   India, Oscar, Romeo, Tango
06 Juliet, Quebec, Sierra,
   Victor, Whisky, Yankee
07 Charlie, Foxtrot, Uniform
08 November

already
06 so soon
07 even now, just now
08 even then, hitherto
09 before now
10 beforehand, previously

also
03 and, too
04 plus
06 as well
07 besides, further
08 as well as, moreover
09 along with, including
10 in addition
11 furthermore

alter
04 turn, vary
05 adapt, amend, emend, shift
06 adjust, change, modify,
   recast, reform, revise
07 convert, remodel, reshape
09 diversify, transform,
   transmute, transpose
12 metamorphose
13 make different

alteration
05 shift
06 change
08 revision, variance
09 amendment, reshaping,
   variation
10 adaptation, adjustment,
   conversion, difference
11 reformation, remodelling,
   vicissitude
12 modification
13 metamorphosis,
   transmutation, transposition
14 transformation

altercation
03 row
05 clash
06 fracas
07 dispute, quarrel, wrangle
08 argument, squabble
09 logomachy
10 dissension
12 disagreement

alternate
04 vary
05 alter
06 change, rotate
08 rotating
09 fluctuate, oscillate, take turns
10 every other, substitute
11 consecutive, every second, intersperse, reciprocate
13 take it in turns

alternative
05 other
06 back-up, choice, fringe, option, second
09 different, selection
10 substitute, unorthodox
14 unconventional

although
05 while
06 albeit, even if, whilst
07 howbeit
11 granted that
15 notwithstanding

altitude
05 depth
06 height
07 stature
09 elevation, loftiness

altogether
05 fully, in all, quite
06 in toto, wholly
07 all told, in total, totally, utterly
08 all in all, entirely
09 perfectly
10 absolutely, thoroughly

altruistic
06 humane
08 generous, selfless
09 unselfish
10 benevolent, charitable
11 considerate
12 humanitarian
13 disinterested, philanthropic
14 public-spirited

always
07 forever
08 evermore
09 endlessly, eternally
10 all the time, constantly, habitually, invariably, repeatedly
11 continually, in perpetuum, perpetually, unceasingly
12 consistently
13 again and again

amalgam
05 alloy, blend, union
06 fusion

07 mixture
08 compound
09 admixture, aggregate, synthesis
10 commixture
11 coalescence, combination

amalgamate
04 ally, fuse
05 alloy, blend, merge, unite
06 mingle
07 combine
08 coalesce, intermix
09 commingle, integrate
10 homogenize, synthesize
11 incorporate

amalgamation
05 blend, union, unity
06 fusion, merger
07 joining
08 alliance, compound
09 admixture, synthesis
11 coalescence, combination, commingling, integration
13 incorporation
14 homogenization

amass
04 gain, heap, pile
05 hoard, store
06 accrue, garner, gather, heap up, pile up
07 acquire, collect, store up
08 assemble
09 aggregate
10 accumulate, foregather

amateur
03 ham
04 buff
06 layman
07 dabbler, fancier
09 lay person
10 dilettante, enthusiast
15 non-professional

amateurish
03 lay
05 crude, inept
06 clumsy, unpaid
08 inexpert
09 unskilful, untrained
11 unqualified
14 unprofessional
15 non-professional

amaze
03 wow
04 daze, stun
05 floor, shock
06 dismay
07 astound, stagger, stupefy
08 astonish, bowl over, confound, gobsmack, surprise

09 dumbfound
10 disconcert, strike dumb
11 flabbergast, knock for six
12 blow your mind

amazement
05 shock
06 dismay, marvel, wonder
08 surprise
09 confusion
10 wonderment
12 astonishment, stupefaction

ambassador
05 agent, envoy
06 consul, deputy, legate
08 delegate, diplomat, emissary, minister
14 representative
15 plenipotentiary

ambience
03 air
04 aura, feel, mood, tone
05 tenor, vibes
06 milieu, spirit
07 feeling, setting
09 character
10 atmosphere, vibrations

ambiguity
05 doubt
06 enigma, puzzle
07 dubiety, paradox
08 polysemy
09 confusion, vagueness
10 woolliness
11 ambivalence, uncertainty
12 equivocality, equivocation
13 double meaning
14 double entendre

ambiguous
05 vague
06 woolly
07 cryptic, dubious, unclear
08 confused, doubtful, puzzling, two-edged
09 confusing, enigmatic, equivocal, uncertain
10 back-handed, indefinite
11 double-edged, paradoxical

ambit
05 range, scope
06 extent
07 compass
08 confines

ambition
03 aim
04 goal, hope, push, wish, zeal
05 dream, drive, ideal
06 design, desire, hunger, intent, object, target, thrust

07 craving, longing, purpose
08 striving, yearning
09 eagerness, objective
10 aspiration, get-up-and-go

ambitious
04 bold, hard, keen
05 eager, pushy
07 arduous, driving, go-ahead, hopeful, zealous
08 aspiring, exacting, full of go
09 demanding, difficult, elaborate
10 formidable, purposeful
11 power-hungry

ambivalence
05 clash, doubt
08 conflict, wavering
09 confusion
10 hesitation, opposition
11 fluctuation, uncertainty, vacillation
13 contradiction, inconsistency
14 irresoluteness

ambivalent
05 mixed
06 unsure
07 opposed, warring
08 clashing, confused, doubtful, hesitant, wavering
09 debatable, uncertain, undecided, unsettled
10 irresolute, unresolved
11 conflicting, fluctuating, vacillating
12 inconclusive, inconsistent
13 contradictory

amble
04 walk
05 drift
06 dawdle, ramble, stroll, toddle, wander
07 meander, saunter
09 promenade
10 mosey along
11 perambulate

ambush
04 jump, trap
05 snare
06 attack, turn on, waylay
07 ensnare
08 pounce on, surprise
09 ambuscade, bushwhack, lie in wait, waylaying

ameliorate
04 ease, mend
05 amend
06 better, remedy
07 benefit, elevate, enhance, improve, promote, relieve
08 mitigate
09 alleviate

amenable
04 open
07 willing
08 flexible
09 agreeable, compliant, tractable
10 responsive, submissive
11 acquiescent, complaisant, persuadable
13 accommodating

amend
03 fix
05 alter, emend
06 adjust, better, change, modify, reform, revise
07 correct, enhance, improve, qualify, rectify, redress
08 emendate
10 ameliorate

amendment
06 change, reform, remedy
07 adjunct
08 addendum, revision
10 adjustment, alteration, correction, emendation
11 corrigendum, enhancement
12 modification
13 qualification, rectification

amends
07 redress
08 requital
09 atonement, expiation, indemnity
10 recompense, reparation
11 restitution, restoration
12 compensation, satisfaction

amenity
07 service, utility
08 facility, resource
09 advantage
11 convenience

American
► *Native American peoples include*:
03 Fox, Ute
04 Cree, Crow, Hopi, Zuni
05 Creek, Huron, Sioux
06 Apache, Cayuga, Dakota, Lakota, Mohawk, Navaho, Navajo, Nootka, Ojibwa, Ottawa, Pawnee, Pueblo, Quapaw, Seneca
07 Arapaho, Chinook, Choctaw, Mohican, Natchez, Shawnee, Tlingit
08 Cherokee, Cheyenne, Comanche, Iroquois, Seminole, Shoshone
09 Algonkian, Blackfoot, Chickasaw, Tuscarora
10 Algonquian, Athabascan

amiable
04 kind, warm
06 genial
07 affable, likable
08 friendly, obliging, pleasant, sociable
09 agreeable, congenial
11 good-natured

amicable
05 civil
07 cordial
08 friendly, peaceful
09 civilized
10 harmonious
11 good-natured

amid
05 among, midst
06 amidst
07 amongst
12 in the midst of, in the thick of

amino acid
► *Types of amino acid*:
04 dopa
06 lysine, serine, valine
07 alanine, cystine, glycine, leucine, proline
08 cysteine, tyrosine
09 glutamine, histidine
10 tryptophan
12 aspartic acid
13 phenylalanine
➤ See also **acid**

amiss
04 awry
05 false, wonky, wrong
06 faulty
08 improper, untoward
09 defective, imperfect
10 inaccurate, out of order
11 out of kilter

amity
05 peace
06 accord, comity
07 concord, harmony
08 goodwill, kindness
10 cordiality, fellowship, fraternity, friendship
12 friendliness, peacefulness
13 brotherliness, understanding

ammunition
04 mine, shot
05 bombs, slugs
06 shells
07 bullets, rockets
08 grenades, missiles
09 gunpowder
10 cartridges

amnesty

05 mercy
06 pardon
08 immunity, lenience, reprieve
09 remission
10 absolution, indulgence
11 forgiveness
12 dispensation

amok

05 crazy, madly
06 wildly
07 berserk
08 frenzied, insanely

among

04 amid, with
05 midst
06 amidst
07 amongst, between
12 in the midst of, in the thick of,
    surrounded by
13 in the middle of

amorous

05 randy
06 erotic, in love, loving, tender
07 amatory, lustful
08 lovesick
10 passionate
11 impassioned

amorphous

05 vague
08 formless, inchoate,
    nebulous
09 irregular, shapeless,
    undefined
10 indistinct
11 featureless

amount

03 lot, sum
04 bulk, mass
05 quota, total, whole
06 extent, number, volume
07 expanse, measure
08 entirety, quantity, sum total
09 aggregate, magnitude

◻amount to

04 make, mean
05 equal, tot up, total
09 aggregate
10 boil down to, come down to
12 correspond to

amphibian

► *Types of amphibian*:
03 eft, olm
04 frog, newt, pipa, toad
07 axolotl, tadpole
08 bullfrog, tree frog
09 caecilian, conger eel
10 hellbender, horned toad,
    natterjack, salamander

11 midwife toad, Surinam toad
15 arrow-poison frog
➤ See also **animal**

ample

03 big
04 full, wide
05 broad, great, large
06 enough, plenty
07 copious, profuse
08 abundant, generous
09 expansive, extensive,
    plentiful
10 commodious, sufficient
11 substantial
12 considerable, unrestricted
14 more than enough

amplify

05 add to, boost, raise, widen
06 deepen, expand, extend
07 augment, broaden, bulk out,
    develop, enhance, fill out
08 flesh out, heighten, increase
09 enlarge on, intensify
10 make louder, strengthen
13 go into details

amplitude

04 bulk, mass
05 width
06 extent, volume
07 expanse
08 capacity, fullness, vastness
09 greatness, magnitude,
    plenitude, profusion

amputate

03 lop
04 dock
05 sever
06 cut off, remove
07 curtail
08 dissever, separate, truncate

amulet

04 juju
05 charm
06 braxas, fetish
07 periapt
08 pentacle, talisman
10 lucky charm, phylactery

amuse

05 charm, cheer, crack, relax
06 crease, divert, occupy,
    please, regale, tickle
07 cheer up, delight, disport,
    engross, enthral, gladden
08 interest, recreate
09 entertain, make laugh

amusement

03 fun
04 game
05 hobby, mirth, sport

07 delight, pastime
08 hilarity, interest, pleasure
09 diversion, merriment
10 recreation
11 distraction
13 entertainment

amusing

05 droll, funny, jolly, witty
07 comical, jocular, waggish
08 charming, humorous
09 enjoyable, facetious,
    hilarious, laughable
12 entertaining

anaemic

03 wan
04 pale, weak
05 ashen, frail, livid, pasty
06 pallid, sallow, sickly
07 insipid
09 bloodless, whey-faced

anaesthetic

06 opiate
07 anodyne
08 epidural, narcotic, sedative
09 analgesic, soporific
10 painkiller, palliative

anaesthetize

04 dope, drug, dull, numb
06 deaden
07 stupefy
11 desensitize

analogous

04 akin, like
07 kindred, similar
08 agreeing, matching, parallel
10 comparable, equivalent
11 correlative
13 corresponding

analogy

06 simile
08 likeness, metaphor, parallel
09 agreement, semblance
10 comparison, similarity
11 correlation, equivalence,
    resemblance
14 correspondence

analyse

04 sift, test
05 assay, judge, study
06 divide, reduce, review
07 dissect, examine, inquire
08 consider, evaluate, separate
09 anatomize, interpret
10 scrutinize
11 investigate

analysis

04 test
05 assay, check, study
06 review

07 inquiry, opinion, sifting
08 division, scrutiny
09 breakdown, judgement, reasoning, reduction
10 dissection, evaluation, exposition, inspection, resolution, separation
11 examination, explanation, explication
13 anatomization, investigation
14 interpretation

analytical
07 in-depth, logical
08 critical, detailed, rational
09 inquiring, searching
10 diagnostic, dissecting, methodical, systematic
11 explanatory, inquisitive, questioning
13 investigative
14 interpretative

anarchic
07 chaotic, lawless, riotous
08 confused, mutinous, nihilist
10 disordered, ungoverned
11 anarchistic, libertarian
12 disorganized
13 revolutionary

anarchist
05 rebel
08 nihilist
09 insurgent, terrorist
11 libertarian
13 revolutionary

anarchy
04 riot
05 chaos
06 mutiny, unrule
07 misrule
08 disorder
09 confusion, rebellion
10 revolution
11 lawlessness, pandemonium
12 insurrection

anathema
04 bane
05 curse, taboo
07 bugbear
08 aversion
09 bête noire
10 abhorrence
11 abomination
12 proscription

anatomy
05 build, frame
06 make-up
07 zootomy
09 framework, structure

➤ *Anatomical terms*:
04 bone, hock, womb

05 aural, elbow, groin, helix, nasal, pedal, renal, spine, uvula, vulva
06 biceps, dental, dorsal, gullet, lumbar, muscle, neural, ocular, tendon, uterus
07 cardiac, gastric, jugular, mammary, optical, triceps
08 cerebral, duodenal, foreskin, ligament, pectoral, voice-box, windpipe
09 cartilage, diaphragm, epidermis, funny bone, hamstring, pulmonary
10 epiglottis, oesophagus
14 Fallopian tubes

➤ *Names of anatomists*:
04 **Baer** (Karl Ernst von), **Bell** (Sir Charles)
05 **Monro** (Alexander)
06 **Adrian** (Edgar Douglas, Lord), **Cuvier** (Georges, Baron), **Stubbs** (George)
07 **Galvani** (Luigi)
08 **Alcmaeon, Malpighi** (Marcello), **Vesalius** (Andreas)
09 **Bartholin** (Caspar), **Fallopius** (Gabriel)
10 **Herophilus**
➢ See also **scientist**

ancestor
08 forebear
09 precursor
10 antecedent, forefather, forerunner, progenitor
11 predecessor
12 primogenitor

ancestral
06 lineal
07 genetic
08 familial, parental
10 hereditary
12 genealogical

ancestry
04 line, race
05 blood, roots, stock
06 family, origin
07 descent, lineage
08 heredity, heritage, pedigree
09 ancestors, forebears, genealogy, parentage
10 extraction, family tree
11 forefathers, progenitors

anchor
03 fix
04 moor
05 affix, berth, tie up
06 attach, fasten
08 make fast

➤ *Types of anchor*:
03 car, sea
04 navy
05 kedge
06 drogue
07 grapnel, killick
08 mushroom

ancient
03 old
04 aged
05 early, olden, passé
06 age-old
07 antique, archaic
08 outmoded, primeval, pristine, time-worn
09 atavistic, out-of-date
10 antiquated, fossilized, primordial
11 prehistoric
12 antediluvian, old-fashioned
13 superannuated
15 as old as the hills

ancillary
05 extra
07 helping
08 adjuvant
09 auxiliary, secondary
10 subsidiary, supporting
11 adminicular, subordinate

and
03 too
04 also, plus, then
06 as well
07 besides
08 as well as, moreover
09 including, what's more
10 in addition
11 furthermore

anecdote
04 tale, yarn
05 story
06 sketch
12 reminiscence

anew
05 again
06 afresh
08 once more
09 once again

angel
03 gem
05 ideal, power, saint
07 darling, paragon
08 treasure
12 principality
13 heavenly being
15 divine messenger

► *Orders of angel*:
05 angel, power
06 cherub, seraph, throne, virtue
08 dominion
09 archangel
10 domination
12 principality
➤ See also **religion**

angelic
04 holy, pure
05 pious
06 divine, lovely
07 saintly
08 cherubic, empyrean, ethereal, heavenly, innocent, seraphic
09 beautiful, celestial

anger
03 ire, irk, vex
04 fury, gall, miff, nark, rage, rile
05 annoy, pique, wrath
06 choler, enrage, madden, needle, nettle, offend, ruffle, temper, wind up
07 chagrin, dudgeon, incense, outrage, provoke, rancour
08 irritate, paroxysm, vexation
09 aggravate, infuriate
10 antagonism, antagonize, bitterness, conniption, exasperate, resentment
11 displeasure, indignation
12 exasperation, irritability

angle
04 bend, edge, face, hook, knee, nook, side, turn
05 elbow, facet, point, slant
06 aspect, corner, direct
07 flexure, outlook
08 approach, gradient, position
09 direction, viewpoint
10 projection, standpoint
11 perspective, point of view
12 intersection

❑**angle for**
03 aim
04 seek
11 make a bid for

angry
03 hot, mad
05 cross, irate, livid
06 bitter, heated, raging
07 annoyed, enraged, furious
08 choleric, foribund, incensed, outraged, seething, up in arms, wrathful
09 indignant, irritated, rancorous, resentful, seeing red, splenetic

10 aggravated, displeased, hopping mad, infuriated
11 disgruntled, exasperated
12 on the warpath

anguish
03 woe
04 dole, pain, pang, rack
05 agony, grief
06 dolour, misery, sorrow
07 anxiety, torment, torture
08 distress
09 heartache, suffering
10 desolation, heartbreak

anguished
08 dolorous, stricken, tortured
09 afflicted, miserable, suffering, tormented
10 distressed

angular
04 bony, lank, lean, thin
05 gaunt, gawky, lanky, spare
06 skinny
07 scrawny
08 rawboned

animal
04 wild, zoic
05 beast, brute, swine
06 bodily, carnal, savage
07 bestial, brutish, fleshly, inhuman, monster, sensual
08 creature, physical
➤ See also **amphibian**; **ape**; **beetle**; **bird**; **butterfly**; **cat**; **cattle**; **chicken**; **crustacean**; **dinosaur**; **dog**; **duck**; **fish**; **insect**; **invertebrate**; **lizard**; **mammal**; **marsupial**; **mollusc**; **monkey**; **moth**; **pig**; **reptile**; **rodent**; **shark**; **sheep**; **snake**; **spider**; **whale**; **worm**

► *Female animals include*:
03 cow, doe, ewe, hen, pen, sow
04 duck, gill, hind, jill, mare
05 bitch, jenny, nanny, queen, vixen
06 peahen
07 lioness, tigress
10 leopardess

► *Male animals include*:
03 cob, dog, ram, tom, tup
04 boar, buck, bull, cock, hart, jack, stag
05 billy, drake
06 gander
07 bullock, peacock
08 stallion

► *Young animals include*:
03 cub, elt, fry, kid, kit
04 brit, calf, colt, eyas, fawn, foal, joey, lamb, parr, peal
05 chick, elver, owlet, puppy, smolt, squab, whelp
06 alevin, cygnet, eaglet, grilse, kitten, lionet, piglet
07 gosling, leveret, tadpole
08 duckling, goatling, nestling
09 fledgling

animate
04 fire, goad, live, move, spur, stir, urge
05 alive, impel, rouse, spark
06 arouse, excite, incite, kindle, living, revive, vivify
07 enliven, inspire, quicken
08 activate, embolden, energize, inspirit, vitalize
09 breathing, conscious, instigate, stimulate
10 invigorate, reactivate

animated
05 alive, eager, quick, vital
06 active, ardent, lively
07 buoyant, excited, fervent, glowing, radiant, vibrant
08 spirited, spritely, vehement
09 ebullient, sprightly
10 passionate
11 full of beans, impassioned
12 enthusiastic

animation
03 pep
04 life, zeal, zest, zing
05 verve
06 action, energy, spirit, vigour
07 fervour, passion, sparkle
08 activity, vibrancy, vitality
10 ebullience, enthusiasm, excitement, liveliness
11 high spirits

animosity
04 feud, hate
05 odium, spite
06 animus, enmity, malice
07 ill-will, rancour
08 acrimony, loathing
09 hostility, malignity
10 antagonism, bitterness, ill feeling, resentment

annals
07 history, memoirs, records
08 archives, journals
09 registers
10 chronicles

annex
03 add
04 join

05 affix, seize, unite, usurp
06 adjoin, append, attach,
   fasten, occupy
07 acquire, connect, conquer
08 arrogate, take over
11 appropriate, incorporate

annexation
07 seizure
08 conquest, takeover,
   usurping
10 arrogation, occupation
11 acquisition
13 appropriation

annexe
04 wing
08 addition
09 expansion, extension
10 attachment, supplement

annihilate
04 raze, rout, slay
05 erase
06 defeat, murder, rub out
07 abolish, conquer, destroy,
   trounce, wipe out
09 eliminate, eradicate
10 extinguish, obliterate
11 assassinate, exterminate

annihilation
06 defeat, murder
07 erasure
09 abolition
10 extinction
11 destruction, elimination,
   eradication
12 obliteration
13 assassination, extermination

anniversary
► *Names of wedding
anniversary:*
03 tin
04 gold, iron, lace, ruby, silk,
   wood, wool
05 china, coral, fruit, ivory,
   linen, paper, pearl, steel,
   sugar
06 bronze, copper, cotton,
   silver, willow
07 crystal, diamond, emerald,
   flowers, leather, pottery
08 platinum, sapphire

annotate
04 note
05 gloss
07 comment, explain
09 elucidate, explicate,
   interpret

annotation
04 note
05 gloss

07 comment
08 exegesis, footnote
10 commentary
11 elucidation, explanation,
   explication

announce
05 state
06 blazon, notify, report, reveal
07 declare, divulge, publish
08 disclose, proclaim,
   propound
09 advertise, broadcast, make
   known, preconize, publicize
10 make public, promulgate

announcement
06 report
07 message
08 bulletin, dispatch
09 broadcast, publicity,
   reporting, statement
10 communiqué, disclosure,
   divulgence, revelation
11 declaration, publication
12 notification, proclamation

announcer
02 MC
04 host
06 herald
07 compère
09 anchorman, messenger,
   presenter, town crier
10 newscaster, newsreader
11 anchorwoman, broadcaster,
   commentator

annoy
03 bug, irk, nag, vex
04 gall, rile
05 anger, tease
06 bother, harass, hassle,
   madden, molest, pester,
   plague, ruffle, wind up
07 disturb, hack off, provoke,
   tick off, trouble
08 brass off, irritate
09 aggravate, cheese off,
   displease, drive nuts
10 drive crazy, exasperate
11 get your goat
13 get on your wick,
   get up your nose,
   get your back up
14 drive up the wall
15 get on your nerves

annoyance
04 bind, bore, drag, pain, pest
05 anger, tease
06 bother
07 trouble
08 headache, irritant, nuisance,
   vexation

10 harassment, irritation
11 aggravation
13 pain in the neck

annoyed
05 angry, cross, upset, vexed
06 bugged, miffed, narked,
   peeved, piqued
07 hassled, in a huff
08 harassed, provoked
09 indignant, irritated
10 cheesed off, got the hump
11 exasperated

annoying
05 pesky
06 trying
07 galling, irksome, teasing
08 tiresome
09 harassing, intrusive,
   maddening, provoking,
   unwelcome, vexatious
10 bothersome, irritating
11 aggravating, troublesome
12 exasperating

annual
06 yearly
07 almanac
08 calendar, register, yearbook

annul
04 void
06 cancel, negate, recall,
   repeal, revoke
07 abolish, nullify, rescind,
   retract, reverse, suspend
08 abrogate
10 invalidate
11 countermand

annulment
06 recall, repeal
07 reverse, voiding
08 negation, quashing
09 abolition
10 abrogation, rescission,
   revocation, suspension
11 countermand, rescindment
12 cancellation, invalidation
13 nullification

anodyne
05 bland
07 neutral
09 deadening
11 inoffensive

anoint
03 oil, rub
04 daub
05 anele, bless, smear
06 grease, ordain
08 apply oil, dedicate, sanctify
09 embrocate, lubricate
10 consecrate

anomalous
03 odd
04 rare
05 freak
07 deviant, unusual
08 abnormal, atypical, freakish, peculiar, singular
09 eccentric, irregular
11 exceptional, incongruous
12 inconsistent

anomaly
05 freak
06 misfit, oddity, rarity
09 deviation, exception
10 aberration, divergence
11 abnormality, incongruity, peculiarity
12 eccentricity, irregularity
13 inconsistency

anonymous
07 unknown, unnamed
08 faceless, nameless, unsigned
09 incognito
10 impersonal, innominate
11 nondescript, unspecified
12 unidentified

another
04 more
05 added, extra, other, spare
06 second
07 further, variant
09 different
10 additional, not the same
11 alternative

answer
03 fit, key
04 fill, meet, pass, suit
05 agree, react, reply, serve
06 fulfil, refute, result, retort
07 respond, riposte, satisfy
08 comeback, reaction, rebuttal, response, solution
09 get back to, rejoinder, retaliate, write back
10 come back to, resolution
11 acknowledge, explanation, retaliation
15 acknowledgement

▫answer back
04 sass
05 argue, rebut
06 retort
07 dispute, riposte
08 disagree, talk back
09 retaliate
10 be cheeky to, contradict

answerable
06 liable
07 to blame
10 chargeable

11 accountable, blameworthy, responsible

antagonism
06 enmity
07 discord, ill-will, rivalry
08 conflict, friction
09 animosity, antipathy, hostility
10 contention, dissension, ill feeling, opposition

antagonist
03 foe
05 enemy, rival
08 opponent
09 adversary, contender
10 competitor, contestant

antagonistic
06 averse
07 adverse, hostile, opposed
10 at variance, unfriendly
11 belligerent, conflicting, contentious, ill-disposed
12 incompatible

antagonize
05 anger, annoy, repel
06 insult, offend
07 incense, provoke
08 alienate, embitter, estrange
09 disaffect

antecedent
09 ancestors, forebears, precedent, precursor
10 extraction, forerunner
11 forefathers

anthem
04 hymn, song
05 chant, paean, psalm
07 chorale
08 canticle
12 song of praise

anthology
06 digest
08 treasury
09 selection, spicilege
10 collection, compendium, miscellany
11 compilation

anthropologist
➤ *Names of anthropologists*:
04 **Buck** (Peter Henry), **Mead** (Margaret)
05 **Tylor** (Sir Edward Burnett)
06 **Frazer** (Sir James George)
09 **Heyerdahl** (Thor)
10 **Malinowski** (Bronislaw)
11 **Lévi-Strauss** (Claude)
➤ See also **scientist**

anticipate
05 await
06 bank on, expect
07 count on, foresee, hope for, obviate, pre-empt, predict
08 beat to it, figure on, forecast, preclude, reckon on
09 intercept, forestall
10 prepare for

anticipation
04 hope
10 excitement, expectancy, prediction
11 bated breath, expectation

anticlimax
06 bathos, fiasco
07 let-down
08 comedown, non-event
09 damp squib
14 disappointment

antics
06 capers, pranks, stunts
07 foolery, frolics
08 clowning, mischief
09 horseplay, silliness
10 skylarking, tomfoolery

antidote
04 cure
06 remedy
07 theriac
09 antitoxin, antivenin
10 corrective, mithridate
12 counter-agent

antipathy
04 hate
05 odium
06 animus, enmity, hatred
07 disgust, dislike, ill-will
08 aversion, bad blood, distaste, loathing
09 animosity, hostility, repulsion
10 abhorrence, antagonism
15 incompatibility

antiquated
05 dated, passé
06 bygone, démodé, old hat
07 ancient, archaic, outworn
08 obsolete, outdated, outmoded
09 out-of-date
12 antediluvian, old-fashioned
13 anachronistic

antique
03 old
05 curio, relic
06 bygone, quaint, rarity
07 ancient, archaic, veteran, vintage
08 heirloom, outdated

antiquity *(continued)*
09 antiquity, curiosity
11 museum piece, period piece
12 old-fashioned

antiquity
03 age
06 old age
07 oldness
08 agedness
09 olden days
11 distant past
12 ancient times
14 time immemorial

antiseptic
04 pure
05 clean
07 aseptic, sterile
08 cleanser, germ-free, hygienic, purifier, sanitary
09 germicide, sanitized
10 sterilized, unpolluted
12 disinfectant
14 uncontaminated

antisocial
07 asocial, hostile, lawless
08 anarchic, reserved, retiring
09 alienated, withdrawn
10 disorderly, disruptive, rebellious, unfriendly
11 belligerent
12 antagonistic, misanthropic

antithesis
07 reverse
08 contrast, converse, opposite, reversal
13 contradiction
15 opposite extreme

anxiety
04 care
05 dread, worry
06 strain, stress
07 anguish, concern, tension
08 disquiet, distress, suspense
09 misgiving, worriment
10 foreboding, uneasiness
11 disquietude, fretfulness, nervousness
12 apprehension, restlessness

anxious
04 keen, taut
05 eager, tense
06 afraid, uneasy
07 fearful, fretful, in a stew, longing, nervous, worried
08 restless, troubled
09 concerned, disturbed, expectant, impatient
10 distressed, solicitous
11 overwrought
12 apprehensive, enthusiastic
13 on tenterhooks

apace
04 fast
07 quickly, rapidly, swiftly
08 speedily
10 at top speed
11 at full speed, double-quick

apart
04 afar, away
05 alone, aloof, aside
06 cut off, in bits, singly, to bits
07 distant
08 distinct, divorced, excluded, in pieces, isolated, separate
09 on your own, privately, separated, to one side
10 by yourself, separately

apart from
05 except
06 but for
08 excepted
09 except for, excluding
11 not counting

apathetic
04 cold, cool, numb
05 blasé
07 passive, unmoved
08 listless, lukewarm
09 impassive, lethargic, unfeeling
10 uninvolved
11 emotionless, half-hearted, indifferent, unambitious, unconcerned, unemotional
12 uninterested, unresponsive

apathy
06 acedia, torpor
07 accidie, inertia, languor
08 coldness, coolness, lethargy
09 passivity, unconcern
11 impassivity
12 indifference, listlessness, sluggishness

ape
04 copy, echo, mock
05 mimic
06 affect, mirror, monkey, parody, parrot, simian
07 imitate, take off
10 caricature

▬ *Apes include:*
05 pongo
06 gibbon
07 gorilla
09 orang-utan
10 chimpanzee
11 orang-outang
➢ See also **animal**

aperture
03 eye, gap

aphorism
03 saw
05 adage, axiom, gnome, maxim
06 dictum, saying
07 epigram, precept, proverb
08 apothegm
09 witticism

aphrodisiac
06 erotic
07 amative, amatory
08 venerous
09 erogenous, stimulant
10 love potion
11 erotogenous

aplomb
05 poise
07 balance
08 audacity, calmness, coolness
09 assurance, composure, sang-froid
10 confidence, equanimity
11 savoir-faire
13 self-assurance
14 self-confidence

apocryphal
08 doubtful, mythical, spurious
09 concocted, equivocal, imaginary, legendary
10 fabricated, fictitious, unverified
11 unsupported
12 questionable

apologetic
05 sorry
06 rueful
08 contrite, penitent
09 regretful, repentant
10 remorseful

apologize
05 plead
06 regret

04 hole, rent, slit, slot, vent
05 chink, cleft, mouth, space
06 breach
07 fissure, foramen, opening, orifice, passage
10 interstice

apex
03 tip, top
04 acme, peak
05 crest, crown, point
06 apogee, climax, height, summit, vertex, zenith
08 pinnacle
09 fastigium, high point
11 culmination
13 crowning point

07 confess, explain, justify
08 say sorry
09 ask pardon
11 acknowledge
12 eat humble pie, eat your words
14 ask forgiveness

apology
04 plea
06 excuse
07 defence, regrets
10 confession, palliation
11 explanation, vindication
13 justification
15 acknowledgement

apostasy
06 heresy
07 perfidy
09 defection, desertion, falseness, recreance, recreancy, treachery
10 disloyalty, recidivism, renegation
12 renunciation

apostate
07 heretic, traitor
08 defector, deserter, recreant, renegade, turncoat
10 recidivist
13 tergiversator

apostle
07 pioneer
08 advocate, champion, crusader, disciple, reformer
09 proponent, supporter
10 evangelist, missionary
12 proselytizer

appal
05 alarm, daunt, scare, shock
06 dismay
07 disgust, horrify, outrage, terrify, unnerve
08 frighten
10 disconcert, intimidate

appalling
04 dire, grim
05 awful
06 horrid
07 ghastly, hideous
08 alarming, daunting, dreadful, horrible, horrific, shocking, terrible
09 atrocious, frightful, harrowing, loathsome
10 disgusting, horrifying, outrageous, terrifying
11 frightening, nightmarish
12 intimidating

apparatus
04 gear
05 means, set-up, tools
06 device, gadget, outfit, system, tackle
07 machine, network
09 appliance, equipment, machinery, materials
10 implements
11 contraption

apparel
04 garb
05 dress
06 outfit
07 clothes, costume
08 clothing, garments, wardrobe

apparent
04 open
05 clear, plain
06 marked, patent
07 evident, obvious, outward, seeming, visible
08 declared, distinct, manifest
10 noticeable, ostensible
11 conspicuous, perceptible, superficial

apparently
07 clearly, plainly
08 patently
09 obviously, outwardly, reputedly, seemingly
10 manifestly, ostensibly
13 on the face of it, superficially

apparition
05 ghost, spook
06 spirit, vision
07 chimera, phantom, spectre
08 presence, visitant
13 manifestation
15 materialization

appeal
03 ask, beg, sue
04 draw, lure, plea, pray, suit
05 apply, charm, claim, plead
06 allure, beauty, engage, entice, invite, invoke, orison, please, prayer
07 beseech, entreat, implore, request, retrial, solicit
08 call upon, charisma, entreaty, interest, petition
09 fascinate, magnetism
10 adjuration, attraction, invocation, supplicate
11 application, enchantment, fascination
12 solicitation, supplication

appear
03 act

04 look, loom, play, seem, show
05 arise, enter, occur, pop up
06 arrive, attend, crop up, emerge, show up, turn up
07 come out, develop, perform, surface, turn out
10 be a guest in
11 come to light, materialize, show signs of
12 come into view

appearance
03 air
04 face, form, look, mien, show
05 début, front, guise, image
06 advent, aspect, façade, figure, manner, visage
07 arrival, bearing
08 illusion, presence, pretence
09 demeanour, semblance
10 attendance, complexion, expression, impression

appease
06 pacify
07 placate, satisfy
08 mitigate
09 reconcile
10 conciliate, propitiate
13 make peace with

appellation
04 name
05 title
07 epithet
09 sobriquet
11 description, designation

append
03 add
04 join
05 affix, annex
06 adjoin, attach, fasten
07 conjoin, subjoin

appendage
07 adjunct
08 addendum, addition, appendix
09 tailpiece
10 supplement

appendix
05 rider
07 adjunct, codicil
08 addendum, addition, epilogue
09 appendage
10 postscript, supplement

appetite
04 lust, zeal, zest
06 desire, hunger, relish, thirst
07 longing, passion, stomach

09 eagerness
11 inclination

appetizing
05 tasty
07 piquant, savoury
08 inviting, tempting
09 appealing, delicious,
   palatable, succulent
11 scrumptious
13 mouthwatering

applaud
04 clap, laud
05 cheer, extol
06 praise
07 acclaim, approve, commend
08 eulogize
12 congratulate
14 give a big hand to

applause
06 bravos, cheers, praise
07 acclaim, ovation
08 a big hand, accolade,
   cheering, clapping
11 acclamation
12 commendation
14 congratulation
15 standing ovation

appliance
04 tool
06 device, gadget
07 machine
09 apparatus, implement
10 instrument
11 contraption, contrivance

applicable
03 apt, fit
06 proper, suited, useful
07 fitting
08 apposite, relevant, suitable
09 pertinent
10 legitimate
11 appropriate

applicant
06 suitor
08 aspirant, claimant, inquirer
09 candidate, postulant
10 petitioner
11 interviewee

application
03 use
04 suit
05 claim, value
06 appeal, demand, effort
07 aptness, bearing, inquiry,
   purpose, request
08 function, hard work,
   industry, keenness, petition
09 assiduity, diligence,
   relevance

10 commitment, dedication,
   pertinence
11 germaneness
12 perseverance,
   sedulousness, significance

apply
03 fit, ply, rub, sue, use
04 give, suit
05 claim, exert, lay on, paint,
   put on, refer, smear, study
06 anoint, appeal, appose, ask
   for, devote, direct, draw on,
   employ, engage, relate
07 address, adhibit, execute,
   harness, inquire, pertain,
   request, solicit, utilize
08 dedicate, exercise, petition,
   practise, put in for, resort to,
   spread on, work hard
09 appertain, implement,
   persevere
10 administer, be relevant,
   buckle down, settle down
11 bring to bear, concentrate,
   requisition, write off for

appoint
03 fix, set
04 hire, name, pick
05 allot, co-opt, elect
06 assign, choose, decide,
   direct, employ, engage,
   ordain, select, settle, take on
07 arrange, command, destine,
   install, recruit
08 delegate, nominate
09 designate, establish
10 commission

appointed
03 set
05 fixed
06 chosen
07 decided, decreed, settled
08 allotted, arranged, assigned,
   destined, ordained
10 designated, determined
11 established, preordained

appointment
03 job
04 date, post
05 place, tryst
06 choice, naming, office
07 meeting
08 choosing, election, position
10 delegation, engagement,
   nomination, rendezvous
11 arrangement, assignation
12 consultation
13 commissioning

apportion
04 deal, mete

05 allot, grant, share
06 assign, divide, ration
07 deal out, dole out, hand out,
   mete out
08 allocate, dispense, share out
09 admeasure, ration out
10 distribute, measure out

apportionment
05 grant, share
06 ration
07 dealing, handout
08 division
09 allotment, rationing
10 allocation, assignment
12 dispensation, distribution

apposite
03 apt
06 suited
07 apropos, germane
08 relevant, suitable
09 befitting, pertinent
10 applicable, to the point
11 appropriate

appraisal
05 assay
06 rating, review, survey
07 opinion
08 estimate, once-over
09 reckoning, valuation
10 assessment, estimation,
   evaluation, inspection
11 examination

appraise
04 rate
05 assay, judge, sum up, value
06 assess, size up, survey
07 examine, inspect
08 estimate, evaluate

appreciable
08 definite
10 noticeable
11 discernible, perceptible,
   significant, substantial
12 considerable, recognizable

appreciate
03 see
04 go up, grow, know, like, rise
05 enjoy, grasp, thank, value
06 admire, esteem, regard,
   relish, savour
07 cherish, enhance, improve,
   inflate, realize
08 increase, perceive, treasure
09 be aware of, recognize
10 comprehend, understand

appreciation
04 gain, rise
06 esteem, growth, liking,
   praise, regard, relish

07 respect, valuing
08 analysis, critique, increase
09 awareness, enjoyment, gratitude, inflation, judgement, knowledge, valuation
10 admiration, assessment, cognizance, escalation, evaluation
11 enhancement, improvement, realization, recognition, sensitivity
12 gratefulness, indebtedness, thankfulness

appreciative
07 mindful, obliged, pleased
08 admiring, beholden, grateful, indebted, thankful
09 conscious, sensitive
10 perceptive, respectful, responsive
11 encouraging
12 enthusiastic
13 knowledgeable

apprehend
03 nab, see
04 bust, grab, nick, twig
05 catch, grasp, run in, seize
06 arrest, collar, detain
07 believe, capture, realize
08 conceive, perceive
09 recognize
10 comprehend, understand

apprehension
04 fear
05 alarm, doubt, dread, qualm, worry
06 arrest, belief, taking
07 anxiety, capture, seizure
08 disquiet, mistrust
09 misgiving, suspicion
10 foreboding, perception, the willies, uneasiness
11 butterflies, nervousness, realization, trepidation
12 perturbation

apprehensive
06 afraid, uneasy
07 alarmed, anxious, fearful, nervous, worried
08 bothered, doubtful
09 concerned
10 suspicious
11 distrustful, mistrustful

apprentice
04 tiro, tyro
05 pupil
06 novice, rookie
07 learner, recruit, starter, student, trainee

08 beginner, newcomer
11 probationer

apprise
04 tell, warn
05 brief
06 advise, inform, notify, tip off
08 acquaint, intimate
09 enlighten

approach
04 meet, near, plea, road
05 begin, drive, greet, means, reach, style, treat
06 accost, arrive, avenue, broach, invite, manner, method, system, tackle
07 address, advance, arrival, catch up, contact, mention, request, speak to, tactics
08 commence, deal with, draw near, driveway, entrance, overture, proposal, sound out, strategy
09 overtures, procedure, technique, threshold
10 come closer, come near to, come nearer
11 application, approximate, come close to, get closer to, move towards, proposition
13 modus operandi
14 course of action

approachable
04 open, warm
07 affable
08 friendly, informal, sociable
09 agreeable, congenial, get-at-able, reachable
10 accessible, attainable

appropriate
03 apt, fit
04 meet, nick, take
05 filch, pinch, right, seize, steal, swipe, usurp
06 pilfer, pocket, proper, seemly, thieve, timely
07 apropos, correct, fitting, germane, impound, purloin
08 accepted, arrogate, becoming, embezzle, peculate, relevant, suitable
09 befitting, opportune, pertinent, well-timed
10 applicable, commandeer, confiscate, felicitous
11 appurtenant, expropriate, make off with, requisition

approval
02 OK
03 nod
04 wink

05 leave
06 assent, esteem, favour, honour, liking, praise, regard
07 consent, go-ahead, licence, mandate, respect, support
08 applause, blessing, sanction, thumbs-up
09 agreement
10 green light, imprimatur, permission, validation
11 concurrence, endorsement, good opinion, rubber stamp
12 confirmation, ratification
13 authorization, certification

approve
02 OK
03 buy
04 back, like, pass
05 adopt, allow, bless, carry
06 accept, admire, concur, esteem, favour, permit, praise, ratify, second
07 acclaim, agree to, applaud, commend, confirm, endorse, mandate, support
08 sanction, validate
09 authorize, consent to
10 appreciate
11 countenance, rubber-stamp, think well of
12 give the nod to

approved
06 proper
07 correct
08 accepted, official, orthodox
09 permitted, preferred
10 authorized, recognized, sanctioned
11 permissible, recommended

approximate
04 like, near
05 close, loose, rough
07 guessed, inexact, similar, verge on
08 approach, ballpark, border on, relative, resemble
09 estimated

approximately
05 about, circa
06 around, nearly
07 close to, loosely, roughly
09 just about, not far off
10 give or take, more or less, round about
11 approaching
13 in the region of, or thereabouts, something like
15 in the vicinity of

approximation
05 guess

08 estimate, likeness
09 rough idea, semblance
10 conjecture
11 guesstimate, resemblance
14 ballpark figure

apropos
02 re
03 apt
05 right
06 proper, seemly, timely
07 correct, fitting
08 accepted, becoming, relevant, suitable
09 befitting, opportune, pertinent, regarding
10 applicable, felicitous, respecting, seasonable, to the point, well-chosen
11 in respect of
12 in relation to, with regard to

apt
03 fit
05 given, prone, ready
06 liable, likely, proper, seemly, spot-on, timely
07 correct, fitting, germane
08 apposite, disposed, inclined, relevant, suitable
10 applicable, seasonable
11 appropriate

aptitude
04 bent, gift
05 flair, skill
06 talent
07 ability, faculty, leaning
08 capacity, facility, tendency
10 capability, cleverness
11 disposition, proficiency
14 natural ability

aquatic
03 sea
05 fluid, river, water
06 liquid, marine, watery
07 fluvial
08 maritime, nautical

arable
06 fecund
07 fertile
08 fruitful, tillable
10 ploughable, productive

arachnid see **spider**

arbiter
05 judge
06 expert, master, umpire
07 referee
09 authority
10 controller
11 adjudicator

arbitrary
06 chance, random
08 despotic, dogmatic
09 illogical, whimsical
10 autocratic, capricious, high-handed, irrational, subjective, unreasoned
11 dictatorial, domineering, instinctive, overbearing
12 inconsistent, unreasonable
13 discretionary

arbitrate
05 judge
06 decide, settle, umpire
07 mediate, referee
09 determine
10 adjudicate
14 sit in judgement

arbitration
08 decision
09 judgement, mediation
10 settlement
11 arbitrament, negotiation
12 adjudication, intervention
13 determination

arbitrator
05 judge
06 umpire
07 arbiter, referee
08 mediator
09 go-between, moderator
10 negotiator
11 adjudicator
12 intermediary

arc
03 bow
04 arch, bend
05 curve
09 curvature

arcade
04 mall, stoa
06 loggia, piazza
07 gallery, portico
08 cloister, precinct
09 colonnade, peristyle

arcane
06 hidden, occult, secret
07 cryptic, obscure
08 abstruse, esoteric, mystical
09 concealed, enigmatic, recondite
10 mysterious

arch
03 arc, bow, sly
04 bend, dome, span
05 curve, vault
06 bridge, camber
07 archway, concave, cunning
09 curvature

► *Types of arch*:
04 keel, ogee, skew
05 round, Tudor
06 convex, corbel, Gothic, lancet, Norman, tented
07 trefoil
09 horseshoe, parabolic
10 shouldered
12 basket handle

archaeology
► *Archaeological terms*:
03 cup, jar, jug, urn
04 bowl, cist, tell
05 blade, burin, cairn, flask, flint, henge, hoard, mound, mummy, stele, whorl
06 barrow, beaker, bogman, dolmen, eolith, mosaic
07 amphora, cave art, handaxe, neolith, obelisk, papyrus, rock art, tumulus
08 artefact, cromlech, hill fort, ley lines, megalith
09 cartouche, earthwork, hypocaust, microlith
10 hieroglyph
11 rock shelter, stone circle
12 amphitheatre

► *Names of archaeologists*:
05 **Evans** (Sir Arthur)
06 **Anning** (Mary), **Breuil** (Henri), **Carter** (Howard), **Daniel** (Glyn), **Layard** (Sir Austen Henry), **Leakey** (Louis Seymour Bazett), **Leakey** (Mary Douglas), **Petrie** (Sir Flinders)
07 **Thomsen** (Christian), **Wheeler** (Sir Mortimer), **Woolley** (Sir Leonard)
08 **Koldewey** (Robert), **Mariette** (Auguste)
10 **Schliemann** (Heinrich)
11 **Champollion** (Jean François)
➤ See also **scientist**

archaic
05 passé
06 old hat
08 outmoded
10 antiquated
11 out of the ark
12 old-fashioned

archbishop
► *Names of archbishops*:
04 **Hope** (David), **Hume** (Basil), **Kemp** (John), **Laud** (William), **Tutu** (Desmond Mpilo)
05 **Carey** (George)

06 **Beaton** (David), **Becket**
(Thomas à), **Coggan**
(Donald), **Fisher**
(Geoffrey), **Morton** (John),
Parker (Matthew), **Ramsay**
(Michael), **Runcie** (Robert),
Temple (William), **Ussher**
(James), **Wolsey** (Thomas)
07 **Arundel** (Thomas),
Cranmer (Thomas),
Dunstan (St), **Habgood**
(John), **Langton** (Stephen),
Mendoza (Pedro Gonzalez
de), **Sheldon** (Gilbert),
Wiseman (Nicholas)
08 **Adalbert**, **Makarios**,
Whitgift (John)
09 **Augustine** (St)
10 **Huddleston** (Trevor)
➤ See also **religion**

archetypal
05 ideal, model, stock
07 classic, typical
08 original, standard
09 exemplary
14 characteristic,
representative

archetype
04 form, type
05 ideal, model
07 classic, epitome, pattern
08 exemplar, original,
paradigm, standard
09 precursor, prototype
10 stereotype

architect
05 maker
06 author, shaper
07 creator, founder, planner
08 designer, engineer, inventor
10 instigator, mastermind,
originator, prime mover
11 constructor, draughtsman
13 master builder

➤ *Names of architects*:
04 **Adam** (Robert), **Loos**
(Adolf), **Nash** (John), **Shaw**
(Norman), **Wren** (Sir
Christopher)
05 **Aalto** (Alvar), **Barry** (Sir
Charles), **Gaudí** (Antonio),
Jones (Inigo), **Nervi** (Pier
Luigi), **Piano** (Renzo),
Pugin (Augustus), **Scott**
(Sir George Gilbert), **Scott**
(Sir Giles Gilbert), **Soane**
(Sir John), **Speer** (Albert)
06 **Casson** (Sir Hugh), **Foster**
(Sir Norman), **Paxton** (Sir
Joseph), **Pisano** (Giovanni),
Rogers (Sir Richard),

Semper (Gottfried), **Serlio**
(Sebastiano), **Wright** (Frank
Lloyd)
07 **Alberti** (Leon Battista),
Asplund (Erik Gunnar),
Behrens (Peter), **Bernini**
(Gian Lorenzo), **Gropius**
(Walter), **Ictinus**, **Imhotep**,
Lutyens (Sir Edwin),
Olmsted (Frederick Law),
Sotsass (Ettore)
08 **Bramante** (Donato),
Jacobsen (Arne), **Palladio**
(Andrea), **Piranesi**
(Giambattista), **Vanbrugh**
(Sir John)
09 **Borromini** (Francesco),
Hawksmoor (Nicholas),
Vitruvius
10 **Mackintosh** (Charles
Rennie)
11 **Le Corbusier**
12 **Brunelleschi** (Filippo)

architecture
05 style
06 design, make-up
08 building, planning
09 designing, framework,
structure
11 arrangement, composition
12 construction

➤ *Architectural and building
terms*:
04 dado, dome, jamb, roof
05 Doric, eaves, groin, Ionic,
ridge, Tudor
06 alcove, annexe, coving,
façade, fascia, finial, frieze,
Gothic, lintel, Norman,
pagoda, plinth, rococo,
scroll, soffit, stucco, Tuscan
07 baroque, cornice, festoon,
fluting, mullion, pantile,
parapet, rafters, Regency,
rotunda
08 baluster, capstone, dry-
stone, gargoyle, Georgian,
pinnacle, wainscot
09 bas relief, Edwardian,
elevation, gatehouse, Queen-
Anne
10 architrave, barge-board,
Corinthian, drawbridge,
flamboyant, groundplan,
Romanesque
11 coping stone, corner-stone,
Elizabethan, Flemish bond
12 Early English, half-timbered

archives
05 deeds
06 annals, papers

07 ledgers, records
09 documents, registers
10 chronicles
11 memorabilia

arctic
05 polar
06 boreal, frozen
07 glacial, subzero
08 far north, freezing
11 hyperborean

ardent
03 hot
04 avid, keen, warm
05 eager, fiery
06 fervid, fierce, strong
07 devoted, fervent, zealous
08 spirited, vehement
09 dedicated
10 passionate
11 impassioned
12 enthusiastic

ardour
04 fire, heat, lust, zeal, zest
06 spirit, warmth
07 avidity, fervour, passion
08 devotion, keenness
09 animation, eagerness,
intensity, vehemence
10 dedication, enthusiasm
12 empressement

arduous
04 hard
05 harsh, heavy, tough
06 severe, taxing, tiring, uphill
07 be a slog, onerous
08 daunting, wearying
09 difficult, gruelling, laborious,
punishing, strenuous
10 burdensome, formidable
12 backbreaking

area
04 part, size, zone
05 field, patch, range, realm,
scope, tract, width, world
06 branch, domain, extent,
parish, region, sector, sphere
07 enclave, expanse, portion,
quarter, section, terrain
08 district, environs, locality,
precinct, province
09 territory
10 department
13 neighbourhood

arena
04 area, bowl, ring
05 field, realm, scene, world
06 domain, ground, sphere
07 stadium
08 coliseum, province
10 department, hippodrome

11 battlefield
12 amphitheatre, battleground

arguable
04 moot
09 debatable, undecided
10 disputable
11 contentious
12 questionable
14 controvertible, open to question

argue
03 row
04 feud, hold, show
05 claim, fight, imply, plead
06 assert, bicker, debate, denote, haggle, reason
07 contend, discuss, dispute, exhibit, fall out, quarrel, suggest, wrangle
08 disagree, have a row, maintain, persuade, question, squabble
09 altercate, have it out, have words, take issue
11 cross swords, demonstrate, expostulate, remonstrate
13 have it out with
15 be at loggerheads, have a bone to pick

argument
03 row
04 case, feud, plot, spat, tiff
05 clash, fight, logic, set-to
06 barney, debate, dust-up, reason, ruckus, rumpus
07 defence, dispute, outline, quarrel, summary, wrangle
08 conflict, ding-dong, squabble
09 argy-bargy, assertion, rationale, reasoning
10 contention, discussion
11 altercation, controversy
12 disagreement
13 expostulation, running battle, shouting-match, slanging-match

argumentative
07 stroppy
08 captious, contrary, perverse
09 litigious, polemical
11 belligerent, contentious, dissentious, quarrelsome
12 cantankerous, disputatious

arid
03 dry
04 drab, dull
05 baked, vapid, waste
06 barren, boring, desert, dreary, jejune, torrid

07 parched, sterile, tedious
08 lifeless
09 infertile, torrefied, waterless
10 colourless, dehydrated, desiccated
12 moistureless, unproductive

aright
05 aptly, fitly, truly
07 exactly, rightly
08 properly, suitably
09 correctly

arise
04 go up, lift, soar, stem
05 begin, climb, ensue, get up, issue, occur, start, tower
06 appear, ascend, come up, crop up, emerge, follow, result, rise up, spring
07 proceed, stand up
08 commence
11 come to light

aristocracy
05 elite
06 gentry
07 peerage
08 nobility
09 gentility, optimates, top drawer
10 haute monde, patricians, patriciate, upper class, upper crust
11 high society, ruling class

aristocrat
04 lady, lord, peer, toff
05 noble
07 grandee, peeress
08 eupatrid, nobleman, optimate
09 patrician
10 noblewoman

aristocratic
05 elite, noble
06 lordly, titled
07 courtly, elegant, refined
08 highborn, well-born
09 dignified, patrician
10 upper-class, upper-crust
11 blue-blooded

arm
03 bay, rig
04 cove, gird, limb, wing
05 array, brace, equip, firth, inlet, issue, prime, steel
06 branch, outfit, supply
07 channel, estuary, forearm, fortify, furnish, prepare, protect, provide, section
08 accoutre, brachium, division, offshoot

09 appendage, extension, reinforce, upper limb
10 department, detachment, projection, strengthen

armada
04 navy
05 fleet
08 flotilla, squadron
10 naval force

armaments
04 arms, guns
06 cannon
07 weapons
08 ordnance, weaponry
09 artillery, munitions
10 ammunition

armistice
05 peace, truce
09 ceasefire
11 peace treaty

armour
04 mail
07 panoply
09 chain mail
12 iron-cladding

armoured
08 iron-clad
09 bomb-proof, protected
10 reinforced
11 bullet-proof, steel-plated
12 armour-plated

armoury
05 depot, stock
07 arsenal
08 magazine
09 arms depot, garderobe, stockpile
10 repository
13 ordnance depot
14 ammunition dump

arms
04 guns
05 crest
06 shield
07 weapons
08 blazonry, firearms, heraldry, insignia, ordnance, weaponry
09 armaments, artillery, munitions
10 ammunition, coat-of-arms, escutcheon

army
03 mob
04 host, pack
05 crowd, horde, swarm
06 throng, troops
07 cohorts, legions, militia
08 infantry, military, soldiers
09 multitude

aroma
05 fumet, odour, scent, smell
07 bouquet, fumette, perfume
09 fragrance, redolence

aromatic
05 balmy, fresh, spicy
07 pungent, savoury, scented
08 fragrant, perfumed, redolent
11 odoriferous
13 sweet-smelling

around
04 near
05 about, circa, close, round
06 at hand, nearby, nearly
07 all over, roughly
08 framed by, to and fro
09 enclosing
10 encircling, everywhere, more or less, on all sides
11 surrounding
12 circumjacent, encompassing
13 approximately, circumambient,
15 in all directions

arouse
04 goad, spur, whet
05 cause, evoke, incur, rouse, spark, waken
06 awaken, excite, incite, induce, kindle, prompt, stir up, turn on, wake up
07 agitate, animate, inflame, provoke, quicken
09 instigate, stimulate

arraign
06 accuse, charge, impugn, indict
07 impeach
09 prosecute
11 incriminate
13 call to account

arrange
03 fix, set
04 file, list, plan, sift, sort, tidy
05 align, array, class, fix up, grade, group, order, set up
06 adjust, codify, decide, design, devise, lay out, line up, set out, settle
07 dispose, marshal, prepare, project, sort out
08 classify, organize, pencil in, position, regulate, settle on
09 catalogue, determine
10 categorize, co-ordinate
11 orchestrate, systematize

arrangement
04 plan

05 array, order, plans, score, set-up, terms
06 design, detail, format, layout, line-up, method, scheme, system
07 details, display, setting
08 contract, grouping, planning, schedule
09 agreement, structure
10 adaptation, compromise, groundwork, settlement
11 disposition, preparation
12 modus vivendi, organization, preparations
13 orchestration
14 classification, interpretation

arrant
04 rank, vile
05 gross, utter
06 brazen
07 blatant, extreme
08 absolute, complete, flagrant, outright, thorough
09 barefaced, downright, egregious, out-and-out
11 unmitigated
12 incorrigible

array
04 deck, robe, show
05 adorn, align, dress, group, order, range
06 attire, clothe, draw up, line up, line-up, muster, parade
07 apparel, arrange, bedizen, display, exhibit, marshal
08 accoutre, assemble, decorate, position
09 formation
10 assemblage, assortment, collection, exhibition, exposition, habilitate
11 arrangement, disposition, marshalling

arrears
04 debt
05 debts
07 balance, deficit
11 liabilities

❑**in arrears**
04 late
05 owing
06 behind, in debt
07 overdue
10 behindhand
11 outstanding

arrest
02 do
03 nab
04 book, bust, grab, grip, halt, nail, nick, slow, stem, stop

05 block, catch, check, delay, rivet, run in, seize, stall
06 collar, detain, hinder, impede, pick up, retard
07 attract, capture, engross, inhibit, seizure
08 restrain, slow down
09 apprehend, interrupt
11 nip in the bud
15 take into custody

❑**under arrest**
09 in custody
11 in captivity

arresting
07 amazing, notable
08 engaging, striking, stunning
10 impressive, noteworthy, remarkable, surprising
11 conspicuous, outstanding
13 extraordinary

arrival
05 entry, guest
06 advent, coming
07 fresher, incomer, visitor
08 approach, débutant, entrance, freshman, newcomer, visitant
09 débutante, emergence
10 appearance, occurrence

arrive
04 come, dock, land, show
05 enter, get to, occur, reach
06 appear, blow in, come in, drop in, happen, make it, roll up, show up, turn up
07 check in, clock in
08 get there
09 be present, touch down
14 come on the scene

arrogance
05 nerve, pride, scorn
06 hubris, vanity
07 conceit, disdain, hauteur
08 boasting, contempt
09 contumely, insolence, lordiness, pomposity
11 haughtiness, presumption
12 snobbishness
13 condescension, imperiousness
14 high-handedness, self-importance

arrogant
05 proud
06 lordly, uppity
07 haughty, stuck-up
08 assuming, boastful, insolent, scornful, snobbish, superior

09 big-headed, conceited, egotistic, hubristic, imperious
10 disdainful, high-handed, hoity-toity
11 overbearing, patronizing, toffee-nosed
12 contemptuous, presumptuous, supercilious
13 condescending, high and mighty, self-important
14 full of yourself

arrogate
05 seize, usurp
06 assume
07 presume
10 commandeer
11 appropriate

arrow
04 bolt, dart
05 shaft
06 flight, marker
07 pointer
08 sagittal
09 indicator

arsenal
05 depot, stock
07 armoury
08 magazine
09 arms depot, garderobe, stockpile
10 repository
13 ordnance depot
14 ammunition dump

arson
09 pyromania
11 fire-raising
12 incendiarism

arsonist
07 fire-bug
10 fire-raiser, incendiary, pyromaniac

art
04 gift
05 craft, flair, guile, knack, skill
06 design, method, talent
07 cunning, drawing, finesse, mastery, slyness
08 aptitude, artistry, facility, painting, trickery, wiliness
09 dexterity, expertise, ingenuity, sculpture
10 adroitness, astuteness, craftiness, profession, shrewdness, virtuosity
➢ See also **artist**; **paint**; **painter**; **painting**; **photograph**; **picture**; **sculpture**

▶ *Schools of art include*:
05 Op Art
06 Cubism, Gothic, Pop Art, Purism, Rococo
07 Art Deco, Baroque, Dadaism, folk art, Realism
08 abstract, Barbizon, Bohemian, Futurism
09 Byzantine, Modernism, Symbolism, Vorticism
10 Art Nouveau, classicism, Minimal Art, Naturalism, Romanesque, Surrealism
11 Hellenistic, renaissance, Romanticism, Suprematism
12 Aestheticism
13 Expressionism, Impressionism, Neoclassicism, Post-Modernism
14 action painting, Constructivism

▶ *Arts and crafts*:
04 film
05 batik, video
06 fresco, mosaic
07 collage, crochet, etching, origami, pottery, weaving
08 ceramics, graphics, knitting, painting, spinning, tapestry
09 engraving, jewellery, marquetry, metalwork, modelling, sculpture, sketching
10 caricature, embroidery, enamelling, needlework
11 calligraphy, lithography, oil painting, photography, portraiture, watercolour, woodcarving
12 architecture, illustration, stained glass

artefact
04 item, tool
05 thing
06 object

artful
03 sly
04 foxy, wily
05 sharp, smart
06 clever, crafty, shrewd, subtle
07 cunning, devious, vulpine
08 masterly, scheming
09 deceitful, ingenious
11 resourceful

article
04 item, part, unit
05 essay, paper, piece, point, story, thing
06 object, report, review

07 account, feature, portion, section, write-up
08 artefact, offprint
09 commodity, monograph, paragraph, thingummy
11 composition, constituent
12 thingummybob, thingummyjig

articulate
03 say
04 talk
05 clear, lucid, speak, state, utter, vocal, voice
06 fluent
07 breathe, express
08 coherent, distinct, eloquent, vocalize
09 enunciate, pronounce, verbalize
10 expressive, meaningful
12 intelligible
14 comprehensible, understandable

articulated
05 joint
06 hinged, joined, linked
07 coupled
08 attached, fastened
09 connected
11 interlocked

articulation
06 saying
07 diction, talking, voicing
08 delivery, speaking
09 utterance
10 expression
11 enunciation
12 vocalization
13 pronunciation, verbalization

artifice
04 ruse, wile
05 craft, dodge, guile, trick
06 deceit, scheme, tactic
07 cunning, slyness
08 strategy, subtlety, trickery
09 chicanery, stratagem
10 artfulness, cleverness, craftiness, subterfuge
11 contrivance

artificial
04 fake, mock, sham
05 bogus, false, pseud
06 made-up, phoney, pseudo
07 assumed, feigned, man-made, plastic, studied
08 affected, mannered, specious, spurious
09 contrived, imitation, insincere
10 non-natural

11 counterfeit
12 manufactured

artisan
06 expert
08 mechanic
09 artificer, craftsman, operative
10 journeyman, technician
11 craftswoman
13 skilled worker

artist

► *Types of artist*:
06 master, potter
07 painter
08 designer, engraver, sculptor
09 architect, craftsman, goldsmith
10 cartoonist
11 craftswoman, draughtsman, illustrator, silversmith
12 photographer
13 draughtswoman
15 graphic designer
➤ See also **art**

artiste
05 actor, comic
06 dancer, player, singer
07 actress, trouper
08 comedian
09 performer
10 comedienne
11 entertainer
12 vaudevillian

artistic
06 gifted
07 elegant, skilled, stylish
08 creative, cultured, talented
09 aesthetic, beautiful, exquisite, sensitive
10 attractive, decorative, harmonious, ornamental
11 imaginative

artistry
05 craft, flair, skill, style, touch
06 genius, talent
07 ability, finesse, mastery
08 deftness
09 expertise
10 brilliance, creativity
11 proficiency, sensitivity, workmanship
13 craftsmanship
14 accomplishment

artless
04 open, pure, true
05 frank, naïve, plain
06 candid, direct, honest, simple, unwary
07 genuine, natural, sincere

08 innocent, trusting
09 guileless, ingenuous

as
04 like, when
05 being, since, while
06 whilst
07 because, owing to, through
10 for example, seeing that
13 at the same time
14 simultaneously

□**as for**
12 with regard to, in relation to
13 with respect to
14 on the subject of
15 with reference to

□**as it were**
06 in a way
07 so to say
09 in some way, so to speak

ascend
04 go up, rise, soar
05 arise, climb, fly up, mount, scale, tower
06 move up
07 float up, lift off, take off

ascendancy
04 edge, sway
05 power
07 command, control, mastery
08 dominion, hegemony
09 authority, dominance, supremacy, upper hand
10 domination, prevalence
11 pre-eminence, superiority

ascent
04 hill, ramp, rise
05 climb, slope
07 advance, incline, scaling
08 climbing, gradient, mounting, progress
09 acclivity, ascending, ascension, elevation
10 escalation

ascertain
03 fix
05 learn
06 detect, locate, settle, verify
07 confirm, find out, pin down
08 discover, identify
09 determine, establish
11 make certain

ascetic
03 nun
04 monk, yogi
05 fakir, harsh, plain, stern
06 hermit, severe, strict
07 austere, dervish, puritan, recluse, Spartan
08 celibate, rigorous, solitary

09 abstainer, abstinent, anchorite
10 abstemious
11 puritanical, self-denying

ascribe
06 assign, credit, impute
07 put down
08 accredit
09 attribute

ashamed
05 sorry
06 guilty, modest
07 abashed, bashful, humbled
08 blushing, contrite, hesitant, red-faced, sheepish
09 mortified, reluctant
10 apologetic, distressed, humiliated, remorseful
11 crestfallen, discomfited, discomposed, embarrassed
13 self-conscious

ashen
03 wan
04 grey, pale
05 livid, pasty, white
06 leaden, pallid
07 anaemic, ghastly
08 blanched, bleached
10 colourless

aside
05 alone, apart
07 whisper
08 secretly
09 alongside, departure, monologue, on one side, privately, soliloquy
10 digression, separately
11 parenthesis
12 stage whisper

asinine
04 daft
05 inane, potty, silly
06 absurd, stupid
07 fatuous, idiotic, moronic
08 gormless
09 imbecilic, senseless
10 half-witted
11 nonsensical

ask
03 beg, bid, sue
04 pray, pump, quiz, seek
05 crave, grill, order, plead, posit, press, query
06 demand, invite, summon
07 beseech, canvass, clamour, entreat, implore, inquire, propose, request, require, solicit, suggest
08 petition, question
09 interview, postulate

10 put forward, supplicate
11 interrogate, requisition
12 cross-examine

askance
08 sideways
09 dubiously, obliquely
10 doubtfully, indirectly
11 sceptically
12 disdainfully, suspiciously
13 distrustfully, mistrustfully
14 disapprovingly

askew
04 skew
07 crooked, oblique
08 lopsided, sideways
09 crookedly, skew-whiff

asleep
04 numb
05 inert
06 dozing
07 dormant, napping, resting
08 comatose, inactive, sleeping, snoozing
09 flaked out
11 unconscious
13 out like a light
14 dead to the world

aspect
03 air
04 face, look, side, view
05 angle, facet, light, point
06 factor, manner
07 bearing, feature, outlook
08 position
09 dimension, direction
10 appearance, expression, standpoint
11 countenance, point of view

asperity
08 acerbity, acrimony, severity, sourness
09 crossness, harshness, roughness, sharpness
10 bitterness, causticity
11 astringency, crabbedness, peevishness
12 churlishness, irascibility, irritability

aspersion
◻ **cast aspersions on**
04 slur
05 smear
06 defame, vilify
07 censure, slander
08 reproach
09 criticize, denigrate, deprecate, disparage
10 sling mud at, throw mud at

asphyxiate
05 choke
06 stifle
07 smother
08 strangle, throttle
09 suffocate
11 strangulate

aspiration
03 aim
04 goal, hope, wish
05 dream, ideal
06 desire, intent, object
07 craving, longing, purpose
08 ambition, yearning
09 endeavour, objective

aspire
03 aim
04 hope, long, seek, wish
05 crave, dream, yearn
06 desire, hanker, pursue

aspiring
04 keen
05 eager
07 budding, hopeful, longing, wishful, would-be
08 aspirant, striving
09 ambitious
10 optimistic
12 endeavouring, enterprising

ass
04 fool, moke, mule, nerd, pony, twit
05 burro, hinny, idiot, ninny, twerp, wally
06 dimwit, donkey, nitwit
07 asinine, jackass
08 dipstick, imbecile, numskull
09 blockhead, numbskull
10 nincompoop

assail
05 beset, worry
06 attack, invade, malign, plague, strike
07 bedevil, bombard, perplex, set upon, torment, trouble
08 maltreat, set about, tear into
09 criticize

assailant
05 enemy
06 abuser, mugger
07 invader, reviler
08 assailer, attacker, opponent
09 adversary, aggressor

assassin
06 gunman, hit-man, killer
08 murderer
09 cut-throat
10 hatchet man, liquidator
11 contract man, executioner

assassinate
03 hit
04 do in, kill, slay
06 murder
07 bump off
08 dispatch
09 eliminate, liquidate

assault
03 GBH, hit, mug
04 raid, rape
05 abuse, blitz, go for, storm
06 attack, beat up, charge, do over, fall on, invade, strike
07 battery, bombard, lay into, mugging, set upon
08 invasion, storming
09 incursion, offensive, onslaught
11 molestation

assemblage
04 mass
05 crowd, flock, group, rally
06 throng
09 gathering, multitude
10 collection
12 accumulation

assemble
04 join, make, mass, meet
05 amass, build, flock, group, rally, set up
06 gather, join up, muster
07 collate, collect, compose, connect, convene, marshal, round up, summons
08 mobilize
09 construct, fabricate
10 accumulate, congregate
11 manufacture, put together

assembly
04 body
05 agora, crowd, flock, gemot, group, rally, synod
06 indaba, kgotla, throng
07 company, council, gorsedd, meeting
08 building, congress, panegyry
09 gathering, multitude
10 assemblage, collection, conference, convention
11 convocation
12 congregation

assent
05 agree, allow, grant, yield
06 accede, accept, accord, comply, concur, permit
07 approve, concede, consent
08 approval, sanction
09 acquiesce, agreement

10 acceptance, compliance, concession, permission
11 approbation, concurrence
12 acquiescence, capitulation

assert
05 argue, claim, state, swear
06 affirm, attest, defend, stress
07 confirm, contend, declare, profess, protest
08 insist on, maintain
09 establish, pronounce, testify to, vindicate

assertion
05 claim
06 avowal
09 statement
10 allegation, contention, insistence, profession
11 affirmation, attestation, declaration, predication, vindication
13 pronouncement

assertive
04 bold, firm
05 pushy
07 decided, forward
08 dominant, emphatic, forceful, positive
09 confident, insistent
10 aggressive
11 self-assured
12 strong-willed
13 self-confident

assess
03 fix, tax
04 levy, rate
05 gauge, judge, value, weigh
06 impose, review, size up
07 compute
08 appraise, check out, consider, estimate, evaluate
09 calculate, determine

assessment
04 levy, rate, toll
05 recce
06 demand, review, tariff
07 opinion, testing
09 appraisal, valuation
10 estimation, evaluation
11 computation

asset
03 aid
04 boon, help, plus
05 funds, goods, money
06 estate, virtue, wealth
07 benefit, capital, savings
08 blessing, holdings, property, reserves, resource, strength
09 advantage, liability, plus point, resources, valuables

10 securities
11 possessions, strong point

assiduous
06 steady
07 devoted
08 constant, diligent, sedulous, studious, untiring
09 attentive, dedicated
10 persistent, unflagging
11 hard-working, industrious
13 conscientious, indefatigable

assign
03 fix, set
04 give, name
05 allot, grant
06 detail, impute, select
07 appoint, ascribe, consign, install, put down, specify
08 accredit, allocate, delegate, dispense, nominate
09 apportion, attribute, chalk up to, designate, determine
10 commission, distribute

assignation
04 date
05 tryst
10 engagement, rendezvous
11 appointment, arrangement

assignment
03 job
04 duty, post, task
06 charge, errand
07 project
08 position
10 allocation, commission, delegation, nomination
11 appointment, designation
12 distribution
14 responsibility

assimilate
03 mix
05 adapt, blend, learn, unite
06 absorb, mingle, take in
08 accustom
09 integrate
11 acclimatize, incorporate

assist
03 aid
04 abet, back, help
05 serve
06 back up, enable, second
07 benefit, further, relieve, succour, support, sustain
08 expedite
09 co-operate, do your bit, encourage, give a hand, lend a hand, reinforce
10 facilitate, give a leg up, rally round
11 collaborate

assistance
03 aid
04 help
05 boost
06 a leg up, relief
07 backing, benefit, service, succour, support
11 co-operation, furtherance
12 a helping hand
13 reinforcement

assistant
04 aide, ally
06 backer, deputy, helper, second
07 abettor, partner
09 accessory, ancillary, associate, auxiliary, colleague, supporter
10 accomplice
11 confederate, subordinate
12 collaborator, driving force, right-hand man
15 second-in-command

associate
03 mix
04 ally, join, link, mate, pair, peer, yoke
05 unite
06 attach, fellow, friend, hobnob, mingle, relate
07 combine, compeer, comrade, connect, consort, hang out, partner
08 co-worker, identify, sidekick
09 affiliate, assistant, colleague, companion, correlate, socialize, syndicate
10 amalgamate, fraternize
11 confederate, keep company
12 collaborator, go hand in hand, rub shoulders

association
03 tie
04 band, bond, club, link
05 group, guild, union
06 cartel, clique, league
07 company, society
08 alliance, relation, sodality
09 coalition, syndicate
10 connection, consortium, federation, fellowship, fraternity, friendship
11 affiliation, confederacy, corporation, correlation, involvement, partnership
12 organization, relationship

assorted
05 mixed
06 motley, sundry, varied
07 diverse, several, various
08 manifold

09 different, differing
10 variegated
12 multifarious
13 heterogeneous, miscellaneous

assortment
03 lot, mix
05 bunch, group
06 choice, jumble, medley
07 farrago, mixture, variety
08 grouping
09 potpourri, selection
10 collection, miscellany, salmagundi
11 arrangement, olla-podrida

assuage
04 calm, ease, lull
05 allay, lower, slake
06 lessen, pacify, quench, reduce, soften, soothe
07 appease, lighten, mollify, relieve, satisfy
08 mitigate, moderate, palliate
09 alleviate

assume
05 adopt, fancy, feign, guess, infer, put on, think, usurp
06 accept, affect, deduce, expect, take on
07 imagine, presume, suppose, surmise
08 arrogate, simulate, take over
09 postulate, undertake
10 commandeer, presuppose, take as read, understand
11 appropriate, counterfeit
14 take for granted

assumed
04 fake, sham
05 bogus, false
06 made-up, phoney
07 feigned
08 affected, putative
09 pretended, simulated
10 fictitious
11 counterfeit

assumption
04 idea
05 fancy, guess
06 belief, notion, theory
07 premise, seizure, surmise
08 adoption, takeover
09 inference, postulate
10 arrogation, conjecture, hypothesis
11 expectation, postulation, presumption, supposition
13 appropriation, commandeering
14 presupposition

assurance
03 vow
04 oath, word
05 nerve
06 aplomb, pledge
07 courage, promise
08 audacity, boldness, security
09 certainty, guarantee
10 confidence, conviction
11 affirmation, assuredness, declaration, undertaking

assure
03 vow
04 seal
05 swear
06 affirm, attest, ensure, pledge, secure, soothe
07 certify, comfort, confirm, hearten, promise, warrant
08 convince, persuade
09 encourage, guarantee

assured
04 bold, sure
05 fixed
06 secure
07 certain, ensured, settled
08 definite, positive, promised
09 assertive, audacious, confident, confirmed
10 guaranteed
11 cut and dried, irrefutable
12 indisputable

astonish
03 wow
04 daze, stun
05 amaze, floor, shock
07 astound, stagger, startle, stupefy
08 bewilder, confound, surprise
09 dumbfound, take aback
11 flabbergast

astonished
05 dazed
06 amazed
07 shocked, stunned
08 startled
09 astounded, staggered, surprised
10 bewildered, bowled over, confounded, taken aback
11 dumbfounded
13 flabbergasted, knocked for six

astonishing
07 amazing
08 shocking, striking, stunning
09 startling
10 astounding, impressive, staggering, surprising
11 bewildering

12 breathtaking, mind-boggling

astonishment
05 shock
06 dismay, wonder
08 surprise
09 amazement, confusion, disbelief
12 bewilderment, stupefaction
13 consternation

astound
04 stun
05 amaze, shock
07 startle, stupefy
08 astonish, bewilder, bowl over, surprise
09 overwhelm
11 knock for six

astounding
07 amazing
08 shocking, stunning
09 startling
10 staggering, stupefying, surprising
11 astonishing, bewildering
12 breathtaking, overwhelming

astray
04 awry, lost, miss
05 amiss, wrong
06 adrift
07 missing
09 off course

astringent
04 acid, hard
05 harsh, stern
06 biting, severe
07 acerbic, caustic, mordant, styptic
08 scathing
09 trenchant

astronaut
08 spaceman
09 cosmonaut
10 spacewoman
14 space traveller

➤ *Names of astronauts:*
04 **Bean** (Alan), **Ride** (Sally)
05 **Foale** (Michael), **Glenn** (John), **Titov** (Gherman), **White** (Edward)
06 **Aldrin** (Edwin Eugene 'Buzz'), **Conrad** (Charles 'Pete'), **Lovell** (James 'Jim')
07 **Chaffee** (Roger), **Collins** (Michael), **Gagarin** (Yuri), **Grissom** (Gus), **Sharman** (Helen), **Shepard** (Alan)
09 **Armstrong** (Neil)
10 **Tereshkova** (Valentina)

astronomer and astrophysicist

➤ *Names of astronomers and astrophysicists*:

04 **Adams** (John Couch), **Airy** (Sir George Biddell), **Biot** (Jean-Baptiste), **Gold** (Thomas), **Hale** (George Ellery), **Oort** (Jan Hendrik), **Saha** (Meghnad), **Webb** (James Edwin)

05 **Adams** (Walter Sydney), **Baade** (Walter), **Baily** (Francis), **Brahe** (Tycho), **Gauss** (Carl Friedrich), **Hoyle** (Sir Fred), **Jeans** (Sir James Hopwood), **Moore** (Patrick), **Sagan** (Carl), **Vogel** (Hermann Carl)

06 **Halley** (Edmond), **Hewish** (Antony), **Hubble** (Edwin Powell), **Jansky** (Karl Guthe), **Kepler** (Johannes), **Kuiper** (Gerard Peter), **Lovell** (Sir Bernard), **Olbers** (Heinrich Wilhelm Matthäus)

07 **Babcock** (Harold Delos), **Barnard** (Edward Emerson), **Burnell** (Jocelyn Bell), **Cassini** (Giovanni Domenico), **Celsius** (Anders), **Galileo**, **Hawking** (Stephen William), **Laplace** (Pierre Simon, Marquis de), **Lockyer** (Sir Norman), **Penrose** (Roger), **Penzias** (Arno Allan), **Ptolemy**, **Seyfert** (Carl Keenan), **Shapley** (Harlow), **Whipple** (Fred Lawrence)

08 **Herschel** (Caroline), **Herschel** (Sir John Frederick William), **Herschel** (Sir William), **Korolyov** (Sergei), **Tombaugh** (Clyde William)

09 **Eddington** (Sir Arthur Stanley), **Fabricius** (David), **Flamsteed** (John), **Sosigenes**

10 **Copernicus** (Nicolaus), **Hipparchos**

11 **Bell Burnell** (Jocelyn), **Tsiolkovsky** (Konstantin)

12 **Schiaparelli** (Giovanni Virginio)

13 **Chandrasekhar** (Subrahmanyan)

➤ See also **scientist**

astute

03 sly
04 keen, wily, wise
05 canny, sharp
06 clever, crafty, shrewd, subtle
07 cunning, knowing, prudent
09 sagacious
10 discerning, perceptive
11 intelligent, penetrating
13 perspicacious

asylum

05 haven
06 refuge
07 retreat, shelter
08 loony bin, madhouse
09 funny farm, sanctuary
11 institution
12 port in a storm

asymmetrical

04 awry
06 uneven
07 crooked, unequal
08 lopsided
09 distorted, irregular
10 unbalanced
13 unsymmetrical

asymmetry

09 imbalance
10 distortion, inequality, unevenness
11 crookedness
12 irregularity, lopsidedness

atheism

07 impiety
08 nihilism, paganism, unbelief
09 disbelief, non-belief
10 heathenism, infidelity, irreligion, scepticism
11 godlessness, rationalism

atheist

05 pagan
07 heathen, heretic, infidel, sceptic
08 humanist, nihilist
10 unbeliever
11 freethinker, non-believer, nullifidian, rationalist

athlete

06 player, runner
07 gymnast
09 contender, sportsman
10 competitor, contestant
11 sportswoman

➤ *Names of athletes*:

03 **Coe** (Sebastian)
04 **Budd** (Zola), **Cram** (Steve), **Koch** (Marita)
05 **Bubka** (Sergei), **Jones** (Marion), **Lewis** (Carl), **Moses** (Ed), **Nurmi**

(Paavo), **Ovett** (Steve), **Owens** (Jesse)

06 **Aouita** (Said), **Beamon** (Bob), **Peters** (Mary)

07 **Ashford** (Evelyn), **Backley** (Steve), **Blondin** (Charles), **Edwards** (Jonathan), **Fosbury** (Dick), **Gunnell** (Sally), **Jackson** (Colin), **Johnson** (Ben), **Johnson** (Michael)

08 **Christie** (Linford), **Pieterse** (Zola), **Thompson** (Daley)

09 **Bannister** (Sir Roger), **Sanderson** (Tessa), **Whitbread** (Fatima)

14 **Griffith-Joyner** (Florence 'Flo-Jo')

➤ See also **sport**

athletic

03 fit
04 wiry
06 active, sinewy, sporty, strong, sturdy
08 muscular, powerful, vigorous, well-knit
09 energetic, gymnastic

➤ *Athletic events include*:

05 relay
06 discus, hammer, sprint
07 javelin, shotput
08 biathlon, high jump, long jump, marathon, tug of war
09 caber toss, decathlon, pole vault, triathlon
10 heptathlon, pentathlon, triple jump
12 half marathon, steeplechase
15 cross-country run, tossing the caber

➤ See also **sport**

athletics

05 games, races
06 sports
10 gymnastics
11 field events, track events
13 callisthenics

atmosphere

03 air, sky
04 aura, feel, mood, tone
05 ether, tenor
06 milieu, spirit
07 climate, feeling, flavour, heavens, quality, setting
09 ambience, character
10 background
11 environment
12 surroundings

➤ *Names of layers of the*
atmosphere:
09 exosphere
10 ionosphere, mesosphere
11 troposphere
12 stratosphere, thermosphere

atom
03 bit, jot
04 hint, iota, mite, spot, whit
05 crumb, grain, scrap, shred, speck, trace
06 morsel
08 fragment, molecule, particle
09 scintilla

➤ *Types of subatomic*
particle:
04 kaon, muon, pion
06 photon, proton
07 neutron
08 electron, neutrino, positron
10 anti-proton
11 anti-neutron, psi particle
12 anti-neutrino

atone
06 offset, pay for, redeem, remedy, repent
07 appease, expiate, redress
08 make good
09 indemnify, make right, make up for, reconcile
10 compensate, make amends, propitiate, recompense

atonement
06 amends
07 payment, penance, redress
08 requital
09 expiation, indemnity, repayment
10 recompense, reparation
11 appeasement, eye for an eye, restitution, restoration
12 compensation, propitiation
13 reimbursement

atrocious
05 cruel
06 brutal, savage, wicked
07 ghastly, heinous, hideous
08 dreadful, fiendish, grievous, horrible, shocking, terrible
09 appalling, merciless, monstrous, nefarious
10 abominable, horrendous

atrocity
04 evil
06 horror
07 cruelty, outrage
08 savagery, vileness, villainy
09 barbarity, brutality, violation
10 wickedness
11 abomination, monstrosity

atrophy
04 fade
05 decay, waste
06 shrink, tabefy, wither
07 decline, shrivel, wasting
08 diminish, emaciate, marasmus
09 waste away, withering
10 degenerate, diminution, emaciation
11 deteriorate, shrivelling, tabefaction, wasting away
12 degeneration
13 deterioration

attach
03 add, fix, pin, put, tie
04 ally, bind, join, link, nail, weld
05 affix, annex, stick, unite
06 adhere, assign, couple, fasten, impute, secure
07 ascribe, connect
09 affiliate, associate, attribute, latch onto

attached
04 fond
06 liking, loving, tender
07 devoted, engaged, married
08 friendly
09 spoken for
11 going steady

attachment
03 tie
04 bond, link, love
07 adjunct, codicil, fitting, fixture, loyalty
08 affinity, devotion, fondness
09 accessory, affection, appendage, extension
10 attraction, friendship, partiality, tenderness
12 accoutrement, appurtenance

attack
03 fit, mug, pan
04 bout, raid, rush, slam
05 abuse, begin, blitz, decry, foray, go for, knock, sally, slate, spasm, start, storm
06 access, ambush, assail, beat up, berate, charge, do over, fall on, impugn, malign, revile, sortie, strike, stroke, tackle, vilify
07 assault, battery, besiege, censure, lay into, seizure, set upon, slag off, slating
08 commence, deal with, denounce, embark on, invasion, knocking, paroxysm, pounce on, set about, slamming, storming

09 criticism, criticize, have a go at, incursion, invective, irruption, offensive, onslaught, undertake
10 calumniate, convulsion, impugnment, revilement
11 bombardment, pick holes in
12 pull to pieces, tear to pieces, tear to shreds, vilification

attacker
06 abuser, critic, mugger, raider
07 invader, reviler
09 aggressor, assailant, detractor
10 persecutor

attain
03 get, hit, net, win
04 earn, find, gain
05 grasp, reach, touch
06 effect, fulfil, obtain, secure
07 achieve, acquire, realize
08 arrive at, complete
10 accomplish

attainable
06 at hand, doable, viable
08 feasible, possible, probable
09 potential, reachable, realistic
10 accessible, achievable, manageable, obtainable
11 conceivable, within reach

attainment
04 feat, gift
05 skill
06 talent
07 ability, mastery, success
08 aptitude, facility
10 capability, competence, completion, fulfilment
11 achievement, acquirement, proficiency, realization
12 consummation
14 accomplishment

attempt
02 go
03 aim, bid, try
04 bash, push, seek, shot, stab
05 crack, trial
06 effort, set out, strive, tackle
07 have a go, venture
09 endeavour, undertake
10 experiment, have a crack
11 try your hand, undertaking
12 give it a whirl
13 try your hand at
15 do your level best

attend
04 go to, hear, heed, help, mark, mind, note, show, tend
05 nurse, serve, visit, watch
06 escort, follow, listen, notice, show up, turn up

07 care for, go along, observe
08 take note, wait upon
09 accompany, be present, chaperone, look after
10 minister to, take notice
12 pay attention

□ attend to
04 heed
06 direct, handle, manage
07 control, oversee, process
08 deal with, follow up
09 look after, supervise

attendance
04 gate
05 crowd, house
07 showing, turnout
08 audience, presence
10 appearance

attendant
04 aide, page
05 guard, guide, usher
06 batman, escort, waiter
07 marshal, related, servant, steward
08 attached, follower, retainer
09 companion, custodian, resultant
10 associated, consequent, incidental, subsequent
11 concomitant
12 accompanying

attention
04 care, heed, help, mind
06 notice, regard
07 service, therapy, thought
08 courtesy
09 alertness, limelight, treatment, vigilance
10 advertence, advertency
11 compliments, observation, recognition
13 concentration, consideration

□ pay attention to
07 focus on
10 take notice
13 concentrate on
14 watch carefully
15 listen carefully

attentive
04 kind
05 alert, awake, aware, civil
07 all ears, careful, devoted, gallant, heedful, mindful
08 gracious, noticing, obliging, vigilant, watchful, watching
09 advertent, courteous, listening, observant
10 chivalrous, thoughtful
11 considerate

12 on the qui vive
13 accommodating, conscientious

attest
04 aver, show
05 prove, swear
06 adjure, affirm, evince, verify
07 certify, confirm, declare, display, endorse
08 evidence, vouch for
10 asseverate
11 corroborate, demonstrate
13 bear witness to

attic
04 loft
06 garret
07 mansard

attire
04 garb, gear, togs, wear
05 dress, habit
06 finery, outfit, rig-out
07 apparel, clothes, costume
08 clothing, garments
11 habiliments
13 accoutrements

attired
07 adorned, arrayed, clothed, dressed
09 decked out, rigged out, turned out
11 habilitated

attitude
04 mood, pose, view
05 stand
06 aspect, manner, stance
07 bearing, feeling, mindset, opinion, outlook, posture
08 approach, carriage, position
09 mentality, world-view
10 deportment
11 disposition, perspective, point of view
13 way of thinking
14 Weltanschauung

attract
04 draw, lure, pull
05 charm, tempt
06 allure, engage, entice, excite, invite, pull in, seduce
07 bewitch, bring in, enchant
08 appeal to, interest
09 captivate, fascinate

attraction
04 bait, draw, lure, pull
05 charm, sight
06 allure, appeal
07 feature
08 affinity, interest
09 magnetism, seduction

10 enticement, inducement, invitation, temptation
11 captivation, fascination
13 entertainment

attractive
04 cute, fair, sexy
05 bonny
06 comely, lovely, pretty
07 dashing, winning, winsome
08 engaging, enticing, fetching, gorgeous, handsome, inviting, magnetic, pleasing, striking, stunning, tempting
09 appealing, beautiful, desirable, seductive
11 captivating, fascinating, good-looking, picturesque
12 irresistible
13 prepossessing

attribute
04 mark, note, side, sign
05 facet, quirk, refer, trait
06 aspect, assign, charge, credit, impute, streak, symbol, virtue
07 ascribe, feature, quality
08 accredit, property
11 peculiarity
12 idiosyncrasy
14 characteristic

attrition
07 chafing, erosion, rubbing
08 abrasion, friction, grinding
09 detrition
10 harassment
11 attenuation, wearing away

attuned
03 set
07 adapted
08 adjusted
09 regulated
10 accustomed, harmonized
11 assimilated, co-ordinated
12 acclimatized, familiarized

atypical
07 deviant, unusual
08 aberrant, abnormal, freakish
09 anomalous, divergent, eccentric, untypical
11 exceptional
13 extraordinary

auburn
04 rust
05 henna, tawny
06 copper, russet, Titian
08 chestnut

audacious
04 bold, pert, rash, rude
05 brave, risky

06 brazen, cheeky, daring
07 assured, forward, valiant
08 fearless, impudent, insolent, intrepid, reckless
09 dauntless, shameless, unabashed
10 courageous
11 adventurous, impertinent, venturesome
12 enterprising, presumptuous

audacity
04 risk
05 cheek, pluck
06 daring, valour
07 bravery, courage
08 boldness, defiance, pertness, rashness, rudeness
09 impudence, insolence
10 brazenness, effrontery, enterprise
11 forwardness, intrepidity, presumption
12 fearlessness, impertinence
13 shamelessness

audible
05 clear, heard
08 distinct, hearable
10 detectable
11 appreciable, discernible, perceptible

audience
04 fans
05 crowd, house
06 public
07 hearing, meeting, ratings, turnout, viewers
08 assembly, devotees, regulars
09 following, gathering, interview, listeners
10 spectators
12 congregation, consultation

audit
05 check
06 go over, review, verify
07 balance, examine, inspect
08 analysis, scrutiny
09 go through, statement
10 inspection, scrutinize
11 examination, investigate

augment
04 grow
05 add to, boost, raise, swell
06 expand, extend
07 amplify, build up, enhance, enlarge, inflate, magnify
08 heighten, increase, multiply
09 intensify, reinforce
10 strengthen

augur
04 bode

06 herald
07 betoken, portend, predict, presage, promise, signify
08 forebode, foretell, prophesy
09 be a sign of, harbinger

augury
04 omen, sign
05 token
06 herald
07 portent, promise, warning
08 prodrome, prophecy
09 harbinger
10 foreboding, prediction
11 forewarning
13 haruspication
15 prognostication

august
05 grand, lofty, noble
06 solemn
07 exalted, stately
08 glorious, imposing, majestic
09 dignified
10 impressive
11 magnificent
12 awe-inspiring

aura
03 air
04 feel, hint, mood
05 vibes
06 nimbus
07 feeling, quality
08 ambience
09 emanation
10 atmosphere, vibrations

auspices
◻**under the auspices of**
11 in the care of
13 in the charge of
15 under the aegis of

auspicious
04 rosy
05 happy, lucky
06 bright, timely
07 hopeful
08 cheerful
09 fortunate, promising
10 favourable, felicitous, optimistic, propitious
11 encouraging

austere
04 cold, grim, hard
05 bleak, grave, harsh, plain, rigid, sober, stark, stern
06 chaste, frugal, severe, solemn, sombre, strict
07 ascetic, serious, spartan
08 exacting, rigorous
09 stringent, unadorned

10 abstemious, economical, forbidding, inflexible
11 puritanical, self-denying

austerity
07 economy
08 coldness, hardness, severity
09 harshness, plainness
10 abstinence, asceticism, puritanism, self-denial
13 inflexibility

authentic
04 real, true
05 legal, valid
06 honest, kosher, lawful
07 certain, factual, genuine
08 accurate, bona fide, credible, faithful, reliable
10 dependable, legitimate
12 the real McCoy

authenticate
05 prove
06 attest, ratify, verify
07 certify, confirm, endorse
08 accredit, validate, vouch for
09 authorize, guarantee
11 corroborate
12 substantiate

authenticity
05 truth
07 honesty
08 accuracy, fidelity, legality, validity, veracity
09 certainty
10 legitimacy
11 correctness, credibility, genuineness, reliability

author
03 pen
04 poet
05 maker, mover
06 parent, writer
07 creator, founder, planner
08 composer, essayist, lyricist, novelist, reporter
09 dramatist, initiator
10 biographer, journalist, librettist, originator, playwright, songwriter
12 screenwriter

authoritarian
05 harsh, rigid, tough
06 severe, strict
08 despotic, dogmatic
09 imperious
10 autocratic, oppressive, tyrannical, unyielding
11 dictatorial, doctrinaire, domineering
12 totalitarian
14 disciplinarian

authoritative
04 bold, true
05 sound, valid
07 factual, learned
08 accepted, accurate, approved, decisive, faithful, official, reliable, truthful
09 authentic, confident, masterful, scholarly
10 authorized, definitive, legitimate, sanctioned
11 self-assured, trustworthy

authority
04 buff, rule, sage, sway, they
05 clout, power, right, state
06 expert, master, muscle, permit, pundit
07 command, control, council, licence, scholar, warrant
08 dominion, sanction
09 influence, supremacy
10 government, management, permission, specialist
11 bureaucracy, connoisseur, credentials, officialdom
12 carte blanche, jurisdiction
13 authorization, establishment
14 administration
15 the powers that be

authorization
02 OK
04 okay
05 leave
06 permit
07 consent, go-ahead, licence, mandate
08 approval, sanction, warranty
10 green light, permission
11 credentials, entitlement
12 confirmation, ratification
13 accreditation

authorize
02 OK
03 let
04 okay
05 allow
06 enable, permit, ratify
07 approve, confirm, empower, entitle, license, warrant
08 legalize, sanction, validate
09 consent to, make legal
10 commission
14 give the go-ahead

autobiography
05 diary
07 journal, memoirs
09 life story

autocracy
07 fascism, tyranny
09 despotism

autocrat
06 despot, Hitler, tyrant
07 fascist
08 dictator
10 absolutist, panjandrum
12 little Hitler, totalitarian
13 authoritarian

10 absolutism
12 dictatorship
15 totalitarianism

autocratic
08 absolute, despotic
09 imperious
10 tyrannical
11 all-powerful, dictatorial, domineering, overbearing
12 totalitarian
13 authoritarian

autograph
04 mark, name, sign
07 endorse, initial
08 initials
09 signature

automatic
06 reflex
07 natural, robotic, routine
08 knee-jerk, unmanned
09 automated, necessary
10 inevitable, mechanical, mechanized, programmed
11 inescapable, instinctive, involuntary, spontaneous
12 computerized

autonomy
07 autarky, freedom
08 free will, home rule, self-rule
11 sovereignty
12 independence
14 self-government
15 self-sufficiency

auxiliary
05 extra, spare
06 helper, second
07 helping, partner, reserve
09 ancillary, assistant, assisting, secondary, supporter
10 foederatus, subsidiary, supporting
11 subordinate
12 right-hand man
13 supplementary
15 second-in-command

available
04 free
05 handy, on tap, ready
06 at hand, on hand, to hand, usable, vacant
07 untaken

10 accessible, convenient, disposable, obtainable, unoccupied, up for grabs
11 forthcoming, within reach
12 up your sleeve
14 at your disposal

avalanche
04 wave
05 flood
06 deluge
07 barrage, cascade, torrent
08 landslip
09 landslide
10 inundation

avant-garde
06 far-out, modern, way-out
07 go-ahead
08 advanced, original
09 inventive
10 futuristic, innovative, innovatory, pioneering
11 progressive
12 contemporary, experimental
14 unconventional

avarice
05 greed
08 meanness
10 greediness
11 materialism, selfishness
12 covetousness
15 acquisitiveness

avaricious
04 mean
06 greedy
08 covetous, grasping
09 mercenary, rapacious
10 pleonectic
11 acquisitive

avenge
05 repay
06 punish
07 pay back, requite
09 get back at, retaliate
11 get even with
14 get your own back, take revenge for

average
03 par, run
04 mean, mode, norm, so-so
05 usual
06 common, medial, median, medium, middle, normal
07 regular, routine, typical
08 everyday, mediocre, middling, ordinary
09 tolerable
11 indifferent, not up to much
12 intermediate, run-of-the-mill, satisfactory

13 no great shakes,
   unexceptional
14 fair to middling,
   nothing special

averse
05 loath
07 hostile, opposed
09 reluctant, unwilling
11 disinclined, ill-disposed
12 antagonistic, antipathetic

aversion
04 hate
06 hatred, horror, phobia
07 disgust, dislike
08 distaste, loathing
09 hostility, repulsion, revulsion
10 abhorrence, antagonism,
   reluctance, repugnance
11 abomination, detestation
13 unwillingness
14 disinclination

avert
04 stop
05 avoid, evade, parry
07 deflect, fend off, head off,
   obviate, prevent, ward off
08 preclude, stave off,
   turn away
09 forestall, frustrate, turn aside

aviation
06 flight, flying
11 aeronautics

aviator

➤ *Names of aviators:*
04 **Byrd** (Richard Evelyn),
   Rust (Mathias), **Udet**
   (Ernst)
05 **Bader** (Sir Douglas Robert
   Stuart), **Brown** (Sir Arthur
   Whitten), **Johns** (Captain
   William Earl)
06 **Alcock** (Sir John William),
   Gibson (Guy), **Harris** (Sir
   Arthur Travers 'Bomber'),
   Hughes (Howard), **Wright**
   (Orville), **Wright** (Wilbur),
   Yeager (Charles Elwood
   'Chuck')
07 **Blériot** (Louis), **Branson**
   (Richard), **Dornier**
   (Claudius), **Douglas**
   (Donald Wills), **Earhart**
   (Amelia), **Fossett** (Steve),
   Goering (Hermann
   Wilhelm), **Johnson** (Amy),
   Piccard (Auguste Antoine),
   Sopwith (Sir Thomas
   Octave Murdoch)
08 **Zeppelin** (Count Ferdinand
   von)

09 **Lindbergh** (Charles
   Augustus)
10 **Lindstrand** (Per),
   Richthofen (Manfred,
   Baron von)
11 **Montgolfier** (Jacques
   Étienne), **Montgolfier**
   (Joseph Michel)
13 **Messerschmitt** (Willy)
➤ See also **military**

avid
03 mad
04 keen
05 crazy, eager, great
06 ardent, greedy, hungry
07 devoted, earnest, fervent,
   intense, thirsty, zealous
08 covetous, grasping
09 dedicated, fanatical
10 insatiable, passionate
12 enthusiastic

avoid
04 balk, duck, shun
05 avert, dodge, elude, evade,
   hedge, shirk
06 bypass, escape, eschew
07 forbear, prevent
08 get round, sidestep
09 give a miss
10 circumvent
11 abstain from, shy away from
12 steer clear of

avoidable
08 eludible
09 avertible, escapable
11 preventable

avowed
04 open
05 overt, sworn
08 admitted, declared
09 confessed, professed
12 acknowledged
13 self-confessed
14 self-proclaimed

await
06 expect
07 hope for, look for

awake
04 stir, wake
05 alert, alive, aware, rouse
06 arouse, wake up
07 aroused, wakeful
08 stirring, vigilant, watchful
09 attentive, conscious,
   observant, sensitive

awakening
05 birth
06 waking
07 arousal, revival, rousing

09 animating
10 activation, enlivening
11 stimulation
12 vivification

award
04 gift, give, gong
05 grant, medal, order, prize
06 bestow, confer, trophy
07 adjudge, present
08 allocate, bestowal, citation
09 allotment, allowance,
   apportion, endowment
10 decoration, distribute
11 certificate
12 commendation,
   dispensation, presentation

➤ *Theatre, television and film
awards include (mostly
trademarks):*
04 Emmy, Tony
05 Bafta, Oscar
06 Grammy
07 Olivier
10 Golden Palm, Golden Rose
11 Golden Globe

aware
05 alert, sharp
06 shrewd
07 heedful, knowing, mindful
08 apprised, familiar, informed,
   sensible, sentient, vigilant
09 attentive, au courant,
   cognizant, conscious,
   in the know, on the ball,
   sensitive
10 acquainted, conversant
11 enlightened
12 appreciative
13 knowledgeable

awe
04 fear
05 dread
06 honour, terror, wonder
07 respect
09 amazement, reverence
10 admiration, veneration
12 apprehension

awe-inspiring
06 moving, solemn
07 amazing, exalted, sublime
08 daunting, majestic,
   numinous, striking, stunning
09 wonderful
10 formidable, impressive
11 magnificent, spectacular
12 breathtaking, overwhelming

awful
04 dire, ugly
05 nasty
06 horrid

07 abysmal, fearful, ghastly, heinous, hideous
08 alarming, dreadful, gruesome, horrible, horrific, shocking, terrible
09 appalling, atrocious, frightful
10 disgusting, horrifying
11 distressing

awkward
03 shy
05 inept
06 clumsy, fiddly, gauche
07 prickly
08 annoying, delicate, inexpert, lubberly, stubborn, ungainly, unwieldy
09 all thumbs, difficult, graceless, ham-fisted, ill at ease, inelegant, irritable, maladroit, obstinate
10 cumbersome, perplexing, ungraceful, unpleasant
11 problematic, troublesome

12 embarrassing, inconvenient
13 uncomfortable

awry
05 amiss, askew, wonky, wrong
06 uneven
07 crooked, oblique, twisted
08 cock-eyed
09 off-centre, skew-whiff
10 misaligned

axe
03 adz, cut, hew
04 adze, chop, fell, fire, sack
06 cancel, cleave, remove
07 chopper, cleaver, cut down, dismiss, hatchet
08 get rid of, tomahawk
09 battle-axe, discharge, eliminate, terminate
11 discontinue

□**get the axe**
10 get the boot, get the chop

axiom
05 adage, maxim, truth
06 byword, dictum, truism
07 precept
08 aphorism

axiomatic
05 given
06 gnomic
07 assumed, certain, granted
08 accepted, manifest
10 aphoristic, proverbial, understood
11 indubitable, self-evident
12 unquestioned
14 apophthegmatic

axis
05 hinge, pivot
08 vertical
10 centre-line, horizontal

axle
03 pin, rod
05 pivot, shaft
07 spindle

babble
05 babel, prate
06 burble, gibber, gurgle, hubbub, jabber, waffle
07 chatter, clamour
08 rabbit on
09 gibberish

babe
04 baby
05 child
06 infant

babel
03 din
05 chaos
06 babble, bedlam, hubbub, tumult, uproar
07 clamour, turmoil
09 commotion, confusion
10 hullabaloo
11 pandemonium

baby
03 tot, wee
04 babe, mini, tiny
05 bairn, child, dwarf, small
06 infant, little, midget, minute
09 miniature
10 diminutive, small-scale

babyish
05 naïve, silly, sissy, young
07 foolish, puerile
08 childish, immature, juvenile
09 infantile

back
03 aid, end
04 abet, help, hind, rear, tail
05 boost, other, spine, stern
06 assist, behind, dorsum, former, recede, recoil, retire, second, tergum
07 bolster, confirm, earlier, endorse, finance, promote, regress, retreat, reverse, sponsor, support, sustain
08 advocate, backbone, backside, champion, hindmost, outdated, previous, sanction, side with, withdraw
09 backtrack, backwards, encourage, subsidize

10 underwrite
11 countenance
12 hindquarters

❏**back away**
06 recede, recoil
07 retreat
08 draw back, fall back, move back, step back, withdraw
10 give ground

❏**back down**
05 yield
06 give in, submit
07 retreat, concede
08 withdraw
09 back-pedal, backtrack, climb down, surrender

❏**back out**
06 cancel, give up, recant, resign
08 go back on, withdraw
10 chicken out
11 get cold feet

❏**back up**
03 aid
06 assist, second
07 bear out, bolster, confirm, endorse, support
09 reinforce
11 corroborate

❏**behind your back**
05 slyly
08 covertly, secretly, sneakily
09 furtively
15 surreptitiously

backbiting
05 abuse, libel, spite
06 gossip, malice
07 calumny, slander
09 cattiness, criticism
10 bitchiness, defamation
11 denigration, mud-slinging, slagging off
12 spitefulness, vilification
13 disparagement

backbone
04 core, grit, guts
05 basis, nerve, pluck, spine
06 bottle, mettle
07 courage, support

08 firmness, mainstay, strength
09 character, toughness, vertebrae, willpower
12 spinal column
13 determination
15 vertebral column

backbreaking
04 hard
07 arduous, killing
09 gruelling, laborious, punishing, strenuous
10 exhausting

backer
06 patron, second
07 sponsor
08 promoter, seconder
09 supporter
10 benefactor, well-wisher
11 underwriter

backfire
04 fail, flop
07 explode, rebound
08 detonate, miscarry, ricochet
14 score an own goal

background
05 scene
06 family, milieu, record, status
07 context, culture, factors, origins, setting
08 backdrop, breeding
09 backcloth, framework, grounding, tradition
10 experience, upbringing
11 credentials, environment, preparation
13 circumstances
14 social standing

backhanded
06 ironic
07 dubious, oblique
08 indirect, two-edged
09 ambiguous, equivocal
11 double-edged

backing
03 aid
04 help
05 funds, grant
07 finance, helpers, subsidy, support
08 advocacy, approval

09 patronage, promotion, seconding
10 assistance
11 championing, endorsement, sponsorship
12 moral support
13 accompaniment, encouragement

backlash
06 recoil
08 backfire, kickback, reaction, reprisal, response
09 boomerang
11 retaliation
12 repercussion

backlog
05 hoard, stock
06 excess, supply
07 reserve
08 mountain, reserves
09 resources
12 accumulation

back-pedal
05 yield, U-turn
06 give in, submit
07 concede, retract, retreat
08 take back, withdraw
09 backtrack, climb down, surrender
12 tergiversate
14 change your mind

backslide
03 sin
04 slip
05 lapse, stray
06 defect, desert, go back, renege, revert
07 default, regress, relapse
10 apostatize
12 tergiversate, turn your back

backslider
07 reneger
08 apostate, defector, deserter, recreant, renegade, turncoat
09 defaulter
10 recidivist
13 tergiversator

backsliding
05 lapse
07 relapse
08 apostasy
09 defection, desertion
10 defaulting, regression
14 tergiversation

bacteriologist
➤ *Names of bacteriologists:*
04 **Cohn** (Ferdinand Julius), **Gram** (Hans Christian

Joachim), **Koch** (Robert), **Roux** (Émile)
05 **Avery** (Oswald Theodore), **Smith** (Theobald)
06 **Enders** (John Franklin)
07 **Behring** (Emil von), **Buchner** (Hans), **Ehrlich** (Paul), **Fleming** (Sir Alexander)
➤ See also **scientist**

backup
03 aid
04 help
07 support
10 assistance
09 equipment, resources
11 endorsement
12 confirmation
13 encouragement, reinforcement

backward
03 shy
04 slow
05 timid
07 bashful, reverse
08 hesitant, immature, rearward, retarded, retiring
09 shrinking, subnormal
10 regressive, retrograde
11 undeveloped
13 retrogressive
14 underdeveloped

backwards
09 rearwards, to the back
12 regressively
15 retrogressively

backwash
04 flow, path, wake, wash
05 swell, waves
06 result
09 aftermath
11 after effect, consequence
13 repercussions

backwoods
04 bush
06 sticks
07 outback
12 back of beyond
15 middle of nowhere

bacteria
04 bugs
05 germs
07 bacilli, viruses
08 microbes
14 micro-organisms

bad
03 ill, off
04 evil, high, poor, sour, vile

05 acute, awful, grave, harsh, lousy, nasty
06 aching, crappy, crummy, faulty, gloomy, mouldy, poorly, putrid, rancid, rotten, severe, sinful, spoilt, unruly, unwell, wicked
07 adverse, botched, corrupt, decayed, harmful, hurtful, immoral, intense, naughty, painful, serious, stroppy, tainted, useless, wayward
08 criminal, critical, damaging, diseased, dreadful, hopeless, inferior, mediocre, pathetic, shameful, terrible
09 appalling, atrocious, dangerous, defective, deficient, dishonest, imperfect, offensive, reprobate, third-rate
10 degenerate, deplorable, ill-behaved, inadequate, indisposed, mismanaged, outrageous, putrescent, refractory, second-rate, unpleasant, unsuitable
11 deleterious, destructive, detrimental, disobedient, distressing, incompetent, ineffective, ineffectual, mischievous, substandard, unwholesome
12 badly-behaved, contaminated, disagreeable, inauspicious, inconvenient, putrefactive, unacceptable, unfavourable
13 inappropriate, reprehensible
14 unsatisfactory

❑**not bad**
02 OK
04 fair, so-so
07 average
08 adequate, all right, passable
09 quite good, tolerable
10 reasonable
12 satisfactory

badge
04 logo, mark, sign
05 brand, crest, stamp, token
06 emblem, ensign, symbol
08 insignia
09 indicator, trademark
10 escutcheon, indication

badger
03 nag
04 bait, goad
05 bully, harry, hound
06 harass, hassle, pester, plague
09 importune

badinage
05 chaff
06 banter, humour
07 ribbing, teasing, waggery
08 drollery, raillery, repartee, word-play
10 jocularity, persiflage

badly
06 deeply, evilly, poorly
07 acutely, awfully, gravely, greatly, wrongly
08 bitterly, faultily, severely, sinfully, terribly, unfairly, very much, wickedly
09 adversely, immorally, intensely, painfully, unhappily, seriously
10 carelessly, criminally, critically, enormously, improperly, shamefully
11 desperately, dishonestly, exceedingly, imperfectly, incorrectly, negligently
12 inadequately, tremendously, unacceptably, unfavourably
13 incompetently, ineffectually

bad-tempered
05 cross, narky, ratty, sulky
06 crabby, grumpy, shirty
07 crabbed, grouchy, stroppy
08 choleric, petulant
09 crotchety, fractious, impatient, irritable
10 in a bad mood
12 cantankerous
13 quick-tempered

baffle
04 daze, foil
05 block, check, stump, upset
06 bemuse, defeat, hinder, puzzle, thwart
07 flummox, mystify, perplex
08 bewilder, confound
09 bamboozle, frustrate

baffling
08 bemusing, puzzling
09 confusing
10 astounding, mysterious, perplexing, stupefying, surprising
11 bewildering
12 unfathomable

bag
03 get
04 grab, kill, land, take, trap
05 catch, shoot
07 acquire, capture, reserve
09 container
10 commandeer, receptacle
11 appropriate

baggage
04 bags, gear
06 things
07 effects, luggage
09 equipment, suitcases
10 belongings
11 impedimenta
13 paraphernalia

baggy
05 loose, roomy, slack
06 droopy, floppy
07 bulging, sagging
08 oversize
09 billowing, shapeless
10 ballooning, ill-fitting
12 loose-fitting

bail
04 bond
06 pledge, surety
08 security, warranty
09 guarantee

❑ **bail out**
03 aid
04 help, quit
06 assist, escape, rescue
07 back out, finance, retreat
09 withdraw

bait
04 goad, lure
05 annoy, bribe, harry, hound, snare, tease
06 badger, harass, hassle, needle, plague
07 provoke, torment
08 irritate
09 incentive, persecute
10 attraction, enticement, inducement, temptation

balance
04 rest
05 level, match, poise, weigh
06 adjust, equate, equity, excess, juggle, parity, square
07 compare, residue, surplus
08 calmness, consider, equality, equalize, evenness, symmetry
09 composure, equipoise, remainder, sangfroid, stability
10 counteract, difference, equanimity, steadiness
11 equilibrium, equivalence
12 counterweigh
13 compensate for
14 correspondence, counterbalance, self-possession

balanced
04 calm, fair

07 assured, healthy
08 sensible, unbiased
09 equitable, impartial, objective
10 cool-headed, even-handed
12 unprejudiced
13 self-possessed

❑ **on balance**
08 all in all
12 in conclusion

balcony
04 gods
06 loggia
07 gallery, terrace, veranda
11 upper circle

bald
04 bare
05 blunt, naked, plain, stark
06 barren, direct, severe, simple, smooth
07 exposed
08 glabrate, glabrous, hairless, outright, straight, treeless
09 depilated, outspoken, unadorned, uncovered
11 bald as a coot, unsheltered
15 straightforward

balderdash
03 rot
04 bunk
05 bilge, trash, tripe
06 bunkum, drivel, hot air, piffle
07 rubbish, twaddle
08 claptrap, cobblers, nonsense, tommyrot
09 gibberish, poppycock

balding
08 receding
09 thin on top
14 losing your hair

baldness
08 alopecia, bareness, psilosis
09 calvities, starkness
12 glabrousness, hairlessness

bale
04 pack
05 truss
06 bundle, parcel
07 package

❑ **bale out**
04 quit
06 escape, get out
07 back out, retreat
08 get clear
09 withdraw

baleful
04 evil
06 deadly

07 harmful, hurtful, noxious, ominous, ruinous
08 menacing, sinister
09 injurious, malignant
10 malevolent, pernicious
11 destructive, threatening

balk, baulk
03 bar, jib
04 foil
05 check, dodge, evade, stall
06 baffle, defeat, eschew, flinch, hinder, impede, recoil, refuse, shrink, thwart
08 hesitate, obstruct
09 forestall, frustrate

ball
03 orb
04 drop, pill, shot, slug
05 dance, globe, party
06 bullet, masque, pellet, sphere
07 globule
11 dinner-dance

❏ **play ball**
07 go along, respond
09 co-operate, play along
11 collaborate, reciprocate

ballad
04 poem, song
05 carol, ditty
08 folk-song

ballet
07 dancing
11 leg-business
➤ See also **choreographer**; **dance**; **dancer**

▬ *Terms used in ballet*:
04 jeté, plié, tutu
05 barre, battu
06 ballon, chassé, écarté, splits
07 à pointe, bourrée, ciseaux, company, fouetté, leotard, pointes
08 attitude, batterie, capriole, coryphée, fish dive, glissade, stulchak
09 arabesque, ballerina, battement, élevation, entrechat, pas de deux, pas de seul, pirouette, point shoe, régisseur
10 ballet shoe, grande jeté, répétiteur
11 ports de bras
12 choreography
13 corps de ballet, five positions, sur les pointes
14 divertissement, prima ballerina

▬ *Names of ballets*:
06 Apollo, Boléro, Façade, Ondine, Onegin, Parade
07 Giselle, Orpheus, Requiem
08 Coppélia, Les Noces, Swan Lake
09 Mayerling, Petrushka, The Sylphs
10 Cinderella, Don Quixote, Pulcinella
11 Billy the Kid, Las Hermanas, The Firebird
12 Les Sylphides
13 Pineapple Poll, The Nutcracker
14 Daphnis et Chloé, Romeo and Juliet, The Prodigal Son
15 The Rite of Spring

balloon
03 bag
05 belly, bulge, swell
06 billow, blow up, dilate
07 distend, inflate, puff out

ballot
04 poll, vote
08 election
10 plebiscite, referendum

ballyhoo
04 fuss, hype, to-do
05 noise
06 hubbub, racket, tumult
07 build-up, clamour
09 commotion, hue and cry, promotion, publicity
10 excitement, hullabaloo
11 advertising, disturbance

balm
05 cream, salve
06 balsam, lotion
07 anodyne, bromide, comfort
08 curative, lenitive, ointment
09 calmative, emollient
10 palliative
11 consolation, embrocation

balmy
04 mild, soft, warm
06 gentle
07 clement, summery
08 pleasant, soothing

bamboozle
03 con
04 daze, dupe, fool, gull
05 cheat, trick, upset
06 bemuse, puzzle
07 confuse, deceive, mystify, perplex, swindle
08 bewilder, confound, hoodwink
10 disconcert

ban
03 bar
04 veto
05 curse, taboo
06 banish, censor, forbid, outlaw
07 boycott, embargo, exclude
08 prohibit, restrict, stoppage
09 proscribe, sanctions
10 disqualify, injunction
11 prohibition, restriction
12 interdiction, proscription

banal
04 dull
05 bland, corny, empty, inane, stale, stock, tired, trite, vapid
06 boring
07 clichéd, humdrum, mundane, trivial
08 everyday, ordinary, overused
09 hackneyed
11 commonplace, stereotyped
13 unimaginative

banality
06 cliché, truism
07 bromide, fatuity
08 dullness, vapidity
09 emptiness, inaneness, tiredness, triteness
11 commonplace
12 ordinariness

band
03 tie
04 belt, body, bond, club, cord, crew, gang, join, tape
05 crowd, group, horde, party, strap, strip, troop, unite
06 clique, fetter, gather, ribbon
07 binding, manacle, shackle
08 ensemble, ligature, pop group
09 affiliate, gathering, orchestra
10 amalgamate, connection, contingent, join forces
12 musical group, pull together
13 stand together

bandage
04 bind
05 cover, dress, gauze
06 bind up, swathe
07 plaster, swaddle
08 compress, dressing, ligature
10 tourniquet

bandit
05 crook, thief
06 cowboy, gunman, outlaw, pirate, robber
07 brigand
08 criminal, gangster, hijacker, marauder

09 buccaneer, desperado
10 highwayman

bandy
04 bent, pass, swap, toss
05 bowed, throw, trade
07 crooked, curved
08 exchange
09 bow-legged, misshapen
11 interchange, reciprocate

bane
03 woe
04 evil, pest, ruin
05 curse, trial
06 blight, misery, plague
07 scourge, torment, trouble
08 distress, nuisance, vexation
09 adversity, annoyance,
   bête noire
10 affliction, irritation,
   misfortune, pestilence
11 destruction

bang
03 hit, pop, rap
04 bash, blow, boom, bump,
   clap, drum, shot, slam, thud
05 burst, clang, crash, knock,
   noise, pound, punch, right,
   smack, stamp, thump,
   whack
06 hammer, report, wallop
07 collide, exactly, explode,
   thunder
08 directly, headlong, straight,
   suddenly
09 explosion, precisely
10 absolutely, detonation

banish
03 ban, bar
04 oust
05 debar, evict, exile, expel
06 deport, dispel, outlaw
07 cast out, dismiss, exclude
08 get rid of, send away
09 drive away, eliminate,
   eradicate, ostracize,
   rusticate, transport
13 excommunicate

banishment
05 exile
08 eviction, outlawry
09 exclusion, expulsion,
   ostracism
11 deportation, extradition
12 expatriation
14 transportation
15 excommunication

banisters
04 rail
08 handrail
10 balustrade

bank
03 row, tip
04 heap, keep, pile, pool, rank,
   rise, save, side, tier, tilt
05 array, bench, cache, drift,
   hoard, knoll, levee, mound,
   pitch, ridge, shore, slant,
   slope, stack, stock, store
06 margin, save up, series
07 deposit, hillock, incline,
   parados, reserve, savings
08 riparian, treasury
09 earthwork, stockpile
10 accumulate, depository,
   embankment, repository
12 finance house, merchant
   bank
14 finance company,
   high-street bank
15 building society

□**bank on**
05 bet on, trust
06 rely on
07 count on
08 depend on
14 pin your hopes on

banknote
04 bill, note
09 greenback
10 paper money
12 treasury note

bankrupt
04 bust, ruin
05 broke, spent
06 beggar, debtor, failed,
   folded, pauper, ruined
08 beggared, in the red
09 destitute, gone under,
   insolvent, penurious
10 on the rocks
11 impecunious
12 impoverished
13 gone to the wall,
   in liquidation

bankruptcy
04 lack, ruin
06 penury
07 beggary, failure
09 ruination
10 exhaustion, insolvency
11 liquidation
12 indebtedness
13 financial ruin

banner
04 flag, sign
06 burgee, ensign, pennon
07 colours, labarum, pennant,
   placard
08 banderol, gonfalon,
   standard

banquet
04 meal
05 feast, party, treat
06 dinner, spread

banter
03 kid, rag, rib
04 jest, joke, mock
05 chaff
06 deride, joking
07 jesting, kidding, ribbing
08 badinage, chaffing, raillery,
   repartee, word play
10 persiflage, pleasantry
15 pull someone's leg

baptism
05 début
06 launch, naming
08 affusion
09 beginning, immersion
10 dedication, initiation,
   sprinkling
11 christening
12 inauguration, introduction

baptize
04 call, name, term
07 cleanse, immerse, recruit
08 christen, initiate, sprinkle

bar
03 ban, inn, pub, rod
04 bolt, cake, lock, lump, pole,
   rail, save, slab, stop
05 block, chunk, court, debar,
   grill, ingot, stick, table
06 batten, boozer, but for,
   except, fasten, forbid,
   lounge, nugget, paling,
   saloon, secure, tavern
07 barrier, counsel, counter,
   exclude, lawyers, prevent,
   railing, suspend, taproom
08 blockade, hostelry, obstacle,
   obstruct, omitting, prohibit,
   restrain, tribunal
09 apart from, barricade,
   brasserie, excepting,
   excluding, lounge bar
10 barristers, crosspiece,
   disqualify, impediment
11 obstruction, public house
12 watering-hole

barb
03 dig
04 gibe
05 arrow, fluke, point, scorn,
   sneer, spike, thorn
06 insult, needle, rebuff
07 bristle, prickle, sarcasm

barbarian
03 oaf
04 boor, lout, wild

05 brute, crude, rough
06 coarse, savage, vulgar
07 brutish, ruffian, uncouth
08 hooligan
09 ignoramus
10 philistine, uncultured
11 uncivilized
12 uncultivated
15 unsophisticated

barbaric
04 rude, wild
05 crude, cruel
06 brutal, coarse, fierce, savage
07 bestial, brutish, inhuman, uncouth, vicious
08 ruthless
09 barbarous, ferocious, murderous, primitive
11 uncivilized

barbarism
07 cruelty
08 ferocity, savagery, wildness
09 brutality, crudeness
10 bestiality, fierceness
11 brutishness, inhumanness, uncouthness, viciousness
12 ruthlessness
13 murderousness

barbarity
07 cruelty, outrage
08 atrocity, enormity, ferocity, savagery, wildness
09 brutality
10 inhumanity
11 brutishness, viciousness
12 ruthlessness
13 barbarousness

barbarous
04 rude, wild
05 crude, cruel, rough
06 brutal, fierce, savage, vulgar
07 bestial, inhuman, vicious
08 barbaric, ignorant, ruthless
09 barbarian, ferocious, heartless, murderous, primitive, unrefined
11 uncivilized
15 unsophisticated

barbed
04 acid
05 nasty, snide, spiny
06 hooked, jagged, spiked, thorny, unkind
07 caustic, cutting, hostile, hurtful, pointed, prickly, pronged, toothed

bare
04 bald, cold, hard, mere, nude
05 basic, bleak, empty, naked, plain, sheer, stark

06 barren, simple, vacant
07 denuded, exposed
08 absolute, desolate, in the raw, stripped, treeless
09 essential, in the nude, unadorned, unclothed, uncovered, undressed
10 defoliated, unforested
11 unfurnished, unsheltered
15 straightforward

barefaced
04 bald, bold, open
05 brash, naked
06 arrant, brazen, patent
07 blatant, glaring, obvious
08 flagrant, insolent, manifest
09 audacious, shameless, unabashed
11 undisguised

barefooted
06 unshod
08 barefoot, shoeless
09 discalced

barely
04 just
06 almost, hardly
08 no sooner, only just, scarcely
12 be a near thing
13 be a close thing

bargain
04 deal, pact, sell, snip
05 steal, trade
06 barter, haggle, treaty
07 good buy, promise, traffic
08 beat down, covenant, discount, giveaway
09 agreement, concordat, negotiate, reduction
11 arrangement, negotiation, transaction
12 special offer
13 understanding

❑**bargain for**
06 expect
07 foresee, imagine, include, look for, plan for
08 consider, reckon on
10 anticipate
13 be prepared for
15 take into account

❑**into the bargain**
06 as well
07 besides
12 additionally

bargaining
08 dealings, haggling
09 bartering
11 negotiation, trafficking
12 horsetrading
14 wheeler-dealing

barge
03 hit
04 bump, push, rush
05 elbow, press, shove, smash
06 jostle, plough, push in
07 collide, lighter
08 flatboat
09 canal-boat, houseboat
10 narrow-boat

❑**barge in**
05 cut in
06 butt in
07 break in, burst in, intrude
09 gatecrash, interrupt

bark
03 bay, cry, yap
04 hide, howl, husk, peel, rind, skin, snap, woof, yell, yelp
05 crust, shell, shout, snarl
06 casing, cortex
08 covering

barmy
03 mad, odd
04 daft, nuts
05 batty, crazy, dippy, dotty, loony, loopy, nutty, silly
06 insane, stupid
07 foolish, idiotic
08 crackers
10 out to lunch
11 off your head
12 round the bend
13 off your nutter, off your rocker, round the twist
14 off your trolley

baroque
05 showy
06 florid, ornate, rococo
08 fanciful, vigorous
09 decorated, elaborate, exuberant, grotesque
10 convoluted, flamboyant
11 embellished, extravagant
13 overdecorated

barrack
04 jeer
06 heckle
09 interrupt, shout down

barracks
04 camp, fort
07 lodging
08 garrison, quarters
10 encampment, guardhouse
13 accommodation

barrage
04 hail, mass, rain
05 burst, flood, salvo, storm
06 attack, deluge, shower
07 assault, battery, gunfire
08 shelling

09 abundance, broadside, cannonade, onslaught
11 bombardment

barrel
03 keg, tun
04 butt, cask
06 tierce
07 rundlet
09 water-butt

barren
03 dry
04 arid, dull, flat
05 empty, vapid, waste
06 desert
07 sterile, useless
08 desolate, infecund
09 childless, fruitless, infertile, pointless, valueless
10 profitless, unfruitful
12 uncultivable, unproductive
13 uninformative

barricade
03 bar
04 shut
05 block, close, fence
06 defend
07 barrier, bulwark, defence, fortify, protect, shut off
08 blockade, obstacle, obstruct, palisade, stockade
10 protection, strengthen

barrier
03 bar
04 boom, gate, wall
05 check, ditch, fence
06 hurdle
07 railing, rampart
08 blockade, handicap, stockade
09 barricade, hindrance, restraint, roadblock
10 difficulty, impediment
11 obstruction, restriction
13 fortification
14 stumbling-block

barring
06 except, unless
09 except for

bartender
06 barman
07 barmaid
08 publican
09 barkeeper

barter
04 deal, sell, swap
05 trade
06 haggle
07 bargain, dealing, trading

08 exchange, haggling, swapping
10 bargaining

base
03 bed, key, low
04 camp, core, evil, foot, home, mean, poor, post, prop, rest, root, site, stay, vile
05 basis, build, found, stand
06 abject, bottom, centre, depend, derive, fundus, ground, origin, plinth, sordid, source, vulgar, wicked
07 corrupt, essence, immoral, install, pitiful, station, support
08 depraved, keystone, pedestal, shameful, wretched
09 essential, establish, low-minded, miserable, principal, reprobate, valueless, worthless
10 despicable, foundation, groundwork, underneath
11 disgraceful, fundamental, ignominious
12 contemptible, disreputable, headquarters, unprincipled
15 foundation stone

baseball

➤ *Names of baseball players*:
03 **Ott** (Mel)
04 **Cobb** (Ty), **Mack** (Connie), **Ruth** (Babe), **Ryan** (Nolan)
05 **Aaron** (Hank), **Bench** (Johnny Lee), **Berra** (Yogi), **Boggs** (Wade), **Paige** (Satchel), **Young** (Cy)
06 **Gehrig** (Lou), **Gibson** (Josh), **Gibson** (Robert), **Gooden** (Dwight), **Koufax** (Sandford 'Sandy'), **Mantle** (Mickey)
07 **Jackson** (Reggie), **Stengel** (Casey)
08 **Clemente** (Roberto Walker), **DiMaggio** (Joe), **Robinson** (Brooks), **Williams** (Ted)
09 **Alexander** (Grover Cleveland), **Mathewson** (Christy)
➤ See also **sport**

baseless
09 unfounded
10 gratuitous, groundless
11 unconfirmed, unjustified
15 unsubstantiated

basement
05 crypt, vault
06 cellar

bash
02 go
03 hit, try
04 belt, shot, slug, sock, stab
05 break, crack, crash, knock, party, punch, smack, smash, whack, whirl
06 rave-up, strike, wallop
07 attempt

bashful
03 coy, shy
05 timid
07 abashed, nervous
08 backward, blushing, hesitant, reserved, reticent, retiring, sheepish, timorous
09 diffident, inhibited, shrinking
10 shamefaced
11 embarrassed
12 self-effacing
13 self-conscious

bashfulness
07 blushes, coyness, modesty, reserve, shyness
08 timidity
09 hesitancy, reticence
10 diffidence, inhibition
11 nervousness
12 sheepishness
13 embarrassment
14 self-effacement

basic
03 key
04 core, root
05 crude, first, plain, stark, vital
06 simple, staple
07 austere, central, minimum, primary, radical, spartan
08 inherent, standard, starting
09 essential, important, intrinsic, necessary, primitive, unadorned
10 elementary, underlying
11 fundamental, preparatory
13 indispensable

basically
07 at heart
09 in essence, in the main, primarily, radically
10 inherently
11 essentially, principally
13 fundamentally, intrinsically

basics
05 facts
07 bedrock
09 realities, rudiments

10 brass tacks, essentials,
   principles, rock bottom
11 necessaries, nitty-gritty
12 fundamentals, introduction,
   nuts and bolts

basin
04 bowl, dish, sink
06 cavity, crater, hollow
10 depression

basis
04 base, core
05 heart, terms
06 bottom, ground, reason
07 bedrock, essence, footing,
   grounds, keynote, premise
08 approach
09 condition, essential,
   principle, rationale
10 conditions, essentials,
   foundation, groundwork
11 arrangement, cornerstone
12 fundamentals, quintessence
13 starting-point
15 first principles

bask
03 lie
04 laze, loll
05 enjoy, lap up, relax, revel
06 relish, savour, wallow
08 sunbathe
09 delight in, luxuriate

basket
04 coop, skep, trug
05 creel
06 hamper, punnet
07 pannier
08 bassinet

bass
03 low
04 deep, rich
09 deep-toned
10 low-pitched

bastard
09 love child
12 illegitimate, natural child

bastardize
06 debase, defile, demean
07 cheapen, corrupt, degrade,
   devalue, distort, pervert
10 adulterate, depreciate
11 contaminate

bastion
04 prop, rock
06 pillar
07 bulwark, citadel, defence
08 fortress, mainstay
10 protection, stronghold

batch
03 lot, set

04 mass, pack
06 amount, parcel
07 cluster
08 quantity
10 collection, contingent
11 consignment

bath
03 dip, spa, tub
04 bath, soak, wash
05 bathe, clean, sauna, scrub
06 douche, hamman, shower
07 balneal, Jacuzzi®, thermae
09 steam room, whirlpool
11 slipper bath, Turkish bath

bathe
03 dip, wet
04 bath, soak, swim, wash
05 cover, flood, rinse, steep
07 cleanse, immerse, suffuse
08 take a dip

bathos
07 let-down
08 comedown
10 anticlimax

baton
03 rod
05 staff, stick
09 truncheon

battalion
04 army, herd, host, mass, unit
05 force, horde
06 legion, throng, troops
07 brigade, company, platoon,
   section
08 division, garrison, regiment
09 multitude

batten
03 bar, fix
05 board, strip
06 fasten, secure
07 board up, tighten
08 nail down
09 barricade, clamp down

batter
03 hit
04 bash, beat, club, dash, lash
05 abuse, pound, smash,
   whack
06 bruise, buffet, pummel,
   strike, thrash, wallop
07 assault, wear out
10 knock about

❑ **batter down**
05 smash, wreck
07 destroy
08 demolish
09 break down

battered
06 abused, beaten, shabby

07 bruised, crushed, damaged
10 ill-treated, tumbledown
11 dilapidated
13 weather-beaten

battery
03 set
04 guns
06 attack, cannon, series
07 beating, mugging
08 striking, violence
09 artillery, thrashing
10 succession
12 emplacements

battle
03 row, war
04 feud, fray, race
05 argue, brawl, clash, fight
06 action, attack, combat,
   debate, strife, strive
07 contest, crusade, dispute,
   quarrel, warfare
08 campaign, conflict,
   disagree, skirmish,
   struggle
09 encounter
10 Armageddon, engagement
11 altercation, competition,
   controversy, hostilities
12 disagreement
13 armed conflict

➤ *Names of battles. We have
omitted the words* **battle of** *and*
battle of the *from names given
in the following list but you may
need to include these words as
part of the solution to some
crossword clues.*
04 Jena, Loos, Neva, Nile, Troy
   (Siege of), Zama
05 Alamo, Anzio, Boyne,
   Bulge, Crécy, Issus, Marne,
   Mylae, Pavia, Rhine, Sedan,
   Somme, Spurs, Varna, Ypres
06 Actium, Amiens, Arnhem,
   Cannae, Kosovo, Midway,
   Mycale, Naseby, Pinkie,
   Shiloh, Tobruk, Verdun,
   Wagram
07 Antwerp, Britain, Bull Run,
   Cambrai, Colenso,
   Corunna, Dresden,
   Flodden, Iwo Jima, Jutland,
   Lepanto, Leuctra, Marengo,
   Orléans (Siege of), Plassey,
   Salamis, Salerno, Thapsus
08 Atlantic, Blenheim,
   Culloden, Fontenoy,
   Hastings, Mafeking (Siege
   of), Marathon, Monmouth,
   Omdurman, Philippi,
   Poitiers, Pyramids,

Saratoga, Spion Kop,
Waterloo
09 Agincourt, Balaclava, Bay of
Pigs, Chaeronea, El
Alamein, Kimberley (Siege
of), Ladysmith (Siege of),
Pharsalus, Ramillies,
Sedgemoor, Seven Days,
Singapore, Solferino,
Trafalgar
10 Aboukir Bay, Adrianople,
Austerlitz, Bunker Hill,
Cold Harbor, Copenhagen,
Gettysburg, Malplaquet,
Oudenaarde, River Plate,
Sevastopol (Siege of),
Stalingrad, Tannenberg, Tel-
El-Kebir
11 Bannockburn,
Guadalcanal, Hohenlinden,
Marston Moor, Navarino
Bay, Prestonpans, Wounded
Knee
12 Monte Cassino, Pearl
Harbour, Tet Offensive
13 Bosworth Field, Cape St
Vincent, Killiecrankie,
Little Bighorn,
Magersfontein, My Lai
Massacre, Passchendaele
14 Fredericksburg
15 Glencoe Massacre

battle-axe
06 dragon, Tartar, virago
08 harridan, martinet
09 termagant

battle-cry
06 slogan, war cry
07 war song
11 rallying cry
12 rallying call

battlefield
05 arena, front
07 war zone
09 front line
10 combat zone
12 battleground

batty
03 mad, odd
04 bats, daft, nuts
05 barmy, crazy, dippy, dotty,
loony, loopy, nutty, silly
07 bonkers, foolish, idiotic
08 crackers, peculiar
09 eccentric
10 out to lunch
11 off your head
12 round the bend
13 off your nutter, off your
rocker, round the twist

bauble
03 toy
06 gewgaw, tinsel, trifle
07 bibelot, flamfew, trinket
08 gimcrack, kickshaw,
ornament
10 knick-knack

baulk see **balk**

bawd
04 pimp
05 madam
09 panderess, procuress
13 brothel-keeper

bawdy
04 blue, lewd, rude
05 dirty, gross
06 coarse, erotic, ribald, risqué,
smutty, vulgar
07 lustful, obscene
08 improper, indecent, prurient
09 lecherous, salacious
10 lascivious, suggestive

bawl
03 cry, sob
04 call, howl, roar, weep, yell
05 shout
06 bellow, snivel, squall

❑**bawl out**
05 scold
06 rebuke, yell at
09 reprimand

bay
03 arm, cry
04 bark, cove, gulf, howl,
roar
05 bight, inlet, niche, sound
06 alcove, bellow, lagoon,
recess
—— *Names of bays. We have
omitted the words* bay *and* bay
of *from names given in the
following list but you may need
to include these words as part of
the solution to some crossword
clues.*
03 Tor
04 Acre, Clew, Daya, Kiel,
Luce, Lyme, Pigs, Tees
05 Algoa, Blind, Enard, Evans,
False, Fundy, Hawke, Shark,
Table
06 Baffin, Bantry, Bengal,
Biscay, Botany, Colwyn,
Drake's, Dublin, Galway,
Hudson, Naples, Plenty,
Tasman, Walvis
07 Aboukir, Bustard, Donegal,
Dundalk, Fortune, Halifax,
Hudson's, Montego,
Thunder, Trinity, Volcano

08 Cardigan, Delaware,
Portland, Tremadoc,
Weymouth
09 Admiralty, Discovery,
Encounter, Frobisher,
Galveston, Hermitage,
Mackenzie, Morecombe,
Placentia
10 Barnstaple, Bridgwater,
Carmarthen, Chesapeake,
Conception, Heligoland,
Robin Hood's
11 Port Jackson, Saint Bride's
12 Saint George's, San
Francisco

bayonet
04 pike, stab
05 blade, knife, spear, stick
06 dagger, impale, pierce
07 poniard

bazaar
04 fair, fête, mart, sale, souk
06 market
08 exchange

be
03 lie
04 form, last, live, make, stay
05 abide, exist, occur, stand
06 endure, happen, remain
07 add up to, breathe, develop,
persist, prevail, survive
08 amount to, continue
09 be located, come about,
take place, transpire
10 come to pass, constitute

beach
04 sand
05 coast, sands, shore
06 strand
07 seaside, shingle
08 littoral, seaboard, seashore
10 water's edge

beachcomber
07 forager
09 scavenger, scrounger

beacon
04 beam, fire, sign
05 fanal, flare, light
06 pharos, rocket, signal
07 bonfire
10 lighthouse, watchtower

bead
04 ball, blob, drip, drop, glob
05 jewel, pearl
06 bubble, pellet
07 droplet, globule

beak
03 neb, nib
04 bill, nose

07 rostrum
09 mandibles, proboscis

beaker
03 cup, jar, mug
05 glass
07 tankard, tumbler

beam
03 aim, bar, ray
04 boom, glow, grin, send, spar
05 glare, joist, plank, relay, shaft, shine, smile
06 direct, girder, lintel, rafter, stream, timber
07 radiate, support, transom
08 transmit, stringer
09 broadcast, scantling, stanchion
10 cantilever

bean
09 fabaceous
10 leguminous

▶ *Varieties of bean and pulse. We have omitted the word* **bean** *from names given in the following list but you may need to include this word as part of the solution to some crossword clues.*
03 dal, pea, soy, wax
04 fava, lima, mung, okra, snap, soya
05 broad, carob, green, pinto, sugar
06 adzuki, butter, chilli, French, kidney, legume, lentil, locust, runner, string
07 alfalfa, haricot
08 borlotti, chick pea, split pea
09 flageolet, mange tout, red kidney
10 beansprout
11 garbanzo pea
12 black-eyed pea, marrowfat pea
➤ See also **food**

bear
03 pay
04 have, hold, hump, like, move, show, take, tote, turn, veer
05 abide, admit, allow, beget, breed, bring, carry, curve, drive, fetch, stand, yield
06 accept, convey, endure, give up, permit, suffer, uphold
07 develop, deviate, display, diverge, harbour, produce, stomach, support, sustain
08 engender, generate, live with, shoulder, tolerate

09 put up with, transport
10 bring forth
11 give birth to

❑ **bear in mind**
04 note
08 consider, remember
11 be mindful of
15 take into account

❑ **bear out**
05 prove
06 back up, ratify, uphold, verify
07 confirm, endorse, support
11 corroborate, demonstrate

❑ **bear up**
04 cope
06 endure, suffer
07 carry on, survive
09 soldier on, withstand

❑ **bear with**
08 tolerate
09 put up with
13 be patient with

bearable
08 passable
09 endurable, tolerable
10 acceptable, manageable
11 supportable, sustainable

beard
04 dare, defy, face, tuft
06 beaver, goatee, oppose
07 bristle, stubble, vandyke
08 confront, imperial, whiskers
09 challenge, sideburns
10 facial hair, sideboards
11 mutton chops
14 stand up against

bearded
05 bushy, hairy
06 shaggy, tufted
07 bristly, hirsute, stubbly
08 unshaven
09 pogoniate, whiskered

bearer
05 payee
06 holder, porter, runner
07 carrier, courier
08 conveyor
09 consignee, messenger, possessor

bearing
04 gait, mien
05 poise, track
06 aspect, course, manner
07 concern, posture, stature
08 carriage, location, position
09 behaviour, demeanour, direction, influence, reference, relevance
10 deportment, pertinence

11 comportment, orientation
12 significance

beast
03 pig
05 brute, devil, fiend, swine
06 animal, savage
07 monster
08 creature

beastly
04 foul
05 awful, cruel, nasty
06 brutal, horrid, rotten
08 horrible, terrible
09 repulsive
10 unpleasant

beat
03 box, hit, mix, tan, way
04 bang, bash, belt, best, biff, blow, cane, club, dash, drub, flap, flay, flog, lash, lick, path, pelt, rout, slap, stir, time, walk, welt, wham, whip
05 birch, clout, forge, knock, knout, metre, outdo, pound, pulse, punch, round, route, shake, smack, stamp, strap, swing, swipe, tempo, throb, thump, tired, whack, whisk
06 batter, bruise, buffet, cudgel, defeat, fill in, hammer, outrun, outwit, pummel, quiver, rhythm, rounds, strike, stroke, subdue, thrash, thwack, wallop, zonked
07 circuit, clobber, combine, conquer, contuse, flutter, knubble, lambast, lay into, measure, outplay, pulsate, surpass, tremble, trounce, vibrate, wearied, worn out
08 fatigued, jiggered, malleate, outsmart, outstrip, overcome, vanquish, vapulate
09 exhausted, overpower, overwhelm, palpitate, subjugate, territory, vibration, zonked out
10 annihilate, transcend

❑ **beat up**
03 mug
06 attack, batter, do over
07 assault, rough up
10 knock about

beaten
05 foamy, mixed
06 forged, formed, frothy
07 blended, stamped, trodden, whipped, whisked, wrought

08 hammered, trampled, well-used, well-worn
11 well-trodden

beatific
06 divine, joyful
07 angelic, blessed, exalted, sublime
08 blissful, ecstatic, heavenly
09 rapturous

beatify
05 bless, exalt
08 macarize, sanctify

beating
04 rout, ruin
06 caning, defeat
07 hitting, lashing, the cane
08 bruising, clubbing, conquest, drubbing, flogging, punching, slapping, the birch, the strap, thumping, whipping
09 battering, hammering, slaughter, thrashing, trouncing, walloping
11 outsmarting, vanquishing
12 overwhelming

beau
05 lover
06 escort, fiancé, suitor
07 admirer
09 boyfriend
10 sweetheart

beautician
07 friseur
09 visagiste
11 cosmetician, hairdresser

beautiful
04 fair, fine
05 bonny
06 comely, lovely, pretty, seemly
07 radiant
08 becoming, gorgeous, graceful, handsome, smashing, striking, stunning
09 exquisite, ravishing
10 voluptuous
11 good-looking, magnificent
15 pulchritudinous

beautify
04 deck, gild
05 adorn, array, grace
06 bedeck, doll up, tart up
07 enhance, improve, smarten
08 decorate, ornament, titivate
09 embellish, glamorize

beauty
05 belle, bonus, glory, grace, merit, peach, siren, Venus
06 allure, appeal, corker, virtue

07 benefit, charmer, cracker, smasher, stunner
08 dividend, knockout, radiance, symmetry
09 advantage, good looks, good point, plus point
10 attraction, excellence, good-looker, loveliness, prettiness, seemliness
11 femme fatale, pulchritude
12 gorgeousness, gracefulness, handsomeness
13 exquisiteness

beaver

❑ beaver away
06 work at
07 persist
08 plug away, work hard
09 persevere, slave away

becalmed
05 still, stuck
08 marooned, stranded
10 motionless
13 at a standstill

because
02 as
03 for
05 due to, since
07 owing to, through
08 seeing as, thanks to
10 by reason of, by virtue of
11 as a result of, on account of

beckon
04 call, coax, draw, lure, pull
05 tempt
06 allure, entice, induce, invite
07 attract, gesture
11 gesticulate

become
03 get, wax
04 grow, suit, turn
05 befit, grace
06 set off
07 enhance, flatter
08 grow into, ornament
09 embellish, harmonize
10 change into, look good on
11 develop into, turn out to be
13 be changed into

becoming
06 comely, pretty
07 elegant, fitting
08 charming, fetching, graceful
10 attractive, compatible, consistent, flattering
11 appropriate

bed
03 fix, hay, kip, row
04 base, bunk, bury, plot, sack

05 couch, divan, embed, floor, layer, patch, plant, strip
06 border, bottom, garden, ground, insert, matrix, settle
07 channel, implant, stratum
10 foundation, substratum
11 watercourse

❑ bed down
05 sleep
06 turn in
07 go to bed, kip down
08 doss down
09 hit the hay
10 hit the sack, settle down

❑ go to bed with
09 sleep with
10 make love to
11 have sex with

bedclothes
06 covers
07 bedding
08 bed-linen

bedeck
04 deck, trim
05 adorn, array
07 festoon, garnish
08 beautify, decorate, ornament, trick out

bedevil
03 irk, vex
04 fret
05 annoy, tease, worry
06 harass, pester, plague
07 afflict, besiege, torment, torture, trouble
08 confound, distress, irritate
09 frustrate

bedlam
05 babel, chaos, noise
06 furore, tumult, uproar
07 anarchy, clamour, turmoil
08 madhouse
09 commotion, confusion
10 hullabaloo
11 pandemonium

bedraggled
03 wet
05 dirty, messy, muddy
06 soaked, soiled, untidy
07 scruffy, soaking, unkempt
08 drenched, dripping
10 disordered, soaking wet
11 dishevelled

bedridden
06 laid up
13 confined to bed, incapacitated
14 flat on your back

bedrock
04 base
05 basis, heart
06 basics, bottom, reason
07 premise, reasons, support
09 rationale
10 essentials, foundation
12 fundamentals
15 first principles

beef
04 moan
05 gripe
06 grouse, object
07 dispute, grumble
08 complain, disagree

▢beef up
07 build up, toughen
09 establish, reinforce
10 invigorate, strengthen
11 consolidate
12 substantiate

beefy
03 fat
05 bulky, burly, heavy, hefty
06 brawny, stocky, sturdy
07 hulking
08 muscular, stalwart
09 corpulent

beer
➤ *Types of beer*:
03 ale, IPA, keg
04 mild, Pils
05 heavy, kvass, lager, plain, sixty, stout
06 bitter, eighty, porter
07 bottled, draught, pale ale, Pilsner, real ale, seventy
08 brown ale, home brew, light ale, Pilsener
09 milk stout, wheat beer
10 Weisse Bier
12 India Pale Ale
13 sixty shilling
14 eighty shilling
15 cask-conditioned, seventy shilling
➤ See also **drink**

beetle
03 nip, run, zip
04 dash, rush, tear
05 hurry, scoot
06 scurry
07 poke out, scamper
➤ *Beetles include*:
03 dor, may, oil
04 bark, dorr, dung, musk, pine, rove, stag
05 click, water
06 chafer, dor-fly, ground, may bug, scarab, weevil

07 burying, cadelle, carabid, goliath, hop-flea, horn-bug, rose-bug
08 bum-clock, Colorado, glowworm, Hercules, ladybird, longhorn, woodworm
09 goldsmith, longicorn, tumble-bug, whirligig
10 bombardier, cockchafer, deathwatch, rhinoceros, rose-chafer, turnip flea
11 typographer
➤ See also **animal**

beetling
07 jutting, pendent
10 projecting, protruding
11 overhanging, sticking out

befall
05 ensue, occur
06 arrive, betide, chance, follow, happen, result
09 supervene, take place

befitting
03 apt, fit
04 meet
05 right
06 decent, proper, seemly
07 correct, fitting
08 becoming, suitable
11 appropriate

before
07 ahead of, already, earlier, in front, prior to
08 formerly
09 in advance, in front of
10 on the eve of, previous to, previously, sooner than
15 in the presence of

beforehand
06 before, sooner
07 already, earlier
09 in advance
10 previously

befriend
03 aid
04 back, help
06 assist, defend, favour, uphold
07 benefit, comfort, protect, stand by, succour, support, sustain, welcome
09 encourage, get to know
10 fall in with, stick up for
11 keep an eye on

befuddle
04 daze
06 baffle, muddle, puzzle
07 confuse, stupefy

08 bewilder
09 disorient

beg
04 pray
05 cadge, crave, mooch, plead
06 appeal, ask for, sponge
07 beseech, entreat, implore
08 petition, scrounge
09 importune
10 supplicate

beget
04 sire
05 breed, cause, spawn
06 create, effect, father
07 produce
08 engender, generate
09 procreate, propagate
10 bring about, give rise to

beggar
03 bum
04 defy
05 tramp
06 cadger, exceed, pauper
07 bludger, moocher, sponger, surpass, vagrant
09 mendicant, schnorrer, scrounger, transcend
10 down-and-out, freeloader, panhandler, supplicant

beggarly
03 low
04 mean
06 abject, meagre, paltry, stingy
07 miserly, pitiful
08 pathetic, wretched
10 despicable, inadequate

begin
04 open
05 arise, found, start
06 appear, crop up, embark, emerge, launch, set off, spring
07 actuate, do first, kick off
08 activate, commence, initiate, set about
09 instigate, institute, introduce, originate
11 get cracking, set in motion

beginner
03 cub
04 tiro
06 novice, rookie
07 fresher, learner, recruit, starter, student, trainee
08 freshman, initiate, neophyte
09 fledgling, greenhorn
10 raw recruit, tenderfoot
11 abecedarian, probationer

beginning
04 dawn, rise, root, seed
05 birth, intro, onset, start
06 day one, launch, origin, outset, source
07 genesis, kick-off, opening
09 first base, first part, inception, square one, the word go
10 conception, fresh start, inchoation, incipience, initiation
11 institution, pastures new
12 commencement, fountainhead, inauguration
13 establishment, starting-point

begrudge
04 envy, mind
05 covet, stint
06 grudge, resent
11 be jealous of

beguile
04 dupe, fool
05 amuse, charm, cheat, cozen, trick
06 delude, divert, seduce
07 attract, bewitch, deceive, delight, enchant, mislead
08 distract, hoodwink
09 captivate, entertain

beguiling
08 alluring, charming, enticing
09 appealing, seductive
10 bewitching, delightful, enchanting, intriguing
11 captivating, interesting

behalf
◻ **on behalf of**
09 acting for
11 in the name of
12 for the sake of, representing
13 to the profit of

behave
03 act
04 work
05 react
06 be good
07 operate, perform, respond
08 function
10 act your age
15 comport yourself, conduct yourself, mind your manners, mind your p's and q's

behaviour
04 ways
06 action, habits, manner
07 conduct, manners
08 dealings, reaction, response

09 attitudes, demeanour
10 deportment
11 comportment, performance

behead
07 execute
10 decapitate, guillotine

behest
◻ **at the behest of**
12 at the order of
13 on the wishes of
14 at the bidding of, at the command of, at the request of

behind
03 ass, bum, for
04 arse, butt, late, next, slow
05 after
06 bottom, in debt
07 backing, causing, overdue
08 backside, buttocks
09 at the back, endorsing, following, in arrears, in the rear, later than, posterior
10 behindhand, explaining, initiating, supporting
11 instigating, running late
12 giving rise to, subsequently
13 at the bottom of
14 responsible for
15 slower than usual

behindhand
04 late, slow
05 tardy
07 delayed
08 backward, dilatory

behold
02 lo
03 see
04 ecce, look, mark, note, view
05 voici, voila, watch
06 gaze at, look at, regard
07 discern, observe, witness
08 consider, perceive

beholden
05 bound, owing
07 obliged
08 grateful, indebted, thankful
09 obligated

behove
05 befit
08 be proper, be seemly
11 be essential, be necessary

beige
03 tan
04 buff, ecru, fawn
05 camel, khaki, sandy
06 coffee, greige

07 neutral, oatmeal
08 mushroom

being
03 man
04 esse, life, soul
05 beast, human, thing, woman
06 animal, entity, mortal, nature, person, spirit
08 creature
09 actuality, existence, haecceity, substance
10 human being, individual

belabour
03 hit
04 beat, belt, flay, flog, whip
06 attack, thrash

belated
04 late
05 tardy
07 delayed, overdue

belch
04 burp, emit, spew, vent
05 eject
06 hiccup
07 give off, give out
08 disgorge, eructate
09 discharge
11 bring up wind

beleaguered
05 beset, vexed
07 plagued, worried
08 badgered, besieged, bothered, harassed, pestered
09 blockaded
10 surrounded, under siege

belie
04 deny
06 negate, refute
07 conceal, confute, deceive, falsify, gainsay, mislead
08 disguise, disprove
10 contradict

belief
03 ism
04 view
05 creed, dogma, faith, tenet, trust
06 credit, notion, theory
07 feeling, opinion
08 doctrine, ideology, sureness
09 assurance, certainty, principle, viewpoint
10 confidence, conviction, impression, persuasion
11 point of view, presumption

believable
06 likely
08 credible, possible, probable

09 plausible
10 acceptable, imaginable
11 conceivable, trustworthy

believe
03 buy
04 deem, hold, wear
05 guess, opine, think, trust
06 accept, assume, reckon
07 imagine, suppose, swallow
08 consider, maintain
10 Adam and Eve, understand
11 be certain of, take on board

◻**believe in**
05 trust
06 favour, rely on
07 swear by
08 depend on
09 approve of, recommend
11 value highly
13 be convinced of,
be persuaded by

believer
06 zealot
07 convert, devotee
08 adherent, disciple, follower
09 proselyte, supporter

belittle
05 decry, scorn
06 demean, deride, lessen
07 dismiss, run down
08 diminish, minimize, play
down, ridicule
09 deprecate, disparage
10 understate, undervalue
11 detract from

bellicose
07 violent, warlike, warring
08 bullying, militant
09 combative
10 aggressive, pugnacious
11 contentious, quarrelsome
12 antagonistic

belligerence
03 war
08 bullying, violence
09 militancy, pugnacity
10 aggression, antagonism
12 war-mongering
13 sabre-rattling

belligerent
07 violent, warlike, warring
08 bullying, militant
09 combative, truculent
10 aggressive, pugnacious
11 contentious, provocative
12 antagonistic, disputatious,
war-mongering
13 argumentative,
sabre-rattling

bellow
03 cry
04 bawl, howl, roar, yell
05 shout
06 holler, scream, shriek
14 raise your voice

belly
03 gut
04 guts
05 tummy
06 paunch, venter
07 abdomen, insides, stomach
08 pot-belly
10 intestines
11 bread basket, corporation

belong
05 fit in
06 go with
07 be yours
08 attach to, be part of
09 be owned by, tie up with
10 be included, link up with
11 be a member of
13 have as its home
14 be affiliated to, be an
adherent of, have as its place
15 be the property of

belonging
05 links
07 kinship, loyalty, rapport
08 affinity
09 closeness
10 acceptance, fellowship
11 association
13 compatibility, fellow-feeling

belongings
04 gear
05 goods, stuff
06 things
07 effects
08 chattels, property
11 possessions
13 accoutrements,
appurtenances,
paraphernalia

beloved
04 dear, love, wife
05 loved, lover, sweet
06 adored, fiancé, spouse
07 darling, dearest, fiancée,
husband, partner, revered
08 precious
09 betrothed, boyfriend,
cherished, favourite,
inamorata, inamorato,
much loved, treasured
10 girlfriend, sweetheart

below
04 down
05 later, lower, under

07 beneath
09 further on, subject to
10 inferior to, lesser than,
underneath
13 subordinate to

belt
03 box, fly, hit, tan, zip
04 area, bang, bash, biff, cane,
dash, flay, flog, lash, pelt,
rush, sash, slap, tear, whip,
zone
05 birch, clout, knock, punch,
smack, speed, strap, strip,
swipe, thump, tract, whack
06 bruise, career, cestus, girdle,
region, strike, swathe,
thwack, wallop
07 baldric, bashing, stretch
08 ceinture, cincture, cingulum,
district
09 waistband
10 cummerbund

◻**belt up**
06 shut up
07 be quiet
08 cut it out, pipe down
12 put a sock in it, shut your
face
13 shut your mouth

bemoan
03 rue
05 mourn
06 bewail, lament, regret
07 deplore, sigh for, weep for
09 grieve for
10 sorrow over

bemuse
07 confuse, perplex, stupefy
08 befuddle, bewilder

bemused
05 dazed
07 muddled, puzzled
08 confused
09 astounded, befuddled,
perplexed, stupefied
10 astonished, bewildered

bench
03 pew
04 form, seat
05 board, judge, ledge, table
06 settle
07 counter
08 tribunal
09 judiciary, workbench
10 judicature, magistrate

benchmark
04 norm
05 level, model, scale
08 standard

09 criterion, guideline, reference, yardstick
10 guidelines, touchstone

bend
03 arc, bow
04 arch, flex, hook, kink, lean, loop, sway, turn, veer, warp
05 angle, crook, curve, elbow, kneel, shape, stoop, twist
06 affect, buckle, corner, crouch, dog-leg, swerve
07 contort, deviate, diverge, flexure, incline, meander
08 persuade
09 curvature, influence
10 deflection, divergence
11 hairpin bend, incurvation

beneath
05 below, lower, under
10 underneath, unworthy of
11 unbefitting

benediction
05 grace
06 favour, prayer
07 benison
08 blessing
10 execration, invocation

benefactor
05 angel, donor, giver
06 backer, friend, helper, patron
07 sponsor
08 promoter, provider
09 supporter
10 subsidizer, well-wisher
11 contributor
14 philanthropist

beneficent
04 kind
06 benign
07 helpful, liberal
08 generous
09 bountiful, unselfish
10 altruistic, benevolent, charitable, munificent

beneficial
06 useful
07 helpful
08 edifying, salutary, valuable
09 improving, promising, rewarding, wholesome
10 favourable, profitable
12 advantageous

beneficiary
04 heir
05 payee
07 heiress, legatee
08 receiver
09 inheritor, recipient

benefit
03 aid, use
04 boon, dole, gain, good, help
05 asset, avail, bonus, serve
06 assist, better, credit, favour, income, pay-off, profit
07 advance, enhance, further, improve, payment, pension, promote, service, sick pay, support, welfare
08 dividend, do good to
09 advantage, allowance
10 assistance
13 be of service to, fringe benefit, income support
14 social security

benevolence
04 care, pity
05 grace, mercy
08 altruism, goodwill, kindness
10 compassion, generosity
11 magnanimity, munificence
12 friendliness, philanthropy
14 charitableness
15 humanitarianism, kind-heartedness

benevolent
04 kind
06 benign, caring, kindly
08 friendly, generous, merciful
10 altruistic, charitable, munificent
11 considerate, kind-hearted, magnanimous, soft-hearted
13 compassionate, philanthropic

benighted
08 backward, ignorant
09 unknowing
10 illiterate, uncultured, uneducated, unschooled
11 unfortunate
13 unenlightened

benign
04 good, kind, mild, warm
06 genial, gentle
07 affable, amiable, cordial, curable, healthy, liberal
08 friendly, gracious, harmless
09 agreeable, temperate, treatable
10 auspicious, beneficial, benevolent, charitable, favourable, propitious
11 restorative, sympathetic
12 non-malignant, providential

bent
04 gift
05 bowed, flair, forte, knack

06 angled, arched, curved, folded, talent, warped
07 ability, corrupt, crooked, faculty, hunched, illegal, leaning, stooped, twisted
08 aptitude, criminal, facility, fondness, penchant, tendency
09 contorted, dishonest
10 fraudulent, preference, proclivity, propensity
11 disposition, inclination, predilecton
13 untrustworthy
14 predisposition

❑**bent on**
05 set on
07 fixed on
08 intent on
10 resolved to
11 insistent on
12 determined to

bequeath
04 give, will
05 endow, grant, leave
06 assign, bestow, commit, impart, pass on
07 consign, entrust
08 hand down, make over

bequest
04 gift
05 trust
06 estate, legacy
07 devisal
08 bestowal, donation, heritage
09 endowment
10 bequeathal, settlement
11 inheritance

berate
05 blast, chide, scold, slate
06 rail at, rebuke, revile
07 censure, chew out, reprove, tell off, upbraid
08 chastise, give hell, reproach
09 castigate, criticize, dress down, fulminate, reprimand
10 vituperate
13 give a rocket to, tear a strip off

bereaved
06 robbed
07 widowed
08 deprived, orphaned
12 dispossessed

bereavement
04 loss
05 death, grief
06 sorrow
07 passing, sadness

11 deprivation, passing-away
13 dispossession

bereft

◻**bereft of**
05 minus
07 lacking, wanting
08 devoid of, robbed of
10 cut off from, deprived of, parted from, stripped of

berserk
03 mad
04 wild
05 crazy, manic, rabid
06 crazed, insane, raging, raving
07 frantic, furious, violent
08 demented, deranged, frenzied, maniacal
10 hysterical
14 uncontrollable

berth
03 bed
04 bunk, dock, land, moor
05 tie up
06 anchor, billet
07 hammock, mooring
09 anchorage
10 cast anchor, drop anchor

beseech
03 ask, beg, sue
04 pray
05 crave, plead
06 adjure, desire, exhort
07 entreat, implore, solicit
08 appeal to, petition
09 importune, obsecrate
10 supplicate

beset
05 hem in, worry
06 assail, attack, harass, hassle, pester, plague
07 bedevil, torment
08 entangle, surround

besetting
08 constant, habitual
09 harassing, recurring
10 inveterate, persistent
11 troublesome
12 irresistible
14 uncontrollable

beside
02 by
04 near
06 next to
07 close to
08 abutting, adjacent
09 abreast of, alongside
10 next door to
12 neighbouring

◻**beside the point**
09 pointless, unrelated
10 extraneous, immaterial, incidental, irrelevant

◻**beside yourself**
03 mad
05 crazy
06 crazed, insane
07 berserk, frantic
08 demented, deranged, frenetic, frenzied, unhinged
09 delirious
10 distraught, unbalanced

besides
03 too
04 also
06 as well
07 further
08 as well as, moreover
09 apart from, aside from, excluding, other than, what's more
10 in addition
11 furthermore
12 additionally, in addition to, over and above

besiege
03 nag
05 beset, hem in, hound, worry
06 assail, badger, bother, harass, pester, plague, shut in
07 confine, trouble
08 blockade, encircle, surround
09 beleaguer, encompass, importune

besmirch
04 soil
05 dirty, smear, stain, sully
06 damage, defame, defile
07 blacken, slander, tarnish
09 dishonour

besotted
06 doting
07 smitten
08 obsessed
09 bewitched, stupefied
10 infatuated, spellbound

bespeak
04 show
05 imply
06 attest, denote, evince, reveal
07 display, exhibit, signify, suggest
08 evidence, indicate, proclaim
11 demonstrate

best
03 ace, top
04 most, pick, rout, star, tops

05 cream, elite, first, ideal, prime, worst
06 choice, finest, outwit, subdue, thrash, utmost
07 clobber, conquer, hardest, highest, largest, leading, optimal, optimum, perfect, supreme, the tops, trounce
08 foremost, greatest, peerless, ultimate
09 damnedest, excellent, extremely, favourite, first-rate, matchless, nonpareil, number one, worthiest
10 first-class, pre-eminent, unequalled, unrivalled
11 excellently, outstanding, superlative, unsurpassed
12 second to none
13 have the edge on, superlatively, unsurpassedly
14 record-breaking

bestial
04 vile
05 cruel, feral, gross
06 animal, brutal, carnal, savage, sordid
07 beastly, brutish, inhuman
08 barbaric, depraved
09 barbarous

bestir
05 exert
06 arouse, awaken, incite
07 actuate, animate
08 activate, energize, motivate
09 galvanize, stimulate

bestow
04 give
05 allot, award, endow, grant
06 accord, commit, confer, donate, impart, lavish
07 entrust, present
08 bequeath, transmit
09 apportion

bestride
08 dominate, straddle
10 bestraddle, overshadow, sit astride

bet
03 bid, lay, put
04 ante, back, punt, risk, view
05 place, stake, wager
06 be sure, chance, choice, expect, gamble, hazard, option, pledge, theory
07 flutter, lottery, venture
09 be certain, intuition, speculate, viewpoint
10 conviction, sweepstake

11 accumulator, alternative, be convinced, speculation
14 not be surprised

➤ *Types of bet and betting system*:
03 TAB
04 tote
06 double, tierce, triple, Yankee
07 each way
08 ante-post, perfecta, quinella, trifecta
09 on the nose, quadrella
10 martingale, pari-mutuel

bête noire
04 bane
05 curse
07 bugbear, pet hate
08 anathema, aversion
11 abomination, pet aversion

betide
05 ensue, occur
06 befall, chance, happen
08 overtake

betoken
04 bode, mark
05 augur
06 denote, signal
07 bespeak, portend, presage, promise, signify, suggest
08 evidence, forebode, indicate, manifest
09 represent

betray
04 dupe, sell, shop, show, tell
05 grass
06 delude, desert, expose, reveal, tell on, unmask
07 deceive, divulge, forsake, let slip, mislead, sell out
08 disclose, give away, inform on, manifest, squeal on
11 double-cross, turn traitor
12 be disloyal to, bring to light
13 stab in the back
14 be unfaithful to, break faith with

betrayal
07 perfidy, sell-out, treason
08 trickery
09 deception, duplicity, falseness, treachery
10 disloyalty
13 double-dealing
14 double-crossing

betrayer
05 grass, Judas
07 traitor
08 apostate, informer, renegade
10 supergrass

13 double-crosser, whistle-blower

betrothal
04 vows
05 troth
07 promise
08 espousal
10 engagement
11 fiançailles

betrothed
07 engaged
08 espoused, promised
09 affianced

better
03 cap, top
04 beat, mend, well
05 cured, finer, outdo, raise
06 bigger, enrich, exceed, fitter, healed, larger, longer, reform
07 correct, enhance, improve, promote, rectify, surpass
08 outstrip, overtake, restored, stronger, superior, worthier
09 a cut above, healthier, on the mend, recovered
10 ameliorate, preferable
11 more fitting, progressing
14 fully recovered

betterment
10 enrichment
11 advancement, edification, enhancement, furtherance, improvement, melioration
12 amelioration

between
03 mid
04 amid
05 among
06 amidst
07 amongst, halfway
11 in the middle

bevel
04 bias, cant, tilt
05 angle, bezel, slant, slope
07 chamfer, oblique

beverage
05 drink
06 liquid, liquor
07 draught, potable
08 potation
11 refreshment

bevy
04 band, pack
05 bunch, crowd, flock, group
06 gaggle, throng, troupe
07 company
08 assembly
09 gathering

bewail
03 rue
04 keen, moan, sigh
05 mourn
06 bemoan, lament, regret
07 cry over, deplore
10 grieve over, sorrow over

beware
04 mind, shun
05 avoid
06 be wary
07 look out, mind out
08 take heed, watch out
09 be careful
10 be cautious
12 guard against, steer clear of
13 be on your guard

bewilder
05 mix up, stump
06 baffle, bemuse, muddle, puzzle
07 confuse, mystify, perplex, stupefy
08 confound
09 bamboozle, disorient
10 disconcert

bewildered
07 baffled, bemused, muddled, puzzled, stunned
08 all at sea, confused
09 mystified, perplexed
10 bamboozled, nonplussed
11 disoriented

bewilderment
03 awe
09 confusion
10 perplexity, puzzlement
12 stupefaction
13 disconcertion, mystification
14 disorientation

bewitch
05 charm
06 allure, obsess, seduce
07 beguile, delight, enchant, enthral, possess
08 entrance, intrigue, transfix
09 captivate, enrapture, fascinate, hypnotize, mesmerize, spellbind

beyond
04 over, past
05 above, after
08 away from
09 later than, upwards of
10 remote from
11 further than, greater than
12 out of range of, out of reach of
14 on the far side of

bias
04 bent, load, sway, warp
05 angle, cross, slant, twist
06 earwig, weight
07 bigotry, distort, leaning
08 diagonal, jaundice,
tendency
09 influence, prejudice
10 distortion, partiality,
predispose, proclivity,
propensity, unfairness
11 favouritism, inclination,
intolerance, load the dice
12 one-sidedness, predilection

biased
06 angled, loaded, swayed,
unfair, warped
07 bigoted, partial, slanted
08 one-sided, partisan,
weighted
09 distorted, jaundiced
10 influenced, prejudiced
11 predisposed, tendentious

Bible
03 law
05 canon
06 manual, primer
07 Gospels, letters, lexicon
08 epistles, good book,
handbook, holy writ,
prophets, textbook, writings
09 Apocrypha, authority,
guidebook, Holy Bible
10 revelation, Scriptures
12 New Testament,
Old Testament
13 reference book
➢ See also **religion**

➤ *Names of biblical
characters*:
03 Dan, Eve, Gad, Ham, Job,
Lot
04 Abel, Adam, Ahab, Amos,
Baal, Cain, Esau, Ezra, Joel,
John, Leah, Levi, Luke,
Mark, Mary, Noah, Paul,
Ruth, Saul, Shem
05 Aaron, Asher, David, Herod
(the Great), Hosea, Isaac,
Jacob, James, Jesus, Jonah,
Judah, Judas, Micah,
Moses, Nahum, Peter,
Sarah, Sheba (Queen of),
Simon, Titus, Tobit
06 Andrew, Baruch, Christ,
Daniel, Elijah, Elisha,
Esther, Gideon, Isaiah,
Joseph, Joshua, Judith,
Philip, Pilate, Rachel,
Reuben, Salome, Samson,
Samuel, Simeon, Thomas

07 Abraham, Absalom,
Delilah, Ezekiel, Gabriel,
Goliath, Ishmael, Japheth,
Jezebel, Lazarus, Malachi,
Matthew, Michael, Rebecca,
Rebekah, Solomon,
Susanna, Timothy, Zebulun
08 Barabbas, Benjamin,
Caiaphas, Habbakuk,
Hezekiah, Issachar,
Jeremiah, Jonathan,
Manasseh, Naphtali,
Nehemiah, Thaddeus,
Zedekiah
09 Bathsheba, Beelzebub,
Nicodemus, Zechariah,
Zephaniah
10 Adam and Eve, Belshazzar,
Methuselah, Simon Magus
11 Bartholomew, Gog and
Magog, Jesus Christ
12 Herod Agrippa, Herod
Antipas
13 Judas Iscariot, Mary
Magdalene, Pontius Pilate
14 Nebuchadnezzar,
Simon the Zealot

➤ *Books of the Bible*:
03 **Job** (Book of)
04 **Amos** (Book of), **Ezra**
(Book of), **Joel** (Book of),
John (Gospel according to),
John (Letters of), **Jude**
(Letter of), **Luke** (Gospel
according to), **Mark**
(Gospel according to), **Ruth**
(Book of)
05 **Hosea** (Book of), **James**
(Letter of), **Jonah** (Book
of), **Kings** (Books of),
Micah (Book of), **Nahum**
(Book of), **Peter** (Letters
of), **Titus** (Letter of Paul to),
Tobit (Book of)
06 **Baruch** (Book of), **Daniel**
(Book of), **Esdras** (Books
of), **Esther** (Book of),
Exodus (Book of), **Haggai**
(Book of), **Isaiah** (Book of),
Joshua (Book of), **Judges**
(Book of), **Judith** (Book
of), **Psalms** (Book of),
Romans (Letter of Paul to
the), **Samuel** (Books of),
Sirach (Book of)
07 **Ezekiel** (Book of), **Genesis**
(Book of), **Gospels**,
Hebrews (Letter of Paul to
the), **Malachi** (Book of),
Matthew (Gospel
according to), **Numbers**
(Book of), **Obadiah** (Book

of), **Susanna** (History of),
Timothy (Letters of Paul
to)
08 **Habakkuk** (Book of),
Jeremiah (Book of),
Jeremiah (Letter of),
Nehemiah (Book of),
Philemon (Letter of Paul
to), **Proverbs** (Book of)
09 **Apocrypha**, **Ephesians**
(Letter of Paul to the),
Galatians (Letter of Paul to
the), **Hexateuch**, **Leviticus**
(Book of), **Maccabees**,
Zechariah (Book of),
Zephaniah (Book of)
10 **Apocalypse**, **Chronicles**
(Books of), **Colossians**
(Letter of Paul to the),
Heptateuch, **Pentateuch**,
Revelation
11 **Corinthians** (Letters of
Paul to the), **Deuteronomy**
(Book of), **Philippians**
(Letter of Paul to the)
12 **Ecclesiastes** (Book of),
Lamentations, **New
Testament**, **Old Testament**
13 **Song of Solomon**,
Thessalonians (Letters of
Paul to the)
14 **Ecclesiasticus** (Book of),
Pauline Letters
15 **Bel and the Dragon**,
Pastoral Letters, **Prayer of
Azariah**, **Wisdom of
Solomon**
16 **Prayer of Manasseh**,
Revelation of John
17 **Acts of the Apostles**
22 **Song of the Three Young
Men**

bibliography
08 book list
09 catalogue

bicker
03 row
04 spar
05 argue, clash, fight,
scrap
07 fall out, quarrel, wrangle
08 disagree, squabble
09 altercate

bicycle
04 bike
05 cycle, racer

➤ *Types of bicycle*:
03 BMX
05 hobby, racer
06 safety, tandem
07 chopper, Raleigh®

08 draisene, draisine, mountain, ordinary, push-bike, tricycle, unicycle
09 recumbent
10 boneshaker, dandy-horse, fixed-wheel, two-wheeler, velocipede
13 penny farthing
14 all-terrain bike
➤ See also **vehicle**

bid
02 go
03 ask, say, sum, try
04 call, tell, wave, wish
05 greet, offer, order, price
06 amount, demand, desire, direct, effort, enjoin, invite, submit, summon, tender
07 advance, attempt, command, proffer, propose, request
08 instruct, proposal
10 put forward, submission

bidding
04 call
05 order
06 behest, charge, desire
07 command, request, summons
11 instruction, requirement

big
03 fat
04 huge, main, mega, tall, vast
05 adult, beefy, bulky, burly, giant, great, hefty, jumbo, large, major, obese, older
06 brawny, bumper, famous
07 eminent, grown-up, leading, serious, sizable, weighty
08 critical, generous, gracious, muscular, spacious
09 cavernous, corpulent, extensive, important, momentous, principal, prominent, unselfish, well-known
10 extra large, voluminous
11 fundamental, kind-hearted, magnanimous, substantial

bigot
03 MCP
06 racist, sexist, zealot
09 dogmatist, sectarian
10 chauvinist

bigoted
06 biased, closed, narrow, swayed, warped
07 partial, twisted
08 dogmatic
09 blinkered, obstinate

10 intolerant, prejudiced
11 opinionated
12 narrow-minded

bigotry
04 bias
06 racism, sexism
08 jingoism
09 dogmatism, injustice, prejudice, racialism
10 chauvinism, partiality
11 intolerance
12 sectarianism

bigwig
03 nob, VIP
05 mogul
06 big gun
07 big shot, notable
08 big noise, somebody
09 big cheese, dignitary
10 panjandrum
11 heavyweight

bile
04 gall
05 anger
06 choler, spleen
07 rancour
09 bad temper, ill-humour
10 bitterness
12 irascibility, irritability

bilge
03 rot
05 trash, tripe
06 drivel, hot air, piffle
07 rubbish, twaddle
08 claptrap, cobblers, nonsense, tommyrot
09 gibberish, poppycock

bilious
04 edgy, sick
05 cross, testy
06 crabby, queasy, sickly
07 grouchy, peevish
08 choleric
09 crotchety, irritable
10 disgusting, nauseating, out of sorts
11 ill-tempered

bilk
02 do
03 con
05 cheat, sting, trick
06 diddle, fleece
07 deceive, defraud, swindle

bill
02 ad
03 act, neb, nib, tab
04 beak, post
05 check, debit, flyer, tally

06 advert, charge, notice, poster
07 account, handout, invoice, leaflet, placard, statute
08 bulletin, circular, handbill, mandible, playbill, proposal
09 advertise, programme, reckoning, statement
11 legislation
13 advertisement

billet
03 job
04 post
05 berth, lodge
07 housing, lodging, quarter
08 barracks, position, quarters
10 employment, occupation
11 accommodate
13 accommodation

billow
04 mass, rise, roll, rush, wave
05 bulge, cloud, surge, swell
07 balloon, breaker, puff out

billowy
07 heaving, rolling, surging, tossing
08 rippling, swelling, swirling
10 undulating

bin
03 box
06 basket
09 container
10 receptacle

bind
03 tie
04 bond, bore, drag, join, lash, rope, spot, tape, wrap, yoke
05 chain, clamp, cover, stick, strap, truss, unify, unite
06 attach, fasten, fetter, hamper, oblige, secure, tether
07 bandage, confine, dilemma, impasse, require, shackle
08 nuisance, restrain, restrict
09 constrain, tight spot
10 difficulty, irritation
11 necessitate, predicament
12 pull together
13 inconvenience

binding
04 tape
05 cover, tight, valid
06 border, edging, strict
07 bandage
08 covering, rigorous, trimming, wrapping
09 mandatory, necessary, permanent, requisite
10 compulsory, conclusive, obligatory

11 irrevocable, unalterable, unbreakable
12 indissoluble

binge
03 jag
04 bout, orgy
05 beano, blind, fling, spree
06 bender, guzzle

biochemist

➤ *Names of biochemists*:
04 **Abel** (John Jacob), **Duve** (Christian René de)
05 **Chain** (Sir Ernst Boris), **Doisy** (Edward Adelbert), **Krebs** (Sir Hans Adolf), **Monod** (Jacques Lucien), **Moore** (Stanford)
06 **Oparin** (Alexandr), **Perutz** (Max Ferdinand), **Porter** (Rodney Robert), **Sanger** (Frederick)
07 **Edelman** (Gerald Maurice), **Hopkins** (Sir Frederick Gowland), **Waksman** (Selman Abraham), **Warburg** (Otto Heinrich)
08 **Anfinsen** (Christian Boehmer), **Chargaff** (Erwin), **Kornberg** (Arthur), **Meyerhof** (Otto Fritz), **Northrop** (John Howard)
09 **Bergström** (Sune), **Butenandt** (Adolf Friedrich Johann)
➤ See also **scientist**

biography
02 cv
04 life
06 biopic, record
07 account, history, profile
09 life story
13 autobiography

➤ *Names of biographers*:
05 **Weems** (Mason Locke)
06 **Wilson** (Andrew Norman)
07 **Ackroyd** (Peter), **Bedford** (Sybille), **Boswell** (James), **Ellmann** (Richard), **Holroyd** (Michael), **Pearson** (Hesketh), **Sitwell** (Sacheverell)
08 **Plutarch**, **Strachey** (Lytton)
09 **Aldington** (Richard), **Kingsmill** (Hugh), **Suetonius**
➤ See also **writer**

biology

➤ *Biological terms include*:
03 DNA, RNA
04 cell, gene
05 class, virus
06 enzyme, fossil
07 meiosis, microbe, mitosis, nucleus, osmosis, protein
08 bacillus, bacteria, genetics, membrane, molecule, mutation, organism, ribosome
09 corpuscle, cytoplasm, ecosystem, ectoplasm, evolution, food chain, symbiosis
10 chromosome, extinction, metabolism, parasitism, protoplasm
11 homeostasis, respiration
12 conservation, reproduction
13 flora and fauna, micro-organism
14 photosynthesis
15 nuclear membrane, ribonucleic acid

➤ *Names of biologists and naturalists*:
03 **His** (Wilhelm)
04 **Berg** (Paul), **Cohn** (Ferdinand Julius), **Gram** (Hans Christian Joachim), **Hess** (Walter Rudolf), **Katz** (Sir Bernard), **Roux** (Emile)
05 **Avery** (Oswald Theodore), **Bacon** (Francis, Viscount), **Bates** (Henry Walter), **Beebe** (Charles William), **Crick** (Francis Harry Compton), **Golgi** (Camillo), **Gould** (Stephen Jay), **Scott** (Sir Peter), **Selby** (Prideaux John), **White** (Gilbert)
06 **Anning** (Mary), **Bordet** (Jules), **Buffon** (George-Louis Leclerc, Comte de), **Cannon** (Walter Bradford), **Carson** (Rachel Louise), **Darwin** (Charles Robert), **Forbes** (Edward), **Huxley** (Sir Julian Sorell), **Huxley** (Thomas Henry), **Lartet** (Edouard Arman Isidore Hippolyte), **Leakey** (Louis Seymour Bazett), **Leakey** (Mary Douglas), **Leakey** (Richard), **Sloane** (Sir Hans), **Watson** (James Dewey), **Wilson** (Edward Osborne)
07 **Adamson** (Joy), **Andrews** (Roy Chapman), **Banting** (Sir Frederick Grant), **Behring** (Emil von), **Dawkins** (Richard), **Haeckel** (Ernst Heinrich Philipp August), **Haldane** (John Burdon Sanderson), **Hershey** (Alfred Day), **Jackson** (Barbara, Lady), **Lamarck** (Jean), **Mantell** (Gideon Algernon), **Pasteur** (Louis), **Wallace** (Alfred Russel)
08 **Cousteau** (Jacques Yves), **Delbrück** (Max), **Franklin** (Rosalind Elsie), **Johanson** (Donald Carl), **Linnaeus** (Carl), **Weismann** (August Friedrich Leopold)
09 **Helmholtz** (Hermann von), **Lederberg** (Joshua)
10 **Darlington** (Cyril Dean)
11 **Leeuwenhoek** (Antoni van), **Spallanzani** (Lazaro)
12 **Attenborough** (Sir David)
➤ See also **scientist**

bird
05 avian, avine
09 ornithoid, volucrine

➤ *Birds include*:
03 ani, auk, emu, hen, jay, kea, moa, owl, roc, tit
04 aves, chat, coot, crow, dodo, dove, duck, erne, fowl, guan, gull, hawk, ibis, kagu, kite, kiwi, lark, loon, lory, myna, rail, rhea, rook, ruff, shag, skua, smee, swan, taha, teal, tern, tody, wren
05 agami, ariel, avian, booby, capon, chick, crane, diver, eagle, egret, eider, finch, fleet, flier, galah, goose, grebe, heron, hobby, macaw, mynah, ousel, piper, pipit, potoo, quail, raven, robin, snipe, squab, stilt, stork, swift, twite, vireo, wader
06 avocet, bantam, barbet, budgie, bulbul, canary, chough, condor, cuckoo, curlew, cushat, darter, dipper, drongo, dunlin, falcon, fulmar, gannet, godwit, grouse, hoopoe, houdan, jabiru, jacana, kakapo, linnet, magpie, martin, merlin, motmot, oriole, osprey, parrot, peahen, peewit, petrel,

pigeon, plover, puffin,
pullet, raptor, redcap, roller,
shrike, siskin, takahe,
thrush, tom-tit, toucan,
trogon, turaco, turkey,
yaffle, zoozoo

07 apteryx, babbler, barn owl,
bittern, blue jay, bluecap,
bluetit, bunting, bustard,
buzzard, chicken, coal-tit,
cotinga, cowbird, creeper,
dottrel, dunnock, fantail,
goshawk, grackle, halcyon,
harrier, jacamar, jackdaw,
kestrel, lapwing, leghorn,
limpkin, mallard, manakin,
moorhen, mudlark, ostrich,
peacock, pelican, penguin,
phoenix, pintail, poultry,
quetzal, redpoll, redwing,
rooster, ruddock, seagull,
skylark, spadger, sparrow,
sunbird, swallow, tanager,
tiercel, tinamou, titlark,
touraco, vulture, wagtail,
warbler, waxbill, wrybill,
wryneck

08 aasvogel, accentor, adjutant,
aigrette, bee-eater, blackcap,
bobolink, cockatoo,
dabchick, dotterel, fish-
hawk, flamingo, great tit,
grosbeak, hornbill, landrail,
laverock, leafbird, lorikeet,
lovebird, lyrebird,
megapode, myna bird,
nightjar, nuthatch, ox-
pecker, palmchat, parakeet,
pheasant, redshank,
redstart, ringtail, sea eagle,
shoebill, starling, water-hen,
whimbrel, white-eye,
woodcock

09 aepyornis, albatross, bald
eagle, blackbird, blackhead,
bowerbird, broadbill,
bullfinch, cassowary,
chaffinch, chickadee,
cockatiel, cormorant,
corncrake, eider duck, fairy
tern, fieldfare, gerfalcon,
goldfinch, goosander,
guillemot, jack-snipe,
kittiwake, little owl,
merganser, mollymawk,
mousebird, mynah bird,
partridge, peregrine,
ptarmigan, razorbill,
sandpiper, scrub-bird,
sheldrake, thornbill,
trumpeter, turnstone, windhover

10 budgerigar, chiff-chaff,
fledgeling, flycatcher,
goatsucker, greenfinch,
greenshank, guinea fowl,
harpy eagle, honeyeater,
honeyguide, kingfisher,
kookaburra, nutcracker,
sanderling, sandgrouse,
shearwater, woodpecker

11 butcherbird, frigatebird,
golden eagle, hummingbird,
mockingbird, nightingale,
reed-warbler, sparrowhawk,
stone-curlew, storm petrel,
thunderbird, tree-creeper

12 adjutant bird,
yellowhammer

13 archaeopteryx, barnacle
goose, oystercatcher,
secretary bird

14 bird of paradise

15 blue-footed booby,
passenger pigeon, peregrine
falcon

➤ See also **animal**; **chicken**;
duck

birth

04 dawn, line, race, rise, root

05 blood, house, start, stock

06 advent, family, labour, origin,
source, strain

07 arrival, descent, genesis,
lineage, origins

08 ancestry, breeding, delivery,
nativity, pedigree

09 beginning, parentage

10 appearance, extraction

11 confinement, parturition

birthday

10 genethliac, natalitial

11 anniversary, date of birth

birthmark

04 mole

06 naevus

07 blemish, naevoid

birthplace

04 home, root

06 cradle, source

08 home town

10 fatherland

12 place of birth

13 mother country, native
country, place of origin

birthright

06 legacy

09 privilege

11 inheritance, prerogative

biscuit

➤ *Biscuits include*:

04 kiss, rusk, tack

05 Marie, wafer, water

06 cookie, parkin

07 Bourbon, cracker, oatcake,
pretzel

08 flapjack, hardtack,
macaroon

09 Abernethy, digestive,
garibaldi, ginger nut

10 Bath Oliver, brandy snap,
florentine, gingersnap,
shortbread

11 ship biscuit

12 ship's biscuit

➤ See also **food**

bisect

04 fork

05 cross, halve, split

06 divide

09 bifurcate, cut in half

bisexual

02 bi

04 AC/DC

07 epicene

11 androgynous, monoclinous

12 ambidextrous

13 hermaphrodite

15 gynandromorphic

bishop

07 prelate, primate

08 diocesan

09 episcopal, patriarch, suffragan

10 archbishop

12 metropolitan

bit

03 jot

04 atom, chip, dash, drop, hint,
iota, lump, mite, part, whit

05 chunk, crumb, flake, grain,
piece, scrap, shred, slice,
speck, touch, trace

06 morsel, sliver, tittle

07 portion, segment, soupçon

08 fragment, mouthful, particle

09 scintilla

❏**a bit**

04 tick

05 jiffy

06 a while, minute, moment,
rather

07 a little, not much, not very

08 slightly

❏**bit by bit**

06 slowly

08 in stages

09 gradually, piecemeal

10 step by step

14 little by little

bitch

03 cat, cow
04 moan
05 gripe, harpy, shrew, vixen
06 virago, whinge
07 grumble, slag off
08 bad-mouth, complain
09 criticize, female dog
13 find fault with

bitchy

04 mean
05 catty, cruel, nasty, snide
07 cutting, vicious
08 shrewish, spiteful, venomous, vixenish
09 malicious, rancorous
10 backbiting, vindictive

bite

03 bit, eat, nip
04 chew, gnaw, grip, hold, kick, peck, rend, snap, tear, work
05 champ, crush, munch, piece, pinch, prick, punch, seize, smart, snack, sting, taste
06 crunch, lesion, morsal, morsel, nibble, pierce, tingle
08 mouthful, piquancy
09 spiciness
10 take effect

biting

03 raw
04 cold, tart
05 harsh, sharp
06 bitter, severe
07 caustic, cutting, hurtful
08 incisive, piercing, scathing
09 trenchant

bitter

03 raw, sad
04 acid, sour, tart
05 acrid, angry, harsh, sharp
06 arctic, biting, fierce, severe
07 acerbic, caustic, cynical, hostile, pungent
08 freezing, piercing, scathing, spiteful, stinging, venomous
09 aggrieved, jaundiced, rancorous, resentful
10 astringent, embittered, vindictive
11 acrimonious, unsweetened
12 freezing cold, vituperative
13 heartbreaking

bitterness

04 bite, pain
05 anger, spite, venom
06 grudge
07 acidity, rancour, rawness

08 acrimony, cynicism, jaundice, pungency, severity, sourness, tartness
09 hostility, sharpness, virulence
10 acerbicity, resentment

bizarre

03 odd
05 queer, wacky, weird
06 way-out
07 comical, curious, oddball, offbeat, strange, unusual
08 abnormal, freakish, peculiar
09 eccentric, fantastic, grotesque, ludicrous
13 extraordinary
14 unconventional

blab

04 leak, tell
06 gossip, reveal, squeal, tattle
07 divulge, let slip
08 blurt out, disclose

black

03 ban, bar, dim, hit, jet, sad
04 dark, inky
05 angry, awful, bleak, dingy, dirty, ebony, grimy, muddy, Negro, pitch, raven, sooty
06 bruise, dismal, filthy, gloomy, grubby, soiled, sombre
07 blacken, boycott, Stygian, subfusc, swarthy, unclean
08 funereal, hopeless, jet-black, menacing, moonless, starless
09 blacklist, Cimmerian, coal-black, depressed, miserable
10 depressing, fuliginous, melanistic, nigrescent
11 dark-skinned, threatening
14 unilluminated

☐black out

05 faint
06 censor, darken
07 conceal, cover up, pass out
08 collapse, flake out, suppress

☐in the black

07 solvent
08 in credit
11 without debt

blackball

03 ban, bar
04 oust, snub, veto
05 expel
06 reject
07 drum out, exclude, shut out
08 throw out
09 blacklist, ostracize

blacken

04 soil

05 cloud, decry, dirty, libel, smear, stain, sully, taint
06 darken, defame, defile, malign, revile, vilify
07 run down, slander, tarnish
08 besmirch
09 discredit, dishonour
10 calumniate

blackguard

05 devil, knave, rogue, swine
06 rascal, rotter, wretch
07 bounder, stinker, villain
08 blighter
09 miscreant, reprobate, scoundrel

blacklist

03 ban, bar
04 snub, veto
05 debar, expel, taboo
06 outlaw, reject
07 boycott, exclude, shut out
09 ostracize, proscribe

blackmail

05 bleed, exact, force
06 coerce, extort, lean on
07 bribery, squeeze
08 chantage, exaction, threaten
09 extortion, hush money
12 hold to ransom, intimidation

blackmailer

07 vampire
11 bloodsucker, extortioner
12 extortionist

☐blackout

04 coma
05 faint, swoon
07 cover-up, secrecy, syncope
08 oblivion, power cut
10 censorship, flaking-out
11 concealment, suppression
12 power failure
15 unconsciousness

blade

04 edge, vane
05 knife, razor, sword
06 dagger
07 scalpel
11 cutting edge

blame

03 rap, tax
04 onus
05 chide, fault, guilt, stick
06 accuse, berate, charge
07 censure, condemn, reprove
08 reproach, tear into
09 criticism, criticize, liability
10 accusation, find guilty
11 culpability
12 condemnation

14 accountability, responsibility
15 hold responsible

blameless
05 clear
07 perfect, sinless, upright
08 innocent, virtuous
09 faultless, guiltless, stainless
11 unblemished
12 without fault
13 unimpeachable
14 irreproachable

blameworthy
06 guilty
07 at fault
08 culpable, shameful
10 flagitious
11 inexcusable
12 indefensible, reproachable
13 discreditable, reprehensible

blanch
04 boil
05 scald
06 whiten
07 go white
08 grow pale, turn pale

bland
04 dull, flat, mild, weak
06 boring
07 humdrum, insipid
08 ordinary
09 tasteless
10 monotonous, unexciting
11 flavourless, inoffensive,
    nondescript, uninspiring
13 characterless, uninteresting

blandishments
07 blarney, coaxing, fawning
08 cajolery, flattery, soft soap
09 sweet talk, wheedling
10 sycophancy
11 compliments, enticements
12 ingratiation, inveiglement

blank
03 gap
04 bare, void
05 clean, clear, empty, space
06 glazed, vacant, vacuum
07 deadpan, vacuity, vacuous
08 lifeless, unfilled, unmarked
09 apathetic, impassive
10 empty space, poker-faced
11 emotionless, indifferent,
    inscrutable, nothingness
14 expressionless
15 uncomprehending

blanket
04 coat, film, hide, mask
05 cloak, cloud, cover, layer,
    sheet, total

06 deaden, global, mantle
07 coating, conceal, overlay
08 bedcover, covering,
    coverlet, envelope,
    surround, sweeping
09 bedspread, inclusive
11 wide-ranging
12 all-embracing, all-inclusive
13 comprehensive
14 across-the-board

blare
04 boom, hoot, roar, toot
05 blast, clang
07 boom out, trumpet
08 blast out
11 sound loudly

blarney
05 spiel
08 cajolery, flattery, soft soap
09 sweet talk, wheedling
13 blandishments
14 persuasiveness

blasé
04 cool
05 bored, jaded, weary
07 offhand, unmoved
09 apathetic, unexcited
10 nonchalant, phlegmatic
11 indifferent, unimpressed
12 uninterested

blaspheme
04 cuss, damn
05 abuse, curse, swear
06 revile
07 profane
09 desecrate, imprecate
10 utter oaths

blasphemous
07 godless, impious, profane
10 irreverent
11 imprecatory, irreligious
12 sacrilegious

blasphemy
05 curse, oaths
08 swearing
09 expletive, profanity,
    sacrilege, violation
11 desecration, imprecation,
    irreverence, profaneness

blast
04 bang, blow, boom, clap,
    gale, gust, honk, hoot, roar
05 blare, burst, crash, sound
06 attack, bellow, blow up,
    volley
07 boom out, clamour, destroy,
    draught, explode, thunder
08 blare out, demolish,
    outburst

09 discharge, explosion
10 detonation
12 blow to pieces

□ **blast off**
07 lift off, take off
10 be launched

blatant
04 open
05 overt, sheer
06 arrant, brazen, patent
07 glaring, obvious
08 flagrant, manifest, outright
09 barefaced, obtrusive, out
    and out, prominent
11 undisguised, unmitigated

blaze
04 beam, burn, fire, glow, rage
05 blast, burst, erupt, flare,
    flash, glare, light, shine
06 flames, see red, seethe
07 bonfire, explode, flare up,
    flare-up, glitter, inferno
09 catch fire, explosion
10 brilliance
13 conflagration
15 burst into flames

blazon
05 vaunt
06 flaunt
07 trumpet
08 announce, proclaim
09 broadcast, celebrate, make
    known, publicize

bleach
04 fade, pale
06 blanch, whiten
07 lighten
08 etiolate, peroxide

bleak
03 raw
04 bare, cold, dark, drab, dull,
    grim, open
05 empty, windy
06 barren, chilly, dismal, dreary
07 exposed, joyless
08 desolate, hopeless
09 cheerless, desperate,
    miserable, windswept
10 depressing
11 comfortless, unpromising
12 discouraging
13 disheartening

bleary
03 dim
05 tired
06 blurry, cloudy, rheumy
07 blurred

bleat
03 baa, cry

04 blat, bray, call, moan
05 whine
06 whinge
08 complain

bleed
03 run, sap
04 flow, gush, milk, ooze, seep, weep
05 drain, exude, spurt
06 extort, reduce
07 extract, suck dry, trickle
09 lose blood, shed blood
11 extravasate, haemorrhage
12 exsanguinate, phlebotomize

blemish
03 mar
04 blot, flaw, mark, spot
05 fault, speck, spoil, stain, sully
06 blotch, damage, defect
09 deformity, disfigure
12 imperfection
13 discoloration, disfigurement

▶ *Types of blemish*:
03 zit
04 acne, boil, bump, corn, mole, scab, scar, spot, wart
06 bunion, callus, naevus, pimple
07 blister, freckle, pustule, verruca
08 pockmark
09 birthmark, blackhead, carbuncle, chilblain, whitehead
14 strawberry mark

blench
03 shy
05 cower, quail, quake, wince
06 falter, flinch, recoil, shrink
07 shudder
08 hesitate

blend
03 fit, mix
04 beat, fuse, stir, suit
05 admix, alloy, match, merge, union, unite, whisk
06 fusion, mingle, set off
07 amalgam, combine, merging, mixture, uniting
08 coalesce, compound
09 composite, synthesis
10 amalgamate, commixture, concoction, go together, homogenize, synthesize
11 combination
12 amalgamation

bless
04 laud
05 exalt, extol, thank
06 anoint, hallow, ordain, praise

08 dedicate, sanctify
10 consecrate

blessed
04 glad, holy
05 happy, lucky
06 divine, graced, sacred
07 endowed, revered
08 favoured, hallowed
09 contented, fortunate
10 prosperous, sanctified

blessing
04 gain, gift, help
05 grace, leave
06 bounty, favour, profit
07 backing, benefit, benison, consent, darshan, godsend, kiddush, service, support
08 approval, sanction, windfall
09 advantage, agreement
10 dedication, permission
11 approbation, benediction, concurrence, good fortune
12 commendation, consecration

blight
03 mar, rot, woe
04 bane, dash, evil, kill, ruin
05 blast, curse, spoil, wreck
06 cancer, canker, damage, fungus, mildew, wither
07 destroy, disease, scourge, shatter, shrivel, trouble
09 frustrate, pollution
10 affliction, misfortune
11 infestation
13 contamination

blind
03 mad
04 mask, rash, slow, trap, wild
05 cover, front, shade, trick
06 closed, dazzle, façade, hidden, screen
07 eyeless, shutter, unaware
08 careless, ignorant, mindless, reckless, unseeing
09 concealed, oblivious, sightless, unsighted
10 obstructed, out of sight, uncritical, unthinking
11 distraction, insensitive, roller blind, smokescreen, unconscious, unobservant
12 imperceptive
13 Austrian blind, inconsiderate, Venetian blind
14 indiscriminate
15 put the eyes out of

blindly
05 madly
06 rashly, wildly

10 mindlessly, unseeingly
11 senselessly, sightlessly
12 uncritically, unthinkingly, without sight
13 thoughtlessly, without vision

blink
04 wink
05 flash, gleam, shine
07 flicker, nictate, twinkle
09 nictitate

bliss
03 joy
06 heaven, utopia
07 ecstasy, elation, nirvana, rapture
08 euphoria, gladness, paradise
09 happiness
11 blessedness
13 seventh heaven

blissful
05 happy
06 elated, joyful, joyous
07 idyllic
08 ecstatic, euphoric
09 enchanted, rapturous

blister
03 wen
04 bleb, boil, cyst, sore
05 bulla, ulcer
06 canker, papula, pimple
07 abscess, pustule, vesicle
08 furuncle, swelling, vesicant
09 carbuncle, pompholyx

blistering
03 hot
05 cruel
06 fierce, savage
07 caustic, extreme, intense, vicious
08 scathing
09 scorching, withering

blithe
06 casual, cheery
08 carefree, careless, cheerful, heedless, uncaring
10 unthinking, untroubled
11 thoughtless, unconcerned
12 light-hearted

blitz
04 raid
06 attack, effort, strike
07 attempt
09 offensive, onslaught
10 blitzkrieg
11 bombardment
12 all-out effort

blizzard
05 storm
06 squall

07 tempest
09 snowstorm

bloated
04 full
05 puffy
07 blown up, stuffed, swollen
08 enlarged, expanded, inflated
09 distended

blob
03 dab, gob
04 ball, drop, glob, lump, spot
05 pearl
07 droplet, globule

bloc
04 axis, ring
05 cabal, group, union
06 cartel, clique, league
07 entente, faction
08 alliance
09 coalition, syndicate
10 federation

block
03 bar, jam, let
04 cake, clog, cube, halt, lump,
   mass, plug, seal, slab, stop
05 brick, choke, chunk, close,
   dam up, delay, piece, wedge
06 bung up, scotch, series,
   square, stop up, thwart
07 barrier, cluster, section
08 blockage, building,
   obstruct, quantity, stoppage
09 frustrate, hindrance, stonewall
10 be in the way, impediment
11 development, obstruction
14 stumbling-block

blockade
04 stop
05 block, check, siege
07 barrier, besiege, closure
08 encircle, obstacle, obstruct,
   surround
09 barricade
11 obstruction, restriction
12 encirclement, prevent using

blockage
03 jam
04 clot
06 log-jam
09 hindrance, occlusion
10 congestion, impediment
11 obstruction

blockhead
04 dork, fool, geek, jerk, nerd,
   twit
05 dunce, idiot, ninny, twerp
06 dimwit, nitwit
08 dipstick, imbecile, numskull
10 nincompoop

bloke
03 boy, guy, man
04 chap, male
06 fellow
09 character
10 individual

blond, blonde
04 fair
06 flaxen, golden
08 bleached
10 fair-haired
11 tow-coloured
12 golden-haired
13 light-coloured

blood
04 gore
05 birth
06 family, haemal, heamic
07 descent, kinship,
   lineage
08 ancestry, haematic
09 lifeblood, relations
10 extraction, vital fluid

bloodcurdling
05 scary
07 fearful
08 chilling, dreadful, horrible
10 horrendous, horrifying,
   terrifying
11 frightening, hair-raising
13 spine-chilling

bloodless
03 wan
04 cold, pale
05 ashen, pasty
06 chalky, pallid, sallow
07 anaemic, drained, insipid
08 lifeless, listless, peaceful
10 colourless, non-violent
11 passionless, unemotional

bloodshed
04 gore
06 murder, pogrom
07 carnage, killing, slaying
08 butchery, massacre
09 blood-bath, slaughter
12 bloodletting

bloodsucker
05 leech
07 sponger
08 parasite
11 blackmailer, extortioner

bloodthirsty
05 cruel
06 brutal, savage
07 inhuman, vicious, warlike
08 barbaric, ruthless
09 barbarous, ferocious
10 sanguinary

bloody
04 gory
05 cruel
06 brutal, fierce, savage
08 bleeding, sanguine
10 sanguinary
11 sanguineous
12 bloodstained, bloodthirsty,
   sanguinolent

bloom
03 bud
04 glow, grow, open
05 blush, flush, prime
06 beauty, flower, health, lustre,
   sprout, thrive
07 blossom, develop, prosper
08 flourish, radiance, rosiness
11 florescence
13 efflorescence

blooming
04 rosy
05 bonny, ruddy
07 healthy
09 flowering
10 blossoming, florescent

blossom
03 bud
05 bloom
06 flower, mature, thrive
07 burgeon, prosper, succeed
08 flourish
11 florescence
13 efflorescence

blot
03 dry, mar
04 blur, flaw, mark, soak, spot
05 dry up, fault, smear, speck,
   spoil, stain, sully, taint
06 absorb, blotch, defect
08 disgrace
12 imperfection

▢blot out
04 hide
06 cancel, darken, delete,
   efface, screen, shadow
07 conceal, expunge, obscure
10 obliterate

blotch
04 blot, mark, spot
05 patch, stain
06 smudge, splash

blotchy
06 smeary, spotty, uneven
08 inflamed, reddened
09 blemished

blow
03 box, fan, hit, rap
04 bang, bash, belt, biff, clip,
   cuff, gale, gust, hook, jolt,

pant, pipe, play, puff, rush, slap, sock, toot, waft, wind

05 blare, blast, clout, knock, punch, shock, smack, sound, spoil, swipe, thump, upset, waste, whack, whirl, wreck

06 buffet, exhale, flurry, squall, stream, stroke, wallop

07 breathe, draught, flutter, puff out, reverse, screw up, setback, tempest, trumpet

08 comedown, misspend

09 bombshell, dissipate

10 affliction, breathe out

11 fritter away, make a mess of

14 disappointment

15 bolt from the blue

◻blow out
07 smother
08 snuff out
10 extinguish

◻blow over
03 end
04 pass
05 cease
06 finish, vanish
07 die down, subside
09 dissipate, fizzle out
11 be forgotten

◻blow up
04 bomb, fill, flip, go up
05 blast, bloat, burst, go ape, go mad, go off, swell
06 expand, puff up, pump up
07 balloon, distend, enlarge, explode, inflate, magnify
08 detonate
09 overstate
10 exaggerate, hit the roof
11 become angry, blow your top, flip your lid, go ballistic
14 lose your temper
15 fly off the handle

blow-out
04 bash, flat, rave
05 binge, feast, party
06 rave-up
07 knees-up
08 flat tyre, puncture
11 celebration

blowy
05 fresh, gusty, windy
06 breezy, stormy
07 squally
08 blustery

blowzy
05 messy
06 sloppy, untidy
07 tousled, unkempt

08 slipshod, slovenly
11 dishevelled

blubber
03 cry, sob
04 blub, weep
06 snivel
07 sniffle, whimper

bludgeon
03 hit
04 beat, club, cosh
05 baton, bully, force
06 batter, coerce, cudgel, harass, hector, strike
08 browbeat, bulldoze
09 terrorize, truncheon
10 intimidate, pressurize

blue
03 low, sad
04 cyan, glum, lewd, navy
05 adult, azure, dirty, fed up
06 coarse, cobalt, erotic, gloomy, indigo, risqué, smutty, steamy, vulgar
07 obscene, raunchy, sky-blue, unhappy
08 cerulean, dejected, downcast, indecent, navy blue, sapphire
09 depressed, miserable, royal blue, turquoise
10 aquamarine, despondent, dispirited, melancholy
11 downhearted, near the bone, ultramarine
12 pornographic
14 down in the dumps

blueprint
04 plan
05 draft, guide, model, pilot
06 design, scheme, sketch
07 outline, pattern, project
09 archetype, prototype

blues
05 dumps, gloom
08 doldrums, miseries
09 dejection, moodiness
10 depression, gloominess, melancholy
11 despondency

bluff
03 lie
04 bank, brow, crag, fake, fool, open, peak, sham, show
05 blind, blunt, cliff, feign, frank, fraud, ridge, scarp, trick
06 candid, deceit, direct, escarp, genial, hearty, height
07 affable, deceive, pretend
08 headland, pretence

09 deception, downright, outspoken, precipice
10 escarpment, promontory
11 good-natured, plain-spoken
15 straightforward

blunder
03 err
04 boob, goof, slip
05 botch, error, fault, fluff, gaffe
06 booboo, bungle, cock-up, howler, slip-up
07 bloomer, clanger, faux pas, go wrong, mistake, screw up, stumble
08 get wrong, solecism
09 mismanage, oversight
10 inaccuracy
12 indiscretion, make a mistake

blunt
04 curt, dull, numb, rude, worn
05 abate, allay, frank, stark
06 abrupt, candid, dampen, direct, honest, weaken
07 brusque, rounded, uncivil
08 edgeless, explicit, hebetate, impolite, not sharp, tactless
09 alleviate, downright, outspoken, pointless
10 forthright
11 unsharpened
13 unceremonious
14 take the edge off
15 straightforward

blur
03 dim, fog
04 haze, mask, mist, spot, veil
05 befog, cloud, smear, stain
06 darken, muddle, smudge
07 becloud, dimness, obscure
09 confusion, fuzziness
10 cloudiness
14 indistinctness

blurb
04 copy, hype, puff
05 spiel
13 advertisement

blurred
03 dim
04 hazy
05 foggy, fuzzy, misty, vague
06 bleary, cloudy
07 clouded, obscure, unclear
08 confused
10 indistinct, out of focus

blurt
◻blurt out
04 blab, gush, leak, tell
05 spout, utter
06 cry out, let out, reveal
07 divulge, exclaim, let slip

08 disclose
09 ejaculate
11 come out with
13 spill the beans

blush
04 glow
05 flush, go red
06 blanch, colour, redden
08 rosiness
09 reddening, ruddiness

blushing
03 red
04 rosy
06 modest
07 ashamed, flushed, glowing
11 embarrassed, erubescence

bluster
04 brag, crow, rant, roar
05 bluff, boast, bully, storm
06 hector
07 bravado, crowing, show off, swagger, talk big
08 boasting, harangue
11 braggadocio, domineering

blustery
04 wild
05 gusty, windy
06 stormy
07 squally, violent
11 tempestuous

board
04 food, grub, jury, slab, slat
05 embus, enter, get in, get on, meals, panel, plank, sheet
06 embark, timber
07 council, emplane, entrain, get into, rations
08 advisers, trustees, victuals
09 committee, directors, governors
10 commission, management, provisions, sustenance
11 directorate

❑**board up**
04 seal, shut
06 shut up
07 close up, cover up

boast
04 brag, crow
05 claim, enjoy, prate, pride, strut, swank, vaunt
06 hot air
07 bluster, crowing, show off, swagger, talk big, trumpet
08 treasure
09 gasconade, gasconism, jactation, loudmouth
10 blustering, self-praise
11 fanfaronade, rodomontade
15 blow your own horn

boastful
04 vain
05 cocky, proud
06 swanky
07 crowing
08 arrogant, bragging
09 big-headed, conceited
10 swaggering
11 egotistical
12 vainglorious
13 swollen-headed

boat
➤ *Types of boat or ship*:
03 cog, cot, gig, hoy, tub, tug
04 bark, brig, dhow, dory, junk, keel, prau, proa, prow, punt, scow, yawl
05 barge, canoe, coper, drake, ferry, kayak, ketch, liner, prore, Q-boat, Q-ship, razee, scull, skiff, sloop, smack, U-boat, whiff, xebec, yacht, zabra
06 barque, bateau, bethel, caique, coaler, convoy, cutter, dinghy, dogger, dugout, galiot, galley, launch, lugger, packet, pedalo, sampan, tanker, wherry
07 bum-boat, caravel, catboat, clipper, coaster, collier, coracle, corsair, cruiser, dredger, felucca, frigate, galleon, galliot, gondola, gunboat, lighter, man-o'-war, mistico, pinnace, steamer, trawler, trireme, warship
08 corocore, corvette, faltboat, foldboat, gallivat, Indiaman, ironclad, lifeboat, longboat, longship, mackinaw, man-of-war, schooner, tall ship, trimaran
09 catamaran, destroyer, freighter, houseboat, hydrofoil, jollyboat, lightship, motor boat, oil-tanker, outrigger, speedboat, steam-boat, steamship, submarine, troop-ship, vaporetto
10 battleship, brigantine, hovercraft, icebreaker, narrow boat, quadrireme, rowing boat, tea clipper, windjammer
11 Berthon-boat, dreadnought, merchant man,

minesweeper, motor launch, quinquereme, torpedo boat
12 cabin cruiser, square-rigger
13 container ship, paddle steamer
15 aircraft carrier
➤ See also **sail**; **ship**; **vehicle**

boatman
05 rower
06 bargee, sailor
07 oarsman
08 ferryman, waterman
09 gondolier, oarswoman, yachtsman
11 yachtswoman

bob
03 bow, hop, nod
04 jerk, jolt, jump, leap, skip
06 bounce, curtsy
09 oscillate
13 move up and down

❑**bob up**
04 rise
05 arise, pop up
06 appear, arrive, show up
07 surface
08 spring up
11 materialize

bode
04 warn
05 augur
06 herald
07 betoken, portend, predict, presage, purport, signify
08 forebode, foreshow, foretell, forewarn, indicate, intimate, prophesy, threaten

bodily
04 real
06 actual, carnal, in toto, wholly
07 en masse, fleshly, totally
08 as a whole, concrete, material, physical, tangible
09 corporeal
11 substantial

body
03 mob
04 band, bloc, bulk, form, mass
05 build, crowd, frame, group, stiff, torso, trunk
06 cartel, corpse, figure, throng
07 cadaver, carcase, council, density, essence, phalanx
08 dead body, firmness, fullness, main part, physique, richness, skeleton, solidity
09 substance, syndicate
11 association, central part, consistency, largest part
12 organization

bodyguard
05 guard
06 minder
08 defender, guardian
09 protector

boffin
05 brain
06 genius, wizard
07 egghead, planner, thinker
08 designer, engineer, inventor
09 intellect, scientist
10 mastermind
11 backroom-boy
12 intellectual

bog
03 fen
04 mire, quag
05 marsh, swamp
06 morass, slough
08 quagmire, wetlands
09 marshland, swampland

❏**bog down**
04 halt, mire, sink
05 delay, stall, stick
06 hold up, impede, slow up
08 encumber, slow down
09 overwhelm

boggle
05 alarm, amaze
07 astound, confuse, stagger
08 bowl over, surprise
09 overwhelm
11 flabbergast

boggy
04 miry, oozy, soft
05 fenny, muddy
06 marshy, spongy, swampy
07 morassy, paludal
11 waterlogged

bogus
04 fake, sham
05 dummy, false, pseud
06 forged, phoney, pseudo
08 spurious
09 imitation
10 artificial, fraudulent
11 counterfeit, make-believe

bohemian
04 arty
07 beatnik, bizarre, drop-out
08 artistic, original
09 eccentric
10 avant-garde, unorthodox
13 nonconformist
14 unconventional

boil
04 brew, cook, fizz, foam,
   fume, heat, rage, rave, stew
05 erupt, froth, steam, ulcer

06 bubble, seethe, simmer
07 abscess, blister, pustule
09 carbuncle, fulminate
10 effervesce, hit the roof
11 blow your top
12 inflammation, fly into a rage
15 go off the deep end

❏**boil down**
06 amount, distil, reduce
08 abstract, condense
09 summarize
11 concentrate

boiling
03 hot
05 angry
06 baking, fuming, torrid
07 enraged, flaming, furious
08 broiling, bubbling, incensed,
   roasting, scalding, steaming
09 indignant, scorching
10 blistering, sweltering

boisterous
04 loud, wild
05 noisy, rough, rowdy
06 active, bouncy, lively, unruly
07 riotous, romping
08 spirited
09 energetic, exuberant
10 disorderly, rollicking

bold
04 loud, pert
05 brash, brave, showy, vivid
06 brassy, brazen, bright,
   daring, heroic, plucky
07 forward, gallant, valiant
08 definite, distinct, fearless,
   insolent, intrepid, outgoing,
   spirited, striking, valorous
09 audacious, barefaced,
   confident, dauntless,
   prominent, shameless,
   unabashed, undaunted
10 courageous, pronounced
11 adventurous, bold as a
   lion, bold as brass,
   eye-catching

bolshie
04 rude
06 touchy
07 awkward, prickly, stroppy
09 difficult, irritable, unhelpful
12 bloody-minded
13 unco-operative

bolster
03 aid
04 help, prop, stay
05 boost, brace
06 buoy up, firm up, pillow
07 augment, cushion, shore up,
   stiffen, support

09 reinforce
10 strengthen, supplement

bolt
03 bar, fly, peg, pin, rod, run
04 dash, flee, gulp, lock, wolf
05 catch, gorge, latch, rivet,
   screw, shaft, stuff
06 devour, escape, fasten,
   gobble, guzzle, hurtle,
   run off, secure, sprint
07 abscond, run away

bomb
04 mine
05 shell
06 attack, blow up, rocket
07 bombard, car bomb,
   grenade, missile, torpedo
08 atom bomb, fire-bomb,
   time bomb
09 bombshell, explosive,
   stink bomb
10 incendiary, letter bomb,
   petrol bomb, projectile
11 depth charge, neutron
   bomb, nuclear bomb
12 hydrogen bomb
15 Molotov cocktail

bombard
04 bomb, pelt, raid
05 blast, pound, shell, stone
06 assail, attack, pester,
   strafe
07 besiege, torpedo

bombardment
04 fire, flak
05 blitz, salvo
06 attack
07 air raid, assault, barrage,
   bombing
08 hounding, shelling
09 besieging, cannonade,
   fusillade, onslaught

bombastic
05 windy, wordy
06 turgid
07 fustian, pompous, verbose
08 affected, inflated
09 grandiose, high-flown
10 euphuistic, portentous
11 pretentious
13 grandiloquent

bona fide
04 real, true
05 legal, valid
06 actual, honest, kosher
07 genuine
09 authentic
10 legitimate
12 the real McCoy

bonanza
04 boon
07 godsend
08 blessing, windfall
12 stroke of luck

bond
03 gum, tie
04 band, bind, cord, fuse, glue, join, link, pact, weld, word
05 chain, stick, union, unite
06 attach, fasten, fetter, pledge
07 binding, connect, manacle, promise, rapport, shackle
08 affinity, contract, covenant
09 agreement, chemistry
10 attachment, connection
12 relationship

bondage
04 yoke
07 serfdom, slavery
08 thraldom
09 captivity, restraint, servitude, vassalage
10 subjection
11 enslavement, subjugation
12 imprisonment, subservience
13 incarceration

bone
06 osteal
07 osseous

► *Human bones. We have omitted the word* **bone** *from names given in the following list but you may need to include this word as part of the solution to some crossword clues.*
02 os
03 jaw, luz, rib
04 coxa, shin, ulna
05 ankle, anvil, costa, femur, funny, hyoid, ilium, incus, jugal, pubis, skull, spine, talus, thigh, tibia, vomer
06 coccyx, fibula, hammer, pecten, pelvis, radius, sacrum, stapes, tarsus
07 cranium, ethmoid, hip-bone, humerus, ischium, kneecap, malleus, ossicle, patella, phalanx, scapula, sternum, stirrup
08 backbone, clavicle, mandible, parietal, scaphoid, vertebra
09 calcaneum, calcaneus, cheekbone, occipital, trapezium, zygomatic
10 breastbone, collarbone, metacarpal, metatarsal

12 pelvic girdle
13 shoulder blade

bonny
04 fair, fine
06 cheery, joyful, lovely, pretty
08 blooming, bouncing
09 beautiful
10 attractive

bonus
03 tip
04 gain, gift, perk, plus
05 extra, prize
06 reward
07 benefit, handout, premium
08 dividend, gratuity
09 advantage, lagniappe
10 honorarium, perquisite

bony
04 lean, thin
05 drawn, gaunt, gawky, lanky
06 skinny
07 angular, scraggy, scrawny
08 gangling, skeletal
09 emaciated

book
04 tome, work
05 blame, order, tract
06 charge, engage, volume
07 arrange, booklet, reserve
08 organize, schedule
11 publication

━━━━━━━━━━━━━━━
► *Terms used in bookbinding:*
03 aeg
04 case, head, limp, tail, yapp
05 bolts, hinge, spine
06 boards, gather, jacket, lining
07 binding, buckram, flyleaf, morocco
08 backbone, endpaper, hardback, tailband
09 backboard, book block, dust cover, embossing, loose-leaf, millboard, paperback, soft-cover
10 pasteboard
11 ring binding
12 quarter bound
14 library binding

❏**book in**
05 enrol
07 check in
08 register

bookish
07 donnish, erudite, learned
08 academic, highbrow, lettered, literary, pedantic, studious, well-read
09 scholarly

10 scholastic
12 bluestocking, intellectual

books
07 ledgers, records
08 accounts
12 balance sheet

boom
04 bang, clap, grow, roar, roll
05 blare, blast, boost, burst, crash, spurt, surge, swell
06 bellow, do well, expand, growth, rumble, thrive
07 explode, prosper, resound, success, thunder, upswing
08 escalate, flourish, increase
09 expansion, explosion
10 escalation, strengthen
11 improvement, reverberate
13 reverberation

boomerang
06 recoil
07 rebound
08 backfire, ricochet
10 bounce back, spring back

boon
04 gift, help, plus
05 bonus, grant
06 favour
07 benefit, godsend, present
08 blessing, kindness, windfall
09 advantage

boor
03 oaf
04 clod, lout
05 yahoo, yokel
06 rustic
07 peasant
09 barbarian, vulgarian
10 clodhopper, philistine

boorish
04 rude
05 crude, gruff, rough
06 coarse, oafish, rustic, vulgar
07 ill-bred, loutish, uncouth
08 ignorant, impolite
09 unrefined
10 uneducated
11 ill-mannered, uncivilized

boost
03 aid
04 help, hype, lift, plug, rise
05 put up, raise
06 assist, expand, fillip, uplift
07 advance, amplify, augment, bolster, develop, ego-trip, enhance, enlarge, further, improve, inspire, promote
08 addition, heighten, increase, maximize, stimulus

09 advertise, encourage, expansion, promotion, publicity, publicize
10 assistance, supplement
11 enhancement, enlargement, furtherance, improvement
12 augmentation, shot in the arm
13 amplification, encouragement

boot
04 kick
05 shove, wader
06 bootee, galosh
07 gumboot
08 overshoe
10 Doc Martens®, riding-boot, wellington
11 walking-boot
12 climbing-boot, football boot

□boot out
04 fire, sack, shed
05 eject, expel
07 dismiss, kick out, suspend
12 give the heave
13 make redundant

□to boot
06 as well
10 in addition
14 into the bargain

booth
03 box, hut
05 kiosk, stall, stand
06 carrel
07 cubicle
11 compartment

bootless
04 vain
06 barren, futile
07 sterile, useless
09 fruitless, pointless, worthless
10 profitless, unavailing
11 ineffective
12 unproductive, unsuccessful

booty
04 haul, loot, swag
05 gains, prize, spoil
06 spoils
07 pillage, plunder, profits
08 pickings, winnings

border
03 bed, hem, rim
04 abut, brim, edge, join, trim
05 bound, frill, skirt, verge
06 adjoin, bounds, frieze, fringe, margin
07 impinge, marches, valance
08 be next to, boundary, confines, frontier, surround

09 perimeter, state line
10 borderline, marchlands
12 be adjacent to, circumscribe

□border on
07 verge on
08 approach, be almost, be nearly, resemble
13 approximate to

borderline
04 iffy
08 doubtful, marginal
09 uncertain
10 ambivalent, indecisive,
13 indeterminate

bore
03 dig, irk, sap, tap, vex
04 bind, drag, mine, sink, tire
05 annoy, drill, weary, worry
06 burrow, dig out, hollow, pall on, pierce, tunnel
07 exhaust, fatigue, trouble, turn off, turn-off, wear out
08 headache, irritate, nuisance
09 hollow out, penetrate, perforate, undermine
11 be tedious to, send to sleep
13 pain in the neck

bored
05 fed up, tired
06 ennuyé, in a rut
07 ennuied, wearied
09 turned off, unexcited
10 bored stiff, brassed off, browned off, cheesed off
12 sick and tired, uninterested

boredom
05 ennui
06 acedia, apathy, tedium
07 humdrum, malaise
08 dullness, monotony, sameness
11 frustration, tediousness
12 listlessness
14 world-weariness

boring
03 dry
04 dull, flat
05 samey, stale, trite
06 dreary, jejune, tiring
07 humdrum, insipid, prosaic, routine, tedious
08 tiresome, unvaried
10 long-winded, monotonous, uneventful, unexciting, uninspired
11 repetitious, stultifying
13 unimaginative, uninteresting
14 soul-destroying

borough
➤ See also **county**; **province**; **state**

▬ *Names of London boroughs*:
05 Brent
06 Barnet, Bexley, Camden, Ealing, Harrow, Merton, Newham, Sutton
07 Bromley, Croydon, Enfield, Hackney, Lambeth
08 Haringey, Havering, Hounslow, Lewisham
09 Greenwich, Islington, Redbridge, Southwark
10 Hillingdon, Wandsworth
12 Tower Hamlets
13 Waltham Forest
17 City of Westminster
18 Barking and Dagenham, Kingston upon Thames, Richmond upon Thames
20 Hammersmith and Fulham, Kensington and Chelsea

▬ *Names of New York boroughs*:
06 Queens
08 Brooklyn, The Bronx
09 Manhattan
12 Staten Island

borrow
04 draw, hire, rent, take
05 adopt, cadge, lease
06 derive, obtain, sponge
07 acquire, charter
08 scrounge, take over
10 have on loan, take on loan
11 appropriate
12 take out a loan
14 use temporarily

borrowing
03 use
04 hire, loan
06 calque, rental
07 charter, leasing
08 adoption, loan-word
11 acquisition
12 temporary use
15 loan-translation

bosom
03 tit
04 boob, bust, dear
05 chest, close, heart
06 breast, loving
07 breasts, bristol, knocker
08 faithful, intimate

boss
04 head
05 bully, chief, owner
06 gaffer, leader, master

bossy

07 captain, foreman, manager, supremo
08 browbeat, bulldoze, director, dominate, domineer, employer, governor, overseer, superior
09 executive, tyrannize
10 push around, supervisor
11 order around
12 give orders to
13 lay down the law

bossy

09 assertive, imperious
10 autocratic, dominating, high-handed, tyrannical
11 dictatorial, domineering, overbearing
13 authoritarian

botanist

> *Names of botanists:*

03 **Mee** (Margaret Ursula), **Ray** (John)
04 **Bary** (Heinrich Anton de), **Bose** (Sir Jagadis Chandra), **Cohn** (Ferdinand Julius), **Gray** (Asa)
05 **Banks** (Sir Joseph), **Sachs** (Julius von)
06 **Haller** (Albrecht von), **Hooker** (Sir Joseph Dalton), **Mendel** (Gregor Johann), **Nägeli** (Karl Wilhelm von)
07 **Bartram** (John), **Bellamy** (David), **Bentham** (George), **De Vries** (Hugo Marie), **Vavilov** (Nikolai)
08 **Candolle** (Augustin Pyrame de)
09 **Schleiden** (Matthias Jakob)
10 **Camerarius** (Rudolph Jacob), **Pringsheim** (Nathaniel)
> See also **scientist**

botch

03 mar
04 goof, hash, mess, muff, ruin
05 farce, fluff, patch, spoil
06 bungle, cock up, foul up, fuck up, mess up, muddle
07 balls up, blunder, failure, louse up, screw up
09 mismanage
11 make a hash of, make a mess of, miscarriage

both

04 each
06 the two
07 the pair

bother

03 bug, nag, vex
04 fuss, pest
05 annoy, pains, upset, worry
06 bustle, dismay, effort, flurry, harass, hassle, molest, pester, plague, put out, strain
07 concern, disturb, problem, trouble
08 distress, exertion, irritate, nuisance, vexation
09 annoyance, incommode
10 difficulty, irritation
11 aggravation
12 make an effort
13 inconvenience, make the effort, pain in the neck
15 concern yourself

bothersome

06 boring, vexing
07 irksome, tedious
08 annoying, tiresome
09 vexatious, wearisome
10 irritating
11 aggravating, distressing, infuriating, troublesome
12 exasperating, inconvenient

bottle

09 container

> *Types of bottle. We have omitted the word* **bottle** *from some names given in the following list but you may need to include this word as part of the solution to some crossword clues.*

04 beer, jack, milk, vial, wine
05 cruet, flask, gourd, phial, scent
06 carafe, carboy, flacon, flagon
07 ampulla, feeding, pitcher
08 calabash, decanter, demijohn, hip flask, hot-water
12 Thermos® flask
> See also **wine**

□ bottle up

04 curb, hide
06 shut in
07 contain, enclose, inhibit
08 hold back, keep back, restrain, restrict, suppress
11 keep in check

bottleneck

05 block
07 snarl-up
08 blockage, clogging
09 narrowing
10 congestion, traffic jam
11 obstruction, restriction
12 constriction

bottom

03 ass, bed, bum, end
04 arse, base, butt, foot, rear, rump, seat, sole, tail
05 floor, lower, nadir
06 behind, depths, far end, ground, lowest, plinth
07 support
08 backside, buttocks, pedestal
09 posterior, underside
10 foundation, underneath

bottomless

04 deep
08 infinite, profound
09 limitless, unlimited
10 fathomless, unfathomed
12 immeasurable
13 inexhaustible

bough

04 limb
06 branch

boulder

04 rock
05 stone

boulevard

04 mall
05 drive
06 avenue, parade
08 prospect
09 promenade
12 thoroughfare

bounce

02 go
03 bob, zip
04 give, jump, leap
05 bound, throw
06 energy, recoil, spring, vigour
07 rebound
08 ricochet, vitality, vivacity
09 animation
10 ebullience, exuberance, get-up-and-go, liveliness, resilience, spring back
11 springiness
12 sprightedness

□ bounce back

07 improve, recover
09 get better
15 get back to normal

bouncing

05 bonny
06 lively, robust, strong
07 healthy

bound

03 bob, hop, off
04 curb, edge, held, jump, leap, line, skip, sure, tied

05 brink, caper, check, dance,
   fated, fixed, flank, frisk,
   going, limit, off to, roped,
   skirt, vault, verge
06 bounce, coming, doomed,
   forced, frolic, gambol,
   headed, lashed, liable,
   prance, spring, tied up
07 certain, chained, clamped,
   confine, contain, enclose,
   heading, obliged, outline,
   pledged, secured, trussed
08 attached, bandaged,
   beholden, destined,
   fastened, fettered, required,
   restrain, shackled, strapped,
   surround, tethered
09 committed, compelled,
   duty-bound, extremity,
   perimeter, restraint
10 limitation, proceeding,
   restricted, travelling
11 constrained, on your way to,
   restriction, termination
12 circumscribe

❑ bound up with

09 related to
10 linked with, tied up with
11 dependent on
13 connected with
14 associated with, hand in
   hand with

❑ out of bounds

05 taboo
06 banned, barred
09 forbidden, off-limits
10 disallowed, prohibited

boundary

04 edge, line
05 brink, verge
06 border, bounds, fringe,
   limits, margin
07 barrier, Rubicon
08 confines, frontier
09 extremity, perimeter
10 borderline, perimetric

bounded

05 edged
07 defined, limited
08 bordered, confined,
   enclosed, hemmed in
09 delimited, encircled
10 controlled, demarcated,
   restrained, surrounded
11 encompassed
13 circumscribed

bounder

03 cad, cur, pig, rat
05 cheat, knave, rogue, swine
06 rotter

08 blighter, dirty dog
09 miscreant
10 blackguard

boundless

04 vast
06 untold
07 endless, immense
08 infinite, unending
09 countless, limitless,
   unbounded, unlimited
10 numberless, unflagging
11 everlasting, illimitable,
   innumerable, never-ending
12 immeasurable, incalculable,
   interminable
13 indefatigable, inexhaustible

bounds

05 edges, scope
06 limits
07 borders, fringes, margins
08 confines
09 perimeter, periphery
10 boundaries, parameters
12 demarcations, restrictions
13 circumference

❑ out of bounds

09 forbidden, off limits
10 not allowed, prohibited

bountiful

05 ample
07 copious, liberal, profuse
08 abundant, generous,
   princely, prolific
09 boundless, bounteous,
   plenteous, plentiful
10 munificent, open-handed
11 magnanimous, overflowing

bounty

04 gift
05 bonus, grant
06 reward
07 charity, premium, present
08 donation, gratuity, kindness,
   largesse
10 almsgiving, generosity,
   liberality, recompense
11 beneficence, munificence
12 philanthropy

bouquet

04 posy
05 aroma, scent, smell, spray
06 wreath
07 corsage, nosegay, perfume
09 fragrance, redolence
15 odoriferousness

bourgeois

04 dull
07 humdrum
08 ordinary
09 hide-bound

10 conformist, uncultured,
   uninspired, unoriginal
11 middle-class, traditional
12 conservative, conventional
13 materialistic, unimaginative
15 money-orientated

bout

02 go
03 fit, run
04 heat, term, time, turn
05 fight, match, round, set-to,
   spell, spree, stint, touch
07 contest, session, stretch
08 struggle
09 encounter
11 competition

bovine

04 dull, dumb, slow
06 stupid
07 cowlike, doltish
09 dim-witted
10 cattlelike, slow-witted

bow

03 arc, bob, nod
04 arch, bend, head, prow
05 crook, crush, curve, defer,
   front, stoop, yield
06 accede, accept, comply,
   crouch, curtsy, give in,
   humble, kowtow, salaam,
   subdue, submit
07 bending, concede, consent,
   incline, rostrum, succumb
09 acquiesce, genuflect, give
   way to, overpower,
   subjugate, surrender
10 capitulate, salutation
11 genuflexion, inclination
13 make obeisance

❑ bow out

04 quit
05 leave
06 defect, desert, give up,
   resign, retire
07 abandon, back out, pull out
08 step down, withdraw
09 stand down

bowdlerize

03 cut
04 edit
05 purge
06 censor, excise, modify
07 clean up, expunge
09 expurgate
10 blue-pencil

bowels

04 core, guts
05 belly, colon, heart
06 centre, depths, inside,
   middle

07 innards, insides, viscera
08 entrails, interior
10 intestines

bower
03 bay
06 alcove, arbour, grotto, recess
07 retreat, shelter
09 sanctuary

bowl
04 dish, hurl, roll, sink, spin
05 basin, pitch, throw, whirl
07 revolve
09 container
10 receptacle

◻**bowl over**
04 fell, stun
05 amaze, floor
07 astound, stagger
08 astonish, push into, surprise
09 dumbfound, knock down
11 flabbergast
14 impress greatly

box
03 hit, pyx
04 case, cuff, pack, slap, slug, sock, spar, wrap
05 bijou, chest, clout, fight, punch, pyxis, thump, whack
06 batter, buffet, carton, casket, packet, strike, wallop
07 coffret, package, present
09 container
10 receptacle

◻**box in**
04 cage, trap
05 hem in
06 coop up, corner, shut in
07 block in, confine, contain, enclose, fence in
08 imprison, restrict, surround
12 circumscribe

boxer
07 fighter
08 pugilist
12 prizefighter
15 sparring partner
➣ See also **sport**

━━ *Weight divisions in professional boxing*:
09 flyweight
11 heavyweight, lightweight, straw-weight
12 bantamweight, middleweight, welterweight
13 cruiserweight, featherweight, mini-flyweight, minimum weight
14 light-flyweight, super-flyweight
15 junior-flyweight

━➤ *Names of boxers, managers and promoters*:
03 **Ali** (Muhammad)
04 **Benn** (Nigel), **Clay** (Cassius), **King** (Don)
05 **Bruno** (Frank), **Hamad** ('Prince' Nasseem), **Lewis** (Lennox), **Louis** (Joe), **Tyson** (Mike)
06 **Cooper** (Henry), **Eubank** (Chris), **Holmes** (Larry), **Liston** (Sonny), **Spinks** (Leon)
07 **Foreman** (George), **Frazier** (Joe), **Leonard** (Sugar Ray)
08 **Marciano** (Rocky), **McGuigan** (Barry), **Robinson** (Sugar Ray)
09 **Holyfield** (Evander), **Honeyghan** (Lloyd)
11 **Fitzsimmons** (Bob)

boxing
08 pugilism, sparring
10 fisticuffs, pugilistic
13 prizefighting

boy
03 kid, lad, son
05 child, youth
06 fellow, junior, nipper
08 teenager, young man
09 schoolboy, stripling, youngster
10 adolescent
14 whippersnapper

boycott
05 avoid, black, spurn
06 eschew, ignore, outlaw, refuse, reject
07 embargo, exclude
09 blacklist, ostracize
12 cold-shoulder
14 send to Coventry

boyfriend
03 man
04 beau, date
05 bloke, lover
06 fiancé, steady, suitor, toyboy
07 admirer, partner
08 young man
10 sweetheart
11 live-in lover

boyish
05 green, young
06 tomboy
07 puerile
08 childish, immature, innocent, juvenile, youthful
09 childlike
10 adolescent, unfeminine

brace
03 duo, tie
04 bind, pair, prop, stay, vice
05 clamp, strap, strut, truss
06 couple, fasten, hold up, prop up, secure, steady
07 bolster, fortify, shore up, shoring, support, twosome
08 buttress, fastener
09 reinforce, stanchion
10 strengthen
13 reinforcement

bracelet
04 band
06 bangle
07 circlet
09 armillary

bracing
05 brisk, crisp, fresh, tonic
07 rousing
08 reviving, vigorous
10 energizing, enlivening, fortifying, refreshing
11 stimulating
12 exhilarating, invigorating
13 strengthening

brackish
04 salt
05 briny, salty
06 bitter, saline

brag
04 crow
05 boast, vaunt
07 bluster, show off, talk big
12 lay it on thick
15 blow your own horn

braggart
06 gascon
07 bluffer, boaster, show-off
08 big mouth, fanfaron
09 blusterer, loud-mouth
11 braggadocio
12 rodomontader

bragging
06 hot air
07 bluster, bravado
08 boasting, vauntery
10 showing-off
12 boastfulness, exaggeration

braid
04 lace, wind
05 plait, twine, twist, weave
07 entwine
09 interlace
10 intertwine, interweave

brain
03 wit
04 head, mind, nous
05 savvy, sense

06 acumen, boffin, brains, genius, pundit, reason
07 egghead, prodigy, scholar
08 brainbox, highbrow
09 intellect, sensorium
10 encephalon, grey matter, mastermind, shrewdness
11 cleverclogs, common sense
12 intellectual, intelligence

➤ *Parts of the brain*:
04 pons
08 cerebrum, midbrain, thalamus
09 brainstem, forebrain, hindbrain
10 cerebellum, grey matter, spinal cord
11 frontal lobe
12 hypothalamus, temporal lobe
14 cerebral cortex, corpus callosum, pituitary gland

brainless
04 daft
05 crazy, inept, silly
06 stupid
07 foolish, idiotic
08 mindless
09 senseless

brainteaser
05 poser
06 puzzle, riddle
07 problem
09 conundrum

brainwashing
09 menticide
11 mind-bending
12 conditioning, pressurizing
14 indoctrination

brainy
04 wise
05 smart
06 bright, clever, gifted
07 sapient
09 brilliant
11 intelligent
12 intellectual

brake
04 curb, drag, halt, slow, stop
05 check
06 pull up, retard
08 moderate
09 restraint
10 constraint, decelerate
11 reduce speed, restriction

branch
03 arm
04 limb, part, stem, wing
05 bough, prong, ramus, shoot
06 office

07 section
08 division, offshoot
10 department, discipline, subsection, subsidiary

❑**branch off**
04 fork
06 divide
07 diverge, furcate
08 separate
09 bifurcate

❑**branch out**
04 vary
06 expand, extend, ramify
07 develop, enlarge
09 diversify, subdivide
10 broaden out
11 proliferate

brand
03 tag
04 burn, kind, line, logo, make, mark, scar, sign, sort, type
05 label, stain, stamp, taint
06 burn in, emblem, symbol
07 censure, species, variety
08 denounce, hallmark, typecast
09 brand-name, discredit, trademark, tradename
10 stigmatize
14 identification
15 identifying mark

brandish
04 wave
05 raise, shake, swing, wield
06 flaunt, parade
07 display, exhibit
08 flourish

brash
04 bold, rash, rude
05 cocky, hasty, pushy
06 brazen
08 impudent, insolent, reckless
09 audacious, foolhardy, impetuous, impulsive
10 incautious, indiscreet
11 impertinent, precipitate
13 self-confident

brass
04 gall
05 cheek, nerve
08 audacity, chutzpah, rudeness, temerity
09 brass neck, impudence, insolence
10 brazenness, effrontery
11 presumption
12 impertinence

brassy
04 bold, hard, loud
05 brash, harsh, noisy, pushy

06 brazen
07 blaring, forward, grating, jarring, raucous
08 insolent, piercing, strident
09 dissonant, shameless
11 loud-mouthed

brat
03 kid
05 puppy
06 nipper, rascal
10 jackanapes
11 guttersnipe
14 whippersnapper

bravado
04 show, talk
05 boast
07 bluster, bombast, swagger
08 boasting, bragging
10 showing-off
11 braggadocio, fanfaronade, rodomontade

brave
04 bear, bold, dare, defy, face
05 gutsy, hardy
06 daring, endure, gritty, heroic, plucky, spunky, suffer
07 doughty, gallant, valiant
08 confront, face up to, fearless, intrepid, unafraid, valorous
09 audacious, dauntless, stand up to, undaunted
10 courageous
11 indomitable, lion-hearted
12 face the music
14 keep your chin up

bravery
04 grit, guts
05 pluck, spunk
06 daring, mettle, spirit, valour
07 courage, heroism
08 audacity, boldness, valiance
09 fortitude, gallantry
11 intrepidity
12 fearlessness, stalwartness
13 dauntlessness

brawl
03 row
04 fray
05 broil, fight, melee, scrap
06 affray, bust-up, dust-up, fracas, ruckus, rumpus
07 dispute, punch-up, quarrel, scuffle, wrangle, wrestle
08 disorder, skirmish
10 Donnybrook, fisticuffs, free-for-all

brawn
04 beef, bulk
05 might, power
06 muscle, sinews

08 strength
11 muscularity

brawny
05 beefy, bulky, burly, hardy, hefty, husky, solid
06 robust, strong, sturdy
07 hulking, massive
08 athletic, muscular, powerful
09 strapping, well-built

bray
05 blare, neigh
06 bellow, heehaw, whinny
07 screech, trumpet

brazen
04 bold, defy, pert
05 brash, pushy, saucy
06 brassy
07 blatant, defiant, forward
08 flagrant, immodest, impudent, insolent
09 audacious, barefaced, be defiant, shameless, unabashed, unashamed

breach
03 gap
04 gulf, hole, rift
05 break, chasm, cleft, crack, lapse, space, split
07 crevice, fissure, opening, parting, quarrel, rupture
08 aperture, breaking, division, infringe, trespass, variance
09 break open, violation
10 contravene, difference, disruption, dissension, infraction, separation
12 burst through, disagreement, dissociation, estrangement, infringement
13 contravention, transgression

bread
03 bap, cob
04 cash, fare, food, loaf, roll
05 funds, money
08 sandwich, victuals
10 provisions, sustenance
11 nourishment

➤ _Types of bread_:
03 nan, rye
04 azym, naan, pita, pone, roti, soda
05 azyme, bagel, matzo, pitta
06 injera
07 bloomer, brioche, challah, chapati, granary, paratha, wheaten
08 baguette, barm cake, chapatti, ciabatta, corn pone, foccacia, leavened, tortilla

09 corn bread, sourdough, wholemeal
10 black bread, brown bread, French loaf, unleavened
11 French stick
12 pumpernickel
➤ See also **food**

breadth
04 size, span
05 range, reach, scope, width
06 extent, spread
07 compass, expanse, measure
08 latitude, vastness, wideness
09 amplitude, broadness
13 extensiveness

break
03 gap
04 fail, gash, halt, hole, luck, lull, open, rend, rest, rift, snap, stop, tame, tear, tell
05 cleft, crack, crash, excel, flout, let-up, outdo, pause, sever, smash, solve, split
06 breach, chance, change, cut off, cut out, divide, exceed, impart, inform, open up, reveal, schism, subdue, weaken, worsen
07 crevice, destroy, disobey, divulge, fissure, fortune, go kaput, holiday, opening, respite, rupture, shatter, surpass, time off, time-out, violate, work out
08 announce, breather, decipher, demolish, disclose, fracture, interval, overcome, puncture, separate, splinter, vacation
09 advantage, figure out, interlude, interrupt, perforate
10 contravene, demoralize, separation
11 discontinue, opportunity
12 bring to an end, disintegrate, estrangement, go on the blink, intermission, stroke of luck

❑**break away**
03 fly
04 flee, quit
05 leave, rebel, split
06 depart, escape, secede
07 run away
08 separate, split off
11 part company

❑**break down**
04 fail, stop
06 detail, pack up

07 analyse, conk out, crack up, give way, itemize, seize up
08 collapse, separate
10 be overcome, go to pieces
11 fall through, lose control, stop working

❑**break in**
05 cut in, train
06 burgle, butt in
07 impinge, intrude
09 condition, get used to, interject, interpose, interrupt, intervene
14 enter illegally

❑**break off**
03 end
04 halt, part, stop
05 cease, pause, sever
06 detach, divide, finish
07 snap off, suspend
11 discontinue
12 bring to an end

❑**break out**
04 bolt, flee
05 begin, erupt, occur, start
06 emerge, escape, happen
08 burst out, commence
09 come out in
13 begin suddenly

❑**break through**
07 succeed
08 overcome, progress
09 penetrate
11 make headway

❑**break up**
04 part, stop
05 sever, split
06 divide, finish
07 adjourn, destroy, disband, divorce, split up, suspend
08 demolish, disperse, separate
09 dismantle, take apart
11 discontinue
12 disintegrate

❑**break with**
04 drop, jilt
05 ditch
06 reject
08 part with, renounce
09 repudiate

breakable
05 frail
06 flimsy
07 brittle, fragile, friable
08 delicate
09 frangible

breakaway
05 rebel

08 apostate, renegade, seceding
09 heretical
10 dissenting, schismatic
12 secessionist

breakdown
07 failure
08 analysis, collapse, stoppage
11 itemization, malfunction
12 interruption
14 classification, disintegration

breaker
04 wave
06 billow, roller
11 white horses

break-in
04 raid
07 larceny, robbery
08 burglary, invasion, trespass
09 intrusion
13 house-breaking

breakthrough
04 find, gain, leap, step
07 advance, finding, headway
08 progress
09 discovery, invention
10 innovation
11 development, leap forward, quantum leap, step forward

break-up
04 rift
05 split
06 finish
07 divorce, parting
09 crumbling, dispersal
10 separation
11 dissolution, splitting-up
14 disintegration

breakwater
04 dock, mole, pier, quay, spur
06 groyne

breast
03 tit
04 boob, bust, teat
05 bosom, chest, front, heart, mamma
06 nipple, thorax
07 bristol, knocker, mammary

breath
03 air
04 gasp, gulp, gust, hint, pant, puff, sigh, waft
05 aroma, odour, smell, whiff
06 breeze, murmur, pneuma
07 whisper
09 breathing, suspicion
10 exhalation, inhalation, suggestion

breathe
04 gasp, pant, puff, sigh, tell
05 imbue, snore, utter, voice
06 exhale, expire, infuse, inhale, inject, instil, murmur
07 inspire, respire, whisper

breather
04 halt, rest, walk
05 break, pause
06 recess
07 respite
14 breathing-space

breathless
04 agog
05 eager
06 puffed, winded
07 anxious, choking, excited, gasping, panting, puffing
08 feverish, wheezing
09 expectant, puffed out
10 in suspense
11 out of breath, short-winded

breathtaking
06 moving
07 amazing
08 exciting, stirring, stunning
09 thrilling
10 impressive
11 astonishing, magnificent, spectacular
12 awe-inspiring

breed
04 kind, line, race, rear, type
05 cause, class, hatch, raise
06 arouse, create, family, foster, hybrid, strain
07 bring up, develop, lineage, nourish, nurture, produce, progeny, species, variety
08 engender, generate, multiply, occasion, pedigree
09 procreate, propagate, pullulate, reproduce
10 bring forth, give rise to

breeding
05 stock
07 culture, lineage, manners, nurture, raising, rearing
08 ancestry, training, urbanity
09 education, gentility
10 politeness, refinement, upbringing
11 development, good manners, procreation
12 reproduction

breeding-ground
04 nest
06 hotbed, school
07 nursery
14 training ground

breeze
03 air
04 flit, gust, puff, waft, wind
06 breath, flurry, wander
07 draught

breezy
04 airy
05 fresh, gusty, light, windy
06 blithe, bright, casual, jaunty
07 blowing, buoyant, squally
08 blustery, carefree, cheerful
09 confident, easy-going

brevity
07 economy
08 curtness, laconism
09 briefness, concision, shortness, terseness
10 abruptness, transience
11 conciseness
12 incisiveness, succinctness

brew
04 cook, plan, plot, soak
05 blend, drink, hatch, steep
06 devise, foment, infuse, liquor, potion, scheme, seethe
07 build up, concoct, develop, ferment, mixture, prepare
08 beverage, contrive, infusion
10 concoction
11 preparation

bribe
03 fix
06 boodle, buy off, grease, pay off, payola, square, suborn
07 corrupt, douceur
08 kickback
09 hush money, incentive, slush fund, sweetener
10 allurement, back-hander, enticement, inducement
15 protection money

bribery
05 graft
10 corruption, protection
12 palm-greasing

bric-à-brac
06 curios
07 baubles
08 antiques, trinkets, trumpery
09 ornaments
11 knick-knacks

brick
04 chum, mate, rock
05 adobe, block, buddy, stone
06 friend, header
07 klinker
09 briquette, firebrick, stretcher
11 breeze block

bridal
07 marital, nuptial, wedding
08 conjugal, marriage
11 matrimonial

bride
04 wife
06 spouse
08 newly-wed, war bride
11 honeymooner
15 marriage partner

bridegroom
05 groom
06 spouse
07 husband
08 newly-wed
11 honeymooner
15 marriage partner

bridge
03 tie
04 arch, bind, bond, fill, join, link, span
05 cross, unite
07 connect
08 causeway, traverse
10 connection
11 reach across

► *Types of bridge. We have omitted the word* **bridge** *from names given in the following list but you may need to include this word as part of the solution to some crossword clues.*
04 arch, rope, toll
05 swing
06 Bailey, flying
07 flyover, pontoon, railway, viaduct
08 aqueduct, humpback, overpass
10 cantilever, drawbridge, footbridge, suspension

bridle
04 curb
05 check
06 halter, master, subdue
07 bristle, contain, control, repress
08 moderate, restrain
09 restraint

brief
04 case, curt, data
05 blunt, crisp, hasty, pithy, prime, quick, remit, sharp, short, surly, swift, terse
06 abrupt, advice, advise, direct, fill in, inform, orders
07 brusque, concise, cursory, defence, dossier, explain, mandate, outline, passing, prepare, summary

08 abridged, abstract, argument, briefing, fleeting, instruct, succinct
09 condensed, directive, fugacious, momentary, temporary, transient
10 aphoristic, directions, short-lived, transitory
12 instructions

briefing
03 gen
06 advice, orders
07 low-down, meeting, priming, run-down
09 filling-in
10 conference, directions
11 information, preparation
12 instructions

briefly
07 in a word, in brief, quickly
09 concisely, cursorily, precisely, summarily
10 succinctly, to the point
11 in a few words, in a nutshell

brigade
04 band, body, crew, team, unit
05 corps, force, squad, troop
07 company
10 contingent

brigand
06 bandit, outlaw, robber
08 gangster, marauder
09 desperado, plunderer
10 freebooter, highwayman

bright
04 fine, glad, keen, rosy
05 acute, happy, jolly, quick, sharp, smart, sunny, vivid
06 astute, brainy, clever, lively
07 beaming, blazing, glaring, hopeful, intense, shining
08 blinding, cheerful, dazzling, flashing, gleaming, glorious, luminous, lustrous, splendid
09 brilliant, cloudless, effulgent, promising, refulgent, sparkling, unclouded
10 auspicious, favourable, glistening, glittering, optimistic, perceptive
11 encouraging, illuminated, intelligent, resplendent
12 incandescent

brighten
05 gleam, pep up, rub up, shine
06 buck up, perk up, polish
07 burnish, cheer up, enliven, gladden, hearten, light up, lighten, liven up

09 encourage
10 illuminate, make bright

brilliance
05 glory, gloss, sheen
06 dazzle, genius, lustre, talent
07 glamour, sparkle
08 aptitude, fulgency, radiance
09 greatness, intensity, splendour, vividness
10 brightness, cleverness, effulgence, excellence, refulgence, virtuosity
11 coruscation, distinction
12 magnificence, resplendence

brilliant
05 great, quick, showy, vivid
06 astute, brainy, bright, clever, expert, glossy, superb
07 blazing, erudite, fulgent, glaring, intense, shining
08 dazzling, glorious, masterly, splendid, talented
09 effulgent, fantastic, refulgent, sparkling
10 celebrated, glittering
11 exceptional, illustrious, intelligent, magnificent, outstanding, resplendent
13 scintillating

brim
03 lip, rim, top
04 edge
05 brink, limit, verge
09 perimeter
10 be full with
12 be filled with, overflow with

bring
04 bear, lead, take
05 carry, cause, fetch, force, guide, usher
06 convey, create, escort
07 deliver, produce, provoke
08 engender, result in
09 accompany, transport

❑ **bring about**
05 cause
06 create, effect, fulfil, manage
07 achieve, produce, realize
08 generate, occasion

❑ **bring down**
04 oust
05 lower
06 defeat, reduce, topple, unseat
07 destroy
08 vanquish
09 overthrow, shoot down
11 cause to drop, cause to fall

❑ **bring forward**
07 advance
11 make earlier

□**bring in**
03 net
04 earn
05 fetch, gross, set up, yield
06 accrue, return
07 pioneer, realize, usher in
08 initiate
09 introduce, originate

□**bring off**
03 win
06 fulfil
07 achieve, execute, pull off
09 discharge, succeed in
10 accomplish

□**bring on**
05 cause
06 foster, induce, lead to
07 advance, improve, inspire, nurture, provoke
08 expedite, occasion
10 accelerate, give rise to
11 precipitate

□**bring out**
05 issue, print
06 launch, stress
07 draw out, enhance, produce, publish
09 emphasize, highlight

□**bring round**
04 coax
05 rouse
06 awaken, cajole, revive
07 bring to, convert, win over
08 convince, persuade
11 resuscitate

□**bring up**
04 form, puke, rear
05 raise, teach, train, vomit
06 broach, foster, submit
07 care for, educate, mention, nurture, propose, throw up
09 introduce
11 regurgitate

brink
03 lip, rim
04 bank, brim, edge
05 limit, verge
09 extremity, threshold

brisk
04 busy, cold, good
05 agile, crisp, fresh, quick
06 active, lively, nimble, snappy
07 bracing
08 bustling, spirited, vigorous
09 energetic
10 no-nonsense, refreshing
11 stimulating
12 businesslike, exhilarating

bristle
03 awn
04 barb, hair
05 quill, spine, thorn
06 seethe
07 prickle, stubble, whisker
08 bridle at, teem with
11 be thick with, horripilate
13 draw oneself up

bristly
05 hairy, rough, spiky, spiny
06 hispid, thorny
07 bearded, hirsute, stubbly
08 unshaven
09 whiskered
10 barbellate

brittle
04 curt, hard
05 crisp, frail, nervy, tense
07 crumbly, fragile, friable
08 delicate, shattery, unstable
09 breakable, crumbling, frangible, irritable
12 easily broken

broach
05 raise
06 hint at
07 mention, propose, suggest
09 introduce

broad
04 vast, wide
05 ample, large, plain, vague
07 general, obvious
08 catholic, spacious, sweeping
09 extensive, inclusive,
10 widespread
11 far-reaching, wide-ranging
12 all-embracing, encyclopedic, latitudinous
13 comprehensive

broadcast
03 air
04 beam, show
05 cable, relay
06 report, spread
07 publish, scatter
08 announce, televise, transmit
09 advertise, circulate, programme, publicize
10 promulgate
11 disseminate
12 transmission

broaden
05 widen
06 expand, extend, open up, spread
07 develop, enlarge, stretch
09 branch out, diversify

broad-minded
07 liberal
08 tolerant, unbiased
09 indulgent, receptive
10 forbearing, open-minded
11 enlightened, progressive
12 free-thinking, unprejudiced

broadside
05 blast, stick
06 attack, volley
07 assault
08 brickbat, diatribe, harangue
09 battering, cannonade
11 bombardment, fulmination

brochure
05 flyer
06 folder
07 booklet, handout, leaflet
08 circular, handbill, pamphlet
10 broadsheet, prospectus

broil
03 fry
04 cook
05 grill, roast
08 barbecue

broiling
06 baking
07 boiling
08 roasting
09 scorching
10 blistering, sweltering

broke
04 bust, poor
05 skint
06 ruined
08 bankrupt, indigent, strapped
09 destitute, insolvent, penniless, penurious
10 cleaned out, stony-broke
11 impecunious
12 impoverished, on your uppers
14 on your beam ends
15 poverty-stricken, strapped for cash

broken
04 bust, down, duff, weak
05 burst, kaput, tamed, wonky
06 beaten, faulty, feeble
07 crushed, damaged, erratic, halting, smashed, subdued
08 defeated, ruptured
09 defective, destroyed, fractured, gone wrong, knackered, separated, shattered, spasmodic
10 disjointed, hesitating, not working, on the blink, out of order, stammering

11 demoralized, fragmentary, inoperative, out of action
12 disconnected, intermittent
13 discontinuous
14 malfunctioning

broken-down
04 bust, duff
05 kaput
06 faulty, ruined
07 damaged, decayed
08 decrepit
09 collapsed, defective
10 on the blink, out of order
11 dilapidated, in disrepair, inoperative

broken-hearted
03 sad
07 forlorn, unhappy
08 dejected, desolate, mournful, wretched
09 miserable, sorrowful
10 despairing, despondent, devastated, prostrated
11 crestfallen, heartbroken
12 disconsolate, inconsolable
13 grief-stricken

broker
05 agent
06 dealer, factor, jobber
07 handler
09 middleman
10 negotiator
11 arbitrageur, stockbroker, stockjobber
12 intermediary

bromide
06 cliché, truism
07 anodyne
08 banality
09 platitude
11 commonplace

bronze
03 tan
04 rust
06 auburn, copper, Titian
08 chestnut
12 reddish-brown
14 copper-coloured

brooch
03 pin
04 clip
05 badge, clasp
06 tiepin

brood
03 sit
04 fret, mope, muse, sulk
05 hatch, issue, worry, young
06 chicks, clutch, family, go over, litter, ponder

07 agonize, dwell on, progeny
08 children, incubate, mull over, rehearse, ruminate
09 offspring

brook
04 bear, beck, burn, gill
05 allow, inlet, stand
06 accept, endure, permit, runnel, stream
07 channel, rivulet, support
08 tolerate
09 put up with, withstand
11 countenance, watercourse

brothel
06 bagnio
08 bordello, cathouse, red light
10 bawdy-house, whorehouse
14 house of ill fame

brother
04 chum, mate, monk
05 friar
06 fellow, friend
07 comrade, partner, sibling
08 relation, relative
09 associate, colleague
12 blood-brother

brotherhood
05 guild, union
06 clique, league
07 society
08 alliance
09 community
10 fellowship, fraternity, friendship
11 association, comradeship

brotherly
04 kind
05 loyal
06 caring, loving
08 amicable, friendly
09 fraternal
10 benevolent
11 sympathetic
12 affectionate
13 philanthropic

brow
03 tip, top
04 peak
05 brink, cliff, ridge, verge
06 summit
07 temples
08 forehead

browbeat
05 bully, force, hound
06 coerce
07 dragoon, oppress
08 bulldoze, threaten
09 tyrannize
10 intimidate

brown
03 bay, fry, tan
04 cook, dark, fawn, rust, seal
05 beige, dusky, hazel, rusty, sepia, tawny, toast, umber
06 auburn, bronze, coffee, ginger, russet, tanned
07 bronzed, browned
08 brunette, chestnut, mahogany, sunburnt
09 chocolate

browned off
05 bored, fed up, weary
10 bored stiff, brassed off, cheesed off
11 discouraged, disgruntled
12 discontented, disheartened

browse
03 eat
04 feed, scan, skim
05 graze
06 nibble, peruse, survey
07 dip into, pasture
11 leaf through

bruise
04 hurt, mark
05 crush, spoil, upset, wound
06 damage, grieve, injure, injury, insult, offend, shiner
07 blacken, blemish
08 black eye
09 contusion, discolour
10 ecchymosis

brunt
05 force, shock
06 burden, impact, strain, thrust, weight
09 main force
10 full weight

brush
03 rub
04 bush, kiss
05 besom, broom, clash, clean, flick, graze, scrub, set-to, shine, sweep, touch, whisk
06 bushes, polish, scrape, shrubs, stroke
07 burnish, contact, sweeper
08 argument, conflict, skirmish
09 brushwood, encounter
11 ground cover, undergrowth
12 disagreement

❑**brush aside**
05 flout
06 ignore
07 dismiss
08 override, pooh-pooh
09 disregard

❑**brush off**
05 spurn

brush-off

06 disown, ignore, rebuff, reject, slight
07 dismiss, repulse
09 disregard, repudiate
12 cold-shoulder

❑**brush up**

04 cram, swot, tidy
05 clean, study
06 read up, revise, tidy up
07 improve, refresh, relearn
08 bone up on, polish up
09 freshen up
15 clean yourself up

brush-off

04 snub
06 rebuff, slight
09 dismissal, rejection
11 repudiation
12 cold shoulder

brusque

04 curt
05 blunt, sharp, short, terse
06 abrupt
07 uncivil
12 discourteous, undiplomatic

brutal

05 cruel, harsh
06 animal, savage, severe
07 beastly, bestial, brutish, callous, inhuman, vicious
08 inhumane, pitiless, ruthless
09 ferocious, heartless, merciless, unfeeling
12 bloodthirsty

brutality

07 cruelty
08 ferocity, savagery, violence
09 barbarism, barbarity
10 coarseness, inhumanity
11 brutishness, callousness, viciousness
12 ruthlessness

brute

04 lout, ogre
05 beast, bully, devil, fiend
06 animal, sadist, savage
08 creature, depraved, mindless, physical
09 senseless
10 unthinking
11 instinctive

brutish

05 crass, crude, cruel, feral, gross
06 brutal, coarse, ferine, savage, stupid, vulgar
07 bestial, loutish, uncouth
08 barbaric
09 barbarian, barbarous
11 uncivilized

bubble

04 fizz, foam, head, suds
05 fraud, froth, spume
06 bounce, burble, gurgle, lather, seethe, trifle, vanity
07 blister, droplet, fantasy, globule, sparkle, vesicle
08 be elated, be filled, illusion
10 effervesce
13 effervescence

bubbly

05 fizzy, happy, merry, sudsy
06 bouncy, elated, frothy, lively
07 excited, foaming
09 ebullient, sparkling
10 carbonated
12 effervescent

buccaneer

06 pirate
07 corsair, sea-wolf
09 privateer, sea-robber
10 filibuster, freebooter

buck

❑**buck up**

05 cheer, hurry, rally
06 hasten, perk up
07 enliven, hearten, hurry up
08 inspirit, step on it
10 encourage, stimulate
15 get a move on
15 get your skates on

bucket

03 can
04 bail, pail
07 pitcher, scuttle

buckle

04 bend, clip, hook, kink, warp
05 bulge, catch, clasp, twist
07 connect, crumple, distort
08 collapse, fastener

bucolic

05 rural
06 rustic
07 country
08 agrarian, pastoral
11 countrified
12 agricultural

bud

04 germ, grow
05 knosp, shoot, sprig
06 embryo, sprout
09 pullulate

budding

07 growing, nascent
09 embryonic, fledgling, incipient, promising

budge

04 give, move, push, roll, stir
05 shift, slide, yield
06 change, give in, remove
07 give way
08 dislodge, persuade

budget

04 plan
05 allot, allow, funds, means
08 allocate, estimate, finances
09 allotment, allowance, apportion, resources
10 allocation

buff

03 fan, rub, tan
04 fawn
05 brush, fiend, freak, khaki, maven, sandy, shine, straw
06 addict, expert, polish
10 aficionado, enthusiast
11 connoisseur

buffer

03 pad
06 bumper, fender, pillow
07 bulwark, cushion
12 intermediary
13 shock-absorber

buffet

03 box, hit, jar
04 bang, beat, blow, bump, café, cuff, jolt, push, slap
05 clout, knock, pound, thump
06 batter, pummel, strike
07 counter
08 cold meal, snackbar
09 cafeteria
11 self-service, smorgasbord

buffoon

04 fool
05 clown, comic, droll, joker
06 jester
08 comedian

buffoonery

07 jesting
08 clowning, nonsense
09 pantomime, silliness
10 tomfoolery

bug

03 fad, irk, tap, vex
04 flaw, flea, germ
05 annoy, craze, error, fault, virus
06 bother, defect, harass, insect, needle, wind up
07 disease, disturb, failing, gremlin, microbe, wire-tap
08 irritate, listen in, phone-tap
09 bacterium, eavesdrop, infection, obsession
12 creepy-crawly, imperfection

13 micro-organism
15 listening device

bugbear
04 bane
05 dread, fiend
06 horror
07 pet hate
08 anathema
09 bête noire, nightmare

build
04 body, form, make, size
05 erect, frame, put up, raise, shape
06 extend, figure
07 develop, enlarge, fashion
08 assemble, escalate, increase, physique
09 construct, fabricate, intensify, structure
11 put together

build up
04 hype, plug
05 boost
06 expand, extend
07 develop, enhance, enlarge, fortify, improve, promote
08 assemble, escalate, heighten, increase
09 intensify, reinforce
13 piece together

building
07 edifice
11 development, fabrication
12 architecture, construction

➤ *Building materials*:
04 clay, sand, tile, wood
05 brick, glass, grout, slate, steel, stone
06 ashlar, cement, girder, gravel, gypsum, lintel, lumber, marble, mortar, tarmac, thatch, timber
07 asphalt, bitumen, fixings, granite, lagging, plaster, plywood, shingle
08 cast iron, concrete, hard core, roof tile
09 chipboard, flagstone, floor tile, hardboard, sandstone
10 glass fibre, insulation
11 breeze block, paving stone
12 plasterboard
13 wattle and daub
14 stainless steel

➤ *Types of building*:
03 inn, pub
04 barn, café, fort, mill, pier, shed, shop, silo
05 abbey, cabin, hotel, house, store, villa

06 castle, chapel, church, cinema, garage, gazebo, mosque, museum, pagoda, palace, prison, school, stable, temple
07 chateau, college, cottage, factory, library, mansion, theatre
08 barracks, beach-hut, bungalow, fortress, hospital, monument, outhouse, pavilion, windmill
09 apartment, boat-house, cathedral, farmhouse, mausoleum, monastery, synagogue, warehouse
10 lighthouse, restaurant, skyscraper, sports hall, tower block
11 condominium, observatory, office block, public house
12 block of flats

➤ *Names of religious buildings*:
04 Kaba
05 Ka'aba
06 Kasbah
07 Abu Mena, al-Azhar
08 Pantheon
09 Acropolis, Borobudur, Eye Temple, Parthenon, Propylaea, Sacred Way, Sun Temple, Temple Bar
10 Blue Mosque, Cluny Abbey, Erechtheum, Meaux Abbey, Sacre Coeur
11 Erechtheion, Great Sphinx, Hagia Sophia, Temple Mount, Wailing Wall, Whitby Abbey, York Minster
12 Ely Cathedral, Golden Temple, Great Pyramid, Temple of Hera, Tintern Abbey
13 Dome of the Rock, Fontenay Abbey, Jedburgh Abbey, Muhammad's Tomb, Rievaulx Abbey, Rila Monastery
14 Belém Monastery, Fountains Abbey, Golden Pavilion, Kazan Cathedral, Reims Cathedral, Ripon Cathedral, Sagrada Familia, Temple of Amon-Ra, Temple of Apollo, Temple of Athena, Wells Cathedral
15 Durham Cathedral, Exeter Cathedral, Pyramid of Cheops, Pyramid of the Sun, Temple of Artemis, Temple of Hathoor, Temple of Solomon

➤ See also **religion**

build-up
04 gain, heap, hype, load, mass
05 drift, stack, store
06 growth
08 increase
09 accretion, promotion, publicity, stockpile
10 escalation
11 development, enlargement
12 accumulation

built-in
06 fitted
08 implicit, included, inherent, integral
09 essential, intrinsic
11 fundamental, inseparable
12 incorporated

bulb
➤ *Plants grown from bulbs and corms*:
04 iris, ixia, lily
05 tulip
06 allium, crocus, garlic, nerine, scilla
07 jonquil
08 amarylis, bluebell, cyclamen, daffodil, gladioli, hyacinth, snowdrop
09 narcissus
10 ranunculus
11 fritillaria
12 autumn crocus
13 crown imperial, grape hyacinth, winter aconite
➤ See also **plant**

bulbous
06 convex
07 bloated, bulging, rounded, swollen
09 distended

bulge
03 sag
04 bump, hump, lump, rise
05 surge, swell
06 dilate, expand
07 distend, enlarge, project, puff out, upsurge
08 increase, protrude, swelling
10 distension, projection
12 protuberance

bulk
04 body, mass, most, size
06 extent, volume, weight
07 bigness
08 majority
09 amplitude, immensity, largeness, magnitude, nearly all, substance
10 dimensions, lion's share
13 preponderance

bulky
03 big
04 huge
05 heavy, hefty, large
07 awkward, hulking, immense, mammoth, massive, weighty
08 colossal, enormous, unwieldy
10 cumbersome, voluminous
11 substantial

bulldoze
04 push, raze
05 bully, clear, force, level
06 coerce
07 flatten
08 browbeat
09 knock down
10 intimidate
11 push through, steamroller

bullet
04 ball, shot, slug
06 pellet
07 missile
09 cartouche, cartridge
10 projectile, propellant

bulletin
06 report
07 leaflet, message
08 dispatch
09 news sheet, newsflash, newspaper, statement
10 communiqué, newsletter
12 announcement, notification

bullish
06 upbeat
07 buoyant, hopeful
08 cheerful, positive, sanguine
09 confident
10 optimistic

bully
04 thug
05 heavy, tough
06 coerce, pick on
07 oppress, ruffian, torment
08 browbeat, bulldoze, bully-boy, bullyrag, domineer
09 persecute, terrorize, tyrannize, victimize
10 browbeater, intimidate, persecutor, push around

bulwark
05 guard
06 buffer
07 bastion, defence, outwork, rampart, redoubt, support
08 buttress, mainstay, security
10 embankment
13 fortification

bumbling
05 inept
06 clumsy
07 awkward, muddled
09 maladroit, stumbling
10 blundering
11 incompetent, inefficient

bump
03 hit, jar
04 bang, blow, hump, jerk, jolt, knur, lump, slam, thud
05 bulge, crash, knock, prang, shake, shock, smash, thump
06 impact, injury, strike
07 collide, papilla
08 swelling
09 collision

◻**bump into**
04 meet
07 run into
09 encounter, light upon
10 chance upon, come across, happen upon

◻**bump off**
03 top
04 do in, kill
06 murder, remove, rub out
09 eliminate, liquidate
11 assassinate

bumper
05 great, large
07 massive
08 abundant, enormous

bumpkin
03 oaf
04 boor, hick
06 rustic
07 hayseed, peasant
09 hillbilly
12 country yokel

bumptious
05 cocky, pushy
07 forward, pompous
08 arrogant, boastful, impudent
09 conceited, officious
10 swaggering
13 self-important
14 full of yourself

bumpy
05 lumpy, rough
06 knobby, uneven
07 knobbly

bunch
03 lot, mob, wad
04 band, crew, gang, heap, mass, pack, pile, posy, tuft
05 batch, clump, crowd, group, party, sheaf, spray, stack
06 bundle, gather, huddle

07 bouquet, cluster, collect, corsage, nosegay
08 assemble, fascicle, quantity
09 fascicule, gathering
10 assortment, collection

bundle
03 bag, box, set, tie
04 bale, bind, heap, mass, pack, pile, roll, rush, wrap
05 batch, bunch, group, hurry, sheaf, shove, stack, truss
06 carton, faggot, fasten, gather, packet, parcel
07 cluster, package
08 fascicle, quantity
09 fascicule
11 consignment, push roughly

bungle
04 boob, muff, ruin
05 bodge, botch, fluff, spoil
06 cock up, foul up, mess up
07 blunder, louse up, screw up
09 mismanage
11 make a mess of

bungler
07 botcher
09 blunderer
11 incompetent
13 butterfingers

bungling
05 inept
06 clumsy
07 awkward
08 botching
09 ham-fisted, maladroit
10 blundering, cack-handed
11 incompetent

bunkum
03 rot
04 bosh, bunk
05 balls, bilge, hooey, trash, tripe
06 piffle
07 baloney, garbage, hogwash, rubbish, twaddle
08 cobblers, nonsense, tommyrot
09 poppycock
10 balderdash

buoy
05 float
06 beacon, marker, signal

◻**buoy up**
04 lift
05 boost, cheer, raise
07 cheer up, hearten, support
09 encourage

buoyant
05 happy, light, peppy

burble
06 afloat, bouncy, bright, lively
07 bullish
08 cheerful, floating
09 floatable, vivacious
10 optimistic, weightless
12 light-hearted

burble
03 lap
06 babble, gurgle, murmur

burden
04 care, duty, load, onus
05 cargo, crush, trial, worry
06 bother, sorrow, weight
07 anxiety, oppress, trouble
08 encumber, handicap, overload, pressure
09 millstone, weigh down
10 affliction, lie heavy on
11 encumbrance

burdensome
05 heavy
06 taxing, trying
07 irksome, onerous, weighty
09 difficult, wearisome
11 troublesome

bureau
04 desk
06 agency, branch, office
07 counter, service
11 writing-desk

bureaucracy
07 red tape
08 ministry
10 government
11 officialdom
12 civil service
14 administration, the authorities

bureaucrat
07 officer
08 mandarin, minister, official
11 apparatchik, functionary
12 civil servant, office-holder
13 administrator
15 committee member

bureaucratic
08 official
10 inflexible, procedural
14 administrative

burglar
05 thief
06 robber
10 cat-burglar, pickpocket
12 housebreaker

burglary
05 heist, theft
07 break-in, larceny, robbery
13 housebreaking

burial
07 burying, funeral
08 exequies
09 interment, obsequies
10 entombment, inhumation

burial place
05 crypt, vault
07 tumulus
08 catacomb, cemetery
09 graveyard, mausoleum
10 churchyard, necropolis

burlesque
04 mock
05 comic, spoof
06 parody, satire, send-up
07 mockery, mocking, take-off
08 ridicule, travesty
10 caricature
12 mickey-taking

burly
03 big
05 beefy, heavy, hefty
06 brawny, strong, sturdy
07 hulking
08 muscular, powerful, thickset
09 strapping, well-built

burn
04 bite, char, fume, glow, hurt, itch, long, sear
05 blaze, brand, flame, flare, parch, scald, singe, smart, smoke, sting, toast, yearn
06 desire, ignite, kindle, scorch
07 consume, corrode, cremate, destroy, flare up, flicker
08 be ablaze, be on fire, burn down, smoulder
09 catch fire, cauterize
10 be in flames, incinerate
11 catch ablaze, conflagrate, go up in smoke, put a match to
15 burst into flames

burning
03 hot, lit
05 acrid, acute, afire, fiery
06 ablaze, aflame, alight, ardent, biting, fervid, urgent
07 blazing, caustic, crucial, earnest, fervent, flaming, frantic, glowing, intense, pungent, searing
08 frenzied, gleaming, piercing, pressing, scalding, smarting, stinging, tingling, vehement
09 consuming, essential, important, prickling, scorching
10 passionate
11 illuminated, smouldering

burnish
04 buff
05 glaze, shine
06 polish
08 brighten, polish up

burp
05 belch
08 eructate
11 bring up wind

burrow
03 den, dig, set
04 hole, lair, mine
05 delve, earth
06 search, tunnel, warren
08 excavate

burst
03 fit, run
04 dart, gush, race, rush, tear
05 barge, break, crack, erupt, hurry, spate, split, surge
07 blow-out, explode, rupture
08 fragment, outbreak, outburst, puncture
09 break in on, break open
10 outpouring

❑**burst out**
03 cry
05 begin, start, utter
06 cry out
07 call out, exclaim
08 blurt out, commence

bury
04 hide, sink
05 cover, embed, inter, plant
06 engulf, entomb, inhume, occupy, shroud
07 conceal, enclose, engross, immerse, implant, inearth
08 enshroud, submerge
09 lay to rest, sepulchre
15 put six feet under

bush
05 brush, hedge, plant, scrub, shrub, wilds
09 backwoods, scrubland

❑**not beat about the bush**
11 speak openly
12 speak plainly

bushy
05 fuzzy, rough, stiff, thick
06 dumose, dumous, fluffy
07 bristly
09 luxuriant, spreading

busily
04 hard
07 briskly
08 actively, speedily
10 diligently

11 assiduously, strenuously
13 energetically, industriously

business

03 job
04 duty, firm, line, task, work
05 issue, point, topic, trade
06 affair, career, matter, métier
07 calling, company, concern, problem, subject, trading
08 commerce, dealings, industry, question, vocation
09 operation, syndicate
10 bargaining, consortium, employment, enterprise, occupation, profession
11 corporation
12 conglomerate, organization, transactions
13 establishment, manufacturing, multinational
14 responsibility

businesslike

07 correct, orderly, precise
09 efficient, organized, practical, pragmatic
10 impersonal, methodical, systematic
11 painstaking, well-ordered
12 matter-of-fact, professional

businessman, businesswoman

06 trader, tycoon
07 magnate
08 employer, merchant
09 executive, financier
10 capitalist
12 entrepreneur
13 industrialist

► *Names of businesspeople*:
04 **Benz** (Karl Friedrich), **Bond** (Alan), **Boot** (Sir Jesse), **Cook** (Thomas), **Ford** (Henry), **Jobs** (Steven), **Mond** (Ludwig), **Shah** (Eddy), **Tate** (Sir Henry), **Wang** (An)
05 **Astor** (John, Lord), **Forte** (Charles, Lord), **Gates** (Bill), **Getty** (Jean Paul), **Grade** (Michael), **Heinz** (Henry John), **Honda** (Soichiro), **Krupp** (Friedrich), **Laker** (Sir Freddie), **Lyons** (Sir Joseph), **Marks** (Simon, Lord), **Rolls** (Charles Stewart), **Royce** (Sir Henry), **Sugar** (Alan), **Zeiss** (Carl)

06 **Boeing** (William Edward), **Butlin** (Billy), **Conran** (Sir Terence), **Cunard** (Sir Samuel), **Du Pont** (Pierre Samuel), **Dunlop** (John Boyd), **Fugger** (Johannes), **Hammer** (Armand), **Hilton** (Conrad Nicholson), **Hoover** (William Henry), **Hughes** (Howard), **Mellon** (Andrew William), **Morgan** (John Pierpont), **Packer** (Kerry), **Ratner** (Gerald Irving), **Turner** (Ted)
07 **Barclay** (Robert), **Branson** (Richard), **Bugatti** (Ettore), **Cadbury** (George), **Citroën** (André Gustave), **Iacocca** (Lee), **Kennedy** (Joseph Patrick), **Maxwell** (Robert), **Murdoch** (Rupert), **Onassis** (Aristotle), **Roddick** (Anita Lucia), **Sotheby** (John), **Tiffany** (Charles Lewis)
08 **Birdseye** (Clarence), **Carnegie** (Andrew), **Christie** (James), **Guinness** (Sir Benjamin Lee), **Michelin** (André), **Nuffield** (William Richard Morris, Viscount), **Olivetti** (Adriano), **Pulitzer** (Joseph), **Rathenau** (Walther), **Rowntree** (Joseph), **Sinclair** (Sir Clive)
09 **Arkwright** (Sir Richard), **Firestone** (Harvey Samuel), **Sainsbury** (Alan, Lord), **Selfridge** (Harry Gordon), **Woolworth** (Frank Winfield)
10 **Leverhulme** (William Hesketh Lever, Viscount), **Pilkington** (Sir Alastair), **Rothschild** (Meyer Amschel), **Vanderbilt** (Cornelius)
11 **Beaverbrook** (Max, Lord), **Harvey-Jones** (Sir John Henry), **Rockefeller** (John Davison)

busker

14 street-musician

bust

04 head, tits
05 boobs, bosom, chest, torso
06 breast, statue
07 breasts
08 bristols, knockers
09 sculpture

bustle

03 ado
04 belt, dash, fuss, rush, stir, tear
05 haste, hurry
06 bestir, flurry, hasten, pother, scurry, tumult
08 activity, rush hour, to and fro
09 agitation, commotion
10 excitement, hurly-burly
15 hustle and bustle

bustling

04 busy, full
05 astir
06 active, hectic, lively
07 buzzing, crowded, humming, rushing, teeming
08 restless, stirring, swarming

busy

06 absorb, active, employ, hectic, lively, occupy, tied up, tiring
07 crowded, engaged, involve, on the go, working
08 bustling, employed, hard at it, interest, involved, occupied
09 energetic, engrossed
10 busy as a bee
11 industrious, unavailable
14 having a lot to do

busybody

03 pry
06 gossip
07 meddler, snooper
08 intruder, quidnunc
10 interferer, nosy parker

butcher

04 kill, slay
06 killer, slayer
08 massacre, murderer, mutilate
09 liquidate, slaughter
11 assassinate, exterminate, meat counter, slaughterer
12 mass murderer, meat retailer

butchery

06 murder
07 carnage, killing
08 massacre
09 bloodshed, slaughter
10 mass murder
12 blood-letting
15 mass destruction

butt

03 bum, end, hit, jab, ram, tip
04 arse, base, bump, foot, haft, mark, prod, push, stub
05 knock, shaft, shove, stock
06 bottom, buffet, dog-end, fag-end, handle, target

07 butt end, subject, tail end
08 buttocks
09 posterior, scapegoat
13 laughing-stock

❑**butt in**
05 cut in
07 intrude
09 interfere, interject,
   interpose, interrupt
12 put your oar in
15 stick your nose in

butter

❑**butter up**
06 cajole, kowtow, praise
07 blarney, flatter, wheedle
08 pander to, soft-soap

butterfly
12 rhopaloceral
13 rhopalocerous
14 papilionaceous

➤ *Types of butterfly*:
05 comma
06 apollo, hermit
07 monarch, peacock, ringlet
08 grayling
09 brimstone, orange-tip
10 common blue, fritillary,
   gatekeeper, hairstreak, red
   admiral
11 meadow brown, painted
   lady, swallowtail
12 cabbage white, white
   admiral
13 tortoiseshell
15 heath fritillary
➤ See also **animal**

buttocks
03 ass, bum
04 arse, butt, rear, rump, seat
05 nates
06 behind, bottom, breech
07 gluteal, gluteus
08 derrière, haunches
09 posterior
12 hindquarters

button
04 disc, knob

06 switch
08 fastener
09 fastening

buttonhole
03 nab
04 grab
05 catch
06 accost, detain, waylay
09 importune, take aside

buttress
04 pier, prop, stay
05 brace, shore, strut
06 back up, hold up, prop up
07 shore up, support, sustain
08 mainstay, underpin
09 bolster up, reinforce,
   stanchion
10 strengthen

buxom
05 ample, busty, plump
06 bosomy, chesty, comely
10 voluptuous
11 well-endowed

buy
03 fix, get
05 bribe
06 buy off, obtain, pay for, pick
   up, snap up, suborn
07 acquire, bargain, procure
08 invest in, purchase
11 acquisition, splash out on

buyer
06 client, emptor, vendee
07 shopper
08 consumer, customer
09 purchaser

buzz
03 hum
04 call, high, kick, race, ring
05 kicks, pulse, throb, whirr
06 bustle, gossip, latest,
   murmur, rumour, thrill
07 buzzing, hearsay, scandal
08 susurrus, tinnitus
09 bombilate, bombinate,
   phone call, susurrate
10 excitement

11 bombilation, bombination,
   stimulation, susurration

by
02 at
03 via
04 away, near, over, past
05 along, aside, close, handy
06 at hand, before, beside,
   beyond, next to
07 close by, close to, through
09 alongside, by means of
11 according to, no later than
12 in relation to

bygone
04 lost, past
05 olden
06 former
07 ancient, one-time
08 departed, forepast, previous
09 erstwhile, forgotten

bypass
05 avoid, dodge, skirt
06 detour, ignore
08 ring road, sidestep
09 diversion
10 circumvent
13 find a way round

by-product
06 result
07 fallout, spin-off
10 derivative, side effect
11 after-effect, consequence
12 repercussion

bystander
07 watcher, witness
08 observer, onlooker
10 eyewitness, rubberneck

byword
05 adage, maxim, motto
06 dictum, saying, slogan
07 precept, proverb
08 aphorism
09 catchword
10 apophthegm

cab

04 taxi
07 minicab, taxicab
08 quarters
11 compartment

cabal

03 set
05 junta, junto, party
06 clique, league
07 coterie, faction
08 conclave, plotters
09 coalition

cabaret

04 show
06 comedy
07 dancing, singing
13 entertainment

cabin

03 hut
04 room, shed
05 berth, bothy, lodge, shack
06 chalet, refuge, shanty
07 cottage, shelter
08 quarters
09 stateroom
11 compartment

cabinet

04 case
05 chest, store
06 closet, locker, senate
07 dresser
08 cupboard
09 executive, ministers
10 government, leadership
14 administration

cable

03 fax, guy
04 cord, flex, lead, rope, wire
05 chain, radio
06 hawser
08 telegram
09 facsimile, telegraph
11 Telemessage®

cache

04 fund
05 hoard, stash, stock, store
06 garner, supply
07 reserve
09 stockpile

10 collection, repository
13 treasure-store

cachet

06 esteem, favour
08 eminence, prestige
10 reputation, street cred

cackle

04 crow
06 giggle, titter
07 chortle, chuckle, snigger

cacophonous

05 harsh
07 grating, jarring, raucous
08 strident
09 dissonant
10 discordant
11 horrisonant

cacophony

07 discord, jarring
09 harshness, stridency
10 disharmony, dissonance
12 caterwauling, horrisonance

cad

03 rat
05 devil, knave, rogue, swine
06 rascal, rotter, wretch
07 bounder, stinker, villain
08 blighter, deceiver
09 reprobate, scoundrel
10 blackguard

cadaver

04 body
05 stiff
06 corpse
07 carcase, remains

cadaverous

03 wan
04 pale, thin
05 ashen, gaunt
07 ghostly, haggard
08 skeletal
09 death-like, emaciated

cadence

04 beat, lilt, rate
05 metre, pulse, swing, tempo
06 accent, rhythm, stress
07 measure, pattern
10 intonation, modulation

cadge

03 beg, bum
06 sponge
08 scrounge

café

06 bistro, buffet
07 tea room, tea shop, wine bar
08 snackbar
09 brasserie, cafeteria, coffee bar, cybercafé
10 coffee shop, restaurant

cafeteria

04 café
06 buffet
07 canteen
10 restaurant

cage

03 pen
04 coop
05 hutch, pound
06 aviary, corral, lock-up
09 enclosure

caged

06 shut up
08 confined, cooped up, fenced in, locked up
09 impounded
10 imprisoned, restrained
12 incarcerated

cagey

04 wary, wily
05 chary
06 shrewd
07 careful, guarded
08 cautious, discreet
09 secretive
11 circumspect

cajole

04 coax, dupe, lure
05 tempt
06 entice, seduce
07 beguile, flatter, wheedle
08 inveigle, persuade, soft-soap
09 sweet-talk

cajolery

06 duping
07 blarney, coaxing
08 flattery, soft soap
09 sweet talk, wheedling

10 enticement, inducement, inveigling, persuasion
11 beguilement, inducements
13 blandishments

cake
04 coat, lump, mass, slab
05 block, chunk, cover
06 harden, pastry
07 congeal, plaster, thicken
08 solidify
09 coagulate
11 consolidate

➤ *Types of cake and pudding*:
03 pie
04 baba, flan, tart
05 bombe, crèpe, fancy, jelly, scone, sweet, torte
06 éclair, gateau, mousse, muffin, parkin, sponge, trifle, waffle
07 baklava, bannock, Bath bun, brioche, brownie, crumble, crumpet, fritter, jam roll, jam tart, pancake, Pavlova, plum pie, ratafia, soufflé, strudel, tartlet, teacake
08 apple pie, doughnut, macaroon, malt loaf, meringue, mince pie, rock cake, seedcake, syllabub, turnover, whim-wham
09 angel cake, fruit tart, fruitcake, fudge cake, lamington, lardy cake, lemon tart, shortcake, Swiss roll
10 Battenburg, carrot cake, cheesecake, Chelsea bun, Dundee cake, Eccles cake, girdle cake, simnel cake, sponge cake
11 baked Alaska, crème brulée, custard tart, gingerbread, hot cross bun, jam roly-poly, Madeira cake, plum pudding, profiterole, rice pudding, sago pudding, spotted dick, treacle tart, wedding cake
12 apfel strudel, Bakewell tart, birthday cake, chocolate log, Danish pastry, figgy pudding, pease pudding
13 apple dumpling, Christmas cake, sponge pudding, summer pudding
14 apple charlotte, charlotte russe, Pontefract cake, upside-down cake, Victoria sponge

15 chocolate éclair, queen of puddings
➤ See also **food**

calamitous
04 dire
05 fatal
06 deadly, tragic, woeful
07 ghastly, ruinous
08 dreadful, grievous, wretched
10 disastrous
11 cataclysmic, devastating
12 catastrophic

calamity
04 ruin
05 trial
06 mishap
07 scourge, tragedy, trouble
08 disaster, distress, downfall
09 adversity, mischance
10 affliction, misfortune
11 catastrophe, tribulation
12 misadventure

calculate
04 make, plan, rate
05 count, gauge, judge, weigh
06 derive, design, figure, reckon
07 compute, measure, work out
08 consider, estimate, reckon up
09 determine, enumerate

calculated
06 wilful
07 planned
08 intended, purposed
10 considered, deliberate, purposeful
11 intentional
12 premeditated

calculating
03 sly
05 sharp
06 crafty, shrewd
07 cunning, devious
08 scheming
09 designing
10 contriving
12 manipulative
13 Machiavellian

calculation
03 sum
06 answer, result
08 estimate, figuring, forecast
09 judgement, reckoning
10 estimation, working-out
11 computation

calibre
04 bore, size

05 gauge, gifts, merit, worth
06 talent
07 ability, faculty, measure, quality, stature
08 capacity, diameter, strength
09 character
10 competence, excellence
11 distinction

call
03 bid, cry, dub, run
04 bawl, bell, buzz, name, need, ring, roar, term, yell
05 brand, label, phone, pop in, shout, style, title, visit
06 appeal, ask for, bellow, call in, come by, cry out, demand, drop in, invite, reason, ring up, signal, stop by, summon, tinkle
07 baptize, command, convene, exclaim, grounds, phone up, send for, summons
08 assemble, christen, occasion
09 pay a visit, telephone
11 exclamation

❑**call for**
04 need
05 fetch, go for
06 demand, entail, pick up
07 collect, involve, justify, push for, require, suggest, warrant
08 occasion, press for

❑**call off**
04 drop
05 scrub
06 cancel, revoke, shelve
07 abandon, rescind
08 break off, withdraw
11 discontinue

❑**call on**
03 ask, bid
04 urge
05 plead, visit
06 appeal, demand, summon
07 entreat, request
08 appeal to, go and see
10 supplicate

❑**on call**
05 ready
10 standing by

call girl
05 whore
06 harlot, hooker
07 hustler
10 loose woman, prostitute
12 street-walker
14 lady of the night

calling
03 job

04 line, work
05 field, trade
06 career, métier
07 mission, pursuit
08 business, province, vocation
10 employment, line of work, occupation, profession
14 line of business

callous
04 cold
05 harsh, stony, tough
08 hardened, obdurate, uncaring
09 heartless, unfeeling
11 cold-blooded, cold-hearted, hard-hearted, indifferent, insensitive
12 thick-skinned
13 unsympathetic

callow
03 raw
05 green, naïve
06 jejune
07 puerile, untried
08 immature, innocent, juvenile
09 guileless, unfledged
11 uninitiated
13 inexperienced

calm
04 cool, lull, mild
05 allay, peace, quiet, relax, still
06 pacify, placid, poised, repose, sedate, serene, settle, soothe, steady
07 appease, assuage, compose, mollify, placate, quieten, relaxed, restful
08 ataraxia, composed, laid back, peaceful, quietude, serenity, tranquil, waveless, windless
09 collected, impassive, placidity, sang-froid, stillness, unclouded, unexcited, unruffled
10 cool-headed, equanimity, untroubled
11 contentment, impassivity, restfulness, undisturbed, unemotional, unexcitable, unflappable, unflustered
12 peacefulness, tranquillity, tranquillize
13 dispassionate, self-possessed
14 self-controlled, unapprehensive

calumny
05 abuse, libel, lying, smear
06 insult
07 obloquy, slander

09 aspersion
10 backbiting, defamation, derogation, revilement
11 denigration, slagging-off
12 vilification, vituperation
13 disparagement

camaraderie
07 rapport
08 affinity, intimacy
09 closeness
10 fellowship
11 brotherhood, comradeship
12 togetherness
13 companionship, esprit de corps

camera
► *Types of camera*:
02 TV
03 SLR, TLR
04 cine, disc, film, Fuji®
05 Canon®, Kodak®, Leica®, Nikon®, plate, still, video
06 Konica®, Pentax®, reflex, Super 8®
07 compact, digital, Minolta®, Olympus®, pinhole
08 Polaroid®, Praktica®, security
09 automatic, binocular, camcorder, miniature
10 box Brownie®, Instamatic®
13 camera obscura, daguerreotype, point-and-press
14 twin-lens reflex

camouflage
04 hide, mask, veil
05 cloak, cover, front, guise
06 façade, screen
07 conceal, cover up, obscure
08 disguise

camp
04 side
05 crowd, group, party
06 caucus, clique
07 bivouac, faction, section
08 affected, mannered
10 artificial, effeminate, over the top, pitch tents, theatrical
12 ostentatious

campaign
03 war
04 push, work
05 drive, fight
06 attack, battle, strive
07 crusade, promote
08 advocate, movement, strategy, struggle

09 offensive, operation, promotion
10 expedition

camp-follower
05 toady
06 lackey
08 hanger-on, henchman

can
03 jar, jug, tin
04 jail, pail, stir
06 prison
08 canister, jerrycan
09 container

canal
05 zanja
07 channel, passage
08 waterway
11 watercourse

cancel
03 axe
04 drop, stop
05 annul, erase, scrap, scrub
06 delete, repeal, revoke, shelve
07 abandon, abolish, call off, nullify, rescind, vitiate
08 abrogate, break off, dissolve, override, postpone
09 eliminate
10 invalidate, obliterate
11 countermand, discontinue

❏**cancel out**
06 offset, redeem
07 balance, nullify
09 make up for
10 compensate, counteract, neutralize
14 counterbalance

cancellation
06 repeal
08 deletion, dropping, quashing, shelving, stopping
09 abolition, annulment, scrubbing
10 abandoning, calling-off, nullifying, revocation
11 abandonment, elimination
12 invalidation
14 neutralization

cancer
03 rot
04 evil
06 blight, canker, growth, plague, tumour
07 disease, scourge
08 sickness
09 carcinoma
10 corruption, malignancy, pestilence

candelabrum
07 menorah
11 candlestick

candid
04 open
05 blunt, clear, frank, plain
06 honest, simple
07 sincere
08 truthful
09 guileless, ingenuous
10 forthright
11 plain-spoken, unequivocal

candidate
06 runner, seeker
07 entrant, nominee
08 aspirant
09 applicant, contender
10 competitor, contestant

candle
05 cerge, taper
08 wax-light

candour
07 honesty, naïvety
08 openness
09 bluntness, frankness,
   plainness, sincerity
10 directness, simplicity
11 artlessness, brusqueness
12 plain-dealing, truthfulness
13 guilelessness,
   ingenuousness,
   outspokenness

candy
06 sweets
07 toffees
10 chocolates
13 confectionery

cane
03 rod
05 crook, staff, stick
06 ferule
10 alpenstock
12 walking-stick

canker
03 rot
04 bane, boil, evil, sore
05 ulcer
06 blight, cancer, lesion, plague
07 disease, scourge
08 sickness
09 corrosion, infection
10 corruption, pestilence

cannabis
03 kef, pot, tea
04 blow, dope, hash, hemp,
   leaf, puff, punk, weed
05 bhang, ganja, grass, skunk
09 marijuana

cannibal
08 man-eater
15 anthropophagite

cannibalism
08 exophagy
09 endophagy, man-eating
13 anthropophagy

cannon
03 gun
06 big gun, mortar
07 battery
08 field gun, howitzer,
   ordnance
09 artillery

cannonade
05 salvo
06 volley
07 barrage
08 pounding, shelling
09 broadside
11 bombardment

canny
03 sly
04 wise
05 acute, pawky, sharp
06 artful, clever, shrewd, subtle
07 careful, knowing, prudent
08 cautious
09 judicious, sagacious
11 circumspect, worldly-wise
13 perspicacious

canon
04 rule
05 vicar
06 priest
07 dictate, precept, statute
08 minister, reverend, standard
09 clergyman, criterion,
   principle, yardstick
10 prebendary, regulation

canonical
07 regular
08 accepted, approved,
   orthodox
10 authorized, recognized,
   sanctioned
13 authoritative

canonical hours
► *Names of canonical hours:*
04 sext
05 lauds, nones, prime, terce
06 matins, tierce
07 vespers
08 compline, evensong

canopy
04 tilt
05 cover, shade
06 awning, tester
07 shelter

08 pavilion, sunshade
09 baldachin

cant
05 argot, lingo, slang
06 jargon
09 hypocrisy
10 vernacular
11 insincerity

cantankerous
05 cross, testy
06 crabby, crusty, grumpy
07 crabbed, grouchy, peevish
08 contrary, perverse
09 crotchety, difficult, irritable
11 bad-tempered, ill-
   humoured, quarrelsome

canter
03 jog, run
04 lope, trot
05 amble
06 gallop
07 jogtrot

canvass
04 poll, scan, sift
05 study
06 debate, survey
07 analyse, examine, explore
08 campaign, evaluate
10 scrutinize
11 electioneer, investigate
13 drum up support

canyon
05 abyss, chasm, gorge, gully
06 ravine, valley

cap
03 hat, lid, top
04 beat, bung, kepi, plug
05 beret, cover, crown, excel,
   limit, outdo, tammy
06 better, bonnet, kalpak
07 control, eclipse, surpass
08 balmoral, outshine, outstrip,
   restrain, restrict, skullcap
09 forage-cap, glengarry,
   muffin-cap, peaked cap,
   school cap, transcend
11 baseball cap, tam-o'-shanter

capability
05 means, power, skill
06 talent
07 ability, faculty
08 aptitude, capacity, facility
09 potential
10 competence, efficiency
11 proficiency, skilfulness
13 qualification
14 accomplishment

capable
04 able

05 adept, apt to, smart
06 clever, fitted, gifted, suited
07 needing, skilful
08 masterly, talented
09 competent, efficient,
   qualified, tending to
10 inclined to, proficient
11 experienced, intelligent
12 accomplished, businesslike

capacious
03 big
04 huge, vast, wide
05 ample, broad, large, roomy
07 liberal, sizable
08 generous, spacious
09 expansive, extensive
10 commodious, voluminous
11 comfortable, substantial

capacity
03 job
04 gift, post, role, room, size
05 power, range, scope, space
06 extent, talent, volume
07 ability, compass, faculty
08 aptitude, function, position
09 largeness, magnitude,
   potential, resources
10 capability, competence,
   dimensions
11 proficiency, proportions
12 intelligence

cape
04 coat, head, ness, robe, wrap
05 cloak, point, shawl
06 mantle, poncho, tongue
07 pelisse
08 headland, pelerine
09 peninsula
10 promontory

caper
03 hop
04 dido, jape, jest, jump, lark,
   leap, romp, skip
05 antic, bound, dance, frisk,
   prank, stunt
06 affair, bounce, cavort, frolic,
   gambol, spring
08 business, escapade
09 high jinks

capital
04 cash, main
05 chief, first, funds, major,
   means, money, prime, stock
06 assets, uncial, wealth
07 central, finance, leading,
   primary, savings, serious
08 cardinal, foremost, reserves
09 majuscule, principal,
   resources, upper-case
10 investment

11 investments, wherewithal
12 liquid assets

capitalism
12 laissez-faire
14 free enterprise

capitalist
05 mogul
06 banker, fat cat, tycoon
07 magnate
08 investor, moneyman
09 financier, moneybags,
   plutocrat

capitalize
□**capitalize on**
07 exploit
08 cash in on
10 profit from
13 make the most of
15 take advantage of

capitulate
05 yield
06 give in, relent, submit
07 succumb
08 back down
09 surrender
15 throw in the towel

capitulation
08 giving-in, yielding
09 relenting, surrender
10 submission, succumbing
11 backing-down

caprice
03 fad
04 whim
05 fancy, quirk
06 notion, vagary, whimsy
07 fantasy, impulse
10 fickleness, fitfulness
11 inconstancy

capricious
03 odd
05 queer
06 fickle, fitful, quirky
07 erratic, wayward
08 fanciful, freakish, variable
09 impulsive, mercurial,
   uncertain, whimsical
10 changeable, inconstant
13 unpredictable

capsize
05 upset
06 invert
07 tip over
08 keel over, overturn, turn over
10 turn turtle

capsule
03 pod
04 pill

05 craft, probe, shell
06 module, sheath, tablet
07 lozenge

captain
04 boss, head
05 chief, pilot
06 leader, master
07 officer, skipper
09 commander

caption
04 note
05 title
06 legend
07 heading, wording
11 inscription

captivate
03 win
04 lure
05 charm
06 allure, dazzle, seduce
07 beguile, bewitch, delight,
   enamour, enchant, enthral
09 enrapture, fascinate,
   hypnotize, mesmerize

captivating
07 winsome
08 alluring, charming, dazzling
09 beautiful, beguiling,
   seductive
10 attractive, bewitching,
   delightful, enchanting
11 enthralling, fascinating

captive
05 caged, slave
06 secure, shut up
07 convict, hostage
08 confined, detained,
   detainee, enslaved,
   interned, internee, jailbird,
   locked up, prisoner
09 enchained, in bondage
10 imprisoned, locked away
12 incarcerated

captivity
06 duress
07 bondage, custody, slavery
09 detention, restraint,
   servitude
10 constraint, internment
11 confinement
12 imprisonment
13 incarceration

capture
03 nab, win
04 nick, take, trap
05 catch, seize, snare
06 arrest, collar, entrap, pick up,
   record, secure
07 embrace, ensnare, seizure

08 hunt down, imprison
09 apprehend, represent
11 encapsulate

car
05 motor
07 vehicle
10 automobile
12 motor vehicle

➤ *Types of car (mostly trademarks)*:
02 MG, VW
03 BMW, cab
04 Audi, auto, Fiat, Ford, jeep, Lada, limo, Merc, Mini, Opel, Polo, taxi
05 Astra, buggy, Buick, coupé, panda, Rolls, stock, Volvo
06 banger, Beetle, Escort, estate, Fiesta, hearse, Jaguar, jalopy, Morris, patrol, Roller, saloon, sports, Toyota, wheels
07 Bentley, Cortina, Daimler, Ferrari, Lagonda, Porsche, Triumph, veteran, vintage
08 Cadillac, Chrysler, Corvette, Maserati, roadster, runabout
09 cabriolet, hatchback, Land Rover, limousine
10 Range Rover, Rolls-Royce, Volkswagen
11 convertible, Silver Ghost
12 Mercedes-Benz, station wagon
14 four-wheel drive

➤ See also **motor**; **vehicle**

carafe
03 jug
05 flask
06 bottle, flagon
07 pitcher
08 decanter

carbuncle
04 boil, sore
06 pimple
07 anthrax
12 inflammation

carcase
04 body, hulk
05 shell
06 corpse
07 cadaver, remains
08 dead body, skeleton
09 framework, structure

card

□ **on the cards**
06 likely
08 possible, probable

11 looking as if, looking like
13 the chances are

cardinal
03 key
04 main
05 chief, first, prime
07 leading, primary
08 foremost, greatest
09 paramount, principal
10 pre-eminent
11 fundamental

➤ *Names of cardinals. We have omitted the word* **cardinal** *from names given in the following list but you may need to include this word as part of the solution to some crossword clues.*
04 **Hume** (Basil)
06 **Borgia** (Rodrigo), **Fisher** (John), **Heenan** (John Carmel), **Medici** (Giovanni de'), **Newman** (John Henry), **Rovere** (Francesco della), **Wolsey** (Thomas)
07 **Mazarin** (Jules), **Mendoza** (Pedro Gonzalez de), **Wiseman** (Nicholas), **Ximenes** (Francisco)
09 **Richelieu** (Armand Jean Duplessis, Duc de), **Wyszynski** (Stefan)
10 **Bellarmine** (Robert), **Breakspear** (Nicolas)

➤ See also **religion**

care
04 heed, keep, mind, tend
05 pains, worry
06 burden, charge, hang-up, regard, strain, stress
07 anxiety, caution, concern, control, custody, trouble
08 accuracy, distress, interest, pressure, tutelage, vexation
09 attention, vigilance
10 affliction, protection
11 forethought, safekeeping, supervision, tribulation
12 guardianship, watchfulness
13 consideration
14 responsibility

□ **care for**
04 like, love, mind, tend, want
05 enjoy, nurse
06 attend, desire
07 cherish, protect
08 be fond of, be keen on, maintain
09 look after, watch over
10 minister to, provide for

career
03 job, run
04 bolt, dash, race, rush, tear
05 shoot, speed, trade
06 gallop, hurtle, métier
07 calling, pursuit
08 life-work, vocation
10 employment, livelihood, occupation, profession

carefree
05 happy
06 blithe, breezy, cheery
08 cheerful, laid back
09 easy-going, unworried
10 insouciant, nonchalant
12 happy-go-lucky, light-hearted

careful
04 wary
05 alert, aware, chary
07 guarded, heedful, mindful, precise, prudent, tactful
08 accurate, cautious, detailed, diligent, discreet, rigorous, thorough, vigilant, watchful
09 assiduous, attentive
10 fastidious, methodical, meticulous, particular, scrupulous, thoughtful
11 circumspect, painstaking

careless
03 lax
05 hasty, messy, slack
06 breezy, casual, remiss, simple, sloppy, untidy
07 artless, cursory, offhand
08 carefree, cheerful, heedless, slapdash, slipshod, tactless
09 easy-going, forgetful, negligent, unguarded
10 disorderly, inaccurate, indiscreet, insouciant, nonchalant, unthinking
11 perfunctory, thoughtless
12 absent-minded, disorganized, happy-go-lucky, light-hearted
13 inconsiderate, irresponsible

caress
03 hug, pat, pet, rub
04 kiss
05 grope, touch
06 cuddle, fondle, nuzzle, stroke
07 embrace, petting
08 canoodle
13 slap and tickle

caretaker
06 keeper, porter, warden

07 curator, janitor, ostiary, steward
08 watchman
09 concierge, custodian
10 doorkeeper

careworn
05 gaunt, tired, weary
07 haggard, worn-out
08 fatigued
09 exhausted

cargo
04 haul, load
05 goods
06 lading
07 baggage, freight, pay-load, tonnage
08 contents, shipment
11 consignment, merchandise

caricature
04 mock
05 mimic
06 parody, satire, send up, send-up
07 cartoon, distort, lampoon, mimicry, take off, take-off
08 ridicule, satirize, travesty
09 burlesque, imitation

carnage
06 murder
07 killing
08 butchery, genocide, massacre
09 bloodbath, bloodshed, holocaust, slaughter
10 mass murder

carnal
04 lewd
06 animal, bodily, erotic, impure, sexual
07 fleshly, lustful, natural, sensual
08 physical
09 corporeal, lecherous
10 lascivious, libidinous, licentious

carnival
04 fair, fête, gala
06 fiesta
07 holiday, jubilee, revelry
08 festival, jamboree
11 celebration, merrymaking

carnivorous
10 meat-eating, zoophagous
11 creophagous

carol
04 hymn, noel, song
06 chorus, strain
07 wassail

carouse
05 booze, drink, party, revel
06 imbibe
07 roister, wassail
09 celebrate, make merry

carousing
08 drinking, partying
11 celebrating, merrymaking

carp
03 nag
05 knock
07 censure, nit-pick, quibble
08 complain, reproach
09 criticize
10 find faults
14 ultracrepidate

carpenter
06 joiner
10 woodworker
12 cabinet-maker

carpet
03 bed, mat, rug
04 kali
05 kilim, layer
06 Wilton
07 blanket, matting
08 Aubusson, covering
09 Axminster
13 Kidderminster

carriage
03 air, cab, car, gig
04 mien, trap
05 coach, guise, wagon
06 hansom, landau, manner
07 bearing, conduct, freight, hackney, postage, posture
08 attitude, presence
09 behaviour, demeanour
10 conveyance, deportment

carrier
06 bearer, porter, runner, vector
07 airline, vehicle
08 conveyor
09 messenger
11 transmitter, transporter

carry
03 lug
04 bear, cart, haul, have, hold, hump, mean, move, pass, pipe, sell, show, take, tote
05 bring, drive, fetch, print, relay, shift, stand, stock
06 accept, convey, entail, ratify, retail, uphold
07 conduct, contain, deliver, display, support, sustain
08 sanction, shoulder, transfer, transmit, underpin

09 authorize, transport
11 communicate, disseminate

❑**carry on**
03 run
04 go on, last
06 endure, keep on, keep up, manage, play up, resume
07 persist, proceed, restart
08 continue, maintain, progress, return to
09 misbehave, persevere
10 administer, mess around

❑**carry out**
02 do
06 effect, fulfil
07 achieve, conduct, deliver, execute, perform, realize
08 bring off
09 discharge, implement, undertake

cart
03 lug
04 bear, dray, haul, hump, move, tote
05 carry, shift, truck, wagon
06 barrow, convey
08 handcart, transfer
11 wheelbarrow

carton
03 box
04 case, pack
06 packet, parcel
07 package
09 container

cartoon
06 parody, send-up, sketch
07 balloon, drawing, lampoon, picture, take-off
09 animation, burlesque
10 caricature, comic strip
12 animated film

cartridge
04 case, tube
05 round, shell
06 charge
08 cassette, magazine

carve
03 cut, hew
04 chip, chop, etch, form, hack
05 cut up, mould, shape, slice
06 chisel, incise, indent, sculpt
07 engrave, fashion, whittle
09 sculpture

❑**carve up**
05 share, split
06 divide
08 separate, share out
09 parcel out, partition
10 distribute

carving
04 bust
06 statue
07 glyptic
08 incision
09 sculpture, statuette
10 lithoglyph, petroglyph
11 dendroglyph

cascade
04 fall, gush, pour, rush
05 chute, falls, flood, surge
06 deluge, shower, tumble
07 descend, torrent, trickle
08 cataract, fountain, overflow
09 avalanche, waterfall
10 outpouring

case
03 bag, box
04 suit
05 chest, cover, crate, event, shell, trial, trunk
06 action, carton, casket, client, sheath, valise, victim
07 attaché, capsule, example, holdall, invalid, lawsuit, patient, wrapper
08 argument, instance, occasion, specimen
09 cartridge, container, flight bag, portfolio, situation, travel bag
10 occurrence, receptacle
11 contingency, hand-luggage, portmanteau
12 illustration, overnight-bag

cash
04 dosh
05 bread, coins, dough, funds, lolly, money, notes, ready
06 change
07 bullion, capital, readies, realize
08 currency, exchange
09 banknotes, hard money
10 ready money
11 legal tender, wherewithal

cashier
04 sack
05 break, clerk, expel
06 banker, bursar, purser, teller
07 discard, dismiss, unfrock
08 get rid of, throw out
09 bank clerk, discharge, treasurer
10 accountant

cask
03 keg, tub, tun, vat
04 butt
06 barrel, firkin

08 hogshead
09 kilderkin

casket
03 box
04 case, kist
05 chest, pyxis
06 coffer, coffin
08 jewel-box
11 sarcophagus

cast
03 lob, put, see, shy
04 emit, form, hurl, look, shed, toss, view, vote
05 drive, fling, found, heave, impel, model, mould, pitch, place, shape, sling, throw
06 actors, direct, glance, launch, look at, record, spread, troupe
07 company, diffuse, fashion, give off, give out, glimpse, players, radiate, scatter
08 covering, register
10 characters, performers

❑**cast down**
05 crush
06 deject, sadden
07 depress
08 desolate
10 discourage, dishearten

caste
04 race, rank
05 class, grade, group, order
06 degree, estate, status
07 lineage, station, stratum
08 position
10 background

castigate
05 chide, scold
06 berate, punish, rebuke
07 censure, chasten, correct, reprove, upbraid
08 chastise
09 criticize, reprimand
10 discipline
13 tear a strip off

castle
04 fort, keep
05 tower
06 kasbah, palace
07 château, citadel, schloss
08 fortress
10 stronghold

▶ *Parts of a castle*:
04 keep, moat, ward
05 ditch, fosse, motte, mound, scarp, tower
06 bailey, chapel, corbel, crenel, donjon, merlon, turret

07 bastion, dungeon, parapet, postern, rampart
08 approach, barbican, buttress, stockade
09 courtyard, gatehouse, inner wall
10 drawbridge, portcullis, watchtower
11 battlements, curtain wall
12 crenellation, lookout tower

▶ *Famous castles include*:
04 York
05 Corfe, Doune, Leeds
06 Cawdor, Glamis, Ludlow
07 Alnwick, Arundel, Caister, Dunster, Harlech, Peveril, Warwick, Windsor
08 Balmoral, Bamburgh, Bastille, Egremont, Elsinore, Stirling, Stokesay, Tintagel
09 Beaumaris, Dunsinane, Edinburgh, Tantallon
10 Caernarvon, Carmarthen, Rockingham
11 Chillingham, Craigmillar, Fotheringay, Lindisfarne, Ravenscraig
12 Conisborough

castrate
04 geld
05 unman, unsex
06 neuter
07 evirate
10 emasculate

casual
05 blasé
06 chance, random
07 cursory, offhand, relaxed
08 informal, laid back
09 apathetic, easy-going, short-term, temporary
10 accidental, incidental, insouciant, nonchalant
11 free-and-easy, indifferent, superficial, unconcerned
12 happy-go-lucky, intermittent
13 lackadaisical, serendipitous
15 couldn't-care-less

casualty
04 loss
05 death
06 injury, victim
07 injured, missing, wounded
08 fatality, sufferer

casuistry
07 sophism
09 chicanery, sophistry
12 equivocation, speciousness

cat
03 mog, tom
04 puss
05 moggy, pussy, tabby
06 feline, kitten, mouser
09 grimalkin
➤ See also **animal**

▶ *Breeds of cat*:
03 Rex
04 Manx
06 Birman, Bombay, Cymric
07 Burmese, Persian, rag-doll, Siamese, Tiffany
09 Singapura, Tonkinese
10 Abyssinian, chinchilla, Turkish Van
11 Egyptian Mau, Russian Blue
12 Scottish Fold
13 Tortoiseshell
15 British longhair, Japanese Bobtail

▶ *Famous cats include*:
03 Tom
04 Bast
05 Dinah, Felix, Korky
06 Arthur, Ginger, Kaspar, Top Cat
07 Bagpuss, Custard, Simpkin
08 Beerbohm, Garfield, Humphrey, Macavity
09 Sylvester, Tom Kitten
10 Heathcliff
11 Cat in the Hat, Cheshire Cat, Pink Panther, Puss in Boots
14 Bustopher Jones, Mr Mistoffelees, Old Deuteronomy

cataclysm
04 blow
07 debacle
08 calamity, disaster, upheaval
11 catastrophe, devastation

catacomb
04 tomb
05 crypt, vault
07 ossuary

catalogue
04 file, list, roll
05 guide, index, table
06 record, roster
08 brochure, bulletin, calendar, classify, register, tabulate
09 checklist, directory, inventory, make a list
10 prospectus

catapult
04 fire, hurl, toss
05 fling, pitch, shoot, sling, throw
06 hurtle, launch, propel

cataract
05 falls, force
06 deluge, rapids
07 cascade, torrent
08 downpour
09 waterfall

catastrophe
04 blow, ruin
06 fiasco
07 debacle, failure, tragedy
08 calamity, disaster, upheaval
09 adversity, cataclysm
10 affliction, misfortune
11 devastation

catastrophic
05 awful, fatal
06 tragic
08 dreadful, terrible
10 calamitous, disastrous
11 cataclysmic, devastating

catcall
03 boo
04 gibe, hiss, jeer, jibe
07 whistle

catch
03 get, nab, net
04 bolt, clip, find, grab, grip, hasp, hear, hold, hook, lock, nick, snag, snare, trap, twig
05 clasp, grasp, hitch, latch, seize, snare, sneck
06 arrest, collar, corner, entrap, expose, fathom, follow, pick up, snatch, take in
07 attract, develop, discern, ensnare, problem, round up, startle
08 contract, discover, drawback, fastener, perceive, surprise
09 apprehend, lay hold of
10 comprehend, difficulty, go down with, understand
12 disadvantage

❏catch on
05 grasp
06 fathom, follow, take in
10 comprehend, understand
13 become popular

❏catch up
06 gain on
08 overtake
09 draw level

catch phrase
05 motto

catch word
06 byword, jingle, saying, slogan
07 formula
08 password
09 catchword, watchword

catching
10 contagious, infectious
12 communicable
13 transmissible, transmittable

catchy
07 melodic, popular, tuneful
08 haunting
09 appealing, memorable
10 attractive
11 captivating
13 unforgettable

catechize
04 test
05 drill, grill
07 examine
08 instruct, question
11 interrogate
12 cross-examine

categorical
05 clear, total, utter
06 direct
07 express
08 absolute, definite, emphatic, explicit, positive
09 downright
10 conclusive, unreserved

categorize
04 list, rank, sort
05 class, grade, group, order
07 arrange
08 classify, tabulate
10 pigeonhole, stereotype

category
04 kind, list, rank, sort, type
05 class, genre, grade, group, order, title
06 rubric
07 chapter, heading, listing, section, variety
08 division, grouping

cater
05 serve
06 pander, supply
07 furnish, provide, victual

caterwaul
03 cry
04 bawl, howl, wail, yowl
05 miaow
06 scream, shriek, squall
07 screech

catharsis
07 purging, release
09 cleansing, epuration, purifying

10 abreaction, abstersion, lustration
12 purification

cathartic
07 lustral, purging, release
09 cleansing, purifying
10 abreactive, abstersive

cathedral
04 dome
05 duomo
07 minster

catholic
04 wide
05 broad
06 global, varied
07 diverse, general, liberal
08 eclectic, tolerant
09 inclusive, universal
10 broad-based, open-minded, widespread
11 broad-minded, wide-ranging
13 comprehensive

cattle
04 cows, oxen
05 bulls, stock
06 beasts, bovine
09 livestock

➤ *Breeds of cattle*:
05 Devon, Luing
06 Ankole, dexter, Durham, Jersey
07 Brahman, Red Poll
08 Ayrshire, Friesian, Galloway, Guernsey, Hereford, Highland, Holstein, Limousin, Longhorn
09 Charolais, Shorthorn, Teeswater
10 Africander
11 Chillingham
12 Simmenthaler
13 Aberdeen Angus
➤ See also **animal**

catty
04 mean
06 bitchy
07 vicious
08 spiteful, venomous
09 malicious, rancorous

caucus
03 set
06 clique, parley
07 meeting, session
08 assembly, conclave
09 gathering
10 convention

causative
04 root
07 causing, factive
09 factitive

cause
03 aim, end
04 make, root
05 agent, basis, begin, breed, force, ideal, maker, mover
06 agency, author, compel, create, effect, factor, incite, induce, lead to, motive, origin, prompt, reason, source, spring
07 grounds, produce, provoke, purpose, trigger
08 generate, motivate, movement, occasion
09 beginning, incentive, originate, stimulate
10 bring about, conviction, enterprise, give rise to, motivation, prime mover, trigger off
11 explanation, precipitate, undertaking

caustic
04 acid, keen
05 snide
06 biting, bitter, severe
07 burning, cutting, mordant, pungent
08 scathing, stinging, virulent
09 corrosive, sarcastic
10 astringent
11 acrimonious, destructive

cauterize
04 burn, sear
05 singe
09 carbonize, disinfect, sterilize

caution
04 care, heed, urge, warn
05 alert, deter
06 advice, advise, caveat
07 counsel, warning
08 admonish, prudence, wariness
09 alertness, vigilance
10 admonition, discretion, injunction
11 carefulness, forethought
12 deliberation, watchfulness
14 circumspection

cautious
04 wary
05 alert, cagey, chary
06 shrewd
07 careful, guarded, heedful, prudent, tactful

08 discreet, gingerly, vigilant, watchful
09 judicious, tentative
11 circumspect
12 softly-softly

cavalcade
05 array, train, troop
06 parade
07 cortège, retinue
09 march-past
10 procession

cavalier
04 curt
05 lofty, spahi
06 casual, escort, knight, lordly
07 gallant, haughty, offhand
08 arrogant, chasseur, horseman, Ironside
09 chevalier, gentleman
10 cavalryman, swaggering
11 Bashi-Bazouk, free-and-easy, patronizing
12 horse soldier, supercilious

cavalry
07 hussars, lancers
08 dragoons, horsemen, troopers
13 horse soldiers

cave
04 hole
06 cavern, cavity, dugout, grotto, hollow, tunnel
07 pothole

❑**cave in**
04 fall, slip
05 yield
07 give way, subside
08 collapse

caveat
05 alarm
07 caution, warning
10 admonition

cavern
03 den
04 cave
05 vault
06 cavity, dugout, grotto, hollow, tunnel
07 pothole

cavernous
04 dark, deep, huge, vast
06 gaping, hollow, sunken
07 immense, yawning
08 resonant, spacious
10 bottomless
12 unfathomable

cavil
03 nag
04 carp

07 censure, nit-pick, quibble
08 complain, reproach
09 criticize, find fault

cavity
03 gap, pit
04 dent, hole, well
05 sinus
06 crater, hollow, lacuna
07 orifice
08 aperture
09 ventricle

cavort
04 romp, skip
05 caper, dance, frisk, sport
06 frolic, gambol, prance

cease
03 die, end
04 fail, halt, quit, stop
05 abate, leave, let up
06 desist, finish, pack in
07 refrain, suspend
08 break off, conclude, leave off, peter out
09 call a halt, fizzle out
11 come to a halt, come to an end, discontinue

ceaseless
07 endless, eternal, non-stop
08 constant, unending, untiring
09 continual, incessant, perpetual, unceasing
10 continuous, persistent
11 everlasting, never-ending, unremitting
12 interminable

cede
05 allow, grant, yield
06 convey, give up, resign
07 abandon, concede, deliver
08 abdicate, hand over, renounce, transfer, turn over
09 surrender
10 relinquish

ceiling
04 most, roof
05 beams, limit, vault
06 awning, canopy
07 maximum, plafond, rafters
10 upper limit
11 cut-off point

celebrate
04 keep, mark, rave
05 binge, extol, revel, toast
06 honour
07 drink to, have fun, observe, perform, rejoice
08 live it up, remember
09 have a ball, whoop it up

11 commemorate, throw a party
14 go out on the town
15 paint the town red

celebrated
05 famed, great, noted
06 famous
07 eminent, notable, popular
08 glorious, renowned
09 acclaimed, legendary, prominent, well-known
11 illustrious, outstanding
13 distinguished

celebration
04 gala, rave
05 binge, party, spree
06 rave-up
07 banquet, revelry
09 festivity
11 merrymaking
13 jollification

▶ *Types of religious celebration and service*:
04 fête, Mass
05 feast
06 May Day
07 baptism, funeral, jubilee, tribute, wedding
08 evensong, festival, High Mass, marriage
09 communion, Eucharist, saint's day
10 bar mitzvah, bat mitzvah, dedication
11 christening, Lord's Supper, nuptial Mass, remembrance, Requiem Mass
12 confirmation, Midnight Mass, thanksgiving
13 Holy Communion, Holy Matrimony
14 evening service, morning prayers, morning service
15 harvest festival, memorial service
➤ See also **religion**

celebrity
03 VIP
04 name, star
06 bigwig, legend, worthy
07 big name, big shot, notable
08 luminary
09 dignitary, superstar
11 personality
12 living legend
13 household name

celerity
05 haste, speed
08 dispatch, fastness, rapidity, velocity

09 fleetness, quickness, swiftness

celestial
06 astral, divine, starry
07 angelic, elysian, eternal, godlike, sublime
08 empyrean, ethereal, heavenly, immortal, seraphic
09 spiritual

celibacy
06 purity
08 chastity
09 virginity
10 abnegation, abstinence, continence, self-denial
12 bachelorhood, spinsterhood
13 self-restraint

celibate
04 pure
06 chaste, single, virgin
08 bachelor, spinster
09 abstinent

cell
04 jail, room, unit
05 crowd, group, party, spore
06 caucus, clique, cytoid, gamete, lock-up, matrix, prison, zygote
07 chamber, cubicle, dungeon, faction, nucleus, section
08 organism
09 cytoplasm, enclosure
10 protoplasm, protoplast
11 compartment

cellar
05 crypt, vault
08 basement
09 storeroom

cement
03 gum
04 bind, bond, glue, join, weld
05 affix, grout, paste, stick
06 attach, cohere, matrix, mortar, screed, solder
07 bonding, combine, plaster
08 adhesive, concrete

cemetery
08 God's acre
09 graveyard
10 churchyard, necropolis
12 burial ground, charnel house

censor
03 ban, cut
04 edit
06 delete, editor
09 expurgate
10 blue-pencil, bowdlerize

censorious
06 severe
07 carping
08 captious, critical
09 cavilling
11 disparaging
12 condemnatory, disapproving, fault-finding
13 hypercritical

censure
05 blame, scold
06 rebuke
07 condemn, obloquy, reproof, reprove, tell off, upbraid
08 admonish, denounce, reproach, scolding
09 castigate, criticism, criticize, reprehend, reprimand
10 admonition, upbraiding
11 castigation, disapproval
12 admonishment, condemnation, denunciation, vituperation
15 come down heavy on

central
03 key, mid
04 core, main
05 basic, chief, focal, inner, major, prime, vital
06 medial, median, middle
07 crucial, pivotal, primary
08 dominant, foremost, interior
09 essential, principal
11 fundamental, significant
13 most important

centralize
05 focus, unify
07 compact
08 condense, converge
10 amalgamate, streamline
11 concentrate, rationalize

centre
03 hub
04 core, crux
05 arena, focus, heart, pivot
06 kernel, middle
07 nucleus, revolve
08 bull's-eye, midpoint
09 gravitate
10 focal point

ceramics
04 raku, ware
06 bisque
08 faience, pottery
09 ironstone, porcelain
11 earthenware

cereal
05 grain
06 muesli
07 oatmeal
08 porridge
10 cornflakes

► *Cereals include*:
03 oat, rye, tef, zea
04 corn, oats, rice, sago, teff
05 emmer, maize, spelt, wheat
06 barley, bulgur, manioc, millet
07 bulghur, cassava, mandioc, manihoc, sorghum, tapioca
08 amelcorn, mandioca, semolina
09 buckwheat, mandiocca, triticale

ceremonial
04 rite
06 custom, formal, ritual
07 stately
08 official, protocol
09 dignified
11 ritualistic

ceremonious
05 civil, exact, grand, stiff
06 formal, polite, ritual, solemn
07 courtly, precise, stately
08 official
09 courteous, dignified

ceremony
04 form, pomp, rite, show
06 custom, parade, ritual
07 decorum, liturgy, service
08 festival, function, protocol
09 etiquette, formality, pageantry, propriety, tradition, unveiling
10 bar mitzvah, dedication, graduation, observance
11 anniversary, investiture
12 inauguration
13 commemoration

certain
04 some, sure, true
05 bound, fated, fixed, plain
07 assured, decided, evident, obvious, precise, settled
08 absolute, definite, destined, in the bag, positive, specific
09 confident, convinced
10 conclusive, convincing, determined, home and dry, individual, inevitable, inexorable, particular
11 cut and dried, established, inescapable, irrefutable, open-and-shut, unavoidable
12 indisputable, no ifs and buts
13 bound to happen

certainly
06 surely
07 clearly, for sure, no doubt
08 of course
09 assuredly, naturally
10 absolutely, by all means, definitely, positively
11 doubtlessly, undoubtedly
13 without a doubt

certainty
04 fact
05 faith, trust, truth
07 reality, safe bet
08 dead cert, sureness, validity
09 assurance, sure thing
10 confidence, conviction

certificate
04 pass
05 award
07 diploma, licence, voucher
08 document
09 guarantee
11 credentials, endorsement, testimonial
13 authorization, qualification

certify
04 aver
05 vouch
06 assure, attest, ratify, verify
07 confirm, endorse, license, testify, warrant, witness
08 accredit, validate
09 authorize, guarantee, pronounce, recognize
11 corroborate
12 authenticate, substantiate
13 bear witness to

certitude
08 sureness
09 assurance, certainty
10 confidence, conviction, plerophory
11 assuredness, plerophoria

cessation
03 end
04 halt, rest, stay
05 break, let-up, pause
06 ending, hiatus, recess
07 ceasing, halting, respite
08 abeyance, interval, stoppage, stopping
09 remission
10 conclusion, desistance, standstill, suspension
11 termination
12 intermission, interruption
15 discontinuation

chafe
03 rub, vex
04 rasp, wear

05 anger, annoy, grate, peeve
06 abrade, enrage, scrape
07 inflame, provoke, scratch
08 irritate
09 excoriate
10 exasperate

chaff
04 pods
05 cases, husks
06 shells

chagrin
03 irk, vex
05 annoy, peeve, shame
07 mortify
08 disquiet, irritate, vexation
09 annoyance, displease, embarrass, humiliate
10 disappoint, dissatisfy, exasperate, irritation
11 displeasure, fretfulness, humiliation, indignation
12 discomfiture, discomposure, exasperation
13 embarrassment, mortification

chain
03 row, set, tie
04 bind, bond, firm, line, link
05 group, hitch, train, union
06 fasten, fetter, secure, series, string, tether
07 company, confine, enslave, manacle, shackle, trammel
08 catenary, coupling, handcuff, restrain, sequence
13 concatenation

chair
02 MC
04 form, lead, seat
05 bench, stool
06 direct
07 convene, speaker
08 convenor, director, recliner
09 president, supervise
11 preside over, toastmaster

chalk

□ **chalk up**
04 gain
05 score, tally
06 attain, charge, credit, record
07 achieve, ascribe, put down
08 register

chalky
03 wan
04 pale
05 ashen, white
06 pallid
07 powdery
10 calcareous, cretaceous

challenge
03 tax, try
04 call, dare, defy, risk, test
05 brave, demur, query, trial
06 accost, hazard, hurdle, invite, summon
07 dispute, problem, provoke, stretch, summons
08 confront, defiance, object to, obstacle, question
09 objection, ultimatum
10 opposition
11 provocation
12 disagree with, disagreement
13 confrontation, interrogation

challenging
06 taxing
07 testing
08 exacting, exciting
09 demanding
10 stretching

chamber
04 hall, room
05 house
06 cavity
07 bedroom, boudoir, council
08 assembly
09 apartment, ventricle
10 auditorium, parliament
11 compartment, legislature
12 assembly room

champion
03 ace
04 back, hero
05 angel, champ
06 backer, defend, patron, uphold, victor, winner
07 espouse, promote, support
08 maintain, upholder
09 conqueror, protector
10 stand up for, vindicator
11 title-holder

chance
03 bet, try
04 fate, luck, odds, risk, time
05 break, fluke, occur, stake
06 casual, follow, flukey, gamble, happen, hazard, random, result
07 destiny, develop, fortune, opening, venture
08 accident, fortuity, prospect
09 arbitrary, haphazard, speculate
10 accidental, fortuitous, likelihood, providence, unexpected
11 bet your life, coincidence, opportunity, possibility, probability, serendipity, speculation

12 bet your boots, push your luck, your best shot
13 serendipitous

□ **chance on, chance upon**
04 meet
07 run into
08 bump into, discover
09 stumble on
10 come across

chancy
05 dicey, dodgy, risky
06 tricky
07 fraught
09 hazardous, uncertain
11 speculative

change
04 cash, move, swap, turn, vary
05 adapt, alter, amend, coins, shift, trade, trend, U-turn
06 adjust, barter, become, evolve, modify, mutate, reform, revise, silver, switch
07 convert, coppers, develop, novelty, remodel, replace, shake-up, variety
08 exchange, mutation, revision, transfer, upheaval
09 about-face, about-turn, amendment, customize, evolution, fluctuate, transform, transpose, turnabout, vacillate, variation, volte-face
10 adaptation, adjustment, difference, ebb and flow, innovation, reorganize, revolution, substitute, transition
11 development, fluctuation, remodelling, replacement, restructure, state of flux, transfigure, transmutate, vacillation, vicissitude
12 metamorphose, modification, substitution
13 chop and change, metamorphosis, restructuring, transmutation, transposition
14 transformation

changeable
05 fluid
06 fickle, labile, mobile
07 erratic, mutable, Protean, varying
08 shifting, unstable, unsteady, variable, volatile, wavering
09 irregular, mercurial, uncertain, unsettled
10 capricious, inconstant

11 fluctuating, vacillating
13 unpredictable

channel
03 way
04 duct, main, neck, path, send
05 agent, canal, flume, guide, gully, means, route, sound
06 agency, avenue, convey, course, direct, furrow, groove, gutter, medium, strait, trough
07 conduct, conduit, passage
08 approach, waterway
11 concentrate, watercourse

chant
03 cry
04 sing, song
05 ditty, psalm, shout
06 chorus, intone, mantra, recite, slogan, warcry
07 refrain
09 plainsong

chaos
04 mess, riot
05 snafu
06 bedlam, tumult, uproar
07 anarchy
08 disorder, madhouse, shambles, tohu bohu, upheaval
09 confusion
11 lawlessness, pandemonium

chaotic
05 snafu
06 unruly
07 lawless, riotous
08 anarchic, confused, deranged
09 disrupted, orderless, shambolic
10 disordered, topsy-turvy, tumultuous
12 disorganized, uncontrolled
14 all over the shop
15 all over the place

chap
03 bod, boy, guy, lad, man
04 cove, gent, sort, type
05 bloke
06 fellow, person

chaperone, chaperon
04 mind
05 guard
06 attend, duenna, escort
07 protect
08 shepherd
09 accompany, companion, safeguard, watch over

chapped
03 raw
04 sore
06 chafed
07 cracked

chapter
04 part, time
05 phase, stage, topic
06 clause, period
07 episode, portion, section
08 division

char
04 burn, sear
05 brown, singe
06 scorch
09 carbonize, cauterize

character
04 case, logo, mark, part, role, rune, sign, sort, type
05 charm, ethos, image, stamp, style, trait
06 appeal, cipher, device, emblem, figure, letter, make-up, nature, oddity, person, psyche, status, symbol
07 calibre, courage, essence, feature, honesty, oddball, persona, quality
08 identity, interest, original, position, property, strength
09 eccentric, ideograph
10 attributes, hieroglyph, moral fibre, reputation
11 disposition, peculiarity, personality, specialness, temperament, uprightness
13 determination, individuality

characteristic
04 mark
05 trait
06 factor
07 feature, quality, special, symptom, typical
08 hallmark, peculiar, property, specific, symbolic
09 attribute, mannerism
11 distinctive, peculiarity
12 idiosyncrasy
13 idiosyncratic

characterize
04 mark
05 brand, stamp
06 typify
07 portray, present, specify
08 describe, identify, indicate
09 designate, represent

charade
04 fake, sham
05 farce
06 parody

07 mockery
08 pretence, travesty
09 pantomime

charge
03 ask, fee, tax
04 bill, care, cost, dues, duty, levy, rate, rent, rush, tear, toll, ward
05 blame, debit, exact, price, storm, trust
06 accuse, amount, ask for, assail, attack, burden, demand, indict, onrush, outlay, rental, sortie
07 arraign, assault, custody, expense, impeach, keeping, payment
08 storming
09 fix a price, incursion, onslaught, set a price
10 accusation, allegation, imputation, indictment, obligation, protection
11 arraignment, impeachment, incriminate, safekeeping
12 guardianship

◻**in charge of**
08 managing
10 overseeing
11 controlling, supervising
12 looking after, taking care of
14 responsible for

charitable
04 kind
06 benign, kindly
07 lenient, liberal
08 generous, gracious, tolerant
09 bounteous, forgiving
10 beneficent, benevolent, open-handed
11 considerate, magnanimous
12 eleemosynary, humanitarian
13 philanthropic

charity
03 aid
04 alms, fund, gift, love
05 trust
06 relief
07 caritas, funding, handout
08 altruism, clemency, goodwill, humanity, kindness, largesse
09 affection, tolerance
10 almsgiving, assistance, benignness, compassion, generosity
11 beneficence, benevolence
12 contribution, philanthropy

charlatan
04 fake, sham

05 cheat, fraud, quack
06 con man, phoney
08 impostor, swindler
09 pretender, trickster
10 mountebank

charm
03 obi, win
04 draw, idol, juju
05 magic, spell
06 allure, amulet, appeal, cajole, fetish, mascot, please, seduce
07 attract, beguile, bewitch, delight, enamour, enchant, periapt, sorcery, trinket
08 grisgris, talisman
09 captivate, enrapture, fascinate, mesmerize
10 allurement, attraction
11 abracadabra
12 desirability, porte-bonheur

charming
04 cute
05 sweet
06 lovely
07 winning, winsome
08 alluring, engaging, fetching, pleasant, pleasing, tempting
09 appealing, seductive
10 attractive, delectable, delightful, enchanting

chart
03 map
04 list, mark, note, plan, plot
05 draft, graph, place, table
06 follow, league, map out, record, sketch
07 diagram, monitor, outline
08 document, nomogram
09 blueprint, delineate, flow sheet, hit parade, nomograph, top twenty

charter
04 bond, deed, hire, rent
05 lease, right
06 employ, engage, permit
07 licence, license, warrant
08 contract, covenant, document, sanction
09 authority, authorize, franchise, indenture, privilege
10 commission, concession

chary
04 slow, wary
05 leery
06 uneasy
07 careful, guarded, heedful, prudent
08 cautious
09 reluctant, unwilling

chase
04 hunt, rush, tail
05 drive, expel, hound, hurry, track, trail
06 follow, pursue, shadow
07 hunting, pursuit
08 coursing, run after

chasm
03 gap
04 gulf, rift, void
05 abyss, cleft, crack, gorge, split
06 breach, canyon, cavity, crater, hollow, ravine
07 fissure, opening
08 crevasse
10 alienation, separation

chassis
05 frame
08 bodywork, fuselage, skeleton
09 framework, structure
13 undercarriage

chaste
04 pure
05 moral, plain
06 modest, simple, single
08 celibate, innocent, virginal, virtuous
09 abstinent, continent
10 immaculate, restrained

chasten
04 curb, tame
06 humble, punish, subdue
07 correct, repress, reprove
08 chastise, moderate, restrain
09 castigate, humiliate
10 discipline

chastise
04 beat, cane, flog, lash, whip
05 scold, smack, spank, strap
06 berate, punish, wallop
07 censure, correct, reprove, scourge, upbraid
08 admonish
09 castigate, dress down, reprimand
10 discipline, take to task

chastity
06 purity, virtue
07 modesty
08 celibacy
09 innocence, virginity
10 abstinence, continence, maidenhood, singleness
13 temperateness

chat
03 gas, jaw
04 talk

06 babble, confab, gossip, jabber, natter, rabbit, waffle
07 chatter, chinwag, prattle
08 converse, rabbit on
09 small talk, tête-à-tête
10 chew the fat, chew the rag
12 conversation, heart-to-heart, tittle-tattle

chatter
03 gab, gas, jaw
04 chat, talk
06 babble, confab, gossip, jabber, natter, rabbit, tattle, waffle, witter
07 chinwag, prattle
08 chit-chat, rabbit on
09 tête-à-tête
12 conversation, tittle-tattle

chatterbox
06 gabber, gasbag, gossip
07 babbler, tattler, windbag
08 big mouth, jabberer, natterer
09 chatterer, gossipper
12 blabbermouth
13 tittle-tattler

chatty
04 glib
07 gossipy, gushing, verbose
08 effusive, friendly, informal
09 garrulous, talkative
10 colloquial, loquacious

chauvinism
04 bias
06 sexism
08 jingoism
09 prejudice
10 flag-waving
11 nationalism
12 partisanship

chauvinist
06 biased, sexist
08 jingoist
10 flag-waving, prejudiced
11 nationalist

cheap
03 low
04 mean, poor, sale
05 a snip, tacky, tatty
06 a steal, budget, paltry, shoddy, sordid, tawdry, two-bit, vulgar
07 bargain, economy, low-cost, reduced, slashed
08 cut-price, giveaway, inferior
09 knock-down, ten a penny, worthless
10 affordable, despicable, discounted, economical, marked-down, reasonable, rock-bottom, second-rate

11 inexpensive, reduced rate
12 contemptible

cheapen
05 lower
06 demean
07 degrade, devalue
08 belittle, derogate
09 denigrate, downgrade
10 depreciate

cheat
02 do
03 con, fix, rig
04 bilk, dupe, fake, fool, gull
05 bluff, check, cozen, crook, fraud, rogue, shark, sting, trick, welsh
06 con man, diddle, dodger, fiddle, fleece, rip off, thwart
07 beguile, cozener, deceive, defraud, deprive, mislead, swindle, two-time
08 deceiver, hoodwink, impostor, swindler
09 bamboozle, charlatan, frustrate, trickster
11 do one over on, double-cross, short-change
12 take for a ride
13 double-crosser

check
03 bar, tab
04 bill, curb, damp, halt, scan, slow, stem, stop, test
05 audit, delay, limit, probe, study, tally
06 arrest, bridle, hinder, impede, police, rein in, screen, thwart, verify
07 analyse, compare, confirm, control, examine, inhibit, inquiry, inspect, invoice, monitor, repress
08 analysis, make sure, obstruct, once-over, research, restrain, scrutiny, slow down, validate
09 go through, take stock
10 inspection, scrutinize
11 corroborate, examination, inquire into, investigate
15 give the once-over

❑ check in
05 enrol
06 book in
08 register

❑ check out
04 test
05 leave, recce, study
07 examine

08 look into
11 investigate

❑ check up
06 assess, verify
07 analyse, confirm, inspect
08 evaluate, make sure
09 ascertain
11 inquire into, investigate

check-up
04 test
05 audit, probe
07 inquiry
08 analysis, research, scrutiny
09 appraisal
10 evaluation, inspection
11 examination
13 investigation

cheek
03 lip
04 gall
05 mouth, nerve, sauce
08 audacity, chutzpah, temerity
09 brass neck, impudence, insolence
10 brazenness, effrontery
12 impertinence

cheeky
04 pert
05 fresh, lippy, sassy, saucy
06 brazen
07 forward
08 impudent, insolent
09 audacious
11 impertinent
12 overfamiliar

cheer
04 clap, hail, warm
05 bravo, elate, shout
06 buck up, buoy up, hurrah, perk up, salute, solace, uplift
07 acclaim, applaud, comfort, console, enliven, fanfare, gladden, hearten, ovation, revelry, root for, support
08 applause, brighten, clapping, gladness
09 celebrate, encourage, happiness, merriment
10 exhilarate, joyfulness
11 high spirits, merrymaking

❑ cheer up
05 liven, rally
06 buck up, perk up
07 comfort, console, hearten
08 brighten
09 encourage, take heart

cheerful
03 gay
04 glad, warm
05 happy, jolly, merry, sunny

06 blithe, bright, chirpy, genial, hearty, jovial, joyful, joyous, lively
07 buoyant, smiling
08 animated, carefree, laughing, spirited, stirring
09 agreeable, contented, exuberant, sparkling
10 delightful, heartening, optimistic
12 happy-go-lucky
13 in good spirits

cheerio
03 bye
04 ta-ta
05 adieu
06 bye-bye, cheers, so long
07 goodbye
08 au revoir, farewell
11 see you later

cheerless
03 sad
04 cold, dark, drab, dull, grim
05 bleak, dingy
06 barren, dismal, dreary, gloomy, lonely, sombre
07 austere, forlorn, joyless, sunless, unhappy
08 dejected, desolate, dolorous, mournful, wintery
09 miserable, sorrowful
10 depressing, uninviting
11 comfortless

cheers
02 ta
03 bye
04 skol, ta-ta
05 adieu
06 bye-bye, prosit, so long
07 goodbye, here's to ..., slàinte
09 bottoms up
10 all the best, here's to you
11 much obliged, see you later
12 down the hatch
13 happy landings
14 your good health
15 to absent friends

cheery
03 gay
04 glad
05 happy, jolly, merry
06 bright, chirpy, genial, hearty, jovial, joyful, lively
07 buoyant, smiling
08 animated, carefree
09 exuberant, sparkling
10 optimistic
12 enthusiastic, light-hearted
13 in good spirits

cheese

► *Varieties of cheese*:

04 Brie, Edam, Feta
05 Caboc, Carré, Derby, Gouda, quark
06 Dunlop, Orkney
07 Boursin, Cheddar, Gruyère, Limburg, Stilton, ricotta
08 Bel Paese, Cheshire, Emmental, Huntsman, Parmesan, raclette
09 Amsterdam, Blue Vinny, Camembert, ewe-cheese, Jarlsberg, Killarney, Leicester, Limburger, Lymeswold, mouse-trap, Port Salut, Roquefort
10 Caerphilly, curd cheese, Danish blue, Dolcelatte, Emmentaler, Gloucester, Gorgonzola, Lancashire, mascarpone, mozzarella, Neufchâtel, Red Windsor, stracchino
11 cream cheese, Wensleydale
12 Red Leicester
13 cottage cheese
➤ See also **food**

chef

► *Names of chefs*:

03 **Hom** (Ken)
04 **Roux** (Albert), **Roux** (Michel), **Spry** (Constance)
05 **Blanc** (Raymond René), **David** (Elizabeth), **Floyd** (Keith), **Leith** (Prue), **Smith** (Delia), **Soyer** (Alexis), **Stein** (Rick), **White** (Marco Pierre)
06 **Beeton** (Mrs Isabella Mary), **Rhodes** (Gary)
07 **Cradock** (Fanny), **Grigson** (Jane), **Grigson** (Sophie), **Jaffrey** (Madhur), **Ladenis** (Nico)
08 **Dimbleby** (Josceline), **Mosimann** (Anton), **Paterson** (Jennifer)
09 **Carluccio** (Antonio), **Escoffier** (Auguste)
12 **Two Fat Ladies**
13 **Dickson Wright** (Clarissa)
15 **Worrall Thompson** (Antony)

chemical

03 tin (Sn)
04 gold (Au), iron (Fe), lead (Pb), neon (Ne), zinc (Zn)
05 argon (Ar), boron (B), radon (Rn), xenon (Xe)
06 barium (Ba), carbon (C), cerium (Ce), cobalt (Co), copper (Cu), curium (Cm), erbium (Er), helium (He), indium (In), iodine (I), nickel (Ni), osmium (Os), oxygen (O), radium (Ra), silver (Ag), sodium (Na)
07 arsenic (As), bismuth (Bi), bromine (Br), cadmium (Cd), caesium (Cs), calcium (Ca), fermium (Fm), gallium (Ga), hafnium (Hf), hahnium (Ha), holmium (Ho), iridium (Ir), krypton (Kr), lithium (Li), mercury (Hg), niobium (Nb), rhenium (Re), rhodium (Rh), silicon (Si), sulphur (S), terbium (Tb), thorium (Th), thulium (Tm), uranium (U), yttrium (Y)
08 actinium (Ac), antimony (Sb), astatine (At), chlorine (Cl), chromium (Cr), europium (Eu), fluorine (F), francium (Fr), hydrogen (H), lutetium (Lu), nitrogen (N), nobelium (No), platinum (Pt), polonium (Po), rubidium (Rb), samarium (Sm), scandium (Sc), selenium (Se), tantalum (Ta), thallium (Tl), titanium (Ti), tungsten (W), vanadium (V)
09 aluminium (Al), americium (Am), berkelium (Bk), beryllium (Be), germanium (Ge), lanthanum (La), magnesium (Mg), manganese (Mn), neodymium (Nd), neptunium (Np), palladium (Pd), plutonium (Pu), potassium (K), ruthenium (Ru), strontium (Sr), tellurium (Te), ytterbium (Yb), zirconium (Zr)
10 dysprosium (Dy), gadolinium (Gd), lawrencium (Lr) (Lw), molybdenum (Mo), phosphorus (P), promethium (Pm), technetium (Tc)
11 californium (Cf), einsteinium (Es), mendelevium (Md)
12 praseodymium (Pr), protactinium (Pa)
13 rutherfordium (Rf)

chemistry

► *Terms used in chemistry* include:

02 pH
03 gas, ion
04 acid, atom, base, bond, mass, mole, salt
05 ester, lipid
06 alkali, isomer, liquid, matter, proton
07 crystal, formula, halogen, isotope, neutron, nucleus, organic, polymer, solvent, valency
08 analysis, catalyst, compound, electron, emulsion, inert gas, molecule, noble gas, reaction, solution
09 allotrope, catalysis, corrosion, diffusion, electrode, inorganic, ionic bond, oxidation, substance, synthesis, titration
10 combustion, hydrolysis, litmus test, suspension
11 free radical, litmus paper
12 atomic number, biochemistry, chemical bond, chlorination, covalent bond, distillation, electrolysis, fermentation, metallic bond
13 chain reaction, decomposition, periodic table, radioactivity
15 atomic structure, chemical element

► *Names of chemists*:

04 **Davy** (Sir Humphry), **Hess** (Germain Henri), **Kuhn** (Richard), **Mond** (Ludwig), **Urey** (Harold Clayton)
05 **Boyle** (Robert), **Curie** (Marie), **Darby** (Abraham), **Dewar** (Sir James), **Haber** (Fritz), **Libby** (Willard Frank), **Nobel** (Alfred), **Soddy** (Frederick)
06 **Baeyer** (Adolf von), **Bunsen** (Robert Wilhelm), **Dalton** (John), **Hevesy** (George Charles von), **Liebig** (Justus von), **Miller** (Stanley Lloyd), **Ramsay** (Sir William)
07 **Bergius** (Friedrich), **Buchner** (Eduard), **Faraday** (Michael), **Fischer** (Emil Hermann), **Fischer** (Hans), **Hodgkin** (Dorothy Mary), **Pasteur** (Louis),

Pauling (Linus Carl),
Scheele (Carl Wilhelm),
Seaborg (Glen Theodore)
08 **Avogadro** (Amedeo),
Chevreul (Michel Eugène),
Klaproth (Martin
Heinrich), **Langmuir**
(Irving), **Lonsdale** (Dame
Kathleen), **Mulliken**
(Robert Sanderson),
Regnault (Henri Victor),
Sidgwick (Nevil Vincent),
Svedberg (Theodor),
Tiselius (Arne Wilhelm
Kaurin)
09 **Arrhenius** (Svante August),
Baekeland (Leo Hendrik),
Berzelius (Jöns Jacob),
Cavendish (Henry),
Lavoisier (Antoine
Laurent), **Priestley** (Joseph),
Prigogine (Ilya, Vicomte),
10 **Mendeleyev** (Dmitri)
12 **Boussingault** (Jean
Baptiste Joseph)
➤ See also **scientist**

chequered
05 mixed
06 varied
07 diverse
15 with ups and downs

cherish
04 love
05 adore, nurse, prize, value
06 foster
07 care for, harbour, nurture,
shelter, support, sustain
08 hold dear, treasure
09 entertain, look after

cherub
05 angel
06 seraph

cherubic
04 cute
05 sweet
06 lovely
07 angelic, lovable
08 adorable, heavenly,
innocent, seraphic

chess
▶ *Names of chess players:*
03 **Tal** (Mikhail)
04 **Euwe** (Max)
05 **Short** (Nigel)
06 **Karpov** (Anatoly), **Lasker**
(Emmanuel), **Polgar** (Judit),
Polgar (Zsuzsa), **Timman**
(Jan)
07 **Fischer** (Bobby), **Spassky**
(Boris)

08 **Alekhine** (Alexander),
Deep Blue, Kasparov
(Gary), **Korchnoi** (Viktor),
Steinitz (Wilhelm)
09 **Botvinnik** (Mikhail),
Petrosian (Tigran)
10 **Capablanca** (José)
➤ See also **sport**

chest
03 box
04 case
05 crate, trunk
06 breast, casket, coffer, thorax
07 sternum

chew
04 bite, gnaw
05 champ, chomp, munch
06 crunch
09 masticate

▢**chew over**
06 muse on, ponder
07 weigh up
08 consider, mull over

chic
05 smart
06 dapper, modish, trendy
07 elegant, stylish, à la mode
11 fashionable
13 sophisticated

chicanery
05 dodge, fraud, guile, wiles
08 artifice, intrigue, trickery
09 deception, duplicity,
sophistry
10 dishonesty, subterfuge
11 deviousness, hoodwinking
13 deceitfulness, double-
dealing, sharp practice
14 jiggery-pokery

chicken
▶ *Breeds of chicken include:*
06 Ancona, bantam, Cochin,
houdan, sultan
07 leghorn, Minorca
08 Langshan
09 Welsummer, wyandotte
10 Australorp, chittagong,
jungle fowl
11 Spanish fowl
12 Plymouth Rock
14 Rhode Island Red
➤ See also **animal; bird**

chide
05 blame, scold
06 berate, rebuke
07 censure, lecture, reprove,
tell off, upbraid
08 admonish, reproach

09 criticize, objurgate,
reprehend, reprimand

chief
03 key
04 arch, boss, head, lord, main
05 grand, major, prime, ruler
06 big gun, gaffer, leader,
master, top dog
07 captain, leading, premier,
primary, supreme, supremo
08 big noise, dominant,
foremost, governor,
overlord, suzerain
09 big cheese, chieftain,
commander, president,
principal, uppermost
10 prevailing, ringleader
11 controlling, outstanding,
predominant, supervising

chiefly
06 mainly, mostly
07 usually
09 generally, in the main
10 especially, on the whole
11 essentially, principally
13 predominantly
14 for the most part

child
03 boy, kid, son, tot
04 baby, brat, girl
05 issue, minor, sprog, youth
06 infant, nipper
07 progeny, tiny tot, toddler
08 daughter, juvenile, young
one
09 offspring, youngster
10 adolescent, descendant

childbirth
06 labour
07 lying-in, travail
08 delivery
09 maternity, pregnancy
11 confinement, parturition
12 accouchement

childhood
05 youth
07 boyhood, infancy
08 babyhood, girlhood,
minority
10 immaturity, schooldays
11 adolescence

childish
05 silly
07 babyish, foolish, puerile
08 immature, juvenile
09 frivolous, infantile
13 irresponsible

childlike
05 naïve

06 simple
07 artless, natural
08 innocent, trustful, trusting
09 credulous, guileless, ingenuous

chill

03 flu, ice, icy, nip, raw
04 bite, cold, cool, fear
05 bleak, dread, fever, nippy, parky, scare, sharp, virus
06 biting, freeze, shiver, wintry
07 anxiety, depress, iciness, rawness, terrify
08 coldness, cool down, coolness, freezing, frighten
09 crispness, influenza
10 discourage, dishearten
11 refrigerate
12 apprehension

❏ chill out

05 relax
08 calm down
10 take it easy

chilly

03 icy, raw
04 cold, cool
05 aloof, brisk, crisp, fresh, nippy, parky, sharp, stony
06 biting, frigid, wintry
07 distant, hostile
08 freezing
10 unfriendly
11 unwelcoming

chime

04 boom, ding, dong, peal, ring, toll
05 clang, sound
06 jingle, strike, tinkle
07 resound
11 reverberate
14 tintinnabulate

❏ chime in

05 agree, blend, cut in, fit in
06 butt in, chip in
09 harmonize, interrupt
10 correspond

chimera

05 dream, fancy
07 fantasy, spectre
08 delusion, illusion
09 idle fancy
12 will-o'-the-wisp
13 hallucination

chimney

03 lum
04 flue, vent
05 cleft, shaft
06 funnel
07 crevice
08 femerall

china

06 dishes, plates
07 ceramic, pottery
08 crockery
09 porcelain, tableware
10 terracotta
11 earthenware

Chinese calendar

➤ *Animals which represent years in the Chinese calendar:*
03 dog, pig, rat
04 goat, hare
05 horse, sheep, snake, tiger
06 dragon, monkey, rabbit
07 buffalo, rooster

chink

03 cut, gap
04 rift, slit, slot
05 cleft, crack, space, split
06 cavity
07 crevice, fissure, opening
08 aperture

chip

04 dent, disc, flaw, gash, nick
05 break, crack, flake, notch, scrap, shard, shred, snick
06 chisel, damage, paring, sliver
07 counter, scratch, shaving
08 break off, fragment, splinter

❏ chip in

03 pay
05 cut in
06 butt in, donate
07 chime in
09 interpose, interrupt
10 contribute
12 club together
13 make a donation
14 have a whip-round

chirp

04 peep, pipe, sing
05 cheep, trill, tweet
06 warble
07 chirrup, twitter, whistle

chirpy

03 gay
05 happy, merry, perky
06 blithe, bright, cheery, jaunty
08 cheerful

chit-chat

04 chat, talk
06 confab, gossip, natter
07 chatter, chinwag
09 small talk, tête-à-tête
10 idle gossip
12 tittle-tattle

chivalrous

04 bold
05 brave, noble

06 heroic, polite
07 gallant, valiant
08 gracious
09 courteous
10 courageous, honourable
11 gentlemanly

chivalry

06 honour
07 bravery, courage
08 boldness, courtesy
09 gallantry, integrity
10 politeness
11 courtliness, good manners
12 graciousness, truthfulness
15 gentlemanliness

chivvy

03 nag
04 goad, prod, urge
05 annoy, hound, hurry
06 badger, harass, hassle, pester, plague
07 hurry up, torment

choice

04 best, fine, plum
05 prime, prize, range
06 answer, option, select
07 picking, special, variety
08 decision, election, superior, valuable
09 excellent, exclusive, exquisite, first-rate, selection
10 first-class, preference

choke

03 bar, dam, gag
04 clog, plug, stop
05 block, close, cough, retch
06 stifle
07 congest, occlude, smother
08 strangle, suppress, throttle
09 constrict, suffocate
10 asphyxiate

❏ choke back

04 curb
05 check
07 control, inhibit, repress
08 restrain, suppress
09 fight back

choleric

05 angry, fiery, testy
06 crabby, rabbed, touchy
08 petulant
09 crotchety, irascible, irritable
11 bad-tempered

choose

04 pick, take, want, wish
05 adopt, elect, fix on, go for
06 decide, desire, favour, opt for, prefer, see fit, select
07 appoint, espouse, pick out

choosy
08 plump for, settle on
09 designate, single out

choosy
05 faddy, fussy, picky
07 finicky
08 exacting
09 selective
10 fastidious, particular, pernickety
14 discriminating

chop
03 axe, cut, hew, lop, saw
04 fell, hack
05 carve, sever, slash, slice, split
06 cleave, divide
07 dissect
08 truncate

◻**chop up**
03 cut
04 cube, dice
05 grate, mince, shred, slice
06 divide

choppy
04 wavy
05 rough
06 broken, stormy, uneven
07 ruffled, squally
08 blustery
09 turbulent
11 tempestuous

chore
03 job
04 duty, task
06 burden, errand

choreographer

➤ *Names of choreographers*:
05 **Cohan** (Robert), **Dolin** (Anton), **Jooss** (Kurt), **Laban** (Rudolf von), **Lifar** (Serge), **Tharp** (Twyla)
06 **Ashton** (Sir Frederick), **Cranko** (John), **Davies** (Siobhan), **Duncan** (Isadora), **Fokine** (Michel), **Graham** (Martha), **Morris** (Mark), **Petipa** (Marius), **Wigman** (Mary)
07 **de Mille** (Agnes George), **Massine** (Léonide)
08 **Berkeley** (Busby), **Nijinska** (Bronislava), **de Valois** (Dame Ninette)
09 **Macmillan** (Sir Kenneth)
10 **Balanchine** (George)
11 **Baryshnikov** (Mikhail)
➤ See also **ballet**; **dance**; **dancer**

chortle
04 crow

05 laugh, snort
06 cackle, guffaw
07 chuckle, snigger

chorus
05 choir, shout
06 burden, strain
07 refrain, singers
08 ensemble, response
09 vocalists
10 choristers

christen
03 dub
04 call, name, term
05 style, title
07 baptize
09 designate
10 begin using, inaugurate

Christmas
04 Noel, Xmas, Yule
08 Yuletide

chronic
05 awful
08 constant, dreadful, habitual, long-term, terrible
09 appalling, atrocious, confirmed, continual, incessant, recurring
10 deep-rooted, deep-seated, inveterate, persistent

chronicle
04 epic, list, saga, tell
05 diary, enter, story
06 annals, record, relate, report
07 account, history, journal, narrate, recount, set down
08 archives, calendar, register
09 narrative, write down

chronicler
06 scribe
07 diarist
08 annalist, narrator, reporter
09 archivist, historian
11 chronologer
13 chronographer
15 historiographer

chronological
06 serial
07 in order, ordered
10 historical, sequential
11 consecutive, progressive

chubby
03 fat
04 full
05 plump, podgy, round, stout, tubby
06 flabby, fleshy, portly, rotund
07 paunchy

chuck
03 shy

04 dump, hurl, jilt, quit, toss
05 fling, pitch, sling, throw
06 give up, pack in, reject
07 abandon, discard, forsake
08 get rid of, jettison
12 give the elbow
15 give the brush-off

chuckle
04 crow
05 laugh, snort
06 cackle, giggle, titter
07 chortle, snigger

chum
03 pal
04 mate
05 buddy, crony
06 friend
07 comrade
09 companion

chummy
05 close, matey, pally, thick
08 friendly, intimate, sociable

chunk
04 hunk, lump, mass, slab
05 block, piece, wedge, wodge
06 dollop
07 portion

church
04 cult, kirk, sect
05 abbey
06 bethel, chapel, shrine
07 chantry, minster
09 cathedral, tradition
10 house of God, tabernacle
12 congregation, meeting-house
13 house of prayer
14 place of worship

➤ *Parts of a church or cathedral*:
03 pew
04 apse, arch, font, nave, rood
05 aisle, altar, choir, crypt, porch, slype, spire, stall, stoup, tower, vault
06 arcade, belfry, chapel, parvis, portal, pulpit, sedile, shrine, squint, vestry
07 almonry, chancel, frontal, gallery, lectern, narthex, piscina, reredos, steeple
08 cloister, credence, crossing, keystone, pinnacle, predella, sacristy, transept
09 bell tower, sanctuary, triforium
10 ambulatory, bell screen, clerestory, fenestella, presbytery, rood screen
12 confessional
➤ See also **religion**

churlish
04 rude
05 harsh, rough, surly
06 morose, oafish, sullen
07 boorish, brusque, crabbed, ill-bred, loutish, uncivil
08 impolite
10 unmannerly, unsociable
11 bad-tempered, ill-mannered, ill-tempered
12 discourteous

churn
04 beat, boil, foam, puke, toss, turn
05 froth, heave, retch, swirl, vomit
06 be sick, seethe, writhe
07 agitate, throw up

chute
04 ramp
05 shaft, slide, slope
06 funnel, gutter, runway, trough
07 channel, incline

cigarette
03 cig, fag
05 cigar, joint, smoke, whiff
06 dog end, fag end, gasper, low-tar, roll-up, spliff
07 high-tar, menthol
08 king-size
09 filter-tip

cinch
04 snip
06 doddle, stroll
08 pushover, walkover
10 child's play
11 piece of cake

cinders
04 coke, slag
05 ashes
06 embers
07 clinker
08 charcoal

cinema
05 films
06 flicks, movies
07 fleapit
08 pictures
09 big screen, multiplex
12 movie theatre, picture-house, silver screen
13 picture-palace

cipher
04 code
06 nobody, yes-man
09 nonentity
10 cryptogram
11 cryptograph
12 coded message

circle
03 set
04 band, belt, club, coil, gang, gird, loop, ring, turn, wind
05 crowd, group, pivot, whirl
06 clique, gyrate, rotate, swivel
07 company, coterie, enclose, envelop, hedge in, revolve
08 assembly, encircle, surround
09 encompass, move round
10 fellowship, fraternity

► *Types of circle*:
03 lap, orb
04 ball, band, belt, coil, curl, disc, eddy, halo, hoop, loop, oval, ring, turn, tyre
05 crown, cycle, globe, orbit, plate, round, wheel
06 cordon, discus, girdle, saucer, sphere, spiral, vortex
07 annulus, circuit, compass, coronet, ellipse

circuit
03 lap
04 area, beat, tour
05 ambit, limit, orbit, range, round, route, track
06 bounds, course, region
07 compass
08 boundary, district
09 race track
10 revolution
12 running-track

circuitous
07 devious, oblique, winding
08 indirect, rambling, tortuous
10 meandering, roundabout
12 labyrinthine, periphrastic

circular
05 flyer, round
06 letter, notice
07 annular, leaflet
08 handbill, pamphlet
09 spherical
10 disc-shaped, ring-shaped
12 announcement
13 advertisement

circulate
04 flow
05 issue, swirl, whirl
06 gyrate, rotate, spread
07 go round, diffuse, give out, publish, revolve
08 go around, transmit
09 broadcast, get around, pass round, propagate, publicize
10 distribute, promulgate
11 disseminate

circulation
04 flow

06 motion, spread
08 circling, movement, rotation
09 blood-flow, publicity
10 readership
11 propagation, publication
12 distribution, transmission
13 dissemination

circumference
03 rim
04 edge
05 girth, verge
06 border, bounds, fringe, limits, margin
07 circuit, outline
08 boundary, confines
09 extremity, perimeter, periphery

circumlocution
08 pleonasm
09 euphemism, prolixity, tautology, verbosity, wordiness
10 redundancy
11 convolution, diffuseness, periphrasis
12 indirectness

circumlocutory
05 wordy
06 prolix
07 diffuse, verbose
08 indirect
09 redundant
10 convoluted, discursive, pleonastic, roundabout
11 euphemistic
12 periphrastic, tautological

circumscribe
05 bound, hem in, limit, pen in
06 define
07 confine, curtail, delimit, enclose
08 encircle, restrain, restrict, surround
09 delineate, demarcate, encompass

circumspect
04 wary, wise
05 canny, chary
07 careful, guarded, prudent
08 cautious, discreet, watchful
09 attentive, judicious, observant, sagacious

circumspection
04 care
07 caution
08 prudence, wariness
09 canniness, chariness, vigilance
10 discretion

circumstance

03 lot
04 case, fact, fate, item
05 event, means, state, thing
06 detail, factor, plight, status
07 element, fortune, respect
08 position
09 condition, happening,
   lifestyle, resources, situation
10 background, occurrence
11 arrangement, environment

circumstantial

07 deduced, hearsay
08 indirect, presumed
10 contingent, evidential,
   incidental
11 conjectural, inferential,
   presumptive, provisional

circumvent

05 avoid, evade
06 bypass, outwit, thwart
07 get past
08 get out of, get round,
   sidestep
12 steer clear of

cistern

03 vat
04 sink, tank
05 basin
09 reservoir

citadel

04 keep
05 tower
06 castle
07 bastion
08 fortress
09 acropolis
10 stronghold
13 fortification

citation

05 award, quote
06 honour, source
07 cutting, mention, passage
09 quotation, reference
12 commendation, illustration

cite

04 name
05 quote
06 adduce
07 advance, bring up, mention,
   refer to, specify
08 allude to, evidence
09 enumerate, exemplify

citizen

05 local, voter
07 burgher, denizen, freeman,
   oppidan, subject
08 resident, taxpayer,
   townsman, urbanite

10 inhabitant, townswoman
11 city-dweller, householder

city

04 town
05 civic, urban
06 ghetto
08 big smoke, downtown,
   precinct, suburbia
09 inner city
10 city centre, metropolis
11 conurbation, megalopolis,
   urban sprawl
12 municipality
13 urban district
14 concrete jungle

► *Ancient cities include*:

02 Ur
04 Susa, Troy, Tula, Tyre, Uruk
05 Aksum, Bosra, Copán,
   Hatra, Huari, Mitla, Moche,
   Petra, Tikal, Uxmal
06 Byblos, Jamnia, Nippur,
   Sardis, Shiloh, Thebes,
   Ugarit
07 Babylon, Ephesus, Miletus,
   Mycenae, Nineveh,
   Pompeii, Samaria, Sybaris
08 Pergamon, Pergamum
09 Byzantium
10 Carchemish, Heliopolis,
   Hierapolis, Persepolis
13 Halicarnassus

► *Names of capital cities*:

04 Apia, Baku, Bern, Doha,
   Kiev, Lima, Lomé, Malé,
   Oslo, Riga, Rome, San'a, Suva
05 Abuja, Accra, Amman,
   Berne, Cairo, Dacca, Dakar,
   Dhaka, Hanoi, Kabul,
   Koror, La Paz, Minsk, Paris,
   Praia, Quito, Rabat, Seoul,
   Sofia, Sucre, Tokyo, Tunis,
   Vaduz
06 Akmola, Ankara, Asmara,
   Athens, Bamako, Bangui,
   Banjul, Beirut, Berlin,
   Bissau, Bogotá, Dodoma,
   Dublin, Harare, Havana,
   Kigali, Lisbon, London,
   Luanda, Lusaka, Madrid,
   Majuro, Malabo, Manama,
   Manila, Maputo, Maseru,
   Moroni, Moscow, Muscat,
   Nassau, Niamey, Ottawa,
   Peking, Prague, Riyadh,
   Roseau, Skopje, Taipei,
   Tarawa, Tehran, Tirana,
   Vienna, Warsaw, Yangon,
   Zagreb
07 Abidjan, Algiers, Alma-Ata,
   Baghdad, Bangkok, Beijing,

Belfast, Bishkek, Caracas,
Cardiff, Cayenne, Colombo,
Conakry, Godthab,
Honiara, Jakarta, Kampala,
Managua, Mbabane,
Nairobi, Nicosia, Palikir,
Papeete, Rangoon, San José,
San Juan, São Tomé, St
John's, Tallinn, Tbilisi,
Teheran, Thimphu, Tripoli,
Valetta, Vilnius, Yaoundé,
Yerevan

08 Abu Dhabi, Asunción,
   Belgrade, Belmopan,
   Brasília, Brussels, Budapest,
   Canberra, Cape Town,
   Castries, Chisinau,
   Damascus, Djibouti,
   Dushanbe, Freetown,
   Gaborone, Helsinki,
   Khartoum, Kingston,
   Kinshasa, Kishinev,
   Lilongwe, Monrovia,
   Ndjamena, New Delhi,
   Port-Vila, Pretoria, Santiago,
   Sarajevo, Tashkent, The
   Hague, Tórshavn, Victoria,
   Windhoek

09 Amsterdam, Ashkhabad,
   Bucharest, Bujumbura,
   Edinburgh, Fongafale,
   Islamabad, Jerusalem,
   Kathmandu, Kingstown,
   Ljubljana, Mogadishu,
   Nuku'alofa, Phnom Penh,
   Port Louis, Porto Novo,
   Pyongyang, Reykjavík, San
   Marino, Singapore, St
   George's, Stockholm, Ulan
   Bator, Vientiane

10 Addis Ababa, Basseterre,
   Bratislava, Bridgetown,
   Copenhagen, Georgetown,
   Kuwait City, Libreville,
   Luxembourg, Mexico
   City, Montevideo,
   Nouakchott, Panama City,
   Paramaribo, Wellington,
   Willemstad

11 Brazzaville, Buenos Aires,
   Kuala Lumpur, Monaco-
   Ville, Ouagadougou,
   Port Moresby, Port of Spain,
   San Salvador, Tegucigalpa,
   Vatican City

12 Antananarivo, Fort-de-
   France, Port-au-Prince,
   Santo Domingo, Washington
   DC, Yamoussoukro

13 Guatemala City

17 Bandar Seri Begawan

► *Names of towns and cities*:

02 Bo

03 Åbo, Ayr, Ely, Fès, Fez, Gao, Hué, Lae, Nis, Pau, Qom, Ufa, Ulm, Vac, Zug

04 Acre, Aden, Agra, Bari, Bath, Bonn, Brno, Bury, Caen, Cali, Cebu, Como, Cork, Deal, Edam, Elat, Eton, Faro, Gent, Gifu, Graz, Györ, Homs, Hove, Hull, Iasi, Icel, Ipoh, Jima, Jixi, Kano, Kiel, Kobe, Köln, Kota, León, Linz, Lódz, Lund, Lvov, Metz, Mold, Mons, Naha, Nara, Nice, Oban, Oita, Omsk, Oran, Pécs, Pegu, Perm, Pisa, Rand, Reno, Rhyl, Ruse, Ryde, Safi, Sian, Sion, Soul, Suez, Tema, Thun, Tula, Tyre, Vasa, Vigo, Waco, Wick, Wien, Wuhu, Wuxi, Xi'an, York, Zibo

05 Adana, Ahvaz, Åland, Al Ayn, Aosta, Aqaba, Argos, Århus, Arles, Arras, Aspen, Aswan, Ávila, Baden, Banff, Baoji, Basle, Basra, Beira, Belém, Benxi, Blyth, Boise, Bondi, Breda, Brest, Bursa, Busan, Cádiz, Chiba, Chita, Colón, Conwy, Cowes, Crewe, Cuzco, Davao, Davos, Delft, Delhi, Derby, Dijon, Dover, Duala, Dubai, Dukou, Eilat, Essen, Fiume, Frome, Fuxin, Genoa, Ghent, Gomel, Gorky, Gouda, Haifa, Halle, Hefei, Hohot, Honan, Iwaki, Izmir, Jaffa, Jedda, Jilin, Jinan, Kandy, Karaj, Kazan, Kelso, Kirov, Kitwe, Kochi, Konya, Kursk, Kyoto, Lagos, Leeds, Lewes, Lhasa, Liège, Lille, Luton, Luxor, Lyons, Mâcon, Mainz, Malmö, Masan, Mecca, Medan, Miami, Milan, Mopti, Mosul, Namur, Nancy, Natal, Ndola, Nîmes, Omagh, Omaha, Omiya, Oryol, Osaka, Otley, Oujda, Padua, Parma, Patna, Pavia, Penza, Perth, Poole, Poona, Pusan, Reims, Ripon, Rouen, Rugby, Sakai, Salem, Sidon, Siena, Sochi, Split, Suita, Surat, Suwon, Taegu, Tampa, Thane, Tomsk, Tours, Trier,

Troon, Truro, Tulsa, Turin, Turku, Ulsan, Urawa, Utica, Vaasa, Varna, Wells, Wigan, Worms, Wuhan, Ypres, Zarqa

06 Aachen, Aarhus, Agadir, Albany, Aleppo, Amiens, Annecy, Anshan, Arezzo, Armagh, Arnhem, Ashdod, Austin, Bangor, Baotou, Bengpu, Bergen, Bhopal, Bilbao, Biloxi, Bochum, Bolton, Bombay, Bootle, Boston, Brasov, Bremen, Bruges, Brugge, Burgos, Buxton, Cairns, Calais, Callao, Camden, Campos, Cannes, Canton, Carlow, Chonju, Cochin, Cracow, Crosby, Dalian, Dallas, Danzig, Daqing, Darwin, Datong, Dayton, Denver, Dieppe, Douala, Dudley, Duluth, Dundee, Durban, Durham, El Gîza, El Paso, Eugene, Evreux, Exeter, Fatima, Fresno, Fushun, Fuzhou, Galway, Gdansk, Geneva, Grozny, Guelph, Gujrat, Handan, Harbin, Harlem, Harlow, Hebron, Hegang, Himeji, Hobart, Howrah, Ibadan, Inchon, Indore, Jaffna, Jaipur, Jarrow, Jeddah, Jiddah, Juneau, Kaluga, Kanpur, Kassel, Kaunas, Kendal, Khulna, Kirkby, Kirkuk, Kosice, Kraków, Kurgan, Lahore, Lanark, Le Mans, Leiden, Leuven, Leyden, Lübeck, Lublin, Ludlow, Lugano, Maceio, Madras, Málaga, Malang, Manaus, Mantua, Medina, Meerut, Meknès, Meshed, Mobile, Mukden, Multan, Munich, Murcia, Mysore, Nablus, Nagano, Nagoya, Nagpur, Nantes, Napier, Naples, Narvik, Newark, Ningbo, Odessa, Oldham, Oporto, Osasco, Ostend, Oviedo, Oxford, Padang, Paphos, Phuket, Pierre, Pilsen, Potosí, Poznan, Puebla, Quebec, Raipur, Rajkat, Ranchi, Recife, Redcar, Reggio, Regina, Rennes, Rheims, Saigon, Santos, Sendai, Shiraz, Slough, Smyrna, Soweto, Sparta, St Ives, St John, St Malo, St

Paul, Stroud, Suzhou, Sydney, Szeged, Tabriz, Tacoma, Taejon, Tainan, Tamale, Tambov, Tarsus, Thurso, Tobruk, Toledo, Topeka, Torbay, Toulon, Toyama, Toyota, Tralee, Trento, Treves, Tubruq, Tucson, Urumqi, Vargas, Venice, Verona, Viborg, Weimar, Whitby, Widnes, Woking, Xining, Xuzhou, Yeovil, Yichun, Zurich

07 Aberfan, Airdrie, Aligarh, Alnwick, Antibes, Antioch, Antwerp, Atlanta, Augusta, Auxerre, Avignon, Baalbek, Badajoz, Banares, Banbury, Bandung, Bedford, Beeston, Benares, Bendigo, Bergamo, Bexhill, Blarney, Bologna, Boulder, Brescia, Bristol, Buffalo, Burnley, Calgary, Calicut, Catania, Cheadle, Cheddar, Chelsea, Chengtu, Chengdu, Chester, Chicago, Chungho, Coblenz, Coimbra, Cologne, Concord, Córdoba, Corinth, Corunna, Crawley, Detroit, Devizes, Donetsk, Douglas, Dresden, Dundalk, Dunedin, Dunkirk, Entebbe, Evesham, Exmouth, Falkirk, Fareham, Ferrara, Fukuoka, Glasgow, Goiânia, Gosport, Granada, Grimsby, Guiyang, Gwalior, Gwangju, Halifax, Hamburg, Hamhung, Hanover, Harwich, Houston, Huainan, Ipswich, Iquique, Iquitos, Irkutsk, Isfahan, Izhevsk, Jackson, Jericho, Jinzhou, Jodhpur, Kalinin, Karachi, Kayseri, Kenitra, Keswick, Kharkov, Kherson, Koblenz, Kunming, La Plata, Lanzhou, Larnaca, Latakia, Le Havre, Leghorn, Leipzig, Lerwick, Limoges, Lincoln, Liuzhou, Livorno, Louvain, Lucerne, Lucknow, Luoyang, Madison, Madurai, Malvern, Maracay, Marburg, Margate, Mashhad, Matlock, Matsudo, Memphis, Mendoza,

Mogilev, Mombasa, Morpeth, Münster, Nanjing, Nanking, Nanning, New York, Newbury, Newport, Newquay, Norfolk, Norwich, Novi Sad, Oakland, Okayama, Okinawa, Olympia, Orlando, Orleans, Paisley, Palermo, Peebles, Penrith, Perugia, Phoenix, Piraeus, Pistoia, Plovdiv, Poltava, Potsdam, Preston, Prizren, Raleigh, Ravenna, Reading, Redwood, Reigate, Roanoke, Rosario, Rostock, Runcorn, Salamis, Salerno, Salford, Sandown, Santa Fe, São Luis, Sapporo, Saratov, Seattle, Segovia, Seville, Shannon, Songnam, Spokane, Spoleto, Staines, Stanley, St Denis, St Louis, Sudbury, Swansea, Swindon, Taiyuan, Tangier, Taunton, Tel Aviv, Telford, Tianjin, Tijuana, Tilbury, Toronto, Torquay, Tournai, Trenton, Trieste, Uppsala, Utrecht, Ventnor, Vicenza, Vitebsk, Walsall, Warwick, Watford, Wexford, Wichita, Windsor, Wrexham, Wroclaw, Yonkers, Zwickau

08 Aberdeen, Acapulco, Adelaide, Alicante, Amarillo, Amritsar, Arbroath, Auckland, Augsburg, Aviemore, Ayia Napa, Bareilly, Barnsley, Bathurst, Bayreuth, Beauvais, Belgorod, Benghazi, Benidorm, Besançon, Biarritz, Bismarck, Blantyre, Bordeaux, Boulogne, Bradford, Braganza, Brighton, Brindisi, Brisbane, Bulawayo, Burgundy, Cagliari, Calcutta, Carlisle, Changsha, Chartres, Chemnitz, Chepstow, Cheyenne, Clevedon, Columbia, Columbus, Coventry, Curitiba, Dartford, Dearborn, Djakarta, Dortmund, Drogheda, Duisburg, Dumfries, Dunleary, Ebbw Vale, Edmonton, Elsinore, Europort, Falmouth,

Florence, Flushing, Freeport, Fribourg, Fukuyama, Grantham, Grasmere, Greenock, Grenoble, Guernica, Haiphong, Hamilton, Hangzhou, Hannover, Hartford, Hastings, Hereford, Hertford, Holyhead, Holywell, Hong Kong, Honolulu, Iowa City, Istanbul, Jabalpur, Kandahar, Karlsbad, Katowice, Kawasaki, Kilkenny, Kirkwall, Kismaayo, Klosters, Konstanz, Las Vegas, Lausanne, Legoland, Limassol, Limerick, Longford, Makassar, Mandalay, Mannheim, Marbella, Medellín, Mercedes, Montreal, Montreux, Montrose, Mulhouse, Murmansk, Nagasaki, Nanchang, Nazareth, New Haven, Newhaven, Novgorod, Nuneaton, Nürnberg, Oak Ridge, Omdurman, Oostende, Oswestry, Pago Pago, Pamplona, Pasadena, Penzance, Peshawar, Piacenza, Plymouth, Poitiers, Port Said, Portland, Portrush, Pristina, Ramsgate, Redditch, Richmond, Rochdale, Rockford, Roskilde, Rosslare, Salonica, Salonika, Salvador, Salzburg, San Diego, Santa Ana, São Paulo, Savannah, Schwerin, Shanghai, Shanklin, Shenyang, Sholapur, Skegness, Smolensk, Solihull, Southend, Srinagar, Stafford, St Albans, Stamford, St David's, St Gallen, St Helens, St Helier, Stirling, St Moritz, Stockton, Strabane, St-Tropez, Surabaya, Swan Hill, Syracuse, Taganrog, Taichung, Tamworth, Tangshan, Teesside, Teresina, Thetford, Tiberias, Timbuktu, Titograd, Toulouse, Trujillo, Tübingen, Ullapool, Vadodara, Valencia, Varanasi, Veracruz,

Vila Real, Vittoria, Vladimir, Voronezh, Wallasey, Wallsend, Weymouth, Winnipeg, Worthing, Würzburg, Yokohama, Yorktown, Zakopane, Zanzibar

09 Adis Abeba, Ahmadabad, Albufeira, Aldershot, Algeciras, Allahabad , Ambleside, Anchorage, Annapolis, Archangel, Astrakhan, Audenarde, Aylesbury, Baltimore, Bangalore, Barcelona, Beersheba, Bethlehem, Blackburn, Blackpool, Botany Bay, Brunswick, Cambridge, Cartagena, Castlebar, Changchun, Charleroi, Charlotte, Cherbourg, Chernobyl, Chiang Mai, Chihuahua, Chongqing, Chungking, Cleveland, Colwyn Bay, Constance, Des Moines, Doncaster, Dordrecht, Dubrovnik, Dumbarton, Dungannon, Dunstable, Eastleigh, Eindhoven, Esztergom, Fairbanks, Famagusta, Fishguard, Fleetwood, Fort Worth, Frankfort, Frankfurt, Fremantle, Galveston, Gateshead, Gaziantep, Gold Coast, Gravesend, Greenwich, Groningen, Guayaquil, Guildford, Harrogate, Haslemere, Heraklion, Hiroshima, Humpty Doo, Hyderabad, Immingham, Innsbruck, Inverness, Ismailiya, Jamestown, Johnstone, Kamchatka, Karlsruhe, Killarney, Kimberley, King's Lynn, Kirkcaldy, Kisangani, Kuybyshev, Lancaster, Leicester, Lexington, Lichfield, Liverpool, Llangefni, Long Beach, Lowestoft, Lymington, Magdeburg, Maidstone, Mansfield, Maracaibo, Marrakesh, Melbourne, Middleton, Milwaukee, Monterrey, Morecambe, Nashville, Neuchâtel, Newcastle, Newmarket, Nuremberg, Osnabrück, Palembang,

Perpignan, Peterhead,
Port Natal, Port Sudan,
Pressburg, Prestwick,
Princeton, Riverside,
Rochester, Rotherham,
Rotterdam, Salisbury,
Samarkand, San Miguel,
Santa Cruz, Santander,
Saragossa, Saskatoon,
Sheerness, Sheffield, Sioux
City, South Bend,
Southport, Southwark,
St Andrews, Stavanger,
Stavropol, St-Étienne,
Stevenage, Stockport,
Stornoway, St-Quentin,
Stranraer, Stuttgart,
Tarragona, Timisoara,
Toamasina, Trondheim,
Tullamore, Vancouver,
Vicksburg, Volgograd,
Wakefield, Walvis Bay,
Waterford, Wiesbaden,
Wimbledon, Wolfsburg,
Worcester, Wuppertal,
Yaroslavl, Zhengzhou

10 Alexandria, Baton Rouge,
Belize City, Birkenhead,
Birmingham, Bridgeport,
Bridgwater, Broken Hill,
Caernarvon, Caerphilly,
Canterbury, Carmarthen,
Carnoustie, Carson City,
Casablanca, Chandigarh,
Charleston, Chelmsford,
Cheltenham, Chichester,
Chittagong, Cincinnati,
Colchester, Concepción,
Darjeeling, Darlington,
Dorchester, Düsseldorf,
Eastbourne, Faisalabad,
Felixstowe, Folkestone,
Fray Bentos, Galashiels,
George Town, Gillingham,
Glenrothes, Gloucester,
Goose Green, Gothenburg,
Haddington, Harrisburg,
Hartlepool, Heidelberg,
Hildesheim, Huntingdon,
Huntsville, Kansas City,
Kenilworth, Kilmarnock,
Kompong Som, Lake
Placid, Launceston,
Leeuwarden, Letchworth,
Linlithgow, Little Rock,
Livingston, Llangollen,
Los Angeles, Louisville,
Lubumbashi, Maastricht,
Maidenhead, Manchester,
Marseilles, Medjugorje,
Miami Beach, Monte Carlo,
Montego Bay, Montgomery,

Montpelier, Motherwell,
New Orleans, Nottingham,
Nova Iguacu, Oudenaarde,
Palmerston, Petersburg,
Pittsburgh, Pontefract,
Portishead, Portsmouth,
Providence, Quezon City,
Rawalpindi, Regensburg,
Sacramento, San Antonio,
San Ignacio, Scunthorpe,
Sebastopol, Shepparton,
Shreveport, Shrewsbury,
Sioux Falls, Strasbourg,
Sunderland, Sverdlovsk,
Tananarive, Thunder Bay,
Townsville, Trivandrum,
Trowbridge, Valladolid,
Valparaíso, Wagga Wagga,
Warrington, Washington,
Whitehorse, Wilmington,
Winchester, Windermere,
Winterthur, Wittenberg,
Wollongong, Workington,
Yogyakarta

11 Aberystwyth, Albuquerque,
Basingstoke, Bognor Regis,
Bournemouth,
Brandenburg, Bremerhaven,
Bridlington, Broadstairs,
Brownsville, Carcassonne,
Charlestown, Chattanooga,
Cirencester, Cleethorpes,
Cockermouth, Coney
Island, Conisbrough,
Constantine, Cumbernauld,
Dar es Salaam,
Downpatrick, Dunfermline,
Enniskillen, Farnborough,
Fort William, Francistown,
Fraserburgh, Fredericton,
Glastonbury, Grangemouth,
Guadalajara, High
Wycombe, Juan-les-Pins,
Kaliningrad, Londonderry,
Lossiemouth, Medicine
Hat, Minneapolis,
Montpellier, New York City,
Northampton, Novosibirsk,
Palm Springs, Pointe-Noire,
Port Augusta, Prestonpans,
Punta Arenas,
Rockhampton, Rostov-on-
Don, Scarborough,
Southampton, Spanish
Town, Springfield,
Stourbridge, Tallahassee,
Trincomalee, Vladivostok,
Westminster, White Plains,
Yellowknife

12 Alice Springs, Atlantic City,
Barranquilla, Beverly Hills,
Bloemfontein, Chesterfield,

Christchurch, East Kilbride,
Great Malvern,
Huddersfield, Indianapolis,
Jacksonville, Johannesburg,
Kota Kinabalu,
Loughborough, Luang
Prabang, Macclesfield,
Magnitogorsk, Milton
Keynes, New Amsterdam,
Oklahoma City,
Peterborough, Philadelphia,
Port Harcourt, Rio de
Janeiro, Salt Lake City, San
Francisco, Santa Barbara,
Skelmersdale, South
Shields, Stoke-on-Trent,
St Petersburg, Tel Aviv-Jaffa,
Tennant Creek,
Thessaloníki, Trichinopoly,
West Bromwich,
Williamsburg,
Winston-Salem

13 Aix-en-Provence,
Charlottetown, Ellesmere
Port, Epsom and Ewell,
Great Yarmouth, Ho Chi
Minh City, Jefferson City,
Kidderminster,
Kirkcudbright,
Kirkintilloch, Leamington
Spa, Lytham St Anne's,
Middlesbrough, Port
Elizabeth, Semipalatinsk,
Sihanoukville, Virginia
Beach, Wolverhampton,
Yekaterinburg

14 Andorra-la-Vella,
Elisabethville, Hemel
Hempstead, Henley-on-
Thames, Santiago de Cuba,
Stockton-on-Tees, Tunbridge
Wells

15 Barrow-in-Furness, Burton-
upon-Trent, Charlottesville,
Chester-le-Street, Clermont-
Ferrand, Colorado Springs,
Frankfurt am Main,
Nizhniy Novgorod, Palma
de Mallorca, Sutton
Coldfield, Weston-super-
Mare

civic
04 city
05 local, urban
06 public
07 borough
08 communal, suburban
09 community, municipal
12 metropolitan

civil
04 home

05 civic, local, state
06 polite, public, urbane
07 affable, courtly, refined, secular
08 domestic, interior, internal, mannerly, national, obliging, polished, well-bred
09 courteous, municipal
10 cultivated, respectful
11 complaisant
12 well-mannered
13 accommodating

civility
04 tact
06 comity
07 amenity, manners, respect
08 breeding, courtesy, urbanity
10 affability, politeness, refinement
11 good manners
12 graciousness, pleasantness
13 courteousness

civilization
07 culture, society
08 progress, urbanity
09 community, education
10 refinement
11 advancement, cultivation
13 enlightenment
14 sophistication

civilize
04 tame
06 polish, refine
07 educate, improve, perfect
08 humanize, instruct
09 cultivate, enlighten, socialize
12 sophisticate

civilized
06 polite, urbane
07 refined
08 advanced, cultured, educated, sensible, sociable
09 developed
10 cultivated, reasonable
11 enlightened
13 sophisticated

clad
07 attired, clothed, covered, dressed, wearing

claim
03 ask
04 aver, avow, call, hold, kill, need, take
05 cause, exact, right, state
06 allege, assert, assume, avowal, demand, insist
07 collect, contend, deserve, pretend, profess, purport, request, require
08 averment, maintain

09 assertion, postulate
10 allegation, contention, insistence, pretension
11 affirmation, application, declaration, entitlement, requirement, requisition

claimant
08 litigant
09 applicant, candidate, pretender, suppliant
10 petitioner, pretendant, supplicant

clairvoyance
03 ESP
09 telepathy
13 psychic powers
14 fortune-telling

clairvoyant
04 seer
05 augur
06 oracle
07 diviner, prophet, psychic
08 telepath
09 prophetic, visionary
10 prophetess, soothsayer
12 extra-sensory
13 fortune-teller

clamber
04 claw, shin
05 climb, mount, scale
06 ascend, shinny
08 scrabble, scramble

clammy
04 damp, dank
05 close, moist, muggy, slimy
06 sticky, sweaty

clamorous
05 lusty, noisy
07 blaring, riotous
08 vehement
09 deafening, insistent
10 tumultuous, vociferous

clamour
03 din
04 urge
05 blare, claim, noise
06 demand, hubbub, insist, outcry, racket, uproar
09 agitation, commotion
12 vociferation

clamp
03 fix
04 grip, hold, vice
05 brace, clasp, press
06 clench, clinch, fasten, secure
07 bracket, squeeze

❏**clamp down on**
04 stop

05 limit
07 confine, control
08 restrain, restrict, suppress
10 put a stop to
11 crack down on
14 come down hard on

clan
03 set
04 band, line, race, sect, sept
05 group, house, tribe
06 circle, clique, family
07 coterie, faction, society
10 fraternity
11 brotherhood

clandestine
03 sly
06 closet, covert, hidden, secret, sneaky
07 furtive, private
08 backroom, stealthy
09 concealed, underhand
10 fraudulent, undercover
11 underground
13 surreptitious
14 cloak-and-dagger
15 under-the-counter

clang
04 bong, peal, ring, toll
05 chime, clank, clash, clunk
06 jangle
07 clatter, resound
11 reverberate

clanger
04 boob, slip
05 error, fault, gaffe
06 booboo, cock-up, howler
07 bloomer, blunder, faux pas, mistake
08 solecism

clank
04 ring, toll
05 clang, clash, clunk
06 jangle
07 clatter, resound
11 reverberate

clannish
06 narrow, select
07 cliquey, insular
08 cliquish
09 exclusive, parochial
10 unfriendly

clap
04 bang, slap
05 cheer, smack, whack
06 strike, wallop
07 acclaim, applaud

claptrap
03 rot

04 bunk
05 bilge, trash, tripe
06 bunkum, drivel, hot air, piffle
07 blarney, rubbish, twaddle
08 nonsense, tommyrot
09 gibberish, poppycock
10 codswallop

clarification
05 gloss
10 definition, exposition
11 elucidation, explanation

clarify
05 clear, gloss
06 define, filter, purify, refine
07 clear up, explain, resolve
08 simplify, spell out
09 elucidate, make clear, make plain
10 illuminate
12 throw light on

clarity
08 lucidity
09 clearness, plainness, precision, sharpness
10 definition, simplicity
12 explicitness, transparency
15 intelligibility, unambiguousness

clash
03 jar, war
04 bang, feud
05 clank, crash, fight, noise
06 jangle, rattle, strike
07 clatter, contend, grapple, quarrel, warring, wrangle
08 coincide, conflict, disagree, fighting, showdown
09 collision, not go with
12 disagreement
13 confrontation

clasp
03 hug, pin
04 clip, grip, hasp, hold, hook
05 catch, grasp, press
06 attach, buckle, clutch, cuddle, enfold, fasten
07 cling to, connect, embrace, grapple, squeeze
08 fastener

class
03 set
04 form, kind, rank, rate, sort, type, year
05 brand, caste, genre, genus, grade, group, order, style
06 course, lesson, period, phylum, sphere, status
07 arrange, lecture, quality, section, seminar, species

08 category, classify, division, elegance, grouping, standing, tutorial, workshop
09 designate
10 background, categorize, department, pigeonhole
11 distinction, social order, stylishness
12 denomination, social status
14 social standing, sophistication

classic
04 best, true
05 great, ideal, model, prime
06 finest
07 abiding, ageless, lasting, regular, typical, undying
08 enduring, exemplar, immortal, masterly, standard, timeless
09 brilliant, exemplary, first-rate, prototype
10 archetypal, consummate, definitive, first-class
11 established, masterpiece, outstanding, traditional
12 paradigmatic
14 quintessential

classical
04 pure
05 Attic, Latin, plain
07 concert, elegant, Grecian, refined, serious
08 Hellenic
09 excellent, symphonic
10 harmonious, restrained
12 ancient Greek, ancient Roman

classification
07 grading, sorting
08 grouping, taxonomy
10 tabulation
11 arrangement, cataloguing
12 codification
14 categorization

classify
04 file, rank, sort, type
05 class, grade, group, order
06 codify
07 arrange, dispose
08 tabulate
09 catalogue
10 categorize, pigeonhole
11 systematize

classy
04 fine, posh
05 grand, ritzy
06 select, swanky
07 elegant, stylish

08 superior, up-market
09 exclusive, high-class
13 sophisticated

clatter
03 jar
04 bang
05 clang, clank, clunk, crash
06 jangle, rattle, strike

clause
04 item, part
05 point, rider
06 phrase
07 article, chapter, heading, passage, proviso, section
08 loophole
09 condition, provision
10 subsection

claw
03 rip
04 maul, nail, tear
05 chela, graze, talon
06 mangle, nipper, pincer, scrape, unguis
07 gripper, scratch
08 lacerate, scrabble

clean
04 fair, good, neat, pure, tidy
05 blank, fresh, fully, moral
06 chaste, decent, honest, proper, simple, smooth, unused, washed
07 aseptic, perfect, regular, sterile, totally, upright
08 flawless, hygienic, innocent, purified, sanitary, spotless, straight, unmarked, unsoiled, virtuous
09 faultless, guiltless, laundered, reputable, righteous, speckless, unstained, unsullied
10 above board, antiseptic, honourable, immaculate, sterilized, unpolluted, upstanding
11 respectable, unblemished, well-defined
12 spick and span

cleaner
04 char
05 daily

cleanse
04 wash
05 bathe, clear, purge, rinse
06 purify
07 absolve, deterge
08 lustrate
09 disinfect, sterilize

cleanser
04 soap
07 cleaner, scourer, solvent
08 purifier
09 detergent
10 soap powder
12 disinfectant
14 scouring powder

clear
03 net, rid
04 earn, fair, fine, free, gain, jump, keen, make, move, open, pass, sure, tidy, wipe
05 allow, bring, clean, empty, erase, let go, light, lucid, plain, quick, sharp, shift, sunny, vault
06 acquit, bright, excuse, glassy, go over, limpid, pardon, patent, permit, refine, remove, unclog, unload, unstop, vacate
07 absolve, approve, audible, bring in, certain, cleanse, evident, logical, obvious, release, unblock
08 apparent, coherent, definite, distinct, evacuate, explicit, get rid of, innocent, jump over, liberate, luminous, manifest, pellucid, sanction, sensible, undimmed
09 authorize, blameless, cloudless, decongest, exculpate, exonerate, extricate, guiltless, unclouded, vindicate
10 colourless, diaphanous, perceptive, pronounced, see-through, unhindered
11 beyond doubt, conspicuous, crystalline, translucent, transparent, unambiguous, unequivocal, well-defined
12 intelligible, recognizable, unmistakable, unobstructed
14 beyond question, comprehensible, give the go-ahead, unquestionable

❏ **clear out**
04 sort, tidy
05 empty, hop it, leave
06 beat it, depart, tidy up
07 get lost, push off, sort out
08 clear off, shove off, throw out, withdraw

❏ **clear up**
04 sort, tidy
05 clear, crack, order, solve
06 answer, remove

07 clarify, explain, improve, iron out, resolve, unravel
08 brighten
09 elucidate, rearrange
10 brighten up, put in order
13 straighten out

clearance
02 OK
03 gap
04 room
05 leave, say-so, space
06 margin, moving
07 consent, freeing, go-ahead
08 emptying, headroom, sanction, vacating
09 allowance, unloading
10 demolition, evacuation, green light, permission
11 endorsement
13 authorization

clear-cut
05 clear, plain
07 precise
08 definite, distinct, explicit
09 trenchant
11 cut and dried, unambiguous, unequivocal, well-defined
15 straightforward

clearing
03 gap
04 dell
05 glade, space
07 opening

clearly
06 openly
07 plainly
08 markedly, patently
09 evidently, obviously
10 distinctly, manifestly, undeniably
11 undoubtedly
12 indisputably, unmistakably, without doubt
13 incontestably

cleave
03 cut, hew
04 chop, hold, open, part, rend
05 cling, crack, halve, sever, slice, split, stick, unite
06 adhere, attach, cohere, divide, remain, sunder
08 dissever, disunite, separate

cleft
03 gap
04 rent
05 chasm, chink, crack, split
06 breach, cranny
07 crevice, fissure, opening
08 fracture

clemency
04 pity
05 mercy
08 leniency, mildness, sympathy
10 compassion, generosity, indulgence, tenderness
11 forbearance, forgiveness, magnanimity

clench
04 grip, grit, hold, seal, shut
05 clasp, close, grasp
06 clutch, double, fasten

clergy
07 clerics
08 ministry, the cloth
09 churchmen, the church
10 holy orders, priesthood

clergyman
04 dean, imam
05 canon, padre, rabbi, vicar
06 cleric, curate, deacon, divine, father, mullah, parson, pastor, priest, rector
07 muezzin
08 chaplain, man of God, minister, reverend
09 churchman, deaconess, presbyter
12 ecclesiastic
13 man of the cloth

clerical
06 filing, office, typing
08 official, pastoral, priestly
09 canonical, episcopal
10 pen-pushing, sacerdotal
11 keyboarding, ministerial, secretarial, white-collar
14 administrative, ecclesiastical

clerk
06 notary, typist, writer
07 copyist
08 official
09 assistant, pen-pusher, secretary
11 protocolist
12 receptionist, record-keeper, stenographer
13 account-keeper, administrator, shop-assistant

clever
03 apt
04 able, keen
05 quick, sharp, smart, witty
06 adroit, brainy, bright, expert, gifted, shrewd
07 capable, cunning, knowing, sapient
08 rational, sensible, talented

cliché

09 brilliant, ingenious, inventive, sagacious
10 discerning, perceptive
11 intelligent, quick-witted, resourceful, sharp-witted
13 knowledgeable

cliché

06 truism
07 bromide
08 banality, chestnut
09 platitude
10 stereotype
11 commonplace, old chestnut

clichéd, clichéed

04 dull, worn
05 banal, corny, stale, stock, tired, trite
06 common
07 routine, worn-out
08 overused, time-worn
09 hackneyed
10 overworked, pedestrian, threadbare
11 commonplace, stereotyped, wearing thin
12 run-of-the-mill
13 platitudinous, unimaginative

click

04 beat, snap, snip, tick, twig
05 clack, clink, snick
08 cotton on
09 make sense
10 understand
13 fall into place

client

06 patron
07 patient, regular, shopper
08 consumer, customer
09 applicant, purchaser

clientèle

06 market
07 clients, patrons
08 business, regulars, shoppers
09 consumers, customers, following, patronage

cliff

03 tor
04 crag, face, scar
05 bluff, scarp
08 overhang, rock-face
09 precipice
10 escarpment, promontory

climactic

07 crucial
08 critical, decisive, exciting
09 paramount

climate

04 mood
05 trend

06 milieu, temper
07 feeling, setting, weather
08 ambience, tendency
10 atmosphere
11 disposition, environment, temperature

climax

03 top
04 acme, apex, head, peak
06 apogee, height, summit, zenith
08 pinnacle
09 high point, highlight

climb

03 top
04 go up, move, rise, soar, stir
05 mount, scale, shift
06 ascend, shin up
07 clamber, shoot up
08 increase, scramble, surmount

▫climb down

07 concede, retract, retreat
08 back down
12 eat your words

clinch

04 land, seal
05 close
06 decide, secure, settle, verify
07 confirm
08 conclude
09 determine

cling

03 hug
04 grip, hold
05 clasp, grasp, stick
06 adhere, cleave, clutch
07 embrace, stick to, support

clinic

07 doctor's
08 hospital
09 infirmary
12 health centre
13 medical centre

clinical

04 cold
05 basic, plain, stark
06 simple
07 austere, medical, patient
08 analytic, detached, hospital
09 impassive, objective
10 impersonal, scientific
11 emotionless, unemotional
12 business-like
13 disinterested, dispassionate

clip

03 box, cut, fix, pin
04 crop, cuff, dock, hold, pare, poll, slap, snip, trim

05 clout, prune, punch, shear, thump, whack
06 attach, fasten, staple, wallop
07 curtail, cutting, excerpt, extract, passage, pollard, section, shorten, snippet
08 citation, cut short, truncate
09 quotation
10 abbreviate

clipping

07 cutting, excerpt, extract, passage, section, snippet
08 citation
09 quotation

clique

03 set
04 band, clan, gang, pack
05 bunch, crowd, group
06 circle
07 coterie, faction, in-crowd
10 fraternity

cloak

04 cape, coat, cope, hide, mask, robe, veil, wrap
05 blind, cover, front, shawl
06 mantle, screen, shroud
07 conceal, obscure, pretext
08 disguise
10 camouflage

clock

▫clock up

05 reach
06 attain, record
07 archive, chalk up, notch up
08 register

clog

03 dam, jam
05 block, choke, dam up
06 bung up, burden, hamper, hinder, impede, stop up
07 congest, occlude
08 encumber, obstruct

cloister

05 aisle
06 arcade
07 portico, walkway
08 corridor, pavement
10 ambulatory

cloistered

08 confined, enclosed, hermitic, isolated, secluded
09 protected, reclusive, sheltered, withdrawn

close

03 bar, end, row
04 bolt, clog, cork, dear, fold, fuse, good, join, lane, like, lock, mean, mews, near, plug, seal, shut, stop, true

05 block, bosom, cease, court, dense, exact, heavy, humid, muggy, place, tight

06 at hand, clinch, ending, fasten, finale, finish, go bust, lock up, loving, narrow, nearby, not far, secret, secure, square, sticky, stingy, stuffy, sultry, wind up

07 airless, careful, compact, confirm, cramped, crowded, devoted, miserly, occlude, padlock, private, similar, terrace

08 adjacent, attached, conclude, cul-de-sac, detailed, faithful, familiar, imminent, intimate, obstruct, shut down, stifling, taciturn

09 adjoining, cessation, condensed, courtyard, determine, establish, impending, niggardly, secretive, terminate

10 comparable, completion, conclusion, dénouement, hard-fought, oppressive, quadrangle, sweltering

11 culmination, draw to an end, go to the wall, inseparable, neck and neck, suffocating, well-matched

12 a stone's throw, bring to an end, concentrated, parsimonious

13 corresponding, evenly matched, in the vicinity, penny-pinching

14 on your doorstep

◻**close in**

08 approach, draw near, encircle, surround

10 come nearer

closet

06 covert, hidden, secret

07 furtive, private

08 cupboard, wardrobe

10 undercover, unrevealed

13 surreptitious

closure

07 failure, folding

08 shutdown

10 bankruptcy, stopping-up

clot

03 gel, set

04 glob, lump, mass

05 clump

06 curdle

07 congeal, thicken

08 coalesce, solidify, thrombus

09 coagulate

10 thrombosis

11 coagulation, obstruction

cloth

03 rag

05 stuff, towel

06 duster, fabric

07 flannel, textile

08 material

clothe

03 rig

04 deck, robe, vest

05 cover, drape, dress, habit

06 attire, fit out, invest, outfit

07 apparel, bedizen

08 accoutre

09 caparison

clothes

04 garb, gear, togs, wear

05 dress, get-up

06 attire, outfit

07 apparel, clobber, costume, raiment, vesture

08 cast-offs, clothing, garments, wardrobe

09 sartorial, vestments

10 habilatory, habilments

11 hand-me-downs

▶ *Types of clothes*:

03 aba, bra, tie

04 abba, belt, gown, kilt, sari, slip, sock, suit, sulu, toga, veil, vest

05 abaya, cloak, cords, dhoti, dress, frock, glove, jeans, Levis®, lungi, pants, parka, scarf, shawl, shift, shirt, skirt, smock, stole, teddy, thong, tunic

06 basque, bikini, blouse, bodice, bow-tie, braces, briefs, caftan, corset, cravat, denims, dirndl, garter, girdle, jersey, jumper, kimono, mitten, poncho, sarong, shorts, slacks, tights, T-shirt

07 doublet, hosiery, leotard, muffler, necktie, nightie, pyjamas, singlet, sweater, twin-set, yashmak, Y-fronts

08 breeches, camisole, cardigan, culottes, earmuffs, flannels, hot pants, jodhpurs, jumpsuit, leggings, lingerie, negligee, pinafore, polo-neck, pullover, swimsuit, tee-shirt, trousers

09 bed-jacket, brassière, dungarees, hair shirt,

housecoat, mini skirt, pantihose, petticoat, plus-fours, separates, shell suit, stockings, tracksuit, waistcoat

10 cummerbund, drainpipes, dress-shirt, flying suit, leg-warmers, nightdress, string vest, suspenders, sweat-shirt, turtle-neck, underpants

11 bell-bottoms, boxer-shorts, pencil-skirt, trouser suit

12 body stocking, camiknickers, dressing-gown, evening-dress

13 Bermuda shorts, liberty bodice, suspender belt

14 bathing-costume, French knickers, swimming trunks

15 swimming costume

cloud

03 dim, fog

04 blur, dull, mist, veil

05 cover, shade

06 darken, mantle, shroud

07 confuse, eclipse, obscure

09 obfuscate

10 overshadow

▶ *Types of cloud*:

06 cirrus, nimbus

07 cumulus, stratus

11 altocumulus, altostratus

12 cirrocumulus, cirrostratus, cumulonimbus, nimbostratus

13 fractocumulus, fractostratus, stratocumulus

cloudy

03 dim

04 dark, dull, grey, hazy

05 foggy, heavy, milky, misty, muddy, murky

06 blurry, gloomy, leaden

07 blurred, obscure, sunless

08 nebulous, overcast

10 indistinct

clout

03 box, hit

04 cuff, pull, slap, slug, sock

05 power, punch, smack, thump, whack

06 muscle, strike, wallop

09 authority, influence

cloven

05 cleft, split

07 divided

08 bisected

clown

04 dork, fool, geek, jerk, jest, joke, nerd, twit, zany
05 comic, idiot, joker, ninny, twerp, wally
06 dimwit, jester, nitwit
07 buffoon, pierrot
08 comedian, dipstick, imbecile, numskull
09 harlequin, muck about
10 act the fool, fool around, mess around, nincompoop
11 play the fool

cloying

06 sickly
07 choking, fulsome
09 oversweet, sickening
10 disgusting, nauseating

club

03 bat, hit, set
04 bash, beat, cosh, mace
05 clout, group, guild, order, staff, stick, union
06 batter, circle, clique, cudgel, league, pummel, strike
07 clobber, company, society
08 bludgeon
09 truncheon
10 federation, fraternity
11 association, brotherhood
12 organization

➤ *Names of clubs. We have omitted the word* **club** *from names given in the following list but you may need to include this word as part of the solution to some crossword clues.*

03 MCC, Ski
04 Arts, Turf
05 Buck's, Naval
06 Cotton, Drones, Kennel, Kitcat, Pratt's, Queen's, Reform, Rotary, Savage, Savile, White's
07 Almack's, Boodle's, Brooks's, Carlton, Country, Farmers, Garrick, Groucho, Kiwanis, Leander, Variety
08 Hell-fire, National, Portland
09 Athenaeum, Beefsteak, East India, Green Room, Lansdowne, Wig and Pen
10 Caledonian, City Livery, Crockford's, Hurlingham, Oddfellows, Roehampton, Travellers
11 Army and Navy, Arts Theatre, Chelsea Arts
12 London Rowing, New Cavendish, Thames Rowing

15 National Liberal, Royal Automobile

❑club together

06 chip in
10 contribute
12 share the cost
14 have a whip-round

clue

03 tip
04 hint, idea, lead, sign
05 trace
06 notion, tip-off
07 inkling, pointer
08 evidence
09 suspicion
10 indication, suggestion

clump

03 lot
04 mass, plod, thud, tuft
05 amass, bunch, clomp, group, stamp, stomp, thump, tramp
06 bundle, lumber, trudge
07 cluster, stumble, thicket
10 accumulate, collection
12 accumulation

clumsy

05 bulky, crude, gawky, heavy, inept, rough
06 gauche, wooden
07 awkward, uncouth
08 bungling, tactless, ungainly, unwieldy
09 all thumbs, ham-fisted, lumbering, maladroit
10 blundering, cumbersome, ungraceful
11 heavy-handed, insensitive
13 accident-prone

cluster

04 band, knot, mass
05 batch, bunch, clump, crowd, flock, group, truss
06 gather, huddle, raceme
07 collect, panicle
08 assemble, assembly
09 gathering
10 assemblage, assortment, collection, congregate

clustered

06 massed
07 bunched, grouped
08 gathered
09 assembled, glomerate

clutch

04 grab, grip, hold, jaws, sway
05 clasp, claws, grasp, group, hands, mercy, power, seize
06 clench, snatch
07 cling to, control, embrace, grapple, keeping, setting

08 dominion
09 get hold of

clutter

04 fill, mess
05 chaos, cover, strew
06 jumble, litter, mess up, muddle
07 scatter
08 disarray, disorder, encumber
09 confusion, make a mess

coach

03 bus, cab, car, gig
04 cram, trap
05 drill, prime, teach, train, tutor, wagon
06 hansom, landau, mentor
07 hackney, teacher, trainer
08 brougham, carriage, educator, instruct
09 charabanc, Greyhound
10 instructor, motor-coach

coagulate

03 gel
04 clot, melt
06 curdle
07 congeal, thicken
08 solidify

coalesce

03 mix
04 fuse, join
05 blend, merge, unite
06 cohere, commix
07 combine
09 affiliate, commingle, integrate
10 amalgamate
11 consolidate, incorporate
12 join together

coalition

04 bloc
05 union
06 fusion, league, merger
07 compact, joining
08 alliance
10 federation
11 affiliation, association, confederacy
12 amalgamation
13 confederation

coarse

04 blue, rank, rude
05 bawdy, crude, gross, hairy, lumpy, rough, scaly
06 earthy, ribald, rugged, smutty, uneven, vulgar
07 boorish, bristly, loutish, obscene, prickly, raunchy
08 immodest, impolite, improper, indecent
09 offensive, unrefined

10 indelicate, unpolished
11 foul-mouthed, ill-mannered, unprocessed

coarsen
06 deaden, harden
07 roughen, thicken
08 indurate
11 desensitize

coarseness
04 smut
07 crudity
08 ribaldry
09 bawdiness, indecency, obscenity, vulgarity
10 crassitude, earthiness, indelicacy, smuttiness
13 offensiveness

coast
04 sail, taxi
05 beach, drift, glide, shore
06 cruise, strand
07 seaside
08 seaboard, seashore
09 foreshore, freewheel

coat
03 fur
04 cake, daub, film, hair, hide, pave, pelt, skin, wool
05 apply, cover, glaze, layer, paint, put on, sheet, smear
06 finish, fleece, mantle, spread, veneer
07 blanket, encrust, varnish
08 cladding, covering, laminate, pellicle

coating
04 film, skin, wash
05 crust, glaze, layer, sheet
06 enamel, finish, patina, veneer
07 blanket, dusting, varnish
08 covering, membrane

coax
05 tempt
06 allure, cajole, entice, induce
07 beguile, flatter, wheedle, win over
08 get round, inveigle, persuade, soft-soap, talk into, win round
09 sweet-talk

cobble

☐**cobble together**
07 knock up
09 improvise
11 put together

cock
03 tip
04 lift

05 capon, point, raise, slant
07 chicken, incline, rooster
11 chanticleer

cock-eyed
04 awry, daft
05 askew, barmy, crazy
06 absurd
07 crooked
08 lopsided
09 ludicrous, skew-whiff

cocktail

➤ *Names of cocktails*:
06 gimlet
07 martini, pink gin, Sazerac®, sidecar, stinger
08 daiquiri, snowball
09 Manhattan, margarita, rusty nail, white lady
10 bloody Mary, margharita, Tom Collins, whisky sour
11 black velvet, screwdriver
12 black Russian, old-fashioned
14 singapore sling
15 brandy Alexander
➤ See also **drink**

cocky
04 vain
05 brash
08 arrogant, cocksure
09 bumptious, conceited, hubristic
10 swaggering
11 egotistical, self-assured
13 self-important, swollen-headed

cocoon
04 wrap
05 cover
07 cushion, envelop, isolate, protect
08 cloister, insulate, preserve

coddle
03 pet
05 spoil
06 cosset, humour, pamper
07 indulge, protect
11 mollycoddle, overprotect

code
04 laws
05 rules, signs
06 cipher, custom, ethics, morals, system
07 bar code, conduct, manners
08 morality, postcode, practice
09 etiquette, Morse code
10 convention, cryptogram
11 cryptograph, regulations

coerce
05 bully, drive, force
06 compel, lean on
07 dragoon
08 bludgeon, browbeat, bulldoze, railroad, threaten
09 pressgang, strongarm
10 intimidate, pressurize

coercion
05 force
06 duress
08 bullying, pressure
10 compulsion, constraint
11 browbeating

coffer
03 box
04 case, safe
05 chest, trunk
06 casket
08 moneybox, treasury
09 strongbox
10 repository

cogent
06 potent, strong, urgent
07 weighty
08 forceful, forcible, powerful
09 effective
10 compelling, persuasive
11 influential
12 irresistible, unanswerable

cogitate
04 muse
06 ponder
07 reflect
08 consider, mull over
10 deliberate
11 contemplate, think deeply

cognate
04 akin
05 alike
06 agnate, allied
07 kindred, related, similar
09 analogous, connected
10 affiliated, associated
13 corresponding

cognition
06 reason
07 insight
08 learning, thinking
09 awareness, knowledge, reasoning
10 perception
11 discernment, rationality
12 apprehension, intelligence
13 comprehension, understanding

cognizance

☐**take cognizance of**
06 accept, regard

09 recognize
11 acknowledge

cognizant
05 aware
06 versed
07 witting
08 familiar, informed
09 conscious
10 acquainted, conversant
13 knowledgeable

cohabit
07 shack up
08 live with
12 live together

cohere
04 bind, fuse, hold
05 agree, cling, stick, unite
06 adhere, square
07 combine
08 coalesce
09 harmonize, make sense
10 correspond
11 consolidate
12 hang together

coherence
05 sense, union, unity
07 harmony
09 agreement, congruity
10 connection, consonance
11 concordance, consistency

coherent
05 clear, lucid
07 logical, orderly
08 rational, reasoned, sensible
09 organized
10 articulate, consistent
12 intelligible
14 comprehensible

cohesion
05 sense, union, unity, whole
07 harmony
09 agreement
10 connection
11 consistency

cohort
04 band, body, mate
05 buddy, squad, troop
06 column, legion
07 brigade, company, partner
08 division, follower,
   myrmidon, regiment,
   sidekick, squadron
09 companion, supporter

coil
04 curl, loop, ring, roll, wind
05 helix, twine, twist, whorl
06 spiral, wreath, writhe
09 convolute, corkscrew

coin
04 cash, mint
05 forge, money, piece
06 change, copper, create,
   devise, invent, make up,
   silver, specie
07 dream up, nummary,
   produce, think up
08 conceive
09 neologise, nummulary,
   originate
11 loose change, small change

▶ *Types of coin*:
02 at, xu
03 bit, bob, fen, hao, ore, pul,
   pya, rap, sen, sou
04 anna, cent, chon, dime, fils,
   jiao, joey, lwei, mite, obol,
   para, quid, real, sent
05 angel, butut, copec, crown,
   ducat, groat, kopek, louis,
   noble, pence, penny, pound
06 aureus, bezant, copeck,
   copper, dollar, florin,
   guinea, kopeck, nickel,
   obolus, satang, stater, talent,
   tanner, thaler
07 centavo, centime, centimo,
   guilder, ha'penny, moidore,
   Pfennig, piastre, quarter,
   solidus
08 australe, denarius,
   doubloon, ducatoon,
   farthing, Groschen,
   imperial, louis d'or,
   millième, napoleon, new
   penny, sesterce, shilling,
   sixpence, ten pence, two
   pence, two pound
09 centesimo, dandiprat, five
   pence, gold crown, half-
   crown, halfpenny, pound
   coin, sovereign
10 fifty pence, half florin, half
   guinea, krugerrand, sestertius
11 double eagle, sixpenny bit,
   twenty pence, twopenny bit
12 silver dollar, two pound coin
13 brass farthing, half
   sovereign, quarter dollar,
   sixpenny piece, ten pence
   piece, tenpenny piece,
   threepenny bit, two pence
   piece, twopenny piece
14 five pence piece
15 fifty pence piece, threepenny
   piece

➤ See also **currency**; **money**

coincide
05 agree, clash, match, tally
06 accord, concur, square

09 be the same, harmonize
10 correspond
11 synchronize

coincidence
04 luck
05 clash, fluke
06 chance
08 accident, clashing, fortuity
11 coexistence, concurrence,
   conjunction, correlation,
   eventuality, serendipity

coincidental
05 lucky
06 casual, chance, flukey
09 unplanned
10 accidental, fortuitous
13 serendipitous, unintentional

coitus
03 sex
05 union
06 mating
07 coition
08 coupling

cold
03 ice, icy, raw
04 cool, keen, rimy, snow
05 aloof, chill, fresh, frore, frost,
   gelid, nippy, parky, polar
06 arctic, biting, bitter, brumal,
   chilly, frigid, frosty, frozen,
   remote, winter, wintry
07 brumous, callous, chilled,
   distant, glacial, hostile
08 clinical, coolness, freezing,
   reserved, Siberian, uncaring
09 frigidity, heartless, unfeeling
10 phlegmatic, unfriendly
11 indifferent, insensitive,
   passionless, standoffish,
   unemotional, unexcitable
12 antagonistic, unresponsive

cold-blooded
05 cruel
06 brutal, savage
07 callous, inhuman
08 barbaric, pitiless, ruthless
09 barbarous, heartless,
   merciless, unfeeling

cold-hearted
04 cold
06 flinty, unkind
07 callous, inhuman
08 detached, uncaring
09 heartless, unfeeling
11 indifferent, insensitive

collaborate
05 unite
06 betray, team up
07 collude

08 conspire
09 co-operate
10 fraternize, join forces
11 participate, turn traitor

collaboration
05 union
08 alliance, teamwork
09 collusion
11 association, co-operation, joint effort, partnership
12 fraternizing

collaborator
07 partner, traitor
08 betrayer, co-worker, colluder, quisling, renegade, team-mate, turncoat
09 assistant, associate, colleague
10 accomplice
11 conspirator, fraternizer

collapse
04 fail, flop, fold, ruin, sink
05 faint, slump, swoon
06 cave in, cave-in, fall in, finish
07 crumble, crumple, debacle, failure, founder, give way, pass out, sinking, subside
08 black out, blackout, downfall, fainting, keel over
10 foundering, subsidence
11 come to an end, fall through
12 disintegrate, fall to pieces
13 come to nothing

collar
03 nab
04 grab, nick, ring, ruff, stop
05 catch, ruche, seize
06 arrest, bertha, gorget, rebato
07 capture
08 neckband
09 apprehend, dog-collar

collate
04 sort
05 order
06 gather
07 arrange, collect, compose
08 organize
10 put in order

collateral
05 funds
06 pledge, surety
07 deposit
08 security
09 assurance, guarantee

colleague
04 aide, ally
06 helper
07 comrade, partner

08 co-worker, confrère, team-mate, workmate
09 assistant, associate, auxiliary, companion
11 confederate

collect
03 get
04 heap, mass, meet, save
05 amass, fetch, hoard, rally
06 gather, muster, pick up
07 acquire, call for, come for, compose, convene, prepare, solicit
08 assemble, converge
09 aggregate, stockpile
10 accumulate, congregate
14 gather together

collected
04 calm, cool
06 placid, poised, serene
08 composed, unshaken
09 unruffled
10 controlled
11 unperturbed
13 self-possessed

collection
03 set
04 gift, heap, mass, pile
05 gifts, group, hoard, store
06 job-lot
07 cluster
08 assembly, donation, offering
09 anthology, offertory, stockpile, whip-round
10 assemblage, assortment
11 compilation
12 accumulation, contribution
14 collected works, conglomeration

collective
05 joint
06 common, moshav, shared, united
07 commune, kibbutz, kolkhoz
08 combined
09 aggregate, community, composite, unanimous
10 cumulative, democratic
11 co-operative
13 collaborative

➤ *Collective nouns*:
03 **gam** (of whales), **nye** (of pheasants), **pod** (of seals)
04 **army** (of frogs), **bask** (of crocodiles), **cete** (of badgers), **dole** (of doves), **herd** (of deer), **pack** (of dogs), **pack** (of hounds),

rout (of wolves), **team** (of ducks), **zeal** (of zebras)
05 **brood** (of chickens), **brood** (of hens), **charm** (of finches), **covey** (of partridges), **crash** (of rhinoceros), **drove** (of cattle), **flock** (of sheep), **pride** (of lions), **shoal** (of fish), **skein** (of geese), **swarm** (of bees), **swarm** (of locusts), **tribe** (of goats), **troop** (of kangaroos), **troop** (of monkeys), **watch** (of nightingales)
06 **colony** (of rats), **gaggle** (of geese), **litter** (of pigs), **murder** (of crows), **muster** (of peacocks), **muster** (of penguins), **parade** (of elephants), **rafter** (of turkeys), **school** (of dolphins), **school** (of porpoises), **string** (of horses)
10 **exaltation** (of larks), **parliament** (of owls), **shrewdness** (of apes), **unkindness** (of ravens)

collector
➤ *Types of collectors and enthusiasts*:
07 gourmet
08 zoophile
09 antiquary
10 audiophile, discophile, gastronome, hippophile, monarchist
11 bibliophile, etymologist, numismatist, philatelist
12 cartophilist, entomologist
13 arachnologist, campanologist, chirographist, lepidopterist, ornithologist
15 conservationist

college
04 poly
06 school
07 academy
08 seminary
09 institute
10 university
11 polytechnic
➤ See also **university**

➤ *Names of Cambridge colleges*:
05 Clare, Jesus, King's
06 Darwin, Girton, Queens', Selwyn
07 Christ's, Downing, New Hall, Newnham, St John's, Trinity, Wolfson

08 Emmanuel, Homerton, Pembroke, Robinson
09 Churchill, Clare Hall, Magdalene, St Edmund's
10 Hughes Hall, Peterhouse
11 Fitzwilliam, Trinity Hall
12 Sidney Sussex, St Catherine's
13 Corpus Christi, Lucy Cavendish
16 Gonville and Caius

➤ *Names of Oxford colleges:*
03 New
05 Green, Jesus, Keble, Oriel
06 Exeter, Merton, Wadham
07 Balliol, Kellogg, Linacre, Lincoln, St Anne's, St Cross, St Hugh's, St John's, Trinity, Wolfson
08 All Souls, Hertford, Magdalen, Nuffield, Pembroke, St Hilda's, St Peter's
09 Brasenose, Mansfield, St Antony's, Templeton, The Queen's, Worcester
10 Greyfriars, Somerville, University
11 Blackfriars, Campion Hall, Regent's Park
12 Christ Church, St Benet's Hall, St Catherine's, St Edmund Hall, Wycliffe Hall
13 Corpus Christi
16 Harris Manchester, Lady Margaret Hall

collide
03 hit, war
04 bump, feud
05 clash, crash, prang, smash
07 grapple, quarrel, run into
08 bump into, conflict, disagree
09 crash into, smash into
10 meet head on, plough into

collision
04 bump, feud
05 brush, clash, crash, fight, prang, smash, wreck
06 impact, pile-up
07 quarrel, warring, wrangle
08 accident, conflict, disaster, fighting, showdown

colloquial
06 casual, chatty
07 demotic, popular
08 everyday, familiar, informal
09 idiomatic
10 vernacular
14 conversational

collude
04 plot

06 scheme
08 conspire, intrigue
09 machinate
11 collaborate

collusion
04 plot
06 deceit, league, scheme
07 cahoots
08 artifice, intrigue, scheming
10 complicity, conspiracy
11 machination
13 collaboration

colonist
07 pioneer, settler
08 colonial, emigrant
09 immigrant

colonize
05 found
06 occupy, people, settle
07 pioneer
08 populate

colonnade
04 stoa
06 arcade
07 portico
09 cloisters, peristyle

colony
05 group
07 outpost
08 dominion, province
09 community, satellite
10 dependency, possession, settlement
12 protectorate

colossal
04 huge, vast
05 great
07 immense, mammoth, massive
08 enormous, gigantic, whopping
09 herculean, monstrous
10 gargantuan, monumental
14 Brobdingnagian

colour
03 dye, hue
04 bias, flag, life, tint, tone
05 blush, flush, go red, paint, shade, slant, taint, tinge
06 affect, banner, crayon, emblem, ensign, redden
07 distort, pigment
08 insignia, standard, tincture
09 highlight, influence, overstate, prejudice
10 complexion, exaggerate, liveliness

➤ *Names of colours:*
03 jet, red, tan

04 anil, blue, ecru, fawn, gold, grey, jade, navy, pink, rose
05 amber, beige, black, brown, coral, cream, ebony, green, khaki, lilac, mauve, ochre, sepia, taupe, umber, white
06 auburn, canary, cerise, cobalt, copper, indigo, maroon, orange, purple, silver, violet, yellow
07 crimson, emerald, gentian, magenta, saffron, scarlet
08 burgundy, charcoal, chestnut, lavender, magnolia, sapphire
09 tangerine, turquoise
10 aquamarine, vermillion

➤ See also **dye**; **pigment**; **rainbow**

colourful
04 deep, rich
05 gaudy, vivid
06 bright, garish, lively
07 graphic, intense, vibrant
08 animated, exciting
11 interesting, picturesque, stimulating

colourless
03 wan
04 drab, dull, pale, tame
05 ashen, faded, plain
06 boring, dreary, sickly
07 anaemic, insipid, neutral
08 bleached
09 washed out
10 lacklustre, monochrome
11 transparent, unmemorable
13 characterless, uninteresting
15 in black and white

column
03 row
04 asta, file, item, line, list, pier, post, rank
05 Atlas, piece, shaft, story
06 parade, pillar, string
07 article, feature, obelisk, support, telamon, upright
08 caryatid, pilaster
10 procession

columnist
06 critic, editor, writer
08 reporter, reviewer
10 journalist
13 correspondent

coma
05 sopor
06 stupor, torpor, trance
08 hypnosis, lethargy, oblivion
09 catalepsy
10 drowsiness, somnolence

comatose
05 dazed
06 drowsy, sleepy, torpid
07 in a coma, out cold, stunned
08 sluggish, soporose
09 lethargic, somnolent
10 cataleptic, insensible
11 unconscious

comb
04 hunt, rake, sift, tidy
05 dress, groom, scour, sweep
06 neaten, screen, search
07 arrange, ransack, rummage

combat
03 war
04 bout, defy, duel
05 clash, fight
06 action, battle, oppose, resist
07 contest, wage war, warfare
08 conflict, do battle, fighting, skirmish, struggle
09 encounter, withstand
10 engagement, take up arms
11 hostilities

combatant
05 enemy
07 fighter, soldier, warrior
08 opponent
09 adversary, contender
10 antagonist

combative
07 warlike
08 militant
09 bellicose, truculent
10 aggressive, pugnacious
11 belligerent, contentious, quarrelsome
12 antagonistic
13 argumentative

combination
03 mix
05 blend, cross, group, union
06 fusion, merger
07 amalgam, mixture
08 alliance, compound
09 coalition, composite, syndicate, synthesis
10 collection, consortium
11 association, coalescence, confederacy, conjunction, integration, unification
12 amalgamation
13 confederation

combine
03 mix
04 ally, bind, bond, fuse, join, link, pool, stir, weld
05 admix, alloy, blend, marry, merge, unify, unite
06 mingle, team up

08 compound
09 associate, integrate
10 amalgamate, homogenize, join forces, synthesize
11 incorporate, put together
13 bring together

combustible
05 tense
06 stormy
07 charged
08 volatile
09 explosive, flammable, ignitable, sensitive
10 incendiary
11 inflammable

combustion
06 firing
07 burning
08 igniting, ignition

come
04 gain, hail, near, stem, turn
05 arise, issue, occur, reach
06 appear, arrive, attain, attend, become, dawn on, evolve, follow, happen, secure
07 achieve, advance, barge in, burst in, develop, get here, occur to, surface, think of
08 approach, draw near, pass into, remember
09 take place, transpire
10 evolve into, result from
11 be a native of, develop into, materialize, move forward, move towards

◻**come about**
05 arise, occur
06 befall, happen, result
09 take place, transpire

◻**come across**
04 find
07 run into
08 bump into, discover
09 encounter
10 chance upon, happen upon
13 stumble across

◻**come along**
05 rally
07 advance, develop, improve, recover
08 progress
09 get better
10 recuperate
11 make headway
12 make progress

◻**come apart**
04 tear
05 break, split
07 break up, crumble
08 collapse, separate

10 fall to bits
12 disintegrate, fall to pieces

◻**come between**
04 part
06 divide
07 split up
08 alienate, estrange, separate

◻**come by**
03 get
06 obtain, secure
07 acquire, procure
09 get hold of

◻**come clean**
05 admit, own up
06 reveal
07 confess, tell all
13 spill the beans

◻**come down**
06 reduce, worsen
07 decline, descend
08 decrease
10 degenerate
11 deteriorate

◻**come down on**
05 blame, chide, slate
06 berate, rebuke
07 reprove, upbraid
08 admonish, tear into
09 criticize, reprimand
13 find fault with

◻**come down to**
04 mean
08 amount to
10 boil down to
12 correspond to

◻**come down with**
03 get
05 catch
06 pick up
07 develop
08 contract
09 succumb to
10 go down with

◻**come forward**
05 offer
09 volunteer

◻**come in**
05 enter
06 arrive, finish, show up

◻**come in for**
03 get
06 endure, suffer
07 receive, undergo
13 be subjected to

◻**come into**
06 be left
07 acquire, inherit, receive

□**come off**
04 work
05 occur
06 go well, happen
07 succeed, work out
11 be effective
12 be successful

□**come out**
05 admit, end up
06 appear, finish, result
10 be produced
11 be published, become known
15 become available

□**come out with**
03 say
05 state
06 affirm
07 declare, divulge, exclaim
08 blurt out, disclose

□**come round**
04 wake
05 agree, allow, awake, yield
06 accede, relent
07 concede, recover
09 be won over
11 be persuaded
14 change your mind

□**come through**
06 endure
07 achieve, prevail, succeed, survive, triumph
09 withstand

□**come to**
04 make, wake
05 awake, equal, run to, total
07 add up to, recover
08 amount to

□**come up**
04 rise
05 arise, occur
06 crop up, happen, turn up

□**come up to**
04 meet
05 reach
08 approach, live up to
09 match up to
11 measure up to
12 make the grade

□**come up with**
05 offer
06 submit
07 advance, dream up, present, propose, suggest, think of
08 conceive
10 put forward

comeback
05 rally
06 return

07 revival
08 recovery
10 resurgence
12 reappearance

comedian
03 wag, wit
05 clown, comic, joker
07 gagster
08 humorist
11 entertainer

➤ *Famous comedians:*
03 **Fry** (Stephen), **Lom** (Herbert), **Sim** (Alastair), **Wax** (Ruby)
04 **Cook** (Peter), **Dodd** (Ken), **Hill** (Benny), **Hope** (Bob), **Idle** (Eric), **Kaye** (Danny), **Marx** (Chico), **Marx** (Groucho), **Marx** (Harpo), **Sims** (Joan), **Tati** (Jacques), **Wise** (Ernie), **Wood** (Victoria)
05 **Allen** (Woody), **Bruce** (Lenny), **Burns** (George), **Cosby** (Bill), **Elton** (Ben), **Emery** (Dick), **Hardy** (Oliver), **Henry** (Lenny), **Inman** (John), **James** (Sid), **Jones** (Terry), **Lewis** (Jerry), **Lloyd** (Harold), **Moore** (Dudley), **Oddie** (Bill), **Palin** (Michael), **Pryor** (Richard), **Sayle** (Alexei), **Starr** (Freddie)
06 **Abbott** (Bud), **Barker** (Ronnie), **Brooks** (Mel), **Cleese** (John), **Cooper** (Tommy), **Dawson** (Les), **Fields** (W C), **French** (Dawn), **Garden** (Graeme), **Howerd** (Frankie), **Keaton** (Buster), **Lauder** (Sir Harry), **Laurel** (Stan), **Laurie** (Hugh), **Martin** (Steve), **Mayall** (Rik), **Merton** (Paul), **Murphy** (Eddie), **Reeves** (Vic), **Ullman** (Tracey), **Wilder** (Gene), **Wisdom** (Norman)
07 **Aykroyd** (Dan), **Bentine** (Michael), **Bremner** (Rory), **Carrott** (Jasper), **Chaplin** (Charlie), **Chapman** (Graham), **Corbett** (Ronnie), **Enfield** (Harry), **Everett** (Kenny), **Feldman** (Marty), **Hancock** (Tony), **Handley** (Tommy), **Manning** (Bernard), **Matthau** (Walter), **Roscius**, **Secombe** (Harry),

Sellers (Peter), **Tarbuck** (Jimmy)
08 **Atkinson** (Rowan), **Connolly** (Billy), **Costello** (Lou), **Grimaldi** (Joseph), **Milligan** (Spike), **Mortimer** (Bob), **Roseanne**, **Saunders** (Jennifer), **Seinfeld** (Jerry), **The Goons**, **Williams** (Kenneth)
09 **Edmondson** (Adrian), **Fernandel**, **Morecombe** (Eric), **Whitfield** (June)
11 **Monty Python**, **Terry-Thomas**
12 **Brooke-Taylor** (Tim)
14 **Laurel and Hardy**, **Little and Large**
15 **The Marx Brothers**
➤ See also **actor**, **actress**

comedown
04 blow
07 decline, descent, let-down
08 demotion, reversal
09 deflation
10 anticlimax
14 disappointment

comedy
03 wit
05 farce
06 humour, joking, satire, sitcom
07 jesting
08 clowning, drollery, hilarity
09 burlesque, funniness, pantomime, slapstick
10 vaudeville

comely
04 fair
05 bonny, buxom
06 lovely, pretty
07 winsome
08 blooming, graceful, pleasing
10 attractive
11 good-looking

come-on
04 lure
10 allurement, enticement, inducement, temptation
13 encouragement

come-uppance
04 dues
05 merit
06 rebuke
07 deserts
08 requital
10 punishment, recompense
11 just deserts, retribution

comfort

03 aid
04 ease, help
05 cheer
06 luxury, relief, solace, soothe
07 assuage, console, enliven,
   gladden, hearten, refresh,
   relieve, succour, support
08 opulence, reassure
09 alleviate, empathize,
   encourage, wellbeing
10 condolence, invigorate,
   relaxation, sympathize
11 alleviation, consolation,
   contentment, reassurance
12 compensation, satisfaction
13 bring solace to

comfortable

04 cosy, easy, safe, snug
05 comfy, happy, roomy
06 at ease
07 opulent, relaxed, restful,
   well-off
08 affluent, well-to-do
09 agreeable, confident,
   contented, luxurious
10 convenient, prosperous

comforting

07 helpful
08 cheering, soothing
09 consoling
10 heartening, reassuring
11 consolatory, inspiriting
12 heart-warming

comic

03 wag, wit
04 rich, zany
05 clown, droll, funny, joker,
   light, witty
06 absurd, joking
07 amusing, buffoon, gagster,
   jocular
08 comedian, farcical,
   humorist, humorous
09 hilarious, laughable,
   ludicrous, priceless
11 entertainer

comical

05 droll, funny, witty
06 absurd
07 amusing
08 farcical, humorous
09 diverting, hilarious,
   laughable, ludicrous
10 ridiculous
12 entertaining

coming

03 due
04 dawn, near, next
05 birth
06 advent, future, rising
07 arrival, nearing
08 approach, aspiring,
   imminent, upcoming
09 accession, advancing,
   impending, promising
11 approaching

command

03 bid, get
04 gain, head, lead, rule, sway
05 edict, order, power, reign
06 adjure, behest, charge,
   compel, decree, demand,
   direct, govern, manage
07 bidding, control, dictate,
   mandate, mastery
08 dominion, instruct
09 authority, direction,
   directive, supervise
10 government, injunction,
   leadership, management
11 instruction, preside over,
   requirement, supervision
12 give orders to
15 superintendence

commandeer

05 seize, usurp
06 hijack
07 impound
08 arrogate
09 sequester
10 confiscate
11 appropriate, expropriate,
   requisition, sequestrate

commander

04 boss, head
05 chief
06 leader
07 admiral, captain, general,
   officer

commanding

05 lofty
06 strong
08 dominant, forceful,
   imposing, powerful,
   superior
09 assertive, confident
10 autocratic, dominating,
   impressive, peremptory
13 authoritative

commemorate

04 keep, mark
06 honour, salute
07 observe
08 remember
09 celebrate, recognize
11 immortalize, memorialize
12 pay tribute to

commemoration

06 honour, memory, salute
07 tribute
08 ceremony
09 honouring
11 celebration, remembrance

commemorative

07 marking
08 memorial, saluting
09 honouring
10 dedicatory, in honour of, in
   memoriam, in memory of
11 celebratory, remembering
12 as a tribute to
15 in remembrance of

commence

04 open
05 begin, start
06 launch
07 go ahead
08 embark on, initiate
10 inaugurate, make a start

commend

04 give, laud
05 extol, trust, yield
06 commit, praise
07 acclaim, applaud, approve,
   confide, consign, deliver,
   entrust, propose, suggest
08 advocate, hand over
13 speak highly of

commendable

05 noble
06 worthy
08 laudable
09 admirable, deserving,
   estimable, exemplary
10 creditable
11 meritorious
12 praiseworthy

commendation

06 credit, praise
07 acclaim
08 accolade, applause,
   approval, encomium
09 panegyric
11 acclamation, approbation,
   good opinion, recognition
13 encouragement
14 special mention

commensurate

03 due
07 fitting
08 adequate
10 acceptable, comparable,
   equivalent, sufficient
11 according to
13 appropriate to
14 compatible with, consistent
   with, in proportion to

comment
03 say
04 note, view
05 opine
06 remark
07 mention, observe, opinion
08 footnote, point out
09 criticism, elucidate, interject, interpret, statement
10 annotation, exposition
11 elucidation, explanation, observation
12 illustration, marginal note

commentary
05 notes
06 report, review
07 account
08 analysis, critique, exegesis, treatise
09 narration, voice-over
10 annotation, exposition
11 description, elucidation, explanation
14 interpretation

commentator
06 critic
07 exegete
08 narrator, reporter
09 annotator, commenter, expositor
11 broadcaster, interpreter

commerce
05 trade
07 dealing, traffic
08 business, dealings, exchange, industry
09 marketing, relations
13 merchandising

commercial
02 ad
04 bill, hype, plug
05 blurb, trade, venal
06 advert, jingle, notice, poster
07 display, handout, leaflet, placard, popular, trading
08 business, circular, handbill, monetary, saleable, sellable
09 marketing, mercenary, promotion, publicity
10 industrial, profitable
12 profit-making
13 advertisement, materialistic
15 entrepreneurial

commiserate
07 comfort, console
10 sympathize, understand
15 send condolences

commiseration
04 pity
06 solace

07 comfort
08 sympathy
09 compassion, condolence
11 consolation
13 consideration, understanding

commission
03 cut, fee, job
04 duty, send, task, work
05 board, order, share, trust
06 assign, charge, depute, employ, engage, errand
07 empower, mandate, rake-off, request, royalty, warrant
08 contract, function, nominate
09 allowance, authority, authorize, committee
10 assignment, deputation, employment, percentage
11 appointment, piece of work
12 advisory body

commit
02 do
04 bind, give
05 enact, trust
06 assign, decide, effect, engage, pledge
07 commend, confide, consign, deliver, deposit, entrust, execute, get up to, perform, promise
08 carry out, covenant, hand over, obligate
10 perpetrate

commitment
03 tie, vow
04 duty, word
06 effort, pledge
07 loyalty, promise
08 covenant, devotion, hard work
09 adherence, assurance, guarantee, liability
10 allegiance, dedication, engagement, obligation
11 involvement, undertaking
14 responsibility

committed
05 loyal
06 active, engagé, red-hot
07 devoted, fervent, zealous
08 diligent, involved, studious
09 dedicated
11 hardworking, industrious
12 card-carrying, enthusiastic

commodious
05 ample, large, roomy
08 spacious
09 capacious, expansive, extensive

commodity
04 item
05 goods, stock, thing, wares
07 article, produce, product
11 merchandise

common
03 low
05 crude, daily, joint, usual
06 coarse, mutual, public, shared, simple, vulgar
07 average, general, ill-bred, loutish, popular, regular, routine, uncouth
08 accepted, communal, everyday, familiar, frequent, habitual, inferior, ordinary, plebeian, workaday
09 customary, prevalent, two a penny, unrefined
10 collective, widespread
12 conventional, run-of-the-mill

commonly
07 as a rule, usually
08 normally
09 generally, routinely, typically
14 for the most part

commonplace
05 banal, stale, stock, trite
06 boring
07 humdrum, mundane, obvious, routine, worn out
08 everyday, frequent, ordinary
09 hackneyed
10 pedestrian, widespread

common sense
04 nous
05 savvy, sense
06 reason, sanity, wisdom
08 gumption, prudence
09 judgement
10 astuteness, experience, pragmatism, shrewdness
11 discernment
12 practicality, sensibleness
13 judiciousness
15 level-headedness

common-sense
04 sane, wise
05 sound
06 astute, shrewd
07 prudent
08 sensible
09 judicious, practical, pragmatic, realistic
10 discerning, reasonable
11 down-to-earth
12 matter-of-fact

commonwealth

➤ *Names of Commonwealth members*:
04 Fiji
05 Ghana, India, Kenya, Malta, Nauru, Samoa, Tonga
06 Belize, Brunei, Canada, Cyprus, Guyana, Malawi, Tuvalu, Uganda, Zambia
07 Grenada, Jamaica, Lesotho, Namibia, Nigeria, St Lucia, Vanuatu
08 Barbados, Botswana, Cameroon, Dominica, Kiribati, Malaysia, Pakistan, Sri Lanka, Tanzania, Zimbabwe
09 Australia, Mauritius, Singapore, Swaziland, The Gambia
10 Bangladesh, Mozambique, New Zealand, Seychelles, The Bahamas
11 Sierra Leone, South Africa, The Maldives
13 United Kingdom
14 Papua New Guinea, Solomon Islands
17 Antigua and Barbuda, Trinidad and Tobago
21 St Christopher and Nevis
25 St Vincent and the Grenadines

commotion
03 ado, row
04 fuss, riot, stir, to-do
06 bust-up, bustle, fracas, furore, hubbub, racket, rumpus, tumult, uproar
07 clamour, ferment, turmoil
08 ballyhoo, brouhaha, disorder, disquiet, upheaval
10 excitement, hullabaloo

communal
05 joint
06 common, public, shared
07 general
10 collective

commune
06 colony
07 kibbutz
08 converse
10 collective, fellowship, get in touch, settlement
11 co-operative, make contact

communicable
08 catching
09 infective

10 contagious, conveyable, infectious, spreadable
12 transferable
13 transmissible, transmittable

communicate
04 talk
05 phone, relay, speak, write
06 convey, impart, inform, notify, pass on, report, reveal, spread, unfold
07 contact, declare, diffuse, divulge, express, publish
08 acquaint, announce, converse, disclose, intimate, proclaim, transmit
09 broadcast, make known
10 correspond, get in touch
11 disseminate

communication
07 contact
10 connection, disclosure
11 information
12 intelligence, transmission
13 dissemination

➤ *Methods of communication*:
02 IT, TV
03 fax
04 memo, note, post, wire, word
05 cable, email, media, press, radar, radio, telex
06 gossip, letter, notice, poster, speech, tannoy, the net
07 bleeper, Braille, journal, leaflet, message, Prestel®
08 aerogram, bulletin, circular, computer, dispatch, Intelsat, intercom, junk mail, mailshot, pamphlet, postcard, telegram, teletext, wireless
09 facsimile, grapevine, mass media, megaphone, Morse code, newsflash, newspaper, satellite, semaphore, telephone
10 communiqué, dictaphone, loud-hailer, television
11 advertising, chain letter, Telemessage®, teleprinter, the Internet
12 broadcasting, conversation, press release, sign language, walkie-talkie, World Wide Web

communicative
04 free, open
05 frank
06 candid, chatty
07 voluble
08 friendly, outgoing, sociable

09 expansive, extrovert, talkative
10 unreserved
11 forthcoming, informative

communion
04 Mass
05 unity
06 accord
07 concord, empathy, harmony
08 affinity, sympathy
09 Eucharist, Sacrament
10 fellowship
11 intercourse, Lord's Supper

communiqué
06 report
07 message
08 bulletin, dispatch
09 newsflash, statement
12 announcement
13 communication

communism
06 Maoism
07 Marxism, Titoism
08 Leninism
09 socialism, Stalinism
10 Bolshevism, Trotskyism
11 revisionism
12 collectivism
15 totalitarianism

community
05 group, state
06 colony, people, public
07 commune, kibbutz, society
08 district, locality, populace
09 residents
10 fellowship, population
13 neighbourhood

commute
05 remit
06 adjust, reduce, soften
07 curtail, journey, lighten, shorten, shuttle
08 decrease, mitigate
12 travel to work

commuter
09 passenger, traveller
11 strap-hanger, suburbanite

compact
04 bond, cram, deal, firm, neat, pact, tamp
05 brief, close, dense, pithy, short, small, solid, terse
06 little, pocket, treaty
07 bargain, concise, entente, flatten, squeeze
08 alliance, compress, condense, contract, covenant, succinct

09 agreement, concordat,
   indenture, press down
10 compressed, settlement
11 consolidate, transaction

companion
03 pal
04 aide, ally, mate
05 buddy, crony
06 escort, fellow, friend
07 comrade, consort, partner
08 follower, intimate, sidekick
09 associate, attendant,
   colleague, confidant
10 accomplice, confidante
11 confederate

companionable
06 genial
07 affable, amiable
08 familiar, friendly, informal,
   outgoing, sociable
09 congenial, convivial
10 gregarious
11 neighbourly, sympathetic
12 approachable

companionship
07 company, rapport, support
08 intimacy, sympathy
10 fellowship, friendship
11 association, camaraderie,
   comradeship, contubernal
12 conviviality, togetherness
13 esprit de corps

company
03 PLC, set
04 band, body, crew, firm, team
05 crowd, party, troop, trust
06 cartel, circle, guests, troupe
07 callers, concern, contact,
   society, support
08 assembly, business,
   ensemble, presence, visitors
09 gathering, syndicate
10 attendance, consortium,
   fellowship, subsidiary
11 association, comradeship,
   corporation, partnership
12 conglomerate, conviviality
13 establishment, multinational

comparable
04 akin, like
05 alike, equal
07 cognate, related, similar
08 parallel
09 analogous
10 equivalent, tantamount
12 commensurate,
   proportional
13 corresponding,
   proportionate

comparative
08 relative

compare
04 link
05 equal, liken, match, weigh
06 equate
07 balance, measure
08 contrast, parallel, resemble
09 analogize, correlate,
   juxtapose

comparison
07 analogy
08 contrast, likeness, parallel
10 similarity
11 correlation, differences,
   distinction, resemblance
12 relationship
13 comparability,
   juxtaposition
15 differentiation

compartment
03 bay
04 area, cell, part
05 berth, booth, niche, stall
06 alcove, carrel, locker
07 chamber, cubicle, section
08 carriage, category, division
09 cubbyhole, partition
10 pigeonhole

compass
04 area, zone
05 field, limit, range, reach,
   realm, scale, scope, space
06 bounds, circle, extent, limits,
   realms, sphere
07 circuit, stretch
08 boundary
09 enclosure

compassion
04 care, pity
05 mercy
06 sorrow
07 concern
08 clemency, kindness,
   leniency, sympathy
10 condolence, tenderness
11 benevolence
13 consideration, fellow-
   feeling, understanding

compassionate
06 caring, gentle, humane,
   kindly, tender
07 clement, lenient, pitying
08 merciful
10 benevolent, supportive
11 kind-hearted, sympathetic,
   warm-hearted
12 humanitarian
13 understanding

compatible
06 suited
07 similar
08 matching, suitable
09 consonant, in harmony
10 consistent, harmonious,
   like-minded, well-suited
11 conformable, sympathetic,
   well-matched

compatriot
10 countryman
12 countrywoman
13 fellow citizen

compel
04 make, urge
05 bully, drive, force, impel
06 coerce, lean on, oblige
07 dragoon
08 browbeat, bulldoze, insist
   on, pressure
09 constrain, press-gang,
   strongarm
10 intimidate, pressurize
14 put the screws on

compelling
06 cogent, urgent
07 weighty
08 forceful, gripping,
   mesmeric, riveting
09 absorbing
10 compulsive, convincing,
   overriding, persuasive
11 enthralling, irrefutable
12 irresistible, spellbinding

compendium
06 digest, manual
07 summary
08 handbook, synopsis
09 companion, vade-mecum

compensate
05 atone, repay
06 cancel, offset, redeem,
   refund, reward
07 balance, nullify, redress,
   restore, satisfy
08 make good
09 indemnify, make up for,
   reimburse
10 counteract, make amends,
   recompense, remunerate
14 make reparation

compensation
06 amends, refund, reward
07 comfort, damages,
   payment, redress
08 requital
09 atonement, indemnity,
   repayment
10 recompense, reparation
11 restitution, restoration

12 remuneration, satisfaction
13 reimbursement
15 indemnification

compère
02 MC
04 host
05 emcee
09 anchorman, presenter
11 anchorwoman

compete
03 run, vie
04 race
05 enter, fight, rival
06 battle, jostle, oppose, strive
07 contend, contest, go in for
08 struggle, take part
09 challenge
11 participate, pit yourself

competence
05 skill
07 ability, fitness
08 aptitude, capacity, facility
09 expertise, technique
10 capability, experience
11 proficiency

competent
03 fit
04 able
05 adept, equal
06 expert
07 capable, skilled, trained
08 adequate, suitable
09 efficient, qualified
10 acceptable, proficient
11 appropriate, experienced
12 accomplished, satisfactory

competition
03 cup
04 bout, meet, quiz, race
05 event, field, match, vying
06 rivals, strife
07 contest, rivalry
08 conflict, struggle
09 challenge, opponents
10 contention, tournament
11 challengers, competitors
12 championship

competitive
04 keen
05 pushy
09 ambitious, combative, cut-throat, dog-eat-dog

competitiveness
07 rat race, rivalry
08 keenness
09 pugnacity, pushiness
10 aggression, antagonism

13 ambitiousness, combativeness

competitor
05 rival
06 player
07 entrant
08 emulator, opponent
09 adversary, candidate, contender
10 antagonist, challenger, contestant, opposition
11 competition, participant

compilation
04 opus, work
05 album
06 corpus
07 omnibus
08 treasury
09 amassment, anthology, collation, selection
10 assemblage, collection, compendium, miscellany

compile
04 edit
05 amass
06 garner, gather
07 arrange, collate, collect, compose, marshal
08 assemble, organize

complacency
05 pride
07 triumph
08 gloating, pleasure, smugness
11 contentment
12 satisfaction

complacent
04 smug
05 proud
07 pleased
08 gloating
09 contented, satisfied
10 triumphant
11 self-assured, unconcerned
13 self-righteous, self-satisfied

complain
03 nag
04 ache, beef, carp, fuss, moan
05 bleat, gripe, groan, whine
06 bemoan, bewail, grouse, repine, whinge
07 grumble, protest
08 be in pain, feel pain
09 belly-ache, criticize
10 suffer from
11 kick up a fuss, remonstrate
15 have a bone to pick

complainer
06 moaner, whiner

07 fuss-pot, grouser, niggler, whinger
08 grumbler
09 nit-picker
10 belly-acher

complaint
04 moan
05 gripe, upset
06 charge, grouse, malady
07 ailment, censure, disease, grumble, illness, malaise, protest, trouble
08 disorder, sickness
09 annoyance, condition, criticism, grievance, objection
10 accusation, affliction

complaisant
06 docile
07 amiable
08 amenable, biddable, obedient, obliging
09 agreeable, compliant, tractable
10 solicitous
11 conformable, deferential
12 conciliatory
13 accommodating

complement
03 sum
05 crown, match, quota, total
06 set off
08 complete, entirety, round off, totality
09 accessory, aggregate, allowance, companion
10 completion, go well with
11 counterpart
12 consummation
14 go well together

complementary
06 fellow
08 matching
09 companion, finishing
10 completing, perfecting, reciprocal
13 corresponding

complete
03 cap, end
04 done, full, over
05 close, crown, ended, total, utter, whole
06 answer, clinch, entire, fill in, finish, fulfil, intact, wind up
07 achieve, execute, fill out, perfect, perform, plenary, realize, settled
08 absolute, conclude, detailed, finalize, finished,

outright, round off, thorough, unbroken
09 concluded, discharge, downright, finalized, out-and-out, polish off, terminate, undivided
10 accomplish, consummate, exhaustive, unabridged
11 unmitigated
13 comprehensive

completely
05 fully, quite
06 in full, wholly
07 solidly, totally, utterly
08 entirely
09 every inch, perfectly
10 absolutely, altogether, thoroughly
12 heart and soul
13 root and branch
14 in every respect

completion
03 end
05 close
06 finish
08 fruition
09 discharge, execution
10 conclusion, fulfilment, perfection, settlement
11 achievement, culmination, realization, termination
12 consummation, finalization

complex
05 mixed, thing
06 hang-up, phobia, scheme, system, varied
07 devious, diverse, network
08 compound, disorder, fixation, involved, multiple, neurosis, ramified, tortuous
09 Byzantine, composite, difficult, elaborate, institute, intricate, obsession, structure
10 circuitous, convoluted
11 development
12 organization
13 establishment, preoccupation

complexion
04 look, skin, tone, type
05 guise, light, stamp
06 aspect, colour, nature
09 character, colouring
10 appearance
12 pigmentation

complexity
09 intricacy

11 convolution, deviousness, diverseness, elaboration, involvement
12 complication, entanglement, multiplicity, ramification, repercussion

compliance
06 assent
08 yielding
09 agreement, deference, obedience, passivity
10 submission
11 concurrence
12 acquiescence, complaisance
14 submissiveness

compliant
06 docile
07 passive, pliable
08 biddable, obedient, yielding
09 agreeable, tractable
10 submissive
11 acquiescent, complaisant, deferential, subservient
13 accommodating

complicate
05 mix up
06 jumble, muddle, tangle
07 confuse, involve
08 compound, entangle
09 elaborate

complicated
06 fiddly
07 complex, cryptic
08 involved, puzzling, tortuous
09 difficult, elaborate, intricate
10 convoluted, perplexing
11 problematic

complication
03 web
04 snag
06 tangle
07 mixture, problem
08 drawback, obstacle
09 confusion, intricacy
10 complexity, difficulty
11 convolution, elaboration
12 ramification, repercussion

complicity
08 abetment, approval
09 agreement, collusion, knowledge
10 connivance
11 concurrence, involvement

compliment
04 laud
05 extol
06 admire, eulogy, homage, honour, praise, salute

07 applaud, commend, devoirs, flatter, tribute
08 accolade, approval, encomium, eulogize, flattery, respects
09 greetings, laudation
10 admiration, best wishes, felicitate, salutation
11 speak well of
12 commendation, congratulate, felicitation
13 speak highly of
15 congratulations

complimentary
04 free
06 gratis
08 admiring, courtesy
09 approving
10 eulogistic, favourable, flattering, on the house
11 panegyrical
12 appreciative, commendatory

comply
04 meet, obey
05 agree, all in, defer, yield
06 accede, accord, assent, follow, fulfil, oblige, submit
07 abide by, conform, consent, observe, perform, satisfy
09 acquiesce, discharge
11 accommodate

component
03 bit
04 item, part, unit
05 basic, piece
06 factor, module
07 element, section
08 inherent, integral
09 essential, intrinsic, spare part
10 ingredient

comport
03 act
04 bear
05 carry
06 acquit, behave, deport
07 conduct, perform

compose
04 calm, form, make
05 frame, quiet, still, write
06 create, devise, invent, make up, pacify, settle, soothe
07 arrange, assuage, collect, concoct, control, produce
08 assemble, calm down
10 constitute

composed
04 calm, cool
06 placid, sedate, serene
07 relaxed

08 tranquil
09 collected, confident, unruffled, unworried
10 calmed down, controlled
11 level-headed, unflappable
13 imperturbable, quietened down, self-possessed
14 self-controlled
15 cool as a cucumber

composer
04 bard, poet
05 maker
06 author, writer
07 creator
08 arranger, musician, producer
09 songsmith, tunesmith
10 originator, songwriter

➤ *Names of composers*:
03 **Bax** (Sir Arnold)
04 **Arne** (Thomas), **Bach** (Johann Sebastian), **Berg** (Alban), **Byrd** (William), **Cage** (John), **Ives** (Charles), **Orff** (Carl)
05 **Bizet** (Georges), **Bliss** (Sir Arthur), **Dukas** (Paul), **Elgar** (Sir Edward), **Falla** (Manuel de), **Fauré** (Gabriel), **Glass** (Philip), **Gluck** (Christoph), **Grieg** (Edvard), **Haydn** (Joseph), **Holst** (Gustav), **Liszt** (Franz), **Lully** (Jean Baptiste), **Parry** (Sir Hubert), **Ravel** (Maurice), **Satie** (Erik), **Verdi** (Giuseppe), **Weber** (Carl Maria von)
06 **Bartók** (Béla), **Boulez** (Pierre), **Brahms** (Johannes), **Casals** (Pablo), **Chopin** (Frédéric), **Coates** (Eric), **Delius** (Frederick), **Dvořák** (Antonín), **Franck** (César), **Glinka** (Mikhail), **Gounod** (Charles), **Handel** (George Frideric), **Ligeti** (György), **Mahler** (Gustav), **Mozart** (Wolfgang Amadeus), **Rameau** (Jean Philippe), **Rubbra** (Edmund), **Varèse** (Edgard), **Wagner** (Richard), **Walton** (Sir William), **Webern** (Anton von)
07 **Albéniz** (Isaac), **Bellini** (Vincenzo), **Berlioz** (Hector), **Borodin** (Alexander), **Britten** (Benjamin), **Copland** (Aaron), **Corelli**
(Arcangelo), **Debussy** (Claude), **Delibes** (Léo), **Dowland** (John), **Janáček** (Leos), **Menotti** (Gian-Carlo), **Nielsen** (Carl), **Poulenc** (Francis), **Puccini** (Giacomo), **Purcell** (Henry), **Rossini** (Gioacchino), **Salieri** (Antonio), **Shankar** (Ravi), **Smetana** (Bedrich), **Strauss** (Johann), **Strauss** (Richard), **Tavener** (John), **Tippett** (Sir Michael), **Vivaldi** (Antonio)
08 **Berkeley** (Sir Lennox), **Bruckner** (Anton), **Couperin** (François), **Grainger** (Percy), **Hoffmann** (Ernst Theodor Wilhelm), **Holliger** (Heinz), **Honegger** (Arthur), **Massenet** (Jules), **Messiaen** (Olivier), **Respighi** (Ottorino), **Schubert** (Franz), **Schumann** (Robert), **Scriabin** (Aleksandr), **Sibelius** (Jean), **Sullivan** (Sir Arthur), **Williams** (John)
09 **Beethoven** (Ludwig van), **Boulanger** (Nadia), **Buxtehude** (Diderik), **Donizetti** (Gaetano), **Hindemith** (Paul), **Meyerbeer** (Giacomo), **Offenbach** (Jacques), **Pachelbel** (Johann), **Prokofiev** (Sergei), **Scarlatti** (Alessandro), **Scarlatti** (Domenico), **Tortelier** (Paul)
10 **Birtwistle** (Sir Harrison), **Monteverdi** (Claudio), **Mussorgsky** (Modeste), **Praetorius** (Michael), **Rubinstein** (Anton), **Saint-Saëns** (Camille), **Schoenberg** (Arnold), **Stravinsky** (Igor), **Villa-Lobos** (Heitor)
11 **Humperdinck** (Engelbert), **Leoncavallo** (Ruggiero), **Mendelssohn** (Felix), **Rachmaninov** (Sergei), **Stockhausen** (Karlheinz), **Tchaikovsky** (Piotr), **Theodorakis** (Mikis)
12 **Shostakovich** (Dmitri)
13 **Khatchaturian** (Aram), **Maxwell Davies** (Sir Peter)
14 **Rimsky-Korsakov** (Nikolai)
15 **Vaughan Williams** (Ralph)
➤ See also **music**

composite
05 alloy, blend, fused, mixed
06 fusion
07 amalgam, blended, complex, mixture
08 compound, pastiche
09 patchwork, synthesis
11 agglutinate, combination, synthesized
12 conglomerate

composition
04 form, opus, poem, work
05 novel, opera, piece, story
06 design, layout, make-up
07 balance, drawing, harmony, mixture, picture, writing
08 creation, devising, exercise, painting, symphony
09 arranging, character, formation, invention, structure, work of art
10 concoction, consonance, production, proportion
11 arrangement, combination, compilation, formulation
12 conformation, constitution, organization

compost
04 peat
05 humus, mulch
06 manure
08 dressing
10 fertilizer

composure
04 calm, ease
05 poise
06 aplomb
07 dignity
08 coolness, serenity
09 assurance, placidity
10 confidence, equanimity
11 impassivity, self-control
12 tranquillity

compound
03 mix, pen
04 fold, fuse, yard
05 add to, alloy, blend, court, fused, mixed, pound, unite
06 corral, fusion, hybrid, medley, mingle, worsen
07 amalgam, combine, complex, magnify, mixture, paddock
08 coalesce, heighten, increase, multiple, stackade

09 admixture, aggravate, composite, enclosure, intensify, intricate, synthesis
10 amalgamate, complicate, exacerbate, synthesize
11 combination, composition, intermingle, synthesized
12 amalgamation, conglomerate

comprehend
03 see
04 know, twig
05 cover, grasp
06 fathom, take in
07 contain, discern, embrace, include, involve, realize
08 comprise, perceive
09 encompass, penetrate
10 appreciate, understand

comprehensible
05 clear, lucid, plain
06 simple
08 coherent, explicit
09 graspable
10 accessible
11 conceivable, discernible
12 intelligible
14 understandable
15 straightforward

comprehension
03 ken
05 grasp, sense
07 insight
09 judgement, knowledge
10 conception, perception
11 discernment, realization
12 appreciation, intelligence
13 understanding

comprehensive
04 full, wide
05 all-in, broad
07 blanket, general, overall
08 complete, thorough
09 extensive, inclusive
10 exhaustive, widespread
14 across-the-board

compress
03 jam
04 cram, tamp
05 crush, press, stuff, wedge
06 impact, reduce, squash
07 abridge, astrict, compact, flatten, shorten, squeeze
08 condense, contract
09 coarctate, constrict, summarize, synopsize
10 abbreviate, pressurize
11 concentrate, consolidate

comprise
06 embody, make up, take in

07 compose, contain, embrace, include, involve
09 consist of, encompass
10 comprehend, constitute
11 incorporate

compromise
05 adapt, agree, shame
06 adjust, damage, expose, settle, weaken
07 balance, bargain, concede, imperil, involve
08 endanger, trade-off
09 agreement, arbitrate, discredit, implicate, mediation, negotiate, prejudice, undermine
10 concession, settlement
11 give and take, meet halfway, negotiation
13 accommodation, understanding

compulsion
04 need, urge
05 drive, force
06 demand, desire, duress
07 impulse, longing
08 coercion, pressure
09 necessity, obsession
10 obligation, temptation

compulsive
06 hooked, urgent
07 driving
08 addicted, gripping, habitual, hardened, hopeless, mesmeric, riveting
09 absorbing, dependent, incurable, obsessive
10 compelling
11 enthralling, fascinating
12 irresistible, overpowering, overwhelming, pathological, spellbinding

compulsory
03 set
06 forced
07 binding
08 required
09 de rigueur, essential, mandatory, necessary, requisite
10 obligatory, stipulated

compunction
05 guilt, qualm, shame
06 regret, sorrow, unease
07 remorse
09 misgiving, penitence
10 contrition, hesitation, repentance, uneasiness

compute
03 sum

04 rate
05 add up, count, tally, total
06 assess, figure, reckon
07 count up, measure
08 estimate, evaluate
09 calculate, enumerate

computer
➤ *Computer terms:*
02 PC, VR
03 bit, CPU, DOS, DTP, FAQ, GUI, ISP, RAM, ROM, VDU, Web, WWW
04 boot, byte, chip, data, disk, game, HTML, icon, ISDN, menu, UNIX®
05 ASCII, BASIC, CD-ROM, COBOL, email, macro, modem, mouse, MS-DOS®, pixel, virus
06 backup, buffer, cursor, DVD-ROM, format, laptop, memory, screen, server, the Net, the Web, toggle, window
07 browser, FORTRAN, hacking, monitor, network, Pentium®, printer, program, toolbar, upgrade, Web page, Web site, Windows®, WYSIWYG
08 Applemac®, bookmark, chat room, databank, database, emoticon, firewall, freeware, function, gigabyte, graphics, hard disk, hardware, home page, joystick, keyboard, kilobyte, megabyte, mouse mat, software, template, terminal, user name, Wordstar®
09 character, directory, disk drive, e-commerce, hypertext, interface, mainframe, newsgroup, scrolling, shareware, video game
10 domain name, floppy disk, multimedia, netiquette, peripheral
11 cut and paste, motherboard, screen saver, silicon chip, the Internet, WordPerfect®, work station
12 laser printer, magnetic disk, search engine, spellchecker, World Wide Web
13 file extension, ink-jet printer, user interface
14 electronic mail, microprocessor, read only

memory, virtual reality,
word-processing
15 operating system

➤ *Names of computer
scientists*:

04 **Cray** (Seymour), **Jobs**
(Steven), **Zuse** (Konrad)
05 **Gates** (William Henry
'Bill'), **Olsen** (Kenneth
Harry), **Sugar** (Alan)
06 **Amdahl** (Gene Myron),
Backus (John), **Eckert**
(John Presper), **Michie**
(Donald), **Turing** (Alan),
Wilkes (Maurice Vincent)
07 **Babbage** (Charles),
Mauchly (John William),
Shannon (Claude Elwood),
Stibitz (George Robert)
08 **Atansoff** (John Vincent),
Lovelace (Ada, Countess
of), **Shockley** (William
Bradford), **Sinclair** (Sir
Clive)
09 **Forrester** (Jay Wright),
Hollerith (Herman)
10 **Von Neumann** (John)
➤ See also **scientist**

comrade
03 pal
04 aide, ally, mate
05 buddy, crony
06 escort, fellow, friend
07 consort, partner
08 follower, intimate, sidekick
09 associate, colleague,
companion, confidant
10 accomplice, confidante
11 confederate

con
02 do
04 dupe, hoax, rook, scam
05 bluff, cheat, fraud, trick
06 fiddle, fleece, racket, rip off
07 deceive, defraud, swindle
08 hoodwink, inveigle
09 bamboozle
11 double-cross

concatenation
05 chain, nexus, trail, train
06 course, series, string, thread
07 linking
08 progress, sequence
10 connection, succession
11 progression
12 interlinking, interlocking

concave
06 cupped, hollow, sunken
07 scooped
08 hollowed, indented

09 depressed, excavated,
incurvate

conceal
04 bury, hide, mask, veil
05 cloak, cover, stash
06 hush up, screen, shroud
07 cover up, obscure, secrete
08 disguise, keep dark,
submerge, suppress
09 keep quiet, whitewash
10 camouflage, keep secret

concealed
06 covert, hidden, latent, unseen
07 covered
08 screened
09 disguised

concealment
04 mask, veil
05 cloak, cover
06 hiding, screen, shroud
07 cover-up, hideout, secrecy
08 disguise, hideaway
09 secretion, whitewash
10 camouflage, protection
11 smokescreen, suppression

concede
03 own
04 cede
05 admit, allow, grant, yield
06 accede, accept, give up
07 confess, forfeit
08 hand over
09 recognize, surrender
10 relinquish
11 acknowledge

conceit
05 pride
06 vanity
07 egotism, swagger
08 self-love
09 arrogance, vainglory
10 narcissism
11 complacency, haughtiness
12 boastfulness
13 conceitedness
14 self-importance

conceited
04 smug, vain
05 cocky, proud
07 haughty, stuck-up
08 arrogant, boastful,
immodest, puffed up
09 big-headed
10 complacent
11 egotistical, toffee-nosed
12 narcissistic, supercilious,
vainglorious
13 self-important, self-satisfied,
swollen-headed
14 full of yourself

conceivable
06 likely
07 tenable
08 credible, possible, probable
09 thinkable
10 believable, imaginable

conceive
05 fancy, grasp, think
06 create, design, devise, invent
07 believe, develop, imagine,
picture, produce, realize
08 contrive, envisage, perceive
09 formulate, originate,
reproduce, visualize
10 appreciate, come up with,
comprehend, understand

concentrate
05 focus, juice, rivet, think
06 apozem, attend, centre,
distil, elixir, gather, reduce
07 cluster, collect, essence,
extract, thicken
08 boil down, compress,
condense, converge
09 decoction, decocture,
evaporate, intensify
10 centralize, congregate
12 distillation, pay attention
13 apply yourself
15 devote attention

concentrated
04 deep, hard, rich
05 dense
06 all-out, strong
07 intense, reduced
08 vigorous
09 condensed, intensive,
thickened, undiluted
10 compressed, evaporated

concentration
04 heed, mind
05 crowd
07 cluster
08 focusing, grouping
09 attention, intensity,
reduction, thickness
10 absorption, collection
11 application, boiling-down,
compression, convergence,
deep thought, evaporation
12 accumulation, distillation

concept
04 idea, plan, view
05 image
06 notion, theory
07 picture, thought
10 hypothesis, impression
13 visualization

conception
04 clue, idea, plan, view

05 birth, image
06 design, notion, origin, outset, theory
07 inkling, picture, thought
09 beginning, formation, invention, knowledge
10 hypothesis, impression, initiation, perception
11 fecundation, origination
12 impregnation, inauguration, insemination, reproduction
13 visualization

concern

03 job
04 busy, care, duty, heed, task
05 alarm, field, touch, worry
06 affair, affect, bear on, bother, charge, devote, matter, regard, strain, unease
07 anxiety, apply to, company, disturb, involve, perturb, problem, refer to, trouble
08 business, disquiet, distress, interest, relate to
09 attention, syndicate
10 enterprise
11 corporation, disturbance, involvement, make anxious, make worried, partnership
12 organization, perturbation

concerned

04 kind
05 upset
06 caring, uneasy
07 anxious, helpful, related, unhappy, worried
08 affected, bothered, gracious, involved, troubled
09 attentive, connected, disturbed, perturbed, sensitive, unselfish
10 altruistic, implicated, interested, thoughtful
11 considerate
12 apprehensive

concerning

02 re
05 about
07 apropos
09 as regards, regarding
10 relating to, respecting
11 referring to
12 with regard to
13 with respect to

concert

03 gig
04 prom, show
05 union
06 accord, soirée, unison
07 concord, harmony, recital
09 agreement, unanimity

10 appearance, consonance, engagement, jam session
11 concordance, performance

concerted

05 joint
06 shared, united
08 combined
10 collective
12 concentrated
13 collaborative

concession

03 cut, sop
05 grant, right
06 ceding, favour
08 decrease, giving-up, handover, yielding
09 admission, allowance, exception, privilege, reduction, sacrifice
10 adjustment, compromise
11 recognition

conciliate

06 disarm, pacify, soothe
07 appease, mollify, placate, satisfy
09 reconcile

conciliation

09 placation
11 appeasement, peacemaking
12 pacification
13 mollification
14 reconciliation

conciliator

04 dove
08 mediator
10 negotiator, peacemaker, reconciler
12 intermediary

conciliatory

06 irenic
07 pacific
09 appeasing, peaceable, placatory
10 mollifying
11 peacemaking
12 pacificatory
14 reconciliatory

concise

05 brief, crisp, pithy, short, terse
07 compact, summary
08 abridged, succinct, synoptic
09 condensed
10 compressed, to the point
11 abbreviated, compendious
12 epigrammatic

conclave

05 cabal
06 parley, powwow

07 council, meeting
08 assembly
10 conference
13 confabulation

conclude

03 end
05 cease, close, infer, judge
06 assume, clinch, decide, deduce, effect, finish, gather, reason, reckon, settle, wind up, wrap up
07 arrange, pull off, resolve, suppose, surmise, work out
08 complete
09 culminate, determine, establish, negotiate, polish off, terminate
11 come to an end, discontinue, draw to an end
12 bring to an end

conclusion

03 end
05 close, issue
06 finale, finish, result, upshot
07 opinion, outcome, verdict
08 decision, settling, solution
09 deduction, inference, judgement
10 completion, conviction, pulling-off, resolution, settlement, working-out
11 arrangement, consequence, culmination, termination
12 consummation

conclusive

05 clear, final
08 decisive, definite, ultimate
10 convincing, definitive,
11 irrefutable
12 indisputable, unanswerable

concoct

03 mix
04 brew, cook, make, plan, plot
05 blend, hatch
06 cook up, devise, invent
07 develop, prepare
08 contrive, rustle up
09 fabricate, formulate

concoction

04 brew
06 potion
07 mixture
08 compound, creation
11 combination, preparation

concomitant

09 attendant, secondary
10 co-existent, concurrent, incidental, side effect
11 associative, synchronous

12 accompanying, coincidental, conterminous, contributing, simultaneous
13 accompaniment
15 contemporaneous

concord
05 amity, peace
06 accord, treaty, unison
07 compact, entente, harmony
09 agreement, consensus, unanimity
10 consonance, friendship

concourse
04 hall
05 crowd, crush, foyer, lobby, plaza, press, swarm
06 lounge, piazza, throng
07 meeting
08 assembly, entrance
09 gathering, multitude

concrete
04 firm, real
05 solid
06 actual
07 factual, genuine, visible
08 definite, material, physical, positive, specific, tangible
11 perceptible, substantial

concubine
05 leman, lover
07 lorette
08 mistress, paramour
09 courtesan, kept woman
11 apple-squire

concupiscence
04 lust
06 desire, libido
07 lechery
08 appetite, lewdness
09 horniness, lubricity
11 lustfulness
14 lasciviousness, libidinousness

concupiscent
04 lewd
05 horny
07 lustful
09 lecherous
10 lascivious, libidinous, lubricious

concur
05 agree
06 accord, assent, comply
07 approve, consent
09 acquiesce, co-operate, harmonize

concurrence
06 assent
08 approval
09 agreement, synchrony

10 acceptance
11 association, coexistence, coincidence, convergence
12 acquiescence, common ground, simultaneity

concurrent
10 coexistent, coexisting, coincident, coinciding
11 concomitant, synchronous
12 simultaneous
15 contemporaneous

condemn
03 ban, bar
04 damn, doom, slam
05 blame, force, judge, slate
06 berate, punish, revile
07 censure, consign, convict, reprove, upbraid
08 demolish, denounce, reproach, sentence
09 castigate, criticize
12 declare unfit

condemnation
05 blame
07 censure, reproof
08 reproach, sentence
09 criticism, damnation, judgement
10 conviction, thumbs-down
11 castigation
12 denunciation

condemnatory
08 accusing, critical
09 damnatory
10 accusatory, censorious
11 deprecatory, reprobatory
12 denunciatory, discouraging, proscriptive, unfavourable
13 incriminating

condensation
06 digest, précis
08 synopsis
09 reduction
11 abridgement, boiling-down, compression, contraction, curtailment, evaporation
12 distillation, liquefaction
13 concentration

condense
03 cut
06 distil, précis, reduce
07 abridge, compact, curtail, cut down, shorten, thicken
08 boil down, compress
09 evaporate, summarize
10 abbreviate, deliquesce
11 concentrate, encapsulate

condensed
03 cut

06 strong
07 clotted, compact, concise, cut down, reduced
09 curtailed, shortened, thickened, undiluted
10 abstracted, coagulated, compressed, contracted, evaporated, summarized
12 concentrated

condescend
05 deign, stoop
06 see fit
09 patronize
10 talk down to
13 lower yourself

condescending
05 lofty
06 lordly, snooty
07 haughty, stuck-up
08 snobbish, superior
09 imperious
10 disdainful
11 patronizing, toffee-nosed
12 supercilious

condescension
04 airs
07 disdain
09 loftiness
10 lordliness
11 haughtiness, superiority
12 snobbishness

condition
04 form, nick, rule, tone, tune
05 equip, groom, limit, mould, order, prime, rider, set-up, shape, state, terms
06 adjust, demand, fettle, health, kilter, malady, milieu, plight, revive
07 ailment, climate, context, disease, factors, fitness, illness, prepare, problem, proviso, restore, setting
08 accustom, quandary, weakness
09 brainwash, complaint, essential, influence, necessity, provision, situation, way of life
10 atmosphere, background, limitation, obligation
11 environment, familiarize, predicament, requirement, restriction, stipulation
12 indoctrinate, prerequisite, surroundings, working order
13 state of health

conditional
04 tied
07 limited, subject
08 relative
09 dependent, qualified
10 contingent, restricted
11 provisional

condolence
04 pity
07 support
08 sympathy
10 compassion
11 consolation
13 commiseration

condom
06 rubber, sheath
07 Femidom®, johnnie
12 French letter

condone
05 allow, brook
06 excuse, ignore, pardon
07 forgive, let pass
08 overlook, tolerate
15 turn a blind eye to

conducive
06 useful
07 helpful, leading, tending
09 promoting
10 beneficial, favourable, productive
11 encouraging
12 advantageous

conduct
02 do
03 act, run
04 bear, lead, show, take, ways
05 bring, carry, chair, guide, pilot, steer, usher
06 acquit, behave, direct, escort, handle, manage
07 actions, bearing, comport, control, manners, perform
08 attitude, carry out, guidance, organize
09 accompany, behaviour, demeanour, operation
10 administer, deportment, leadership, management
11 comportment, orchestrate, supervision

conductor
➤ *Names of conductors:*
04 **Böhm** (Karl), **Wood** (Sir Henry)
05 **Boult** (Sir Adrian), **Bülow** (Hans von), **Davis** (Sir Colin), **Hallé** (Sir Charles), **Kempe** (Rudolf), **Solti** (Sir Georg), **Sousa** (John Philip)

06 **Abbado** (Claudio), **Previn** (André), **Rattle** (Sir Simon), **Walter** (Bruno)
07 **Beecham** (Sir Thomas), **Haitink** (Bernard), **Karajan** (Herbert von), **Lambert** (Constant), **Richter** (Hans), **Sargent** (Sir Malcolm)
08 **Goossens** (Sir Eugene)
09 **Ashkenazy** (Vladimir), **Barenboim** (Daniel), **Bernstein** (Leonard), **Klemperer** (Otto), **Tortelier** (Paul), **Toscanini** (Arturo)
10 **Barbirolli** (Sir John)
11 **Furtwängler** (Wilhelm)
12 **Rostropovich** (Mstislav)
➤ See also **music**

conduit
04 duct, main, pipe, tube
05 canal, chute, ditch, drain, flume
06 gutter, tunnel
07 channel, culvert, passage
08 waterway
10 passageway
11 watercourse

confectionery
04 rock
05 candy, fudge
06 bonbon, sweets, tablet
07 toffees, truffle
10 chocolates

confederacy
05 union
06 league
07 compact
08 alliance
09 coalition
10 federation
11 partnership

confederate
04 ally
06 allied, friend, united
07 abettor, federal, partner
08 combined, federate
09 accessory, associate, colleague, supporter
10 accomplice, associated

confederation
05 union
06 league
07 compact
08 alliance
09 coalition
10 federation
11 association, partnership
12 amalgamation

confer
04 give, lend, talk
05 award, grant
06 accord, bestow, impart
07 consult, discuss, present
08 converse
10 deliberate

conference
05 forum
06 debate, summit
07 meeting, seminar
08 congress, dialogue
09 symposium
10 colloquium, discussion
11 convocation

confess
03 own
05 admit, grant, own up
06 assert, expose
07 concede, declare, divulge, profess, tell all, unbosom
08 disclose, unburden
09 come clean, make known
11 accept blame, acknowledge
13 spill the beans
15 get off your chest

confession
08 exposure, owning-up
09 admission, assertion
10 disclosure, divulgence, profession, revelation
11 declaration, unburdening
15 acknowledgement

confidant, confidante
03 pal
04 mate
05 crony
06 friend
08 intimate
09 companion
11 bosom friend, close friend

confide
04 tell
05 admit
06 impart, reveal
07 confess, divulge
08 disclose, intimate, unburden
11 tell a secret
15 get off your chest

confidence
05 faith, poise, trust
06 aplomb, belief, secret
07 courage
08 boldness, calmness, credence, intimacy, reliance
09 certainty, composure
10 conviction, dependence
12 self-reliance
13 self-assurance
14 self-possession

□in confidence
08 in secret
09 entre nous, in privacy, in private, privately
15 between you and me

confident
04 bold, calm, cool, sure
06 upbeat
07 assured, certain
08 composed, positive
09 dauntless, unabashed
10 courageous, optimistic
11 self-assured, self-reliant
12 unhesitating
13 self-possessed
14 sure of yourself

confidential
05 privy
06 secret
07 private
08 hush-hush, intimate
09 sensitive, top secret
10 classified, restricted
12 off-the-record

confidentially
08 in camera, in secret
09 entre nous, in privacy, in private, privately
10 on the quiet, personally
15 between you and me

configuration
04 cast, form
05 shape
06 figure
07 contour, outline
11 arrangement, composition

confine
04 bind, cage, edge, shut
05 bound, limit, scope
06 border, coop up, immure, intern, lock up, shut up
07 enclose, impound, inhibit, repress, shackle, trammel
08 boundary, frontier, imprison, lock away, restrain, restrict
09 constrain, parameter, perimeter
10 limitation
11 hold captive, incarcerate
12 circumscribe, hold prisoner

confined
06 narrow
07 limited
08 enclosed
10 housebound, restricted
11 constrained
13 circumscribed

confinement
05 birth

06 labour
07 custody
09 captivity, detention
10 childbirth, internment
11 house arrest, parturition
12 imprisonment
13 incarceration

confirm
05 check, prove
06 affirm, assert, assure, clinch, harden, ratify, settle, verify
07 approve, endorse, fortify, promise, support, warrant
08 evidence, sanction, validate
09 authorize, establish, guarantee, reinforce
10 asseverate, strengthen
11 corroborate, demonstrate

confirmation
05 proof
07 backing, support
08 approval, sanction
09 agreement, testimony
10 acceptance, validation
11 affirmation, endorsement
12 ratification, verification
13 accreditation, corroboration

confirmed
03 set
05 fixed
06 inured, rooted
07 chronic
08 hardened, seasoned
09 incurable
10 entrenched, inveterate
11 established
12 incorrigible, long-standing
13 dyed-in-the-wool

confiscate
05 seize
07 impound
08 arrogate, take away
09 sequester
10 commandeer
11 appropriate, expropriate

confiscation
07 escheat, removal, seizure
09 distraint
10 forfeiture
12 distrainment
13 appropriation, expropriation, sequestration

conflagration
04 fire
05 blaze
07 inferno
09 holocaust
12 deflagration

conflict
03 row, war
04 feud
05 brawl, clash, fight, set-to
06 battle, bust-up, combat, differ, fracas, oppose, strife, strive, unrest
07 contend, contest, dispute, ill-will, quarrel, warfare
08 be at odds, disagree, friction, skirmish, struggle, variance
09 antipathy, hostility
10 antagonism, contradict, dissension, opposition
12 disagreement
13 confrontation

confluence
05 union
07 conflux, meeting
08 junction
10 watersmeet
11 concurrence, convergence
12 meeting-point

conform
04 obey
05 adapt, agree, match, tally
06 adjust, comply, follow
07 observe
09 be uniform, harmonize
10 correspond, toe the line
13 go with the flow
14 follow the crowd

conformist
06 yes-man
11 rubber-stamp
13 stick-in-the-mud
14 traditionalist
15 conventionalist

conformity
07 harmony
08 affinity, likeness
09 agreement, congruity, obedience, orthodoxy
10 compliance, consonance, observance, uniformity
11 resemblance
13 accommodation
14 correspondence

confound
04 beat, ruin, stun
05 amaze, upset
06 baffle, defeat, puzzle, thwart
07 astound, confuse, destroy, flummox, mystify, nonplus, perplex, startle, stupefy
08 astonish, bewilder, demolish, surprise
09 bamboozle, discomfit, dumbfound, frustrate
11 flabbergast

confront
04 defy, face, meet, show
05 brave
06 accost, attack, oppose, resist, tackle
07 address, assault, present
08 deal with, face up to
09 challenge, encounter, stand up to, withstand
10 meet head on, reckon with
12 face the music
14 get to grips with

confrontation
05 clash, fight, set-to
06 battle
07 contest, quarrel
08 conflict, showdown
09 collision, encounter
10 engagement
12 disagreement

confuse
05 floor, mix up, throw, upset
06 baffle, bemuse, mingle, muddle, puzzle, tangle
07 fluster, involve, mistake, mortify, mystify, perplex
08 bewilder, confound, disorder, entangle
09 disorient, elaborate
10 complicate, decompose, disconcert, tie in knots

confused
05 dazed
07 baffled, bemused, chaotic, floored, in a flap, jumbled, mixed-up, muddled, puzzled
08 all at sea
09 flummoxed, flustered, mystified, perplexed
10 bewildered, confounded, nonplussed, up a gumtree
11 disarranged, in a flat spin
12 disconcerted, disorganized
13 disorientated

confusing
07 cryptic, unclear
08 baffling, involved, muddling, puzzling, tortuous
09 ambiguous, difficult
10 misleading, perplexing
11 bewildering, complicated

confusion
04 mess
05 chaos, mix-up
06 jumble, muddle
07 clutter, turmoil
08 disarray, shambles, upheaval
09 commotion
10 bafflement, perplexity, puzzlement, untidiness

12 bewilderment
13 mystification

congeal
03 gel, set
04 cake, clot, fuse
06 curdle, freeze, harden
07 stiffen, thicken
08 coalesce, solidify
09 coagulate

congenial
06 genial, homely
08 friendly, pleasant, relaxing
09 agreeable
10 compatible, favourable, like-minded, well-suited
11 complaisant, sympathetic

congenital
05 utter
06 inborn, inbred, innate
07 chronic, connate, natural
08 complete, habitual, hardened, inherent, seasoned, thorough
09 incurable, inherited
10 hereditary, inveterate

congested
04 full
06 choked, jammed, packed
07 blocked, clogged, crammed, crowded, stuffed
11 overcrowded, overflowing

congestion
03 jam
07 choking, snarl-up
08 blockage, blocking, clogging, gridlock
10 bottleneck, traffic jam
12 overcrowding

conglomerate
04 firm
06 cartel, merger
07 company, concern
08 business
10 consortium
11 association, corporation, partnership
13 establishment, multinational

conglomeration
04 mass
06 medley
09 composite
10 collection, hotchpotch
11 aggregation
12 accumulation
13 agglomeration

congratulate
06 praise
08 wish well

10 compliment, felicitate
12 pat on the back

congratulations
09 greetings
10 best wishes, good wishes
11 compliments
12 pat on the back
13 felicitations

congregate
04 form, mass, meet
05 clump, crowd, flock, rally
06 gather, muster, throng
07 cluster, collect, convene
08 assemble, converge
10 accumulate, rendezvous

congregation
04 host, mass
05 crowd, flock, group, laity
06 parish, throng
07 meeting
08 assembly
09 multitude
10 fellowship
12 parishioners

congress
04 diet
05 forum, synod
07 council, meeting
08 assembly, conclave
09 gathering
10 convention, parliament
11 convocation, legislature

congruence
07 harmony
09 agreement
10 concinnity, similarity
11 coincidence, concurrence, consistency, parallelism
13 compatibility
14 correspondence

conical
07 pointed, tapered
08 tapering
09 pyramidal, turbinate
10 cone-shaped
12 funnel-shaped, infundibular
13 infundibulate

conjectural
07 assumed, posited
08 supposed, surmised
09 tentative
10 postulated
11 speculative, theoretical
12 hypothetical

conjecture
05 fancy, guess, infer
06 notion, reckon, theory
07 imagine, presume, suppose, surmise, suspect

08 estimate, theorize
09 guesswork, inference, speculate, suspicion
10 conclusion, hypothesis, projection
11 hypothesize, presumption, speculation, supposition
13 extrapolation

conjugal
06 bridal, wedded
07 marital, married, nuptial, spousal
08 hymeneal
09 connubial
11 epithalamic, matrimonial

conjunction
05 union
11 association, coexistence, combination, unification
12 amalgamation

❑**in conjunction with**
04 with
09 along with, alongside
12 together with

conjure
05 charm, evoke, raise, rouse
06 call up, invoke, summon
07 bewitch, do magic
08 do tricks
09 fascinate

❑**conjure up**
05 evoke
06 awaken, create, excite, recall
07 produce
09 recollect
10 call to mind
11 bring to mind

conjurer
06 wizard
08 magician, sorcerer
11 illusionist, thaumaturge
12 prestigiator
15 prestidigitator

conk

❑**conk out**
04 fail
06 pack up
09 break down, go haywire
12 go on the blink

connect
03 tie
04 ally, fuse, join, link
05 affix, clamp, unite
06 attach, bridge, couple, fasten, relate, secure
07 bracket, combine
08 identify, relate to
09 associate, correlate
11 concatenate

connected
04 akin, tied
06 allied, joined, linked, united
07 coupled, related, secured
08 combined, fastened
10 affiliated, associated

connection
03 tie
04 bond, link
05 clasp, joint
07 analogy, contact, sponsor
08 alliance, coupling, junction, parallel, relation, relative
09 fastening, relevance
10 attachment
11 association, correlation
12 acquaintance, relationship

connivance
07 consent
08 abetment, abetting
09 collusion, condoning
10 complicity

connive
04 plot
05 allow, cabal, coact, let go
06 ignore, scheme, wink at
07 collude, condone, let pass
08 conspire, overlook, tolerate
09 disregard, gloss over
15 turn a blind eye to

conniving
05 nasty
07 corrupt, immoral
08 plotting, scheming
09 colluding
10 conspiring

connoisseur
04 buff
05 judge
06 expert, pundit
07 devotee, epicure, gourmet
08 aesthete, virtuoso
09 authority
10 aficionado, specialist
11 cognoscente

connotation
04 hint
06 nuance
08 allusion, overtone
09 colouring, undertone
10 intimation, suggestion
11 implication, insinuation

connote
05 imply
06 hint at, import
07 purport, signify, suggest
08 allude to, indicate, intimate
09 associate, insinuate

conquer
03 win
04 beat, best, rout, take
05 annex, crush, quell, seize
06 defeat, humble, master, obtain, occupy, subdue
07 overrun, succeed, trounce
08 overcome, vanquish
09 overpower, overthrow, rise above, subjugate
11 triumph over
14 get the better of

conqueror
04 hero, lord
06 master, victor, winner
08 champion
10 subjugator, vanquisher
12 conquistador

conquest
03 win
04 coup, rout
05 catch, lover
06 defeat
07 capture, mastery, success, triumph, victory
08 crushing, invasion
09 overthrow
10 annexation, occupation
11 acquisition, subjugation
12 vanquishment
13 appropriation

conscience
06 ethics, morals, qualms
08 scruples
09 moral code, standards
10 moral sense, principles

conscience-stricken
05 sorry
06 guilty
07 ashamed
08 contrite, penitent, troubled
09 regretful, repentant
10 remorseful
11 guilt-ridden
12 compunctious

conscientious
06 honest
07 careful, dutiful, upright
08 diligent, faithful, thorough
09 assiduous, dedicated
10 methodical, meticulous, particular, scrupulous
11 hard-working, painstaking

conscious
05 alert, alive, awake, aware
06 wilful
07 heedful, knowing, studied
08 rational, sensible, sentient
09 cognizant, reasoning

10 calculated, deliberate, responsive, volitional
11 intentional
12 premeditated

consciousness
04 mind
09 alertness, awareness, intuition, sentience
10 cognizance, perception
11 realization, recognition, sensibility, wakefulness

conscript
05 draft
06 call up, enlist, muster
07 draftee, recruit, round up
08 enlistee

consecrate
05 bless, exalt
06 anoint, devote, hallow, ordain, revere
08 dedicate, make holy, sanctify, venerate

consecutive
06 in turn, serial
07 running, seriate
08 straight, unbroken
09 following, on the trot
10 back to back, continuous, sequential, successive

consensus
05 unity
07 concord, consent, harmony
09 agreement, unanimity
11 concurrence

consent
05 agree, allow, grant, yield
06 accede, accept, assent, comply, concur, permit
07 concede, go-ahead
08 approval, sanction
09 acquiesce, agreement, authorize, clearance
10 acceptance, compliance, concession, consensual, green light, permission
11 concurrence, go along with
12 acquiescence
13 authorization
14 give the go-ahead
15 give the thumbs-up

consequence
03 end
05 issue, value
06 effect, import, moment, result, upshot, weight
07 concern, outcome
09 substance
10 importance, side effect
11 eventuality, implication

12 repercussion, significance
13 reverberation

consequent
07 ensuing
09 following, resultant
10 sequential, subsequent

consequently
04 ergo, then, thus
05 hence
09 as a result, therefore
11 accordingly, necessarily
12 subsequently

conservation
06 saving, upkeep
07 custody, economy, keeping
09 husbandry
10 protection
11 maintenance, safe-keeping
12 preservation, safeguarding

conservatism
09 orthodoxy
14 traditionalism
15 conventionalism

conservative
04 Tory
05 sober
07 careful, die-hard, guarded
08 cautious, moderate, orthodox
09 hidebound, right-wing
10 inflexible
11 reactionary, traditional
12 conventional
13 set in your ways, stick-in-the-mud, unprogressive
14 traditionalist
15 middle-of-the-road

conservatory
06 school
07 academy, college
08 hothouse
10 glasshouse, greenhouse
11 music school
13 conservatoire

conserve
04 keep, save
05 guard, hoard
07 protect, store up
08 keep back, maintain
09 safeguard
10 take care of

consider
04 deem, feel, hold, muse, note, rate
05 count, judge, study, think, weigh
06 ponder

07 believe, examine, reflect, respect, toy with, weigh up
08 chew over, cogitate, meditate, mull over
10 bear in mind, deliberate
11 contemplate

considerable
03 big
04 tidy
05 ample, great, large
06 lavish, marked
07 sizable
08 abundant, generous
09 important, plentiful
10 noteworthy, reasonable
11 appreciable, perceptible, significant, substantial

considerably
04 much
07 greatly
08 markedly
10 noticeably, remarkably
11 appreciably
13 significantly, substantially

considerate
04 kind
06 caring
07 helpful, tactful
08 discreet, generous, gracious, obliging, selfless
09 attentive, concerned, sensitive, unselfish
10 altruistic, charitable, solicitous, thoughtful
11 sympathetic
13 compassionate

consideration
04 care, fact, heed, tact
05 issue, point
06 factor, notice, regard, review
07 concern, respect, thought
08 altruism, analysis, kindness, scrutiny, sympathy
09 attention, reckoning
10 cogitation, compassion, generosity, meditation, reflection, rumination
11 examination, sensitivity
12 circumstance, deliberation, graciousness, selflessness
13 contemplation
14 thoughtfulness

considering
08 all in all, in view of
12 in the light of
13 bearing in mind

consign
04 ship
06 assign, banish, convey
07 commend, deliver, entrust

08 give over, hand over, relegate, transfer, transmit

consignment
04 load
05 batch, cargo, goods
08 delivery, shipment

consist
03 lie
06 embody, inhere, reside
07 embrace, include, involve
08 amount to, comprise
11 be contained, incorporate

consistency
07 density, harmony
08 cohesion, evenness, firmness, identity, sameness
09 agreement, constancy, thickness, viscosity
10 accordance, consonance, regularity, uniformity
11 persistence, reliability
13 dependability, steadfastness
14 correspondence

consistent
04 same
06 steady, stable
07 logical, regular, uniform
08 constant, matching
09 accordant, congruous, consonant, unfailing
10 compatible, conforming, dependable, harmonious, unchanging
13 corresponding

consolation
04 ease, help
05 cheer
06 relief, solace
07 comfort, succour, support
08 soothing, sympathy
11 alleviation, reassurance
13 commiseration

console
04 calm, help
05 board, cheer, dials, panel
06 levers, solace, soothe
07 buttons, comfort, hearten, relieve, succour, support
08 controls, keyboard, reassure
09 dashboard, encourage
11 instruments
12 control panel

consolidate
04 fuse, join
05 merge, unify, unite
06 cement, secure
07 combine, fortify
09 reinforce, stabilize
10 amalgamate, strengthen

consolidation
06 fusion, merger
07 joining, uniting
08 alliance, securing
09 cementing
10 federation
11 affiliation, association, combination, unification
12 amalgamation
13 confederation, reinforcement, stabilization, strengthening

consonance
07 concord, harmony
09 agreement, congruity
10 accordance, conformity
11 consistency, suitability
14 correspondence

consonant
08 agreeing, suitable
09 accordant, according, congruous, in harmony
10 consistent, harmonious
12 in accordance
13 correspondent

consort
03 mix
04 wife
06 escort, mingle, spouse
07 husband, partner
09 associate, companion
10 fraternize

consortium
04 bloc, bond, pact
05 guild, union
06 cartel, league, treaty
07 compact, company
08 alliance, marriage
09 coalition, syndicate
10 federation
11 affiliation, association, corporation, partnership
12 conglomerate, organization
13 confederation

conspicuous
05 clear, showy
06 flashy, garish, marked, patent
07 blatant, evident, glaring, obvious, visible
08 flagrant, manifest, striking
09 prominent
10 noticeable, observable
11 discernible, perceptible
12 ostentatious, recognizable

conspiracy
04 plot
05 cabal
06 league, scheme
07 frame-up, treason
08 intrigue

09 collusion, stratagem
10 connivance
11 machination
13 collaboration

conspirator
07 plotter, schemer, traitor
08 colluder
09 conspirer, intriguer
12 collaborator

conspire
04 ally, join, link, plot
06 scheme
07 collude, connect, connive
08 intrigue
09 associate, co-operate, machinate, manoeuvre
10 hatch a plot, join forces
11 act together, collaborate

constancy
07 loyalty
08 devotion, fidelity, firmness
09 stability
10 permanence, resolution, steadiness, uniformity
12 faithfulness, perseverance
13 dependability, steadfastness
15 trustworthiness

constant
04 even, firm, true
05 loyal
06 stable, steady
07 devoted, endless, eternal, non-stop, staunch, uniform
08 faithful, resolute, unbroken
09 ceaseless, continual, incessant, perpetual, steadfast, unvarying
10 changeless, continuous, dependable, persistent, unchanging, unwavering
11 everlasting, never-ending, trustworthy, unremitting
12 interminable
13 uninterrupted
14 without respite

constantly
06 always
07 for ever, non-stop
09 ad nauseam, endlessly
10 all the time, invariably
11 ceaselessly, continually, incessantly, perpetually
12 continuously, interminably, relentlessly

constellation
► *Names of constellations:*
03 Ara, Fly, Fox, Leo, Net, Ram
04 Crab, Crow, Crux, Dove, Harp, Lion, Lynx, Lyra, Pavo, Swan, Vela, Wolf

05 Altar, Aries, Arrow, Cetus, Clock, Crane, Draco, Eagle, Hydra, Lepus, Libra, Lupus, Mensa, Musca, Norma, Orion, Pyxis, Sails, Table, Twins, Virgo, Whale

06 Antlia, Aquila, Archer, Auriga, Boötes, Cancer, Corvus, Crater, Cygnus, Dragon, Fishes, Gemini, Hydrus, Lizard, Octans, Octant, Pictor, Pisces, Scales, Taurus, Virgin

07 Centaur, Cepheus, Columba, Dolphin, Giraffe, Lacerta, Peacock, Pegasus, Perseus, Phoenix, Sagitta, Serpens, Serpent, Sextans, Sextant, Unicorn

08 Aquarius, Eridanus, Great Dog, Hercules, Herdsman, Leo Minor, Scorpion, Scorpius

09 Andromeda, Centaurus, Chameleon, Delphinus, Great Bear, Little Dog, Monoceros, Swordfish, Telescope, Ursa Major, Ursa Minor

10 Canis Major, Canis Minor, Cassiopeia, Chamaeleon, Charioteer, Little Bear, Little Lion, Microscope, Sea Serpent, Triangulum

11 Capricornus, Sagittarius, Telescopium, Water Bearer, Winged Horse

12 Microscopium

13 Northern Crown, River Eridanus, Southern Cross, Southern Crown

14 Camelopardalis, Corona Borealis

15 Corona Australis, Mariner's Compass

➢ See also **star**

consternation

04 fear

05 alarm, dread, panic, shock

06 dismay, fright, horror, terror

07 anxiety

11 disquietude, trepidation

12 bewilderment, perturbation

constituent

03 bit

04 part, unit

05 basic, voter

07 content, elector, element

08 inherent, integral

09 component, principle

10 ingredient

13 component part

constitute

02 be

04 form, make, mean

05 found, set up

06 create, make up

07 add up to, appoint, charter, compose, empower

08 amount to, comprise

09 authorize, establish, institute, represent

10 commission

constitution

04 code, laws

05 rules

06 health, make-up, nature

07 charter

08 physique, statutes

09 character, condition, formation, structure

11 codified law, composition, disposition, temperament

12 bill of rights, organization

constitutional

04 turn, walk

05 amble, by law, legal

06 airing, lawful, stroll, vested

08 codified, ratified

09 promenade, statutory

10 authorized, legitimate

11 legislative

12 governmental

constrain

04 bind, curb, urge

05 check, force, impel, limit

06 coerce, compel, oblige

07 confine

08 hold back, pressure, restrict

09 constrict

10 pressurize

constrained

05 stiff

06 forced, uneasy

07 guarded

08 reserved, reticent

09 inhibited, unnatural

constraint

04 curb

05 check, force

06 damper, demand, duress

08 coercion, pressure

09 necessity, restraint

10 compulsion, impediment, limitation, obligation

11 restriction

constrict

04 bind, curb

05 check, cramp, limit, pinch

06 hamper, hinder, impede, narrow, shrink

07 confine, inhibit, squeeze, tighten

08 compress, contract, hold back, restrict, strangle

09 constrain

constriction

04 curb

05 check, cramp

08 blockage, pressure, stenosis

09 hindrance, narrowing, reduction, squeezing, stricture, tightness

10 constraint, impediment, limitation, tightening

11 compression, restriction

construct

04 form, make

05 build, erect, found, model, put up, raise, set up, shape

06 create, design, devise

07 compose, elevate, fashion

08 assemble, engineer

09 establish, fabricate

11 manufacture, put together

construction

04 form

05 model, shape

06 fabric, figure, making

07 edifice, meaning, reading

08 assembly, building, erection

09 elevation, framework, inference, structure

11 fabrication, manufacture

14 interpretation

constructive

06 useful

07 helpful

08 positive, valuable

09 practical

10 beneficial, productive

construe

04 read

05 infer, see as

06 deduce, render

07 analyse, explain, expound

08 regard as

09 interpret

10 take to mean, understand

consult

06 confer, look up, turn to

07 discuss, refer to

08 question

09 ask advice

10 deliberate, seek advice

consultant

06 expert

07 adviser

09 authority
10 specialist

consultation
04 talk
05 forum
07 hearing, meeting, session
08 dialogue
09 interview
10 conference, discussion
11 appointment, examination
12 deliberation

consultative
08 advising, advisory
11 counselling
12 recommending

consume
03 eat, gut, use
04 grip, take
05 drain, drink, eat up, scoff, spend, touch, use up, waste
06 absorb, devour, expend, gobble, guzzle, ingest, obsess, ravage, tuck in
07 deplete, destroy, drink up, engross, swallow, utilize
08 demolish, dominate, lay waste, squander
09 go through, overwhelm, polish off, preoccupy
10 annihilate, get through

consumer
04 user
05 buyer
06 client, patron
07 end-user, shopper
08 customer

consuming
08 gripping
09 absorbing, devouring, obsessive
10 compelling, dominating, engrossing, tormenting
12 overwhelming, preoccupying

consummate
03 cap, end
05 crown, total, utter
06 finish, fulfil, gifted, superb
07 perfect, perform, realize, skilled, supreme
08 absolute, complete, polished, ultimate
09 matchless, practised, terminate
10 accomplish, proficient
12 accomplished, transcendent
13 distinguished

consummation
03 end
06 finish
07 capping
08 crowning
09 execution
10 completion, conclusion, fulfilment, perfection
11 achievement, culmination, realization, termination
13 actualization
14 accomplishment

consumption
05 waste
06 eating
07 using-up
08 draining, drinking, guzzling, scoffing, spending
09 devouring, expending, ingestion, tucking-in
10 exhaustion, swallowing
11 expenditure, utilization

contact
03 fax
04 call, meet, ring
05 phone, reach, touch, union
06 friend, impact, notify
07 speak to, sponsor, write to
08 approach
09 get hold of, proximity, telephone
10 connection, contiguity
11 association
12 acquaintance
13 communication
14 get in touch with

contagious
08 catching, epidemic, pandemic
09 spreading
10 compelling, infectious
12 communicable, irresistible
13 transmissible, transmittable

contain
04 curb, hold, seat, stop, take
05 carry, check, limit
06 embody, stifle, take in
07 control, embrace, enclose, include, involve, repress
08 comprise, keep back, restrain, suppress
11 incorporate, keep in check

container
06 holder, vessel
10 receptacle, repository

contaminate
04 foul, harm, soil
05 decay, spoil, stain, sully, taint
06 debase, defile, infect
07 corrupt, pollute, tarnish
10 adulterate, make impure

contamination
05 decay, filth, stain, taint
07 soiling, tarnish
08 impurity, spoiling, sullying
09 infection, pollution, vitiation
10 corruption, debasement, defilement, rottenness
12 adulteration

contemplate
04 muse, plan, view
05 dwell, study, weigh
06 design, expect, intend, look at, ponder, regard, survey
07 examine, foresee, inspect, observe, propose, weigh up
08 cogitate, consider, envisage, meditate, mull over, ruminate
09 reflect on
10 deliberate, think about

contemplation
05 dwell, study
06 gazing, musing, regard
07 thought
08 scrutiny, weighing
09 pondering
10 cogitation, meditation, reflection, rumination
11 cerebration, mulling-over
12 deliberation
13 consideration

contemplative
06 intent, musing
07 pensive
08 cerebral
10 meditative, reflective, ruminative, thoughtful
13 deep in thought

contemporary
06 coeval, latest, modern, recent, trendy, with it
07 current, present, topical
08 up-to-date
10 avant-garde, coetaneous, futuristic, new-fangled, present-day
11 fashionable, present-time, synchronous, ultra-modern
13 up-to-the-minute

contempt
05 scorn
06 hatred
07 disdain, dislike, neglect
08 derision, loathing, ridicule
09 dishonour, disregard
10 disrespect
11 detestation

contemptible
03 low
04 base, mean, vile
06 abject, paltry
07 pitiful
08 shameful, wretched
09 loathsome, worthless
10 degenerate, despicable, detestable, lamentable
11 ignominious

contemptuous
07 cynical, jeering, mocking
08 arrogant, derisive, derisory, insolent, scornful, sneering
09 insulting, withering
10 disdainful
12 contumelious, supercilious
13 condescending, disrespectful

contend
03 vie, war
04 aver, cope, deal, hold
05 argue, brave, claim, clash, fight, state
06 affirm, allege, assert, battle, combat, oppose, reckon, strive, tackle, tussle
07 address, compete, contest, declare, dispute, grapple, profess, wrestle
08 face up to, maintain, struggle
09 challenge
10 asseverate, meet head on

content
04 ease, gist, glad, load, size
05 happy, ideas, items, parts, peace, theme, topic
06 at ease, matter, pacify, please, volume
07 appease, comfort, delight, essence, gratify, meaning, placate, pleased, satisfy, section, subject, willing
08 capacity, cheerful, elements, gladness, material, pleasure
09 fulfilled, happiness, satisfied, substance, unworried
10 components
11 comfortable, ingredients

contented
04 glad
05 happy
07 pleased, relaxed
08 cheerful
09 fulfilled, satisfied, unworried
10 untroubled
11 comfortable

contention
04 view

05 claim, stand
06 belief, debate, enmity, notion, strife, theory, thesis
07 discord, dispute, feeling, feuding, opinion, rivalry
08 argument, position, struggle
09 assertion, hostility, intuition, judgement, viewpoint
10 conviction, dissension, impression, persuasion
11 controversy, point of view
12 disagreement

contentious
07 hostile
08 disputed, doubtful, perverse
09 debatable, polemical
10 disputable, pugnacious
11 quarrelsome
12 antagonistic, questionable
13 argumentative, controversial

contentment
04 ease
05 peace
07 comfort
08 gladness, pleasure, serenity
09 happiness
10 equanimity, fulfilment
11 complacency
12 cheerfulness, peacefulness, satisfaction

contest
03 vie
04 deny, game, race
05 doubt, event, fight, match, set-to, vying
06 battle, combat, debate, oppose, refute, strive, tussle
07 compete, contend, dispute
08 conflict, litigate, question, skirmish, struggle
09 challenge, encounter
10 tournament
11 competition, controversy
12 championship

contestant
05 rival
06 player
07 entrant
08 aspirant, opponent
09 adversary, contender
10 competitor

context
07 factors, setting
09 framework, situation
10 background, conditions
12 surroundings
13 circumstances

contiguous
04 near, next
05 close

06 beside
07 vicinal
08 abutting, adjacent, touching
09 adjoining, bordering
10 conjoining, tangential
12 conterminous, neighbouring

continent
► *Names of continents:*
04 Asia
06 Africa, Europe
09 Australia
10 Antarctica
12 North America, South America

contingency
05 event
06 chance
08 accident, fortuity, incident
09 emergency, happening
10 randomness
11 chance event, eventuality, possibility, uncertainty

contingent
04 body
05 batch, group, party, quota
07 company, mission, section, subject
09 dependent
10 complement, delegation, deputation, detachment
11 conditional
15 representatives

continual
07 eternal, regular
08 constant, frequent, repeated
09 incessant, perpetual, recurrent
10 persistent, repetitive
11 everlasting
12 interminable

continually
06 always
07 forever, non-stop
09 endlessly, eternally, regularly
10 all the time, constantly, habitually, repeatedly
11 ceaselessly, incessantly, perpetually, recurrently
12 interminably, persistently

continuance
04 term
06 period
08 duration
10 permanence
11 persistence, protraction
12 continuation

continuation
06 sequel

07 renewal
08 addition
09 extension
10 resumption, supplement
11 development, furtherance, lengthening, protraction
12 prolongation

continue
04 go on, last, rest, stay
05 abide, renew
06 endure, extend, keep on, pursue, remain, resume
07 carry on, hold out, persist, press on, proceed, prolong, survive, sustain
08 lengthen, maintain, progress
09 keep going, soldier on
10 keep on with, recommence, start again
11 persevere in

continuity
04 flow
07 linkage
08 cohesion, sequence
10 connection, succession
11 progression

continuous
05 solid
07 endless, lasting, non-stop
08 constant, extended, unbroken, unending
09 ceaseless, unceasing
11 consecutive, never-ending, unremitting, with no let-up
12 interminable
13 uninterrupted

contort
04 knot, warp
05 gnarl, twist
06 deform, wrench, writhe
07 distort, wriggle
08 misshape
09 convolute, disfigure
14 bend out of shape

contortionist
07 acrobat, gymnast, tumbler
09 aerialist
10 rope-dancer, rope-walker
11 equilibrist, funambulist

contour
04 form
05 curve, lines, shape
06 aspect, figure, relief
07 outline, profile
10 silhouette

contraband
08 hot goods, smuggled
11 banned goods, bootlegging

contract
03 get
04 bond, deal, pact
05 agree, catch, tense
06 draw in, engage, lessen, narrow, pick up, pledge, reduce, settle, shrink, treaty
07 abridge, arrange, bargain, compact, curtail, develop, promise, shorten, shrivel, tighten, wrinkle
08 compress, condense, decrease, diminish
09 agreement, concordat, constrict, negotiate, stipulate, succumb to, undertake
10 abbreviate, agree terms, go down with, settlement
11 arrangement, transaction
12 come down with

contraction
07 tensing
09 drawing-in, lessening, narrowing, reduction, shrinkage
10 shortening, tightening
11 abridgement, astringency, compression, curtailment, shrivelling
12 abbreviation, constriction
13 shortened form

contradict
04 deny
05 clash, rebut
06 impugn, negate, refute
07 confute, counter, gainsay
08 be at odds, conflict, contrast, disagree
09 disaffirm, go against
14 fly in the face of

contradiction
07 dispute, paradox
08 conflict, negation, rebuttal, variance
09 challenge
10 antithesis, refutation
11 confutation, incongruity
12 disagreement
13 disaffirmance, inconsistency
14 disaffirmation
15 counter-argument

contradictory
08 clashing, contrary, opposing, opposite
11 conflicting, dissentient, incongruous, paradoxical
12 antagonistic, antithetical, incompatible, inconsistent

contraption
03 rig
06 device, gadget
07 machine
09 apparatus, mechanism
11 contrivance, thingumajig

contrary
07 adverse, awkward, counter, hostile, opposed, reverse, stroppy, wayward
08 clashing, converse, opposing, opposite, perverse, stubborn
09 difficult, obstinate
10 antithesis, headstrong
11 disobliging, intractable
12 antagonistic, cantankerous, incompatible, inconsistent
14 just the reverse

❑**on the contrary**
15 just the opposite, quite the reverse

contrast
04 foil
06 differ, oppose, relief
07 compare
08 be at odds, conflict, disagree, opposite
09 disparity, go against
10 contradict, difference, divergence, opposition
11 distinction, distinguish

❑**in contrast to**
09 as against, opposed to
10 rather than

contravene
04 defy
05 break, flout
06 breach
07 disobey, violate
08 infringe
10 transgress

contretemps
04 tiff
05 brush, clash, hitch
06 mishap
08 accident
10 difficulty, misfortune
11 predicament
12 misadventure

contribute
04 edit, give, help, make
05 add to, cause, endow, grant
06 bestow, chip in, create, donate, lead to, supply
07 compile, compose, conduce, furnish, produce, promote, provide
08 generate, occasion, result in
09 originate, subscribe

10 bring about, give rise to
11 play a part in

contribution
04 gift, item
05 grant, input, piece, story
06 column, report, review
07 article, feature, handout
08 addition, bestowal, donation, gratuity, offering
09 endowment
12 subscription

contributor
05 donor, giver
06 author, backer, patron, writer
07 sponsor
08 compiler, reporter, reviewer
09 columnist, freelance
10 benefactor, journalist, subscriber
13 correspondent

contrite
05 sorry
06 humble
08 penitent
09 chastened, regretful, repentant
10 remorseful
11 guilt-ridden, penitential

contrition
05 shame
06 regret, sorrow
07 remorse
09 penitence
10 repentance
11 compunction, humiliation

contrivance
04 plan, plot, ploy, ruse, tool
05 dodge, trick
06 device, gadget, scheme
07 machine, project
08 artifice, intrigue
09 apparatus, appliance, implement, invention, mechanism, stratagem
11 contraption, machination

contrive
04 plan, plot
06 design, devise, invent, manage, scheme, wangle
07 arrange, concoct, succeed
08 engineer, find a way
09 construct, manoeuvre
11 orchestrate, stage-manage

contrived
05 false, set-up
06 forced
08 laboured, mannered, overdone, strained

09 elaborate, unnatural
10 artificial

control
03 run
04 curb, dial, head, keep, knob, lead, rule, sway, work
05 brake, check, lever, limit, power, reign
06 direct, govern, manage, subdue, switch, verify
07 command, contain, mastery, monitor, oversee, repress
08 dominate, guidance, regulate, restrain, restrict
09 be the boss, constrain, dominance, hindrance, influence, restraint, supervise, supremacy
10 constraint, discipline, government, limitation, management, regulation, repression, run the show
11 call the tune, preside over, restriction, supervision
12 call the shots, jurisdiction, rule the roost
14 pull the strings
15 wear the trousers

controversial
07 at issue
08 disputed, doubtful
09 debatable, polemical
10 disputable
11 contentious

controversy
06 debate, strife
07 discord, dispute, eristic, polemic, quarrel, wrangle
08 argument, friction, squabble
10 contention, discussion, dissension, war of words
11 altercation
12 disagreement

contusion
04 bump, lump, mark
05 knock
06 bruise, injury
07 blemish
08 swelling
10 ecchymosis

conundrum
05 poser
06 enigma, puzzle, riddle
07 anagram, problem
08 word game
11 brainteaser

convalescence
08 recovery
11 improvement, restoration

12 recuperation
14 rehabilitation

convene
04 call, meet
05 rally
06 gather, muster, summon
07 collect, convoke
08 assemble
10 congregate
12 call together

convenience
03 use
06 device, gadget
07 amenity, benefit, fitness, service, utility
08 facility, resource
09 advantage, appliance, ease of use, handiness
10 expediency, usefulness
11 propinquity, suitability
13 accessibility, opportuneness
14 propitiousness, serviceability

convenient
05 handy
06 at hand, fitted, nearby, suited, timely, useful
07 adapted, fitting, helpful
08 suitable
09 available, expedient, opportune, well-timed
10 accessible, near at hand
11 close at hand, within reach
12 labour-saving

convention
04 bond, code, deal, pact
05 synod, usage
06 custom, treaty
07 compact, council, meeting
08 assembly, conclave, practice, protocol
09 agreement, concordat, delegates, etiquette, formality, gathering, propriety, punctilio, tradition
10 conference, settlement
11 convocation, transaction

conventional
05 trite, usual
06 normal, proper, ritual
07 correct, regular, routine
08 accepted, expected, ordinary, orthodox, received, standard, straight
09 customary, prevalent
10 conformist, mainstream, pedestrian, unoriginal
11 commonplace, stereotyped
12 conservative, run-of-the-mill
14 common or garden

converge
04 form, join, mass, meet
05 focus, merge, unite
07 close in, combine
08 approach, coincide
11 concentrate, move towards
12 come together

convergence
05 union
07 meeting, merging
08 blending, junction
10 confluence
11 coincidence, combination
12 intersection

conversant

❏**conversant with**
08 versed in
09 skilled in
10 apprised of, au fait with
11 practised in
12 familiar with, proficient in
13 experienced in
14 acquainted with

conversation
04 chat, talk
06 confab, gossip, natter
07 chinwag
08 colloquy, cosy chat, dialogue, exchange
09 discourse, tête-à-tête
10 discussion
12 heart-to-heart

conversational
06 casual, chatty
07 relaxed
08 informal
10 colloquial
13 communicative

converse
04 chat, talk
06 confer, gossip
07 chatter, commune, counter, discuss, obverse, reverse
08 contrary, opposing, opposite, reversed
09 discourse
10 antithesis, transposed
11 communicate

conversion
06 change, switch
07 rebirth, turning
08 exchange, mutation
09 preaching, reshaping
10 adaptation, adjustment, alteration, persuasion
11 reformation, remodelling
12 modification, regeneration
13 metamorphosis, transmutation

14 reconstruction, transformation

convert
04 make, turn
05 adapt, alter
06 adjust, change, modify, mutate, reform, revise, switch
07 rebuild, remodel, reshape, restyle, win over
08 adherent, believer, disciple, exchange, go over to, neophyte, persuade, transfer
09 proselyte, refashion, transform, transmute
11 reconstruct
12 metamorphose
13 changed person

convertible
09 adaptable
10 adjustable, modifiable, permutable
15 interchangeable

convex
07 bulging, gibbous, rounded
08 swelling
11 protuberant

convey
04 bear, move, pipe, send, tell
05 carry, drive, fetch, guide
06 impart, relate, reveal
07 conduct, deliver, express
08 disclose, transfer, transmit
09 make known, transport
11 communicate

conveyance
03 bus, car, van
05 coach, lorry, truck, wagon
06 ceding
07 bicycle, vehicle
08 carriage, delivery, granting, movement, transfer
09 transport
10 bequeathal, motorcycle

convict
03 lag
05 crook, felon, judge, thief
06 inmate, robber
07 burglar, condemn, villain
08 criminal, imprison, jailbird, offender, prisoner, sentence
09 wrongdoer
10 find guilty, law-breaker

conviction
05 creed, faith, tenet
06 belief
07 fervour, opinion
08 firmness, sentence

09 assurance, certainty, certitude, judgement
10 confidence, persuasion
12 condemnation, imprisonment

convince
04 sway
06 assure, prompt
07 prove to, win over
08 persuade, talk into
09 influence
10 bring round

convincing
06 cogent, likely
07 telling
08 credible, forceful, powerful
09 plausible
10 compelling, conclusive, impressive, persuasive

convivial
05 jolly, merry
06 genial, hearty, jovial, lively
07 cordial, festive
08 cheerful, friendly, sociable
09 fun-loving

conviviality
05 cheer, mirth
06 gaiety
07 jollity
08 bonhomie
09 festivity, geniality, joviality
10 cordiality, liveliness
11 merrymaking, sociability

convocation
04 diet
05 synod
07 council, meeting
08 assembly, conclave, congress
10 assemblage, convention
12 congregation, forgathering

convoluted
07 complex, winding
08 involved, tortuous, twisting
11 complicated

convolution
04 coil, loop, turn
05 gyrus, helix, twist, whorl
06 spiral
07 coiling, winding
08 curlicue
09 intricacy, sinuosity
10 complexity
11 involvement
12 complication

convoy
04 line
05 fleet, group, guard, train
06 escort

07 caravan
10 attendance, protection

convulse
04 jerk
05 seize
07 disturb
08 unsettle

convulsion
03 fit, tic
05 cramp, spasm
06 attack, furore, tremor, tumult, unrest
07 seizure, turmoil
08 disorder, eruption, outburst, paroxysm, upheaval
09 agitation, commotion

convulsive
05 jerky
06 fitful
07 violent
08 sporadic
09 spasmodic
12 uncontrolled

cook
04 burn, heat, warm
07 prepare
08 rustle up

► *Cooking methods*:
03 fry
04 bake, boil, stew
05 broil, brown, grill, poach, roast, sauté, steam, toast
06 braise, coddle, simmer
07 deep-fry, parboil, stir-fry
08 barbecue, scramble
09 casserole, fricassee

□ **cook up**
04 brew, plan, plot
06 devise, invent, scheme
07 concoct, prepare

cool
03 fan, ice
04 calm, cold, iced
05 abate, allay, aloof, chill, crisp, fresh, great, nippy, poise
06 chilly, dampen, frigid, frosty, placid, poised, sedate, temper, trendy
07 assuage, bracing, chilled, control, distant, elegant, relaxed, stylish, unmoved
08 composed, diminish, laid back, moderate, reserved,
09 apathetic, collected, composure, crispness, excellent, fantastic, freshness, impassive, unexcited, unruffled
10 refreshing, unfriendly, untroubled

11 fashionable, half-hearted, level-headed, refrigerate, self-control, standoffish, unwelcoming
12 uninterested
13 defervescence, defervescency

cooling
08 chilling, freezing
11 refrigerant, ventilation
13 defervescence, defervescency, refrigeration, refrigerative, refrigeratory

coop
03 box, pen
04 cage
05 hutch, pound
09 enclosure

□ **coop up**
03 pen
04 cage, shut
06 immure, keep in, lock up, shut up
07 enclose, impound
08 imprison, lock away
11 incarcerate

co-operate
03 aid
04 help, pool
05 share, unite
06 assist, team up
07 combine
08 conspire, play ball
10 contribute, join forces
11 collaborate, participate
12 band together

co-operation
03 aid
04 help
05 unity
08 teamwork
10 assistance
11 give-and-take
13 collaboration, participation

co-operative
05 joint
06 shared, united
07 helpful, helping, willing
08 combined, obliging
09 assisting, compliant
10 supportive
11 co-ordinated
13 accommodating, collaborative

co-ordinate
04 mesh
05 match, order
07 arrange
08 organize, regulate, tabulate

09 co-operate, correlate, harmonize, integrate
11 collaborate, synchronize

cope
05 get by
06 make do, manage
07 carry on, succeed, survive

□ **cope with**
06 endure, handle, manage
07 weather
08 deal with
09 encounter
11 contend with, grapple with, wrestle with

copious
04 full, huge, rich
05 ample, great
06 bags of, lavish
07 liberal, profuse
08 abundant, generous
09 bounteous, bountiful, extensive, plentiful

cop-out
05 alibi, dodge, fraud
07 evasion, pretext
08 pretence, shirking
14 passing the buck

copse
04 bush, wood
05 brush, grove
07 coppice, thicket

copulate
03 bed, lay
04 have, line, mate
08 make love

copy
03 ape, fax
04 crib, echo, fake, scan
05 forge, image, issue, mimic, model, print, trace, Xerox®
06 borrow, mirror, parrot, pirate, repeat, sample
07 emulate, example, forgery, imitate, replica, tracing
08 likeness, simulate, specimen
09 duplicate, facsimile, imitation, photocopy, Photostat®, replicate, reproduce
10 carbon copy, plagiarism, plagiarize, transcribe
11 counterfeit, impersonate
12 reproduction

coquettish
06 flirty
07 flighty, teasing, vampish
08 dallying, inviting
10 come-hither
11 flirtatious

cord
03 tie
04 bond, flex, line, link, rope
05 cable, twine
06 string
07 funicle

cordial
04 warm
06 genial, hearty
07 affable, earnest
08 amicable, cheerful, friendly, pleasant, sociable
09 agreeable, heartfelt, welcoming

cordiality
06 warmth
07 earnest, welcome
09 affection, geniality, sincerity
10 affability, heartiness
11 sociability
12 cheerfulness, friendliness
13 agreeableness

cordon
04 line, ring
05 chain, fence
07 barrier

❑cordon off
07 enclose, isolate
08 close off, encircle, fence off, separate, surround

core
03 nub
04 crux, gist
05 heart
06 centre, kernel, middle
07 essence, nucleus
11 nitty-gritty
12 quintessence

corn
03 rye
04 oats
05 grain, maize, wheat
06 barley, cereal

corner
03 hog
04 bend, fork, hole, nook, trap
05 angle, catch, crook, curve, joint, niche
06 cavity, cranny, cut off, pickle, plight, recess
07 confine, control, crevice, retreat, straits, turning
08 hardship, hideaway, hunt down, junction
09 situation, tight spot
10 monopolize, run to earth
11 predicament

corny
04 dull

05 banal, stale, trite
06 feeble
07 clichéd, maudlin, mawkish
08 overused
09 hackneyed
11 commonplace, sentimental

corollary
06 result, upshot
08 illation
09 deduction, inference
10 conclusion
11 consequence

coronation
08 crowning
12 enthronement

coronet
05 crown, tiara
06 diadem, wreath
07 circlet, garland

corporal
06 bodily, carnal
07 fleshly, somatic
08 material, physical, tangible
09 corporeal

corporate
05 joint
06 allied, merged, pooled, shared, united
08 combined, communal
10 collective
13 collaborative

corporation
04 firm
05 house, trust
06 cartel
07 company, concern, council
08 business, industry
09 authority, syndicate
10 consortium
11 association, partnership
12 conglomerate, organization
13 establishment, governing body, multinational
14 holding company

corporeal
05 human
06 actual, bodily, mortal
07 fleshly
08 material, physical, tangible
11 substantial

corps
04 band, body, crew, team, unit
05 squad
07 brigade, company
08 division, regiment, squadron
10 contingent, detachment

corpse
04 body
05 mummy, stiff

06 zombie
07 cadaver, carcase, remains
08 dead body, skeleton

corpulent
03 fat
05 beefy, burly, large, obese, plump, podgy, stout, tubby
06 fleshy, portly, rotund
07 adipose
10 overweight, pot-bellied

corpus
04 body
05 whole
08 entirety
10 collection

corral
03 sty
04 coop, fold
05 kraal, pound, stall
09 enclosure

correct
04 cure, just, real, true
05 amend, debug, emend, exact, right, scold
06 actual, adjust, proper, punish, rebuke, reform, remedy, revise, seemly
07 fitting, improve, precise, rectify, redress, reprove
08 accepted, accurate, admonish, put right, regulate, standard, suitable
09 faultless, reprimand
10 ameliorate, discipline
11 appropriate, put straight, word-perfect

correction
06 rebuke
07 reproof
08 scolding
09 amendment, reprimand
10 alteration, discipline, emendation, punishment
11 improvement, reformation
12 amelioration, modification
13 rectification

corrective
08 curative, punitive, remedial
09 medicinal
10 emendatory, palliative
11 reformatory, therapeutic
12 disciplinary

correlate
04 link
05 agree, tie in
06 equate, relate
07 compare, connect
08 interact, parallel
10 co-ordinate, correspond

correlation
04 link
10 connection
11 interaction, interchange, reciprocity
12 relationship
14 correspondence

correspond
03 fit, pen
05 agree, match, tally, write
06 accord, answer, concur
07 conform, match up
08 coincide, dovetail
09 correlate, harmonize
11 communicate, fit together, keep in touch

correspondence
04 mail, post
05 match
07 analogy, harmony, letters
08 relation
09 agreement, congruity
10 consonance, similarity
11 coincidence, concurrence, correlation, resemblance
13 communication

correspondent
06 writer
08 reporter
10 journalist
11 contributor

corresponding
04 like
07 similar
08 matching, parallel
09 analogous, identical
10 reciprocal
13 complementary

corridor
04 hall
05 aisle, lobby
07 hallway, passage
10 passageway

corroborate
06 back up, ratify, uphold, verify
07 bear out, certify, confirm, endorse, support, sustain
08 document, evidence, underpin, validate
12 authenticate, substantiate

corroborative
09 endorsing, verifying
10 confirming, supporting, supportive, validating
14 substantiating

corrode
03 rot
04 rust
05 erode, waste

06 abrade, impair
07 consume, crumble, destroy, eat away, oxidize, tarnish
08 wear away
11 deteriorate
12 disintegrate

corrosive
04 acid
07 caustic, cutting, erosive, wasting, wearing
08 abrasive
09 consuming, corroding
11 destructive

corrugated
06 fluted, folded, ridged
07 creased, grooved, striate
08 crinkled, furrowed, wrinkled
10 channelled

corrupt
03 buy, mar
04 bent, evil, lure, warp
05 bribe, shady, taint, venal
06 blight, buy off, debase, defile, infect, rotten, suborn
07 debauch, deprave, immoral, pervert, pollute, vitiate
08 bribable, depraved
09 dishonest, dissolute
10 adulterate, degenerate, fraudulent, lead astray
11 contaminate
12 contaminated

corruption
04 evil, vice
05 fraud, graft
07 bribery
08 impurity, iniquity, villainy
09 depravity, extortion, pollution, shadiness
10 debauchery, dishonesty, distortion, immorality, perversion, rottenness, wickedness
11 criminality, crookedness, degradation, subornation
12 degeneration
13 contamination

corset
04 belt
05 stays
06 bodice, girdle
08 corselet
11 panty girdle

cortège
05 suite, train
06 column, parade
07 retinue
09 cavalcade, entourage
10 procession

cosmetic
05 minor
06 beauty, make-up, slight
07 shallow, surface, trivial
08 external
10 peripheral
11 beautifying, superficial

cosmic
04 huge, vast
07 immense, in space
08 infinite
09 grandiose, limitless, universal, worldwide

cosmonaut
08 spaceman
09 astronaut
14 space traveller

cosmopolitan
06 urbane
07 worldly
08 cultured
09 universal
11 broad-minded, multiracial
13 international, multicultural, sophisticated, well-travelled

cosmos
06 galaxy, system, worlds
08 creation, universe

cosset
03 pet
04 baby
05 spoil
06 coddle, fondle, pamper
07 cherish, indulge
11 mollycoddle

cost
04 harm, hurt, loss, rate
05 quote, value, worth
06 amount, budget, charge, come to, damage, figure, injure, injury, outlay
07 expense, payment, penalty
08 estimate, expenses
09 calculate, detriment, outgoings, overheads, quotation, sacrifice, valuation
11 asking price, expenditure
12 disbursement, selling price

costly
04 dear, rich
05 steep
06 lavish, pricey
07 harmful, ruinous
08 precious, splendid, valuable
09 expensive, priceless
10 disastrous, exorbitant, high-priced, loss-making
11 destructive, detrimental

costume
05 dress, get-up, habit, robes
06 attire, livery, outfit
07 apparel, clothes, uniform
08 clothing, ensemble, garments
09 vestments
10 fancy dress

cosy
04 safe, snug, warm
05 comfy
06 homely, secure
08 intimate
09 congenial, sheltered

coterie
03 set
04 camp, club, gang
05 cabal, group
06 caucus, circle, clique
07 faction

cottage
03 hut
05 bothy, cabin, lodge, shack
06 chalet
08 bungalow

couch
03 bed, set
04 bear, sofa, word
05 divan, frame, utter
06 cradle, day bed, settee
07 express, ottoman, sofa bed
12 chaise-longue, chesterfield

cough
03 hem
04 bark, hack, hawk
06 tussis

❑cough up
03 pay
04 give
06 pay out
07 fork out, stump up
08 shell out

council
04 body, jury
05 board, group, panel, rally
06 senate, throng
07 cabinet, company, meeting
08 advisers, assembly, congress, ministry, trustees
09 committee, gathering, governors, multitude
10 commission, convention, government, parliament
11 convocation, directorate
12 advisory body, working party
13 governing body
14 administration, local authority

counsel
04 urge, warn
05 guide
06 advice, advise, direct, exhort, lawyer
07 caution, opinion, suggest
08 admonish, advocate, attorney, guidance, instruct
09 barrister, solicitor
10 admonition, suggestion
11 exhortation, information
12 consultation
14 recommendation

count
03 add, sum
04 deem, hold, list, poll, tell
05 add up, check, judge, score, tally, think, tot up, total
06 esteem, matter, number, reckon, regard
07 compute, include
08 consider, look upon
09 calculate, enumerate, reckoning, totting-up
10 cut some ice, full amount
11 calculation, computation, enumeration
15 make a difference

❑count on
05 trust
06 bank on, expect, rely on
08 depend on, reckon on

❑count out
04 omit
06 ignore
07 exclude
08 leave out, pass over
09 disregard, eliminate

countenance
04 back, face, look, mien
05 agree, allow, brook
06 endure, visage
07 approve, condone, endorse
08 features, sanction, tolerate
09 put up with
10 appearance, expression
11 physiognomy

counter
04 chip, coin, disc, meet
05 parry, piece, table, token
06 answer, combat, marker, offset, oppose, resist, return
07 adverse, against, dispute, opposed, respond, surface
08 contrary, opposing, opposite
09 hit back at, retaliate
10 contrary to, conversely
11 work surface

counteract
04 foil, undo
05 annul, check
06 defeat, hinder, negate, offset, oppose, resist, thwart
09 frustrate
10 invalidate, neutralize

counterbalance
04 undo
06 offset
08 equalize
09 make up for
10 counteract, neutralize
11 countervail
12 counterpoise
13 compensate for

counterfeit
04 copy, fake, sham
05 bogus, faked, false, feign, forge, fraud, pseud
06 forged, phoney, pirate
07 falsify, feigned, forgery, imitate, pretend
08 simulate, spurious
09 fabricate, imitation, reproduce, simulated
10 artificial, fraudulent
12 reproduction

countermand
05 annul, quash
06 cancel, repeal, revoke
07 rescind, reverse
08 abrogate, override, overturn

counterpart
04 copy, mate, twin
05 equal, match
06 fellow
07 obverse
08 parallel
09 duplicate
14 opposite number

countless
06 myriad, untold
07 endless, umpteen
08 infinite
09 boundless, limitless
10 numberless, without end
11 innumerable, measureless
12 immeasurable, incalculable

countrified
04 hick
05 rural
06 rustic
07 bucolic, idyllic, outback
08 agrarian, pastoral
10 provincial
12 agricultural

country
04 area, bush, land

05 realm, rural, state, wilds
06 landed, nation, people, region, rustic, sticks, voters
07 bucolic, idyllic, kingdom, outback, terrain
08 agrarian, citizens, electors, moorland, pastoral, republic
09 backwater, backwoods, green belt, provinces, residents, territory
10 population, provincial
12 agricultural, back of beyond, principality

▶ *Countries of the world*:
02 UK
03 USA
04 Chad, Cuba, Fiji, Iran, Iraq, Laos, Mali, Oman, Peru, Togo, USSR
05 Benin, Burma, Chile, China, Congo, Egypt, Gabon, Ghana, Haiti, India, Italy, Japan, Kenya, Libya, Malta, Nauru, Nepal, Niger, Palau, Qatar, Samoa, Spain, Syria, Tonga, Yemen, Zaire
06 Angola, Belize, Bhutan, Brazil, Brunei, Canada, Ceylon, Cyprus, France, Greece, Guinea, Guyana, Israel, Jordan, Kuwait, Latvia, Malawi, Mexico, Monaco, Norway, Panama, Poland, Russia, Rwanda, Taiwan, Turkey, Tuvalu, Uganda, Zambia, Sweden
07 Albania, Algeria, Andorra, Armenia, Austria, Bahrain, Belarus, Belgium, Bolivia, Burundi, Comoros, Croatia, Denmark, Ecuador, Eritrea, Estonia, Finland, Georgia, Germany, Grenada, Holland, Hungary, Iceland, Ireland, Jamaica, Lebanon, Lesotho, Liberia, Moldova, Morocco, Myanmar, Namibia, Nigeria, Romania, Senegal, Somalia, St Lucia, Tunisia, Ukraine, Uruguay, Vanuatu, Vietnam
08 Barbados, Botswana, Bulgaria, Cambodia, Cameroon, Colombia, Djibouti, Dominica, Ethiopia, Honduras, Kiribati, Malaysia, Maldives, Mongolia, Pakistan, Paraguay, Portugal, Rhodesia, Slovakia, Slovenia, Sri Lanka, Suriname, Tanzania,

Thailand, The Sudan, Zimbabwe
09 Argentina, Australia, Cape Verde, Greenland, Guatemala, Indonesia, Kampuchea, Lithuania, Macedonia, Mauritius, Nicaragua, San Marino, Singapore, Swaziland, The Gambia, Venezuela
10 Azerbaijan, Bangladesh, El Salvador, Ivory Coast, Kazakhstan, Kyrgyzstan, Luxembourg, Madagascar, Martinique, Mauritania, Micronesia, Mozambique, New Zealand, North Korea, Puerto Rico, Seychelles, South Korea, Tajikistan, The Bahamas, Uzbekistan, Yugoslavia
11 Afghanistan, Burkina Faso, Côte d'Ivoire, Philippines, Saudi Arabia, Sierra Leone, South Africa, Switzerland, Vatican City
12 Faroe Islands, French Guiana, Guinea-Bissau, Turkmenistan, Western Samoa
13 Czech Republic, Liechtenstein, United Kingdom
14 Papua New Guinea, Solomon Islands, The Netherlands
15 French Polynesia, Marshall Islands, St Kitts and Nevis
16 Equatorial Guinea
17 Antigua and Barbuda, Bosnia-Herzegovina, Dominican Republic, São Tomé and Príncipe, Trinidad and Tobago
18 United Arad Emirates
19 Netherlands Antilles
21 United States of America
22 Central African Republic
25 Democratic Republic of Congo, St Vincent and the Grenadines

countryman, countrywoman
04 boor, hick, hind
05 yokel
06 farmer, rustic
07 bumpkin, hayseed, peasant
09 hillbilly
10 clodhopper, compatriot
11 bushwhacker
12 backwoodsman

countryside
08 farmland, moorland
09 green belt, landscape

county
04 area
05 shire, state
06 region
08 district, province
09 territory
➤ See also **borough**; **state**; **province**

▶ *Names of counties and provinces of Eire*:
04 Cork, Leix, Mayo
05 Cavan, Clare, Kerry, Laois, Louth, Meath, Sligo
06 Carlow, Dublin, Galway, Offaly
07 Donegal, Kildare, Leitrim, Munster, Wexford, Wicklow
08 Connacht, Kilkenny, Laoighis, Leinster, Limerick, Longford, Monaghan
09 Connaught, Roscommon, Tipperary, Waterford, Westmeath

▶ *Names of counties of England*:
04 Avon, Kent
05 Devon, Essex
06 Dorset, Durham, Surrey
07 Cumbria, Norfolk, Suffolk
08 Cheshire, Cornwall, Somerset
09 Berkshire, Cleveland, Hampshire, Wiltshire
10 Derbyshire, East Sussex, Humberside, Lancashire, Merseyside, Shropshire, West Sussex
11 Isle of Wight, Oxfordshire, Tyne and Wear
12 Bedfordshire, Lincolnshire, Warwickshire, West Midlands
13 Greater London, Herefordshire, Hertfordshire, Staffordshire, West Yorkshire
14 Cambridgeshire, Leicestershire, North Yorkshire, Northumberland, South Yorkshire, Worcestershire
15 Buckinghamshire, Gloucestershire, Nottinghamshire
16 Northamptonshire
17 Greater Manchester
20 Hereford and Worcester

► *Counties and council areas of Scotland*:

04 Fife
05 Angus, Moray
07 Borders, Falkirk, Lothian, Tayside
08 Galloway, Grampian, Highland
09 Edinburgh
10 Dundee City, Inverclyde, Midlothian
11 East Lothian, Glasgow City, Strathclyde, West Lothian
12 Aberdeen City, East Ayrshire, Renfrewshire, West Stirling, Western Isles
13 Aberdeenshire, Argyll and Bute, Central Region, North Ayrshire, Orkney Islands, South Ayrshire
15 Perth and Kinross, Scottish Borders, Shetland Islands
16 Clackmannanshire, East Renfrewshire, North Lanarkshire, South Lanarkshire
18 East Dunbartonshire, West Dunbartonshire
19 Dumfries and Galloway

► *Counties and council areas of Wales*:

04 Taff
05 Clwyd, Conwy, Cynon, Dyfed, Gwent, Powys
07 Cardiff, Gwynedd, Newport, Rhondda, Swansea, Torfaen, Wrexham
08 Anglesey, Bridgend
10 Caerphilly, Ceredigion, Flintshire
12 Blaenau Gwent, Denbighshire, Mid Glamorgan
13 Merthyr Tydfil, Monmouthshire, Pembrokeshire, West Glamorgan
14 Isle of Anglesey, South Glamorgan
15 Carmarthenshire, Neath Port Talbot, Vale of Glamorgan

coup
04 deed, feat
05 stunt
06 action, putsch, revolt, stroke
07 exploit
08 takeover, uprising
09 coup d'état, manoeuvre, overthrow, rebellion
10 revolution

coup de grâce
04 kill
06 kibosh
07 quietus
08 clincher
09 death blow
11 come-uppance

coup d'état
04 coup
06 putsch, revolt
08 takeover, uprising
09 overthrow, rebellion
10 revolution

couple
03 duo, wed
04 ally, bind, join, link, pair, yoke
05 brace, hitch, marry
06 attach, buckle, fasten, lovers
07 conjoin, connect, twosome
08 partners
09 associate, newlyweds

coupon
04 form, slip, stub
05 check, token
06 ticket
07 voucher
11 certificate

courage
04 grit, guts
05 nerve, pluck, spunk
06 bottle, mettle, spirit, valour
07 bravery, heroism
08 audacity, backbone
09 fortitude, gallantry

courageous
04 bold
05 brave, gutsy, hardy
06 daring, heroic, plucky, spunky
07 gallant, valiant
08 fearless, intrepid, valorous
09 audacious, dauntless
10 determined
11 indomitable, lion-hearted

courier
05 envoy, guide
06 bearer, escort, herald, legate, nuncio, runner
07 carrier
08 emissary
09 estafette, messenger
10 pursuivant
13 dispatch rider

course
03 run, way
04 dish, flow, gush, hunt, lane, line, path, plan, pour, race, rise, road, tack, term, time
05 chase, lapse, march, orbit, order, route, spell, stage, surge, sweet, track, trail
06 afters, entrée, follow, ground, manner, period, policy, pursue, remove, series, stream, system
07 channel, circuit, dessert, passage, process, pudding, regimen, studies
08 approach, duration, progress, run after, schedule, sequence, starters, syllabus
09 appetizer, direction, entremets, procedure, programme, racetrack
10 curriculum, flight path, succession, trajectory
11 development, furtherance, progression
12 hors d'oeuvres

□in due course
07 finally
10 eventually
13 sooner or later

□of course
06 surely
07 no doubt
08 to be sure
09 certainly, naturally
10 by all means, definitely
11 doubtlessly, indubitably, undoubtedly
13 needless to say

court
03 bar, woo
04 date, quad, ring, seek, yard
05 arena, bench, green, patio, plaza, train, trial
06 castle, incite, invite, palace, prompt, pursue
07 assizes, attract, cortège, flatter, provoke, retinue, session, solicit
08 cloister, go steady, lawcourt, tribunal
09 cultivate, enclosure, entourage, esplanade, household, judiciary
10 attendants, quadrangle
14 royal residence

► *Names of courts*:

07 assizes
09 High Court, Old Bailey
10 civil court, crown court
11 county court, family court
12 court-martial, federal court, House of Lords, Privy Council, sheriff court, Supreme Court

13 coroner's court, criminal court, juvenile court
14 court of appeals, court of justice, Court of Session,
➤ See also **legal**

courteous
04 kind
05 civil
06 polite, urbane
07 courtly, gallant, refined
08 debonair, obliging, polished, well-bred
09 attentive
10 chivalrous, respectful
11 considerate, gentlemanly
12 well-mannered

courtesy
04 tact
06 favour
07 manners, respect
08 breeding, chivalry, civility, kindness, urbanity
09 deference, gallantry
10 politeness, refinement
11 good manners

courtier
04 lady, lord, page
05 noble, toady
07 steward, subject
08 follower, liegeman, nobleman
09 attendant, cup-bearer, flatterer, sycophant
11 train-bearer
13 lady-in-waiting

courtly
05 civil
06 formal, lordly, polite
07 elegant, gallant, refined, stately
08 decorous, gracious, high-bred, obliging, polished
09 dignified
10 chivalrous, flattering

courtship
06 affair, dating, wooing
07 chasing, pursuit, romance
08 courting, going-out
11 going steady

courtyard
04 area, quad, yard
05 court, patio, plaza
06 atrium, square
08 cloister
09 enclosure, esplanade
10 quadrangle

cove
03 bay
05 bight, creek, fiord, firth, inlet
07 estuary

covenant
04 bond, deed, pact
05 agree, trust
06 engage, pledge, treaty
07 compact, promise
08 contract
09 concordat, indenture, stipulate, undertake
10 commitment
11 arrangement, stipulation, undertaking

cover
03 cup, lid, top
04 bury, cake, case, coat, daub, film, hide, skin, veil, wrap
05 cross, dress, duvet, front, guard, layer, treat
06 attire, canopy, carpet, clothe, encase, insure, jacket, mantle, screen, shield, shroud
07 binding, blanket, coating, conceal, envelop, obscure, overlay, plaster, replace, shelter, stretch, swaddle, wrapper, wreathe
08 accoutre, blankets, clothing, deal with, describe, disguise, envelope, go across, pretence
09 assurance, bedspread, encompass, indemnify, indemnity, insurance, safeguard, whitewash
10 bedclothes, camouflage, conspiracy, provide for, recompense, stand in for, travel over
11 concealment, hiding-place, incorporate, investigate, smokescreen
12 compensation
15 indemnification

❏ **cover up**
06 hush up
07 conceal, repress
08 keep dark, suppress
09 dissemble, gloss over, whitewash
10 keep secret

coverage
04 item
05 story
06 report
07 account, reports
08 analysis
09 reportage, reporting

covering
03 top
04 case, coat, film, roof, skin
05 cover, crust, layer, shell

06 carpet, casing, veneer
07 blanket, coating, housing, overlay, roofing, shelter
08 clothing, wrapping
10 protection
11 descriptive, explanatory

covert
06 hidden, secret, veiled
07 private
08 sidelong, stealthy, ulterior
09 concealed, underhand
10 dissembled
11 clandestine, unsuspected
13 subreptitious, surreptitious

cover-up
05 front
06 façade, screen
09 whitewash
10 complicity, conspiracy
11 concealment, smokescreen

covet
04 envy, want
05 crave, fancy
06 desire
07 long for
08 begrudge, yearn for
09 hanker for, hunger for, lust after, thirst for

covetous
06 greedy
07 craving, envious, jealous, longing, wanting
08 desirous, grasping, yearning
09 hankering, hungering, rapacious, thirsting
10 avaricious, insatiable

covey
03 nid
04 bevy
05 flock, group, skein
06 flight
07 cluster

cow
05 bully, daunt, scare
06 dismay, rattle, subdue
07 overawe, unnerve
08 browbeat, domineer
10 dishearten, intimidate

coward
04 sook, wimp
05 sissy
07 chicken, cry-baby
08 deserter, poltroon, recreant
10 faint-heart, scaredy-cat
11 yellow-belly

cowardice
13 pusillanimity, spinelessness

cowardly
04 soft, weak

cowboy *(continued)*

06 craven, scared, yellow
07 chicken, gutless, jittery
08 timorous, unheroic
09 spineless, weak-kneed
11 lily-livered
12 faint-hearted
13 pusillanimous, yellow-bellied

cowboy

05 rogue, waddy
06 drover, gaucho, herder
07 bungler, cowhand, cowpoke, rancher, vaquero
08 buckaroo, herdsman, ranchero, stockman
09 cattleman, scoundrel
12 bronco-buster, cattleherder

cower

05 quail, quake, shake, skulk, wince
06 cringe, crouch, flinch, grovel, recoil, shiver, shrink
07 tremble

coy

03 shy
04 arch, prim
05 timid
06 demure, modest
07 bashful, evasive, prudish
08 backward, reserved, retiring, skittish
09 shrinking, withdrawn
10 coquettish
11 flirtatious

crabbed, crabby

04 sour, tart
05 acrid, cross, surly, testy
06 morose, snappy
07 awkward, fretful, grouchy, iracund, prickly
08 captious, churlish, perverse, petulant, snappish
09 crotchety, difficult, irascible, irritable, splenetic
11 acrimonious, bad-tempered, ill-tempered
12 cantankerous, iracundulous

crack

02 go
03 dig, gag, gap, hit, pop, try
04 bump, chip, clap, flaw, gibe, joke, line, quip, rift, shot, slap, snap, stab
05 break, chink, cleft, smack, solve, split
06 breach, cavity, choice, cranny, expert, report
07 attempt, crevice, fissure, rupture, shatter, unravel

08 collapse, decipher, fracture, one-liner, splinter, superior, top-notch
09 break down, brilliant, excellent, explosion, figure out, first-rate, witticism
10 first-class, go to pieces, hand-picked

❑ **crack down on**

04 stop
05 check, crush, limit
07 confine, control, repress
08 restrict, suppress
10 act against, put a stop to
11 clamp down on

❑ **crack up**

05 go mad
09 break down
10 go to pieces
11 lose control

crackdown

05 check
08 crushing
09 clampdown
10 repression
11 suppression

cracked

04 daft, nuts, torn
05 barmy, batty, crazy, loony, nutty, split
06 broken, crazed, faulty, flawed, insane
07 damaged, foolish, idiotic
08 crackpot, deranged, fissured
09 defective, imperfect
12 round the bend
13 off your rocker

crackers

03 mad
04 daft, nuts
05 batty, crazy, loony, nutty
07 cracked, foolish, idiotic
08 crackpot
12 round the bend

crackle

04 snap
06 rustle, sizzle
09 crepitate
11 crepitation, decrepitate
13 decrepitation

crackpot

04 dork, fool
05 freak, idiot, loony
06 nutter, weirdo
07 oddball

cradle

03 bed, cot
04 crib, hold, lull, rock, tend
05 fount, nurse

06 nestle, origin, source, spring
07 nurture, shelter, support
08 bassinet, carry-cot
10 birthplace, wellspring

craft

03 art, job
04 boat, line, ship, work
05 flair, knack, skill, trade
06 talent, vessel
07 ability, calling, pursuit
08 aptitude, artistry
09 dexterity, expertise, handiwork, spaceship, technique
10 employment, handicraft, occupation, spacecraft
11 skilfulness, workmanship

craftsman, craftswoman

05 maker, smith
06 artist, expert, master, wright
07 artisan
10 technician
13 skilled worker

craftsmanship

05 skill
07 mastery
08 artistry
09 dexterity, expertise, technique
11 workmanship

crafty

03 sly
04 foxy, wily
05 canny, sharp
06 artful, astute, shrewd, subtle
07 crooked, cunning, devious
08 scheming
09 conniving, designing
11 calculating, duplicitous

crag

03 tor
04 peak, rock
05 bluff, cliff, ridge, scarp
08 pinnacle
10 escarpment

craggy

05 rocky, rough, stony
06 jagged, rugged, uneven
07 cragged
11 precipitous

cram

03 jam, ram
04 fill, glut, pack, swot
05 crowd, crush, force, gorge, grind, mug up, press, stuff
06 fill up, revise
07 compact, squeeze
08 bone up on, compress

cramp
04 ache, pain, pang
05 check, crick, limit, spasm
06 arrest, bridle, hamper, hinder, impede, stitch, stymie, thwart, twinge
07 confine, inhibit, shackle
08 handicap, obstruct, restrict
09 frustrate
14 pins and needles

cramped
04 full, poky
05 small, tight
06 narrow, packed
07 crowded
08 closed in, confined, squashed, squeezed
09 congested, jam-packed
11 overcrowded
13 uncomfortable

crane
05 davit, hoist, winch
06 tackle
07 derrick
14 block and tackle

crank
05 freak, idiot, loony
06 madman, nutter, weirdo
07 oddball
08 crackpot
09 character, eccentric

cranky
05 cross, surly, testy
06 crabby, snappy
07 awkward, prickly
08 freakish, peculiar
09 crotchety, difficult, eccentric, irritable
11 bad-tempered, ill-tempered
12 cantankerous
13 idiosyncratic
14 unconventional

cranny
03 gap
04 hole, nook, rent
05 chink, cleft, crack
07 crevice, fissure, opening
10 interstice

crash
03 din, hit
04 bang, boom, bump, dash, fail, fall, fold, ruin, thud
05 clang, clank, clash, prang, rapid, smash, thump
06 batter, cut out, fold up, go bust, pack up, pile-up, plunge, topple
07 clatter, collide, founder, go under, run into, shatter
08 accident, collapse, downfall

09 collision, drive into, explosion
10 bankruptcy, depression
11 go to the wall, stop working
12 go on the blink

crass
04 rude
05 crude, dense
06 coarse, oafish, stupid
08 tactless, unsubtle
09 unrefined
10 blundering, indelicate
11 insensitive
15 unsophisticated

crate
03 box
04 case
08 tea chest
09 container
11 packing-case

crater
03 dip, pit
04 hole
05 abyss, chasm
06 cavity, hollow
10 depression

crave
04 need, want, wish
05 covet, fancy
06 desire
07 long for, pine for
08 yearn for
09 hunger for, lust after

craven
06 afraid, scared, yellow
07 chicken, fearful, gutless
08 cowardly, poltroon, recreant, timorous, unheroic
09 spineless, weak-kneed
11 lily-livered
12 faint-hearted, mean-spirited
13 pusillanimous

craving
04 lust, need, urge, wish
06 desire, hunger, pining, thirst
07 longing, panting, sighing
08 appetite, yearning
09 hankering

crawl
04 drag, edge, fawn, inch, teem
05 creep, swarm, toady
06 cringe, grovel, seethe, squirm, suck up, writhe
07 bristle, flatter, slither, wriggle
11 curry favour
12 bow and scrape

craze
03 fad
04 mode, rage, whim

05 mania, thing, trend, vogue
06 frenzy
07 fashion, novelty, passion
09 obsession, the latest

crazed
03 mad
04 nuts, wild
05 crazy, loony
06 insane
07 berserk, lunatic
08 demented, deranged, unhinged
10 unbalanced
12 round the bend
13 off your rocker, out of your mind, round the twist

crazy
03 mad, odd
04 avid, daft, keen, nuts, wild
05 barmy, batty, loony, loopy, nutty, potty, silly
06 absurd, ardent, insane
07 berserk, bonkers, idiotic, lunatic, smitten, zealous
08 crackpot, demented, deranged, doolally, unhinged
09 disturbed, fanatical, foolhardy, half-baked, ludicrous
10 infatuated, out to lunch, ridiculous, unbalanced
11 hare-brained, nonsensical, not all there, unrealistic
12 crackbrained, round the bend
13 off your rocker, out of your mind, round the twist

❑**go crazy**
04 flip
05 go ape, go mad
11 flip your lid, go ballistic
15 lose your marbles

creak
04 rasp
05 grate, grind, groan
06 scrape, squeak, squeal
07 scratch, screech

creaky
05 rusty
07 grating, rasping, squeaky
08 grinding, groaning, scraping
09 squeaking, squealing
10 scratching, screeching

cream
04 best, pale, pick
05 elite, paste, prime, salve
06 flower, lotion
07 unguent

08 emulsion, liniment, off-
white, ointment
09 emollient
10 choice part, select part
14 crème de la crème, pick of
the bunch

creamy
04 oily, pale, rich
05 milky, pasty, thick
06 creamy, smooth
07 buttery, velvety
08 off-white

crease
04 fold, line, ruck, tuck
05 crimp, pleat, ridge
06 furrow, groove, pucker
07 crinkle, crumple, wrinkle
09 corrugate
11 corrugation

❏**crease up**
05 amuse
09 make laugh

create
04 coin, form, make
05 build, erect, found, frame,
hatch, mould, set up, shape
06 design, devise, invent,
invest, lead to, ordain
07 appoint, compose, concoct,
develop, install, produce
08 engender, generate, occasion
09 construct, establish,
fabricate, formulate,
institute, originate
10 bring about, inaugurate
14 bring into being

creation
04 life, work
05 birth, world
06 cosmos, design, making,
nature, origin
07 concept, genesis, product
08 universe
09 formation, invention
10 brainchild, conception,
concoction, foundation,
initiation, innovation
11 achievement, chef d'oeuvre,
fabrication, institution,
masterpiece, origination
12 constitution, construction
13 establishment

creative
06 clever, gifted
07 fertile
08 artistic, inspired, talented
09 ingenious, intuitive,
inventive, visionary
10 productive
11 imaginative, resourceful

creativity
06 talent, vision
08 artistry
09 fertility, ingenuity
10 cleverness
11 imagination, inspiration
13 inventiveness

creator
03 God
05 maker
06 author, father, mother
07 builder, founder
08 composer, designer,
inventor, producer
09 architect, initiator
10 originator, prime mover

creature
03 man
04 bird, body, fish, soul
05 beast, being, human
06 animal, insect, person
11 living thing

credence
05 faith, trust
06 belief, credit
10 confidence,
dependence

credentials
04 deed
05 title
06 papers, permit
07 diploma, licence, warrant
09 documents, reference
11 certificate, testimonial
12 identity card
15 proof of identity

credibility
09 integrity
10 likelihood
11 probability, reliability
12 plausibility

credible
06 honest, likely
07 sincere, tenable
08 possible, probable, reliable
09 plausible, thinkable
10 believable, convincing,
persuasive, reasonable
11 conceivable, trustworthy

credit
04 fame
05 asset, glory, pride, trust
06 accept, assign, belief,
charge, esteem, honour,
impute, praise, thanks
07 acclaim, ascribe, believe, fall
for, put down, tribute
08 approval, credence
09 attribute, laudation

10 confidence, estimation, in
the black, reputation
11 distinction, pride and joy,
recognition, subscribe to
15 acknowledgement

❏**on credit**
06 on tick
09 on account
10 on the slate
13 by instalments
15 on the never-never

creditable
04 good
06 worthy
08 laudable
09 admirable, deserving,
estimable, excellent,
exemplary, reputable
10 honourable
11 commendable, respectable
12 praiseworthy

creditor
06 debtee, lender
09 loan shark

credulity
07 naïvety
09 silliness, stupidity
10 dupability, simplicity
11 gullibility

credulous
05 naïve
07 dupable
08 gullible, trusting, wide-eyed
12 overtrusting, unsuspecting

creed
05 canon, credo, dogma, faith
06 belief, tenets
08 articles, doctrine, teaching
09 catechism
10 persuasion, principles

creek
03 bay
04 cove
05 bight, fiord, firth, inlet
07 estuary

creep
04 edge, fear, inch, worm
05 crawl, slink, sneak, toady
06 fawner, grovel, tiptoe,
writhe, yes-man
07 slither, wriggle
09 sycophant
10 bootlicker

creeper
04 vine
05 liana, plant
06 runner
07 climber, rambler, trailer
13 climbing plant, trailing plant

creepy
05 eerie, scary, weird
06 spooky
07 macabre, ominous
08 gruesome, horrible, horrific, menacing, sinister
10 disturbing, horrifying, terrifying, unpleasant
11 frightening, hair-raising, nightmarish, threatening
13 bloodcurdling, spine-chilling

crescent-shaped
06 lunate
07 falcate, lunated, lunular
08 falcated
09 bow-shaped, falciform
12 sickle-shaped

crest
03 top
04 apex, comb, mane, peak
05 badge, crown, plume, ridge
06 device, emblem, summit, symbol, tassel
07 panache, regalia
08 aigrette, caruncle, insignia, pinnacle
09 cockscomb
10 coat of arms

crestfallen
03 sad
08 dejected, downcast
09 depressed
10 despondent, dispirited
11 discouraged, downhearted
12 disappointed, disheartened
13 in the doldrums
14 down in the dumps

crevasse
05 abyss, chasm, cleft, crack
07 fissure
11 bergschrund

crevice
03 gap
04 hole, rift, slit
05 chink, cleft, crack, split
06 cranny
07 fissure, opening
10 interstice

crew
03 lot, mob, set
04 band, gang, pack, team, unit
05 bunch, corps, crowd, force, group, party, squad, troop
07 company
10 complement

crib
03 bed, cot

04 copy, lift
05 cheat, pinch, steal
06 pirate
07 purloin
08 bassinet, carry-cot
10 plagiarize

crick
05 cramp, spasm
06 twinge
10 convulsion

cricket
➢ See also **sport**

► *Cricket terms include*:
02 lb
03 bat, cut, lbw, six, ton
04 bail, deep, duck, edge, four, grub, hook, over, pair, poke, pull, slip, tail, tice, wide
05 catch, dolly, glide, gully, knock, mid-on, plumb, point, silly, skyer, snick, stump
06 beamer, bowled, crease, glance, googly, howzat, leg bye, long on, maiden, mid-off, middle, no ball, not out, opener, play on, run out, single, square, stumps, the leg, umpire, whites, wicket, yorker
07 batsman, bouncer, declare, dismiss, grubber, infield, last man, leg side, leg slip, leg spin, long hop, long leg, long off, off-spin, on the up, spinner, striker, wrong 'un
08 bodyline, boundary, Chinaman, flannels, follow on, full toss, how's that, leg break, leg guard, long slip, long stop, misfield, off guard, off-break, off-drive, outfield, short leg, sledging, third man
09 batswoman, deep field, fieldsman, hit wicket, inswinger, leg before, leg theory, long field, mid-wicket, overpitch, short slip, square leg, tip and run
10 cover drive, draw stumps, fast bowler, leg spinner, maiden over, pace-bowler, right guard, seam bowler, silly mid-on, skittle out, spin-bowler, twelfth man
11 clean bowled, fast bowling, fieldswoman, grass-cutter, pace-bowling, seam bowling, sight screen, silly mid-off, spin-bowling

12 carry your bat, wicket-keeper
13 keep your end up, maiden century, night-watchman, popping crease
14 off the back foot
15 bowl a maiden over, caught and bowled, leather on willow, leg before wicket, square leg umpire

► *Names of cricketers*:
04 **Ames** (Leslie), **Bedi** (Bishan), **Bird** (Richard 'Dicky'), **Hall** (Wesley), **Hick** (Graham), **Khan** (Imran), **Lara** (Brian)
05 **Akram** (Wasim), **Amiss** (Dennis Leslie), **Evans** (Godfrey), **Gooch** (Graham), **Gough** (Darren), **Gower** (David Ivon), **Grace** (William Gilbert), **Greig** (Tony), **Hobbs** (Sir Jack), **Knott** (Alan), **Laker** (Jim), **Lloyd** (Clive Hubert), **Warne** (Shane)
06 **Bailey** (Trevor), **Benaud** (Richie), **Border** (Allan), **Botham** (Ian), **Dexter** (Ted), **Edrich** (John), **Hadlee** (Sir Richard), **Hutton** (Len), **Lillie** (Dennis Keith), **Rhodes** (Wilfred), **Sobers** (Sir Garfield), **Titmus** (Fred), **Warner** (Sir Pelham 'Plum')
07 **Ambrose** (Curtley), **Boycott** (Geoffrey), **Bradman** (Sir Donald), **Compton** (Dennis), **Cowdrey** (Sir Colin), **Gatting** (Mike), **Holding** (Michael), **Hussain** (Nasser), **Jardine** (Douglas Robert), **Larwood** (Harold), **Pollock** (Graham), **Stewart** (Alec), **Trueman** (Fred)
08 **Atherton** (Michael), **Chappell** (Greg), **Chappell** (Ian), **Gavaskar** (Sunil), **Kapil Dev** (Nihanj), **Richards** (Vivian), **Sheppard** (David Stewart)
09 **D'Oliveira** (Basil Lewis)
11 **Heyhoe Flint** (Rachel), **Illingworth** (Raymond)

crier
06 herald
09 announcer, messenger
10 proclaimer

crime
03 sin
04 vice
06 felony
07 misdeed, offence, outrage
07 atrocity, iniquity, villainy
09 violation
10 misconduct, wrongdoing
11 delinquency, law-breaking, lawlessness, malfeasance
12 misdemeanour
13 transgression

➤ *Types of crime:*
03 ABH, GBH
05 rape
05 arson, fraud, theft
06 hijack, murder, piracy
07 assault, battery, bribery, forgery, larceny, mugging, perjury, robbery, treason
08 burglary, homicide
09 blackmail, extortion, joy-riding, pilfering, terrorism, vandalism
10 corruption, kidnapping
11 hooliganism
12 drink-driving, embezzlement, manslaughter
13 drug-smuggling
14 counterfeiting
➤ See also **legal**

criminal
04 bent, evil, gang, ring
05 felon, wrong
06 wicked
07 convict, corrupt, crooked, culprit, illegal, illicit, lawless, obscene, villain
08 culpable, offender, prisoner, unlawful
09 felonious, miscreant, nefarious, wrongdoer
10 delinquent, indictable, iniquitous, law-breaker, malefactor, scandalous, underworld, villainous
11 disgraceful, law-breaking
13 reprehensible

➤ *Types of criminal:*
03 lag
04 hood, thug
05 crook, thief
06 bandit, forger, gunman, killer, mugger, pirate, rapist, robber, vandal
07 brigand, burglar, hoodlum, mobster, poacher, rustler
08 arsonist, assassin, bigamist, car-thief, gangster, hijacker, jailbird, joyrider, murderer, perjurer, smuggler, swindler

09 buccaneer, embezzler, kidnapper, larcenist, racketeer, terrorist
10 bootlegger, cat burglar, dope pusher, fire-raiser, highwayman, pickpocket, shoplifter, trespasser
11 armed robber, blackmailer, safecracker, war criminal
12 drug-smuggler, extortionist, housebreaker
13 counterfeiter

➤ *Names of criminals:*
03 **Ray** (James Earl)
04 **Aram** (Eugene), **Hare** (William), **Hood** (Robin), **Kray** (Reginald), **Kray** (Ronald), **Rais** (Gilles de), **Todd** (Sweeney)
05 **Biggs** (Ronald), **Blood** (Thomas), **Booth** (John Wilkes), **Brady** (Ian), **Burke** (William), **Ellis** (Ruth), **James** (Jesse), **Kelly** (Ned), **Lucan** (Richard John Bingham, Earl of)
06 **Barrow** (Clyde), **Bonney** (William H), **Borden** (Lizzie Andrew), **Capone** (Al), **Corday** (Charlotte), **Nilsen** (Dennis), **Oswald** (Lee Harvey), **Parker** (Bonnie), **Rob Roy, Sirhan** (Sirhan), **Turpin** (Dick)
07 **Crippen** (Hawley Harvey), **Hindley** (Myra), **Luciano** (Charles 'Lucky'), **Shipman** (Harold)
08 **Barabbas, Christie** (John Reginald Halliday), **Hanratty** (James)
09 **Berkowitz** (David), **Sutcliffe** (Peter)
11 **Billy the Kid**
13 **Jack the Ripper**
15 **Yorkshire Ripper**

crimp
04 fold, tuck
05 flute, pleat, ridge
06 crease, furrow, gather, groove, pucker, rumple
07 crinkle, crumple, wrinkle
09 corrugate

cringe
03 bow, shy
04 bend, fawn
05 cower, crawl, creep, quail, start, stoop, toady, wince
06 blench, crouch, flinch, grovel, recoil, shrink

07 flatter, tremble
08 draw back

crinkle
04 curl, fold, line, ruck, tuck, wave
05 crimp, pleat, ridge, twist
06 crease, furrow, groove, pucker, ruffle, rumple
07 crinkle, crumple, wrinkle
09 corrugate
11 corrugation

crinkly
05 curly, kinky
06 fluted, frizzy, ridged, tucked
07 creased, crimped, grooved, pleated, rumpled, wrinkly
08 crumpled, furrowed, puckered, wrinkled
10 corrugated

cripple
04 lame, maim, ruin
05 spoil
06 damage, hamper, impair, impede, injure, weaken
07 destroy, disable, vitiate
08 handicap, paralyse, sabotage
09 hamstring
10 debilitate
12 incapacitate

crippled
04 lame
08 disabled
09 paralysed
11 handicapped
13 incapacitated

crisis
03 fix, jam
04 hole, mess
06 crunch, pickle, scrape
07 dilemma, problem, trouble
08 hot water, quandary
09 emergency, extremity

crisp
04 cool, firm, hard
05 brisk, clear, fresh, short, terse
06 chilly, crispy, snappy
07 bracing, brittle, crumbly, crunchy, friable
08 incisive, succinct
10 refreshing

criterion
04 norm, rule, test
05 canon, gauge, model, scale
07 measure
08 exemplar, standard
09 benchmark, yardstick
10 touchstone

critic
05 judge
06 carper, censor, pundit
07 analyst, knocker
08 attacker, censurer, reviewer
09 backbiter, nit-picker
11 commentator, fault-finder

critical
05 grave, major, vital
06 urgent
07 carping, crucial, exigent, pivotal, probing, serious
08 captious, deciding, decisive, historic, niggling, perilous, pressing, scathing
09 cavilling, essential, important, momentous, quibbling, vitriolic
10 analytical, censorious, derogatory, diagnostic, discerning, nit-picking, precarious
11 disparaging, explanatory, judgemental, penetrating
12 all-important, disapproving, fault-finding, vituperative

criticism
04 flak
05 blame, stick
06 niggle, review
07 censure, reproof, slating
08 analysis, bad press, brickbat, critique, knocking
09 appraisal, judgement
10 assessment, commentary, evaluation, nit-picking
11 disapproval, explanation
12 condemnation, fault-finding

criticize
03 nag, pan
04 carp, slam
05 blame, decry, judge, knock, slate, snipe
06 assess, attack, review
07 analyse, censure, condemn, explain, nit-pick, rubbish, run down, slag off
08 appraise, badmouth, denounce, evaluate
09 denigrate, disparage, excoriate, interpret
10 go to town on, vituperate
11 pick holes in
12 pull to pieces, tear to shreds
13 find fault with, tear a strip off
15 do a hatchet job on

critique
05 essay
06 review
07 write-up
08 analysis

09 appraisal, judgement
10 assessment, commentary, evaluation, exposition
11 explanation, explication
14 interpretation

croak
03 caw
04 crow, gasp, rasp
06 squawk, wheeze

crock
03 jar, pot
06 vessel

crockery
05 china
06 dishes
07 pottery
09 porcelain, tableware
11 earthenware

croft
04 farm, plot
12 smallholding

crony
03 pal
04 ally, chum, mate
05 buddy
06 friend
07 comrade
08 follower, sidekick
09 associate, companion
10 accomplice

crook
03 bow
04 bend, flex, hook, warp
05 cheat, curve, fraud, rogue, shark, thief, twist
06 con man, deform, robber
07 distort, villain
08 criminal, swindler
10 law-breaker

crooked
04 awry, bent
05 askew, bowed, shady
06 curved, hooked, shifty, uneven, warped, zigzag
07 corrupt, illegal, illicit, sinuous, twisted, winding
08 criminal, deformed, lopsided, slanting, unlawful
09 contorted, deceitful, dishonest, distorted, irregular, misshapen, nefarious, off-centre, skew-whiff, underhand
10 asymmetric, fraudulent

croon
03 hum
04 lilt, sing
06 warble

crop
03 cut, lop, lot, mow, set
04 clip, pare, snip, trim
05 batch, prune, shear, yield
06 fruits, growth, reduce
07 curtail, harvest, produce, reaping, shorten, vintage

❑crop up
05 arise, occur
06 appear, arrive, come up, emerge, happen, turn up
09 take place
10 come to pass

cross
03 mix, woe
04 foil, ford, join, lace, load, meet, pain, span
05 angry, blend, check, short, surly, trial, vexed, worry
06 bridge, burden, crabby, grumpy, hybrid, impede, oppose, peeved, put out, shirty, snappy, thwart
07 annoyed, grouchy, mixture, mongrel, prickly
08 converge, diagonal, obstruct, pass over, snappish, traverse
09 crotchety, difficult, fractious, hybridize, intersect, irascible, irritable, splenetic
10 affliction, crossbreed, criss-cross, interbreed, interweave, transverse
11 bad-tempered, combination, ill-tempered, tribulation
12 cantankerous, disagreeable

▶ *Types of cross:*
03 tau
04 ankh, rood
05 Greek, Latin, papal
06 botoné, Celtic, fleury, fylfot, moline, potent, Y-cross
07 Calvary, capital, Cornish, Maltese, Russian, saltire
08 cardinal, crosslet, crucifix, Lorraine, quadrate, St Peter's, swastika
09 encolpion, Jerusalem, St Andrew's, St George's
11 patriarchal
13 Constantinian

cross-examine
04 pump, quiz
05 grill
07 examine
08 question
11 interrogate

crossing
04 trip
06 voyage
07 journey, passage
08 junction
13 zebra crossing
14 Toucan crossing
15 pelican crossing

crosswise
04 awry, over
06 across, aslant
07 athwart
08 sideways
09 crossways, obliquely
10 crisscross, diagonally

crotchety
05 cross, surly, testy
06 crabby, crusty, grumpy
07 awkward, crabbed, grouchy, iracund, peevish, prickly
08 contrary, petulant
09 difficult, fractious, irritable
11 bad-tempered
12 cantankerous, disagreeable, iracundulous, obstreperous

crouch
03 bow
04 bend, duck
05 cower, kneel, squat, stoop
06 cringe

crow
04 brag
05 boast, exult, gloat, vaunt
07 bluster, rejoice, show off
15 blow your own horn

crowd
03 jam, lot, mob, set
04 army, cram, gate, herd, host, mass, pack, pile, push
05 bunch, crush, drove, flock, group, horde, press, shove, stuff, surge, swarm
06 circle, clique, gather, huddle, jostle, masses, people, rabble, squash, throng
07 cluster, company, congest, squeeze, turnout, viewers
08 assembly, audience, overflow, populace, riff-raff
09 listeners, multitude
10 congregate, fraternity, spectators

crowded
04 busy, full
06 filled, jammed, packed
07 crammed, cramped, crushed, teeming
08 overfull, swarming
09 congested, jam-packed

11 chock-a-block
14 full to bursting

crown
03 cap, tip, top
04 acme, apex, king, peak
05 adorn, crest, glory, kudos, prize, queen, ruler, tiara
06 anoint, climax, diadem, height, honour, invest, summit, trophy, wreath
07 circlet, coronet, dignify, emperor, empress, festoon, garland, install, laurels, monarch, perfect, royalty
08 complete, enthrone, finalize, monarchy, pinnacle
09 sovereign

crowning
03 top
05 final
07 perfect, supreme
08 ultimate
09 climactic, paramount, sovereign, unmatched
10 consummate, coronation
11 culminating, investiture
12 enthronement

crucial
03 key
05 major, vital
06 trying, urgent
07 central, pivotal, testing
08 critical, decisive, historic
09 essential, important

crucify
05 slate
06 punish
07 execute, torment, torture
08 ridicule
09 criticize, persecute

crude
03 hot, raw
04 blue, lewd, rude
05 basic, bawdy, dirty, rough
06 coarse, earthy, risqué, simple, smutty, vulgar
07 obscene, raunchy, uncouth
08 indecent
09 makeshift, offensive, primitive, unrefined

cruel
04 evil, grim, mean
05 nasty
06 bitter, brutal, fierce, flinty, savage, severe, unkind
07 callous, cutting, hellish, inhuman, painful, vicious
08 barbaric, fiendish, indurate, inhumane, pitiless, ruthless, sadistic, spiteful, vengeful

09 barbarous, heartless, merciless, unfeeling
10 malevolent
11 cold-blooded, hard-hearted, remorseless, unrelenting
12 bloodthirsty

cruelty
05 abuse, spite, venom
06 malice, sadism
07 tyranny
08 bullying, ferocity, meanness, savagery, severity, violence
09 barbarity, brutality, harshness
10 inhumanity
11 callousness, viciousness
12 ruthlessness
13 heartlessness

cruise
04 sail, taxi, trip
05 coast, drift, glide, slide
06 travel, voyage
07 holiday, journey
09 freewheel

crumb
03 bit, jot
04 atom, iota, mite
05 flake, grain, piece, scrap, shred, speck
06 morsel, sliver, titbit
07 snippet, soupçon
08 particle

crumble
03 rot
05 crush, decay, grind, pound
06 powder
07 break up
08 collapse, fragment
09 break down, decompose, fall apart, pulverize
12 disintegrate, fall to pieces

crumbly
05 short
07 brittle, friable, powdery
11 pulverulent

crummy
06 grotty, rotten, shoddy, trashy
07 useless
08 inferior, pathetic, rubbishy
09 half-baked, worthless

crumple
04 fall, fold
05 crush
06 crease, pucker, rumple
07 crinkle, wrinkle
08 collapse

crunch
04 bite, chew, crux, test

05 champ, chomp, crush, grind, munch, pinch, smash
06 crisis
09 emergency, masticate
13 moment of truth

crusade
04 push, work
05 cause, drive, fight, jihad
06 attack, battle, strive
07 holy war, promote
08 advocate, campaign, movement, struggle

crusader
06 zealot
07 fighter, pilgrim
08 champion, promoter
10 campaigner, enthusiast

crush
03 jam
04 mash, mill, pash, pulp
05 abash, break, crowd, grind, pound, press, quash, quell, shame, smash, upset
06 crunch, squash, subdue
07 conquer, crumble, passion, put down, screw up, shatter, squeeze, wrinkle
08 demolish, overcome, suppress, vanquish
09 devastate, humiliate, overpower, overwhelm, pulverize, triturate
11 infatuation

crust
04 coat, husk, rind, scab, skin
05 layer, shell
06 caking, casing, mantle
07 coating, surface, topping
08 covering, exterior

crustacean
➤ *Types of crustacean*:
04 crab
05 krill, prawn
06 shrimp
07 camaron, lobster
08 barnacle, crawfish, crayfish
09 centipede, langouste, millipede, water flea, woodlouse
10 hermit crab, sand hopper, spider crab
11 fiddler crab, langoustine
➤ See also **animal**

crusty
04 firm, hard
05 cross, gruff, surly, testy
06 crabby, grumpy, touchy
07 brusque, crabbed, crunchy, grouchy, peevish, prickly

08 contrary, petulant
09 breakable, difficult, fractious, irascible, irritable, splenetic, well-baked
11 bad-tempered
12 cantankerous, disagreeable, obstreperous

crux
03 nub
04 core
05 heart
06 centre, kernel
07 essence, nucleus
13 the bottom line

cry
03 sob
04 bawl, call, howl, plea, roar, wail, weep, yell
05 shout, tears, whine
06 scream, shriek, snivel
07 blubber, call out, screech, sobbing, weeping, whimper

◻**cry off**
06 cancel
07 back out
08 withdraw
14 change your mind, excuse yourself

◻**cry out for**
04 need, want
06 demand
07 call for, require
11 necessitate

crypt
04 tomb
05 vault
08 catacomb
09 mausoleum
10 undercroft
13 burial chamber

cryptic
04 dark
06 hidden, occult, secret
07 bizarre, obscure, strange
08 abstruse, esoteric, puzzling
09 ambiguous, enigmatic
10 mysterious, perplexing

crystallize
04 form
06 appear, emerge, harden
07 clarify
08 solidify

cub
03 pup
04 baby, tiro
05 puppy, whelp, youth
06 novice, rookie
07 fresher, learner, recruit, starter, student, trainee

08 beginner, freshman, initiate, neophyte
09 fledgling, greenhorn, offspring, youngster
10 apprentice, raw recruit, tenderfoot

cubbyhole
03 den
04 hole, slot
05 niche
06 recess
08 hideaway

cube
03 die
04 dice
05 block, solid
10 hexahedron

cuddle
03 hug, pet
04 hold, neck, snog
05 clasp, nurse
06 caress, enfold, fondle, nestle, smooch
07 embrace, snuggle
08 canoodle

cuddly
04 cosy, soft, warm
05 plump
07 lovable
08 huggable

cudgel
03 bat, hit
04 bash, beat, club, cosh, mace
05 clout, pound, stick
06 alpeen, batter, strike, thwack
07 clobber
08 bludgeon
09 bastinado, truncheon
10 shillelagh

cue
03 nod
04 hint, sign
06 prompt, signal
08 reminder, stimulus
10 indication, intimation, suggestion

cuff
03 box, hit
04 beat, belt, biff, clip, slap
05 clout, smack, thump, whack
06 buffet, strike
07 clobber

◻**off the cuff**
05 ad lib
09 extempore, impromptu
10 improvised, unprepared
11 unrehearsed
13 spontaneously

cuisine
07 cookery, cooking
10 cordon bleu
12 haute cuisine
15 nouvelle cuisine

cul-de-sac
07 dead end
10 blind alley
13 no through road

cull
04 kill, pick, sift, thin
05 amass, glean, pluck
06 choose, gather, select
07 destroy, pick out, thin out

culminate
03 end
05 close, end up
06 climax, finish, wind up
08 conclude

culmination
03 top
04 acme, apex, peak
05 crown
06 climax, finale, height, summit, zenith
08 pinnacle
09 high point
10 completion, conclusion

culpable
06 guilty, liable, sinful
07 at fault, peccant, to blame
09 offending
10 answerable, censurable
11 blameworthy, responsible

culprit
05 felon
07 convict, villain
08 criminal, offender
09 miscreant, wrongdoer
10 delinquent, law-breaker
11 guilty party

cult
03 fad
04 sect
05 craze, faith, trend, vogue
06 belief, school
07 faction, fashion, in-thing
08 movement, religion
09 obsession

cultivate
03 aid, dig, sow, woo
04 farm, grow, help, till, work
05 court, plant, raise, train
06 assist, foster, plough, polish, pursue, refine, work on
07 develop, enhance, forward, further, harvest, improve, nurture, prepare, produce
09 encourage, enlighten

cultivated
06 urbane
07 genteel, refined
08 cultured, educated, polished, well-read
09 civilized, scholarly
10 discerning
11 enlightened
13 sophisticated

cultural
04 folk
06 ethnic, tribal
07 liberal
08 artistic, communal, edifying, national, societal
09 aesthetic, educative, elevating, improving
10 broadening, civilizing, humanizing
11 educational, traditional

culture
05 mores, music
06 growth, habits
07 customs, society, the arts
08 heritage, learning, painting
09 behaviour, lifestyle, way of life
10 humanities, literature, philosophy, traditions
12 civilization

cultured
04 arty
06 polite, urbane
07 erudite, genteel, learned, refined
08 artistic, educated, polished, tasteful, well-bred, well-read
09 civilized, scholarly
10 cultivated
11 enlightened
12 intellectual, well-educated, well-informed
13 sophisticated

culvert
04 duct
05 drain, sewer
06 gutter
07 channel, conduit
11 watercourse

cumbersome
04 slow
05 bulky, heavy
06 clumsy
07 awkward, weighty
08 cumbrous, unwieldy
10 burdensome
11 complicated, inefficient

cumulative
07 growing
08 mounting
09 enlarging
10 collective, increasing
11 multiplying, snowballing

cunning
03 sly
04 deep, deft, foxy, wily
05 canny, sharp, skill, wiles
06 artful, astute, clever, crafty, shifty, shrewd, subtle, tricky
07 devious, skilful, slyness
08 deftness, fiendish, guileful, subtlety, trickery
09 deceitful, dexterous, ingenious
10 artfulness, astuteness, cleverness, craftiness

cup
03 mug
04 wine
05 award, medal, prize, punch
06 beaker, goblet, trophy
07 chalice, tankard

cupboard
05 chest, press
06 closet, locker, pantry
07 cabinet, dresser, tallboy
08 wardrobe
09 sideboard
12 Welsh dresser

cupidity
05 greed
06 hunger
07 avarice, avidity, longing
08 rapacity, voracity, yearning
09 eagerness, hankering
10 greediness
12 covetousness

curative
05 tonic
07 healing
08 remedial, salutary
09 healthful, medicinal, vulnerary
10 corrective, febrifugal
11 restorative, therapeutic
12 health-giving

curator
06 keeper, warden, warder
07 steward
08 guardian
09 attendant, caretaker, custodian

curb
04 rein
05 brake, check
06 bridle, damper, hinder, impede
07 control, inhibit, repress

curdle
08 hold back, moderate, restrain, restrict, suppress
09 constrain
10 constraint, impediment, limitation, repression

curdle
04 clot, sour, turn
07 congeal, ferment, thicken
08 solidify, turn sour
09 coagulate

cure
03 dry, fix
04 ease, heal, help, mend, salt
05 smoke, treat
06 elixir, kipper, pickle, remedy
07 correct, cure-all, healing, panacea, rectify, relieve, restore, therapy
08 antidote, make well, medicine, preserve
09 alleviate, treatment
11 restorative

curio
06 bygone
07 antique, bibelot, trinket
09 curiosity, objet d'art
10 knick-knack

curiosity
05 curio, freak
06 bygone, marvel, oddity, rarity, wonder
07 antique, exotica, inquiry, novelty, trinket
08 interest, nosiness, snooping
09 objet d'art, spectacle
10 knick-knack, phenomenon

curious
03 odd
04 nosy, rare
05 funny, novel, queer, weird
06 exotic, prying, quaint, unique
07 bizarre, strange, unusual
08 peculiar, puzzling, querying, snooping
09 inquiring, intrigued, searching
10 mysterious, remarkable, unorthodox
11 inquisitive, interfering, questioning
13 extraordinary
14 unconventional

curl
04 bend, coil, kink, loop, ring, turn, wave, wind
05 crimp, curve, frizz, helix, snake, swirl, twine, twirl, twist, whorl
06 ripple, scroll, spiral
07 crinkle, ringlet, wreathe

08 curlicue
09 corkscrew

curly
04 wavy
05 fuzzy, kinky
06 curled, frizzy, permed
07 coiling, crimped, curling, looping, turning, winding
08 twirling, twisting
09 corkscrew, spiralled
10 spiralling

currency
04 cash
05 bills, coins, money, notes
07 coinage
09 publicity
10 acceptance, popularity, prevalence
11 circulation, legal tender
13 dissemination

➤ *Names of currencies include*:
03 ecu, kip, lei, lek, leu, lev, som, sum, won, yen
04 baht, birr, cedi, dong, dram, euro, kina, kuna, kyat, lari, lats, lira, loti, mark, peso, pula, punt, rand, real, rial, riel, taka, tala, vatu, yuan
05 colon, dinar, dobra, franc, frank, krona, krone, kroon, kunar, leone, litas, manat, marka, naira, nakfa, pence, pound, riyal, rupee, sucre, tenge, tolar, zloty
06 balboa, dalasi, dirham, dollar, escudo, forint, gourde, gulden, hryvna, koruna, kwacha, kwanza, markka, new sol, pa'anga, pataca, peseta, rouble, rupiah, shekel, tugrik
07 Afghani, bolivar, cordoba, drachma, guarani, guilder, lempira, metical, ouguiya, quetzal, ringgit, rufiyaa
08 ngultrum, shilling, sterling, US dollar
09 boliviano, lilangeni, schilling
10 Swiss franc
11 Deutschmark, French franc, karbovanets, Turkish lira
12 Belgian franc, Deutsche mark
14 Canadian dollar
➤ See also **coin**; **money**

current
02 in
03 ebb, jet

04 flow, mood, tide
05 drift, swirl, tenor, trend
06 common, course, extant, modern, stream, trendy
07 draught, feeling, general, in vogue, ongoing, present
08 accepted, reigning, undertow, up-to-date
09 in fashion, prevalent
10 mainstream, present-day, prevailing, widespread
11 fashionable
12 contemporary

curriculum
06 course, module
08 subjects, syllabus
09 programme, timetable

curse
04 bane, cuss, damn, jinx, oath
05 beset, blast, spell, swear
06 blight, ordeal, plague
07 scourge, torment, trouble
08 anathema, calamity, denounce, disaster
09 blaspheme, expletive, imprecate, obscenity, profanity, swear-word
10 affliction, execration
11 bad language, imprecation, malediction, tribulation
14 four-letter word

cursed
04 vile
06 damned, dashed, odious
07 blasted, hateful
08 fiendish, infernal
09 execrable, loathsome
10 abominable, confounded

cursory
05 brief, hasty, quick, rapid
06 casual, slight
07 offhand, passing, summary
08 careless, fleeting, slapdash
09 desultory
10 dismissive
11 perfunctory, superficial

curt
04 rude, tart
05 blunt, brief, gruff, pithy, sharp, short, terse
06 abrupt
07 brusque, concise, laconic, offhand, summary, uncivil
08 snappish, succinct

curtail
03 cut
04 pare, slim, trim
05 limit, prune
06 lessen, reduce, shrink
07 abridge, shorten

08 cut short, decrease, restrict, truncate

curtailment
03 cut
06 paring
07 cutback, docking, pruning
08 decrease
09 lessening, reduction
10 shortening, truncation
11 abridgement, contraction

curtain
05 blind, cover, drape
06 screen
07 drapery, hanging, shutter
08 backdrop, portière, tapestry
13 window hanging

curtsy
03 bob, bow
06 kowtow, salaam
09 genuflect

curvaceous
05 buxom, curvy
06 bosomy, comely
07 shapely
10 voluptuous

curve
03 arc, bow
04 arch, bend, coil, hook, kink, loop, turn, wind
05 helix, round, swell, twist
06 camber, circle, spiral
07 flexure, incurve, winding
08 crescent

curved
04 bent
05 bowed
06 arched, convex, cupped, humped, warped
07 arcuate, bending, concave, rounded, sinuous, twisted
08 sweeping, swelling
10 serpentine

cushion
03 mat, pad
05 squab
06 absorb, buffer, dampen, deaden, lessen, muffle, pillow, reduce, soften
07 beanbag, bolster, hassock, padding, protect, support
08 buttress, diminish, headrest, mitigate, suppress

cushy
04 easy, plum, soft
05 jammy
11 comfortable, undemanding

custodian
05 guard

06 keeper, warden, warder
07 curator
08 guardian, overseer, watchdog, watchman
09 caretaker, castellan, protector
11 conservator

custody
04 care
06 arrest, charge
07 keeping
08 guidance, wardship
09 captivity, detention
10 possession, protection
11 confinement, safekeeping
12 guardianship, imprisonment, preservation

custom
03 use, way
04 form, rite
05 habit, style, trade, usage
06 manner, policy, ritual
07 fashion, routine
08 business, practice
09 etiquette, patronage, procedure, tradition
10 convention, observance

customarily
07 as a rule, usually
08 commonly, normally
09 generally
10 habitually, ordinarily
13 traditionally
14 conventionally

customary
03 set
05 usual
06 common, normal
07 general, regular, routine
08 accepted, everyday, familiar, habitual, ordinary
11 established, traditional
12 conventional

customer
05 buyer
06 client, patron, punter
07 regular, shopper
08 consumer, prospect
09 clientele, purchaser

customize
03 fit
04 suit
05 adapt, alter
06 adjust, modify, tailor
07 convert
08 fine-tune

cut
03 axe, bit, hew, lop, mow, row

04 chop, clip, crop, dice, dock, edit, form, gash, hack, nick, omit, pare, slit, snip, snub, stab, trim
05 carve, grate, mince, notch, prune, quota, score, scorn, sever, share, shave, shear, shred, slash, slice, split, style, wound
06 chisel, chop up, cleave, divide, excise, ignore, incise, insult, pierce, ration, rebuff, reduce, slight
07 abridge, curtail, dissect, engrave, fashion, portion, section, shorten
08 decrease, diminish, incision, lacerate
09 expurgate, lessening, reduction, summarize
10 abbreviate, laceration
14 send to Coventry, slice of the cake

❑**cut across**
08 go beyond, surmount
09 rise above, transcend

❑**cut and dried**
05 clear, fixed
06 sewn up
07 certain, settled
08 definite
13 predetermined

❑**cut back**
03 lop
04 crop, curb, trim
05 check, lower, prune, slash
06 lessen, reduce
07 curtail
08 decrease, downsize, retrench
09 economize, scale down

❑**cut down**
03 hew, lop, saw
04 curb, fell, raze
05 level, lower, prune
06 lessen, reduce
07 curtail
08 decrease, diminish

❑**cut in**
06 butt in
07 barge in, break in, intrude
09 interject, interpose, interrupt, intervene

❑**cut off**
03 end
04 halt, stop
05 block, sever
06 detach, remove, unhook
07 isolate, seclude, shelter

08 amputate, break off,
 separate
09 intercept, interrupt

◻**cut out**
04 drop, edit, fail, omit, stop
05 cease
06 delete, desist, excise, lay off,
 pack in, pack up, remove
07 conk out, exclude, extract
09 break down
11 discontinue, malfunction,
 stop working

◻**cut out for**
04 good, made
05 right
06 suited
08 suitable
09 qualified

◻**cut up**
04 chop, dice
05 carve, mince, slash, slice
06 chop up, divide
07 dissect, slice up
09 dismember

cutback
06 saving
07 economy
08 decrease, lowering, slashing
09 lessening, reduction
11 curtailment
12 retrenchment

cut-price
04 sale
05 cheap
07 bargain, cut-rate, reduced
08 discount
09 low-priced

cutter
► *Types of cutter*:
03 axe, saw
05 blade, knife, mower, plane,
 razor, sword

06 chisel, jigsaw, lopper, scythe,
 shears, sickle
07 chopper, fretsaw, hacksaw,
 machete, scalpel
08 billhook, chainsaw, clippers,
 penknife, scissors,
 Strimmer®
09 lawnmower, secateurs
10 flick knife, guillotine
11 pocket knife
12 hedgetrimmer, Stanley
 knife®
13 pinking shears
14 Swiss army knife
➤ See also **saw**; **weapon**

cut-throat
04 keen
05 cruel
06 brutal, fierce
08 pitiless, ruthless
09 dog-eat-dog

cutting
03 raw
04 acid, keen
05 chill, piece, sharp, snide
06 bitchy, biting, bitter
07 caustic, excerpt, extract,
 hurtful, mordant, pointed
08 clipping, incisive, piercing,
 scathing, wounding
09 sarcastic, trenchant
11 penetrating

cycle
03 age, era
04 aeon, rota
05 epoch, order, phase, round
06 circle, period, rhythm, series
07 pattern
08 rotation, sequence
09 biorhythm, body clock
10 revolution, succession
11 oscillation

cyclone
05 storm
07 monsoon, tempest, tornado,
 typhoon
09 hurricane, whirlwind
13 tropical storm

cylinder
04 drum, reel
05 spool
06 barrel, bobbin, column
07 spindle

cynic
07 doubter, killjoy, knocker,
 sceptic, scoffer
09 pessimist
10 spoilsport

cynical
07 mocking
08 critical, derisive, doubtful,
 doubting, negative,
 sardonic, scoffing, scornful,
 sneering
09 sarcastic, sceptical
10 suspicious
11 distrustful, pessimistic

cynicism
05 doubt, irony, scorn
07 mocking, sarcasm
08 contempt, distrust, scoffing,
 sneering
09 disbelief, pessimism,
 suspicion
10 scepticism
11 misanthropy

cyst
03 sac, wen
04 bleb
06 growth
07 bladder, blister, utricle,
 vesicle
08 atheroma

dab
03 bit, pat, tap
04 daub, spot, swab, wipe
05 press, smear, tinge, touch
06 dollop, smudge, stroke

◻dab hand
03 ace
05 adept
06 expert, wizard

dabble
03 dip, toy, wet
04 play
05 dally
06 dampen, paddle, potter, splash, tinker, trifle
07 moisten
08 splatter, sprinkle

dabbler
07 amateur, dallier, trifler
09 lay person
10 dilettante

daft
03 mad, odd
04 avid, daft, dumb, keen, nuts
05 barmy, batty, crazy, dotty, inane, loony, loopy, nutty, potty, silly, sweet, wacky
06 absurd, crazed, insane, mental, stupid, unwise
07 berserk, bonkers, devoted, foolish, idiotic, lunatic, smitten, touched, zealous
08 crackpot, demented, deranged, peculiar
09 disturbed, enamoured, fanatical, foolhardy, imprudent, senseless
10 infatuated, irrational, outrageous, passionate, ridiculous, unbalanced
11 hare-brained, nonsensical
12 enthusiastic, round the bend
13 off your rocker, out of your mind, round the twist

dagger
04 dirk, kris
05 blade, knife, kukri, skean
07 bayonet, jambiya, poniard
08 skene-dhu, stiletto

daily
07 diurnal, regular, routine
08 day by day, every day, everyday, habitual, ordinary
09 circadian, quotidian
11 commonplace, day after day

dainty
04 fine, neat, trim
05 fancy, fussy, juicy, small, tasty
06 bonbon, choosy, little, petite, pretty, titbit
07 elegant, refined, savoury
08 delicacy, delicate
09 exquisite, sweetmeat
10 fastidious, particular
11 bonne-bouche

dais
05 stage, stand
06 podium
07 rostrum
08 platform

dale
04 dell, gill, glen, vale
06 dingle, strath, valley

dally
03 toy
04 play
05 delay, flirt, tarry
06 dawdle, linger, loiter, trifle
13 procrastinate

dam
04 stem, wall
05 block, check
07 barrage, barrier, staunch
08 blockage, obstruct, restrict
09 barricade, hindrance
10 embankment
11 obstruction

► *Names of dams*:
04 Guri, Kiev
05 Aswan, Rogun
06 Bratsk, Hoover, Itaipu, Kariba
07 Boulder
08 Akosombo, Gezhouba
09 Aswan High, Owen Falls
13 Grande Dixence
14 Afsluitdijk Sea

damage
03 mar
04 fine, harm, hurt, loss, ruin
05 abuse, havoc, spoil, wreck
06 deface, impair, injure, injury
08 mischief, mutilate, sabotage
09 desecrate, detriment, vandalism, vandalize
10 defacement, impairment, mutilation, reparation
11 devastation, restitution
12 compensation, incapacitate
13 reimbursement

damaging
03 bad
07 harmful, hurtful, ruinous
09 injurious
11 deleterious, detrimental, prejudicial
12 unfavourable
15 disadvantageous

dame
04 lady
05 broad, woman
06 female
07 dowager, peeress
08 baroness

damn
03 jot, pan
04 dash, doom, slam, toss
05 blast, curse, decry, knock, slate, swear
07 accurse, censure, condemn, inveigh, monkey's, run down
08 denounce, execrate, maledict, two hoots
09 blaspheme, castigate, criticize, denigrate, excoriate, fulminate, imprecate
10 come down on, denunciate
13 brass farthing

damnable
06 cursed, wicked
08 horrible, infernal
09 execrable, offensive
10 abominable, detestable

damnation
04 doom, hell
09 perdition

12 condemnation,
   denunciation

damned
04 lost, vile
06 cursed, darned, doomed
07 blasted, hateful
08 accursed, annoying,
   blooming, dratting, infernal
09 condemned
10 abominable, confounded

damning
09 damnatory
10 condemning
11 implicating, inculpatory
12 accusatorial, condemnatory
13 incriminating

damp
03 dew, fog, wet
04 dank, dewy, mist, rain
05 humid, misty, moist, muggy
06 clammy, rheumy, vapour
07 drizzle, drizzly, wetness
08 moisture, vaporous
10 clamminess

◻**damp down**
04 calm, dull
05 check
06 deaden, lessen, reduce
08 decrease, diminish,
   moderate, restrain

dampen
03 wet
04 damp, dash, dull
05 check, deter, spray
06 deaden, dismay, lessen,
   muffle, reduce, stifle
07 inhibit, moisten, smother
08 damp down, decrease,
   diminish, moderate, restrain
12 put a damper on

damper

◻**put a damper on**
04 dash, dull
05 check, deter
06 dismay, lessen, reduce
07 depress, inhibit, smother
08 damp down, decrease,
   diminish, moderate, restrain
10 discourage, dishearten

dampness
03 dew, fog, wet
04 damp, mist, rain
06 vapour
07 drizzle, wetness
08 dankness, humidity,
   moisture
10 clamminess

damsel
04 girl, lass

06 maiden
09 young lady
10 young woman

dance
03 hop, jig
04 ball, play, rock, skip, sway
05 caper, flash, frisk, stomp,
   swing, twirl, waver, whirl
06 bounce, frolic, gambol, hoof
   it, prance, social
07 flicker, knees-up, shindig
08 kantikoy
09 pirouette, shake a leg
13 tread a measure
➤ See also **ballet**;
   choreographer; **dancer**

▶ *Names of dances:*
03 bop, jig
04 jive, reel
05 conga, mambo, polka,
   rumba, samba, stomp,
   tango, twist, waltz
06 bolero, can-can, cha-cha,
   minuet, valeta
07 beguine, foxtrot, gavotte,
   hoe-down, Lancers,
   mazurka, one-step
08 fandango, flamenco,
   galliard, hornpipe
09 bossanova, clog dance,
   jitterbug, paso doble, Paul
   Jones, quadrille, quickstep,
   rock 'n' roll
10 belly-dance, Charleston,
   hokey-cokey, turkey-trot
11 black bottom, Lambeth
   Walk, morris-dance
12 mashed potato
13 Highland fling
15 military two-step

▶ *Types of dancing:*
03 tap
04 folk
05 disco, Irish
06 ballet
07 country, old-time
08 ballroom, flamenco,
   Highland, robotics
11 clog-dancing
12 break-dancing, limbo-
   dancing
13 Latin-American, morris
   dancing

▶ *Types of dance function:*
03 hop
04 ball, prom, rave
05 dance, disco
06 social
07 ceilidh
08 hunt ball, tea dance
09 barn dance

11 charity ball

dancer
07 danseur
08 coryphee, danseuse
09 ballerina, tap-dancer
11 belly-dancer
12 ballet dancer

▶ *Names of dancers:*
04 **Bull** (Deborah), **Edur**
   (Thomas), **Oaks** (Agnes)
05 **Baker** (Josephine), **Cohan**
   (Robert), **Dolin** (Anton),
   Kelly (Gene), **Laban**
   (Rudolf von), **Lifar** (Serge),
   Tharp (Twyla)
06 **Ashton** (Sir Frederick),
   Béjart (Maurice), **Blasis**
   (Carlo), **Davies** (Siobhan),
   Dowell (Anthony),
   Duncan (Isadora), **Fokine**
   (Michel), **Graham**
   (Martha), **Petipa** (Marius),
   Rogers (Ginger), **Sibley**
   (Antoinette), **Wigman**
   (Mary)
07 **Astaire** (Fred), **Bussell**
   (Darcey), **Fonteyn** (Dame
   Margot), **Guillem** (Sylvie),
   Markova (Dame Alicia),
   Massine (Léonide),
   Nureyev (Rudolf), **Pavlova**
   (Anna), **Rambert** (Dame
   Marie), **Seymour** (Lynn),
   Ulanova (Galina)
08 **Danilova** (Alexandra), **De
   Valois** (Dame Ninette),
   Helpmann (Sir Robert),
   Humphrey (Doris),
   Nijinska (Bronislava),
   Nijinsky (Vaslav)
09 **Diaghilev** (Sergei),
   Macmillan (Sir Kenneth)
10 **Balanchine** (George),
   Cunningham (Merce)
11 **Baryshnikov** (Mikhail),
   Mistinguett

dandy
03 fop
04 beau, dude, fine, toff
05 blade, great, swell
08 popinjay, splendid
09 excellent, exquisite, first-rate
12 man about town

danger
04 risk
05 peril
06 hazard, menace, threat
07 pitfall
08 jeopardy
13 vulnerability

dangerous
05 dicey, grave, hairy, risky
06 chancy, severe, unsafe
07 exposed, ominous, serious
08 critical, high-risk, menacing, perilous, reckless
09 hazardous, minacious
10 precarious, vulnerable
11 threatening, treacherous

dangle
04 flap, hang, lure, sway
05 droop, swing, trail, tempt
06 entice, flaunt
09 tantalize

dank
03 wet
04 damp, dewy
05 moist, slimy, soggy
06 clammy, sticky

dapper
04 chic, neat, spry, trim
05 brisk, natty, smart
06 dainty, nimble, spruce
07 stylish
11 well-dressed, well-groomed
13 well-turned-out

dappled
04 pied
06 dotted
07 flecked, mottled, spotted
08 freckled, speckled, stippled

dare
04 defy, face, goad, risk
05 brave, flout, stake, taunt
06 gamble, hazard, resist
09 adventure, challenge
12 be bold enough
13 be brave enough
14 have the courage

daredevil
04 bold, rash
05 brave
06 daring, madcap, plucky
08 fearless, intrepid, stuntman
09 audacious, dauntless, desperado, impetuous
10 adventurer
11 adventurous

daring
04 bold, gall, guts, rash, wild
05 brave, nerve, pluck
06 plucky, spirit, valour
07 bravery, courage, valiant
08 audacity, boldness, defiance, intrepid, reckless
09 audacious, dauntless
10 courageous
12 fearlessness

dark
03 dim, fog, sad
04 drab, dusk, grim, mist
05 awful, black, brown, dingy, dusky, gloom, murky, night, shade, shady, unlit
06 dismal, gloomy, hidden, morose, secret, sombre
07 dimness, evening, mystery, obscure, ominous, secrecy, shadows, shadowy, sunless
08 abstruse, badly lit, brunette, darkness, dimly lit, hopeless, menacing, overcast, sinister, twilight
09 blackness, cheerless, enigmatic, half-light, ignorance, murkiness, night-time, nightfall, obscurity, shadiness
10 cloudiness, dark-haired, forbidding, mysterious
13 unilluminated

darken
03 dim, fog
04 fade
05 cloud, frown, shade
06 deject, sadden, shadow
07 blacken, depress, eclipse
09 cloud over, grow angry
10 grow darker, make gloomy, obnubilate, overshadow

darling
03 pet
04 dear, love
05 angel, honey
06 adored
07 beloved, dearest
08 precious, treasure
09 cherished, favourite
10 sweetheart
11 blue-eyed boy, teacher's pet
14 apple of your eye

darn
04 mend
05 sew up
06 repair, stitch

dart
03 fly, run
04 barb, bolt, dash, flit, hurl, leap, race, rush, send, tear
05 arrow, flash, shoot, throw
07 feather, project

dash
03 bit, fly, nip, pop, run
04 beat, bolt, dart, hurl, lash, race, ruin, rush, slam, tear
05 break, crash, crush, fling, hurry, pound, smash, speed, spoil, throw, touch, trace

06 blight, dampen, flavour, hurtle, little, sprint, strike
07 shatter, smidgen, soupçon
08 confound
10 disappoint, suggestion

◻**dash off**
06 scrawl
08 scribble

dashing
04 bold
05 showy, smart
06 daring, lively, plucky
07 elegant, gallant, stylish
08 debonair, spirited, vigorous
10 attractive, flamboyant
11 fashionable

dastardly
03 low
04 base, mean, vile
06 craven, wicked
08 cowardly
09 underhand
10 despicable
12 contemptible, faint-hearted

data
05 facts, input
07 details, figures
08 material, research
10 statistics
11 information, particulars

date
03 age, day, era
04 time, week, year
05 court, go out, month
06 decade, escort, friend, go back, period, steady
07 meeting, partner, take out
08 come from, go steady
09 boyfriend, exist from, go out with, obsolesce, originate
10 be together, engagement, girlfriend, go out of use, millennium, rendezvous
11 appointment, assignation

◻**out of date**
05 dated, passé
06 old hat
07 archaic
08 obsolete, outdated, outmoded
10 antiquated, superseded
11 obsolescent
12 old-fashioned
13 unfashionable

◻**to date**
05 so far
07 up to now
08 until now
14 up to the present

□up to date
06 trendy, modern
07 current
11 fashionable
12 contemporary
13 up to the minute

dated
05 passé
06 old hat
07 archaic
08 obsolete, outdated, outmoded
09 out-of-date
10 antiquated, superseded
11 obsolescent
12 old-fashioned
13 unfashionable

daub
04 blot, coat, spot
05 paint, smear, stain, sully
06 blotch, smudge, splash
07 plaster, splodge, splotch

daughter
04 girl, lass
05 child
06 lassie
08 disciple
09 offspring
10 descendant, inhabitant

daunt
03 cow
05 alarm, deter, scare
06 dismay, put off
07 overawe, unnerve
08 dispirit, frighten
09 take aback
10 demoralize, disconcert, discourage, dishearten, intimidate

dauntless
04 bold
05 brave
06 daring, plucky
07 valiant
08 fearless, intrepid, resolute
09 undaunted
10 courageous

dawdle
03 lag
05 dally, delay, tarry, trail
06 linger, loiter, potter
09 hang about
10 dilly-dally
15 go at a snail's pace

dawn
04 open, rise
05 begin, birth, onset, start
06 advent, appear, be born
07 arrival, genesis, glimmer, lighten, morning, sunrise
08 brighten, commence, daybreak, daylight
09 beginning, originate
10 break of day, first light
12 commencement

□dawn on
03 hit
05 click
06 sink in, strike
07 occur to, realize

day
03 age, era
04 date, time
05 epoch
06 period
07 daytime, diurnal
08 daylight

□day after day
09 endlessly, regularly
11 continually, perpetually
12 monotonously, persistently

□day by day
08 steadily
09 gradually
13 progressively
15 slowly but surely

□have had its day
08 be past it
11 be out of date

daybreak
04 dawn
05 sun-up
07 morning, sunrise
08 cock-crow, daylight
10 break of day, first light
11 crack of dawn

daydream
04 muse, wish
05 dream, fancy
06 musing, vision
07 fantasy, imagine, reverie
09 fantasize, switch off
13 be lost in space
14 stare into space
15 castles in the air

daylight
03 day
04 dawn
05 light
07 daytime, morning, sunrise
08 daybreak, sunlight
10 break of day, first light
11 crack of dawn
12 natural light

daze
04 numb, stun
05 amaze, blind, shock
06 baffle, dazzle, stupor, trance
07 confuse, perplex, stupefy
08 bewilder, numbness, paralyse, surprise
09 confusion, dumbfound, take aback
12 bewilderment

dazed
06 amazed, numbed
07 baffled, dazzled, shocked, stunned
08 confused, startled
09 paralysed, perplexed, staggered, stupefied
10 astonished, bewildered, speechless, taken aback
11 dumbfounded, unconscious

dazzle
03 awe, wow
05 amaze, blind, glare, gleam
07 bewitch, confuse, impress, overawe, sparkle, stupefy
08 astonish, bedazzle, bowl over, knock out
09 dumbfound, fascinate, hypnotize, splendour
10 brightness, brilliance, razzmatazz
11 scintillate
12 magnificence
13 scintillation

dazzling
05 grand
06 superb
07 glaring, radiant, shining
08 glorious, splendid, stunning
09 brilliant, ravishing, sparkling
11 sensational, spectacular
12 awe-inspiring, breathtaking
13 scintillating

dead
04 dull, gone, late, numb, very
05 dated, exact, inert, passé, quiet, quite, tired, total, utter
06 no more, old hat
07 defunct, exactly, extinct, humdrum, perfect, tedious, totally, utterly, worn out
08 absolute, complete, dead beat, deceased, departed, entirely, lifeless, obsolete, perished, tired out
09 exanimate, exhausted, inanimate, insensate, knackered, out of date, paralysed, precisely
10 absolutely, completely, insentient, thoroughly
11 dead as a dodo, gone to sleep, ready to drop
12 discontinued, unresponsive

14 no longer spoken
15 dead as a doornail

deaden
04 dull, hush, mute, numb
05 abate, allay, blunt, check
06 dampen, lessen, muffle, reduce, soothe, subdue
07 assuage, quieten, smother
08 diminish, mitigate, paralyse, suppress
09 alleviate
12 anaesthetize
14 take the edge off

deadlock
04 halt
07 dead end, impasse
08 stoppage
09 checkmate, stalemate
10 standstill

deadly
04 dull, grim, sure, true
05 fatal, great, quite, toxic
06 boring, lethal, mortal
07 intense, noxious, precise, serious, totally, utterly
08 accurate, entirely, venomous
09 dangerous, malignant, murderous, perfectly
10 absolutely, completely, dreadfully, implacable, pernicious, thoroughly
11 destructive

deadpan
05 blank, empty
09 impassive
10 poker-faced
11 inscrutable
12 inexpressive, unexpressive
13 dispassionate, straight-faced
14 expressionless

deaf
07 unmoved
08 heedless
09 oblivious, stone-deaf
10 impervious
11 deaf as a post, indifferent, unconcerned
13 hard of hearing

deafening
07 booming, ringing, roaring
08 piercing, very loud
09 very noisy
10 resounding, thunderous
12 ear-splitting, overwhelming

deal
03 buy, lot
04 hand, load, mete, pact
05 allot, round, share, trade

06 assign, direct, divide, export, handle, market
07 bargain, contract, deliver, dole out, give out, inflict, mete out, operate, traffic
08 dispense, quantity
09 agreement, apportion
10 administer, buy and sell, distribute, do business
11 arrangement, transaction
12 distribution

❑**deal with**
05 cover, see to, treat
06 handle, manage, tackle
07 concern, process, sort out
08 attend to, cope with
10 take care of
14 get to grips with

dealer
04 tout
06 pusher, trader, vendor
08 marketer, merchant, retailer, salesman
10 saleswoman, trafficker, wholesaler
11 salesperson
12 merchandiser

dealings
05 trade, truck
07 traffic
08 business, commerce
09 relations
10 operations
12 negotiations, transactions

dear
03 pet
05 close, honey, loved, steep
06 adored, costly, pricey, valued
07 beloved, darling
08 esteemed, favoured, high-cost, loved one, not cheap, precious, treasure
09 cherished, endearing, expensive, favourite, respected, treasured
10 exorbitant, high-priced, overpriced, sweetheart

dearly
06 deeply, fondly
07 greatly
08 lovingly, tenderly, very much
09 adoringly, extremely
10 profoundly, with favour
12 at a great cost, at a high price
13 with great loss
14 affectionately

dearth
04 lack, need, want
06 famine

07 absence, paucity, poverty
08 scarcity, shortage, sparsity
10 deficiency, scantiness
13 insufficiency

death
03 end
04 loss, ruin
06 demise, finish, mortal
07 decease, passing, quietus
08 curtains, fatality, the grave
09 departure, perishing
10 expiration, extinction, loss of life
11 destruction, eradication, passing away, termination
12 annihilation, last farewell
13 extermination

❑**put to death**
04 kill, hang
05 shoot
06 behead, martyr
07 execute
10 guillotine
11 electrocute, exterminate

deathless
07 eternal, undying
08 immortal, timeless
11 everlasting, never-ending

deathly
04 grim, pale
05 ashen, fatal
06 deadly, mortal, pallid
07 extreme, ghastly, intense
10 cadaverous, colourless

debacle
05 farce, havoc
06 defeat, fiasco
07 failure, turmoil
08 collapse, disaster, reversal
09 cataclysm, overthrow

debar
03 ban, bar
04 deny, stop
05 eject, expel
06 forbid, hamper, hinder
07 exclude, keep out, prevent, shut out
08 obstruct, preclude, prohibit
09 blackball, proscribe

debase
05 alloy, lower, shame, taint
06 defile, demean, humble
07 cheapen, corrupt, degrade, devalue, pollute, vitiate
08 disgrace
09 discredit, dishonour
10 adulterate
11 contaminate

debased
03 low
04 base, vile
06 fallen, impure, shamed
07 corrupt, defiled, tainted
08 degraded, devalued,
   polluted
09 cheapened, disgraced
10 degenerate, humiliated
11 adulterated, discredited
12 contaminated

debasement
05 shame
08 disgrace
09 abasement, dishonour,
   pollution
10 cheapening, corruption,
   defilement, perversion
11 degradation, depravation,
   devaluation, humiliation
12 adulteration, degeneration
13 contamination

debatable
04 moot
06 unsure
08 arguable, doubtful
09 uncertain, undecided
10 disputable
11 contentious, contestable
12 questionable
13 controversial, problematical
14 open to question

debate
05 argue, forum, weigh
06 ponder, reason
07 contend, contest, discuss,
   dispute, polemic, wrangle
08 argument, consider
09 altercate, talk about
10 contention, discussion
11 altercation, controversy

debauch
04 ruin
06 ravish, seduce
07 corrupt, deprave, pervert,
   pollute, subvert, violate
10 lead astray

debauched
04 lewd
06 wanton
07 corrupt, debased, immoral
08 decadent, degraded,
   depraved
09 abandoned, carousing,
   corrupted, dissolute,
   excessive, perverted
10 degenerate, dissipated,
   licentious
11 intemperate, promiscuous
13 overindulgent

debauchery
04 lust, orgy, riot
06 excess
08 carousal, lewdness
09 decadence, depravity
10 corruption, degeneracy,
   immorality, wantonness
11 degradation, dissipation,
   libertinism
12 intemperance
13 dissoluteness
14 licentiousness,
   overindulgence

debilitate
06 impair, weaken
07 cripple, exhaust, wear out
08 enervate, enfeeble
09 undermine
10 devitalize
12 incapacitate

debilitating
06 tiring
09 crippling, fatiguing,
   impairing, weakening
10 enervating, enervative,
   enfeebling, exhausting
11 undermining
14 incapacitating

debility
05 atony
07 fatigue, frailty, malaise
08 asthenia, weakness
09 atonicity, faintness, infirmity
10 feebleness, incapacity
11 decrepitude
12 enfeeblement

debonair
05 suave
06 breezy, smooth, urbane
07 dashing, elegant, refined
08 charming, well-bred
12 light-hearted

debris
04 bits
05 ruins, trash, waste, wreck
06 litter, pieces, rubble
07 remains, rubbish
08 detritus, wreckage
09 fragments, sweepings

debt
03 due
04 bill, duty, hock
05 claim, debit, score
06 the red
07 arrears
09 liability, overdraft
10 money owing
11 Queer Street

debtor
08 bankrupt, borrower
09 defaulter, insolvent

debunk
06 expose, show up
07 deflate, explode, lampoon
08 disprove, puncture, ridicule
13 cut down to size

début
08 entrance, première
09 beginning, coming-out, first
   time, launching
10 first night, initiation
12 inauguration, introduction
15 first appearance

decadence
09 depravity
10 debauchery, degeneracy,
   immorality, perversion
11 dissipation, dissolution
14 degenerateness,
   licentiousness, self-
   indulgence

decadent
07 corrupt, debased, immoral
08 degraded, depraved
09 debauched, dissolute
10 degenerate, dissipated,
   licentious
13 self-indulgent

decamp
04 bolt, flee, flit
06 desert, escape
07 abscond, do a bunk, make
   off, run away, scarper, take
   off, vamoose
09 do a runner, skedaddle
10 hightail it
12 absquatulate

decapitate
06 behead, unhead
07 execute
10 guillotine

decay
03 rot
04 fail, rust, sink
05 go bad, spoil
06 fester, perish, wither
07 atrophy, corrode, crumble,
   decline, failing, putrefy,
   rotting, shrivel, wasting
08 collapse, going bad
09 decadence, decompose,
   putridity, waste away
10 degenerate
11 deteriorate, putrescence
12 degeneration, disintegrate,
   putrefaction

13 decomposition, deterioration
14 disintegration

decayed
03 bad, off
04 rank, sour
05 stale
06 addled, mouldy, putrid, rotten, wasted
07 carious, carrion, spoiled
08 corroded, perished
09 putrefied
10 decomposed

decease
05 death, dying
06 demise
07 passing
09 departure
10 expiration
11 dissolution, passing away

deceased
04 dead, gone, late, lost
06 former
07 defunct, expired, extinct
08 departed, finished

deceit
04 fake, ruse, sham, wile
05 abuse, feint, fraud, guile
07 cunning, slyness, swindle
08 artifice, cheating, pretence, trickery, wiliness
09 chicanery, deception, duplicity, hypocrisy
10 subterfuge
11 fraudulence
13 double-dealing
15 underhandedness

deceitful
05 false, lying
06 crafty, sneaky, tricky
07 cunning, knavish
08 guileful, illusory, two-faced
09 deceiving, deceptive, designing, dishonest, insincere, underhand
10 fraudulent, mendacious, perfidious, untruthful
11 counterfeit, dissembling, duplicitous, treacherous
13 double-dealing

deceive
03 con, kid
04 dupe, fool, gull, hoax
05 abuse, bluff, cheat, trick
06 betray, delude, entrap, have on, lead on, outwit, seduce
07 beguile, cheat on, ensnare, mislead, swindle, two-time
08 hoodwink, misguide
09 bamboozle, dissemble

11 double-cross, string along
12 put one over on, take for a ride
14 pull a fast one on
15 pull someone's leg

deceiver
05 cheat, crook, fraud
06 abuser, con man, hoaxer
08 betrayer, impostor, swindler
09 charlatan, trickster
10 dissembler, mountebank
12 double-dealer

decelerate
05 brake
08 slow down
11 reduce speed
14 put the brakes on

decency
07 decorum, fitness, modesty
08 civility, courtesy
09 etiquette, good taste, integrity, propriety
10 seemliness
11 helpfulness, uprightness
14 respectability

decent
02 OK
03 fit
04 kind, nice, pure
06 chaste, modest, polite, proper, seemly, worthy
07 ethical, helpful, upright
08 adequate, becoming, decorous, generous, gracious, obliging, suitable, tasteful, virtuous
09 befitting, courteous
10 acceptable, thoughtful
11 presentable, respectable
12 satisfactory
13 accommodating

decentralize
07 devolve
08 delegate, localize
11 regionalize
13 deconcentrate
14 spread outwards

deception
03 con, lie
04 hoax, ruse, sham, wile
05 bluff, cheat, fraud, guile, snare, trick
06 deceit
07 cunning, leg-pull, swindle
08 artifice, cheating, pretence, put-up job, trickery
09 chicanery, duplicity, imposture, treachery
10 craftiness, subterfuge
11 dissembling, fraudulence

13 double-dealing
15 underhandedness

deceptive
04 fake, mock, sham
05 bogus, false
06 crafty
07 crooked, cunning
08 cheating, illusive, illusory, specious, spurious
09 dishonest, underhand
10 fallacious, misleading
11 dissembling, duplicitous

decide
03 fix
04 pick, rule
05 go for, judge
06 choose, opt for, select, settle
07 resolve
08 conclude, plump for
09 arbitrate, determine
10 adjudicate
11 give a ruling
13 make a decision
14 give a judgement, make up, your mind, reach a decision

decided
04 firm
05 clear
06 marked
07 certain, express, obvious
08 absolute, clear-cut, decisive, definite, positive, resolute
10 deliberate, determined, forthright, purposeful, unswerving, unwavering
11 categorical, unequivocal
12 unhesitating, unmistakable

decidedly
04 very
05 quite
07 clearly
09 certainly, downright
10 decisively, definitely, distinctly, positively
12 unmistakably
13 unequivocally
14 unquestionably

decider
08 clincher
10 determiner
11 coup de grâce

deciding
05 chief, final, prime
06 crunch
07 crucial, supreme
08 critical, decisive
10 conclusive
11 determining, significant

decipher
05 crack
06 decode
07 make out, unravel, work out
09 figure out, interpret,
   translate
10 understand, unscramble
13 transliterate

decision
06 decree, result, ruling
07 finding, opinion, outcome,
   purpose, resolve, verdict
08 firmness
09 judgement
10 conclusion, resolution
12 adjudication, decisiveness
13 determination

decisive
04 firm
05 final, prime
06 strong
07 crucial, decided, fateful
08 critical, deciding, definite,
   forceful, positive, resolute
10 conclusive, definitive,
   determined, forthright,
   unswerving, unwavering
11 determining, influential
12 strong-minded

deck
04 trim
05 adorn, array, grace
06 bedeck, enrich, tart up
07 festoon, garland, garnish
08 beautify, decorate,
   ornament, prettify, trick out
09 embellish

declaim
04 rant
05 orate, spiel, spout
07 lecture
08 harangue, proclaim
09 hold forth, sermonize

declamation
04 rant
06 sermon, speech, tirade
07 address, lecture, oration
08 harangue
12 speechifying

declamatory
04 bold
07 fustian, orotund, pompous
08 dramatic, inflated
09 bombastic, grandiose, high-
   flown, overblown
10 oratorical, theatrical
12 magniloquent
13 grandiloquent

declaration
05 edict
06 avowal, decree
08 averment
09 affidavit, assertion,
   broadcast, manifesto,
   statement, testimony
10 confession, disclosure,
   profession, revelation
11 affirmation, attestation
12 announcement,
   confirmation, notification,
   proclamation, promulgation
13 pronouncement

declare
04 aver, avow, show
05 claim, state, swear
06 affirm, assert, attest, decree
07 certify, confess, profess,
   publish, testify, witness
08 announce, disclose,
   maintain, proclaim, validate
09 make known, pronounce
10 promulgate

decline
03 dip, ebb, rot
04 balk, deny, drop, fade, fall,
   flag, hill, sink, slip, wane
05 abate, decay, forgo, lapse,
   slant, slide, slope, slump
06 forego, go down, lessen,
   refuse, reject, waning,
   weaken, wither, worsen
07 descend, descent, dwindle,
   failing, failure, fall off, get
   less, incline, plummet,
   regress, say no to, subside
08 decrease, diminish,
   downturn, turn down
09 abatement, declivity,
   dwindling, lessening,
   recession, reduction,
   weakening, worsening
10 degenerate, diminution,
   divergence, falling-off
11 declination, deteriorate
12 degeneration
13 deterioration

decode
05 crack
07 make out, unravel, work out
08 construe, decipher
09 figure out, interpret,
   translate
10 understand, unscramble
13 transliterate

decomposable
10 degradable
12 destructible
13 biodegradable

decompose
03 rot
05 decay, spoil
06 fester
07 break up, crumble, putrefy
09 break down
12 disintegrate

decomposition
03 rot
05 decay
07 rotting
08 going bad
09 perishing, putridity
11 dissolution, putrescence
12 putrefaction
14 disintegration

décor
07 scenery
10 decoration
11 furnishings
12 colour scheme

decorate
04 cite, deck, do up, trim
05 adorn, grace, paint, paper
06 bedaub, colour, honour
07 bedizen, bemedal, festoon,
   garland, garnish, smarten
08 beautify, ornament,
   renovate, prettify, trick out
09 embellish, refurbish
12 give a medal to
13 give a honour to

decoration
04 star
05 award, badge, cross, crown,
   décor, frill, medal, mural,
   order, title
06 bauble, emblem, honour,
   laurel, ribbon, scroll, wreath
07 bunting, colours, garland,
   garnish, trinket
08 flourish, ornament,
   trimming
09 adornment
11 elaboration, enhancement
12 colour scheme
13 embellishment,
   ornamentation
14 beautification

decorative
05 fancy
06 ornate, pretty, rococo
09 elaborate, enhancing
10 ornamental
13 non-functional

decorous
03 fit
05 staid
06 decent, modest, polite,
   proper, sedate, seemly

07 correct, courtly, refined
08 becoming, suitable
09 befitting, dignified
11 comme il faut, well-behaved

decorum
05 grace
07 decency, dignity, modesty
08 breeding, good form
09 etiquette, propriety
10 conformity, deportment, politeness, seemliness
11 good manners
14 respectability

decoy
04 bait, draw, lead, lure, trap
05 dummy, snare, tempt
06 allure, entice, entrap, seduce
07 attract, deceive, ensnare
09 diversion
10 allurement, attraction, temptation
11 ensnarement

decrease
03 ebb
04 drop, fall, loss, slim, wane
05 abate, let up, lower, slide
06 go down, lessen, plunge, reduce, shrink
07 cut back, cut down, cutback, decline, dwindle, fall off, plummet, slacken, subside
08 come down, contract, diminish, downturn, lowering, make less, slim down, step-down, taper off
09 abatement, dwindling, lessening, reduction, scale down, shrinkage
10 become less, diminution, falling-off, subsidence
11 contraction

decree
03 act, law
04 fiat, rule
05 edict, enact, irade, order
06 decide, direct, enjoin, firman, ordain, ruling
07 command, dictate, lay down, precept, statute
08 proclaim, psephism, rescript
09 determine, enactment, manifesto, ordinance, prescribe, pronounce
11 hatti-sherif
12 proclamation

decrepit
03 old
04 aged, weak
05 frail

06 feeble, infirm
07 elderly, run-down, worn-out
08 battered
09 crumbling, doddering, senescent, tottering
10 broken-down, clapped-out, in bad shape, ramshackle, tumbledown
11 dilapidated
12 falling apart
13 falling to bits

decrepitude
04 ruin
05 decay
06 dotage, old age
08 debility, senility, weakness
09 infirmity
10 disability, feebleness, incapacity, senescence
12 degeneration, dilapidation

decry
03 pan
05 blame, knock, slate, snipe
06 attack
07 censure, condemn, devalue, nit-pick, run down, traduce
08 belittle, denounce, derogate
09 criticize, denigrate, disparage, underrate
10 animadvert, come down on
12 pull to pieces, tear to shreds
13 find fault with, tear a strip off
14 inveigh against
15 do a hatchet job on

dedicate
04 give, name
05 bless, offer
06 assign, commit, devote, hallow, pledge
07 address, present
08 inscribe, make holy, sanctify, set apart
10 consecrate, give over to

dedicated
07 bespoke, devoted, zealous
08 diligent
09 committed
10 customized, purposeful
11 custom-built, given over to, hard working, industrious
12 enthusiastic, single-minded, wholehearted

dedication
04 zeal
07 address, loyalty
08 blessing, devotion
09 adherence, hallowing
10 allegiance, commitment
11 inscription
12 consecration, faithfulness

13 self-sacrifice

deduce
04 draw
05 glean, infer
06 derive, gather, reason
07 surmise
08 conclude
10 understand

deduct
06 remove
07 take off
08 knock off, reduce by, subtract, take away
10 decrease by

deduction
07 finding, removal
08 decrease, discount
09 abatement, allowance, corollary, inference, reasoning, reduction, surmising, taking off
10 assumption, conclusion, diminution, taking away
11 subtraction, presumption

deed
03 act
04 fact, feat
05 title, truth
06 action, record
07 exploit, reality
08 activity, contract, document

deem
04 hold
05 judge, think
06 esteem, reckon, regard
07 account, adjudge, believe, imagine, suppose
08 conceive, consider, estimate

deep
03 far, low, sea
04 bass, dark, rich, warm, wise
05 briny, grave, ocean, quiet
06 ardent, severe, strong
07 booming, earnest, extreme, fervent, glowing, intense, obscure, serious, yawning
08 abstruse, esoteric, high seas, immersed, profound, reserved
09 brilliant, cavernous, difficult, heart-felt, recondite, sagacious, unplumbed
10 bottomless, discerning, fathomless, low-pitched, mysterious, passionate, perceptive, unfathomed
13 perspicacious

deepen
04 grow
06 dig out, extend, worsen

07 build up, magnify
08 excavate, get worse, heighten, increase
09 intensify, reinforce
10 strengthen
11 deteriorate

deeply
05 sadly
07 acutely, gravely
08 ardently, movingly, severely, strongly, very much
09 earnestly, extremely,, fervently, intensely, seriously
10 completely, profoundly, thoroughly, to the quick
12 passionately

deep-seated
04 deep
05 fixed
07 settled
09 confirmed, ingrained
10 deep-rooted, entrenched

deer
03 doe, roe
04 buck, hart, stag
07 cervine
08 reindeer

deface
03 mar
05 spoil, sully
06 damage, deform, injure
07 blemish, destroy, tarnish
08 mutilate
09 disfigure, vandalize

de facto
04 real
06 actual, really
08 actually, existing, in effect

defamation
04 slur
05 libel, smear
07 calumny, obloquy, scandal, slander
08 innuendo
09 aspersion
10 backbiting, opprobrium
11 denigration, malediction
12 vilification
13 smear campaign

defamatory
09 insulting, libellous, vilifying
10 calumnious, derogatory, pejorative, slanderous
11 denigrating, disparaging, maledictory
12 contumelious

defame
05 libel, smear
06 infame, malign, vilify

07 asperse, blacken, run down, slander, traduce
09 denigrate, discredit, dishonour, disparage
10 calumniate, sling mud at, stigmatize, vituperate
11 speak evil of
14 cast aspersions

default
04 fail, lack, want
05 dodge, evade, fault, lapse
06 defect
07 absence, defraud, failure
08 omission
09 backslide
10 negligence, non-payment

defaulter
08 absentee, non-payer, offender

defeat
04 balk, beat, foil, lick, rout
05 block, crush, excel, quell, repel, smash, thump, worst
06 baffle, hammer, reject, subdue, thrash, thwart
07 beating, conquer, debacle, failure, setback, trounce
08 confound, conquest, downfall, overcome, vanquish
09 checkmate, devastate, frustrate, overpower, overthrow, overwhelm, rejection, repulsion, slaughter, thrashing, thwarting, trouncing
12 vanquishment
14 get the better of
15 make mincemeat of

defeatist
06 gloomy
07 quitter, yielder
08 helpless, hopeless, resigned
09 pessimist
10 despondent, fatalistic
11 doomwatcher, pessimistic
13 prophet of doom

defecate
03 poo
05 egest
07 excrete
08 evacuate
11 do number two, pass a motion
12 ease yourself
14 move your bowels
15 empty your bowels

defect
03 bug
04 flaw, lack, snag, spot, want

05 error, fault, rebel, taint
06 desert, renege, revolt
07 abandon, absence, blemish, failing, frailty, mistake
08 weak spot, weakness
09 deformity, shortfall
10 apostatize, break faith, deficiency, inadequacy
11 change sides, shortcoming, turn traitor
12 imperfection, tergiversate

defection
06 mutiny, revolt
07 perfidy, treason
08 apostasy, betrayal
09 desertion, rebellion
11 abandonment, dereliction
14 tergiversation

defective
04 bust, duff
06 broken, faulty, flawed
09 deficient, imperfect
10 on the blink, out of order
14 malfunctioning

defector
03 rat
05 Judas, rebel
07 traitor
08 apostate, betrayer, deserter, mutineer, quisling, recreant, renegade, turncoat
13 tergiversator

defence
04 army, case, keep, navy, plea
05 alibi, cover, guard
06 screen, shield, troops
07 bastion, bulwark, outpost, rampart, shelter, weapons
08 air force, apologia, argument, buttress, fortress, garrison, immunity, military, pleading, security, soldiers
09 armaments, barricade, deterrent, safeguard
10 deterrence, protection, resistance, stronghold
11 armed forces, explanation, explication, vindication
13 justification, fortification

defenceless
04 weak
07 exposed, unarmed
08 helpless, impotent
09 powerless, unguarded
10 undefended, vulnerable
11 unprotected
12 open to attack

defend
04 back
05 cover, deter, guard, plead

06 resist, screen, uphold
07 contest, explain, fortify, justify, protect, stand by
08 argue for, buttress, champion, garrison
09 barricade, exonerate, safeguard, vindicate
10 speak up for, stand up for, stick up for
12 keep from harm

defendant
07 accused
08 litigant, offender, prisoner
09 appellant
10 respondent

defender
05 guard
06 backer, keeper, patron
08 advocate, champion, endorser, guardian
09 apologist, bodyguard, protector, supporter

defensible
07 tenable
08 arguable
09 plausible
10 pardonable, vindicable
11 justifiable, permissible

defensive
04 wary
08 cautious, watchful
09 defending
10 apologetic, protective
14 self-justifying

defer
03 bow
05 delay, waive, yield
06 accede, comply, give in, put off, shelve, submit
07 give way, put back, respect
08 hold over, postpone, prorogue, put on ice
09 acquiesce, surrender
10 capitulate

deference
06 esteem, honour, regard
07 respect
08 civility, courtesy, yielding
09 obedience, reverence
10 compliance, politeness
12 acquiescence
13 attentiveness, consideration

deferential
05 civil
06 polite
07 dutiful
08 obeisant, reverent
09 attentive, courteous

10 morigerous, obsequious, respectful, thoughtful
11 considerate, reverential
12 ingratiating

deferment
04 stay
05 delay
07 waiving
08 shelving
10 moratorium, suspension
11 adjournment, prorogation
12 postponement
15 procrastination

defiance
08 contempt
09 challenge, disregard
10 opposition, resistance
12 disobedience
13 confrontation, recalcitrance
14 rebelliousness
15 insubordination

defiant
04 bold
08 insolent, militant, scornful
09 obstinate, resistant
10 aggressive, rebellious
11 challenging, disobedient
12 antagonistic, contumacious, intransigent, recalcitrant
13 insubordinate

deficiency
04 flaw, lack, want
05 fault
06 dearth, defect
07 absence, deficit, failing
08 scarcity, shortage, weakness
10 inadequacy, scantiness
11 shortcoming
12 imperfection
13 insufficiency

deficient
04 weak
05 short
06 meagre, scarce, skimpy
07 lacking, wanting
08 exiguous, inferior
10 inadequate, incomplete
12 insufficient
14 unsatisfactory

deficit
04 lack, loss
07 arrears, default
08 shortage
09 shortfall
10 deficiency

defile
04 pass, soil
05 dirty, gorge, gully, spoil, stain, sully, taint

06 debase, defame, infect, ravine, valley
07 blacken, corrupt, degrade, passage, pollute, profane, tarnish, violate, vitiate
08 disgrace
09 denigrate, desecrate, dishonour, inquinate
10 make impure
11 contaminate, make unclean

definable
08 definite, specific
10 explicable
11 describable, perceptible
12 determinable, identifiable
13 ascertainable

define
03 fix
05 bound, limit
07 delimit, explain, mark out
08 describe, spell out
09 delineate, demarcate, establish, interpret
12 characterize, circumscribe

definite
04 firm, sure
05 clear, exact, fixed
06 marked
07 assured, certain, decided, obvious, precise, settled
08 clear-cut, explicit, positive
10 determined, guaranteed

definitely
06 easily, indeed, surely
07 clearly, plainly
09 certainly, doubtless, no denying, obviously
10 absolutely, positively
11 indubitably, undoubtedly
12 unmistakably, without doubt
13 categorically
14 unquestionably
15 without question

definition
05 focus, sense
07 clarity, meaning
08 contrast
09 clearness, precision, sharpness
11 description, explanation
12 distinctness, significance

definitive
05 exact, final
07 correct, perfect
08 absolute, complete, standard, ultimate
11 categorical
13 authoritative

deflate
04 dash, void
05 empty, lower
06 debunk, humble, lessen, reduce, shrink, squash
07 chasten, depress, devalue, exhaust, flatten, let down, mortify, put down, squeeze
08 collapse, contract, diminish, dispirit, puncture
09 humiliate
10 depreciate, disappoint

deflect
04 bend, turn, veer, wind
05 avert, drift, twist
07 deviate, diverge
08 ricochet
09 glance off, turn aside
12 change course

deflection
04 bend, veer
06 swerve
08 ricochet, twisting
09 deviation
10 divergence, refraction
11 glancing-off
12 sidetracking, turning aside
14 changing course

deflower
03 mar
04 harm, rape, ruin
05 force, spoil
06 defile, ravish, seduce
07 assault, despoil, violate
09 desecrate

deform
03 mar
04 maim, ruin, warp
05 spoil, twist
06 buckle, damage, deface
07 contort, distort, pervert
08 misshape, mutilate
09 disfigure

deformation
04 bend, warp
05 curve, twist
06 buckle
08 twisting
10 contortion, defacement, distortion, mutilation
12 diastrophism, malformation
13 misshapenness

deformed
04 bent
06 maimed, marred, warped
07 buckled, crooked, defaced, gnarled, mangled, twisted
08 crippled

09 contorted, distorted, malformed, misshapen, mutilated, perverted
10 disfigured

deformity
06 defect
08 ugliness, vileness
09 grossness
10 defacement, distortion
11 abnormality, crookedness
12 imperfection, malformation
13 disfigurement, misshapenness

defraud
02 do
03 con, rob
04 dupe, fool, rook
05 cheat, cozen, sting, trick
06 delude, diddle, fiddle, fleece, outwit, rip off
07 deceive, mislead, swindle
08 embezzle, hoodwink

defray
03 pay
05 repay
06 refund, settle

deft
04 able, neat
05 adept, agile, handy, nifty
06 adroit, expert, nimble
07 skilful
09 dexterous

defunct
04 dead, gone
05 passé
06 bygone
07 expired, extinct, invalid
08 obsolete, outmoded
11 inoperative

defy
04 dare, face, foil
05 avoid, beard, brave, elude, flout, repel, scorn, spurn
06 baffle, defeat, slight, thwart
07 despise, disobey, provoke
08 confront
09 challenge, disregard, stand up to, withstand
12 rebel against

degeneracy
08 vileness
09 decadence
10 corruption, debasement, debauchery, immorality, sinfulness, wickedness
11 degradation, depravation
13 deterioration, dissoluteness

degenerate
03 low, rot

04 base, mean, sink, slip, vile
05 decay, lapse
06 effete, fallen, wicked, worsen
07 corrupt, debased, decline, fall off, go to pot, ignoble, immoral, regress
08 decadent, decrease, degraded, depraved
09 debauched, dissolute
10 go downhill, profligate
11 degenerated, deteriorate
13 go down the tube

degeneration
04 drop, slip
05 decay, lapse, slide
07 atrophy, decline, sinking
08 decrease
09 worsening
10 debasement, regression
13 deterioration

degradation
05 shame
07 decline
08 demotion, disgrace, ignominy, vileness
09 abasement, dishonour
10 corruption, debasement, debauchery, degeneracy, fallenness, immorality, sinfulness, wickedness
11 downgrading, humiliation
12 degeneration
13 deterioration, dissoluteness

degrade
05 abase, lower, shame, sully
06 debase, defile, demean, demote, depose, humble, impair, unseat, weaken
07 cashier, cheapen, corrupt, deprive, devalue
08 belittle, disgrace, relegate
09 discredit, dishonour, downgrade, humiliate
10 adulterate
11 deteriorate, lower in rank
12 reduce in rank

degrading
04 base
07 ignoble
08 debasing, shameful
09 demeaning
10 belittling, cheapening
11 disgraceful, humiliating
13 dishonourable

degree
04 mark, rank, rung, step, unit
05 class, grade, level, limit, order, point, range, stage
06 amount, extent, status

07 measure
08 position, standing, strength
09 intensity

dehydrate
03 dry
05 drain, dry up, parch
06 dry out
09 desiccate, lose water

deification
07 worship
09 elevation, extolling
10 apotheosis, exaltation
11 ennoblement, idolization
12 divinization, idealization
13 glorification
14 divinification
15 immortalization

deify
05 exalt, extol
07 elevate, ennoble, glorify, idolize, worship
08 idealize, venerate
11 immortalize

deign
05 stoop
10 condescend
13 lower yourself
14 demean yourself

deity
03 god
04 idol
05 power
06 spirit
07 eternal, goddess, godhead
08 divinity, immortal
11 divine being

dejected
03 low, sad
04 blue, down, glum
06 dismal, gloomy, morose
07 crushed, doleful
08 cast down, downcast, wretched
09 depressed, miserable
10 despondent, dispirited, melancholy, spiritless
11 crestfallen, demoralized, discouraged, downhearted
12 disconsolate, disheartened
14 down in the dumps

dejection
05 blues, dumps, gloom
06 misery, sorrow
07 despair, sadness
10 depression, gloominess, low spirits, melancholy
11 despondency, dolefulness
12 wretchedness

14 disconsolation, dispiritedness
15 downheartedness

de jure
05 legal
07 legally
08 rightful
10 rightfully

delay
03 lag
04 halt, keep, mora, stay, wait
05 check, defer, stall, tarry
06 detain, dither, hinder, hold up, impede, linger, loiter, put off, shelve
07 adjourn, set back, suspend
08 dawdling, hold back, hold over, obstruct, postpone, put on ice, reprieve, restrain, stalling, stoppage
09 deferment, hindrance, lag behind, lingering, stonewall
10 cunctation, dilly-dally, filibuster, moratorium, putting-off, suspension
11 adjournment, holding-over
12 interruption, postponement
15 procrastination

delectable
05 tasty, yummy
06 dainty
07 savoury
08 adorable, charming, engaging, exciting, luscious
09 agreeable, delicious, palatable, succulent
10 appetizing, delightful
11 flavoursome, scrumptious
13 mouth-watering

delectation
06 relish
07 comfort, delight
08 pleasure
09 amusement, diversion, enjoyment, happiness
12 satisfaction
13 entertainment, gratification

delegate
04 give, name
05 agent, envoy, leave, proxy
06 assign, charge, commit, depute, deputy, pass on
07 appoint, consign, devolve, empower, entrust
08 emissary, nominate
09 authorize, designate, messenger, spokesman
10 ambassador, commission
11 spokeswoman

12 commissioner, spokesperson
14 representative

delegation
07 embassy, mission
08 legation
09 committal, passing on
10 commission, contingent, deputation, devolution
11 consignment, empowerment
15 representatives

delete
03 cut
04 edit
05 erase
06 cancel, cut out, efface, excise, remove, rub out, strike
07 blot out, expunge, take out
08 cross out
09 strike out
10 blue-pencil, obliterate

deleterious
03 bad
07 harmful, hurtful, noxious
08 damaging
09 injurious
10 pernicious
11 destructive, detrimental

deliberate
04 muse, slow
05 think, weigh
06 debate, ponder, steady
07 careful, planned, prudent, reflect, studied, weigh up
08 cautious, consider, designed, measured, meditate, mull over, resolute, ruminate
09 conscious, think over
10 calculated, considered, methodical, preplanned
11 circumspect, intentional
12 premeditated

deliberately
06 slowly
08 by design, steadily, wilfully
09 carefully, knowingly, on purpose, pointedly
11 consciously, in cold blood
12 methodically, thoughtfully
13 intentionally

deliberation
04 care
05 study
06 debate, musing
07 caution, mulling, thought
09 pondering

10 cogitation, discussion, meditation, reflection, rumination, weighing-up
11 calculation, forethought
13 consideration
14 circumspection, thoughtfulness

delicacy
04 care, tact
05 taste, treat
06 dainty, luxury, relish, titbit
07 finesse, savoury
08 elegance, subtlety
09 diplomacy, fragility, sweetmeat
10 daintiness, discretion, speciality
11 sensitivity

delicate
04 fine, mild, pale, soft, weak
05 bland, faint, frail, muted
06 ailing, dainty, flimsy, infirm, pastel, sickly, slight, subtle, touchy, tricky, unwell
07 awkward, brittle, fragile
08 critical, discreet, graceful
09 breakable, difficult, exquisite, sensitive
11 debilitated, problematic
12 easily broken, in poor health, softly-softly
13 controversial, easily damaged, insubstantial

delicious
04 good
05 juicy, tasty, yummy
06 choice, morish
09 ambrosial, palatable, succulent, toothsome
10 appetizing, delectable, enchanting, nectareous
11 captivating, scrumptious
13 mouth-watering

delight
03 joy
04 glee, like, love
05 amuse, bliss, charm, cheer
06 excite, please, ravish, relish, savour, thrill, tickle
07 ecstasy, elation, enchant, gladden, gratify, rapture
08 euphoria, gladness, pleasure, wallow in
09 amusement, captivate, enjoyment, enrapture, entertain, happiness
10 appreciate, tickle pink
13 entertainment, gratification
14 take pleasure in

delighted
04 glad
05 happy
06 elated, joyful, joyous
07 charmed, excited, gleeful
08 ecstatic, jubilant, thrilled
09 enchanted, entranced, gratified, overjoyed
10 captivated, enraptured
11 over the moon, tickled pink
12 happy as Larry
14 pleased as Punch
15 happy as a sandboy

delightful
07 amusing, the tops
08 charming, engaging, exciting, pleasant, pleasing
09 diverting, enjoyable, thrilling
10 delectable, enchanting
11 captivating, fascinating
12 entertaining

delimit
03 fix
04 mark
05 bound
06 define
09 demarcate, determine, establish

delineate
03 fix
04 draw, mark
05 bound, chart, trace
06 define, depict, design
07 outline, portray
08 describe, set forth
09 determine, establish, represent

delinquency
05 crime
07 misdeed, offence
10 misconduct, wrongdoing
11 criminality, law-breaking
12 misbehaviour

delinquent
06 guilty, remiss, vandal
07 culprit, lawless, ruffian
08 criminal, hooligan, offender
09 miscreant, offending
10 law-breaker
11 law-breaking
13 young offender

delirious
03 mad
04 wild
05 crazy
06 elated, insane, raving
07 frantic
08 babbling, demented, deranged, ecstatic,

euphoric, frenzied, jubilant, unhinged
09 overjoyed
10 incoherent, irrational
11 carried away, light-headed, over the moon
13 out of your mind
14 beside yourself

delirium
03 joy
05 fever
06 frenzy, lunacy, raving
07 ecstasy, elation, jimjams, madness, passion
08 euphoria, hysteria, wildness
10 excitement, jubilation
11 derangement, incoherence

deliver
02 do
04 give, make, save, send, take
05 bring, carry, grant, speak
06 commit, convey, direct, launch, ransom, redeem, rescue, strike, supply
07 entrust, give out, inflict, provide, release, set free
08 announce, carry out, dispatch, hand over, liberate
09 implement, pronounce
10 distribute, emancipate

deliverance
06 escape, ransom, rescue
07 freedom, release
09 salvation
10 liberation, redemption
11 extrication
12 articulation, emancipation

delivery
06 labour, speech, supply
08 carriage, dispatch, shipment, transfer
09 elocution, transport
10 childbirth, conveyance
11 confinement, consignment, enunciation, parturition
12 articulation, distribution, transmission
14 transportation

dell
04 dean, vale
06 dingle, hollow, valley

delude
04 dupe, fool, hoax
05 cheat, trick
06 have on, lead on, take in
07 beguile, deceive, mislead
08 hoodwink, misguide
09 bamboozle, misinform
12 take for a ride

deluge
04 rush, soak, wave
05 drown, flood, spate, swamp
06 drench, engulf
07 torrent
08 downpour, inundate
10 inundation

delusion
05 fancy
07 fallacy
08 illusion, tricking
09 deception, misbelief
11 false belief
13 hallucination, misconception
14 misinformation
15 false impression, misapprehension

de luxe, deluxe
04 fine, rich
05 grand, plush
06 choice, costly, lavish, luxury, select
07 elegant, opulent, quality, special
08 palatial, splendid, superior
09 exclusive, expensive, luxurious, sumptuous

delve
04 poke, root
05 probe
06 burrow, go into, hunt in, search
07 dig into, examine, explore, ransack, rummage
08 look into, research
11 hunt through, investigate

demagogue
06 orator
08 agitator
09 firebrand, haranguer
10 tub-thumper
12 rabble-rouser

demand
03 ask, big
04 call, need, take, tell, want
05 claim, exact, order
07 call for, clamour, dictate, inquire, inquiry, require
08 exigency, insist on, petition, press for, pressure, question
09 cry out for, stipulate
10 hold out for, insistence
11 interrogate, necessitate
13 interrogation

◻ in demand
03 big
06 trendy
07 popular
08 asked for
09 requested
11 fashionable, sought after

demanding
04 hard
05 tough
06 taxing, trying, urgent
07 exigent, nagging, testing, wearing
09 difficult, harassing, insistent
11 challenging

demarcate
04 mark
05 bound
06 define
07 delimit, mark out
09 determine, establish

demarcation
04 line
05 bound, limit
08 boundary, division
09 enclosure
10 marking off, marking out
12 delimitation
13 determination, establishment

demean
05 abase, lower, stoop
06 debase, demote, humble
07 degrade, descend
08 belittle
09 deprecate, humiliate

demeanour
03 air
04 mien
06 manner
07 bearing, conduct
09 behaviour
10 deportment
11 comportment

demented
03 mad
04 nuts, wild
05 loony, loopy, nutty
06 crazed, insane
07 berserk, bonkers, lunatic
08 deranged, unhinged
10 unbalanced
12 round the bend
13 out of your mind

demise
03 end
05 death
07 decease, failure, passing
08 collapse, downfall
10 expiration

democracy
08 autonomy, republic
12 commonwealth
14 self-government

democratic
07 popular
08 populist
10 autonomous, republican
11 egalitarian
13 self-governing

demolish
04 beat, raze, rout, ruin, undo
05 crush, level, repel, wreck
06 hammer, subdue, thrash
07 break up, destroy, flatten
08 bulldoze, overturn, pull down, tear down
09 devastate, dismantle, knock down, pulverize, slaughter, subjugate
10 annihilate

demolition
04 rout
06 razing
07 beating, licking
09 hammering, levelling, slaughter, thrashing
10 breaking-up, flattening
11 destruction, dismantling, pulling-down, tearing-down
12 knocking-down

demon
03 ace, imp
05 afrit, beast, brute, devil, fiend, freak, ghoul, rogue
06 addict, daemon, wizard
07 dab hand, fanatic, incubus, monster, rakshas, villain
08 succubus
09 cacodemon
10 evil spirit

demonic
03 mad
05 manic
06 crazed
07 furious, hellish, satanic
08 devilish, fiendish, frenetic, frenzied, infernal, maniacal
10 diabolical

demonstrable
05 clear
07 certain, evident, obvious
08 arguable, positive, provable
09 evincible
10 attestable, verifiable
11 self-evident

demonstrate
04 show
05 march, rally, prove, sit in
06 betray, evince, parade, picket, verify

07 bespeak, betoken, display,
     exhibit, express, protest
08 indicate, manifest, validate
09 make clear, testify to
10 illustrate
12 substantiate
13 bear witness to

demonstration
04 demo, test
05 march, proof, rally, sit-in, trial
06 parade, picket
07 display, protest
08 evidence
09 mass rally, testimony
10 evincement, exhibition,
     indication, validation
11 affirmation, explanation
12 confirmation, illustration,
     presentation, verification
13 manifestation
14 substantiation

demonstrative
04 open, warm
06 loving
07 gushing
08 effusive
09 emotional, extrovert
10 expressive, unreserved
12 affectionate

demoralize
05 crush, daunt, lower
06 debase, deject, weaken
07 corrupt, deprave, depress,
     pervert
08 cast down, dispirit
09 undermine
10 discourage, dishearten

demote
06 humble
07 cashier, degrade
08 relegate
09 downgrade

demotic
06 vulgar
07 popular
08 enchoric
09 enchorial
10 colloquial, vernacular

demur
04 balk
05 cavil, doubt, qualm
06 object, refuse
07 dissent, protest, scruple
08 demurral, disagree, hesitate
09 misgiving, objection
10 hesitation
11 compunction, reservation
12 disagreement
13 express doubts

demure
03 coy, shy
04 prim
05 grave, quiet, staid, timid
06 modest, prissy
07 prudish, serious
08 reserved, reticent, retiring
11 strait-laced

den
04 dive, hole, lair
05 haunt, joint, pitch, study
06 hollow
07 hideout, retreat, shelter
08 hideaway
09 sanctuary

denial
04 veto
06 rebuff
07 dissent, refusal
08 negation
09 disavowal, dismissal,
     disowning, rejection
10 abjuration, disclaimer
11 prohibition, repudiation
12 disagreement, renunciation
13 contradiction

denigrate
05 abuse, decry
06 assail, defame, impugn,
     malign, revile, vilify
07 run down, slander
08 belittle, besmirch, vilipend
09 criticize, deprecate, disparage
10 calumniate

denizen
07 citizen, dweller, habitué
08 habitant, occupant, resident
10 inhabitant

denomination
04 cult, kind, sect, sort, unit
05 class, creed, faith, grade,
     order, value, worth
09 communion, face value
10 persuasion

denote
04 mark, mean, show
05 imply
06 typify
07 betoken, express, refer to,
     signify, suggest
08 indicate, stand for
09 represent, symbolize

dénouement
05 close
06 climax, finale, finish, upshot
07 last act, outcome
08 solution
10 conclusion, resolution
13 clarification

denounce
05 decry
06 accuse, attack, betray,
     impugn, indict, revile, vilify
07 arraign, censure, condemn
09 castigate, criticize,
     fulminate, inculpate
13 inform against

dense
03 dim
04 dull, slow
05 close, heavy, solid, thick
06 opaque, packed, stupid
07 compact, crammed
09 close-knit, condensed, dim-
     witted
10 compressed, slow-witted
12 concentrated, impenetrable
13 tightly packed

density
04 body, bulk, mass
09 closeness, denseness,
     solidness, thickness,
     tightness
11 compactness, consistency

dent
03 dip, pit
04 dint
06 crater, dimple, hollow,
     indent, push in
07 depress
09 concavity
10 depression
11 indentation

denude
04 bare
05 strip
06 divest, expose
07 uncover
08 deforest
09 defoliate

denunciation
06 attack
07 censure, decrial, obloquy
09 criticism, invective
10 accusation
11 castigation, fulmination
12 condemnation,
     denouncement

deny
04 veto
05 rebut
06 abjure, disown, forbid,
     negate, oppose, rebuff,
     recant, refuse, refute, reject
07 decline, disavow, dismiss,
     gainsay, nullify
08 disclaim, disprove, prohibit,
     renounce, turn down,
     withhold

09 disaffirm, repudiate

deodorant
08 fumigant
09 fumigator
10 deodorizer
12 air-freshener, disinfectant
14 anti-perspirant

deodorize
06 aerate, purify
07 freshen, refresh, sweeten
08 fumigate
09 disinfect, ventilate

depart
02 go
04 exit, quit, scat, vary, veer
05 leave, scoot, scram, split
06 decamp, differ, escape, remove, retire, set off, set out, swerve, vanish
07 deviate, digress, diverge, make off, migrate, pull out, push off, retreat, scarper, take off, vamoose
08 clear off, get going, shove off, start out, up sticks
09 branch off, disappear, do a runner, skedaddle
10 hit the road, make tracks
13 sling your hook, take your leave
15 make a break for it, take to your heels

departed
04 dead, gone, late
07 expired
08 deceased
10 passed away

department
04 area, line, unit, wing
05 field, realm
06 agency, branch, bureau, domain, office, region
07 concern, section, station
08 district, division, province
11 subdivision

departure
04 exit
05 going, shift
06 change, escape, exodus
07 leaving, removal, retreat
09 branching, deviation, going away, variation
10 difference, digression, divergence, innovation, retirement, setting-off, setting-out, withdrawal
11 leave-taking

depend
04 need

06 bank on, hang on, lean on, rely on, rest on, turn on
07 count on, hinge on, trust in
09 be based on, build upon
11 be decided by, be subject to,
13 be dependent on, revolve around
14 be contingent on, be determined by

dependable
04 sure
06 honest, stable, steady, trusty
07 certain
08 faithful, reliable
09 steadfast, unfailing
11 responsible, trustworthy
13 conscientious
14 tried and tested

dependant
04 ward
05 child, minor
06 charge, client, minion
07 protégé
08 hanger-on, parasite
11 subordinate

dependence
04 need
05 abuse, faith, trust
08 reliance
09 addiction
12 helplessness, subservience
13 subordination

dependency
05 abuse, habit
06 colony
07 support
08 province, reliance, weakness
09 addiction
10 attachment, immaturity
12 helplessness, protectorate
13 subordination

dependent
04 weak
05 based
07 decided, reliant, subject
08 helpless, immature, relative
09 supported, sustained
10 contingent, controlled, determined, influenced
11 conditional, subordinate

depict
04 draw, show
05 paint, trace
06 detail, record, render, sketch
07 outline, picture, portray
08 describe
09 delineate, represent
10 illustrate

depiction
05 image
07 drawing, outline, picture
08 likeness
09 portrayal, rendering
10 caricature
11 delineation, description
12 illustration
14 representation

deplete
05 drain, empty, spend, use up
06 lessen, reduce, weaken
07 eat into, exhaust, run down
08 decrease, diminish
09 attenuate
10 impoverish
11 whittle away

depletion
08 decrease, lowering
09 dwindling, lessening, reduction, shrinkage, weakening
10 diminution, exhaustion
11 attenuation, consumption

deplorable
04 dire
08 grievous, shameful, wretched
09 appalling, miserable
10 abominable, despicable, disastrous, lamentable, outrageous, scandalous
11 blameworthy, disgraceful, distressing, regrettable
12 disreputable
13 dishonourable, reprehensible

deplore
03 cry, rue
05 blame, mourn, slate
06 bemoan, berate, bewail, lament, regret, revile
07 censure, condemn, reprove
08 denounce, reproach
09 castigate, criticize, deprecate, grieve for
12 disapprove of

deploy
03 use
07 arrange, station, utilize
08 position
09 spread out
10 distribute

depopulate
05 empty

deport
03 act
04 bear, hold, oust
05 carry, exile, expel

06 acquit, banish, behave
07 comport, conduct
09 extradite, transport
10 repatriate

deportation
05 exile
07 ousting
09 expulsion, ostracism
10 banishment
11 extradition
12 repatriation
14 transportation

deportment
03 air
04 mien, pose
06 aspect, manner, stance
07 bearing, conduct, posture
08 carriage
09 behaviour, demeanour,
   etiquette
10 appearance
11 comportment

depose
04 fire, oust, sack
06 remove, topple, unseat
08 dethrone, displace
09 discharge, overthrow

deposit
03 lay, put, set, sit
04 bank, drop, dump, file, gage,
   lees, park, save, silt, stow
05 dregs, hoard, lodge, place,
   plant, put by, stake, store
06 locate, pledge, settle
07 consign, entrust, put away,
   put down, set down
08 retainer, security, sediment
11 down payment

deposition
07 ousting, removal
08 evidence, toppling
09 affidavit, statement,
   testimony, unseating
11 declaration, information
12 dethronement,
   displacement

depository
05 depot, store
07 arsenal
09 warehouse
10 repository, storehouse
15 bonded warehouse

depot
05 cache, store
06 garage
07 arsenal, station
08 terminal, terminus
09 warehouse

10 depository, repository,
   storehouse

deprave
06 debase, defile, infect
07 corrupt, debauch, degrade,
   pervert, pollute, subvert
10 demoralize, lead astray
11 contaminate

depraved
04 base, evil, vile
06 sinful, wicked
07 corrupt, debased, immoral
09 debauched, dissolute,
   perverted, reprobate,
   shameless
10 degenerate, licentious

depravity
04 evil, vice
08 baseness, iniquity, vileness
09 reprobacy, turpitude
10 corruption, debasement,
   debauchery, degeneracy,
   immorality, perversion
13 dissoluteness

deprecate
04 slam
05 blame, knock, slate
06 berate, reject, revile
07 censure, condemn, deplore
08 denounce, reproach
09 castigate, criticize,
   disparage, reprehend
12 disapprove of

deprecatory
09 regretful
10 apologetic, censorious,
   dismissive, protesting
11 reproachful
12 condemnatory,
   disapproving

depreciate
06 defame, lessen, malign,
   reduce, revile, slight
07 decline, deflate, devalue,
   run down
09 belittle, denigrate,
   disparage, downgrade
11 make light of
13 go down in value

depreciation
04 fall
05 slump
08 mark-down
09 deflation
10 cheapening, depression
11 denigration, devaluation
12 belittlement
13 disparagement
15 underestimation

depredation
05 theft
07 looting, pillage, plunder,
   raiding, robbery
08 harrying, ravaging
09 marauding
10 denudation, despoiling
11 destruction, devastation,
   laying waste

depress
05 daunt, lower, press, weary
06 deject, lessen, reduce
07 devalue, get down, oppress
08 cast down, enervate
09 bring down, weigh down
10 discourage, dishearten

depressant
06 downer
07 calmant
08 relaxant, sedative
09 calmative
13 tranquillizer

depressed
03 low, sad
04 blue, down, glum, poor
05 fed up, moody, needy
06 dented, gloomy, hollow,
   morose, sunken
07 concave, unhappy
08 cast down, dejected,
   deprived, downcast,
   indented, pushed in
10 despondent, dispirited,
   distressed, melancholy
11 crestfallen, discouraged,
   downhearted, low-spirited
12 disheartened, low in spirits
13 disadvantaged
14 down in the dumps

depressing
03 sad
04 grey
05 black, bleak, grave
06 dismal, dreary, gloomy
08 daunting, hopeless
09 cheerless, dejecting
10 melancholy
11 dispiriting, distressing
12 discouraging
13 disheartening

depression
03 dip, pit
04 bowl, dent, dint, hole, sink
05 blues, dumps, gloom, slump
06 cavity, dimple, hollow, valley
07 decline, despair, sadness
08 doldrums, glumness
09 concavity, dejection, hard
   times, pessimism, recession

10 desolation, excavation, gloominess, impression, low spirits, melancholy
11 despondency, indentation, melancholia, unhappiness
12 hopelessness
14 discouragement
15 downheartedness

deprivation
04 lack, need, want
06 denial, penury
07 poverty, removal
08 hardship
09 privation
10 withdrawal
11 destitution, withholding
12 disadvantage
13 dispossession

deprive
03 rob
04 deny
05 strip
06 denude, divest, refuse
08 take away, withhold
10 confiscate, dispossess
11 expropriate

deprived
04 poor
05 needy
06 bereft, in need
07 lacking
12 impoverished
13 disadvantaged
15 underprivileged

depth
04 deep, drop, glow, gulf
05 abyss, floor, midst, scope
06 acumen, amount, bottom, extent, warmth, wisdom
07 measure, passion
08 darkness, deepness, richness, severity, strength
09 intensity, intuition
10 profundity, shrewdness
11 discernment, earnestness, penetration, seriousness
12 profoundness, remotest area, thoroughness
13 extensiveness

◻in depth
08 in detail
10 thoroughly
11 extensively
12 exhaustively
15 comprehensively

deputation
07 embassy, mission
08 legation
09 committee
10 commission, delegation

15 representatives

depute
06 charge, second
07 appoint, consign, empower, entrust, mandate
08 accredit, delegate, hand over, nominate
09 authorize, designate
10 commission

deputize
05 cover
06 act for, double, sub for
07 relieve, replace
10 stand in for, substitute, understudy
14 take the place of

deputy
04 vice-
05 agent, envoy, locum, proxy
06 depute, legate
07 stand-in
08 delegate
09 assistant, coadjutor, suffragan, surrogate
10 ambassador, substitute
11 subordinate
12 commissioner
13 vice-president
14 representative
15 second-in-command

deranged
03 mad
04 nuts
05 crazy, loony, loopy, nutty
06 insane
07 berserk, bonkers, lunatic
08 demented, unhinged
09 delirious, disturbed
10 distraught, irrational, out to lunch, unbalanced
12 round the bend
13 of unsound mind, off your rocker, out of your mind, round the twist
15 non compos mentis

derangement
05 mania
06 frenzy, lunacy
07 madness
08 delirium, dementia, disorder, insanity
11 distraction, disturbance

derelict
04 hobo
05 tramp
06 beggar, dosser, wretch
07 drifter, no-hoper, outcast, run-down, vagrant
08 deserted, desolate, forsaken
09 abandoned, neglected

10 down-and-out, ramshackle, tumbledown
11 dilapidated, in disrepair
15 falling to pieces

dereliction
04 ruin
05 ruins
07 evasion, failure, neglect
08 apostasy, betrayal
09 desertion, disrepair
10 abdication, renegation
11 abandonment
12 dilapidation, renunciation

deride
03 rag
04 gibe, jeer, mock
05 knock, scoff, scorn, sneer, taunt, tease
06 insult
08 belittle, pooh-pooh, ridicule, satirize
09 disparage, make fun of

de rigueur
04 done
05 right
06 decent, proper
07 correct, fitting
08 decorous, required
09 necessary
12 conventional, the done thing

derision
05 scorn
06 insult, satire
07 mockery, ragging, teasing
08 contempt, ridicule, scoffing, sneering, taunting
10 disrespect
13 disparagement

derisive
07 jeering, mocking
08 scoffing, scornful, taunting
09 insulting
10 disdainful, irreverent
12 contemptuous
13 disrespectful

derisory
04 tiny
06 absurd, paltry
07 risible
09 insulting, laughable, ludicrous
10 outrageous, ridiculous
12 contemptible, preposterous

derivation
04 root
05 basis
06 origin, source
07 descent

08 ancestry
09 beginning, etymology, genealogy, inference
10 extraction, foundation

derivative

06 branch, copied
07 cribbed, derived, spin-off
08 rehashed
09 by-product, imitative
10 derivation, descendant, second-hand, unoriginal

derive

03 get
04 draw, flow, gain, stem
05 arise, issue
06 borrow, evolve, follow
07 descend, develop, emanate, proceed, procure, receive
09 originate
14 have its roots in
15 have as the source

derogatory

08 critical
09 injurious, insulting, offensive, slighting, vilifying
10 defamatory, pejorative
11 denigratory, disparaging
12 depreciative, disapproving, unfavourable
15 uncomplimentary

descend

03 dip
04 drop, fall, sink, stem
05 deign, slope, stoop, swoop
06 alight, arrive, go down, invade, plunge, tumble
07 decline, emanate, incline, plummet, proceed, subside
08 dismount, move down
09 originate
10 degenerate, go downhill
11 deteriorate, go to the dogs
14 arrive suddenly

descendants

04 line, seed
05 issue
06 scions
07 lineage, progeny
08 children
09 offspring, posterity
10 successors

descent

03 dip
04 drop, fall, line
05 slant, slope, stock
06 origin, plunge
07 decline, incline, lineage
08 ancestry, heredity

09 decadence, declivity, genealogy, parentage, subsiding
10 debasement, degeneracy, extraction, family tree
11 degradation
13 deterioration

describe

04 call, draw, hail, talk, tell
05 brand, label, style, think
06 depict, detail, relate, report
07 explain, mark out, narrate, portray, recount, specify
09 delineate, designate
12 characterize
13 give details of

description

04 kind, make, sort, type
05 brand, breed, class, order
06 report, sketch
07 account, outline, profile
09 depiction, narration, portrayal
10 commentary, exposition
11 delineation, designation
14 representation

descriptive

05 vivid
07 graphic
08 detailed, striking
09 colourful, pictorial
10 expressive

descry

03 see
04 espy, mark, spot
06 detect, notice
07 discern, glimpse, observe
08 discover, perceive
09 recognize
11 distinguish
12 catch sight of

desecrate

05 abuse
06 debase, defile, insult
07 pervert, pollute, profane, violate
09 blaspheme, vandalize

desecration

06 insult
07 impiety
09 blasphemy, pollution, sacrilege, violation
10 debasement, defilement
11 profanation

desert

03 dry, due, fly
04 arid, bare, flee, jilt, quit
05 empty, leave, merit, rat on, right, waste, wilds, worth

06 barren, betray, decamp, defect, give up, go AWOL, maroon, recant, reward
07 abandon, abscond, cast off, deserts, dried up, forsake, parched, payment, run away
08 desolate, renounce, run out on, solitary
09 infertile, walk out on
10 apostasize, recompense, relinquish, wilderness
11 change sides, come-uppance, retribution
12 moistureless, tergiversate, uncultivated
14 turn your back on, what you deserve
15 leave high and dry, leave in the lurch

➤ *Names of deserts*:
04 Gobi, Thar
05 Kavir, Namib, Ordos, Sturt
06 Nubian, Sahara, Syrian, Ust'-Urt
07 Alashan, Arabian, Atacama, Kara Kum, Simpson, Sonoran
08 Kalahari, Kyzyl-Kum
09 Dzungaria
10 Chihuahuan, Great Basin, Great Sandy, Patagonian, Takla Makan
13 Great Victoria
14 Bolson de Mapimi

deserted

04 left
05 empty
06 bereft, lonely, vacant
08 derelict, desolate, forsaken, isolated, solitary, stranded
09 abandoned, neglected
10 unoccupied
11 God-forsaken, uninhabited

deserter

03 rat
06 truant
07 escapee, runaway, traitor
08 apostate, betrayer, defector, fugitive, renegade, turncoat
09 absconder

desertion

06 denial, flight, give up
07 jilting, leaving, truancy
08 apostasy, betrayal, giving-up, quitting
09 defection, forsaking
10 absconding, renegation
11 abandonment, dereliction
12 renunciation
14 tergiversation

deserve
04 earn, rate
05 incur, merit
07 justify, warrant
10 be worthy of
12 be entitled to, have a right to

deserved
03 apt, due
04 fair, just, meet
05 right
06 earned, proper
07 condign, fitting, merited
08 apposite, rightful, suitable
09 justified, warranted
10 legitimate, well-earned

deserving
06 worthy
07 upright
08 laudable, virtuous
09 admirable
11 commendable, meritorious
12 praiseworthy

desiccated
03 dry
05 dried
07 drained, parched, sterile
08 lifeless, powdered
10 dehydrated, exsiccated

desiccation
07 aridity, dryness
08 parching, xeransis
11 dehydration, exsiccation

design
03 aim, end, map
04 draw, form, gear, goal, hope, logo, make, mean, plan, plot
05 draft, dream, guide, hatch, model, motif, shape, style
06 cipher, create, device, devise, draw up, emblem, figure, format, intend, invent, make-up, object, scheme, sketch, tailor
07 develop, diagram, fashion, meaning, pattern, purpose
08 conceive, contrive, monogram
09 blueprint, construct, fabricate, intention, objective, originate, prototype, structure
11 arrangement, composition
12 construction, organization

◻by design
08 wilfully
09 knowingly, on purpose, pointedly, wittingly
11 consciously
12 deliberately
13 calculatingly, intentionally

designate
03 dub
04 call, name, show, term
05 elect, style, title
06 assign, choose, select
07 appoint, earmark, specify
08 christen, describe, indicate, nominate, set aside
09 stipulate

designation
03 tag
04 name, term
05 label, style, title
07 epithet, marking
08 category, denoting, election, nickname
10 definition, nomination
11 appellation, appointment
14 classification

designer
05 maker
06 author
07 creator, planner, stylist
08 inventor, producer
09 architect, contriver

designing
03 sly
04 wily
06 artful, crafty, shrewd, tricky
07 cunning, devious
08 guileful, plotting, scheming
09 deceitful, underhand
10 conspiring, intriguing
11 calculating

desirability
05 merit, worth
06 allure, profit
07 benefit
08 sexiness
09 advantage
10 attraction, popularity, preference, usefulness
12 advisability
13 seductiveness
14 attractiveness

desirable
04 good, sexy
07 popular
08 alluring, fetching, in demand, sensible, tempting
09 advisable, agreeable, expedient, seductive
10 attractive, beneficial, preferable, profitable
11 appropriate, sought-after
12 advantageous

desire
03 yen
04 itch, lust, need, want, wish
05 covet, crave, fancy

06 ardour, hunger, libido
07 craving, longing, passion
08 appetite, sex drive, yearning
09 hankering, sexuality
10 aspiration, preference, proclivity, sensuality
11 hanker after
12 have a crush on, predilection
13 concupiscence
14 lasciviousness, predisposition, set your heart on
15 give the world for

desired
05 exact, right
07 correct, fitting
08 accurate, expected, required
09 necessary
11 appropriate

desirous
04 avid, keen
05 eager, ready
06 hoping
07 anxious, burning, craving, hopeful, itching, longing, willing, wishing
08 aspiring, yearning
09 ambitious

desist
03 end
04 halt, stop
05 cease, pause, remit
06 give up
07 forbear, refrain, suspend
08 break off, leave off, peter out
11 discontinue

desk
04 ambo
06 bureau
07 lectern
09 davenport, écritoire
10 escritoire, secretaire
11 reading-desk
12 writing-table

desolate
03 sad
04 arid, bare
05 bleak, floor, upset, waste
06 barren, bereft, dismal, dreary, gloomy, lonely
07 forlorn, get down, nonplus, shatter, unhappy
08 dejected, deserted, downcast, forsaken, isolated, solitary, wretched
09 abandoned, depressed, devastate, miserable, overwhelm, take aback

10 depressing, despondent, distressed, unoccupied
11 heartbroken, uninhabited
12 God-forsaken
13 broken-hearted

desolation
04 ruin
05 gloom, grief
06 misery, sorrow
07 anguish, despair, sadness
08 distress, solitude, wildness
09 bleakness, dejection, emptiness, isolation
10 depression, loneliness, melancholy, remoteness
11 despondency, devastation, laying waste, unhappiness
12 wretchedness

despair
05 gloom
06 give in, give up, misery
07 anguish
08 collapse, distress, lose hope
09 lose heart, surrender
10 depression, melancholy
11 desperation, despondency
12 hopelessness, wretchedness
13 hit rock bottom
15 throw in the towel

despairing
08 dejected, desolate, dismayed, downcast, hopeless, suicidal, wretched
09 anguished, depressed, desperate, miserable
10 despondent, distraught
11 heartbroken, pessimistic
12 disheartened, inconsolable

despatch see **dispatch**

desperado
04 thug
06 bandit, gunman, outlaw
07 brigand, hoodlum, ruffian
08 criminal, gangster
09 cut-throat, terrorist
10 law-breaker

desperate
04 bold, dire, rash, wild
05 acute, grave, great, risky
07 crucial, do-or-die, extreme, frantic, serious, violent
08 dejected, desolate, dismayed, frenzied, hopeless, reckless, suicidal, wretched
09 abandoned, dangerous, miserable, sorrowful
10 compelling, despondent, determined, distraught
11 in great need
12 crying out for, inconsolable

15 needing very much, wanting very much

desperately
05 badly
07 acutely, gravely, greatly
08 severely, urgently
09 extremely, fearfully, seriously
10 critically, dreadfully, hopelessly
11 dangerously, frightfully

desperation
05 agony, gloom, worry
06 misery, sorrow
07 anguish, despair, trouble
11 despondency
12 hopelessness, wretchedness

despicable
04 mean, vile
07 caitiff
08 shameful, wretched
09 loathsome, reprobate
10 abominable, detestable
11 disgraceful
12 contemptible, disreputable
13 reprehensible

despise
04 hate, mock, shun
05 abhor, scorn, sneer, spurn
06 deride, detest, loathe, revile
07 condemn, deplore, disdain

despite
07 against, defying
09 in spite of
11 in the face of
12 regardless of, undeterred by
15 notwithstanding

despoil
03 rob
04 loot
05 rifle, strip, wreck
06 denude, maraud, ravage
07 deprive, destroy, pillage, plunder, ransack
08 spoliate
09 depredate, devastate, vandalize
10 dispossess

despondency
05 blues, gloom, grief
06 misery, sorrow
07 despair, sadness
08 distress, glumness
09 dejection, heartache
10 depression, melancholy
11 desperation, melancholia
12 hopelessness, wretchedness
14 discouragement, dispiritedness
15 downheartedness, inconsolability

despondent
03 low, sad
04 blue, down, glum
06 gloomy
07 doleful
08 dejected, downcast, mournful, wretched
09 depressed, miserable, sorrowful
10 despairing, distressed, melancholy
11 discouraged, heartbroken
12 disheartened, inconsolable
14 down in the dumps

despot
04 boss
06 tyrant
08 autocrat, dictator
09 oppressor
10 absolutist
13 absolute ruler

despotic
08 absolute, arrogant
09 arbitrary, imperious
10 autocratic, high-handed, oppressive, tyrannical
11 dictatorial, domineering
13 authoritarian

despotism
07 tyranny
09 autocracy
10 absolutism, oppression, repression
12 dictatorship
15 totalitarianism

dessert
03 pud
05 sweet
06 afters
07 pudding

destination
03 aim, end
04 goal, stop
06 design, object, target
08 ambition, terminus
09 intention, objective
11 journey's end
12 end of the line
15 final port of call

destined
05 bound, fated, meant
06 doomed, headed, routed
07 certain, en route, heading
08 assigned, intended, ordained, set apart
09 appointed, scheduled
10 inevitable
11 inescapable, unavoidable
13 predetermined

destiny
03 lot
04 doom, fate, luck
05 karma
06 future, kismet
07 fortune, portion
10 predestiny
14 predestination

destitute
04 poor
05 broke, needy, skint
06 bereft, hard up
07 lacking, wanting
08 badly off, bankrupt, devoid of, indigent
09 penniless, penurious
10 cleaned out, down and out, stony-broke
11 impecunious
12 impoverished
14 on the breadline, on your beam-ends
15 poverty-stricken

destitution
06 penury
07 beggary, poverty, straits
09 indigence, pauperdom
10 bankruptcy, starvation
13 pennilessness
14 impoverishment, on the breadline
15 impecuniousness

destroy
03 gut
04 kill, raze, ruin, slay, undo
05 break, crush, level, smash, spoil, waste, wreck
07 flatten, nullify, put down, shatter, unshape, vitiate
08 decimate, demolish, lay waste, sabotage, stamp out, tear down
09 devastate, eliminate, eradicate, extirpate, knock down, slaughter
10 annihilate, put to sleep

destroyer
06 locust, vandal
07 ravager, wrecker
09 despoiler, ransacker
11 annihilator, kiss of death

destruction
03 end
04 ruin
05 havoc
06 defeat, murder, razing
07 killing, undoing, wastage
08 crushing, downfall, smashing, wreckage
09 levelling, ruination, slaughter, vandalism
10 demolition, desolation, extinction, ravagement
11 depredation, devastation, dismantling, elimination, eradication, liquidation
12 annihilation, knocking-down, obliteration
13 extermination, nullification

destructive
05 fatal
06 deadly, lethal
07 harmful, hostile, hurtful, noxious, ruinous, vicious
08 damaging, negative
09 injurious, malignant
10 disastrous, disruptive, nullifying, pernicious, subversive, unfriendly
11 deleterious, denigrating, detrimental, devastating, mischievous, undermining
12 catastrophic, slaughterous

desultory
05 loose
06 fitful, random
07 aimless, chaotic, erratic
09 haphazard, irregular
11 half-hearted
12 disconnected, inconsistent, unmethodical, unsystematic
13 unco-ordinated

detach
04 free, undo
05 sever, split, unfix
06 cut off, divide, loosen, remove
07 disjoin, isolate, take off, tear off, unhitch
08 estrange, separate, uncouple, unfasten
09 disengage, segregate
10 disconnect, dissociate
11 disentangle

detached
04 cold, free
05 aloof, loose
06 remote
07 divided, neutral, severed
08 clinical, discrete, separate
09 impartial, objective
10 impersonal
11 dissociated, independent, indifferent, unconcerned, unemotional
12 disconnected
13 disinterested, dispassionate

detachment
04 unit
05 corps, force, squad
06 patrol
07 brigade, removal, undoing
08 coolness, disunion, fairness
09 aloofness, isolation, loosening, severance, task force, unconcern
10 neutrality, remoteness, separation, withdrawal
11 objectivity, unfastening
12 impartiality, indifference
13 disconnection, disengagement, disentangling

detail
04 fact, item, list
05 count, point
06 aspect, assign, charge, factor, nicety, set out
07 appoint, element, feature, itemize, recount, specify
08 allocate, delegate, describe, minutiae, point out, specific, spell out, tabulate
09 attribute, component, enumerate, intricacy
10 complexity, ins and outs, particular, refinement, small print, triviality
11 elaboration, nitty-gritty
12 complication, technicality
13 specification

❑**in detail**
05 fully
07 in depth
08 at length
09 carefully
10 item by item, thoroughly
12 exhaustively, point by point
15 comprehensively

detailed
04 full
05 exact
07 complex, in-depth, precise
08 itemized, specific, thorough
09 elaborate, intricate
10 blow-by-blow, convoluted, exhaustive, meticulous
13 comprehensive

detain
04 hold, keep, slow, stay, stop
05 check, delay
06 arrest, hinder, hold up, impede, intern, lock up
07 confine, inhibit
08 hold back, imprison, keep back, make late, restrain
11 incarcerate, put in prison
13 hold in custody

detect
04 find, note, spot
06 expose, notice, reveal, turn up, unmask
07 discern, make out, observe, uncover, unearth
08 disclose, discover, identify, perceive
09 ascertain, track down
12 bring to light

detection
06 exposé
08 exposure, sighting, noticing
09 discovery, unmasking
10 disclosure, perception, revelation, uncovering, unearthing
11 discernment, observation
12 ascertaining, tracking-down
14 distinguishing, identification

detective
04 dick, tail
06 shamus, sleuth
07 gumshoe
10 private eye
12 investigator
13 police officer

▶ *Names of famous detectives:*
04 **Chan** (Charlie)
05 **Brown** (Father), **Dupin** (C Auguste), **Mason** (Perry), **Morse** (Inspector), **Queen** (Ellery), **Spade** (Sam)
06 **Holmes** (Sherlock), **Marple** (Miss Jane), **Poirot** (Hercule), **Wimsey** (Lord Peter)
07 **Cadfael** (Brother), **Columbo** (Lieutenant), **Maigret** (Inspector), **Marlowe** (Philip)
08 **Bergerac** (Jim), **Lestrade** (Inspector)

detention
05 delay
07 custody
09 captivity, hindrance, restraint, slowing-up
10 constraint, detainment, internment, punishment, quarantine
11 confinement, holding-back
12 imprisonment
13 incarceration

deter
04 stop, warn
05 check, daunt
06 hinder, put off
07 inhibit, prevent, turn off
08 dissuade, frighten, restrain
09 talk out of
10 discourage, disincline

detergent
04 soap
07 cleaner
08 cleanser
10 abstergent
13 washing powder
15 washing-up liquid

deteriorate
05 decay, go bad, lapse, slide
06 weaken, worsen
07 break up, decline, fall off, go to pot, relapse
08 get worse, go to seed
09 decompose, fall apart
10 degenerate, depreciate, go downhill, retrograde, retrogress
12 disintegrate, fall to pieces

deterioration
05 lapse, slide
06 waning
07 decline, failure, relapse
08 downturn, slipping
09 corrosion, worsening
10 debasement, pejoration
11 degradation
12 degeneration, exacerbation
13 retrogression

determinate
05 fixed
07 certain, decided, defined, express, precise, settled
08 absolute, clear-cut, decisive, definite, distinct, explicit
09 specified
10 conclusive, definitive, quantified
11 established

determination
04 grit, guts, push, will
05 drive
07 purpose, resolve, stamina
08 backbone, decision, firmness, tenacity
09 fortitude, willpower
10 conclusion, insistence, moral fibre, resolution
11 persistence
12 perseverance, resoluteness
13 steadfastness

determine
05 fix on, guide, impel, learn
06 affect, choose, clinch, decide, detect, direct, govern, ordain, settle, verify
07 agree on, control, dictate, find out, purpose, resolve
08 conclude, discover, identify
09 ascertain, influence
14 make up your mind

determined
03 out, set
04 bent, firm
05 fixed
06 dogged, intent, strong
07 dead set, decided
08 hell-bent, resolute, resolved, stubborn
09 convinced, insistent, steadfast, tenacious
10 persistent, unwavering
11 persevering, unflinching
12 single-minded, strong-minded, strong-willed
14 uncompromising

deterrent
03 bar
04 curb
05 block, check
07 barrier
08 obstacle
09 hindrance, repellent
12 disincentive
14 discouragement

detest
04 hate
05 abhor
06 loathe
07 deplore, despise, dislike
08 execrate
09 abominate, can't stand

detestable
04 vile
06 odious, sordid
07 hateful, heinous
08 accursed, shocking
09 abhorrent, execrable, loathsome, obnoxious, offensive, repellent, repugnant, repulsive
10 abominable, despicable
12 contemptible

detestation
04 hate
05 odium
06 hatred
08 anathema, aversion, loathing
09 animosity, revulsion
10 abhorrence, execration, repugnance
11 abomination

dethrone
04 oust
06 depose, topple, unseat
07 uncrown
08 unthrone

detonate
05 blast
06 blow up, let off, set off
07 explode
08 spark off
09 discharge, fulminate

detonation
04 bang, boom
05 blast, burst
06 blow-up, report
08 igniting, ignition
09 discharge, explosion
11 fulmination

detour
05 byway
06 bypass, bypath, byroad
09 deviation, diversion
10 digression
11 scenic route
13 indirect route

detract
03 mar
05 lower, spoil
06 lessen, reduce
08 belittle, diminish
09 devaluate, disparage
10 depreciate
12 take away from

detractor
07 defamer, reviler
08 traducer, vilifier
09 backbiter, belittler, muck-
   raker, slanderer
10 denigrator, disparager

detriment
03 ill
04 evil, harm, hurt, loss
05 wrong
06 damage, injury
08 mischief
09 prejudice
10 disservice, impairment
12 disadvantage

detrimental
07 adverse, harmful, hurtful
08 damaging, inimical
09 injurious
10 pernicious
11 destructive, prejudicial
15 disadvantageous

detritus
04 junk, scum
05 waste
06 debris, litter, rubble
07 garbage, remains,
   rubbish
08 wreckage
09 fragments

devalue
05 lower
06 reduce
07 deflate
08 decrease
09 devaluate

devastate
04 raze, ruin, sack
05 floor, level, waste,
   wreck
06 ravage
07 despoil, destroy, flatten,
   pillage, ransack, shatter
08 desolate, lay waste

devastating
07 harmful
08 incisive, stunning
09 effective
10 disastrous, shattering
11 destructive
12 catastrophic, overwhelming

devastation
04 ruin
05 havoc, ruins, waste
06 pillage, plunder, ravages
08 wreckage
10 desolation, spoliation
11 destruction
12 annihilation

develop
03 get
04 grow
05 arise, begin, catch, ensue
06 create, evolve, expand,
   happen, invent, mature, pick
   up, spread, unfold
07 acquire, advance, enhance,
   enlarge, improve, nurture,
   produce, prosper, work
   out
08 commence, contract,
   expand on, flourish,
   generate, progress
09 branch out, come about,
   elaborate, establish
10 go down with

development
06 centre, change, estate,
   growth, result, spread
07 advance, complex, outcome
08 incident, increase, maturity,
   progress
09 evolution, expansion,
   extension, happening,
   promotion, unfolding
10 blossoming, refinement
11 elaboration, enlargement,
   flourishing, furtherance,
   improvement, progression

deviant
04 bent, geek, goof, kook
05 crank, freak, kinky
06 misfit, oddity, quirky, weirdo
07 bizarre, dropout, odd sort,
   oddball, pervert, twisted,
   variant, wayward
08 aberrant, abnormal,
   freakish, perverse
09 anomalous, disparity,
   divergent, eccentric,
   irregular, perverted

deviate
03 err, yaw
04 part, turn, vary, veer
05 drift, stray
06 change, depart, differ,
   swerve, wander
07 deflect, digress, diverge
08 go astray
09 turn aside

deviation
05 drift, freak, quirk, shift
06 change, detour
07 anomaly
08 variance
09 disparity, variation
10 aberration, deflection,
   digression, divergence
11 abnormality, fluctuation
12 eccentricity, irregularity
13 inconsistency

device
04 logo, plan, ploy, ruse, wile
05 gizmo, motif, trick
06 design, emblem, gadget,
   gambit, scheme, symbol
07 machine, utensil
08 artifice, insignia, strategy
09 apparatus, appliance,
   implement, mechanism
10 coat of arms, instrument
11 contraption, contrivance

devil
03 imp
04 ogre
05 beast, brute, demon, fiend,
   rogue, Satan
06 rascal, savage, terror, wretch
07 Evil One, Lucifer, Old Nick
08 diabolic, Old Harry
09 arch-fiend, Beelzebub
10 evil spirit
14 Mephistopheles

devilish
04 evil, vile
06 wicked
07 demonic, hellish, satanic
08 damnable, diabolic,
   dreadful, fiendish, infernal

09 execrable, nefarious
10 diabolical, outrageous

devil-may-care
06 casual
08 careless, cavalier, flippant, heedless, reckless
09 easy-going, frivolous
10 insouciant, nonchalant
11 unconcerned
12 happy-go-lucky

devious
03 sly
04 wily
06 artful, crafty, tricky
07 crooked, cunning, erratic, evasive, winding
08 indirect, rambling, scheming, slippery, tortuous
09 deceitful, designing, deviating, insidious, insincere, wandering
10 circuitous, roundabout
11 calculating, treacherous
12 disingenuous, unscrupulous
13 double-dealing, surreptitious

devise
04 form, plan, plot
05 forge, frame, hatch, shape
06 cook up, create, design, invent, scheme
07 arrange, compose, concoct, dream up, imagine, project, think up, work out
08 conceive, contrive
09 construct, fabricate, formulate, originate
10 come up with
11 put together

devoid
04 bare, free, void
05 empty
06 barren, bereft, vacant
07 lacking, wanting, without

devolution
08 dispersal
12 distribution

devolve
06 convey, depute, fall to
07 consign, deliver, entrust
08 delegate, hand down, rest with, transfer

devote
04 give
05 allot, apply, offer, put in
06 assign, commit, pledge
08 dedicate, enshrine, set aside
09 sacrifice, surrender
10 consecrate

devoted
04 fond, true
05 loyal
06 caring, devout, loving
08 constant, faithful, tireless
09 attentive, committed, dedicated, steadfast
10 unswerving

devotee
03 fan
05 fiend, freak, hound
06 addict, zealot
08 adherent, disciple, follower
09 supporter
10 aficionado, enthusiast

devotion
04 love, zeal
05 faith, piety
06 ardour, prayer, regard
07 loyalty, passion, worship
08 fidelity, trueness, warmness
09 adherence, adoration, affection, constancy
10 admiration, allegiance, attachment, commitment, dedication, devoutness
11 earnestness, staunchness
12 faithfulness, spirituality
13 steadfastness

devotional
04 holy
06 devout, sacred, solemn
09 pietistic, religious, spiritual
11 reverential

devour
03 eat
04 bolt, cram, gulp
05 eat up, gorge, scoff, stuff
06 gobble, guzzle, relish
07 consume, destroy, envelop, feast on, put away, swallow
08 tuck into, wolf down
09 finish off, knock back
10 appreciate, gormandize

devout
04 deep, holy
05 godly, pious
06 ardent
07 devoted, earnest, fervent, intense, saintly, serious, sincere, staunch, zealous
08 constant, faithful, orthodox, profound, reverent
09 committed, heartfelt, prayerful, religious, steadfast
10 passionate, practising
12 wholehearted

devoutly
06 deeply
07 piously

08 ardently
09 earnestly, fervently, sincerely, staunchly, zealously
10 faithfully, reverently
11 prayerfully, steadfastly
12 passionately
14 wholeheartedly

dewy
05 roral, roric, rorid
06 roscid
08 innocent, youthful
10 starry-eyed

dexterity
03 art
05 knack, skill
07 ability, address, agility, finesse, mastery, sleight
08 aptitude, artistry, deftness
09 adeptness, expertise, handiness, ingenuity
10 adroitness, expertness, nimbleness
11 legerdemain, proficiency, skilfulness

dexterous
04 able, deft
05 adept, agile, handy, nifty
06 adroit, expert, nimble
07 skilful
10 neat-handed, proficient
12 accomplished
14 nimble-fingered

diabolical
04 evil, vile
05 nasty
06 sinful, wicked
07 demonic, hellish, satanic
08 damnable, devilish, fiendish, infernal
09 execrable, monstrous

diadem
05 crown, mitre, round, tiara
07 circlet, coronet
08 headband

diagnose
06 detect
07 analyse, explain, isolate
08 identify, pinpoint
09 determine, recognize

diagnosis
06 answer
07 opinion, verdict
08 analysis, scrutiny
09 detection, judgement
10 conclusion
11 examination, recognition
13 investigation

14 identification, interpretation

diagnostic
10 analytical, indicative
10 distinguishing, interpretative

diagonal
05 cross
06 angled
07 crooked, oblique, sloping
08 crossing, slanting
09 crosswise

diagonally
06 aslant
09 at an angle, crosswise,
   obliquely, on the bias
10 on the cross, on the
   slant

diagram
04 plan
05 chart, draft, graph, table
06 figure, layout, schema
07 drawing, outline, picture
08 bar chart, pie chart
09 flow chart
12 exploded view, illustration

diagrammatic
07 graphic, tabular
09 schematic

dial
04 call, disc, face, ring
05 clock, phone
09 give a bell, give a buzz,
   telephone

dialect
05 argot, idiom, lingo
06 jargon, patois, speech
07 diction, variety
08 language, localism
10 vernacular

dialectic
05 logic
06 debate
07 logical
08 analysis, logistic, polemics
09 rationale, reasoning
10 analytical, dialectics
11 dialectical, disputation
13 argumentation,
   ratiocination, rationalistic

dialogue
04 chat, talk
06 debate, gossip, script
08 colloquy, converse
09 discourse, tête-à-tête
10 conference, discussion
11 interchange
12 conversation
13 interlocution

diametrically
07 utterly
08 directly
10 absolutely, completely

diaphanous
04 fine, thin
05 filmy, gauzy, light, sheer
08 delicate, gossamer, pellucid
10 see-through
11 translucent, transparent

diarrhoea
07 the runs
08 the trots
09 dysentery
10 Delhi belly, gippy tummy
12 Spanish tummy

diary
07 day-book, Filofax®, journal,
   logbook
09 chronicle
14 engagement book
15 appointment book

▶ *Names of diarists:*
04 **Byrd** (William), **Gide**
   (André)
05 **Frank** (Anne), **Pepys**
   (Samuel), **Reyes** (Alfonso),
   Scott (Robert Falcon),
   Torga (Miguel)
06 **Burney** (Fanny), **Evelyn**
   (John)
07 **Régnier** (Paule)
08 **Greville** (Charles
   Cavendish Fulke),
   Robinson (Henry Crabb)
➤ See also **writer**

diatribe
05 abuse
06 attack, insult, rebuke, tirade
07 reproof, slating
08 harangue, knocking
09 criticism, invective,
   onslaught, philippic
10 upbraiding
12 denunciation, vituperation

dicey
04 iffy
05 dodgy, hairy, risky
06 chancy, tricky
09 dangerous, uncertain
13 unpredictable

dicky
04 weak
07 unsound
08 unsteady

dictate
03 law, say
04 read, rule, word
05 edict, order, speak, utter

06 behest, charge, decree,
   demand, direct, ruling
07 bidding, command, lay
   down, mandate, precept,
   read out, set down, statute
08 announce, instruct, transmit
09 direction, ordinance,
   prescribe, pronounce, read
   aloud, ultimatum
11 requirement

dictator
06 despot, tyrant
07 supremo
08 autocrat
09 oppressor
10 autarchist, Big Brother
13 absolute ruler

dictatorial
05 bossy
08 absolute, despotic
09 autarchic, imperious
10 autocratic, oppressive,
   repressive, tyrannical
11 all powerful, domineering
12 totalitarian, unrestricted
13 authoritarian

dictatorship
07 fascism, tyranny
09 autocracy, despotism
11 police state
12 absolute rule
13 reign of terror
15 totalitarianism

diction
06 speech
08 delivery, language, phrasing
09 elocution
10 expression, inflection,
   intonation
11 enunciation
12 articulation
13 pronunciation

dictionary
07 lexicon
08 glossary, wordbook
09 thesaurus
10 vocabulary
11 concordance
12 encyclopedia

dictum
04 fiat
05 axiom, edict, maxim, order
06 decree, ruling, saying
07 command, dictate, precept,
   proverb
08 aphorism
09 utterance
13 pronouncement

didactic
05 moral
08 pedantic
09 educative, pedagogic
10 moralizing
11 educational, instructive
12 prescriptive

die
03 ebb, end
04 fade, pass, stop, wane, wilt
05 be mad, decay, lapse, yearn
06 depart, desire, expire, finish,
   pass on, peg out, perish, pop
   off, vanish, wither
07 conk out, dwindle, long for,
   pine for, snuff it, subside
08 decrease, dissolve,
   pass away, peter out
09 break down, lose power
11 be desperate, bite the dust,
   come to an end
12 lose your life
13 kick the bucket, meet your
   maker, push up daisies
14 depart this life, give up the
   ghost
15 breathe your last, cash in
   your chips

❑**die away**
04 fade
09 disappear
10 become weak
11 become faint

❑**die down**
04 stop
07 decline, quieten, subside
08 decrease

❑**die out**
06 vanish
08 peter out
09 disappear

die-hard
05 blimp
06 zealot
08 old fogey, rightist
09 hardliner
11 reactionary
12 intransigent
13 stick-in-the-mud

diet
04 fare, fast, food, slim
06 reduce, viands
07 abstain, rations, regimen
08 victuals
09 nutrition
10 foodstuffs, lose weight,
   provisions, sustenance
11 comestibles, weight-watch

differ
05 argue, clash, vary

06 debate, oppose
07 deviate, diverge, quarrel
08 be unlike, contrast, disagree
12 be at odds with, be at
   variance, be dissimilar
14 not see eye to eye

difference
03 row
04 rest
05 clash, set-to
07 balance, dispute, quarrel
08 argument, conflict, contrast,
   variance
09 deviation, disparity, diversity,
   remainder, variation
10 divergence, unlikeness
11 altercation, controversy,
   discrepancy, disputation,
   distinction, singularity
12 disagreement, distinctness
13 dissimilarity, dissimilitude

different
03 odd
05 other
06 at odds, sundry, unique,
   unlike, varied
07 a far cry, another, diverse,
   opposed, several, special,
   strange, unusual, various
08 assorted, discrete, distinct,
   peculiar, separate
09 disparate, divergent
10 at variance, dissimilar,
   individual, poles apart
11 contrasting, distinctive,
   worlds apart
13 extraordinary,
   miscellaneous
14 unconventional

differentiate
07 mark off
08 contrast, separate
09 tell apart
11 distinguish
12 discriminate

differentiation
08 contrast
10 separation
11 demarcation, distinction
14 discrimination

difficult
04 dark, hard
05 tough
06 arcane, knotty, thorny, tiring,
   tricky, trying, uphill
07 arduous, awkward
08 abstruse, baffling, esoteric,
   exacting, perverse,
   puzzling, stubborn,
   tiresome

09 demanding, gruelling,
   intricate, laborious,
   obstinate, recondite
10 exhausting, formidable,
   perplexing, refractory
11 intractable, troublesome
12 back-breaking, recalcitrant,
   unmanageable
13 problematical,
   unco-operative

difficulty
03 fix, jam
04 hole, mess, snag, spot
05 bitch, block, devil, trial
06 hiccup, hurdle, plight
07 barrier, catch-22, dilemma,
   pitfall, problem, trouble
08 distress, exigency, hardship,
   obstacle, quandary
09 deep water, hindrance,
   objection, shit creek
10 cleft stick, impediment,
   perplexity, pretty pass
11 arduousness, dire straits,
   predicament, tribulation
12 complication
13 embarrassment, pain in the
   arse, strenuousness
14 stumbling-block

❑**in difficulties**
06 in a fix, in a jam
07 in a hole, in a mess
09 in a scrape, in trouble
11 in deep water, up against it,
   up shit creek
12 in a tight spot
13 in dire straits
14 having problems, out of your
   depth

diffidence
07 modesty, reserve, shyness
08 humility, meekness,
   timidity
09 hesitancy, self-doubt
10 inhibition, reluctance
11 bashfulness
12 backwardness, self-distrust
14 self-effacement
15 unassertiveness

diffident
03 shy
04 meek
05 timid
06 modest, unsure
07 abashed, bashful, nervous
08 hesitant, insecure, reserved,
   sheepish
09 inhibited, reluctant,
   shrinking, tentative
11 unassertive
12 self-effacing

13 self-conscious

diffuse
05 vague, wordy
06 prolix, spread
07 profuse, scatter, verbose
08 diffused, dispense, disperse, rambling, waffling
09 dispersed, imprecise, propagate, scattered
10 discursive, distribute, long-winded, loquacious, promulgate
11 disseminate
12 disconnected, periphrastic
14 circumlocutory

dig
03 jab
04 gibe, jeer, mine, till
05 delve, gouge, probe, scoop
06 burrow, go into, harrow, hollow, insult, pierce, plough, quarry, tunnel
08 excavate, research, turn over
09 cultivate, make a hole
11 insinuation, investigate

dig up
04 find
06 exhume, expose
07 root out, uncover, unearth
08 discover, disinter, retrieve
12 bring to light

digest
05 grasp, study
06 absorb, macera, ponder, reduce, take in
07 process, shorten, summary
08 abstract, compress, condense, consider, dissolve, macerate, meditate, mull over
09 break down, reduction
10 assimilate, compendium, comprehend, understand
11 abridgement, compression, contemplate, incorporate

digestion
08 eupepsia
09 ingestion
10 absorption
12 assimilation, breaking-down

dignified
05 grand, grave, lofty, noble
06 august, formal, solemn
07 courtly, exalted, stately
08 imposing, majestic
11 ceremonious
13 distinguished

dignify
05 adorn, exalt, grace, raise
06 honour

07 advance, elevate, enhance, ennoble, glorify, promote
10 aggrandize
11 apotheosize, distinguish

dignitary
03 VIP
06 bigwig, high-up, worthy
07 big name, big shot, notable
08 luminary, somebody, top brass
09 personage

dignity
05 poise, pride
06 honour, status
07 decorum, majesty
08 eminence, grandeur, nobility, standing
09 elevation, greatness, loftiness, solemnity
10 self-esteem
11 courtliness, self-respect
14 respectability

digress
05 drift, stray
06 depart, ramble, wander
07 deviate, diverge
09 turn aside
13 be sidetracked
15 go off at a tangent, go off the subject

digression
05 aside
08 excursus, footnote, straying
09 departure, deviation, diversion, wandering
10 apostrophe, divagation, divergence
11 parenthesis
12 obiter dictum

dilapidated
05 shaky
06 ruined, shabby
07 decayed, in ruins, rickety, run-down, worn-out
08 decaying, decrepit
09 crumbling, neglected
10 broken-down, ramshackle, tumbledown, uncared-for
12 falling apart

dilapidation
04 ruin
05 decay, waste
08 collapse
09 disrepair
13 deterioration
14 disintegration

dilate
05 bloat, swell, widen
06 expand, extend, spread

07 distend, enlarge, inflate
08 increase
09 spread out

dilatory
04 lazy, slow
05 slack, tardy
08 dawdling, delaying, sluggish, stalling, tarrying
09 lingering, snail-like
11 time-wasting
13 lackadaisical
15 procrastinating

dilemma
04 mess, spot
06 plight, puzzle
07 catch-22, problem
08 conflict, quandary
10 difficulty, perplexity
11 predicament, tight corner
13 embarrassment

dilettante
07 amateur, dabbler, trifler
08 aesthete, potterer, sciolist

diligence
04 care
08 industry
09 assiduity, attention, constancy
10 dedication, intentness
11 application, earnestness
12 perseverance, sedulousness, thoroughness
13 assiduousness, attentiveness, laboriousness

diligent
04 busy
07 careful, earnest
08 constant, sedulous, studious, thorough, tireless
09 assiduous, attentive, dedicated
10 meticulous, persistent
11 hard-working, industrious, painstaking, persevering
13 conscientious

dilly-dally
05 dally, delay, hover, tarry
06 dawdle, dither, linger, potter
08 hesitate
09 vacillate
12 shilly-shally, take your time

dilute
04 thin
06 lessen, reduce, weaken
07 diffuse, thin out
08 decrease, diminish, mitigate, moderate, tone down
09 attenuate, water down
10 adulterate, make weaker

11 make thinner

dim
04 blur, dark, dull, dumb, fade, grey, hazy, pale, weak
05 cloud, dense, dingy, dusky, faint, foggy, fuzzy, misty, shade, thick, unlit, vague
06 cloudy, darken, feeble, gloomy, leaden, obtuse, sombre, stupid
07 adverse, blurred, doltish, obscure, shadowy, tarnish
08 gormless, overcast
09 dim-witted, tenebrous
10 ill-defined, indistinct, lacklustre, obfuscated, slow-witted
11 crepuscular, unpromising
13 become blurred

dimension
04 area, bulk, mass, side, size
05 depth, facet, range, scale, scope, width
06 aspect, extent, factor, height, length, volume
07 breadth, element, feature, measure
08 capacity
09 greatness, largeness, magnitude
11 measurement, proportions

diminish
03 cut, ebb
04 fade, sink, wane
05 abate, lower
06 defame, lessen, recede, reduce, shrink, weaken
07 decline, deflate, devalue, dwindle, slacken, subside
08 belittle, contract, decrease, derogate, grow less, peter out, retrench, taper off
09 denigrate, deprecate, disparage
10 become less, grow weaker

diminution
03 cut, ebb
05 decay
07 cutback, decline
08 decrease
09 abatement, lessening, reduction, shrinkage
10 shortening, subsidence
11 contraction, curtailment

diminutive
03 wee
04 mini, tiny
05 dinky, elfin, pygmy, small
06 little, midget, minute, petite, pocket
07 compact
08 dwarfish, pint-size
09 miniature, pint-sized
10 homuncular, small-scale, teeny-weeny, undersized
11 Lilliputian, microscopic, pocket-sized

dimple
04 dint
05 fovea
06 hollow
09 concavity, umbilicus
10 depression

dimwit
04 fool, twit
05 dunce, idiot
06 nitwit
07 dullard
08 bonehead, numskull
09 blockhead, ignoramus
10 dunderhead

din
03 row
05 clash, crash, noise, shout
06 babble, hubbub, outcry, racket, tumult, uproar
07 clamour, clatter, yelling
08 brouhaha, clangour
09 commotion, loud noise
10 hullabaloo

dine
03 eat, sup
04 feed
05 feast, lunch
07 banquet
10 have dinner

dingy
03 dim
04 dark, drab, dull, worn
05 dirty, dusky, faded, grimy, murky, seedy
06 dismal, dreary, gloomy, shabby, soiled, sombre
09 cheerless
11 discoloured

dinky
04 fine, mini, neat, trim
05 natty, small
06 dainty, petite
09 miniature

dinner
03 tea
04 meal
05 feast
06 repast, spread, supper
07 banquet, blow-out
08 main meal, prandial
09 refection
11 evening meal

dinosaur

➤ *Types of dinosaur:*
04 T Rex
08 Sauropod, Theropod
09 Hadrosaur, Iguanodon
10 Allosaurus, Barosaurus, Diplodocus, Saurischia, Torosaurus
11 Apatosaurus, Coelophysis, Deinonychus, Dromaeosaur, Polacanthus, Stegosaurus, Triceratops
12 Ankylosaurus, Brontosaurus, Camptosaurus, Megalosaurus, Ornithischia, Ornithomimus, Plateosaurus, Velociraptor
13 Brachiosaurus, Compsognathus, Corythosaurus,, Edmontosaurus, Ornitholestes, Styracosaurus, Tyrannosaurus
15 Parasaurolophus
➤ See also **animal**

dint
04 blow, dent
06 hollow, stroke
09 concavity
10 depression, impression
11 indentation

❑ **by dint of**
09 by means of
10 by virtue of

dip
04 dent, dive, drop, duck, dunk, fall, hole, sink, soak, swim
05 basin, bathe, douse, lower, sauce, slope, slump, souse
06 go down, hollow, plunge
07 descend, descent, ducking, immerse, soaking, subside
08 decrease, dressing, infusion, lowering, submerge
09 concavity, immersion
10 depression
11 indentation

❑ **dip into**
04 skim
06 browse, draw on, look at
11 leaf through, look through
12 flick through, thumb through

diplomacy
04 tact
07 finesse
08 delicacy, politics, subtlety

10 discretion, statecraft
11 manoeuvring, negotiation, savoir-faire, tactfulness
13 judiciousness, statesmanship

diplomat
05 envoy
06 consul, legate
07 attaché
08 emissary, mediator
09 moderator, statesman
10 ambassador, arbitrator, negotiator, politician
11 conciliator
15 chargé d'affaires, plenipotentiary

diplomatic
06 clever, subtle
07 politic, prudent, tactful
08 consular, discreet
13 ambassadorial

dire
05 awful, grave, vital
06 urgent
07 crucial, drastic, extreme
08 alarming, dreadful, horrible, pressing, shocking, terrible
09 appalling, atrocious, desperate, frightful
10 calamitous, disastrous
12 catastrophic

direct
03 aim, run
04 lead, mean, show, turn
05 bluff, blunt, frank, guide, order, point, steer, usher
06 adjure, candid, escort, govern, handle, manage
07 command, conduct, control, non-stop, through, up-front
08 explicit, instruct, organize, personal, straight, unbroken
09 first-hand, immediate, outspoken, supervise
10 administer, face-to-face, forthright, give orders, show the way, unswerving
11 plainspoken, point the way, preside over, superintend, undeviating, unequivocal
12 be in charge of, call the shots
13 be in control of
15 straightforward

direction
04 way
04 line, path, plan, road
05 brief, drift, route, track, trend
06 course, orders

07 bearing, control, running
08 briefing, guidance, handling, tendency
10 government, guidelines, indication, leadership, management, regulation
11 inclination, orientation, regulations, supervision
12 instructions
14 administration

directive
04 fiat
05 edict, order
06 charge, decree, notice
07 bidding, command, dictate, mandate
09 ordinance
10 imperative, injunction
11 instruction

directly
04 soon
05 right
06 at once, pronto
07 bluntly, clearly, exactly, frankly, plainly, quickly
08 candidly, honestly, promptly, speedily, straight
09 forthwith, instantly, presently, right away
10 explicitly
11 immediately
12 straightaway, without delay
13 unequivocally
15 instantaneously

director
04 boss, head
05 chair, chief
06 leader, top dog
07 manager
08 chairman, governor
09 conductor, executive, organizer, president, principal, régisseur
10 chairwoman, controller
11 chairperson
13 administrator
14 chief executive

➤ *Names of film and theatre directors*:
03 Lee (Spike), Ray (Satyajit)
04 Ford (John), Hall (Sir Peter), Hare (David), Lang (Fritz), Lean (Sir David), Nunn (Trevor), Reed (Sir Carol), Roeg (Nicolas), Todd (Mike)
05 Allen (Woody), Brook (Peter), Capra (Frank), Carné (Marcel), Cohen (Ethan), Cohen (Joel), Cukor (George Dewey),

Dante (Joe), Hawks (Howard), Ivory (James Francis), Kazan (Elia), Korda (Sir Alexander), Leigh (Mike), Lucas (George), Lynch (David), Malle (Louis), Mayer (Louis Burt), Roach (Hal), Scott (Ridley), Stone (Oliver), Vadim (Roger), Wyler (William)
06 Altman (Robert), Artaud (Antoni), Besson (Luc), Brecht (Bertolt), Brooks (Mel), Burton (Tim), Buñuel (Luis), Corman (Roger), De Sica (Vittorio), Disney (Walt), Forbes (Bryan), Forman (Milos), Frears (Stephen), Godard (Jean-Luc), Herzog (Werner), Hughes (Howard), Huston (John), Jarman (Derek), Ophuls (Max), Parker (Alan), Powell (Michael), Renoir (Jean), Warner (Jack), Welles (Orson), Wilder (Billy), Zanuck (Darryl Francis)
07 Aldrich (Robert), Bergman (Ingmar), Boorman (John), Chabrol (Claude), Coppola (Francis Ford), De Mille (Cecil Blount), De Palma (Brian), Fellini (Federico), Gaumont (Léon), Gilliam (Terry), Goldwyn (Samuel), Kubrick (Stanley), Pollack (Sydney), Redford (Robert), Resnais (Alain), Russell (Ken), Sennett (Mack), Wenders (Wim)
08 Berkeley (Busby), Eastwood (Clint), Friedkin (William), Kurosawa (Akira), Lubitsch (Ernst), Merchant (Ismail), Pasolini (Pier Paulo), Polanski (Roman), Scorsese (Martin), Selznick (David Oliver), Truffaut (François), Visconti (Luchino)
09 Almodovar (Pedro), Antonioni (Michelangelo), Greenaway (Peter), Grotowski (Jerzy), Hitchcock (Sir Alfred), Peckinpah (Sam),

Preminger (Otto),
Spielberg (Steven),
Strasberg (Lee),
Tarantino (Quentin)
10 **Bertolucci** (Bernardo),
Cronenberg (David),
Eisenstein (Sergei),
Fassbinder (Rainer
Werner), **Kieslowski**
(Krzystof), **Rossellini**
(Roberto), **Zeffirelli**
(Franco)
11 **Bogdanovich** (Peter),
Pressburger (Emeric),
Riefenstahl (Leni),
Schlesinger (John)
12 **Stanislavsky**

dirge
05 elegy
06 lament, monody
07 requiem
08 coronach, threnody
09 dead-march
11 funeral song

dirt
03 mud
04 clay, crap, crud, dust, grot,
   gunk, loam, mire, muck,
   smut, soil, soot, yuck
05 earth, filth, grime, gunge
06 grunge, sleaze, sludge,
   smudge
08 impurity, lewdness
09 excrement, indecency,
   obscenity, pollution
11 pornography
13 salaciousness

dirty
04 blue, dull, foul, lewd, soil
05 bawdy, dusty, grimy, messy,
   mucky, muddy, slimy, sooty,
   spoil, stain, sully, yucky
06 coarse, cruddy, defile, filthy,
   greasy, grotty, grubby, mess
   up, ribald, risqué, sleazy,
   smudge, smutty, soiled,
   sordid, splash, vulgar
07 begrime, blacken, corrupt,
   defiled, obscene, pollute,
   squalid, stained, sullied,
   tarnish, unclean
08 besmirch, indecent,
   polluted, unwashed
09 salacious, tarnished
10 suggestive, unhygienic
11 contaminate
12 contaminated,
   pornographic

disability
06 defect, malady
07 ailment, illness

08 disorder, handicap,
   weakness
09 complaint, inability,
   infirmity, unfitness
10 affliction, impairment,
   incapacity

disable
04 lame, stop
06 damage, impair, weaken
07 cripple
08 enfeeble, handicap, paralyse
09 hamstring, make unfit
10 deactivate, debilitate,
   immobilize, invalidate
12 incapacitate
14 put out of action

disabled
04 lame, weak
05 unfit
06 infirm, maimed
07 wrecked
08 crippled, impaired
09 bed-ridden, enfeebled,
   paralysed
10 indisposed
11 debilitated, handicapped,
   immobilized, out of action
13 incapacitated

disadvantage
04 flaw, lack, loss, snag
06 damage, defect, injury
07 penalty, trouble
08 downside, drawback,
   handicap, weakness
09 detriment, hindrance,
   liability, prejudice, privation
10 impediment, limitation

disadvantaged
04 poor
06 in need, in want
08 deprived
10 in distress, struggling
11 handicapped
15 poverty stricken,
   underprivileged

disadvantageous
07 adverse, harmful, hurtful
08 damaging, ill-timed
09 injurious
11 deleterious, detrimental,
   inopportune, prejudicial
12 inconvenient, unfavourable

disaffected
07 hostile
08 disloyal, mutinous
09 alienated, estranged
10 rebellious, unfriendly
11 disgruntled
12 antagonistic, discontented,
   dissatisfied

disaffection
07 discord, dislike, ill-will
08 aversion, coolness
09 animosity, hostility
10 alienation, antagonism,
   disloyalty, resentment
12 disagreement,
   estrangement
14 discontentment,
   unfriendliness

disagree
05 argue, clash, fight, upset
06 bicker, differ, object, oppose
07 contend, contest, dispute,
   dissent, diverge, fall out,
   quarrel, wrangle
09 be against, take issue
10 contradict, make unwell
11 beg to differ
12 argue against, be at odds
   with, cause illness
13 agree to differ, take issue
   with

disagreeable
04 rude
05 cross, nasty, surly
07 brusque, grouchy, peevish
08 churlish, contrary, impolite
09 difficult, irritable, obnoxious,
   offensive, repellent,
   repugnant, repulsive,
   unhelpful, unsavoury
10 disgusting, ill-natured,
   unfriendly, unpleasant
11 bad-tempered, disobliging,
   ill-humoured
13 objectionable

disagreement
03 row
04 tiff
05 clash
06 strife
07 discord, dispute, dissent,
   quarrel, wrangle
08 argument, conflict, friction,
   squabble, variance
09 deviation, disparity, diversity
10 contention, difference,
   dissension, falling-out
11 altercation, discrepancy,
   disputation, incongruity
13 dissimilarity, inconsistency
15 incompatibility

disallow
03 ban
04 veto
05 debar
06 abjure, cancel, disown,
   forbid, rebuff, refuse, reject
07 exclude, say no to
08 disclaim, prohibit

09 proscribe, repudiate

disappear
02 go
03 ebb, end, fly
04 exit, fade, flee, hide, wane
05 cease
06 depart, perish, recede
07 die away, get lost, scarper, vamoose
08 dissolve, evanesce, melt away, withdraw
09 evaporate, go missing
12 go out of sight
13 become extinct, dematerialize

disappearance
03 end
04 exit, loss
06 expiry, fading, flight
07 passing
08 dying-out
09 desertion, vanishing
10 extinction, withdrawal
11 evanescence, evaporation

disappoint
04 fail, foil
06 dismay, hamper, hinder, sadden, thwart
07 deceive, depress, let down
08 dispirit
09 frustrate
10 disenchant, dishearten
11 disillusion

disappointed
05 upset, vexed
06 miffed
07 let-down
08 cast down, deflated, saddened, thwarted
09 depressed
10 despondent, frustrated
11 discouraged, downhearted
12 disenchanted, disheartened
13 disillusioned

disappointing
03 sad
05 sorry
08 inferior, pathetic, unworthy
10 depressing, inadequate
12 discouraging, insufficient
13 anticlimactic, underwhelming
14 unsatisfactory

disappointment
04 blow, swiz
07 chagrin, failure, let-down, sadness, setback, swizzle, washout, wipeout
08 comedown, non-event
09 damp squib

10 anticlimax, bitter pill
11 cold comfort, frustration
14 disenchantment
15 disillusionment

disapprobation
05 blame
07 censure, dislike, reproof
08 reproach
09 criticism, objection
11 approbation, disapproval, displeasure
12 condemnation
13 disparagement
15 dissatisfaction

disapproval
04 veto
05 blame
06 rebuke
07 censure, dislike, reproof
08 reproach
09 criticism, exception, objection, rejection
11 displeasure
12 condemnation, denunciation
13 disparagement, remonstration, the thumbs-down
14 disapprobation
15 dissatisfaction

disapprove
04 veto
05 blame, spurn
06 reject
07 censure, condemn, deplore, dislike, frown on
08 disallow, object to
09 deprecate, disparage
10 animadvert, look down on
11 not hold with
12 think badly of
14 discountenance, take a dim view of
15 take exception to

disapproving
08 critical
10 censorious, derogatory, pejorative
11 deprecatory, disparaging, improbative, improbatory, reproachful
12 condemnatory
14 disapprobative, disapprobatory

disarm
05 charm, unarm
07 appease, disable, disband, mollify, placate, win over
10 conciliate, deactivate, demobilize, immobilize

11 lay down arms
12 demilitarize
13 make powerless
14 put out of action

disarmament
11 arms control
12 deactivation
13 arms reduction
14 arms limitation, demobilization

disarming
07 winning
08 charming, likeable
12 conciliatory, irresistible

disarrange
04 mess
06 jumble, untidy
07 confuse, disturb, shuffle
08 disorder, unsettle
11 disorganize

disarray
04 mess
05 chaos, upset
06 jumble, muddle, tangle
07 clutter
08 disorder, shambles
09 confusion
10 unruliness, untidiness
12 dishevelment, indiscipline
15 disorganization

disaster
04 blow, flop, ruin
06 fiasco, mishap, stroke
07 debacle, failure, reverse, tragedy, trouble, wash out
08 accident, act of God, calamity, reversal
09 adversity, cataclysm, mischance, ruination
10 misfortune
11 catastrophe

disastrous
04 dire
05 fatal
06 tragic
07 adverse, ruinous, unlucky
08 dreadful, terrible
09 appalling, injurious
10 calamitous, ill-starred
11 cataclysmic, devastating
12 catastrophic

disavowal
06 denial
07 dissent
09 rejection
10 abjuration
11 repudiation
12 renunciation
13 contradiction

14 disaffirmation

disband
05 demob
07 break up, dismiss, scatter
08 disperse, dissolve, separate
10 demobilize
11 part company
14 go separate ways

disbelief
05 doubt
07 dubiety
08 distrust, mistrust, unbelief
09 discredit, suspicion
10 scepticism
11 incredulity, questioning

disbelieve
05 doubt
06 reject
07 suspect
08 distrust, mistrust, question
09 discredit, repudiate
13 be unconvinced

disbeliever
07 atheist, doubter, sceptic
08 agnostic
10 questioner, unbeliever
11 nullifidian
14 doubting Thomas

disburse
05 spend
06 expend, lay out, pay out
07 cough up, fork out
08 shell out

disbursement
06 outlay
07 payment
08 disposal, spending
09 disbursal
11 expenditure

disc
02 CD, LP
04 disk, face, ring
05 album, CD-ROM, plate, vinyl
06 circle, discus, record, saucer
07 counter
08 diskette, hard disk
10 floppy disk
11 compact disk, microfloppy

discard
04 drop, dump, shed
05 ditch, scrap
06 reject, remove
07 abandon, forsake, toss out
08 chuck out, get rid of, jettison, throw out
09 cast aside, chuck away, dispose of, throw away
12 dispense with

discern
03 see
05 judge
06 descry, detect, notice
07 make out, observe
08 discover, perceive
09 ascertain, recognize
11 distinguish
12 discriminate
13 differentiate

discernible
05 clear, plain
06 patent
07 obvious, visible
08 apparent, distinct, manifest
10 detectable, noticeable, observable
11 appreciable, conspicuous, perceptible
15 distinguishable

discerning
04 wise
05 acute, quick, sharp, sound
06 astute, clever, shrewd, subtle
07 prudent, sapient
08 critical, piercing
09 eagle-eyed, sensitive
10 perceptive, percipient
11 intelligent, penetrating
12 clear-sighted
13 perspicacious
14 discriminating

discernment
05 taste
07 insight
08 keenness, sagacity
09 acuteness, awareness, good taste, judgement, sharpness
10 perception, shrewdness
11 penetration, percipience
12 intelligence, perspicacity
13 understanding
14 discrimination, perceptiveness

discharge
02 do
03 axe, pay, pus
04 emit, fire, flow, free, gush, leak, meet, ooze, oust, sack
05 clear, doing, eject, expel, exude, let go, shoot
06 acquit, firing, fulfil, honour, let off, let out, pardon, remove, set off, settle
07 absolve, boot out, discard, dismiss, excrete, explode, give off, perform, release, relieve, removal, sacking, set free, the boot, the sack
08 carry out, detonate, disgorge, dispense, emission, get rid of, liberate, the elbow
09 acquittal, dismissal, excretion, exculpate, execution, exonerate, expulsion, secretion
10 absolution, disembogue, fulfilment, liberation
11 exculpation, exoneration, performance, suppuration

disciple
05 pupil
06 votary
07 devotee, learner, student
08 adherent, believer, follower, upholder
09 proselyte, supporter

disciplinarian
06 despot, tyrant
08 autocrat, martinet, stickler
10 taskmaster
13 authoritarian

discipline
05 check, drill, inure, limit, train
06 branch, punish, rebuke
07 chasten, control, correct, educate, regimen, reprove, routine, subject
08 chastise, exercise, instruct, penalize, practice, regulate, restrain, restrict, training
09 castigate, inculcate, reprimand, restraint
10 correction, punishment, regulation, strictness
11 area of study, castigation
12 chastisement, field of study

disclaim
04 deny
06 abjure, disown, refuse, reject
07 abandon, decline, disavow
08 renounce
09 repudiate
15 wash your hands of

disclaimer
06 denial
09 disavowal, rejection
10 disownment, retraction
11 repudiation
12 renunciation
14 disaffirmation

disclose
04 blab, leak, show, tell
06 expose, impart, relate, reveal, squeal, unveil
07 confess, divulge, lay bare, let slip, publish, uncover
08 blurt out, discover
09 broadcast, make known
10 make public

12 bring to light
13 spill the beans

disclosure
04 leak
06 exposé
08 exposure
09 admission, broadcast
10 confession, divulgence,
   revelation, uncovering
11 declaration, publication
12 announcement

discoloration
04 blot, mark, spot
05 patch, stain
06 blotch, streak
07 blemish, splotch
08 dyschroa
10 ecchymosis

discolour
04 fade, mark, rust, soil
05 stain, tinge
06 streak
07 tarnish, weather

discomfit
04 faze
06 outwit, rattle, ruffle, thwart
07 confuse, fluster, perplex
08 confound, unsettle
09 embarrass, frustrate
10 discompose, disconcert

discomfiture
06 unease
09 abashment, confusion
11 frustration, humiliation
12 discomposure
13 embarrassment

discomfort
04 ache, hurt, pain, pang
06 bother, twinge, unease
07 malaise, trouble
08 disquiet, distress, nuisance,
   soreness, vexation
13 embarrassment

discomposure
05 upset
06 unease
07 anxiety, fluster
09 agitation, annoyance
10 inquietude, irritation
11 disquietude, disturbance
12 perturbation, restlessness

disconcert
04 faze
05 alarm, shake, upset
06 dismay, put off, rattle, ruffle
07 confuse, disturb, fluster,
   perturb, startle, unnerve
08 bewilder, surprise, unsettle
09 embarrass, take aback

14 discombobulate
15 throw off balance

disconcerting
07 awkward
08 alarming, baffling, daunting
09 confusing, unnerving
10 disturbing, off-putting,
   perturbing
11 bewildering, distracting

disconnect
04 part, undo
05 sever, split
06 cut off, detach, divide,
   unhook, unplug
07 unhitch
08 separate, uncouple
09 disengage

disconnected
05 loose
07 garbled, jumbled, mixed-up
08 confused, staccato
09 illogical, wandering
10 disjointed, incoherent

disconsolate
03 low, sad
04 down
06 gloomy
07 crushed, forlorn, unhappy
08 dejected, desolate,
   downcast, hopeless,
   wretched
09 depressed, miserable
10 despondent, dispirited,
   melancholy
11 heartbroken, low-spirited
12 heavy-hearted,
14 down in the dumps

discontent
06 misery, regret, unrest
08 disquiet, vexation
10 impatience, uneasiness
11 displeasure, fretfulness,
   unhappiness
12 disaffection, restlessness
15 dissatisfaction

discontented
05 fed up
07 unhappy
08 restless, wretched
09 miserable, pissed off
10 browned off, cheesed off
11 complaining, disaffected,
   disgruntled, exasperated
12 dissatisfied

discontinue
03 end
04 drop, halt, quit, stop
05 cease, scrap
06 cancel, finish

07 abandon, abolish, refrain,
   suspend
08 break off
09 interrupt, terminate
11 come to an end

discontinuity
07 rupture
10 disruption
11 incoherence
12 interruption
13 disconnection
14 disjointedness

discontinuous
06 broken, fitful
08 periodic
09 irregular, spasmodic
11 interrupted
12 disconnected, intermittent

discord
03 row
05 split
06 jangle, strife
07 dispute, dissent, jarring
08 argument, clashing, conflict,
   disunity, division, friction
09 cacophony, wrangling
10 contention, difference,
   disharmony, dissension,
   dissonance, opposition
12 disagreement
15 incompatibility

discordant
04 flat
05 harsh, sharp
06 at odds, atonal
07 grating, hostile, jarring
08 clashing, jangling, strident
09 differing, dissonant
10 at variance, dissenting
11 cacophonous
12 incompatible, inconsistent

discount
03 cut
05 slash
06 deduct, ignore, reduce
07 take off
08 cut price, knock off, mark
   down, overlook
09 deduction, disregard, gloss
   over, reduction
10 concession, disbelieve

discourage
05 daunt, deter
06 dampen, dismay, put off
07 depress, prevent, unnerve
08 cast down, dispirit, dissuade
09 talk out of
10 demoralize, dishearten
12 put a damper on
13 advise against

discouraged
04 glum
06 dashed
07 daunted, let-down
08 deflated, dejected, dismayed, downcast
09 depressed
10 dispirited
11 crestfallen, demoralized, pessimistic
12 disheartened

discouragement
04 curb
05 gloom
06 damper, dismay, rebuff
07 barrier, despair, setback
09 deterrent, pessimism
10 depression, impediment
12 disincentive, hopelessness

discouraging
08 daunting
09 dampening
10 depressing, dissuasive, dissuasory, off-putting
11 dehortatory, dispiriting
12 demoralizing, inauspicious, unfavourable, unpropitious
13 disheartening

discourse
04 chat, talk
05 essay, speak
06 confer, debate, homily, preach, sermon, speech
07 discuss, lecture, oration
08 converse, dialogue
10 discussion
12 conversation, dissertation
13 confabulation

discourteous
04 curt, rude
05 gruff, short
07 boorish, brusque, ill-bred, offhand, uncivil, uncouth
08 impolite, impudent, insolent
10 ungracious, unmannerly
11 bad-mannered, ill-mannered, impertinent
13 disrespectful

discourtesy
04 snub
06 insult, rebuff, slight
07 affront
08 curtness, rudeness
09 indecorum, insolence
10 bad manners, incivility
12 impertinence, impoliteness
14 ungraciousness, unmannerliness

discover
03 see

04 find, spot, twig
05 dig up, learn
06 detect, devise, fathom, invent, locate, notice, reveal, rumble, turn up
07 discern, get onto, light on, pioneer, realize, suss out, uncover, unearth, work out
08 disclose, perceive
09 ascertain, determine, establish, fathom out, ferret out, get wind of, stumble on
10 come across, come to know
13 stumble across

discoverer
06 author, finder
07 deviser, founder, pioneer
08 explorer, inventor
09 initiator
10 originator

discovery
04 find
07 finding
08 devising, learning, research
09 detection, invention
10 disclosure, revelation
11 discernment, exploration, realization, recognition
12 breakthrough, introduction

discredit
04 deny, slur
05 blame, doubt, shame, smear
06 damage, debunk, defame, infamy, stigma, vilify
07 censure, degrade, tarnish
08 belittle, disgrace, distrust, ignominy, mistrust, reproach
09 aspersion, dishonour, disparage, disrepute
10 disbelieve, invalidate, opprobrium
11 humiliation
14 put in a bad light, reflect badly on

discreditable
08 improper, infamous, shameful
09 degrading
10 scandalous
11 blameworthy, disgraceful
12 disreputable
13 dishonourable, reprehensible

discreet
04 wary, wise
07 careful, guarded, politic, prudent, tactful
08 cautious, delicate, reserved
10 diplomatic
11 circumspect, considerate

discrepancy
08 conflict, variance
09 deviation, disparity, variation
10 difference, divergence
11 discordance, incongruity
12 disagreement
13 contradiction, inconsistency

discrete
08 detached, distinct, separate
10 individual, unattached
12 disconnected
13 discontinuous

discretion
04 care, tact, will, wish
06 choice, desire, wisdom
07 caution, freedom, reserve
08 prudence, volition, wariness
09 good sense, judgement
11 discernment, inclination
13 consideration, judiciousness
14 circumspection

discretionary
04 open
08 elective, optional
09 voluntary

discriminate
07 discern
08 be biased, separate
09 segregate, tell apart, victimize
11 distinguish
12 be intolerant, be prejudiced
13 differentiate

discriminating
04 keen
06 astute, shrewd
08 critical, tasteful
09 selective, sensitive
10 discerning, fastidious, particular, perceptive

discrimination
04 bias
05 taste
06 ageism, racism, sexism
07 bigotry, insight
08 inequity, keenness, subtlety
09 judgement, prejudice
10 astuteness, homophobia, perception, unfairness
11 discernment, favouritism, intolerance, segregation
12 perspicacity
14 male chauvinism

discriminatory
06 biased, loaded, unfair, unjust
07 partial
08 one-sided, partisan, weighted
09 favouring
10 prejudiced

11 inequitable, prejudicial
12 preferential

discursive
05 wordy
06 prolix
07 diffuse, verbose
08 rambling
10 circuitous, digressing, long-winded, meandering

discuss
05 argue, study
06 confer, debate, parley
07 analyse, consult, weigh up
08 consider, converse, talk over
09 discourse, talk about
10 deliberate, kick around
11 confabulate

discussion
04 talk
05 forum, study, talks
06 debate, parley, powwow
07 seminar
08 analysis, argument, dialogue, exchange, scrutiny
09 discourse, symposium
10 colloquium, conference
11 examination
12 consultation, conversation, deliberation, negotiations

disdain
04 snub
05 scorn, spurn
06 deride, rebuff, reject, slight
07 despise, dislike, sneer at
08 belittle, contempt, derision, pooh-pooh, sneering
09 arrogance, disregard
10 look down on, undervalue
11 deprecation, haughtiness
12 cold shoulder, snobbishness
13 disparagement

disdainful
05 aloof, proud
07 haughty, pompous
08 arrogant, derisive, insolent, scornful, sneering, superior
09 slighting
11 disparaging
12 contemptuous, supercilious

disease
03 bug
05 virus
06 malady
07 ailment, illness
08 disorder, epidemic, sickness
09 complaint, contagion, infection, infirmity
10 affliction, disability

► *Names of diseases. We have omitted the word* **disease** *from names given in the following list, but you may need to include this word as part of the solution to some crossword clues.*
02 ME, MS, TB
03 flu
04 AIDS, mono
05 croup, mumps, polio
06 angina, asthma, autism, cancer, chorea, dropsy, herpes, rabies, scurvy, thrush, typhus
07 anaemia, anthrax, Bright's, bulimia, cholera, leprosy, lockjaw, malaria, Marburg, measles, rickets, rubella, scabies, tetanus, typhoid, vertigo
08 alopecia, anorexia, beriberi, botulism, diabetes, gangrene, glaucoma, Hodgkin's, impetigo, ringworm, shingles, smallpox, syphilis, tapeworm, tinnitus
09 arthritis, bilharzia, cirrhosis, dysentery, emphysema, enteritis, hepatitis, influenza, leukaemia, pneumonia, psoriasis, silicosis
10 Alzheimer's, asbestosis, Black Death, bronchitis, chickenpox, common cold, diphtheria, gingivitis, gonorrhoea, laryngitis, Lassa fever, meningitis, Parkinson's, thrombosis
11 brucellosis, consumption, dengue fever, farmer's lung, green monkey, haemophilia, Huntington's, hydrophobia, peritonitis, psittacosis, septicaemia, tonsillitis, yellow fever
12 appendicitis, athlete's foot, encephalitis, foot-and-mouth, osteoporosis, scarlet fever, tuberculosis
13 bubonic plague, cerebral palsy, endometriosis, German measles, mononucleosis,

osteomyelitis, poliomyelitis, schizophrenia, whooping cough
14 conjunctivitis, cystic fibrosis, glandular fever, rheumatic fever
15 anorexia nervosa, gastroenteritis, schistosomiasis

diseased
03 ill
04 sick
08 blighted, infected
09 unhealthy
12 contaminated

disembark
04 land
05 leave
06 alight, arrive, debark, get off
07 deplane, detrain, step off

disembodied
07 ghostly, phantom
08 bodiless, spectral
09 spiritual
10 discarnate, intangible
11 incorporeal

disembowel
03 gut
04 draw
06 paunch
08 disbowel, gralloch
10 eviscerate, exenterate

disenchanted
05 blasé, fed up
06 soured
07 cynical, let down
09 jaundiced
11 discouraged, indifferent
13 disillusioned

disenchantment
08 cynicism
11 disillusion
15 disillusionment

disengage
04 free, undo
05 untie
06 detach, loosen, unhook
07 release, unhitch
08 liberate, separate, uncouple, unfasten, withdraw
09 extricate
10 disconnect
11 disentangle

disengaged
04 free
05 freed, loose
08 detached, released
09 separated, unhitched
10 unattached

11 unconnected
12 disentangled

disentangle
04 free, undo
05 loose
06 detach, unknot, unwind
07 clarify, release, resolve, unravel, unsnarl, untwist
08 separate, simplify, untangle
09 disengage, extricate
11 distinguish

disfavour
07 dislike
08 distaste, ignominy
09 disregard, disrepute
10 low opinion, opprobrium
11 disapproval, displeasure
12 unpopularity
14 disapprobation

disfigure
03 mar
04 flaw, maim, ruin, scar
05 spoil
06 damage, deface, deform
07 blemish, distort
08 make ugly, mutilate

disfigurement
04 scar, spot
05 stain
06 blotch, defect, injury
07 blemish
09 deformity
10 defacement, distortion

disgorge
04 spew
05 belch, eject, empty, expel, spout, vomit
07 throw up
09 discharge, surrender
10 relinquish
11 regurgitate

disgrace
04 blot, slur
05 abase, blame, shame, smear, stain, sully, taint
06 defame, infamy, stigma
07 degrade, obloquy, scandal
08 belittle, ignominy, reproach
09 black mark, discredit, dishonour, disparage, disrepute, humiliate
10 debasement, defamation, disrespect, opprobrium, put to shame, stigmatize
11 degradation, humiliation
12 bring shame on
15 cause to lose face

disgraced
06 shamed

07 branded
08 degraded
10 humiliated
11 discredited, dishonoured, stigmatized
13 in the doghouse

disgraceful
05 awful
08 culpable, dreadful, shameful, shocking, terrible, unworthy
09 appalling
10 despicable, outrageous, scandalous
11 blameworthy, ignominious
12 contemptible, disreputable
13 dishonourable, reprehensible

disgruntled
05 fed up, sulky, testy, vexed
06 grumpy, peeved, put out
07 annoyed, peevish
08 petulant
09 hacked off, irritated, resentful
10 brassed off, browned off, cheesed off, displeased
12 discontented, dissatisfied

disguise
04 fake, hide, mask, veil
05 cloak, cover, feign, front
06 façade, screen, shroud
07 conceal, costume, cover up, dress up, falsify, pretend
08 pretence, suppress, travesty
09 deception, dissemble, gloss over, whitewash
10 camouflage, masquerade
12 be under cover

disguised
04 fake
05 false
06 covert, hidden, made up, masked, veiled
07 cloaked, feigned
09 incognito
10 undercover
11 camouflaged

disgust
05 repel
06 hatred, nausea, offend, put off, revolt, sicken
07 outrage, turn off
08 aversion, nauseate
09 repulsion, revulsion
10 abhorrence, repugnance
11 detestation
15 turn your stomach

disgusted
06 put off

08 appalled, offended, repelled, repulsed, revolted, sickened

disgusting
03 bad
04 foul, vile
05 gross, nasty, yucky
06 odious
07 obscene
08 nauseous, shocking
09 offensive, repellent, repugnant, repulsive, revolting, sickening
10 nauseating, off-putting, outrageous, unpleasant
11 disgraceful, distasteful, rebarbative, unpalatable
13 objectionable

dish
04 bowl, fare, food
05 plate
06 course, recipe
10 speciality

❑**dish out**
07 dole out, give out, hand out, inflict, mete out
08 allocate, share out
09 hand round, pass round
10 distribute

❑**dish up**
05 ladle, scoop, serve, spoon
07 present

disharmony
05 clash
07 discord
08 conflict, friction
09 disaccord
10 dissonance
11 discordance
15 incompatibility

dishearten
05 crush, daunt, deter
06 dampen, deject, dismay
07 depress
08 cast down, dispirit
09 weigh down
10 disappoint, discourage

disheartened
07 crushed, daunted
08 dejected, dismayed, downcast
09 depressed
10 dispirited
11 crestfallen, discouraged, downhearted

dishevelled
05 messy
06 untidy

07 in a mess, ruffled, rumpled, tousled, unkempt
08 slovenly, uncombed
10 bedraggled, disordered
11 disarranged

dishonest
03 sly
04 bent, iffy
05 false, fishy, lying, shady
06 crafty, shifty
07 corrupt, crooked, devious
08 cheating
09 deceitful, deceptive
10 fraudulent, mendacious, perfidious, untruthful
11 duplicitous, treacherous
13 dishonourable, double-dealing, untrustworthy

dishonesty
05 fraud
06 deceit
07 falsity, perfidy
08 cheating, trickery
09 chicanery, duplicity, falsehood, improbity, shadiness, treachery
10 corruption, dirty trick
11 criminality, crookedness, fraudulence, insincerity
13 double-dealing, sharp practice
14 untruthfulness

dishonour
04 slur
05 abuse, shame, stain, sully
06 debase, defame, defile, demean, infamy, insult, offend, slight, stigma
07 degrade, outrage, scandal
08 disgrace, ignominy
09 abasement, aspersion, discredit, disfavour, disrepute, indignity
10 debasement, opprobrium
11 degradation, humiliation

dishonourable
05 shady
07 corrupt, ignoble
08 shameful, unworthy
09 shameless, unethical
10 despicable, perfidious, scandalous
11 disgraceful, ignominious
12 disreputable, unscrupulous
13 discreditable, untrustworthy

disillusion
08 disabuse
10 disappoint, disenchant

disillusioned
07 let-down
09 disabused

10 undeceived
12 disappointed, disenchanted

disincentive
08 obstacle
09 determent, deterrent, hindrance, repellent
10 dissuasion, impediment
11 restriction
14 discouragement

disinclination
09 loathness, objection
10 averseness, hesitation, opposition, reluctance, repugnance, resistance
13 unwillingness

disinclined
05 loath
06 averse
07 opposed
08 hesitant
09 reluctant, resistant, unwilling
14 unenthusiastic

disinfect
05 clean, purge
06 purify
07 cleanse
08 fumigate, sanitize
09 sterilize
13 decontaminate

disinfectant
08 fumigant
09 germicide, sanitizer
10 antiseptic, sterilizer
11 bactericide
13 decontaminant

disingenuous
03 sly
04 wily
06 artful, crafty, shifty
07 cunning, devious, feigned
08 guileful, two-faced
09 designing, dishonest, insidious, insincere
11 duplicitous

disinherit
06 cut off, reject
08 renounce
09 repudiate
10 dispossess, impoverish
14 turn your back on

disintegrate
03 rot
05 decay, smash
07 break up, crumble, moulder, shatter
08 separate, splinter
09 decompose, fall apart
10 break apart
12 fall to pieces

disinterest
08 fairness
10 detachment, neutrality
12 impartiality, unbiasedness

disinterested
04 fair, just
07 neutral
08 detached, unbiased
09 equitable, impartial, objective, unselfish
10 even-handed, open-minded, uninvolved
12 unprejudiced
13 dispassionate

disjointed
05 bitty, loose, split
06 broken, fitful
08 confused, rambling
09 separated, spasmodic
10 dislocated, disordered, incoherent
11 unconnected
12 disconnected
14 disarticulated

dislike
06 animus, detest, enmity
07 despise, disgust
08 aversion, distaste, object to
09 animosity, antipathy, disesteem, disfavour, disrelish
10 antagonism, disapprove, repugnance, resentment
11 disapproval, displeasure
14 disapprobation

dislocate
04 do in, pull
05 shift, twist
06 luxate, put out, sprain, strain
07 confuse, disrupt, disturb
08 disjoint, disorder, displace
09 disengage
10 disconnect
11 disorganize
13 put out of joint, put out of place

dislocation
08 disarray, disorder
10 disruption
11 disturbance
15 disorganization

dislodge
04 move, oust
05 eject, shift
06 remove, uproot
08 displace, force out
09 extricate

disloyal
05 false

06 untrue
08 apostate, two-faced
09 deceitful, faithless
10 perfidious, traitorous, unfaithful
11 treacherous, unpatriotic
13 double-dealing

disloyalty
06 deceit
07 falsity, perfidy, treason
08 adultery, apostasy, betrayal, sedition
09 falseness, treachery
10 infidelity
11 inconstancy
13 breach of trust, double-dealing
14 perfidiousness, unfaithfulness

dismal
04 dark, drab, dull
05 bleak, dingy
06 dreary, gloomy, sombre
07 forlorn
08 desolate, hopeless
09 cheerless, long-faced, miserable, sorrowful
10 depressing, despondent, lugubrious, melancholy

dismantle
05 strip
08 demolish, separate
09 pull apart, strip down, take apart
11 disassemble
12 take to pieces

dismay
04 fear
05 alarm, daunt, dread, scare, shock, upset, worry
06 fright, horror, put off, terror
07 concern, depress, disturb, horrify, perturb, unnerve
08 cast down, dispirit, distress, frighten, unsettle
09 agitation, take aback
10 disappoint, disconcert, discourage, dishearten
11 disillusion, trepidation
13 consternation
14 disappointment, discouragement

dismember
06 divide
07 break up, dissect
08 amputate, mutilate, separate

dismiss
04 drop, fire, free, sack
05 expel, let go, spurn
06 lay off, reject, remove

07 boot out, cashier, release
08 discount, dissolve, relegate, send away, set aside
09 discharge, disregard
10 give notice
11 send packing
13 make redundant
15 pour cold water on

dismissal
04 boot, push, sack
05 elbow
06 firing, notice, papers
07 removal, sacking
09 discharge, expulsion, laying-off
10 redundancy
14 marching-orders

dismissive
07 off-hand
08 scornful, sneering
10 disdainful, dismissory
12 contemptuous

dismount
06 alight, get off
07 descend, get down

disobedience
06 mutiny, revolt
08 defiance
09 contumacy, rebellion
10 infraction, unruliness, wilfulness
11 contumacity, waywardness
12 contrariness, indiscipline
13 recalcitrance
15 insubordination

disobedient
06 unruly, wilful
07 defiant, froward, naughty, wayward
08 contrary, recusant
10 rebellious, refractory
11 intractable, mischievous
12 contumacious, obstreperous, recalcitrant
13 insubordinate

disobey
04 defy
05 flout, rebel
07 violate
08 infringe, overstep
10 contravene, transgress
13 step out of line

disobliging
04 rude
07 awkward, uncivil
09 unhelpful, unwilling
12 bloody-minded, disagreeable, discourteous
13 unco-operative

disorder
04 mess, riot, rout
05 brawl, chaos, fight, melee
06 fracas, malady, muddle, tumult, unrest, uproar
07 ailment, clamour, clutter, disease, illness, quarrel
08 brouhaha, disarray, shambles, sickness
09 commotion, complaint, condition, confusion
10 affliction, disability, disruption, untidiness
11 disturbance

disordered
05 messy, upset
06 untidy
07 jumbled, muddled
08 confused, troubled
09 cluttered, disturbed
10 unbalanced, upside-down
11 maladjusted
12 disorganized

disorderly
04 wild
05 messy, rough, rowdy
06 unruly, untidy
07 chaotic, jumbled, lawless
08 confused
09 cluttered, irregular, turbulent
10 in disarray, rebellious, refractory, tumultuous
12 disorganized, obstreperous
13 undisciplined

disorganization
05 chaos
06 muddle
08 disarray, disorder, shambles
09 confusion
10 disruption, untidiness

disorganize
05 mix up, upset
06 jumble, mess up, muddle
07 confuse, disrupt, disturb
08 disorder, unsettle
10 disarrange, decompose
13 play havoc with

disorganized
07 chaotic, jumbled, muddled
08 careless, confused, unsorted
09 haphazard, shambolic
10 disordered, topsy-turvy
12 unstructured, unsystematic

disorientate
04 faze
05 upset
06 muddle, puzzle
07 confuse, mislead, perplex

disorientated
04 lost
05 at sea, upset
06 adrift, astray
07 mixed up, muddled, puzzled
08 confused
09 perplexed, unsettled
10 bewildered, unbalanced
11 disoriented

disown
04 deny
06 reject
07 abandon, disavow, forsake
08 abnegate, disclaim, renounce
09 repudiate
14 turn your back on

disparage
05 decry, scorn
06 defame, malign, vilify
07 disdain, run down, slander
08 belittle, derogate, minimize, ridicule, vilipend
09 criticize, denigrate, deprecate, discredit
10 calumniate, undervalue

disparagement
05 scorn
07 decrial, disdain, slander
08 contempt, decrying
09 aspersion, contumely, criticism, discredit
10 debasement, derogation, detraction
11 degradation, deprecation
12 belittlement, denunciation, vilification

disparaging
05 snide
07 mocking
08 critical, derisive, scornful
09 insulting
10 derogatory, dismissive
11 deprecatory

disparate
06 unlike
07 diverse, unequal
08 contrary, distinct
09 different
10 discrepant, dissimilar

disparity
03 gap
04 bias, gulf
08 contrast, inequity
09 imbalance
10 difference, inequality
11 discrepancy, distinction
13 dissimilarity, dissimilitude

dispassionate
04 calm, cool, fair
07 neutral
08 detached, unbiased
09 equitable, impartial, objective, unexcited
10 impersonal
11 unemotional
12 unprejudiced
13 disinterested, self-possessed
14 self-controlled

dispatch, despatch
04 do in, kill, mail, post, send
05 haste, piece, remit, speed
06 convey, finish, letter, report
07 account, article, bump off, consign, execute, express, forward, message, perform
08 alacrity, celerity, conclude, expedite, transmit
09 discharge, dispose of, slaughter, swiftness
10 accelerate, communiqué, expedition, promptness
11 assassinate, promptitude
13 communication

dispel
03 rid
04 rout
05 allay, expel
06 banish
07 dismiss, scatter
08 disperse, get rid of
09 dissipate, eliminate
11 disseminate

dispensable
07 useless
10 disposable, expendable
11 inessential, replaceable, superfluous, unnecessary
12 non-essential

dispensation
04 plan
05 issue, order
06 relief, scheme, system
07 economy, licence, release
08 immunity, reprieve
09 authority, direction, endowment, exception, exemption, remission
10 allocation, permission
12 distribution, organization
13 apportionment
14 administration

dispense
05 allot, apply, share
06 assign, bestow, confer
07 deal out, dole out, execute, give out, hand out, mete out
08 allocate, carry out, share out
09 apportion, discharge, divide out, implement
10 administer, distribute

◻ dispense with
04 omit
05 waive
06 cancel, forego, revoke
07 abolish, discard, rescind
08 get rid of, renounce
09 dispose of, disregard, do without

disperse
06 dispel, spread
07 break up, diffuse, disband, dismiss, scatter, thin out
08 dissolve, melt away, separate
09 dissipate
10 distribute
11 disseminate

dispersion
08 diaspora
09 broadcast, diffusion, dispersal, spreading
10 scattering
11 circulation, dissipation
12 distribution
13 dissemination

dispirit
04 damp, dash
06 dampen, deject, sadden
07 depress
10 discourage, dishearten
12 put a damper on

dispirited
03 low, sad
04 down, glum
05 fed up
06 gloomy, morose
08 cast down, dejected, downcast
09 depressed
10 brassed off, browned off, cheesed off, despondent
11 crestfallen, discouraged
12 disheartened
14 down in the dumps

displace
04 move, oust
05 eject, evict, expel, shift
06 depose, remove
07 boot out, dismiss, turf out
08 dislodge, force out
09 dislocate, supersede

displacement
06 ectopy, moving
07 ectopia
08 shifting
10 dislodging
11 dislocation, disturbance, heterotaxis, heterotopia
14 disarrangement

display
04 show
05 array, boast
06 blazon, evince, expose, flaunt, parade, reveal
07 exhibit, pageant, present, promote, show off
08 disclose, evidence, manifest
09 advertise, publicize, put on show, spectacle
10 exhibition, revelation
11 demonstrate
12 presentation
13 demonstration, manifestation

displease
03 bug, irk, vex
05 anger, annoy, upset
06 offend, put out
07 incense, perturb, provoke
10 discompose, dissatisfy

displeased
05 angry, upset
06 peeved, piqued, put out
07 annoyed, furious
08 offended
09 irritated
11 disgruntled, exasperated

displeasure
03 ire
05 anger, pique, wrath
07 chagrin, disgust, offence
09 annoyance, disfavour
10 irritation, resentment
11 disapproval, indignation
14 disapprobation, discontentment
15 dissatisfaction

disport
04 play, romp
05 amuse, cheer, frisk, revel
06 cavort, divert, frolic, gambol
07 delight
09 entertain

disposable
09 throwaway
10 expendable
13 non-returnable

disposal
07 command, control, removal
08 grouping, riddance
09 clearance, scrapping
10 discarding
11 arrangement, jettisoning
12 throwing-away

□at someone's disposal
05 on tap, ready
06 at hand, to hand
09 available
10 obtainable

dispose
03 put
04 do in, dump, kill, shed
05 align, group, order, place
06 decide, finish, handle, line up, murder, settle, tackle
07 arrange, bump off, destroy, discard, situate, sort out
08 attend to, clear out, deal with, get rid of, jettison, organize, position, throw out
09 determine, throw away
10 do away with, put to death

disposed
03 apt
05 eager, prone, ready
06 liable, likely, minded
07 subject, willing
08 inclined, prepared

disposition
04 bent, mood
05 habit, order
06 humour, line-up, make-up, nature, spirit, temper
07 leaning, pattern, placing
08 disposal, grouping, sequence, tendency
09 alignment, character
10 allocation, conveyance,, proclivity, propensity
11 arrangement, inclination, positioning, temperament
12 constitution, distribution, predilection

dispossess
03 rob
04 oust
05 eject, evict, expel, strip
06 divest
07 deprive
08 dislodge, take away

disproportion
09 asymmetry, imbalance
10 inadequacy, inequality, unevenness
11 discrepancy
12 lopsidedness
13 insufficiency

disproportionate
06 uneven
07 unequal
09 excessive
10 unbalanced
12 unreasonable
14 incommensurate
15 out of proportion

disprove
04 deny
05 rebut

06 debunk, negate, refute
07 confute
09 discredit
10 contradict, controvert, invalidate, prove false
12 give the lie to

disputable
04 moot
07 dubious
08 arguable, doubtful
09 debatable, uncertain
12 questionable
13 controversial

disputation
06 debate
07 dispute
08 argument, polemics
10 dissension
11 controversy

disputatious
08 captious
09 litigious, polemical
10 pugnacious
11 contentious, quarrelsome
13 argumentative

dispute
03 row
05 argue, clash, doubt
06 bicker, debate, strife
07 contend, contest, discuss, quarrel, wrangle
08 argument, conflict, question, squabble
09 challenge
11 altercation, controversy
12 disagreement

disqualified
08 debarred
09 precluded, struck off
10 eliminated, ineligible

disqualify
05 debar
07 disable, rule out, suspend
08 handicap, preclude, prohibit
09 eliminate, strike off
10 immobilize, invalidate

disquiet
03 vex
04 fear, fret
05 alarm, shake, upset, worry
06 bother, harass, ruffle
07 anxiety, concern, disturb, perturb, trouble, unnerve
08 distress, unsettle
09 agitation, incommode
10 discompose, foreboding, uneasiness
11 disquietude, disturbance, nervousness

disquisition
05 essay, paper
06 sermon, thesis
08 treatise
09 discourse, monograph
10 exposition
11 explanation
12 dissertation

disregard
05 flout
06 ignore, insult, slight
07 disdain, disobey, neglect
08 brush-off, contempt,
    discount, laugh off,
    overlook, set aside
09 denigrate, disparage
10 brush aside, negligence
11 denigration, make light of
12 carelessness, indifference
14 take no notice of
15 turn a blind eye to

disrepair
04 ruin
05 decay
10 shabbiness
11 rack and ruin
12 dilapidation
13 deterioration

disreputable
03 low
04 base, mean
05 dodgy, seedy, shady
06 shabby, shifty, untidy
07 corrupt, dubious, scruffy
08 infamous, shameful,
    slovenly, unworthy
10 outrageous, scandalous
11 disgraceful, ignominious
13 dishonourable,
    unrespectable

disrepute
05 shame
06 infamy
07 obloquy
08 disgrace, ignominy
09 discredit, dishonour

disrespect
05 cheek, scorn
08 contempt, rudeness
09 dishonour, disregard,
    impudence, insolence
11 discourtesy, irreverence
12 impertinence, impoliteness

disrespectful
04 rude
05 sassy
06 cheeky
08 impolite, impudent, insolent
09 insulting
10 irreverent, unmannerly

11 impertinent
12 contemptuous,
    discourteous

disrobe
04 bare, shed
05 strip
06 denude, divest, remove
07 take off, uncover, undress
08 unclothe
10 disapparel

disrupt
05 upset
07 break up, confuse, disturb
08 sabotage, unsettle
09 interrupt
10 disarrange
11 disorganize
13 interfere with

disruption
05 upset
07 turmoil
08 disorder, stoppage,
    upheaval
09 confusion
11 disturbance
12 interference, interruption
14 disorderliness
15 disorganization

disruptive
05 noisy
06 unruly
09 turbulent, upsetting
10 boisterous, disorderly,
    disturbing, unsettling
11 distracting, troublesome

dissatisfaction
06 regret
07 chagrin, dislike
08 vexation
09 annoyance
10 discomfort, discontent,
    irritation, resentment
11 disapproval, displeasure,
    frustration, unhappiness
12 exasperation, restlessness
14 disappointment,
    disapprobation

dissatisfied
05 angry, fed up
07 annoyed, unhappy
09 irritated, pissed off
10 brassed off, cheesed off,
    displeased, frustrated
11 disgruntled, exasperated
12 disappointed, discontented

dissatisfy
03 vex
05 anger, annoy
06 put out

08 irritate
09 displease, frustrate
10 disappoint, discontent

dissect
05 cut up, probe, study
07 analyse, examine, inspect
08 pore over, vivisect
09 anatomize, break down,
    dismember
10 scrutinize
11 investigate

dissection
05 probe, study
07 autopsy
08 analysis, necropsy, scrutiny
09 breakdown, cutting up
10 inspection
11 examination, vivisection
13 dismemberment,
    investigation

dissemble
04 fake, hide, mask, sham
05 cloak, feign
06 affect
07 conceal, falsify, pretend
08 disguise, simulate
10 camouflage, play possum
11 counterfeit, dissimulate

dissembler
04 fake
05 fraud
07 feigner
08 deceiver, impostor
09 charlatan, pretender

disseminate
03 sow
06 spread
07 diffuse, publish, scatter
08 disperse, proclaim
09 broadcast, circulate
10 distribute, promulgate

dissemination
06 spread
09 diffusion
10 dispersion, publishing
11 circulation, propagation
12 broadcasting, distribution,
    promulgation

dissension
06 strife
07 discord, dissent, quarrel
08 argument, conflict, friction
12 disagreement

dissent
06 differ, object, refuse
07 discord, dispute, protest
08 disagree, friction
09 objection

10 difference, dissension, opposition, resistance
12 disagreement

dissenter
05 rebel
07 heretic, sectary
08 objector, recusant
09 dissident, protester
10 protestant, schismatic
13 nonconformist, revolutionary

dissentient
08 opposing, recusant
09 differing, dissident, heretical
10 dissenting, rebellious
11 conflicting, disagreeing

dissertation
05 essay, paper
06 thesis
08 critique, treatise
09 discourse, monograph
10 exposition
12 disquisition, propaedeutic

disservice
04 harm, hurt
05 wrong
06 injury
07 bad turn
09 disfavour, injustice
10 dirty trick, unkindness
14 kick in the teeth

dissidence
04 feud
06 schism
07 dispute, dissent, rupture
08 variance
09 recusancy
11 discordance
12 disagreement

dissident
05 rebel
07 heretic
08 agitator, objector, recusant
09 differing, dissenter, protester
10 discordant, dissenting, protesting, rebellious
11 conflicting, disagreeing
13 nonconformist, revolutionary

dissimilar
06 unlike
07 diverse, various, varying
08 distinct
09 different, disparate, divergent, unrelated
13 heterogeneous

dissimilarity
09 disparity, diversity
10 difference, unlikeness

11 discrepancy, distinction
13 dissimilitude, heterogeneity

dissimulate
03 lie
04 fake, hide, mask
05 cloak, feign
06 affect
07 conceal, cover up, pretend
08 disguise
09 dissemble

dissipate
05 drain, spend, use up, waste
06 burn up, dispel, vanish
07 break up, consume, deplete, diffuse, exhaust, scatter
08 disperse, dissolve, melt away, squander
09 disappear, evaporate
11 fritter away

dissipated
04 wild
06 rakish, wasted
08 depraved
09 debauched, dissolute
10 degenerate, licentious, profligate
11 intemperate

dissipation
06 excess
07 licence
09 depletion, depravity, diffusion, dispersal
10 corruption, debauchery
11 consumption, evaporation, expenditure, prodigality, squandering
12 extravagance, intemperance
13 disappearance
14 licentiousness, self-indulgence

dissociate
04 part, quit
05 sever
06 cut off, detach, secede
07 break up, disband, disrupt, divorce, isolate
08 break off, distance, disunite, separate, withdraw
09 disengage, segregate
10 disconnect
12 disassociate

dissociation
05 break, split
07 divorce, parting
08 disunion, division, severing
09 isolation, severance
10 cutting-off, detachment, distancing, separation
11 dissevering, segregation

13 disconnection, disengagement

dissolute
04 lewd, wild
06 rakish, wanton
07 corrupt, immoral
08 depraved
09 abandoned, debauched
10 degenerate, dissipated, licentious, profligate
11 intemperate
13 self-indulgent

dissolution
06 ending
07 break-up, divorce
08 collapse, disposal, division
09 annulment, overthrow
10 conclusion, suspension
11 destruction, evaporation
13 decomposition
14 disintegration
15 discontinuation

dissolve
03 end
04 melt
05 begin, break, burst, start
06 finish, vanish, wind up
07 break up, disband, liquefy
08 collapse, disperse, evanesce, melt away
09 dissipate, evaporate
10 deliquesce
12 bring to an end, disintegrate

dissonance
05 clash
06 jangle
07 discord, grating, jarring
08 variance
09 cacophony, harshness
10 disharmony, dissension
11 discordance, incongruity
12 disagreement
13 inconsistency

dissonant
05 harsh
07 grating, jarring, raucous
08 clashing, jangling, tuneless
09 anomalous, unmusical
10 discordant
11 cacophonous, disagreeing
12 incompatible, inconsistent

dissuade
04 stop
05 deter
06 put off
09 talk out of
10 discourage, disincline

dissuasion
09 deterring

distance

10 deterrence
12 remonstrance
13 expostulation, remonstration
14 discouragement

distance

03 gap
04 span
05 break, depth, range, reach, space, width
06 cut off, extent, height, length, remove, secede
07 breadth, reserve, stretch
08 coldness, coolness, separate
09 aloofness, formality, stiffness
10 dissociate, separation
14 unfriendliness

distant

03 far
04 cold, cool
05 aloof, stiff
06 far-off, formal, remote
07 faraway
08 detached, far-flung, not close, outlying, reserved
10 antisocial, unfriendly
11 out-of-the-way, stand-offish
12 unresponsive
14 unapproachable
15 uncommunicative

distaste

06 horror
07 disgust, dislike
08 aversion, loathing
09 antipathy, revulsion
10 abhorrence, repugnance
11 displeasure

distasteful

09 loathsome, obnoxious, offensive, repellent, repugnant, repulsive, revolting, unsavoury
10 disgusting, unpleasant
11 displeasing, undesirable
12 disagreeable
13 objectionable

distend

04 puff
05 bloat, bulge, swell, widen
06 dilate, expand
07 balloon, enlarge, fill out, inflate, stretch
09 intumesce

distended

05 puffy
07 bloated, dilated, swollen
08 enlarged, expanded, inflated, varicose
09 puffed-out, stretched, tumescent

distension

06 spread
08 bloating, dilation, swelling
09 expansion, extension
10 tumescence
11 enlargement
12 intumescence

distil

04 drip, flow, leak
06 derive, purify, refine
07 draw out, express, extract
08 condense, vaporize
09 evaporate, sublimate

distillation

06 spirit
07 essence, extract
10 extraction
11 evaporation
12 condensation

distinct

05 clear, plain, sharp
06 marked
07 defined, evident, obvious
08 apparent, clear-cut, definite, discrete, separate
09 different, disparate
10 dissimilar, noticeable
11 unambiguous, well-defined
12 recognizable, unmistakable

distinction

04 fame, mark
05 merit, worth
06 credit, renown, repute
07 feature, quality
08 eminence, prestige
09 celebrity, greatness
10 difference, importance, reputation, separation
11 discernment, peculiarity
12 significance
13 dissimilarity, individuality
14 discrimination
15 differentiation

distinctive

07 special, typical
08 original, peculiar, singular
09 different
10 individual, particular
13 extraordinary, idiosyncratic
14 characteristic, distinguishing

distinctly

07 clearly, plainly
08 markedly
09 evidently, obviously
10 definitely, noticeably
12 unmistakably
13 unambiguously

distinguish

03 see

04 mark
05 excel, stamp
06 descry, detect, notice
07 discern, make out, pick out
08 classify, identify, perceive
09 ascertain, determine, recognize, tell apart
10 categorize
12 characterize, discriminate
13 differentiate

distinguishable

07 evident, obvious
10 noticeable, observable
11 appreciable, conspicuous, discernible, perceptible
12 recognizable

distinguished

05 famed, noble, noted
06 famous, marked
07 eminent, notable, refined
08 esteemed, renowned
09 acclaimed, well-known
10 celebrated
11 conspicuous, illustrious
13 extraordinary

distinguishing

06 marked, unique
07 typical
08 peculiar, singular
09 different
10 individual
11 diacritical, distinctive
14 characteristic, discriminatory
15 differentiating

distort

04 bend, bias, warp
05 slant, twist
06 buckle, colour, deform
07 contort, falsify, pervert
08 misshape
09 disfigure
12 misrepresent

distorted

03 wry
04 awry, bent, skew
06 biased, skewed, warped
07 twisted
08 deformed
09 misshapen, perverted
10 disfigured, out of shape

distortion

04 bend, bias, skew, warp
05 slant, twist
06 buckle
08 garbling, twisting
09 colouring, deformity
10 contortion, perversion
11 crookedness

distract
05 amuse
06 divert, put off, puzzle
07 confuse, deflect, disturb, engross, fluster, perplex
08 bewilder, confound, draw away, turn away
09 entertain, sidetrack
10 discompose, disconcert

distracted
03 mad
04 wild
05 crazy, upset
06 raving
07 anxious, frantic
08 agitated, worked up
09 miles away, not with it
10 abstracted, distraught, distressed, hysterical
11 inattentive, overwrought, preoccupied
12 absent-minded
14 beside yourself

distracting
08 annoying
09 confusing
10 disturbing, irritating, off-putting, perturbing
13 disconcerting

distraction
04 game
05 hobby, sport
07 pastime
09 amusement, diversion
10 recreation
11 derangement, disturbance
13 entertainment
14 divertissement

❑**drive someone to distraction**
05 anger, annoy, upset
06 madden
10 drive crazy, exasperate

distraught
03 mad
04 wild
05 crazy, het up, upset
06 raving
07 anxious, frantic
08 agitated, in a state, worked up
10 distracted, distressed, hysterical
11 overwrought
14 beside yourself

distress
03 vex, woe
04 hurt, need, pain
05 agony, trial, upset, worry

06 grieve, harrow, penury, sadden, sorrow, unease
07 afflict, agonize, anguish, anxiety, disturb, perturb, sadness, trouble
08 calamity, hardship
09 adversity, heartache, indigence, suffering
10 affliction, desolation
11 make anxious, tribulation
12 difficulties, perturbation

distribute
04 deal
05 allot, issue, share
06 divide, spread, supply
07 deal out, deliver, diffuse, dish out, dole out, give out, hand out, mete out, scatter
08 allocate, dispense, disperse
09 circulate, pass round
11 disseminate

distribution
06 supply
07 dealing, sharing
08 delivery, division, handling,
09 placement, spreading
10 allocation, conveyance, dispersal, scattering
11 arrangement, circulation
13 dissemination

district
04 area, ward, zone
05 block, place
06 parish, region, sector
07 quarter
08 locality, precinct, vicinity
12 constituency
13 neighbourhood

distrust
05 doubt, qualm
07 suspect
08 mistrust, question, wariness
09 chariness, discredit, misgiving, suspicion
10 disbelieve, scepticism
11 questioning
12 doubtfulness
14 be suspicious of
15 have doubts about

distrustful
04 wary
05 chary
06 uneasy
07 cynical, dubious
08 doubtful, doubting
09 sceptical
10 suspicious, untrusting
12 disbelieving

disturb
04 stir

05 annoy, upset, worry
06 bother, dismay, pester
07 agitate, confuse, disrupt, fluster, perturb, trouble
08 distract, distress, unsettle
09 discomfit, interrupt
10 disarrange, disconcert
11 disorganize, make anxious

disturbance
03 row
04 fray, riot
05 brawl, upset
06 bother, fracas, racket, rumpus, tumult, uproar
07 illness, trouble, turmoil
08 disorder, neurosis, upheaval
09 agitation, annoyance, commotion, intrusion
10 disruption, hullabaloo
11 distraction
12 interference, interruption

disturbed
05 upset
06 hung-up, uneasy
07 anxious, worried
08 bothered, confused, neurotic, paranoid, troubled
09 concerned, flustered, psychotic, screwed-up
10 unbalanced
11 discomposed, maladjusted

disturbing
08 alarming, worrying
09 agitating, confusing, dismaying, startling, troubling, upsetting
10 perturbing, unsettling
11 bewildering, disquieting, distressing, frightening
13 disconcerting

disunited
05 split
07 divided
09 alienated, disrupted, estranged, separated

disunity
05 split
06 breach, schism, strife
07 discord, dissent, rupture
08 conflict, division
10 alienation, dissension
12 disagreement, estrangement

disuse
07 neglect
09 desuetude
11 abandonment

disused
06 unused
09 abandoned, neglected

ditch
04 drop, dump, dyke, moat
05 canal, drain, gully, scrap
06 furrow, gutter, trench
07 abandon, channel, discard
08 get rid of, jettison, throw out
09 dispose of, throw away
11 watercourse

dither
04 flap, stew
05 delay, panic, tizzy, waver
06 bother, pother
07 fluster, flutter
08 hang back, hesitate
09 vacillate
10 dilly-dally, indecision
12 be in two minds, shilly-shally, take your time

divan
04 sofa
05 couch
06 day bed, lounge, settee
07 lounger, ottoman
12 chaise-longue, chesterfield

dive
03 bar, dip, fly, pub
04 bolt, club, dart, dash, drop, fall, hole, rush, tear
05 hurry, joint, lunge, swoop
06 go down, header, plunge
07 descend, go under, plummet
08 nose-dive, submerge
09 nightclub

diverge
04 fork, part, vary
05 clash, drift, split, stray
06 branch, depart, differ, divide, spread, wander
07 deviate, digress, radiate
08 disagree, divagate, separate
09 bifurcate, branch off
10 contradict
12 be at variance

divergence
05 clash
07 parting
08 conflict
09 departure, deviation
10 deflection, difference, digression, separation
12 branching-out

divergent
07 diverse, variant, varying
08 separate
09 deviating, different, differing
10 tangential

divers
04 many, some
07 several, various, varying
08 manifold, numerous

diverse
05 mixed
06 sundry, unlike, varied
07 several, various, varying
08 assorted, discrete, distinct
09 different, differing
10 all means of, dissimilar
13 heterogeneous, miscellaneous

diversify
04 vary
06 assort, change, expand, extend, modify
09 branch out, spread out, variegate

diversion
03 fun
04 game, play
05 hobby, sport
06 change, detour
07 pastime
09 amusement, deviation
10 recreation, rerouteing
11 distraction, redirection
13 entertainment
14 divertissement

diversionary
09 divertive
11 distracting

diversity
05 range
06 medley
07 mixture, variety
10 assortment, difference
11 variegation
13 dissimilarity, dissimilitude, heterogeneity

divert
05 amuse, avert
06 absorb, occupy, switch
07 deflect, delight, reroute
08 distract, draw away, interest, intrigue, redirect, turn away
09 entertain, sidetrack

diverting
03 fun
05 funny, witty
07 amusing
08 humorous, pleasant
09 enjoyable
11 pleasurable
12 entertaining

divest
04 doff
05 strip

06 denude, remove
07 deprive, disrobe, undress
10 dispossess

divide
03 cut
04 fork, part, rank, sort
05 cut up, group, sever, split
06 bisect, branch, detach
07 arrange, break up, deal out, diverge, hand out, split up
08 alienate, classify, dispense, disunite, estrange, separate
09 break down, segregate
10 disconnect, distribute
11 come between

❑**divide up**
05 allot, share
07 dole out
08 allocate, share out
10 measure out

dividend
03 cut
04 gain, plus
05 bonus, extra, share, whack
07 benefit, portion, surplus

divination
05 -mancy
06 augury, mantic
07 presage
08 prophecy, taghairm
10 dukkeripen, prediction
11 foretelling, hariolation, rhabdomancy, second sight, soothsaying
12 clairvoyance
14 fortune-telling
15 prognostication

divine
04 holy
05 godly, guess, infer
06 cleric, deduce, intuit, lovely, parson, pastor, priest, sacred
07 angelic, exalted, godlike, prelate, saintly, suppose, supreme, surmise, suspect
08 heavenly, minister, mystical, perceive, reverend, seraphic
09 beautiful, celestial, churchman, clergyman,, religious, spiritual
10 sanctified, understand
11 clergywoman, consecrated
12 ecclesiastic, supernatural, transcendent
13 prognosticate

diviner
04 seer
05 augur, sibyl

06 dowser, oracle
07 prophet
08 haruspex
09 divinator
10 astrologer, soothsayer

divinity
03 god
05 deity
06 spirit
07 goddess, godhead
08 holiness, religion, sanctity, theology
09 godliness

division
03 arm
04 feud, part, rift
05 class, group, split
06 border, branch, breach, divide, schism, sector
07 cutting, discord, parting, rupture, section, segment
08 boundary, category, conflict, disunion, dividing, frontier
09 allotment, cutting up, partition, severance
10 alienation, allocation, department, separation
11 compartment
12 disagreement, distribution, dividing-line, estrangement

divisive
08 damaging
09 injurious
10 alienating, discordant, disruptive, estranging
11 troublesome
13 troublemaking

divorce
04 part
05 annul, sever, split
06 breach, detach, divide
07 break up, rupture, split up
08 dissolve, disunite, separate
09 annulment, partition, severance
10 disconnect, dissociate, separation

divulge
04 leak, tell
06 betray, impart, reveal
07 confess, declare, let slip, publish, uncover
08 disclose, proclaim
09 broadcast, make known
11 blow the gaff, communicate
12 break the news
13 spill the beans

dizzy
05 dazed, ditsy, faint, giddy, shaky, silly, woozy

07 foolish, muddled, reeling
08 confused
10 bewildered, off-balance
11 light-headed, vertiginous
14 feather-brained, scatterbrained

do
03 act, con, end, fix
04 bash, dupe, fare, go at, have, make, read, take, work
05 cause, cheat, crack, event, get on, learn, offer, party, put on, reach, serve, study, trick
06 affair, behave, come on, create, finish, fleece, fulfil, manage, master, rave-up, rip off, soirée, supply, tackle, work as, work at, work on
07 achieve, arrange, deceive, defraud, execute, knees-up, perform, prepare, present, proceed, produce, provide, satisfy, suffice, swindle
08 be enough, carry out, complete, conclude, deal with, function, get along, hoodwink, occasion, organize, progress,
09 discharge, gathering, implement, undertake
10 accomplish, be adequate, effectuate, fit the bill
11 celebration
12 be sufficient, take for a ride
14 be satisfactory

◻**do away with**
04 do in, kill, slay
06 murder, remove
07 abolish, bump off, discard
08 get rid of, knock off
09 dispose of, eliminate
11 assassinate, discontinue, exterminate

◻**do down**
05 blame
07 censure, condemn
08 critcize
13 find fault with

◻**do in**
04 kill, slay
06 murder
07 bump off
08 knock off
09 slaughter
11 assassinate, exterminate

◻**do out of**
06 fleece
08 con out of
09 deprive of
10 cheat out of, trick out of

11 diddle out of
12 swindle out of

◻**dos and don'ts**
04 code
05 rules
07 customs
09 etiquette, standards
11 regulations
12 instructions

◻**do up**
03 tie
04 lace, pack
05 zip up
06 button, fasten, repair
07 restore
08 decorate, renovate
09 modernize
10 redecorate
11 recondition

◻**do without**
05 forgo
06 forego, give up
09 go without
10 relinquish
11 abstain from
12 deny yourself, dispense with
13 manage without

docile
08 amenable, obedient, obliging, yielding
09 compliant, tractable
10 controlled, manageable
11 co-operative
12 controllable

docility
07 pliancy
08 meekness
09 ductility, obedience
10 compliance, pliability
11 amenability
12 biddableness, complaisance, tractability
13 manageability
14 submissiveness

dock
03 cut
04 clip, crop, moor, pier, quay
05 berth, jetty, tie up, wharf
06 anchor, deduct, lessen, marina, reduce, remove
07 curtail, harbour, shorten
08 boat-yard, decrease, subtract, truncate, withhold
10 drop anchor, waterfront

docket
03 tab, tag
04 bill, chit, file, mark
05 index, label, tally
06 chitty, ticket
07 receipt

09 catalogue, paperwork
11 certificate, counterfoil
13 documentation

doctor
04 drug, lace, spay
05 bones, medic, quack, spike
06 dilute, neuter, weaken
07 falsify, pervert
08 castrate, disguise
09 clinician, physician, sterilize
10 adulterate, consultant
11 add poison to, contaminate
13 interfere with
14 medical officer
➢ See also **medical**

▬ *Types of doctor*:
02 GP, MO
05 locum
06 intern
08 houseman, resident
09 registrar
10 consultant
12 family doctor
14 medical officer

▬ *Names of doctors*:
04 **Bell** (Sir Charles), **Koch**
(Robert), **Lind** (James),
Reed (Walter), **Ross** (Sir
Ronald)
05 **Broca** (Paul Pierre), **Bruce**
(Sir David), **Galen**, **Paget**
(Sir James), **Steno**
(Nicolaus)
06 **Bichat** (Marie François
Xavier), **Bright** (Richard),
Carrel (Alexis), **Celsus**
(Aulus Cornelius), **Cooper**
(Sir Astley), **Garrod** (Sir
Archibald Edward), **Harvey**
(William), **Hunter** (John),
Jenner (Edward), **Lister**
(Joseph, Lord), **Manson**
(Sir Patrick), **Mesmer**
(Franz Anton)
07 **Addison** (Thomas),
Barnard (Christian
Neethling), **Cushing**
(Harvey Williams), **Gilbert**
(William), **Winston**
(Robert, Lord)
08 **Anderson** (Elizabeth
Garrett), **Beaumont**
(William), **Billroth**
(Theodor), **Charnley** (Sir
John), **Duchenne**
(Guillaume Benjamin
Amand), **Tournier** (Paul)
09 **Bartholin** (Erasmus),
Dutrochet (Henri),
Hahnemann (Samuel),
Parkinson (James)

10 **Paracelsus**, **Sanctorius**
11 **Hippocrates**
12 **Erasistratus**
➢ See also **surgeon**

doctrinaire
05 rigid
08 dogmatic, pedantic
09 fanatical, insistent
10 inflexible

doctrine
05 canon, credo, creed,
dogma, tenet
08 teaching
09 principle

document
04 cite, deed, form, list
05 chart, paper, proof, prove
06 record, report, verify
07 charter, support
08 evidence, register, validate
09 affidavit, chronicle
11 certificate, corroborate, put
on record
12 give weight to, keep on
record, substantiate

documentary
07 charted, written
08 detailed, recorded
10 chronicled

doddering
04 aged, weak
05 frail
06 feeble, infirm
08 decrepit
09 tottering

doddery
04 aged, weak
05 shaky
06 feeble, infirm
07 tottery
08 unsteady
09 doddering, faltering

dodge
04 duck, ploy, ruse, shun, wile
05 avoid, elude, evade, shift,
shirk, trick
06 bypass, scheme, swerve
08 get out of, get round, jump
away, side-step
09 deception, manoeuvre
10 subterfuge
11 contrivance, machination

dodger
06 evader, skiver
07 dreamer, shirker, slacker
08 layabout, slyboots
09 lazybones, trickster
11 lead-swinger

dodgy
05 dicey, dicky, risky
06 chancy, shifty, tricky, unsafe
07 dubious, suspect
08 delicate, ticklish
09 dangerous, uncertain
10 unreliable
12 disreputable

doer
06 dynamo, worker
08 achiever, activist, executor
09 organizer
10 power-house

doff
03 tip
04 lift, shed
05 raise, touch
06 remove
07 discard, take off

dog
03 cur, pup
04 mutt, tail
05 bitch, harry, hound, pooch,
puppy, track, trail, worry
06 canine, follow, plague,
pursue, shadow, wretch
07 mongrel, trouble, villain
09 scoundrel
➢ See also **animal**

▬ *Breeds of dog*:
03 Pom, pug
04 chow, Peke
05 boxer, corgi, dingo, husky
06 beagle, borzoi, collie, gun dog,
poodle, saluki, setter, Westie
07 bulldog, griffon, lurcher,
Maltese, mastiff, pointer,
Scottie, sheltie, shih tzu,
spaniel, terrier, whippet
08 Airedale, Alsatian,
Doberman, foxhound,
Labrador, Pekinese,
Sealyham, sheepdog
09 chihuahua, dachshund,
Dalmatian, Great Dane,
greyhound, Pekingese,
retriever, Schnauzer, St
Bernard, wolf-hound
10 bloodhound, fox-terrier,
Pomeranian, Rottweiler,
sausage-dog
11 Afghan hound, basset-
hound, bull-mastiff, bull-
terrier, Jack Russell
12 Border collie, cairn terrier,
Newfoundland
13 cocker spaniel
14 German Shepherd, Irish
wolfhound, pit bull terrier
15 golden retriever, Scottish
terrier, springer spaniel

► *Names of famous dogs*:
04 Nana, Odie, Shep, Toto
05 Butch, Goofy, Laika, Petra,
     Pluto, Pongo, Snowy
06 Droopy, Gromit, Hector,
     Lassie, Nipper, Snoopy
07 Gnasher, Perdita, Roobarb
08 Bullseye, Cerberus
09 Rin Tin Tin, Scooby Doo
10 Deputy Dawg, Fred Basset
15 Greyfriars Bobby

dogged
06 intent, steady
08 obdurate, resolute,
     stubborn, tireless
09 obstinate, steadfast,
     tenacious
10 determined, persistent,
     relentless, unflagging,
     unshakable, unyielding
11 persevering, unfaltering
12 pertinacious, single-minded
13 indefatigable

doggedness
08 firmness, tenacity
09 endurance, obstinacy
10 resolution, steadiness
11 persistence, pertinacity
12 perseverance, stubbornness
13 determination,
     steadfastness, tenaciousness
14 indomitability, relentlessness

dogma
04 code
05 credo, creed, maxim, tenet
06 belief
07 article, opinion, precept
08 doctrine, teaching
09 principle
10 conviction
12 code of belief
14 article of faith

dogmatic
08 arrogant, emphatic, positive
09 arbitrary, assertive,
     canonical, doctrinal,
     imperious, insistent
10 ex cathedra, pontifical
11 categorical, doctrinaire,
     domineering, opinionated
13 authoritarian, authoritative

dogmatism
07 bigotry
11 presumption
13 arbitrariness, assertiveness,
     imperiousness
14 peremptoriness

dogsbody
05 gofer, slave
06 drudge, menial, skivvy

07 doormat
08 factotum
11 galley-slave
12 man-of-all-work
13 maid-of-all-work

doings
04 acts
05 deeds, feats
06 events
07 actions, affairs
08 concerns, dealings, exploits
09 handiwork
10 activities, adventures
11 enterprises, proceedings
12 achievements, transactions

doldrums
05 blues, dumps, ennui, gloom
06 acedia, apathy, torpor
07 boredom, inertia, malaise
08 dullness
09 dejection, lassitude
10 depression, stagnation
12 listlessness, sluggishness

dole
03 JSA
06 credit, income
07 benefit, payment, support
09 allowance
14 social security

❑ **dole out**
04 deal
05 allot, issue, share
06 assign, divide, ration
07 deal out, dish out, give out,
     hand out, mete out
08 allocate, dispense, divide
     up, share out
09 apportion
10 administer, distribute

doleful
03 sad
04 blue
06 dismal, dreary, gloomy,
     rueful, sombre, woeful
07 forlorn, painful, pitiful
08 dolorous, mournful,
     pathetic, wretched
09 cheerless, miserable,
     sorrowful, woebegone
10 depressing, lugubrious,
     melancholy
12 disconsolate
14 down in the dumps

doll
03 toy
05 dolly, Sindy®
06 Barbie®, figure, puppet
08 figurine
09 plaything
10 marionette

❑ **doll up**
05 preen, primp
06 tart up
07 deck out, dress up
08 titivate, trick out

dollop
03 gob
04 ball, blob, glob, lump
06 gobbet

dolorous
03 sad
06 rueful, sombre, woeful
07 doleful, painful
08 grievous, mournful,
     wretched
09 anguished, harrowing,
     miserable, sorrowful,
     woebegone
10 lugubrious, melancholy
12 heart-rending

dolour
05 grief
06 misery, sorrow
07 anguish, sadness
08 distress, mourning
09 heartache, suffering
10 heartbreak
11 lamentation

dolt
03 ass
04 clot, dope, fool, nerd, twit
05 chump, idiot, ninny, twerp,
     wally
06 dimwit, nitwit
08 dipstick, imbecile, numskull
09 blockhead, simpleton
10 nincompoop

domain
04 area
05 field, lands, realm, world
06 empire, region, sphere
07 concern, kingdom, section
08 dominion, province
09 territory
10 discipline, speciality
12 jurisdiction

dome
05 mound, vault
06 cupola
07 rotunda
10 hemisphere

domestic
03 pet
04 char, home, maid, tame
05 daily
06 au pair, family, native
07 private, servant
08 internal, personal

09 charwoman, daily help, household
10 home-loving, indigenous
11 domiciliary
12 house-trained

domesticate
04 tame
05 break, train
07 break in
09 habituate
10 house-train, naturalize
11 acclimatize, familiarize

domesticated
03 pet
04 tame
05 tamed
08 broken in, domestic
11 housewifely, naturalized
12 house-trained

domesticity
09 homecraft
10 homemaking, housecraft
12 housekeeping
13 home economics
15 domestic science

domicile
04 home
05 abode, house
07 lodging, mansion
08 dwelling, lodgings, quarters
09 residence, residency
10 habitation, settlement
15 take up residence

dominance
04 rule, sway
05 power
07 command, control, mastery
08 hegemony
09 authority, supremacy
10 ascendancy, government
11 pre-eminence

dominant
03 key
04 main
05 chief, major, prime
06 ruling, strong
07 leading, primary, supreme
09 assertive, prevalent, principal, prominent
10 pre-eminent, prevailing
11 outstanding, predominant
13 authoritative

dominate
04 lead, rule
06 direct, govern, master
07 control, eclipse, prevail
08 domineer, overbear, overlook, overrule
09 tower over, tyrannize

10 monopolize, overshadow
11 predominate

domination
04 rule, sway
05 power
07 command, control, tyranny
09 despotism, supremacy
10 ascendancy, oppression, repression, subjection
11 pre-eminence, superiority, suppression
12 dictatorship, predominance
13 subordination

domineering
05 bossy, pushy
08 arrogant, coercive, despotic, forceful
09 imperious, masterful
10 autocratic, high-handed, oppressive, tyrannical
11 dictatorial, overbearing
13 authoritarian

dominion
04 rule, sway
05 power, realm
06 colony, domain, empire
07 command, control, country, kingdom, mastery
08 lordship, province
09 authority, direction, supremacy, territory
11 sovereignty
12 jurisdiction

don
05 put on, tutor
07 dress in, scholar, teacher
08 academic, lecturer, slip into
09 professor

Don Juan
05 lover, romeo
06 gigolo
08 Casanova
09 ladies' man, philander, womanizer
10 lady-killer
11 philanderer

donate
04 give
06 bestow, chip in, pledge
07 cough up, fork out, present
08 give away, shell out
09 make a gift, subscribe
10 contribute

donation
04 alms, gift
07 bequest, charity, largess, present
08 gratuity, largesse, offering

11 benefaction
12 contribution, presentation

done
02 OK
04 over
05 baked, ended, ready, right
06 agreed, boiled, cooked, proper, seemly, stewed
07 decided, fitting, settled
08 accepted, arranged, complete, decorous, executed, finished, prepared, realized, suitable
09 completed, concluded, fulfilled
10 acceptable, terminated
11 appropriate, consummated
12 accomplished, conventional

□**done for**
04 lost
06 broken, dashed, doomed, foiled, ruined, undone
07 wrecked
08 defeated, finished
09 destroyed

□**done in**
04 dead
05 all in, weary
06 bushed, pooped, zonked
08 dead beat, dog-tired, fatigued, tired out
09 exhausted, fagged out, knackered, shattered
14 on your last legs

□**have done with**
08 over with
12 finished with

donkey
03 ass
04 moke, mule
05 burro, hinny, jenny
07 jackass

donnish
07 bookish, erudite, learned
08 academic, pedantic
09 pedagogic, scholarly
10 scholastic
12 intellectual

donor
05 angel, giver
06 backer
07 donator
10 benefactor
11 contributor
14 fairy godmother

doom
03 lot
04 damn, fate, ruin
05 death, judge

07 condemn, consign, destine, destiny, portion, verdict
09 judgement, ruination
11 destruction, rack and ruin

doomed
05 fated
06 cursed, damned, ruined
07 unlucky
08 destined, hopeless, ill-fated, luckless
09 condemned
10 bedevilled, ill-omened
11 star-crossed

door
04 exit, road
05 entry, hatch, route, way in
06 access, portal
07 doorway, gateway, opening
08 entrance, open door

doorkeeper
06 porter
07 doorman, janitor, ostiary
09 concierge
10 gatekeeper
14 commissionaire

dope
01 E
03 gen, LSD, pot
04 acid, clot, coke, dolt, drug, fool, hash, info, twit, weed
05 crack, drugs, dunce, facts, grass, idiot, ninny, speed
06 dimwit, doctor, inject, nitwit, opiate, sedate
07 Ecstasy, half-wit, low-down
08 cannabis, narcotic
09 blockhead, marijuana
10 nincompoop
11 amphetamine, barbiturate, information, particulars
12 anaesthetize, hallucinogen

dopey
04 daft, dozy
06 drowsy, groggy, simple, sleepy, stupid, torpid
07 foolish, nodding
09 lethargic, somnolent

dormant
05 inert
06 asleep, fallow, latent, torpid
07 resting
08 comatose, inactive, sleeping, sluggish
10 slumbering, unrealized
11 hibernating, undeveloped

dose
04 shot
06 amount, dosage, potion

07 draught, measure, portion
08 medicate, quantity

dot
03 dab, jot
04 atom, iota, mark, spot, stud
05 fleck, point, speck
07 scatter, speckle, stipple
08 full stop, particle, pin-point
12 decimal point

❑**on the dot**
05 sharp
08 promptly
09 precisely
10 punctually
13 exactly on time

dotage
06 old age
08 senility, weakness
10 feebleness, imbecility
11 decrepitude
15 second childhood

dote

❑**dote on**
05 adore, spoil
06 admire, pamper
07 idolize, indulge, worship
08 hold dear, treasure

doting
04 fond, soft
06 loving, tender
07 adoring, devoted
09 indulgent
12 affectionate

dotty
04 daft
05 barmy, batty, crazy, potty
07 touched
08 peculiar
09 eccentric

double
04 copy, dual, fold, twin
05 binal, clone, match, twice
06 binate, paired, repeat, ringer, two-ply
07 coupled, doubled, magnify, replica, stand in, twofold
09 bifarious, duplicate, facsimile, lookalike
10 substitute, understudy
11 counterpart, double-edged
12 doppelgänger
13 have a dual role, multiply by two, spitting image
14 be an understudy
15 have a second role

❑**at the double**
06 at once
07 quickly
09 right away

11 at full speed, immediately
12 straight away, without delay

❑**double back**
04 loop
06 circle, return
07 reverse
09 backtrack

double-cross
03 con
05 cheat, trick
06 betray
07 defraud, swindle, two-time
08 hoodwink
12 take for a ride
14 pull a fast one on

double-dealing
07 perfidy
08 betrayal, cheating, tricking
09 duplicity, mendacity, swindling, treachery, two-timing
10 defrauding, misleading
11 crookedness, hoodwinking
12 two-facedness

double entendre
03 pun
08 innuendo, wordplay
09 ambiguity
11 play on words
13 double meaning
14 suggestiveness

doubly
03 bis
05 again, extra, twice
07 twofold

doubt
04 fear
05 demur, qualm, query, waver
07 dilemma, problem, suspect
08 distrust, mistrust, question
09 ambiguity, be dubious, misgiving, suspicion
10 difficulty, disbelieve, hesitation, indecision, scepticism, uneasiness
11 be uncertain, be undecided, incredulity, reservation, uncertainty
12 apprehension, be suspicious, mixed feeling
15 have qualms about

❑**in doubt**
09 ambiguous, debatable, uncertain, undecided
10 in question, unreliable, unresolved, up in the air
12 questionable
14 open to question

❑no doubt
06 surely
08 of course, probably
09 certainly, doubtless
10 definitely, presumably
11 undoubtedly
12 without doubt
14 unquestionably

doubter
05 cynic
07 sceptic, scoffer
08 agnostic
10 questioner, unbeliever
11 disbeliever
14 doubting Thomas

doubtful
04 iffy
05 fishy, shady, vague
06 uneasy, unsure
07 dubious, in doubt, unclear
08 hesitant, unlikely, wavering
09 debatable, tentative, uncertain, undecided
10 improbable, in two minds, irresolute, suspicious
11 distrustful, vacillating
12 inconclusive, questionable

doubtless
05 truly
06 surely
07 clearly, no doubt
08 of course, probably
09 certainly, seemingly
10 most likely, presumably
11 undoubtedly
12 indisputably, without doubt
14 unquestionably

dour
04 grim, hard, sour
05 gruff, harsh, rigid, stern
06 dismal, dreary, gloomy, morose, severe, strict, sullen
07 austere
08 churlish, rigorous
09 obstinate, unsmiling
10 forbidding, inflexible

douse, dowse
03 dip, wet
04 duck, dunk, soak
05 flood, snuff, souse, steep
06 deluge, drench, plunge, put out, quench, splash
07 blow out, immerge, immerse, smother
08 saturate, submerge
10 extinguish

dovetail
04 join, link
05 agree, match, tally
08 coincide

09 harmonize, interlock
10 correspond
11 fit together

dowdy
04 drab
05 dingy, tacky, tatty
08 frumpish, slovenly
12 old-fashioned
13 unfashionable

down
03 low, nap, sad
04 blue, bust, fell, flue, fuzz, gulp, pile, shag, swig, wool
05 bloom, drink, floor, fluff
07 consume, crashed, floccus, pappose, pappous, put away, swallow, unhappy
08 dejected, wretched
09 depressed, knock back, miserable, prostrate
10 dispirited, melancholy, not working, out of order
11 inoperative, out of action
12 soft feathers
13 to a lower level
14 down in the dumps

❑down with
08 away with, get rid of

down-and-out
04 hobo
05 loser, tramp
06 dosser, ruined
07 vagrant
08 derelict, vagabond
09 destitute, penniless
12 impoverished, on your uppers

down-at-heel
04 drab, poor
05 dingy, seedy, tacky, tatty
06 frayed, ragged, shabby
08 slovenly, tattered

downbeat
03 low
04 calm
06 casual, gloomy
07 cynical, relaxed
08 informal, laid back
09 cheerless, depressed, unhurried, unworried
10 insouciant, nonchalant
11 pessimistic

downcast
03 low, sad
04 blue, down, glum
05 fed up
06 gloomy
07 daunted, unhappy
08 dejected, wretched
09 depressed, miserable

10 despondent, dispirited
11 crestfallen, discouraged
12 disappointed, disconsolate

downfall
04 fall, ruin
07 debacle, failure, undoing
08 collapse, disgrace
10 debasement
11 degradation, destruction

downgrade
06 demote, depose, humble
07 deflate, degrade, run down
08 belittle, minimize, relegate
09 denigrate, disparage
11 lower in rank, make light of

downhearted
03 sad
04 glum
06 gloomy
07 daunted, unhappy
08 dejected, downcast
09 depressed
10 despondent, dispirited
11 discouraged, low-spirited
12 disconsolate, disheartened

downpour
05 flood
06 deluge
07 torrent
09 rainstorm
10 cloudburst, inundation

downright
05 clear, plain, sheer, total, utter
07 clearly, plainly, totally, utterly
08 absolute, complete, outright, thorough
09 out-and-out, wholesale
10 absolutely, completely, thoroughly
11 categorical, unequivocal, unqualified
13 categorically

down-to-earth
04 sane
07 mundane
08 sensible
09 practical, realistic
10 hard-headed, no-nonsense
11 commonsense
12 matter-of-fact
13 unsentimental
14 commonsensical

down-trodden
06 abused
07 bullied
09 exploited, oppressed
10 subjugated, trampled on, tyrannized, victimized
11 subservient

downward
07 sliding
08 downhill, slipping
09 declining, going down
10 descending, moving down

dowry
04 gift
05 dower, share
07 faculty, portion
09 endowment, provision
11 inheritance
12 wedding-dower
15 marriage portion

dowse see **douse**

doze
03 kip, nap
04 zizz
05 go off, sleep
06 catnap, nod off, siesta, snooze
07 drop off, shut-eye
08 drift off, take a nap
10 forty winks

drab
04 dull, flat, grey
05 dingy
06 boring, dismal, dreary, gloomy, shabby, sombre
08 lifeless
09 cheerless
10 colourless, lacklustre

draft
04 draw, plan
05 rough
06 cheque, draw up, sketch
07 compose, drawing, outline
08 abstract, protocol
09 blueprint, formulate
10 money order
11 delineation, postal order
14 bill of exchange, letter of credit

drag
03 lag, lug, pest, tow, tug
04 bind, bore, draw, haul, pain, pull, yank
05 crawl, creep, trail
08 go slowly, nuisance
09 annoyance, go on and on
13 pain in the neck

❑**drag out**
06 extend, hang on
07 draw out, prolong, spin out
08 lengthen, protract

❑**drag up**
05 raise
06 rake up, remind, revive
07 bring up, mention

dragoon
05 bully, drive, force, impel
06 coerce, compel, harass
08 browbeat
09 constrain, strongarm
10 intimidate

drain
03 dry, sap, tap, tax
04 duct, leak, milk, pipe, void
05 bleed, ditch, empty, sewer
06 effuse, gutter, outlet, remove, strain, trench
07 channel, conduit, consume, culvert, deplete, draw off, drink up, exhaust, extract, flow out, pump off, seep out, swallow, trickle
10 exhaustion
11 consumption

drama
04 play, show
05 piece, scene
06 acting, comedy, crisis, thrill
07 tension, theatre, tragedy
09 dramatics, sensation
10 excitement, stagecraft
11 histrionics

dramatic
05 stage, tense, vivid
06 abrupt, marked, sudden
07 graphic
08 distinct, exciting, stirring, striking, Thespian
09 effective, thrilling
10 expressive, flamboyant, histrionic, noticeable, theatrical, unexpected
11 sensational, spectacular
12 melodramatic

dramatist
08 comedian
09 tragedian
10 dramaturge, play-writer, playwright
12 dramaturgist, screen writer, scriptwriter

dramatize
03 act, ham
05 adapt, ham up, put on, stage
06 overdo
07 play-act
09 overstate
10 arrange for, exaggerate
12 lay it on thick

drape
04 drop, fold, hang, veil, wrap
05 adorn, cloak, cover, droop
06 shroud
07 envelop, overlay, suspend
08 decorate

drapery
05 arras, blind, cloth
06 blinds
07 curtain, hanging, valance
08 backdrop, covering, curtains, hangings, tapestry

drastic
04 dire
05 harsh
06 severe, strong
07 extreme, radical
09 desperate, Draconian
11 far-reaching

draught
03 cup
05 drink
06 influx, potion
07 current, drawing, pulling
08 dragging, traction

draw
02 go
03 get, lug, tie, tug
04 bait, come, drag, haul, lure, move, pull
05 chart, paint, trace, trail
06 allure, appeal, come to, deduce, depict, design, doodle, elicit, entice, gather, inhale, map out, obtain, pencil, remove, sketch
07 advance, attract, bring in, extract, portray, produce, pull out, respire, take out
08 approach, breath in, bring out, conclude, dead heat, progress, scribble, withdraw
09 delineate, magnetism, represent, stalemate
10 attraction, enticement

❑**draw back**
05 wince
06 flinch, recoil, shrink
07 retract, retreat
08 withdraw

❑**draw on**
03 use
05 apply
07 exploit, utilize
08 put to use
09 make use of
14 have recourse to

❑**draw out**
05 leave, start
06 depart, extend
07 move out, prolong, pull out, spin out, stretch
08 elongate, lengthen, protract

❑**draw up**
04 halt, stop
06 pull up

07 compose, prepare
08 write out
09 formulate

drawback
04 flaw, snag
05 catch, fault, hitch
06 damper, defect, hurdle
07 barrier, problem, trouble
08 handicap, nuisance,
   obstacle, weak spot
10 deficiency, difficulty,
   impediment, limitation
12 disadvantage, imperfection
14 stumbling-block

drawing
05 study
06 sketch
07 cartoon, diagram, graphic,
   outline, picture
08 portrait
09 depiction, portrayal
11 composition, delineation
12 illustration
14 representation

drawl
05 drone, twang
06 haw-haw

drawn
04 taut, worn
05 gaunt, tense, tired
07 fraught, haggard, pinched
08 fatigued, strained, stressed
09 washed out

dread
04 dire, fear, funk
05 alarm, awful, quail, worry
06 dismay, feared, flinch, fright,
   grisly, horror, terror
07 ghastly, shudder, tremble
08 disquiet, dreadful,
   gruesome, horrible, terrible
09 cold sweat, frightful
10 blind panic, shrink from,
   terrifying
11 fit of terror, trepidation
12 awe-inspiring
13 be terrified by

dreadful
04 dire, grim
05 awful, nasty
07 ghastly, heinous, hideous
08 alarming, grievous, horrible,
   horrific, shocking, terrible
09 appalling, frightful
10 horrendous, outrageous,
   terrifying, unpleasant
11 frightening

dream
03 aim, joy

04 goal, hope, muse, plan, wish
05 fancy, ideal, model, yearn
06 beauty, design, desire,
   superb, trance, vision
07 fantasy, imagine, reverie
08 ambition, daydream,
   delusion, envisage, illusion
09 fantasize, nightmare, pipe
   dream, switch off
10 aspiration
11 hallucinate, inattention
13 hallucination
14 phantasmagoria, stare into
   space
15 castles in the air

❏**dream up**
04 spin
05 hatch
06 create, devise, invent
07 concoct, imagine, think up
08 conceive, contrive
09 conjure up, fabricate

❏**not dream of**
08 not think
10 not imagine
11 not conceive, not consider

dreamer
07 Utopian
08 idealist, romancer, romantic
09 fantasist, star-gazer,
   theorizer, visionary
10 daydreamer

dreamlike
06 unreal
07 phantom, surreal
08 ethereal, illusory
09 visionary
10 chimerical, trance-like
13 hallucinatory, insubstantial,
   unsubstantial
14 phantasmagoric

dreamy
03 dim
04 hazy, soft
05 faint, misty, vague
06 absent, gentle, unreal
07 calming, faraway, lulling,
   pensive, shadowy, unclear
08 ethereal, fanciful, relaxing,
   romantic, soothing
09 fantastic, imaginary,
   visionary
10 abstracted, idealistic,
   indistinct, thoughtful
11 fantasizing, preoccupied
12 absent-minded

dreary
03 sad
04 dark, drab, dull
05 bleak

06 boring, dismal, gloomy,
   sombre
07 humdrum, routine, tedious
08 lifeless, mournful, overcast
09 cheerless, wearisome
10 colourless, depressing,
   monotonous, uneventful

dredge

❏**dredge up**
05 dig up, raise
06 drag up, fish up, rake up
07 scoop up, uncover, unearth
08 discover

dregs
04 lees, scum
05 dross, trash, waste
07 deposit, grounds, residue
08 detritus, residuum, sediment
09 scourings, sublimate

drench
03 wet
04 duck, soak
05 douse, drown, flood, imbue,
   souse, steep, swamp
08 inundate, permeate, saturate
13 soak to the skin

dress
02 do
03 don, fit, rig
04 comb, deck, garb, gear,
   gown, robe, tend, tidy, togs,
   trim, wear
05 adorn, array, clean, cover,
   drape, frock, get-up, groom,
   preen, primp, put on, treat
06 adjust, attire, bind up,
   clothe, fit out, outfit, swathe
07 apparel, bandage, clothes,
   costume, garment, garnish,
   prepare, throw on, turn out
08 accoutre, clothing,
   decorate, garments
13 put a plaster on

❏**dress down**
05 chide, scold
06 berate, carpet, rebuke
07 reprove, tell off, upbraid
09 castigate, reprimand
13 tear off a strip

❏**dress up**
04 deck, gild
05 adorn, tog up
06 doll up, tart up
07 improve
09 decorate, disguise,
   ornament

dressing
03 pad
04 lint

dressmaker
05 gauze, sauce, spica
07 bandage, plaster
08 compress, ligature, poultice
10 tourniquet
11 Elastoplast®

dressmaker
06 tailor
07 modiste
09 couturier, tailoress
10 seamstress
11 needlewoman

dressy
05 natty, ritzy, smart, swish
06 classy, formal, ornate
07 elegant, stylish
09 elaborate

dribble
03 run
04 drip, drop, leak, ooze, seep
05 drool, exude
06 drivel, slaver
07 seepage, slobber, trickle

dried
04 arid
07 drained, parched, wizened
08 withered
09 mummified
10 dehydrated, desiccated, exsiccated, shrivelled

drift
04 bank, core, flow, gist, heap, mass, pile, roam, rove, waft
05 amass, coast, drive, float, mound, point, stray, sweep
06 course, gather, import, pile up, thrust, wander
07 current, essence, meaning
08 movement, tendency
09 direction, intention, substance, variation
10 accumulate, digression
12 accumulation, significance
14 be carried along
15 go with the stream

drifter
04 hobo
05 nomad, rover, tramp
07 swagman, vagrant
08 vagabond, wanderer
09 itinerant, traveller
11 beachcomber
12 rolling stone

drill
03 awl, bit
04 bore
05 borer, coach, teach, train
06 gimlet, ground, school
07 routine, tuition
08 coaching, exercise, instruct, practice, rehearse, training
09 inculcate, procedure
10 discipline, repetition
11 inculcation, instruction

drink
03 sip, sup, tot
04 brew, down, gulp, lush, swig
05 booze, quaff, swill, toast
06 absorb, guzzle, imbibe, liquid, liquor, salute, tipple
07 alcohol, carouse, draught, indulge, spirits, swallow
08 beverage, infusion
09 hard stuff, knock back, partake of, polish off, soft drink, stiffener, the bottle
11 refreshment, strong drink
12 hit the bottle
13 knock back a few
14 be a hard drinker, drink like a fish, thirst-quencher
15 be a heavy drinker

➤ *Types of non-alcoholic drink*:
03 pop
04 coke, milk
05 Assam, cocoa, float, julep, latte, mixer, Pepsi®
06 coffee, Indian, Ribena®, squash, tisane
07 cordial, limeade, mineral, Perrier®, seltzer
08 café noir, China tea, Coca Cola®, Earl Grey, espresso, expresso, fruit tea, green tea, Horlicks®, lemon tea, lemonade, Lucozade®, Ovaltine®, root beer
09 Canada Dry®, cherryade, cream soda, ginger ale, herbal tea, milk shake, mint-julep, soda water
10 café au lait, café filtre, cappuccino, fizzy drink, fruit juice, ginger beer, rosehip tea, tonic water, Vichy water
11 barley water, bitter lemon, camomile tea
12 hot chocolate, mineral water, sarsaparilla
13 peppermint tea, Turkish coffee
15 lapsang souchong

➤ See also **beer**; **cocktail**; **liqueur**; **spirits**; **wine**

drinkable
07 potable
10 fit to drink

drinker
04 lush, soak, wino
05 alkie, dipso, drunk, toper
06 boozer
07 imbiber, tippler, tosspot
08 drunkard
09 inebriate
10 piss artist
11 dipsomaniac

drip
03 wet
04 bead, bore, drop, leak, ooze, plop, tear, weep, wimp
06 filter, splash
07 dribble, drizzle, trickle
09 percolate

drive
02 go
03 dig, ram, run, tax, vim, zip
04 come, dash, goad, herd, lead, move, need, prod, push, ride, road, send, sink, spin, spur, take, trip, urge, will
05 carry, fight, force, guide, impel, jaunt, knock, motor, power, press, steer, verve
06 action, appeal, avenue, coerce, compel, convey, direct, effort, energy, hammer, incite, manage, oblige, outing, plunge, propel, strike, thrust, vigour
07 actuate, control, crusade, dragoon, go by car, journey, operate, overtax, provoke, resolve, roadway, round up
08 ambition, campaign, instinct, motivate, overdo it, overwork, persuade, pressure, struggle, tenacity
09 chauffeur, come by car, excursion, transport
10 enterprise, get-up-and-go, initiative, motivation, pressurize, propulsion
11 travel by car, work too hard
12 be at the wheel
13 determination
14 propeller shaft
15 be at the controls

❑**drive at**
04 hint, mean
05 aim at, get at, imply
06 intend
07 refer to, signify, suggest
08 allude to, indicate, intimate
09 insinuate
10 have in mind

drivel
03 rot

04 crap
05 tripe
06 bunkum, waffle
07 garbage, hogwash, rubbish, twaddle
08 claptrap, nonsense
09 gibberish, poppycock
10 balderdash, mumbo-jumbo
12 gobbledygook

driver
05 rider
06 cabbie
07 trucker
08 motorist
09 chauffeur
12 motorcyclist

driving
05 heavy
07 dynamic, violent
08 forceful, sweeping, vigorous
09 energetic
10 compelling, forthright

drizzle
04 mist, rain, spit, spot
06 mizzle, shower
09 light rain

droll
03 odd
04 zany
05 comic, funny, queer, witty
07 amusing, comical, jocular,
08 clownish, farcical, humorous, peculiar
09 diverting, eccentric, laughable, ludicrous
10 ridiculous
12 entertaining

drone
03 hum
04 buzz, purr
05 chant, idler, leech, whirr
06 intone, loafer
07 slacker, sponger, vibrate
08 hanger-on, layabout, parasite, whirring
09 bombilate, bombinate, go on and on, murmuring, scrounger, vibration
10 lazy person

drool
04 dote, gush
06 drivel, slaver
07 dribble, enthuse, slobber
08 salivate
11 slobber over
15 water at the mouth

droop
03 bow, sag
04 bend, drop, flag, sink, wilt

05 faint, slump, stoop
06 dangle, falter, slouch, wither
08 fall down, hang down

drop
03 bit, dab, end, nip, sip, tad, tot
04 bead, blob, dash, dive, drip, fall, jilt, leak, omit, plop, quit, sack, sink, spot, stop, tear
05 abyss, chasm, chuck, ditch, droop, gutta, let go, lower, pinch, slope, slump, trace
06 bubble, disown, finish, forego, give up, goutte, lessen, little, plunge, reject, splash, tumble, weaken
07 abandon, cutback, decline, descend, descent, dismiss, droplet, dwindle, exclude, fall-off, forsake, globule, let fall, miss out, plummet, smidgen, trickle, turf out
08 decrease, downturn, globulet, leave out
09 declivity, precipice, reduction, terminate, throw over, walk out on
10 falling-off, relinquish, slacken off
11 devaluation, discontinue
12 depreciation, dispense with
13 make redundant

❑drop back
03 lag
07 retreat
08 fall back
09 lag behind
10 fall behind

❑drop in
04 call
05 pop in, visit
06 call by, come by
08 come over
09 call round, come round

❑drop off
04 doze, sink
06 catnap, hand in, lessen, nod off, snooze, unload
07 decline, deliver, deposit, dwindle, fall off, set down
08 decrease, drift off
10 fall asleep, slacken off
14 have forty winks

❑drop out
04 quit
05 leave
06 cry off, give up
07 abandon, back out, forsake
08 renounce, withdraw

❑drop out of
04 quit

05 leave
07 abandon, pull out
08 opt out of, renounce
09 back out of
10 cry off from
12 withdraw from

dropout
05 loner, rebel
06 hippie
07 deviant
08 Bohemian, renegade
09 dissenter
10 malcontent
11 dissentient
13 non-conformist

droppings
04 dung
06 egesta, faeces, manure, ordure, stools
07 excreta, spraint
09 excrement

dross
05 dregs, trash, waste
06 debris, refuse, scoria
07 remains, rubbish

drought
04 want
07 aridity, dryness
08 shortage
11 dehydration, desiccation

drove
03 mob
04 herd, host, pack
05 crowd, flock, horde, swarm
06 throng
09 gathering, multitude

drown
04 sink
05 flood, swamp
06 deluge, drench, engulf
07 go under, immerse, wipe out
08 inundate, overcome, submerge
09 overpower, overwhelm

drowsiness
06 torpor
08 dopiness, doziness, lethargy
09 oscitancy, weariness
10 sleepiness, somnolence

drowsy
04 dozy
05 dopey, tired, weary
06 dreamy, sleepy, torpid
07 nodding, yawning
09 lethargic, somnolent
10 half-asleep

drubbing
06 defeat
07 beating, licking

08 flogging, whipping
09 hammering, thrashing,
    trouncing, walloping

drudge
04 hack, plod, slog, toil, work
05 grind, slave
06 beaver, labour, lackey,
    menial, skivvy, toiler, worker
07 servant
08 dogsbody, factotum,
    labourer

drudgery
04 slog, toil
05 chore, grind, sweat
06 labour
07 slavery
09 skivvying
10 donkeywork, menial work
13 sweated labour

drug
04 cure, dope, dose, numb
06 potion, remedy, sedate
07 stupefy
08 knock out, medicine
10 medication
12 anaesthetize, tranquillize

► *Types of drug*:
03 LSD
04 acid, dope
05 crack, opium, smack, speed
06 downer, heroin, opiate,
    peyote, Valium®
07 aspirin, cocaine, codeine,
    ecstasy, insulin, quinine,
    steroid
08 cannabis, diazepam,
    laudanum, morphine,
    narcotic, sedative
09 analgesic, cortisone,
    digitalis, marijuana,
    oestrogen, stimulant
10 antibiotic, chloroform,
    penicillin
11 amphetamine, anaesthetic,
    barbiturate, paracetamol
12 progesterone
13 antihistamine, tranquillizer
14 antidepressant,
    hallucinogenic
➤ See also **medicine**

drug addict
04 head, user
05 freak
06 junkie
07 tripper
08 coke-head
09 dope-fiend, mainliner

drugged
04 high
05 doped

06 stoned, zonked
07 on a trip
09 spaced out, stupefied
10 knocked out

drum
03 rap, tap
04 beat
05 knock, throb, thrum
06 tattoo
07 pulsate

❏**drum into**
06 hammer, harp on, instil
07 din into
09 drive home, inculcate

❏**drum out**
05 expel
08 throw out
09 discharge

❏**drum up**
03 get
06 gather, obtain, summon
07 attract, canvass, collect,
    round up, solicit
08 petition

drunk
03 sot
04 lush, soak, wino
05 alkie, dipso, happy, merry,
    tight, tipsy, toper, woozy
06 blotto, bombed, boozer,
    canned, loaded, pissed,
    soused, stewed, stoned,
    tiddly, wasted
07 bevvied, drinker, drunken,
    legless, pickled, sloshed,
    smashed, sozzled, squiffy,
    tippler, tosspot, wrecked
08 bibulous, drunkard
09 alcoholic, paralytic,
    plastered, well-oiled
10 blind drunk, inebriated, piss
    artist
11 dipsomaniac, hard drinker,
    have had a few, intoxicated
12 drunk as a lord, heavy
    drinker, roaring drunk
13 under the table

drunkard
03 sot
04 lush, soak, wino
05 alkie, dipso, drunk, toper
06 boozer
07 drinker, tippler, tosspot
09 alcoholic
10 inebriated, piss artist
11 dipsomaniac, hard drinker
12 heavy drinker

drunken
05 boozy, drunk, merry
07 riotous, sloshed

09 crapulent, debauched
11 baccanalian, intoxicated

drunkenness
09 inebriety, tipsiness
10 alcoholism, crapulence,
    debauchery, insobriety
11 inebriation
12 bibulousness, intoxication

dry
04 arid, dull, flat, wilt
05 drain, droll, witty, xeric
06 barren, boring, dreary,
    ironic, subtle, wither
07 cutting, cynical, laconic,
    parched, shrivel, thirsty
08 rainless, scorched, withered
09 dehydrate, desiccate, dry as
    dust, sarcastic, wearisome
10 dehydrated, desiccated, dry
    as a bone, shrivelled
12 moistureless

❏**dry up**
04 fade, fail, stop
06 die out, shut up
09 disappear
11 come to an end, stop talking
15 forget your lines

dryness
06 thirst
07 aridity, drought
08 aridness
10 barrenness
11 dehydration, thirstiness

dual
04 twin
06 binary, double, paired
07 coupled, matched, twofold

dub
03 tag
04 call, name, term
05 label, style
06 bestow, confer
07 entitle
08 christen, nickname
09 designate

dubiety
05 doubt, qualm
08 mistrust
09 misgiving, suspicion
10 hesitation, indecision,
    scepticism
11 incertitude, uncertainty
12 doubtfulness

dubious
04 iffy
05 fishy, shady
06 shifty, unsure
07 obscure, suspect

duck

09 ambiguous, debatable, sceptical, uncertain
10 suspicious, unreliable
12 questionable
13 untrustworthy

duck

03 bob, dip, wet
04 bend, dive, drop, dunk, shun
05 avoid, dodge, douse, elude, evade, lower, shirk, souse, squat, stoop
06 crouch, plunge
07 bow down, immerse
08 sidestep, submerge
12 steer clear of, wriggle out of

➤ *Breeds of duck include*:

04 blue, musk, smee, smew, teal
05 eider, scaup
06 garrot, hareld, herald, runner, scoter, smeath, smeeth, wigeon
07 gadwall, mallard, muscovy, pintail, pochard, widgeon
08 baldpate, garganey, mandarin, oldsquaw, shelduck
09 Aylesbury, golden-eye, goosander, harlequin, shellduck, sheldrake, shieldduck, shoveller
10 canvasback, shelldrake

➤ See also **animal**; **bird**

duct

04 pipe, tube
05 canal
06 funnel, vessel
07 channel, conduit, passage

ductile

06 pliant
07 plastic, pliable
08 amenable, biddable, flexible, yielding
09 compliant, malleable, tractable
10 manageable, refractory

dud

04 bust, duff, flop
05 kaput
06 broken, failed
07 failure, washout
08 nugatory
09 valueless, worthless

due

03 fee
04 dead, levy, owed
05 ample, owing, right
06 charge, direct, enough, merits, proper, rights, unpaid
07 charges, correct, deserts, fitting, merited, payable

08 adequate, deserved, expected, plenty of, required, rightful, straight, suitable
09 in arrears, justified, privilege, requisite, scheduled
10 birthright, sufficient
11 anticipated, appropriate, come-uppance, just deserts, long-awaited, outstanding, prerogative
12 contribution, subscription
13 membership fee

❏ **due to**

07 owing to
08 caused by
09 because of
11 as a result of

duel

05 clash, fight
06 battle, combat
07 contest, rivalry
10 engagement
11 competition
14 affair of honour

duffer

03 oaf
04 clod, clot, dolt, fool
05 idiot
06 dimwit
08 bonehead
09 blunderer, ignoramus

dulcet

04 soft
05 sweet
06 gentle, mellow
08 pleasant, soothing
09 agreeable, melodious
10 harmonious
11 mellifluous
13 sweet-sounding

dull

03 dim
04 dark, drab, drug, dumb, fade, flat, grey, idle, matt, mild, numb, slow, weak
05 allay, bland, blunt, dense, faint, heavy, inert, murky, muted, plain, thick
06 boring, cloudy, dampen, darken, deaden, dismal, dreary, feeble, gloomy, leaden, lessen, reduce, sadden, soften, sombre, stupid, subdue, torpid
07 assuage, humdrum, insipid, muffled, obscure, relieve, stupefy, tedious, wash out
08 decrease, diminish, edgeless, inactive, lifeless, mitigate,

moderate, overcast, tiresome, tone down
09 alleviate, lethargic, ponderous, wearisome
10 indistinct, lacklustre, monotonous, pedestrian, uneventful, unexciting
11 stereotyped, stultifying, troublesome, unsharpened
13 unimaginative, uninteresting
15 slow on the uptake

dullard

03 oaf
04 clod, clot, dolt, dope
05 chump, dunce, idiot, moron
06 dimwit, nitwit
08 bonehead, imbecile
09 blockhead, simpleton
10 dunderhead

dullness

06 tedium, torpor
07 dryness, vacuity
08 flatness, monotony, slowness, vapidity
10 dreariness
12 sluggishness

duly

05 fitly
08 properly, suitably
09 correctly, fittingly
10 decorously, deservedly, rightfully, sure enough
11 accordingly, befittingly
13 appropriately

dumb

03 mum
04 mute
05 dense, thick
06 shtoom, silent, stupid
07 foolish
08 gormless
09 brainless, dim-witted
10 speechless, tongue-tied
12 inarticulate, lost for words
13 unintelligent, without speech

dumbfounded

04 dumb
06 amazed, thrown
07 baffled, floored, stunned
08 overcome, startled
09 astounded, paralysed, staggered
10 astonished, bewildered, bowled over, confounded, gobsmacked, nonplussed, speechless, taken aback
11 overwhelmed
12 lost for words
13 flabbergasted

dummy
03 oaf
04 clot, copy, fake, fool, form, mock, sham, teat
05 bogus, chump, false, idiot, model, trial
06 dimwit, figure, nitwit
08 numskull, pacifier, practice
09 blockhead, imitation, lay-figure, mannequin
10 artificial, substitute

dump
03 tip
04 drop, mess, park, slum
05 chuck, ditch, hovel, joint, leave, place, plonk, scrap
06 pigsty, tip out, unload
07 abandon, deposit, discard, forsake, let fall, offload, pour out, put down
08 empty out, get rid of, jettison, junkyard, throw out
09 chuck away, discharge, dispose of, fling down, scrapyard, throw away
11 rubbish heap

□ **down in the dumps**
03 low, sad
04 blue
07 unhappy
08 dejected, downcast
09 depressed, miserable
10 dispirited, melancholy
11 downhearted

dumpy
05 plump, podgy, pudgy, short, squab, squat, stout, tubby
06 chubby, chunky, stubby

dun
04 dull
05 dingy
11 mud-coloured
12 greyish-brown

dunce
04 fool, nerd, twit
05 idiot, ninny, twerp, wally
06 dimwit, nitwit
08 bonehead, dipstick, imbecile, numskull
09 blockhead
10 nincompoop

dung
06 faeces, manure, ordure
07 spraint
09 droppings, excrement
11 animal waste

dungeon
04 cage, cell, gaol, jail, keep
05 vault

06 lock-up, prison
09 oubliette

dupe
03 con, mug
04 fool, gull, hoax, pawn
05 cheat, trick
06 delude, outwit, rip off, stooge, sucker, take in, victim
07 deceive, defraud, swindle
08 hoodwink, push-over
09 bamboozle, simpleton

duplicate
03 fax
04 copy, echo, mate, twin
05 clone, model, Xerox®
06 carbon, double, paired, repeat, ringer
07 do again, forgery, matched, replica, twofold
08 matching
09 facsimile, identical, lookalike, photocopy, replicate, reproduce
10 carbon copy, dead ringer
12 reproduction
13 spitting image

duplication
04 copy
05 clone
07 cloning, copying
08 doubling
09 photocopy
10 gemination, repetition
11 dittography, replication
12 photocopying, reproduction

duplicity
05 fraud, guile
06 deceit
07 perfidy
08 artifice, betrayal
09 chicanery, deception, falsehood, hypocrisy, mendacity, treachery
10 dishonesty
13 dissimulation, double-dealing

durability
08 strength
09 constancy, endurance, longevity, stability
10 permanence
11 durableness, lastingness
15 imperishability

durable
04 fast, firm
05 fixed, solid, sound, tough
06 robust, stable, strong, sturdy
07 abiding, lasting

08 constant, enduring, reliable
09 heavy-duty, permanent
11 hard-wearing, long-lasting

duration
04 span, time
05 spell
06 extent, length, period
07 stretch
08 fullness, time span
09 time scale
12 continuation, length of time

duress
05 force
06 threat
08 coercion, exaction, pressure
10 compulsion, constraint
11 arm-twisting, enforcement

during
02 in
10 throughout
11 all the while, at the time of
13 in the course of

dusk
05 gloom, shade
06 sunset
07 evening, shadows, sundown
08 darkness, gloaming, twilight
09 nightfall

dusky
03 dim
04 dark, hazy
05 black, brown, murky
06 cloudy, gloomy, twilit
07 shadowy, subfusc, swarthy
09 tenebrous
10 fuliginous
11 crepuscular, dark-skinned

dust
04 clay, dirt, grit, smut, soil, soot, wipe
05 clean, cover, earth, spray
06 ground, powder, spread
08 sprinkle
09 particles

dust-up
05 brawl, brush, fight, scrap
06 fracas, tussle
07 punch-up, quarrel, scuffle
08 argument, conflict, skirmish
09 argy-bargy, commotion
11 disturbance

dusty
05 dirty, grimy, sandy, sooty
06 chalky, filthy, grubby
07 crumbly, friable, powdery

dutiful
06 filial
08 obedient
10 respectful, submissive

11 deferential, reverential
13 conscientious

duty
03 job, tax
04 dues, levy, onus, part, role, task, toll, work
05 charge, excise, tariff
07 calling, customs, loyalty, mission, respect, service
08 business, fidelity, function
10 allegiance, obligation
11 requirement
12 faithfulness
14 responsibility

⊃off duty
03 off
04 free
07 off work, resting
09 on holiday

⊃on duty
06 active, at work, on call
07 engaged, working

dwarf
04 baby, mini, tiny
05 check, gnome, pygmy, small, stunt
06 goblin, midget, pocket
07 atrophy, stunted
08 dominate, Tom Thumb
09 miniature, tower over
10 diminutive, overshadow, undersized
11 Lilliputian

dwell
04 live, rest, stay
05 abide, lodge
06 people, reside, settle
07 hang out, inhabit
08 populate

⊃dwell on
07 brood on
09 elaborate, emphasize, expatiate, reflect on
10 linger over, meditate on

dweller
07 denizen
08 occupant, occupier, resident
10 inhabitant

dwelling
03 hut
04 home, tent
05 abode, house, lodge
06 shanty
07 cottage, lodging
08 domicile, quarters
09 residence
10 habitation
13 dwelling-house, establishment

dwindle
03 ebb
04 fade, fall, wane
06 die out, lessen, shrink, vanish, weaken, wither
07 decline, subside, tail off
08 decrease, diminish, grow less, peter out, taper off
09 disappear, waste away

dye
03 hue
04 tint, wash
05 imbue, shade, stain, tinge
06 colour
07 pigment

▶ *Dyes include*:
04 anil, wald, weld, woad
05 chica, eosin, henna, mauve
06 anatto, archil, corkir, flavin, fustic, indigo, kamala, korkir, madder, orchil
07 alkanet, annatto, azurine, cudbear, flavine, magenta, mauvein, mauvine, para-red, saffron
08 amaranth, fuchsine, mauveine, orchella, safranin, turnsole
09 cochineal, nigrosine, primuline, safranine, Saxon blue, Turkey red, Tyrian red
10 tartrazine, Saxony blue
12 Tyrian purple
➤ See also **colour**; **pigment**

dyed-in-the-wool
05 fixed
07 die-hard, settled

08 complete, hard-core, hardened, thorough
09 confirmed
10 deep-rooted, entrenched, inveterate, unshakable
12 card-carrying, long-standing, unchangeable

dying
05 final, going
06 ebbing, fading, mortal
07 failing, passing
08 deathbed, moribund
12 at death's door
14 on your last legs

dynamic
05 vital
06 active, lively, potent, strong
07 driving, go-ahead
08 forceful, magnetic, powerful, spirited, vigorous
09 energetic, go-getting
11 high-powered
12 full of energy

dynamism
02 go
03 pep, vim, zap, zip
04 push
05 drive
06 energy, vigour
07 pizzazz
10 enterprise, get-up-and-go, initiative, liveliness
12 forcefulness

dynasty
04 line, rule
05 house
06 empire, regime
09 authority
10 government, succession
11 sovereignty

dyspeptic
05 testy
06 crabby, gloomy, touchy
07 crabbed, grouchy, peevish
08 snappish
09 crotchety
10 indigested
11 bad-tempered
13 short-tempered

each
05 every
06 apiece, singly
07 each one, per head
09 per capita, per person
12 individually, respectively
15 every individual

eager
04 avid, keen
06 ardent, hungry, intent
07 earnest, thirsty, zealous
08 diligent, yearning
09 impatient
12 enthusiastic, wholehearted

eagerly
06 avidly, keenly
08 ardently, greedily, intently
09 earnestly, zealously
11 impatiently
14 wholeheartedly

eagerness
04 zeal
06 ardour, hunger, thirst
07 avidity, fervour, longing
08 fervency, keenness, yearning
09 fervidity
10 enthusiasm, impatience
11 earnestness, impetuosity

ear
05 skill, taste
07 ability, hearing
10 perception
11 sensitivity
12 appreciation
14 discrimination

► *Parts of the ear*:
04 lobe
05 anvil, helix, incus, pinna
06 concha, hammer, stapes, tragus
07 auricle, cochlea, eardrum, malleus, stirrup
08 tympanum
09 labyrinth, vestibule
13 auditory canal, auditory nerve
14 eustachian tube

❏ play it by ear
05 ad-lib
09 improvise
11 extemporize

early
05 first
06 at dawn
07 ancient, initial, opening
08 advanced, primeval
09 premature, primitive
10 beforehand, in good time, precocious, primordial
11 ahead of time, prematurely
13 autochthonous
15 ahead of schedule

earmark
03 tag
05 label
07 mark out, reserve
08 put aside, set aside
09 designate

earn
03 get, net, win
04 draw, gain, make, rate, reap
05 clear, gross, merit
06 attain, be paid, pocket
07 achieve, bring in, deserve, get paid, receive, warrant
08 take home

earnest
04 firm, keen
05 eager, grave, token, truth
06 intent, solemn, steady
07 deposit, devoted, fervent, intense, promise, serious, sincere, zealous
08 resolute, security
09 assurance, committed, dedicated, guarantee, heartfelt, sincerity
10 resolution, thoughtful
11 down payment, seriousness

❏ in earnest
07 genuine, serious, sincere
08 ardently, intently, steadily
09 not joking, seriously
10 resolutely
14 wholeheartedly
15 conscientiously

earnestly
06 firmly, keenly, warmly
07 eagerly
08 intently

09 seriously, sincerely, zealously
10 resolutely

earnestness
04 zeal
06 ardour, warmth
08 devotion, keenness
09 eagerness, sincerity
10 enthusiasm, resolution
11 seriousness

earnings
03 fee, pay
05 wages
06 income, reward, salary
07 profits, revenue, stipend
08 gross pay, proceeds, receipts
09 emolument
10 honorarium
12 remuneration

earth
03 orb, sod
04 clay, dirt, land, loam, soil, turf
05 globe, humus, world
06 ground, planet, sphere

earthenware
04 pots
07 pottery
08 ceramics, crockery
09 stoneware

earthly
05 human
06 likely, mortal
07 fleshly, sensual, worldly
08 feasible, material, physical, possible, telluric, temporal
10 imaginable
11 conceivable, terrestrial

earthquake
05 quake, seism, shake
06 tremor
07 seismal, seismic
10 aftershock
11 earth-tremor, terremotive

earthy
04 blue, rude
05 bawdy, crude, rough
06 coarse, ribald, robust, vulgar
07 natural, raunchy
11 down-to-earth, uninhibited
15 unsophisticated

ease
04 edge, inch, rest
05 abate, allay, guide, peace, quiet, relax, salve, steer
06 lessen, reduce, relent, repose, smooth, soothe
07 assuage, comfort, leisure, lighten, quieten, relieve
08 deftness, diminish, facility, grow less, mitigate
09 alleviate, happiness
10 adroitness, ameliorate, bed of roses, facilitate, prosperity, relaxation
11 contentment, lap of luxury, life of Riley, naturalness
14 effortlessness

❑**at ease**
04 calm
06 at home, secure
07 relaxed, natural
11 comfortable

❑**ease off**
04 wane
05 abate
06 relent
07 die down, slacken, subside
08 decrease, diminish
10 become less

easily
04 well
05 by far
06 simply, surely
07 clearly, readily
09 certainly
10 definitely, far and away
11 comfortably, undoubtedly
12 effortlessly, indisputably

easy
04 calm
05 cushy
06 a cinch, casual, simple
07 a doddle, natural, relaxed
08 informal, laid-back
09 a pushover, easy as ABC, foolproof, leisurely
10 child's play, effortless
11 comfortable, undemanding
12 a piece of cake
15 straightforward

easy-going
04 calm
06 placid, serene
07 lenient, relaxed
08 amenable, carefree, laid-back, tolerant
10 insouciant, nonchalant
12 happy-go-lucky

eat
04 chew, dine, feed

05 decay, erode, graze, lunch, munch, scoff, snack
06 devour, gobble, ingest
07 consume, corrode, swallow
08 bolt down, dissolve, wear away, wolf down
09 breakfast, partake of

eatable
04 good
06 edible
09 palatable, wholesome

eavesdrop
03 bug, spy, tap
05 snoop
08 listen in, overhear

eavesdropper
03 spy
05 snoop
07 monitor, snooper
08 listener

ebb
04 drop, fall, flag, sink, wane
05 abate, decay, go out
06 lessen, recede, weaken
07 decline, dwindle, low tide, retreat, slacken, subside
08 decrease, diminish, fade away, fall back, flow back, going out, low water
09 dwindling, lessening, retrocede, weakening
10 degenerate, slackening

ebony
03 jet
04 dark
05 black, jetty, sable, sooty
08 jet-black

ebullience
04 zest
07 elation
08 buoyancy, vivacity
10 brightness, enthusiasm, excitement, exuberance
11 high spirits
12 effusiveness, exhilaration

ebullient
06 breezy, bright, chirpy, elated
07 buoyant, excited, zestful
09 exuberant, vivacious
11 exhilarated
12 effervescent, enthusiastic
13 irrepressible

eccentric
03 nut, odd
04 case, geek, kook
05 crank, kooky, loony, loopy, nutty, queer, wacky, weird
06 oddity, quirky, way-out

07 bizarre, erratic, odd fish, oddball, off-beat, strange
08 aberrant, abnormal, freakish, peculiar, singular
09 character
13 idiosyncratic, nonconformist
14 unconventional

eccentricity
05 quirk
06 oddity
07 anomaly
09 weirdness
10 aberration
11 abnormality, peculiarity, singularity, strangeness
12 freakishness, idiosyncrasy
13 nonconformity

ecclesiastic
04 dean
05 canon, padre, vicar
06 cleric, curate, deacon, father, parson, pastor, priest, rector
08 chaplain, man of God, minister, reverend
09 churchman, clergyman, deaconess, presbyter
10 woman of God
11 churchwoman, clergywoman
13 man of the cloth
15 woman of the cloth

ecclesiastical
04 holy
06 church, divine
08 churchly, clerical, priestly
09 religious, spiritual
10 sacerdotal

echelon
04 rank, rung, tier
05 grade, level, place
06 degree, status
08 position

echo
04 copy, hint, ring
05 clone, image, mimic, trace
06 memory, parrot, repeat
07 imitate, reflect, resound
08 allusion, reminder, resemble
09 duplicate, evocation, reiterate, reproduce
10 reflection, repetition
11 reiteration, reverberate
12 reproduction

éclat
04 fame, show
05 glory
06 effect, lustre, renown
07 acclaim, display, success

08 applause, approval, plaudits
09 celebrity, splendour
10 brilliance
11 acclamation, distinction

eclectic
05 broad
06 varied
07 diverse, general, liberal
08 catholic
09 many-sided, selective
11 diversified, wide-ranging
12 all-embracing, multifarious
13 heterogeneous

eclipse
03 dim, ebb
04 fall, loss, veil
05 cloud, cover, dwarf, outdo
06 darken, exceed, shroud
07 blot out, conceal, decline, dimming, failure, obscure, shading, surpass, veiling
09 darkening, transcend
10 concealing, overshadow
11 blotting-out, obscuration
13 overshadowing
15 cast a shadow over, put into the shade

economic
05 trade
06 fiscal, viable
08 business, monetary
09 budgetary, financial
10 commercial,, profitable
11 money-making
12 profit-making, remunerative
13 cost-effective

economical
05 cheap
06 budget, frugal, modest
07 low-cost, sparing, thrifty
08 skimping
09 efficient, low-budget, low-priced, scrimping
10 reasonable
11 inexpensive
13 cost-effective

economize
04 save
06 budget
07 cut back, use less
08 cut costs, retrench
10 buy cheaply, cut corners
13 scrimp and save
14 cut expenditure
15 tighten your belt

economy
04 care
06 saving, thrift
08 prudence, skimping

09 husbandry, parsimony, restraint, scrimping
10 providence
11 carefulness
15 financial system

➤ *Names of economists*:
04 **Ward** (Dame Barbara), **Webb** (Sidney)
05 **Meade** (James Edward), **Smith** (Adam), **Solow** (Robert Merton), **Tobin** (James)
06 **Cobden** (Richard), **Cripps** (Sir Stafford), **Debreu** (Gerard), **Erhard** (Ludwig), **Frisch** (Ragnar), **Keynes** (John Maynard), **Myrdal** (Gunnar), **Tawney** (Richard Henry)
07 **Bagehot** (Walter), **Kuznets** (Simon), **Malthus** (Thomas Robert), **Ricardo** (David), **Toynbee** (Arnold)
08 **Friedman** (Milton), **Mirrlees** (James), **Schiller** (Karl)
09 **Beveridge** (William, Lord), **Galbraith** (John Kenneth), **Tinbergen** (Jan)
➤ See also **scientist**

ecstasy
03 joy
05 bliss
07 elation, fervour, rapture
08 euphoria, pleasure
10 exultation, jubilation

ecstatic
06 elated, joyful
07 fervent
08 blissful, euphoric, jubilant
09 delirious, overjoyed, rapturous, rhapsodic
10 enraptured
11 high as a kite, on cloud nine, over the moon, tickled pink
13 jumping for joy
15 in seventh heaven

eddy
05 swirl, twist, whirl
06 vortex
08 swirling
09 maelstrom, whirlpool

edge
03 lip, rim
04 bite, brim, inch, line, side
05 brink, crawl, creep, elbow, limit, sidle, steal, sting, verge
06 border, fringe, margin
07 outline

08 acerbity, boundary, frontier, keenness, severity
09 advantage, dominance, extremity, perimeter, periphery, sharpness, threshold, upper hand
10 ascendancy, outer limit
11 pick your way, superiority

❏ on edge
04 edgy
05 nervy, tense
06 touchy
07 keyed-up, nervous, uptight
09 ill at ease, irritable
12 apprehensive

edgy
05 nervy, tense
06 on edge, touchy
07 anxious, keyed-up, nervous, uptight
09 ill at ease, irritable

edible
04 good
07 eatable
08 fit to eat, harmless
10 comestible, digestible

edict
03 act, law
04 fiat, rule
05 order, ukase
06 decree, ruling
07 command, mandate, statute
10 injunction, regulation
12 proclamation
13 pronouncement

edification
08 guidance, teaching
09 education, uplifting
11 improvement, instruction
13 enlightenment

edifice
08 building, erection
09 structure
12 construction

edify
05 coach, guide, teach, tutor
06 inform, school, uplift
07 educate, improve, nurture
08 instruct
09 enlighten

edit
05 adapt, check, emend
06 modify, redact, revise, select
07 compile, correct, reorder
08 annotate, rephrase
09 rearrange
10 blue pencil

edition
04 copy

05 issue
06 number, volume
07 version
08 printing
10 impression
11 publication

educable
09 teachable, trainable
12 instructible

educate
05 coach, drill, edify, prime, teach, train, tutor
06 inform, school
07 develop, improve, prepare
08 instruct
09 enlighten, inculcate
12 indoctrinate

educated
04 wise
06 brainy, taught
07 erudite, learned, refined, trained, tutored
08 cultured, informed, lettered, literate, schooled, well-read
10 cultivated, instructed
11 enlightened
13 knowledgeable

education
07 letters, nurture, tuition
08 coaching, drilling, guidance, teaching, training, tutoring
09 knowledge, schooling
10 upbringing
11 development, edification, improvement, inculcation, instruction, scholarship
13 enlightenment
14 indoctrination

educational
08 academic, cultural, didactic, edifying, learning, teaching
09 educative, pedagogic
10 scholastic
11 informative, instructive, pedagogical
12 enlightening

educative
08 didactic, edifying
09 improving
11 catechismal, catechistic, informative, instructive
12 enlightening
13 catechistical

educator
05 coach, tutor
07 teacher, trainer
08 academic, lecturer
09 pedagogue, professor
10 instructor

12 schoolmaster
13 schoolteacher
14 schoolmistress

eerie
05 scary, weird
06 creepy, spooky
07 ghostly, strange, uncanny
09 unearthly, unnatural
10 mysterious
11 frightening
13 spine-chilling

efface
05 erase
06 cancel, delete, excise, remove, rub out
07 blot out, expunge, wipe out
08 blank out, cross out
09 eradicate, extirpate
10 obliterate

effect
04 gear, make
05 cause, drift, force, fruit, goods, issue, power, stuff
06 create, fulfil, impact, import, result, things, upshot
07 achieve, baggage, execute, luggage, outcome, perform, produce
08 carry out, chattels, complete, efficacy, generate, initiate, property, strength
09 aftermath, influence
10 accomplish, belongings, bring about, conclusion, give rise to, impression
11 consequence, possessions
12 significance
13 accoutrements, paraphernalia

◻**in effect**
06 in fact, really
07 in truth
08 actually
09 in reality, virtually
10 in practice
11 effectively, essentially
12 in actual fact

◻**take effect**
04 work
05 begin
08 function
11 become valid, be effective
13 come into force
15 become operative

effective
05 valid
06 active, actual, potent
07 capable, current, in force
08 adequate, powerful, striking
09 efficient, operative

10 attractive, convincing, impressive, persuasive, productive, successful
11 efficacious, functioning

effectiveness
03 use
05 clout, force, power
07 cogency, potency, success
08 efficacy, strength, validity
09 influence
10 capability, efficiency

effectual
05 legal, sound, valid
06 lawful, useful
07 binding, capable
08 forcible, powerful
09 effective, operative
10 productive, successful

effeminate
05 sissy
07 unmanly, wimpish, womanly
08 delicate, feminine

effervesce
04 boil, fizz, foam
05 froth
06 bubble
07 ferment, sparkle
09 ebullient

effervescence
04 fizz, foam, zing
05 froth
07 bubbles, ferment, foaming
08 bubbling, buoyancy, frothing, vitality, vivacity
09 animation
10 ebullience, excitement, exuberance, liveliness
11 excitedness, high spirits
12 exhilaration, fermentation

effervescent
05 fizzy, vital
06 bubbly, frothy, lively
07 excited, fizzing, foaming
08 animated, bubbling
09 ebullient, exuberant, sparkling, vivacious
10 carbonated, fermenting

effete
04 weak
05 spent
06 barren, feeble, wasted
07 corrupt, debased, decayed, drained, sterile, worn out
08 decadent, decrepit
09 enervated, enfeebled, exhausted, fruitless
10 degenerate, unfruitful
12 unproductive

efficacious
06 active, potent, strong, useful
07 capable
08 adequate, powerful
09 competent, effective, effectual, operative
10 productive, successful

efficacy
03 use
05 force, power
06 effect, energy, virtue
07 ability, potency, success
08 strength
09 influence
10 capability, usefulness
13 effectiveness

efficiency
05 skill
07 ability
09 expertise
10 capability, competence
11 proficiency, skilfulness
13 effectiveness

efficient
04 able
07 capable, skilful, well-run
08 powerful
09 competent, effective
10 productive, proficient
11 streamlined, well-ordered
12 businesslike, rationalized
13 well-organized

effigy
03 guy
04 icon, idol
05 dummy, image
06 figure, statue
07 carving, picture
08 likeness, portrait
14 representation

effluent
05 waste
06 efflux, sewage
07 outflow
08 emission
09 discharge, emanation, pollutant, pollution

effort
02 go
03 try
04 bash, beef, deed, feat, opus, shot, stab, toil, work
05 crack, force, power, sweat
06 energy, labour, strain, stress
07 attempt, travail, trouble
08 creation, exertion, hard work, striving, struggle
09 endeavour

11 application, elbow grease, muscle power
15 sweat of your brow

effortless
04 easy
06 facile, simple, smooth
08 painless
11 undemanding

effrontery
03 lip
04 face, gall
05 brass, cheek, nerve
08 audacity, boldness, chutzpah, temerity
09 arrogance, brashness, impudence, insolence
10 brazenness, cheekiness
11 presumption
12 impertinence

effulgent
07 glowing, radiant, shining
09 brilliant, refulgent
11 resplendent
12 incandescent

effusion
04 gush
07 outflow
08 outburst, voidance
09 discharge, effluence
10 outpouring

effusive
03 OTT
05 gabby, gassy
07 fulsome, gushing, profuse
08 all mouth
09 expansive, exuberant, rhapsodic, talkative
10 big-mouthed, unreserved
11 extravagant, overflowing
12 enthusiastic, unrestrained
13 demonstrative

egg
❏ **egg on**
04 coax, goad, push, spur, urge
06 exhort, incite, prompt
08 talk into
09 encourage, stimulate

egghead
05 brain
06 boffin, genius
07 know-all, scholar, thinker
08 academic, Einstein
09 intellect, know-it-all
12 intellectual

ego
04 self
08 identity
09 self-image, self-worth
10 self-esteem

14 self-confidence, self-importance

egoism
07 egotism
08 egomania, self-love
10 narcissism, self-regard
11 amour-propre, selfishness
12 self-interest
13 egocentricity
14 self-absorption, self-importance
15 self-centredness

egoist
07 egotist
09 egomaniac
10 narcissist, self-seeker

egoistic
09 egotistic
10 egocentric, egoistical
11 egomaniacal, egotistical, self-centred, self-seeking
12 narcissistic, self-absorbed
13 self-important

egotism
05 pride, swank
06 egoism, vanity
08 egomania, self-love
10 narcissism, self-regard
11 braggadocio, selfishness
12 boastfulness
13 bigheadedness, conceitedness, egocentricity
14 self-admiration, self-importance
15 self-centredness

egotist
06 egoist
07 bighead, boaster, show-off
08 big mouth, braggart
09 egomaniac, smart alec
10 clever dick
11 braggadocio, self-admirer

egotistic
04 vain
05 proud
07 selfish
08 boasting, bragging, egoistic
09 bigheaded, conceited
10 egocentric
11 self-centred
12 narcissistic, self-admiring
13 self-important

egregious
04 rank
05 gross
06 arrant
07 glaring, heinous
08 flagrant, infamous, shocking
09 monstrous, notorious

egress

10 outrageous, scandalous
11 intolerable
12 insufferable

egress

04 exit, vent
06 escape, outlet, way out
07 leaving
09 departure, emergence

ejaculate

03 cry
04 call, come, emit, yell
05 blurt, shout, spurt, utter
06 cry out, scream
07 call out, exclaim, release
08 blurt out, shout out
09 discharge

ejaculation

03 cry
04 call, yell
05 shout, spurt
06 climax, coming, orgasm
08 ejection, emission
09 discharge, expulsion
11 exclamation

eject

04 emit, fire, oust, sack, spew
05 evict, expel, exude, spout
06 banish, deport, get out,
   propel, remove
07 boot out, dismiss, excrete,
   kick out, release, turn out
08 chuck out, disgorge, drive
   out, get rid of, throw out
09 discharge, thrust out

ejection

05 exile
06 firing
07 ousting, removal, sacking
08 eviction
09 discharge, expulsion
10 banishment
11 deportation

eke

❏**eke out**

05 add to, get by
06 scrape
07 scratch, spin out, stretch
13 scrimp and save

elaborate

05 exact, fancy, fussy, showy
06 ornate, refine, rococo
07 amplify, complex, develop,
   enhance, explain, improve
08 detailed, expand on, flesh
   out, involved, laboured
09 decorated, enlarge on,
   expatiate, extensive,
   intricate, perfected
11 complicated, extravagant

élan

04 brio, dash, zest
05 flair, oomph, style, verve
06 esprit, spirit, vigour
07 panache, pizzazz
08 flourish, vivacity
10 confidence, liveliness

elapse

04 go by, go on, pass
05 lapse
06 slip by

elastic

04 easy
05 fluid
06 bouncy, pliant, supple
07 buoyant, plastic, pliable,
   rubbery, springy
08 flexible, stretchy, yielding
09 adaptable, compliant
10 adjustable
13 accommodating

elasticity

04 give
06 bounce
07 stretch
09 tolerance
10 plasticity, pliability,
   resilience, suppleness
11 flexibility, springiness
12 adaptability, stretchiness
13 adjustability

elated

06 joyful, joyous
07 excited
08 blissful, ecstatic, euphoric,
   exultant, jubilant
09 delighted, overjoyed,
   rapturous, rhapsodic
11 exhilarated, on cloud nine,
   over the moon

elation

03 joy
04 glee
05 bliss
07 delight, ecstasy, rapture
08 euphoria
10 exultation, joyfulness,
   joyousness, jubilation
11 high spirits
12 exhilaration

elbow

04 bump, push
05 barge, knock, nudge, shove
08 shoulder

elbow-room

04 play, room
05 scope, space
06 leeway
07 freedom

elder

05 older
06 senior
09 first-born

elderly

03 old
04 aged, OAPs
05 aging, hoary
06 oldies, past it, senile
09 senescent, wrinklies
10 grey-haired, pensioners
11 older adults, over the hill
13 retired people
14 long in the tooth, senior
   citizens
15 older generation

eldest

05 first
06 oldest
09 first-born

elect

04 pick, to be
05 adopt, elite
06 choice, choose, chosen, opt
   for, picked, prefer, select
07 appoint, vote for
08 decide on, plump for
09 cast a vote, designate
11 prospective

election

04 poll, vote
06 ballot, choice, voting
08 choosing, decision, hustings
09 selection
10 preference, referendum

elector

05 voter
10 electorate
11 constituent

electric

04 live
05 tense
07 charged, dynamic,
   powered, rousing
08 cordless, exciting, stirring
09 startling, thrilling
11 stimulating
12 electrifying

electrify

04 fire, jolt, stir
05 amaze, rouse, shock
06 charge, excite, thrill
07 animate, astound, stagger
08 astonish
09 galvanize, stimulate
10 invigorate

elegance
04 chic
05 grace, poise, style, taste
06 beauty, luxury, polish
07 dignity
08 grandeur
09 gentility, propriety
10 politeness, refinement
11 discernment, distinction
12 gracefulness, tastefulness
14 sophistication
15 fashionableness

elegant
04 chic, fine, neat
05 smart
06 lovely, modish, smooth
07 genteel, refined, stylish
08 delicate, graceful, handsome, polished, tasteful
09 beautiful, exquisite
10 cultivated
11 fashionable
13 sophisticated

elegiac
03 sad
07 doleful, keening
08 funereal, mournful
09 lamenting, plaintive, threnetic, threnodic
10 threnodial
11 melancholic, threnetical

elegy
05 dirge
06 lament, plaint
07 requiem
08 threnode, threnody
09 epicedial, epicedian
11 funeral poem, funeral song

element
04 hint, part, rain, wind
05 grain, piece, touch, trace
06 basics, clique, factor, member, storms, strand
07 faction, feature, weather
09 component, rudiments
10 essentials, individual, ingredient, principles
11 constituent, foundations, individuals, small amount
12 fundamentals

elemental
05 basic
07 immense, natural, radical
08 forceful, powerful
09 primitive
11 fundamental, rudimentary

elementary
04 easy
05 basic, clear
06 simple
07 primary
09 principal
11 fundamental, rudimentary
12 introductory
13 uncomplicated
15 straightforward

elephantine
04 huge, vast
05 bulky, heavy, large
06 clumsy
07 awkward, hulking, immense, massive, weighty
08 enormous
09 lumbering

elevate
04 lift
05 boost, exalt, hoist, raise
06 buoy up, hike up, uplift
07 advance, ennoble, gladden, magnify, promote, upgrade
08 brighten, heighten
10 aggrandize
15 move up the ladder

elevated
04 high
05 grand, great, lofty, noble
06 lifted, raised, rising
07 exalted, hoisted, sublime
08 advanced, lifted up, uplifted
09 dignified, important

elevation
04 hill, rise
05 leg-up, mound, mount
06 height
08 altitude, eminence, grandeur, nobility, tallness
09 loftiness, promotion, sublimity, upgrading
10 exaltation, preferment
11 advancement
14 aggrandizement
15 step up the ladder

elf
03 imp
04 puck
05 elfin, elvan, fairy, gnome
06 elfish, elvish, goblin, sprite
07 banshee, brownie
09 hobgoblin
10 leprechaun

elfin
05 small
06 elfish, impish, petite
07 elflike, playful, puckish
08 charming, delicate
09 sprightly
11 mischievous

elicit
05 educe, evoke, exact, wrest
06 derive, extort, obtain
07 draw out, extract, worm out
08 bring out

eligible
03 fit
06 proper, worthy
07 fitting
08 suitable
09 desirable, qualified
11 appropriate

eliminate
04 beat, do in, drop, kill, omit
05 expel
06 cut out, defeat, delete, hammer, murder, reject, remove, rub out, thrash
07 exclude, take out, wipe out
08 get rid of, stamp out
09 dispose of, disregard, eradicate, liquidate
10 do away with, extinguish, put a stop to, put an end to
11 exterminate
12 dispense with

elite
04 best, pick
05 cream, elect, noble
06 choice, gentry, jet set
08 nobility, selected
09 exclusive
10 first-class, upper-class
11 aristocracy, high society
12 aristocratic, upper classes
14 crème de la crème, pick of the bunch

elixir
05 syrup
06 potion, remedy
07 cure-all, essence, extract, mixture, nostrum, panacea
08 solution, tincture
11 concentrate
12 quintessence

elliptical
04 oval
05 ovoid, terse
07 concise, cryptic, laconic, obscure, oviform, ovoidal
08 abstruse
09 ambiguous, condensed, egg-shaped, recondite
12 concentrated

elocution
06 speech
07 diction, oratory
08 delivery, phrasing, rhetoric
11 enunciation
12 articulation

13 pronunciation
15 voice production

elongate
06 extend
07 draw out, prolong, stretch
08 lengthen, protract
10 make longer

elongated
04 long
08 extended
09 prolonged, stretched
10 lengthened, protracted

elope
04 bolt, flee
06 decamp, escape, run off
07 abscond, do a bunk, make off, run away
08 slip away

eloquence
07 blarney, fluency, oratory
08 facility, rhetoric
09 facundity, gassiness
11 flow of words
12 forcefulness, gift of the gab
14 articulateness, expressiveness

eloquent
05 vivid, vocal
06 fluent, moving
07 voluble
08 forceful, graceful, stirring
09 effective, plausible
10 articulate, persuasive
13 well-expressed

elsewhere
06 abroad, absent
07 not here, removed
12 another place
13 somewhere else

elucidate
06 fill in, unfold
07 clarify, clear up, explain
08 simplify, spell out
09 exemplify, explicate, interpret, make clear
10 illuminate, illustrate
11 shed light on, state simply
12 throw light on
13 give an example

elucidation
05 gloss
08 footnote
10 annotation, commentary, exposition, marginalia
11 explanation, explication
12 illumination, illustration
13 clarification
14 interpretation

elude
04 duck, flee, foil
05 avoid, dodge, evade, shirk
06 baffle, escape, thwart
08 confound, shake off
09 frustrate
10 circumvent
11 get away from

elusive
05 dodgy
06 shifty, subtle, tricky
07 evasive
08 baffling, puzzling, slippery
09 deceptive, transient
10 intangible, transitory
11 hard to catch, indefinable
15 difficult to find

emaciated
04 lean, thin
05 drawn, gaunt
06 meagre, skinny, wasted
07 haggard, pinched, scrawny
08 anorexic, skeletal
10 attenuated, cadaverous
11 thin as a rake
14 all skin and bone

emaciation
07 atrophy
08 leanness, thinness
09 gauntness
11 haggardness, scrawniness

emanate
04 come, emit, flow, stem
05 arise, issue
06 derive, emerge, spring
07 give off, give out, proceed, radiate, send out
09 discharge, originate

emanation
04 flow
06 efflux
08 effluent, effusion, emission
09 discharge, effluence, effluvium, radiation

emancipate
04 free
05 loose, untie
06 unyoke
07 deliver, manumit, release, set free, unchain
08 liberate, set loose, unfetter
09 discharge, unshackle

emancipation
07 freedom, liberty, release
10 liberation, unchaining
11 deliverance, manumission, setting free, unfettering
15 enfranchisement

emasculate
04 geld, spay
06 neuter, soften, weaken
07 cripple
08 castrate, enervate
10 debilitate, impoverish

embalm
05 store
06 lay out
07 cherish, mummify
08 conserve, enshrine, preserve, treasure

embankment
03 dam
05 levee
07 rampart
08 causeway
09 earthwork

embargo
03 ban, bar
04 stop
05 block, check, seize
06 impede
07 barrier, seizure
08 blockage, obstruct, prohibit, restrain, restrict, stoppage
09 hindrance, restraint
10 impediment
11 prohibition, restriction

embark
05 board
08 go aboard, take ship

◻**embark on**
05 begin, enter, start
07 enter on
08 commence, initiate, set about
09 undertake
10 launch into

embarrass
05 shame, upset
06 show up
07 confuse, fluster, mortify
08 distress
09 discomfit, humiliate
10 discompose, disconcert
14 discountenance

embarrassed
05 upset
06 guilty, shamed
07 abashed, ashamed, awkward, shown up
08 confused, sheepish
09 mortified
10 distressed, humiliated
11 discomfited
12 disconcerted
13 self-conscious, uncomfortable

embarrassing
06 touchy, tricky
07 awkward, painful, shaming
08 delicate, shameful
09 sensitive, upsetting
10 indelicate, mortifying
11 distressing, humiliating
12 compromising, discomfiting
13 disconcerting, uncomfortable

embarrassment
06 excess, pickle, plight, scrape
07 chagrin, dilemma, surplus
08 distress
09 confusion, profusion
10 constraint, difficulty
11 awkwardness, bashfulness, humiliation, predicament
12 discomfiture, discomposure
13 mortification
14 superabundance

embassy
07 mission
08 legation, ministry
09 consulate
10 delegation, deputation

embed
04 root, sink
05 drive, plant
06 hammer, insert
07 implant

embellish
04 deck, gild, trim
05 adorn, grace
06 bedeck, enrich
07 dress up, enhance, garnish
08 decorate, ornament
09 elaborate, embroider

embellishment
07 garnish, gilding
08 ornament, trimming
09 adornment
10 decoration, embroidery, enrichment
11 elaboration, enhancement
13 ornamentation

embers
05 ashes
07 cinders, residue

embezzle
05 filch, pinch, steal
06 pilfer, rip off
07 purloin, swindle
08 peculate
09 defalcate
11 appropriate
14 misappropriate

embezzlement
05 fraud, theft
08 filching, stealing
09 pilfering
11 defalcation
13 appropriation

embezzler
05 cheat, crook, fraud, thief
09 peculator
10 defalcator

embittered
04 sour
05 angry
06 bitter, piqued
09 resentful
11 disaffected, exasperated
12 disenchanted
13 disillusioned

emblazon
05 adorn, extol, paint
06 colour, depict, praise
07 glorify, publish, trumpet
08 decorate, ornament
09 embellish, publicize

emblem
04 logo, mark, sign
05 badge, crest, image, token
06 device, figure, symbol
08 insignia

emblematic
08 symbolic
10 figurative, symbolical
14 representative

embodiment
05 model
07 epitome, example
10 expression
11 incarnation, realization
13 manifestation
15 exemplification, personification

embody
06 take in, typify
07 combine, contain, include
08 manifest, stand for
09 exemplify, personify, represent, symbolize
11 incorporate

embolden
05 cheer, nerve, rouse
07 hearten, inflame, inspire
08 make bold, reassure, vitalize
09 encourage, make brave
10 invigorate, strengthen
13 give courage to

embrace
03 hug
04 hold, neck, span
05 clasp, cover, grasp
06 accept, clinch, take in
07 contain, include, involve, necking, squeeze, welcome
09 encompass
11 incorporate, take on board

embrocation
05 cream, salve
06 lotion
07 epithem
08 ointment

embroider
03 sew
06 colour, enrich, stitch
07 dress up, enhance, garnish
08 decorate
09 elaborate, embellish
10 exaggerate

embroidery
06 sewing
08 tapestry
10 needlework
11 needlepoint

▶ *Types of embroidery stitch*:
04 moss, stem, tent
05 chain, cross, satin
07 blanket, chevron, feather, running
08 fishbone, straight
09 half-cross, lazy-daisy
10 backstitch, French knot, longstitch
11 herringbone
12 long-and-short

embroil
05 mix up
06 enmesh
07 involve
08 draw into, entangle
09 catch up in, implicate

embryo
04 germ, root
06 basics, foetus
11 unborn child

embryonic
05 early
08 germinal, inchoate
09 beginning, incipient
11 rudimentary, undeveloped

emend
04 edit
05 alter, amend
06 polish, redact, refine, revise
07 correct, improve, rectify

emendation
07 editing
08 revision
09 amendment, redaction
10 alteration, correction
13 rectification

emerge

05 arise, issue
06 appear, crop up, turn up
07 come out, develop, emanate, proceed, surface
09 come forth, transpire
11 come to light, materialize
12 come into view

emergence

06 advent, coming
07 arrival
09 unfolding
11 appearance, disclosure
11 development, springing-up

emergency

06 back-up, crisis, danger, pickle, plight, scrape, strait
07 dilemma, reserve
08 accident, calamity, disaster, exigency, fall-back, hot water, quandary
10 difficulty, substitute
11 alternative, catastrophe

emergent

06 coming, rising
07 budding
08 emerging
10 developing

emetic

08 emetical, vomitary, vomitive, vomitory

emigrate

07 migrate
08 relocate, resettle
10 move abroad

emigration

06 exodus
07 journey, removal
09 departure, migration
10 relocation
12 expatriation, moving abroad

eminence

04 fame, note, rank
06 esteem, renown
08 prestige
09 celebrity, greatness
10 importance, notability, prominence, reputation
11 distinction, pre-eminence

eminent

05 grand, great
06 famous
07 notable
08 elevated, esteemed, renowned, superior
09 important, prominent, respected, well-known
10 celebrated, noteworthy
11 conspicuous, high-ranking, illustrious, prestigious
13 distinguished

eminently

04 very, well
06 highly
07 greatly, notably
08 signally
09 extremely
10 remarkably, strikingly
11 exceedingly, prominently
13 exceptionally, outstandingly

emissary

03 spy
05 agent, envoy, scout
07 courier
08 delegate
09 go-between, messenger
10 ambassador
12 intermediary
14 representative

emission

05 issue
07 release
08 ejection
09 diffusion, discharge, emanation, exudation, giving-out, radiation

emit

04 leak, ooze, shed, vent
05 eject, exude, issue
06 let out
07 diffuse, emanate, excrete, express, give off, produce, radiate, release, send out
08 throw out
09 discharge, send forth

emollient

03 oil
04 balm
05 cream, salve
06 lotion
07 calming, unguent
08 balsamic, lenitive, liniment, ointment, poultice, soothing
09 appeasing, assuaging, placatory, softening
10 mitigative, mollifying
11 moisturizer

emolument

03 fee, pay
05 wages
06 profit, return, reward, salary
07 benefit, payment, stipend
08 earnings
10 honorarium, recompense
12 compensation, remuneration

emotion

03 joy
04 fear, hate
05 anger, dread, grief, sense
06 ardour, sorrow, warmth
07 despair, ecstasy, feeling, fervour, passion, sadness
09 happiness, sensation, sentiment, vehemence
10 excitement

emotional

04 warm
05 fiery, moved, soppy
06 ardent, heated, loving, moving, roused, tender
07 emotive, feeling, fervent
08 exciting, stirring, touching
09 excitable, thrilling
10 hot-blooded, passionate
11 impassioned, sentimental, tear-jerking, tempestuous
12 enthusiastic, heart-warming, soul-stirring
13 demonstrative, temperamental

emotionless

04 cold, cool
05 blank
06 frigid, remote
07 distant, glacial
08 clinical, detached, toneless
09 impassive, unfeeling
10 phlegmatic
11 indifferent, unemotional
15 undemonstrative

emotive

06 touchy
09 sensitive
12 inflammatory
13 controversial

empathize

05 share
07 comfort, feel for, support
10 understand
12 identify with

emperor

04 tsar
05 ruler
06 kaiser, mikado, shogun
09 imperator, sovereign

► *Names of emperors. We have omitted the word* **emperor** *from names given in the following list but you may need to include this word as part of the solution to some crossword clues. The regnal numerals of individual emperors have also been omitted.*

03 Leo
04 John, Nero, Otho, Otto, Paul, Pu Yi

05 Akbar (the Great), Babur,
   Basil, Boris, Galba, Henry,
   Louis, Murad, Nerva, Pedro,
   Peter, Selim, Titus
06 Julian, Justin, Mehmet,
   Philip (the Arab), Trajan
07 Agustín (de Itúrbide),
   Akihito, Alamgir, Alexius,
   Charles (the Bald), Charles
   (the Fat), Gordian, Hadrian,
   Leopold, Lothair, Marcian,
   Severus
08 Augustus, Aurelius,
   Caligula, Claudius,
   Commodus, Constans,
   Domitian, Galerius,
   Hirohito, Honorius,
   Jahangir, Maximian,
   Napoleon, Nicholas,
   Süleyman, Tiberius, Valerian
09 Alexander, Antoninus,
   Aurangzeb, Caracalla,
   Carausius, Ferdinand,
   Frederick, Justinian,
   Maxentius, Montezuma,
   Sigismund, Vespasian,
   Vitellius
10 Andronicus, Diocletian,
   Elagabalus, Kublai Khan,
   Maximilian, Theodosius
11 Charlemagne, Constantine,
   Valentinian
12 Chandragupta,
   Heliogabalus
13 Antoninus Pius, Haile
   Selassie
14 Marcus Aurelius

► *Names of empresses. We*
have omitted the word **empress**
from names given in the
following list but you may need
to include this word as part of
the solution to some crossword
clues. The regnal numerals of
individual empresses have also
been omitted.
02 Lu, Wu
03 Zoë
04 Anna, Ci-xi
05 Irene, Livia
06 Helena (Saint)
08 Faustina, Theodora, Victoria
09 Alexandra, Catherine (the
   Great), Elizabeth, Joséphine
   (de Beauharnais),
   Kunigunde (Saint),
   Messalina
11 Marie Louise
12 Maria Theresa

emphasis
04 mark

05 force, power
06 accent, stress, weight
07 urgency
08 priority, strength
09 attention, intensity
10 importance, insistence
12 accentuation, underscoring

emphasize
06 accent, play up, stress
08 heighten, insist on
09 highlight, press home,
   spotlight, underline
10 accentuate, strengthen

emphatic
06 direct, marked, strong
07 certain, decided, earnest
08 definite, forceful, positive,
   powerful, striking, vigorous
09 energetic, insistent
10 pronounced, punctuated
11 categorical, distinctive,
   significant, unequivocal

empire
04 rule, sway
05 power, realm
06 domain
07 command, control, kingdom
08 dominion, province
09 authority, supremacy
11 sovereignty
12 commonwealth, jurisdiction

empirical
08 observed
09 practical, pragmatic
12 experiential, experimental

employ
03 ply, use
04 fill, hire
05 apply, exert
06 draw on, engage, enlist,
   occupy, retain, sign up, take
   on, take up
07 appoint, exploit, utilize
08 exercise, put to use
09 make use of
10 apprentice, commission
11 bring to bear

employed
04 busy
05 hired
06 active, in work
07 earning, engaged, working
08 occupied, with a job
12 in employment

employee
04 hand
06 worker
07 artisan
08 labourer

09 assistant, operative
10 wage-earner, working man
12 office worker, working
   woman
13 member of staff, working
   person

employer
04 boss, firm, head
05 owner
06 gaffer
07 company, manager, skipper
08 business, director
09 executive
10 management, proprietor
12 organization

employment
03 job
04 hire, line, work
05 craft, trade
06 employ, hiring, métier
07 calling, pursuit, service
08 business, vocation
09 signing-up, situation
10 occupation, profession

emporium
04 fair, mart, shop
05 store
06 bazaar, market

empower
05 equip
06 enable, permit
07 entitle, license, warrant
09 authorize
10 commission

emptiness
04 void
06 hiatus, hunger, vacuum
08 bareness, futility, voidness
10 desolation, hollowness
13 senselessness, worthlessness
15 meaninglessness,
   purposelessness

empty
03 gut
04 bare, free, idle, vain, void
05 blank, clear, drain, go out,
   inane, issue, leave, use up
06 barren, futile, hollow,
   unload, vacant, vacate
07 pour out, turn out, vacuous
08 deserted, desolate,
   evacuate, unfilled
09 available, discharge,
   fruitless, insincere,
   senseless, worthless
10 unoccupied
11 ineffective, ineffectual,
   meaningless, purposeless
14 expressionless
15 with nothing in it

empty-headed
04 daft
05 dopey, dotty, inane, silly
06 scatty, stupid
07 foolish
09 frivolous
14 feather-brained

emulate
04 copy, echo
05 match, mimic, rival
06 follow
07 imitate, vie with
15 model yourself on

emulation
06 strife
07 copying, mimicry, rivalry
08 matching
09 challenge, following, imitation

enable
04 help
05 allow, endue, equip
06 permit
07 empower, entitle, license, prepare, qualify, warrant
08 accredit, sanction, validate
09 authorize
10 commission, facilitate
12 make possible

enact
04 pass, play, rule
06 act out, decree, depict
07 command, make law, perform, portray
09 establish, legislate

enactment
03 act, law
04 bill, play, rule
06 acting, decree
07 command, passing, playing, staging, statute
09 ordinance, portrayal
10 performing, regulation
11 legislation, performance
12 ratification
14 representation

enamoured
07 charmed, smitten
09 entranced
10 captivated, enthralled, fascinated, in love with, infatuated

encampment
04 base, camp
05 tents
07 bivouac
08 campsite, quarters
13 camping-ground

encapsulate
05 sum up
06 digest, précis, take in, typify
07 capture, contain, include
08 compress, condense
09 epitomize, exemplify, represent, summarize

enchant
05 charm
07 attract, beguile, bewitch, delight, enamour, enthral
08 entrance
09 captivate, enrapture, fascinate, hypnotize, mesmerize, spellbind

enchanter
05 magus, witch
06 wizard
07 warlock
08 conjurer, magician, sorcerer
09 mesmerist
10 reim-kennar
11 necromancer, spellbinder

enchanting
06 lovely
08 alluring, charming, pleasant
09 appealing, endearing, ravishing, wonderful
10 attractive, bewitching, delightful, entrancing
11 captivating, fascinating, mesmerizing

enchantment
05 bliss, charm, magic, spell
07 delight, ecstasy, glamour, rapture, sorcery
08 wizardry
09 hypnotism, mesmerism
10 necromancy, witchcraft
11 fascination, incantation

enchantress
04 vamp
05 Circe, lamia, siren, witch
07 charmer
08 conjurer, magician
09 sorceress
10 seductress
11 femme fatale, necromancer

encircle
04 gird, ring
05 crowd, hem in, orbit
06 circle, enfold, girdle
07 close in, compass, enclose, envelop
08 surround
09 encompass
12 circumscribe

enclose
03 pen

encourage
04 cage, hold, ring, wrap
05 bound, cover, fence, frame, hedge, hem in, put in
06 circle, cocoon, corral, encase, insert, shut in
07 confine, contain, embrace, envelop, include
08 encircle, send with, surround
09 encompass
12 circumscribe

enclosure
03 pen, run, sty
04 area, fold, ring, yard
05 arena, court, kraal, pound
06 corral
07 fencing, paddock
08 addition, cloister, compound, stockade
09 inclusion, insertion

encompass
04 gird, hold, ring, span
06 circle, shut in, take in
07 close in, confine, contain, embrace, enclose, envelop, include, involve
08 comprise, encircle, surround
11 incorporate
12 circumscribe

encore
06 repeat
10 repetition

encounter
04 face, meet
05 brush, clash, run-in, set-to
06 action, battle, tussle
07 contact, meeting, run into
08 bump into, conflict, confront, happen on, skirmish
09 collision, run across
10 chance upon, come across, engagement, experience
11 be up against, grapple with
13 come up against, stumble across
15 cross swords with

encourage
04 back, help, spur, sway, urge
05 cheer, egg on, rally, rouse
06 exhort, foster, incite, prompt
07 comfort, console, hearten, inspire, promote, support
08 advocate, embolden, motivate, reassure
09 influence, stimulate
10 strengthen
14 be supportive to

encouragement
05 boost, cheer

06 urging
07 backing, pep talk, support
08 stimulus
09 incentive, promotion
10 assistance, incitement, motivation, persuasion
11 consolation, exhortation, furtherance, inspiration, reassurance, stimulation
12 shot in the arm

encouraging
04 rosy
06 bright
07 hopeful
08 cheerful, cheering
09 inspiring, promising
10 auspicious, heartening
11 stimulating

encroach
05 usurp
06 invade
07 impinge, intrude, overrun
08 infringe, overstep, trespass
10 infiltrate, muscle in on
11 make inroads

encroachment
08 invasion
09 incursion, intrusion
11 trespassing
12 infiltration, infringement

encumber
06 burden, hamper, hinder, impede, retard, saddle
07 congest, oppress, prevent
08 handicap, overload, restrain, slow down
09 constrain, weigh down
13 inconvenience

encumbrance
04 load
06 burden, strain, stress, weight
08 handicap, obstacle
09 albatross, hindrance, millstone, restraint
10 constraint, difficulty, impediment, obligation
13 inconvenience

encyclopedic
04 vast
05 broad
08 complete, thorough
09 universal
10 exhaustive
11 compendious
12 all-embracing, all-inclusive
13 comprehensive
15 all-encompassing

end
03 aim, tip

04 area, butt, doom, edge, goal, part, ruin, side, stop, stub
05 cease, close, death, field, issue, limit, point, scrap
06 be over, demise, design, die out, ending, expire, finale, finish, intent, motive, object, reason, result, run out, upshot, wind up
07 abolish, outcome, purpose, remnant, section, vestige
08 break off, conclude, dissolve, downfall, epilogue, fade away, fragment, left-over, round off
09 cessation, culminate, extremity, intention, objective, terminate
10 annihilate, completion, conclusion, dénouement, extinction, extinguish
11 consequence, culmination, destruction, discontinue, dissolution, exterminate, termination
13 extermination

□**the end**
06 enough
07 too much
08 the limit, the worst
10 unbearable
11 intolerable, unendurable
12 insufferable, the final blow, the last straw
15 beyond endurance

endanger
04 risk
06 expose, hazard
07 imperil
08 threaten
09 put at risk
10 compromise, jeopardize
11 put in danger
13 put in jeopardy

endearing
05 sweet
07 lovable, winsome
08 adorable, charming, engaging
09 appealing
10 attractive, delightful

endearment
04 love
07 pet-name
08 fondness
09 affection
10 diminutive, hypocorism
12 sweet nothing

endeavour
02 go

03 aim, try
04 bash, seek, shot, stab
05 crack
06 aspire, effort, labour, strive
07 attempt, venture
08 striving, struggle
09 take pains, undertake
10 do your best, enterprise
11 undertaking

ending
03 end
05 close
06 climax, finale, finish
08 epilogue
09 cessation
10 completion, conclusion, dénouement, resolution
11 culmination, termination
12 consummation

endless
06 boring, entire
07 eternal, undying
08 constant, infinite, unbroken, unending
09 boundless, ceaseless, continual, limitless, perpetual, unlimited
10 continuous, without end
11 everlasting, measureless
12 interminable
13 uninterrupted

endorse
04 back, sign
06 affirm, favour, ratify, uphold
07 approve, confirm, support, sustain, warrant
08 advocate, be behind, sanction, vouch for
09 authorize, get behind, recommend
11 countersign, subscribe to

endorsement
02 OK
07 backing, support, warrant
08 advocacy, approval, sanction
09 signature
11 affirmation, testimonial
12 commendation, confirmation, ratification
13 authorization
14 recommendation, seal of approval

endow
04 fund, give, have, will
05 award, boast, grant, leave
06 bestow, confer, donate
07 furnish, present, provide
08 bequeath, make over

endowment
04 fund, gift
05 award, dowry, flair, grant
06 income, legacy, talent
07 ability, bequest, finance, present, quality, revenue
08 aptitude, bestowal, donation
09 attribute, provision
10 capability, settlement
11 benefaction
13 qualification

endurable
08 bearable
09 tolerable
10 manageable, sufferable
11 supportable, sustainable

endurance
07 stamina
08 patience, stoicism, tenacity
09 fortitude, stability
10 resolution, toleration
11 persistence, resignation
12 perseverance, staying power, stickability

endure
04 bear, face, hold, last, stay
05 abide, brave, stand, stick
06 permit, remain, suffer
07 persist, prevail, survive, sustain, undergo, weather
08 continue, tolerate
09 encounter, go through, put up with, withstand
10 experience

enduring
04 firm
06 stable, steady
07 abiding, chronic, durable, eternal, lasting
08 immortal
09 permanent, perpetual, remaining, steadfast, surviving
10 continuing, persistent, persisting, prevailing
11 long-lasting, unfaltering
12 imperishable, long-standing

enemy
03 foe
05 rival
08 opponent
09 adversary, other side
10 antagonist, competitor

energetic
05 brisk, zippy
06 active, lively, potent, punchy
07 dynamic, zestful
08 animated, forceful, powerful, spirited, vigorous
09 go-getting, strenuous

10 boisterous
11 full of beans, high-powered

energize
04 stir
05 liven, pep up
06 arouse, vivify
07 animate, enliven, quicken
08 activate, motivate, vitalize
09 electrify, galvanize, stimulate
10 invigorate

energy
03 zip
04 brio, fire, life, push, zeal, zest
05 drive, force, power, verve
06 ardour, spirit, vigour
07 pizzazz, sparkle, stamina
08 activity, dynamism, exertion, strength, vitality, vivacity
09 animation, intensity
10 efficiency, enthusiasm, get-up-and-go, liveliness
12 forcefulness
13 effectiveness, effervescence

enervated
04 limp, weak
05 spent, tired
06 done in, effete, sapped
07 run-down, worn out
08 fatigued, unmanned, unnerved, weakened
09 exhausted, washed-out
11 debilitated, devitalized
13 incapacitated

enfeeble
03 sap
04 geld
06 reduce, weaken
07 deplete, exhaust, fatigue, unhinge, unnerve, wear out
08 diminish, enervate
09 undermine
10 debilitate, devitalize

enfold
03 hug
04 fold, hold, wrap
05 clasp
06 shroud, swathe, wrap up
07 embrace, enclose, envelop
08 encircle
09 encompass

enforce
05 apply, force
06 coerce, compel, fulfil, impose, oblige
07 execute, require
08 carry out, insist on, pressure
09 discharge, implement, prosecute, reinforce
10 administer, pressurize
11 necessitate

enforced
06 forced
07 binding, imposed, obliged
09 compelled, necessary
10 compulsory, prescribed
11 involuntary, unavoidable

enforcement
08 coaction, coercion, pressure
09 discharge, execution
10 compulsion, imposition, insistence, obligation
11 prosecution, requirement
14 implementation

enfranchise
04 free
07 manumit, release
08 liberate
10 emancipate
13 give the vote to
14 give suffrage to

enfranchisement
07 freedom, freeing, release
08 suffrage
10 liberating, liberation
11 manumission
12 emancipation, voting rights

engage
03 win
04 busy, draw, fill, gain, grip, hire, hold, join, mesh
05 catch, charm, fight, tie up
06 allure, attach, attack, employ, enlist, enmesh, join in, occupy, sign up, take on, take up
07 appoint, involve, recruit
08 contract, embark on, interact, practise, take part
09 captivate, clash with, encounter, enter into, interlock, undertake
10 battle with, commission
11 fit together, participate
12 interconnect
15 put on the payroll

engaged
04 busy
05 in use, taken
06 active, tied up
07 pledged
08 employed, espoused, involved, occupied, plighted, promised
09 affianced, betrothed, committed, spoken for
11 preoccupied, unavailable

engagement
04 bond, date
05 clash, fight, troth
06 action, battle, pledge

07 contest, fixture, meeting
08 conflict, contract, struggle
09 agreement, assurance, betrothal, encounter, interview, offensive
10 commitment, rendezvous
11 appointment, assignation
13 confrontation

engaging
05 sweet
07 lovable, winning, winsome
08 adorable, charming, fetching, pleasant, pleasing
09 agreeable, appealing
10 attractive, delightful
11 captivating, fascinating

engender
05 beget, breed, cause
06 arouse, create, effect, excite, incite, induce, kindle, lead to
07 inspire, produce, provoke
08 generate, occasion
09 instigate, propagate
10 bring about, give rise to

engine
05 motor
06 device, dynamo
07 machine
09 appliance, generator, machinery, mechanism
10 instrument, locomotive

► *Engine parts include*:
04 sump
05 choke
06 con-rod, gasket, piston, tappet
07 fan belt, oil pump, push-rod
08 camshaft, flywheel, radiator, rotor arm
09 air filter, drive belt, oil filter, rocker arm, spark plug
10 alternator, cooling fan, crankshaft, inlet valve, petrol pump, piston ring, timing belt
11 carburettor
12 cylinder head, exhaust valve, fuel injector, ignition coil, starter motor, turbocharger
13 connecting rod, cylinder block, inlet manifold
15 exhaust manifold

► *Types of engine*:
03 jet
05 steam
06 diesel, donkey, petrol
07 turbine
08 turbojet
09 turboprop
13 fuel-injection

engineer
03 rig
04 plan, plot
05 cause
06 create, devise, direct, driver, effect, manage, scheme
07 arrange, builder, control, deviser, planner
08 contrive, designer, inventor, mechanic, operator
09 architect, manoeuvre
10 bring about, manipulate, mastermind, technician
11 orchestrate, stage-manage

► *Names of engineers*:
04 **Bell** (Alexander Graham), **Benz** (Karl), **Eads** (James Buchanan), **Ford** (Henry), **Page** (Sir Frederick Handley), **Watt** (James)
05 **Baird** (John Logie), **Braun** (Wernher von), **Maxim** (Sir Hiram Stevens), **Rolls** (Charles Stewart), **Royce** (Sir Henry), **Tesla** (Nikola)
06 **Brunel** (Isambard Kingdom), **Brunel** (Sir Marc Isambard), **Diesel** (Rudolf Christian Karl), **Eckert** (John Presper), **Edison** (Thomas Alva), **Eiffel** (Gustave), **Fokker** (Anthony Herman Gerard), **Fuller** (Buckminster), **Jansky** (Karl Guthe), **McAdam** (John Loudon), **Rennie** (John), **Savery** (Thomas), **Taylor** (Frederick Winslow), **Vauban** (Sebastien le Prestre de), **Wallis** (Sir Barnes Neville), **Wankel** (Felix), **Wright** (Orville), **Wright** (Wilbur)
07 **Citroën** (André Gustave), **Daimler** (Gottlieb), **Dornier** (Claude), **Eastman** (George), **Fleming** (Sir John Ambrose), **Goddard** (Robert Hutchings), **Lesseps** (Ferdinand Marie, Vicomte de), **Nasmyth** (James), **Parsons** (Sir Charles Algernon), **Porsche** (Ferdinand), **Rankine** (William John Macquorn), **Siemens** (Sir William), **Siemens** (Werner von), **Sopwith** (Sir Thomas Octave Murdoch), **Telford** (Thomas), **Tupolev**

(Andrei), **Whittle** (Sir Frank)
08 **Bessemer** (Sir Henry), **De Forest** (Lee), **Ericsson** (John), **Ferranti** (Sebastian Ziani de), **Korolyov** (Sergei), **Poncelet** (Jean Victor), **Sikorsky** (Igor), **Sinclair** (Sir Clive), **Zeppelin** (Ferdinand, Graf von)
09 **Cockerell** (Sir Christopher Sydney), **Issigonis** (Sir Alec), **Trésaguet** (Pierre Marie Jerome), **Whitworth** (Sir Joseph)
10 **Bazalgette** (Sir Joseph William), **Lilienthal** (Otto), **Stephenson** (George), **Stephenson** (Robert), **Trevithick** (Richard)
11 **De Havilland** (Sir Geoffrey), **Montgolfier** (Joseph Michel)
12 **Westinghouse** (George)
13 **Messerschmitt** (Willy)
➤ See also **scientist**

engrave
03 cut, fix, set
04 etch, mark
05 brand, carve, chase, embed
06 chisel, incise
07 engrain, impress, imprint
08 inscribe

engraving
03 cut
04 mark
05 block, plate, print
07 carving, cutting, etching, imprint, woodcut
08 dry-point, intaglio
10 chiselling, impression
11 inscription

engross
04 grip, hold
05 rivet
06 absorb, engage, occupy
07 enthral, involve
08 interest, intrigue
09 captivate, fascinate

engrossed
04 lost, rapt
06 intent
07 engaged, fixated, gripped, riveted, taken up, wrapped
08 absorbed, caught up, immersed, occupied
09 intrigued
10 captivated, enthralled, fascinated, mesmerized

engrossing
08 gripping, riveting
09 absorbing
10 compelling, intriguing
11 captivating, enthralling, fascinating, interesting
13 unputdownable

engulf
04 bury
05 drown, flood, swamp
06 absorb, devour, plunge
07 consume, engross, envelop, immerse, overrun
08 inundate, overtake, submerge
09 overwhelm, swallow up

enhance
04 lift
05 add to, boost, exalt, raise
06 enrich, stress
07 augment, improve, upgrade
08 heighten, increase
09 embellish, emphasize, intensify, reinforce
10 strengthen

enhancement
05 boost
06 stress
08 emphasis, increase
10 enrichment
11 heightening, improvement
12 augmentation
13 reinforcement
15 intensification

enigma
05 poser
06 puzzle, riddle
07 mystery, paradox, problem
09 conundrum
11 brain-teaser

enigmatic
06 arcane
07 cryptic, obscure, strange
08 baffling, esoteric, puzzling
09 recondite
10 mysterious, mystifying, perplexing
11 paradoxical
12 inexplicable, unfathomable

enjoin
04 urge
05 order
06 advise, charge, decree, demand, direct, ordain
07 command, require
08 disallow, instruct, prohibit
09 interdict, proscribe

enjoy
04 have, like, love

06 relish, savour
07 possess, revel in
08 be fond of
09 delight in, rejoice in
14 take pleasure in

❏ enjoy yourself
07 have fun
08 live it up
09 make merry
13 have a good time
15 let your hair down

enjoyable
03 fun
04 fine, good, nice
06 lovely
07 amusing
08 pleasant, pleasing
09 agreeable, delicious
10 gratifying, satisfying
11 pleasurable
12 entertaining

enjoyment
03 fun, joy, use
04 zest
06 favour, relish
08 blessing, gladness, pleasure
09 advantage, amusement, diversion, happiness
10 indulgence, recreation
11 delectation
12 satisfaction
13 entertainment, gratification

enlarge
05 add to, swell, widen
06 blow up, dilate, expand, extend
07 amplify, augment, broaden, develop, distend, inflate, magnify, stretch
08 elongate, expand on, heighten, increase, lengthen
09 intumesce
10 make bigger, supplement
11 elaborate on, expatiate on
12 become bigger

enlargement
06 blow up, oedema
08 dilation, increase, swelling
09 expansion, extension, inflation
10 distension, stretching
11 development
12 augmentation, intumescence
13 amplification, magnification

enlighten
05 edify, teach, tutor
06 advise, inform
07 apprise, counsel, educate
08 instruct

09 cultivate, make aware
10 illuminate

enlightened
04 wise
05 aware
07 erudite, learned, liberal
08 educated, informed
09 civilized
10 conversant, cultivated
13 knowledgeable

enlightenment
06 wisdom
07 insight
08 learning, teaching
09 awareness, education, erudition, knowledge
11 cultivation, edification, information, instruction
13 comprehension, understanding

enlist
04 hire, join
05 enrol, enter
06 employ, engage, join up, muster, sign up, take on
07 procure, recruit
08 register
09 conscript, volunteer

enliven
05 cheer, liven, pep up, rouse
06 buoy up, excite, kindle, perk up, vivify, wake up
07 animate, cheer up, hearten, inspire, liven up, quicken
08 brighten
10 invigorate, revitalize
11 give a lift to

en masse
05 as one
06 en bloc
07 in a body
08 as a group, as a whole, ensemble, together
09 all at once, wholesale
11 all together

enmity
04 feud, hate
05 venom
06 hatred, malice, strife
07 discord, ill-will, rancour
08 acrimony, bad blood
09 animosity, antipathy, hostility
10 antagonism, bitterness
11 malevolence

ennoble
05 exalt, raise
06 honour, uplift

07 dignify, elevate, enhance, glorify, magnify
10 aggrandize, nobilitate

ennui
06 acedia, tedium
07 accidie, boredom, languor
09 lassitude, tiredness
12 listlessness
15 dissatisfaction

enormity
04 evil
06 horror
07 outrage
08 atrocity, iniquity, vileness
09 depravity, violation
10 wickedness
11 abomination, monstrosity
13 atrociousness
14 outrageousness

enormous
04 huge, vast
05 gross, jumbo
07 immense, mammoth, massive
08 colossal, gigantic, great big
09 monstrous
10 astronomic, gargantuan, stupendous, tremendous

enormously
06 hugely
09 immensely, massively
11 exceedingly
12 tremendously
13 to a huge extent
15 extraordinarily

enormousness
07 expanse
08 hugeness, vastness
09 greatness, magnitude
11 immenseness, massiveness
13 extensiveness

enough
05 ample, amply
06 fairly, plenty
08 abundant, adequacy, adequate, passably
09 abundance, amplitude
10 adequately, moderately, reasonably, sufficient
11 ample supply, sufficiency
12 sufficiently
14 satisfactorily

en passant
08 by the way
09 cursorily, in passing
12 incidentally

enquire, enquirer, enquiring, enquiry see **inquire, inquirer, inquiring, inquiry**

enrage
04 rile
05 anger, annoy
06 incite, madden
07 agitate, incense, inflame
09 infuriate, make angry
10 exasperate, push too far

enraged
03 mad
04 wild
05 angry, irate, livid
06 fuming, raging
07 angered, annoyed, furious
08 incensed, storming
10 aggravated, infuriated
11 exasperated

enrapture
05 charm
06 ravish, thrill
07 beguile, bewitch, delight, enchant, enthral
08 entrance
09 captivate, fascinate, spellbind, transport

enrich
04 gild
05 add to, adorn, endow, grace
07 enhance, garnish, improve
08 decorate, ornament
09 cultivate, embellish
10 aggrandize, supplement

enrol
05 admit, enter
06 engage, enlist, join up, record, sign on, sign up
07 go in for, put down, recruit
08 inscribe, register
15 put your name down

enrolment
09 admission, enlisting, joining up, signing on, signing up
10 acceptance, enlistment
11 recruitment
12 registration

en route
08 on the way
09 in transit, on the move, on the road

ensconce
05 lodge, place
06 nestle, screen, settle, shield
07 install, protect, shelter
08 entrench
09 establish

ensemble
03 set, sum

04 band, cast, suit
05 get-up, group, total, whole
06 chorus, outfit, rig-out, troupe
07 company, costume
08 entirety
10 collection, whole shoot
11 co-ordinates

enshrine
05 exalt, guard
06 embalm, hallow, revere
07 cherish, idolize, protect
08 preserve, sanctify, treasure
10 consecrate
11 apotheosize, immortalize

enshroud
04 hide, pall, veil, wrap
05 cloak, cloud, cover
06 enfold, enwrap, shroud
07 enclose, envelop, obscure

ensign
04 flag, jack
05 badge, crest
06 banner, shield
07 colours, pennant
08 standard
10 coat of arms

enslave
04 bind, trap, yoke
07 enchain, subject
09 subjugate

enslavement
07 bondage, serfdom, slavery
08 thraldom
09 captivity, servitude
10 oppression, repression, subjection
11 enthralment, subjugation

ensnare
03 net
04 trap
05 catch, snare
06 enmesh, entrap
07 capture, embroil
08 entangle

ensue
04 flow, stem
05 arise, issue, occur
06 befall, derive, follow, happen, result
07 proceed, succeed, turn out
08 come next
09 transpire

ensure
05 guard
06 effect, secure
07 certify, protect, warrant
08 make safe, make sure

entail
09 guarantee, safeguard
11 make certain

entail
04 need
05 cause
06 demand, lead to
07 involve, produce, require
08 occasion, result in
10 bring about, give rise to
11 necessitate

entangle
05 mix up, ravel, snare, twist
06 enmesh, jumble, muddle
07 embroil, ensnare, involve
10 complicate, intertwine

entanglement
04 knot, mesh, mess, trap
05 mix-up, snare
06 affair, muddle, tangle
07 liaison, snarl-up
09 confusion
11 involvement, predicament
12 complication
13 embarrassment

entente
04 deal, pact
06 treaty
07 compact
09 agreement
10 friendship
11 arrangement
13 understanding
15 entente cordiale

enter
03 log
04 go in, join, list, note
05 begin, board, enrol, get in, input, lodge, pop in, start
06 arrive, enlist, go in to, insert, occupy, record, sign up, submit, take up
07 break in, burst in, get in to, go in for, put down
08 engage in, inscribe, register, take down, take part
09 introduce, penetrate
10 embark upon, infiltrate
11 participate, put on record
15 become a member of

enterprise
04 firm, plan, push, task
05 drive, oomph
06 effort, energy, scheme, spirit
07 company, project, venture
08 boldness, business, industry
09 endeavour, operation
10 get-up-and-go, initiative
11 undertaking
13 establishment

15 adventurousness, resourcefulness

enterprising
04 bold, keen
05 eager, pushy
06 active, daring
07 go-ahead, zealous
08 aspiring, spirited, vigorous
09 ambitious, energetic
11 adventurous, imaginative, resourceful, self-reliant
15 entrepreneurial

entertain
04 host
05 amuse, charm, cheer
06 divert, engage, foster, occupy, please, regale
07 delight, engross, harbour, imagine, nurture, receive
08 consider, interest
09 captivate, have round
10 have guests, think about
11 contemplate, countenance

➤ *Types of entertainer*:
02 DJ
05 actor, clown, comic, mimic
06 busker, dancer, jester, player, singer
07 acrobat, actress, artiste, juggler
08 comedian, conjuror, magician, minstrel, musician, stripper
09 hypnotist, performer, presenter
10 disc jockey, mime artist, mind-reader
12 escapologist, stand-up comic
13 impressionist, trapeze-artist, ventriloquist
15 song-and-dance act, tight-rope walker

➤ See also **actor, actress**; **comedian**; **musician**; **singer**

entertaining
03 fun
05 funny, witty
07 amusing, comical
08 humorous, pleasing
09 diverting, enjoyable
11 interesting, pleasurable

entertainment
03 fun
04 play, show
05 hobby, sport
07 leisure, pastime
08 activity, pleasure

09 amusement, diversion, enjoyment, spectacle
10 recreation
11 distraction, performance
12 extravaganza, presentation

➤ *Types of entertainment*:
03 zoo
04 fête
05 dance, disco, opera, radio, revue, rodeo, video
06 casino, cinema, circus
07 cabaret, concert, karaoke, musical, pageant, recital, show biz, theatre
08 carnival, festival, gymkhana, waxworks
09 magic-show, music hall, night-club, pantomime
10 puppet show, television
11 discothèque, variety show
12 show business

➤ See also **theatrical**

enthral
04 grip
05 charm, rivet
06 absorb, thrill
07 beguile, bewitch, delight, enchant, engross
08 entrance, intrigue
09 captivate, fascinate, hypnotize, mesmerize

enthralling
08 charming, gripping, mesmeric, riveting
09 beguiling, thrilling
10 compelling, compulsive, enchanting, entrancing
11 captivating, fascinating, hypnotizing, mesmerizing
12 spellbinding

enthuse
04 fire, gush, rave
05 drool
06 excite, praise
07 inspire
08 motivate
10 bubble over, wax lyrical

enthusiasm
04 fire, rage, zeal, zest
05 craze, hobby, mania, thing
06 ardour, frenzy, relish, spirit
07 fervour, passion, pastime
08 devotion, interest, keenness
09 eagerness, vehemence
10 commitment, excitement

enthusiast
03 fan
04 buff
05 fiend, freak, lover
06 zealot

07 admirer, devotee, fanatic
09 supporter
10 aficionado

enthusiastic
03 mad
04 avid, daft, keen, nuts, wild
05 crazy, eager, potty
06 ardent
07 excited, fervent, zealous
08 spirited, vehement, vigorous
09 ebullient, fanatical
10 passionate
12 wholehearted

entice
04 coax, draw, lure
05 tempt
06 cajole, induce, lead on, seduce
07 attract, beguile
08 inveigle, persuade
09 sweet-talk

enticement
04 bait, lure
05 decoy
06 come-on
07 coaxing
08 cajolery
09 seduction, sweet-talk
10 allurement, attraction, inducement, temptation

entire
04 full
05 sound, total, whole
08 absolute, complete

entirely
04 only
05 fully
06 in toto, solely, wholly
07 totally, utterly
09 every inch, perfectly
10 absolutely, altogether, completely, thoroughly
11 exclusively
12 unreservedly

entirety
05 whole
08 fullness, totality
09 wholeness
12 completeness

entitle
03 dub
04 call, name, term
05 allow, label, style, title
06 enable, know as, permit
07 license, qualify, warrant
08 accredit, christen, sanction
09 authorize, designate

entity
04 body

05 being, thing
06 object
08 creature, organism
09 existence, substance

entombment
06 burial
09 interment, sepulture
10 inhumation

entourage
05 court, staff, suite, train
06 escort
07 company, cortège, retinue
09 followers, retainers
10 attendants, companions

entrails
04 guts
05 offal
06 bowels, umbles
07 giblets, innards, insides, viscera
10 intestines

entrance
04 door, gate, hall
05 charm, debut, drive, entry, foyer, lobby, porch, way in
06 access, entrée, ravish
07 arrival, beguile, bewitch, delight, doorway, enchant, enthral, gateway, ingress
08 approach, driveway
09 admission, captivate, enrapture, fascinate, hypnotize, mesmerize, spellbind, threshold, transport, vestibule
10 admittance, appearance
12 introduction, right of entry

entrant
05 entry, pupil, rival
07 convert, fresher, learner, starter, student, trainee
08 beginner, freshman, initiate, newcomer, opponent
09 applicant, candidate, contender
10 competitor, contestant
11 participant, probationer

entrap
03 net
04 lure, trap
05 catch, snare, trick
06 allure, ambush, delude, enmesh, entice, seduce
07 beguile, capture, deceive, embroil, ensnare
08 entangle, inveigle

entreat
03 ask, beg
04 pray

07 beseech, implore, request
08 appeal to, petition
09 importune, plead with
10 supplicate

entreaty
03 cry
04 plea, suit
06 appeal, prayer
07 request
08 petition
10 invocation
12 solicitation, supplication

entrench
03 fix, set
04 root, seat
05 dig in, embed, lodge, plant
06 anchor, settle
07 ingrain, install
08 ensconce, stop a gap
09 establish

entrenched
03 set
04 firm
05 fixed
06 inbred, rooted
07 diehard
09 indelible, ingrained
10 deep-rooted, deep-seated, inflexible, unshakable
12 ineradicable, intransigent
13 dyed-in-the-wool
15 well-established

entrepreneur
05 agent
06 broker, dealer, tycoon
07 magnate, manager
08 promoter
09 financier, middleman
10 impresario, speculator
11 businessman
13 businesswoman, industrialist

entrepreneurial
08 business, economic
09 budgetary, financial
10 commercial, managerial

entrust
05 trust
06 charge, commit, invest
07 commend, confide, consign
08 delegate, hand over
09 authorize
11 put in charge

entry
04 door, gate, hall, item, note
05 foyer, lobby, porch, way in
06 access, minute, record
07 doorway, entrant, gateway, listing, opening, passage
08 approach, entrance

09 admission, applicant, candidate, statement, threshold, vestibule
10 admittance, appearance, competitor, contestant
12 introduction

entwine
04 knit, knot, wind
05 braid, plait, ravel, twine, twist, weave
07 embroil, intwine, wreathe
08 entangle
09 interlace, interlink
10 intertwine, interweave

enumerate
04 cite, list, name, tell
05 count, quote
06 detail, number, recite, reckon, relate
07 itemize, recount, specify
09 calculate

enunciate
03 say
05 sound, speak, state, voice
07 declare, express
08 announce, vocalize
09 pronounce
10 articulate, put forward

envelop
04 hide, veil, wrap
05 cloak, cover
06 encase, enfold, engulf, enwrap, shroud, swathe
07 conceal, enclose, obscure
08 encircle, surround
09 encompass

envelope
04 case, skin
05 cover, shell
06 casing, jacket, sheath
07 coating, wrapper
09 covering, wrapping

enviable
05 lucky
08 favoured
09 desirable, fortunate
10 privileged
11 sought-after
12 advantageous

envious
05 green
07 jealous
08 covetous, grudging
09 green-eyed, jaundiced, resentful
10 begrudging
12 dissatisfied
13 green with envy

environment
06 locale, medium, milieu
07 climate, context, element, habitat, setting
08 ambience
09 situation, territory
10 atmosphere, background, conditions, influences
12 surroundings
13 circumstances

environmentalist
05 green
09 ecologist
15 conservationist, preservationist

environs
07 suburbs
08 locality, purlieus, vicinity
09 outskirts, precincts
12 surroundings
13 neighbourhood

envisage
03 see
07 foresee, imagine, picture, predict, think of
09 see coming, visualize
10 anticipate, conceive of
11 contemplate, preconceive

envoy
05 agent
06 consul, deputy, legate
07 attaché, courier
08 delegate, diplomat, emissary, mediator, minister
09 go-between, messenger
10 ambassador
12 intermediary
14 representative

envy
05 covet, crave, spite
06 grudge, malice, resent
08 begrudge, jealousy
10 resentment
12 covetousness
13 resentfulness

ephemeral
05 brief, short
07 fungous, passing
08 fleeting, flitting
09 fugacious, momentary, temporary, transient
10 evanescent, short-lived, transitory

epic
04 huge, long, myth, saga, vast
05 grand, great, large, lofty
06 heroic, legend
07 exalted, history, sublime

08 colossal, elevated, long poem, majestic
09 ambitious, long story
10 impressive, large-scale

epicure
07 glutton, gourmet
08 gourmand, hedonist, Sybarite
09 bon vivant, bon viveur, epicurean
10 gastronome, sensualist
11 connoisseur

epicurean
07 gourmet, sensual
08 luscious
09 libertine, luxurious, Sybaritic
10 gluttonous, hedonistic
11 gastronomic
12 unrestrained
13 gourmandizing

epidemic
04 rash, rife, rise, wave
05 spate
06 growth, plague, spread
07 rampant, scourge, upsurge
08 increase, pandemic
09 pervasive, prevalent
10 prevailing, widespread
11 wide-ranging

epigram
04 quip
05 gnome, maxim
06 bon mot, saying
07 proverb
08 aphorism
09 witticism
10 apophthegm

epigrammatic
05 pithy, sharp, short, witty
06 ironic
07 concise, laconic, piquant, pointed, pungent
08 incisive, succinct
10 aphoristic

epilogue
02 PS
04 coda
08 appendix, swan song
09 afterword
10 conclusion, postscript

episode
04 part
05 event, scene
06 affair, matter
07 chapter, passage, section
08 business, incident, occasion
09 adventure, happening
10 experience, instalment

episodic
08 periodic, sporadic
09 anecdotal, irregular
10 occasional, picaresque
12 disconnected, intermittent

epistle
04 line, note
06 letter
07 message, missive
08 bulletin
13 communication
14 correspondence

epitaph
03 RIP
08 obituary
11 inscription, rest in peace

epithet
03 tag
04 name
05 title
08 nickname
09 sobriquet
11 appellation, description

epitome
04 type
05 model
06 digest, précis, résumé
07 essence, example, summary
08 abstract, exemplar, synopsis
10 embodiment
11 abridgement
12 quintessence
14 representation
15 personification

epitomize
03 cut
05 sum up
06 embody, précis, typify
07 abridge, curtail, shorten
08 abstract, compress,
   condense, contract
09 exemplify, personify,
   represent, summarize
11 encapsulate

epoch
03 age, era
04 date, time
06 period

equable
04 calm, even
06 placid, serene, smooth,
   stable, steady
08 composed, constant, laid-
   back, moderate, tranquil
09 easy-going, temperate
10 consistent, unchanging
11 level-headed, unflappable
12 even-tempered
13 imperturbable

equal
03 fit
04 able, even, fair, just, like,
   make, mate, peer, twin
05 alike, level, match, rival, total
07 add up to, balance, capable,
   matched, regular, the same
08 adequate, amount to,
   balanced, come up to,
   equalize, parallel, suitable
09 competent, identical, tally
   with
10 comparable, equate with,
   equivalent, fifty-fifty, square
   with, sufficient, unchanging
11 be level with, be the same
   as, counterpart, measure up
   to, neck and neck, non-
   partisan, symmetrical
12 be on a par with, coincide
   with, commensurate,
   correspond to
13 corresponding, evenly
   matched

equality
03 par
06 parity
07 balance, justice
08 evenness, fairness, likeness,
   sameness, symmetry
10 similarity, uniformity
11 equal rights, equivalence
13 comparability
14 correspondence,
   egalitarianism

equalize
05 equal, level, match
06 equate, even up, square
07 balance, even out
08 keep pace, make even
09 draw level
10 compensate, regularize
11 standardize

equanimity
04 calm, ease, pose
06 aplomb
07 dignity
08 coolness, serenity
09 assurance, composure,
   placidity, sangfroid
10 confidence
11 impassivity, self-control
12 tranquillity
13 self-assurance
14 self-possession,
   unflappability
15 level-headedness

equate
06 offset
07 balance, be equal, liken to
08 equalize, pair with, parallel

09 agree with, tally with
10 correspond, square with
15 bracket together

equation
05 match
07 pairing
08 equality, identity, likeness,
   matching, parallel
09 agreement, balancing
10 comparison, similarity
11 equivalence
14 correspondence

equestrian
05 rider
06 cowboy, equine, herder,
   hussar, jockey, knight, riding
07 courier, cowgirl, mounted,
   rancher, trooper
08 cavalier, horseman
10 cavalryman, horsewoman
11 horse-riding

equilibrium
05 poise
06 aplomb, stasis
07 balance, dignity
08 calmness, coolness,
   evenness, symmetry
09 assurance, composure,
   sangfroid, stability
10 equanimity, steadiness
11 self-control
14 self-possession
15 level-headedness

equip
03 arm, rig
05 array, dress, endow, fit up,
   issue, stock
06 fit out, kit out, supply
07 furnish, prepare, provide
08 accoutre

equipment
03 kit
04 gear
05 stuff, tools
06 outfit, rig-out, tackle, things
08 material, supplies
09 apparatus, furniture
11 accessories, furnishings
13 accoutrements,
   paraphernalia

equipoise
07 balance, ballast
08 evenness, symmetry
09 stability
11 equibalance, equilibrium
12 counterpoise
13 counter-weight
14 counterbalance

equitable
03 due
04 fair, just
05 right
06 honest, proper, square
07 ethical
08 rightful, unbiased
09 impartial, objective
10 even-handed, reasonable
12 unprejudiced
13 disinterested, fair-and-square

equity
07 honesty, justice
08 fair play, fairness, justness
13 equitableness
14 even-handedness, reasonableness

equivalence
06 parity
08 equality, sameness
11 correlation
13 comparability
14 correspondence

equivalent
04 even, like, peer, same, twin
05 alike, equal, match
08 parallel
09 homologue, identical
10 comparable, tantamount
11 correlative, counterpart
12 commensurate
13 correspondent, corresponding
14 opposite number
15 interchangeable

equivocal
05 vague
07 evasive, oblique, obscure
09 ambiguous, uncertain
10 ambivalent, suspicious

equivocate
05 dodge, evade, fence, hedge
06 waffle
09 pussyfoot, vacillate
11 prevaricate
12 shilly-shally, tergiversate
13 hedge your bets

equivocation
06 waffle
07 evasion, hedging
10 double talk
11 weasel words
12 pussyfooting
13 prevarication
14 tergiversation
15 dodging the issue

era
03 age, day

04 aeon, date, days, time
05 cycle, epoch, stage, times
06 period, season
07 century
10 generation

eradicate
05 erase
06 efface, remove, uproot
07 abolish, destroy, expunge, root out, weed out, wipe out
08 get rid of, stamp out
09 eliminate, extirpate
10 annihilate, obliterate
11 crack down on, exterminate

eradication
07 removal
08 riddance
09 abolition
10 effacement, extinction
11 destruction, elimination
12 annihilation, obliteration
13 extermination

erasable
09 removable
10 effaceable, eradicable

erase
06 cancel, delete, efface, excise, remove, rub out
07 blot out, expunge, wipe out
08 get rid of
09 eradicate
10 obliterate

erasure
07 removal
08 deletion
09 cleansing, erasement
11 elimination, eradication
12 cancellation, obliteration

erect
04 firm, form, hard, lift, rear
05 build, mount, pitch, put up, raise, rigid, set up, stiff
06 create, raised
07 elevate, upright
08 standing, straight, vertical
09 construct, establish, institute
10 upstanding

erection
04 pile
07 edifice, raising
08 assembly, building, rigidity
09 elevation, structure
10 tumescence
12 construction
13 establishment

ergo
02 so
04 then, thus
05 hence

09 therefore
11 accordingly
12 consequently
13 for this reason

erode
05 spoil
06 abrade
07 consume, corrode, deplete, destroy, eat away, eat into
08 wear away, wear down
09 excoriate, grind down, undermine
11 deteriorate
12 disintegrate

erosion
04 wear
08 abrasion
10 denudation
11 destruction, excoriation, undermining, wearing away
13 deterioration
14 disintegration

erotic
04 blue, sexy
05 adult, dirty
06 carnal, steamy
07 lustful, raunchy, sensual
09 erogenous, seductive
10 lascivious, suggestive
11 stimulating, titillating
12 pornographic

err
03 sin
06 cock up, offend, slip up
07 be wrong, deviate, mistake
08 go astray, misjudge
09 make a slip, misbehave
10 transgress
11 be incorrect, misconstrue
12 miscalculate
13 fall from grace, misunderstand

errand
03 job
04 duty, task
06 charge
07 message, mission
10 assignment, commission
11 undertaking

errant
05 loose, stray, wrong
06 erring, roving, sinful
07 deviant, lawless, nomadic, roaming, sinning, wayward
08 aberrant, criminal, straying
09 itinerant, offending
10 journeying
11 disobedient, peripatetic

erratic
06 fitful
07 varying
08 sporadic, unstable, unsteady, variable, volatile
09 desultory, eccentric, irregular, unsettled
10 capricious, changeable, inconstant, unreliable
11 fluctuating
12 inconsistent, intermittent
13 unpredictable

erring
05 loose, stray, wrong
06 errant, guilty, sinful
07 deviant, lawless, peccant, sinning, wayward
08 criminal, straying

erroneous
05 false, wrong
06 faulty, flawed, untrue
07 inexact, invalid
08 mistaken, specious, spurious
09 incorrect, misguided, misplaced, unfounded
10 fallacious, inaccurate

error
04 boob, flaw, slip
05 fault, gaffe, lapse, mix-up
06 howler, slip-up
07 blunder, literal, mistake
08 misprint, omission, solecism
09 oversight
10 aberration, inaccuracy
12 misjudgement
13 misconception
14 miscalculation
15 misapprehension, slip of the tongue, spelling mistake

ersatz
04 fake, sham
05 bogus
06 phoney
07 man-made
09 imitation, synthetic
10 artificial, substitute
11 counterfeit

erstwhile
02 ex
03 old
04 late, once, past
06 bygone, former
07 one-time
08 previous, sometime

erudite
06 brainy
07 learned
08 academic, cultured, educated, highbrow, lettered, profound, well-read
09 scholarly
12 intellectual, well-educated
13 knowledgeable

erudition
05 facts
06 wisdom
07 culture, letters
08 learning
09 education, knowledge
10 profundity
11 learnedness, scholarship

erupt
04 emit, gush, spew, vent
05 belch, break, burst, eject, eruct, expel, spout, vomit
07 explode, flare up
08 break out, eructate
09 discharge, pour forth

eruption
04 rash
07 flare-up, venting
08 ejection, emission, outbreak, outburst
09 discharge, explosion
12 inflammation

escalate
04 grow, rise, soar
05 climb, mount, raise
06 ascend, extend, spiral
07 develop, enlarge, magnify
08 heighten, increase
09 intensify
10 accelerate, hit the roof

escalator
04 lift
08 elevator
10 travolator
13 moving walkway
15 moving staircase

escapable
09 avertible, avoidable

escapade
04 lark, romp
05 caper, fling, prank, stunt
07 exploit
09 adventure
10 skylarking

escape
03 fly
04 bolt, bunk, duck, flee, flit, flow, gush, leak, ooze, pass, scat, seep, shun, skip, slip
05 avoid, dodge, drain, elude, evade, issue, scoot, scram
06 decamp, efflux, flight, forget
07 abscond, do a bunk, evasion, fantasy, getaway, leakage, run away, scarper, seepage, trickle

08 breakout, dreaming, emission, shake off, sidestep, slip away
09 avoidance, break free, discharge, diversion, do a runner, emanation, jailbreak
10 break loose, decampment, recreation, relaxation
11 distraction, fantasizing
13 circumvention
14 make a bolt for it
15 make a break for it, not be remembered, take to your heels

escapee
06 truant
07 refugee, runaway
08 defector, deserter, fugitive
09 absconder
11 jailbreaker

escapism
07 fantasy, pastime
08 dreaming
09 diversion
10 recreation, relaxation
11 distraction, fantasizing
15 wishful thinking

escapist
07 dreamer, ostrich
10 daydreamer, fantasizer

eschew
04 shun
05 avoid, forgo, spurn
06 abjure, give up
07 abandon, disdain
08 forswear, renounce
09 repudiate
11 abstain from, keep clear of

escort
04 aide, beau, date, lead, take
05 bring, guard, train, usher
07 company, conduct, cortège, partner, protect, retinue
08 attend on, chaperon, come with, defender, shepherd
09 accompany, attendant, bodyguard, chaperone, companion, entourage
10 attendants

esoteric
06 arcane, hidden, inside, mystic, occult, secret
07 cryptic, obscure, private
08 abstruse, mystical
09 recondite
10 mysterious
11 inscrutable
12 confidential

especial
06 marked, signal, unique
07 express, notable, special
08 peculiar, singular, specific
09 exclusive
10 noteworthy, particular, pre-eminent, remarkable
11 exceptional, outstanding
13 extraordinary

especially
04 very
06 mainly
07 chiefly, notably
08 markedly, uniquely
09 expressly, primarily, supremely, unusually
10 remarkably, strikingly, uncommonly
11 exclusively, principally
12 particularly, pre-eminently
13 exceptionally, outstandingly
15 extraordinarily

espionage
06 spying
07 bugging, probing
08 snooping
11 fifth column, wiretapping
12 infiltration, intelligence, intercepting, surveillance
14 reconnaissance, undercover work

espousal
07 backing, defence, support
08 adoption, advocacy
09 embracing, promotion
11 championing, maintenance

espouse
04 back
05 adopt
06 defend, opt for, take up
07 embrace, support
08 advocate, champion
09 patronize
10 stand up for

espy
03 see, spy
04 spot
05 sight
06 behold, detect, notice
07 discern, glimpse, make out
08 discover, perceive
11 distinguish
12 catch sight of

essay
03 try
04 test
05 go for, paper, piece, tract
06 leader, review, take on, thesis
07 article, attempt, have a go

08 critique, struggle, treatise
09 discourse, undertake
10 assignment, commentary
11 composition
12 disquisition, dissertation

➤ *Names of essayists:*
04 **Hunt** (Leigh), **Lamb** (Charles)
05 **Bacon** (Francis), **Couch** (Sir Arthur Quiller), **Gould** (Stephen Jay), **Pater** (Walter Horatio), **Smith** (Sydney)
06 **Borges** (Jorge Luis), **Orwell** (George), **Ruskin** (John), **Steele** (Sir Richard)
07 **Addison** (Joseph), **Calvino** (Italo), **Carlyle** (Thomas), **Emerson** (Ralph Waldo), **Hazlitt** (William), **Montagu** (Lady Mary Wortley), **Thoreau** (Henry David)
08 **Beerbohm** (Sir Max), **Macaulay** (Thomas Babington, Lord)
09 **De Quincey** (Thomas), **Montaigne** (Michel Eyquem de)
10 **Chesterton** (Gilbert Keith)
➤ See also **writer**

essence
04 core, crux, life, pith, soul
05 being, heart, point
06 centre, entity, kernel, marrow, nature, spirit
07 extract, reality, spirits
09 character, substance
11 concentrate
12 distillation, quintessence
13 concentration

◻**in essence**
09 basically
11 essentially
13 fundamentally, substantially

◻**of the essence**
05 vital
06 needed
07 crucial
08 required
09 important, necessary, requisite
13 indispensable

essential
03 key
04 gist, main, must
05 basic, vital
06 innate, needed
07 central, crucial, typical
08 inherent, key point, required

09 important, intrinsic, necessary, necessity, principal, principle, requisite
10 definitive, sine qua non
11 fundamental, requirement
12 prerequisite
13 indispensable

establish
04 base, form, open, show
05 begin, found, lodge, plant, prove, set up, start
08 affirm, attest, create, ratify, secure, settle, verify
09 institute, introduce
11 corroborate, demonstrate
12 authenticate, substantiate
14 bring into being

established
05 fixed
06 proved, proven, secure
07 settled
10 entrenched
11 experienced, traditional
12 conventional
14 tried and tested

establishment
04 firm, shop
07 company, concern, forming
08 business, creation, founding
09 formation, inception, institute, the system
10 enterprise, foundation
11 corporation, institution
12 inauguration, installation
14 the authorities
15 the powers that be

estate
04 area, land, rank
05 goods, lands, manor, place
06 assets, centre, region, status
07 effects
08 holdings, position, property
09 condition, situation
10 belongings, real estate
11 development, possessions

estate agent
07 realtor
13 property agent
15 real-estate agent

esteem
04 deem, hold, love, rate, view
05 count, judge, think, value
06 admire, credit, honour, reckon, regard, revere
07 adjudge, believe, respect
08 consider, treasure, venerate
09 judgement, reckoning
10 admiration, estimation
11 approbation, good opinion

esteemed

12 appreciation, regard highly
13 consideration

esteemed

06 prized, valued, worthy
07 admired, revered
08 honoured
09 admirable, excellent, reputable, respected, treasured, venerated
10 honourable
11 respectable
13 distinguished, well-respected, well-thought-of
14 highly-regarded

estimable

04 good
06 valued, worthy
07 notable
08 esteemed, valuable
09 admirable, excellent, reputable, respected
10 creditable, honourable
11 commendable, meritorious
12 praiseworthy
13 distinguished

estimate

05 gauge, guess, value
06 assess, belief, reckon
07 opinion
08 evaluate, thinking
09 judgement, quotation, reckoning, valuation
10 assessment, estimation, evaluation, rough guess
11 computation, guesstimate
13 approximation
14 ballpark figure

estimation

05 guess
06 belief, credit, esteem, regard
07 feeling, opinion, respect
08 estimate, thinking
09 judgement, valuation
10 assessment, conclusion, evaluation, rough guess
11 calculation, computation
13 consideration

estrange

04 part
05 sever
06 divide
07 break up, divorce, split up
08 alienate, disunite, separate
09 disaffect
10 antagonize, drive apart
13 set at variance

estranged

07 divided
08 divorced, separate

09 alienated, separated
11 antagonized, disaffected

estrangement

05 split
06 breach
07 break-up, parting
08 disunity, division
09 antipathy, hostility
10 alienation, separation
12 disaffection, dissociation
14 antagonization

estuary

03 arm, bay
05 firth, fjord, inlet, mouth
07 sea-loch

et cetera

03 etc
04 et al
07 and so on
10 and so forth, and the like, and the rest, or whatever
11 and suchlike, and whatever
14 and what have you

etch

03 cut, dig
04 bite, burn
05 carve, stamp
06 furrow, groove, incise
07 corrode, engrave, impress, imprint, ingrain
08 inscribe

etching

03 cut
05 print
06 sketch
07 carving, imprint
09 engraving
10 impression
11 inscription

eternal

07 abiding, endless, lasting, non-stop, undying
08 constant, enduring, immortal, infinite, timeless, unending
09 ceaseless, deathless, limitless, perpetual
10 continuous, persistent, relentless, unchanging
11 everlasting, never-ending
12 imperishable, interminable
14 indestructible

eternally

06 always
07 for ever
09 endlessly, lastingly
10 constantly
11 ceaselessly, perpetually
12 interminably
13 everlastingly

eternity

06 heaven
08 infinity, long time, paradise
09 after-life, hereafter, next world
10 perpetuity
11 ages and ages, endlessness
12 immutability, timelessness
15 everlasting life, world without end

ethereal

04 fine
05 light
06 dainty, subtle
07 refined, tenuous
08 delicate, empyreal, empyrean, gossamer, heavenly, rarefied
09 airy-fairy, celestial, exquisite, spiritual, unearthly, unworldly
10 diaphanous, intangible
13 insubstantial

ethical

04 fair, good, just
05 moral, noble, right
06 decent, honest, seemly
07 correct, fitting, upright
08 decorous, virtuous
10 honourable, principled

ethics

04 code
05 rules
06 equity, morals, values
07 beliefs
08 morality
09 moral code, standards
10 conscience, principles
11 moral values
14 moral standards
15 moral philosophy

ethnic

04 folk
06 native, racial, tribal
08 cultural, national
10 aboriginal, indigenous
11 traditional

ethos

04 code
05 tenor
06 ethics, spirit
07 beliefs, flavour, manners
08 attitude, morality
09 character, rationale
10 principles
11 disposition

etiquette

04 code, form
05 rules

07 customs, decency, decorum, manners
08 ceremony, civility, courtesy, good form, protocol
09 propriety, standards
10 politeness
11 conventions, correctness, formalities, good manners
12 unwritten law
13 code of conduct
14 code of practice
15 code of behaviour

etymology
06 origin, source
08 word-lore
09 philology, semantics
10 derivation, lexicology
11 linguistics, word history, word origins

eulogize
04 hype, laud, plug
05 exalt, extol
06 honour, praise
07 acclaim, applaud, approve, commend, glorify, magnify
10 panegyrize, wax lyrical

eulogy
04 laud
05 paean
06 praise
07 acclaim, plaudit, tribute
08 accolade, encomium
09 laudation, panegyric
10 compliment, exaltation
11 acclamation
12 commendation
13 glorification

euphemism
07 evasion
09 softening
10 genteelism, polite term
12 substitution

euphemistic
05 vague
06 polite
07 evasive, genteel, neutral
08 indirect
11 understated

euphonious
04 soft
05 clear, sweet
06 dulcet, mellow
07 melodic, musical, silvery
09 consonant, melodious
10 harmonious, sweet-toned
11 dulcifluous, mellifluous
13 sweet-sounding

euphoria
03 joy

04 glee, high
05 bliss
07 ecstasy, elation, rapture
08 buoyancy
09 transport, well-being
10 exultation, jubilation
11 high spirits
12 cheerfulness, exhilaration, intoxication

euphoric
04 high
05 happy
06 elated, joyful, joyous
07 buoyant, exulted, gleeful
08 blissful, cheerful, ecstatic, exultant, jubilant
09 rapturous
11 exhilarated, intoxicated

euthanasia
07 quietus, release
12 happy release, mercy killing
15 merciful release

evacuate
04 quit, void
05 clear, eject, empty, expel, leave, purge
06 decamp, depart, desert, remove, vacate
07 abandon, excrete, forsake
08 clear out, defecate
09 discharge, eliminate, make empty, pull out of

evacuation
06 exodus, flight
07 leaving, purging, removal
08 ejection, emptying, vacating
09 clearance, desertion, discharge, expulsion, forsaking, urination
10 defecation, retirement
11 abandonment, elimination

evade
04 balk, duck, shun
05 avoid, dodge, elude, fudge, hedge, parry, shirk, skive
06 cop out, escape
08 get round, sidestep
10 circumvent, equivocate
11 prevaricate
12 steer clear of

evaluate
04 rank, rate
05 gauge, judge, value, weigh
06 assess, reckon, size up
07 compute, measure
08 appraise, estimate
09 calculate, determine

evaluation
07 opinion

08 estimate
09 appraisal, judgement, reckoning, valuation
10 assessment, estimation
11 calculation, computation

evanescent
05 brief
06 fading
07 passing
08 fleeting, unstable
09 ephemeral, momentary, temporary, transient, vanishing
10 short-lived, transitory
12 disappearing
13 insubstantial

evangelical
07 zealous
08 biblical, orthodox
09 crusading
10 missionary, scriptural
11 campaigning
12 Bible-bashing, evangelistic
13 Bible-punching, Bible-thumping, proselytizing
14 fundamentalist

evangelist
08 crusader, preacher
10 campaigner, missionary

evangelize
06 preach
07 baptize, convert, crusade
08 campaign
11 proselytize
13 spread the word

evaporate
03 dry
04 fade, melt
06 dispel, exhale, vanish
08 disperse, dissolve, evanesce, melt away, vaporize
09 dehydrate, dissipate

evaporation
06 drying, fading
07 melting
09 vanishing
11 dehydration, desiccation
12 condensation, distillation, vaporization

evasion
05 dodge
06 deceit, escape, excuse
07 dodging, ducking, fencing, fudging, hedging, quibble
08 shirking, shunning, trickery
09 avoidance, deception
12 equivocation
13 circumvention, prevarication

14 tergiversation
15 steering clear of

evasive
05 cagey, vague
07 cunning, devious, oblique
08 indirect, slippery, waffling
09 deceitful, secretive
12 equivocating
13 prevaricating

eve
07 evening
09 day before, threshold

even
03 too
04 also, calm, cool, fair, flat,
   just, like, more, same,
   true
05 at all, equal, flush, level,
   match, oddly, plane, still
06 as well, hardly, indeed,
   placid, serene, smooth,
   square, stable, steady
07 equable, flatten, regular
08 balanced, composed,
   constant, matching, parallel,
   scarcely, tranquil
09 equitable, impartial, make
   equal, stabilize, still more,
   unruffled, unvarying
10 all the more, consistent,
   fifty-fifty, straighten,
   unchanging, unwavering
11 neck and neck, non-
   partisan, symmetrical,
   unexcitable, unflappable
12 even-tempered, surprisingly
13 more precisely

❑ **even so**
03 but, yet
05 still
07 however
10 all the same
11 despite that, nonetheless
12 nevertheless
13 in spite of that

even-handed
04 fair, just
06 square
07 neutral
08 balanced, unbiased
09 equitable, impartial
10 reasonable
12 unprejudiced
13 disinterested, dispassionate

evening
03 eve
04 dusk
06 sunset
07 sundown
08 eventide, twilight

09 nightfall
10 close of day

event
04 case, fact, game, item, race
05 issue, match, round
06 affair, matter, result, upshot
07 contest, episode, fixture,
   meeting, outcome
08 business, incident, occasion
09 adventure, aftermath,
   happening, milestone
10 experience, occurrence
11 competition, possibility
12 circumstance

even-tempered
04 calm, cool
06 placid, serene, stable, steady
07 equable, unfazed
08 composed, laid-back,
   peaceful, tranquil
09 peaceable
13 imperturbable

eventful
04 busy, full
06 active, lively
09 important, memorable
11 interesting, significant
12 action-packed

eventual
04 last
05 final, later
06 future
07 closing, ensuing, planned
08 ultimate
09 impending, projected, resulting
10 concluding, subsequent

eventuality
04 case
05 event
06 chance, crisis, mishap
07 outcome
09 emergency, happening
10 likelihood
11 contingency, possibility
12 circumstance

eventually
06 at last
07 finally
08 after all, at length, in the end
10 ultimately
12 in the long run
13 sooner or later

ever
05 at all
06 always
07 for ever
08 evermore
09 at any time, endlessly,
   eternally, in any case

10 at all times, constantly
11 continually, incessantly,
   permanently, perpetually
12 on any account
13 on any occasion

❑ **ever so**
04 very
06 really
08 very much
09 extremely

everlasting
07 endless, eternal, undying
08 constant, immortal, timeless
09 permanent, perpetual
10 continuous, persistent
11 never-ending, unremitting
12 imperishable, interminable
14 indestructible

evermore
04 ever
06 always
07 for ever
09 eternally, ever after, hereafter
10 henceforth
11 in perpetuum, unceasingly
14 for ever and a day, for ever
   and ever, to the end of time

every
03 all
04 each, full
11 all possible, every single
15 every individual

everybody
08 everyone
09 one and all
10 each person
11 every person
12 all and sundry
13 the whole world

everyday
05 basic, daily, plain, usual
06 common, normal, simple
07 average, regular, routine
08 day-to-day, familiar,
   frequent, habitual, ordinary,
   standard, workaday
11 commonplace
13 run-of-the-mill
14 common-or-garden

everyone
07 each one
09 everybody, one and all
10 each person
11 every person
12 all and sundry, every man
   Jack
13 the whole world

everything
03 all

06 the lot, the sum
08 the total, the works
09 all things, each thing
11 the entirety, the whole lot
15 the whole shebang

everywhere
07 all over
09 all around
10 every place, far and near, far and wide, high and low, near and far, throughout
11 in all places, to all places
12 the world over
14 right and centre

evict
04 oust
05 eject, expel
06 put out, remove
07 kick out, turf out, turn out
08 chuck out, dislodge, force out, throw out
10 dispossess
11 expropriate
12 force to leave

eviction
07 removal, the boot, the push
08 ejection, the elbow
09 clearance, expulsion
11 the bum's rush
12 dislodgement
13 dispossession, expropriation

evidence
04 data, hint, mark, show, sign
05 proof, prove, token, trace
07 exhibit, grounds, support, symptom, witness
09 affidavit, testimony
10 indication, suggestion
11 affirmation, declaration
12 confirmation, verification
13 corroboration, documentation
14 substantiation

◻**in evidence**
05 clear, plain
06 patent
07 obvious, visible
08 apparent, clear-cut
10 noticeable
11 conspicuous

evident
05 clear, plain
06 patent
07 obvious, visible
08 apparent, manifest, tangible
10 noticeable
11 conspicuous, discernible, perceptible
12 indisputable, unmistakable

evidently
07 clearly, plainly
08 patently
09 doubtless, obviously, outwardly, seemingly
10 apparently, manifestly, ostensibly
11 so it appears

evil
03 bad, ill, sin, woe
04 base, blow, dire, foul, harm, hurt, pain, ruin, vice, vile
05 black, cruel, curse, wrong
06 injury, misery, sinful, wicked
07 badness, corrupt, demonic, harmful, heinous, immoral, noxious, ruinous, vicious
08 baseness, depraved, devilish, diabolic, iniquity, mischief, sinister, vileness
09 adversity, depravity, malicious, malignant, malignity, nefarious
10 affliction, calamitous, corruption, immorality, iniquitous, malevolent, pernicious, sinfulness, wickedness
11 catastrophe, deleteriousl, heinousness, viciousness
12 catastrophic, devilishness

evildoer
05 rogue
06 sinner
07 villain
08 criminal, offender
09 miscreant, reprobate, scoundrel, wrongdoer

evince
04 show
06 attest, betray, reveal
07 bespeak, betoken, declare, display, exhibit, express
08 evidence, indicate, manifest
11 demonstrate

eviscerate
03 gut
04 draw
08 gralloch
10 disembowel, exenterate

evocation
04 echo
08 inducing, kindling, stirring
10 activation, excitation, invocation, suggestion
11 elicitation, stimulation, summoning-up

evocative
05 vivid
07 graphic

08 redolent
09 memorable
10 expressive, indicative, suggestive
11 reminiscent

evoke
04 call, stir
05 cause, raise
06 arouse, awaken, call up, elicit, excite, induce, invoke, kindle, recall, summon
07 provoke
08 summon up
09 call forth, conjure up

evolution
06 growth
07 descent
08 increase, progress, ripening
09 unfolding, unrolling
10 derivation, opening-out
11 development, progression

evolve
04 grow
06 derive, emerge, expand, mature, result, unfold, unroll
07 descend, develop, unravel

exacerbate
03 vex
06 deepen, enrage, worsen
07 inflame, provoke, sharpen
08 heighten, increase, irritate
09 aggravate, infuriate, intensify, make worse
10 exaggerate, exasperate
15 make things worse

exact
04 just, milk, true
05 bleed, claim, close, force, right, wrest, wring
06 bang on, compel, demand, extort, impose, spot on
07 call for, careful, command, correct, extract, literal, precise, require, squeeze
08 accurate, definite, detailed, explicit, faithful, flawless, insist on, specific, thorough
09 identical, on the nail
10 blow-by-blow, methodical, meticulous, scrupulous
11 on the button, painstaking, punctilious, word-perfect

exacting
04 firm, hard
05 harsh, stern, tough
06 severe, strict, taxing, tiring
07 arduous, onerous
08 rigorous

09 demanding, difficult, laborious, stringent
11 challenging, painstaking

exactitude
04 care
06 detail, rigour
08 accuracy
09 exactness, precision
10 strictness
11 carefulness, correctness, orderliness
14 meticulousness

exactly
04 dead, just, to a T, true
05 plumb, quite, right, truly
06 agreed, bang on, indeed, just so, spot on
08 of course, on the dot, strictly, verbatim
09 correctly, expressly, literally, on the nail, precisely
10 absolutely, accurately, definitely, faithfully, unerringly
11 faultlessly, on the button, religiously, to the letter
12 particularly, scrupulously, specifically, without error

exactness
08 accuracy
09 precision
10 exactitude, strictness
11 correctness, orderliness
12 rigorousness, thoroughness
14 meticulousness

exaggerate
06 colour, overdo, stress
07 amplify, enlarge, magnify
08 overplay, oversell, pile it on
09 dramatize, embellish, embroider, overstate
10 aggrandize, shoot a line
12 lay it on thick
13 overdramatize, pile it on thick
15 stretch the truth

exaggerated
04 tall
08 inflated, overdone
09 amplified, excessive
10 hyperbolic, overstated
11 caricatured, embellished

exaggeration
06 excess, parody
09 burlesque, hyperbole
10 caricature
11 enlargement
12 extravagance, overemphasis

13 amplification, magnification, overstatement
14 overestimation

exalt
04 laud
05 adore, bless, extol, raise
06 honour, praise, prefer, revere
07 acclaim, applaud, elevate, glorify, magnify, promote, upgrade, worship
08 eulogize, venerate
09 reverence, transport

exaltation
03 joy
05 bliss, glory
06 eulogy, honour, praise
07 acclaim, ecstasy, elation, rapture, worship
09 adoration, reverence
10 jubilation, veneration
11 high spirits
12 exhilaration
13 glorification

exalted
04 high
05 grand, lofty, noble, regal
06 elated, joyful, lordly
07 eminent, stately
08 blissful, ecstatic, elevated
09 rapturous
13 in high spirits
15 in seventh heaven

exam
04 oral, quiz, test, viva
05 final, paper
09 practical, questions
11 examination

examination
04 exam, oral, scan, test, viva
05 audit, check, probe, study
06 review, search, survey
07 check-up, inquiry, perusal
08 analysis, critique, once-over, research, scrutiny
09 appraisal
10 assessment, inspection, post-mortem
11 exploration, inquisition, observation, questioning
13 interrogation, investigation

examine
03 vet
04 case, pump, quiz, scan, sift, test
05 assay, audit, check, grill, probe, study
06 assess, look at, peruse, ponder, review, survey

07 analyse, explore, inquire, inspect, observe, weigh up
08 appraise, check out, consider, look into, pore over, question, research
11 interrogate, investigate
12 cross-examine
13 cross-question

examinee
07 entrant
09 applicant, candidate
10 competitor, contestant
11 interviewee

examiner
05 judge
06 censor, critic, marker, tester
07 analyst, arbiter, auditor
08 assessor, reviewer
09 examinant, inspector
10 questioner, scrutineer
11 adjudicator, interviewer
12 interlocutor

example
04 case, type
05 guide, ideal, model
06 lesson, sample
07 epitome, pattern, warning
08 exemplar, instance, paradigm, specimen
09 archetype, precedent, prototype, role model
11 case in point, typical case
12 illustration
15 exemplification

❏**for example**
02 eg
03 say
11 as an example, for instance
12 as an instance, to illustrate

exasperate
04 gall, goad, rile
05 anger, annoy, get to, rouse
06 enrage, madden, rankle
07 incense, provoke
09 infuriate
14 drive up the wall

exasperated
05 angry, fed up, irked, riled
06 bugged, galled, goaded
07 angered, annoyed, needled
08 incensed, maddened
10 aggravated, infuriated

exasperating
09 maddening, provoking
10 bothersome, pernicious
11 aggravating, infuriating

excavate
03 cut, dig
04 mine

05 delve, dig up, gouge, scoop
06 burrow, dig out, exhume, hollow, quarry, reveal, tunnel
07 uncover, unearth
08 disinter

excavation
03 dig, pit
04 hole, mine
05 ditch, shaft
06 burrow, cavity, crater, dugout, hollow, quarry, trench, trough
08 colliery, diggings

exceed
03 cap, top
04 beat, pass
05 outdo
06 better, go over, outrun
07 eclipse, surpass
08 go beyond, outshine, outstrip, overstep
09 outnumber, transcend
10 be more than
12 be larger than
13 be greater than

exceedingly
04 very
06 highly, hugely, vastly
07 greatly
08 very much
09 amazingly, extremely, immensely, unusually
10 enormously, especially
11 excessively
12 inordinately, surpassingly
13 astonishingly, exceptionally
15 extraordinarily

excel
04 beat
05 outdo, shine
07 eclipse, outrank, surpass
08 outclass, outrival, stand out
10 outperform
11 be excellent, predominate
12 be better than
13 be outstanding

excellence
05 merit, skill, value, worth
06 purity, virtue
08 fineness, goodness
09 greatness, supremacy
10 perfection
11 distinction, pre-eminence
13 transcendence

excellent
03 ace
04 cool, fine, good, mega, neat
05 brill, great, noted, prime
06 groovy, select, superb, way-out, wicked, worthy

07 crucial, eminent, notable, perfect, radical, shit-hot
08 flawless, inspired, splendid, sterling, top-notch, very good
09 admirable, brilliant, exemplary, fantastic, faultless, first-rate, matchless, wonderful
10 first-class, marvellous, noteworthy, pre-eminent, remarkable, unequalled
11 commendable, exceptional, outstanding, superlative
12 praiseworthy, second to none, unparalleled
13 distinguished
14 out of this world

except
03 bar, but
04 less, omit, save
05 minus
06 but for, reject
07 barring, besides, rule out
08 leave out, omitting
09 apart from, aside from, except for, excepting, excluding, other than
10 leaving out
11 not counting

exception
05 freak, quirk
06 oddity, rarity
07 anomaly
11 abnormality, peculiarity, special case
12 irregularity
13 inconsistency

❑**with the exception of**
03 bar, but
04 less, save
05 minus
07 barring, besides
08 omitting
09 apart from, except for, excepting, excluding, other than
10 leaving out
11 not counting

exceptionable
09 abhorrent, offensive, repugnant
10 deplorable, disgusting, unpleasant
12 disagreeable, unacceptable
13 objectionable

exceptional
03 odd
04 rare
07 notable, special, unusual

08 aberrant, abnormal, atypical, peculiar, singular, superior, uncommon
09 anomalous, brilliant, excellent, irregular
10 marvellous, noteworthy, phenomenal, prodigious, remarkable, unequalled
11 outstanding
13 extraordinary

exceptionally
06 rarely
07 notably
09 extremely, unusually
10 abnormally, especially, remarkably, uncommonly
13 outstandingly
15 extraordinarily

excerpt
04 clip, part
05 piece, quote, scrap
07 cutting, extract, passage
08 citation, clipping, fragment,
09 quotation, selection

excess
04 glut
05 extra, spare
07 backlog, residue, surfeit, surplus, too much
08 bellyful, left-over, overflow, overkill, plethora, residual
09 leftovers, redundant, remainder, remaining
10 additional, debauchery
11 dissipation, prodigality, superfluity, superfluous
12 extravagance, intemperance
13 dissoluteness
14 more than enough, overindulgence, superabundance

excessive
03 OTT
05 steep, undue
07 extreme, too much
08 needless, overdone
10 exorbitant, immoderate, inordinate, over the top
11 extravagant, superfluous, uncalled-for, unnecessary
12 unreasonable
13 superabundant

excessively
06 overly, unduly
07 too much
08 overmuch, to a fault
09 extremely
10 needlessly
12 exorbitantly, immoderately, inordinately, unreasonably

13 extravagantly, intemperately, superfluously, unnecessarily

exchange
04 chat, swap
05 bandy, trade
06 barter, change, switch
07 commute, convert, replace
08 argument, trade-off
09 transpose
11 catallactic, give and take, interchange, reciprocate, reciprocity, replacement
12 conversation, substitution

excise
03 cut, tax, VAT
04 duty, levy, toll
05 erase
06 cut out, delete, impost, remove, tariff
07 customs, destroy, expunge, extract, rescind
09 eradicate, expurgate, extirpate, surcharge

excision
07 removal
08 deletion
11 destruction, eradication, expurgation, extirpation

excitable
05 fiery, hasty
07 nervous
08 choleric, volatile
09 emotional, hot-headed, irascible, mercurial, sensitive
11 hot-tempered, susceptible
12 highly-strung
13 quick-tempered, temperamental

excite
04 fire, move, sway
05 evoke, rouse, touch, upset
06 arouse, awaken, ignite, incite, induce, kindle, stir up, thrill, turn on
07 agitate, animate, impress, inflame, inspire, provoke
08 engender, generate
09 stimulate, titillate

excited
04 high, wild
05 eager, hyper, moved
06 elated, roused
07 aroused, fired up, stirred
08 agitated, animated, frenzied, restless, turned on, worked up
10 stimulated
11 exhilarated, overwrought
12 enthusiastic
13 in high spirits
14 thrilled to bits

excitement
03 ado
04 fuss, kick, stir
05 fever, kicks
06 action, furore, thrill, tumult
07 elation, emotion, passion
09 adventure, agitation, animation, commotion
10 enthusiasm
11 stimulation
12 exhilaration, perturbation

exciting
04 sexy
06 moving
07 rousing
08 dramatic, stirring, striking
09 inspiring, thrilling
10 nail-biting
11 enthralling, provocative, sensational, stimulating
12 action-packed, breathtaking, cliff-hanging, electrifying, exhilarating

exclaim
03 cry
04 call, roar, yell
05 blurt, shout, utter
06 bellow, cry out, shriek
07 declare
08 blurt out, proclaim
09 ejaculate

exclamation
03 cry
04 call, roar, yell
05 shout
06 bellow, outcry, shriek
09 expletive, utterance
11 ejaculation
12 interjection

exclude
03 ban, bar
04 drop, omit, skip, veto
05 eject, evict, expel
06 delete, forbid, ignore, refuse, reject, remove
07 keep out, miss out, rule out
08 disallow, leave out, preclude, prohibit
09 blacklist, eliminate, ostracize
13 excommunicate

exclusion
03 ban, bar
04 veto
07 boycott, embargo, refusal
08 ejection, eviction, omission
09 exception, expulsion, interdict, ruling out
10 preclusion
11 elimination, prohibition
12 proscription

exclusive
04 chic, only, posh, sole
05 plush, ritzy, total, whole
06 choice, classy, closed, select, single, unique
07 cliquey, limited, private
08 complete, peculiar, snobbish, up-market
09 undivided
10 individual, restricted
11 fashionable, restrictive

❏**exclusive of**
06 except
07 barring
08 omitting
09 debarring, except for, excepting, ruling out
10 leaving out
11 not counting
12 not including

excommunicate
03 ban, bar
05 debar, eject, expel
06 banish, outlaw, remove
07 exclude
08 denounce, unchurch
09 blacklist, proscribe
12 anathematize

excoriate
05 blame, decry, knock, slate
06 attack
07 censure, condemn, run down
08 denounce
09 denigrate, disparage
10 animadvert, vituperate

excrement
04 dung, poop, turd
05 frass, guano, scats, stool
06 egesta, faeces, ordure
09 droppings, excretion
11 waste matter

excrescence
04 boil, bump, knob, lump, wart
06 cancer, growth, tumour
08 swelling
09 appendage, outgrowth
10 projection, prominence
12 intumescence, protuberance
13 disfigurement

excrete
04 pass, void
05 eject, expel, exude
07 secrete, urinate
08 defecate, evacuate
09 discharge

excretion
04 dung
05 stool

06 faeces, ordure
07 excreta
09 discharge, droppings, excrement, urination
10 defecation, evacuation
12 perspiration

excruciating
05 acute, sharp
06 bitter, savage, severe
07 intense, painful, racking
09 agonizing, atrocious
10 tormenting, unbearable
11 intolerable
12 insufferable

exculpate
05 clear
06 acquit, excuse, let off, pardon
07 absolve, forgive, release
09 exonerate, vindicate

excursion
04 ride, tour, trip, walk
05 drive, jaunt
06 detour, outing, ramble
07 day trip, journey
09 departure, diversion
10 digression, expedition

excusable
09 allowable
10 defensible, forgivable, pardonable
11 explainable, justifiable
14 understandable

excuse
04 free, plea
05 alibi, front, shift, spare
06 acquit, cop-out, exempt, let off, pardon, reason
07 absolve, cover-up, defence, evasion, forgive, grounds, indulge, justify, release
08 mitigate, overlook, tolerate
09 discharge, exculpate, exonerate, vindicate
11 explanation, vindication
13 justification

execrable
04 foul, vile
06 odious
07 hateful, heinous
08 accursed, damnable, horrible, shocking
09 abhorrent, appalling, atrocious, loathsome, obnoxious, offensive, repulsive, revolting
10 abominable, deplorable, despicable, disgusting

execrate
04 damn, hate
05 abhor, blast, curse
06 detest, loathe, revile, vilify
07 condemn, deplore, despise
08 denounce
09 abominate, excoriate, fulminate, imprecate

execute
02 do
04 hang, kill
05 enact, serve, shoot, stage
06 behead, effect, finish, fulfil
07 achieve, crucify, deliver, enforce, perform, realize
08 bring off, carry out, complete, dispatch, engineer, expedite, validate
09 discharge, liquidate
10 accomplish, decapitate, guillotine, put to death
11 electrocute
15 put into practice

execution
07 killing, staging
08 delivery, dispatch
09 discharge, operation, rendition, technique
10 completion, fulfilment
11 achievement, enforcement, performance, realization
12 death penalty
13 death sentence
14 accomplishment, implementation, putting to death

▶ *Methods of execution*:
07 burning, gassing, hanging, stoning
08 lynching, shooting
09 beheading
10 garrotting
11 crucifixion, firing squad
12 decapitation, guillotining
13 electrocution
15 lethal injection

executioner
06 axeman, hit man, killer
07 hangman
08 assassin, murderer
12 exterminator

executive
06 leader
07 guiding, leading, manager
08 director, governor, official
09 directing, governing, hierarchy, organizer
10 controller, government, leadership, management, managerial, organizing

11 controlling, directorial
13 administrator
14 administrative, decision-making, organizational

exegesis
10 exposition, expounding
11 explanation, explication
13 clarification
14 interpretation

exemplar
04 copy, type
05 ideal, model
07 epitome, example, paragon
08 instance, paradigm, specimen, standard
09 archetype, criterion, prototype, yardstick
10 embodiment
12 illustration
15 exemplification

exemplary
04 good
05 ideal, model
06 worthy
07 correct, perfect, warning
08 flawless, laudable
09 admirable, estimable, excellent, faultless
10 cautionary, honourable
11 commendable, meritorious
12 praiseworthy

exemplify
04 cite, show
06 depict, embody, typify
08 instance, manifest
09 epitomize, represent
10 illustrate
11 demonstrate
12 characterize
13 be an example of

exempt
05 clear, spare, waive
06 excuse, let off, spared
07 absolve, dismiss, exclude, excused, release, relieve
08 absolved, excluded, released
09 dismissed, exonerate, liberated, not liable
10 discharged, not subject
15 grant immunity to, make an exception

exemption
07 freedom, release
08 immunity
09 discharge, exception, exclusion, privilege
10 absolution, indulgence
11 exoneration
12 dispensation

exercise
02 PE, PT
03 try, use, vex
04 task, work
05 annoy, apply, drill, exert, train, upset, wield, worry
06 burden, effort, employ, lesson, sports, warm-up
07 afflict, disturb, exploit, jogging, keep fit, keep-fit, perturb, running, trouble, utilize, work out, workout
08 activity, aerobics, distress, exertion, movement, practice, practise, training
09 implement, make use of, operation, preoccupy
10 assignment, discipline, employment, fulfilment, gymnastics, isometrics
11 application, bring to bear, eurhythmics, piece of work
13 bring into play, callisthenics, exert yourself, physical jerks
14 implementation

exert
03 use
05 apply, spend, wield
06 employ, expend
08 exercise
11 bring to bear

◻**exert yourself**
04 toil, work
05 sweat
06 labour, strain, strive
07 try hard
08 go all out, struggle
09 endeavour, take pains
10 do your best
11 give your all
12 do your utmost
13 apply yourself
15 make every effort

exertion
03 use
04 toil, work
05 pains, trial
06 effort, labour, strain, stress
07 attempt, travail
08 exercise, industry, struggle
09 endeavour, operation
11 application, utilization

exhale
04 blow, emit
05 expel, issue, steam
06 expire
07 breathe, emanate, give off, respire
10 breathe out

exhaust
03 dry, sap, tax
04 do in, tire
05 drain, empty, fumes, smoke, spend, steam, use up, waste
06 expend, fag out, finish, strain, vapour, weaken
07 consume, deplete, fatigue, overtax, tire out, wear out
08 bankrupt, emission, enervate, knock out, overwork, squander
09 discharge, dissipate
10 exhalation, impoverish

exhausted
03 dry
04 done, void, weak
05 all in, empty, jaded, spent
06 bushed, done in, used up
07 drained, whacked, worn out
08 burnt out, consumed, dead-beat, depleted, dog-tired, fatigued, finished, tired out
09 dead tired, enervated, fagged out, knackered
11 ready to drop

exhausting
04 hard
06 severe, taxing, tiring
07 arduous, testing, wearing
08 draining
09 gruelling, laborious, punishing, strenuous
10 enervating, formidable

exhaustion
07 fatigue
09 tiredness, weariness
10 enervation, feebleness

exhaustive
04 full
05 total
06 all-out
07 in-depth
08 complete, detailed, sweeping, thorough
09 extensive, full-scale
10 definitive
11 far-reaching
12 all-embracing, all-inclusive
13 comprehensive

exhibit
03 air
04 show
05 array, model, offer
06 expose, flaunt, parade, reveal, set out, unveil
07 display, express, present
08 disclose, indicate, manifest
11 demonstrate

12 illustration, presentation
13 demonstration

exhibition
04 expo, fair, show
06 airing
07 display, exhibit, showing
09 spectacle
10 disclosure, exposition, indication, revelation
12 presentation
13 demonstration

exhibitionist
05 poser
06 poseur
07 show-off
09 extrovert

exhilarate
04 lift
05 elate
06 excite, perk up, thrill
07 animate, cheer up, delight, enliven, gladden
08 brighten, vitalize
10 invigorate, revitalize

exhilarating
05 heady
08 cheerful, cheering, exciting
09 thrilling
10 enlivening, gladdening
11 mind-blowing, stimulating
12 breathtaking, invigorating, revitalizing

exhilaration
03 joy
04 dash, glee, zeal, élan
06 ardour, gaiety, thrill
07 delight, elation
08 gladness, hilarity, vivacity
09 animation, happiness
10 enthusiasm, excitement, joyfulness, liveliness
11 high spirits, stimulation
12 cheerfulness, invigoration
14 revitalization

exhort
03 bid
04 goad, spur, urge, warn
05 press
06 advise, enjoin, prompt
07 beseech, caution, counsel, entreat, implore, inspire
08 admonish, persuade
09 encourage, instigate

exhortation
06 advice, sermon, urging
07 bidding, caution, counsel, goading, lecture, warning
08 entreaty
09 enjoinder

10 admonition, beseeching, incitement, paraenesis, persuasion, protreptic
13 encouragement

exhume
05 dig up
07 unearth
08 disinter, excavate
09 disentomb, resurrect

exigency
04 need
06 crisis, demand, plight, stress
07 urgency
08 distress, pressure, quandary
09 emergency, necessity
10 difficulty
11 predicament, requirement

exigent
06 urgent
07 crucial
08 critical, exacting, pressing
09 demanding, insistent, necessary, stringent

exiguous
04 bare, slim
05 scant
06 meagre, scanty, slight
10 negligible
12 insufficient

exile
03 ban, bar
04 oust
05 eject, ex-pat, expel
06 banish, deport, outlaw, pariah, uproot, émigré
07 cast out, outcast, refugee
08 deportee, drive out
09 expulsion, extradite, ostracism, ostracize
10 banishment, expatriate, repatriate, separation
11 deportation
12 expatriation
14 transportation
15 displaced person

exist
02 be
04 last, live
06 endure, happen, remain
07 breathe, subsist, survive
08 continue, have life
09 be present, have being
10 have breath

existence
04 fact, life
05 being, thing
06 breath, entity, living
07 reality
08 creation, creature, survival

09 actuality, endurance, lifestyle, way of life
11 continuance, subsistence

existent
04 real
05 alive
06 actual, around, extant, living
07 abiding, current, present
08 enduring, existing, standing
09 remaining, surviving
10 prevailing

exit
02 go
04 door, gate, vent
05 going, issue, leave
06 depart, egress, exodus, flight, outlet, retire, way out
07 doorway, leaving, retreat
08 farewell, withdraw
09 departure
10 retirement, withdrawal
11 leave-taking
13 take your leave

exodus
04 exit
06 escape, flight, hegira
07 fleeing, leaving, retreat
09 departure, migration
10 evacuation, withdrawal

exonerate
04 free
05 clear, spare
06 acquit, excuse, exempt, let off, pardon
07 absolve, justify, release
09 exculpate, vindicate

exoneration
06 pardon, relief
07 amnesty, freeing, release
08 excusing, immunity
09 acquittal, dismissal, exemption, indemnity
10 absolution, liberation
11 exculpation, vindication

exorbitant
05 undue
07 a rip-off
09 excessive, monstrous
11 extravagant, unwarranted
12 extortionate, unreasonable
15 daylight robbery

exorcism
07 freeing
09 expulsion
10 adjuration, casting out
11 deliverance
12 exsufflation, purification

exorcize
04 free

05 expel
06 adjure, purify
07 cast out
08 drive out
10 exsufflate

exotic
05 alien
07 bizarre, curious, foreign, strange, unusual
08 external, imported, peculiar, striking, tropical
09 colourful, different, glamorous, non-native
10 impressive, introduced, outlandish, outrageous, remarkable, unfamiliar
11 extravagant, fascinating
13 extraordinary

expand
04 grow
05 swell, widen
06 blow up, dilate, extend, fatten, spread, unfold, unfurl
07 amplify, broaden, develop, distend, enlarge, fill out, inflate, magnify, open out, puff out, stretch, thicken
08 escalate, increase, lengthen
09 branch out, diversify, intensify, intumesce

❏**expand on**
09 embroider, enlarge on
11 elaborate on, expatiate on
13 go into details

expanse
04 area
05 field, plain, range, space, sweep, tract
06 extent, region
07 breadth, stretch
13 extensiveness

expansion
06 growth, spread
07 expanse
08 dilation, increase, swelling
09 diffusion, extension, inflation, unfolding
10 broadening, dilatation, distension, thickening
11 development, enlargement, lengthening
12 augmentation
13 amplification, magnification
14 multiplication
15 diversification

expansive
04 open, warm, wide
05 broad
06 genial
07 affable, growing

08 effusive, friendly, outgoing,
   sociable, thorough
09 enlarging, expanding,
   extensive, talkative
10 developing, increasing,
   loquacious, widespread
11 uninhibited, wide-ranging
12 all-embracing, diversifying
13 comprehensive

expatiate
06 dilate, expand
07 amplify, develop, dwell on,
   enlarge, expound
09 elaborate, embellish

expatriate
04 oust
05 ex-pat, exile, expel
06 banish, deport, exiled,
   uproot, émigré
07 outcast, refugee
08 banished, deported, drive
   out, emigrant, expelled
09 extradite, ostracize
15 displaced person

expect
04 want, wish
05 await, guess, think, trust
06 assume, bank on, demand,
   reckon, rely on
07 believe, call for, count on,
   foresee, hope for, imagine,
   look for, predict, presume,
   project, require, suppose
08 envisage, forecast, insist on
10 anticipate, bargain for
11 contemplate
13 look forward to

expectancy
04 hope
07 waiting
08 suspense
09 curiosity, eagerness
10 conjecture
11 expectation
12 anticipation

expectant
05 eager, ready
06 gravid
07 anxious, curious, hopeful
08 awaiting, enceinte,
   preggers, pregnant, watchful
09 expecting, in the club, with
   child
10 in suspense
12 anticipating, apprehensive
13 on tenterhooks
14 in the family way
15 with bated breath

expectantly
07 eagerly

09 hopefully
10 in suspense
14 apprehensively, in
   anticipation, optimistically

expectation
04 hope, want, wish
05 trust
06 belief, demand
07 outlook, promise, surmise
08 forecast, optimism,
   prospect, reliance, suspense
09 assurance, eagerness
10 assumption, confidence,
   conjecture, insistence,
   prediction, projection
11 calculation, possibility,
   presumption, probability,
   requirement, supposition
12 anticipation

expecting
06 gravid
08 enceinte, pregnant
09 expectant, in the club, with
   child
14 in the family way

expedience
07 aptness, benefit, fitness
09 advantage, propriety
10 expediency, pragmatism,
   properness, usefulness
11 convenience, suitability
12 desirability, practicality
13 effectiveness, profitability

expedient
04 plan, ploy
05 dodge, means, shift, trick
06 device, method, scheme,
   tactic, useful
07 fitting, politic, prudent
08 sensible, suitable, tactical
09 advisable, opportune,
   practical, pragmatic
10 convenient, profitable
11 appropriate, contrivance
12 advantageous

expedite
05 hurry, press
06 assist, hasten, step up
07 further, quicken, speed up
08 dispatch
09 discharge
10 accelerate, facilitate
11 precipitate
12 hurry through

expedition
04 crew, hike, raid, sail, team,
   tour, trek, trip
05 haste, party, quest, speed
06 outing, ramble, safari
07 crusade, journey, mission

08 alacrity, campaign, celerity
09 adventure, excursion
10 enterprise, pilgrimage
11 exploration, undertaking

expeditious
04 fast
05 alert, brisk, hasty, quick,
   rapid, ready, swift
06 active, prompt, speedy
08 diligent, meteoric
09 efficient, immediate

expel
03 ban, bar
04 oust, void
05 belch, eject, evict, exile
06 banish, outlaw, reject
07 boot out, cast out, dismiss,
   kick out, spew out
08 chuck out, drive out,
   evacuate, throw out
09 discharge, proscribe
10 expatriate

expend
03 buy, pay, sap, use
05 empty, spend, use up, waste
06 afford, employ, lay out
07 consume, deplete, exhaust,
   fork out, fritter, utilize
08 shell out, squander
09 dissipate, go through,
   overspend, splash out

expendable
10 disposable
11 dispensable, inessential,
   replaceable, unnecessary
12 non-essential

expenditure
03 use
05 costs, waste
06 outlay, output
07 expense, payment, sapping
08 expenses, spending
09 outgoings
11 consumption, dissipation,
   squandering, utilization
12 disbursement

expense
03 fee
04 cost, harm, loss, rate
05 costs, price
06 charge, outlay
07 payment
08 spending
09 detriment, outgoings,
   overheads, paying-out,
   sacrifice, sumptuary
11 expenditure, incidentals
12 disadvantage, disbursement

expensive
04 dear
05 steep
06 costly, lavish, pricey
10 exorbitant, overpriced
12 costing a bomb, extortionate
15 costing the earth, daylight robbery

experience
03 try
04 case, face, feel, know, meet
06 affair, endure, ordeal, suffer
07 contact, episode, know-how, sustain, undergo
08 exposure, incident, learning, perceive, practice, training
09 adventure, encounter, go through, knowledge
11 familiarity, involvement, live through, observation
13 participate in, participation

experienced
04 wise
05 adept, tried
06 au fait, expert, mature
07 capable, skilful, skilled, trained, veteran
08 familiar, seasoned
09 au courant, competent, practised, qualified
10 streetwise, well-versed
11 worldly wise
12 accomplished, professional

experiment
03 try
04 test
05 proof, trial
06 dry run, try out, verify
07 attempt, examine, explore, observe, testing, venture
08 analysis, dummy run, piloting, research, trial run
10 pilot study
11 examination, investigate
13 carry out tests, investigation, trial and error
15 experimentation

experimental
04 test
05 pilot, trial
09 empirical, peirastic
11 exploratory, preliminary, provisional, speculative
13 investigative, trial-and-error
15 at the trial stage

expert
03 ace, pro
04 able, buff, up on
05 adept, crack, maven, mavin

06 master, pundit
07 dab hand, egghead, maestro, old hand, skilful, skilled, wise guy
08 masterly, top-notch, virtuoso, well up on
09 authority, brilliant, dexterous, excellent, old master, practised, qualified
10 proficient, specialist
11 connoisseur, experienced
12 accomplished, professional

expertise
05 knack, skill
07 ability, command, know-how, mastery
08 deftness, facility
09 dexterity, knowledge
10 cleverness, virtuosity
11 proficiency, skilfulness
15 professionalism

expiate
05 purge
06 pay for
07 redress
08 atone for
09 make up for
12 do penance for
13 make amends for

expiation
06 amends, ransom, shrift
07 penance, redress
09 atonement
10 recompense, reparation

expire
03 die, end
04 stop
05 cease, close, lapse
06 depart, finish, pass on, peg out, perish, pop off, run out
07 decease, snuff it
08 conclude, pass away
09 have had it, terminate
11 bite the dust, come to an end, discontinue
12 lose your life
13 kick the bucket, meet your maker
14 depart this life, give up the ghost
15 be no longer valid, breathe your last, cash in your chips

expiry
03 end
05 close, lapse
06 finish
09 cessation
10 conclusion, expiration
11 termination

explain
05 solve, teach
06 decode, defend, define, excuse, set out, unfold
07 clarify, expound, justify, resolve, unravel
08 decipher, describe, disclose, simplify, spell out, untangle
09 delineate, elaborate, elucidate, explicate, interpret, lie behind, make clear, translate, vindicate
10 account for, illustrate
11 demonstrate, explain away, rationalize, shed light on
12 throw light on
14 give a reason for

explanation
05 alibi, gloss
06 answer, excuse, reason
07 account, comment, defence, meaning, warrant
08 apologia, decoding, exegesis, footnote
10 annotation, commentary, definition, expounding
11 deciphering, delineation, description, elucidation
13 demonstration, justification
14 interpretation
15 rationalization

explanatory
10 exegetical, justifying
11 elucidatory, explicative
12 illustrative, interpretive
13 demonstrative
14 interpretative

expletive
04 oath
05 curse
09 blasphemy, obscenity, profanity, swear-word
10 execration
11 bad language, imprecation
14 four-letter word

explicable
08 solvable
10 resolvable
11 explainable, justifiable
12 determinable, intelligible
13 interpretable
14 understandable

explicate
06 define, unfold
07 clarify, explain, expound, unravel, work out
08 describe, spell out, untangle
09 elucidate, make clear
10 illustrate
11 demonstrate

explicit
04 open
05 clear, exact, frank, plain
06 candid, direct, stated
07 certain, express, precise
08 declared, definite, detailed, distinct, positive, specific
09 outspoken
10 forthright, unreserved
11 categorical, plain-spoken, unambiguous, unequivocal
15 straightforward

explode
04 boom, go up, leap
05 blast, burst, erupt, go off
06 blow up, debunk, go bang, refute, rocket, see red, set off
08 burst out, detonate, disprove, escalate, mushroom
09 blow a fuse, discharge, do your nut, repudiate
10 hit the roof, invalidate
11 blow your top, go up the wall, lose your rag
12 fly into a rage, give the lie to, lose your cool
13 hit the ceiling
15 fly off the handle, go off the deep end

exploit
03 act, tap, use
04 deed, feat, milk
05 abuse, apply, bleed, stunt
06 action, draw on, employ, fleece, misuse, rip off
07 oppress, utilize
08 activity, cash in on, ill-treat, impose on, profit by
09 adventure, profiteer
10 attainment, manipulate
11 achievement, walk all over
12 capitalize on, put to good use, take for a ride
13 take liberties
14 play off against
15 take advantage of

exploration
04 tour, trip
05 probe, study
06 safari, search, survey, travel
08 analysis, research, scrutiny
10 expedition, inspection
11 examination, observation
13 investigation
14 reconnaissance

exploratory
05 pilot, trial
07 probing
08 analytic
09 searching, tentative

11 fact-finding
12 experimental
13 investigative

explore
05 probe, scout, study
06 review, search, survey, travel
07 analyse, examine, inspect
08 look into, research
11 inquire into, investigate, reconnoitre, see the world

explorer
05 scout
08 surveyor
09 navigator, traveller
10 discoverer, prospector
12 reconnoitrer

► *Names of explorers and pioneers*:
04 **Byrd** (Richard Evelyn), **Cano** (Juan Sebastian del), **Cook** (James), **Diaz** (Bartolomeu), **Eyre** (Edward John), **Gama** (Vasco da), **Park** (Mungo), **Polo** (Marco), **Ross** (Sir James Clark), **Soto** (Fernando de), **Soto** (Hernando de)
05 **Barth** (Heinrich), **Boone** (Daniel), **Cabot** (John), **Clark** (William), **Drake** (Francis), **Fuchs** (Sir Vivian Ernest), **Hanno**, **Lewis** (Meriwether), **Newby** (Eric), **Oates** (Lawrence), **Peary** (Robert Edwin), **Scott** (Robert Falcon), **Speke** (John Hanning)
06 **Balboa** (Vasco Núñez de), **Burton** (Sir Richard), **Carson** (Kit), **Nansen** (Fridtjof), **Tasman** (Abel Janszoon)
07 **Fiennes** (Sir Ranulph Twistleton-Wykeham), **Pytheas**, **Raleigh** (Walter), **Stanley** (Sir Henry Morton)
08 **Amundsen** (Roald), **Columbus** (Christopher), **Flinders** (Matthew), **Linnaeus** (Carolus), **Magellan** (Ferdinand), **Standish** (Myles), **Thesiger** (Wilfred), **Vespucci** (Amerigo)
09 **Heyerdahl** (Thor), **Rasmussen** (Knud), **Vancouver** (George)
10 **Erik the Red, Shackleton** (Sir Ernest Henry), **Van der Post** (Sir Laurens)

11 **Livingstone** (David)
12 **Leif Eriksson, Younghusband** (Sir Francis)
14 **Blashford-Snell** (Colonel John), **Hanbury-Tenison** (Robin Airling)

explosion
03 fit
04 bang, boom, clap, rage, roll
05 blast, burst, crack, surge
06 report, rumble
07 flare-up, tantrum, thunder
08 eruption, outbreak, outburst, paroxysm
09 discharge
10 detonation
14 dramatic growth, sudden increase

explosive
03 TNT
05 angry, fiery, jelly, rapid, tense
06 abrupt, Semtex®, touchy
07 charged, cordite, fraught, violent
08 critical, dramatic, dynamite, unstable, volatile
09 gelignite, gunpowder, hazardous, sensitive
10 burgeoning, unexpected
11 mushrooming, overwrought
14 nitroglycerine

exponent
06 backer, expert, master
08 adherent, advocate, champion, defender, promoter, upholder
09 performer, proponent, spokesman, supporter
11 spokeswoman
12 practitioner, spokesperson

export
05 trade
08 deal with, transfer
09 traffic in, transport
10 sell abroad
12 foreign trade, sell overseas

expose
04 risk, show
06 betray, detect, hazard, reveal, unmask, unveil
07 display, divulge, exhibit, imperil, lay bare, present, uncover, unearth
08 denounce, disclose, endanger, manifest
09 lay open to, make known, put at risk, subject to
11 introduce to
12 acquaint with, bring to light

13 take the lid off
14 blow the whistle

exposé
07 account, article
08 exposure
10 disclosure, divulgence, revelation, uncovering

exposed
04 bare, open
06 on show, on view
08 laid bare, revealed
09 in the open, on display
10 vulnerable
11 susceptible, unprotected

exposition
04 expo, fair, show
05 paper, study
06 thesis
07 account, display
08 analysis, critique, exegesis
09 discourse, monograph
10 commentary, exhibition
11 description, elucidation, explanation, explication
12 illumination, presentation
13 clarification, demonstration
14 interpretation

expository
08 exegetic
11 declaratory, descriptive, elucidative, explanatory, explicatory, hermeneutic
12 illustrative, interpretive
14 interpretative

expostulate
05 argue, plead
06 reason
07 protest
08 dissuade
11 remonstrate

exposure
04 hype, plug, risk
06 airing, danger, exposé
07 contact, display, showing
09 awareness, detection, discovery, publicity, unmasking, unveiling
10 disclosure, divulgence, exhibition, experience, revelation, uncovering
11 advertising, familiarity
12 denunciation, presentation
15 public attention

expound
06 preach, set out, unfold
07 analyse, clarify, dissect, explain, unravel
08 describe, set forth, spell out

09 elucidate, explicate
10 illuminate, illustrate

express
03 air, say
04 fast, show, sole, tell, vent
05 plain, quick, rapid, speak, state, swift, utter, voice
06 assert, convey, denote, reveal, speedy, stated
07 certain, declare, non-stop, precise, put over, signify
08 announce, clear-cut, definite, distinct, explicit, indicate, intimate, manifest, point out, specific, stand for
09 enunciate, high-speed, pronounce, put across, represent, symbolize
10 articulate, particular
11 categorical, communicate, give voice to, well-defined
12 put into words

expression
04 look, mien, show, sign, term, tone, word
05 idiom, power, scowl, style
06 aspect, phrase, saying, speech, symbol, vigour
07 diction, gesture, grimace, passion, voicing, wording
08 artistry, delivery, language, locution, phrasing
09 assertion, set phrase, statement, utterance
10 appearance, exhibition, indication, intimation, intonation, modulation
11 countenance, declaration, enunciation, imagination
12 announcement, articulation, illustration, turn of phrase
13 communication, demonstration, manifestation
14 representation

expressionless
05 blank, empty
06 glassy
07 deadpan, vacuous
09 impassive
10 poker-faced
11 emotionless, inscrutable
13 straight-faced

expressive
05 vivid
06 lively, moving
07 showing, telling
08 animated, eloquent, emphatic, forceful
09 evocative, revealing
10 articulate, meaningful, suggestive, thoughtful

11 significant, sympathetic
13 communicative, demonstrative

expressly
06 solely
07 clearly, exactly, plainly
09 decidedly, on purpose, pointedly, precisely, purposely, specially
10 definitely, distinctly, especially, explicitly
12 particularly, specifically
13 categorically, intentionally

expropriate
04 take
05 annex, seize, usurp
08 arrogate, disseise, take away
09 sequester
10 commandeer, confiscate
11 appropriate, requisition

expulsion
05 exile
07 removal, sacking, the boot, the sack, voiding
08 belching, ejection, eviction
09 discharge, exclusion, excretion, rejection
10 banishment, evacuation

expunge
05 annul, erase
06 cancel, delete, efface, remove, rub out
07 abolish, blot out, wipe out
08 cross out, get rid of
09 eradicate, extirpate
10 annihilate, obliterate
11 exterminate

expurgate
03 cut
05 emend, purge
06 censor, purify
07 clean up
08 sanitize
10 blue-pencil, bowdlerize

exquisite
04 fine, keen, rare
05 acute, sharp
06 choice, dainty, lovely, pretty
07 elegant, fragile, intense, perfect, refined
08 charming, cultured, delicate, flawless, piercing, precious
09 beautiful, excellent
10 delightful, impeccable

extant
05 alive
06 living
08 existent, existing
09 remaining, surviving

10 subsistent, subsisting
11 in existence

extempore
05 ad lib, ad-lib
09 impromptu, unplanned
10 improvised, off the cuff, unprepared, unscripted
11 spontaneous, unrehearsed
13 spontaneously
14 extemporaneous

extemporize
05 ad-lib
06 make up
09 improvise
11 play it by ear
15 think on your feet

extend
03 run
04 give, last
05 grant, offer, reach, widen
06 bestow, come to, confer, expand, go up to, impart, spread, step up, unwind
07 amplify, augment, broaden, carry on, develop, drag out, draw out, enlarge, hold out, present, proffer, prolong, spin out, stretch
08 continue, elongate, go down to, increase, lengthen, protract, reach out
09 go as far as, intensify

extended
04 long
07 lengthy
08 enlarged, expanded
09 developed, increased
10 lengthened

extension
04 wing
05 add-on, delay
06 annexe
07 adjunct
08 addendum, addition, appendix, increase
09 expansion
10 broadening, elongation, stretching, supplement
11 development, lengthening, protraction
12 continuation, postponement, prolongation

extensive
04 huge, long, vast, wide
05 broad, large, roomy
07 general, lengthy
08 complete, extended, sizeable, spacious, thorough

09 boundless, capacious, universal, unlimited
10 commodious, widespread
11 far-reaching, wide-ranging
12 all-inclusive
13 comprehensive

extent
04 area, bulk, size, term, time
05 level, limit, range, reach, scope, sweep, width
06 amount, bounds, degree, length, sphere, spread
07 breadth, compass, expanse, lengths, measure, stretch
08 coverage, duration, quantity
09 magnitude, dimension

extenuate
06 excuse, lessen, soften
07 qualify
08 diminish, minimize, mitigate

extenuating
08 excusing
09 lessening, softening
10 justifying, minimizing, mitigating, moderating, palliative, qualifying
11 diminishing, exculpatory, extenuative, extenuatory

exterior
04 face, skin
05 outer, shell
06 façade, finish
07 coating, outside, surface
08 covering, external
09 extrinsic, outermost
10 appearance, peripheral
11 superficial, surrounding
12 outer surface
15 external surface

exterminate
04 kill
07 abolish, destroy, wipe out
08 massacre
09 eliminate, eradicate, extirpate, slaughter
10 annihilate

extermination
07 killing
08 genocide, massacre
11 destruction, elimination, eradication, extirpation
12 annihilation

external
05 outer
07 outside, outward, surface
08 apparent, exterior, visiting
10 extramural, peripheral
11 independent, superficial

extinct
04 dead, gone, lost
06 bygone
07 defunct, died out, expired
08 burnt out, inactive, quenched, vanished, wiped out
11 non-existent
12 exterminated, extinguished

extinction
05 death
08 dying-out, excision
09 abolition, vanishing
11 destruction, eradication
12 annihilation, obliteration
13 extermination

extinguish
04 kill
05 choke, douse, erase
06 put out, quench, stifle
07 abolish, blow out, destroy, expunge, smother, stub out
08 snuff out, suppress
09 eliminate, extirpate
10 annihilate, dampen down
11 exterminate

extirpate
05 erase
06 cut out, remove, uproot
07 abolish, destroy, expunge, root out, wipe out
09 eliminate, eradicate
10 annihilate, deracinate, extinguish
11 exterminate

extol
04 laud
05 exalt
06 praise
07 acclaim, applaud, commend, glorify, magnify
08 eulogize

extort
04 milk
05 bleed, exact, wrest, wring
06 coerce
07 extract, squeeze
09 blackmail

extortion
05 force
06 demand
07 milking
08 coercion, exaction
09 blackmail
12 racketeering

extortionate
08 exacting, grasping
09 excessive, rapacious

10 exorbitant, immoderate, inordinate, outrageous
12 preposterous, unreasonable

extra
03 new, too
04 also, more
05 added, bonus, fresh, spare
06 as well, excess, unused
07 adjunct, another, besides, further, reserve, surplus
08 addendum, addition, additive, left-over, let alone
09 accessory, along with, ancillary, appendage, auxiliary, extension, redundant, unusually
10 additional, attachment, in addition, especially, remarkably, supplement
11 superfluous, unnecessary
12 additionally, particularly, spear-carrier, together with
13 exceptionally, not forgetting, supernumerary, supplementary
14 above and beyond
15 extraordinarily

extract
03 get
04 cite, clip, copy, cull, draw
05 exact, glean, juice, pluck, prize, quote, wrest, wring
06 choose, cut out, derive, distil, elicit, gather, get out, obtain, remove, select, uproot, wrench
07 draw out, essence, excerpt, pull out, spirits, take out
08 abstract, citation, clipping
09 quotation, selection
10 deracinate, distillate
11 concentrate
12 distillation

extraction
04 race
05 birth, blood, stock
06 family, origin
07 descent, drawing, lineage, pulling, removal
08 ancestry, pedigree
09 parentage, taking out
10 derivation, withdrawal

extradite
05 exile, expel
06 banish, deport
08 send back, send home
10 repatriate

extradition
05 exile
09 expulsion

10 banishment
11 deportation, sending back

extraneous
05 alien, extra, inapt
07 foreign, strange
08 exterior, needless, unneeded
09 extrinsic, redundant
10 additional, immaterial, incidental, irrelevant, peripheral, tangential
11 inessential, superfluous, unconnected, unnecessary
12 inapplicable, non-essential
13 inappropriate, supplementary

extraordinary
03 odd
04 rare
06 unique
07 amazing, bizarre, curious, notable, special, strange, unusual
08 peculiar, uncommon
09 fantastic, wonderful
10 astounding, marvellous, noteworthy, remarkable, surprising, unexpected
11 exceptional, outstanding
14 out of this world

extravagance
05 folly, waste
06 excess
08 wildness
10 lavishness, profligacy
11 prodigality, squandering
12 immoderation, improvidence, overspending, recklessness, wastefulness
14 thriftlessness

extravagant
03 OTT
04 dear, wild
06 costly, flashy, lavish, ornate
08 prodigal, reckless, wasteful
09 excessive, expensive, fantastic, imprudent
10 exorbitant, flamboyant, immoderate, outrageous, over the top, profligate
11 improvident, spendthrift
12 ostentatious, unrestrained

extravaganza
04 show
07 display, pageant
09 spectacle
11 spectacular

extreme
03 end, top

04 acme, apex, dire, edge, last, line, mark, peak, pole
05 acute, depth, final, great, harsh, limit, rigid, stern
06 climax, excess, height, severe, utmost, zenith
07 distant, drastic, faraway, highest, intense, maximum, radical, supreme, zealous
08 farthest, greatest, pinnacle, remotest, terminal, ultimate
09 Draconian, excessive, extremist, extremity, fanatical, out-and-out, outermost, stringent, uttermost
10 immoderate, most remote
14 uncompromising

❏ **in the extreme**
04 very
06 highly
07 greatly, utterly
09 intensely
10 remarkably, uncommonly
11 exceedingly, excessively
12 immoderately, inordinately
13 exceptionally
15 extraordinarily

extremely
04 very
06 highly, really
07 acutely, greatly, utterly
08 severely, terribly
09 decidedly, intensely
10 dreadfully, remarkably, thoroughly, uncommonly
11 exceedingly, excessively
12 immoderately, inordinately, terrifically, unreasonably
13 exceptionally
15 extraordinarily

extremism
04 zeal
08 zealotry
10 fanaticism, radicalism
13 excessiveness

extremist
05 ultra
06 zealot
07 diehard, fanatic, radical
08 militant
09 hardliner, terrorist
14 fundamentalist

extremity
03 arm, end, leg, tip, toe, top
04 acme, apex, edge, foot, hand, limb, peak, pole
05 brink, depth, limit, verge

06 apogee, border, crisis, danger, excess, finger, height, margin, plight, zenith
07 maximum, minimum
08 boundary, exigency, frontier, hardship, pinnacle, terminal, terminus, ultimate
09 adversity, emergency, indigence, periphery
11 termination

extricate
04 free
05 clear
06 detach, get out, rescue
07 deliver, extract, release
08 let loose, liberate, withdraw
09 disengage
11 disentangle

extrinsic
05 alien
06 exotic
07 foreign, outside
08 exterior, external, imported
10 extraneous

extrovert
10 socializer
14 outgoing person, sociable person

extroverted
06 hearty
07 amiable
08 amicable, friendly, outgoing, sociable
09 exuberant
13 demonstrative

extrude
05 mould
08 force out, press out
10 squeeze out

exuberance
04 life, zest
06 energy, vigour
07 elation, pizzazz
08 buoyancy, rankness, richness, vitality, vivacity
09 plenitude, profusion
10 ebullience, excitement, lavishness, liveliness
11 copiousness, fulsomeness, high spirits, prodigality
12 cheerfulness, effusiveness, exaggeration, exhilaration
13 effervescence

exuberant
04 lush, rank, rich
06 elated, lavish, lively

07 buoyant, excited, fulsome, profuse, zestful
08 abundant, animated, cheerful, effusive, spirited, thriving, vigorous
09 ebullient, energetic, luxurious, plenteous, sparkling, vivacious
10 full of life
11 exaggerated, exhilarated
12 effervescent, enthusiastic, high-spirited, unrestrained
13 irrepressible

exude
04 emit, leak, ooze, seep, weep
05 bleed, issue, sweat
07 display, emanate, excrete, exhibit, secrete, trickle
08 manifest, perspire

exult
04 crow
05 gloat, glory, revel
06 relish
07 delight, rejoice, triumph
08 be joyful
09 celebrate

exultant
06 elated, joyful, joyous
07 gleeful
08 exulting, jubilant
09 cock-a-hoop, delighted, overjoyed, rejoicing
10 enraptured, triumphant
11 over the moon

exultation
03 joy
04 glee
05 glory, paean
06 eulogy
07 crowing, elation, triumph
08 gloating, glorying
09 merriness, rejoicing, revelling, transport
10 joyfulness, joyousness, jubilation
11 celebration

eye
04 scan, view
05 sight, study, taste, watch
06 assess, gaze at, look at, peruse, regard, survey
07 examine, inspect, observe, opinion, stare at
08 eyesight, glance at
09 awareness, judgement, viewpoint, vigilance
10 estimation, perception, scrutinize

11 contemplate, discernment, observation, point of view, recognition, sensitivity
12 appreciation, surveillance
13 look up and down
14 discrimination

► *Parts of the eye*:
03 rod
04 cone, iris, lens
05 fovea, pupil
06 cornea, retina, sclera
07 choroid, eyelash, papilla
09 blind spot
10 optic nerve
11 ciliary body, conjunctiva, lower eyelid, upper eyelid
12 lacrimal duct, ocular muscle
13 aqueous humour
14 vitreous humour
15 anterior chamber

❑**keep an eye on**
04 mind
08 attend to
07 monitor
09 look after
10 keep tabs on, take care of
12 watch closely

❑**see eye to eye**
05 agree
07 be at one
11 be of one mind, go along with

❑**set eyes on**
03 see
04 meet
06 behold, notice
07 observe
09 encounter, lay eyes on
10 clap eyes on, come across

❑**up to your eyes**
04 busy
06 tied up
08 involved, occupied
09 engrossed, inundated
11 overwhelmed, snowed under
14 fully stretched

eye-catching
08 gorgeous, imposing, striking, stunning
09 arresting, prominent
10 attractive, impressive, noticeable
11 captivating, conspicuous, spectacular

eyesight
04 view
05 sight
06 ocular, vision, visual

07 optical
11 observation
13 power of seeing
14 faculty of sight

eyesore
04 blot, mess, scar

06 blight, horror
08 atrocity, disgrace, ugliness
09 carbuncle
10 defacement
11 monstrosity
13 disfigurement

eyewitness
07 watcher, witness
08 looker-on, observer,
    onlooker, passer-by
09 bystander, spectator

fable
03 lie
04 epic, myth, saga, tale, yarn
05 story
06 legend
07 fiction, parable, untruth
08 allegory, apologue
09 falsehood, invention, moral tale, tall story
11 fabrication
12 old wives' tale

➤ *Names of fable writers:*
03 **Fay** (András), **Gay** (John)
05 **Aesop, Torga** (Miguel)
06 **Dryden** (John), **Krylov** (Ivan), **Ramsay** (Allan)
07 **Babrius, Fénelon** (François de Salignac de la Mothe), **Kipling** (Rudyard)
08 **Phaedrus, Saltykov** (Michail)
10 **La Fontaine** (Jean de)
➤ See also **writer**

fabled
05 famed
06 famous
08 renowned
09 legendary

fabric
05 cloth, stuff
07 textile, texture
08 material
09 framework, structure
11 foundations
14 infrastructure

➤ *Types of fabric:*
03 kid, net, rep
04 cord, felt, jean, lamé, lawn, repp, silk, wool
05 camel, chino, crêpe, denim, gauze, linen, lisle, llama, loden, Lurex®, Lycra®, nylon, piqué, rayon, satin, scrim, serge, suede, terry, toile, tulle, tweed, twill, voile
06 alpaca, angora, burlap, calico, canvas, chintz, cotton, Dacron®, damask, Dralon®, duffel, fleece, jersey, merino, mohair, muslin, sateen, velour, velvet, vicuña
07 brocade, buckram, cambric, chamois, chiffon, flannel, fustian, gingham, hessian, kidskin, leather, morocco, nankeen, organza, orleans, paisley, taffeta, ticking, veiling, Viyella®, webbing, woolsey, worsted
08 barathea, buckskin, cashmere, chenille, corduroy, gossamer, moleskin, oilcloth, organdie, quilting, Terylene®, waxcloth
09 astrakhan, bombasine, Crimplene®, gaberdine, haircloth, horsehair, polyester, sackcloth, sailcloth, sharkskin, sheepskin, velveteen
10 candlewick, seersucker, winceyette
11 cheesecloth, flannelette, Harris tweed®
12 Brussels lace, butter-muslin, cavalry twill, crêpe de chine, Shetland wool
14 terry towelling

fabricate
04 fake, form, make
05 erect, forge, frame, shape
06 cook up, create, devise, invent, make up
07 concoct, falsify, fashion, produce, trump up
08 assemble
09 construct
11 counterfeit, manufacture

fabrication
04 fake, myth
05 fable, story
07 fiction, forgery, untruth
08 assembly, building, erection
09 falsehood, invention
10 assemblage, concoction, fairy story, production
11 manufacture
12 construction

fabulous
04 cool
05 great, magic, super
06 fabled, made-up, superb, unreal, way-out
08 invented, mythical
09 fantastic, fictional, imaginary, legendary
10 astounding, fictitious, incredible, marvellous, phenomenal, remarkable
11 astonishing, spectacular
12 unbelievable, unimaginable
13 inconceivable
14 out of this world

façade
04 face, mask, show, veil
05 cloak, cover, front, guise
06 veneer
08 disguise, exterior, frontage
09 semblance
10 appearance

face
03 air, mug, pan
04 clad, coat, dial, look, meet, name, phiz, puss, side
05 brave, clock, cover, dress, front, frown, looks, scowl
06 aspect, façade, facial, honour, kisser, oppose, polish, resist, smooth, tackle, veneer, visage
07 grimace, outside, surface
08 confront, cope with, deal with, exterior, face up to, features, frontage, overlook, prestige, standing
09 encounter, go against
10 appearance, expression, be opposite, reputation
11 countenance, physiognomy
12 be at variance, be in conflict
13 come up against

□ **face to face**
06 facing

08 eye to eye, opposite
13 confronting
15 in confrontation

◻**face up to**
06 accept
08 confront, cope with, deal with
09 recognize, stand up to
10 meet head-on
11 acknowledge
15 come to terms with

◻**fly in the face of**
05 clash
06 oppose
07 disagree
08 be at odds, conflict, contrast
09 contradict, go against
12 be at variance, be in conflict

◻**on the face of it**
09 obviously, outwardly, reputedly, seemingly
10 apparently, manifestly, ostensibly
12 on the surface
13 superficially

◻**pull a face**
03 lour, pout, sulk
05 frown
06 glower
07 grimace
13 knit your brows

facelift
10 renovation
11 restoration
14 plastic surgery
15 cosmetic surgery

facet
04 face, side
05 angle, plane, point, slant
06 aspect, factor
07 element, feature, surface
14 characteristic

facetious
05 comic, droll, funny, witty
06 jocose, joking
07 amusing, jesting, jocular
08 flippant, humorous
09 frivolous
12 light-hearted
13 tongue-in-cheek

facile
04 easy, glib
05 hasty, quick, ready, slick
06 fluent, simple, smooth
07 shallow
10 simplistic
11 superficial
13 uncomplicated

facilitate
04 ease, help
06 assist, smooth
07 advance, forward, further, promote, speed up
08 expedite
12 smooth the way

facility
04 ease, gift
05 knack, means, skill
06 mod con, talent
07 ability, amenity, fluency, service, utility
08 resource
09 appliance, dexterity, eloquence, equipment, quickness, readiness
11 convenience, opportunity, proficiency, skilfulness

facing
06 façade, lining, veneer
07 coating, overlay, surface
08 cladding, covering, trimming
09 revetment
10 false front

facsimile
03 fax
04 copy
05 image, print, repro, Xerox®
07 replica
09 duplicate, imitation, photocopy, Photostat®
10 mimeograph, transcript
12 reproduction

fact
04 deed, info, item
05 datum, point, score, truth
06 detail, factor
07 feature, low-down, reality
09 actuality, certainty, component, happening
11 information
12 circumstance, fait accompli

◻**in fact**
05 truly
06 indeed, really
07 in truth
08 actually
09 in reality
10 in practice
12 in actual fact
13 in point of fact
15 as a matter of fact

faction
03 set
04 band, camp, ring, side
05 cabal, junta, lobby, party
06 caucus, clique, sector, strife
07 coterie, discord, section

08 argument, conflict, division, friction, minority, quarrels
10 contention, contingent, disharmony, infighting
12 disagreement
13 splinter group

factious
05 rival
06 at odds
07 warring
08 clashing, divisive, mutinous
09 seditious, turbulent
10 discordant, rebellious, refractory, tumultuous
11 conflicting, contentious, quarrelling, quarrelsome
12 disputatious
13 at loggerheads

factor
04 fact, item, part
05 cause, facet, point
06 aspect, detail
07 element, feature
09 component, influence
10 ingredient
11 constituent, contingency
13 consideration
14 characteristic

factory
04 mill
05 plant, works
07 foundry
08 workshop
09 shop floor
12 assembly line

factotum
08 handyman
09 Man Friday, odd-jobman
10 Girl Friday
13 maid-of-all-work
15 jack-of-all-trades

factual
04 real, true
05 close, exact
06 actual, strict
07 correct, genuine, precise
08 accurate, detailed, faithful, truthful, unbiased
09 authentic, realistic
10 historical, true-to-life

faculties
04 wits
06 powers, reason, senses
07 ability
12 capabilities, intelligence

faculty
04 bent, gift
05 flair, knack, power, skill
06 talent

07 ability, section
08 aptitude, capacity, facility
10 capability, department
11 proficiency

fad

04 mode, rage, whim
05 craze, fancy, mania, trend
07 fashion
10 enthusiasm
11 affectation

faddy

05 exact, fussy, picky
06 choosy
07 finicky
10 fastidious, nit-picking,
   particular, pernickety

fade

03 die, dim, ebb
04 fail, flag, melt, pale, wane
06 blanch, bleach, blench,
   perish, recede, vanish,
   weaken, whiten, wither
07 decline, die away, dwindle,
   ebb away, shrivel, wash out
08 diminish, dissolve, etiolate,
   evanesce, peter out
09 disappear, discolour, fizzle
   out, waste away
10 lose colour
11 become paler
12 become weaker

faeces

04 crap, dung, shit, turd
06 ordure, stools
07 excreta
09 body waste, droppings,
   excrement
11 waste matter

fag

03 cig
04 bind, bore, drag, pest
05 chore, joint, smoke, whiff
06 dog end, gasper, roll-up
08 king-size, nuisance
09 cigarette, filter-tip
10 coffin-nail, irritation
11 cancer-stick, roll-your-own

fagged

05 all in, jaded, weary
07 worn out
08 fatigued
09 exhausted, knackered
14 on your last legs

fail

04 bomb, fade, flag, flop, fold,
   omit, sink, stop, wane
05 crash, droop, flunk, leave
06 blow it, cut out, forget, go
   bust, pack up, weaken

07 abandon, conk out, decline,
   forsake, founder, go kaput,
   go under, go wrong, let
   down, neglect, not work
08 diminish, fall flat, not start
09 break down, not make it
10 disappoint, get nowhere, go
   bankrupt, not come off
11 bite the dust, come to grief,
   come unstuck, fall through,
   go to the wall, malfunction
12 come a cropper
13 come to nothing
14 be unsuccessful
15 become insolvent, blow
   your chances

▫**without fail**

08 reliably
09 regularly
10 constantly, dependably,
   faithfully, punctually
11 predictably, religiously,
   unfailingly
13 like clockwork

failing

04 flaw
05 error, fault, lapse
06 defect, foible
07 blemish, lacking, without
08 drawback, weakness
10 deficiency
11 in default of, shortcoming
12 imperfection
14 in the absence of

failure

04 flop, mess, miss, no go, ruin
05 crash, loser
06 defeat, fiasco, misfit, reject,
   slip-up, victim, waning
07 also-ran, decline, default,
   dropout, has-been, let-
   down, neglect, no-hoper,
   sinking, washout, wipeout
08 abortion, collapse, dead
   loss, disaster, downfall,
   omission, shutdown,
   stalling, stopping, write-off
09 born loser, breakdown,
   packing-up, weakening
10 bankruptcy, conking-out,
   cutting-out, foundering,
   going under, insolvency,
   negligence, non-starter
11 dereliction, miscarriage
13 deterioration, lack of success
14 disappointment, going to
   the wall, malfunctioning
15 coming to nothing

faint

03 dim, low
04 drop, dull, pale, soft, weak

05 dizzy, faded, giddy, light,
   muted, swoon, vague
06 feeble, hushed, slight
07 blurred, muffled, obscure,
   pass out, syncope, unclear
08 black out, collapse, flake
   out, keel over
10 indistinct
11 half-hearted, light-headed
15 unconsciousness

faint-hearted

04 weak
05 timid
06 yellow
08 timorous
09 diffident
10 irresolute, spiritless
11 half-hearted, lily-livered

faintly

04 a bit
06 feebly, softly, weakly
07 a little, vaguely
08 slightly

fair

02 OK
03 dry
04 expo, fête, fine, gala, just,
   pale, show, so-so
05 blond, clear, cream, legit,
   light, right, sunny
06 bazaar, blonde, bright,
   decent, honest, kosher,
   lawful, market, modest, not
   bad, proper, square, yellow
08 adequate, all right, carnival,
   detached, mediocre,
   middling, moderate,
   nundinal, passable,
   sporting, unbiased
09 cloudless, equitable,
   impartial, objective,
   tolerable, unclouded
10 above board, acceptable,
   even-handed, fair-haired,
   on the level, reasonable,
   straight up, sufficient
11 respectable, trustworthy
12 satisfactory, unprejudiced
13 disinterested, dispassionate
15 played by the book

fairly

05 fully, quite
06 justly, pretty, rather, really
07 legally
08 honestly, lawfully, somewhat
09 equitably, tolerably, veritably
10 absolutely, adequately,
   moderately, positively,
   reasonably, unbiasedly
11 impartially, objectively

fairness
06 equity
07 decency, justice
12 impartiality, unbiasedness
13 equitableness
14 even-handedness

fairy
03 elf, fay, fée, hob, imp
04 peri, Puck
05 nymph, pixie
06 sprite
07 brownie, rusalka
09 hobgoblin
10 leprechaun
15 Robin Goodfellow

fairy tale
03 lie
04 myth
07 fantasy, fiction, untruth
08 folk-tale
11 fabrication

faith
04 sect
05 creed, dogma, trust
06 belief, church, fealty, honour
07 honesty, loyalty
08 credence, devotion,
   doctrine, fidelity, reliance,
   religion, teaching
09 assurance, sincerity
10 allegiance, commitment,
   confidence, conviction,
   dedication, persuasion
12 denomination, truthfulness

faithful
04 true
05 close, exact, loyal
06 strict, trusty
07 devoted, precise, staunch
08 accurate, brethren, constant,
   obedient, reliable, truthful
09 adherents, believers,
   committed, dedicated,
   followers, steadfast
10 dependable, supporters
11 trustworthy
12 communicants,
   congregation

faithfulness
06 fealty
07 loyalty
08 accuracy, devotion, fidelity
09 closeness, constancy
10 allegiance, commitment,
   dedication, strictness
11 reliability, staunchness
13 dependability, steadfastness

faithless
05 false
06 fickle, untrue

08 disloyal, doubting
10 adulterous, inconstant,
   perfidious, traitorous,
   unfaithful, untruthful
11 treacherous, unbelieving
12 disbelieving, false-hearted

faithlessness
06 deceit
07 perfidy
08 adultery, apostasy, betrayal
09 treachery
10 disloyalty, infidelity
11 inconstancy

fake
04 copy, hoax, mock, sham
05 bogus, false, feign, forge,
   fraud, pseud, put on, quack
06 affect, assume, forged,
   phoney, pirate, pseudo
07 forgery, pretend, replica
08 affected, impostor, simulate
09 charlatan, fabricate,
   imitation, simulated
10 artificial, fraudulent,
   mountebank, simulation
11 counterfeit
12 reproduction

fall
03 cut, die
04 dive, drop, grow, pass, ruin,
   sink, slip, trip, turn
05 crash, occur, pitch, slant,
   slide, slope, slump, yield
06 become, defeat, demise,
   give in, go down, happen,
   lessen, perish, plunge,
   recede, topple, tumble
07 be slain, be taken, capture,
   decline, descend, dwindle,
   failure, fall off, incline,
   plummet, stumble, subside
08 be killed, collapse,
   decrease, diminish,
   downfall, giving-in, grow
   into, keel over, yielding
09 come about, dwindling,
   lessening, overthrow,
   reduction, surrender
10 be defeated, plummeting
11 be conquered, destruction,
   keeling-over, resignation
12 be vanquished, capitulation,
   lose your life, pitch forward

❑ fall apart
05 break, decay
07 break up, crack up, crumble,
   shatter
08 collapse, come away,
   dissolve, go to bits
09 decompose
10 fall to bits, go to pieces

12 come to pieces, disintegrate,
   fall to pieces
15 break into pieces

❑ fall back
06 depart, recoil
07 retreat
08 draw back, pull back,
   withdraw
09 disengage

❑ fall back on
06 call on, look to, turn to
08 resort to
09 make use of
12 call into play
14 have recourse to

❑ fall behind
03 lag
05 trail
08 drop back
09 lag behind, not keep up

❑ fall for
03 buy
05 fancy
06 accept, desire, take to
07 swallow
10 be fooled by
11 be taken in by
12 be attached to, be deceived
   by, have a crush on
14 fall in love with

❑ fall in
04 sink
05 crash
06 cave in
07 give way, subside
08 collapse, come down

❑ fall in with
06 accept
07 support
08 assent to
09 agree with
10 comply with
11 go along with
13 co-operate with

❑ fall off
04 drop, slow
05 slump
06 lessen, worsen
07 decline, drop off, slacken
08 decrease
11 deteriorate

❑ fall on
06 assail, attack, snatch
07 assault, lay into, set upon
08 pounce on
09 descend on

❑ fall out
05 argue, clash, fight
06 bicker, differ

07 quarrel
08 disagree, squabble

▢fall through
04 fail
08 collapse, miscarry
11 come to grief
13 come to nothing

▢fall to
05 begin, set to, start
06 set about
10 get stuck in
13 apply yourself

fallacious
05 false, wrong
06 untrue
08 illusory, mistaken, spurious
09 deceptive, erroneous, illogical, incorrect, sophistic
10 fictitious, inaccurate
11 casuistical, sophistical

fallacy
04 flaw, myth
07 mistake, sophism
08 delusion, illusion
09 casuistry, false idea, falsehood, sophistry
13 misconception
14 miscalculation
15 misapprehension

fallen
04 dead, died, lost
05 loose, slain
06 killed, shamed
07 immoral
08 perished
09 disgraced
10 degenerate
11 promiscuous, slaughtered

fallible
04 weak
05 frail, human
06 errant, erring, flawed, mortal
09 imperfect, uncertain

fallow
04 idle
06 barren, unsown, unused
07 dormant, resting
08 inactive
09 unplanted
10 unploughed
11 undeveloped
12 uncultivated, unproductive

false
04 fake, mock, sham
05 bogus, lying, wrong
06 forged, phoney, untrue
07 assumed, feigned, pretend
08 disloyal, illusory, two-faced

09 deceitful, dishonest, erroneous, faithless, imitation, incorrect, insincere, pretended, simulated, synthetic
10 artificial, fabricated, fallacious, fictitious, fraudulent, inaccurate, misleading, perfidious, traitorous, unfaithful
11 counterfeit, treacherous
12 hypocritical
13 double-dealing, untrustworthy

falsehood
03 fib, lie
05 story
06 deceit
07 fiction, perfidy, untruth
08 bullshit
09 deception, duplicity, hypocrisy, invention, tall story, treachery
10 dishonesty, fairy story
11 fabrication, insincerity
12 two-facedness
13 double dealing
14 untruthfulness

falsification
06 change, deceit
07 forgery
10 alteration, perversion
12 adulteration
13 dissimulation

falsify
03 rig
04 cook, fake
05 alter, forge, twist
06 doctor, fiddle
07 distort, massage, pervert
10 adulterate, tamper with
11 counterfeit
12 misrepresent

falter
04 fail, flag
05 delay, quail, shake, waver
06 flinch, totter
07 stammer, stumble, stutter
08 hesitate
10 be unsteady, dilly-dally
12 be in two minds, drag your feet, shilly-shally

faltering
04 weak
05 timid
06 broken
07 failing
08 flagging, hesitant, unsteady
09 tentative, uncertain
10 irresolute, stammering

fame
04 name, note
05 glory
06 esteem, honour, renown
07 stardom
08 eminence
09 celebrity, greatness
10 importance, notability, prominence, reputation
11 distinction

famed
05 noted
06 famous
08 esteemed, renowned
09 acclaimed, well-known
10 celebrated, recognized
11 widely-known

familiar
04 bold, dear, easy, free, near
05 close, known, pally, usual
06 au fait, casual, chummy, common, smarmy, versed
07 natural, relaxed, routine
08 everyday, friendly, habitual, informal, intimate, ordinary
09 au courant, customary, household, well-known
10 accustomed, acquainted, conversant, unreserved
11 commonplace, free-and-easy, impertinent
12 over-friendly, presumptuous, recognizable, run-of-the-mill
13 disrespectful

familiarity
04 ease
07 liberty, mastery
08 boldness, intimacy, nearness, openness
09 closeness, impudence, knowledge, pushiness
10 casualness, chumminess, disrespect, experience
11 forwardness, informality, presumption, sociability
12 acquaintance, friendliness, impertinence

familiarize
05 brief, coach, prime, teach, train
08 accustom, instruct
09 habituate, make aware
11 acclimatize
14 make acquainted

family
03 kin
04 clan, folk, kids, line, race

05 birth, blood, class, genus, house, issue, stock, tribe
06 people, scions, stirps, strain
07 descent, dynasty, kindred, kinsmen, lineage, parents, progeny, species
08 ancestry, children, pedigree
09 ancestors, forebears, household, next of kin, offspring, parentage, relations, relatives
11 descendants, you and yours

⊐ family tree
04 line
07 lineage
08 ancestry, pedigree
09 genealogy
10 background, extraction

famine
04 lack, want
05 death
06 dearth, hunger
08 scarcity
10 starvation
11 deprivation, destitution
12 malnutrition
14 shortage of food

famished
06 hungry
07 starved
08 ravenous, starving
09 famishing, voracious

famous
05 famed, great, noted
07 eminent, notable, popular
08 esteemed, honoured, infamous, renowned
09 acclaimed, legendary, notorious, prominent, venerable, well-known
10 celebrated, remarkable
11 illustrious
13 distinguished

fan
03 air, nut
04 blow, buff, cool, vane
05 fiend, freak, lover, rouse
06 addict, arouse, backer, blower, cooler, incite, kindle, stir up, whip up, work up
07 admirer, air-cool, devotee, freshen, provoke, refresh
08 adherent, follower, increase
09 air cooler, propeller, stimulate, supporter, ventilate
10 aficionado, enthusiast, ventilator
14 air-conditioner

⊐ fan out
06 unfold, unfurl
07 move out, open out
09 spread out

fanatic
05 bigot, fiend, freak
06 addict, maniac, zealot
07 devotee, radical
08 activist, militant
09 extremist, visionary
10 enthusiast
14 fundamentalist

fanatical
03 mad
04 wild
07 bigoted, burning, extreme, fervent, radical, zealous
08 activist, frenzied, militant
09 extremist, obsessive
10 immoderate, passionate
12 narrow-minded, single-minded
14 fundamentalist

fanaticism
04 zeal
06 frenzy
07 bigotry, fervour, madness
08 activism, wildness
09 dogmatism, extremism, militancy, monomania
13 obsessiveness
14 fundamentalism

fanciful
04 wild
06 ornate, unreal
07 curious, flighty
08 creative, fabulous, illusory, mythical, romantic
09 airy-fairy, decorated, elaborate, fairy-tale, fantastic, imaginary, legendary, whimsical
11 extravagant, imaginative, make-believe, unrealistic

fancy
03 yen
04 idea, itch, like, urge, want, whim, wish
05 dream, guess, showy, think
06 desire, favour, lavish, liking, notion, ornate, reckon, rococo, take to, vision
07 adorned, baroque, believe, caprice, dream of, elegant, fantasy, imagine, long for, not mind, opinion, picture, suppose, surmise, thought
08 conceive, delusion, fanciful, feel like, fondness, illusion, penchant, yearn for

09 decorated, elaborate, fantastic, lust after
10 be mad about, conjecture, creativity, far-fetched, have in mind, not say no to, ornamented, preference
11 embellished, extravagant, imagination, inclination
12 be attracted to, have a crush on, ostentatious
14 be interested in, find attractive, have the hots for

fanfare
06 tucket
08 flourish
09 fanfarade
11 trumpet call

fang
04 tang, tusk
05 prong, tooth
10 venom-tooth

fantasize
05 dream
06 invent
07 imagine, romance
08 daydream
11 hallucinate
12 live in a dream

fantastic
03 ace, odd
04 cool, neat, wild
05 brill, great, magic, weird
06 exotic, superb, unreal
07 amazing, bizarre, strange
08 fabulous, fanciful, illusory, romantic, terrific
09 brilliant, eccentric, first-rate, imaginary, visionary, wonderful
10 impressive, incredible, marvellous, outlandish
11 extravagant, imaginative
12 unbelievable
14 out of this world

fantasy
04 myth
05 dream, fancy
06 mirage, vision
07 reverie
08 daydream, delusion, illusion
09 invention, nightmare, pipe-dream, unreality
10 apparition, creativity
11 imagination, originality, pie in the sky, speculation
13 flight of fancy, hallucination

far
04 much
05 miles, other
06 far-off, remote

07 distant, faraway, further, greatly, removed
08 a good way, a long way, far-flung, markedly, opposite, outlying, secluded
09 decidedly, extremely
11 God-forsaken, nowhere near, out-of-the-way
12 considerably, immeasurably, in the boonies, inaccessible, incomparably
13 great distance
14 in the boondocks

□**far and wide**
06 widely
07 broadly
08 all about
09 worldwide
10 far and near
11 extensively, in all places
13 from all places

□**far out**
05 weird
06 exotic, way out
07 bizarre, extreme, strange
10 outlandish

□**go far**
05 get on
08 go places
12 be successful
14 achieve success
15 get on in the world

□**so far**
06 to date
07 up to now, thus far, till now
08 hitherto
13 up to this point

faraway
06 absent, dreamy, remote
07 distant
08 far-flung, outlying
10 abstracted
11 preoccupied
12 absent-minded

farce
04 joke, sham
06 comedy, parody, satire
07 mockery
08 nonsense, travesty
09 absurdity, slapstick
10 buffoonery
14 ridiculousness

farcical
05 comic, silly
06 absurd, stupid
08 derisory
09 laughable, ludicrous
10 ridiculous
11 nonsensical
12 preposterous

fare
02 be, do, go
03 fee
04 cost, diet, eats, food, menu
05 get on, meals, price, table
06 charge, ticket, viands
07 make out, passage, prosper, rations, succeed
08 eatables, get along, progress, victuals
10 provisions, sustenance
11 nourishment

far-fetched
05 crazy
07 dubious
08 fanciful, unlikely
09 fantastic
10 improbable, incredible
11 implausible, unrealistic
12 preposterous, unbelievable

farm
04 land, till
05 acres, croft, plant, ranch
06 grange, plough
07 acreage, holding, station
08 farmland
09 cultivate, homestead
11 co-operative, work the land

□**farm out**
08 delegate
11 contract out, subcontract

farmer
06 yeoman
07 crofter, grazier, rancher
10 agronomist, husbandman
11 smallholder
13 agriculturist

farming
07 tilling
08 agronomy, crofting
09 geoponics, husbandry
11 agriculture, cultivation

farrago
04 hash
06 jumble, medley
07 mixture, mélange
08 mishmash
09 pot-pourri
10 hotchpotch, miscellany, salmagundi
11 gallimaufry
13 dog's breakfast

far-reaching
04 wide
05 broad
08 sweeping, thorough
09 extensive, important
10 widespread
11 significant, wide-ranging
13 comprehensive

far-sighted
05 acute, canny
06 shrewd
07 politic, prudent
09 far-seeing, judicious, prescient, provident
10 discerning
11 circumspect
14 forward-looking

farther
07 further, remoter
11 more distant, more extreme

farthest
08 furthest, remotest
11 most distant, most extreme

fascinate
04 draw, lure
05 charm, rivet
06 absorb, allure, entice
07 attract, beguile, delight, enchant, engross, enthral
08 intrigue, transfix
09 captivate, hypnotize, mesmerize, spellbind

fascinated
06 hooked
07 charmed, curious, smitten
08 absorbed, beguiled
09 bewitched, engrossed, entranced, intrigued
10 captivated, enthralled, hypnotized, infatuated, mesmerized, spellbound

fascinating
08 alluring, charming, engaging, enticing, exciting, gripping, riveting, tempting
09 absorbing, seductive
10 bewitching, compelling, delightful, enchanting, engrossing, intriguing
11 captivating, interesting, mesmerizing, stimulating

fascination
04 draw, lure, pull
05 charm, magic, spell
06 allure, appeal
08 interest
09 magnetism
10 attraction, compulsion
11 captivation, enchantment

fascism
09 autocracy, Hitlerism
10 absolutism
12 dictatorship
15 totalitarianism

fascist
08 autocrat
09 Hitlerist, Hitlerite

10 absolutist, autocratic,
   Blackshirt
12 totalitarian
13 authoritarian

fashion
03 cut, fad, fit, way
04 form, kind, line, look, make,
   mode, rage, sort, suit, type
05 adapt, alter, craze, mould,
   shape, style, trend, vogue
06 adjust, create, custom,
   design, latest, manner,
   method, system, tailor
07 clothes, couture, pattern
08 approach, rag trade
12 haute couture
15 clothes industry

➤ *Names of fashion
designers*:
04 **Dior** (Christian), **Muir**
   (Jean)
05 **Farhi** (Nicole), **Karan**
   (Donna), **Kenzo** (Takada),
   Klein (Calvin), **Pucci**
   (Emilio), **Quant** (Mary)
06 **Armani** (Giorgio), **Ashley**
   (Laura), **Cardin** (Pierre),
   Chanel (Coco), **Conran**
   (Jasper), **Lauren** (Ralph),
   Miyake (Issey), **Ozbeck**
   (Rifat), **Rhodes** (Zandra)
07 **Hamnett** (Katharine),
   Lacroix (Christian),
   Laroche (Guy), **Versace**
   (Gianni)
08 **Galliano** (John), **Gaultier**
   (Jean-Paul), **Givenchy**
   (Hubert James Marcel
   Taffin de), **Hilfiger**
   (Tommy), **Oldfield** (Bruce),
   Westwood (Vivienne),
   Yamamoto (Yohji)
09 **Lagerfeld** (Karl),
   McCartney (Stella),
   Valentino
12 **Saint Laurent** (Yves),
   Schiaparelli (Elsa)

◻**after a fashion**
11 not very well
13 to some extent

fashionable
02 in
03 hip
04 chic, cool
05 funky, natty, ritzy, smart
06 latest, modern, modish,
   snazzy, trendy, with it
07 current, elegant, in vogue,
   popular, stylish, à la mode
08 designer, up-to-date
10 all the rage, prevailing

12 contemporary
13 up-to-the-minute

fast
04 diet, firm, shut, slim
05 apace, brisk, fixed, fully,
   hasty, nippy, quick, rapid,
   sound, swift, tight
06 deeply, firmly, flying, presto,
   secure, speedy, starve
07 express, fixedly, hastily,
   hurried, like mad, quickly,
   rapidly, refrain, swiftly, tightly
08 doggedly, go hungry, in a
   hurry, securely, speedily
09 high-speed, hurriedly,
   immovable, like a shot
10 abstinence, like a flash,
   resolutely, starvation
11 lickety-spit, like the wind
13 like lightning
14 at a rate of knots, hell for
   leather
15 like the clappers

fasten
03 fix, pin, tie
04 bind, bolt, clip, do up, grip,
   join, lace, link, lock, nail,
   seal, shut, tack
05 affix, chain, clamp, close,
   focus, hitch, rivet, zip up
06 anchor, attach, buckle,
   button, direct, secure, tether
07 connect

fastener
➤ *Types of fastener*:
03 tie, zip
04 bond, clip, frog, hasp, hook,
   knot, lace, link, lock, loop,
   nail, stud
05 catch, clasp, hinge, latch,
   rivet, screw
06 button, eyelet, holder, staple,
   stitch, toggle, Velcro®,
   zipper
08 cufflink, shoelace, split pin
09 paperclip, press stud
10 collar stud, hook-and-eye
11 treasury tag

fastidious
05 faddy, fussy, picky
06 choosy, dainty
07 finicky, precise
10 meticulous, particular,
   persnickety
11 punctilious
12 hard-to-please
13 hypercritical

fat
03 big, pot
04 bulk, flab, lard, suet, wide

05 broad, buxom, cream,
   dumpy, gross, heavy, large,
   obese, plump, podgy, round,
   solid, sonsy, stout, thick,
   tubby
06 butter, cheese, chubby,
   flabby, fleshy, greasy, portly,
   rotund, tallow
07 adipose, blubber, fatness,
   obesity, paunchy, pinguid
08 pot belly, sizeable
09 corpulent, fat as a pig,
   margarine, plumpness,
   sebaceous, solidness,
   stoutness
10 chubbiness, corpulence,
   oleaginous, overweight,
   pot-bellied
12 considerable, steatopygous

fatal
05 final
06 deadly, lethal, mortal
07 killing
08 terminal
09 incurable, malignant
10 calamitous, disastrous
12 catastrophic

fatalism
08 stoicism
09 endurance, passivity
10 acceptance
11 resignation
13 preordination
14 predestination

fatality
04 dead, loss
05 death
08 casualty, disaster
09 lethality, mortality
10 deadliness

fate
03 end, lot
04 doom, luck, ruin
05 death, issue, karma, stars
06 chance, future, kismet
07 destiny, fortune, outcome
08 disaster, God's will
09 horoscope
10 providence
11 catastrophe, destruction

fated
04 sure
06 doomed
07 certain
08 destined
10 inevitable
11 ineluctable, inescapable,
   predestined, preordained

fateful
07 crucial, pivotal

08 critical, decisive
09 important, momentous

father
02 pa
03 dad, pop
04 abbé, curé, papa, sire
05 beget, daddy, padre, pater
06 leader, old man, parent,
   parson, pastor, priest
07 creator, founder, produce
08 ancestor, begetter,
   engender, forebear,
   inventor, paternal
09 architect, clergyman,
   initiator, patriarch, procreate
10 forefather, give life to,
   originator, prime mover,
   procreator, progenitor
11 predecessor
13 paterfamilias

fatherland
04 home
08 homeland
10 motherland, native land, old
   country
13 mother-country

fatherly
06 benign, kindly, tender
08 paternal
09 avuncular, indulgent
10 benevolent, forbearing,
   protective, supportive
11 patriarchal
12 affectionate

fathom
05 gauge, plumb, probe, sound
07 measure, work out
08 estimate, perceive
09 interpret, penetrate
10 comprehend, understand

fatigue
03 sap, tax
04 tire
05 drain, weary
06 weaken
07 exhaust, wear out
08 enervate, lethargy,
   weakness
09 lassitude, tiredness,
   weariness
10 debilitate, enervation,
   exhaustion
11 take it out of
12 listlessness

fatigued
04 beat
05 all in, jaded, tired, weary
06 bushed, done in, fagged,
   wasted, zonked
07 whacked

08 dead-beat, tired out
09 exhausted, fagged out,
   knackered, overtired

fatness
04 bulk, flab
07 obesity
09 bulkiness, grossness,
   largeness, plumpness,
   podginess, rotundity,
   stoutness, tubbiness
10 corpulence, overweight

fatten
04 cram, feed
05 bloat, stuff, swell, widen
06 expand, feed up, spread
07 broaden, build up, fill out,
   nourish, nurture, thicken

fatty
03 fat
04 oily, waxy
06 creamy, fleshy, greasy, lipoid
07 adipose, buttery, pinguid
08 unctuous
09 sebaceous
10 oleaginous

fatuous
05 dense, inane, silly
06 absurd, stupid
07 asinine, foolish, idiotic,
   lunatic, moronic, puerile,
   vacuous, witless
08 mindless
09 brainless, ludicrous
10 ridiculous, weak-minded

fault
03 bug, sin
04 boob, flaw, slam, slip
05 blame, error, hitch, knock,
   lapse, slate, wrong
06 booboo, defect, foible,
   glitch, impugn, slip-up
07 blemish, censure, failing,
   misdeed, mistake, offence
09 criticize, liability, weak point
10 deficiency, negligence,
   peccadillo, wrongdoing
11 culpability, pick holes in
12 imperfection, indiscretion,
   misdemeanour, pull to
   pieces
14 accountability, responsibility
15 blameworthiness

□**at fault**
05 wrong
06 guilty
07 to blame
08 culpable
10 in the wrong
11 accountable, blameworthy,
   responsible

□**to a fault**
06 unduly
07 too much
09 extremely
10 over the top, to extremes
11 excessively
12 immoderately, in the
   extreme, inordinately
13 unnecessarily

fault-finding
07 carping, nagging
08 captious, critical, niggling
09 cavilling, criticism,
   querulous, quibbling
10 censorious, nit-picking
12 pettifogging
13 hair-splitting, hypercritical
14 finger-pointing

faultless
04 pure
07 correct, perfect
08 accurate, flawless, spotless
09 blameless, exemplary,
   unsullied
10 immaculate, impeccable
11 unblemished

faulty
04 bust, duff, weak
05 kaput, wrong
06 broken, flawed
07 damaged, invalid
09 casuistic, defective,
   erroneous, illogical,
   imperfect, incorrect
10 inaccurate, not working, on
   the blink, out of order
11 inoperative, out of action
14 malfunctioning

faux pas
04 boob, goof
05 gaffe
06 booboo, howler, slip-up
07 blunder, clanger, mistake
12 indiscretion

favour
04 back, help, like, pick
06 assist, choose, esteem,
   prefer, opt for, select
07 benefit, endorse, indulge,
   service, succour, support
08 approval, champion,
   courtesy, good deed, good
   turn, kindness, sympathy
09 patronage, recommend
10 partiality, preference
11 approbation, favouritism

□**in favour of**
03 for, pro
06 all for, behind
07 backing

10 supporting
11 on the side of

favourable
04 fair, good, kind
08 pleasing, positive, suitable
09 opportune, promising
10 auspicious, beneficial, convenient, heartening, propitious, reassuring
11 encouraging, sympathetic
12 advantageous, well-disposed
13 complimentary

favourably
04 well
09 agreeably, helpfully
10 positively, profitably
11 approvingly, opportunely
12 auspiciously, propitiously
14 advantageously
15 sympathetically

favoured
05 elite
06 chosen
07 blessed
08 selected
09 favourite, preferred
10 advantaged, privileged
11 predilected, recommended

favourite
03 pet
04 idol, pick
06 choice, chosen
07 beloved, darling, dearest
08 esteemed, favoured
09 best-loved, most-liked, number one, preferred
11 blue-eyed boy, first choice, teacher's pet

favouritism
04 bias
08 inequity, nepotism
09 injustice, prejudice
10 inequality, partiality, preference, unfairness
12 one-sidedness, partisanship

fawn
04 buff
05 beige, court, crawl, creep, khaki, sandy, smarm, toady
06 cringe, grovel, kowtow
07 flatter
08 bootlick, butter up, pay court, soft-soap, suck up to
11 curry favour
12 bow and scrape
14 yellowish-brown
15 dance attendance

fawning
06 abject
07 servile
08 crawling, toadying, toadyish, unctuous
09 cringing
10 flattering, grovelling, obsequious
11 deferential, sycophantic
12 ingratiating

fear
03 awe
04 fear, risk
05 alarm, doubt, dread, panic, scope, worry
06 chance, dismay, expect, fright, honour, horror, phobia, qualms, revere, terror, unease, wonder
07 anxiety, concern, suspect
08 aversion, be afraid, disquiet, distress, prospect, venerate
09 agitation, bête noire, fear of God, nightmare, reverence, shudder at, suspicion
10 anticipate, be afraid of, be scared of, foreboding, misgivings, tremble for, uneasiness, veneration
11 fearfulness, possibility, probability, trepidation
12 apprehension, get the wind up, stand in awe of, take fright at
13 be uneasy about, consternation, have a horror of, lose your nerve
14 be anxious about, be in a cold sweat, lose your bottle
15 have qualms about

fearful
04 dire, grim
05 awful, nervy, tense, timid
06 afraid, scared, uneasy
07 alarmed, anxious, ghastly, hideous, in dread, nervous, panicky, shaking
08 agitated, dreadful, fearsome, hesitant, horrible, horrific, shocking, terrible
09 appalling, atrocious, frightful, harrowing, monstrous, petrified, spineless, trembling
10 frightened
12 apprehensive, faint-hearted

fearfully
07 awfully, timidly
08 terribly
09 anxiously, extremely, intensely, nervously

10 dreadfully, hesitantly
11 exceedingly, frightfully
14 apprehensively

fearless
04 bold, game
05 brave, gutsy
06 daring, gritty, heroic, plucky
07 doughty, gallant, valiant
08 intrepid, unafraid, valorous
09 confident, dauntless, unabashed, undaunted
10 courageous, unblinking
11 indomitable, lion-hearted, unblenching, unflinching

fearsome
05 awful
07 awesome
08 alarming, daunting, horrible, horrific, menacing, terrible
09 frightful, unnerving
10 formidable, horrifying
11 frightening, hair-raising

feasibility
09 viability
11 possibility, workability
13 achievability
14 practicability

feasible
06 doable, likely, viable
08 possible, workable
09 practical, realistic
10 achievable, attainable, realizable, reasonable
11 practicable

feast
04 fête, gala
05 beano, binge, gorge, treat
06 dinner, festal, junket, repast, revels, spread, wealth
07 banquet, holiday, holy day
08 feast day, festival
09 abundance, partake of, profusion, saint's day
10 cornucopia, slap-up meal
11 celebration, eat your fill

feat
03 act
04 deed
06 action
07 exploit
10 attainment
11 achievement, performance
14 accomplishment

feather
04 down, tuft
05 crest, penna, plume, quill
07 plumula, plumule
08 aigrette

feathery
04 soft
05 downy, light, plumy, wispy
06 fleecy, fluffy, plumed
07 plumate, plumose, plumous
09 feathered, penniform
10 pennaceous

feature
03 act, mug, pan
04 dial, face, item, mark, phiz, show, side, star
05 clock, point, story, trait
06 appear, aspect, factor, figure, play up, report, visage
07 article, comment, perform, present, promote, quality
08 hallmark, property
09 attribute, emphasize, highlight, spotlight
10 accentuate, attraction, focal point, lineaments, speciality
11 countenance, participate, peculiarity, physiognomy
14 characteristic

febrile
03 hot
05 fiery
07 burning, febrile, fevered, flushed, pyretic
08 feverish, inflamed
09 delirious

feckless
04 weak
06 feeble, futile
07 aimless, useless
08 hopeless
09 worthless
11 incompetent, ineffectual
13 irresponsible

fecund
07 fertile, teeming
08 fruitful, prolific
09 feracious, fructuous
10 productive
12 fructiferous

fecundity
08 feracity
09 fertility
12 fruitfulness
14 productiveness

fed up
04 blue, down, glum
05 bored, tired, weary
06 dismal, gloomy
09 depressed, hacked off
10 brassed off, cheesed off
12 discontented, dissatisfied, sick and tired
13 have had enough

federal
06 allied, united
07 unified
08 combined, in league
10 associated, integrated
11 amalgamated
12 confederated

federate
05 unify, unite
07 combine
09 integrate, syndicate
10 amalgamate
11 confederate
12 join together

federation
05 union
06 league
08 alliance, federacy
09 coalition, syndicate
11 association, confederacy
12 amalgamation
13 confederation

fee
04 bill, cost, hire, rent, toll
05 price, terms
06 charge, reward
07 account, payment
08 retainer
09 emolument
10 honorarium, recompense
12 remuneration, subscription

feeble
03 wet
04 poor, puny, tame, thin, weak
05 faint, frail
06 ailing, effete, flimsy, futile, infirm, sickly, slight
07 failing, wimpish
08 decrepit, delicate, helpless
09 enervated, exhausted
11 debilitated, ineffectual
12 unconvincing, unsuccessful

feeble-minded
06 simple, stupid
09 deficient, dim-witted
10 half-witted, slow-witted, weak-minded
13 soft in the head
15 slow on the uptake

feed
03 eat, put
04 crop, dine, food, fuel, slip
05 graze, slide
06 browse, dine on, fodder, forage, foster, silage, suckle
07 consume, gratify, nourish, nurture, pasture, provide
08 cater for, ruminate
09 encourage, partake of
10 provide for, strengthen

feel
02 be
03 air, paw, rub
04 aura, bear, deem, hold, know, look, maul, mood, seem
05 enjoy, flair, grasp, grope, judge, knack, nurse, sense, skill, think, touch, vibes
06 appear, caress, clutch, endure, finger, finish, fondle, fumble, handle, notice, reckon, stroke, suffer, talent
07 ability, believe, contact, faculty, feeling, massage, observe, quality, realize, surface, texture, undergo
08 ambience, aptitude, consider, perceive
09 be aware of, go through
10 atmosphere, experience, impression, understand
11 consistency, live through

❑**feel for**
04 pity
06 weep for
09 be moved by, grieve for
10 be sorry for, sympathize
11 commiserate
13 empathize with

❑**feel like**
04 want, wish
05 fancy
06 desire

feeler
04 horn, palp
05 probe
06 palpus
07 advance, antenna
08 approach, overture, tentacle

feeling
03 air, ego
04 aura, feel, idea, mood, pity
05 hunch, sense, vibes
06 ardour, notion, warmth
07 emotion, fervour, inkling, opinion, passion, quality
08 emotions, fondness, instinct, passions, sympathy
09 affection, intuition, sensation, suspicion
10 affections, atmosphere, compassion, impression, perception, self-esteem
11 sensibility, sensitivity
12 appreciation
13 sensitivities, understanding
14 sentimentality, susceptibility

feign
03 act

04 fake, sham
05 forge, put on
06 affect, assume, invent
07 imitate, pretend, put it on
08 simulate
09 dissemble, fabricate
11 counterfeit, dissimulate

feint
04 play, ruse, wile
05 blind, bluff, dodge
06 gambit
08 artifice, pretence
09 deception, expedient,
   manoeuvre, stratagem
10 subterfuge
11 distraction, mock-assault

felicitous
03 apt
05 happy
06 timely
07 apropos, fitting
08 apposite, inspired, suitable
09 fortunate, opportune
10 delightful, propitious
11 appropriate

felicity
03 joy
05 bliss
07 aptness, delight, ecstasy
09 eloquence, happiness
11 delectation, suitability
12 suitableness
13 applicability
15 appropriateness

feline
05 sleek
06 slinky, smooth
07 catlike, leonine, sinuous
08 graceful, stealthy
09 seductive

fell
03 hew
04 raze
05 floor, level
07 cut down, flatten
08 demolish
09 knock down, overthrow
10 strike down

fellow
02 co-
03 boy, guy, lad, man, pal
04 chap, like, male, mate,
   peer
05 bloke, buddy, crony, equal
06 double, friend, person
07 comrade, partner, related
08 co-worker, confrère
09 associate, character,
   colleague, companion
10 associated, individual

11 counterpart
12 contemporary

fellow feeling
07 empathy
08 sympathy
10 compassion
13 commiseration

fellowship
04 club
05 guild, order, union
06 league
07 society
08 intimacy, matiness
09 communion, palliness
10 affability, amiability,
   friendship, sisterhood
11 affiliation, association,
   brotherhood, camaraderie,
   comradeship, familiarity
13 companionship

female
03 she-
07 girlish, womanly
08 feminine, ladylike

feminine
05 sissy
06 female, gentle, pretty, tender
07 girlish, unmanly, womanly
08 delicate, graceful, ladylike
10 effeminate

femininity
08 delicacy
09 sissiness, womanhood
10 effeminacy, gentleness,
   prettiness, tenderness
11 girlishness, womanliness
12 feminineness, gracefulness

feminism
09 women's lib
12 women's rights
14 women's movement

feminist
━━ *Names of feminists:*
04 **Daly** (Mary), **Hite** (Shere),
   Mott (Lucretia), **Shaw**
   (Anna Howard), **Wolf**
   (Naomi)
05 **Astor** (Nancy, Viscountess),
   Greer (Germaine)
06 **Callil** (Carmen), **Faludi**
   (Susan), **Friday** (Nancy),
   Gilman (Charlotte Anna
   Perkins), **Rankin**
   (Jeannette), **Stopes** (Marie),
   Weldon (Fay)
07 **Anthony** (Susan Brownell),
   Davison (Emily), **Fawcett**
   (Dame Millicent), **Friedan**
   (Betty), **Goldman** (Emma),

Kennedy (Helena Ann),
   Lenclos (Ninon de),
   Steinem (Gloria), **Tennant**
   (Emma)
08 **Beauvoir** (Simone de),
   Brittain (Vera)
09 **Blackwell** (Elizabeth),
   Pankhurst (Emmeline)
14 **Wollstonecraft** (Mary)

femme fatale
04 vamp
05 siren
07 charmer
09 temptress
10 seductress
11 enchantress

fen
03 bog
04 moss, quag
05 marsh, swamp

fence
03 pen
04 coop, rail, wall
05 bound, dodge, evade,
   guard, hedge, parry
06 paling, secure, shut in
07 barrier, confine, defence,
   enclose, fortify, protect,
   quibble, railing, rampart
08 encircle, palisade, restrict,
   stockade, surround
09 barricade, enclosure,
   pussyfoot, windbreak
10 equivocate

◻**sit on the fence**
06 dither
08 be unsure
09 vacillate
11 be uncertain, be undecided
12 be irresolute, shilly-shally
13 be uncommitted

fencing
━━ *Fencing terms:*
03 hit
04 épée, foil, pink, volt
05 feint, forte, lunge, parry,
   prime, sabre, sixte, touch
06 attack, foible, octave, quarte,
   quinte, remise, thrust, tierce,
   touché
07 barrage, en garde, on guard,
   reprise, riposte, seconde,
   septime
08 plastron, tac-au-tac
09 disengage
12 counter-parry
14 counter-riposte

fend
05 avert, parry, repel

07 beat off, deflect, keep off, provide, repulse, shut out, support, sustain, ward off
08 maintain, stave off
09 hold at bay, turn aside

feral
04 wild
06 brutal, fierce, savage
07 bestial, untamed, vicious
08 unbroken
09 ferocious
14 undomesticated

ferment
04 boil, brew, foam, fuss, heat, rise, stew, stir, work
05 cause, fever, froth, rouse
06 bubble, excite, fester, foment, frenzy, furore, hubbub, incite, seethe, stir up, tumult, unrest, uproar
07 agitate, provoke, turmoil
08 brouhaha, smoulder
09 agitation, commotion
10 disruption, effervesce, excitement, turbulence

ferocious
04 deep, wild
05 cruel, feral
06 bitter, brutal, fierce, savage, severe, strong
07 extreme, inhuman, intense, untamed, vicious, violent
08 barbaric, pitiless, vigorous
09 barbarous, murderous
12 bloodthirsty

ferocity
06 sadism
07 cruelty
08 savagery, violence, wildness
09 barbarity, brutality
10 fierceness, inhumanity
11 viciousness

ferret
04 hunt
05 rifle, scour
06 forage, search
07 rummage
09 go through

❑**ferret out**
04 find
05 dig up, trace
07 extract, root out, unearth
08 discover, hunt down
09 search out, track down
10 run to earth

ferry
03 ply, run
04 boat, move, ship, take, taxi
06 convey, packet, vessel
07 shuttle

08 car ferry
09 ferry-boat, transport

fertile
04 rich
06 fecund, potent, virile
08 creative, fruitful, prolific
09 inventive, luxuriant
10 generative, productive
11 imaginative, resourceful

fertility
07 potency
08 richness, virility
09 abundance, fecundity
10 luxuriance
12 fruitfulness, prolificness
14 productiveness

fertilization
11 fecundation, pollination, procreation, propagation
12 implantation, impregnation, insemination

fertilize
04 dung, feed
05 dress, mulch
06 enrich, manure
08 fructify, top-dress
09 fecundate, pollinate
10 impregnate, inseminate
12 make fruitful, make pregnant

fertilizer
04 dung
05 humus, mulch
06 manure
07 compost
08 bone meal, dressing
11 top-dressing

fervent
04 warm
05 eager, fiery
06 ardent, devout
07 earnest, excited, intense, sincere, zealous
08 spirited, vehement, vigorous
09 emotional, heartfelt
10 passionate
11 full-blooded, impassioned
12 enthusiastic, wholehearted

fervour
04 fire, zeal
05 verve
06 ardour, energy, spirit, warmth
07 emotion, passion
09 eagerness, intensity, sincerity, vehemence
10 enthusiasm, excitement
11 earnestness

fester
03 irk, rot

05 anger, chafe, decay, go bad
06 gather, infect, perish, rankle
07 putrefy
08 maturate, smoulder, ulcerate
09 decompose, suppurate

festival
04 fair, fête, gala
05 feast, party
06 fiesta
07 gala day, holiday, jubilee
08 carnival
11 anniversary, celebration
13 commemoration, entertainment

➤ _Names of religious festivals:_
02 Id
03 Eid
04 Holi, Lent, Obon
05 Purim
06 Advent, Divali, Diwali, Easter, Pesach, Sukkot
07 Beltane, New Year, Ramadan, Sukkoth
08 All Souls, Dipavali, Epiphany, Hanukkah, Id al-Fitr, Passover
09 All Saints, Ascension, Candlemas, Christmas, Deepavali, Easter Day, Eid al-Fitr, Mardi Gras, Pentecost, Up-Helly-Aa, Yom Kippur
10 Assumption, Good Friday, Lupercalia, Michaelmas, Palm Sunday, saturnalia, Whit Sunday
11 All Souls Day, Rosh Hashana
12 All Saints' Day, Annunciation, Ascension Day, Ash Wednesday, Christmas Day, Easter Sunday, Holy Saturday, Night of Power, Rosh Hashanah
13 Corpus Christi, Holy Innocents, Night of Ascent, Passion Sunday, spring equinox, Trinity Sunday, vernal equinox
14 Chinese New Year, Day of Atonement, Easter Saturday, summer solstice, winter solstice
15 autumnal equinox, Lantern Festival, Transfiguration
➤ See also **religion**

festive
05 happy, jolly, merry
06 cheery, joyful, joyous
07 cordial, holiday

08 carnival, cheerful, jubilant
09 convivial
11 celebratory
12 light-hearted

festivity
03 fun
05 party, revel, sport
07 jollity, revelry
08 carousal, feasting, festival
09 amusement, enjoyment, joviality, merriment
10 banqueting, jubilation
11 celebration, fun and games, merrymaking
12 cheerfulness, conviviality
13 entertainment

festoon
04 deck, hang, swag
05 adorn, array, drape
06 bedeck, swathe, wreath
07 garland, garnish, wreathe
08 decorate, ornament

fetch
03 get
05 bring, carry, go for, yield
06 convey, escort
07 bring in, collect, conduct, deliver, realize, sell for
08 go and get

fetching
04 cute
05 sweet
06 pretty
07 winsome
08 alluring, charming
10 attractive, enchanting
11 captivating, fascinating

fête
04 fair, gala
06 bazaar, honour, regale
07 lionize, welcome
08 carnival, festival
10 sale of work
11 garden party

fetid
04 foul, rank
06 filthy, rancid, sickly, smelly
07 noisome, noxious, odorous, reeking
08 mephitic, stinking
10 malodorous, nauseating

fetish
04 idol, ju-ju
05 charm, image, mania, thing
06 amulet
08 fixation, idée fixe, talisman
09 obsession

fetter
04 bind, curb

05 chain, tie up, truss
06 hamper, hinder, impede
07 confine, manacle, shackle
08 encumber, obstruct, restrain, restrict
09 constrain, hamstring

fetters
05 bonds, curbs, irons
06 chains, checks
07 bondage
08 manacles, shackles
09 bracelets, handcuffs
11 constraints, inhibitions

feud
03 row, war
05 argue, brawl, clash, fight
06 bicker, enmity, strife
07 contend, discord, dispute, ill will, quarrel, rivalry, wrangle
08 argument, bad blood, be at odds, conflict, vendetta
09 altercate, animosity, bickering, hostility
10 antagonism, bitterness

fever
04 ague, heat
06 frenzy, unrest
07 ecstasy, febrile, ferment, passion, pyrexia, turmoil
09 agitation, calenture
10 excitement
12 feverishness, restlessness
15 high temperature

feverish
03 hot, red
06 hectic, rushed
07 burning, excited, flushed, frantic, hurried, nervous
08 agitated, frenzied, in a tizzy, troubled, worked up
09 delirious, flustered
11 overwrought
14 hot and bothered

few
04 rare, some, thin
05 scant
06 meagre, scanty, scarce
07 a couple, handful, not many
08 one or two, uncommon
09 a minority, hardly any
10 inadequate, infrequent, scattering, sprinkling
11 scarcely any
12 insufficient
15 thin on the ground

fiancé, fiancée
08 intended, wife-to-be
09 betrothed, bride-to-be
10 future wife
11 husband-to-be

13 future husband
14 bridegroom-to-be
15 prospective wife

fiasco
04 flop, mess, rout, ruin
07 debacle, failure, washout
08 calamity, collapse, disaster
09 damp squib

fiat
02 OK
05 edict, order
06 decree, dictum, diktat
07 command, dictate, mandate, precept, warrant
08 sanction
09 directive, ordinance
10 injunction, permission
12 proclamation
13 authorization

fib
03 lie
04 tale, yarn
05 evade, story
07 evasion, falsify, fantasy, fiction, untruth, whopper
08 sidestep, white lie
09 dissemble, falsehood
10 concoction

fibre
05 cloth, nerve, sinew, stuff
06 fibril, nature, strand, thread
07 calibre, courage, stamina
08 backbone, filament, firmness, material, strength
09 character, substance, toughness, willpower
11 disposition, temperament
12 resoluteness
13 determination

fickle
07 flighty
08 disloyal, unstable, unsteady, variable, volatile
09 faithless, mercurial
10 capricious, changeable, inconstant, irresolute, unfaithful, unreliable
13 unpredictable

fickleness
10 fitfulness, volatility
11 flightiness, inconstancy
13 changeability, faithlessness, unreliability
14 capriciousness, unfaithfulness

fiction
03 fib, lie
04 myth, tale, yarn
05 fable, story

06 legend, novels
07 fantasy, romance, untruth
09 falsehood, tall story
10 concoction
11 fabrication

▶ *Names of works of non-fiction*:
06 Walden
07 Capital
08 Self-Help
09 Kama Sutra, Leviathan, TableTalk, The Phaedo
10 Das Kapital, The Annales, The Gorgias, The Poetics, The Timaeus
11 Down the Mine, Mythologies, The Analects, The Phaedrus, The Republic
12 Novum Organum, Silent Spring, The City of God, The Second Sex, The Symposium
13 The Story of Art
14 A Room of One's Own, Birds of America, Eudemian Ethics, Modern Painters, Past and Present, Sartor Resartus, The Age of Reason, The Golden Bough, The Life of Jesus, The Rights of Man, The Selfish Gene
15 Lives of the Poets, Roget's Thesaurus, The Essays of Elia, The Female Eunuch

fictional
06 made-up, unreal
08 fabulous, invented, literary, mythical
09 imaginary, legendary
11 make-believe, non-existent
12 mythological

▶ *Fictional places include*:
02 Ix, Oz
04 Alph (River), Rhun
05 Arnor, Moria, Rohan
06 Baucis, Gondor, Icaria, Laputa, Lorien, Mordor, Narnia, Titipu, Utopia, Vulcan, Xanadu
07 Camelot, Camford, Erewhon, Midwich, Mole End, Prydain, Toyland
08 Blefuscu, Calormen, Earthsea, Llaregyb, Mirkwood, New Crete, Polyglot, Ragnarok, Stepford, Sylvania, Tartarus, The Shire, Toad Hall
09 Barataria, Concordia, Discworld, Freedonia,
Ringworld, Rivendell, River Alph, Ruritania, Shangri-La
10 Archenland, Moominland, Vanity Fair, Wonderland
11 Airstrip One, Brobdingnag, Gormenghast, Middle-Earth, Orbitsville, The Wild Wood
12 Alderley Edge, Celesteville, Jurassic Park, Sleepy Hollow
13 Christminster
14 Doubting-Castle, Never-Never Land, Nightmare Abbey, Oroonoko Island, Treasure Island

fictitious
04 fake, sham
05 bogus, false
06 made-up, untrue
08 invented, spurious
09 concocted, imaginary
10 apocryphal, fabricated

fiddle
03 con, fix, toy
04 fuss, play
05 cheat, fraud, graft
06 diddle, fidget, juggle, meddle, racket, rip-off, tamper, tinker, trifle
07 falsify, swindle
09 manoeuvre, racketeer
10 fool around, mess around
12 cook the books
13 sharp practice

fiddling
06 paltry
07 trivial
08 trifling
10 negligible
13 insignificant

fidelity
07 loyalty
08 accuracy, devotion
09 adherence, closeness, constancy, exactness
10 allegiance, strictness
11 devotedness, reliability
12 authenticity, faithfulness

fidget
03 toy
04 fret, fuss, jerk, jump
06 fiddle, jiggle, squirm, twitch
07 shuffle, twiddle, wriggle
10 play around

fidgety
05 jumpy
06 on edge, uneasy
07 jittery, nervous, twitchy
08 agitated, restless
09 impatient

field
03 lea
04 area, lawn, line, mead, stop
05 catch, forte, glebe, green, pitch, range, scope, sward
06 answer, domain, ground, handle, meadow, pick up, regime, return, sphere
07 deflect, paddock, pasture
08 cope with, deal with, entrants, province
09 grassland, opponents, possibles, territory
10 applicants, candidates, contenders, discipline, speciality
11 competitors, contestants
12 participants, playing-field

fiend
03 fan, nut
04 buff, ogre
05 beast, brute, demon, devil
06 addict, savage
07 devotee, fanatic, monster
10 aficionado, enthusiast

fiendish
06 brutal, clever, wicked
07 complex, cunning, inhuman
08 barbaric, devilish, infernal, involved, ruthless
09 difficult, ferocious, ingenious, intricate
10 aggressive, diabolical, horrendous, malevolent
11 challenging, complicated, imaginative, resourceful

fierce
03 hot
04 grim, keen, wild
05 cruel, grave, stern
06 brutal, raging, savage, severe, strong
07 intense, vicious, violent
08 menacing, powerful, ruthless, terrible
09 cut-throat, dangerous, ferocious, murderous
10 aggressive, passionate
11 frightening, threatening
12 bloodthirsty, uncontrolled

fiercely
06 keenly, wildly
07 cruelly, sternly
08 bitterly, brutally, savagely, severely, strongly, terribly
09 intensely, viciously, violently
10 implacably, menacingly, powerfully, ruthlessly
11 dangerously, fanatically, ferociously, murderously

12 aggressively, passionately, relentlessly, tooth and nail

fiery
03 hot
05 afire, aglow, sharp, spicy
06 ablaze, aflame, ardent, fierce, heated, red-hot, spiced, sultry, torrid
07 blazing, burning, fervent, flaming, flushed, glowing, piquant, pungent, violent
08 inflamed, seasoned
09 excitable, hot-headed, impetuous, impulsive
10 passionate

fight
03 box, hit, row, war
04 defy, duel, feud, fray, riot
05 aggro, argue, brawl, brush, clash, drive, fence, joust, melee, punch, scrap, set-to
06 action, attack, battle, bicker, bovver, combat, dust-up, engage, fracas, oppose, resist, ruckus, ruffle, shindy, spirit, strive, take on, tussle
07 be at war, contend, contest, crusade, dispute, fall out, grapple, lay into, make war, punch-up, quarrel, scuffle, wage war, wrangle, wrestle
08 argument, campaign, champion, conflict, do battle, have a row, movement, object to, set about, skirmish, squabble, struggle, tenacity
09 altercate, encounter, stand up to, weigh into, willpower, withstand
10 aggression, dissension, Donnybrook, engagement, free-for-all, will to live
11 altercation, come to blows, cross swords, hostilities
12 disagreement, resoluteness
13 confrontation, determination
15 campaign against

□**fight back**
05 check, reply
06 resist, retort
07 contain, control, repress
08 bottle up, hold back, restrain, suppress
09 force back, retaliate
11 put up a fight
13 counter-attack
14 defend yourself

□**fight off**
04 rout

05 repel
06 rebuff, resist
07 beat off, hold off, ward off
08 stave off
09 hold at bay, keep at bay

fighter
05 boxer, rival
07 soldier, trouper, warrior
08 opponent, pugilist, wrestler
09 adversary, contender, disputant, gladiator, mercenary, swordsman
10 antagonist, contestant

figment
□**a figment of your imagination**
05 fable, fancy
08 delusion, illusion
09 falsehood, invention
11 fabrication

figurative
08 symbolic
09 parabolic, pictorial
11 allegorical, descriptive
12 metaphorical, naturalistic

figure
03 sum
04 body, form, sign
05 build, digit, guess, image, shape, think, torso, total
06 amount, appear, crop up, design, emblem, figure, leader, number, person, reckon, sketch, symbol
07 believe, diagram, drawing, feature, imagery, integer, numeral, outline, picture
08 consider, estimate
09 celebrity, character, dignitary, personage
11 mathematics, personality
12 be included in, illustration
13 be mentioned in
14 representation

□**figure out**
03 see
05 count
06 fathom, reason, reckon
07 compute, make out, work out
08 decipher, estimate
09 calculate, puzzle out
10 understand

figurehead
04 bust, name
05 dummy, image, token
06 figure, puppet
08 front man
10 man of straw, mouthpiece

figure of speech
05 image
06 figure
07 imagery
12 turn of phrase

filament
04 cord, hair, pile, wire
05 cable, fibre
06 strand, string, thread

filch
04 crib, lift, nick, palm, take
05 pinch, steal, swipe
06 pilfer, rip off, snitch, thieve
07 purloin, snaffle
08 embezzle, knock off, peculate
14 misappropriate

file
03 box, row, rub
04 case, data, hone, line, make, note, rasp, sand, whet
05 enter, march, put in, queue, shape, store, trail, train
06 abrade, binder, column, folder, papers, polish, record, scrape, smooth, stream, string, submit
07 details, dossier, rub down
08 classify, document
09 catalogue, portfolio
10 categorize, pigeonhole, procession, walk in line
11 information, particulars

filial
05 loyal
06 loving
07 devoted, dutiful
10 daughterly, respectful
12 affectionate

filibuster
06 hinder, impede, put off
08 obstruct, perorate
09 hindrance, speechify
10 impediment, peroration
12 speechifying
13 procrastinate
15 procrastination

filigree
04 lace
07 lattice, tracery
08 fretwork, wirework
09 interlace
10 scrollwork

fill
04 bung, clog, cork, cram, hold, pack, plug, seal, soak, stop
05 ample, block, close, crowd, imbue, stock, stuff

06 charge, fulfil, occupy, stop up, supply, take up
07 congest, perform, pervade, provide, satisfy, suffuse
08 complete, saturate
09 abundance, replenish
10 all you want, impregnate
11 sufficiency
14 more than enough

❑ fill in

05 brief
06 act for, answer, inform
07 fill out, replace, stand in
08 complete, deputize
10 substitute, understudy
13 bring up to date

❑ fill out

06 answer, fill in
08 complete
10 gain weight, grow fatter
11 put on weight

filling

05 ample, heavy, large, solid
06 filler, inside, square, stodgy
07 padding, wadding
08 contents, generous, stuffing
10 nutritious, satisfying
11 substantial

fillip

04 goad, prod, push, spur
05 boost, shove
07 impetus
08 stimulus
09 incentive
13 encouragement

film

04 coat, mist, reel, skin, veil
05 cloud, cover, flick, glaze, layer, movie, sheet, shoot, short, spool, video
07 blanket, coating, dusting, footage, picture
08 cassette, covering, membrane, televise
09 cartridge, videotape
11 documentary, feature film
13 motion picture, videocassette

➢ See also **director**

► *Kinds of film*:

03 war
04 blue, cult, epic
05 adult, buddy, farce, short, weepy
06 action, biopic, B-movie, comedy, Disney, family, horror, re-make, silent, weepie
07 Carry-on, cartoon, classic, diorama, fantasy, musical, new wave, tragedy, western
08 animated, disaster, film noir, gangster, newsreel, romantic, thriller
09 adventure, burlesque, flashback, Hitchcock, Hollywood, James Bond, love story, low-budget, melodrama, Spielberg, whodunnit
10 avant-garde, tear-jerker, travelogue
11 black comedy, blockbuster, cliff-hanger, documentary, kitchen sink, period drama, tragicomedy
12 cinéma-vérité, Ealing comedy, pornographic
13 murder mystery
14 Charlie Chaplin, rites of passage, romantic comedy, science-fiction
15 cowboy and Indian

► *Names of films*:

02 ET, If
03 JFK, Kes, Ran
04 Babe, Bird, Diva, Gigi, Jaws, Reds, Tess
05 Alfie, Alien, Bambi, Crash, Dumbo, Ghost, Giant, Greed, Klute, Marty, Rocky, Shane
06 Ben-Hur, Blow-Up, Brazil, Gandhi, Grease, Heimat, Mad Max, Patton, The Fly, The Kid, Top Gun
07 Amadeus, Die Hard, Dracula, L'Age d'Or, Platoon, Rain Man, Rebecca, Robocop, The Boat, The Omen, The Robe, Titanic, Tootsie
08 Born Free, Duck Soup, Fantasia, High Noon, Key Largo, King Kong, Star Wars, The Piano, The Sting, The Thing, Toy Story
09 Annie Hall, Betty Blue, Cat Ballou, GoldenEye, Home Alone, Local Hero, Manhattan, Ninotchka, Nosferatu, Notorious, Pinocchio, Spartacus
10 Bagdad Café, Blue Velvet, Braveheart, Casablanca, Dirty Harry, East of Eden, Goldfinger, GoodFellas, Grand Hotel, Jungle Book, Mrs Miniver, Now, Voyager, Raging Bull, Rear Window, Safety Last, Taxi Driver, The Hustler, The Mission, The Servant, The Shining, The Wild One, Unforgiven, Wall Street, Way Out West
11 All About Eve, American Pie, Blade Runner, Citizen Kane, Deliverance, Forrest Gump, Heaven's Gate, Jungle Fever, La Dolce Vita, Mary Poppins, Modern Times, Notting Hill, Out of Africa, Paris, Texas, Pretty Woman, Pulp Fiction, The Exorcist, The Graduate, The Lion King, The Music Man, The Third Man, Wayne's World, Yellow Earth
12 A View to a Kill, Delicatessen, Eyes Wide Shut, Frankenstein, Ghostbusters, Jurassic Park, The Apartment, The Go-Between, The Godfather, The Naked City, Whisky Galore, Withnail and I
13 Apocalypse Now, Babette's Feast, Basic Instinct, Death in Venice, Doctor Zhivago, Educating Rita, Live and Let Die, Reservoir Dogs, Scent of a Woman, Some Like It Hot, Sophie's Choice, The Dam Busters, The Deer Hunter, The Dirty Dozen, The Jazz Singer, The Longest Day, The Right Stuff, Trainspotting, West Side Story, Zorba the Greek
14 American Beauty, Animal Crackers, Black Narcissus, Brief Encounter, Chariots of Fire, Cinema Paradiso, Enter the Dragon, In Which We Serve, Midnight Cowboy, Schindler's List, The Commitments, The Elephant Man, The King of Kings, The Ladykillers, The Last Emperor, The Music Lovers
15 Back to the Future, Company of Wolves, Crocodile Dundee, Double Indemnity, Fantastic Voyage, Forbidden Planet, Full Metal Jacket, Gone With the Wind, Independence Day, Midnight Express, On the Waterfront, Return of the Jedi, Tarzan the Ape Man, The African Queen, The Bicycle Thief, The King of Comedy, The Lady Vanishes,

Thelma and Louise, The
Sound of Music

❑**film over**
05 glaze
08 mist over
09 cloud over
13 become blurred

filmy
04 fine, thin
05 gauzy, light, sheer
06 flimsy, floaty
08 delicate, gossamer
10 diaphanous, see-through,
   shimmering
11 translucent, transparent
13 insubstantial

filter
04 leak, mesh, ooze, seep, sift
05 drain, gauze, leach, sieve
06 purify, refine, screen, strain
07 dribble, netting, trickle
08 membrane, strainer
09 percolate

filth
04 crap, crud, dirt, grot, gunk,
   muck, porn, smut, yuck
05 grime, gunge, slime, trash
06 grunge, sleaze, sludge
07 garbage, rubbish, squalor
08 effluent, foulness, hard porn
09 blue films, excrement,
   indecency, obscenity,
   pollution, vulgarity
10 coarseness, defilement
11 pornography, putrescence,
   raunchiness, uncleanness
12 putrefaction
13 sexploitation

filthy
04 base, blue, foul, lewd, vile
05 adult, bawdy, black, dirty,
   grimy, gross, mucky, muddy,
   nasty, slimy, sooty, yucky
06 coarse, faecal, grubby,
   impure, putrid, rotten,
   smutty, soiled, sordid, vulgar
07 corrupt, obscene, squalid
08 decaying, depraved,
   indecent, polluted,
   unwashed
09 offensive, worthless
10 despicable, putrefying,
   suggestive
11 foul-mouthed
12 contemptible, pornographic

final
03 end
04 last
05 dying
07 closing, settled

08 decisive, definite, eventual,
   terminal, ultimate
09 finishing
10 concluding, conclusive,
   definitive, last-minute
11 irrevocable, terminating

finale
03 end
05 close
06 climax, ending
08 epilogue, final act
10 conclusion, dénouement
11 culmination
13 crowning glory

finality
08 firmness, ultimacy
09 certitude
10 conviction, resolution
12 decisiveness, definiteness
14 conclusiveness,
   irrevocability, unavoidability
15 irreversibility

finalize
05 agree, close, sew up
06 clinch, decide, finish, settle,
   wrap up
07 resolve, work out
08 complete, conclude, round
   off

finally
06 at last, lastly
07 for ever, for good
08 at length, in the end
10 decisively, eventually, to
   conclude, ultimately
11 irrevocably, permanently
12 in conclusion, irreversibly
13 once and for all

finance
04 back, cash, fund
05 float, funds, means, money
06 assets, pay for, wealth
07 affairs, banking, capital,
   funding, revenue, savings,
   sponsor, subsidy, support
08 accounts, commerce
09 economics, liquidity,
   resources, subsidize
10 investment, underwrite
11 sponsorship, wherewithal
15 money management

financial
05 money
06 fiscal
08 economic, monetary
09 budgetary, pecuniary
10 commercial
15 entrepreneurial

financier
06 banker
08 investor
10 money-maker, speculator
11 stockbroker

find
03 get, win
04 boon, deem, earn, gain
05 catch, judge, think, trace
06 attain, come by, detect, dig
   out, locate, notice, obtain,
   regain, reveal, turn up
07 achieve, acquire, declare,
   get back, godsend, good
   buy, observe, procure,
   realize, recover, uncover,
   unearth
08 consider, discover, perceive
09 discovery, encounter,
   stumble on, track down
10 chance upon, come across,
   happen upon
12 bring to light
13 stumble across

❑**find out**
05 get at, learn
06 detect, expose, reveal,
   rumble, show up, unmask
07 realize, suss out, uncover
08 disclose, discover, identify,
   perceive, pinpoint
09 ascertain, establish, get
   wind of
12 bring to light

finding
04 find
07 verdict
08 decision
09 discovery, judgement
10 conclusion, innovation
12 breakthrough
13 pronouncement

fine
02 OK
03 dry, fit
04 fair, nice, slim, thin, well
05 clear, exact, gauzy, great,
   light, mulct, sheer, sunny
06 amerce, bright, choice,
   dainty, flimsy, ground, lovely,
   narrow, select, slight, strong
07 clement, crushed, damages,
   elegant, forfeit, fragile,
   healthy, penalty, powdery,
   precise, slender, stylish
08 accurate, all right, critical,
   delicate, gossamer,
   handsome, penalize,
   splendid, superior, vigorous
09 admirable, beautiful,
   brilliant, cloudless,

excellent, expensive,
exquisite
10 acceptable, amercement,
attractive, forfeiture
11 exceptional, fashionable,
fine-grained, magnificent
12 in good health, satisfactory

finery
08 frippery, glad rags
09 jewellery, ornaments,
splendour, trappings
10 Sunday best
11 bedizenment, best clothes

finesse
05 bluff, evade, flair, skill, trick
06 polish
07 know-how
08 deftness, delicacy, elegance,
neatness, subtlety
09 adeptness, diplomacy,
expertise, quickness
10 adroitness, cleverness,
manipulate, refinement
14 sophistication

finger
03 paw
04 feel
05 place, touch
06 caress, fondle, handle,
locate, recall, stroke
07 hit upon, isolate, toy with
08 identify, indicate, pinpoint
10 fiddle with, manipulate
13 play about with

❏**put your finger on**
06 locate, recall
07 hit upon, isolate, pin down
08 discover, identify, indicate,
pinpoint, remember

finicky
05 faddy, fussy, picky
06 choosy, fiddly, tricky
09 difficult, finickety, intricate
10 fastidious, meticulous,
nit-picking, particular,
pernickety, scrupulous
13 hypercritical

finish
03 eat, end, use
04 rout, ruin, stop
05 cease, close, crush, drain,
drink, empty, glaze, gloss,
grain, sew up, shine, use up
06 attain, be over, defeat,
devour, ending, expend,
finale, fulfil, lustre, pack in,
polish, settle, veneer, wind
up, wind-up, wrap up

07 achieve, coating, deplete,
destroy, exhaust, lacquer,
surface, texture, wipe out
08 carry out, complete,
conclude, curtains, deal
with, get rid of, round off
09 be through, cessation,
culminate, get shot of,
overpower, overthrow,
polish off, terminate
10 accomplish, annihilate, be
done with, call it a day,
completion, conclusion,
perfection, smoothness
11 achievement, come to an
end, culmination,
destruction, discontinue,
exterminate, termination
12 bring to an end

finished
04 over
05 empty, spent
06 doomed, expert, ruined,
sewn up, undone, urbane
07 at an end, done for, drained,
perfect, refined, through
08 complete, defeated,
masterly, polished,
unwanted
09 completed, concluded,
dealt with, exhausted,
played out, wrapped up
10 consummate, proficient
12 accomplished, professional
13 sophisticated
15 over and done with

finite
05 fixed
07 bounded, limited
08 numbered
09 countable, definable
10 calculable, measurable,
restricted, terminable

fire
04 flak, heat, hurl, sack, stir,
whet
05 blaze, eject, light, rouse,
salvo, shoot, verve
06 ardour, arouse, attack,
energy, excite, flames,
heater, incite, kindle, launch,
let off, set off, spirit, stir up
07 animate, bombing, bonfire,
boot out, burning, dismiss,
enliven, explode, fervour,
gunfire, igneous, inferno,
inflame, inspire, passion,
sniping, sparkle, trigger
08 detonate, get rid of,
motivate, shelling, spark off

09 animation, convector,
discharge, galvanize,
holocaust, intensity, set
ablaze, set alight, set fire to,
set on fire, stimulate
10 combustion, creativity,
enthusiasm, excitement,
liveliness, trigger off
11 bombardment, put a match
to
13 conflagration, inventiveness

❏**on fire**
05 eager, fiery
06 ablaze, aflame, alight,
ardent
07 blazing, burning, excited,
flaming, ignited
08 creative, in flames, inspired
10 passionate

firearm
03 gun
05 rifle
06 musket, pistol, weapon
07 handgun, shotgun
08 revolver
09 automatic

fireworks
04 rage, rows
06 sparks, temper, uproar
07 trouble
08 outburst
09 hysterics
10 explosions
12 pyrotechnics
13 feux d'artifice, illuminations

► *Types of firework*:
04 pioy
05 devil, gerbe, peeoy, squib,
wheel
06 banger, fisgig, fizgig,
maroon, petard, rocket
07 cracker, volcano
08 fountain, pinwheel, sparkler,
whizbang
09 girandola, girandole,
sky-rocket, whizz-bang
11 firecracker, jumping-jack,
Roman candle, tourbillion
14 Catherine wheel, indoor
firework

firm
03 set
04 fast, hard, sure, true
05 close, dense, fixed, rigid,
solid, stiff, tight
06 dogged, secure, stable,
steady, strict, strong, sturdy
07 adamant, compact,
company, concern, decided,
riveted, settled, staunch

08 anchored, business,
constant, definite,
embedded, fastened,
hardened, obdurate,
resolute, resolved, stubborn
09 committed, immovable,
obstinate, steadfast,
syndicate, tenacious
10 compressed, dependable,
determined, enterprise,
inflexible, solidified,
unshakable, unswerving,
unwavering, unyielding
11 corporation, established,
institution, long-lasting,
partnership, unalterable,
unfaltering, unflinching
12 conglomerate, long-
standing, organization
13 establishment

firmly
06 stably
07 tightly
08 robustly, securely, steadily,
strictly, strongly, sturdily
09 immovably, staunchly
10 decisively, inflexibly,
resolutely, unshakably
11 steadfastly, unalterably
12 unchangeably, unwaveringly

firmness
07 density, resolve, tension
08 hardness, obduracy, rigidity,
solidity, strength, tautness
09 constancy, stability, stiffness
10 conviction, resolution,
steadiness, strictness
11 compactness, reliability
12 immovability, inelasticity
13 dependability,
determination, inflexibility,
steadfastness
14 indomitability, strength of
will

first
04 best, head, main
05 basic, chief, prime, prior
06 eldest, oldest, outset, senior
07 at first, earlier, highest, initial,
leading, opening, origins,
primary, supreme
08 earliest, foremost, greatest,
original, première, primeval
09 beginning, inaugural,
initially, paramount,
primitive, principal,
prototype, sovereign,
square one, the word go,
unveiling, uppermost

10 beforehand, elementary,
first of all, originally, pre-
eminent, primordial
11 at the outset, fundamental,
predominant, preliminary,
to begin with, to start with
12 in preference, introduction,
introductory
15 in the first place

first-born
04 aîné
05 aînée, eigne, elder, older
06 eldest, oldest, senior
12 primogenital
13 primogenitary

firsthand
06 direct
08 directly, on the job, personal
10 personally

first name
08 forename
09 given name
13 baptismal name, Christian
name

first-rate
02 A1
03 ace, top
04 cool, fine, mega
05 crack, prime, super
07 leading, premier, supreme
08 peerless, superior,
top-notch
09 admirable, excellent,
matchless, top-flight
10 first-class
11 outstanding, superlative
12 second-to-none

fiscal
05 money
07 capital
08 economic, monetary
09 financial, pecuniary

fish
05 angle, delve, grope, trawl
09 go fishing

► *Names of and types of fish
and shellfish:*
03 cod, dab, eel, ray
04 bass, carp, chub, clam, crab,
dace, dory, hake, pike, sole,
tuna
05 bream, brill, coley, guppy,
perch, prawn, roach, shark,
skate, smelt, sprat, squid,
tench, trout, whelk
06 cockle, dorado, kipper,
marlin, minnow, mullet,
mussel, oyster, plaice,
salmon, shrimp, turbot,
wrasse

07 anchovy, bloater, catfish,
dogfish, grouper, gurnard,
haddock, halibut, herring,
lobster, octopus, piranha,
sardine, scallop, sea bass,
snapper, whiting
08 brisling, crayfish, crawfish,
flounder, goldfish, mackerel,
monkfish, Moray eel,
pilchard, sea bream,
seahorse, stingray, sturgeon
09 angel-fish, barracuda,
conger eel, Dover sole, king
prawn, lemon sole, red
mullet, swordfish, whitebait
10 angler fish, Bombay duck,
cuttlefish, damsel fish, flying
fish, jellied eel
11 electric eel, stickleback
12 rainbow trout
➤ See also **animal**;
crustacean

▢**fish out**
07 extract, haul out, produce,
pull out, take out
08 dredge up, retrieve
10 come up with

fisherman
06 angler, fisher, rodman
07 rodsman, rodster
08 piscator
09 rodfisher
11 piscatorian

fishing
07 angling
08 trawling
09 halieutic, piscatory
11 piscatorial

fishy
05 funny, queer, shady
07 dubious, piscine, suspect
08 doubtful, fish-like
09 irregular, piscatory
10 improbable, suspicious
11 implausible, piscatorial
12 questionable

fission
06 schism
07 parting, rending, rupture
08 breaking, cleavage, division
09 severance, splitting

fissure
03 gap
04 gash, hole, rent, rift, slit
05 break, chasm, chink, cleft,
crack, fault, grike, split
06 breach, cranny, sulcus
07 crevice, opening, rupture
08 cleavage, crevasse, scissure
10 interstice

fist
04 hand, mitt, palm

fit
02 go
03 apt, arm, due, fix
04 able, bout, meet, suit, well
05 alter, equip, hardy, ictus, prime, put in, ready, right, spasm, spell, surge, tally
06 adjust, attach, attack, belong, change, in trim, insert, proper, robust, seemly, strong, sturdy, tailor
07 arrange, be right, capable, conform, connect, get into, healthy, in shape, install, qualify, seizure, tantrum
08 decorous, outbreak, outburst, paroxysm, position, prepared, suitable, vigorous
09 competent, explosion, harmonize, interlock
10 able-bodied, correspond, in good form, put in place
11 accommodate, appropriate, convulsion, flourishing, in good shape, put together
12 be consistent, in good health
13 fit like a glove, hale and hearty, put in position
15 in good condition

◻ **fit in**
04 slot
05 agree, match
06 accord, belong, square
07 conform, squeeze

◻ **fit out**
03 arm
05 equip
06 kit out, outfit, rig out, supply
07 furnish, prepare, provide
08 accoutre

◻ **in fits and starts**
08 brokenly, fitfully, off and on
11 erratically, irregularly
12 occasionally, sporadically
14 intermittently

fitful
06 broken, uneven
07 erratic
08 sporadic
09 disturbed, haphazard, irregular, spasmodic
12 disconnected, intermittent

fitness
06 health, vigour
07 aptness
08 adequacy, strength

09 condition, readiness
10 competence, good health, pertinence, robustness
11 healthiness, suitability
12 preparedness
13 applicability

fitted
05 armed, fixed, right
06 cut out, suited
07 built-in
08 equipped, prepared, provided, suitable, tailored
09 furnished, permanent

fitting
03 apt, fit
04 meet, part, unit
06 extras, proper, seemly
07 correct, fitment, fixture
08 decorous, deserved, fitments, fixtures, suitable
09 accessory, furniture
10 attachment, connection
11 appropriate, furnishings
13 accoutrements, installations

fix
03 aim, hit, jam, pin, rig, set, tie
04 bind, cook, dose, glue, join, link, make, mend, nail, shot, slug, spot, tidy, turn
05 clamp, embed, focus, order, rivet, screw, see to, stick
06 adjust, anchor, attach, cement, decide, define, fasten, harden, muddle, pickle, plight, remedy, repair, secure, settle
07 agree on, arrange, connect, correct, dilemma, falsify, patch up, prepare, rectify, resolve, restore, situate, station, stiffen, the soup
08 arrive at, finalize, position, put right, quandary, solidify
09 determine, injection, stabilize, tight spot
10 difficulty, put in order, straighten, tamper with
11 predicament, put together

◻ **fix up**
05 equip, lay on
06 settle, supply
07 agree on, arrange, furnish, produce, provide, sort out
08 organize

fixation
05 mania, thing
06 fetish, hang-up, phobia
07 complex
08 idée fixe
09 obsession

11 infatuation
13 preoccupation

fixed
03 set
04 fast, firm
06 rooted, secure, steady
07 decided, planned, settled
08 arranged, constant, definite
09 permanent
10 inflexible, set in stone
11 cast in stone, established

fixity
09 constancy, stability
10 permanence, steadiness
11 persistence
12 immutability

fixture
04 game, race
05 event, match, round
07 contest, meeting
09 equipment, furniture
11 competition, furnishings
13 installations

fizz
04 foam, hiss
05 froth
06 bubble, fizzle
07 sparkle
10 effervesce

fizzle

◻ **fizzle out**
04 fail, flop, fold, stop
07 die away, die down, subside
08 collapse, peter out, taper off
09 disappear, dissipate, evaporate
13 come to nothing

fizzy
05 gassy
06 bubbly, frothy
07 aerated, foaming
08 bubbling
09 sparkling
10 carbonated
12 effervescent

flabbergasted
06 amazed
07 stunned
09 astounded, staggered
10 astonished, bowled over, nonplussed, speechless
11 dumbfounded

flabby
03 fat, lax
04 limp, soft, weak
05 loose, plump, slack
06 feeble, fleshy, floppy
07 flaccid, hanging, sagging
08 drooping, yielding

flaccid
04 limp, soft, weak
05 loose, slack
06 clammy, flabby, floppy
07 relaxed, sagging
08 drooping, toneless

flag
03 die, ebb, sag, tag
04 fade, fail, flop, hail, mark, sink, slow, tire, wane, wave
05 droop, faint, label, slump
06 falter, salute, signal, weaken
07 decline, dwindle, fall off
08 diminish, indicate, peter out, taper off, wave down
09 grow tired, vexillary
12 signal to stop

► *Types of flag:*
04 jack
06 banner, burgee, ensign
07 bunting, colours, pennant
08 banderol, gonfalon, standard, streamer, vexillum
09 oriflamme, pilot flag
10 signal flag
11 swallow tail

► *Names of flags:*
07 Saltire
08 Crescent, Old Glory
09 Blue Peter, Red Ensign, Rising Sun, Tricolour, Union Jack
10 Blue Ensign, Jolly Roger, Yellow Jack
11 Olympic Flag, White Ensign
15 Cross of St George, Hammer and Sickle, Stars and Stripes

flagellation
07 flaying, lashing, whaling
08 flogging, whipping
09 scourging, thrashing
11 castigation, verberation

flagging
06 ebbing, fading, tiring
07 abating, failing, sagging, sinking, slowing, wilting
09 declining, dwindling, faltering, lessening, subsiding, weakening

flagon
03 jug
04 ewer
05 flask
06 bottle, carafe, vessel
07 pitcher

flagrant
04 bold, open, rank
06 arrant, brazen
07 blatant, glaring, heinous
08 dreadful, enormous
09 atrocious, audacious, barefaced, egregious, notorious, shameless
10 outrageous, scandalous
11 conspicuous, undisguised
12 ostentatious

flail
04 beat, whip
06 batter, strike, thrash, thresh

flair
04 bent, feel, gift
05 knack, skill, style, taste
06 acumen, genius, talent
07 ability, faculty, panache
08 aptitude, elegance, facility
11 discernment, stylishness

flak
05 abuse, blame, stick
09 brickbats, criticism, invective
10 complaints, opposition
12 condemnation, fault-finding
14 disapprobation

flake
03 bit
04 chip, peel
06 furfur, paring, sliver
07 blister, peeling, shaving
11 exfoliation

▢ flake out
05 faint
07 pass out
08 collapse, keel over
10 fall asleep

flaky
07 laminar, layered
08 scabrous
11 exfoliative

flamboyance
04 dash, élan
07 glamour, panache, pizzazz
09 showiness
10 brilliance
12 extravagance
13 theatricality

flamboyant
05 gaudy, showy
06 bright, flashy, florid, ornate
08 dazzling, exciting, striking
09 brilliant, colourful, elaborate, glamorous
10 theatrical
11 extravagant

flame
04 beam, burn, fire, heat, zeal
05 blaze, flare, flash, glare, gleam, light, lover, shine
07 fervour, partner, passion, radiate, sparkle
08 fervency, keenness, radiance
09 boyfriend, catch fire, eagerness, intensity
10 enthusiasm, excitement, girlfriend, sweetheart

flaming
03 mad
05 angry, fiery, vivid
06 aflame, alight, bright, on fire, raging, red-hot
07 blazing, burning, enraged, furious, intense, violent
08 incensed, in flames
09 brilliant
10 infuriated

flammable
09 ignitable
11 combustible, inflammable

flank
04 edge, line, loin, side, wing
05 bound, skirt, thigh
06 border, haunch, screen
07 confine, quarter

flannel
06 waffle
07 blarney, rubbish
08 flattery, nonsense, soft soap
09 sweet talk

flap
03 fly, lug, tab, tag, wag
04 beat, fold, fuss, tail, wave
05 apron, lapel, panic, skirt, state, swing, swish, tizzy
06 dither, lappet, thrash, waggle
07 agitate, aileron, fluster, flutter, overlap, vibrate
08 covering, overhang
09 agitation, commotion

flare
04 beam, burn, glow
05 blaze, burst, erupt, flame, flash, glare, splay, widen
06 beacon, dazzle, rocket, signal, spread
07 broaden, explode, flicker
10 broadening
13 warning signal
14 distress signal

▢ flare up
06 blow up
07 explode
08 break out, burst out
11 lose control
12 lose your cool
14 lose your temper

flash
03 fly, ray
04 beam, bolt, dart, dash, race, rush, show, tear, zoom
05 blaze, bound, burst, dance, flare, gaudy, glare, gleam, glint, shaft, shine, shoot, showy, smart, spark, speed
06 career, flaunt, kitsch, streak
07 flicker, glimmer, glisten, glitter, light up, shimmer, show off, sparkle, twinkle
08 flourish, outbreak, outburst
09 coruscate, expensive, fulgurate, glamorous
11 fashionable, pretentious
12 ostentatious

◻**in a flash**
06 pronto
08 in a jiffy, in a trice, in no time
09 in a moment
11 in an instant
12 in a twinkling
13 in no time at all
14 in a split second

flashy
04 bold, loud
05 flash, gaudy, showy, tacky
06 garish, glitzy, kitsch, vulgar
09 glamorous, tasteless
10 flamboyant
11 pretentious
12 ostentatious

flask
06 bottle, carafe, flagon
07 flacket, matrass
08 decanter, lekythos

flat
04 dead, down, dull, even, firm, slow, weak
05 bland, burst, empty, final, fixed, level, plain, plane, prone, rigid, rooms, slack, stale, suite, total, vapid
06 bed-sit, boring, direct, smooth, supine, watery
07 exactly, flatlet, insipid, not deep, not tall, plainly, planned, shallow, tedious, totally, uniform, utterly
08 blown-out, definite, deflated, dejected, directly, downcast, entirely, explicit, levelled, lifeless, not thick, outright, positive, ruptured, straight, unbroken
09 apartment, bed-sitter, collapsed, depressed, downright, miserable, out and out, penthouse, prostrate, punctured, reclining, recumbent
10 homaloidal, horizontal, monotonous, point-blank, spiritless, unexciting
11 categorical, discouraged, unequivocal, unqualified
13 categorically, uninteresting
14 flat as a pancake

◻**flat out**
06 all out
10 at top speed
11 at full speed

flatly
10 absolutely, completely, point-blank, positively
12 peremptorily
13 categorically
15 unconditionally

flatness
06 tedium
07 boredom, languor
08 dullness, evenness, monotony, vapidity
09 emptiness, staleness
10 insipidity, uniformity

flatten
04 fell, iron, raze, roll
05 crush, floor, level, press
06 smooth, squash, subdue
07 even out
08 compress, demolish, make even, make flat, tear down
09 knock down, overwhelm, prostrate

flatter
04 fawn, suit
05 befit, court, creep, toady
06 become, kowtow, praise
08 butter up, eulogize, inveigle, make up to, play up to, soft-soap, suck up to
09 embellish, sweet-talk
10 compliment, look good on
12 sycophantize

flatterer
05 toady
06 fawner, lackey
07 crawler, creeper
09 encomiast, eulogizer, groveller, sycophant
10 bootlicker

flattering
07 fawning, fulsome, honeyed
08 effusive, unctuous
09 adulatory, enhancing
10 favourable, obsequious
11 sycophantic

12 honey-tongued, ingratiating, smooth-spoken
13 complimentary

flattery
06 eulogy, praise
07 blarney, fawning, flannel
08 cajolery, soft soap, toadyism
09 servility, sweet talk
10 sycophancy
11 compliments, fulsomeness
13 blandishments

flatulence
03 gas
04 wind
06 flatus
07 farting
09 gassiness, ventosity
10 eructation
11 borborygmus

flatulent
05 gassy, windy
07 ventose

flaunt
03 air
05 boast, flash, sport, vaunt
06 dangle, parade
07 display, disport, show off
08 brandish, flourish

flavour
04 feel, hint, lace, soul, tang, tone, zest, zing
05 aroma, imbue, odour, smack, spice, style, taste, tinge, touch
06 aspect, infuse, quality, relish, season, spirit
07 essence, feeling, quality
08 ginger up, piquancy
10 atmosphere, suggestion

flavouring
04 tang, zest, zing
07 essence, extract, flavour
08 additive, piquancy
09 seasoning

flaw
04 chip, mark, rent, rift, slip
05 break, cleft, crack, error, fault, lapse, speck, split
06 defect, foible
07 blemish, crevice, failing, fallacy, fissure, mistake
08 weak spot, weakness
11 shortcoming
12 imperfection

flawed
06 broken, faulty, marked, marred, spoilt
07 cracked, damaged, unsound

09 blemished, defective, erroneous, imperfect
10 fallacious

flawless
05 sound, whole
07 perfect
08 spotless, unbroken
09 faultless, stainless, undamaged
10 immaculate, impeccable
11 unblemished

flay
04 flog, skin
07 lambast, scourge, upbraid
08 execrate
09 excoriate, skin alive
12 pull to pieces
13 tear a strip off

fleck
03 dot
04 dust, mark, spot
05 point, speck
06 dapple, mottle, streak
07 freckle, spatter, speckle

fledgling
06 novice, rookie
07 learner, recruit, trainee
08 neophyte, newcomer
09 greenhorn, novitiate
10 apprentice, tenderfoot

flee
03 fly
04 bolt, rush
05 leave, scoot, scram
06 decamp, escape, vanish
07 abscond, get away, make off, retreat, run away, scarper, take off, vamoose
08 clear off, withdraw
09 cut and run, disappear
10 take flight
15 take to your heels

fleece
03 con, rob
04 bilk, coat, down, gull, wool
05 bleed, cheat, steal, sting
06 diddle, fiddle, rip off
07 defraud, plunder, swindle
10 overcharge
12 pull a fast one, take for a ride
13 have someone on

fleecy
04 soft
05 downy, hairy, nappy
06 fluffy, pilose, shaggy, woolly
07 velvety
08 floccose
10 flocculate, lanuginose
11 eriophorous

fleet
04 fast, navy
05 quick, rapid, swift
06 armada, speedy, winged
08 flotilla, meteoric, squadron
09 mercurial, task force
10 naval force
11 expeditious, light-footed

fleeting
05 brief, quick, short
06 flying, rushed, sudden
07 passing
09 ephemeral, fugacious, momentary, temporary, transient
10 short-lived, transitory

flesh
03 fat, kin
04 body, meat, pith, pulp, skin
05 brawn, folks, stuff
06 family, matter, muscle, tissue, weight
08 relative, solidity
09 carnality, substance
11 human nature, physicality
12 carnal nature, corporeality, in actual life, significance

❑**flesh and blood**
03 kin
05 folks
06 family
08 relative
09 relations

❑**flesh out**
09 elaborate
10 add details
11 give details
12 make complete

❑**in the flesh**
08 in person
10 in real life
12 in actual life

fleshly
05 human
06 animal, bodily, carnal, earthy, erotic, sexual, wordly
07 bestial, brutish, earthly, lustful, sensual
08 corporal, material, physical
09 corporeal

fleshy
03 fat
05 ample, hefty, meaty, obese, plump, podgy, stout, tubby
06 brawny, chubby, chunky, flabby, portly, rotund
09 corpulent
10 overweight, well-padded

flex
03 bow, ply
04 bend, cord, lead, wire
05 angle, cable, crook, curve
07 stretch, tighten
08 contract, double up

flexibility
04 give
06 spring
07 flexion, pliancy
10 elasticity, pliability, resilience, suppleness
11 amenability, springiness
12 adaptability, complaisance

flexible
05 agile, bendy, lithe
06 limber, pliant, supple
07 elastic, plastic, pliable
08 amenable, bendable, stretchy, variable, yielding
09 adaptable, malleable, mouldable, open-ended
10 adjustable, manageable
13 accommodating

flick
03 dab, hit, rap, tap
04 flip, jerk, lash, snap, whip
05 click, swish, touch

❑**flick through**
04 scan, skim, skip
08 glance at
10 glance over
11 flip through, leaf through
12 thumb through
13 browse through

flicker
03 bat
04 atom, drop, iota, wink
05 blink, flare, flash, gleam, glint, spark, trace, waver
06 gutter, quiver
07 flutter, glimmer, glitter, shimmer, sparkle, twinkle
10 indication

flight
03 set
05 steps
06 escape, exodus, flying, stairs, voyage
07 fleeing, getaway, journey, retreat, shuttle
08 aviation, stairway
09 departure, staircase
10 absconding, running off
11 aeronautics, running away

❑**take flight**
03 fly
05 leave
06 depart, escape, vanish

07 abscond, get away, make off, retreat, run away, take off
09 cut and run, disappear

flighty
05 silly
06 fickle
08 skittish, unsteady, volatile
09 frivolous, impetuous, impulsive, mercurial
10 capricious, changeable, inconstant, unbalanced
11 bird-brained, hare-brained, light-headed, thoughtless
13 irresponsible, rattle-brained
14 scatterbrained

flimsy
04 fine, poor, thin, weak
05 filmy, light, shaky, sheer
06 feeble, meagre, slight
07 fragile, rickety, shallow, trivial
08 delicate, ethereal, trifling
10 inadequate, jerry-built
11 implausible, lightweight
13 insubstantial

flinch
04 balk, duck, flee
05 avoid, cower, dodge, quail, quake, shirk, start, wince
06 blench, cringe, crouch, recoil, shiver, shrink
07 retreat, shy away, tremble
08 draw back, pull back

fling
02 go
03 lob, try
04 cast, hurl, send, shot, toss
05 chuck, crack, dance, heave, pitch, sling, spree, throw
06 gamble, let fly, propel
07 attempt, venture
08 catapult
10 indulgence, send flying

flip
04 cast, flap, spin, toss, turn
05 flick, pitch, throw

◻**flip through**
04 scan, skim, skip
10 glance over
11 leaf through
12 thumb through
13 browse through

flippancy
05 cheek
06 levity
08 glibness, pertness
09 frivolity, sauciness
10 cheekiness, disrespect, persiflage
11 irreverence, shallowness

12 impertinence
13 facetiousness

flippant
04 flip, glib, pert, rude
06 cheeky
07 offhand, shallow
09 facetious, frivolous
10 insouciant, irreverent
11 impertinent, superficial
12 light-hearted
13 disrespectful, irresponsible

flirt
04 ogle, vamp
05 dally, eye up, hussy, tease
06 chat up, chippy, coquet, gillet, lead on, wanton
08 coquette, make up to
09 gillflirt, philander
10 make eyes at
11 make a pass at, philanderer
12 heart-breaker

◻**flirt with**
03 try
07 toy with
08 dabble in, play with
09 entertain
10 trifle with

flirtation
05 amour, sport
06 affair, toying
08 coquetry, dallying, trifling
09 dalliance
10 chatting up
12 philandering

flirtatious
06 come-on, flirty, wanton
07 amorous, teasing
10 come-hither, coquettish
11 promiscuous, provocative

flit
03 bob, fly
04 dart, dash, pass, rush, skim
05 dance, flash, speed, whisk
07 flitter, flutter

float
03 bob
04 hang, sail, swim, waft
05 drift, glide, set up, slide
06 launch, submit, wander
07 present, promote, propose, suggest, suspend
08 get going, initiate
09 be buoyant, recommend

floating
06 afloat
07 bobbing, buoyant, movable, sailing, wafting
08 drifting, hovering, swimming, variable

09 migratory, unsettled
10 transitory, unattached
11 fluctuating, uncommitted

flock
04 fold, herd, host, mill, pack
05 bunch, crowd, drove, group, swarm, troop
06 gather, huddle, throng
07 cluster, collect
08 assemble, converge
09 gathering, multitude
10 collection, congregate
12 congregation

flog
04 beat, belt, cane, drub, flay, hawk, lash, sell, whip
05 birch, strap, trade, whack
06 deal in, handle, peddle, punish, thrash, wallop
07 scourge
09 horsewhip
10 flagellate

flogging
06 caning, hiding
07 beating, flaying, lashing
08 birching, whipping
09 scourging, strapping, thrashing, walloping
12 flagellation
13 horsewhipping

flood
04 fill, flow, glut, gush, pour, rush, soak, tide
05 drown, spate, surge, swell
06 deluge, drench, engulf, excess, stream
07 immerse, smother, torrent
08 brim over, downpour, inundate, overflow, plethora, saturate, submerge
09 abundance, overwhelm
10 inundation, outpouring

floor
04 base, beat, deck, fell, tier
05 basis, level, stump, throw
06 baffle, defeat, ground, puzzle, storey
07 landing, nonplus, perplex
08 bewilder, confound, flooring
09 discomfit, dumbfound, frustrate, knock down, overwhelm, prostrate
10 disconcert, strike down

flop
04 bomb, drop, fail, fall, fold, hang, sink
05 crash, droop, slump
06 dangle, fiasco, go bust, pack up, slip-up, topple, tumble

07 debacle, failure, founder, misfire, wash-out
08 collapse, disaster, shambles
10 non-starter
11 go to the wall
12 go into the red

floppy
04 limp, soft
05 baggy, loose
06 droopy, flabby
07 hanging, sagging
08 dangling

flora
06 botany, plants
07 herbage
08 plantage
09 plant life
10 vegetation

florid
03 red
05 fussy, ruddy
06 ornate, purple, rococo
07 baroque, flowery, flushed, pompous, reddish, verbose
08 red-faced, rubicund
09 bombastic, elaborate
10 flamboyant, melismatic
11 embellished, extravagant

flotsam
04 junk
06 debris, jetsam
07 rubbish
08 detritus, wreckage
11 odds and ends

flounce
04 jerk, toss
05 fling, frill, stamp, storm, throw, twist
06 bounce, fringe, ruffle, spring
07 falbala, valance
08 furbelow, trimming

flounder
06 dither, falter, fumble, wallow
07 blunder, go under, stumble
10 be confused, flail about
11 thresh about

flourish
03 wag, wax
04 boom, show, wave, élan
05 bloom, get on, serif, shake, sweep, swing, swirl, swish, twirl, twist, vaunt, wield
06 do well, flaunt, flower, parade, thrive
07 blossom, burgeon, develop, display, exhibit, fanfare, gesture, panache, pizzazz, prosper, show off, succeed

08 be strong, brandish, curlicue, increase, ornament, progress
10 decoration

flourishing
07 booming
08 blooming, thriving
10 prosperous, successful

flout
04 defy, mock
05 break, scorn, spurn
06 jeer at, reject
07 disdain, disobey, laugh at, scoff at, sneer at, violate
09 disregard
15 show contempt for

flow
03 jet, run
04 drip, flux, gush, pour, rush, spew, stem, teem, tide, well
05 flood, issue, spate, spill, spout, spurt, surge, swirl
06 babble, bubble, course, deluge, emerge, gurgle, ripple, spring, squirt, stream
07 cascade, current, emanate, proceed, trickle
08 effusion, overflow, plethora
09 circulate, originate
10 outpouring

flower
03 bud
04 best, grow, open, pick
05 bloom, cream, elite
06 choice, finest, floral, floret, mature, select, sprout, thrive
07 blossom, burgeon, come out, develop, prosper
08 flourish, floweret
11 florescence
13 efflorescence, inflorescence
➤ See also **plant**
━━━━━━━━━━━━━━━━━━━
▶ *Parts of a flower*:
05 calyx, ovary, ovule, petal, sepal, spike, stalk, style, torus, umbel
06 anther, carpel, corymb, pistil, spadix, stamen, stigma
07 corolla, nectary
08 filament, thalamus
09 capitulum, gynoecium
10 receptacle
━━━━━━━━━━━━━━━━━━━
▶ *Names of flowers*:
04 flag, iris, lily, pink, rose
05 aster, daisy, lupin, pansy, phlox, poppy, stock, tulip, viola
06 azalea, crocus, dahlia, orchid, salvia, violet, zinnia

07 alyssum, anemone, begonia, cowslip, freesia, fuchsia, lobelia, nemesia, nigella, petunia, primula, verbena
08 bluebell, cyclamen, daffodil, dianthus, foxglove, gardenia, geranium, gladioli, hyacinth, marigold, primrose, snowdrop, sweet pea
09 aubrietia, calendula, candytuft, carnation, digitalis, hollyhock, impatiens, narcissus, nicotiana, sunflower
10 busy lizzie, cornflower, delphinium, nasturtium, poinsettia, polyanthus, snapdragon, wallflower
11 antirrhinum, forget-me-not, love-in-a-mist
12 sweet william
13 African violet, chrysanthemum
15 lily-of-the-valley
━━━━━━━━━━━━━━━━━━━
▶ *Wild flowers include*:
05 clary, daisy, poppy
06 clover, oxslip, teasel, violet, yarrow
07 ale hoof, bistort, campion, comfrey, cowslip, goldcup, heather
08 bluebell, crowfoot, foxglove, harebell, lungwort, primrose, rock rose, self-heal, toadflax, wild iris
09 Aaron's rod, birth-wort, broomrape, buttercup, celandine, columbine, edelweiss, goldenrod, horsetail, stonecrop, water lily, wild pansy
10 crane's bill, goatsbeard, heartsease, lady's smock, oxeye daisy, pennyroyal, wild endive, wild orchid
11 ragged robin, wild chicory, wood anemone
12 common mallow, cuckoo flower, lady's slipper, solomon's seal, white campion, yellow rocket
13 butter-and-eggs, shepherd's club
14 black-eyed susan, bladder campion, common toadflax

flowery
05 fancy
06 florid, ornate
07 baroque, pompous, verbose
09 elaborate, high-flown

10 euphuistic, rhetorical
13 grandiloquent

flowing
04 easy
06 fluent, moving, smooth
07 falling, gushing, hanging, pouring, rolling, rushing, seeping, surging, welling
08 sweeping, unbroken
09 cascading, streaming
10 continuous, effortless
13 uninterrupted

fluctuate
04 sway, vary
05 alter, shift, swing, waver
06 change, seesaw
08 hesitate, undulate
09 alternate, oscillate, vacillate
10 ebb and flow
11 go up and down, rise and fall
13 chop and change

fluctuation
05 shift, swing
06 change
10 fickleness
11 alternation, inconstancy, instability, oscillation, vacillation, variability
12 irresolution, unsteadiness

flue
04 duct, pipe, vent
05 shaft
07 channel, chimney, passage

fluency
04 ease
07 command, control
08 facility, glibness
09 assurance, eloquence, facundity, slickness
10 smoothness, volubility
14 articulateness

fluent
04 easy, glib
05 fluid, ready, slick
06 smooth
07 elegant, flowing, natural
08 eloquent, graceful
10 articulate, effortless
11 mellifluous
13 silver-tongued

fluff
03 nap
04 blow, boob, down, dust, fuzz, lint, muff, pile
05 botch, floss, spoil
06 bungle, cock up, foul up, fumble, mess up, muck up
07 balls up, do badly, screw up
11 make a mess of

fluffy
04 soft
05 downy, furry, hairy, silky
06 fleecy, shaggy, woolly
08 feathery

fluid
04 easy, open
05 juice, runny
06 liquid, liquor, melted, mobile, molten, smooth
07 aqueous, elegant, flowing, natural, protean, running
08 flexible, graceful, shifting, unstable, unsteady, variable
09 adaptable, unsettled
10 adjustable, changeable, effortless, inconstant

fluke
05 break, freak, quirk
06 chance, stroke
08 accident, fortuity, windfall
10 lucky break
11 coincidence, serendipity
12 stroke of luck

fluky
05 lucky
09 fortunate, uncertain
10 accidental, fortuitous
12 coincidental, incalculable
13 serendipitous

flummox
03 fox
05 stump
06 baffle, puzzle, stymie
07 mystify, nonplus, perplex
08 bewilder, confound
09 bamboozle

flummoxed
05 at sea, foxed
07 at a loss, baffled, puzzled, stumped, stymied
09 mystified, perplexed
10 confounded, nonplussed

flunkey
05 slave, toady, valet
06 drudge, lackey, menial, minion, yes-man
07 cringer, footman
08 hanger-on
09 assistant, underling
10 bootlicker, manservant

flurry
04 bout, flap, fuss, gust, stir
05 blast, burst, hurry, spell, spurt, upset, whirl
06 bother, bustle, hassle, hubbub, hustle, rattle, ruffle, shower, squall, tumult

07 agitate, confuse, disturb, fluster, flutter, perturb
08 bewilder, outbreak, unsettle
09 agitation, commotion
10 disconcert, excitement
11 disturbance

flush
04 burn, even, flat, full, glow, hose, rich, swab, true, wash
05 bloom, blush, clear, eject, empty, evacuate, generous, rosiness, well-to-do
06 colour, lavish, redden, smooth, square, vigour
07 cleanse, crimson, moneyed, redness, suffuse, turn red, uncover, wealthy, well-off
08 discover, drive out, force out, evacuate, generous, rosiness, well-to-do
09 freshness, ruddiness
10 prosperous, well-heeled

flushed
03 hot, red
04 rosy
05 aglow, ruddy
06 ablaze, aflame, elated
07 aroused, burning, crimson, excited, glowing, scarlet
08 animated, blushing, exultant, inspired, rubicund
11 embarrassed, intoxicated

fluster
04 faze, flap, tizz
05 panic, state, tizzy, upset
06 bother, bustle, dither, flurry, put off, rattle, ruffle
07 agitate, confuse, disturb, perturb, turmoil, unnerve
08 confound, distract, unsettle
09 confusion, embarrass
10 discompose, disconcert
13 embarrassment

fluted
06 ribbed, ridged
10 channelled, corrugated

flutter
03 bat, bet
04 beat, flap, risk, toss, wave
05 dance, hover, wager, waver
06 gamble, quiver, ripple, ruffle, shiver, tremor, twitch
07 agitate, flicker, flitter, pulsate, shudder, tremble, vibrate
09 fluctuate, palpitate, vibration
11 palpitation, speculation

flux
04 flow
06 change, motion, unrest
08 fluidity, movement

fly

10 alteration, transition
11 development, instability
12 modification

fly

03 jet
04 bolt, dart, dash, flit, race, rise, rush, show, soar, tear, wave, wing, zoom
05 canny, glide, hover, hurry, pilot, sharp, shoot, speed
06 artful, ascend, astute, hasten, shrewd, slip by, sprint
07 careful, cunning, display, exhibit, flutter, operate, present, prudent, take off
09 go quickly, manoeuvre
11 nobody's fool, pass quickly

❑**fly at**

03 hit
05 go for
06 attack, charge, let fly, strike
07 lay into
08 fall upon
09 lash out at

fly-by-night

05 shady
06 cowboy
07 dubious
09 ephemeral
10 short-lived, unreliable
12 disreputable, questionable
13 discreditable, untrustworthy

flying

04 fast
05 brief, hasty, rapid
06 rushed, speedy, winged
07 hurried, soaring, winging
08 airborne, flapping, fleeting, floating, hovering
09 wind-borne

foam

04 boil, fizz, head, suds
05 froth, spume
06 bubble, lather, seethe
07 bubbles
10 effervesce
13 effervescence

foamy

05 spumy, sudsy
06 bubbly, frothy
07 foaming, lathery
10 spumescent

fob

❑**fob off**

05 foist
06 impose, put off, unload
07 inflict, palm off, pass off
08 get rid of

focus

03 aim, fix, hub
04 axis, core, crux, join, meet
05 heart, hinge, pivot
06 centre, direct, home in, kernel, zero in, zoom in
07 nucleus
08 converge, linchpin, pinpoint
09 spotlight
10 focal point
11 concentrate

❑**in focus**

05 clear, sharp
08 distinct
11 well-defined

❑**out of focus**

04 hazy
06 blurry
07 blurred
10 ill-defined, indistinct

fodder

04 feed, food
06 forage, silage
07 lucerne, pabulum, rations
09 foodstuff, provender
11 nourishment

foe

05 enemy, rival
08 opponent
09 adversary, combatant
10 antagonist

foetus

06 embryo, foetal
11 unborn child

fog

04 blur, daze, haze, mist, smog
05 cloud, gloom
06 baffle, darken, muddle
07 confuse, obscure, steam up
08 bewilder, haziness
09 mistiness, murkiness, obfuscate, obscurity, pea-souper, vagueness
10 perplexity, puzzlement
12 bewilderment
14 disorientation

foggy

03 dim
04 dark, grey, hazy
05 misty, murky, vague
06 cloudy, gloomy, smoggy
07 clouded, obscure, unclear
10 indistinct

foible

05 fault, habit, quirk
06 defect, oddity
07 failing, oddness
08 weakness

11 peculiarity, shortcoming
12 eccentricity, imperfection

foil

04 stop
05 baulk, block, check, elude
06 baffle, defeat, hamper, hinder, outwit, relief, thwart
07 counter, nullify, prevent, scupper, scuttle, setting
08 contrast, obstruct
09 frustrate
10 antithesis, circumvent

foist

05 force
06 fob off, impose, thrust, unload, wish on
07 palm off, pass off
08 get rid of

fold

03 hug, pen, ply
04 bend, fail, flop, line, ring, tuck, turn, wrap, yard
05 clasp, close, crash, crimp, flock, kraal, layer, pleat
06 crease, double, enfold, furrow, gather, go bust, pack up, pucker, wrap up
07 crinkle, crumple, embrace, enclose, envelop, overlap, paddock, squeeze, wrinkle
08 collapse, shut down, stockade, turn down
09 enclosure, gathering, knife-edge, turn under
11 corrugation, go to the wall
12 congregation, parishioners
15 go out of business

folder

04 file
05 folio
06 binder, pocket, wallet
08 envelope
09 portfolio

foliage

06 leaves
07 leafage, verdure
08 greenery
09 foliation, foliature, vernation
10 vegetation
12 frondescence

folk

03 kin
04 clan, race
05 tribe
06 ethnic, family, nation, native, people, public, tribal
07 kindred, parents, popular
08 national
09 ancestral, relations, relatives

10 indigenous, population
11 ethnic group, traditional

folklore
05 myths, tales
06 fables
07 beliefs, customs, legends, stories
09 mythology, tradition
13 superstitions

follow
03 dog
04 flow, heed, hunt, mind, note, obey, tail, twig
05 arise, chase, ensue, hound, issue, stalk, track, trail
06 accept, escort, fathom, go with, pursue, result, shadow, spring, take in
07 develop, emanate, go after, observe, proceed, replace, succeed, support, yield to
08 adhere to, be a fan of, carry out, come next, go behind, run after, supplant, tag along
09 accompany, conform to, give chase, supersede
10 appreciate, comply with, keep up with, understand
14 be a supporter of, be interested in

❑ **follow through**
06 finish, fulfil, pursue
08 complete, conclude
09 implement
10 see through

❑ **follow up**
06 pursue
08 check out, continue, look into, research
09 reinforce
11 consolidate, investigate

follower
03 fan
05 freak, pupil
06 backer, escort, helper
07 admirer, apostle, devotee
08 adherent, believer, disciple, emulator, hanger-on, imitator, retainer, sidekick
09 attendant, supporter
10 enthusiast

following
04 fans, next
05 later, suite
06 circle, public
07 backers, backing, coterie, ensuing, retinue, support
08 admirers, audience

09 adherents, clientèle, entourage, followers, patronage, resulting
10 consequent, subsequent, succeeding, successive

folly
04 whim
05 tower
06 gazebo, idiocy, lunacy
07 inanity, madness
08 insanity, monument, nonsense, rashness
09 absurdity, belvedere, craziness, silliness, stupidity
10 imbecility, imprudence
11 fatuousness, foolishness
12 indiscretion, recklessness
13 ludicrousness, senselessness

foment
04 brew, goad, spur
05 raise, rouse
06 arouse, foster, incite, kindle, prompt, stir up, whip up
07 agitate, promote, provoke
08 activate
09 encourage, instigate, stimulate

fond
04 vain, warm
05 naïve
06 absurd, caring, doting, keen on, liking, loving, tender
07 adoring, amorous, deluded, devoted, foolish
09 indulgent, partial to
10 addicted to, attached to
11 enamoured of, impractical
12 affectionate

fondle
03 hug, pat, pet
06 caress, cuddle, stroke
07 touch up

fondness
04 love
05 fancy, taste
06 liking
08 devotion, kindness, penchant, soft spot
09 affection
10 attachment, enthusiasm, partiality, tenderness
12 predilection

food
04 chow, diet, dish, eats, fare, feed, grub, menu, nosh, tuck
05 board, meals, scoff, table
06 fodder, stores, viands
07 cooking, cuisine, rations
08 delicacy, eatables, victuals
09 nutriment, nutrition

10 foodstuffs, provisions, speciality, sustenance
11 comestibles, nourishment
12 refreshments

► *Types of food include*:
03 poi
04 hash, luau, olio, soss
05 balti, brose, champ, grits, gumbo, kebab, kofta, pilau, pilaw, pilow, pizza, ramen, salmi, satay, sushi, tikka
06 borsch, caviar, faggot, fondue, haggis, hotpot, hummus, kipper, mousse, paella, pakora, pilaff, quiche, ragout, samosa, scampi, tamale
07 biryani, borscht, burrito, compote, crowdie, fajitas, falafel, fritter, friture, gnocchi, goulash, gravlax, lasagne, ramakin, ramekin, rarebit, risotto, sashimi, soufflé, tempura, terrine, timbale, tostada
08 biriyani, calamari, chop suey, chow mein, consommé, coq au vin, couscous, fishcake, gado-gado, gazpacho, kedgeree, moussaka, omelette, porridge, pot-roast, raclette, ramequin, souvlaki, tandoori, teriyaki, tzatziki, vindaloo, yakitori
09 cassoulet, fricassee, galantine, gravadlax, guacamole, jambalaya, meatballs, nut cutlet, souvlakia, succotash
10 cannelloni, cottage pie, enchiladas, fish-finger, minestrone, mixed grill, salmagundi, salmagundy, sauerkraut, stroganoff
11 cockaleekie, French fries, fritto misto, gefilte fish, ratatouille, smorgasbord, vichyssoise
12 fish and chips, mulligatawny, shepherd's pie, taramasalata, Waldorf salad, welsh rarebit
13 bouillabaisse, prawn cocktail, salade niçoise, toad-in-the-hole
14 chilli con carne, macaroni cheese, pickled herring
15 bubble-and-squeak, Wiener schnitzel

➤ See also **bean**; **biscuit**; **bread**; **cake**; **cheese**;

fruit; herbs and spices; meat; mushroom; nut; pasta; pastry; sauce; sausage; vegetable

fool
03 ass, con, git, kid, mug, nit
04 butt, clot, dope, dork, dupe, geek, gull, hoax, jerk, jest, joke, prat, sham, twit
05 bluff, chump, clown, comic, dunce, idiot, moron, ninny, prick, trick, twerp, wally
06 cretin, delude, dimwit, jester, nitwit, stooge, take in
07 buffoon, fat-head, deceive, halfwit, mislead, pillock, plonker, pretend, swindle
08 hoodwink, imbecile
09 bamboozle, birdbrain, blockhead, lark about, mess about, play about, simpleton
10 act the fool, mess around, nincompoop, play tricks
11 clown around, horse around, make believe, monkey about, string along
12 put one over on
13 laughing-stock

❑**play the fool**
09 fool about, mess about
10 fool around, mess around
11 clown around
12 monkey around

foolery
05 farce, folly, larks
06 antics, capers, pranks
07 carry-on, fooling, waggery
08 clowning, drollery, nonsense
09 high jinks, horseplay, silliness
10 buffoonery, tomfoolery
11 shenanigans
12 childishness, monkey tricks
14 practical jokes

foolhardy
04 bold, rash
08 reckless
09 daredevil, imprudent
10 ill-advised, incautious
13 irresponsible

foolish
03 mad
04 daft, dumb
05 barmy, batty, crazy, dotty, inane, inept, nutty, potty, silly
06 simple, stupid, unwise
07 fatuous, idiotic, moronic
08 gormless, ignorant
09 half-baked, ludicrous, pointless, senseless

10 half-witted, ill-advised
11 hare-brained, injudicious
12 short-sighted, simple-minded, unreasonable
13 ill-considered

foolishly
08 absurdly, stupidly, unwisely
09 fatuously
11 idiotically, imprudently
12 ill-advisedly, incautiously, indiscreetly, ridiculously
13 injudiciously

foolishness
04 bunk, crap
05 balls, bilge, folly
06 bunkum, lunacy, piffle
07 baloney, foolery, hogwash, inanity, madness, rubbish
08 claptrap, cobblers, daftness, nonsense, weakness
09 absurdity, craziness, incaution, poppycock, silliness, stupidity
10 imprudence, ineptitude
13 senselessness

foolproof
04 safe, sure
07 certain
08 fail-safe, sure-fire
09 unfailing
10 dependable, guaranteed, idiot-proof, infallible

foot
03 end, leg, pad, paw, pes, toe
04 heel, hoof, sole
05 limit, pedal
06 border, bottom, far end
07 trotter
09 extremity

football
➢ See also **sport**

━ *English and Scottish Premier League football club nicknames*:
04 Boro, Dons, Gers, Owls, Rams, Reds, Well
05 Blues, Foxes, Hoops, Spurs, Villa
06 Hibees, Jambos, Killie, Saints, United
07 Gunners, Hammers, Hornets, Magpies, Toffees
08 Filberts, Jam tarts, Sky blues
09 Dark blues, Red devils, Toffeemen
10 Light blues, Tangerines

━ *Names of football players*:
03 Fry (Charles Burgess), Law (Dennis)

04 Best (George), **Didi**, **Owen** (Michael), **Pele**, **Rush** (Ian)
05 **Adams** (Tony), **Banks** (Gordon), **Busby** (Sir Matt), **Giggs** (Ryan), **Greig** (John), **Hurst** (Geoff), **James** (Alex), **Moore** (Sir Bobby), **Revie** (Don), **Stein** (Jock)
06 **Baggio** (Roberto), **Barnes** (John), **Clough** (Brian), **Cruyff** (Johann), **Finney** (Tom), **Ginola** (David), **Graham** (George), **Gullit** (Ruud), **Hoddle** (Glen), **Keegan** (Kevin), **McStay** (Paul), **Muller** (Gerd), **Ramsay** (Sir Alf), **Robson** (Bobby), **Robson** (Brian), **Seaman** (David), **Wenger** (Arsene), **Wright** (Ian)
07 **Beckham** (David), **Bremner** (Billy), **Cantona** (Eric), **DiCanio** (Paulo), **Eastham** (George), **Eusebio** (Silva), **Greaves** (Jimmy), **Lineker** (Gary), **Macleod** (Ally), **McCoist** (Ally), **McNeill** (Billy), **Paisley** (Bob), **Rivaldo**, **Ronaldo**, **Shankly** (Bill), **Shearer** (Alan), **Shilton** (Peter), **Souness** (Graeme), **Toshack** (John)
08 **Bergkamp** (Dennis), **Charlton** (Bobby), **Charlton** (Jackie), **Dalglish** (Kenny), **Docherty** (Tommy), **Ferguson** (Sir Alex), **Jennings** (Pat), **Maradona** (Diego), **Matthaus** (Lothar), **Matthews** (Sir Stanley)
09 **Collymore** (Stan), **DiStefano** (Alfredo), **Gascoigne** (Paul 'Gazza'), **Greenwood** (Ron), **Klinsmann** (Jurgen), **Van Basten** (Marco)
10 **Battistuta** (Gabriel)
11 **Beckenbauer** (Franz)
12 **Blanchflower** (Danny)

━ *Names of American footballers*:
04 **Camp** (Walter Chauncy), **Monk** (Art), **Rice** (Jerry)
05 **Elway** (John), **Fouts** (Dan), **Halas** (George)
06 **Blanda** (Frederick), **Butkus** (Dick), **Graham** (Otto), **Grange** (Red), **Greene** (Joe), **Marino** (Dan), **Namath** (Joe Willie),

Payton (Walter), **Sayers** (Gale), **Unitas** (Johnny Constantine)
07 **Montana** (Joe), **Simpson** (Orenthal James)
08 **Lombardi** (Vince)
09 **Tarkenton** (Frank)

footing
04 base, grip, rank
05 basis, grade, state, terms
07 balance, support
08 foothold, position, standing
10 conditions, foundation
12 relationship

footling
05 minor, petty
06 paltry
07 trivial
08 piffling, trifling
10 irrelevant
13 insignificant

footnotes
04 note
05 gloss
07 scholia
10 annotation, commentary, marginalia

footprint
04 step
05 trace, track, trail, tread

footstep
04 plod, step
05 track, tramp, tread
08 footfall, footmark

footwear
➤ *Types of footwear:*
04 boot, clog, mule, pump, shoe
05 sabot, wader, welly
06 bootee, brogue, casual, galosh, lace-up, sandal, slip-on
07 gumboot, slipper, sneaker, trainer
08 flip-flop, moccasin, overshoe, plimsoll, snow-shoe
09 court-shoe, rugby boot, slingback
10 ballet shoe, Doc Martens®, espadrille, kitten-heel, riding-boot, tennis shoe
11 walking-boot
12 football boot, platform heel, stiletto heel
14 wellington boot
15 brothel-creepers

fop
04 beau, dude, toff
05 dandy, swell

07 coxcomb, peacock
08 muscadin, popinjay

foppish
04 vain
06 dainty, dapper, la-di-da
08 affected, dandyish, preening
09 dandified
11 overdressed

forage
04 feed, food, hunt, loot, raid
06 fodder, ravage, search
07 assault, plunder, ransack, rummage, scratch
08 scavenge
09 cast about, provender
10 foodstuffs

foray
04 raid
05 sally, swoop
06 attack, inroad, ravage, sortie
09 incursion, offensive
14 reconnaissance

forbear
04 hold, omit, stay, stop
05 avoid, cease, pause
06 desist, eschew
07 abstain, decline, refrain
08 hesitate, hold back

forbearance
08 clemency, leniency, mildness, patience
09 avoidance, endurance, restraint, tolerance
10 abstinence, moderation, refraining, sufferance, temperance, toleration
11 resignation, self-control
13 long-suffering

forbearing
04 easy, mild
07 clement, lenient, patient
08 merciful, moderate, tolerant
09 forgiving, indulgent
10 restrained
14 self-controlled

forbid
03 ban
04 deny, veto
05 block, debar
06 hinder, not let, outlaw, refuse
07 inhibit, prevent, rule out
08 disallow, not allow, preclude, prohibit
09 blacklist, interdict, proscribe

forbidden
05 taboo
06 banned, vetoed
07 illicit

08 debarred, excluded, outlawed
10 prohibited, proscribed
11 out of bounds

forbidding
04 grim
05 harsh, stern
06 severe
07 awesome, ominous
08 daunting, menacing, sinister
10 formidable, off-putting, unfriendly, uninviting
11 frightening, threatening

force
04 army, body, make, push, unit
05 blast, bully, corps, drive, impel, might, power, prise, squad, troop, wrest, wring
06 coerce, compel, duress, dynamo, effort, energy, extort, impose, lean on, muscle, oblige, propel, stress, vigour, wrench
07 binding, current, essence, extract, impetus, inflict, meaning, passion, platoon
08 bulldoze, coercion, division, dynamism, emphasis, exertion, momentum, pressure, railroad, regiment, squadron, strength, violence, vitality
09 battalion, constrain, intensity, pressgang
10 aggression, compulsion, constraint, pressurize
11 arm-twisting, enforcement, functioning, necessitate
13 determination, put pressure on
14 in great numbers, persuasiveness, put the screws on, the third degree

❑**in force**
05 valid
07 binding, current, working
08 in crowds, in droves
09 effective, operative
10 in strength
11 functioning, in operation

forced
05 false, stiff
06 wooden
07 feigned, stilted
08 affected, laboured, overdone, strained
09 compelled, contrived, insincere, mandatory
10 artificial, obligatory

forceful
06 cogent, mighty, potent,
   strong, urgent
07 dynamic, telling, weighty
08 emphatic, powerful,
   vehement, vigorous
09 assertive, effective
10 compelling, convincing,
   impressive, persuasive

forcible
06 cogent, forced, mighty,
   potent, strong
07 by force, violent, weighty
08 coercive, forceful, powerful
09 effective, energetic
10 aggressive, compelling,
   compulsory, impressive

forcibly
07 by force
09 violently
10 vehemently, vigorously
11 under duress
12 compulsorily, emphatically

ford
08 causeway, crossing

forebear
06 father
08 ancestor
10 antecedent, forefather,
   forerunner, progenitor
11 predecessor
12 primogenitor

foreboding
04 fear, omen, sign
05 dread, token, worry
07 anxiety, feeling, warning
09 misgiving, suspicion
10 prediction, sixth sense
11 premonition
12 apprehension, presentiment

forecast
03 tip
05 augur, guess
06 augury, expect, tip off
07 foresee, outlook, predict
08 estimate, foretell, forewarn,
   prophecy, prophesy
09 calculate, prognosis
10 anticipate, conjecture,
   prediction, projection
11 expectation, forewarning,
   guesstimate, speculation
15 prognostication

forefather
06 father
08 ancestor, forebear
10 antecedent, progenitor
11 predecessor
12 primogenitor

forefront
03 van
04 fore, lead
05 front
08 vanguard
09 front line, spearhead
10 avant-garde, firing line
15 leading position

forego
05 waive, yield
06 eschew, give up, pass up
07 abandon, forfeit
08 renounce
09 do without, go without,
   sacrifice, surrender
10 relinquish
11 abstain from, refrain from

foregoing
05 above, prior
06 former
07 earlier
08 previous
09 precedent, preceding
10 antecedent
14 aforementioned

foregone
05 fixed
08 foreseen
10 inevitable
11 anticipated, cut-and-dried,
   predictable, preordained
13 predetermined

foreground
04 fore
05 front
06 centre
09 forefront, limelight
10 prominence
15 leading position

forehead
04 brow
05 front
06 metope
07 frontal, metopic, temples

foreign
03 odd
05 alien
06 ethnic, exotic, remote
07 distant, faraway, migrant,
   outside, strange, unknown
08 borrowed, external,
   imported, overseas, peculiar
09 immigrant
10 extraneous, inapposite,
   outlandish, unfamiliar
11 incongruous, unconnected
13 international

foreigner
05 alien

07 incomer, visitor
08 outsider, stranger
09 immigrant

foreknowledge
09 foresight, prevision
10 prescience
11 forewarning, premonition
12 clairvoyance, precognition
15 prognostication

foreman
04 boss
06 gaffer, ganger, honcho
07 manager, overman, steward
08 overseer
10 charge hand, supervisor
14 superintendent

foremost
03 top
04 main
05 chief, first, front, prime
07 central, highest, leading,
   premier, primary, supreme
08 advanced, cardinal
09 principal, uppermost
10 pre-eminent
13 most important

foreordained
05 fated
08 destined
09 appointed
11 prearranged, predestined,
   preordained
13 predetermined

forerunner
05 envoy, token
06 herald
08 ancestor
09 harbinger, precursor
10 antecedent, forefather
11 predecessor

foresee
06 divine, expect
07 predict
08 envisage, forebode,
   forecast, foretell, prophesy
10 anticipate
13 prognosticate

foreshadow
04 bode, mean
05 augur
07 portend, predict, presage,
   promise, signify, suggest
08 indicate, prophesy
09 prefigure

foresight
06 vision
08 planning, prudence
09 provision, readiness
11 discernment, forethought

12 anticipation, perspicacity
14 circumspection, far-
sightedness
15 forward planning

forest
04 wood
05 monte, trees, urman, woods
08 woodland
09 greenwood
10 plantation

forestall
04 balk, stop
05 avert, parry
06 hinder, impede, thwart
07 head off, obviate, pre-empt,
prevent, ward off
08 obstruct, preclude, stave off
09 frustrate, intercept
10 anticipate, get ahead of

forestry
09 woodcraft
10 dendrology
11 forestation, woodmanship
12 silviculture
13 afforestation, arboriculture

foretaste
05 whiff
06 sample
07 example, preview, trailer
08 specimen
09 appetizer, foretoken
11 forewarning, premonition

foretell
06 divine
07 foresee, predict, presage
08 forecast, forewarn,
prophesy
10 foreshadow
13 prognosticate

forethought
08 planning, prudence
09 foresight, provision
11 discernment, preparation
12 anticipation, perspicacity
14 circumspection, far-
sightedness
15 forward planning

forever
04 ever
06 always
07 for good
08 evermore
09 endlessly, eternally
10 constantly, for all time
11 continually, incessantly,
permanently, perpetually
12 interminably, persistently
15 till kingdom come

forewarn
05 alert
06 advise, tip off
07 apprise, caution, previse
08 admonish, dissuade

foreword
07 preface, prelims
08 prologue
11 frontmatter
12 introduction

forfeit
04 fine, lose, loss
06 forego, give up
07 abandon, damages, penalty
08 hand over, renounce
09 sacrifice, surrender
10 amercement, relinquish

forfeiture
04 loss
07 escheat
08 giving up
09 attainder, déchéance,
sacrifice, surrender
12 confiscation
13 sequestration
14 relinquishment

forge
04 cast, copy, fake, make, work
05 feign, frame, mould, shape
06 create, devise, invent
07 beat out, falsify, fashion
08 construct, hammer out
11 counterfeit, put together

□ forge ahead
07 advance
08 progress
09 go forward
11 make headway, move
forward, push forward
12 make progress

forger
05 faker
06 coiner, framer
09 contriver, falsifier
13 counterfeiter

forgery
03 dud
04 copy, fake, sham
05 fraud
06 faking, phoney
07 replica
09 imitation
11 counterfeit
12 reproduction
13 falsification

forget
04 fail, omit
06 ignore
07 dismiss, let slip, neglect

08 overlook, put aside
09 disregard
11 lose sight of
12 slip your mind

□ forget yourself
09 misbehave
11 behave badly

forgetful
06 dreamy, remiss
08 careless, heedless
09 negligent, oblivious
10 abstracted, distracted
11 inattentive, preoccupied
12 absent-minded
14 scatterbrained

forgetfulness
05 lapse
07 amnesia, laxness
10 dreaminess
11 abstraction, inattention
12 carelessness, heedlessness
13 wool-gathering

forgivable
05 minor, petty
06 slight, venial
08 innocent, trifling
09 excusable
10 pardonable

forgive
05 clear, remit, spare
06 excuse, let off, pardon
07 absolve, condone, let it go
08 overlook
09 exculpate, exonerate
14 bury the hatchet

forgiveness
05 mercy
06 pardon
07 amnesty
08 clemency, leniency
09 acquittal, remission
10 absolution
11 exoneration

forgiving
04 kind, mild
06 humane
07 clement, lenient
08 merciful, tolerant
09 indulgent
10 forbearing
11 magnanimous, soft-hearted
13 compassionate

forgo see **forego**

forgotten
04 gone, lost, past
06 buried, bygone
07 ignored, omitted
09 neglected, out of mind
10 overlooked, unrecalled

11 disregarded, obliterated
13 irrecoverable, irretrievable
fork
04 part
05 split
06 branch, divide
07 diverge
08 division, junction, separate
09 bifurcate, branching
10 divergence, separation
11 bifurcation
□ **fork out**
03 pay
04 give
05 pay up
07 cough up, stump up
08 shell out
forked
05 split, tined
06 furcal
07 divided, furcate, Y-shaped
08 branched, furcular
09 bifurcate, branching,
 forficate, separated
11 divaricated
forlorn
03 sad
04 lost
06 bereft, lonely
07 unhappy
08 deserted, desolate,
 forsaken, helpless,
 homeless, hopeless,
 pathetic, pitiable, wretched
09 abandoned, cheerless,
 desperate, destitute,
 forgotten, miserable
10 despairing, friendless
12 disconsolate
form
03 cut
04 cast, grow, kind, make, sort,
 trim, type, year
05 build, class, forge, found,
 frame, genre, genus, guise,
 model, mould, order, paper,
 set up, shape, sheet, style
06 create, custom, design,
 devise, fettle, figure, format,
 make up, manner, nature,
 show up, stream, system
07 acquire, arrange, compose,
 develop, fashion, fitness,
 manners, outline, produce,
 species, spirits, variety
08 assemble, comprise,
 document, organize,
 planning, protocol
09 be a part of, behaviour,
 condition, construct,

 establish, etiquette,
 formation, framework,
 structure, take shape
10 appearance, constitute,
 convention, silhouette
11 application, arrangement,
 crystallize, disposition,
 manufacture, materialize
12 construction, organization,
 the done thing
13 configuration, manifestation,
 questionnaire
formal
04 prim
05 aloof, exact, fixed, rigid, stiff
06 proper, remote, ritual,
 solemn, strict
07 correct, ordered, regular,
 starchy, stately, stilted
08 approved, official,
 orthodox, reserved
09 organized, unbending
10 ceremonial, controlled,
 inflexible, prescribed
11 ceremonious, established,
 punctilious, strait-laced,
 symmetrical, traditional
formality
04 form, rule
06 custom, ritual
07 decorum, red tape
08 ceremony, protocol
09 etiquette, procedure,
 propriety, punctilio
10 convention, politeness
11 bureaucracy, correctness
format
04 form, look, plan, type
05 order, shape, style
06 design, layout, make-up
09 structure
10 appearance, dimensions
11 arrangement
12 construction, presentation
13 configuration
formation
05 order
06 design, figure, format,
 layout, make-up, making
07 pattern, phalanx, shaping
08 creation, founding, grouping
09 structure
10 appearance, production
11 arrangement, composition,
 development, disposition,
 institution, manufacture
12 construction, organization
13 configuration, establishment
formative
06 pliant

07 growing, guiding, shaping
08 dominant, moulding
09 malleable, teachable
11 controlling, determining,
 influential, susceptible
13 developmental
14 impressionable
former
02 ex-
03 old
04 late, past
05 above, first, prior
06 bygone, of yore
07 ancient, earlier, old-time,
 one-time, quondam
08 departed, long-gone,
 previous, sometime
09 erstwhile, preceding
10 antecedent, historical
14 first-mentioned
formerly
04 erst, once
06 before
07 earlier
08 hitherto
09 erstwhile, in the past
10 heretofore, previously
12 historically
formidable
04 huge
05 great, scary
07 awesome, fearful
08 alarming, colossal,
 daunting, dreadful, horrific,
 menacing, powerful, terrific
10 horrifying, impressive,
 prodigious, staggering,
 terrifying, tremendous
11 challenging, frightening,
 redoubtable, threatening
12 intimidating, overwhelming
formless
05 vague
07 chaotic
08 confused, inchoate,
 indigest, nebulous
09 amorphous, shapeless
10 incoherent, indefinite
12 disorganized
13 indeterminate
formula
03 way
04 code, form, rule
06 method, recipe, rubric
09 blueprint, principle,
 procedure, technique
12 prescription
15 fixed expression
formulate
04 form, plan

05 found, frame, state
06 create, define, design, devise, draw up, evolve, invent
07 compose, develop, express, itemize, prepare, put down, set down, specify, think up
08 conceive
09 originate
10 articulate, give form to

fornication
03 sex
06 coitus
10 copulation, love-making, making love
15 sexual relations

forsake
04 jilt, quit
05 ditch, leave
06 desert, disown, forego
07 abandon, cast off, discard
08 jettison, renounce, set aside
09 repudiate, surrender
10 relinquish
15 leave in the lurch

forsaken
06 dreary, jilted, lonely, remote
07 cast off, forlorn, ignored
08 derelict, deserted, desolate, disowned, rejected
09 abandoned, destitute, discarded, neglected
10 friendless

forswear
03 lie
04 deny, drop
06 abjure, cut out, disown, forego, give up, jack in, pack in, recant, reject, renege
07 abandon, forsake, retract
08 disclaim, renounce
09 do without, repudiate
15 perjure yourself

fort
04 camp, keep
05 tower
06 castle, donjon, turret
07 citadel, redoubt, station
08 fortress, garrison
10 stronghold, watchtower
13 fortification

forte
04 bent, gift
06 métier, talent
08 aptitude, strength
10 speciality
11 strong point

forth
03 off, out

07 onwards, outside
08 forwards, into view
13 into existence

forthcoming
04 open
05 frank, on tap, ready
06 chatty, coming, future
08 imminent, sociable
09 available, expansive, impending, talkative
10 accessible, loquacious
11 approaching, prospective
13 communicative
14 conversational

forthright
04 bold, open
05 blunt, frank, plain
06 candid, direct, honest
09 outspoken
11 plain-spoken
15 straightforward

forthwith
06 at once, pronto
07 quickly
08 directly
09 instantly, right away
11 immediately
12 straightaway, without delay

fortification
04 fort, keep
06 castle
07 bastion, bulwark, citadel, defence, parapet, rampart
08 fortress, palisade, stockade
09 barricade, earthwork
10 protection, stronghold
11 battlements, buttressing
12 entrenchment
13 reinforcement, strengthening

fortify
05 boost, cheer, cover, guard
06 defend, revive, secure
07 hearten, protect, shore up, support, sustain
08 buttress, energize, garrison
09 encourage, reinforce
10 invigorate, strengthen

fortitude
04 grit
05 nerve, pluck, spine
06 mettle, valour
07 bravery, courage
08 backbone, firmness, patience, stoicism, tenacity
09 endurance, willpower
10 resolution
11 forbearance
12 perseverance
13 determination

fortress
04 keep
05 tower
06 castle
07 citadel
08 fastness, garrison
10 stronghold
13 fortification

fortuitous
05 fluky, lucky
06 casual, chance, random
09 arbitrary, fortunate
10 accidental, unforeseen
12 providential

fortunate
05 happy, lucky
06 timely
07 blessed, well-off
08 favoured
09 opportune, promising
10 auspicious, convenient, favourable, felicitous, profitable, propitious
11 encouraging, flourishing
12 advantageous, providential

fortunately
07 happily, luckily
12 conveniently
14 providentially

fortune
03 cup, lot
04 bomb, doom, fate, luck, pile
06 assets, bundle, chance, estate, future, income, packet, riches, wealth
07 destiny, history, success
08 accident, big bucks, opulence, property
09 affluence, condition, megabucks, situation
10 prosperity, providence
11 coincidence, serendipity
13 circumstances

fortune-teller
04 seer
05 augur, sibyl
06 oracle
07 diviner, prophet, psychic
09 visionary
10 prophetess, soothsayer

forum
05 arena, stage
07 meeting, rostrum
08 assembly
09 symposium
10 conference, discussion
12 meeting-place

forward
02 on

03 aid, out
04 back, bold, fore, head, help, mail, post, send, ship
05 ahead, brash, cocky, forth, fresh, front, pushy, speed
06 assist, brazen, cheeky, favour, future, hasten, onward, send on, step up
07 advance, deliver, frontal, further, go-ahead, leading, onwards, promote
08 advanced, dispatch, expedite, familiar, foremost, forwards, impudent
09 advancing, audacious, barefaced, confident, premature, presuming, thrusting, transport
10 accelerate, aggressive, facilitate, precocious
11 impertinent, progressive
12 enterprising, overfamiliar, presumptuous
13 over-confident

forward-looking
06 modern
07 dynamic, go-ahead, liberal
09 go-getting, reforming
10 avant-garde, far-sighted, innovative
11 enlightened, progressive
12 enterprising

forwardness
05 cheek
08 audacity, boldness, pertness
09 impudence, pushiness
10 brazenness, cheekiness
11 presumption
12 impertinence
14 over-confidence

forwards
02 on
03 out
05 ahead, forth
07 forward, onwards

fossil
05 relic
07 remains, remnant
08 ammonite
09 coprolite, reliquiae, trilobite
10 graptolite

fossilized
04 dead
05 passé, stony
07 archaic, extinct
08 hardened, obsolete, ossified, outmoded
09 out of date, petrified
11 prehistoric

12 antediluvian, old-fashioned
13 anachronistic

foster
03 aid
04 back, feed, help, hold, rear
05 boost, nurse, raise
06 assist, uphold
07 advance, bring up, care for, cherish, further, harbour, nourish, nurture, support
09 cultivate, encourage, look after, stimulate
10 take care of

foul
03 bad, jam, low, wet
04 base, blue, clog, lewd, mean, rank, soil, vile, wild
05 block, catch, choke, crime, dirty, fetid, gross, muddy, nasty, rainy, rough, snarl, stain, sully, taint, twist
06 coarse, defile, filthy, impure, odious, putrid, ribald, rotten, smelly, smutty, soiled, tangle, vulgar, wicked
07 abusive, blacken, decayed, defiled, ensnare, heinous, obscene, pollute, profane, rotting, squalid, squally, tainted, unclean, vicious
08 blustery, entangle, horrible, indecent, infected, obstruct, polluted, shameful, stinking
09 abhorrent, execrable, loathsome, nefarious, off-colour, offensive, repulsive, revolting, sickening
10 abominable, despicable, disgusting, iniquitous, nauseating, putrescent
11 blasphemous, contaminate
12 contaminated, contemptible, putrefactive

◻**foul play**
05 crime
09 deception, dirty work
13 double-dealing, funny business, sharp practice

foul-mouthed
06 coarse
07 abusive, obscene, profane
09 offensive
11 blasphemous

found
03 fix, set
04 base, rest, root
05 build, endow, erect, plant, raise, set up, start
06 bottom, locate, settle
08 initiate, organize, position

09 construct, establish, institute, originate
10 constitute, inaugurate

foundation
03 key
04 base, core, foot
05 basis, heart
06 bottom, ground, reason
07 bedrock, footing, keynote, premise, reasons, support
08 creation, founding
09 endowment, principle, rationale, setting-up
10 groundwork, hypostasis, initiation, substratum
11 fundamental, institution
12 constitution, fundamentals, inauguration, organization, substructure, underpinning
13 establishment
14 understructure
15 first principles

founder
04 fail, fall, sink
05 abort, maker
06 father, go down, mother
07 builder, capsize, creator, go wrong, misfire, subside
08 collapse, miscarry, submerge
09 architect, developer, initiator, organizer
10 benefactor, discoverer, originator, prime mover
11 come to grief, fall through

foundling
04 waif
05 stray
06 orphan, urchin
07 outcast
12 enfant trouvé

fountain
03 jet
04 rise, well
05 fount, spout, spray, spurt
06 origin, source, spring
09 beginning, inception
10 waterworks, wellspring
12 commencement, fountainhead

four-square
06 firmly
07 frankly, solidly
08 honestly, squarely
10 resolutely

fowl
03 hen
04 bird, cock, duck
05 goose
06 bantam, turkey

07 chicken, poultry
08 pheasant, wildfowl
12 gallinaceous

foxy
03 fly, sly
04 wily
05 canny, sharp
06 artful, crafty, shrewd, tricky
07 cunning, devious, knowing
08 guileful

foyer
04 hall
05 lobby
09 reception, vestibule
11 antechamber
12 entrance hall

fracas
03 row
04 riot, rout
05 aggro, brawl, fight, melee
06 affray, barney, ruckus, ruffle, rumpus, shindy, uproar
07 quarrel, scuffle, trouble
10 Donnybrook, free-for-all
11 disturbance

fraction
03 bit
04 part
05 ratio
06 amount
11 subdivision

fractious
05 cross, testy
06 crabby, grumpy, touchy
07 awkward, fretful, grouchy
08 captious, choleric, petulant
09 crotchety, irritable
10 refractory
11 bad-tempered, quarrelsome
12 recalcitrant

fracture
03 gap
04 chip, rent, rift, slit
05 break, cleft, crack, split
06 breach, schism
07 fissure, opening, rupture
08 aperture, breakage, splinter
09 splitting

fragile
04 fine, weak
05 frail
06 dainty, flimsy, infirm, slight
07 brittle
08 delicate, unstable
09 breakable, frangible
13 insubstantial

fragility
07 frailty
08 delicacy, weakness

11 brittleness
12 frangibility

fragment
03 bit
04 chip, part, snip
05 break, chink, crumb, piece, scrap, shard, shred, split
06 divide, morsel, shiver, sliver
07 break up, crumble, portion, remains, remnant, shatter, snippet, split up
08 disunite, particle, splinter
12 come to pieces, disintegrate

fragmentary
05 bitty
06 broken, uneven
07 partial, scrappy, sketchy
09 piecemeal, scattered
10 disjointed, incomplete
12 disconnected

fragrance
04 balm, otto
05 aroma, attar, odour, scent, smell
07 bouquet, perfume
09 redolence

fragrant
05 balmy, sweet
07 odorous, scented
08 aromatic, perfumed, redolent
11 odoriferous
13 sweet-smelling

frail
04 puny, weak
06 feeble, infirm, slight, unwell
07 brittle, fragile, unsound
09 breakable, frangible
10 vulnerable
11 susceptible
13 insubstantial

frailty
04 flaw
05 fault
06 defect, foible
07 blemish, failing
08 delicacy, weakness
09 fragility, infirmity, weak point
10 deficiency
11 fallibility, shortcoming
12 imperfection
13 vulnerability

frame
04 body, case, edge, form, make, plan, plot, size, trap
05 build, fit up, mould, mount, pin on, plant, set up, shell

06 border, casing, cook up, create, devise, encase, figure, map out, sketch
07 carcase, chassis, compose, enclose, setting, support
08 bodywork, conceive, mounting, physique, skeleton, surround
09 construct, formulate, framework, structure
11 incriminate, manufacture, put together
12 construction, substructure

◻**frame of mind**
04 mood
05 state
06 humour, spirit, temper
07 outlook
08 attitude
09 condition
11 disposition, state of mind

frame-up
03 fix
04 trap
05 fit-up
08 put-up job
11 fabrication
15 trumped-up charge

framework
04 plan, rack
05 frame, shell
06 casing, fabric, scheme
07 lattice, outline, trestle
08 skeleton
09 bare bones, structure
10 foundation, groundwork
12 substructure

franchise
05 right
07 charter, consent, freedom, liberty, licence, warrant
08 immunity, suffrage
09 exemption, privilege
10 concession, permission
13 authorization
15 enfranchisement

frank
04 free, mark, open
05 bluff, blunt, plain, stamp
06 candid, direct, honest
07 genuine, sincere, up-front
08 explicit, postmark, truthful
09 downright, outspoken
10 forthright
11 plain-spoken
15 straightforward

frankly
06 freely, openly
07 bluntly, in truth, plainly
08 candidly, directly, honestly

09 to be blunt, to be frank
10 explicitly, truthfully

frankness
07 candour
08 openness
09 bluntness, sincerity
10 directness
12 truthfulness
13 outspokenness, plain speaking
14 forthrightness

frantic
03 mad
04 wild
06 hectic, raging, raving
07 berserk, fraught, furious
08 agitated, frenetic, frenzied
09 desperate
10 distracted, distraught
11 overwrought
13 at your wits' end, panic-stricken

fraternity
04 clan, club
05 guild, order, union
07 company, kinship, society
10 fellowship
11 association, brotherhood, camaraderie, comradeship

fraternize
03 mix
05 unite
06 hobnob, mingle
07 consort
09 associate, socialize
11 keep company
12 rub shoulders

fraud
03 con, fix
04 fake, hoax, scam, sham
05 cheat, guile, quack, trick
06 deceit, diddle, hoaxer, phoney, racket, rip-off
07 bluffer, forgery
08 cheating, impostor, swindler, trickery
09 charlatan, chicanery, deception, pretender, swindling, trickster
10 mountebank
11 counterfeit, fraudulence
12 embezzlement
13 double-dealing, sharp practice

fraudulent
04 sham
05 bogus, false, shady
06 phoney
07 crooked
08 cheating, criminal

09 deceitful, deceptive, dishonest, swindling
11 counterfeit, duplicitous
13 double-dealing

fraught
04 full
05 laden, tense
06 filled
07 anxious, charged, uptight
08 agitated, attended
09 abounding, bristling
10 distraught, distressed
11 accompanied, overwrought, stressed out

fray
03 row, tax, vex
04 riot, wear
05 brawl, clash, fight, set-to
06 battle, combat, dust-up, rumpus, strain, stress
07 overtax, scuffle, unravel
08 conflict, irritate, wear thin
09 challenge, put on edge
10 excitement, free-for-all
12 become ragged

frayed
04 thin, worn
06 ragged
08 tattered, worn thin
10 threadbare, unravelled

freak
03 fan, nut, odd
04 buff, turn, whim
05 fiend, fluky, quirk, twist
06 addict, chance, mutant, oddity, vagary, weirdo
07 anomaly, bizarre, erratic, monster, oddball, unusual
08 aberrant, abnormal, atypical, mutation, surprise
09 curiosity, deformity
10 aberration, unexpected
11 exceptional, monstrosity
12 irregularity, malformation

freakish
03 odd
05 weird
06 fitful, freaky
07 erratic, strange, unusual
08 aberrant, abnormal, fanciful
09 fantastic, grotesque, malformed, monstrous
10 capricious, outlandish
13 unpredictable
14 unconventional

free
03 out, rid
04 easy, idle, open, save
05 clear, empty, fluid, let go, loose, spare, untie, vague

06 acquit, casual, exempt, freely, giving, gratis, lavish, let out, ransom, rescue, tied up, unbind, vacant
07 absolve, at large, clear of, deliver, for love, inexact, lacking, liberal, natural, relaxed, release, relieve, unchain, untaken, without
08 at no cost, buckshee, devoid of, generous, lavishly, liberate, set loose, unburden
09 at liberty, available, copiously, disengage, easy-going, extricate, imprecise, liberally, liberated, sovereign, turn loose
10 abundantly, autonomous, charitable, democratic, emancipate, exempt from, for nothing, generously, munificent, on the house, on the loose, open-handed, unattached, unconfined, unemployed, unhampered, unoccupied, unstinting
11 disentangle, emancipated, free as a bird, independent, spontaneous, uninhibited
12 free of charge, unaffected by, unrestrained
13 at no extra cost, complimentary, self-governing

◻**free and easy**
06 casual
07 relaxed
08 carefree, informal
09 easy-going
11 spontaneous
12 happy-go-lucky

◻**free hand**
05 power, scope
07 freedom, liberty
08 latitude
10 discretion
12 carte blanche

free will
07 autarky, freedom, liberty
08 autonomy, volition
11 spontaneity
12 independence
15 self-sufficiency

freedom
04 play
05 power, range, right, scope
06 leeway, margin
07 liberty, licence, release
08 autonomy, free hand, free rein, home rule, immunity, impunity, latitude

freely
09 democracy, exemption
11 deliverance, flexibility, informality, sovereignty
12 emancipation, independence
14 self-government

freely
05 amply
06 easily, openly
07 bluntly, plainly, readily
08 candidly, lavishly
09 liberally, willingly
10 abundantly, generously
11 voluntarily
12 unreservedly
13 spontaneously

freethinker
05 deist
07 doubter, infidel, sceptic
08 agnostic
10 unbeliever
11 rationalist

freeze
03 fix, ice, peg, set
04 cool, halt, hold, stay, stop
05 chill, frost, ice up
06 harden, quiver, shiver
07 congeal, embargo, get cold, ice over, stiffen, suspend
08 freeze-up, glaciate, shutdown, solidify, stoppage
10 deep-freeze, immobilize, moratorium, stand still, standstill, suspension

freezing
03 icy, raw
04 cold, numb
05 polar
06 arctic, biting, bitter, chilly, frosty, wintry
07 cutting, glacial, numbing
08 piercing, Siberian, stinging
12 bitterly cold

freight
04 load
05 cargo, goods
06 lading
07 haulage, payload, portage
08 carriage, contents, shipment
10 conveyance, freightage
11 consignment, merchandise
14 transportation

frenetic
03 mad
04 wild
06 hectic, insane
07 berserk, excited, frantic
08 demented, frenzied
10 distraught, hysterical
11 hyperactive, overwrought

frenzied
03 mad
04 amok, wild
06 crazed, hectic, raving
07 berserk, frantic, furious
08 demented, feverish, frenetic
09 desperate, obsessive
10 distracted, distraught
11 overwrought
12 out of control, uncontrolled
13 at your wits' end
14 beside yourself

frenzy
03 fit
04 bout, fury, rage
05 burst, fever, mania, spasm
07 madness, seizure, turmoil
08 hysteria, insanity, outburst, paroxysm, wildness
09 agitation, transport
11 derangement, distraction

frequency
09 constancy, incidence
10 commonness, prevalence, recurrence, repetition
12 frequentness

frequent
05 haunt, usual, visit
06 attend, common, normal
08 everyday, familiar, habitual, numerous, repeated
09 countless, customary, hang out at, patronize, prevalent, recurring
11 commonplace
13 go to regularly
14 go to frequently, happening often

frequenter
06 client, patron
07 habitué, haunter, regular
08 customer
14 regular visitor

frequently
04 much
05 often
08 commonly
09 many a time, many times
10 oftentimes, repeatedly
11 customarily, over and over

fresh
03 new, raw
04 bold, cool, fair, keen, more, pert, pink, pure, rosy
05 alert, brisk, clean, clear, cocky, crisp, crude, extra, novel, other, saucy, vital
06 brazen, bright, cheeky, chilly, latest, recent, rested

07 bracing, forward, glowing, healthy, natural, renewed, revived, unfaded, unusual
08 blooming, bouncing, brand-new, exciting, familiar, impudent, insolent, original, up-to-date, vigorous
09 different, refreshed
10 additional, innovative, raring to go, unpolluted
11 unpreserved, unprocessed
12 overfamiliar, presumptuous, ready for more
13 disrespectful, fresh as a daisy, supplementary
14 unconventional

freshen
03 air
05 clean, clear, liven, rouse
06 purify, revive, tart up
07 enliven, refresh, restore
09 deodorize, ventilate
10 revitalize
12 reinvigorate

▢freshen up
09 get washed
12 wash yourself
14 tidy yourself up

freshman
07 fresher
09 first-year
13 underclassman

freshness
04 glow
05 bloom, shine
07 newness, novelty, sparkle
09 cleanness, clearness
10 brightness
11 originality
13 wholesomeness

fret
03 vex
04 mope, pine, rile
05 anger, annoy, brood, worry
06 bother, nettle
07 anguish, be upset, trouble
08 irritate
09 be anxious, make a fuss
12 be distressed

fretful
04 edgy
05 tense, upset
06 uneasy
07 anxious, fearful, unhappy, uptight, worried
08 restless, troubled
09 disturbed
10 distressed

friable
05 crisp
07 brittle, crumbly, powdery

friar
04 monk
05 abbot, prior
07 brother
09 mendicant, religious
10 religioner

friction
06 strife
07 arguing, chafing, discord, erosion, gnawing, grating, rasping, rivalry, rubbing
08 bad blood, clashing, conflict, scraping, traction
09 animosity, attrition, hostility
10 antagonism, bad feeling, disharmony, dissension, ill feeling, irritation, resentment, resistance
11 disputation, excoriation, quarrelling, wearing away
12 disagreement

friend
03 pal
04 ally, chum, mate
05 buddy, crony
06 backer, patron
07 comrade, partner, sponsor
08 familiar, intimate, playmate
09 associate, companion, confidant, supporter
10 benefactor, confidante, subscriber, well-wisher
11 bosom friend, close friend
12 acquaintance

friendless
05 alone
06 lonely
07 forlorn, shunned, unloved
08 isolated, lonesome, solitary
09 abandoned, unpopular
10 by yourself, ostracized
12 unbefriended
13 companionless
14 cold shouldered

friendliness
06 warmth
08 kindness, matiness
09 geniality
10 affability, amiability
11 sociability
12 congeniality, conviviality
13 Gemütlichkeit
15 approachability

friendly
04 fond, kind, maty, warm
05 close, pally, thick, tight
06 chummy, genial, kindly

07 amiable, cordial, helpful
08 amicable, familiar, intimate, outgoing, sociable
09 agreeable, comradely, congenial, convivial, receptive, welcoming
10 favourable, hospitable
11 good-natured, inseparable, neighbourly, sympathetic
12 affectionate, approachable
13 companionable

friendship
04 love
05 amity
06 warmth
07 concord, harmony, rapport
08 affinity, alliance, fondness, goodwill, intimacy
09 affection, closeness
10 amiability, kindliness
11 comradeship, familiarity
12 friendliness
13 companionship, understanding

fright
04 fear, funk
05 alarm, panic, scare, shock
06 creeps, dismay, horror, terror
07 jitters, shivers, willies
09 bombshell, cold sweat
10 blind panic
11 fearfulness, trepidation
12 apprehension, perturbation
13 consternation, heebie-jeebies, knocking knees
15 bolt from the blue

frighten
05 alarm, appal, daunt, panic, scare, shock, unman
06 dismay, rattle
07 petrify, startle, terrify, unnerve
09 terrorize
10 intimidate, scare stiff
12 put the wind up

frightened
05 cowed
06 afraid, frozen, scared
07 alarmed, panicky, trembly
08 startled, unnerved
09 petrified, terrified
10 terrorized
11 in a blue funk, scared stiff
13 having kittens, panic-stricken, scared to death
14 terror-stricken

frightening
04 grim
05 hairy, scary
06 creepy, spooky

08 alarming, fearsome
09 traumatic
10 forbidding, formidable, petrifying, terrifying
11 hair-raising
13 bloodcurdling, spine-chilling

frightful
04 dire, grim
05 awful, nasty
06 grisly, horrid, odious
07 fearful, ghastly, hideous
08 alarming, dreadful, gruesome, horrible, shocking, terrible
09 abhorrent, appalling, harrowing, loathsome, repulsive, revolting

frigid
03 icy
04 cold, cool
05 aloof, chill, polar
06 arctic, bitter, chilly, formal, frosty, frozen, wintry
07 distant, glacial, passive
08 freezing, Siberian, unloving
09 unfeeling
11 passionless
12 unresponsive

frigidity
05 chill
07 iciness
08 coldness
09 aloofness, passivity, stiffness
10 chilliness, frostiness
15 cold-heartedness

frill
04 fold, ruff, tuck
05 extra, ruche
06 finery, fringe, purfle, ruffle
07 flounce, orphrey, valance
08 frippery, furbelow, trimming
09 accessory, fanciness, fandangle, gathering
10 decoration, frilliness
11 ostentation, superfluity
13 embellishment, ornamentation

frilly
04 lacy
05 fancy
06 ornate
07 frilled, ruffled, trimmed
08 gathered

fringe
03 rim
04 edge, trim
05 frill, limit, skirt, verge
06 border, edging, margin
08 surround, trimming

09 outskirts, perimeter, periphery
10 borderline, unofficial
11 alternative
12 experimental

fringed
05 edged
07 trimmed
08 bordered, tasselly
09 tasselled
10 fimbriated

frippery
05 froth
06 finery, frills, trivia
07 baubles, gewgaws, trifles
08 glad rags, nonsense, trinkets
09 fussiness, gaudiness, ornaments, showiness
10 adornments, fandangles, flashiness, frilliness, tawdriness, triviality
11 decorations, knickknacks
15 pretentiousness

frisk
03 hop
04 leap, play, romp, skip, trip
05 caper, check, dance, sport
06 bounce, cavort, frolic, gambol, prance, search
09 shake down
10 body-search

frisky
04 high
05 hyper
06 active, bouncy, lively
07 dashing, playful, romping
08 spirited
09 exuberant
10 frolicsome, rollicking
11 full of beans
12 high-spirited
13 in high spirits

fritter
04 blow, idle
05 waste
06 misuse
08 misspend, squander
09 dissipate, go through
10 get through, overspend
14 spend like water

frivolity
03 fun
04 jest
05 folly
06 gaiety, levity
08 nonsense
09 flippancy, pettiness, silliness
10 triviality
11 foolishness
13 facetiousness, senselessness
14 superficiality

frivolous
04 idle, vain, zany
05 inane, light, merry, petty, silly
07 flighty, foolish, jocular, puerile, shallow, trivial
08 flippant, juvenile, trifling
09 facetious, pointless
11 superficial, unimportant
12 light-hearted

frizzy
04 wiry
05 crisp, curly
06 curled
07 crimped, frizzed

frolic
03 fun, hop
04 game, lark, leap, romp, skip
05 caper, dance, frisk, mirth, prank, revel, sport, spree
06 antics, bounce, cavort, gaiety, gambol, prance
08 escapade
09 amusement, high jinks, make merry, merriment

frolicsome
03 gay
05 merry
06 frisky, lively
07 coltish, playful
08 skittish, sportive

front
03 air, bow, top
04 face, fore, head, lead, look, mask, meet, show
05 blind, cover, first
06 aspect, before, faade, facing, manner, oppose
07 leading, outside, pretext
08 confront, disguise, exterior, foremost, forepart, frontage pretence, vanguard
09 forefront, front line
10 appearance, foreground
11 countenance

□**in front**
05 ahead, first
06 before
07 leading
09 in advance, preceding, to the fore

frontier
04 edge
05 limit, verge
06 border, bounds
08 boundary, confines
09 perimeter
10 borderline

frost
04 rime
06 freeze

08 coldness, freeze-up
09 hoar-frost, Jack Frost

frosty
03 icy
04 cold, cool, rimy
05 aloof, nippy, parky, polar, stiff
06 arctic, chilly, frozen, wintry
07 glacial, hostile
08 freezing, Siberian
10 unfriendly
11 standoffish, unwelcoming
12 bitterly cold, discouraging

froth
04 fizz, foam, head, scum, suds
05 spume, spumy
06 bubble, lather
07 bubbles, ferment, spumous
13 effervescence

frothy
04 vain
05 empty, fizzy, foamy, sudsy
06 bubbly, slight, yeasty
07 foaming, spumous, trivial
08 bubbling, trifling
09 frivolous
10 spumescent
12 insubstantial

frown
04 lour, pout
05 glare, scowl
06 glower
07 grimace
09 dirty look
13 look daggers at

□**frown on**
07 dislike, grimace
08 object to
10 discourage
12 disapprove of, think badly of
14 take a dim view of

frowsy
05 dirty, messy
06 frumpy, sloppy, untidy
07 unkempt
08 frumpish, sluttish, unwashed
09 ungroomed
10 slatternly
11 dishevelled

frozen
03 icy, raw
04 hard, iced, numb
05 fixed, polar, rigid, stiff
06 arctic, frigid, frosty
07 chilled, frosted, ice-cold
08 freezing, icebound, Siberian
10 ice-covered, solidified
12 bitterly cold

frugal
06 meagre, paltry, scanty

07 careful, sparing, thrifty
09 penny-wise, provident
10 economical, inadequate

fruit
04 crop
05 yield
06 effect, profit, result, return
07 benefit, harvest, outcome, produce, product
09 advantage
11 consequence

Types of fruit:
03 fig
04 date, kaki, lime, pear, plum, sloe
05 apple, grape, guava, Jaffa, lemon, mango, melon, olive, peach
06 banana, cherry, damson, lychee, orange, papaya, pawpaw, pomelo, quince, tomato
07 apricot, avocado, Bramley, kumquat, rhubarb, satsuma
08 bilberry, goosegog, honeydew, mandarin
09 blueberry, crab apple, cranberry, greengage, kiwi fruit, nectarine, persimmon, pineapple, raspberry, star fruit, tangerine, ugli® fruit
10 blackberry, cantaloupe, clementine, Conference, elderberry, gooseberry, grapefruit, loganberry, redcurrant, strawberry, watermelon
11 boysenberry, Granny Smith, pomegranate
12 blackcurrant, custard apple, passion fruit
15 Golden Delicious
➢ See also **food**

fruitful
04 rich
06 fecund, useful
07 fertile, teeming
08 abundant, prolific
09 effective, feracious, rewarding, well-spent
10 beneficial, productive, profitable, worthwhile
11 efficacious
12 advantageous, fruit-bearing

fruitfulness
08 feracity
09 fecundity, fertility
10 usefulness
13 profitability

fruition
07 success
08 maturity, ripeness
10 attainment, completion, fulfilment, perfection
11 achievement, realization
12 consummation

fruitless
04 idle, vain
06 barren, futile
07 sterile, useless
08 abortive, hopeless
09 pointless, worthless
11 ineffectual
12 unproductive, unsuccessful

fruity
04 blue, full, racy, rich, sexy
05 bawdy, juicy, saucy, spicy
06 mellow, risqué, smutty
08 indecent, resonant
09 salacious
10 indelicate, suggestive

frumpy
04 drab
05 dated, dingy, dowdy
06 dreary
09 out of date

frustrate
04 balk, foil, stop
05 anger, annoy, block, check
06 defeat, hamper, hinder, impede, stymie, thwart
07 counter, inhibit, nullify
08 embitter, irritate, obstruct
09 forestall
10 circumvent, disappoint, dissatisfy, neutralize

frustrated
05 angry
07 annoyed
08 blighted, thwarted
09 repressed, resentful
10 embittered
12 disappointed, discontented, disheartened, dissatisfied

frustration
05 anger
06 defeat
07 balking, failure, foiling
08 blocking, vexation
09 annoyance, thwarting
10 irritation, resentment
11 obstruction
13 non-fulfilment
14 disappointment
15 dissatisfaction

fuddled
04 hazy
05 drunk, muzzy, tipsy, woozy

06 groggy
07 bemused, muddled, sozzled
08 confused
10 inebriated
11 intoxicated

fuddy-duddy
04 prim
06 fossil, square, stuffy
08 old fogey
11 museum piece, old-fogeyish
12 conservative, old-fashioned, stuffed shirt
13 stick-in-the-mud

fudge
04 cook, fake
05 dodge, evade, hedge, stall
06 fiddle
07 falsify, shuffle
10 equivocate
12 misrepresent

fuel
03 fan
04 feed, fire
07 inflame, nourish, stoke up
09 encourage, incentive
10 ammunition, propellant
11 combustible, provocation
13 encouragement

Types of fuel:
03 gas, oil
04 coal, coke, derv, peat, wood
06 butane, diesel, petrol
07 methane, propane
08 calor gas®, charcoal, firewood, gasoline, kerosene, kindling, paraffin
10 fossil fuel
11 electricity
12 nuclear power

fug
05 stink
09 fetidness, fustiness, staleness
10 stuffiness
11 frowstiness

fuggy
04 foul
05 close, fetid, fusty, stale
06 stuffy
07 airless, noisome, noxious
11 suffocating
12 unventilated

fugitive
05 brief, short
06 flying
07 escapee, refugee, runaway
08 deserter, fleeting
09 ephemeral, fugacious, temporary, transient
10 short-lived, transitory

fulfil
04 fill, keep, meet, obey
06 answer, effect, finish
07 achieve, execute, satisfy
08 carry out, complete
09 conform to, discharge,
    implement
10 accomplish, comply with

fulfilled
05 happy
07 content, pleased
09 gratified, satisfied

fulfilment
07 success
09 discharge, execution
10 completion, observance
11 achievement, realization
12 consummation, satisfaction
14 accomplishment

full
03 fat, top
04 busy, deep, loud, rich, wide
05 ample, buxom, clear, laden,
    large, plump, round, sated,
    stout, total, whole
06 active, entire, filled, gorged,
    jammed, loaded, packed,
    rotund, strong, utmost
07 bulging, copious, crammed,
    crowded, highest,
    maximum, replete, shapely,
    stuffed
08 abundant, bursting,
    complete, detailed, directly,
    generous, resonant,
    satiated, squarely, straight,
    thorough
09 corpulent, extensive,
    packed out, satisfied
10 exhaustive, sufficient,
    unabridged, voluminous
11 overflowing, well-stocked
12 all-inclusive, loose-fitting
13 comprehensive

◻**in full**
05 fully, uncut
06 wholly
07 in total
08 in detail
10 completely
13 in its entirety

◻**to the full**
05 fully
07 utterly
08 entirely
10 thoroughly
11 to the utmost

full-blooded
06 hearty
07 devoted

08 thorough, vigorous
09 committed, dedicated
12 enthusiastic, wholehearted

full-grown
04 ripe
05 adult, of age
06 mature
07 grown-up
09 developed, full-blown
12 fully-fledged

fullness
04 fill, glut
06 growth, plenty, wideth
07 breadth, satiety, variety
08 dilation, loudness, richness,
    strength, swelling, totality
09 abundance, ampleness,
    largeness, repletion,
    resonance, satedness,
    satiation, wholeness
10 tumescence
11 enlargement, shapeliness
12 completeness
13 extensiveness

◻**in the fullness of time**
07 finally
08 in the end
10 eventually, ultimately
11 in due course

full-scale
05 major
06 all-out
07 in-depth
08 complete, thorough
09 extensive, intensive
10 exhaustive
11 wide-ranging
13 comprehensive
15 all-encompassing

fully
05 quite
06 wholly
07 totally, utterly
08 entirely
09 perfectly
10 altogether, completely,
    positively, thoroughly
13 in all respects
14 without reserve

fully-fledged
06 mature, senior
07 trained
08 graduate
09 full-blown, qualified
14 fully-developed

fulminate
04 fume, rage, rail
05 curse, decry
07 condemn, declaim, inveigh
08 denounce

09 criticize
10 animadvert, vituperate

fulmination
06 tirade
07 decrial, obloquy
08 diatribe
09 criticism, invective, philippic
12 condemnation,
    denunciation

fulsome
05 gross, slimy
07 buttery, cloying, fawning
08 effusive, nauseous,
    overdone, unctuous
09 excessive, insincere,
    offensive, sickening
10 inordinate, nauseating, over
    the top, saccharine
11 extravagant, sycophantic
12 ingratiating

fumble
04 feel
05 botch, grope, spoil
08 flounder, scrabble
09 mishandle, mismanage

fume
04 boil, rage, rant, rave
05 smoke, steam, storm
06 seethe
07 be livid
08 smoulder
09 be furious
11 rant and rave

fumes
03 fog, gas
04 haze, reek, smog
05 smell, smoke, stink
06 stench, vapour
07 exhaust

fumigate
06 purify
07 cleanse
08 sanitize
09 deodorize, disinfect

fuming
05 angry, livid
06 raging
07 boiling, enraged, furious
08 incensed, seething

fun
03 joy
04 game, play, romp
05 mirth, sport, witty
06 joking, laughs, lively
07 amusing, jesting, jollity
08 hilarity, laughter, pleasure
09 amusement, diverting,
    enjoyable, enjoyment

10 recreation, relaxation, skylarking, tomfoolery
11 celebration, distraction, merrymaking, pleasurable
12 entertaining, recreational
13 entertainment

□for fun
08 for kicks
09 for a laugh
12 for enjoyment
14 for the hell of it

□in fun
06 in jest
07 as a joke, to tease
08 jokingly
09 for a laugh, teasingly
13 tongue in cheek

□make fun of
03 rib
04 mock
05 taunt, tease
06 deride, jeer at, send up
07 scoff at, sneer at
08 ridicule
09 humiliate, poke fun at
11 take the piss
13 take the mickey
15 pull someone's leg

function
02 do, go
03 act, job, run, use
04 duty, post, role, task, work
05 chore, party, serve
06 affair, behave, dinner
07 operate, perform, purpose
08 capacity, luncheon
09 gathering, reception
14 responsibility

functional
06 useful
07 running, utility, working
09 operative, practical
11 hard-wearing, operational, serviceable, utilitarian

functionary
07 officer
08 employee, official
09 dignitary
10 bureaucrat
12 office-bearer, office-holder

fund
04 back, cash, mine, pool, well
05 cache, endow, float, hoard, kitty, money, stock, store
06 assets, supply, wealth
07 capital, finance, reserve, savings, sponsor, support
09 endowment, reservoir, resources, subsidize

10 capitalize, collection, foundation, repository, storehouse, underwrite
12 accumulation

fundamental
03 key
04 main
05 basic, chief, first, prime
07 central, crucial, primary
08 integral, original, profound
09 elemental, essential, important, principal
10 elementary, underlying
11 rudimentary
13 indispensable

fundamentally
07 at heart
08 at bottom, deep down
09 basically, primarily
10 inherently
11 essentially
13 intrinsically

fundamentals
04 laws
05 facts, rules
06 basics
09 rudiments
10 brass tacks, essentials
11 necessaries, nitty-gritty
15 first principles

funeral
04 wake
06 burial
08 exequies
09 cremation, interment
10 entombment, inhumation

funereal
04 dark
05 grave
06 dismal, dreary, gloomy, solemn, sombre, woeful
07 serious
08 exequial, funebral, mournful
09 deathlike, funebrial
10 depressing, sepulchral

fungus
07 fungous

➤ *Types of fungus*:
04 rust, scab, smut
05 ergot, yeast
06 blight
07 candida
08 botritis, mushroom
09 black spot, grey mould, toadstool
10 slime mould
11 penicillium
12 brewer's yeast, potato blight
➤ See also **mushroom**

funk
05 dodge
06 balk at, blench, cop out
09 duck out of, shirk from
10 flinch from, recoil from
12 chicken out of

funnel
04 move, pass, pour
06 convey, direct, filter, siphon

funny
03 odd, rum
05 a hoot, comic, droll, queer, shady, wacky, weird, witty
06 absurd, way-out
07 a scream, amusing, bizarre, comical, curious, dubious, killing, oddball, off-beat, risible, strange, unusual
08 farcical, humorous, peculiar
09 hilarious, laughable
10 hysterical, perplexing, suspicious, uproarious
12 entertaining
13 side-splitting

fur
04 coat, down, fell, hair, hide, pelt, skin, wool
06 fleece, pelage

furious
03 mad
04 wild
05 angry, irate, livid
06 fierce, fuming, raging
07 boiling, enraged, in a huff, in a stew, intense, violent
08 incensed, inflamed, seething, sizzling, up in arms, vehement, vigorous
10 hopping mad, infuriated
11 tempestuous

furnish
03 rig
04 give
05 endue, equip, grant, offer, stock
06 afford, bestow, fit out, supply
07 appoint, present, provide

furniture
07 effects
08 fitments, fittings, movables
10 appliances
11 furnishings, possessions
12 appointments
14 household goods

➤ *Types of furniture*:
03 bed, cot
04 bunk, desk, sofa
05 chair, chest, couch, divan, stool, suite, table

06 buffet, bureau, cradle, daybed, fender, lowboy, pouffe, settee
07 armoire, bean-bag, cabinet, camp-bed, commode, ottoman, tallboy
08 armchair, bookcase, cupboard, wardrobe, water-bed
09 bed-settee, card table, easy chair, fireplace, footstool, hallstand, high-chair, side-table, sideboard, washstand
10 chiffonier, dumb-waiter, escritoire, firescreen, four-poster, secretaire
11 coffee-table, dining-chair, dining-table, swivel-chair
12 chaise-longue, chesterfield, china cabinet, gateleg table, kitchen chair, rocking-chair, Welsh dresser
13 dressing-table, umbrella-stand
14 chest-of-drawers, refectory table
15 occasional table

► *Styles of furniture*:
04 Adam, buhl
06 boulle, Empire, Gothic, rococo
07 Art Deco, Baroque, Regency, Windsor
08 Colonial, Georgian, Sheraton
09 Edwardian, Shibayama,
10 Art Nouveau, provincial
11 Anglo-Indian, Biedermeier, Chippendale, Hepplewhite, Louis-Quinze
12 Gainsborough, Vernis Martin
13 Anglo-Colonial, Arts and Crafts, Dutch Colonial, Louis Philippe, Louis-Quatorze

furore
04 fury, fuss, rage, stir, to-do
05 storm
06 outcry, tumult, uproar
08 outburst
09 commotion
10 excitement, hullabaloo
11 disturbance

furrow
03 rut
04 knit, line, seam
05 flute, gouge, track
06 crease, groove, plough, trench, trough
07 channel, crinkle, wrinkle
12 draw together

further
03 aid, new, too
04 also, ease, help, more, push
05 extra, fresh, other, speed
06 as well, assist, foster, hasten
07 advance, besides, farther, forward, promote, remoter
08 champion, expedite, moreover
09 encourage, what's more
10 accelerate, additional, facilitate, in addition
11 furthermore
12 additionally
13 supplementary

furtherance
04 help
07 backing, pursuit
08 advocacy, boosting
09 advancing, promotion
10 preferment
11 advancement, carrying-out
12 championship, facilitation
13 encouragement

furthermore
03 too
04 also
06 as well
07 besides, further
08 moreover
10 in addition, what's more
12 additionally

furthest
06 utmost
07 extreme, outmost
08 farthest, remotest, ultimate
09 outermost, uttermost

furtive
03 sly
06 covert, secret, sneaky
07 cloaked
08 stealthy
09 secretive, underhand
11 clandestine
13 surreptitious

fury
03 ire
04 rage
05 anger, force, power, wrath
06 frenzy
07 madness, passion
08 ferocity, violence, wildness
09 intensity, vehemence
10 fierceness, turbulence

fuse
04 join, meld, melt, weld
05 blend, merge, smelt, unite
06 solder
08 coalesce, intermix
10 amalgamate, synthesize

fusillade
04 fire, hail
05 burst, salvo
06 volley
07 barrage
08 outburst
09 broadside, discharge

fusion
05 union
06 merger
07 melting, welding
08 blending, smelting
09 synthesis
12 amalgamation

fuss
03 row
04 flap, fret, stir, to-do
05 hoo-ha, panic, tizzy, upset
06 bother, fidget, flurry, furore
07 carry-on, fluster, palaver
08 ballyhoo, squabble
09 commotion, confusion, kerfuffle, take pains
10 be in a tizzy, excitement
13 a song and dance
14 storm in a teacup

fussiness
08 busyness, niceness, niggling
10 choosiness, finicality
13 particularity, perfectionism
14 pernicketiness

fusspot
06 fidget
07 worrier
08 old woman, stickler
09 nit-picker
11 hyper-critic
13 perfectionist

fussy
05 faddy, fancy, picky
06 choosy, ornate, rococo
07 baroque, finical, finicky
08 pedantic
09 cluttered, difficult, elaborate, quibbling
10 fastidious, nit-picking, particular, pernickety
12 hard to please, pettifogging
13 overdecorated

fusty
04 damp, dank, rank
05 fuggy, musty, passé, stale
06 mouldy, stuffy
07 airless, archaic, frowsty
10 malodorous, mouldering
11 ill-smelling, old-fogeyish
12 unventilated, old-fashioned

futile
04 idle, vain
05 empty
06 barren, in vain, wasted
07 forlorn, useless
09 fruitless, pointless, to no
   avail, worthless
11 ineffective, ineffectual
12 unproductive, unprofitable

futility
05 waste
06 vanity
09 emptiness
11 aimlessness, uselessness

13 fruitlessness, pointlessness
15 ineffectiveness

future
04 next, to be
05 fated, later
06 coming, to come, unborn
07 outlook, planned
08 destined, eventual
09 designate, hereafter,
   impending, prospects
11 approaching, forthcoming,
   in the offing, prospective
12 expectations

fuzz
03 fug, nap
04 down, hair, lint, pile
05 fibre, flock, floss, fluff

fuzzy
04 hazy
05 downy, faint, foggy, frizzy,
   furry, linty, muzzy, vague
06 fleecy, fluffy, frizzy, woolly
07 blurred, fuddled, muffled,
   shadowy, unclear, velvety
10 ill-defined, indistinct

gab
03 jaw, yak
04 blab, chat, talk
06 babble, gossip
07 blether, chatter, prattle
08 chitchat
09 loquacity, prattling, small talk
10 blethering, yackety-yak
12 conversation, tittle-tattle

gabble
04 blab
05 spout
06 babble, cackle, drivel, gaggle, gibber, jabber, waffle
07 blabber, blether, chatter, prattle, sputter, twaddle
08 cackling, nonsense, splutter
09 gibberish
10 blethering

gad

□ **gad about**
04 roam, rove
05 range, stray
06 ramble, travel, wander
09 flit about, gallivant

gadabout
05 rover
07 rambler
10 stravaiger
11 gallivanter
14 pleasure-seeker

gadget
04 tool
05 gismo
06 device, widget
07 whatnot, whatsit
09 appliance, implement, invention, thingummy
10 instrument
11 contraption, contrivance

gaffe
04 boob, goof, slip
05 brick
06 boo-boo, howler
07 bloomer, blunder, clanger, faux pas, mistake
08 solecism
12 indiscretion

gaffer
04 boss
06 ganger
07 foreman, manager, overman
08 overseer

gag
03 pun
04 clog, jest, joke, quip
05 block, choke, heave, retch
06 muffle, muzzle, stifle
07 silence, smother
08 one-liner, suppress, throttle
09 wisecrack, witticism

gaiety
03 fun, joy
04 glee, show
05 mirth
07 delight, glitter, jollity, sparkle
08 pleasure, vivacity
09 festivity, happiness, joviality, merriment, showiness
10 brightness, brilliance, exuberance, liveliness
11 high spirits, joie de vivre
12 cheerfulness
13 colourfulness

gaily
07 happily, merrily
08 blithely, brightly, joyfully
10 cheerfully
11 brilliantly, colourfully
14 light-heartedly

gain
03 add, get, net, win
04 earn, make, reap, rise
05 clear, gross, reach, yield
06 attain, gather, growth, income, obtain, profit, return, reward, secure
07 achieve, acquire, advance, benefit, collect, headway, improve, procure, produce, realize, revenue, takings
08 addition, dividend, earnings, increase, progress, winnings
09 accretion, advantage, emolument, increment
11 advancement, improvement

□ **gain on**
07 catch up
08 approach, overtake
09 close with
12 narrow the gap

□ **gain time**
05 delay, stall
09 temporize
10 dilly-dally
13 procrastinate

gainful
06 paying, useful
09 fructuous, lucrative, rewarding
10 worthwhile
12 advantageous, remunerative

gainsay
04 deny
07 dispute
09 challenge, disaffirm
10 contradict, controvert

gait
04 pace, step, walk
07 bearing
08 carriage

gala
04 fair, fête
07 jubilee, pageant
08 carnival, festival, jamboree
09 festivity
10 procession

galaxy
04 host, mass
05 array, group, stars
08 assembly
09 gathering
10 collection, star system
11 solar system, the Milky Way
13 constellation

gale
04 wind
05 blast, burst, storm
06 squall
07 cyclone, tornado, typhoon
09 hurricane

gall
03 irk, nag, vex
04 neck, rile
05 annoy, cheek, nerve, peeve

06 animus, bother, harass, nettle, plague, rankle
07 provoke, rancour
08 acrimony, chutzpah, irritate
09 aggravate, animosity, antipathy, brass neck, impudence, insolence
10 bitterness, brazenness, effrontery, exasperate
12 impertinence

gallant
05 brave, manly, noble
06 daring, heroic, plucky, polite
07 courtly, dashing, valiant
08 fearless, gracious, intrepid
09 attentive, audacious, courteous, dauntless
10 chivalrous, courageous, honourable, thoughtful
11 considerate, gentlemanly

gallantry
05 pluck
06 daring, honour, spirit, valour
07 bravery, courage, heroism
08 audacity, boldness, chivalry, courtesy, nobility, valiance
09 manliness
10 politeness
11 courtliness, intrepidity
12 fearlessness, graciousness
13 attentiveness, consideration, courteousness, dauntlessness
14 thoughtfulness
15 gentlemanliness

gallery
04 gods, walk
06 arcade, circle, museum
07 balcony, passage
10 art gallery, spectators
➤ See also **museum**

galling
06 bitter, vexing
07 irksome
08 annoying, nettling, plaguing, rankling
09 harassing, provoking, vexatious
10 bothersome, irritating
11 aggravating, infuriating
12 exasperating

gallivant
04 roam, rove
05 range, stray
06 ramble, travel, wander
08 dot about, gad about, stravaig
09 flit about, run around

gallop
03 run

04 dash, race, rush, tear, zoom
05 hurry, shoot, speed
06 scurry, sprint

gallows
06 gibbet
08 scaffold

galore
06 lots of, tons of
07 heaps of
08 plenty of, stacks of
10 everywhere, millions of

galvanize
04 fire, jolt, move, prod, spur, stir, urge
05 rouse, shock
06 arouse, awaken, excite
07 animate, enliven, provoke
08 energize, vitalize
09 electrify, stimulate

gambit
04 move, play, ploy, ruse, wile
06 device, tactic
07 tactics
08 artifice
09 manoeuvre, stratagem

gamble
03 bet
04 back, game, play, punt, risk
05 stake, wager
06 chance, hazard
07 flutter, lottery, pot luck, venture
09 speculate, take a risk
10 put money on
11 speculation, take a chance, try your luck
12 have a flutter, play for money
13 leap in the dark

gambler
06 better, punter
09 daredevil, risk-taker

gambol
04 jump, leap, romp, skip
05 bound, caper, dance, frisk
06 cavort, frolic, prance

game
03 bag, fun
04 bold, bout, jest, joke, line, meat, meet, play, plot, ploy, prey, romp, ruse
05 eager, event, flesh, match, prank, ready, sport, trade
06 daring, frolic, quarry, scheme, spoils, tactic
07 contest, pastime, tactics, valiant, willing
08 activity, business, fearless, inclined, prepared, spirited, strategy

09 diversion, intention, stratagem
10 courageous, enterprise, interested, occupation, profession, recreation
11 competition, distraction
12 enthusiastic
13 entertainment

➤ *Types of game animal*:
03 elk, fox
04 bear, boar, deer, duck, hare, lion, stag, wolf
05 hyena, moose, quail, snipe
06 grouse, rabbit
07 caribou, red deer, roe deer
08 antelope, pheasant, wild boar, woodcock
09 partridge, waterfowl
10 fallow deer, wood grouse
12 capercaillie

➤ *Names of games*:
03 nap
04 brag, crib, dice, faro, I-spy, ludo, pool, snap
05 bowls, chess, craps, darts, halma, jacks, poker, rummy, whist
06 bridge, Cluedo®
07 bezique, bowling, canasta, hangman, mah-jong, old maid, picquet, pinball, pontoon, snooker
08 baccarat, charades, checkers, cribbage, dominoes, draughts, forfeits, gin rummy, Monopoly®, patience, ping pong, roulette, sardines, Scrabble®
09 bagatelle, billiards, blackjack, newmarket, Simon says, solitaire, stud poker, twenty-one, vingt-et-un
10 back-gammon
11 battleships, chemin de fer, hide-and-seek, table tennis, tiddlywinks
12 consequences, shove ha'penny
13 blind man's buff, happy families, musical chairs, pass the parcel, postman's knock, spin the bottle, ten-pin bowling
14 nine men's morris, Trivial Pursuit®
15 Chinese whispers

gamekeeper
06 keeper, warden
07 venerer

gamut
04 area
05 field, range, scope, sweep
06 series
07 compass, variety
08 sequence, spectrum

gang
03 lot, mob, set
04 band, club, crew, herd, pack, ring, team
05 crowd, group, horde, squad
06 circle, clique, troupe
07 company, coterie

gangling
04 bony, tall
05 gawky, lanky, rangy
06 gangly, gauche, skinny
07 angular, awkward, spindly
08 raw-boned, ungainly

gangster
04 thug
05 crook, heavy, rough, tough
06 bandit, robber
07 hoodlum, mobster, ruffian
08 criminal
09 desperado, racketeer

gaol see **jail**

gaoler see **jailer**

gap
04 gulf, hole, lull, rent, rift, void
05 blank, break, chink, cleft, crack, pause, space
06 breach, cavity, cranny, divide, hiatus, lacuna, recess
07 crevice, opening, vacuity
08 aperture, fracture, interval
09 disparity, interlude
10 difference, divergence
12 intermission, interruption
13 discontinuity

gape
04 gawk, gawp, gaze, open, part, yawn
05 crack, split, stare
06 goggle, wonder
10 rubberneck

gaping
04 open, vast, wide
05 broad
07 yawning
09 cavernous

garage
06 lock-up
07 car port

garb
04 gear, robe, togs, wear
05 array, dress, get-up, robes
06 attire, clothe, outfit, rig-out

07 apparel, clothes, costume, garment, raiment, uniform
08 clothing
09 vestments
10 appearance, habiliment

garbage
03 rot
04 bunk, junk, muck, shit
05 bilge, filth, trash, tripe, waste
06 bunkum, hot air, piffle, refuse
07 remains, rubbish, twaddle
08 claptrap, cobblers, detritus, nonsense, tommyrot
09 gibberish, poppycock
11 odds and ends
13 bits and pieces

garble
05 mix up, slant, twist
06 doctor, jumble, muddle
07 confuse, corrupt, distort
08 mutilate, scramble

garden
04 park, plot, yard
08 backyard

gargantuan
04 huge, vast
05 giant, large
07 immense, mammoth, massive, titanic
08 colossal, enormous, gigantic, towering
09 leviathan, monstrous
11 elephantine
14 Brobdingnagian

garish
04 loud
05 cheap, flash, gaudy, lurid, showy
06 flashy, glitzy, tawdry, vulgar
07 glaring, raffish

garland
03 lei
05 adorn, crown
06 stemma, wreath
07 chaplet, coronal, coronet, festoon, flowers, honours, laurels, wreathe
08 decorate, headband

garments
04 garb, gear, togs, wear
05 dress, get-up
06 attire, outfit
07 apparel, clothes, costume, uniform
08 clothing

garner
04 cull, heap, save
05 amass, hoard, store

06 gather
07 collect, deposit, husband, reserve
08 assemble, stow away
10 accumulate

garnish
04 deck, trim
05 adorn, grace
07 deck out, enhance, festoon
08 decorate, ornament
09 adornment, embellish
10 decoration
11 enhancement
13 embellishment, ornamentation

garret
04 loft
05 attic

garrison
03 man
04 base, camp, fort, post, unit
05 guard, mount, place
06 assign, casern, defend, occupy, troops, zareba
07 command, furnish, protect, station
08 barracks, fortress, position
10 detachment, encampment, stronghold
13 fortification

garrulous
04 glib
05 gabby, gassy, windy, wordy
06 chatty, mouthy, prolix
07 prating, verbose, voluble
08 babbling, effusive
09 gossiping, prattling, talkative, yabbering
10 chattering, long-winded, loquacious

gas
09 pneumatic

▶ *Types of gas:*
04 neon
05 CS gas, ether, ozone, radon, xenon
06 butane, helium
07 ammonia, krypton, methane, propane, tear gas
08 fire damp, marsh gas, nerve gas
09 acetylene
10 chloroform, mustard gas, natural gas
11 laughing gas
12 nitrous oxide
13 carbon dioxide
14 carbon monoxide

gash
03 cut

04 nick, rend, rent, slit, tear
05 gouge, score, slash, wound
06 incise
08 incision, lacerate
10 laceration

gasp
04 blow, gulp, pant, puff
06 breath, wheeze
07 breathe
11 exclamation

gastric
09 abdominal
10 intestinal

gate
04 door, exit
06 access, portal
07 barrier, doorway, gateway, opening, passage
08 entrance

gather
04 crop, cull, draw, fold, gain, grow, heap, hear, mass, meet, pick, reap, tuck
05 amass, build, crowd, glean, group, hoard, infer, learn, pleat, pluck, rally, shirr
06 assume, deduce, garner, muster, pick up, pile up, pucker, pull in, ruffle, summon
07 advance, attract, believe, build up, cluster, collect, convene, harvest, hoard up, marshal, round up, surmise
08 assemble, conclude, converge, increase
09 stash away, stockpile
10 accumulate, congregate, understand
12 come together
13 bring together

gathering
03 mob
05 crowd, flock, group, horde, party, rally
06 throng
07 company, meeting
08 assembly, conclave, jamboree
10 assemblage, convention
11 convocation, get-together
12 congregation

gauche
03 shy
05 gawky, inept
06 clumsy
07 awkward, ill-bred
08 farouche, ignorant, tactless, ungainly
09 graceless, inelegant

10 uncultured, ungraceful, unpolished
15 unsophisticated

gaudy
04 loud
05 flash, harsh, showy, stark
06 bright, flashy, garish, glitzy, kitsch, snazzy, tawdry, vulgar
07 glaring, raffish
08 tinselly
09 brilliant, colourful, tasteless
12 meretricious, ostentatious
13 multicoloured

gauge
04 area, bore, norm, rate, rule, size, span, test
05 basic, check, count, depth, guess, guide, judge, meter, scope, value, weigh, width
06 assess, degree, extent, height, reckon, sample
07 apprise, calibre, compute, example, measure, pattern
08 estimate, evaluate, exemplar
09 ascertain, benchmark, calculate, criterion, determine, guideline, indicator, yardstick

➤ *Types of gauge. We have omitted the word* **gauge** *from names given in the following list but you may need to include this word as part of the solution to some crossword clues.*
04 rain, ring, snap, tide
05 drill, paper, steam, taper, water
06 feeler, radius, strain, vacuum
07 cutting, marking, mortise
08 gauge rod, pressure
➤ See also **measuring instrument**

gaunt
04 bare, bony, grim, lean, thin
05 bleak, harsh, stark
06 skinny, wasted
07 angular, forlorn, haggard
08 desolate, skeletal
09 emaciated
10 cadaverous, hollow-eyed
12 skin and bones

gauzy
05 filmy, light, sheer
06 flimsy
08 delicate, gossamer
10 diaphanous, see-through
11 transparent

gawk
04 gape, gaze, look, ogle

05 stare
06 goggle

gawky
05 inept, lanky
06 clumsy, gauche
07 awkward
08 gangling, ungainly
09 graceless
13 unco-ordinated

gay
03 fag
04 bent, camp, dyke, homo, poof
05 butch, fairy, gaudy, happy, nancy, pansy, queen, queer, showy, vivid
06 blithe, bright, faggot, flashy, garish, joyful, lively
07 festive, lesbian, woofter
08 animated, bisexual, carefree, cheerful, debonair
09 brilliant, colourful, fun-loving, sparkling, sprightly, vivacious
10 flamboyant, homosexual
12 light-hearted
15 pleasure-seeking

gaze
04 gape, gawk, look, view
05 stare, watch
06 goggle, regard, wonder
11 contemplate

gazebo
08 pavilion
09 belvedere
11 summerhouse

gazette
05 organ, paper
06 notice
07 journal
08 dispatch, magazine
09 news-sheet, newspaper

gear
03 cog, fit, kit
05 stuff, tools
06 attire, outfit, tackle
07 baggage, clothes, effects, gearing, luggage, prepare
08 clothing, cogwheel, organize, supplies, utensils
09 engrenage, equipment, gearwheel, machinery, mechanism
10 belongings, implements
11 accessories, instruments, possessions
12 contrivances
13 accoutrements, paraphernalia

gel, jell
03 set
07 congeal, thicken
08 solidify
09 coagulate, take shape
12 come together

gelatinous
05 gluey, gooey, gummy
06 sticky, viscid
07 jellied, rubbery, viscous
09 congealed, glutinous
12 mucilaginous

geld
06 neuter
08 castrate
10 emasculate

gem
05 jewel, prize, stone
08 gemstone, treasure
11 masterpiece, pride and joy
13 precious stone

▶ *Types of gemstone*:
03 jet
04 jade, onyx, opal, ruby
05 agate, amber, beryl, coral, pearl, topaz
06 garnet, jasper, zircon
07 cat's eye, citrine, crystal, diamond, emerald, peridot
08 amethyst, fire opal, sapphire
09 cairngorm, carbuncle, carnelian, cornelian, malachite, moonstone, tiger's eye, turquoise
10 aquamarine, bloodstone, chalcedony, chrysolite, rhinestone
11 chrysoberyl, lapis lazuli
13 mother-of-pearl, white sapphire

gen
04 data, dope, info
05 facts
07 details, low-down
09 knowledge
10 background
11 information

❑**gen up on**
05 study
08 bone up on, read up on, research, swot up on

genealogy
05 birth
06 family
07 descent, dynasty, lineage
08 ancestry, pedigree
09 parentage
10 family tree
13 family history

general
05 broad, loose, mixed, rough, total, usual, vague
06 common, global, normal, public, varied
07 blanket, overall, typical
08 accepted, assorted, everyday, habitual, ordinary, standard, sweeping
09 customary, extensive, imprecise, panoramic, prevalent, universal
10 ill-defined, indefinite, prevailing, unspecific, variegated, widespread
11 approximate, wide-ranging
12 all-inclusive
13 comprehensive, heterogeneous
14 across-the-board

generality
07 breadth
09 looseness, vagueness
10 commonness, popularity, prevalence
11 catholicity, ecumenicity, inexactness
12 universality
13 impreciseness
14 generalization, indefiniteness
15 approximateness

generally
06 mainly, mostly
07 as a rule, at large, broadly, chiefly, largely, usually
08 commonly, normally
09 in general
10 by and large, habitually, on the whole, ordinarily
11 customarily, in most cases, universally
14 for the most part

generate
04 form, make
05 breed, cause
06 arouse, create, whip up
07 produce
08 engender, initiate, occasion
09 originate, propagate
10 bring about, give rise to

generation
05 epoch
07 genesis
08 age group, breeding, creation
09 formation
10 production
11 procreation, propagation
12 reproduction

generic
06 common
07 blanket, general
09 inclusive, unbranded, universal
10 collective
12 all-inclusive
13 comprehensive

generosity
06 bounty
07 charity
08 goodness, kindness
10 lavishness, liberality
11 benevolence, magnanimity, munificence
12 philanthropy
14 big-heartedness, open-handedness

generous
03 big
04 free, full, good, kind, rich
05 ample, lofty, noble
06 lavish
07 copious, liberal
08 abundant, selfless
09 bountiful, plentiful, unselfish, unsparing
10 benevolent, big-hearted, charitable, munificent
11 magnanimous, overflowing
13 philanthropic

genesis
04 dawn, root
05 birth, start
06 origin, outset, source
08 creation, founding
09 beginning, formation, inception
10 generation
11 engendering, propagation

geneticist
▶ *Names of geneticists*:
05 **Jones** (Steve)
06 **Beadle** (George Wells), **Boveri** (Theodor Heinrich), **Fisher** (Sir Ronald Aylmer), **Galton** (Sir Francis), **Zinder** (Norton David)
07 **Bateson** (William), **De Vries** (Hugo Marie), **Lysenko** (Trofim)
08 **Yanofsky** (Charles)
09 **Lederberg** (Joshua)
10 **Darlington** (Cyril Dean), **Kettlewell** (Henry Bernard David), **McClintock** (Barbara), **Sturtevant** (Alfred Henry)
➤ See also **scientist**

genial
04 kind, warm
05 happy, jolly
06 hearty, jovial, kindly
07 affable, amiable, cordial
08 cheerful, pleasant, sociable
09 convivial, easy-going
11 good-natured
12 good-humoured

geniality
06 warmth
07 jollity
08 gladness, kindness
09 happiness, joviality
10 affability, amiability, cheeriness, cordiality, good nature, kindliness
12 cheerfulness, pleasantness

genie
04 jann
05 demon, fairy, jinni
06 jinnee, spirit

genitals
08 privates
09 genitalia
12 private parts, sexual organs

genius
04 bent, gift, nous, sage
05 adept, brain, flair, knack
06 boffin, brains
07 ability, egghead, faculty, maestro, prodigy
08 aptitude, capacity, fine mind, virtuoso
09 intellect
10 brilliance, cleverness, grey matter, mastermind
12 intellectual, intelligence
15 little grey cells

genocide
08 massacre
09 ethnocide, slaughter
15 ethnic cleansing

genre
04 form, kind, sort, type
05 brand, class, genus, group, style
06 school, strain
07 fashion, variety
08 category
09 character

genteel
05 civil
06 formal, polite, urbane
07 courtly, elegant, refined, stylish
08 cultured, graceful, ladylike, mannerly, polished, well-bred

09 courteous
10 cultivated
11 fashionable, gentlemanly, respectable
12 aristocratic, well-mannered

gentility
06 gentry, nobles
07 culture, decorum, manners
08 breeding, civility, courtesy, elegance, nobility, urbanity
09 blue blood, high birth, propriety
10 good family, politeness, refinement, upper class
11 aristocracy, courtliness, gentle birth

gentle
04 calm, easy, kind, mild, slow, soft
05 balmy, light, quiet
06 benign, humane, kindly, placid, serene, slight, smooth, tender
07 amiable, gradual, lenient
08 merciful, moderate, peaceful, pleasant, soothing, tranquil
11 soft-hearted, sympathetic
13 compassionate, imperceptible, tender-hearted

gentlemanly
05 civil, noble, suave
06 polite, urbane
07 gallant, genteel, refined
08 mannerly, obliging, polished, well-bred
09 civilized, courteous, reputable
10 cultivated, honourable

gentry
08 nobility
09 gentility
10 upper class
11 aristocracy

genuine
04 open, pure, real, true
05 frank, legal, pukka, sound
06 actual, candid, honest, lawful
07 earnest, factual, natural, sincere
08 bona fide, original, truthful
09 authentic, real McCoy, veritable
10 legitimate
13 unadulterated, with integrity

genus
03 set
04 kind, race, sort, type

05 breed, class, genre, group, order, taxon
07 species
08 category, division
11 subdivision

geography

➤ *Terms used in geography include:*
03 bay, col, cwm
04 arid, crag, mesa, tail, veld, wadi, wady
05 butte, delta, taiga, veldt
06 canyon, tundra, valley
07 caldera, equator, glacial, isthmus, volcano
08 alluvium, altitude, landmass, landslip, latitude, meridian
09 accretion, antipodes, billabong, deviation, ethnology, landslide, longitude, relief map
10 coordinate, glaciation, landlocked, topography
11 archipelago, cartography, conurbation, hydrography, vulcanology
13 shield volcano
14 plate tectonics

➤ *Names of geographers:*
03 **Dee** (John)
04 **Cary** (John)
05 **Barth** (Heinrich), **Cabot** (Sebastian)
06 **Strabo**
07 **Hakluyt** (Richard)
08 **Humboldt** (Alexander, Baron von), **Mercator** (Gerhardus), **Ortelius**
➤ See also **scientist**

geological

➤ *Names of geological periods:*
06 Eocene (Epoch)
07 Miocene (Epoch), Permian (Period)
08 Cambrian (Period), Cenozoic (Era), Devonian (Period), Holocene (Epoch), Jurassic (Period), Mesozoic (Era), Pliocene (Epoch), Silurian (Period), Tertiary (Period), Triassic (Period)
09 Oligocene (Epoch)
10 Cretaceous (Period), Ordovician (Period), Palaeocene (Epoch), Palaeozoic (Era), Quaternary (Period)

11 Pleistocene (Epoch),
Precambrian (Era)
13 Carboniferous (Period)

germ
03 bud, bug
04 root, seed
05 cause, spark, start, virus
06 embryo, origin, source,
sprout
07 microbe, nucleus
08 bacillus, fountain, rudiment
09 bacterium, beginning,
inception
13 micro-organism

germane
03 apt
04 akin
06 allied, proper
07 apropos, fitting, related
08 apposite, material, relevant,
suitable
09 connected, pertinent
10 applicable
11 appropriate

germinal
07 seminal
09 embryonic
10 developing, generative
11 rudimentary

germinate
03 bud
04 grow
05 shoot, swell
06 sprout
07 burgeon, develop
08 spring up, take root
09 originate

gestation
08 drafting, planning, ripening
09 evolution, pregnancy
10 conception, incubation,
maturation
11 development

gesticulate
04 sign, wave
06 motion, signal
07 gesture
08 indicate

gesticulation
04 sign, wave
06 motion, signal
07 gesture
08 movement
09 chironomy
10 indication

gesture
04 sign, wave
05 point
06 beckon, motion, signal

08 indicate, movement
11 gesticulate

get
03 buy, vex, win
04 coax, come, earn, gain,
make, take, trap, twig, urge
05 annoy, catch, fetch, get it,
grasp, reach, seize, snare
06 arrest, arrive, become,
bother, collar, come by,
fathom, induce, manage,
obtain, secure
07 achieve, acquire, capture,
collect, develop, procure,
provoke, realize, receive,
succeed
08 contract, convince, irritate,
organize, persuade,
purchase, talk into
09 influence, infuriate
10 comprehend, understand

❏**get about**
06 travel
09 move about
10 move around

❏**get across**
06 convey, impart
07 get over, put over
08 transmit
09 put across
11 communicate

❏**get ahead**
05 get on
06 thrive
07 advance, prosper, succeed
08 flourish, go places, progress
12 make your mark
14 go up in the world

❏**get along**
04 cope, fare
05 agree, get on
06 manage
07 develop, survive
08 hit it off, progress

❏**get at**
04 find, hint, mean, slam
05 imply, knock, slate
06 attack, intend, pick on
07 suggest
08 discover
09 criticize, insinuate
11 pick holes in
13 find fault with

❏**get away**
05 leave
06 depart, escape
07 run away

❏**get back**
06 recoup, regain, return

07 recover
08 retrieve
09 repossess, retaliate

❏**get by**
04 cope, fare
06 hang on, manage
07 subsist, survive
12 make ends meet

❏**get down**
06 alight, get off, sadden
07 depress, descend
08 dismount
09 disembark
10 dishearten

❏**get even**
05 repay
07 pay back, requite
11 reciprocate
12 settle a score
14 get your own back

❏**get in**
04 land
05 enter
06 arrive, embark

❏**get off**
04 shed
05 leave
06 alight, detach, remove
07 descend, get down
08 dismount, separate
09 disembark

❏**get on**
04 cope, fare
05 board, mount
06 ascend, embark, manage
07 advance, make out, press
on, proceed
08 continue, progress
12 hit it off with

❏**get out**
04 flee, quit
05 leave
06 depart, escape, vacate
07 produce
08 evacuate, withdraw
09 circulate

❏**get out of**
05 avoid, dodge, evade, shirk,
skive
06 escape

❏**get over**
06 convey, defeat, impart,
master
07 explain, put over, survive
08 complete, deal with,
overcome
11 communicate, pull through,
recover from

❑ get ready
07 arrange, prepare
08 rehearse

❑ get rid of
04 dump
05 eject, expel
06 remove, unload
08 jettison, shake off
09 eliminate, dispose of, get shot of, throw away
10 do away with
12 dispense with

❑ get round
04 coax, sway
05 avoid, evade
06 bypass, induce
07 win over
08 persuade
10 circumvent
11 prevail upon

❑ get there
06 arrive, make it
07 advance, prosper, succeed
08 go places, make good

❑ get together
04 join, meet
05 rally, unite
06 gather
07 collect
08 assemble, organize
10 congregate
11 collaborate

❑ get up
04 rise
05 arise, climb, mount, scale, stand
06 ascend
07 stand up

getaway
05 start
06 escape, flight
10 absconding, decampment

get-together
02 do
05 party, rally
06 social, soirée
07 meeting, reunion
08 assembly, function
09 gathering, reception

get-up
04 gear, togs
06 outfit, rig-out
07 clothes

ghastly
03 bad, ill
04 grim
05 awful, grave, nasty
06 horrid
07 hideous, serious

08 critical, dreadful, gruesome, horrible, shocking, terrible
09 appalling, frightful, loathsome, repellent
10 horrendous, terrifying
11 frightening

ghost
04 hint, soul
05 shade, spook, trace
06 shadow, spirit, wraith
07 phantom, spectre
08 presence, visitant
09 semblance
10 apparition, suggestion

ghostly
05 eerie, weird
06 creepy, spooky
07 phantom, shadowy
08 illusory, spectral
09 ghostlike, unearthly
10 wraith-like
12 supernatural

ghoulish
06 grisly, morbid
07 macabre
08 gruesome

giant
04 huge, ogre, vast
05 jumbo, large, titan
07 Cyclops, Goliath, immense, mammoth, massive, monster, titanic
08 behemoth, colossal, colossus, enormous, gigantic, king-size, whopping
10 gargantuan
14 Brobdingnagian

gibber
04 blab, cant
06 babble, cackle, gabble, jabber
07 blabber, chatter, prattle

gibberish
06 bunkum, drivel
07 prattle, rubbish, twaddle
08 cobblers, nonsense, tommyrot
10 balderdash, mumbo-jumbo
12 gobbledygook

gibe, jibe
03 dig
04 jeer, mock, poke, quip
05 crack, scoff, sneer, taunt, tease
06 deride
07 mockery, teasing
08 derision, ridicule

giddiness
06 frenzy, nausea, thrill
07 vertigo
09 animation, dizziness, faintness, wooziness
10 excitement, wobbliness
12 exhilaration
15 light-headedness

giddy
04 high, wild
05 dizzy, faint, woozy
06 elated
07 excited, reeling, stirred
08 frenzied, thrilled, unsteady
11 exhilarated, light-headed, vertiginous

gift
03 tip
04 bent, turn
05 bonus, flair, knack, offer, power, skill
06 bestow, bounty, confer, donate, genius, legacy, talent
07 ability, aptness, bequest, faculty, freebie, present
08 aptitude, donation, facility, gratuity, largesse, offering
09 attribute, endowment
10 capability, contribute
11 inheritance, proficiency
12 contribution

gifted
05 adept, sharp, smart
06 bright, clever, expert
07 capable, endowed, skilful, skilled
08 masterly, talented
09 brilliant
10 proficient
12 accomplished

gigantic
04 huge, vast
05 giant, jumbo
07 immense, mammoth, massive, titanic
08 colossal, enormous, king-size, whopping
10 gargantuan, monumental
14 Brobdingnagian

giggle
06 titter
07 snicker, snigger

gild
04 coat, deck, trim
05 adorn, array, grace, paint
06 bedeck, enrich
07 enhance, festoon, garnish
08 beautify, brighten, ornament

gilded
04 gilt, gold
06 golden
10 gold-plated

gimcrack
05 cheap, tacky
06 shoddy, tawdry, trashy

gimmick
04 ploy, ruse
05 dodge, stunt, trick
06 device, gadget, scheme
09 publicity, stratagem
10 attraction

gingerly
06 warily
07 charily
09 carefully, prudently
10 cautiously, delicately, hesitantly, watchfully
11 tentatively

Gipsy see **Gypsy**

gird
04 belt, bind, ring
05 brace, hem in, ready, steel
06 enfold, fasten, girdle
07 enclose, fortify, prepare
08 encircle, get ready, surround
09 encompass

girdle
04 band, belt, bind, gird, sash
06 cestus, circle, corset
07 enclose, go round
08 ceinture, cincture, cingulum, encircle, surround
09 waistband
10 cummerbund

girl
04 lass
06 au pair, maiden
08 daughter, teenager
09 young lady
10 adolescent, girlfriend, schoolgirl, sweetheart, young woman

girlfriend
04 bird, date, girl, lass
05 chick, lover
07 fiancée, partner
08 mistress, old flame
09 cohabitee, young lady
10 sweetheart

girlish
08 childish, immature, innocent, youthful
09 childlike
11 unmasculine

girth
04 band, bulk, size

05 strap
09 perimeter
13 circumference

gist
03 nub
04 core, crux, idea, pith
05 drift, point, sense
06 import, marrow, matter
07 essence, keynote, meaning
09 direction, substance
12 quintessence, significance

give
04 bend, cede, gift, lead, lend, move, sink, slip, tell
05 admit, allow, award, endow, grant, lay on, leave, put on, throw, utter, yield
06 accord, bestow, buckle, confer, convey, create, devote, direct, donate, impart, induce, prompt, reveal, supply
07 arrange, concede, declare, display, dispose, entrust, exhibit, furnish, give way, incline, present, produce, proffer, provide, publish
08 announce, bequeath, collapse, estimate, hand over, indicate, make over, manifest, occasion, organize, set forth, transfer, transmit, turn over
09 break down, pronounce
10 contribute, distribute
11 communicate, concentrate

❏**give away**
04 leak
06 betray, expose, reveal
07 concede, divulge, let slip
08 disclose, inform on

❏**give in**
04 quit
05 yield
06 give up, jack in, submit
07 concede, give way, succumb
08 pack it in
09 chuck it in, surrender
10 call it a day, capitulate
11 admit defeat
15 throw in the towel

❏**give off**
04 emit, vent
05 exude
06 exhale
07 give out, produce, release
08 throw out
09 discharge

❏**give on to**
06 lead to
08 open on to, overlook

❏**give out**
04 deal
05 allot
06 impart, notify, pack up
07 conk out, declare, dish out, dole out, hand out, mete out, publish
08 announce, transmit
09 advertise, break down, broadcast, circulate
10 distribute
11 communicate, disseminate

❏**give up**
04 quit, stop
05 cease, waive
06 cut out, give in, resign
07 abandon, concede
08 forswear, leave off, renounce
09 sacrifice, surrender
10 capitulate, relinquish
11 discontinue
15 throw in the towel

give-and-take
10 compliance, compromise
11 flexibility, negotiation
12 adaptability

given
05 prone
06 liable, likely
08 assuming, definite, disposed, distinct, inclined
09 specified
10 individual, particular
11 considering
12 in the light of
13 bearing in mind

giver
05 angel, donor
06 backer, friend, helper, patron
07 sponsor
08 promoter, provider
09 supporter
10 benefactor, subsidizer
11 contributor
14 philanthropist

glacial
03 icy, raw
04 cold
05 chill, gelid, polar, stiff
06 arctic, biting, bitter, chilly, frigid, frosty, frozen, wintry
07 brumous, hostile
08 freezing, inimical, piercing, Siberian

glad
04 keen

05 eager, happy, merry, ready
06 bright, cheery, elated, joyful
07 chuffed, gleeful, pleased, welcome, willing
08 cheerful, disposed, inclined, prepared, thrilled
09 contented, delighted, gratified

gladden
05 cheer, elate
06 buck up, please
07 delight, enliven, gratify, hearten, rejoice
08 brighten
09 encourage

gladly
04 fain
06 freely
07 happily, readily
09 willingly
10 cheerfully
12 with pleasure

gladness
03 joy
05 mirth
06 gaiety
07 delight, jollity
08 felicity, pleasure
09 happiness
10 brightness, joyousness
12 cheerfulness

glamorous
05 ritzy, smart
06 flashy, glitzy, glossy, lovely
07 elegant
08 alluring, charming, dazzling, exciting, gorgeous
09 appealing, beautiful
10 attractive, glittering
11 well-dressed

glamour
05 charm, magic
06 allure, appeal, beauty
07 glitter
08 elegance, prestige
10 attraction, excitement
14 attractiveness

glance
04 flip, leaf, look, peek, peep, scan, skim, view
05 dekko, flick
06 browse, gander
07 glimpse
08 butcher's

▫glance off
07 rebound
08 ricochet
09 bounce off

gland

━ *Types of gland:*

05 lymph, ovary
06 cortex, pineal, thymus
07 adrenal, eccrine, mammary, medulla, parotid, thyroid
08 pancreas, prostate, testicle
09 endocrine, lachrymal, lymph node, pituitary, sebaceous

glare
04 beam, glow, look
05 blaze, flame, flare, frown, scowl, shine, stare
06 dazzle, glower
07 daggers, reflect
09 black look, dirty look, spotlight
10 brightness, brilliance

glaring
05 gross, lurid, overt
06 patent
07 blatant, obvious
08 flagrant, manifest
10 outrageous
11 conspicuous

glass
04 lens
05 specs
06 beaker, goblet
07 crystal, monocle, tumbler, vitrics
08 pince-nez
09 lorgnette
10 spectacles

glassy
03 icy
04 cold, dull
05 blank, clear, dazed, empty, fixed, shiny
06 glazed, glossy, smooth, vacant
07 deadpan, vacuous
08 lifeless, polished, slippery, unmoving
11 transparent
12 crystal clear
14 expressionless

glaze
05 cover, gloss, shine
06 enamel, finish, lustre, polish
07 burnish, lacquer, varnish

gleam
03 ray
04 beam, glow
05 flare, flash, glint, gloss, shine
06 glance, lustre
07 flicker, glimmer, glisten, glitter, radiate, shimmer, sparkle

10 brightness
11 scintillate

glean
04 cull, pick, reap
05 amass, learn
06 garner, gather, pick up
07 collect, find out, harvest
10 accumulate

glee
07 delight, elation, triumph
08 pleasure
10 exultation
12 exhilaration

gleeful
05 happy
06 elated, joyful
07 pleased
08 exultant, jubilant
09 cock-a-hoop, delighted, exuberant, gratified, overjoyed
10 triumphant

glib
04 easy
05 slick, suave
06 facile, fluent, smooth
07 voluble
09 insincere, plausible
13 silver-tongued, smooth-talking, smooth-tongued

glide
03 fly, run
04 flow, pass, roll, sail, skim, slip
05 coast, drift, float, skate, slide

glimmer
03 ray
04 glow, hint, wink
05 blink, flash, gleam, glint, grain, shine, trace
07 glisten, inkling, shimmer, twinkle
10 suggestion

glimpse
03 spy
04 espy, look, peek, peep, spot, view
05 sight
06 glance, squint
08 sighting
12 catch sight of

glint
05 flash, gleam, shine
07 glimmer, glisten, twinkle
10 glistening
11 scintillate

glisten
05 flash, gleam, glint, shine
07 glimmer, shimmer
09 coruscate

glitter
05 gleam, glint, glitz, shine
06 dazzle, lustre, tinsel
07 glamour, glimmer, glisten, shimmer, sparkle, twinkle
09 coruscate, showiness, splendour
10 brightness, brilliance, flashiness, razzmatazz
11 coruscation, scintillate
12 razzle-dazzle

gloat
04 crow
05 boast, exult, glory, vaunt
06 relish
07 rejoice, revel in, rub it in, triumph

global
05 total
07 general
08 thorough
09 universal, worldwide
10 exhaustive
11 encylopedic, wide-ranging
13 comprehensive, international

globe
03 orb
04 ball
05 earth, round, world
06 planet, sphere

globular
05 round
07 globate
08 spheroid
09 orbicular, spherical

globule
04 ball, bead, drop
05 pearl
06 bubble, pellet
07 droplet, vesicle
08 globulet, particle, vesicula

gloom
03 woe
04 dark, dusk
05 cloud, grief, shade
06 misery, shadow, sorrow
07 despair, dimness, sadness
08 darkness, dullness, glumness, the blues, twilight
09 blackness, dejection, murkiness, pessimism
10 depression, desolation, low spirits, melancholy
11 despondency, unhappiness

gloomy
03 dim, low, sad
04 dark, down, dull, glum
05 dingy, drear, unlit
06 dismal, dreary, morose, sombre
08 dejected, desolate, downcast, overcast
09 depressed, miserable, sorrowful, tenebrous
10 depressing, despondent, dispirited, melancholy
11 crepuscular, down-hearted, pessimistic
12 disconsolate, in low spirits
14 down in the dumps

glorify
04 hail, laud
05 adore, bless, exalt, extol
06 honour, praise, revere, vilify
07 idolize, lionize, worship
08 eulogize, sanctify, venerate
09 celebrate
10 panegyrize
11 immortalize, romanticize

glorious
04 fine
05 famed, grand, great, noble, noted, super
06 bright, famous, superb
07 eminent, perfect, radiant, shining, supreme
08 dazzling, gorgeous, heavenly, honoured, majestic, renowned, splendid, terrific
09 beautiful, brilliant, excellent, wonderful
10 celebrated, marvellous, triumphant, victorious
11 illustrious, magnificent

glory
04 fame, pomp
05 boast, exult, gloat, kudos
06 honour, praise, renown
07 acclaim, majesty, rejoice, tribute, triumph, worship
08 accolade, blessing, eminence, grandeur, prestige, radiance
09 adoration, celebrity, gratitude, greatness, splendour
10 exaltation, veneration
12 magnificence, resplendence, thanksgiving
15 illustriousness

gloss
04 mask, note, show, veil
05 front, gleam, sheen, shine
06 define, façade, lustre, polish, veneer
07 comment, explain, shimmer, sparkle, varnish
08 annotate, construe, disguise, footnote, scholion
09 elucidate, interpret, semblance, translate
10 appearance, brightness, brilliance, commentary, definition
11 elucidation, explanation, explication, translation
14 interpretation, window-dressing

❑gloss over
04 hide, mask, veil
05 avoid, evade
06 ignore
07 conceal, cover up
08 disguise
09 whitewash
10 camouflage, smooth over
11 explain away
13 draw a veil over

glossy
05 shiny, silky, sleek
06 bright, glassy, glazed, sheeny, smooth
07 shining
08 gleaming, lustrous, polished
09 brilliant, burnished, enamelled, sparkling

glove
04 gage, mitt
06 mitten
08 gauntlet

glow
04 burn
05 blush, flush, gleam, light, shine
06 ardour, colour, redden, warmth
07 burning, fervour, glimmer, passion, radiate, redness
08 grow pink, look pink, pinkness, radiance, richness, rosiness, smoulder
09 intensity, splendour, vividness
10 brightness, brilliance, enthusiasm, luminosity
12 satisfaction

glower
04 look
05 frown, glare, scowl, stare
09 black look, dirty look
11 look daggers

glowing
04 rave, rich, warm
05 ruddy, vivid
06 bright
07 flaming, flushed, vibrant
08 ecstatic, luminous

09 laudatory, rhapsodic
10 eulogistic, favourable
11 panegyrical, smouldering
12 enthusiastic, incandescent
13 complimentary

glue
03 fix, gum
04 bond, seal, size
05 affix, paste, stick
06 cement, mortar
08 adhesive, fixative
11 agglutinate

gluey
05 gummy
06 sticky, viscid
07 viscous
08 adhesive
09 glutinous

glum
03 low, sad
04 down, sour
05 gruff, moody, sulky, surly
06 gloomy, morose, sullen
07 crabbed, doleful, unhappy
09 depressed, miserable
10 despondent
14 down in the dumps

glut
04 clog, cram, fill, sate
05 choke, flood, gorge, stuff
06 deluge, excess
07 satiate, surfeit, surplus
10 oversupply
11 superfluity
14 superabundance

glutinous
05 gluey, gummy
06 mucous, sticky, viscid
07 viscous
08 adhesive, cohesive

glutton
03 pig
07 gobbler, guzzler
08 gourmand
10 greedy guts

gluttonous
05 gutsy
06 greedy
07 hoggish, piggish
10 gluttonish, insatiable, omnivorous
12 gormandizing

gluttony
05 greed
08 voracity
10 greediness
11 gourmandism, piggishness

gnarled
05 bumpy, lumpy, rough

06 gnarly, knotty, rugged
07 knotted, twisted
08 leathery, wrinkled
09 contorted, distorted
13 weather-beaten

gnash
04 grit
05 grate, grind

gnaw
03 eat, nag
04 bite, chew, fret, prey, wear
05 erode, harry, haunt, munch, worry
06 crunch, devour, harass, nibble, niggle, plague
07 consume, torment, trouble
09 masticate

go
03 act, bid, fit, get, run, try
04 bash, fare, head, lead, move, pass, quit, scat, shot, span, stab, suit, turn, walk, work
05 begin, drive, end up, fit in, leave, match, occur, reach, scoot, scram, sound, start
06 accord, be axed, become, depart, effort, energy, extend, manage, repair, result, set off, set out, spirit, travel, vanish, vigour
07 advance, attempt, give off, journey, operate, perform, pizzazz, proceed, stretch
08 continue, dynamism, function, progress, vitality, withdraw
09 animation, disappear, endeavour, harmonize
10 co-ordinate, complement, correspond, get-up-and-go, make a sound, make tracks
13 take your leave

❑**go about**
06 tackle
07 address, perform
08 approach, attend to, engage in, set about
09 undertake

❑**go ahead**
05 begin
07 advance, carry on, proceed
08 continue, progress

❑**go along with**
04 obey
06 accept, follow
07 abide by, support
09 agree with
10 comply with, concur with

❑**go around**
09 circulate

❑**go at**
05 argue, blame
06 attack, tackle
08 set about
09 criticize

❑**go away**
05 leave
06 depart, vanish
07 abscond, retreat
08 withdraw
09 disappear

❑**go back**
06 return, revert
07 retreat

❑**go back on**
04 deny
08 renege on
09 default on

❑**go by**
04 flow, heed, obey, pass
05 lapse
06 elapse, follow
07 observe
10 comply with

❑**go down**
04 drop, fail, fall, fold, lose, sink
07 decline, descend, founder
08 be beaten, collapse, decrease, fall down, submerge
10 degenerate
11 deteriorate
12 come a cropper

❑**go for**
04 like
05 enjoy
06 aim for, attack, choose, prefer, rush at, select
07 assault, lunge at
08 set about

❑**go in for**
05 adopt, enter
06 follow, pursue, take up
07 embrace, espouse
08 engage in, practise
09 undertake

❑**go into**
05 probe, study
06 review
07 analyse, dissect, examine
08 check out, consider, look into, research
09 delve into
10 scrutinize
11 investigate

❑**go off**
03 rot
04 quit, sour, turn
05 blast, burst, go bad, leave

06 blow up, depart
07 abscond, explode
08 detonate
09 disappear
11 deteriorate

☐ **go on**
03 gab, gas
04 last, stay
05 occur
06 endure, happen, natter,
   rabbit, remain, witter
07 carry on, chatter, persist,
   proceed
08 continue, ramble on
09 take place

☐ **go out**
04 date, exit
05 court, leave
06 depart
08 go steady, withdraw

☐ **go over**
04 list, read, scan
05 check, study
06 peruse, review, revise
07 discuss, examine, inspect
08 look over, rehearse

☐ **go through**
04 bear, hunt
05 check, use up
06 endure, suffer
07 consume, examine, undergo
08 squander
10 experience
11 investigate, look through

☐ **go together**
03 fit
04 suit
05 blend, match
06 accord
09 harmonize
10 co-ordinate, complement

☐ **go under**
04 fail, flop, fold, sink
06 go bust
07 founder, succumb
08 collapse, submerge

☐ **go with**
03 fit
04 suit, take
05 blend, match, usher
06 escort
09 accompany, harmonize
10 co-ordinate, complement

☐ **go without**
04 lack, want
06 forego
07 abstain
09 do without

goad
03 nag, vex
04 jolt, prod, push, spur, urge
05 annoy, drive, hound, impel,
   prick, taunt
06 arouse, harass, incite,
   induce, prompt
07 inspire, provoke
08 irritate, motivate
09 instigate, stimulate
10 pressurize

go-ahead
02 OK
05 pushy
07 consent, dynamic, forward
08 approval, sanction, thumbs-
   up, vigorous, warranty
09 ambitious, clearance,
   energetic, go-getting
10 aggressive, green light,
   permission, pioneering
11 opportunist, progressive
12 confirmation, enterprising
13 authorization
14 forward-looking

goal
03 aim, end
06 design, object, target
07 purpose
08 ambition
09 intention, objective
10 aspiration

gobble
04 bolt, cram, gulp, wolf
05 gorge, scoff, stuff
06 devour, guzzle

gobbledygook
06 drivel, jargon
07 prattle, rubbish, twaddle
08 nonsense
10 balderdash, journalese
12 psychobabble

go-between
05 agent
06 broker, medium
08 mediator
09 messenger, middleman
12 intermediary

goblin
03 elf, imp
05 bogey, demon, fiend,
   gnome, nixie
06 kelpie, kobold, red-cap,
   spirit, sprite
07 brownie, gremlin
09 hobgoblin

God
04 King, Lord, Zeus
05 Allah, Deity

06 Brahma, Father, Yahweh
07 Holy One, Jehovah
08 Almighty
12 Supreme Being

god, goddess
04 icon, idol
05 deity, power
06 spirit
08 divinity
11 divine being, graven image
➤ See also **mythology**

► *Names of Egyptian gods*:
03 Geb, Nut
04 Apis, Aten, Ptah, Seth
05 Horus, Thoth
06 Amun-Re, Anubis, Osiris

► *Names of Egyptian
goddesses*:
04 Isis, Maat
06 Hathor
07 Sekhmet
08 Nephthys

► *Names of Greek gods*:
03 Pan
04 Ares, Eros, Zeus
05 Atlas, Hades
06 Adonis, Aeolus, Apollo,
   Boreas, Cronus, Helios,
   Hermes
07 Nemesis, Oceanus
08 Dionysus, Ganymede,
   Morpheus, Poseidon,
   Thanatos
09 Asclepius
10 Hephaestus

► *Names of Greek goddesses*:
03 Eos
04 Gaia, Hebe, Hera, Iris, Nike,
   Rhea
06 Athene, Cybele, Hecate,
   Selene
07 Artemis, Demeter
08 Arethusa
09 Aphrodite
10 Persephone

► *Names of Hindu gods*:
04 Agni, Kama, Rama, Siva
05 Indra, Shiva, Surya
06 Brahma, Ganesa, Varuna,
   Vishnu
07 Ganesha, Hanuman, Krishna
08 Nataraja
09 Prajapati
10 Jagannatha

► *Names of Hindu goddesses*:
04 Kali, Maya, Sita
05 Aditi, Durga, Sakti
06 Shakti
07 Lakshmi, Parvati
09 Sarasvati, Saraswati

➤ *Names of Norse gods*:
03 Bor, Otr, Tyr, Ull
04 Frey, Logi, Loki, Njord, Thor
05 Aegir, Alcis, Mimir, Njord,
   Vidar, Woden, Wotan
06 Balder, Fafnir, Weland
07 Wayland, Weiland
08 Heimdall

➤ *Names of Norse goddesses*:
03 Hel, Ran, Sif
05 Frigg, Idunn, Nanna, Norns
06 Freyja, Gefion
07 Nerthus
09 Valkyries

➤ *Names of Roman gods*:
04 Mars
05 Cupid, Fides, Janus, Lares,
   Pluto
06 Apollo, Faunus, Genius,
   Saturn, Vulcan
07 Bacchus, Jupiter, Mercury,
   Mithras, Neptune, Penates
08 Silvanus

➤ *Names of Roman
goddesses*:
03 Ops
04 Juno, Maia
05 Ceres, Diana, Epona,
   Fauna, Flora, Venus, Vesta
06 Pomona
07 Bellona, Egreria, Fortuna,
   Minerva
08 Victoria
10 Prosperina

God-forsaken
05 bleak
06 lonely, remote
08 deserted, desolate, isolated
09 miserable
10 depressing

godless
05 pagan
06 sinful, unholy, wicked
07 heathen, impious, profane,
   ungodly
08 agnostic
09 atheistic, faithless
10 irreverent
11 irreligious, nullifidian

godlike
04 holy
06 divine, sacred
07 deiform, exalted, sublime
08 heavenly
09 celestial
10 superhuman
11 theomorphic
12 transcendent

godly
04 good, holy, pure
05 moral, pious
06 devout
07 saintly
09 believing, religious,
   righteous
10 God-fearing

godsend
04 boon
07 bonanza, miracle
08 blessing, windfall

goggle
04 gawk, gawp, gaze
05 stare

going-over
05 check, study
06 attack, review, survey
07 beating, check-up, chiding,
   pasting
08 analysis, scolding, scrutiny,
   whipping
09 criticism, reprimand,
   thrashing, trouncing
10 inspection
11 castigation, examination
12 chastisement

goings-on
08 business, mischief
10 activities, happenings
11 occurrences
12 misbehaviour
13 funny business

gold
06 nugget
07 bullion

golden
04 fair, gilt, gold, rosy
05 blond, happy
06 blonde, flaxen, gilded,
   yellow
08 glorious, lustrous
09 brilliant, promising,
   treasured
10 auspicious, favourable,
   propitious
11 flourishing, resplendent

golf
➤ *Types of golf club*:
04 iron, wood
05 spoon
06 driver, mashie, putter
07 brassie, midiron, niblick
09 sand wedge
10 mashie iron
11 driving iron
13 mashie niblick

➤ *Names of golfers*:
04 **Lyle** (Sandy)

05 **Braid** (James), **Davis**
   (Laura), **Faldo** (Nick),
   Hagen (Walter), **Hogan**
   (Ben), **Jones** (Bobby),
   Snead (Sam Jackson),
   Woods (Tiger)
06 **Garcia** (Sergio), **Nelson**
   (Byron), **Norman** (Greg),
   Palmer (Arnold), **Player**
   (Gary), **Vardon** (Harry)
07 **Jacklin** (Tony), **Sarazen**
   (Gene), **Stewart** (Payne),
   Trevino (Lee Buck),
   Woosnam (Ian)
08 **Nicklaus** (Jack), **Olazabal**
   (Jose Maria), **Torrance**
   (Sam)
09 **Whitworth** (Kathy)
11 **Ballesteros** (Severiano),
   Montgomerie (Colin)
➤ See also **sport**

gone
04 away, dead, done, lost, over,
   past, used
05 spent
06 absent, astray
07 elapsed, missing
08 departed, finished, vanished
11 disappeared
15 over and done with

goo
03 mud
04 crud, grot, gunk, mire,
   muck, ooze, scum, yuck
05 grime, gunge, slime, slush
06 grease, matter, sludge
10 stickiness

good
04 able, gain, kind, nice, sake
05 adept, large, merit, moral,
   noble, right, sound, valid
06 behalf, honest, honour,
   loving, polite, profit, useful,
   virtue, worthy
07 benefit, capable, fitting,
   genuine, honesty, purpose,
   skilful, skilled, upright
08 adequate, complete,
   goodness, gracious, interest,
   intimate, passable, pleasant,
   pleasing, reliable, sensible,
   suitable, superior, talented,
   thorough, vigorous, virtuous
09 advantage, agreeable,
   competent, compliant,
   efficient, enjoyable,
   excellent, fantastic,
   fortunate, righteous,
   tolerable, wellbeing
10 acceptable, auspicious,
   beneficial, benevolent,

dependable, favourable, good as gold, honourable, proficient, propitious, reasonable, satisfying, usefulness, worthwhile
11 appropriate, commendable, kind-hearted, pleasurable, substantial, uprightness, well-behaved
12 advantageous, considerable, satisfactory
13 philanthropic, righteousness
14 salt of the earth

□ for good
04 ever
06 always
07 for ever
08 evermore
09 eternally
10 for all time
11 permanently

□ make good
02 do
05 go far
06 effect, fulfil
07 succeed
08 carry out, get ahead, live up to, progress, put right
12 be successful
13 compensate for, make amends for, put into action
15 get on in the world

goodbye
03 bye
04 ciao, ta-ta
05 adieu, adios
06 bye-bye, cheers, so long
07 cheerio, parting
08 au revoir, farewell, sayonara, swan song, take care
11 arrivederci, be seeing you, leave-taking, valediction
14 auf Wiedersehen

good-for-nothing
03 bum
04 idle, lazy
05 idler
06 loafer, no-good, waster
07 useless, wastrel
08 feckless, indolent, layabout
09 lazy-bones, reprobate, worthless
10 black sheep, ne'er-do-well, profligate

good-humoured
05 happy
06 genial, jovial
07 affable, amiable
08 cheerful, friendly, pleasant

09 congenial
12 good-tempered

good-looking
04 fair
06 comely, lovely, pretty
08 handsome
09 beautiful
10 attractive
11 presentable

goodly
04 good, tidy
05 ample, large
08 sizeable
10 sufficient
11 significant, substantial
12 considerable

good-natured
04 kind
06 gentle, kindly
07 helpful, patient
08 friendly, generous, tolerant
10 benevolent
11 kind-hearted, sympathetic, warm-hearted
12 good-tempered

goodness
06 virtue
07 benefit, honesty, probity
08 goodwill, kindness
10 compassion, generosity
11 helpfulness, uprightness
13 righteousness, wholesomeness

goods
04 gear
05 stuff, wares
07 effects, freight
08 chattels, products, property
10 belongings
11 merchandise, possessions

goodwill
05 amity
06 favour
08 kindness
10 compassion, friendship, generosity
11 benevolence
12 friendliness

goody-goody
05 pious
08 priggish
13 sanctimonious, self-righteous

gooey
04 soft
05 gluey, gungy, tacky, thick
06 sloppy, sticky, syrupy, viscid
07 maudlin, mawkish, viscous

09 glutinous
11 sentimental

gore
04 stab
05 blood, cruor, grume, spear, stick, wound
06 impale, pierce
09 bloodshed, slaughter
10 bloodiness

gorge
03 gap
04 bolt, cram, feed, fill, glut, pass, rift, sate, wolf
05 abyss, chasm, cleft, gully
06 canyon, defile, devour, ravine
07 overeat, surfeit

gorgeous
04 rich, sexy
05 grand, showy
06 lovely, pretty, superb
07 opulent
08 dazzling, glorious, splendid, stunning
09 beautiful, glamorous, luxurious, ravishing, sumptuous
10 attractive, delightful, impressive, marvellous
11 good-looking, magnificent, resplendent

gory
06 bloody, brutal, grisly, savage
10 sanguinary
12 bloodstained

gospel
05 credo, creed, truth
06 verity
08 doctrine, good news, teaching
09 certainty
12 New Testament

gossamer
04 airy, fine, thin
05 gauzy, light, sheer, silky
06 flimsy
08 cobwebby, delicate
10 diaphanous, see-through
11 translucent, transparent

gossip
03 gas, jaw
04 chat, talk
06 natter, rabbit, report, rumour, tattle
07 blether, chinwag, hearsay, scandal, tattler, whisper
08 busybody, chitchat, idle talk
09 tell tales, whisperer
10 chew the fat, talebearer

11 mud-slinging
12 tittle-tattle
13 scandalmonger

gouge
03 cut, dig
04 claw, gash, hack
05 scoop, score, slash
06 chisel, groove, hollow, incise

gourmand
03 hog, pig
07 glutton, guzzler
08 omnivore
11 gormandizer

gourmet
06 foodie
07 epicure
09 bon vivant, epicurean
10 gastronome
11 connoisseur

govern
04 curb, head, lead, rule
05 check, quell, reign, steer
06 direct, manage
07 command, conduct, contain, control, preside
08 dominate, regulate, restrain
09 be in power, influence
10 administer, hold office
11 keep in check, superintend

governess
06 duenna, mentor
07 teacher, tutress
08 tutoress
11 gouvernante
12 instructress

governing
06 ruling
07 guiding, leading
09 dominant, reigning
10 commanding, regulatory
11 controlling, predominant

government
04 rule, sway
05 power, state
06 charge, régime
07 command, control
08 dominion, ministry
09 authority, restraint
10 domination, leadership, management, parliament
11 authorities, sovereignty
12 powers that be
14 administration

➤ *Types of government*:
05 junta
06 empire
07 kingdom
08 monarchy, republic

09 autocracy, communism, democracy, despotism, theocracy
10 absolutism, federation, hierocracy, plutocracy
11 triumvirate
12 commonwealth, dictatorship
➤ See also **politics**

governor
04 boss, head
05 chief, guide, ruler
06 leader, master, warden
07 manager, viceroy
08 director, overseer
09 commander, president
10 controller, supervisor
12 commissioner
13 administrator

gown
04 garb, robe
05 dress, frock, habit
07 costume, garment

grab
03 bag, nab
04 grip, nail, take
05 catch, grasp, pluck, seize
06 clutch, collar, snap up, snatch
07 capture
10 commandeer, take hold of
11 appropriate, catch hold of

❑ **up for grabs**
07 to be had
09 available
10 obtainable

grace
05 adorn, charm, mercy, poise
06 beauty, enrich, favour, honour, pardon, polish, prayer, set off, virtue
07 charity, decency, decorum, dignify, enhance, finesse, fluency
08 blessing, breeding, clemency, courtesy, decorate, elegance, goodness, goodwill, leniency, ornament
09 embellish, etiquette, good taste, propriety
10 compassion, generosity, indulgence, kindliness, loveliness, refinement
11 beneficence, benevolence, cultivation, forgiveness, shapeliness
13 consideration
14 attractiveness

➤ *Names of the Three Graces*:
06 Aglaia, Thalia
10 Euphrosyne
➤ See also **mythology**

graceful
05 agile, fluid
06 nimble, smooth, supple
07 elegant, flowing, slender
08 charming, cultured, polished, tasteful
09 appealing, beautiful
10 attractive, cultivated

graceless
04 rude
05 crude, gawky, rough
06 clumsy, coarse, forced, gauche, vulgar
07 awkward, uncouth
08 impolite, improper, ungainly
09 barbarous, inelegant, shameless
10 indecorous
11 ill-mannered
12 unattractive
15 unsophisticated

gracious
04 kind, mild
06 kindly, polite
07 elegant, lenient, refined
08 friendly, generous, merciful, obliging, pleasant, tasteful
09 courteous, luxurious, sumptuous
10 beneficent, hospitable
11 considerate, kind-hearted
13 accommodating

gradation
04 mark, rank, step
05 array, level, stage
06 change, degree, series
07 grading, shading, sorting
08 ordering, sequence
10 succession
11 arrangement, progression

grade
04 mark, rank, rate, rung, size, sort, step, type
05 brand, class, order, place, range, stage
06 assess, degree, rating, status
07 arrange, echelon, quality, station
08 category, classify, evaluate, position, standard, standing
10 categorize, pigeonhole
14 classification

❑ **make the grade**
04 pass
07 succeed

gradient
04 bank, hill, rise
05 grade, slope
07 incline
09 acclivity, declivity

gradual
04 easy, even, slow
06 gentle, steady
07 regular
08 measured, moderate
10 continuous, step-by-step

gradually
06 evenly, gently, slowly
08 bit by bit
09 by degrees, piecemeal
10 cautiously, inch by inch, moderately, step by step
12 continuously, successively
13 imperceptibly, progressively
14 little by little

graduate
04 pass, rank, sort
05 grade, group, order, range
06 alumna, fellow, master, move up
07 advance, alumnus, mark off, qualify
08 bachelor, graduand, progress
09 calibrate

graft
03 bud
04 join, scam, slog, toil
05 affix, scion, shoot, sting
06 effort, growth, insert, labour, rip-off, splice, sprout
07 bribery, engraft, implant
08 hard work
09 con tricks, extortion
10 corruption, dishonesty, transplant
11 dirty tricks
12 implantation
14 sharp practices
15 sweat of your brow

grain
03 bit, jot, nap, rye
04 atom, corn, iota, oats, seed
05 crumb, maize, scrap, speck, trace, wheat
06 barley, kernel, morsel
07 cereals, granule, modicum, pattern, soupçon, texture
08 fragment, molecule, particle
09 scintilla
10 suggestion

grand
04 arch, fine, head, main
05 chief, final, great, large, lofty, noble, regal, showy, super

06 lavish, lordly, senior, superb
07 highest, leading, opulent, pompous, stately, supreme
08 glorious, imposing, majestic, palatial, smashing, splendid, striking, terrific
09 ambitious, enjoyable, excellent, fantastic, first-rate, grandiose, luxurious, principal, sumptuous, wonderful
10 impressive, marvellous, monumental, pre-eminent
11 illustrious, magnificent, outstanding, pretentious
12 ostentatious

grandeur
07 dignity, majesty
08 eminence, nobility, opulence
09 greatness, splendour
10 importance, lavishness, prominence
11 stateliness
12 magnificence
13 luxuriousness
14 impressiveness

grandfather
07 grandad, grandpa
08 granddad

grandiloquent
07 flowery, fustian, orotund, pompous
08 inflated
09 bombastic, high-flown
10 euphuistic, rhetorical
11 exaggerated, pretentious
12 high-sounding, magniloquent

grandiose
05 grand, lofty, showy
07 pompous, stately
08 imposing, majestic, splendid, striking
09 ambitious, high-flown
10 flamboyant, monumental
11 extravagant, magnificent, pretentious
12 high-sounding, ostentatious

grandmother
03 nan
04 gran
06 granny
07 grandma

grant
04 gift, give
05 admit, allow, award
06 accept, bestow, confer, donate, permit, supply

07 agree to, annuity, bequest, bursary, concede, furnish, pension, present, provide, subsidy
08 accede to, donation
09 allowance, apportion, consent to, endowment, vouchsafe
10 concession, contribute, honorarium
11 acknowledge, scholarship

granule
03 jot
04 atom, bead, iota, seed
05 crumb, grain, piece, scrap, speck
06 pellet
08 fragment, molecule, particle

granular
05 lumpy, rough, sandy
06 grainy, gritty
07 crumbly, friable

graph
04 grid, plot
05 chart, curve, table
07 diagram
08 bar chart, pie chart

graphic
05 clear, drawn, lucid, vivid
06 cogent, lively, visual
08 detailed, explicit, specific, striking
09 effective, pictorial, realistic
10 blow-by-blow, expressive
11 delineative
12 diagrammatic, illustrative

grapple
04 grab, grip, hold
05 clasp, fight, grasp, seize
06 clutch, combat, engage
07 address, contend, wrestle
08 confront, cope with, deal with, struggle
09 encounter, lay hold of
14 get to grips with

grasp
03 get, see
04 grab, grip, hold
05 catch, clasp, seize
06 clutch, master, take in
07 catch on, command, embrace, grapple, mastery, realize
08 clutches, perceive
09 awareness, knowledge, lay hold of
10 comprehend, perception, possession, understand
11 familiarity

13 comprehension, understanding

grasping
06 greedy
08 covetous
09 mercenary, rapacious
10 avaricious
11 acquisitive

grass
03 lea
04 lawn, mead, turf
05 downs, field, green, sward
06 common, meadow
07 pasture

► *Types of grass*:
03 rye
04 bent, cane, corn, oats, reed, rice
05 maize, paddy, wheat
06 bamboo, barley, fescue, millet
07 esparto, papyrus, sorghum, wild oat
08 ryegrass
09 buckwheat, cocksfoot, knot grass, marijuana, sugar cane
10 couch grass
11 marram grass, meadow grass, pampas grass, twitch grass
13 kangaroo grass
➢ See also **plant**

grate
03 irk, jar, vex
04 gall, rasp
05 annoy, grind, peeve, shred
06 rankle, scrape
07 scratch
08 irritate
09 aggravate

grateful
07 obliged
08 beholden, indebted, thankful
09 obligated
12 appreciative

gratification
05 kicks
06 relish, thrill
07 delight, elation
08 pleasure
09 enjoyment
10 indulgence
12 satisfaction

gratify
06 cosset, favour, fulfil, humour, pamper, please
07 delight, gladden, indulge, placate, satisfy
08 pander to

grating
04 grid
05 frame, grate, harsh
06 grille
07 irksome, jarring, rasping
08 annoying, grinding, scraping
10 discordant, irritating, scratching

gratis
04 free
08 at no cost, buckshee
10 for nothing, on the house
12 free of charge
13 complimentary

gratitude
06 thanks
10 obligation
12 appreciation, gratefulness, indebtedness, thankfulness

gratuitous
04 free
06 gratis, unpaid, wanton
08 needless
09 unmerited, voluntary
10 for nothing, unasked-for, undeserved
11 superfluous, uncalled-for, unjustified, unnecessary, unsolicited, unwarranted
12 free of charge
13 complimentary

gratuity
03 tip
04 boon, gift, perk
05 bonus
06 bounty, reward
07 present
08 donation, largesse
09 baksheesh, pourboire
10 perquisite, recompense

grave
04 grim, tomb
05 acute, cairn, crypt, death, quiet, sober, staid, vault
06 barrow, gloomy, solemn, sombre, urgent
07 crucial, exigent, pensive, serious, subdued, weighty
08 critical, fatality, perilous, pressing, reserved
09 dangerous, dignified, hazardous, important, long-faced, mausoleum, sepulchre
10 burial site
11 burial mound, burial place, significant, threatening

gravel
04 grit
06 stones
07 pebbles, shingle

gravelly
05 gruff, harsh, rough, thick
06 grainy, gritty, hoarse, pebbly
07 grating, shingly, throaty
08 granular, guttural

gravestone
08 memorial

graveyard
08 cemetery, God's acre
10 churchyard, necropolis
12 burial ground, charnel house

gravitate
04 drop, fall, lean, move, sink, tend
05 drift
06 settle
07 descend, head for, incline
09 be drawn to
11 precipitate

gravity
04 pull
06 danger, hazard, weight
07 dignity, reserve, urgency
08 exigency, grimness, severity, sobriety
09 acuteness, heaviness, restraint, solemnity
10 attraction, importance
11 gravitation, seriousness, weightiness
12 significance
13 momentousness

graze
03 rub
04 crop, feed, kiss, skim, skin
05 brush, chafe, shave, touch
06 abrade, browse, scrape
07 pasture, scratch
08 abrasion

grease
03 fat, oil
04 lard
06 tallow
08 dripping
11 lubrication

greasy
04 oily, waxy
05 fatty, lardy, oleic, slimy
07 adipose, buttery
08 slippery, unctuous
09 sebaceous
10 oleaginous

great
03 ace, big
04 able, cool, huge, mega, vast
05 chief, crack, famed, grand, jumbo, large, major, noted
06 august, expert, famous, superb, wicked

07 crucial, eminent, extreme, immense, leading, mammoth, massive, notable, primary, salient, serious, skilful, skilled

08 colossal, critical, enormous, fabulous, gigantic, imposing, masterly, renowned, sizeable, smashing, spacious, splendid, terrific, top-notch, virtuoso, whopping

09 admirable, boundless, brilliant, dexterous, essential, excellent, excessive, extensive, fantastic, first-rate, ginormous, important, momentous, practised, principal, prominent, wonderful

10 celebrated, impressive, inordinate, marvellous, proficient, remarkable, tremendous

11 illustrious, magnificent, outstanding, substantial

12 accomplished, considerable

13 distinguished

greatly
04 much
06 highly, hugely, vastly
08 markedly, mightily
09 extremely, immensely
10 abundantly, enormously
11 exceedingly
12 considerably
13 significantly, substantially

greatness
04 fame, note
05 glory, power
06 genius, renown, weight
08 eminence, grandeur
09 intensity, magnitude
10 excellence, importance
11 distinction, seriousness
12 significance

greed
07 avarice, edacity
08 cupidity, gluttony, rapacity, voracity
09 esurience
11 gourmandism, hoggishness, piggishness
12 covetousness, ravenousness
13 insatiability
15 acquisitiveness

greedy
06 grabby, hungry
07 hoggish, piggish, selfish

08 covetous, desirous, edacious, esurient, grabbing, grasping
09 rapacious, voracious
10 avaricious, cupidinous, gluttonous, insatiable
12 gormandizing

green
03 lea, new, raw
04 lawn, lush, turf
05 field, fresh, grass, leafy, naïve, sward, young
06 common, grassy, meadow, recent, tender, unripe
07 budding, envious, healthy, jealous, pasture, verdant
08 covetous, glaucous, ignorant, immature, inexpert, unversed
09 grassland, resentful, untrained
10 ecological, unseasoned
11 eco-friendly, flourishing, unqualified
13 environmental, inexperienced
15 conservationist, unsophisticated

greenery
07 foliage, verdure
08 verdancy
10 vegetation, virescence

greenhorn
04 tiro
06 novice, rookie
07 learner
08 beginner, initiate, neophyte, newcomer
09 fledgling
10 apprentice, tenderfoot

greenhouse
08 hothouse
10 glasshouse

greet
04 hail, kiss, meet
05 nod to
06 accost, salute, wave to
07 address, receive, welcome
10 say hello to
11 acknowledge

greeting
03 nod
04 wave
05 hallo
07 address, welcome
09 handshake, reception
10 salutation
15 acknowledgement

greetings
04 love
07 regards
08 respects
10 best wishes, good wishes
11 salutations

gregarious
06 social
07 affable, cordial
08 friendly, outgoing, sociable
09 convivial, extrovert
13 companionable

grey
03 dim, wan
04 dark, dull, pale
05 ashen, bleak, foggy, misty, murky
06 cloudy, dismal, dreary, gloomy, leaden, pallid
07 neutral, unclear
08 doubtful, overcast
09 ambiguous, cheerless, debatable, uncertain
10 colourless, depressing
13 uninteresting
14 open to question

grid
05 frame, grill
06 grille
07 grating, lattice, trellis
08 gridiron

grief
03 woe
04 pain
05 agony
06 misery, regret, sorrow
07 anguish, despair, remorse, sadness
08 distress, mourning
09 heartache, suffering
10 affliction, depression, desolation, heartbreak
11 bereavement, despondency, lamentation, tribulation, unhappiness

grief-stricken
03 sad
07 unhappy
08 desolate, grieving, mourning, wretched
09 anguished, sorrowful, sorrowing
10 devastated, distressed
11 heartbroken
12 inconsolable
13 broken-hearted

grievance
05 gripe, trial, wrong
06 grouse

07 grumble, offence, protest, trouble
09 complaint, objection
10 bone to pick, resentment

grieve
04 ache, hurt, mope, pain, weep
05 brood, crush, mourn, shock, upset, wound
06 dismay, lament, offend, sadden, sorrow, suffer
07 afflict, horrify
08 distress

grievous
05 grave
06 severe, tragic
08 damaging, dreadful, shocking
09 appalling, atrocious, injurious, monstrous
10 deplorable, outrageous, unbearable
11 devastating, distressing

grim
04 dire, dour
05 awful, harsh, stern, surly
06 dogged, fierce, gloomy, grisly, horrid, morose, severe, sullen
07 ghastly
08 dreadful, fearsome, gruesome, horrible, menacing, obdurate, resolute, shocking, sinister, stubborn, terrible
09 appalling, harrowing, tenacious
10 depressing, determined, forbidding, formidable, horrendous, inexorable, persistent, unpleasant, unshakable, unyielding
11 frightening, threatening

grimace
04 face, pout
05 frown, mouth, scowl, smirk, sneer
09 make a face, pull a face

grime
03 mud
04 crud, dirt, dust, grot, muck, soot, yuck
05 filth, gunge
06 grunge

grimy
05 dirty, dusty, mucky, muddy, sooty
06 filthy, grubby, smudgy, smutty, soiled

grind
03 rub
04 file, mill, rasp, sand, toil, whet
05 crush, grate, grind, pound
06 abrade, kibble, labour, polish, powder
07 crumble, slavery
08 drudgery, levigate
09 comminute, granulate, pulverize, triturate

▢grind down
05 crush
08 wear down

grip
03 bag, hug
04 case, grab, hold
05 catch, clasp, cling, grasp, power, rivet, seize
06 clench, clutch, compel, engage, kitbag, valise
07 command, control, embrace, engross, enthral, hold-all, involve, mastery
08 clutches, entrance, suitcase
09 fascinate, get hold of, hypnotize, influence, latch onto, mesmerize, spellbind
10 domination, grab hold of
11 catch hold of, shoulder-bag
12 overnight bag
13 travelling bag

▢come to grips with, get to grips with
05 grasp
06 tackle, take on
08 confront, cope with, deal with, face up to

gripe
03 nag
04 beef, carp, moan
05 bitch, groan, whine
06 grouch, grouse, whinge
07 griping, grumble, protest
08 complain
09 bellyache, complaint, grievance, objection
15 have a bone to pick

gripping
08 exciting, riveting
09 absorbing, thrilling
10 compelling, compulsive, engrossing, entrancing
11 enthralling, fascinating
12 spellbinding
13 unputdownable

grisly
04 gory, grim
05 awful
06 horrid

07 ghastly, hideous, macabre
08 dreadful, gruesome, horrible, shocking, terrible
09 abhorrent, appalling, frightful, loathsome, repulsive, revolting
10 abominable, disgusting, horrifying

grit
04 dust, guts, rasp, sand
05 gnash, grate, grind
06 clench, gravel, mettle, scrape
07 bravery, courage, pebbles, resolve, shingle
08 backbone, hardness, strength, tenacity
09 endurance, toughness
10 doggedness, resolution
12 perseverance
13 determination, steadfastness

gritty
05 brave, hardy, sandy, tough
06 dogged, grainy, plucky, spunky
08 abrasive, granular, gravelly, resolute, spirited
09 steadfast, tenacious
10 courageous, determined, mettlesome

grizzle
04 fret, moan
05 whine
06 snivel, whinge
07 grumble, sniffle, snuffle, whimper
08 complain

grizzled
04 grey
05 hoary
07 greying
09 canescent
10 grey-haired, grey-headed
13 pepper-and-salt

groan
04 moan
05 whine
06 grouch, grouse, lament, object, outcry, whinge
07 griping, grumble, protest
08 complain
09 bellyache, complaint, grievance

grocer
10 victualler
11 greengrocer, supermarket

groggy
- 05 dazed, dizzy, dopey, faint, muzzy, shaky, woozy
- 06 wobbly
- 07 stunned
- 08 confused, unsteady
- 09 befuddled, stupefied
- 10 bewildered, punch-drunk

groom
- 03 fix
- 04 tidy
- 05 brush, coach, curry, drill, preen, prime, train, tutor
- 06 school, tidy up
- 07 arrange, husband, prepare, smarten
- 08 instruct, spruce up
- 09 stableboy, stable lad
- 10 bridegroom, stable hand, stable lass

groove
- 03 cut, rut
- 04 slot
- 05 canal, ditch, gouge, ridge, score, track
- 06 furrow, gutter, rabbet, rebate, sulcus, trench, trough
- 07 chamfer, channel
- 11 indentation

grooved
- 06 fluted, rutted, scored, sulcal
- 07 exarate, sulcate
- 08 furrowed, rabbeted
- 09 chamfered
- 10 channelled
- 12 scrobiculate

grope
- 04 feel, fish, hunt, pick
- 06 fumble, search
- 08 flounder, scrabble
- 09 cast about

gross
- 03 big, fat
- 04 blue, earn, huge, lewd, make, rude, take
- 05 bawdy, bulky, crude, dirty, heavy, large, obese, plain, sheer, total, utter, whole
- 06 coarse, earthy, entire, filthy, ribald, risqué, smutty, vulgar
- 07 blatant, boorish, glaring, hulking, immense, massive, obscene, obvious, serious
- 08 colossal, complete, flagrant, grievous, improper, indecent, manifest, outright, shameful, shocking

- 09 aggregate, before tax, corpulent, egregious, offensive, tasteless
- 10 outrageous, overweight, uncultured
- 11 insensitive

grotesque
- 03 odd
- 04 ugly
- 05 weird
- 07 bizarre, hideous, macabre, strange, surreal, twisted
- 08 deformed, fanciful, freakish
- 09 distorted, fantastic, ludicrous, malformed, misshapen, monstrous, unnatural, unsightly, whimsical
- 10 outlandish, ridiculous
- 11 extravagant

grotto
- 04 cave
- 06 cavern
- 08 catacomb

grouch
- 04 moan
- 05 gripe
- 06 grouse, moaner, whiner, whinge
- 07 grumble, whinger
- 08 grumbler
- 09 complaint, grievance, objection
- 10 belly-acher, complainer, crosspatch, malcontent
- 11 fault-finder

grouchy
- 05 cross, sulky, surly, testy
- 06 grumpy
- 08 captious, churlish, petulant
- 09 crotchety, grumbling, irascible, irritable, querulous, truculent
- 11 bad-tempered
- 12 cantankerous

ground
- 04 base, call, clay, dirt, dust, land, lees, loam, park, plot, soil
- 05 acres, arena, basis, coach, dregs, earth, field, found, pitch, score, train, tutor
- 06 bottom, campus, domain, estate, excuse, fields, inform, motive, reason, settle
- 07 account, deposit, dry land, educate, gardens, holding, prepare, residue, stadium, surface, terrain

- 08 initiate, instruct, property, sediment
- 09 establish, introduce, principle, scourings, territory
- 10 foundation, terra firma
- 11 precipitate, vindication
- 12 acquaint with, surroundings
- 13 justification

groundless
- 05 empty, false
- 08 baseless, illusory
- 09 imaginary, unfounded
- 11 unjustified, unsupported
- 15 unsubstantiated

groundwork
- 04 base
- 05 basis
- 07 footing
- 08 homework, research
- 09 spadework
- 10 essentials, foundation
- 11 preparation

group
- 03 lot, set
- 04 band, body, club, crew, gang, knot, link, mass, pack, rank, sort, team, unit
- 05 batch, bunch, class, crowd, flock, genus, order, party, troop
- 06 circle, clique, family, gather, huddle
- 07 arrange, cluster, collect, company, coterie, element, faction, marshal
- 08 assemble, assembly, category, classify, organize
- 09 associate, formation, gathering
- 10 categorize, collection, congregate, contingent
- 11 association, combination
- 12 congregation, organization

grouse
- 04 beef, carp, moan
- 05 bitch, gripe, groan, whine
- 06 grouch, whinge
- 07 grumble, protest
- 08 complain
- 09 bellyache, complaint, find fault, grievance, objection

grove
- 04 wood
- 05 copse
- 06 arbour, avenue, covert
- 07 coppice, spinney, thicket

grovel
- 04 fawn

05 cower, crawl, creep, defer, kneel, stoop, toady
06 cringe, crouch, kowtow, lie low, suck up
07 bow down, flatter, lie down
08 kiss up to
12 bow and scrape
14 demean yourself

grow
03 bud, get, sow, wax
04 farm, rise, stem, turn
05 arise, breed, issue, plant, raise, shoot, swell, widen
06 become, change, expand, extend, mature, spread, spring, sprout, thrive
07 advance, burgeon, develop, enlarge, fill out, improve, produce, stretch, thicken
08 flourish, increase, lengthen, multiply, mushroom, progress
09 cultivate, germinate, originate, propagate
11 proliferate

growl
03 yap
04 bark, howl, roar, snap, yelp
05 snarl
06 rumble

grown-up
03 man
05 adult, of age, woman
06 mature
09 full-grown
10 fully-grown

growth
04 lump, rise
06 spread, tumour
07 advance
08 increase, progress, swelling
09 evolution, expansion, extension, flowering, outgrowth, sprouting
10 burgeoning, maturation
11 development, enlargement, excrescence
13 amplification, magnification, proliferation
14 multiplication

grub
03 dig
04 eats, food, hunt, lava, nosh, pupa, root, tuck, worm
05 delve, meals
06 burrow, ferret, forage, maggot, search
07 rummage
08 excavate
10 sustenance

11 caterpillar
12 refreshments

grubby
05 dirty, grimy, messy, mucky, seedy
06 filthy, shabby, soiled
07 scruffy, squalid

grudge
04 envy, hate, mind
05 covet, pique, spite, venom
06 animus, enmity, hatred, malice, resent
07 dislike, ill-will, rancour
08 aversion, begrudge, jealousy, object to
09 animosity, antipathy, grievance
10 antagonism, bitterness, resentment
12 hard feelings

grudging
07 envious, jealous
09 reluctant, resentful, unwilling
11 half-hearted

gruelling
04 hard
05 harsh, tough
06 severe, taxing, tiring, trying
07 arduous
08 crushing, draining, grinding
09 demanding, difficult, laborious, punishing, strenuous
10 exhausting
12 backbreaking

gruesome
04 grim
05 awful
06 grisly, horrid
07 ghastly, hideous, macabre
08 dreadful, horrible, horrific, shocking, terrible
09 abhorrent, appalling, frightful, loathsome, monstrous, repellent, repugnant, repulsive, revolting, sickening
10 abominable, disgusting

gruff
04 curt, rude, sour
05 blunt, harsh, husky, rough, surly, testy, thick
06 abrupt, grumpy, hoarse, sullen, tetchy
07 brusque, rasping, throaty
08 croaking, impolite
11 bad-tempered
12 discourteous

grumble
04 beef, carp, moan
05 bitch, gripe, growl, whine
06 grouch, grouse, object, whinge
07 protest
08 complain
09 bellyache, complaint

grumpy
05 cross, ratty, sulky, surly
06 snappy, sullen, tetchy
07 crabbed, grouchy, in a huff, in a sulk
09 crotchety, irritable
11 bad-tempered, ill-tempered
12 cantankerous, discontented

guarantee
04 back, bond, oath
06 assure, ensure, insure, pledge, secure, surety
07 certify, earnest, endorse, promise, protect, warrant
08 contract, covenant, make sure, security, vouch for, warranty
09 assurance, insurance
10 collateral, underwrite
11 make certain
12 word of honour

guarantor
05 angel
06 backer, surety
08 bailsman, bondsman
09 guarantee, warrantor
10 covenantor
11 underwriter

guard
04 mind, save, wall
05 cover, fence, scout, watch
06 beware, buffer, bumper, defend, escort, fender, keeper, minder, patrol, picket, police, screen, secure, sentry, shield, warder
07 barrier, be alert, cushion, defence, look out, lookout, oversee, protect, shelter
08 defender, guardian, preserve, security, sentinel, take care, watchman
09 bodyguard, conductor, custodian, keep watch, protector, safeguard, supervise
10 protection

□ off your guard
06 unwary
07 napping, unaware
08 careless, unawares

10 unprepared
11 inattentive
12 unsuspecting

▢on your guard
04 wary
05 alert, ready
07 careful
08 cautious, vigilant, watchful
09 attentive, wide awake
10 on the alert
11 circumspect
12 on the lookout

guarded
04 wary
05 cagey, chary
07 careful
08 cautious, discreet, reserved, reticent, watchful
09 reluctant, secretive
10 restrained
11 circumspect
12 non-committal

guardian
05 guard
06 escort, keeper, warden, warder
07 curator, steward, trustee
08 champion, defender
09 attendant, caretaker, custodian, preserver, protector

guardianship
04 care
05 aegis, guard, hands, trust
07 custody, defence, keeping
08 guidance, wardship
09 patronage
10 wardenship
11 curatorship, safekeeping, stewardship, trusteeship

guerrilla
08 partisan
09 irregular, maquisard, terrorist
11 bushwhacker, franc-tireur
14 freedomfighter

guess
05 fancy, hunch, judge, think
06 assume, reckon, theory
07 suppose, surmise
08 consider, estimate
09 judgement, postulate, reckoning, speculate
10 assumption, conjecture, hypothesis, make a guess, prediction
11 guesstimate, hypothesize, speculation, supposition
13 shot in the dark
14 ballpark figure

guesswork
06 theory
07 surmise
09 intuition, reckoning
10 assumption, conjecture, estimation, hypothesis
11 guesstimate, speculation, supposition

guest
06 lodger
07 boarder, visitor
08 resident, visitant

guesthouse
03 inn
05 hotel
06 hostel
07 pension
08 hostelry
12 rooming-house
13 boarding-house

guidance
03 tip
04 help, hint, rule, tips
05 hints
06 advice, charge
07 control, counsel, pointer
08 teaching
09 direction
10 assistance, directions, guidelines, indication, leadership, suggestion
11 counselling, indications, information, instruction, suggestions

guide
03 ABC, key
04 guru, lead, mark, norm, rule, show, sign
05 gauge, model, pilot, point, steer, teach, train, tutor, usher
06 advise, attend, beacon, direct, escort, govern, leader, manage, manual, marker, mentor, ranger, signal
07 adviser, command, conduct, control, counsel, courier, educate, example, measure, oversee, pattern, pointer, teacher
08 chaperon, director, exemplar, handbook, instruct, navigate, signpost, standard
09 archetype, attendant, benchmark, catalogue, companion, conductor, criterion, directory, guidebook, guideline,

influence, manoeuvre, yardstick
10 counsellor, indication, instructor, show the way
11 preside over, superintend

guideline
05 terms
06 advice
07 measure
08 standard
09 benchmark, criterion, direction, framework, parameter, principle, procedure, yardstick
10 constraint, regulation, suggestion, touchstone
11 information, instruction
14 indication rule, recommendation

guild
07 company, society
08 alliance, sorority
10 fellowship, fraternity
11 association, brotherhood, corporation
12 organization

guile
04 ruse
05 craft, fraud
06 deceit
07 cunning, knavery, slyness
08 artifice, trickery, wiliness
10 artfulness, cleverness, craftiness, trickiness
11 deviousness
12 gamesmanship
13 double-dealing

guileless
04 open
05 frank, naïve
06 direct, honest, simple
07 artless, genuine, sincere
08 innocent, straight, trusting, truthful
09 ingenuous, unworldly
11 transparent
15 straightforward, unsophisticated

guilt
05 blame, shame, wrong
06 regret
07 remorse
08 disgrace
09 dishonour, penitence
10 conscience, contrition, misconduct, repentance, wrongdoing
11 compunction, criminality, culpability
12 self-reproach, unlawfulness

14 responsibility, self-
accusation
15 blameworthiness

guiltless
04 pure
05 clean, clear
07 sinless
08 innocent, spotless
09 blameless, faultless,
stainless, undefiled,
unspotted, unsullied,
untainted
10 impeccable, inculpable
11 untarnished
13 above reproach,
unimpeachable

guilty
03 bad
04 evil
05 sorry, wrong
06 sinful, wicked
07 ashamed, at fault, to blame
08 blamable, contrite, criminal,
culpable, sheepish
09 convicted, offending
10 shamefaced
11 blameworthy, responsible
12 compunctious

guise
04 face, form, mask, show
05 front, shape
06 aspect, custom, façade,
manner
08 disguise, likeness, pretence
09 behaviour, demeanour,
semblance
10 appearance

gulf
03 bay
04 cove, hole, rift, void
05 abyss, basin, bight, chasm,
cleft, gorge, inlet, split
06 canyon, hollow, ravine
07 crevice, fissure, opening
10 separation

gullet
03 maw
04 craw, crop
06 throat
10 oesophagus

gullibility
07 naïvety
09 credulity, innocence
10 simplicity
12 trustfulness

gullible
05 green, naïve
07 foolish
08 innocent, trustful, trusting

09 credulous, ingenuous
12 unsuspecting
13 inexperienced
14 impressionable
15 unsophisticated

gully
05 ditch, gorge
06 canyon, gutter, ravine, valley
07 channel

gulp
04 bolt, swig, wolf
05 quaff, stuff, swill
06 devour, gobble, guzzle
07 draught, swallow
08 mouthful, tuck into

gum
03 fix
04 clog, glue, seal
05 affix, paste, resin, stick
06 cement
08 adhesive, fixative

▢**gum up**
04 clog
05 choke
06 hinder, impede
08 obstruct

gummy
05 gluey, gooey, tacky
06 sticky, viscid
07 viscous

gumption
03 wit
04 nous
05 savvy
06 acumen
07 ability
08 sagacity
09 acuteness
10 astuteness, cleverness,
shrewdness
11 common sense,
discernment

gun
04 Colt®
05 fusil, rifle
06 airgun, cannon, mortar,
musket, pistol
07 bazooka, carbine, firearm,
shooter
08 howitzer, revolver
09 flintlock
10 Winchester®
11 blunderbuss

gunman
06 hit man, killer, sniper
08 assassin, murderer, shootist
10 gunslinger

gurgle
04 crow

05 plash
06 babble, bubble, burble,
murmur, ripple, splash

guru
04 sage
05 swami, tutor
06 expert, leader, master,
mentor, pundit
07 teacher
08 luminary, Svengali
09 authority, maharishi
10 instructor
12 guiding light

gush
03 jet, run
04 flow, fuss, go on, pour, rush,
tide, well
05 burst, flood, issue, spate,
spout, spurt, surge
06 babble, drivel, effuse, jabber,
stream
07 cascade, chatter, enthuse
08 outburst
10 outpouring

gushing
05 gushy
06 sickly
07 cloying, fulsome, mawkish
08 effusive
09 emotional, excessive
10 saccharine
11 sentimental

gust
03 fit
04 blow, gale, puff, rush, wind
05 blast, burst, surge
06 breeze, flurry, squall
07 bluster

gusto
04 élan, zeal, zest
05 verve
06 energy, relish
07 delight, fervour
09 enjoyment
10 enthusiasm, exuberance
12 exhilaration

gusty
05 blowy, windy
06 breezy
07 squally
08 blustery

gut
04 draw, grit, loot, sack
05 basic, belly, clean, clear,
empty, nerve, pluck, rifle,
spunk, strip
06 bottle, bowels, innate,
mettle, ravage

07 bravery, courage, enteral, enteric, innards, insides, plunder, ransack, stomach, viscera

08 audacity, backbone, boldness, clean out, clear out, entrails

09 devastate, fortitude, heartfelt, intuitive

10 deep-seated, disembowel, eviscerate, intestines

11 instinctive, vital organs

gutless
04 weak
06 abject, craven, feeble
07 chicken
08 cowardly
09 spineless
11 lily-livered
12 faint-hearted
14 chicken-hearted, chicken-livered

gutsy
04 bold, game
05 brave
06 plucky
07 gallant, staunch
08 resolute, spirited
10 courageous, determined, mettlesome

gutter
04 duct, pipe, tube
05 ditch, drain, sewer
06 sluice, trench, trough
07 channel, conduit, culvert

guttersnipe
04 waif
05 gamin
06 urchin
07 mudlark
10 ragamuffin

guttural
03 low
04 deep
05 gruff, harsh, husky, thick
06 hoarse
07 grating, rasping, throaty
08 croaking, gravelly

guy
03 boy, lad, man
04 chap
05 bloke, youth
06 fellow, person

guzzle
04 bolt, cram, gulp, swig, wolf
05 quaff, scoff, stuff, swill
06 devour, gobble
07 put away, swallow
08 tuck into
09 knock back, polish off

gymnastics
➢ See also **sport**
► *Gymnastic events include*:
04 beam
05 clubs, rings
07 high bar
08 tumbling
10 horse vault
11 pommel horse
12 parallel bars, trampolining

13 horizontal bar
14 asymmetric bars, floor exercises
► *Names of gymnasts*:
03 **Kim** (Nellie), **Ono** (Takashi)
06 **Korbut** (Olga), **Retton** (Mary Lou)
08 **Comaneci** (Nadia), **Latynina** (Larissa)
09 **Andrianov** (Nikolai), **Caslavska** (Vera)

Gypsy, Gipsy
03 rom, rye
05 nomad, rover
06 hawker, Romany, tinker
07 rambler, tzigany
08 Bohemian, diddicoy, huckster, wanderer
09 traveller

gyrate
04 spin, turn
05 swirl, twirl, wheel, whirl
06 circle, rotate, spiral, swivel
07 revolve
09 pirouette

gyration
04 spin, turn
05 swirl, twirl, whirl
06 circle, spiral, swivel
08 rotation, spinning, wheeling, whirling
09 pirouette
10 revolution

H

habit
- 03 way
- 04 bent, mode, robe, ways, wont
- 05 dress, quirk, usage
- 06 custom, manner, outfit
- 07 costume, leaning, routine
- 08 clothing, practice, tendency, vestment
- 09 addiction, mannerism
- 10 dependence, proclivity, propensity
- 11 inclination
- 12 second nature
- 14 matter of course

habitable
- 11 fit to live in, inhabitable

habitat
- 04 home
- 06 domain
- 07 element, terrain
- 08 dwelling, locality
- 09 territory
- 11 environment
- 12 surroundings

habitation
- 03 pad
- 04 home
- 05 abode, house
- 07 housing, lodging, mansion
- 08 domicile, dwelling, quarters
- 09 occupancy, residence, residency
- 13 accommodation, dwelling-place
- 14 living quarters

habitual
- 03 set
- 05 fixed, usual
- 06 common, normal, wonted
- 07 chronic, regular, routine
- 08 addicted, constant, hardened
- 09 confirmed, customary
- 10 inveterate, persistent
- 11 established, traditional

habituate
- 05 adapt, inure, train
- 06 harden, school, season
- 07 break in

- 08 accustom
- 09 condition
- 10 make used to
- 11 acclimatize, familiarize

habitué
- 06 patron
- 07 denizen, regular
- 10 frequenter

hack
- 03 cut, hew, saw
- 04 chop, fell, gash
- 05 clear, notch, slash, slave
- 06 mangle, writer
- 08 lacerate, mutilate
- 09 scribbler
- 10 journalist

hackle

□ make somone's hackles rise
- 03 bug, irk, vex
- 04 gall, miff, rile
- 05 anger, annoy
- 06 bother, enrage, hassle, madden, needle, nettle, offend, ruffle
- 07 affront, incense, outrage, provoke
- 08 irritate
- 09 aggravate, infuriate
- 10 antagonize, exasperate
- 15 get on your nerves

hackneyed
- 05 banal, corny, stale, stock, tired, trite
- 06 common
- 07 clichéd, worn-out
- 08 overused, time-worn
- 10 overworked, pedestrian, uninspired, unoriginal
- 11 commonplace, stereotyped
- 12 cliché-ridden, run-of-the-mill
- 13 platitudinous, unimaginative

hag
- 05 crone, harpy, shrew, witch
- 06 gorgon, virago
- 08 harridan
- 09 battle-axe, termagant

haggard
- 03 wan
- 04 pale, thin
- 05 drawn, gaunt
- 06 pallid, wasted
- 07 drained, ghastly, pinched
- 08 careworn, shrunken
- 13 hollow-cheeked

haggle
- 06 barter, bicker, dicker, higgle
- 07 bargain, dispute, wrangle
- 08 beat down, squabble
- 09 negotiate

hail
- 04 come, laud, pelt, rain
- 05 cheer, exalt, greet, storm
- 06 batter, honour, praise, salute, shower, volley, wave to
- 07 acclaim, bombard, welcome
- 08 flag down, signal to
- 09 call out to, originate
- 11 acknowledge, bombardment
- 14 have your home in
- 15 have your roots in

hair
- 03 fur, mop
- 04 coat, hide, mane, pelt, wool
- 05 locks, shock
- 06 fleece
- 07 tresses
- 10 Barnet fair

□ let your hair down
- 05 relax
- 08 chill out, loosen up
- 09 hang loose
- 13 let yourself go
- 15 let it all hang out

□ not turn a hair
- 08 stay cool
- 12 keep your cool
- 14 not bat an eyelid

□ split hairs
- 05 cavil
- 07 nit-pick, quibble
- 09 find fault

hair's-breadth
- 04 hair, inch
- 07 whisker

hairdo
03 cut, set
05 style
08 coiffure

hairdresser
06 barber
07 stylist
08 coiffeur
09 coiffeuse

hairless
04 bald
05 shorn
06 shaven
08 tonsured
09 beardless

hair-raising
05 eerie, scary
06 creepy
08 alarming, exciting, shocking
09 startling, thrilling
10 horrifying, petrifying,
   terrifying
11 frightening

hairstyle
03 cut, set
08 coiffure

► *Hairstyles include:*
02 DA
03 bob, bun, wig
04 Afro, crop, perm
05 bangs, braid, plait, quiff
06 curled, fringe, pouffe, toupee
07 beehive, chignon, cowlick,
   crewcut, crimped, mohican,
   pageboy, pigtail, shingle,
   tonsure, topknot
08 bouffant, Eton crop,
   ponytail, ringlets, skinhead
09 duck's arse, hair-piece,
   pompadour
10 dreadlocks

hairy
05 bushy, furry, fuzzy
06 fleecy, pilose, shaggy,
   woolly
07 bearded, hirsute
08 unshaven

halcyon
04 calm, mild
05 balmy, happy, quiet, still
06 gentle, golden, placid,
   serene
07 pacific
08 carefree, peaceful, tranquil
10 prosperous
11 flourishing, undisturbed

hale
03 fit
04 well

05 sound
06 hearty, robust, strong
07 healthy
09 in the pink
10 able-bodied
12 in fine fettle

half
04 part, semi-
05 share
06 barely, halved, partly, slight
07 divided, limited, partial,
   portion, section, segment
08 bisected, fraction,
   moderate, slightly
09 bisection, equal part,
   partially
10 equal share, fractional,
   hemisphere, incomplete,
   moderately, semicircle
12 divided in two, fifty per cent
13 hemispherical

□ **by half**
03 too
04 very
11 excessively
12 considerably

□ **by halves**
12 inadequately, incompletely

□ **not half**
04 very
06 indeed, really
09 not nearly

half-baked
05 crazy, silly
06 stupid
07 foolish
09 ill-judged, senseless
11 impractical, undeveloped
12 ill-conceived

half-caste
06 Creole, mestee
07 mestiza, mestizo, mulatta,
   mulatto
08 quadroon
09 quintroon
10 quarteroon

half-hearted
04 weak
06 feeble
08 listless, lukewarm
09 apathetic
10 lacklustre
11 indifferent, unconcerned
14 unenthusiastic

halfway
03 mid
04 mean
06 median, middle, midway
07 central

09 centrally
11 equidistant, in the middle
12 intermediate

□ **meet someone halfway**
09 make a deal, negotiate
11 give and take
15 make concessions

halfwit
03 ass, mug, nit
04 clot, dope, dork, dupe, fool,
   geek, prat, twit
05 chump, dumbo, dunce,
   moron, ninny, twerp, wally
06 cretin, dimwit, nitwit,
   stooge
07 buffoon, fat-head, pillock,
   plonker
08 imbecile
09 birdbrain, blockhead,
   ignoramus, simpleton
10 nincompoop

half-witted
04 dull, dumb
05 barmy, batty, crazy, dotty,
   nutty, potty, silly
06 simple, stupid
07 foolish, idiotic, moronic
08 crackpot
09 dim-witted
12 crack-brained, feeble-
   minded, simple-minded

hall
05 foyer, lobby
07 chamber, passage
08 corridor
09 vestibule
10 auditorium, passageway
12 assembly room

hallmark
04 mark, sign
05 badge, stamp
06 device, emblem, symbol
09 brand-name, trademark
10 indication

hallowed
04 holy
06 sacred
07 blessed, revered
09 dedicated
10 inviolable, sacrosanct,
   sanctified
11 consecrated

hallucinate
04 trip
05 dream
08 daydream, freak out
09 fantasize, see things
13 imagine things

hallucination
04 trip
05 dream
06 mirage, vision
07 fantasy, figment
08 daydream, delirium, delusion, freak-out, illusion
10 apparition
14 phantasmagoria

halo
04 aura, ring
05 crown, glory
06 corona, gloria, nimbus
07 aureola, aureole
08 gloriole, halation, radiance

halt
03 end
04 curb, quit, rest, stem, stop
05 break, cease, check, pause
06 arrest, desist, draw up, finish, impede, pull up
08 deadlock, hold back, stoppage
09 cessation, terminate
10 call it a day, put an end to, standstill
11 come to a stop, discontinue, termination
12 interruption
13 bring to a close

halting
06 broken
07 awkward
08 hesitant, laboured, unsteady
09 faltering, imperfect, stumbling, uncertain
10 stammering, stuttering

halve
05 share, split
06 bisect, divide
07 cut down
10 split in two
11 dichotomize

halved
06 shared
07 divided
08 bisected

hammer
03 din, hit
04 bang, bash, beat, drum, form, lick, make, plug, rout, slam, slap, slog
05 drive, force, grind, knock, mould, pound, shape
06 attack, batter, beetle, defeat, drudge, instil, keep on, labour, mallet, strike, thrash
07 clobber, outplay, persist, run down, trounce
08 overcome

09 criticize, denigrate, drive home, overwhelm, persevere, reiterate,
10 annihilate

▫ hammer out
06 finish, settle
07 resolve, sort out, work out
09 negotiate, thrash out
10 accomplish

hamper
03 box
04 curb, foil, stop
05 block, check, cramp
06 basket, bridle, fetter, hinder, hold up, impede, retard, stymie, thwart
07 inhibit, pannier, prevent, shackle
08 encumber, handicap, obstruct, restrain, restrict
09 frustrate, hamstring

hamstring
04 foil, stop
05 check, cramp
06 hinder, hold up, impede, stymie, thwart
07 cripple, disable
08 encumber, handicap, paralyse, restrain, restrict
09 frustrate
12 incapacitate

hand
03 aid, fin, paw
04 care, fist, give, help, mitt, palm, part, pass
05 arrow, offer, power, yield
06 charge, convey, marker, worker
07 acclaim, command, conduct, control, custody, deliver, ovation, pointer, present, succour, support, workman, writing
08 applause, cheering, clapping, clutches, employee, farm-hand, hand over, handclap, hireling, labourer, transmit
09 authority, indicator, influence, operative
10 assistance, management, penmanship, possession
11 calligraphy, handwriting, helping hand, supervision

▫ at hand
04 near
05 close, handy, ready
06 to hand
08 imminent
10 accessible

▫ by hand
08 manually

▫ from hand to mouth
12 precariously
14 on the breadline

▫ hand down
04 give, will
05 grant, leave
06 pass on
08 bequeath, pass down

▫ hand in glove
11 very closely

▫ hand in hand
14 closely related
15 closely together

▫ hand out
07 deal out, dish out, give out, mete out, pass out
08 dispense, share out
10 distribute

▫ hand over
04 give, pass
05 yield
06 donate
07 consign, deliver, present
08 transfer, turn over
09 surrender
10 relinquish

▫ in hand
05 put by, ready, spare
08 under way
09 available, in reserve
12 under control

▫ to hand
04 near
05 close, handy, ready
06 at hand
08 imminent
09 available
10 accessible
13 about to happen

▫ try your hand
07 attempt, have a go
09 have a shot, have a stab
10 have a crack

▫ win hands down
09 win easily
15 win effortlessly

handbill
05 flyer
06 letter, notice
07 leaflet
08 circular, pamphlet
13 advertisement

handbook
03 ABC
06 manual
09 companion, guidebook

10 prospectus
15 instruction book

handcuff
06 fasten, fetter, secure
07 manacle, shackle

handcuffs
07 darbies, fetters
08 manacles, shackles

handful
03 few
04 pain, pest
06 bother, little
08 nuisance
10 smattering
11 small amount, small number
13 pain in the neck
15 thorn in the flesh

handicap
04 curb
05 block, check, limit
06 defect, hamper, hinder, impair, impede, retard
07 barrier, disable, penalty
08 drawback, encumber, hold back, obstacle, restrict
09 hindrance
10 constraint, disability, impediment, limitation
11 abnormality, encumbrance, restriction
14 stumbling-block

handicraft
03 art
05 craft, skill
09 craftwork

handiwork
03 art
05 craft, doing, skill
07 product
08 creation
09 invention
11 achievement
14 responsibility

handle
03 paw
04 feel, grip, haft, hilt, hold, knob, work
05 drive, grasp, shaft, steer, stock, touch, treat
06 deal in, finger, fondle, manage, market, tackle
07 control, trade in, traffic
08 cope with, deal with
09 supervise
10 take care of

handling
07 conduct, running
08 approach

09 direction, operation, treatment
10 discussion, management
12 manipulation
14 administration

handout
04 alms, dole
05 gifts, issue, share
07 charity, freebie, leaflet
08 brochure, circular, pamphlet
10 free sample, literature
12 press release

hand-picked
05 elect, elite
06 choice, chosen, select
08 screened, selected

handsome
04 fair, fine
05 dishy, hunky, large
06 lavish
07 elegant, liberal
08 abundant, generous, gorgeous, sizeable
09 plentiful
10 attractive, personable
11 good-looking, magnanimous
12 considerable

handsomely
06 richly
08 lavishly
09 liberally
10 abundantly, generously
11 plentifully
12 munificently
13 magnanimously

handwriting
04 fist, hand
06 scrawl, script
07 writing
08 scribble
09 autograph
10 penmanship
11 calligraphy

handy
04 near
05 adept, ready
06 adroit, at hand, clever, expert, to hand, useful
07 skilful, skilled
09 available, dexterous, practical
10 accessible, convenient
11 practicable, within reach

handyman
09 odd-jobber, odd-jobman
15 Jack-of-all-trades

hang
03 fix, sag
04 bend, drop, flop, lean

05 affix, cling, drape, drift, droop, float, hover, put up, stick, swing
06 append, attach, dangle, fasten, linger, remain
07 flutter, suspend
08 hang down, string up

❑ **get the hang**
04 twig
05 grasp
06 fathom
10 comprehend, understand
13 get the knack of

❑ **hang about**
05 haunt
06 dawdle, linger, loiter
08 frequent
09 waste time
10 hang around

❑ **hang back**
06 recoil
07 shy away
08 hesitate, hold back
10 shrink back, stay behind

❑ **hang fire**
04 stop, wait
05 delay, stall, stick
08 hold back
09 vacillate
13 procrastinate

❑ **hang on**
04 grip, wait
05 cling, grasp
06 clutch, endure, hold on, remain, rest on, turn on
07 carry on, hinge on, hold out, persist
08 continue, depend on, hold fast
09 persevere

❑ **hang over**
04 loom
06 impend, menace
08 approach, threaten

hangdog
05 cowed
06 abject, guilty
08 cringing, defeated, downcast, sneaking, wretched
09 miserable
10 browbeaten, shamefaced

hanger-on
05 toady
06 lackey, minion
08 follower, henchman, parasite
09 dependant, sycophant
10 freeloader

hanging
04 drop
05 drape, loose
06 floppy
07 drapery, pendent
08 dangling, drooping, flapping, flopping, swinging
09 pendulous, suspended
11 unsupported

hang-out
03 den
05 haunt, joint, local, patch
12 meeting-place

hangover
12 after-effects, morning after

hang-up
05 block, thing
06 phobia
07 problem
08 fixation, idée fixe
09 obsession
10 difficulty, inhibition
11 mental block

hank
04 coil, fank, loop, roll
05 piece, skein, twist
06 length

hanker

□**hanker after, hanker for**
05 covet, crave
07 itch for, long for, pine for, wish for
08 yearn for
09 hunger for, thirst for
10 be dying for

hankering
04 itch, urge, wish
06 desire, hunger, pining, thirst
07 craving, longing
08 yearning

hanky-panky
08 mischief, trickery
09 chicanery, deception
10 dishonesty, subterfuge
11 shenanigans
13 funny business, jiggery-pokery
14 monkey business

haphazard
06 casual, chance, random
07 aimless
08 careless, slapdash, slipshod
09 arbitrary, hit-or-miss, irregular
12 disorganized, unmethodical, unsystematic
14 indiscriminate

hapless
06 cursed, jinxed
07 unhappy, unlucky
08 ill-fated, luckless, wretched
09 miserable
11 star-crossed, unfortunate

happen
04 fall, find, go on
05 arise, ensue, hit on, occur
06 appear, crop up, follow, result, turn up
07 develop, light on, turn out
08 chance on, come true, discover
09 come about, eventuate, stumble on, supervene, take place, transpire
10 come across
11 materialize
13 come into being

happening
05 event, scene
06 action, affair, chance
07 episode
08 accident, incident, occasion
10 experience, occurrence, phenomenon
11 eventuality, proceedings
12 circumstance

happily
06 gladly
07 luckily, merrily
08 by chance, heartily, joyfully, joyously
09 agreeably, fittingly, gleefully, willingly
10 cheerfully
11 contentedly, delightedly, fortunately, opportunely
12 auspiciously, propitiously
14 providentially

happiness
03 joy
05 bliss
06 gaiety
07 delight, ecstasy, elation
08 felicity, gladness, pleasure
09 enjoyment, merriment, merriness
10 blitheness, cheeriness, exuberance, joyfulness
11 contentment, good spirits
12 cheerfulness

happy
03 apt, gay
04 glad
05 jolly, lucky, merry
06 blithe, elated, jovial, joyful, joyous, proper

07 content, fitting, gleeful, helpful, pleased, radiant
08 apposite, carefree, cheerful, ecstatic, euphoric, thrilled
09 cock-a-hoop, contented, delighted, fortunate, gratified, opportune, overjoyed, rapturous, satisfied, unworried
10 auspicious, beneficial, favourable, felicitous, propitious
11 appropriate, in a good mood, on cloud nine, over the moon, tickled pink
12 advantageous, light-hearted, walking on air
13 floating on air, in good spirits, in high spirits
15 in seventh heaven, on top of the world

happy-go-lucky
06 blithe, casual
08 carefree
09 easy-going
10 insouciant, nonchalant
11 improvident
12 devil-may-care, light-hearted

harangue
05 spout
06 preach, speech, tirade
07 address, declaim, lecture
08 diatribe
09 hold forth
10 peroration
11 exhortation

harass
03 nag, vex
04 fret, tire
05 annoy, harry, hound, worry
06 badger, bother, hassle, pester, plague, stress
07 disturb, dragoon, exhaust, fatigue, provoke, torment, trouble, wear out
08 irritate
09 persecute
10 antagonize, exasperate
12 put the wind up

harassed
05 vexed
07 harried, hassled, hounded, plagued, uptight, worried
08 careworn, pestered, strained, stressed, troubled
09 pressured, tormented
11 pressurized, stressed out
13 under pressure

harassment
06 bother, hassle
07 torment, trouble
08 distress, nuisance, vexation
09 annoyance, badgering, pestering
10 irritation, pressuring
11 aggravation, persecution

harbinger
04 omen, sign
06 herald
07 portent, warning
09 foretoken, messenger, precursor
10 forerunner, indication

harbour
04 dock, hide, hold, port, quay
05 haven, house, nurse, wharf
06 foster, marina, refuge, shield
07 cherish, cling to, mooring, nurture, protect, shelter
09 anchorage, entertain

hard
04 busy, cold, firm, grim, keen, real, true
05 cruel, dense, harsh, heavy, rigid, sharp, solid, stern, stiff, tough
06 actual, bitter, knotty, potent, severe, strict, strong, tiring
07 arduous, austere, callous, certain, complex, harmful, heavily, intense, onerous, painful, violent, zealous
08 exacting, forceful, obdurate, pitiless, powerful, puzzling, rigorous, ruthless
09 addictive, assiduous, condensed, difficult, energetic, intricate, laborious, merciless, resistant, strenuous, unfeeling, unsparing
10 compressed, exhausting, implacable, inflexible, oppressive, perplexing, tyrannical, unpleasant, unyielding
11 bewildering, cold-hearted, complicated, distressing, industrious, unrelenting
12 backbreaking, disagreeable, enthusiastic, habit-forming, impenetrable, indisputable
13 conscientious, uncomfortable, unsympathetic
14 with difficulty

□ **hard and fast**
03 set
05 fixed, rigid, strict

07 binding
08 definite
09 immutable, stringent
10 inflexible, invariable, unchanging
11 unalterable
12 unchangeable
14 uncompromising

□ **hard up**
04 bust
05 broke, short, skint
08 bankrupt, in the red
09 penniless
10 cleaned out, stony broke
11 impecunious
12 impoverished, on your uppers
14 on your beam ends
15 strapped for cash

hard-bitten
05 tough
06 inured, shrewd
07 callous, cynical
08 ruthless
09 practical, realistic, toughened
10 hard-boiled, hard-headed
11 down-to-earth
12 matter-of-fact
13 unsentimental

hard-boiled
05 tough
07 cynical
11 down-to-earth
13 unsentimental

hard-core
05 rigid
07 blatant, diehard, extreme
08 explicit
09 dedicated, steadfast

harden
03 set
04 bake, cake, gird
05 inure, nerve, steel
06 anneal, deaden, freeze, season, temper
07 congeal, fortify, petrify, stiffen, toughen
08 accustom, solidify
09 habituate, reinforce, vulcanize
10 strengthen

hardened
03 set
06 inured
07 callous, chronic
08 habitual, obdurate, seasoned
09 reprobate, toughened

10 accustomed, habituated, inveterate
12 incorrigible, irredeemable

hard-headed
05 sharp, tough
06 astute, shrewd
08 rational, sensible
09 hard-nosed, practical, pragmatic, realistic
10 hard-bitten, hard-boiled
11 down-to-earth
13 unsentimental

hard-hearted
04 cold
05 cruel, stony
06 unkind
07 callous, inhuman
08 pitiless, uncaring
09 heartless, merciless, unfeeling
13 unsympathetic

hard-hitting
05 tough
08 critical, directly, forceful, straight, vigorous
12 condemnatory
13 no-holds-barred
14 uncompromising

hardiness
09 fortitude, toughness
10 resilience, robustness, ruggedness, sturdiness
11 intrepidity

hardline
05 tough
06 strict
07 extreme
08 militant
10 inflexible, unyielding
12 intransigent

hardly
04 just
06 barely
08 not at all, not quite, only just, scarcely
08 coldness, firmness, rigidity, severity
09 harshness, sternness, toughness
10 difficulty, inhumanity
12 pitilessness

hard-pressed
06 pushed
07 hard put, harried
08 harassed
09 overtaxed
10 hard-pushed
11 up against it
12 overburdened

hardship
04 need, pain, want
05 trial
07 burdens, poverty, trouble
09 adversity, austerity, privation, suffering
10 affliction, misfortune
11 deprivation, destitution, tribulation

hard-wearing
05 stout, tough
06 rugged, strong, sturdy
07 durable, lasting
08 well-made
09 resilient
11 built to last

hard-working
04 busy
11 industrious

hardy
05 stout, tough
06 plucky, robust, strong, sturdy
07 durable, healthy, stoical
08 intrepid, stalwart, vigorous
09 heavy-duty, undaunted
11 indomitable
12 stout-hearted

hare-brained
04 daft, rash, wild
05 giddy, inane, silly
06 scatty, stupid
07 foolish
08 careless, crackpot, reckless
14 scatterbrained

hark
04 hear, mark, note
06 listen, notice
07 give ear, hearken, pay heed

◻**hark back**
06 go back, recall, revert
07 regress
08 remember, turn back
09 recollect

harlequin
04 fool, zany
05 clown, comic, joker
06 jester
07 buffoon

harlot
03 pro
04 tart
05 hussy, tramp, whore
06 hooker
08 callgirl, scrubber, strumpet
10 loose woman, prostitute
11 fallen woman
12 streetwalker

harm
03 ill, mar

04 hurt, loss, pain, ruin
05 abuse, spoil, wound, wrong
06 damage, impair, injure, injury, misuse, molest
07 blemish, destroy
08 ill-treat, maltreat
09 adversity, detriment, suffering
10 impairment, misfortune
11 destruction, work against

harmful
03 bad
05 toxic
07 noxious
08 damaging, wounding
09 dangerous, hazardous, injurious, poisonous, unhealthy
10 pernicious
11 deleterious, destructive, detrimental, unwholesome

harmless
04 mild, safe
06 gentle
08 innocent, non-toxic
09 blameless, innocuous
11 inoffensive

harmonious
06 mellow
07 cordial, musical, tuneful
08 amicable, balanced, friendly, matching, peaceful, pleasant, rhythmic
09 congruous, melodious
10 compatible, concordant, euphonious, like-minded
11 mellifluous, sympathetic, symphonious

harmonize
03 mix
04 suit, tone
05 agree, blend, fit in, match
06 accord
07 balance, compose
08 coincide
10 co-ordinate, correspond, go together

harmony
04 tune
05 amity, peace, unity
06 accord, melody, unison
07 balance, concord, euphony, oneness, rapport
08 goodwill, symmetry
09 agreement, unanimity
10 conformity, consonance
11 co-operation, concurrence, tunefulness
12 co-ordination, friendliness

13 compatibility, melodiousness
14 like-mindedness
15 mellifluousness

harness
04 gear, tack
05 reins
06 straps, tackle
07 channel, control, exploit, utilize
09 equipment, make use of
13 accoutrements

◻**in harness**
08 together
11 co-operating
13 collaborating, in co-operation

harp

◻**harp on**
03 nag
05 press, renew
06 labour, repeat
07 dwell on
09 reiterate

harpoon
04 barb, dart
05 arrow, spear
07 trident

harridan
03 nag
04 fury
05 harpy, scold, shrew, witch
06 dragon, gorgon, tartar, virago
07 hell-cat
09 battle-axe, termagant, Xanthippe

harried
05 beset
07 anxious, hassled, plagued, ravaged, worried
08 agitated, bothered, harassed, troubled
09 pressured, tormented
11 hard-pressed, pressurized

harrowing
08 alarming, daunting
09 agonizing, traumatic, upsetting
10 disturbing, perturbing, terrifying, tormenting
11 distressing, frightening
12 excruciating, heart-rending, nerve-racking

harry
03 nag, vex
05 annoy, worry

06 badger, bother, chivvy, harass, hassle, molest, pester, plague
07 oppress, torment
09 persecute

harsh
04 grim, hard, wild
05 bleak, cruel, gaudy, gruff, lurid, rough, sharp, showy, stark, stern
06 barren, bitter, bright, brutal, coarse, flashy, garish, hoarse, savage, severe, strict
07 acerbic, austere, glaring, grating, inhuman, jarring, rasping, raucous, Spartan
08 abrasive, croaking, dazzling, desolate, grinding, guttural, pitiless, ruthless, strident
09 dissonant, Draconian, merciless, unfeeling
10 discordant, unpleasant
11 comfortless, ear-piercing
12 inhospitable

harshness
06 rigour
08 acerbity, acrimony, asperity, hardness, severity
09 brutality, ill-temper, roughness, starkness, sternness
10 bitterness, coarseness, strictness
12 abrasiveness

harum-scarum
04 rash, wild
05 hasty
06 scatty
07 erratic
08 careless, reckless
09 haphazard, impetuous
11 hare-brained, precipitate
13 ill-considered, irresponsible
14 scatterbrained

harvest
04 crop, gain, pick, reap
05 amass, glean, horde, pluck, stock, store, yield
06 fruits, garner, gather, obtain, return
07 acquire, collect, produce, product, reaping, returns
08 gather in
10 accumulate, collection
11 consequence, ingathering
12 accumulation

hash
04 mess, stew
05 botch, mix-up
06 bungle, hotpot, muddle

07 goulash
08 mishmash
09 confusion
10 hotchpotch, lob's course

hashish
03 pot
04 dope, hash, hemp
05 bhang, ganja, grass
08 cannabis
09 marijuana

hassle
03 bug
05 aggro, annoy, harry, hound,
06 badger, bother, chivvy, harass, pester
07 dispute, problem, quarrel, trouble, wrangle
08 nuisance, struggle
09 bickering
13 inconvenience

haste
04 rush
05 hurry, speed
07 urgency
08 alacrity, celerity, rapidity, rashness, velocity
09 quickness, swiftness
11 impetuosity
15 expeditiousness

hasten
03 aid, fly, run
04 bolt, dash, race, rush, tear
05 boost, hurry, press, speed
06 assist, sprint
07 advance, hurry up, quicken, speed up
08 dispatch, expedite, step on it
09 hotfoot it, make haste
10 accelerate, get a move on
11 precipitate, push forward
12 step on the gas

hastily
04 fast
05 apace
06 rashly
07 quickly, rapidly
08 chop-chop, speedily
09 hurriedly
10 heedlessly, recklessly
11 double-quick, impetuously, impulsively
13 precipitately

hasty
04 fast, rash
05 brief, brisk, quick, rapid, short, swift
06 prompt, rushed, speedy
07 cursory, hurried
08 careless, fleeting, headlong, heedless, reckless

09 hot-headed, impatient, impetuous, impulsive
11 precipitate, thoughtless

hat
► *Types of hat:*
03 fez
04 hood
05 beret, busby, derby, mitre, snood, toque
06 beanie, boater, bonnet, bowler, cloche, fedora, helmet, mob-cap, panama, sunhat, top-hat, trilby, turban
07 biretta, flat-cap, Homburg, pill-box, stetson
08 bearskin, sombrero, straw hat
09 glengarry, peaked cap, sailor-hat, sou'wester
10 hunting-cap, poke-bonnet, pork-pie hat
11 baseball cap, deerstalker, mortar-board, tam-o'- shanter
12 stovepipe hat, ten-gallon hat

hatch
04 plan, plot
05 breed, brood, sit on
06 design, devise, invent, scheme
07 concoct, dream up, project, think up
08 conceive, contrive, incubate
09 formulate, originate

hatchet
03 axe
07 chopper, cleaver, machete, mattock, pickaxe
08 tomahawk
09 battle-axe

hate
05 abhor
06 detest, enmity, grudge, hatred, loathe, regret
07 despise, ill-will, rancour
08 aversion, execrate, loathing
09 abominate, animosity, apologize, hostility
10 abhorrence, antagonism, bitterness, resentment
11 abomination

hateful
04 evil, foul, vile
06 horrid, odious
07 heinous
09 abhorrent, execrable, loathsome, obnoxious, offensive, repellent,

repugnant, repulsive, revolting
10 abominable, despicable, detestable, disgusting
12 contemptible

hatred
04 hate
06 animus, enmity, grudge
07 ill-will, rancour
08 aversion, loathing
09 animosity, antipathy, hostility, revulsion
10 abhorrence, antagonism, execration, repugnance
11 abomination, detestation

haughtiness
04 airs
05 pride
07 conceit, disdain, hauteur
08 contempt
09 aloofness, arrogance, loftiness
10 snootiness
12 snobbishness

haughty
04 vain
05 lofty, proud
06 snooty
07 stuck-up
08 arrogant, snobbish, superior
09 conceited, imperious
10 disdainful
11 overbearing, patronizing
12 supercilious
13 condescending, high and mighty, swollen-headed

haul
03 lug, tow, tug
04 cart, drag, draw, find, gain, hump, loot, move, pull, push, ship, swag
05 booty, carry, heave, trail, yield
06 convey, convoy, spoils
07 plunder, takings
09 transport

haunches
04 hips
05 hucks, nates
06 thighs
07 huckles, hunkers
08 buttocks

haunt
03 den
05 beset, curse, harry, local, recur, spook, visit, worry
06 burden, obsess, plague, prey on
07 hangout, oppress, possess, torment, trouble

08 frequent
09 patronize
11 hang about in, materialize
12 hang around in, meeting-place
14 stamping-ground

haunted
06 cursed, jinxed, spooky
07 ghostly, plagued, worried
08 obsessed, troubled
09 hag-ridden, possessed, tormented

haunting
08 poignant
09 evocative, memorable, nostalgic, recurrent
11 atmospheric
13 unforgettable

have
.03 ask, bid, con, eat, get, own, use
04 bear, down, dupe, feel, find, fool, gain, gulp, hold, keep, make, meet, must, show, take, tell
05 abide, allow, beget, brook, cheat, drink, enjoy, force, order, ought, stand, trick
06 accept, compel, devour, diddle, embody, endure, enjoin, guzzle, oblige, obtain, permit, secure, should, suffer, take in
07 acquire, arrange, command, consume, contain, deceive, embrace, exhibit, express, include, possess, procure, receive, request, require, swallow, swindle, undergo
08 comprise, manifest, organize, persuade, submit to, talk into, tolerate, tuck into
09 consist of, encounter, go through, knock back, partake of, put up with
10 comprehend, experience, take part in
11 demonstrate, give birth to, incorporate, prevail upon
13 participate in

❑ **have done with**
04 stop
05 cease
06 desist, give up
09 throw over
10 finish with
13 be through with
15 wash your hands of

❑ **have had it**
10 be defeated, have no hope
11 be exhausted, bite the dust

❑ **have on**
03 kid, rag
04 wear
05 tease, trick
11 play a joke on
15 pull someone's leg

haven
04 dock, port
05 oasis
06 asylum, refuge
07 harbour, retreat, shelter
09 anchorage, sanctuary

haversack
06 kitbag
08 backpack

havoc
04 ruin
05 chaos, wreck
06 damage, mayhem
08 shambles, wreckage
11 rack and ruin

hawk
03 cry
04 bark, kite, sell, tout, vend
06 falcon, market, peddle, tercel
07 buzzard, haggard, harrier

hawker
06 coster, pedlar, vendor
07 chapman
08 huckster
09 barrow-boy
12 costermonger

haywire
03 mad
04 wild
05 crazy, wrong
07 chaotic, tangled
10 disordered, topsy-turvy
12 disorganized, out of control

hazard
04 luck, risk
05 offer, peril, stake
06 chance, danger, gamble, menace, submit, threat
07 pitfall, suggest, venture
08 accident
09 put at risk, speculate
10 jeopardize
13 put in jeopardy
14 expose to danger

hazardous
05 hairy, risky
06 chancy, tricky, unsafe
08 insecure, perilous
09 dangerous

10 precarious
11 threatening

haze
03 fog
04 blur, film, mist, smog
05 cloud, steam
06 muddle, vapour
09 confusion, fogginess, mistiness, obscurity, smokiness, vagueness
10 cloudiness
12 bewilderment
14 indistinctness

hazy
03 dim
05 faint, foggy, fuzzy, milky, misty, muzzy, smoky, vague
06 cloudy, veiled
07 blurred, clouded, obscure
08 overcast
10 ill-defined, indefinite, indistinct

head
03 nut, run, tip, top, van, wit
04 apex, boss, conk, fizz, flap, foam, fore, lead, loaf, main, mind, peak, rise, rule, wits
05 bonce, brain, chair, chief, crest, crown, first, fount, front, froth, guide, prime, ruler, sense, skull
06 brains, charge, climax, crisis, crunch, direct, govern, height, leader, manage, noddle, origin, source, spring, summit, wisdom
07 bubbles, captain, command, control, cranium, dilemma, go first, highest, leading, premier, supreme, topmost
08 calamity, chairman, controls, director, dominant, foremost, governor, vanguard
09 commander, emergency, forefront, intellect, president, principal, reasoning, supervise
10 administer, chairwoman, controller, grey matter, leadership, management, pre-eminent, supervisor, wellspring
11 catastrophe, chairperson, common sense, loaf of bread, superintend, supervision, upper storey
12 be in charge of, directorship, headmistress, intelligence

13 administrator, be in control of, critical point, understanding
14 be at the front of, superintendent
15 little grey cells

◻**go to your head**
06 puff up
08 befuddle
09 inebriate, make drunk, make dizzy, make proud, make woozy
10 intoxicate
12 make arrogant
13 make conceited

◻**head for**
06 aim for
07 make for, point to, turn for
08 steer for
09 go towards
11 move towards
13 direct towards

◻**head off**
05 avert
06 cut off, divert
07 deflect, fend off, prevent, ward off
09 forestall, intercept, interpose, intervene, turn aside

◻**head over heels**
07 utterly
09 intensely
10 completely, recklessly, thoroughly
14 uncontrollably

◻**head up**
04 lead
06 direct, manage
12 be in charge of, take charge of

◻**keep your head**
08 keep calm
12 keep your cool

◻**lose your head**
05 panic
12 lose your cool

headache
04 bane, pest
05 worry
06 bother, hassle
07 problem, trouble
08 migraine, nuisance, vexation

heading
04 head, name
05 class, title
06 rubric
07 caption, section, subject
08 category, division, headline

headland
04 cape, head, ness
05 point
10 promontory

headlong
04 rash
05 hasty
06 rashly, wildly
07 hastily
08 reckless
09 breakneck
10 recklessly
11 precipitate
13 precipitately

headman
05 chief, ruler
06 leader, sachem
07 captain

head-on
06 direct
08 straight
11 full-frontal

headquarters
02 HQ
04 base
10 head office, main office
11 nerve centre

headstrong
06 unruly, wilful
07 wayward
08 obdurate, stubborn
09 obstinate, pigheaded
10 refractory, self-willed

headway
06 ground
07 advance
08 progress

heady
07 rousing
08 euphoric, exciting
11 stimulating
12 exhilarating, intoxicating, invigorating, overpowering

heal
04 cure, mend
05 salve, treat
06 remedy, settle, soothe
07 assuage, comfort, improve, patch up, restore
08 make good, make well, palliate, put right, set right
09 reconcile
10 make better

health
04 form, tone, trim
05 shape, state
06 fettle, vigour
07 fitness, welfare

08 strength
09 condition, good shape, soundness, wellbeing
10 robustness
12 constitution

healthy
03 fit
04 fine, good, well
05 hardy, sound
06 robust, strong, sturdy
07 bracing
08 blooming, sensible, thriving, vigorous
09 in the pink, judicious, wholesome
10 beneficial, nourishing, nutritious, refreshing, salubrious, successful
11 flourishing, in condition, in good shape, stimulating
12 fit as a fiddle, in fine fettle, invigorating
13 hale and hearty

heap
03 lot, pot
04 a lot, bank, load, lots, mass, pile, pots, tons
05 amass, build, hoard, loads, mound, stack, store
06 bestow, bundle, burden, confer, gather, lavish, oodles, plenty, scores, shower, stacks, supply
08 assemble, lashings, millions, mountain
09 abundance, great deal, stockpile
10 quantities

hear
03 try
04 heed
05 catch, judge, learn
06 be told, gather, listen, pick up, take in
07 examine, find out, inquire, make out
08 consider, discover, perceive
09 ascertain, eavesdrop
10 adjudicate, be informed, understand
11 investigate
12 pay attention

hearing
03 ear
05 range, reach, sound, trial
06 review
07 earshot, inquest, inquiry
08 audience, audition
09 interview, judgement
10 perception
11 examination, inquisition

12 adjudication
13 investigation

hearsay
04 buzz, talk
06 gossip, report, rumour
11 word of mouth
12 tittle-tattle

heart
03 nub
04 core, crux, guts, love, mind, pith, pity
05 pluck
06 centre, kernel, marrow, middle, warmth
07 bravery, concern, courage, emotion, essence, feeling, nucleus, passion
08 boldness, keenness, kindness, sympathy
09 affection, character, eagerness, fortitude, sentiment, substance
10 compassion, enthusiasm, resolution, tenderness
12 quintessence
13 determination

➤　*Parts of the heart:*
10 left atrium, myocardium
11 aortic valve, mitral valve, right atrium
13 bicuspid valve, carotid artery, left ventricle
14 ascending aorta, pulmonary valve, right ventricle, tricuspid valve

▢ **at heart**
08 at bottom
09 basically, in essence
11 essentially
13 fundamentally

▢ **by heart**
03 pat
06 by rote, off pat
08 verbatim
11 word for word
13 parrot-fashion

▢ **change of heart**
07 rethink
14 second thoughts

▢ **from the bottom of your heart**
09 earnestly, sincerely
10 profoundly

▢ **heart and soul**
08 entirely, heartily
09 devotedly
10 absolutely, completely

▢ **set your heart on**
05 crave, yearn

06 desire
07 long for, wish for

▢ **take heart**
06 buck up, perk up, revive
07 cheer up
10 brighten up

▢ **take to heart**
12 be affected by
13 be disturbed by

heartache
04 pain
05 agony, grief, worry
06 sorrow
07 anguish, anxiety, despair, remorse, torment, torture
08 distress
09 dejection, suffering
10 affliction, bitterness

heartbreak
04 pain
05 agony, grief
06 misery, sorrow
07 anguish, despair, sadness

heartbreaking
03 sad
06 tragic
07 painful, pitiful
08 grievous, poignant
09 agonizing, harrowing
12 excruciating
13 disappointing

heartbroken
03 sad
09 anguished, miserable, sorrowful, suffering
10 despondent, dispirited
11 crestfallen
12 disappointed, in low spirits

hearten
05 boost, cheer, pep up, rouse
06 buck up
07 animate, cheer up, comfort, console, inspire
08 energize, reassure
09 encourage, stimulate

heartfelt
04 deep
06 ardent, devout, honest
07 earnest, fervent, genuine, sincere
08 profound

heartily
06 deeply, gladly
07 totally
09 cordially, earnestly, genuinely, sincerely
10 absolutely, completely, profoundly, thoroughly

heartless
04 cold, hard
05 cruel, harsh
06 brutal, unkind
07 callous, inhuman, unmoved
08 pitiless, ruthless, uncaring
09 merciless, unfeeling
11 cold-blooded
13 inconsiderate, unsympathetic

heart-rending
03 sad
06 moving, tragic
07 piteous, pitiful
08 pathetic, poignant
09 affecting, agonizing, harrowing
11 distressing

heartsick
03 sad
08 dejected, downcast
09 depressed
10 despondent, melancholy
12 disappointed

heart-throb
04 idol, star
05 pin-up
09 dreamboat

heart-to-heart
08 cosy chat
09 tête-à-tête

heartwarming
06 moving
08 cheering, pleasing, touching
09 affecting, rewarding, uplifting
10 gratifying, satisfying
11 encouraging

hearty
04 warm
05 ample, large, sound
06 jovial, robust, strong
07 affable, cordial, filling, genuine, healthy, sincere
08 abundant, cheerful, effusive, friendly, generous, sizeable, stalwart, vigorous
09 ebullient, energetic, exuberant, heartfelt, unfeigned
10 boisterous, nourishing
11 substantial
12 enthusiastic, wholehearted

heat
04 bake, boil, cook, fury, glow, stir, warm, zeal
05 anger, annoy, fever, flush, roast, rouse, toast

06 ardour, calefy, enrage, excite, warm up, warmth
07 animate, fervour, hotness, inflame, passion, swelter
08 fervency
09 fieriness, intensity, microwave, stimulate, vehemence
10 enthusiasm, excitement
12 feverishness
15 high temperature

heated
05 angry, fiery, fired
06 fierce, raging, roused, stormy
07 enraged, furious, stirred
08 inflamed, vehement, worked-up
10 passionate, stimulated
11 impassioned, tempestuous

heathen
05 pagan
06 savage
07 godless, infidel, nations
08 barbaric, idolater
09 barbarian
10 idolatress, idolatrous, philistine, unbeliever
11 irreligious

heave
03 gag, tug
04 cast, drag, haul, hurl, lift, pull, spew, toss
05 chuck, fling, hitch, hoist, lever, pitch, raise, retch, sling, surge, throw, utter, vomit
07 breathe, express, throw up

heaven
03 joy, sky
04 Zion
05 bliss, ether, skies
06 Asgard, Swarga, utopia
07 ecstasy, Elysium, nirvana, Olympus, the blue, up there
08 paradise, Valhalla
09 afterlife, firmament, hereafter, next world
10 abode of God, life to come
13 elysian fields, fiddler's green, seventh heaven

heavenly
04 holy
06 cosmic, divine, lovely
07 angelic, blessed, godlike, perfect, sublime
08 beatific, blissful, cherubic, empyreal, empyrean, glorious, immortal, seraphic

09 beautiful, celestial, enjoyable, exquisite, rapturous, spiritual, unearthly, wonderful
10 enchanting
14 out of this world

heavily
04 hard
05 thick
06 slowly
07 closely, densely, solidly, soundly, thickly, utterly
08 clumsily, to excess, woodenly
09 copiously, weightily
10 abundantly, completely, decisively, sluggishly, thoroughly
11 excessively, laboriously

heaviness
04 bulk
06 weight
07 density, languor
08 deadness, solidity
09 heftiness, lassitude, thickness
10 drowsiness, oppression, sleepiness, somnolence
11 despondency, onerousness, seriousness, weightiness
12 sluggishness
13 ponderousness
14 burdensomeness, oppressiveness

heavy
05 bulky, close, dense, grave, harsh, hefty, humid, laden, large, muggy, solid, thick
06 cloudy, gloomy, leaden, loaded, severe, sombre, steamy, sticky, stodgy, strong, sultry, taxing, trying
07 arduous, awkward, crushed, extreme, filling, hulking, intense, irksome, massive, onerous, serious, starchy, tedious, violent, weighty
08 burdened, crushing, exacting, forceful, groaning, overcast, powerful, profound
09 demanding, difficult, laborious, ponderous, strenuous, wearisome
10 burdensome, cumbersome, despondent, encumbered, immoderate, inordinate, oppressive, unbearable
11 discouraged, intolerable, substantial, troublesome, weighed down

12 considerable, indigestible
13 uninteresting

heavy-handed
05 harsh, stern
06 clumsy, severe
07 awkward
08 bungling, despotic, forceful, tactless, unsubtle
09 ham-fisted, maladroit
10 autocratic, blundering, cack-handed, oppressive
11 domineering, overbearing

heavy-hearted
03 sad
04 glum
06 gloomy, morose
08 downcast, mournful
09 depressed, miserable, sorrowful
10 despondent, melancholy

heckle
04 bait, gibe, jeer
06 pester
07 barrack, catcall, disrupt

hectic
04 busy, fast, wild
06 heated
07 chaotic, excited, frantic, furious
08 bustling, feverish, frenetic, frenzied

hector
05 bully
06 badger, chivvy
08 browbeat, bulldoze, bullyrag, threaten
10 intimidate

hedge
04 duck, dyke, edge
05 cover, dodge, evade, fence, guard, hem in, limit, stall
06 insure, screen, shield
07 barrier, confine, enclose, fortify, protect, quibble
08 boundary, encircle, restrict, sidestep, surround
09 safeguard, temporize, windbreak
10 equivocate, protection
11 prevaricate

hedonism
09 dolce vita, epicurism
10 sensualism, sensuality, sybaritism
13 gratification, luxuriousness
14 self-indulgence, voluptuousness
15 pleasure-seeking

hedonist
08 sybarite
09 bon vivant, bon viveur
10 sensualist, voluptuary
14 pleasure-seeker

hedonistic
09 sybaritic
10 voluptuous
13 self-indulgent
15 pleasure-seeking

heed
04 care, mark, mind, note, obey
06 follow, listen, notice, regard
07 caution, observe, respect, thought
08 attend to, consider, take note
09 attention
10 bear in mind, take notice
12 pay attention, watchfulness
13 animadversion, consideration
15 take into account

heedful
07 careful, mindful, prudent
08 cautious, vigilant, watchful
09 attentive, observant, regardful

heedless
04 rash
06 unwary
08 careless, reckless
09 foolhardy, negligent, oblivious, unmindful
11 inattentive, precipitate, thoughtless, unconcerned, unobservant

hefty
03 big
04 hard, huge
05 ample, beefy, bulky, burly, heavy, large, solid, stout
06 brawny, robust, strong
07 hulking, immense, massive, weighty
08 colossal, forceful, generous, muscular, powerful, sizeable, unwieldy
09 strapping
11 substantial
12 considerable

height
03 top
04 apex, peak
05 crest, crown, limit
06 apogee, climax, summit, vertex, zenith
07 hill top, maximum, stature
08 altitude, highness, pinnacle, tallness, ultimate

09 elevation, extremity, loftiness, uttermost
11 culmination, mountain top

heighten
04 lift
05 add to, boost, exalt, raise
07 amplify, augment, build up, elevate, enhance, improve, magnify, sharpen
08 increase
09 intensify
10 strengthen

heinous
04 evil
06 odious, wicked
07 hateful, hideous, vicious
08 flagrant, infamous, shocking
09 abhorrent, atrocious, execrable, loathsome, monstrous, nefarious
10 abominable, despicable, detestable, iniquitous, outrageous, villainous
11 unspeakable
12 contemptible

heir, heiress
05 scion
07 legatee
09 inheritor, successor
10 inheritrix
11 beneficiary, inheritress

helix
04 coil, curl, loop
05 screw, twist, whorl
06 spiral, volute

hell
04 fire
05 abyss, agony, Hades
06 blazes, misery, ordeal, Tophet
07 inferno, torment, torture
09 down there, nightmare, perdition, suffering
10 underworld
11 nether world, tribulation
12 lower regions
13 bottomless pit
15 infernal regions

❑**give someone hell**
04 beat, flog
05 annoy, scold
06 harass, pester, punish
07 torment, trouble

❑**hell for leather**
07 quickly, rapidly, swiftly
08 very fast
09 hurriedly, post-haste
13 precipitately

◻**raise hell**
09 be furious
10 hit the roof

hell-bent
05 fixed
06 dogged, intent
08 obdurate, resolved
09 tenacious
10 determined, inflexible, unwavering
12 intransigent, unhesitating

hellish
06 savage, wicked
07 awfully, demonic, satanic
08 accursed, barbaric, damnable, devilish, dreadful, fiendish, infernal
09 atrocious, execrable, extremely, monstrous, nefarious
10 abominable, diabolical, dreadfully

helm
05 wheel
06 rudder, tiller

◻**at the helm**
07 leading
08 in charge
09 directing, in command, in control
11 in the saddle
15 holding the reins

help
03 aid, use
04 back, balm, ease
05 avail, boost, guide, serve
06 advice, assist, backup, oblige, remedy
07 assuage, backing, be of use, benefit, charity, further, healing, improve, relieve, service, stand by, succour, support, utility
08 guidance, mitigate
09 advantage, alleviate, co-operate, do your bit, encourage, lend a hand
10 ameliorate, assistance, facilitate, rally round
11 alleviation, co-operation, helping hand
12 amelioration, contribute to, give a boost to, shot in the arm
13 encouragement

helper
02 PA
04 aide, ally, maid, mate
06 deputy, second, worker
07 partner, servant

08 adjutant, co-worker, employee, helpmate
09 assistant, associate, attendant, auxiliary, colleague, man Friday, supporter
10 accomplice, girl Friday, subsidiary
11 subordinate
12 collaborator, right-hand man
14 right-hand woman

helpful
04 kind
05 of use
06 caring, useful
08 friendly, obliging, valuable
09 of service, practical
10 beneficial, benevolent, charitable, supportive
11 considerate, neighbourly
12 advantageous, constructive
13 accommodating

helping
05 piece, share
06 amount, dollop, ration
07 bowlful, portion, serving
08 plateful, spoonful

helpless
06 feeble, infirm
07 forlorn
08 disabled, impotent
09 dependent, incapable, paralysed, powerless
10 friendless, vulnerable
11 debilitated, defenceless, incompetent, unprotected

helpmate
04 wife
06 helper, spouse
07 consort, husband, partner, support
09 assistant, associate, companion, other half
10 better half

helter-skelter
08 headlong, pell-mell
09 hurriedly
10 recklessly

hem
04 bind, edge, fold, trim
05 frill, skirt
06 border, edging, fringe, margin
07 fimbria, flounce, valance
08 trimming

◻**hem in**
04 trap
05 box in, limit, pen in
06 shut in

07 close in, confine, enclose, hedge in
08 restrict, surround
09 constrain

hence
04 ergo, thus
09 therefore
11 accordingly
12 consequently

henceforth
05 hence
09 from now on, hereafter
11 hereinafter, in the future
12 henceforward

henchman
04 aide
05 crony, heavy
06 lackey, minder, minion
08 follower, sidekick
09 associate, attendant, bodyguard, supporter, underling
11 subordinate

henpecked
04 meek
05 timid
09 dominated
10 browbeaten, subjugated

herald
04 omen, show, sign
05 augur, crier, token, usher
06 augury, signal
07 courier, portend, portent, precede, promise, trumpet, usher in
08 announce, proclaim
09 announcer, broadcast, harbinger, make known, messenger, precursor
10 forerunner, foreshadow, make public, pave the way

heraldry
▶ *Heraldry terms include*:
04 arms, lion, orle, pall, pile
05 badge, crest, eagle, field, motto
06 bezant, blazon, canton, centre, charge, dexter, emblem, ensign, helmet, impale, mullet, sejant, shield, volant, wivern
07 bordure, chevron, dormant, griffin, lozenge, martlet, passant, phoenix, quarter, rampant, roundel, statant, tierced, unicorn, urinant
08 caboched, couchant, insignia, sinister
09 displayed
10 cinquefoil, coat of arms,

cockatrice, escutcheon,
fleur-de-lis, quatrefoil

herbs and spices

➤ *Names of herbs and spices:*
03 bay
04 dill, mace, mint, sage
05 anise, basil, caper, cumin,
curry, thyme
06 borage, chilli, chives, cloves,
fennel, garlic, ginger, hyssop,
lovage, nutmeg, pepper,
sesame, sorrel
07 catmint, chervil, comfrey,
mustard, oregano, paprika,
parsley, saffron, vanilla
08 allspice, angelica, bergamot,
camomile, cardamon,
cinnamon, lavender,
marjoram, rosemary,
tarragon, turmeric
09 coriander, fenugreek
13 cayenne pepper
➤ See also **food**

herculean

04 hard, huge
05 great, heavy, large, tough
06 strong
07 arduous, mammoth,
massive, onerous
08 colossal, enormous,
exacting, gigantic, powerful
09 demanding, difficult,
gruelling, laborious,
strenuous
10 formidable, tremendous

herd

03 mob
04 goad, host, lead, mass, pack,
urge
05 crowd, crush, drive, drove,
flock, force, guide, horde,
plebs, press, rally, swarm
06 gather, huddle, muster,
proles, rabble, throng
07 collect, round up
08 assemble, riff-raff
09 multitude, the masses
10 collection, congregate
11 get together

herdsman

06 cowman, drover
07 cowherd, grazier, vaquero
08 stockman, wrangler

here

03 now
07 present
10 at this time
11 at this place, at this point,
at this stage, in this place,
to this place

here and there

08 to and fro
12 sporadically

hereafter

05 hence, later
09 afterlife, from now on, next
world
10 eventually, henceforth, life
to come
11 in the future
12 henceforward

hereditary

06 family, inborn, inbred, innate
07 genetic, natural
08 inherent
09 ancestral, inherited
10 bequeathed, congenital,
handed down
13 transmissible

heresy

07 atheism, dissent
08 apostasy, unbelief
09 blasphemy
10 dissidence, heterodoxy,
scepticism
11 agnosticism, revisionism

heretic

07 atheist, sceptic
08 agnostic, apostate,
renegade
09 dissenter, dissident
10 unbeliever
11 free-thinker, revisionist
13 nonconformist

heretical

07 impious
08 agnostic, recusant,
renegade
09 atheistic, dissident,
heterodox, sceptical,
sectarian
10 dissenting, irreverent,
schismatic, separatist,
unorthodox
11 blasphemous, revisionist,
unbelieving
12 free-thinking, iconoclastic
13 rationalistic

heritage

04 past
06 estate, family, legacy
07 bequest, culture, descent,
dynasty, history, lineage
08 ancestry, cultural
09 tradition
10 background, birthright,
extraction, traditions
11 inheritance

hermetic

06 sealed
08 airtight
10 watertight

hermit

04 monk
07 ancress, ascetic, eremite,
recluse, stylite
08 solitary
09 anchoress, anchorite

hermitage

05 haven
06 asylum, refuge
07 hideout, retreat, shelter
08 cloister, hideaway
09 sanctuary
11 hiding-place

hero

04 idol, lead, lion, star
05 goody, ideal, pin-up
06 victor
07 paragon
08 cavalier, champion
09 conqueror
11 protagonist

heroic

04 bold
05 brave, noble
06 daring
07 doughty, gallant, valiant
08 fearless, intrepid, selfless,
valorous
09 dauntless, undaunted
10 chivalrous, courageous,
determined
11 adventurous, lion-hearted
12 stout-hearted

heroine

04 diva, idol, lead, lion, star
05 goody, ideal, pin-up
06 victor
07 paragon
08 champion
09 conqueror
10 prima donna
11 leading lady, protagonist

heroism

06 daring, valour
07 bravery, courage
08 boldness, chivalry
09 fortitude, gallantry
12 fearlessness, selflessness
15 lion-heartedness

hero-worship

09 adoration, adulation
10 admiration, veneration
11 deification, idolization
12 idealization

hesitancy
05 demur, doubt
08 wavering
10 indecision, reluctance
11 reservation, uncertainty
12 doubtfulness, irresolution
13 unwillingness
14 disinclination

hesitant
03 shy
04 wary
05 timid
06 unsure
07 dubious, halting
08 doubtful, stalling, wavering
09 demurring, reluctant,
   tentative, uncertain
10 indecisive, irresolute,
   stammering, stuttering
11 disinclined, vacillating

hesitate
04 halt, wait
05 delay, demur, pause, stall,
   waver
06 boggle, dither, falter
07 stammer, stumble, stutter
08 hang back, hold back
09 vacillate
10 dilly-dally, think twice
12 shilly-shally

hesitation
05 delay, doubt, pause
07 waiting
08 stalling, wavering
09 faltering, hesitance,
   stumbling
10 indecision, reluctance,
   scepticism, stammering,
   stuttering, unsureness
11 holding-back, uncertainty,
   vacillation
12 doubtfulness, irresolution
13 dilly-dallying, unwillingness
14 second thoughts
15 shilly-shallying

heterodox
09 dissident, heretical
10 dissenting, unorthodox
12 free-thinking, iconoclastic

heterogeneous
05 mixed
06 motley, unlike, varied
07 diverse, opposed
08 assorted, catholic, contrary
09 different, disparate,
   divergent, multiform,
   unrelated
10 dissimilar
11 diversified, polymorphic
13 miscellaneous

heterosexual
06 hetero
08 straight

hew
03 axe, cut, lop, saw
04 chip, chop, fell, hack,
   trim
05 carve, model, prune, sever
06 chisel, hammer, sculpt
07 fashion, whittle
09 sculpture

heyday
04 peak
05 bloom, flush, prime
09 flowering, golden age

hiatus
03 gap
04 lull, rest, rift, void
05 break, lapse, pause, space
06 breach, lacuna
08 aperture, interval
10 suspension
12 interruption

hidden
04 dark
05 close
06 arcane, covert, latent,
   masked, occult, secret,
   unseen, veiled
07 covered, cryptic, obscure
08 abstruse, mystical, shrouded
09 concealed, disguised,
   recondite
10 indistinct, mysterious, out of
   sight, under wraps
11 camouflaged

hide
03 fur
04 bury, coat, fell, lurk, mask,
   pelt, skin, stow, veil
05 cloak, cloud, cover, store
06 darken, fleece, hole up, lie
   low, screen, shadow, shroud
07 conceal, eclipse, leather,
   obscure, secrete, shelter
08 bottle up, disguise, keep
   dark, lie doggo, obstruct,
   suppress, withhold
09 dissemble, stash away, take
   cover
10 camouflage, go to ground
12 go into hiding
13 draw a veil over
14 keep out of sight, keep
   under wraps
15 keep a low profile

hideaway
03 den
04 hole, lair, nest
07 retreat, shelter

08 cloister
09 hermitage, sanctuary

hidebound
03 set
05 fixed, rigid
06 narrow
07 bigoted
10 entrenched, intolerant
11 intractable, reactionary

hideous
04 grim, ugly
05 awful
06 horrid
07 ghastly, macabre
08 dreadful, gruesome,
   horrible, shocking, terrible
09 appalling, frightful,
   grotesque, monstrous,
   repellent, repulsive,
   revolting, unsightly
10 disgusting, horrendous,
   horrifying, terrifying

hideout
03 den
04 hole, lair, nest
05 haven
06 refuge
07 retreat, shelter
08 cloister, hideaway
09 hermitage, sanctuary

hiding
04 mask, veil
05 cover
06 caning, shroud
07 beating, belting, licking,
   tanning, veiling
08 disguise, drubbing, flogging,
   spanking, whacking,
   whipping
09 battering, screening,
   thrashing, walloping
10 camouflage
11 concealment

hiding-place
03 den
04 hole, lair, nest
05 cache, cover, haven
07 retreat
08 cloister
09 sanctuary

hierarchy
05 scale
06 ladder, series, strata, system
07 grading, ranking
08 echelons
09 structure
12 pecking order

higgledy-piggledy
06 anyhow, untidy

07 jumbled, muddled
08 confused, untidily
09 any old how, haphazard
10 confusedly, disorderly, topsy-turvy
11 haphazardly
12 disorganized

high
03 bad, off, top
04 dear, fine, good, peak, tall
05 acute, chief, doped, great, lofty, moral, sharp, steep
06 bombed, choice, classy, costly, de luxe, height, loaded, piping, putrid, rancid, select, shrill, stoned, strong, summit, tiptop, treble, wasted, worthy, zenith
07 blitzed, decayed, eminent, exalted, extreme, intense, leading, notable, out of it, perfect, quality, rotting, soaring, upright, violent
08 advanced, elevated, falsetto, forceful, inflated, piercing, powerful, smelling, top-class, towering, turned on, vigorous, virtuous
09 excellent, excessive, exemplary, expensive, first-rate, gilt-edged, important, principal, prominent, spaced out
10 exorbitant, first-class, honourable, noteworthy, surpassing, unequalled
11 influential, outstanding, penetrating, superlative, ultra-modern
12 extortionate, unparalleled
13 distinguished

▫**high and dry**
08 marooned, stranded
09 abandoned, destitute

▫**high and mighty**
05 proud
06 swanky
07 haughty, stuck-up
08 arrogant, snobbish, superior
09 conceited, egotistic, imperious
11 overbearing, overweening, patronizing
13 condescending

high spirits
06 bounce, capers, spirit
07 sparkle
08 buoyancy, hilarity, vivacity
09 animation, good cheer
10 ebullience, exuberance, liveliness
11 joie de vivre
12 exhilaration
14 boisterousness

high-born
05 noble
08 well-born
09 patrician
11 blue-blooded
12 aristocratic, thoroughbred

highbrow
07 bookish, serious
08 academic, cultured, profound
09 scholarly
10 cultivated
12 intellectual
13 sophisticated

high-class
04 posh
05 super, élite
06 choice, classy, de luxe, select
07 elegant, quality
08 superior, top-class
09 excellent, exclusive, first-rate, luxurious, top-flight
10 upper-class

highfalutin, highfaluting
05 lofty
06 la-di-da, swanky
07 pompous
08 affected
09 bombastic, grandiose
11 pretentious
12 magniloquent, supercilious

high-flown
05 lofty
06 florid, la-di-da, ornate
07 pompous
08 affected
09 bombastic, elaborate, grandiose
10 artificial, flamboyant
11 exaggerated, extravagant, pretentious
12 ostentatious
13 grandiloquent

high-handed
05 bossy
07 haughty
08 arrogant, despotic
09 arbitrary, imperious
10 autocratic, oppressive, peremptory, tyrannical
11 dictatorial, domineering, overbearing

highland
04 hill, rise
05 mound, mount, ridge
06 height, upland
07 plateau
08 mountain
09 elevation

highlight
04 best, peak
05 cream, focus
06 accent, climax, play up, set off, show up, stress
07 feature, focus on, point up
09 emphasize, underline
10 accentuate, illuminate
13 put emphasis on

highly
04 very, well
06 hugely, vastly, warmly
07 greatly
09 certainly, decidedly, extremely
10 favourably
12 considerably, tremendously
13 exceptionally
14 appreciatively

highly-strung
04 edgy
05 jumpy, nervy, tense
06 on edge
07 nervous, uptight, wound up
08 neurotic, restless, stressed
09 excitable, sensitive
13 temperamental

high-minded
04 fair, good, pure
05 lofty, moral, noble
07 ethical, upright
08 elevated, virtuous
09 righteous
10 honourable, idealistic, principled

high-pitched
05 acute, sharp, tinny
06 piping, shrill, treble
08 falsetto, piercing
11 penetrating

high-powered
07 driving, dynamic, go-ahead
08 forceful, powerful, vigorous
09 ambitious, assertive, energetic, insistent
10 aggressive
12 enterprising

high-priced
04 dear
05 steep, stiff
06 costly, pricey
09 excessive, expensive
10 exorbitant
12 extortionate, unreasonable

high-sounding
06 florid
07 orotund, pompous, stilted
09 bombastic, grandiose, overblown, ponderous
11 extravagant, pretentious
12 magniloquent, ostentatious
13 grandiloquent

high-spirited
06 active, bouncy, daring, lively
07 dashing, dynamic, vibrant
08 animated, spirited, vigorous
09 ebullient, exuberant, vivacious
10 boisterous, frolicsome
11 full of beans

highwayman
06 bandit, robber
07 footpad
15 knight of the road

hijack
05 seize
08 take over
10 commandeer
11 expropriate

hike
04 lift, pull, trek, walk, yank
05 hitch, hoist, march, put up, raise, tramp
06 jack up, pull up, push up, ramble, trudge, wander
08 increase

hilarious
05 funny, jolly, merry, noisy
07 a scream, amusing, comical, killing, riotous, risible
08 farcical, humorous
10 boisterous, hysterical, rollicking, uproarious
13 side-splitting

hilarity
03 fun
05 mirth
06 comedy, levity
07 jollity
08 laughter
09 amusement, merriment
10 exuberance
11 high spirits

hill
03 tor
04 down, drop, fell, mesa, ramp, rise
05 knoll, mound, mount, slope
06 ascent, height
07 descent, hummock, incline
08 eminence, gradient, mountain
09 acclivity, declivity, elevation
10 prominence
12 rising ground

➤ *The seven hills of Rome*:
07 Caelian, Viminal
08 Aventine, Palatine, Quirinal
09 Esquiline
10 Capitoline

hillock
04 dune, knap, knob, tump
05 knoll, knowe, mound
06 barrow
07 hummock

hilt
04 grip, haft, heft
05 helve, shaft
06 handle

❑to the hilt
05 fully
06 wholly
07 utterly
08 entirely, to the end
10 completely
15 from first to last

hind
04 back, rear, tail
05 after
06 caudal, hinder
09 posterior

hinder
04 balk, curb, foil, halt, stop
05 block, check, delay
06 arrest, hamper, hold up, impede, oppose, retard, stymie, thwart
07 inhibit, prevent
08 encumber, handicap, hold back, obstruct, slow down
09 forestall, frustrate, hamstring, interrupt

hindmost
04 last, tail
07 endmost
08 furthest, rearmost, remotest, terminal, trailing, ultimate
10 concluding

hindrance
03 bar
04 curb, drag, foil, snag
05 block, check, delay, hitch
06 hold-up
07 barrier
08 handicap, obstacle, stoppage
09 deterrent, restraint
10 difficulty, impediment
11 encumbrance, obstruction, restriction
14 stumbling-block

hinge
04 hang, rest, turn
05 pivot
06 centre, depend
07 revolve

hint
03 tip, cue
04 clue, dash, help, sign
05 imply, speck, taste, tinge, touch, trace, whiff
06 advice, allude, nuance, prompt, signal, tip off
07 inkling, mention, pointer, soupçon, suggest, whisper,
08 allusion, indicate, innuendo, intimate, reminder
09 insinuate, suspicion
10 indication, suggestion
11 implication, insinuation

hinterland
08 interior
10 hinderland
11 back-country

hip
04 loin, rump
05 croup
06 haunch, pelvis

hippy, hippie
07 beatnik, deviant, dropout
08 bohemian
11 flower child

hire
03 fee, let, pay
04 book, cost, rent, wage
05 lease, price
06 charge, employ, engage, enlist, rental, retain, salary, sign on, sign up, take on
07 appoint, charter, reserve
10 commission

hire-purchase
09 easy terms
10 never-never
14 instalment plan

hirsute
05 hairy
06 shaggy
07 bearded, bristly
08 unshaven
11 bewhiskered

hiss
03 boo
04 buzz, hoot, jeer, mock
05 scorn, taunt, whizz
06 deride, shrill, sizzle
07 catcall, hissing, mockery, scoff at, whistle
08 contempt, derision, ridicule, scoffing, sibilate, taunting

09 shout down, sibilance
10 sibilation
15 blow raspberries

historian
07 diarist
08 annalist, narrator, recorder
09 archivist
10 chronicler
11 chronologer

historic
05 famed
06 famous
07 notable
08 renowned
09 memorable, momentous
10 celebrated, remarkable
11 epoch-making, outstanding, significant
13 extraordinary

historical
03 old
04 past
05 prior
06 actual, bygone, former, of yore
07 ancient
08 recorded, verified
10 chronicled, documented

history
04 life, past, saga, tale
05 story, study
06 annals, family, record, report
07 account, memoirs, records
08 archives
09 antiquity, biography, chronicle, days of old, olden days, yesterday
10 background, bygone days, chronology, days of yore, experience, the old days, yesteryear
11 credentials, former times
13 autobiography, circumstances

──➤ *Names of historians*:
04 **Bede** (Saint 'The Venerable'), **Livy**, **Read** (Sir Herbert Edward), **Webb** (Sidney)
05 **Blunt** (Anthony Frederick), **Clark** (Kenneth, Lord), **Ensor** (Sir Robert), **Nepos** (Cornelius), **Paris** (Matthew), **Ranke** (Leopold von), **Renan** (Ernest), **Stone** (Norman)
06 **Arrian**, **Berlin** (Sir Isaiah), **Eliade** (Mircea), **Gibbon** (Edward), **O'Brien** (Conor Cruise), **Strabo**, **Strong** (Sir

Roy), **Tawney** (Richard Henry), **Taylor** (Alan John Percivale), **Terkel** (Studs), **Vasari** (Giorgio)
07 **Bullock** (Alan, Lord), **Carlyle** (Thomas), **Mommsen** (Theodor), **Pevsner** (Sir Nikolaus Bernhard), **Sallust**, **Tacitus**, **Toynbee** (Arnold), **William** (of Malmesbury), **William** (of Tyre)
08 **Foucault** (Michel), **Geoffrey** (of Monmouth), **Gombrich** (Sir Ernst Hans Josef), **Josephus** (Flavius), **Las Casas** (Emmanuel), **Macaulay** (Thomas Babington, Lord), **Michelet** (Jules), **Palgrave** (Sir Francis), **Panofsky** (Erwin), **Plutarch**, **Polybius**, **Xenophon**
09 **Dionysius** (of Halicarnassus), **Herodotus**, **Holinshed** (Raphael), **Pausanias**, **Procopius**, **Suetonius**, **Trevelyan** (George Macaulay)
10 **Burckhardt** (Jacob Christopher), **Dio Cassius**, **Thucydides**
11 **Trevor-Roper** (Hugh Redwald)
15 **Diodorus Siculus**
➢ See also **writer**

histrionic
03 ham
08 affected, dramatic
09 insincere, unnatural
10 artificial, theatrical
11 exaggerated, sensational
12 melodramatic

histrionics
05 scene
08 tantrums
09 dramatics, staginess
10 overacting
11 affectation, performance
13 artificiality, theatricality, unnaturalness

hit
03 bat, box, tap, zap
04 bang, bash, beat, belt, biff, blow, bump, cuff, harm, move, shot, slap, sock
05 clout, crash, knock, pound, punch, smack, smash, thump, touch, upset, whack

06 affect, batter, buffet, come to, damage, dawn on, impact, strike, stroke, thrash, wallop, winner
07 beating, clobber, disturb, occur to, perturb, run into, success, triumph, trouble
09 collision, overwhelm, smash into, thrashing
10 clobbering, come to mind, meet head-on, plough into
11 collide with, knock for six
12 be remembered
14 have an effect on

❑**hit back**
09 retaliate
10 strike back
13 counter-attack

❑**hit it off**
06 warm to
09 get on with
10 grow to like
12 get along with
13 get on well with

❑**hit on**
05 guess
07 light on, realize, think of, uncover
08 arrive at, chance on, discover
09 stumble on

❑**hit out**
04 rail
06 assail, attack, vilify
07 condemn, inveigh, lash out
08 denounce
09 criticize, strike out

hitch
03 tie, tug
04 bind, hike, jerk, join, pull, snag, yank, yoke
05 block, catch, check, delay, heave, hoist, unite
06 attach, couple, fasten, hiccup, hike up, hold-up, mishap, tether
07 barrier, connect, harness, problem, setback, trouble
08 drawback, obstacle
09 hindrance
10 difficulty, impediment
11 obstruction

hitherto
05 so far
07 thus far, till now, up to now
08 until now
10 beforehand, heretofore

hit-or-miss
06 casual, random
07 aimless

08 careless
09 haphazard
10 undirected
12 disorganized
13 trial-and-error
14 indiscriminate

hoard
04 fund, heap, mass, pile, save
05 amass, buy up, cache, stash, store
06 gather, supply
07 collect, put away, reserve, stack up, stock up
09 reservoir, stash away, stockpile
10 accumulate, collection
11 aggregation
12 accumulation
13 treasure-trove

hoarder
05 miser, saver
06 magpie
08 gatherer, squirrel
09 collector

hoary
03 old
04 aged, grey
05 white
06 old-hat
07 ancient, antique, archaic, silvery
08 familiar, grizzled
09 venerable
10 antiquated

hoarse
05 gruff, harsh, husky, raspy, rough
07 grating, rasping, raucous, throaty
08 croaking, gravelly, growling
10 discordant

hoax
03 con
04 dupe, fake, fool, gull, jest, joke, ruse, scam
05 bluff, cheat, fraud, prank, put-on, spoof, trick
06 delude, have on
07 deceive, fast one, leg-pull, swindle
08 hoodwink, put-up job
09 bamboozle, deception
12 take for a ride
14 pull a fast one on
15 pull someone's leg

hoaxer
09 mystifier, prankster, trickster
10 bamboozler, hoodwinker

hobble
04 limp, reel
06 dodder, falter, totter
07 shuffle, stagger, stumble

hobby
04 game
05 sport
07 leisure, pastime, pursuit
08 activity, interest, sideline
09 amusement, diversion
10 recreation, relaxation
13 entertainment

hobgoblin
03 elf, imp
05 bogey, dwarf, gnome
06 goblin, spirit, sprite
07 bugaboo, bugbear, spectre
10 apparition, evil spirit

hobnob
03 mix
06 mingle
07 consort
09 associate, socialize
10 fraternize

hocus-pocus
04 cant, hoax
06 deceit, humbug, jargon
07 swindle
08 artifice, delusion, nonsense, trickery
09 chicanery, conjuring, deception, imposture
10 mumbo-jumbo
11 abracadabra, legerdemain
13 sleight of hand

hog
03 pig
04 boar
05 swine
06 corner, porker
07 control, grunter
08 dominate, wild boar
10 monopolize

hogwash
03 rot
04 bunk, tosh
05 bilge, hooey, trash, tripe
06 bunkum, drivel, hot air, piffle
07 eyewash, rubbish, twaddle
08 claptrap, cobblers, nonsense, tommyrot
10 balderdash

hoi polloi
07 the herd
08 riff-raff, the plebs
09 the masses, the proles, the rabble
11 the peasants, the populace

14 the proletariat
15 the common people

hoist
04 jack, lift, rear
05 crane, erect, heave, raise, winch
06 jack up, pulley, tackle, uplift
07 capstan, elevate, winch up
08 elevator

hoity-toity
06 snooty, uppity
07 haughty, pompous, stuck-up
08 arrogant, snobbish
10 disdainful
11 overweening, toffee-nosed
12 supercilious
13 high and mighty

hold
03 hug, own, run
04 bear, call, curb, deem, fill, grip, have, keep, last, stay, stop, sway, take, view
05 apply, carry, catch, check, clasp, cling, grasp, judge, power, prize, rivet, seize, stick, think, treat, value
06 absorb, adhere, arrest, assume, clutch, detain, enfold, engage, esteem, fulfil, lock up, occupy, prop up, reckon, regard, remain, retain, summon, take up
07 believe, carry on, cherish, cling to, conduct, confine, contain, control, convene, embrace, engross, enthral, impound, mastery, possess, support, sustain
08 assemble, buttress, consider, continue, dominion, hold dear, hold down, imprison, leverage, maintain, organize, restrain, treasure
09 authority, dominance, fascinate, influence
10 compromise, monopolize
11 accommodate, incarcerate, preside over
13 hold in custody
14 have in your hand
15 have in your hands

❑**get hold of**
05 reach
06 obtain
07 acquire, contact, speak to

❑**hold back**
03 bar
04 curb, stop
05 check, delay
06 impede, retain, retard, stifle

07 contain, control, forbear, inhibit, prevent, refrain, repress
08 hesitate, obstruct, restrain, suppress, withhold

▢ hold down
04 have, keep
06 occupy
07 oppress
08 dominate, suppress
09 tyrannize

▢ hold forth
05 orate, speak, spout
06 preach
07 declaim, lecture
08 harangue

▢ hold off
04 wait
05 avoid, defer, delay, repel
06 put off, rebuff
07 fend off, keep off, ward off
08 fight off, postpone, stave off
09 keep at bay

▢ hold on
04 grip
05 clasp, grasp, seize
06 endure, hang on, remain
07 carry on, cling to, survive
09 keep going, persevere

▢ hold out
04 give, last
05 offer
06 extend, hang on, resist
07 carry on, last out, persist, present, proffer
09 persevere, stand fast, stand firm, withstand

▢ hold over
05 defer, delay
06 put off, shelve
08 postpone

▢ hold up
03 mug, rob
04 bear, hold, lift, slow
05 brace, carry, delay, raise
06 detain, hinder, impede, nobble, prop up, retard
07 put back, set back, shore up, stick up, support, sustain
08 knock off, obstruct
09 knock over, steal from

▢ hold water
04 wash, work
07 stand up
08 convince, ring true

▢ hold with
07 support
09 agree with, approve of

11 countenance, go along with, subscribe to

▢ hold your own
09 stand fast, stand firm, withstand
15 stand your ground

▢ put on hold
05 defer, delay
06 put off
08 postpone

holder
04 case, rest
05 cover, owner, stand
06 casing, keeper, sheath
07 housing
08 occupant
09 container, custodian, incumbent, possessor
10 proprietor, receptacle

holdings
04 land
06 assets
08 property
09 resources
10 real estate
11 investments, possessions

hold-up
03 jam
04 raid, snag, wait
05 delay, heist, hitch, theft
07 break-in, mugging, problem, robbery, setback, stick-up, trouble
08 burglary, stoppage
10 bottleneck, difficulty, stick-up job, traffic jam
11 obstruction

hole
03 den, fix, gap, jam, pit, set, tip
04 cave, dent, dump, flaw, gash, lair, mess, mine, nest, pore, rent, rift, slit, slot, slum, snag, spot, stab, tear, vent
05 break, chasm, crack, error, fault, hovel, notch, scoop, shack, shaft, space, spike, split
06 breach, burrow, cavern, cavity, covert, crater, defect, dimple, eyelet, hollow, outlet, pickle, pierce, pigsty, plight, pocket, recess
07 chamber, fissure, mistake, opening, orifice, pothole
08 aperture, hot water, loophole, puncture, quandary, weakness
09 deep water, perforate
10 depression, difficulty, excavation, pretty pass

11 discrepancy, perforation, predicament
13 inconsistency

▢ hole up
06 lie low
09 take cover
10 go to ground
12 go into hiding

▢ pick holes in
07 nit-pick, run down
09 criticize
13 find fault with

hole-and-corner
06 covert, secret, sneaky
07 furtive
08 back-door, hush-hush, stealthy
09 secretive, underhand
11 clandestine
13 surreptitious
15 under-the-counter

holiday
04 rest, trip
05 break, leave
06 day off, recess
07 holy day, time off
08 feast day, festival, furlough, half-term, vacation
09 saint's day
11 anniversary, bank holiday, celebration
12 legal holiday
13 public holiday
14 leave of absence

holier-than-thou
05 pious
08 priggish
11 goody-goody,
13 sanctimonious, self-righteous

holiness
05 piety
08 divinity, goodness, sanctity
09 godliness
10 devoutness, sacredness
11 blessedness, saintliness
12 spirituality, virtuousness
13 religiousness, righteousness

holler
03 cry
04 bawl, howl, roar, yell, yelp, yowl
05 cheer, shout, whoop
06 bellow, shriek
07 clamour

hollow
03 cup, dig, dip, low, pit

04 bowl, cave, dale, deep, dell, dent, dull, flat, glen, hole, nook, sham, vain, void, well
05 empty, false, niche, scoop
06 burrow, cavern, cavity, cirque, cranny, crater, dimple, groove, indent, recess, sunken, trough, vacant, valley
07 channel, concave, deep-set, echoing, muffled, Pyrrhic
08 excavate, indented, rumbling, unfilled
09 concavity, incurvate, insincere, pointless, valueless, worthless
10 artificial, depression, excavation, profitless, unavailing
11 indentation, meaningless
12 hypocritical

❏beat someone hollow
04 lick, rout
06 hammer, thrash
07 trounce
09 devastate, overwhelm, slaughter
10 annihilate

holocaust
06 flames, pogrom
07 carnage, inferno
08 genocide, massacre
09 sacrifice, slaughter
10 extinction, mass murder
11 destruction, devastation
12 annihilation
13 conflagration, extermination

holy
05 godly, moral, pious
06 devout, divine, sacred
07 blessed, saintly, sinless
08 faithful, hallowed, virtuous
09 pietistic, religious, righteous, spiritual, venerated
10 sacrosanct, sanctified
11 consecrated

homage
06 esteem, honour, praise, regard
07 respect, tribute, worship
08 devotion
09 adoration, adulation
10 admiration, veneration

home
03 pad
04 digs, flat
05 abode, house, local, roots
06 asylum, cradle, family, hostel, native, refuge, source
07 address, habitat, retreat

08 domestic, domicile, dwelling, interior, internal, national
09 household, residence, safe place
10 birthplace, fatherland, habitation, motherland
11 institution, nursing home
13 dwelling-place, mother country, native country, place of origin
15 country of origin

❏at home
06 at ease
07 relaxed, skilled
08 familiar
09 competent
10 conversant
11 comfortable, experienced

❏bring home
06 instil
07 impress
09 emphasize, inculcate

❏home in on
03 aim
05 focus
08 pinpoint, zero in on, zoom in on

❏nothing to write home about
06 boring
08 inferior, mediocre, ordinary
13 no great shakes

homeland
10 fatherland, motherland, native land
13 mother country, native country
15 country of origin

homeless
07 dossers, nomadic, vagrant
08 forsaken, rootless, vagrants
09 destitute, displaced, itinerant, vagabonds, wandering
10 down-and-out
11 down-and-outs
12 dispossessed
14 of no fixed abode

homely
04 cosy, snug, ugly
05 homey, plain
06 folksy, modest, simple
07 natural, relaxed
08 cheerful, domestic, everyday, familiar, friendly, informal, intimate, ordinary, unlovely
09 welcoming
10 hospitable

11 comfortable
12 unattractive
13 unpretentious
15 not much to look at

homespun
05 crude, plain, rough
06 coarse, folksy, rustic, simple
07 artless
09 inelegant, unrefined
15 unsophisticated

homicidal
07 violent
08 maniacal
09 murderous
10 sanguinary
12 bloodthirsty

homicide
06 murder
07 killing, slaying
09 bloodshed, slaughter
12 manslaughter

homily
04 talk
05 spiel
06 postil, sermon, speech
07 address, lecture, oration
09 discourse, preaching

homogeneity
07 oneness
08 likeness, sameness
09 agreement
10 consonancy, similarity, similitude, uniformity

homogeneous
05 alike
07 cognate, the same, uniform
08 unvaried
10 all the same
11 all of a piece
13 of the same kind

homogenize
04 fuse
05 blend, merge, unite
07 combine
08 coalesce
10 amalgamate

homologous
04 like
07 related, similar
08 matching, parallel
09 analogous
10 comparable, equivalent
13 correspondent, corresponding

homosexual
03 fag, gay
04 bent, camp, dyke, homo, poof

05 butch, dykey, fairy, nancy, pansy, queen, queer
06 faggot, invert
07 lesbian, woofter

hone
04 edge, file, whet
05 grind, point
06 polish
07 develop, sharpen

honest
04 fair, just, open, real, true
05 blunt, frank, legal, plain
06 candid, direct, lawful, simple
07 ethical, genuine, sincere, up front, upright
08 straight, truthful, virtuous
09 equitable, impartial, objective, outspoken, reputable
10 above-board, forthright, honourable, law-abiding, legitimate, on the level, principled, scrupulous, upstanding
11 respectable, trustworthy
13 fair and square, incorruptible, plain-speaking
14 straight as a die
15 straightforward

honestly
05 truly
06 fairly, justly, openly, really
07 frankly, legally, plainly
08 directly, lawfully, outright
10 honourably, on the level, straight up, truthfully
11 in good faith, objectively
12 legitimately

honesty
06 ethics, honour, virtue
07 balance, candour, probity
08 legality, morality, openness, veracity
09 bluntness, frankness, integrity, rectitude
10 legitimacy
11 genuineness, objectivity, uprightness
12 explicitness, truthfulness
13 plain-speaking, righteousness
14 forthrightness
15 trustworthiness

honorarium
03 fee, pay
06 reward, salary
09 emolument
12 remuneration

honorary
06 formal, unpaid
07 nominal, titular
09 ex officio, honorific
10 in name only, unofficial

honour
04 fame, keep
05 award, clear, crown, exalt, glory, pride, prize, title, value
06 accept, credit, esteem, ethics, favour, fulfil, homage, laurel, morals, praise, renown, repute, revere, reward, trophy, virtue
07 acclaim, applaud, commend, decency, dignity, glorify, honesty, probity, respect, tribute, worship
08 accolade, applause, decorate, good name, goodness, morality, remember, venerate
09 adoration, celebrate, discharge, integrity, privilege, recognize, rectitude, reverence
10 compliment, decoration, principles, reputation
11 acclamation, acknowledge, commemorate, distinction, pay homage to, recognition, self-respect, uprightness
12 commendation, pay tribute to, truthfulness
13 righteousness
15 trustworthiness

honourable
04 fair, good, just, true
05 great, moral, noble, noted, right
06 decent, famous, honest, trusty, worthy
07 eminent, ethical, notable, sincere, upright
08 reliable, renowned, straight, truthful, virtuous
09 admirable, reputable, respected, righteous
10 dependable, high-minded, principled, upstanding
11 illustrious, prestigious, respectable, trustworthy
13 distinguished

hood
04 cowl
05 scarf
07 capuche
08 capeline

hoodlum
03 yob
04 hood, lout, thug

05 brute, felon, rowdy, tough
06 gunman, mugger, vandal
07 mobster, ruffian
08 criminal, gangster, hooligan
09 bovver boy

hoodwink
03 con
04 dupe, fool, gull, hoax
05 cheat, trick
06 delude, take in
07 deceive, mislead, swindle
09 bamboozle
12 take for a ride
14 pull a fast one on

hoof
04 foot
07 trotter
10 cloven hoof

hoofed
08 ungulate
12 cloven-footed, cloven-hoofed

hook
03 arc, bag, bow, box, fix, hit, peg, rap
04 barb, bend, blow, clip, cuff, curl, grab, hasp, loop, trap
05 angle, catch, clasp, clout, crook, curve, elbow, hitch, knock, punch, snare, thump
06 enmesh, entrap, fasten, scythe, secure, sickle, stroke, wallop
07 capture, ensnare
08 entangle, fastener

❑ **off the hook**
07 cleared
09 acquitted
10 exonerated, in the clear

hooked
04 bent
06 barbed, beaked, curled, curved
08 addicted, aquiline, hamulate, obsessed, unciform, uncinate
09 dependent, enamoured

hooligan
03 yob
04 lout, thug
05 rough, rowdy, tough
06 vandal
07 hoodlum, ruffian
09 bovver boy
10 delinquent

hoop
04 band, loop, ring
06 circle, girdle
07 circlet

hoot
03 boo, cry
04 beep, call, hiss, howl, jeer, mock, toot
05 shout, sneer, taunt, whoop
06 shriek
07 screech, ululate, whistle

hop
04 jump, leap, limp, rave, skip, step, trip
05 bound, dance, disco, frisk, jaunt, party, vault
06 bounce, flight, hobble, prance, social, spring
07 journey, knees-up, shindig
09 excursion

hope
04 long, rely, wish
05 await, crave, dream, faith, trust, yearn
06 aspire, assume, belief, desire, expect
07 believe, craving, foresee, longing, promise
08 ambition, optimism, prospect, reckon on, yearning
09 assurance, be hopeful
10 anticipate, aspiration, assumption, confidence, conviction
11 contemplate, expectation
12 anticipation
13 look forward to
14 have confidence
15 hope against hope

hopeful
06 bright
07 assured, bullish, buoyant
08 aspirant, aspiring, cheerful, pleasant, positive, sanguine
09 confident, expectant, promising
10 auspicious, favourable, optimistic, propitious
11 encouraging

hopefully
05 I hope
08 probably, with hope, with luck
10 expectedly, sanguinely
11 expectantly
14 optimistically

hopeless
04 lost, poor, vain, weak
05 awful, grave, lousy
06 futile, gloomy
07 foolish, forlorn, useless
08 dejected, downcast, helpless, pathetic, wretched

09 defeatist, desperate, incurable, pointless, worthless
10 despairing, despondent, impossible
11 downhearted, incompetent, irreparable, pessimistic
12 beyond repair, irremediable, unachievable, unattainable

horde
03 mob
04 army, band, crew, gang, herd, host, mass, pack
05 crowd, drove, flock, swarm, troop
06 throng
09 multitude

horizon
05 range, scope, vista
07 compass, outlook, skyline
08 prospect
10 perception
11 perspective
13 range of vision

horizontal
04 flat
05 level, plane
06 smooth, supine
09 on its side

hormone
▶ *Hormones include*:
05 kinin
07 gastrin, insulin, relaxin
08 androgen, autacoid, estrogen, florigen, glucagon, oxytocin, secretin
09 adrenalin, cortisone, melatonin, oestrogen, prolactin
10 adrenaline
11 vasopressin
12 progesterone, testosterone

horny
04 hard, sexy
05 corny, randy
06 ardent
07 callous, lustful, ruttish
08 ceratoid, corneous
09 lecherous
10 lascivious, libidinous
12 concupiscent

horrendous
08 dreadful, horrific, shocking, terrible
09 appalling, frightful
10 horrifying, terrifying
11 frightening

horrible
04 grim

05 awful, nasty, scary
06 horrid, unkind
07 ghastly, hideous
08 dreadful, gruesome, horrific, shocking, terrible
09 appalling, frightful, harrowing, loathsome, obnoxious, offensive, repulsive, revolting
10 abominable, detestable, disgusting, horrifying, terrifying, unpleasant
11 frightening, hair-raising
12 disagreeable
13 bloodcurdling

horrid
04 grim, mean
05 awful, cruel, nasty
07 beastly, ghastly, hateful, hideous
08 dreadful, gruesome, horrific, shocking, terrible
09 appalling, frightful, obnoxious, repulsive, revolting
10 abominable, horrifying, terrifying
11 frightening, hair-raising

horrific
05 awful, scary
07 ghastly
08 dreadful, gruesome, shocking, terrible
09 appalling, frightful, harrowing
10 horrifying, terrifying
11 frightening

horrify
05 alarm, appal, panic, repel, scare, shock
06 dismay, offend, revolt, sicken
07 disgust, outrage, startle, terrify
08 frighten, nauseate
09 terrorize
10 intimidate, scandalize
12 put the wind up, scare to death

horror
04 fear, hate
05 alarm, dread, panic, shock
06 dismay, fright, terror
07 disgust, outrage
08 distaste, loathing
09 awfulness, revulsion
10 abhorrence, repugnance
11 abomination, detestation, ghastliness, hideousness, trepidation
12 apprehension

13 consternation, frightfulness
14 unpleasantness

horror-struck
06 aghast
07 shocked, stunned
08 appalled
09 horrified, petrified, terrified
10 frightened
14 horror-stricken

horse
03 bay, cob, nag
04 colt, hack, mare, roan
05 filly, mount, steed
06 bronco, dobbin, sorrel
07 broncho, centaur, charger, hackney, mustang
08 stallion

➤ *Horse and pony breeds*:
03 Don
04 Arab, Barb, Fell
05 Dales, Iomud, Pinto, Shire, Toric, Waler
06 Breton, Brumby, Exmoor, Morgan, Tersky
07 Furioso, Hackney, Hispano, Jutland, Mustang, Salerno
08 Danubian, Dartmoor, Friesian, Highland, Holstein, Karabair, Karabakh, Lusitano, Palomino, Shetland, Welsh Cob
09 Alter-Réal, Anglo-Arab, Appaloosa, Calabrese, Connemara, Knabstrup, New Forest, Oldenburg, Percheron, Welsh Pony
10 Brabançon, Clydesdale, Gelderland, Lipizzaner, Mangalarga
11 Anglo-Norman, Irish Hunter
12 Dutch Draught, East Friesian, Irish Draught, Suffolk Punch, Thoroughbred
13 French Trotter, German Trotter
15 American Trotter

➤ *Names of horseriders, jockeys and trainers*:
04 **Anne** (Princess), **Hern** (Major Dick), **Leng** (Virginia), **Tait** (Blyth), **Todd** (Mark)
05 **Cecil** (Henry), **Green** (Lucinda), **Meade** (Richard), **Smith** (Harvey)
06 **Arcaro** (Eddie), **Carson** (Willie), **Eddery** (Pat), **Fallon** (Keiron), **O'Brien**

(Vincent), **O'Neill** (Jonjo), **Pitman** (Jenny)
07 **Dettori** (Frankie), **Francis** (Richard Stanley 'Dick'), **Gifford** (Josh), **Piggott** (Lester), **Winkler** (Hans Gunter)
08 **Champion** (Bob), **Donoghue** (Steve), **Dunwoody** (Richard), **Phillips** (Captain Mark), **Richards** (Sir Gordon)
09 **Scudamore** (Peter), **Shoemaker** (Willie)
➤ See also **sport**

━━━━━━━━━━━━━━━━
▬ *Famous racehorses include*:
05 Arkle, Cigar, Pinza
06 Red Rum, Sir Ken
07 Alleged, Dawn Run, Eclipse, Pharlap, Sceptre, Shergar, Sir Ivor
08 Aldaniti, Corbiere, Hyperion, Istabraq, Mill Reef
09 John Henry, L'Escargot, Oh So Sharp
10 Night Nurse, Persian War, See You Then, Sun Chariot
11 Cottage Rake, Pretty Polly
12 Dancing Brave, Desert Orchid
➤ See also **sport**

horseman, horsewoman
05 rider
06 hussar, jockey, knight
07 dragoon
10 cavalryman, equestrian

horseplay
06 antics, capers, pranks
08 clowning
09 high jinks
10 buffoonery, skylarking, tomfoolery
11 fun and games
13 fooling around
14 rough-and-tumble

hortatory
03 pep
08 didactic, edifying
09 homiletic, hortative
10 heartening, preceptive
11 encouraging, exhortative, exhortatory, inspiriting, instructive, stimulating

horticulture
09 gardening
11 cultivation

hosanna
06 praise, save us

08 alleluia
09 laudation

hose
04 duct, pipe, tube
06 tubing
07 channel, conduit

hosiery
04 hose
05 socks
06 tights
08 leggings
09 stockings
12 leg-coverings

hospitable
04 kind, warm
06 genial
07 cordial, helpful, liberal
08 amicable, friendly, generous, gracious, sociable
09 bountiful, congenial, convivial, receptive, welcoming
10 open-handed
11 kind-hearted, neighbourly

hospital
06 clinic
07 hospice
09 infirmary, institute
10 sanatorium

hospitality
05 cheer
06 warmth
07 welcome
08 kindness
10 generosity, liberality
11 helpfulness, sociability
12 congeniality, conviviality, friendliness
13 accommodation, entertainment
14 open-handedness
15 neighbourliness

host
02 MC
03 mob
04 army, band, give, herd, mass, pack
05 array, crowd, crush, emcee, horde, swarm, troop
06 myriad, throng
07 compère, present
08 landlady, landlord, publican
09 innkeeper, introduce, multitude, presenter
10 proprietor

hostage
07 captive
08 prisoner

hostel
03 inn
05 hotel, motel
07 pension
09 dosshouse, residence
10 guesthouse

hostile
07 adverse, opposed, warlike
08 contrary, inimical, opposite
09 bellicose
10 malevolent, unfriendly
11 belligerent, ill-disposed
12 antagonistic, inauspicious, inhospitable, unfavourable
13 unsympathetic

hostilities
03 war
06 battle, strife
07 warfare
08 conflict, fighting
09 bloodshed

hostility
04 hate
06 enmity, hatred, malice
07 cruelty, dislike, ill-will
08 aversion
09 animosity, militancy
10 aggression, antagonism, resentment
11 bellicosity, malevolence
12 belligerence, estrangement
14 unfriendliness

hot
03 new, red
04 keen, warm
05 angry, eager, fiery, fresh, livid, sharp, spicy
06 baking, fierce, fuming, heated, latest, piping, raging, recent, stolen, strong, sultry, torrid
07 boiling, burning, devoted, earnest, enraged, flushed, furious, intense, peppery, piquant, pungent, searing, violent, zealous
08 diligent, exciting, feverish, incensed, inflamed, parching, pilfered, roasting, scalding, seething, sizzling, steaming, tropical
09 indignant, scorching
10 blistering, contraband, sweltering

◻**hot air**
03 gas
04 bosh, bunk
05 bilge, froth
06 bunkum, piffle, vapour

07 blather, blether, bluster, bombast
08 bullshit, claptrap, cobblers, nonsense, verbiage
09 empty talk, mere words
10 balderdash

hotbed
03 den
04 hive, nest
06 cradle, school
07 nursery, seedbed
12 forcing-house
14 breeding-ground

hot-blooded
04 bold, rash, wild
05 fiery, lusty
07 fervent, lustful, sensual
09 impulsive, perfervid
10 passionate
13 temperamental

hotchpotch
03 mix
04 mess
06 jumble, medley
07 melange, mixture
08 mishmash
09 confusion
10 collection, miscellany

hotel
03 inn
05 motel
06 hostel, tavern
07 pension
08 hostelry

hotfoot
07 hastily, in haste, quickly, rapidly, swiftly
08 pell-mell, speedily
09 hurriedly, posthaste
10 at top speed

hothead
06 madcap, madman, terror
07 hotspur
08 tearaway
09 daredevil, desperado

hotheaded
04 rash, wild
05 fiery, hasty
08 reckless, volatile, volcanic
09 excitable, explosive, foolhardy, impetuous, impulsive, irascible
10 headstrong

hothouse
10 glasshouse, greenhouse
12 conservatory

hot-tempered
05 fiery, hasty, testy
07 violent

08 choleric, petulant, volcanic
09 explosive, irascible, irritable

hound
03 nag
04 goad, hunt, prod, urge
05 bully, chase, drive, force, harry, stalk, track, trail
06 badger, harass, pursue
07 disturb, provoke
09 persecute

house
04 body, clan, firm, hold, home, keep, line, race
05 blood, guard, lodge, place, put up, store, train
06 billet, family, ménage, strain
07 chamber, company, contain, dynasty, kindred, lineage, quarter, sheathe, shelter
08 ancestry, assembly, audience, congress, domestic, domicile, dwelling
09 gathering, residence
10 auditorium, enterprise, habitation, parliament, spectators
11 accommodate, corporation, legislature
12 family circle, organization

► *Types of house*:
03 hut
04 flat, hall, semi
05 croft, igloo, lodge, manor, manse, shack, villa
06 bedsit, chalet, duplex, grange, prefab, shanty, studio
07 cottage, mansion, rectory
08 bungalow, detached, hacienda, log cabin, terraced, vicarage
09 apartment, farmhouse, homestead, parsonage, penthouse, town-house
10 maisonette, pied-à-terre, ranchhouse
11 condominium
12 council house, semi-detached
➤ See also **accommodation**

◻**on the house**
04 free
06 gratis
08 at no cost
10 for nothing
11 without cost
12 free of charge
13 without charge

household
06 family, ménage
08 domestic
12 family circle, ménage à trois
13 establishment

householder
05 owner
06 tenant
08 landlady, landlord,
    occupant, occupier, resident
09 home-owner
10 freeholder, proprietor
11 leaseholder

housekeeping
10 homemaking
11 housewifery
12 domestic work, running a
    home
13 home economics
15 domestic matters, domestic
    science

houseman
06 doctor, intern
07 interne
08 resident

house-trained
11 house-broken
12 domesticated

housing
04 case
05 cover, guard
06 casing, holder, jacket,
    sheath
07 shelter
08 covering
09 container, dwellings
10 habitation, protection
13 accommodation

hovel
04 dump, hole, shed
05 cabin, shack
06 shanty

hover
04 flap, hang
05 drift, float, pause, poise,
    waver
06 linger, seesaw
07 flutter
08 hesitate
09 alternate, fluctuate, hang
    about, oscillate, vacillate

however
03 yet
05 still
06 anyhow, even so, though
10 regardless
11 just the same, nonetheless
12 nevertheless
15 notwithstanding

howl
03 bay, cry
04 bawl, hoot, moan, roar, wail,
    yell, yelp, yowl
05 groan, shout
06 bellow, scream, shriek

howler
04 boob
05 error, gaffe
07 bloomer, clanger, mistake
08 solecism

hub
04 axis, core
05 focus, heart, pivot
06 centre, middle
08 linchpin
11 nerve centre

hubbub
03 din
04 riot
05 chaos, noise
06 racket, tumult, uproar
07 clamour
09 commotion, confusion
10 hullabaloo, hurly-burly
11 disturbance, pandemonium

huckster
06 barker, dealer, hawker,
    pedlar, tinker, vendor
07 haggler, packman, pitcher

huddle
04 cram, knot, mass, pack
05 crowd, flock, hunch, press
06 crouch, gather, muddle,
    nestle
07 cluster, snuggle, squeeze
10 conference, discussion

hue
03 dye
04 tint, tone
05 light, shade, tinge
06 aspect, colour, nuance
10 complexion

hue and cry
03 ado
04 fuss, to-do
06 furore, outcry, rumpus,
    uproar
07 clamour, ruction
08 brouhaha
10 hullabaloo

huff
04 mood, rage
05 anger, pique, sulks
07 bad mood, passion

huffy
05 moody, sulky, surly, testy
06 grumpy, miffed
07 peevish, waspish

08 petulant
09 querulous, resentful

hug
04 grip, hold
05 clasp, press
06 clinch, clutch, cuddle, enfold
07 cling to, embrace, enclose
11 stay close to

huge
04 vast
05 bulky, giant, great, jumbo
07 immense, mammoth,
    massive, titanic
08 colossal, enormous,
    gigantic, unwieldy
09 extensive, monstrous
10 gargantuan, prodigious,
    stupendous, tremendous

hulk
03 oaf
04 clod, hull, lout, lump
05 frame, shell, wreck
06 lubber
09 shipwreck

hulking
05 bulky, heavy
06 clumsy
07 awkward, massive, weighty
08 ungainly, unwieldy
09 lumbering

hull
03 pod
04 body, husk, pare, peel, rind,
    skin, trim
05 frame, shell, shuck, strip
06 casing, legume
07 capsule, epicarp
08 covering, skeleton
09 framework, structure

hullabaloo
03 din
04 fuss, to-do
05 noise
06 furore, hubbub, outcry,
    racket, tumult, uproar
08 brouhaha
09 commotion, hue and cry
11 disturbance, pandemonium

hum
04 buzz, purr, sing
05 croon, drone, pulse, throb,
    thrum, whirr
06 mumble, murmur
07 buzzing, purring, vibrate
08 whirring
09 pulsation, throbbing,
    vibration

human
03 man

04 body, soul
05 child, woman
06 humane, mortal, person
07 fleshly
08 fallible
10 anthropoid, individual
11 homo sapiens, sympathetic
13 flesh and blood

humane
04 good, kind, mild
06 benign, gentle, kindly, loving, tender
07 lenient
08 generous, merciful
09 forgiving
10 benevolent, charitable, forbearing
11 considerate, good-natured, kind-hearted, sympathetic
12 humanitarian
13 compassionate, understanding

humanitarian
04 kind
06 humane
08 altruist, do-gooder
10 altruistic, charitable
13 good Samaritan, philanthropic
14 philanthropist, public-spirited

humanitarianism
07 charity
08 goodwill, humanism
10 generosity
11 beneficence, benevolence
12 philanthropy
14 charitableness

humanity
03 man
06 people
07 mankind, mortals
08 goodness, sympathy
09 humankind, human race, womankind
10 compassion, humaneness
11 benevolence, homo sapiens
13 brotherly love, fellow-feeling
15 kind-heartedness

humanize
04 tame
05 edify
06 better, polish, refine
07 educate, improve
08 civilize
09 cultivate, enlighten
11 domesticate

humble
03 low

04 mean, meek, poor
05 abase, crush, lower, lowly, plain
06 common, demean, modest, simple, subdue
07 chasten, deflate, mortify, servile
08 belittle, bring low, disgrace, inferior, ordinary
09 bring down, disparage, humiliate, unrefined
10 low-ranking, obsequious, put to shame, respectful, submissive, unassuming
11 commonplace, deferential, subservient, sycophantic, unassertive, unimportant
12 self-effacing
13 insignificant, unpretentious
14 unostentatious

humbly
06 meekly, simply
08 docilely, modestly
09 cap in hand, servilely
12 obsequiously, respectfully, submissively, unassumingly
13 deferentially, subserviently

humbug
03 con, rot
04 cant, fake, hoax, sham
05 actor, bluff, cheat, fraud, poser, rogue, swank, trick
06 bunkum, con man, deceit
07 baloney, bluffer, eyewash, rubbish, swindle
08 cheating, claptrap, cobblers, impostor, nonsense, pretence, swindler, trickery
09 charlatan, deception, hypocrisy, poppycock, trickster
10 balderdash

humdrum
04 dull
05 banal
06 boring, dreary
07 mundane, routine, tedious
08 ordinary, unvaried
10 monotonous, uneventful
11 commonplace, repetitious
12 run-of-the-mill
13 uninteresting

humid
03 wet
04 damp, dank
05 close, heavy, moist, muggy
06 clammy, steamy, sticky, sultry
10 oppressive

humidity
03 dew
04 damp, mist
07 wetness
08 dampness, dankness, moisture
09 closeness, heaviness, humidness, moistness, mugginess, sogginess
10 clamminess, steaminess, stickiness, sultriness

humiliate
05 abase, abash, break, crush, shame
06 demean, humble
07 chasten, deflate, degrade, mortify, put down
08 bring low, confound, disgrace
09 discomfit, discredit, embarrass

humiliating
07 shaming
08 humbling
09 degrading
10 disgracing, mortifying
11 disgraceful, ignominious
12 discomfiting, embarrassing

humiliation
04 snub
05 shame
06 rebuff
07 affront, put-down
08 crushing, disgrace, humbling, ignominy
09 abasement, deflation, discredit, dishonour, humble pie, indignity
10 chastening, loss of face
11 confounding, degradation
12 discomfiture
13 embarrassment, mortification

humility
07 modesty
09 deference, servility
10 diffidence, humbleness
13 self-abasement
14 self-effacement, submissiveness

hummock
04 hump
05 knoll, mound
06 barrow
07 hillock
10 prominence

humorist
03 wag, wit
05 clown, comic, joker

06 jester
08 comedian, satirist

humorous
04 zany
05 comic, droll, funny, witty
06 absurd
07 amusing, comical, jocular, playful, risible, waggish
08 farcical
09 facetious, hilarious, laughable, ludicrous, satirical, whimsical
10 ridiculous
12 entertaining
13 side-splitting

humour
03 fun, wit
04 gags, mood
05 farce, jokes, spoil
06 comedy, favour, pamper, please, satire, temper
07 flatter, gratify, indulge, jesting, mollify, satisfy, spirits
08 drollery, hilarity, pander to
09 amusement, wittiness
10 jocularity, wisecracks
11 disposition, frame of mind, go along with, state of mind, temperament

▶ *The four bodily humours*:
05 blood
06 choler, phlegm
09 black bile
10 melancholy, yellow bile

humourless
03 dry
04 dull, glum, grim
05 grave
06 boring, morose, solemn, sombre
07 serious, tedious
09 long-faced, unsmiling
10 unlaughing

hump
03 lug
04 arch, bump, knob, lift, lump
05 bulge, carry, crook, curve, gloom, heave, hoist, hunch, mound
08 shoulder, swelling, vexation
09 annoyance, outgrowth
10 prominence, protrusion

hump-backed
07 crooked, gibbous, hunched, stooped
08 deformed, kyphotic
09 misshapen

humped
04 bent

06 arched, curved
07 crooked, gibbous, hunched

hunch
04 bend, hump, idea
05 curve, guess, stoop
06 crouch
07 feeling, inkling
08 intuition, suspicion
11 premonition
12 presentiment

hunger
03 yen
04 ache, itch, long, pine, wish
05 crave, greed, yearn
06 desire, famine, hanker, pining, starve, thirst
07 craving, longing
08 appetite, voracity, yearning
09 emptiness, esurience, esuriency, hankering
10 greediness, hungriness, starvation
12 malnutrition, ravenousness

hungry
04 avid
05 eager, empty
06 aching, greedy, hollow, pining
07 craving, itching, longing, needing, peckish, thirsty
08 covetous, desirous, famished, ravenous, starving, underfed, yearning
09 hankering, voracious
12 malnourished
14 could eat a horse, undernourished

hunk
04 clod, lump, mass, slab
05 block, chunk, piece, wedge

hunt
04 fish, seek
05 chase, hound, quest, scour, stalk, track, trail
06 ferret, forage, pursue, search
07 look for, pursuit, rummage
08 stalking, tracking
09 try to find
11 investigate
13 investigation

hunter
08 huntsman, woodsman

hurdle
04 jump, wall
05 fence, hedge
07 barrier, problem, railing
08 handicap, obstacle
09 barricade, hindrance
10 difficulty, impediment

11 obstruction
14 stumbling-block

hurl
04 cast, fire, send, toss
05 chuck, fling, heave, pitch, sling, throw
06 launch, let fly, propel
07 project
08 catapult

hurly-burly
05 chaos
06 bustle, hubbub, hustle, tumult
08 brouhaha, disorder
09 commotion, confusion
11 pandemonium

hurricane
04 gale
05 storm
07 cyclone, tempest, tornado, typhoon

hurried
05 brief, hasty, quick, rapid, swift
06 hectic, rushed, speedy
07 cursory, offhand, shallow
08 careless, fleeting, slapdash
09 breakneck, transient
10 transitory
11 perfunctory, precipitate, superficial

hurry
03 fly, run
04 dash, push, rush
05 haste, speed
06 bustle, hasten, hustle
07 quicken, speed up, urgency
08 celerity, dispatch, go all out, rapidity, step on it
09 commotion, confusion, cut and run, make haste, quickness, shake a leg
10 accelerate, get a move on
11 get cracking, run like hell
13 show your heels
15 put your foot down

hurt
03 cut, mar, sad
04 ache, harm, pain, sore
05 annoy, grief, smart, spoil, sting, throb, upset, wound
06 aching, blight, bruise, damage, grieve, impair, injure, injury, maimed, misery, offend, sadden, sorrow
07 afflict, annoyed, blemish, bruised, burning, disable, injured, painful, sadness,

scarred, scratch, torture, wounded
08 distress, ill-treat, maltreat, offended, smarting, soreness
09 affronted, aggrieved, be painful, in anguish, lacerated, miserable, sorrowful, suffering, throbbing
10 affliction, debilitate, discomfort, distressed
13 grief-stricken

hurtful
06 unkind
07 cutting, harmful, vicious
08 damaging, scathing, wounding
09 injurious, upsetting
11 destructive, distressing

hurtle
03 fly
04 dash, dive, race, rush, tear
05 crash, shoot, speed
06 career, charge, plunge, rattle

husband
04 mate, save
05 groom, hoard, hubby, store
06 budget, eke out, ration, save up, spouse
07 partner, reserve
08 conserve, put aside
09 economize, other half
12 use carefully, use sparingly

husbandry
06 saving, thrift
07 economy, farming, tillage
09 frugality
10 management
11 cultivation, thriftiness
12 conservation

hush
04 calm
05 peace, quiet, shush, still
06 repose, settle, shut up, soothe, subdue
07 quieten, silence
08 calmness, pipe down
09 quietness, stillness
12 peacefulness, tranquillity
14 hold your tongue, not another word

◻**hush up**
03 gag
07 conceal, cover up, smother
08 keep dark, suppress
10 keep secret

hush-hush
06 secret
09 top-secret

10 classified, under wraps
12 confidential

husk
03 pod
04 bran, case, hull, rind
05 chaff, shell, shuck
07 capsule, epicarp
08 covering

husky
03 low
04 deep
05 beefy, burly, gruff, harsh
06 brawny, coarse, hoarse
07 rasping, throaty
08 gravelly, muscular
09 strapping, well-built

hussy
04 minx, slag, slut, tart, vamp
05 tramp
07 floosie
08 scrubber

hustle
03 fly
04 dash, fuss, push, rush, stir
05 crowd, elbow, force, hurry, nudge, shove
06 bundle, bustle, hasten, jostle, thrust, tumult
08 activity
09 agitation, commotion
10 hurly-burly, pressurize

hut
04 shed
05 booth, cabin, shack
06 lean-to, shanty

hybrid
05 cross, mixed
07 amalgam, mixture, mongrel
08 combined, compound
09 composite, crossbred, half-blood, half-breed
10 crossbreed
11 combination
13 heterogeneous
14 conglomeration

hybridize
05 cross
10 crossbreed, interbreed

hydrocarbon
▶ *Hydrocarbons include*:
03 wax
05 halon
06 aldrin, alkane, alkene, alkyne, butane, cetane, decane, ethane, hexane, nonane, octane, olefin, picene, pyrene
07 benzene, heptane, methane, pentane, propane, styrene

08 camphene, diphenyl, stilbene
09 butadiene
10 mesitylene
11 naphthalane

hygiene
06 purity
09 sterility
10 sanitation
11 cleanliness

hygienic
04 pure
05 clean
07 aseptic, healthy, sterile
08 germ-free, sanitary
10 salubrious, sterilized
11 disinfected

hymn
04 song
05 carol, chant, paean, psalm
06 anthem, choral, chorus
07 cantata, chorale, introit
08 canticle, doxology
09 offertory, spiritual
12 song of praise

hype
04 fuss, plug
06 racket
07 build up, build-up, promote, puffing
08 ballyhoo, plugging
09 advertise, promotion, publicity, publicize
10 razzmatazz

hyperbole
06 excess
08 overkill
12 exaggeration, extravagance
13 magnification, overstatement

hypercritical
05 picky
07 carping, finicky
09 cavilling, quibbling
10 censorious, nit-picking, pernickety
14 over-particular

hypnotic
07 numbing
08 magnetic, sedative
09 soporific
10 compelling
11 fascinating, mesmerizing, somniferous
12 irresistible, spellbinding
13 sleep-inducing

hypnotism
09 mesmerism
10 suggestion
14 auto-suggestion

hypnotize
07 beguile, bewitch, enchant
08 entrance
09 captivate, fascinate, magnetize, mesmerize, spellbind

hypochondria
08 neurosis
15 hypochondriasis

hypochondriac
08 neurotic
14 valetudinarian

hypocrisy
04 cant
06 deceit
07 falsity
08 pretence
09 deception, duplicity
10 dishonesty, double-talk, lip service, pharisaism, phoneyness
11 dissembling, insincerity
12 two-facedness
13 deceitfulness, double-dealing

hypocrite
05 fraud, pseud
06 canter, phoney, pseudo
08 Pharisee
09 pretender
10 Holy Willie
15 whited sepulchre

hypocritical
08 two-faced
09 insincere
10 fraudulent, perfidious
11 dissembling, duplicitous, pharisaical
12 Pecksniffian

hypothesis
05 axiom
06 theory, thesis
07 premise, theorem
09 postulate
10 assumption, conjecture
11 presumption, proposition, speculation, supposition

hypothetical
07 assumed
08 imagined, presumed, proposed, supposed

09 imaginary
11 conjectural, speculative, theoretical

hysteria
05 mania, panic
06 frenzy
07 habdabs, madness
08 delirium, neurosis
09 agitation, hysterics

hysterical
03 mad
06 crazed, raving
07 berserk, frantic
08 demented, frenzied, in a panic, neurotic
09 delirious, hilarious, priceless
10 uproarious
11 overwrought
13 side-splitting
14 beside yourself, uncontrollable

hysterics
06 frenzy
07 habdabs, madness
08 delirium, hysteria, neurosis

ice
04 rime
05 chill, frost, glaze
06 freeze, icicle
07 glacier, iciness
10 freeze over, frostiness
11 frozen water, refrigerate

❑ put on ice
05 defer, delay
08 postpone
06 put off, shelve
14 hold in abeyance
15 leave in abeyance

ice-cold
03 icy, raw
04 iced, numb
05 algid, gelid, polar
06 arctic, frigid, frosty, frozen
07 chilled, frosted, glacial
08 freezing, Siberian
11 frozen-stiff
12 bitterly cold

icon
04 idol
05 image
06 figure, symbol
14 representation

iconoclast
07 heretic, radical, sceptic
09 dissenter, dissident
10 questioner, unbeliever
11 denunciator
12 image-breaker

iconoclastic
08 critical
09 dissident, heretical,
   sceptical
10 irreverent, subversive
11 dissentient, questioning
12 denunciatory

icy
03 raw
04 cold, rimy
05 chill, gelid, polar
06 arctic, biting, bitter, chilly,
   frigid, frosty, frozen, glassy
07 glacial, hostile
08 freezing, Siberian
10 frostbound

idea
03 aim, end
04 clue, goal, plan, view
05 fancy, guess, image, point
06 belief, notion, object,
   reason, theory, vision
07 concept, feeling, inkling,
   opinion, purpose, thought
08 proposal
09 brainwave, intention,
   judgement, objective,
   suspicion, viewpoint
10 conception, conjecture,
   hypothesis, impression,
   perception, suggestion
11 abstraction, proposition
13 understanding
14 interpretation

ideal
04 acme, best
05 dream, image, model
06 ethics, morals
07 epitome, optimal, optimum,
   paragon, pattern, perfect,
   supreme, utopian
08 exemplar
09 archetype, nonpareil,
   yardstick
10 archetypal, consummate,
   perfection
11 moral values, theoretical
12 hypothetical
13 ethical values
14 moral standards

idealism
10 utopianism
11 romanticism
13 perfectionism

idealist
08 optimist, romantic
11 romanticist
13 perfectionist

idealistic
07 utopian
08 romantic
10 optimistic, starry-eyed
13 perfectionist

idealization
10 apotheosis
11 idolization

13 glamorization, glorification
15 romanticization

idealize
07 glorify, idolize, worship
09 glamorize
11 romanticize

ideally
06 at best
08 in theory
09 perfectly
13 theoretically
15 in a perfect world

idée fixe
06 hang-up
08 fixation
09 fixed idea, leitmotiv,
   monomania, obsession

identical
04 like, same, twin
05 alike, equal
08 matching, self-same
09 duplicate
13 one and the same
15 interchangeable

identifiable
10 detectable, noticeable
11 discernible, perceptible
12 recognizable, unmistakable
15 distinguishable

identification
02 ID
05 badge
06 papers
07 empathy, rapport
08 sympathy
09 detection, diagnosis,
   documents, labelling
11 credentials, recognition
12 identity card
13 fellow feeling

identify
03 tag
04 know, name, spot
05 label, place
06 detect, notice, relate
07 discern, feel for, find out,
   make out, pick out, specify

08 classify, diagnose, discover, perceive, pinpoint, point out, relate to
09 ascertain, catalogue, establish, recognize, single out
11 distinguish
13 empathize with
14 sympathize with

identity
03 ego
04 name, self
08 likeness, sameness, selfhood
09 character, existence
10 uniqueness
11 personality, resemblance
13 individuality, particularity
15 distinctiveness

ideologist
07 teacher, thinker
08 theorist
09 ideologue, visionary
11 doctrinaire, philosopher

ideology
05 credo, creed, dogma, faith, ideas
06 belief, tenets, theory, thesis
07 beliefs, opinion
08 doctrine, opinions, teaching
09 doctrines, world-view
10 philosophy, principles
11 convictions

idiocy
08 daftness, insanity
09 absurdity, craziness, silliness, stupidity
11 fatuousness
13 foolhardiness, senselessness

idiom
05 style, usage
06 jargon, phrase, speech
08 language, locution
10 expression, vernacular
11 phraseology
12 turn of phrase

idiomatic
07 correct
09 dialectal
10 idiolectal, vernacular
11 dialectical, grammatical

idiosyncrasy
05 freak, habit, quirk, trait
06 oddity
07 feature, quality
09 mannerism
11 peculiarity, singularity
12 eccentricity
13 individuality
14 characteristic

idiosyncratic
03 odd
06 quirky
08 peculiar, personal, singular
09 eccentric
10 individual
11 distinctive
14 characteristic

idiot
03 ass, mug, nit
04 clot, dope, dork, fool, prat, twit
05 chump, clown, dumbo, dunce, ninny, twerp, wally
06 cretin, dimwit, nitwit, sucker
07 fat-head, halfwit, pillock
08 imbecile, numskull
09 birdbrain, ignoramus, numbskull, simpleton
10 nincompoop

idiotic
03 mad
04 daft, dumb
05 barmy, batty, crazy, dotty, inane, inept, nutty, potty, silly
06 absurd, simple, stupid
07 fatuous, foolish, moronic, risible
09 half-baked, ludicrous, pointless, senseless
10 half-witted, ridiculous
11 hare-brained, nonsensical, thick-headed
12 crack-brained, simple-minded, unreasonable
13 ill-considered, unintelligent

idle
04 laze, lazy, loaf
05 dally, empty, petty, relax, shirk, skive, slack, waste
06 casual, dawdle, futile, loiter, lounge, potter
07 fritter, jobless, loafish, trivial, work-shy
08 inactive, indolent, kill time, slothful, sluggish, tick over
09 bum around, do nothing, lethargic, on the dole, pointless, redundant
10 take it easy, unemployed, unoccupied
11 ineffectual, inoperative
12 unproductive
13 insignificant, lackadaisical

idleness
04 ease
05 sloth
06 lazing, torpor
07 inertia, leisure, loafing, skiving
08 inaction, laziness

09 indolence
10 inactivity
12 slothfulness, unemployment
13 shiftlessness

idler
05 drone, sloth
06 loafer, skiver, waster
07 dawdler, laggard, lounger, shirker, slacker, wastrel
08 layabout, sluggard
09 do-nothing, lazybones
10 malingerer

idol
03 god
04 hero, icon, star
05 deity, image, pin-up
06 effigy, fetish, mammet
07 beloved, darling, heroine
09 favourite, superstar
11 blue-eyed boy, graven image

idolater
06 adorer, votary
07 admirer, devotee
10 iconolater, worshipper

idolatrous
05 pagan
07 adoring
09 adulatory, heretical, lionizing
10 glorifying, uncritical
11 reverential, worshipping

idolatry
08 paganism
09 adoration, adulation, fetishism, reverence
10 admiration, exaltation, heathenism, iconolatry
11 deification, hero-worship
13 glorification

idolize
05 adore, deify, exalt
06 admire, dote on, revere
07 adulate, glorify, lionize, worship
08 venerate
09 reverence
11 hero-worship
14 put on a pedestal

idyllic
05 happy
07 perfect
08 blissful, charming, heavenly, pastoral, peaceful, romantic
09 idealized, unspoiled, wonderful
10 delightful

if
08 as long as, assuming, in case
   of, provided, so long as
09 providing, supposing
12 assuming that, in the event
   of
13 supposing that
15 on condition that

iffy
05 dodgy
07 dubious
08 doubtful
09 uncertain

ignite
04 burn, fire
05 light
06 kindle
07 flare up, inflame
08 spark off, touch off
09 catch fire, set alight, set fire
   to
11 conflagrate, put a match to
15 burst into flames

ignoble
03 low
04 base, mean, vile
06 vulgar
08 shameful, wretched
10 despicable
11 disgraceful
12 contemptible
13 dishonourable

ignominious
04 base
06 abject
08 infamous, shameful
09 degrading
10 despicable, mortifying
11 disgraceful, humiliating
12 contemptible, disreputable,
   embarrassing
13 discreditable, dishonourable

ignominy
05 odium, shame
06 infamy, stigma
07 obloquy
08 contempt, disgrace
09 dishonour, indignity
10 opprobrium
11 degradation, humiliation
13 mortification

ignoramus
04 dolt, fool
05 dunce
06 dimwit, duffer
07 dullard, halfwit
08 bonehead, imbecile,
   numskull
09 blockhead, simpleton

ignorance
07 naïvety
09 greenness, innocence,
   stupidity, thickness
12 inexperience

ignorant
05 blind, dense, naïve, thick
06 stupid
07 unaware
08 backward, clueless,
   innocent
09 in the dark, oblivious,
   unwitting
10 illiterate, innumerate,
   uneducated
11 unconscious, uninitiated
12 unacquainted
13 inexperienced

ignore
03 cut
04 snub
05 spurn
06 reject, slight
07 cut dead, neglect
08 overlook, pass over
09 disregard
10 brush aside
12 cold-shoulder
14 shut your eyes to, take no
   notice of, turn a deaf ear to
15 look the other way, turn a
   blind eye to

ilk
04 kind, make, sort, type
05 brand, breed, class
07 variety

ill
03 bad
04 evil, harm, hurt, pain, sick,
   weak
05 amiss, badly, harsh, rough,
   seedy
06 ailing, barely, groggy, hardly,
   infirm, injury, laid up, poorly,
   queasy, sorrow, trials,
   unkind, unwell
07 adverse, cruelty, harmful,
   hostile, ominous, problem,
   ruinous, run down, trouble,
   unlucky
08 damaging, disaster,
   diseased, scantily, scarcely,
   sinister, unkindly
09 adversely, afflicted,
   bedridden, by no means,
   difficult, off-colour,
   suffering, unhealthy
10 affliction, indisposed,
   misfortune, out of sorts,
   unpleasant

11 deleterious, destruction,
   destructive, detrimental,
   tribulation, unfortunate,
   unpromising
12 inauspicious, unfavourable,
   unpropitious
14 inauspiciously, insufficiently,
   unpleasantness,
   unsuccessfully
15 under the weather

◻**ill at ease**
04 edgy
05 tense
06 on edge, uneasy, unsure
07 anxious, fidgety, nervous
08 hesitant, restless
09 disturbed, unsettled
13 on tenterhooks,
   uncomfortable
14 self-conscious

ill-advised
04 rash
05 hasty
06 unwise
07 foolish
08 careless, reckless
09 imprudent, misguided
11 injudicious, thoughtless

ill-assorted
08 unsuited
10 discordant, mismatched
11 incongruous
12 incompatible, inharmonious

ill-bred
04 rude
05 crass, crude
06 coarse, vulgar
07 boorish, loutish, uncivil,
   uncouth
08 impolite, unseemly
11 bad-mannered, uncivilized
12 discourteous

ill-considered
04 rash
05 hasty
06 unwise
07 foolish
08 careless, heedless
09 imprudent, overhasty
11 improvident, injudicious

ill-defined
03 dim
04 hazy
05 fuzzy, vague
06 blurry, woolly
07 blurred, shadowy, unclear
08 nebulous
09 imprecise
10 indefinite, indistinct

ill-disposed
06 averse
07 against, hostile, opposed
08 inimical
10 unfriendly
12 antagonistic

illegal
06 banned, barred
07 illicit
08 criminal, outlawed, unlawful, wrongful
09 felonious, forbidden
10 prohibited, proscribed
11 black-market, interdicted
15 under-the-counter

illegality
05 crime
11 criminality, illicitness, lawlessness
12 unlawfulness, wrongfulness

illegible
05 faint
07 obscure
10 indistinct, unreadable
12 hieroglyphic
14 indecipherable

illegitimate
04 love
07 bastard, illicit, invalid, lawless, natural, unsound
08 improper, spurious, unlawful
09 illogical, incorrect
10 adulterine
11 misbegotten, unauthorized

ill-fated
06 doomed
07 hapless, unhappy, unlucky
08 blighted, luckless
11 unfortunate

ill-favoured
04 ugly
05 plain
06 homely
08 unlovely
09 unsightly
12 unattractive
15 unprepossessing

ill-feeling
05 anger, odium, spite, wrath
06 animus, enmity, grudge, malice
07 dudgeon, rancour
08 bad blood, sourness
09 animosity, hostility
10 antagonism, bitterness, resentment
14 disgruntlement

ill-founded
08 baseless

10 groundless
11 unjustified, unsupported

ill-humoured
05 cross, huffy, moody, testy
06 crabby, grumpy, morose, snappy, sullen
07 crabbed, grouchy, peevish, waspish
08 petulant, snappish
09 crotchety, irascible, irritable
11 acrimonious, bad-tempered
12 cantankerous, disagreeable
13 quick-tempered

illiberal
04 mean
05 petty, tight
06 stingy
07 bigoted, miserly
09 hidebound, niggardly
10 intolerant, prejudiced
11 close-fisted, reactionary, small-minded, tight-fisted
12 narrow-minded, parsimonious

illicit
06 banned, barred
07 furtive, illegal
08 criminal, unlawful
09 forbidden, ill-gotten
10 contraband, prohibited, unlicensed
11 black-market, clandestine
12 illegitimate, unauthorized
15 under-the-counter

illiterate
08 ignorant, untaught
09 unlearned, untutored
10 uncultured, uneducated, unlettered, unschooled
12 analphabetic

ill-judged
04 daft, rash
06 unwise
07 foolish
08 reckless
09 foolhardy, impolitic, imprudent, misguided
10 incautious
11 injudicious, wrong-headed

ill-mannered
04 rude
05 crude
06 coarse
07 boorish, loutish, uncivil, uncouth
08 churlish, impolite, insolent
10 unmannerly
11 insensitive
12 badly-behaved, discourteous

ill-natured
05 cross, nasty, sulky, surly
06 sullen
07 crabbed, vicious
08 churlish, petulant, spiteful
09 malicious, malignant
10 malevolent, unfriendly, unpleasant, vindictive
11 bad-tempered

illness
06 attack, malady
07 ailment, disease
08 disorder, sickness
09 complaint, condition, infirmity
10 affliction, disability, poor health
13 indisposition

illogical
06 absurd, faulty
07 invalid, unsound
08 specious, spurious
09 senseless, untenable
10 fallacious, irrational
11 meaningless, sophistical
12 inconsistent, unscientific

illogicality
09 absurdity
10 invalidity
11 unsoundness
12 speciousness
13 irrationality, senselessness
14 fallaciousness

ill-starred
06 doomed
07 hapless, unhappy, unlucky
08 blighted
11 star-crossed, unfortunate
12 inauspicious

ill-tempered
04 curt
05 cross, sharp, testy
06 grumpy, tetchy, touchy
07 vicious
08 choleric, spiteful
09 impatient, irascible, irritable
11 bad-tempered

ill-timed
08 untimely
11 inopportune
12 inconvenient, unseasonable
13 inappropriate

ill-treat
04 harm
05 abuse, wrong
06 damage, injure, misuse
07 neglect
08 maltreat, mistreat

ill-treatment
04 harm
05 abuse
06 damage, injury, misuse
07 neglect
12 maltreatment, mistreatment

illuminate
05 light
07 clarify, clear up, explain, light up, shine on
08 brighten, illumine, ornament
09 elucidate, enlighten
10 floodlight, illustrate
12 throw light on

illuminating
08 edifying
09 revealing
10 revelatory
11 explanatory, instructive
12 enlightening

illumination
03 ray
04 beam
05 light
07 insight
08 lighting, radiance
10 brightness, decoration, perception, revelation
11 irradiation
13 enlightenment, understanding

illusion
05 error, fancy
06 mirage
07 chimera, fallacy, fantasy, phantom, spectre
08 delusion
09 deception
10 apparition
13 hallucination, misconception
15 false impression, misapprehension

illusory
05 false
06 unreal, untrue
07 fancied, seeming
08 apparent, deluding, delusive, delusory, illusive, imagined, mistaken, specious
09 deceptive, erroneous
10 chimerical, fallacious, misleading
11 illusionary
13 unsubstantial

illustrate
04 draw, show
06 depict, sketch
07 clarify, explain, picture

08 decorate, ornament
09 elucidate, embellish, exemplify, interpret
10 illuminate
11 demonstrate

illustrated
09 decorated, pictorial
11 embellished, illuminated

illustration
04 case
05 chart, plate
06 design, sample, sketch
07 analogy, artwork, diagram, drawing, example, picture
08 exemplar, specimen
10 decoration, photograph
11 elucidation, explanation
13 clarification, demonstration
14 representation
15 exemplification

illustrative
07 graphic, typical
08 specimen
09 pictorial
11 delineative, descriptive, explanatory, explicatory
12 diagrammatic, exemplifying, illustratory
14 illustrational, representative

illustrious
05 famed, great, noble, noted
07 eminent, exalted, notable
08 esteemed, glorious, honoured, renowned, splendid
09 acclaimed, prominent, well-known
10 celebrated, pre-eminent
11 magnificent, outstanding
13 distinguished

ill-will
05 anger, odium, spite, wrath
06 animus, enmity, grudge, hatred, malice
07 dislike, rancour
08 aversion, bad blood
09 animosity, antipathy, hostility
10 antagonism, resentment
11 indignation, malevolence
12 hard feelings

image
04 copy, doll, icon, idol, twin
06 double, effigy, figure, notion, ringer, simile, statue, vision
07 imagery, picture, replica
08 figurine, likeness, portrait
09 facsimile, lookalike
10 dead ringer, perception, photograph, reflection

11 resemblance
12 doppelgänger, reproduction
14 representation

imaginable
06 likely
08 credible, feasible
09 plausible, thinkable
10 believable, supposable
11 conceivable

imaginary
06 dreamy, made-up, unreal
07 fancied, pretend, shadowy
08 fabulous, fanciful, illusory, imagined, invented, mythical, spectral
09 fantastic, fictional, visionary
10 fictitious
11 make-believe, non-existent
12 hypothetical, mythological
13 hallucinatory

imagination
05 dream, fancy
06 vision
07 chimera, insight
08 illusion, mind's eye
09 ingenuity
10 creativity
11 inspiration, originality
12 fancifulness
13 inventiveness
15 resourcefulness

imaginative
08 creative, fanciful, inspired, original
09 fantastic, ingenious, inventive, visionary, whimsical
11 full of ideas, resourceful

imagine
03 see
04 deem, plan
05 dream, fancy, guess, think
06 assume, create, devise, gather, invent, reckon, scheme, take it
07 believe, dream up, picture, presume, suppose, surmise
08 conceive, envisage
09 conjure up, fantasize, visualize
10 conjecture
11 make believe

imbalance
04 bias
09 disparity
10 inequality, unevenness
13 disproportion

imbecile
03 ass

04 clot, daft, fool, twit
05 barmy, crazy, dopey, dunce, idiot, inane, moron, thick
06 cretin, dimwit, stupid
07 asinine, foolish, halfwit, idiotic, moronic, witless
09 blockhead, simpleton

imbecility
06 idiocy
07 amentia, fatuity, inanity
09 asininity, cretinism, stupidity
11 foolishness

imbibe
05 drink, lap up, quaff
06 absorb, soak up, take in
07 consume, drink in, receive, swallow

imbroglio
04 mess
06 muddle, scrape, tangle
09 confusion
11 embroilment, involvement
12 entanglement

imbue
04 fill, tint
05 steep, tinge
06 charge, inject, instil
07 ingrain, pervade, suffuse
08 permeate, saturate
09 inculcate
10 impregnate

imitate
03 ape
04 copy, echo, fake, mock
05 forge, mimic, spoof
06 follow, mirror, parody, parrot, repeat, send up
07 emulate, take off
08 simulate
09 duplicate, replicate, reproduce
10 caricature
11 counterfeit, impersonate

imitation
04 copy, fake, faux, mock, sham
05 apery, aping, dummy, spoof
06 ersatz, parody, phoney, pseudo, send-up
07 forgery, mimicry, replica, take-off
09 simulated, synthetic
10 artificial, impression, reflection, simulation
11 counterfeit
13 impersonation

imitative
04 mock
07 copying, mimetic
09 mimicking, simulated
10 parrot-like

imitator
03 ape
04 echo
05 mimic
06 copier, parrot
07 copycat
08 emulator, follower, parodist
12 impersonator
13 impressionist

immaculate
04 pure
05 clean
07 perfect, sinless
08 flawless, innocent, spotless, unsoiled
09 blameless, faultless, guiltless, incorrupt, stainless, undefiled, unsullied, untainted
10 impeccable
11 unblemished
12 spick and span

immaterial
10 irrelevant
11 of no account, unimportant
15 inconsequential

immature
05 green, naïve, young
06 callow, unripe
07 babyish, puerile
08 childish, juvenile
09 infantile
10 adolescent
13 inexperienced

immaturity
05 youth
09 greenness, puerility
10 callowness, juvenility, unripeness
11 adolescence, babyishness
12 childishness, inexperience

immeasurable
04 vast
07 endless, immense
08 infinite
10 bottomless
11 inestimable, never ending
12 incalculable, interminable, unfathomable

immediacy
07 urgency
08 instancy
09 imminence
10 directness, promptness
11 spontaneity

immediate
04 near, next
05 chief, close, swift
06 prompt, speedy, sudden, urgent

07 closest, crucial, instant, nearest, primary
08 abutting, adjacent, critical, next-door, pressing
09 important, principal
11 fundamental
12 without delay
13 instantaneous

immediately
03 now
06 at once
08 as soon as, directly, promptly, right now, speedily
09 forthwith, instantly, right away, yesterday
10 this minute
11 this instant
12 no sooner than, straight away, without delay
14 unhesitatingly
15 instantaneously

immemorial
06 age-old, of yore
07 ancient, archaic
08 timeless
09 ancestral
12 long-standing, time-honoured

immense
04 huge, mega, vast
05 giant, great, jumbo
06 bumper, cosmic
07 mammoth, massive, titanic
08 colossal, enormous, gigantic, whopping
09 extensive, ginormous, herculean, humungous
10 monumental, tremendous
11 elephantine
14 Brobdingnagian

immensely
07 greatly
09 extremely, massively
10 enormously
15 extraordinarily

immensity
07 expanse
08 hugeness, vastness
09 greatness, magnitude
11 massiveness
12 enormousness

immerse
03 dip
04 bury, duck, dunk, sink, soak
05 bathe, douse, souse
06 absorb, drench, engulf, occupy, plunge
07 baptize, engross, involve

08 saturate, submerge, submerse, wrap up in
09 preoccupy

immersed
04 rapt, sunk
06 buried
08 absorbed, consumed, involved, occupied
09 engrossed, wrapped up
11 preoccupied

immersion
03 dip
05 bathe
07 baptism, dipping, dousing, ducking, dunking, sinking, soaking
08 plunging
10 absorption, engrossing, saturation, submersion
11 involvement
13 preoccupation

immigrant
05 alien
07 incomer, migrant, settler
08 newcomer
10 new arrival

immigrate
06 settle
07 migrate
08 resettle

imminence
08 approach, instancy, nearness
09 closeness, immediacy
11 propinquity

imminent
04 near
05 close
06 at hand, coming
08 in the air, on the way
09 impending
11 approaching, forthcoming, in the offing
12 on the horizon
13 about to happen
14 round the corner

immobile
05 fixed, rigid, stiff, still
06 at rest, frozen, rooted, static
08 unmoving
09 immovable
10 motionless, stationary, stock-still

immobility
06 fixity
09 fixedness, inertness, stability, stillness
10 steadiness
12 immovability
14 motionlessness

immobilize
04 halt, stop
06 freeze
07 cripple, disable
08 paralyse, transfix
10 inactivate
14 put out of action

immoderate
03 OTT
06 lavish, wanton
07 extreme, fulsome
08 enormous, uncurbed
09 egregious, excessive, hubristic, unbridled, unlimited
10 inordinate, outrageous, over the top
11 extravagant, intemperate
12 distemperate, uncontrolled, unreasonable, unrestrained, unrestricted
14 unconscionable

immoderately
08 wantonly
09 extremely
11 excessively
12 inordinately, unreasonably
13 exaggeratedly, extravagantly
14 unrestrainedly

immoderation
06 excess
10 lavishness
11 prodigality, unrestraint
12 extravagance, intemperance
13 excessiveness
14 overindulgence

immodest
04 bold, lewd
05 cocky, fresh, saucy
06 brazen, cheeky, coarse, risqué
07 immoral, obscene
08 boastful, improper, impudent, indecent
09 revealing, shameless
10 indecorous

immodesty
08 audacity, boldness, impurity, lewdness, temerity
09 bawdiness, impudence, indecorum, obscenity
10 coarseness, indelicacy
13 shamelessness
14 indecorousness

immoral
03 bad
04 base, blue, evil, lewd, vile
05 loose, wrong
06 impure, sinful, wicked
07 corrupt, obscene, raunchy

08 depraved, indecent
09 debauched, dishonest, dissolute, nefarious, reprobate, unethical
10 degenerate, iniquitous, licentious
12 unprincipled, unscrupulous

immorality
03 sin
04 evil, vice
05 wrong
07 badness
08 impurity, iniquity, lewdness, vileness
09 depravity, indecency, obscenity, turpitude
10 corruption, debauchery, dishonesty, profligacy, sinfulness, wickedness, wrongdoing
13 dissoluteness
14 licentiousness

immortal
03 god
05 deity, great
07 abiding, ageless, endless, eternal, goddess, undying
08 divinity, enduring, Olympian, timeless, unfading
09 deathless, memorable, perennial, perpetual
11 everlasting, sempiternal
12 imperishable
13 unforgettable
14 indestructible

immortality
06 honour, renown
08 eternity
09 celebrity, greatness
10 perpetuity
11 distinction, eternal life
12 timelessness
13 deathlessness, glorification
15 everlasting life, imperishability

immortalize
04 laud
07 glorify
08 enshrine
10 eternalize, perpetuate
11 commemorate, memorialize

immovable
03 set
04 fast, firm
05 fixed, stuck
06 jammed, rooted, secure
07 adamant, riveted

immune

08 anchored, immobile, resolute, stubborn
09 obstinate, steadfast
10 inflexible, unshakable, unswerving, unwavering, unyielding
12 intransigent
14 uncompromising

immune

06 exempt, spared
08 absolved, released, relieved
09 protected, resistant
13 unsusceptible

immunity

07 licence, release
09 exception, exemption, indemnity
10 permission, protection, resistance
11 exoneration, inoculation, vaccination
12 immunization

immunization

03 jab
09 injection
11 inoculation, vaccination

immunize

06 inject, shield
07 protect
09 inoculate, vaccinate

immure

06 shut up, wall in
07 confine, enclose
08 cloister, imprison
11 incarcerate

immutability

09 constancy, fixedness
10 durability, permanence
14 changelessness
15 unalterableness

immutable

05 fixed
08 constant
09 permanent, perpetual, steadfast
10 changeless, inflexible, invariable
11 unalterable
12 unchangeable

imp

04 brat, minx, puck
05 demon, devil, gamin, gnome, rogue, scamp
06 goblin, rascal, sprite, urchin
09 hobgoblin, prankster, trickster
12 troublemaker
13 mischief-maker
15 flibbertigibbet

impact

03 hit
04 bang, blow, bump
05 brunt, crash, force, knock, shock, smash, whack
06 affect, effect, strike
07 apply to, collide, impinge
09 collision, influence
12 consequences, significance
13 repercussions
14 have an effect on

impair

03 mar
04 harm
05 spoil
06 damage, hinder, injure, weaken
07 cripple, disable, vitiate
08 decrease, diminish, enfeeble
10 debilitate
11 deteriorate

impaired

04 poor, weak
06 spoilt
07 damaged, unsound
08 disabled, vitiated
09 defective

impairment

04 flaw, harm, hurt, ruin
05 fault
06 damage, injury
08 weakness
09 vitiation
10 disability
11 disablement, dysfunction

impale

04 spit, stab
05 lance, prick, spear, spike, stick
06 pierce, skewer
08 transfix
10 run through

impalpable

07 elusive, shadowy, tenuous
10 indistinct, intangible
11 incorporeal
13 imperceptible, insubstantial, unsubstantial

impart

04 give, lend, tell
06 bestow, confer, convey, pass on, relate, reveal
07 divulge
08 disclose, transmit
10 contribute
11 communicate

impartial

04 fair, just

07 neutral
08 detached, unbiased
09 equitable, objective
10 even-handed, fair-minded
11 non-partisan
12 unprejudiced

impartiality

07 justice
08 equality, fairness
10 detachment, neutrality
11 objectivity
12 unbiasedness
14 even-handedness
15 non-partisanship

impassable

07 blocked
10 obstructed, unpassable
11 insuperable, unnavigable
12 impenetrable

impasse

07 dead end
08 deadlock
09 checkmate, stalemate
10 standstill

impassioned

05 eager, fiery
06 ardent, fervid, heated
07 blazing, excited, fervent, furious, glowing, intense, rousing, violent
08 animated, forceful, inflamed, inspired, spirited, stirring, vehement, vigorous
09 emotional
10 passionate
12 enthusiastic

impassive

04 calm, cool
07 stoical, unmoved
08 composed, laid back
09 unruffled
10 phlegmatic
11 emotionless, indifferent, unconcerned, unemotional, unexcitable, unflappable
13 dispassionate, imperturbable
14 expressionless

impatience

05 haste
08 curtness, keenness, rashness
09 agitation, eagerness, shortness, tenseness
11 brusqueness, impetuosity, intolerance, nervousness
12 irritability, restlessness

impatient

04 keen

05 eager, hasty, short, tense, testy
07 brusque, fidgety, fretful, jittery, nervous, restive
08 agitated, restless
09 impetuous, irritable, querulous
10 intolerant
11 precipitate

impeach
05 blame
06 accuse, attack, charge, impugn, indict, revile
07 arraign, censure
08 denounce
09 criticize, disparage

impeachment
06 charge
10 accusation, indictment
11 arraignment
13 disparagement

impeccable
04 pure
07 correct, perfect, precise
08 flawless
09 blameless, exemplary, faultless, stainless
10 immaculate
11 unblemished
14 irreproachable

impecunious
04 poor
05 broke, needy
08 indigent
09 destitute, insolvent, penniless, penurious
12 impoverished
15 poverty-stricken

impede
03 bar
04 clog, curb, slow, stop
05 block, check, delay
06 hamper, hinder, hold up
08 handicap, hold back, obstruct, slow down

impediment
03 bar
04 curb, snag
05 block, check
06 burden, defect
07 barrier, setback, stammer, stutter
08 handicap, obstacle
09 hindrance
11 encumbrance, obstruction
14 stumbling-block

impedimenta
04 gear
07 baggage, effects, luggage

09 equipment
10 belongings
13 accoutrements

impel
04 goad, move, prod, push, spur, urge
05 drive, force, press
06 compel, excite, incite, oblige, prompt, propel
07 inspire
08 motivate, pressure
09 constrain, instigate, stimulate

impending
04 near
05 close
06 at hand, coming
07 brewing, looming
08 imminent, in the air, on the way
11 approaching, forthcoming, in the offing
12 on the horizon

impenetrable
05 dense, solid, thick
07 cryptic, obscure
08 abstruse, baffling, puzzling
09 enigmatic, recondite
10 impassable, mysterious
11 inscrutable
12 unfathomable
14 unintelligible

impenitence
08 defiance, obduracy
12 stubbornness
15 incorrigibility

impenitent
08 hardened, obdurate
09 unabashed, unashamed
10 uncontrite, unreformed
11 remorseless, unrepentant
12 incorrigible

imperative
05 vital
07 crucial
08 critical, pressing
09 essential, necessary
10 compulsory, obligatory

imperceptible
04 fine, tiny
05 faint, small, vague
06 minute, slight, subtle
07 obscure, unclear
09 inaudible, minuscule
10 impalpable, indefinite, indistinct, negligible
11 microscopic
12 undetectable
13 indiscernible, infinitesimal

imperceptibly
06 slowly, subtly, unseen
08 bit by bit
09 gradually
13 inappreciably, indiscernibly, unobtrusively
14 little by little

imperfect
06 faulty, flawed
07 damaged
08 impaired
09 blemished, defective

imperfection
04 blot, dent, flaw, spot, tear
05 break, crack, fault, stain, taint
06 blotch, defect, foible
07 blemish, failing, scratch
08 weakness
09 deformity
10 deficiency, impairment, inadequacy
11 shortcoming

imperial
05 grand, great, lofty, noble, regal, royal
06 kingly
07 queenly, stately, supreme
08 absolute, glorious, majestic, splendid
09 sovereign
11 magnificent, monarchical

imperialism
12 expansionism
14 empire-building

imperil
04 risk
06 expose, hazard
08 endanger, threaten
10 compromise, jeopardize
12 expose to risk
13 put in jeopardy

imperious
06 lordly
07 haughty
08 arrogant, despotic
09 assertive, masterful
10 autocratic, commanding, high-handed, peremptory, tyrannical
11 dictatorial, domineering, overbearing, overweening

imperishable
07 abiding, eternal, undying
08 enduring, immortal, unfading
09 deathless, perennial, permanent, perpetual
11 everlasting
14 indestructible

impermanent
06 flying, mortal
07 elusive, passing
08 fleeting, fugitive
09 ephemeral, fugacious, temporary, transient
10 evanescent, fly-by-night, inconstant, transitory

impermeable
05 proof
06 sealed
08 hermetic
09 damp-proof, non-porous, resistant
10 impassable, impervious, waterproof
12 impenetrable

impersonal
04 cold, cool
05 aloof, stiff
06 formal, frigid, remote, stuffy
07 distant, neutral
08 clinical, detached, official, unbiased
09 objective, unfeeling
11 unemotional
13 dispassionate

impersonate
03 act, ape
05 mimic
06 parody, pose as
07 imitate, portray, take off
09 pass off as
10 caricature
12 masquerade as

impersonation
05 apery, aping
06 parody
07 mimicry, take-off
09 burlesque, imitation
10 caricature, impression

impertinence
03 lip
04 face, gall
05 brass, cheek, nerve, sauce
08 audacity, boldness, rudeness
09 brass neck, impudence, insolence
10 brazenness, disrespect, effrontery
11 discourtesy
12 impoliteness
13 shamelessness

impertinent
04 bold, pert, rude
05 brash, fresh, sassy, saucy
06 brazen, cheeky
08 impolite, impudent, insolent
09 audacious, shameless
11 ill-mannered

12 discourteous
13 disrespectful

imperturbability
08 calmness, coolness
09 composure
10 equanimity
12 tranquillity

imperturbable
04 calm, cool
07 unmoved
08 composed, tranquil
09 collected, impassive, unruffled
10 untroubled
11 unexcitable, unflappable

impervious
05 proof
06 closed, immune, sealed
08 hermetic
09 damp-proof, non-porous
10 waterproof, watertight
11 impermeable
12 impenetrable

impetuosity
05 haste
08 rashness
09 hastiness
10 impatience
12 recklessness
13 foolhardiness, impetuousness, impulsiveness
15 precipitateness, thoughtlessness

impetuous
04 rash
05 hasty
08 headlong, reckless
09 foolhardy, impatient, impulsive, unplanned
11 precipitate, spontaneous, thoughtless
14 unpremeditated
15 spur-of-the-moment

impetuously
06 rashly
10 recklessly
11 impulsively
13 precipitately

impetus
04 goad, push, spur
05 boost, drive, force, power
06 energy, urging
07 impulse
08 momentum, stimulus
09 incentive, influence
10 motivation
13 encouragement

impiety
09 blasphemy, profanity, sacrilege
10 irreligion, unholiness
11 godlessness, irreverence, profaneness, ungodliness

impinge
05 touch
06 affect, invade
07 intrude, touch on
08 encroach, infringe, trespass
09 influence

impious
06 sinful, unholy
07 godless, profane, ungodly
10 irreverent
11 blasphemous, irreligious
12 sacrilegious

impish
05 elfin, gamin
07 naughty, roguish, waggish
10 frolicsome
11 mischievous

implacability
12 pitilessness, ruthlessness
13 inexorability, inflexibility, intransigence, mercilessness
14 intractability, relentlessness
15 remorselessness

implacable
07 adamant
08 pitiless, ruthless
09 heartless, merciless
10 inexorable, inflexible, relentless, unyielding
11 intractable, remorseless, unforgiving, unrelenting
12 intransigent

implant
03 fix, sow
04 root
05 embed, graft
06 insert, instil
07 engraft
09 inculcate

implausible
06 flimsy
07 dubious, suspect
08 doubtful, unlikely
10 far-fetched, improbable, incredible
12 questionable, unbelievable, unconvincing
13 hard to believe, inconceivable

implement
02 do
04 tool
06 device, effect, fulfil, gadget

07 execute, perform, utensil
08 carry out
09 apparatus, appliance
10 instrument
11 contrivance
13 put into action, put into effect

implementation
09 effecting, operation
10 fulfilling, fulfilment, performing
11 carrying out, performance

implicate
07 embroil, include, involve
08 entangle
09 associate, be a part of, be party to, inculpate
10 be a party to
11 incriminate

implicated
07 party to
08 included, involved
09 embroiled, entangled
10 associated, inculpated
12 incriminated

implication
06 effect
07 meaning
08 overtone
09 deduction, inference, undertone
10 suggestion
11 association, consequence, embroilment, inculpation, insinuation, involvement
12 entanglement, ramification, repercussion, significance
13 incrimination

implicit
04 full
05 sheer, tacit, total, utter
06 entire, hidden, hinted, latent, unsaid
07 implied, perfect
08 absolute, complete, indirect, inferred, inherent, positive, unspoken, unstated
09 deducible, steadfast, suggested
10 insinuated, understood, unreserved
11 unexpressed, unqualified
12 unhesitating, wholehearted
13 unconditional, unquestioning

implicitly
06 firmly
07 totally, utterly
10 absolutely, completely
11 steadfastly

12 unreservedly
14 unhesitatingly, wholeheartedly
15 unconditionally, unquestioningly

implied
05 tacit
06 hinted
08 indirect, unspoken, unstated
09 suggested
10 insinuated

implore
03 beg
04 pray
05 crave, plead
06 appeal
07 beseech, entreat
09 importune

imply
04 hint, mean
06 denote, entail, signal
07 involve, point to, require, signify, suggest
08 indicate, intimate
09 insinuate

impolite
04 rude
05 crude, rough
06 cheeky, coarse, vulgar
07 boorish, loutish, uncivil
08 insolent
09 unrefined
10 indecorous, unmannerly
11 bad-mannered, ill-mannered, impertinent
12 discourteous
13 disrespectful, inconsiderate

impoliteness
08 rudeness
09 insolence, roughness
10 bad manners, coarseness, incivility, indelicacy
11 boorishness, discourtesy
12 churlishness, impertinence

impolitic
06 unwise
07 foolish
09 ill-judged, imprudent, maladroit, misguided
10 ill-advised, indiscreet
11 inexpedient, injudicious
12 undiplomatic
13 ill-considered

import
04 gist, mean
05 drift, imply, sense
06 thrust, weight
07 bring in, content, essence, meaning, message, signify

08 indicate
09 intention, substance
10 importance
11 consequence, implication
12 significance

importance
05 power, value, worth
06 esteem, status, weight
07 concern, urgency
08 eminence, interest, prestige, standing
09 graveness
10 prominence, usefulness
11 consequence, distinction
12 criticalness, significance
13 momentousness
14 noteworthiness

important
03 key
04 main
05 chief, grave, major, vital
06 urgent, valued
07 central, crucial, eminent, fateful, leading, notable, pivotal, primary, salient, seminal, serious, weighty
08 critical, esteemed, foremost, historic, material, powerful, priority, relevant, valuable
09 essential, momentous, principal, prominent
10 meaningful, noteworthy, pre-eminent
11 high-ranking, influential, outstanding, prestigious, substantial
13 distinguished

importunate
06 dogged, urgent
08 pressing
09 impatient, insistent, tenacious
10 persistent

importune
04 urge
05 beset, hound, press
06 appeal, badger, cajole, harass, pester, plague
07 request, solicit
09 plead with

importunity
06 urging
08 cajolery, hounding, pressing
09 harassing, pestering
10 entreaties, harassment, insistence
11 persistence
12 solicitation

impose
03 fix, lay, put, set

04 levy
05 apply, exact, foist, force, lay on, place, put on
06 burden, decree, saddle
07 enforce, exploit, inflict, intrude, obtrude, place on, presume, put upon
08 encroach, encumber, trespass
09 institute, introduce
13 take liberties
15 take advantage of

imposing
05 grand, lofty
06 august
07 stately
08 majestic, splendid, striking
09 dignified
10 impressive

imposition
03 tax
04 duty, load, task, toll
06 burden, charge, decree, tariff
07 levying
10 constraint, infliction
11 application, encumbrance, enforcement, institution, trespassing
12 encroachment, introduction
13 establishment

impossibility
09 absurdity
11 unviability
12 hopelessness, untenability
13 ludicrousness

impossible
06 absurd
08 hopeless
09 insoluble, ludicrous
10 incredible, unworkable
11 intolerable, unthinkable
12 preposterous, unattainable, unbelievable, unobtainable, unreasonable
13 impracticable, inconceivable

impostor
04 fake, sham
05 cheat, fraud, quack, rogue
06 con man, phoney
08 deceiver, swindler
09 charlatan, pretender
10 hoodwinker, mountebank
12 impersonator

imposture
03 con
05 cheat, fraud, trick
07 swindle
08 con trick, quackery

09 deception
13 impersonation

impotence
09 inability, infirmity, paralysis
10 disability, enervation, inadequacy, incapacity
11 impuissance, uselessness
12 helplessness, incompetence
13 powerlessness
15 ineffectiveness

impotent
06 infirm, unable
07 useless
08 crippled, disabled, helpless
09 enervated, incapable, paralysed, powerless
10 impuissant
11 ineffective
13 incapacitated

impound
05 seize
06 lock up, remove, shut up
07 confine
08 take away
10 commandeer, confiscate
11 appropriate, expropriate, incarcerate

impoverish
04 ruin
06 beggar
07 deplete
08 bankrupt
09 pauperize

impoverished
04 bust, poor
05 empty, needy, skint
06 barren, ruined
07 drained
08 bankrupt, desolate, indigent
09 destitute, penniless, penurious
10 down-and-out, stony-broke
11 impecunious
12 on your uppers
14 on your beam ends
15 poverty-stricken

impracticability
11 unviability, uselessness
12 hopelessness
13 impossibility, infeasibility, unworkability
14 unsuitableness

impracticable
08 unviable
10 impossible, inoperable, unfeasible, unworkable
12 unachievable, unattainable

impractical
08 academic, romantic

10 idealistic, impossible, unworkable
11 unrealistic
13 impracticable, unserviceable

impracticality
08 idealism
13 impossibility, infeasibility, unworkability

imprecation
05 abuse, curse
08 anathema
09 blasphemy, profanity
10 execration
11 malediction

imprecise
04 hazy
05 loose, rough, vague
06 sloppy, woolly
07 blurred, inexact
09 ambiguous, equivocal
10 ill-defined, inaccurate, indefinite, inexplicit

impregnable
06 secure, strong
09 fortified
10 invincible, inviolable, unbeatable
11 irrefutable
12 impenetrable, invulnerable, unassailable
13 unconquerable
14 indestructible, unquestionable

impregnate
04 fill, soak
05 imbue, steep
06 drench, infuse
07 pervade, suffuse
08 permeate, saturate
09 fertilize, penetrate
10 inseminate

impregnation
10 saturation
11 fertilizing
12 insemination
13 fertilization
14 fructification

impresario
08 director, producer, promoter
09 organizer

impress
04 mark, move, stir, sway
05 print, stamp, touch
06 affect, indent, instil, strike
07 engrave, imprint, inspire
09 bring home, emphasize, inculcate, influence, underline

impressed
05 moved, taken
06 marked, struck
07 excited, grabbed, stamped, stirred, touched
08 affected, overawed
10 influenced, knocked out

impression
04 dent, idea, mark, sway
05 fancy, hunch, power, print, sense, stamp, vibes
06 belief, effect, impact, memory, notion, parody
07 control, feeling, imprint, mimicry, opinion, outline, take-off, thought
08 illusion, pressure
09 awareness, burlesque, imitation, influence, sensation, suspicion
10 caricature, conviction
11 indentation
13 impersonation

impressionability
07 naïvety
09 greenness
11 gullibility, receptivity
13 receptiveness
14 suggestibility, susceptibility

impressionable
05 naïve
07 pliable
08 gullible
09 mouldable, receptive
11 persuadable, susceptible

impressive
05 grand
07 awesome
08 imposing, powerful
09 inspiring
11 spectacular
12 awe-inspiring

imprint
03 fix
04 etch, logo, mark, sign
05 badge, brand, print, stamp
06 emblem, emboss
07 engrave, impress
08 colophon
10 impression
11 indentation

imprison
03 pen
04 cage, jail
06 detain, intern, lock up
07 confine
11 incarcerate

imprisoned
05 caged

06 inside, jailed
07 captive, immured, put away
08 confined, locked up, sent down
09 doing bird, doing time
10 behind bars
12 incarcerated
13 doing porridge

imprisonment
09 captivity, detention
10 internment
11 confinement
13 incarceration

improbability
05 doubt
07 dubiety
11 dubiousness, uncertainty
12 doubtfulness, unlikelihood, unlikeliness
14 implausibility, ridiculousness

improbable
08 doubtful, unlikely
10 far-fetched, incredible
11 implausible
12 questionable, unconvincing

impromptu
05 ad lib, ad-lib
09 extempore
10 improvised, off the cuff, unprepared, unscripted
11 spontaneous, unrehearsed

improper
04 rude
05 false, wrong
06 risqué, vulgar
08 indecent, unseemly
09 incorrect, unfitting
10 indecorous, indelicate, unbecoming, unsuitable
11 incongruous
13 inappropriate

impropriety
07 blunder, faux pas, mistake
08 bad taste, solecism
09 gaucherie, immodesty, indecency, indecorum, vulgarity
12 unseemliness
13 unsuitability
14 indecorousness

improve
04 do up, help, mend
05 amend, fix up
06 better, enrich, look up, perk up, pick up, polish
07 enhance, perfect, recover, rectify, touch up, upgrade
08 progress, put right, set right
09 get better, modernize

10 ameliorate, convalesce, make better, recuperate, streamline

improvement
04 gain, rise
07 upswing
08 increase, progress, recovery
09 amendment, upgrading
10 betterment, rectifying
11 enhancement, furtherance, modernizing
12 amelioration

improvident
08 careless, prodigal, wasteful
09 imprudent, unthrifty
10 profligate, thriftless
11 extravagant, Micawberish, spendthrift
12 uneconomical

improvisation
04 vamp
05 ad-lib
09 ad-libbing, impromptu, invention
11 spontaneity
13 extemporizing

improvise
04 vamp
05 ad-lib, rig up, run up
06 devise, invent, make do
07 knock up
08 contrive
09 play by ear
11 extemporize
13 throw together
14 cobble together
15 speak off the cuff

improvised
05 ad-lib
09 extempore, makeshift
10 off-the-cuff, unprepared, unscripted
11 spontaneous, unrehearsed
12 extemporized
14 extemporaneous

imprudent
04 rash
06 unwise
07 foolish
08 careless, heedless, reckless
09 foolhardy, impolitic
10 unthinking
11 improvident, injudicious, thoughtless

impudence
03 lip
05 cheek, mouth, nerve
08 boldness, pertness, rudeness

09 brass neck, insolence,
sauciness
10 brazenness, effrontery
12 impertinence

impudent
04 bold, pert, rude
05 cocky, fresh, saucy
06 brazen, cheeky
07 forward
08 insolent
09 audacious, shameless
11 impertinent
13 disrespectful

impugn
06 assail, attack, berate,
oppose, resist, revile, vilify
07 censure, dispute, traduce
08 question
09 challenge, criticize
10 vituperate

impulse
04 push, urge, whim, wish
05 drive, force, surge
06 desire, motive, notion,
thrust
07 caprice, feeling, impetus,
passion
08 instinct, momentum,
pressure, stimulus
09 impulsion, incentive
10 incitement, inducement,
motivation, propulsion
11 inclination, stimulation

impulsive
04 rash
05 hasty, quick
06 madcap
08 reckless
09 foolhardy, ill-judged,
impetuous, intuitive
10 headstrong, unthinking
11 instinctive, precipitate,
spontaneous, thoughtless
13 ill-considered

impulsiveness
05 haste
08 rashness
09 hastiness, quickness
10 impatience
11 impetuosity
12 recklessness
13 foolhardiness,
impetuousness,
intuitiveness, precipitation
15 thoughtlessness

impunity
07 amnesty, excusal, freedom,
liberty, licence
08 immunity, security
09 exemption

10 permission
12 dispensation

impure
04 foul, lewd
05 bawdy, crude, dirty
06 coarse, filthy, smutty, vulgar
07 corrupt, debased, defiled,
immoral, sullied, tainted,
unclean
08 improper, indecent,
polluted, unchaste
09 shameless
11 adulterated
12 contaminated

impurity
04 dirt, mark, smut, spot
05 filth, grime, taint
08 foulness, lewdness
09 dirtiness, immodesty,
indecency, pollutant,
pollution
10 corruption, debasement,
immorality
11 contaminant, foreign body,
impropriety
12 adulteration
13 contamination,
shamelessness

impute
05 refer
06 assign, charge, credit
07 ascribe
08 accredit
09 attribute, put down to

in
06 modish, trendy
07 in vogue, popular, stylish
10 all the rage
11 fashionable

inability
08 handicap, weakness
09 impotence
10 disability, inadequacy,
incapacity, ineptitude
12 incapability, incompetence
13 powerlessness
15 ineffectiveness

inaccessible
06 remote
08 isolated
10 out of reach
11 beyond reach, out of the
way, unavailable,
unreachable
12 impenetrable, unattainable

inaccuracy
04 slip
05 error, fault, gaffe
06 defect, howler, slip-up

07 blunder, erratum, mistake
11 corrigendum, inexactness
12 mistakenness
13 erroneousness

inaccurate
03 out
05 false, wrong
06 faulty, flawed, untrue
07 inexact, unsound
08 mistaken
09 defective, erroneous,
incorrect

inaccurately
07 falsely, wrongly
09 inexactly
10 carelessly
11 defectively, erroneously,
incorrectly

inaction
06 torpor
07 inertia
08 idleness, lethargy
10 immobility, inactivity,
stagnation
14 motionlessness

inactivate
04 stop
07 cripple, disable, scupper
10 immobilize

inactive
04 idle, lazy, slow
05 inert
06 sleepy, torpid, unused
07 dormant, passive
08 immobile, indolent, lifeless,
sluggish, stagnant
09 lethargic, quiescent,
sedentary
10 motionless, stationary,
unemployed
11 inoperative

inactivity
05 sloth
06 stasis, torpor
07 inertia, languor
08 abeyance, dormancy,
idleness, inaction, laziness,
lethargy
09 indolence, inertness,
passivity
10 immobility, quiescence,
stagnation
11 hibernation
12 lifelessness, sluggishness,
unemployment

inadequacy
04 flaw, lack, want
06 dearth, defect
07 deficit, failing, paucity

08 scarcity, shortage
10 deficiency, inefficacy, meagreness, scantiness
11 shortcoming
12 incapability, incompetence
13 insufficiency

inadequate
05 scant, short, unfit
06 meagre, scanty, scarce, skimpy, sparse
07 unequal, wanting
09 defective, deficient, incapable, niggardly, too little
11 incompetent, substandard
12 insufficient
13 disappointing, inefficacious, not good enough
14 not up to scratch

inadequately
06 poorly, thinly
08 meagrely, scantily, skimpily, sparsely
09 sketchily
14 insufficiently

inadmissible
10 disallowed, immaterial, inapposite, irrelevant, prohibited
12 unacceptable
13 inappropriate

inadvertent
09 unplanned, unwitting
10 accidental, unintended
11 involuntary, thoughtless, unconscious
13 unintentional
14 unpremeditated

inadvertently
09 by mistake
10 by accident, mistakenly
11 unwittingly
12 accidentally, unthinkingly
13 involuntarily, unconsciously
15 unintentionally

inadvisable
09 ill-judged, imprudent, misguided
10 ill-advised, indiscreet
11 inexpedient, injudicious
13 ill-considered

inalienable
08 absolute, inherent
10 inviolable, sacrosanct
11 unremovable
12 unassailable
13 non-negotiable

inane
05 empty, silly, vapid

06 absurd, stupid
07 fatuous, foolish, idiotic, puerile, vacuous
08 mindless, trifling
09 frivolous, senseless, worthless
10 ridiculous
11 nonsensical

inanimate
04 dead
05 inert
06 torpid
07 defunct, dormant, extinct
08 immobile, lifeless, stagnant
09 insensate
10 insentient

inanity
05 folly
07 fatuity, vacuity
08 vapidity
09 absurdity, asininity, emptiness, frivolity, puerility, silliness, stupidity
10 imbecility
11 foolishness

inapplicable
05 inapt
08 unsuited
09 unrelated
10 immaterial, irrelevant, unsuitable
11 unconnected
12 inconsequent
13 inappropriate

inapposite
10 immaterial, irrelevant, out of place, unsuitable
13 inappropriate

inappropriate
08 ill-timed, improper, tactless, unseemly, untimely
09 ill-fitted, ill-suited, tasteless, unfitting
10 inapposite, indecorous, irrelevant, out of place, unbecoming, unsuitable
11 incongruous, inopportune

inapt
08 ill-timed, unsuited
09 ill-fitted, ill-suited
10 inapposite, irrelevant, out of place, unsuitable
11 inopportune, unfortunate

inarticulacy
08 mumbling
09 hesitancy, stumbling
10 stammering, stuttering
11 incoherence
14 indistinctness

inarticulate
04 dumb, mute
07 halting, muffled, mumbled, quavery, shaking, unclear
09 faltering, soundless, stumbling, trembling, voiceless
10 disjointed, incoherent, indistinct, stammering, stuttering, tongue-tied
14 unintelligible

inattention
10 dreaminess, negligence
11 daydreaming, distraction
12 heedlessness
13 forgetfulness, preoccupation
15 inattentiveness

inattentive
06 dreamy, remiss
08 distrait, heedless
09 forgetful, miles away, negligent, unmindful
10 distracted, regardless
11 daydreaming, preoccupied
12 absent-minded
13 wool-gathering

inaudible
06 silent
09 noiseless, whispered
10 indistinct
13 imperceptible

inaugural
05 first
06 maiden
07 initial, opening
08 exordial, original
12 introductory

inaugurate
04 open
05 begin, set up, start
06 induct, invest, launch, ordain
07 install, instate, usher in
08 commence, dedicate, enthrone, get going, initiate
09 institute, introduce, originate
10 commission, consecrate
11 set in motion
14 open officially

inauguration
06 launch
07 opening
09 induction, setting up
10 initiation, ordination
11 institution, investiture
12 commencement, consecration, enthronement, installation

inauspicious
- 03 bad
- 07 ominous, unlucky
- 08 ill-fated, untimely
- 10 ill-starred
- 11 unpromising
- 12 discouraging, infelicitous, unfavourable, unpropitious

inborn
- 06 inbred, innate
- 07 connate, natural
- 08 inherent
- 09 ingrained, inherited, intuitive
- 10 congenital, hereditary
- 11 instinctive

inbred
- 06 innate, native
- 07 connate, natural
- 08 inherent
- 09 ingrained
- 14 constitutional

incalculable
- 07 endless, immense
- 08 enormous, infinite
- 09 boundless, countless, limitless, unlimited
- 10 numberless
- 11 inestimable, innumerable
- 12 immeasurable
- 13 without number

incandescent
- 05 aglow
- 07 glowing
- 08 dazzling, white-hot

incantation
- 05 chant, spell
- 06 mantra
- 07 formula, mantram
- 10 invocation
- 11 conjuration

incapable
- 05 inept, unfit
- 06 feeble, unable
- 08 helpless, impotent, unfitted, unsuited
- 10 inadequate
- 11 incompetent, ineffective, ineffectual, unqualified

incapacitate
- 05 lay up
- 07 cripple, disable, scupper
- 08 paralyse
- 10 debilitate, immobilize
- 14 put out of action

incapacitated
- 05 drunk, tipsy, unfit
- 06 laid up, unwell
- 08 crippled, disabled

- 09 hamstrung, paralysed, prostrate, scuppered
- 10 indisposed
- 11 immobilized, out of action

incapacity
- 09 impotence, inability, unfitness
- 10 disability, feebleness, inadequacy, ineptitude
- 12 incapability, incompetence, incompetency
- 14 ineffectuality
- 15 ineffectiveness

incarcerate
- 04 cage, gaol, jail
- 06 commit, coop up, detain, intern, lock up
- 07 confine, impound, put away
- 08 imprison, send down
- 09 put in jail
- 11 put in prison

incarceration
- 04 jail
- 07 bondage, custody
- 09 captivity, detention
- 10 internment
- 11 confinement
- 12 imprisonment

incarnate
- 08 embodied, typified
- 09 corporeal, made flesh
- 10 in the flesh
- 11 personified

incarnation
- 10 embodiment
- 13 manifestation
- 15 personification

incautious
- 04 rash
- 05 hasty
- 06 unwary
- 07 foolish
- 08 careless, reckless
- 09 foolhardy, ill-judged, imprudent, impulsive
- 10 unthinking, unwatchful
- 11 inattentive, injudicious, precipitate, thoughtless

incendiary
- 04 bomb, mine
- 06 charge
- 07 firebug, grenade
- 08 agitator, arsonist, fire-bomb, inciting, stirring
- 09 explosive, firebrand, flammable, insurgent, seditious
- 10 fire-raiser, petrol bomb, pyromaniac

- 11 combustible, dissentious, fire-raising, provocative
- 12 inflammatory, rabble-rouser
- 13 rabble-rousing, revolutionary

incense
- 03 irk, vex
- 04 rile
- 05 anger, aroma, scent
- 06 enrage, excite, nettle
- 07 agitate, bouquet, inflame, perfume, provoke
- 09 aggravate, fragrance, infuriate, joss-stick
- 10 exasperate
- 14 drive up the wall

incensed
- 03 mad
- 05 angry, irate
- 06 fuming, ireful
- 07 enraged, furious
- 08 furibund, in a paddy, maddened, up in arms, wrathful
- 09 indignant, steamed up
- 10 infuriated
- 12 on the warpath

incentive
- 04 lure, spur
- 06 carrot, motive, reward
- 09 sweetener
- 10 enticement, incitement, inducement, motivation
- 13 encouragement

inception
- 04 dawn, rise
- 05 birth, start
- 06 origin, outset
- 07 opening
- 09 beginning
- 12 commencement, inauguration

incessant
- 07 non-stop
- 08 constant, unbroken, unending
- 09 ceaseless, continual, unceasing
- 10 continuous, persistent
- 11 never-ending, unremitting
- 12 interminable
- 13 uninterrupted

incidence
- 06 amount, degree, extent
- 09 frequency
- 10 occurrence, prevalence

incident
- 05 scene, upset
- 06 affair, fracas, matter, mishap

07 episode
08 conflict, instance, occasion, skirmish
09 commotion, happening
10 occurrence, proceeding
11 disturbance
12 circumstance
13 confrontation

incidental
05 minor, petty, small
06 chance, random
07 related, trivial
08 by chance
09 ancillary, attendant, secondary
10 accidental, fortuitous, peripheral, subsidiary
11 concomitant, subordinate
12 accompanying, contributory, non-essential

incidentally
07 apropos, by the by
08 by chance, by the way, casually
09 en passant, in passing
10 by accident
12 accidentally, unexpectedly
14 coincidentally
15 parenthetically

incinerate
04 burn
07 cremate
13 reduce to ashes

incipient
07 nascent, newborn
08 inchoate, starting
09 beginning, embryonic, inaugural, inceptive
10 commencing, developing
11 originating, rudimentary

incise
03 cut
04 etch, gash, nick, slit
05 carve, notch, slash
06 chisel, sculpt
07 cut into, engrave
09 sculpture

incision
03 cut
04 gash, nick, slit
05 notch, slash

incisive
04 acid, keen
05 acute, sharp
06 astute, biting, shrewd
07 caustic, cutting, mordant
09 sarcastic, trenchant
11 penetrating
13 perspicacious

incisiveness
07 acidity, sarcasm
08 keenness
09 acuteness, sharpness
10 astuteness, trenchancy
11 penetration
12 perspicacity

incite
04 goad, prod, spur, urge
05 drive, egg on, impel, rouse
06 arouse, excite, foment, induce, prompt, stir up, whip up, work up
07 agitate, animate, inflame, provoke
09 encourage, instigate, stimulate

incitement
04 goad, prod, spur
05 drive
07 impetus, rousing
08 stimulus
09 agitation, animation, incentive, prompting
10 inducement, motivation
11 instigation, provocation, stimulation
13 encouragement

inciting
08 stirring
09 seditious
10 incendiary, subversive
11 provocative
12 inflammatory
13 rabble-rousing

incivility
08 rudeness
09 roughness, vulgarity
10 bad manners, coarseness, disrespect
11 boorishness, discourtesy
12 impoliteness

inclemency
08 foulness, severity
09 harshness, roughness

inclement
05 harsh, nasty, rough
06 severe
11 intemperate, tempestuous

inclination
03 bow, nod
04 bank, bend, bias, ramp, tilt
05 angle, pitch, slant, slope, taste, trend
06 ascent, liking
07 incline, leaning
08 affinity, fondness, gradient, penchant, tendency

09 acclivity, affection, declivity, steepness
10 attraction, partiality, preference, proclivity, propensity
11 disposition
12 predilection
14 predisposition

incline
03 bow, dip, nod, tip
04 bank, bend, bias, hill, lean, list, ramp, rise, sway, tend, tilt, veer
05 curve, slant, slope, stoop, swing
06 affect, ascent
07 descent, deviate, dispose
08 gradient, persuade
09 acclivity, influence, prejudice

inclined
03 apt
04 wont
05 given
06 liable, likely
07 of a mind, tending, willing
08 disposed

include
03 add
04 hold, span
05 admit, cover, enter, put in
06 embody, insert, rope in, take in
07 contain, embrace, enclose, involve, let in on, subsume, throw in
08 allow for, comprise
09 encompass, introduce
10 comprehend
11 incorporate
15 take into account

including
04 with
08 counting, included

inclusion
08 addition
09 insertion
10 embodiment
11 involvement
12 encompassing
13 comprehension, incorporation

inclusive
04 full
05 all-in
07 blanket, general, overall
08 catch-all, sweeping
12 all-embracing, all-inclusive
13 comprehensive
14 across-the-board

incognito
06 masked, veiled
07 unknown
08 nameless, unmarked
09 disguised
10 in disguise
14 unidentifiable
15 under a false name

incognizant
07 unaware
08 ignorant
09 unknowing
11 inattentive, unconscious
12 unacquainted
13 unenlightened

incoherence
05 mix-up
06 jumble, muddle, mumble, mutter
07 stammer, stutter
09 confusion
11 garbledness
13 inconsistency
14 disjointedness

incoherent
07 garbled, jumbled, mixed-up, muddled, mumbled, unclear
08 confused, muttered, rambling
09 wandering
10 disjointed, disordered, stammering, stuttering
12 disconnected, inarticulate
14 unintelligible

incombustible
09 fireproof
10 flameproof
12 non-flammable
13 fire-resistant
14 flame-resistant

income
03 pay
05 gains, means, wages
06 salary
07 profits, returns, revenue
08 earnings, proceeds
12 remuneration

incoming
03 new
06 coming
07 ensuing
08 arriving, entering
09 returning
11 approaching

incommensurate
07 extreme, unequal
09 excessive
10 inadequate, inordinate
11 extravagant, inequitable
12 insufficient

incommunicable
09 ineffable
11 unspeakable, unutterable
12 unimpartable
13 indescribable, inexpressible

incomparable
07 supreme
08 peerless
09 matchless, nonpareil, paramount, unmatched
10 inimitable, unequalled, unrivalled
11 unsurpassed
12 unparalleled, without equal
13 beyond compare
15 without parallel

incomparably
08 superbly
09 eminently, supremely
10 far and away, infinitely
12 immeasurably
13 beyond compare, superlatively

incompatibility
08 mismatch, variance
09 disparity
10 difference
11 discrepancy, incongruity
12 disagreement
13 contradiction, disparateness, inconsistency

incompatible
08 unsuited
09 disparate
10 at variance, discordant, ill-matched, mismatched
11 incongruous, uncongenial
12 antagonistic, inconsistent
13 contradictory
14 irreconcilable

incompetence
08 bungling
09 ineptness, unfitness
10 inadequacy, ineptitude
11 uselessness
13 insufficiency, unsuitability
15 ineffectiveness

incompetent
05 unfit
06 clumsy, unable
07 awkward, botched, useless
08 bungling, fumbling, inexpert
09 deficient, unskilful
10 inadequate
11 ineffective, unqualified
12 insufficient

incomplete
07 lacking, partial, wanting
08 abridged

09 deficient, imperfect, piecemeal, shortened
10 unfinished
11 fragmentary, undeveloped

incomprehensible
06 opaque
07 complex, obscure
08 abstruse, baffling, puzzling
09 enigmatic, recondite
10 mysterious, perplexing
11 complicated, inscrutable
12 impenetrable, unfathomable
14 unintelligible

inconceivable
09 ludicrous
10 impossible, incredible, staggering
11 implausible, unthinkable
12 mind-boggling, unbelievable, unimaginable

inconclusive
05 vague
09 ambiguous, uncertain, undecided, unsettled
10 indecisive, indefinite, up in the air
11 left hanging
13 indeterminate
14 open to question

incongruity
05 clash
08 conflict
09 disparity, inaptness
13 contradiction, inconsistency, unsuitability
15 incompatibility

incongruous
03 odd
06 absurd, at odds
07 jarring, strange
08 clashing, contrary
10 out of place, unsuitable
11 conflicting
12 incompatible, inconsistent, out of keeping
13 contradictory

inconsequential
05 minor, petty
07 trivial
08 trifling
10 immaterial, negligible
11 unimportant
13 insignificant

inconsiderable
05 minor, petty, small
06 slight
07 trivial
08 trifling

10 negligible
11 unimportant
13 insignificant

inconsiderate
04 rude
06 unkind
07 selfish
08 careless, heedless, tactless, uncaring
10 intolerant, unthinking
11 insensitive, self-centred, thoughtless, unconcerned
12 uncharitable

inconsiderateness
08 rudeness
09 unconcern
10 unkindness
11 intolerance, selfishness
12 carelessness, tactlessness
13 insensitivity
15 self-centredness, thoughtlessness

inconsistency
07 paradox
08 conflict, variance
09 disparity
10 divergence, fickleness
11 contrariety, discrepancy, incongruity
12 disagreement, unsteadiness
13 contradiction, unreliability
14 changeableness

inconsistent
06 at odd
07 erratic, varying
08 contrary, variable
09 differing, irregular, mercurial
10 at variance, capricious, changeable, inconstant, out of place
11 conflicting, incongruous
12 in opposition, incompatible, out of keeping
13 contradictory, unpredictable
14 irreconcilable

inconsolable
10 despairing, devastated
11 heartbroken
12 disconsolate
13 brokenhearted, grief-stricken

inconspicuous
06 hidden, low-key, modest
08 discreet, ordinary, retiring
09 concealed
10 indistinct, unassuming
11 camouflaged, unobtrusive
12 unremarkable
13 insignificant
15 in the background

inconstant
06 fickle
07 erratic, mutable, varying, wayward
08 variable, volatile, wavering
09 mercurial, unsettled
10 capricious, changeable, irresolute, unfaithful, unreliable
11 fluctuating, vacillating
12 inconsistent, undependable

incontestable
04 sure
07 certain, evident, obvious
10 undeniable
11 indubitable, irrefutable
12 indisputable
14 unquestionable

incontinent
06 wanton
09 dissolute, unbridled, unchecked
10 ungoverned
11 promiscuous
12 uncontrolled, ungovernable, unrestrained
14 uncontrollable

incontrovertible
10 undeniable
11 beyond doubt, indubitable, irrefutable, self-evident
12 indisputable
14 beyond question, unquestionable

inconvenience
04 bind, bore, drag, fuss, pain
06 bother, burden, put out
07 disrupt, disturb
08 nuisance, vexation
09 annoyance, hindrance
10 difficulty, discommode, disruption, impose upon
11 awkwardness, disturbance
12 disadvantage

inconvenient
07 awkward
08 ill-timed, untimely, unwieldy
10 cumbersome, unsuitable
11 inopportune
12 unmanageable

incorporate
03 mix
04 fuse
05 blend, merge, unify, unite
06 absorb, embody, take in
07 combine, contain, embrace, include, subsume
08 coalesce
09 integrate
10 amalgamate, assimilate
11 consolidate

incorporation
05 blend
06 fusion, merger
07 company, society
08 unifying
09 inclusion, subsuming
10 absorption, embodiment, federation
11 association, coalescence, combination, integration, unification
12 amalgamation, assimilation

incorporeal
07 ghostly
08 ethereal, illusory, spectral
10 phantasmal, phantasmic

incorrect
05 false, wrong
06 faulty, untrue
07 inexact, off beam
08 improper, mistaken
09 erroneous, imprecise
10 fallacious, inaccurate

incorrectness
05 error
09 falseness, wrongness
10 faultiness, inaccuracy
11 imprecision, inexactness
12 mistakenness, speciousness
13 erroneousness

incorrigible
08 hardened, hopeless
09 incurable
10 beyond hope, inveterate
12 irredeemable
13 dyed-in-the-wool

incorruptibility
06 honour, virtue
07 honesty, probity
08 justness, morality, nobility
09 integrity
11 uprightness
15 trustworthiness

incorruptible
04 just
05 moral
06 honest
07 ethical, upright
08 straight, virtuous
10 honourable, unbribable
11 trustworthy
14 high-principled

increase
04 gain, go up, grow, hike, rise
05 add to, boost, breed, climb, raise, surge, swell
06 bump up, expand, growth, hike up, rocket, spiral, step up, step-up, upturn

07 advance, augment,
broaden, build up, build-up,
develop, enhance, enlarge,
magnify, scale up, upsurge
08 addition, escalate, heighten,
multiply, mushroom,
progress, snowball
09 expansion, extension,
increment, propagate
10 accumulate, escalation
11 enlargement, heightening,
mushrooming, proliferate,
snowballing
12 augmentation
13 proliferation
15 intensification

increasingly
11 more and more
12 cumulatively
13 progressively

incredible
07 amazing
09 fantastic, wonderful
10 astounding, improbable,
marvellous, past belief,
remarkable
11 astonishing, implausible
12 beyond belief,
preposterous, unbelievable
13 inconceivable

incredulity
09 disbelief
10 scepticism

incredulous
08 doubtful, doubting
09 sceptical
11 unconvinced
12 disbelieving

increment
04 gain
06 growth, step-up
07 accrual
08 addition, increase
09 accretion, accrument
10 supplement
11 advancement
12 augmentation

incriminate
06 accuse, charge, indict
07 arraign, impeach
09 implicate, inculpate
13 put the blame on

inculcate
05 teach
06 infuse, instil
07 din into, implant, impress,
imprint, ingrain
08 drum into
09 drill into

10 hammer into
12 indoctrinate

inculpate
05 blame
06 accuse, charge, indict
07 arraign, censure
09 implicate
11 incriminate
13 put the blame on

incumbent
06 member
07 binding, officer
08 official
09 mandatory, necessary
10 compulsory, obligatory,
prescribed
11 functionary
12 office-bearer, office-holder

incur
04 earn, gain
05 run up
06 arouse, suffer
07 provoke, sustain
10 experience

incurable
05 fatal
08 hardened, hopeless,
terminal
10 beyond hope, inoperable,
inveterate, unhealable
11 untreatable
12 incorrigible
13 dyed-in-the-wool

incursion
05 foray, sally
06 sortie
07 inroads
08 invasion
09 irruption
11 penetration
12 infiltration

indebted
07 obliged
08 beholden, grateful

indecency
07 crudity
08 foulness, impurity, lewdness
09 grossness, immodesty,
indecorum, obscenity,
vulgarity
10 coarseness
13 offensiveness
14 licentiousness

indecent
04 foul, lewd
05 bawdy, crude, dirty, gross
06 coarse, filthy, impure, ribald,
risqué, smutty, vulgar
07 corrupt, immoral, obscene

08 depraved, immodest,
improper, shocking,
unseemly
09 offensive, perverted
10 degenerate, indecorous,
indelicate, licentious,
outrageous, suggestive,
unbecoming, unsuitable
12 pornographic
13 inappropriate

indecipherable
07 unclear
09 illegible
10 indistinct, unreadable
14 unintelligible

indecision
05 doubt
08 wavering
09 hesitancy
10 hesitation
11 ambivalence, fluctuation,
uncertainty, vacillation
12 irresolution
14 indecisiveness
15 shilly-shallying

indecisive
06 unsure
07 unclear
08 doubtful, hesitant,
wavering
09 faltering, tentative,
uncertain, undecided,
unsettled
10 ambivalent, hesitating, in
two minds, indefinite,
irresolute, wishy-washy
11 fluctuating, vacillating
12 inconclusive, pussyfooting
13 indeterminate
15 shilly-shallying

indecorous
04 rude
05 crude, rough
06 coarse, vulgar
07 boorish, uncivil, uncouth
08 churlish, immodest,
impolite, improper,
indecent, unseemly,
untoward
09 tasteless
10 in bad taste, unmannerly
11 ill-mannered, undignified
13 inappropriate

indecorum
07 crudity
08 bad taste, rudeness
09 immodesty, indecency,
roughness, vulgarity
10 coarseness, uncivility
11 impropriety

12 impoliteness, unseemliness
13 tastelessness

indeed
05 truly
06 in fact, really
07 for sure, in truth
08 actually, to be sure
09 certainly
10 absolutely, positively, undeniably
11 doubtlessly, undoubtedly
12 without doubt

indefatigable
06 dogged
07 patient, undying
08 diligent, tireless, untiring
09 unfailing, unresting, unwearied
10 unflagging, unwearying
11 persevering, unremitting
13 inexhaustible

indefensible
07 exposed
09 unguarded, untenable
10 vulnerable
11 defenceless, inexcusable, unprotected
12 unforgivable, unpardonable
13 insupportable, unjustifiable

indefinable
03 dim
04 hazy
05 vague
06 subtle
07 obscure, unclear
10 impalpable, indistinct, unrealized
13 indescribable, inexpressible

indefinite
04 hazy
05 fuzzy, loose, vague
07 blurred, general, inexact, obscure, unclear, unfixed, unknown
08 confused, doubtful
09 ambiguous, equivocal, imprecise, uncertain, undecided, undefined, unlimited, unsettled
10 ambivalent, ill-defined, indistinct, unresolved
11 nondescript, unspecified
12 inconclusive, undetermined
13 indeterminate

indefinitely
07 for ever
09 endlessly, eternally
11 ad infinitum, continually

indelible
04 fast
07 lasting
08 enduring, unfading
09 ingrained, permanent
12 imperishable, ineffaceable, ineradicable
14 indestructible

indelicacy
07 crudity
08 bad taste, rudeness
09 grossness, immodesty, indecency, obscenity, vulgarity
10 coarseness, smuttiness
11 impropriety
13 offensiveness, tastelessness
14 suggestiveness

indelicate
04 blue, rude
05 crude, gross
06 coarse, risqué, vulgar
07 obscene
08 immodest, improper, indecent, unseemly
09 off-colour, offensive, tasteless
10 in bad taste, indecorous, suggestive, unbecoming

indemnify
04 free
06 exempt, insure, secure
07 protect, satisfy
09 guarantee,
10 compensate, underwrite

indemnity
07 redress
08 immunity, security
09 assurance, exemption, guarantee, insurance, safeguard
10 protection, reparation
12 compensation
13 reimbursement

indent
03 cut
04 dent, dint, mark, nick, pink
05 notch, order
07 request, scallop, serrate
11 requisition

indentation
03 cut, dip, pit
04 dent, nick
05 notch
06 dimple, furrow, groove, hollow
09 serration
10 depression

indenture
04 bond, deal, deed
08 contract, covenant
09 agreement
10 commitment, settlement

independence
07 autarky, freedom, liberty
08 autonomy, home rule, self-rule
11 sovereignty
12 self-reliance
13 individualism
14 self-government
15 self-sufficiency

independent
04 free
07 neutral, unaided
08 autarkic, distinct, separate
09 autarchic, freelance, impartial, liberated, sovereign, unrelated
10 autonomous, individual, self-ruling
11 self-reliant, unconnected
12 free-standing, free-thinking
13 individualist, self-contained, self-governing
14 self-sufficient, self-supporting
15 individualistic

independently
04 solo
05 alone
07 unaided
09 on your own, on your tod
10 by yourself, separately
12 autonomously, individually

indescribable
07 amazing
09 ineffable
10 incredible
11 exceptional, indefinable, unspeakable, unutterable
13 extraordinary, inexpressible

indestructible
07 durable
11 everlasting, infrangible, unbreakable
12 imperishable

indeterminate
05 vague
07 inexact, unclear, unknown
09 ambiguous, equivocal, imprecise, uncertain, undecided, undefined
10 ambivalent, ill-defined, indefinite
11 unspecified

index
03 key
04 list, mark, sign
05 guide, table, token
07 pointer, symptom
09 catalogue, directory

indicate
04 mark, mean, read, show, tell
05 imply
06 denote, evince, record
07 display, express, point to, signify, specify, suggest
08 manifest, point out, register
09 designate, represent

indicated
06 needed
08 required
09 called-for, necessary, suggested
11 recommended

indication
04 clue, hint, mark, note, omen, sign
06 augury, record, signal
07 portent, symptom, warning
08 evidence, register
10 intimation, suggestion
11 explanation
13 manifestation

indicative
08 symbolic
10 denotative, suggestive
11 significant, symptomatic
13 demonstrative
14 characteristic

indicator
04 dial, hand, mark, sign
05 gauge, index, meter, token
06 needle, signal, symbol
07 display, pointer
08 signpost

indict
06 accuse, charge, summon
07 arraign, impeach, summons
09 inculpate, prosecute
10 put on trial

indictment
06 charge
07 summons
10 accusation, allegation
11 arraignment, impeachment, inculpation, prosecution

indifference
06 apathy
09 disregard, unconcern
10 negligence, neutrality
11 impassivity, nonchalance
13 lack of concern
14 lack of interest

indifferent
02 OK
03 bad
04 cold, cool, easy, fair, so-so
05 aloof, blasé
06 medium
07 average, neutral, unmoved
08 detached, heedless, mediocre, middling, moderate, ordinary, passable, uncaring
09 apathetic, impassive
10 nonchalant, uninvolved
11 unconcerned, unemotional
12 run of the mill, uninterested
13 disinterested

indigence
04 need, want
06 penury
07 poverty
09 privation
11 deprivation, destitution

indigenous
06 native
08 original
09 home-grown
10 aboriginal
13 autochthonous

indigent
04 poor
05 broke, needy, skint
06 in need, in want
09 destitute, penniless, penurious
10 down and out, stony-broke
11 impecunious
12 impoverished, on your uppers
13 in dire straits
14 on your beam ends
15 poverty-stricken

indigestion
07 acidity, pyrosis
08 dyspepsy
09 dyspepsia, heartburn

indignant
05 angry, irate, livid, riled
06 miffed, narked, peeved
07 annoyed, in a huff
08 up in arms, wrathful
10 got the hump, infuriated
11 disgruntled

indignation
03 ire
05 anger, pique, wrath
07 outrage
09 annoyance

indignity
06 injury, insult, slight

07 affront, obloquy, offence
08 disgrace, reproach
09 contumely, dishonour
10 opprobrium
11 humiliation
13 slap in the face
14 kick in the teeth

indirect
07 curving, devious, oblique, winding
08 rambling, tortuous
09 divergent, wandering
10 circuitous, discursive, meandering, roundabout
12 periphrastic
14 circumlocutory

indirectly
09 deviously, obliquely
10 second-hand

indiscernible
06 hidden, minute
07 obscure, unclear
09 invisible, minuscule
10 impalpable, indistinct
11 microscopic
12 undetectable
13 imperceptible, undiscernible

indiscreet
06 unwary, unwise
08 careless, tactless
09 impolitic, imprudent, shameless
10 unthinking
11 injudicious
12 undiplomatic

indiscretion
04 boob, slip
05 error, folly, gaffe, lapse
06 slip-up
07 blunder, faux pas, mistake
10 imprudence
12 tactlessness

indiscriminate
05 mixed
06 motley, random, varied
07 aimless, chaotic, diverse, general
08 careless, confused, sweeping
09 haphazard, hit or miss, wholesale
10 hit and miss
11 unselective
12 unsystematic
13 miscellaneous

indiscriminately
08 randomly

09 aimlessly, generally, in the mass, wholesale
10 carelessly
11 haphazardly
13 unselectively

indispensable
05 basic, vital
06 needed
07 crucial, needful
08 required
09 essential, important, necessary, requisite
10 imperative
11 fundamental

indisposed
03 ill
04 sick
05 loath
06 ailing, averse, groggy, laid up, poorly, unwell
09 reluctant, unwilling
10 not of a mind, not willing, out of sorts
11 disinclined
12 not of a mind to
13 incapacitated
15 under the weather

indisposition
06 malady
07 ailment, disease, illness
08 aversion, disorder, sickness
09 complaint, ill health
10 reluctance
13 unwillingness
14 disinclination

indisputable
07 certain
08 absolute, definite, positive
10 undeniable, undisputed
11 indubitable, irrefutable
13 incontestable
14 beyond question, unquestionable

indissoluble
05 fixed, solid
10 inviolable
11 inseparable, unbreakable
12 imperishable
13 incorruptible
14 indestructible

indistinct
03 dim
04 hazy, pale
05 faded, faint, fuzzy, misty, muted, vague
06 woolly
07 blurred, muffled, obscure, shadowy, unclear
08 confused, muttered
09 ambiguous, undefined

10 ill-defined, indefinite, out of focus
14 indecipherable, unintelligible

indistinguishable
04 same
06 cloned
09 identical
10 tantamount
15 interchangeable

individual
03 own
04 lone, sole, sort, type
05 being, party
06 person, single, unique
07 several, special, typical
08 distinct, original, peculiar, personal, separate, singular
09 character, exclusive
10 human being, particular
11 distinctive
12 personalized
13 idiosyncratic
14 characteristic

individualism
06 egoism
11 freethought, originality
12 freethinking, independence, self-interest, self-reliance
13 egocentricity
14 libertarianism

individualist
05 loner
06 egoist
08 lone wolf, maverick
10 egocentric, free spirit
11 freethinker, independent

individualistic
06 unique
07 special, typical
08 original
09 eccentric
10 particular, unorthodox
11 independent, self-reliant
13 idiosyncratic

individuality
09 character
10 uniqueness
11 distinction, originality, peculiarity, personality, singularity
15 distinctiveness

individually
06 singly
08 one by one
09 severally
10 separately
13 independently

indivisible
10 impartible
11 inseparable, undividable
12 indissoluble
14 indiscerptible

indoctrinate
05 drill
07 impress
09 brainwash, inculcate

indoctrination
08 drilling
10 catechesis, instilling
11 catechetics, inculcation
12 brainwashing

indolence
05 sloth
06 apathy, torpor
07 inertia, languor
08 idleness, laziness, lethargy, shirking, slacking
09 inertness, torpidity
10 inactivity, torpidness
11 languidness
12 listlessness, sluggishness

indolent
04 idle, lazy, slow
05 inert, slack
06 torpid
07 languid, lumpish
08 fainéant, inactive, listless, slothful, sluggard, sluggish
09 apathetic, do-nothing, lethargic, shiftless
13 lackadaisical

indomitable
07 staunch, valiant
08 fearless, intrepid, resolute, stalwart
09 steadfast, undaunted
10 determined, invincible, unbeatable, unyielding
11 lion-hearted, unflinching
12 intransigent, unassailable, undefeatable
13 unconquerable

indubitable
07 certain, evident, obvious
08 absolute
09 undoubted
10 unarguable, undeniable
11 beyond doubt, irrefutable, undoubtable
12 indisputable, unanswerable
13 beyond dispute, incontestable
14 unquestionable

induce
04 coax, draw, move, urge
05 cause, impel, press, tempt

06 effect, incite, lead to, prompt
07 actuate, inspire, produce, provoke
08 generate, motivate, occasion, persuade, talk into
09 encourage, influence, instigate, originate
10 bring about, give rise to
11 prevail upon, set in motion

inducement
04 bait, goad, lure, spur
06 carrot, motive, reason, reward
07 impetus
08 stimulus
09 incentive, sweetener
10 enticement, incitement
13 encouragement

induct
06 invest, ordain
07 install, swear in
08 enthrone, initiate
09 introduce
10 consecrate, inaugurate

induction
10 conclusion, initiation, ordination
11 institution, investiture
12 consecration, enthronement, inauguration, installation, introduction
14 generalization

indulge
03 pet
05 spoil, treat
06 cosset, favour, humour, pamper, regale
07 cater to, gratify, revel in, satisfy, yield to
08 give in to, pander to, wallow in
09 give way to
11 go along with, mollycoddle

indulgence
05 treat
06 excess, favour, luxury, pardon
08 lenience
09 remission, tolerance
10 fulfilment, generosity
11 dissipation
12 extravagance, immoderation, intemperance, satisfaction
13 dissoluteness, gratification

indulgent
04 fond, kind
06 humane, tender
07 lenient, liberal, patient

08 generous, spoiling, tolerant
09 cosseting, forgiving, humouring, pampering
10 forbearing, permissive
13 mollycoddling, understanding

industrial
05 trade
08 business
10 commercial
13 manufacturing

industrialist
06 tycoon
07 magnate
08 producer
09 financier
12 manufacturer

industrious
04 busy
06 active
09 energetic, laborious
10 busy as a bee, productive
11 hard-working

industriously
04 hard

industry
04 toil
05 field, trade
06 effort, energy, labour, vigour
08 activity, business, commerce, hard work, sedulity
10 enterprise, production
11 application, persistence
13 laboriousness, manufacturing
14 productiveness

inebriated
05 drunk, happy, lit up, merry, tight, tipsy, woozy
06 blotto, bombed, canned, loaded, soused, stewed, stoned, tiddly, wasted
07 bevvied, drunken, legless, pickled, sloshed, smashed, sozzled, squiffy, wrecked
08 bibulous, tanked up
09 crapulant, paralytic, plastered, well-oiled
10 blind drunk
11 have had a few, intoxicated
12 drunk as a lord, drunk as a newt, roaring drunk
13 under the table
15 one over the eight

inedible
09 uneatable
11 not fit to eat, unpalatable
12 indigestible, unconsumable

ineducable
11 unteachable
12 incorrigible

ineffable
11 beyond words, unspeakable, unutterable
12 unimpartible
13 indescribable, inexpressible
14 incommunicable

ineffective
04 idle, lame, vain, weak
05 inept
06 feeble, futile
07 useless
08 abortive, impotent
09 fruitless, powerless, to no avail, worthless
10 inadequate, profitless, unavailing
11 incompetent, ineffectual
12 unproductive, unsuccessful

ineffectual
04 lame, vain, weak
05 inept
06 feeble, futile
07 useless
08 abortive, impotent
09 fruitless, powerless, worthless
10 inadequate, unavailing
11 incompetent

inefficacy
08 futility
10 inadequacy
11 uselessness
15 ineffectiveness, ineffectualness

inefficiency
06 laxity, muddle
10 ineptitude, sloppiness
12 incompetence, wastefulness
15 disorganization

inefficient
03 lax
05 inept, slack
06 sloppy
08 careless, inexpert, slipshod, wasteful
09 negligent
11 incompetent, ineffective, time-wasting, unorganized
12 disorganized

inelegant
04 ugly
05 crude, rough
06 clumsy, gauche, vulgar
07 awkward, ill-bred, uncouth
08 laboured, ungainly
09 graceless, unrefined

ineligible
05 unfit
08 ruled out, unfitted
11 unqualified
12 disqualified, unacceptable

inept
06 clumsy
07 awkward, useless
08 bungling, inexpert
09 ham-fisted, incapable, maladroit, unskilful
10 cack-handed, inadequate
11 heavy-handed, incompetent
12 unsuccessful

ineptitude
08 bungling
09 gaucherie, unfitness
10 clumsiness, gaucheness
11 awkwardness, unhandiness
12 incompetence, inexpertness
13 unskilfulness

inequality
04 bias
08 contrast
09 disparity, diversity, imbalance, prejudice, roughness, variation
10 difference, unevenness
11 discrepancy, unequalness
12 irregularity
13 disproportion, nonconformity
14 discrimination

inequitable
06 biased, unfair, unjust
07 bigoted, partial, unequal
08 one-sided, partisan
10 intolerant, prejudiced
14 discriminatory

inequity
04 bias
09 injustice, prejudice
10 inequality, partiality, unfairness, unjustness
12 one-sidedness, wrongfulness

inert
04 dead, idle
05 still
06 sleepy, static, torpid
07 dormant, passive
08 immobile, inactive, indolent, lifeless, listless, sluggish, stagnant, unmoving
09 inanimate, lethargic
10 motionless, stationary, stock-still

inertia
05 sloth
06 apathy, torpor
07 languor
08 idleness, inaction, laziness, lethargy
09 indolence, passivity, stillness
10 immobility, inactivity
12 listlessness, slothfulness
14 motionlessness

inescapable
04 sure
05 fated
07 assured, certain
10 inevitable, inexorable
11 ineluctable, irrevocable, unalterable, unavoidable

inessential
05 extra, spare
08 needless, optional
09 extrinsic, redundant, secondary
10 expendable, extraneous, irrelevant
11 dispensable, superfluity, superfluous, uncalled-for, unessential, unimportant, unnecessary
12 extravagance, non-essential

inestimable
04 vast
06 untold
07 immense
08 infinite
09 unlimited
10 invaluable, prodigious
11 uncountable
12 immeasurable, incalculable, unfathomable

inevitable
05 fated
07 assured, certain, decreed, settled
08 definite, destined, ordained
09 automatic, necessary
10 inexorable
11 inescapable, predestined, unalterable, unavoidable

inevitably
06 surely
09 assuredly, certainly
10 definitely, inexorably
11 inescapably, irrevocably, necessarily, unavoidably
13 automatically

inexact
05 fuzzy, loose
06 woolly
07 muddled
09 imprecise

10 fallacious, inaccurate, indefinite, indistinct
11 approximate
13 indeterminate

inexactitude
07 blunder, mistake
09 looseness
10 inaccuracy, woolliness
11 imprecision, inexactness
13 approximation, impreciseness
14 indefiniteness

inexcusable
10 outrageous
11 blameworthy, intolerable
12 indefensible, unacceptable, unforgivable, unpardonable

inexhaustible
07 endless
08 abundant, infinite, tireless, untiring
09 boundless, limitless, unlimited
10 unflagging, unwearying
11 illimitable, measureless, never-ending
13 indefatigable

inexorable
09 immovable
10 relentless, unyielding
11 ineluctable, remorseless, unalterable, unrelenting, unstoppable
12 irresistible
13 unpreventable

inexorably
10 implacably, inevitably, pitilessly
11 ineluctably, inescapably, irrevocably, mercilessly
12 relentlessly
13 remorselessly

inexpedient
05 wrong
06 unwise
07 foolish
09 ill-chosen, ill-judged, impolitic, imprudent, misguided, senseless
10 ill-advised, indiscreet, unsuitable
11 detrimental, impractical, inadvisable, injudicious, unadvisable, undesirable
12 inconvenient, undiplomatic, unfavourable
13 inappropriate
15 disadvantageous

inexpensive
05 cheap
06 budget, modest
07 bargain, cut-rate, low-cost, reduced
08 low-price
09 low-priced
10 discounted, economical, reasonable

inexperience
07 newness, rawness
09 freshness, ignorance, innocence, naïveness
10 immaturity
12 inexpertness
13 unfamiliarity

inexperienced
03 new, raw
05 fresh, green, naïve, young
06 callow
08 ignorant, immature, innocent
10 apprentice, unseasoned
11 new to the job
12 probationary, unaccustomed, unacquainted
15 unsophisticated

inexpert
03 ham
05 inept
06 clumsy
07 amateur, awkward, unhandy
08 bungling
09 ham-fisted, maladroit, unskilful, untrained,
10 amateurish, cack-handed
11 incompetent, unpractised
13 unworkmanlike

inexplicable
05 weird
07 strange
08 abstruse, baffling, puzzling
09 enigmatic
10 mysterious, mystifying, perplexing
12 unfathomable
13 unaccountable, unexplainable

inexplicably
09 strangely
10 bafflingly, incredibly, puzzlingly
12 mysteriously, mystifyingly
13 unaccountably, unexplainably

inexpressible
08 nameless
09 ineffable, unsayable
11 unspeakable, unutterable

13 indescribable
14 incommunicable

inexpressive
05 blank, empty
06 vacant
07 deadpan
09 impassive
10 poker-faced
11 emotionless, inscrutable

inextinguishable
11 unquellable
12 imperishable, unquenchable
13 irrepressible
14 indestructible

inextricable
11 indivisible, inseparable
12 indissoluble, irreversible
13 irretrievable

inextricably
11 indivisibly, inseparably,
12 indissolubly, irreversibly
13 irretrievably

infallibility
09 inerrancy, supremacy
10 perfection
11 omniscience, reliability
12 unerringness
13 faultlessness
14 irrefutability

infallible
07 perfect
08 accurate, fail-safe, flawless, reliable, sure-fire, unerring
09 faultless, foolproof, unfailing
10 dependable

infamous
04 base, evil, vile
06 wicked
08 ill-famed, shameful, shocking
09 dastardly, egregious, nefarious, notorious
10 iniquitous, outrageous, scandalous
11 disgraceful, ignominious
12 disreputable
13 discreditable, dishonourable

infamy
04 evil
05 shame
08 baseness, disgrace, ignominy, vileness, villainy
09 depravity, discredit, dishonour, disrepute, notoriety, turpitude
10 wickedness

infancy
04 dawn, rise

05 birth, start, youth
07 genesis, origins
08 babyhood
09 beginning, childhood, emergence, inception

infant
04 babe, baby
05 bairn, child, early, young
07 dawning, nascent, newborn
08 emergent, immature, juvenile, youthful
09 beginning, little one
10 babe in arms

infantile
05 young
07 babyish, puerile
08 childish, immature, juvenile

infatuated
03 mad
04 daft, nuts, sold, wild
05 crazy
06 in love
07 far gone, smitten
08 besotted, obsessed
09 bewitched, enamoured
10 captivated, enraptured, fascinated, mesmerized, spellbound
11 carried away

infatuation
04 love, pash
05 craze, crush, mania, thing
07 passion
08 fixation, fondness
09 obsession
11 fascination
12 besottedness

infect
03 mar
05 spoil, taint, touch
06 affect, blight, defile, excite, pass on, poison
07 animate, corrupt, inspire, pervert, pollute
08 spread to
09 influence, stimulate
11 contaminate

infection
03 bug
04 germ
05 virus
06 blight, poison, sepsis
07 disease, illness
08 bacteria, epidemic
09 contagion, influence, pollution
10 corruption, defilement, pestilence
13 contamination

infectious
05 toxic
06 deadly, septic
07 noxious
08 catching, epidemic, virulent
09 infective, polluting, spreading
10 compelling, contagious, corrupting
12 communicable, irresistible
13 transmissible, transmittable

infelicitous
07 unhappy, unlucky
08 untimely, wretched
09 miserable, sorrowful, unfitting
10 despairing, unsuitable
11 incongruous, inopportune, unfortunate
13 inappropriate

infer
06 allude, assume, deduce, derive, gather, reason
07 presume, surmise
08 conclude
09 figure out
10 conjecture, understand
11 extrapolate

inference
07 reading, surmise
09 corollary, deduction, reasoning
10 assumption, conclusion, conjecture
11 consequence, presumption
13 extrapolation
14 interpretation

inferior
03 bad, low
04 naff, poor, ropy
05 cheap, lower, lowly, minor
06 humble, junior, menial, minion, shoddy, vassal
08 mediocre, slipshod
09 secondary, underling
10 low-quality, second-rate, subsidiary
11 second-class, subordinate, subservient, substandard

inferiority
08 meanness
09 lowliness
10 faultiness, humbleness, low quality, mediocrity, shoddiness
12 imperfection, slovenliness, subservience
13 subordination

infernal
04 evil, vile

06 cursed, damned, darned, dashed, Hadean, wicked
07 blasted, demonic, hellish, satanic
08 accursed, devilish, fiendish, wretched
09 atrocious, execrable
10 confounded, diabolical, malevolent

infertile
06 barren, effete
07 sterile
08 infecund
09 childless
10 unfruitful
11 unfructuous
12 unproductive

infertility
09 sterility
10 barrenness, effeteness
11 infecundity
14 unfruitfulness

infest
05 beset, crawl, flood, swarm
06 invade, plague, throng
07 bristle, overrun, pervade
08 permeate, take over
09 penetrate
10 infiltrate

infested
05 alive, beset
06 ridden
07 overrun, plagued, ravaged, teeming
08 crawling, pervaded, swarming
09 bristling, permeated
11 infiltrated

infidel
05 pagan
07 atheist, heathen, heretic, sceptic
10 unbeliever
11 disbeliever, freethinker
13 irreligionist

infidelity
06 affair
07 liaison, perfidy, romance
08 adultery, betrayal, cheating, intrigue
09 duplicity, falseness, treachery
10 disloyalty
13 faithlessness, fooling around, playing around
14 unfaithfulness

infiltrate
04 seep, soak
05 enter

06 filter, invade
07 intrude, pervade
08 permeate
09 creep into, insinuate, penetrate, percolate

infiltration
08 invasion
09 intrusion, pervasion
10 permeation
11 insinuation, penetration, percolation

infiltrator
03 spy
07 entrist
08 entryist, intruder
10 penetrator, subversive
11 seditionary

infinite
04 huge, vast
06 untold
07 endless, immense
08 absolute, enormous
09 boundless, countless, extensive, limitless, unbounded, unlimited
10 bottomless, fathomless, numberless
11 inestimable, innumerable, never-ending, uncountable
12 immeasurable, incalculable, interminable, unfathomable
13 inexhaustible, without number
14 indeterminable

infinitesimal
03 wee
04 tiny
05 teeny
06 minute
09 minuscule
10 negligible
11 microscopic
13 imperceptible
14 inconsiderable

infinity
08 eternity, vastness
09 immensity
11 endlessness
12 enormousness

infirm
03 ill, old
04 lame, weak
05 frail, shaky
06 ailing, feeble, poorly, sickly, unwell, wobbly
07 doddery, failing
08 decrepit, disabled, unsteady
09 faltering

infirmity
07 ailment, disease, failing, frailty, illness
08 debility, disorder, sickness, weakness
09 complaint, ill health
10 feebleness, sickliness
11 decrepitude, dodderiness, instability

inflame
04 fire, fuel, heat, rile, stir
05 anger, rouse
06 arouse, enrage, excite, foment, ignite, kindle, madden, stir up, whip up
07 agitate, incense, provoke
09 aggravate, impassion, infuriate, stimulate
10 exacerbate, exasperate

inflamed
03 hot, red
05 angry
06 heated, septic
07 fevered, flushed
08 festered, infected, poisoned

inflammable
08 burnable
09 flammable, ignitable, ignitible
11 combustible

inflammation
04 heat, rash, sore
06 sepsis
07 abscess, empyema, redness
08 erythema, swelling
09 erruption, festering, infection, septicity
10 irritation, tenderness

inflammatory
05 fiery, rabid
06 septic, tender
07 painful, riotous, swollen
08 allergic, inciting, infected
09 demagogic, explosive, festering, seditious
10 incendiary, incitative
11 instigative, provocative
13 rabble-rousing

inflate
05 bloat, boost, raise, swell
06 aerate, blow up, dilate, expand, extend, hike up, pump up, push up, step up
07 enlarge, magnify, puff out
08 escalate, increase, overrate
09 intensify, overstate
10 aggrandize, exaggerate
12 overestimate

inflated
05 tumid
07 bloated, blown up, dilated, pompous, swollen
08 extended, tumefied
09 ballooned, bombastic, distended, increased, overblown, puffed out
10 euphuistic
11 exaggerated, intensified
12 magniloquent, ostentatious
13 grandiloquent

inflation
04 rise
08 increase
09 expansion

inflection
05 pitch
06 rhythm, stress
08 emphasis
10 modulation
12 change of tone

inflexibility
08 hardness, obduracy, rigidity
09 obstinacy, stiffness
12 immovability, immutability, inelasticity, stubbornness, unsuppleness
13 immutableness, intransigence
14 intractability

inflexible
04 firm, hard, taut
05 fixed, rigid, solid, stiff
06 steely, strict
07 adamant
08 obdurate, resolute, rigorous, stubborn, unsupple
09 immovable, immutable, merciless, obstinate, unbending, unvarying
10 entrenched, implacable, unbendable, unyielding
11 intractable
12 intransigent, unchangeable
13 dyed-in-the-wool
14 uncompromising

inflict
05 apply, exact, wreak
06 burden, impose
07 deal out, deliver, enforce, mete out
10 administer, perpetrate

infliction
06 burden
07 penalty, trouble
08 exaction, wreaking
10 affliction, imposition, punishment
11 application, castigation, enforcement, retribution
12 chastisement, perpetration

influence
04 drag, hold, move, pull, rule, sway
05 alter, clout, guide, impel, mould, power, rouse, shape
06 affect, arouse, change, colour, direct, effect, impact, induce, prompt, weight
07 control, impress, incline
08 guidance, impact on, motivate, persuade, pressure, standing, whip hand
09 authority, condition, determine, direction, dominance, instigate, manoeuvre, prejudice, supremacy, transform
10 importance, manipulate
11 carry weight, pull strings
14 have an effect on

influential
06 moving, potent, strong
07 guiding, leading, telling, weighty
08 dominant, powerful
09 effective, inspiring
10 compelling, convincing, meaningful, persuasive
11 charismatic, controlling, far-reaching, prestigious, significant
12 instrumental
13 authoritative

influx
04 flow, rush
05 flood
06 inflow, inrush, stream
07 arrival, ingress
08 invasion
10 inundation

inform
03 rat
04 blab, leak, shop, tell
05 brand, brief, grass, split, stamp
06 advise, betray, clue up, fill in, impart, notify, relate, snitch, squeal, tell on, tip off, wise up
07 apprise, put wise
08 acquaint, announce, denounce, identify, instruct
09 enlighten
10 illuminate, keep posted
11 communicate, incriminate
15 put in the picture

informal
04 easy, free
06 casual
07 natural, relaxed
09 easygoing
10 colloquial, unofficial, vernacular

informality
04 ease
07 freedom
10 casualness, homeliness, relaxation, simplicity
11 familiarity, naturalness

informally
06 easily, freely, simply
08 casually
10 familiarly, on the quiet
12 colloquially, unofficially
14 confidentially

information
03 gen
04 bumf, data, dope, file, info, news, word
05 clues, facts, input
06 advice, record, report
07 details, dossier, low-down, message, tidings
08 briefing, bulletin, databank, database, evidence
09 knowledge
10 communiqué, propaganda
11 instruction, particulars
12 intelligence

informative
05 newsy
06 chatty, useful
07 gossipy, helpful
08 edifying
09 revealing
11 educational, instructive
12 enlightening, illuminating
13 communicative

informed
06 au fait, expert, posted, primed, versed
07 abreast, briefed, erudite, learned
08 familiar, up to date
09 in the know
10 acquainted, conversant
11 enlightened
13 knowledgeable

informer
03 rat, spy
04 mole, nark
05 grass, Judas, sneak
06 snitch
07 traitor
08 betrayer, squealer, tell-tale
09 informant

10 supergrass
11 stool pigeon
13 whistle-blower

infraction
06 breach
08 breaking
09 violation
12 infringement
13 contravention, transgression

infrequent
06 scanty, sparse
08 sporadic, uncommon
09 spasmodic
10 occasional
12 intermittent

infringe
04 defy
05 break, flout
06 ignore, invade
07 disobey, impinge, intrude, violate
10 contravene, transgress

infringement
06 breach
07 evasion
08 breaking, defiance, invasion, trespass
09 intrusion, violation
10 infraction
12 disobedience, encroachment
13 contravention, non-compliance, non-observance, transgression

infuriate
03 bug, get, vex
04 rile
05 anger, annoy, rouse
06 enrage, madden
07 incense, inflame, provoke
10 antagonize, exasperate

infuriated
05 angry, irate, vexed
06 heated, roused
07 enraged, flaming, furious, violent
08 agitated, incensed, maddened, provoked
11 exasperated
14 beside yourself

infuriating
07 galling
08 annoying
09 maddening, provoking, vexatious
11 aggravating, frustrating
12 exasperating

infuse
04 brew, draw, fill, soak

05 imbue, steep
06 inject, instil
08 impart to, saturate
09 inculcate, introduce

infusion
04 brew
07 soaking
08 steeping
11 inculcation
12 instillation

ingenious
04 wily
05 adept, sharp, smart
06 astute, clever, crafty, shrewd
07 cunning, skilful
08 creative, talented
09 inventive
10 innovative
11 imaginative

ingenuity
05 flair, knack, skill
06 genius
07 cunning, faculty
08 deftness
09 invention, sharpness
10 astuteness, shrewdness
11 originality, skilfulness
12 creativeness
13 inventiveness
14 innovativeness
15 resourcefulness

ingenuous
04 open
05 frank, naïve, plain
06 candid, direct, honest, simple
07 artless, genuine, sincere
08 innocent
09 guileless

ingenuousness
07 candour, honesty, naïvety
08 openness
09 frankness, innocence, unreserve
10 directness
11 artlessness, genuineness
13 guilelessness

inglorious
07 ignoble, obscure, unknown
08 infamous, shameful, unheroic
10 mortifying
11 disgraceful, ignominious
12 disreputable
13 discreditable, dishonourable

ingrain
05 embed, imbue, infix
06 instil

07 build in, engrain, implant, impress, imprint

ingrained
06 inborn, inbred
07 built-in, inbuilt
08 embedded, inherent
09 immovable, implanted, permanent
10 deep-rooted, deep-seated

ingratiate
04 fawn
05 crawl, creep, toady
06 grovel
07 flatter
08 play up to, suck up to
11 curry favour
12 bow and scrape

ingratiating
07 fawning, servile
08 crawling, toadying, unctuous
10 flattering, obsequious
11 bootlicking, sycophantic, time-serving

ingratitude
13 thanklessness
14 ungratefulness

ingredient
04 item, part, unit
06 factor
07 element, feature
09 component
11 constituent

ingress
05 entry
06 access
08 entrance
09 admission
10 admittance
12 means of entry, right of entry

inhabit
06 live in, occupy, people, settle, stay in
07 dwell in
08 colonize, populate, reside in

inhabitant
06 inmate, lodger, native, tenant
07 citizen, dweller, settler
08 habitant, occupant, occupier, resident

inhabited
07 lived-in, peopled, settled
08 occupied, tenanted
09 colonized, populated

inhalation
06 breath
08 inhaling

09 breathing, spiration
11 inspiration, respiration

inhale
04 draw
06 draw in, suck in
07 inspire, respire
09 breathe in, inbreathe

inharmonious
06 atonal
07 grating, jarring, raucous
08 clashing, jangling, strident
09 dissonant, untuneful
10 discordant, unfriendly
11 cacophonous, inconsonant, unmelodious
12 unharmonious

inherent
06 inborn, inbred, innate, native
07 built-in, inbuilt, natural
09 essential, ingrained, inherited, intrinsic
10 hereditary, in the blood

inherit
06 be left
07 receive
08 accede to, come into
09 succeed to

inheritance
06 legacy
07 bequest
08 heredity, heritage
09 accession, endowment
10 birthright, succession

inheritor
04 heir
07 heiress, heritor, legatee
08 heritrix, legatary
09 heritress, successor
10 inheritrix
11 beneficiary, inheritress

inhibit
04 balk, curb, stem, stop
05 check
06 hamper, hinder, impede, rein in, thwart
07 prevent, repress
08 hold back, obstruct, restrain, restrict, slow down, suppress
09 constrain, frustrate
10 discourage

inhibited
07 guarded, subdued, uptight
08 reserved, reticent
09 repressed, withdrawn
10 frustrated, restrained
11 constrained, introverted
13 self-conscious

inhibition
04 curb

05 check
06 hang-up
07 reserve
09 hampering, hindrance, restraint, reticence
10 impediment, repression
11 obstruction, restriction

inhospitable
04 bare, cold, cool
05 aloof, bleak, empty
06 barren, lonely, unkind
07 hostile, uncivil
08 desolate, inimical
10 forbidding, unfriendly, unsociable, xenophobic
11 uncongenial, unwelcoming
13 uninhabitable, unneighbourly

inhuman
05 cruel
06 animal, brutal, savage
07 bestial, strange, vicious
08 barbaric, sadistic
09 barbarous, merciless
10 diabolical

inhumane
05 cruel, harsh
06 unkind
07 callous
08 pitiless, uncaring
09 heartless, unfeeling
11 cold-hearted, hard-hearted, insensitive

inhumanity
06 sadism
07 cruelty
08 atrocity
09 barbarism, barbarity, brutality
10 savageness
11 brutishness, callousness, viciousness
12 pitilessness, ruthlessness
13 heartlessness

inimical
07 adverse, harmful, hostile, opposed
08 contrary
09 injurious
10 pernicious, unfriendly
11 unwelcoming
12 antagonistic, unfavourable

inimitable
08 peerless
09 matchless, nonpareil, unmatched
10 unequalled, unexampled, unrivalled
11 unsurpassed
12 incomparable, unparalleled
13 unsurpassable

iniquitous
04 base, evil
06 sinful, unjust, wicked
07 heinous, immoral, vicious
08 accursed, criminal, dreadful, infamous
09 atrocious, nefarious, reprobate
10 abominable
13 reprehensible

iniquity
03 sin
04 evil, vice
05 crime, wrong
07 misdeed, offence
08 baseness, enormity
09 evil-doing, injustice
10 sinfulness, wickedness, wrongdoing
11 abomination, heinousness, lawlessness, viciousness
13 transgression

initial
05 basic, early, first, prime
07 opening, primary
08 inchoate, original, starting
09 beginning, formative, inaugural, inceptive, incipient
10 commencing, elementary
12 introductory

initially
07 at first, firstly
10 at the start, first of all, originally
11 to begin with, to start with
14 at the beginning

initiate
04 open
05 admit, begin, drill, enrol, let in, set up, start, teach, train
06 induct, instil, invest, launch, novice, ordain, prompt, rookie, sign up
07 convert, entrant, kick off, learner, pioneer, recruit
08 activate, beginner, commence, instruct, neophyte, newcomer
09 authority, greenhorn, inculcate, instigate, institute, introduce, novitiate, originate, proselyte
10 catechumen, inaugurate, tenderfoot
11 get under way, probationer, set in motion
15 get off the ground

initiation
05 debut, entry, start

07 baptism, opening
08 entrance
09 admission, beginning, enrolment, inception, induction, setting-up
10 admittance, enlistment, ordination
11 investiture, origination
12 inauguration, installation, introduction
13 rite of passage

initiative
02 go
04 lead
05 drive
08 ambition, dynamism
09 first move, first step
10 enterprise, get-up-and-go
11 opening move, originality
13 inventiveness
14 innovativeness
15 resourcefulness

inject
03 jab
06 infuse, insert, instil
07 shoot up, syringe
08 immunize, mainline
09 inoculate, introduce, vaccinate

injection
03 jab
04 dose, shot
08 addition, infusion
09 insertion
10 instilling
11 inoculation, vaccination
12 immunization, introduction

injudicious
04 rash
05 hasty
08 ill-timed
09 ill-judged, impolitic, imprudent, misguided
10 ill-advised, unthinking
11 inadvisable

injunction
05 order
06 dictum, ruling
07 command, dictate, mandate
09 directive

injure
03 cut, mar
04 harm, hurt, lame, maim, ruin
05 abuse, break, spoil, upset, wound, wrong
06 damage, deface, deform, impair, offend, put out
07 blemish, cripple, disable
08 fracture, ill-treat, maltreat

injured
04 hurt, lame
05 upset
06 abused, harmed, pained, put out
07 damaged, grieved, misused, wounded, wronged
08 crippled, disabled, insulted, maligned, offended
09 aggrieved
10 ill-treated, maltreated
13 cut to the quick

injurious
03 bad
06 unjust
07 adverse, harmful, hurtful
08 damaging
09 insulting, libellous
10 calumnious, corrupting, iniquitous, pernicious
11 deleterious, destructive, detrimental

injury
04 harm, hurt, ruin
05 abuse, wound, wrong
06 damage, insult
07 offence
09 grievance, injustice
10 impairment
12 ill-treatment

injustice
05 wrong
08 inequity
09 disparity, prejudice
10 inequality, unfairness, unjustness
12 one-sidedness, partisanship
14 discrimination

inkling
04 clue, hint, idea, sign
07 pointer
08 allusion, faintest, foggiest
09 suspicion
10 glimmering, suggestion

inky
05 black, sooty
08 dark-blue, jet-black
09 coal-black
10 pitch-black

inlaid
05 inset, lined, tiled
07 studded
08 enchased
09 empaestic, enamelled
10 damascened
11 tessellated

inland
05 inner
07 central

inlay
08 interior, internal
09 up-country

inlay
05 inset
06 enamel, lining, mosaic, tiling
09 damascene
12 tessellation

inlet
03 bay
04 cove
05 bight, creek, fiord, firth, sound
07 opening

inmate
07 convict, patient
08 detainee, prisoner

inn
03 bar, pub
05 hotel, local
06 tavern
08 hostelry
11 public house

innards
04 guts
05 works
06 entera, organs, umbles, vitals
07 insides, viscera
08 entrails, interior
09 mechanism
10 intestines
13 inner workings
14 internal organs

innate
06 inborn, inbred, native
07 connate, natural
08 inherent
09 inherited, intrinsic, intuitive
10 congenital, hereditary
11 instinctive

inner
06 hidden, inside, inward, mental, middle, secret
07 central, obscure, private
08 esoteric, interior, internal, intimate
09 concealed, emotional, innermost
13 psychological

innermost
05 basic
06 inmost, secret
07 central, closest, dearest, deepest
08 esoteric, intimate
09 essential

innkeeper
08 hotelier, landlady, landlord, publican
09 bar-keeper

innocence
06 purity, virtue
07 honesty, naïvety
08 chastity
09 credulity, ignorance, naïveness, virginity
10 simplicity
11 artlessness, gullibility
13 ingenuousness, unworldliness

innocent
04 babe, open, pure
05 child, green, naïve
06 chaste, honest, infant, novice, simple
07 artless, ingénue, sinless, upright
08 gullible, spotless, trustful, trusting, virginal, virtuous
09 childlike, credulous, faultless, greenhorn, guileless, guiltless, ingenuous, righteous, untainted, unworldly
10 babe in arms, immaculate, tenderfoot
11 inoffensive, unblemished, uncorrupted
13 inexperienced
14 above suspicion, irreproachable
15 unsophisticated

innocently
07 naïvely
09 artlessly
10 trustfully, trustingly
11 credulously, ingenuously

innocuous
04 mild, safe
05 bland
08 harmless, innocent
11 inoffensive
15 unobjectionable

innovation
07 newness, novelty
09 neologism, variation
10 alteration
12 introduction
13 modernization

innovative
03 new
05 fresh
07 go-ahead
08 creative, original
09 inventive
11 adventurous, imaginative, progressive

innuendo
04 hint, slur
08 allusion
09 aspersion
10 intimation, suggestion
11 implication, insinuation

innumerable
04 many
06 untold
07 umpteen
08 infinite, numerous
09 countless
10 numberless, unnumbered
11 uncountable

inoculate
06 inject
08 immunize
09 safeguard, vaccinate

inoculation
03 jab
04 shot
09 injection
11 vaccination
12 immunization

inoffensive
04 mild, safe
05 bland, quiet
08 harmless, retiring
09 innocuous, peaceable
15 unobjectionable

inoperable
08 hopeless, terminal
09 incurable
11 intractable, irremovable, unremovable, untreatable

inoperative
04 idle
05 kaput
06 broken, futile
09 defective, worthless
10 broken-down, not working, out of order
11 out of action
12 out of service
14 non-functioning
15 out of commission

inopportune
08 ill-timed, mistimed, untimely
10 unsuitable, wrong-timed
11 unfortunate
12 inconvenient, unseasonable
13 inappropriate

inordinate
05 great, undue
09 excessive
10 exorbitant, immoderate
11 unwarranted
12 unreasonable, unrestrained, unrestricted

input
04 code, data

05 facts, key in
06 feed in, insert
07 details, figures

inquest

07 hearing, inquiry
10 inspection, post-mortem
11 examination
13 investigation

inquietude

05 worry
06 unease
07 anxiety
08 disquiet
09 agitation, jumpiness
10 solicitude, uneasiness
11 disquietude, nervousness
12 apprehension,
   discomposure,
   perturbation, restlessness

inquire, enquire

03 ask
04 quiz
05 probe, query, snoop, study
06 search
07 examine, explore, inspect
08 look into, question, research
10 scrutinize
11 interrogate, investigate

inquirer, enquirer

10 questioner, researcher
12 interrogator, investigator

inquiring, enquiring

04 nosy
05 eager
06 prying
07 curious, probing, zetetic
09 sceptical, searching,
   wondering
10 analytical, interested
11 inquisitive, questioning
13 interrogatory, investigative,
   investigatory

inquiry, enquiry

05 probe, query, study
06 search, survey
07 hearing, inquest
08 question, scrutiny, sounding
10 inspection
11 examination, exploration,
   inquisition
13 interrogation, investigation

inquisition

07 enquiry, inquest, inquiry
08 grilling, quizzing
09 witch hunt
11 examination, questioning,
   third degree
13 interrogation, investigation

inquisitive

04 nosy
06 prying, snoopy, spying
07 curious, probing
08 snooping
09 enquiring, inquiring,
   intrusive, searching
10 meddlesome
11 interfering, questioning

inroad

05 foray, sally
06 attack, charge, sortie
07 advance, assault
08 invasion, progress, trespass
09 incursion, intrusion,
   onslaught
12 encroachment

insane

03 mad
04 daft, nuts
05 barmy, crazy, loony, loopy,
   nutty, potty
06 absurd, mental, stupid
07 bonkers, lunatic
08 crackers, demented,
   deranged, unhinged
09 disturbed
11 mentally ill, not all there
12 round the bend
13 off your rocker, out of your
   mind, round the twist
14 off your trolley
15 non compos mentis

insanitary

06 filthy, impure
07 noisome, unclean
08 infected, polluted
09 unhealthy
10 unhygienic, unsanitary
12 contaminated, insalubrious

insanity

05 folly, mania
06 frenzy, lunacy
07 madness
08 daftness, delirium,
   dementia, neurosis
09 craziness, psychosis
11 derangement
13 mental illness

insatiable

06 greedy, hungry
08 ravenous
09 rapacious, voracious
10 gluttonous
12 unappeasable,
   unquenchable
13 unsatisfiable

inscribe

03 cut
04 etch, mark, sign

05 carve, stamp, write
06 incise, record
07 address, engrave, impress,
   imprint
08 dedicate
09 autograph

inscription

06 legend
07 caption, epitaph, etching,
   message, writing
09 autograph, engraving,
   lettering, signature
10 dedication

inscrutable

04 deep
07 cryptic
08 baffling, puzzling
09 enigmatic
10 mysterious, unreadable
12 impenetrable, inexplicable,
   unfathomable

insect

➤ *Types of insect*:
03 ant, bee, fly, nit
04 flea, gnat, moth, tick, wasp
05 aphid, louse, midge, roach,
   thrip
06 cicada, earwig, hornet,
   locust, mantis, mayfly,
   sawfly
07 cricket, termite
08 blackfly, bookworm,
   greenfly, honey bee, horsefly,
   lacewing, mosquito
09 bumblebee, butterfly,
   cockroach, damselfly,
   dragonfly, tsetse-fly,
   woodlouse
10 boll-weevil, silverfish,
   springtail
11 grasshopper, stick insect
12 water boatman
13 daddy longlegs,
   leatherjacket, praying
   mantis
➤ See also **animal**

➤ *Parts of an insect*:
04 head, legs
06 thorax
07 abdomen, antenna, segment
08 forewing, hindwing,
   mandible
09 mouthpart
10 ovipositor
11 compound eye

insecure

04 weak
05 frail, loose, shaky
06 flimsy, unsafe, unsure
07 anxious, nervous, worried

08 hesitant, unstable, unsteady
09 hazardous, uncertain
10 precarious, vulnerable
11 defenceless, unprotected
12 apprehensive

insecurity
05 worry
07 anxiety
08 weakness, unsafety
09 frailness, shakiness
10 flimsiness, uneasiness, unsafeness, unsureness
11 instability, nervousness, uncertainty
12 apprehension, unsteadiness
13 vulnerability
14 precariousness

insensible
04 cold, deaf, hard, numb
05 aloof, blind, faint
06 zonked
07 distant, unaware, unmoved
08 comatose, ignorant
09 oblivious, senseless, unfeeling, untouched
10 insentient, knocked out, unaffected
11 insensitive, unconscious
12 unresponsive
13 anaesthetized, imperceptible, indiscernible
14 dead to the world, out for the count

insensitive
05 crass, tough
07 callous, unmoved
08 hardened, tactless, uncaring
09 heartless, impassive, oblivious, unfeeling
10 impervious, unaffected
11 indifferent, unconcerned
12 thick-skinned, unresponsive
13 unsusceptible

insensitivity
08 hardness, immunity
09 toughness, unconcern
10 obtuseness, resistance
12 indifference, tactlessness
14 hard-headedness

inseparable
05 close
07 devoted
08 constant, intimate
11 indivisible, undividable

insert
03 put, set
05 embed, enter, infix, inlay, inset, place, press, put in
06 push in, slip in

07 enclose, engraft, implant, slide in, stick in
08 addition, circular, thrust in
09 enclosure, insertion, interject, interpose, introduce
10 interleave, supplement
11 intercalate, interpolate
13 advertisement

insertion
05 entry
07 implant
08 addition
09 inclusion, intrusion
12 introduction, intromission
13 interpolation

inside
04 core, guts
05 belly, heart, inner
06 centre, inward, middle
07 content, indoors, private
08 contents, interior, internal, inwardly, secretly
09 innermost, intrinsic
10 restricted

insider
06 member
07 one of us
11 participant, staff member
15 one of the in-crowd

insides
04 guts
05 belly
06 bowels, organs
07 abdomen, innards, stomach, viscera
08 entrails
10 intestines
14 internal organs

insidious
03 sly
04 wily
06 artful, subtle, tricky
07 cunning, devious, furtive
08 sneaking, stealthy
09 deceitful, deceptive
10 perfidious

insight
06 acumen, vision
09 intuition, judgement, sharpness
10 perception, shrewdness
11 discernment, penetration
12 perspicacity
13 comprehension, understanding

insightful
05 acute, sharp
06 astute, shrewd

10 discerning, perceptive, percipient
11 penetrating
13 perspicacious

insignia
04 mark, sign
05 badge, brand, crest
06 emblem, ensign, ribbon, symbol
08 hallmark
09 hallmarks, medallion, trademark

insignificance
09 pettiness, smallness
10 paltriness, triviality
12 nugatoriness, unimportance
13 immateriality, inconsequence, negligibility, worthlessness

insignificant
05 minor, petty, small
06 meagre, paltry, scanty, slight
07 trivial
08 nugatory, piddling, trifling
10 negligible, peripheral
11 unimportant
13 insubstantial
15 inconsequential

insincere
05 false, lying
06 phoney, untrue
07 feigned
09 faithless, pretended
10 mendacious, perfidious
11 dissembling, duplicitous, treacherous
12 disingenuous, hypocritical

insincerity
04 cant
07 falsity, perfidy
08 pretence
09 duplicity, falseness, hypocrisy, mendacity, phoniness
10 lip service
11 deviousness, dissembling, evasiveness
13 dissimulation, faithlessness

insinuate
04 hint
05 get at, imply
06 allude
07 suggest, whisper

❑**insinuate yourself**
04 work, worm
05 sidle
09 get in with
10 ingratiate
11 curry favour

insinuation
04 hint, slur
05 slant
08 allusion, innuendo
09 aspersion
10 intimation, suggestion
11 implication

insipid
04 drab, dull, flat, tame, weak
05 banal, bland, trite, vapid
06 boring, jejune, watery
07 anaemic
08 lifeless
10 colourless, monotonous, spiritless, wishy-washy
11 flavourless
13 unimaginative, uninteresting

insist
04 aver, hold, urge
05 swear
06 assert, demand, harp on, repeat, stress
07 contend, declare, entreat, persist, require
08 maintain
09 emphasize, stand firm
11 state firmly
15 put your foot down

insistence
06 demand, stress, urging
08 emphasis, firmness
09 assertion
10 contention
11 declaration, exhortation, persistence, requirement
13 determination

insistent
06 dogged, urgent
07 adamant, exigent
08 emphatic, forceful, pressing
09 incessant, tenacious
10 determined, inexorable, persistent, relentless
11 importunate, persevering, unrelenting, unremitting

insobriety
09 inebriety, tipsiness
10 crapulence
11 drunkenness, inebriation
12 intemperance, intoxication

insolence
03 lip
04 gall
05 abuse, cheek, mouth, nerve, sauce
06 hubris
08 audacity, boldness, chutzpah, defiance, pertness, rudeness
09 impudence, sauciness

10 cheekiness, effrontery
11 forwardness, presumption
12 impertinence

insolent
04 bold, rude
05 brash, fresh, saucy
06 brazen, cheeky
07 abusive, defiant, forward
08 impudent
09 audacious
11 ill-mannered, impertinent
12 presumptuous

insoluble
07 complex, obscure
08 baffling, involved, puzzling
09 enigmatic, intricate
10 mysterious, mystifying, perplexing, unsolvable
11 inscrutable
12 impenetrable, inexplicable, unfathomable
13 unexplainable
14 indecipherable

insolvency
04 ruin
07 failure
10 bankruptcy
11 destitution, liquidation

insolvent
04 bust
05 broke, skint
06 failed, ruined
08 bankrupt, in the red
09 gone under
10 liquidated, on the rocks
13 gone to the wall, in queer street

insomnia
11 wakefulness
12 insomnolence, restlessness
13 sleeplessness

insouciance
04 ease
08 airiness
09 flippancy, unconcern
10 breeziness, jauntiness
11 nonchalance
12 carefreeness

insouciant
04 airy
06 breezy, casual, jaunty
07 buoyant
08 carefree, flippant, heedless
09 easy-going, unworried
10 nonchalant, untroubled
11 free and easy, unconcerned

inspect
03 vet
04 scan, tour, view

05 audit, check, study
06 assess, go over, survey
07 examine, oversee, see over
08 look over, pore over
10 scrutinize
11 investigate, reconnoitre

inspection
04 scan, tour
05 audit, check, recce, study
06 review, search, survey
07 check-up, vetting
08 once-over, scrutiny
11 examination
13 investigation

inspector
07 auditor, checker
08 assessor, examiner, overseer, reviewer, surveyor
10 scrutineer, supervisor

inspiration
04 goad, idea, muse, spur
06 fillip, genius
08 arousing, stimulus, stirring
09 awakening, brainwave
10 bright idea, creativity, motivation
11 imagination, originality, stimulation
12 illumination
13 encouragement, enlightenment, inventiveness

inspire
05 imbue, rouse
06 arouse, excite, infuse, kindle, prompt, thrill
07 animate, breathe, enliven, enthral, hearten, impress, inflame, quicken, trigger
08 energize, motivate, spark off, touch off
09 galvanize, instigate, stimulate
10 bring about, exhilarate

inspired
09 brilliant, memorable
10 marvellous, remarkable
11 enthralling, superlative

inspiring
07 rousing
08 exciting, stirring
09 affecting, memorable, thrilling, uplifting
10 heartening, impressive
11 enthralling, stimulating
12 exhilarating

inspirit
04 move

07 animate, enliven, gladden, hearten, inspire, quicken, refresh
08 embolden
09 encourage, galvanize, stimulate
10 exhilarate, invigorate
12 reinvigorate

instability
09 shakiness
10 flimsiness, insecurity, transience, unsafeness, volatility
11 fluctuation, inconstancy, uncertainty, vacillation, variability
12 unsteadiness
14 capriciousness, changeableness, precariousness

install
03 fit, fix, lay, put
05 lodge, place, plant, put in, set up
06 induct, insert, invest, locate, ordain, settle
07 instate, situate, station
08 position
09 establish, institute, introduce
10 consecrate, inaugurate

installation
05 plant
06 siting, system
07 fitting, placing, station
08 location
09 equipment, induction, insertion, machinery
10 ordination, settlement
11 instatement, investiture
12 inauguration
13 establishment

instalment
04 part
07 chapter, episode, payment, portion, section, segment
08 division
11 part payment

instance
04 case, cite, give, name
05 quote
06 adduce, sample
07 example, mention, point to, refer to, request, specify
08 citation, occasion
09 exemplify, prompting
10 incitement, occurrence
11 case in point
12 illustration
15 exemplification

instant
04 fast, tick, time
05 flash, jiffy, quick, rapid, swift, trice
06 direct, minute, moment, prompt, second, urgent
08 juncture, occasion
09 immediate, on-the-spot, twinkling
11 convenience, split second
13 instantaneous

instantaneous
05 rapid
06 direct, prompt, sudden
07 instant
09 immediate, on-the-spot

instantaneously
06 at once, pronto
07 quickly, rapidly
08 directly, promptly, speedily
09 forthwith, on the spot, right away
11 immediately
12 straight away, there and then, without delay

instantly
06 at once, pronto
08 directly
09 forthwith, on the spot, right away
11 immediately
12 straight away, there and then, without delay

instead
04 else
06 rather
10 by contrast, in contrast
13 alternatively
15 as an alternative

▢instead of
08 in lieu of
09 in place of
10 rather than

instigate
04 goad, move, prod, spur, urge
05 begin, cause, egg on, press, rouse, set on, start
06 excite, foment, incite, induce, kindle, prompt, stir up, whip up
07 inspire, provoke
08 generate, initiate, persuade
09 encourage, stimulate
10 bring about

instigation
06 behest, urging
07 bidding
09 incentive, prompting

10 incitement, inducement, initiation, initiative, insistence
13 encouragement

instigator
04 goad, spur
06 leader
07 inciter
08 agitator, fomenter, provoker
09 firebrand, motivator
10 prime mover, ringleader

instil
05 drill, imbue, teach
06 infuse
07 din into, implant, impress
09 inculcate, introduce

instinct
04 bent, feel, gift, urge
05 drive, flair, hunch, knack
06 talent
07 ability, faculty, feeling, impulse
08 aptitude, tendency
09 intuition
10 gut feeling, sixth sense
11 gut reaction
14 predisposition

instinctive
03 gut
06 inborn, innate, native, reflex
07 natural
08 inherent, visceral
09 automatic, impulsive, intuitive
11 involuntary, spontaneous

instinctively
09 naturally
11 intuitively
13 automatically, spontaneously

institute
03 law
04 rule
05 begin, enact, found, set up, start
06 create, custom, decree, induct, invest, launch, ordain, school
07 academy, appoint, college, develop, install
08 commence, initiate, organize, seminary
09 establish, introduce, originate, principle
10 foundation, inaugurate
11 institution
12 conservatory

institution
04 club, home, rule

05 guild, usage
06 centre, custom, league, ritual, system
07 society
08 creation, founding, hospital, practice
09 enactment, formation, inception, institute, setting-up, tradition
10 convention, foundation, initiation
11 association, corporation
12 commencement, installation, introduction, organization
13 establishment

institutional
04 cold, drab, dull
06 dreary, formal
07 orderly, routine, uniform
08 accepted, clinical, orthodox
09 cheerless, customary
10 forbidding, impersonal, methodical, monotonous, regimented, systematic
11 established, ritualistic
12 bureaucratic, conventional

instruct
03 bid
04 tell
05 coach, drill, guide, order, prime, teach, train, tutor
06 advise, charge, direct, inform, notify, school
07 command, educate, mandate, require

instruction
03 key
05 brief, order, rules
06 advice, charge, legend, lesson, manual, orders, ruling
07 classes, command, mandate, priming, tuition
08 briefing, coaching, drilling, guidance, teaching, training, tutelage, tutoring
09 direction, directive, education, schooling
10 directions, guidelines, injunction
11 information, preparation
13 enlightenment
14 recommendation

instructive
09 educative, uplifting
11 educational, informative
12 enlightening, illuminating

instructor
04 guru

05 coach, guide, tutor
06 master, mentor
07 adviser, teacher, trainer
08 educator, exponent, lecturer, mistress
09 pedagogue

instrument
04 tool
05 agent, gismo, gauge, means, meter, organ
06 device, gadget, medium
07 channel, utensil
09 apparatus, appliance, implement, indicator, yardstick
11 contraption, contrivance

➤ *Musical instruments include*:
04 bell, drum, fife, gong, harp, horn, kora, lute, lyre, Moog®, oboe, pipe, tuba, viol
05 Amati, banjo, bells, bongo, bugle, cello, chime, flute, hi-hat, kazoo, organ, piano, pipes, rebec, shawm, sitar, tabla, tabor, vibes, viola, zirna, zurna
06 cornet, cymbal, Fender, fiddle, guitar, spinet, tom-tom, violin, zither
07 alphorn, bagpipe, bassoon, bodhran, buccina, celeste, cowbell, maracas, marimba, ocarina, Pianola®, piccolo, sackbut, serpent, sistrum, tambura, theorbo, timpani, trumpet, ukulele, whistle
08 bagpipes, bass drum, bouzouki, cimbalom, clappers, clarinet, crumhorn, dulcimer, handbell, jew's harp, keyboard, mandolin, melodeon, Pan-pipes, recorder, side-drum, Steinway, theramin, triangle, trombone, virginal
09 accordion, balalaika, banjolele, castanets, euphonium, flageolet, harmonica, harmonium, saxophone, snare-drum, tenor-drum, wood block, Wurlitzer®, xylophone
10 bass guitar, bongo-drums, clavichord, concertina, cor anglais, didgeridoo, double bass, flugelhorn, French horn, grand piano, hurdy-gurdy, kettle-drum, mouth-

organ, pianoforte, sousaphone, squeeze-box, tambourine, thumb piano, tin whistle, vibraphone
11 aeolian harp, barrel organ, harpsichord, player-piano, synthesizer, violoncello
12 glockenspiel, Stradivarius, tubular bells, viola da gamba
13 slide trombone
14 acoustic guitar, electric guitar
➤ See also **music**

instrumental
06 active, useful
07 helpful
08 involved
09 auxiliary, conducive
11 influential, significant
12 contributory

insubordinate
04 rude
06 unruly
07 defiant, riotous
09 seditious, turbulent
10 disorderly, rebellious, refractory
11 disobedient, impertinent
12 contumacious, recalcitrant, ungovernable
13 undisciplined

insubordination
06 mutiny, revolt
09 rebellion
12 disobedience, insurrection, mutinousness

insubstantial
04 poor, thin, weak
06 feeble, flimsy, slight, unreal
07 tenuous
08 fanciful, illusory, vaporous
09 ephemeral
10 chimerical, immaterial
11 incorporeal

insufferable
10 unbearable
11 intolerable, unendurable

insufficiency
04 lack, need, want
06 dearth
08 scarcity, shortage
10 deficiency, inadequacy

insufficient
05 scant, short
06 meagre, scanty, scarce, sparse
07 lacking, wanting
09 deficient, not enough
10 inadequate

insular
06 closed, cut off, narrow
08 detached, isolated, separate, solitary
09 blinkered, insulated, parochial, withdrawn
10 parish-pump, prejudiced, provincial, xenophobic
12 narrow-minded
13 inward-looking

insularity
09 isolation, pettiness, prejudice
10 detachment, xenophobia
12 parochiality, solitariness
13 parochialness

insulate
03 lag, pad
04 wrap
06 cocoon, cut off, detach, encase, shield
07 cushion, envelop, isolate, protect, shelter

insulation
05 cover
06 shield
07 lagging, padding, shelter
08 cladding, stuffing, wrapping
09 cocooning, isolation
10 cushioning, protection

insult
04 bait, barb, gibe, hurt, slur, snub
05 abuse, libel, taunt, wound
06 impugn, injure, malign, offend, rebuff, revile, slight
07 affront, mortify, offence, outrage, put-down, slander, traduce
08 ridicule, rudeness
09 aspersion, call names, disparage, indignity
10 calumniate, defamation
12 cold shoulder
13 slap in the face
14 kick in the teeth

insulting
04 rude
07 abusive, hurtful
08 insolent
09 degrading, injurious, libellous, offensive
10 outrageous, scurrilous, slanderous
11 disparaging
12 contemptuous

insuperable
10 invincible
12 overwhelming, unassailable
13 unconquerable
14 insurmountable

insupportable
09 untenable
11 intolerable, unendurable
12 indefensible, insufferable, unacceptable
13 unjustifiable

insuppressible
06 lively
09 energetic
11 unstoppable, unsubduable
12 ungovernable
13 irrepressible

insurance
05 cover
06 policy, surety
08 security, warranty
09 assurance, guarantee, indemnity, safeguard
10 protection
15 indemnification

insure
05 cover
06 assure
07 protect, warrant
09 guarantee, indemnify
10 underwrite

insurer
07 assurer
09 guarantor, warrantor
11 indemnifier, underwriter

insurgent
05 rebel
06 rioter
08 mutineer, partisan, resister
09 seditious
11 seditionist
13 revolutionary, revolutionist
15 insurrectionary, insurrectionist

insurmountable
10 impossible, invincible
11 insuperable
13 unconquerable

insurrection
04 coup, riot
06 mutiny, putsch, revolt, rising
08 sedition, uprising
09 coup d'état, rebellion

intact
05 whole
06 entire
07 perfect
08 complete, flawless, integral, unbroken, unharmed
09 faultless, undamaged
10 in one piece

intangible
04 airy
05 vague

07 elusive, obscure, shadowy, unclear
08 abstract, fleeting
09 invisible
10 indefinite
11 undefinable
13 insubstantial

integral
04 full
05 basic
08 inherent
09 component, elemental, essential, intrinsic, necessary, requisite
11 constituent, fundamental

integrate
03 mix
04 fuse, join, knit, mesh
05 blend, merge, unite
06 mingle
07 combine
10 amalgamate, assimilate, homogenize
11 desegregate, incorporate

integrated
05 fused, mixed
06 joined, merged, meshed, united
07 blended, mingled, unified
08 cohesive, combined
11 amalgamated, assimilated, unseparated
12 desegregated, incorporated
13 part and parcel

integration
03 mix
05 blend
06 fusion, merger
07 harmony
11 combination, unification
12 amalgamation, assimilation
13 desegregation, incorporation

integrity
05 unity
06 honour, purity, virtue
07 decency, honesty, probity
08 cohesion, morality
09 coherence, principle, rectitude
11 unification, uprightness
12 completeness

intellect
04 mind
05 brain, sense
06 brains, genius, reason, wisdom
07 egghead, thinker, thought
08 academic, highbrow
09 judgement

10 brainpower, brilliance, mastermind
12 intellectual, intelligence
13 comprehension, understanding

intellectual
06 mental
07 bookish, egghead, erudite, learned, logical, thinker
08 academic, cerebral, highbrow, studious
09 scholarly

intelligence
03 gen, wit
04 data, dope, news, nous, wits
05 brain, facts
06 acumen, advice, brains, report, spying, tip-off
07 low-down, thought
09 espionage, intellect, knowledge, sharpness
10 brainpower, brightness, brilliance, cleverness, grey matter, perception
11 information
12 surveillance
15 little grey cells

intelligent
05 acute, alert, quick, sharp, smart
06 brainy, bright, clever
08 all there, rational, sensible
09 brilliant, sagacious
10 discerning, perceptive
11 quick-witted
13 using your loaf

intelligentsia
08 literati
09 academics
11 cognoscenti
13 intellectuals

intelligibility
07 clarity
08 lucidity
09 clearness, plainness
10 legibility
12 distinctness, explicitness

intelligible
05 clear, lucid
07 legible
08 distinct, explicit
14 comprehensible, understandable

intemperance
06 excess
07 licence
10 crapulence, insobriety
11 drunkenness, inebriation, unrestraint

12 extravagance, immoderation, intoxication
14 overindulgence

intemperate
04 wild
07 drunken, extreme, violent
08 prodigal
09 dissolute, excessive
10 immoderate, inebriated, licentious, over the top, profligate
11 extravagant, incontinent, intoxicated, tempestuous
12 uncontrolled, ungovernable, unreasonable, unrestrained

intend
03 aim
04 mean, plan, plot
06 design, devise, scheme
07 destine, earmark, propose, purpose, resolve
09 determine, have a mind
10 have in mind

intended
06 fiancé, future
07 fiancée, planned
08 destined, wife-to-be
09 betrothed
11 husband-to-be, intentional, prospective

intense
04 deep, keen
05 acute, eager, heavy
06 ardent, fervid, fierce, potent, severe, strong
07 burning, earnest, excited, fervent, nervous, serious, violent, zealous
08 forceful, powerful, profound, vigorous
09 consuming, emotional, energetic
10 passionate, thoughtful
12 concentrated, enthusiastic

intensely
06 deeply
08 ardently, fiercely, strongly
09 fervently
10 profoundly
12 passionately
14 with a vengeance

intensification
07 build-up
08 emphasis, increase
09 deepening, worsening
10 escalation, stepping-up
11 heightening
12 acceleration, augmentation
13 concentration, magnification, reinforcement, strengthening

intensify
03 fan
04 fire, fuel, whet
05 add to, boost
06 deepen, step up, worsen
07 augment, build up, enhance, magnify, quicken, sharpen
08 escalate, increase
09 aggravate, emphasize, reinforce
10 exacerbate, strengthen
11 concentrate
12 bring to a head

intensity
04 fire, zeal
05 depth, force, power
06 ardour, energy, strain, vigour
07 emotion, fervour, passion, potency
08 fervency, keenness, severity
09 acuteness, eagerness, extremity
10 fierceness, profundity
11 earnestness
13 concentration

intensive
07 in-depth, intense
08 detailed, thorough
10 exhaustive
12 concentrated
13 thoroughgoing

intent
03 aim, end, set
04 bent, firm, goal, hard, idea, keen, plan, rapt, view
05 alert, eager, fixed
06 design, enrapt, object, steady, target
07 focused, meaning, purpose
08 absorbed, occupied, resolved, watchful
09 attentive, committed, engrossed, objective, wrapped up
10 determined
11 preoccupied
13 concentrating

□**to all intents and purposes**
08 as good as
09 virtually
10 pretty much, pretty well
11 practically

intention
03 aim, end
04 goal, idea, plan,
06 design, intent, object, target
07 meaning, purpose
08 ambition

09 objective
10 aspiration

intentional
05 meant
07 planned, studied
08 designed, intended
09 conscious, on purpose
10 calculated, considered,
   deliberate, purposeful

intentionally
08 by design
09 on purpose
12 deliberately

intently
04 hard
06 keenly
07 closely, fixedly
08 steadily

inter
04 bury
06 entomb, inhume
09 lay to rest, sepulchre

interbreed
05 cross
09 hybridize
10 crossbreed, mongrelize
14 cross-fertilize

interbreeding
08 crossing
13 cross-breeding,
   hybridization

intercede
07 mediate
09 interpose, intervene

intercept
04 stop
05 block, check, delay
06 ambush, arrest, cut off,
   impede, thwart
07 deflect, head off
08 obstruct
09 frustrate

intercession
06 agency
09 mediation
11 arbitration
12 intervention
13 interposition

interchange
04 swap
05 trade
06 barter, switch
07 replace, reverse, trading
08 crossing, exchange,
   junction
09 crossroad, transpose
10 crossroads, substitute
11 alternation, reciprocate

12 intersection
13 reciprocation

interchangeable
09 identical
10 reciprocal, synonymous
12 exchangeable, transposable

intercourse
03 sex
05 trade
06 coitus, nookie
07 coition, contact, traffic
08 commerce, congress,
   converse, dealings, intimacy
09 communion
10 copulation, love-making
12 conversation
13 communication
14 correspondence
15 sexual relations

interdict
03 ban, bar
04 veto
05 debar, taboo
06 forbid, outlaw
07 embargo, prevent, rule out
08 disallow, preclude, prohibit
09 proscribe
10 injunction, preclusion
11 prohibition
12 proscription

interest
04 care, gain, grip, heed, note
05 amuse, bonus, charm,
   hobby, share, stake, stock,
   value
06 absorb, allure, appeal,
   divert, engage, equity,
   moment, notice, occupy,
   profit, regard, return, weight
07 attract, concern, credits,
   engross, involve, pastime,
   portion, premium, pursuit,
   revenue
08 activity, business, dividend,
   priority, proceeds, receipts
09 advantage, amusement,
   attention, captivate,
   curiosity, diversion,
   fascinate, relevance
10 attraction, engagement,
   importance, investment,
   percentage, prominence,
   recreation
11 consequence, fascination,
   involvement, seriousness
12 significance
13 attentiveness, consideration,
   participation

❑**in the interests of**
10 on behalf of

12 for the sake of
15 for the benefit of

interested
04 keen
06 intent
07 curious, gripped, riveted
08 absorbed, affected, involved
09 attentive, concerned,
   engrossed
10 fascinated, implicated
12 enthusiastic

interesting
07 amusing, curious, unusual
08 engaging
09 absorbing, appealing
10 attractive, compelling,
   engrossing, intriguing
11 fascinating, stimulating
12 entertaining

interfere
03 pry
04 balk, rape
05 abuse, block, check, clash,
   cramp
06 butt in, impede, meddle,
   molest, tamper
07 assault, intrude
08 conflict, handicap, obstruct
09 interrupt, intervene
10 muscle in on
12 put your oar in
13 get in the way of
14 poke your nose in, stick your
   oar in
15 stick your nose in

interference
06 prying
08 meddling
09 intrusion
11 obstruction
12 interruption, intervention
14 meddlesomeness

interim
06 acting, pro tem
07 stand-in, stopgap
08 interval, meantime
09 caretaker, meanwhile
11 interregnum

interior
04 core
05 heart, inner
06 centre, depths, inland,
   inside, inward, mental,
   middle
07 central, nucleus
08 internal, intimate
09 innermost, intrinsic,
   intuitive, spiritual,
   up- country

11 instinctive, involuntary, spontaneous
13 psychological

interject
03 cry
04 call
05 shout, utter
07 exclaim
09 ejaculate, interrupt

interjection
03 cry
04 call
05 shout
09 utterance
11 ejaculation, exclamation
12 interruption
13 interpolation

interlace
04 knit
05 braid, cross, plait, twine
07 entwine
10 intertwine, interweave, reticulate

interlink
04 knit, link, mesh
12 interconnect

interlock
04 link
12 interconnect
13 clasp together

interloper
08 intruder
10 trespasser
11 gate-crasher

interlude
04 halt, rest, stop, wait
05 break, let-up, pause, spell
06 hiatus, recess
08 breather, interval, stoppage
12 intermission
14 breathing-space

intermediary
05 agent
06 broker
08 mediator
09 go-between, middleman
10 arbitrator

intermediate
03 mid
04 mean
06 medial, median, middle, midway
07 halfway
09 in-between
12 intermediary

interment
06 burial

07 burying, funeral
10 inhumation

interminable
04 dull, long
06 boring, prolix
07 endless, eternal, tedious
08 dragging
09 boundless, ceaseless, limitless, perpetual, unlimited, wearisome
10 long-winded, loquacious, monotonous, without end
11 everlasting, never-ending
12 long-drawn-out

intermingle
03 mix
04 fuse
05 blend, merge, mix up
06 commix
07 combine
08 intermix
09 commingle, interlace
10 amalgamate, interweave
11 mix together

intermission
04 halt, lull, rest, stop
05 break, let-up, pause
06 recess
07 respite
08 breather, interval, stoppage
09 cessation, interlude, remission
10 suspension
12 interruption
14 breathing-space

intermittent
07 erratic
08 off and on, periodic, sporadic
09 irregular, spasmodic

intern
04 hold, jail
06 detain
07 confine
08 imprison

internal
05 inner
06 inside, inward, mental
07 in-house, private
08 domestic, interior, intimate, personal
09 emotional, spiritual
10 subjective
13 psychological

international
06 global
07 general
09 universal, worldwide
12 cosmopolitan

internecine
05 civil, fatal
06 bloody, deadly, family, mortal
08 internal
09 murderous
13 exterminating

interplay
08 exchange
11 alternation, give-and-take, interaction, interchange
13 reciprocation, transposition

interpolate
03 add
05 put in
06 insert
09 interject, interpose

interpolation
06 insert
08 addition
09 insertion
12 interjection

interpose
05 put in
06 butt in, insert, step in
07 barge in, intrude, mediate
08 muscle in, thrust in
09 arbitrate, intercede, interject, intervene
11 come between, interpolate
12 put your oar in
14 poke your nose in

interpret
05 solve
06 decode, define, render
07 clarify, explain, expound
08 construe, decipher
09 elucidate, explicate, make clear, translate
10 paraphrase, understand
11 make sense of, shed light on
12 throw light on

interpretation
05 sense
07 anagogy, meaning, opinion, reading, version
08 analysis, construe, decoding, exegesis
09 rendering
10 exposition, paraphrase
11 deciphering, elucidation, explanation, translation
13 clarification, understanding

interpretative
08 exegetic
10 expository
11 explanatory, explicatory, hermeneutic
12 interpretive

interpreter
07 exegete
08 exponent, linguist
09 annotator, expositor
10 elucidator, translator
12 hermeneutist

interrogate
04 pump, quiz
05 grill
07 debrief, examine
08 question
12 cross-examine
13 cross-question

interrogation
07 inquest, inquiry
08 grilling, quizzing
09 going-over
11 examination, inquisition,
   questioning, third degree

interrogative
07 curious, probing
08 erotetic
09 inquiring, quizzical
11 inquisitive, questioning
12 catechetical
13 inquisitional, interrogatory

interrupt
05 block, break, cut in, delay
06 butt in, cancel, chip in, cut
   off, heckle, hold up
07 barge in, barrack, break in,
   disrupt, disturb, intrude,
   suspend
08 cut short, postpone
09 punctuate
12 put your oar in

interruption
04 halt, stop
05 break, delay, pause
06 recess, remark
08 breather, interval
09 cessation, cutting-in,
   intrusion
10 disruption, suspension
11 disturbance, obstruction
12 interference, interjection,
   intermission
13 interpolation
14 discontinuance

intersect
05 cross
06 bisect, divide
09 cut across
10 criss-cross

intersection
08 crossing, junction
10 crossroads
11 interchange

intersperse
03 dot
06 pepper
07 scatter
08 intermix, sprinkle
09 interlard, interpose

intertwine
05 twine, twirl, twist, weave
07 connect, entwine
10 interweave

interval
04 lull, rest, time, wait
05 break, delay, pause
06 recess
07 interim
08 breather, meantime
09 interlude, meanwhile
12 intermission

intervene
04 pass
05 arise, occur
06 befall, elapse, happen,
   step in
07 intrude, mediate
09 arbitrate, intercede,
   interfere, interrupt
10 come to pass

intervening
07 between, mediate
11 interjacent, interposing

intervention
06 agency
09 intrusion, mediation
10 stepping-in
11 arbitration, involvement,
   negotiation
12 intercession, interference,
   interruption

interview
03 vet
04 talk, viva
06 assess, talk to
07 examine, meeting
08 audience, dialogue,
   evaluate, question,
   sound out
09 appraisal
10 assessment, conference,
   discussion, evaluation
11 interrogate
12 consultation, cross-examine
13 cross-question
15 oral examination, press
   conference

interviewer
08 assessor, examiner, reporter
09 appraiser, evaluator
10 inquisitor, questioner
11 interrogant

12 interlocutor, interrogator,
   investigator
13 correspondent

interweave
04 coil, knit
05 blend, braid, cross, twine,
   twist, weave
07 connect, entwine
10 criss-cross, reticulate

intestinal
05 ileac
07 coeliac, enteric, gastric
08 duodenal, internal, visceral
09 abdominal, stomachic

intestines
04 guts
05 colon, offal
06 bowels, vitals
07 innards, insides, viscera
08 entrails

intimacy
04 love
06 coitus, warmth
07 coition, privacy
09 affection, closeness
10 confidence, copulation,
   friendship, love-making
11 familiarity
15 carnal knowledge,
   confidentiality, sexual
   relations

intimate
04 cosy, dear, deep, hint, mate,
   near, tell, warm
05 bosom, buddy, close, imply,
   state, thick, tight
06 friend, impart, secret, signal
07 declare, in-depth, private,
   suggest
08 announce, detailed, familiar,
   friendly, indicate, informal,
   internal, personal, profound,
   thorough
09 associate, cherished,
   confidant, innermost,
   insinuate, make known
10 best friend, confidante,
   exhaustive
11 bosom friend, close friend,
   communicate, penetrating
12 affectionate, confidential,
   let it be known

intimately
05 fully
06 deeply, warmly
07 closely
08 in detail, tenderly
09 inside out, privately
10 familiarly, personally,
   thoroughly

11 confidingly
12 exhaustively
14 affectionately, confidentially

intimation
06 notice, signal
07 inkling, warning
08 allusion, reminder
09 reference, statement
10 indication, suggestion
11 declaration
12 announcement
13 communication

intimidate
03 cow
05 bully, daunt
06 extort, lean on, menace
07 overawe, terrify
08 browbeat, bulldoze, domineer, frighten, pressure, threaten
09 blackmail, terrorize, tyrannize

intimidation
04 fear
07 menaces, threats
08 bullying
10 compulsion
11 arm-twisting, browbeating, frighteners
13 terrorization, tyrannization

intolerable
10 impossible, unbearable
11 unendurable
12 insufferable, unacceptable
13 insupportable

intolerance
07 bigotry
09 dogmatism, prejudice
10 chauvinism, impatience, insularity
12 illiberality
14 discrimination

intolerant
06 biased, narrow
07 bigoted, insular
08 dogmatic, partisan
09 extremist, fanatical, illiberal, impatient, racialist
10 jingoistic, prejudiced, provincial, xenophobic
12 chauvinistic, narrow-minded, uncharitable

intonation
04 lilt, tone
05 pitch
06 stress, timbre
07 cadence
08 emphasis
10 inflection, modulation

intone
03 say
04 sing
05 chant, croon, speak, utter, voice
06 recite
07 declaim
09 enunciate, pronounce

intoxicate
06 excite, fuddle, thrill
07 inflame, inspire, stupefy
08 befuddle
09 inebriate, make drunk
10 exhilarate

intoxicated
05 drunk, happy, lit up, merry, moved, tight, tipsy, woozy
06 blotto, elated, loaded, soused, stewed, stoned, tiddly
07 bevvied, drunken, excited, legless, pickled, sloshed, smashed, sozzled, squiffy
08 bibulous
09 crapulent, paralytic, plastered, well-oiled
10 blind drunk, inebriated
11 exhilarated, have had a few
12 drunk as a lord, roaring drunk
13 in high spirits, under the table
15 one over the eight

intoxicating
05 heady
07 rousing
08 stirring
09 alcoholic, inebriant, stimulant
11 enthralling
12 exhilarating
15 going to your head

intoxication
07 elation, rapture
08 euphoria, pleasure
09 inebriety, tipsiness
10 crapulence, excitement, insobriety
11 drunkenness, inebriation
12 bibulousness, exhilaration, intemperance
15 serious drinking

intractability
08 obduracy
09 obstinacy
12 stubbornness
13 pig-headedness

intractable
04 wild
06 unruly, wilful

07 awkward, wayward
08 contrary, obdurate, perverse, stubborn
09 difficult, fractious, obstinate, pig-headed, unbending
10 headstrong, refractory, self-willed, unamenable, unyielding
11 disobedient
12 cantankerous, intransigent, ungovernable, unmanageable
13 unco-operative, undisciplined
14 uncontrollable

intransigent
08 hardline, obdurate, stubborn
09 immovable, obstinate, tenacious, unbending
10 determined, implacable

intrepid
04 bold
05 brave, gutsy
06 daring, gritty, heroic, plucky, spunky
07 doughty, gallant, valiant
08 fearless, spirited, stalwart, valorous
09 audacious, dauntless, undaunted
10 courageous, undismayed
11 lion-hearted, unflinching
12 stout-hearted

intrepidness
04 guts
05 nerve, pluck
06 daring, spirit, valour
07 bravery, courage, heroism, prowess
08 audacity, boldness
09 fortitude, gallantry
11 doughtiness, intrepidity
12 fearlessness
13 dauntlessness, undauntedness
15 lion-heartedness

intricacy
09 obscurity
10 complexity, knottiness
11 complexness, convolution, involvement
12 complication
13 elaborateness, intricateness

intricate
05 fancy
06 knotty, ornate, rococo
07 complex, tangled
08 baffling, involved, puzzling, tortuous

09 elaborate, enigmatic, entangled
10 convoluted, perplexing
11 complicated

intrigue
04 draw, plot, pull, ruse, wile
05 amour, cabal, dodge
06 puzzle, scheme
07 attract, connive, liaison, romance
08 artifice, conspire, trickery
09 collusion, conniving, fascinate, machinate, manoeuvre, stratagem
10 conspiracy, love affair
11 machination
13 double-dealing, sharp practice

intriguer
07 plotter, schemer, wangler
08 conniver
09 intrigant
10 intrigante, machinator, wire-puller
11 conspirator
12 collaborator
13 Machiavellian, wheeler-dealer

intriguing
08 puzzling, riveting
09 absorbing, appealing, beguiling, diverting
10 attractive, compelling
11 captivating, fascinating, interesting

intrinsic
06 inborn, inbred, native
07 built-in, central, genuine, in-built, natural
08 inherent, interior
09 elemental, essential
11 fundamental
14 constitutional

introduce
05 begin, found, offer, start
06 launch, lead in, submit
07 advance, bring in, develop, precede, preface, present, propose, suggest, usher in
08 acquaint, announce, commence, initiate, lead into, organize
09 establish, institute, originate
10 inaugurate, put forward
11 put in motion, set in motion

introduction
05 debut, intro, proem, start
06 launch, lead-in
07 opening, preface, prelude

08 exordium, foreword, overture, preamble, prologue
09 beginning
12 commencement, inauguration
13 establishment, preliminaries
15 first principles

introductory
05 basic, early, first
07 initial, opening
08 exordial, isagogic, starting
09 beginning, essential, inaugural, prefatory
10 elementary, initiatory, precursory
11 fundamental, preliminary, preparatory, rudimentary

introspection
08 brooding
11 navel-gazing, pensiveness
12 introversion, self-analysis
13 contemplation, soul-searching
14 heart-searching, thoughtfulness
15 self-examination

introspective
06 musing
07 pensive
08 brooding, reserved
09 withdrawn
10 meditative, thoughtful
11 introverted
12 self-absorbed
13 contemplative, inward-looking

introverted
03 shy
05 quiet
08 reserved
09 withdrawn
12 self-absorbed
13 introspective, inward-looking

intrude
06 butt in, chip in, meddle
07 barge in, obtrude, violate
08 encroach, infringe, trespass
09 gatecrash, interfere, interject, interlope, interrupt

intruder
06 raider, robber
07 burglar, prowler
10 interloper, trespasser
11 gatecrasher, infiltrator
12 housebreaker
14 unwelcome guest

intrusion
08 meddling, trespass
09 incursion, obtrusion, violation
12 encroachment, gatecrashing, infringement, interference, interruption

intrusive
04 nosy
05 pushy
08 invasive, snooping, unwanted
09 obtrusive, officious, uninvited, unwelcome
10 meddlesome
11 impertinent, importunate, interfering, trespassing
12 interrupting, presumptuous

intuition
05 hunch
07 feeling, insight
08 instinct
10 gut feeling, perception, sixth sense
12 presentiment

intuitive
06 inborn, innate
09 automatic
11 instinctive, intuitional

inundate
05 drown, flood, swamp
06 deluge, engulf
07 immerse
08 overflow, saturate, submerge

inundation
05 flood, spate, swamp
06 deluge, excess
07 surplus, torrent
08 overflow
09 tidal wave

inure
06 harden, temper
07 toughen
08 accustom
09 habituate
11 acclimatize, familiarize

invade
05 enter, seize, storm
06 attack, infest, maraud, occupy
07 assault, burst in, intrude, obtrude, overrun, pervade
08 encroach, infringe, take over, trespass
09 descend on, march into, penetrate, swarm over
10 infiltrate
12 enter by force

invader
08 attacker, intruder, marauder
09 aggressor, infringer
10 trespasser

invalid
03 ill
04 null, sick, void, weak
05 false, frail
06 ailing, feeble, infirm, poorly, sickly, unwell
07 patient, quashed, unsound
08 disabled, sufferer
09 bedridden, erroneous, illogical, incorrect, unfounded, untenable
10 fallacious, groundless, ill-founded, irrational
11 debilitated, inoperative, null and void, unjustified, unwarranted
12 convalescent, unacceptable

invalidate
04 void
05 annul
06 cancel, negate, revoke
07 nullify, rescind, vitiate

invalidity
07 fallacy, falsity, sophism
08 voidness
11 unsoundness
12 illogicality, speciousness
13 inconsistency, incorrectness, irrationality
14 fallaciousness

invaluable
08 precious, valuable
13 indispensable

invariable
03 set
05 fixed, rigid
06 stable, steady
07 regular, uniform
08 constant, habitual
09 immutable, permanent
10 changeless, consistent, inflexible, unchanging

invariably
06 always
09 regularly
10 constantly, habitually, inevitably, repeatedly
11 unfailingly, without fail
12 consistently

invasion
06 attack, breach
09 incursion, intrusion, offensive, onslaught, violation
10 occupation

11 penetration
12 encroachment, infiltration, infringement, interference, interruption

invective
05 abuse
06 tirade
07 censure, obloquy, sarcasm
08 berating, diatribe, scolding
09 contumely, philippic, reprimand
11 castigation, fulmination
12 denunciation, vilification, vituperation
13 recrimination, tongue-lashing

inveigh
04 rail
05 blame, scold
06 berate
07 censure, condemn, lambast, upbraid
08 denounce, reproach, sound off
09 castigate, criticize, fulminate
10 tongue-lash, vituperate

inveigle
03 con
04 coax, lure, wile
06 cajole, entice, lead on, seduce
07 beguile, wheedle
08 persuade
09 manoeuvre, sweet-talk
10 manipulate

invent
04 coin
06 cook up, create, design, devise, make up
07 concoct, dream up, hit upon, imagine, pioneer, think up, trump up
08 conceive, contrive, discover, innovate
09 fabricate, formulate, improvise, originate
10 come up with

invention
03 fib, lie
04 fake, myth
06 deceit, design, device, gadget, genius
07 fantasy, fiction, figment, forgery, machine, untruth
08 artistry, creation
09 discovery, falsehood, ingenuity, tall story
10 brainchild, concoction, contriving, creativity, innovation

11 contrivance, development, fabrication, imagination, inspiration, originality
12 construction
13 falsification, inventiveness

inventive
07 fertile, skilful
08 artistic, creative, original
09 ingenious
10 innovative
11 imaginative, resourceful

inventor
05 maker
07 creator, deviser
08 designer, producer
09 architect, innovator
10 discoverer, originator

► *Names of inventors:*
04 Bell (Alexander Graham), Benz (Karl), Biro (Laszlo), Colt (Samuel), Hood (Thomas), Otis (Elisha Graves), Swan (Sir Joseph Wilson), Tull (Jethro), Watt (James)
05 Baird (John Logie), Boyle (Robert), Hertz (Heinrich), Maxim (Sir Hiram Stevens), Morse (Samuel), Nobel (Alfred), Sousa (John Philip), Tesla (Nikola), Volta (Alessandro), Zeiss (Carl)
06 Ampère (André Marie), Brunel (Isambard Kingdom), Bunsen (Robert Wilhelm), Diesel (Rudolf), Dunlop (John), Eckert (John Presper), Edison (Thomas Alva), McAdam (John Loudon), Newton (Sir Isaac), Pascal (Blaise), Pitman (Sir Isaac), Savery (Thomas), Schick (Jacob), Talbot (William Henry Fox), Wallis (Sir Barnes Neville), Wright (Orville), Wright (Wilbur)
07 Babbage (Charles), Daimler (Gottlieb), Eastman (George), Faraday (Michael), Huygens (Christiaan), Lumière (Auguste), Marconi (Guglielmo, Marchese), Maxwell (James Clerk), Pasteur (Louis), Whittle (Sir Frank)
08 Bessemer (Sir Henry), Birdseye (Clarence), Daguerre (Louis Jacques Mandé), De Forest (Lee),

Ericsson (John), **Ferranti**
(Sebastian Ziani de),
Franklin (Benjamin),
Goodyear (Charles),
Newcomen (Thomas),
Sandwich (John Montagu,
Earl of), **Sinclair** (Sir Clive),
Zamenhof (Lazarus
Ludwig), **Zeppelin**
(Ferdinand, Graf von)
09 **Arkwright** (Sir Richard),
Cockerell (Sir Christopher
Sydney), **Ctesibius**,
Gutenberg (Johannes),
Hollerith (Herman),
Whitworth (Sir Joseph)
10 **Archimedes**, **Fahrenheit**
(Gabriel), **Pilkington** (Sir
Alastair), **Stephenson**
(George), **Torricelli**
(Evangelista), **Trevithick**
(Richard)
11 **Montgolfier** (Joseph
Michel)
➤ See also **scientist**

inventory
04 list, roll
05 stock, tally
06 record, roster, supply
07 account, listing
08 register, schedule
09 catalogue, checklist
11 description

inverse
05 other
07 counter
08 contrary, opposite
10 transposed, upside down

inversion
08 contrary, opposite
10 antithesis, transposal
13 transposition
14 contraposition

invert
06 upturn
07 capsize
08 overturn
09 transpose
10 turn turtle
14 turn upside down

invertebrate
▸ *Types of invertebrate*:
05 coral, fluke, hydra, leech
06 insect, spider, sponge
07 bivalve, crinoid, mollusc
08 arachnid, flatworm,
nematode, starfish,
tapeworm
09 arthropod, centipede,
earthworm, gastropod,

jellyfish, millipede,
roundworm, sea urchin,
trilobite
10 cephalopod, crustacean,
echinoderm, sand dollar,
sea anemone
11 annelid worm, sea
cucumber
13 horseshoe crab
➤ See also **animal**; **butterfly**;
crustacean; **insect**;
mollusc; **moth**; **worm**

invest
04 fund, give, sink, vest
05 endow, grant, put in, spend
06 bestow, confer, devote, lay
out, ordain
07 empower, entrust, install,
provide
10 contribute, inaugurate

investigate
05 probe, study
06 go into, search
07 analyse, examine, explore,
inspect, suss out
08 check out, consider,
look into, research
09 delve into
10 scrutinize
11 inquire into
15 give the once-over

investigation
05 probe, study
06 review, search, survey
07 hearing, inquest, inquiry
08 analysis, research, scrutiny
10 inspection
11 examination, exploration

investigative
10 analytical, inspecting
11 exploratory, fact-finding,
researching
13 investigating

investigator
06 prober, sleuth
07 analyst
08 analyser, examiner, explorer,
inquirer, reviewer, searcher
09 detective, inspector
10 private eye, questioner,
researcher, scrutineer
11 scrutinizer

investiture
09 admission, induction
10 coronation, ordination
11 instatement
12 enthronement,
inauguration, installation

investment
05 stake, stock
06 outlay
07 capital, finance, venture
11 expenditure, speculation
12 contribution

inveterate
07 chronic, diehard
08 hard-core, hardened
09 confirmed, incurable
10 entrenched
12 incorrigible, irreformable,
long-standing
13 dyed-in-the-wool

invidious
09 difficult, obnoxious,
offensive, repugnant
13 objectionable
14 discriminating,
discriminatory

invigorate
05 brace, pep up, rouse
06 buck up, perk up
07 animate, enliven, fortify,
freshen, inspire, liven up,
quicken, refresh
08 energize, motivate, vitalize
10 exhilarate, rejuvenate,
revitalize, strengthen

invigorating
05 fresh, tonic
07 bracing
09 animating, healthful,
uplifting, vivifying
10 energizing, refreshing,
salubrious
11 restorative, stimulating
12 exhilarating, rejuvenating

invincible
10 unbeatable
11 indomitable, insuperable
12 impenetrable, invulnerable,
unassailable, undefeatable
13 unconquerable

inviolability
08 sanctity
10 sacredness
14 sacrosanctness
15 invulnerability

inviolable
04 holy
06 sacred
08 hallowed
10 intemerate, sacrosanct
11 inalienable, unalterable,
untouchable

inviolate
04 pure
05 whole

06 entire, intact, sacred, unhurt, virgin
08 complete, unbroken, unharmed
09 stainless, undamaged, undefiled, uninjured, unspoiled, unstained, unsullied, untouched
10 intemerate, unpolluted, unprofaned

invisible
06 hidden, unseen
09 concealed, imaginary
10 out of sight, unobserved
11 microscopic, non-existent
12 undetectable
13 indiscernible, infinitesimal

invitation
04 bait, call, draw, lure
06 appeal, come-on
07 bidding, request, summons
08 overture, petition
09 challenge
10 allurement, attraction, enticement, incitement, inducement, temptation
11 provocation
12 solicitation
13 encouragement

invite
03 ask, bid
04 call, draw, lead, seek
05 tempt
06 allure, appeal, ask for, entice, summon
07 attract, bring on, look for, provoke, request, solicit, welcome
08 petition
09 encourage, entertain

inviting
08 alluring, enticing, tempting
09 appealing, beguiling, seductive, welcoming
10 attractive, bewitching, enchanting
11 fascinating

invocation
06 appeal, prayer
07 request
08 entreaty, petition
09 epiclesis
10 beseeching
11 conjuration, imploration
12 solicitation, supplication

invoice
04 bill
07 account, charges
09 reckoning

invoke
03 beg
04 pray
07 beseech, conjure, entreat, implore, request, solicit
08 appeal to, call upon, petition, resort to
09 imprecate
10 supplicate

involuntary
06 forced, reflex
07 coerced
09 automatic, compelled, unwilling
10 mechanical, unthinking
11 conditioned, instinctive, spontaneous, unconscious
13 unintentional

involve
04 mean
05 cover, imply, mix up
06 absorb, affect, denote, draw in, engage, entail, occupy, take in
07 concern, embrace, embroil, engross, include, require
08 interest
09 associate, encompass, implicate
11 incorporate, necessitate

involved
06 knotty
07 complex, jumbled, mixed up, tangled
08 caught up, tortuous
09 concerned, confusing, difficult, elaborate
10 associated, convoluted, implicated, taking part
11 complicated
13 participating

involvement
04 part
05 share
07 concern
08 interest
10 connection
11 association, implication
12 entanglement
13 participation

invulnerability
13 invincibility, inviolability
14 impregnability
15 impenetrability, unassailability

invulnerable
06 secure
10 invincible
12 impenetrable, unassailable
14 indestructible

inward
05 inner
06 inmost, inside
08 entering, incoming, interior, internal
09 innermost

inwardly
06 inside, within
07 at heart
08 deep down, secretly
09 privately

iota
03 bit, jot, tad
04 atom, hint, mite, whit
05 grain, scrap, speck, trace
06 morsel
08 fraction, particle

irascibility
09 bad temper, crossness, petulance, shortness, testiness
10 crabbiness, impatience, irritation, touchiness
12 irritability, snappishness

irascible
05 cross, testy
06 crabby
07 crabbed, prickly
08 choleric
09 irritable
10 ill-natured
11 bad-tempered, ill-tempered
12 cantankerous
13 quick-tempered, short-tempered

irate
03 mad
05 angry, livid, vexed
06 fuming, raging
07 annoyed, enraged, furious
08 incensed, up in arms, worked up
09 indignant, irritated
10 infuriated

ire
04 fury, rage
05 anger, wrath
06 choler
07 passion
09 annoyance
11 displeasure, indignation

iridescent
04 shot
07 rainbow
09 prismatic, sparkling
10 glittering, shimmering, variegated
11 rainbow-like

irk
03 bug, get, vex
04 gall, miff, rile
05 anger, annoy, get to, peeve
06 hassle, nettle, put out, ruffle
07 disgust, incense, provoke
08 distress, irritate
09 aggravate, infuriate
10 exasperate

irksome
06 boring, trying, vexing
08 annoying, tiresome
09 vexatious
10 bothersome, burdensome, irritating
11 aggravating, infuriating, troublesome
12 disagreeable, exasperating

iron
04 firm, hard
05 press, rigid, tough
06 smooth, steely, strong
07 adamant, flatten
10 determined, inflexible

◻iron out
06 settle
07 clear up, resolve, sort out
08 deal with, get rid of, put right
09 eliminate, eradicate, harmonize, reconcile
13 straighten out

ironic
03 wry
07 mocking
08 derisive, ironical, sardonic, scoffing, scornful, sneering
09 sarcastic, satirical
11 paradoxical

irons
05 bonds
06 chains
07 fetters
08 manacles, shackles

irony
05 scorn
06 satire
07 mockery, paradox, sarcasm

irradiate
06 illume
07 light up, lighten, shine on
08 brighten, illumine
10 illuminate

irrational
06 absurd, unwise
07 foolish, invalid, unsound
09 arbitrary, illogical, senseless
10 groundless, ridiculous
11 implausible, nonsensical
12 inconsistent, unreasonable

irrationality
08 unreason
09 absurdity
12 illogicality
13 senselessness
14 groundlessness, ridiculousness

irreconcilable
06 at odds
08 clashing, contrary, opposite
11 conflicting, incongruous
12 incompatible, inconsistent
13 contradictory

irrecoverable
04 lost
11 irreparable
12 irredeemable, irremediable
13 irreclaimable, irretrievable, unsalvageable

irrefutable
04 sure
07 certain
08 decisive, definite, positive
10 undeniable
11 beyond doubt, indubitable
12 indisputable, unanswerable
13 incontestable
14 beyond question, unquestionable

irregular
03 odd
05 bumpy, false, lumpy, rough
06 fitful, jagged, pitted, ragged, random, uneven
07 crooked, erratic, lawless, strange, unusual
08 aberrant, abnormal, improper, lopsided, peculiar, sporadic, variable, wavering
09 anomalous, haphazard, spasmodic
10 asymmetric, disorderly, fraudulent, immoderate, occasional, out of order, unofficial, unorthodox
11 exceptional, fluctuating
12 disorganized, inconsistent, intermittent, unmethodical, unprincipled, unsystematic
13 extraordinary
14 unconventional

irregularity
06 oddity
07 anomaly
08 cheating
09 asymmetry, deviation, roughness
10 aberration, dishonesty, randomness, unevenness
11 abnormality, fluctuation, inconstancy, malpractice, peculiarity, singularity, uncertainty, unorthodoxy, variability
12 eccentricity, lopsidedness
13 haphazardness, inconsistency, unpunctuality
14 disorderliness

irregularly
08 fitfully, off and on, unevenly
11 erratically, haphazardly, now and again
12 occasionally
13 spasmodically
14 intermittently
15 by fits and starts, in fits and starts

irrelevance
09 inaptness
10 red herring
12 unimportance
13 inconsequence, unrelatedness
14 inappositeness

irrelevant
05 inapt
09 unrelated
10 immaterial, inapposite, out of place
12 inapplicable, inconsequent
13 inappropriate
14 beside the point
15 having no bearing

irreligious
05 pagan
06 sinful, unholy, wicked
07 godless, heathen, impious, profane, ungodly
08 agnostic
09 atheistic, heretical
11 unbelieving, unrighteous

irremediable
08 hopeless
09 incurable
11 irreparable
12 irreversible
13 irretrievable

irremovable
03 set
05 fixed, stuck
06 rooted
08 obdurate
09 immovable, ingrained, obstinate, permanent

irreparable
09 incurable
12 irreversible
13 irretrievable

irreplaceable
08 peerless, precious
09 essential, matchless, priceless, unmatched
13 indispensable

irrepressible
06 bubbly
07 buoyant
08 animated
09 ebullient, resilient, vivacious
10 boisterous
11 unstoppable

irreproachable
07 perfect, sinless
08 flawless, spotless
09 blameless, faultless, guiltless
10 immaculate, impeccable
11 unblemished
13 unimpeachable
14 beyond reproach

irresistible
06 potent, urgent
08 alluring, charming, enticing, forceful, pressing, tempting
09 ravishing, seductive
10 compelling, enchanting, imperative
11 captivating, fascinating, inescapable, tantalizing, unavoidable
12 overpowering, overwhelming
13 irrepressible, unpreventable
14 uncontrollable

irresolute
06 fickle, unsure
08 doubtful, hesitant, shifting, unstable, unsteady, variable, wavering
09 dithering, tentative, uncertain, undecided, unsettled
10 ambivalent, hesitating, in two minds, indecisive, on the fence
11 fluctuating, half-hearted, vacillating
12 faint-hearted, pussyfooting, undetermined
15 shilly-shallying

irrespective
□ **irrespective of**
07 however, whoever
08 ignoring, no matter, whatever
09 never mind, whichever
12 disregarding, not affecting, regardless of
15 notwithstanding

irresponsible
04 rash, wild
06 unwise
07 erratic, flighty
08 carefree, careless, heedless, reckless
09 negligent
11 injudicious, thoughtless
13 ill-considered, untrustworthy

irretrievable
04 lost
08 hopeless
11 irreparable, irrevocable
12 irredeemable, unrecallable
13 irrecoverable, unsalvageable

irreverence
05 cheek, sauce
06 heresy, levity
07 impiety, mockery
08 rudeness
09 blasphemy, flippancy, impudence, insolence, profanity, sacrilege
10 cheekiness, disrespect, irreligion
11 discourtesy, godlessness, ungodliness
12 impertinence, impoliteness

irreverent
04 rude
05 saucy
06 cheeky
07 godless, impious, mocking, profane, ungodly
08 flippant, impolite, impudent, insolent
09 heretical
11 blasphemous, impertinent, irreligious
12 discourteous, sacrilegious
13 disrespectful

irreversible
05 final
09 incurable, permanent
11 irreparable, irrevocable, unalterable
12 irremediable
13 irretrievable, unrectifiable

irrevocable
05 final, fixed
07 settled
09 immutable
11 unalterable
12 irreversible, unchangeable

irrigate
03 wet
04 soak
05 flood, spray, water

07 moisten
08 sprinkle

irritability
09 bad temper, crossness, ill-temper, petulance, testiness
10 grumpiness, tetchiness
11 peevishness, prickliness
12 irascibility

irritable
05 cross, ratty, short, testy
06 crabby, crusty, grumpy, shirty, snappy, touchy
07 peevish, prickly, stroppy
08 snappish
09 crotchety, irascible
11 bad-tempered
12 cantankerous
13 quick-tempered, short-tempered

irritant
04 goad, pain
06 bother, menace
07 trouble
08 nuisance, vexation
09 annoyance
11 provocation
15 thorn in the flesh

irritate
03 bug, get, irk, jar, rub, vex
04 fret, goad, hurt, itch, rile
05 anger, annoy, chafe, grate, peeve, rouse
06 enrage, harass, nettle
07 incense, inflame, provoke
09 aggravate, drive nuts, infuriate
10 drive crazy, exasperate
13 get your back up
14 drive up the wall
15 get on your nerves

irritated
04 edgy
05 angry, cross, irked, ratty, riled, vexed
06 miffed, narked, peeved, piqued, put out
07 annoyed, nettled, ruffled
10 displeased
11 discomposed, exasperated

irritating
04 sore
05 itchy, pesky
06 thorny, trying, vexing
07 chafing, galling, irksome
08 abrasive, annoying, tiresome
09 maddening, provoking
10 bothersome, disturbing
11 aggravating, displeasing, infuriating, troublesome

irritation

04 bind, drag, fury, pain, pest
05 anger, pique
08 nuisance, vexation
09 annoyance, crossness, testiness
10 impatience, snappiness
11 aggravation, displeasure, provocation
12 exasperation, irritability
13 pain in the neck
15 dissatisfaction, thorn in the flesh

island

03 cay, key
04 eyot, holm, isle
05 atoll, islet
06 skerry
11 archipelago

▶ *Names of islands and island groups. We have omitted the words* **island** *and* **islands** *from names given in the following list but you may need to include one of these words as part of the solution to some crossword clues.*

03 Cos, Fyn, Ios, Rab, Rum
04 Bali, Coll, Cook, Cuba, Eigg, Elba, Fiji, Gozo, Guam, Holy, Iona, Java, Jura, Line, Long, Mahe, Muck, Maui, Mull, Oahu, Sark, Skye, Wake
05 Arran, Barra, Capri, Chios, Cocos, Coney, Corfu, Crete, Ellis, Faroe, Ibiza, Islay, Kuril, Lundy, Luzon, Malta, Melos, Nauru, Naxos, North, Palau, Paros, Samoa, Samos, South, Sunda, Timor, Tiree, Tonga
06 Aegean, Andros, Azores, Baffin, Bikini, Borneo, Caicos, Canary, Chagos, Comino, Cyprus, Devil's, Easter, Euboea, Flores, Hainan, Harris, Hawaii, Honshu, Icaria, Ionian, Jersey, Komodo, Kyushu, Lemnos, Lesbos, Midway, Orkney, Patmos, Rhodes, Sicily, Skiros, Staffa, Staten, Tahiti, Taiwan, Tobago, Tuvalu, Virgin
07 Bahamas, Bahrain, Bermuda, Celebes, Channel, Comoros, Corsica, Curaçao, Frisian, Gilbert, Gotland, Grenada, Iceland, Ireland, Iwo Jima,

Jamaica, Leeward, Madeira, Majorca, Menorca, Mikonos, Mindoro, Minorca, Nicobar, Norfolk, Okinawa, Phoenix, Praslin, Rathlin, Réunion, Society, Solomon, Stewart, St Kilda, St Lucia, Sumatra, Surtsey, Vanuatu, Zealand
08 Aleutian, Anglesey, Anguilla, Balearic, Coral Sea, Cyclades, Dominica, Falkland, Guernsey, Hawaiian, Hebrides, Hokkaido, Hong Kong, Kiribati, Maldives, Marshall, Mindanao, Moluccas, Pitcairn, Sakhalin, Sandwich, Sardinia, Shetland, Sri Lanka, Sulawesi, Tenerife, Trinidad, Victoria, Windward, Zanzibar
09 Admiralty, Ascension, Australia, Benbecula, Cape Verde, Christmas, Ellesmere, Galápagos, Greenland, Indonesia, Irian Jaya, Isle of Man, Lanzarote, Las Palmas, Manhattan, Marquesas, Mauritius, Melanesia, Nantucket, New Guinea, North Uist, Santorini, Singapore, South Seas, South Uist, Stromboli
10 Basse-Terre, Cephalonia, Cook Strait, Dodecanese, Heligoland, Hispaniola, Kalimantan, Madagascar, Martinique, Micronesia, Montserrat, New Britain, New Ireland, Puerto Rico, Samothrace, Seychelles, West Indies
11 Gran Canaria, Grand Bahama, Grand Cayman, Guadalcanal, Isle of Wight, Saint Helena, Scilly Isles, South Orkney
12 Bougainville, Grande Comore, Newfoundland, Prince Edward, Prince Rupert, South Georgia
13 American Samoa, British Virgin, Inner Hebrides, Isles of Scilly, Outer Hebrides, South Shetland
14 Papua New Guinea, Tierra del Fuego, Tristan da Cunha, Turks and Caicos
15 French Polynesia, Martha's Vineyard, Wallis and Futuna

isolate

06 cut off, detach, maroon, remove, strand
07 exclude, seclude, shut out
08 alienate, insulate, separate, set apart, shut away
09 keep apart, ostracize, segregate, sequester
10 disconnect, quarantine
12 cold-shoulder
14 send to Coventry

isolated

05 alone, apart
06 cut off, lonely, remote, unique
08 abnormal, atypical, deserted, detached, outlying, secluded, solitary, uncommon
09 anomalous, separated, unrelated, untypical
10 segregated
11 exceptional, God-forsaken, out-of-the-way

isolation

05 exile
08 solitude
09 aloneness, seclusion
10 alienation, detachment, insulation, loneliness, quarantine, remoteness, separation
11 abstraction, segregation
12 dissociation, separateness, solitariness
13 disconnection, sequestration

issue

04 copy, emit, flow, gush, ooze, rise, rush, seed, seep, stem
05 arise, exude, heirs, point, spurt, topic, young
06 affair, debate, effect, emerge, family, finale, matter, number, put out, result, scions, spring, supply
07 come out, concern, deal out, deliver, dispute, edition, emanate, give out, outcome, outflow, problem, proceed, produce, progeny, publish, release, subject, version
08 announce, argument, children, delivery, effusion, printing, proclaim
09 broadcast, circulate, discharge, effluence, offspring, originate
10 burst forth, conclusion, distribute, impression, instalment, promulgate, successors

11 circulation, controversy, descendants, disseminate, publication

12 announcement, distribution, promulgation

13 dissemination

▫at issue

10 in question

15 under discussion

▫take issue

05 argue, fight

06 object

07 contest, dispute, quarrel, protest

09 challenge

13 take exception

itch

04 ache, burn, long, pine

05 crave, crawl, yearn

06 desire, hanker, hunger, thirst, tickle, tingle

07 craving, longing, prickle

08 irritate, keenness, pruritis, tingling, yearning

09 eagerness, hankering, prickling

10 irritation

itching

05 dying, eager

06 aching, greedy, raring

07 burning, longing

09 hankering, impatient

item

05 entry, piece, point, story, thing

06 detail, factor, object

07 account, element, feature

09 component

10 ingredient, particular

13 consideration

itemize

04 list

05 count

06 detail, number, record

08 instance, tabulate

09 enumerate

13 particularize

15 make an inventory

itinerant

06 roving

07 nomadic, roaming, vagrant

08 drifting, rambling, vagabond

09 wandering, wayfaring

10 journeying, travelling

11 peripatetic

itinerary

04 plan, tour

05 route

06 course

07 circuit, journey

J

jab
04 poke, prod, push, shot, stab
05 elbow, lunge, nudge, punch
09 injection

jabber
03 gab, jaw, yap
06 babble, gabble, mumble, rabbit, ramble, rattle, witter
07 blether, chatter, prattle

jack
▫**jack up**
04 hike, lift
05 hoist, raise
07 elevate, inflate
08 increase

jacket
04 case, skin, wrap
05 cover, shell
06 casing, folder, sheath
07 wrapper
08 covering, wrapping

jackpot
07 big time, bonanza
10 first prize

jaded
05 bored, fed up, spent, tired, weary
06 bushed, done in, dulled
07 wearied, worn out
08 fatigued, tired out
09 exhausted, played-out

jag
04 barb, snag, spur
05 notch, point, tooth
10 projection, protrusion

jagged
06 barbed, broken, ragged, snaggy, spiked, uneven
07 notched, toothed
08 indented, saw-edged, serrated
09 irregular

jail, gaol
03 can, jug
04 nick, quod
05 choky, clink
06 cooler, detain, inside, intern, lock up, prison

07 confine, custody, impound, put away, slammer
08 imprison, send down
11 incarcerate
12 penitentiary, send to prison

jailer, gaoler
05 guard, screw
06 keeper, warden, warder
13 prison officer

jam
03 fix, mob, ram
04 bind, clog, cram, herd, hole, pack, push, spot
05 block, close, crowd, crush, force, horde, jelly, press, stick, stuff, wedge
06 hold-up, pickle, plight, scrape, spread, squash, throng, thrust
07 confine, congest, squeeze, straits, the soup, trouble
08 conserve, gridlock, obstruct, preserve, quandary
09 confiture, marmalade, multitude, tight spot
10 bottleneck, congestion
11 obstruction, predicament

jamboree
04 fête
05 party, rally, spree
06 frolic, junket
07 carouse, revelry, shindig
08 carnival, festival, field day
09 festivity, gathering
10 convention
11 celebration, get-together

jangle
03 din, jar
05 clang, clash, clank, clink
06 bother, jingle, racket, rattle
07 clatter, discord, jarring
08 clangour, irritate
09 cacophony
10 dissonance
13 reverberation

janitor
09 caretaker, concierge

jar
03 irk

04 jerk, jolt
05 annoy, clash, grate, shake, upset
06 bicker, jangle, nettle, offend, rattle
07 agitate, disturb, quarrel, trouble, vibrate
08 be at odds, disagree, irritate
12 be at variance, be in conflict

jargon
04 cant
05 argot, idiom, slang, usage
08 legalese, parlance
09 buzz words, gibberish
10 journalese, mumbo-jumbo
11 computerese
12 gobbledegook, psychobabble
13 computerspeak

jarring
05 harsh
07 grating, jolting, rasping
08 jangling, strident
10 discordant, irritating
11 cacophonous

jaundiced
05 jaded
06 biased, bitter
07 bigoted, cynical, hostile
09 resentful, sceptical
10 prejudiced, suspicious
11 distrustful, pessimistic
12 misanthropic
14 unenthusiastic

jaunt
04 ride, spin, tour, trip
05 drive
06 outing, ramble, stroll
09 excursion

jaunty
04 airy, trim
05 perky, showy, smart
06 bouncy, breezy, dapper, lively
07 buoyant, stylish
08 carefree, debonair
09 energetic, sprightly
13 self-confident

jaw
04 chat, talk, trap

jazz

05 chops, claws, mouth
06 babble, confab, gabble, gossip, jabber, muzzle, natter, rabbit
07 chatter, chinwag, maxilla
08 clutches, mandible
10 discussion
12 conversation

jazz

➤ *Types of jazz*:
03 bop
04 jive
05 bebop, blues, swing
06 fusion, modern
07 hot jazz, post-bop, ragtime
08 acid jazz, free-form
09 Afro-Cuban, Dixieland, West Coast
10 avant-garde, mainstream, New Orleans
12 boogie-woogie
➤ See also **music**

❑**jazz up**
07 enliven, liven up
09 smarten up

jazzy

05 fancy, gaudy, smart
06 flashy, lively, snazzy
08 spirited, swinging

jealous

05 green
07 careful, envious, mindful
08 covetous, desirous, grudging, vigilant, watchful
09 green-eyed, resentful
10 begrudging, possessive, protective, suspicious

jealousy

04 envy
05 spite
06 grudge
09 suspicion, vigilance
10 bitterness, resentment
11 carefulness, mindfulness
12 covetousness
14 possessiveness, protectiveness

jeer

03 boo
04 gibe, hiss, hoot, mock, razz
05 abuse, chaff, knock, scoff, scorn, sneer, taunt, tease
06 banter, deride, heckle
07 barrack, catcall, mockery
08 derision, ridicule
09 make fun of, shout down

jejune

04 arid, dull
05 banal, naïve, silly, vapid

06 barren, callow, meagre
07 insipid, prosaic, puerile
08 childish, immature, juvenile
10 colourless, spiritless
15 unsophisticated

jell see **gel**

jeopardize

04 risk
05 stake
06 gamble, hazard
07 imperil
08 endanger, threaten
09 put at risk
11 take a chance
14 expose to danger

jeopardy

04 risk
05 peril
06 danger, hazard, threat
09 liability
12 endangerment
13 vulnerability
14 precariousness

jerk

03 jar, jog, tug
04 clot, dope, fool, geek, jolt, nerd, prat, pull, twit, yank
05 idiot, lurch, twerp, wally
06 twitch, wrench

jerky

05 bumpy, jumpy, rough, shaky
06 bouncy, fitful
07 jolting, shaking, twitchy
08 lurching
09 spasmodic
10 convulsive, incoherent
12 disconnected, uncontrolled
13 unco-ordinated

jerry-built

06 faulty, flimsy, shoddy
07 rickety
08 slipshod, unstable
09 cheapjack, defective
10 ramshackle
14 thrown together

jersey

06 jumper, woolly
07 sweater
08 pullover

jest

03 gag, kid
04 fool, hoax, joke, mock, quip
05 crack, prank, tease, trick
06 banter
07 fooling, kidding, leg-pull
09 tell jokes, wisecrack, witticism

❑**in jest**
05 in fun

07 as a joke, to tease
08 jokingly

jester

03 wag, wit
04 fool
05 clown, comic, droll, joker
06 mummer
07 buffoon, juggler
08 comedian, humorist, quipster
09 prankster
11 merry-andrew

jet

03 fly
04 flow, gush, inky, rush, zoom
05 black, ebony, raven, sable, shoot, spout, spray, spurt
06 spring, squirt, stream
08 fountain
10 pitch-black
09 sprinkler

jettison

04 dump
05 chuck, ditch, eject, expel, heave, scrap
06 unload
07 abandon, discard, offload
08 get rid of
09 throw away

jetty

04 dock, mole, pier, quay
05 wharf
07 harbour

jewel

03 gem
04 rock
05 pearl, prize
08 gemstone, ornament, sparkler, treasure
09 jewellery, showpiece
11 masterpiece, pride and joy
13 precious stone

jewellery

04 gems
05 gauds
06 bijoux, jewels
07 gemmery, regalia
08 treasure, trinkets
09 ornaments
10 bijouterie

➤ *Types of jewellery*:
04 ring, stud
05 beads, cameo, chain, tiara
06 amulet, anklet, bangle, brooch, choker, diadem, hatpin, locket, tiepin, torque
07 coronet, earring, necklet, pendant
08 bracelet, cufflink, necklace, nose-ring

10 signet-ring
13 charm bracelet

Jewish calendar

➤ *Months in the Jewish calendar*:
02 Av
04 Adar, Elul, Iyar
05 Nisan, Sivan, Tevet
06 Kislev, Shevat, Tammuz, Tishri
07 Heshvan
09 Adar Sheni

Jezebel
04 jade, tart, vamp
05 hussy, whore, witch
06 harlot, wanton
10 loose woman, seductress
11 femme fatale
12 scarlet woman

jib
04 balk
05 stall
06 recoil, refuse, shrink
09 stop short

jiffy
03 sec
04 tick
05 flash, trice
06 minute, moment, second
07 instant
08 two ticks
09 twinkling
11 split second

jig
03 bob, hop
04 jerk, jump, leap, skip
05 caper, shake
06 bounce, prance, twitch, wiggle, wobble

jigger
04 ruin
05 break, spoil, wreck
07 botch up, destroy, louse up, scupper, vitiate
09 undermine
14 make a pig's ear of

jiggery-pokery
05 fraud
06 deceit
08 mischief, trickery
09 chicanery, deception
10 hanky-panky, subterfuge
13 funny business
14 monkey business

jiggle
03 jog
04 jerk, jump
05 shake

06 bounce, fidget, twitch, waggle, wiggle, wobble
07 agitate

jilt
05 chuck, ditch, leave, spurn
06 betray, desert, pack in, reject
07 abandon, discard
09 cast aside, throw over

jingle
04 ding, poem, ring, song, tune
05 chime, chink, clang, clink, ditty, rhyme, verse
06 chorus, jangle, melody, rattle, tinkle
07 clatter, refrain, ringing
14 tintinnabulate

jingoism
10 chauvinism, flag-waving, insularity, patriotism
11 imperialism, nationalism

jinx
03 hex
05 charm, curse, spell
06 hoodoo, voodoo
07 bad luck, bedevil, bewitch, evil eye, gremlin
10 affliction, black magic
12 cast a spell on

jitters
06 nerves
07 anxiety, fidgets, habdabs, jimjams
09 agitation, the creeps, the shakes, trembling
10 the shivers, the willies,
11 nervousness
13 heebie-jeebies

jittery
04 edgy
05 jumpy, nervy, shaky
07 anxious, fidgety, nervous, panicky, quaking, shivery
08 agitated
09 flustered, perturbed, quivering, trembling

job
04 duty, part, post, role, task, work
05 chore, share, stint, trade
06 affair, career, charge, errand, métier, office
07 calling, mission, problem, project, pursuit, venture
08 activity, business, capacity, function, position, province, vocation
10 assignment, employment, line of work, livelihood, occupation, profession

11 consignment, piece of work, undertaking
14 line of business, responsibility

jobless
04 idle
08 inactive, workless
09 on the dole, out of work, redundant
10 unemployed

jockey
04 coax, ease
05 rider
06 cajole, induce
07 wheedle
08 horseman
09 manoeuvre, negotiate
10 equestrian, horsewoman, manipulate

jocose
05 droll, funny, merry, witty
06 jovial, joyous
07 comical, jesting, playful, teasing, waggish
08 humorous, mirthful

jocular
05 comic, droll, funny, witty
06 jocose, joking, jovial
07 amusing, comical, jesting, playful, waggish
08 humorous

jocularity
03 wit
06 gaiety, humour
07 fooling, jesting, teasing
08 jocosity, laughter
09 amusement, funniness, jolliness, joviality, merriment
10 jocoseness
11 playfulness, waggishness
12 sportiveness, whimsicality
13 facetiousness

jog
03 jar, run
04 bump, jerk, jolt, push, trot
05 elbow, nudge, shove
06 arouse, bounce, canter, joggle, jostle, prompt, remind
09 stimulate

joie de vivre
03 joy
04 zest
05 gusto, mirth
06 bounce, gaiety, relish
08 buoyancy
09 enjoyment, merriment
10 ebullience, enthusiasm, joyfulness

join
03 add, tie
04 abut, ally, bind, fuse, glue, knit, link, meet, weld, yoke
05 annex, enrol, enter, marry, merge, touch, unify, unite
06 adhere, adjoin, attach, border, cement, couple, enlist, fasten, sign up, splice
07 combine, connect, verge on
08 border on, converge
09 accompany, affiliate, associate, co-operate
10 amalgamate, team up with
11 collaborate

▫**join in**
06 chip in, muck in
07 partake, pitch in
09 co-operate
10 contribute, take part in
11 participate

▫**join up**
05 enrol, enter
06 enlist, sign up

joint
03 bar, fit, pub
04 club, dive, join, knot, seam
05 carve, cut up, haunt, hinge, nexus, place, roach, sever, stick, union, unite
06 common, couple, divide, fasten, joined, mutual, reefer, shared, spliff, united
07 connect, dissect
08 combined, communal, coupling, junction, juncture
09 dismember, nightclub
10 articulate, collective
11 amalgamated
12 articulation, intersection

joke
03 fun, gag, kid, pun
04 fool, hoax, hoot, jape, jest, lark, mock, play, quip, yarn
05 clown, crack, laugh, prank, spoof, sport, tease, trick
06 banter, whimsy
08 one-liner, repartee
09 wisecrack, witticism
10 fool around, funny story
12 take for a ride
13 have someone on
15 pull someone's leg

joker
03 wag, wit
04 card
05 clown, comic, droll, sport
06 jester, kidder
08 comedian, humorist, quipster

09 prankster, trickster
11 wisecracker

jolly
03 gay
04 glad, very
05 happy, merry
06 cheery, hearty, highly, jovial, joyful, lively
07 festive, gleeful, greatly
08 cheerful, mirthful
09 enjoyable, extremely, intensely
10 delightful
11 pleasurable
13 exceptionally

jolt
03 hit, jar, jog
04 bang, blow, bump, jerk, push, stun
05 amaze, knock, lurch, nudge, shake, shock, shove, start
06 bounce, jostle, jounce
07 astound, disturb, perturb, shake up, startle
08 astonish, reversal, surprise

jostle
03 jog, vie
04 bang, bump, jolt, push
05 crowd, elbow, shove
06 hustle, joggle
07 collide, compete
08 shoulder, struggle

jot
03 ace, bit
04 atom, hint, iota, mite, whit
05 grain, scrap, speck, trace
06 detail, morsel, tittle, trifle
07 glimmer, smidgen
08 fraction, particle
09 scintilla

▫**jot down**
04 list, note
06 record
08 scribble

journal
03 log
05 diary, paper
06 record, review, weekly
07 account, daybook, gazette, monthly
08 magazine, register
09 chronicle, newspaper
10 periodical
11 publication

journalism
04 news
05 media, press
07 writing
09 reportage, reporting
11 copy-writing, Fleet Street

12 broadcasting, fourth estate, news coverage
14 correspondence, feature-writing

journalist
03 sub
04 hack
06 editor, journo, scribe
08 reporter, reviewer, stringer
09 columnist, newshound, paparazzo, subeditor
10 news-writer
11 broadcaster, commentator
13 correspondent, feature-writer

➤ *Names of journalists, editors and newspaper proprietors*:
03 **Day** (Sir Robin), **Mee** (Arthur)
04 **Adie** (Kate), **Amis** (Martin), **Bell** (Martin), **Birt** (John), **Ford** (Anna), **Gall** (Sandy), **Jane** (Frederick Thomas), **King** (Cecil), **Neil** (Andrew), **Rook** (Jean), **Snow** (Peter), **Wark** (Kirsty)
05 **Astor** (William, Viscount), **Black** (Conrad), **Buerk** (Michael), **Cooke** (Alistair), **Evans** (Harold), **Frost** (David), **James** (Clive), **Junor** (Sir John), **Laski** (Marghanita), **Levin** (Bernard), **Reith** (John Charles Walsham, Lord), **Waugh** (Auberon)
06 **Bierce** (Ambrose), **Burnet** (Sir Alastair), **Deedes** (Bill, Lord), **Gallup** (George), **Greene** (Sir Hugh), **Hislop** (Ian), **Hutton** (Will), **Isaacs** (Jeremy), **Morgan** (Piers), **O'Brien** (Conor Cruise), **Paxman** (Jeremy), **Pilger** (John), **Proops** (Marjorie), **Reuter** (Paul Julius, Baron von), **Rippon** (Angela), **Savile** (Sir Jimmy)
07 **Boycott** (Rosie), **Bradlee** (Ben), **Buckley** (William Frank), **Cameron** (James), **Cobbett** (William), **Ingrams** (Richard), **Kennedy** (Helena Ann), **Kennedy** (Ludovic), **Leeming** (Jan), **Malcolm** (Derek), **Maxwell** (Robert), **Mencken** (Henry Louis), **Murdoch** (Rupert),

Rowland ('Tiny'), **Stanley** (Sir Henry Morton)
08 **Burchill** (Julie), **Cronkite** (Walter), **Dimbleby** (David), **Dimbleby** (Jonathan), **Dimbleby** (Richard), **Gellhorn** (Martha), **Hanrahan** (Brian), **Lippmann** (Walter), **McCarthy** (John), **McDonald** (Trevor), **Naughtie** (James), **Pulitzer** (Joseph), **Rees-Mogg** (William, Lord), **Robinson** (Henry Crabb), **Woodward** (Bob)
09 **Bernstein** (Carl), **Bosanquet** (Reginald), **Humphreys** (John), **Macdonald** (Gus, Lord), **Magnusson** (Magnus), **Plekhanov** (Giorgiy), **Streicher** (Julius)
10 **Greenslade** (Roy), **Muggeridge** (Malcolm), **Rothermere** (Harold Harmsworth, Viscount), **Rusbridger** (Alan), **Waterhouse** (Keith), **Worsthorne** (Sir Peregrine)
11 **Beaverbrook** (William Maxwell Aitken, Lord), **Northcliffe** (Alfred Harmsworth, Viscount)
12 **Street-Porter** (Janet)
➢ See also **writer**

journey
02 go
03 fly
04 hike, ride, roam, rove, sail, tour, trek, trip
05 drive, jaunt, range, tramp
06 cruise, flight, ramble, roving, safari, travel, voyage
07 odyssey, passage, proceed
08 crossing, progress
09 excursion
10 expedition, wanderings
11 peregrinate
13 peregrination

journeyer
07 pilgrim, rambler, tourist, trekker, tripper, voyager
08 wanderer, wayfarer
09 traveller
12 peregrinator

joust
03 vie
04 spar, tilt
05 fight, trial
07 compete, contest, quarrel, tourney, wrangle
08 skirmish
10 engagement, tournament

jovial
05 happy, jolly, merry
06 cheery, genial
07 affable, buoyant, gleeful
08 animated, cheerful, mirthful
13 in good spirits

joviality
03 fun
04 glee
05 mirth
07 jollity
08 buoyancy, hilarity
09 happiness, merriment
10 affability, ebullience
12 cheerfulness

joy
04 glee
05 bliss
06 thrill
07 delight, ecstasy, elation, rapture, success, victory
08 gladness, pleasure, treasure
09 cloud nine, felicitiy, happiness, rejoicing
10 exultation
13 gratification, seventh heaven

joyful
04 glad
05 happy, merry
06 elated
07 gleeful, pleased
08 cheerful, ecstatic, euphoric
09 delighted, gratified, overjoyed
11 on cloud nine, over the moon, tickled pink
15 in seventh heaven, on top of the world

joyless
03 sad
04 dour, glum, grim
05 bleak
06 dismal, dreary, gloomy, sombre
07 doleful, forlorn, unhappy
09 cheerless, miserable

joyous
04 glad
05 happy, merry
06 festal, joyful
07 festive, gleeful
08 cheerful, ecstatic, gladsome, jubilant
09 rapturous

jubilant
06 elated, joyful
07 excited
08 ecstatic, euphoric, exultant, thrilled
09 exuberant, overjoyed, rejoicing, rhapsodic
10 triumphant

jubilation
07 ecstasy, elation, jubilee, triumph
08 euphoria, jamboree
10 excitement, exultation
11 celebration

jubilee
04 fête, gala
08 carnival, feast day, festival
09 festivity
11 anniversary, celebration
13 commemoration

Judas
07 traitor
08 betrayer, quisling, turncoat
13 tergiversator

judge
03 try
04 beak, damn, doom, rate
05 gauge, think, value, weigh
06 assess, critic, decide, decree, expert, reckon, review, umpire
07 adjudge, arbiter, condemn, convict, coroner, discern, examine, justice, Law Lord, mediate, sheriff, weigh up
08 appraise, assessor, conclude, consider, estimate, evaluate, mediator
09 arbitrate, ascertain, criticize, determine, evaluator, moderator, ombudsman, seneschal
10 adjudicate, arbitrator, magistrate
11 adjudicator, connoisseur, distinguish
13 form an opinion
14 sit in judgement

► *Names of judges*:
04 **Coke** (Sir Edward)
05 **Burgh** (Hubert de), **Draco**, **Solon**
06 **Gideon**, **Irvine** (Alexander, Lord), **Mackay** (James, Lord), **Warren** (Earl)
07 **Brennan** (William Joseph), **Denning** (Alfred, Lord), **Erskine** (Thomas, Lord), **Scarman** (Leslie, Lord)

08 **Gardiner** (Gerald, Lord),
Hailsham (Douglas
McGarel Hogg, Viscount),
Hailsham (Quintin
McGarel Hogg, Viscount),
Jeffreys (George, Lord)
09 **Vyshinsky** (Andrei)

judgement
04 doom, fate, view
05 taste
06 acumen, decree, ruling,
wisdom
07 finding, opinion, verdict
08 decision, estimate,
prudence, sagacity,
sentence
09 appraisal, damnation,
diagnosis, good sense,
mediation
10 assessment, conclusion,
conviction, evaluation,
perception, punishment,
shrewdness
11 arbitration, common sense,
discernment, penetration,
retribution
12 adjudication, perspicacity
14 discrimination

judicial
05 legal
08 critical, forensic
09 impartial, judiciary, magistral
14 discriminating

judicious
04 wise
05 smart, sound
06 astute, clever, shrewd
07 careful, prudent
08 cautious, informed, sensible
09 sagacious
10 considered, discerning,
reasonable, thoughtful
11 circumspect, common-sense
14 discriminating

jug
03 jar, urn
04 ewer
05 crock
06 carafe, flagon, vessel
07 pitcher, Toby jug
08 decanter

juggle
06 adjust, change, doctor
07 balance, falsify, massage
08 disguise, equalize
09 rearrange
10 manipulate, tamper with

juice
03 sap
05 fluid, serum

06 liquid, liquor, nectar
07 essence, extract

juicy
04 lush, racy
05 lurid, spicy, vivid
06 risqué, watery
09 colourful, succulent, thrilling
10 scandalous, suggestive
11 interesting, sensational

jumble
03 mix
04 mess
05 chaos, mix-up
06 medley, muddle, tangle
07 clutter, mixture, shuffle
08 disarray, disorder, shambles
09 confusion, potpourri
10 disarrange, hotch-potch
11 disorganize

jumbled
06 untidy
07 chaotic, mixed-up,
muddled, tangled
08 confused, shuffled, unsorted
10 disarrayed, disordered
12 disorganized

jumbo
04 huge, vast
05 giant
07 immense, mammoth
08 colossal, enormous,
gigantic, whopping

jump
03 gap, hop, jar, mug
04 gate, go up, hike, jolt, leap,
miss, omit, rail, rise, romp,
skip
05 avoid, boost, bound, break,
caper, clear, fence, frisk,
hedge, lapse, lurch, mount,
quail, shake, shock, space,
spasm, sport, start, surge,
vault, wince
06 ascend, attack, beat up,
bounce, breach, bypass,
cavort, cut out, flinch, frolic,
gambol, go over, hiatus,
hurdle, ignore, lacuna,
pounce, prance, spiral,
spring, switch, twitch,
upturn
07 advance, assault, barrier, set
upon, swoop on, upsurge
08 escalate, increase, interval,
leave out, obstacle,
omission, overlook, pass
over, pounce on
09 barricade, elevation,
increment
10 appreciate, escalation

❑**jump at**
04 grab
05 seize
08 pounce on

❑**jump on**
05 blame, chide, fly at, scold
06 berate, rebuke, revile
07 censure, reprove, tick off,
upbraid
08 reproach
09 castigate, criticize,
reprimand

jumper
06 jersey, woolly
07 sweater
08 pullover

jumpy
04 edgy
05 bumpy, jerky, rough, shaky,
tense
06 bouncy, fitful, on edge,
uneasy
07 anxious, fidgety, jittery,
jolting, nervous, panicky,
restive, shaking, twitchy
08 agitated, lurching
09 spasmodic
10 convulsive, incoherent
12 apprehensive,
disconnected, uncontrolled
13 unco-ordinated

junction
04 bond, join, link, seam
05 joint, union
07 joining, linking, welding
08 coupling, crossing, juncture
10 confluence, crossroads
11 interchange
12 intersection

juncture
04 crux, time
05 point, stage
06 minute, moment, period
08 occasion

jungle
04 bush, maze
05 chaos, snarl
06 medley, tangle
08 disarray, disorder, mishmash
09 confusion, labyrinth
10 hotch-potch, miscellany,
rainforest

junior
05 lower, minor
06 lesser, minion
07 servant, younger
08 inferior

junk
04 dump

05 chuck, ditch, dregs, scrap,
   trash, waste
06 debris, litter, refuse
07 clutter, discard, garbage,
   rubbish, rummage
08 get rid of, jettison,
   oddments, throw out
09 bric-à-brac, dispose of

junta
04 gang, ring
05 cabal, group
06 cartel, clique, league
07 coterie, council, faction
09 camarilla

jurisdiction
04 area, rule, sway, zone
05 field, orbit, power, range,
   reach, right, scope
06 bounds, sphere
07 command, control, mastery
08 dominion, province
09 authority, influence
10 domination, leadership
11 prerogative, sovereignty
14 administration

jury
05 panel
06 jurors

just
03 apt, due
04 fair, good, only
05 legal, moral, quite, valid
06 barely, hardly, honest, lawful,
   proper, purely, simply,
   spot on
07 ethical, exactly, fitting,
   merited
08 deserved, recently, rightful,
   scarcely, suitable, unbiased
09 equitable, impartial,
   objective, perfectly,
   precisely, righteous
10 a moment ago, absolutely,
   completely, even-handed,

fair-minded, honourable,
legitimate, principled,
reasonable, upstanding
11 appropriate, well-founded
12 unprejudiced
13 a short time ago,
   disinterested

◻**just about**
06 all but, almost, nearly
08 as good as, well-nigh
10 more or less
11 practically

justice
02 JP
03 law
05 judge, right
06 equity, honour, morals
07 penalty, redress, sheriff
08 fairness, fair play
09 integrity, propriety,
   rectitude, rightness
10 lawfulness, legitimacy,
   magistrate, punishment,
   recompense, reparation
11 objectivity, uprightness
12 compensation, impartiality
13 equitableness,
   righteousness

justifiable
05 legal, right, sound, valid
06 lawful, proper
09 excusable, warranted
10 acceptable, defensible,
   forgivable, legitimate,
   pardonable, reasonable
11 sustainable, well-founded
12 within reason
14 understandable

justification
04 plea
05 basis
06 excuse, reason
07 apology, defence, grounds,
   warrant

10 mitigation
11 explanation, vindication
15 rationalization

justify
05 clear, prove
06 acquit, defend, excuse,
   pardon, uphold, verify
07 absolve, bear out, confirm,
   deserve, explain, forgive,
   support, sustain, warrant
09 exculpate, vindicate
10 stand up for
11 rationalize
12 substantiate

justly
06 fairly
07 equally, rightly
08 honestly, lawfully, properly
10 rightfully, with reason
11 impartially, objectively
12 even-handedly, legitimately

jut, jut out
06 beetle, extend
07 extrude, project
08 protrude, stick out

juvenile
03 boy, kid
04 girl
05 child, minor, young, youth
06 callow, infant, junior
07 babyish, puerile
08 childish, immature,
   teenager, youthful
09 infantile, youngster
10 adolescent
11 young person

juxtapose
11 put together
15 place side by side

juxtaposition
08 nearness
09 closeness, proximity

kaleidoscopic
06 motley
10 changeable, poikilitic, polychrome, variegated
12 ever-changing, many-coloured, multifarious
13 multicoloured, polychromatic

kaput
06 broken, ruined
07 defunct, extinct, wrecked
09 conked out, destroyed

keel

❑keel over
04 drop, fall
05 faint, swoon, upset
07 capsize, founder, pass out
08 black out, collapse, overturn
10 topple over, turn turtle

keen
03 cry, sob
04 avid, howl, wail, wild
05 acute, eager, mourn, sharp
06 astute, biting, clever, fierce, fond of, grieve, lament, liking, shrewd, sorrow, strong
07 devoted, earnest, fervent, mordant, pointed, pungent
08 incisive, piercing, ruthless
09 assiduous, cut-throat, devoted to, sensitive, trenchant
10 attached to, discerning, perceptive
11 industrious, penetrating, quick-witted, sharp-witted
12 enthusiastic
13 conscientious, perspicacious
14 discriminating

keenness
06 wisdom
08 industry, sagacity, sapience, sedulity
09 diligence, eagerness, sharpness
10 astuteness, cleverness, enthusiasm, shrewdness, trenchancy
11 discernment, earnestness, penetration, sensitivity
12 incisiveness

keep
04 feed, food, fort, hold, mind, save, tend
05 board, deter, guard, hoard, stock, store, tower, watch
06 castle, deal in, detain, foster, fulfil, hold up, honour, living, remain, shield
07 abide by, care for, carry on, citadel, collect, confinel, deposit, dungeon, furnish, inhibit, nurture, observe, perform, persist, possess, protect, respect, shelter, store up, support, sustain
08 adhere to, carry out, conserve, continue, fortress, hang on to, hold on to, maintain, obstruct, preserve
09 celebrate, look after, persevere, safeguard, subsidize, watch over
10 accumulate, comply with, effectuate, livelihood, perpetuate, provide for, stronghold, sustenance
11 commemorate, maintenance, subsistence

❑for keeps
06 always
07 for ever, for good
10 for all time

❑keep at
04 last, stay, toil
05 grind
06 drudge, endure, finish, labour, remain, slog at
07 carry on, persist, stick at
08 continue, maintain
09 persevere
11 be steadfast

❑keep back
04 curb, hide, stop
05 check, delay, limit
06 hush up, impede, retard
07 conceal, control, reserve
08 restrain, restrict, withhold
09 constrain

❑keep from
04 halt, stop
06 desist, resist
07 forbear, prevent

❑keep in
04 hide
05 quell
06 coop up, detain, shut in, stifle, stop up
07 conceal, confine, repress
08 bottle up, restrain, suppress

❑keep off
05 avoid
07 stay off
09 not go near
12 stay away from, steer clear of

❑keep on
04 last, stay
06 endure, hold on, retain
07 carry on, persist
08 continue, maintain
09 persevere, stick at it
13 stay the course

❑keep on at
03 nag
05 harry
06 badger, chivvy, harass, pester, plague, pursue

❑keep secret
04 hide
07 conceal
08 keep dark
14 keep under wraps

❑keep to
04 obey
06 fulfil
07 observe, respect, stick to
08 adhere to
10 comply with

❑keep track of
05 trace, watch
06 follow, record
07 monitor, oversee

❑keep up
03 vie
05 equal, match, rival
07 compete, contend, emulate, support, sustain

08 continue, keep pace,
maintain, preserve
09 persevere
11 go along with

keeper
05 guard
06 jailer, minder, warden,
warder
07 curator, steward
08 defender, governor,
guardian, overseer, surveyor
09 attendant, caretaker,
custodian
10 supervisor
11 conservator
14 superintendent

keeping
04 care, cure, ward
05 aegis, trust
06 accord, charge
07 custody, harmony
08 auspices, tutelage
09 agreement, retention
10 conformity, protection
11 maintenance, supervision
12 guardianship, surveillance

keepsake
05 relic, token
06 emblem, pledge
07 memento
08 reminder, souvenir
11 remembrance

keg
03 tun, vat
04 butt, cask, drum
06 barrel, firkin
08 hogshead

ken
05 grasp, range, reach
06 notice
07 compass
09 awareness, knowledge
10 cognizance, perception
13 comprehension,
understanding

kernel
03 nub, nut
04 core, crux, germ, gist, seed
05 grain, heart, stone
06 centre, marrow
07 essence, innards, nucleus

key
04 clue, code, main, sign
05 chief, gloss, guide, index,
major, pitch, table, vital
06 answer, legend, secret
07 central, crucial, leading,
pointer
08 decisive, glossary, solution

09 essential, important,
indicator, necessary,
principal
11 explanation, explication,
fundamental, translation
14 interpretation

keynote
04 core, gist, pith
05 heart, theme
06 accent, centre, marrow,
stress
07 essence
09 substance

keystone
04 base, core, crux, root
05 basis
06 ground, motive, source,
spring
08 linchpin
10 foundation, mainspring
11 cornerstone

kick
03 fun, hit, pep, zip
04 bite, blow, boot, buzz, high,
jolt, knee, quit, stop, zing
05 break, power, punch
06 effect, give up, recoil, strike,
thrill
07 abandon, potency
08 leave off, pleasure, stimulus,
strength, striking
10 desist from, excitement
11 stimulation

◻**kick against**
05 rebel, spurn
06 oppose, resist
14 hold out against

◻**kick around**
07 discuss, toy with
08 play with
09 talk about

◻**kick off**
04 open
05 begin, start
08 commence, initiate
09 introduce
10 inaugurate
11 get under way

◻**kick out**
04 oust, sack
05 eject, evict, expel
06 reject, remove
07 boot out, dismiss
08 chuck out, get rid of,
throw out
09 discharge

kick-off
05 start
06 outset, word go

07 opening
09 beginning, inception
12 commencement,
introduction

kid
03 boy, con, lad, tot
04 dupe, fool, girl, gull, hoax,
jest, joke
05 child, tease, trick, youth
06 delude, have on, humbug,
infant, nipper
07 deceive, pretend, toddler
08 hoodwink, juvenile,
teenager, young one
09 little one, youngster
10 adolescent
15 pull someone's leg

kidnap
05 seize, steal
06 abduct, hijack, snatch
12 hold to ransom

kill
03 end, sap, use, zap
04 ache, do in, fill, hang, hurt,
pass, ruin, slay
05 death, pound, quash, quell,
shoot, smart, smite, spend,
throb, use up, waste
06 be sore, behead, climax,
deaden, finish, murder,
occupy, rub out, suffer
07 abolish, bump off, butcher,
destroy, execute, put down,
smother, take out, wipe out
08 blow away, decimate,
dispatch, knock off,
massacre, suppress
09 death-blow, devastate, do to
death, eliminate, eradicate,
finish off, liquidate, polish
off, slaughter, while away
10 annihilate, decapitate, do
away with, dénouement,
guillotine, put to death,
put to sleep
11 assassinate, coup de grâce,
electrocute, exterminate

killer
06 gunman, hit-man, slayer
07 butcher
08 assassin, homicide,
murderer
09 cut-throat
10 hatchet man, liquidator
11 executioner, slaughterer
12 exterminator

killing
03 hit
04 coup, gain, hard
05 booty

06 absurd, big hit, murder, profit, taxing
07 amusing, arduous, bonanza, carnage, clean-up, fortune, slaying, success
08 butchery, draining, fatality, genocide, homicide, massacre, windfall
09 bloodshed, execution, fatiguing, hilarious, matricide, patricide, slaughter, uxoricide
10 enervating, exhausting, fratricide, sororicide
11 destruction, elimination, infanticide, liquidation
12 debilitating, manslaughter
13 assassination, extermination

killjoy
06 damper, grouch, misery, moaner, whiner
08 dampener
10 complainer, spoilsport, wet blanket

kin
04 clan
05 blood, stock, tribe
06 family, people
07 cousins, kindred, lineage
09 relations, relatives
13 consanguinity, flesh and blood

kind
03 set
04 good, mild, nice, race, sort, type, warm
05 brand, breed, class, genre, genus, stamp, style
06 benign, family, genial, gentle, giving, humane, kindly, loving, manner, nature, strain
07 amiable, cordial, helpful, patient, species, variety
08 amicable, category, friendly, generous, gracious, obliging
09 character, congenial, indulgent, unselfish
10 altruistic, benevolent, big-hearted, charitable, persuasion
11 considerate, description, good-hearted, good-natured, magnanimous, neighbourly, soft-hearted, sympathetic, warm-hearted
12 affectionate, humanitarian
13 compassionate, philanthropic, tender-hearted, understanding

◻**in kind**
09 similarly, tit for tat
10 in exchange
12 in like manner

kind-hearted
04 warm
06 benign, humane
07 helpful
08 generous, obliging
10 altruistic
11 considerate, good-natured, sympathetic
12 humanitarian
13 compassionate, philanthropic, tender-hearted

kindle
04 fire, stir
05 light, rouse
06 arouse, awaken, excite, ignite, incite, induce, thrill
07 inflame, inspire, provoke
09 set alight, set fire to, set on fire, stimulate

kindliness
06 warmth
07 charity
08 sympathy
09 benignity
10 compassion, generosity
11 beneficence, benevolence

kindly
04 good, warm
06 giving, humane
07 cordial, helpful, patient
08 amicable, friendly, generous, pleasant
09 indulgent
10 benevolent, big-hearted, charitable, thoughtful
11 considerate, good-natured
13 compassionate

kindness
04 help, love
05 grace
06 favour, warmth
07 charity, service
08 altruism, good turn, good will, goodness, humanity
09 affection, tolerance
10 assistance, compassion, generosity, humaneness, indulgence
11 benevolence, helpfulness, hospitality
12 friendliness, philanthropy
13 consideration, fellow feeling
14 thoughtfulness

15 considerateness, humanitarianism, warm-heartedness

kindred
04 akin, clan, folk, like
06 allied, common, family, people
07 cognate, lineage, related
09 connected, relations, relatives
10 affiliated
11 connections
12 relationship
13 consanguinity, corresponding, flesh and blood

king
04 lord, star
05 chief, ruler
06 leader, master, prince, top dog
07 big shot, emperor, kingpin, majesty, monarch, supremo
08 big noise
09 big cheese, chieftain, sovereign

➤ *Names of kings. We have omitted the word* **king** *from names given in the following list but you may need to include this word as part of the solution to some crossword clues. The regnal numerals of individual kings have also been omitted.*
03 Zog
04 Fahd, Ivan, Ivan (the Terrible), John, Knut, Offa, Olav, Otto, Paul
05 Boris, Brian, Capet (Hugo), Carol, Creon, David, Edgar, Edred, Edwin (Saint), Henry, Herod (the Great), James, Louis, Murat (Joachim), Penda, Pepin (the Short)
06 Alaric, Albert, Alfred, Attila, Canute, Clovis, Darius, Duncan, Edmund, Edward, Edward (the Confessor), Edward (the Elder), Edward (the Martyr), Egbert, Faisal, Farouk, Faysal, George, Harald, Harold, Khalid, Philip, Philip (Augustus), Robert, Robert (the Bruce), Rudolf, Sargon, Xerxes
07 Alfonso, Charles, Croesus, Emanuel, Francis, Hussein, Leopold, Macbeth, Malcolm, Ptolemy, Richard,

Romulus, Stephen, Tarquin,
William, William (the Silent)
8 Ethelred, Ethelred (the
Unready), Leonidas,
Ramesses, Thutmose
9 Akhenaton, Alexander,
Amenhotep, Antiochus,
Atahualpa, Athelstan,
Cymbeline, Ethelbert,
Ethelwulf, Ferdinand,
Frederick, Hammurabi,
Hardaknut, Hugo Capet,
Sigismund, Stanislaw,
Theodoric, Vortigern,
Wenceslas
0 Artaxerxes, Esarhaddon,
Juan Carlos, Tarquinius
1 Charlemagne, Constantine,
Hardicanute, Mithridates,
Sennacherib, Shalmaneser,
Tutankhamen
2 Assurbanipal, Boris
Godunov, Herod Agrippa
3 Francis Joseph, Louis-
Philippe
4 Edmund Ironside, Harold
Harefoot, Nebuchadnezzar,
Victor Emmanuel

kingdom
04 land
5 realm, reign, state
6 domain, empire, nation
7 country, dynasty
8 dominion, monarchy,
province
9 territory
1 sovereignty

kingly
5 regal, royal
6 august
8 imperial, majestic, splendid
9 imperious, sovereign
1 monarchical

kink
4 bend, curl, dent, loop, whim
5 crimp, curve, quirk, twist
6 fetish, foible
7 caprice, crinkle, wrinkle
9 deviation
0 perversion

kinky
4 wavy
5 curly, queer, weird
6 curled, frizzy, quirky,
warped
7 crimped, deviant, twisted
8 depraved, freakish
9 perverted, unnatural,
whimsical
0 degenerate, outlandish

kinsfolk
04 clan
06 family
07 cousins
09 relations, relatives

kinship
05 blood
06 family
07 lineage
08 affinity, alliance, ancestry,
likeness, relation
09 community
10 conformity, connection
11 association, equivalence
12 relationship
13 consanguinity

kiosk
05 booth, cabin, stall, stand
09 bookstall, news-stand

kismet
03 lot
04 doom, fate
05 karma
07 destiny, fortune

kiss
04 lick, neck, peck, snog
05 brush, graze, smack, touch
06 caress, scrape, smooch
07 smacker
08 canoodle, osculate
09 glance off
10 bill and coo, osculation

kit
03 rig, set
04 gear, togs
05 get-up, strip, stuff, tools
06 outfit, rig-out, tackle, things
07 baggage, effects, luggage
08 clothing, supplies, utensils
09 apparatus, equipment
10 implements, provisions
11 instruments
13 accoutrements,
paraphernalia

◻kit out
03 arm
05 dress, equip, fix up
06 fit out, outfit, rig out, supply

kittenish
07 playful
10 coquettish, frolicsome
11 flirtatious

knack
04 bent, gift, hang, turn
05 flair, forte, skill, trick
06 genius, talent
07 ability, faculty
08 aptitude, capacity, facility

09 dexterity, expertise,
handiness, quickness
10 adroitness, capability,
competence, propensity
11 proficiency, skilfulness

knapsack
04 pack
06 kitbag
08 backpack, rucksack
09 duffel bag, haversack
11 shoulder-bag

knave
05 cheat, rogue, scamp, swine
06 rascal, rotter
07 bounder, dastard, villain
08 blighter, swindler
09 reprobate, scallywag,
scoundrel

knavery
05 fraud
06 deceit
07 devilry, roguery
08 mischief, trickery, villainy
09 chicanery, deception,
duplicity, imposture
10 corruption, dishonesty,
hanky-panky
13 double-dealing

knavish
06 wicked
07 corrupt, roguish
08 devilish, fiendish, rascally
09 dastardly, deceitful,
dishonest, reprobate
10 fraudulent, villainous
11 mischievous, scoundrelly
12 contemptible, unscrupulous
13 dishonourable

knead
03 ply, rub
04 form, work
05 malax, mould, press, shape
07 knuckle, massage, squeeze
10 manipulate

kneel
03 bow
04 bend
05 stoop
06 curtsy, kowtow, revere
07 bow down, defer to
09 genuflect
13 make obeisance

knell
04 peal, ring, toll
05 chime, knoll, sound
07 ringing

knickers
05 pants
06 briefs, smalls

07 drawers, panties
08 bloomers, lingerie
12 bikini briefs, camiknickers
14 knickerbockers

knick-knack
06 bauble, gewgaw, trifle
07 trinket
08 gimcrack, ornament
09 bagatelle, bric-à-brac

knife
03 cut, rip
04 dirk, stab
05 blade, slash, wound
06 carver, cutter, dagger, pierce
07 bayonet, machete, scalpel
08 lacerate, penknife,
   skene-dhu
09 jackknife
10 craft knife, flick knife
11 pocket knife, switchblade

knight
07 gallant, soldier, warrior
08 banneret, cavalier,
   champion, horseman
09 chevalier, freelance,
   man-at-arms
10 cavalryman, equestrian

knightly
05 noble
06 heroic
07 courtly, gallant, valiant
08 gracious, intrepid, valorous
09 dauntless, soldierly
10 chivalrous, courageous

knit
04 ally, bind, join, knot, link,
   loop, mend, purl
05 unite, weave
06 fasten, gather, secure
08 crotchet
12 draw together

knob
03 nub
04 ball, boss, knot, lump, umbo
05 gnarl, knurl, swell, tuber
06 handle, switch, tumour
08 swelling, tubercle
09 capitulum
10 door-handle, protrusion
12 protuberance

knock
03 box, hit, pan, rap, tap
04 bang, bash, belt, blow,
   bump, clip, cuff, dash, jolt,
   slam, slap
05 clout, crash, pound, punch,
   slate, smack, stamp, swipe,
   thump, whack

06 attack, batter, defeat, rebuff,
   strike, wallop
07 bad luck, banging, censure,
   collide, condemn, failure,
   run down, setback
08 pounding, reversal
09 criticize, deprecate, disparage,
   hammering, rejection
10 misfortune
11 pick holes in
12 pull to pieces, tear to pieces
13 find fault with

▢knock about
03 gad, hit
04 bash, hurt, roam, rove
05 abuse, punch, range, wound
06 batter, beat up, bruise,
   buffet, damage, injure,
   ramble, strike, travel, wander
07 consort, saunter, traipse
08 go around, maltreat, mistreat
09 associate, manhandle
10 hang around

▢knock down
04 fell, raze
05 clout, floor, level, lower,
   pound, smash, wreck
06 batter, reduce, wallop
07 destroy, run down, run over
08 decrease, demolish

▢knock off
03 rob
04 do in, kill, lift, nick, slay, stop
05 cease, filch, pinch, steal,
   swipe, waste
06 deduct, finish, murder, pack
   in, pilfer, rip off, snitch
07 bump off, snaffle
08 clock off, clock out, get rid
   of, pack it in, stop work,
   take away
09 terminate
10 do away with, finish work
11 assassinate

▢knock out
02 KO
04 beat, fell, rout, stun
05 amaze, crush, floor
06 defeat, hammer, thrash
07 astound, impress, startle
08 astonish, bowl over
09 eliminate, prostrate
11 knock for six

▢knock up
09 improvise
10 jerry-build

knockout
07 stunner, success, triumph
08 smash-hit
09 sensation

knoll
04 hill
05 knowe, mound
06 barrow, koppie
07 hillock, hummock

knot
03 tie
04 band, bind, bond, knit, knob,
   knub, lash, loop, lump, ring
05 bunch, clump, crowd, gnarl,
   group, joint, knurl, leash,
   ravel, twist, weave
06 circle, secure, splice, tangle,
   tether
07 cluster, entwine
08 entangle, ligature, swelling
09 fastening, gathering

➤ *Types of knot. We have
omitted the word* **knot** *from
names given in the following list
but you may need to include this
word as part of the solution to
some crossword clues.*
03 bow, tie
04 bend, flat, loop, reef, wall
05 hitch, thumb
06 granny, square
07 bowline, weaver's, Windsor
08 overhand, slipknot,
   surgeon's
09 half hitch, sheet bend, Turk's
   head
10 clove hitch, common bend,
   fisherman's, sheepshank
11 carrick bend, Englishman's,
   timber hitch
12 rolling hitch
13 figure of eight
14 fisherman's bend, running
   bowline

knotty
05 bumpy, rough
06 nodose, thorny, tricky
07 complex, gnarled, nodular
08 baffling, puzzling
09 Byzantine, difficult, intricate
10 mystifying, perplexing
11 complicated, troublesome

know
05 sense
06 fathom, notice
07 be aware, discern, make out,
   realize, undergo
08 identify, perceive
09 apprehend, be clued up,
   go through, recognize
10 comprehend, experience,
   understand
11 distinguish
12 discriminate
13 associate with, differentiate

know-all

07 wise guy
08 wiseacre
09 know-it-all, smart alec
10 clever dick
11 clever clogs, smartypants

know-how

05 knack, savvy, skill
07 ability, faculty
09 expertise, knowledge
10 capability, competence
11 savoir-faire

knowing

05 aware
06 astute, shrewd
07 cunning
09 conscious
10 discerning, perceptive
11 significant

knowingly

08 by design, wilfully
09 on purpose, purposely
10 designedly
11 consciously
12 calculatedly, deliberately
13 intentionally

knowledge

04 data
05 facts, grasp, skill
06 wisdom
07 ability, know-how
08 intimacy, learning
09 awareness, cognition,
   education, erudition,
   expertise, schooling
10 cognizance
11 conversance, discernment,
   familiarity, information,
   proficiency, scholarship
12 acquaintance,
   apprehension, intelligence
13 consciousness, enlightenment

knowledgeable

06 au fait, expert
07 erudite, learned
08 educated, familiar,
   informed, lettered, well-read
09 scholarly
10 conversant, well-versed
12 well-informed

known

05 noted, plain
06 avowed, famous, patent
07 obvious
08 admitted, familiar, revealed
09 confessed, published
10 celebrated, proclaimed,
   recognized
12 acknowledged

knuckle

□ knuckle down

10 buckle down
15 start to work hard

□ knuckle under

05 defer, yield
06 accede, give in, submit
07 give way, succumb
09 acquiesce, surrender

kowtow

04 fawn
05 defer, kneel, toady
06 cringe, grovel, pander, suck
   up
11 curry favour
12 bow and scrape

kudos

04 fame
05 glory
06 esteem, honour, praise,
   regard, renown, repute
07 acclaim, laurels
08 plaudits, prestige

label
03 dub, tab, tag
04 call, mark, name, term
05 badge, brand, stamp, title
06 define, docket, marker, ticket
07 epithet, sticker
08 classify, identify, nickname
09 brand name, trademark
10 categorize
11 description, designation
12 characterize
14 categorization, classification, identification
15 proprietary name

laborious
04 hard
05 heavy, tough
06 tiring, uphill
07 arduous, careful, onerous, tedious
08 diligent, tiresome, toilsome, wearying
09 assiduous, difficult, fatiguing, strenuous, wearisome
11 hard-working, industrious, painstaking
12 backbreaking

labour
03 job
04 plod, roll, slog, task, toil, toss, turn, work
05 birth, chore, grind, hands, pangs, pitch, slave, sweat
06 drudge, effort, overdo, strain, strive, suffer, throes
07 travail, workers, workmen
08 delivery, drudgery, exertion, go all out, hard work, struggle, work hard
09 diligence, elaborate, employees, endeavour, labourers, workforce
10 childbirth, employment, overstress
11 parturition
12 contractions
13 exert yourself, overemphasize
15 industriousness

laboured
06 forced
07 awkward, stilted, studied
08 affected, overdone, strained
09 contrived, ponderous, unnatural
11 complicated, overwrought

labourer
04 hand
05 navvy
06 menial, worker
07 workman
12 manual worker

labyrinth
04 maze
06 enigma, jungle, puzzle, riddle, tangle, warren
09 confusion, intricacy
12 complication, entanglement

labyrinthine
07 complex, tangled, winding
08 confused, involved, mazelike, puzzling, tortuous
09 Byzantine, intricate
10 convoluted, perplexing

lace
04 cord, do up
05 mix in, spike, thong, twine
06 fasten, lacing, string, thread
07 fortify, tatting
08 bootlace, shoelace
10 intertwine, interweave

▬ *Types of lace*:
04 gold
05 filet, jabot
06 trolly
07 galloon, guipure, Honiton, Mechlin, pearlin, tatting, torchon, trolley
08 Brussels, dentelle, duchesse
09 Chantilly, point-lace, reticella
10 Colbertine, mignonette, pillow-lace, thread-lace

lacerate
03 cut, rip
04 claw, gash, rend, tear
05 slash, wound
06 harrow, injure, mangle
07 afflict, cut open, torture

08 distress, mutilate

laceration
03 cut, rip
04 gash, maim, rent, tear
05 slash, wound
10 mutilation

lachrymose
05 teary, weepy
06 crying, woeful
07 sobbing, tearful, weeping

lack
04 miss, need, void, want
06 dearth
07 absence, not have, paucity, require, vacancy
08 scarcity, shortage
09 emptiness, privation
10 deficiency, have need of, scantiness
11 deprivation, destitution
13 be deficient in, insufficiency
15 not have enough of

lackadaisical
04 dull, idle, lazy, limp
08 indolent, listless
09 enervated, lethargic
10 languorous

lackey
05 toady, valet
06 menial, minion, yes-man
07 servant, steward
10 instrument, manservant

lacking
05 minus
07 missing, needing, short of, wanting, without
09 defective, deficient

lacklustre
04 drab, dull, flat
05 vapid
06 boring, leaden
07 insipid, tedious
08 lifeless
10 spiritless, uninspired
13 unimaginative, uninteresting

laconic
05 blunt, brief, crisp, pithy, short, terse
06 abrupt

07 concise
08 incisive, succinct, taciturn
10 economical, to the point

lacuna
03 gap
04 void
05 blank, break, space
06 cavity, hiatus
08 omission

lad
03 boy, guy, kid, son
04 chap
05 bloke, youth
06 fellow
09 schoolboy, youngster

laden
04 full
05 taxed
06 jammed, loaded, packed
07 charged, fraught, stuffed
08 burdened, hampered,
   weighted
09 oppressed
10 encumbered
11 weighed down

la-di-da
04 posh
06 snooty
07 foppish, stuck-up
08 affected, mannered,
   snobbish
11 highfalutin, over-refined,
   pretentious, toffee-nosed

ladle
03 dip
04 bail, dish, lade
05 scoop, spoon
06 shovel

◻**ladle out**
07 dish out, dole out, hand out
10 distribute

lady
04 dame
05 woman
06 damsel, female, matron
10 noblewoman
11 gentlewoman

ladylike
06 modest, polite, proper
07 genteel, refined
08 polished, well-bred
11 respectable
12 well-mannered

lag
05 dally, delay, tarry, trail
06 dawdle, linger, loiter
08 hang back, straggle
10 fall behind
12 drag your feet, shilly-shally

14 bring up the rear

laggard
05 snail
07 dawdler
08 lingerer, loiterer
09 slowcoach, straggler

lagoon
04 lake, pond, pool
05 bayou, marsh, swamp

laid up
03 ill
04 sick
07 injured
09 bedridden
11 immobilized, out of action
12 hors de combat
13 incapacitated, on the sick list

laid-back
06 at ease, casual
07 relaxed
09 easy-going, leisurely,
   unhurried, unworried
10 untroubled
11 free and easy, unflappable
13 imperturbable

lair

► *Lairs and homes of*
animals:
03 den, pen, sty
04 byre, coop, drey, fold, form,
   hive, hole, holt, nest, sett
05 earth, eyrie, lodge
06 burrow, warren
08 dovecote, vespiary

laissez-faire
09 free-trade
10 free-market
14 free-enterprise

lake
04 loch, mere, pond, pool,
   tarn
05 basin, bayou
06 lagoon

► *Names of lakes. We have*
omitted the word **lake** *from*
names given in the following list
but you may need to include this
word as part of the solution to
some crossword clues.
03 Van
04 Abbé, Biwa, Bled, Chad,
   Como, Erie, Eyre, Kivu,
   Tana
05 Garda, Great, Huron,
   Nyasa, Ohrid, Onega, Patos,
   Poopó
06 Albert, Baikal, Crater,
   Finger, Geneva, Ladoga,
   Malawi, Nasser, Saimaa,

Taimyr, Taymyr, Vänern
07 Balaton, Chapala, Lucerne,
   Ontario, Rannoch, Scutari,
   Torrens, Turkana
08 Balkhash, Bodensee, Lac
   Léman, Loch Earn, Loch
   Ness, Maggiore, Michigan,
   Superior, Tiberias, Titicaca,
   Victoria, Winnipeg
09 Constance, Great Bear,
   Great Salt, Loch Leven,
   Loch Morar, Maracaibo,
   Neuchâtel, Nicaragua,
   Ullswater, Zeller See
10 Great Slave, Loch Lomond,
   Lough Foyle, Lough Neagh,
   Okeechobee, Tanganyika,
   Windermere
11 Great Bitter
12 Derwent Water, Kielder
   Water
13 Coniston Water

lam
03 hit
04 beat, pelt
05 clout, knock, pound, thump,
   whack
06 batter, pummel, strike,
   thrash, wallop
07 leather

lambaste
03 tan
04 beat, drub, flay, flog, whip
05 oast, scold
06 batter, berate, strike, thrash
07 censure, upbraid
09 castigate, criticize

lame
04 hurt, poor, thin, weak
05 gammy
06 feeble, maimed, poorly
07 halting, injured, limping
08 crippled, disabled, hobbling
12 unconvincing
14 unsatisfactory

lament
03 cry, sob
04 howl, keen, moan, wail
05 dirge, elegy, mourn, tears
06 bemoan, bewail, grieve,
   regret, sorrow
07 requiem, ululate, weeping
08 grieving, threnody
09 complaint

lamentable
04 mean, poor
06 meagre, tragic, woeful
07 pitiful
08 grievous, mournful, terrible,
   wretched

09 miserable, niggardly, sorrowful
10 deplorable, inadequate
11 regrettable

lamentation
04 keen, moan
05 dirge, elegy, grief
06 plaint, sorrow
07 keening, sobbing, wailing, weeping
08 grieving, jeremiad, mourning, threnody
09 ululation

laminate
04 coat, face
05 cover, flake, layer, plate, split
06 veneer

lamp
04 bulb
05 light
07 lantern
09 light bulb

lampoon
04 mock, skit
05 spoof
06 parody, satire, send up
07 take off
08 ridicule, satirize, travesty
09 burlesque, make fun of
10 caricature, pasquinade

lampooner
08 parodist, satirist
09 pasquiler
11 pasquinader
12 caricaturist

lance
03 cut
04 pike, slit
05 prick, spear
06 incise, lancet, pierce
07 bayonet, harpoon, javelin
08 puncture

land
03 get, hit, net, tax, win
04 area, deal, dock, drop, gain, give, loam, soil
05 acres, berth, catch, earth, end up, fetch, manor, reach, realm, state, tract
06 alight, arrive, burden, direct, domain, estate, fields, ground, nation, obtain, region, saddle, secure, settle, unload
07 achieve, acquire, acreage, capture, country, deliver, deposit, grounds, inflict, procure, terrain, trouble

08 dismount, district, encumber, farmland, go ashore, property, province, take down
09 disembark, territory, touch down
10 come to rest, real estate, terra firma
11 countryside
13 native country

landlady, landlord
04 host
05 owner
08 hotelier, mine host, publican
09 innkeeper
10 freeholder, proprietor

landmark
05 cairn
06 beacon
07 feature
08 boundary, monument
12 turning-point

landscape
04 view
05 scene, vista
06 aspect
07 outlook, scenery
08 panorama, prospect
11 countryside, perspective

landslide
08 decisive, emphatic, landslip, rockfall
09 avalanche
12 overwhelming

lane
03 way
04 path
05 alley, byway, track
06 avenue, byroad
07 footway, pathway, towpath
08 alleyway, driveway, footpath

language
04 talk
05 style
06 speech
07 diction, wording
08 parlance, phrasing, rhetoric
09 discourse, utterance
10 expression, vocabulary, vocalizing
11 phraseology, terminology, verbalizing
12 conversation
13 communication

➤ *Language terms include*:
04 cant
05 argot, idiom, lingo, slang, usage

06 brogue, creole, jargon, patois, patter, pidgin, syntax, tongue
07 dialect, grammar
08 buzz word, localism
09 etymology, phonetics, semantics
10 journalese, vernacular
11 doublespeak, linguistics, orthography, regionalism
12 lexicography, lingua franca
13 colloquialism

➤ *Languages of the world include*:
04 Lapp, Manx, Thai, Urdu, Zulu
05 Bantu, Croat, Czech, Dutch, Farsi, Greek, Hindi, Iraqi, Irish, Latin, Malay, Maori, Swiss, Tamil, Welsh
06 Afghan, Arabic, Basque, Celtic, Danish, Eskimo, French, Gaelic, German, Hebrew, Magyar, Polish, Romany, Slovak, Somali
07 Bengali, Burmese, Catalan, Chinese, Cornish, English, Finnish, Flemish, Iranian, Italian, Kurdish, Latvian, Maltese, Mexican, Persian, Punjabi, Russian, Serbian, Spanish, Swahili, Swedish, Tibetan, Turkish, Volapük, Yiddish
08 Estonian, Hawaiian, Japanese, Mandarin, Romanian, Sanskrit, Scottish
09 Aborigine, Afrikaans, Esperanto, Ethiopian, Hottentot, Hungarian, Icelandic, Norwegian, Sinhalese, Slovenian, Ukrainian
10 Hindustani, Indonesian, Lithuanian, Portuguese, Vietnamese

languid
04 dull, lazy, limp, slow, weak
05 faint, heavy, inert, weary
06 feeble, pining, sickly, torpid
08 drooping, inactive, listless, sluggish
09 enervated, lethargic
10 languorous, spiritless
11 debilitated, indifferent
13 lackadaisical
14 unenthusiastic

languish
04 fade, fail, flag, long, mope, pine, sigh, sink, want, wilt

05 brood, droop, faint, waste, yearn
06 desire, grieve, hanker, hunger, sicken, sorrow, weaken, wither

languor
05 ennui, sloth
06 torpor
07 fatigue, inertia
08 debility, laziness, lethargy
09 heaviness, indolence, lassitude, weariness
10 drowsiness, enervation, relaxation, sleepiness
12 listlessness

lank
04 lean, limp, slim, thin
05 gaunt, lanky
06 skinny
07 scraggy, scrawny, slender
08 drooping, lifeless, rawboned
10 lustreless, straggling

lanky
04 lean, slim, thin
05 gaunt
07 scraggy, scrawny, slender
08 gangling

lap
03 leg, sip, sup
04 fold, lick, wind, wrap
05 cover, drink, round, stage
06 circle, course, encase, enfold, swathe
07 circuit, compass, envelop, overlap, section, swaddle
08 distance, surround

❑ **lap up**
06 absorb

lapse
03 end, gap
04 drop, fail, fall, go by, go on, lull, pass, sink, slip, stop
05 break, cease, drift, error, fault, pause, slide
06 elapse, expire, hiatus, run out, slip by, worsen
07 decline, descent, failing, go to pot, mistake, relapse
08 downturn, interval, omission, slip away, slipping
09 backslide, oversight, terminate, worsening
10 aberration, degenerate, negligence
11 backsliding, dereliction, deteriorate, go to the dogs
12 degeneration, indiscretion, intermission, interruption

lapsed
06 run out

07 expired, invalid
08 finished, obsolete, outdated
09 out of date, unrenewed

larceny
05 theft
06 piracy
07 robbery
08 burglary, stealing

larder
06 pantry
09 storeroom
11 storage room

large
03 big
04 full, high, huge, tall, vast
05 ample, broad, bulky, giant, grand, great, heavy, jumbo, roomy
06 bumper
07 immense, liberal, mammoth, massive, sizable
08 colossal, enormous, generous, gigantic, spacious, sweeping, whopping
09 extensive, ginormous, grandiose, humungous, king-sized, plentiful
10 commodious, dirty great, exhaustive, monumental, prodigious, stupendous, voluminous
11 far-reaching, substantial
12 considerable
13 comprehensive

❑ **at large**
04 free
08 on the run
09 at liberty, generally, in general
10 on the loose, on the whole
11 independent

❑ **by and large**
06 mostly
07 as a rule
09 generally
10 on the whole
14 for the most part

largely
06 mainly, mostly
07 chiefly, greatly
09 generally, in the main, primarily
10 by and large
11 principally
13 predominantly
14 for the most part

large-scale
04 epic, vast, wide
05 broad

08 sweeping
09 expansive, extensive, wholesale
11 far-reaching, wide-ranging

largesse
04 alms, gift
06 bounty
07 charity, handout, present
08 donation, kindness
10 generosity, liberality
11 benefaction, munificence
12 philanthropy
14 open-handedness

lark
03 job
04 game, play, romp, task
05 antic, caper, chore, fling, prank, revel, sport
06 cavort, frolic, gambol
07 fooling, have fun, skylark
08 activity, escapade, mischief
09 cavorting, fool about, horseplay, mess about

lascivious
04 blue, lewd
05 bawdy, horny, randy
06 ribald, smutty, vulgar, wanton
07 lustful, obscene, sensual
08 indecent, prurient, unchaste
09 lecherous, salacious
10 libidinous, licentious, scurrilous, suggestive

lash
03 hit, tie, wag
04 beat, bind, blow, dash, flog, join, rope, whip
05 affix, break, flail, flick, pound, scold, strap, swipe
06 attack, batter, berate, buffet, fasten, rebuke, secure, strike, stroke, switch, tether, thrash
07 bawl out, censure, lay into, reprove, scourge
08 make fast
09 criticize, fulminate

❑ **lash out**
08 hit out at
09 have a go at
11 splash out on
15 speak out against

lass
04 bird, girl, miss
05 chick
06 damsel, lassie, maiden
10 schoolgirl, young woman

lassitude
06 apathy, torpor
07 fatigue, languor
09 heaviness, tiredness

10 drowsiness
12 listlessness, sluggishness

last
03 end
04 go on, keep, stay, take, wear
05 abide, after, close, exist, final
06 behind, ending, endure, finish, hold on, keep on, latest, remain, utmost
07 carry on, closing, extreme, finally, hold out, persist, stand up, subsist, survive
08 continue, furthest, hindmost, previous, rearmost, terminal, ultimate
10 completion, concluding, conclusion, most recent, ultimately

□**at last**
07 finally
08 at length, in the end
10 eventually, ultimately
11 in due course
12 in conclusion

□**last word**
04 best, pick, rage
05 cream, vogue
08 final say, ultimate
10 dernier cri, perfection
11 ne plus ultra
12 quintessence
13 final decision
14 crème de la crème

last-ditch
05 final
06 all-out
07 frantic
08 frenzied, last-gasp
09 desperate, straining
12 eleventh-hour

lasting
07 abiding, durable, undying
08 enduring, long-term, unending
09 ceaseless, long-lived, permanent, perpetual, surviving, unceasing
10 persisting, unchanging
11 everlasting, never-ending
12 interminable, long-standing

lastly
07 finally, to sum up
08 in the end
12 in conclusion

latch
03 bar
04 bolt, hasp, hook, lock
05 catch
06 fasten
09 fastening

□**latch on to**
05 grasp, learn
06 follow
07 realize
10 comprehend, understand

late
03 new, old
04 dead, past, slow
05 fresh, tardy
06 behind, former, latest, recent, slowly
07 current, delayed, overdue
08 deceased, departed, formerly, previous, recently, up-to-date
09 belatedly, in arrears, preceding
10 behindhand, dilatorily, last-minute, unpunctual
12 unpunctually
14 behind schedule

□**of late**
06 lately
08 latterly, recently
10 not long ago

lately
05 newly
06 of late
08 latterly, recently
10 not long ago

lateness
09 tardiness
11 belatedness
12 dilatoriness

latent
06 hidden, unseen, veiled
07 dormant, lurking, passive
08 inactive, possible
09 concealed, invisible, potential, quiescent
10 underlying, unrevealed
11 undeveloped, unexpressed

later
05 after
08 in a while
09 following
10 afterwards, subsequent, succeeding
11 in due course, in the future
12 subsequently, successively
13 at a future date, at a future time, some other time

lateral
04 side
07 oblique
08 edgeways, flanking, indirect, sideward, sideways

latest
02 in

03 now
06 modern, newest, with it
08 ultimate, up-to-date
10 most recent
13 up-to-the-minute

lather
04 flap, foam, fuss, soap, stew, suds
05 fever, froth, sweat, tizzy
06 dither, whip up
07 anxiety, bubbles, fluster, flutter, shampoo
08 soapsuds

latitude
04 play, room, span
05 field, range, reach, scope, space, sweep, width
06 extent, laxity, leeway
07 freedom, liberty, licence
12 carte blanche

latter
03 end
04 last
05 final, later
07 closing, ensuing
10 concluding, succeeding, successive
13 last-mentioned

latter-day
06 modern
10 present-day
12 contemporary

latterly
06 lately, of late
08 hitherto

lattice
03 web
04 grid, mesh
07 network, tracery, trellis
08 fretwork, openwork
12 reticulation

laud
04 hail
05 extol
06 admire, honour, praise
07 acclaim, applaud, approve, glorify, magnify

laudable
09 admirable, estimable, excellent, exemplary
11 commendable, meritorious
12 praiseworthy

laudation
05 glory, kudos, paean
06 eulogy, homage, praise
07 acclaim, tribute
08 accolade, encomion, encomium

laudatory
09 adulation, extolment, panegyric
10 veneration
11 acclamation

laudatory
09 adulatory, approving
10 eulogistic
11 acclamatory, approbatory, encomiastic, panegyrical
13 encomiastical

laugh
03 fun
04 hoot, jest, joke, lark, roar
05 prank, sport, trick
06 cackle, giggle, guffaw, scream, titter
07 chortle, chuckle, snigger
08 crease up
09 fall about
12 be in stitches
14 split your sides

□**laugh at**
04 jeer, mock
05 scorn, taunt
06 deride
07 scoff at
08 ridicule

□**laugh off**
06 ignore
07 dismiss
08 pooh-pooh, shrug off
10 brush aside
12 make little of

laughable
05 comic, droll, funny
06 absurd
07 amusing, comical
08 derisive, derisory, farcical, humorous
09 hilarious, ludicrous
10 ridiculous, uproarious
11 nonsensical
12 entertaining, preposterous
13 side-splitting

laughing-stock
04 butt, dupe
06 stooge, target, victim
09 Aunt Sally

laughter
04 glee
05 mirth
08 giggling, hilarity, laughing
09 amusement, chortling, chuckling, guffawing, merriment, tittering
10 sniggering
11 convulsions

launch
04 fire, open

05 begin, float, found, set up, start
06 propel
07 project, send off
08 commence, dispatch, embark on, initiate, organize
09 discharge, instigate, introduce, set afloat
10 inaugurate
11 set in motion

laundry
04 wash
07 clothes, washing
10 laundrette, Laundromat®
11 launderette
12 dirty clothes

lavatory
02 WC
03 bog, loo
04 john, kazi
05 privy
06 toilet, urinal
07 latrine
08 bathroom, rest room, the gents, washroom
09 cloakroom, the ladies
10 ladies' room, powder room
11 water closet

lavish
04 free, heap, pour, rich
05 grand, spend, waste
06 bestow, deluge, shower
07 copious, liberal, profuse
08 abundant, generous, prolific, splendid, squander
09 bountiful, dissipate, excessive, luxuriant, plentiful, unlimited, unsparing
10 immoderate, open-handed, profligate, thriftless, unstinting
11 extravagant, intemperate

law
03 act
04 code, rule
05 axiom, canon, edict, maxim, order, tenet
06 decree
07 charter, command, formula, lawsuit, precept, statute
09 criterion, directive, enactment, ordinance, principle
10 litigation, regulation
11 commandment, legislation
12 constitution
13 jurisprudence

law-abiding
06 decent, honest

07 dutiful, upright
10 honourable, upstanding

law-breaker
05 crook, felon
06 outlaw, sinner
07 convict
08 criminal, offender
09 infractor, miscreant
10 delinquent, trespasser
12 transgressor

lawful
05 legal, licit, valid
09 legalized, warranted
10 authorized, legitimate, sanctioned

lawless
06 unruly
07 illegal
08 anarchic, criminal, mutinous
09 insurgent, seditious
10 anarchical, rebellious
11 law-breaking
13 revolutionary
15 insurrectionary

lawlessness
06 piracy
07 anarchy, mob-rule
08 disorder, sedition
09 mobocracy, rebellion
10 insurgency, ochlocracy, revolution
12 insurrection, racketeering

lawsuit
04 case
05 cause, trial
06 action
10 indictment, litigation
11 legal action, proceedings, prosecution

lawyer
02 QC
05 brief
07 counsel
08 advocate, attorney
09 barrister, solicitor

➤ *Names of lawyers:*
03 **Lie** (Trygve)
04 **John** (Otto)
05 **Mills** (Barbara Jean Lyon), **Nader** (Ralph), **Vance** (Cyrus Roberts)
06 **Darrow** (Clarence), **Martin** (Richard)
07 **Acheson** (Dean), **Kennedy** (Helena Ann), **Mondale** (Walter Frederick), **O'Connor** (Sandra Day)
08 **Marshall** (Thurgood)
09 **La Guardia** (Fiorello Henry)

10 **Dershowitz** (Alan)
11 **Hore-Belisha** (Leslie, Lord)

lax
05 loose, slack, vague
06 casual, remiss, sloppy
07 inexact, lenient
08 careless, heedless, slipshod
09 easy-going, imprecise, indulgent, negligent
10 neglectful, permissive

laxative
05 purge, salts, senna
08 aperient, evacuant
09 cathartic, purgative
11 ipecacuanha

laxity
08 latitude, leniency, softness
09 looseness, slackness
10 indulgence, negligence, sloppiness
11 imprecision, inexactness, nonchalance
12 carelessness, heedlessness, laissez-faire, slovenliness
14 permissiveness

lay
03 bet, ode, put, set
04 bear, have, laic, make, plan, poem, risk, song
05 allot, apply, beget, breed, leave, lodge, lyric, offer, place, plant, posit, wager
06 assign, ballad, burden, chance, charge, design, devise, gamble, hazard, impose, impute, locate, saddle, set out, settle, submit, thrust
07 amateur, arrange, ascribe, deposit, dispose, inflict, oppress, prepare, present, produce, secular, set down, work out
08 encumber, engender, madrigal, oviposit, position
09 attribute, establish, weigh down
10 make it with, put forward
11 give birth to, go to bed with, have sex with
12 make love with
13 have it off with, non-specialist
15 non-professional

❑**lay aside**
04 keep, save
05 store
06 put off, reject, shelve

07 abandon, discard, dismiss
08 postpone

❑**lay bare**
04 show
06 expose, reveal, unveil
07 exhibit, uncover
08 disclose

❑**lay down**
04 drop, give
05 state, yield
06 affirm, assert, give up, ordain
07 discard
09 establish, formulate, postulate, prescribe, stipulate, surrender
10 relinquish

❑**lay down the law**
07 dictate
11 pontificate
14 read the riot act

❑**lay hands on**
03 get
04 find, grab, grip
05 bless, clasp, grasp, seize
06 clutch, locate, ordain
07 acquire, confirm, unearth
08 discover
09 get hold of
10 consecrate
12 bring to light

❑**lay in**
05 amass, hoard, store
07 build up, collect, stock up, store up
09 stockpile

❑**lay into**
06 assail, attack
08 let fly at, set about, tear into
09 have a go at, pitch into

❑**lay it on**
07 flatter
08 butter up, overdo it, soft-soap
09 sweet-talk

❑**lay off**
04 drop, quit, sack, stop
05 cease, let go, let up
06 desist, give up, pay off
07 dismiss, refrain
08 leave off
11 discontinue
13 make redundant

❑**lay on**
04 give
05 cater, set up
06 supply
07 furnish, provide
08 organize

❑**lay out**
03 pay
04 fell, give, plan
05 floor, spend
06 design, invest
07 arrange, display, exhibit, flatten
08 demolish, disburse
10 contribute

❑**lay up**
04 keep, save
05 amass, hoard
07 put away, store up
10 accumulate

❑**lay waste**
04 rape, raze, ruin, sack
06 ravage
07 despoil, destroy, pillage
09 devastate, vandalize

layabout
05 idler
06 loafer, skiver, waster
07 laggard, lounger, shirker
09 lazy-bones

layer
03 bed, ply, row
04 band, coat, film, seam, tier, vein
05 cover, plate, sheet
06 lamina, mantle
07 blanket, coating, deposit, stratum
08 covering
09 thickness

layman, laywoman, layperson
07 amateur
11 parishioner
15 non-professional

lay-off
04 boot, push, sack
05 elbow
07 sacking
09 discharge, dismissal
10 redundancy

layout
03 map
04 plan
05 draft
06 design, format, sketch
07 outline
09 geography
11 arrangement

laze
04 idle, loaf, loll
05 relax
06 lounge

laziness
05 sloth

08 idleness, lethargy, slowness
09 fainéance, indolence
12 slothfulness, sluggishness

lazy
04 idle, slow
05 inert, slack, tardy
06 torpid
07 languid, work-shy
08 bone idle, fainéant, inactive, indolent, slothful, sluggish
09 lethargic
10 languorous, slow-moving

lazy-bones
05 idler
06 loafer, skiver, slouch
07 laggard, lounger, shirker
08 layabout, sluggard

leach
04 seep
06 filter, osmose
08 filtrate
09 lixiviate, percolate

lead
03 gap, tip, top, van
04 clue, edge, have, head, hint, live, main, move, pass, rule, shot, star, sway
05 balls, cause, chief, excel, first, guide, model, outdo, pilot, plumb, prime, slugs, spend, start, steer, usher
06 direct, escort, exceed, govern, induce, manage, margin, outrun, prompt, sinker, tip-off, weight
07 bring on, bullets, command, conduct, dispose, eclipse, example, incline, leading, pattern, pellets, premier, primary, produce, provoke, surpass, undergo
08 be in lead, foremost, guidance, interval, outstrip, persuade, priority, regulate, result in, vanguard
09 advantage, be in front, call forth, come first, direction, forefront, indicator, influence, principal, supervise, supremacy, title role, transcend
10 ammunition, bring about, experience, first place, indication, leadership, precedence, suggestion
11 heavy weight, leading role, outdistance, pre-eminence, preside over, tend towards
12 be in charge of, call the shots

□ **lead off**
04 open
05 begin, start
08 commence, initiate
10 inaugurate

□ **lead on**
04 lure
05 tempt, trick
06 entice, seduce
07 beguile, deceive, mislead
11 string along

□ **lead the way**
04 show
05 guide
07 go first
09 go in front

□ **lead up to**
08 approach
09 introduce
10 pave the way, prepare for

leaden
04 dull, grey, lead
05 dingy, heavy, inert, stiff
06 cloudy, dismal, dreary, gloomy, sombre, wooden
07 greyish, onerous, stilted
08 laboured, lifeless, listless, overcast, plodding, sluggish
10 lacklustre, oppressive, spiritless

leader
04 boss, head
05 chief, guide, ruler
07 captain, pioneer, skipper
08 director, governor
09 chieftain, commander, conductor, principal
10 figurehead, pathfinder, ringleader
11 front-runner, trailblazer
12 guiding light, leading light
13 groundbreaker

leadership
04 rule
07 command
08 guidance, headship
09 authority, captaincy
11 pre-eminence, premiership
12 directorship, governorship

leading
04 main
05 chief, first, front
07 primary, supreme, top-rank
08 foremost, greatest
09 number one, paramount, principal
10 pre-eminent

leaf
03 pad

04 flip, page, skim
05 blade, bract, calyx, folio, frond, sepal, sheet, thumb
06 browse, glance, needle
07 leaflet
09 cotyledon
12 thumb through
➤ See also **plant**

▬ *Parts of a leaf* :
03 tip
04 vein
05 blade
06 margin, midrib
07 petiole, stipule
08 leaf axil
09 epidermis, leaf cells
12 auxiliary bud

▬ *Leaf shapes* :
05 lobed, ovate
06 entire, linear, lyrate
07 ciliate, cordate, crenate, dentate, hastate, obovate, palmate, peltate, pinnate, ternate
08 digitate, elliptic, subulate
09 runcinate, sagittate
10 lanceolate, trifoliate
13 doubly dentate

leaflet
04 bill
05 flyer, tract
07 handout
08 circular, handbill, pamphlet

leafy
05 bosky, green, shady, woody
06 shaded, wooded
07 foliose, verdant

league
04 ally, band, link
05 class, guild, union, unite
06 cartel
07 combine, compact, consort
08 alliance, category, conspire
09 associate, co-operate, coalition, syndicate
10 consortium, federation, fellowship
11 affiliation, association, co-operative, collaborate, combination, confederacy, confederate, corporation, partnership
12 conglomerate
13 confederation

□ **in league**
06 allied, linked
09 in cahoots
10 conspiring, in alliance

11 co-operating, hand in glove, in collusion
13 collaborating

leak
03 cut
04 drip, ooze, seep, tell
05 break, crack, exude
06 escape, exposé, impart, oozing, reveal, squeal
07 divulge, leakage, leaking, let slip, seepage, seeping, trickle
08 disclose, exposure, give away, puncture
09 discharge, make known
10 disclosure, divulgence, make public, revelation, uncovering
11 percolation
13 spill the beans

leaky
05 holey, split
06 porous
07 cracked, leaking
09 permeable, punctured
10 perforated

lean
04 arid, bank, bare, bend, bony, lank, list, poor, prop, rest, slim, tend, thin, tilt
05 gaunt, slant, slope
06 barren, favour, prefer, scanty, skinny, sparse, repose
07 angular, incline, recline, scraggy, scrawny, slender
10 inadequate, unfruitful
12 insufficient, unproductive

◻**lean on**
06 rely on
08 depend on, persuade
10 pressurize
13 put pressure on

leaning
04 bent, bias
06 liking
08 aptitude, fondness, penchant, tendency
10 attraction, partiality, proclivity, propensity
11 disposition, inclination
12 predilection

leap
03 hop
04 jump, rise, romp, skip, soar
05 bound, caper, clear, dance, frisk, mount, surge, vault
06 bounce, cavort, frolic, gambol, rocket, spring
07 soaring, upsurge, upswing

08 escalate, increase, jump over
09 entrechat, skyrocket
10 escalation

◻**by leaps and bounds, in leaps and bounds**
07 quickly, rapidly, swiftly
08 in no time
13 in no time at all

◻**leap at**
04 grab
05 seize
06 jump at, snatch
07 agree to, fall for, swallow
08 pounce on

learn
04 hear
05 grasp, study, train
06 absorb, digest, gather, master, pick up, take in
07 acquire, discern, find out, realize
08 discover, memorize
09 ascertain, determine, get wind of
10 assimilate, comprehend, have off pat, understand
14 commit to memory

learned
06 versed
07 erudite
08 academic, cultured, lettered, literary, studious, well read
09 scholarly
10 widely read
12 intellectual, well-informed
13 knowledgeable

learner
04 tiro
05 pupil
06 novice, rookie
07 scholar, student, trainee
08 beginner, neophyte
09 greenhorn
10 apprentice

learning
05 study
06 wisdom
07 culture, letters, tuition
09 education, erudition, knowledge, schooling
11 edification, scholarship

lease
03 let
04 hire, loan, rent
06 sublet
07 charter

leash
04 curb, hold, lead, lyam, rein

05 check
06 tether
09 restraint
10 discipline

least
06 fewest, lowest
08 smallest
09 slightest

leathery
05 rough, tough
07 corious, wizened
08 hardened, wrinkled
10 coriaceous

leave
02 go
04 damp, drop, exit, jilt, move, quit, will
05 allot, break, cease, chuck, ditch, endow, say-so, scoot
06 assign, day off, decamp, depart, desert, go away, retire, set out
07 abandon, consent, consign, deliver, do a bunk, entrust, forsake, freedom, holiday, liberty, pull out, push off, retreat, take off, time off, warrant
08 bequeath, emigrate, furlough, hand down, hand over, run out on, sanction, transmit, up sticks, vacation, withdraw
09 disappear
10 green light, indulgence, make tracks, permission, sabbatical
11 leave behind
12 dispensation
13 authorization

◻**leave off**
03 end
04 halt, quit, stop
05 cease
06 desist, lay off
07 abstain, refrain
08 break off, give over, knock off
09 terminate
11 discontinue

◻**leave out**
03 bar, cut
04 omit
06 except, ignore, reject
07 exclude, neglect
08 overlook, pass over
09 disregard

leaven
05 raise, swell
06 expand, puff up

07 ferment, inspire, lighten,
09 stimulate

leavings
05 dregs, dross, spoil, waste
06 debris, refuse, scraps
07 remains, residue, rubbish
08 detritus
09 leftovers, remainder

lecher
04 goat, rake, roué, wolf
07 Don Juan, seducer
08 Casanova
09 adulterer, debauchee,
    libertine, womanizer
10 fornicator
11 dirty old man

lecherous
04 lewd
05 horny, randy
06 carnal, wanton
07 lustful, raunchy
08 prurient
09 salacious
10 lascivious, libidinous,
    licentious, womanizing
12 concupiscent

lechery
09 carnality, prurience,
    randiness
10 debauchery, rakishness,
    sensuality, wantonness
13 concupiscence,
    salaciousness
14 lasciviousness,
    libidinousness,
    licentiousness

lecture
04 talk
05 chide, scold, speak, teach
06 berate, homily, lesson,
    rebuke, sermon, speech
07 address, censure, chiding,
    expound, reproof, reprove,
    tell off
08 admonish, berating, harangue,
    instruct, reproach, scolding
09 discourse, give a talk, hold
    forth, reprimand, talking-to
10 telling-off, upbraiding
11 instruction, make a speech
12 disquisition, dressing-down,
    pull to pieces, tear to pieces

lecturer
05 tutor
06 orator, reader, talker
07 speaker, teacher
08 academic, preacher
09 declaimer, expounder,
    haranguer, pedagogue
11 speech-maker, speechifier

ledge
04 sill, step
05 ridge, shelf
06 mantel
08 overhang
10 projection
11 mantelpiece, mantelshelf

lee
06 refuge
07 shelter
09 sanctuary
10 protection

leech
07 sponger
08 hanger-on, parasite
09 scrounger
10 freeloader
11 bloodsucker, extortioner

leer
03 eye
04 grin, ogle, wink
05 gloat, smirk, sneer, stare
06 goggle, squint

leery
04 wary
05 chary
07 careful, dubious, guarded
08 cautious, doubting
11 distrustful, on your guard

lees
05 draff, dregs
07 deposit, grounds, residue
08 sediment

leeway
04 play, room
06 margin
08 latitude

left
03 red
04 port
07 liberal, radical
08 left-hand, left-wing
09 communist, sinistral, socialist

left-handed
09 sinistral
12 corrie-fisted

left-over
06 unused
07 uneaten

leftovers
05 dregs
06 excess, refuse, scraps
07 remains, residue, surplus
08 leavings, remnants
09 remainder, sweepings

leg
03 bit, lap, peg, pin
04 crus, limb, part, prop

05 brace, shank, stage, stump
06 member
07 portion, section, segment,
    stretch, support, upright
12 underpinning

❑**leg it**
03 run
04 walk
05 hurry

❑**not have a leg to stand
on**
11 lack support

❑**on its last legs**
04 weak
06 ailing
07 failing
12 at death's door

❑**pull someone's leg**
03 kid, rib
04 fool, joke
05 tease, trick
06 have on, wind up
11 play a joke on

legacy
04 gift
06 estate
08 heirloom, heritage
09 heritance, patrimony
11 inheritance

legal
05 licit, right, sound, valid
06 lawful, proper
07 allowed
08 forensic, judicial, licensed,
    rightful
09 allowable, judiciary,
    legalized, permitted,
    statutory, warranted
10 above-board, acceptable,
    admissible, authorized,
    legitimate, sanctioned
11 permissible
12 within the law
14 constitutional

► *Legal terms:*
02 JP, QC
03 bar, DPP, sue
04 bail, deed, dock, fine, jury,
    oath, will, writ
05 alibi, asset, bench, brief,
    by-law, claim, felon,
    judge, lease, party,
    proof, proxy, title, trial
06 appeal, arrest, bigamy,
    charge, equity, estate, guilty,
    lawyer, legacy, pardon,
    parole, patent, remand,
    repeal, waiver
07 accused, alimony, amnesty,
    caution, charter, codicil,

convict, coroner, custody, damages, defence, divorce, hearing, inquest, inquiry, Law Lord, lawsuit, mandate, probate, sheriff, statute, summons, verdict, warrant, witness

08 act of God, advocate, civil law, contract, covenant, criminal, easement, eviction, evidence, executor, freehold, hung jury, innocent, judgment, juvenile, legal aid, offender, prisoner, receiver, reprieve, sanction, sentence, subpoena, tribunal

09 accessory, acquittal, affidavit, annulment, barrister, common law, court case, defendant, endowment, fee simple, indemnity, intestacy, judiciary, leasehold, liability, plaintiff, precedent, probation, solicitor, testimony

10 accomplice, allegation, confession, conveyance, decree nisi, indictment, injunction, magistrate, settlement

11 adjournment, extradition, foreclosure, inheritance, maintenance, plead guilty, proceedings, ward of court

12 Bill of Rights, court martial, cross-examine, misadventure, notary public

13 public inquiry, Queen's Counsel, young offender

14 decree absolute, plead not guilty

15 Act of Parliament, clerk of the court, contempt of court, power of attorney

➤ See also **court**; **crime**

legality
08 validity
09 rightness, soundness
10 lawfulness, legitimacy

legalize
06 permit, ratify
07 license, warrant
08 sanction, validate
10 legitimize
13 decriminalize

legate
05 agent, envoy
06 deputy, nuncio
08 delegate, emissary

10 ambassador
12 commissioner

legatee
04 heir
06 co-heir
09 co-heiress, inheritor
10 inheritrix
11 beneficiary

legation
07 embassy, mission
09 consulate
10 delegation, deputation

legend
03 key
04 myth, saga, tale
05 fable, motto, story
06 cipher
07 caption, fiction, romance
08 folk-tale
09 narrative
11 explanation, inscription

➤ *The Arthurian legend includes*:
03 Kay
04 Bors
06 Arthur, Avalon, Elaine, Gareth (of Orkney), Gawain, Merlin, Modred
07 Camelot, Galahad, Igraine, Tristan
08 Bedivere, Lancelot, Parsifal, Perceval, Tristram
09 Excalibur, Guinevere
11 Morgan le Fay
14 Launcelot du Lac, Uther Pendragon
➤ See also **mythology**

legendary
06 fabled, famous
08 fabulous, fanciful, glorious, honoured, immortal, mythical, renowned
09 acclaimed, fictional, story-book, well-known
10 celebrated, fictitious, remembered
11 illustrious, traditional

legerdemain
08 artifice, trickery
09 chicanery,deception,sophistry
10 hocus-pocus
11 contrivance, manoeuvring
12 manipulation
13 sleight of hand

legible
04 neat
05 clear, plain
08 distinct, readable
12 decipherable, intelligible

legion
04 army, host, mass
05 horde, swarm, troop
06 cohort, myriad, throng
07 brigade, company
08 division, numerous, regiment
09 battalion, countless, multitude
10 numberless

legislate
05 enact, order
06 codify, decree, ordain
09 authorize, prescribe

legislation
03 act, law
04 bill, code
07 charter, measure, statute
09 enactment, law-making, ordinance
11 formulation
12 codification, prescription
13 authorization

legislative
09 law-giving, law-making
10 senatorial
13 congressional, parliamentary

legislator
07 senator
08 law-giver, law-maker
11 congressman
13 congresswoman
15 parliamentarian

legislature
05 house
06 senate
07 chamber
08 assembly, congress
10 parliament

legitimate
04 fair, real, true
05 legal, licit, sound, valid
06 lawful, proper
07 correct, genuine, logical
08 credible, rightful
09 justified, plausible, statutory, warranted
10 acceptable, admissible, authorized, sanctioned
11 justifiable, well-founded

legitimize
07 charter, entitle, license, warrant
08 legalize, sanction, validate
09 authorize

leisure
04 ease, rest
05 break

07 freedom, holiday, liberty, time off, time out
08 free time, vacation
09 spare time
10 recreation, relaxation, retirement

❑**at your leisure**
11 unhurriedly
13 in your own time

leisurely
04 easy, slow
07 relaxed, restful, unhasty
08 carefree, laid-back, tranquil
09 easy-going, unhurried

lend
04 give, loan
05 grant
06 bestow, confer, impart
07 advance, furnish, provide
10 contribute

❑**lend an ear**
04 heed
06 listen
07 hearken

❑**lend a hand**
03 aid
04 help
06 assist

❑**lend itself to**
13 be suitable for

length
04 span, term
05 piece, reach, space
06 extent, period
07 measure, portion, section, segment, stretch
08 distance, duration

❑**at length**
06 at last
10 eventually
11 in due course
12 exhaustively
13 in great detail

❑**go to any lengths**
10 do anything
12 go to extremes

lengthen
03 eke
06 expand, extend
07 draw out, prolong, spin out, stretch
08 continue, elongate, increase, protract

lengthwise
07 endlong, endways, endwise
10 lengthways, vertically
12 horizontally

lengthy
04 long
05 wordy
06 prolix
07 diffuse, tedious, verbose
08 drawn-out, extended, overlong, rambling
09 prolonged
10 long-winded, protracted
12 long-drawn-out

leniency
05 mercy
08 clemency, lenience
09 tolerance
10 compassion, gentleness, humaneness
11 forbearance, forgiveness
14 permissiveness

lenient
06 gentle, humane
07 liberal, sparing
08 merciful, moderate
09 forgiving, indulgent
10 forbearing
11 magnanimous, soft-hearted

lenitive
06 easing
08 soothing
10 mitigating, palliative

leper
05 lazar
06 pariah
07 outcast
11 undesirable, untouchable
13 social outcast

lesbian
03 gay, les, lez
04 dyke
05 butch, dykey, lezzy, queer
07 Sapphic, tribade
08 sapphist, tribadic

lesion
03 cut
04 gash, hurt, sore
05 wound
06 bruise, injury, scrape, trauma
07 scratch
08 abrasion
09 contusion
10 impairment, laceration

less
05 fewer
09 not as many, not as much, not so many, not so much
13 smaller amount

lessen
03 ebb
04 dull, ease, fail, flag, wane
05 abate, let up, lower, slack

06 deaden, go down, impair, narrow, plunge, reduce, shrink, weaken
07 abridge, curtail, decline, die down, dwindle, ease off, lighten, plummet, relieve, slacken, subside
08 come down, decrease, diminish, moderate, slow down

lessening
05 let-up
06 easing, ebbing, waning
07 decline, erosion, failure
08 decrease, flagging
09 abatement, dwindling, reduction, weakening
10 diminution, moderation, slackening
11 contraction, curtailment, petering out
12 de-escalation, minimization

lesser
05 lower, minor
07 smaller
08 inferior, slighter
09 secondary
11 subordinate

lesson
05 class, model, moral
06 course, period, sermon
07 example, lecture, seminar, warning
08 coaching, teaching, tutorial
09 deterrent
11 instruction

let
04 hire, make, rent
05 allow, cause, check, grant, lease
06 enable, permit
07 agree to
08 assent to, obstacle, sanction, tolerate
09 authorize, consent to, hindrance, restraint
10 constraint, give the nod, impediment
11 obstruction, restriction
12 interference

❑**let alone**
04 also
08 as well as
09 apart from, never mind
12 not to mention
13 not forgetting

❑**let down**
04 fail
06 betray, desert
07 abandon

09 fall short
10 disappoint, disenchant, dissatisfy
11 disillusion
15 leave in the lurch

□ **let go**
04 free
06 unhand
07 manumit, release, set free
08 liberate

□ **let in**
05 admit, greet
06 accept, take in
07 include, receive, welcome
11 incorporate
12 allow to enter

□ **let off**
04 emit, fire
06 acquit, excuse, exempt, ignore, pardon
07 explode, give off, release
08 detonate, reprieve
09 discharge, exonerate

□ **let on**
04 blab, tell
06 reveal, squeal
07 divulge, let slip
08 disclose, give away
13 spill the beans

□ **let out**
04 blab, free, leak
06 betray, reveal, squeal
07 let slip, release
08 disclose
09 discharge, make known
13 spill the beans

□ **let up**
03 end
04 ease, halt, stop
05 abate, cease
06 lessen
07 die down, ease off, subside
08 decrease, diminish

□ **let-down**
07 washout
10 anticlimax
14 disappointment

lethal
05 fatal, toxic
06 deadly, mortal
07 deathly, noxious, ruinous
09 dangerous, murderous

lethargic
04 dull, idle, lazy, slow
05 heavy, inert, weary
06 drowsy, sleepy, torpid
07 languid
08 listless, slothful, sluggish
09 enervated

lethargy
05 sloth
06 torpor
07 inertia, langour
08 dullness, idleness, laziness, slowness
09 lassitude
12 listlessness, sluggishness

letter
04 line, sign
05 reply
06 symbol
07 culture, epistle, message, missive, writing
08 dispatch, grapheme, learning
09 character, education, erudition
10 literature
13 belles-lettres, communication
14 correspondence

□ **to the letter**
07 exactly
08 strictly
09 by the book, literally
11 religiously, word for word
13 in every detail, punctiliously

lettered
06 versed
07 erudite, learned
08 cultured, educated, highbrow, literary, literate, well-read
09 scholarly
10 cultivated, widely read

let-up
04 lull
05 break, pause
06 recess
07 respite
08 breather, interval
09 abatement, cessation, lessening, remission
10 slackening

level
03 aim
04 avow, calm, even, flat, mark, rank, raze, size, tell, zone
05 admit, class, equal, flush, focus, grade, layer, plane, point, stage, train
06 amount, degree, direct, even up, extent, height, stable, status, steady, storey, volume
07 aligned, confess, destroy, divulge, echelon, even out, flatten, measure, station, stratum, tell all, uniform

08 altitude, balanced, bulldoze, constant, demolish, equalize, lay waste, matching, position, pull down, quantity, standard, standing, tear down
09 come clean, devastate, elevation, knock down, magnitude, stabilize
10 horizontal, unchanging
11 concentrate, neck and neck, unemotional, unflappable
12 level pegging, speak plainly
13 self-possessed
14 tell it like it is
15 raze to the ground

□ **on the level**
04 fair, open
06 candid, honest
07 upfront
08 straight
10 above board, straight-up
13 fair and square

level-headed
04 calm, cool, sane
06 steady
07 prudent
08 balanced, composed, rational, sensible
10 cool-headed, dependable, reasonable
11 circumspect, unflappable
12 even-tempered
13 imperturbable

lever
03 bar, pry
04 lift, move, pull
05 force, heave, hoist, jemmy, prise, raise, shift
06 handle, switch
07 crowbar
08 dislodge, joystick
09 handspike

leverage
04 pull, rank
05 clout, force, power
06 weight
08 purchase, strength
09 advantage, influence

leviathan
04 hulk
05 giant, Titan, whale
07 mammoth, monster
08 behemoth, colossus
10 sea monster

levitate
03 fly
04 hang, waft
05 drift, float, glide, hover

levity
03 fun
08 hilarity
09 flippancy, frivolity, silliness
10 triviality
11 irreverence
12 carefreeness
13 facetiousness

levy
03 due, fee, tax
04 duty, toll
05 exact, raise, tithe
06 charge, demand, duties, excise, gather, impose, impost, tariff
07 collect, customs
10 assessment, collection
12 contribution, subscription

lewd
05 bawdy, randy
06 carnal, impure, smutty, vulgar
07 lustful, obscene, raunchy
08 indecent, unchaste
09 lecherous, salacious
10 lascivious, licentious

lewdness
04 smut
07 crudity, lechery
09 bawdiness, carnality, depravity, indecency, obscenity, randiness, vulgarity
10 smuttiness
11 lustfulness
13 salaciousness
14 lasciviousness, licentiousness

lexicographer
➤ *Names of lexicographers and philologists:*
04 Bopp (Franz)
05 Sapir (Edward), Skeat (Walter William)
06 Brewer (Ebenezer Cobham), Fowler (Henry Watson), Freund (Wilhelm), Hornby (Albert Sidney), Murray (Sir James Augustus Henry), Onions (Charles Talbut)
07 Chomsky (Noam), Craigie (Sir William Alexander), Diderot (Denis), Johnson (Samuel), Mencken (Henry Louis), Ventris (Michael George Francis), Webster (Noah)
08 Chambers (Ephraim), Larousse (Pierre

Athanase), Saussure (Ferdinand de)
09 Furnivall (Frederick James), Jespersen (Otto), Partridge (Eric Honeywood)
10 Amarasimha, Burchfield (Robert William),
➤ See also **writer**

lexicon
08 word-list, wordbook
09 thesaurus
10 dictionary, phrase book, vocabulary

liability
05 debit
06 burden
07 arrears
08 drawback, nuisance
09 hindrance
10 impediment
11 culpability, encumbrance
12 disadvantage, indebtedness
14 accountability, responsibility

liable
03 apt
04 open
05 prone
06 likely
07 subject, tending
08 disposed, inclined
10 answerable
11 accountable, predisposed, responsible, susceptible

liaise
07 network
09 co-operate, interface
11 collaborate, communicate
12 work together

liaison
06 affair
07 contact, romance
08 intrigue
09 go-between
10 connection, love affair
11 co-operation, interchange
12 entanglement, relationship
13 collaboration
15 working together

liar
06 fibber
08 deceiver, perjurer
09 falsifier
12 false witness, prevaricator

libation
08 oblation
09 sacrifice
13 drink offering

libel
04 slur
05 smear
06 defame, malign, revile, vilify
07 calumny, traduce
08 badmouth
09 aspersion
10 calumniate, defamation, muck-raking, throw mud at
11 mudslinging
12 vilification

libellous
05 false
06 untrue
09 injurious, maligning, traducing, vilifying
10 defamatory, scurrilous
12 calumniatory

liberal
06 lavish
07 copious, lenient, profuse, radical
08 abundant, catholic, generous, handsome, tolerant, unbiased
09 bountiful, plentiful, unsparing
10 broad-based, munificent, open-handed, open-minded
11 broad-minded, enlightened, libertarian, progressive
14 forward-looking

liberalism
10 radicalism
12 free-thinking
13 progressivism
14 libertarianism
15 humanitarianism

liberality
06 bounty
07 breadth, charity
08 altruism, kindness, largesse
09 tolerance
10 generosity, toleration
11 beneficence, benevolence, catholicity, magnanimity, munificence
12 impartiality, philanthropy
13 progressivism
14 open-handedness, open-mindedness, permissiveness
15 broad-mindedness

liberate
04 free
05 let go
06 let out, redeem, rescue
07 deliver, manumit, release, set free, unchain
08 let loose, set loose, unfetter

09 discharge, unshackle
10 emancipate

liberation
07 freedom, freeing, release
10 redemption
11 deliverance, manumission
12 emancipation
15 enfranchisement

liberator
07 rescuer, saviour
08 ransomer, redeemer
09 deliverer
10 manumitter
11 emancipator

libertine
04 rake, roué
06 lecher
07 Don Juan, lustful, seducer
08 Casanova
09 debauched, debauchee, dissolute, lecherous, reprobate, salacious, voluptary, womanizer
10 licentious, profligate, sensualist, womanizing

liberty
05 right
07 freedom, licence, release
08 autonomy, sanction
09 franchise, impudence, insolence
10 disrespect, permission
11 deliverance, entitlement, familiarity, manumission, prerogative, presumption
12 emancipation, impertinence, independence
15 overfamiliarity

◻**at liberty**
04 free
07 allowed
09 permitted

libidinous
04 lewd
06 carnal, wanton
07 lustful, ruttish, sensual
08 prurient
09 debauched, lecherous, salacious
10 cupidinous, lascivious
12 concupiscent

libido
04 lust
06 ardour
07 passion, the hots
08 sex drive
09 eroticism, randiness
10 sexual urge
12 erotic desire, sexual desire
14 sexual appetite

libretto
04 book, text
05 lines, words
06 lyrics, script

➤ *Names of librettists*:
04 **Jouy** (Victor Joseph Étienne de)
05 **Rolli** (Paolo Antonio)
07 **Gilbert** (Sir William Schwenck), **Harwood** (Gwen), **Sedaine** (Michel-Jean)
08 **Meredith** (William Morris)
➤ See also **music**

licence
04 pass
05 grant, leave, right
06 excess, permit
07 abandon, anarchy, charter, consent, freedom, liberty
08 approval, document, sanction, warranty
09 authority, decadence, exemption, privilege
10 debauchery, immorality, imprimatur, indulgence, permission
11 certificate, dissipation, entitlement, prerogative
12 carte blanche, dispensation, immoderation, independence
13 accreditation, authorization, certification, dissoluteness
14 licentiousness

license
05 allow
06 permit
07 certify, warrant
08 accredit, sanction
09 authorize, franchise
14 give permission

licentious
04 lewd
06 impure, wanton
07 immoral, lustful
08 depraved
09 abandoned, debauched, dissolute, lecherous, libertine
10 lascivious
11 promiscuous

licentiousness
04 lust
07 abandon, lechery
08 impurity, lewdness, salacity
10 debauchery, immorality, wantonness
11 dissipation, promiscuity
13 dissoluteness, salaciousness

lichen see **algae**

lick
03 bit, dab, lap, wet
04 beat, dart, hint, spot, wash
05 brush, clean, flick, speck, taste, touch
06 defeat, hammer, little, ripple, sample, stroke, thrash, tongue
07 conquer, flicker, moisten, trounce
08 play over, smidgeon, vanquish

◻**lick your lips**
05 enjoy
06 relish, savour
09 drool over

licking
06 defeat, hiding
07 beating, tanning
08 drubbing
09 thrashing

lid
03 cap, top
05 cover
07 stopper
08 covering

lie
03 fib
04 keep, laze, rest, stay, trap
05 couch, dwell, exist, porky, reach, stand, rebut
06 belong, deceit, extend, invent, lounge, remain, repose
07 falsify, falsity, fiction, perjure, perjury, recline, stretch, untruth, whopper
08 continue, disprove
09 dissemble, fabricate, falsehood, half-truth, invention, sprawl out, tall story
10 equivocate, stretch out
11 dissimulate, fabrication, prevaricate
12 make up a story, misrepresent
13 falsification

◻**give the lie to**
05 rebut
08 disprove
10 contradict, prove false

◻**lie in wait for**
06 ambush, attack, waylay
08 surprise
09 ambuscade

◻**lie low**
04 hide, lurk

05 skulk
06 hole up
07 hide out
08 hide away, lie doggo
09 go to earth, take cover
12 go into hiding
15 keep a low profile

lieutenant
06 deputy
09 assistant
12 right-hand man
14 right-hand woman
15 second-in-command

life
04 soul, span, time, zest, élan
05 being, fauna, flora, verve
06 breath, career, course, energy, entity, person, spirit, vigour
07 pizzazz, sparkle
08 activity, duration, lifespan, lifetime, vitality, vivacity
09 aliveness, animation, biography, existence, human life, life story, viability
10 enthusiasm, experience, exuberance, human being, liveliness
11 continuance, high spirits
12 cheerfulness, living things
13 autobiography, fauna and flora

❑**come to life**
06 wake up
09 come alive
12 become active, become lively
14 become exciting

❑**give your life**
06 die for

life-and-death
05 vital
07 crucial, serious
08 critical

lifeblood
04 core, soul
05 heart
06 centre, spirit
09 life-force
11 inspiration

lifeless
04 dead, dull, gone
05 stiff
06 barren, wooden
07 defunct, sterile
08 deceased, desolate
09 inanimate, lethargic
10 colourless, insensible, lacklustre, uninspired

11 unconscious, uninhabited, uninspiring

lifelike
04 real, true
05 exact, vivid
07 natural
09 authentic, realistic
10 true-to-life

lifelong
07 abiding, lasting
08 constant, enduring, lifetime
09 permanent
10 persistent

lifestyle
04 life
09 way of life
11 way of living

lifetime
04 life, span, time
06 career, course, period
08 duration, lifespan
09 existence

lift
03 end, fly, run
04 copy, crib, move, pick, ride, spur, stop
05 annul, boost, clear, dig up, drive, exalt, hitch, hoist, raise, relax, shift, steal
06 borrow, buoy up, cancel, fillip, hold up, pick up, pull up, remove, revoke, uplift
07 airlift, elevate, rescind, root out, scatter, thin out, unearth, upraise
08 disperse, dissolve, elevator, hold high, pick-me-up
09 disappear, escalator, terminate, transport
10 plagiarize
11 reassurance
12 shot in the arm

ligature
03 tie
04 band, bond, cord, link, rope
05 strap, thong
06 string
07 bandage, binding
08 ligament
10 connection, tourniquet

light
03 day, gay, ray
04 airy, beam, bulb, dawn, easy, fair, fine, fire, glow, lamp, mild, pale, thin, weak
05 agile, angle, blaze, blond, cheer, faded, faint, flash, funny, glare, gleam, glint, happy, loose, match, merry,

petty, put on, quick, shaft, shine, small, style, sunny, taper, torch, witty
06 aspect, beacon, blithe, blonde, bright, candle, cheery, flimsy, floaty, gentle, ignite, kindle, lively, lustre, manner, modest, nimble, pastel, porous, slight, turn on
07 amusing, animate, buoyant, cheer up, crumbly, daytime, glowing, insight, lantern, lenient, light up, lighten, lighter, shining, sunrise, trivial, well-lit, whitish
08 bleached, brighten, carefree, cheerful, cockcrow, daybreak, daylight, delicate, feathery, graceful, humorous, lambency, luminous, moderate, pleasing, portable, radiance, switch on, trifling, untaxing
09 brilliant, dimension, diverting, easily dug, irradiate, knowledge, set alight, set fire to
10 brightness, brilliance, digestible, effortless, effulgence, illuminate, luminosity
11 crack of dawn, easily moved, elucidation, explanation, illuminated, lightweight, point of view, superficial, undemanding, unimportant
12 entertaining, illumination, light-hearted, luminescence
13 comprehension, enlightenment, incandescence, insubstantial, understanding
14 inconsiderable
15 inconsequential

❑**bring to light**
06 expose, notice, reveal
07 uncover
08 discover

❑**come to light**
09 be exposed, be noticed
11 be uncovered
12 be discovered

❑**in the light of**
08 in view of
09 because of
11 considering, remembering
13 bearing in mind, keeping in mind

❑**light on, light upon**
04 find, spot

05 hit on
08 chance on, discover
09 encounter, stumble on
10 come across, happen upon

❑ **shed light on, throw light on, cast light on**
07 clarify, explain
09 elucidate, make clear
10 illuminate

lighten
04 calm, ease, glow, lift
05 allay, cheer, elate, shine
06 buoy up, lessen, reduce, revive, unload, uplift
07 assuage, cheer up, gladden, hearten, inspire, relieve
08 brighten, illumine
09 alleviate, encourage
10 illuminate
11 make lighter
12 make brighter

light-fingered
03 sly
06 crafty, shifty
07 crooked, furtive
08 filching, stealing, thieving, thievish
09 dishonest, pilfering
11 shoplifting

light-footed
04 spry
05 agile, lithe, swift
06 active, nimble
08 graceful
09 sprightly

light-headed
04 airy
05 dizzy, faint, giddy, silly, woozy
07 flighty, foolish, shallow, vacuous
08 flippant, trifling, unsteady
09 delirious, frivolous
11 empty-headed, superficial, vertiginous
14 feather-brained, scatter-brained

light-hearted
03 gay
04 glad, high
05 happy, jolly, merry, sunny
06 blithe, bouncy, bright, chirpy, elated, jovial, joyful
07 amusing, playful
08 carefree, cheerful
10 frolicsome, untroubled
12 entertaining, happy-go-lucky
13 in good spirits, in high spirits

lighthouse
06 beacon, pharos

lightly
05 gaily
06 airily, easily, gently, mildly, softly, thinly
07 faintly, readily
08 breezily, slightly, sparsely
09 leniently, sparingly
10 carelessly, delicately
12 effortlessly

lightness
06 levity
07 agility
08 airiness, buoyancy, delicacy, mildness, thinness
09 litheness
10 blitheness, flimsiness, gentleness, nimbleness, triviality
12 delicateness, gracefulness
14 weightlessness

lightning
07 hastily, quickly, rapidly
08 speedily, wildfire
11 immediately, thunderbolt
13 electric storm
14 sheet lightning
15 forked lightning

lightweight
05 light, petty
06 flimsy, paltry, slight
08 delicate, feathery
10 negligible, weightless
13 insignificant, insubstantial

like
03 dig
04 akin, peer, twin, want, wish
05 adore, alike, enjoy, equal, fancy, go for, match
06 admire, desire, esteem, prefer, select, take to
07 approve, care for, of a kind, similar, welcome
08 be fond of, be keen on, decide on, hold dear,
09 analogous, similar to
10 appreciate, comparable, equivalent, resembling
11 counterpart, go a bundle on, much the same
12 feel inclined, on the lines of, take kindly to
13 approximating, corresponding
14 in the same way as, take pleasure in
15 along the lines of

likeable
06 genial

likemise

07 amiable, winning, winsome
08 pleasant, pleasing
09 agreeable, congenial

likelihood
06 chance
08 prospect
10 likeliness
11 possibility, probability

likely
03 fit
05 prone, right
06 liable, odds-on, proper
07 fitting, hopeful, no doubt, tending
08 credible, expected, feasible, inclined, pleasing, possible, probable, probably
09 in the wind, like as not, plausible, promising
10 acceptable, believable, on the cards, presumably
11 anticipated, appropriate, as like as not, doubtlessly, foreseeable, predictable
12 to be expected

like-minded
08 agreeing, in accord
09 in harmony
10 compatible, harmonious

liken
05 match
06 equate, relate
07 compare
09 analogize, associate, correlate, juxtapose

likeness
04 bust, copy, form, icon
05 guise, image, shape, study
06 effigy, sketch, statue
07 drawing, picture, replica
08 affinity, painting, portrait
09 facsimile, semblance
10 appearance, comparison, photograph, similarity, similitude
11 counterpart, parallelism, resemblance
12 reproduction
14 correspondence, representation

likewise
03 too
04 also
07 besides
09 similarly
12 in like manner, in the same way
14 by the same token

liking
04 bent, bias, love
05 fancy, taste, thing
06 desire
07 leaning
08 affinity, fondness, penchant, soft spot, tendency, weakness
09 affection
10 attraction, partiality, preference, proclivity, propensity
11 inclination
12 appreciation, predilection

lilt
03 air
04 beat, song, sway
06 rhythm
07 cadence, measure
11 rise and fall

lily
➤ *Types of lily*:
04 aloe, arum, pond, sego
05 calla, camas, lotus, regal, tiger, torch, yucca
06 camash, camass, crinum, Easter, Nuphar, smilax
07 candock, day-lily, may-lily, quamash, Tritoma
08 asphodel, hyacinth, martagon, nenuphar, Phormium, trillium, victoria
09 amaryllis, herb-Paris, kniphofia, Richardia
10 agapanthus, aspidistra, belladonna, fritillary
11 Convallaria, Madonna-lily, red-hot poker
12 Annunciation, Solomon's seal
13 butcher's broom, lily of the nile
15 lily of the valley
➤ See also **plant**

lily-white
04 pure
06 chaste, virgin
08 innocent, spotless, virtuous
09 blameless, faultless, untainted
14 irreproachable

limb
03 arm, leg
04 fork, part, spur, wing
05 bough
06 branch, member
07 section
08 offshoot
09 appendage, extension, extremity
10 projection

◻**out on a limb**
07 exposed
08 isolated
10 vulnerable

limber
05 agile, lithe
06 lissom, pliant, supple
07 elastic, plastic, pliable
08 flexible, graceful

◻**limber up**
06 warm up
08 exercise, loosen up

limbo
◻**in limbo**
10 in abeyance
11 left hanging
12 left in the air
15 on the back burner

limelight
04 fame
06 notice, renown
07 stardom
09 attention, celebrity, public eye, publicity, spotlight

limit
03 end, lid, rim
04 brim, curb, edge
05 bound, brink, check, verge
06 border, bounds, hinder, impede, ration, reduce, utmost
07 ceiling, compass, confine, control, extreme, maximum
08 boundary, confines, deadline, frontier, restrain, restrict, terminus, ultimate
09 constrain, extremity, perimeter, restraint
10 constraint, limitation, parameters
11 cut-off point, restriction, termination
12 circumscribe

◻**the limit**
06 enough, the end
07 too much
11 intolerable
12 the last straw

limitation
04 curb, snag
05 block, check
07 control
08 drawback, weakness
09 hindrance, restraint, weak point
10 constraint, impediment
11 restriction, shortcoming
12 disadvantage, incapability

limited
05 basic, fixed, small
06 finite, narrow, scanty
07 checked, defined, minimal
08 confined
10 controlled, restricted
11 constrained
13 circumscribed

limitless
04 vast
07 endless
08 infinite, unending
09 boundless, countless, unbounded, undefined
11 measureless, never-ending
12 interminable

limp
03 hop, lax
04 soft, weak
05 frail, hitch, loose, slack, spent, tired, weary
06 falter, feeble, flabby, floppy, hobble, limber, totter
07 flaccid, pliable, relaxed, shamble, shuffle, stagger, stumble
08 drooping, fatigued, flexible, lameness
09 lethargic
11 debilitated
12 claudication

limpid
04 pure
05 clear, lucid, still
06 bright, glassy
07 flowing
11 translucent, transparent
12 crystal-clear, intelligible

line
03 bar, job, pad, rim, row, way
04 area, axis, back, band, bank, belt, book, card, cord, dash, draw, edge, face, file, fill, firm, kind, make, mark, memo, note, part, path, race, rank, rope, rule, seam, sort, talk, text, tier, type, wire, word, work
05 bound, brand, breed, cable, chain, cover, field, forte, front, hatch, inlay, limit, pitch, queue, route, score, shape, slash, spiel, stock, strip, stuff, style, track, trade, twine, verge, words
06 avenue, belief, border, career, column, course, crease, encase, family,

figure, fringe, furrow, groove, letter, margin, method, parade, patter, policy, report, scheme, script, series, strain, strand, streak, string, stripe, stroke, system, thread

07 calling, channel, company, conform, contour, descent, lineage, message, outline, pattern, profile, pursuit, scratch, variety, wrinkle

08 activity, ancestry, approach, attitude, boundary, business, defences, frontier, heritage, ideology, inscribe, interest, libretto, pedigree, position, postcard, practice, province, sequence, vocation

09 direction, formation, front line, parentage, perimeter, periphery, procedure, reinforce, sales talk, specialty, underline

10 appearance, battle zone, crow's feet, employment, extraction, firing-line, line of work, occupation, profession, silhouette, specialism, speciality, trajectory

11 battlefield, delineation, demarcation

13 configuration

14 course of action, specialization

□**draw the line**
07 rule out
09 stand firm
11 stop short of
15 put your foot down

□**in line**
03 due
06 in a row, in step, likely
08 in accord
09 in harmony
10 on the cards
11 in agreement
12 in the running

□**lay on the line, put on the line**
04 risk
07 imperil
08 endanger
10 jeopardize

□**line up**
05 align, array, group, lay on, order, range
06 fall in, obtain, secure
07 arrange, marshal, prepare, procure, produce
08 assemble, organize

09 form ranks
10 straighten

□**toe the line**
07 conform
12 keep the rules
14 be conventional, follow the rules

lineage
04 line, race
05 birth, breed, house, stock
06 family
07 descent
08 ancestry, heredity, pedigree
09 ancestors, forebears, genealogy, offspring
11 descendants

lineaments
05 lines
06 aspect, traits, visage
07 outline, profile
08 features, outlines

lined
05 feint, ruled
07 creased
08 furrowed, wrinkled

linen
06 sheets
10 white goods
11 pillowcases, tablecloths

line-up
03 row
04 bill, cast, line, list, team
05 array, queue
11 arrangement

linger
03 lag
04 idle, last, stay, stop, wait
05 dally, delay, tarry
06 dawdle, endure, hang on, loiter, remain
07 hold out, persist, survive
10 dilly-dally, hang around
12 take your time
13 procrastinate

lingerie
03 bra
04 slip
05 teddy
06 smalls, undies
07 panties
08 camisole, frillies, knickers
09 brassiere, underwear
11 panty girdle
12 body stocking, camiknickers, underclothes
13 suspender belt, underclothing, undergarments
14 unmentionables

lingering
08 dragging
09 prolonged
10 protracted
12 long-drawn-out

lingo
04 cant, talk
05 argot, idiom
06 jargon, patois, patter, speech, tongue
07 dialect
08 language, parlance
10 vernacular, vocabulary
11 terminology

liniment
05 cream, salve
06 balsam, lotion
07 unguent
08 ointment
09 emollient

lining
07 backing, padding
11 interfacing
13 reinforcement

link
03 tie
04 ally, bind, bond, join, knot, loop, part, ring, yoke
05 joint, merge, piece, tie-up, union, unite
08 attach, couple, fasten, hook up, team up
07 bracket, connect, liaison
10 amalgamate, attachment, connection, join forces
11 association, constituent, partnership
12 relationship
13 communication

□**link up**
04 ally, dock, join
05 merge, unify
06 hook up, team up
07 connect
10 amalgamate, join forces

link-up
05 tie-in, union
06 merger
10 connection
11 association, partnership

lion-hearted
04 bold
05 brave
06 daring, heroic
07 gallant, valiant
08 fearless, intrepid, resolute, stalwart, valorous
10 courageous

lionize
05 exalt
06 honour, praise
07 acclaim, adulate, glorify, idolize
10 aggrandize
11 hero-worship
14 put on a pedestal

lip
03 rim
04 brim, edge
05 brink, cheek, sauce, verge
06 border, margin
08 backchat, rudeness
09 impudence, insolence
12 impertinance

liquefaction
07 melting, thawing
10 dissolving
13 deliquescence

liquefy
04 flux, melt, thaw
05 smelt
08 dissolve, fluidize
10 deliquesce

liqueur
➤ *Types of liqueur (mostly trademarks):*
06 kirsch, kümmel
07 curaçao, ratafia
08 advocaat, amaretto, Drambuie, Tia Maria
09 Cointreau
10 chartreuse, maraschino
11 Benedictine
12 cherry brandy, kirschwasser
13 crème de menthe
➤ See also **drink**

liquid
03 wet
05 clear, drink, fluid, juice, runny
06 liquor, lotion, melted, molten, sloppy, thawed, watery
07 aqueous, flowing, running
08 solution
09 liquefied

liquidate
04 kill, sell
06 cash in, murder, remove, rub out, wind up
07 abolish, break up, destroy, disband, sell off, wipe out
08 dispatch, dissolve, massacre
09 close down, eliminate, terminate
10 annihilate, do away with, put an end to
11 assassinate, exterminate

liquidize
05 blend, crush, purée
07 process

liquor
04 grog, vino
05 booze, broth, drink, gravy, juice, sauce, stock
06 hootch, liquid
07 alcohol, essence, spirits
08 infusion
10 intoxicant
11 strong drink

lissom
05 agile, light, lithe
06 limber, nimble, pliant, supple
07 pliable, willowy
08 flexible, graceful

list
03 tip
04 bill, book, cant, file, heel, lean, note, roll, rota, tilt
05 enrol, enter, index, slant, slope, table, tally
06 agenda, record, roster,
07 compile, incline, invoice, itemize, listing, set down
08 calendar, classify, contents, heel over, lean over, register, schedule, syllabus, tabulate
09 catalogue, checklist, directory, enumerate, inventory, programme
10 tabulation
11 enumeration

listen
04 hark, hear, heed, mind
07 give ear, hearken
09 lend an ear
15 prick up your ears

▢listen in
03 bug, tap
07 monitor, wiretap
09 eavesdrop
15 pin back your ears, prick up your ears

listless
04 dull, limp
05 inert
06 torpid
07 languid, passive
08 inactive, indolent, sluggish
09 apathetic, impassive, lethargic
10 spiritless
11 indifferent

listlessness
05 ennui, sloth
06 apathy, torpor
07 languor

08 lethargy
09 indolence, torpidity
11 inattention, languidness

litany
04 list
06 prayer
07 account, recital
09 catalogue
10 invocation, recitation, repetition
11 enumeration

literacy
08 learning
09 education, erudition, knowledge
10 articulacy
11 cultivation, learnedness, proficiency, scholarship

literal
04 dull, true
05 close, exact
06 actual, boring, strict
07 factual, genuine, humdrum, precise, prosaic, tedious
08 accurate, faithful, verbatim
10 colourless, uninspired
11 unvarnished, word-for-word
12 matter-of-fact

literally
05 truly
06 really
07 closely, exactly, plainly
08 actually, strictly, verbatim
09 certainly, precisely
10 faithfully
11 to the letter, word for word

literary
06 formal, poetic
07 bookish, erudite, learned, refined
08 cultured, educated, lettered, literate, well-read
09 scholarly
10 colloquial, cultivated, widely-read
12 old-fashioned

➤ *Names of literary characters:*
03 **Eva** (Little), **Fox** (Brer), **Jim** (Lord), **Kaa**, **Kim**, **Lee** (Lorelei), **Pan** (Peter), **Pip**, **Roo**, **Tom** (Uncle), **Una**
04 **Ahab** (Captain), **Bede** (Adam), **Bond** (James), **Budd** (Billy), **Eyre** (Jane), **Finn** (Huckleberry), **Fogg** (Phileas), **Gamp** (Sarah), **Gray** (Dorian), **Gunn** (Ben), **Heep** (Uriah), **Hood** (Robin), **Hook** (Captain),

Hyde (Mister), Jack, Mole, Pooh, Pope (Giant), Slop (Doctor), Tigg (Montague), Toad (Mister), Trim (Corporal), Troy (Sergeant Francis), Tuck (Friar)

05 Akela, Aslan, Athos, Baloo, Bates (Miss), Bloom (Leopold), Bloom (Molly), Boxer, Brown (Father), Chips (Mister), Darcy (Fitzwilliam), Doone (Lorna), Drood (Edwin), Flint (Captain), Geste (Beau), Jones (Tom), Kanga, Kipps (Arthur), Loman (Willy), Lucky, March (Amy), Maria (Mad), Mitty (Walter), Moore (Mrs), Mosca, Nancy, O'Hara (Kimball), O'Hara (Scarlett), Piggy, Polly (Alfred), Porgy, Pozzo, Price (Fanny), Quilp (Daniel), Ralph, Ratty, Remus (Uncle), Rudge (Barnaby), Satan, Sharp (Becky), Sikes (Bill), Slope (Reverend Obadiah), Sloth, Smike, Smith (Winston), Spade (Sam), Stubb, Tarka (the Otter), Titus, Topsy, Trent (Little Nell), Twist (Oliver)

06 Aramis, Arthur (King), Badger, Barkis, Belial, Bennet (Elizabeth), Bourgh (Lady Catherine de), Bovary (Emma), Brodie (Miss Jean), Brooke (Dorothea), Bumble (Mister), Bumppo (Natty), Bunter (Billy), Butler (Rhett), Crusoe (Robinson), Dombey (Paul), Dorrit (Amy), Dorrit (William), Du Bois (Blanche), Eeyore, Friday (Man), Gatsby (Jay), Gawain, Hannay (Richard), Holmes (Sherlock), Jeeves (Reginald), Jekyll (Doctor Henry), Legree (Simon), Marley (Jacob), Marner (Silas), Marple (Jane), Moreau (Doctor), Mowgli, Omnium (Duke of), Pickle (Gamaliel), Piglet, Pinkie, Pliant (Dame), Poirot (Hercule), Rabbit, Rabbit (Brer), Random

(Roderick), Rob Roy, Sawyer (Bob), Sawyer (Tom), Shandy (Tristram), Silver (Long John), Subtle, Tarzan, Tigger, Tybalt, Varden (Dolly), Wadman (Widow), Watson (Doctor John), Weller (Samuel), Wimsey (Lord Peter), Wopsle (Mister), Yahoos

07 Andrews (Pamela), Ayeesha, Baggins (Bilbo), Beowulf, Biggles, Bramble (Matthew), Brer Fox, Clinker (Humphry), Crackit (Toby), Danvers (Mrs), Dawkins (Jack), Dedalus (Stephen), Deronda (Daniel), Despair (Giant), Don Juan, Dorigen, Dorothy, Dracula (Count), Estella, Fairfax (Jane), Gandalf (the Grey), Gargery (Joe), Grendel, Harding (Reverend Septimus), Harlowe (Clarissa), Hawkins (Jim), Higgins (Professor Henry), Hopeful, Humbert (Humbert), Ishmael, Jaggers (Mister), Jellyby (Mrs), Le Fever (Lieutenant), Maigret (Jules), Marlowe (Philip), Newsome (Chad), Obadiah, Peachum (Thomas), Pierrot, Porthos, Proudie (Doctor), Raffles, Rebecca, Scarlet (Will), Scrooge (Ebenezer), Shalott (Lady of), Shipton (Mother), Slumkey (Samuel), Squeers (Wackford), Surface (Charles), Surface (Joseph), Tiny Tim, Wemmick (Mister), Wickham (George), William, Witches (The Three), Wooster (Bertie), Would-be (Sir Politic)

08 Absolute (Captain), Anderson (Pastor Anthony), Backbite (Sir Benjamin), Bagheera, Bedivere (Sir), Black Dog, Casaubon (Reverend Edward), Cratchit (Bob), Criseyde, Faithful, Flanders (Moll), Flashman, Gloriana,

Griselda (Patient), Gulliver (Lemuel), Havisham (Miss), Hrothgar, Jarndyce (John), Knightly (George), Kowalski (Stanley), Ladislaw (Will), Lancelot (Sir), Lestrade (Inspector), MacHeath (Captain), Magwitch (Abel), Malaprop (Mrs), Micawber (Wilkins), Moriarty (Professor James), Napoleon, Nickleby (Nicholas), Paradise (Sal), Peggotty (Clara), Peterkin, Pickwick (Samuel), Queequeg, Snowball, Starbuck, Svengali, Tashtego, Thatcher (Becky), The Clerk, The Friar, The Reeve, Trotwood (Betsey), Tulliver (Maggie), Twitcher (Jemmy), Vladimir

09 Archimago, Bounderby (Josiah), Britomart, Bulstrode (Nicholas), Caulfield (Holden), Cheeryble (Charles), Christian, Churchill (Frank), Constance, D'Artagnan, Doolittle (Eliza), Fezziwigg (Mister), Gradgrind (Thomas), Grandison (Sir Charles), harlequin, Lismahago (Obadiah), Lochinvar, Minnehaha, Pecksniff (Seth), Pendennis (Arthur), Pollyanna, Rochester (Edward Fairfax), Scudamour (Sir), Shere Khan, The Knight, The Miller, The Squire, The Walrus, Tiger Lily, Trelawney (Squire), Van Winkle (Rip), Woodhouse (Emma), Yossarian (Captain John), Zenocrate

10 Allan-a-Dale, Big Brother, Brer Rabbit, Challenger (Professor), Chuzzlewit (Martin), Evangelist, Fauntleroy (Little Lord), Great-heart (Mister), Heathcliff, Hornblower (Horatio), Houyhnhnms, Little John, Little Nell, Maid Marian, Quatermain

(Allan), **The Red King, The Tar Baby, Tinkerbell, Tweedledee, Tweedledum**

11 **Copperfield** (David), **D'Urberville** (Alec), **Durbeyfield** (Tess), **Mickey Mouse, Mutabilitie, Pumblechook** (Mister), **Ready-to-Halt** (Mister), **The Dormouse, The Franklin, The Man of Law, The Merchant, The Pardoner, The Prioress, The Red Queen, The Summoner, Tiggy-Winkle** (Mrs)

12 **Blatant Beast, Chaunticleer, Frankenstein** (Victor), **Humpty-Dumpty, Lilliputians, Rip Van Winkle, The Carpenter, The Mad Hatter, The March Hare, The Pied Piper** (of Hamelin), **The Red Knight, The Scarecrow**

13 **The Jabberwock, The Mock Turtle, The Tin Woodman, The Wife of Bath, Winnie-the-Pooh**

14 **Mephistopheles, Rikki-Tikki-Tavi, The White Rabbit, Worldly Wiseman** (Mister)

15 **The Artful Dodger, The Cowardly Lion, The Three Witches, Valiant-for-Truth**

➢ See also **Shakespeare**

▶ *Names of literary critics*:
04 **Bell** (Clive Howard), **Blum** (Léon)
05 **Hicks** (Granville), **Lodge** (David), **Stead** (Christian Karlson)
06 **Arnold** (Matthew), **Calder** (Angus), **Empson** (Sir William), **Leavis** (Frank Raymond), **Leavis** (Queenie Dorothy), **Lukacs** (György Szegedy von), **Sontag** (Susan), **Wilson** (Edmund)
07 **Alvarez** (Alfred), **Barthes** (Roland), **Derrida** (Jacques), **Hoggart** (Richard), **Kermode** (Frank)
08 **Bradbury** (Malcolm Stanley), **Longinus, Nicolson** (Sir Harold

George), **Richards** (Ivor Armstrong), **Trilling** (Lionel), **Williams** (Raymond)

literate
07 learned
08 cultured, educated
10 able to read, proficient
11 able to write, intelligent
12 intellectual, well-educated
13 knowledgeable

literature
04 bumf, data
05 facts, paper
06 papers
07 hand-out, leaflet, letters
08 brochure, circular, hand-outs, leaflets, pamphlet, writings
09 brochures, circulars, pamphlets
11 information
12 printed works
13 printed matter
14 published works

▬ *Types of literature*:
04 epic, saga
05 drama, essay, novel, prose, verse
06 parody, poetry, satire, thesis
07 epistle, fiction, lampoon, novella, polemic, tragedy, trilogy
08 allegory, libretto, pastiche, treatise
09 anti-novel, biography, criticism
10 magnum opus, non-fiction
11 Gothic novel
13 autobiography, belles-lettres, penny dreadful
15 picaresque novel

lithe
05 agile
06 limber, lissom, pliant, supple
07 pliable
08 flexible

litigant
05 party
08 claimant
09 contender, disputant, litigator, plaintiff
11 complainant

litigation
04 case, suit
06 action
07 dispute, lawsuit, process
11 prosecution

litigious
11 belligerent, contentious, quarrelsome
12 disputatious
13 argumentative

litter
04 grot, junk, mess, muck
05 brood, strew, trash, young
06 debris, family, refuse
07 garbage, rubbish, scatter
08 detritus
09 confusion, offspring

little
03 bit, dab, wee
04 baby, cute, dash, drop, hint, mini, nice, spot, tiny
05 brief, dwarf, minor, petty, pinch, scant, short, small, taste, teeny, touch, trace
06 barely, hardly, meagre, midget, minute, paltry, petite, rarely, seldom, skimpy, slight, sparse, trifle
07 modicum, nominal, peanuts, slender, soupçon, trickle, trivial, younger
08 fragment, nugatory, particle, pint-size, trifling
09 ephemeral, miniature, momentary, pint-sized, transient
10 attractive, diminutive, negligible, short-lived, smattering, transitory
11 Lilliputian, microscopic, small amount, unimportant
12 infrequently, insufficient
13 infinitesimal, insignificant, next to nothing
14 inconsiderable
15 a drop in the ocean

◻**little by little**
06 slowly
08 bit by bit
09 by degrees, gradually, piecemeal
10 step by step
13 imperceptibly, progressively

liturgical
06 formal, ritual, solemn
08 hieratic
10 ceremonial, sacerdotal
11 eucharistic, sacramental

liturgy
04 form, rite
06 office, ritual
07 service, worship
09 ordinance, sacrament
10 observance

live
02 be
03 hot
04 last, lead, pass, stay
05 abide, alive, dwell, exist, lodge, revel, spend, vital
06 active, alight, behave, endure, lively, reside, urgent
07 animate, be alive, burning, breathe, current, dynamic, flaming, glowing, ignited, inhabit, persist, survive, topical
08 continue, existent, relevant, vigorous, volatile
09 breathing, connected, enjoy life, explosive, pertinent
10 draw breath, unexploded
12 have your home
13 controversial
14 earn your living
15 support yourself

◻**live it up**
05 revel
09 have a ball, make merry
11 make whoopee
15 paint the town red

◻**live on**
04 feed
05 exist
06 rely on
07 live off, subsist

◻**live wire**
06 dynamo
08 go-getter, whizz kid

liveable
09 habitable
11 inhabitable

◻**liveable with**
08 bearable, passable, sociable
09 congenial, tolerable
10 compatible, harmonious
13 companionable

livelihood
05 means
06 income, living, upkeep
07 support
11 maintenance, subsistence
14 means of support, source of income

liveliness
04 brio
05 oomph
06 energy, spirit
08 dynamism, vitality, vivacity
09 animation, quickness
13 sprightliness

livelong
05 whole
06 entire

lively
04 busy, keen, racy, spry
05 agile, alert, alive, brisk, merry, perky, quick, rapid, vivid
06 active, blithe, bouncy, breezy, bright, chirpy, frisky, heated, hectic, jaunty, nimble, strong
07 buoyant, buzzing, crowded, dynamic, graphic, playful, teeming
08 animated, bustling, cheerful, eventful, exciting, spirited, stirring, striking, vigorous
09 colourful, energetic, sprightly, vivacious
10 frolicsome, refreshing
11 imaginative, interesting, stimulating
12 enthusiastic, high-spirited, invigorating

liven
05 hot up, pep up, rouse, spice
06 buck up, perk up, stir up
07 animate, enliven, spice up
08 brighten, energize, vitalize
10 invigorate

liverish
05 testy
06 crabby, crusty, grumpy, snappy, tetchy
07 crabbed, peevish
09 crotchety, irascible, irritable, splenetic
12 disagreeable
13 quick-tempered

livery
04 garb, gear, suit, togs
05 dress, get-up, habit
06 attire
07 apparel, clobber, clothes, costume, regalia, uniform
08 clothing, garments
09 vestments
10 habiliments

livid
03 mad, wan
04 pale, waxy
05 angry, ashen, irate, pasty
06 fuming, leaden, pallid, purple, raging
07 bruised, enraged, furious, ghastly, greyish
08 blanched, incensed, outraged, purplish, seething
09 bloodless, indignant
10 infuriated
11 deathly pale, discoloured, exasperated
12 black-and-blue

living
04 life, live
05 alive, being, exact, vital
06 active, extant, income, lively
07 animate, current, precise, support
08 animated, benefice, existing, vigorous
09 animation, breathing, existence, lifestyle, surviving
10 continuing, livelihood, sustenance
11 going strong, subsistence
14 means of support, source of income

living-room
06 lounge
11 drawing-room, sitting-room

lizard
➤ *Types of lizard*:
05 gecko, skink
06 agamid, iguana
08 basilisk, slowworm
09 chameleon
10 sand lizard
11 gila monster
12 flying lizard, Komodo dragon
13 monitor lizard
➤ See also **animal**

load
03 tax
04 heap, lade, lots, pile, tons
05 cargo, goods, heaps
06 burden, dozens, hordes, lading, scores, strain, weight
07 freight, oppress, trouble
08 encumber, hundreds, millions, shipment
09 millstone, thousands, weigh down
10 overburden, saddle with
11 consignment, encumbrance

loaded
04 full, rich
05 drunk, flush, laden, piled, tight, tipsy
06 biased, filled, heaped, packed, stoned, tiddly
07 charged, drunken, legless, pickled, sloshed, smashed, sozzled, squiffy, stacked, wealthy, well-off
08 affluent, burdened, tanked up, weighted
09 plastered, well-oiled
10 blind drunk, in the money, inebriated, well-heeled
11 rolling in it, snowed under

12 drunk as a lord, roaring
drunk

loaf
04 cake, cube, head, idle, laze,
lump, mass, nous, slab
05 block, brick, mooch, sense
06 brains, loiter, noddle
10 hang around, take it easy
11 common sense
12 lounge around

loafer
05 idler
07 lounger, shirker, wastrel
08 layabout, sluggard
10 ne'er-do-well

loan
04 lend
06 credit
07 advance, lending
08 mortgage

loath
06 averse
08 grudging, hesitant
09 reluctant, resisting, unwilling
10 indisposed
11 disinclined

loathe
04 hate
05 abhor
06 detest
07 despise, dislike
08 execrate, not stand
09 abominate
10 recoil from
15 feel revulsion at

loathing
04 hate
05 odium
06 hatred, horror
07 disgust, dislike, ill-will
08 aversion
09 antipathy, repulsion,
revulsion
10 abhorrence, execration,
repugnance
11 abomination, detestation

loathsome
04 vile
06 odious
07 hateful
09 execrable, obnoxious,
offensive, repellent,
repugnant, revolting
10 abominable, despicable,
detestable, disgusting,
nauseating
12 contemptible, disagreeable

lob
04 hurl, lift, loft, toss

05 chuck, fling, heave, pitch,
throw

lobby
04 hall
05 foyer, porch
07 call for, hallway, passage,
promote, push for, solicit
08 anteroom, campaign,
corridor, entrance, press for,
pressure
09 influence, vestibule
10 passageway
11 campaign for, ginger group,
waiting-room
12 entrance hall
13 pressure group

local
03 bar, inn, pub
06 native, parish
07 limited
08 hostelry, resident
09 community, parochial
10 inhabitant, parish-pump,
vernacular
11 public house
13 neighbourhood

locale
04 area, site, spot, zone
05 locus, place, scene, venue
08 locality, location, position
11 environment
13 neighbourhood

locality
04 area, site, spot
05 place, scene
06 locale, region
08 district, position, vicinity
11 environment
13 neighbourhood

localize
05 limit
07 confine, contain, delimit,
specify
08 pinpoint, zero in on
10 delimitate, narrow down
11 concentrate

locate
03 fix, put, set
04 find, seat, site
05 build, place
06 detect, settle
07 hit upon, situate, station,
uncover, unearth
08 discover, pinpoint, position
09 establish, track down
10 come across, run to earth

location
04 site, spot
05 locus, place, scene, venue

06 locale
07 setting
08 bearings, position
09 situation
11 whereabouts

lock
03 bar, hug, jam
04 bolt, curl, join, link, mesh,
seal, shut, tuft
05 catch, clasp, grasp, latch,
plait, tress, unite
06 clench, clutch, engage,
fasten, secure, strand
07 embrace, enclose, entwine,
grapple, padlock, ringlet
08 encircle, entangle
09 fastening, interlock

➤ *Parts of a lock*:
03 key, pin
04 bolt, hasp, knob, rose, sash
05 latch
06 barrel, keyway, spring, staple
07 key card, keyhole, spindle
08 cylinder, dead bolt, sash bolt
09 face plate, latch bolt
10 escutcheon, latch lever
11 mortise bolt, spindle hole,
strike plate

❑**lock out**
03 bar
05 debar
07 exclude

❑**lock up**
03 pen
04 cage, jail
06 detain, secure, shut in,
shut up, wall in
07 close up, confine
08 imprison
11 incarcerate
13 put behind bars

locker
07 cabinet
08 cupboard

lock-up
03 can, jug
04 cell, gaol, jail, quod
05 clink
06 cooler, garage, prison
09 storeroom, warehouse
10 depository
12 penitentiary

locomotion
06 action, motion, travel
07 headway, walking
08 movement, progress
10 ambulation, travelling

locution
05 idiom

06 accent, phrase
07 diction, wording
10 expression, inflection, intonation
12 articulation, turn of phrase

lodge
03 den, fix, hut, put
04 bank, club, file, lair, live, make, nest, room, stay
05 board, cabin, dwell, house, imbed, put up
06 billet, branch, reside, submit
07 chapter, deposit, implant, quarter, section, shelter, society, sojourn
08 register
09 gatehouse
11 accommodate, association
12 meeting-place

lodger
06 inmate, roomer, tenant
07 boarder
11 paying guest

lodgings
04 digs
05 abode, board, place, rooms
06 billet
08 quarters
13 accommodation, boarding-house

lofty
04 high, tall
05 grand, noble, proud
06 lordly, raised, snooty
07 exalted, haughty, sky-high, soaring, stately, sublime
08 arrogant, elevated, imperial, imposing, majestic, superior, towering
09 dignified
10 disdainful
11 illustrious, patronizing, toffee-nosed
12 supercilious
13 condescending, high and mighty

log
04 book, file, note
05 chart, diary, tally, trunk
06 record, timber
07 account, daybook, journal, logbook, set down, write up
08 register

loggerheads

□**at loggerheads**
06 at odds
11 disagreeing, quarrelling
14 at daggers drawn

logic
05 sense
06 reason
08 argument
09 deduction, rationale, reasoning
10 dialectics

logical
05 clear, sound, valid
06 cogent
08 coherent, rational, reasoned, sensible
09 deducible, judicious
10 methodical, reasonable
14 well-thought-out

logistics
08 planning, strategy
10 management
12 co-ordination, organization
13 masterminding, orchestration

logo
04 mark, sign
05 badge, image
06 device, emblem, symbol
08 insignia
09 trademark

loiter
03 lag
04 idle, loaf
05 dally, delay, mooch, tarry
06 dawdle, linger, lounge
09 hang about, waste time
10 dilly-dally

loll
04 flap, flop, hang
05 droop, relax, slump
06 dangle, lounge, slouch, sprawl
07 recline

lone
03 one
04 only, sole
05 alone
06 single
08 divorced, forsaken, isolated, separate, solitary
09 abandoned, on your own, separated, unmarried
10 by yourself, unattached

loneliness
08 solitude
09 aloneness, isolation, seclusion
12 lonesomeness, solitariness

lonely
04 lone
05 alone
06 barren, remote

07 outcast
08 deserted, desolate, isolated, lonesome, secluded, solitary, wretched
09 abandoned, destitute, miserable, reclusive
10 friendless
11 God-forsaken, out-of-the-way, uninhabited
12 unfrequented

loner
06 hermit
07 recluse
08 lone wolf, solitary
13 individualist
14 solitudinarian

lonesome
04 lone
05 alone
06 barren, lonely, remote
07 outcast, unhappy
08 deserted, desolate, forsaken, isolated, lonesome, rejected, secluded, solitary, wretched
09 abandoned, destitute, miserable, reclusive
10 friendless
11 out-of-the-way, uninhabited
12 unfrequented

long
04 hope, itch, pine, want, wish
05 covet, crave, yearn
06 desire, hanker, hunger, thirst
07 lengthy, spun out, verbose
08 extended, marathon
09 elongated, extensive, prolonged, spread out, stretched
10 protracted
12 interminable, long-drawn-out, stretched out

□**before long**
04 soon
07 shortly
15 in the near future

long-drawn-out
06 prolix
07 lengthy, spun out, tedious
08 marathon, overlong
09 prolonged
10 long-winded, protracted
12 interminable, overextended

longing
03 yen
04 avid, hope, itch, urge, wish
05 dream, eager
06 ardent, desire, hunger, hungry, pining, thirst

07 anxious, craving, wanting, wishful, wistful
08 ambition, coveting, desirous, yearning
09 hankering, hungering
10 aspiration

long-lasting
07 abiding, chronic
08 enduring, unfading
09 lingering, prolonged
10 continuing, protracted

long-lived
07 durable, lasting
08 enduring
09 longevous, macrobian
11 macrobiotic

long-standing
07 abiding
08 enduring
09 long-lived
11 established, long-lasting, traditional
12 time-honoured
15 long-established

long-suffering
07 patient, stoical
08 resigned, tolerant
10 forbearing
13 uncomplaining

long-winded
05 wordy
06 prolix
07 diffuse, lengthy, tedious, verbose, voluble
10 discursive, protracted
12 long-drawn-out

long-windedness
08 longueur
09 garrulity, prolixity, verbosity, wordiness
11 lengthiness, tediousness
14 discursiveness

look
04 face, gape, gawp, gaze, mien, peek, peep, seem, show, view
05 dekko, front, guise, sight, stare, study, watch
06 appear, aspect, effect, eyeful, façade, gander, give on, glance, manner, review, shufti, squint, survey
07 bearing, display, exhibit, eyeball, front on, glimpse
08 butcher's, features, give on to, once-over
09 semblance

10 appearance, complexion, expression, impression, inspection
11 examination, observation
12 butcher's hook, take a dekko at
13 get an eyeful of, take a gander at, take a shufti at, take a squint at

◻look after
04 mind, tend
05 guard, nurse
07 babysit, care for, protect
08 attend to, maintain
09 childmind, watch over

◻look back
06 recall
08 remember
09 reminisce, think back

◻look down on
05 scorn, spurn
07 despise, disdain, sneer at
09 disparage, patronize
14 hold in contempt

◻look for
04 seek
05 quest
07 hunt for, hunt out
09 forage for, search for, try to find

◻look forward to
05 await
06 expect
07 hope for, long for, wait for
08 envisage, envision
10 anticipate

◻look into
03 dig
05 delve, plumb, probe, study
06 fathom, go into
07 examine, explore, inspect
08 ask about, check out, look over, research
10 scrutinize, search into
11 investigate
12 inquire about

◻look like
08 resemble
09 take after

◻look on, look upon
05 count, judge, think
06 regard
08 consider

◻look out
06 beware
07 be alert
08 watch out
09 be careful

12 keep an eye out, pay attention
13 be on your guard
14 be on the qui vive

◻look over
04 scan, view
05 check
07 examine, inspect, monitor
08 check out
09 go through
11 read through
13 cast an eye over

◻look to
05 await
06 expect, rely on, turn to
07 count on
10 anticipate, think about

◻look up
04 find, seek
05 visit
06 call on, drop by, perk up, pick up, stop by
07 advance, consult, develop, hunt for, improve
08 drop in on, look in on, progress, research
09 come along, get better, search for, track down
10 ameliorate
11 make headway, pay a visit to
12 make progress

◻look up to
06 admire, esteem, honour, revere
07 respect
13 think highly of

look-alike
04 spit, twin
05 clone, image
06 double, ringer
10 dead ringer
12 doppelgänger
13 spitting image

lookout
05 watch
06 affair, pigeon, sentry
07 concern, problem
08 sentinel, watchman
10 watch-tower
15 observation post

◻keep a lookout
05 watch
10 be vigilant
11 remain alert
14 be on the qui vive

loom
06 appear, emerge, impend, menace
08 overhang, threaten

09 take shape
10 be imminent, overshadow

loop
03 tie
04 bend, coil, curl, hoop, knot, ring, turn, wind
05 braid, noose
06 circle, eyelet, spiral
08 encircle, loophole, surround
11 convolution

loophole
06 escape, excuse, let-out
07 evasion, mistake, pretext
08 omission, pretence

loose
03 lax, off
04 ease, fast, free, undo
05 baggy, broad, let go, relax, slack, unpen, untie, vague
06 detach, loosen, unbind, undone, unhook, unlock, untied, wanton, weaken
07 at large, escaped, flowing, general, hanging, immoral, inexact, movable, release, sagging, set free, slacken, unclasp, unleash
08 rambling, released, unchaste, uncouple, unfasten, unsteady
09 abandoned, debauched, disengage, dissolute, imprecise, shapeless, uncoupled
10 degenerate, disconnect, ill-defined, inaccurate, indefinite, indistinct, unattached, unconfined, unfastened, untethered
11 promiscuous
12 disreputable, loose-fitting

❑ **at a loose end**
04 idle
05 bored, fed up
14 with time to kill

loosen
04 ease, free, undo
05 let go, loose, relax, untie
06 let out, unbind, weaken
07 deliver, release, set free, slacken
08 diminish, moderate, set loose, unfasten

❑ **loosen up**
05 let up, relax
06 cool it, ease up, go easy, lessen, unwind, warm up
07 prepare, work out
08 chill out, exercise, limber up
09 hang loose

loot
03 rob
04 haul, raid, sack, swag
05 booty, prize, rifle, steal
06 burgle, maraud, ravage, riches, spoils
07 despoil, pillage, plunder, ransack
11 stolen goods, stolen money

lop
03 cut
04 chop, clip, crop, dock, trim
05 prune, sever
06 cut off, detach, reduce, remove
07 curtail, shorten, take off
08 truncate

lope
03 run
05 bound
06 lollop, spring, stride

lop-sided
05 askew
06 squint, uneven
07 crooked, tilting, unequal
08 one-sided
10 off balance, unbalanced
12 asymmetrical

loquacious
05 gabby, gassy, wordy
06 chatty
07 gossipy, voluble
09 garrulous, talkative
10 blathering, chattering

loquacity
09 garrulity, gassiness
10 chattiness, volubility
12 effusiveness
13 talkativeness

lord
03 God
04 duke, earl, king, peer
05 baron, chief, count, noble, ruler
06 Christ, Father, leader, master, prince, Yahweh
07 captain, emperor, Eternal, monarch
08 governor, nobleman, overlord, superior, viscount
09 sovereign
10 aristocrat
11 Jesus Christ

❑ **lord it over**
07 oppress, repress, swagger
08 domineer, pull rank
09 put on airs, tyrannize
10 boss around
11 order around, queen it over

lordly
05 grand, lofty, noble, proud
07 haughty, stately, stuck-up
08 arrogant, imperial, majestic
09 dignified, grandiose, hubristic, imperious
10 disdainful, high-handed, hoity-toity
11 domineering, magnificent, overbearing, patronizing
12 aristocratic, supercilious
13 condescending, high and mighty

lore
06 wisdom
07 legends, sayings, stories
08 folklore, learning, teaching
09 erudition, knowledge
10 traditions
13 superstitions

lorry
05 float, truck, wagon
06 pick-up
10 juggernaut, removal van
12 pantechnicon

lose
04 drop, fail, miss
05 drain, elude, evade, spend, use up, waste
06 expend, forget, go down, ignore, mislay, outrun
07 consume, deplete, exhaust, forfeit, fritter, get lost, neglect, not find
08 be beaten, go astray, misplace, shake off, squander, throw off
09 disregard, dissipate
10 be defeated, depart from, stop having, wander from
11 be conquered, be taken away, come to grief, fail to grasp, leave behind
12 suffer defeat
14 be unsuccessful
15 throw in the towel

❑ **lose out**
06 suffer
07 miss out
14 be unsuccessful
15 be disadvantaged

❑ **lose yourself in something**
12 be absorbed in
13 be engrossed in, be taken up with
14 be captivated by, be enthralled by

loser
07 also-ran, failure, has-been, no-hoper, washout
08 dead loss, runner-up, write-off
10 non-starter

loss
04 dead, debt
05 waste
07 deficit, missing
09 death toll, mislaying, privation
10 casualties, deficiency, fatalities, forfeiture
11 bereavement, deprivation
12 disadvantage, misplacement
13 disappearance

at a loss
07 puzzled
09 mystified, perplexed
10 bewildered

lost
04 dead, past
06 astray, bygone, damned, doomed, dreamy, fallen, missed
07 at a loss, baffled, defunct, extinct, mislaid, missing, puzzled, strayed, wrecked
08 absorbed, vanished
09 destroyed, engrossed, misplaced, off course, perplexed
10 bewildered, captivated, enthralled, fascinated, spellbound, squandered
11 disappeared, disoriented, preoccupied, untraceable
12 absent-minded, irredeemable
13 disorientated, unrecoverable

lot
03 cut, set
04 fate, many, part, plot, tons
05 batch, bunch, crowd, group, heaps, loads, miles, piece, piles, quota, share
06 bundle, dozens, masses, oodles, parcel, ration, stacks
07 destiny, fortune, portion
08 hundreds, millions, quantity
09 a good deal, a quantity, allotment, allowance, situation, thousands
10 assortment, collection
11 consignment, great number, large amount
13 circumstances

a lot
04 much
05 often
10 frequently
14 to a great degree, to a great extent

throw your lot in with
10 join forces, team up with
11 combine with

lotion
04 balm
05 cream, salve
06 balsam
08 liniment, ointment
09 emollient
11 embrocation

lottery
04 draw, risk
05 bingo
06 gamble, hazard, raffle
07 tombola, venture
10 sweepstake
11 speculation

loud
04 bold
05 brash, flash, gaudy, noisy, rowdy, showy
06 brazen, flashy, garish, shrill, vulgar
07 blaring, booming, glaring, raucous, roaring
08 emphatic, piercing, resonant, strident, vehement
09 clamorous, deafening, insistent, obtrusive, tasteless
10 aggressive, flamboyant, resounding, stentorian, thundering, vociferous
11 loud-mouthed
12 ostentatious

loudly
07 lustily, noisily, shrilly
10 fortissimo, stridently, vehemently, vigorously
11 clamorously, deafeningly
12 resoundingly, uproariously, vociferously

loudmouth
07 boaster, windbag
08 big mouth, braggart
09 blusterer, swaggerer
11 braggadocio

loud-mouthed
05 noisy
08 boasting, bragging

lounge
04 idle, laze, loll
05 relax, slump
06 repose, sprawl
07 day-room, lie back, parlour, recline
09 lie around, loll about, waste time
10 living-room, take it easy
11 drawing-room, sitting-room

lour, lower
04 loom
05 frown, glare, scowl
06 darken, glower, menace
07 blacken
08 threaten
09 be brewing, cloud over

louring, lowering
04 dark, grey, grim
05 black, heavy
06 cloudy, gloomy
07 ominous
08 menacing, overcast
09 darkening
11 threatening

lousy
03 bad, ill, low
04 crap, poor, sick
05 awful, mingy, seedy
06 poorly, rotten, unwell
08 inferior, terrible
09 miserable
10 out of sorts, second-rate
12 contemptible
15 under the weather

lout
03 oaf, yob
04 boor
05 yahoo, yobbo
09 barbarian

loutish
04 rude
05 crude, rough
06 coarse, oafish, vulgar
07 boorish, uncouth
11 ill-mannered, uncivilized

lovable
04 dear
07 winsome
08 adorable, charming
09 appealing, endearing

love
03 pet
04 care, dear, lust
05 adore, angel, enjoy, fancy, honey, prize, taste
06 ardour, desire, dote on, liking, regard, relish, savour, warmth
07 be mad on, beloved, care for, cherish, concern, darling, dear one, dearest,

delight, idolize, long for,
passion, rapture, worship
08 be daft on, be fond of,
be nuts on, be sold on,
devotion, fondness, hold
dear, intimacy, kindness,
pleasure, soft spot,
sympathy, treasure,
weakness
09 adoration, adulation,
affection, be sweet on,
delight in, enjoyment,
favourite
10 appreciate, attachment,
friendship, partiality,
sweetheart, tenderness
11 amorousness, be devoted
to, be partial to,
brotherhood, inclination,
infatuation
12 appreciation, have a crush
on, like very much
13 be attracted to
14 have a liking for, have the
hots for, take pleasure in
15 think the world of

◻**fall in love with**
05 fancy
07 fall for
12 be crazy about, have a
crush on, take a shine to
13 have a thing for
15 lose your heart to

◻**in love with**
06 doting, hooked, soft on
07 charmed, smitten, stuck on,
sweet on
08 besotted, mad about
09 enamoured, nuts about,
wild about
10 crazy about, infatuated
12 have a crush on

◻**love affair**
05 amour
06 affair
07 liaison, passion, romance

◻**make love**
09 sleep with
11 go to bed with
13 sleep together

loveless
04 cold, hard
06 frigid
08 forsaken, unloving
09 unfeeling
11 insensitive, passionless

lovelorn
06 pining
07 longing
08 desiring, lovesick, yearning

lovely
04 fair
06 pretty
08 adorable, charming,
handsome, pleasant
09 beautiful, enjoyable,
exquisite, wonderful
10 attractive, delightful,
enchanting, marvellous
11 good-looking

love-making
03 sex
06 coitus, mating
07 coition
08 congress, foreplay, intimacy
10 copulation
11 intercourse, sexual union
15 carnal knowledge, sexual
relations

lover
03 fan
04 bird, buff, date, vamp, wolf
05 fella, fiend, flame, freak
06 fiancé, suitor, toy boy
07 admirer, beloved, devotee,
fanatic, fiancée, partner
08 follower, mistress
09 boyfriend
10 enthusiast, girlfriend,
heart-throb, sweetheart
12 bit on the side

lovesick
06 pining
07 longing
08 desiring, lovelorn, yearning

loving
04 fond, kind, warm
06 ardent, caring, doting,
tender
07 adoring, amorous, devoted
10 passionate
11 sympathetic, warm-hearted
12 affectionate

low
03 bad, moo, sad
04 base, bass, blue, deep,
down, dull, evil, flat, glum,
mean, meek, mild, poor,
rich, sale, slow, soft
05 cheap, fed up, lowly, muted,
nadir, nasty, plain, quiet,
scant, short, small, squat
06 bellow, bottom, coarse,
common, gentle, gloomy,
humble, hushed, junior, little,
meagre, modest, paltry,
scanty, simple, smutty,
sparse, sunken, vulgar,
wicked

07 adverse, foolish, heinous,
hostile, immoral, muffled,
obscene, obscure, peasant,
reduced, shallow, slashed,
stunted, subdued, unhappy
08 depraved, downcast,
indecent, inferior, mediocre,
moderate, negative,
opposing, ordinary,
plebeian, resonant, sea-
level, sonorous, trifling
09 dastardly, deficient,
depressed, miserable,
quietened, whispered
10 cheesed off, despicable,
despondent, inadequate,
rock-bottom, submissive
11 downhearted, ground-level,
inexpensive, subordinate,
unimportant
12 contemptible, disconsolate,
disheartened, insufficient,
unfavourable
13 dishonourable, insignificant
14 down in the dumps

low-born
05 lowly
06 humble
07 obscure, peasant
08 mean-born, plebeian
10 low-ranking

lowbrow
05 crude
09 unlearned, unrefined
10 uncultured
12 uncultivated

low-down
03 gen
04 data, dope, info, news
05 facts
11 information, inside story
12 intelligence

lower
04 drop, hush, sink
05 abase, lowly, minor, under
06 debase, demean, junior,
lessen, lesser, nether, reduce
07 cheapen, curtail, degrade,
depress, descend, let down,
let fall, quieten, set down
08 belittle, decrease, diminish,
disgrace, inferior, take down
09 bring down, dishonour,
disparage, secondary,
undermost
11 second-class, subordinate

lower see **lour**

lowering see **louring**

low-grade
04 poor
08 inferior
09 cheap-jack, third-rate
11 poor-quality, substandard
14 not up to scratch

low-key
04 soft
05 muted, quiet
07 relaxed, subdued
10 restrained
11 understated

lowly
04 mean, meek, mild, poor
06 common, humble, junior,
   modest, simple
07 low-born, obscure, peasant
08 inferior, ordinary, plebeian
10 low-ranking, submissive
11 subordinate, unimportant

low-pitched
03 low
04 bass, deep, rich
08 resonant, sonorous

low-spirited
03 low, sad
04 down, glum
05 fed up, moody
06 gloomy
07 unhappy
08 dejected
09 depressed, miserable
10 cheesed off, despondent
11 downhearted
14 down in the dumps

loyal
04 firm, true
06 trusty
07 devoted, sincere, staunch
08 constant, faithful, reliable
09 patriotic, steadfast
10 dependable, unchanging

loyalty
06 fealty
08 devotion, fidelity
09 constancy
10 allegiance, patriotism
11 reliability, staunchness
12 faithfulness
13 dependability, steadfastness

lozenge
06 jujube, tablet
07 gumdrop
08 pastille
09 cough-drop

lubber
04 clod, dolt, hick, lout,
   slob
07 bumpkin
10 clodhopper

lubberly
06 clumsy, coarse, oafish
07 awkward, doltish, loutish,
   lumpish, uncouth
08 ungainly
09 lumbering
11 clodhopping

lubricant
03 fat, oil
04 lard
06 grease
11 lubrication

lubricate
03 oil, wax
04 lard
05 smear
06 grease, polish

lucid
04 pure, sane
05 clear, plain, sober, sound
06 bright, glassy, limpid
07 beaming, radiant, shining
08 distinct, explicit, gleaming,
   luminous, pellucid, rational,
   sensible
09 brilliant, effulgent
10 diaphanous, reasonable
11 clear-headed, crystalline, of
   sound mind, resplendent,
   translucent, transparent
12 compos mentis, intelligible
14 comprehensible

luck
04 fate
06 chance, hazard
07 destiny, fortune, godsend,
   success
08 accident, fortuity
10 prosperity
11 good fortune
14 predestination

❑**in luck**
08 favoured
09 fortunate, opportune
10 auspicious, successful

❑**out of luck**
07 hapless, unlucky
08 luckless
11 unfortunate
12 inauspicious, unsuccessful
13 disadvantaged

luckily
08 by chance
10 by accident, by good luck

11 fortunately
12 fortuitously

luckless
06 cursed, doomed, jinxed
07 hapless, unhappy, unlucky
08 hopeless, ill-fated
10 calamitous, disastrous,
   ill-starred
11 star-crossed, unfortunate
12 unpropitious, unsuccessful

lucky
05 jammy
06 in luck, timely
07 charmed
09 expedient, fortunate,
   opportune, promising
10 auspicious, fortuitous,
   propitious
12 providential

lucrative
07 gainful
08 well-paid
10 high-paying, productive,
   profitable, worthwhile
11 money-making
12 advantageous, profit-
   making, remunerative

lucre
04 cash, dosh
05 bread, dough, money
06 mammon, riches, wealth

ludicrous
04 zany
05 crazy, droll
06 absurd
07 comical, risible
08 farcical, humorous
09 eccentric, hilarious
10 outlandish, ridiculous
12 preposterous

lug
03 tow, tug
04 drag, haul, hump, pull, tote
05 carry, heave

luggage
04 gear
05 stuff
06 things
07 baggage
10 belongings
11 impedimenta
13 paraphernalia

lugubrious
03 sad
04 glum
06 dismal, dreary, gloomy,
   morose, sombre, woeful
07 doleful, serious
08 funereal, mournful

09 sorrowful, woebegone
10 melancholy, sepulchral

lukewarm
05 tepid
07 warmish
09 apathetic, Laodicean
11 half-hearted
14 unenthusiastic

lull
04 calm, ease, hush
05 allay, let-up, pause, peace, quell, quiet, still
06 pacify, soothe, subdue
07 assuage, compose, silence
08 calmness
09 stillness
12 tranquillity

lullaby
08 berceuse
10 cradle song

lumber
04 junk, land, load, plod, wood
05 clump, stamp, stump, trash
06 burden, charge, hamper, impose, jumble, refuse, saddle, timber, trudge
07 clutter, rubbish, shamble, shuffle, stumble, trundle
08 encumber

lumbering
05 heavy
06 bovine, clumsy
07 awkward, hulking, lumpish, massive
08 ungainly, unwieldy
09 ponderous
11 elephantine, heavy-footed

luminary
03 VIP
04 star
06 bigwig, expert, leader
07 big name, notable
09 authority, celebrity, dignitary, superstar
12 leading light

luminescent
06 bright
07 glowing, radiant, shining
08 luminous
09 effulgent
10 luciferous
11 fluorescent
14 phosphorescent

luminous
03 lit
06 bright
07 glowing, radiant, shining
08 dazzling, lustrous
09 brilliant, effulgent

11 fluorescent, illuminated, luminescent

lump
03 dab, wad
04 ball, bear, bump, cake, clod, fuse, hunk, mass, pool, take
05 blend, brook, bulge, bunch, chunk, clump, group, piece, stand, thole, unite, wedge
06 endure, gather, growth, nugget, suffer, tumour
07 cluster, collect, combine, stomach, swallow
08 bear with, coalesce, swelling, tolerate
09 carbuncle, put up with
10 protrusion, tumescence
11 consolidate, mix together, put together
12 conglomerate, protuberance

lumpish
05 gawky, heavy
06 clumsy, oafish, obtuse, stolid, stupid
07 awkward, boorish, doltish, hulking
08 bungling, ungainly
09 lethargic, lumbering
10 dull-witted
11 elephantine

lumpy
05 bumpy
06 nodose, nodous
07 bunched, clotted, curdled, knobbly
08 granular

lunacy
05 folly, mania
06 idiocy
07 inanity, madness
08 dementia, insanity
09 absurdity, craziness, stupidity
10 aberration, imbecility
11 derangement, foolishness
12 dementedness, illogicality
13 irrationality, senselessness

lunatic
03 mad
04 daft, nuts
05 barmy, crazy, inane, loony, loopy, nutty, potty, silly
06 absurd, insane, madman, maniac, nutter, psycho
07 bonkers, foolish, idiotic, nutcase, oddball
08 crackpot, demented, deranged, dipstick,

headcase, imbecile, madwoman, neurotic
09 disturbed, fruitcake, psychotic, senseless
10 psychopath, unbalanced
11 hare-brained
12 round the bend
13 off your rocker, round the twist
15 manic-depressive

lunch
06 brunch
08 luncheon
10 midday meal

lunge
03 cut, hit, jab
04 dart, dash, dive, grab, leap, pass, poke, stab
05 bound, hit at
06 charge, grab at, plunge, pounce, spring, strike, thrust
08 fall upon, strike at
09 pitch into

lurch
04 reel, rock, roll, sway, veer
05 pitch
06 swerve, totter
07 stagger, stumble

lure
04 bait, draw
05 decoy, tempt
06 allure, carrot, entice, induce, lead on, seduce
07 attract, beguile, ensnare
08 inveigle
09 seduction
10 allurement, attraction, enticement, inducement, temptation

lurid
04 gory, loud
05 showy, vivid
06 garish, grisly
07 ghastly, graphic, macabre
08 dazzling, explicit, gruesome, horrific, shocking
09 brilliant, revolting, startling
11 exaggerated, sensational
12 melodramatic

lurk
05 prowl, skulk, slink, sneak, snoop
06 crouch, lie low
09 lie in wait

luscious
04 sexy
05 juicy, sweet, tasty, yummy
08 sensuous

lush
09 delicious, desirable, succulent
10 appetizing, delectable
11 scrumptious
13 mouth-watering

lush
03 sot
04 rich, soak, wino
05 alkie, dense, dipso, green
06 boozer, lavish, ornate
07 opulent, profuse, teeming, verdant
08 abundant, drunkard, palatial, prolific
09 alcoholic, luxuriant, sumptuous
11 dipsomaniac, extravagant, flourishing, hard drinker

lust
05 greed
06 desire, hunger, libido
07 avidity, craving, lechery, longing, passion, the hots
08 appetite, cupidity, yearning
09 horniness, prurience, randiness
10 greediness, sensuality
11 sexual drive
12 covetousness, sexual desire
13 concupiscence
14 lasciviousness, licentiousness

◻**lust after**
04 need, want
05 covet, crave
06 desire
07 long for
08 yearn for
09 hunger for, thirst for

lustful
04 lewd
05 horny, randy
06 carnal, wanton
07 craving, raunchy, sensual
08 prurient, unchaste
09 hankering, lecherous, lickerish, salacious
10 cupidinous, lascivious, libidinous, licentious, passionate
12 concupiscent

lustily
08 robustly, strongly
10 forcefully, powerfully, vigorously

lustiness
06 energy, health, vigour
08 haleness, strength, virility

10 robustness, sturdiness
11 healthiness

lustre
04 fame, glow
05 gleam, glint, glory, gloss, merit, sheen, shine
06 credit, honour, renown
07 burnish, glitter, shimmer, sparkle
08 lambency, prestige, radiance
10 brightness, brilliance, refulgence

lustrous
05 shiny
06 bright, glossy
07 glowing, lambent, radiant
08 dazzling, gleaming, luminous
09 burnished, sparkling, twinkling
10 glistening, glittering, shimmering

lusty
04 hale
05 gutsy
06 hearty, robust, sturdy, virile
07 healthy
08 powerful, vigorous
09 energetic, strapping
13 hale and hearty

luxuriance
08 lushness, rankness, richness
09 abundance, denseness, fecundity, fertility, profusion
10 exuberance, lavishness

luxuriant
04 lush, rank, rich
05 ample, dense
06 fecund, florid, lavish, ornate
07 abundant, fertile, flowery, profuse, riotous, teeming
08 prolific, thriving
09 elaborate, plentiful
10 flamboyant, productive
11 extravagant, overflowing
13 superabundant

luxuriate
04 bask
05 bloom, enjoy, revel
06 abound, relish, wallow
07 burgeon, indulge, prosper
08 flourish

luxurious
04 posh, rich
05 cushy, grand, plush
06 de luxe, glitzy, lavish
07 opulent

08 affluent, splendid
09 sumptuous
11 comfortable, magnificent
13 well-appointed

luxury
05 extra, treat
07 comfort
08 grandeur, hedonism, opulence, richness
09 affluence, grandness, splendour
10 costliness, indulgence
12 extravagance, magnificence, satisfaction
13 expensiveness, gratification, sumptuousness

lying
05 false
06 deceit
07 crooked, falsity, fibbing, perjury
08 two-faced
09 deceitful, dishonest, duplicity, invention
10 dishonesty, mendacious, untruthful
11 crookedness, dissembling, fabrication
13 dissimulating, double-dealing, falsification
14 untruthfulness

lynch
04 hang, kill
07 execute
08 string up
10 put to death

lyric
06 direct, poetic, strong
07 musical
09 emotional
10 passionate, subjective

lyrical
06 poetic
07 musical
08 ecstatic, romantic
09 emotional, rapturous, rhapsodic
10 expressive, passionate
11 carried away, impassioned
12 enthusiastic

lyricist see **songwriter**

lyrics
04 book, text
05 words
08 libretto

M m

macabre
04 gory, grim
05 eerie
06 grisly, morbid
07 ghastly, ghostly, hideous
08 chilling, dreadful, gruesome

mace
03 rod
04 club
05 staff, stick
06 cudgel

macerate
04 mash, pulp, soak
05 blend, steep
06 soften
07 liquefy

Machiavellian
04 foxy, wily
06 artful, astute, crafty, shrewd
07 cunning, devious
08 guileful, scheming
09 underhand
10 intriguing, perfidious
11 calculating, opportunist
13 double-dealing

machination
04 plot, ploy, ruse, wile
06 design, device, scheme, tactic
08 artifice, intrigue
09 manoeuvre, stratagem

machine
04 tool
05 motor, organ, robot
06 agency, device, engine, gadget, system, zombie
07 android, vehicle
08 catalyst, hardware
09 apparatus, appliance, automaton, mechanism
10 instrument
11 contraption, contrivance
12 organization

machinery
04 gear
05 tools
06 system, tackle
08 gadgetry, workings
09 apparatus, equipment, mechanism

11 instruments
12 organization

machinist
08 mechanic, operator
09 operative

machismo
08 maleness, virility
09 manliness, toughness
11 masculinity

macrocosm
05 world
06 system
07 culture, society
08 totality, universe
09 community
11 solar system

mad
04 avid, daft, fond, nuts, wild
05 angry, batty, crazy, irate, livid, loony, loopy, manic, nutty, potty, rapid
06 absurd, crazed, fuming, insane, raging
07 bananas, blazing, bonkers, enraged, frantic, furious, hurried, idiotic, lunatic, zealous
08 crackers, demented, deranged, frenzied, incensed, maniacal, reckless, unhinged
09 energetic, fanatical, foolhardy, ludicrous, psychotic, seeing red
10 infatuated, infuriated, off the wall, out to lunch, passionate, unbalanced
11 nonsensical, off your head
12 preposterous, round the bend, uncontrolled
13 of unsound mind, off your rocker, out of your mind, round the twist
14 off your trolley
15 non compos mentis

□**like mad**
06 avidly, wildly
09 furiously, hurriedly, zealously
11 fanatically, frantically

madcap
04 fury, rash, wild
05 crazy, silly
07 flighty, hothead
08 heedless, reckless, tearaway
09 daredevil, desperado, firebrand, foolhardy, hotheaded, impulsive
11 bird-brained, thoughtless

madden
03 bug, irk, vex
05 anger, annoy, upset
06 enrage, hassle
07 agitate, incense, inflame, provoke
09 aggravate, drive nuts, infuriate
10 drive crazy, exasperate
14 drive up the wall
15 get your dander up

maddening
07 galling
08 annoying
09 upsetting, vexatious
10 disturbing, irritating
11 infuriating, troublesome
12 exasperating

made-up
05 false
06 done up, unreal, untrue
07 painted
08 invented, powdered
09 fairy-tale, fictional, imaginary, trumped-up
10 fabricated
11 make-believe

madhouse
05 Babel, chaos
06 asylum, bedlam
08 loony bin, nut-house
09 funny farm
11 pandemonium
13 lunatic asylum
14 mental hospital

madly
06 wildly
07 crazily, hastily, rapidly, utterly
08 insanely
09 devotedly, excitedly, extremely, fervently,

furiously, hurriedly, intensely, violently
10 dementedly, frenziedly, recklessly
11 deliriously, exceedingly, frantically
12 distractedly, hysterically, unreasonably
13 energetically, exceptionally

madman, madwoman
03 nut
05 crank, loony
06 maniac, nutter
07 lunatic, nutcase, oddball
08 crackpot, headcase
09 fruitcake, psychotic, screwball
10 basket case, psychopath

madness
03 ire
04 fury, rage, riot, zeal
05 anger, mania, wrath
06 frenzy, lunacy, raving
07 abandon, passion
08 dementia, hysteria, insanity, wildness
09 craziness, psychosis
11 derangement, enthusiasm, infatuation

maelstrom
05 chaos
06 bedlam, vortex
07 turmoil
09 Charybdis, whirlpool
11 pandemonium

maestro
03 ace
06 expert, genius, master, wizard
08 virtuoso

magazine
05 depot, paper
06 weekly
07 arsenal, journal, monthly
09 quarterly
10 periodical, storehouse, supplement
11 publication
14 ammunition dump
➢ See also **newspaper**

magic
05 charm, curse, great, spell
06 allure, hoodoo, occult, voodoo
07 demonic, glamour, sorcery
08 black art, charming, illusion, magnetic, terrific, trickery, wizardry

09 conjuring, deception, excellent, magnetism, occultism, wonderful
10 bewitching, black magic, enchanting, entrancing, marvellous, mysterious, necromancy, witchcraft
11 captivating, enchantment, fascinating, fascination, legerdemain, thaumaturgy
12 spellbinding, supernatural
13 magical powers, sleight of hand, wonder-working

magician
05 witch
06 expert, wizard
07 warlock
08 conjurer, sorcerer
09 enchanter
11 illusionist, necromancer, spellworker, thaumaturge
12 wonder-worker
13 miracle-worker

magisterial
06 lordly
08 arrogant, despotic
09 assertive, imperious, masterful
10 commanding, high-handed, peremptory
11 dictatorial, domineering, overbearing
13 authoritarian, authoritative

magistrate
02 JP
04 beak
05 judge
07 bailiff, justice, tribune
11 stipendiary

magnanimity
05 mercy
07 charity
08 altruism, kindness, largesse, nobility
10 generosity, liberality
11 beneficence, benevolence, forgiveness, munificence
12 philanthropy, selflessness
13 bountifulness, unselfishness
14 big-heartedness, charitableness

magnanimous
04 kind
05 noble
07 liberal
08 generous, merciful, selfless
09 bountiful, forgiving, unselfish
10 altruistic, beneficent, benevolent, big-hearted,

charitable, munificent, ungrudging
13 philanthropic

magnate
05 baron, mogul
06 bigwig, fat cat, leader, tycoon
07 big shot, notable
09 executive, financier, plutocrat
13 industrialist

magnet
04 bait, draw, lure
05 charm, focus
06 appeal
10 allurement, attraction, enticement, focal point

magnetic
08 alluring, charming, hypnotic, tempting
09 seductive
10 attractive, bewitching, enchanting
11 captivating, charismatic, fascinating, mesmerizing, tantalizing
12 irresistible

magnetism
04 draw, grip, lure, pull
05 charm, magic, power, spell
06 allure
08 charisma
09 hypnotism, mesmerism
10 attraction, temptation
11 captivation, enchantment, fascination
12 drawing power
13 seductiveness

magnification
08 dilation, increase
09 expansion, inflation
11 enhancement, enlargement
12 augmentation, exaggeration, overemphasis
13 amplification
15 intensification

magnificence
04 pomp
05 glory
06 luxury
07 majesty
08 grandeur, opulence
09 splendour
10 brilliance, lavishness
13 luxuriousness, sumptuousness

magnificent
05 grand, royal
06 august, lavish, superb

07 elegant, exalted, opulent, sublime
08 dazzling, glorious, imposing, majestic, splendid, striking
09 brilliant, grandiose, luxurious, sumptuous, wonderful
10 impressive, marvellous
11 resplendent

magnify
06 blow up, deepen, dilate, expand, extend, overdo
07 amplify, broaden, build up, enhance, enlarge, greaten
08 increase, overplay
09 intensify, overstate
10 exaggerate
13 overemphasize

magniloquence
07 bombast, fustian
08 euphuism, rhetoric
09 loftiness, pomposity
10 orotundity
14 grandiloquence
15 pretentiousness

magniloquent
05 lofty
07 exalted, fustian, orotund, pompous, stilted
08 elevated, sonorous
09 bombastic, high-flown,
10 euphuistic, rhetorical
11 declamatory, pretentious
13 grandiloquent

magnitude
04 bulk, mass, note, size
06 amount, extent, moment
07 expanse, measure
08 eminence, quantity, strength
09 amplitude, greatness, intensity
10 dimensions, importance
11 consequence, proportions
12 significance

magnum opus
10 masterwork
11 chef d'oeuvre, masterpiece

maid
04 girl
06 au pair, skivvy
07 abigail, servant
08 domestic, waitress
09 soubrette

maiden
03 new
04 girl, lass, miss, pure
05 first, nymph, unwed

06 chaste, damsel, female, lassie, vestal, virgin
07 girlish, initial
08 virginal, virtuous
09 inaugural, unmarried, young girl, young lady
10 young woman
12 introductory

maidenly
04 pure
05 unwed
06 chaste, decent, demure, female, gentle, modest, proper, seemly, vestal, virgin
07 girlish
08 virginal, virtuous
09 unmarried

mail
04 post, send
05 e-mail
06 armour
07 airmail, forward, letters, packets, panoply, parcels
08 delivery, dispatch, packages
10 Post Office
12 postal system
13 postal service
14 correspondence, electronic mail

maim
04 hurt, lame
05 wound
06 impair, injure
07 cripple, disable
08 mutilate
12 incapacitate
14 put out of action

main
03 key
04 head, pipe
05 cable, chief, first, major, prime, vital
07 central, channel, conduit, crucial, leading, pivotal, premier, primary, supreme
08 cardinal, foremost
09 essential, paramount, principal
10 pre-eminent
11 outstanding, predominant
13 most important

❏in the main
06 mostly
07 as a rule, chiefly, largely, usually
09 generally, in general
10 by and large, especially, on the whole
14 for the most part

mainly
06 mostly
07 as a rule, chiefly, largely, overall, usually
09 generally, in general
10 by and large, especially, on the whole
11 principally
14 for the most part

mainspring
05 cause
06 motive, origin, reason, source
07 impulse
09 generator, incentive
10 motivation, prime mover
11 inspiration
12 driving force, fountainhead

mainstay
04 base, prop
05 basis
06 anchor, pillar
07 bulwark, support
08 backbone, buttress, linchpin
10 foundation

mainstream
07 average, central, general, regular, typical
08 accepted, mainline, orthodox, standard
11 established
12 conventional

maintain
04 aver, avow, feed, hold, keep
05 claim, state
06 affirm, assert, insist, keep up, retain, supply
07 believe, care for, carry on, contend, declare, profess, stand by, support, sustain
08 announce, conserve, continue, fight for, preserve
09 keep going, look after
10 asseverate, perpetuate, provide for, take care of

maintenance
04 care, keep
06 living, upkeep
07 aliment, alimony, nurture, repairs, support
09 allowance, financing
10 livelihood, sustenance
11 continuance, subsistence
12 conservation, continuation, perpetuation, preservation

majestic
05 grand, noble, regal, royal
06 august, kingly, lordly, superb
07 queenly, stately, sublime

08 glorious, imperial, imposing, princely, splendid
09 dignified
10 impressive, monumental

majesty
04 pomp
05 glory
07 dignity, royalty
08 grandeur, nobility, regality
09 splendour, sublimity
11 exaltedness

major
04 main
05 chief, great, older, prime, vital
06 senior
07 crucial, leading, notable, serious, supreme, weighty
08 superior
09 important, paramount
10 pre-eminent
11 outstanding, significant

majority
04 bulk, many, mass, most
08 legal age, maturity
09 adulthood
11 greater part, lion's share
12 age of consent

make
03 net, win
04 cook, earn, form, gain, kind, mark, name, sort, type, urge, vote
05 act as, brand, build, cause, clear, drive, elect, erect, force, frame, gross, impel, model, mould, press, put up, score, shape, style, total, write
06 become, coerce, come to, compel, create, devise, draw up, effect, ordain, reckon, render, secure
07 achieve, acquire, add up to, appoint, arrange, bring in, chalk up, compose, compute, deliver, dragoon, execute, fashion, install, notch up, perform, prepare, produce, realize, require, turn out, variety, work out
08 amount to, assemble, bulldoze, carry out, comprise, engender, estimate, generate, occasion, pressure, reckon up, take home
09 calculate, constrain, construct, designate, discharge, fabricate, get down to, originate,

strongarm, structure, undertake
10 accomplish, bring about, give rise to, pressurize
11 manufacture, mass-produce, prevail upon, put together

❑ **make away with**
04 do in, kill, nick
05 pinch, seize, steal, swipe
06 kidnap, murder, snatch
07 bump off
10 do away with, run off with
11 assassinate, walk off with

❑ **make believe**
04 play
05 dream, enact, feign
07 imagine, play-act, pretend
09 fantasize

❑ **make do**
04 cope
05 get by
06 manage
07 make out, survive
08 get along, scrape by
09 improvise

❑ **make for**
06 aim for, lead to
07 head for, produce, promote
10 facilitate
12 contribute to
13 be conducive to

❑ **make it**
05 reach
06 arrive
07 prosper, succeed, survive
11 come through, pull through

❑ **make off**
05 leave
06 depart, run off
07 run away, scarper
08 clear off
09 cut and run, skedaddle
12 make a getaway
15 take to your heels

❑ **make off with**
04 nick
05 filch, pinch, steal, swipe
06 abduct, kidnap, pilfer
07 purloin
10 run off with
11 appropriate, walk off with

❑ **make out**
03 see
04 aver, cope, espy, fare
05 claim, get by, get on, imply, prove
06 affirm, assert, detect, draw up, fathom, fill in, manage

07 declare, discern, fill out, succeed, work out
08 decipher, describe, get along, maintain, perceive, progress, write out
10 comprehend, understand
11 distinguish

❑ **make over**
05 leave
06 assign, convey
08 bequeath, sign over, transfer

❑ **make up**
05 paint, rouge
06 create, devise, doll up, invent, tart up
07 compose, concoct, dream up, think up
08 complete
09 construct, fabricate, formulate, make peace
10 constitute, shake hands, supplement
12 be reconciled
14 bury the hatchet

❑ **make up for**
06 offset
08 atone for
13 compensate for, make amends for

❑ **make up to**
06 chat up, fawn on
07 toady to
08 butter up
15 curry favour with, make overtures to

❑ **make up your mind**
06 decide
07 resolve
09 determine

❑ **make way**
11 allow to pass, make room for

make-believe
05 dream
06 made-up, unreal
07 charade, fantasy, pretend
08 dreaming, pretence, role-play
09 imaginary, pretended,
10 masquerade, play-acting
11 daydreaming, imagination

maker
06 author
07 builder, creator
08 director, producer
09 architect
10 fabricator
11 constructor
12 manufacturer

makeshift
06 make-do
07 stand-by, stopgap
09 expedient, temporary
10 improvised, substitute
13 rough and ready
14 thrown together
15 cobbled together

make-up
04 form
05 paint, style
06 format, nature, powder
08 assembly, war paint
09 character, cosmetics, formation, structure
10 maquillage
11 arrangement, composition, disposition, greasepaint, personality, temperament
12 construction, organization

making
06 income
07 forging, profits, promise, returns, revenue, takings
08 assembly, building, capacity, creating, creation, earnings, moulding, proceeds
09 materials, modelling, potential, qualities
10 beginnings, capability, production
11 composition, fabrication, ingredients, manufacture
12 construction, potentiality
13 possibilities

◻**in the making**
06 coming
07 budding, nascent
08 emergent
09 incipient, potential
10 burgeoning, developing
11 up and coming

maladjusted
08 neurotic, unstable
09 disturbed, screwed-up

maladministration
07 misrule
08 bungling
10 corruption, misconduct
11 malfeasance, malpractice, misfeasance, mishandling
12 incompetence, inefficiency
13 mismanagement

maladroit
05 inept
06 clumsy, gauche
07 awkward, unhandy
08 bungling, ill-timed, inexpert, tactless, untoward

09 graceless, ham-fisted, inelegant, unskilful
10 cack-handed
11 insensitive, thoughtless
12 undiplomatic

malady
07 ailment, disease, illness, malaise
08 disorder, sickness
09 breakdown, complaint, infirmity
10 affliction
13 indisposition

malaise
05 angst
07 disease, illness
09 sickness, weakness

malapropism
06 misuse
09 wrong word
14 misapplication

malapropos
05 inapt
08 ill-timed, tactless, untimely
10 inapposite, misapplied, unsuitable
11 inopportune, uncalled-for
13 inappropriate

malcontent
05 rebel
06 grouch, moaner, morose
07 unhappy, whinger
08 agitator, grumbler
09 nit-picker, resentful
10 complainer, rebellious
11 belly-aching, disaffected, disgruntled
12 discontented, troublemaker
13 mischief-maker

male
02 he-
05 manly
06 boyish, virile
07 manlike
09 masculine

malediction
05 curse
07 damning, malison
08 anathema
09 damnation
10 execration
11 imprecation

malefactor
05 crook, felon
06 outlaw
07 convict, culprit, villain
08 criminal, evildoer, offender
09 miscreant, misfeasor, wrongdoer

10 delinquent, law-breaker
12 transgressor

malevolence
04 hate
05 spite, venom
06 hatred, malice
07 ill-will, rancour
09 hostility, malignity
10 malignancy
11 viciousness
12 spitefulness, vengefulness
13 maliciousness
14 vindictiveness

malevolent
06 malign
07 baleful, hostile, vicious
08 spiteful, vengeful, venomous
09 malicious, rancorous, resentful
10 evil-minded, maleficent, vindictive

malformation
09 deformity
10 distortion
13 disfigurement, misshapenness

malformed
04 bent
06 warped
07 crooked, twisted
08 deformed
09 distorted

malfunction
04 fail, flaw
05 fault
06 defect, pack up
07 conk out, go kaput, go wrong
09 break down, breakdown

malice
04 hate
05 spite, venom
06 animus, hatred
07 rancour
09 animosity, hostility
10 bitchiness
11 malevolence
13 maliciousness
14 vindictiveness

malicious
04 evil
06 bitter, malign
07 vicious
08 spiteful, vengeful, venomous
10 evil-minded, malevolent

malign
03 bad
04 evil, harm, slur
05 abuse, libel, smear

malignant *(continued)*

06 defame, injure, insult, vilify
07 harmful, hostile, hurtful, run down, slander, traduce
08 badmouth
09 disparage, injurious, malignant
10 calumniate, malevolent
11 destructive

malignant
04 evil
05 fatal
06 deadly, lethal
07 harmful, hostile, vicious
08 spiteful, venomous, virulent
09 cancerous, incurable, malicious
10 malevolent, pernicious
11 destructive
15 life-threatening

malignity
04 gall, hate
05 spite, venom
06 animus, hatred, malice
08 bad blood
09 animosity, hostility
10 deadliness, wickedness
11 hurtfulness, malevolence, viciousness
13 maliciousness

malinger
05 dodge, shirk, skive, slack
12 swing the lead

malingerer
06 dodger, skiver
07 shirker, slacker

mall
05 plaza
08 galleria
14 shopping centre

malleable
06 pliant, supple
07 ductile, plastic, pliable
08 biddable, flexible, tractile, workable
09 compliant, tractable
11 persuadable, susceptible
14 impressionable

malnutrition
06 hunger
08 anorexia
09 inanition
10 starvation
12 underfeeding
15 anorexia nervosa

malodorous
04 rank
05 fetid, niffy
06 putrid, smelly
07 miasmal, miasmic, reeking

08 miasmous, stinking
09 miasmatic, offensive
12 evil-smelling, foul-smelling

malpractice
10 misconduct, negligence, wrongdoing
11 impropriety
12 carelessness
13 mismanagement

maltreat
04 harm, hurt
05 abuse, bully
06 injure, misuse
07 torture
08 ill-treat, mistreat

maltreatment
04 harm, hurt
05 abuse
06 damage, ill-use, injury, misuse
07 torture
08 bullying, ill-usage

mammals

➤ *Types of mammal*:

03 ape, ass, bat, cat, cow, dog, elk, fox, gnu, pig, rat, yak
04 bear, boar, cavy, deer, goat, hare, ibex, kudu, lion, lynx, mink, mole, paca, puma, seal, vole, wolf, zebu
05 aguti, bison, camel, civet, coney, coypu, dingo, eland, genet, horse, human, hyena, hyrax, koala, lemur, llama, loris, moose, mouse, okapi, otter, ounce, panda, potto, rhino, sheep, shrew, skunk, sloth, stoat, tapir, tiger, whale, zebra
06 aye-aye, baboon, badger, beaver, beluga, bobcat, colugo, cougar, coyote, cuscus, dugong, duiker, ermine, ferret, galago, gerbil, gibbon, gopher, hacker, impala, jackal, jaguar, jerboa, langur, marmot, marten, monkey, ocelot, possum, rabbit, rhebok, sea cow, serval, tenrec, vicuna, walrus, wapiti, weasel, wombat
07 ant-bear, buffalo, caracal, caribou, chamois, cheetah, dolphin, echidna, fur seal, gazelle, giraffe, gorilla, grampus, grizzly, guanaco, guereza, gymnura, hamster, lemming, leopard, macaque, manatee, meercat, mole rat,

muntjac, muskrat, narwhal, opossum, pack rat, panther, peccary, polecat, primate, raccoon, red deer, roe deer, sea lion, tamarin, tarsier, wallaby, warthog, wild ass, wildcat
08 aardvark, aardwolf, anteater, antelope, bushbaby, bushbuck, capybara, chipmunk, dormouse, elephant, fruit bat, grey wolf, harp seal, hedgehog, house bat, kangaroo, mandrill, marmoset, mongoose, musk deer, pacarana, pangolin, platypus, porpoise, reedbuck, reindeer, sea otter, sewer rat, squirrel
09 Arctic fox, armadillo, bandicoot, black bear, blue whale, brown bear, dromedary, flying fox, grey whale, guinea pig, mouse-deer, orang utan, phalanger, polar bear, porcupine, springbok, waterbuck, wolverine
10 Barbary ape, chimpanzee, chinchilla, coatimundi, common seal, fallow deer, field mouse, giant panda, house mouse, human being, jack rabbit, kodiak bear, pilot whale, pine marten, prairie dog, rhinoceros, sperm whale, springbuck, vampire bat, white whale, wildebeest
11 grizzly bear, honey badger, killer whale, muntjac deer, pipistrelle, red squirrel, snow leopard
12 elephant seal, grey squirrel, harvest mouse, hippopotamus, mountain goat, mountain lion, rhesus monkey, spider monkey, two-toed sloth, vervet monkey, water buffalo
13 colobus monkey, elephant shrew, howling monkey, humpback whale, spiny anteater, Tasmanian wolf, thylacine wolf
14 capuchin monkey, edible dormouse, flying squirrel, Indian elephant, squirrel monkey, Tasmanian devil, three-toed sloth
15 African elephant, black rhinoceros, humpbacked

whale, proboscis monkey,
ring-tailed lemur,
Thomson's gazelle, white
rhinoceros

➤ See also **animal**; **ape**; **cat**;
cattle; **dog**; **marsupial**;
monkey; **pig**; **rodent**;
sheep; **whale**

mammoth
04 huge, vast
05 giant, jumbo
06 mighty
07 immense, massive
08 colossal, enormous,
gigantic, whopping
09 ginormous, herculean,
leviathan
10 gargantuan, prodigious

man
03 boy, guy, lad
04 chap, crew, hand, male
05 adult, bloke, human, lover,
staff, valet
06 fellow, mortal, people,
person, spouse, worker
07 husband, mankind, partner,
servant, soldier, workman
08 employee, factotum,
houseboy, humanity,
labourer
09 attendant, boyfriend,
gentleman, human race,
humankind, odd-jobman
10 human being, individual,
manservant
11 Homo sapiens

◻**to a man**
05 as one
07 bar none
09 one and all
11 unanimously
12 with one voice

manacle
04 bind, curb
05 chain, check
06 fetter, hamper
07 inhibit, shackle
08 handcuff, restrain
11 put in chains

manacles
05 bonds, cuffs, gyves, irons
06 chains
07 darbies, fetters
08 shackles
09 bracelets, handcuffs

manage
03 run, use
04 cope, fare, head, lead, rule,
work

05 get by, get on, guide
06 direct, effect, govern,
handle, head up, make do,
master
07 achieve, command,
conduct, control, make out,
operate, oversee, succeed,
survive
08 be head of, bring off, deal
with, engineer, get along,
organize
09 influence, supervise
10 accomplish, administer,
bring about, manipulate
11 preside over, superintend
12 be in charge of

manageable
06 doable, docile, pliant, viable
07 pliable
08 amenable, feasible
09 tolerable, tractable
10 attainable, reasonable
11 practicable
13 accommodating

management
04 care
05 board
06 bosses, charge, owners
07 command, control, running
08 handling, managers
09 direction, directors,
executive, governors
10 executives, government,
leadership, overseeing
11 directorate, supervision,
supervisors
12 organization
14 administration

manager
03 guv
04 boss, head
05 chief
06 gaffer, honcho
08 director, governor, overseer
09 executive, organizer
10 controller, supervisor
11 comptroller
12 commissioner
13 administrator
14 chief executive

mandate
03 law
05 edict, order
06 decree, ruling
07 command, statute, warrant
08 sanction
09 authority, direction,
directive, ordinance
10 commission, injunction
11 instruction
13 authorization

mandatory
09 essential
10 compulsory, imperative,
obligatory

manful
04 bold
05 brave, hardy, manly, noble
06 daring, heroic, strong
07 gallant, valiant
08 stalwart, vigorous
10 courageous, determined
11 indomitable, lion-hearted,
unflinching
12 stout-hearted

manfully
04 hard
07 bravely, stoutly
09 gallantly, valiantly
10 heroically, stalwartly,
vigorously
12 courageously, determinedly

manger
04 crib
06 trough

mangle
04 hack, maim, maul, rend, ruin
05 botch, crush, spoil, twist,
wreck
06 bungle, deform, mess up
07 destroy, distort
08 mutilate
09 disfigure
11 make a mess of

mangy
05 dirty, seedy, tatty
06 filthy, scabby, shabby, shoddy
07 scruffy
09 moth-eaten

manhandle
04 haul, maul, pull, push
05 abuse, heave
06 misuse
07 rough up
10 knock about
13 handle roughly

manhood
08 maleness, virility
09 adulthood, manliness
11 masculinity

mania
04 rage
05 craze
06 desire, fetish, frenzy, lunacy
07 craving, madness, passion
08 dementia, fixation, insanity
09 obsession, psychosis
10 compulsion, enthusiasm
11 fascination, infatuation
13 preoccupation

► *Types of mania*:
08 egomania
09 monomania, pyromania, theomania
10 dipsomania, hippomania, narcomania, necromania
11 ablutomania, bibliomania, hedonomania, kleptomania, megalomania, nymphomania
12 thanatomania

maniac
05 crank, loony
06 nutter, psycho
07 fanatic, lunatic, nutcase
08 crackpot, headcase
09 fruitcake, psychotic, screwball
10 enthusiast, psychopath

manifest
04 open, show
05 clear, plain, prove
06 evince, expose, patent, reveal
07 blatant, display, evident, exhibit, express, obvious, visible
08 apparent, distinct, indicate
09 establish, make clear, make plain
10 illustrate
11 conspicuous, demonstrate

manifestation
04 mark, show, sign
05 token
07 display
08 evidence, exposure
10 appearance, exhibition, exposition, expression, indication
12 illustration
13 demonstration
15 exemplification

manifesto
08 platform, policies
09 statement
11 declaration, publication
12 announcement, proclamation

manifold
04 many
06 varied
07 diverse, several, various
08 multiple, numerous
12 multifarious

manipulate
05 guide, knead, steer, wield
06 direct, docto, fiddle, handle, wangle
07 control, exploit, falsify, massage, operate, process, utilize

08 engineer
09 influence
10 juggle with, tamper with
11 pull strings

manipulator
07 handler, schemer, wielder
08 director, engineer, operator
09 exploiter
10 controller, manoeuvrer, negotiator
13 wheeler-dealer

mankind
03 man
06 people
08 humanity
09 human race, humankind
11 Homo sapiens, human beings

manliness
07 bravery, courage
08 boldness, machismo, maleness, strength, virility
10 manfulness, resolution
11 masculinity
12 fearlessness, stalwartness

manly
04 bold
05 brave, macho, tough
06 rugged, strong, virile
08 powerful, vigorous
09 masculine
10 courageous, determined

man-made
06 ersatz
09 imitation, simulated, synthetic
10 artificial
12 manufactured

manner
03 air, way
04 form, look, mien, mode
05 means, style
06 aspect, method, stance
07 bearing, conduct, decorum, fashion, posture, process, p's and q's, routine, variety
08 approach, attitude, courtesy, practice, protocol
09 behaviour, character, demeanour, etiquette, procedure, propriety, technique
10 appearance, deportment, politeness
11 formalities
12 social graces, the done thing
13 way of behaving

mannered
05 posed, put-on

06 pseudo
07 stilted
08 affected, precious
10 artificial, euphuistic
11 pretentious

mannerism
05 habit, quirk, trait
06 foible
11 peculiarity
12 idiosyncrasy
14 characteristic

mannerly
05 civil
06 polite
07 genteel, refined
08 decorous, gracious, polished, well-bred
09 civilized, courteous
10 respectful
11 deferential
12 well-mannered

mannish
05 butch
07 laddish
09 Amazonian, masculine, tomboyish
10 unfeminine, unladylike

mannishness
08 virilism
09 butchness
11 masculinity

manoeuvre
04 move, plan, plot, ploy, ruse
05 dodge, drive, guide, pilot, steer, trick
06 action, device, devise, direct, gambit, handle, jockey, manage, scheme, tactic, wangle
08 contrive, engineer, intrigue, movement, navigate
09 negotiate, stratagem
10 deployment, manipulate, subterfuge
11 machination, pull strings
12 manipulation

manor
03 Hof
04 hall, seat
05 house, villa
06 barony
07 château, Schloss
12 country house

manse
07 deanery, rectory
08 vicarage
09 parsonage
10 glebe-house

manservant
05 valet
06 butler
08 retainer

mansion
04 hall, seat
05 house, manor, villa
10 manor-house

manslaughter
06 murder
07 killing, slaying
08 homicide
09 matricide, patricide, uxoricide
10 fratricide, sororicide
11 infanticide

mantle
04 cape, hide, hood, mask, veil
05 cloak, cover, layer, shawl
06 screen, shroud
07 blanket, conceal, envelop
08 covering, disguise, envelope

manual
03 ABC
05 bible, guide
06 by hand
08 handbook, physical
09 companion, guidebook, vade-mecum
10 directions, prospectus
12 hand-operated, instructions
15 instruction book

manufacture
04 form, make
05 build, forge, frame, model
06 create, devise, invent
07 concoct, dream up, fashion, produce, think up
08 assemble, assembly, building, creation
09 construct, fabricate
10 production
11 fabrication, mass-produce
12 construction
14 mass-production

manufacturer
05 maker
07 builder, creator
08 producer
11 constructor
13 industrialist

manure
04 dung, muck
05 guana
06 ordure
09 droppings
10 fertilizer

manuscript
04 text

05 paper
06 scroll, vellum
08 document
09 parchment

many
04 tons, wads
05 heaps, piles, scads
06 lots of, masses, oodles, scores, stacks
07 copious, diverse, umpteen
08 billions, hundreds, manifold, millions, multiple, numerous, zillions
09 countless, thousands
11 innumerable
13 multitudinous

map
04 plan, plot
05 atlas, chart, graph
06 sketch
08 town plan
09 delineate, gazetteer
10 street plan

◻**map out**
05 draft
06 draw up, sketch
07 outline, work out

mar
04 harm, hurt, maim, ruin, scar
05 spoil, stain, taint, wreck
06 damage, deface, impair
07 blemish, tarnish
08 mutilate
09 disfigure
11 detract from

maraud
04 loot, raid, sack
07 despoil, pillage, plunder, ransack
08 spoliate
09 depredate

marauder
06 bandit, looter, pirate, raider
07 brigand, rustler
08 pillager, predator
09 buccaneer, plunderer
10 freebooter, highwayman

march
04 demo, file, gait, hike, pace, step, trek, walk
05 stalk, strut, tramp, tread
06 parade, stride
07 headway, passage
08 footslog, progress
10 procession
11 development, make headway
13 demonstration

margin
03 rim
04 brim, edge, play, room, side
05 brink, limit, scope, skirt, space, verge
06 border, leeway, limits
07 confine, surplus
08 boundary, confines, latitude
09 allowance, perimeter, periphery
10 difference
12 differential

marginal
05 minor, small
06 minute, slight
07 minimal
09 on the edge
10 borderline, negligible, peripheral
13 insignificant

marijuana
03 kef, pot
04 blow, dope, hash, hemp, leaf, weed
05 bhang, ganja, grass, skunk
07 hashish
08 cannabis

marina
04 dock, port
07 harbour, mooring

marinade
04 soak
05 imbue, souse, steep
07 immerse
08 marinate, permeate, saturate

marine
03 sea
05 naval
07 aquatic, oceanic, pelagic
08 maritime, nautical, seagoing, seawater
09 saltwater, seafaring, thalassic
10 ocean-going, thalassian

mariner
03 tar
04 salt
05 limey
06 sailor, sea dog, seaman
07 Jack Tar, matelot
08 deckhand, seafarer
09 navigator

marital
06 wedded
07 married, nuptial, wedding
08 conjugal, marriage
09 connubial
11 matrimonial

maritime
03 sea
05 naval
06 marine
07 coastal, oceanic, pelagic
08 littoral, nautical, seagoing
09 seafaring

mark
03 aim, cut, end, see, tag
04 blot, chip, clue, dent, flag,
   goal, heed, hint, keep, line,
   logo, mind, name, nick,
   note, scar, seal, sign, spot,
   tick
05 badge, brand, grade, label,
   level, motto, notch, patch,
   point, print, proof, score,
   smear, speck, stage, stain,
   stamp, token, trace, track
06 assess, blotch, bruise,
   device, emblem, notice,
   number, object, pimple,
   regard, smudge, stigma,
   symbol, target, tracks, typify
07 blemish, correct, discern,
   feature, freckle, imprint,
   observe, purpose, quality,
   scratch, specify, symptom
08 appraise, bull's-eye,
   evidence, evaluate, identify,
   indicate, monogram
09 attribute, celebrate,
   character, designate,
   discolour, objective,
   recognize, trademark,
   write down
10 assessment, evaluation,
   impression, indication,
   percentage, take heed of
11 commemorate, distinguish
12 characterize, fingerprints
14 characteristic,
   pay attention to

❑ make one's mark
05 get on
06 make it
07 prosper, succeed
12 be successful

❑ mark down
03 cut
05 lower, slash
06 reduce

❑ mark out
03 fix
07 delimit
08 set apart
09 demarcate, draw lines,
   single out, tell apart
11 distinguish
13 differentiate

❑ mark up
05 put up, raise
06 hike up, jack up

❑ wide of the mark
09 incorrect, off target
10 inaccurate, irrelevant
14 beside the point

marked
05 clear
06 doomed, signal, spotty
07 blotchy, bruised, decided,
   evident, obvious, scarred,
   spotted, stained
08 apparent, blotched, distinct,
   emphatic, striking
09 blemished, condemned,
   prominent, scratched,
   suspected
10 noticeable, pronounced
11 conspicuous

markedly
07 clearly
08 signally
09 blatantly, decidedly,
   evidently, glaringly,
   obviously
10 noticeably, strikingly
11 prominently
12 unmistakably
13 conspicuously

market
04 call, fair, hawk, mall, mart,
   sell
05 agora, trade
06 bazaar, buying, demand,
   desire, outlet, peddle, retail
08 business, dealings,
   exchange, industry
12 offer for sale

❑ on the market
06 on sale
07 for sale
09 available, up for sale

marketable
08 in demand, saleable,
   sellable, vendible

marksman, markswoman
06 sniper
09 crack shot
11 bersagliere
12 sharpshooter

maroon
06 desert, strand
07 abandon, forsake, isolate
08 cast away
09 put ashore

marriage
04 link
05 union

06 fusion, merger
07 wedding, wedlock
08 alliance, coupling, nuptials,
   spousage
09 matrimony
10 connection
11 affiliation, association,
   combination, partnership,
   unification
12 amalgamation, married state
13 confederation

married
03 wed
05 wived, yoked
06 joined, united, wedded
07 hitched, marital, nuptial,
   spliced, spousal
08 conjugal
09 connubial
11 matrimonial

marrow
03 nub
04 core, gist, pith, soul
05 heart, quick, stuff
06 centre, kernel, spirit
07 essence, nucleus
09 substance
12 nuts and bolts, quintessence

marry
03 wed
04 ally, fuse, join, knit, link, weld
05 elope, match, merge, unite
06 couple
07 combine, connect
10 get hitched, get married,
   get spliced, tie the knot
13 take the plunge
14 lead to the altar
15 join in matrimony

marsh
03 bog, fen
04 mire
05 bayou, swamp
06 morass, slough
08 quagmire

marshal
04 lead, rank, take
05 align, array, group, guide,
   order, usher
06 deploy, draw up, escort,
   gather, line up, muster
07 arrange, collect, conduct
08 assemble, organize,
   shepherd

marshy
03 wet
04 miry
05 boggy, fenny, muddy
06 quaggy, slumpy, spongy,
   swampy

07 fennish
08 squelchy
11 waterlogged

marsupial

➤ *Types of marsupial*:
05 koala
06 cuscus, wombat
07 opossum, wallaby
08 kangaroo, wallaroo
09 bandicoot, pademelon, phalanger
11 rat kangaroo, rock wallaby
12 tree kangaroo
13 Tasmanian wolf
14 Tasmanian devil
➤ See also **animal**; **mammal**

martial
04 army
07 warlike
08 militant, military
09 bellicose, soldierly
10 aggressive, pugnacious
11 belligerent

martinet
06 tyrant
08 stickler
10 taskmaster
11 slave-driver
12 taskmistress
14 disciplinarian

martyr
07 crucify, torment, torture
09 persecute
10 put to death
14 burn at the stake
15 throw to the lions

martyrdom
05 agony, death
07 anguish, torment, torture
09 suffering
11 persecution
12 excruciation

marvel
04 gape, gawp, gaze
05 stare
06 genius, wonder
07 miracle, prodigy
09 sensation, spectacle
10 be amazed at, phenomenon

marvellous
05 great, magic, super
06 superb
07 amazing, awesome
08 glorious, splendid, terrific
09 excellent, fantastic, wonderful
10 astounding, incredible, miraculous, stupendous

11 magnificent, sensational, spectacular
13 extraordinary

masculine
04 male
05 butch, macho, manly
06 strong, virile
07 mannish

masculinity
07 manhood
08 machismo, maleness, virility
09 manliness

mash
03 pap
04 beat, mush, pulp
05 crush, grind, pound, purée
06 pummel, squash
09 pulverize

mask
04 hide, veil
05 blind, cloak, cover, front, guise, visor
06 screen, shield, veneer, façade
07 conceal, cover up, obscure
08 disguise, pretence

masquerade
04 play, pose
06 masque
07 cover-up, pretend
08 disguise, pretence
09 deception
10 masked ball
11 costume ball, counterfeit, dissimulate, impersonate
15 fancy-dress party, pass yourself off

mass
03 lot, mob, sum
04 bags, band, body, bulk, heap, herd, hunk, load, lots, lump, most, pile, size, tons
05 amass, batch, block, bunch, chunk, crowd, group, heaps, horde, loads, piece, piles, rally, swarm, troop, wedge
06 gather, muster, rabble, scores, throng
07 cluster, collect, general, popular
08 assemble, majority, quantity
09 abundance, aggregate, Communion, dimension, Eucharist, extensive, hoi polloi, immensity, magnitude, multitude, wholesale
10 accumulate, assemblage, collection, congregate, large-scale

11 greater part, Lord's Supper, proletariat
12 accumulation, come together, common people, working class
13 bring together, Holy Communion
14 conglomeration, the rank and file, working classes

massacre
04 kill, slay
06 murder, pogrom
07 butcher, carnage, wipe out
08 butchery, decimate, genocide, homicide
09 bloodbath, holocaust, liquidate, slaughter
10 decimation
11 exterminate, liquidation
15 ethnic cleansing

massage
03 rub
05 knead
06 pummel
07 Jacuzzi®, rub down, shiatsu
10 manipulate, osteopathy, pummelling
11 acupressure, reflexology
13 physiotherapy

massive
03 big
04 huge, vast
05 bulky, great, heavy, hefty, jumbo, large, solid
06 mighty
07 hulking, immense, mammoth, weighty
08 colossal, enormous, gigantic, whopping
09 extensive, ginormous
10 monumental
11 substantial

mast
03 bar, rod
04 boom, heel, pole, post, spar, yard
05 shaft, staff, stick
07 support, upright

master
03 pro
04 buff, curb, guru, head, lord, main, rule, tame
05 adept, chief, grand, grasp, great, learn, owner, prime, quell, ruler, tutor
06 bridle, defeat, expert, genius, govern, manage, mentor, pundit, subdue

07 acquire, captain, conquer, control, leading, maestro, skilled, skipper, teacher
08 foremost, overcome, overlord, overseer, vanquish, virtuoso
09 commander, overpower, pedagogue, preceptor, principal, subjugate
10 controller, proficient
11 controlling, predominant, triumph over
12 get the hang of, professional, schoolmaster
13 schoolteacher
14 schoolmistress, superintendent

masterful
08 arrogant, powerful
10 autocratic, dominating, high-handed, tyrannical
11 controlling, dictatorial, domineering, overbearing
13 authoritative

masterly
03 ace
05 adept, crack
06 adroit, expert
07 skilful, skilled
08 polished, superior
09 dexterous, excellent
10 consummate
12 accomplished, professional

mastermind
04 plan
05 forge, frame, hatch
06 brains, direct, genius
07 creator, dream up
08 be behind, conceive
09 architect, intellect, organizer
10 prime mover

masterpiece
09 work of art
10 magnum opus, masterwork
11 chef d'oeuvre

mastery
05 grasp, skill
07 ability, command, control, know-how, prowess
08 dominion
09 authority, dexterity, expertise, knowledge, upper hand
10 domination, virtuosity
11 proficiency, sovereignty
13 comprehension, understanding

masticate
03 eat

04 chew
05 champ, chomp, knead, munch
06 crunch

masturbate
04 frig, wank
07 jack off, jerk off, toss off

masturbation
04 frig, wank
07 onanism, tribady, wanking
08 frigging, frottage
09 self-abuse, tribadism
11 hand release
13 autoeroticism
15 self-stimulation

mat
03 rug
04 felt, knot, mass
06 carpet, tangle
07 cluster, coaster, drugget

match
03 fit, vie
04 ally, bout, copy, fuse, game, join, link, mate, meet, pair, peer, suit, team, test, twin, yoke
05 adapt, agree, blend, equal, event, light, marry, rival, spill, tally, taper, trial, union, unite, vesta
06 accord, couple, double, fellow, go with, merger, oppose, pair up, relate
07 combine, compare, compete, connect, contest, pairing, replica
08 alliance, coupling, marriage, parallel, tone with
09 accompany, companion, duplicate, harmonize
10 co-ordinate, competitor, complement, correspond, dead ringer, equivalent, go together, keep up with, one of a pair, pit against, tournament
11 affiliation, combination, competition, counterpart, measure up to, partnership

matching
04 like, same, twin
06 double, paired
07 coupled, similar
08 blending, parallel
09 analogous, identical
10 comparable, equivalent
11 harmonizing
12 co-ordinating
13 complementary, corresponding

matchless
06 unique
07 perfect
08 peerless
10 inimitable
12 incomparable, without equal
13 beyond compare

mate
03 pal, wed
04 chum, join, pair, twin, wife
05 breed, buddy, china, crony, marry, match
06 couple, fellow, friend, helper, spouse
07 compeer, comrade, husband, partner
08 copulate, co-worker, workmate
09 assistant, colleague, companion, other half
10 accomplice, apprentice, better half, equivalent
11 counterpart
12 fellow worker

material
05 cloth, stuff, vital
06 bodily, fabric, matter
07 earthly, germane, serious, textile, weighty, worldly
08 apposite, concrete, palpable, physical, relevant, tangible
09 corporeal, essential, important, momentous, pertinent, substance
11 significant, substantial
13 consequential, indispensable

materialistic
09 mercenary
11 mammonistic
13 money-grabbing

materialize
06 appear, happen, turn up
09 take place, take shape
13 become visible, come into being

materially
07 greatly
09 basically
11 essentially
12 considerably
13 fundamentally, substantially

maternal
06 caring, doting, loving
08 motherly
09 nurturing
10 motherlike, nourishing, protective

mathematics

➤ *Terms used in mathematics include*:

02 pi
03 arc, set
04 apex, area, axes, axis, base, cube, edge, face, line, mean, mode, plus, root, side, sine, skew, unit, zero
05 angle, chaos, chord, curve, depth, equal, graph, helix, locus, minus, point, ratio, solid, speed, total, width
06 binary, chance, convex, cosine, degree, factor, height, length, linear, matrix, median, number, origin, radius, sample, sector, spiral, square, subset, vector, vertex, volume
07 algebra, average, bearing, bounded, breadth, chaotic, concave, decimal, divisor, formula, fractal, integer, maximum, measure, minimum, oblique, product, segment, tangent
08 addition, analysis, bar chart, bar graph, binomial, calculus, constant, converse, cube root, diameter, discrete, dividend, division, equation, exponent, fraction, function, geometry, gradient, identity, infinity, multiple, parabola, pie chart, quadrant, quartile, quotient, rotation, symmetry, variable, variance, vertical
09 algorithm, Cartesian, congruent, factorial, histogram, hyperbola, logarithm, numerator, odd number, operation, parameter, perimeter, remainder
10 acute angle, arithmetic, coordinate, covariance, derivative, even number, horizontal, hypotenuse, percentage, percentile, place value, proportion, protractor, reciprocal, reflection, right-angle, square root, statistics, subtractor
11 coefficient, coordinates, correlation, denominator, determinant, equidistant, exponential, magic square, mirror image, Möbius strip, obtuse angle, permutation, plane figure, prime number, probability, Pythagorean, Venn diagram, whole number
12 asymmetrical, cross section, random sample, trigonometry
13 circumference, complex number, Mandelbrot set, natural number, ordinal number, perpendicular, quadrilateral, triangulation
14 axis of symmetry, cardinal number, mirror symmetry, multiplication, negative number, positive number, rational number, vulgar fraction
15 imaginary number, scalene triangle

➤ *Names of mathematicians*:

03 **Dee** (John), **Lie** (Sophus)
04 **Hero** (of Alexandria), **Venn** (John)
05 **Boole** (George), **Euler** (Leonhard), **Gauss** (Carl Friedrich), **Gödel** (Kurt), **Klein** (Felix), **Peano** (Giuseppe)
06 **Euclid**, **Fermat** (Pierre de), **Fisher** (Sir Ronald Aylmer), **Galois** (Évariste), **Möbius** (August Ferdinand), **Napier** (John), **Newton** (Sir Isaac), **Pappus** (of Alexandria), **Pascal** (Blaise), **Turing** (Alan Mathison), **Wiener** (Norbert)
07 **Alhazen**, **Babbage** (Charles), **Cardano** (Girolamo), **Eudoxus** (of Cnidus), **Fourier** (Jean Baptiste Joseph, Baron de), **Hilbert** (David), **Laplace** (Pierre Simon, Marquis de), **Leibniz** (Gottfried Wilhelm), **Poisson** (Siméon Denis), **Riemann** (Bernhard), **Russell** (Bertrand, Earl)
08 **Dedekind** (Julius Wilhelm Richard), **Lagrange** (Joseph Louis de, Comte), **Lovelace** (Ada, Countess of), **Poincaré** (Jules Henri)
09 **Bernoulli** (Daniel), **Bronowski** (Jacob), **Descartes** (René), **Fibonacci** (Leonardo), **Minkowski** (Hermann), **Whitehead** (Alfred North)
10 **Apollonius** (of Perga), **Archimedes**, **Diophantus**, **Pythagoras**, **Torricelli** (Evangelista)
11 **al-Khwarizmi**
12 **Eratosthenes**
➤ See also **scientist**

mating

06 fusing
07 coition, pairing, uniting
08 breeding, coupling, matching
10 copulating

matrimonial

06 wedded
07 marital, nuptial, wedding
08 conjugal, marriage

matrimony

07 wedlock
08 marriage, nuptials, spousage
09 espousals
12 married state

matted

06 tangly
07 knotted, tangled, tousled
08 uncombed

matter

03 pus
04 body, case, note
05 count, event, issue, stuff, topic, upset, value
06 affair, bother, import, medium, weight
07 concern, content, episode, problem, subject, trouble
08 business, incident, interest, material, nuisance, question
09 discharge, happening, purulence, secretion, situation, substance
10 be relevant, importance, occurrence, proceeding
11 be important, carry weight, consequence, suppuration
12 circumstance, significance
13 have influence, inconvenience, mean something
15 make a difference

❑ **as a matter of fact**
06 in fact, really
08 actually
11 as it happens
12 in actual fact

❑ **no matter**
09 never mind
15 it does not matter, it is unimportant

matter-of-fact

04 dull, flat
05 sober

07 deadpan, prosaic
08 lifeless
10 pedestrian
11 down-to-earth,
emotionless, unemotional
13 unimaginative,
unsentimental
15 straightforward

mature
03 age
04 ripe, wise
05 adult, bloom, grown, of age,
ready, ripen
06 evolve, grow up, mellow
07 develop, fall due, grown-up,
perfect, ripened
08 balanced, complete,
finished, seasoned,
sensible
09 come of age, finalized,
full-grown, perfected
11 experienced, responsible
13 well-developed
14 well-thought-out

maturity
06 wisdom
07 manhood
08 majority, ripeness
09 adulthood, womanhood
10 experience, mellowness
11 coming of age
14 responsibility

maudlin
05 drunk, gushy, mushy, soppy,
tipsy, weepy
06 sickly, slushy
07 fuddled, mawkish, tearful
09 emotional, half-drunk,
schmaltzy
10 lachrymose
11 sentimental

maul
03 mug, paw
04 beat, belt, claw
05 abuse
06 attack, batter, mangle,
molest, thrash, wallop
07 assault
08 lacerate, maltreat, mutilate
09 manhandle

maunder
06 babble, gabble, jabber,
mutter, natter, rabbit,
ramble, waffle, witter
07 blather, chatter, prattle
08 rabbit on

mausoleum
04 tomb
05 crypt, vault
08 catacomb

09 sepulchre
13 burial chamber

maverick
05 rebel
08 agitator, outsider
13 individualist, nonconformist

maw
04 jaws
05 abyss, chasm, mouth
06 gullet, throat

mawkish
05 gushy, mushy, soppy
06 feeble, sickly, slushy
07 maudlin
09 emotional, schmaltzy
11 sentimental

maxim
03 saw
04 rule
05 adage, axiom, gnome, motto
06 byword, saying
07 epigram, precept, proverb
08 aphorism

maximum
04 acme, most, peak
06 apogee, height, summit,
utmost, zenith
07 biggest, ceiling, highest,
largest, supreme, topmost
08 greatest, pinnacle
09 extremity
10 upper limit

maybe
07 perhaps
08 possibly
09 perchance
12 peradventure

mayhem
05 chaos
06 bedlam, tumult, uproar
07 anarchy
08 disorder, madhouse

maze
06 jungle, puzzle, tangle
07 complex, network
09 confusion, intricacy,
labyrinth

meadow
03 lea
04 mead
05 field, grass, green
07 paddock, pasture
09 grassland
11 pastureland

meagre
04 poor, puny, thin
06 measly, paltry, scanty,
skimpy, slight, sparse, stingy

08 exiguous
09 niggardly
10 negligible

meagreness
08 puniness
10 measliness, scantiness,
sparseness, stinginess
13 insufficiency

meal

➤ *Meals include*:
03 tea
04 bite
05 feast, lunch, snack
06 brunch, buffet, dinner, nosh-
up, picnic, repast, spread,
supper, tiffin
07 banquet, blow-out, high-tea
08 barbecue, cream-tea,
luncheon, take-away,
tea-party, TV dinner
09 breakfast, elevenses
10 midday meal, slap-up meal
11 dinner party, evening meal
12 afternoon tea

mealy-mouthed
04 glib, prim
07 mincing
08 indirect, reticent
09 equivocal, plausible
10 flattering
11 euphemistic
13 smooth-tongued

mean
03 aim
04 fate, mode, norm, plan,
show, wish, wont
05 cause, cross, cruel, dirty,
imply, lowly, mingy, nasty,
tight
06 aspire, common, convey,
denote, design, dismal,
entail, humble, intend, lead
to, median, medium,
middle, ordain, shabby,
stingy, unkind
07 appoint, average, betoken,
connote, destine, express,
halfway, involve, miserly,
obscure, produce, propose,
purport, purpose, selfish,
signify, squalid, suggest
08 grasping, indicate, intimate,
middling, mid-point,
ordinary, result in, stand for,
wretched
09 designate, miserable,
niggardly, represent,
symbolize

10 bring about, compromise, give rise to, have in mind, unpleasant
11 close-fisted, happy medium, tight-fisted
12 intermediate, parsimonious
13 penny-pinching

meander
04 bend, roam, wind
05 amble, mosey, snake
06 ramble, stroll, wander, zigzag

meandering
07 sinuous, snaking, winding
08 indirect, tortuous, twisting
10 serpentine

meaning
03 aim
04 gist, goal, idea, plan, wish
05 drift, point, sense, trend, value, worth
06 import, object, thrust
07 essence, message, purpose
09 intention, objective, substance
10 aspiration, definition, expression
11 connotation, elucidation, explanation, explication, implication
12 significance
13 signification
14 interpretation

meaningful
07 pointed, warning
08 eloquent, material, pregnant, relevant
10 purposeful, worthwhile
11 significant

meaningless
05 empty
06 absurd, futile, hollow
07 aimless, useless, vacuous
09 pointless, senseless, worthless
10 motiveless
14 unintelligible

meanness
09 parsimony
10 stinginess
11 miserliness
15 close-fistedness, tight-fistedness

means
03 way
05 funds, money
06 agency, assets, avenue, course, income, manner,

medium, method, riches, wealth
07 capital, channel, fortune, process, vehicle
09 affluence, resources, substance
11 wherewithal

□**by all means**
08 of course
09 certainly, naturally

□**by means of**
03 via
05 using
08 by dint of
12 with the aid of
13 with the help of

□**by no means**
05 never, no way
08 not at all
12 certainly not

meantime, meanwhile
06 for now
12 for the moment, in the interim
15 for the time being

measly
04 mean, poor, puny
05 mingy, petty
06 meagre, paltry, scanty, skimpy, stingy
07 miserly, pitiful
08 beggarly, pathetic, piddling
09 miserable, niggardly
12 contemptible

measurable
10 assessable, computable, fathomable
11 appreciable, perceptible
12 quantifiable, quantitative

measure
04 area, bulk, deed, mass, norm, part, rate, read, rule, size, step, time, unit
05 depth, gauge, judge, level, meter, piece, plumb, quota, range, ruler, scale, scope, share, sound, units, value, weigh, width
06 action, amount, assess, course, degree, extent, fathom, height, length, ration, record, size up, survey, system, volume, weight
07 compute, expanse, portion, rake-off, statute
08 appraise, capacity, division, estimate, evaluate, quantify, quantity, standard

09 allotment, benchmark, calculate, criterion, determine, magnitude, procedure, yardstick
10 allocation, dimensions, proceeding, touchstone
11 proportions

□**beyond measure**
09 endlessly, immensely
10 infinitely
12 beyond belief, incalculably

□**for good measure**
06 as well
08 as a bonus
10 in addition
11 furthermore
12 over and above

□**measure off**
07 mark out, measure, pace out
10 measure out

□**measure out**
05 allot, issue
07 deal out, dole out, hand out
08 dispense, share out
09 apportion, parcel out
10 distribute

□**measure up**
07 shape up
10 fit the bill, pass muster
12 make the grade
15 come up to scratch

□**measure up to**
05 equal, match, touch
08 come up to, live up to
09 match up to
11 compare with

measured
04 slow
06 steady
07 careful, planned, precise
09 unhurried
10 considered, deliberate
14 well-thought-out

measureless
07 endless, immense
08 infinite
10 bottomless

measurement
04 area, bulk, mass, size, unit
05 depth, range, width
06 amount, extent, height, length, sizing, volume, weight
07 expanse, reading
08 capacity, quantity
09 appraisal, dimension, judgement
10 estimation, evaluation, proportion

11 calculation, calibration, computation, proportions
14 quantification

➤ *Measurements include*:
03 bar, day, erg, ohm, rod, ton
04 acre, foot, gill, gram, hand, hour, inch, knot, mile, mole, pint, span, volt, watt, week, yard, year
05 cable, chain, farad, hertz, joule, litre, lumen, metre, month, ounce, pound, stone, therm, tonne
06 ampere, bushel, decade, degree, fathom, gallon, kelvin, league, minute, newton, pascal, radian, second
07 calorie, candela, century, coulomb, decibel, furlong, hectare
08 angstrom, kilogram, millibar
09 becquerel, cubic foot, cubic inch, cubic yard, foot-pound, kilometre
10 atmosphere, centimetre, cubic metre, fluid ounce, horsepower, micrometre, millennium, millilitre, square foot, square inch, square mile, square yard
11 square metre
12 nautical mile
13 hundredweight
15 cubic centimetre, square kilometre

measuring instruments
➤ *Types of measuring instrument*:
04 rule
05 gauge, meter
06 octant
07 ammeter, balance, burette, pipette, sextant
08 quadrant
09 altimeter, barometer, callipers, hourglass, optometer, pedometer, plumb line, pyrometer, steelyard, stopwatch, voltmeter
10 anemometer, audiometer, bathometer, gravimeter, hydrometer, micrometer, photometer, protractor, tachometer, tachymeter, theodolite
11 seismograph, speedometer, tape measure, tensiometer, thermometer, weighbridge

12 Breathalyser®, galvanometer
13 Geiger counter
➤ See also **gauge**

meat
03 nub
04 core, crux, gist, grub, pith
05 flesh, heart, point
06 kernel, marrow, viands
07 essence, nucleus
09 substance
➤ See also **food**

➤ *Cuts of meat*:
03 leg, rib
04 chop, hock, loin, neck, rump, shin
05 chine, flank, scrag
06 breast, collar, cutlet, fillet, saddle
07 brisket, sirloin, topside
08 escalope, shoulder, spare-rib
10 silverside

➤ *Some types of meat*:
03 ham
04 beef, duck, hare, lamb, paté, pork
05 bacon, brawn, goose, heart, liver, offal, steak, tripe
06 brains, faggot, gammon, kidney, mutton, oxtail, pigeon, rabbit, tongue, turkey
07 chicken, rissole, sausage, venison
08 trotters
09 hamburger
10 beefburger, minced beef, sweetbread
11 pig's knuckle
12 black pudding

meaty
05 beefy, burly, heavy, hunky, pithy, solid
06 brawny, fleshy, hearty, sturdy
08 profound
10 meaningful
11 substantial

mechanic
08 engineer, operator
09 repairman
10 technician

mechanical
07 routine
08 habitual
09 automated, automatic
11 emotionless, instinctive, involuntary, machine-like, power-driven, unconscious
14 machine-powered

mechanism
05 gears, means, motor, works
06 device, engine, gadget
07 channel, machine, process
08 movement, workings
09 apparatus, appliance, machinery, procedure, structure, technique
11 contraption, contrivance

medal
04 gong
05 award, prize
09 medallion
10 decoration
➤ See also **military**

meddle
06 butt in, tamper
07 intrude
09 interfere, intervene
12 put your oar in
14 poke your nose in, stick your oar in
15 stick your nose in

meddlesome
04 nosy
09 intruding, intrusive
11 interfering, mischievous

mediate
06 umpire
07 referee
08 moderate
09 arbitrate, intercede, interpose, intervene
10 conciliate

mediation
11 arbitration, good offices, peacemaking
12 conciliation, intercession, intervention

mediator
06 umpire
07 arbiter, referee
09 go-between, middleman, moderator, ombudsman
10 arbitrator, interceder, peacemaker
11 conciliator, intercessor
12 intermediary

medical
➤ *Types of medical equipment*:
03 ECG, MRI
05 clamp, swabs
06 scales
07 cannula, curette, forceps, inhaler, scalpel, scanner, syringe

08 catheter, iron lung, speculum, tweezers, X-ray unit
09 CT scanner, aspirator, auriscope, autoclave, endoscope, incubator, nebulizer, retractor
10 CAT scanner, audiometer, ear syringe, hypodermic, kidney dish, microscope, oxygen mask, respirator, sterilizer, ultrasound
11 body scanner, first aid kit, stethoscope, stomach pump, thermometer
12 resuscitator, surgical mask
13 defibrillator
14 operating table, ophthalmoscope, oxygen cylinder

➤ *Types of medical specialist*:
06 doctor
07 dentist
08 optician
09 dietician
10 homoeopath, oncologist, pharmacist
11 chiropodist, neurologist, optometrist, pathologist
12 anaesthetist, cardiologist, chiropractor, embryologist, geriatrician, obstetrician, orthodontist, orthopaedist, psychiatrist, psychologist, toxicologist
13 dermatologist, gynaecologist, haematologist, paediatrician
14 bacteriologist, pharmacologist
15 endocrinologist, ophthalmologist, physiotherapist

➤ See also **doctor**; **nurse**

medicinal
07 healing, medical
08 curative, remedial
11 restorative, therapeutic

medicine
04 cure, drug
06 remedy
07 panacea
09 analeptic
10 medicament, medication
12 prescription
14 pharmaceutical

➤ See also **therapy**

➤ *Types of medicine*:
04 pill
05 tonic

06 arnica, emetic, gargle, tablet
07 antacid, capsule, inhaler, linctus, lozenge
08 ear drops, eye drops, laxative, ointment, pastille
09 paregoric
10 antibiotic, gripe-water, nasal spray, painkiller, penicillin
11 suppository

➤ See also **drug**

medieval
07 antique, archaic
08 historic, obsolete, old-world, outmoded
09 primitive
10 antiquated
12 antediluvian, old-fashioned
13 unenlightened

mediocre
04 so-so
07 average
08 adequate, inferior, middling, ordinary, passable
10 pedestrian, uninspired
11 commonplace, indifferent
12 run-of-the-mill
13 insignificant, no great shakes, unexceptional
15 undistinguished

mediocrity
08 dead loss, poorness
09 nonentity
11 inferiority
12 indifference, ordinariness unimportance

meditate
04 muse, plan
05 brood, study, think
06 devise, ponder
07 reflect
08 cogitate, consider, mull over, ruminate
09 think over
10 deliberate
11 contemplate

meditation
05 study
06 musing
07 reverie, thought
08 brooding
09 pondering
10 brown study, cogitation, reflection, rumination
11 cerebration, mulling over, speculation
12 deliberation, excogitation
13 concentration, contemplation

meditative
07 museful, pensive

08 ruminant, studious
10 cogitative, reflective, ruminative, thoughtful
12 deliberative
13 contemplative

medium
03 way
04 mean, mode, norm
05 means, organ
06 agency, avenue, centre, median, middle, midway
07 average, channel, habitat, psychic, vehicle
08 ambience, middling, midpoint, standard
09 spiritist
10 atmosphere, compromise, golden mean, instrument
11 clairvoyant, environment, necromancer
12 intermediate, middle ground, spiritualist

medley
03 mix
06 jumble
07 farrago, melange, mixture, variety
08 mixed bag
09 potpourri
10 assortment, hodge-podge, hotchpotch, miscellany
14 conglomeration, omnium-gatherum

meek
04 mild, tame, weak
05 lowly, quiet, timid
06 docile, gentle, humble, modest
07 patient
08 peaceful, resigned, yielding
09 compliant, spineless
10 forbearing, spiritless, submissive, unassuming
11 deferential
13 long-suffering, unpretentious

meekness
08 docility, humility, mildness, softness, timidity, weakness
09 deference
10 gentleness, humbleness, submission
12 acquiescence, peacefulness
14 submissiveness

meet
04 abut, bear, face, join, link
05 cross, equal, match, rally, touch, unite

06 adjoin, answer, fulfil, gather, handle, link up, manage, muster, pay for, suffer, tackle
07 collect, connect, convene, execute, perform, run into, satisfy
08 assemble, bump into, come up to, converge, cope with, deal with
09 discharge, encounter, forgather, intersect, look after, run across
10 come across, comply with, congregate, experience, happen upon, join up with, rendezvous
11 get together, measure up to
12 come together

meeting
04 date
05 tryst, union, venue
07 contact, session
08 abutment, junction
09 concourse, encounter, gathering, interface
10 confluence, rendezvous
11 appointment, assignation, conjunction, convergence
12 intersection, introduction
13 confrontation
14 point of contact

megalomania
13 conceitedness
14 self-importance
15 folie de grandeur

melancholy
03 low, sad
04 blue, down, glum
05 blues, dumps, gloom, moody
06 dismal, gloomy, sorrow, woeful
07 sadness, unhappy
08 dejected, doldrums, downcast, mournful
09 pessimism, woebegone
10 depression, despondent, dispirited, low spirits, lugubrious
11 downhearted, unhappiness
12 disconsolate, heavy-hearted
14 down in the dumps

melange
06 jumble
07 farrago, mixture, variety
08 mixed bag
10 assortment, collection, hodge-podge, hotchpotch, miscellany, salmagundi
14 conglomeration

melee
04 fray, mess
05 brawl, broil, chaos, fight, mix-up, scrum, set-to
06 affray, fracas, jumble, ruckus, rumpus, tussle
07 clutter, ruction, scuffle
08 disorder, stramash
09 confusion
10 free-for-all

mellifluous
05 sweet
06 dulcet, mellow, smooth
07 honeyed, silvery, tuneful
10 euphonious, harmonious
13 sweet-sounding

mellow
05 juicy, ripen, sweet
06 dulcet, genial, mature, placid, serene, smooth, soften, temper
07 affable, amiable, improve, relaxed, rounded, sweeten, tuneful
08 luscious, pleasant, tranquil
09 easy-going, melodious
10 harmonious
13 full-flavoured

melodious
05 sweet
06 dulcet
07 melodic, musical, tuneful
10 euphonious, harmonious
13 sweet-sounding

melodramatic
05 hammy, stagy
10 histrionic, theatrical
11 exaggerated, sensational
12 overdramatic
13 overemotional

melody
03 air
04 song, tune
05 music, theme
06 rhythm, strain
07 euphony, harmony, refrain
11 musicalness, tunefulness
14 harmoniousness

melt
04 fuse, thaw
06 soften
07 defrost, liquefy
08 dissolve, unfreeze
10 deliquesce

❑ **melt away**
08 disperse, dissolve, evanesce, fade away
09 disappear, evaporate

member
03 arm, leg
04 limb
05 organ
09 appendage, associate, extremity
14 representative

membership
09 adherents, enrolment
10 associates, fellowship
11 affiliation, subscribers
15 representatives

membrane
04 film, skin
05 hymen, velum
06 septum, tissue
09 diaphragm

memento
05 relic, token
06 record, trophy
08 keepsake, memorial, reminder, souvenir
11 remembrance

memoir
07 account, journal
09 biography, chronicle

memoirs
06 annals
07 diaries, records
08 journals, memories
09 life story
10 chronicles
11 confessions, experiences
13 autobiography, recollections, reminiscences

memorable
10 impressive, noteworthy, remarkable
11 distinctive, outstanding, significant
13 consequential, distinguished, extraordinary, unforgettable

memorandum
04 memo, note
07 message
08 reminder

memorial
06 plaque, shrine
07 memento
08 cenotaph, monument, souvenir
09 mausoleum
11 remembrance
13 commemorative

memorize
05 learn
08 remember
11 learn by rote

12 learn by heart
14 commit to memory

memory
06 honour, recall
07 tribute
11 recognition, remembrance
13 commemoration
12 recollection, reminiscence
14 powers of recall

menace
04 loom, lour, pain, pest, risk
05 alarm, appal, bully, daunt, peril, press, scare
06 bother, coerce, danger, dismay, hazard, threat
07 terrify, warning
08 browbeat, bullying, coercion, jeopardy, nuisance, pressure, threaten
09 terrorize
10 intimidate, pressurize
11 frighteners, ominousness, terrorizing
15 thorn in your side

menacing
07 looming, louring, ominous
08 alarming, minatory, sinister
09 Damoclean, impending
10 portentous
11 threatening
12 intimidating, intimidatory

mend
03 fix, sew
04 cure, darn, heal
05 amend, emend, patch, refit, renew, stick
06 cobble, reform, remedy, repair, revise
07 correct, improve, patch up, recover, rectify, restore
08 put right, renovate
09 get better, make whole
10 ameliorate, recuperate

□ **on the mend**
07 healing
09 improving
10 recovering
12 convalescent, convalescing, recuperating

mendacious
05 false, lying
06 untrue
09 deceitful, deceptive, dishonest, insincere
10 fictitious, perfidious, untruthful
11 duplicitous

mendacity
05 lying
06 deceit

07 perfidy, perjury, untruth
09 duplicity, falsehood
10 dishonesty, distortion
13 deceitfulness, falsification
14 untruthfulness

mendicant
06 beggar, cadger
07 begging, cadging, moocher
09 scrounger
10 scrounging, supplicant
11 petitionary

menial
05 lowly, slave
06 drudge, minion, skivvy
07 humdrum, servant, servile, slavish
08 dogsbody
09 attendant, degrading, demeaning, underling, unskilled

menstruation
06 menses, period
08 the curse
09 monthlies
10 menorrhoea
11 monthly flow
14 menstrual cycle

mensuration
09 measuring, surveying, valuation
10 assessment, estimation, evaluation
11 calculation, calibration, computation, measurement

mental
03 mad
04 nuts
05 barmy, crazy, loony
06 insane
07 bonkers, lunatic
08 abstract, cerebral
09 cognitive, disturbed, psychotic
10 conceptual, unbalanced
11 off your head, theoretical
12 intellectual
14 off your trolley

mentality
04 mind
06 brains, make-up
07 faculty, mindset, outlook
08 attitude
09 character, intellect
10 grey matter, psychology
11 disposition, frame of mind
12 intelligence
13 comprehension, understanding, way of thinking

mentally
08 inwardly
09 in the mind
11 emotionally
14 intellectually
15 psychologically, temperamentally

mention
03 say
04 cite, name
05 quote, state
06 broach, impart, remark, report
07 bring up, declare, divulge, refer to, speak of, touch on
08 allude to, allusion, citation, disclose, intimate, point out
09 reference, statement
11 acknowledge, communicate, observation
12 announcement, notification
15 acknowledgement

□ **don't mention it**
08 not at all
08 forget it
09 don't worry
12 it's a pleasure, it was nothing

□ **not to mention**
07 besides
08 as well as, let alone
12 not including
13 not forgetting
14 to say nothing of

mentioned
05 cited
06 quoted, stated
08 foresaid, reported
09 aforesaid, forenamed
13 forementioned
14 above-mentioned

mentor
04 guru
05 coach, guide, swami, tutor
07 adviser, teacher
09 pedagogue, therapist
10 counsellor, instructor

menu
04 card, list
06 tariff
10 bill of fare
11 carte du jour

mercantile
07 trading
08 saleable
10 commercial, marketable

mercenary
05 hired, venal
06 greedy, sordid
08 covetous, grasping, hireling

09 freelance, on the make
10 avaricious, galloglass
11 acquisitive, condottiere
12 hired soldier
13 materialistic,
   money-grubbing
15 money-orientated

merchandise
04 hype, plug, push, sell, vend
05 cargo, carry, goods, stock,
   trade, wares
06 deal in, market, peddle,
   retail, supply
07 freight, produce, promote
08 products, shipment
09 advertise, publicize, traffic
   in, vendibles
10 buy and sell

merchant
06 broker, dealer, seller, trader,
   vendor
08 retailer, salesman
10 saleswoman, shopkeeper,
   trafficker, wholesaler
11 distributor, salesperson
14 sales executive

merciful
04 kind
06 humane
07 lenient, liberal
08 generous, gracious, tolerant
09 forgiving
10 forbearing
13 compassionate,
   tender-hearted

merciless
05 cruel, harsh, rigid, stern
06 severe
07 callous, inhuman
08 inhumane, pitiless, ruthless
09 heartless, unpitying,
   unsparing
10 implacable, inexorable,
   intolerant, relentless
11 hard-hearted, remorseless,
   unforgiving

mercurial
07 erratic, flighty
08 spirited, unstable,
   volatile
10 capricious, inconstant
13 temperamental,
   unpredictable

mercy
04 boon, pity
05 grace
06 favour, relief
07 godsend
08 blessing, clemency, leniency,
   mildness

10 compassion, humaneness
11 forbearance, forgiveness
◻ **at the mercy of**
09 exposed to
11 at the whim of
12 in the power of, vulnerable
   to

mere
04 bare, pure
05 petty, plain, sheer, utter
06 common, paltry, simple
08 absolute, complete
10 no more than
13 pure and simple

merely
04 just, only
06 barely, hardly, purely, simply
08 scarcely
10 nothing but

merge
03 mix
04 fuse, join, meet, meld
05 blend, unite
06 mingle, team up
07 combine, run into
08 coalesce, converge, intermix
10 amalgamate, join forces
11 consolidate, incorporate

merger
05 blend, union
06 fusion
08 alliance
09 coalition
11 combination, convergence
12 amalgamation, assimilation
13 confederation,
   consolidation,
   incorporation

merit
05 asset, claim, value, worth
06 credit, reward, talent, virtue
07 deserts, deserve, justify,
   quality, warrant
08 goodness
09 advantage
10 excellence, worthiness
11 high quality, strong point
13 justification

merited
03 due
04 just
06 earned, worthy
07 condign, fitting
08 deserved, entitled, rightful
09 justified, warranted
11 appropriate

meritorious
08 laudable, virtuous
09 deserving, estimable

10 creditable, honourable
11 commendable
12 praiseworthy

merriment
03 fun
05 mirth
06 frolic, gaiety
07 jollity, revelry
08 hilarity, laughter
09 festivity, jocundity
11 high spirits

merry
04 glad
05 happy, jolly, tipsy
06 blithe, cheery, jovial, joyful
07 amusing, festive
08 carefree, cheerful, mirthful
09 convivial
12 light-hearted
◻ **make merry**
04 sing
05 dance, drink
07 carouse, have fun
09 celebrate
10 have a party
13 enjoy yourself

merry-go-round
08 carousel
09 whirligig
10 roundabout

merrymaking
03 fun
05 party, revel
06 gaiety
07 revelry
08 carousal
09 festivity, merriment
11 celebration
13 jollification

mesh
03 net, web
04 trap
05 match, snare
06 engage, tangle
07 combine, connect, lattice,
   netting, network, tracery,
   trellis
09 harmonize, interlock
10 co-ordinate, go together
11 fit together, latticework

mesmerize
07 enthral, stupefy
08 entrance, transfix
09 captivate, fascinate,
   hypnotize, magnetize,
   spellbind

mess
03 fix, jam
04 hash, hole, spot, stew

05 botch, chaos, farce, filth, mix-up

06 bungle, cock-up, hiccup, jumble, litter, muddle, pickle, plight

07 balls-up, clutter, dilemma, failure, squalor, trouble, turmoil

08 disarray, disorder, hot water, quandary, shambles

09 confusion, deep water, dirtiness, tight spot

10 difficulty, dog's dinner, filthiness, pretty pass, untidiness

11 predicament

13 dog's breakfast, pig's breakfast

❏ mess about, mess around

09 faff about, muck about, play about

10 faff around, fool around, play around

11 potter about

❏ mess about with, mess around with

05 upset

06 bother

07 trouble

08 play with

10 meddle with, tamper with

13 fool about with, inconvenience, interfere with, play about with

14 fool around with, play around with

❏ mess up

04 foul, muff, ruin

05 bodge, botch, dirty, fluff, spoil

06 bungle, cock up, foul up, jumble, muck up, muddle, tangle, untidy

07 confuse, disrupt, louse up, screw up

08 dishevel

10 disarrange

11 make a hash of

message

03 fax

04 gist, idea, memo, note, word

05 cable, drift, moral, point, sense, theme

06 errand, notice, thrust

07 epistle, essence, meaning, missive, purport

08 bulletin, dispatch

10 communiqué, memorandum

11 implication

12 significance

13 communication

❏ get the message

06 follow, take in

07 catch on

08 cotton on

10 comprehend, get the idea, understand

11 get the point

13 catch the drift

messenger

05 agent, envoy

06 bearer, herald, Hermes, runner

07 carrier, courier

08 emissary

09 errand-boy, go-between, harbinger

messy

05 dirty

06 filthy, grubby, sloppy, untidy

07 chaotic, muddled, unkempt

08 confused, littered, slobbish, slovenly

09 cluttered, shambolic

10 disordered, in disarray

11 dishevelled

metal

➤ *Names of metal alloys. We have omitted the word* **metal** *from names given in the following list but you may need to include this word as part of the solution to some crossword clues.*

03 pot

04 type

05 brass, Dutch, Invar ®, Muntz, potin, steel, terne, white

06 bronze, latten, occamy, ormolu, oroide, pewter, solder, tambac, tombac, tombak, Y-alloy

07 amalgam,, chromel, shakudo, similor, tutania, tutenag

08 cast iron, gunmetal, Nichrome ®, orichalc, speculum, zircaloy, Zircoloy ®

09 Britannia, Duralumin ®, Dutch gold, Dutch leaf, magnalium, pinchbeck, shibuichi, white gold

10 constantan, ferro-alloy, mischmetal, white brass

11 chrome steel, cupro-nickel, nicrosilial, white copper

14 stainless steel

metallic

03 tin

04 gold, iron, lead

05 harsh, rough, shiny, steel

06 copper, nickel, silver

07 grating, jarring

08 gleaming, jangling, polished

➤ *Names of metallic elements and their symbols:*

03 tin (Sn)

04 gold (Au), iron (Fe), lead (Pb), zinc (Zn)

06 barium (Ba), cerium (Ce), cobalt (Co), copper (Cu), curium (Cm), erbium (Er), indium (In), nickel (Ni), osmium (Os), radium (Ra), silver (Ag), sodium (Na)

07 bismuth (Bi), cadmium (Cd), caesium (Cs), calcium (Ca), fermium (Fm), gallium (Ga), hafnium (Hf), holmium (Ho), iridium (Ir), lithium (Li), mercury (Hg), niobium (Nb), rhenium (Re), rhodium (Rh), terbium (Tb), thorium (Th), thulium (Tm), uranium (U), wolfram (W), yttrium (Y)

08 actinium (Ac), antimony (Sb), chromium (Cr), europium (Eu), francium (Fr), lutetium (Lu), nobelium (No), platinum (Pt), polonium (Po), rubidium (Rb), samarium (Sm), scandium (Sc), tantalum (Ta), thallium (Tl), titanium (Ti), tungsten (W), vanadium (V)

09 aluminium (Al), americium (Am), berkelium (Bk), beryllium (Be), germanium (Ge), lanthanum (La), magnesium (Mg), manganese (Mn), neodymium (Nd), neptunium (Np), palladium (Pd), plutonium (Pu), potassium (K), ruthenium (Ru), strontium (Sr), ytterbium (Yb), zirconium (Zr)

10 dysprosium (Dy), gadolinium (Gd), lawrencium (Lr) (Lw), molybdenum (Mo), promethium (Pm), technetium (Tc)

11 californium (Cf), einsteinium (Es)

12 mendeleevium (Md),
   praseodymium (Pr),
   protactinium (Pa)

metamorphose
05 alter
06 change, mutate
09 transform, transmute
12 transmogrify

metamorphosis
06 change
07 rebirth
08 mutation
10 alteration
14 transformation
15 transfiguration

metaphor
05 image, trope
06 emblem, symbol, visual
07 analogy, picture
08 allegory
10 emblematic
14 figure of speech,
   representation

metaphorical
08 symbolic
10 analogical, emblematic,
   figurative
11 allegorical

metaphysical
07 eternal
08 abstract, abstruse, esoteric,
   profound
09 recondite, spiritual, universal
10 immaterial, impalpable,
   intangible, subjective
11 incorporeal, theoretical
12 supernatural
13 insubstantial, philosophical
14 transcendental

mete

◻**mete out**
05 allot
06 assign
07 deal out, dole out, hand out,
   portion
08 dispense, share out
09 apportion, divide out
10 administer, distribute,
   measure out

meteor
05 comet
06 bolide
08 aerolite, aerolith, fireball
12 shooting star

meteoric
05 brief, quick, rapid, swift
06 speedy, sudden
09 brilliant, momentary, overnight
11 spectacular

meteorologist
10 weatherman
11 weathergirl, weatherlady
13 climatologist
14 weather prophet

method
03 way
04 form, mode, plan, rule
05 means, order, route,
   style
06 course, design, manner,
   scheme, system
07 fashion, pattern, process
08 approach, practice
09 procedure, programme,
   structure, technique
11 arrangement
13 modus operandi

methodical
04 neat, tidy
07 logical, ordered, orderly,
   planned, precise, regular
09 efficient, organized
10 deliberate, meticulous,
   scrupulous, systematic
11 disciplined, painstaking,
   well-ordered

meticulous
05 exact, fussy
06 strict
07 careful, precise
08 accurate, detailed, rigorous,
   thorough
10 fastidious, particular,
   scrupulous
11 painstaking, punctilious
13 conscientious

métier
04 line
05 craft, field, forte, trade
06 sphere
07 calling, pursuit
08 business, vocation
09 specialty
10 occupation, profession,
   speciality
14 line of business

metropolis
04 city
07 capital
11 megalopolis
12 municipality

mettle
05 nerve, pluck, spunk
06 daring, make-up, nature,
   spirit, valour, vigour
07 bravery, calibre, courage,
   resolve
08 backbone, boldness
09 character, fortitude

11 personality, temperament
13 determination

mew
04 meow, mewl
05 miaow, whine
09 caterwaul

mewl
05 whine
06 snivel, whinge
07 blubber, grizzle, whimper

miasma
04 reek
05 fetor, odour, smell, stink
06 stench
08 mephitis
09 effluvium, pollution

miasmal
04 foul
05 fetid
06 putrid, smelly
07 noisome, noxious, reeking
08 mephitic
10 malodorous
11 unwholesome

microbe
03 bug
04 germ
05 virus
08 bacillus, pathogen
09 bacterium
13 micro-organism

microscopic
04 tiny
06 minute
09 minuscule
10 negligible
13 infinitesimal
14 extremely small

midday
04 noon
06 twelve
07 noonday
08 noontide
09 lunchtime
10 twelve noon
12 twelve o'clock

middle
03 mid
04 core, mean
05 heart, inner, midst
06 centre, inside, medial,
   median, medium, midway
07 central, halfway
08 bull's eye, midpoint
11 equidistant, intervening
12 halfway point, intermediate

◻**in the middle of**
05 among, while
06 during

middle-class (cont.)
08 busy with
09 engaged in
12 in the midst of, surrounded by
14 in the process of

middle-class
08 suburban
09 bourgeois
10 gentrified
11 white-collar
12 conventional, professional

middleman
06 broker
09 go-between
10 negotiator
11 distributor
12 entrepreneur, intermediary

middling
02 OK
04 fair, so-so
06 medium, modest
07 average
08 adequate, mediocre, moderate, passable
09 tolerable
11 indifferent
12 run-of-the-mill, unremarkable
13 unexceptional

midget
04 baby, tiny
05 dwarf, gnome, pygmy, small, teeny
06 little, minute, pocket
07 manikin
08 TomThumb
09 itsy-bitsy, miniature
10 diminutive, homunculus, teeny-weeny
11 Lilliputian, pocket-sized

midst
03 hub
04 core
05 bosom, heart, thick
06 centre, depths, middle
07 nucleus
08 interior, midpoint

□in the midst
05 among
06 during
12 in the thick of
13 in the middle of

midway
07 halfway
11 in the centre, in the middle
13 at the midpoint

mien
03 air
04 aura, look
06 aspect, manner
07 bearing
08 carriage, presence
09 demeanour
10 appearance, complexion, deportment, expression
11 countenance

miffed
05 irked, upset, vexed
06 narked, peeved, piqued, put out
07 annoyed, in a huff, nettled
08 offended
09 aggrieved, irritated, resentful
10 displeased

might
04 sway
05 clout, force, power
06 energy, muscle, valour, vigour
07 ability, potency, prowess, stamina
08 capacity, efficacy, strength
09 heftiness, puissance
10 capability
11 muscularity
12 forcefulness, powerfulness

mightily
04 much, very
06 highly, hugely
07 greatly, lustily
08 strongly, very much
09 extremely, intensely
10 forcefully, powerfully
11 exceedingly, strenuously

mighty
04 huge, vast
05 bulky, grand, great, hardy, hefty, large, lusty, stout, tough
06 potent, robust, strong
07 immense, massive, titanic
08 colossal, dominant, enormous, forceful, gigantic, powerful, puissant, towering, vigorous
10 monumental, prodigious

migrant
05 Gypsy, nomad, rover
06 roving, tinker
07 drifter, nomadic, vagrant
08 drifting, emigrant, wanderer
09 immigrant, itinerant, traveller, wandering
10 travelling
11 peripatetic

migrate
04 hike, move, roam, rove, trek
05 drift
06 travel, voyage, wander
07 journey
08 emigrate, relocate, resettle

migration
04 trek
06 roving, travel, voyage
08 diaspora, movement
09 wandering
10 emigration
12 transhumance

migratory
05 Gypsy
06 roving
07 migrant, nomadic, vagrant
08 drifting, shifting
09 immigrant, itinerant, transient, wandering
10 travelling
11 peripatetic

mild
04 calm, fair, kind, meek, soft, warm
05 balmy, bland
06 gentle, humane, mellow, placid, smooth, subtle
07 amiable, clement, insipid, lenient
08 merciful, moderate, pleasant, soothing
09 easy-going, peaceable, sensitive
10 forbearing
11 good-natured

mildewy
05 fetid, fusty, mucid, musty
06 rotten
10 mucedinous

mildness
05 mercy
06 lenity, warmth
08 calmness, clemency, docility, kindness, leniency, meekness, softness, sympathy
09 blandness, passivity, placidity
10 gentleness, indulgence, mellowness, moderation, smoothness
11 forbearance, insipidness
12 tranquillity

milieu
05 arena, scene
06 locale, medium, sphere
07 element, setting
08 location
10 background
11 environment
12 surroundings

militant
07 fighter, soldier, warring, warrior
08 activist, fighting, partisan
09 aggressor, assertive, combatant, combative
10 aggressive, pugnacious
11 belligerent

military
04 army, navy
05 armed
06 forces
07 martial, militia, service, warlike
08 air force, services, soldiers
09 soldierly
11 armed forces, disciplined
➤ see also **aviator**; **rank**; **sailor**; **soldier**

▬ *Names of military decorations:*
02 GC, GM, MC, MM, VC
03 BEM, DCM, DFC, DFM, DSC, DSM, DSO
10 Bronze Star, Silver Star
11 George Cross, George Medal, Purple Heart
13 Legion of Merit, Military Cross, Military Medal, Victoria Cross
14 Oak-leaf Cluster

▬ *Types of military unit:*
04 file, post
05 corps, flank, troop
06 cohort, legion, patrol
07 company, militia, phalanx, platoon
08 division, regiment, squadron
09 battalion, effective
10 rifle-corps
11 flying party
12 flying column
13 guard of honour

militate

▢**militate against**
06 damage, oppose, resist
07 contend, counter
09 go against, prejudice
10 act against, counteract
11 be harmful to, tell against
15 be detrimental to

▢**militate for**
03 aid
04 back, help
07 advance, further, promote

militia
08 yeomanry
09 fencibles, minutemen
10 reservists

13 National Guard
15 Territorial Army

milk
03 tap, use
04 draw, pump
05 bleed, drain, press, wring
06 rip off, siphon
07 draw off, exploit, express, extract, oppress, squeeze
10 manipulate
15 take advantage of

milksop
04 wimp
05 pansy, sissy
06 coward
08 weakling
09 mummy's boy
10 namby-pamby

milky
05 white
06 chalky, cloudy, opaque
07 clouded

mill
04 roll
05 crush, grate, grind, pound, press, quern
06 crunch, powder, roller
07 crusher, foundry, grinder
09 comminute, pulverize
15 processing plant

▢**mill around**
05 swarm
06 stream, throng
11 crowd around, press around

millstone
04 duty, load, onus
06 burden, weight
10 affliction, grindstone, obligation, quernstone
11 cross to bear, encumbrance

mime
05 mimic
06 act out, signal
07 charade, gesture, imitate, mimicry, mummery
08 dumb show, indicate, simulate
09 pantomime, represent
11 impersonate

mimic
03 ape
04 copy, echo
06 parody, parrot, send up
07 copycat, copyist, emulate, imitate, take off
08 imitator, resemble, simulate
10 caricature
11 impersonate

12 caricaturist, impersonator
13 impressionist

mimicry
05 aping
06 parody
07 copying, take-off
09 burlesque, imitating, imitation
10 caricature, impression
13 impersonation

mince
04 chop, dice, hash, pose
05 grind, ponce, spare
06 simper, soften
08 diminish, hold back, moderate, tone down
11 strike a pose
12 attitudinize

mincing
05 poncy, sissy
06 dainty, la-di-da
07 foppish, minikin
08 affected, precious
10 effeminate

mind
04 head, heed, mark, note, obey, urge, view, will, wish, wits
05 brain, guard, sense, watch
06 belief, brains, desire, ensure, expert, follow, genius, memory, notion, object, psyche, reason, recall, regard, resent, spirit
07 dislike, egghead, opinion, scholar, thinker
08 attend to, attitude, listen to, make sure, object to, remember, take care, tendency, thinking, thoughts
09 attention, be careful, care about, intellect, intention, judgement, look after, mentality, not forget, pay heed to, sentiment, viewpoint, watch over
10 disapprove, grey matter, take care of
11 be annoyed by, inclination, keep an eye on, make certain, point of view, remembrance, take offense
12 be bothered by, be offended by, have charge of, intellectual, intelligence, pay attention, subconscious
13 comprehension, concentrate on, concentration, ratiocination, understanding, way of thinking
15 little grey cells

□ be in two minds
05 waver
06 dither
08 be unsure, hesitate
09 vacillate
12 shilly-shally

□ bear in mind, keep in mind
08 remember
15 take into account

□ cross your mind
06 come to, strike
07 occur to, think of

□ make up your mind
06 choose, decide, settle
07 resolve
09 determine
13 make a decision

□ mind out
05 watch
06 beware
07 look out
08 take care, watch out
09 be careful
12 pay attention

□ mind's eye
04 head, mind
10 imagination

□ never mind
08 as well as, forget it, let alone
09 apart from, don't worry
12 not to mention

mindful
04 wary
05 alert, alive, aware, chary
07 alive to, careful, heedful
08 sensible, watchful
09 cognizant, conscious

mindless
06 stupid
07 foolish, tedious
09 senseless
10 gratuitous, mechanical
11 bird-brained, thoughtless
13 unintelligent

mine
03 pit
04 bomb, fund, lode, seam, vein, well
05 delve, dig up, hoard, shaft, stock, store
06 dig for, quarry, trench, tunnel, wealth
07 deposit, extract, reserve, unearth
08 colliery, excavate, treasury
09 coalfield, explosive, reservoir, undermine
10 excavation, repository
11 depth charge

miner
06 pitman
07 collier
09 coalminer

mineral
▸ *Types of mineral*:
04 alum, mica, ruby, salt, talc
05 beryl, topaz, umber
06 blende, galena, garnet, gypsum, halite, jasper, natron, pyrite, quartz, rutile, spinel, zircon
07 apatite, calcite, crystal, cuprite, diamond, jadeite, olivine
08 chromite, cinnabar, corundum, dolomite, feldspar, fluorite, graphite, ilmenite, nephrite, pyroxene, rock salt, sapphire, siderite, sodalite
09 aragonite, cairngorm, fluorspar, lodestone, magnetite, malachite, marcasite, muscovite, pearl spar, soapstone, turquoise
10 aquamarine, bloodstone, chalcedony, glauconite, hornblende, meerschaum, orthoclase, pyrolusite, serpentine, sphalerite, tourmaline
11 chrysoberyl, lapis lazuli, pitchblende, sal ammoniac
13 precious stone
14 sodium chloride

mingle
03 mix
04 fuse, join
05 alloy, blend, merge, unite
07 combine
08 coalesce, compound, intermix
09 associate, circulate, commingle, socialize
10 amalgamate

miniature
03 toy, wee
04 baby, mini, tiny
05 dwarf, small
06 little, midget, minute
08 pint-size
09 pint-sized
10 diminutive, scaled-down

minimal
05 least, token
06 minute

07 minimum, nominal
08 littlest, smallest
09 slightest
10 negligible

minimize
03 cut
06 reduce, shrink
07 curtail
08 belittle, discount, play down
09 deprecate, disparage
10 trivialize
11 make light of
12 make little of
13 underestimate

minimum
05 least, nadir
06 bottom, lowest
07 minimal, tiniest
08 littlest, smallest
09 slightest

minion
06 drudge, lackey, menial
07 flunkey, servant
08 follower, hanger-on, hireling
09 attendant, dependant, underling

minister
04 dean, tend
05 agent, elder, envoy, nurse, padre, serve, vicar
06 attend, cleric, consul, curate, deacon, divine, legate, parson, pastor, priest, rector, verger, wait on
07 cater to
08 chaplain, delegate, diplomat, emissary, official, preacher
09 churchman, clergyman, dignitary, executive, look after
10 administer, ambassador, politician, take care of
11 accommodate
12 ecclesiastic, office-holder
14 representative

▸ *Names of prime ministers*:
02 **Nu** (U)
03 **Kok** (Wim), **Rao** (Pamulaparti Venkata Narasimha)
04 **Bute** (John Stuart, Earl of), **Dini** (Lamberto), **Eden** (Sir Anthony), **Grey** (Charles, Earl), **Home** (Alec Douglas-Home, Lord), **Meir** (Golda), **Moro** (Aldo), **Peel** (Sir Robert), **Pitt** (William, the younger), **Tojo** (Hideki)

05 **Ahern** (Bertie), **Assad**
(Hafez al-), **Banda**
(Hastings Kamuzu), **Barak**
(Ehud), **Begin** (Menachem),
Blair (Anthony 'Tony'),
Botha (Louis), **Botha**
(Pieter Willem), **Cecil**
(Robert), **Derby** (Edward
Geoffrey Smith Stanley, Earl
of), **Hawke** (Robert James
Lee), **Heath** (Sir Edward),
Hoxha (Enver), **Nehru**
(Jawaharlal), **North**
(Frederick, Lord), **Obote**
(Milton), **Peres** (Shimon),
Prodi (Romano), **Putin**
(Vladimir), **Rabin**
(Yitzhak), **Sadat** (Anwar
al-), **Smith** (Ian), **Smuts**
(Jan)

06 **Attlee** (Clement, Earl),
Bhutto (Benazir), **Bhutto**
(Zulfikar Ali), **Bruton**
(John), **Castro** (Fidel),
Chirac (Jacques), **Fabius**
(Laurent), **Gaidar** (Yegor),
Gandhi (Indira), **Gandhi**
(Rajiv), **Gaulle** (Charles de),
Howard (John), **Hun Sen**,
Jospin (Lionel), **Manley**
(Michael), **Mugabe**
(Robert), **Pelham** (Henry),
Pétain (Philippe), **Pol Pot**,
Shamir (Yitzhak), **Sharif**
(Muhammad Nawaz),
Wilson (Harold, Lord)

07 **Asquith** (Herbert, Earl of),
Baldwin (Stanley, Earl),
Balfour (Arthur, Earl),
Canning (George),
Cresson (Édith), **Dehaene**
(Jean-Luc), **Grafton**
(Augustus Henry Fitzroy,
Duke of), **Halifax** (Charles
Montagu, Earl of),
Haughey (Charles),
Keating (Paul), **Kosygin**
(Alexei), **Lubbers** (Ruud),
Molotov (Vyacheslav),
Muldoon (Robert David),
Nkrumah (Kwame),
Nyerere (Julius), **Russell**
(John, Earl), **Trudeau**
(Pierre Elliott), **Vorster**
(John), **Walpole** (Robert),
Whitlam (Gough), **Yeltsin**
(Boris)

08 **Aberdeen** (George
Hamilton Gordon, Earl of),
Bentinck (William, Lord),
Bismarck (Otto Edward
Leopold, Fürst von), **Bonar**

Law (Andrew), **Bulganin**
(Nikolai), **Daladier**
(Édouard), **de Valera**
(Éamon), **Disraeli**
(Benjamin), **Goderich**
(Frederick John Robinson,
Viscount), **González**
(Felipe), **Kenyatta** (Jomo),
Mahathir (bin Mohamad),
Mulroney (Brian),
Nakasone (Yasuhiro),
Perceval (Spencer),
Poincaré (Raymond),
Pompidou (Georges),
Portland (William Henry
Cavendish, Duke of),
Quisling (Vidkun),
Reynolds (Albert),
Rosebery (Archibald Philip
Primrose, Earl of),
Sidmouth (Henry
Addington, Viscount),
Thatcher (Margaret, Lady),
Verwoerd (Hendrik)

09 **Andreotti** (Giulio), **Ben-
Gurion** (David),
Callaghan (James, Lord),
Churchill (Sir Winston),
Gladstone (William
Ewart), **Grenville** (George),
Grenville (William
Wyndham, Lord), **Kim Il-
sung, Kim Jong-Il**,
Liverpool (Robert Banks
Jenkinson, Earl of),
MacDonald (Ramsay),
Macmillan (Sir Harold),
Melbourne (William
Lamb, Viscount), **Mussolini**
(Benito), **Netanyahu**
(Binyamin), **Newcastle**
(Thomas Pelham-Holles,
Duke of), **Salisbury**
(Robert Gascoyne-Cecil,
Marquess of), **Shelburne**
(William Petty Fitzmaurice,
Earl of)

10 **Berlusconi** (Silvio),
Clemenceau (Georges),
Devonshire (William
Cavendish, Duke of),
Fitzgerald (Doctor
Garrett), **Jaruzelski**
(General Wojciech), **Lee
Kuan Yew**, **Palmerston**
(Henry John Temple,
Viscount), **Rockingham**
(Charles Watson Wentworth,
Marquess of), **Wilmington**
(Spencer Compton, Earl of)

11 **Chamberlain** (Neville),
Douglas-Home (Alec),

Lloyd-George (David,
Earl)

13 **Brookeborough** (Basil
Stanlake Brooke, Viscount)

➤ See also **politics**

ministration
03 aid
04 care, help
06 favour, relief
07 service, succour, support
09 patronage
10 assistance

ministry
06 bureau, office
07 cabinet
09 the church
10 department, government,
holy orders
13 the priesthood
14 administration

minor
05 light, petty, small
06 junior, lesser, slight
07 smaller, trivial, unknown,
younger
08 inferior, trifling
09 secondary
11 subordinate, unimportant
13 insignificant
14 inconsiderable

minstrel
04 bard
06 rhymer, singer
08 jongleur, musician
09 joculator
10 troubadour

mint
03 new
04 bomb, cast, coin, pile
05 as new, forge, stack, stamp
06 bundle, packet, riches,
strike, unused, wealth
07 fashion, fortune, million,
perfect, produce
08 brand-new
09 construct, undamaged
10 first-class, immaculate
11 manufacture, unblemished

minuscule
04 fine, tiny
05 teeny
06 little, minute
09 itsy-bitsy, miniature
10 diminutive, teeny-weeny
11 Lilliputian, microscopic
13 infinitesimal

minute
04 tick, tiny
05 close, exact, flash, jiffy

06 moment, second, slight
07 instant, precise
08 accurate, as soon as, critical, detailed, directly, no sooner
09 miniature, minuscule, short time, the moment
10 diminutive, meticulous, negligible, the instant
11 immediately, Lilliputian, microscopic, painstaking
13 infinitesimal, insignificant

▫in a minute
04 soon
06 pronto
07 in a tick, shortly
08 in a flash, in a jiffy, very soon
09 in a moment
15 in the near future

▫up to the minute
02 in
06 latest, newest, with it
10 all the rage
11 fashionable

minutely
07 closely, exactly
08 in detail
09 precisely
10 critically
12 meticulously
13 painstakingly

minutes
05 notes
07 details, records
10 memorandum, transcript

minutiae
07 details, trifles
08 niceties
10 small print, subtleties
11 finer points, particulars

miracle
06 marvel, wonder
07 prodigy
10 phenomenon

miraculous
07 amazing
09 wonderful
10 astounding, incredible, marvellous, phenomenal, remarkable
11 astonishing
12 unbelievable
13 extraordinary

mirage
08 illusion, phantasm
13 hallucination
14 phantasmagoria
15 optical illusion

mire
03 bog, fen, fix, jam, mud

04 dirt, hole, mess, muck, ooze, quag, sink, spot, stew
05 glaur, marsh, slime, swamp
06 morass, pickle, slough
07 bog down, trouble
08 quagmire
09 marshland

mirror
03 ape
04 copy, echo, show, twin
05 clone, glass, image, mimic
06 depict, follow
07 emulate, imitate, reflect
08 likeness
09 reflector, represent
10 dead ringer, reflection
12 looking-glass
13 spitting image

mirth
03 fun
04 glee
06 gaiety
07 frolics, jollity, revelry
08 hilarity, laughter, pleasure
09 amusement, enjoyment, merriment

mirthful
05 funny, happy, jolly, merry
06 jocund, jovial
07 amusing
09 hilarious, laughable
10 uproarious

miry
04 oozy
05 boggy, mucky, muddy, slimy
06 glaury, marshy, swampy

misadventure
06 mishap
07 bad luck, debacle, failure, ill luck, reverse, setback, tragedy
08 accident, calamity, disaster, hard luck
09 cataclysm, mischance
10 ill fortune, misfortune
11 catastrophe

misanthropic
05 surly
10 antisocial, malevolent, unfriendly, unsociable
13 unsympathetic

misanthropy
11 malevolence
13 antisociality
14 unsociableness

misapply
06 misuse
09 misemploy
14 misappropriate

misapprehend
11 misconstrue
12 misinterpret
13 misunderstand
15 get the wrong idea

misapprehension
05 error
07 fallacy, mistake
08 delusion
09 wrong idea
13 misconception
15 false impression

misappropriate
03 nab, rob
04 nick
05 abuse, filch, pinch, steal
06 pilfer, pocket, thieve
07 swindle
08 embezzle, peculate
09 defalcate

misappropriation
05 theft
07 robbing
08 stealing
09 pilfering, pocketing
10 peculation
11 defalcation
12 embezzlement

misbegotten
05 shady
06 stolen
07 bastard
09 ill-gotten, purloined
10 ill-advised
12 disreputable, ill-conceived, illegitimate

misbehave
05 act up
06 play up
07 carry on, disobey
10 transgress
15 get up to mischief

misbehaviour
08 mischief
10 bad manners, misconduct
11 impropriety, naughtiness
12 disobedience, misdemeanour

misbelief
05 error
07 fallacy, mistake
08 delusion, illusion
13 misconception
15 misapprehension

miscalculate
03 err
06 slip up
07 blunder
08 miscount, misjudge

12 make a mistake,
  overestimate
13 underestimate

miscarriage
05 error
07 failure
08 aborting, abortion
09 breakdown
10 perversion
13 mismanagement

miscarry
04 fail, flop, fold
05 abort
07 founder, go amiss, go wrong,
  misfire
10 not come off
11 come to grief
13 come to nothing

miscellaneous
05 mixed
06 motley, sundry, varied
07 diverse, jumbled, various
08 assorted
10 variegated
11 diversified
12 multifarious
13 heterogeneous

miscellany
03 mix
06 jumble, medley
07 farrago, mixture, variety
08 mishmash, mixed bag,
  pastiche
09 patchwork, potpourri
10 assortment, collection,
  hotch-potch
11 gallimaufry, salmangundi,
  smorgasbord

mischance
04 blow
06 mishap
07 ill-luck, tragedy
08 accident, bad break,
  calamity, disaster
10 ill-fortune, infelicity,
  misfortune
12 misadventure

mischief
04 evil, harm, hurt
06 damage, injury, pranks,
  tricks
07 carry-on, trouble
08 escapade, nuisance
09 devilment
10 hanky-panky, impishness
11 naughtiness, roguishness,
  shenanigans
12 bad behaviour,
  misbehaviour

13 funny business, jiggery-
  pokery
14 monkey business

mischievous
03 bad
04 evil
06 impish, wicked
07 harmful, hurtful, naughty,
  playful, roguish, teasing,
  vicious
08 rascally, spiteful
09 injurious, malicious,
  malignant
11 destructive, detrimental,
  disobedient, misbehaving,
  troublesome
12 badly-behaved

misconceive
12 misapprehend, misinterpret
13 misunderstand

misconception
05 error
07 fallacy, mistake
08 delusion
09 wrong idea
15 false impression,
  misapprehension

misconduct
10 wrongdoing
11 impropriety, malpractice
12 bad behaviour

misconstrue
07 misread, mistake
08 misjudge
12 misinterpret
15 take the wrong way

miscreant
05 knave, rogue, scamp
06 rascal, sinner, wretch
07 dastard, villain
08 criminal, evildoer, vagabond
09 reprobate, scallywag,
  scoundrel, wrongdoer
10 malefactor, profligate

misdeed
03 sin
05 crime, error, fault, wrong
06 felony
07 offence
10 misconduct, wrongdoing
13 transgression

misdemeanour
07 misdeed, offence
10 misconduct, wrongdoing
11 malfeasance
13 transgression

miser
06 meanie
07 niggard, Scrooge

08 tightwad
09 skinflint, tight arse
10 cheapskate
11 cheeseparer
12 money-grubber, penny-
  pincher

miserable
03 low, sad
04 base, blue, down, glum,
  mean, poor
06 dismal, dreary, gloomy,
  grumpy, meagre, measly,
  paltry, scanty, shabby, sullen
07 forlorn, grouchy, joyless,
  pitiful, squalid, unhappy
08 dejected, desolate,
  downcast, pathetic,
  shameful, wretched
09 cheerless, depressed,
  niggardly, sorrowful,
  worthless
10 depressing, despondent
11 downhearted, low-spirited,
  melancholic
12 disconsolate, impoverished
14 down in the dumps

miserliness
08 meanness
09 frugality, minginess,
  parsimony, tightness
10 stinginess
12 cheeseparing
13 niggardliness, penny-
  pinching, penuriousness
15 close-fistedness, tight-
  fistedness

miserly
04 mean
05 mingy, tight
06 stingy
09 niggardly, penurious
11 close-fisted, tight-fisted
12 cheeseparing, parsimonious
13 money-grubbing, penny-
  pinching

misery
03 woe
04 want
05 agony, gloom, grief
06 grouch, moaner, penury,
  sorrow, whiner
07 anguish, despair, killjoy,
  poverty, sadness, whinger
08 distress, hardship, Jeremiah,
  sourpuss
09 indigence, pessimist,
  suffering
10 affliction, complainer,
  depression, melancholy,
  spoilsport, wet blanket

11 deprivation, destitution, unhappiness
12 wretchedness
13 prophet of doom

misfire
04 fail, flop
05 abort
06 go awry
07 founder, go amiss, go wrong
08 miscarry
11 come to grief, fall through
12 come a cropper

misfit
05 freak, loner
06 weirdo
07 dropout, oddball
08 lone wolf, maverick
09 eccentric, odd one out

misfortune
03 woe
04 blow
05 trial
06 mishap, sorrow
07 bad luck, ill-luck, reverse, setback, tragedy
08 accident, calamity, disaster, hard luck, hardship
09 adversity, mischance
11 tribulation

misgiving
05 doubt, qualm, worry
06 unease
07 anxiety, scruple
08 distrust
10 hesitation
11 reservation, uncertainty
12 apprehension

misguided
04 rash
05 wrong
06 misled
07 deluded, foolish
09 ill-judged, imprudent
10 fallacious, ill-advised
13 ill-considered

mishandle
04 muff
05 botch
06 bungle, mess up
07 balls up, screw up
09 mismanage
11 make a hash of
14 make a pig's ear of

mishap
07 reverse, setback, trouble
08 accident, calamity, disaster, incident
09 adversity

10 ill-fortune, misfortune
11 catastrophe, tribulation
12 misadventure

mishmash
04 hash, mess, olio
06 jumble, medley, muddle
07 farrago
08 pastiche
09 potpourri
10 hodge-podge, hotchpotch, salmagundi

misinform
07 deceive, mislead
08 hoodwink, misguide
13 give a bum steer

misinformation
04 dope, guff, hype, lies
05 bluff
07 baloney, eyewash
08 bum steer, nonsense
14 disinformation

misinterpret
07 distort, mistake
11 misconstrue
12 misapprehend
13 misunderstand
15 take the wrong way

misjudge
12 miscalculate
13 misunderstand

mislay
04 lose, miss
08 misplace

mislead
04 fool
06 delude
07 deceive
08 hoodwink
09 misinform
10 lead astray
12 misrepresent, take for a ride
14 pull a fast one on

misleading
09 ambiguous, confusing, deceiving, deceptive, equivocal
10 fallacious, unreliable

mismanage
06 bungle, foul up, mess up
09 mishandle
11 make a hash of, make a mess of
14 make a pig's ear of

mismatched
08 clashing, unsuited
10 discordant, unmatching
11 ill-assorted, incongruous
12 antipathetic, incompatible

misogynist
03 MCP
10 misogamist, woman-hater
12 anti-feminist
15 male supremacist

misplace
04 lose, miss
06 mislay

misprint
04 typo
05 error
07 erratum, literal, mistake
11 corrigendum
13 printing error

misquote
06 garble, muddle
07 distort, falsify, pervert
09 misreport

misrepresent
05 slant, twist
07 distort, falsify, pervert
08 misquote, misstate
09 misreport
10 exaggerate
11 misconstrue
12 misinterpret

misrule
05 chaos
07 anarchy, turmoil
08 disorder
11 lawlessness
12 indiscipline
13 misgovernment, mismanagement
15 disorganization

miss
02 Ms
03 err
04 blow, fail, flop, girl, lass, lose, maid, omit, skip
05 avoid, dodge, evade, fault, let go, mourn
06 damsel, forego, lament, maiden, not see, regret
07 ache for, failure, let slip, long for, mistake, neglect, not go to, not spot, pine for
08 leave out, omission, overlook, pass over, sidestep, yearn for
09 disregard, fail to get, fail to hit, not notice, oversight, young lady
10 schoolgirl, young woman
11 fail to catch
12 be absent from, fail to notice, mademoiselle
13 feel the loss of, misunderstand, not take part in

◻miss out
04 jump, omit, skip
06 bypass, ignore
08 leave out, pass over
09 disregard
12 dispense with

missal
08 breviary, Triodion
09 formulary
10 prayerbook
11 euchologion, servicebook

misshapen
04 bent, ugly
06 warped
07 crooked, twisted
08 crippled, deformed
09 contorted, distorted, grotesque, malformed

missile
04 bomb, dart, shot
05 arrow, shaft, shell
06 rocket, weapon
07 grenade, missile, torpedo
09 ballistic
10 flying bomb, projectile

missing
04 gone, lost
06 absent, astray
07 lacking, mislaid, strayed, wanting
09 misplaced
11 disappeared
14 unaccounted-for

mission
03 aim, job
04 duty, goal, task, work
05 chore, quest
06 charge, errand, office
07 calling, crusade, embassy, purpose, pursuit
08 business, campaign, legation, ministry, vocation
09 operation, task-force
10 assignment, commission, delegation, deputation
11 raison d'être, undertaking

missionary
05 envoy
07 apostle
08 champion, crusader, emissary, minister, preacher
10 ambassador, evangelist

▶ *Names of missionaries:*
03 Fox (George)
05 Carey (William), David (Père Armand), Moody (Dwight Lyman), Ricci (Matteo), Smith (Eli)

06 Damien (Father Joseph), Wesley (John)
07 Aylward (Gladys), Liddell (Eric Henry), Theresa (Mother)
10 Huddleston (Trevor), Schweitzer (Albert)
11 Livingstone (David)
➤ See also **religion**

missive
06 letter, report
07 epistle, message
08 dispatch
10 communiqué
13 communication

misspent
06 wasted
07 misused
08 prodigal
10 dissipated, squandered, thrown away

misstate
07 distort, falsify
08 misquote
09 misrelate, misreport
12 misrepresent

mist
03 dew, fog
04 film, haze, smog, veil
05 cloud, spray, steam
06 mizzle, vapour
07 dimness, drizzle
12 condensation

◻mist over, mist up
03 dim, fog
04 blur, veil
05 fog up, glaze
07 obscure, steam up
09 cloud over

mistake
03 err
04 boob, goof, muff, slip
05 error, fault, fluff, gaffe, lapse, mix up
06 booboo, howler, slip up
07 bloomer, blunder, botch-up, clanger, confuse, erratum, faux pas, misread
08 confound, get wrong, misjudge, misprint, muddle up, solecism
09 oversight
10 aberration, inaccuracy, misreading
11 corrigendum, misconstrue, misspelling
12 indiscretion, miscalculate, misjudgement
13 misunderstand
14 miscalculation

15 misapprehension, put your foot in it, slip of the tongue

mistaken
05 false, wrong
06 faulty, misled, untrue
07 at fault, deluded, in error
08 deceived
09 erroneous, ill-judged, incorrect, misguided, unfounded
10 fallacious, inaccurate
11 inauthentic, misinformed
15 get the wrong idea

mistakenly
07 falsely, wrongly
08 unfairly, unjustly
11 erroneously, incorrectly, misguidedly
12 fallaciously, inaccurately

mistimed
08 ill-timed, tactless, untimely
10 malapropos
11 inopportune
12 inconvenient, unseasonable
14 unsynchronized

mistreat
04 harm, hurt, maul
05 abuse, bully
06 batter, beat up, ill-use, injure, misuse, molest
08 ill-treat, maltreat
09 mishandle
10 knock about, treat badly

mistreatment
04 harm, hurt
05 abuse
06 ill-use, injury, misuse
07 cruelty, mauling
08 bullying, ill-usage
09 battering
11 mishandling, molestation
12 ill-treatment, maltreatment

mistress
05 lover, tutor, woman
07 hetaera, partner, teacher
08 lady-love, paramour
09 concubine, courtesan, governess, inamorata, kept woman
10 girlfriend
13 schoolteacher

mistrust
05 doubt, qualm
06 caution, suspect
08 be wary of, distrust, wariness
09 chariness, hesitancy, misgiving, suspicion
12 apprehension, reservations
13 have no faith in

14 be suspicious of, have misgivings
15 have doubts about

mistrustful
04 wary
05 chary, leery
07 cynical, dubious, fearful
08 cautious, doubtful, hesitant
10 suspicious
11 distrustful

misty
03 dim
04 hazy
05 foggy, fuzzy, murky, smoky, vague
06 cloudy, opaque, veiled
07 blurred, obscure, unclear
08 nebulous
10 indistinct

misunderstand
08 get wrong
12 misapprehend, misinterpret
15 get the wrong idea

misunderstanding
04 rift, tiff
05 clash, error, mix-up
06 breach
07 discord, dispute, mistake, quarrel
08 argument, conflict
09 wrong idea
10 difference, misreading
12 crossed wires, misjudgement
13 misconception
15 false impression, misapprehension

misunderstood
07 misread
09 ill-judged, misjudged
12 misconstrued
13 unappreciated
14 misinterpreted

misuse
04 harm, hurt
05 abuse, waste, wrong
06 ill-use, injure, injury
07 corrupt, pervert
08 ill-treat, misapply, mistreat, squander
10 corruption
11 mishandling
12 exploitation, ill-treatment, maltreatment, mistreatment

mite
03 bit, jot, tad
04 atom, iota, whit
05 grain, ounce, scrap, spark, touch, trace

06 morsel
07 modicum, smidgen

mitigate
04 ease
05 abate, allay, blunt, remit
06 lessen, modify, pacify, reduce, soften, soothe, temper
07 appease, assuage, lighten, mollify, placate
08 decrease, diminish, moderate, palliate, tone down
09 alleviate, extenuate

mitigating
09 modifying, tempering
10 justifying, palliative
11 extenuating

mitigation
08 allaying, decrease, easement
09 abatement, lessening, reduction, remission, tempering
10 diminution, moderation, palliation
11 alleviation, assuagement

mix
04 fuse, join, mash, stir, suit
05 agree, alloy, blend, get on, merge, union, unite
06 fold in, fusion, hobnob, medley, merger, mingle
07 amalgam, combine
08 coalesce, compound, emulsify, get along
09 associate, coalition, composite, harmonize, introduce, socialize, synthesis
10 amalgamate, assortment, complement, fraternize, homogenize, synthesize
11 combination, incorporate, intermingle

□**mix in**
05 add in, blend, merge
09 introduce
11 incorporate, interpolate

□**mix up**
06 garble, jumble, muddle, puzzle
07 confuse, disturb, involve, mistake, perplex, snarl up
08 bewilder, confound, muddle up
09 implicate
10 complicate

mixed
05 fused
06 hybrid, motley, varied

07 alloyed, blended, diverse, mingled, mongrel
08 assorted, combined, compound
09 composite, crossbred, equivocal, interbred, uncertain
10 ambivalent
11 amalgamated, diversified
13 miscellaneous

□**mixed up**
04 in on
05 upset
07 chaotic, muddled, puzzled
08 caught up, confused, involved
09 disturbed, embroiled, entangled, perplexed, screwed up
10 bewildered, disordered, distracted, implicated, inculpated
11 disoriented, maladjusted

mixer
05 whisk
06 beater, joiner
07 blender, meddler, stirrer
08 busybody, makebate
10 interferer, liquidizer
12 troublemaker
13 food processor, mischief-maker

mixing
05 union
06 fusion
08 blending, mingling
09 interflow, synthesis
11 association, coalescence, combination, socializing
12 amalgamation
13 hybridization

mixture
05 alloy, blend, cross, union
06 fusion, medley
07 amalgam, melange, variety
08 compound
09 composite, potpourri, synthesis
10 assortment, concoction
11 combination
12 amalgamation
14 conglomeration

mix-up
04 mess
05 chaos, snafu
06 foul-up, jumble, muddle, tangle
07 balls-up, mistake, snarl-up
08 disorder, nonsense
09 confusion

moan
03 sob
04 beef, carp, howl, sigh, wail, weep
05 bleat, gripe, groan, mourn, whine
06 charge, grieve, grouse, lament, whinge
07 censure, grumble, whimper
08 complain
09 annoyance, belly-ache, complaint, criticism
12 fault-finding

mob
03 set
04 body, crew, fill, gang, herd, host, mass, pack
05 brood, crowd, drove, flock, group, horde, plebs, press, swarm, tribe, troop
06 attack, charge, jostle, masses, pester, rabble, throng
07 besiege, overrun, set upon
08 canaille, populace, riff-raff
09 descend on, gathering, hoi polloi, multitude
10 assemblage, collection, crowd round, swarm round
13 great unwashed

mobile
05 agile
06 active, lively, motile, moving, nimble, roving, supple
07 migrant, movable, roaming
08 changing, flexible, portable
09 itinerant, wandering
10 able to move, ambulatory, expressive, locomotive, travelling
11 peripatetic
13 transportable

mobility
06 motion
07 agility
08 motility, motivity, vivacity
10 locomotion, movability, suppleness
11 flexibility, portability
12 locomobility, locomotivity
14 expressiveness

mobilize
05 rally, ready
06 summon
07 animate, marshal
08 activate, assemble, get ready, organize
09 galvanize, make ready
14 call into action

mob rule
08 lynch law
09 mobocracy
10 ochlocracy

mock
03 ape, kid, rag, rib
04 fake, gibe, jeer, sham
05 bogus, chaff, dummy, faked, false, knock, mimic, scoff, scorn, sneer, taunt, tease
06 deride, ersatz, forged, insult, parody, phoney, pseudo, send up
07 emulate, feigned, imitate, lampoon, laugh at, pretend, take off
08 ridicule, satirize, simulate
09 burlesque, imitation, make fun of, poke fun at, pretended, simulated
10 artificial, caricature, fraudulent, substitute
11 counterfeit

mocker
05 tease
06 critic, jeerer
07 derider, scoffer, sneerer
08 satirist
09 lampooner, ridiculer
10 lampoonist
11 pasquinader

mockery
05 farce, scorn, sneer, spoof
06 parody, satire, send-up
07 apology, disdain, jeering, lampoon, ragging, ribbing, sarcasm, take-off, teasing
08 ridicule, scoffing, sneering, taunting
09 burlesque, contumely
10 caricature
12 mickey-taking

mocking
05 snide
07 cynical
08 derisive, derisory, sardonic, scoffing, scornful, sneering
09 sarcastic, satirical
10 disdainful, irreverent
12 contemptuous
13 disrespectful

mode
03 fad, way
04 form, look, plan, rage
05 craze, style, trend, vogue
06 custom, manner, method, system
07 fashion, process
08 approach, practice

model
04 base, cast, copy, form, kind, make, mark, mode, plan, pose, sort, type, wear, work
05 carve, dummy, ideal, image, mould, poser, shape, sport, style
06 create, design, mock-up, sample, sculpt, sitter
07 display, epitome, example, fashion, paragon, pattern, perfect, show off, subject, version
08 exemplar, original, paradigm, standard, template
09 archetype, exemplary, facsimile, imitation, mannequin, prototype
10 archetypal, embodiment
12 prototypical
14 perfect example, representation

moderate
04 calm, cool, curb, ease, fair, just, mild, so-so, tame
05 abate, allay, check, sober
06 lessen, medium, modest, pacify, soften, steady, subdue
07 average, control, fairish, liberal, slacken, subside
08 adequate, centrist, decrease, diminish, middling, mitigate, modulate, palliate, play down, regulate, restrain, sensible, tone down
09 alleviate, attenuate, soft-pedal, temperate, tolerable
10 controlled, reasonable
11 keep in check
12 nonextremist
13 no great shakes
14 fair to middling
15 middle-of-the-road

moderately
05 quite
06 fairly, rather
08 passably, slightly, somewhat
10 reasonably
12 to some extent, within reason

moderation
07 caution, control, curbing
08 decrease, sobriety

09 abatement, composure, lessening, reduction, restraint
10 mitigation, temperance
11 alleviation, attenuation, self-control
13 self-restraint, temperateness
14 abstemiousness, reasonableness

◻**in moderation**
10 moderately
12 within bounds, within limits, within reason
15 with self-control

modern
02 in
03 new
05 fresh, novel
06 latest, modish, recent, trendy, with it
07 current, present
08 advanced, up-to-date
09 in fashion, the latest
10 innovative, present-day
11 progressive
12 contemporary
13 state-of-the-art, up-to-the-minute

modernity
07 newness, novelty
09 freshness
10 innovation, recentness

modernize
05 renew
06 reform, revamp, update
07 refresh, remodel
08 progress, renovate
09 get with it
10 regenerate, rejuvenate
13 bring up-to-date

modest
03 shy
05 plain, quiet, small, timid
06 chaste, demure, humble, simple
07 bashful
08 decorous, discreet, moderate, reserved, retiring, virtuous
10 reasonable, unassuming
11 inexpensive
12 self-effacing
13 unpretentious
15 self-deprecating

modesty
07 coyness, decency, decorum, reserve, shyness
08 humility, timidity
09 plainness, reticence

10 chasteness, demureness, seemliness, simplicity
11 bashfulness
14 self-effacement
15 self-deprecation

modicum
03 bit, tad
04 atom, dash, drop, hint, inch, iota, mite
05 crumb, grain, ounce, pinch, scrap, shred, speck, tinge, touch, trace
06 degree, little
08 fragment, molecule, particle
09 little bit
10 suggestion
11 small amount

modification
06 change
08 mutation, revision
09 recasting, reworking, tempering, variation
10 adaptation, adjustment, alteration, limitation, moderation, modulation, refinement, remoulding
11 improvement, reformation, restriction
13 qualification

modify
04 dull, vary
05 abate, adapt, alter, limit
06 adjust, change, lessen, recast, reduce, reform, revise, rework, soften, temper
07 convert, improve, qualify, remould, reshape
08 decrease, diminish, mitigate, moderate, redesign, tone down

modish
02 in
03 hip, mod, now
06 modern, trendy, with it
07 stylish, voguish, à la mode
10 all the rage, avant-garde
11 fashionable, modernistic
13 up-to-the-minute

modulate
04 tune, vary
05 alter, lower
06 adjust, change, modify, soften, temper
07 balance, inflect
08 moderate, regulate
09 harmonize

modulation
04 tone
05 shade, shift

06 accent, change, tuning
08 lowering
09 inflexion, softening
10 adjustment, alteration, inflection, intonation
13 harmonization

modus operandi
06 manner, method, praxis, system
08 practice
09 procedure, technique
11 rule of thumb

mogul
03 VIP
05 baron, Mr Big
06 big gun, big pot, bigwig, top dog, tycoon
07 big shot, magnate, supremo
08 big noise, big wheel
09 big cheese, potentate

moist
03 wet
04 damp, dank, dewy
05 humid, muggy, rainy, soggy
06 clammy, marshy, watery
07 drizzly, wettish
08 dripping
09 drizzling

moisten
03 wet
04 damp, lick, soak
05 water
06 dampen, humify
07 make wet
08 humidify, irrigate
10 moisturize

moisture
03 dew, wet
04 damp, rain
05 spray, steam, sweat, water
06 liquid, vapour
07 drizzle, soaking, wetness
08 dampness, humidity
12 condensation, perspiration

mole
03 spy
04 dyke, pier, spot
05 agent, jetty
06 blotch, groyne
07 barrier, blemish, freckle
08 causeway
10 breakwater, embankment
11 double agent, infiltrator, secret agent

molest
04 harm, hurt, rape
05 abuse, harry, hound, tease
06 accost, assail, attack, injure, plague, ravish

07 assault, disturb, torment, trouble
08 ill-treat, maltreat, mistreat
13 interfere with
15 sexually assault

mollify
04 calm, ease, lull
05 abate, allay, blunt, quell, quiet, relax
06 lessen, mellow, modify, pacify, soften, soothe, temper
07 appease, assuage, compose, cushion, placate, relieve, sweeten
08 mitigate, moderate
10 conciliate, propitiate

mollusc
➤ *Types of mollusc*:
04 clam, slug
05 conch, snail, squid, whelk
06 cockle, cowrie, limpet, mussel, oyster
07 abalone, octopus, scallop, sea slug
08 nautilus, shipworm
09 land snail
10 cuttlefish, nudibranch, periwinkle
➤ See also **animal**; **crustacean**

mollycoddle
03 pet
04 baby, ruin
05 spoil
06 coddle, cosset, pamper
08 pander to
09 spoon-feed
11 overprotect

moment
02 mo
03 sec
04 note, tick
05 flash, jiffy, trice, value, worth
06 import, minute, second, weight
07 concern, gravity, instant
08 as soon as, directly, interest, no sooner, two ticks
09 short time, substance, the minute
10 importance, the instant
11 consequence, immediately, point in time, seriousness, split second, weightiness
12 significance
13 very short time
14 less than no time

momentarily
07 briefly

10 fleetingly, for a moment, for a second
11 temporarily
12 for an instant
13 for a short time

momentary
05 brief, hasty, quick, short
08 fleeting
09 ephemeral, transient
10 evanescent, short-lived, transitory

momentous
07 crucial, fateful, pivotal, serious, weighty
08 critical, decisive, historic
11 epoch-making, significant
12 earth-shaking
15 earth-shattering, world-shattering

momentum
04 push, urge
05 drive, force, power, speed
06 energy, impact, thrust
07 impetus, impulse
08 stimulus, strength, velocity
09 incentive
10 propulsion

monarch
04 king, tsar
05 queen, ruler
06 prince
07 emperor, empress
08 princess
09 potentate, sovereign
11 crowned head

monarchy
05 realm
06 domain, empire
07 kingdom, tyranny
08 dominion, kingship, royalism
09 monocracy
11 sovereignty
12 principality
14 sovereign state

monastery
05 abbey
06 friary, priory
07 convent, nunnery
08 cloister
09 coenobium
12 charterhouse

monastic
07 ascetic, austere
08 celibate, eremitic, secluded
09 reclusive, withdrawn
10 anchoritic, cloistered, coenobitic, meditative
11 sequestered
13 contemplative

➤ *Names of monastic orders*:
04 Sufi
05 Taizé
06 Culdee, Essene, Jesuit,
08 Buddhist, Capuchin, Grey nuns, Minorite, Trappist, Ursuline
09 Carmelite, Dominican, mendicant
10 Bernardine, Carthusian, Cistercian, Conventual, Franciscan, Grey friars, Norbertine, Poor Clares
11 Augustinian, Benedictine, Black friars, Camaldolite, Ignorantine, White friars
12 Austin friars
14 Knights Templar, Society of Jesus
➤ See also **religion**

monasticism
09 austerity, eremitism
10 asceticism
11 coenobitism

monetary
04 cash
05 money
06 fiscal
07 capital
08 economic
09 budgetary, financial, pecuniary

money
04 cash, coin, dosh, gelt, loot
05 brass, bread, dough, funds, gravy, lolly, means, rhino
06 assets, greens, moolah, riches, wealth
07 capital, readies, savings, shekels
08 currency, finances
09 affluence, banknotes, megabucks, resources
10 prosperity
11 legal tender, spondulicks
12 the necessary
➤ See also **coin**; **currency**

⬚**in the money**
04 rich
05 flush
06 loaded
07 wealthy
08 affluent, well-off, well-to-do
10 prosperous, well-heeled
11 rolling in it

money-box
04 safe
05 chest
06 coffer
07 cash box
09 piggy-bank

moneyed
04 rich
07 opulent, wealthy, well-off
08 affluent, well-to-do
10 prosperous, well-heeled

money-grubbing
07 miserly
08 grasping
09 mercenary
11 acquisitive, mammonistic

money-making
09 lucrative
10 commercial, profitable
12 profit-making, remunerative

mongrel
03 cur
05 cross, mixed
06 hybrid
08 half-bred
09 crossbred, half-breed
10 crossbreed, ill-defined,
   mixed breed

monitor
03 VDU
04 CCTV, note, plot, scan
05 check, track, watch
06 record, survey
07 observe, oversee, prefect,
   scanner
08 observer, overseer, watchdog
09 supervise
10 supervisor
11 invigilator, keep an eye on,
   keep track of
14 security camera

monk
05 abbot, friar, prior
06 beguin, frater, hermit
07 brother
09 anchorite, coenobite,
   gyrovague, mendicant
10 cloisterer, conventual,
   religioner
13 contemplative

monkey
03 imp
04 brat, fool, mess, play
05 rogue, scamp
06 fiddle, meddle, potter,
   rascal, simian, tamper, tinker
07 primate
09 interfere, scallywag
13 mischief-maker

► *Monkeys include:*
03 pug, sai
04 douc, mico, mona, saki, titi,
   zati
05 Diana, magot, sajou
06 baboon, bandar, coaita,
   grivet, guenon, howler,

langur, malmag, rhesus,
sagoin, saguin, spider,
uakari, vervet
07 colobus, guereza, hanuman,
   macaque, sagouin, saimiri,
   sapajou, tamarin, tarsier
08 capuchin, durukuli, entellus,
   mangabey, marmoset,
   squirrel, talapoin,
   wanderoo
09 proboscis
10 Barbary ape
➤ See also **animal**

◻**monkey business**
06 pranks
07 carry-on, foolery
08 clowning, mischief, trickery
09 chicanery
10 hanky-panky, tomfoolery
11 legerdemain, shenanigans,
   skulduggery
12 monkey tricks
13 funny business, jiggery-
   pokery, sleight-of-hand

monochrome
08 monotone
09 unicolour
11 unicolorate, unicoloured
13 black-and-white

monocle
08 eyeglass

monogamous
10 monandrous, monogynous

monogamy
08 monandry, monogyny

monolingual
08 monoglot
10 unilingual

monolith
06 menhir, sarsen
08 megalith
13 standing stone

monolithic
04 huge, vast
05 giant, rigid, solid
07 massive
08 colossal, faceless, gigantic,
   immobile, unmoving,
   unvaried
09 immovable
10 fossilized, monumental,
   unchanging

monologue
05 spiel
09 soliloquy

monomania
06 fetish
08 fixation, idée fixe

09 obsession
10 hobby-horse

monopolize
03 hog
05 tie up
06 corner
08 dominate, take over
14 keep to yourself

monopoly
06 corner
09 monopsony, sole right
10 domination, sole rights
14 exclusive right

monotonous
05 samey
06 boring, deadly
07 humdrum, routine, tedious,
   uniform
08 tiresome, unvaried
09 unvarying, wearisome
10 all the same, repetitive
11 repetitious
12 run-of-the-mill
13 uninteresting

monotony
06 tedium
07 boredom, routine
08 dullness, sameness
10 repetition, uniformity
13 wearisomeness
14 repetitiveness

monster
04 huge, mega, ogre, vast
05 beast, brute, devil, fiend,
   freak, giant, jumbo, troll
06 dragon, Gorgon, kraken,
   Medusa, mutant, ogress,
   savage, Sphinx, wivern
07 cyclops, immense,
   mammoth, massive, villain,
   windigo
08 behemoth, colossal,
   colossus, enormous,
   gigantic, Minotaur, teratism,
   whopping
09 barbarian, ginormous,
   leviathan, monstrous
10 tremendous
11 hippocampus, miscreation,
   monstrosity
12 Frankenstein, malformation
13 freak of nature
14 Brobdingnagian

monstrosity
05 freak, teras
06 horror, mutant
07 eyesore, monster
08 atrocity, enormity
11 hideousness

monstrous
04 evil, foul, huge, vast, vile
07 heinous, hideous, immense, inhuman, mammoth, massive
08 abnormal, colossal, deformed, dreadful, enormous, freakish, gigantic, horrible, shocking, teratoid, terrible
09 frightful, grotesque, malformed, misshapen
10 abominable, tremendous

monument
05 cairn, cross, relic, token
06 barrow, column, marker, pillar, record, shrine, statue
07 memento, obelisk, witness
08 cenotaph, evidence, memorial, reminder
09 headstone, mausoleum, testament, tombstone
10 gravestone

▶ *Monuments include*:
04 Eros
06 Sphinx
08 Cenotaph,, Lion Gate, Monument, Taj Mahal
09 Tsar's Bell
10 Berlin Wall, Ishtar Gate, London Wall, Marble Arch, Stonehenge
11 Eiffel Tower, Grande Arche, Great Sphinx, Machu Picchu, Silbury Hill
12 Antonine Wall, Eleanor Cross, Hadrian's Wall, Spanish Steps, Statue of Zeus, Tower of Babel
13 Admiralty Arch, Arc de Triomphe, Nelson's Column, Trajan's Column, Trevi Fountain
14 Albert Memorial, Glastonbury Tor, Stone of Destiny, Tomb of Mausolus, Wayland's Smithy
15 Brandenburg Gate, Lincoln Memorial, Rollright Stones, Statue of Liberty

monumental
04 huge, vast
05 great
07 abiding, awesome, immense, lasting, massive
08 colossal, enduring, enormous, historic, immortal, imposing, majestic, memorial, striking
09 important, memorable
10 impressive, tremendous

11 celebratory, epoch-making, exceptional, magnificent, outstanding, significant
12 awe-inspiring, overwhelming
13 commemorative, extraordinary, unforgettable

mood
04 feel, sulk, tone, vein, whim
05 blues, dumps, pique, tenor
06 humour, spirit, temper
07 climate, feeling
08 ambience, doldrums, the sulks
09 bad temper
10 atmosphere, depression, low spirits, melancholy
11 disposition, frame of mind, state of mind

◻ **in the mood for**
07 eager to
09 willing to
10 disposed to, inclinded to
11 feeling like

moody
04 glum, mopy
05 angry, sulky, testy
06 broody, crabby, crusty, fickle, gloomy, morose, sullen, touchy
07 doleful, in a huff, in a mood
08 downcast, petulant, unstable, volatile
09 crotchety, impulsive, irascible, irritable, miserable
10 capricious, changeable, in a bad mood, melancholy
13 temperamental, unpredictable

moon
05 brood, dream, mooch
08 daydream, languish

◻ **once in a blue moon**
06 seldom
08 not often
10 hardly ever, very rarely

◻ **over the moon**
06 elated, joyful
08 blissful, ecstatic, euphoric, frenzied, jubilant
09 delirious, overjoyed
11 on cloud nine, tickled pink
13 jumping for joy
15 in seventh heaven

moonlike
05 lunar
06 lunate
07 lunular, selenic
08 crescent
10 crescentic, moon-shaped

moonshine
03 rot
04 bosh, bunk, crap, guff, tosh
05 hooch, stuff, tripe
06 bunkum, hootch, hot air, liquor, piffle, poteen
07 baloney, blather, blether, bootleg, eyewash, fantasy, hogwash, potheen, rubbish
08 bullshit, claptrap, nonsense, tommyrot

moor
04 bind, dock, fell, lash
05 berth, heath, hitch, tie up
06 anchor, fasten, secure, upland
08 make fast, moorland
10 drop anchor

moot
04 open, pose
05 argue, vexed
06 broach, debate, knotty, submit
07 advance, bring up, propose, suggest
08 academic, arguable, disputed, doubtful
09 debatable, introduce
10 disputable, put forward
12 open to debate, questionable
13 controversial

mop
04 mane, mass, soak, swab
06 absorb, sponge
10 head of hair

◻ **mop up**
06 absorb, soak up, wipe up
07 clean up, round up
09 finish off

mope
04 fret, pine, sulk
05 brood, droop, grump
06 grieve, grouch, misery, moaner
07 despair, killjoy
08 languish
09 introvert, pessimist

◻ **mope about**
04 idle, loll, moon
05 mooch
06 lounge, wander
08 languish

moral
04 good, just, pure
05 adage, maxim, right
06 chaste, decent, dictum, honest, lesson, proper, saying

07 epigram, ethical, meaning, message, precept, proverb, upright
08 aphorism, virtuous
09 righteous
10 high-minded, honourable, principled, upstanding
11 clean-living

morale
05 heart
06 spirit
07 spirits
10 confidence, self-esteem
11 hopefulness, state of mind
13 esprit de corps
14 self-confidence

morality
06 ethics, ideals, morals, virtue
07 decency, honesty
08 chastity, goodness
09 integrity, propriety, rectitude, standards
10 principles
13 righteousness

moralize
06 preach
07 lecture
09 sermonize
11 pontificate

morals
06 ethics, habits, ideals
07 conduct
08 morality, scruples
09 integrity, moral code, standards
10 principles
11 moral values

morass
03 bog, fen
04 mess, mire, moss, quag
05 chaos, marsh, swamp
06 slough
08 quagmire
09 confusion, marshland, quicksand

moratorium
03 ban
04 halt, stay
05 delay
06 freeze
07 embargo, respite
08 stoppage
10 standstill, suspension
12 postponement

morbid
06 ailing, gloomy, grisly, horrid, morose, sombre
07 ghastly, hideous, macabre

08 diseased, ghoulish, gruesome, horrible
09 unhealthy
10 lugubrious
11 unwholesome
12 insalubrious

mordant
04 acid
05 edged, harsh, sharp
06 biting, bitter
07 acerbic, caustic, cutting, pungent, vicious, waspish
08 critical, incisive, scathing, stinging, venomous, wounding
09 sarcastic, trenchant
10 astringent

more
03 new
05 added, again, extra, fresh, other, spare
06 better, longer
07 another, besides, further
09 increased
10 additional
13 supplementary

moreover
04 also
06 as well
07 besides, further
10 in addition, what is more
11 furthermore
12 additionally

morgue
08 mortuary
12 charnel house
14 funeral parlour

moribund
05 dying
06 doomed, ebbing, fading, feeble, senile, waning
07 failing
08 comatose, expiring, lifeless, stagnant
10 in extremis, stagnating
11 obsolescent, on the way out, wasting away
14 on your last legs

morning
02 a.m.
04 dawn
07 sunrise
08 daybreak, daylight
10 before noon, break of day

moron
04 clot, dolt, dope fool
05 dumbo, dunce, idiot
06 cretin, dimwit
07 buffoon, halfwit

08 imbecile
09 simpleton

moronic
04 dumb
06 stupid, unwise
08 gormless, ignorant
09 ludicrous, pointless, senseless
10 half-witted
12 simple-minded
13 unintelligent

morose
04 glum, grim, sour
06 gloomy
08 mournful, taciturn
09 depressed, saturnine
10 lugubrious
11 bad-tempered, ill-tempered, melancholic

morsel
03 bit
04 atom, bite, part
05 crumb, grain, piece, scrap, slice, taste
06 nibble, titbit
07 modicum, segment, soupçon
08 fraction, fragment, mouthful, particle

mortal
03 man
04 body, dire
05 awful, being, cruel, fatal, grave, great, human, woman
06 bitter, bodily, deadly, lethal, person, severe
07 earthly, extreme, fleshly, intense, killing, worldly
08 creature, temporal, terrible, vengeful
09 corporeal, earthling, ephemeral, transient
10 human being, implacable, individual, perishable, relentless, unbearable

mortality
05 death
07 carnage, killing
08 casualty, fatality, humanity
09 death rate, slaughter
10 loss of life, transience
11 earthliness, worldliness
13 perishability

mortgage
04 bond, lien, loan
06 pledge, wadset
08 security
09 debenture

mortification
05 shame
07 chagrin, control
08 disgrace, ignominy, vexation
09 abasement, annoyance, dishonour
10 asceticism, chastening, conquering, discipline, loss of face, punishment, self-denial
11 confounding, humiliation, self-control, subjugation
12 discomfiture
13 embarrassment

mortified
06 shamed
07 ashamed, crushed, humbled
09 disgraced, horrified
10 confounded, humiliated
11 dishonoured, embarrassed

mortify
03 die
04 deny
05 abash, annoy, crush, shame
06 humble, offend, subdue
07 affront, chagrin, chasten, conquer, control, deflate, horrify
08 bring low, chastise, confound, disgrace, restrain, suppress
09 discomfit, dishonour, embarrass, humiliate
10 disappoint, discipline, put to shame

mortifying
07 shaming
11 humiliating, ignominious
12 embarrassing

mortuary
06 morgue
09 deadhouse
12 charnel house
14 funeral parlour

most
04 bulk, mass
08 majority
09 almost all, nearly all
10 lion's share
13 preponderance

mostly
06 mainly
07 as a rule, chiefly, largely, overall, usually
08 above all
09 generally, in general, in the main
10 especially, on the whole
11 principally

13 predominantly
14 for the most part

moth
➤ *Types of moth*:
03 wax
04 puss
05 gypsy
06 burnet, carpet, lackey, lappet, magpie, turnip, winter
07 buff-tip, clothes, emperor, silver-Y, six-spot
08 cinnabar, peppered, silkworm
11 garden tiger, pale tussock, swallowtail
12 peach blossom, red underwing
➤ See also **animal**

moth-eaten
03 old
04 worn
05 dated, mangy, musty, seedy, stale
06 mouldy, ragged, shabby
07 ancient, archaic, decayed, outworn, worn-out
08 decrepit, tattered
10 threadbare

mother
02 ma
03 dam, mam, mom, mum
04 baby, base, bear, rear, tend
05 cause, fount, mamma, mater, mommy, mummy, mumsy, nurse, raise, roots, spoil
06 matron, origin, pamper, parent, source, spring
07 care for, cherish, indulge, nurture, produce
08 ancestor, fuss over, old woman
09 look after, matriarch
10 bring forth, derivation, foundation, procreator, take care of, wellspring
11 overprotect
12 progenitress
13 materfamilias

motherly
04 fond, kind, warm
06 caring, gentle, loving, tender
08 maternal
10 comforting, protective
12 affectionate

motif
04 form, idea, logo
05 shape, theme, topic
06 design, device, emblem

08 ornament

motion
03 bid, nod
04 sign, wave
05 usher
06 action, beckon, direct, signal
07 gesture, project
08 activity, mobility, motility, movement, progress, proposal
10 indication, suggestion
11 gesticulate, proposition

❑in motion
05 going
06 moving
07 on the go, running
08 under way
09 on the move
10 in progress, travelling
11 functioning, operational

motionless
05 fixed, inert, rigid, still
06 at rest, frozen, halted, static
07 resting
08 immobile, lifeless, stagnant, standing, unmoving
09 inanimate, paralysed, unmovable
10 stationary, stock-still, transfixed
13 at a standstill

motivate
04 draw, goad, lead, move, push, spur, stir, urge
05 bring, cause, drive, impel
06 arouse, excite, incite, induce, kindle, prompt, propel
07 actuate, inspire, provoke, trigger
08 activate, initiate, persuade
09 encourage, stimulate

motivation
04 push, spur, urge
05 drive
06 desire, motive, reason
07 impulse
08 momentum, stimulus
09 incentive, prompting
10 incitement, inducement
11 inspiration, instigation

motive
04 goad, lure, spur, urge
05 basis, cause
06 design, desire, ground, object, reason
07 grounds, impulse, purpose
08 occasion, stimulus, thinking
09 incentive, influence, intention, rationale

10 attraction, incitement, inducement, motivation
11 inspiration
13 consideration, encouragement

motley
07 dappled, diverse, mottled, piebald, spotted, striped
08 assorted, many-hued
09 colourful
10 variegated
11 diversified
12 multifarious
13 heterogeneous, multicoloured, particoloured

motor

➤ *Names of motor racers:*
04 Hill (Damon), Hill (Graham), Hunt (James), Ickx (Jacky), Moss (Stirling)
05 Clark (Jim), Lauda (Niki), Olsen (Ole), Prost (Alain), Senna (Ayrton), Unser (Al)
06 Alessi (Jean), Berger (Gerhard), Briggs (Barry), Dunlop (Joey), Fangio (Juan Manuel), Irvine (Eddie), Piquet (Nelson), Sheene (Barry), Walker (Murray)
07 Brabham (Jack), Brundle (Martin), Ferrari (Enzo), Mansell (Nigel), McLaren (Bruce), Segrave (Sir Henry), Stewart (Jackie), Surtees (John)
08 Agostini (Giacomo), Andretti (Mario), Campbell (Donald), Campbell (Sir Malcolm), Hakkinen (Mikka), Williams (Frank)
09 Blomquist (Stig), Coulthard (David), Chevrolet (Louis)
10 Fittipaldi (Emerson), Schumacher (Michael), Schumacher (Ralph), Villeneuve (Jacques)
12 Rickenbacker (Edward Vernon)
➤ See also **sport**

➤ *Parts of a motor vehicle:*
03 ABS
04 axle, boot, gear, hood, horn, jack, tyre, vent, wing
05 grill, shaft, trunk, wheel
06 airbag, bonnet, bumper, clutch, engine, fender, hub-cap, towbar

07 battery, chassis, fog lamp, gas tank, gearbox, spoiler, sunroof
08 air brake, air inlet, bodywork, brake pad, car phone, car radio, headrest, ignition, jump lead, oil gauge, roof rack, seat belt, silencer, solenoid, track rod
09 brake drum, brake shoe, crankcase, dashboard, disc brake, drum brake, fuel gauge, gear-lever, gear-stick, handbrake, headlight, indicator, monocoque, prop shaft, rear light, reflector, sidelight, spare tyre, stoplight, wheel arch
10 brake light, drive shaft, petrol tank, power brake, rev counter, side mirror, stick shift, suspension, windscreen, windshield, wing mirror
11 accelerator, anti-roll bar, exhaust pipe, ignition key, number plate, speedometer
12 license plate, parking-light, transmission
13 cruise control, pneumatic tyre, rack and pinion, radial-ply tyre, shock absorber, side-impact bar, steering-wheel
14 central locking, electric window, four-wheel drive, hydraulic brake, rear-view mirror, reversing light, steering-column
15 child-safety seat, instrument panel, windscreen-wiper
➤ See also **car**; **vehicle**

mottled
07 blotchy, dappled, flecked
08 blotched, speckled, splotchy, stippled
10 variegated

motto
05 adage, axiom, gnome, maxim
06 byword, dictum, slogan
09 catchword, watchword
10 golden rule

mould
03 cut, die, rot
04 cast, form, kind, line, make, must, sort, type, work
05 brand, forge, model, shape, stamp, style
06 create, design, format, fungus, mildew, sculpt

07 calibre, fashion, pattern
08 template
09 character, formation, mustiness, structure
12 construction
13 configuration

moulder
03 rot
05 decay, waste
06 humify, perish
07 corrupt, crumble
09 decompose
10 turn to dust
12 disintegrate

mouldy
03 bad
05 fusty, musty, stale
06 putrid, rotten
08 blighted, mildewed

mound
03 lot
04 bank, dune, heap, hill, pile, rise, tump
05 hoard, knoll, ridge, stack, store
06 barrow, bundle, supply
07 hillock, hummock, tumulus
08 mountain
09 abundance, earthwork, elevation, stockpile
10 collection, embankment
12 accumulation

mount
04 base, go up, grow, rise, soar
05 build, climb, frame, get on, get up, horse, put on, scale, set up, stage, stand, steed, swell
06 accrue, ascend, jump on, launch, pile up
07 arrange, backing, build up, climb on, climb up, display, exhibit, fixture, install, prepare, produce, support
08 escalate, increase, jump onto, mounting, multiply, organize
09 clamber up, climb on to, intensify
10 accumulate, get astride

mountain
03 alp, lot, tor
04 fell, heap, hill, mass, peak, pile
05 mound, mount, stack
06 height, massif
07 backlog
08 pinnacle
09 abundance, elevation
12 accumulation

▶ *Names of mountaineers*:
04 Hunt (John, Lord)
05 Munro (Sir Hugh Thomas),
   Scott (Doug)
06 Irvine (Andrew), Necker
   (Louis Albert), Tilman
   (Harold William), Uemura
   (Naomi)
07 Hillary (Sir Edmund),
   Mallory (George), Shipton
   (Eric Earle), Simpson
   (Myrtle Lillias), Tenzing
   (Sherpa), Whymper
   (Edward)
08 Coolidge (William
   Augustus Brevoort),
   MacInnes (Hamish),
   Whillans (Don)
09 Bonington (Chris)
13 Tenzing Norgay
➤ See also **sport**

▶ *Names of mountains and
mountain ranges. We have
omitted the words* mount,
mountain *and* mountains
*from names given in the
following list but you may need
to include one of these words as
part of the solution to some
crossword clues.*
02 K2
03 Dom
04 Alps, Blue, Cook, Fuji, Jura,
   Ossa, Rila, Sion, Ural
05 Altai, Andes, Atlas, Downs,
   Eiger, Ghats, Kenya, Logan,
   Matra, Ozark, Rocky, Table,
   Tatra
06 Ararat, Deccan, Egmont,
   Elbert, Elbrus, Hoggar,
   Lhotse, Makalu, Mourne,
   Musala, Pindus, Taurus,
   Vosges, Zagros
07 Beskids, Everest, Lebanon,
   Olympus, Rainier,
   Rhodope, Roraima, Scafell,
   Skiddaw, Snowdon, Stanley,
   Troödos
08 Ben Nevis, Cameroon,
   Catskill, Caucasus,
   Cévennes, Five Holy,
   Jungfrau, Kinabalu, Mauna
   Kea, Mauna Loa,
   McKinley, Pennines,
   Pyrenees, Rushmore,
   St Helens
09 Allegheny, Annapurna,
   Apennines, Blue Ridge,
   Dolomites, Grampians,
   Helvellyn, Himalayas,
   Hindu Kush, Lenin Peak,

Mont Blanc, Tirol Alps,
   Zugspitze
10 Adirondack, Cader Idris,
   Cairngorms, Cantabrian,
   Carpathian, Chimborazo,
   Great Smoky, Matterhorn,
   Pobedy Peak
11 Appalachian, Arthur's Pass,
   Black Forest, Kilimanjaro,
   Mendip Hills
12 Bavarian Alps, Cascade
   Range, Cheviot Hills,
   Darling Range,
   Popocatepetl, Sierra
   Nevada, Southern Alps,
   Tibet Plateau, Victoria Peak
13 Chiltern Hills, Communism
   Peak, Kangchenjunga,
   Stirling Range
14 Australian Alps, Bavarian
   Forest, Bohemian Forest,
   Fichtelgebirge, Flinders
   Ranges, Grand St Bernard,
   Hamersley Range,
   Mackenzie Range,
   Musgrave Ranges
15 Guiana Highlands

mountainous
04 high, huge, vast
05 hilly, lofty, rocky, steep
06 alpine, craggy, upland
07 immense, massive, soaring
08 colossal, enormous,
   gigantic, highland,
   towering

mountebank
04 fake
05 cheat, fraud, pseud, quack
06 con man, phoney
08 impostor, swindler
09 charlatan, trickster

mourn
04 keen, miss, wail, weep
06 bemoan, bewail, grieve,
   lament, regret, sorrow

mourner
04 mute
06 keener
08 bereaved

mournful
03 sad
06 tragic, woeful
07 elegiac, unhappy
08 dejected, desolate,
   downcast, funereal
09 depressed, sorrowful
10 lugubrious, melancholy
11 heartbroken
12 disconsolate, heavy-
   hearted

13 broken-hearted,
   grief-stricken

mourning
05 grief
06 sorrow
07 keening, wailing, weeping
08 grieving
09 sorrowing
11 bereavement, lamentation

moustache
06 walrus
08 whiskers
09 mustachio
10 face fungus

mousy
03 shy
04 drab, dull
05 plain, quiet, timid
07 greyish
08 brownish, timorous
09 diffident, withdrawn
10 colourless

mouth
03 gas, gob, lip, say
04 door, form, gall, jaws, lips,
   trap, vent
05 chops, delta, inlet, utter
06 babble, hot air, kisser, outlet
07 estuary, opening, orifice,
   whisper
08 aperture, boasting,
   bragging, cakehole, idle
   talk, rudeness, traphole
09 empty talk, enunciate,
   insolence, pronounce
10 articulate, embouchure

▶ *Parts of the mouth*:
03 gum
05 uvula
06 tongue, tonsil
07 hare lip
08 lower lip, upper lip
10 hard palate, soft palate
11 cleft palate
➤ See also **teeth**

mouthful
03 bit, sip, sup
04 bite, drop, gulp, slug
05 taste
06 morsel, nibble, sample, titbit

mouthpiece
05 agent, organ
07 journal
08 delegate
09 spokesman
10 periodical
11 publication, spokeswoman
12 propagandist, spokesperson
14 representative

movable
06 mobile
08 flexible, portable
09 alterable, portative
10 adjustable, changeable
12 transferable
13 transportable

movables
04 gear
05 goods, stuff
06 things
07 effects
08 chattels, property
09 furniture
10 belongings
11 impedimenta, plenishings, possessions

move
02 go
03 act
04 lead, pass, push, stir, tack, take, urge, walk
05 bring, budge, carry, cause, drive, fetch, impel, leave, rouse, shift, shunt, swing, touch, upset
06 action, affect, arouse, change, decamp, depart, device, excite, go away, incite, induce, motion, prompt, propel, remove, switch, travel
07 actuate, advance, agitate, disturb, gesture, impress, incline, inspire, measure, migrate, proceed, propose, provoke, removal, request, step out, suggest
08 activity, advocate, motivate, move away, movement, persuade, progress, relocate, transfer
09 influence, manoeuvre, migration, move house, recommend, stimulate, stratagem, transport, transpose
10 put forward, relocation, take action
11 make strides
13 gesticulation, repositioning
15 change of address

□ get a move on
07 hurry up, speed up
09 make haste, shake a leg
11 get cracking
15 put your foot down

□ on the move
06 active, moving
07 on the go
08 under way

09 advancing
11 progressing

movement
03 act, bit
04 fall, flow, guts, move, part, rise, wing
05 drift, drive, group, party, piece, shift, swing, trend, works
06 action, change, moving, system
07 advance, crusade, current, faction, gesture, passage, portion, section
08 activity, campaign, division, progress, shifting, stirring, tendency, transfer, workings
09 agitation, coalition, evolution, mechanism, variation
10 relocation
11 development, improvement, progression
12 breakthrough, organization
13 gesticulation, repositioning
14 transportation

movie
04 film
05 flick, video
06 silent, talkie
07 picture
11 feature film
13 motion picture

moving
05 astir
06 active, mobile, motile, urging
07 driving, dynamic, emotive, kinetic, leading
08 arousing, exciting, in motion, pathetic, poignant, stirring, touching, worrying
09 affecting, emotional, inspiring, thrilling, upsetting
10 disturbing, impressive, motivating, persuasive
11 influential, stimulating
12 manoeuvrable
13 inspirational

mow
03 cut
04 clip, crop, trim
05 shear
06 scythe

□ mow down
07 butcher, cut down
08 decimate, massacre
09 shoot down, slaughter
11 cut to pieces

much
04 a lot, lots
05 ample, great, heaps, loads, often
06 plenty
07 copious, greatly
08 abundant, lashings
09 extensive, plentiful
10 a great deal, frequently, widespread
11 substantial
12 considerable, considerably
14 to a great extent

muck
03 mud
04 crud, dirt, dung, mire, scum, yuck
05 filth, grime, guano, gunge, slime
06 faeces, grunge, manure, ordure, sewage, sludge
09 excrement

□ muck about, muck around
05 upset
06 bother, mess up, tamper
08 dishevel, disorder
09 interfere, mess about
10 disarrange, fool around, lark around, mess around, play around
15 lead a merry dance

□ muck up
04 ruin
05 botch, spoil, wreck
06 bungle, cock up, mess up
07 louse up, screw up

mucky
05 dirty, grimy, messy, muddy, slimy
06 filthy, soiled

mucous
05 slimy
06 snotty, viscid
07 viscous
12 mucilaginous

mud
04 mire, ooze, silt
06 sludge

muddle
04 daze, mess
05 chaos, mix up, mix-up
06 bemuse, jumble
07 clutter, confuse, perplex
08 befuddle, bewilder, confound, disarray, disorder, jumble up, scramble
09 confusion
11 disorganize

muddle through
05 get by
08 get along

muddled
06 woolly
07 chaotic, mixed-up, unclear
08 confused
09 befuddled, perplexed
10 bewildered, disarrayed, disordered, incoherent
13 disorientated

muddy
04 dull, foul, hazy, miry, oozy, soil
05 boggy, cloud, dingy, dirty, fuzzy, grimy, mucky, murky
06 cloudy, filthy, grubby, jumble, marshy, opaque, quaggy, slushy, swampy, tangle, turbid
07 begrime, blurred, obscure
10 indistinct
11 disorganize, make unclear

muff
05 botch, fluff, spoil
06 bungle, mess up, mishit

muffle
03 gag
06 dampen, deaden, muzzle, soften, stifle, wrap up
07 envelop, quieten, smother
08 suppress

mug
03 cup, pot, rob
04 bash, face, fool, gull
05 chump
06 attack, batter, beaker, beat up, do over, jump on, kisser, sucker, visage, waylay
07 assault, muggins, tankard
08 features
09 simpleton, soft touch
10 knock about
11 countenance

mug up
04 cram, swot
06 bone up

muggy
04 damp
05 close, humid, moist
06 clammy, sticky, stuffy, sultry
07 airless
10 oppressive, sweltering

mulish
07 defiant
08 perverse, stubborn
09 difficult, obstinate, pig-headed

10 headstrong, inflexible, refractory, self-willed
11 intractable
12 intransigent

mull

mull over
06 muse on, ponder
08 chew over, consider, meditate, ruminate
09 reflect on, think over
10 deliberate, think about
11 contemplate

multicoloured
06 motley
10 variegated

multifarious
04 many
06 legion, varied
07 diverse
08 manifold, multiple, numerous
09 different, multiform

multiple
04 many
07 several, various
08 manifold, numerous

multiplicity
03 lot
04 host, lots, mass, tons
05 heaps, loads, piles
06 myriad, oodles, scores
09 profusion

multiply
04 grow
05 boost, breed
06 expand, extend, spread
07 augment, build up
08 increase
09 propagate, reproduce
11 proliferate

multitude
03 lot, mob
04 herd, host, lots, mass
05 crowd, horde, plebs, swarm
06 legion, people, public, rabble, throng
08 assembly, populace, riff-raff
09 hoi polloi
10 common herd

multitudinous
04 many
06 legion, myriad
07 teeming, umpteen
08 manifold, numerous, swarming
09 abounding, countless
11 innumerable

mum
04 dumb, mute
05 quiet
06 silent
11 close-lipped, tight-lipped
12 close-mouthed

mumble
06 murmur, rumble
11 speak softly
14 speak unclearly, talk to yourself

mumbo-jumbo
04 cant, rite
05 chant, charm, magic, spell
06 humbug, jargon, ritual
08 claptrap, nonsense
09 gibberish, rigmarole
10 hocus-pocus
12 gobbledygook, superstition

munch
03 eat
04 chew
05 champ, chomp
06 crunch
09 masticate

mundane
05 banal
06 boring
07 earthly, humdrum, prosaic, routine
08 everyday, ordinary, temporal, workaday
11 commonplace, terrestrial

municipal
04 city, town
05 civic, civil, urban

municipality
04 city, town
05 burgh
07 borough

munificence
08 largesse
10 generosity, liberality
12 generousness, philanthropy
13 bounteousness
14 open-handedness

munificent
06 lavish
07 liberal
08 generous, princely
09 bounteous, bountiful
10 free-handed, open-handed
11 magnanimous
15 philanthropical

murder
04 beat, do in, hell, kill, slay
05 agony, spoil, waste, wreck
06 misery, ordeal, rub out

07 anguish, bump off, butcher,
clobber, destroy, killing,
slaying, take out, torment,
torture, wipe out

08 blow away, butchery,
homicide, knock off,
massacre

09 bloodshed, eliminate,
execution, liquidate, matricide,
patricide, slaughter, uxoricide

10 annihilate, fratricide, put to
death, sororicide

11 infanticide, liquidation

12 manslaughter

13 assassination

murderer
06 killer, slayer
07 butcher
08 assassin, homicide
09 cut-throat
11 slaughterer

murderous
06 bloody, deadly, lethal,
mortal
07 arduous, killing
09 cut-throat, ferocious,
homicidal
12 bloodthirsty

murky
03 dim
05 dingy, dirty, foggy, misty,
shady
06 cloudy, dismal, dreary,
gloomy, turbid
07 obscure
08 overcast
10 mysterious, suspicious

murmur
03 hum
04 buzz, carp, purl, purr
05 gripe, whine
06 grouse, intone, mumble,
mutter, object, rumble, whinge
07 carping, grumble,
humming, protest, whisper
08 complain
09 belly-ache, complaint,
criticize, find fault,
grievance, muttering,
objection, undertone,
whingeing
15 dissatisfaction

murmuring
04 buzz, purr
06 mumble, rumble
07 buzzing, purring, whisper
08 mumbling, rumbling, susurrus
09 muttering
10 whispering
11 murmuration

muscle
04 beef
05 brawn, clout, force, might,
power, sinew
06 tendon, weight
08 ligament, strength

➤ *Names of muscles:*
05 psoas
06 biceps, rectus, soleus
07 deltoid, gluteus, triceps
08 scalenus
09 abdominal, sartorius, trapezius
10 quadriceps
13 gastrocnemius
15 pectoralis major, pectoralis
minor, peroneal muscles

☐ **muscle in**
05 shove
06 butt in, jostle, push in
09 strongarm

muscular
05 beefy, burly, hefty, husky
06 brawny, rugged, sinewy,
strong, sturdy
07 fibrous
08 athletic, powerful, stalwart,
vigorous
09 strapping

muse
05 brood, dream, think, weigh
06 ponder, review
07 reflect
08 cogitate, consider,
meditate, mull over,
ruminate
09 speculate, think over
10 deliberate
11 contemplate

➤ *Names of the Nine Muses:*
04 Clio
05 Aoede, Erato, Mneme
06 Melete, Thalia, Urania
07 Euterpe
08 Calliope
09 Melpomene
10 Polyhymnia
11 Terpsichore
➤ See also **mythology**

museum

➤ *Names of galleries and
museums. We have omitted the
words* gallery *and* museum
*from names given in the
following list but you may need
to include these words as part of
the solution to some crossword
clues.*
03 ICA
04 Tate
05 Prado, Terme

06 Correr, London, Louvre,
Uffizi
07 British, Fogg Art, Hofburg,
Pushkin, Science, Vatican
08 Bargello, Borghese,
National, Pergamum
09 Accademia, Albertina,
Arnolfini, Ashmolean,
Belvedere, Cloisters,
Deutsches, Hermitage,
Holocaust, Sans Souci,
Tretyakov
10 Guggenheim, Pinakothek,
Pitt-Rivers, Serpentine
11 Fitzwilliam, Imperial War,
Musée d'Orsay, Pitti Palace,
Rijksmuseum
12 Whitworth Art
13 Jean Paul Getty
14 Barbican Centre, Natural
History, State Hermitage
15 Frick Collection, Museum
of Mankind, South Bank
Centre

mush
03 pap
04 corn, mash, pulp
05 paste, purée, slush, swill
08 schmaltz
11 mawkishness
14 sentimentality

mushroom
04 boom, grow
06 expand, spread, sprout
07 burgeon, shoot up
08 flourish, increase, spring up
11 proliferate

➤ *Types of mushrooms and
toadstools:*
03 cep
05 morel
06 ink cap
07 amanita, blewits, boletus,
truffle
08 death cap, shiitake
09 earth ball, fairy ring, fly
agaric
10 champignon, false morel,
lawyer's wig, panther cap
11 chanterelle, common morel,
honey fungus, sulphur tuft,
velvet shank
12 common ink cap, horn of
plenty, wood hedgehog
13 copper trumpet,, gypsy
mushroom, horse
mushroom, shaggy milk
cap, shaggy parasol, woolly
milk cap
14 button mushroom,
man on horseback,

oyster mushroom,
satan's mushroom

15 beefsteak fungus, destroying
angel, parasol mushroom,
stinking parasol

➤ See also **food**; **fungus**

mushy

05 pappy, pulpy, weepy
06 doughy, sloppy, slushy,
sugary, syrupy
07 mawkish, squashy, squidgy
08 squelchy
09 schmaltzy
10 saccharine
11 sentimental

music

➤ *Types of music*:

03 pop, rap, ska
04 folk, funk, jazz, jive, rock,
soul
05 blues, dance, disco, house,
R and B, swing
06 ballet, choral, doo-wop,
garage, gospel, grunge,
hip-hop, reggae, sacred
07 chamber, karaoke, ragtime,
skiffle
08 ballroom, folk rock, hard
rock, jazz-funk, operatic,
oratorio, punk rock
09 acid house, bluegrass,
classical, Dixieland,
honky-tonk
10 electronic, heavy metal,
incidental, orchestral
11 rock and roll
12 boogie-woogie,
instrumental
14 rhythm and blues

➤ See also **composer**;
conductor; **instrument**;
jazz; **libretto**; **musical**;
musician; **opera**;
oratorio; **singer**; **song**;
songwriter

musical

06 dulcet, mellow
07 lyrical, melodic, tuneful
09 melodious
10 euphonious, harmonious
11 mellifluous

➤ See also **instrument**;
music

➤ *Musicals include*:

04 Cats, Hair, Rent
05 Annie, Chess, Evita, Zorba
06 Grease, Kismet, Oliver!,
The Wiz
07 Cabaret, Camelot, Follies

08 Carnival, Carousel,
Godspell, Oklahoma!, Peter
Pan, Show Boat
09 Brigadoon, Funny Girl, Girl
Crazy, On the Town
10 Hello Dolly!, Kiss Me Kate,
Miss Saigon, My Fair Lady
11 A Chorus Line, Babes in
Arms, Carmen Jones, Me
and My Girl, Sweeney Todd,
The King and I, The Music
Man
12 Anything Goes, Guys and
Dolls, South Pacific, The
Boy Friend
13 Aspects of Love, Blood
Brothers, Les Miserables,
Man of La Mancha, The
Pajama Game, West Side
Story
15 Annie Get Your Gun, La
Cage aux Folles, Sunset
Boulevard, The Sound of
Music

➤ *Types of musical*
composition:

03 jig, lay, rag
04 aria, hymn, lied, opus, raga,
song, tune
05 canon, carol, étude, fugue,
gigue, march, opera, piece,
rondo, round, suite, tango,
track, waltz
06 aubade, ballad, bolero,
lieder, masque, minuet,
number, shanty, sonata
07 ballade, bourrée, cantata,
fanfare, gavotte, mazurka,
partita, prelude, requiem,
scherzo, toccata
08 concerto, fandango,
fantasia, galliard, hornpipe,
madrigal, nocturne,
operetta, overture, rhapsody,
serenade, sonatina,
symphony
09 allemande, arabesque,
bagatelle, capriccio,
écossaise, impromptu,
invention, pastorale,
polonaise, sarabande,
spiritual, voluntary
10 barcarolle, humoresque,
intermezzo, opera buffa,
tarantella
11 composition, sinfonietta
12 divertimento
14 chorale prelude, concerto
grosso

➤ *Names of musical*
compositions:

04 Saul
05 Rodeo
06 Bolero, Elijah, Études,
Façade
07 Mazeppa, Messiah
08 Ballades, Caprices,
Creation, Drum Mass, Ode
to Joy, Peer Gynt
09 Capriccio, Fantaisie,
Finlandia, Jerusalem,
Nocturnes
10 Arabesques, Bacchanale,
Bagatelles, Concertino, The
Planets, The Seasons, Water
Music
11 Curlew River, Minute Waltz,
Requiem Mass, Stabat
Mater, Winterreise
12 A Sea Symphony, Danse
Macabre, Schéhérézade,
Trout Quintet
13 Carmina Burana, Choral
Fantasy, Faust Symphony,
Fêtes Galantes, Missa
Solemnis, On Wenlock
Edge, The Art of Fugue
14 Choral Symphony, Eroica
Symphony, Glagolitic Mass,
Prague Symphony,
Rhapsody in Blue, Slavonic
Dances, The Four Seasons
15 A Child of our Time,
Children's Corner, Emperor
Concerto, Jupiter Symphony,
Manfred Symphony, Peter
and the Wolf

➤ *Musical terms include*:

03 bar, bis, cue, key, tie
04 a due, alto, bass, beat, clef,
coda, fine, flat, fret, hold,
mode, mute, note, part, rest,
root, slur, solo, tone, tune,
turn
05 ad lib, breve, buffo, chord,
dolce, drone, forte, grave,
largo, lento, lyric, major,
metre, minim, minor, pause,
piano, piece, pitch, scale,
score, shake, sharp, staff,
stave, swell, tacet, tempo,
tenor, theme, triad, trill, tutti
06 a tempo, adagio, al fine, da
capo, encore, finale, legato,
medley, melody, octave,
phrase, presto, quaver,
rhythm, sempre, subito,
tenuto, timbre, treble,
tuning, unison, upbeat,
vivace

07 al segno, allegro, amoroso, andante, animato, attacca, cadence, con brio, con moto, concert, descant, harmony, marcato, mordent, natural, recital, refrain, soprano, tremolo, triplet, vibrato

08 acoustic, alto clef, arpeggio, baritone, bass clef, con fuoco, crotchet, diatonic, doloroso, dominant, downbeat, ensemble, interval, maestoso, moderato, movement, ostinato, ritenuto, semitone, semplice, sequence, staccato, vigoroso, virtuoso

09 alla breve, cantabile, chromatic, contralto, crescendo, glissando, harmonics, imitation, larghetto, orchestra, pizzicato, semibreve, sextuplet, sostenuto, sotto voce, spiritoso, tenor clef

10 accidental, affettuoso, allegretto, diminuendo, dissonance, double flat, fortissimo, intonation, mezzo forte, modulation, pentatonic, pianissimo, resolution, semiquaver, simple time, supertonic, tonic sol-fa, treble clef, two-two time

11 accelerando, arrangement, decrescendo, double sharp, fingerboard, leading note, quarter tone, rallentando, subdominant, syncopation

12 acciaccatura, alla cappella, appoggiatura, compound time, counterpoint, four-four time, key signature, six-eight time

13 accompaniment, improvisation, major interval, minor interval, orchestration, three-four time, time signature, transposition

14 demisemiquaver

15 perfect interval

musician

➤ *Types of musician*:

03 duo

04 band, bard, diva, duet, trio

05 choir, group, octet, piper

06 bugler, busker, oboist, player, sextet, singer

07 cellist, drummer, fiddler, harpist, maestro, pianist, quartet, quintet, soloist

08 composer, ensemble, flautist, organist, virtuoso, vocalist

09 balladeer, conductor, guitarist, orchestra, performer, trumpeter, violinist

10 prima donna, trombonist

11 accompanist

12 backing group, clarinettist

15 instrumentalist

➤ *Names of classical musicians*:

02 **Ma** (Yo-Yo)

03 **Pré** (Jacqueline du)

04 **Hess** (Dame Myra)

05 **Bream** (Julian), **Bülow** (Hans von), **Grove** (Sir George), **Ogdon** (John), **Sharp** (Cecil), **Stern** (Isaac)

06 **Casals** (Pablo), **Galway** (James), **Köchel** (Ludwig Ritter von), **Rizzio** (David)

07 **Blondel**, **Glennie** (Evelyn), **Heifetz** (Jascha), **Kennedy** (Nigel), **Menuhin** (Yehudi), **Perlman** (Itzhak), **Segovia** (Andrés), **Shankar** (Ravi)

08 **Paganini** (Niccolo), **Sarasate** (Martin Meliton), **Steinway** (Heinrich Engelhard), **Williams** (John)

09 **Ashkenazy** (Vladimir), **Barenboim** (Daniel), **Boulanger** (Nadia), **Guarnieri**, **Tortelier** (Paul)

10 **Cristofori**, **Paderewski** (Ignacy Jan), **Rubinstein** (Anton), **Rubinstein** (Artur), **Stradivari** (Antonio), **Villa-Lobos** (Heitor)

11 **Theodorakis** (Mikis)

12 **Rostropovich** (Mstislav)

➤ See also **music**

musing

07 reverie

08 dreaming, thinking

10 brown study, cogitation, meditation, rumination

11 cerebration, daydreaming

13 contemplation, introspection, wool-gathering

muss

06 ruffle, tousle

08 dishevel

10 disarrange

11 make a mess of

must

09 essential, necessity, requisite

10 imperative, sine qua non

11 requirement

muster

04 mass, meet

05 enrol, group, rally

06 gather, parade, summon

07 collect, marshal, meeting, round up

08 assemble, summon up

09 gathering

10 assemblage, congregate

12 call together, come together

13 bring together

14 gather together

❑**pass muster**

07 shape up

09 measure up

12 be acceptable, make the grade

15 come up to scratch

musty

05 fusty, stale

06 mouldy, smelly, stuffy

07 airless, decayed

08 mildewed

mutability

12 alterability

13 permutability

14 changeableness

mutable

08 changing, variable, volatile

09 alterable

10 changeable, permutable

15 interchangeable

mutation

06 change

07 anomaly

09 deviation, variation

10 adaptation

12 modification

14 transformation

mute

03 mum

04 dumb

05 lower

06 dampen, deaden, muffle, silent, stifle

07 aphasic, quieten, silence

08 suppress, tone down, wordless

09 noiseless, voiceless

10 speechless

11 unexpressed

muted

06 low-key, subtle

07 muffled, stifled, subdued

08 dampened, softened
10 restrained, suppressed

mutilate
03 cut, mar
04 hack, lame, maim, ruin
05 cut up, spoil
06 damage, impair, injure
07 butcher, disable
08 lacerate
09 disfigure, dismember
11 cut to pieces

mutilation
06 damage
07 maiming
10 amputation
12 detruncation,
   dismembering
13 disfigurement

mutinous
07 bolshie, riotous
09 insurgent, seditious
10 rebellious, subversive
11 anarchistic, disobedient
13 insubordinate, revolutionary

mutiny
04 defy, riot
05 rebel
06 resist, revolt, rise up, strike
08 defiance, uprising
09 rebellion
10 revolution
12 disobedience, insurrection

mutt
03 cur, dog
05 bitch, hound, pooch
07 mongrel

mutter
04 beef, carp, fuss
05 gripe, whine
06 grouse, mumble, murmur,
   object, rumble, whinge
07 grumble, protest, stutter
08 complain
09 belly-ache
14 talk to yourself

mutual
05 joint
06 common, shared
09 exchanged

muzzle
03 gag
05 check, choke
06 censor, fetter, stifle
07 inhibit, silence
08 restrain, suppress

muzzy
04 hazy
05 dazed, faint, fuzzy, tipsy
06 addled, groggy

07 blurred, muddled, unclear
08 confused
09 befuddled, unfocused
10 bewildered, indistinct

myopic
06 narrow
08 purblind
11 near-sighted, thoughtless
12 narrow-minded, short-
   sighted

myriad
04 army, host
05 flood, horde, swarm
06 scores, throng
09 countless, multitude,
   thousands
11 innumerable
13 multitudinous

mysterious
04 dark
05 weird
06 arcane, secret, veiled
07 cryptic, obscure, strange
08 abstruse, baffling, mystical,
   puzzling
09 enigmatic, recondite,
   secretive
10 mystifying, perplexing
11 inscrutable
12 inexplicable, unfathomable

mystery
06 enigma, puzzle, riddle,
   secret
07 problem, secrecy
08 mystique, question
09 ambiguity, conundrum,
   curiosity, obscurity,
   reticence, weirdness
11 furtiveness, strangeness
12 question mark
14 inscrutability
15 inexplicability,
   unfathomability

mystical
06 arcane, mystic, occult
08 abstruse, baffling, esoteric
09 recondite, spiritual
10 mysterious, paranormal
12 metaphysical, other-worldly,
   supernatural
13 preternatural
14 transcendental

mystify
06 baffle, puzzle
07 confuse, perplex
08 bewilder, confound

mystique
05 charm, magic, spell
07 glamour, mystery, secrecy

08 charisma
11 fascination

myth
03 lie
04 saga, tale
05 fable, story
06 legend
07 fantasy, fiction, untruth
08 folk tale
09 fairy tale, invention, tall story
10 fairy story

mythical
06 fabled, made-up
07 fantasy, pretend
08 fabulous, fanciful, invented
09 fairytale, fantastic,
   imaginary, legendary
10 fictitious
11 make-believe, non-existent

➤ *Mythical places include*:
03 Dis, Hel
04 Hell, Styx (River)
05 Argos, Babel, Hades, Lethe
   (River), Pluto, Thule
06 Albion, Asgard, Avalon,
   Heaven, Utgard
07 Alfheim, Arcadia, Elysium,
   Lemuria, Nirvana
08 Amazonia, Atlantis, El
   Dorado, Niflheim, Paradise,
   Valhalla, Vanaheim
09 Cockaigne, Fairyland,
   Purgatory, River Styx
10 River Lethe
11 Ultima Thule
13 Jewel Mountain,
   The Underworld
15 Cloudcuckooland, The
   Garden of Eden, The Isle
   of Avalon, The Tower of
   Babel

➤ See also **mythology**

mythological
06 fabled, mythic
08 fabulous
09 fairytale, folkloric,
   legendary
10 fictitious

➤ *Names of mythological*
creatures and spirits:
03 elf, imp, orc, roc
04 faun, fury, jinn, ogre, yeti
05 devil, demon, djinn, dryad,
   fairy, genie, ghost, ghoul,
   gnome, golem, harpy, lamia,
   naiad, nymph, pixie, satyr,
   shade, Siren, sylph, troll
06 bunyip, dragon, dybbuk,
   Furies, goblin, Gorgon,
   kraken, Lilith, Medusa,

merman, nereid, ogress,
Sphinx, sprite, wivern
07 banshee, brownie, centaur,
Chimera, Cyclops, gremlin,
griffin, lorelei, mermaid,
Pegasus, phoenix, unicorn,
windigo
08 basilisk, Cerberus,
Minotaur, succubus,
werewolf
09 hobgoblin, sasquatch
10 cockatrice, hippogriff,
leprechaun, sea serpent
11 hippocampus
15 Loch Ness monster
➤ See also **mythology**

mythology
04 lore
05 tales
06 legend
08 folklore
09 folk tales, tradition
10 traditions
➤ See also **god, goddess**;
grace; **legend**; **muse**;
mythical; **mythological**;
sage

▶ *Celtic mythology includes*:
03 Anu, Lug
04 Bran, Danu, Lugh, Ogma
05 Balor, Boann, Dagda,
Macha, Maeve, Neman,
Nuada, Oisin, Pwyll
06 Brigit, Danaan, Deidre,
Imbolc, Isolde, Ogmios,
Ossian
07 Beltane, Branwen, Brighid,
Samhain, Tristan
08 Manannan, Morrigan,
Rhiannon, Tir nan-Og
09 Cernunnos, Conchobar

10 Cú Chulainn
11 Finn mac Cool
14 Bran the Blessed, Finn mac
Cumhail

▶ *Characters from Greek
mythology*:
02 Io
04 Ajax, Dido, Echo, Leda,
Leto
05 Atlas, Chloe, Circe, Creon,
Danae, Helen, Hydra, Irene,
Jason, Kreon, Laius, Lamia,
Medea, Midas, Minos,
Niobe, Orion, Priam
06 Aeneas, Aeolus, Amazon,
Atreus, Cadmus, Castor,
Charon, Chiron, Cronus,,
Daphne, Dryads, Europa,
Europe, Furies, Hector,
Hecuba, Icarus, Kronos,
Medusa, Megara, Memnon,
Naiads, Nestor, Nymphs,
Oreads, Phoebe, Pollux,
Satyrs, Scylla, Semele,
Sileni, Sirens, Syrinx, Titans,
Triton, Typhon
07 Actaeon, Arachne, Ariadne,
Calypso, Chimera, Cyclops,
Daphnis, Diomede, Electra,
Galatea, Gorgons, Griffin,
Gryphon, Harpies, Jocasta,
Laocoon, Lapiths,
Maenads, Nereids, Oceanus,
Oedipus, Orestes, Orpheus,
Pandora, Pegasus, Perseus,
Phaedra, Silenus, Theseus,
Titania, Troilus, Ulysses
08 Achilles, Alcestis,
Alcmaeon, Antigone,
Arethusa, Atalanta,
Basilisk, Centaurs,

Cerberus, Chimaera,
Cressida, Cyclopes,
Daedalus, Diomedes,
Endymion, Eurydice,
Ganymede, Gigantes,
Heracles, Hercules,
Hyperion, Lycurgus,
Meleager, Menelaus,
Minotaur, Nausicaa,
Odysseus, Pasiphae,
Penelope, Phaethon,
Pleiades, Sisyphus, Tantalus,
Tiresias
09 Agamemnon, Andromeda,
Argonauts, Autolycus,
Cassandra, Charybdis,
Deucalion, Lotophagi,
Myrmidons, Narcissus,
Patroclus, Pygmalion,
Semiramis
10 Amphitryon, Andromache,
Cassiopeia, Cockatrice,
Erechtheus, Hamadryads,
Hesperides, Hippolytus,
Iphigeneia, Polyphemus,
Procrustes, Prometheus,
Telemachus
11 Bellerophon,
Lotus-eaters
12 Clytemnestra,
Hyperboreans
14 Hero and Leander

▶ *Characters from Roman
mythology*:
05 Lamia, Lares, Manes,
Remus, Sibyl
07 Latinus, Lemures, Lucrece,
Penates, Romulus, Sibylla,
Tarpeia
08 Lucretia
10 Rhea Silvia, Rhea Sylvia

nab
04 grab, nail, nick
05 catch, seize
06 arrest, collar, nobble, snatch
07 capture
09 apprehend

nabob
03 VIP
06 bigwig, tycoon
08 luminary
09 celebrity, personage
11 billionaire, millionaire

nadir
06 bottom, depths
08 low point
10 all-time low, rock bottom
11 lowest point

nag
03 bug, rip, vex
04 hack, jade, moan, plug
05 harry, horse, scold, worry
06 badger, berate, bother,
   harass, hassle, keffel, niggle,
   pester, pick on, plague
07 henpeck, torment, upbraid
08 complain, irritate, keep on at

nagging
06 aching
07 moaning, painful
08 critical, niggling, scolding,
   shrewish, worrying
10 continuous, irritating,
   nit-picking, persistent

nail
03 fix, nab, pin
04 brad, claw, grab, nick, tack
05 catch, clout, rivet, screw,
   seize, spike, sprig, talon
06 arrest, attach, collar, corner,
   fasten, hammer, nobble,
   pincer, secure, skewer
07 capture, pin down, toenail
08 fastener, identify, sparable
09 apprehend
10 fingernail

naïve
04 open
05 frank, green
06 candid, jejune, simple
07 artless, natural

08 gullible, innocent, wide-
   eyed
09 childlike, credulous,
   guileless, ingenuous,
   unworldly
10 unaffected
12 unsuspecting, unsuspicious
13 born yesterday,
   inexperienced
15 unsophisticated

naïvety
09 credulity, innocence
10 immaturity, simplicity
11 artlessness, gullibility
12 inexperience

naked
04 bald, bare, nude, open
05 overt, plain, stark
06 barren, patent, simple
07 blatant, denuded, glaring
08 disrobed, flagrant, in the
   raw, starkers, stripped,
   treeless
09 grassless, in the buff,
   unadorned, unclothed,
   uncovered, undressed
10 stark-naked, vulnerable
11 undisguised, unprotected
12 not a stitch on
13 with nothing on
15 in the altogether

nakedness
06 nudity
07 the buff, undress
08 baldness, bareness
09 plainness, starkness
10 barrenness, simplicity

namby-pamby
03 wet
04 prim, weak
05 vapid, weedy
06 feeble, prissy
07 anaemic, insipid, mawkish
09 spineless
11 sentimental
12 pretty-pretty

name
03 dub, tag, VIP
04 call, cite, fame, hero, note,
   pick, star, term

05 label, style, title
06 bigwig, choose, esteem,
   expert, handle, honour,
   renown, repute, select
07 appoint, baptize, entitle,
   epithet, mention, specify
08 big noise, christen, classify,
   cognomen, eminence,
   identify, luminary, monicker,
   nickname, nominate
09 a somebody, celebrity,
   character, dignitary
10 commission, popularity,
   prominence, reputation
11 appellation, designation,
   distinction

► *Boys' names:*
02 Al, Cy, Ed, Jo
03 Abe, Alf, Ali, Asa, Baz, Ben,
   Bob, Dai, Dan, Del, Den,
   Don, Gaz, Gil, Gus, Guy,
   Hew, Huw, Ian, Ike, Ira, Ivo,
   Jay, Jem, Jim, Joe, Jon, Ken,
   Kim, Kit, Lee, Len, Leo,
   Lew, Mat, Max, Nat, Ned,
   Nye, Pat, Pip, Rab, Rae, Ray,
   Reg, Rex, Rob, Rod, Roy,
   Sam, Sol, Tam, Ted, Tim,
   Tom, Vic, Viv, Wat, Wyn
04 Adam, Alan, Alec, Aled,
   Alex, Algy, Alun, Andy,
   Anil, Arun, Bart, Bert, Bill,
   Bram, Bryn, Carl, Chad,
   Chay, Clem, Colm, Dave,
   Davy, Dean, Dick, Dirk,
   Doug, Drew, Egon, Eric,
   Evan, Ewan, Ewen, Ezra,
   Finn, Fred, Gabe, Gary,
   Gene, Glen, Glyn, Gwyn,
   Hank, Huey, Hugh, Hugo,
   Iain, Ifor, Ivan, Ivon, Ivor,
   Jack, Jake, Jeff, Jock, Joel,
   Joey, John, Josh, Joss, Jude,
   Karl, Kirk, Kurt, Liam,
   Luke, Mark, Matt, Mick,
   Mike, Neal, Neil, Nick,
   Noam, Noel, Omar, Owen,
   Paul, Pete, Phil, Ravi, René,
   Rhys, Rick, Rolf, Rory,
   Ross, Ryan, Saul, Sean,
   Seth, Theo, Toby, Tony, Walt,
   Will, Yves, Zach, Zack

05 Aaron, Abd-al, Abdul, Abram, Adnan, Ahmad, Ahmed, Aidan, Aiden, Alfie, Allan, Allen, Angus, Anwar, Archy, Arran, Barry, Basil, Bazza, Benny, Billy, Bobby, Boris, Brent, Brett, Brian, Bruce, Bruno, Bryan, Calum, Cecil, Chaim, Chris, Chuck, Claud, Clint, Clive, Clyde, Colin, Colum, Conor, Corin, Cosmo, Craig, Cyril, Cyrus, Damon, Danny, David, Davie, Denis, Denny, Denys, Derek, Dicky, Dilip, Donal, Duane, Dwane, Dylan, Eddie, Edgar, Edwin, Elroy, Elton, Elvis, Elwyn, Emlyn, Emrys, Enoch, Ernie, Errol, Faruq, Felix, Floyd, Frank, Gabby, Garry, Gavin, Geoff, Gerry, Giles, Glenn, Gopal, Harry, Hasan, Henry, Homer, Humph, Husni, Hywel, Idris, Ieuan, Inigo, Isaac, Jacob, Jamal, James, Jamie, Jamil, Jared, Jason, Jerry, Jesse, Jimmy, Jools, Kamal, Kasim, Keith, Kenny, Kevin, Kumar, Lance, Larry, Leigh, Lenny, Leroy, Lewis, Linus, Lloyd, Louie, Louis, Lucas, Manny, Micky, Miles, Moses, Moshe, Mungo, Murdo, Myles, Neale, Neddy, Niall, Nicky, Nigel, Ollie, Orson, Oscar, Ozzie, Paddy, Percy, Perry, Peter, Piers, Rajiv, Ralph, Randy, Ricky, Roald, Robin, Roddy, Roger, Rowan, Rufus, Sacha, Sammy, Sandy, Sasha, Scott, Shane, Shaun, Shawn, Silas, Simon, Solly, Steve, Sunil, Taffy, Tariq, Teddy, Terry, Tommy, Vijay, Waldo, Wally, Wasim, Wayne, Willy, Wynne

06 Adrian, Albert, Alexei, Alexis, Alfred, Andrew, Antony, Archie, Arnold, Arthur, Ashley, Aubrey, Austin, Barney, Bernie, Bertie, Blaise, Callum, Calvin, Caspar, Cedric, Ciaran, Clancy, Claude, Clovis, Connor, Conrad, Dafydd, Damian, Damien, Daniel, Darren, Declan, Delroy, Dennis, Denzil, Dermot, Dicken, Dickie,

Dickon, Donald, Donnie, Dougal, Dudley, Dugald, Duggie, Duncan, Dustin, Eamonn, Edmund, Edward, Ernest, Eugene, Faisal, Faysal, Fergus, Finbar, Fingal, Finlay, Finley, Freddy, Gareth, George, Gerald, Gerard, Gideon, Gordon, Govind, Graeme, Graham, Gussie, Hamish, Harold, Haroun, Harvey, Hassan, Hayden, Haydon, Hector, Herbie, Hilary, Horace, Howard, Hubert, Hughie, Husain, Isaiah, Ismail, Israel, Jarvis, Jasper, Jeremy, Jerome, Jervis, Jethro, Jolyon, Jordan, Joseph, Joshua, Julian, Julius, Justin, Kelvin, Kieran, Kieron, Laurie, Lawrie, Leslie, Lester, Lionel, Lorcan, Lucius, Luther, Magnus, Mahmud, Marcel, Marcus, Marlon, Martin, Martyn, Marvin, Melvin, Melvyn, Mervyn, Milton, Morgan, Morris, Murray, Nathan, Nichol, Ninian, Norman, Oliver, Osbert, Oswald, Pascal, Pearce, Philip, Pierce, Randal, Ranulf, Reggie, Reuben, Richie, Robbie, Robert, Rodney, Roland, Ronald, Rudolf, Rupert, Samuel, Sanjay, Seamas, Seamus, Seumas, Shamus, Sidney, Sorley, St John, Steven, Stevie, Stuart, Sydney, Thomas, Timmie, Tobias, Trevor, Tyrone, Vernon, Victor, Vikram, Virgil, Vivian, Walter, Willie, Xavier

07 Abraham, Ambrose, Aneurin, Anthony, Auberon, Barnaby, Bernard, Bertram, Brendan, Chandra, Charles, Charley, Charlie, Christy, Clement, Crispin, Derrick, Desmond, Dominic, Douglas, Eustace, Finbarr, Francis, Frankie, Freddie, Gabriel, Geordie, Geraint, Gervase, Gilbert, Godfrey, Grahame, Gwillym, Herbert, Humphry, Hussain, Hussein, Ibrahim, Isadore, Isidore, Jeffrey, Johnnie,

Kenneth, Killian, Krishna, Lachlan, Leonard, Leopold, Lindsay, Lindsey, Ludovic, Malcolm, Matthew, Maurice, Michael, Murdoch, Mustafa, Neville, Nicolas, Orlando, Patrick, Peredur, Phillip, Quentin, Quintin, Quinton, Randall, Randolf, Ranulph, Raymond, Reynold, Richard, Rudolph, Russell, Shelley, Solomon, Stanley, Stephen, Stewart, Terence, Timothy, Torquil, Tristan, Vaughan, Vincent, Wilfred, Wilfrid, William, Winston, Zachary

08 Alasdair, Alastair, Algernon, Alistair, Augustus, Barnabas, Benedick, Benjamin, Beverley, Christie, Clarence, Clifford, Crispian, Cuthbert, Emmanuel, Frederic, Geoffrey, Humphrey, Jonathan, Jonathon, Kimberly, Kingsley, Lancelot, Laurence, Lawrence, Llewelyn, Matthias, Meredith, Mordecai, Muhammad, Nicholas, Perceval, Percival, Randolph, Reginald, Roderick, Terrance, Theodore, Tristram

09 Alexander, Archibald, Augustine, Christian, Ferdinand, Frederick, Kimberley, Launcelot, Nathaniel, Peregrine, Sebastian, Siegfried, Sylvester

10 Maximilian

11 Bartholomew, Christopher

▶ *Girls' names*:

02 Di, Jo, Mo

03 Ada, Ali, Amy, Ann,, Bea, Bee, Bel, Bet, Cis, Con, Deb, Dee, Dot, Emm, Ena, Eva, Eve, Fay, Flo, Gay, Ida, Isa, Ivy, Jan, Jay, Jen, Joy, Kay, Kim, Kit, Lea, Lee, Liv, Liz, Lou, Mae, May, Meg, Mia, Nan, Pat, Peg, Rae, Ray, Ria, Ros, Roz, Sal, Sue, Una, Val, Viv, Win, Zoë

04 Abby, Addy, Afra, Aggy, Alex, Ally, Alma, Anna, Anne, Babs, Bess, Beth, Cara, Caro, Cass, Ceri,

Cher, Cleo, Cora, Dana, Dawn, Dian, Dora, Edie, Edna, Ella, Elma, Emma, Emmy, Enid, Erin, Evie, Faye, Gabi, Gaia, Gail, Gale, Gaye, Gert, Gill, Gina, Gita, Gwen, Hope, Ines, Inez, Inga, Inge, Iona, Iris, Irma, Isla, Jade, Jane, Jean, Jess, Jill, Joan, Jodi, Jody, Joey, Joni, Joss, Jozy, Jude, Judy, June, Kate, Kath, Katy, Kaye, Lara, Leah, Lena, Lian, Lily, Lisa, Lise, Liza, Lois, Lola, Lucy, Lynn, Maev, Mary, Maud, Moll, Mona, Myra, Nell, Nina, Nita, Noel, Nora, Olga, Page, Phyl, Poll, Prue, Rana, Rene, Rita, Rona, Rosa, Rose, Ruby, Ruth, Sara, Sian, Sìne, Suky, Susy, Suzy, Tess, Thea, Tina, Toni, Trix, Vera, Vita, Zara, Zena, Zola

05 Adela, Adèle, Aggie, Agnes, Ailsa, Aisha, Alice, Allie, Amber, Anaïs, Angel, Angie, Anita, Annie, April, Avril, Aysha, Becky, Bella, Belle, Beryl, Bessy, Betsy, Betty, Biddy, Bunty, Candy, Carla, Carly, Carol, Cathy, Celia, Chloe, Chris, Cindy, Cissy, Clara, Clare, Coral, Daisy, Debby, Debra, Delia, Della, Diana, Diane, Dilys, Dinah, Dolly, Donna, Doris, Edith, Effie, Eliza, Ellen, Ellie, Elsie, Emily, Emmie, Erica, Ethel, Faith, Fanny, Farah, Ffion, Fiona, Fleur, Flora, Freda, Freya, Gabby, Gayle, Geeta, Gemma, Gerda, Ginny, Golda, Golde, Grace, Greta, Haley, Hatty, Hazel, Heidi, Helen, Helga, Hetty, Hilda, Holly, Honor, Ilana, Ilona, Irena, Irene, Ivana, Jamie, Janet, Janis, Jemma, Jenna, Jenny, Jessy, Jinny, Jodie, Joely, Josie, Joyce, Julia, Julie, Karen, Karin, Karla, Kathy, Katie, Katya, Kelly, Kerry, Kiera, Kitty, Kylie, Lalla, Laura, Leigh, Leila, Leona, Letty, Liana, Libby, Linda, Lindy, Lorna, Louie, Lucia, Lydia, Lynda, Lynne, Mabel, Madge, Maeve, Magda, Mamie, Mandy, Margo, Maria,

Marie, , Maude, Mavis, Megan, Mercy, Meryl, Moira, Molly, Morag, Morna, Moyra, Myrna, Nadia, Nancy, Nelly, Nerys, Nesta, Netty, Ngaio, Niamh, Nicky, Norah, Norma, Nuala, Olive, Olwen, Olwyn, Oprah, Paige, Pansy, Patsy, Patty, Paula, Pearl, Peggy, Penny, Petra, Pippa, Polly, Raine, Renée, Rhian, Rhoda, Rhona, Robin, Robyn, Rosie, Sadie, Sally, Sarah, Sasha, Shona, Shula, Sibyl, Sindy, Sonia, Sonya, Sophy, Stacy, Sukie, Susan, Susie, Sybil, Tammy, Tania, Tanya, Tessa, Thora, Tibby, Tilly, Tracy, Trina, Trish, Trixy, Trudy, Unity, Viola, Wanda, Wendy, Wilma, Zelda

06 Adella, Agatha, Aileen, Alexia, Alexis, Alicia, Alison, Althea, Amabel, Amanda, Amelia, Andrea, Angela, Anneka, Annika, Anthea, Aretha, Ashley, Astrid, Audrey, Auriel, Auriol, Aurora, Aurore, Averil, Ayesha, Barbie, Bertha, Bessie, Bianca, Blanch, Bonnie, Brenda, Bridie, Brigid, Brigit, Briony, Bryony, Carina, Carmel, Carmen, Carola, Carole, Carrie, Cassie, Cathie, Cecily, Celina, Cherie, Cherry, Cicely, Cissie, Claire, Connie, Daphne, Davina, Deanna, Deanne, Debbie, Denise, Dervla, Dianne, Dionne, Doreen, Dottie, Dulcie, Eartha, Edwina, Eileen, Eilidh, Elaine, Elinor, Eloisa, Eloise, Elspet, Elvira, Esther, Eunice, Evadne, Evelyn, Evonne, Fatima, Fedora, Flavia, Frieda, Gaynor, Gertie, Gladys, Glenda, Glenys, Gloria, Glynis, Goldie, Gracie, Gudrun, Gwenda, Hannah, Hattie, Hayley, Helena, Hermia, Hester, Hilary, Honora, Honour, Imelda, Imogen, Indira, Ingrid, Isabel, Iseult, Ishbel, Isobel, Isolda, Isolde, Jamila, Jancis, Janice, Janina, Janine, Jeanie, Jemima,

Jennie, Jessie, Joanie, Joanna, Joanne, Joelle, Joleen, Jolene, Judith, Juliet, Kamala, Karina, Kirsty, Laurel, Lauren, Laurie, Leanne, Leonie, Lesley, Lettie, Lianna, Lianne, Lilian, Lilias, Lisbet, Lizzie, Lolita, Lottie, Louisa, Louise, Lynsey, Madhur, Maggie, Maisie, Marcia, Marian, Marina, Marion, Marsha, Martha, Mattie, Maxine, Melody, Meriel, Millie, Minnie, Miriam, Monica, Morven, Muriel, Myriam, Myrtle, Nadine, Nellie, Nicola, Nicole, Noelle, Noreen, Odette, Olivia, Olwyne, Paloma, Pamela, Petula, Phoebe, Rachel, Raquel, Regina, Renata, Rhonda, Roisin, Rosina, Rowena, Roxana, Roxane, Sabina, Sabine, Salome, Sandra, Saskia, Selina, Serena, Sharon, Sheela, Sheena, Sheila, Sherry, Sheryl, Silvia, Simone, Sinéad, Sophia, Sophie, Stacey, Stella, Sylvia, Tamara, Tamsin, Teresa, Thelma, Tracey, Tricia, Trisha, Trixie, Ulrica, Ursula, Violet, Vivian, Vivien, Winnie, Winona, Xanthe, Yasmin, Yvette, Yvonne, Zainab, Zaynab

07 Abigail, Annabel, Annette, Antonia, Ariadne, Augusta, Barbara, Beatrix, Belinda, Bernice, Bethany, Bettina, Blanche, Bridget, Bronagh, Bronwen, Caitlín, Camilla, Candace, Candice, Candida, Carolyn, Cecilia, Chandra, Chantal, Charity, Charley, Chelsea, Chelsey, Christy, Clarice, Claudia, Colette, Colleen, Corinna, Corinne, Crystal, Cynthia, Daniela, Deborah, Deirdre, Désirée, Dolores, Dorothy, Eleanor, Elspeth, Emerald, Estella, Estelle, Eugenia, Eugénie, Felicia, Fenella, Floella, Florrie, Flossie, Frances, Frankie, Georgia, Georgie, Gillian, Giselle, Gwenyth, Gwyneth, Harriet, Heather, Heloise, Isadora, Isidora, Jacinta,

Jacinth, Janetta, Janette,
Jasmine, Jeannie, Jessica,
Jillian, Jocasta, Jocelin,
Jocelyn, Jonquil, Josette,
Juliana, Justina, Justine,
Kathryn, Katrina, Kirstin,
Lakshmi, Lavinia, Leonora,
Letitia, Lettice, Lillian,
Lillias, Lindsay, Lindsey,
Linette, Lisbeth, Lisette,
Lizbeth, Loretta, Lucilla,
Lucille, Lucinda, Lynette,
Madonna, Margery,
Marilyn, Marjory, Marlene,
Martina, Martine, Matilda,
Maureen, Melanie, Melissa,
Mildred, Miranda,
Myfanwy, Nanette, Natalia,
Natalie, Natasha, Nichola,
Nigella, Ninette, Ophelia,
Pandora, Parvati, Pascale,
Paulina, Pauline, Phyllis,
Queenie, Rachael, Rebecca,
Roberta, Rosabel, Rosalie,
Rosanna, Rosetta, Roxanne,
Sabrina, Saffron, Shelagh,
Shelley, Shirley, Sidonie,
Silvana, Siobhán, Susanna,
Sybilla, Tabitha, Theresa,
Tiffany, Valerie, Vanessa,
Venetia, Yolanda, Zuleika

08 Adelaide, Adrianne,
Adrienne, Angelica,
Angelina, Angharad,
Arabella, Beatrice,
Berenice, Beverley, Caroline,
Catriona, Charlene,
Charmian, Chrissie,
Christie, Clarinda, Clarissa,
Claudine, Cordelia,
Courtney, Cressida,
Daniella, Danielle,
Dorothea, Eleanore,
Emmeline, Felicity,
Florence, Francine,
Georgina, Germaine,
Gertrude, Griselda,
Hermione, Isabella,
Jacintha, Jacinthe, Jeanette,
Jennifer, Joceline, Joscelin,
Katerina, Kathleen,
Kimberly, Lauretta,
Lorraine, Madeline,
Magdalen, Margaret,
Marigold, Marjorie,
Mathilda, Meredith,
Michaela, Michelle,
Morwenna, Ottoline,
Patience, Patricia, Paulette,
Penelope, Philippa,
Primrose, Prudence,
Prunella, Rhiannon,

Rosalind, Rosamond,
Rosamund, Roseanna,
Roseanne, Rosemary,
Samantha, Scarlett,
Susannah, Theodora,
Tomasina, Veronica,
Victoria, Virginia, Winifred

09 Albertina, Alexandra,
Anastasia, Annabella,
Annabelle, Cassandra,
Catharine, Catherina,
Catherine, Charlotte,
Charmaine, Christina,
Christine, Claudette,
Cleopatra, Constance,
Elisabeth, Elizabeth,
Frederica, Gabrielle,
Genevieve, Georgette,
Georgiana, Geraldine,
Ghislaine, Guinevere,
Gwendolen, Henrietta,
Jaqueline, Jeannette,
Josephine, Katharine,
Katherine, Kimberley,
Madeleine, Magdalene,
Mélisande, Millicent,
Nicolette, Priscilla,
Sigourney, Silvestra,
Stephanie, Sylvestra,
Thomasina

10 Antoinette, Bernadette,
Christabel, Clementina,
Clementine, Jacqueline,
Wilhelmina

named
05 cited
06 called, chosen, dubbed,
picked, styled, termed, titled
08 baptized, entitled, labelled
09 appointed, mentioned,
nominated, specified
10 christened, classified,
identified, singled out
11 by the name of
12 commissioned

nameless
07 unknown, unnamed
08 untitled
09 anonymous, unheard-of
10 innominate, unlabelled
11 unspecified, unutterable
12 undesignated, unidentified
13 indescribable, inexpressible,
unmentionable

namely
02 ie
03 viz
05 to wit
06 that is
11 that is to say
12 in other words, specifically

nap
03 kip, nod
04 doze, fuzz, pile, rest, shag
05 fibre, grain, sleep, weave
06 catnap, siesta, snooze
07 drop off, lie down, texture
10 forty winks, light sleep
12 sleep lightly
14 get some shut-eye, have
forty winks

nappy
05 towel
06 diaper, napkin

narcissism
06 vanity
07 conceit, egotism
08 egomania, self-love
10 self-regard
13 egocentricity
15 self-centredness

narcissistic
04 vain
09 conceited, egotistic
10 egocentric, self-loving
11 egomaniacal, self-centred

narcotic
04 drug
06 downer, opiate
07 anodyne, calming, numbing
08 hypnotic, sedative
09 analgesic, somnolent
10 painkiller, palliative,
stupefying
11 anaesthetic, painkilling
12 sleeping pill, stupefacient
13 sleep-inducing, tranquillizer

narked
05 irked, riled, vexed
06 bugged, galled, miffed,
peeved, piqued
07 annoyed, nettled
09 irritated

narrate
04 read, tell
06 recite, relate, report, set out
07 explain, portray, recount
08 describe, rehearse, set forth

narration
04 tale
05 story
06 detail, report, sketch
07 account, history, telling
09 chronicle, portrayal,
recountal, rehearsal,
statement, voice-over
11 description, explanation
12 story-telling

narrative
04 tale

05 story
06 detail, report, sketch
07 account, history, reading
09 portrayal, statement
11 description

narrator
06 author, writer
08 annalist, reporter
09 describer, raconteur
10 anecdotist, chronicler
11 commentator, storyteller

narrow
04 fine, slim, thin, true
05 close, limit, petty, rigid,
   small, spare, taper, tight
06 biased, reduce, strict
07 bigoted, cramped, insular,
   limited, precise, tighten
08 confined, diminish,
   dogmatic, exiguous, restrict,
   simplify, tapering
09 constrict, hidebound
10 attenuated, intolerant,
   prejudiced, restricted
11 constricted, reactionary,
   small-minded, strait-laced
12 circumscribe, conservative,
   narrow-minded
13 dyed-in-the-wool

narrowing
08 stenosis, tapering, thinning
11 attenuation, contraction
12 constipation, constriction

narrowly
04 just
06 barely
07 closely, exactly
08 only just, scarcely, strictly
09 carefully, precisely
10 by a whisker
15 by a hair's breadth

narrow-minded
05 petty, rigid
07 bigoted, diehard, insular
08 blimpish
09 exclusive, hidebound,
   jaundiced, parochial
10 entrenched, inflexible,
   intolerant, prejudiced
11 opinionated, petty-minded,
   reactionary, small- minded
12 conservative, unreasonable
13 dyed in the wool

narrowness
07 bigotry
08 nearness, rigidity, thinness
09 prejudice, tightness
10 insularity, limitation
11 attenuation, slenderness
12 conservatism, constriction,

13 exclusiveness
15 small-mindedness

narrows
05 sound
07 channel, passage, straits

nascent
05 young
06 rising
07 budding, growing
08 evolving, naissant
09 advancing, beginning,
   embryonic, incipient
10 burgeoning, developing

nastiness
05 filth, spite
06 malice
08 foulness, impurity
09 dirtiness, pollution
10 filthiness, smuttiness
11 malevolence, viciousness
12 horribleness, spitefulness
13 offensiveness,
   unsavouriness
14 unpleasantness

nasty
04 blue, foul, mean, rank, vile
05 awful, cruel, dirty, foggy,
   grave, rainy, yucky
06 filthy, grotty, odious, ribald,
   smutty, stormy, tricky, unkind
07 hateful, noisome, obscene,
   serious, squalid, vicious
08 alarming, horrible, indecent,
   polluted, spiteful, worrying
09 dangerous, difficult,
   malicious, obnoxious,
   offensive, repellent,
   repugnant, repulsive,
   revolting, sickening
10 disgusting, malevolent,
   malodorous, unpleasant
11 bad-tempered, distasteful
12 disagreeable, pornographic
13 objectionable

nation
04 land, race
05 realm, state, tribe
06 people
07 country, kingdom, society
10 population

national
05 civic, civil, state
06 native, public, social
07 citizen, federal, subject
08 domestic, internal, resident
10 inhabitant, nationwide
11 countrywide
12 governmental

nationalism
08 jingoism
10 allegiance, chauvinism,
   patriotism, xenophobia

nationalistic
05 loyal
09 patriotic
10 jingoistic, xenophobic
12 chauvinistic
13 ethnocentrist

nationality
04 clan, race
05 birth, tribe
06 nation

nationwide
05 state
08 national
10 widespread
11 countrywide
12 coast-to-coast

native
04 home
05 local, natal
06 inborn, inbred, mother
07 citizen, connate, natural
08 domestic, inherent, original
09 aborigine, home-grown,
   inherited, intuitive
10 aboriginal, autochthon,
   congenital, hereditary,
   indigenous, vernacular
11 instinctive
13 autochthonous

nativity
05 birth
08 delivery
10 childbirth
11 parturition

natter
03 gab, jaw
04 chat, talk
06 confab, gossip, jabber
07 blather, blether, chatter,
   chinwag, prattle
08 chit-chat, rabbit on
12 conversation

natty
04 chic, neat, trim
05 ritzy, smart
06 dapper, snazzy, spruce
07 elegant, stylish

natural
03 raw
04 open, pure, real
05 frank, plain, usual, whole
06 candid, common, inborn,
   inbred, innate, native,
   normal, simple, virgin

07 artless, built-in, connate, genuine, organic, routine, sincere, typical, unmixed
08 everyday, inherent, ordinary
09 authentic, guileless, ingenuous, inherited, intuitive, unrefined
10 congenital, indigenous, unaffected
11 instinctive, spontaneous, unprocessed
12 additive-free, chemical-free, run-of-the-mill
13 unpretentious
15 unsophisticated

naturalist
08 botanist
09 biologist, Darwinist, ecologist, zoologist
11 creationist
12 evolutionist
13 life scientist

naturalistic
07 factual, graphic, natural
08 lifelike, real-life
09 realistic
10 true-to-life
12 photographic

naturalize
05 adapt, adopt
06 accept
08 accustom
09 acclimate, endenizen, habituate, introduce
10 assimilate
11 acclimatize, domesticate, familiarize, incorporate

naturally
05 natch
06 simply
08 candidly, normally, of course
09 artlessly, certainly, genuinely, obviously, sincerely, typically
10 absolutely
11 ingenuously
13 instinctively, spontaneously

naturalness
06 purity
07 realism
08 openness, pureness
09 frankness, plainness, sincerity, wholeness
10 candidness, simplicity
11 artlessness, spontaneity
13 ingenuousness
14 unaffectedness
15 spontaneousness

nature
04 kind, mood, sort, type
05 earth, stamp, style, world

06 humour, make-up, temper
07 country, essence, scenery
08 creation, identity, universe
09 character, chemistry
11 countryside, description, disposition, environment, mother earth, personality, temperament
12 constitution, mother nature
14 natural history

naught
03 nil
04 zero
05 zilch
06 nought
07 nothing
11 nothingness

naughty
03 bad
04 blue, lewd
05 bawdy
06 risqué, smutty, unruly
07 defiant, obscene, playful, roguish, wayward
08 indecent, perverse
10 refractory
11 disobedient, misbehaving, mischievous
12 badly behaved, exasperating, incorrigible
13 undisciplined

nausea
06 hatred, puking
07 disgust, gagging
08 retching, sickness, vomiting
09 revulsion
10 abhorrence, queasiness, repugnance, throwing up
11 airsickness, biliousness, carsickness, seasickness
14 motion sickness, travel sickness
15 morning sickness

nauseate
05 repel
06 offend, revolt, sicken
07 disgust, turn off
08 gross out, make sick
15 turn your stomach

nauseating
06 odious
09 offensive, repellent, repugnant, repulsive, revolting, sickening
10 detestable, disgusting

nauseous
03 ill
04 sick
06 queasy
07 airsick, carsick, seasick

09 nauseated
10 travel sick

nautical
05 naval
07 boating, oceanic, sailing
08 maritime, seagoing, yachting

naval
03 sea
06 marine
08 maritime, nautical, seagoing
09 seafaring

navel
03 hub
06 centre, middle
08 omphalos
09 umbilical, umbilicus
11 belly-button, tummy-button

navigable
04 open
05 clear
08 passable
09 crossable, unblocked
10 negotiable

navigate
04 helm, plan, plot, sail
05 drive, guide, pilot, steer
06 cruise, direct, voyage
07 journey, skipper
09 manoeuvre, negotiate

navigation
07 guiding, sailing
08 cruising, guidance, nautical, piloting, steering, voyaging
10 seamanship
12 helmsmanship

► *Navigational aids*:
03 GPS, log
05 chart, loran, pilot, radar
07 compass, sextant
08 bell buoy, dividers, VHF radio
09 lightship
10 depth gauge, lighthouse, marker buoy
11 chronometer, echo-sounder, gyrocompass
13 nautical table
15 astro-navigation, magnetic compass

navigator
05 pilot
06 seaman
07 mariner
08 helmsman

navvy
06 digger, ganger, worker
07 workman

08 labourer
12 manual worker

navy
05 fleet, ships
06 armada
08 flotilla, warships

nay
06 in fact, indeed, really
08 actually, to be sure

near
04 akin, dear, like
05 alike, close, handy, local
06 at hand, coming, nearby
07 close by, close to, looming
08 approach, imminent,
 intimate
09 alongside, close in on,
 immediate, impending
10 accessible, come closer,
 comparable, contiguous,
 draw near to, not far away
11 approaching, bordering on,
 come towards, forthcoming,
 get closer to, in the offing,
 move towards, within reach
12 contiguous to, neighbouring
14 advance towards
15 at close quarters

□**near thing**
08 near miss
09 close call
10 close shave
11 nasty moment
12 narrow escape

nearby
04 near
05 close, handy
10 accessible, not far away
11 close at hand, within reach
12 neighbouring
13 in the vicinity
14 on your doorstep
15 at close quarters

nearly
06 all but, almost
07 close to, closely, roughly
08 as good as, well-nigh
09 just about, virtually
10 more or less
11 practically
13 approximately

nearness
08 dearness, intimacy, vicinity
09 closeness, immediacy,
 imminence, proximity
11 familiarity, propinquity
13 accessibility

near-sighted
06 myopic

08 purblind
09 half-blind
12 short-sighted

neat
03 apt
04 deft, nice, pure, tidy, trim
05 handy, natty, nifty, smart
06 adroit, clever, dainty,
 dapper, nimble, simple,
 spruce, superb, wicked
07 compact, elegant, ordered,
 orderly, skilful, unmixed
08 straight, terrific, well-made
09 admirable, dexterous,
 efficient, ingenious,
 organized, shipshape,
 undiluted, wonderful
10 convenient, marvellous
11 well-ordered
12 spick-and-span, user-
 friendly, well-designed
13 unadulterated
15 in apple-pie order

neaten
04 edge, tidy, trim
05 clean, groom
06 tidy up
07 arrange, clean up, smarten
08 round off, spruce up
09 smarten up
10 straighten

neatly
05 aptly
06 deftly, nicely, nimbly, tidily
07 adeptly, agilely, smartly
08 adroitly, cleverly, daintily
09 elegantly, precisely, stylishly
10 accurately, gracefully
11 dexterously, efficiently
12 conveniently, methodically
14 systematically

neatness
05 grace, skill, style
07 agility, aptness
08 accuracy, deftness,
 elegance, niceness, tidiness
09 adeptness, dexterity,
 precision, smartness
10 adroitness, cleverness,
 daintiness, efficiency,
 nimbleness, spruceness
11 orderliness, stylishness
14 methodicalness

nebulous
03 dim
04 hazy
05 fuzzy, misty, vague
06 cloudy
07 obscure, shadowy, unclear

08 abstract, confused,
 unformed
09 amorphous, imprecise,
 shapeless, uncertain
10 indefinite, indistinct

necessarily
08 of course, perforce
09 certainly, naturally, therefore
10 inevitably, willy-nilly
11 ineluctably, inescapably
12 by definition, consequently
13 automatically, axiomatically

necessary
04 sure
05 vital
06 needed
07 certain, crucial, needful
08 required
09 de rigueur, essential,
 mandatory, requisite
10 compulsory, imperative,
 inevitable, obligatory
11 ineluctable, inescapable,
 unavoidable
13 indispensable

necessitate
04 need, take
05 exact, force
06 compel, demand, entail
07 call for, involve, require

necessity
04 must, need, want
06 demand, penury
09 certainty, essential,
 indigence, requisite
10 obligation, sine
 qua non
11 desideratum, fundamental,
 needfulness, requirement
12 prerequisite

neck
04 kiss, nape, snog
05 halse, scrag
06 cervix, scruff, smooch
08 canoodle, cervical

necklace
04 band, torc
05 beads, chain
06 choker, gorget, jewels,
 locket, pearls, string, torque
07 pendant, rivière

necromancer
05 witch
06 wizard
07 diviner, warlock
08 conjurer, magician, sorcerer
09 sorceress, spiritist
12 spiritualist

necromancy
05 magic
06 hoodoo, voodoo
07 sorcery
08 black art, witchery, wizardry
09 spiritism
10 black magic, demonology, divination, witchcraft
12 spiritualism
13 magical powers

necropolis
08 cemetery, God's acre
09 graveyard
10 burial site, churchyard
11 burial place
12 burial ground, charnel house

need
04 call, lack, miss, must, want
06 demand, have to, rely on
07 call for, pine for, require
08 depend on, exigency, shortage, yearn for
09 cry out for, essential, necessity, neediness, requisite
10 have need of, inadequacy, obligation
11 be reliant on, desideratum, necessitate, requirement
12 prerequisite
13 be compelled to, be dependent on, insufficiency
14 be desperate for

◻**in need**
04 poor
06 hard up
08 deprived, indigent
09 destitute, penniless, penurious
11 impecunious
12 impoverished
13 disadvantaged
14 on the breadline
15 poverty-stricken, underprivileged

needed
06 wanted
07 desired, lacking
08 required
09 called for, essential, necessary, requisite
10 compulsory, obligatory

needful
05 needy, vital
08 required
09 necessary, requisite
10 stipulated

needle
03 irk, nag, nib, pin
04 bait, barb, goad, hand, rile

05 annoy, arrow, prick, quill, spike, spine, sting, taunt
06 bodkin, harass, marker, nettle, niggle, stylus, wind up
07 bristle, pointer, prickle, provoke, spicule, torment
08 irritate, splinter
09 aggravate, indicator

needless
07 useless
09 pointless, redundant
10 expendable, gratuitous
11 purposeless, superfluous, uncalled-for, unnecessary

needlework
06 sewing
08 knitting, tapestry
09 fancywork, stitching
10 crocheting, embroidery
11 needlepoint

needy
04 poor
06 hard up, in need
08 deprived, indigent
09 destitute, penurious
12 impoverished
15 underprivileged

ne'er-do-well
05 idler
06 loafer, skiver, waster
07 shirker, wastrel
08 layabout
10 black sheep
14 good-for-nothing

nefarious
04 base, evil, foul, vile
06 odious, sinful, wicked
07 heinous, satanic, vicious
08 criminal, depraved, infamous, infernal, shameful
09 execrable, monstrous
10 abominable, iniquitous, outrageous, villainous
11 opprobrious

negate
04 deny, undo, void
05 annul, quash
06 cancel, refute, reject, repeal, revoke, squash
07 explode, gainsay, nullify, rescind, retract, reverse
09 abrogate, disprove
09 discredit, repudiate
10 contradict, invalidate
11 countermand

negation
04 veto
06 denial, repeal

07 inverse, reverse
08 contrary, converse, opposite
09 disavowal, rejection
10 abrogation, disclaimer
12 cancellation, renunciation
13 contradiction, nullification
14 countermanding

negative
06 denial, gloomy
07 cynical, denying, refusal
08 contrary, critical, refusing
09 annulling, defeatist, rejection, unhelpful
10 dissension, dissenting, gainsaying, nullifying
11 pessimistic
12 invalidating, uninterested
13 contradiction, contradictory, unco-operative

neglect
04 fail, omit
05 scorn, shirk, skimp, spurn
06 fail in, forget, ignore, laxity
07 abandon, default, failure
08 ignoring, let slide, overlook
09 disrepair, oversight
10 be lax about, disrespect, negligence, remissness
12 carelessness, heedlessness, indifference
13 forgetfulness

neglected
08 derelict, untended, untilled
09 abandoned, overgrown
10 uncared-for
11 disregarded, undervalued
12 uncultivated, unmaintained
13 unappreciated
14 underestimated

neglectful
03 lax
06 remiss, sloppy
08 careless, heedless, uncaring
09 forgetful, negligent, oblivious, unmindful
11 indifferent, thoughtless

negligence
07 default, failure, neglect
09 oversight, slackness
10 remissness, sloppiness
11 inattention, shortcoming
12 carelessness, heedlessness, indifference
13 forgetfulness
15 thoughtlessness

negligent
03 lax
05 slack
06 casual, remiss, sloppy
08 careless, dilatory, heedless

09 forgetful, unmindful
11 indifferent, thoughtless

negligible
04 tiny
05 minor, petty, small
06 minute, paltry
07 trivial
08 trifling
11 unimportant
13 imperceptible, insignificant

negotiable
04 open
08 arguable, passable
09 debatable, navigable,
    undecided, unsettled
11 contestable, traversable
12 surmountable

negotiate
04 deal, pass, talk
05 agree, clear, cross
06 confer, debate, fulfil, haggle,
    manage, parley, settle
07 arrange, bargain, discuss,
    mediate, resolve, work out
08 conclude, contract, get
    round, pass over, surmount,
    transact, traverse
09 arbitrate, hammer out,
    intercede, thrash out
12 wheel and deal

negotiation
05 talks
06 debate, parley
08 haggling
09 diplomacy, mediation
10 bargaining, discussion
11 arbitration, transaction
12 thrashing-out

negotiator
06 broker
07 haggler
08 diplomat, mediator, parleyer
09 go-between, moderator
10 ambassador, arbitrator
11 adjudicator, intercessor
12 intermediary
13 wheeler-dealer

neigh
04 bray
05 hinny
06 nicker, whinny

neighbourhood
04 area, part
06 locale, region
07 quarter
08 district, environs, locality,
    precinct, purlieus, vicinity
09 community, proximity

□**in the neighbourhood of**
04 near
05 about
06 almost, nearby, next to
07 close to, roughly
13 approximately

neighbouring
04 near, next
05 local
06 nearby
07 nearest
08 abutting, adjacent
09 adjoining, bordering
10 connecting, contiguous

neighbourly
04 kind, warm
06 genial
07 amiable, cordial, helpful
08 friendly, obliging, sociable
11 considerate

nemesis
04 fate, ruin
08 downfall
09 vengeance
10 punishment
11 destruction, retribution

neologism
07 coinage, new word, novelty
09 new phrase, vogue word
10 innovation

neophyte
04 tiro
06 novice, rookie
07 learner, recruit, trainee
08 beginner, newcomer
09 greenhorn, new member,
    noviciate, novitiate
10 apprentice, raw recruit
11 probationer

nepotism
04 bias
10 partiality
11 favouritism
12 old-school tie
13 old-boy network
14 jobs for the boys

nerve
03 lip
04 gall, grit, guts, neck, will
05 brace, cheek, force, mouth,
    pluck, sauce, spunk, steel
06 bottle, daring, mettle, spirit,
    valour, vigour
07 bolster, bravery, courage,
    fortify, hearten
08 audacity, boldness,
    chutzpah, temerity

09 brass neck, encourage,
    endurance, fortitude,
    impudence, insolence
10 brazenness, effrontery
11 intrepidity, presumption
12 fearlessness, impertinence
13 determination
14 cool-headedness

nerveless
04 calm, weak
05 inert, slack, timid
06 afraid, feeble, flabby
08 cowardly, unnerved
09 enervated, spineless

nerve-racking
05 tense
06 trying
08 worrying
09 difficult, harrowing,
    maddening, stressful
10 nail-biting
11 distressing, frightening

nerves
05 worry
06 neural, strain, stress
07 anxiety, jitters, tension
11 butterflies, nervousness
12 collywobbles
13 heebie-jeebies

nervous
04 edgy
05 het up, jumpy, tense, timid
06 on edge, uneasy
07 anxious, fearful, fidgety,
    fretful, in a stew, jittery, keyed
    up, quaking, twitchy,
    uptight, worried, wound up
08 agitated, in a sweat, in a
    tizzy, neurotic, timorous
09 excitable, screwed-up
12 apprehensive, highly-strung
13 on tenterhooks

nervous breakdown
06 crisis
08 neurosis
10 cracking-up, depression
11 melancholia
15 mental breakdown

nervousness
05 worry
06 strain, stress
07 anxiety, fluster, tension
08 disquiet, edginess, timidity
09 agitation
10 touchiness, uneasiness
12 excitability, perturbation,
    restlessness, timorousness
13 heebie-jeebies

nervy
04 edgy
05 het up, jumpy, shaky, tense
06 on edge, uneasy
07 anxious, fearful, fidgety,
jittery, keyed up, twitchy,
uptight, worried, wound up
08 agitated, neurotic, strained
09 excitable, flustered
12 apprehensive, highly-strung

nescient
06 stupid, unread
07 unaware
08 backward, clueless,
ignorant, untaught
09 unlearned, unwitting
10 illiterate, innumerate,
uneducated, unschooled

nest
03 den, mew
04 cote, lair
05 eyrie, haunt, nidal, roost
07 hideout, retreat, shelter
08 dovecote, vespiary
10 nesting-box
12 nidification
14 breeding-ground

nest egg
04 fund
05 cache, funds, store
07 deposit, reserve, savings
08 reserves
12 bottom drawer

nestle
06 cuddle, curl up, nuzzle
07 snuggle
08 cuddle up
09 snuggle up

nestling
04 baby
05 chick
08 suckling, weanling
09 fledgling

net
03 bag, get, nab, web
04 drag, earn, gain, lace, make,
mesh, nett, nick, take, trap
05 broad, catch, clear, drift,
final, raise, seine, snare, total
06 enmesh, lowest, obtain,
pocket, pull in, rake in
07 bring in, capture, dragnet,
drop-net, ensnare, fishnet,
lattice, netting, network,
overall, receive, retiary
08 after tax, drift-net,
meshwork, open work,
seine net, take home,
take-home, ultimate
09 inclusive, reticular, reticulum

10 accumulate
15 after deductions

nether
05 basal, below, lower, under
06 bottom
07 beneath, hellish, Stygian
08 inferior, infernal
10 lower-level, underworld
11 underground

nettle
03 bug, vex
04 fret, goad
05 annoy, chafe, pique, sting
06 harass, hassle, needle, ruffle
07 incense, provoke, torment
08 irritate

nettled
05 angry, cross, huffy, riled,
stung, vexed
06 galled, goaded, miffed,
narked, peeved, piqued
07 annoyed, needled, ruffled
08 harassed, offended
09 aggrieved, irritable, irritated

network
03 net, web
04 grid, lace, maze, mesh
06 matrix, system, tracks
07 complex, lattice, netting,
network, tracery, webbing
08 channels, filigree,
meshwork, open work
09 circuitry, grapevine,
labyrinth, structure
11 arrangement, latticework
12 old-school tie, organization
13 bush telegraph

neurosis
06 phobia
08 disorder, fixation
09 deviation, obsession
11 abnormality, derangement,
disturbance, instability
14 mental disorder

neurotic
06 phobic
07 anxious, deviant, nervous
08 deranged, paranoid
09 disturbed, obsessive
10 compulsive, irrational

neuter
03 fix
04 geld, spay
06 doctor
08 caponize, castrate
09 sterilize
10 emasculate

neutral
04 drab, dull, fawn, grey, pale

05 beige, bland
07 anodyne, insipid
08 detached, unbiased
09 impartial, objective
10 colourless, even-handed,
indefinite, non-aligned,
open-minded, uninvolved
11 indifferent, inoffensive, non-
partisan, uncommitted
12 non-committal,
unprejudiced, unremarkable
13 disinterested, dispassionate
14 expressionless

neutrality
10 detachment
11 disinterest
12 impartiality, non-alignment
14 non-involvement
15 non-intervention

neutralize
04 undo
05 annul
06 cancel, negate, offset
07 balance, nullify
09 cancel out, make up for
10 counteract, invalidate
12 incapacitate
14 counterbalance

never
05 no way
07 not ever
08 at no time, not at all
11 on no account, when pigs fly
13 not for a moment, not on
your life
15 not on your nellie

never-ending
07 endless, eternal, non-stop
08 constant, infinite, unending
09 boundless, incessant,
limitless, permanent,
perpetual, unceasing
10 continuous, persistent,
relentless, without end
11 everlasting, unremitting
12 interminable

nevertheless
03 but, yet
05 still
06 anyhow, anyway, even so
07 however
09 in any case
10 all the same, for all that,
in any event, regardless
11 just the same, nonetheless
15 notwithstanding

new
04 mint, more
05 added, extra, fresh, novel

06 latest, modern, recent, trendy, unused, virgin
07 altered, another, changed, current, further, newborn, renewed, strange, unknown
08 advanced, brand-new, original, up-to-date
09 born-again, different, ingenious, refreshed
10 additional, avant-garde, futuristic, innovative, modernized, newfangled, pioneering, redesigned, remodelled, unfamiliar
11 imaginative, ultra-modern
12 contemporary, experimental
13 revolutionary, state-of-the-art, up-to-the-minute
14 ground-breaking

newcomer
06 novice, rookie
07 arrival, incomer, learner, recruit, settler, trainee
08 beginner, colonist, intruder, neophyte, outsider, stranger
09 foreigner, immigrant
10 apprentice, new arrival
11 probationer

newfangled
03 new
05 novel
06 modern, recent, trendy
08 gimmicky
11 modernistic, ultra-modern
12 contemporary
13 state-of-the-art

newly
04 anew, just
06 afresh, lately, of late
07 freshly
08 latterly, recently

newness
06 oddity
07 novelty, recency
09 freshness
10 innovation, uniqueness
11 originality, strangeness
13 unfamiliarity

news
03 gen
04 data, dope, info, word
05 facts, story
06 advice, exposé, gossip, latest, report, rumour
07 account, scandal, tidings
08 bulletin, dispatch, news item, newscast
09 newsflash, statement

10 communiqué, disclosure, revelation
12 announcement, developments, intelligence, press release
13 communication

newspaper
03 rag
05 daily, organ, press, sheet
06 weekly
07 gazette, journal, tabloid
10 broadsheet, periodical
11 publication

➤ *Names of newspapers and magazines*:
02 GQ, OK!
03 FHM, Red, She, Viz
04 Best, Chat, Chic, Elle, Mind, Mojo, More!, Time
05 Bella, Bunty, Hello!, Prima, Punch, Vogue, Which?, Wired, Woman
06 Forbes, Granta, Lancet, Loaded, Nature, The Sun, War Cry
07 Company, Esquire, Fortune, Hustler, Mayfair, Men Only, Newsday, Playboy, Science, TV Times, The Face, The Lady, The Star, Time Out, Tribune
08 Gay Times, Newsweek, Scotsman, The Beano, The Dandy, The Eagle, The Month, The Times, USA Today
09 Daily Mail, Daily Star, Ideal Home, Penthouse, Red Pepper, Smash Hits, The Friend, The Grocer, The Herald, The Mirror, The People, The Tablet, The Tatler, Woman's Own
10 Daily Sport, Private Eye, Racing Post, Radio Times, Sunday Post, The Express, Vanity Fair
11 Church Times, Country Life, Daily Record, Melody Maker, Morning Star, Sunday Sport, The Big Issue, The European, The Guardian, The Observer, The Universe
12 Cosmopolitan, Mail on Sunday, New Scientist, New Statesman, The Economist, The Pink Paper, The Spectator, Time Magazine
13 Catholic Times, Daltons Weekly, Horse and Hound,

Just Seventeen, People's Friend, Reader's Digest, The Bookseller, The Watchtower
14 Catholic Herald, Financial Times, Literary Review, News of the World, The Independent, The New York Post
15 Evening Standard, Exchange and Mart, Harpers and Queen, The New York Times

newsworthy
07 notable, unusual
09 arresting, important
10 noteworthy, remarkable
11 interesting, significant

next
04 then
05 along, later
06 beside
07 closest, ensuing, nearest
08 adjacent
09 adjoining, alongside, bordering, following
10 afterwards, contiguous, subsequent, succeeding, successive, thereafter
12 neighbouring, subsequently

nibble
03 bit, eat
04 bite, gnaw, nosh, peck
05 piece, snack, taste
06 morsel, pick at, titbit

nice
04 fine, good, kind
05 civil, close, exact, sweet
06 genial, kindly, lovely, minute, polite, strict, subtle
07 amiable, amusing, welcome
08 charming, delicate, friendly, likeable, pleasant
09 agreeable, appealing, courteous, enjoyable
10 acceptable, attractive, delightful, satisfying
11 good-natured, pleasurable, respectable, sympathetic
12 entertaining, good-humoured, well-mannered
13 understanding

nicely
04 well
08 properly
09 agreeably
10 pleasantly, pleasingly
12 delightfully
14 satisfactorily

niceness
05 charm

08 kindness
10 amiability, politeness
12 friendliness, pleasantness
13 agreeableness
14 attractiveness, respectability

nicety
06 nuance
07 finesse
08 accuracy, delicacy, subtlety
09 fine point, precision
10 minuteness, refinement

niche
04 nook, slot
05 place
06 alcove, corner, cranny, hollow, métier, recess
08 position, vocation
09 cubbyhole

nick
03 cut, jug, lag, nab
04 chip, jail, mark, scar, take
05 catch, clink, notch, pinch, run in, score, steal, swipe
06 arrest, collar, cooler, fettle, groove, health, indent, inside, pick up, pilfer, pocket, prison, snitch
07 capture, scratch, slammer
08 knock off
09 apprehend, condition
13 police station

nickname
07 epithet, pet name
09 sobriquet
10 diminutive, soubriquet
12 familiar name

nifty
04 chic, deft, neat
05 agile, nippy, quick, sharp
06 adroit, clever, spruce
07 skilful, stylish

niggardliness
08 meanness
09 closeness, parsimony, smallness
10 inadequacy, meagreness, paltriness, scantiness, skimpiness, stinginess
11 miserliness
12 cheese-paring
13 insufficiency
15 tight-fistedness

niggardly
04 mean
05 close, small
06 meagre, measly, paltry, scanty, skimpy, stingy
07 miserly, sparing
09 miserable

10 hard-fisted, inadequate
11 tight-fisted
12 cheese-paring, insufficient, parsimonious

niggle
03 bug, nag
04 carp, moan
05 annoy, upset, worry
06 bother, hassle, pick on
07 nit-pick, quibble, trouble
08 complain, irritate, keep on at

night
04 dark
08 darkness
09 night-time, nocturnal
15 hours of darkness

nightclub
04 club
05 disco
06 nitery
07 cabaret, niterie
09 nightspot
11 discotheque

nightfall
04 dark, dusk
06 sunset
07 evening, sundown
08 gloaming, twilight
10 crepuscule

nightmare
05 agony, trial
06 horror, ordeal
07 anguish, incubus, torture
08 bad dream, calamity
09 ephialtes

nightmarish
06 creepy, unreal
08 alarming, horrible, horrific
10 disturbing, terrifying
11 frightening

nihilism
06 denial
07 anarchy, atheism, nullity
08 cynicism, negation, oblivion
09 disbelief, emptiness, pessimism, rejection
10 abnegation, negativism
11 agnosticism, lawlessness, nothingness, repudiation

nihilist
05 cynic
07 atheist, sceptic
08 agitator, agnostic
09 anarchist, pessimist
10 antinomian, negativist
11 disbeliever, negationist
13 revolutionary

nil
04 duck, love, none, zero

05 zilch
06 naught, nought
07 nothing

nimble
04 deft, spry
05 agile, alert, brisk, lithe, nippy, quick, ready, smart, swift
06 active, clever, lively, prompt
09 sharp-eyed, sprightly
11 light-footed, quick-moving

nimbleness
05 grace, skill
07 agility, finesse
08 alacrity, deftness, spryness
09 dexterity, niftiness, nippiness, smartness
10 adroitness
13 sprightliness

nimbly
04 fast
06 deftly, easily, spryly
07 agilely, alertly, briskly, quickly, readily, sharply, smartly, swiftly
08 snappily, speedily
11 dexterously

nincompoop
04 clot, dolt, fool, nerd, twit
05 chump, dunce, idiot, twerp, wally
06 dimwit, nitwit
07 plonker
08 numskull
09 blockhead, simpleton

nip
02 go
03 fly, lop, pop, run, sip
04 bite, clip, dash, dock, dram, drop, grip, rush, shot, snip
05 catch, hurry, pinch, tweak
07 draught, portion, squeeze

❑**nip in the bud**
04 halt, stem, stop
05 block, check
06 arrest, impede
08 obstruct
09 frustrate

nipple
03 dug, pap, tit
04 teat
05 udder
06 breast
07 mamilla, papilla

nippy
03 raw
04 cold, fast, spry
05 agile, brisk, quick, sharp
06 active, biting, chilly, nimble
08 piercing, stinging

nirvana

03 joy
05 bliss, peace
07 ecstasy
08 paradise, serenity
12 tranquillity
13 enlightenment

nit-picking

05 fussy
07 carping, finicky
08 captious, pedantic
09 cavilling, quibbling
12 pettifogging
13 hair-splitting, hypercritical

nitty-gritty

06 basics
10 bottom line, brass tacks, essentials, main points
12 fundamentals, nuts and bolts

nitwit

04 fool, twit
05 dummy, idiot, ninny
06 dimwit
09 numbskull, simpleton
10 nincompoop

no

04 nope
05 no way
08 no thanks, not at all
11 of course not
13 absolutely not, not on your life
14 over my dead body

nob

03 VIP
04 toff
06 bigwig, fat cat
07 big shot
09 personage
10 aristocrat

nobble

03 buy, nab
04 dope, drug, foil, grab, nick
05 bribe, catch, check, get at, pinch, seize, steal, swipe
06 arrest, buy off, collar, defeat, hinder, pilfer, snitch, thwart
07 disable, warn off
08 knock off, threaten
09 frustrate, hamstring
10 intimidate
12 incapacitate
13 interfere with

Nobel Prize

► *Names of Nobel Prize winners*:

02 Fo (Dario), Oë (Kenzaburo)

03 Paz (Octavio)

04 Belo (Carlos), Bohr (Niels Henrik David), Böll (Heinrich), Born (Max), Buck (Pearl Sydenstricker), Cela (Camilo José), Duve (Christian René de), Gide (André), Hume (John), Katz (Sir Bernard), Mann (Thomas), Mott (Sir Nevill Francis), Shaw (George Bernard), Tutu (Desmond), Urey (Harold Clayton)

05 Bethe (Hans Albrecht), Bloch (Felix), Bragg (Sir Lawrence), Bragg (Sir William Henry), Bunin (Ivan), Camus (Albert), Crick (Francis Harry Compton), Curie (Marie), Curie (Pierre), Debye (Peter Joseph Wilhelm), Dirac (Paul Adrien Maurice), Eliot (Thomas Stearns), Euler (Ulf Svante von), Fermi (Enrico), Golgi (Camillo), Grass (Günter), Haber (Fritz), Hesse (Hermann), Klerk (Frederik Willem de), Krebs (Sir Hans Adolf), Lewis (Sinclair), Libby (Willard Frank), Monod (Jacques Lucien), Pauli (Wolfgang), Peres (Shimon), Rabin (Yitzhak), Sachs (Nelly), Salam (Abdus), Simon (Claude), Soddy (Frederick), Stern (Otto), Yeats (William Butler)

06 Arafat (Yasser), Bellow (Saul), Bordet (Jules), Carrel (Alexis), Debreu (Gerard), France (Anatole), Frisch (Ragnar), Glaser (Donald Arthur), Hamsun (Knut), Heaney (Seamus), Hevesy (George Charles von), Hewish (Antony), Lorenz (Konrad Zacharias), Myrdal (Gunnar), Nernst (Walther Hermann), Neruda (Pablo), O'Neill (Eugene), Pavlov (Ivan), Perutz (Max Ferdinand), Planck (Max Karl Ernst), Porter (George, Lord), Sanger (Frederick), Sartre (Jean-Paul), Singer (Isaac Bashevis), Tagore (Rabindranath), Walesa (Lech), Watson (James Dewey), Wiesel (Elie), Wilson (Robert Woodrow)

07 Alvarez (Luis Walter), Axelrod (Julius), Banting (Sir Frederick Grant), Beckett (Samuel), Brodsky (Joseph), Canetti (Elias), Ehrlich (Paul), Feynman (Richard Phillips), Fleming (Sir Alexander), Glashow (Sheldon Lee), Golding (William), Hodgkin (Dorothy Mary), Hodgkin (Sir Alan Lloyd), Jiménez (Juan Ramón), Khorana (Har Gobind), Kipling (Rudyard), Laxness (Halldór), Mahfouz (Naguib), Mandela (Nelson), Marconi (Guglielmo, Marchese), Mauriac (François), Medawar (Sir Peter Brian), Mistral (Frédéric), Mommsen (Theodor), Pauling (Linus Carl), Penzias (Arno Allan), Röntgen (Wilhelm Konrad von), Rotblat (Joseph), Russell (Bertrand, Earl), Seaborg (Glen Theodore), Seifert (Jaroslav), Soyinka (Wole), Trimble (David), Waksman (Selman Abraham), Walcott (Derek)

08 Appleton (Sir Edward Victor), Asturias (Miguel Angel), Chadwick (Sir James), Delbrück (Max), Einstein (Albert), Faulkner (William), Friedman (Milton), Gajdusek (Daniel Carleton), Gell-Mann (Murray), Gordimer (Nadine), Langmuir (Irving), Leontief (Wassily), Meyerhof (Otto Fritz), Millikan (Robert Andrews), Milstein (Cesar), Morrison (Toni), Mulliken (Robert Sanderson), Northrop (John Howard), Saramago (José), Shockley (William Bradford), Tiselius (Arne Wilhelm Kaurin), Weinberg (Steven)

09 Arrhenius (Svante August), Becquerel (Antoine Henri), Cherenkov (Pavel), Churchill (Sir Winston), Dalai Lama, Gorbachev

(Mikhail), **Hemingway**
(Ernest), **Michelson**
(Albert Abraham),
Sholokhov (Mikhail),
Steinbeck (John),
Tinbergen (Jan), **Tinbergen**
(Nikolaas)
10 **Galsworthy** (John),
Heisenberg (Werner Karl),
Hofstadter (Robert),
Lagerkvist (Pär),
Pirandello (Luigi),
Ramos-Horta (José),
Rutherford (Ernest, Lord),
Szymborska (Wislawa)
11 **Joliot-Curie** (Frédéric),
Joliot-Curie (Irène),
Maeterlinck (Count
Maurice), **Ramón y Cajal**
(Santiago), **Schrödinger**
(Erwin)
12 **Solzhenitsyn** (Aleksandr)
13 **Aung San Suu Kyi** (Daw),
Chandrasekhar
(Subrahmanyan), **García
Márquez** (Gabriel)

nobility
04 nobs
05 elite, lords, peers, toffs
06 gentry, honour, nobles
07 dignity, majesty, peerage
09 grandness, integrity
10 excellence, generosity,
worthiness
11 aristocracy, high society
15 illustriousness

━ *Titles of the nobility*:
04 dame, duke, earl, lady, lord,
peer
05 baron, count, laird, liege,
noble, ruler, thane
06 knight, squire
07 baronet, dowager, duchess,
marquis, peeress
08 baroness, countess, life peer,
marquess, nobleman,
seigneur, viscount
09 grand duke, liege lord
10 aristocrat, noblewoman
11 marchioness, viscountess

noble
04 fine, lady, lord, peer
05 grand, great, lofty
06 landed, titled, worthy
07 eminent, exalted, stately
08 elevated, generous, high-
born, imposing, majestic,
virtuous
09 dignified, excellent,
patrician, unselfish
10 aristocrat, honourable

11 blue-blooded, high-
ranking, magnificent
12 aristocratic
15 self-sacrificing

nobody
05 no one
06 cipher, menial
07 nothing
09 nonentity
10 mediocrity

nod
03 bow, dip, nap
04 beck, doze, sign
05 agree, sleep
06 accept, assent, drowse,
salute, signal
07 approve, doze off, drop off,
gesture, incline, slumber
08 greeting, indicate, say yes to
10 fall asleep, indication
15 acknowledgement

node
03 bud
04 bump, knob, knot, lump
06 growth, nodule
08 swelling
09 carbuncle
12 protuberance

noise
03 cry, din, row
05 blare, clash, sound
06 babble, hubbub, outcry,
racket, report, rumour,
tumult, uproar
07 clamour, clatter
11 pandemonium

noiseless
04 mute
05 quiet, still
06 hushed, silent
09 inaudible, soundless

noisome
03 bad
04 foul
05 fetid
06 putrid, smelly
07 hurtful, noxious, reeking
08 mephitic, stinking
09 obnoxious, offensive,
poisonous, repulsive
10 disgusting, malodorous,
nauseating, pernicious
11 deleterious, pestiferous
12 disagreeable, pestilential

noisy
04 loud
05 rowdy, vocal
07 blaring, booming, roaring
08 blasting, piercing

09 clamorous, deafening
10 boisterous, thundering,
tumultuous, vociferous
12 ear-splitting, obstreperous

nomad
05 rover
06 roamer
07 migrant, rambler, vagrant
08 vagabond, wanderer
09 itinerant, transient, traveller

nomadic
05 Gypsy
06 roving
07 migrant, roaming, vagrant
08 drifting
09 itinerant, migratory,
unsettled, wandering
10 travelling
11 peripatetic
13 peregrinating

nom-de-plume
05 alias
07 pen-name
09 pseudonym
11 assumed name

nomenclature
06 naming
08 locution, taxonomy
10 vocabulary
11 phraseology, terminology
12 codification
14 classification

nominal
05 small, token
06 formal, puppet
07 minimal, titular, trivial
08 so-called, supposed,
symbolic, trifling
09 professed, purported
10 in name only, ostensible
11 theoretical
13 insignificant

nominate
04 name, term
05 elect, put up
06 assign, choose, select
07 appoint, propose, suggest
09 designate, recommend
10 commission

nomination
06 choice
08 election, proposal
09 selection
10 submission, suggestion
11 appointment, designation
14 recommendation

nominee
06 runner
07 entrant

08 assignee
09 appointee, candidate

non-aligned
07 neutral
09 impartial, undecided
10 uninvolved
11 independent, non-partisan

nonchalance
04 calm, cool
06 aplomb
09 sang-froid, unconcern
10 detachment, equanimity
11 insouciance
12 indifference
13 pococurantism
14 self-possession

nonchalant
04 calm, cool
05 blasé
06 casual
07 offhand
08 detached, laid-back
10 insouciant
11 indifferent, unconcerned
13 dispassionate,
   imperturbable
15 cool as a cucumber

non-committal
04 wary
05 vague
07 careful, evasive, guarded,
   neutral, prudent, tactful
08 cautious, discreet, reserved
09 equivocal, tentative
10 diplomatic, indefinite
11 circumspect, unrevealing

non compos mentis
05 crazy
06 insane
08 deranged, unhinged
10 unbalanced
11 mentally ill
13 of unsound mind

nonconformist
05 rebel
07 heretic, radical, seceder
08 maverick
09 dissenter, dissident,
   eccentric, heretical
10 iconoclast
11 dissentient
12 secessionist
13 individualist
14 fish out of water

nonconformity
06 heresy
07 dissent
09 deviation, secession
10 heterodoxy

11 originality
12 eccentricity

nondescript
04 dull
05 bland, plain, vague
07 anaemic, insipid, outrage
11 featureless, uninspiring
12 run of the mill, unremarkable
13 indeterminate, undistinctive,
   unexceptional, uninteresting
15 undistinguished

none
03 nil
04 zero
05 no one
06 nobody, not any, not one
07 nothing
08 not a soul

nonentity
06 cipher, menial, nobody
07 nothing
10 mediocrity

non-essential
09 excessive, redundant
10 expendable, extraneous,
   peripheral
11 dispensable, inessential,
   superfluous, unimportant,
   unnecessary
13 supplementary

nonetheless
03 but, yet
05 still
06 anyhow, anyway, even so
07 however
10 regardless
12 nevertheless
15 notwithstanding

non-existence
05 fancy
07 chimera, unbeing
08 illusion
09 unreality

non-existent
06 unreal
07 fancied, fantasy, missing
08 fanciful, illusory, imagined,
   mythical
09 fictional, imaginary
10 chimerical, fictitious
11 incorporeal
12 hypothetical
13 hallucinatory, insubstantial

non-flammable
09 fire-proof
13 fire-resistant, incombustible
14 flame-resistant

non-intervention
08 inaction

09 passivity
12 laissez-faire, non-alignment
14 hands-off policy, non-
   involvement
15 non-interference

nonpareil
06 unique
09 matchless
10 inimitable, unequalled,
   unrivalled
12 incomparable, unparalleled,
   without equal
13 beyond compare

non-partisan
07 neutral
08 detached, unbiased
09 impartial, objective
10 even-handed
11 independent
12 unprejudiced
13 dispassionate

nonplus
04 faze, stun
05 stump
06 baffle, dismay, puzzle
07 astound, confuse, flummox,
   mystify, perplex
08 astonish, bewilder,
   confound
09 discomfit, dumbfound,
   embarrass, take aback
10 disconcert
11 flabbergast
14 discountenance

nonplussed
05 fazed
07 at a loss, baffled, floored,
   puzzled, stumped, stunned
09 astounded, flummoxed,
   perplexed
10 astonished, bewildered,
   confounded, taken aback
11 dumbfounded
12 disconcerted
13 flabbergasted
14 out of your depth

nonsense
03 rot
04 bosh, bull, bunk, crap,
   tosh
05 balls, hooey, trash, tripe
06 bunkum, drivel, humbug
07 baloney, blather, flannel,
   rubbish, twaddle
08 claptrap, cobblers
09 gibberish, poppycock,
   silliness, stupidity
10 balderdash, codswallop,
   mumbo-jumbo
11 double Dutch, foolishness

12 gobbledygook
13 senselessness

nonsensical
05 barmy, crazy, dotty, inane, nutty, potty, silly, wacky
06 absurd, stupid
09 ludicrous, senseless
10 irrational, ridiculous
11 hare-brained, meaningless
14 unintelligible

non-stop
07 endless, ongoing
08 constant, steadily, unbroken
09 ceaseless, endlessly, incessant, unceasing
10 constantly, continuous, persistent, relentless
11 ceaselessly, incessantly, never-ending, unceasingly
12 continuously, interminable, interminably, relentlessly
13 round-the-clock, unfalteringly, uninterrupted, unrelentingly, unremittingly
15 uninterruptedly

non-violent
06 dovish, irenic
07 passive
08 pacifist, peaceful
09 peaceable

nook
05 niche
06 alcove, cavity, corner, cranny, refuge, recess
07 hideout, opening, shelter
09 cubbyhole

noon
06 midday
09 lunchtime
10 twelve noon
12 twelve o'clock

norm
04 mean, rule, type
07 average, measure, pattern
08 standard
09 benchmark, criterion
10 touchstone

normal
05 usual
06 common
07 average, general, natural, regular, routine, typical
08 accepted, everyday, habitual, ordinary, rational, standard, straight
10 accustomed, mainstream
11 commonplace
12 conventional, well-adjusted

normality
06 reason
07 balance, routine
11 averageness, naturalness
12 ordinariness
15 conventionality

normally
07 as a rule, as usual, usually
08 commonly
09 generally, naturally, regularly, routinely, typically
10 ordinarily
14 conventionally

northern
05 north, polar
06 Arctic, boreal
09 northerly
11 hyperborean
13 septentrional

nose
03 neb
04 beak, bill, boko, conk, push
05 flair, nasal, snoot, snout
06 hooter, rhinal, snitch
08 instinct
09 proboscis, schnozzle

❑**nose around**
03 pry
05 snoop
06 search
10 poke around, rubberneck

❑**nose out**
06 detect, reveal
07 find out, inquire, uncover
08 discover, sniff out

nosedive
04 dive, drop
05 swoop
06 header, plunge, purler
07 decline, plummet
08 get worse, submerge

nosegay
04 posy
05 bunch, spray
07 bouquet

nosh
04 diet, dish, eats, fare, feed, food, grub, menu, tuck
05 board, meals, table
06 fodder, stores, viands
07 cooking, cuisine, rations
08 delicacy, eatables, victuals
09 nutriment, nutrition
10 provisions, sustenance
11 nourishment, subsistence
12 refreshments

nostalgia
06 pining, regret
07 longing, regrets

11 remembrance, wistfulness
12 recollection, reminiscence

nostalgic
06 pining
07 longing, wistful
08 homesick, yearning
09 emotional, regretful
11 reminiscent, sentimental

nostrum
04 cure, drug, pill
06 elixir, potion, remedy
07 cure-all, panacea
08 medicine
13 universal cure
14 cure for all ills

nosy
06 prying
07 curious, probing
08 snooping
10 meddlesome
11 inquisitive, interfering
13 eavesdropping

notability
04 fame
06 esteem, renown, worthy
08 eminence, luminary
09 celebrity, personage
10 importance
11 distinction, heavyweight
12 significance

notable
03 VIP
04 rare, star
05 great
06 famous, marked, worthy
07 eminent, special, unusual
08 luminary, renowned, somebody, striking
09 celebrity, dignitary, important, memorable, momentous, notorious, personage, well-known
10 celebrated, impressive, notability, noteworthy, noticeable, particular, pre-eminent, remarkable
11 illustrious, outstanding, significant
13 distinguished, extraordinary, unforgettable

notably
08 markedly, signally
09 eminently
10 distinctly, especially, noticeably, remarkably, strikingly, uncommonly
12 impressively, particularly
13 outstandingly, significantly
15 extraordinarily

notation
04 code
05 signs
06 cipher, script, system
07 symbols
08 alphabet
09 shorthand
10 characters
13 hieroglyphics

notch
03 cut
04 gash, mark, nick, snip, step
05 gouge, grade, level, stage
06 degree, groove, indent
07 scratch
08 incision

◻**notch up**
04 gain, make
05 score
06 attain, record
07 achieve, chalk up
08 register

notched
05 erose, jaggy
06 eroded, jagged, pinked
08 serrated
10 emarginate, serrulated
11 crenellated

note
03 log, see
04 care, fame, mark, memo, tone
05 enter, gloss, token
06 detect, letter, notice, record, regard, remark, renown
07 comment, element, jot down, jotting, mention, message, missive, observe, put down, refer to, touch on
08 eminence, footnote, perceive, prestige, register
09 greatness, write down
10 annotation, commentary, indication, inflection, marginalia, memorandum
11 consequence, distinction
13 communication
15 illustriousness

noted
05 great
06 famous, of note
07 eminent, notable
08 renowned
09 prominent, respected, well-known
10 celebrated, recognized
11 illustrious
13 distinguished

notes
05 draft

06 record, report, sketch
07 minutes, outline
08 jottings, synopsis
10 commentary, transcript
11 impressions

noteworthy
07 notable, unusual
08 striking
09 important, memorable
10 impressive, remarkable
11 exceptional, significant
13 extraordinary

nothing
04 void, zero
05 zilch
06 cipher, menial, naught, nobody, nought, sod all
08 oblivion
09 bugger all, emptiness, nonentity, not a thing
11 lightweight, nothingness
15 sweet Fanny Adams

◻**for nothing**
04 free
06 gratis, in vain
08 at no cost, futilely
09 to no avail
10 needlessly, on the house
12 free of charge, with no result

nothingness
04 void
06 vacuum
07 nullity
08 nihilism, nihility, oblivion
09 emptiness
12 non-existence

notice
03 see
04 bill, crit, espy, heed, mark, mind, news, note, sign, spot
05 order
06 advice, behold, detect, poster, remark, review
07 comment, discern, observe, warning, write-up
08 bulletin, critique, handbill, interest, pamphlet, perceive
09 attention, awareness
10 cognizance, intimation
11 declaration, information
12 announcement, notification
13 advertisement, become aware of
14 pay attention to

noticeable
05 clear, plain
06 patent
07 evident, obvious, visible
08 distinct, manifest, striking
10 detectable, observable

11 appreciable, conspicuous, discernible, perceptible
15 distinguishable

notification
06 advice, notice
07 message, telling, warning
09 informing, statement
11 declaration, publication
12 announcement, intelligence
13 communication

notify
04 tell, warn
05 alert
06 advise, inform, reveal
07 apprise, caution, declare, divulge, publish
08 acquaint, announce
09 broadcast, make known
11 communicate

notion
04 idea, view, whim, wish
05 fancy
06 belief, desire, theory
07 caprice, concept, thought
10 assumption, conception, hypothesis, impression
11 inclination
12 apprehension
13 understanding

notional
06 unreal
07 fancied
08 abstract, fanciful, thematic
09 imaginary, unfounded
10 conceptual, ideational
11 speculative, theoretical
12 hypothetical

notoriety
06 infamy
07 obloquy, scandal
08 disgrace, ignominy
09 dishonour, disrepute
10 opprobrium

notorious
07 blatant, glaring
08 flagrant, ill-famed, infamous
09 egregious, well-known
10 scandalous
11 disgraceful, ignominious, of ill repute, opprobrious
12 disreputable

notoriously
06 openly
07 notably, overtly
08 arrantly, patently
09 blatantly, glaringly, obviously
10 flagrantly, infamously
12 disreputably, scandalously
13 disgracefully, ignominiously

notwithstanding

03 yet
06 even so, though
07 despite, however
08 although
09 in spite of
11 nonetheless
12 nevertheless, regardless of

nought

03 nil
04 zero
05 zilch
06 naught
07 nothing
11 nothingness

nourish

03 aid
04 feed, have, help, rear, tend
05 boost, nurse
06 assist, foster
07 cherish, forward, further, nurture, promote, support
08 attend to, maintain
09 cultivate, encourage, stimulate
10 provide for, strengthen

nourishing

04 good
09 wholesome
10 beneficial, nutritious
11 substantial
12 health-giving, invigorating
13 strengthening

nourishment

04 diet, food, grub, nosh, tuck
09 nutriment, nutrition
10 sustenance
11 subsistence

novel

03 new
04 book, rare, tale
05 fresh, story
06 modern, unique
07 fiction, strange, unusual
08 creative, original
09 different, ingenious, inventive, narrative
10 innovative, unorthodox
11 imaginative, resourceful
14 ground-breaking

► *Names of novelists and short-story writers*:

03 Eco (Umberto), Kee (Robert), Lee (Harper), Lee (Laurie), Poe (Edgar Allan), Pym (Barbara), Roy (Arundhati)

04 Amis (Kingsley), Amis (Martin), Behn (Aphra), Böll (Heinrich), Buck

(Pearl Sydenstricker), Cary (Joyce), Dahl (Roald), Ford (Ford Madox), Gide (André), Grey (Zane), Hogg (James), Hugo (Victor), King (Stephen), Levi (Primo), Mann (Thomas), Okri (Ben), Puzo (Mario), Rhys (Jean), Roth (Philip), Sade (Marquis de), Saki, Sand (George), Seth (Vikram), Snow (Charles Percy), Wain (John), West (Dame Rebecca), Zola (Emile)

05 Adams (Douglas), Adams (Richard), Banks (Iain), Bates (Herbert Ernest), Behan (Brendan), Bragg (Melvyn), Brink (André), Brown (George Mackay), Bunin (Ivan), Byatt (Antonia Susan), Camus (Albert), Chase (James Hadley), Crane (Stephen), Defoe (Daniel), Desai (Anita), Doyle (Roddy), Doyle (Sir Arthur Conan), Dumas (Alexandre, fils), Dumas (Alexandre, père), Eliot (George), Ellis (Alice Thomas), Elton (Ben), Genet (Jean), Gogol (Nikolai), Gorky (Maxim), Grass (Günter), Hardy (Thomas), Hesse (Hermann), Heyer (Georgette), Innes (Hammond), James (Henry), James (Phyllis Dorothy), Joyce (James), Kafka (Franz), Keane (Molly), Kesey (Ken), Laski (Marghanita), Lewis (Clive Staples), Lewis (Sinclair), Lewis (Wyndham), Lodge (David), Lowry (Malcolm), Marsh (Dame Ngaio), Milne (Alan Alexander), Moore (Brian), Munro (Hector Hugh), Peake (Mervyn), Plath (Sylvia), Queen (Ellery), Sagan (Françoise), Scott (Paul), Scott (Sir Walter), Shute (Nevil), Simon (Claude), Smith (Stevie), Smith (Wilbur), Spark (Dame Muriel), Staël (Madame de), Stowe (Harriet Beecher), Swift (Graham), Swift

(Jonathan), Twain (Mark), Verne (Jules), Vidal (Gore), Waugh (Auberon), Waugh (Evelyn), Wells (Herbert George), White (Patrick), White (Terence Hanbury), Wilde (Oscar), Wolfe (Thomas Clayton), Wolfe (Tom), Woolf (Virginia), Yates (Dornford), Yonge (Charlotte Mary)

06 Achebe (Chinua), Alcott (Louisa May), Aldiss (Brian), Aragon (Louis), Archer (Jeffrey), Asimov (Isaac), Atwood (Margaret), Austen (Jane), Balzac (Honoré de), Barker (Pat), Barrie (Sir James Matthew), Bellow (Saul), Binchy (Maeve), Blixen (Karen, Lady), Blyton (Enid), Borges (Jorge Luis), Braine (John), Brontë (Anne), Brontë (Charlotte), Brontë (Emily), Bryson (Bill), Buchan (John), Bunyan (John), Burney (Fanny), Butler (Samuel), Capote (Truman), Carter (Angela), Cather (Willa), Clancy (Tom), Clarke (Arthur Charles), Conrad (Joseph), Cooper (James Fenimore), Cooper (Jilly), Cronin (Archibald Joseph), Faulks (Sebastian), Fowles (John), France (Anatole), Gibbon (Lewis Grassic), Godden (Rumer), Godwin (William), Goethe (Johann Wolfgang von), Graham (Winston), Graves (Robert), Greene (Graham), Hamsun (Knut), Heller (Joseph), Holtby (Winifred), Hornby (Nick), Hughes (Thomas), Huxley (Aldous), Jerome (Jerome Klapka), Kelman (James), Laclos (Pierre Choderlos de), Larkin (Philip), Lively (Penelope), London (Jack), Mailer (Norman), McEwan (Ian), Miller (Henry), Nesbit (Edith), O'Brien (Edna), O'Brien (Flann), Orwell (George), Powell (Anthony), Proust (Marcel), Sapper, Sartre (Jean-Paul), Sayers (Dorothy Leigh), Sewell

(Anna), **Sharpe** (Tom),
Singer (Isaac Bashevis),
Steele (Danielle), **Sterne**
(Laurence), **Stoker** (Bram),
Tagore (Rabindranath),
Thomas (Dylan), **Updike**
(John), **Walker** (Alice),
Warner (Marina), **Warren**
(Robert Penn), **Weldon**
(Fay), **Wesley** (Mary),
Wilder (Thornton), **Wilson**
(Sir Angus)

07 **Ackroyd** (Peter), **Angelou**
(Maya), **Baldwin** (James),
Ballard (James Graham),
Beckett (Samuel), **Bennett**
(Arnold), **Burgess**
(Anthony), **Burnett**
(Frances Hodgson),
Calvino (Italo), **Canetti**
(Elias), **Carroll** (Lewis),
Chatwin (Bruce),
Chekhov (Anton), **Clavell**
(James), **Cleland** (John),
Cocteau (Jean), **Coetzee**
(John Michael), **Colette**,
Collins (Wilkie), **Cookson**
(Catherine), **Dickens**
(Charles), **Diderot** (Denis),
Dineson (Isaac), **Drabble**
(Margaret), **Durrell**
(Gerald), **Durrell**
(Lawrence), **Fleming** (Ian),
Forster (Edward Morgan),
Forster (Margaret),
Forsyth (Frederick),
Francis (Dick), **Gaskell**
(Mrs Elizabeth), **Gautier**
(Théophile), **Gibbons**
(Stella), **Gissing** (George),
Golding (William),
Grahame (Kenneth),
Grisham (John), **Haggard**
(Sir Henry Rider),
Hammett (Dashiell),
Hartley (Leslie Poles),
Kerouac (Jack), **Kipling**
(Rudyard), **Kundera**
(Milan), **Lardner** (Ring),
Laxness (Halldór), **Le
Carré** (John), **Lessing**
(Doris), **Maclean** (Alistair),
Mahfouz (Naguib),
Malamud (Bernard),
Malraux (André), **Marryat**
(Captain Frederick),
Maugham (William
Somerset), **Mauriac**
(François), **Mishima**
(Yukio), **Mitford** (Nancy),
Moravia (Alberto),
Murdoch (Dame Iris),

Nabokov (Vladimir),
Naipaul (Vidiadhar
Surajprasad), **Peacock**
(Thomas Love), **Prévost**
(l'Abbé), **Pushkin**
(Alexander), **Pynchon**
(Thomas), **Ransome**
(Arthur), **Raphael**
(Frederic), **Renault** (Mary),
Rendell (Ruth), **Richler**
(Mordecai), **Robbins**
(Harold), **Rowling** (J K),
Rushdie (Salman),
Sassoon (Siegfried),
Shelley (Mary), **Simenon**
(Georges), **Sitwell** (Sir
Osbert), **Soyinka** (Wole),
Spender (Sir Stephen),
Surtees (Robert Smith),
Theroux (Paul), **Tolkien**
(John Ronald Reuel),
Tolstoy (Leo, Count),
Tremain (Rose), **Walpole**
(Sir Hugh), **Wharton**
(Edith), **Wyndham** (John)

08 **Andersen** (Hans
Christian), **Apuleius**
(Lucius), **Barbusse** (Henri),
Beckford (William
Thomas), **Beerbohm** (Sir
Max), **Bradbury**
(Malcolm), **Bradbury**
(Ray), **Bradford** (Barbara
Taylor), **Brittain** (Vera),
Brookner (Anita),
Bulgakov (Mikhail),
Cartland (Barbara),
Chandler (Raymond),
Christie (Dame Agatha),
Cornwell (Patricia),
Crompton (Richmal),
Day-Lewis (Cecil), **De La
Mare** (Walter), **Deighton**
(Len), **Disraeli** (Benjamin),
Donleavy (James Patrick),
Faulkner (William),
Fielding (Henry), **Flaubert**
(Gustave), **Forester** (Cecil
Scott), **Goncourt** (Edmond
de), **Gordimer** (Nadine),
Huysmans (Joris Karl),
Ishiguro (Kazuo),
Jhabvala (Ruth Prawer),
Keneally (Thomas),
Kingsley (Charles),
Koestler (Arthur),
Lawrence (David Herbert),
Macaulay (Dame Rose),
Melville (Herman),
Meredith (George),
Michener (James Albert),
Milligan (Spike),

Morrison (Toni),
Mortimer (John),
Ondaatje (Michael),
Remarque (Erich Maria),
Rousseau (Jean Jacques),
Salinger (Jerome David),
Sillitoe (Alan), **Sinclair**
(Upton), **Smollett** (Tobias),
Spillane (Mickey),
Stendhal, **Trollope**
(Anthony), **Trollope**
(Joanna), **Turgenev** (Ivan),
Voltaire (François-Marie
Arouet de), **Vonnegut**
(Kurt, Junior)

09 **Allingham** (Margery),
Bernières (Louis de),
Burroughs (Edgar Rice),
Burroughs (William
Seward), **Cervantes**
(Miguel de), **Charteris**
(Leslie), **D'Annunzio**
(Gabriele), **De Quincey**
(Thomas), **Delafield** (E M),
Dos Passos (John), **Du
Maurier** (Dame Daphne),
Du Maurier (George),
Edgeworth (Maria),
Gerhardie (William
Alexander), **Goldsmith**
(Oliver), **Grossmith**
(George), **Grossmith**
(Weedon), **Hawthorne**
(Nathaniel), **Hemingway**
(Ernest), **Highsmith**
(Patricia), **Hölderlin**
(Friedrich), **Isherwood**
(Christopher), **Lampedusa**
(Giuseppe Tomasi de),
Lermontov (Mikhail),
Linklater (Eric),
Mackenzie (Sir Compton),
Mankowitz (Wolf),
Mansfield (Katherine),
Masefield (John),
McCullers (Carson),
Mitchison (Naomi),
Monsarrat (Nicholas),
Pasternak (Boris),
Pratchett (Terry), **Priestley**
(John Boynton), **Radcliffe**
(Ann), **Santayana** (George),
Sholokhov (Mikhail),
Steinbeck (John),
Stevenson (Robert Louis),
Thackeray (William
Makepeace), **Wodehouse**
(Sir Pelham Grenville)

10 **Bainbridge** (Beryl),
Ballantyne (Robert
Michael), **Chesterton**
(Gilbert Keith), **De**

Beauvoir (Simone),
Dostoevsky (Fyodor),
Fitzgerald (Francis Scott),
Galsworthy (John),
Lagerkvist (Pär),
Maupassant (Guy de),
Pirandello (Luigi),
Richardson (Dorothy
Miller), **Richardson**
(Samuel), **Strindberg**
(August), **Van der Post** (Sir
Laurens), **Waterhouse**
(Keith)
11 **Vargas Llosa** (Mario)
12 **Quiller-Couch** (Sir
Arthur), **Robbe-Grillet**
(Alain), **Saint-Exupéry**
(Antoine de), **Solzhenitsyn**
(Aleksandr)
13 **Alain-Fournier** (Henri),
García Márquez (Gabriel),
Sackville-West (Vita)
14 **Compton-Burnett** (Dame
Ivy)
15 **Somerset Maugham**
(William)
➤ See also **writer**

▶ *Names of novels and
fictional works*:
03 Kim, She
04 Emma, Nana, Voss
05 Kipps, Money, Scoop, Sybil
06 Herzog, Lolita, Nausea,
Pamela, Rob Roy, Trilby,
Utopia, Walden
07 Babbitt, Beloved, Candide,
Catch-22, Dracula,
Erewhon, Ivanhoe, Justine,
Lord Jim, Orlando,
Rebecca, The Bell, The Fall,
Ulysses
08 Adam Bede, Clarissa,
Germinal, Jane Eyre,
Lavengro, Lucky Jim, Moby
Dick, Nostromo, Oroonoko,
Peter Pan, Rasselas, The
Idiot, The Trial, The Waves,
Tom Jones, Tom Thumb,
Villette, Waverley
09 Beau Geste, Billy Budd,
Billy Liar, Dead Souls,
Dubliners, Hard Times,
Kidnapped, On the Road,
Rogue Male, The Devils, The
Hobbit, Tom Sawyer
10 Animal Farm, Bleak House,
Cancer Ward, Cannery Row,
Don Quixote, East of Eden,
Edwin Drood, Goldfinger,
Howards End, Lorna
Doone, Persuasion, Rural
Rides, The Rainbow, The Tin

Drum, Titus Alone, Titus
Groan, Uncle Remus, Vanity
Fair, Westward Ho!
11 A Tale of a Tub, Black Beauty,
Burmese Days, Cakes and
Ale, Daisy Miller,
Gormenghast, Little
Women, Middlemarch, Mrs
Dalloway, Oliver Twist, Silas
Marner, Steppenwolf, The
Big Sleep, The Outsider, The
Third Man, War and Peace,
Women in Love
12 Anna Karenina, A Suitable
Boy, Barnaby Rudge,
Brighton Rock, Casino
Royale, Dombey and Son,
Fear of Flying,
Frankenstein, Little Dorrit,
Madame Bovary, Moll
Flanders, Of Mice and Men,
Rip Van Winkle, Room at the
Top, The Go-Between, The
Golden Ass, The Lost
World, The Sea, the Sea
13 A Kind of Loving, Arabian
Nights, Brave New World,
Call of the Wild, Daniel
Deronda, Doctor Zhivago,
Finnegans Wake, Joseph
Andrews, Just So Stories,
Les Misérables, Mansfield
Park, Metamorphosis,
North and South,
Schindler's Ark, Sketches By
Boz, Smiley's People, Sons
and Lovers, Tarka the Otter,
The Awkward Age, The
Bostonians, The Golden
Bowl, The Jungle Book, The
Last Tycoon, The
Mabinogion, The Naked
Lunch, The Odessa File, The
Virginians, Under Milk
Wood, Winnie-the-Pooh,
Zuleika Dobson
14 A Handful of Dust, A Room
with a View, A Town Like
Alice, Cider with Rosie,
Death on the Nile, Decline
and Fall, Fathers and Sons,
Humphry Clinker, Jude the
Obscure, Lord of the Flies,
Robinson Crusoe, Roderick
Random, The Ambassadors,
The Coral Island, The
Forsyte Saga, The Great
Gatsby, The Kraken Wakes,
The Long Goodbye, The
Secret Agent, The Time
Machine, The Water-Babies,
The Woodlanders, Treasure

Island, Tristram Shandy,
Tropic of Cancer, Uncle
Tom's Cabin, What Maisie
Knew
15 A Christmas Carol, A
Farewell to Arms, A Passage
to India, Cold Comfort
Farm, Daphnis and Chloe,
Gone with the Wind,
Huckleberry Finn,
Northanger Abbey, Our
Mutual Friend, Peregrine
Pickle, Tarzan of the Apes,
The African Queen, The
Invisible Man, The Little
Prince, The Secret Garden,
The Woman in White, Three
Men in a Boat, To the
Lighthouse, Under the
Volcano, Where Eagles Dare
➤ See also **fiction**

novelty
06 bauble, gadget, trifle
07 newness, trinket
08 gimcrack, rareness,
souvenir
09 curiosity, freshness
10 difference, innovation,
knick-knack, uniqueness
11 originality, strangeness

novice
04 tiro
05 pupil
06 rookie
07 amateur, learner, recruit
08 beginner, neophyte,
newcomer
09 greenhorn, noviciate
10 apprentice, raw recruit
11 probationer

noviciate
08 training
10 initiation
11 trial period
13 trainee period
14 apprenticeship

now
04 next
05 today
06 at once
08 directly, nowadays
09 at present, currently,
instantly, presently, right
away, these days
10 at this time
11 at the moment, immediately
12 straight away, without delay
15 for the time being

❑**now and then**
07 at times

08 on and off
09 sometimes
10 on occasion
11 desultorily, now and again
12 infrequently, occasionally, once in a while, periodically, sporadically
13 spasmodically
14 from time to time, intermittently

nowadays
09 today
09 at present, currently, presently, these days
11 at the moment
15 in this day and age

noxious
04 foul
05 toxic
06 deadly
07 harmful, noisome, ruinous
09 poisonous, unhealthy
10 disgusting, pernicious
11 destructive, detrimental

nuance
04 hint
05 shade, tinge, touch, trace
07 shading
08 overtone, subtlety
10 refinement, suggestion

nub
04 core, crux, gist, meat, pith
05 focus, heart, pivot, point
06 centre, kernel, marrow
07 essence, nucleus

nubile
04 sexy
05 adult
06 mature
09 desirable
10 attractive, voluptuous
12 marriageable

nucleus
03 nub
04 core, crux, meat
05 basis, focus, heart, pivot
06 centre, kernel, marrow

nude
04 bare
05 naked
07 exposed
08 in the raw, starkers, stripped
09 in the buff, unclothed, uncovered, undressed
10 stark-naked
12 not a stitch on
13 with nothing on
15 in the altogether

nudge
03 dig, jab, jog
04 bump, poke, prod, push
05 elbow, shove
06 prompt

nudity
06 nudism
07 undress
08 bareness
09 nakedness
10 dishabille, déshabillé
15 in the altogether

nugatory
04 vain
06 futile
07 invalid, trivial, useless
08 trifling
09 valueless, worthless
10 inadequate, unavailing
11 inoperative, null and void
13 insignificant

nugget
04 hunk, lump, mass
05 chunk, clump, piece, wodge

nuisance
04 bore, drag, pain, pest
06 bother, plague, weight
07 problem, trouble
08 drawback, irritant, vexation
09 annoyance
10 affliction, difficulty, irritation
13 inconvenience

null
04 vain, void
07 invalid, revoked, useless
08 annulled
09 abrogated, cancelled, nullified, worthless
11 inoperative, invalidated

nullify
04 void
05 annul, quash
06 cancel, negate, repeal
07 abolish, rescind, reverse
08 abrogate, renounce
10 counteract, invalidate
11 countermand, discontinue

nullity
08 voidness
10 invalidity
12 non-existence
13 worthlessness

numb
04 dead, drug, dull, stun
05 dazed
06 deaden, freeze, frozen
07 drugged, in shock, stunned
09 insensate, paralysed

10 immobilize, insensible
12 anaesthetize
13 anaesthetized
14 without feeling

number
03 add, sum
04 copy, data, many, unit
05 count, digit, group, horde, issue, score, tally, total
06 amount, cipher, figure
07 add up to, company, compute, decimal, delimit, edition, imprint, include, integer, numeral, several
08 fraction, quantity, restrict
09 aggregate, calculate, character, enumerate
10 impression, statistics

numberless
04 many
06 myriad, untold
07 endless
08 infinite, unsummed
09 countless, uncounted
10 unnumbered
11 innumerable
12 immeasurable

numbness
06 stupor, torpor
08 deadness, dullness
09 paralysis
12 stupefaction
13 insensateness, insensibility

numeral
04 unit
05 digit
06 cipher, figure, number
07 integer
09 character

▶ *Roman numerals include:*
01 **C** (hundred), **D** (five hundred), **I** (one), **L** (fifty), **M** (thousand), **V** (five), **X** (ten)
02 **II** (two), **IV** (four), **IX** (nine), **VI** (six), **XI** (eleven), **XV** (fifteen), **XX** (twenty)
03 **III** (three), **VII** (seven), **XII** (twelve), **XIV** (fourteen), **XIX** (nineteen), **XVI** (sixteen)
04 **VIII** (eight), **XIII** (thirteen), **XVII** (seventeen)
05 **XVIII** (eighteen)

numerous
04 many
06 legion, sundry
07 copious, endless, profuse
08 abundant, manifold
09 countless, plentiful

11 innumerable
13 multitudinous

numerousness
08 multeity
09 abundance, profusion
11 copiousness
12 manifoldness, multiplicity
13 countlessness, plentifulness

numskull
03 nit
04 clot, fool, twit
05 dummy, dunce, twerp
06 dimwit, nitwit
07 fat head
09 birdbrain, simpleton

nun
06 abbess, sister, vestal, vowess
07 ancress
08 canoness, prioress
09 anchoress
14 mother superior

nuncio
05 envoy
06 legate
10 ambassador
14 representative

nunnery
05 abbey
06 priory
07 convent
08 cloister

nuptial
06 bridal, wedded
07 marital, wedding
08 conjugal, hymeneal
09 connubial
11 epithalamic, matrimonial
12 epithalamial

nuptials
06 bridal
07 wedding
08 espousal, marriage, spousals
09 matrimony

nurse
03 aid
04 feed, help, keep, tend
05 boost, treat
06 assist, foster, suckle
07 advance, care for, cherish,
   further, harbour, nourish,
   nurture, support, sustain
08 attend to, wet-nurse
09 encourage, look after
10 breast-feed, take care of
➤ See also **medical**

➤ *Types of nurse. We have
omitted the word* **nurse** *from
names in this list but you may
need to include this word as part
of the solution to some
crossword clues.*
03 RGN, SEN, SRN, wet
04 home
05 nanny, night, staff
06 charge, dental, matron,
   school, sister
07 midwife, nursery
08 district
09 children's, Macmillan,
   nursemaid
10 ward sister
11 night sister, psychiatric
13 health visitor, State Enrolled
15 State Registered

➤ *Names of nurses*:
05 **Kenny** (Elizabeth)
06 **Cavell** (Edith), **Sanger**
   (Margaret Louise)
07 **Seacole** (Mary)
08 **Pattison** (Dorothy
   Wyndlow)
10 **Stephenson** (Elsie)
11 **Nightingale** (Florence)

nurture
04 care, feed, help, rear, tend
05 boost, coach, train, tutor
06 assist, foster, school
07 advance, bring up, care for,
   develop, educate, feeding,
   further, nourish, rearing,
   support, sustain, tending
09 cultivate, education,
   fostering, nutrition
10 sustenance, upbringing
11 cultivation, development,
   furtherance, nourishment

nut
03 fan, pip
04 buff, seed
05 fiend, freak, loony, stone
06 kernel, madman, maniac,
   nutter, psycho, zealot
07 admirer, devotee, fanatic,
   lunatic, nutcase, oddball
08 headcase, madwoman
09 fruitcake, supporter
10 enthusiast, psychopath
➤ *Types of nut*:
05 pecan
06 almond, cashew, cobnut,
   peanut, walnut
07 coconut, filbert

08 beech nut, chestnut,
   hazelnut
09 brazil nut, macadamia,
   monkey nut, pistachio
➤ See also **food**

nutriment
04 diet, food, grub, nosh, tuck
09 nutrition
10 sustenance
11 nourishment, subsistence

nutrition
04 diet, food, grub, nosh, tuck
07 trophic
09 nutriment
10 sustenance
11 nourishment, subsistence

nutritious
04 good
09 nutritive, wholesome
10 beneficial, nourishing
12 health-giving, invigorating
13 strengthening

nuts
03 mad
04 avid, daft, fond, keen, wild
05 crazy, loony, loopy, nutty
06 ardent, crazed, insane
07 berserk, bonkers, devoted,
   lunatic, smitten, zealous
08 demented, deranged,
   doolally, unhinged
09 disturbed, fanatical
10 infatuated, out to lunch,
   passionate, unbalanced
12 enthusiastic, round the bend
13 off your rocker, out of your
   mind, round the twist

nuts and bolts
06 basics
07 details
10 components, essentials
11 nitty-gritty
12 fundamentals
14 practicalities

nuzzle
03 pet
05 nudge
06 burrow, cuddle, nestle
07 snuggle

nymph
04 girl, lass, maid
05 dryad, naiad, oread, sylph
06 damsel, sprite, undine
09 hamadryad

oaf
04 clod, dolt, gawk, hick, lout
05 yahoo, yobbo
06 lubber
07 bumpkin
11 hobbledehoy

oafish
05 gawky, gross, rough
06 coarse, lumpen, stolid
07 doltish, ill-bred, uncouth
08 bungling, churlish, lubberly
10 unmannerly
11 clodhopping, ill-mannered

oasis
05 haven
06 island, refuge, spring
07 hideout, retreat, sanctum
12 watering-hole

oath
03 vow
05 curse
06 avowal, pledge
07 promise
09 assurance, blasphemy,
   expletive, obscenity,
   profanity, swear-word
11 attestation, bad language,
   imprecation, malediction

obdurate
04 firm, iron
05 stony
06 dogged, wilful
07 adamant
08 stubborn
09 immovable, obstinate,
   pig-headed, steadfast,
   unbending, unfeeling
10 determined, headstrong,
   implacable, inflexible, self-
   willed, unyielding
11 hard-hearted, intractable,
   stiff-necked, unrelenting
12 bloody-minded,
   intransigent, strong-minded

obedience
04 duty
07 respect
08 docility
09 deference, passivity
10 allegiance, compliance,
   observance, submission
11 amenability, dutifulness
12 acquiescence,
   subservience, tractability
14 submissiveness

obedient
06 docile
07 dutiful, pliable
08 amenable, biddable
09 compliant, tractable
10 law-abiding
11 acquiescent, disciplined,
   subservient, well-trained

obeisance
03 bow
06 curtsy, homage, kowtow,
   salaam, salute
07 respect
09 deference, reverence
10 salutation, submission
12 genuflection

obelisk
06 column, needle, pillar
08 memorial, monument

obese
03 big, fat
05 bulky, gross, heavy, large,
   plump, round, stout
06 flabby, fleshy, portly, rotund
07 outsize, paunchy
09 corpulent, ponderous
10 overweight

obesity
07 fatness
09 grossness, stoutness
10 chubbiness, corpulence,
   flabbiness, overweight,
   portliness, rotundness

obey
04 heed, keep, mind
05 bow to, defer, yield
06 comply, follow, fulfil,
   keep to
07 abide by, act upon, conform,
   defer to, execute, give way
08 adhere to, carry out
09 consent to, surrender
10 toe the line
11 acquiesce in, go by the book
14 do as you are told
15 stick to the rules

obfuscate
04 blur, hide, mask, veil
05 cloak, cloud, cover, shade
06 muddle, shadow, shroud
07 conceal, confuse, obscure
10 complicate, overshadow

object
03 aim, end
04 body, butt, goal, idea, item
05 argue, demur, point, thing
06 design, device, gadget,
   intent, motive, oppose,
   resist, target, victim
07 article, protest, purpose
08 ambition, complain
09 intention, something,
   take issue
11 beg to differ, expostulate,
   remonstrate
13 take exception

objection
05 demur
07 dissent, protest, scruple
09 challenge, complaint,
   grievance
10 opposition
11 disapproval
13 remonstration

objectionable
09 loathsome, obnoxious,
   offensive, repellent,
   repugnant, repulsive,
   revolting, sickening
10 deplorable, detestable,
   nauseating, unpleasant
12 disagreeable, unacceptable
13 reprehensible

objective
03 aim, end
04 fair, goal, idea, real, true
06 intent, object, target
07 factual, neutral, purpose
08 detached, unbiased
09 equitable, impartial
10 even-handed, open-
   minded, uninvolved
12 unprejudiced
13 disinterested, dispassionate

objectively
06 fairly, justly
09 equitably, neutrally
11 impartially
12 even-handedly
14 with an open mind
15 disinterestedly, dispassionately

objectivity
08 fairness, justness, open mind
10 detachment
11 disinterest
12 impartiality
13 equitableness
14 even-handedness, open-mindedness

obligate
04 bind, make
05 force, impel, press
06 coerce, compel
09 constrain
10 pressurize

obligation
04 debt, duty, onus, task
06 burden, charge, demand
08 contract, covenant
09 agreement, liability
10 commitment, compulsion
11 requirement
12 indebtedness
14 accountability, responsibility

obligatory
07 binding
08 enforced, required
09 mandatory, necessary, requisite, statutory
10 compulsory, imperative
11 unavoidable

oblige
04 bind, help, make
05 force, impel, press, serve
06 assist, compel, please
07 gratify, require
10 pressurize
11 accommodate, necessitate

obliged
05 bound
06 forced, in debt
08 beholden, grateful, in debt to, indebted, thankful
09 compelled, duty-bound, gratified, obligated
11 constrained, honour-bound

obliging
04 kind
05 civil
06 polite
07 helpful, willing
08 friendly, generous, pleasant

09 agreeable, courteous
11 co-operative, complaisant, considerate, good-natured
13 accommodating

oblique
05 slant, slash
06 angled, stroke, tilted, zigzag
07 devious, sloping, virgule
08 diagonal, inclined, slanting
09 divergent
10 circuitous, discursive, meandering, roundabout
12 periphrastic
14 circumlocutory

obliquely
06 askant, aslant, aslope
07 askance
09 at an angle, evasively
10 diagonally, indirectly
12 circuitously

obliterate
05 erase
06 delete, efface, rub out
07 blot out, destroy, expunge, wipe out
09 eliminate, eradicate, extirpate, strike out
10 annihilate

obliteration
07 erasure
10 effacement, expunction
11 blotting out, destruction, elimination, eradication, extirpation
12 annihilation

oblivion
07 lethean
08 darkness, deafness
09 blindness, obscurity
11 nothingness, unawareness
12 carelessness, non-existence
15 unconsciousness

oblivious
04 deaf
05 blind
07 unaware
08 careless, heedless, ignorant
09 unheeding, unmindful
10 insensible
11 inattentive, preoccupied, unconcerned, unconscious

obloquy
05 abuse, blame, odium, shame
06 attack, stigma
07 calumny, censure, slander
08 disgrace, ignominy

09 aspersion, contumely, criticism, dishonour, invective
10 defamation, opprobrium
11 humiliation
12 vilification

obnoxious
04 vile
05 nasty
06 horrid, odious
08 horrible
09 abhorrent, loathsome, offensive, repellent, repugnant, repulsive, revolting, sickening
10 deplorable, detestable, disgusting, nauseating
12 contemptible, disagreeable

obscene
04 blue, foul, lewd, rude, vile
05 bawdy, dirty, gross
06 carnal, coarse, filthy, risqué, sleazy, smutty, vulgar
07 immoral, raunchy
08 improper, indecent, prurient, shocking
09 offensive, shameless
10 disgusting, licentious, lubricious, outrageous, scurrilous, suggestive
12 pornographic

obscenity
05 curse
06 sleaze
07 offence, outrage
08 atrocity, impurity, lewdness
09 bawdiness, dirtiness, eroticism, expletive, indecency, lubricity, profanity, prurience, swear-word, vulgarity
10 coarseness, filthiness, immorality, wickedness
11 bad language, heinousness, imprecation, impropriety, malediction, pornography
13 salaciousness
14 four-letter word, lasciviousness, licentiousness

obscure
03 dim
04 blur, dark, hazy, hide, mask
05 cloak, cloud, cover, dusky, faint, fuzzy, minor, misty, murky, shade, shady, vague
06 arcane, gloomy, hidden, opaque, remote, screen, shadow, shroud, unsung

obscurity
07 blurred, complex, conceal, confuse, cryptic, eclipse, shadowy, unclear, unknown
08 abstruse, esoteric, nameless
09 confusing, enigmatic, obfuscate, recondite, uncertain, unheard-of
10 complicate, indefinite, indistinct, mysterious, overshadow, perplexing
11 God-forsaken, little-known, out-of-the-way
12 impenetrable, inexplicable
13 inconspicuous, insignificant
15 undistinguished

obscurity
07 mystery
09 ambiguity, confusion
11 unclearness
12 abstruseness
13 reconditeness
14 insignificance
15 impenetrability

obsequious
04 oily
06 abject, creepy, smarmy
07 fawning, servile, slavish
08 cringing, toadying, unctuous
10 flattering, grovelling
11 arse-licking, bootlicking, deferential, subservient, sycophantic
12 ingratiating

observable
05 clear
06 patent
07 evident, obvious, visible
08 apparent
10 detectable, noticeable
11 appreciable, discernible, perceivable, perceptible
12 recognizable

observance
04 rite
06 custom, notice, ritual
07 heeding, keeping, service
08 ceremony, festival, practice
09 adherence, attention, following, formality, honouring, tradition
10 compliance, fulfilment
11 celebration, performance

observant
05 alert, sharp
07 heedful, mindful, on guard
08 hawk-eyed, obedient, orthodox, vigilant, watchful
09 attentive, eagle-eyed, sharp-eyed, wide-awake

observation
04 data, note
05 study
06 remark, result, seeing
07 comment, finding, thought
08 noticing, scrutiny, watching
09 attention, statement
10 annotation, monitoring, perception, reflection
11 description, discernment, examination, information
13 consideration

observe
03 say, see
04 espy, keep, mark, note, obey
05 state, study, utter, watch
06 behold, detect, follow, fulfil, honour, notice, remark
07 comment, declare, discern, examine, execute, mention, monitor, perform, respect
08 perceive, remember
09 celebrate, conform to
10 comply with, keep tabs on
11 commemorate, keep an eye on, keep watch on, miss nothing
12 catch sight of

observer
06 viewer
07 watcher, witness
08 beholder, looker-on, onlooker, reporter
09 bystander, spectator
10 eyewitness
11 commentator

obsess
04 grip, rule
05 haunt, hound
06 plague, prey on
07 bedevil, consume, control, engross, possess, torment
09 preoccupy
10 monopolize

obsessed
05 beset
07 gripped, haunted, plagued
08 hung up on
10 immersed in, infatuated
11 in the grip of, preoccupied

obsession
05 mania, thing
06 fetish, hang-up, phobia
07 complex, passion
09 fixation, idée fixe
11 fascination, infatuation
12 one-track mind
13 preoccupation

obsessive
08 gripping, haunting

09 consuming, maddening
10 compulsive, tormenting

obsolescent
05 dated
06 ageing, fading, waning
08 dying out, outdated
09 declining, on the wane
11 on the way out
12 disappearing, old-fashioned, on the decline, past its prime

obsolete
03 old
04 dead
05 dated, passé
06 bygone, old hat
07 ancient, disused, extinct
08 in disuse, outmoded
09 discarded, out of date
10 antiquated, on the shelf
11 out of the ark
12 antediluvian, discontinued, old-fashioned
13 superannuated

obstacle
03 bar
04 curb, no-no, snag, stop
05 catch, check, hitch
06 hiccup, hurdle
07 barrier
08 blockade, blockage, drawback, handicap
09 barricade, deterrent
10 difficulty, impediment
11 obstruction
14 stumbling-block

obstinacy
08 firmness, obduracy, tenacity
10 doggedness, mulishness, perversity, wilfulness
11 frowardness, persistence
12 resoluteness, stubbornness
13 inflexibility, intransigence, pig-headedness

obstinate
04 firm
06 dogged, wilful
07 adamant
08 stubborn
09 immovable, pig-headed, steadfast, unbending
10 determined, headstrong, inflexible, refractory, self-willed, unyielding
11 intractable, persevering
12 bloody-minded, intransigent, recalcitrant, strong-minded

obstreperous
04 loud, wild

obstruct
05 noisy, rough, rowdy
06 unruly
07 bolshie, raucous, restive, riotous, stroppy
09 clamorous, out of hand
10 boisterous, disorderly, refractory, tumultuous, uproarious, vociferous
11 intractable, tempestuous
12 uncontrolled, unmanageable
13 undisciplined

obstruct
03 bar
04 clog, curb, halt, stop
05 block, check, choke, stall
06 hamper, hinder, hold up, impede, retard, thwart
07 inhibit, obscure, prevent
08 restrict, slow down
09 frustrate, hamstring

obstruction
03 bar
04 stop
05 check
07 barrier, embargo
08 blockage, obstacle, sanction, stoppage
09 barricade, deterrent
10 difficulty, impediment
14 stumbling-block

obstructive
07 awkward
08 blocking, delaying, stalling
09 difficult, hindering
11 restrictive
13 unco-operative

obtain
03 get
04 earn, gain, hold, rule
05 exist, reign, seize, stand
06 attain, come by, secure
07 achieve, acquire, procure
09 be in force, be the case
11 be effective, be prevalent
14 get your hands on

obtainable
05 on tap, ready
06 at hand, on call
07 to be had
09 available
10 attainable, realizable

obtrusive
04 bold, nosy
05 pushy
07 blatant, forward, obvious
08 flagrant, meddling
09 intrusive, prominent
10 noticeable, projecting
11 conspicuous, interfering

obtuse
03 dim
04 dull, dumb, slow
05 crass, dense, thick
06 stolid, stupid
09 dim-witted
10 dull-witted, slow-witted
12 thick-skinned
13 unintelligent

obviate
05 avert
06 divert, remove
07 counter, prevent
08 preclude
09 forestall
10 anticipate, counteract

obvious
04 open
05 clear, plain
06 patent
07 evident, glaring, visible
08 apparent, distinct, manifest
10 noticeable, pronounced, undeniable
11 conspicuous
12 crystal clear, unmistakable
15 self-explanatory, straightforward

obviously
07 clearly, plainly
08 of course, patently
09 certainly, evidently
10 manifestly, noticeably
11 undoubtedly
12 unmistakably, without doubt

occasion
02 do
04 call, case, make, time
05 cause, event, evoke, party
06 affair, create, effect, elicit, lead to, prompt, reason
07 bring on, episode, grounds, inspire, produce, provoke
08 engender, function, generate, instance
09 happening, influence
10 bring about, experience, give rise to, occurrence
11 celebration, get-together, opportunity

occasional
03 odd
04 rare
06 casual
07 periodic, sporadic
09 irregular
10 incidental, infrequent
12 intermittent

occasionally
07 at times

08 off and on, on and off
09 sometimes
10 now and then, on occasion
11 irregularly, now and again
12 every so often, infrequently, once in a while, periodically, sporadically
14 from time to time, intermittently

occult
05 magic
06 hidden, secret, veiled
07 magical, obscure
08 abstruse, esoteric, mystical
09 black arts, mysticism
10 mysterious
12 supernatural
13 preternatural
14 transcendental

occupancy
03 use
06 tenure
07 holding, tenancy
09 ownership, residence
10 habitation, occupation, possession
11 inhabitancy
13 domiciliation

occupant
04 user
06 holder, inmate, lessee, renter, tenant
08 occupier, resident, squatter
10 inhabitant
11 householder, leaseholder
13 owner-occupier

occupation
03 job, use
04 line, post, work
05 craft, field, trade
06 career, employ, métier
07 calling, capture, control, pursuit, seizure, tenancy
08 activity, business, conquest, invasion, province, takeover
09 occupancy, residence
10 employment, habitation, possession, profession
11 foreign rule, subjugation

occupational
04 work
05 trade
06 career
08 business
10 employment, job-related, vocational
12 professional

occupied
04 busy, full
05 in use, taken

occupy
06 tied up
07 engaged, taken up, working
08 employed, tenanted

occupy
03 own, use
04 busy, fill, have, hold
05 amuse, seize, use up
06 divert, employ, invade, live in, people, settle, stay in, take up, tenant
07 capture, dwell in, inhabit, involve, overrun, possess
08 interest, reside in, take over
09 entertain, preoccupy

occur
05 arise, exist
06 appear, befall, chance, crop up, dawn on, happen, result, strike, turn up
07 be found, develop, turn out
09 be present, come about, take place, transpire
10 come to mind, come to pass
12 spring to mind
13 cross your mind, enter your head, suggest itself

occurrence
04 case
05 event
06 action, affair
07 arising, episode
08 incident, instance
09 happening, incidence
10 appearance
11 development, proceedings
12 circumstance
13 manifestation

ocean
03 sea
04 main
05 briny
07 pelagic, the deep
08 profound, the drink

➤ *Names of oceans. We have omitted the word* **ocean** *from names given in the following list but you may need to include this word as part of the solution to some crossword clues.*
06 Arctic, Indian
07 Pacific
08 Atlantic, Southern
09 Antarctic
➤ See also **sea**

odd
03 rum
04 rare, wild, zany
05 barmy, funny, kinky, queer, spare, wacky, weird

06 far-out, freaky, random, single, sundry, way-out
07 bizarre, curious, deviant, oddball, strange, surplus, uncanny, unusual, various
08 abnormal, atypical, left-over, peculiar, periodic, singular, uncommon
09 different, eccentric, haphazard, irregular, remaining, unmatched
10 incidental, occasional, off the wall, outlandish
11 exceptional, superfluous
13 extraordinary, idiosyncratic, miscellaneous
14 unconventional

❏**odd one out**
05 freak
06 oddball, odd bod, weirdo
09 eccentric
13 nonconformist
14 fish out of water

oddity
05 freak, quirk, twist
06 misfit, rarity
07 anomaly
09 character, curiosity
10 phenomenon
11 abnormality, peculiarity
12 eccentricity, idiosyncrasy

oddment
03 bit, end
05 patch, piece, scrap, shred
06 offcut
07 remnant, snippet
08 fragment, leftover

odds
04 edge, lead
07 chances
09 advantage, supremacy
10 ascendancy, likelihood
11 probability, superiority

❏**at odds**
07 arguing
09 differing
10 in conflict
11 disagreeing, quarrelling
13 at loggerheads
14 in disagreement

❏**odds and ends**
04 bits, junk, tatt
06 debris, litter, scraps
07 rubbish
08 oddments, remnants, snippets
11 odds and sods, this and that
13 bits and pieces

odious
04 foul, vile
06 horrid
07 hateful, heinous
08 horrible
09 abhorrent, execrable, loathsome, obnoxious, offensive, repugnant, repulsive, revolting
10 abominable, despicable, detestable, disgusting
12 contemptible, disagreeable
13 objectionable

odium
06 hatred, infamy
07 censure, dislike, obloquy
08 contempt, disgrace
09 animosity, antipathy, discredit, disfavour, dishonour, disrepute
10 abhorrence, execration, opprobrium
11 detestation, disapproval
12 condemnation

odorous
05 balmy
07 pungent, scented
08 aromatic, fragrant, perfumed, redolent
11 odoriferous
13 sweet-smelling

odour
04 niff, pong
05 aroma, scent, smell, stink
06 stench
07 bouquet, perfume
09 fragrance, redolence

odyssey
04 trek
06 voyage
07 journey, travels
09 adventure, wandering
13 peregrination

off
03 bad, ill, out
04 away, gone, high, sick, sour
05 apart, aside, slack, wrong
06 absent, mouldy, poorly, rancid, rotten, spoilt, turned
08 below par, scrapped
09 abandoned, called off, cancelled, elsewhere
10 decomposed
11 unavailable
14 unsatisfactory
15 under the weather

offbeat
05 kooky, wacky, weird
06 far-out, freaky, way-out
07 bizarre, oddball, strange

10 unorthodox
14 unconventional

off-colour
03 ill
04 rude, sexy, sick
05 dirty
06 coarse, filthy, poorly, risqué, smutty, unwell, vulgar
07 immoral, off form, run down
08 improper, indecent
10 indisposed, out of sorts, suggestive
12 pornographic
15 under the weather

off-duty
03 off
04 free
07 off work
09 not at work, on holiday

offence
03 ire, sin
05 anger, crime, pique, wrong
06 injury, insult, slight
07 affront, outrage, umbrage
08 atrocity, trespass
09 annoyance, antipathy, indignity, violation
10 illegal act, infraction, resentment, wrongdoing
11 disapproval, indignation
12 hard feelings, infringement, misdemeanour
13 transgression

□**take offence**
06 be hurt, resent
07 be angry, be upset
08 be miffed, be put out
09 be annoyed
10 be insulted, be offended
11 be indignant, take umbrage
13 take exception
14 take personally

offend
03 err, sin
04 hurt, miff, snub
05 anger, annoy, repel, upset, wound, wrong
06 injure, insult, revolt, sicken
07 affront, disgust, do wrong, incense, outrage, provoke
08 go astray, nauseate
09 displease
10 exasperate, transgress
11 break the law

offended
04 hurt
05 huffy, stung, upset
06 miffed, piqued, put out
07 angered, annoyed, in a huff, wounded

08 incensed, outraged
09 affronted, disgusted

offender
07 culprit
08 criminal
09 miscreant, wrongdoer
10 delinquent, law-breaker
11 guilty party
12 transgressor

offensive
04 foul, push, raid, rude, vile
05 drive, nasty
06 attack, charge, odious
07 abusive, assault, hurtful
08 annoying, impolite, insolent, invasion, wounding
09 abhorrent, incursion, insulting, loathsome, obnoxious, onslaught, repellent, repugnant, revolting, sickening
10 abominable, affronting, detestable, disgusting, nauseating, unpleasant
11 displeasing, impertinent
12 disagreeable
13 disrespectful, objectionable

offer
03 bid, try
04 give, sell, show
06 extend, submit, tender
07 advance, attempt, express, hold out, present, proffer, propose, suggest
08 approach, dedicate, proposal, propound
09 put in a bid, sacrifice, volunteer
10 consecrate, put forward, submission, suggestion
11 come forward, proposition
14 put on the market

offering
04 gift
05 tithe
07 handout, present
08 donation, oblation
09 dedication, sacrifice
12 consecration, contribution

offhand
04 curt, rude
05 ad lib, blasé, terse
06 abrupt, casual
07 brusque, cursory
08 careless, cavalier, laid-back
09 extempore, impromptu
10 off the cuff
11 free-and-easy, indifferent, perfunctory, unconcerned

12 discourteous, happy-go-lucky, uninterested
13 unceremonious
15 couldn't-care-less, take-it-or-leave-it

office
04 base, duty, help, post, role
05 aegis, place
06 bureau, charge, favour
07 backing, service, support
08 advocacy, auspices, business, function, position
09 mediation, workplace
10 commission, employment, obligation, occupation
11 appointment
12 intercession, intervention
14 responsibility
15 place of business

officer
05 agent, envoy
06 deputy
08 official
09 executive, messenger
10 bureaucrat
11 board member, functionary
12 office-bearer, office-holder
13 administrator, public servant
14 representative

official
05 legal
06 formal, kosher, lawful, proper, ritual, solemn
07 officer, stately
08 accepted, approved, bona fide, endorsed, licensed
09 authentic, certified, dignified, validated
10 accredited, authorized, ceremonial, legitimate, recognized, sanctioned
11 functionary
12 office-bearer, office-holder
13 authenticated, authoritative

officiate
05 chair
06 manage
07 conduct, oversee, preside
10 be in charge, take charge
11 superintend
12 take the chair

officious
05 bossy, pushy
08 bustling, meddling
09 intrusive, obtrusive
11 dictatorial, domineering, opinionated, over-zealous
13 self-important

offing

◻**in the offing**
04 near
06 at hand
07 in sight
08 imminent, on the way
10 coming soon, on the cards
11 close at hand
12 on the horizon

offish
04 cool
05 aloof
07 haughty, stuck-up
10 unsociable
11 standoffish

off-key
07 jarring
09 dissonant, out of tune
10 discordant, unsuitable
13 inappropriate

offload
04 drop, dump
05 chuck, shift
06 unload
07 deposit
08 get rid of, jettison, unburden
09 disburden, discharge

off-putting
08 daunting
09 unnerving, upsetting
10 disturbing, formidable
11 dispiriting, frightening
12 demoralizing, discomfiting, discouraging, intimidating
13 disconcerting, disheartening

offset
07 balance
09 cancel out, make up for
10 balance out, counteract
12 counterpoise
13 compensate for
14 counterbalance

offshoot
03 arm
04 limb
06 branch, result
07 outcome, product, spin-off
09 appendage, by-product
11 consequence, development

offspring
04 heir, kids
05 brood, child,, issue, young
07 nippers, progeny
08 children, young one
10 successors
11 descendants

often
04 much

09 generally, many a time, many times, regularly
10 frequently, repeatedly
12 time and again

ogle
03 eye
04 leer, look
05 eye up, stare
10 make eyes at

ogre
05 beast, bogey, brute, demon, devil, fiend, giant, troll
06 savage
07 monster, villain
09 barbarian

oil
04 balm
05 cream, salve
06 anoint, grease, lotion
07 unguent
08 liniment, ointment
09 lubricant, lubricate

oily
04 glib
05 fatty, suave
06 greasy, smarmy, urbane
07 buttery, servile
08 unctuous
10 obsequious, oleaginous
11 subservient
12 ingratiating
13 smooth-talking

ointment
03 gel
04 balm
05 cream, salve
06 lotion
08 liniment
09 emollient
11 embrocation

OK
03 yes
04 fair, fine, good, pass, so-so
05 right
06 agreed, not bad
07 approve, consent, correct, go-ahead, in order, up to par
08 accurate, adequate, all right, approval, passable, sanction, thumbs-up
09 agreement, authorize, consent to, permitted, tolerable
10 acceptable, green light, permission, reasonable
11 approbation, endorsement, rubber-stamp, up to scratch
12 satisfactory
13 authorization

old
02 ex-
04 aged, gaga, grey, torn, wise
05 early, passé
06 age-old, ageing, bygone, former, mature, past it, primal, senile, shabby
07 ancient, antique, archaic, cast-off, classic, decayed, earlier, elderly, lasting, one-time, quondam, veteran, vintage, worn out
08 decaying, decrepit, earliest, obsolete, original, outdated, previous, primeval, pristine, sensible, sometime
09 crumbling, erstwhile, getting on, long-lived, out of date, primitive, senescent
10 antiquated, broken down, Dickensian, primordial
11 out of the ark, over the hill, prehistoric, traditional
12 antediluvian, long-standing, time-honoured
13 old as the hills, past your prime, unfashionable
14 long in the tooth
15 advanced in years, long-established, no spring chicken

old age
03 age
06 dotage
08 agedness, senility
07 oldness
09 geriatric
10 senescence
11 elderliness
14 advancing years
15 second childhood

old-fashioned
04 dead, past
05 dated, passé
06 old hat, past it, square
07 ancient, archaic, old-time
08 obsolete, outdated, outmoded
09 moth-eaten, out of date
10 antiquated, fuddy-duddy
11 obsolescent, on the way out, out of the ark
12 antediluvian, out of fashion
13 unfashionable
14 behind the times

old man
03 OAP
04 boss
05 elder
06 father, gaffer, geezer, grouch
07 husband, oldster

08 employer, grumbler, old-timer
09 greybeard, old codger
10 fuddy-duddy, white-beard
11 grandfather
13 senior citizen
14 elder statesman
➤ See also **old woman**

old-time
03 old
04 past
05 dated, passé
06 bygone
07 archaic
08 outdated, outmoded
09 out of date
10 antiquated
12 old fashioned, out of fashion
13 unfashionable

old woman
03 OAP
03 bag, hag
04 wife
06 granny, grouch, mother
07 old dear, oldster
08 fusspot, grumbler
10 complainer
11 grandmother
13 senior citizen
➤ See also **old man**

old-world
04 past
06 bygone, quaint
07 archaic
10 antiquated
11 picturesque, traditional
12 old fashioned

omen
04 sign
05 token
06 augury
07 auspice, portent, warning
09 harbinger, prodromus
10 foreboding, prediction
11 premonition

ominous
07 fateful, unlucky
08 menacing, minatory, sinister
10 foreboding, portentous
11 threatening, unpromising
12 inauspicious, unpropitious

omission
03 gap
04 lack
06 lacuna
07 default, failure, neglect
09 avoidance, exception, exclusion, oversight
10 leaving-out, negligence
11 dereliction

omit
04 drop, fail, miss, skip
05 erase
06 delete, forget, rub out
07 edit out, exclude, expunge, miss out, neglect
08 cross out, leave out, overlook, pass over
09 disregard, eliminate
13 fail to mention

omnibus
09 anthology, inclusive
10 collection, compendium
11 compendious, compilation
12 encyclopedia
13 comprehensive

omnipotence
07 mastery
09 supremacy
10 total power
11 divine right, sovereignty
12 almightiness, plenipotence
13 absolute power, invincibility

omnipotent
07 supreme
08 almighty
10 invincible
11 all-powerful, plenipotent

omnipresent
08 infinite
09 pervasive, universal
10 all-present, ubiquitous
12 all-pervasive

omniscient
07 all-wise
09 all-seeing, pansophic
10 all-knowing

omnivorous
10 gluttonous
14 indiscriminate

on

❑**on and off**
08 fitfully, off and on
09 sometimes
10 now and then, on occasion
11 at intervals, irregularly, now and again
12 every so often, occasionally, periodically, sporadically
13 spasmodically
14 from time to time, intermittently

once
04 when
05 after
07 long ago, one time
08 as soon as, formerly
09 at one time, in the past
10 at one point

11 in times past
12 in the old days
13 in times gone by, on one occasion, once upon a time

❑**at once**
03 now
06 pronto
08 directly, promptly, right now
09 forthwith, instantly, like a shot, right away, yesterday
11 immediately
12 straightaway, without delay
13 at the same time
14 simultaneously
15 at the same moment

❑**once and for all**
07 finally, for good
11 permanently
10 decisively, positively
12 conclusively, definitively
14 for the last time

❑**once in a while**
07 at times
08 on and off
09 sometimes
10 now and then, on occasion
11 now and again
12 occasionally, periodically
14 from time to time

oncoming
07 looming, nearing
08 upcoming
09 advancing, gathering
11 approaching

one
03 ace
04 lone, only, sole
05 alike, equal, fused, whole
06 entire, joined, single, united
08 complete, solitary
10 individual, like-minded

oneness
05 unity
08 identity, sameness
09 wholeness
10 singleness
12 completeness

onerous
04 hard
05 heavy
06 taxing, tiring
07 arduous, exigent, weighty
08 exacting, wearying
09 demanding, difficult, fatiguing, laborious
10 burdensome, exhausting
12 back-breaking

oneself

❑**by oneself**
04 solo
05 alone
06 lonely, singly
07 forlorn, unaided
08 deserted, forsaken, isolated, lonesome
09 abandoned, on your own
10 by yourself, unassisted
11 without help
12 single-handed
13 independently, unaccompanied

one-sided
06 biased, unfair, unjust
07 bigoted, partial, unequal
08 lopsided, partisan, separate
10 prejudiced, unbalanced
11 independent, inequitable
12 narrow-minded

one-time
02 ex-
04 late
06 former
07 quondam
08 previous, sometime
09 erstwhile

ongoing
07 current, growing, non-stop
08 constant, evolving
09 incessant, unfolding
10 continuing, developing, in progress, unfinished
11 progressing

onlooker
06 gawper, viewer
07 watcher, witness
08 looker-on, observer
09 bystander, spectator
10 eyewitness, rubberneck

only
04 just, lone, sole
06 at most, barely, merely, purely, simply, single, solely
10 individual, no more than, nothing but, one and only
11 exclusively, not more than

onrush
04 flow, push, rush
05 flood, onset, surge
06 career, charge, stream
08 stampede
09 onslaught

onset
05 start
06 attack, charge, outset
08 outbreak

09 beginning, inception
12 commencement

onslaught
04 push, raid
05 blitz, drive, foray
06 attack, charge, thrust
07 assault
08 storming
09 offensive
11 bombardment

onus
04 duty, load, task
06 burden, charge, weight
09 albatross, liability, millstone
10 obligation
14 responsibility

onwards
02 on
05 ahead, forth
06 beyond
07 forward, in front
08 forwards

oodles
04 bags, lots, tons
05 heaps, loads
06 masses
08 lashings

oomph
03 pep
04 zing
06 bounce, energy, vigour
07 pizzazz, sparkle
08 sexiness, vitality, vivacity
09 animation
10 get-up-and-go

ooze
04 drip, drop, emit, leak, seep
05 bleed, drain, exude, slime
06 escape, filter, sludge
07 deposit, dribble, excrete, secrete, trickle
08 alluvium, filtrate, sediment
09 discharge, percolate

oozy
04 dewy, miry
05 moist, mucky, muddy, slimy
06 sloppy, sludgy, sweaty
07 weeping
08 dripping
09 uliginous

opacity
07 density
09 filminess, milkiness, murkiness, obscurity
10 cloudiness, opaqueness
11 obfuscation, unclearness
15 impenetrability

opalescent
04 shot

06 pearly
07 rainbow
10 iridescent, shimmering
11 rainbow-like
13 multicoloured, polychromatic

opaque
03 dim
05 dense, misty, muddy, murky
07 blurred, clouded, cryptic, muddied, obscure, unclear
08 abstruse, baffling, esoteric
09 enigmatic, recondite
12 as clear as mud, impenetrable, unfathomable
14 unintelligible

open
04 airy, ajar, free, moot, undo
05 begin, blunt, clear, crack, frank, holey, overt, plain, split, start, untie
06 broach, candid, direct, flower, gaping, honest, launch, liable, patent, porous, public, simple, spread, unbolt, uncork, unfold, unfurl, unlock, unroll, unseal, vacant
07 blatant, divulge, evident, exposed, general, kick off, lay bare, natural, obvious, pour out, unblock, uncover, unlatch, visible, yawning
08 apparent, arguable, cellular, commence, disclose, disposed, flagrant, manifest, separate, unbarred, unbolted, unfasten, unfenced, unlocked, unsealed, wide open
09 available, come apart, debatable, guileless, ingenuous, navigable, receptive, spread out, unblocked, uncovered, undecided, unlatched, unsettled, well known
10 forthright, inaugurate, unfastened, unreserved, unresolved, vulnerable
11 honeycombed, set in motion, susceptible, unconcealed, undisguised, unprotected, widely known
12 loosely woven, unobstructed, unrestricted

❑**open onto**
04 face
06 lead to
08 give onto, overlook

open-air
06 afield
07 outdoor, outside
08 alfresco
10 out-of-doors

open-and-shut
05 clear
06 simple
07 obvious
12 easily solved
13 easily decided
15 straightforward

open-handed
04 free
06 lavish
07 liberal
08 generous
09 bounteous, bountiful
10 munificent, unstinting
12 eleemosynary, large-hearted

opening
03 gap, job
04 cave, dawn, hole, slot, vent
05 break, chasm, chink, cleft, crack, early, first, inlet, onset, place, space, split, start
06 breach, chance, outlet
07 crevice, fissure, initial, kick-off, orifice, rupture, vacancy
08 aperture, occasion, position, starting
09 beginning, inaugural, inception, the word go
10 commencing, interstice
11 opportunity
12 inauguration, introductory

openly
07 frankly, overtly, plainly
08 brazenly, candidly, directly, honestly, in public
09 blatantly, glaringly
10 flagrantly, in full view
11 shamelessly, unashamedly
12 forthrightly, unreservedly

open-minded
07 liberal
08 catholic, tolerant, unbiased
09 impartial, objective
11 broad-minded, enlightened
12 unprejudiced
13 dispassionate
14 latitudinarian

open-mouthed
06 amazed
07 shocked
09 astounded, expectant
11 dumbfounded
13 flabbergasted, thunderstruck

opera
▶ *Names of operas and operettas:*
04 Aida
05 Faust, Norma, Tosca
06 Carmen, Otello, Salome
07 Fidelio, Macbeth, Nabucco, The Ring, Werther, Wozzeck
08 Falstaff, Idomeneo, Iolanthe, La Bohème, Parsifal, Patience, Turandot
09 Billy Budd, Capriccio, Lohengrin, Rigoletto, Ruddigore, Siegfried, The Mikado, Véronique
10 Cinderella, I Pagliacci, La Traviata, Oedipus Rex, Tannhäuser
11 Don Giovanni, Don Pasquale, HMS Pinafore, Il Trovatore, Peter Grimes, Princess Ida, The Sorceror, Trial by Jury, William Tell
12 Boris Godunov, Così Fan Tutte, Das Rheingold, Eugene Onegin, Manon Lescaut, Nixon in China, Porgy and Bess, The Grand Duke, The Valkyries
13 Albert Herring, Dido and Aeneas, Die Fledermaus, La Belle Hélène, The Fairy Queen, The Gondoliers, The Magic Flute
14 Ariadne on Naxos, Le Grand Macabre
15 Götterdämmerung, Hansel and Gretel, Madame Butterfly, The Beggar's Opera, The Pearl Fishers
➤ See also **music**

operate
03 act, run, use
04 work
06 employ, handle, manage
07 control, perform, utilize
08 function

operation
03 job, use
04 deal, raid, task
06 action, attack, charge, motion
07 control, process, running
08 activity, business, campaign, exercise, handling
09 manoeuvre, procedure
10 enterprise, management
11 functioning, performance, undertaking, utilization
12 manipulation

in operation
05 going, valid
06 active, viable
07 in force, working
08 in action, workable
09 effective, efficient, in service
10 functional
11 functioning, serviceable

operational
05 going, in use, ready
06 usable, viable
07 working
08 in action, workable
09 in service
10 functional
11 functioning
14 in working order

operative
03 key, spy
04 dick, hand, mole
05 agent, valid, vital
06 shamus, sleuth, worker
07 artisan, crucial, gumshoe, in force, working, workman
08 employee, in action, labourer, mechanic, operator, relevant, workable
09 detective, machinist
10 functional, private eye
11 double agent, functioning, in operation, operational, secret agent, significant
12 investigator

operator
05 mover
06 dealer, driver, trader, worker
07 handler, manager, shyster
08 director, mechanic
09 machinist, operative
10 contractor, manoeuvrer, speculator, technician
13 wheeler-dealer

operetta see **opera**

opiate
04 drug
06 downer
07 anodyne, bromide
08 narcotic, nepenthe, pacifier, sedative
09 soporific
10 depressant
12 stupefacient
13 tranquillizer

opine
05 guess, judge, think
07 believe, declare, presume, suggest, suppose, surmise, suspect, venture
08 conceive, conclude

09 volunteer
10 conjecture

opinion
04 idea, mind, view
06 belief, notion, stance, theory
07 feeling, thought
08 attitude, feelings, thoughts
09 judgement, viewpoint
10 assessment, assumption, conviction, estimation, persuasion, standpoint
11 point of view
13 way of thinking
15 school of thought

opinionated
07 adamant, bigoted, pompous
08 arrogant, cocksure, dogmatic, stubborn
09 obstinate, pigheaded
10 inflexible, pontifical
11 dictatorial, doctrinaire
12 single-minded
13 self-important
14 uncompromising

opponent
03 foe
05 enemy, rival
09 adversary, contender
10 antagonist, challenger, competitor, contestant
11 dissentient

opportune
03 apt, fit
04 good
05 happy, lucky
06 proper, timely
07 fitting
08 suitable
09 fortunate, pertinent, well-timed
10 auspicious, convenient, favourable, felicitous, propitious, seasonable
11 appropriate
12 advantageous, providential

opportunism
07 realism
10 expediency, pragmatism
12 exploitation
15 taking advantage

opportunity
05 break
06 chance, look-in, moment
07 opening

oppose
04 defy, face
05 check, fight, match

06 attack, combat, hinder, offset, resist, thwart
07 contest, counter, play off
08 confront, contrast, obstruct
09 be against, challenge, juxtapose, stand up to
10 contradict, set against
12 argue against, disapprove of
13 take issue with
14 counterbalance, fly in the face of

opposed
04 anti
06 averse
07 against, hostile
08 clashing, contrary, inimical, opposing, opposite
11 conflicting, disagreeing
12 antagonistic, in opposition

opposing
05 enemy, rival
06 at odds
07 hostile, opposed, warring
08 clashing, contrary, opposite
09 combatant, differing, oppugnant
10 at variance, contending
11 conflicting, contentious
12 antagonistic, antipathetic, disputatious, incompatible
14 irreconcilable

opposite
06 at odds, facing, unlike
07 adverse, hostile, inverse, opposed, reverse
08 clashing, contrary, converse, flip side, fronting
09 different, differing, dissident
10 antithesis, contrasted, face to face, poles apart
12 antithetical, inconsistent
13 contradiction, contradictory, corresponding
14 irreconcilable

opposition
03 foe
05 enemy, rival
08 opponent
09 adversary, other side
10 antagonism, resistance
11 competition, disapproval
15 obstructiveness

oppress
05 abuse, crush, quash, quell
06 burden, deject, harass, sadden, subdue
07 afflict, depress, enslave, repress, torment, trample
08 dispirit, maltreat, suppress

09 overpower, overwhelm, persecute, subjugate, tyrannize, weigh down
10 discourage, lie heavy on

oppressed
06 abused
07 crushed, misused, subject
08 burdened, enslaved, harassed, troubled
09 repressed
10 maltreated, persecuted, subjugated, tyrannized
11 downtrodden
13 disadvantaged
15 underprivileged

oppression
05 abuse
07 cruelty, tyranny
08 hardship
09 brutality, despotism, harshness, injustice
10 repression, subjection
11 persecution, subjugation
12 maltreatment

oppressive
05 close, cruel, heavy, muggy
06 brutal, stuffy, sultry, unjust
07 airless, inhuman, onerous
08 crushing, despotic, pitiless, ruthless, stifling
09 Draconian, merciless
10 burdensome, iron-fisted, repressive, tyrannical
11 domineering, intolerable, overbearing, suffocating

oppressor
05 bully
06 despot, tyrant
08 autocrat, dictator, torturer
10 persecutor, subjugator
11 intimidator, slave-driver

opprobrious
07 abusive
08 insolent, venomous
09 insulting, invective, offensive, vitriolic
10 calumnious, defamatory, derogatory, scurrilous
12 calumniatory, contemptuous, contumelious, vituperative

opprobrium
04 slur
05 odium, shame
06 infamy, stigma
07 calumny, censure, obloquy
08 disgrace, ignominy, reproach
09 contumely, discredit, dishonour, disrepute

10 debasement, scurrility
11 degradation

opt
04 pick
05 elect, go for
06 choose, decide, select
08 plump for, settle on

optical instrument
▶ *Types of optical instrument*:
05 laser
06 camera
07 sextant
08 spyglass
09 endoscope, periscope, telescope
10 binoculars, opera-glass, theodolite
12 field-glasses
13 film projector
14 slide projector
15 magnifying glass, telescopic sight

optimistic
06 bright, upbeat
07 bullish, buoyant, hopeful
08 cheerful, positive, sanguine
09 confident, expectant
11 Panglossian, pollyannish

optimum
03 top
04 best
05 ideal, model
07 highest, optimal, perfect
11 superlative
14 most favourable

option
06 choice
09 selection
10 preference
11 alternative, possibility

optional
04 free
08 elective, unforced
09 voluntary
13 discretionary

opulence
06 luxury, plenty, riches, wealth
07 fortune
08 fullness, richness
09 abundance, affluence
10 cornucopia, prosperity
11 copiousness
13 sumptuousness
14 superabundance

opulent
04 posh, rich
05 plush
06 lavish

07 copious, moneyed, profuse, wealthy, well-off
08 abundant, affluent, prolific, well-to-do
09 luxuriant, luxurious, plentiful, sumptuous
10 prosperous, well-heeled
11 rolling in it
13 superabundant

opus
04 work
05 piece
06 oeuvre
08 creation
11 composition

oracle
04 guru, sage, seer
05 augur, sibyl
06 augury, expert, mentor, pundit, vision, wizard
07 adviser, prophet
08 prophecy
09 authority
10 divination, high priest, prediction, revelation, soothsayer, specialist
15 prognostication

oracular
04 sage, wise
05 grave
06 arcane
07 cryptic, Delphic, obscure
08 abstruse, dogmatic, positive, two-edged
09 ambiguous, equivocal, prescient, prophetic
10 auspicious, haruspical, mysterious, portentous
11 dictatorial, significant
13 authoritative

oral
04 said
05 vocal
06 spoken, verbal
07 uttered
09 unwritten

orate
04 talk
05 speak
07 declaim
08 harangue
09 discourse, hold forth, sermonize, speechify

oration
05 spiel
06 homily, sermon, speech
07 address, lecture
09 discourse
11 declamation

orator
07 speaker, spieler
08 lecturer
09 declaimer, demagogue
11 rhetorician, spellbinder
13 public speaker

oratorical
08 eloquent, sonorous
09 bombastic, high-flown
10 Ciceronian, rhetorical
11 declamatory, Demosthenic
12 elocutionary, magniloquent
13 grandiloquent

oratorio
▶ *Names of oratorios*:
04 Saul
06 Elijah, Esther, Joshua, Samson, Semele
07 Athalia, Deborah, Jephtha, Messiah, Solomon, Susanna
08 Christus, Hercules, Theodora
10 Belshazzar, Oedipus Rex, The Seasons
11 The Creation
13 Israel in Egypt
15 Judas Maccabaeus
➤ See also **music**

oratory
06 speech
07 diction
08 rhetoric
09 elocution, eloquence
11 declamation
12 speechifying
14 grandiloquence, public speaking

orb
04 ball, ring
05 globe, mound, round
06 circle, sphere

orbit
04 path
05 ambit, range, scope, track
06 circle, course, domain
07 circuit, compass, revolve
10 revolution, trajectory
14 circumnavigate

orchestrate
03 fix
05 score
07 arrange, compose, prepare
08 organize
10 co-ordinate, mastermind
11 put together, stage-manage

ordain
03 fix, set
04 call, fate, rule, will
05 elect, frock, order

06 anoint, decree, invest
07 appoint, destine, dictate
09 prescribe, pronounce
10 consecrate, predestine
12 predetermine

ordeal
04 pain, test
05 agony, trial
07 anguish, torment, torture
09 nightmare, suffering
11 persecution, tribulation

order
03 bid, law
04 book, call, calm, form, kind, rota, rule, sect, sort, writ
05 array, class, edict, genus, grade, quiet, set-up, union
06 codify, decree, demand, direct, lay out, line-up, manage, method, system
07 arrange, call for, command, control, dictate, dispose, harmony, mandate, marshal, pattern, request, request, require, reserve, society, sort out, species, summons, variety, warrant
08 classify, instruct, neatness, organize, regulate, sequence, sorority, symmetry, tidiness
09 catalogue, directive, hierarchy, legislate, ordinance, prescribe, structure
10 discipline, fraternity, injunction, lawfulness, regularity, regulation, sisterhood, uniformity
11 application, arrangement, brotherhood, disposition, instruction, law and order, requisition, reservation, send away for, stipulation, systematize, write off for
12 codification, denomination, organization, pecking order
13 secret society
14 categorization, classification

☐ **in order**
02 OK
04 done, neat, tidy
05 right
06 lawful, mended, proper
07 allowed, correct, fitting, ordered, orderly, regular
08 all right, arranged, suitable
09 permitted, shipshape
10 acceptable, classified, in sequence, systematic
11 appropriate, categorized
12 well-organized

☐ **in order to**
06 so that
11 intending to, with a view to
13 with the result
14 with the purpose

☐ **order around**
05 bully
08 browbeat, bulldoze, dominate, domineer
09 tyrannize
10 boss around, order about, push around

☐ **out of order**
06 broken, untidy
07 haywire, muddled
08 confused, gone phut, improper, unseemly
10 broken down, disordered, not working, on the blink
11 inoperative, un-called-for
12 disorganized, unacceptable
13 out of sequence
14 not functioning
15 out of commission

orderly
04 neat, ruly, tidy, trim
07 in order, ordered, regular
10 controlled, law-abiding, methodical, restrained, systematic
11 disciplined, well-behaved
13 well-organized, well-regulated
15 in apple-pie order

ordinance
03 law
04 fiat, rite, rule
05 canon, edict, order
06 decree, dictum, ritual, ruling
07 command, statute
08 ceremony, practice
09 directive, sacrament
10 injunction, observance, regulation
11 institution

ordinarily
07 as a rule, usually
08 commonly, normally
09 generally, in general
11 customarily

ordinary
04 dull, fair
05 banal, bland, plain, usual
06 common, normal, simple
07 average, mundane, prosaic, regular, routine, typical
08 everyday, familiar, habitual, standard, workaday
09 customary, quotidian
10 mainstream, pedestrian

11 commonplace, indifferent, nondescript, unmemorable
12 conventional, run-of-the-mill, unremarkable
13 unexceptional
14 common-or-garden
15 undistinguished

☐ **out of the ordinary**
04 rare
06 unique
07 unusual
09 different, memorable
10 noteworthy, remarkable, surprising, unexpected
11 exceptional, outstanding
13 extraordinary

ordnance
04 arms, guns
06 cannon
07 big guns, weapons
09 artillery, munitions

ordure
04 crap, dirt, dung, poop, shit
05 filth, frass, guano, scats, stool
06 egesta, faeces
09 droppings, excrement, excretion
11 waste matter

ore

► *Ores include*:
03 wad
04 wadd
06 bog-ore, galena, rutile
07 bauxite, bog-iron, bornite, cuprite, iron ore, oligist, schlich, uranite
08 hematite, limonite, tenorite
09 coffinite, haematite, hedyphane, ironstone, magnetite, malachite, manganite, minestone, proustite, tantalite
10 melaconite, peacock-ore, pyrolusite, ruby silver, stephanite
11 cassiterite, pyrargyrite
12 babingtonite, chalcopyrite, pyromorphite, tetrahedrite
13 copper pyrites, horseflesh ore
15 stilpnosiderite

organ
04 part, tool, unit
05 forum, paper, voice
06 agency, medium, member
07 journal, process, vehicle
09 component, implement
10 instrument, mouthpiece
11 constituent, publication

organic
06 biotic, living
07 animate, natural, ordered
09 organized
10 biological, harmonious, structured
11 non-chemical
12 additive-free
13 not artificial, pesticide-free

organism
04 body, cell
05 being, plant, set-up, unity
06 animal, entity, system
08 creature
09 bacterium, structure

organization
04 body, club, firm, plan
05 group, order, set-up, union
06 design, outfit, system
07 company, concern, society
08 grouping
09 authority, formation, operation, structure
10 consortium, management
11 arrangement, association, composition, corporation, development, institution
12 co-ordination
13 configuration
14 administration, classification

organize
03 run
05 begin, found, group, order, see to, set up, shape, start
06 create, manage
07 arrange, develop, dispose, marshal, prepare, sort out
08 assemble, classify, tabulate
09 catalogue, structure
10 administer, co-ordinate
11 standardize, systematize

organized
04 neat, tidy
07 ordered, orderly, planned
08 arranged
09 efficient
10 structured, systematic
11 well-ordered
12 businesslike
13 well-regulated

orgy
04 bout
05 binge, party, revel, spree
06 excess, frenzy, revels
07 debauch, revelry, splurge
08 carousal
09 wild party
11 bacchanalia

orient
05 adapt, align

06 adjust
08 accustom
09 habituate, orientate
11 acclimatize, familiarize
15 get your bearings

orientation
07 guiding, leading
08 bearings, location, position
09 alignment, direction, induction, placement
10 adaptation, adjustment, initiation, settling-in
11 inclination
15 acclimatization, familiarization

orifice
04 hole, pore, rift, slit, slot, vent
05 cleft, crack, inlet, mouth
07 crevice, fissure, opening
08 aperture
11 perforation

origin
04 base, dawn, root
05 basis, birth, cause, fount, roots, start, stock
06 family, launch, source, spring
07 dawning, descent, genesis
08 ancestry, creation, pedigree
09 beginning, emergence, etymology, inception, parentage, paternity
10 conception, derivation, extraction, foundation, provenance, well-spring
12 commencement

original
03 new
04 real, true, type
05 early, first, model, novel
06 master, primal, unique
07 genuine, initial, opening, pattern, primary, unusual
08 creative, paradigm, standard
09 archetype, authentic, ingenious, inventive, primitive, prototype
10 archetypal, innovative, pioneering, unorthodox
11 imaginative, resourceful
13 autochthonous
14 ground-breaking

originality
07 newness, novelty
09 freshness, ingenuity
10 creativity, innovation
11 imagination, singularity
12 creativeness, eccentricity
13 individuality, inventiveness
14 creative spirit
15 resourcefulness

originally
05 first
07 at first, by birth
09 initially
10 at the start
11 at the outset, to begin with
14 in the beginning

originate
04 come, flow, form, rise, stem
05 arise, begin, issue, start
06 be born, create, derive, emerge, evolve, invent
07 develop, emanate, pioneer
09 establish, introduce
11 give birth to, set in motion
13 be the father of, be the mother of

originator
06 author, father, mother
07 creator, founder, pioneer
08 designer, inventor
09 architect, developer, initiator, innovator

ornament
04 deck, gild, trim
05 adorn, frill, jewel
06 bauble, fallal, gewgaw
07 dress up, garnish, trinket
08 decorate, furbelow, trimming
09 accessory, adornment, embellish
10 decoration
13 embellishment

ornamental
05 fancy, showy
10 attractive, decorative
12 embellishing, embroidering

ornamentation
09 adornment, fallalery, garniture
10 decoration, embroidery
11 elaboration
13 embellishment

ornate
04 busy
05 fancy, flash, fussy, showy
06 florid, rococo
07 baroque, flowery
09 decorated, elaborate
10 flamboyant, ornamented
11 embellished

orotund
04 deep, full, loud, rich
06 ground, ornate, strong
07 booming, pompous
08 imposing, powerful, sonorous, strained
09 dignified

10 resonating
11 pretentious
12 magniloquent

orthodox
05 sound, usual
06 devout, strict
07 correct, regular
08 accepted, faithful, official, received
10 conformist, recognized
11 established, traditional
12 conservative, conventional
15 well-established

orthodoxy
08 devotion, trueness
10 conformism, conformity, devoutness, strictness
11 correctness
12 conservatism, faithfulness
13 inflexibility
14 received wisdom, traditionalism
15 conventionality

oscillate
04 sway, vary, yo-yo
05 swing, waver
06 seesaw, wigwag
09 fluctuate, vacillate

oscillation
08 swinging, wavering
09 seesawing, variation
11 fluctuation, vacillation
15 shilly-shallying

ossify
06 harden
07 petrify
08 indurate, rigidify, solidify
09 fossilize

ostensible
07 alleged, claimed, feigned, outward, seeming
08 apparent, presumed, so-called, specious, supposed
09 pretended, professed, purported
11 superficial

ostensibly
09 allegedly, outwardly, reputedly, seemingly
10 apparently, supposedly
11 professedly, purportedly
13 superficially

ostentation
04 pomp, show
05 swank
07 display
08 boasting, flourish, vaunting
09 flaunting, pageantry, showiness, trappings

10 flashiness, pretension, showing off
11 affectation, flamboyance
13 exhibitionism
15 pretentiousness

ostentatious
03 OTT
04 loud
05 flash, gaudy, showy
06 flashy, glitzy, kitsch, vulgar
08 affected
10 flamboyant, over the top
11 conspicuous, extravagant

ostracism
05 exile
09 exclusion, expulsion, isolation, rejection
10 banishment
12 cold-shoulder, proscription
15 excommunication

ostracize
03 bar, cut
04 shun, snub
05 avoid, exile, expel
06 banish, outlaw, reject
07 boycott, exclude, isolate
12 cold-shoulder
13 excommunicate
14 send to Coventry

other
04 more
05 extra, spare
07 further, variant
08 distinct, separate
09 different, disparate
10 additional, dissimilar
11 alternative, contrasting

otherwise
02 or
05 if not
06 or else, unless

otherworldly
03 fey
06 dreamy
07 bemused
08 ethereal
11 preoccupied

ounce
03 jot
04 atom, drop, iota, spot, whit
05 crumb, scrap, shred, trace
06 morsel, uncial
08 particle

oust
04 fire, sack
05 eject, evict, expel
06 depose, put out, topple, unseat
07 boot out, dismiss, turn out

08 displace, drive out, force out, get rid of, throw out
09 overthrow, thrust out
10 disinherit, dispossess

out
03 KO'd, set
04 away, bent, dead, gone
05 dated, known, passé, ready
06 démodé, old hat, public
07 evident, exposed, in bloom, in print, out cold, outside
08 blooming, comatose, divulged, excluded, in flower
09 available, disclosed, in the open, insistent, not at home, out-of-date, published
10 antiquated, blossoming, determined, disallowed, impossible, insensible, knocked out, obtainable, unsuitable
11 in full bloom, unconscious
12 extinguished, inadmissible, old-fashioned
13 unfashionable

out-and-out
05 total, utter
06 arrant
07 perfect
08 absolute, complete, outright, thorough
09 downright
10 consummate, inveterate
11 unmitigated, unqualified
13 dyed-in-the-wool

outbreak
04 rash
05 burst, flash
07 flare-up, upsurge
08 epidemic, eruption
09 explosion
13 recrudescence

outburst
03 fit
04 gale, gush
05 burst, spasm, storm, surge
06 attack
07 flare-up, seizure
08 eruption, paroxysm
09 explosion
10 outpouring
11 fit of temper

outcast
05 exile, leper
06 pariah, reject
07 evacuee, refugee
08 castaway, outsider
11 untouchable
15 persona non grata

outclass
03 top
04 beat
05 outdo
07 eclipse, outrank, surpass
08 outrival, outshine, outstrip
10 overshadow
13 leave standing, put in the shade

outcome
05 issue
06 effect, result, sequel, upshot
07 product
09 end result
10 conclusion
11 after-effect, consequence

outcry
03 cry, row
04 fuss
05 noise
06 racket, tumult, uproar
07 clamour, dissent, protest
08 outburst
09 commotion, complaint, hue and cry, objection
11 exclamation, hullaballoo, indignation

outdated
05 dated, passé
06 démodé, old hat, square
08 obsolete, outmoded
09 out of date
10 antiquated, superseded
12 old-fashioned, out of fashion
13 unfashionable
14 behind the times

outdistance
04 pass
06 outrun
07 outpace, surpass
08 outstrip, overtake
11 leave behind, pull ahead of
13 leave standing

outdo
03 cap, top
04 beat
06 defeat, exceed
07 eclipse, surpass
08 outclass, outshine, outstrip
11 outdistance
13 run rings round
14 get the better of
15 run circles round

outdoors
03 out
07 outside
08 alfresco, outdoors
10 en plein air, out-of-doors
12 in the open air

outer
06 fringe, remote
07 outside, outward, surface
08 exterior, external, outlying
09 outermost
10 peripheral
11 superficial

outface
04 defy
05 beard, brave
08 confront, outstare
09 brazen out, stare down

outfit
03 kit, rig, set
04 crew, firm, gang, garb, gear, suit, team, togs, unit
05 dress, equip, fit up, get-up, group, set-up, stock, tools
06 attire, fit out, kit out, supply
07 apparel, appoint, clothes, company, costume, coterie, furnish, provide, turn out
08 accoutre, business, ensemble
09 equipment, trappings
12 organization

outfitter
06 sartor, tailor
07 clothier, costumer
09 costumier, couturier
10 couturière, dressmaker
11 haberdasher

outflow
04 gush, rush
06 efflux
07 outfall, outrush
08 drainage, effluent, effusion
09 discharge, effluence, effluvium, emanation
10 outpouring

outflowing
07 gushing, leaking, rushing
08 effluent, spurting
10 debouching
11 discharging

outgoing
02 ex-
04 last, open, past, warm
06 former, genial
07 affable, amiable, cordial
08 friendly, retiring, sociable
09 departing, easy-going, extrovert, talkative
10 gregarious, unreserved
13 communicative

outgoings
05 costs
06 outlay

08 expenses, spending
09 disbursal, overheads
11 expenditure

outgrowth
05 shoot
06 effect, sprout
07 product, spin-off
08 offshoot, swelling
12 protuberance

outing
04 spin, tour, trip
05 jaunt
06 picnic
09 excursion
12 pleasure trip

outlandish
03 odd
05 alien, wacky, weird
06 exotic, far-out, way-out
07 bizarre, curious, foreign, strange, unknown, unusual
08 peculiar
09 eccentric, unheard-of
10 unfamiliar
13 extraordinary
14 unconventional

outlandishness
07 oddness
09 queerness, weirdness
10 exoticness, quaintness
11 bizarreness, strangeness
12 eccentricity

outlast
04 ride
07 outlive, survive, weather
11 come through

outlaw
03 ban, bar
05 debar, exile
06 bandit, forbid, pirate, robber
07 brigand, condemn, embargo, exclude, outcast
08 criminal, fugitive, prohibit
09 desperado, proscribe
10 highwayman
13 excommunicate

outlay
04 cost
05 price
07 payment
08 expenses, spending
09 outgoings
11 expenditure
12 disbursement

outlet
04 duct, exit, shop, vent
05 store, valve
06 egress, escape, way out
07 conduit, culvert, opening

outline
08 retailer, supplier
11 safety valve

outline
04 form, plan
05 draft, shape, trace
06 layout, précis, résumé
07 profile, summary, tracing
08 abstract, rough out, synopsis
09 bare bones, bare facts,
delineate, lineament, rough
idea, sketch out, summarize
10 main points, silhouette

outlive
07 outlast, survive, weather
11 come through, live through

outlook
04 view
05 angle, slant
06 aspect, future
07 opinion
08 forecast, prospect
09 prognosis, viewpoint
11 frame of mind, perspective,
point of view
12 expectations

outlying
05 outer
06 far-off, remote
07 distant, far-away
08 far-flung, isolated
10 provincial
11 out-of-the-way
12 inaccessible

outmanoeuvre
04 beat
05 outdo
06 outfox, outwit
08 outflank, outsmart,
outthink
14 get the better of

outmoded
05 dated, passé
06 démodé, old hat, square
07 archaic
08 obsolete
10 antiquated, superseded
11 obsolescent, old-fogeyish
12 antediluvian, old-fashioned,
out of fashion
13 unfashionable
14 behind the times

out of date
05 dated, passé
06 démodé, old hat, square
07 archaic
08 obsolete, outdated
10 antiquated, superseded
11 obsolescent, old-fogeyish
12 antediluvian, old-fashioned

13 unfashionable
14 behind the times

out-of-the-way
06 far-off, lonely, remote
07 distant, far-away, obscure
08 far-flung, isolated, outlying
11 little-known
12 inaccessible, unfrequented

out of work
04 idle
07 jobless, laid off, unwaged
08 workless
09 on the dole, out of a job,
redundant
10 unemployed

outpace
04 beat, pass
05 outdo
06 outrun
08 outstrip, overhaul, overtake

outpouring
04 flow, flux
05 flood, spate, spurt
06 deluge, efflux, stream
07 cascade, outflow, torrent
08 effusion
09 effluence, emanation
11 debouchment
14 disemboguement

output
04 gain
05 yield
06 fruits, return
07 harvest, product
10 production
11 achievement, performance
12 productivity

outrage
04 evil, fury, rage
05 abuse, anger, shock, wrath
06 enrage, horror, injury,
madden, offend, ravage
07 affront, assault, disgust,
horrify, incense, scandal
08 atrocity, enormity
09 barbarism, brutality,
infuriate, violation
10 scandalize
11 indignation

outrageous
04 foul, vile
07 ghastly, heinous, obscene
08 horrible, shocking, terrible
09 excessive, monstrous
10 exorbitant, inordinate,
scandalous, unbearable
11 intolerable, unspeakable
12 extortionate, insufferable,
preposterous

outré
03 odd
05 weird
06 far-out, freaky, way-out
07 bizarre, strange, unusual
09 eccentric
10 outrageous
13 extraordinary
14 unconventional

outrider
05 guard
06 escort, herald
09 attendant, bodyguard

outright
04 pure
05 clear, total, utter
06 at once, direct, openly
07 perfect, totally, utterly
08 absolute, complete, entirely
09 downright, out-and-out
10 positively, thoroughly
11 categorical, unequivocal,
unmitigated, unqualified
12 straight away
13 categorically, unconditional

outrun
04 beat, lose, pass
05 excel, outdo
07 outpace, surpass
08 outstrip, overtake, shake off
11 leave behind, outdistance

outset
05 start
07 kick-off, opening
09 beginning, inception
12 commencement

outshine
04 beat, best
05 dwarf, excel, outdo
07 eclipse, outrank, upstage
08 outclass, outstrip
10 overshadow, put to shame
13 put in the shade

outside
05 cover, faint, front, outer,
small, vague
06 façade, remote, slight
07 distant, outdoor, outward
08 exterior, external, unlikely
09 outermost
10 appearance, extraneous,
improbable, negligible
11 superficial

outsider
05 alien
06 misfit, émigré
08 emigrant, intruder,
newcomer, stranger

09 foreigner, immigrant, non-
member, odd one out
10 interloper
11 gatecrasher, non-resident

outskirts
04 edge
06 margin
07 borders, fringes, suburbs
08 boundary, suburbia
09 perimeter, periphery

outsmart
03 con, kid
04 beat, best, dupe
05 trick
06 have on, outfox, outwit
07 deceive
08 out-think
12 take for a ride
14 get the better of, pull a fast
one on

outspoken
04 free, rude
05 blunt, frank, plain
06 candid, direct
08 explicit
10 forthright, unreserved
11 plain-spoken, unequivocal
15 straightforward

outspread
04 open, wide
06 flared, opened
08 extended, unfolded
09 fanned out, spread out
12 outstretched

outstanding
03 due
05 famed, great, owing
06 famous, superb, unpaid
07 eminent, notable, ongoing,
payable, pending, special
08 left-over, superior
09 excellent, important,
memorable, prominent,
remaining, unsettled
10 celebrated, impressive,
noteworthy, pre-eminent,
remarkable, unfinished
11 exceptional, superlative
13 distinguished, extraordinary

outstandingly
07 greatly, notably
09 amazingly, extremely
10 especially, remarkably
13 exceptionally
15 extraordinarily

outstrip
03 top
04 beat, pass
05 outdo

06 better, exceed, outrun
07 eclipse, surpass
08 outshine, overtake
09 transcend
11 leave behind, outdistance
13 leave standing

outward
05 outer
06 public
07 evident, outside, visible
08 apparent, exterior, external
10 noticeable, ostensible
11 discernible, perceptible,
superficial

outwardly
07 visibly
09 seemingly
10 apparently, externally,
supposedly
12 at first sight, on the surface
13 on the face of it, superficially

outweigh
06 exceed
07 surpass
08 overcome, override
11 predominate, prevail over
12 preponderate
13 be greater than,
compensate for

outwit
03 con, kid
04 beat, dupe
05 cheat, trick
07 deceive, defraud, swindle
08 outsmart, outthink
12 outmanoeuvre, take for
a ride
14 be cleverer than, get the
better of, pull a fast one on

outworn
07 defunct, disused
08 outmoded, rejected
09 hackneyed, moth-eaten
11 discredited, obsolescent
12 old-fashioned

oval
05 ovate, ovoid
07 obovate, oviform
09 egg-shaped, vulviform
10 elliptical

ovation
06 bravos, cheers, praise
07 acclaim, praises, tribute
08 accolade, applause,
cheering, clapping, plaudits
09 laudation
11 acclamation

oven
04 kiln

05 stove
06 cooker
09 microwave

over
02 on, up
04 gone, left, past, upon
05 above, aloft, ended, extra
06 beyond, no more, unused
07 at an end, settled, surplus
08 done with, finished, in
excess, more than, overhead
09 completed, concluded,
exceeding, forgotten, in the
past, remaining, unclaimed
10 higher than, in addition,
in charge of, in excess of
11 in command of,
superfluous
14 ancient history
15 over and done with

❏ **over and above**
04 plus
07 added to, besides, on top of
08 as well as, let alone
09 along with
12 in addition to, not to
mention, together with

❏ **over and over (again)**
05 often
09 ad nauseam, endlessly
10 frequently, repeatedly
11 ad infinitum, continually
12 time and again
13 again and again

overabundance
04 glut
06 excess
07 surfeit, surplus
08 plethora
09 profusion
11 superfluity
14 superabundance
15 embarras de choix

overact
03 ham
06 overdo
07 lay it on
08 overplay, pile it on
10 exaggerate
12 lay it on thick

overall
05 broad, total
06 global
07 all-over, blanket, general
08 complete, umbrella
09 in general, inclusive
10 by and large, on the whole
13 comprehensive

overalls
08 coverall, workwear

09 dungarees
10 boiler suit

overawe
03 awe, cow
05 abash, alarm, daunt, scare
07 petrify, terrify, unnerve
10 disconcert, intimidate

overbalance
04 slip, trip
05 upset
07 capsize, tip over
08 fall over, keel over, overturn
10 somersault, topple over
15 lose your balance

overbearing
05 bossy, proud
06 snobby, snooty, snotty
08 arrogant, cavalier, despotic,
   dogmatic, smart-ass
09 imperious, officious
10 autocratic, disdainful,
   high-handed, oppressive
11 dictatorial, domineering
12 contemptuous

overblown
03 OTT
08 inflated, overdone
09 amplified, bombastic,
   excessive
10 overcharge, overstated
11 extravagant, pretentious
13 self-important

overcast
04 dark, dull, grey, hazy
05 foggy, misty
06 cloudy, dismal, dreary,
   gloomy, leaden, sombre
08 darkened

overcharge
02 do
04 rook
05 cheat, sting
06 diddle, extort, fleece, rip off
07 swindle
11 short-change

overcome
04 beat, best, lick, rout
05 moved, worst
06 broken, defeat, hammer,
   master, subdue, thrash
07 conquer, prevail, trounce
08 affected, vanquish
09 overpower, overthrow,
   overwhelm, rise above
10 bowled over, speechless
11 overpowered,
   overwhelmed, triumph over
12 lost for words

over-confident
04 rash
05 brash, cocky
08 arrogant, cocksure
09 foolhardy, hubristic
10 blustering, swaggering
11 overweening, self-assured
14 over-optimistic

overcritical
07 carping, Zoilean
08 captious, pedantic
09 cavilling
10 nit-picking, pernickety
12 fault-finding, hard to please
13 hair-splitting, hypercritical

overcrowded
06 packed
07 overrun, teeming
08 swarming
09 chock-full, congested
10 overloaded
11 crammed full
13 overpopulated

overdo
05 ham it
07 lay it on, overact
08 go too far, pile it on
09 overstate
10 exaggerate
11 go overboard, overindulge
12 lay it on thick

▫**overdo it**
07 crack up
08 overwork
09 do too much
10 sweat blood
11 work too hard
14 strain yourself
15 burn yourself out

overdone
05 burnt, undue
07 charred, dried up, spoiled
08 effusive
09 excessive, overbaked
10 histrionic, inordinate,
   overcooked, over the top,
   overplayed, overstated
11 exaggerated, unnecessary
14 burnt to a cinder
15 burnt to a frazzle

overdraft
04 debt
07 arrears, deficit

overdue
03 due
04 late, slow
05 owing, tardy
06 unpaid
07 belated, delayed, pending
09 unsettled

10 behindhand, unpunctual
14 behind schedule

overeat
05 binge, gorge
06 guzzle, pig out
10 go on a binge, gormandize
11 overindulge
13 stuff yourself

overeating
07 bulimia
08 bingeing, gluttony, guzzling
10 gormandism
11 gourmandism,
   hyperphagia
14 overindulgence

overemphasize
06 labour
08 belabour
10 exaggerate, overstress
13 overdramatize

overexert

▫**overexert yourself**
08 overdo it, overwork
11 work too hard
14 strain yourself
15 overtax yourself, wear
   yourself out

overflow
05 cover, flood, spill, swamp
06 deluge, shower
07 overrun, run over, surplus
08 brim over, flow over,
   inundate, spillage, well
   over
09 overspill, spill over
10 bubble over, inundation

overflowing
04 full, rife
07 brimful, profuse, teeming
08 inundant, thronged
09 abounding, bountiful
13 superabundant

overgrowth
10 escalation
11 hypertrophy
13 overabundance
14 superabundance
15 overdevelopment

overhang
03 jut
05 bulge
06 beetle, extend, jut out
07 project
08 bulge out, protrude, stand
   out, stick out

overhanging
07 bulging, jutting, pensile
08 beetling

10 bulging out, jutting out, projecting, protruding
11 standing out, sticking out

overhaul
03 fix
04 mend, pass
05 check
06 repair, revamp, survey
07 check up, examine, inspect, outpace, service
09 check over, going-over
10 inspection, renovation
11 examination, recondition
14 reconditioning

overhead
05 above
06 aerial, on high, raised, upward
07 up above
11 overhanging

overheads
06 burden, oncost
08 expenses
09 outgoings
11 expenditure
12 disbursement, regular costs, running costs
14 operating costs

overheated
05 angry, fiery
07 excited, flaming
08 agitated, inflamed
11 overexcited, overwrought

overindulge
05 binge, booze, gorge, spoil
06 guzzle, pander, pig out
07 debauch, satiate
08 pamper
09 spoon-feed
10 gluttonize, gormandize
11 mollycoddle

overindulgence
05 binge
06 excess
07 debauch, surfeit
10 overeating
12 intemperance

overjoyed
06 elated, joyful
08 ecstatic, euphoric, jubilant, thrilled
09 delighted, rapturous
10 enraptured, in raptures
11 high as a kite, on cloud nine, over the moon, tickled pink
14 pleased as Punch
15 in seventh heaven, on top of the world

overlap
07 overlay, overlie, shingle
08 coincide, flap over
09 imbricate

overlay
04 wrap
05 adorn, cover, inlay
06 veneer
07 blanket, envelop, varnish
08 decorate, laminate

overload
03 tax
06 burden, lumber, strain
07 oppress, overtax
10 overburden, overcharge

overlook
04 face, miss, omit
06 excuse, forget, ignore, pardon, slight, wink at
07 condone, forgive, let pass
08 look onto, look over
09 disregard, front onto
14 take no notice of
15 turn a blind eye to

overlooked
08 unheeded, unvalued
10 unregarded, unremarked

overly
03 too
06 unduly
11 exceedingly, excessively
12 inordinately, unreasonably

overnice
10 nit-picking, pernickety
11 overprecise
13 oversensitive
14 overparticular, overscrupulous

overplay
06 colour, overdo, stress
07 amplify, enhance, enlarge, lay it on, magnify
08 oversell, pile it on
09 dramatize, embroider, emphasize, overstate
10 aggrandize, exaggerate
13 lay it on thick
13 overdramatize, overemphasize
15 stretch the truth

overpopulated
07 overrun, teeming
08 swarming
09 chock-full, congested
11 crammed full, overcrowded

overpower
04 beat, daze, move, rout
05 crush, floor, quash, quell
06 defeat, master, subdue

07 conquer, stagger, trounce
08 bowl over, overcome, vanquish
09 dumbfound, overwhelm, subjugate, take aback
10 immobilize
11 flabbergast, knock for six
15 gain mastery over

overpowering
06 strong
07 extreme
08 forceful, powerful, stifling
09 sickening
10 compelling, nauseating, oppressive, unbearable
11 irrefutable, suffocating
12 irresistible, overwhelming
14 uncontrollable

overrate
06 blow up
07 magnify
09 overprize, overvalue
10 overpraise
12 overestimate

overreach
◻ **overreach yourself**
08 go too far, overdo it
14 strain yourself
15 burn yourself out

override
05 annul, quash
06 cancel, exceed, ignore
07 nullify, rescind, surpass
08 abrogate, outweigh, overcome, overrule
09 disregard, supersede
11 countermand, prevail over, trample over

overriding
05 final, first, major, prime, prior
06 ruling
07 pivotal, primary, supreme
08 cardinal, dominant, ultimate
09 essential, number one, paramount, principal
10 compelling, prevailing
11 determining, predominant
13 most important
15 most significant

overrule
05 annul
06 cancel, reject, revoke
07 nullify, rescind, reverse
08 abrogate, disallow, override, overturn, vote down
10 invalidate
11 countermand

overrun
05 storm, swamp

06 attack, exceed, go over, infest, invade, occupy
07 besiege, run riot
08 inundate, overgrow
09 overshoot, overwhelm, surge over, swarm over
10 spread over

overseas
06 abroad, exotic, remote
07 distant, faraway, foreign
08 external
10 far and wide
12 foreign parts
13 international
15 out of the country

overseer
04 boss
05 chief
06 gaffer
07 foreman, manager
09 forewoman
10 manageress, supervisor
14 superintendent

overshadow
03 dim, mar
05 cloud, dwarf, excel, spoil
06 blight, darken
07 eclipse, obscure, surpass
08 dominate, outshine
10 tower above
12 put a damper on
13 put in the shade
14 take the edge off

oversight
04 boob, care
05 error, fault, lapse
06 charge, howler, slip-up
07 blunder, control, mistake
08 handling, omission
10 management
11 dereliction, supervision
12 carelessness, surveillance

overstate
06 colour, overdo, stress
07 amplify, enhance, enlarge, lay it on, magnify
08 oversell, pile it on
09 dramatize, emphasize
10 aggrandize, exaggerate
12 lay it on thick
13 overdramatize, overemphasize
15 stretch the truth

overstatement
06 excess, parody
09 burlesque, hyperbole
10 caricature
11 enlargement
12 exaggeration, extravagance, overemphasis

13 amplification, embellishment
14 overestimation
15 pretentiousness

overt
04 open
05 plain
06 patent, public
07 evident, obvious, visible
08 apparent, manifest
10 noticeable, observable
11 unconcealed, undisguised

overtake
04 pass
06 befall, engulf, go past, strike
08 happen to, outstrip
09 drive past, overwhelm
11 leave behind, pull ahead of
13 catch unawares
14 take by surprise

overthrow
03 end
04 beat, fall, oust, rout, ruin
05 crush, quash, quell, upset
06 defeat, depose, invert, master, subdue, topple, unseat, upturn
07 abolish, conquer, ousting
08 dethrone, displace, downfall, overcome, turn over, vanquish
09 bring down, overpower, overwhelm, unseating
10 deposition
11 destruction, humiliation, suppression, vanquishing
12 dethronement

overtone
04 hint
05 sense
06 nuance
07 feeling, flavour
08 innuendo
10 intimation, suggestion
11 implication, insinuation
12 undercurrent
13 hidden meaning

overture
05 moves, offer
06 gambit, motion, signal
07 prelude
08 approach
08 advances, proposal
10 invitation, suggestion
11 opening move, proposition
12 introduction
13 opening gambit

overturn
04 beat, oust, veto
05 annul, crush, quash, upset

06 cancel, defeat, depose, invert, repeal, revoke, topple, unseat, upturn
07 abolish, capsize, destroy, nullify, rescind, tip over
08 abrogate, dethrone, displace, keel over, override, overrule, set aside, turn over, vanquish
09 bring down, overpower, overthrow, overwhelm
11 overbalance

overused
04 worn
05 stale, tired, trite
07 clichéd
08 bromidic
09 hackneyed, played out
10 overworked, threadbare
11 commonplace, stereotyped
13 platitudinous

overweening
04 vain
05 cocky, proud
07 haughty, pompous, swollen
08 arrogant, cavalier, cocksure, inflated, insolent
09 conceited, excessive, hubristic, overblown
10 high-handed, immoderate
11 egotistical, extravagant, opinionated
12 presumptuous, supercilious
13 self-confident

overweight
03 fat
04 huge
05 bulky, buxom, gross, heavy, hefty, obese, podgy, stout
06 chunky, flabby, portly
07 massive, outsize
09 corpulent
10 pot-bellied, well-padded

overwhelm
04 beat, best, daze, lick, rout
05 crush, quash, quell, swamp
06 defeat, deluge, engulf, outwit, subdue, thrash
07 clobber, confuse, destroy, outplay, overrun, prevail, stagger, trounce
08 bowl over, inundate, outsmart, overcome, submerge, vanquish
09 devastate, overpower, overthrow, slaughter, snow under, subjugate
10 overburden
11 knock for six
14 get the better of

overwhelming

04 huge, vast
05 great, large
07 extreme, immense
08 forceful, powerful, stifling
10 compelling, nauseating,
   oppressive, unbearable,
   undeniable
11 irrefutable, suffocating
12 irresistible, overpowering
14 uncontrollable

overwork

05 weary
06 burden, strain
07 exhaust, exploit, oppress,
   overtax, overuse, wear out
08 overdo it, overload
09 do too much
10 overstrain, sweat blood
11 work too hard
15 burn yourself out

overworked

04 worn
05 stale, tired, trite
07 clichéd, worn out
08 bromidic
09 exhausted, hackneyed,
   overtaxed, played out
10 threadbare, unoriginal
11 commonplace, stereotyped,
   stressed out
13 platitudinous

overwrought

04 edgy

05 nervy, tense
06 highly, on edge, strung
07 excited, frantic, keyed up,
   nervous, uptight, wound up
08 agitated, worked up
10 distraught
11 overcharged, overexcited
14 beside yourself

owe

10 be in debt to, be in the red
11 be overdrawn, get into debt
12 be indebted to
13 be in arrears to

owing

03 due
04 owed
06 unpaid
07 overdue, payable
09 in arrears, unsettled
11 outstanding

▫ owing to

08 thanks to
09 because of
11 as a result of, on account of

own

03 use
04 have, hold, keep
05 enjoy
07 have got, possess, private
08 personal
10 individual, monopolize
13 idiosyncratic

▫ on your own

05 alone
06 singly
07 unaided
09 on your tod
10 by yourself, unassisted
13 independently,
   unaccompanied, off your
   own bat

▫ own up

05 admit
07 confess
09 come clean
11 acknowledge
12 tell the truth

owner

06 holder, keeper, master
08 landlady, landlord, mistress
09 home-owner, possessor
10 freeholder, proprietor
11 householder
12 proprietress

ownership

05 title
06 rights
08 dominion, freehold
10 possession
14 proprietorship

ox

03 yak
04 bull
05 bison, steer
07 buffalo, bullock

pace
04 gait, rate, step, walk
05 march, speed, tempo
06 patrol, stride
07 mark out, measure
08 celerity, rapidity
09 quickness, swiftness

pacific
04 calm, mild
05 quiet, still
06 dovish, irenic, placid, serene
07 equable, halcyon
08 dovelike, peaceful, tranquil
09 peaceable, placatory, unruffled
10 non-violent
11 peace-loving, peacemaking
12 conciliatory, pacificatory
14 nonbelligerent

pacifism
10 pacifism, satyagraha
11 non-violence

pacifist
04 dove
06 conchy
10 pacificist, peace-lover

pacify
04 calm, lull, tame
05 quiet, still
06 defuse, soothe
07 appease, assuage, compose, mollify, placate, put down, quieten, silence
08 calm down, moderate
10 conciliate

pack
03 bag, jam, mob, ram, set
04 bale, band, cram, fill, load, stow, wrap
05 bunch, cover, crate, crowd, drove, flock, group, press, store, stuff, tie up, wedge
06 bundle, burden, carton, kitbag, packet, parcel, wrap up
07 compact, package, squeeze
08 compress, knapsack, rucksack
09 container, haversack

❏pack in
03 end, jam, mob, ram
04 stop
05 chuck, crowd, stuff, wedge
06 cram in, give up, jack in, resign, throng
07 squeeze, throw in

❏pack off
04 send
07 dismiss
08 dispatch

❏pack up
03 end
04 fail, stop
06 finish, give up, jack in, tidy up, wrap up
07 conk out, seize up
09 break down
10 call it a day
11 malfunction, stop working

package
03 box, set
04 bale, pack, unit, wrap
05 batch, group, whole
06 carton, entity, packet, parcel
08 gift-wrap
09 container
11 consignment, package deal

packaging
06 packet
07 packing, wrapper
08 wrapping
09 container

packed
04 full
06 filled, jammed
07 brimful, crammed, crowded
09 congested, jam-packed
11 chock-a-block

packet
04 a lot, lots, mint, pack, pots
06 bundle, carton, parcel
07 fortune, package, packing, tidy sum
09 a bob or two, container
11 king's ransom, pretty penny
12 small fortune

pact
04 bond, deal

06 cartel, treaty
07 compact, entente
08 alliance, contract, covenant
09 agreement, concordat

pad
03 paw, run, wad
04 fill, flat, foot, home, pack, sole, step, walk
05 stuff, tramp, tread
06 jotter, tiptoe, trudge
07 cushion, hang-out, padding, protect, wadding
08 notebook, quarters
09 apartment, footprint
10 protection

❏pad out
06 expand
07 augment, fill out, spin out, stretch
08 flesh out, lengthen, protract
09 elaborate

padding
06 hot air, lining, waffle
07 filling, packing, wadding
08 stuffing, verbiage
09 wordiness
10 cushioning, protection

paddle
03 oar, row
04 pull, punt, slop, wade
05 scull, steer, sweep
06 dabble, propel, splash

paddock
03 pen
04 fold, yard
05 field, pound
06 corral
08 compound, stockade
09 enclosure

paddy
03 pet
04 bate, fury, rage, tiff
06 temper
07 passion, tantrum

padlock
04 bolt
05 catch, clasp
09 fastening

padre
05 vicar
06 cleric, curate, deacon, parson, pastor, priest, rector
08 chaplain, minister, reverend
09 clergyman

paean
04 hymn
05 psalm
06 anthem, eulogy
08 doxology, encomium, ode to joy
09 dithyramb, panegyric
12 song of praise

pagan
07 atheist, godless, heathen
10 unbeliever
11 pantheistic

page
04 call, leaf, side
05 epoch, event, folio, phase, recto, sheet, stage, verso
06 ask for, period, summon
07 bell-boy, bell-hop, chapter, episode, pageboy, send for
08 announce, incident
09 attendant, messenger

pageant
04 play, show
06 parade
07 display, tableau
09 cavalcade, spectacle
10 procession
14 representation

pageantry
04 pomp, show
06 parade
07 display, glamour, glitter
08 ceremony, flourish, grandeur
09 spectacle, splendour
12 extravagance, magnificence
13 theatricality

pail
03 can, tub
04 bail
05 churn
06 bucket, piggin

pain
03 woe
04 ache, bore, drag, hurt, pang, pest, rack, stab
05 agony, cramp, grief, smart, spasm, sting, throb, worry
06 aching, be sore, bother, burden, grieve, misery, sadden, sorrow, twinge
07 afflict, agonize, anguish, torment, torture

08 distress, headache, nuisance, vexation
09 annoyance, heartache
10 discomfort, heartbreak, tenderness
13 make miserable

pained
04 hurt
05 stung, upset, vexed
07 grieved, injured, wounded
08 offended, saddened
09 aggrieved
10 distressed
11 reproachful

painful
04 hard, sore
05 tough
06 aching, tender, touchy
07 arduous, hurting, tedious
08 inflamed, rigorous, shameful, smarting, stabbing
09 agonizing, difficult, harrowing, laborious, miserable, sensitive, strenuous, throbbing, upsetting
10 mortifying, unpleasant
11 distressing
12 disagreeable, excruciating
13 uncomfortable

painfully
05 sadly
08 pitiably, terribly, woefully
09 pitifully
10 alarmingly, deplorably, dreadfully
11 agonizingly, excessively
13 distressingly, unfortunately
14 excruciatingly

painkiller
07 anodyne
08 lenitive, sedative
09 analgesic
10 palliative
11 anaesthetic

painless
05 cushy
08 pain-free
10 child's play, effortless
11 trouble-free, undemanding
12 a piece of cake, plain sailing

pains
06 effort, labour
07 trouble
09 diligence

□ be at pains
06 bother
07 try hard
08 take care
15 make every effort

painstaking
07 careful, devoted
08 diligent, sedulous, thorough
09 assiduous, attentive
10 meticulous, scrupulous
11 hardworking, industrious, persevering, punctilious
13 conscientious

paint
04 coat, daub, tell, tint, wash
05 evoke, glaze, spray, stain
06 colour, depict, sketch
07 lacquer, narrate, pigment, plaster, portray, recount
08 colorant, decorate, describe
09 colouring, represent, whitewash
10 redecorate

► *Types of paint*:
03 oil
04 matt, oils
05 glaze, gloss
06 enamel, pastel, poster, primer
07 acrylic, gouache, lacquer, scumble, varnish
08 eggshell, emulsion
09 distemper, undercoat, whitewash
10 colourwash
11 watercolour
➤ See also **art**

□ paint the town red
04 rave
05 binge, go out
07 have fun, rejoice
08 live it up
09 celebrate, have a ball, whoop it up
13 go on the razzle

painter
06 artist, dauber, limner
09 colourist
10 oil painter
11 miniaturist
14 watercolourist

► *Some names of painters, printmakers, illustrators and graphic artists*:
03 **Arp** (Jean), **Dix** (Otto), **Ray** (Man)
04 **Bell** (Vanessa), **Dali** (Salvador), **Doré** (Gustave), **Dufy** (Raoul), **Eyck** (Jan van), **Goya** (Francisco de), **Gris** (Juan), **Hals** (Frans), **Hunt** (Holman), **John** (Augustus), **John** (Gwen), **Klee** (Paul), **Long** (Richard), **Marc** (Franz), **Miró** (Joan), **Nash** (Paul)

05 **Bacon** (Francis), **Blake**
(Peter), **Blake** (William),
Bosch (Hieronymus),
Brown (Ford Madox),
Burra (Edward), **Corot**
(Camille), **David** (Jacques
Louis), **Degas** (Edgar),
Dürer (Albrecht), **Ernst**
(Max), **Freud** (Lucien),
Gorky (Arshile), **Greco**
(El), **Grosz** (George), **Hirst**
(Damien), **Johns** (Jasper),
Kahlo (Frida), **Kitaj**
(Ronald Brooks), **Klimt**
(Gustav), **Kline** (Franz),
Léger (Fernand), **Lewis**
(Wyndham), **Lippi**
(Filippino), **Lippi** (Fra
Filippo), **Lowry** (Laurence
Stephen), **Manet** (Edouard),
Monet (Claude), **Mucha**
(Alphonse), **Munch**
(Edvard), **Piper** (John),
Riley (Bridget), **Sarto**
(Andrea del)

06 **Braque** (Georges), **Bratby**
(John), **Cassat** (Mary),
Claude, Derain (André
Louis), **Escher** (Maurits
Cornelis), **Fuseli** (Henri),
Giotto, Ingres (Jean
Auguste Dominique),
Jarman (Derek), **Mabuse,
Massys** (Quentin), **Millet**
(Jean François), **Morris**
(William), **Newman**
(Barnett), **O'Keefe**
(Georgia), **Palmer**
(Samuel), **Pisano** (Nicola),
Renoir (Pierre Auguste),
Rivera (Diego), **Rothko**
(Mark), **Rubens** (Sir Peter
Paul), **Scarfe** (Gerald),
Searle (Ronald), **Seurat**
(Georges), **Sisley** (Alfred),
Stubbs (George), **Tanguy**
(Yves), **Titian, Turner**
(Joseph Mallord William),
Warhol (Andy), **Wright**
(Joseph)

07 **Attwell** (Mabel Lucie),
Bellini (Giovanni),
Bonnard (Pierre), **Boucher**
(François), **Cézanne** (Paul),
Chagall (Marc), **Chirico**
(Giorgio de), **Christo,
Cimabué, Courbet**
(Gustave), **Cranach** (Lucas,
the Elder), **Daumier**
(Honoré), **Delvaux** (Paul),
Duchamp (Marcel), **El
Greco, Gauguin** (Paul),

Hobbema (Meindert),
Hockney (David),
Hodgkin (Sir Howard),
Hogarth (William),
Holbein (Hans), **Keating**
(Tom), **Matisse** (Henri),
Millais (Sir John Everett),
Morisot (Berthe), **Picabia**
(Francis), **Picasso** (Pablo),
Pollock (Jackson), **Poussin**
(Nicolas), **Rackham**
(Arthur), **Raeburn** (Sir
Henry), **Raphael, Sargent**
(John Singer), **Schiele**
(Egon), **Sickert** (Walter),
Spencer (Sir Stanley),
Tenniel (Sir John), **Tiepolo**
(Giovanni Battista),
Uccello (Paolo), **Utrillo**
(Maurice), **Van Eyck** (Jan),
Van Gogh (Vincent),
Vermeer (Jan), **Watteau**
(Antoine), **Wearing**
(Gillian)

08 **Angelico** (Fra), **Auerbach**
(Frank), **Breughel** (Pieter),
Brueghel (Pieter),
Delaunay (Robert),
Dubuffet (Jean), **Goncourt**
(Edmond de), **Hamilton**
(Richard), **Hilliard**
(Nicholas), **Landseer** (Sir
Edwin), **Leonardo,
Magritte** (René),
Mantegna (Andrea),
Masaccio, Mondrian
(Piet), **Perugino, Piranesi**
(Giovanni Battista),
Pissarro (Camille),
Reynolds (Sir Joshua),
Rossetti (Dante Gabriel),
Rousseau (Henri, 'Le
Douanier'), **Ruisdael**
(Jacob van), **Ruysdael**
(Jacob van), **Veronese**
(Paolo), **Vlaminck**
(Maurice de), **Whistler**
(James McNeill)

09 **Beardsley** (Aubrey),
Canaletto, Constable
(John), **Correggio, De
Kooning** (Willem),
Delacroix (Eugène),
Fragonard (Jean Honoré),
Friedrich (Caspar David),
Géricault (Théodore),
Giorgione, Greenaway
(Kate), **Grünewald**
(Matthias), **Kandinsky**
(Wasily), **Kokoschka**
(Oskar), **Lancaster** (Sir
Osbert), **Nicholson** (Ben),

**Pisanello, Rembrandt,
Velázquez** (Diego)

10 **Alma-Tadema** (Sir
Lawrence), **Botticelli**
(Sandro), **Burne-Jones** (Sir
Edward), **Caravaggio**
(Michelangelo),
Giacometti (Alberto),
Modigliani (Amedeo),
Motherwell (Robert),
Sutherland (Graham),
Tintoretto

12 **Gainsborough** (Thomas),
Lichtenstein (Roy),
Michelangelo

14 **Andrea del Sarto, Claude
Lorraine, Lucas van
Leyden**

15 **Leonardo da Vinci,
Toulouse-Lautrec** (Henri
de)

➢ See also **art**

painting
03 oil
05 mural
06 fresco
08 likeness, portrait
09 landscape, miniature,
portrayal, still life
11 watercolour
➢ See also **art**

━ *Painting terms:*
04 icon, tint, tone, wash
05 bloom, brush, easel, gesso,
mural, paint, pieta, tondo
06 canvas, fresco, frieze,
primer, sketch
07 cartoon, collage, diptych,
drawing, gallery, gouache,
impasto, montage, palette,
pastels, picture, pigment,
scumble, sfumato, stipple,
tempera
08 abstract, aquatint, bleeding,
charcoal, frottage, hard
edge, pastoral, portrait,
seascape, thinners, triptych,
vignette
09 aquarelle, capriccio,
encaustic, flat brush,
grisaille, grotesque,
landscape, mahlstick,
miniature, sgraffito, still life
10 art gallery, craquelure,
figurative, monochrome,
pentimento, sable brush,
silhouette, turpentine
11 chiaroscuro, composition,
oil painting, perspective,
pointillism, trompe l'oeil,
watercolour

12 brush strokes, illustration, palette knife

13 genre painting, underpainting

14 foreshortening

➤ *Some well known paintings, drawings, etchings and engravings*:

04 Flag

05 Manga, Pietà

06 Spring

07 Bubbles, Erasmus, Gin Lane, Olympia, Targets

08 Guernica, Maja Nude, Mona Lisa

09 Bacchanal, Black Iris, Haystacks, Jerusalem, Night Café, Primavera, The Scream

10 Adam and Eve, Assumption, Beer Street, Blue Horses, Las Meninas, Sunflowers, The Angelus, The Hay Wain

11 A Shrimp Girl, Crucifixion, Limp Watches, Maja Clothed, Starry Night, The Gleaners, Water Lilies

12 Peasant Dance, The Nightmare, The Scapegoat, The Umbrellas

13 A Bigger Splash, Christ in Glory, Sleeping Gypsy, The Last Supper, The Night Watch

14 A Rake's Progress, Disasters of War, Peasant Wedding, Sistine Madonna, The Ambassadors, The Card Players, The Four Seasons, The Rokeby Venus

15 Flight into Egypt, Madonna and Child, Madonna del Prato, Marriage à la Mode, The Annunciation, The Birth of Venus, The Dance of Death, The Death of Marat, The Flagellation, The Potato Eaters, The Raft of Medusa, The Rape of Europa

pair

03 duo, set, two, wed

04 join, link, mate, team, twin

05 brace, marry, match, twins

06 couple, splice

07 bracket, match up, twosome

10 two of a kind

11 put together

paired

05 mated, yoked

06 double, in twos, joined

07 coupled, matched, twinned

09 bracketed

pal

04 chum, mate

05 buddy, crony

06 friend

07 comrade

palace

06 castle

07 château, mansion

palaeontologists

➤ *Names of palaeontologists and palaeoanthropologists*:

04 **Cope** (Edward Drinker)

05 **Gould** (Stephen Jay), **Marsh** (Othniel Charles)

06 **Forbes** (Edward), **Leakey** (Louis Seymour Bazett), **Leakey** (Mary Douglas), **Leakey** (Richard)

07 **Mantell** (Gideon Algernon)

08 **Johanson** (Donald Carl)

➤ See also **scientist**

palatable

05 tasty, yummy

06 edible, morish

07 eatable, savoury, scrummy

09 agreeable, enjoyable, flavorous, succulent

10 appetizing, delectable

11 flavoursome, scrumptious

13 mouth-watering

palate

04 gout

05 taste

08 appetite

palatial

04 posh

05 grand, plush, regal, ritzy

06 de luxe

07 opulent, stately

08 imposing, splendid

09 grandiose, luxurious, sumptuous

palaver

04 flap, fuss, to-do

06 bother, bustle

07 carry-on, fluster

08 activity, business

09 commotion, rigmarole

12 song and dance

pale

03 dim, wan

04 ashy, fade, waxy, weak

05 ashen, faded, faint, light, muted, pasty, peaky, waxen, white

06 blanch, bleach, chalky, feeble, lessen, pallid, pastel, sallow, whiten

07 anaemic, drained, insipid

08 bleached, diminish

09 etoliated, washed-out

10 colourless, pasty-faced

❑**beyond the pale**

08 improper, unseemly

11 intolerable

12 inadmissible, unacceptable

13 inappropriate

palisade

05 fence

06 paling

08 stockade

09 barricade, enclosure

pall

04 cloy, jade, sate, tire, veil

05 cloak, cloud, gloom, weary

06 damper, mantle, shadow, shroud, sicken

07 satiate, wear off

❑**cast a pall over**

03 mar

05 spoil, upset

06 impair

palliate

04 ease

05 abate, allay, cloak, cover

06 lenify, soothe, temper

07 assuage, mollify, relieve

08 mitigate, moderate

09 alleviate, extenuate

palliative

07 anodyne, calming

08 lenitive, sedative, soothing

09 analgesic, calmative, demulcent

10 painkiller

11 alleviative

13 tranquillizer

pallid

03 wan

04 ashy, pale, waxy, weak

05 ashen, bland, pasty, waxen

06 sallow

07 anaemic, insipid

09 bloodless, etiolated, whey-faced

10 colourless, pasty-faced, spiritless

11 peelie-wally

pallor

07 wanness

09 whiteness

10 chalkiness, etiolation, pallidness, sallowness

13 bloodlessness

pally
05 close, thick
06 chummy
08 familiar, friendly, intimate

palm
03 paw
04 grab, hand, mitt, take
06 snatch
11 appropriate

► *Types of palm*:
03 ita
04 atap, coco, nipa
05 areca, assai, bussu, nikau, Sabal
06 buriti, cohune, corozo, Elaeis, gomuti, gru-gru, jupati, kentia, kittul, raffia, Raphia, rattan, troely
07 babassu, calamus, coquito, Corypha, Euterpe, moriche, oil-palm, palmyra, paxiuba, pupunha, talipat, talipot, troelie, troolie, wax palm
08 carnauba, coco-palm, coco-tree, date-palm, date-tree, groo-groo, sago-palm
09 macaw-palm, sugar palm, toddy-palm
10 Chamaerops
11 coconut-palm
12 chiquichiqui, Washingtonia
➤ See also **plant**

❏**palm off**
05 foist
06 fob off, thrust, unload
07 offload, pass off
08 get rid of

palmist
11 clairvoyant
13 fortune-teller

palmistry
10 chirognomy, chiromancy
12 clairvoyancy
14 fortune-telling

palmy
06 golden, joyous
07 halcyon
08 carefree, glorious, thriving
10 prosperous, successful

palpable
05 clear, plain, solid
08 concrete, material, tangible
09 touchable
11 substantial

palpitate
04 beat, thud
05 pound, pulse, throb, thump
07 flutter, pulsate

paltry
04 mean, poor, puny
05 minor, petty, small, sorry
06 meagre, measly, slight
07 trivial
08 derisory, piddling, trifling
09 miserable, worthless
10 negligible
12 contemptible
13 insignificant

pamper
03 pet
05 spoil
06 coddle, cosset, pander
07 indulge
09 spoon-feed
11 mollycoddle, overindulge

pampered
06 petted, spoilt
07 coddled
08 cosseted, indulged
12 mollycoddled

pamphlet
06 folder, notice
07 booklet, handout, leaflet
08 brochure, circular

pan
03 pot, wok
04 flay, scan, slam
05 fryer, knock, roast, slate, sweep, swing, track
06 hammer, vessel
07 censure, rubbish, skillet
08 pancheon, traverse
09 casserole, container, criticize
12 pull to pieces
13 find fault with

❏**pan out**
06 happen, result
07 turn out, work out

panacea
06 elixir
07 cure-all, nostrum
12 panpharmacon
15 universal remedy

panache
04 brio, dash, zest, élan
05 flair, style, verve
06 energy, spirit, vigour
08 flourish
11 flamboyance, ostentation

pancake
05 blini, crêpe
06 waffle
07 bannock
08 flapjack, tortilla
10 battercake
11 griddle-cake

pandemic
06 common, global
07 general
09 extensive, universal
10 widespread
11 far-reaching

pandemonium
03 din
04 to-do
05 chaos
06 bedlam, hubbub, rumpus, tumult, uproar
09 commotion, confusion, hue and cry
10 hullabaloo, turbulence
11 hullaballoo

pander

❏**pander to**
06 humour, pamper
07 gratify, indulge

panegyric
05 paean
06 eulogy, homage, praise
07 glowing, tribute
08 accolade, citation, encomium, eulogium
09 laudatory
10 eulogistic
11 encomiastic
12 commendation
13 complimentary

panel
04 beam, jury, slab, team
05 board, dials, knobs, sheet
06 levers
07 buttons, console, council
08 controls, switches
09 cartouche, committee, dashboard
10 commission
11 directorate, instruments

panelling
04 dado
08 wainscot
11 wainscoting
12 wainscotting

pang
04 ache, pain, stab
05 agony, gripe, prick, qualm, spasm, sting, throe
07 anguish, scruple
08 distress
10 discomfort, uneasiness

panic
04 flap
05 alarm
06 frenzy, fright, terror
08 hysteria
09 agitation, overreact

10 go to pieces
11 have kittens
12 lose your cool, lose your head
13 lose your nerve

panic-stricken
07 frantic, panicky
08 frenzied
09 petrified, terrified
10 frightened, hysterical
11 scared stiff
12 in a cold sweat

panoply
05 array, get-up, range
06 armour, attire
07 raiment, regalia, turn-out
09 equipment, trappings

panorama
04 view
05 scene, vista
06 survey
07 scenery
08 overview, prospect
09 landscape
11 perspective

panoramic
04 wide
05 broad
06 scenic
07 general, overall
08 sweeping
09 extensive, universal
11 far-reaching, wide-ranging

pant
04 ache, blow, gasp, huff, long, pine, puff, sigh, want
05 covet, crave, heave, yearn
06 desire, hanker, thirst
11 huff and puff

panting
05 eager
06 puffed, winded
07 anxious, craving, gasping, longing, puffing
09 hankering, puffed out
10 breathless
11 out of breath, short-winded

pantomime
05 farce, panto
06 masque
07 charade
12 harlequinade

pants
05 jeans
06 briefs, shorts, slacks, smalls, trunks, undies
07 drawers, panties, Y-fronts
08 frillies, knickers, trousers
10 underpants

11 boxer shorts
12 camiknickers

pap
03 goo, rot
04 crap, mush, pulp
05 purée, trash
06 drivel
07 rubbish
08 claptrap, nonsense
09 gibberish

paper
03 rag
04 deed, work
05 daily, essay, organ, study
06 record, report, thesis, weekly
07 article, journal, tabloid
08 document, magazine, treatise
09 monograph, newspaper
10 broadsheet, credential, periodical
11 certificate, composition, examination
12 dissertation, identity card
14 identification

► *Paper sizes*:
03 pot
04 demy, post, pott
05 atlas, crown, folio, jésus, royal
06 medium, quarto
07 emperor
08 elephant, foolscap, imperial
09 antiquary, music-demy
10 super-royal

❑ **on paper**
08 in theory, recorded
09 in writing
10 officially
11 on the record, written down
13 theoretically
14 hypothetically
15 in black and white

❑ **paper over**
04 hide
07 conceal, cover up, obscure
08 disguise
10 camouflage

papery
04 thin
05 frail, light
06 flimsy
07 fragile
08 delicate
09 paper-thin
13 insubstantial

par
04 mean, norm
05 level, usual

06 median, parity
07 average, balance
08 equality, standard
11 equilibrium, equivalence
12 equal footing

❑ **below par**
05 tired
06 unwell
10 out of sorts
12 below average
14 not up to scratch, unsatisfactory
15 under the weather

❑ **on a par with**
07 equal to
08 as good as

❑ **par for the course**
05 usual
06 normal
07 typical
08 standard

parable
05 fable, story
06 lesson
08 allegory
09 moral tale

parade
04 file, show
05 array, march, train, vaunt
06 column, flaunt, review
07 display, exhibit, show off
08 brandish, ceremony, file past
09 cavalcade, motorcade, spectacle
10 exhibition, procession

paradigm
05 ideal, model
07 example, pattern
08 exemplar, original
09 archetype, framework, prototype

paradise
04 Eden
05 bliss
06 heaven, utopia
07 Elysium, rapture
09 afterlife, hereafter, next world, Shangri-La
12 Garden of Eden
13 elysium fields, seventh heaven

paradox
06 enigma, puzzle, riddle
07 anomaly
11 incongruity
13 contradiction, inconsistency

paradoxical
08 baffling, puzzling

09 anomalous, enigmatic, illogical
11 incongruous
12 inconsistent
13 contradictory

paragon
05 ideal, model
07 epitome, pattern
08 exemplar, standard
09 archetype, criterion, nonpareil, prototype
12 quintessence, the bee's knees

paragraph
04 item, part
07 passage, portion, section, segment
10 subsection
11 subdivision

parallel
05 agree, equal, liken, match
07 aligned, analogy, compare, conform, similar, uniform
08 analogue, likeness, matching, resemble
09 alongside, analogous, correlate, duplicate
10 collateral, comparable, comparison, correspond, equivalent, homologous, resembling, similarity
11 coextensive, correlation, equidistant
13 corresponding

paralyse
04 halt, lame, numb, stop
06 deaden, freeze
07 cripple, disable
08 transfix
10 immobilize

paralysed
04 numb
08 crippled, disabled
09 paralytic
10 paraplegic
12 quadriplegic

paralysis
04 halt
05 palsy
07 paresis
08 deadness, numbness, shutdown, stoppage
10 immobility, paraplegia, standstill
12 debilitation, quadriplegia
13 powerlessness

paralytic
05 drunk
07 legless, palsied

08 crippled, disabled
09 paralysed
10 hemiplegic, monoplegic
12 quadriplegic

parameter
08 boundary, variable
09 criterion, framework, guideline
10 limitation
11 restriction
14 limiting factor

paramount
04 main
05 chief, first, prime
07 highest, supreme, topmost
08 cardinal
11 outstanding, predominant

paramour
04 beau
05 lover
07 beloved, hetaera
08 fancy man, mistress
09 inamorata, inamorato
10 fancy woman
12 bit on the side

paranoia
09 delusions, obsession, psychosis

paranoid
10 bewildered, suspicious
11 distrustful

parapet
04 rail, wall
05 fence, guard
06 paling
07 barrier, bastion, bulwark, defence, railing, rampart
08 barbican
10 battlement, embankment

paraphernalia
04 gear
05 stuff, tools
06 tackle, things
07 baggage, effects
09 apparatus, equipment, materials, trappings
10 belongings, implements
11 accessories, odds and ends, possessions
13 accoutrements, bits and pieces

paraphrase
05 gloss
06 rehash, render, reword
07 restate, version
09 interpret, rendering, rewording, translate
11 restatement, translation
14 interpretation

parasite
05 leech
07 epizoan, epizoon, sponger
08 endozoon, entozoon, epiphyte
09 endophyte, passenger
10 freeloader
11 bloodsucker

parasitic
07 epizoan, epizoic
08 sponging
09 biogenous, leechlike
11 freeloading, parasitical
12 bloodsucking

parcel
03 box, lot, mob
04 area, band, deal, gang, herd, pack, plot, wrap
05 crowd, flock, group, patch, piece, tie up, tract, troop
06 bundle, carton, pack up, packet, wrap up
07 company, package, portion
08 bundle up, gift-wrap
09 allotment
10 collection

□ **parcel out**
05 allot
06 divide
07 carve up, deal out, dole out, hand out, mete out
08 allocate, dispense, share out
09 apportion, divide out
10 distribute

parch
04 bake, burn, sear
05 dry up
06 scorch, wither
07 blister, shrivel
09 dehydrate, desiccate

parched
03 dry
04 arid, sear, sere
05 baked
06 burned, seared
07 dried up, gasping, thirsty
08 scorched, withered
09 waterless
10 dehydrated, desiccated, dry as a bone, shrivelled

parchment
06 scroll, vellum
07 charter, diploma
08 document
10 palimpsest
11 certificate

pardon
05 mercy, remit
06 acquit, excuse, let off

07 absolve, amnesty, condone, forgive, release
08 clemency, lenience, liberate, overlook, reprieve
09 acquittal, discharge, exculpate, exonerate, vindicate
10 absolution, indulgence
11 forbearance, forgiveness
13 let off the hook

pardonable
06 venial
09 excusable
10 condonable, forgivable
11 justifiable

pare
04 peel, skin, trim
06 reduce
07 cut back, whittle
08 decrease

parent
03 dam
04 root, sire
05 beget, raise
06 author, create, father, foster, mother, origin, source
07 bring up, creator, nurture
08 begetter, guardian
09 look after, procreate
10 originator, procreator, progenitor, take care of

parentage
04 line, race
05 birth, stock
06 family, origin, source, stirps
07 descent, lineage
08 ancestry, pedigree
09 filiation, paternity
10 derivation, extraction

parenthetical
08 inserted
09 bracketed
10 incidental, interposed
11 intervening
13 in parenthesis

pariah
05 exile, leper
06 outlaw
07 Ishmael, outcast
08 castaway, unperson
11 undesirable, untouchable

paring
04 peel, rind, skin
05 flake, shred, slice
06 sliver
07 cutting, flaught, peeling, shaving, snippet
08 clipping, trimming

parish
04 fold, town
05 flock
06 church
07 village
08 district
09 community
11 churchgoers
12 congregation, parishioners

parity
03 par
07 analogy
08 affinity, equality
09 agreement, congruity
10 congruence, consonance
11 consistency, parallelism

park
03 put, set
04 stop
05 leave, place, plonk
07 deposit, grounds
08 position, woodland
09 grassland

parlance
04 cant, talk
05 argot, idiom, lingo
06 jargon, speech, tongue
11 phraseology

parley
04 talk
05 speak, talks
06 confab, confer, powwow
07 consult, council, discuss
08 colloquy, dialogue
09 negotiate, tête-à-tête
10 conference, discussion
11 negotiation

parliament
04 diet
05 house
06 senate
07 council
08 assembly, congress
10 lower house, upper house
11 convocation, legislature

➤ *Names of parliaments and political assemblies*:
04 Dáil, Diet, Duma
05 Forum, Lords
06 Cortes, Majlis, Senate, Soviet
07 Commons, Knesset, Riksdag, Tynwald
08 Assembly, Congress, Lok Sabha, Storting
09 Bundesrat, Bundestag, Directory, Eduskunta, Reichstag, State Duma
10 Convention, lower house, upper house

11 House of Keys, Star Chamber
12 House of Lords
13 Supreme Soviet
14 Council of State, Estates General, House of Commons, Long Parliament, Rump Parliament
15 People's Assembly, People's Congress
➤ See also **politics**

parliamentary
09 law-giving, law-making
10 democratic, republican, senatorial
11 legislative
12 governmental
13 congressional, legislatorial

parlour
06 lounge
09 front room
10 living-room
11 drawing-room, sitting-room

parochial
04 hick
06 narrow
07 insular, limited
09 blinkered, small-town
10 parish-pump, provincial
12 narrow-minded
13 inward-looking

parochialism
10 insularity, narrowness
13 provincialism

parody
04 skit
05 spoof
06 satire, send up, send-up
07 imitate, lampoon, take off
08 satirize, travesty
09 burlesque
10 caricature, distortion, pasquinade

paroxysm
05 spasm
07 seizure
10 convulsion

parrot
03 ape
04 copy, echo
05 mimic
06 repeat
07 copy-cat, imitate, phraser
08 imitator

parrot-fashion
06 by rote
10 mindlessly

parry
05 avert, avoid, block, evade, field
07 deflect, fend off, ward off
08 stave off
09 turn aside

parsimonious
04 mean
05 close, mingy, tight
06 frugal, stingy
07 miserly
09 niggardly, penurious
11 close-fisted, tight-fisted
12 cheese-paring
13 penny-pinching

parsimony
08 meanness
09 frugality, minginess, tightness
10 stinginess
11 miserliness
13 niggardliness, penny-pinching
15 tight-fistedness

parson
05 vicar
06 cleric, pastor, priest, rector
08 minister, preacher, reverend
09 churchman, clergyman

part
03 bit, job
04 area, book, duty, gift, half, role, side, tear, wing, work
05 break, chore, facet, piece, scrap, sever, share, skill, slice, split
06 aspect, branch, cleave, detach, divide, factor, module, office, region, volume
07 break up, chapter, disband, disjoin, diverge, element, excerpt, extract, faculty, limited, partial, portion, quarter, scatter, section, segment, split up
08 capacity, disperse, district, division, fraction, fragment, function, get going, particle, separate
09 character, come apart, component, dimension, dismantle, imperfect, take apart, territory
10 depart from, department, disconnect, go away from, ingredient, instalment, percentage, proportion, say goodbye
11 constituent, involvement, not complete

12 separate from
13 take your leave
14 accomplishment, responsibility

◻**for the most part**
06 mainly, mostly
09 in the main
10 by and large, on the whole

◻**in part**
06 partly
10 up to a point
12 to some degree, to some extent

◻**part with**
05 yield
06 forego, give up
07 discard, let go of
10 relinquish

◻**take part in**
06 join in
07 partake, share in
08 assist in, engage in, help with
12 be involved in, contribute to
13 participate in

partake
05 share
08 take part
10 be involved
11 participate

◻**partake of**
03 eat
05 drink, evoke, share
06 evince
07 consume, receive, suggest
11 demonstrate

partial
04 part
06 biased, in part, unfair, unjust
07 limited
08 coloured, one-sided, partisan
10 incomplete, prejudiced
11 inequitable, predisposed
14 discriminatory

◻**partial to**
06 fond of, keen on
09 taken with

partiality
04 bias
08 fondness, inequity
09 prejudice
10 preference, proclivity
11 inclination
12 partisanship, predilection
14 predisposition

partially
06 in part, partly
08 not fully, somewhat
12 incompletely

participant
05 party
06 helper, member, worker
07 entrant, partner
09 associate
10 competitor, contestant
11 contributor, shareholder

participate
05 enter, share
06 assist, engage, join in
07 partake
08 take part
09 co-operate, play a part
10 be involved, contribute

participation
09 partaking
11 co-operation, involvement, partnership
12 contribution

particle
03 bit, jot
04 atom, drop, iota, mite, whit
05 crumb, grain, shred, speck
06 morsel, tittle
07 smidgen
08 molecule

parti-coloured
06 motley
07 piebald
10 variegated
13 versicoloured

particular
04 fact, item
05 exact, fussy, picky, point
06 choosy, detail
07 certain, feature, finicky, precise, special
08 detailed, distinct, especial, exacting, peculiar, specific, thorough
10 fastidious, individual, meticulous, pernickety
11 painstaking
12 circumstance
14 discriminating

◻**in particular**
07 exactly
08 in detail
09 precisely
10 especially
12 particularly, specifically

particularity
04 fact, item
05 point, quirk, trait
06 detail
07 feature
08 instance, property
10 uniqueness
11 peculiarity, singularity
12 circumstance, idiosyncrasy

13 individuality
14 characteristic
15 distinctiveness

particularize
06 detail
07 itemize, specify
09 enumerate, stipulate
13 individualize

particularly
08 markedly
09 expressly, unusually
10 distinctly, especially, remarkably
12 specifically
13 exceptionally
15 extraordinarily

parting
05 adieu, dying, final, split
07 closing, goodbye, leaving, rupture
08 breaking, division, farewell
09 departing, departure
10 breaking-up, concluding, divergence, separation
11 leave-taking, valediction, valedictory

partisan
03 fan
06 backer, biased, unfair, votary
07 devotee, partial
08 adherent, one-sided, stalwart
09 factional, guerrilla, sectarian, supporter
10 prejudiced
14 freedom fighter

partisanship
04 bias
09 prejudice
10 partiality
12 factionalism, sectarianism

partition
04 wall
05 panel, share
06 divide, screen
07 barrier, break up, divider, parting, split up, wall off
08 divide up, division, separate
09 diaphragm, screen off, separator, subdivide
11 room-divider, separate off
12 dividing wall

partly
06 in part
07 a little
08 slightly, somewhat
09 partially
10 moderately, relatively, up to a point

12 incompletely, to some degree, to some extent
13 in some measure

partner
04 ally, mate, wife
06 friend, helper, spouse
07 comrade, consort, husband
08 co-worker, sidekick, team-mate
09 associate, boyfriend, colleague, companion, other half
10 accomplice, girlfriend
11 confederate

partnership
04 firm
05 union
07 company, society
08 alliance
09 syndicate
10 fellowship, fraternity
11 affiliation, association, brotherhood, corporation
13 confederation

party
04 band, body, camp, crew, gang, side, team, unit
05 group, squad
06 league, person
07 company, faction
08 alliance, grouping, litigant
09 defendant, gathering, plaintiff
10 contingent, detachment, individual
11 celebration, get-together

► *Types of party*:
02 do
03 hen
04 bash, rave, stag
05 beano, disco
06 dinner, garden, hooley
07 ceilidh
08 barbecue, birthday, cocktail
09 acid-house, beanfeast, Hallowe'en
11 discotheque
12 housewarming

parvenu
07 climber, new rich, upstart
09 arriviste, pretender
12 nouveau riche

pass
03 col, gap, lap, run
04 emit, fill, flow, hand, move, play, visa
05 enact, expel, occur, outdo, spend, throw
06 accept, become, befall, canyon, defile, elapse,

exceed, go past, happen, let out, occupy, permit, ratify, ravine, slip by, take up, ticket, travel
07 agree to, approve, excrete, licence, passage, proceed, qualify, release, run past, succeed, surpass, vote for
08 advances, go beyond, graduate, outstrip, overhaul, overtake, passport, progress, sanction, transfer, transmit, traverse
09 authorize, come about, discharge, drive past, get across, go through, take place, transpire, while away
10 get through, permission, suggestion
11 leave behind, make your way, outdistance, proposition, pull ahead of, sail through
13 authorization, breeze through, draw level with
14 be successful in, identification

❑**pass as, pass for**
10 be taken for
12 be regarded as
13 be mistaken for

❑**pass away**
03 die
06 expire, pass on, peg out, pop off
07 decease
13 kick the bucket
14 give up the ghost

❑**pass for** see **pass as**

❑**pass off**
05 feign, go off, occur
06 happen, vanish
07 die down, palm off, wear off
08 fade away
09 disappear, take place
11 counterfeit

❑**pass out**
05 faint, swoon
07 deal out, give out, hand out
08 allocate, black out, collapse, flake out, keel over
10 distribute

❑**pass over**
04 miss
06 forget, ignore
08 overlook
09 disregard

❑**pass up**
04 miss
06 ignore, refuse, reject
07 let slip, neglect

passable
02 OK
04 fair, so-so
05 clear
08 adequate, all right
09 navigable, tolerable
10 acceptable
11 traversable

passably
06 fairly
09 tolerably
10 moderately, reasonably

passage
03 way
04 duct, exit, flow, hall, lane, neck, path, road, text, trip
05 aisle, alley, flume, gully, lobby, route, track, verse
06 access, avenue, course, furrow, groove, gutter, strait, trough, voyage
07 channel, conduit, excerpt, extract, hallway, journey
08 citation, corridor, entrance, movement, progress, waterway
09 enactment, paragraph, vestibule
10 transition
11 safe conduct, watercourse
12 thoroughfare

passageway
04 hall, lane, path
05 aisle, alley, lobby
07 hallway, passage
08 corridor

passé
06 démodé, old hat
07 outworn
08 obsolete, outdated, outmoded
09 out-of-date
11 past its best
12 old-fashioned

passenger
04 fare
05 rider
07 voyager
08 commuter, hanger-on
09 fare-payer, traveller
10 freeloader, hitchhiker

passer-by
06 gawper
07 witness
08 looker-on, observer, onlooker
09 bystander, spectator
10 eyewitness, rubberneck

passing
03 end
05 brief, death, hasty, quick, short
06 casual, demise, slight
07 cursory, decease, quietus
09 departure, ephemeral, temporary, transient
10 incidental, short-lived
11 superficial, termination
12 transitional

❑**in passing**
07 by the by
08 by the bye, by the way
09 en passant
12 incidentally
15 parenthetically

passion
03 fit
04 fire, fury, heat, love, lust, rage, zeal, zest
05 anger, craze, mania, wrath
06 ardour, desire, spirit, temper
07 avidity, craving, emotion, feeling, fervour, tantrum
09 adoration, eagerness, intensity, obsession, vehemence
10 enthusiasm, fanaticism
11 infatuation
12 sexual desire

passionate
03 hot
04 avid, keen, sexy, wild
05 eager, fiery, randy
06 erotic, fierce, stormy, sultry
07 aroused, fervent, lustful, sensual, violent, zealous
08 frenzied, inflamed, turned on, vehement
09 emotional, excitable, fanatical, hot-headed, impetuous, impulsive
11 impassioned, tempestuous
12 enthusiastic
13 quick-tempered

passionless
04 calm, cold
06 frigid, frosty
07 callous
08 detached
09 apathetic, impassive, unfeeling
11 cold-blooded, cold-hearted, emotionless
13 dispassionate

passive
06 docile
07 patient, unmoved
08 inactive, lifeless, resigned

09 apathetic, compliant
10 non-violent, submissive
11 indifferent, unassertive

passport
02 ID
03 key, way
04 door, visa
05 entry, route
06 avenue, papers, permit
07 doorway
09 admission
12 identity card
13 authorization, laissez-passer, means of access
15 travel documents

password
03 key
04 word
06 parole, signal
09 watchword
10 open sesame, shibboleth

past
04 done, gone, last, late, life, over
05 early, ended, olden
06 bygone, former, gone by, latter, no more, recent
07 ancient, defunct, elapsed, extinct, history, long ago
08 finished, foregone, previous, sometime
09 antiquity, completed, erstwhile, foregoing, forgotten, olden days, preceding
10 background, bygone days, days gone by, days of yore, experience, olden times
11 bygone times, former times, good old days, track record
15 over and done with

pasta
➤ *Types of pasta*:
04 ziti
05 penne
06 noodle, trofie
07 fusilli, lasagna, lasagne, pennine, ravioli
08 bucatini, fedelini, linguini, macaroni, rigatoni, stelline
09 agnolotti, fiochetti, manicotti, spaghetti
10 angel's hair, bombolotti, cannelloni, conchiglie, farfalline, fettuccine, tagliarini, tortellini, vermicelli
11 tagliatelle
➤ See also **food**

paste
03 fix, gum, pap
04 glue, mush, pulp
05 blend, purée, putty, stick
06 cement, mastic
08 adhesive

pastel
04 pale, soft
05 chalk, faint, light, muted
06 crayon, low-key, subtle
07 subdued
08 delicate, pastille, soft-hued

pastiche
03 mix
06 jumble, medley
07 farrago, melange, mixture
08 mishmash, mixed bag
09 potpourri
10 assortment, collection, hodge-podge, hotchpotch, miscellany, salmagundi
11 gallimaufry, smorgasbord
14 conglomeration

pastille
05 sweet
06 jujube, pastel, tablet, troche
07 lozenge
09 cough drop
10 cough sweet

pastime
04 game, play
05 hobby, sport
08 activity
09 amusement, diversion
10 recreation, relaxation
13 entertainment
15 leisure activity

past master
03 ace
05 adept
06 artist, expert, wizard
07 dab hand, old hand
08 virtuoso

pastor
05 canon, vicar
06 cleric, divine, parson, priest, rector
08 minister
09 churchman, clergyman
10 prebendary
12 ecclesiastic

pastoral
05 rural
06 rustic, simple
07 bucolic, country, idyllic
08 agrarian, clerical, priestly
12 agricultural
14 ecclesiastical

pastry
➤ *Types of pastry:*
04 filo, puff
05 choux, flaky, short
06 Danish
09 rough-puff, suetcrust
10 flan pastry, shortcrust
12 biscuit-crumb
13 American crust, hot-water crust, pork-pie pastry
14 one-stage pastry
➤ See also **food**

pasture
05 field, grass
06 meadow
07 grazing, paddock
09 grassland, pasturage
11 grazing land

pasty
03 wan
04 pale
06 pallid, sallow, sickly
07 anaemic
09 unhealthy

pat
03 dab, pet, tap
04 clap, easy, glib, slap
05 ready, slick, touch
06 caress, facile, fluent, smooth
07 exactly
09 perfectly, precisely
10 flawlessly, simplistic
11 faultlessly

□ **pat someone on the back**
06 praise
10 compliment
12 congratulate

patch
03 bed, fix, lot, sew
04 area, mend, plot, spot, term, time
05 cloth, cover, phase, piece, spell, tract
06 parcel, period, repair, stitch
08 covering, material

patchwork
06 jumble, medley
07 farrago, mixture
08 mishmash, pastiche
10 hotchpotch

patchy
05 bitty
06 fitful, random, spotty, uneven
07 blotchy, erratic, sketchy
09 irregular
12 inconsistent

patent
04 open
05 clear, overt, plain, right
07 blatant, evident, glaring, licence, obvious
08 apparent, flagrant
09 copyright, invention, privilege
11 certificate, conspicuous, transparent, unequivocal

paternal
08 fatherly
10 benevolent, protective

path
03 way
04 lane, road, walk
05 route, track, trail
06 avenue, course
07 circuit, passage
08 approach
09 bridleway, direction

pathetic
03 sad
04 poor
05 sorry
06 dismal, feeble, meagre, moving, woeful
07 pitiful, useless
08 derisory, pitiable, poignant, touching, wretched
09 affecting, miserable, plaintive, worthless
10 deplorable, inadequate, lamentable
12 heart-rending
13 heartbreaking

pathological
07 chronic
08 addicted, habitual, hardened
09 confirmed, obsessive
10 compulsive, inveterate

pathos
06 misery
07 sadness
09 poignancy
11 pitifulness

patience
04 cool
08 calmness, serenity, stoicism
09 composure, diligence, endurance, tolerance
10 doggedness, equanimity
11 forbearance, self-control
12 perseverance, tranquillity
13 long-suffering

patient
04 calm, case, cool, mild
06 serene
07 invalid, lenient, stoical
08 composed, sufferer, tolerant

09 forgiving
10 forbearing
11 persevering
12 even-tempered
13 imperturbable, long-suffering, philosophical, uncomplaining
14 hanging in there

patois
04 cant
05 argot, lingo, slang
06 jargon, patter
07 dialect
10 vernacular
12 lingua franca
13 local parlance

patriarch
04 sire
05 elder
06 father
07 founder
09 greybeard
11 grand old man, grandfather
13 paterfamilias

patrician
04 peer
05 noble
06 lordly
07 grandee
08 high-born, nobleman
09 gentleman, high-class
10 aristocrat
11 blue-blooded
12 aristocratic, thoroughbred

patrimony
06 estate, legacy
07 bequest, portion
08 heritage, property
10 birthright
11 inheritance, possessions

patriot
08 jingoist, loyalist
09 flag-waver
10 chauvinist
11 nationalist

patriotic
05 loyal
08 loyalist
10 flag-waving, jingoistic
11 nationalist
12 chauvinistic
13 nationalistic

patriotism
07 loyalty
08 jingoism
10 chauvinism, flag-waving
11 nationalism

patrol
04 beat, tour

05 guard, round, vigil, watch
06 police, sentry
07 inspect, monitor
08 policing, sentinel, watchman
11 be on the beat, do the rounds, go the rounds, keep guard on, keep watch on
13 keep watch over, make the rounds, night-watchman, police officer, security guard

patron
05 angel, buyer
06 backer, client, helper
07 regular, shopper, sponsor
08 advocate, champion, customer, guardian, promoter
09 purchaser, supporter
10 benefactor
13 guardian angel
14 fairy godmother

patronage
05 trade
06 buying, custom
07 backing, funding, support
08 business
11 sponsorship
12 subscription

patronize
03 aid
04 back, fund, help
06 assist, foster, shop at
07 buy from, finance, promote, sponsor, support
08 deal with, frequent
10 look down on, talk down to
12 be a regular at

patronizing
05 lofty
06 snooty
07 haughty, stuck up
08 superior
10 high-handed
12 supercilious
13 condescending, high-and-mighty

patter
03 pat, tap, yak
04 beat, drum, line, pelt, trip
05 lingo, pitch, spiel
06 jargon, scurry
07 chatter, scuttle, tapping
09 monologue

pattern
04 copy, form, norm, plan, trim
05 guide, ideal, match, model, motif, mould, order, shape, style

06 design, device, figure, follow, method, sample, swatch, system
07 emulate, example, imitate
08 decorate, markings, original, standard, template
09 blueprint, prototype
10 decoration
11 arrangement, instruction
13 ornamentation

patterned
05 moiré
07 figured, printed, watered
09 decorated
10 ornamented

paucity
04 lack, want
06 dearth
07 fewness, poverty
08 scarcity, shortage, sparsity
09 smallness
10 meagreness, paltriness, scantiness, sparseness

paunch
05 belly
07 abdomen
08 pot-belly
09 beer-belly

paunchy
03 fat
05 podgy, pudgy, tubby
06 portly, rotund
09 corpulent
10 pot-bellied

pauper
06 beggar
07 have-not
08 bankrupt, indigent
09 insolvent, mendicant
10 down-and-out
11 church-mouse

pause
03 gap
04 halt, lull, rest, stay, stop, wait
05 break, cease, delay, let up
06 desist
07 adjourn, respite, time out
08 break off, breather, hesitate, hold back, interval, stoppage, take five
09 cessation, interlude, interrupt
10 hesitation
11 discontinue
12 intermission, interruption
14 breathing space

pave
03 tar
04 flag, tile

05 cover, floor
06 tarmac
07 asphalt, surface
08 concrete
10 macadamize

◻**pave the way for**
08 lead up to
09 introduce, take steps
10 prepare for
11 get ready for
12 make ready for
14 clear the ground

pavement
04 path
07 footway
08 causeway, footpath, sidewalk

paw
03 pad
04 foot, hand, maul
05 touch
06 molest, stroke
07 touch up
09 manhandle, mishandle

pawn
04 dupe, hock, tool
06 pledge, puppet, stooge
07 cat's paw, deposit
08 mortgage
09 plaything
10 instrument
11 impignorate
13 lay in lavender

pawnbroker
05 uncle
06 lender, usurer
08 pawnshop

pay
03 fee
05 atone, remit, spend, wages
06 expend, income, invest, lay out, outlay, profit, rake in, refund, return, reward, salary, settle
07 benefit, bring in, cough up, fork out, produce, stipend
08 disburse, earnings, hand over, settle up, shell out
09 discharge, reimburse
10 commission, compensate, emoluments, honorarium, make amends, remunerate
11 foot the bill
12 compensation, pick up the tab, remuneration
13 meet the cost of, reimbursement

◻**pay back**
05 repay

06 pay off, punish, refund, settle, square
09 reimburse, retaliate
11 get even with, take revenge
13 counter-attack
14 get your own back

◻**pay for**
05 atone
09 answer for
10 compensate, cost dearly, make amends
12 face the music
13 be punished for
14 count the cost of, get your deserts

◻**pay off**
04 fire, sack
05 bribe, clear, repay
06 buy off, grease, lay off, settle, square
07 dismiss
09 discharge, pay in full
10 get results
12 be successful
13 make redundant

◻**pay out**
05 remit, spend
06 lay out
07 fork out
08 disburse, hand over, part with, shell out

payable
03 due
04 owed
05 owing
06 unpaid
11 outstanding

payment
03 fee, pay
04 fare, hire, toll
06 outlay, reward
07 advance, deposit, premium
08 donation
10 instalment, remittance, settlement
12 contribution, remuneration

pay-off
05 bribe
06 result, reward
07 benefit, outcome
09 hush money, slush fund, sweetener
10 back-hander, inducement
11 consequence
13 moment of truth
15 protection money

peace
04 calm, hush, rest
05 amity, quiet, still
06 accord, repose

07 concord, harmony, silence
08 calmness, serenity
09 agreement, armistice, cease-fire, quietness, stillness
10 relaxation
11 non-violence, restfulness
12 amicableness, tranquillity
13 non-aggression

peaceable
04 mild
06 gentle, irenic, placid
07 pacific
08 amicable, friendly
09 unwarlike
10 non-violent
11 inoffensive, peace-loving
12 conciliatory
13 non-aggressive

peaceful
04 calm
05 quiet, still
06 gentle, placid, serene, sleepy
07 pacific, restful
08 in repose, tranquil
09 peaceable, unruffled
11 undisturbed

peacemaker
08 appeaser, pacifier, pacifist
11 conciliator, peace-monger

peacemaking
06 irenic
07 pacific
08 irenical
09 appeasing
12 conciliatory

peak
03 tip, top
04 apex, hill
05 crest, crown, mount, point
06 apogee, climax, summit, zenith
07 maximum
08 mountain, pinnacle
09 culminate, elevation, high point
11 come to a head

peaky
03 ill, wan
04 pale, sick
06 pallid, poorly, sickly, unwell
09 off-colour, washed-out
15 under the weather

peal
04 boom, clap, ring, roll, toll
05 chime, clang, knell
06 rumble
07 resound, ring out, ringing
08 carillon, resonate
11 reverberate

peasant
03 oaf
04 boor, lout
05 churl, yokel
06 rustic
08 bumpkin
10 provincial
14 country bumpkin

pebble
04 chip
05 agate, stone
06 gallet

peccadillo
05 error, fault, lapse
07 misdeed
10 infraction
11 delinquency
12 indiscretion, minor offence, misdemeanour

peck
03 hit, jab, nip, rap, tap
04 bite, kiss

peculiar
03 odd
05 droll, funny, queer, weird
06 quaint, way-out
07 bizarre, curious, offbeat, strange, unusual
08 abnormal, distinct, freakish, singular, specific
09 eccentric
10 individual, outlandish, particular
11 distinctive
13 idiosyncratic
14 characteristic, unconventional
15 individualistic

❑peculiar to
08 unique to
09 typical of

peculiarity
04 mark
05 quirk, trait
06 foible, oddity
08 hallmark
09 mannerism, weirdness
11 abnormality, bizarreness
12 eccentricity, idiosyncrasy
14 characteristic

pecuniary
06 fiscal
08 monetary
09 financial

pedagogic
08 academic, didactic, teaching
09 tuitional
11 educational
13 instructional

pedagogue
06 master, pedant
07 dominie, teacher
08 educator, mistress
09 dogmatist, preceptor
10 instructor
12 educationist, schoolmaster
14 educationalist, schoolmistress

pedagogy
07 tuition
08 teaching, training, tutelage
09 didactics
10 pedagogics

pedant
06 purist
07 casuist
08 quibbler
09 dogmatist, nit-picker
10 literalist, scholastic
11 pettifogger
12 hair-splitter, precisionist

pedantic
05 exact, fussy
06 purist, stuffy
07 bookish, erudite, finical, pompous, precise, stilted
09 quibbling
10 literalist, meticulous, nit-picking, particular, scrupulous
13 hair-splitting, perfectionist

pedantry
09 cavilling, exactness, quibbling
10 finicality, nit-picking
13 hair-splitting
14 meticulousness
15 punctiliousness

peddle
04 flog, hawk, push, sell, tout, vend
05 trade
06 market
07 traffic
12 offer for sale

pedestal
04 base, foot
05 stand
06 column, pillar, plinth, podium
07 support
08 mounting, platform
10 foundation

❑put on a pedestal
05 exalt
06 admire, revere
07 adulate, idolize
11 hero-worship

pedestrian
04 dull, flat
05 banal
06 boring, turgid, walker
07 humdrum, mundane, prosaic
08 mediocre, plodding
11 commonplace
13 foot-traveller

pedigree
04 line, race
05 blood, breed, stock
06 family, stirps, strain
07 descent, lineage
08 ancestry, pedigree, pure-bred
09 genealogy, parentage
10 derivation, extraction, family tree
11 full-blooded
12 aristocratic, thoroughbred

pedlar
06 hawker, seller, vendor
07 chapman
08 huckster
09 cheap-jack
10 colporteur
12 street-trader

peek
03 spy
04 look, peep, peer
05 blink, dekko
06 gander, glance, shufti
07 glimpse, look-see

peel
04 pare, rind, skin, zest
05 flake, scale, strip
06 remove
07 epicarp, exocarp, take off
08 flake off
10 desquamate, integument
11 decorticate

❑keep your eyes peeled
07 be alert
12 watch closely
15 keep a lookout for

peep
04 look, peek, peer, pipe, word
05 cheep, dekko, sound, tweet
06 emerge, gander, glance, shufti, squeak, squint
07 chirrup, look-see, twitter

peephole
05 chink, cleft, crack
07 keyhole, pinhole, spyhole
09 Judas-hole

peer
04 duke, earl, gaze, look, lord, peep, scan

peerage
05 baron, count, equal, noble
06 fellow, squint
07 examine, inspect, marquis
08 confrère, marquess, nobleman, viscount
10 aristocrat, scrutinize
11 counterpart

peerage
08 nobility
09 top drawer
10 upper crust
11 aristocracy

peeress
04 dame, lady
05 noble
07 duchess
08 baroness, countess
10 aristocrat, noblewoman
11 marchioness, viscountess

peerless
06 unique
09 matchless, nonpareil, unmatched
10 unequalled, unrivalled
11 unsurpassed
12 incomparable, second to none, unparalleled, without equal
13 beyond compare

peeve
03 irk, vex
04 gall
05 annoy
10 exasperate
14 drive up the wall

peeved
05 irked, riled, upset, vexed
06 galled, miffed, narked, piqued, put out
07 annoyed, in a huff, nettled
10 got the hump

peevish
05 cross, moody, ratty, sulky, surly, testy
06 crusty, grumpy, snappy, sullen, tetchy, touchy
07 crabbed, fretful
08 churlish, petulant
09 crotchety, fractious, querulous
10 in a bad mood
11 complaining, ill-tempered
12 cantankerous

peevishness
05 pique
09 petulance, testiness
12 captiousness
13 querulousness

peg
03 fix, pin, set
04 brad, hook, join, knob, mark, nail, post
05 dowel, limit, screw, spike, stake
06 attach, fasten, freeze, marker, secure
07 control
09 stabilize

◻**peg away**
07 persist
08 keep at it, plug away,
09 persevere, stick at it
10 beaver away

◻**take down a peg or two, bring down a peg or two**
09 humiliate
13 cut down to size
15 bring down to size

pejorative
08 negative
09 slighting
10 belittling, derogatory
11 deprecatory, disparaging
12 unflattering
15 uncomplimentary

pellet
04 ball, drop, pill, shot, slug
06 bullet
07 capsule, lozenge

pell-mell
07 hastily
09 hurriedly, posthaste
10 at full tilt, feverishly, heedlessly, recklessly
11 hurry-scurry, impetuously
13 helter-skelter, precipitously

pellucid
04 pure
05 clear
06 bright, glassy, limpid
11 translucent, transparent

pelt
03 fur, hit, run
04 beat, belt, coat, dash, fell, hide, hurl, pour, race, rush, skin, tear, teem
05 hurry, speed, throw
06 assail, attack, batter, bucket, career, charge, fleece, shower, sprint, strike
07 bombard
10 bucket down
15 rain cats and dogs

pen
03 mew, sty
04 Biro®, cage, coop, fold, shut

05 draft, fence, hedge, hem in, hutch, pound, stall, write
06 corral, shut up
07 compose, confine, enclose, felt-tip, jot down
08 compound, scribble
09 ballpoint, enclosure

penal
08 punitive
10 corrective
11 retributive
12 disciplinary

penalize
04 fine
06 punish
07 correct
08 chastise, handicap
09 castigate
10 discipline
12 disadvantage

penal servitude
03 lag
04 bird, time
07 stretch
08 porridge
10 hard labour

penalty
04 fine, snag
05 mulct
07 forfeit
08 handicap, sentence
10 punishment
12 disadvantage

penance
09 atonement
10 punishment, reparation
13 mortification

penchant
04 bent, bias
05 taste
06 liking
07 leaning
08 affinity, fondness, soft spot, tendency, weakness
10 partiality, preference, proclivity, propensity
11 disposition, inclination
12 predilection

pendant
06 locket
08 necklace
09 medallion

pendent
06 nutant
07 hanging, pensile
08 dangling, drooping, swinging
09 pendulous, suspended

pending
04 near, till
05 until, while
06 before, coming, whilst
08 imminent
09 impending
10 throughout, up in the air
11 approaching, forthcoming, in the offing
12 in the balance

pendulous
07 hanging, pendent, sagging, swaying
08 dangling, drooping, swinging

penetrable
06 porous
08 passable, pervious
09 permeable
10 accessible, fathomable
14 comprehensible, understandable

penetrate
03 see
04 bore, seep, sink, stab
05 crack, enter, grasp, imbue, prick, probe, spike
06 fathom, pierce, sink in
07 get into, make out, pervade, suffuse, work out
08 cotton on, permeate, puncture, register, saturate
09 perforate
10 comprehend, infiltrate, understand

penetrating
04 deep, keen, loud, wise
05 acute, clear, sharp
06 biting, shrewd, shrill
07 probing
08 carrying, incisive, piercing, profound, stinging, strident
09 observant, searching
10 discerning, perceptive

penetration
03 wit
05 entry
06 acumen, inroad
07 insight
08 entrance, incision, invasion, keenness, piercing, pricking, stabbing
09 acuteness, pervasion, sharpness
10 astuteness, perception, permeation, puncturing
11 discernment, perforation
12 infiltration, perspicacity

peninsula
04 cape, doab, mull

05 point
06 tongue
10 chersonese

penis
04 cock, dick, knob, tool
05 prick, willy
06 pecker, winkle
07 phallus
13 membrum virile

penitence
05 shame
06 regret, sorrow
07 remorse
10 contrition, repentance
11 compunction
12 self-reproach

penitent
05 sorry
07 ashamed
08 contrite
09 regretful, repentant
10 apologetic, remorseful

pen-name
07 allonym
09 false name, pseudonym
10 nom de plume
11 assumed name

pennant
04 flag, jack
06 banner, ensign
07 colours
08 banderol, gonfalon, standard, streamer

penniless
04 bust, poor
05 broke, skint
08 indigent
09 destitute
10 cleaned out, down and out, stony-broke
12 impoverished
14 on the breadline, on your beam-ends
15 poverty-stricken, strapped for cash

penny-pincher
05 miser
06 meanie
07 niggard, Scrooge
09 skinflint
10 cheapskate
11 cheeseparer
12 money-grubber

penny-pinching
04 mean
05 close, mingy
06 frugal, stingy
07 miserly
09 niggardly, scrimping

11 tight-fisted
12 cheeseparing, parsimonious

pension
06 income
07 annuity, benefit, support, welfare
09 allowance
14 superannuation

pensioner
13 retired person, senior citizen
15 old-age pensioner

pensive
06 dreamy, musing, solemn
07 serious, wistful
08 absorbed, thinking
09 pondering
10 cogitative, meditative, ruminative, thoughtful
11 preoccupied
13 contemplative

pent-up
06 curbed, held in
09 bottled-up, inhibited, repressed
10 restrained, suppressed

penurious
04 bust, mean, poor
05 close, tight
06 hard up, stingy
07 miserly
08 beggarly, grudging, indigent
09 destitute, flat broke, niggardly, penniless
11 close-fisted, impecunious, tight-fisted
12 cheeseparing, impoverished, parsimonious
15 poverty-stricken

penury
07 beggary, poverty, straits
09 indigence, pauperism
11 destitution
14 impoverishment

people
04 clan, folk, race
05 folks, tribe
06 family, humans, nation, occupy, public, settle
07 inhabit, mankind, mortals, parents, persons, society
08 citizens, colonize, humanity, populace, populate
09 community, humankind, relations, relatives
10 electorate, kith and kin, population
11 human beings, individuals
12 the human race
13 general public

pep
05 verve
06 energy, spirit, vigour
07 sparkle
08 vitality
10 ebullience, exuberance, get-up-and-go, liveliness
11 high spirits
13 effervescence

❑**pep up**
07 inspire, liven up
08 energize, vitalize
09 stimulate
10 exhilarate, invigorate

pepper
03 dot
04 pelt
05 blitz, strew
06 shower
07 bombard, scatter, spatter
08 sprinkle
09 bespatter

peppery
03 hot
05 fiery, sharp, spicy, testy
06 biting, grumpy, touchy
07 caustic, piquant, pungent
08 seasoned, stinging
09 irascible, sarcastic, trenchant

perceive
03 see
04 espy, feel, know, note, spot, view
05 grasp, learn, sense
06 detect, notice, remark
07 discern, glimpse, make out, observe, realize
09 apprehend, be aware of, recognize
10 appreciate, comprehend, understand
11 distinguish
12 catch sight of
13 be cognizant of

perceptible
05 clear, plain
06 patent
07 evident, obvious, visible
08 apparent, distinct, tangible
10 detectable, noticeable, observable
11 appreciable, conspicuous, discernible

perception
04 idea, view
05 grasp, sense
07 feeling, insight
09 awareness, knowledge
10 cognizance, conception, impression
11 discernment, observation
13 consciousness, understanding

perceptive
04 keen
05 alert, aware, quick, sharp
06 astute, shrewd
09 observant, sharp-eyed
10 discerning
13 perspicacious

perch
04 land, rest
05 roost
06 alight, settle
07 balance

perchance
05 maybe
07 perhaps
08 feasibly, possibly

percipience
07 insight
09 awareness, intuition, judgement
10 astuteness, perception
11 discernment, penetration
12 perspicacity

percipient
05 alert, alive, aware, sharp
06 astute
09 observant, wide-awake
10 discerning, perceptive
11 penetrating
13 perspicacious
14 discriminating

percolate
04 drip, leak, ooze, seep
05 drain, leach, sieve
06 filter, strain
14 trickle through

perdition
04 doom, hell, ruin
08 downfall, hellfire
09 damnation, ruination
12 annihilation

peregrination
04 tour, trek, trip
06 roving, travel, voyage
07 journey, odyssey, roaming
09 wandering, wayfaring
10 expedition, travelling

peremptory
04 curt
06 abrupt, lordly
07 summary
08 absolute, dogmatic
09 arbitrary, imperious
10 autocratic, commanding, high-handed, tyrannical
11 dictatorial, domineering, irrefutable, overbearing

perennial
07 lasting, undying
08 enduring, immortal
09 perpetual, unceasing
11 everlasting, never-ending

perfect
04 pure, true
05 exact, ideal, model, right, sheer, total, utter
06 better, entire, expert, finish, fulfil, polish, refine, superb
07 correct, improve, precise, sinless, skilful
08 absolute, accurate, complete, faithful, flawless, peerless, spotless, textbook, thorough, ultimate, unmarred
09 downright, excellent, exemplary, faultless, matchless, out and out, wonderful
10 consummate, immaculate, impeccable, just the job
11 superlative, unblemished

perfection
04 acme
05 crown, ideal, model
07 paragon
08 pinnacle, ultimate
10 excellence, refinement
11 improvement, ne plus ultra
12 consummation, flawlessness
13 faultlessness, impeccability, one in a million
14 immaculateness

perfectionist
06 pedant, purist
08 idealist, stickler

perfectly
05 fully, quite
06 wholly
07 exactly, ideally, totally, utterly
08 entirely, superbly
10 absolutely, altogether, completely, flawlessly, impeccably, thoroughly
11 faultlessly, wonderfully
12 immaculately, to perfection
14 without blemish

perfidious
05 false, Punic
08 disloyal, two-faced
09 deceitful, dishonest, faithless

10 traitorous, treasonous,
   unfaithful
11 double-faced, duplicitous,
   treacherous
13 double-dealing,
   Machiavellian,
   untrustworthy

perfidy
06 deceit
07 falsity, treason
08 betrayal
09 duplicity, treachery
10 disloyalty, infidelity
13 double-dealing,
   faithlessness
14 perfidiousness,
   traitorousness

perforate
04 bore, gore, hole, stab, tear
05 burst, drill, prick, punch,
   spike, split
06 pierce
07 rupture
08 puncture
11 make holes in

perforated
06 porous
07 drilled, pierced
09 punctured

perforation
04 hole
05 prick
07 foramen
08 puncture
10 dotted line

perforce
10 inevitably, willy-nilly
11 necessarily, of necessity,
   unavoidably

perform
02 do, go
03 act, run
04 play, work
05 enact, put on, stage
06 behave, effect, fulfil
07 conduct, execute, produce,
   pull off
08 bring off, carry out,
   complete, function
09 discharge, represent
10 accomplish, bring about

performance
04 show
06 acting, action
07 conduct
09 behaviour, discharge,
   execution, portrayal
10 appearance, conducting,
   fulfilment, production

11 carrying out, functioning
12 presentation
14 interpretation,
   representation

performer
04 doer
05 actor, clown, comic
06 author, dancer, player, singer
07 actress, artiste, trouper
08 comedian, executor,
   musician, Thespian
11 entertainer

perfume
04 balm
05 aroma, odour, scent, smell
07 bouquet, cologne, essence,
   incense
09 fragrance
11 toilet water
12 eau-de-cologne
13 eau-de-toilette

perfunctory
05 brief
07 cursory, hurried, offhand,
   quickly
08 slipshod, slovenly
10 mechanical

perhaps
05 maybe
08 feasibly, possibly
09 perchance
11 conceivably

peril
04 risk
06 danger, hazard, menace,
   threat
08 jeopardy

perilous
04 dire
05 risky
06 chancy, unsafe, unsure
09 dangerous, hazardous
10 precarious, vulnerable

perimeter
04 edge
05 limit
06 border, bounds, fringe,
   limits, margin
08 boundary, confines, frontier
09 periphery
11 outer limits

period
03 age, end, eon, era
04 date, span, stop, term, time,
   turn
05 class, cycle, epoch, phase,
   point, shift, space, spell,
   stage, stint, while, years

06 finish, lesson, menses,
   season
07 session, stretch
08 duration, full stop, interval,
   the curse
09 full point, monthlies
12 menstruation

periodic
06 cyclic
08 cyclical, seasonal
09 recurrent, recurring
10 infrequent, occasional
12 intermittent, once in a while

periodical
06 review, weekly
07 journal, monthly
08 magazine
09 quarterly

peripatetic
06 mobile, roving
07 migrant, nomadic, roaming
09 itinerant, migratory,
   wandering
10 ambulatory, journeying,
   travelling

peripheral
05 minor, outer
06 lesser
08 marginal, outlying
09 ancillary, outermost
10 borderline, incidental,
   irrelevant, subsidiary
11 surrounding
14 beside the point

periphery
03 hem, rim
04 brim, edge
05 ambit, brink, skirt, verge
06 border, fringe, margin
07 circuit
08 boundary
09 outskirts, perimeter

periphrastic
07 oblique
08 indirect, rambling, tortuous
10 circuitous, discursive,
   roundabout
14 circumlocutory

perish
03 die, rot
04 fail, fall
05 decay, go off
06 depart, expire, peg out, pop
   off, vanish
07 crumble, die away
08 collapse, pass away
09 decompose, disappear,
   have had it

11 bite the dust, come to an end
12 disintegrate, lose your life
13 kick the bucket
15 breathe your last

perishable
10 short-lived
13 biodegradable

perjure

□ **perjure yourself**
03 lie
13 commit perjury

perjury
12 false witness
13 false evidence
14 false testimony

perk
03 tip
05 bonus, extra
07 benefit, freebie
10 perquisite
13 fringe benefit
15 golden handshake

□ **perk up**
05 pep up, rally
06 buck up, look up, revive
07 cheer up, liven up, recover
08 brighten
09 take heart
10 brighten up

perky
05 peppy, sunny
06 bouncy, bright, bubbly, cheery, jaunty, lively
09 ebullient, sprightly, vivacious

permanence
09 endurance, stability
10 durability, perpetuity
11 persistence
15 imperishability

permanent
05 fixed
06 stable
07 durable, eternal, lasting
08 constant, enduring
09 indelible, perennial, perpetual
10 invariable, unchanging
11 established, everlasting, long-lasting
12 imperishable, unchangeable
14 indestructible

permanently
06 always
07 for ever
08 ever more, for keeps
09 endlessly, eternally, indelibly
10 for all time, unendingly

11 continually, perpetually
12 in perpetuity, till doomsday
14 for ever and ever
15 till kingdom come

permeable
06 porous, spongy
09 absorbent
10 absorptive, penetrable

permeate
04 fill
05 imbue
07 diffuse, pervade
08 saturate
09 penetrate, percolate
10 impregnate, infiltrate
11 seep through, soak through
13 spread through

permissible
02 OK
06 kosher, lawful, proper
07 allowed
08 all right
09 allowable, permitted, tolerable
10 acceptable, admissible, legitimate, sanctioned

permission
05 leave
06 assent, permit
07 consent, go-ahead, licence, warrant
08 approval, sanction, thumbs up
09 agreement, clearance
10 green light
11 approbation
12 dispensation
13 authorization

permissive
03 lax
07 lenient, liberal
08 tolerant
09 easy-going, indulgent
10 forbearing
11 broad-minded
14 latitudinarian

permit
03 let
04 pass, visa
05 admit, agree, allow, grant
07 consent, licence, license, warrant
08 passport, sanction
09 authorize
12 give the nod to
13 authorization

permutation
06 change
09 variation

10 alteration
11 commutation
13 transmutation
14 transformation

pernicious
03 bad
04 evil
05 fatal, toxic
06 deadly, wicked
07 harmful, noxious
08 damaging
09 injurious, malignant, pestilent, poisonous
10 maleficent
11 deleterious, destructive, detrimental, unwholesome

pernickety
04 nice
05 fussy, picky
06 choosy, fiddly, tricky
07 carping, finical, finicky
08 detailed, exacting
10 fastidious, nit-picking
11 over-precise, punctilious
13 hair-splitting
14 over-particular

peroration
04 talk
06 speech
07 address, lecture, summary
08 diatribe
09 recapping, summing-up
10 conclusion
11 declamation, reiteration
14 closing remarks, recapitulation

perpendicular
05 erect, plumb, sheer, steep
07 upright
08 straight, vertical
13 at right angles

perpetrate
02 do
05 wreak
06 commit, effect
07 execute, inflict, perform
08 carry out

perpetual
07 abiding, endless, eternal, lasting, undying
08 constant, enduring, infinite, unending
09 ceaseless, continual, incessant, perennial, recurrent, unceasing, unfailing
10 continuous, persistent
11 everlasting, never-ending

perpetually
09 endlessly, eternally
10 constantly
11 ceaselessly, continually, incessantly, unceasingly
12 persistently

perpetuate
06 keep up
07 sustain
08 continue, maintain
09 keep alive, keep going
11 immortalize, memorialize

perpetuity

◻**in perpetuity**
06 always
07 for ever
08 ever more
09 endlessly, eternally
10 for all time
11 perpetually
14 for ever and ever

perplex
06 baffle, muddle, puzzle
07 confuse, mystify, nonplus
08 bewilder, confound
09 bamboozle, dumbfound

perplexed
07 at a loss, baffled, muddled, puzzled
08 confused
09 mystified
10 bamboozled, bewildered, confounded, nonplussed

perplexing
06 knotty, taxing, thorny
07 amazing, complex, strange
08 baffling, involved, puzzling
09 enigmatic, intricate
10 mysterious, mystifying
11 bewildering, complicated, paradoxical

perplexity
06 puzzle
07 dilemma, mystery, paradox
09 intricacy, labyrinth
10 complexity, puzzlement
12 bewilderment, complication
13 mystification
15 incomprehension

perquisite
03 tip
04 perk, plus
05 bonus, extra
07 benefit, freebie
08 dividend, gratuity
13 fringe benefit

persecute
05 abuse, annoy, hound, worry

06 badger, harass, hassle, martyr, pester, pursue
07 oppress, torment, torture
09 tyrannize, victimize

persecution
05 abuse
07 torture, tyranny
09 martyrdom
10 harassment, oppression
11 subjugation, suppression
13 victimization
14 discrimination

perseverance
07 resolve, stamina
08 tenacity
09 constancy, diligence, endurance
10 doggedness, resolution
11 persistence
12 stickability
13 determination

persevere
04 go on
06 hang on, hold on, remain
07 carry on, persist
08 continue, plug away
09 keep going, soldier on
11 hang in there
12 be persistent
15 stick to your guns

persist
04 go on, hold, last
05 abide
06 endure, hang on, hold on, insist, keep on, linger, remain
07 carry on
08 continue, keep at it
09 keep going, persevere, stand fast, stand firm
12 be determined, be persistent

persistence
04 grit
07 stamina
08 sedulity, tenacity
09 constancy, endurance
10 doggedness, resolution
11 pertinacity
12 perseverance, stickability
13 determination, steadfastness

persistent
06 dogged, steady
07 endless, lasting, zealous
08 constant, enduring, obdurate, resolute, tireless
09 assiduous, continual, incessant, obstinate, perpetual, steadfast, tenacious

10 determined, relentless, unflagging
11 never-ending, persevering, unrelenting, unremitting
12 interminable, pertinacious

person
03 man
04 body, soul, type
05 being, human, woman
06 mortal
07 someone
08 somebody
09 character
10 human being, individual

◻**in person**
10 face to face, in the flesh
13 as large as life

persona
04 face, mask, part, role
05 front, image
06 façade
09 character
10 public face
11 personality

personable
07 affable, amiable, winning
08 charming, handsome, likeable, pleasant
10 attractive
11 good-looking, presentable

personage
03 VIP
04 name
06 bigwig, worthy
07 big shot, notable
08 big noise, luminary
09 celebrity, dignitary
11 personality
12 public figure

personal
03 own
06 secret, unique
07 abusive, hurtful, private
08 critical, in person, intimate, peculiar, wounding
09 exclusive, offensive
10 individual, particular, subjective
12 confidential
14 characteristic

personality
03 VIP
04 star
05 charm
06 make-up, temper, worthy
08 charisma
09 celebrity, character, dignitary, magnetism
11 disposition, temperament

personally
05 alone
06 solely
08 in person
09 privately
11 exclusively
12 individually, particularly, subjectively
14 confidentially

personification
05 image
07 essence
08 likeness
09 portrayal, semblance
10 embodiment
11 incarnation
13 manifestation

personify
06 embody, mirror, typify
09 epitomize, exemplify, represent, symbolize

personnel
04 crew
05 staff
06 people
07 members, workers
08 liveware, manpower
09 employees, workforce
11 labour force
14 human resources

perspective
04 view
05 angle, scene, slant, vista
06 aspect
07 outlook
08 attitude, prospect, relation
09 viewpoint
10 proportion, standpoint
11 frame of mind, point of view
12 vantage point

perspicacious
05 alert, aware, quick, sharp
06 astute, shrewd
09 observant, sagacious, sharp-eyed
10 discerning, percipient
11 penetrating
14 discriminating

perspicacity
06 acumen, brains
07 insight
09 acuteness, sharpness
10 astuteness, shrewdness
11 discernment, penetration
14 discrimination

perspicuity
07 clarity
08 lucidity
09 clearness, plainness

12 distinctness, transparency
13 penetrability

perspicuous
05 clear, lucid, plain
07 obvious
08 apparent, distinct
11 self-evident, transparent, unambiguous
12 crystal-clear
14 comprehensible
15 straightforward

perspiration
05 sudor, sweat
08 hidrosis
09 exudation, secretion
11 diaphoresis

perspire
04 drip
05 sweat
06 sudate
07 secrete, swelter

persuadable
07 pliable
08 amenable, flexible
09 malleable, receptive
10 susceptive

persuade
04 coax, lure, sway, urge
05 lobby, tempt
06 cajole, coerce, induce, lead on, lean on
07 satisfy, wheedle, win over
08 convince, inveigle, soft-soap, talk into
09 influence, sweet-talk
10 bring round
11 prevail upon

persuasion
04 pull, sect, side, sway, view
05 clout, faith, party, power
06 belief, school, urging
07 coaxing, faction, opinion
08 cajolery, coercion
09 influence, prompting, viewpoint, wheedling
10 conviction, inducement, philosophy
11 affiliation, arm-twisting, point of view, winning over
12 denomination
15 school of thought

persuasive
05 pushy, slick
06 cogent
07 weighty
08 forceful
09 effective, effectual, plausible
10 compelling, convincing
13 smooth-talking

pert
04 bold
05 brash, brisk, cocky, fresh, perky, saucy, tossy
06 cheeky, daring, jaunty, lively
07 forward
08 impudent, spirited
11 impertinent
12 presumptuous

pertain
05 apply, befit, refer
06 bear on, belong, relate
07 concern
09 appertain
10 be relevant
14 have a bearing on

pertinacious
06 dogged, mulish, wilful
08 obdurate, perverse, resolute, stubborn
09 obstinate, tenacious
10 determined, headstrong, persistent, relentless, self-willed, unyielding
11 intractable, persevering
12 strong-willed
14 uncompromising

pertinent
03 apt
05 ad rem
07 apropos, fitting, germane
08 apposite, material, relevant
10 applicable, to the point
11 appropriate

pertness
05 brass, cheek
08 audacity, boldness, chutzpah
09 brashness, cockiness, impudence, sauciness
10 cheekiness, effrontery
11 forwardness, presumption
12 impertinence

perturb
05 alarm, upset, worry
06 bother, ruffle
07 agitate, disturb, fluster
08 disquiet, unsettle
10 discompose, disconcert

perturbed
05 upset
07 anxious, nervous, worried
08 agitated, flurried
09 flustered, unsettled

perusal
04 look, read, skim
05 check, study
06 browse, glance
10 inspection
11 examination

peruse
04 read, scan, skim
05 check, study
06 browse
07 examine, inspect
11 look through

pervade
04 fill
05 imbue
06 affect, charge, infuse
07 diffuse, suffuse
08 permeate, saturate
09 penetrate, percolate
11 pass through
13 spread through

pervasive
09 extensive, prevalent, universal
10 ubiquitous, widespread
11 inescapable, omnipresent

perverse
06 cussed, unruly, wilful
07 awkward, bolshie, stroppy
08 contrary, obdurate, stubborn
09 difficult, obstinate, pig-headed
10 headstrong, rebellious, refractory, unyielding
11 disobedient, intractable, troublesome, wrong-headed
12 bloody-minded, cantankerous, intransigent

perversion
04 vice
08 deviance, twisting, travesty
09 depravity, deviation, kinkiness
10 aberration, corruption, debauchery, immorality
11 abnormality

perversity
08 obduracy
09 contumacy, obstinacy
10 cussedness, wilfulness
11 awkwardness, waywardness
12 contrariness, disobedience, stubbornness
13 intransigence
14 rebelliousness

pervert
04 perv, warp
05 abuse, avert, twist
06 debase, misuse, weirdo
07 corrupt, debauch, degrade, deprave, deviant, distort
09 debauchee, misdirect
10 degenerate, lead astray
12 misrepresent

perverted
05 kinky
06 warped, wicked
07 corrupt, debased, deviant, immoral, twisted
08 abnormal, depraved
09 corrupted, debauched, distorted, unnatural

pessimism
05 gloom
07 despair
08 cynicism, distrust, fatalism, glumness
10 gloominess
11 Weltschmerz
12 hopelessness

pessimist
05 cynic
07 killjoy
08 alarmist, doomster, fatalist
10 wet blanket
11 dismal Jimmy, doomwatcher, gloom-monger
13 prophet of doom
14 doubting Thomas

pessimistic
05 bleak
06 gloomy
08 alarmist, doubting, hopeless, negative, resigned
10 despairing, fatalistic, suspicious
11 distrustful
12 discouraging

pest
03 bug
04 bane, pain
05 curse, trial
06 blight, bother
07 scourge
08 irritant, nuisance
09 annoyance
13 pain in the neck
15 thorn in the flesh

pester
03 irk, nag
05 annoy, get at, hound, worry
06 badger, hassle, plague
07 torment
08 irritate
14 drive up the wall

pestilence
04 lues
06 plague
07 cholera, disease
08 epidemic, pandemic, sickness
09 contagion, infection

pestilent
07 harmful, irksome, ruinous
08 annoying, diseased, infected
09 poisonous
10 contagious, infectious, pernicious
11 destructive, infuriating
12 plague-ridden
13 disease-ridden

pestilential
07 irksome
08 annoying
10 bothersome, irritating, pernicious
11 infuriating, troublesome

pet
04 dear, huff, hump, idol, kiss, neck, snog, stew, sulk
05 jewel, paddy, sulks
06 caress, cuddle, fondle, smooch, stroke, temper
07 bad mood, darling, dearest, special, tantrum
08 canoodle, favoured, personal, treasure
09 cherished, favourite
10 particular
11 blue-eyed boy, teacher's pet
12 blue-eyed girl
14 apple of your eye

peter
□**peter out**
04 fade, fail, stop, wane
05 cease
07 die away, dwindle
08 diminish, taper off
09 evaporate, fizzle out

petite
05 bijou, dinky, small
06 dainty, little, slight
08 delicate

petition
03 ask, beg, bid, sue
04 plea, pray, urge
05 crave, plead, press
06 adjure, appeal, prayer
07 beseech, entreat, implore, protest, request, solicit
08 call upon, entreaty
10 round robin, supplicate
12 solicitation, supplication

pet name
08 nickname
10 diminutive, endearment
11 hypocorisma

petrified
04 numb
06 aghast, frozen

07 shocked, stunned
08 appalled, benumbed
09 horrified, stupefied, terrified
10 speechless, transfixed
11 dumbfounded, scared stiff
14 horror-stricken, terror-stricken

petrify
04 numb, stun
05 alarm, appal, panic
06 ossify
07 horrify, stupefy, terrify
08 frighten, paralyse
09 dumbfound, fossilize
11 turn to stone

petticoat
04 slip
06 kirtle
10 underskirt

pettifogging
05 petty
06 paltry
08 captious, niggling
09 cavilling, quibbling
10 nit-picking
11 over-refined, sophistical
13 hair-splitting

pettish
05 cross, huffy, sulky
06 grumpy, tetchy, touchy
07 fretful, peevish, waspish
08 petulant, snappish
09 irritable, querulous
11 bad-tempered

petty
04 mean
05 small, minor
06 little, measly, paltry, slight
07 trivial
08 grudging, piddling, trifling
10 negligible, ungenerous
11 small-minded, unimportant
13 insignificant, no great shakes
15 inconsequential

petulance
05 pique
09 procacity, sulkiness
10 sullenness
11 peevishness, waspishness
13 querulousness

petulant
05 cross, moody, ratty, sulky
06 sullen
07 fretful, peevish
08 in a paddy
09 crotchety, irritable, querulous
11 complaining

phantom
05 ghost, spook
06 spirit, vision, wraith
07 spectre
10 apparition
13 hallucination

pharisaical
12 hypocritical
13 sanctimonious, self-righteous
14 holier-than-thou

Pharisee
09 hypocrite
15 whited sepulchre

phase
04 form, part, step, time
05 point, shape, spell, stage, state
06 aspect, period, season
08 juncture, position

❑**phase in**
05 start
06 ease in
09 introduce

❑**phase out**
04 stop
06 wind up
07 run down
08 taper off, wind down
09 eliminate

phenomenal
07 amazing, unusual
08 singular
09 fantastic, wonderful
10 astounding, incredible, marvellous, remarkable, stupendous
11 astonishing, exceptional
12 breath-taking, mind-boggling, unbelievable
13 extraordinary

phenomenon
04 fact
05 event, sight
06 marvel, rarity, wonder
07 miracle, prodigy
09 sensation, spectacle
10 appearance, experience, occurrence
12 circumstance

philander
05 dally, flirt
08 womanize
11 sleep around

philanderer
04 stud, wolf
07 Don Juan, playboy
08 Casanova

09 ladies' man, libertine, womanizer
10 lady-killer

philanthropic
06 humane
08 generous
09 bounteous, bountiful
10 alms-giving, altruistic, benevolent, charitable, munificent, open-handed
12 humanitarian
14 public-spirited

philanthropist
05 donor, giver
06 helper, patron
09 alms-giver
10 benefactor
12 humanitarian

philanthropy
04 help
06 giving
07 charity
08 altruism
09 patronage
10 alms-giving, generosity
11 benevolence, munificence
12 beneficence
13 bounteousness, bountifulness
14 open-handedness
15 humanitarianism

philippic
05 abuse
06 attack, insult, rebuke, tirade
08 diatribe, harangue
09 criticism, onslaught
10 upbraiding
12 denunciation, vituperation

philistine
04 boor, lout
05 crass, yahoo
07 boorish, lowbrow
09 barbarian, tasteless, unrefined, vulgarian
10 uncultured
12 uncultivated

philosopher
04 guru, sage
07 scholar, thinker
08 analyser, logician, theorist
12 dialectician
13 deipnosophist, metaphysicist
14 epistemologist

➤ *Names of philosophers:*
04 **Ayer** (Sir Alfred Jules), **Hume** (David), **Joad** (Cyril Edwin Mitchinson), **Kant** (Immanuel), **Mach** (Ernst),

Marx (Karl), **Mill** (John
Stuart), **Otto** (Rudolf), **Ryle**
(Gilbert), **Weil** (Simone)
05 **Bacon** (Francis), **Bacon**
(Roger), **Bayle** (Pierre),
Bruno (Giordano), **Buber**
(Martin), **Burke** (Edmund),
Comte (Auguste), **Croce**
(Benedetto), **Frege**
(Gottlob), **Gödel** (Kurt),
Hegel (Georg Wilhelm
Friedrich), **James**
(William), **Locke** (John),
Moore (George Edward),
Plato
06 **Anselm** (Saint), **Berlin** (Sir
Isaiah), **Carnap** (Rudolf),
Engels (Friedrich), **Fichte**
(Johann Gottlieb), **Herder**
(Johann Gottfried von),
Hobbes (Thomas), **Lukács**
(Georg), **Popper** (Sir Karl),
Pyrrho, **Sartre** (Jean-Paul),
Strato, Thales
07 **Aquinas** (St Thomas),
Bentham (Jeremy),
Derrida (Jacques), **Diderot**
(Denis), **Erasmus**
(Desiderius), **Gorgias**,
Husserl (Edmund),
Hypatia, **Jaspers** (Karl),
Leibniz (Gottfried
Wilhelm), **Marcuse**
(Herbert), **Mencius**,
Proclus, **Russell** (Bertrand,
Earl), **Sankara**, **Spencer**
(Herbert), **Spinoza**
(Baruch), **Steiner** (Rudolf),
Tillich (Paul)
08 **Alcmaeon**, **Averroës**,
Avicenna, **Berkeley**
(Bishop George), **Boethius**
(Anicius Manlius
Severinus), **Epicurus**,
Foucault (Michel),
Hobhouse (Leonard),
Longinus (Dionysius),
Plotinus, **Porphyry**, **Ram
Singh**, **Rousseau** (Jean
Jacques), **Sidgwick** (Henry),
Socrates, **Spengler**
(Oswald)
09 **Althusser** (Louis),
Aristotle, **Bronowski**
(Jacob), **Confucius**,
Descartes (René),
Feuerbach (Ludwig),
Heidegger (Martin),
Nietzsche (Friedrich),
Santayana (George),
Schelling (Friedrich),
Whitehead (Alfred North)

10 **Anaxagoras**, **Aristippus**,
De Beauvoir (Simone),
Democritus, **Duns Scotus**
(John), **Empedocles**,
Heraclitus, **Maimonides**
(Moses), **Parmenides**,
Posidonius, **Protagoras**,
Pythagoras, **Schweitzer**
(Albert), **Xenocrates**,
Xenophanes, **Zeno of
Elea**
11 **Anaximander**,
Kierkegaard (Sören),
Montesquieu (Charles-
Louis, Baron de),
Reichenbach (Hans)
12 **Philo Judaeus**,
Schopenhauer (Arthur),
Theophrastus,
Wittgenstein (Ludwig),
Zeno of Citium
14 **Schleiermacher** (Friedrich)
15 **William of Ockham**

philosophical
04 wise
05 stoic
07 logical, patient, stoical
08 abstract, composed
09 collected, realistic, unruffled
10 analytical, meditative,
phlegmatic, thoughtful
12 metaphysical
13 contemplative, dispassionate,
imperturbable

philosophy
04 view
06 tenets, values, wisdom
07 beliefs, thought
08 attitude, doctrine, ideology,
thinking
09 viewpoint, world-view
10 principles
11 convictions, point of view

► *Terms used in philosophy
include*:
05 deism, logic
06 egoism, ethics, monism,
theism
07 a priori, atheism, atomism,
dualism, realism
08 altruism, asceticism, fatalism,
hedonism, humanism,
idealism, identity, nihilism,
ontology, stoicism
09 deduction, dogmatism,
induction, intuition,
pantheism, sense data,
solipsism, substance,
syllogism, teleology
10 absolutism, aesthetics,
empiricism, entailment,

positivism, pragmatism,
relativism, scepticism
11 a posteriori, agnosticism,
determinism, historicism,
materialism, metaphysics,
rationalism
12 behaviourism,
Epicureanism,
epistemology, reductionism
13 antinomianism,
phenomenology,
scholasticism, structuralism
14 existentialism,
libertarianism,
utilitarianism

phlegmatic
04 calm
06 placid, stolid
07 stoical
09 impassive
11 unemotional
13 dispassionate

phobia
04 fear
05 dread
06 hang-up, horror, terror
07 anxiety, dislike
08 aversion, loathing, neurosis
09 antipathy, obsession,
repulsion, revulsion
14 irrational fear

► *Types of phobia*:
09 apiphobia, panphobia,
zoophobia
10 acrophobia, autophobia,
cynophobia, pyrophobia,
toxiphobia, xenophobia
11 agoraphobia, astraphobia,
hippophobia, hydrophobia,
necrophobia, tachophobia
12 ailurophobia,
entomophobia
13 arachnophobia
14 claustrophobia

phone
04 bell, buzz, call, dial, ring
06 blower, call up, ring up,
mobile, tinkle
07 contact, handset
08 receiver
09 telephone

phoney
04 fake, mock, sham
05 bogus, false, pseud, quack
06 ersatz, forged, pseudo
07 assumed, feigned, forgery
08 affected, impostor, spurious
09 imitation, simulated
10 fraudulent, mountebank
11 counterfeit

phosphorescent
08 luminous
09 refulgent
11 luminescent, noctilucent, noctilucous

photocopy
05 print, Xerox®
06 run off
09 duplicate, facsimile, Photostat®

photograph
04 film, shot, snap, take
05 image, photo, print, shoot, slide, still, video
07 mug shot, picture
08 likeness, snapshot
12 transparency

▶ _Names of photographers_:
03 **Ray** (Man)
04 **Capa** (Robert), **Hill** (David Octavius)
05 **Arbus** (Diane), **Hardy** (Bert)
06 **Arnold** (Eve), **Bailey** (David), **Beaton** (Sir Cecil), **McBean** (Angus), **Miller** (Lee), **Niepce** (Joseph Nicéphore), **Talbot** (William Henry Fox), **Warhol** (Andy)
07 **Brassai**, **Cameron** (Julia Margaret), **Carroll** (Lewis), **Dodgson** (Charles Lutwidge), **Eastman** (George), **Lumière** (Auguste), **Snowdon** (Antony Armstrong-Jones, Earl of)
08 **Daguerre** (Louis), **McCullin** (Don)
09 **Leibovitz** (Annie), **Lichfield** (Patrick, Earl of), **Muybridge** (Eadweard James), **Rodchenko** (Alexander), **Stieglitz** (Alfred), **Winogrand** (Garry)
14 **Cartier-Bresson** (Henri)
➤ See also **art**

photographic
05 exact, vivid
06 filmic
07 graphic, natural, precise
08 accurate, detailed, faithful, lifelike
09 cinematic, pictorial, realistic, retentive
12 naturalistic

phrase
03 put, say

04 word
05 couch, frame, idiom, usage, utter
06 clause, remark, saying
07 comment, express, present
09 formulate, pronounce
10 expression
11 phraseology
12 construction

phraseology
04 cant
05 argot, idiom, style
06 patois, phrase, speech, syntax
07 diction, wording, writing
08 language, parlance, phrasing
10 expression
11 terminology

physical
04 real
05 solid
06 actual, bodily, carnal, mortal
07 earthly, fleshly, somatic, visible
08 concrete, material, palpable, tangible
09 corporeal, incarnate
11 substantial

physician
02 GP
03 doc
05 medic, quack
06 doctor, healer, intern, medico
08 houseman
09 registrar
10 consultant, specialist

physics
▶ _Terms used in physics include_:
03 gas, ion, law
04 atom, heat, lens, mass, wave, work, X-ray
05 field, force, laser, lever, light, power, quark, ratio, sound, speed
06 charge, couple, energy, moment, optics, photon, proton, SI unit, volume, weight
07 circuit, density, digital, entropy, formula, gravity, inertia, neutron, nuclear, nucleus, statics, tension
08 dynamics, electron, equation, friction, gamma ray, half-life, infrared, molecule, momentum, particle, polarity, pressure, spectrum, velocity
09 acoustics, frequency, magnetism, mechanics,

radiation, radio wave, resonance, sound wave, viscosity, white heat
10 elasticity, flash point, heavy water, hydraulics, latent heat, Mach number, microwaves, reflection, refraction, relativity, resistance, ultrasound
11 diffraction, electricity, equilibrium, evaporation, light source, oscillation, periodic law, sensitivity, temperature, ultraviolet
12 absolute zero, acceleration, boiling point, critical mass, hydrostatics, interference, laws of motion, luminescence, radioisotope, spectroscopy
13 beta particles, Big Bang theory, bubble-chamber, chain reaction, freezing point, hydrodynamics, incandescence, kinetic energy, magnetic field, nuclear fusion, quantum theory, radioactivity, semiconductor, supersymmetry
14 alpha particles, analogue signal, applied physics, circuit-breaker, nuclear fission, nuclear physics, surface tension, thermodynamics, transverse wave
15 capillary action, centre of gravity, charged particle, electric current, electrodynamics, perpetual motion, potential energy, visible spectrum

▶ _Names of physicists_:
02 **Wu** (Chien-Shiung)
03 **Lee** (Tsung-Dao), **Ohm** (Georg Simon)
04 **Abbe** (Ernst), **Bohr** (Niels Henrik David), **Born** (Max), **Bose** (Satyendra Nath), **Hess** (Victor Francis), **Katz** (Sir Bernard), **Land** (Edwin Herbert), **Laue** (Max Theodor Felix von), **Lenz** (Heinrich Friedrich Emil), **Mach** (Ernst), **Mott** (Sir Nevill Francis), **Rabi** (Isidor Isaac), **Saha** (Meghnad), **Wien** (Wilhelm)
05 **Bethe** (Hans Albrecht), **Bloch** (Felix), **Bondi** (Sir

Hermann), **Boyle** (Robert),
Bragg (Sir Lawrence),
Bragg (Sir William Henry),
Curie (Marie), **Curie**
(Pierre), **Dewar** (Sir James),
Dirac (Paul Adrien
Maurice), **Fermi** (Enrico),
Fuchs (Klaus), **Gamow**
(George), **Hertz** (Heinrich
Rudolf), **Hooke** (Robert),
Jeans (Sir James Hopwood),
Joule (James Prescott),
Milne (Edward Arthur),
Pauli (Wolfgang), **Raman**
(Sir Chandrasekhara
Venkata), **Salam** (Abdus),
Segrè (Emilio), **Stern**
(Otto), **Tesla** (Nikola), **Volta**
(Alessandro Giuseppe
Anastasio, Count)

06 **Ampère** (André Marie),
Bunsen (Robert Wilhelm),
Dalton (John), **Edison**
(Thomas Alva), **Frisch**
(Otto Robert), **Geiger**
(Hans Wilhelm), **Glaser**
(Donald Arthur), **Huxley**
(Hugh Esmor), **Kelvin**
(William Thomson, Lord),
Newton (Sir Isaac), **Pascal**
(Blaise), **Planck** (Max),
Rohrer (Heinrich), **Stokes**
(Sir George Gabriel), **Taylor**
(Sir Geoffrey Ingram), **Teller**
(Edward), **Wilson** (Robert
Woodrow)

07 **Alvarez** (Luis Walter),
Broglie (Louis-Victor Pierre
Raymond de), **Compton**
(Arthur Holly), **Coulomb**
(Charles Augustin de),
Doppler (Christian
Johann), **Eastman**
(George), **Faraday**
(Michael), **Feynman**
(Richard Phillips), **Fresnel**
(Augustin Jean), **Galilei**
(Galileo), **Galileo**,
Glashow (Sheldon Lee),
Goddard (Robert
Hutchings), **Hawking**
(Stephen William), **Huygens**
(Christiaan), **Langley**
(Samuel Pierpont), **Lorentz**
(Hendrik Antoon),
Marconi (Guglielmo,
Marchese), **Maxwell** (James
Clerk), **Meitner** (Lise),
Peierls (Sir Rudolf Ernst),
Penzias (Arno Allan),
Poisson (Siméon Denis),
Réaumur (René Antoine

Ferchault de), **Richter**
(Burton), **Röntgen**
(Wilhelm Konrad von),
Seaborg (Glen Theodore),
Szilard (Leo), **Vernier**
(Pierre)

08 **Ångström** (Anders Jonas),
Appleton (Sir Edward
Victor), **Avogadro**
(Amedeo), **Beaufort** (Sir
Francis), **Chadwick** (Sir
James), **De Forest** (Lee),
Delbrück (Max), **Einstein**
(Albert), **Gell-Mann**
(Murray), **Langevin** (Paul),
Lemaître (Georges Henri),
Millikan (Robert
Andrews), **Mulliken**
(Robert Sanderson),
Regnault (Henri Victor),
Sakharov (Andrei),
Shockley (William
Bradford), **Tomonaga** (Sin-
Itiro), **Van Allen** (James
Alfred), **Weinberg** (Steven)

09 **Aristotle**, **Bartholin**
(Erasmus), **Becquerel**
(Antoine Henri), **Birkeland**
(Kristian Olaf Bernhard),
Boltzmann (Ludwig),
Cavendish (Henry),
Cherenkov (Pavel),
Heaviside (Oliver),
Helmholtz (Hermann von),
Michelson (Albert
Abraham)

10 **Anaximenes**, **Fahrenheit**
(Daniel), **Heisenberg**
(Werner Karl), **Rutherford**
(Ernest, Lord), **Torricelli**
(Evangelista), **Xenocrates**

11 **Chamberlain** (Owen),
Joliot-Curie (Frédéric),
Joliot-Curie (Irène),
Leeuwenhoek (Antoni
van), **Oppenheimer**
(Robert), **Schrödinger**
(Erwin), **Tsiolkovsky**
(Konstantin), **Van de
Graaff** (Robert Jemison)

13 **Chandrasekhar**
(Subrahmanyan), **Thomson
Kelvin** (William, Lord)

➤ See also **scientist**

physiognomy

03 mug
04 dial, face, look, phiz
05 clock
06 kisser, phizog, visage
07 visnomy
08 features
11 countenance

physiologist

► *Names of physiologists*:
05 **Hubel** (David Hunter),
Marey (Etienne-Jules),
Prout (William), **Yalow**
(Rosalyn)
06 **Adrian** (Edgar Douglas,
Lord), **Bordet** (Jules),
Haller (Albrecht von),
Pavlov (Ivan), **Pincus**
(Gregory Goodwin)
07 **Banting** (Sir Frederick
Grant), **Beddoes** (Thomas
Lovell), **Diamond** (Jared
Mason), **Galvani** (Luigi),
Haldane (John Scott),
Hodgkin (Sir Alan Lloyd),
Schwann (Theodor)
08 **Mariotte** (Edmé),
Meyerhof (Otto Fritz)
09 **Blakemore** (Colin),
Einthoven (Willem),
Helmholtz (Hermann von)
➤ See also **scientist**

physique

04 body, form
05 build, frame, shape
06 figure, make-up
09 structure
12 constitution

pick

04 best, cull
05 cause, cream, elect, elite, fix
on, go for, pluck
06 choice, choose, favour,
flower, gather, lead to, opt
for, option, prefer, prompt,
select, take in
07 collect, harvest, produce
08 choicest, decide on,
decision, plump for, settle on
09 selection, single out
10 preference
14 crème de la crème

❑**pick at**
04 peck
06 nibble
07 toy with
08 play with

❑**pick off**
04 kill
05 shoot
06 detach, fire at, remove
07 take out

❑**pick on**
04 bait
05 blame, bully, get at
06 needle
07 torment
09 persecute

□**pick out**
06 choose, notice, select
07 discern, make out
08 hand-pick, perceive
09 recognize, single out

□**pick up**
03 buy, get
04 find, gain, go on, hear, lift
05 fetch, hoist, learn, rally
06 arrest, collar, detect, gather,
   obtain, perk up, resume
07 acquire, carry on, collect,
   improve, receive
08 contract, purchase
09 get better, give a lift
10 begin again, go down with,
   start again
15 take into custody

picket
04 pale, pike, post
05 guard, rebel, spike, stake,
   watch
06 paling, patrol, sentry
07 boycott, enclose, lookout,
   outpost, protest, striker,
   upright
08 blockade, objector, picketer,
   surround
09 dissident, protester,
   stanchion
11 demonstrate
12 demonstrator

pickings
04 loot, take
05 booty, gravy, yield
06 spoils
07 plunder, profits, returns,
   rewards
08 earnings, proceeds

pickle
03 fix, jam
04 bind, cure, mess, salt
05 sauce, souse, steep
06 relish, scrape
07 chutney, dilemma, straits,
   vinegar
08 conserve, hot water,
   marinade, preserve,
   quandary
09 condiment, tight spot
11 predicament

pick-me-up
05 boost, tonic
06 fillip
07 cordial
11 restorative
12 shot in the arm

pick-pocket
03 dip
05 thief

08 snatcher
09 pick-purse

picnic
05 cinch
06 doddle, outing
08 pushover, walkover
09 excursion, wayzgoose
10 child's play
11 outdoor meal, piece of cake

pictorial
05 vivid
06 scenic
07 graphic
09 schematic
11 illustrated, picturesque
12 diagrammatic

picture
03 see
04 draw, film, show, tale
05 flick, paint, story
06 appear, cinema, depict,
   flicks, movies, report, sketch
07 account, epitome, essence,
   imagine, portray
08 conceive, envisage
09 delineate, depiction,
   portrayal, represent,
   reproduce, visualize
10 call to mind, illustrate,
   impression, photograph
11 delineation, description
12 quintessence
13 motion picture
15 personification

► *Types of picture*:
04 icon, snap
05 cameo, image, mural, pin-
   up, plate, print, slide, still
06 canvas, design, doodle,
   fresco, mosaic, sketch
07 cartoon, collage, drawing,
   etching, montage, mugshot,
   tableau
08 abstract, graffiti, graphics,
   likeness, negative, painting,
   Photofit®, portrait,
   snapshot, tapestry, triptych,
   vignette
09 engraving, identikit,
   landscape, miniature, old
   master, still life
10 caricature, photograph,
   silhouette
11 oil-painting, trompe l'oeil,
   watercolour
12 illustration, self-portrait,
   transparency
13 passport photo
➢ See also **art**

□**get the picture**
03 see
05 get it, grasp
08 cotton on
10 comprehend, get the idea,
   understand
11 get the point
13 get the message

□**put someone in the
picture**
06 clue up, fill in, inform, notify,
   update
10 keep posted

picturesque
06 pretty, quaint, scenic
08 charming, pleasant,
   pleasing, striking
09 beautiful, colourful
10 attractive, delightful,
   impressive
11 descriptive

piddling
04 mean, poor, puny
05 minor, petty, small, sorry
06 meagre, measly, paltry, slight
07 trivial
08 derisory, piffling, trifling
09 miserable, worthless
12 contemptible

pie
03 pie
04 tart
06 pastry

□**pie in the sky**
05 dream
06 hot air, mirage, notion
07 fantasy, reverie, romance
08 daydream, delusion
13 castle in Spain
14 castle in the air

piebald
04 pied
07 dappled, mottled, spotted
10 variegated
13 black and white

piece
03 bar, bit, cut
04 bite, chip, hunk, item, lump,
   opus, part, slab, unit, work
05 block, chunk, crumb, flake,
   fleck, quota, scrap, share,
   shred, slice, speck, story,
   study, wedge
06 dollop, length, morsel,
   offcut, report, review,
   sample, sliver, tidbit, titbit
07 article, element, example,
   portion, section, segment,
   snippet

08 division, fraction, fragment, mouthful, quantity, specimen, splinter
09 allotment, component
10 allocation, percentage, smithereen
11 composition, constituent
12 illustration

◻**all in one piece**
05 whole
06 entire, intact, unhurt
08 complete, integral, unbroken, unharmed
09 undamaged, uninjured

◻**go to pieces**
07 crack up
08 collapse
09 break down
11 lose control

◻**in pieces**
05 kaput
06 broken, in bits, ruined
07 damaged, smashed
09 shattered
13 disintegrated, in smithereens

◻**piece together**
03 fit, fix
04 join, mend
05 patch, unite
06 attach, repair
07 compose, restore
08 assemble

pièce de résistance
05 jewel, prize
09 showpiece
10 magnum opus, masterwork
11 chef-d'oeuvre, masterpiece

piecemeal
06 patchy, slowly
07 partial
08 bit by bit, discrete, fitfully, sporadic
09 by degrees, partially, scattered
10 parcel-wise
11 at intervals, fragmentary
12 intermittent, unsystematic
14 intermittently, little by little
15 in dribs and drabs

pied
06 motley
07 brindle, dappled, flecked, mottled, piebald, spotted
08 brindled, skewbald, streaked
10 variegated
12 varicoloured
13 multicoloured

pier
04 dock, pile, post, quay

05 jetty, wharf
06 column, pillar
07 support, upright
10 breakwater
12 landing-stage

pierce
04 bore, fill, hurt, move, pain, stab
05 drill, enter, lance, prick, probe, punch, spear, spike, sting
06 impale, skewer
07 bayonet
08 puncture, transfix
09 penetrate, perforate
13 cut to the quick

pierced
07 impaled, pertuse
08 pertused
09 pertusate, punctured
10 perforated

piercing
03 raw
04 cold, keen, loud
05 alert, sharp
06 Arctic, astute, biting, bitter, fierce, frosty, severe, shrewd, shrill, wintry
07 painful, intense, probing
08 freezing
09 searching
10 discerning, lacerating
11 high-pitched, penetrating
12 ear-splitting, excruciating

piety
05 faith
07 respect
08 devotion, holiness, sanctity
09 godliness, piousness
10 devoutness
11 saintliness

piffle
03 rot
04 bunk, guff, tosh
05 balls, hooey, trash, tripe
06 bunkum, drivel
07 rubbish, twaddle
08 nonsense, tommy-rot
09 poppycock
10 balderdash, codswallop

pig
03 hog, sow
04 boar, boor, wolf
05 beast, brute, piggy, swine
06 animal, guzzle, piglet
07 glutton, grunter, guzzler
08 gourmand
10 greedy guts

► *Pigs include*:
05 Duroc

07 Old Spot
08 landrace, Tamworth, wild boar
09 Berkshire, Hampshire, Yorkshire
10 Large White, potbellied, saddleback
11 Middle White
➤ See also **animal**

pigeonhole
03 box, tag
04 file, slot, sort
05 label, niche
06 locker
07 cubicle, section
08 category, classify
09 catalogue, cubby-hole
10 categorize
11 compartment
14 classification

pig-headed
06 mulish, stupid, wilful
07 froward
08 contrary, perverse, stubborn
09 obstinate
10 bull-headed, headstrong, inflexible
11 intractable, wrong-headed
12 intransigent

pigment
03 dye, hue
04 tint
05 paint, stain
06 colour
08 tincture
09 colouring

► *Pigments include*:
03 hem
04 haem, heme
05 henna, ochre, sepia, umber
06 bister, bistre, cobalt, cyanin, madder, sienna, zaffer, zaffre
07 carmine, etiolin, gamboge, melanin, sinopia
08 cinnabar, orpiment, rose-pink, verditer, viridian
09 anthocyan, bilirubin, Indian red, lamp-black, lithopone, quercetin, zinc white
10 Berlin blue, Chinese red, chlorophyl, green earth, Paris-green, pearl white, terre verte, vermillion
11 anthochlore, anthocyanin, chlorophyll, King's-yellow, ultramarine, Venetian red
12 Cappagh-brown, Chinese white, chrome yellow, Naples-yellow, phycoxanthin, Prussian blue, xanthopterin

13 cadmium yellow, Scheele's green, titanium white

➤ See also **colour**; **dye**

pile
03 bar, fur, jam, nap
04 a lot, down, fuzz, heap, load, lots, mass, mint, pack, post, rush, shag, tons, wool
05 amass, crowd, crush, flock, flood, fluff, heaps, hoard, loads, mound, plush, stack, store
06 bundle, column, gather, packet, piling, riches, stacks, wealth
07 build up, collect, edifice, fortune, squeeze, support, surface, texture, upright
08 assemble, lashings, mountain
10 a great deal, accumulate, assemblage, assortment, collection, foundation, quantities
12 accumulation

❑**pile it on**
06 overdo, stress
07 lay it on, magnify
09 dramatize, overstate
10 exaggerate
12 lay it on thick

❑**pile up**
07 mount up
08 escalate, increase, multiply
10 accumulate

pile-up
05 crash, prang, smash, wreck
07 smash-up
09 collision

pilfer
03 rob
04 lift, nick
05 filch, pinch, steal, swipe
06 nobble, snitch, thieve
07 purloin, snaffle
08 knock off, peculate, shoplift

pilgrim
05 hadji
06 palmer
07 devotee
08 crusader, wanderer, wayfarer
09 traveller
10 worshipper

pilgrimage
04 hadj, tour, trip
07 crusade, journey, mission

pill
04 ball

06 pellet, tablet
07 capsule, lozenge

pillage
03 rob
04 loot, raid, raze, sack
05 booty, rifle, spoil, strip
06 maraud, rapine, ravage, spoils
07 despoil, plunder, ransack, robbery, seizure
08 freeboot, harrying, spoliate
09 depredate, marauding
10 spoliation
11 depredation, devastation

pillar
04 mast, pier, pile, pole, post, prop, rock
05 shaft
06 cippus, column
07 bastion, support, upright
08 mainstay
09 stanchion
15 tower of strength

pillory
04 lash, mock
05 brand
06 show up
07 laugh at
08 denounce, ridicule
10 stigmatize
11 cast a slur on, pour scorn on
13 hold up to shame

pillow
07 bolster, cushion
08 headrest

pilot
05 flyer, guide, steer, trial
06 airman, direct, leader
07 aircrew, aviator, captain, conduct, control, operate
08 airwoman, coxswain, navigate
09 commander, manoeuvre, navigator, steersman

pimp
08 procurer
09 go-between, solicitor
11 fleshmonger, whoremonger

pimple
03 zit
04 boil, spot
06 papula, papule
07 pustule
08 swelling

pin
03 fix, lay, peg, put
04 bolt, clip, join, nail, tack
05 affix, dowel, place, press, rivet, screw, spike, stick

06 attach, brooch, fasten, impute, secure, staple
07 ascribe
08 fastener, hold down, hold fast, restrain
09 attribute, constrain
10 immobilize

❑**pin down**
05 force, press
06 compel, define
08 hold down, identify, nail down, pinpoint, restrain
09 constrain, determine
10 pressurize
15 put your finger on

pincers
06 forfex
07 forceps
08 tweezers

pinch
03 bit, jot, nab, nip, tad
04 book, bust, dash, grip, hurt, lift, mite, nail, nick, save
05 catch, cramp, crush, filch, grasp, press, run in, seize, speck, steal, taste, touch, trace, tweak
06 arrest, budget, collar, crisis, detain, pick up, pilfer, snatch, stress
07 capture, confine, cut back, purloin, smidgen, soupçon, squeeze
08 compress, hardship, peculate, pressure
09 economize, emergency
10 difficulty
11 appropriate, predicament, walk off with
13 keep costs down, scrape a living, scrimp and save

❑**at a pinch**
11 if necessary
13 in an emergency

pinched
04 pale, thin, worn
05 drawn, gaunt, peaky
07 haggard, starved
08 careworn, narrowed
12 straightened

pine
04 ache, fade, fret, long, sigh, wish
05 crave, mourn, yearn
06 desire, grieve, hanker, hunger, thirst, weaken
08 languish
09 waste away

pinion
04 bind

05 chain, truss
06 fetter, hobble
07 confine, manacle, pin down, shackle
10 immobilize

pink
04 acme, best, peak, rose, rosy
06 flower, height, incise, salmon, summit, tiptop
07 extreme, flushed, reddish, roseate, scallop, serrate

❑**in the pink**
03 fit
04 well
07 healthy
11 in good shape, right as rain
12 in fine fettle
15 in perfect health

pinnacle
03 cap, top
04 acme, apex, cone, peak
05 crest, crown, spire
06 apogee, height, needle, summit, turret, vertex, zenith
07 obelisk, pyramid, steeple

pinpoint
06 define, locate
07 pin down, specify
08 discover, home in on, identify, nail down, zero in on
11 distinguish
15 put your finger on

pint-size
03 wee
04 tiny
05 dwarf, small
06 little, midget, pocket
09 miniature
10 diminutive

pioneer
05 begin, found, set up, start
06 create, invent, launch, leader, open up
07 develop, founder, settler
08 colonist, discover, explorer, initiate, inventor
09 developer, innovator, instigate, introduce, originate, spearhead
10 discoverer, lead the way, pathfinder, pave the way
11 blaze a trail, trail-blazer
12 frontiersman
13 ground-breaker
14 break new ground, founding father, frontierswoman

pious
04 good, holy

05 godly, moral
06 devout
07 devoted, saintly
08 faithful, reverent, virtuous
09 dedicated, insincere, religious, righteous, spiritual
12 hypocritical
13 sanctimonious, self-righteous
14 holier-than-thou

pipe
04 clay, duct, flue, hose, main, peep, play, sing, tube
05 brier, cheep, chirp, sound, trill, tweet
06 convey, dudeen, funnel, hookah, kalian, siphon, supply, tubing, warble
07 calumet, channel, chirrup, conduct, conduit, deliver, passage, twitter, whistle
08 claypipe, conveyor, cylinder, narghile, overflow, transmit
10 meerschaum
12 hubble-bubble

❑**pipe down**
06 shut up
07 be quiet
11 stop talking

pipe dream
06 mirage, notion
07 fantasy, romance
08 daydream, delusion
11 pie in the sky
13 castle in Spain
14 castle in the air

pipeline
04 duct, line, pipe, tube
07 channel, conduit, passage
08 conveyor

❑**in the pipeline**
07 planned
08 under way
13 in preparation

pipsqueak
05 creep, twerp
06 nobody, squirt
07 nothing, upstart
09 nonentity
11 hobbledehoy
14 whippersnapper

piquancy
03 pep, zip
04 bite, edge, kick, tang, zest
05 punch, spice
06 ginger, relish, vigour
07 flavour, pizzazz
08 interest, pungency, raciness, vitality
09 sharpness, spiciness

10 excitement, liveliness
11 pepperiness

piquant
04 racy, tart
05 juicy, salty, sharp, spicy, tangy, zesty
06 biting, lively
07 peppery, pungent, savoury
08 seasoned, spirited, stinging
09 colourful, sparkling
10 intriguing
11 provocative, stimulating
14 highly seasoned

pique
03 get, irk, vex
04 gall, goad, huff, miff, rile, spur, stir, whet
05 anger, annoy, peeve, rouse, sting, wound
06 arouse, excite, grudge, kindle, nettle, offend, put out
07 affront, incense, mortify, offence, provoke, umbrage
08 vexation
09 annoyance, galvanize, stimulate
11 displeasure

piqued
05 angry, riled, vexed
06 miffed, peeved, put out
07 annoyed
08 offended

piracy
05 theft
06 rapine
09 hijacking
10 plagiarism
11 bootlegging, freebooting
12 buccaneering, infringement

pirate
04 copy, crib, lift, nick
05 pinch, poach, rover, steal
06 marque, raider, sea rat
07 brigand, corsair, sea wolf
08 marauder, picaroon, sea rover, water rat
09 buccaneer, infringer, sallee-man, sea robber
10 filibuster, freebooter, plagiarist, plagiarize
11 appropriate, plagiarizer

► *Names of pirates*:
03 **Tew** (Thomas)
04 **Gunn** (Ben), **Hook** (Captain), **Kidd** (William), **Read** (Mary), **Smee**
05 **Bones** (Billy), **Bonny** (Anne), **Drake** (Sir Francis), **Every** (Henry), **Teach** (Edward)

06 **Morgan** (Sir Henry), **Silver** (Long John)
07 **Dampier** (William), **Lafitte** (Jean)
08 **Black Dog, Blind Pew, Redbeard**
09 **Black Bart**
10 **Barbarossa** (Khair-ed-din), **Blackbeard, Calico Jack**

pirouette
04 spin, turn
05 pivot, twirl, whirl

pistol
03 gun, rod
04 iron
05 Luger®, piece
07 handgun, sidearm
08 revolver
09 derringer
10 six-shooter

pit
04 dent, gulf, hole, mine, scar
05 abyss, chasm, ditch, notch
06 cavity, crater, dimple, hollow, indent, quarry, trench
07 depress, pothole
08 coalmine, diggings, pockmark, workings
10 depression
11 excavations, indentation

❑**pit against**
06 oppose
10 set against

pitch
03 aim, fix, lob, tar, yak
04 bowl, cant, cast, dive, drop, fall, fire, hurl, keel, line, list, mark, park, reel, roll, sway, talk, tilt, tone, toss
05 angle, arena, chuck, erect, field, fling, grade, heave, level, lurch, place, point, put up, set up, slant, sling, slope, sound, spiel, throw
06 degree, direct, extend, gabble, ground, height, jargon, launch, patter, plunge, settle, timbre, topple, tumble, wallow
07 asphalt, bitumen, chatter, incline, plummet, stadium, station
08 flounder, gradient, position, tonality
09 frequency, intensity, steepness
10 modulation
11 inclination, sports field
12 fall headlong, playing-field

❑**pitch in**
04 help
06 join in, muck in
09 do your bit, lend a hand
10 be involved
11 participate

pitch-black
04 dark, inky
05 black, unlit
08 jet-black
09 coal-black, pitch-dark

pitcher
03 can, jar, jug, urn
04 ewer
05 crock
06 bottle, vessel
09 container

piteous
06 moving, woeful
07 pitiful
08 pathetic, pitiable, poignant, wretched
11 distressing
12 heart-rending
13 heart-breaking

pitfall
04 snag, trap
05 catch, peril, snare
06 danger, hazard
08 drawback
14 stumbling-block

pith
03 nub
04 core, crux, gist, meat
05 heart, point
06 import, kernel, marrow, matter, moment, vigour, weight
07 essence
09 substance
11 consequence
12 quintessence, salient point, significance

pithy
05 brief, short, terse
06 cogent
07 compact, concise, pointed, summary, telling
08 forceful, incisive, succinct
09 condensed, trenchant
10 expressive, meaningful

pitiable
03 sad
05 sorry
07 doleful, piteous
08 pathetic, wretched
09 miserable
10 lamentable
11 distressing

pitiful
03 low, sad
04 base, mean, poor, vile
06 meagre, moving, paltry, shabby, woeful
07 doleful, piteous
08 hopeless, mournful, pathetic, pitiable, wretched
09 miserable, worthless
10 deplorable, despicable, inadequate, lamentable
12 contemptible, heart-rending
13 heart-breaking, insignificant

pitiless
05 cruel, harsh
06 brutal, severe
07 callous, inhuman
08 inhumane, ruthless
09 heartless, merciless
10 inexorable, relentless
11 cold-blooded, cold-hearted, hard-hearted, unremitting

pittance
06 trifle
07 modicum, peanuts
11 chickenfeed
14 drop in the ocean

pitted
05 holey, rough
06 dented, marked
07 notched, scarred
08 indented, potholed
09 blemished, depressed
10 pockmarked

pity
05 mercy, shame
06 regret, sorrow
07 sadness, weep for
08 distress, sympathy
10 compassion, condolence
11 crying shame
13 commiseration, understanding

❑**take pity on**
05 spare
06 pardon
07 feel for
09 show mercy
11 have mercy on
12 feel sorry for

pivot
03 hub, lie
04 axis, axle, hang, rely, turn
05 focus, heart, hinge, swing
06 centre, rotate, swivel
07 fulcrum, kingpin, spindle
08 linchpin
10 focal point

pivotal
05 axial, focal, vital
07 central, crucial
08 critical, decisive
09 climactic, important
11 determining

pixie
03 elf
05 fairy
06 goblin, sprite
07 brownie
10 leprechaun

placard
02 ad
04 bill, sign
06 advert, notice, poster
07 sticker
13 advertisement

placate
04 calm, lull
06 pacify, soothe
07 appease, mollify, win over
08 calm down
10 conciliate, propitiate

placatory
07 calming
08 soothing
09 appeasing
10 mollifying
11 peace-making
12 conciliatory, pacificatory, propitiative, propitiatory

place
03 fix, job, lay, pad, put, set
04 area, city, digs, duty, flat, home, know, part, rank, rest, role, room, seat, site, sort, spot, task, town
05 abode, class, grade, group, hotel, house, leave, lodge, niche, plant, point, scene, space, stand, state, venue
06 assign, hamlet, locale, locate, region, settle, status
07 arrange, concern, country, deposit, install, lay down, put down, set down, setting, situate, station, village
08 allocate, building, business, classify, district, domicile, dwelling, identify, locality, location, pinpoint, position, property, standing
09 apartment, recognize, residence, situation
11 appointment, whereabouts
13 accommodation, establishment
14 responsibility

▫in place
05 set up
07 in order, working
08 arranged

▫in place of
08 in lieu of
09 instead of
13 in exchange for

▫out of place
08 tactless, unseemly
09 unfitting
10 inapposite, unsuitable
13 inappropriate

▫put someone in their place
05 crush, shame
06 humble
07 deflate
09 humiliate

▫take place
05 occur
06 befall, be held, betide, happen
08 come about
09 transpire
10 come to pass

▫take the place of
07 replace
09 supersede
10 stand in for
13 substitute for

placement
03 job
07 ranking
08 locating, location, ordering
10 deployment, employment, engagement, stationing
11 appointment, arrangement, disposition, positioning
12 distribution, installation

placid
04 calm, cool, mild
05 quiet, still
06 gentle, serene
07 equable, pacific, restful
08 composed, peaceful, tranquil
09 easy-going, peaceable, unruffled
10 untroubled
11 unemotional, unflappable
12 even-tempered
13 imperturbable

plagiarism
05 theft
06 piracy
07 copying, lifting
08 cribbing

plagiarist
05 thief
06 copier, pirate, robber

plagiarize
04 copy, crib, lift, nick
05 poach, steal
06 borrow, pirate
07 imitate
09 reproduce
11 appropriate, counterfeit

plague
03 bug, dog, vex
05 annoy, curse, haunt, hound, swarm, trial, upset, worry
06 bother, hamper, harass, hassle, hinder, influx, pester
07 afflict, cholera, disease, scourge, torment, torture
08 epidemic, invasion, irritate, nuisance, pandemic
09 aggravate, annoyance, contagion, infection, persecute
10 Black Death, pestilence
11 infestation
13 pain in the neck
15 thorn in the flesh

plain
04 flat, open, ugly
05 basic, blunt, clear, frank, lucid, overt, stark
06 candid, direct, homely, honest, modest, pampas, patent, simple, simply
07 austere, evident, lowland, obvious, prairie, sincere, visible
08 apparent, flatland, manifest, ordinary, savannah, unlovely
09 grassland, unadorned
10 accessible, forthright, noticeable, restrained
11 discernible, perceptible, transparent, unambiguous, undecorated
12 intelligible, self-coloured, unattractive
13 uncomplicated, unembellished
15 straightforward, unprepossessing, unsophisticated

plain-spoken
05 blunt, frank
06 candid, direct, honest
08 explicit, outright, truthful
09 downright, outspoken
10 forthright
11 unequivocal
15 straightforward

plaintive
03 sad
06 woeful
07 doleful, piteous, pitiful, unhappy, wistful
08 mournful, wretched
09 sorrowful
10 melancholy
11 heart-broken
12 disconsolate, heart-rending

plan
03 aim, map, way
04 idea, mean, plot, seek, want, wish
05 chart, draft, frame, means, shape
06 design, devise, intend, invent, layout, map out, method, policy, scheme, sketch, system
07 arrange, develop, diagram, drawing, foresee, formula, outline, prepare, project, propose, purpose, resolve, think of, work out
08 contrive, envisage, organize, proposal, scenario, schedule, strategy
09 blueprint, formulate, intention, procedure, programme
10 mastermind, suggestion
11 arrangement, contemplate, delineation, proposition
12 illustration, scale drawing
14 representation

plane
03 fly, jet
04 even, flat, rank, rung, sail, skim, VTOL, wing
05 class, flush, glide, jumbo, level, plain, skate, stage
06 bomber, degree, glider, planar, smooth
07 echelon, fighter, footing, regular, stratum, uniform
08 aircraft, airliner, jumbo jet
09 swing-wing
11 flat surface
12 level surface

planet
➤ *Names of planets:*
04 Mars
05 Earth, Pluto, Venus
06 Saturn, Uranus
07 Jupiter, Mercury, Neptune

plant
03 fix, put, set, sow
04 bury, gear, hide, mill, root, seed, shop, yard

05 found, imbed, lodge, place, works
06 insert, settle
07 conceal, factory, foundry, implant, scatter, secrete, situate
08 disguise, position, workshop
09 apparatus, equipment, establish, machinery

➤ *Types of plant:*
04 bulb, bush, corm, fern, herb, moss, tree, vine, weed
05 algae, grass, shrub
06 annual, cactus, cereal, flower, fungus, hybrid, lichen
07 climber, sapling
08 biennial, cultivar, pot plant, seedling
09 evergreen, perennial, succulent, vegetable
10 house plant, water-plant, wild flower
➤ See also **algae**; **bulb**; **flower**; **grass**; **leaf**; **lily**; **palm**; **poisonous**; **seaweed**; **shrub**; **tree**; **weed**

plaque
04 sign
05 badge, brass, medal, plate
06 shield, tablet
09 cartouche, medallion

plaster
04 coat, daub
05 cover, patch, smear
06 bedaub, gypsum, mortar, spread, stucco
07 bandage, Band-aid®
08 dressing
11 Elastoplast®

plastic
04 soft
05 false
06 phoney, pliant, supple
07 ductile, man-made, pliable
08 flexible
09 compliant, malleable, mouldable, receptive, shapeable, synthetic, tractable, unnatural
10 artificial, manageable
14 impressionable

➤ *Types of plastic:*
03 PVC
04 PTFE, uPVC
05 vinyl
06 Teflon®
07 Perspex®
08 Bakelite®, silicone

09 celluloid®, Plexiglas®, polyester, polythene
10 epoxy resin
11 polystyrene
12 polyethylene, polyurethane
13 polypropylene

plasticity
07 pliancy
10 pliability, suppleness
11 flexibility, pliableness
12 malleability, tractability

plate
03 tin
04 coat, dish, gild, pane, sign, slab
05 ashet, cover, panel, print
06 lamina, plaque, salver, silver, tablet, veneer
07 anodize, helping, overlay, picture, platter, portion, serving
08 laminate
09 galvanize, platinize
10 lithograph, photograph
12 electroplate, illustration

plateau
04 mesa
05 table
06 upland
08 highland
09 tableland

platform
04 dais
05 stage, stand
06 podium, policy
07 rostrum, soapbox
08 strategy
09 manifesto, party line, programme

platitude
06 cliché, truism
07 bromide, inanity
08 banality, chestnut
11 commonplace

platitudinous
05 banal, corny, inane, stale, stock, tired, trite, vapid
07 clichéd
08 truistic, well-worn
09 hackneyed
10 overworked
11 commonplace, stereotyped

platonic
09 non-sexual, spiritual
10 idealistic
11 incorporeal, non-physical
12 intellectual, transcendent

platoon
04 team

05 group, squad
06 outfit, patrol
07 battery, company
08 squadron

platter
04 dish, tray
05 plate
06 salver
07 charger
08 trencher

plaudits
06 praise
07 acclaim, hurrahs, ovation
08 accolade, applause
09 good press
10 rave review
11 acclamation, approbation
12 pat on the back
15 congratulations, standing ovation

plausible
04 glib
07 logical
08 credible, possible, probable
10 believable, convincing, persuasive
11 conceivable
13 smooth-talking

play
03 act, fun
04 game, give, jest, plot, room, romp, show
05 caper, dance, drama, farce, flash, frisk, hobby, kicks, laugh, range, revel, rival, scope, slack, space, sport
06 action, cavort, comedy, frolic, gambol, join in, joking, leeway, margin, oppose, take on
07 compete, flicker, freedom, have fun, leisure, liberty, licence, pastime, perform, portray, teasing, tragedy, twinkle, vie with
08 exercise, free rein, latitude, movement, take part
09 amusement, challenge, diversion, enjoyment, interplay, looseness, melodrama, operation, play games, represent
10 recreation
11 flexibility, impersonate, interaction, move lightly, participate, performance
13 amuse yourself, enjoy yourself, entertainment, play the part of
14 compete against

► *Names of plays*:
04 Loot
05 Equus, Faust, Le Cid, Medea, Médée, Roots, Yerma
06 Becket, Phèdre
07 Amadeus, Electra, Endgame, Galileo, Oleanna
08 Antigone, Betrayal, Everyman, Huis Clos, Oresteia, Peer Gynt, Tartuffe, The Birds, The Flies, The Frogs, The Miser, The Wasps
09 Miss Julie, Pygmalion, Saint Joan, The Clouds, The Rivals
10 Andromaque, Lysistrata, No Man's Land, Oedipus Rex, The Bacchae, The Seagull, Uncle Vanya
11 A Doll's House, Hedda Gabler, The Crucible, The Wild Duck, Trojan Women
12 Blithe Spirit, Blood Wedding, Major Barbara, Private Lives, Punch and Judy, The Alchemist, The Caretaker, The Mousetrap
13 Arms and the Man, Doctor Faustus, Le Misanthrope, The Jew of Malta, The White Devil, The Winslow Boy
14 Can't Pay, Won't Pay, Krapp's Last Tape, Man and Superman, Orlando Furioso, The Country Wife
15 Bartholomew Fair, Look Back in Anger, Prometheus Bound, The Beggar's Opera, The Iceman Cometh, The Three Sisters, Waiting For Godot
➤ See also **Shakespeare**

❑**play around with**
07 toy with
08 fool with
09 dally with, flirt with
10 fiddle with, fidget with, meddle with, tamper with, trifle with
13 interfere with
14 mess around with

❑**play at**
06 affect
07 make out, pretend
10 put on an act

❑**play down**
08 downplay, minimize
09 gloss over, underplay
10 understate, undervalue
11 make light of
13 underestimate

❑**play on**
07 exploit, trade on
08 profit by
12 capitalize on

❑**play out**
03 act
04 go on
05 enact
06 unfold

❑**play up**
06 bother, stress
07 go wrong, point up, trouble
09 be naughty, highlight, misbehave, spotlight
10 accentuate, exaggerate
11 give trouble, malfunction
12 go on the blink

❑**play up to**
05 toady
07 flatter
08 blandish, bootlick, butter up, soft-soap, suck up to
15 curry favour with

playboy
04 rake, roué
09 ladies' man, libertine, socialite, womanizer
10 lady-killer
11 philanderer
12 man about town

player
05 actor
06 artist, player
07 actress, artiste, trouper
08 comedian, musician
09 performer, sportsman
10 competitor, contestant
11 accompanist, entertainer, participant, sportswoman
15 instrumentalist

playful
06 frisky, impish, joking, lively
07 jesting, puckish, roguish, teasing, waggish
08 humorous, spirited, sportive
09 facetious, fun-loving, kittenish
10 frolicsome
11 mischievous

playground
04 park
08 play area
12 playing-field
13 amusement park
14 pleasure ground

playmate
10 playfellow

plaything
03 toy
06 bauble, gewgaw, trifle
07 pastime, trinket
08 gimcrack
09 amusement

playwright
06 writer
09 dramatist, tragedian
10 dramaturge
12 dramaturgist

➤ *Names of playwrights and screenwriters*:
02 Fo (Dario)
03 Fry (Christopher), Gay (John), Kyd (Thomas)
04 Bolt (Robert), Bond (Edward), Dane (Clemence), Ford (John), Hare (David), Shaw (George Bernard), Vega (Lope de)
05 Albee (Edward), Allen (Woody), Arden (John), Behan (Brendan), Dumas (Alexandre), Eliot (Thomas Stearns), Genet (Jean), Gogol (Nikolai), Havel (Vaclav), Ibsen (Henrik), Lorca (Federico García), Mamet (David), Nashe (Thomas), Odets (Clifford), Orton (Joe), Sachs (Hans), Sachs (Nelly), Smith (Dodie), Synge (John Millington), Wilde (Oscar), Yeats (William Butler)
06 Barrie (Sir James Matthew), Brecht (Bertolt), Coward (Sir Noël), Dekker (Thomas), Dryden (John), Galdós (Benito Pérez), Goethe (Johann Wolfgang von), Greene (Robert), Herzog (Werner), Huston (John), Jerome (Jerome Klapka), Jonson (Ben), Lerner (Alan Jay), Mercer (David), Miller (Arthur), O'Casey (Sean), O'Neill (Eugene), Pinero (Sir Arthur Wing), Pinter (Harold), Powell (Michael), Sartre (Jean-Paul), Steele (Sir Richard), Wesker (Arnold), Wilder (Thornton)
07 Anouilh (Jean), Beckett (Samuel), Chapman (George), Chekhov⁻ (Anton), Cocteau (Jean),

Coppola (Francis Ford), Ionesco (Eugène), Kubrick (Stanley), Lardner (Ring), Marlowe (Christopher), Marston (John), Mishima (Yukio), Molière, Novello (Ivor), Osborne (John), Plautus (Titus Maccius), Richler (Mordecai), Rostand (Edmond), Russell (Willy), Shaffer (Peter), Shepard (Sam), Ustinov (Sir Peter), Webster (John)
08 Beaumont (Francis), Congreve (William), Davenant (Sir William), Fielding (Henry), Fletcher (John), Menander, Mortimer (John), Polanski (Roman), Rattigan (Sir Terence), Schiller (Friedrich), Sheridan (Richard Brinsley), Stoppard (Tom), Suckling (Sir John), Tourneur (Cyril), Vanbrugh (Sir John), Wedekind (Frank), Williams (Emlyn), Williams (Tennessee)
09 Aeschylus, Ayckbourn (Alan), Corneille (Pierre), D'Annunzio (Gabriele), Euripides, Goldsmith (Oliver), Isherwood (Christopher), Mankowitz (Wolf), Marinetti (Filippo Tommaso), Middleton (Thomas), Priestley (John Boynton), Sophocles, Wycherley (William)
10 Galsworthy (John), Pirandello (Luigi), Strindberg (August)
11 Shakespeare (William)
12 Aristophanes, Beaumarchais (Pierre-Augustin Caron de)
➤ *See also* **writer**

plea
06 appeal, excuse, prayer
07 defence, request
08 entreaty, petition
10 invocation
11 imploration
13 justification

plead
03 ask, beg
05 argue, claim, state
06 adduce, allege, appeal, assert

07 beseech, entreat, implore, request, solicit
08 maintain, petition

pleasant
04 fine, nice
07 affable, amiable, amusing
08 charming, friendly, likeable
09 agreeable, congenial, enjoyable
10 delightful, satisfying
12 good-humoured

pleasantry
04 jest, joke, quip
06 banter, bon mot
08 badinage

please
04 like, suit, want, will, wish
05 amuse, charm, cheer
06 choose, desire, divert, fulfil, humour, prefer, see fit
07 delight, gladden, gratify, indulge, satisfy
08 appeal to, think fit
09 captivate, entertain
14 give pleasure to

pleased
04 glad
05 happy
07 chuffed
09 contented, delighted, gratified, satisfied
11 tickled pink

pleasing
07 amusing, winning
08 charming, engaging
09 agreeable, enjoyable
10 attractive, delightful, gratifying, satisfying

pleasurable
03 fun
07 amusing
09 congenial, diverting, enjoyable
10 delightful, gratifying
12 entertaining

pleasure
03 fun, joy
04 will, wish
06 choice, desire
07 delight, leisure
09 amusement, enjoyment
10 preference, recreation
12 satisfaction
13 entertainment, gratification

pleat
04 fold, tuck
05 crimp, flute
06 crease, gather, pucker

plebeian
03 low
04 base, mean, non-U
05 prole
06 coarse, common, worker
07 ignoble, low-born, peasant
08 commoner
10 lower-class, uncultured
11 proletarian
12 uncultivated, working-class

plebiscite
04 poll, vote
06 ballot
09 straw poll
10 referendum

pledge
03 vow
04 bail, bond, gage, oath, pawn, word
05 swear, vouch
06 surety
07 deposit, promise, warrant
08 covenant, security
09 assurance, guarantee, undertake
10 collateral, take an oath
11 undertaking
12 give your word, word of honour

plenary
04 full, open
05 whole
06 entire
07 general
08 absolute, complete, integral, sweeping, thorough
09 unlimited
12 unrestricted
13 unconditional

plenipotentiary
05 envoy
06 legate, nuncio
08 emissary, minister
09 dignitary
10 ambassador

plenitude
06 bounty, plenty, wealth
08 fullness, plethora
09 abundance, amplitude, profusion, repletion
10 cornucopia, entireness
11 copiousness
13 plenteousness, plentifulness

plenteous
06 bumper, lavish
07 copious, fertile, liberal, profuse
08 abundant, fruitful, generous
09 abounding, bounteous, bountiful, luxuriant, plentiful
10 productive

plentiful
05 ample
06 bumper, lavish
07 copious, liberal, profuse
08 abundant, fruitful, generous, infinite
09 bounteous, bountiful
10 production, productive
11 overflowing
13 inexhaustible

plenty
04 fund, mass, mine
06 riches, volume, wealth
07 fortune
08 fullness, plethora, quantity
09 abundance, affluence, profusion
10 prosperity
11 sufficiency, wealthiness

◻**plenty of**
04 lots, many
05 heaps, loads, piles
06 enough, masses, stacks
11 large amount, large number
14 more than enough

plethora
04 glut
06 excess
07 surfeit, surplus
09 profusion
11 superfluity
13 overabundance
14 superabundance

pliability
08 docility
10 compliance, elasticity, plasticity
11 amenability, flexibility
12 adaptability, malleability
13 tractableness

pliable
05 bendy, lithe
06 docile, pliant, supple
07 elastic, plastic
08 bendable, biddable, flexible, yielding
09 adaptable, compliant, malleable, receptive, tractable
10 manageable, responsive
11 persuadable
14 impressionable

pliant
05 bendy, lithe
06 docile, supple
07 elastic, plastic, pliable
08 bendable, flexible, yielding
09 compliant, malleable, tractable
11 persuadable, susceptible

plight
03 jam, vow
05 state, swear, vouch
06 pickle, pledge, scrape
07 dilemma, promise, propose, straits, trouble
08 contract, covenant, quandary
09 condition, extremity, guarantee, tight spot
10 difficulty
11 dire straits, predicament
13 circumstances

plod
04 slog, toil
05 clump, grind, stomp, stump, tramp
06 drudge, lumber, trudge
07 peg away
08 plug away
09 persevere, soldier on

plodder
03 mug, sap
06 drudge, toiler
07 dullard, slogger

plot
03 lay, lot, map
04 area, draw, mark, plan, ruse
05 cabal, chart, draft, frame, hatch, patch, story, theme, tract
06 action, cook up, design, devise, locate, map out, parcel, scheme, sketch
07 collude, concoct, connive, outline, project, subject
08 conspire, contrive, intrigue, scenario
09 allotment, calculate, machinate, narrative, storyline, stratagem
10 conspiracy
11 machination

plotter
07 planner, schemer
09 intriguer
10 machinator
11 conspirator

plough
04 till, work
05 break
06 furrow, turn up
09 cultivate

◻**plough into**
07 collide, run into
08 bump into
09 crash into, smash into

◻**plough through**
11 plod through, wade through
13 trudge through

ploy
04 game, move, ruse, wile
05 dodge, trick
06 device, scheme, tactic
08 artifice
09 manoeuvre, stratagem
10 subterfuge
11 contrivance

pluck
04 draw, grit, guts, pick, pull, yank
05 nerve, strum
06 daring, gather, mettle, remove, snatch, valour
07 bravery, courage, harvest
08 backbone, boldness
09 fortitude
11 intrepidity
12 fearlessness

plucky
04 bold
05 brave, gutsy
06 daring, gritty, heroic, spunky
07 valiant
08 fearless, intrepid, spirited
10 courageous, determined

plug
02 ad
03 wad
04 bung, cake, chew, cork, fill, hype, pack, puff, push, seal, stop, tout
05 block, blurb, choke, close, stuff, twist
06 market, spigot, stop up
07 mention, promote, stopper
08 good word
09 advertise, promotion, publicity, publicize
10 commercial
13 advertisement

❑**plug away**
06 plod on
07 peg away
08 slog away
09 soldier on

plum
04 best
06 choice
10 first-class

plumb
05 gauge, probe, sheer, sound
06 fathom, search
07 exactly, explore, measure
08 sound out
09 delve into, penetrate, up and down
10 straight up, vertically
12 straight down
15 perpendicularly

❑**plumb the depths of**
15 reach rock bottom

plume
04 tuft
05 crest, quill
06 pappus, pinion
07 feather
08 aigrette

❑**plume yourself on**
07 exult in
10 boast about

plummet
04 dive, drop, fall
06 hurtle, plunge, tumble
08 nose-dive

plump
03 fat
04 drop, dump, flop, full, sink
05 ample, buxom, dumpy, podgy, round, stout, tubby
06 chubby, portly, rotund
07 deposit, put down, set down
09 corpulent
11 well-rounded
15 well-upholstered

❑**plump for**
06 choose, favour, opt for, prefer, select

plumpness
07 fatness
09 podginess, pudginess, rotundity, stoutness, tubbiness
10 chubbiness, corpulence, portliness

plunder
03 rob
04 loot, raid, sack, swag
05 booty, prize, rifle, steal, strip
06 fleece, maraud, ravage, spoils
07 despoil, pillage, ransack
08 lay waste, pickings
09 depredate, devastate
14 ill-gotten gains

plunge
03 dip, jab, ram
04 dash, dive, drop, fall, jump, push, rush, sink, stab, tear
05 drive, pitch, shove, stick, swoop, throw
06 career, charge, go down, hurtle, thrust, tumble
07 descend, descent, immerse, plummet
08 dive-bomb, nose-dive, submerge
11 drop rapidly, fall rapidly

plurality
04 bulk, mass, most
06 galaxy, number
07 variety
08 majority
09 diversity, profusion
12 multiplicity, numerousness
13 preponderance

plus
03 and
04 gain, perk, with
05 asset, bonus, extra
07 benefit, surplus
08 as well as
09 advantage, good point
12 in addition to, not to mention, over and above, together with

plush
04 posh, rich
05 ritzy
06 costly, de luxe, glitzy, lavish, luxury, swanky
07 opulent, stylish
08 affluent, palatial
09 luxurious, sumptuous

plutocrat
05 Dives
06 fat cat, tycoon
07 Croesus, magnate, rich man
09 moneybags
10 capitalist

ply
04 feed, fold, leaf
05 ferry, layer, sheet
06 assail, employ, follow, handle, harass, lavish, pursue, strand, supply, travel, work at
07 bombard, carry on, utilize
08 exercise, practise
09 importune, thickness

poach
04 copy, lift, nick, take
05 steal
06 borrow, pilfer
08 encroach, infringe, trespass
11 appropriate

pocket
03 bag
04 gain, lift, mini, nick, take
05 filch, funds, means, money, patch, pinch, pouch, small, steal
06 assets, budget, cavity, hollow, little, pilfer, potted
07 capital, compact, concise, purloin
08 abridged, envelope, finances, pint-size, portable

09 miniature, resources
10 receptacle, small group
11 appropriate, compartment

pockmark
03 pit
04 pock, scar
07 blemish, pockpit

pod
04 case, hull, husk
05 shell
06 legume

podgy
05 plump, tubby
06 chubby, chunky, rotund
08 roly-poly

podium
04 dais
05 stage, stand
07 rostrum
08 platform

poem

▶ *Types of poem*:
03 lay, ode
04 epic, song
05 ditty, elegy, epode, haiku,
   idyll, lyric, rhyme, tanka,
   verse
06 ballad, monody, sonnet
07 couplet, eclogue, epigram,
   georgic, rondeau, triolet
08 clerihew, limerick, madrigal,
   pastoral, versicle
09 roundelay
11 epithalmium
12 nursery rhyme,
   prothalamion
➤ See also **song**

▶ *Poems and poetry
collections include*:
02 If
04 Crow, Days, Edda, Hope,
   Howl, Maud, Odes
05 Comus, Lamia
06 Hellas, Marina, The Fly,
   Villon
07 Beowulf, Don Juan, Façade,
   Lycidas, Mariana,
   Marmion, Requiem,
   Ulysses
08 Bermudas, Endymion,
   Georgics, Gunga Din,
   Hiawatha, Hudibras,
   Kalevala, Lupercal, Queen
   Mab, Ramayana, The Iliad,
   The Pearl, The Tyger,
   Tithonus, To Autumn
09 Decameron, Jerusalem,
   Kubla Khan, The Aeneid,
   The Cantos

10 Cherry Ripe, Christabel,
   Dream Songs, In
   Memoriam, Lalla Rookh,
   The Dunciad, The Odyssey,
   The Poetics, The Prelude,
   The Village, View of a Pig
11 A Red, Red Rose, Ars
   Amatoria, High Windows,
   Holy Sonnets, Humming-
   Bird, Jabberwocky,
   Mahabharata, Ode to
   Autumn, Remembrance,
   Song of my Cid, Tam
   O'Shanter, The Eclogues,
   The Extasie, The Sick
   Rose, The Sluggard, The
   Woodlark
12 A Song to Celia, Ash
   Wednesday, Auld Lang
   Syne, Bhagavad Gita,
   Eugene Onegin, Faith
   Healing, Four Quartets,
   Goblin Market, Hawk
   Roosting, Homage to Clio,
   Jubilate Agno, Mercian
   Hymns, Morte d'Arthur,
   Ode to Evening, Paradise
   Lost, Piers Plowman, The
   Lucy Poems, The Waste
   Land, The Windhover
13 Arms and the Boy,
   Gilgamesh Epic, Leaves of
   Grass, Metamorphoses,
   Missing the Sea, Naming of
   Parts, Roman de la Rose,
   September Song, The Book
   of Thel
14 A Shropshire Lad, Divina
   Commedia, Leda and the
   Swan, Les Fleurs du Mal,
   Love Songs in Age, Lyrical
   Ballads, Orlando Furioso,
   Song of Hiawatha, Strange
   Meeting, The Lotus-Eaters
15 Canterbury Tales,
   Cautionary Tales, Idylls of
   the King, Ode on
   Melancholy, Summoned by
   Bells, The Age of Anxiety,
   The Divine Comedy, The
   Eve of St Agnes, The Faerie
   Queene, The Second
   Coming

poet
04 bard
06 rhymer
07 elegist, rhymist
08 idyllist, lyricist, minstrel
09 balladeer, poetaster,
   poeticule, rhymester,
   sonneteer, versifier
➤ See also **writer**

▶ *Names of poets*:
03 **Gay** (John), **Lee** (Laurie),
   Paz (Octavio), **Poe** (Edgar
   Allan)
04 **Amis** (Kingsley), **Blok**
   (Alexander), **Dunn**
   (Douglas), **Gray** (Thomas),
   Gunn (Thom), **Hill**
   (Geoffrey), **Hogg** (James),
   Hood (Thomas), **Hunt**
   (Leigh), **Lear** (Edward),
   Muir (Edwin), **Nash**
   (Ogden), **Ovid**, **Owen**
   (Wilfred), **Pope**
   (Alexander), **Rich**
   (Adrienne), **Seth** (Vikram),
   Vega (Lope de)
05 **Auden** (Wystan Hugh),
   Basho (Matsuo), **Benét**
   (Stephen Vincent), **Blake**
   (William), **Burns** (Robert),
   Byron (George, Lord),
   Clare (John), **Crane** (Hart),
   Dante, **Donne** (John),
   Duffy (Carol Ann), **Eliot**
   (Thomas Stearns), **Frost**
   (Robert), **Hardy** (Thomas),
   Harte (Brett), **Heine**
   (Heinrich), **Henri** (Adrian),
   Hesse (Hermann), **Homer**,
   Ibsen (Henrik), **Keats**
   (John), **Lorca** (Federico
   García), **O'Hara** (Frank),
   Opitz (Martin), **Plath**
   (Sylvia), **Pound** (Ezra),
   Raine (Craig), **Rilke**
   (Rainer Maria), **Sachs**
   (Hans), **Sachs** (Nelly), **Scott**
   (Sir Walter), **Smart**
   (Christopher), **Smith**
   (Stevie), **Spark** (Dame
   Muriel), **Tasso** (Torquato),
   Yeats (William Butler)
06 **Adcock** (Fleur), **Aragon**
   (Louis), **Arnold** (Matthew),
   Artaud (Antoni), **Barnes**
   (William), **Belloc** (Hilaire),
   Benoît, **Binyon** (Laurence),
   Bishop (Elizabeth), **Brecht**
   (Bertolt), **Brontë** (Anne),
   Brontë (Emily), **Brooke**
   (Rupert), **Carver**
   (Raymond), **Cowper**
   (William), **Crabbe**
   (George), **Dunbar**
   (William), **Eluard** (Paul),
   Empson (Sir William),
   Ennius (Quintus), **Fuller**
   (Roy), **Goethe** (Johann
   Wolfgang von), **Graves**
   (Robert), **Gurney** (Ivor),
   Heaney (Seamus), **Hesiod**,

Horace, **Larkin** (Philip),
Lowell (Amy), **Lowell**
(Robert), **Millay** (Edna
Saint Vincent), **Milosz**
(Czeslaw), **Milton** (John),
Morris (William), **Neruda**
(Pablo), **Ossian, Patten**
(Brian), **Pindar, Porter**
(Peter), **Racine** (Jean),
Riding (Laura), **Sappho,
Sidney** (Sir Philip), **Tagore**
(Rabindranath), **Thomas**
(Dylan), **Thomas** (Edward),
Thomas (Ronald Stuart),
Valéry (Paul), **Villon**
(François), **Virgil, Waller**
(Edmund)

07 **Addison** (Joseph),
Aneurin, Angelou (Maya),
Aretino (Pietro), **Ariosto**
(Ludovico), **Ashbery**
(John), **Beckett** (Samuel),
Blunden (Edmund
Charles), **Brodsky** (Joseph),
Büchner (Georg),
Caedmon, Campion
(Thomas), **Causley**
(Charles), **Chapman**
(George), **Chaucer**
(Geoffrey), **Cocteau** (Jean),
Durrell (Lawrence),
Emerson (Ralph Waldo),
Gautier (Théophile),
Herbert (George), **Herrick**
(Robert), **Hopkins** (Gerard
Manley), **Housman** (Alfred
Edward), **Jiménez** (Juan
Ramón), **Johnson**
(Samuel), **Kipling**
(Rudyard), **Layamon,
MacCaig** (Norman),
MacLean (Sorley),
Macbeth (George),
Manzoni (Alessandro),
Martial, Marvell
(Andrew), **McGough**
(Roger), **Mishima** (Yukio),
Novalis, Pushkin
(Alexander), **Rimbaud**
(Arthur), **Roethke**
(Theodore), **Ronsard**
(Pierre de), **Rostand**
(Edmond), **Sassoon**
(Siegfried), **Seferis, Seifert**
(Jaroslav), **Shelley** (Percy
Bysshe), **Sitwell** (Dame
Edith), **Sitwell** (Sir
Sacheverell), **Skelton**
(John), **Spender** (Sir
Stephen), **Spenser**
(Edmund), **Stevens**
(Wallace), **Terence,**

Thoreau (Henry David),
Vaughan (Henry), **Vicente**
(Gil), **Walcott** (Derek),
Whitman (Walt)

08 **Anacreon, Ausonius**
(Decimus Magnus),
Banville (Théodore de),
Berryman (John),
Brentano (Clemens),
Brittain (Vera), **Browning**
(Elizabeth Barrett),
Browning (Robert),
Catullus (Gaius Valerius),
Claudian, Congreve
(William), **cummings** (e e),
Cynewulf, De La Mare
(Walter), **Ginsberg** (Allen),
Laforgue (Jules),
Langland (William),
Lawrence (David Herbert),
Leopardi (Giacomo),
Lovelace (Richard),
MacLeish (Archibald),
MacNeice (Louis),
Macaulay (Dame Rose),
Macaulay (Thomas),
Mallarmé (Stéphane),
Menander, Milligan
(Spike), **Palgrave** (Francis
Turner), **Petrarch,
Robinson** (Edwin
Arlington), **Rossetti**
(Christina), **Rossetti**
(Dante Gabriel), **Sandburg**
(Carl), **Schiller** (Friedrich),
Schlegel (August Wilhelm
von), **Suckling** (Sir John),
Taliesin, Tibullus, Verlaine
(Paul), **Whittier** (John
Greenleaf)

09 **Aeschylus, Akhmatova**
(Anna), **Bronowski** (Jacob),
Coleridge (Samuel Taylor),
D'Annunzio (Gabriele),
Dickinson (Emily),
Froissart (Jean),
Goldsmith (Oliver),
Hölderlin (Friedrich),
Lamartine (Alphonse de),
Lucretius, Marinetti
(Filippo Tommaso),
Pasternak (Boris),
Rochester (John Wilmot,
Earl of), **Rosenberg** (Isaac),
Santayana (George),
Southwell (Robert),
Swinburne (Algernon
Charles), **Ungaretti**
(Giuseppe), **Zephaniah**
(Benjamin)

10 **Baudelaire** (Charles),
Bradstreet (Anne),

Chatterton (Thomas),
Chesterton (Gilbert Keith),
Empedocles, FitzGerald
(Edward), **La Fontaine**
(Jean de), **Lagerkvist** (Pär),
Longfellow (Henry
Wadsworth), **MacDiarmid**
(Hugh), **Mayakovsky**
(Vladimir), **McGonagall**
(William), **Propertius**
(Sextus), **Theocritus**

11 **Apollinaire** (Guillaume),
**Omar Khayyám,
Shakespeare** (William),
Yevtushenko (Yevegeny)

13 **Sackville-West** (Vita)

14 **Dante Alighieri, Saint-
John Perse**

► *Names of poets laureate*:
03 **Pye** (Henry)
04 **Rowe** (Nicholas), **Tate**
(Nahum)
06 **Austin** (Alfred), **Cibber**
(Colley), **Dryden** (John),
Eusden (Laurence),
Hughes (Ted), **Jonson**
(Ben), **Motion** (Andrew),
Warton (Thomas)
07 **Bridges** (Robert), **Southey**
(Robert)
08 **Betjeman** (Sir John),
Davenant (Sir William),
Day-Lewis (Cecil),
Shadwell (Thomas),
Tennyson (Alfred, Lord)
09 **Masefield** (John),
Whitehead (William)
10 **Wordsworth** (William)

poetic
07 flowing, lyrical, prosaic,
rhyming
08 creative, metrical, symbolic
09 sensitive
10 expressive, figurative

poetry
04 muse
05 poems, poesy, rhyme, verse
06 lyrics
07 iambics, pennill, rhyming,
versing
09 free verse, Parnassus, vers
libre
13 versification

pogrom
08 genocide, homicide
09 holocaust, slaughter
11 liquidation
12 annihilation
13 extermination
15 ethnic cleansing

poignancy
04 pain
06 misery, pathos
07 emotion, feeling, sadness
08 distress, keenness, piquancy
09 intensity, sentiment
10 bitterness, tenderness
11 painfulness, piteousness
12 wretchedness

poignant
03 sad
06 moving, tender, tragic
07 painful, piteous, tearful
08 pathetic, touching
09 affecting, upsetting
12 heart-rending
13 heartbreaking

point
03 aim, dot, end, nib, nub, tip, top, use
04 area, cape, core, crux, gist, goal, head, hits, item, mark, meat, ness, pith, runs, show, site, spot, stop, time, tine, vein
05 drift, facet, goals, heart, issue, level, place, score, sense, speck, spike, stage, taper, tenor, theme, topic, total, train, trait
06 burden, denote, detail, direct, marrow, matter, moment, motive, object, period, reason, signal, thrust
07 essence, feature, instant, keynote, meaning, outlook, purpose, quality, signify, subject, suggest
08 evidence, foreland, full stop, headland, indicate, juncture, locality, location, property, question, sharp end
09 attribute, designate, extremity, full point, gesture at, intention, main point, objective, situation
10 particular, promontory
12 significance
14 characteristic

□beside the point
10 immaterial, irrelevant, out of place

□in point of fact
06 in fact
08 actually
15 as a matter of fact

□on the point of
07 about to, going to, ready to
12 on the verge of

□point of view
05 angle, slant
06 aspect, belief
07 feeling, opinion, outlook
08 approach, attitude, position
09 judgement, viewpoint
10 standpoint
11 perspective

□point out
04 show
06 remind, reveal
07 mention, point to, specify
08 allude to, identify, indicate
15 draw attention to

□point up
06 stress
09 emphasize, highlight, underline
15 call attention to

□to the point
07 germane
08 apposite, relevant
09 pertinent
11 appropriate

□up to a point
06 partly
08 slightly, somewhat
12 to some degree, to some extent

point-blank
06 direct, openly
07 bluntly, close to, closely, frankly, plainly
08 abruptly, candidly, directly, outright, straight
10 explicitly, forthright, unreserved
12 at close range
15 straightforward

pointed
04 keen
05 clear, edged, sharp
06 barbed, biting
07 cutting, obvious, telling
08 aculeate, incisive, tapering
09 trenchant
10 fastigiate, lanceolate
11 penetrating

pointer
03 rod, tip
04 cane, clue, hand, hint, pole, sign
05 arrow, guide, stick
06 advice, needle
07 caution, warning
09 guideline, indicator
10 indication, suggestion
14 recommendation

pointless
04 vain
06 absurd, futile
07 aimless, foolish, useless
09 a mug's game, fruitless, senseless, to no avail, valueless, worthless
11 meaningless, nonsensical
12 a waste of time, unproductive, unprofitable
14 a waste of effort

poise
04 cool, hang
05 grace, hover
06 aplomb, steady
07 balance, dignity, support, suspend
08 calmness, coolness, elegance, position, serenity
09 assurance, composure
10 equanimity
11 equilibrium, self-control
13 self-assurance
14 self-possession

poised
04 calm, cool
05 ready, suave
06 all set, serene, urbane
07 assured, waiting
08 composed, graceful, prepared
09 collected, dignified, expectant, unruffled
11 unflappable
13 self-confident, self-possessed
14 self-controlled

poison
04 bane, warp
05 spoil, taint, toxin, venom
06 blight, cancer, defile, infect
07 corrupt, deprave, pervert, pollute
09 contagion, pollution
10 adulterate, corruption, malignancy

poisonous
05 fatal, toxic
06 deadly, lethal, mortal
07 harmful, noxious, vicious
08 spiteful, venomous, virulent
09 cancerous, malignant
10 corrupting, pernicious

► *Names of poisonous plants:*
05 dwale
07 aconite, amanita, anemone, cowbane, hemlock
08 banewort, foxglove, laburnum, oleander, wild arum

poke

09 digitalis, monkshood, poison ivy, stinkweed, wolfsbane
10 belladonna, cuckoo pint, thorn apple, windflower
12 helmet flower
13 meadow saffron
14 castor oil plant, lords-and-ladies
15 black nightshade
➤ See also **plant**

poke

03 dig, hit, jab
04 butt, prod, push, stab
05 elbow, nudge, punch, shove, stick
06 thrust

poke around

07 look for
09 search for
11 grope around, rake through
13 rummage around

poke fun at

03 rag, rib
04 jeer, mock
05 spoof, tease
06 parody, send up
08 ridicule
13 take the mickey

poke out

06 beetle, extend
07 project
08 protrude, stick out

poke your nose into

08 meddle in
11 interfere in
12 put your oar in
14 stick your oar in

poky

04 tiny
05 small, tight
06 narrow
07 cramped, crowded
08 confined
12 incommodious

polar

04 cold
03 icy
06 arctic, frozen
07 glacial
08 freezing, opposite, Siberian
10 ambivalent
11 conflicting, dichotomous
12 antithetical
13 contradictory

polarity

07 duality, paradox
09 dichotomy
10 antithesis, opposition

11 ambivalence, contrariety
12 oppositeness
13 contradiction

pole

03 bar, rod
04 mast, post, spar
05 limit, shaft, staff, stake, stick
06 pillar
07 extreme, support, upright
09 extremity

poles apart

11 worlds apart
12 incompatible
14 irreconcilable

polemic

06 debate
07 dispute, eristic
08 argument
09 eristical, polemical
11 contentious, controversy
12 disputatious
13 argumentative, controversial

polemicist

06 arguer
07 debater
08 disputer
09 disputant
11 logomachist

polemics

06 debate
07 dispute
08 argument
09 logomachy
11 controversy, disputation

police

04 cops, fuzz, pigs
05 check, garda, guard, watch
06 defend, gardai, mounty, patrol, peeler, the Law
07 control, monitor, mountie, observe, oversee, protect, rozzers, the Bill, the fuzz
08 gendarme, the Force
09 keep watch, supervise
11 police force
12 constabulary, keep the peace

police officer

03 cop, pig
04 bull, nark
05 bobby
06 copper, rozzer, the Law
07 officer, the Bill, the fuzz
08 flatfoot
09 constable, policeman
10 bluebottle, boys in blue, the old Bill
11 policewoman

policy

04 line, plan
05 rules
06 course, custom, method, scheme, stance, system
08 approach, position, practice, protocol, schedule
09 procedure, programme
10 guidelines
14 code of practice

polish

03 rub, wax
04 buff
05 class, clean, glaze, gloss, grace, poise, rub up, sheen, shine, style
06 finish, lustre, refine, veneer
07 brush up, burnish, enhance, finesse, furbish, improve, perfect, sparkle, touch up, varnish
08 breeding, elegance
09 cultivate
10 brightness, brilliance, refinement, smoothness
11 cultivation
14 sophistication

polish off

04 bolt, down, kill, wolf
06 devour, finish, gobble, murder, rub out
07 bump off, consume
08 complete
09 dispose of, eliminate, liquidate

polished

05 adept, shiny, suave, waxed
06 expert, glassy, glossy, polite, smooth, urbane
07 elegant, genteel, perfect, refined, shining, skilful
08 flawless, gleaming, lustrous, masterly, slippery, well-bred
09 burnished, civilized, excellent, faultless, perfected
10 cultivated, impeccable, proficient
11 outstanding, superlative
12 accomplished, professional, well-mannered
13 sophisticated

polite

05 civil, suave
06 polite, urbane
07 elegant, gallant, genteel, refined, tactful
08 cultured, gracious, ladylike, obliging, well-bred
09 civilized, courteous

10 chivalrous, diplomatic,
respectful, thoughtful
11 considerate, deferential,
gentlemanly, well-behaved
12 well-mannered
13 sophisticated

politeness
04 tact
05 grace
06 polish
07 culture, manners, respect
08 civility, courtesy, elegance
09 diplomacy, gentility
10 cordiality, discretion,
refinement
11 courtliness, cultivation,
good manners
12 graciousness, mannerliness
14 respectfulness, thoughtfulness
15 considerateness,
gentlemanliness

politic
04 sage, wise
06 shrewd
07 prudent, tactful
08 sensible
09 advisable, expedient,
opportune
10 diplomatic
12 advantageous

political
05 civil
06 public
08 judicial
09 executive
11 ministerial
12 bureaucratic, governmental
13 parliamentary
14 administrative,
constitutional

politics
06 civics
09 diplomacy, power game
10 government, statecraft
13 power struggle, public
affairs, statesmanship
14 affairs of state
➤ See also **government**;
minister; **parliament**;
president

▶ *Names of politicians*:
03 Coe (Sebastian), **Fox**
(Charles James), **Fox** (Sir
Marcus), **Jay** (Margaret,
Lady), **Lee** (Jennie, Lady),
Lie (Trygve), **Pym** (John),
Wet (Christian de), **Yeo**
(Timothy)
04 Aziz (Tariq), **Bell** (Martin),
Benn (Anthony Wedgwood

'Tony'), **Cato** (Marcus
Porcius), **Cook** (Robin),
Debs (Eugene Victor), **Dole**
(Robert), **Foot** (Michael),
Gore (Albert), **Haig**
(Alexander), **Hess** (Rudolf),
Howe (Geoffrey, Lord),
Hume (John), **Hurd**
(Douglas, Lord), **Koch**
(Ed), **Kohl** (Helmut), **More**
(Sir Thomas), **Nagy** (Imre),
Owen (David, Lord), **Pitt**
(William, the elder), **Reno**
(Janet), **Röhm** (Ernst),
Rusk (Dean)
05 Adams (Gerry), **Agnew**
(Spiro Theodore), **Astor**
(Nancy, Viscountess), **Bacon**
(Francis), **Baker** (James
Addison), **Baker** (Kenneth,
Lord), **Bevan** (Aneurin),
Bevin (Ernest), **Brown**
(George), **Brown** (Gordon),
Cimon, **Clark** (Alan),
Cleon, **Dayan** (Moshe),
Dewar (Donald), **Field**
(Frank), **Freud** (Sir
Clement), **Hague** (William),
Kirov (Sergey), **Krenz**
(Egon), **Lenin** (Vladimir
Ilyich), **Marat** (Jean Paul),
Maude (Francis), **Nkomo**
(Joshua), **Perón** (Eva),
Perón (Isabelita), **Scott** (Sir
Nicholas), **Scott** (Sir
Richard), **Short** (Clare),
Smith (Chris), **Smith**
(John), **Solon**, **Steel** (David,
Lord), **Straw** (Jack), **Sulla**
(Lucius Cornelius), **Sully**
(Maximilien de Béthune
Duc de), **Tambo** (Oliver),
Vance (Cyrus Roberts)
06 Abacha (Sanni), **Abbott**
(Diane), **Antony** (Mark),
Archer (Jeffrey), **Benton**
(Thomas Hart), **Boyson**
(Sir Rhodes), **Brandt**
(Willy), **Bright** (John),
Butler (Richard, Lord),
Caesar (Julius), **Castle**
(Barbara, Lady), **Cicero**
(Marcus Tullius), **Clarke**
(Kenneth), **Cobden**
(Richard), **Cripps** (Sir
Stafford), **Curzon** (George,
Marquis), **Danton**
(Georges), **Davies** (Denzil),
Dobson (Frank), **Dubcek**
(Alexander), **Dulles** (John
Foster), **Erhard** (Ludwig),
Fowler (Sir Norman),

Gummer (John), **Hardie**
(Keir), **Harman** (Harriet),
Healey (Denis, Lord),
Hitler (Adolf), **Horthy**
(Miklós), **Howard**
(Michael), **Hughes** (Simon),
Irvine (Alexander, Lord),
Jinnah (Muhammad Ali),
Joseph (Keith, Lord),
Jowell (Tessa), **Kaunda**
(Kenneth), **Lamont**
(Norman), **Lawson** (Nigel,
Lord), **Lilley** (Peter),
Mallon (Seamus), **Marius**
(Gaius), **Mellor** (David),
Mosley (Sir Oswald),
Mowlam (Doctor Marjorie
'Mo'), **Nansen** (Fridtjof),
Necker (Jacques), **Norris**
(Steven), **Pompey**, **Powell**
(Enoch), **Prasad**
(Rajendra), **Quayle** (Dan),
Tebbit (Norman, Lord),
Thorpe (Jeremy), **Warren**
(Earl), **Wilkes** (John),
Wolsey (Thomas)

07 Acheson (Dean), **Allende**
(Salvador), **Ashdown**
(Paddy), **Beckett**
(Margaret), **Boateng** (Paul),
Bormann (Martin),
Brittan (Sir Leon),
Canning (George),
Cassius, **Collins** (Michael),
Crassus (Marcus Licinius),
Dalyell (Tam), **Darling**
(Alistair), **De Klerk**
(Frederik William), **Dorrell**
(Stephen), **Fischer**
(Joschka), **Grimond** (Jo,
Lord), **Hussein** (Saddam),
Jackson (Glenda), **Jackson**
(Jesse), **Jameson** (Sir
Leander Starr), **Jenkins**
(Roy, Lord), **Kaufman**
(Gerald), **Kennedy**
(Charles), **Kennedy**
(Edward Moore), **Kennedy**
(Robert Francis), **Kinnock**
(Neil), **Lepidus** (Marcus
Aemilius), **MacLeod** (Iain),
Malraux (André), **Mazarin**
(Jules, Cardinal), **Meacher**
(Michael), **Milburn** (Alan),
Mondale (Walter
Frederick), **Paisley**
(Reverend Ian), **Profumo**
(John), **Redwood** (John),
Rifkind (Sir Malcolm),
Salmond (Alexander),
Schmidt (Helmut), **Sithole**
(Reverend Ndabaningi),

Skinner (Dennis), **Trimble** (David)

08 **Adenauer** (Konrad), **Albright** (Madeleine), **Antonius** (Marcus), **Blunkett** (David), **Catiline**, **Constant** (Benjamin), **Cromwell** (Oliver), **Cromwell** (Thomas), **Daladier** (Edouard), **Franklin** (Benjamin), **Goebbels** (Joseph), **Hailsham** (Quintin McGarel Hogg, Viscount), **Honecker** (Erich), **Humphrey** (Hubert Horatio), **Karadzic** (Radovan), **Khomeini** (Ayatollah Ruhollah), **Lansbury** (George), **Lucullus** (Lucius Licinius), **Malenkov** (Giorgiy), **Marshall** (George Catlett), **Maudling** (Reginald), **McCarthy** (Joseph Raymond), **McGovern** (George Stanley), **McNamara** (Robert Strange), **Mirabeau** (Honoré Gabriel Riqueti Comte de), **Montfort** (Simon de), **Morrison** (Herbert, Lord), **Pericles**, **Polignac** (Auguste Jules Armand Marie, Prince de), **Portillo** (Michael), **Prescott** (John), **Rathenau** (Walther), **Schröder** (Gerhard), **Schüssel** (Wolfgang), **Shephard** (Gillian), **Shinwell** (Manny, Lord), **Whitelaw** (William 'Willie', Viscount), **Williams** (Shirley, Lady), **Zinoviev** (Grigoriy)

09 **Boothroyd** (Betty), **Bottomley** (Virginia), **Buthelezi** (Chief Mangosuthu), **Ceausescu** (Nicolae), **Churchill** (Randolph, Lord), **Gaitskell** (Hugh), **Goldwater** (Barry Morris), **Heseltine** (Michael), **Kissinger** (Henry Alfred), **Kitchener** (Herbert, Earl), **La Guardia** (Fiorello Henry), **Lafayette** (Marie Joseph, Marquis de), **Luxemburg** (Rosa), **Mandelson** (Peter), **Miltiades**, **Parkinson**

(Cecil, Lord), **Podgorniy** (Nikolay), **Ramaphosa** (Cyril), **Richelieu** (Armand Jean du Plessis, Cardinal and Duc de), **Robertson** (George, Lord), **Stevenson** (Adlai), **Streicher** (Julius), **Vyshinsky** (Andrei)

10 **Alcibiades**, **Carrington** (Peter, Lord), **Cunningham** (Doctor Jack), **Enver Pasha**, **Hattersley** (Roy, Lord), **McGuinness** (Martin), **Metternich** (Klemens Fürst von), **Ribbentrop** (Joachim von), **Stresemann** (Gustav), **Talleyrand** (Charles Maurice de), **Waldegrave** (William), **Walsingham** (Sir Francis), **Weinberger** (Caspar), **Widdecombe** (Ann)

11 **Beaverbrook** (Max Aitken, Lord), **Bolingbroke** (Henry St John, Viscount), **Castlereagh** (Robert Stewart, Viscount), **Chamberlain** (Joseph), **Chamberlain** (Sir Austen), **Cincinnatus** (Lucius Quinctius), **Demosthenes**, **George-Brown** (Lord), **Hore-Belisha** (Leslie, Lord), **Livingstone** (Ken), **Machiavelli** (Niccolo dei), **Mountbatten** (Louis, Earl), **Wilberforce** (William)

12 **Boutros-Ghali** (Boutros), **Hammarskjöld** (Dag), **Themistocles**

13 **Chateaubriand** (François Auguste René Viscount of), **Fabius Maximus** (Quintus)

poll
03 cut, dod, get, net, win
04 clip, gain, trim, vote
05 count, shear, tally
06 ballot, census, sample, survey, voting
07 canvass, dishorn, pollard
08 question, sampling
09 ballot-box, head count
10 plebiscite, referendum
11 electioneer, show of hands
14 market research

pollute
03 mar
04 foul, soil, warp
05 dirty, spoil, stain, sully, taint

06 befoul, debase, defile, infect, poison
07 blacken, corrupt, deprave, tarnish, vitiate
10 adulterate
11 contaminate

pollution
05 taint
07 fouling
08 foulness, impurity, staining, sullying
09 depravity, dirtiness, infection, muckiness
10 blackening, corruption, debasement, defilement, filthiness, tarnishing
12 adulteration
13 contamination

polychromatic
06 motley
07 rainbow
08 many-hued
12 many-coloured, varicoloured
13 kaleidoscopic, multicoloured

polyglot
08 linguist
12 cosmopolitan, multilingual
13 international, multilinguist

polymath
06 oracle
07 know-all
10 all-rounder, pansophist, polyhistor

pomp
04 show
05 glory, state
06 parade, ritual
07 display, glitter, majesty
08 ceremony, flourish, grandeur
09 formality, pageantry, solemnity, spectacle, splendour
10 brilliance, ceremonial
11 ostentation
12 magnificence
15 ceremoniousness

pomposity
07 bombast, fustian
08 euphuism, rhetoric
09 arrogance, turgidity
10 pretension, stuffiness
11 affectation, haughtiness, preachiness
14 self-importance

pompous
05 proud, windy
06 stuffy, turgid

07 haughty, preachy
08 affected, arrogant
09 bombastic, conceited, grandiose
10 euphuistic
11 overbearing, patronizing, pretentious
12 ostentatious, supercilious
13 self-important

pond
04 lake, mere, pond, pool, tarn
06 puddle
09 waterhole
12 watering-hole

ponder
04 muse
05 brood, study, think, weigh
06 reason
07 analyse, examine, reflect
08 cogitate, consider, meditate, mull over
09 cerebrate
10 deliberate, excogitate, puzzle over
11 contemplate, ratiocinate
12 ruminate over
13 give thought to

ponderous
04 dull, huge
05 bulky, heavy, hefty
06 clumsy, dreary, prolix, stodgy, stolid
07 awkward, massive, serious, stilted, tedious, verbose, weighty
08 laboured, lifeless, pedantic, plodding, unwieldy
09 graceless, laborious, lumbering
10 cumbersome, long-winded, pedestrian, slow-moving
11 elephantine, heavy-footed, heavy-handed

ponderousness
06 tedium
09 heaviness, stolidity
11 seriousness, weightiness
13 laboriousness

pontifical
05 papal
07 pompous, preachy
08 didactic, dogmatic, prelatic
09 apostolic, imperious
10 portentous
11 magisterial, overbearing, pretentious, sermonizing
13 condescending

pontificate
06 preach
07 declaim, expound, lecture

08 harangue, moralize, perorate, sound off
09 dogmatize, hold forth, pronounce, sermonize
13 lay down the law

pooh-pooh
05 scoff, scorn, sneer, spurn
06 deride, reject, slight
07 disdain, dismiss, sniff at
08 belittle, minimize, play down, ridicule
09 disparage, disregard

pool
03 pot
04 ante, bank, fund, lake, mere, pond, ring, tarn, team
05 group, kitty, merge, purse, share
06 cartel, chip in, muck in, puddle, supply
07 combine, jackpot, reserve
09 syndicate, waterhole
10 amalgamate, collective, consortium, contribute
12 swimming-bath, watering-hole
13 swimming-baths

poor
03 bad, low, sad
04 mean, naff, ropy, weak
05 broke, lowly, needy, skint
06 barren, faulty, feeble, hard-up, humble, in need, meagre, measly, paltry, scanty, shoddy, sparse
07 hapless, lacking, reduced, unlucky
08 badly off, below par, exiguous, indigent, inferior, low-grade, mediocre, pathetic, wretched
09 deficient, destitute, imperfect, miserable, penniless, penurious, third-rate, worthless
10 inadequate, low-quality, stony-broke, straitened
11 impecunious, substandard, unfortunate
12 impoverished, insufficient, on your uppers, without means
13 below standard
14 on the breadline, on your beam ends, unsatisfactory
15 poverty-stricken

poorly
03 ill
04 sick
05 badly, seedy

06 ailing, feebly, meanly, sickly, unwell
08 below par
09 off colour
10 indisposed, out of sorts
12 inadequately
13 incompetently
15 under the weather

pop
03 nip, put
04 bang, boom, dash, drop, push, rush, slip, snap, soda
05 burst, crack, go off, hurry, shove, slide
06 insert, report, thrust
07 explode
09 explosion
10 fizzy drink

❏**pop off**
03 die
06 pass on, peg out
07 snuff it
08 pass away
09 have had it
13 kick the bucket

❏**pop up**
05 occur
06 appear, crop up, show up, turn up
11 materialize

pope
07 pontiff
10 Holy Father
11 His Holiness
12 Bishop of Rome
13 Vicar of Christ

▶ *Names of popes. We have omitted the word* **pope** *from names given in the following list but you may need to include this word as part of the solution to some crossword clues. The regnal numerals of individual popes have also been omitted.*
03 Leo
04 Cono, Joan, John, Mark, Paul, Pius
05 Felix, Lando, Linus, Peter, Soter, Urban
06 Adrian, Agatho, Albert, Fabian, Julius, Lucius, Martin, Philip, Sixtus, Victor
07 Clement, Damasus, Gregory, Hadrian, Hilarus, Marinus, Paschal, Pontian, Romanus, Sergius, Stephen, Ursinus, Zosimus
08 Agapetus, Benedict, Boniface, Calixtus, Eugenius, Eusebius,

Formosus, Gelasius,
Honorius, Innocent, John
Paul, Liberius, Nicholas,
Novatian, Pelagius,
Theodore, Vigilius
09 Alexander, Anacletus,
Callistus, Celestine,
Cornelius, Deusdedit,
Dionysius, Dioscorus,
Marcellus, Severinus,
Silverius, Sylvester,
Symmachus, Theodoric,
Valentine, Zacharias
10 Anastasius, Hippolytus,
Laurentius, Militiades,
Simplicius, Zephyrinus
11 Christopher, Constantine
➤ See also **religion**

popinjay
03 fop
04 beau, dude, toff
05 dandy, pansy, swell
07 coxcomb, peacock

poppycock
03 rot
04 bosh, bull, bunk, crap, tosh
05 balls, bilge, folly, hooey,
trash, tripe
06 drivel, humbug, piffle, waffle
07 baloney, blather, flannel,
rubbish, twaddle
08 claptrap, cobblers,
nonsense, tommy-rot
09 gibberish, silliness, stupidity
10 balderdash, codswallop
12 gobbledygook

populace
03 mob
04 folk
05 crowd, plebs
06 masses, people, public,
rabble
07 natives, punters, society
08 canaille, citizens
09 hoi polloi, multitude,
residents
10 common herd
11 inhabitants, proletariat, rank
and file
13 general public

popular
02 in
03 big, hip
04 cool
05 liked, noted, stock, usual
06 common, famous, modish,
simple, trendy, wanted
07 admired, current, desired,
general

08 accepted, approved,
favoured, idolized, in
demand, in favour, ordinary,
renowned, standard
09 acclaimed, customary,
favourite, household,
prevalent, universal, well-
known, well-liked
10 accessible, all the rage,
celebrated, mass-market,
prevailing, simplified,
widespread
11 fashionable, sought-after
12 conventional, non-technical
13 non-specialist
14 understandable

popularity
04 fame
05 glory, kudos, vogue
06 esteem, favour, regard,
renown, repute
07 acclaim, worship
09 adoration, adulation
10 acceptance, mass appeal
11 approbation, idolization,
lionization

popularize
06 spread
10 generalize
11 democratize, familiarize

popularly
06 widely
08 commonly
09 generally, regularly
10 ordinarily
11 customarily, universally
13 traditionally
14 conventionally

populate
05 dwell
06 live in, occupy, people, settle
07 inhabit, overrun
08 colonize

population
04 folk
06 people
07 natives, society
08 citizens, populace
09 community, occupants,
residents
11 inhabitants

populous
06 packed
07 crowded, teeming
08 crawling, swarming

porcelain
➤ *Types of porcelain*:
05 Imari, Kraak
06 bisque, Canton, Parian

07 biscuit, faience, nankeen
08 eggshell, Kakiemon
09 bone china, copper red,
hard paste, soft paste
11 Capodimonte, chinoiserie,
famille-rose
12 blue and white, famille-verte
14 soapstone paste

➤ *Famous makes of
porcelain*:
03 Bow
04 Ming
05 Arita, Derby
06 Minton, Sèvres, Vienna
07 Belleek, Bristol, Chelsea,
Dresden, Limoges, Meissen,
Nanking, Satsuma
08 Caughley, Coalport,
Wedgwood
09 Chantilly, Worcester
10 Rockingham
12 Royal Doulton
14 Royal Worcester

porch
04 hall
05 foyer, lobby
07 hallway
09 vestibule
12 entrance-hall

pore
04 hole, vent
06 outlet
07 foramen, opening, orifice
08 aperture
11 perforation

❑**pore over**
04 read, scan
05 brood, study
06 go over, peruse, ponder
07 examine
10 scrutinize

pornographic
04 blue, lewd, porn
05 bawdy, dirty, gross
06 coarse, erotic, filthy, risqué
07 obscene
08 indecent, prurient
11 titillating

pornography
04 dirt, porn, smut
05 filth, porno
07 erotica
08 facetiae
09 indecency, obscenity

porous
04 airy, open
05 holey
06 spongy
07 foveate
08 cellular, pervious

09 absorbent, permeable
10 foraminous, spongelike

port

04 dock
05 haven, hithe, jetty, roads
07 harbour, seaport
09 anchorage, roadstead
10 harbourage

► *Names of ports*:

03 Gao, Lae, Vac
04 Aden , Apia, Baku, Bari, Caen, Cebu, Ciba, Cork, Doha, Elat, Faro, Hull, Kiel, Kobe, Linz, Lomé, Lüda, Nice, Oban, Omsk, Oran, Oslo, Oulu, Pula, Riga, Safi, Sfax, Suez, Suva, Tyre, Vigo, Wick
05 Accra, Agana, Aqaba, Arica, Basle, Basra, Beira, Belém, Blyth, Brest, Busan , Colón, Dakar, Davao, Dover, Dubai, Emden, Gavle, Genoa, Ghent, Haifa, Ibiza, Izmir, Kazan, Lagos, Larne, Leith, Liège, Macao, Malmo, Masan, Miami, Nampo, Natal, Omaha, Osaka, Ostia, Palma, Paris , Poole, Praia, Pusan, Rouen, Sakai, Salem, Sitra, Split, Tampa, Tanga, Tokyo, Tomsk, Tulsa, Tunis, Turku, Ulsan, Vaasa, Varna, Worms, Wuhan
06 Aarhus, Abadan, Agadir, Ancona, Annaba, Ashdod, Avarua, Aveira, Aviles, Balboa, Bamako, Banjul, Batumi, Beirut, Bergen, Bissau, Bombay, Boston, Bremen, Bruges, Calais, Callao, Cannes, Cochin, Dalian, Dammam, Darwin, Denver, Dieppe, Douala, Dublin, Duluth, Dundee, Durban, Durres, El Paso, Galway, Gdansk, Gdynia, Havana, Hobart, Inchon, Jarrow, Jeddah, Juneau, Kandla, Kaunas, Khulna, Lisbon, Lobito, London, Luanda, Lübeck, Madras, Malabo, Malaga, Manama, Manaus, Manila, Maputo, Mersin, Mobile, Muscat, Nacala, Nagoya, Nantes, Napier, Naples, Narvik, Nassau, Nelson, Newark, Niamey, Ningbo, Nouméa, Nyborg, Odense, Odessa,

Oporto, Ostend, Penang, Phuket, Quebec, Recife, Rijeka, Rimini, Samara, Samsun, Santos, Sasebo, Sittwe, Sousse, St John, St-Malo, Sydney, Szeged, Tacoma, Thurso, Timaru, Toledo, Toulon, Toyama, Treves, Velsen, Venice, Warsaw, Whitby, Xiamen, Yangon

07 Aalborg, Abidjan, Ajaccio, Algiers, Almeria, Antibes, Antwerp, Bangkok, Belfast, Bizerta, Bristol, Buffalo, Cabinda, Calabar, Caldera, Calicut, Cardiff, Catania, Cayenne, Chicago, Cologne, Colombo, Conakry, Corinth, Corinto, Dampier, Detroit, Douglas, Dunedin, Dunkirk, Esbjerg, Funchal, Geelong, Glasgow, Grimsby, Halifax, Hamburg, Harstad, Harwich, Hodeida, Honiari, Houston, Ipswich, Iquique, Jakarta, Karachi, Kowloon, Kuching, Kushiro, La Plata, Larnaca, Le Havre, Livorno, Marsala, Memphis, Messina, Mindelo, Mombasa, Newport, Oakland, Okayama, Palermo, Papeete, Paradip, Piraeus, Rangoon, Ravenna, Rosaria, Rostock, Salerno, San José, San Juan, San Remo, Santa Fe, Sao Tomé, Seattle, Seville, Shimizu, Stanley, St John's, St Louis, Swansea, Tallinn, Tampico, Tangier, Taranto, Tel Aviv, Tianjin, Tilbury, Toronto, Trieste, Tripoli, Vitebsk, Vitoria, Wroclaw, Zhdanov

08 Aberdeen, Abu Dhabi, Acapulco, Adelaide, Alicante, Arbroath, Asunción, Auckland, Benghazi , Bordeaux, Boulogne, Brindisi, Brisbane, Cagliari , Calcutta, Cape Town, Castries, Djibouti, Dortmund, Duisburg, Dunleary, Falmouth, Flushing, Freeport, Freetown, Godthaab, Greenock, Guyaquil, Halmstad, Hamilton, Hay Point, Helsinki, Holyhead, Honolulu, Istanbul,

Kawasaki, Kingston, Kinshasa, Kirkaldy, Kirkwall, Kismaayo, La Coruna, Lattakia, Limassol, Limerick, Mandalay, Mannheim, Marbella, Monrovia, Montreal, Montrose, Moulmein, Mulhouse, Murmansk, Nagasaki, New Haven, Newhaven, Pago Pago, Plymouth, Port Said, Port-Vila, Portland, Ramsgate, Richmond, Roskilde, Rosslare, Salonica, Salvador, San Diego, San Pedro, Savannah, Shanghai, Simbirsk, Smolensk, St Helier, Stockton, St-Tropez, Surabaya, Syracuse, Tauranga, Torshavn, Ullapool, Valencia, Valletta, Veracruz, Voronezh, Weymouth, Yokohama, Zanzibar

09 Algeciras, Amsterdam, Anchorage, Archangel, Astrakhan, Baltimore, Barcelona, Bujumbura, Cartagena, Cherbourg, Cleveland, Constance, Constanta, Dordrecht, Dubrovnik, Europoort, Famagusta, Fleetwood, Flensburg, Fortaleza, Frankfurt, Fremantle, Galveston, Gateshead, Gibraltar, Gravesend, Heraklion, Hiroshima, Immingham, Kagoshima, Karlsruhe, King's Lynn, Kingstown, Langesund, Las Palmas, Launceston, Liverpool, Long Beach, Lowestoft, Magdeburg, Maracaibo, Melbourne, Milwaukee, Mogadishu, Nashville, Newcastle, Nuku'alofa, Palembang, Palm Beach, Paranagua, Peterhead, Phnom Penh, Port Limon, Port Louis, Port Sudan, Reykjavík, Rio Grande, Rochester, Rotterdam, Santander, Sassandra, Sheerness, Singapore, Stavanger, St-Nazaire, Stockholm, Stornoway, Stralsund, Stranraer, Sundsvall, Tarragona, Toamasina, Trebizond, Trondheim,

Vancouver, Volgograd, Walvis Bay, Yaroslavl, Zeebrugge

10 Alexandria, Basseterre, Baton Rouge, Belize City, Bratislava, Bridgeport, Bridgetown, Cap Haitian, Casablanca, Charleston, Chittagong, Cienfuegos, Copenhagen, Felixstowe, Folkestone, Fray Bentos, Fredericia, George Town, Georgetown, Gothenburg, Hartlepool, Hildesheim, Iskenderun, Kansas City, Kompong Som, Kuwait City, Libreville, Los Angeles, Manchester, Manzanillo, Marseilles, Montego Bay, Montevideo, New Orleans, Nouakchott, Oranjestad, Paramaribo, Pittsburgh, Port Talbot, Portishead, Portsmouth, Providence, Sacramento, San Lorenzo, Sebastopol, Sevastopol, Strasbourg, Sunderland, Thunder Bay, Townsville, Valparaiso, Wellington, Willemstad, Wilmington, Workington

11 Antofagasta, Bahia Blanca, Bandar Abbas, Brazzaville, Bridlington, Buenos Aires, Charlestown, Chattanooga, Dar es Salaam, Grangemouth, Helsingborg, Livingstone, Lossiemouth, Mar del Plata, New Plymouth, New York City, Novosibirsk, Panama Canal, Point-a-Pitre, Pointe-Noire, Pondicherry, Port Cartier, Port Moresby, Port of Spain, Punta Arenas, Richards Bay, Rostov-on-Don, Southampton, Three Rivers, Vladivostok

12 Barranquilla, Buenaventura, Fort de France, Frederikstad, Jacksonville, Kota Kinabalu, Kristiansand, New Amsterdam, New Mangalore, Philadelphia, Ponta Delgada, Port Adelaide, Port Harcourt, Port Victoria, Port-au-Prince, Puerto Cortes, Rio de Janeiro, Saint George's, San Francisco, San Sebastian, Santo Domingo, St Petersburg, Tel Aviv-Jaffa, Villahermosa

13 Ellesmere Port, Frederikshavn, Great Yarmouth, Ho Chi Minh City, Hook of Holland, Middlesbrough, Port Elizabeth

14 Port Georgetown, Santiago de Cuba

15 Barrow-in-Furness, Frankfurt am Main

portable
07 movable
10 conveyable
13 transportable

portend
04 bode
05 augur
06 herald, warn of
07 point to, predict, presage, promise
08 announce, forecast, foretell, forewarn, indicate, threaten
09 adumbrate, be a sign of, foretoken, harbinger
10 foreshadow

portent
04 omen, sign
06 augury, threat
07 presage, warning
08 forecast, prodrome
09 harbinger
10 indication
11 forewarning, premonition
15 prognostication

portentous
06 solemn
07 fateful, ominous, pompous, weighty
08 menacing, sinister
09 important, momentous
10 foreboding, pontifical, remarkable
11 significant, threatening
13 self-important

porter
06 bearer
07 carrier, doorman, janitor
09 caretaker, concierge
10 door-keeper, gatekeeper
13 door attendant
14 baggage-carrier, baggage-handler, commissionaire

portion
03 bit, cut, lot
04 deal, fate, luck, part
05 allot, piece, quota, share, slice, wedge, whack
06 divide, morsel, parcel, ration
07 carve up, destiny, dole out, fortune, helping, measure,

section, segment, serving, slice up, tranche
08 allocate, division, fragment, quantity, share out
09 allowance, partition
10 allocation, distribute

portliness
07 fatness, obesity
09 plumpness, rotundity, roundness, stoutness, tubbiness
10 chubbiness, corpulence

portly
05 ample, plump, round, stout
06 rotund, stocky
09 corpulent
10 overweight

portrait
04 icon
06 sketch
07 account, profile
08 likeness, vignette
09 depiction, miniature, portrayal
10 caricature
11 description
14 representation
15 thumbnail sketch

portray
03 act
04 draw, play
05 evoke, paint
06 depict, sketch
07 perform, picture
08 describe
09 personify, represent
10 illustrate
11 impersonate
12 act the part of, characterize
13 play the part of

portrayal
05 study
07 drawing, picture
08 painting
09 depiction, evocation, rendering
11 delineation, description, performance
14 representation

pose
03 act, air, ask, put, set, sit
04 aim, role, sham
05 feign, front, model, posit
06 affect, create, façade, lead to, stance, submit
07 advance, arrange, bearing, posture, present, pretend, produce, propose, suggest
08 attitude, carriage, position, pretence, propound

09 postulate, put on airs
10 deportment, give rise to, masquerade, put forward, put on an act
11 affectation, impersonate
12 attitudinize

poser
04 sham
05 pseud
06 enigma, phoney, poseur, puzzle, riddle
07 dilemma, mystery, poseuse, problem, show-off
08 impostor, posturer
09 conundrum
11 brainteaser
13 exhibitionist, vexed question

poseur
04 sham
05 poser, pseud
06 phoney
07 poseuse, show-off
08 impostor, posturer
13 exhibitionist

posh
05 grand, plush, smart, swish
06 classy, de-luxe, la-di-da, lavish, luxury, select, swanky
07 elegant, opulent, stylish
08 up-market
09 exclusive, high-class, luxurious, sumptuous
10 upper-class

posit
04 pose
06 assert, assume, submit
07 advance, presume
08 propound
09 postulate, predicate
10 put forward

position
03 fix, job, put, set
04 area, case, duty, pose, post, rank, role, site, spot, view
05 array, grade, level, place, point, scene, stand, state
06 belief, deploy, factor, lay out, locate, office, plight, settle, stance, status
07 arrange, bearing, dispose, factors, install, opinion, outlook, posture, ranking, setting, situate, station
08 attitude, capacity, locality, location, standing
09 condition, establish, influence, situation, viewpoint

10 background, employment, occupation, standpoint
11 appointment, arrangement, disposition, point of view, predicament, whereabouts
13 circumstances
14 state of affairs

positive
04 firm, rank, real, sure
05 clear, sheer, utter
06 actual, direct, upbeat, useful
07 assured, certain, express, helpful, hopeful, precise
08 absolute, cheerful, clear-cut, complete, concrete, decisive, definite, emphatic, explicit, outright, thorough
09 confident, convinced, out-and-out, veritable
10 conclusive, consummate, encouraged, optimistic, productive, undeniable
11 categorical, encouraging, irrefutable, unequivocal, unmitigated
12 constructive, indisputable
13 incontestable

positively
06 firmly, surely
09 assuredly, certainly, expressly
10 absolutely, decisively, definitely, undeniably
12 conclusively, emphatically, indisputably
13 categorically, incontestably, unequivocally
14 unquestionably

possess
03 get, own
04 gain, have, hold, take
05 enjoy, haunt, seize
06 obsess, obtain, occupy
07 bewitch, control, enchant
08 dominate, take over
09 infatuate, influence
13 be endowed with

possessed
06 crazed, cursed, raving
07 berserk, haunted
08 besotted, demented, frenzied, obsessed
09 bewitched, dominated, enchanted, hag-ridden
10 bedevilled, controlled, infatuated, mesmerized

possession
04 grip, hold
05 title
06 tenure

07 control, custody, holding, tenancy
09 ownership
10 occupation
14 proprietorship

possessions
04 gear
05 goods, stuff
06 assets, estate, things
07 baggage, effects, luggage
08 chattels, movables, property
10 belongings
13 worldly wealth

possessive
06 greedy
07 jealous, selfish
08 clinging, covetous, grasping
10 dominating

possibility
04 hope, odds, risk
06 chance, choice, danger, hazard, option, talent
07 promise
08 prospect, recourse
09 potential, prospects
10 advantages, likelihood, preference
11 alternative, feasibility, probability
12 capabilities, expectations, potentiality
13 attainability
14 conceivability, practicability

possible
06 doable, likely, odds-on
07 tenable
08 credible, feasible, probable
09 potential, promising
10 achievable, attainable, on the cards
11 conceivable, practicable
14 accomplishable

possibly
05 at all, maybe
07 perhaps
09 hopefully
10 by any means
11 by any chance, conceivably
12 peradventure

post
03 job, leg, pin, put
04 beat, mail, move, pale, pole, prop, send
05 affix, assign, e-mail, locate, newel, office, pin up, place, put up, second, shaft, stake, strut
06 column, picket, pillar, report
07 airmail, appoint, display, forward, letters, packets,

parcels, publish, situate,
station, upright, vacancy
08 announce, delivery,
dispatch, junk mail,
packages, position,
standard, transfer, transmit
09 publicize, situation, snail
mail, stanchion
10 direct mail, employment
11 appointment, surface mail
12 recorded mail
14 correspondence, electronic
mail, registered mail
15 special delivery

□**keep someone posted**
06 fill in, inform
12 keep up to date

poster
02 ad
04 bill, sign
06 advert, notice
07 placard, sticker
08 bulletin
12 announcement
13 advertisement

posterior
03 ass, bum
04 arse, back, butt, hind, rear,
rump, seat, tail
06 behind, bottom, dorsal,
hinder, latter
08 backside, buttocks,
haunches, rearward
09 hinder end, posticous
12 hindquarters

posterity
10 successors
11 descendants

posthaste
06 at once, pronto
07 hastily, quickly, swiftly
08 directly, full tilt, promptly,
speedily
11 double-quick, immediately
12 straightaway, with all speed

postman, postwoman
06 postie
07 mailman
11 mail handler, mail-carrier
12 postal worker
13 letter-carrier

post-mortem
07 autopsy
08 analysis, necropsy
10 dissection
11 examination

postpone
05 defer, delay
06 freeze, put off, shelve

07 adjourn, put back,
suspend
08 hold over, prorogue, put on
ice
10 pigeonhole, reschedule
13 procrastinate

postponed
05 on ice
06 frozen, put off
07 shelved
08 deferred
09 adjourned, suspended
10 in abeyance
15 on the back burner

postponement
04 stay
05 delay
06 freeze, put-off
08 deferral
09 deferment
10 moratorium, suspension
11 adjournment, prorogation

postscript
02 PS
07 codicil
08 appendix, epilogue
09 afterword
12 afterthought

postulate
05 posit
07 advance, lay down,
presume, propose,
suppose
08 theorize
10 presuppose
11 hypothesize

posture
04 pose, view
05 stand, strut
06 affect, belief, stance
07 bearing, opinion, show off
08 attitude, carriage, position
10 deportment, standpoint
11 disposition, point of view
12 attitudinize
15 strike attitudes

posy
05 spray
07 bouquet, corsage, nosegay

pot
03 jar, pan, urn
04 bowl, fund, vase
05 basin, kitty, purse
06 teapot, vessel
08 cauldron, crucible
09 coffee pot
10 receptacle

pot-bellied
06 portly

07 bloated, paunchy
09 corpulent, distended

pot-belly
03 gut, pot
06 paunch
09 beer belly

potency
04 kick, sway
05 force, might, power, punch
06 energy, muscle, vigour
08 capacity, efficacy, strength
09 potential, puissance
13 effectiveness
15 efficaciousness

potent
06 mighty, strong
07 dynamic, pungent
08 eloquent, forceful,
powerful, puissant, vigorous
10 commanding, compelling,
convincing, impressive
11 efficacious, influential
12 intoxicating, overpowering

potentate
04 king
05 chief, mogul, queen, ruler
06 despot, prince, tyrant
07 emperor, empress, monarch
08 autocrat, dictator, overlord
11 head of state

potential
06 hidden, latent, talent
07 ability, promise, would-be
08 capacity, inherent, possible,
probable
09 embryonic, promising
10 capability, developing
11 possibility, prospective

potentiality
07 ability, promise
08 aptitude, capacity,
prospect
10 capability, likelihood
13 possibilities

potion
04 brew, dose
05 drink, tonic
06 elixir
07 draught, mixture, philtre
08 medicine, potation
10 concoction

potpourri
06 jumble, medley
07 melange, mixture
08 mishmash, pastiche
09 confusion, patchwork
10 assortment, collection,
hotchpotch, miscellany
11 gallimaufry, smorgasbord

potter
05 amble
06 dawdle, loiter, toddle
10 dilly-dally

potter about
11 fiddle about, tinker about
12 fiddle around, tinker around

pottery
05 china
08 ceramics, crockery

Pottery terms:
04 kiln, slip
05 delft, glaze
06 basalt, enamel, firing, flambé, ground, jasper, lustre, sagger
07 celadon, ceramic, crazing, faience, fairing
08 armorial, bronzing, flatback, maiolica, majolica, monogram, slip-cast
09 china clay, creamware, ironstone, overglaze, porcelain, sgraffito, stoneware
10 maker's mark, spongeware, terracotta, underglaze
11 crackleware, earthenware
12 blanc-de-chine
13 Staffordshire, Willow pattern
➤ See also **porcelain**

potty
04 daft, nuts, soft
05 barmy, crazy, dippy, dotty, nutty, silly
07 bananas, bonkers, touched
08 crackers, demented
09 eccentric

pouch
03 bag, sac
04 poke, sack
05 purse
06 pocket, wallet
07 sporran
08 reticule
09 container, marsupium
10 receptacle

pounce
04 dive, drop, grab, jump, leap
05 bound, lunge, swoop
06 snatch, spring, strike
12 take unawares
13 catch off guard, catch unawares
14 take by surprise

pound
03 pen
04 bang, beat, drum, fold, mash, pelt, quid, thud, yard

05 crush, grind, smash, stomp, throb, thump, tread
06 batter, corral, hammer, pestle, pummel, strike
09 comminute, enclosure, palpitate, pulverize, triturate

pour
03 jet, run, tip
04 emit, flow, gush, leak, ooze, rain, rush, spew
05 crowd, flood, issue, serve, spill, spout, spurt, swarm
06 decant, stream, throng
07 cascade, come out
08 disgorge, pelt down, piss down, team down
09 discharge
10 bucket down, disembogue
15 rain cats and dogs

pout
04 moue, sulk
07 grimace
08 long face
09 pull a face

poverty
04 lack, need, want
06 dearth, penury
07 paucity
08 poorness, scarcity, shortage
09 indigence, privation
10 bankruptcy, deficiency, insolvency, meagreness
11 deprivation, destitution
13 impecuniosity, pennilessness
14 impoverishment

poverty-stricken
04 poor
05 broke, needy, skint, stony
08 indigent, strapped
09 destitute, penurious
10 stony-broke
11 impecunious
12 impoverished, on your uppers

powder
04 bran, bray, dust, mash, talc
05 crush, grind
06 pestle, pounce, powder, pulvil
08 levigate, pulvilio, pulville, sprinkle
09 comminute, pulverize, pulvillio, triturate

powdery
03 dry
04 fine
05 dusty, loose
06 chalky, floury, ground

08 levigate
10 pulverized

power
04 pull, rule, sway
05 clout, force, juice, might, right, teeth
06 energy, muscle, vigour
07 ability, command, control, faculty, potency, warrant
08 capacity, clutches, dominion, strength
09 authority, intensity, potential, supremacy
10 ascendancy, capability, competence, domination
11 prerogative, sovereignty
12 forcefulness, potentiality, powerfulness
13 authorization

powerful
05 burly, tough
06 brawny, mighty, potent, robust, strong
08 dominant, forceful, muscular, puissant
09 effective, energetic, strapping
10 commanding, compelling, convincing, persuasive
11 influential
13 authoritative

powerfully
08 cogently, forcibly, mightily, potently, strongly
10 forcefully, vigorously
12 convincingly, impressively, persuasively

powerless
04 weak
05 frail, unfit
06 feeble, infirm, unable
07 unarmed
08 disabled, helpless, impotent
09 incapable, paralysed
11 defenceless, ineffectual

practicability
03 use
05 value
07 utility
09 handiness
10 usefulness
11 operability, workability

practicable
06 doable, viable
08 workable
10 achievable, attainable

practical
05 handy
06 actual, strong, useful

07 applied, hands on, skilled, trained, working
08 feasible, suitable, workable, workaday
09 effective, efficient, hard-nosed, pragmatic, realistic
10 functional, hard-headed
11 commonsense, down-to-earth, serviceable, utilitarian
12 matter-of-fact

practicality
06 basics
07 realism, utility
08 practice
10 usefulness
11 common sense, feasibility, nitty-gritty, workability
12 nuts and bolts
14 serviceability

practically
06 all but, almost, nearly
08 in effect, sensibly, well-nigh
09 just about, virtually
10 pretty much, pretty well
11 essentially, in principle
13 pragmatically, realistically
14 matter-of-factly

practice
05 drill, habit, study, usage
06 career, custom, dry run, method, policy, warm-up
07 pursuit, reality, routine, work-out
08 business, dummy run, exercise, training
09 actuality, procedure, rehearsal, tradition
10 occupation, profession, run-through
11 application, performance, preparation

practise
05 apply, drill, study, train
06 follow, polish, pursue, refine, work at, work on
07 execute, observe, prepare
08 carry out, engage in, exercise, rehearse
09 implement, undertake
10 run through

practised
05 adept
06 expert, versed
07 skilful, skilled, trained
08 finished, masterly, seasoned
10 consummate, proficient
11 experienced
12 accomplished

pragmatic
08 sensible

09 efficient, hard-nosed, practical, realistic
10 hard-headed
12 businesslike, matter-of-fact

pragmatism
07 realism
08 humanism
12 practicalism, practicality
14 hard-headedness

pragmatist
07 realist
11 opportunist, utilitarian
12 practicalist

praise
04 hail, laud
05 cheer, exalt, extol, glory
06 eulogy, homage, honour
07 acclaim, applaud, commend, flatter, glorify, ovation, tribute, worship
08 accolade, applause, approval, encomium, eulogize, flattery, plaudits, rave over
09 laudation, panegyric
10 admiration, compliment, hallelujah, wax lyrical
11 approbation, speak well of, testimonial
12 commendation, congratulate, pay tribute to
13 speak highly of

praiseworthy
08 laudable, sterling
09 admirable, deserving, estimable, exemplary
10 honourable
11 commendable

praising
09 adulatory, laudative, laudatory, panegyric
10 eulogistic, flattering, plauditory, worshipful
11 approbatory, encomiastic
12 commendatory
13 complimentary
14 congratulatory

prance
04 jump, leap, romp, skip
05 bound, caper, dance, frisk, stalk, strut, swank, vault
06 cavort, curvet, frolic, gambol, parade, spring

prank
04 joke, lark
05 antic, caper, stunt, trick
08 escapade
13 practical joke

prattle
03 gab, jaw
04 chat, talk
06 babble, drivel, gabble, gossip, hot air, jabber, rattle, tattle, witter
07 blather, blether, chatter, prating, twaddle, twitter
08 nonsense
09 gibberish
11 foolishness

prattler
06 gossip, magpie, talker, tatler
07 babbler, blether, gabbler, tattler, windbag
09 chatterer
10 chatterbox

pray
03 ask, beg
05 adore, crave, plead, thank
06 call on, invoke, praise, talk to
07 beseech, entreat, implore, request, solicit, worship
08 petition
10 say a prayer, supplicate
14 say your prayers

prayer
04 plea
05 adore, thank
06 appeal, litany
07 collect, request
08 Ave Maria, devotion, entreaty, Hail Mary, petition
09 communion, Our Father
10 invocation
11 Paternoster
12 intercession, supplication
14 the Lord's Prayer

prayer-book
06 mahzor, missal
07 ordinal
08 breviary, Triodion
09 euchology, formulary
11 euchologion, service-book

preach
04 urge
05 teach
06 advise, exhort
07 address, lecture
08 admonish, advocate, harangue, moralize
09 sermonize
10 evangelize
11 give a sermon, pontificate

preacher
06 parson, ranter
08 homilist, minister, pulpiter
09 clergyman, moralizer, pulpiteer

10 evangelist, sermonizer
12 pontificater

preaching
05 dogma
06 gospel
07 evangel, kerygma, sermons
08 doctrine, homilies, precepts, teaching
10 evangelism, homiletics
11 exhortation, sermonizing
13 pontificating

preachy
08 didactic, dogmatic, edifying
09 homiletic, hortatory, pharisaic, pietistic, religiose
10 moralizing, pontifical
11 exhortatory, sermonizing
13 pontificating

preamble
05 proem
06 lead-in
07 preface, prelude
08 exordium, foreword, overture, prologue
11 preparation
12 introduction
13 preliminaries

precarious
05 dicey, hairy, risky, shaky
06 chancy, unsafe, wobbly
08 insecure, unstable, unsteady
09 dangerous, hazardous, uncertain, unsettled
10 unreliable, vulnerable
11 treacherous

precaution
08 prudence
09 foresight, insurance, provision, safeguard
10 protection, providence
11 forethought

precautionary
07 prudent
08 cautious
09 judicious, provident
10 protective
12 preventative

precede
04 head, lead
07 preface, prevene
08 antecede, antedate, go before
09 come first, go ahead of, introduce
10 come before
14 take precedence

precedence
04 lead, rank
08 eminence, priority

09 seniority, supremacy
10 ascendancy, preference
11 pre-eminence, superiority
12 pride of place

◻**take precedence over**
10 come before

precedent
05 model
07 example, pattern
08 exemplar, paradigm, standard
09 criterion, yardstick

preceding
05 above, prior, supra
06 former
07 earlier
08 anterior, previous
09 aforesaid, foregoing
10 antecedent, precursive
14 aforementioned

precept
03 law
04 rule
05 axiom, canon, maxim, motto, order
06 charge, decree, dictum, rubric, saying
07 command, mandate, statute
09 guideline, ordinance, principle
10 injunction, regulation
11 commandment, instruction

precinct
04 area, mall, zone
05 bound, close, court, limit
06 milieu, sector
07 confine, quarter, section
08 boundary, district, division, environs, galleria, locality, purlieus, vicinity
09 enclosure, surrounds
13 neighbourhood
14 shopping centre

preciosity
06 chichi
08 tweeness
11 affectation, floweriness
15 pretentiousness

precious
04 dear, fine, rare, twee
05 loved
06 adored, chichi, choice, costly, prized, valued
07 beloved, darling, dearest, flowery, revered
08 affected, idolized, mannered, valuable
09 cherished, contrived, expensive, favourite,

priceless, simulated, treasured
10 artificial, high-priced
11 overrefined, pretentious

precipice
04 crag, drop
05 bluff, brink, cliff, scarp, steep
06 escarp, height, krantz
09 cliff face
10 escarpment

precipitate
04 hurl, rash
05 brief, cause, fling, hasty, hurry, quick, rapid, speed, swift, throw
06 abrupt, plunge, speedy, sudden, thrust
07 advance, bring on, frantic, further, hurried, quicken, speed up, trigger, violent
08 expedite, hasten, headlong, heedless, occasion, reckless
09 breakneck, hot-headed, impatient, impetuous, impulsive
10 accelerate, bring about, indiscreet, unexpected

precipitous
04 high
05 sharp, sheer, steep
06 abrupt, sudden
08 vertical
13 perpendicular

précis
05 sum up, table
06 digest, résumé, sketch
07 abridge, epitome, outline, shorten, summary
08 abstract, condense, contract, synopsis
09 epitomize, summarize, synopsize
10 abbreviate
11 abridgement

precise
04 nice
05 exact, fixed, right, rigid
06 actual, minute, strict
07 express, factual, literal
08 accurate, clear-cut, definite, faithful, rigorous, specific
10 fastidious, meticulous, particular, scrupulous
11 punctilious, unequivocal, word-for-word
13 conscientious

precisely
04 to a T
05 plumb, smack
06 spot on

07 exactly
08 on the dot, verbatim
09 correctly, literally
10 accurately, distinctly
11 word for word

precision
06 detail, rigour
08 accuracy
09 exactness
10 exactitude
11 correctness
12 distinctness, explicitness
14 fastidiousness,
meticulousness

preclude
04 stop
05 check, debar
06 hinder
07 obviate, prevent, rule out
08 prohibit
09 forestall

precocious
05 ahead, early, quick, smart
06 bright, clever, gifted, mature
07 forward
08 advanced, far ahead
09 brilliant, premature

preconceive
07 presume, project
10 anticipate, presuppose

preconception
10 assumption, conjecture
11 expectation, presumption
12 anticipation

precondition
09 necessity
10 sine qua non
11 requirement, stipulation
12 prerequisite

precursor
06 herald
07 prelude
09 harbinger, messenger
10 antecedent, forerunner
11 trailblazer
13 curtain-raiser

precursory
05 prior
07 warning
08 anterior, previous
09 preceding
10 antecedent, prevenient
12 introductory

predatory
06 greedy, lupine
07 hunting, preying, wolfish
08 covetous, ravaging, thieving
09 rapacious, raptorial,
voracious

10 avaricious, predacious
11 acquisitive, carnivorous,
raptorial

predecessor
08 ancestor, forebear
10 antecedent, forefather,
forerunner, progenitor

predestination
03 lot
04 doom, fate
07 destiny

predestine
04 doom, fate, mean
07 destine
09 preordain
10 foreordain

predetermined
03 set
05 fated, fixed
06 agreed, doomed
07 settled
08 destined, ordained
11 prearranged, predestined
12 foreordained

predicament
03 fix, jam
04 hole, mess, spot, stew
06 crisis, pickle, plight, scrape
07 dilemma, impasse, trouble
08 hot water, quandary
09 deep water, emergency,
situation, tight spot

predicate
04 base, rest
05 build, found, posit
06 ground
07 premise
09 establish
11 be dependent

predict
05 augur
06 divine
07 foresee, portend, presage,
project
08 forecast, foretell, prophesy
11 second-guess
13 prognosticate

predictable
04 sure
06 likely, odds-on
07 certain
08 expected, foregone,
foreseen, probable, reliable
10 dependable, on the cards
11 anticipated, foreseeable

prediction
06 augury
08 forecast, prophecy
09 prognosis

10 divination
11 auspication, soothsaying
14 fortune-telling
15 prognostication

predictive
07 augural
09 prophetic
10 divinatory, prognostic
11 foretelling

predilection
04 bent, bias, love
05 fancy, taste
07 leaning
08 fondness, penchant, soft
spot, tendency, weakness
10 partiality, preference,
proclivity, propensity
11 inclination
14 predisposition

predispose
04 bias, make, move, sway
06 affect, induce, prompt
07 dispose, incline
09 influence, prejudice

predisposed
05 prone, ready
06 biased, minded
07 subject
08 amenable, inclined
09 agreeable
10 favourable, prejudiced
11 susceptible

predisposition
04 bent, bias
07 leaning
08 penchant, tendency
09 prejudice, proneness
10 likelihood, preference,
proclivity, propensity
11 inclination
12 potentiality, predilection
14 susceptibility

predominance
04 edge, hold, sway
05 power
06 weight
07 control, mastery, numbers
08 dominion, hegemony
09 dominance, influence,
supremacy, upper hand
10 ascendancy, prevalence
11 paramountcy, superiority

predominant
04 main
05 chief, prime
06 potent, ruling, strong
07 capital, leading, primary,
supreme
08 forceful, powerful

09 ascendant, important, in control, paramount, principal, sovereign
10 prevailing
11 controlling, influential
12 preponderant
15 in the ascendancy

predominate
04 rule, tell
05 reign
06 obtain
07 prevail
08 dominate, outweigh, override, overrule
09 outnumber, transcend
12 preponderate

pre-eminence
04 fame
06 renown, repute
08 prestige
09 supremacy
10 excellence, prominence
11 paramountcy, superiority

pre-eminent
05 chief, first
07 leading, supreme
08 foremost, superior
09 excellent, matchless
10 inimitable, unequalled, unrivalled
11 exceptional, outstanding, superlative, unsurpassed
12 incomparable, transcendent
13 most important

pre-eminently
08 signally
09 supremely
10 especially
13 par excellence

pre-empt
05 seize, usurp
06 assume, secure
07 acquire, prevent
08 arrogate
09 forestall
10 anticipate
11 appropriate

preen
04 bask, deck, do up, trim
05 adorn, array, clean, exult, gloat, groom, pique, plume, pride, primp, prink, slick
06 doll up, smooth, tart up
07 dress up
08 beautify, prettify, trick out
12 congratulate

preface
04 open
05 begin, proem, start

06 launch, prefix
07 precede, prelims, prelude
08 exordium, foreword, lead up to, preamble, prologue
09 introduce
11 frontmatter
12 introduction

prefatory
07 opening
08 exordial, proemial
09 preludial, prelusive, prelusory
10 antecedent, precursory
11 explanatory, prefatorial, preliminary, preparatory
12 introductory, prolegomenal
13 preambulatory

prefect
07 monitor
08 praefect
10 praeposter, prepositor, supervisor
13 administrator

prefer
03 opt
04 back, file, pick, want, wish
05 adopt, bring, elect, exalt, fancy, go for, lodge, place, press, raise
06 choose, desire, favour, honour, move up, opt for, select
07 advance, elevate, pick out, present, promote, support
08 advocate, plump for
09 recommend, single out
10 aggrandize, like better
11 be partial to, would rather, would sooner

preferable
05 nicer
06 better, chosen
08 favoured, superior
09 advisable, desirable

preferably
06 rather, sooner
09 for choice
10 from choice

preference
04 bent, bias, pick, wish
05 fancy
06 choice, desire, liking, option
07 leaning
08 cup of tea, priority
09 selection, favourite
10 partiality, precedence
11 favouritism, first choice, inclination
12 predilection
14 discrimination

preferential
07 partial, special
08 favoured, partisan, superior
10 favourable, privileged

preferment
04 rise
06 step up
07 dignity
09 elevation, promotion, upgrading
10 betterment, exaltation
11 advancement, furtherance

preferred
06 choice, chosen
07 desired
08 approved, favoured, selected
09 predilect
10 authorized, sanctioned
11 recommended

pregnancy
09 family way, gestation, gravidity
10 conception
11 parturition
12 child-bearing, impregnation
13 fertilization

pregnant
04 full, rich
05 heavy
06 loaded
08 eloquent, enceinte, preggers
09 expectant, expecting, in the club, with child
10 parturient, suggestive, up the spout
11 significant
14 in the family way

prehistoric
07 ancient, archaic
08 earliest, primeval
09 primitive
10 antiquated, primordial
11 out of the ark
12 antediluvian
14 before the flood

prejudge
07 presume
10 anticipate, presuppose
12 predetermine

prejudice
04 bias, harm, hurt, ruin, sway
05 slant, spoil, wreck
06 colour, damage, hinder, impair, injure, injury
07 bigotry, distort
09 detriment, influence

10 chauvinism, partiality, predispose, preference
11 intolerance, misanthropy
12 disadvantage, one-sidedness, partisanship
14 discrimination
15 be detrimental to

prejudiced
06 biased, unfair, unjust
07 bigoted, partial
08 one-sided, partisan
09 distorted, jaundiced
10 chauvinist, influenced
11 predisposed
12 chauvinistic
14 discriminatory

prejudicial
07 harmful, hurtful, noxious
08 damaging, inimical
09 injurious
11 deleterious, detrimental
15 disadvantageous

preliminary
05 early, first, pilot, proem
07 opening, prelude
08 exordial, exordium, preamble
09 inaugural, prefatory
10 groundwork, precursory
11 formalities, foundations, preparation, preparatory
12 introduction, introductory

prelude
05 proem, start
06 herald, opener
07 opening, preface
08 exordium, foreword, overture, preamble, prologue
09 beginning, harbinger, precursor
10 forerunner
11 preliminary, preparation
12 introduction
13 curtain-raiser

premature
04 rash, soon
05 early, green, hasty
06 unripe
07 too soon
08 abortive, ill-timed, too early, untimely
09 embryonic, impetuous, impulsive
10 half-formed, incomplete
11 inopportune, precipitate, undeveloped
13 ill-considered, jumping the gun

premeditated
07 planned
08 intended
10 calculated, deliberate
11 intentional

premeditation
06 design
07 purpose
08 planning, plotting, scheming
09 intention
11 forethought
12 deliberation

premier
03 top
04 head, main
05 chief, first, prime
07 highest, initial, leading, primary, supreme
08 cardinal, foremost
09 paramount, principal
10 chancellor, pre-eminent
13 chief minister, first minister, prime minister

première
05 début
07 opening
10 first night
12 first showing, opening night

premise
05 basis, posit, state
06 assert, assume, thesis
07 lay down
08 argument
09 assertion, postulate, predicate, statement, stipulate
10 assumption, hypothesis, presuppose, take as true
11 hypothesize, proposition, supposition
14 presupposition

premises
04 site
05 place
06 estate, office
07 grounds
08 building, property
13 establishment

premium
09 surcharge
10 instalment
11 extra charge
12 overcharging

□ **at a premium**
06 scarce
12 hard to come by, like gold dust
13 in short supply

□ **put a premium on**
06 favour
08 hold dear, treasure
12 regard highly, value greatly
15 set great store by

premonition
04 fear, idea, omen, sign
05 hunch, worry
07 anxiety, feeling, portent, presage, warning
09 intuition, misgiving, suspicion
10 foreboding, gut feeling, sixth sense
12 apprehension, funny feeling, presentiment

preoccupation
05 thing
07 concern, reverie
08 fixation, interest, oblivion
10 absorption, hobby-horse
11 abstraction, daydreaming, distraction
15 bee in your bonnet, inattentiveness

preoccupied
07 engaged, faraway, pensive, taken up
08 absorbed, distrait
10 abstracted, distracted
11 daydreaming
12 absent-minded
13 deep in thought

preoccupy
06 absorb, engage, obsess, occupy, take up
07 involve

preordain
04 doom, fate
07 destine
10 foreordain, predestine

preparation
04 plan
05 study
06 basics, lotion, potion, supply
07 mixture
08 assembly, coaching, compound, cosmetic, homework, medicine, planning, practice, revision, training
09 provision, readiness, spadework
10 concoction, groundwork
11 application, arrangement, composition, development
13 preliminaries

preparatory
05 basic

07 initial, opening, primary
09 prefatory
10 elementary, precursory
11 fundamental, preliminary, rudimentary
12 introductory

❏**preparatory to**
06 before
07 prior to
10 previous to
11 in advance of
15 in expectation of

prepare
03 fix
04 make, plan
05 coach, draft, equip, prime, set up, study, tee up, train
06 adjust, devise, draw up, fit out, gear up, rig out, supply, warm up
07 arrange, compose, concoct, fashion, produce, provide, psych up
08 assemble, contrive, exercise, get ready, organize, practise
09 construct, make ready
10 pave the way
12 get into shape
14 set the scene for

❏**prepare yourself**
12 gird yourself
13 brace yourself, steel yourself
15 fortify yourself, gird up your loins

prepared
03 fit, set
05 fixed, ready
07 in order, planned, waiting, willing
08 arranged, disposed, inclined
09 organized

preparedness
07 fitness
09 alertness, readiness
12 anticipation

preponderance
04 bulk, mass, sway
05 force, power
06 weight
08 majority
09 dominance, supremacy
10 lion's share, prevalence
12 predominance

preponderant
06 larger
07 greater
08 foremost, superior
09 important
10 overriding, overruling
11 controlling, predominant

preponderate
04 rule, tell
07 prevail
08 dominate, override, overrule
09 outnumber, weigh with
11 predominate
13 turn the scales
14 turn the balance

prepossessing
04 fair
06 taking
07 winning, winsome
08 alluring, charming, engaging, fetching, handsome, pleasing, striking
09 appealing, beautiful
10 attractive, enchanting
11 captivating, good-looking

preposterous
05 crazy
06 absurd
08 farcical, shocking
09 ludicrous, senseless
10 impossible, incredible, irrational, ridiculous
11 nonsensical, unthinkable
12 unbelievable, unreasonable

prerequisite
04 must
05 basic, vital
07 needful, proviso
09 essential, necessary, necessity, requisite
10 imperative, sine qua non
11 requirement
12 precondition

prerogative
03 due
05 claim, droit, right
07 liberty, licence
08 sanction
09 authority, privilege
10 birthright

presage
04 bode, omen, sign
05 augur
06 augury, herald, warn of
07 point to, portend, portent, predict, promise, warning
08 forecast, foretell, forewarn, indicate
09 adumbrate, be a sign of, harbinger
10 foreshadow
11 forewarning, premonition

prescience
08 prophecy
09 foresight, prevision
11 second sight

12 precognition
14 far-sightedness

prescient
07 psychic
08 divining
09 far-seeing, prophetic
10 discerning, divinatory, far-sighted, perceptive
11 foresighted

prescribe
04 rule
05 limit, order
06 advise, decree, ordain
07 dictate, lay down, specify
09 stipulate

prescribed
07 decreed
08 assigned, laid down, ordained
09 specified
10 stipulated

prescription
04 drug
06 advice, recipe, remedy
07 formula, mixture
08 medicine
11 instruction, preparation

prescriptive
05 rigid
08 didactic, dogmatic
09 customary
10 preceptive
11 dictatorial, legislating, prescribing
13 authoritarian

presence
03 air
04 aura
05 being, ghost
06 appeal, shadow, spirit
07 bearing, phantom, spectre
08 carriage, charisma, nearness, vicinity, visitant
09 closeness, demeanour, existence, magnetism, occupancy, proximity, residence
10 apparition, appearance, attendance

❏**presence of mind**
04 cool
05 poise
06 aplomb
08 calmness, coolness
09 composure, sang-froid
14 unflappability

present
03 tip

04 gift, give, here, host, near, perk, show

05 award, grant, mount, offer, put on, ready, stage, there

06 at hand, bestow, bounty, confer, depict, donate, extend, favour, nearby, submit, tender, to hand

07 compère, current, display, entrust, exhibit, hold out, perform, picture, portray, proffer

08 announce, describe, donation, existent, existing, gratuity, hand over, largesse, offering, organize

09 attending, available, delineate, endowment, immediate, introduce, make known, represent, sweetener

11 benefaction, demonstrate

12 characterize, contemporary, contribution, put on display

◻**at present**

03 now

09 currently

11 at the moment

10 at this time

◻**for the present**

06 for now, pro tem

12 for the moment

13 in the meantime

15 for the time being

◻**present oneself**

06 appear, emerge, happen, show up, turn up

11 come to light, materialize

◻**the present day**

03 now

05 today

08 nowadays

09 currently

presentable

04 neat, tidy

05 clean, smart

06 decent, proper, spruce

12 satisfactory

14 smartly dressed

presentation

04 show, talk

05 award

06 layout

07 display, showing, staging

08 bestowal, donating, granting

09 rendition

10 exhibition, production

11 performance

12 disquisition, introduction

13 demonstration

present-day

06 living, modern

07 current, present

08 existing, up-to-date

11 fashionable

12 contemporary

presenter

02 MC

04 host

05 emcee

07 compère

08 frontman

09 anchorman, announcer

11 anchorwoman

presentiment

05 hunch

07 feeling, presage

09 intuition, misgiving

10 foreboding

11 premonition

presently

03 now

04 soon

07 by and by, shortly

09 at present, currently, in a minute, these days

11 before long

11 at the moment

13 in a short while

preservation

06 safety

08 guarding, security

09 upholding

10 protection

11 maintenance, safekeeping

12 conservation, safeguarding

preserve

03 can, dry, jam, tin

04 area, cure, keep, salt, save

05 field, guard, jelly, realm, smoke, store

06 bottle, defend, domain, pickle, retain, shield, sphere

07 protect, reserve, shelter

08 conserve, maintain

09 look after, marmalade, safeguard, sanctuary

10 take care of

preside

04 head, lead, rule

05 chair

06 direct, govern, head up

07 conduct, control

09 officiate

12 be in charge of, be in the chair, call the shots

president

04 boss, head

05 chief, ruler

06 leader

08 director, governor

11 head of state

➤ *Names of presidents. We have omitted the word* **president** *from names given in the following list but you may need to include this word as part of the solution to some crossword clues.*

03 **Moi** (Daniel arap), **Rau** (Johannes), **Zia** (Muhammad)

04 **Amin** (Idi), **Bush** (George), **Díaz** (Porfirio), **Ford** (Gerald Rudolph), **Khan** (Ayub), **Ozal** (Turgut), **Polk** (James Knox), **René** (France-Albert), **Rhee** (Syngman), **Taft** (William Howard), **Tito** (Josip Broz)

05 **Adams** (John Quincy), **Adams** (John), **Assad** (Hafez al-), **Banda** (Hastings Kamuzu), **Botha** (Pieter Willem), **Grant** (Ulysses Simpson), **Havel** (Vaclav), **Hayes** (Rutherford Birchard), **Klerk** (Frederick Willem de), **Mbeki** (Thabo), **Menem** (Carlos), **Nixon** (Richard Milhous), **Obote** (Milton), **Perón** (Juan), **Putin** (Vladimir), **Ramos** (Fidel), **Sadat** (Mohammed Anwar el-), **Tyler** (John)

06 **Aideed** (Mohammed), **Aquino** (Corazon), **Arthur** (Chester Alan), **Banana** (Canaan), **Bhutto** (Zulfikar Ali), **Biswas** (Abdur Rahman), **Carter** (Jimmy), **Castro** (Fidel), **Chirac** (Jacques), **Gaulle** (Charles de), **Herzog** (Chaim), **Hoover** (Herbert), **Juárez** (Benito), **Kruger** (Paul), **Marcos** (Ferdinand), **Mobutu**, **Monroe** (James), **Mugabe** (Robert), **Nasser** (Gamal Abdel), **Ortega** (Daniel), **Pierce** (Franklin), **Rahman** (Ziaur), **Reagan** (Ronald), **Somoza** (Anastasio), **Somoza** (Luis), **Taylor** (Zachary), **Truman** (Harry S), **Valera** (Éamon de), **Walesa** (Lech), **Wilson** (Woodrow)

07 **Atatürk** (Mustapha Kemal), **Batista** (Fulgencio), **Bolívar**

(Simón), **Clinton** (William
Jefferson 'Bill'), **Demirel**
(Süleyman), **Gaddafi**
(Colonel Muammar),
Gemayel (Amin),
Gromyko (Andrei),
Habibie (Jusuf), **Harding**
(Warren Gamaliel),
Hussein (Saddam), **Iliescu**
(Ion), **Jackson** (Andrew),
Johnson (Andrew),
Johnson (Lyndon Baines),
Kennedy (John Fitzgerald),
Khatami (Sayed Ayatollah
Mohammad), **Lincoln**
(Abraham), **Madison**
(James), **Mancham**
(James), **Mandela**
(Nelson), **Mubarak**
(Hosni), **Nkrumah**
(Kwame), **Parnell** (Charles
Stewart), **Suharto**
(Thojib N J), **Sukarno**
(Ahmed), **Tudjman**
(Franjo), **Weizman** (Ezer),
Yanayev (Gennady),
Yeltsin (Boris), **Zhivkov**
(Todor)

08 **Andropov** (Yuri), **Aristide**
(Jean-Bertrand), **Brezhnev**
(Leonid), **Buchanan**
(James), **Chamorro**
(Violeta), **Childers**
(Erskine), **Coolidge**
(Calvin), **Cosgrave**
(William Thomas),
Duvalier (François 'Papa
Doc'), **Duvalier** (Jean-
Claude 'Baby Doc'),
Fillmore (Millard),
Fujimori (Alberto),
Galtieri (Leopoldo),
Garfield (James Abram),
Harrison (Benjamin),
Harrison (William Henry),
Karadzic (Radovan),
Kenyatta (Jomo),
Khamenei (Sayed Ali),
Kravchuk (Leonid),
Makarios (Cyprus Enosis),
McAleese (Mary),
McKinley (William),
Mengistu (Haile Mariam),
Museveni (Yoweri),
Napoleon, Pinochet
(Augusto), **Poincaré**
(Raymond), **Pompidou**
(Georges), **Rawlings**
(Jerry), **Robinson** (Mary),
Van Buren (Martin),
Waldheim (Kurt),
Weizmann (Chaim)

09 **Ceausescu** (Nicolae),
Chernenko (Konstantin),
Cleveland (Grover),
Gorbachev (Mikhail), **Ho
Chi Minh, Jefferson**
(Thomas), **Kim Il-sung,
Kim Jong Il, Mao
Zedong, Milosevic**
(Slobodan), **Roosevelt**
(Franklin Delano),
Roosevelt (Theodore), **Sun
Yat-Sen**
10 **Eisenhower** (Dwight
David), **Hindenburg** (Paul
von), **Jaruzelski** (Wojciech),
Jiang Zemin, Khrushchev
(Nikita), **Mitterrand**
(François), **Najibullah**
(Mohammad), **Rafsanjani**
(Ali Akbar Hashemi),
Stroessner (Alfredo),
Washington (George)
14 **Mobutu Seze Seko**
15 **Giscard d'Estaing** (Valéry)
➢ See also **politics**

press
03 hug, jam, mob
04 cram, iron, mash, pack,
push, roll, urge
05 clasp, crowd, crush, flock,
force, grasp, horde, knead,
pinch, plead, stuff, surge,
swarm, troop, worry
06 caress, coerce, compel,
cuddle, demand, enfold,
exhort, harass, papers,
praise, smooth, squash,
throng
07 afflict, besiege, call for,
depress, embrace, entreat,
flatten, push for, reviews,
squeeze, trample, trouble
08 articles, campaign,
compress, coverage, insist
on, petition, pressmen,
pressure, push down, the
media
09 constrain, criticism,
multitude, news media,
paparazzi, reporters,
smooth out, treatment
10 journalism, newspapers,
pressurize, presswomen,
supplicate
11 Fleet Street, journalists
12 fourth estate,
newspapermen
13 photographers, printing
press, put pressure on
14 correspondents,
newspaperwomen
15 printing-machine

❏ **press on**
04 go on
07 carry on, go ahead, proceed
08 continue

pressed
06 forced, pushed, rushed
07 bullied, coerced, hurried,
lacking, short of
08 harassed
10 browbeaten
11 constrained, deficient in,
pressurized

pressing
06 urgent
07 burning, serious
08 critical
09 demanding, essential,
important
12 high-priority

pressure
04 load
05 force, power
06 burden, demand, duress,
hassle, strain, stress, weight
07 tension
08 bullying, coercion, crushing
09 heaviness, squeezing
10 compulsion, constraint
11 compression

pressurize
05 bully, drive, force, press
06 coerce, compel, lean on,
oblige
07 dragoon
08 browbeat, bulldoze
09 constrain
14 put the screws on

prestige
04 fame
05 kudos
06 credit, esteem, honour,
regard, renown, status
07 stature
08 eminence, standing
10 importance

prestigious
05 great
06 famous
07 eminent, exalted
08 blue-chip, esteemed,
renowned, up-market
09 important, prominent,
reputable, respected, well-
known
10 celebrated, impressive
11 high-ranking, illustrious,
influential
13 distinguished

presumably
08 probably
09 doubtless, seemingly
10 apparently, very likely
11 as like as not, doubtlessly

presume
04 dare
06 assume, deduce, take it
07 believe, go so far, imagine, suppose, surmise, venture
10 make so bold, presuppose
11 hypothesize
14 take for granted, take the liberty
15 have the audacity

◻**presume on**
05 trust
06 bank on, rely on
07 count on, exploit
08 depend on
15 take advantage of

presumption
05 cheek, guess, nerve
07 opinion, surmise
08 audacity, boldness, temerity
09 arrogance, assurance, impudence, inference, insolence
10 assumption, conjecture, effrontery, hypothesis
11 probability, supposition
12 impertinence

presumptive
06 likely
07 assumed
08 believed, expected, inferred, probable, supposed
09 designate
10 understood
11 conceivable, prospective

presumptuous
04 bold
05 cocky, pushy
06 cheeky
07 forward
08 arrogant, cocksure, impudent, insolent
09 audacious
11 impertinent
12 over-familiar
13 over-confident

presuppose
06 assume
07 presume
14 take for granted

presupposition
10 assumption
11 presumption

pretence
03 lie
04 mask, ruse, sham, show, veil, wile
05 bluff, cloak, cover, front, guise
06 acting, deceit, façade, faking
07 charade, display, pretext
08 feigning, trickery
09 deception, false show, falsehood, hypocrisy, invention, posturing, semblance, showiness
10 appearance, masquerade, play-acting, simulation
11 affectation, dissembling, fabrication, make-believe
13 dissimulation

pretend
03 act
04 fake, mime, sham
05 bluff, claim, feign, put on
06 affect, allege, assume
07 imagine, play-act, profess, purport, suppose
08 simulate
09 dissemble, fabricate
10 put on an act
11 counterfeit, impersonate, make believe
15 pass yourself off

pretended
04 fake, sham
05 bogus, false, put on
06 avowed, phoney, pseudo
07 alleged, feigned, pretend
08 so-called
09 imaginary
10 artificial, fictitious
11 counterfeit

pretender
07 claimer
08 aspirant, claimant

pretension
04 airs, show
05 claim
06 demand, vanity
07 conceit
08 ambition, pretence
09 showiness
10 aspiration
11 affectation, floweriness, ostentation
13 magniloquence
14 self-importance
15 pretentiousness

pretentious
03 OTT
04 twee

05 showy
08 affected, immodest, inflated, mannered
09 ambitious, bombastic, conceited, elaborate, flaunting, grandiose
10 artificial, flamboyant, over-the-top
11 exaggerated, extravagant
12 high-sounding, magniloquent, ostentatious, vainglorious
13 overambitious, self-important

pretentiousness
04 show
10 floridness, pretension
11 floweriness, ostentation
13 theatricality
14 attitudinizing

preternatural
07 unusual
08 abnormal
11 exceptional
13 extraordinary

pretext
04 mask, ploy, ruse, sham, show, veil
05 cloak, cover, guise
06 excuse
08 pretence
09 semblance
10 appearance, red herring

prettify
04 deck, do up, gild, trim
05 adorn
06 bedeck, doll up, tart up
07 deck out, garnish
08 beautify, decorate, ornament, trick out
09 embellish, smarten up

pretty
04 cute, fair, fine, nice
05 bonny, quite
06 comely, dainty, fairly, lovely
07 elegant, winsome
08 charming, delicate, engaging, graceful, handsome, pleasant, pleasing, somewhat
09 appealing, beautiful, tolerably
10 attractive, moderately, personable, reasonably

prevail
03 win
04 rule
05 occur, reign
06 abound, obtain
07 conquer, succeed, triumph

08 hold sway, overcome,
overrule
11 carry the day, predominate
12 preponderate

prevail upon
04 sway, urge
06 induce, lean on, prompt
07 incline, win over
08 convince, persuade,
pressure, soft-soap, talk into
09 influence, sweet-talk
10 bring round, pressurize
11 pull strings

prevailing
04 main
05 chief, usual
06 common, ruling
07 current, general, in style, in
vogue, popular, supreme
08 dominant, reigning
09 ascendant, most usual,
prevalent
10 most common, widespread
11 established, predominant
12 preponderant

prevalence
04 hold, rule, sway
07 mastery, primacy
08 currency, ubiquity
09 frequency, profusion
10 acceptance, commonness,
regularity
12 omnipresence,
predominance, universality
13 pervasiveness,
preponderance

prevalent
04 rife
06 common
07 current, general, rampant
08 accepted, dominant,
everyday, frequent
09 customary, extensive,
pervasive, universal
10 prevailing, ubiquitous,
widespread
11 established

prevaricate
03 lie
05 cavil, dodge, evade, hedge,
shift
06 waffle
07 deceive, quibble, shuffle
09 pussy-foot
10 equivocate
12 shilly-shally, tergiversate
13 sit on the fence

prevarication
03 fib, lie
04 fibs

06 deceit
07 evasion, fibbing, untruth
09 cavilling, deception,
falsehood, half-truth,
quibbling

prevaricator
06 dodger, evader, fibber
07 casuist, sophist
08 caviller, quibbler
09 hypocrite
10 dissembler
11 pettifogger

prevent
03 bar
04 balk, foil, halt, stop
05 avert, avoid, block, check,
deter
06 arrest, hamper, hinder,
impede, thwart
07 fend off, head off, inhibit,
obviate, ward off
08 hold back, keep from,
obstruct, preclude, restrain,
stave off
09 forestall, frustrate, intercept
10 anticipate

prevention
03 bar
05 check
07 balking, foiling, halting
08 obstacle
09 arresting, avoidance,
hampering, hindrance,
obviation, safeguard
10 deterrence, impediment,
precaution, preclusion
11 elimination, prophylaxis

preventive
06 remedy, shield
08 obstacle
09 deterrent, hindrance,
safeguard
10 impediment, inhibitory, pre-
emptive, prevention,
protection, protective
11 neutralizer, obstruction,
obstructive
12 anticipatory, preventative,
prophylactic
13 counteractive,
precautionary

previous
05 prior
06 former
07 earlier, one-time, quondam
09 erstwhile, foregoing,
preceding

previously
04 erst, once
06 before

07 earlier
08 formerly, hitherto, until now
09 at one time, in the past
10 beforehand, heretofore

prey
04 game, kill
06 quarry, target, victim
07 fall guy

prey on
04 hunt, kill
05 catch, haunt, seize
06 devour, feed on, plague
07 exploit, oppress, trouble
15 take advantage of

price
03 fee, sum
04 bill, cost, levy, rate, toll
05 value, worth
06 amount, assess, charge,
figure, outlay, result, reward
07 expense, forfeit, payment,
penalty
08 appraise, estimate, evaluate,
expenses, valorize
09 quotation, sacrifice,
valuation
10 assessment
11 expenditure
12 consequences

at a price
09 expensive
11 at a high cost
12 at a high price

at any price
09 at any cost
15 whatever it takes, whatever
the cost

priceless
04 dear, rare, rich
05 comic, funny
06 costly, prized
07 a scream, amusing, killing,
riotous
08 precious, valuable
09 cherished, expensive,
hilarious, treasured
10 invaluable
13 side-splitting

pricey
04 dear
05 steep
06 costly
09 excessive, expensive
10 exorbitant, high-priced
11 over the odds
12 extortionate

prick
03 jab, jag

04 bite, bore, gash, hole, itch, nick, pain, pang, slit, stab
05 harry, punch, smart, spike, sting, worry, wound
06 gnaw at, harass, pierce, plague, prey on, tingle, twinge
07 pinhole, prickle, torment, trouble
08 distress, puncture, smarting
09 perforate
11 perforation

prickle
04 barb, itch, pang, spur, tine
05 point, spike, spine, sting, thorn
06 needle, tingle, twinge
07 itching
08 smarting, stinging
14 pins and needles

prickly
04 edgy
05 ratty, spiky, spiny
06 spiked, thorny, touchy, tricky
07 bristly, pronged, stroppy
08 scratchy
09 crotchety, difficult, irritable
11 complicated, troublesome

pride
03 ego
06 honour, vanity
07 conceit, dignity, egotism
08 snobbery
09 arrogance, self-image, self-worth
10 self-esteem
11 haughtiness, presumption, self-conceit, self-respect
12 boastfulness, satisfaction
13 big-headedness, gratification
14 self-importance

◻**pride yourself on**
05 vaunt
07 exult in, glory in, revel in
09 brag about, crow about
10 boast about
15 flatter yourself

priest
05 padre, vicar
06 deacon, father, parson, pastor
08 man of God, minister
09 churchman, clergyman, deaconess
10 woman of God
11 churchwoman, clergywoman
13 man of the cloth
15 woman of the cloth

priestess
03 nun
05 mambo
06 abbess, sister, vestal
08 canoness, prioress
09 deaconess
11 clergywoman

priestly
07 Aaronic
08 clerical, hieratic, pastoral
09 Aaronical, canonical
10 priestlike, sacerdotal
14 ecclesiastical

prig
05 prude
07 killjoy, puritan
09 Mrs Grundy, precisian
10 goody-goody

priggish
04 prim, smug
06 stuffy
07 prudish, starchy
10 goody-goody
11 puritanical, strait-laced
12 narrow-minded
13 sanctimonious, self-righteous
14 holier-than-thou

prim
05 fussy
06 demure, formal, prissy, proper, stuffy
07 precise, prudish, starchy
08 priggish
10 fastidious, fuddy-duddy, old-maidish, particular
11 puritanical, strait-laced
13 school-marmish

primacy
07 command
08 dominion
09 dominance, supremacy
10 ascendancy, paramouncy
11 pre-eminence, superiority

primal
04 main
05 basic, chief, first, major, prime
07 central, highest, initial, primary
08 earliest, original, primeval
09 paramount, primitive
10 primordial

primarily
05 first
06 mainly, mostly
07 chiefly, firstly
09 basically, in essence, in the main

10 especially
11 essentially, principally
12 particularly
13 fundamentally, predominantly
15 in the first place

primary
04 main
05 basic, chief, first, prime
06 simple
07 capital, highest, initial, leading, radical, supreme
08 cardinal, dominant, earliest, foremost, greatest, original, primeval, ultimate
09 beginning, elemental, essential, paramount, principal
10 elementary, primordial
11 fundamental, predominant, rudimentary
12 introductory

prime
03 top
04 acme, best, fill, main, peak
05 bloom, brief, chief, coach, equip, gen up, train
06 choice, clue up, fill in, flower, height, heyday, inform, notify, select, zenith
07 highest, leading, prepare, quality, supreme
08 best part, foremost, get ready, maturity, pinnacle, standard, top-grade
09 excellent, first-rate, principal
10 first-class, pre-eminent

primer
06 manual
08 textbook
12 introduction

primeval
05 early, first
07 ancient
08 earliest, original
10 primordial
11 instinctive, prehistoric
12 autochthonal

primitive
05 crude, early, first, rough
06 savage, simple
07 ancient, natural
08 earliest, original, primeval
10 primordial, uncultured
11 rudimentary, uncivilized, undeveloped

primordial
05 early, first
07 ancient
08 earliest, original, primeval

09 primitive
11 instinctive, prehistoric
12 autochthonal

primp
05 groom, preen
06 doll up, tart up
07 dress up, smarten
08 beautify, spruce up, titivate

prince, princess
04 lord
05 ruler
07 monarch
09 potentate, sovereign

► *Names of princes. We have omitted the word* **prince** *from names given in the following list but you may need to include this word as part of the solution to some crossword clues.*
04 Ivan, John (of Gaunt)
05 Edgar (the Atheling), Harry, Henry (the Navigator), James
06 Albert, Andrew, Arthur, Edward, Edward, Edward (the Black Prince), Philip
07 Charles, Michael (of Kent), Rainier, Richard, William
08 Vladimir
15 Alexander Nevski

► *Names of princesses. We have omitted the word* **princess** *from names given in the following list but you may need to include this word as part of the solution to some crossword clues.*
04 Anne
05 Alice, Diana, Grace
06 Salome
07 Eugenie, Jezebel, Matilda
08 Beatrice, Caroline, Margaret
09 Alexandra, Charlotte, Elizabeth, Stephanie
10 Pocahontas

princely
05 grand, noble, regal, royal
07 liberal, stately
08 generous, handsome, imperial, imposing, majestic, splendid
09 bounteous, sovereign
11 magnanimous, magnificent

principal
03 key
04 arch, boss, head, main
05 chief, first, major, money, prime, ruler
06 assets, leader, rector

07 capital, highest, leading, primary, supreme
08 cardinal, dominant, foremost, in charge
09 essential, paramount
10 capital sum, headmaster, pre-eminent
11 controlling, head teacher
12 capital funds, headmistress
13 most important

principally
06 mainly, mostly
07 chiefly
08 above all
09 in the main, primarily
10 especially
14 for the most part

principle
03 law
04 code, idea, rule
05 axiom, basis, canon, creed, dogma, maxim, tenet, truth
06 dictum, ethics, honour, morals, theory, virtue
07 decency, formula, precept
08 doctrine, morality, scruples, standard
09 criterion, essential, integrity, rectitude, standards
10 conscience
11 uprightness

▢**in principle**
07 ideally
08 in theory
09 in essence
10 en principe
13 theoretically

principled
05 moral
06 decent
07 ethical, upright
09 righteous
10 high-minded, honourable, scrupulous
11 right-minded
13 conscientious

print
04 copy, etch, mark, snap, type
05 fount, issue, photo, stamp
06 design, run off
07 engrave, impress, imprint, letters, picture, publish, replica
08 snapshot, typeface
09 footprint, lettering
10 characters, impression, lithograph, photograph, typescript
11 fingerprint
12 reproduction

► *Printing methods:*
05 litho
07 etching, gravure
08 intaglio
09 collotype, engraving
10 xerography
11 die-stamping, duplicating, letterpress, lithography, rotary press, stencilling
12 lino blocking
13 laser printing
14 ink-jet printing, offset printing, photoengraving, screen printing
15 copper engraving

► *Printing terms:*
02 em, en
04 copy, font, kern, stet, text, tint, type, typo
05 flong, forme, proof, roman, widow, zinco
06 galley, gutter, indent, italic, margin, matrix, orphan, Ozalid®
07 bromide, carding, cast-off, compose, end even, leaders, leading, reprint, strip in, woodcut
08 bad break, bold face, Linotype®, logotype, misprint, Monotype®, offprint, take over, type spec, typeface
09 catchword, condensed, Intertype®, letterset, lower-case, makeready, newsprint, overprint, sans serif, signature, trim marks, type scale, upper-case, web offset
10 collograph, compositor, first proof, hard hyphen, impression, large print, manuscript, ragged left, see-through, soft hyphen, stereotype, typescript
11 electrotype, initial caps, line printer, ragged right, running head, running text, typesetting, typographer
12 author's proof, expanded type, flat-bed press, inking roller, specimen page
13 composing room, cylinder press, justification, printing press, small capitals, wood engraving
14 relief printing, thermal printer
15 camera-ready copy

in print
09 available, published
10 obtainable
13 in circulation

prior
06 former
07 earlier
08 previous
09 foregoing

prior to
05 until
06 before
09 preceding
11 earlier than

priority
04 rank
07 the lead
09 essential, main thing, seniority, supremacy
10 first place, paramouncy, precedence, right of way
11 pre-eminence, requirement, superiority
12 first concern, highest place, pole position, primary issue, top of the tree
13 supreme matter

priory
05 abbey
06 friary
07 convent, nunnery
08 cloister
09 béguinage, monastery

prise
03 pry
04 lift, move
05 force, hoist, jemmy, lever
06 winkle
08 dislodge

prison
03 can, jug
04 cage, cell, jail, nick, quod
05 choky, clink
06 cooler, inside, lock-up
07 custody, dungeon, slammer
09 detention
11 confinement
12 imprisonment, penitentiary

prisoner
03 con, lag, POW
05 lifer
06 inmate, old lag
07 captive, convict, hostage
08 detainee, internee, jailbird, yardbird
13 prisoner of war

prissy
04 prim
05 fussy

06 demure, formal, proper, stuffy
07 finicky, po-faced, precise, prudish, starchy
08 priggish
10 fastidious, old-maidish, particular
11 puritanical, strait-laced
13 school-marmish

pristine
05 first
06 former, primal, virgin
07 initial, primary
08 earliest, original, primeval
09 primitive, undefiled, unspoiled, unsullied, untouched
10 immaculate, primordial
11 primigenial, uncorrupted

privacy
07 retreat, secrecy
08 solitude
09 isolation, quietness, seclusion
10 retirement
11 concealment, privateness
12 independence
13 sequestration
15 confidentiality

private
05 quiet, Tommy
06 hidden, remote, secret
07 special, squaddy
08 in secret, intimate, isolated, personal, reserved, retiring, secluded, solitary
09 concealed, exclusive, innermost
10 classified, individual, privatized
11 enlisted man, independent, out-of-the-way, sequestered, Tommy Atkins, undisturbed
12 confidential, off the record
14 denationalized, free-enterprise

in private
07 sub rosa
08 in camera, secretly
12 in confidence

private detective
06 shamus
09 pinkerton
10 private eye

private parts
05 penis
06 vagina
07 pudenda
08 genitals, privates

09 genitalia

privateer
06 marque, pirate
07 brigand, corsair, sea wolf
09 buccaneer, sea robber
10 filibuster, freebooter

privation
04 lack, loss, need, want
06 misery, penury
07 poverty
08 distress, hardship
09 indigence, suffering
11 deprivation, destitution

privilege
03 due
05 right, title
07 benefit, licence
08 immunity, sanction
09 advantage, authority, exemption, franchise
10 birthright, concession
11 entitlement, prerogative

privileged
05 elite
06 exempt, immune, ruling
07 private, special
08 favoured, powerful
10 advantaged, classified, sanctioned
12 confidential, off the record

privy
02 WC
03 bog, loo
06 toilet
07 latrine
08 lavatory
11 water closet

privy to
04 in on
10 apprised of
11 cognizant of
13 informed about
14 in the know about

prize
03 aim, top
04 best, gain, goal, hope, loot, love
05 award, booty, medal, purse, reward, stake, value
06 desire, esteem, honour, revere, reward, spoils, stakes, trophy
07 capture, cherish, jackpot, laurels, pennant, pillage, plunder, premium, winning
08 accolade, champion, hold dear, pickings, smashing, terrific, top-notch, treasure, winnings
09 excellent, first-rate

10 appreciate
11 outstanding
12 award-winning
13 think highly of
14 out of this world
15 set great store by

prize-winner
03 dux
05 champ
08 champion
09 cup-winner, medallist

probability
04 odds
07 chances
08 prospect
10 likelihood, likeliness
11 expectation, possibility

probable
06 likely, odds-on
08 a fair bet, feasible, possible
10 forseeable, on the cards
11 anticipated, predictable
12 to be expected

probably
05 maybe
06 likely
07 perhaps
08 a fair bet, possibly
09 doubtless, like as not
10 most likely, presumably
11 as like as not, it looks like
13 as likely as not, the chances
    are
15 in all likelihood

probation
04 test
05 trial
10 test period
11 supervision, trial period
14 apprenticeship

probe
04 bore, poke, prod, sift, test
05 check, drill, plumb, sound,
    study
06 go into, pierce, search
07 analyse, examine, explore,
    inquest, inquire, inquiry
08 analysis, look into, research,
    scrutiny
09 penetrate
10 scrutinize
11 examination, exploration,
    investigate
13 investigation
14 scrutinization

probity
05 worth
06 equity, honour, virtue
07 honesty, justice

08 fairness, fidelity, goodness,
    morality
09 integrity, rectitude, sincerity
11 uprightness
12 truthfulness
13 righteousness
14 honourableness
15 trustworthiness

problem
03 fix
04 hole, mess, snag
05 poser, worry
06 enigma, pickle, plight,
    puzzle, riddle
07 catch-22, dilemma, trouble
08 quandary, question
09 conundrum, difficult, tight
    spot
10 delinquent, difficulty
11 brain-teaser, dire straits,
    predicament, troublesome
12 complication,
    unmanageable
14 no-win situation

problematic
04 hard, moot
06 thorny, tricky
07 awkward, dubious
08 doubtful, involved, puzzling
09 debatable, difficult,
    enigmatic, intricate,
    uncertain
10 a minefield, perplexing
11 a can of worms,
    troublesome
12 questionable
13 problematical

procedure
03 way
04 move, step
05 means
06 course, custom, method,
    policy, scheme, system
07 conduct, formula, measure,
    process, routine
08 practice, strategy
09 operation, technique
11 methodology, performance
12 plan of action
13 modus operandi
14 course of action

proceed
04 come, flow, go on, stem
05 arise, begin, ensue, start
06 derive, follow, move on,
    result, spring
07 advance, carry on, go ahead
08 continue, progress
09 go forward, take steps
11 get under way, make your
    way, set in motion

proceedings
04 case
05 deeds, moves, steps, trial
06 action, annals, doings,
    events, report
07 account, affairs, lawsuit,
    matters, minutes, process,
    records
08 archives, business, dealings,
    measures
10 activities, happenings,
    litigation, manoeuvres,
    operations, procedures
12 transactions

proceeds
05 yield
06 income, profit
07 profits, returns, revenue
08 earnings

process
03 way
04 mode, step
05 alter, means, stage, treat
06 action, change, course,
    growth, handle, manner,
    method, refine, system
07 advance, changes, convert,
    prepare
08 deal with, movement,
    practice, progress
09 evolution, formation,
    operation, procedure,
    technique, transform
10 proceeding
11 development, progression

❑ **in the process of**
05 being
13 in preparation, in the course
    of, in the middle of

procession
04 file
05 march, train
06 column, parade, series
07 cortège
08 sequence
09 cavalcade, motorcade

proclaim
06 affirm, blazon, notify
07 declare, give out, profess,
    publish, testify, trumpet
08 announce, indicate
09 advertise, broadcast,
    circulate, make known,
    pronounce

proclamation
05 edict, order
06 decree, notice
07 command
09 broadcast, manifesto
11 declaration, publication

12 announcement
13 advertisement, pronouncement

proclivity
04 bent, bias
07 leaning
08 penchant, tendency, weakness
10 propensity
11 disposition, inclination
12 predilection
14 predisposition

procrastinate
05 dally, defer, delay, stall
06 put off, retard
08 postpone, protract
09 temporize
10 dilly-dally
11 play for time
12 drag your feet

procrastination
08 deferral, delaying, stalling
11 temporizing
13 dilly-dallying
15 delaying tactics

procreate
04 sire
05 beget, breed, spawn
06 father, mother
07 produce
08 conceive, engender, generate, multiply
09 propagate, reproduce

procure
03 buy, get, win
04 earn, find, gain
06 come by, hustle, obtain, pick up, secure
07 acquire, solicit
08 purchase
09 get hold of, importune
10 lay hands on
11 appropriate, requisition

procurer
04 bawd, pimp
05 madam
11 whoremonger

prod
03 dig, jab
04 butt, goad, move, poke, push, spur, stir, urge
05 egg on, elbow, nudge, shove
06 incite, prompt, thrust
07 motivate, reminder, stimulus
09 encourage, prompting, stimulate

prodigal
06 lavish, wanton, waster
07 copious, profuse, wastrel
08 reckless, spendall, wasteful

09 bounteous, bountiful, excessive, exuberant, luxuriant, sumptuous, unsparing, unthrifty
10 big spender, immoderate, profligate, squanderer
11 extravagant, improvident, spendthrift

prodigality
06 excess, plenty
09 abundance, profusion
10 exuberance, lavishness, luxuriance, profligacy, wantonness
11 copiousness, dissipation, squandering
12 extravagance, immoderation, intemperance, recklessness, wastefulness

prodigious
04 huge, vast
05 giant
07 amazing, immense, mammoth, massive
08 colossal, enormous, gigantic, striking
09 wonderful
10 astounding, inordinate, phenomenal, remarkable, stupendous, tremendous
11 exceptional, spectacular
13 extraordinary

prodigy
06 genius, marvel, rarity, wonder
08 virtuoso, whizz kid
09 curiosity, sensation
10 mastermind, phenomenon

produce
04 bear, crop, eggs, food, give, grow, make, show
05 breed, cause, evoke, mount, offer, put on, stage, yield
06 create, direct, effect, invent, manage, output, supply
07 advance, develop, exhibit, fashion, furnish, harvest, perform, prepare, present, proffer, provide, provoke
08 assemble, bring out, generate, occasion, organize, products, result in
09 construct, fabricate, originate
10 bring about, bring forth, come up with, foodstuffs, give rise to, put forward
11 demonstrate, manufacture, put together
12 bring forward

producer
06 farmer, grower
09 presenter, régisseur
10 impresario
12 manufacturer

product
05 goods, wares, yield
06 effect, output, result, upshot
07 article, outcome, spin-off
08 artefact, creation, offshoot
09 commodity, invention
11 consequence, merchandise

production
04 film, play, show
05 opera, yield
06 fruits, making, output
07 harvest, musical, returns
08 building, creation
09 formation
11 fabrication, manufacture, performance
12 presentation, productivity
13 manufacturing

productive
06 fecund
07 fertile
08 creative, fruitful, prolific
09 inventive
12 fructiferous, high-yielding

productivity
05 yield
06 output
08 capacity, work rate
10 efficiency, production
14 productiveness

profane
04 foul
05 abuse, crude
06 debase, defile, unholy, vulgar
07 godless, impious, secular, ungodly, worldly
08 temporal
09 desecrate
10 idolatrous, irreverent
11 blasphemous, irreligious
12 sacrilegious, unsanctified
13 unconsecrated

profanity
05 abuse, curse
07 cursing, impiety
08 swearing
09 blasphemy, expletive, obscenity, sacrilege, swear-word
11 imprecation, irreverence
14 four-letter word

profess
03 own

04 aver, avow
05 admit, claim, state
06 affirm, allege, assert
07 declare, make out, pretend
08 announce, maintain, proclaim
09 dissemble
10 lay claim to
11 acknowledge

professed
06 avowed
08 declared, so-called
09 pretended, purported, soi-disant
10 ostensible, self-styled

profession
03 job
04 line, post
05 claim, craft, trade
06 avowal, career, métier, office
07 calling
08 business, position
09 situation, statement, testimony
10 employment, line of work, occupation, walk of life

professional
03 ace, pro
06 expert, master, wizard
07 trained
08 educated, licensed
09 practised, qualified
10 specialist

proffer
04 hand
05 offer
06 extend, submit, tender
07 hold out, present, propose

proficiency
05 knack, skill
06 talent
07 ability, mastery
08 aptitude
09 adeptness, dexterity, expertise
10 capability, competence
11 skilfulness

proficient
04 able
05 adept
06 clever, expert, gifted
07 capable, skilful, skilled, trained
08 masterly, talented
09 competent, effective, efficient, qualified
11 experienced
12 accomplished

profile
02 CV
07 contour, outline
08 portrait, side view, vignette
09 biography
10 silhouette
15 curriculum vitae, thumbnail sketch

profit
04 gain
05 avail, value, worth, yield
06 return
07 rake-off, revenue
08 dividend, earnings, proceeds, winnings
09 advantage, make money
10 bottom line
15 line your pockets

❑ **profit by, profit from**
07 exploit
08 cash in on
12 capitalize on
15 take advantage of, turn to advantage

profitable
07 gainful
08 economic, fruitful, valuable
09 lucrative, rewarding
10 beneficial, in the black, productive
11 money-making

profiteer
06 extort, fleece
07 exploit
09 exploiter, racketeer
10 overcharge
12 extortionist
13 make a fast buck

profiteering
09 extortion
10 Rachmanism
12 exploitation, racketeering

profitless
06 futile
08 gainless
09 fruitless, thankless
12 unproductive, unprofitable

profligacy
05 waste
06 excess
10 debauchery, lavishness, wantonness
11 dissipation, prodigality, promiscuity, squandering
12 extravagance, improvidence, recklessness, wastefulness
13 dissoluteness

profligate
04 rake, roué
06 wanton, waster
07 wastrel
08 prodigal, reckless, wasteful
09 debauched, debauchee, dissolute, excessive
10 dissipated, immoderate, squanderer
11 extravagant, improvident, promiscuous, spendthrift

profound
04 deep, wise
07 extreme, intense, learned, serious, weighty
08 abstruse, esoteric, thorough
09 heartfelt
10 discerning, thoughtful
11 far-reaching, penetrating
13 philosophical, thoroughgoing

profoundly
06 deeply, keenly
07 acutely, greatly
08 heartily
09 extremely, intensely
10 thoroughly

profundity
05 depth
06 acumen, wisdom
08 learning, severity
09 extremity, intensity
11 penetration
12 abstruseness

profuse
06 lavish
07 copious, fulsome, liberal
08 abundant, generous
09 excessive, luxuriant, plentiful
11 extravagant, overflowing
12 overabundant
13 superabundant

profusion
04 glut, lots, riot, tons
05 heaps, loads
06 excess, plenty, wealth
08 plethora
09 abundance, plenitude
11 copiousness, superfluity
14 superabundance

progenitor
06 father, mother, parent, source
08 ancestor, begetter, forebear
10 forefather, forerunner, originator, procreator
12 primogenitor

progeny
04 race, seed

05 breed, issue, stock, young
06 family, scions
08 children
09 offspring, posterity, quiverful
11 descendants

prognosis
07 outlook
08 forecast, prospect
10 prediction, projection
11 expectation
15 prognostication

prognosticate
05 augur
06 divine, herald
07 betoken, portend, predict, presage
08 forecast, foretell, indicate, prophesy, soothsay
09 harbinger
10 foreshadow

prognostication
07 surmise
08 forecast, prophecy
09 horoscope, prognosis
10 prediction, projection

programme
04 book, list, plan, show
05 lay on
06 agenda, design, line up, line-up, map out, scheme
07 arrange, episode, itemize, listing, project, work out
08 calendar, schedule, syllabus
09 broadcast, formulate, simulcast, timetable
10 curriculum, prearrange, production, prospectus
11 performance
12 plan of action

progress
03 way
04 go on, grow
05 going
06 better, come on, growth, mature
07 advance, blossom, develop, headway, improve, journey, passage, proceed, prosper, recover, shape up
08 continue, flourish, increase, movement
09 evolution, go forward, promotion, upgrading
10 betterment, forge ahead
11 advancement, development, improvement, make headway, make strides,

make your way, move forward, progression
12 breakthrough, make progress

◻**in progress**
07 going on
08 under way
09 happening, occurring
10 continuing, proceeding
11 not finished, on the stocks
12 not completed
13 in the pipeline

progression
05 chain, cycle, order, train
06 course, series, stream, string
07 advance, headway, passage
08 progress, sequence
10 succession
11 advancement, development

progressive
06 modern
07 dynamic, go-ahead, growing, liberal, radical
08 advanced
09 advancing, reformist
10 avant-garde, continuing, developing, escalating, increasing, innovative
11 enlightened, up-and-coming
12 accelerating, enterprising, intensifying
13 revolutionary
14 forward-looking
15 forward-thinking

prohibit
03 ban, bar
04 stop, veto
06 forbid, hamper, hinder, impede, outlaw
07 exclude, prevent, rule out
08 obstruct, preclude, restrict
09 interdict, proscribe

prohibited
05 taboo
06 banned, barred, vetoed
08 verboten
09 embargoed, forbidden
10 disallowed, proscribed
11 interdicted

prohibition
03 ban, bar
04 veto
07 embargo
08 negation
09 exclusion, forbiddal, interdict
10 constraint, forbidding, injunction, prevention
11 forbiddance, obstruction
12 interdiction, proscription

prohibitionist
11 teetotaller
12 abolitionist

prohibitive
09 excessive
10 exorbitant
12 extortionate, preposterous, proscriptive

project
03 job
04 cast, hurl, idea, plan, task, work
05 bulge, fling, gauge, throw
06 design, expect, extend, jut out, launch, map out, propel, reckon, scheme
07 obtrude, predict, propose, venture
08 activity, campaign, contract, estimate, forecast, overhang, proposal, protrude, stand out, stick out
09 calculate, discharge, programme
10 assignment, conception, enterprise, occupation
11 extrapolate, undertaking
12 predetermine

projectile
04 ball, shot
05 shell
06 bullet, rocket
07 grenade, missile
10 mortar-bomb

projecting
08 beetling
09 exsertile, extrusive
10 protrudent, protruding, protrusive
11 overhanging

projection
04 plan, sill
05 bulge, ledge, ridge, shelf
07 jutting
08 estimate, forecast, overhang
10 prediction
11 expectation
12 protuberance

proletariat
04 herd
05 plebs
06 masses, proles, rabble
08 canaille, riff-raff
09 commoners, hoi polloi
10 commonalty
12 common people, lower classes, working class
13 great unwashed

proliferate
05 breed
06 expand, extend, spread, thrive
07 build up, burgeon
08 escalate, increase, multiply, mushroom

proliferation
06 spread
07 build-up
08 increase
09 expansion, extension
11 mushrooming
14 multiplication

prolific
06 fecund
07 copious, fertile, profuse
08 abundant, fruitful
09 luxuriant
10 productive

prolix
05 prosy, wordy
07 lengthy, verbose
08 rambling, tiresome
10 digressive, discursive, long-winded, pleonastic

prolixity
08 pleonasm, rambling, verbiage
09 verbosity, wordiness
11 verboseness
14 discursiveness, long-windedness

prologue
05 proem
07 preface, prelude
08 exordium, foreword, preamble
11 preliminary, prolegomena
12 introduction

prolong
06 extend
07 drag out, draw out, spin out, stretch
08 continue, elongate, lengthen, protract

promenade
04 prom, turn, walk
06 airing, parade, stroll
07 saunter, swagger, walkway
09 boulevard, esplanade
11 perambulate
14 constitutional

prominence
04 fame, lump, note, rank
05 bulge, mound
06 height, renown
08 eminence, headland, prestige, standing, swelling

09 celebrity
10 importance, projection, promontory, reputation
11 distinction, pre-eminence
12 protuberance
15 illustriousness

prominent
06 famous
07 bulging, eminent, jutting, leading, notable, obvious, popular
08 foremost, renowned, striking
09 acclaimed, important, obtrusive, respected, well-known
10 celebrated, jutting out, noticeable, pre-eminent, projecting, protruding, protrusive
11 conspicuous, eye-catching, illustrious, outstanding, protuberant, standing out, sticking out
12 unmistakable
13 distinguished

promiscuity
09 depravity, looseness
10 debauchery, immorality, profligacy, protervity, wantonness
14 licentiousness

promiscuous
04 fast
05 loose
06 casual, random, wanton
07 immoral
09 debauched, dissolute
10 licentious, profligate
12 of easy virtue
14 indiscriminate

promise
03 vow
04 bond, hint, oath, sign, word
05 augur, flair, swear, vouch
06 assure, denote, hint at, pledge, talent
07 ability, betoken, compact, presage, signify, suggest, warrant
08 aptitude, contract, covenant, evidence, indicate
09 assurance, be a sign of, guarantee, potential, undertake
10 capability, commitment, engagement, indication, suggestion, take an oath
11 undertaking

12 give your word, word of honour

promised land
04 Zion
08 paradise
09 Shangri-la
➢ See also **heaven**

promising
04 able, rosy
06 bright, gifted
07 budding, hopeful
10 auspicious, favourable, optimistic, propitious

promontory
04 cape, head, naze, ness, spur
05 bluff, cliff, point, ridge
08 foreland, headland
09 peninsula, precipice
10 projection, prominence

promote
03 aid
04 back, help, hype, plug, push, sell, urge
05 boost, exalt, raise
06 assist, foster, honour, market, move up, prefer, puff up
07 advance, elevate, endorse, espouse, forward, further, nurture, sponsor, support, upgrade
08 advocate, champion
09 advertise, encourage, publicize, recommend, stimulate
10 aggrandize, popularize
12 contribute to

promotion
04 hype, rise
06 move-up, urging
07 backing, pushing, support
08 advocacy, boosting, campaign, espousal, plugging
09 elevation, fostering, marketing, publicity, upgrading
10 exaltation, preferment, propaganda
11 advancement, advertising, development, furtherance
12 contribution
13 encouragement
14 aggrandizement, recommendation

prompt
03 cue
04 lead, prod, spur, urge
05 cause, quick, rapid, sharp, swift

06 elicit, incite, induce, on time, remind, speedy, timely
07 inspire, produce, provoke
08 motivate, on the dot, punctual, reminder, result in, stimulus
09 call forth, encourage, instigate, stimulate
10 give rise to, punctually
11 expeditious, to the minute
13 encouragement

prompting
04 hint
06 advice, urging
07 jogging, pushing
08 prodding, reminder
10 incitement, persuasion

promptly
03 pdq
04 asap
05 sharp
06 on time, pronto
07 quickly, swiftly
08 speedily
09 forthwith, posthaste
10 punctually
15 pretty damn quick

promptness
05 haste, speed
08 alacrity, dispatch
09 alertness, briskness, eagerness, quickness, readiness, swiftness
10 expedition
11 promptitude, punctuality, willingness

promulgate
05 issue
06 decree, notify, spread
07 declare, promote, publish
08 announce, proclaim
09 advertise, broadcast, circulate, publicize
11 communicate, disseminate

promulgation
11 publication, publicizing
12 announcement, proclamation, promulgating
13 dissemination

prone
03 apt
04 bent, flat
05 given
06 liable, likely
07 subject
08 disposed, inclined
09 prostrate, recumbent
10 full-length, horizontal, procumbent, vulnerable
11 predisposed, susceptible

proneness
07 aptness, leaning
08 penchant, tendency
09 liability
10 proclivity, propensity
11 disposition, inclination
14 susceptibility

prong
04 fork, spur, tine
05 grain, point, spike
10 projection

pronounce
03 say
05 judge, speak, utter, voice
06 affirm, assert, decree, stress
07 declare, express
08 announce, proclaim, vocalize
09 enunciate
10 articulate

pronounceable
07 sayable, vocable
09 speakable, utterable
10 enunciable

pronounced
05 broad, clear, thick
06 marked, strong
07 decided, evident, obvious
08 definite, distinct, positive, striking
10 noticeable
11 conspicuous

pronouncement
05 edict
06 decree, dictum
09 assertion, ipse dixit, judgement, statement
11 declaration
12 announcement, proclamation

pronunciation
06 accent, speech, stress
07 diction, voicing
08 delivery, uttering
09 elocution
10 inflection, intonation, modulation
11 enunciation
12 articulation, vocalization

proof
08 evidence
09 repellent, resistant
10 impervious, validation
11 attestation
12 confirmation, verification
13 certification, corroboration, demonstration, documentation

14 authentication, substantiation

prop
03 set
04 lean, post, rest, stay
05 brace, shaft, shore, stand, stick, strut, truss
06 anchor, column, hold up, pillar, steady, uphold
07 balance, bolster, shore up, support, sustain, upright
08 buttress, mainstay, maintain, underpin
09 bolster up, stanchion, supporter

propaganda
04 hype
09 promotion, publicity
11 advertising, information
14 disinformation, indoctrination

propagandist
07 plugger
08 advocate, promoter
09 proponent, publicist
11 pamphleteer
12 proselytizer

propagate
04 grow
05 beget, breed, spawn
06 spread
07 diffuse, produce, promote, publish
08 generate, increase, multiply, proclaim, transmit
09 broadcast, circulate, procreate, publicize, reproduce
10 distribute, promulgate
11 communicate, disseminate, proliferate

propagation
06 spread
08 breeding, increase, spawning
09 diffusion, promotion, spreading
10 generation
11 circulation, procreation
12 distribution, promulgation, reproduction, transmission
13 dissemination, proliferation
14 multiplication

propel
04 move, push, send
05 drive, force, impel, shoot, shove
06 launch, thrust
11 push forward

propensity
04 bent, bias
06 foible
07 aptness, leaning
08 penchant, tendency, weakness
09 liability, proneness, readiness
10 proclivity
11 disposition, inclination
14 predisposition, susceptibility

proper
04 prim, real, true
05 exact, right
06 actual, decent, formal, polite, strict
07 correct, fitting, genteel, genuine, precise, prudish, refined
08 accepted, accurate, ladylike, orthodox, suitable
10 acceptable
11 appropriate, established, gentlemanly, respectable
12 conventional

property
04 gear, land, mark
05 acres, goods, house, means, quirk, trait
06 assets, estate, houses, riches, wealth
07 capital, effects, feature, holding, quality
08 chattels, holdings, premises
09 attribute, buildings, resources
10 belongings, real estate
11 peculiarity, possessions
12 idiosyncrasy
13 paraphernalia
14 characteristic

prophecy
06 augury
08 forecast
09 prognosis
10 divination, prediction
11 second sight, soothsaying
14 fortune-telling
15 prognostication

prophesy
05 augur
07 foresee, predict
08 forecast, foretell, forewarn
13 prognosticate

prophet
04 seer
06 oracle
10 forecaster, foreteller, soothsayer

11 clairvoyant
13 fortune-teller
14 prognosticator

◻ **prophet of doom**
08 Jeremiah
09 Cassandra, pessimist

prophetic
03 fey
05 vatic
06 mantic
07 augural
08 oracular
09 fatidical, presaging, prescient, sibylline, vaticidal
10 divinatory, predictive, prognostic
11 forecasting
13 foreshadowing

prophylactic
10 preventive, protective
12 preventative

propinquity
03 tie
08 nearness
09 closeness, proximity
10 connection, contiguity
11 affiliation

propitiate
07 appease, mollify, placate, satisfy

propitiation
09 placation
11 appeasement
13 mollification

propitiatory
09 appeasing, assuaging, pacifying, placatory
10 mollifying

propitious
05 happy, lucky
06 benign, bright, kindly, timely
08 friendly, gracious
09 fortunate, opportune, promising
10 auspicious, beneficial, benevolent, favourable, prosperous, reassuring
11 encouraging
12 advantageous, well-disposed

proponent
06 backer, friend, patron
08 advocate, champion, defender, exponent, partisan, proposer, upholder
09 apologist, supporter
10 enthusiast, propounder, subscriber, vindicator

proportion
03 cut
04 bulk, mass, part, size
05 depth, quota, ratio, scale, share, split, whack, width
06 amount, extent, height, length, volume
07 balance, breadth, measure, portion, segment
08 capacity, division, fraction, quotient, symmetry
09 magnitude
10 dimensions, percentage
12 distribution, measurements, relationship
14 correspondence, slice of the cake

proportional
04 even
08 relative
09 analogous, equitable
10 comparable, consistent, equivalent
12 commensurate
13 corresponding, proportionate

proportionally
06 evenly
07 pro rata
10 comparably, relatively
14 commensurately
15 correspondingly, proportionately

proposal
03 bid
04 plan
05 offer, terms
06 design, motion, scheme, tender
07 project
09 manifesto, programme
10 suggestion
11 proposition
12 presentation
14 recommendation

propose
03 aim
04 mean, move, name, plan
05 offer, put up, table
06 design, intend, submit, tender
07 advance, bring up, present, proffer, purpose, suggest
08 advocate, nominate, propound
09 introduce, recommend
10 have in mind, put forward
14 pop the question
15 plight your troth

proposition
04 pass, plan, task
06 accost, motion, scheme, tender, theory
07 advance, project, solicit, theorem, venture
08 activity, approach, overture, proposal
09 manifesto, programme
10 suggestion
11 make a pass at, undertaking
14 recommendation

propound
07 advance, contend, lay down, present, propose, suggest
08 advocate, set forth
09 postulate
10 put forward

proprietor, proprietress
05 owner
08 landlady, landlord
09 landowner, possessor
10 deed holder, freeholder
11 leaseholder, title-holder

propriety
06 nicety
07 decency, decorum, fitness, manners, modesty, p's and q's
08 breeding, civility, courtesy, delicacy, protocol, standard
09 etiquette, punctilio, rectitude, rightness
10 convention, politeness, refinement, seemliness
11 correctness, good manners
12 becomingness, ladylikeness, suitableness, the done thing
14 respectability
15 appropriateness, gentlemanliness

propulsion
04 push
06 thrust
07 impetus, impulse
09 impulsion

prosaic
04 dull, flat, tame
05 banal, bland, stale, trite
06 boring
07 humdrum, mundane
08 everyday, ordinary
10 monotonous, pedestrian, uninspired
11 commonplace
12 matter-of-fact
13 unimaginative

proscribe
03 ban, bar
04 damn, doom
05 black, exile, expel
06 banish, deport, forbid, outlaw, reject
07 boycott, censure, condemn, embargo, exclude
08 denounce, disallow, prohibit
09 blackball, interdict, ostracize
10 expatriate
13 excommunicate

proscription
03 ban, bar
05 exile
07 barring, boycott, censure, damning, embargo
08 ejection, eviction, outlawry
09 exclusion, expulsion, interdict, ostracism, rejection
10 banishment
11 deportation, prohibition
12 condemnation, denunciation, expatriation
15 excommunication

prosecute
03 sue, try
06 accuse, charge, indict, summon
07 arraign
08 litigate
10 put on trial
11 take to court
12 bring charges
13 prefer charges

proselytize
07 convert, win over
08 persuade
10 bring to God, evangelize
12 make converts

prosody
➤ *Forms of prosody*:
04 foot, iamb
05 canto, envoy, epode, Ionic, metre, paeon
06 dactyl, rondel, sonnet
07 ballade, caesura, couplet, elision, pyrrhic, rondeau, Sapphic, spondee, strophe, triolet, trochee, virelay
08 anapaest, choriamb, cinquain, eye rhyme, Pindaric, quatrain, tribrach, trimeter
09 anacrusis, assonance, catalexis, dispondee, ditrochee, free verse, hexameter, macaronic, monometer, monorhyme
10 amphibrach, amphimacer, blank verse, enjambment, galliambic, heptameter, pentameter, rhyme royal, tetrameter, villanelle
11 Alcaic verse, alexandrine, broken rhyme, linked verse, long-measure
12 alliteration, Leonine rhyme, Pythian verse, sprung rhythm
13 abstract verse, heroic couplet, hypermetrical
15 poulters' measure

prospect
04 hope, nose, odds, seek, view
05 quest, scene, vista
06 aspect, chance, future, search, survey
07 chances, examine, explore, fossick, inspect, look for, opening, outlook, promise
08 likeness, panorama
09 landscape, spectacle
10 likelihood
11 expectation, perspective, possibility, probability
12 anticipation

prospective
04 -to-be
06 coming, future, likely
07 awaited, would-be
08 aspiring, destined, expected, hoped-for, imminent, intended, possible, probable
09 designate, potential
11 anticipated, approaching, forthcoming

prospectus
04 list, plan
06 scheme
07 leaflet, outline
08 brochure, pamphlet, syllabus, synopsis
09 catalogue, manifesto, programme
10 conspectus, literature

prosper
06 do well, flower, thrive
07 advance, burgeon
08 flourish, get ahead, grow rich
09 get on well
14 go up in the world
15 get on in the world

prosperity
06 plenty, riches, wealth
07 fortune, success
09 affluence, well-being
11 good fortune, lap of luxury, the good life

prosperous
07 opulent, wealthy, well-off
08 affluent, thriving, well-to-do
10 burgeoning, well-heeled
11 flourishing, rolling in it

prostitute
03 pro
04 bawd, drab, moll, tart
05 brass, whore
06 debase, harlot, hooker
07 cocotte, degrade, floosie, hustler, rent-boy, trollop
08 call-girl, strumpet
09 courtesan
10 loose woman
11 fallen woman, fille de joie
12 street-walker

prostitution
07 the game, whoring
08 harlotry, whoredom
13 street-walking

prostrate
04 flat, ruin, tire
05 prone
06 fallen, lay low
07 exhaust, laid low, wear out
09 knock down, lying down, lying flat, paralysed
10 devastated, horizontal

❑**prostrate yourself**
05 kneel
06 cringe, grovel, kowtow, submit
07 bow down
13 abase yourself

prostration
03 bow
05 grief
06 kowtow
07 despair
08 collapse, kneeling, weakness
09 abasement, dejection, obeisance, paralysis, weariness
10 depression, desolation, exhaustion, submission
11 despondency
12 genuflection, helplessness
15 slough of despond

protagonist
04 hero, lead
06 banker, leader
07 heroine
08 adherent, advocate, champion, exponent, mainstay
09 principal, proponent, supporter, title role
10 prime mover

12 moving spirit
13 main character
14 chief character, standard-bearer

protean
07 amoebic, mutable
08 variable, volatile
09 many-sided, mercurial, multiform, versatile
10 changeable, inconstant
11 polymorphic
12 ever-changing, polymorphous

protect
04 keep, save
05 cover, guard
06 defend, escort, screen, secure, shield
07 care for, harbour, shelter
08 conserve, keep safe, preserve
09 look after, safeguard, watch over
10 take care of

protection
04 care
05 cover, guard
06 armour, buffer, charge, refuge, safety, screen, shield
07 barrier, bulwark, custody, defence, shelter
08 security
09 insurance, safeguard
11 safekeeping
12 conservation, guardianship, preservation

protective
04 wary
08 covering, vigilant, watchful
09 defensive, fireproof, shielding
10 insulating, waterproof

protector
06 minder, patron
08 defender, guardian
09 bodyguard, safeguard

protégé, protégée
04 ward
05 pupil
06 charge
07 student
09 dependant, discovery
11 blue-eyed boy

protein
➤ *Types of protein*:
04 zein
05 abrin, actin, renin
06 avidin, casein, fibrin, globin, myosin

07 albumen, albumin, elastin, gliadin, histone, hordein, sericin, tubulin
08 aleurone, amandine, collagen, cytokine, globulin
09 fibrillin, prolamine, protamine, sclerotin
10 conchiolin, dystrophin, fibronogen, interferon
11 interleukin, lipoprotein, transferrin
12 immunoglobin

protest
04 avow, demo, fuss, riot
05 argue, demur, gripe, march
06 affirm, appeal, assert, attest, avowal, insist, object, oppose, outcry, reject, whinge
07 boycott, contend, declare, dissent, profess
08 announce, complain, demurral, disagree, proclaim, speak out
09 assertion, complaint, exception, objection, take issue
10 contention, disapprove, opposition
11 affirmation, declaration, demonstrate, kick up a fuss, remonstrate
12 proclamation, protestation
13 demonstration, remonstration, take exception

protestation
03 vow
04 oath
06 avowal, outcry, pledge
07 dissent, protest
09 assurance, complaint, objection, statement
10 profession
11 affirmation, declaration
12 asseveration, remonstrance
13 expostulation, remonstration

protester
05 rebel
07 opposer, striker
08 agitator, objector, opponent
09 dissenter, dissident
10 complainer
12 demonstrator

protocol
06 custom
07 manners, p's and q's
09 etiquette, propriety
10 civilities, convention

11 formalities
15 code of behaviour

prototype
04 type
05 model
06 mock-up
07 example, pattern
08 exemplar, original, paradigm, standard
09 archetype, precedent

protract
06 extend
07 drag out, draw out, prolong, spin out, sustain
08 continue, lengthen
09 keep going
10 make longer, stretch out

protracted
04 long
07 lengthy
08 drawn-out, extended
09 prolonged
12 long-drawn-out

protrude
05 bulge
06 beetle, extend, jut out
07 obtrude, poke out, project
08 stand out, stick out

protruding
05 proud
07 jutting
09 extrusive, prominent
11 protuberant

protrusion
03 jut
04 bump, knob, lump
05 bulge
08 swelling
09 obtrusion, outgrowth
10 projection
12 protuberance

protuberance
04 bulb, bump, knob, lump, wart, welt
05 bulge, tuber
06 tumour
08 swelling, tubercle
09 apophysis, outgrowth
10 protrusion
11 excrescence

protuberant
05 proud
07 bulbous, bulging, jutting, popping
08 beetling, swelling
09 prominent
10 protrudent, protruding, protrusive

proud
04 glad, smug, vain
05 cocky, grand
07 haughty, pompous, stuck-up
08 arrogant, boastful, jumped-up, puffed up, snobbish, splendid, thrilled
09 big headed, conceited, dignified, gratified, hubristic, imperious, red-letter, wonderful
10 high-handed
11 egotistical, outstanding, overbearing, overweening
12 presumptuous, supercilious
13 high and mighty, self-important
14 full of yourself

provable
10 attestable, verifiable
11 confirmable
12 demonstrable

prove
04 show, test
06 attest, pan out, try out, verify
07 bear out, confirm, justify, turn out
08 validate
09 ascertain, determine, establish, transpire
11 demonstrate
12 authenticate, substantiate
13 bear witness to

proven
08 accepted, attested, verified
09 confirmed, undoubted
11 established

provenance
06 origin, source
10 birthplace, derivation

provender
04 fare, food
06 fodder, forage
07 edibles, rations
08 eatables, supplies, victuals
10 foodstuffs, provisions
11 comestibles

proverb
03 saw
05 adage, gnome, maxim
06 byword, dictum, saying
07 precept
08 aphorism, paroemia
10 apophthegm

proverbial
06 famous
07 typical
08 accepted, renowned

09 axiomatic, customary, legendary
10 archetypal

provide
04 give, lend
05 bring, cater, serve, yield
06 afford, impart, supply
07 furnish, present
09 take steps
10 arrange for, contribute, prepare for
11 accommodate
12 make plans for, take measures
13 make provision

❑**provide for**
04 fend, keep
05 endow
07 support, sustain
08 maintain

provided
05 given
08 as long as, so long as
11 on condition
14 with the proviso

providence
04 fate, luck
06 thrift, wisdom
07 destiny, economy, fortune
08 God's will, prudence
09 foresight, judgement
11 forethought

provident
07 careful, prudent, thrifty
10 economical, far-sighted

providential
05 happy, lucky
06 timely
07 welcome
09 fortunate, opportune
10 fortuitous, heaven-sent

provider
05 angel, donor, giver
06 earner, funder, source
08 supplier
10 benefactor, wage-earner
11 breadwinner

providing
05 given
08 as long as, provided
11 on condition
14 with the proviso

province
04 area, duty, line, role, zone
05 field, shire, state
06 charge, colony, county, domain, office, pigeon, region, sphere
07 concern

08 business, district, function
09 territory
10 department, dependency
14 responsibility

───────
Names of Canadian
provinces and territories:
05 Yukon
06 Quebec
07 Alberta, Nunavut, Ontario
08 Labrador, Manitoba
10 Nova Scotia
12 New Brunswick,
Newfoundland,
Saskatchewan
14 Yukon Territory
15 British Columbia
18 Prince Edward Island
20 Northwest Territories
23 Newfoundland and
Labrador
➤ See also **borough**; **county**;
state

provincial
04 hick
06 narrow
07 insular, limited
08 outlying, regional
09 home-grown, parochial,
small-town
10 intolerant, parish-pump
12 narrow-minded
15 unsophisticated

provincialism
12 parochialism
13 provinciality

provision
04 food, plan, step, term
06 stocks, stores, supply
07 measure, proviso, rations
08 eatables, services, supplies
09 allowance, condition,
foodstuff, groceries
10 facilities, precaution,
sustenance
11 arrangement, preparation,
requirement, stipulation
13 qualification, specification

provisional
06 pro tem
07 interim, stopgap
09 makeshift, temporary,
tentative
11 conditional
12 transitional

provisionally
06 pro tem
07 interim
09 meanwhile
15 for the time being

proviso
06 clause
07 strings
09 condition, provision
10 limitation
11 requirement, stipulation
13 qualification

provocation
04 dare
05 cause, taunt
06 injury, insult, motive, reason
07 affront, grounds, offence
08 stimulus
10 generation, incitement,
inducement, motivation
11 aggravation, inspiration,
instigation, stimulation

provocative
04 sexy
06 erotic
07 galling, teasing
08 alluring, annoying, arousing,
exciting, inviting, tempting
09 insulting, offensive,
seductive
10 irritating, suggestive
11 aggravating, stimulating,
tantalizing, titillating

provoke
04 move, goad, prod, rile, spur,
stir
05 anger, annoy, cause, egg on,
evoke, pique, rouse, taunt,
tease
06 elicit, excite, harass, hassle,
incite, induce, insult,
madden, needle, nettle,
prompt, wind up
07 incense, inflame, inspire,
produce, promote
08 engender, generate, motivate
09 aggravate, call forth,
instigate, stimulate
10 exasperate, give rise to

provoking
06 irking, vexing
07 galling, irksome
11 aggravating

prow
03 bow
04 bows, fore, head, nose, stem
05 front

prowess
05 skill
06 genius, talent
07 ability, command, mastery
08 aptitude, facility
09 adeptness, dexterity,
expertise
11 proficiency, skilfulness

prowl
04 hunt, lurk, nose, roam, rove
05 creep, skulk, slink, sneak
06 cruise, patrol, search
14 move stealthily

proximity
08 nearness, vicinity
09 adjacency, closeness
10 contiguity
11 propinquity

proxy
05 agent
06 deputy, factor
07 stand-in
08 attorney, delegate
09 surrogate
10 substitute
14 representative

prude
04 prig
07 old maid, puritan
09 Mrs Grundy
10 school-marm

prudence
06 thrift, wisdom
07 caution, economy
09 canniness, foresight,
frugality, good sense,
husbandry
11 common sense, forethought
13 judiciousness

prudent
04 wise
06 frugal
07 careful, politic, thrifty
08 cautious, discreet, sensible
10 economical

prudery
08 primness
09 Grundyism
10 prissiness, puritanism
11 overmodesty
12 priggishness

prudish
04 prim
06 prissy
08 overnice, priggish
09 Victorian
10 old-maidish, overmodest
11 puritanical, strait-laced
13 school-marmish

prune
03 cut, lop
04 clip, dock, pare, snip, trim
05 shape
07 shorten

prurient
04 lewd
06 erotic, smutty

07 obscene
08 desirous, indecent
09 salacious
12 concupiscent, pornographic

pry
03 dig
04 nose, peep, peer
05 delve, snoop
06 ferret, meddle
07 intrude
09 interfere
12 put your oar in
14 poke your nose in
15 stick your nose in

prying
04 nosy
08 meddling, snooping
09 intrusive
10 meddlesome
11 inquisitive, interfering

psalm
04 hymn, poem, song
05 chant, paean
06 prayer
08 canticle

pseud
05 fraud, poser
06 phoney, poseur

pseudo
04 fake, mock, sham
05 bogus, false, pseud, quasi-
06 ersatz, phoney
08 spurious
09 imitation, pretended
10 artificial

pseudonym
05 alias
07 allonym, pen-name
09 false name, incognito, stage name
10 nom de plume
11 assumed name

psyche
04 mind, self, soul
05 anima
06 pneuma, spirit
09 awareness, intellect
12 subconscious
13 consciousness, heart of hearts

psychiatrist
06 shrink
07 analyst
09 therapist
10 head doctor
12 headshrinker, psychologist, trick cyclist
13 psychoanalyst
15 psychotherapist

psychic
06 mental, mystic, occult
08 mystical
09 cognitive, spiritual
10 telepathic
11 clairvoyant, telekinetic
12 extrasensory, supernatural
13 psychological

psychological
06 mental
08 cerebral
09 cognitive, imaginary
10 irrational, subjective
11 unconscious
12 subconscious
13 psychosomatic

psychology
04 mind
06 habits, make-up
07 mindset, motives
09 attitudes

➤ *Names of psychologists:*
04 **Beck** (Aaron Temkin), **Jung** (Carl)
05 **Adler** (Alfred), **Binet** (Alfred), **Freud** (Anna), **Freud** (Sigmund), **James** (William), **Klein** (Melanie), **Laing** (Ronald David), **Meyer** (Adolf), **Rhine** (Joseph Banks)
06 **Bowlby** (John), **De Bono** (Edward), **Kinsey** (Alfred Charles), **Piaget** (Jean)
07 **Eysenck** (Hans Jürgen), **Persaud** (Raj), **Skinner** (Burrhus Frederic)
08 **Wernicke** (Carl)
09 **Alexander** (Franz Gabriel), **Alzheimer** (Alois), **Rorschach** (Hermann)
➤ See also **scientist**

psychopath
06 maniac, psycho
07 lunatic
09 psychotic, sociopath

psychopathic
03 mad
06 insane
07 lunatic
08 demented, maniacal
09 psychotic

pub see **public house**

puberty
05 teens
10 pubescence
11 adolescence
12 teenage years

public
04 fans
05 civic, civil, overt, plain
06 masses, nation, people, voters
07 country, exposed, patrons, popular
08 audience, citizens, national, populace
09 clientèle, community, consumers, customers, followers, multitude, published, universal
10 celebrated, electorate, population, spectators, supporters
11 illustrious, influential
12 nationalized

❑**in public**
06 openly
08 publicly
09 in the open
11 for all to see

publican
06 barman
07 barmaid
08 hotelier, landlady, landlord, mine host, taverner
09 innkeeper
11 hotel-keeper

publication
04 book
05 daily, issue
06 weekly
07 booklet, journal, leaflet, monthly, release
08 brochure, handbill, magazine, pamphlet
09 newspaper, quarterly
10 disclosure, periodical, production, publishing
12 announcement, notification, proclamation

public house
03 bar, inn, pub
06 boozer, tavern
12 watering-hole

publicity
04 hype, plug, puff
06 splash
07 build-up
09 limelight, promotion
10 propaganda
11 advertising

publicize
04 hype, plug, push
07 promote
08 announce
09 advertise, broadcast, make known, spotlight
10 make public

public-spirited
10 altruistic, charitable
12 humanitarian
13 philanthropic

publish
05 issue, print
06 report, reveal
07 declare, release
08 announce, bring out, disclose, proclaim
09 advertise, circulate, make known, publicize
10 distribute, make public
11 communicate, disseminate

pucker
04 fold, ruck
05 pleat, purse, shirr
06 crease, gather, ruffle
07 crinkle, crumple, screw up, shrivel, wrinkle
08 compress, contract

puckered
05 pursy
06 rucked
07 creased, ruckled
08 gathered, wrinkled

puckish
03 sly
06 impish
07 naughty, playful
09 whimsical
10 frolicsome
11 mischievous

pudding
03 pie, pud
04 tart
05 sweet
06 afters, pastry
07 dessert

puddle
04 pool, slop
05 plash

puerile
07 babyish, foolish, trivial
08 childish, immature, juvenile
09 infantile
10 adolescent

puff
04 blow, drag, draw, gasp, gulp, gust, pant, plug, pull, push, suck, waft
05 blast, smoke, swell, whiff
06 breath, expand, flurry, market, praise, wheeze
07 breathe, promote
09 promotion, publicity, publicize

puffed
06 winded

07 gasping, panting
10 breathless
11 out of breath

□puffed up
05 proud
08 arrogant
09 big-headed
13 swollen-headed
14 full of yourself

puffy
07 bloated, dilated, swollen
08 enlarged, inflated, puffed up
09 distended

pugilism
06 boxing
07 the ring
08 fighting, fistiana, the fancy
11 the noble art
13 prize-fighting

pugilist
05 boxer
07 bruiser, fighter
12 prize-fighter

pugnacious
09 bellicose
10 aggressive
11 belligerent, contentious, quarrelsome
13 argumentative

puke
04 spew
05 heave, retch, vomit
07 throw up
11 regurgitate

pull
03 rip, tow, tug
04 drag, draw, haul, jerk, lure, tear, yank
05 heave, pluck, power, tempt
06 allure, entice, pull in, pull up, remove, sprain, strain, uproot, weight
07 attract, bring in, draw out, extract, pull out, take out
09 dislocate, influence, magnetism, magnetize
10 allurement, attraction
12 drawing power, forcefulness

□pull apart
08 separate
09 criticize, dismantle, dismember
12 pull to pieces, take to pieces

□pull back
07 back out, retreat
08 withdraw
09 disengage

□pull down
07 destroy

08 bulldoze, demolish
09 dismantle, knock down
15 raze to the ground

□pull in
04 book, draw, earn, lure, make, stop
05 clear, run in, seize
06 arrest, arrive, be paid, detain, entice, rake in
07 attract, bring in, receive
15 take into custody

□pull off
06 detach, remove, rip off
07 achieve, succeed
08 bring off, carry off, carry out
10 accomplish

□pull out
04 quit
05 leave
06 depart, desert
07 abandon, back out, move out, retreat
08 evacuate, withdraw

□pull through
07 recover, survive, weather
10 recuperate

□pull together
09 co-operate
11 collaborate
12 work together

□ pull yourself together
15 control yourself

□pull up
04 halt, park, stop
06 carpet, draw up, rebuke
07 tell off, tick off
10 take to task

pulp
03 pap
04 mash, mush
05 crush, flesh, paste, purée
06 marrow, squash
09 liquidize, pulverize, triturate

pulpit
04 dais
07 lectern, rostrum, soapbox
08 platform

pulpy
04 soft
05 mushy, pappy
06 fleshy
07 squashy

pulsate
04 beat, drum, thud
05 pound, pulse, throb, thump
06 hammer, quiver
07 vibrate
09 oscillate

pulsating
09 vibratile, vibrating, vibrative
11 oscillating, palpitating

pulsation
05 ictus
09 vibration
11 oscillation, palpitation
12 vibratiuncle

pulse
04 beat, drum, thud, tick
05 pound, throb, thump
06 rhythm, stroke
07 vibrate
11 oscillation
➤ See also **bean**

pulverize
05 crush, grind, pound, smash
06 powder, squash, thrash
09 triturate

pummel
05 knock, pound, punch, thump
06 batter, hammer, strike

pump
04 draw, push, quiz, send
05 drain, drive, force, grill
06 inject
11 interrogate
12 cross-examine
13 cross-question

❏**pump out**
05 drain, empty
07 draw off
08 force out

❏**pump up**
06 blow up, puff up
07 inflate

pun
04 quip
09 witticism
11 paronomasia, play on words
14 double entendre

punch
03 bop, box, cut, hit, jab
04 bash, biff, bite, blow, bore, cuff, hole, slug, sock
05 clout, knock, power, thump, verve
06 impact, pummel, strike, vigour, wallop
07 panache, pizzazz
08 puncture, strength
09 perforate
12 forcefulness

punch-drunk
05 dazed, dizzy, woozy
06 groggy
07 reeling

08 confused, unsteady
09 befuddled, stupefied

punch-up
05 brawl, fight, scrap, set-to
06 dust-up, ruckus, shindy
08 argument, ding-dong
10 free-for-all
12 stand-up fight

punchy
05 zappy
08 forceful, incisive, powerful, spirited, vigorous

punctilio
06 nicety
09 exactness
11 finickiness
14 scrupulousness
15 punctiliousness

punctilious
05 exact, fussy, picky
06 choosy, formal, proper, strict
07 careful, finicky, precise
10 meticulous, nit-picking, particular, pernickety, scrupulous
13 conscientious

punctual
05 early, exact, on cue
06 on time, prompt
07 precise
08 on the dot
09 well-timed
10 bang on time, dead on time, in good time

punctuality
10 promptness, regularity
11 promptitude

punctually
06 bang on, dead on, on time, prompt, spot on
08 on the dot, promptly
09 precisely
11 to the minute

punctuate
05 break, point
06 pepper
08 sprinkle
09 emphasize, interject, interrupt
10 accentuate
11 intersperse

puncture
04 flat, hole, slit
05 burst, prick, spike
06 pierce
07 blow-out, deflate, flatten, let down, rupture
08 flat tyre

09 penetrate, perforate
11 perforation

pundit
04 buff, guru, sage
06 expert, master, savant
07 maestro, teacher
09 authority

pungent
03 hot
04 acid, keen, sour, tart
05 acrid, acute, fiery, sharp, spicy, tangy
06 biting, bitter, strong
07 burning, caustic, cutting, peppery, piquant, pointed
08 piercing, scathing, stinging

punish
04 beat, cane, fine, flog, hang, harm, lash, slap, whip
05 abuse, scold, smack, spank
06 batter, damage, defeat, hammer, misuse, thrash
07 correct, crucify, knee-cap, rough up, scourge, trounce
08 chastise, imprison, maltreat, penalize
09 castigate
10 discipline
11 bring to book
14 make someone pay, throw the book at
15 give someone hell, make an example of

punishable
08 criminal, culpable, unlawful
10 chargeable, indictable
11 blameworthy, convictable

punishing
04 hard
05 cruel, harsh
06 severe, taxing, tiring
07 arduous
09 crippling, demanding, fatiguing, gruelling, strenuous
12 backbreaking

punishment
07 deserts, penalty, revenge
08 sentence
10 correction, discipline
11 retribution
12 chastisement

punitive
04 hard
05 cruel, harsh, penal
06 severe
09 crippling, punishing
10 burdensome
11 retributive
12 disciplinary

punter
06 client, fellow, person
07 gambler, wagerer
08 consumer, customer
10 individual

puny
04 tiny, weak
05 frail, minor, petty, small
06 feeble, little, measly, sickly
07 stunted, trivial
08 piddling, trifling
10 diminutive, undersized
13 insignificant
14 underdeveloped
15 inconsequential

pupil
07 learner, protégé, scholar, student
08 disciple, protégée
09 schoolboy
10 apprentice, schoolgirl

puppet
04 doll, dupe, gull, pawn, tool
06 stooge
07 cat's-paw
08 creature, quisling
10 figurehead, instrument, marionette, mouthpiece

purchase
03 buy, get
04 gain, grip, hold
05 grasp
06 assets, pay for, pick up, secure, snap up
07 acquire, procure, shop for
08 foothold, leverage
09 advantage
10 go shopping
11 acquisition, splash out on

purchaser
05 buyer
06 client, emptor, vendee
07 shopper
08 consumer, customer

pure
04 good, neat, real, true
05 clean, clear, fresh, moral, sheer, total, utter
06 chaste, decent, honest, simple, virgin
07 aseptic, natural, sterile, unmixed
08 absolute, abstract, academic, flawless, germ-free, hygienic, innocent, sanitary, spotless, thorough, virginal, virtuous
09 downright, unalloyed, undefiled, undiluted, unsullied

10 antiseptic, immaculate, sterilized, uninfected, unpolluted
11 theoretical, unblemished, unmitigated
13 unadulterated
14 uncontaminated

pure-bred
07 blooded
08 pedigree
09 pedigreed, pure-blood
11 full-blooded, pure-blooded
12 thoroughbred

purely
06 simply, solely, wholly
11 exclusively

purgative
05 enema, purge
06 emetic
08 aperient, evacuant, laxative
09 cathartic, cleansing
10 abstersive, depurative, eccoprotic

purge
03 rid
04 kill, oust
05 clear, eject, expel, scour
06 purify
07 absolve, cleanse, dismiss, wipe out
08 clean out, clear out, get rid of
09 cleansing, eradicate, expulsion
11 eradication, exterminate
13 extermination

purification
05 purge
08 cleaning
09 cleansing, epuration, purgation
10 absolution, depuration, filtration, redemption
12 disinfection, sanitization
14 sanctification

purify
05 clean, purge
06 distil, filter, redeem
07 absolve, cleanse
08 depurate, filtrate, fumigate, sanctify, sanitize
09 disinfect, sterilize

purifying
07 purging
09 cathartic, cleansing, purgative
10 depurative
12 purificatory

purism
08 pedantry
14 fastidiousness

purist
06 pedant
07 finicky
08 pedantic, puristic, stickler
09 nit-picker, over-exact
10 fastidious, nit-picking
11 over-precise
14 over-fastidious, over-meticulous, over-particular

puritan
05 prude
06 zealot
07 fanatic, killjoy, pietist
08 moralist, rigorist
14 disciplinarian

puritanical
04 prim
05 rigid, stern, stiff
06 proper, severe, strict, stuffy
07 ascetic, austere, bigoted, prudish, puritan, zealous
09 fanatical
10 abstemious, moralistic
11 strait-laced
12 narrow-minded

puritanism
08 primness, rigidity, severity, zealotry
09 austerity, stiffness
10 abstinence, asceticism, self-denial, strictness
11 prudishness
14 abstemiousness

purity
06 honour, virtue
07 clarity, decency
08 chastity, goodness, morality
09 cleanness, freshness, innocence, virginity
11 cleanliness, uprightness
12 virtuousness

purlieus
06 bounds, limits
07 borders, fringes, suburbs
08 confines, environs, vicinity
09 outskirts, perimeter, periphery, precincts
12 surroundings
13 neighbourhood

purloin
03 rob
04 lift, nick, take
05 filch, pinch, steal, swipe
06 finger, nobble, pilfer, pocket, remove, snitch, thieve

07 snaffle
11 appropriate

purport
04 gist, idea, mean, seem, show
05 claim, drift, imply, point, tenor, theme
06 allege, assert, convey, denote, import, intend, pose as, spirit, thrust
07 bearing, betoken, declare, express, meaning, portend, pretend, profess, signify, suggest
08 indicate, maintain, proclaim, tendency
09 direction, substance
11 implication
12 significance

purpose
03 aim, end, use
04 gain, goal, good, hope, idea, mean, plan, wish, zeal
05 basis, drive, point, value
06 aspire, decide, design, desire, effect, intend, motive, object, reason, result, settle, target, vision
07 outcome, propose, resolve
08 ambition, firmness, function, tenacity
09 advantage, determine, intention, objective, principle, rationale
10 aspiration, dedication, doggedness, motivation, resolution, usefulness
11 application, contemplate, persistence
12 perseverance
13 determination, justification, steadfastness

☐**on purpose**
08 by design, wilfully
09 knowingly, purposely
12 deliberately
13 intentionally

purposeful
04 firm
06 dogged
07 decided
08 constant, resolute, resolved
09 steadfast, tenacious
10 deliberate, determined, persistent, unwavering
11 persevering, unfaltering
12 single-minded, strong-willed

purposefully
10 resolutely
11 steadfastly, tenaciously

12 persistently, unwaveringly
13 perseveringly, unfalteringly
14 single-mindedly

purposeless
04 vain
07 aimless, useless, vacuous
09 pointless, senseless
10 gratuitous, motiveless

purposely
08 by design, wilfully
09 expressly, on purpose
10 designedly
12 calculatedly, deliberately
13 intentionally

purse
05 award, funds, money, pouch, prize
06 pucker, reward
07 coffers
08 compress, contract, finances, money-bag, treasury
09 exchequer, resources

pursuance
09 discharge, execution, following
10 fulfilment
11 performance, prosecution

pursue
03 dog
04 hunt, seek, tail
05 chase, harry, hound, stalk, track, trail
06 follow, harass, shadow
07 carry on, conduct, go after, perform
08 aspire to, engage in, maintain, practise, run after
09 persist in, strive for
11 investigate, persevere in, work towards

pursuit
04 goal, hunt, line
05 chase, craft, hobby, quest, trade, trail
07 pastime, tailing
08 activity, interest, stalking, tracking
09 following, hue and cry, shadowing
10 occupation, speciality
13 investigation

purvey
04 sell
05 cater, stock
06 deal in, retail, supply
07 furnish, provide, trade in
08 put about, transmit
09 provision, publicize

purveyor
06 dealer, trader
08 provider, provisor, retailer, stockist, supplier
10 victualler
11 transmitter
12 communicator

push
02 go
03 ram
04 butt, cram, goad, hype, jolt, plug, poke, prod, raid, spur, urge
05 boost, bully, drive, egg on, elbow, foray, force, impel, knock, nudge, press, shove
06 charge, coerce, effort, energy, hustle, incite, jostle, market, plunge, propel, squash, thrust, vigour
07 advance, assault, depress, promote, squeeze
08 ambition, dynamism, invasion, persuade, press for, vitality
09 advertise, constrain, encourage, incursion, influence, manhandle, offensive, publicize
10 enterprise, get-up-and-go, initiative, pressurize
12 forcefulness
13 determination
14 put the screws on

☐**push around**
05 bully
07 torment
09 terrorize, victimize
10 intimidate

☐**push off**
04 move
05 leave
06 beat it, depart, go away
07 buzz off
08 clear off, clear out, shove off
09 make a move, push along
10 make tracks

pushed
06 hard-up, rushed
07 harried, hurried, pinched, pressed, short of
08 harassed, strapped
11 hard-pressed
13 under pressure

pushover
03 mug
04 dupe, gull
05 cinch
06 doddle, picnic, sucker
08 walk-over

09 soft touch
10 child's play
11 piece of cake, sitting duck

pushy
04 bold
05 bossy, brash
07 forward
08 arrogant, assuming, forceful
09 ambitious, assertive
10 aggressive
11 impertinent
12 presumptuous
13 over-confident

pusillanimity
08 timidity, weakness
10 cravenness, feebleness
11 fearfulness, gutlessness
12 cowardliness, timorousness
13 spinelessness

pusillanimous
04 weak
05 timid
06 craven, feeble, scared, yellow
07 chicken, fearful, gutless, wimpish
08 cowardly, timorous
09 spineless, weak-kneed
11 lily-livered
12 faint-hearted

pussyfoot
03 pad
05 creep, hedge, prowl, slink, steal
06 tiptoe
09 mess about
10 equivocate

pustule
04 boil, pock
05 ulcer
06 fester, papule, pimple
07 abscess, blister, whitlow
08 eruption
09 carbuncle

put
03 bet, fix, lay, pin, say, set
04 dump, give, levy, post, rank, rest, risk, sink, sort, turn, word
05 apply, class, couch, exact, frame, grade, group, offer, place, plonk, speak, spend, stand, state, utter, voice
06 assign, attach, chance, charge, demand, devote, gamble, impose, impute, invest, locate, phrase, render, settle, submit, tender
07 arrange, ascribe, convert, deposit, dispose, express,

inflict, lay down, present, proffer, propose, require, set down, situate, station, subject, suggest
08 classify, dedicate, position, set forth
09 attribute, establish, formulate, lay before, pronounce, set before, translate
10 categorize, contribute, transcribe
12 bring forward

◻ **put about**
04 tell
06 spread
09 circulate, make known
11 disseminate

◻ **put across**
06 convey
07 explain, get over, put over
09 get across, make clear
11 communicate
12 get through to
14 make understood

◻ **put aside**
04 keep, save, stow
05 hoard, lay by, put by, stash, store
06 retain
07 reserve
08 lay aside, salt away, set aside
09 stockpile
13 keep in reserve

◻ **put away**
03 eat
04 jail, save, stow, wolf
05 drink, lay by, put by, scoff, store
06 commit, devour, guzzle, lock up
07 certify, confine, consume, reserve, swallow
08 imprison, put aside, send down
09 polish off, stockpile

◻ **put back**
05 defer, delay
06 freeze, return, shelve
07 replace, restore
08 postpone, put on ice
09 reinstate

◻ **put down**
03 fix, lay, log
04 kill, list, snub, stop
05 blame, crush, enter, quash, quell, shame
06 attach, charge, defeat, humble, record

07 ascribe, deflate, destroy, jot down, set down
08 note down, register, stamp out, suppress
09 ascribe, attribute, deprecate, disparage
10 put to sleep, transcribe

◻ **put forward**
05 offer, table
06 submit, tender
07 advance, present, proffer, propose, suggest
08 nominate
09 recommend

◻ **put in**
05 enter, input
06 insert, submit
07 install

◻ **put off**
05 daunt, defer, delay, deter
06 dismay, divert, shelve, sicken
07 adjourn, confuse, deflect
08 dissuade, distract, postpone, put on ice
09 turn aside
10 discourage, dishearten, reschedule
13 procrastinate

◻ **put on**
03 add, don
04 fake, sham, wear
05 affix, apply, feign, mount, place, stage
06 affect, assume, attach
07 dress in, perform, present, pretend, produce
08 simulate

◻ **put out**
04 faze
05 annoy, douse, issue, upset
06 bother, quench
07 disturb, perturb, publish, smother
08 announce, disclose, impose on, irritate, unsettle
09 broadcast, circulate, make known
10 extinguish
13 inconvenience

◻ **put through**
06 manage
07 achieve, execute
08 bring off, complete, conclude, finalize
10 accomplish

◻ **put together**
04 join
05 build
08 assemble
09 construct

11 fit together
13 piece together

▫put up
05 build, erect, float, house, lodge, offer, raise
06 bump up, choose, hike up, invest, pledge, supply
07 advance, propose, provide, shelter, suggest
08 increase, nominate
09 construct, recommend
11 accommodate

▫put up to
04 goad, urge
05 egg on
06 incite, prompt
08 persuade
09 encourage

▫put upon
07 exploit
08 impose on
13 inconvenience, take liberties
14 take for granted
15 take advantage of

▫put up with
04 bear, take
05 abide, allow, brook, stand
06 accept, endure, suffer
07 stomach, swallow
08 stand for, tolerate
13 take lying down

putative
07 alleged, assumed, reputed
08 presumed, reported, supposed
10 reputative
11 conjectural, theoretical
12 hypothetical

put-down
03 dig
04 gibe, snub
05 sneer
06 insult, rebuff, slight
07 affront, sarcasm
11 humiliation
13 disparagement, slap in the face

put-off
06 damper
09 deterrent, hindrance

12 disincentive
14 discouragement

putrefy
03 rot
05 addle, decay, go bad, mould, spoil, stink, taint
06 fester, perish
07 corrupt
08 gangrene
09 decompose
11 deteriorate

putrescent
07 rotting
08 decaying, mephitic, stinking
09 festering, perishing
10 putrefying
11 decomposing

putrid
03 bad, off
04 foul, rank
05 fetid
06 addled, mouldy, rancid, rotten
07 corrupt, decayed, tainted
08 polluted, stinking
10 decomposed
12 contaminated

put-upon
06 abused
09 exploited, imposed on
10 maltreated, persecuted
14 inconvenienced

puzzle
04 beat
05 brood, floor, poser, rebus, stump, think
06 baffle, enigma, figure, ponder, riddle
07 anagram, confuse, dilemma, flummox, mystery, mystify, nonplus, paradox, perplex, stagger
08 acrostic, bewilder, confound, consider, meditate, mull over, muse over, question
09 conundrum, crossword
10 deliberate, mind-bender
11 brainteaser
14 rack your brains

▫puzzle out
04 suss

05 crack, solve
06 decode
07 suss out, unravel, work out
08 decipher
09 figure out

puzzled
05 at sea
07 at a loss, baffled, stumped
09 flummoxed, mystified, perplexed
10 bewildered, confounded, nonplussed

puzzlement
05 doubt
09 confusion
10 bafflement, perplexity
11 incertitude, uncertainty
12 bewilderment
13 mystification

puzzling
06 knotty
07 bizarre, cryptic, curious, strange, unclear
08 abstruse, baffling, peculiar, tortuous
09 confusing, enigmatic, intricate
10 mysterious, mystifying, perplexing, Sphynx-like
11 bewildering, mind-bending
12 impenetrable, inexplicable, labyrinthine, mind-boggling, unfathomable

pygmy
03 toy, wee
04 baby, tiny
05 dwarf, elfin, small
06 midget, minute, pocket
07 manikin, stunted
08 dwarfish, half-pint
09 miniature, minuscule, pint-sized, thumbling
10 diminutive, fingerling, homunculus, undersized
11 Lilliputian

pyromaniac
07 firebug
08 arsonist
10 fire-raiser, incendiary

quack
04 fake, sham
05 bogus, false, fraud, pseud
06 cowboy, humbug, phoney
08 impostor, so-called
09 charlatan, trickster

quackery
04 sham
05 fraud
06 humbug
09 imposture, phoniness
12 charlatanism
13 mountebankery

quaff
04 down, gulp, swig
05 booze, drain, drink, swill
06 guzzle, imbibe, tipple
07 carouse, swallow, toss off
09 knock back

quagmire
03 bog, fen, fix
04 hole, mess, mire, quag
05 marsh, swamp
06 morass, pickle, slough
09 deep water, tight spot

quail
05 cower, quake, shake
06 blench, cringe, falter, flinch, recoil, shiver, shrink
07 shudder, shy away, tremble
08 back away, draw back

quaint
03 odd
04 twee
05 droll, sweet
07 bizarre, curious, strange
08 charming, old-world
09 whimsical
10 antiquated, olde-worlde
11 picturesque
12 old-fashioned

quake
04 move, rock, sway
05 heave, quail, shake, throb
06 quiver, shiver, wobble
07 shudder, tremble, vibrate
08 convulse

qualification
05 rider, skill

06 caveat, degree
07 diploma, fitness, proviso
09 condition, exception, exemption, provision
10 competence, limitation
11 certificate, eligibility, proficiency, reservation, restriction, stipulation
13 certification

qualified
04 able
06 expert, fitted
07 capable, guarded, limited, skilful, skilled, trained
08 eligible, licensed, prepared, reserved, talented
09 certified, chartered, competent, efficient
10 proficient, restricted
11 conditional, experienced
12 accomplished, professional

qualify
04 ease, pass
05 allow, equip, limit, train
06 adjust, lessen, modify, reduce, soften, weaken
07 certify, delimit, empower, entitle, license, warrant
08 graduate, moderate, restrain, restrict, sanction
09 alleviate, authorize

quality
04 kind, make, rank, sort, type
05 class, grade, level, merit, trait, value, worth
06 make-up, nature, status
07 calibre, feature, variety
08 eminence, standard
09 attribute, character
10 excellence, refinement
11 distinction, peculiarity, pre-eminence, superiority
14 characteristic

qualm
04 fear
05 doubt, worry
07 anxiety, concern, scruple
08 disquiet
09 hesitancy, misgiving

10 hesitation, reluctance, uneasiness
11 compunction, uncertainty
12 apprehension

quandary
03 fix, jam
04 hole, mess
06 muddle, pickle
07 dilemma, impasse, problem
10 difficulty, perplexity
11 predicament

quantity
03 lot, sum
04 area, bulk, dose, lots, many, mass, much, part, size
05 heaps, loads, quota, total
06 amount, extent, length, number, volume, weight
07 breadth, expanse, measure
08 capacity
09 aggregate, magnitude
10 proportion

quarantine
09 detention, isolation
11 segregation

quarrel
03 row
04 feud, slam, tiff
05 argue, brawl, clash, set-to
06 bicker, differ, fracas, schism
07 censure, dispute, dissent, fall out, punch-up, wrangle
08 argument, conflict, disagree, squabble, vendetta
10 contention, difference
11 altercation, controversy
12 disagreement, pull to pieces
13 slanging match
15 be at loggerheads

quarrelling
06 at odds, rowing, strife
07 discord, feuding, warring
09 bickering, scrapping, wrangling
10 at variance, contention, discordant, disharmony, dissension, squabbling
11 altercation, disputation
12 argy-bargying

13 at loggerheads
14 vitilitigation

quarrelsome
09 bellicose, irascible, irritable
11 belligerent, contentious
12 disputatious
13 argumentative
14 ready for a fight

quarry
04 game, goal, kill, prey
05 prize
06 object, target, victim

quarter
04 area, digs, part, pity, post, side, spot, zone
05 board, grace, house, mercy, point, put up, rooms
06 billet, pardon, sector
07 section, shelter, station
08 barracks, clemency, district, division, dwelling, leniency, locality, lodgings, vicinity
09 residence, territory
10 compassion, habitation
11 accommodate, forgiveness
13 accommodation, neighbourhood

quash
04 void
05 annul, crush, quell
06 cancel, defeat, revoke
07 nullify, rescind, reverse
08 abrogate, override, overrule, overturn, set aside, suppress
09 overthrow
10 invalidate
11 countermand

quaver
05 break, quake, shake, waver
06 quiver, tremor, warble
07 flutter, shudder, tremble, tremolo, vibrate
09 oscillate, vibration

quay
04 dock, pier
05 jetty, wharf
07 harbour

queasy
03 ill
04 sick
05 faint, green, queer, rough
06 groggy, unwell
07 bilious
08 sickened
09 nauseated, squeamish
10 out of sorts
15 under the weather

queen
04 idol

05 belle, charm, ruler, Venus
06 beauty
07 consort, empress, majesty, monarch
08 princess
09 sovereign

► *Names of queens. We have omitted the word* **queen** *from names given in the following list but you may need to include this word as part of the solution to some crossword clues. The regnal numerals of individual queens have also been omitted.*

04 Anne (of Cleves), Grey (Lady Jane), Mary (of Teck), Mary (Queen of Scots), Parr (Catherine)
05 Maria, Marie (de Médici)
06 Boleyn (Anne), Howard (Catherine)
07 Beatrix, Eleanor (of Aquitaine), Eleanor (of Castile), Juliana, Seymour (Jane), Zenobia
08 Adelaide, Boadicea, Boudicca, Caroline (of Ansbach), Caroline (of Brunswick), Isabella (of Castile), Margaret (of Anjou), Victoria
09 Alexandra, Brunhilde, Catherine (de' Medici), Catherine (of Aragon), Catherine (of Braganza), Cleopatra, Elizabeth, Fredegond, Nefertiti, Semiramis
10 Anne Boleyn, Hatshepsut
11 Jane Seymour
13 Catherine Parr, Margaret Tudor
14 Henrietta Maria
15 Catherine Howard, Marie Antoinette

queenly
05 grand, noble, regal, royal
06 august
07 stately, sublime
08 gracious, imperial, majestic
09 imperious, sovereign
11 monarchical

queer
03 gay, ill, mar, odd
04 foil, harm, iffy, ruin, sick
05 botch, dizzy, faint, fishy, funny, giddy, rough, shady, spoil, upset, weird, wreck
06 queasy, shifty, stymie, unwell
07 curious, deviant, lesbian, strange, suspect, unusual

08 abnormal, bisexual, peculiar, puzzling, singular
09 eccentric, frustrate, unnatural
10 homosexual, mysterious, out of sorts, outlandish, remarkable, suspicious
11 light-headed
15 under the weather

queerness
11 abnormality, bizarreness, curiousness, peculiarity, singularity, strangeness
12 eccentricity, irregularity
13 anomalousness

quell
04 calm, hush, rout
05 allay, crush, quash, quiet
06 defeat, pacify, soothe, squash, stifle, subdue
07 appease, conquer, put down, silence
08 moderate, overcome, suppress, vanquish
10 extinguish

quench
04 cool, sate
05 douse, slake
06 put out, stifle
07 satiate, satisfy, smother
08 snuff out, stamp out
10 extinguish

querulous
05 cross, fussy, ratty, testy
07 carping, fretful, grouchy, peevish
08 captious, critical, petulant
09 fractious, grumbling, irascible, irritable
11 complaining
12 cantankerous, discontented, dissatisfied, fault-finding

query
03 ask
07 dispute, inquire, inquiry, problem, quibble, suspect
08 distrust, mistrust, question
09 challenge, suspicion
10 disbelieve, scepticism
11 reservation, uncertainty

quest
03 aim
04 goal, hunt
06 search, voyage
07 crusade, inquiry, journey, mission, purpose, pursuit
09 adventure
10 expedition, pilgrimage
11 exploration, undertaking
13 investigation

question
04 pump, quiz
05 doubt, grill, issue, point, poser, probe, query, theme, topic
06 debate, matter, motion
07 debrief, dispute, examine, inquire, inquiry, problem
08 argument, proposal
09 catechize, challenge, interview
10 difficulty, disbelieve
11 controversy, interrogate, investigate, uncertainty
12 cross-examine
13 cross-question

◻ **out of the question**
06 absurd
10 impossible, ridiculous
11 unthinkable
12 unacceptable, unbelievable

◻ **without question**
11 immediately
14 unhesitatingly, unquestionably

questionable
04 iffy
05 fishy, shady, vexed
07 dubious, suspect
08 arguable, doubtful, unproven
09 debatable, uncertain
10 disputable, suspicious

questioner
07 doubter, sceptic
08 agnostic, examiner, inquirer
09 catechist
10 catechizer, inquisitor
11 disbeliever, interviewer
12 interlocutor, interrogator

questionnaire
04 form, quiz, test
06 survey
11 opinion poll
14 market research

queue
03 row
04 file, line
06 column, series, string
08 sequence, tailback
09 crocodile
10 procession, succession
13 concatenation

quibble
04 carp
05 cavil, query
06 niggle
07 nit-pick, protest
08 pettifog

09 complaint, criticism, objection
10 equivocate, split hairs

quibbler
07 casuist, niggler, sophist
08 caviller
09 nit-picker
12 hair-splitter

quibbling
07 carping, evasive
08 captious, critical, niggling
09 casuistic, cavilling
10 nit-picking
13 hair-splitting

quick
04 fast, keen
05 agile, alive, brief, brisk, rapid, ready, sharp, smart, swift
06 astute, clever, nimble, prompt, speedy, sudden
07 cursory, express, instant
08 fleeting
09 immediate, sprightly
10 discerning, perceptive
11 expeditious, intelligent, perfunctory, sharp-witted
12 without delay
13 instantaneous

quicken
04 stir, whet
05 hurry, rouse, speed
06 arouse, excite, hasten, incite, kindle, revive, stir up
07 advance, animate, enliven, hurry up, inspire, speed up
08 energize, expedite, revivify
09 galvanize, stimulate
10 accelerate, invigorate, revitalize, strengthen

quickly
04 fast, soon
05 apace, quick
06 presto, pronto
07 briskly, express, hastily, rapidly, readily, swiftly
08 abruptly, promptly, speedily
09 cursorily, hurriedly, instantly, posthaste
11 at the double, immediately
12 lickety-split
14 at a rate of knots, hell for leather, unhesitatingly
15 instantaneously

quickness
05 speed
07 agility
08 keenness, rapidity
09 acuteness, briskness, hastiness, readiness, sharpness, swiftness

10 astuteness, expedition, promptness, speediness, suddenness
12 intelligence
13 precipitation

quick-tempered
05 fiery, testy
06 snappy, touchy
07 waspish
08 choleric, petulant, shrewish
09 excitable, explosive, impatient, impulsive, irascible, irritable, splenetic
11 hot-tempered, quarrelsome
13 temperamental

quick-witted
04 keen
05 acute, alert, sharp, smart
06 astute, bright, clever, crafty
11 intelligent, penetrating

quiescent
04 calm
05 inert, quiet, still
06 asleep, at rest, latent, placid, serene, silent
07 dormant, passive, resting
08 inactive, peaceful, tranquil
10 in abeyance, motionless

quiet
03 low, shy
04 calm, hush, lull, rest, soft
05 faint, muted, peace, still
06 gentle, hushed, lonely, low-key, placid, repose, serene, silent, sleepy, subtle
07 muffled, silence, subdued
08 discreet, peaceful, reserved, reticent, retiring, secluded, taciturn, tranquil
09 inaudible, introvert, noiseless, soundless, stillness, withdrawn
10 restrained, thoughtful
11 sequestered, undisturbed
12 tranquillity, unfrequented
13 unforthcoming, without a sound
15 uncommunicative

quieten
04 calm, dull, hush, mute
05 quell, quiet, shush, still
06 deaden, muffle, pacify, reduce, shut up, smooth, soften, soothe, stifle, subdue
07 compose, silence
08 calm down, diminish
12 tranquillize

quietly
06 calmly, gently, meekly, mildly, mutely, softly

08 placidly, secretly, silently
09 inaudibly, privately
10 peacefully, tranquilly
11 noiselessly, soundlessly
13 unobtrusively
15 surreptitiously

quietness
04 calm, hush, lull
05 peace, quiet, still
06 repose
07 inertia, silence
08 calmness, serenity
09 composure, placidity, stillness
10 inactivity, quiescence
12 tranquillity

quietus
03 end
05 death
06 demise
07 decease, release
08 dispatch
09 death-blow, discharge
10 extinction
11 acquittance, coup de grâce, death-stroke

quilt
05 duvet
08 bedcover, coverlet
09 bedspread, eiderdown
11 counterpane

quintessence
04 core, gist, pith, soul
05 heart
06 kernel, marrow, spirit
07 essence, extract, pattern
08 exemplar, quiddity
12 distillation

quintessential
05 ideal
07 perfect
08 complete, ultimate
10 consummate, definitive
12 archetypical, prototypical

quip
04 gibe, jest, joke
05 crack, quirk
07 epigram, riposte
08 one-liner
09 wisecrack, witticism

quirk
04 kink, turn, whim
05 freak, habit, thing, trait, twist
06 foible, hang-up, oddity
07 caprice, feature

09 curiosity, mannerism
11 peculiarity
12 eccentricity, idiosyncrasy

quisling
05 Judas
07 traitor
08 betrayer, renegade, turncoat
12 collaborator
14 fifth columnist

quit
03 end
04 drop, exit, stop
05 cease, leave
06 depart, desert, give up, go away, pack in, resign
07 abandon, abstain, forsake
08 leave off, withdraw
11 discontinue

quite
05 fully
06 fairly, rather, wholly
07 exactly, totally, utterly
08 entirely, somewhat
09 perfectly, precisely
10 absolutely, completely, moderately, relatively
12 to some extent
13 comparatively

quits
04 even
05 equal, level
06 square

□**call it quits**
04 stop
05 cease
08 break off
09 make peace
11 discontinue
12 stop fighting
14 bury the hatchet

quitter
03 rat
06 skiver
07 shirker
08 apostate, defector, deserter, recreant, renegade
10 delinquent

quiver
05 quake, shake, throb
06 quaver, shiver, tingle, tremor
07 flicker, flutter, pulsate, shudder, tremble, vibrate
09 oscillate, palpitate, pulsation, vibration

quixotic
07 Utopian
08 fanciful, romantic
09 impetuous, impulsive, unworldly, visionary
10 chivalrous, idealistic
11 fantastical, unrealistic
13 impracticable

quiz
04 pump, test
05 grill
11 competition, examination, interrogate, questioning
12 cross-examine
13 cross-question

quizzical
06 amused
07 baffled, curious, mocking, puzzled, teasing
08 humorous, sardonic
09 inquiring, perplexed, satirical, sceptical

quota
04 part
05 share, slice, whack
06 ration
07 portion
09 allowance
10 allocation, proportion

quotation
04 cost, line, rate
05 piece, price, quote
06 charge, figure, tender
07 cutting, excerpt, extract
08 allusion, citation, estimate

quote
04 cite, echo, name
06 recall, recite, repeat
08 allude to
09 recollect, reproduce

quoted
05 cited
06 stated
08 reported
10 referred to, reproduced
14 above-mentioned

quotidian
05 daily
06 common, normal
07 diurnal, regular, routine
08 day-to-day, everyday, habitual, ordinary, repeated, workaday
09 customary, recurrent
11 commonplace

R

rabbit
04 cony
05 bunny, daman, hyrax
06 dassie
10 cottontail

▭rabbit on
06 babble, natter, waffle, witter
07 blather, blether, maunder
08 witter on
09 go on and on, maunder on

rabble
03 mob
05 crowd, horde, plebs
06 masses, throng
08 populace, riff-raff
09 hoi polloi
11 proletariat

rabble-rouser
08 agitator
09 demagogue, firebrand
10 incendiary, ringleader
12 troublemaker

Rabelaisian
04 lewd, racy
05 bawdy, gross
06 coarse, ribald, risqué, vulgar
08 indecent
09 exuberant, satirical
11 extravagant, uninhibited

rabid
03 mad
06 ardent, crazed, raging
07 berserk, bigoted, burning, extreme, fervent, frantic, furious, violent, zealous
08 frenzied, maniacal
09 fanatical, obsessive
10 hysterical, irrational
11 hydrophobic, unreasoning
12 narrow-minded

rabies
11 hydrophobia

race
03 fly, run
04 bolt, clan, dart, dash, line, rush, tear, zoom
05 blood, chase, house, hurry, quest, speed, stock, tribe

06 colour, ethnic, family, gallop, hasten, people, stirps
07 contest, dynasty, kindred, lineage, pursuit, species
10 accelerate, contention, extraction, get a move on
11 competition, ethnic group, racial group, run like hell
➢ See also **sport**

▶ *Types of race*:
03 ski
04 dash, road, sack
05 cycle, horse, relay, yacht
06 rowing, slalom, sprint
07 hurdles, pancake, pursuit, regatta, walking
08 downhill, marathon, scramble, speedway, stock car, swimming
09 Grand Prix, greyhound, motocross, time trial
10 cyclo-cross, motorcycle, track event
11 egg-and-spoon
12 cross-country, steeplechase

▶ *Names of famous races*:
02 TT
04 Oaks
05 Derby
06 Le Mans
07 St Leger
08 Boat Race, Milk Race
11 Admiral's Cup, America's Cup
12 Melbourne Cup, Tour de France
13 Grand National, Kentucky Derby
14 Greyhound Derby, London Marathon
15 Indianapolis 500, Monte Carlo Rally

racecourse
04 turf
05 track
07 circuit
08 speedway

racial
04 folk
06 ethnic, tribal

07 genetic
09 ancestral, inherited
12 ethnological, genealogical

raciness
04 zest
06 energy
08 dynamism, ribaldry
09 animation, bawdiness, freshness, indecency
10 coarseness, ebullience, liveliness, smuttiness
11 naughtiness, zestfulness
12 exhilaration
14 suggestiveness

racism
04 bias
08 jingoism
09 apartheid, prejudice, racialism
10 chauvinism, xenophobia
14 discrimination

racist
05 bigot
07 bigoted
09 racialist
10 chauvinist, intolerant
13 discriminator
14 discriminatory

rack
04 pain, tear
05 agony, frame, pangs, shake, shelf, stand, wrest, wring
06 harass, harrow, holder, misery, strain, stress, wrench
07 afflict, anguish, crucify, oppress, stretch, support, torment, torture, trestle
08 convulse, distress, lacerate
09 framework, suffering
11 persecution

racket
03 con, din, row
04 fuss, game
05 dodge, fraud, noise, trick
06 fiddle, scheme, uproar
07 clamour, swindle, yelling
09 commotion, deception
11 disturbance, pandemonium

raconteur
07 relater

08 narrator, reporter
10 anecdotist, chronicler
11 commentator, storyteller

racy
04 blue, rude
05 bawdy, crude, dirty, zippy
06 coarse, lively, ribald, risqué, smutty, vulgar
07 buoyant, dynamic, naughty
08 animated, indecent, spirited
09 sparkling, vivacious
10 boisterous, fast-moving, indelicate, suggestive

raddled
05 drawn, gaunt
06 wasted
07 haggard, unkempt
11 dishevelled
15 the worse for wear

radiance
03 joy
04 glow
05 bliss, gleam, light, shine
07 delight, ecstasy, elation, glitter, rapture
09 happiness, splendour
10 brightness, brilliance, effulgence, luminosity
13 incandescence

radiant
06 bright, elated, joyful
07 beaming, glowing, shining
08 blissful, ecstatic, gleaming, glorious, luminous, splendid
09 brilliant, delighted, effulgent, sparkling
11 illuminated, over the moon

radiate
04 emit, glow, pour, shed
05 gleam, issue, shine
06 branch, spread
07 diffuse, diverge, emanate, give off, scatter, send out
09 send forth, spread out
10 divaricate
11 disseminate

radiation
04 rays
05 waves
08 emission
09 emanation
10 insolation
12 transmission

radical
05 basic, rebel, total, utter
06 entire, innate, native
07 drastic, extreme, primary
08 militant, profound, reformer, sweeping, thorough

09 elemental, essential, extremist, fanatical, intrinsic
10 deep-seated, elementary
11 far-reaching, fundamental
13 comprehensive, revolutionary

raffish
04 loud
05 cheap, gaudy, gross, showy
06 casual, coarse, flashy, garish, jaunty, rakish, trashy, vulgar
07 dashing, uncouth
08 bohemian, improper
09 dissolute, tasteless
10 dissipated, flamboyant
12 devil-may-care, disreputable, meretricious

raffle
04 draw
05 sweep
07 lottery, tombola
10 sweepstake

rag
03 kid, rib
04 bait, duds, jeer, mock, tats
05 cloth, taunt, tease, towel
06 clouts, duster, shreds
07 duddery, flannel, tatters
08 remnants, ridicule

ragamuffin
04 waif
05 gamin
06 urchin
10 street arab
11 guttersnipe

ragbag
06 jumble, medley
07 mixture
08 pastiche
09 confusion, potpourri
10 assemblage, assortment, hotchpotch, miscellany
14 omnium-gatherum

rage
04 fume, fury, rant, rave
05 anger, go mad, storm, wrath
06 frenzy, raving, see red, seethe, temper, tumult
07 explode, madness, rampage, tantrum, thunder
09 blow a fuse, do your nut
11 blow your top, flip your lid, go up the wall, lose your rag
12 lose your cool
14 foam at the mouth
15 fly off the handle, go off the deep end

❏**all the rage**
06 trendy
07 in vogue, popular, stylish

10 the in thing
11 fashionable

ragged
04 poor, rent, torn
05 holey, rough, tatty
06 frayed, ripped, rugged, shabby, uneven, untidy
07 erratic, in holes, notched, scruffy, unkempt, worn-out
08 indigent, serrated, tattered
09 destitute, in tatters, irregular
10 down and out, down-at-heel, fragmented, straggling
12 disorganized

raging
03 mad
04 wild
05 angry, irate
06 fuming, ireful, raving, stormy
07 enraged, furious, violent
08 furibund, incensed, seething
09 turbulent
10 infuriated, tumultuous
11 fulminating

raid
04 bust, loot, rush, sack
05 blitz, foray, onset, rifle, swoop
06 assail, attack, charge, forage, hold-up, inroad, invade, maraud, sortie, strike
07 assault, break-in, pillage, plunder, ransack
09 break into, descend on, incursion, onslaught

raider
05 crook, shark, thief
06 looter, pirate, robber
07 brigand, invader, villain
08 attacker, marauder, pillager
09 plunderer, ransacker

rail
04 jeer, mock
05 abuse, decry, scoff
06 attack, revile
07 arraign, censure, inveigh, protest, upbraid
09 castigate, criticize, fulminate
10 vituperate, vociferate

railing
05 fence, rails
06 paling
07 barrier, fencing, parapet
10 balustrade

raillery
04 joke
05 chaff, irony, sport
06 banter, joking, satire

07 jesting, kidding, mockery, ragging, ribbing, teasing
08 badinage, diatribe, dicacity, repartee, ridicule
09 chiacking, invective
10 persiflage, pleasantry

railway
04 line, rail
05 rails, track
08 railroad

rain
04 pelt, pour, spit, teem
06 bucket, deluge, hyetal, mizzle, shower, squall
07 drizzle, pluvial, torrent
08 downpour, piss down, pour down, rainfall, sprinkle
10 cloudburst
12 thunderstorm
13 precipitation
15 rain cats and dogs

rainbow
03 arc, bow
04 arch, iris
08 irisated, spectral, spectrum
09 prismatic
10 iridescent, opalescent
13 kaleidoscopic

➤ *Colours of the rainbow:*
03 red
04 blue
05 green
06 indigo, orange, violet, yellow
➤ See also **colour**

rainy
03 wet
04 damp
07 drizzly, pluvial, showery

raise
04 grow, lift, moot, rear, stir
05 amass, boost, breed, build, cause, erect, hoist, put up, rally, rouse, set up, weigh
06 arouse, broach, create, excite, gather, jack up, lift up, muster, step up, uplift
07 amplify, collect, develop, educate, elevate, enhance, nurture, produce, provoke, recruit, suggest, upgrade
08 assemble, heighten, increase
09 construct, cultivate, intensify, introduce
10 accumulate, put forward
11 get together

raised
05 cameo
06 relief

07 applied, relievo
08 appliqué, embossed

rake
03 hoe
04 comb, hunt, roué
05 amass, graze, rifle, scour
06 scrape, search, smooth
07 collect, playboy, ransack, rummage, scratch, swinger
08 hedonist, prodigal
09 debauchee, libertine
10 degenerate, profligate
14 pleasure-seeker

❑**rake in**
04 earn, make
07 bring in, get paid, receive

❑**rake up**
05 raise
06 drag up, remind, revive
07 bring up, mention
09 introduce

rake-off
03 cut
04 part
05 share, slice
07 portion

rakish
05 loose, natty, sharp, smart
06 breezy, casual, dapper, flashy, jaunty, sinful, snazzy
07 dashing, immoral, raffish
08 debonair, depraved
09 debauched, dissolute, lecherous, libertine
10 degenerate, flamboyant, nonchalant, profligate
12 devil-may-care

rally
05 group, march, unite
06 gather, muster, perk up, pick up, reform, revive, summon
07 collect, convene, get well, improve, marshal, meeting, recover, regroup, renewal, reunion, revival, round up
08 assemble, assembly, comeback, jamboree, mobilize, organize, recovery
10 bounce back, conference, congregate, convention, recuperate, resurgence
11 convocation, get together, improvement, mass meeting, pull through
13 bring together, demonstration

ram
03 hit, jam
04 beat, bump, butt, cram, dash, drum, pack, slam

05 crash, crowd, drive, force, pound, smash, stuff, wedge

ramble
04 hike, roam, rove, tour, trek, trip, walk, wind
05 amble, range, stray, tramp
06 babble, rabbit, stroll, waffle, wander, witter, zigzag
07 blether, digress, diverge, meander, saunter, traipse
09 excursion, expatiate
15 go off at a tangent

rambler
05 hiker, rover
06 roamer, walker
08 stroller, wanderer, wayfarer

rambling
05 wordy
06 errant
07 verbose
09 sprawling, spreading
10 circuitous, disjointed, incoherent, long-winded, roundabout, straggling
12 disconnected, long-drawn-out, periphrastic

ramification
06 branch, effect, result, sequel, upshot
07 outcome
11 consequence, development, implication
12 complication, divarication

ramp
04 rise
05 grade, slope
07 incline
08 gradient
09 acclivity

rampage
04 fury, rage, rant, rave, rush
05 storm
06 charge, frenzy, furore, mayhem, uproar
07 run amok, run riot, run wild
09 go berserk

❑**on the rampage**
04 amok, wild
07 berserk, violent
08 frenzied
09 in a frenzy, violently
12 out of control

rampant
04 rank, rife, wild
06 fierce, raging, wanton
07 profuse, riotous, violent
08 epidemic, pandemic
09 excessive, out of hand, unbridled, unchecked

10 widespread
12 out of control, uncontrolled

rampart
04 bank, fort, wall
05 fence, guard
06 vallum
07 bulwark, defence, parapet
09 barricade, earthwork
10 embankment, stronghold
13 fortification

ramshackle
06 flimsy, ruined, unsafe
07 rickety, run-down
08 decrepit, derelict, unsteady
09 crumbling, neglected
10 broken-down, tumbledown
11 dilapidated

ranch
04 farm
06 estate
07 station
08 estancia, hacienda
10 plantation

rancid
03 bad, off
04 foul, high, rank, sour
05 fetid, musty, stale
06 putrid, rotten, turned
07 noisome, noxious
10 malodorous, unpleasant

rancorous
06 bitter
07 acerbic, hostile
08 spiteful, vengeful,
    venomous, virulent
09 resentful, splenetic
10 malevolent, vindictive
11 acrimonious

rancour
05 spite, venom
06 animus, enmity, grudge,
    hatred, malice, spleen
08 acrimony
09 animosity, antipathy,
    hostility, malignity
10 bitterness, ill-feeling,
    resentment
11 malevolence
13 resentfulness
14 vindictiveness

random
06 casual, chance
09 arbitrary, haphazard, hit-or-
    miss, irregular, unplanned
10 accidental, incidental
12 unmethodical, unsystematic
13 serendipitous
14 indiscriminate

▫**at random**
09 aimlessly
11 arbitrarily, haphazardly
12 fortuitously, incidentally
14 unmethodically

randy
07 amorous, aroused, goatish,
    lustful, raunchy, satyric
08 turned-on
09 lecherous
10 lascivious
12 concupiscent

range
04 area, file, kind, line, oven,
    rank, roam, sort, span, type
05 align, amble, array, class,
    cover, field, gamut, genus,
    group, order, reach, scale,
    scope, stove, stray, sweep
06 bounds, cooker, domain,
    extend, extent, limits, line
    up, radius, ramble, series,
    spread, string, stroll, wander
07 arrange, compass, species
08 classify, distance, spectrum
09 catalogue, diversity,
    fluctuate, selection
10 assortment, parameters

rangy
05 lanky, leggy, weedy
06 skinny
08 gangling, rawboned
10 long-legged

rank
03 row
04 file, foul, line, lush, mark,
    rate, sort, tier, type, vile
05 acrid, align, caste, class,
    dense, fetid, grade, gross,
    level, order, place, range,
    sheer, stale, total, utter
06 arrant, coarse, column,
    degree, line up, putrid,
    rancid, series, status, string
07 arrange, blatant, echelon,
    glaring, marshal, profuse,
    pungent, station, stratum
08 absolute, classify, complete,
    division, flagrant, mephitic,
    organize, position, standing,
    stinking, thorough, vigorous
09 downright, formation,
    offensive, out-and-out,
    repulsive, revolting
10 disgusting, graveolent,
    malodorous, outrageous
11 unmitigated, unqualified
12 disagreeable, evil-smelling
14 classification
➢ See also **military**

► *Ranks in the British and
American air forces*:
05 major
07 captain, colonel, general
08 corporal, sergeant
10 air-marshal
11 aircraftman
12 air-commodore,
    aircraftsman, group captain,
    major-general, pilot officer
13 aircraftwoman, flying
    officer, wing commander
14 air-vice-marshal,
    aircraftswoman, squadron
    leader, warrant officer
15 air-chief-marshal, first-
    lieutenant
16 brigadier-general, flight
    lieutenant, second-
    lieutenant
17 lieutenant-colonel,
    lieutenant-general
20 general of the air force
25 marshal of the Royal Air
    Force

► *Ranks in the British and
American armies*:
05 major
07 captain, colonel, general,
    private
08 corporal, sergeant
09 brigadier
10 lieutenant
12 field marshal, major general
13 lance-corporal
14 warrant officer
15 first-lieutenant
16 brigadier-general, general of
    the army, second-lieutenant
17 lieutenant colonel,
    lieutenant-general

► *Ranks in the British and
American navies*:
06 ensign, rating
07 admiral, captain
09 captain RN, commander,
    commodore
10 able seaman, lieutenant,
    midshipman
11 rear admiral, vice-admiral
12 fleet admiral, petty officer
13 sublieutenant
16 commodore admiral
17 admiral of the fleet, chief
    petty officer
19 lieutenant-commander
21 lieutenant junior grade

▫**rank and file**
03 mob
05 crowd, plebs
06 masses, rabble

08 populace, riff-raff, soldiers
09 hoi polloi
11 ordinary men, proletariat
15 private soldiers

rankle
03 bug, irk, vex
04 gall, rile
05 anger, annoy, peeve
08 embitter, irritate

ransack
04 comb, loot, raid, sack
05 harry, rifle, scour, strip
06 maraud, ravage, search
07 despoil, pillage, plunder
09 depredate, devastate
13 turn inside out
14 turn upside down

ransom
04 free
05 money, price
06 pay-off, redeem, rescue
07 deliver, payment, release
08 liberate
11 deliverance, restoration

rant
04 rave, roar, yell
05 shout, storm
06 bellow, crying, tirade
07 bluster, bombast, declaim
08 diatribe, harangue, rhetoric, shouting, tub-thump
09 philippic
10 vociferate

rap
03 hit, tap
04 bang, blow, clip, cuff, slam
05 blame, clout, knock, scold, slate, stick, thump, whack
06 punish, rebuke, strike
07 censure, reprove, slating
09 castigate, reprimand
10 punishment
11 castigation

rapacious
06 greedy
07 preying, wolfish, wolvish
08 esurient, grasping, ravenous, usurious
09 marauding, predatory, voracious, vulturous
10 avaricious, insatiable, plundering

rapacity
05 greed, usury
07 avarice, avidity
08 voracity
09 esurience, esuriency
10 greediness
13 voraciousness

rape
03 rob
04 loot, raid, sack
05 abuse, strip
06 defile, rapine, ravage, ravish
07 assault, despoil, looting, pillage, plunder, ransack
08 maltreat, ravaging, spoliate
09 depredate, stripping
10 plundering, spoliation
12 despoliation, maltreatment
13 sexual assault

rapid
04 fast
05 brisk, hasty, quick, swift
06 lively, prompt, speedy
07 express, hurried
11 expeditious, precipitate

rapidity
04 rush
05 haste, hurry, speed
08 alacrity, celerity, dispatch, velocity
09 briskness, fleetness, quickness, swiftness
10 promptness, speediness
15 expeditiousness

rapidly
07 briskly, hastily, swiftly
08 promptly, speedily
09 hurriedly
12 lickety-split
13 expeditiously, precipitately

rapine
04 rage, raid
07 looting, sacking
08 ravaging
09 stripping, violation
10 defilement, plundering, ransacking, spoliation
11 depredation, devastation
12 despoliation

rapport
04 bond, link
07 empathy, harmony
08 affinity, sympathy
12 relationship
13 understanding

rapprochement
07 détente, reunion
09 agreement, softening
13 harmonization
14 reconciliation

rapt
06 intent
07 charmed, gripped
08 absorbed, thrilled
09 delighted, enchanted, engrossed, entranced

10 captivated, enthralled, fascinated, spellbound

rapture
03 joy
05 bliss
07 delight, ecstasy, elation
08 euphoria, felicity
09 cloud nine, transport
11 delectation, enchantment
13 seventh heaven, top of the world

rapturous
06 joyful, joyous
07 exalted
08 blissful, ecstatic, euphoric
09 delighted, entranced, overjoyed, rhapsodic
11 on cloud nine, over the moon, tickled pink, transported

rare
06 scarce, sparse, superb
07 unusual
08 sporadic, uncommon
09 exquisite, matchless
10 infrequent, remarkable
11 exceptional, outstanding
12 like gold dust
15 thin on the ground

rarefied
04 high
05 noble
06 select
07 private, refined, special
08 esoteric
09 exclusive

rarely
06 hardly, little, seldom
08 scarcely
10 hardly ever
12 infrequently, occasionally
15 once in a blue moon

raring
04 keen
05 eager, ready
07 itching, longing, willing
09 desperate, impatient
12 enthusiastic

rarity
04 find
05 curio, pearl
06 marvel, wonder
08 scarcity, shortage, treasure
09 curiosity, nonpareil
11 strangeness, unusualness

rascal
03 imp
05 devil, rogue, scamp
07 villain, wastrel

09 scallywag, scoundrel
10 ne'er-do-well
13 mischief-maker
14 good-for-nothing

rascally
03 bad, low
07 crooked, knavish, vicious
11 furciferous, mischievous
12 disreputable, unscrupulous
14 good-for-nothing

rash
03 run
04 rush, wave
05 flood, hasty, hives, spate
06 deluge, madcap, plague
08 careless, epidemic,
   eruption, outbreak, reckless
09 foolhardy, hot-headed,
   impetuous, imprudent,
   impulsive, pompholyx,
   unguarded, urticaria
10 headstrong, ill-advised,
   indiscreet, nettlerash
11 adventurous, hare-brained,
   precipitate, temerarious
13 ill-considered

rashness
08 audacity, temerity
09 hastiness, incaution
12 carelessness, heedlessness,
   precipitance, recklessness
13 foolhardiness,
   impulsiveness, precipitation
15 thoughtlessness

rasp
03 bug, jar, rub
04 file, sand
05 croak, grate, grind, peeve
06 abrade, cackle, scrape
07 grating, scratch, screech
08 grinding, irritate
09 excoriate, harshness
10 hoarseness
15 get on your nerves

rasping
05 gruff, harsh, husky, rough
06 croaky, hoarse
07 grating, jarring, raucous
08 creaking, croaking, scratchy
10 stridulant

rate
03 fee, pay, tax
04 cost, deem, rank, toll
05 basis, class, count, grade,
   judge, merit, price, prize,
   ratio, scale, speed, tempo,
   value, weigh, worth
06 admire, amount, assess,
   charge, degree, figure,
   reckon, regard, tariff

07 adjudge, deserve, measure,
   payment, warrant, weigh up
08 appraise, classify, consider,
   estimate, evaluate, relation,
   standard, velocity
10 be worthy of, categorize,
   percentage, proportion
12 be entitled to, have a right to

❑**at any rate**
06 anyway
09 in any case
10 in any event, regardless
12 nevertheless

rather
04 a bit, very
05 quite
06 fairly, pretty, sooner
07 a little, instead
08 slightly, somewhat
10 moderately, much sooner,
   preferably, relatively
13 for preference, significantly

ratify
06 affirm, uphold
07 agree to, approve, certify,
   confirm, endorse, warrant
08 legalize, sanction, validate
11 corroborate, countersign

rating
04 mark, rank
05 class, grade, order, score
06 degree, status
07 grading, placing
08 category, position, standing
10 assessment, evaluation

ratio
07 balance
08 fraction, relation, symmetry
10 percentage, proportion
12 relationship

ration
03 lot
04 food, part, save
05 allot, issue, limit, share
06 amount, budget, viands
07 control, dole out, hand out,
   helping, measure, portion
08 allocate, conserve,
   dispense, restrict, victuals
09 allowance, apportion
10 allocation, distribute,
   foodstuffs, percentage,
   proportion, provisions

rational
04 sane, wise
05 lucid, sound
07 logical, prudent
08 cerebral, sensible, thinking
09 cognitive, judicious, realistic,
   reasoning, sagacious

10 reasonable
11 circumspect, clear-headed,
   intelligent, well-founded
13 ratiocinative

rationale
05 basis, logic
06 motive, reason, theory
07 grounds, purpose, reasons
09 principle, reasoning
10 motivation, philosophy
11 explanation, raison d'être

rationalize
04 trim
07 explain, justify
09 cut back on, modernize
10 reorganize, streamline

rattle
04 bang, bump, faze, jolt
05 alarm, clang, clank, clink,
   knock, shake, upset
06 jangle, jingle, put off
07 clatter, confuse, disturb,
   unnerve, vibrate
08 unsettle
10 disconcert
15 throw off balance

❑**rattle off**
04 list
06 recite, repeat
07 reel off

❑**rattle on**
03 gab
04 yack
05 prate
06 gabble, jabber, witter
07 blether, chatter, prattle
08 rabbit on

ratty
05 angry, cross, short, testy
06 peeved, snappy, touchy
07 annoyed, crabbed
09 impatient, irritable
13 short-tempered

raucous
04 loud
05 harsh, noisy, rough, sharp
06 hoarse, shrill
07 grating, jarring, rasping
08 piercing, strident
10 scratching, screeching
11 ear-piercing

ravage
04 loot, raze, ruin, sack
05 havoc, level, spoil, wreck
06 damage, maraud
07 despoil, destroy, looting,
   pillage, plunder
08 lay waste, wreckage
09 depredate, devastate

10 desolation, ransacking, spoliation
11 depredation, destruction, devastation

ravaged
07 war-torn, war-worn, wrecked
08 desolate
09 destroyed, ransacked
10 battle-torn, devastated

rave
02 do
04 bash, fume, hail, orgy, rage, rant, roar, yell
05 disco, extol, party, storm
06 ramble, rave-up, seethe
07 acclaim, blow-out, enthuse, explode, knees-up, thunder
08 boil over, carousal, praising
09 excellent, laudatory, rapturous, wonderful
10 be mad about, favourable, wax lyrical
11 celebration, flip your lid
12 enthusiastic, lose your cool
14 acid-house party, lose your temper

ravenous
06 greedy, hungry
07 starved, wolfish
08 famished, starving
10 insatiable

rave-up
02 do
04 bash, orgy
05 party
07 blow-out, debauch, shindig
08 carousal
11 celebration

ravine
04 pass
05 abyss, gorge, gully
06 canyon

raving
03 mad
04 wild
05 barmy, batty, crazy, loony
06 insane
07 berserk, furious
08 demented, deranged
09 delirious
10 hysterical, unbalanced
13 out of your mind

ravish
04 rape
05 abuse, charm
06 defile
07 assault, delight, enchant, enthral, overjoy, violate

08 entrance, maltreat
09 captivate, enrapture, fascinate, spellbind

ravishing
06 lovely
08 gorgeous, stunning
09 beautiful, seductive
10 bewitching, enchanting

raw
03 new, wet
04 bare, cold, damp, open, sore
05 bleak, chill, crude, green, harsh, naked, naïve, plain
06 biting, bitter, bloody, callow, chafed, grazed
07 abraded, exposed, natural
08 immature, uncooked
09 unrefined, unskilled, untrained, untreated
10 excoriated, unprepared
11 unpractised, unprocessed
13 inexperienced

ray
04 beam, hint
05 flash, gleam, glint, shaft
06 streak, stream
10 indication, suggestion

raze
04 fell, ruin
05 level, wreck
07 destroy, flatten
08 bulldoze, demolish, pull down, tear down
09 knock down

re
05 about
09 regarding
10 concerning
12 with regard to
14 on the subject of
15 with reference to

reach
04 call, hold, make, ring, span
05 ambit, get to, grasp, phone, power, range, scope, touch
06 attain, extend, extent
07 achieve, command, compass, contact, stretch
08 amount to, arrive at, distance, latitude
09 authority, extension, get hold of, go as far as
12 get through to, jurisdiction
14 get in touch with

react
05 rebel, reply
06 answer, oppose, rise up
07 dissent, respond

09 retaliate
11 acknowledge, reciprocate

reaction
05 reply
06 answer, recoil, reflex
08 backlash, feedback, kickback, response, reversal
11 retaliation
12 repercussion
13 counteraction, reciprocation
15 acknowledgement

reactionary
07 diehard
09 right-wing
11 right-winger, traditional
12 conservative
14 traditionalist

read
04 look, scan, show, skim
05 speak, study, utter
06 decode, peruse, recite
07 declaim, deliver, display, examine, perusal, measure
08 construe, decipher, indicate, pore over, register
09 interpret
10 comprehend, scrutinize, understand
11 leaf through
12 flick through, thumb through

▫ **read into**
05 infer
06 deduce, reason
08 construe
09 interpret
12 misinterpret

readable
05 clear
07 legible
08 gripping
11 captivating, enthralling, interesting, stimulating
12 decipherable, entertaining, intelligible, worth reading
13 unputdownable
14 comprehensible

readily
06 easily, freely, gladly
07 eagerly, happily, quickly, rapidly, swiftly
08 promptly, smoothly, speedily, with ease
09 willingly
14 unhesitatingly

readiness
08 aptitude, facility, keenness
09 eagerness, handiness

10 promptness
11 preparation, willingness

□in readiness
06 on call
08 prepared
09 available, on standby
10 standing by
11 on full alert
13 in preparation

reading
04 scan
05 study
06 figure, lesson, record
07 display, edition, passage, perusal, recital, version
08 browsing, decoding
09 rendering, rendition
10 indication, inspection
11 deciphering, examination, measurement
13 understanding
14 interpretation

ready
03 fit, set
04 easy, game, keen, near
05 alert, eager, equip, handy, happy, prime, rapid, swift
06 all set, astute, on hand, prompt, speedy, to hand
07 arrange, prepare, willing
08 arranged, disposed, equipped, geared up, organize, prepared
09 available, completed, organized, psyched up
10 accessible, convenient, discerning, perceptive
11 predisposed, resourceful
12 enthusiastic, on the point of

real
04 sure, true
05 right, utter, valid
06 actual, honest
07 certain, factual, fervent, genuine, sincere
08 absolute, bona fide, complete, concrete, existing, material, official, physical, positive, rightful, tangible, thorough, truthful
09 authentic, heartfelt, unfeigned, veritable
10 legitimate, unaffected
11 substantial

realism
09 actuality
10 pragmatism
11 genuineness, naturalness
12 authenticity, faithfulness, lifelikeness, truthfulness

realistic
04 real, true
05 close, vivid
07 genuine, logical, natural
08 faithful, lifelike, rational, real-life, sensible, truthful
09 hard-nosed, objective, practical, pragmatic
10 hard-boiled, hard-headed, true-to-life, unromantic
11 commonsense, down-to-earth, level-headed
12 businesslike, clear-sighted, matter-of-fact
13 unsentimental

reality
04 fact
05 truth
08 real life, validity
09 actuality, certainty, existence, real world
11 genuineness, tangibility
12 authenticity, corporeality

realization
04 gain
05 grasp
06 making
07 earning, selling
09 awareness
10 acceptance, cognizance, completion, fulfilment, perception
11 achievement, discernment, performance, recognition
12 appreciation, apprehension
13 comprehension, understanding
14 accomplishment

realize
03 net
04 earn, gain, make, sell, twig
05 clear, fetch, grasp, learn
06 accept, effect, fulfil, take in
07 achieve, bring in, catch on, discern, produce, sell for
08 complete, cotton on, discover, perceive, tumble to
09 apprehend, ascertain, implement, recognize
10 accomplish, appreciate, bring about, comprehend, effectuate, understand
13 become aware of

really
04 very
05 truly
06 highly, in fact, indeed, surely
08 actually, honestly, severely
09 certainly, extremely, genuinely, sincerely

10 absolutely, remarkably
13 categorically, exceptionally

realm
04 area, land
05 field, orbit, state, world
06 domain, empire, sphere
07 country, kingdom
08 monarchy, province
12 principality

reap
03 cut, get, mow, win
04 crop, gain
06 derive, garner, gather, obtain, secure
07 collect, harvest, realize

rear
03 end
04 back, grow, hind, last, lift, loom, rise, rump, soar, tail
05 breed, hoist, nurse, raise, stern, tower, train
06 behind, bottom, foster
07 bring up, care for, educate, elevate, nurture, tail-end
08 backside, buttocks, hindmost, instruct, rearmost
09 cultivate, posterior

rearrange
04 vary
05 alter, rejig, shift
06 adjust, change
07 reorder
10 reposition, reschedule

reason
03 aim, end, wit
04 case, goal, mind, nous
05 basis, brain, cause, infer, logic, sense, solve, think
06 deduce, excuse, motive, object, reckon, sanity
07 defence, grounds, impetus, purpose, thought, work out
08 argument, cogitate, conclude, gumption
09 cerebrate, incentive, intellect, intention, judgement, rationale, reasoning, syllogize
10 inducement, motivation
11 common sense, explanation, raison d'être
12 intelligence, use your brain
13 comprehension, justification, ratiocination, understanding

□reason with
04 coax, move, urge
08 persuade
09 argue with, plead with
10 debate with

1 discuss with
5 remonstrate with

within reason
0 moderately
2 in moderation, within bounds, within limits

easonable
3 low
4 fair, just, sane, wise
5 sound
6 modest, viable
7 average, logical
8 credible, moderate, possible, rational, sensible
9 judicious, plausible, practical, sagacious
0 acceptable
1 inexpensive, intelligent
3 no great shakes

easoned
5 clear, sound
7 logical
8 rational, sensible
9 judicious, organized
0 methodical, systematic
4 well-thought-out

easoning
5 logic, proof
8 analysis, argument, thinking
9 deduction, rationale
0 hypothesis, logistical
1 cerebration, supposition
3 ratiocination
4 interpretation
5 rationalization

eassure
5 brace, cheer, nerve, rally
6 buoy up
7 cheer up, comfort, hearten
9 encourage

ebate
6 refund
9 allowance, deduction, reduction, repayment

ebel
4 defy, riot
6 flinch, mutiny, oppose, recoil, resist, revolt, rise up
7 defiant, disobey, dissent, heretic, run riot, shy away
8 agitator, apostate, mutineer, mutinous, recusant
9 dissenter, guerrilla, insurgent
0 malcontent, schismatic
3 insubordinate, nonconformist, revolutionary
4 freedom fighter
5 insurrectionary

rebellion
04 coup, riot
06 heresy, mutiny, revolt, rising
07 dissent
08 defiance, uprising
09 coup d'état
10 insurgence, opposition, resistance, revolution
12 disobedience, insurrection
15 insubordination

rebellious
06 unruly
07 defiant, rioting
08 mutinous
09 insurgent, obstinate, rebelling, resistant, seditious
11 disobedient, intractable
12 contumacious, recalcitrant, unmanageable
13 insubordinate, revolutionary
15 insurrectionary

rebirth
07 renewal, revival
11 renaissance, restoration
12 regeneration, rejuvenation, resurrection
13 reincarnation
14 revitalization

rebound
06 bounce, recoil, return, spring
08 backfire, ricochet
09 boomerang
10 backfiring, bounce back
15 come home to roost

rebuff
03 cut
04 snub
05 check, spurn
06 refuse, reject, slight
07 decline, put down, put-down, refusal, repulse
08 brush-off, spurning
09 rejection, repudiate
11 repudiation
12 cold shoulder
13 slap in the face
14 discouragement, kick in the teeth

rebuild
06 remake
07 re-edify, remodel, restore
08 renovate
10 reassemble
11 reconstruct

rebuke
04 rate
05 blame, chide, scold
06 carpet
07 censure, reproof, reprove, tell off, tick off, upbraid

08 admonish, reproach, scolding
09 carpeting, castigate, dress down, reprimand
10 admonition, ticking-off
11 castigation, remonstrate
12 give an earful
13 remonstration, tear off a strip

rebut
05 quash
06 defeat, negate, refute
07 confute, explode
08 disprove, overturn
09 discredit
12 give the lie to

rebuttal
06 defeat
08 disproof, negation
10 refutation
11 confutation
12 invalidation

recalcitrant
06 unruly, wilful
07 defiant, wayward
08 contrary, renitent, stubborn
09 obstinate, unwilling
10 refractory
11 disobedient, intractable
12 contumacious, unmanageable
13 insubordinate, unco-operative
14 uncontrollable

recall
05 annul, evoke
06 call up, cancel, memory, repeal, revoke, summon
07 nullify, rescind, retract
08 abrogate, call back, recision, remember, withdraw
09 annulment, order back, recollect, reminisce
10 abrogation, call to mind, revocation, withdrawal
11 remembrance, think back to
12 cancellation, recollection

recant
04 deny
06 abjure, disown, revoke
07 disavow, rescind, retract
08 abrogate, disclaim, forswear, renounce, withdraw
09 repudiate
10 apostatize

recantation
06 denial, revoke
08 apostasy
09 disavowal

10 abjuration, disclaimer, disownment, revocation, withdrawal
11 repudiation
12 renunciation, retraction

recapitulate
05 recap, sum up
06 go over, repeat, review
07 recount, restate, run over
09 reiterate, summarize

recede
03 ebb
04 drop, fade, sink, wane
06 go back, lessen, shrink
07 decline, dwindle, fall off, retreat, slacken, subside
08 decrease, diminish, move away, withdraw

receipt
04 slip, stub
06 income, return, ticket
07 profits, returns, takings
08 delivery, earnings, proceeds
09 receiving, reception
10 acceptance
11 counterfoil
15 proof of purchase

receive
03 get
04 bear, gain, hear, hold, take
05 admit, greet, let in
06 accept, derive, gather, obtain, pick up, suffer
07 acquire, collect, inherit, sustain, undergo, welcome
08 meet with, perceive
09 apprehend, encounter, entertain, respond to
10 experience, learn about
11 accommodate

receiver
05 donee, radio, tuner
07 grantee, handset, legatee
08 assignee, wireless
09 recipient
11 beneficiary

recent
03 new
04 late
05 fresh, novel, young
06 latest, modern
08 up-to-date
10 present-day
13 up-to-the-minute

recently
05 newly
06 lately, of late
10 not long ago

receptacle
06 holder, vessel
09 container
10 repository

reception
02 do
04 bash
05 beano, party
06 at-home, rave-up, social
07 receipt, shindig, welcome
08 function, greeting, reaction
09 admission, gathering
11 get-together, recognition
13 entertainment

receptive
04 open
07 willing
08 amenable, flexible, friendly
09 sensitive, welcoming
10 hospitable, interested, open-minded, responsive
11 susceptible, sympathetic
12 approachable
13 accommodating

recess
03 bay
04 nook, rest
05 break, heart, niche, oriel
06 alcove, bowels, cavity, corner, depths, hollow
07 holiday, innards, reaches, respite, time off, time out
08 interior, interval, vacation
10 depression, penetralia
11 indentation
12 intermission

recession
05 crash, slide, slump
06 trough
07 decline, failure
08 collapse, downturn
10 depression

recherché
04 rare
06 arcane, choice, select
07 refined
08 abstruse, esoteric

recipe
05 guide, means
06 method, system
07 formula, process
09 procedure, technique
10 directions
11 ingredients
12 instructions, prescription

recipient
05 donee
07 grantee, legatee

08 assignee, receiver
11 beneficiary

reciprocal
05 joint
06 mutual, shared
08 requited, returned
09 exchanged
11 alternating, correlative
13 complementary, corresponding
14 interdependent

reciprocate
04 swap
05 match, repay, reply, trade
06 return
07 requite, respond
08 exchange
10 correspond

recital
04 show
07 account, concert, reading
09 narration, rendering, rendition
10 recitation, repetition
11 declamation, performance
14 interpretation

recitation
04 poem, tale
05 piece, story, verse
07 passage, reading, telling
09 monologue, narration
10 party piece

recite
04 tell
06 relate, repeat
07 declaim, deliver, itemize, narrate, recount, reel off
08 say aloud
09 enumerate, rattle off
10 articulate

reckless
04 rash, wild
05 hasty
06 madcap
08 careless, heedless, tearaway
09 daredevil, foolhardy, imprudent, negligent
10 ill-advised, incautious
11 precipitate, thoughtless
12 devil-may-care
13 irresponsible

recklessness
07 madness
08 rashness
10 imprudence, negligence
12 carelessness, heedlessness
13 foolhardiness

reckon
04 deem, rate

reckoning

05 add up, count, gauge, guess, judge, tally, think, total
06 assess, assume, esteem, number, regard
07 compute, imagine, suppose, surmise, think of, work out
08 consider, estimate, evaluate
09 calculate, figure out
10 conjecture

reckon on

06 bank on, expect, rely on
07 count on, plan for, trust in
08 depend on, figure on
10 anticipate, bargain for
14 take for granted
15 take into account

reckon with

04 cope, deal, face
06 expect, handle
07 foresee, plan for
08 consider
10 anticipate, bargain for
15 take into account

reckoning

04 bill, doom
05 score, tally, total
06 charge, number, paying
07 account, opinion, payment
08 addition, estimate
09 appraisal, judgement
10 assessment, estimation, evaluation, punishment, settlement, working-out
11 calculation, computation, enumeration, retribution

reclaim

06 redeem, regain, rescue
07 get back, recover, salvage
08 retrieve, take back
09 recapture, reinstate

recline

04 loll, rest
06 lounge, repose, sprawl
07 lie down
08 lean back
10 stretch out

recluse

05 loner
06 hermit
07 ascetic, eremite, stylite
08 anchoret, solitary
09 anchoress, anchorite
10 solitarian

reclusive

07 ascetic, recluse
08 eremitic, isolated, retiring, secluded, solitary
09 withdrawn
10 anchoritic, cloistered, hermitical

recognition

06 honour, reward, salute
07 knowing, placing, respect
08 allowing, approval
09 admission, awareness, detection, discovery, gratitude, knowledge
10 acceptance, admittance, cognizance, confession, perception, validation
11 endorsement, realization
12 appreciation, thankfulness
13 understanding
15 acknowledgement

recognize

03 own, see
04 know, spot, tell
05 admit, adopt, allow, grant
06 accept, honour, notice, recall, salute
07 approve, concede, confess, discern, endorse, not miss, pick out, realize, respect
08 identify, perceive, remember, validate
09 apprehend, be aware of
10 appreciate, understand
11 acknowledge
13 be conscious of, be thankful for

recoil

04 kick
05 quail, react
06 falter, flinch, shrink
07 misfire, rebound, shy away
08 backfire, backlash, reaction
10 spring back
12 repercussion

recollect

06 recall
08 remember
09 reminisce
10 call to mind

recollection

06 memory, recall
08 souvenir
11 remembrance
12 reminiscence

recommend

04 plug, urge
06 advise, exhort, praise
07 advance, approve, commend, counsel, endorse, propose, suggest
08 advocate, vouch for
10 put forward

recommendation

03 tip
04 plug
06 advice, praise, urging

07 counsel
08 advocacy, approval, blessing, good word, guidance, proposal
09 reference
10 suggestion
11 endorsement, testimonial

recompense

03 pay
05 repay, wages
06 amends, reward
07 damages, guerdon, payment, redress, requite
08 requital
09 indemnify, reimburse, repayment
10 compensate, remunerate, reparation
11 restitution
12 compensation, remuneration, satisfaction

reconcile

04 mend
06 accept, adjust, make up, pacify, remedy, settle, square
07 appease, mollify, patch up, placate, resolve, reunite
08 face up to, put right
09 harmonize, make peace
10 conciliate, shake hands
13 make your peace
14 bury the hatchet

reconciliation

05 peace
06 accord
07 détente, harmony, reunion
10 adjustment, compromise, resolution, settlement
11 appeasement, harmonizing
13 accommodation, mollification, rapprochement

recondite

04 dark, deep
06 arcane, hidden, secret
07 obscure
08 abstruse, esoteric, mystical
09 concealed, difficult, intricate
10 mysterious

recondition

05 renew
06 repair, revamp
07 remodel, restore
08 overhaul, renovate
09 refurbish

reconnaissance

05 probe, recce
06 patrol, search, survey
08 scouting, scrutiny
10 expedition, inspection

11 exploration, observation
13 investigation, reconnoitring

reconnoitre
04 scan
05 probe, recce
06 patrol, spy out, survey
07 explore, inspect, observe
08 check out
11 investigate

reconsider
06 modify, review, revise
07 rethink
08 reassess
09 re-examine, think over
10 think twice
13 think better of

reconstruct
04 redo
06 reform, remake, revamp
07 rebuild, remodel, restore
08 recreate, renovate

record
02 CD, LP
03 cut, log
04 data, disc, edit, file, keep,
   list, note, read, show, tape
05 album, chart, diary, entry,
   notes, trace, video, vinyl
06 annals, career, memoir,
   minute, report, single
07 account, display, history,
   journal, logbook, minutes,
   put down, release
08 archives, cassette,
   document, evidence,
   indicate, inscribe, memorial,
   preserve, register
09 catalogue, chronicle,
   documents, testimony,
   videotape, write down
10 background, memorandum,
   tape-record, transcribe
11 compact disc, fastest time,
   photography, put on record
12 personal best

◻**off the record**
07 private, sub rosa
09 privately
10 unofficial
12 confidential, unofficially
14 confidentially

◻**on record**
05 noted
10 documented
11 written down
13 publicly known

recorder
05 clerk, video
06 scorer, scribe
07 camera, diarist

08 annalist
09 archivist, registrar, secretary
10 chronicler
11 chronologer, score-keeper
12 stenographer

recount
04 tell
06 depict, detail, impart, recite,
   relate, repeat, report, unfold
07 narrate, portray
08 describe, rehearse
11 communicate

recoup
05 repay
06 refund, regain
07 get back, recover, win back
08 make good, retrieve
09 reimburse, repossess

recourse
06 access, appeal, choice,
   option, refuge, remedy,
   resort, way out
09 turning to
11 alternative, possibility

recover
04 heal, mend
05 rally
06 pick up, recoup, regain,
   retake, revive
07 get back, get over, get well,
   improve, reclaim, win back
08 retrieve
09 come round, get better,
   recapture, repossess
10 ameliorate, bounce back,
   convalesce, recuperate
11 be on the mend

recovery
05 rally
06 upturn
07 healing, mending, salvage
08 rallying
09 recapture, recouping,
   recycling, retrieval
11 improvement, reclamation
12 amelioration, recuperation,
   repossession
13 convalescence

recreation
03 fun
04 game, play
05 hobby, sport
07 leisure, pastime
08 pleasure
09 diversion, enjoyment
10 relaxation
11 distraction, refreshment
13 entertainment

recrimination
08 reprisal
11 retaliation
13 counter-attack,
   countercharge

recruit
05 draft, enrol, raise
06 engage, enlist, novice,
   rookie, sign up, take on
07 acquire, convert, draftee,
   learner, procure, trainee
08 beginner, initiate, newcomer
09 conscript, greenhorn
10 apprentice, new entrant

rectify
03 fix
04 cure, mend
05 amend, emend, right
06 adjust, better, reform,
   remedy, repair
07 correct, improve, redress
08 make good, put right

rectitude
06 honour, virtue
07 honesty, justice, probity
09 exactness, integrity
11 correctness, uprightness
13 righteousness
14 scrupulousness

recumbent
04 flat
05 lying, prone
06 supine
07 leaning, resting
08 lounging
09 lying down, prostrate,
   reclining, sprawling
10 horizontal

recuperate
04 mend
06 pick up, revive
07 get well, improve, recover
08 get better
10 bounce back, convalesce
11 be on the mend

recur
06 return
08 reappear
11 happen again

recurrent
07 chronic, regular
08 cyclical, frequent, periodic
10 persistent, repetitive
12 intermittent

recycle
04 save
05 reuse
07 reclaim, recover, salvage
09 reprocess

red

04 pink, rose, rosy, ruby
05 ruddy
06 auburn, cherry, florid, ginger, maroon, russet, Titian
07 carroty, crimson, flushed, glowing, leftist, scarlet
08 blushing, chestnut, inflamed, rubicund
09 bloodshot, Bolshevik, communist, rufescent, socialist, vermilion
10 shamefaced
11 embarrassed

◻in the red

05 broke
06 in debt
08 bankrupt
09 in arrears, insolvent, overdrawn, penniless
10 on the rocks, owing money
13 gone to the wall

◻see red

05 go mad
07 explode
08 boil over
11 become angry, blow your top, lose your rag
12 blow your cool, fly into a rage, lose your cool
14 lose your temper
15 fly off the handle

red-blooded

05 lusty, manly
06 hearty, robust, strong, virile
08 vigorous

redden

05 blush, flush, go red
06 colour
07 crimson, suffuse

reddish

04 pink, rosy
05 ruddy, sandy
06 ginger, rufous, russet
08 rubicund
09 bloodshot, rufescent

redeem

04 cash, free, save
06 cash in, offset, ransom, recoup, regain, rescue
07 absolve, buy back, convert, deliver, expiate, get back, reclaim, recover, release, salvage, set free, trade in
08 atone for, exchange, liberate, outweigh, retrieve
09 make up for, repossess
10 emancipate, repurchase
13 compensate for

redemption

06 ransom, rescue
07 freedom, release, trade-in
08 exchange, recovery
09 atonement, expiation, retrieval, salvation
10 liberation, reparation
11 deliverance, reclamation
12 emancipation, repossession

redolent

07 odorous, scented
08 fragrant, perfumed
09 evocative, remindful
10 suggestive
11 reminiscent

redoubtable

06 mighty, strong
08 dreadful, fearsome, powerful, resolute, terrible
10 formidable

redound

04 tend
05 ensue
06 effect, result
07 conduce, reflect
10 contribute

redress

05 amend, right
06 adjust, relief, remedy
07 balance, correct, justice, payment, rectify, requite
08 put right, regulate, requital
10 assistance, correction, recompense, reparation
12 compensation, satisfaction

reduce

04 diet, slim, trim
05 halve, lower, slash
06 demote, humble, lessen, shrink, subdue, weaken
07 curtail, deplete, shorten
08 contract, decrease, diminish, discount, downsize, make less, minimize, mitigate
09 bring down, downgrade, go on a diet, humiliate, knock down, overpower
10 abbreviate, lose weight

reduction

03 cut
04 drop, fall, loss
07 cutback, decline
08 decrease, discount
09 allowance, deduction, lessening, narrowing, shrinkage, weakening
10 concession, diminution, downsizing, limitation

11 compression, contraction, discounting, subtraction

redundancy

04 boot, push, sack
06 excess, firing, notice, papers
07 removal, sacking, surplus
08 pleonasm
09 discharge, dismissal, expulsion, laying-off, prolixity, tautology, verbosity, wordiness
11 superfluity, uselessness

redundant

05 extra, fired, wordy
06 excess, padded, sacked
07 jobless, laid off, surplus
08 unneeded, unwanted
09 dismissed, out of work
10 pleonastic, unemployed
11 superfluous, unnecessary
12 periphrastic, tautological
13 supernumerary

reef

03 cay, key
05 ridge
07 sandbar
08 sandbank

reek

03 hum
04 fume, pong
05 fetor, odour, smell, stink
06 exhale, stench, vapour
08 malodour, mephitis
09 effluvium

reel

04 rock, roll, spin, sway, swim
05 fling, lurch, pitch, swirl, twirl, waver, wheel, whirl
06 falter, gyrate, totter, wobble
07 revolve, stagger, stumble

refer

04 cite, send
05 apply, guide, point, quote
06 allude, belong, direct, hand on, hint at, look at, look up, pass on, relate, turn to
07 bring up, concern, consult, deliver, mention, pertain, speak of, touch on
09 recommend

referee

03 ref
05 judge
06 umpire
07 mediate
08 mediator
09 arbitrate, intercede
10 adjudicate, arbitrator
11 adjudicator

reference
04 hint, note
06 regard, remark, source
07 bearing, mention, respect
08 allusion, citation, footnote
09 character, quotation
10 connection, pertinence
11 credentials, testimonial
13 applicability
14 recommendation

referendum
04 poll, vote
06 survey, voting
10 plebiscite

refine
04 hone, sift
05 clear, exalt, treat
06 distil, filter, polish, purify
07 clarify, cleanse, elevate,
improve, perfect,
process
08 civilize

refined
04 fine
05 civil, clear, exact
06 polite, subtle, urbane
07 courtly, elegant, genteel,
precise, stylish, treated
08 cultured, delicate, filtered,
gracious, ladylike, polished,
purified, well-bred
09 civilized, distilled,
processed, sensitive
10 cultivated
11 gentlemanly
12 well-mannered
13 sophisticated

refinement
05 grace, style, taste
06 polish
07 culture, finesse
08 addition, breeding, civility,
elegance, subtlety, urbanity
09 amendment, gentility
10 alteration
11 cultivation, good manners,
improvement
12 amelioration, modification
14 sophistication

reflect
04 echo, mull, muse, show
05 brood, dwell, image, think
06 mirror, ponder, reveal
07 bespeak, display, exhibit,
express, imitate, portray
08 cogitate, consider, indicate,
manifest, meditate, mull
over, ruminate, send back
09 bounce off, cerebrate,
reproduce, throw back

10 deliberate
11 contemplate, demonstrate

reflection
04 echo, idea, slur, view
05 blame, image, shame, study
07 feeling, opinion, thought
08 likeness, reproach, thinking
09 aspersion, criticism,
discredit, disrepute
10 cogitation, expression,
meditation, rumination
11 cerebration, mirror image,
observation
12 deliberation
13 consideration, contemplation

reflective
06 dreamy
07 pensive
08 absorbed
09 pondering, reasoning
10 cogitating, meditative,
ruminative, thoughtful
12 deliberative
13 contemplative

reflex
08 knee-jerk, unwilled
09 automatic
11 involuntary, spontaneous
14 uncontrollable

reform
05 amend, purge
06 change, revamp, revise
07 improve, rebuild, rectify,
remodel, shake up
08 renovate, revision
09 amendment, refashion
10 ameliorate, reorganize
11 improvement, reconstruct
12 reconstitute, rehabilitate
14 rehabilitation,
reorganization

reformer
08 do-gooder
13 revolutionary, whistle-
blower

refractory
06 mulish, unruly, wilful
07 defiant, naughty, restive
08 perverse, stubborn
09 difficult, obstinate, resistant
10 headstrong
11 disobedient, intractable
12 cantankerous,
contumacious, disputatious,
recalcitrant, unmanageable
13 unco-operative
14 uncontrollable

refrain
04 quit, song, stop, tune

05 avoid, cease
06 burden, chorus, desist,
eschew, give up, melody
07 abstain, forbear
08 renounce, response

refresh
04 cool, prod, stir
05 brace, renew
06 prompt, remind, revive
07 enliven, freshen, restore
08 activate, energize, revivify
09 reanimate, stimulate
10 invigorate, rejuvenate,
revitalize

refreshing
03 new
04 cool
05 fresh, novel
07 bracing
08 original, reviving
09 different, inspiring
10 energizing, freshening
11 stimulating
12 exhilarating, invigorating

refreshment
04 food
05 drink, snack
07 renewal, revival
10 freshening, sustenance
11 restoration, stimulation
12 invigoration
14 reinvigoration, revitalization

refreshments
04 eats, food, grub, nosh
06 drinks, snacks
10 provisions, sustenance

refrigerate
04 cool
05 chill
06 freeze

refuge
05 haven
06 asylum, island, resort
07 hideout, retreat, shelter
08 bolthole, hide-away
09 sanctuary
10 protection
13 place of safety

refugee
05 exile
06 émigré
07 escapee, runaway
08 fugitive
15 displaced person

refulgent
06 bright
07 beaming, lambent, radiant,
shining
08 gleaming, lustrous

09 brilliant, irradiant
10 glistening, glittering
11 resplendent

refund
05 repay
06 rebate, return
07 pay back, restore
09 reimburse, repayment

refurbish
04 do up, mend
05 refit
06 repair, revamp
07 re-equip, remodel, restore
08 overhaul, renovate
10 redecorate
11 recondition

refusal
02 no
06 denial, rebuff
08 negation, spurning
09 rejection
11 repudiation, turning-down

refuse
04 deny, junk, scum
05 draff, dregs, dross, repel, say no, spurn, trash, waste
06 debris, litter, pass up, rebuff, reject, scoria
07 decline, garbage, rubbish
08 turn down, withhold
13 draw the line at

refutation
08 disproof, elenchus, negation, rebuttal
11 confutation

refute
05 rebut
06 negate
07 confute, counter, silence
08 disprove
09 discredit, overthrow
12 deny strongly, give the lie to

regain
06 recoup, retake
07 get back, reclaim, recover
08 retrieve, return to, take back
09 recapture, repossess

regal
05 noble, royal
06 kingly, lordly
07 queenly, stately
08 imperial, majestic, princely
09 sovereign

regale
03 ply
05 amuse, feast, serve
06 divert
07 delight, gratify, refresh
09 captivate, entertain

regard
03 eye, see
04 care, heed, note, view
05 judge, think, value, watch
06 aspect, behold, esteem, follow, gaze at, honour, look at, matter, notice
07 observe, respect, suppose
08 appraise, approval, consider, estimate, listen to, look upon, respects, sympathy
09 affection, attention, deference, greetings
10 admiration, best wishes, good wishes, scrutinize
11 approbation, compliments, contemplate, salutations
13 consideration

❑**with regard to, in regard to**
02 re
04 as to
05 about
07 apropos
09 as regards
10 concerning
12 in relation to
13 with respect to
14 on the subject of
15 with reference to

regardful
07 careful, dutiful, mindful
08 noticing, watchful
09 attentive, observant
10 respectful, thoughtful
11 circumspect, considerate

regarding
02 re
04 as to
05 about
07 apropos
09 as regards
10 concerning, in regard to
12 in relation to, with regard to
13 with respect to
14 on the subject of
15 with reference to

regardless
06 anyhow, anyway
09 at any cost, unmindful
10 at any price, neglectful
11 come what may, inattentive, indifferent
12 no matter what

regenerate
05 renew
06 change, revive, uplift
07 refresh, restore
08 reawaken, rekindle, renovate
10 invigorate, rejuvenate

11 re-establish, reconstruct
12 reconstitute, reinvigorate

regeneration
07 renewal
10 renovation
11 restoration
12 rejuvenation, reproduction
14 reconstitution, reconstruction, reinvigoration

regime
06 system
07 command, control
10 government, leadership, management
13 establishment
14 administration

regiment
04 army, band, body, crew, gang
06 cohort
07 brigade, company, platoon
08 squadron

regimented
06 strict
07 ordered
09 organized, regulated
11 disciplined

region
04 land, part
05 place, range, scope
06 sector, sphere
07 expanse, section, terrain
13 neighbourhood

❑**in the region of**
04 some
05 about, circa
06 around, nearly
07 close to, loosely, roughly
09 just about, not far off
10 give or take, more or less
11 approaching
13 approximately, or thereabouts, something like
14 in round numbers

regional
05 local, zonal
08 district
09 localized, parochial
10 provincial

register
03 log, say
04 file, list, note, roll, show
05 diary, enrol, enter, files, index
06 annals, betray, enlist, ledger, record, reveal, roster, sign on
07 almanac, check in, display, exhibit, express, listing
08 indicate, manifest

09 catalogue, chronicle, directory

registrar
05 clerk
08 annalist, official, recorder
09 archivist, secretary
10 cataloguer, chronicler

regress
03 ebb
05 lapse
06 recede, return, revert
07 relapse, retreat
09 backslide, retrocede
10 degenerate, retrogress
11 deteriorate

regret
03 rue
06 bemoan, grieve, lament, repent, sorrow
07 deplore, remorse
09 feel sorry, penitence
10 contrition, repentance
12 be distressed, self-reproach
14 disappointment

regretful
03 sad
05 sorry
06 rueful
07 ashamed
08 contrite, penitent
09 repentant, sorrowful
10 apologetic, remorseful
12 disappointed

regrettable
03 sad
05 sorry, wrong
07 unhappy, unlucky
10 ill-advised, lamentable
11 distressing, unfortunate
13 disappointing, reprehensible

regular
04 even, flat
05 daily, fixed, level, usual
06 hourly, normal, smooth, steady, weekly, yearly
07 monthly, orderly, routine, typical, uniform
08 approved, balanced, constant, frequent, habitual, official, periodic, rhythmic, standard
09 recurring, unvarying
10 consistent, methodical, systematic, unchanging
11 established, symmetrical
12 conventional, evenly spread

regulate
03 run, set
04 rule, tune

05 guide, order
06 adjust, direct, govern, handle, manage, settle
07 arrange, balance, conduct, control, monitor, oversee
08 moderate, organize
09 supervise
11 superintend, synchronize

regulation
03 act, law, set
04 rule
05 by-law, edict, order, usual
06 decree, dictum, ruling
07 command, control, dictate, precept, statute
08 guidance, official, orthodox, required, standard
09 direction, directive, mandatory, statutory
10 management, obligatory, prescribed
11 commandment, requirement, supervision
14 administration
15 superintendence

regurgitate
04 puke, spew
05 vomit
06 repeat
07 bring up, restate, throw up
08 disgorge, say again
09 reiterate, tell again

rehabilitate
04 mend, save
06 adjust, redeem, reform
07 convert, rebuild, restore
08 renovate
09 normalize, reinstate
11 re-establish, recondition, reconstruct, reintegrate

rehash
05 alter, rejig
06 change, rework
08 rejigger
09 rearrange, refashion, reshuffle, reworking
13 rearrangement

rehearsal
05 drill
06 dry run
07 reading, recital
08 dummy run, exercise, practice, trial run
10 run-through

rehearse
05 drill, train
06 go over, recite, repeat
07 narrate, prepare, recount
08 practise
10 run through

reign
04 rule, sway
05 exist, occur, power
06 empire, govern, obtain
07 control, prevail
08 dominion, hold sway
10 ascendancy
11 predominate, sovereignty
14 sit on the throne

reimburse
05 repay
06 refund, return
07 pay back, restore
08 give back
10 compensate, recompense

rein
04 curb, halt, hold, stop
05 brake, check, limit
06 arrest, bridle
07 control, harness
08 hold back, restrain, restrict
09 overcheck, restraint

reindeer

➤ *Father Christmas's reindeer:*
05 Comet, Cupid, Vixen
06 Dancer, Dasher, Donner
07 Blitzen, Prancer, Rudolph

reinforce
04 prop, stay
05 brace, shore, steel
07 augment, fortify, stiffen, support, toughen
08 buttress, increase
09 emphasize, underline
10 strengthen, supplement

reinforcement
04 help, prop, stay
05 brace, shore
06 back-up
07 support
08 buttress, emphasis, reserves
11 auxiliaries, enlargement
12 augmentation
13 fortification, strengthening

reinstate
06 recall, return
07 replace, restore
09 reappoint, reinstall
11 re-establish

reinstatement
06 recall, return
11 replacement, restoration
15 re-establishment

reiterate
05 recap, resay
06 repeat, retell, stress
07 iterate, restate

09 emphasize
12 recapitulate

reject
04 deny, jilt, veto
05 repel, scrap, spurn
06 rebuff, refuse, second
07 cast off, decline, discard, exclude, forsake, outcast
08 brush off, disallow, jettison, set aside, turn down
09 eliminate, throw away
14 turn your back on
15 wash your hands of

rejection
04 veto
06 denial, rebuff
07 refusal
08 brush-off
09 dismissal, exclusion
11 elimination, jettisoning
12 cold shoulder, renunciation
14 Dear John letter

rejoice
05 exult, glory, revel
07 be happy, delight, triumph
08 be joyful
09 be pleased, celebrate
10 jump for joy
11 be delighted

rejoicing
03 joy
07 delight, elation, triumph
08 euphoria, gladness, pleasure
09 festivity, happiness
10 exultation, jubilation
11 celebration, merrymaking

rejoin
04 quip
05 reply
06 answer, retort
07 respond, riposte

rejoinder
04 quip
05 reply
06 answer, retort
07 riposte
08 repartee, response

rejuvenate
05 renew
06 revive
07 refresh, restore
08 recharge, rekindle, revivify
09 freshen up, reanimate
10 regenerate, revitalize
12 reinvigorate

relapse
04 fail, sink
06 revert, weaken, worsen
07 regress, setback

09 backslide, reversion, weakening, worsening
10 degenerate, recurrence, regression, retrogress
11 backsliding, deteriorate
13 deterioration, retrogression

relate
04 ally, join, link, tell
05 apply, refer
06 couple, detail, recite, report
07 concern, connect, narrate, pertain, present, recount
08 describe, hit it off, identify
09 appertain, associate, correlate, empathize
10 be relevant, sympathize
14 have a bearing on

related
04 akin
05 joint
06 agnate, allied, linked, mutual
07 cognate, kindred
08 relevant
09 connected
10 affiliated, associated
11 concomitant
12 accompanying, interrelated
14 consanguineous, interconnected

relation
03 kin
04 bond, link
06 family, regard
07 bearing, kindred, kinsman
08 alliance, kinsfolk, relative
09 kinswoman, relevance
10 comparison, connection
11 affiliation, correlation

relations
03 kin, sex
05 folks, terms
06 coitus, family
07 coition, contact, kindred
08 dealings, intimacy, kinsfolk
09 relatives
10 copulation, love-making
11 interaction, intercourse
12 associations, relationship
15 carnal knowledge

relationship
03 tie
04 bond, link, ties
05 fling, ratio, tie-up
06 affair
07 liaison, rapport, romance
08 affinity, alliance, intimacy, parallel
09 chemistry, closeness

10 connection, friendship, love affair, proportion, similarity
11 association, correlation

relative
03 kin
06 family
07 germane, kindred, kinsman
08 kinsfolk, parallel, relation
09 kinswoman, pertinent
10 reciprocal, respective
11 comparative, correlative
12 commensurate, proportional
13 corresponding, proportionate

relatively
05 quite
06 fairly, rather
08 somewhat
12 by comparison, in comparison
13 comparatively

relax
04 calm, cool, ease, rest
05 abate, lower, remit
06 lessen, loosen, reduce, sedate, unwind, weaken
07 ease off, slacken
08 calm down, chill out, diminish, wind down
09 hang loose
10 take it easy
13 put your feet up
14 take things easy
15 let your hair down

relaxation
03 fun
04 rest
05 let-up
06 easing, repose
07 détente, leisure
09 abatement, amusement, enjoyment, lessening, loosening, unwinding
10 moderation, recreation
11 loosening up, refreshment

relaxed
04 calm, cool
06 at ease, casual
08 carefree, composed, informal, laid-back
09 collected, easy-going, leisurely, unhurried

relay
04 send, time, turn
05 carry, shift, spell, stint
06 hand on, pass on, period
07 message
08 dispatch, transmit
09 broadcast, programme

11 communicate
12 transmission

release
04 free, undo
05 issue, let go, loose, untie
06 acquit, excuse, exempt, launch, let off, loosen, reveal, unbind, unlock
07 absolve, deliver, divulge, publish, set free, unchain, unleash, unloose
08 announce, bulletin, disclose, liberate, unfasten
09 acquittal, discharge, make known, unshackle
10 absolution, disclosure, emancipate, liberation, publishing, revelation
11 deliverance, exoneration, manumission, publication
12 announcement, emancipation, proclamation

relegate
05 eject, exile, expel, refer
06 assign, banish, demote, deport, reduce
07 consign, degrade, entrust
08 delegate, dispatch, transfer
09 downgrade
10 expatriate

relent
05 abate, let up, relax, yield
06 give in, soften, weaken
07 die down, give way, slacken
09 come round
10 capitulate

relentless
04 grim, hard
05 cruel, harsh
08 pitiless, ruthless
09 incessant, merciless, punishing, unceasing
10 implacable, inexorable, inflexible, persistent
11 cold-hearted, hard-hearted, remorseless, unforgiving, unrelenting, unremitting
14 uncompromising

relevant
03 apt
07 apropos, fitting, germane
08 apposite, material, suitable
09 congruous, pertinent
10 applicable, to the point
11 appropriate, significant

reliable
04 safe, sure, true
05 solid, sound
06 honest, stable, tested, trusty
07 certain, regular, staunch

08 constant, faithful
09 unfailing
10 dependable
11 predictable, trustworthy

reliance
05 faith, trust
06 belief, credit
09 assurance
10 confidence, dependence

relic
05 scrap, token, trace
07 antique, memento, remains, remnant, vestige
08 artefact, fragment, keepsake, survival
11 remembrance

relief
03 aid
04 cure, help, rest
05 break, let-up, locum, proxy
06 back-up, easing, remedy, rescue, saving, supply
07 comfort, respite, stand-by, stand-in, succour, support
08 allaying, breather, soothing
09 abatement, assuaging, diversion, lessening, reduction, remission
10 assistance, palliation, relaxation, substitute
11 alleviation, deliverance, refreshment, replacement
12 interruption

relieve
03 aid
04 cure, free, heal, help, save
05 abate, allay, break, pause
06 assist, excuse, exempt, lessen, reduce, remove, rescue, soften, soothe
07 assuage, break up, comfort, console, deliver, dismiss, release, replace, set free, slacken, succour, support
08 liberate, palliate, unburden
09 alleviate, interrupt
10 stand in for, substitute
12 take over from

religion
➤ *Names of religions:*
03 Bon, Zen
04 Shi'a
05 Amish, Baha'i, Druze, Islam, Sunni
06 Sufism, Taoism, voodoo
07 animism, Baha'ism, Essenes, Jainism, Jesuits, Judaism, Lamaism, Moonies, Opus Dei, Quakers, Sikhism

08 Baptists, Buddhism, Druidism, Hasidism, Hinduism, paganism, Tantrism
09 Cabbalism, Calvinism, Methodism, Mithraism, Mormonism, occultism, Parseeism, shamanism, Shintoism, Vedantism
10 Adventists, Brahmanism, Evangelism, Gnosticism, Iconoclasm, Puritanism
11 Anabaptists, Anglicanism, Catholicism, Creationism, Freemasonry, Hare Krishna, Lutheranism, Manichaeism, Scientology, Zen Buddhism
12 Christianity, Confucianism, Unitarianism
13 Church in Wales, Protestantism, Reform Judaism, Salvation Army
14 Fundamentalism, Oxford Movement, Pentecostalism, Rastafarianism, Society of Jesus, Zoroastrianism
15 ancestor-worship, Church of England, Presbyterianism
➤ See also **angel**; **archbishop**; **bible**; **building**; **cardinal**; **celebration**; **church**; **festival**; **missionary**; **monastic**; **pope**; **religious**; **scripture**; **theologian**; **vestment**; **worship**

religious
04 holy
05 godly, pious
06 devout, divine, sacred, strict
09 believing, committed, doctrinal, righteous, spiritual
10 devotional, God-fearing, meticulous, scriptural
11 church-going, theological
13 conscientious
➤ See also **religion**

➤ *Names of religious figures:*
03 Fry (Elizabeth), Hus (Jan), Roy (Ram Mohan)
04 Huss (John), John (of Leyden), King (Martin Luther), Knox (John), Penn (William), Shaw (Anna Howard), Weil (Simone)
05 Booth (William), Jesus, Lao Zi, Lewis (Clive Staples), Mahdi (El), Paris

(Matthew), **Smith** (Joseph), **Waite** (Terry), **Young** (Brigham)

06 **Besant** (Annie), **Borgia**, **Browne** (Robert), **Browne** (Sir Thomas), **Buddha**, **Bunyan** (John), **Calvin** (John), **Christ**, **Gandhi** (Mohandas), **Garvey** (Marcus), **Graham** (Billy), **Hillel**, **Hutter** (Leonhard), **Julian** (of Norwich), **Kempis** (Thomas à), **Lao-tzu**, **Luther** (Martin), **Mather** (Cotton), **Mesmer** (Franz Anton), **Olcott** (Colonel Henry Steel), **Pilate** (Pontius), **Ridley** (Nicholas), **Wesley** (John)

07 **Aga Khan**, **Ayeshah**, **Cranmer** (Thomas), **Crowley** (Aleister), **Erasmus** (Desiderius), **Falwell** (Jerry), **Fénelon** (François), **Hubbard** (L Ron), **Jackson** (Jesse), **Latimer** (Hugh), **Mahatma**, **Mahomet**, **Paisley** (Reverend Ian), **Photius**, **Russell** (Charles Taze), **Sithole** (Reverend Ndabaningi), **Spooner** (William Archibald), **Steiner** (Rudolf), **Tyndale** (William), **William** (of Malmesbury), **William** (of Ockham), **William** (of Tyre), **Zwingli** (Huldreich)

08 **Andrewes** (Lancelot), **Barabbas**, **Caiaphas**, **Khomeini** (Ayatollah Ruhollah), **Mahavira** (Vardhamana), **Mohammed**, **Muhammad**, **Pelagius**, **Rasputin** (Grigoriy), **Selassie** (Emperor Haile), **Wycliffe** (John)

09 **Akhenaten**, **Bar Kokhba** (Simon), **Blavatsky** (Madame Helena), **Confucius**, **Dalai Lama**, **Guru Nanak**, **McPherson** (Aimee Semple), **Niemöller** (Martin), **Zoroaster**

10 **Belshazzar**, **Manichaeus**, **Savonarola** (Girolamo), **Swedenborg** (Emmanuel), **Torquemada** (Tomás de)

11 **Bodhidharma**, **Jesus Christ**, **Prester John**, **Ramakrishna**

12 **Krishnamurti** (Jiddu)
13 **Judas Iscariot**

► *Types of religious officer*:
03 nun
04 dean, guru, imam, monk, pope
05 abbot, canon, elder, friar, padre, prior, rabbi, vicar
06 abbess, bishop, curate, deacon, father, mullah, parson, pastor, priest, rector
07 muezzin, prelate, proctor
08 cardinal, chaplain, minister
09 ayatollah, clergyman, Dalai Lama, deaconess, Monsignor
10 archbishop, archdeacon, chancellor
11 clergywoman
14 mother superior

relinquish
04 cede, drop, quit
05 cease, let go, waive, yield
06 desist, forego, give up
07 abandon, forsake, release
08 abdicate, hand over
09 repudiate, surrender

relish
04 like, love, tang, zest
05 enjoy, gusto, sauce, spice
06 pickle, savour, vigour
07 chutney, delight, revel in
08 piquancy, pleasure, vivacity
09 enjoyment, seasoning
10 appreciate, flavouring
12 appreciation, satisfaction

reluctance
07 dislike
08 aversion, distaste, loathing
10 hesitation, repugnance
13 recalcitrance, unwillingness
14 disinclination

reluctant
04 slow
05 loath
06 averse
08 grudging, hesitant
09 unwilling
11 disinclined
14 unenthusiastic

rely
04 bank, lean
05 count, trust
06 be sure, depend, reckon
07 swear by

remain
04 bide, last, rest, stay, wait
05 abide, dwell, stand, tarry
06 endure, linger
07 persist, prevail, survive
10 be left over, stay behind

remainder
04 rest
06 excess
07 balance, remains, remnant, residue, surplus
08 residuum, vestiges
09 leftovers

remaining
04 last, left
05 spare
06 unused
07 abiding, lasting, unspent
08 left over, residual
09 lingering, surviving
10 persisting, unfinished

remains
04 body, rest
05 ashes, dregs
06 corpse, crumbs, debris, relics, scraps, traces
07 cadaver, carcase, residue
08 dead body, detritus, remnants, vestiges
09 fragments, leftovers, reliquiae, remainder

remark
03 say
04 note
05 state
07 assert, notice
07 comment, mention, observe
09 reference, utterance
10 reflection
11 declaration, observation

remarkable
03 odd
04 rare
06 signal
07 notable, strange, unusual
08 singular, striking
09 memorable, momentous
10 impressive, noteworthy, phenomenal, surprising
11 conspicuous, exceptional, outstanding, significant
13 distinguished, extraordinary

remedy
03 fix
04 cure, ease, heal, help, mend
06 physic, relief, repair, soothe
07 control, correct, nostrum, panacea, rectify, redress, relieve, restore, sort out
08 antidote, medicine, mitigate
09 treatment
10 corrective, counteract, medicament, medication
11 restorative

remember
04 keep, mark
05 learn, place
06 honour, recall, retain
08 hark back, memorize
09 celebrate, recognize, recollect, reminisce
10 call to mind
11 commemorate

remembrance
05 relic, token
06 memory, recall
07 memento, thought
08 keepsake, memorial, reminder, souvenir
09 nostalgia
11 recognition, testimonial
12 recollection, reminiscence
13 commemoration

remind
06 call up, prompt
10 call to mind
11 bring to mind
13 jog your memory

reminder
04 hint, memo, note
06 prompt
07 memento
08 souvenir
10 memorandum, suggestion
11 aide-mémoire

reminisce
06 recall, review
08 look back, remember
09 recollect, think back
10 retrospect

reminiscence
06 memoir, memory, recall
08 anecdote
11 remembrance
12 recollection
13 retrospection

reminiscent
08 redolent
09 evocative, nostalgic
10 suggestive

remiss
03 lax
04 slow
05 slack, tardy
06 casual, sloppy
07 wayward
08 careless, culpable, dilatory, slipshod
09 forgetful, negligent
11 inattentive, thoughtless
13 lackadaisical

remission
04 lull

05 annul, let-up
06 excuse, pardon, repeal
07 amnesty, release, respite
08 decrease, reprieve
09 abatement, acquittal, discharge, exemption, lessening, weakening
10 abrogation, absolution, indulgence, moderation, relaxation, rescinding, revocation, slackening
11 alleviation, exoneration
12 cancellation

remit
03 pay
04 mail, post, send
05 brief, refer, scope
06 cancel, direct, orders, pass on, repeal, revoke, settle
07 forward, rescind, suspend
08 abrogate, dispatch, hold over, set aside, transfer
10 guidelines
12 instructions
14 responsibility

remittance
03 fee
07 payment, sending
08 dispatch
09 allowance
13 consideration

remnant
03 bit, end
05 piece, scrap, shred, trace
06 offcut
07 oddment, remains, vestige
08 fragment, leftover
09 remainder

remonstrance
07 protest, reproof
08 petition
09 complaint, exception, grievance, objection
10 opposition
12 protestation
13 expostulation

remonstrate
05 argue, gripe
06 object, oppose
07 dispute, dissent, protest
08 complain
09 challenge
11 expostulate

remorse
05 grief, guilt, shame
06 regret, sorrow
10 contrition, repentance
12 self-reproach
13 bad conscience

remorseful
03 sad
05 sorry
06 guilty, rueful
07 ashamed
08 contrite, penitent
09 regretful, repentant
10 apologetic
11 guilt-ridden

remorseless
05 cruel, harsh, stern
07 callous
08 inhumane, pitiless, ruthless
09 merciless
10 implacable, inexorable, relentless, unmerciful
11 hard-hearted, unforgiving, unrelenting, unremitting

remote
03 far
04 poor, slim
05 aloof, faint, small
06 far-off, lonely, meagre, slight
07 distant, outside, slender
08 detached, doubtful, isolated, outlying, secluded
10 improbable, uninvolved
11 God-forsaken, out-of-the-way, standoffish
12 inaccessible
14 unapproachable

removal
04 boot, move, push, sack
05 elbow, shift
07 ousting, purging, sacking
08 ejection, eviction, riddance
09 abolition, dismissal, expulsion, uprooting
10 conveyance, detachment, extraction, relegation, relocation, withdrawal
12 dislodgement, transporting

remove
04 doff, fire, oust, sack, shed
05 carry, eject, erase, evict, expel, purge, shift, strip
06 convey, cut off, cut out, delete, depose, detach, efface, excise, lop off
07 abolish, expurge, extract
08 amputate, get rid of, take away, withdraw
09 discharge, eliminate, strike out, transport
10 blue-pencil, obliterate

remunerate
03 pay
05 repay
06 reward
07 redress

09 indemnify, reimburse
10 compensate, recompense

remuneration
03 fee, pay
05 wages
06 income, profit, salary
07 payment, stipend
08 earnings, retainer
09 emolument, indemnity
10 honorarium, remittance
12 compensation
13 reimbursement

remunerative
04 rich
06 paying
07 gainful
09 lucrative, rewarding
10 profitable, worthwhile
11 moneymaking

renaissance
07 new dawn, rebirth, renewal
08 new birth
09 awakening
10 renascence, resurgence
11 reawakening, restoration
12 reappearance, regeneration,
   rejuvenation, resurrection
13 recrudescence

renascent
06 reborn
07 renewed, revived
09 born again, redivivus, resurgent
10 re-emergent, reanimated,
   reawakened
11 resurrected

rend
03 rip
04 stab, tear
05 break, burst, sever, split
06 cleave, divide, pierce
07 rupture, shatter
08 fracture, separate, splinter

render
04 give, make, play, show, sing
05 leave
06 change, depict, supply
07 deliver, display, exhibit,
   perform, present, proffer
08 describe, manifest
09 cause to be, represent

rendezvous
04 date, meet
05 haunt, rally, tryst, venue
06 gather, muster, resort
07 collect, convene, meeting
08 assemble, converge
10 engagement
11 appointment, assignation
12 meeting-place

rendition
07 reading, version
08 delivery
09 depiction, execution,
   portrayal, rendering
11 arrangement, explanation,
   performance, translation
12 construction, presentation
14 interpretation

renegade
05 rebel
06 outlaw
07 runaway, traitor
08 apostate, betrayer, defector,
   deserter, disloyal, mutineer,
   mutinous, recreant, turncoat
09 dissident
10 perfidious, rebellious,
   traitorous, unfaithful
13 tergiversator

renege
05 welsh
07 default
09 backslide, repudiate
10 apostatize

renew
06 extend, reform, repair,
   repeat, resume, revive
07 prolong, refresh, replace,
   restart, restock, restore
08 overhaul, reaffirm, renovate
09 modernize, refurbish,
   replenish, transform
10 recommence, regenerate,
   rejuvenate, revitalize
11 re-establish, recondition
12 reconstitute, reinvigorate

renewal
06 repair
10 re-creation, renovation,
   repetition, resumption
11 reiteration, restatement
12 rejuvenation, resurrection
13 refurbishment,
   replenishment, resuscitation
14 recommencement,
   reconstruction,
   reinvigoration, revitalization

renounce
04 deny, shun
05 spurn, waive
06 abjure, disown, eschew,
   forego, give up, recant
07 abandon, abstain, forsake
08 abdicate, disclaim
09 repudiate, surrender
10 disinherit, relinquish

renovate
04 do up
05 refit, renew

renovation
05 refit
06 repair
07 renewal
08 facelift
11 improvement, restoration
13 modernization,
   refurbishment
14 reconditioning

renown
04 fame, mark, note
06 esteem, honour, repute
07 acclaim, stardom
08 eminence, prestige
09 celebrity
10 prominence, reputation
11 distinction, pre-eminence

renowned
05 famed, noted
06 famous
07 eminent, notable
09 acclaimed, well-known
10 celebrated, pre-eminent
13 distinguished

rent
03 cut, fee, let, rip
04 hire, hole, rift, slit, tear, torn
05 cleft, crack, lease, split
06 breach, let out, sublet
07 charter, hire out, severed
08 cleavage, disunion, division
10 dissension
11 perforation

renunciation
06 denial
07 waiving
08 giving up, shunning,
   spurning
09 disowning, forsaking,
   rejection, surrender
10 abdication, abnegation,
   abstinence, desistance,
   discarding
11 abandonment, disclaiming,
   repudiation
13 disinheriting
14 relinquishment

repair
03 fix, sew
04 darn, form, heal, mend,
   move, nick, turn
05 patch, refit, renew, state
06 kilter, remove, resort, retire

repair (continued, right column)
06 reform, repair, revamp
07 improve, remodel, restore
08 overhaul
09 modernize, refurbish
10 redecorate
11 recondition
13 give a facelift

07 patch up, rectify, redress, restore, service
08 make good, overhaul, put right, renovate, withdraw
09 condition
11 improvement, restoration

reparable
07 curable, savable
10 corrigible, restorable
11 recoverable, rectifiable, retrievable, salvageable

reparation
06 amends
07 damages, redress, renewal
08 requital, solatium
09 atonement, indemnity
10 recompense
11 restitution
12 compensation, propitiation

repartee
03 wit
06 banter, retort
07 jesting, riposte
08 badinage

repast
04 feed, food, meal
06 spread
08 victuals
09 collation, refection
11 nourishment

repay
06 avenge, refund, reward, settle, square
09 reimburse, retaliate
10 compensate, recompense, remunerate
11 get even with, reciprocate
12 settle up with

repayment
06 rebate, refund, reward
07 payment, redress, revenge
09 tit for tat, vengeance
10 recompense, reparation
11 retaliation, retribution
12 compensation, remuneration
13 reciprocation, reimbursement

repeal
04 void
05 annul, quash
06 abjure, cancel, recall, revoke
07 abolish, nullify, rescind, retract, reverse
08 abrogate, withdraw
09 abolition, annulment
10 abrogation, invalidate, rescinding, rescission, revocation, withdrawal

11 countermand, rescindment
12 cancellation, invalidation
13 nullification

repeat
04 copy, echo, redo
05 ditto, quote, recap, rerun
06 go over, parrot, recite, relate, replay, reshow, retell
08 rehearse, say again
09 duplicate, reiterate, reproduce, reshowing
10 repetition
12 recapitulate, reproduction
14 recapitulation

repeated
07 regular
08 constant, frequent, periodic
09 recurrent, recurring
10 persistent, rhythmical

repeatedly
10 frequently
11 over and over
12 time and again
13 again and again, time after time

repel
05 check, fight, parry, spurn
06 oppose, rebuff, refuse, reject, resist, revolt, sicken
07 disgust, hold off, repulse
08 beat back, nauseate
09 drive back, keep at bay

repellent
04 foul, vile
07 hateful
08 shocking
09 abhorrent, loathsome, obnoxious, offensive, repugnant, repulsive, revolting, sickening
10 abominable, despicable, disgusting, nauseating
11 distasteful
12 contemptible, disagreeable

repent
03 rue
06 lament, recant, regret
07 be sorry, confess, deplore
09 be ashamed
10 be contrite
11 feel remorse, see the light
14 beat your breast

repentance
05 grief, guilt, shame, U-turn
06 regret, sorrow
07 penance, remorse
10 contrition, conversion
11 compunction, recantation

repentant
05 sorry
06 guilty, rueful
07 ashamed
08 contrite, penitent
09 chastened, regretful
10 apologetic, remorseful

repercussion
06 effect, recoil, result, ripple
07 rebound
08 backlash
09 shock wave
11 consequence
13 reverberation

repertoire
05 range, stock, store
06 supply
07 reserve
09 repertory, reservoir
10 collection, repository

repetition
04 echo
07 copying, echoing, reprise
09 echolalia, iteration, rehearsal, tautology
10 recurrence, redundancy
11 duplication, reiteration
14 recapitulation

repetitious
06 boring, prolix
07 tedious, verbose
10 long-winded, monotonous, pleonastic, unchanging
12 pleonastical, tautological

repetitive
05 samey
08 unvaried
09 automatic, recurrent
10 mechanical, monotonous

rephrase
06 recast, reword
07 rewrite
10 paraphrase

repine
04 beef, fret, moan, mope, sulk
05 brood
06 grieve, grouse, lament
07 grumble
08 complain, languish

replace
04 oust
06 act for, follow, return
07 put back, relieve, restore
08 deputize, supplant
09 reinstate, supersede
10 stand in for, substitute

replacement
05 proxy
06 fill-in, supply

07 reserve, stand-in
09 successor, surrogate
10 substitute, understudy

replenish
05 renew, stock, top up
06 fill up, make up, refill, reload
07 replace, restock, restore
08 recharge

replete
04 full
05 sated
06 filled, full up, jammed
07 brimful, charged, crammed, glutted, stuffed, teeming
08 brimming, satiated
09 abounding, chock-full
11 well-stocked

repletion
04 glut
07 satiety
08 fullness, plethora
09 satiation
12 completeness, overfullness
14 superabundance

replica
04 copy
05 clone, model
09 duplicate, facsimile
12 reproduction

replicate
03 ape
04 copy
05 clone, mimic
06 follow, repeat
08 recreate
09 duplicate, reproduce

reply
04 echo
05 react
06 answer, rejoin, retort, return
07 counter, respond, riposte
08 comeback, repartee, response
09 rejoinder, retaliate
11 acknowledge, reciprocate
15 acknowledgement

report
04 bang, boom, fame, file, item, name, news, note, shop, shot, tale, talk, tell, word
05 brief, cover, crack, crash, grass, noise, piece, relay, split, state, story
06 credit, detail, esteem, gossip, honour, notify, pass on, record, relate, renown, repute, rumour, squeal
07 account, article, declare, divulge, dossier, hearsay,

message, minutes, narrate, recount, stature, write-up
08 bulletin, describe, disclose, document, register, set forth
09 broadcast, chronicle, explosion, narrative
10 communiqué, reputation
11 communicate, declaration, description, information
13 communication, reverberation

reporter
04 hack
09 announcer, columnist
10 journalist, newscaster
11 commentator
12 newspaperman
13 correspondent
14 newspaperwoman

repose
03 lay, lie, put, set
04 calm, ease, laze, lean, rest
05 lodge, peace, place, poise, quiet, relax, sleep, store
06 aplomb, invest
07 deposit, dignity, entrust, recline, respite, slumber
08 calmness, quietude, serenity
09 composure, quietness
10 inactivity, relaxation
11 restfulness
12 tranquillity

repository
04 bank, safe
05 depot, store, vault
07 archive
08 magazine, treasury
09 container, warehouse
10 depository, receptacle

reprehensible
03 bad
06 errant, erring, remiss
07 ignoble
08 shameful, unworthy
10 censurable, delinquent
11 blameworthy, disgraceful, opprobrious

represent
02 be
04 draw, mean, show
05 act as, enact, evoke
06 act for, denote, depict, embody, sketch, typify
07 perform, picture, portray
08 describe, speak for, stand for
09 epitomize, exemplify, personify, symbolize
10 constitute, illustrate
12 characterize, correspond to
13 act on behalf of

representation
04 bust, icon, play, show
05 envoy, image, model, proxy
06 deputy, sketch, statue
07 account, picture, stand-in
08 delegate, likeness, portrait
09 complaint, depiction, portrayal, spectacle
10 allegation, delegation, deputation, production
11 delineation, description, explanation, performance
12 illustration, presentation

representative
02 MP
03 rep
05 agent, envoy, proxy, usual
06 chosen, deputy, normal
07 elected, stand-in, typical
08 delegate, elective, symbolic
09 exemplary, spokesman
10 ambassador, archetypal, authorized, councillor, delegation, deputation, indicative, saleswoman
11 spokeswoman
12 commissioner, illustrative, spokesperson
14 characteristic

repress
04 curb
05 check, crush, quash, quell
06 master, muffle, stifle, subdue
07 control, inhibit, oppress, put down, silence, smother
08 bottle up, dominate, overcome, restrain, suppress, vanquish
09 overpower, subjugate

repressed
07 uptight
09 inhibited, withdrawn
10 frustrated

repression
07 control, gagging, tyranny
08 coercion, muffling, quashing, quelling, stifling
09 despotism, restraint
10 censorship, constraint, domination, inhibition, oppression, smothering
11 holding-back, subjugation, suffocation, suppression
12 dictatorship

repressive
05 cruel, harsh, tough
06 severe, strict
08 absolute, coercive, despotic
10 autocratic, dominating, oppressive, tyrannical

11 dictatorial
12 totalitarian
13 authoritarian

reprieve
05 let-up, spare
06 acquit, let off, pardon, redeem, relief, rescue
07 amnesty, relieve, respite
09 remission, show mercy
13 let off the hook

reprimand
05 blame, chide, scold, slate
06 berate, rebuke, rocket
07 censure, lecture, reproof, reprove, tell off, tick off
08 admonish, reproach
09 castigate, criticize
10 admonition, telling-off, ticking-off, upbraiding
11 castigation
12 dressing-down

reprisal
06 ultion
07 redress, revenge
09 tit for tat, vengeance
11 retaliation, retribution
13 recrimination

reproach
04 blot, slur
05 blame, chide, scold, scorn, shame, smear, stain
06 defame, rebuke, stigma
07 censure, condemn, obloquy, reproof, reprove, upbraid
08 admonish, contempt, disgrace, ignominy, scolding
09 criticism, criticize, discredit, dishonour, disparage, reprehend, reprimand
10 admonition, opprobrium
11 degradation, disapproval
12 condemnation

reproachful
08 critical, scolding, scornful
09 reproving
10 censorious, upbraiding
11 castigating, disparaging, opprobrious
12 disappointed, fault-finding

reprobate
03 bad
04 base, rake, roué, vile
05 knave, rogue, scamp
06 damned, rascal, sinful, sinner, wicked, wretch
07 corrupt, immoral, villain
08 criminal, depraved, evildoer
09 dissolute, miscreant, scallywag, scoundrel

10 degenerate, profligate, ne'er-do-well
12 incorrigible, troublemaker

reproduce
03 ape
04 copy, echo, redo
05 breed, spawn, Xerox®
06 mirror, remake, repeat
07 emulate, imitate
08 multiply, recreate, simulate
09 bear young, duplicate, give birth, photocopy, Photostat®, procreate, propagate, replicate
10 transcribe
11 proliferate, reconstruct

reproduction
04 copy
05 clone, print, Xerox®
07 genital, picture, replica
08 breeding
09 duplicate, facsimile, imitation, photocopy, Photostat®
11 procreation, propagation

reproductive
06 sexual
07 genital
10 generative
11 procreative, progenitive, propagative

reproof
06 rebuke, rocket
08 berating, reproach, scolding
09 criticism, reprimand
10 admonition, telling-off, ticking-off, upbraiding
12 dressing-down

reprove
05 chide, scold, slate
06 berate, rebuke
07 tell off, tick off, upbraid
08 admonish, reproach
09 criticize, reprimand

reptile
► *Types of reptile*:
06 caiman, cayman, turtle
07 tuatara
08 terrapin, tortoise
09 alligator, crocodile
11 green turtle
13 giant tortoise
14 snapping turtle
➤ See also **animal; dinosaur; lizard; snake**

repudiate
04 deny
06 abjure, desert, disown, reject, revoke

07 abandon, cast off, disavow, divorce, forsake, rescind
08 disclaim, renounce
09 disaffirm

repudiation
06 denial
09 disavowal, disowning, rejection
10 abjuration, retraction
11 recantation
12 renunciation
14 disaffirmation

repugnance
05 odium
06 hatred, horror, nausea
07 disgust, dislike
08 aversion, distaste, loathing
09 repulsion, revulsion
10 abhorrence, reluctance

repugnant
04 foul, vile
06 averse, horrid, odious
07 adverse, hateful, opposed
09 abhorrent, loathsome, obnoxious, offensive, repellent, revolting, sickening
10 abominable, disgusting, nauseating
12 antagonistic, antipathetic, incompatible, inconsistent

repulse
04 snub
05 check, repel, spurn
06 defeat, rebuff, refuse, reject
07 beat off, refusal, reverse
08 spurning
09 drive back, rejection
11 repudiation

repulsion
06 hatred
07 disgust
08 aversion, distaste, loathing
09 disrelish, revulsion
10 abhorrence, repellence, repellency, repugnance
11 detestation

repulsive
04 foul, ugly, vile
05 nasty
06 horrid
07 hateful, heinous, hideous
08 shocking
09 abhorrent, loathsome, obnoxious, offensive, repellent, repugnant, revolting, sickening
10 abominable, despicable, disgusting, nauseating, off-putting, unpleasant

11 distasteful
12 contemptible, disagreeable

reputable
04 good
06 honest, worthy
07 upright
08 esteemed, reliable, virtuous
09 admirable, estimable, excellent, respected
10 dependable, honourable
11 respectable, trustworthy
13 well-thought-of

reputation
04 fame, name, rank
05 image
06 credit, esteem, honour, infamy, renown, repute
07 opinion, respect, stature
08 good name, position, prestige, standing
09 character, notoriety
11 distinction
14 respectability

repute
04 fame, name
06 esteem, renown
07 stature
08 good name, standing
09 celebrity
10 estimation, reputation
11 distinction

reputed
04 held, said
07 alleged, seeming, thought
08 apparent, believed, presumed, reckoned, regarded, rumoured, supposed
10 considered, ostensible

reputedly
09 allegedly, seemingly
10 apparently, ostensibly, supposedly

request
03 beg
04 call, plea, seek, suit
06 appeal, ask for, behest, demand, desire, prayer
07 beseech, entreat, solicit
08 apply for, entreaty, petition
10 supplicate
11 application, petitioning
12 solicitation, supplication

require
04 lack, miss, need, want
05 crave, force, order
06 demand, enjoin, entail
07 command, involve, request

08 insist on, instruct
09 be short of, constrain

required
03 set
05 vital
06 needed
08 demanded
09 essential, mandatory, necessary, requisite
10 compulsory, obligatory, prescribed, stipulated

requirement
04 lack, must, need, term, want
06 demand
07 proviso
09 condition, essential, necessity, provision
10 sine qua non
11 stipulation
12 precondition, prerequisite
13 qualification, specification

requisite
03 due, set
06 needed
08 required
09 condition, essential, mandatory, necessary, necessity
10 compulsory, obligatory, prescribed, sine qua non
11 desideratum, requirement
12 precondition, prerequisite
13 qualification, specification

requisition
03 use
04 call, take
05 order, seize
06 demand, occupy
07 request, seizure, summons
08 put in for, take over, takeover
10 commandeer, confiscate
11 application, appropriate
12 confiscation
13 appropriation, commandeering

requital
06 amends, pay-off
07 payment, redress
09 indemnity, quittance, repayment
10 recompense, reparation
11 restitution
12 compensation, satisfaction
15 indemnification

requite
05 repay
06 avenge, return, reward
07 redress, respond, satisfy
09 reimburse, retaliate
11 reciprocate

rescind
04 void
05 annul, quash
06 cancel, negate, recall, repeal, revoke
07 nullify, retract, reverse
08 abrogate, overturn, set aside
11 countermand

rescission
06 recall, repeal
08 negation, reversal, voidance
09 annulment
10 abrogation, revocation
11 rescindment
12 cancellation, invalidation
13 nullification

rescue
04 free, save
06 ransom, redeem
07 deliver, relieve, set free
08 liberate, recovery
09 extricate, salvation
10 liberation, redemption
11 deliverance

research
05 probe, study, tests
06 assess, review, search
07 analyse, examine, explore, inquiry, inspect, testing
08 analysis, look into, scrutiny
10 experiment, scrutinize
11 examination, exploration, fact-finding, investigate
13 investigation
15 experimentation

researcher
06 boffin
07 analyst, student
11 field worker
12 investigator

resemblance
06 parity
07 analogy
08 affinity, likeness, parallel
09 agreement, facsimile
10 comparison, similarity, similitude, uniformity
13 comparability
14 correspondence

resemble
06 be like, favour, mirror
08 approach, look like, parallel
09 duplicate, take after

resent
04 envy
06 grudge
07 dislike
08 begrudge, object to

13 take offence at, take
umbrage at
15 take exception to

resentful
04 hurt
05 angry, irked
06 bitter, miffed, peeved,
piqued, put out
07 envious, jealous, wounded
08 grudging, offended
09 aggrieved, indignant
10 embittered, vindictive

resentment
03 ire
04 envy, hurt
05 anger, pique, spite
06 grudge, malice
07 dudgeon, ill-will, offence,
umbrage
08 jealousy, vexation
09 animosity, annoyance
10 bitterness, ill-feeling
11 high dudgeon, indignation

reservation
04 park
05 doubt, demur, order, qualm
07 booking, enclave, proviso,
reserve, scruple
08 homeland, preserve
09 hesitancy, misgiving
10 hesitation, scepticism
11 arrangement, stipulation
13 qualification
14 prearrangement

reserve
04 area, bank, book, fund,
keep, park, pool, save
05 cache, extra, hoard, spare,
stock, store, tract
06 fill-in, retain, shelve, supply
07 earmark, modesty, shyness
08 coldness, coolness,
distance, hold back, keep
back, lay aside, postpone,
set aside
09 aloofness, auxiliary,
reservoir, reticence,
sanctuary, stockpile
10 accumulate, additional,
detachment, remoteness,
substitute, understudy
11 alternative, replacement
13 secretiveness, self-restraint

❑**in reserve**
05 spare
06 in hand, stored, unused
08 set aside

reserved
03 shy
04 cold, cool, held, kept

05 aloof, meant, saved, taken
06 booked, modest, remote
07 distant, engaged, ordered
08 arranged, destined,
intended, retained, reticent,
retiring, set aside
09 diffident, earmarked,
secretive, spoken for
10 designated, restrained,
unsociable
11 prearranged, standoffish
12 unresponsive
13 unforthcoming
15 uncommunicative

reservoir
03 vat
04 bank, fund, lake, loch, pond,
pool, tank
05 basin, stock, store
06 holder, source, supply
07 cistern
08 reserves
09 container, stockpile
10 receptacle, repository
11 reservatory

reshuffle
05 shift
06 change, revise
07 realign, regroup, shake up
09 rearrange
10 regrouping, reorganize
11 realignment, restructure
13 rearrangement,
restructuring
14 redistribution,
reorganization

reside
03 lie
04 live, rest, stay
05 abide, board, dwell, lodge
06 occupy, remain, settle
07 inhabit, sojourn

residence
03 pad
04 digs, flat, hall, home, seat
05 abode, house, manor, place
06 palace
07 lodging, mansion, sojourn
08 domicile, dwelling,
lodgings, quarters
10 habitation
11 country seat
12 country house

resident
05 guest, local
06 client, inmate, live-in,
lodger, tenant
07 citizen, dweller, en poste,
gremial, patient, resider
08 occupant, occupier

10 inhabitant, inhabiting
11 householder

residential
07 exurban
08 commuter, suburban
09 dormitory

residual
03 net
06 excess, unused
07 surplus
08 left-over
09 remaining
10 unconsumed

residue
04 lees, rest
05 dregs, extra
06 excess
07 balance, remains, surplus
08 overflow, residuum
09 leftovers, remainder

resign
04 quit
05 leave, waive
06 forego, give up, retire, vacate
07 abandon, forsake
08 abdicate, step down
09 stand down, surrender
10 relinquish

❑**resign yourself**
03 bow
05 yield
06 accept, comply, submit
09 acquiesce
11 come to terms

resignation
06 notice
07 waiving
08 patience, stoicism
09 defeatism, departure,
passivity, surrender
10 abdication, acceptance,
compliance, retirement,
submission
12 acquiescence, standing-
down, stepping-down

resigned
07 passive, patient, stoical
08 yielding
09 defeatist
10 reconciled, submissive
11 acquiescent, unresisting
12 unprotesting
13 philosophical

resilience
04 give
06 bounce, recoil, spring
08 buoyancy, strength
09 hardiness, toughness
10 elasticity, plasticity

11 flexibility, springiness
12 adaptability
14 unshockability

resilient
05 hardy, tough
06 bouncy, strong, supple
07 buoyant, elastic, plastic, pliable, rubbery, springy
08 flexible
09 adaptable
13 irrepressible

resist
04 curb, defy, halt, stem, stop
05 avoid, check, fight, repel
06 impede, oppose, thwart
07 contend, counter, prevent
08 confront, obstruct, restrain
09 stand up to, withstand
14 hold out against

resistance
05 fight
06 battle, combat, thwart
07 refusal
08 defiance, fighting, struggle
09 repulsion, restraint
10 contention, impediment, opposition, prevention
11 obstruction
12 withstanding
13 confrontation

resistant
05 proof, tough
06 immune, strong
07 defiant, opposed
09 unwilling
10 impervious, unaffected
12 antagonistic, intransigent

resolute
03 set
04 bold, firm
05 fixed
06 dogged, intent
07 adamant, decided, earnest
08 constant, obdurate, resolved, stalwart, stubborn
09 dedicated, obstinate, steadfast, tenacious, undaunted
10 determined, relentless, unswerving, unwavering
11 persevering, unflinching
12 single-minded, strong-willed

resolution
06 answer, decree, motion
07 courage, finding, resolve, solving, verdict
08 boldness, decision, devotion, firmness, solution, tenacity

09 constancy, willpower
10 dedication, doggedness, intentness, working out
11 persistence, proposition
12 perseverance
13 determination, steadfastness

resolve
03 fix
04 zeal
05 solve
06 answer, decide, settle
07 courage, sort out, work out
08 boldness, conclude, firmness, settle on, tenacity
09 break down, constancy, determine, willpower
10 dedication, doggedness
11 disentangle, earnestness, persistence, seriousness
12 disintegrate, perseverance
13 determination, steadfastness

resonant
04 deep, full, rich
06 plummy, strong
07 booming, ringing, vibrant
08 canorous, sonorous
10 resounding
11 reverberant

resort
03 spa
04 spot, step
05 haunt, visit
06 centre, chance, course
08 frequent, recourse
09 expedient, patronize
11 alternative, possibility
13 holiday centre
14 course of action

❑ **resort to**
03 use
06 employ, turn to
07 utilize
08 exercise
09 make use of
10 fall back on
14 have recourse to

resound
04 boom, echo, ring
05 sound
06 re-echo
07 thunder
08 resonate
11 reverberate

resounding
04 full, loud, rich
07 booming, echoing, notable, ringing, vibrant

08 decisive, emphatic, resonant, sonorous, striking
10 conclusive, impressive, resonating, thunderous
13 reverberating

resource
03 wit
04 fund, pool
05 funds, means, money, power, store
06 assets, course, riches, supply, talent, wealth
07 ability, capital, reserve
08 holdings, property, reserves
09 expedient, ingenuity, materials, stockpile
10 enterprise, initiative
11 imagination, wherewithal
13 inventiveness
15 resourcefulness

resourceful
04 able
05 sharp, witty
06 adroit, bright, clever
07 capable
08 creative, original, talented
09 ingenious, inventive, versatile
10 innovative
11 imaginative, quick-witted
12 enterprising

resourceless
07 useless
08 feckless, helpless, hopeless
10 inadequate

respect
03 way
04 heed, obey
05 facet, point, sense, value
06 admire, aspect, detail, esteem, follow, fulfil, homage, honour, matter, notice, praise, regard, revere
07 devoirs, feature, observe
08 courtesy, relation, venerate
09 approve of, deference, greetings, obeisance, reference, reverence
10 admiration, best wishes, connection, high regard, politeness, veneration
11 approbation, compliments, high opinion, salutations
13 consideration, show regard for, think highly of
14 thoughtfulness
15 set great store by

respectable
02 OK
04 fair, good, neat, tidy

05 clean
06 decent, honest, worthy
07 upright
08 adequate, all right, decorous, passable
09 dignified, reputable, respected, tolerable
10 above-board, acceptable, honourable, reasonable
11 appreciable, clean-living, presentable, trustworthy
12 considerable

respected
06 valued
07 admired
08 esteemed
14 highly regarded
15 thought highly of

respectful
05 civil
06 humble, polite
07 courtly, dutiful
08 reverent
09 courteous
11 deferential, reverential, subservient

respecting
05 about
09 regarding
10 concerning
11 considering
12 with regard to

respective
03 own
07 several, special, various
08 personal, relevant, specific
10 individual, particular
13 corresponding

respite
03 gap
04 halt, lull, rest, stay
05 break, delay, let-up, pause
06 hiatus, recess, relief
08 breather, interval, reprieve
09 abatement, remission
10 moratorium, relaxation
11 adjournment
12 intermission, interruption

resplendent
06 bright
07 fulgent, radiant, shining
08 glorious, luminous, lustrous, splendid
09 brilliant, effulgent, irradiant, refulgent
13 splendiferous

respond
05 react, reply
06 answer, rejoin, retort, return

07 counter
10 answer back
11 acknowledge, reciprocate

response
05 reply
06 answer, retort, return
07 riposte
08 comeback, feedback, reaction
09 rejoinder
15 acknowledgement

responsibility
04 care, duty, onus, role, task
05 blame, fault, guilt
06 affair, burden, charge, pidgin
07 concern, honesty
08 business, maturity
09 adulthood, authority
10 obligation, power trust
11 culpability, reliability
13 answerability, dependability
14 accountability

responsible
04 sane
05 adult, sober, sound
06 guilty, liable, stable, steady
07 at fault, leading, to blame
08 culpable, powerful, rational, reliable, sensible
09 executive, high-level
10 answerable, dependable, in charge of, reasonable
11 accountable, blameworthy, controlling, level-headed
13 authoritative, conscientious
14 decision-making

responsive
04 open
05 alert, awake, aware, sharp
06 with it
08 amenable, reactive
09 on the ball, receptive, sensitive
11 forthcoming, susceptible, sympathetic
14 impressionable

rest
03 lie, nap, sit
04 base, calm, doze, ease, halt, hang, last, laze, lean, lull, prop, rely, stay, stop
05 break, cease, hinge, pause, relax, sleep, stand
06 depend, endure, excess, holder, lounge, others, recess, remain, repose, siesta, snooze, steady
07 balance, holiday, leisure, lie down, persist, recline,

remains, remnant, residue, respite, support, surplus
08 breather, continue, idleness, interval, quietude, remnants, residuum, vacation
09 cessation, interlude, leftovers, remainder, stillness
10 inactivity, relaxation, standstill, take it easy
12 intermission, tranquillity
13 put your feet up
14 breathing-space

restful
04 calm
05 quiet, still
06 placid, serene
07 calming, languid, relaxed
08 peaceful, relaxing, soothing, tranquil

restitution
06 amends, refund, return
07 damages, redress
08 requital
09 indemnity, repayment
10 recompense, reparation
11 restoration
12 compensation, remuneration, satisfaction
13 reimbursement

restive
04 edgy
05 jumpy, tense
06 uneasy, unruly, wilful
07 anxious, fidgety, fretful, nervous, uptight, wayward
08 agitated, restless
09 impatient, unsettled
10 refractory
12 recalcitrant, unmanageable
13 undisciplined

restless
04 edgy
05 jumpy
06 broken, uneasy, unruly
07 anxious, fidgety, fretful, jittery, nervous, restive, uptight, worried
08 agitated, troubled
09 disturbed, impatient, sleepless, unsettled

restlessness
06 bustle, unrest
07 anxiety, jitters, turmoil
08 activity, disquiet, edginess, insomnia, movement
09 agitation, jumpiness
10 fitfulness, inquietude

11 disturbance, fretfulness,
  inconstancy, instability,
  nervousness, restiveness
13 heebie-jeebies

restoration
06 repair, return
07 renewal, revival
08 recovery
10 rebuilding, renovation
11 refreshment, restitution
12 refurbishing, rejuvenation
13 reinstatement
14 reconstruction
15 re-establishment

restore
03 fix
04 do up, mend
05 renew
06 repair, return, revamp, revive
07 build up, rebuild, recover,
  refresh, replace, retouch
08 give back, hand back,
  renovate, revivify
09 refurbish, reinstate
10 redecorate, rejuvenate
11 re-establish, recondition,
  reconstruct, reintroduce

restrain
03 tie
04 bind, curb, jail, stop
05 chain, check
06 arrest, bridle, detain, fetter,
  hinder, impede, subdue
07 confine, control, inhibit,
  manacle, prevent, repress
08 bottle up, imprison, restrict,
  suppress
11 hold in check

restrained
04 calm, cold, mild, soft
05 aloof, muted, quiet
06 formal, low-key, subtle
07 subdued
08 discreet, moderate, tasteful
09 temperate
10 controlled
11 unemotional, unobtrusive
14 self-controlled
15 uncommunicative

restraint
03 tie
04 curb, grip, hold, rein
05 block, bonds, check, limit
06 bridle, chains, duress, limits
07 bondage, control, fetters
09 captivity, hindrance
10 constraint, inhibition,
  limitation, moderation
11 confinement, restriction,
  self-control, suppression

12 restrictions, straitjacket
14 self-discipline

restrict
03 tie
05 bound, cramp, hem in, limit
06 hamper, hinder, impede
07 confine, control, curtail
08 handicap, regulate, restrain
09 constrain, demarcate

restricted
05 small, tight
06 narrow, secret
07 cramped, limited, private
08 confined
09 exclusive, regulated
10 controlled

restriction
03 ban
04 curb, rule
05 bound, check, limit, stint
07 confine, embargo, proviso
08 handicap
09 condition, restraint
10 constraint, limitation
13 qualification

result
03 end
04 flow, mark, stem
05 arise, ensue, fruit, grade,
  issue, occur, score
06 effect, emerge, evolve,
  finish, follow, pay-off,
  sequel, spring, upshot
07 develop, emanate, outcome,
  proceed, spin-off, verdict
08 decision, reaction
09 by-product, culminate,
  judgement, terminate
10 conclusion, end-product
11 consequence, implication

resume
04 go on
06 reopen, take up
07 carry on, proceed, restart
08 continue, re-occupy
09 reconvene
10 recommence

résumé
06 digest, précis, review, sketch
07 outline, summary
08 abstract, overview, synopsis
09 breakdown
14 recapitulation

resumption
07 renewal, restart
09 reopening
12 continuation
14 recommencement
15 re-establishment

resurgence
06 return
07 rebirth, revival
10 renascence, resumption
11 re-emergence, renaissance
12 re-appearance,
  resurrection, risorgimento
14 revivification

resurrect
05 renew
06 revive
07 restore
10 reactivate, revitalize
11 re-establish, reintroduce,
  resuscitate

resurrection
07 rebirth, renewal, revival
08 comeback
10 resurgence
11 renaissance, restoration
12 reappearance
13 resuscitation
14 revitalization
15 re-establishment

resuscitate
05 renew
06 rescue, revive
07 quicken, restore
08 revivify
09 reanimate, resurrect
10 bring round, revitalize
12 reinvigorate

resuscitated
07 revived
08 restored
09 redivivus
11 resurrected

retain
03 pay
04 grip, hire, hold, keep, save
06 employ, engage, recall
07 reserve
08 continue, hang on to, hold
  back, memorize, remember
10 keep hold of, keep in mind

retainer
03 fee
05 valet
06 lackey, menial, vassal
07 advance, deposit, servant
08 domestic
09 attendant, dependant,
  supporter

retaliate
06 avenge
07 hit back
09 fight back, get back at
10 strike back
11 reciprocate, take revenge

13 counter-attack
14 get your own back

retaliation
06 ultion
07 revenge
08 reprisal
09 tit for tat, vengeance
11 like for like, retribution
13 counter-attack,
   reciprocation

retard
04 curb
05 brake, check, delay
06 hinder, hold up, impede
08 handicap, obstruct, restrict

retardation
03 lag
05 delay
07 slowing
09 hindering, hindrance
10 deficiency, incapacity
11 obstruction

retch
03 gag
04 puke, spew
05 heave, reach, vomit
07 throw up
08 disgorge
11 regurgitate

retching
06 nausea, puking
07 gagging
08 reaching, vomiting
12 vomiturition

reticence
07 reserve, silence
09 quietness, restraint
10 diffidence
11 taciturnity
13 secretiveness

reticent
03 shy
05 quiet
06 silent
08 reserved, taciturn
09 diffident, secretive
10 restrained
11 tight-lipped
13 unforthcoming
15 uncommunicative

retinue
05 aides, staff, suite, train
06 escort
07 cortège
08 servants
09 entourage, followers,
   following, personnel
10 attendants

retire
05 leave
06 bow out, decamp, depart
07 retreat
08 stop work, withdraw

retired
02 ex-
04 past
06 former
08 emeritus

retirement
04 exit
07 privacy, retreat
08 solitude
09 departure, obscurity,
   seclusion
10 loneliness, withdrawal

retiring
03 coy, shy
05 quiet, timid
06 humble, modest
07 bashful
08 reserved, reticent
09 diffident, shrinking
10 unassuming
12 self-effacing

retort
04 quip
05 reply
06 answer, rejoin, return
07 counter, respond, riposte
08 repartee, response
09 rejoinder, retaliate

retract
04 deny
06 abjure, cancel, recant,
   renege, repeal, revoke
07 disavow, rescind, reverse
08 abrogate, renounce, take
   back, withdraw

retreat
03 den
04 flee, quit
05 haven, leave
06 asylum, decamp, depart,
   flight, refuge, retire, shrink
07 hideout, privacy, shelter
08 draw back, fall back,
   hideaway, pull back,
   solitude, turn tail, withdraw
09 departure, sanctuary
10 evacuation, give ground,
   retirement, withdrawal

retrench
03 cut
04 pare, save, trim
05 limit, prune
06 lessen, reduce
07 curtail, cut back, husband

08 decrease, slim down
09 economize
15 tighten your belt

retrenchment
07 cutback, economy, pruning
09 reduction, shrinkage
11 cost-cutting, cutting back

retribution
06 reward, talion
07 justice, Nemesis, payment,
   redress, revenge
08 reprisal, requital
09 repayment, vengeance
10 punishment, recompense
11 just deserts, retaliation
12 compensation, satisfaction

retrieve
04 mend, save
05 fetch
06 recoup, redeem, regain,
   repair, rescue, return
07 reclaim, recover, salvage
09 bring back, recapture,
   repossess

retrograde
07 reverse
08 backward, downward,
   negative
09 declining, worsening
13 deteriorating, retrogressive

retrogress
04 drop, fall, sink, wane
06 recede, revert, worsen
07 decline, regress, relapse
09 backslide
10 degenerate, retrograde
11 deteriorate

retrogression
03 ebb
04 drop, fall
06 return
07 decline, regress, relapse
09 worsening
10 recidivism, regression
13 deterioration

retrospect
06 review, survey
09 hindsight
10 reflection
12 recollection, thinking back
13 re-examination

▫**in retrospect**
11 looking back
12 on reflection, thinking back
13 with hindsight

retrospective
11 retro-active
14 retro-operative
15 backward-looking

return
04 gain
05 equal, match, recur, remit, repay, reply, yield
06 answer, go back, income, profit, refund, rejoin, retort, revert, reward
07 benefit, counter, deliver, put back, regress, replace, requite, respond, restore, revenue, riposte, takings
08 come home, comeback, delivery, exchange, give back, hand back, interest, proceeds, reappear, send back, take back
09 come again, pronounce, reimburse, reinstate, repayment
10 home-coming, recompense
11 handing back, reciprocate, replacement, restoration
12 reappearance
13 reciprocation, reinstatement

re-use
07 recycle
12 reconstitute

revamp
04 do up
05 refit
06 recast, repair, revise
07 rebuild, restore
08 overhaul, renovate
09 refurbish
11 recondition, reconstruct

reveal
04 leak, show, tell
06 betray, expose, let out
07 display, divulge, exhibit, lay bare, let slip, publish, uncover, unearth
08 announce, disclose, give away, manifest, proclaim
09 broadcast, make aware, make known, publicize
10 make public
12 bring to light, expose to view

revealing
05 sheer
06 daring, low-cut
08 give-away
10 diaphanous, indicative, revelatory, see-through

revel
04 bask, crow, gala, rave
05 enjoy, glory, lap up, party
06 relish, savour, wallow
07 carouse, debauch, delight, indulge, rejoice, roister

09 bacchanal, celebrate, festivity, luxuriate
10 have a party, saturnalia
11 celebration, merrymaking
13 jollification
15 paint the town red

revelation
04 fact, leak, news, show
07 display
08 exposure, giveaway
09 admission, unmasking
10 confession, disclosure, divulgence, exhibition, uncovering, unearthing
11 information, publication
12 announcement, bring to light, broadcasting

reveller
08 carouser
09 bacchanal, party-goer, roisterer, wassailer
10 celebrator, merrymaker
14 pleasure-seeker

revelry
03 fun
05 party
07 jollity
08 carousal
09 festivity
10 debauchery
11 celebration, merrymaking
13 jollification

revenge
06 avenge
07 hit back, redress
08 reprisal, requital, vendetta
09 fight back, retaliate, tit for tat, vengeance
11 get even with, retaliation, retribution
12 satisfaction, settle a score
14 get your own back

revengeful
06 bitter
08 pitiless, spiteful, vengeful
09 merciless, resentful
10 malevolent, vindictive
11 unforgiving

revenue
04 gain
05 yield
06 income, profit, return
07 profits, rewards, takings
08 interest, proceeds, receipts

reverberate
04 boom, echo, ring
06 re-echo
07 resound, vibrate
08 resonate

reverberation
04 echo, wave
06 effect, recoil, result, ripple
07 rebound, ringing
09 re-echoing, resonance, shock wave, vibration
10 reflection, resounding
11 consequence
12 repercussion

revere
05 adore, exalt
06 admire, esteem, honour
07 respect, worship
08 look up to, venerate
09 reverence
11 pay homage to

reverence
03 awe
06 admire, esteem, homage, honour, revere
07 respect, worship
08 devotion, venerate
09 adoration, deference
10 admiration, veneration

reverent
04 awed
05 pious
06 devout, humble, solemn
10 respectful
11 deferential, reverential, worshipping

reverie
06 musing, trance
08 daydream
11 abstraction, daydreaming
13 preoccupation, woolgathering

reversal
04 blow
05 check, delay, trial, U-turn
06 defeat, mishap, repeal
07 failure, problem, setback
08 hardship, negation
09 adversity, annulment, turnabout, volte-face
10 misfortune, rescinding, revocation, turnaround
13 nullification
14 countermanding

reverse
04 back, blow, rear, swap, undo
05 annul, check, delay, quash, up-end, upset, verso
06 cancel, change, defeat, invert, mishap, negate, repeal, revoke
07 counter, failure, inverse, rescind, retract, setback

08 backward, contrary, converse, inverted, opposite, reversal, withdraw
09 adversity, backtrack, other side, turn round, underside
10 antithesis, difficulty, invalidate, misfortune
11 change round, countermand, vicissitude
12 misadventure
14 put back to front, turn upside-down

revert
05 lapse
06 go back, resume, return
07 regress, relapse

review
05 judge, study, weigh
06 assess, report, revise, survey
07 analyse, discuss, examine, inspect, rethink, weigh up
08 analysis, appraise, critique, evaluate, magazine, reassess, revision, scrutiny
09 appraisal, criticism, criticize, judgement, re-examine
10 assessment, commentary, evaluation, periodical, re-evaluate, reconsider, scrutinize
11 examination, take stock of
12 re-evaluation, reassessment, recapitulate
13 re-examination

reviewer
05 judge
06 critic
07 arbiter
08 essayist, observer
11 commentator, connoisseur

revile
05 abuse, libel, scorn, smear
06 defame, malign, vilify
07 despise, slander, traduce
09 denigrate
10 blackguard, calumniate, vituperate

revise
04 cram, edit, swot
05 alter, amend, emend, learn, mug up, study
06 change, modify, revamp, review, reword, update
07 correct, redraft, rewrite
10 reconsider

revision
06 change, recast, review
07 editing
08 studying, swotting, updating

09 amendment, recasting, rereading, rewriting
10 alteration, correction
12 modification

revitalize
05 renew
06 revive
07 refresh, restore
08 revivify
09 reanimate, resurrect
10 reactivate, rejuvenate

revival
06 upturn
07 rebirth, renewal, upsurge
08 comeback
10 resurgence
11 reawakening, renaissance
12 resurrection
13 resuscitation, the kiss of life
14 reintroduction, revitalization

revive
05 rally, renew, rouse
07 animate, cheer up, quicken, recover, refresh, restore
08 reawaken, rekindle
09 reanimate
10 bring round, invigorate, reactivate, revitalize
11 re-establish, reintroduce

revivify
05 renew
06 revive
07 refresh, restore
08 inspirit
09 reanimate
10 invigorate, reactivate, revitalize
11 resuscitate

reviving
05 tonic
07 bracing
11 reanimating, revivescent, reviviscent, stimulating
12 enheartening, exhilarating, invigorating, refreshening
14 reinvigorating

revocation
06 repeal
08 quashing, reversal, revoking
09 abolition, annulment, repealing
10 rescinding, rescission, retraction, withdrawal
11 repudiation
12 cancellation, invalidation
13 nullification

revoke
05 annul, quash
06 cancel, negate, repeal

07 abolish, nullify, rescind, retract, reverse
08 abrogate, withdraw
10 invalidate
11 countermand

revolt
04 coup, riot, rise
05 rebel, repel, shock
06 defect, mutiny, putsch, resist, rise up, rising, sicken
07 disgust, dissent, outrage
08 nauseate, uprising
09 coup d'état, rebellion
10 revolution, take up arms
12 insurrection
15 turn your stomach

revolting
04 foul, vile
05 nasty
07 hateful, heinous
08 horrible, shocking
09 abhorrent, appalling, loathsome, obnoxious, offensive, repellent, repugnant, repulsive, sickening
10 disgusting, nauseating
11 distasteful

revolution
04 coup, spin, turn
05 cycle, orbit, round, wheel
06 change, circle, mutiny, putsch, revolt, rising
07 circuit
08 gyration, rotation, uprising
09 coup d'état, rebellion
10 innovation, insurgence
12 insurrection

revolutionary
03 new
05 rebel
07 drastic, radical
08 mutineer, mutinous
09 anarchist, extremist, insurgent, seditious
10 avant-garde, innovative, rebellious, subversive
11 anarchistic, progressive
15 insurrectionary, insurrectionist

► *Names of revolutionaries:*
04 **Biko** (Steve), **Cade** (Jack), **Kett** (Robert), **Marx** (Karl)
05 **Allen** (Ethan), **Fanon** (Frantz), **Kirov** (Sergey), **Lenin** (Vladimir Ilyich), **Marat** (Jean Paul), **Paine** (Tom), **Sands** (Bobby), **Sucre** (Antonio José de), **Tyler** (Wat), **Villa** (Pancho)

06 **Arafat** (Yasser), **Baader**
(Andreas), **Castro** (Fidel),
Corday (Charlotte),
Danton (Georges), **Fawkes**
(Guy), **Fuller** (Margaret),
Stalin (Joseph), **Zapata**
(Emiliano)
07 **Bakunin** (Mikhail),
Bolívar (Simón), **Catesby**
(Robert), **Goldman**
(Emma), **Guevara** (Che),
Mandela (Nelson),
Meinhof (Ulrike Marie),
Princip (Gavrilo), **Sandino**
(Augusto César), **Savimbi**
(Jonas)), **Trotsky** (Leon),
Wallace (William)
08 **Abu Nidal**, **Bukharin**
(Nikolay), **Hereward** (the
Wake), **Kerensky**
(Alexander), **Lilburne**
(John), **Mirabeau** (Honoré
Gabriel Riqueti Comte de),
Proudhon (Pierre Joseph),
Zinoviev (Grigoriy)
09 **Christian** (Fletcher),
Garibaldi (Giuseppe),
Guillotin (Joseph),
Kropotkin (Knyaz Peter),
Luxemburg (Rosa), **Mao
Zedong**, **Spartacus**, **Sun
Yat-Sen**
11 **Robespierre** (Maximilien
de)
13 **Chiang Kai-Shek**

revolutionize
06 reform
09 transform
10 reorganize
11 restructure, transfigure
14 turn upside-down

revolve
04 move, spin, turn
05 orbit, pivot, wheel, whirl
06 circle, gyrate, hang on,
rotate, swivel, turn on
08 centre on

revolver
03 gun
06 airgun, pistol
07 firearm, handgun, shooter
10 six-shooter

revolving
07 turning
08 gyrating, gyratory, rotating,
spinning, whirling

revulsion
04 hate
06 hatred, nausea, recoil
07 disgust, dislike

08 aversion, distaste, loathing
09 repulsion
10 abhorrence, repugnance
11 abomination, detestation

reward
03 pay
04 gain
05 bonus, medal, merit, prize
06 desert, profit, return
07 benefit, payment, premium
08 decorate, requital
10 decoration, punishment,
recompense, remunerate
11 just deserts, retribution
12 compensation,
remuneration

rewarding
08 edifying, fruitful, pleasing
09 enriching, lucrative
10 beneficial, fulfilling,
gratifying, profitable,
satisfying, worthwhile
12 advantageous, remunerative

rewording
08 revision
10 paraphrase, rephrasing
11 metaphrasis

rewrite
04 edit
05 emend
06 revise, reword, rework
07 correct, redraft

rhetoric
07 bombast, fustian, oratory
09 eloquence, hyperbole,
pomposity, prolixity,
verbosity, wordiness
13 magniloquence
14 grandiloquence

rhetorical
05 grand, showy, wordy
06 florid, prolix
07 flowery, pompous, verbose
09 bombastic, high-flown
10 flamboyant, long-winded
11 declamatory, pretentious
12 high-sounding,
magniloquent
13 grandiloquent

▶ *Types of rhetorical device*:
03 pun
05 irony, trope
06 bathos, climax, simile,
zeugma
07 epigram, litotes, meiosis,
paradox
08 anaphora, chiasmus,
diegesis, ellipsis, innuendo,
metaphor, metonymy,
oxymoron, parabole

09 dissimile, euphemism,
hyperbole, prolepsis,
syllepsis, tautology
10 anastrophe, anticlimax,
antithesis, apostrophe,
dysphemism, epistrophe,
metalepsis, synchrysis,
synecdoche
11 anacoluthon, antiphrasis,
catachresis, enumeration,
hypostrophe, parenthesis
12 alliteration, onomatopoeia
13 amplification, dramatic
irony, mixed metaphor
14 double entendre, figure of
speech
15 pathetic fallacy,
personification

rhyme
04 poem, song
05 ditty, verse
06 jingle, poetry
08 limerick

rhythm
04 beat, flow, lilt, time
05 metre, pulse, swing, throb
07 measure, pattern
08 movement

rhythmic
06 metric, steady
07 flowing, lilting, regular
08 metrical, periodic, repeated
09 pulsating, throbbing
10 rhythmical

rib
03 bar
04 band, bone, vein, wale,
welt
05 costa, ridge, shaft
07 ribbing, support

ribald
03 low
04 base, blue, lewd, racy, rude
05 bawdy, gross
06 coarse, earthy, filthy, risqué,
smutty, vulgar
07 jeering, mocking, naughty
08 derisive, indecent
09 off-colour, satirical
10 irreverent, licentious
11 foul-mouthed, Rabelaisian

ribaldry
04 smut
05 filth
07 jeering, lowness, mockery
08 baseness, raciness, rudeness
09 bawdiness, grossness,
indecency, vulgarity
10 coarseness, earthiness,
scurrility, smuttiness

11 naughtiness
14 licentiousness

ribbon
04 band, cord, line, sash
05 braid, cloth, shred, strip

rich
04 deep, fine, full, lush, oily
05 fatty, flush, grand, heavy, spicy, sweet, vivid
06 costly, creamy, fecund, ironic, lavish, loaded, mellow, ornate, strong
07 fertile, intense, moneyed, opulent, profuse, steeped, vibrant, wealthy, well-off
08 abundant, affluent, fruitful, gorgeous, luscious, palatial, prolific, resonant, sonorous, splendid
09 abounding, elaborate, laughable, luxurious, plenteous, plentiful, sumptuous
10 full-bodied, outrageous, productive, prosperous, ridiculous, well-heeled
11 made of money, magnificent, mellifluous, overflowing, rolling in it
13 full-flavoured

riches
04 gold
05 lucre, means, money
06 assets, wealth
08 opulence, property, treasure
09 affluence, resources
10 prosperity

richly
04 well
05 fully
08 lavishly, strongly, suitably
09 elegantly, opulently
10 completely, gorgeously, palatially, splendidly
11 elaborately, expensively, exquisitely, luxuriously, sumptuously

rickety
05 shaky
06 flimsy, wobbly
08 decrepit, derelict, insecure, unstable, unsteady
10 broken-down, jerry-built, ramshackle
11 dilapidated

rid
04 free
05 clear, purge
06 purify

07 cleanse, deliver, relieve
08 unburden

□ **get rid of**
04 dump, junk
05 chuck, ditch, scrap
07 abolish, discard
08 chuck out, jettison
09 dispose of, eliminate
10 do away with, put an end to

riddance
06 relief
07 freedom, release, removal
08 disposal, ejection
09 clearance, expulsion
11 deliverance, elimination

riddle
03 mar
04 fill, koan, sift
05 poser, sieve
06 enigma, filter, infest, pepper, puzzle, strain, winnow
07 mystery, pervade, problem
08 permeate, puncture
09 conundrum, perforate
11 brainteaser

ride
03 sit
04 lift, move, spin, trip, trot
05 drive, jaunt, pedal, steer
06 gallop, handle, manage
08 bestride, dominate, progress

ridge
04 band, hill, reef, wale, welt
05 arête, costa, esker, knurl
06 ripple, saddle
07 crinkle, drumlin, hummock, yardang
08 hog's back, sastruga
10 escarpment

ridicule
03 kid, rag, rib
04 gibe, jeer, mock
05 chaff, irony, scoff, scorn, sneer, taunt, tease
06 banter, deride, parody, satire, send up
07 jeering, lampoon, laugh at, mockery, sarcasm, teasing
08 badinage, derision, laughter, pooh-pooh, satirize
09 burlesque, humiliate, make fun of
10 caricature

ridiculous
05 droll, funny, silly
06 absurd, stupid
07 comical, foolish, risible
08 derisory, farcical, humorous
09 laughable, ludicrous
11 nonsensical

12 contemptible, preposterous, unbelievable

rife
06 common, raging
07 general, rampant, teeming
08 abundant, epidemic, frequent, swarming
09 abounding, prevalent
10 ubiquitous, widespread

riff-raff
03 mob
04 scum
05 dregs
06 rabble
08 canaille, rent-a-mob
09 hoi polloi
12 undesirables

rifle
03 gun, gut, rob
04 loot, sack
05 fusil, strip
06 maraud, musket, search
07 bundook, carbine, despoil, firearm, pillage, plunder, ransack, rummage, shotgun
08 firelock
09 flintlock

rift
03 gap, row
04 feud, hole, slit
05 break, chink, cleft, crack, fault, fight, space, split
06 breach, cranny, schism
07 crevice, fissure, opening
08 conflict, division, fracture
10 alienation, separation
11 altercation
12 disagreement, estrangement

rig
03 kit
04 cook, fake, gear
05 forge, twist
06 doctor, fiddle, outfit, tackle
07 distort, falsify, pervert
08 fittings, fixtures
09 apparatus, equipment
10 manipulate, tamper with
12 misrepresent
13 accoutrements

□ **rig out**
03 fit
04 garb, robe, trim, wear
05 array, dress, equip, get up
06 attire, clothe, outfit, supply
07 dress up, furnish, provide

□ **rig up**
05 build, erect, fit up, fix up
07 arrange, knock up
08 assemble

09 construct, improvise
11 put together
14 cobble together

right
03 due, fit, fix
04 good, just, lien, real, Tory, true
05 claim, droit, exact, legal, moral, power, valid
06 actual, avenge, bang on, ethics, fairly, honest, honour, lawful, proper, repair, seemly, settle, spot on, unfair, virtue, wholly
07 correct, ethical, exactly, factual, fitting, genuine, honesty, justice, precise, rectify, redress, warrant
08 accurate, complete, entirely, fairness, goodness, legality, morality, properly, slap bang, straight, suitable, thorough, true-blue, virtuous
09 authentic, authority, correctly, equitable, factually, opportune, precisely, privilege, propriety, rectitude
10 absolutely, accurately, auspicious, birthright, completely, favourable, favourably, honourable, lawfulness, permission, principled, propitious, reasonable, straighten
11 appropriate, entitlement, prerogative, reactionary, uprightness
12 conservative, satisfactory, the done thing, truthfulness

❑**by rights**
06 de jure, justly
07 legally, rightly
08 lawfully, properly
10 rightfully
11 justifiably
12 legitimately

❑**in the right**
05 right
09 justified, warranted
10 vindicated

❑**put to rights, set to rights**
03 fix
06 settle
07 correct, rectify
10 put in order, straighten
13 straighten out

❑**right away**
03 now
06 at once

08 directly, promptly
09 forthwith, instantly
11 immediately
12 straight away, without delay
13 from the word go

❑**within your rights**
05 right
07 allowed
08 entitled
09 justified, permitted

righteous
04 fair, good, just, pure
05 legal, moral, valid
06 honest, lawful, proper
07 ethical, sinless, upright
08 virtuous
09 blameless, equitable, guiltless, incorrupt, justified, warranted
10 acceptable, defensible, God-fearing, honourable, law-abiding, legitimate
11 justifiable, supportable
14 irreproachable

righteousness
06 dharma, equity, honour, purity, virtue
07 honesty, justice, probity
08 goodness, holiness, morality
09 integrity, rectitude
11 ethicalness, uprightness

rightful
03 due
04 just, real, true
05 legal, valid
06 lawful, proper
07 correct, genuine
08 bona fide, suitable
10 authorized, legitimate

rightfully
06 de jure, justly
07 legally, rightly
08 by rights, lawfully, properly
11 justifiably
12 legitimately

rigid
03 set
04 firm, hard
05 fixed, harsh, stern, stiff
08 cast-iron, rigorous
09 inelastic, stringent
10 inflexible, invariable
11 unalterable, unrelenting
12 intransigent
14 uncompromising

rigmarole
04 fuss, to-do
06 bother, hassle, jargon
07 carry-on, palaver, process
11 performance

rigorous
04 firm, hard
05 exact, harsh, rigid, tough
06 severe, strict
07 austere, precise, Spartan
08 exacting, thorough
09 laborious, stringent
10 meticulous, scrupulous
11 painstaking, punctilious
14 uncompromising

rigour
05 trial
06 ordeal
08 accuracy, firmness, hardness, hardship, rigidity
09 austerity, exactness, harshness, precision, suffering, toughness
10 strictness, stringency
12 thoroughness
13 meticulousness
15 punctiliousness

rig-out
04 garb, gear, togs
05 dress, get-up, habit
06 livery, outfit
07 apparel, clobber, clothes, costume, raiment, uniform
08 clothing, garments

rile
03 bug, irk, vex
05 anger, annoy, pique, upset
06 nettle, put out
08 irritate
09 aggravate

rim
03 lip
04 brim, edge
05 brink, verge
06 border, margin
13 circumference

rind
04 husk, peel, skin
05 crust
07 epicarp
10 integument

ring
03 mob
04 band, bell, belt, buzz, call, ding, disc, echo, gang, gird, halo, hoop, loop, peal, toll
05 arena, atoll, chime, clang, clink, knell, phone
06 cartel, circle, clique, collar, girdle, league, tinkle
07 circlet, circuit, combine, coterie, enclose, resound
08 ding-dong, encircle, resonate, surround

09 enclosure, encompass, phone call, syndicate

11 give a tinkle, reverberate

ringleader

05 chief

06 brains, leader

09 spokesman

10 bell-wether, mouthpiece

11 spokeswoman

12 spokesperson

rinse

05 bathe, clean, flush, swill

07 cleanse

09 flush away, wash clean

riot

03 row

04 fray, hoot, rage, rant, rave

05 brawl, fight, laugh, rebel

06 affray, fracas, mutiny, rave-up, revolt, rise up, rising, scream, tumult, uproar

07 anarchy, rampage, revelry, run wild, turmoil

08 disorder, feasting, uprising

09 commotion, confusion, go berserk, rebellion

10 debauchery, insurgence, turbulence

11 disturbance, lawlessness

12 extravaganza, insurrection

14 go on the rampage

❏**run riot**

04 rage, rant, rave, tear

05 storm

06 charge

07 rampage, run amok, run wild

09 go berserk

riotous

04 loud, wild

05 noisy, rowdy

06 unruly, wanton

07 lawless, violent

08 mutinous

10 boisterous, disorderly, rebellious, tumultuous, uproarious

12 ungovernable, unrestrained

13 insubordinate

14 uncontrollable

15 insurrectionary

rip

03 cut

04 hole, rend, rent, slit, tear

05 burst, shred, slash, split

07 rupture

08 cleavage, lacerate, separate

❏**rip off**

02 do

03 con

04 dupe

05 cheat, sting, trick

06 diddle, fleece

07 defraud, exploit, swindle

10 overcharge

ripe

03 fit

05 grown, ready, right

06 mature, mellow, timely

07 perfect, ripened

09 developed, opportune

10 auspicious, favourable, fully-grown, propitious

14 fully-developed

ripen

03 age

06 mature, mellow, season

07 develop

14 come to maturity

rip-off

03 con

05 cheat, fraud, sting, theft

06 diddle

07 robbery, swindle

08 con trick

12 exploitation

15 daylight robbery

riposte

04 quip

05 reply, sally

06 answer, rejoin, retort, return

07 respond

08 comeback, response

09 rejoinder

11 reciprocate

ripple

04 eddy, flow, purl, wave

06 burble, crease, gurgle, result, ruffle, wimple

07 lapping, ripplet, wrinkle

08 undulate

09 shock wave

10 undulation

11 consequence, disturbance

12 repercussion

13 reverberation

rise

04 flow, go up, grow, hill, leap, loom, riot, soar

05 arise, begin, climb, get up, issue, mount, raise, rebel, slope, start, swell, tower

06 appear, ascend, ascent, emerge, mutiny, resist, revolt, rocket, spring, upturn

07 advance, emanate, improve, incline, react to, respond, slope up, stand up, upsurge

08 escalate, increase, progress, spring up, towering

09 acclivity, elevation, get higher, increment, intensify, originate, promotion

10 escalation, take up arms

11 advancement, get out of bed, improvement

12 amelioration, make progress

13 get to your feet

risible

05 comic, droll, funny

06 absurd

07 amusing, comical

08 farcical, humorous

09 hilarious, laughable, ludicrous

10 ridiculous

11 rib-tickling

rising

04 riot

06 revolt

08 emerging, mounting, swelling, uprising

09 advancing, ascending

10 increasing, revolution

12 insurrection, intensifying

risk

04 dare

06 chance, danger, gamble

07 imperil, venture

08 endanger, jeopardy

10 go for broke, jeopardize

11 possibility, speculation

12 play with fire, put on the line

risky

04 iffy

05 dicey, dodgy

06 chancy, tricky, unsafe

08 high-risk, perilous

09 dangerous, hazardous

10 precarious, touch-and-go

risqué

04 blue, racy, rude

05 adult, bawdy, crude, dirty

06 coarse, earthy, ribald, smutty

07 naughty

08 immodest, indecent

09 off-colour

10 indelicate, suggestive

14 near the knuckle

rite

04 form

05 custom, office, ritual

07 liturgy, service, worship

08 ceremony, practice

09 formality, ordinance, procedure, sacrament

10 ceremonial, observance

ritual

03 act, set

rival
04 form, rite, wont
05 habit, usage
06 custom, formal
07 liturgy, routine, service
08 ceremony, habitual, practice
09 customary, formality, ordinance, sacrament, solemnity, tradition
10 ceremonial, observance, prescribed, procedural
11 celebration, traditional

rival
04 peer, vier
06 fellow, oppose
07 emulate, opposed, vie with
08 opponent, opposing
09 adversary, contender
10 antagonist, challenger, competitor, contestant, in conflict, opposition
11 competitive, conflicting

rivalry
05 vying
07 contest
10 contention, opposition
11 competition
15 competitiveness

river
07 fluvial, potamic
08 waterway
11 watercourse

► *Types of river*:
03 cut
04 beck, burn, rill, wadi
05 bourn, brook, canal, creek, delta, firth, inlet, mouth
06 broads, runnel, source, stream
07 channel, estuary, rivulet
08 waterway
09 billabong, tributary
10 confluence

► *Names of rivers*:
02 Ob, Po
03 Don, Ems, Red, San, Tay, Wye
04 Aare, Amur, Avon, Bann, East, Ebro, Eden, Elbe, Kemi, Lena, Nile, Oder, Ohio, Ouse, Oxus, Ravi, Ruhr, Saar, Spey, Styx, Swan, Tees, Towy, Tyne, Vaal, Yalu
05 Adige, Argun, Boyne, Clyde, Congo, Donau, Douro, Fleet, Forth, Indus, Jumna, Loire, Marne, Meuse, Mosel, Negro, Niger, Peace, Pearl, Pecos, Plata, Plate, Rhine, Rhône, Seine, Snake,

Somme, Tagus, Tiber, Trent, Tweed, Volga, Volta, Weser, Yukon, Zaire
06 Amazon, Danube, Dnestr, Gambia, Ganges, Grande, Hudson, Humber, Irtysh, Jordan, Kolyma, Liffey, Mekong, Mersey, Murray, Orange, Ottawa, Pahang, Paraná, Ribble, Severn, Thames, Tigris, Ubangi, Vltava, Wabash, Yellow
07 Darling, Dnieper, Garonne, Huang Ho, Lachlan, Limpopo, Lualaba, Madeira, Orinoco, Pechora, Potomac, Salween, Selenga, Sénégal, Shannon, Ucayali, Uruguay, Vistula, Yangtze, Yenisei, Zambezi
08 Achelous, Arkansas, Blue Nile, Canadian, Colorado, Columbia, Delaware, Dniester, Dordogne, Missouri, Okavango, Paraguay, Tunguska, Wanganui
09 Euphrates, Irrawaddy, Mackenzie, Rio Grande, Tennessee, White Nile
10 Albert Nile, Bass Strait, Sacramento, San Joaquin, Shenandoah
11 Mississippi, Shatt al-Arab
12 Murrumbidgee, Saskatchewan
13 Saint Lawrence

riveting
08 exciting, gripping, hypnotic
09 absorbing, arresting
10 engrossing
11 captivating, enthralling, fascinating, interesting
12 spellbinding

roam
04 rove, trek, walk
05 drift, prowl, range, tramp
06 ramble, stroll, travel, wander
08 ambulate, traverse
11 perambulate, peregrinate

roar
03 cry
04 bawl, hoot, howl, yell
05 blare, crash, laugh, shout
06 bellow, guffaw, rumble
07 break up, thunder
15 laugh like a drain

rob
02 do
03 mug
04 loot, raid, sack

05 cheat, heist, rifle, sting
06 burgle, hold up, rip off
07 defraud, deprive, pillage, plunder, ransack, swindle

robber
05 cheat, fraud, thief
06 bandit, con man, looter, mugger, pirate, raider
07 brigand, burglar, stealer
10 highwayman

robbery
04 raid
05 fraud, heist, theft
06 hold-up, rip-off
07 break-in, larceny, mugging, pillage, plunder, stick-up
08 burglary, stealing
09 pilferage
12 embezzlement
13 housebreaking

robe
04 garb, gown, vest, wrap
05 drape, dress, habit
07 apparel, costume, wrapper
08 bathrobe, peignoir
09 housecoat
12 dressing-gown

robot
06 zombie
07 android, machine
09 automaton

robust
03 fit, raw
04 rude, well
05 crude, hardy, tough
06 coarse, earthy, strong, sturdy
07 healthy
08 athletic, forceful, muscular, powerful, stalwart, vigorous
09 energetic, strapping
10 no-nonsense

rock
04 crag, roll, sway, tilt, toss
05 lurch, pitch, shake, stone
06 pebble, totter, wobble
07 astound, boulder, outcrop
08 take back, undulate
09 dumbfound, oscillate
12 move to and fro

► *Types of rock*:
03 ore
04 coal, lava, marl
05 chalk, flint, shale, slate
06 basalt, gabbro, gneiss, gravel, marble, schist
07 granite
08 obsidian, porphyry
09 limestone, sandstone
11 pumice stone
12 conglomerate

rocket
04 soar
07 shoot up
08 escalate, increase

rocky
04 hard, weak
05 rough, shaky, stony
06 craggy, rugged, wobbly
08 unstable, unsteady

rod
03 bar
04 cane, mace, pole, wand
05 baton, shaft, staff, stick, strut
07 sceptre
08 rhabdoid

rodent
➤ *Types of rodent*:
03 rat
04 cavy, cony, hare, pika, vole
05 aguti, coypu, mouse
06 agouti, beaver, ferret, gerbil, gopher, jerboa, marmot, rabbit
07 hamster, lemming, meerkat, muskrat, ondatra, potoroo
08 black rat, brown rat, capybara, chipmunk, dormouse, hedgehog, musquash, sewer-rat, squirrel, water rat
09 bandicoot, groundhog, guinea pig, porcupine, water vole, woodchuck
10 chinchilla, fieldmouse, prairie dog
11 kangaroo rat, red squirrel
12 grey squirrel, harvest mouse
➤ See also **animal**

rogue
05 cheat, crook, fraud, scamp
06 con man, rascal
07 villain, wastrel
08 deceiver, swindler
09 fraudster, miscreant, reprobate, scoundrel
10 ne'er-do-well
14 good-for-nothing

roguish
05 shady
06 cheeky, impish
07 crooked, knavish, playful
08 criminal, rascally
09 deceitful, dishonest
10 coquettish, frolicsome
11 mischievous

roister
04 brag, romp

05 boast, revel, strut
06 frolic
07 bluster, carouse, rollick
09 celebrate, make merry
15 paint the town red

roisterer
06 ranter
07 boaster, roister
08 braggart, carouser, reveller
09 blusterer, swaggerer

roisterous
04 loud, wild
05 noisy, rowdy
09 clamorous, exuberant
10 boisterous, disorderly
12 obstreperous

role
03 job
04 duty, part, post, task
08 capacity, function, position
09 character, situation
13 impersonation
14 representation

roll
03 run
04 boom, coil, curl, drum, file, furl, list, reel, roar, rock, spin, sway, toss, turn, wind, wrap
05 index, lurch, pitch, spool, swell, twirl, twist, wheel
06 billow, bobbin, census, gyrate, record, roller, roster, rotate, rumble, scroll, tumble
07 envelop, flatten, reeling, resound, revolve, rocking, stagger, thunder, tossing
08 cylinder, gyration, pitching, register, rotation, undulate
09 billowing, catalogue, chronicle, directory, inventory, press down
10 revolution, undulation

❑**roll up**
06 arrive, gather
07 convene
08 assemble
10 congregate

rollicking
05 merry, noisy
06 hearty, jovial, joyous, lively
07 playful, romping
08 roisting, spirited, sportive
09 cavorting, exuberant
10 boisterous, frolicsome, rip-roaring, roisterous
12 devil-may-care
13 swashbuckling

rolling
06 waving

07 heaving, surging
10 undulating

roly-poly
03 fat
05 buxom, plump, podgy, pudgy, tubby
06 chubby, rotund
10 overweight

romance
03 lie, see
04 date, tale
05 amour, novel, story
06 affair, legend, whimsy
07 fantasy, fiction, glamour, liaison, mystery, passion
08 intrigue
09 adventure, fairytale, fantasize, love story, melodrama, sentiment
10 attachment, exaggerate, excitement, love affair

romantic
04 fond, wild
05 mushy, soppy
06 loving, sloppy, tender
07 amorous, dreamer, idyllic
08 exciting, fanciful, idealist
09 fairy-tale, fantastic, imaginary, legendary
10 fictitious, idealistic, improbable, lovey-dovey, mysterious, optimistic, passionate, starry-eyed
11 extravagant, fascinating, impractical, sentimental
14 sentimentalist

Romeo
05 lover
06 gigolo
07 Don Juan
08 Casanova
09 ladies' man
10 lady-killer

romp
04 lark, skip
05 caper, frisk, revel, sport
06 cavort, frolic, gambol
07 roister, rollick

roof
09 tectiform
➤ *Types of roof*:
03 hip
04 bell, dome, flat, helm, ogee, span
05 gable
06 cupola, lean-to, saddle
07 gambrel, mansard, monitor, pitched
08 imperial, pavilion, sawtooth, thatched

09 onion dome
10 imbricated, saucer dome
12 geodesic dome

rook
02 do
03 con
04 bilk
05 cheat, sting
06 diddle, fleece, rip off
07 defraud, swindle
10 overcharge

room
05 range, scope, space
06 extent, leeway, margin
07 expanse, legroom
08 capacity, headroom, latitude
09 allowance, elbow-room

roomy
04 wide
05 ample, broad, large
08 generous, sizeable, spacious
09 capacious, extensive
10 commodious, voluminous

root
03 fix, nub, set
04 base, core, germ, hail, home, moor, pull, seat, seed, stem
05 basis, cause, cheer, embed, fount, heart, radix, tuber
06 anchor, bottom, fasten, kernel, origin, source
07 applaud, cheer on, essence, nucleus, origins, radical, radicle, rhizome, support
09 beginning, establish
10 background, beginnings, derivation, foundation
11 fundamental
12 fountainhead
13 starting point

◻**root and branch**
06 wholly
07 finally, totally, utterly
08 entirely
09 radically
10 completely, thoroughly

◻**root around**
03 dig, pry
04 hunt, nose, poke
05 delve
06 burrow, ferret, forage
07 rummage

◻**root out**
06 dig out, remove, uproot
07 destroy, uncover, unearth
08 discover, get rid of
09 clear away, extirpate
10 put an end to
11 exterminate

rooted
04 deep, felt, firm
05 fixed, rigid
06 deeply
07 radical
09 confirmed, ingrained
10 deep-seated, entrenched
11 established

rope
03 tie
04 bind, lash, moor
05 hitch
06 fasten, tether
09 funicular

━ *Types of rope*:
03 guy
04 cord, line, stay, tack, vang, warp
05 brace, cable, lasso, noose, widdy
06 halter, hawser, lariat, strand, string, tether
07 bobstay, bowline, cordage, cringle, guy-rope, halyard, lanyard, lashing, marline, painter, towrope
08 buntline, clew-line, dragline, dragrope, gantline
09 hackamore

◻**rope in**
06 engage, enlist
07 involve
08 inveigle, persuade, talk into

ropy
04 poor
05 rough
06 unwell
08 below par, inferior
09 deficient, off colour
11 substandard
14 unsatisfactory

roster
04 list, roll, rota
05 index
07 listing
08 register, schedule
09 directory

rostrum
04 dais
05 stage
06 podium
08 platform

rosy
03 red
04 pink, rose
05 fresh, ruddy, sunny
06 bright, florid
07 flushed, glowing, hopeful, reddish, rose-red, roseate

08 blooming, blushing, roselike, rubicund
10 auspicious, favourable
14 healthy-looking

rot
04 bosh, bunk, rust, tosh
05 decay, go bad, go off, mould
06 bunkum, drivel, fester, go sour, humbug, perish, piffle
07 baloney, putrefy, rubbish
08 claptrap, nonsense
09 decompose, poppycock
10 codswallop, degenerate
12 disintegrate, putrefaction
13 decomposition

rotary
07 turning
08 gyrating, gyratory, rotating, spinning, whirling
09 revolving

rotate
04 reel, roll, spin, turn
05 pivot, whirl
06 gyrate, swivel
07 go round, revolve
09 alternate, move round
13 take it in turns

rotation
04 spin, turn
05 cycle, orbit, whirl
06 swivel
07 turning
08 gyration, sequence, spinning, whirling
10 revolution, succession, swivelling

rotten
03 bad, ill, off
04 evil, foul, rank, sick, sour
05 awful, dirty, fetid, lousy
06 addled, crummy, grotty, mouldy, poorly, putrid, spoilt, unwell, wicked
07 beastly, corrupt, decayed, immoral, rotting, tainted
08 decaying, horrible, inferior, low-grade, stinking
10 decomposed, despicable, mouldering, putrescent
14 disintegrating

rotter
03 cad, cur, rat
04 fink
05 louse, swine
07 bounder, dastard, stinker
08 blighter
09 scoundrel
10 blackguard

rotund
03 fat
04 full, rich
05 heavy, obese, plump, podgy, round, stout, tubby
06 chubby, fleshy, portly
07 bulbous, rounded, spheric
08 globular, roly-poly
09 corpulent, orbicular, rotundate, spherular

roué
04 rake
06 lecher, wanton
08 rakehell
09 debauchee, libertine
10 profligate, sensualist

rough
03 ill, yob
04 hard, hazy, sick, thug, wild
05 bully, bumpy, crude, draft, gruff, harsh, hasty, husky, noisy, quick, rowdy, scaly, stony, tough, vague, yobbo
06 brutal, choppy, coarse, craggy, grotty, hoarse, jagged, mock-up, poorly, rotten, rugged, severe, shaggy, sketch, stormy
07 bristly, brusque, brutish, cursory, general, gnarled, inexact, outline, prickly, rasping, raucous, ruffian, sketchy, throaty, violent
08 below par, croaking, forceful, guttural, hooligan, scratchy, strident
09 estimated, imprecise, irregular, off colour, roughneck, turbulent, unhealthy, unrefined
10 boisterous, incomplete, unfinished, unpolished
11 approximate, insensitive, rudimentary, tempestuous

❏**rough out**
05 draft
06 mock up, sketch
07 outline
14 give a summary of

❏**rough up**
03 mug
04 bash, do in
06 beat up
08 maltreat, mistreat
09 manhandle
10 knock about

rough-and-ready
05 crude
06 make-do, simple
07 hurried, sketchy, stop-gap

09 makeshift, unrefined
10 unpolished
11 approximate, provisional

rough-and-tumble
05 brawl, fight, melee, scrap
06 affray, dust-up, fracas
07 punch-up, scuffle
08 struggle

roughen
04 chap, rasp
05 chafe, graze, rough, scuff
06 abrade, ruffle
07 coarsen, harshen
08 asperate
09 granulate

roughneck
04 lout, thug
05 rough, rowdy, tough
06 keelie
07 bruiser, ruffian
08 bully boy, hooligan

round
03 lap, orb
04 ball, band, beat, bout, disc, game, heat, hoop, path, ring
05 cycle, globe, plump, rough, route, skirt, stage, stout
06 bypass, circle, course, curved, period, portly, rotund, series, sphere
07 circlet, circuit, discoid, globate, go round, rounded, routine, session
08 circular, cylinder, globular, sequence, spheroid
09 corpulent, discoidal, estimated, imprecise, orbicular, spherical
10 ring-shaped, succession
11 approximate, cylindrical

❏**round off**
03 cap, end
05 close, crown
06 finish, top off
08 complete, conclude
09 finish off

❏**round on**
06 attack, turn on
07 lay into, set upon

❏**round up**
04 herd
05 group, rally
06 gather, muster
07 collect, marshal
08 assemble
13 bring together

roundabout
07 evasive, oblique, winding
08 indirect, tortuous, twisting

10 circuitous, meandering
14 circumlocutory

roundly
06 openly
08 fiercely, severely
09 intensely, violently
10 completely, forcefully, thoroughly, vehemently
11 outspokenly

round-up
05 rally
06 muster, précis, survey
07 herding, summary
08 assembly, overview
09 collation, gathering
10 collection

rouse
04 call, move, stir, wake
05 anger, evoke, get up, start
06 arouse, awaken, excite, incite, induce, wake up, whip up
07 agitate, disturb, provoke
09 galvanize, stimulate

rousing
08 exciting, spirited, stirring
09 inspiring
11 stimulating

rout
04 beat, lick
05 chase, crush
06 defeat, dispel, flight, hammer, thrash
07 conquer, retreat, trounce
08 conquest, drubbing
09 overthrow, slaughter, thrashing, trouncing
11 put to flight, subjugation

route
03 run, way
04 beat, path, road, send
06 avenue, course, direct
07 circuit, journey, passage
09 direction, itinerary
10 flight path

routine
03 act, rut, way, yak
05 banal, habit, piece, spiel
06 boring, common, custom, method, normal, system
07 formula, humdrum, pattern
08 everyday, familiar, habitual, ordinary, practice, schedule
09 customary, hackneyed, procedure, programme
11 performance, predictable
12 conventional

rove
04 roam

05 drift, range, stray
06 cruise, ramble, stroll, wander
08 stravaig
09 gallivant

rover
05 Gypsy, nomad
06 ranger
07 drifter, rambler, vagrant
08 gadabout, wanderer
09 itinerant, transient, traveller
10 stravaiger

row
03 din
04 bank, file, line, rank, tier, tiff
05 argue chain, fight, noise,
   queue, range, scrap, set-to
06 bicker, column, fracas,
   hubbub, racket, rumpus,
   series, string, uproar
07 dispute, quarrel, wrangle
08 argument, conflict,
   sequence, squabble
09 commotion
10 falling-out
11 altercation, arrangement,
   controversy, disturbance
12 disagreement
13 slanging match

rowdy
03 yob
04 loud, lout, wild
05 noisy, rough, tough, yahoo
06 apache, keelie, unruly
07 brawler, hoodlum, riotous
08 hooligan, tearaway
10 boisterous, disorderly
12 obstreperous, unrestrained

royal
05 grand, regal
06 august, kingly, superb
07 queenly, stately
08 imperial, majestic, princely
09 sovereign
11 magnificent, monarchical

rub
04 buff, snag, wipe
05 catch, chafe, clean, grate,
   put on, scour, scrub, smear
06 abrade, buff up, fondle,
   polish, scrape, smooth,
   spread, stroke, work in
07 burnish, massage, scratch
08 drawback, kneading
09 embrocate, hindrance
10 difficulty, impediment

❏**rub in**
06 harp on, stress
09 emphasize, underline
10 make much of

❏**rub off on**
06 affect, change
09 influence, transform
14 have an effect on

❏**rub out**
04 do in, kill
05 erase
06 delete, efface, murder
09 eliminate, finish off, liquidate
10 obliterate, put to death
11 assassinate

❏**rub up the wrong way**
03 bug, get, irk, vex
05 anger, annoy, get to, peeve
06 needle, niggle
08 irritate
11 get one's goat

rubbish
03 rot
04 bull, bunk, crap, junk, tosh
05 dross, scrap, trash, waste
06 bunkum, debris, drivel, litter,
   piffle, refuse, rubble
07 garbage, twaddle
08 claptrap, cobblers, detritus,
   nonsense
09 gibberish, poppycock
10 balderdash
12 gobblydegook

rubbishy
05 cheap, petty, tatty
06 grotty, paltry, shoddy,
   tawdry, trashy
08 gimcrack
09 third-rate, throw-away

ruction
03 row
04 fuss, rout, to-do
05 brawl, scrap, storm
06 fracas, rumpus, uproar
07 dispute, protest, quarrel
09 commotion
11 altercation, disturbance

ruddy
03 red
04 rosy
05 fresh
06 florid
07 crimson, flushed, glowing,
   healthy, reddish, scarlet
08 blooming, blushing

rude
04 curt, lewd
05 bawdy, crude, dirty, gross,
   nasty, rough, sharp, short
06 cheeky, coarse, filthy, ribald,
   risqué, simple, vulgar
07 abusive, brusque, ill-bred,
   obscene, uncivil, uncouth

08 ignorant, impolite,
   improper, impudent,
   indecent, insolent
09 insulting, primitive,
   unrefined, untutored
10 indelicate, uneducated,
   unpleasant, unpolished
11 bad-tempered, ill-
   mannered, impertinent,
   near the bone, uncivilized
12 disagreeable, discourteous
13 rough-and-ready

rudimentary
05 basic, crude, rough
06 simple
09 embryonic, primitive
10 elementary
11 fundamental, undeveloped
12 introductory

rudiments
03 ABC
06 basics
08 elements
10 essentials, principles
12 fundamentals

rue
05 mourn
06 bemoan, bewail, grieve,
   lament, regret, repent
07 be sorry, deplore
11 be regretful

rueful
03 sad
05 sorry
06 dismal, woeful
07 doleful, pitiful
08 contrite, grievous,
   mournful, penitent,
   pitiable
09 plaintive, repentant,
   sorrowful, woebegone
10 apologetic, lugubrious,
   melancholy, remorseful
15 self-reproachful

ruffian
03 yob
04 lout, thug
05 bully, rowdy, tough, yobbo
07 bruiser, hoodlum, villain
08 bully-boy, hooligan
09 cut-throat, miscreant,
   roughneck, scoundrel

ruffle
03 bug, irk, vex
04 rile
05 anger, annoy, upset
06 crease, hassle, nettle, rattle,
   rumple, tousle
07 confuse, crumple, fluster,
   perturb, trouble, wrinkle

08 dishevel, irritate
10 disarrange, discompose

rugby

➤ *Names of rugby players*:
04 **Hare** (William Henry
   'Dusty'), **John** (Barry),
   Lomo (Jonah), **Sole** (David
   Michael Barclay)
05 **Batty** (Grant), **Botha**
   (Naas), **Ellis** (William
   Webb), **Meads** (Colin),
   Sella (Philippe)
06 **Blanco** (Serge), **Brooke**
   (Zinzan), **Gibson** (Mike),
   Irvine (Andy), **Kirwan**
   (John)
07 **Andrews** (Rob), **Bennett**
   (Phil), **Campese** (David),
   Carling (Will), **Edwards**
   (Gareth Owen), **Edwards**
   (Shaun), **Gregory** (Andy),
   Guscott (Jeremy),
   McBride (Willie John)
08 **Beaumont** (Bill), **Hastings**
   (Gavin), **Scotland** (Ken),
   Slattery (Fergus), **Sullivan**
   (Jim), **Williams** (John 'JJ'),
   Williams (John Peter Rhys
   'JPR')
09 **McGeechan** (Ian),
   Underwood (Rory)
10 **Rutherford** (John)
➤ See also **sport**

rugged

05 rocky, stark, stony, tough
06 craggy, jagged, robust,
   sinewy, strong, uneven
08 furrowed, muscular
09 irregular, well-built
13 weather-beaten

ruin

03 mar
04 fall, harm, loss, raze
05 havoc, smash, spoil, wreck
06 debris, mess up, penury,
   relics, rubble, traces
07 cripple, destroy, failure,
   remains, shatter, undoing
08 bankrupt, collapse,
   demolish, detritus, disaster,
   downfall, lay waste, vestiges,
   wreckage
09 indigence, overwhelm,
   ruination
10 bankruptcy, impoverish,
   insolvency, wreak havoc
11 destruction, devastation

ruinous

07 damaged, in ruins, wrecked
08 decrepit

09 crippling, excessive
10 broken-down, calamitous,
   devastated, ramshackle
11 cataclysmic, devastating
12 catastrophic, extortionate

rule

03 law
04 find, form, lead, sway, wont
05 axiom, canon, guide, maxim,
   order, power, reign, tenet
06 decree, govern, manage,
   regime, ruling, settle, truism
07 control, formula, lay down,
   precept, prevail, statute
08 dominate, dominion,
   kingship, practice, protocol,
   regulate, standard
09 authority, criterion,
   determine, guideline,
   officiate, ordinance,
   principle, pronounce,
   queenship, supremacy
10 adjudicate, administer,
   convention, government,
   leadership, regulation
11 commandment, preside
   over, restriction, sovereignty
12 call the shots, jurisdiction
14 administration

□as a rule

06 mainly
07 usually
08 normally
09 generally, in general
10 by and large, on the whole,
   ordinarily
14 for the most part

□rule out

03 ban
06 forbid, reject
07 dismiss, exclude, prevent
08 disallow, preclude, prohibit
09 eliminate

ruler

➤ *Types of ruler*:
03 aga
04 duce, emir, head, khan, king,
   lord, rani, shah, tsar
05 nawab, nizam, queen, rajah
06 caesar, caliph, consul,
   Führer, kaiser, leader,
   mikado, prince, regent,
   sheikh, shogun, sultan
07 emperor, empress, monarch,
   pharaoh, sultana, viceroy
08 governor, maharani,
   overlord, princess, suzerain
09 commander, maharajah,
   potentate, president,
   sovereign

11 head of state
15 governor-general

ruling

06 decree
07 finding, supreme, verdict
08 decision, dominant, in
   charge, reigning
09 governing, in control,
   judgement, sovereign
10 commanding, resolution
11 controlling, on the throne
12 adjudication
13 pronouncement

rum

03 odd
05 funny, queer, weird
07 curious, strange, unusual
08 abnormal, peculiar, singular
10 suspicious

rumbustious

04 loud, wild
05 noisy, rough, rowdy
06 robust, unruly, wilful
09 clamorous, exuberant
10 boisterous, disorderly,
   refractory, roisterous,
   uproarious
12 unmanageable

ruminate

04 muse
05 brood, think
06 ponder
07 reflect
08 chew over, cogitate,
   consider, mull over
10 deliberate
11 contemplate

rummage

04 hunt, junk, root
05 delve, rifle
06 forage, jumble, search
10 poke around, root around

rumour

04 buzz, news, talk, tell, word
05 bruit, story
06 gossip, report
07 hearsay, scandal, whisper
09 circulate, grapevine
11 information, speculation
13 bush telegraph

rump

03 bum
04 butt, dock, rear, seat
05 croup, nache, trace
06 bottom, haunch
07 remains, residue, vestige
08 backside, buttocks
09 posterior, remainder
12 hindquarters

rumple
05 crush
06 crease, pucker, ruffle, tousle
07 crumple, derange, wrinkle
08 dishevel, disorder

rumpus
03 row
04 fuss, rout
05 brawl, noise
06 fracas, furore, tumult, uproar
07 ruction
08 brouhaha
09 commotion, confusion, kerfuffle
10 disruption
11 disturbance

run
03 jog, rip, set, sty, use, way
04 bolt, coop, dart, dash, drip, flow, gash, go on, gush, lead, line, pass, pour, race, ride, road, rush, snag, spin, tear, trip, trot, work
05 carry, cross, cycle, drive, enter, hurry, jaunt, print, range, reach, round, route, scoot, score, slide, speed, spurt, track
06 career, convey, course, direct, extend, gallop, ladder, manage, outing, period, scurry, series, sprint, stream, string, travel
07 carry on, cascade, compete, conduct, contend, control, operate, oversee, perform, publish, scamper, scuttle, stretch, trickle
08 be played, be staged, carry out, continue, organize, progress, regulate, sequence, step on it
09 broadcast, challenge, enclosure, excursion, supervise, transport
10 administer, co-ordinate, succession, take part in
12 be in charge of
13 be in operation

☐**in the long run**
06 at last
08 in the end
10 eventually, ultimately

☐**run across**
04 meet
07 run into
08 bump into
09 encounter
10 chance upon, come across

☐**run after**
04 tail
05 chase
06 follow, pursue

☐**run away**
04 bolt, flee, lift, nick
05 elope, leave, pinch, steal
06 beat it, decamp, escape
07 abscond, make off, scarper
08 clear off
13 make a run for it

☐**run down**
03 cut, hit
05 knock, slate, weary
06 attack, reduce, weaken
07 curtail, exhaust, rubbish, run over, slag off
08 belittle, decrease, denounce
09 criticize, denigrate, disparage, knock down

☐**run for it**
04 bolt, flee
05 scram
06 escape
07 do a bunk, make off, retreat, scarper
09 skedaddle

☐**run in**
03 nab
04 book, bust, jail, lift, nick
05 pinch
06 arrest, collar, pick up
09 apprehend

☐**run into**
03 hit, ram
04 meet
05 crash
08 bump into
09 encounter, run across
10 chance upon
11 collide with

☐**run off**
04 bolt
05 elope, print, xerox
06 decamp, escape
07 abscond, make off, produce, run away, scarper
09 duplicate, photostat, skedaddle

☐**run off with**
09 elope with
11 make off with, run away with

☐**run on**
04 go on, last
05 reach
06 extend
07 carry on
08 continue

☐**run out**
03 end
05 cease, close, dry up
06 expire, finish
07 exhaust, give out
09 terminate

☐**run out on**
04 dump, jilt
05 chuck, ditch, leave
07 abandon, forsake
09 walk out on
15 leave in the lurch

☐**run over**
03 hit
06 go over, repeat, review
07 run down
08 overflow, practise, rehearse
09 knock down, reiterate
10 run through

☐**run through**
04 read
05 spend, waste
06 review, survey
07 examine, exhaust, run over
08 practise, rehearse, squander
09 dissipate, go through
11 fritter away

☐**run to**
06 afford, come to
07 add up to
08 amount to
12 have enough of

☐**run together**
03 mix
04 fuse, join
05 blend, merge, unite
06 mingle
07 combine
10 amalgamate

runaway
05 loose
07 escaped, escapee, refugee
08 deserter, fugitive
09 absconder
12 out of control, uncontrolled

run-down
05 peaky, seedy, tired, weary
06 grotty, review, résumé
07 outline, summary, worn-out
08 analysis, briefing, fatigued
09 exhausted, neglected
10 ramshackle, run-through
11 debilitated, dilapidated

run-in
05 brush, fight, set-to
06 dust-up, tussle
07 dispute, quarrel, wrangle
08 argument, skirmish

11 altercation, contretemps
13 confrontation

runner
05 racer, shoot, sprig
06 bearer, jogger, sprout, stolon
07 athlete, courier, tendril
08 offshoot, sprinter
09 flagellum, messenger, sarmentum
13 dispatch rider

running
06 charge, in a row, racing
07 contest, control, flowing, jogging, rushing, working
08 constant, unbroken
09 ceaseless, incessant, on the trot, perpetual, sprinting, unceasing
10 continuous, leadership, management, successive
11 consecutive, controlling, functioning, supervision
12 co-ordination, in succession
13 uninterrupted
14 administration

runny
05 fluid
06 liquid, melted, molten
07 diluted, flowing
09 liquefied

run-of-the-mill
06 common, normal
07 average
08 everyday, mediocre, middling, ordinary
12 unimpressive, unremarkable
13 no great shakes, unexceptional
15 undistinguished

rupture
04 rend, rent, rift, tear
05 break, burst, crack, split
06 breach, divide, schism
08 breaking, puncture, separate
12 disagreement

rural
06 rustic, sylvan
07 bucolic, country
08 agrarian, pastoral
12 agricultural

ruse
04 hoax, plan, ploy, sham, wile
05 blind, dodge, trick
06 device, scheme, tactic
08 artifice
09 deception, imposture, manoeuvre, stratagem
10 subterfuge

rush
03 fly, run
04 bolt, dart, dash, flow, gush, push, race, raid, stir, tear
05 flood, haste, hurry, press, shoot, speed, storm, surge
06 attack, charge, flurry, hasten, sprint, stream
07 assault, clamour, urgency
08 activity, dispatch, pressure, rapidity, stampede
09 commotion, make haste, onslaught, swiftness
10 get a move on, hurly-burly
14 hive of activity
15 hustle and bustle

rushed
04 busy, fast
05 hasty, quick, rapid, swift
06 prompt, urgent
07 cursory, hurried
08 careless
09 emergency
11 expeditious, superficial

rust
05 decay, stain
07 corrode, oxidize, tarnish
09 corrosion, oxidation, verdigris

rust-coloured
03 red
05 brown, rusty, sandy, tawny
06 auburn, copper, ginger, russet, Titian
07 coppery, gingery, reddish
08 chestnut
12 reddish-brown

rustic
03 oaf
04 boor, clod, hick, rude
05 churl, rough, rural, yokel
06 coarse, simple, sylvan
07 artless, awkward, bucolic, bumpkin, country, peasant

08 homespun, pastoral
09 hillbilly, unrefined
10 provincial, uncultured
11 countrified, countryside
13 country cousin
15 unsophisticated

rustle
07 crackle, whisper
08 crepitus, rustling, susurrus
09 crinkling, susurrate
10 whispering
11 crepitation, susurration

rusty
03 red
04 dull, poor, weak
05 brown, dated, sandy, stale, stiff, tawny
06 auburn, copper, ginger, russet, rusted, Titian
07 coppery, gingery, reddish
08 chestnut, corroded, outmoded, oxidized
09 deficient, tarnished
10 antiquated
11 discoloured, unpractised
12 old-fashioned, reddish-brown, rust-coloured
13 out of practice

rut
05 grind, habit, ditch, track
06 furrow, groove, gutter, system, trough
07 channel, humdrum, pattern, pothole, routine
09 treadmill, wheelmark
10 daily grind
11 indentation
12 same old round

ruthless
04 grim, hard
05 cruel, harsh, stern
06 brutal, fierce, savage, severe
07 callous, inhuman, vicious
08 pitiless
09 barbarous, cut-throat, dog-eat-dog, draconian, ferocious, heartless, merciless, unfeeling, unsparing
10 implacable, inexorable, relentless, unmerciful
11 hard-hearted, remorseless, unforgiving, unrelenting

sable
03 jet
04 dark, inky
05 black, dusky, ebony
06 pitchy, sombre
09 coal-black, pitch-dark
10 pitch-black

sabotage
04 ruin
05 spoil, wreck
06 damage, thwart, weaken
07 destroy, disable, scupper
09 undermine, vandalism, vandalize
11 destruction

sac
03 bag
04 cyst
05 bursa, pouch, theca
06 pocket, vesica
07 bladder, saccule, vesicle
08 follicle, vesicula

saccharine
05 mushy, soppy, sweet
06 sugary, syrupy
07 cloying, honeyed, mawkish
09 schmaltzy
11 sentimental, sickly-sweet

sack
03 axe, rob
04 fire, loot, raid, raze
05 rifle, strip, waste
06 despoil, destroy, maraud, papers, pillage, plunder, rapine, ravage, the axe
07 dismiss, the boot, the chop, the push
08 lay waste, the elbow
09 dismissal, marauding, your cards
11 destruction, send packing
12 despoliation
13 make redundant
14 marching orders

sacred
04 holy
05 godly
06 divine
07 blessed, revered, saintly
08 hallowed, heavenly

09 religious, respected, spiritual, venerable
10 devotional, inviolable, sacrosanct, sanctified
11 consecrated, untouchable
14 ecclesiastical

sacredness
08 divinity, holiness, sanctity
09 godliness, solemnity
11 saintliness
13 inviolability, sacrosanctity

sacrifice
04 loss
05 let go
06 forego, give up
07 abandon, forfeit, offer up
08 immolate, oblation, offering
09 surrender
10 immolation, relinquish
11 abandonment, destruction

sacrificial
06 votive
08 oblatory, piacular
09 expiatory
12 propitiatory

sacrilege
06 heresy
07 impiety, mockery, outrage
09 blasphemy, profanity, violation
10 disrespect
11 desecration, irreverence, profanation

sacrilegious
07 impious, profane
09 heretical
10 irreverent
11 blasphemous, desecrating, profanatory
13 disrespectful

sacrosanct
06 sacred, secure
08 hallowed
09 protected
10 inviolable
11 impregnable, untouchable

sad
03 low
04 blue, down, glum

05 fed up, grave, sorry, upset
06 dismal, gloomy, tragic
07 doleful, joyless, pitiful, serious, unhappy, wistful
08 downcast, grievous, mournful, pathetic, pitiable, poignant, touching, wretched
09 depressed, long-faced, miserable, sorrowful, upsetting, woebegone
10 depressing, despondent, distressed, lamentable, melancholy, rock bottom
11 distressing, down-hearted, regrettable, unfortunate
12 disconsolate, heavy-hearted, in low spirits
13 grief-stricken
14 down in the dumps

sadden
06 dismay, grieve
08 cast down, dispirit, distress
10 discourage, dishearten
14 break your heart, drive to despair, get someone down

saddle
04 land, load
06 burden, impose, lumber
08 encumber

sadism
07 cruelty
09 barbarity, brutality
10 bestiality, inhumanity
11 callousness, viciousness
13 heartlessness, sado-masochism, unnaturalness

sadistic
05 cruel
06 brutal
07 bestial, inhuman, vicious
09 barbarous, merciless, perverted, unnatural

sadness
03 woe
05 grief
06 misery, pathos, regret, sorrow
08 distress, glumness
09 heartache, poignancy

10 dismalness, gloominess, low spirits, melancholy, sombreness
11 despondency, dolefulness, joylessness, unhappiness
12 mournfulness, wretchedness
13 sorrowfulness
14 lugubriousness

safe
04 sure
05 chest, tried, vault
06 coffer, honest, immune, intact, proven, secure, tested, unhurt
07 cash box, guarded, prudent
08 defended, harmless, non-toxic, unharmed
09 protected, sheltered, strongbox, undamaged, uninjured, unscathed
10 dependable, deposit box, depository, repository
11 impregnable, in good hands, out of danger, trustworthy
12 invulnerable, non-poisonous, safe as houses, unassailable
13 out of harm's way
14 uncontaminated

safe-conduct
04 pass
06 convoy, permit
07 licence, warrant
08 passport
13 authorization, laissez-passer

safeguard
06 defend, screen, secure, shield, surety
07 defence, protect, shelter
08 preserve, security
09 assurance, guarantee, insurance
10 precaution, protection

safekeeping
04 care, ward
06 charge
07 custody, keeping
08 wardship
10 protection
12 guardianship

safety
05 cover
06 refuge
07 shelter, welfare
08 fail-safe, immunity, security
09 safeguard, sanctuary
10 protection, protective
13 precautionary
14 impregnability

sag
03 bag, dip, low
04 bend, drop, fail, fall, flag, flop, hang, sink, slip
05 droop, slide, slump
06 falter, weaken
07 decline, subside

saga
04 epic, epos, tale, yarn
05 story
06 epopee
07 epopeia, history, romance
09 adventure, chronicle, narrative, soap opera
11 roman fleuve

sagacious
04 sage, wise
05 acute, canny, quick, sharp
06 astute, shrewd
07 knowing
10 far-sighted, insightful, perceptive, percipient
11 penetrating
13 perspicacious

sagacity
06 acumen, wisdom
07 insight
08 sapience
09 acuteness, canniness, foresight, sharpness
10 astuteness, shrewdness
11 knowingness, penetration, percipience
12 perspicacity
13 understanding

sage
04 guru, wise
05 canny, elder, hakam
06 expert, master, savant
07 knowing, learned, mahatma, prudent, sapient, wise man
08 sensible, wiseacre
09 judicious, maharishi, sagacious, wise woman
11 intelligent, philosopher
13 knowledgeable, perspicacious

► *The seven sages*:
04 **Bias** (of Priene in Caria)
05 **Solon** (of Athens)
06 **Chilon** (of Sparta), **Thales** (of Miletus)
08 **Pittacus** (of Mitylene)
09 **Cleobulus** (tyrant of Lindus in Rhodes), **Periander** (tyrant of Corinth)
➤ See also **mythology**

sail
03 fly

04 boat, scud, ship, skim, wing
05 coast, drift, float, glide, pilot, plane, steer, sweep, yacht
06 cruise, embark, voyage
07 captain, skipper
08 navigate, put to sea
09 leave port
11 weigh anchor

► *Types of sail*:
03 jib, rig
04 kite
05 genoa, royal
06 canvas, course, jigger, mizzen
07 foretop, jury rig, lugsail, skysail, spanker, topsail, trysail
08 foresail, gaff sail, headsail, mainsail, staysail
09 foreroyal, moonraker, spinnaker, spritsail
10 Bermuda rig, lateen sail, main course, square sail, topgallant
11 fore-topsail, gaff-topsail, maintopsail
12 forestaysail, studdingsail
13 fore-and-aft rig
14 fore-topgallant

❑ **sail into**
06 attack, let fly, turn on
07 assault, lay into
08 set about, tear into

❑ **sail through**
10 pass easily
11 romp through

sailor
06 seaman
07 mariner
08 seafarer
➤ See also **military**; **pirate**

► *Types of sailor*:
02 AB
03 cox, gob, tar
04 mate, salt, Wren
05 bosun, limey, pilot, rower
06 bargee, hearty, lascar, marine, master, pirate, purser, rating, seadog
07 boatman, captain, crewman, Jack tar, matelot, oarsman, skipper
08 cabin boy, coxswain, deck hand, helmsman, water rat
09 boatswain, buccaneer, fisherman, navigator, yachtsman
10 able seaman, bluejacket
11 yachtswoman

► *Names of sailors:*

04 **Byng** (George), **Byng** (John), **Cook** (James), **Diaz** (Bartolomeu), **Gama** (Vasco da), **Hood** (Samuel, Viscount), **Kidd** (William), **Ross** (Sir James Clark), **Ross** (Sir John), **Spee** (Count Maximilian von)

05 **Bligh** (William), **Cabot** (John), **Cabot** (Sebastian), **Doria** (Andrea), **Drake** (Sir Francis), **Henry** (the Navigator), **Jones** (Paul), **Peary** (Robert Edwin)

06 **Baffin** (William), **Beatty** (David, Earl), **Benbow** (John), **Bering** (Vitus), **Dönitz** (Karl), **Hudson** (Henry), **Nelson** (Horatio, Viscount), **Nimitz** (Chester), **Tasman** (Abel Janszoon), **Vernon** (Edward)

07 **Barentz** (William), **Hawkins** (Sir John), **Hawkyns** (Sir John), **Marryat** (Captain Frederick), **Pytheas**, **Raleigh** (Sir Walter), **Selkirk** (Alexander), **Tirpitz** (Alfred von), **Weddell** (James)

08 **Beaufort** (Sir Francis), **Columbus** (Christopher), **Cousteau** (Jacques Yves), **Jellicoe** (John Rushworth, Earl), **Magellan** (Ferdinand), **Pitcairn** (Robert), **Vespucci** (Amerigo)

09 **Christian** (Fletcher), **Frobisher** (Sir Martin), **Grenville** (Sir Richard), **Vancouver** (George)

10 **Chichester** (Sir Francis), **Erik the Red**

11 **Mountbatten** (Louis, Earl)

12 **Themistocles**

saint

► *Names of saints. We have omitted the word* **saint** *from names given in the following list but you may need to include this word as part of the solution to some crossword clues.*

03 Leo

04 Anne, Bede, Gall, Joan (of Arc), John, John (of the Cross), John (Chrysostom), John (the Baptist), Jude,

Lucy, Luke, Mark, Mary, Mary (Magdalene), Paul

05 Agnes, Aidan, Alban, Basil (the Great), Clare, David, Denis, Giles, James, Peter, Titus, Vitus

06 Andrew, Anselm, Antony, Antony (of Padua), Aquila, Cosmas, Damian, George, Helena, Hilary (of Poitiers), Jerome, Joseph, Joseph (of Arimathea), Justin, Martha, Martin, Monica, Oswald, Philip, Prisca, Simeon, Teresa (of Avila), Thomas, Thomas (à Becket), Thomas (Aquinas), Thomas (Becket), Thomas (More), Ursula

07 Ambrose, Anthony, Anthony (of Padua), Bernard (of Clairvaux), Bridget, Cecilia, Clement, Columba, Crispin, Cyprian, Dominic, Dunstan, Francis (of Assisi), Francis (Xavier), Gregory (of Nazianzus), Gregory (of Tours), Isidore (of Seville), Matthew, Michael, Patrick, Stephen, Swithin, Theresa (of Lisieux), Timothy, Vincent (de Paul), Wilfrid

08 Barnabas, Benedict (of Nursia), Boniface, Cuthbert, Ignatius (of Loyola), Lawrence, Margaret, Nicholas, Polycarp, Veronica, Walpurga

09 Alexander (Nevsky), Augustine (of Canterbury), Augustine (of Hippo), Catherine, Genevieve, Kentigern, Ladislaus, Methodius, Sebastian, Valentine

10 Bernadette, Stanislaus, Wenceslaus

11 Bonaventure, Christopher

12 Justin Martyr

15 Aquila and Prisca, Cosmas and Damian

saintliness

05 faith, piety

06 purity, virtue

08 chastity, goodness, holiness, morality, sanctity

10 asceticism, devoutness

11 blessedness

12 spirituality

13 righteousness, self-sacrifice

saintly

04 good, holy, pure

05 godly, moral, pious

06 devout, worthy

07 angelic, blessed, sinless

08 spotless, virtuous

09 religious, righteous, saintlike, spiritual

sake

04 gain, goal, good

06 behalf

07 account, benefit, welfare

08 interest

09 advantage, wellbeing

salacious

04 blue, lewd

05 bawdy, horny, randy

06 coarse, ribald, smutty

07 lustful, obscene, raunchy

09 lecherous

10 lascivious, libidinous, lubricious

salaried

04 paid

05 waged

11 emolumental, remunerated, stipendiary

salary

03 fee, pay

05 wages

06 income

07 stipend

08 earnings

09 emolument

10 honorarium

12 remuneration

sale

04 deal

05 trade

07 selling, traffic, vending

09 marketing

11 transaction

◻for sale

06 on sale

09 available, up for sale

10 in the shops, obtainable

11 on the market

saleable

08 vendible

09 desirable

10 marketable

12 merchantable

salesperson

03 rep

07 shop-boy

08 salesman, shop-girl

09 salesgirl, saleslady

10 salesclerk, saleswoman, shopkeeper

13 shop assistant
14 representative, sales assistant

salient
04 main
05 chief
08 striking
09 principal, prominent
10 noticeable, pronounced
11 conspicuous, significant

sallow
05 pasty, waxen
06 pallid, sickly
09 jaundiced, yellowish
10 colourless

sally
04 dash, jest, joke, quip, raid
05 erupt, foray, issue, retort
06 attack, charge, sortie, thrust
07 assault, riposte, venture
09 promenade, wisecrack, witticism

salt
03 wit, zip
04 zest
05 briny, punch, smack, taste
06 marine, rating, relish, sailor, saline, savour, seaman, vigour
07 flavour, mariner
08 brackish, piquancy, pungency, seafarer
09 seasoning
10 liveliness, trenchancy

□**salt away**
04 bank, hide, save
05 amass, cache, hoard, stash

salty
05 briny, spicy, tangy, witty
06 saline
07 piquant, savoury
08 brackish
09 trenchant

salubrious
07 healthy
08 hygienic, pleasant, sanitary
09 healthful, wholesome
10 beneficial, refreshing
12 health-giving, invigorating

salutary
06 timely, useful
08 valuable
10 beneficial, profitable
12 advantageous

salutation
06 homage, salute
07 address, welcome
08 greeting, respects

salute
03 bow, nod
04 hail, mark, wave
05 greet
06 homage, honour
07 address, tribute
08 greeting
09 celebrate, handshake, recognize
11 acknowledge, celebration, present arms, recognition
15 acknowledgement

salvage
04 save
06 redeem, rescue
07 reclaim, recover, restore
08 conserve, preserve, retrieve

salvation
06 rescue, saving
08 lifeline
10 liberation, redemption
11 deliverance, reclamation, soteriology
12 preservation

salve
04 balm, calm, ease
05 cream
06 lotion, soothe
07 comfort, lighten, relieve
08 liniment, ointment
11 embrocation

same
04 like, twin, very
05 alike, ditto, equal
06 mutual
07 similar, uniform
08 matching, selfsame
09 duplicate, identical, unchanged, unvarying
10 carbon copy, changeless, comparable, consistent, equivalent, reciprocal, synonymous, unchanging, unvariable
12 the aforesaid
13 corresponding
15 interchangeable

□**all the same**
03 but, yet
05 still
06 anyhow, anyway, even so
07 however
09 in any case
10 by any means, for all that, in any event, regardless
11 nonetheless
12 nevertheless
15 notwithstanding

sameness
07 oneness

08 identity, likeness, monotony
10 repetition, uniformity
11 consistency, duplication
14 changelessness, predictability
15 standardization

sample
05 dummy, model, piece, taste, trial
06 swatch
07 example
08 specimen
09 foretaste
12 illustration, illustrative
13 demonstration, demonstrative
14 representative

sanctify
05 bless, exalt
06 anoint, hallow, purify, ratify
07 absolve, cleanse
08 canonize, dedicate, make holy, sanction, set apart
10 consecrate, make sacred

sanctimonious
05 pious
09 pietistic
10 goody-goody, moralizing
11 pharisaical
12 hypocritical
13 self-righteous
14 holier-than-thou

sanctimoniousness
04 cant
06 humbug
09 hypocrisy
10 moralizing, pharisaism
11 complacency, preachiness
12 priggishness, unctuousness

sanction
02 OK
03 ban
04 back
05 allow
06 permit, ratify
07 approve, boycott, embargo, endorse, go-ahead, licence, license, penalty, warrant
08 accredit, approval, sentence, thumbs-up
09 agreement, authority, authorize, deterrent
10 green light, legitimize, permission
11 approbation, endorsement, prohibition, restriction
12 confirmation, ratification

sanctity
05 grace, piety
06 purity, virtue

08 devotion, goodness, holiness
10 sacredness
12 spirituality
13 inviolability

sanctuary
04 area, park
05 altar, haven, tract
06 asylum, church, refuge, safety, shrine, temple
07 enclave, hideout, reserve, retreat, sanctum, shelter
08 hideaway, immunity
09 holy place, safeguard
10 protection, tabernacle
12 holy of holies
14 place of worship

sanctum
03 den
06 refuge, shrine
07 hideout, retreat
08 hideaway
09 holy place, sanctuary
12 holy of holies

sand
04 grit, rock
05 beach, sands, shore
06 desert, strand

sandbank
03 bar, key
04 dune, reef
07 sand bar, yardang

sandy
03 red
05 rusty, tawny
06 ginger, gritty, yellow
07 coppery, gingery, reddish, yellowy
09 psammitic, yellowish
10 arenaceous
13 reddish-yellow

sane
04 wise
05 lucid, sober, sound
08 all there, moderate, rational, sensible
09 judicious
11 level-headed, of sound mind
15 in your right mind

sang-froid
04 cool
05 nerve, poise
06 aplomb, phlegm
08 calmness, coolness
09 assurance, composure
10 dispassion, equanimity
11 nonchalance, self-control
12 indifference

sanguinary
04 gory, grim
06 bloody, brutal, savage
09 merciless, murderous
12 bloodthirsty

sanguine
03 red
04 pink, rosy
05 fresh, ruddy
06 ardent, florid, lively
07 assured, buoyant, flushed, hopeful, unbowed
08 animated, cheerful
09 confident, expectant, unabashed
10 optimistic

sanitary
05 clean
07 aseptic, healthy, sterile
08 germ-free, hygienic
09 wholesome
10 antiseptic, salubrious
11 disinfected

sanity
06 reason, wisdom
08 lucidity, prudence
09 good sense, normality, soundness, stability
11 common sense, rationality
15 level-headedness, right-mindedness

sap
04 clot, fink, fool, jerk, prat, twit
05 bleed, drain, erode, juice
06 energy, impair, nitwit, reduce, vigour, weaken
07 deplete, essence, exhaust
08 diminish, enervate, enfeeble, imbecile
09 lifeblood, undermine
10 debilitate, vital fluid

sarcasm
05 irony, scorn
06 gibing, satire
07 acidity, mockery
08 derision, ridicule, scoffing, sneering
10 bitterness, trenchancy
12 spitefulness

sarcastic
05 sarky, snide
06 biting
07 acerbic, caustic, cynical, jeering, mocking, mordant
08 ironical, sardonic, scathing, scoffing, scornful, sneering
09 satirical

sardonic
03 dry

06 biting, bitter
07 cynical, mocking, mordant
08 derisive
09 sarcastic

sash
04 belt
06 girdle
08 cincture
09 waistband
10 cummerbund

Satan
06 Belial
07 Abaddon, Lucifer, Old Nick
08 Apollyon, the Devil
09 Beelzebub
10 the Evil One, the Tempter
14 Mephistopheles

satanic
04 dark, evil
05 black
06 damned, sinful, wicked
07 demonic, hellish, inhuman
08 accursed, devilish, fiendish, infernal
10 diabolical, malevolent

sate
04 cloy, fill, glut
05 gorge, slake
06 sicken
07 gratify, satiate, satisfy, surfeit
08 overfill, saturate

satellite
04 aide, moon
06 lackey, minion, planet, puppet, vassal
07 sputnik
08 adherent, disciple, follower, hanger-on, sidekick
09 attendant, dependant, spaceship, sycophant
10 spacecraft

satiate
04 cloy, glut, jade, sate
05 gorge, slake, stuff
07 engorge, satisfy, surfeit
08 overfeed, overfill

satiety
07 surfeit
08 fullness
09 repletion
10 saturation
11 repleteness
12 over-fullness, satisfaction

satire
03 wit
04 skit
05 irony, spoof
06 parody, send-up

07 lampoon, sarcasm, take-off
10 caricature, piss-taking

satirical
06 biting, bitter
07 acerbic, caustic, cutting, cynical, mocking, mordant
08 derisive, incisive, ironical, sardonic, taunting
10 irreverent, ridiculing
11 acrimonious

satirist
06 mocker
08 parodist
09 lampooner
10 cartoonist, lampoonist, pasquilant
11 pasquinader
12 caricaturist

➤ *Names of satirists*:
03 **Loy** (Mina)
04 **Isla** (José Francisco de), **Pope** (Alexander)
05 **Brown** (Thomas), **Cooke** (Ebenezer), **Ellis** (George), **Swift** (Jonathan)
06 **Butler** (Samuel), **Giusti** (Giuseppe), **Horace**, **Lucian**, **Murner** (Thomas), **Pindar** (Peter)
07 **Barclay** (John), **Juvenal**, **Marston** (John), **Mencken** (Henry Louis), **Persius**, **Thurber** (James)
08 **Apuleius** (Lucius), **Beerbohm** (Max), **Lucilius** (Gaius), **Rabelais** (François)
09 **Petronius** (Arbiter)
10 **Mandeville** (Bernard)
➤ See also **writer**

satirize
04 mock
06 deride, parody, send up
07 lampoon, take off
08 ridicule
09 burlesque, criticize
10 caricature

satisfaction
07 comfort, damages, redress
08 pleasure, requital
09 enjoyment, happiness, indemnity, well-being
10 fulfilment, recompense, reparation, settlement
11 contentment, restitution
12 compensation
13 gratification, reimbursement

satisfactory
02 OK
07 average

08 adequate, all right, passable, suitable
09 competent
10 acceptable, sufficient

satisfied
04 full, smug, sure
05 happy, sated
07 certain, content, replete
08 pacified, positive, satiated
09 contented, convinced, persuaded, reassured

satisfy
04 fill, meet, sate
06 answer, assure, fulfil, please, quench, settle
07 appease, assuage, content, delight, gratify, indulge, placate, qualify, requite, satiate, suffice, surfeit
08 convince, persuade
09 discharge, indemnify
10 comply with
13 compensate for

satisfying
08 cheering, pleasing
10 fulfilling, gratifying, persuasive, refreshing
11 pleasurable

saturate
03 wet
04 fill, glut, sate, soak
05 flood, imbue, souse, steep
06 drench
07 pervade, suffuse, surfeit
08 overfill, permeate, waterlog
10 impregnate

saturated
06 imbued, soaked, sodden, soused
07 flooded, soaking, sopping, steeped
08 drenched, wringing
09 permeated
11 impregnated, waterlogged

saturnine
04 dour, dull, glum
05 grave, heavy, moody, stern
06 dismal, gloomy, morose, severe, sombre
08 taciturn
10 melancholy, phlegmatic, unfriendly
15 uncommunicative

sauce
03 dip, lip
05 brass, cheek, mouth, nerve
08 audacity, backchat, dressing, pertness, rudeness

09 condiment, flippancy, impudence, insolence
10 brazenness, cheekiness, disrespect, flavouring
11 presumption
12 impertinence, malapertness

➤ *Types of sauce*:
03 jus, red, soy
04 mint, soja, soya
05 bread, brown, caper, garum, gravy, pesto, salsa, satay, shoyu, white
06 coulis, mornay, panada, tamari, tartar, tomato
07 custard, ketchup, rouille, sabayon, soubise, supreme, Tabasco®, tartare
08 béchamel, piri-piri
09 béarnaise, cranberry, espagnole, remoulade, Worcester
10 chaudfroid, mayonnaise, mousseline
11 Cumberland, hollandaise, horseradish
12 sweet-and-sour
13 crème anglaise
14 Worcestershire
➤ See also **food**

saucy
04 pert, rude
05 fresh, lippy, sassy
06 brazen, cheeky
08 flippant, impudent, insolent
11 impertinent
12 presumptuous
13 disrespectful

saunter
04 walk
05 amble, mooch, mosey
06 ramble, stroll, wander
09 promenade
14 constitutional

sausage
➤ *Sausages include*:
05 snags, wurst
06 banger, polony, salami, Wiener
07 baloney, Bologna, cabanos, chorizo, saveloy, zampone
08 cervelat, drisheen
09 bierwurst, bratwurst, chipolata, pepperoni, saucisson
10 Cumberland, knackwurst, knockwurst, liverwurst, mortadella
11 frankfurter, Wienerwurst
12 andouillette
➤ See also **food**

savage
04 bite, boor, claw, fell, grim, maul, slam, tear, wild
05 beast, brute, churl, cruel, feral, harsh, slate
06 attack, bloody, brutal, mangle
07 beastly, inhuman, monster, run down, untamed, vicious
08 barbaric, denounce, lacerate, pitiless, ruthless, sadistic, terrible
09 barbarian, barbarous, cut-throat, dog-eat-dog, ferocious, merciless, murderous, primitive
11 uncivilized
12 bloodthirsty

savagery
06 ferity, sadism
07 cruelty
08 ferocity, wildness
09 barbarity, brutality
10 bestiality, inhumanity
11 viciousness

savant
04 guru, sage
06 master, pundit
09 authority
10 mastermind
12 intellectual

save
04 free, hold, keep
05 guard, hoard, lay up, put by, spare, stash, store
06 budget, gather, hinder, redeem, rescue, retain, screen, scrimp, shield
07 bail out, collect, cut back, deliver, obviate, prevent, protect, reclaim, recover, release, reserve, salvage
08 conserve, cut costs, keep safe, liberate, preserve, put aside, set aside
09 economize, safeguard, stockpile
14 live on the cheap
15 tighten your belt

saving
06 frugal, thrift
07 bargain, capital, careful, nest egg, thrifty
08 discount, reserves
09 reduction, resources
10 economical, mitigating, qualifying
11 investments
12 compensatory, conservation, preservation

saviour
07 rescuer
08 champion, Emmanuel, Mediator, redeemer
09 deliverer, Lamb of God, liberator
11 emancipator

savoir-faire
04 tact
05 poise
07 ability, finesse, know-how
08 urbanity
09 assurance, diplomacy, expertise
10 capability, confidence, discretion

savour
04 hint, like, salt, tang, zest
05 aroma, enjoy, smack, smell, spice, taste, touch, trace
06 relish
07 bouquet, flavour, perfume, revel in, suggest
08 piquancy, seem like
09 delight in, fragrance
10 appreciate, smattering, suggestion

savoury
05 salty, snack, spicy, tangy, tasty, yummy
06 canapé
07 piquant
08 aromatic, luscious
09 appetizer, delicious
10 appetizing
11 bonne-bouche, flavoursome, hors d'oeuvre
13 mouthwatering

saw
03 mot
05 adage, axiom, maxim
06 byword, dictum, saying
07 epigram, proverb
08 aphorism
──────────────────
► *Types of saw*:
06 jigsaw, ripsaw
07 band-saw, fretsaw, hacksaw, handsaw
08 bench saw, chainsaw, panel saw, tenon saw
09 coping-saw, rabbet saw, scroll-saw
10 compass saw, pruning-saw
11 circular saw, crosscut saw
➤ See also **tool**

say
04 aver, call, tell
05 reply, speak, state, utter, voice

06 affirm, allege, answer, assert, convey, finish, inform, insist, recite, rejoin, relate, remark, render, repeat, report, retort, reveal
07 comment, declare, divulge, exclaim, express, mention, observe, suggest, suppose, venture
08 announce, disclose, indicate, intimate, maintain
09 make known, pronounce, volunteer
10 articulate
11 acknowledge, come out with, communicate
12 put into words

❑**that is to say**
02 ie
06 that is
12 in other words

saying
05 adage, axiom, maxim, motto
06 cliché, dictum, phrase, remark, slogan
07 epigram, precept, proverb
08 aphorism
09 platitude, quotation, statement
10 apophthegm, expression
11 catch phrase

say-so
02 OK
04 word
06 dictum
07 backing, consent
08 approval, sanction
09 agreement, assurance, authority
10 permission
13 authorization

scaffold
05 tower
06 gantry, gibbet
07 gallows, the rope
09 framework
11 scaffolding

scald
04 burn, sear
06 scorch
07 blister
09 cauterize

scale
04 coat, film, go up
05 climb, crust, flake, gamut, layer, level, mount, order, plate, range, ratio, reach, scope, scurf
06 ascend, degree, extent, furfur, ladder, lamina,

plaque, series, shin up, spread, squama, tartar
07 clamber, compass, conquer, deposit, measure
08 scramble, sequence, spectrum, surmount
09 hierarchy, limescale
10 graduation, proportion
11 calibration, progression
12 encrustation

□**scale down**
04 drop
06 lessen, reduce, shrink
07 cut back, cut down
08 contract, decrease, make less

scaliness
06 furfur
08 dandruff
09 flakiness
10 scurfiness, squamosity
12 scabrousness

scaly
05 flaky, rough
06 branny, scabby, scurfy
08 lepidote, scabrous
09 furfurous

scamp
03 imp
06 monkey, rascal, wretch
09 scallywag
12 troublemaker
13 mischief-maker
14 whippersnapper

scamper
04 dart, dash, race, romp, rush
06 frolic, gambol, scurry
07 scuttle

scan
05 check, probe, study, sweep
06 go over, search, survey
07 examine, inspect
08 glance at, scrutiny
09 screening
10 inspection, scrutinize
11 examination, investigate
14 run your eye over

scandal
04 blot, dirt, pity, slur
05 libel, shame, smear, stain
06 furore, gossip, outcry, uproar
07 calumny, obloquy, offence, outrage, rumours, slander
08 disgrace, ignominy, reproach
09 discredit, dishonour
10 defamation, opprobrium
11 crying shame

scandalize
05 appal, repel, shock

06 dismay, insult, offend, revolt
07 affront, disgust, horrify, outrage

scandalmonger
07 defamer
08 quidnunc, traducer
09 muck-raker
11 calumniator
12 gossip-monger

scandalous
08 infamous, shameful, shocking, unseemly
09 appalling, atrocious, malicious
10 defamatory, outrageous, slanderous
11 disgraceful
12 disreputable

scant
04 bare
06 little, measly, sparse
07 limited, minimal
08 exiguous
09 deficient, hardly any
10 inadequate, little or no
12 insufficient

scanty
04 bare, poor, thin
05 scant, short
06 little, meagre, narrow, skimpy, sparse
07 limited
09 deficient
10 inadequate, restricted
12 insufficient

scapegoat
05 patsy
06 sucker, victim
07 fall guy
11 whipping-boy

scar
04 mark
05 brand, shock, spoil, wound
06 damage, deface, injure, injury, lesion, stigma, trauma
07 blemish
09 disfigure
10 defacement, stigmatize, traumatize
13 disfigurement

scarce
03 few
04 rare
06 meagre, scanty, sparse
07 lacking, unusual
08 uncommon
09 deficient
10 inadequate, infrequent
12 insufficient, like gold dust
13 in short supply

scarcely
06 barely, hardly
08 not at all, only just
12 certainly not
13 definitely not

scarcity
04 lack, want
06 dearth, rarity
07 paucity
08 exiguity, rareness, shortage
10 deficiency

scare
05 alarm, panic, start
06 fright, menace, terror
07 perturb, petrify, startle, terrify, unnerve
08 frighten, threaten
10 intimidate, make afraid
12 put the wind up

scared
06 afraid, shaken
07 alarmed, anxious, fearful, jittery, nervous, panicky, quivery, worried
08 startled, unnerved
09 petrified, terrified
10 frightened, terrorized
11 in a blue funk
13 having kittens, panic-stricken
14 terror-stricken

scaremonger
08 alarmist
09 Cassandra, pessimist
13 prophet of doom

scarf
05 shawl, stole
06 cravat
07 muffler, necktie
08 babushka, kerchief
10 headsquare
11 neckerchief

scarper
04 bolt, flee, flit
06 beat it, decamp, depart, escape, vanish
07 abscond, bunk off, do a bunk, run away, vamoose
09 disappear, skedaddle
10 hightail it

scary
05 eerie, hairy
06 creepy, spooky
08 alarming, chilling, daunting, fearsome, shocking
10 disturbing, formidable, petrifying, terrifying
11 frightening, hair-raising

13 bloodcurdling, spine-chilling

scathing
04 acid
05 harsh
06 biting, bitter, brutal, fierce, savage, severe
07 caustic, cutting, mordant
08 critical, scornful, stinging
09 ferocious, trenchant, vitriolic

scatter
03 sow
05 fling, strew
06 dispel, divide, spread
07 break up, diffuse, disband
08 disperse, separate, sprinkle
09 broadcast, dissipate
11 disseminate

scatterbrained
08 carefree, careless
09 forgetful, frivolous, impulsive, slaphappy
11 empty-headed, hare-brained, thoughtless
12 absent-minded
13 wool-gathering
14 feather-brained

scattering
03 few
07 break-up, handful
10 smattering, sprinkling

scavenge
04 hunt, rake
06 forage, search

scavenger
05 raker
07 forager

scenario
04 plan, plot
05 scene, state
06 résumé, scheme, script
07 outline, summary
08 sequence, synopsis
09 situation, storyline
10 projection, screenplay

scene
03 act, set
04 area, clip, fuss, part, show, site, spot, to-do, view
05 arena, drama, field, place, sight, stage, vista
06 furore, locale, milieu
07 context, display, episode, outlook, pageant, picture, scenery, setting, tableau
08 backdrop, division, incident, locality, location, outburst, panorama, position, prospect

09 commotion, kerfuffle, landscape, situation, spectacle
10 background, exhibition, proceeding, speciality
11 environment, performance
14 area of activity, area of interest

scenery
03 set
04 view
05 scene, vista
08 backdrop, panorama, prospect
09 landscape
10 background
11 mise-en-scène

scenic
05 grand
09 beautiful, panoramic
10 attractive, impressive
11 picturesque, spectacular

scent
04 nose
05 aroma, odour, smell, sniff
06 detect
07 cologne, discern, essence, perfume
08 perceive, sniff out
09 fragrance
11 toilet water
12 eau-de-cologne

scented
08 aromatic, fragrant, perfumed
13 sweet-smelling

sceptic
05 cynic
07 atheist, doubter, scoffer
08 agnostic
11 disbeliever, rationalist
14 doubting Thomas

sceptical
07 cynical, dubious
08 doubtful, doubting
11 distrustful, incredulous, questioning, unbelieving, unconvinced
12 disbelieving

scepticism
05 doubt
07 atheism, dubiety
08 cynicism, distrust, unbelief
09 disbelief
11 agnosticism, incredulity

schedule
04 book, list, plan
05 diary
06 agenda, scheme

08 calendar, organize, syllabus
09 catalogue, inventory, itinerary, programme, timetable

schematic
07 graphic
08 symbolic
12 diagrammatic, illustrative

scheme
03 map
04 idea, plan, plot, ploy, ruse
05 chart, draft, frame
06 design, device, devise, layout, method, schema, sketch, system, tactic
07 connive, diagram, project, tactics, work out
08 conspire, contrive, intrigue, proposal, schedule, strategy
09 blueprint, manoeuvre, procedure, programme, stratagem
10 conspiracy, manipulate, mastermind, suggestion
11 arrangement, proposition
14 course of action

schemer
03 fox
07 plotter, wangler
08 conniver, deceiver
09 intriguer
10 machinator, mastermind, politician, wire-puller
11 Machiavelli
13 éminence grise

scheming
03 sly
04 foxy, wily
06 artful, crafty, tricky
07 cunning, devious
08 slippery
09 conniving, underhand
11 calculating, duplicitous
13 Machiavellian

schism
04 rift, sect
05 break, group, split
06 breach
07 discord, faction, rupture
08 disunion, division, splinter
10 detachment, separation

scholar
05 pupil
06 expert, pundit
07 egghead, learner, student
08 academic, bookworm
09 authority, schoolboy
10 mastermind, schoolgirl
11 philosopher, schoolchild
12 intellectual

scholarly
06 school
07 bookish, erudite, learned
08 academic, highbrow, lettered, studious, well-read
10 scholastic, scientific
12 intellectual
13 knowledgeable

scholarship
05 award, grant
06 wisdom
07 bursary
09 education, erudition, knowledge
10 exhibition, fellowship

scholastic
07 bookish, learned, precise
08 academic
09 pedagogic, scholarly
11 educational

school
05 class, coach, drill, guild, teach, train, tutor, verse
06 circle, clique, league, pupils
07 academy, college, company, coterie, educate, faction, faculty, prepare, society
08 instruct, seminary, students
09 institute
10 university

► *Names of famous schools*:
04 Eton
05 Rugby, Slade
06 Harrow
07 Roedean, St Paul's
08 Bluecoat
10 Ampleforth, Shrewsbury, Stonyhurst, Winchester
11 Giggleswick, Gordonstoun, Marlborough, Westminster
12 Charterhouse

schooling
05 drill
07 tuition
08 coaching, guidance, learning, teaching, training
09 education, grounding
11 instruction, preparation
12 book-learning

schoolteacher
06 master
07 teacher
08 educator, mistress
09 pedagogue
10 instructor, schoolmarm
12 schoolmaster
14 schoolmistress

science
03 art
05 skill

09 expertise, technique
10 discipline, technology

► *Sciences include*:
06 botany
07 anatomy, biology, ecology, geology, physics, zoology
08 genetics, robotics
09 acoustics, astronomy, chemistry, dietetics, economics, mechanics, pathology, sociology
10 biophysics, entomology, geophysics, hydraulics, metallurgy, mineralogy, morphology, physiology, psychology, toxicology
11 aeronautics, archaeology, climatology, cybernetics, electronics, engineering, food science, life science, linguistics, mathematics, meteorology, ornithology
12 aerodynamics, anthropology, astrophysics, biochemistry, earth science, geochemistry, macrobiotics, microbiology, pharmacology
14 medical science, natural science, nuclear physics, thermodynamics
15 computer science, domestic science, electrodynamics, space technology

scientific
05 exact
07 orderly, precise
08 accurate, thorough
09 regulated, scholarly
10 methodical, systematic
12 mathematical

► *Names of scientific instruments*:
06 strobe
07 coherer, vernier
08 barostat, cryostat, rheocord, rheostat
09 heliostat, hydrostat, hygrostat, image tube, microtome, slide-rule, telemeter, tesla coil
10 centrifuge, collimator, eudiometer, heliograph, humidistat, hydrophone, hydroscope, hygrograph, pantograph, radarscope, radiosonde, tachograph, thermostat
11 chronograph, fluoroscope, stroboscope, transformer, transponder, tunnel diode

12 oscillograph, oscilloscope, spectroscope
14 image converter, interferometer

scientist see **anatomy**; **anthropologist**; **archaeology**; **astronomer**; **bacteriologist**; **biochemist**; **biology**; **botanist**; **chemistry**; **computer**; **economist**; **engineer**; **geneticist**; **geography**; **inventor**; **mathematics**; **palaeontologist**; **physics**; **physiologist**; **psychology**; **zoologist**

scintillate
05 blaze, flash, gleam, glint, shine, spark
07 glisten, glitter, sparkle, twinkle
09 coruscate

scintillating
05 witty
06 bright, lively
07 shining
08 animated, dazzling
09 brilliant, sparkling, vivacious
10 glittering
12 exhilarating, invigorating

scion
04 heir, twig
05 child, graft, shoot
06 branch, sprout
08 offshoot
09 offspring, successor
10 descendant

scoff
03 eat, rib
04 bolt, eats, food, gibe, grub, gulp, jeer, mock, wolf
05 scorn, sneer
06 deride, gobble, guzzle
07 consume, laugh at, poke fun
08 eatables, ridicule
09 disparage, finish off, nutriment
10 foodstuffs, provisions
11 comestibles, nourishment

scoffing
07 cynical, mocking
08 derisive, scathing, sneering
11 disparaging

scold
03 nag
05 blame, chide
06 berate, rebuke
07 censure, lecture, reprove, tell off, tick off, upbraid

08 lambaste, reproach
09 castigate, reprimand
10 take to task

scolding
06 rebuke
07 lecture, reproof, wigging
09 reprimand, talking-to
10 telling-off, ticking-off
12 dressing-down

scoop
03 dig, dip
04 bail, coup
05 empty, gouge, ladle, spoon
06 bailer, bucket, dipper, exposé, hollow, latest, remove, scrape, shovel
08 excavate
09 exclusive, sensation
10 revelation
11 inside story

scoot
03 run, zip
04 bolt, dart, dash, rush, scud
05 hurry, shoot
06 beat it, career, scurry, sprint, tootle
07 scarper, scuttle, vamoose
09 skedaddle

scope
04 area, room, span
05 ambit, field, orbit, range, reach, realm, space, sweep
06 extent, leeway, limits, sphere
07 breadth, compass, freedom, liberty
08 capacity, confines, coverage, latitude
09 elbow-room
11 opportunity

scorch
04 burn, char, sear
05 dry up, parch, roast, scald, singe
06 wither
07 blacken, shrivel
09 discolour

scorching
06 baking, red-hot, torrid
07 boiling, burning, searing
08 roasting, sizzling, tropical
10 blistering, sweltering

score
03 cut, get, set, sum, win
04 case, earn, gain, gash, hits, line, lots, make, mark, nick, runs, slit
05 adapt, basis, count, goals, gouge, graze, hosts, issue,

marks, notch, slash, tally, total, write
06 aspect, attain, crowds, droves, groove, grudge, incise, indent, masses, matter, points, reason, record, result, scrape
07 achieve, arrange, be one up, chalk up, concern, dispute, engrave, grounds, notch up, outcome, quarrel, scratch, subject
08 argument, hundreds, incision, millions, question, register
09 complaint, grievance, thousands
10 instrument, keep a tally, multitudes
11 explanation, have the edge, orchestrate
13 hit the jackpot

❑score off
09 humiliate
11 have the edge
12 get one over on

❑score out
05 erase
06 cancel, delete, efface, remove
07 expunge
08 cross out
09 strike out
10 obliterate

scorn
04 mock, shun
05 spurn
06 deride, rebuff
07 disdain, disgust, dismiss, mockery, sarcasm, scoff at, sneer at, sniff at
08 contempt, derision, ridicule
09 contumely, disparage
10 look down on
11 haughtiness

scornful
07 haughty, jeering, mocking
08 arrogant, derisive, scathing, scoffing, sneering
09 insulting, sarcastic, slighting
10 disdainful, dismissive
11 disparaging
12 contemptuous, supercilious

scornfully
09 haughtily
10 arrogantly, scathingly
12 disdainfully, dismissively
13 disparagingly
14 contemptuously

scot-free
04 safe
06 unhurt
08 unharmed
09 uninjured, unscathed
10 unpunished
15 without a scratch

scoundrel
03 rat
04 scab
05 cheat, louse, rogue, scamp, swine
06 rascal, rotter
07 bounder, dastard, ruffian, stinker, villain
08 blighter, vagabond
09 miscreant, reprobate, scallywag
10 ne'er-do-well
14 good-for-nothing

scour
03 rub
04 comb, drag, hunt, rake, wash, wipe
05 clean, flush, purge, scrub
06 abrade, forage, polish, scrape, search
07 burnish, cleanse, rummage

scourge
04 bane, beat, cane, evil, flog, lash, whip
05 birch, curse, flail, strap, trial
06 burden, menace, plague, punish, switch, terror, thrash
07 afflict, torment, torture
08 chastise, nuisance
09 devastate, flagellum
10 affliction, discipline, misfortune, punishment
13 cat-o'-nine-tails

scout
03 spy
04 case, hunt, look, seek
05 probe, recce, snoop, watch
06 escort, search, spy out, survey
07 explore, inspect, look for, lookout, observe, spotter
08 check out, vanguard
11 investigate, reconnoitre
13 talent spotter

scowl
04 lour, pout
05 frown, glare
06 glower
07 grimace

scrabble
03 dig, paw
04 claw, grub, root
05 grope

06 scrape
07 clamber, scratch

scraggy
04 bony, lean, thin
06 skinny, wasted
07 angular, scrawny
09 emaciated

scram
04 bolt, flee, quit
06 beat it, depart, go away
07 do a bunk, scarper
08 clear off, clear out, shove off
09 disappear, skedaddle
15 take to your heels

scramble
03 mix, run, vie
04 dash, push, race, rush
05 climb, crawl, grope, hurry,
   mix up, mêlée, scale, vying
06 battle, bustle, hasten, hustle,
   infuse, jockey, jostle, jumble,
   muddle, scurry, strive, tussle
07 clamber, compete, contend,
   disturb, scaling, shuffle
10 free-for-all

scrap
03 axe, bit, row
04 atom, bite, bits, drop, dump,
   iota, junk, mite, shed, tiff
05 argue, brawl, crumb, ditch,
   fight, grain, piece, set-to,
   shred, trace, waste
06 bicker, cancel, dust-up,
   fracas, morsel, sliver, tatter
07 abandon, discard, dispute,
   punch-up, quarrel, remains,
   remnant, scuffle, snippet,
   vestige, wrangle
08 argument, chuck out,
   disagree, fraction, fragment,
   jettison, leavings, mouthful,
   particle, squabble, write off
09 leftovers
11 odds and ends, odds and sods
13 bits and pieces

❑**on the scrap heap**
09 discarded, forgotten,
   redundant
10 jettisoned, written off

scrape
03 cut, fix, rub
04 bark, file, rasp, skin
05 clean, erase, grate, graze,
   grind, scour, scuff, shave
06 abrade, pickle, plight
07 dilemma, scratch, trouble
08 abrasion, distress, scrabble
09 tight spot
10 difficulty
11 predicament

❑**scrape by**
05 get by, skimp
06 scrimp

❑**scrape through**
08 just pass
09 barely win

❑**scrape together**
07 round up
11 get together
12 pool together

scrappy
05 bitty
06 untidy
07 sketchy
08 slapdash, slipshod
09 piecemeal
10 disjointed, incomplete
11 fragmentary

scratch
03 cut, rub
04 claw, etch, gash, line, mark,
   nick, skin, tear
05 gouge, graze, rough, score,
   scuff, wound
06 abrade, incise, scrape
07 engrave
08 abrasion, lacerate
09 haphazard, impromptu
10 improvised, laceration
13 rough-and-ready

❑**up to scratch**
02 OK
08 adequate
09 competent, tolerable
10 acceptable, good enough
12 satisfactory

scrawl
03 jot, pen
06 doodle
07 dash off, jot down, scratch,
   writing
08 scrabble, scribble, squiggle
10 cacography
11 handwriting

scrawny
04 bony, lean, thin
05 lanky
06 skinny
07 angular, scraggy
08 raw-boned
09 emaciated

scream
03 cry, wit
04 bawl, hoot, howl, riot, roar,
   wail, yawp, yell, yelp
05 comic, joker, laugh, shout
06 holler, shriek, squeal
07 screech
08 comedian

screech
03 cry
04 howl, yell, yelp
06 shriek, squeal

screen
03 net, vet
04 hide, mask, mesh, scan,
   show, sift, sort, test, veil
05 blind, check, cloak, cover,
   front, gauge, grade, guard,
   shade, sieve
06 awning, canopy, defend,
   façade, filter, riddle, shield,
   shroud
07 conceal, curtain, divider,
   netting, protect, shelter
08 disguise, evaluate
09 partition, safeguard
10 camouflage, protection

❑**screen off**
04 hide
06 divide
07 conceal
08 fence off, separate
09 divide off
12 partition off

screenwriter see
playwright

screw
03 fix, pin
04 bolt, brad, milk, nail, tack,
   turn, wind
05 bleed, force, rivet, twist
06 adjust, extort, fasten
07 distort, extract, squeeze,
   tighten, wrinkle
08 compress, contract, fastener

❑**put the screws on**
05 force
06 coerce, compel, lean on
07 dragoon

❑**screw up**
05 botch, spoil
06 bungle, mess up
07 contort, crumple, distort,
   louse up, tighten, wrinkle
09 mishandle, mismanage
11 make a hash of

screwy
03 mad, odd
04 daft
05 batty, crazy, dotty, nutty,
   queer, weird
08 crackers
09 eccentric
12 round the bend
13 round the twist

scribble
03 jot, pen

scribbler

05 write
06 doodle, scrawl
07 dash off, jot down, writing
08 scrabble, squiggle
10 cacography
11 handwriting

scribbler

04 hack
06 writer
09 pen-pusher, pot-boiler

scribe

04 hack
05 clerk
06 author, writer
07 copyist
08 recorder, reporter
09 pen-pusher, secretary
10 amanuensis

scrimmage

03 row
04 fray, riot
05 brawl, fight, melee, scrap, set-to
07 scuffle
08 skirmish, squabble, struggle
10 free-for-all
11 disturbance

scrimp

04 save
05 limit, pinch, skimp, stint
06 reduce, scrape
07 curtail
08 restrict
09 cut back on, economize
15 tighten your belt

script

07 letters, writing
08 dialogue, libretto, longhand
10 manuscript, screenplay
11 calligraphy, handwriting

scripture

➤ *Sacred writings of religions*:
02 NT, OT
05 Bayan, Bible, Koran, Qur'an, Torah, Vedas, Zohar, sutra
06 Gemara, Granth, Hadith, I Ching, Mishna, Talmud, Tantra, gospel
07 Puranas, Shari'ah, epistle
08 Haft Wadi, Halakhah, Ramayana
09 Adi Granth, Apocrypha, Decalogue, Digambara, Hexateuch, Tripitaka, scripture
10 Heptateuch, Lotus Sutra, Pentateuch, Svetambara, Tao-te-ching, Upanishads, Zend-Avesta

11 Bardo Thodol, Mahabharata
12 Bhagavad Gita, New Testament, Old Testament
14 Dead Sea Scrolls, Mahayana Sutras, Revised Version
15 Ten Commandments
➤ See also **religion**

scroll

04 list, roll
05 paper
06 volume
09 inventory, parchment

Scrooge

05 miser
06 meanie
07 niggard
08 tightwad
09 skinflint
10 cheapskate
12 money-grubber, penny-pincher

scrounge

03 beg, bum
05 cadge
06 bludge, borrow, sponge

scrounger

03 bum
06 beggar, cadger
07 bludger, moocher, sponger
10 freeloader

scrub

03 axe, rub
04 bush, drop, wash, wipe
05 brush, clean, scour
06 cancel, delete, forget
07 abandon, abolish, cleanse
09 backwoods, scrubland

scruffy

06 ragged, shabby
07 run-down, unkempt
09 ungroomed
10 bedraggled, down-at-heel
11 dishevelled

scrumptious

05 tasty, yummy
09 delicious
10 delectable, delightful
13 mouth-watering

scrunch

04 chew, mash
05 champ, crush
06 crunch, squash
07 crumple, screw up

scruple

04 balk
05 doubt, qualm
06 ethics, morals, shrink
08 hesitate, hold back
09 misgiving, standards

10 principles, reluctance, think twice, uneasiness
11 compunction, reservation
14 second thoughts

scrupulous

04 nice
05 exact, moral
06 honest, minute, strict
07 careful, ethical, precise
08 rigorous, thorough
10 fastidious, meticulous
11 painstaking, punctilious
13 conscientious

scrutinize

04 scan, sift
05 probe, study
06 go over, peruse, search
07 analyse, examine, explore, inspect, run over
08 look over

scrutiny

05 probe, study
06 search
07 inquiry, perusal
08 analysis
10 inspection
11 examination, exploration

scud

03 fly
04 blow, dart, race, sail, skim
05 shoot, speed

scuff

04 drag
05 brush, graze
06 abrade, scrape
07 scratch

scuffle

03 row
04 fray
05 brawl, clash, fight, scrap, set-to
06 affray, dust-up, rumpus, tussle
08 struggle
09 commotion
11 disturbance

sculpt

03 cut, hew
04 cast, form
05 carve, model, mould, shape
06 chisel
07 fashion
09 sculpture

sculpture

➤ See also **art**

➤ *Names of sculptors*:
03 **Arp** (Hans)

04 **Caro** (Sir Anthony), **Gabo** (Naum), **Mach** (David), **Rude** (François)
05 **Andre** (Carl), **Beuys** (Joseph), **Frink** (Dame Elizabeth), **Manzú** (Giacomo), **Moore** (Henry), **Myron**, **Rodin** (Auguste)
06 **Calder** (Alexander), **Canova** (Antonio), **Deacon** (Richard), **Kapoor** (Anish), **Marini** (Marino), **Pisano** (Andrea), **Pisano** (Giovanni), **Scopas**
07 **Bernini** (Gianlorenzo), **Cellini** (Benvenuto), **Christo**, **Duchamp** (Marcel), **Epstein** (Sir Jacob), **Gormley** (Antony), **Phidias**
08 **Brancusi** (Constantin), **Chadwick** (Lynn), **Ghiberti** (Lorenzo), **Hepworth** (Dame Barbara), **Landseer** (Sir Edwin), **Paolozzi** (Eduardo Luigi), **Pheidias**, **Tinguely** (Jean)
09 **Borromini** (Francesco), **Bourgeois** (Louise), **Donatello**, **Roubiliac** (Louis François), **Whiteread** (Rachel)
10 **Giacometti** (Alberto), **Polyclitus**, **Praxiteles**, **Schwitters** (Kurt), **Verrocchio** (Andrea del)
11 **Goldsworthy** (Andy)
12 **Michelangelo**
15 **Leonardo da Vinci**

► *Names of sculptures:*
04 Adam
05 Angel, Cupid, David, House, Medea, Pieta, Torso
07 Bacchus, Genesis, Mercury, Merzbau, Spiders, The Kiss, The Wall
08 Ecce Homo, Have Pity!, Piscator
09 A Universe, Seated Man, Slate Cone
10 Double Talk, Ledge Piece, Running Man, Single Form, The Thinker
11 Kiss and Tell
12 Feast of Herod
13 Fallen Warrior
14 Cosimo de' Medici, Fontana Magiore, Japanese War God, Sailing Tonight, The Age of Bronze, The Gates of Hell

15 Athena Promachos, Christ in Majesty, Figure and Clouds, Recumbent Figure

scum
04 film, foam
05 dregs, dross, froth, trash
06 rabble
07 rubbish
08 riff-raff
10 impurities
14 dregs of society, lowest of the low

scupper
04 foil, ruin, sink
05 wreck
07 destroy, disable, scuttle
08 demolish, submerge
09 overthrow, overwhelm

scurf
05 scale
06 furfur
08 dandruff
09 flakiness, scaliness
12 scabrousness

scurfy
05 flaky, scaly
06 scabby
09 furfurous

scurrility
05 abuse
07 obloquy
08 foulness, rudeness
09 nastiness, vulgarity
10 coarseness
11 abusiveness
12 vituperation
13 offensiveness

scurrilous
04 foul, rude
06 coarse, vulgar
07 abusive, obscene
09 insulting, libellous, offensive
10 defamatory, scandalous, slanderous
11 disparaging
12 vituperative

scurry
04 dart, dash, race, rush, scud, skim, trot
05 hurry, scoot, whirl
06 bustle, flurry, hasten, sprint
07 scamper, scuttle

scurvy
04 base, mean, vile
05 dirty, sorry
06 abject, rotten, shabby
07 low-down
10 despicable
12 contemptible

scuttle
05 hurry
06 bustle, hasten, scurry
07 scamper, scutter
08 scramble

sea
04 deep, host, main, mass, salt
05 briny, ocean
06 afloat
07 aquatic, expanse, oceanic
09 abundance, multitude, profusion, saltwater, seafaring

► *Names of seas. We have omitted the word* **sea** *from names given in the following list but you may need to include this word as part of the solution to some crossword clues.*
03 Red
04 Aral, Azov, Dead, Java, Kara, Ross
05 Black, Coral, Irish, Japan, North, South, Timor, White
06 Aegean, Baltic, Bering, Ionian, Tasman, Yellow
07 Andaman, Arabian, Barents, Caspian, Celebes, Galilee, Marmara, Okhotsk, Weddell
08 Adriatic, Beaufort, Bismarck, Labrador, Ligurian, Sargasso
09 Caribbean, Greenland, Norwegian
10 South China, Tyrrhenian
13 Mediterranean
➢ See also **ocean**

❑**at sea**
06 adrift
07 baffled, puzzled
08 confused
09 mystified, perplexed
10 bewildered

seafaring
05 naval
06 marine
07 oceanic, sailing
08 maritime, nautical
10 ocean-going

seal
04 cork, plug, shut, stop
05 close, stamp
06 clinch, fasten, ratify, secure, settle, signet, stop up
07 close up, stopper, tighten
08 conclude, finalize, insignia
09 assurance
10 imprimatur, waterproof

11 attestation
12 ratification
14 authentication

□**seal off**
06 cut off
07 block up, isolate, shut off
08 close off, fence off
09 cordon off, segregate
10 quarantine

sealed
04 shut
06 closed, corked
08 hermetic

seam
04 join, line, lode, vein, weld
05 joint, layer
07 closure, stratum
08 junction

seaman
02 AB
03 tar
06 rating, sailor, sea dog
07 Jack tar, matelot
08 deck hand, seafarer

seamy
05 nasty, rough
06 sleazy, sordid
07 squalid
09 unsavoury
12 disreputable

sear
03 fry
04 burn, char, seal, wilt
05 brand, brown, singe
06 scorch, sizzle, wither
09 cauterize

search
03 pry
04 comb, hunt, look, seek, sift
05 check, frisk, probe, quest,
   rifle, scour
06 forage, survey
07 examine, explore, inquire,
   inquiry, inspect, pursuit,
   ransack, rifling, rummage
08 research, scrutiny
10 inspection, ransacking,
   scrutinize
11 examination, exploration,
   investigate, look through
13 investigation

searching
06 intent, minute
07 probing
08 piercing, thorough
11 penetrating

seaside
05 beach, coast, sands, shore
08 littoral, seashore

season
03 age
04 salt, span, term, time
05 pep up, phase, ripen, spell,
   spice, treat
06 harden, mature, mellow,
   period, temper
07 flavour, prepare, toughen

□**in season**
09 available
10 obtainable
11 on the market

seasonable
06 timely
07 fitting, welcome
09 opportune, well-timed
12 providential

seasoned
06 mature
07 veteran
08 hardened
09 practised, weathered
10 habituated
11 conditioned, established,
   experienced, long-serving
12 acclimatized

seasoning
04 salt
05 herbs, sauce, spice
06 pepper, relish
09 condiment
10 flavouring

seat
03 fit, fix, hub, pew, put, set, sit
04 axis, base, form, hold, site,
   take
05 bench, cause, chair, heart,
   house, place, stall, stool
06 bottom, centre, ground,
   locate, origin, reason, settle,
   source, throne
07 contain, deposit, footing,
   install, mansion
08 location, position
09 residence, situation
10 foundation
11 accommodate, stately home

seating
05 seats
06 chairs, places
13 accommodation

seaweed
04 alga
05 varec, vraic
06 varech
07 seaware

► *Types of seaweed*:
05 laver, wrack
06 tangle

07 oarweed, sea moss
08 gulfweed, sargasso
09 carrageen, coral weed, Irish
   moss
12 bladder wrack, peacock's
   tail
► See also **plant**

secede
04 quit
05 break, leave
06 resign, retire
08 separate, split off, withdraw
09 break away

secession
05 break, split
06 schism
09 breakaway, defection
10 withdrawal

secluded
06 hidden, lonely, remote
07 private
08 isolated, shut away, solitary
09 concealed, sheltered
10 cloistered
11 out-of-the-way, sequestered
12 unfrequented

seclusion
06 hiding
07 privacy, retreat, secrecy,
   shelter
08 solitude
09 isolation
10 remoteness, retirement
13 sequestration

second
03 aid
04 back, help, move, next,
   send, tick, twin
05 extra, flash, jiffy, lower, other,
   shift, trice
06 assign, assist, back up, back-
   up, backer, change, double,
   helper, lesser, minute,
   moment
07 advance, approve, endorse,
   forward, further, instant,
   promote, support
08 inferior, relocate, repeated,
   transfer
09 agree with, alternate,
   assistant, attendant,
   duplicate, encourage,
   following, secondary,
   supporter, twinkling
10 additional, subsequent,
   succeeding, supporting
11 alternative, split second,
   subordinate
13 supplementary

secondary
05 extra, lower, minor, spare
06 back-up, lesser, relief, second
07 derived, reserve
08 indirect, inferior
09 ancillary, auxiliary, resulting
10 derivative, subsidiary, supporting
11 alternative, subordinate, unimportant

second-class
08 inferior, mediocre
11 indifferent, unimportant
15 undistinguished

second-hand
03 old
04 used, worn
08 borrowed, indirect
09 nearly-new, vicarious
10 hand-me-down

second-in-command
06 backer, helper
09 assistant, attendant, supporter

second-rate
04 poor, ropy
05 cheap, lousy, tacky
06 lesser, shoddy, tawdry, tinpot
08 inferior, low-grade, mediocre
11 substandard

secrecy
07 mystery, privacy, stealth
09 seclusion
10 confidence, covertness
11 concealment, furtiveness
15 confidentiality

secret
03 key, sly
04 code, deep
05 close
06 answer, arcane, closet, covert, cut off, enigma, hidden, lonely, occult, recipe, remote, unseen
07 cryptic, furtive, mystery, private, unknown
08 abstruse, discreet, hush-hush, isolated, secluded, shrouded, shut away, stealthy
09 concealed, disguised, recondite, sensitive, sheltered, underhand
10 backstairs, classified, cloistered, confidence, mysterious, restricted, undercover, unrevealed

11 camouflaged, clandestine, inside story, underground, undisclosed, unpublished
12 confidential, unfrequented
13 hole-and-corner, private matter, surreptitious
14 cloak-and-dagger
15 between you and me, under-the-counter

▢**in secret**
07 on the q.t., privily, quietly
08 covertly, in camera
10 on the quiet, under cover, unobserved
12 hugger-mugger

secretary
02 PA
05 clerk
06 typist
10 amanuensis

secrete
04 bury, emit, hide, leak, ooze, take
05 cache, cover, exude, leach
06 screen, shroud
07 conceal, cover up, emanate, excrete, give off, produce, release, send out
09 discharge, stash away

secretion
07 leakage, osmosis, release
08 emission
09 discharge, emanation, exudation

secretive
04 deep
05 cagey, close, quiet
07 cryptic
08 reserved, reticent, taciturn
09 enigmatic, withdrawn
11 tight-lipped
15 uncommunicative

secretly
07 on the q.t., privily, quietly
08 covertly, in camera
09 furtively, in private, privately
10 on the quiet, stealthily, under cover, unobserved
12 in confidence
13 clandestinely
14 confidentially
15 surreptitiously

sect
04 camp, cult, wing
05 group, order, party
06 school
07 faction
12 denomination
13 splinter group

sectarian
05 bigot
06 narrow, zealot
07 bigoted, fanatic, insular
08 cliquish, partisan
09 exclusive, factional, fanatical, parochial
12 narrow-minded
13 fractionalist

section
03 bit
04 area, part, wing, zone
05 piece, slice
06 branch, region, sector
07 chapter, passage, portion, segment
08 district, division, fraction, fragment
09 component, paragraph
10 department, instalment

sectional
05 class, local
06 racial
07 divided, partial
08 regional, separate
09 exclusive, factional, localized, sectarian
10 separatist

sector
04 area, part, zone
05 field
06 branch, region
07 quarter, section
08 category, district, division
11 subdivision

secular
03 lay
05 civil, state
07 earthly, profane, worldly
08 temporal
12 non-religious, non-spiritual

secure
03 fix, get, tie
04 bolt, fast, firm, gain, land, lash, lock, moor, nail, safe, shut, sure
05 chain, close, fixed, guard, rivet, solid, tight
06 assure, attach, closed, come by, defend, ensure, fasten, locked, screen, sealed, steady, sturdy
07 acquire, assured, certain, confirm, padlock, procure, relaxed, settled, sponsor
08 definite, fastened, make fast, make safe, unharmed
09 confident, contented, establish, get hold of, guarantee, protected,

reassured, safeguard, steadfast
10 batten down, conclusive, underwrite
11 impregnable, well-founded

security
04 care, ease, gage
05 cover
06 asylum, pledge, refuge, safety, surety
07 custody, defence
08 immunity, warranty
09 assurance, guarantee, insurance, safeguard
10 collateral, protection, safeguards
11 peace of mind, precautions, safe-keeping
12 preservation, surveillance
15 invulnerability

sedate
04 calm
05 quiet, sober, staid, stiff
06 demure, pacify, seemly, serene, soothe
08 composed, tranquil
09 collected, dignified
11 unflappable
12 tranquillize

sedative
06 downer, opiate
07 anodyne, calming
08 lenitive, narcotic, relaxing, soothing
09 calmative, soporific
11 barbiturate
12 sleeping-pill
13 tranquillizer

sedentary
05 still
06 seated
07 sitting
08 immobile, inactive
09 desk-bound

sediment
04 lees, silt
05 dregs
07 deposit, grounds, residue
08 residuum
11 precipitate

sedition
06 mutiny, revolt
07 treason
09 agitation, rebellion
10 disloyalty, subversion
11 fomentation
13 rabble-rousing

seditious
08 disloyal, inciting, mutinous

09 agitating, dissident, fomenting
10 rebellious, subversive
13 revolutionary
15 insurrectionist

seduce
04 lure, ruin
05 charm, tempt
06 allure, entice
07 attract, beguile, corrupt, deceive, deprave, ensnare, mislead
08 inveigle

seducer
04 goat, wolf
05 flirt
07 charmer, Don Juan
08 Casanova, Lothario
09 libertine, womanizer
11 philanderer

seduction
04 lure
06 allure, appeal, come-on
10 allurement, corruption, enticement, temptation
11 beguilement

seductive
04 sexy
06 sultry
08 alluring, enticing, inviting
09 beguiling
10 attractive, bewitching, come-hither
11 flirtatious, provocative

seductress
04 vamp
05 Circe, siren
07 Lorelei
09 temptress
11 femme fatale

sedulous
08 diligent, tireless, untiring
09 assiduous, laborious
10 determined, persistent
11 industrious, persevering
13 conscientious

see
04 espy, know, lead, meet, note, show, spot, view
05 grasp, sight, visit, watch
06 behold, decide, fathom, follow, look at, notice, regard, take in
07 discern, find out, glimpse, make out, observe, picture, realize, witness
08 consider, envisage, forecast, perceive

09 ascertain, interview, recognize, set eyes on, visualize
10 appreciate, comprehend, get a look at, understand
11 distinguish, investigate
12 catch sight of

❑ see about
06 manage, repair
07 arrange, sort out
08 attend to, deal with, organize
09 look after
10 take care of

❑ see through
07 persist, realize
08 stick out
09 get wise to, not give up, persevere
14 not be taken in by
15 not be deceived by

❑ see to
03 fix
06 ensure, manage, repair
07 arrange, sort out
08 attend to, deal with, make sure, organize
09 look after
10 take care of
11 make certain

seed
03 egg, pip
04 germ, ovum, root
05 cause, child, grain, heirs, ovule, semen, spawn, sperm, start, stone, young
06 embryo, family, kernel, origin, reason, source
07 nucleus, reasons
08 children, young one
09 beginning, offspring, young ones
10 successors
11 descendants
12 spermatozoon

❑ go to seed, run to seed
05 decay
07 decline
08 get worse
10 degenerate, go downhill

seedy
03 ill
04 sick
05 dirty, mangy, rough, tatty
06 ailing, grotty, poorly, shabby, unwell
07 run-down, scruffy, squalid
09 off-colour
10 out of sorts
11 dilapidated

seek
03 aim, ask, beg, try
04 want
06 aspire, desire, follow, invite, pursue, strive
07 attempt, entreat, hunt for, inquire, look for, request, solicit
09 endeavour, search for

seeker
05 chela
06 novice
07 student, zetetic
08 disciple, inquirer, searcher

seem
04 feel, look
05 sound
06 appear
08 look like
11 pretend to be

seeming
05 quasi-
06 pseudo
07 assumed, outward, surface
08 apparent, external, specious, supposed
09 pretended
10 ostensible
11 superficial

seemingly
10 apparently, ostensibly
12 on the surface
13 on the face of it, superficially

seemly
03 fit
04 meet, nice
06 decent, proper
07 fitting
08 becoming, decorous, suitable
09 befitting
11 appropriate

seep
04 drip, leak, ooze, soak, well
08 permeate
09 percolate

seepage
04 leak
06 oozing
07 leakage, osmosis
08 dripping
11 percolation

seer
05 augur, sibyl
07 prophet, spaeman
08 spaewife
10 soothsayer

seesaw
04 yo-yo

05 pitch, swing
09 alternate, fluctuate, oscillate

seethe
04 boil, fizz, foam, fume, rage, rise, teem
05 froth, storm, surge, swarm, swell
06 bubble, see red, simmer
07 be livid, explode, ferment
08 boil over, smoulder
10 effervesce

see-through
05 filmy, gauzy, sheer
06 flimsy
08 gossamer
11 translucent, transparent

segment
05 slice, wedge
06 divide
07 portion, section
08 division, separate
11 compartment

segregate
06 cut off
07 exclude, isolate
08 separate, set apart
09 keep apart
10 dissociate, quarantine

segregation
09 apartheid, isolation
10 quarantine, separation
12 dissociation, setting apart
13 sequestration
14 discrimination

seize
03 nab
04 grab, grip, hold, nail, take
05 annex, catch, grasp, usurp
06 abduct, arrest, clutch, collar, hijack, kidnap, snatch
07 capture, impound
09 apprehend, get hold of
10 commandeer, confiscate
11 appropriate, sequestrate

seizure
03 fit
05 spasm
06 arrest, attack, hijack, taking
07 capture
08 paroxysm
10 convulsion

seldom
06 rarely
10 hardly ever
12 infrequently
15 once in a blue moon

select
03 top
04 best, pick, posh

05 elect, prime, élite
06 choice, choose, favour, finest, invite, opt for, prefer
07 appoint, limited, special
08 decide on, selected, settle on, superior
09 excellent, exclusive, first-rate, single out
10 first-class, hand-picked, privileged
11 high-quality

selection
04 pick
06 choice, line-up, medley, option
09 anthology, potpourri
10 assortment, collection, miscellany, preference

selective
05 fussy, picky
06 choosy
07 careful, finicky
10 fastidious, particular
14 discriminating

self
01 I
03 ego
04 soul
08 identity
11 personality

self-assertive
05 bossy, pushy
07 pushing
08 forceful
10 aggressive, commanding, high-handed, peremptory
11 overbearing, overweening

self-assurance
06 aplomb
09 assurance, cockiness
10 confidence
12 cocksureness
14 self-confidence

self-assured
05 cocky
09 confident
13 sure of oneself

self-centred
07 selfish
09 egotistic
10 egocentric
11 egotistical
12 narcissistic

self-confident
04 bold, cool
07 assured
08 composed, fearless, positive
09 confident, unabashed

self-conscious
03 coy, shy
05 timid
07 awkward, bashful, nervous
08 blushing, insecure, retiring, sheepish, timorous
09 diffident, ill at ease, shrinking
11 embarrassed
13 uncomfortable

self-control
04 cool
08 calmness, patience
09 composure, restraint, willpower
10 temperance
14 self-discipline

self-denial
10 asceticism, moderation, temperance
12 selflessness
13 self-sacrifice, unselfishness
14 abstemiousness, self-abnegation

self-esteem
03 ego
05 pride
07 dignity
11 amour-propre, self-respect

self-evident
08 manifest
09 axiomatic
10 undeniable

self-glorification
07 egotism
09 egotheism

self-government
08 autarchy, autonomy, home rule
09 democracy
12 independence

self-importance
06 vanity
07 conceit, donnism
09 arrogance, cockiness, pomposity, pushiness
13 big-headedness, bumptiousness, conceitedness

self-important
04 vain
05 cocky, proud, pushy
07 pompous
08 arrogant, egoistic
09 conceited, strutting
10 swaggering
13 swollen-headed

self-indulgence
08 hedonism
10 profligacy, sensualism

11 dissipation
12 extravagance, intemperance
13 dissoluteness

self-indulgent
10 dissipated, hedonistic, immoderate, profligate
11 extravagant, intemperate

self-interest
11 self-serving, selfishness

selfish
04 mean
06 greedy
08 covetous
09 egotistic, mercenary
10 egocentric
11 egotistical, self-centred, self-seeking, self-serving
13 inconsiderate

selfishness
05 greed
07 egotism
08 meanness

selfless
08 generous
09 unselfish
10 altruistic
13 philanthropic
15 self-sacrificing

self-possessed
04 calm, cool
06 poised
08 composed, together
09 collected, confident
11 unflappable

self-possession
04 cool
05 poise
06 aplomb
08 calmness, coolness
09 composure, sang-froid
10 confidence
14 unflappability

self-reliance
07 autarky
11 self-support
12 independence
15 self-sufficiency

self-reliant
08 autarkic
10 autarkical
11 independent
14 self-sufficient

self-respect
05 pride
07 dignity
11 amour-propre

self-restraint
07 encraty

08 patience
09 willpower
10 moderation, temperance
11 forbearance
14 abstemiousness

self-righteous
02 pi
04 smug
05 pious
08 priggish, superior
10 complacent, goody-goody
12 hypocritical
13 sanctimonious
14 holier-than-thou

self-righteousness
09 piousness
12 priggishness
14 goody-goodiness
15 pharisaicalness

self-sacrifice
08 altruism
10 generosity
12 selflessness
13 unselfishness

self-satisfaction
05 pride
08 smugness
11 complacency, contentment

self-satisfied
04 smug
05 proud
08 puffed up
10 complacent

self-seeking
07 selfish
09 careerist, mercenary, on the make
11 acquisitive, calculating, gold-digging
13 opportunistic
14 fortune-hunting

self-styled
07 would-be
08 so-called
09 pretended, professed, soi-disant

self-supporting
11 independent
14 self-sufficient

self-willed
06 cussed, wilful
08 stubborn
09 obstinate, pig-headed
10 headstrong, refractory
11 intractable, stiff-necked
12 ungovernable

sell
04 flog, hawk, hype, push, tout, vend
05 carry, stock, trade
06 barter, deal in, export, handle, import, market, peddle, retail
07 auction, promote, trade in, win over
08 exchange, persuade
09 advertise, dispose of, traffic in
11 merchandise

❏ sell out
04 fail
05 rat on
06 betray, fink on
08 run out of
11 double-cross
12 be out of stock
13 stab in the back

seller
06 trader, vendor
08 merchant, stockist, supplier

selling
07 dealing, trading, traffic
09 marketing, promotion
11 trafficking
13 merchandising

semblance
03 air
04 look, mask, show
05 front, guise, image
06 aspect, façade, veneer
08 likeness, pretence
10 apparition, appearance, similarity
11 resemblance

seminal
05 major
08 creative, original, seminary
09 formative, important
10 innovative, productive
11 imaginative, influential

seminary
06 school
07 academy, college
09 institute
15 training-college

send
04 beam, cast, emit, fire, hurl, mail, move, post
05 drive, fling, radio, relay, remit, shoot, throw
06 arouse, convey, direct, excite, get off, launch, propel, thrill, turn on
07 address, consign, deliver, forward, project
08 dispatch, transmit

09 broadcast, discharge
11 communicate
12 put in the mail, put in the post

❏ send for
05 order
06 summon
07 call for, command, request

❏ send up
04 mock
05 mimic
06 parody
07 imitate, take off
08 ridicule, satirize

send-off
05 start
07 goodbye
08 farewell
09 departure
11 leave-taking

send-up
04 skit
05 spoof
06 parody, satire
07 mockery, take-off
09 imitation

senile
03 old
04 aged, gaga
08 confused, decrepit
09 doddering, senescent

senility
06 dotage, old age
09 infirmity
10 senescence
11 decrepitude
14 senile dementia

senior
05 chief, doyen, elder, first, major, older
07 doyenne
08 superior
11 high-ranking

seniority
03 age
04 rank
06 status
08 priority, standing
10 importance, precedence
11 superiority

sensation
05 sense, vibes
06 furore, thrill
07 feeling, success, triumph
09 commotion
10 impression, perception
13 consciousness

sensational
05 lurid
07 amazing
08 dramatic, exciting, stirring
09 startling, thrilling
10 astounding, impressive, scandalous
12 breathtaking, electrifying, melodramatic

sense
03 wit
04 feel, mind, nous, wits
05 brain, drift, grasp, logic, point, savvy, tenor
06 brains, detect, divine, import, intuit, notice, nuance, pick up, reason, wisdom
07 discern, faculty, feeling, meaning, observe, purport, purpose, realize, suspect
08 gumption, perceive, prudence
09 awareness, be aware of, intuition, judgement, sensation, substance
10 appreciate, comprehend, impression, perception
11 common sense
12 appreciation, apprehension, intelligence, significance
13 understanding
14 interpretation

❏ make sense of
05 grasp
06 fathom
07 make out
09 comprehend, figure out

senseless
03 mad, out
04 daft, numb
05 batty, crazy, dotty, silly
06 absurd, futile, stupid, unwise
07 fatuous, foolish, idiotic, moronic, out cold, stunned
08 deadened, mindless
09 illogical, insensate, ludicrous, pointless
10 insensible, irrational, ridiculous
11 nonsensical, unconscious
12 unreasonable
13 anaesthetized

sensibility
05 taste
07 insight
08 delicacy, emotions, feelings
09 awareness, intuition
10 sentiments
11 discernment
12 appreciation
14 susceptibility

sensible
04 sane, wise
05 aware, sharp, sober, sound, tough
06 clever, mature, shrewd, strong
07 logical, prudent, working
08 everyday, ordinary, rational
09 judicious, practical, realistic, sagacious, sensitive
10 discerning, far-sighted, functional, perceptive, reasonable, responsive, vulnerable
11 commonsense, down-to-earth, level-headed, susceptible, well-advised
14 commonsensical

◻**sensible of**
07 alive to, aware of
09 mindful of
11 cognizant of, conscious of, sensitive to

sensitive
04 fine, soft
05 aware, exact
06 tender, touchy, tricky
07 awkward, careful, fragile, precise, tactful
08 delicate, discreet, reactive, sentient
09 difficult, emotional, irritable
10 diplomatic, perceptive, responsive, vulnerable
11 considerate, problematic, susceptible, sympathetic, thin-skinned

sensitivity
08 delicacy, fineness, softness, sympathy
09 awareness, fragility
11 discernment
12 appreciation
14 responsiveness, susceptibility

sensual
04 lewd, sexy
06 animal, bodily, carnal, erotic, sexual, sultry
07 fleshly, lustful, worldly
08 physical
13 self-indulgent

sensuality
08 sexiness
09 animalism, carnality
10 debauchery, profligacy
11 gourmandize, libertinism

sensuous
04 lush, rich
09 pleasant, pleasing

09 aesthetic, luxurious
10 gratifying, voluptuous

sentence
04 doom
05 judge, order
06 decree, punish, ruling
07 condemn, verdict
08 decision, penalize
10 punishment
13 pronouncement
15 pass judgement on

sententious
05 brief, pithy, short, terse
06 gnomic
07 canting, compact, concise, laconic, pointed, pompous, preachy
08 succinct
09 axiomatic
10 aphoristic, moralistic, moralizing
11 judgemental
12 epigrammatic
13 sanctimonious

sentient
04 live
05 aware
09 conscious, sensitive
10 responsive

sentiment
04 idea, view
07 emotion, feeling, opinion, romance, thought
08 attitude, softness
09 judgement
10 persuasion, tenderness
11 mawkishness, point of view, romanticism, sensibility

sentimental
05 corny, gushy, mushy, soppy, weepy
06 loving, sickly, sloppy, slushy, sugary, tender
07 gushing, maudlin, mawkish
08 pathetic, romantic, touching
09 emotional, schmaltzy
10 lovey-dovey
11 soft-hearted, tear-jerking

sentimentality
05 slush
06 bathos
08 schmaltz
10 sloppiness, tenderness
11 mawkishness, romanticism

sentry
05 guard, watch
06 picket
07 lookout
08 sentinel, watchman

separable
09 divisible
10 detachable, particular
11 independent
15 distinguishable

separate
04 part
05 alone, apart, sever, split
06 cut off, detach, divide, remove, single, sunder
07 diverge, divorce, isolate, several, split up
08 abstract, break off, discrete, distinct, disunite, solitary, uncouple, withdraw
09 come apart, disparate, disunited, partition, segregate, take apart, unrelated
10 autonomous, disconnect, disjointed, individual, particular, segregated, unattached
11 disentangle, independent, part company, unconnected
15 become estranged

separated
05 apart
06 parted
07 divided, split up
08 isolated, sundered
09 disunited
10 segregated
12 disconnected

separately
05 alone, apart
06 singly
09 severally
10 discretely, personally
12 individually

separating
08 dividing, divisive
09 isolating
11 intervening, segregating
12 partitioning

separation
03 gap
04 rift
05 split
06 schism
07 break-up, divorce, parting, split-up
09 apartheid, severance
10 detachment, divergence, uncoupling
11 leave-taking, segregation
12 dissociation, estrangement
13 disconnection, disengagement

septic
06 putrid
08 infected, poisoned
09 festering
10 putrefying
11 suppurating
12 putrefactive

sepulchral
05 grave
06 dismal, gloomy, morbid, solemn, sombre, woeful
08 funereal, mournful
10 lugubrious, melancholy

sepulchre
04 tomb
05 grave, vault
09 mausoleum
11 burial place

sequel
06 pay-off, result, upshot
07 outcome
08 follow-up
11 consequence, development
12 continuation

sequence
05 chain, cycle, order, train
06 course, series, string
10 procession, succession
11 consequence, progression

sequester
06 detach, remove
07 impound, isolate, seclude, shut off
08 insulate, set apart
10 commandeer, confiscate

sequestered
06 lonely, remote
07 outback, private, retired
08 isolated, secluded
10 cloistered
11 out-of-the-way

sequestrate
05 seize
07 impound
09 sequester
10 commandeer, confiscate

seraphic
07 angelic, saintly, sublime
08 beatific, blissful, heavenly
09 celestial

serendipity
04 luck
06 chance
07 fortune
08 accident, fortuity
11 coincidence, good fortune

serene
04 calm, cool

08 peaceful, tranquil
09 unclouded, unruffled
11 undisturbed, unflappable
13 imperturbable

serenity
04 calm, cool
05 peace
08 calmness, quietude
09 placidity
12 peacefulness, tranquillity
14 unflappability

serf
05 helot, slave
06 thrall
07 bondman, servant, villein
08 bondmaid, bondsman
09 bond-slave, bondwoman
10 bondswoman
11 bondservant

series
03 row, run, set
04 line
05 chain, cycle, order, train
06 course, stream, string
08 sequence
10 succession
11 arrangement, progression
13 concatenation

serious
04 deep, dour, grim
05 grave, heavy, sober, stern
06 no joke, severe, solemn, sombre
07 crucial, earnest, genuine, pensive, sincere, weighty
08 critical, pressing, worrying
09 difficult, long-faced, momentous, unsmiling
10 humourless, precarious
11 preoccupied, significant
12 life-and-death
13 consequential, of consequence

seriously
05 badly
06 sorely
07 acutely, gravely
08 severely, solemnly
09 earnestly, sincerely
10 critically, grievously
11 dangerously, joking apart
12 thoughtfully
13 distressingly

seriousness
06 moment, weight
07 gravity, urgency
08 gravitas, sobriety
09 solemnity, staidness, sternness
10 importance, sedateness

11 earnestness
14 humourlessness

sermon
06 homily
07 address, lecture, message, oration
08 harangue
09 discourse, talking-to
11 declamation, exhortation

serpentine
05 snaky
07 coiling, crooked, sinuous, snaking, winding
08 tortuous, twisting
09 snakelike
10 meandering

serrated
06 jagged
07 notched, sawlike, toothed
08 indented, saw-edged
10 saw-toothed, serrulated

serried
05 close, dense
06 massed
07 compact, crowded

servant
04 help
06 helper, menial
08 hireling, retainer
09 ancillary, assistant, attendant

serve
03 act, aid
04 help, wait
06 answer, assist, attend, dish up, fulfil, supply, wait on
07 benefit, deliver, dole out, further, give out, perform, present, provide, satisfy, succour, suffice, support, work for
08 carry out, complete, function
09 discharge, go through
10 distribute, minister to, take care of

service
03 job, use
04 army, duty, help, navy, rite, tune, turn, work
06 duties, forces, ritual
07 benefit, repairs, worship
08 air force, ceremony, function, maintain, overhaul
09 advantage, amenities, ordinance, resources, sacrament, servicing, utilities
10 assistance, employment, facilities, usefulness

serviceable
06 usable, useful
09 practical
10 functional
11 utilitarian

servile
03 low
04 base, mean
05 lowly
06 abject, humble, menial
07 fawning, slavish, subject
08 cringing, toadying
10 grovelling, obsequious, submissive
11 bootlicking, subservient, sycophantic

servility
08 baseness, meanness, toadyism
09 abjection
10 sycophancy
12 subservience
13 self-abasement

serving
05 share
06 amount, ration
07 bowlful, helping, portion
08 plateful, spoonful

servitude
06 chains, thrall
07 bondage, serfdom, slavery
08 thraldom
09 obedience, vassalage
10 villeinage
11 enslavement, subjugation

session
04 time, year
05 spell
06 period
07 hearing, meeting, sitting
08 assembly, semester
10 conference, discussion
➤ See also **term**

set
03 fix, gel, kit, lay, put
04 band, firm, gang, give, look, turn, plan, sink
05 batch, begin, class, crowd, fixed, grant, group, place, plonk, ready, rigid, scene, score, start, stock, usual, write
06 adjust, agreed, all set, assign, circle, clique, create, decide, devise, go down, harden, impose, insert, locate, ordain, outfit, prompt, select, series, settle, strict, vanish

07 agree on, appoint, arrange, confirm, congeal, decided, deposit, faction, install, lay down, prepare, produce, provide, regular, resolve, scenery, settled, situate, specify, stiffen, thicken
08 allocate, arranged, backdrop, everyday, finished, get ready, habitual, ordained, organize, position, prepared, regulate, sequence, solidify, standard
09 appointed, coagulate, customary, designate, determine, disappear, establish, ingrained, make ready, prescribe, scheduled, specified, stipulate
10 assemblage, assortment, background, collection, compendium, entrenched, give rise to, inflexible, prescribed
11 crystallize, established, mise-en-scène, prearranged, stereotyped, traditional
12 conventional
13 predetermined

❑**set about**
05 begin, start
06 attack, tackle
08 commence, embark on
09 get down to, undertake

❑**set against**
05 weigh
06 divide, oppose
07 balance, compare
08 contrast, disunite
09 juxtapose

❑**set apart**
07 mark off
08 put aside, separate
11 distinguish
13 differentiate

❑**set aside**
04 keep, save
06 cancel, reject, revoke
07 discard, reserve, reverse
08 abrogate, discount, keep back, lay aside, overrule, overturn, put aside, separate
09 stash away
13 keep in reserve

❑**set back**
04 slow
05 check, delay
06 hinder, hold up, impede, retard, thwart

❑**set down**
04 note
06 affirm, assert, record
07 lay down
08 note down
09 establish, formulate, prescribe, stipulate
12 put in writing

❑**set forth**
05 leave
06 depart
07 expound, present
08 start out
09 delineate, elucidate

❑**set in**
05 begin, start
06 arrive
08 commence

❑**set off**
05 begin, leave, start
06 depart, ignite, prompt
07 display, enhance, explode, show off, trigger
08 activate, contrast, detonate, initiate, start out, touch off
10 trigger off
11 set in motion
15 throw into relief

❑**set on**
06 attack, beat up, turn on
07 assault, lay into, set upon

❑**set out**
05 begin, leave, start
06 depart, lay out
07 arrange, display, exhibit, explain, present
08 describe, start out

❑**set up**
05 array, begin, build, erect, fit up, found, frame, raise, start
07 arrange, elevate, prepare
08 assemble, initiate, organize
09 construct, establish
10 inaugurate
11 incriminate

setback
04 blow, snag
05 delay, hitch, upset
06 hiccup, hold-up
07 reverse
08 reversal
10 impediment

setting
04 site
05 frame, scene
06 locale, milieu
07 context, scenery
08 location, position
10 background

11 environment, mise-en-scène, perspective
12 surroundings

setting-up
08 creation, founding
10 foundation, initiation
12 inauguration, introduction
13 establishment

settle
03 fix, pay
04 drop, fall, foot, land, live, sink
05 agree, clear, order, solve
06 adjust, alight, choose, clinch, decide, occupy, reside, square
07 agree on, appoint, arrange, confirm, cough up, descend, fork out, inhabit, patch up, resolve, subside
08 colonize, complete, conclude, decide on, organize, populate, square up
09 determine, discharge, establish, light upon, reconcile
10 compromise, put in order
12 put down roots

□ **settle down**
05 still
06 soothe
07 compose, quieten
08 calm down

settlement
04 camp
06 colony, hamlet
07 kibbutz, payment, village
08 contract, decision, defrayal
09 agreement, discharge
10 completion, encampment, resolution
11 arrangement, termination
12 colonization
13 establishment
14 reconciliation

settler
07 incomer, pioneer
08 colonist, newcomer, squatter
09 colonizer, immigrant

set-to
03 row
04 spat
05 brush, fight, scrap
06 barney, dust-up, fracas
07 contest, quarrel, wrangle
08 argument, squabble
09 argy-bargy
11 altercation
13 slanging-match

set-up
06 format, system
08 business
09 framework, structure
11 arrangement, disposition
12 organization

sever
03 cut, end
04 chop, hack, part, rend
05 cease, split
06 cleave, cut off, detach, divide, lop off
07 chop off, disjoin, tear off
08 amputate, break off, dissolve, separate
09 terminate
10 disconnect

several
04 a few, many, some
06 sundry
07 diverse, various
08 assorted, distinct, separate
09 a number of, different, disparate, quite a few

severally
06 apiece, singly
08 seriatim
10 discretely, separately
12 individually, particularly, respectively, specifically

severe
04 grim, hard
05 acute, grave, harsh, plain, rigid, stern, tough
06 fierce, strict, strong, taxing
07 arduous, austere, drastic, extreme, intense, serious, Spartan, violent
08 exacting, forceful, pitiless, powerful, rigorous
09 dangerous, demanding, difficult, draconian, merciless, stringent, unbending, unsmiling
10 burdensome, inexorable, relentless, tyrannical
11 strait-laced

severely
04 hard
05 badly
06 grimly, sorely
07 acutely, gravely, harshly, sharply, sternly
08 bitterly, strictly
09 extremely, intensely
10 critically, rigorously
11 dangerously

severity
06 rigour
07 gravity

08 grimness, hardness, strength
09 extremity, harshness, intensity, plainness, sharpness
10 fierceness, Spartanism, strictness, stringency
11 seriousness
12 forcefulness

sew
03 hem
04 darn, mend, seam, tack
05 baste
06 stitch
09 embroider

sex
02 it
05 union
06 coitus, gender, libido
07 coition
08 intimacy, nubility, sexiness
09 sexuality
10 copulation, lovemaking
11 fornication, intercourse
12 reproduction
15 sexual relations

sexless
06 neuter
07 asexual, unsexed
08 unsexual
15 parthenogenetic

sexton
06 fossor, verger
09 caretaker, sacristan
10 grave-maker
11 grave-digger

sexual
06 carnal, coital, erotic
07 genital, sensual
08 venereal
12 reproductive

sexuality
06 desire
08 sexiness, virility
09 carnality, eroticism
10 sensuality
12 sexual desire

sexy
06 erotic, nubile, slinky
07 raunchy, sensual
08 alluring, arousing, beddable
09 desirable, provoking, salacious, seductive
10 suggestive, voluptuous
11 provocative, titillating
12 pornographic

shabby
04 worn
05 dowdy, faded, tatty

06 frayed, ragged, shoddy, unfair
07 scruffy, worn-out
08 shameful, tattered
10 despicable, threadbare
12 contemptible, disreputable
13 dishonourable

shack
03 hut
04 dump, hole, shed
05 cabin, hovel, hutch
06 lean-to, shanty

shackle
03 tie
04 bind, bond, gyve, iron, rope
05 chain, limit
06 fetter, hamper, impede, secure, tether, thwart
07 darbies, manacle, trammel
08 encumber, handcuff, handicap, restrain, restrict
09 bracelets, constrain

shade
03 dim, hue, tad
04 dash, dusk, hide, hint, tint, tone, veil
05 blind, cover, ghost, gloom, tinge, touch, trace, visor
06 awning, canopy, colour, darken, degree, memory, nuance, screen, shadow, shroud, spirit
07 conceal, curtain, dimness, parasol, phantom, protect, shadows, shelter, spectre
08 covering, darkness, gloaming, twilight
09 gradation, obscurity, suspicion
10 apparition, gloominess, overshadow, suggestion
12 semi-darkness

❑ **a shade**
06 a touch
07 a little, a trifle
08 slightly

❑ **put in the shade**
05 dwarf, excel
07 eclipse, outrank, surpass
08 outclass, outshine

shadow
03 dog
04 dusk, hint, tail
05 cloud, gloom, shade, shape, trail, trace
06 darken, follow
07 dimness, remnant, vestige
08 darkness, follower, gloaming, twilight
09 companion, obscurity

10 foreboding, silhouette, suggestion
11 tenebrosity

❑ **a shadow of your former self**
07 remnant, vestige
13 poor imitation

shadowy
03 dim
04 dark, hazy
05 faint, murky, vague
06 gloomy, unreal
07 ghostly, obscure, phantom
08 ethereal, nebulous, spectral
09 tenebrose, tenebrous
10 ill-defined, indistinct, mysterious, tenebrious
11 crepuscular

shady
03 dim
04 cool, dark, iffy
05 fishy, leafy
06 dubious, veiled
07 covered, dubious, obscure, shadowy, suspect, umbrous
08 screened, shielded, shrouded
09 tenebrous, underhand
10 caliginous, suspicious, tenebrious, umbrageous
11 umbratilous, umbriferous
12 disreputable, questionable
13 untrustworthy

shaft
03 bar, ray, rod
04 beam, dart, duct, flue, pole, stem, well
05 arrow, shank, stick, winze
06 handle, pencil, pillar, tunnel

shaggy
05 bushy, hairy
06 woolly
07 crinose, hirsute, unshorn
10 long-haired

shake
03 wag
04 bump, faze, jerk, jolt, rock, roll, stir, sway, wave
05 alarm, heave, lower, quake, rouse, shock, swing, throb, upset, wield
06 bounce, judder, lessen, quiver, rattle, reduce, shiver, totter, weaken, wobble
07 agitate, disturb, perturb, quaking, shudder, tremble, unnerve, vibrate
08 brandish, convulse, diminish, distress, flourish, frighten, unsettle

09 oscillate, undermine, vibration
10 convulsion, discompose, intimidate
11 disturbance, oscillation

❑ **shake a leg**
08 step on it
10 get a move on, look lively
11 get cracking

❑ **shake off**
04 lose
05 elude
06 escape
08 dislodge, get rid of, outstrip
11 give the slip, leave behind

❑ **shake up**
05 alarm, shock, upset
06 rattle
07 unnerve
08 distress, unsettle
10 reorganize

Shakespeare

➤ *Characters in Shakespeare's plays*:
03 Hal (Prince), Nym, Sly (Christopher)
04 Dull, Fool (The), Ford (Mistress), Hero, Iago, John (Don), John (King), Kate, Kent (Earl of), Lear (King), Moth, Page (Mistress), Puck, Snug
05 Ariel, Belch (Sir Toby), Celia, Diana, Edgar, Feste, Flute, Gobbo (Launcelot), Julia, Maria, Nurse, Paris (Count), Pedro (Don), Regan, Romeo, Snout, Timon, Titus, Viola
06 Alonso, Angelo, Antony (Mark), Armado (Don Adriano de), Audrey, Banquo, Bianca, Bottom (Nick), Brutus, Cassio, Cloten, Cobweb, Dromio, Duncan (King), Edmund, Emilia, Fabian, Hamlet, Hecate, Hector, Helena, Hermia, Imogen, Jaques, Juliet, Oberon, Oliver (de Bois), Olivia, Orsino, Oswald, Pistol, Porter, Portia, Quince, Silvia, Thisbe, Yorick
07 Adriana, Antonio, Caliban, Capulet, Claudio, Costard, Fleance, Goneril, Gonzalo, Horatio, Hotspur, Iachimo, Jessica, Laertes, Leontes, Lorenzo, Macbeth,

Macbeth (Lady), Macduff,
Malcolm, Mariana, Martext
(Sir Oliver), Miranda,
Octavia, Ophelia, Orlando,
Othello, Paulina, Perdita,
Proteus, Pyramus, Quickly
(Mistress), Shylock,
Sycorax, Theseus, Titania,
Troilus
08 Bardolph, Bassanio,
Beatrice, Benedick,
Benvolio, Claudius,
Cordelia, Cressida,
Dogberry, Falstaff (Sir
John), Florizel, Fluellen,
Gertrude, Hermione,
Isabella, Laurence (Friar),
Lucretia, Lysander,
Malvolio, Mercutio,
Montague, Pericles,
Polonius, Prospero,
Rosalind, Rosaline,
Stephano, Trinculo
09 Aguecheek (Sir Andrew),
Antigonus, Cleopatra,
Cornelius, Cymbeline,
Demetrius, Desdemona,
Enobarbus, Frederick
(Duke), Hippolyta,
Hortensio, Katharina,
Katharine (Princess of
France), Petruchio,
Polixenes, Sebastian,
Valentine, Vincentio (Duke)
10 Coriolanus, Fortinbras,
Gloucester (Earl of),
Holofernes, Jaquenetta,
Starveling, Touchstone
11 Mustard-seed,
Peasblossom, Rosencrantz
12 Guildenstern, Julius Caesar,
Three Witches
15 Robin Goodfellow, Titus
Andronicus

► *Names of Shakespeare's*
plays:
06 Hamlet (Prince of
Denmark), Henry V
07 Henry IV (Parts 1 and 2),
Henry VI (Parts 1, 2 and 3),
Macbeth, Othello (The
Moor of Venice)
08 King John, King Lear,
Pericles
09 Cymbeline, Henry VIII,
Richard II
10 Coriolanus, Richard III, The
Tempest
11 As You Like It
12 Julius Caesar, Twelfth Night
(or What You Will)
13 Timon of Athens

14 Romeo and Juliet, The
Winter's Tale
15 Titus Andronicus
16 Love's Labours Lost
17 Measure for Measure, The
Comedy of Errors
18 Antony and Cleopatra,
Troilus and Cressida
19 Much Ado About Nothing,
The Merchant of Venice, The
Taming of the Shrew
20 All's Well That Ends Well
21 A Midsummer Night's
Dream
22 The Merry Wives of
Windsor
23 The Two Gentlemen of
Verona

shake-up
08 upheaval
11 disturbance
13 rearrangement
14 reorganization

shaky
04 weak
05 rocky
06 flimsy, wobbly
07 rickety, tottery, unsound
08 insecure, unstable, unsteady
09 doddering, faltering,
quivering, tentative,
tottering, tremulous,
uncertain
10 precarious, unreliable
12 questionable

shallow
04 idle
05 empty, petty
06 flimsy, simple, slight
07 foolish, surface, trivial
08 ignorant, skin-deep, trifling
09 frivolous, insincere
11 meaningless, superficial

sham
04 copy, fake, hoax, mock
05 bogus, cheat, false, feign,
fraud, put on, put-on
06 humbug, phoney
07 forgery, imitate, pretend
08 deceiver, imposter, pretence
09 charlatan, dissemble,
imposture, simulated,
synthetic
10 artificial, simulation
11 counterfeit, make-believe

shaman
05 pawaw
06 powwow
07 angekok
08 magician, sorcerer

11 medicine man, witch doctor
13 medicine woman

shamble
04 drag, limp
06 hobble, scrape, toddle
07 shuffle

shambles
04 mess
05 chaos, havoc, wreck
06 bedlam, muddle, pigsty
08 abbattoir, butchery, disarray,
disorder, madhouse
14 slaughterhouse
15 disorganization

shambling
06 clumsy
08 lurching, ungainly, unsteady
09 lumbering, shuffling

shame
04 pity
05 abash, guilt, stain, sully, taint
06 debase, humble, infamy,
show up, stigma
07 degrade, mortify, remorse
08 confound, disgrace,
ignominy, ridicule
09 discredit, dishonour,
embarrass, humiliate
10 misfortune, opprobrium
11 degradation, humiliation
13 embarrassment,
mortification
14 disappointment

❑**put to shame**
06 humble, show up
07 eclipse, mortify, surpass
08 disgrace, outclass, outshine
09 embarrass, humiliate

shamefaced
07 abashed, ashamed
08 blushing, contrite, penitent,
red-faced, sheepish

shameful
04 base, mean, vile
07 heinous, ignoble, shaming
08 shocking, unworthy
09 atrocious
10 mortifying, outrageous,
scandalous
11 disgraceful, ignominious
12 contemptible, embarrassing
13 discreditable, reprehensible

shameless
06 brazen, wanton
07 blatant, defiant
08 flagrant, hardened,
immodest
09 audacious, barefaced,
unabashed, unashamed

10 impenitent, indecorous, unbecoming
12 incorrigible, unprincipled

shanty
03 hut
04 shed
05 bothy, cabin, hovel, hutch, shack
06 lean-to

shape
03 cut
04 cast, form, make, plan, trim
05 adapt, alter, block, build, carve, forge, frame, guise, model, mould, state
06 create, design, devise, fettle, figure, format, kilter, sculpt
07 fashion, outline, pattern, profile, remodel, whittle
08 contours, likeness, physique
09 character, condition, construct, influence, sculpture, structure
10 appearance, silhouette
13 configuration

➤ *Names of shapes*:
04 cone, cube, oval
06 circle, cuboid, oblong, sphere, square
07 diamond, ellipse, hexagon, nonagon, octagon, polygon, pyramid, rhombus
08 crescent, cylinder, heptagon, pentagon, quadrant, triangle
09 rectangle, trapezium
10 hemisphere, octahedron, polyhedron, semicircle
11 tetrahedron
13 parallelogram, quadrilateral
15 scalene triangle

❑**shape up**
07 develop
08 flourish, progress
09 take shape
11 make headway, move forward
12 make progress

shapeless
08 formless, nebulous, unformed
09 amorphous, irregular
12 unstructured

shapely
04 neat, trim
07 elegant
10 attractive, curvaceous, voluptuous, well-turned

shard
04 chip, part
05 piece

06 shiver
08 fragment, particle, splinter

share
03 cut, due, lot
04 part
05 allot, quota, split, whack
06 assign, divide, ration
07 carve up, deal out, dole out, give out, go Dutch, partake, portion
08 allocate, dividend, division, go halves
09 allotment, allowance, apportion
10 allocation, distribute, percentage, proportion
12 contribution, go fifty-fifty
14 slice of the cake

❑**share out**
05 allot
06 assign
07 give out, hand out, mete out
08 divide up
09 apportion, parcel out
10 distribute

shark
05 crook
08 swindler
11 extortioner
13 wheeler-dealer

➤ *Types of shark*:
03 fox, saw
04 blue, mako
05 ghost, nurse, tiger, whale
07 basking, dogfish, leopard, requiem
08 mackerel, thresher
09 man-eating, porbeagle
10 great white, hammerhead
➤ See also **animal**

sharp
03 sly
04 acid, keen, sour, tart, wily
05 acrid, acute, alert, clear, edged, harsh, natty, quick, rapid, smart, spiky, tight
06 abrupt, acidic, artful, astute, barbed, biting, clever, crafty, fierce, jagged, severe, shrewd, snappy, sudden
07 acerbic, cunning, exactly, extreme, intense, piquant, pointed, pungent, stylish
08 clear-cut, distinct, incisive, on the dot, piercing, promptly, scathing, serrated, stabbing, suddenly, venomous, vinegary
09 dishonest, observant, precisely, trenchant, vitriolic

10 discerning, knife-edged, needle-like, perceptive, punctually, razor-edged, razor-sharp, unexpected
11 intelligent, penetrating, quick-witted, well-defined
12 unexpectedly

sharpen
04 edge, file, hone, keen, whet
05 grind, strop
09 acuminate

sharp-eyed
08 hawk-eyed
09 eagle-eyed, observant
11 keen-sighted

sharpness
05 venom
07 clarity, cruelty, sarcasm, vitriol
08 keenness, severity
09 acuteness, harshness, intensity
10 astuteness, definition, fierceness, shrewdness
11 penetration
12 incisiveness
14 perceptiveness

shatter
04 dash, ruin
05 burst, crack, smash, split, upset, wreck
06 shiver
07 destroy, explode
08 demolish, overturn, splinter
09 devastate, overwhelm, pulverize

shattered
05 all in, weary
06 broken, done in, zonked
07 crushed, worn out
08 dead beat, dog-tired, tired out
09 exhausted, knackered
10 devastated

shattering
06 severe
08 crushing, damaging
10 paralysing
11 devastating

shave
03 cut
04 crop, pare, trim
05 graze, plane, shear
06 barber, fleece, scrape

sheaf
05 bunch, truss
06 armful, bundle

sheath
04 case

05 shell
06 casing, condom, sleeve
08 envelope, scabbard
12 French letter, prophylactic

shed
03 hut
04 cast, drop, emit
05 moult, shack, spill
06 lean-to, slough
07 cast off, discard, scatter
08 building, get rid of, outhouse

sheen
05 gleam, gloss, shine
06 lustre, patina, polish
07 burnish

sheep
03 ewe, ram, tup
04 lamb
06 wether
07 jumbuck
10 bell-wether

➤ *Sheep include*:
04 Soay
05 ammon, ancon, Jacob, Texel, urial
06 aoudad, argali, bharal, burhel, burrel, merino, muflon
07 bighorn, burrell, burrhel, caracul, Cheviot, karakul, mouflon, Suffolk
08 Cotswold, herdwick, Loaghtan, moufflon
09 blackface, Leicester, Marco Polo, Southdown
11 Wensleydale
➤ See also **animal**

sheepish
07 abashed, ashamed, foolish
09 chastened, mortified
10 shamefaced
11 embarrassed

sheer
04 fine, mere, pure, thin, veer
05 gauzy, sharp, steep, utter
06 abrupt, flimsy, swerve
07 deviate
08 absolute, gossamer, thorough, vertical
09 downright, out-and-out, veritable
10 diaphanous, see-through
11 precipitous, transparent, unmitigated
13 perpendicular, thoroughgoing

sheet
04 coat, film, leaf, page, pane, skin, slab

05 cover, folio, layer, panel, piece, plate, reach, sweep
06 lamina, veneer
07 blanket, expanse, overlay, stratum, surface
08 bed-linen

shelf
03 bar
04 bank, reef, sill, step
05 bench, ledge, shoal
07 counter, sand bar, terrace
08 sandbank
11 mantelpiece, mantelshelf

shell
03 pod
04 bomb, case, hull, husk, rind
05 blitz, crust, frame, shuck
06 bullet, casing, fire on, chassis, grenade, missile
08 carapace, skeleton
10 integument

❑ **shell out**
04 ante, give
05 spend
06 donate, expend, lay out, pay out
07 cough up, fork out
10 contribute

shellfish see **crustacean**; **mollusc**

shelter
04 hide, roof
05 cover, guard, haven, put up
06 asylum, refuge, safety, shield
07 harbour, lodging, protect
08 security
09 safeguard, sanctuary
10 protection

sheltered
04 cosy, snug, warm
05 quiet, shady
07 covered
08 shielded
09 protected, unworldly
10 cloistered

shelve
05 defer
06 put off
07 suspend
08 lay aside, mothball, postpone, put on ice
10 pigeonhole

shepherd
04 herd, lead
05 guide, steer, usher
06 convoy, escort
07 conduct, marshal
08 guardian, herdsman

09 protector
11 shepherdess

shield
05 cover, guard, shade, targe
06 defend, screen, shadow
07 buckler, bulwark, defence, protect, rampart, shelter, support
09 protector, safeguard
10 escutcheon, protection

shift
04 move, span, time, vary, veer
05 alter, budge, carry, spell, stint, U-turn
06 adjust, change, modify, period, remove, swerve, switch
07 removal, stretch
08 dislodge, displace, get rid of, movement, relocate, transfer
09 fluctuate, rearrange, transpose, variation
10 alteration, relocation, reposition
11 fluctuation
12 displacement, modification

shiftless
04 idle, lazy
05 inept
07 aimless
08 feckless, goalless, indolent
11 incompetent, ineffectual, inefficient, unambitious
13 directionless, irresponsible, lackadaisical
14 good-for-nothing

shifty
04 iffy, wily
05 shady
06 crafty, tricky
07 cunning, devious, dubious, evasive, furtive
08 scheming, slippery
09 deceitful, dishonest, underhand
11 duplicitous
13 untrustworthy

shilly-shally
05 waver
06 dither, falter, seesaw, teeter
08 hesitate
09 fluctuate, hem and haw, mess about, vacillate
10 dilly-dally
11 prevaricate

shimmer
04 glow
05 gleam, glint
06 lustre

07 flicker, glimmer, glisten, glitter, sparkle, twinkle
11 iridescence, scintillate

shimmering
05 shiny
07 glowing, shining
08 gleaming, luminous, lustrous
10 aventurine, glistening, glittering, iridescent
12 incandescent

shin
04 soar
05 climb, mount, scale, shoot, swarm
06 ascend
07 clamber
08 scramble

shine
03 rub, wax
04 beam, buff, glow
05 excel, flash, gleam, glint, gloss, light, rub up, sheen
06 dazzle, lustre, patina, polish
07 burnish, flicker, glimmer, glisten, glitter, radiate, shimmer, sparkle, twinkle
08 lambency, radiance
10 brightness, effulgence, incandesce
12 luminescence
13 incandescence

shininess
05 gleam, sheen, shine
06 lustre, polish
07 burnish, glitter

shining
06 bright
07 beaming, eminent, glowing, leading, radiant
08 flashing, gleaming, glinting, glorious, luminous, splendid
09 brilliant, effulgent, sparkling, twinkling
10 glistening, glittering, pre-eminent, shimmering
11 illustrious, outstanding, resplendent
12 incandescent
13 distinguished

shiny
05 silky, sleek
06 bright, glossy
08 gleaming, lustrous, polished
09 burnished
10 glistening, shimmering

ship
04 boat
05 craft, ferry, liner, yacht

06 tanker, vessel
07 steamer, trawler
➤ See also **boat**; **sail**; **vehicle**

▶ *Parts of a ship*:
03 oar
04 brig, bunk, deck, head, hold, keel, mast, port, prow, sail
05 berth, bilge, cabin, cleat, davit, hatch, stern, wheel, winch
06 anchor, bridge, fo'c'sle, funnel, galley, gunnel, hawser, rigger, rudder, tiller
07 bollard, capstan, gangway, gun deck, gunwale, hammock, rowlock, top deck, transom
08 boat deck, bulkhead, bulwarks, hatchway, main deck, poop deck, porthole, wardroom
09 after deck, crow's nest, gangplank, lower deck, stanchion, starboard, stateroom, waterline
10 boiler room, engine room, figurehead, flight deck, forecastle, pilot house
11 paddle wheel, quarter deck
12 Plimsoll line
13 promenade deck

▶ *Names of famous ships*:
03 QE2
04 Ajax, Argo, Hood, Nina
05 Argus, Pinta
06 Beagle, Bounty, Oriana, Pequod, Renown
07 Amistad, Belfast, Blücher, Pelican, Potomac, Repulse, Tirpitz, Titanic, Victory
08 Ark Royal, Bismarck, Canberra, Graf Spee, Mary Rose
09 Aquitania, Brittania, Brittanic, Cutty Sark, Discovery, Endeavour, Gneisenau, Lusitania, Mayflower, Queen Mary, Sheffield, Téméraire, Terranova
10 Golden Hind, Hispaniola, Mauretania, Prinz Eugen, Santa Maria
11 Dawn Treader, Dreadnought, Scharnhorst
12 Great Britain, Great Eastern, Great Western, Marie Celeste
14 Flying Dutchman, Queen Elizabeth
15 Admiral Graf Spee, General Belgrano, Queen Elizabeth 2

shipping
▶ *Shipping forecast areas include*:
04 Sole, Tyne
05 Dover, Forth, Lundy, Malin, Wight
06 Bailey, Biscay, Dogger, Faroes, Fisher, Humber, Thames, Viking
07 Fastnet, Forties, Rockall, Shannon
08 Cromarty, Fair Isle, Hebrides, Irish Sea, Plymouth, Portland
09 Trafalgar
10 Finisterre
11 German Bight, North Utsire, South Utsire

shipshape
04 neat, tidy, trig, trim
07 orderly
12 businesslike, spick and span
13 well-organized

shirk
04 duck, shun
05 avoid, dodge, evade, skive, slack
08 get out of
10 play truant, shrink from

shirker
05 idler
06 dodger, loafer, skiver, truant
07 quitter, slacker
10 malingerer

shiver
05 break, crack, quake, shake, shard, shred, smash, split
06 quiver, sliver, tremor, twitch
07 flutter, shatter, shaving, shudder, tremble, vibrate
08 fragment, splinter
09 palpitate, vibration
10 smithereen
11 smithereens

shivery
06 chilly
07 chilled, nervous, quaking, quivery, shaking, trembly
08 fluttery, shuddery

shoal
04 mass
05 flock, group, horde, swarm

shock
03 jar
04 blow, daze, jerk, jolt, numb, stun
05 amaze, appal, crash, repel, shake, start, upset

06 dismay, fright, horror, impact, offend, revolt, sicken, trauma
07 agitate, astound, disgust, jarring, outrage, perturb, startle, unnerve
08 bewilder, bowl over, paralyse, surprise
09 bombshell, collision, dumbfound, take aback
10 scandalize, traumatize
13 rude awakening
15 bolt from the blue

shocking
07 ghastly, hideous
08 dreadful, horrific
09 appalling, atrocious, frightful, loathsome, monstrous
10 abominable, horrifying, outrageous, scandalous
11 unspeakable

shoddy
04 poor, ropy
05 cheap, tacky, tatty
06 tawdry, trashy
08 inferior, slapdash, slipshod

shoemaker
07 cobbler
09 bootmaker

shoemaking
08 cobblery, cobbling
10 bootmaking

shoot
03 aim, bud, fly, hit, lob, zap
04 bolt, dart, dash, film, fire, grow, hurl, kick, kill, race, rush, slip, snap, tear, twig
05 blast, fling, graft, hurry, scion, shell, speed, sprig, throw, video, whisk, wound
06 branch, charge, direct, hurtle, injure, launch, let off, propel, sprint, sprout, streak
07 bombard, burgeon, cutting, gun down, pick off, project, snipe at, stretch, tendron
08 offshoot, open fire
09 discharge, germinate
10 photograph

shop
03 buy, get, rat
05 grass, split, store
06 betray, squeal, tell on
08 emporium, inform on, purchase
09 buy things, stock up on
10 go shopping
12 retail outlet

shore
04 bank, hold, prop, sand, stay
05 beach, brace, coast, front, sands
06 hold up, prop up, strand
07 seaside, shingle, support
08 buttress, lakeside, littoral, seaboard, seashore, underpin
09 foreshore, promenade, reinforce
10 strengthen, waterfront

shorn
03 cut
04 bald
06 shaved, shaven
07 crew-cut, cropped
08 deprived, stripped

short
03 low, wee
04 curt, poor, rude
05 blunt, brief, crisp, gruff, pithy, scant, sharp, small, squat, teeny, terse, tight
06 abrupt, direct, little, meagre, petite, scanty, scarce, slight, snappy, sparse, stubby
07 brusque, compact, concise, cursory, summary, uncivil
08 abridged, abruptly, fleeting, pint-size, succinct, suddenly
09 condensed, curtailed, deficient, ephemeral, minuscule, momentary, pint-sized, temporary, truncated
10 diminutive, evanescent, inadequate, summarized, to the point, transitory
11 abbreviated
12 discourteous, insufficient

◻**fall short**
09 be lacking
12 be inadequate
14 be insufficient

◻**in short**
07 in a word, in brief
09 concisely
11 in a few words, in a nutshell

◻**short of**
05 low on
07 lacking, missing, short on, wanting
08 less than
09 other than, pushed for

shortage
04 lack, need, want
06 dearth
07 absence, deficit, paucity, poverty
08 scarcity

10 deficiency, inadequacy
13 insufficiency

shortcoming
04 flaw
05 fault
06 defect, foible
07 failing, frailty
08 drawback, weakness
12 imperfection

shorten
03 cut
04 crop, dock, pare, trim
05 prune
06 lessen, reduce, take up
07 abridge, curtail, cut down
08 condense, contract, decrease, pare down, truncate
10 abbreviate

shortened
08 abridged
09 condensed
11 abbreviated

short-lived
05 brief, short
08 caducous, fleeting
09 ephemeral, fugacious, momentary
10 evanescent

shortly
04 soon
06 curtly
07 by and by, tersely
08 abruptly, directly, in a while
09 presently
10 before long
14 in a little while

short-sighted
04 rash
05 hasty
06 myopic, unwise
08 careless, heedless
09 impolitic, imprudent
10 ill-advised, unthinking
11 improvident, injudicious, near-sighted, thoughtless

short-staffed
11 shorthanded
12 understaffed
13 below strength

short-tempered
05 fiery, ratty, testy
06 crusty, touchy
08 choleric
09 impatient, irascible, irritable

short-winded
07 gasping, panting, puffing
10 breathless

shot
02 go
03 fix, hit, jab, lob, try
04 ball, bang, bash, dose, kick, slug, snap, stab, turn
05 blast, crack, fling, image, moiré, photo, print, throw
06 bullet, effort, pellet
07 attempt, gunfire, missile, mottled, picture, watered
09 discharge, endeavour, explosion, injection
10 ammunition, iridescent, photograph, projectile
11 inoculation, vaccination
12 immunization

□ **call the shots**
04 head, lead
06 direct, head up, manage
07 command
09 give a lead, supervise
10 be in charge

□ **like a shot**
06 at once
07 eagerly
09 instantly, willingly
11 immediately

□ **shot in the arm**
05 boost
06 fillip, uplift
08 stimulus

□ **shot in the dark**
05 guess
09 guesswork, wild guess
10 blind guess, conjecture
11 speculation

shoulder
04 bear, push
05 carry, elbow, force, press, shove
06 accept, assume, jostle, take on, thrust
07 support, sustain

□ **rub shoulders with**
07 mix with
10 hobnob with
13 associate with, socialize with
14 fraternize with

□ **shoulder to shoulder**
07 closely
10 hand in hand, side by side
13 co-operatively

shout
03 bay, cry
04 bawl, call, howl, roar, yell
05 cheer
06 bellow, cry out, holler, scream, shriek, squawk
07 call out
11 rant and rave
14 raise your voice

shove
04 jolt, push
05 barge, crowd, drive, elbow, force, press
06 jostle, propel, thrust

□ **shove off**
05 leave, scram
06 beat it, depart
07 do a bunk, get lost, push off, scarper, vamoose
08 clear off, clear out
09 skedaddle

shovel
03 dig
04 heap, move
05 clear, scoop, shift, spade
06 bucket, dredge

show
03 air
04 expo, fair, lead, mean, sign
05 array, front, guide, prove, steer, teach, usher
06 affair, appear, arrive, attend, depict, direct, escort, expose, façade, parade, record, reveal, set out, turn up
07 clarify, conduct, display, divulge, exhibit, explain, expound, express, panache, pizzazz, portray, present, produce, showing, signify, staging, suggest, uncover
08 disclose, indicate, instruct, manifest, point out, register
09 elucidate, exemplify, make clear, make known, operation, programme, spectacle
10 appearance, exhibition, exposition, illustrate, production, profession
11 affectation, demonstrate, flamboyance, ostentation, performance, undertaking
12 extravaganza, presentation
13 entertainment, manifestation
14 representation, window dressing

□ **show off**
04 brag
05 boast, strut, swank
06 flaunt, parade, set off
07 display, enhance, exhibit, swagger
11 demonstrate

□ **show up**
04 come, show
05 shame
06 appear, arrive, expose, reveal, turn up, unmask
07 lay bare, let down, mortify
08 disgrace, pinpoint
09 embarrass, highlight, humiliate
10 put to shame
11 make visible

showdown
07 face-off
10 dénouement
13 confrontation, moment of truth

shower
04 fall, hail, heap, load, pour, rain
05 spray
06 deluge, lavish, stream, volley
07 barrage, torrent
08 inundate, sprinkle
09 drizzling, overwhelm
10 sprinkling

showiness
05 glitz, swank
07 glitter, pizzazz
10 flashiness, razzmatazz
11 flamboyance, ostentation
12 razzle-dazzle

showing
06 record
07 account, display, staging
08 evidence
10 appearance, exhibition
11 performance, track record
12 presentation
14 representation

showing-off
05 swank
07 egotism, swagger
08 boasting, bragging
09 vainglory
10 peacockery
11 braggadocio
13 exhibitionism

showman
09 performer, publicist
10 impresario, ring-master
11 entertainer

show-off
05 poser
06 poseur
07 boaster, egotist, know-all, peacock, swanker
08 braggart
09 swaggerer
13 exhibitionist

showy
04 loud
05 fancy, flash, gaudy
06 flashy, garish, ornate, swanky, tawdry
10 flamboyant, glittering
12 ostentatious

shred
03 bit, jot, rag
04 atom, iota, mite, whit
05 grain, piece, scrap, speck, trace, whisp
06 ribbon, sliver, tatter
07 modicum, remnant, snippet
08 fragment, particle

shred
04 chop, tear
05 cut up, rip up, slice
06 tear up

shrew
03 nag
04 Fury
05 bitch, scold, vixen
06 dragon, virago
08 harridan, spitfire
09 henpecker, termagant, Xanthippe

shrewd
03 sly
04 keen, wily
05 acute, alert, canny, sharp
06 artful, astute, crafty
07 cunning
10 calculated, discerning
11 calculating, intelligent
14 discriminating

shrewdly
05 slyly
06 wisely
07 cannily
08 artfully, astutely, craftily

shrewdness
06 acumen, wisdom
08 astucity
09 acuteness, canniness, sharpness
10 astuteness
11 penetration

shrewish
07 nagging
08 captious, scolding, vixenish
10 henpecking
12 fault-finding, sharp-tongued

shriek
04 howl, wail, yell
06 cry out, scream, squawk, squeal
07 screech

shrill
04 high
05 acute, sharp
06 treble
08 piercing, strident
11 high-pitched, penetrating
12 ear-splitting

shrine
04 dome, fane, tope
05 darga, stupa
06 chapel, church, dagoba, temple, vimana
09 holy place, sanctuary
10 tabernacle

shrink
04 balk, shun
05 cower, quail, wince
06 cringe, flinch, lessen, narrow, recoil, reduce, retire, wither
07 atrophy, dwindle, shorten, shrivel, shy away
08 back away, contract, decrease, withdraw

shrivel
03 dry
04 burn, sear, wilt
05 dry up, parch
06 gizzen, pucker, scorch, shrink, wither
07 dwindle, frizzle, wrinkle
08 pucker up
09 dehydrate, desiccate

shrivelled
03 dry
04 sere
07 dried up, wizened
08 puckered, shrunken, withered, wrinkled, writhled
09 emaciated
10 desiccated

shroud
04 hide, pall, veil, wrap
05 cloak, cloth, cloud, cover
06 mantle, screen, swathe
07 blanket, conceal, envelop
08 cerement
09 cerecloth
12 graveclothes, winding-sheet

shrouded
06 hidden, veiled
07 cloaked, clouded, covered, swathed, wrapped
09 concealed, enveloped

shrug
□ **shrug off**
06 ignore
07 dismiss, neglect
09 disregard
14 take no notice of

shrub
➤ *Names of shrubs*:
03 ivy
04 hebe, rose
05 broom, holly, lilac, peony
06 azalea, daphne, laurel, mallow, mimosa, privet
07 dogwood, fuchsia, heather, jasmine
08 buddleia, camellia, clematis, japonica, laburnum, lavender, magnolia, musk rose, viburnum, wistaria
09 forsythia, hydrangea
10 witch hazel
11 honeysuckle
12 rhododendron
➤ See also **plant**

shrunken
05 gaunt
09 emaciated
10 cadaverous, shrivelled

shudder
05 heave, quake, shake, spasm
06 quiver, shiver, tremor
07 tremble
08 convulse
10 convulsion

shuffle
03 mix
04 drag, limp
05 mix up
06 doddle, falter, hobble, jumble, scrape, switch, toddle
07 confuse, scuffle, shamble
08 intermix, jumble up
09 rearrange
10 move around, reorganize

shun
05 avoid, elude, evade, spurn
06 eschew, ignore
09 ostracize
11 shy away from
12 cold-shoulder, keep away from, steer clear of

shut
03 bar
04 bolt, lock, seal, slam
05 close, latch
06 fasten, secure
11 put the lid on

□ **shut down**
04 halt, stop
05 cease, close
07 suspend
09 close down, switch off, terminate

10 inactivate
11 discontinue

□shut in
04 cage
05 box in, hem in
06 cage in, immure, keep in
07 confine, enclose, fence in
08 imprison, restrain

□shut off
06 cut off
07 isolate, seclude
08 separate
09 segregate

□shut out
03 bar
04 hide, mask, veil
05 cover, debar, exile
06 banish, outlaw, screen
07 conceal, exclude
09 ostracize

□shut up
03 gag
04 hush, jail
05 quiet
06 clam up, coop up, hush up, immure, intern, lock up
07 confine, keep mum, quieten, silence
08 imprison, pipe down
11 incarcerate
14 hold your tongue

shutter
05 blind, shade
06 louvre, screen
08 jalousie

shuttle
03 ply
05 shunt
06 seesaw, travel
09 alternate
11 shuttlecock

shy
03 coy
05 chary, mousy, timid
06 demure, modest
07 bashful, nervous
08 reserved, reticent, retiring, timorous
09 diffident, inhibited, shrinking
11 embarrassed, introverted
13 self-conscious

□fight shy of
04 shun
05 avoid, spurn
06 eschew
12 steer clear of

□shy away
04 balk, buck, rear
05 avoid, quail, start, wince

06 flinch, recoil, shrink, swerve
08 back away

shyness
07 coyness, modesty
08 timidity
09 mousiness, timidness
10 diffidence

sibling
04 twin
06 german, sister
07 brother

sibyl
04 seer
06 oracle, Pythia
07 seeress
09 pythoness, sorceress, wise woman
10 prophetess

sick
03 ill
04 weak
05 angry, black, bored, cruel, fed up, gross, tired, weary
06 ailing, groggy, laid up, poorly, puking, queasy, unwell
07 annoyed, bilious, enraged
08 nauseous, retching, vomiting
09 hacked off, nauseated, off colour, tasteless
10 browned off, cheesed off, indisposed, out of sorts
12 sick and tired
15 under the weather

sicken
03 get
05 appal, catch, repel
06 pick up, put off, revolt
07 develop, disgust, turn off
08 contract, nauseate
09 succumb to
15 turn your stomach

sickening
04 foul, vile
08 nauseous, shocking
09 appalling, loathsome, offensive, repellent, repulsive, revolting
10 disgusting, nauseating, off-putting
11 distasteful
14 stomach-turning

sickly
03 wan
04 pale, sick, weak
05 faint, frail, gushy, mushy, soppy, sweet

06 ailing, feeble, infirm, pallid, slushy, syrupy
08 delicate

sickness
03 bug
06 malady, nausea, puking
07 ailment, disease, illness
08 disorder, retching, vomiting
09 complaint, ill-health
10 affliction, queasiness, throwing up
11 biliousness
13 indisposition

side
03 end, rim
04 area, bank, camp, edge, face, hand, jamb, sect, team, view, wing, zone
05 angle, brink, cause, facet, flank, limit, minor, party, shore, slant, verge
06 aspect, border, fringe, lesser, margin, region, sector
07 faction, lateral, oblique, profile, section
08 boundary, district, flanking, interest, marginal, sidelong, wideward, wideways
09 secondary, viewpoint
10 standpoint, subsidiary
11 point of view, subordinate

□side by side
15 next to each other

□side with
04 back
06 favour, prefer
07 support, vote for
08 join with
09 agree with
10 team up with
13 be on the side of

sidelong
06 covert
07 oblique
08 indirect, sideward, sideways

sidestep
05 avoid, dodge, elude, evade, shirk, skirt
06 bypass
10 circumvent

sidetrack
06 divert
07 deflect, head off
08 distract

sideways
07 askance, athwart, lateral, oblique, slanted

sidle
08 crabwise, edgeways, edgewise, indirect, sidelong, sideward
09 laterally, obliquely

sidle
04 edge, inch
05 creep, slink, sneak

siege
08 blockade
11 besiegement
12 encirclement
13 beleaguerment

siesta
03 nap
04 doze, rest
05 sleep
06 catnap, repose, snooze
10 forty winks, relaxation

sieve
04 sift, sort
06 filter, remove, riddle, screen, sifter, strain, winnow
08 colander, separate, strainer

sift
04 sort
06 filter, riddle, strain, winnow
08 pore over, separate

sigh
04 moan
05 swish
06 exhale, grieve, lament, rustle
07 breathe, suspire, whisper
08 complain
09 susurrate

□**sigh for**
04 long, pine, weep
05 mourn, yearn
06 grieve, lament

sight
03 see
04 espy, look, show, spot, view
05 range, scene
06 behold, fright, glance, seeing, vision
07 eyesore, glimpse, make out, wonders
08 beauties, features, perceive
09 spectacle
10 appearance, exhibition, perception
11 curiosities, distinguish, monstrosity, observation
13 field of vision, range of vision

► *Ways of describing sight impairment*:
06 myopic
08 purblind
09 amaurotic, half-blind, sand-blind, snow-blind
10 astigmatic, far-sighted, night-blind, stone-blind
11 blind as a bat, colour-blind, hemeralopic, long-sighted, near-sighted
12 short-sighted

□**catch sight of**
03 see
04 mark, note, spot, view
06 look at, notice
07 glimpse, make out
08 identify, perceive

□**lose sight of**
04 omit
06 forget, ignore
07 neglect
08 overlook, put aside
09 disregard

□**set your sights on**
05 aim at
09 strive for
11 work towards
13 aspire towards

sightseer
07 tourist, tripper, visitor
10 rubberneck
12 excursionist, holidaymaker

sign
03 act, nod
04 clue, code, hint, logo, mark, omen, show, wave, wink
05 badge, board, proof, token, trace, write
06 action, augury, beckon, cipher, emblem, figure, marker, motion, notice, poster, signal, symbol
07 endorse, express, gesture, initial, placard, pointer, portent, presage, symptom
08 evidence, indicate, inscribe, insignia, movement
09 autograph, character, harbinger, indicator
10 foreboding, indication, suggestion
11 communicate, forewarning, gesticulate
13 gesticulation, manifestation
14 representation
15 prognostication

□**sign over**
06 convey
07 consign, deliver, entrust
08 make over, transfer, turn over

□**sign up**
04 hire, join
05 enrol
06 employ, engage, enlist, join up, sign on, take on
07 recruit
08 register
09 volunteer
15 join the services

signal
03 nod
04 clue, hint, mark, show, sign, wave, wink
05 alert, light, token
06 beckon, motion, tip-off
07 eminent, express, gesture, message, notable, pointer, signify, symptom, warning
08 evidence, indicate, striking
09 important, momentous
10 impressive, indication, noteworthy, remarkable
11 communicate, conspicuous, gesticulate, outstanding, significant
13 distinguished, extraordinary

signature
04 mark, name
08 initials
09 autograph
11 endorsement, inscription, John Hancock

significance
04 gist
05 force, point, sense
06 import, matter, weight
07 essence, meaning, message, purport
08 interest
09 magnitude, relevance, solemnity
10 importance
11 consequence, implication, seriousness
12 implications, significance
13 consideration

significant
03 key
05 vital
06 marked
07 crucial, fateful, ominous, serious, weighty
08 critical, eloquent, material, pregnant, relevant, symbolic
09 important, memorable, momentous
10 expressive, indicative, meaningful, noteworthy, suggestive

significantly
10 noticeably
11 appreciably, perceptibly
12 considerably

signify
04 mean, show

05 count, imply
06 convey, denote, matter, signal
07 betoken, declare, exhibit, express, portend, suggest
08 indicate, intimate, proclaim, stand for, transmit
09 represent, symbolize
10 be relevant
11 be important, carry weight, communicate

signpost
04 clue, sign
06 marker
07 placard, pointer
09 indicator

silence
03 gag
04 calm, hush, lull, mute
05 abate, peace, quell, quiet, still
06 deaden, muffle, muzzle, stifle, subdue
07 quieten, reserve
08 calmness, dumbness, muteness, suppress
09 dumbfound, quietness, reticence, stillness
10 strike dumb
12 peacefulness, tranquillity

silent
03 mum
04 calm, dumb, mute
05 muted, quiet, still, tacit
08 implicit, peaceful, reserved, reticent, taciturn, unspoken, unvoiced, wordless
09 inaudible, noiseless, soundless, voiceless
10 speechless, tongue-tied, understood
11 tight-lipped

silently
06 calmly, dumbly, mutely
07 quietly, tacitly, unheard
11 noiselessly, soundlessly

silhouette
04 form
05 shape
06 shadow
07 contour, outline, profile
08 stand out
09 delineate
11 delineation

silky
05 sleek
06 glossy, satiny, silken, smooth
07 velvety

silly
04 clot, daft, dope, fool, rash, soft, twit
05 barmy, dotty, dumbo, goose, idiot, inane, loony, loopy, ninny, nutty, potty, wally
06 absurd, duffer, stupid, unwise
07 fatuous, foolish, half-wit, idiotic, puerile
08 childish, immature, reckless
09 foolhardy, illogical, imprudent, ludicrous, pointless, senseless, simpleton
10 irrational, ridiculous
11 injudicious, meaningless, thoughtless
12 preposterous, unreasonable
13 irresponsible, unintelligent
14 scatterbrained

silt
03 mud
04 ooze
06 sludge
07 deposit, residue
08 alluvium, sediment

◻**silt up**
04 clog
05 block, choke

silvan
05 leafy
06 wooded
08 forestal, forested, woodland
09 arboreous, forestine
11 tree-covered

similar
04 akin, like
05 alike, close
07 related, uniform
09 analogous
10 comparable, homologous
11 homogeneous, much the same
13 corresponding

similarity
07 analogy, kinship
08 likeness, sameness
09 agreement, closeness
10 congruence
11 concordance, homogeneity, resemblance
13 comparability, compatibility
14 correspondence

similarly
08 likewise
09 by analogy, uniformly
12 in the same way
14 by the same token
15 correspondingly

similitude
07 analogy
08 affinity, likeness, relation, sameness
09 agreement, closeness
10 congruence
11 resemblance
14 correspondence

simmer
04 burn, fume, rage, stew
06 bubble, seethe
08 smoulder
10 boil gently, cook gently

◻**simmer down**
06 lessen
07 subside
08 calm down, cool down

simpering
03 coy
05 silly
07 missish
08 affected, giggling
13 schoolgirlish, self-conscious

simple
04 bald, easy
05 basic, clear, crude, cushy, naïve, plain, silly, stark
06 a cinch, honest, stupid
07 a doddle, artless, classic, foolish, idiotic, natural, sincere, unfussy
08 backward, innocent, no-frills, ordinary, retarded
09 a pushover, easy-peasy, ingenuous, unadorned
10 effortless, elementary, half-witted
11 rudimentary, undecorated
12 a piece of cake, feeble-minded
13 uncomplicated, unembellished, unpretentious
14 comprehensible
15 straightforward, unsophisticated

simple-minded
05 idiot
07 foolish, moronic, natural
08 imbecile
09 dim-witted
12 addle-brained, feeble-minded

simpleton
04 dolt, dope, fool, twit
05 booby, dunce, idiot, ninny
06 nitwit
07 dullard
08 imbecile, numskull
09 blockhead

simplicity
04 ease
06 purity
07 candour, clarity, honesty, naïvety
08 easiness, facility, lucidity, openness
09 frankness, innocence, plainness, restraint, sincerity, starkness
10 clean lines, directness, simpleness
11 artlessness, naturalness
13 guilelessness
14 elementariness
15 intelligibility

simplify
07 clarify, explain, unravel
08 make easy, untangle
10 make easier
11 disentangle

simplistic
03 pat
05 naïve
06 facile, simple
07 shallow
08 sweeping
14 oversimplified

simply
04 just, only
05 quite
06 merely, purely, solely
07 clearly, lucidly, plainly
10 altogether, completely

simulate
03 act
04 copy, echo, fake, sham
05 feign, mimic, put on
06 affect, assume, parrot
07 imitate, pretend, reflect
08 parallel
09 duplicate, reproduce
11 counterfeit, make believe

simulated
04 fake, mock, sham
05 bogus, put-on
06 phoney, pseudo
07 man-made
09 imitation, insincere, pretended, synthetic
10 artificial, substitute
11 inauthentic, make-believe

simultaneous
10 concurrent, synchronic
15 contemporaneous

sin
04 evil, fall
05 crime, error, fault, guilt, lapse, stray, wrong

07 impiety, misdeed, offence
08 go astray, iniquity, trespass
10 immorality, sinfulness, transgress, wickedness
13 fall from grace, transgression

➤ *The seven deadly sins*:
04 envy, lust
05 anger, pride, sloth, wrath
06 acedia
07 accidie, avarice
08 gluttony
12 covetousness

sincere
04 open, pure, real, true
05 frank
06 candid, direct, honest, simple
07 artless, earnest, fervent, genuine, natural, serious, unmixed, up front
08 bona fide, truthful
09 guileless, heartfelt, ingenuous, unfeigned
10 above board, no-nonsense, unaffected
11 plain-spoken, trustworthy
12 wholehearted
13 unadulterated
15 straightforward

sincerely
05 truly
08 honestly
09 earnestly, genuinely, in earnest,
10 truthfully

sincerity
05 truth
06 honour
07 candour, honesty, probity
08 openness
09 frankness, integrity
10 directness
11 artlessness, earnestness, genuineness, seriousness, uprightness
12 truthfulness
13 guilelessness, ingenuousness
15 trustworthiness

sinecure
07 plum job
08 cushy job
10 gravy train, soft option

sinewy
04 wiry
06 strong
07 stringy
08 athletic, muscular

sinful
03 bad

04 evil
05 wrong
06 erring, fallen, guilty, unholy, wicked
07 corrupt, immoral, impious, ungodly
08 criminal, depraved, wrongful
10 iniquitous
11 irreligious, unrighteous

sinfulness
03 sin
05 guilt
07 impiety
08 iniquity, peccancy
09 depravity
10 corruption, immorality, wickedness
11 peccability, ungodliness
13 transgression
15 unrighteousness

sing
03 hum
04 pipe
05 chant, chirp, croon, trill, yodel
06 intone, quaver, warble
08 serenade, vocalize

❑sing out
04 bawl, call, yell
05 cooee, shout
06 bellow, cry out, holler

singe
04 burn, char, sear
06 scorch
07 blacken

singer
➤ See also **music**

➤ *Types of singer*:
04 alto, bass, diva
05 mezzo, tenor
06 chorus, treble
07 crooner, pop star, soloist, soprano, warbler
08 baritone, castrato, choirboy, falsetto, minstrel, songster, vocalist
09 balladeer, chanteuse, choirgirl, chorister, contralto, pop singer, precentor
10 folk-singer, prima donna, songstress, troubadour
11 carol-singer, opera singer
12 counter-tenor, mezzo-soprano
13 basso profondo, basso profundo

➤ *Names of classical singers*:
04 **Butt** (Dame Clara), **Lind** (Jenny), **Popp** (Lucia)

05 **Baker** (Dame Janet), **Evans** (Sir Geraint), **Gigli** (Beniamino), **Lanza** (Mario), **Lenya** (Lotte), **Melba** (Dame Nellie), **Patti** (Adelina), **Pears** (Sir Peter)

06 **Callas** (Maria), **Caruso** (Enrico), **Turner** (Dame Eva)

07 **Caballé** (Montserrat), **Domingo** (Plácido), **Ferrier** (Kathleen), **Hammond** (Dame Joan), **Lehmann** (Lotte), **Nilsson** (Birgit)

08 **Carreras** (José), **Te Kanawa** (Dame Kiri)

09 **Chaliapin** (Fyodor), **Pavarotti** (Luciano)

10 **Söderström** (Elisabeth), **Sutherland** (Dame Joan)

11 **Schwarzkopf** (Dame Elisabeth)

► *Names of folk musicians and singers*:

03 **Gow** (Niel)

04 **Baez** (Joan), **Bain** (Aly)

05 **Sharp** (Cecil James)

06 **Fisher** (Archie), **Foster** (Stephen Collins), **Fraser** (Marjory Kennedy), **Mackay** (Charles), **Nairne** (Carolina), **Pogues**, **Runrig**, **Seeger** (Pete)

07 **Clannad**, **Donegan** (Lonnie), **Gaughan** (Dick), **Guthrie** (Woody), **MacColl** (Ewan), **Robeson** (Paul), **Skinner** (James Scott), **Thomson** (George)

08 **Rafferty** (Gerry)

09 **Dubliners**, **Henderson** (Hamish), **Leadbelly**, **Robertson** (Jeannie)

► *Names of jazz musicians and singers*:

03 **Guy** (Buddy), **Ory** (Kid)

04 **Cole** (Nat 'King'), **Getz** (Stan), **King** (B B), **Monk** (Thelonius), **Pine** (Courtney), **Shaw** (Artie)

05 **Basie** (Count), **Corea** (Chick), **Davis** (Miles), **Evans** (Gil), **Hines** (Earl), **Jones** (Quincy), **Roach** (Max), **Smith** (Bessie), **Sun Ra**, **Tatum** (Art)

06 **Barber** (Chris), **Bechet** (Sidney), **Blakey** (Art), **Dorsey** (Tommy), **Garner** (Errol), **Gordon** (Dexter),

Herman (Woody), **Hooker** (John Lee), **Joplin** (Scott), **Kenton** (Stan), **Miller** (Glenn), **Mingus** (Charles), **Morton** (Jelly Roll), **Oliver** (King), **Parker** (Charlie), **Powell** (Bud), **Simone** (Nina), **Tracey** (Stan), **Walker** (T-Bone), **Waller** (Thomas 'Fats'), **Waters** (Muddy)

07 **Bennett** (Tony), **Brubeck** (Dave), **Charles** (Ray), **Coleman** (Ornette), **Goodman** (Benny), **Hampton** (Lionel 'Hamp'), **Hancock** (Herbie), **Hawkins** (Coleman), **Holiday** (Billie 'Lady Day'), **Hot Five**, **Ibrahim** (Abdullah), **Jackson** (Milt), **Jarrett** (Keith), **Metheny** (Pat), **Mezzrow** (Mezz), **Rollins** (Sonny), **Shorter** (Wayne), **Vaughan** (Sarah)

08 **Adderley** (Cannonball), **All Stars**, **Calloway** (Cab), **Coltrane** (John), **Gershwin** (George), **Hot Seven**, **Marsalis** (Wynton), **Mulligan** (Gerry), **Peterson** (Oscar)

09 **Armstrong** (Louis 'Satchmo'), **Dankworth** (John), **Ellington** (Duke), **Gillespie** (Dizzy), **Grappelli** (Stephane), **Leadbelly**, **Lyttelton** (Humphrey), **Reinhardt** (Django), **Teagarden** (Jack)

10 **Fitzgerald** (Ella), **McLaughlin** (John)

11 **Beiderbecke** (Bix), **Howling Wolf**

12 **Jazz Warriors**

► *Names of pop musicians*:

03 **Eno** (Brian), **Jam**, **Lee** (Peggy), **Pop** (Iggy), **REM**, **Yes**

04 **Abba**, **Baez** (Joan), **Blur**, **Bush** (Kate), **Cash** (Johnny), **Cher**, **Cray** (Robert), **Cure**, **Devo**, **Dury** (Ian), **Gaye** (Marvin), **Joel** (Billy), **John** (Sir Elton), **Kiss**, **Lulu**, **Piaf** (Edith), **Pulp**, **Reed** (Lou), **Ross** (Diana), **Sade**, **UB40**, **Vega** (Suzanne), **Wham!**

05 **Adams** (Bryan), **Berry** (Chuck), **Black** (Cilla), **Bolan** (Marc), **Bowie**

(David), **Brown** (James), **Byrds**, **Carey** (Mariah), **Clash**, **Cohen** (Leonard), **Davis** (Sammy, Junior), **Doors**, **Dylan** (Bob), **Ferry** (Bryan), **Flack** (Roberta), **Haley** (Bill, and the Comets), **Jones** (Grace), **Jones** (Tom), **Kinks**, **Lewis** (Jerry Lee), **Oasis**, **Queen**, **Simon** (Paul), **Starr** (Ringo), **Waits** (Tom), **White** (Barry), **Wings**, **Young** (Neil), **ZZ Top**, **Zappa** (Frank)

06 **Bassey** (Shirley), **Cooper** (Alice), **Crosby** (Bing), **Damned**, **Denver** (John), **Domino** (Fats), **Eagles**, **Jolson** (Al), **Joplin** (Janis), **Knight** (Gladys, and the Pips), **Lennon** (John), **Marley** (Bob), **Midler** (Bette), **Newman** (Randy), **Pitney** (Gene), **Pogues**, **Police**, **Prince**, **Richie** (Lionel), **Simone** (Nina), **Smiths**, **Summer** (Donna), **The Who**, **Turner** (Tina), **Wonder** (Stevie)

07 **Animals**, **Beatles**, **Bee Gees**, **Blondie**, **Bon Jovi**, **Charles** (Ray), **Clapton** (Eric), **Cochran** (Eddie), **Collins** (Phil), **Diamond** (Neil), **Diddley** (Bo), **Gabriel** (Peter), **Garland** (Judy), **Genesis**, **Hendrix** (Jimi), **Hollies**, **Houston** (Whitney), **Jackson** (Janet), **Jackson** (Michael), **Madonna**, **Mercury** (Freddie), **Michael** (George), **Minogue** (Kylie), **Monkees**, **Orbison** (Roy), **Osmonds**, **Pickett** (Wilson), **Presley** (Elvis), **Redding** (Otis), **Richard** (Sir Cliff), **Shadows**, **Sinatra** (Frank), **Stevens** (Cat), **Stewart** (Rod), **Vincent** (Gene), **Warwick** (Dionne)

08 **Costello** (Elvis), **Franklin** (Aretha), **Harrison** (George), **Liberace**, **Mitchell** (Joni), **Morrison** (Van), **Oldfield** (Mike), **Van Halen**, **Vandross** (Luther), **Williams** (Robbie)

09 **Aerosmith**, **Beach Boys**, **Garfunkel** (Art),

Kraftwerk, McCartney
(Paul), **Motorhead, Pink
Floyd, Radiohead, Roxy
Music, Simply Red, Status
Quo, Steely Dan,
Streisand** (Barbra), **Thin
Lizzy**
10 **Carpenters, Deep Purple,
Duran Duran,
Eurythmics, Guns 'n'
Roses, Iron Maiden,
Moody Blues, Portishead,
Pretenders, Sex Pistols,
Spice Girls, Stranglers**
11 **Armatrading** (Joan),
**Culture Club, Dire
Straits, Human League,
Judas Priest, Led
Zeppelin, Public Enemy,
Simple Minds,
Springfield** (Dusty),
Springsteen (Bruce),
Temptations
12 **Black Sabbath,
Fleetwood Mac, Grateful
Dead, Talking Heads**
13 **Little Richard, Rolling
Stones, Spandau Ballet**
14 **Everly Brothers, Pointer
Sisters, Public Image Ltd**
15 **Neville Brothers**

single
03 one
04 free, lone, only, sole
06 unique
08 distinct, isolated, separate,
singular, solitary, unbroken
09 on your own, unmarried
10 individual, one and only,
particular, unattached

□single out
06 choose, select
07 isolate
08 identify, pinpoint, separate,
set apart
09 highlight
11 distinguish, separate out

single-handed
04 solo
05 alone
07 unaided
09 on your own
10 by yourself, unassisted

single-minded
03 set
05 fixed
06 dogged
08 resolute, tireless
09 dedicated, obsessive
10 unswerving, unwavering
12 monomaniacal

singly
06 solely
08 one by one
10 on their own, one at a time,
separately
12 individually

singular
03 odd
06 unique
07 curious, strange, unusual
08 atypical, peculiar,
uncommon
09 eccentric
10 remarkable
11 exceptional, outstanding
13 extraordinary

singularity
06 oddity
07 oddness
10 uniqueness
11 peculiarity, strangeness
12 eccentricity, idiosyncrasy
13 particularity

singularly
08 signally
09 unusually
10 especially, remarkably,
uncommonly
12 particularly
13 exceptionally, outstandingly
15 extraordinarily

sinister
07 harmful, ominous
08 menacing
10 malevolent, portentous
11 disquieting, threatening
12 inauspicious

sink
03 dig, dip, ebb, lay, sag, set
04 bore, dive, drop, fail, fall,
flag, risk, ruin, slip
05 drill, droop, drown, embed,
lapse, lower, put in, slump,
stoop, wreck
06 engulf, go down, invest,
lessen, plough, plunge,
weaken, worsen
07 decline, degrade, descend,
dwindle, founder, immerse,
plummet, scupper, scuttle,
subside, succumb
08 collapse, decrease,
diminish, submerge
09 disappear, penetrate
10 degenerate, go downhill

sinless
04 pure
08 innocent, virtuous
09 faultless, guiltless
11 uncorrupted

sinner
08 criminal, evil-doer, offender
09 miscreant, reprobate,
wrongdoer
10 malefactor
12 transgressor

sinuous
06 curved, slinky
07 bending, coiling, curling,
curving, turning, winding
08 tortuous, twisting
10 meandering, serpentine,
undulating

sip
03 sup
05 drink, taste
06 sample
08 mouthful, spoonful

siren
04 vamp
05 alarm, Circe
06 tocsin
07 charmer, Lorelei
08 car alarm
09 fire alarm, temptress
10 seductress
11 femme fatale
12 burglar alarm

sissy
03 wet
04 baby, soft, weak, wimp
05 pansy, softy
06 coward, feeble
07 milksop, unmanly, wimpish
08 cowardly, weakling
09 mummy's boy
10 effeminate, namby-pamby

sister
03 nun
06 abbess, fellow, friend
07 comrade, partner, sibling
08 prioress, relation, relative
09 associate, colleague,
companion

sit
03 lie
04 hang, hold, meet, pose, rest,
seat
05 brood, perch, place, roost,
squat, stand
06 gather, locate, settle
07 consult, contain, convene,
deposit, situate
08 assemble, position
10 deliberate
11 accommodate, be in session

site
03 lot, put, set
04 area, plot, spot

05 place, scene
06 ground, locate
07 install, setting, situate, station
08 locality, location, position
09 situation

sitting
05 spell
06 period
07 hearing, meeting, session
08 assembly
12 consultation

situate
05 place
06 locate
07 install, station
08 position

situation
03 job
04 case, post, rank, seat, site, spot
05 place, score, set-up, state
06 locale, milieu, office, status
07 affairs, climate, picture, setting, station
08 locality, location, position, scenario
09 condition
10 conditions, employment
11 environment, predicament, state of play
12 lie of the land, what's going on
13 circumstances
14 state of affairs

size
04 area, bulk, mass
05 range, scale
06 amount, extent, height, length, volume
07 expanse
08 vastness
09 immensity, magnitude
10 dimensions
11 measurement, proportions
12 measurements

◻**size up**
04 rate
05 gauge, judge
06 assess
07 measure, suss out, weigh up
08 appraise, estimate, evaluate

sizeable
11 substantial
12 considerable

sizzle
03 fry
04 hiss, spit
07 crackle, frizzle, sputter

skeletal
05 drawn, gaunt
06 wasted
07 haggard
08 shrunken
09 emaciated, fleshless
10 cadaverous
11 skin-and-bone
13 hollow-cheeked

skeleton
04 plan
05 basic, bones, draft, frame
06 lowest, sketch
07 minimum, outline, support
08 smallest
09 bare bones, framework, structure

sketch
04 draw, plan
05 draft, paint
06 depict, design, pencil
07 croquis, diagram, drawing, outline, portray, ébauche
08 abstract, block out, esquisse, rough out, skeleton, vignette
09 delineate, represent
11 delineation, description
14 representation

sketchily
07 hastily, roughly, vaguely
08 patchily
09 cursorily
11 imperfectly
12 inadequately, incompletely
13 perfunctorily

sketchy
05 bitty, crude, hasty, rough, vague
06 meagre, patchy, slight
07 cursory, scrappy
09 defective, deficient, imperfect
10 inadequate, incomplete, unfinished, unpolished
11 perfunctory, provisional, superficial
12 insufficient

skier
▶ *Names of skiers:*
04 **Hess** (Erica)
05 **Killy** (Jean Claude), **Tomba** (Alberto)
06 **Figini** (Michela), **Sailer** (Toni)
07 **Edwards** (Eddie 'The Eagle'), **Klammer** (Franz), **Nykanen** (Matti)
08 **Stenmark** (Ingemark), **Walliser** (Maria)

09 **Schneider** (Vreni)
10 **Girardelli** (Marc), **Moser-Proll** (Annemarie), **Zurbriggen** (Pirmin)
➤ See also **sport**

skilful
04 able, deft, good
05 adept, handy, smart
06 adroit, clever, expert, gifted, versed
07 capable, cunning, skilled, trained
08 masterly, tactical, talented
09 competent, dexterous, efficient, practised
10 proficient, well-versed
11 experienced
12 accomplished, professional

skill
03 art
05 knack
07 ability, finesse, mastery
08 deftness, facility
09 adeptness, expertise, handiness, technique
10 adroitness, cleverness, competence, efficiency, experience, expertness
11 proficiency
14 accomplishment
15 professionalism

skilled
04 able, good
05 adept
06 expert, gifted
07 capable, skilful, trained
08 masterly, schooled, talented
09 competent, efficient, practised, qualified
10 proficient
11 experienced
12 accomplished, professional

skim
03 fly
04 sail, scan, skip
05 brush, cream, float, glide, graze, plane, skate, touch
06 bounce
07 run over
08 glance at, separate
09 despumate
10 run through

skimp
06 scrimp
09 cut back on, economize
10 cut corners
12 be economical
15 tighten your belt

skimpy
04 thin

skin

05 short, small, tight
06 meagre, measly, scanty, sparse
09 niggardly
10 inadequate

skin

03 pod
04 fell, film, flay, hide, hull, husk, peel, pelt, rind
05 cover, crust, cutis, derma, graze, layer, strip
06 casing, corium, dermis, fleece, scrape
07 coating, cuticle, outside, surface
08 covering, membrane, tegument
09 epidermis
10 integument

◻ **by the skin of your teeth**

06 barely
08 narrowly, only just
10 a near thing
11 a close thing

skin-deep

07 outward, shallow, surface
08 external
10 artificial
11 superficial

skinflint

05 miser
06 meanie
07 niggard, Scrooge
08 tightwad
11 cheeseparer
12 penny-pincher

skinny

04 lean, thin
07 scraggy, scrawny
08 skeletal, underfed
09 emaciated
11 skin-and-bone
14 undernourished

skip

03 bob, cut, hop
04 dart, jump, leap, miss, omit, pass, race, rush, tear
05 bound, caper, dance, dodge, frisk
06 bounce, cavort, gambol, prance, spring
07 miss out
08 leave out

skirmish

05 argue, brawl, brush, clash, fight, mêlée, scrap, set-to
06 affray, battle, combat, dust-up, fracas, tussle
07 scuffle
08 argument, conflict

11 altercation
13 confrontation

skirt

04 edge
05 avoid, evade, flank
06 border, bypass, circle
07 go round
10 circumvent

skit

05 spoof
06 parody, satire, send-up, sketch
07 take-off
09 burlesque
10 caricature

skittish

07 fidgety, playful, restive
09 excitable, frivolous
12 highly-strung

skittles

04 pins
06 tenpin
08 ninepins
10 kettle-pins

skive

04 idle, laze
05 dodge, shirk, skulk, slack
12 swing the lead

skiver

05 idler
06 dodger, loafer
07 shirker, slacker

skulduggery

08 trickery
09 chicanery, duplicity
13 double-dealing, jiggery-pokery
15 underhandedness

skulk

04 hide, lurk
05 prowl, slink, sneak, steal
09 lie in wait, pussyfoot

sky

03 air
05 space
06 welkin
07 heavens, the blue
08 empyreal, empyrean, supernal
09 celestial, firmament
10 atmosphere
13 vault of heaven

slab

04 hunk, lump
05 block, brick, chunk, piece, slice, wedge, wodge

slack

03 lax

04 give, idle, lazy, limp, play, slow
05 loose, quiet, shirk, skive
06 excess, leeway, sloppy
07 flaccid, relaxed, sagging
08 inactive, malinger, sluggish
09 negligent
10 neglectful, permissive

slacken

◻ **slacken off**

04 ease, slow
05 abate, relax
06 lessen, loosen, reduce
07 get less, release
08 decrease, diminish, moderate, slow down
10 take it easy

slacker

05 idler
06 loafer, skiver
07 dawdler, shirker
08 layabout
10 malingerer
12 clock-watcher

slag

◻ **slag off**

05 abuse, slate
06 berate, deride, insult, malign
08 lambaste
09 criticize

slake

04 sate
06 quench, reduce
07 assuage, gratify, satiate, satisfy
10 extinguish

slam

03 pan
04 bang, dash, hurl, slap
05 crash, fling, slate, smash, throw, thump
06 attack
07 rubbish, run down
08 denounce
09 criticize
12 pull to pieces, tear to shreds

slander

05 smear
06 defame, malign, vilify
07 calumny, obloquy, scandal, traduce
08 badmouth, vilipend
09 aspersion
10 calumniate, defamation, sling mud at
11 mudslinging, traducement
12 vilification
13 smear campaign

slanderous
06 untrue
07 abusive
09 aspersive, aspersory, insulting, malicious
10 calumnious, defamatory
12 calumniatory

slang
04 cant
05 argot, lingo
06 jargon, patois, patter
09 vulgarism
11 doublespeak
13 colloquialism

slanging match
05 set-to
06 barney
07 dispute, quarrel
08 argument
09 argy-bargy
11 altercation

slant
04 bend, bias, lean, list, ramp, skew, tilt, view, warp
05 angle, pitch, slope, twist
06 camber, shelve
07 distort, incline, leaning
08 attitude, diagonal, gradient
09 prejudice, viewpoint
10 distortion
11 inclination, point of view

slanting
05 askew
06 tilted
07 oblique
08 diagonal
11 on an incline

slap
03 hit
04 bang, biff, clap, cuff, daub, dead, slam, sock
05 apply, clout, plonk, plumb, plump, punch, right, smack, spank, stick, thump, whack
06 spread, strike, wallop
07 clobber, exactly, plaster, put down, set down
08 directly, straight
09 precisely

□slap in the face
04 blow, snub
06 insult, rebuff, rebuke
07 affront, put-down, repulse
11 humiliation

slapdash
04 rash
05 hasty, messy
06 clumsy, sloppy, untidy
07 hurried, offhand
08 careless, slipshod, slovenly

11 perfunctory, thoughtless
14 thrown-together

slap-happy
06 casual
08 reckless, slapdash
09 haphazard, hit-or-miss
10 nonchalant
13 irresponsible

slapstick
05 farce
09 horseplay
10 buffoonery, knockabout

slap-up
06 lavish, superb
08 princely, splendid
09 sumptuous

slash
03 axe, cut, rip
04 curb, gash, hack, rend, rent, slit, tear
05 knife, prune, score
08 decrease, incision, lacerate

slate
03 pan
04 slam
06 berate, rebuke
07 censure, rubbish, run down
09 criticize, reprimand
12 pull to pieces, tear to pieces, tear to shreds

slatternly
05 dirty, dowdy
06 frowzy, frumpy, untidy
07 unclean, unkempt
08 slipshod, slovenly, sluttish
10 bedraggled

slaughter
04 kill, slay
06 murder
07 butcher, carnage, killing
08 butchery, massacre
09 blood-bath, bloodshed, liquidate
10 annihilate, put to death
11 exterminate

slave
04 serf, slog, toil
05 grind, sweat
06 drudge, labour, lackey, menial, skivvy, thrall, vassal
07 bondman, servant, villein
08 bondsman
09 bond-slave, bondwoman
10 bondswoman
11 bondservant

slaver
05 drool
06 drivel

07 dribble, slobber
08 salivate

slavery
04 yoke
06 thrall
07 bondage, serfdom
08 thraldom
09 captivity, servitude, vassalage
11 enslavement, subjugation

slavish
03 low
04 mean
06 abject, menial, strict
07 fawning, literal, servile
08 cringing
10 grovelling, obsequious, submissive
11 deferential, sycophantic

slay
04 kill
06 murder, rub out
07 butcher, destroy, execute
08 dispatch, massacre
09 eliminate, slaughter

slaying
06 murder
07 killing
08 butchery, dispatch, massacre
09 mactation, slaughter
11 destruction, elimination

sleazy
05 seedy, tacky
06 crummy, sordid
07 run-down, squalid
12 disreputable

sleek
05 shiny, silky
06 glossy, silken, smooth
11 well-groomed

sleep
03 kip, nap
04 doss, doze, rest
06 catnap, nod off, repose, siesta, snooze
07 drop off, shut-eye, slumber
08 be asleep, crash out, doss down, drift off, flake out
09 hibernate
10 fall asleep, forty winks
11 have a snooze, hibernation
14 have forty winks
15 go out like a light

sleepiness
06 torpor
07 languor
09 heaviness, oscitancy
10 drowsiness, somnolence

sleeping
04 idle
06 asleep
07 dormant, passive, unaware
08 inactive, off guard
10 slumbering
11 daydreaming, hibernating, inattentive

sleepless
05 alert, awake
07 wakeful
08 restless, vigilant, watchful
09 disturbed, insomniac, wide-awake

sleeplessness
08 insomnia
11 wakefulness
12 insomnolence

sleepwalker
12 noctambulist, somnambulist

sleepwalking
12 noctambulism, somnambulism

sleepy
04 dull, slow
05 heavy, quiet, still, tired, weary
06 drowsy, torpid
07 languid
08 comatose, hypnotic, peaceful, sluggish
09 lethargic, somnolent, soporific
10 languorous

sleight of hand
05 magic, skill
08 artifice, trickery
09 deception, dexterity
10 adroitness
11 legerdemain

slender
04 lean, slim, thin, trim
05 faint, scant, small
06 feeble, flimsy, little, meagre, remote, scanty, slight, svelte
07 tenuous, willowy
08 graceful
09 sylphlike, willowish
10 inadequate
12 insufficient
14 inconsiderable

sleuth
04 dick, tail
06 shadow
07 gumshoe, tracker
09 detective
10 bloodhound, private eye

slice
03 cut
04 chop, hunk, part, slab
05 carve, chunk, cut up, piece, sever, share, wafer, wedge, whack
06 divide, rasher, sliver
07 helping, portion, section, segment, tranche
09 allotment

slick
04 deft, easy, glib
05 quick, sharp, shiny, sleek, suave
06 adroit, smarmy, smooth
07 skilful
08 masterly, polished, unctuous
09 dexterous, efficient, plausible, well-oiled
11 streamlined
13 smooth-talking, sophisticated, well-organized

slide
03 ski
04 drop, fall, skid, skim, slip
05 coast, glide, plane, skate
06 lessen, plunge, worsen
07 decline, plummet, slither
08 decrease
10 depreciate
11 deteriorate

slight
03 cut
04 slim, slur, snub
05 elfin, frail, minor, petty, scant, scorn, small, spurn
06 dainty, ignore, insult, little, minute, modest, offend, paltry, petite, rebuff, subtle
07 affront, despise, disdain, fragile, slender, trivial
08 delicate, rudeness
09 disparage
10 diminutive, negligible
11 discourtesy, unimportant
13 insubstantial, slap in the face
14 kick in the teeth

slighting
07 abusive
08 scornful
09 insulting, offensive
10 belittling, disdainful, slanderous
11 disparaging
15 uncomplimentary

slightly
04 a bit
06 rather
07 a little

slim
04 diet, lean, poor, thin, trim
05 faint, scant, small
06 flimsy, little, meagre, reduce, remote, scanty, slight, svelte
07 slender, tenuous, willowy
09 go on a diet, sylphlike, willowish
10 inadequate, lose weight

slime
03 goo, mud
04 gunk, mess, muck, ooze, yuck

slimy
04 miry, oily, oozy
05 muddy
06 greasy, mucous, sludgy, smarmy, sticky
07 servile, viscous
08 creeping, slippery, toadying, unctuous

sling
03 lob, shy
04 band, hang, hurl, loop, toss
05 chuck, fling, heave, pitch, strap, swing, throw
07 bandage, support, suspend
08 catapult

slink
04 lurk, slip
05 creep, prowl, sidle, skulk, sneak, steal

slinky
05 sleek
07 sinuous
08 clinging
09 skin-tight
12 close-fitting
13 figure-hugging

slip
04 boob, fall, note, sink, skid, slim, trip, wear
05 error, fault, glide, jupon, lapse, paper, skate, slide, slink, slump, steal, strip
06 cock-up, coupon, howler, kirtle, plunge, slight, worsen
07 bloomer, blunder, clanger, decline, failure, get into, go to pot, mistake, slender, slither, take off, voucher
08 decrease, omission
09 oversight, petticoat
10 change into, underskirt
11 certificate, deteriorate
12 indiscretion
15 lose your balance, lose your footing

◘**give someone the slip**
04 duck

05 dodge
08 shake off
10 escape from

☐**let slip**
04 leak, tell
06 betray, let out, reveal
07 divulge

☐**slip up**
03 err
04 boob, goof
05 botch, fluff
06 bungle, cock up
07 blunder, stumble
08 get wrong
12 miscalculate

slipper
04 mule, pump
06 loafer, panton, sandal
08 flip-flop, moccasin,
    pabouche, pantable,
    pantofle
09 houseshoe, pantoffle,
    pantoufle

slippery
03 icy, wet
04 foxy, oily
05 slimy
06 clever, crafty, greasy, shifty,
    smarmy, smooth
07 cunning, devious, evasive
09 deceitful, dishonest
10 perfidious, unreliable
11 duplicitous, treacherous
13 untrustworthy

slipshod
03 lax
06 casual, sloppy, untidy
08 careless, slapdash, slovenly
09 negligent

slip-up
04 boob, slip
05 error, fault
06 booboo, cock-up, howler
07 bloomer, blunder, mistake

slit
03 cut, rip
04 gash, rend, rent, tear, vent
05 knife, lance, slash, slice, split
06 pierce
07 fissure, opening
08 aperture, incision

slither
04 skid, slip, worm
05 creep, slide, snake

sliver
04 chip
05 flake, piece, scrap, shard,
    shred, slice, wafer
06 paring, shiver

07 shaving
08 fragment, splinter

slob
03 oaf, yob
04 boor, lout
06 sloven

slobber
05 drool
06 drivel, slaver
07 dribble
08 salivate

slog
04 bash, belt, hike, plod, slug,
    sock, toil, trek, work
05 grind, slave, slosh, thump
06 effort, labour, trudge
08 exertion, struggle
13 plough through

slogan
05 motto
06 jingle, war cry
09 battle-cry, catchword,
    watchword
11 catch phrase, rallying cry

slop
05 slosh, spill
08 overflow, splatter

slope
03 dip, tip
04 drop, fall, lean, rise, tilt
05 pitch, slant
07 incline

☐**slope off**
08 slip away, sneak off

sloping
05 askew
06 angled
07 canting, leaning, oblique,
    tilting
08 bevelled, inclined, slanting
09 inclining
11 acclivitous, declivitous

sloppy
03 wet
05 corny, gushy, hasty, messy,
    mushy, runny, soggy, soppy
06 clumsy, sickly, slushy, watery
07 hurried, splashy
08 careless, slapdash, slipshod,
    slovenly
09 hit-or-miss, schmaltzy
11 sentimental

slosh
04 bash, biff, pour, slap, slog,
    slop, slug, sock, wade
05 swipe, thump
06 splash, thwack, wallop

slot
03 fit, gap, put
04 hole, slit, spot, time, vent
05 crack, niche, notch, place,
    space
06 assign, groove, insert, window
07 channel, install, opening,
    vacancy
08 aperture, position
10 pigeonhole

sloth
06 acedia, torpor
07 accidie, inertia
08 idleness, laziness
09 fainéance, indolence

slothful
04 idle, lazy
06 torpid
07 skiving, workshy
08 fainéant, inactive, indolent

slouch
04 bend, loll
05 droop, hunch, slump, stoop
06 lounge
07 shamble, shuffle

slovenly
05 dirty, messy
06 sloppy, untidy
07 scruffy, unclean, unkempt
08 careless, slipshod, sluttish
10 slatternly
12 disorganized

slow
04 curb, dull, dumb, late, lazy
05 brake, check, delay, quiet,
    slack, tardy, thick
06 averse, ease up, hold up,
    retard, stupid
07 gradual, tedious
08 creeping, dilatory, handicap,
    keep back, measured,
    plodding, retarded, sluggish,
    stagnant
09 ponderous, prolonged,
    unhurried, unwilling
10 decelerate, dull-witted,
    protracted, uneventful
11 reduce speed
12 long-drawn-out
13 at a snail's pace,
    time-consuming
14 put the brakes on

slowly
05 largo, lento
06 adagio, lazily
09 by degrees, larghetto
10 ploddingly, sluggishly
11 ponderously, unhurriedly
13 at a snail's pace
14 little by little

sludge
03 mud
04 gunk, mire, muck, ooze, silt, slag, slop
05 dregs, gunge, slime, slush, swill
07 residue
08 sediment

sluggish
04 dull, idle, lazy, slow
06 torpid
07 languid
08 inactive, indolent, lifeless, listless, slothful
09 apathetic, lethargic
10 languorous, slow-moving

sluggishness
06 apathy, phlegm, torpor
07 inertia, languor
08 dullness, lethargy, slowness
09 indolence, lassitude
10 drowsiness, stagnation
12 listlessness, slothfulness

sluice
04 wash
05 drain, flush, slosh, swill
06 drench
08 irrigate

slumber
03 kip, nap
04 doze, rest
05 sleep
06 drowse, repose, snooze
10 forty winks

slummy
07 decayed, run-down, squalid
08 wretched
10 ramshackle

slump
03 low, sag
04 bend, fail, fall, flop, loll, sink
05 crash, droop, slide
06 plunge, slouch, trough
07 decline, plummet, subside
08 collapse, downturn, nosedive
09 recession
10 depression

slur
05 libel, smear, stain
06 insult, slight, stigma
07 affront, calumny, slander
08 disgrace, innuendo
09 aspersion, discredit
11 insinuation

slush
04 gush, mush, pulp, snow
08 schmaltz
10 sloppiness

11 mawkishness
14 sentimentality

slut
04 drab, slag, tart
06 hooker, sloven
07 floosie, trollop
08 scrubber, slattern
10 loose woman, prostitute

sly
04 foxy, wily
05 canny, smart
06 artful, astute, covert, crafty, shifty, sneaky, subtle, tricky
07 devious, furtive
08 guileful, scheming, stealthy
09 conniving, underhand

❏**on the sly**
07 on the q.t.
08 covertly, in secret
09 furtively, in private

smack
03 box, hit
04 bang, belt, blow, clap, cuff, dash, hint, slap, tang, thud, zest
05 crash, evoke, punch, spank, speck, taste, tinge, touch, trace, whack, whiff
06 hint at, nuance, relish, savour, strike, thwack
07 exactly, flavour, suggest
08 directly, piquancy, savour of, slap-bang, straight
09 precisely
11 bring to mind, remind you of

❏**smack your lips**
06 relish, savour
09 delight in, drool over

small
03 wee
04 mean, mini, poky, puny, tiny
05 minor, petty, short, teeny
06 little, meagre, minute, paltry, petite, pocket, slight
07 ashamed, compact, trivial
08 degraded, pint-size, trifling
09 miniature, minuscule, pint-sized
10 diminutive, humiliated, inadequate, negligible
11 microscopic, unimportant
13 insignificant

small-minded
04 mean
05 petty, rigid
06 biased
07 bigoted, insular
09 parochial
12 narrow-minded

small-time
05 minor, petty
08 piddling

smarminess
07 suavity
08 oiliness, toadying
09 servility
10 sycophancy, unctuosity
12 unctuousness
14 obsequiousness

smarmy
04 oily
05 suave
07 fawning, servile
08 crawling, toadying, unctuous
10 obsequious
11 bootlicking, sycophantic
12 ingratiating

smart
03 nip
04 ache, burn, chic, cool, hurt, neat, posh, tidy, trim
05 acute, sharp, sting, throb
06 astute, bright, clever, dapper, glitzy, modish, shrewd, snazzy, spruce, tingle, twinge
07 elegant, stylish
11 fashionable, intelligent, presentable, well-dressed, well-groomed

smart alec
07 know-all, wise guy
08 wiseacre
10 clever dick
11 clever clogs, smartypants

smarten
05 clean, groom
06 neaten, polish
08 spruce up

smash
03 hit, run
04 bang, bash, bump, dash, ruin
05 break, crack, crash, crush, drive, knock, prang, thump, wreck
06 defeat, pile-up, strike
07 collide, destroy, shatter
08 accident, demolish
09 collision, pulverize
12 disintegrate

smashing
05 great, super
08 fabulous, terrific
09 excellent, fantastic, first-rate, wonderful
10 first-class, tremendous

smattering
04 dash
07 modicum
09 rudiments
10 sprinkling

smear
03 rub
04 blot, coat, daub, slap, slur, spot
05 cover, libel, patch, stain, sully, taint
06 blotch, defame, malign, smudge, spread, streak, vilify
07 blacken, obloquy, slander, tarnish
08 badmouth
09 aspersion
10 calumniate, defamation
11 mudslinging

smell
03 fug, hum
04 niff, nose, pong, ponk, reek
05 aroma, odour, scent, sniff, snuff, stink, trace, whiff
06 savour, stench
07 perfume
08 mephitis

smelly
03 bad, off
04 foul, high
05 fetid, pongy
06 putrid
07 humming, noisome, reeking
08 mephitic, stinking
10 malodorous

smile
04 beam, grin, leer
05 laugh, smirk, sneer
06 giggle, simper, titter
07 chuckle, snigger

smirk
04 grin, leer
05 sneer

smitten
07 charmed, plagued
09 afflicted, enamoured
10 bowled over, captivated, infatuated

smog
03 fog
04 haze, mist
05 fumes, smoke
09 pea-souper, pollution

smoke
03 dry, fog, gas
04 cure, puff, smog
05 fumes
07 light up
08 preserve, smoulder

smoky
04 dark, grey, hazy
05 black, foggy
06 cloudy, smoggy

smooth
04 calm, ease, easy, even, flat, glib, help, iron, roll, sand
05 allay, flush, level, plane, press, sleek, slick, suave
06 assist, glassy, pacify, polish, silken, smarmy, soothe, steady, urbane
07 appease, assuage, even out, flatten, mollify, plaster, rub down, velvety
08 calm down, mitigate, palliate, polished, tranquil
09 alleviate, burnished, encourage, plausible
10 effortless, facilitate, make easier, persuasive
11 like a mirror, trouble-free, undisturbed
12 ingratiating, plain sailing
13 over-confident, sophisticated, uninterrupted

smoothly
06 calmly, easily, evenly, mildly
07 equably
08 fluently
10 peacefully, tranquilly
12 effortlessly

smoothness
04 ease, flow
07 fluency
08 calmness, evenness, facility
10 efficiency, regularity

smooth-talking
04 glib
05 bland, slick, suave
06 facile, smooth
09 plausible
10 persuasive
13 silver-tongued

smother
04 damp
05 choke, cover, snuff
06 dampen, muffle, put out, stifle
07 repress
08 suppress
09 overwhelm, suffocate
10 asphyxiate, extinguish

smoulder
04 boil, burn, foam, fume, rage
06 fester, seethe, simmer

smudge
04 blot, blur, daub, mark, soil, spot

05 dirty, smear, stain
06 blotch, smutch, streak
07 blacken, blemish
08 besmirch

smug
08 priggish, superior
10 complacent
13 self-righteous, self-satisfied
14 holier-than-thou

smuggler
04 mule
06 runner
10 bootlegger, moonshiner
13 contrabandist

smutty
04 blue, lewd, racy
05 bawdy, crude, dirty
06 ribald, risqué, vulgar
07 obscene, raunchy
08 improper, indecent, prurient
09 off colour, salacious
10 indelicate, suggestive

snack
04 bite
06 buffet, titbit
07 nibbles
08 sandwich
09 bite to eat, elevenses, light meal
12 refreshments

snag
04 hole, tear
05 catch, hitch
07 problem
08 drawback, obstacle
10 difficulty
12 complication
14 stumbling-block

snake

➤ *Types of snake:*
03 asp, boa
05 adder, cobra, mamba, viper
06 python, taipan
08 anaconda, pit viper
09 king cobra, puff adder, tree snake
10 copperhead, coral snake, fer-de-lance, grass snake, sidewinder
11 rattlesnake, smooth snake
14 boa constrictor
➤ See also **animal**

snap
03 nip
04 bark, bite, film, grip, shot, span, take, time
05 break, catch, crack, flick, grasp, growl, photo, print,

seize, shoot, snarl, spell, split, still, stint
06 abrupt, bark at, fillip, period, record, retort, snatch, sudden
07 crackle, growl at, instant, picture, snarl at, stretch
08 fracture, separate, snapshot, splinter
09 immediate, lash out at, on-the-spot
10 photograph
14 speak sharply to

□snap up
03 nab
04 grab
05 grasp, pluck, seize
06 pick up, snatch
08 pounce on

snappy
04 chic, edgy
05 brisk, cross, natty, quick, smart, testy
06 lively, snazzy, touchy, trendy
07 brusque, stylish
09 crotchety, energetic, irascible, irritable
11 bad-tempered, fashionable
13 quick-tempered

snare
03 gin, net
04 trap, wire
05 catch, noose, seize
06 entrap
07 capture, ensnare, springe

snarl
04 bark, howl, knot, snap, yelp
05 growl, ravel, twist
06 enmesh, tangle
07 confuse, embroil, entwine
08 complain, entangle
10 complicate

snarl-up
04 mess
05 mix-up
06 tangle
08 gridlock
10 traffic jam
12 entanglement

snatch
03 bag, nab
04 gain, grab, grip, pull
05 grasp, pluck, seize, steal, swipe, wrest
06 abduct, kidnap, wrench
07 section, segment, snippet
08 fragment
11 make off with

snazzy
05 jazzy, ritzy, showy, smart

06 flashy, snappy, sporty, with it
07 dashing, raffish, stylish

sneak
03 pad, rat
04 lurk, mole, shop, slip
05 creep, grass, prowl, slink, split, steal
06 covert, secret, snitch, squeal
07 furtive, grass on, smuggle
08 inform on, informer, squealer, tell-tale
09 tell tales
13 whistle-blower

sneaking
06 hidden, secret
07 furtive, lurking, nagging
08 grudging, unvoiced
09 intuitive
11 unexpressed
13 surreptitious, uncomfortable

sneaky
03 low, sly
04 base, mean
05 nasty, shady, snide
07 devious, furtive, low-down
08 cowardly, guileful, slippery
09 deceitful, malicious
12 unscrupulous
13 double-dealing, untrustworthy

sneer
04 gibe, jeer, mock
05 laugh, scoff, scorn, taunt
06 deride, insult, slight
07 disdain, mockery
08 derision, ridicule
10 look down on

snicker
05 laugh, sneer
06 giggle, titter
07 chortle, chuckle, snigger

snide
04 mean
05 nasty
06 biting, unkind
07 jeering, mocking
08 derisive, scathing, scoffing, spiteful, taunting
09 malicious, sarcastic

sniff
04 hint, nose
05 aroma, scent, smell, snuff, trace, whiff
06 inhale
07 breathe, snuffle
10 suggestion
11 get a whiff of

□sniff at
04 mock, shun
05 spurn
06 deride, refuse, reject, slight
07 disdain, dismiss, laugh at, scoff at, sneer at

sniffy
06 snobby
07 haughty
08 scoffing, scornful, sneering, snobbish, superior
10 disdainful
12 supercilious

snigger
05 laugh, smirk, sneer
06 giggle, titter
07 chortle, chuckle, snicker

snip
03 bit, cut
04 clip, crop, trim
05 piece, prune, steal
07 bargain, good buy, snippet
08 clipping, fragment
12 special offer
13 value for money

snippet
03 bit
04 part
05 piece, scrap, shred
06 snatch
07 cutting, portion, section, segment
08 clipping, fragment, particle

snivel
03 cry, sob
04 bawl, blub
05 sniff, whine
06 whinge
07 grizzle, sniffle, snuffle

snivelling
06 crying
07 whining
09 sniffling, snuffling, whingeing

snobbery
04 airs, side
09 arrogance, loftiness
10 pretension, snootiness, uppishness
11 haughtiness, superiority
13 airs and graces

snobbish
05 lofty, proud
06 snooty, uppity
07 haughty, stuck-up
08 affected, jumped-up, superior
10 hoity-toity
11 pretentious, toffee-nosed

12 supercilious
13 high and mighty

snoop
03 pry, spy
07 Paul Pry, snooper
08 busybody, meddling
10 nosy parker
12 interference
14 poke your nose in
15 stick your nose in

snooper
03 pry, spy
05 snoop
07 Paul Pry
10 nosy parker

snooze
03 kip, nap
04 doze
05 sleep
06 catnap, nod off, siesta
07 drop off, shut-eye, slumber
14 have forty winks

snout
03 neb
04 nose
05 trunk
06 muzzle, snitch
09 proboscis, schnozzle

snow
05 sleet, slush
08 blizzard

snub
03 cut
04 shun
06 ignore, insult, slight
07 affront, mortify
12 cold-shoulder
13 slap in the face

snug
04 cosy, warm
05 comfy, tight
06 homely, secure
08 friendly, intimate
09 sheltered, skintight
11 comfortable
12 close-fitting

snuggle
06 cuddle, curl up, nestle, nuzzle

soak
03 wet
05 bathe, imbue, souse, steep
06 drench, infuse
07 immerse
08 marinate, permeate, saturate, submerge
09 penetrate

soaking
06 soaked, sodden
07 sopping
08 drenched, dripping, wringing
09 saturated, streaming
10 sopping wet, wet through
11 waterlogged

soar
03 fly
04 rise, wing
05 climb, glide, tower
06 ascend, rocket, spiral
07 take off
08 escalate
09 skyrocket

sob
03 cry
06 boohoo, snivel
07 blubber

sober
03 dry
04 calm, dark, drab
05 grave, plain, quiet, staid
06 sedate, serene, solemn, sombre, steady
07 serious, subdued
08 composed, rational
09 abstinent, dignified, practical, realistic, temperate
10 abstemious, on the wagon, restrained, thoughtful
14 self-controlled

sobriety
07 gravity
08 calmness
09 composure, restraint, solemnity, staidness
10 abstinence, temperance
14 abstemiousness

so-called
07 alleged, nominal, would-be
08 supposed
09 professed, soi-disant
10 self-styled

sociability
10 affability, chumminess
12 congeniality, conviviality, friendliness
14 gregariousness

sociable
06 chummy, genial
07 affable
08 familiar, friendly, outgoing
09 convivial
10 gregarious
13 companionable

social
05 civic, dance, group, party
06 common, public
07 general
09 community, gathering
11 get-together
13 entertainment

socialism
07 leftism, Marxism
08 Leninism
09 communism, Stalinism, welfarism
10 Trotskyism

socialist
03 red
04 Trot
06 commie, leftie
07 leftist
08 left-wing
09 communist
10 left-winger, Trotskyist, Trotskyite

socialize
03 mix
06 hobnob, mingle
09 entertain
10 be sociable, meet people
11 get together

society
04 band, body, club, nobs
05 elite, group, guild, union
06 circle, gentry, league, nation, people, public, swells
07 company, culture, mankind
08 alliance, humanity, sorority
09 community, human race, humankind
10 federation, fellowship, fraternity, friendship, population, sisterhood
11 aristocracy, association, brotherhood, camaraderie, corporation, high society, the smart set
12 civilization
13 companionship, the upper crust

sodden
03 wet
05 boggy, soggy
06 marshy, soaked
09 saturated
11 waterlogged

soft
03 dim, lax, low
04 easy, kind, mild, pale, weak
05 bland, cushy, downy, faint, furry, light, mushy, muted, pulpy, quiet, silky, sweet

06 dulcet, fleecy, gentle,
hushed, low-key, mellow,
pastel, pliant, silken, smooth,
spongy, tender

07 diffuse, ductile, elastic,
flowing, lenient, liberal,
plastic, pliable, squashy,
squishy, subdued, velvety

08 delicate, merciful, soothing,
squelchy, tolerant, yielding

09 easy-going, forgiving,
indulgent, malleable,
sensitive, spineless

10 forbearing, restrained

11 comfortable, soft-hearted,
sympathetic

12 affectionate

soften
03 pad
04 calm, ease, melt
05 abate, lower, quell, relax, still
06 lessen, muffle, reduce,
soothe, subdue, temper
07 appease, assuage, cushion,
lighten, liquefy, mollify
08 diminish, mitigate,
moderate, palliate
09 alleviate

◻**soften up**
04 melt
06 disarm, weaken
07 win over
08 butter up, soft-soap
10 conciliate

soft-hearted
06 gentle, tender
11 sentimental, sympathetic,
warm-hearted
12 affectionate
13 compassionate

soft-pedal
06 go easy, subdue
08 moderate, play down, tone
down

soft spot
08 penchant, weakness
10 partiality

soggy
03 wet
04 damp
05 boggy, heavy, moist, pulpy
06 soaked, sodden, spongy
11 waterlogged

soil
04 clay, dirt, dust, foul, land,
loam, spot
05 dirty, earth, humus, muddy,
smear, stain, sully
06 defile, ground, region,
smudge

07 begrime, country, pollute,
tarnish
08 besmirch
09 territory
10 terra firma

soiled
05 dirty, grimy, manky
07 spotted, stained, sullied
08 maculate, polluted

sojourn
04 rest, stay, stop
05 abide, lodge, tarry, visit
06 reside
08 stopover
13 peregrination

solace
05 allay, cheer
06 relief, soften, soothe
07 comfort, console
10 condolence
11 alleviation, consolation

soldier
➤ See also **military**
─────────────────────
▶ *Types of soldier*:
02 GI
03 NCO
05 cadet, tommy
06 gunner, hussar, lancer,
marine, sapper, sentry,
troops
07 dragoon, fighter, officer,
orderly, private, recruit,
regular, trooper, warrior
08 commando, fusilier,
partisan, rifleman
09 centurion, conscript,
guardsman, guerrilla,
mercenary
10 cavalryman, serviceman
11 infantryman, legionnaire,
paratrooper, Territorial
─────────────────────
▶ *Names of soldiers*:
03 Cid (El), Lee (Robert
Edward), Ney (Michel), Wet
(Christian de), Zia
(Muhammad)
04 Cade (Jack), Foch
(Ferdinand), Haig
(Alexander), Haig
(Douglas, Earl), Jodl
(Alfred), John (Don), Khan
(Ayub), Röhm (Ernst), Tojo
(Hideki)
05 Allen (Ethan), Bader (Sir
Douglas), Botha (Louis),
Bowie (James), Bruce
(Robert), Cimon, Clive
(Robert, Lord), Dayan
(Moshe), Essex (Robert
Devereux, Earl of), Gates

(Horatio), Grant (Ulysses
Simpson), Inönü (Ismet),
Monck (George), Murat
(Joachim), Perón (Juan),
Pride (Sir Thomas), Smuts
(Jan), Sucre (Antonio José
de), Sully (Maximilien de
Béthune Duc de), Timur,
Zhu De

06 Antony (Mark), Arnold
(Benedict), Brutus (Marcus
Junius), Caesar (Julius),
Cortés (Hernán), Custer
(George Armstrong),
Edward (the Black Prince),
Egmont (Graaf van Gavre),
Eugene (of Savoy), Franco
(Francisco), Gaulle
(Charles de), Gordon
(Charles George), Granby
(John Manners, Marquis
of), Greene (Nathanael),
Marius (Gaius), Moltke
(Helmuth, Graf von),
Napier (Robert, Lord),
Nasser (Gamal Abd al-),
Patton (George), Pétain
(Philippe), Pompey,
Raglan (Fitzroy James
Henry Somerset, Lord),
Revere (Paul), Rommel
(Erwin), Rupert (Prince),
Scipio (Publius Cornelius),
Zhukov (Giorgiy)

07 Agrippa (Marcus
Vipsanius), Allenby
(Edmund, Viscount),
Atatürk (Mustapha
Kemal), Baldwin, Blücher
(Gebbard Leberecht von
Fürst von), Bourbon
(Charles), Boycott (Charles
Cunningham), Bradley
(Omar Nelson), Cassius,
Coligny (Gaspard de),
Dreyfus (Alfred), Farnese
(Alessandro), Gaddafi
(Muammar), Gemayel
(Bashir), Jackson (Thomas
Jonathan), Kutuzov
(Mikhail, Knyaz), Lambert
(John), Maurice (Prince),
Metaxas (Ioannis), Pizarro
(Francisco), Ptolemy,
Sherman (William
Tecumseh), Tancred,
Warwick (Richard Neville,
Earl of), William (Prince of
Orange)

08 Agricola (Gnaeus Julius),
Antonius (Marcus),
Arminius, Badoglio

(Pietro), **Bentinck** (William, Lord), **Boadicea**, **Burnside** (Ambrose Everett), **Campbell** (Sir Colin), **Cardigan** (James Thomas Brudenell, Earl of), **Cromwell** (Oliver), **Eichmann** (Adolf), **Harrison** (William Henry), **Hereward** (the Wake), **Horrocks** (Sir Brian), **Ironside** (William, Lord), **Itúrbide** (Agustín de), **Lawrence** (Thomas Edward), **Lucullus** (Lucius Licinius), **Marshall** (George Catlett), **Mengistu** (Haile Mariam), **Montfort** (Simon de), **Montrose** (James Graham, Marquis of), **Napoleon**, **Pershing** (John Joseph), **Potemkin** (Grigoriy), **Seleucus**, **Sheridan** (Philip Henry), **Sikorski** (Wladyslaw), **Stanhope** (James, Earl), **Tokugawa** (Ieyasu), **Wolseley** (Garnet, Viscount), **Xenophon**, **Yamagata** (Prince Aritomo)

09 **Alexander** (Harold, Earl), **Antonescu** (Ion), **Bonaparte** (Jérôme), **Carausius** (Marcus Aurelius Mausaeus), **Cavendish** (William), **Gneisenau** (August, Graf Neithardt von), **Hasdrubal**, **Hideyoshi** (Toyotomi), **Kim Il-sung**, **Kitchener** (Herbert, Earl), **Lafayette** (Marie Joseph, Marquis de), **MacArthur** (Douglas), **Miltiades**, **Spartacus**

10 **Abercromby** (Sir Ralph), **Alanbrooke** (Alan Francis Brooke, Viscount), **Alcibiades**, **Auchinleck** (Sir Claude), **Belisarius**, **Clausewitz** (Karl von), **Cornwallis** (Charles, Marquis), **Cumberland** (William Augustus, Duke of), **Eisenhower** (Dwight David), **Germanicus**, **Hindenburg** (Paul von), **Karageorge**, **Montgomery** (Bernard, Viscount), **Schlieffen** (Alfred, Graf von), **Stroessner** (Alfredo), **Washington** (George),

Wellington (Arthur Wellesley, Duke of)

11 **Baden-Powell** (Robert, Lord), **Black Prince**, **Genghis Khan**, **Marlborough** (John Churchill, Duke of), **Mohammed Ali**, **Münchhausen** (Baron von)

12 **Ptolemy Soter**, **Stauffenburg** (Claus, Graf von)

13 **Fabius Maximus** (Quintus)

15 **Scipio Africanus** (Publius Cornelius), **Seleucus Nicator**

❑**soldier on**
06 hold on, keep on
08 continue, keep at it, plug away
09 keep going, persevere, stick at it

sole
03 one
04 lone, only
06 single, unique
08 singular, solitary
10 individual

solecism
04 boob
05 error, gaffe, lapse
06 booboo, howler
07 blunder, faux pas, mistake
08 cacology
09 gaucherie
11 anacoluthon, incongruity

solely
04 only
05 alone
06 merely, singly
08 entirely, uniquely
11 exclusively

solemn
04 glum
05 grave, sober
06 formal, sombre
07 earnest, genuine, pompous, serious, sincere, stately
08 imposing, majestic
09 dignified, venerable
10 ceremonial, thoughtful
11 ceremonious, reverential
12 awe-inspiring

solemnity
04 rite
06 ritual
07 dignity, gravity
08 ceremony, grandeur, sanctity
10 ceremonial, observance,

11 celebration, formalities, proceedings

solemnize
06 honour
07 dignify, observe
09 celebrate

solicit
03 ask, beg, sue
04 pray, seek, tout
05 apply, crave, plead
06 ask for, hustle
07 canvass, request
08 apply for, petition
09 importune

solicitor
02 QC
06 lawyer
08 advocate, attorney
09 barrister

solicitous
05 eager
06 caring, uneasy
07 anxious, worried, zealous
08 troubled
09 attentive, concerned
12 apprehensive

solicitude
04 care
07 concern
13 attentiveness, consideration

solid
04 firm, hard, pure, real
05 dense, sound, thick, valid
06 cogent, decent, stable, strong, sturdy, trusty, worthy
07 compact, durable, genuine, unmixed, upright, weighty
08 concrete, reliable, sensible, tangible, unbroken
09 steadfast, well-built
10 continuous, dependable, unshakable
11 level-headed, long-lasting, respectable, substantial, trustworthy, well-founded
12 well-grounded
13 authoritative

solidarity
05 unity
06 accord
07 concord, harmony
08 cohesion
09 soundness, stability, unanimity
14 like-mindedness

solidify
03 gel, set
04 cake, clot, jell
06 go hard, harden

07 congeal
09 coagulate
10 become hard
11 crystallize

solitary
04 lone, monk, sole
05 alone, loner
06 hermit, lonely, single
07 ancress, ascetic, eremite, recluse, retired
08 desolate, lone wolf, lonesome, separate
09 anchoress, anchorite, reclusive, withdrawn
10 by yourself, cloistered, friendless, hermitical, unsociable
13 companionless, individualist

solitude
07 privacy
09 aloneness
10 loneliness
12 introversion, lonesomeness
13 reclusiveness, unsociability

solution
03 key
06 answer, remedy, way out
07 cure-all, panacea, solvent
08 quick fix
10 resolution, suspension
11 elucidation, explanation, unravelling
13 clarification

solve
05 crack
06 answer, fathom, settle
07 clear up, explain, rectify, resolve, unravel, work out
08 decipher, put right
09 figure out, interpret, puzzle out

solvent
10 in the black

sombre
04 dark, drab, dull
05 dingy, grave, shady, sober
06 dismal, gloomy, solemn
07 joyless, serious
08 funereal
10 lugubrious, melancholy

somebody
03 VIP
04 name, star
05 mogul, nabob
06 bigwig
07 big shot, magnate, notable, someone
08 luminary

09 celebrity, dignitary, personage, superstar
10 panjandrum
13 household name

someday
05 later
06 one day
07 by and by
08 sometime
10 eventually, ultimately
11 in due course
13 sooner or later
14 one of these days

somehow
11 by some means, come what may
15 by hook or by crook, one way or another

sometime
02 ex
04 late, then
06 former, one day
07 earlier, one-time, quondam, retired, someday
08 emeritus, previous
09 erstwhile, in the past

sometimes
07 at times
08 off and on, on and off
10 now and then, on occasion
11 now and again
12 every so often, occasionally, once in a while
14 from time to time

somnolent
04 dozy
06 drowsy, sleepy, torpid
08 comatose, oscitant
09 half-awake, heavy-eyed, soporific

son
03 boy, lad
05 child
06 laddie, native
08 disciple
09 offspring
10 descendant, inhabitant

song
► *Types of song*:
03 air, lay, ode
04 aria, hymn, lied, lilt, tune
05 blues, carol, chant, dirge, ditty, elegy, lyric, psalm, yodel
06 anthem, ballad, chorus, jingle, lyrics, melody, number, shanty
07 calypso, cantata, canzone, chanson, descant, lullaby,

pop song, refrain, requiem, war song, wassail
08 bird call, bird song, canticle, folk-song, love-song, madrigal, serenade, threnody
09 barcarole, cantilena, plainsong, roundelay, spiritual
10 gospel song, plainchant, recitative
11 rock and roll
12 nursery rhyme
14 Negro spiritual
➢ See also **poem**

► *Titles of pop songs include*:
05 Fever, Layla, Money, Relax, Think
06 Apache, Exodus
07 Hey Jude, Imagine
08 Parklife, Peggy Sue, Spaceman, Waterloo
09 Billy Jean, China Girl, Jean Genie, Never Ever, Penny Lane, Release Me, Stand By Me, Stand By Me, Two Tribes
10 All Shook Up, Bright Eyes, Bye Bye Love, Jealous Guy, Moving On Up, Perfect Day, Purple Haze, Purple Rain, Secret Love, Sex Machine, Tenderness, Wonderwall
11 From Me To You, Light My Fire, Mrs Robinson, Set Them Free, She Loves You, Space Oddity, Tutti Frutti, Voodoo Child
12 Ashes To Ashes, Baby Come Back, Born in the USA, Born to be Wild, Come on Eileen, Common People, Dancing Queen, Dock of the Bay, Eleanor Rigby, Johnny B Goode, Mack The Knife, Magic Moments, No Woman, No Cry, Paint It Black, Pretty Vacant, The Passenger, The Young Ones
13 Blueberry Hill, Can't Buy Me Love, Get Off My Cloud, Hard Day's Night, Jailhouse Rock, Mull of Kintyre, Oh, Pretty Woman, Only the Lonely
14 Good Vibrations, Karma Chameleon, Love on the Rocks, That'll Be The Day, The Power of Love, Wonderful World
15 Blowin' in the Wind, Candle in the Wind, I Shot the

Sheriff, In the Name of Love,
Jumpin' Jack Flash, Killing
Me Softly, Love is All
Around, Money for
Nothing, Mr Tambourine
Man, Paperback Writer,
Puppet on a String, Rivers of
Babylon, Smoke on the
Water, Too Much Too Young,
Unchained Melody, Wish
You Were Here, Yellow
Submarine

➢ See also **music**

song and dance
03 ado
04 flap, fuss, stir, to-do
05 hoo-ha, tizzy
06 bother, furore
09 commotion, kerfuffle
11 performance

songster
06 singer
07 crooner, warbler
08 minstrel, vocalist
09 balladeer, chanteuse,
    chorister
10 troubadour

songwriter

➤ *Names of songwriters and
lyricists*:
04 **Bart** (Lionel), **Cahn**
    (Sammy), **Cash** (Johnny),
    John (Elton), **Kern**
    (Jerome), **Rice** (Tim),
    Reed (Lou)
05 **Berry** (Chuck), **Brown**
    (James), **Cohan** (George
    Michael), **Davis** (Miles),
    Dylan (Bob), **Holly**
    (Buddy), **Loewe**
    (Frederick), **Simon** (Paul),
    Sousa (John Philip),
    Weill (Kurt)
06 **Berlin** (Irving), **Coward**
    (Sir Noël), **Lennon** (John),
    Lerner (Alan Jay), **Marley**
    (Bob), **Mercer** (Johnny H),
    Oliver (King), **Parker**
    (Charlie), **Porter** (Cole),
    Seeger (Pete), **Waller**
    (Thomas 'Fats')
07 **Gilbert** (Sir Wiliam),
    Guthrie (Woody),
    Loesser (Frank), **MacColl**
    (Ewan), **Mancini** (Henry),
    Novello (Ivor), **Rodgers**
    (Richard), **Romberg**
    (Sigmund)
08 **Coltrane** (John), **Gershwin**
    (George), **Mitchell** (Joni),
    Sondheim (Stephen)

09 **Bernstein** (Leonard),
    Ellington (Duke),
    McCartney (Paul)
11 **Hammerstein** (Oscar),
    Lloyd Webber (Sir
    Andrew)

➢ See also **music**

sonorous
04 full, loud, rich
07 orotund, ringing, rounded
08 plangent, resonant
10 resounding

soon
06 pronto
07 in a tick, shortly
08 in a jiffy, in no time
09 any minute, in a minute, in a
    moment, presently
10 before long
12 any minute now, in a short
    time
13 in no time at all
14 in a little while, in a moment
    or two
15 in the near future

soothe
04 calm, ease, hush, lull
05 allay, quiet, salve, still
06 pacify, settle, soften, temper
07 appease, assuage, comfort,
    mollify, quieten, relieve
08 calm down, mitigate, palliate
09 alleviate
12 tranquillize

soothing
05 balmy
06 anetic
07 calming, easeful, restful
08 balsamic, lenitive, relaxing
09 demulcent, emollient
10 palliative

soothsayer
04 seer
05 augur, sibyl
07 Chaldee, diviner, prophet
08 haruspex

sophisticated
05 suave
06 subtle, urbane
07 complex, elegant, refined,
    stylish, worldly
08 advanced, cultured
09 elaborate, intricate
10 cultivated
11 complicated, experienced,
    worldly-wise
12 cosmopolitan

sophistication
05 poise

07 culture, finesse
08 elegance, urbanity
10 experience
11 savoir-faire, savoir-vivre,
    worldliness

sophistry
07 fallacy, quibble, sophism
08 elenchus
09 casuistry

soporific
06 hypnic, opiate, sleepy
08 hypnotic, narcotic, sedative
09 somnolent
12 sleeping pill
13 sleep-inducing, tranquillizer
14 tranquillizing

soppy
03 wet
04 daft, soft, wild
05 corny, mushy, silly, weepy
06 sloppy, slushy
07 cloying, wimpish
09 schmaltzy
10 lovey-dovey
11 sentimental

sorcerer
05 magus, witch
06 magian, voodoo, wizard
07 angekok, warlock
08 angekkok, magician
09 enchanter, sorceress
10 reim-kennar
11 necromancer
13 thaumaturgist

sorcery
05 charm, magic, spell
06 voodoo
08 pishogue, wizardry
10 black magic, necromancy,
    witchcraft
11 thaumaturgy

sordid
03 low
04 base, foul, mean, vile
05 dirty, mucky, seamy, seedy
06 filthy, shabby, sleazy
07 corrupt, debased, immoral,
    miserly, squalid, unclean
08 degraded, shameful
09 debauched, mercenary
11 ignominious, self-seeking

sore
03 cut, raw, red
04 boil, hurt
05 angry, chafe, graze, ulcer,
    upset, vexed, wound
06 aching, bitter, chafed, lesion,
    scrape, tender

07 abscess, annoyed, bruised,
   burning, injured, painful
08 inflamed, offended,
   smarting, stinging, swelling
09 aggrieved, resentful

sorrow
03 woe
05 grief, mourn, trial
06 bewail, dolour, grieve,
   lament, misery
07 agonize, anguish, feel sad,
   remorse, sadness, trouble
08 distress, hardship, mourning
09 heartache, suffering
10 affliction, heartbreak
11 tribulation, unhappiness
12 wretchedness
13 feel miserable

sorrowful
03 sad, wae
06 rueful, woeful
07 doleful, painful, piteous,
   tearful, unhappy
08 dejected, grievous,
   mournful, wretched
09 afflicted, depressed,
   miserable, woebegone
10 lamentable, lugubrious,
   melancholy
12 disconsolate, heart-rending,
   heavy-hearted

sorry
03 sad
04 down, poor
05 moved, upset
06 dismal
07 ashamed, pitiful, pitying,
   unhappy
08 contrite, grievous, pathetic,
   penitent, shameful,
   wretched
09 concerned, miserable,
   regretful, repentant
10 apologetic, distressed,
   remorseful, shamefaced
11 guilt-ridden, sympathetic
12 heart-rending

sort
03 ilk, set
04 kind, make, race, rank, sift,
   type
05 brand, breed, class, genre,
   genus, grade, group, order,
   stamp, style
06 divide, family, nature, screen
07 arrange, quality, species,
   variety
08 category, classify, organize,
   separate
09 catalogue, character,
   segregate

10 categorize, distribute, put in
   order
11 description, systematize
12 denomination

□**out of sorts**
03 ill
04 sick, weak
05 cross, narky, ratty
06 ailing, crabby, groggy,
   grumpy, poorly, queasy,
   snappy, unwell
07 grouchy, in a mood, run
   down
08 below par
09 irritable, off-colour
10 in a bad mood
14 down in the dumps,
   down in the mouth
15 under the weather

□**sort out**
04 rank
05 class, grade, group, order,
   solve
06 choose, divide, select
07 arrange, resolve
08 classify, put right, separate
10 categorize, put in order

sortie
04 raid, rush
05 foray, sally
06 attack, charge
09 offensive

so-so
02 OK
04 fair
06 not bad
07 average, neutral
08 adequate, middling,
   passable
09 tolerable
11 indifferent, respectable
12 run-of-the-mill
13 unexceptional
14 fair to middling
15 undistinguished

soul
03 man
04 life, mind
05 model, woman
06 person, psyche, spirit
07 epitome, essence, example
08 creature, humanity
09 character, inner self, intellect
10 compassion, embodiment,
   human being, individual,
   inner being
11 inspiration, sensitivity
13 heart of hearts,
   understanding
15 personification

soulful
06 moving
08 eloquent, mournful,
   profound
09 emotional, heartfelt,
   sensitive
10 expressive, meaningful

soulless
04 cold, dead, mean
07 callous, ignoble, inhuman
09 unfeeling
10 mechanical, spiritless
12 mean-spirited
13 unsympathetic
14 soul-destroying

sound
03 din, fit, say, voe
04 echo, firm, good, peal, ring,
   sane, test, toll, tone, true,
   well
05 chime, firth, fiord, go off,
   inlet, noise, plumb, probe,
   right, solid, tenor, utter, valid,
   voice, whole
06 cogent, fathom, intact,
   report, robust, secure, strait,
   sturdy, timbre, unhurt
07 channel, estuary, examine,
   express, healthy, inspect,
   logical, measure, passage,
   perfect, resound, weighty
08 complete, orthodox,
   rational, reliable, resonate,
   thorough, unbroken,
   vigorous
09 enunciate, judicious,
   pronounce, resonance,
   undamaged, uninjured
10 articulate, dependable,
   reasonable, unimpaired
11 description, disease-free, in
   good shape, investigate,
   reverberate, substantial,
   trustworthy, well-founded
12 in fine fettle, in good health,
   sound as a bell,
   well-grounded
13 authoritative, reverberation
15 in good condition

▶ *Types of sound:*
03 cry, hum, pip, pop, sob, tap
04 bang, beep, boom, buzz,
   clap, echo, fizz, hiss, honk,
   hoot, moan, peal, ping, plop,
   ring, roar, sigh, slam, snap,
   thud, tick, toot, wail, yell
05 blare, blast, bleep, chime,
   chink, clack, clang, clank,
   clash, click, clink, crack,
   crash, creak, drone, grate,
   groan, knock, skirl, smack,

sniff, snore, snort, swish, throb, thump, twang, whine, whirr, whoop
06 bubble, crunch, gurgle, hiccup, jangle, jingle, murmur, patter, rattle, report, rumble, rustle, scrape, scream, sizzle, splash, squeak, squeal, tinkle
07 clatter, crackle, grizzle, screech, squelch, thunder, whimper, whistle
08 splutter
11 reverberate

► *Sounds animals make:*
03 bay, caw, coo, low, mew, moo, yap
04 bark, bray, crow, hiss, hoot, howl, purr, roar, woof, yelp
05 bleat, chirp, cluck, croak, growl, grunt, miaow, neigh, quack, snarl, tweet
06 bellow, cackle, gobble, squawk, squeak, warble, whinny
07 chirrup, twitter

❑**sound out**
03 ask
04 pump
05 probe
06 survey
07 canvass, examine, suss out
08 question, research

soup
05 broth, stock
06 bisque, borsch, potage
07 chowder
08 consommé, gazpacho
12 cockieleekie, mulligatawny

sour
03 bad, off
04 acid, tart
05 acidy, nasty, ratty, sharp, spoil, surly, tangy
06 acetic, bitter, rancid, turned
07 crabbed, curdled, pungent
08 aciduous, alienate, embitter, vinegary
09 resentful
10 embittered, unpleasant
11 acrimonious
12 disagreeable

source
04 mine, rise, root, ylem
05 cause, start
06 author, origin, spring, supply
08 wellhead
09 beginning, informant

10 originator, primordium, provenance, wellspring
12 fountainhead

sourpuss
05 grump, shrew
06 grouse, kvetch, misery
07 killjoy, whinger
10 crosspatch

souse
04 dunk, sink, soak
05 douse, steep
06 drench, pickle, plunge
07 immerse
08 marinade, marinate, saturate, submerge

souvenir
05 relic, token
06 trophy
07 memento
08 keepsake, reminder
11 remembrance

sovereign
04 king, tsar
05 chief, queen, royal, ruler
06 kingly, ruling, utmost
07 emperor, empress, monarch
08 imperial, majestic, princely
09 paramount, potentate, principal
10 autonomous, self-ruling, unequalled, unrivalled
11 independent
13 self-governing

sovereignty
03 raj
07 primacy
08 autonomy, dominion, imperium, kingship, regality
09 queenship, supremacy
10 ascendancy, domination, suzerainty
12 independence

sow
04 seed
05 lodge, plant, strew
06 spread
07 bestrew, implant, scatter
08 disperse
09 broadcast
10 distribute
11 disseminate

space
03 gap
04 area, play, room, seat, span, time
05 array, blank, break, chasm, range, scope, shift, spell
06 cosmos, extent, galaxy, lacuna, margin, volume

07 arrange, be apart, dispose, expanse, opening, stretch
08 capacity, interval, latitude, omission, set apart, universe
09 clearance, elbow-room, expansion, string out
10 interstice, stretch out
11 solar system, the Milky Way
12 intermission
13 accommodation

spacious
03 big
04 huge, open, vast, wide
05 ample, broad, large, roomy
07 immense, sizable
09 capacious, extensive
10 commodious

spadework
06 labour
08 drudgery, homework
10 foundation, groundwork
11 preparation

span
04 arch, last, link, term, time
05 cover, cross, range, reach, scope
06 bridge, extend, extent, length, period, spread
07 compass, include, stretch
08 bestride, duration, traverse

spank
03 tan
04 cane, slap
05 smack, whack
06 thrash, thwack, wallop

spanking
04 fast, fine
05 brisk, quick, smart, swift
06 lively, snappy, speedy
07 exactly, totally, utterly
08 gleaming, vigorous
10 absolutely, completely, strikingly
12 invigorating

spar
03 box
04 spat, tiff
05 argue, scrap
06 bicker
07 contend, contest, dispute
08 skirmish, squabble

spare
04 bony, free, give, lank, lean, over, save, slim, thin
05 allow, extra, scant
06 afford, defend, frugal, let off, meagre, pardon, scanty, unused

07 forgive, leisure, protect, release, reserve, scraggy, scrawny, sparing, surplus
08 leftover, reprieve, unwanted
09 auxiliary, emergency, safeguard
10 additional, unoccupied
11 show mercy to, superfluous
12 dispense with
13 supernumerary, supplementary
15 all skin and bones

❑**to spare**
05 extra
06 unused
07 surplus
08 left over

sparing
05 mingy
06 frugal, meagre, stingy
07 careful, prudent, thrifty
10 economical

spark
03 bit, jot
04 atom, hint, iota
05 flash, gleam, glint, trace
07 flicker, glimmer, vestige
10 suggestion

❑**spark off**
04 stir
05 cause, start
06 excite, incite, prompt
07 inspire, provoke, trigger
08 occasion, start off, touch off
10 trigger off
11 precipitate

sparkle
03 vim
04 beam, dash, fizz, glow, life
05 gleam, glint, shine, spark
06 bubble, dazzle, energy, spirit
07 be witty, flicker, glimmer, glisten, glitter, pizzazz, shimmer, twinkle
08 radiance, vitality, vivacity
09 animation, coruscate
10 brilliance, ebullience, effervesce, enthusiasm, get-up-and-go, liveliness
11 coruscation, scintillate

sparkling
05 fizzy, witty
06 bubbly, lively
08 flashing, gleaming
10 carbonated, glittering
11 coruscating
12 effervescent
13 scintillating

sparse
06 meagre, scanty, scarce

08 sporadic
09 scattered
10 infrequent

spartan
05 bleak, harsh, plain
06 frugal, severe, simple, strict
07 ascetic, austere
11 disciplined, self-denying

spasm
03 fit, tic
04 bout, jerk
05 burst, cramp
06 access, attack, frenzy, twitch
07 seizure
08 eruption, paroxysm
10 convulsion
11 contraction

spasmodic
05 jerky
06 fitful
07 erratic
08 periodic, sporadic
12 intermittent

spate
04 flow, rush
05 flood
06 deluge
07 torrent
10 outpouring

spatter
04 daub, soil
05 dirty, spray
06 bedaub, shower, splash
07 bestrew, scatter, speckle
08 splatter, sprinkle

spay
04 geld
06 doctor, neuter
08 castrate
09 sterilize

speak
03 gab, say, yak
04 chat, talk, tell
05 state, utter, voice
07 address, declaim, declare, express
08 converse
09 enunciate, hold forth, pronounce
10 articulate
11 communicate

❑**speak for**
06 act for
08 stand for
09 represent
15 speak on behalf of

❑**speak of**
07 discuss, mention, refer to

13 make mention of
15 make reference to

❑**speak out, speak up**
06 defend
07 protest, support

❑**speak to**
04 warn
05 scold
06 accost, rebuke
07 address, lecture, tell off, upbraid
08 admonish
09 dress down, reprimand

❑**speak up**
10 talk loudly
14 raise your voice, talk more loudly
➤ See also **speak out**

speaker
06 orator, talker
08 lecturer
10 mouthpiece, prolocutor

spearhead
03 van
04 head, lead
05 front, guide
08 initiate, overseer, vanguard
11 cutting edge, trailblazer

special
06 choice, select, unique
07 notable, precise, unusual
08 detailed, peculiar, singular
09 different, exclusive, important, memorable, momentous, red-letter
10 noteworthy, particular, remarkable
11 distinctive, exceptional, outstanding, significant
13 distinguished, extraordinary
14 characteristic

specialist
06 brains, expert, master
11 connoisseur
12 professional

speciality
05 field, forte
06 talent
08 strength
09 specialty

specially
08 uniquely
09 expressly
10 distinctly, explicitly
11 exclusively
12 particularly, specifically

species
04 kind, sort, type

05 breed, class, genus, group
07 variety
08 category

specific
03 set
05 exact, fixed
07 limited, precise, special
08 clear-cut, definite, detailed
10 particular
11 unambiguous, unequivocal

specification
06 detail
10 particular
11 delineation, description, instruction, stipulation

specify
04 cite, list, name
06 define, detail, set out
07 itemize
08 describe, spell out
09 designate, stipulate
13 particularize

specimen
04 copy, type
06 sample
07 example, exhibit, pattern
08 exemplar, paradigm

specious
05 false
06 untrue
07 unsound
09 deceptive, plausible
10 fallacious, misleading
11 sophistical

speck
03 bit, dot, jot
04 atom, blot, mark, spot, whit
05 fleck, shred, stain, trace
07 blemish, speckle
08 particle

speckled
06 dotted, spotty
07 dappled, flecked, spotted
08 freckled, stippled

spectacle
04 show
05 scene, sight
06 marvel, parade, wonder
07 display, pageant, picture
09 curiosity
10 exhibition, phenomenon
12 extravaganza

spectacular
04 show
05 grand
06 daring
07 amazing, opulent, pageant
08 dazzling, dramatic, glorious, splendid, striking, stunning

09 colourful, spectacle
10 exhibition, impressive, remarkable, staggering
11 astonishing, eye-catching, magnificent, outstanding, resplendent, sensational
12 breathtaking, extravaganza, ostentatious
13 extraordinary

spectator
06 viewer
07 watcher, witness
08 beholder, observer, onlooker
09 bystander
10 eye-witness, rubberneck

spectral
05 eerie, weird
06 spooky
07 ghostly, phantom
09 unearthly
11 disembodied, incorporeal
12 supernatural

spectre
04 fear
05 ghost, shade, spook
06 menace, shadow, spirit, threat, vision, wraith
07 phantom
08 presence, revenant, visitant
10 apparition

speculate
04 muse, risk
05 guess
06 gamble, hazard, wonder
07 reflect, suppose, surmise, venture
08 cogitate, consider, theorize
10 conjecture, deliberate
11 contemplate, hypothesize

speculation
04 risk
05 guess
06 gamble, hazard, theory
07 surmise
09 guesswork
10 conjecture, hypothesis
11 supposition
13 flight of fancy

speculative
04 iffy
05 dicey, risky, vague
06 chancy
08 notional, unproven
09 hazardous, tentative, uncertain
10 indefinite
11 conjectural, theoretical
12 hypothetical
13 suppositional

speech
04 talk
05 lingo, spiel, voice
06 jargon, patter, tirade, tongue
07 address, dialect, diction, lecture, oration
08 delivery, dialogue, diatribe, language
09 discourse, monologue, philippic, soliloquy
11 enunciation
12 articulation, conversation
13 communication, pronunciation

speechless
03 mum
04 dumb, mute
06 silent
10 dumbstruck, tongue-tied
11 dumbfounded, obmutescent
12 inarticulate
13 thunderstruck

speed
04 belt, dash, pace, pelt, race, rate, rush, tear, zoom
05 haste, hurry, tempo
06 career, gallop, hurtle, sprint
07 quicken
08 alacrity, celerity, dispatch, momentum, rapidity, step on it, velocity
09 bowl along, quickness, swiftness
10 accelerate, promptness
12 acceleration, step on the gas
15 put your foot down

❑**speed up**
05 hurry
06 hasten, spur on, step up
07 advance, forward, quicken
08 expedite, go faster, step on it
09 stimulate
10 accelerate, facilitate
11 precipitate, put on a spurt
12 gain momentum
14 step on the juice
15 put your foot down

speedily
04 fast
07 hastily, quickly, rapidly, swiftly
08 promptly
09 hurriedly, posthaste

speedy
04 fast
05 hasty, quick, rapid, swift
06 nimble, prompt
07 cursory, express, hurried

09 immediate
11 expeditious, precipitate

spell
04 bout, span, term, time, turn
05 augur, charm, magic, patch
06 allure, course, extent,
   herald, period, trance
07 portend, presage, session,
   signify, sorcery, stretch
08 indicate, interval, witchery
09 magnetism
10 attraction
11 abracadabra, bewitchment,
   enchantment, fascination,
   incantation

□**spell out**
06 detail
07 clarify, explain, specify
09 elucidate, emphasize, make
   clear, stipulate

spellbinding
08 gripping, riveting
10 bewitching, entrancing
11 captivating, enthralling,
   mesmerizing

spellbound
04 rapt
07 charmed, gripped, riveted
09 bewitched, entranced
10 captivated, enraptured,
   enthralled, hypnotized,
   mesmerized, transfixed

spend
02 do
03 use
04 blow, fill, kill, pass
05 apply, put in, use up, waste
06 devote, expend, finish,
   invest, lay out, occupy, pay
   out
07 consume, exhaust, fork out,
   fritter
08 disburse, shell out, squander
09 splash out, while away

spendthrift
07 wastrel
08 prodigal, wasteful
10 profligate, squanderer
11 extravagant, improvident

spent
05 all in, weary
06 bushed, done in, effete,
   used up
07 drained, worn out
08 burnt out, consumed,
   dead beat, expended,
   finished, tired out
09 exhausted

spew
04 gush, puke
05 issue, retch, spurt, vomit
07 spit out, throw up
08 disgorge
11 regurgitate

sphere
03 orb, set
04 area, ball, band, rank
05 class, crowd, field, globe,
   group, realm, round, scope
06 circle, clique, domain, extent
07 compass, globule
08 capacity, function, province
09 territory
10 department, speciality

spherical
05 round
06 rotund
07 globate, globoid, globose
08 globular
09 orbicular

spice
03 pep, zap, zip
04 kick, life, stir, tang, zest
05 gusto, hot up, liven, pep up,
   rouse
06 buck up, colour, perk up,
   relish, savour, stir up
07 animate, enliven, liven up
08 brighten, energize,
   piquancy, vitalize
09 seasoning
10 excitement, flavouring,
   invigorate
11 put life into
➤ See also **herbs and spices**

spick and span
04 neat, tidy, trim
05 clean
06 spruce
08 polished, scrubbed,
   spotless, well-kept
10 immaculate

spicy
03 hot
04 racy, tart
05 juicy, sharp, tangy
06 ribald, risqué
07 peppery, piquant, pungent
08 aromatic, seasoned
10 scandalous, suggestive
11 flavoursome, sensational

spider
➤ *Types of arachnid and
spider:*
04 mite, tick
06 katipo, mygale
07 araneid, redback

08 scorpion
09 harvester, tarantula
10 bird-spider, black widow,
   harvestman, wolf spider
11 bolas spider, money spider,
   water spider
12 book-scorpion, diadem
   spider, whip scorpion
13 harvest spider
14 trapdoor spider
15 funnel-web spider
➤ See also **animal**

spiel
05 pitch
06 patter, speech
07 oration, recital

spike
03 add
04 barb, drug, lace, nail, spit,
   tine
05 mix in, point, prick, prong,
   rowel, spear, spine, stake,
   stick
06 impale, skewer

spill
04 fall, flow, pour, shed, slop,
   well
05 upset
06 run out, tumble
07 run over, scatter
08 accident, disgorge,
   overflow, overturn
09 discharge

□**spill the beans**
03 rat
04 blab, tell
05 grass, split
06 inform, squeal, tell on
11 blow the gaff
15 give the game away

spin
03 run
04 flap, reel, ride, tell, tizz, trip,
   turn
05 drive, jaunt, panic, state,
   swirl, tizzy, twirl, twist,
   wheel, whirl, whirr
06 circle, dither, gyrate, invent,
   make up, outing, relate,
   rotate, swivel
07 dream up, fluster, revolve
08 gyration, rotation
09 fabricate, pirouette, turn
   round
10 revolution

□**spin out**
06 extend, pad out
07 amplify, prolong
08 lengthen, protract

spindle
03 pin, rod
04 axis, axle
05 arbor, fusee, pivot

spindly
04 long, thin
05 lanky, weedy
06 gangly, skinny
07 spidery
08 gangling, skeletal
10 attenuated

spine
04 barb, grit, guts
05 pluck, quill, spike, thorn
06 dorsum, needle, rachis
07 bristle, courage, prickle
08 backbone
09 fortitude, vertebrae
12 spinal column
15 vertebral column

spine-chilling
05 eerie, scary
10 horrifying, terrifying
11 frightening, hair-raising
13 bloodcurdling

spineless
04 soft, weak
05 timid
06 feeble, yellow
07 chicken, wimpish
08 cowardly, timorous
11 lily-livered
12 faint-hearted

spiny
06 briery, thorny
07 prickly, spinous, thistly
09 acanthous, spiculate
12 acanthaceous

spiral
04 coil, go up, gyre, rise, soar, wind
05 climb, helix, screw, twist, whorl
06 circle, coiled, gyrate, rocket, volute, wreath
07 cochlea, helical, voluted, whorled, winding, wreathe
08 circular, cochlear, curlicue, escalate, increase, scrolled, twisting, volution
09 cochleate, corkscrew
11 convolution

spire
03 tip, top
04 peak
05 crest, point, spike, tower
06 belfry, summit, turret
07 steeple
08 pinnacle

spirit
03 air, zip
04 fire, gist, grit, guts, kick, life, mind, mood, soul, zeal, zest
05 angel, demon, devil, fairy, fiend, force, ghost, pluck, shade, spook, spunk, tenor
06 ardour, energy, humour, make-up, mettle, morale, psyche, shadow, sprite, temper, vigour, wraith
07 bravery, courage, essence, feeling, meaning, outlook, phantom, pizzazz, purport, quality, sparkle, spectre
08 attitude, backbone, feelings, tendency, visitant, vivacity
09 animation, character, principle, substance, willpower
10 apparition, atmosphere, complexion, enterprise, enthusiasm, liveliness, motivation, resolution
11 disposition, implication, temperament
13 determination
14 characteristic

❑spirit away
05 carry, seize, steal, whisk
06 abduct, convey, kidnap, remove
07 capture, purloin, snaffle

spirited
05 fiery
06 feisty, lively, plucky
07 valiant
08 animated, vigorous
09 energetic, vivacious
10 courageous, determined

spiritless
07 anaemic, languid
08 lifeless, listless
09 apathetic
10 despondent, lacklustre, wishy-washy

spirits
04 mood
06 humour, liquor, temper
07 alcohol
08 attitude, emotions, feelings
09 fire-water, moonshine
11 strong drink, temperament
12 strong liquor, the hard stuff

➤ *Types of liquid spirit*:
03 gin, rum
05 vodka
06 brandy, cognac, grappa, poteen, Scotch, whisky
07 aquavit, bourbon, tequila, whiskey
08 Armagnac, Calvados, schnapps
09 aqua vitae, slivovitz
10 malt whisky, usquebaugh
➤ See also **drink**

spiritual
04 holy
06 divine, sacred
08 ethereal, heavenly
09 religious, unworldly
10 devotional, intangible
11 incorporeal
12 otherworldly

spit
04 hawk, hiss, rasp
05 drool, eject, issue
06 phlegm, saliva, slaver, sputum
07 dribble, spittle
08 splutter
11 expectorate

spite
03 irk, vex
04 evil, gall, hate, hurt
05 annoy, upset, venom, wound
06 grudge, hatred, injure, malice, offend, put out
07 ill-will, provoke, rancour
09 animosity, vengeance
10 bitterness, ill-feeling, resentment
11 malevolence

❑in spite of
07 against, defying, despite
12 regardless of, undeterred by
15 notwithstanding

spiteful
05 catty, cruel, nasty, snide
06 barbed, bitchy, bitter
08 vengeful, venomous
09 malicious, resentful
10 vindictive

spitting image
04 spit, twin
05 clone
06 double, ringer
07 picture, replica
08 dead spit, likeness
09 lookalike
10 dead ringer
13 exact likeness

splash
03 wet
04 beat, dash, daub, plop, slop, spot, stir, wade, wash
05 bathe, break, burst, patch, slosh, smack, spray, stain, surge, touch

06 batter, blazon, buffet, dabble, effect, impact, paddle, plunge, shower, spread, squirt, streak, strike, wallow
07 exhibit, scatter, spatter, splodge, splotch, trumpet
08 splatter, sprinkle
09 publicity, publicize, sensation

❑**splash out**
05 spend
07 lash out, splurge
08 invest in
14 push the boat out

spleen
04 bile, gall
05 spite, venom
06 animus, hatred, malice
07 ill-will, rancour
08 acrimony
09 animosity, bad temper, hostility, malignity
10 bitterness, resentment
11 biliousness, malevolence
12 spitefulness
14 vindictiveness

splendid
04 fine, rich
05 grand, great, super
06 bright, lavish, superb
07 glowing, opulent, radiant, stately, sublime, supreme
08 dazzling, fabulous, glorious, imposing, renowned
09 brilliant, luxurious, refulgent, sumptuous, wonderful
10 glittering, impressive, marvellous
11 magnificent, outstanding, resplendent

splendour
04 glow, pomp, show
05 gleam, glory
06 dazzle, lustre, luxury
07 display, majesty
08 ceremony, grandeur, opulence, radiance, richness
09 spectacle
10 brightness, brilliance
12 magnificence, resplendence
13 sumptuousness

splenetic
04 acid, sour
05 angry, cross, ratty, testy
06 crabby, morose, touchy
07 bilious, crabbed
08 choleric, churlish, spiteful
09 irascible, rancorous

splice
03 tie
04 bind, join, knit, mesh
05 braid, graft, marry, plait
06 fasten
07 connect

❑**get spliced**
03 wed
10 get hitched, get married, tie the knot
13 take the plunge

splinter
04 chip
05 break, flake, piece, shard, shred, smash, split
06 cleave, paring, shiver, sliver
07 crumble, shatter, shaving
08 fracture, fragment
11 smithereens
12 disintegrate

split
03 cut, gap, rat, rip
04 chop, dual, open, part, rend, rent, rift, shop, slit, tear
05 allot, break, burst, cleft, crack, halve, share, slash
06 betray, bisect, breach, broken, cleave, cloven, divide, schism, shiver, squeal, tell on
07 break up, break-up, carve up, cracked, crevice, disband, discord, divorce, dole out, fissure, hand out, rupture, twofold
08 allocate, bisected, disunion, disunite, division, inform on, ruptured, separate, set apart, splinter
09 apportion, fractured, parcel out, partition
10 alienation, difference, dissension, distribute, divergence, separation
11 incriminate, part company
12 estrangement

❑**split hairs**
05 cavil
07 nit-pick, quibble
08 pettifog
09 find fault
10 over-refine

❑**split up**
04 part
07 break up, disband, divorce
08 separate
11 get divorced, part company

split-up
07 break-up, divorce, parting

10 alienation, separation
12 estrangement

spoil
03 mar, rot
04 foul, harm, hurt, sour, turn
05 go bad, go off, taint, upset
06 coddle, cosset, damage, deface, deform, go sour, impair, injure, mess up, pamper
07 blemish, destroy, indulge, pollute, tarnish
08 go rotten
09 decompose, disfigure,
11 contaminate, deteriorate, overindulge
12 put a damper on

❑**spoil for**
10 be eager for, be intent on

spoils
04 gain, haul, loot, swag
05 booty
06 prizes, profit
07 benefit, plunder
08 pickings, winnings
10 spoliation

spoilsport
06 damper, misery, wowser
07 killjoy, meddler
10 wet blanket
11 party-pooper
14 dog in the manger

spoken
04 oral, said, told
06 stated, verbal, voiced
07 uttered
08 phonetic
09 expressed

spokesman, spokes-woman
05 voice
08 delegate
10 mouthpiece
12 spokesperson

sponge
03 beg, bum, mop
04 swab, wash, wipe
05 cadge, clean
08 freeload, scrounge

sponger
03 bum
06 beggar, cadger
08 hanger-on, parasite
09 scrounger
10 freeloader

spongy
04 soft
05 light
06 porous

07 elastic, springy, squashy
09 absorbent, cushioned, resilient

sponsor
04 back, fund
05 angel
06 backer, friend, patron, surety
07 finance, promote, support
08 bankroll, promoter
09 guarantee, guarantor, supporter
10 underwrite
11 be a patron of, underwriter

spontaneous
07 natural, willing
08 unforced
09 extempore, impromptu, impulsive, unplanned, voluntary
10 unprompted
11 instinctive, unrehearsed
14 unpremeditated
15 spur of the moment

spontaneously
09 extempore, impromptu, on impulse, unplanned
10 off the cuff, unprompted
11 impulsively, voluntarily
13 instinctively
15 of your own accord

spoof
04 fake, game, hoax, joke
05 bluff, prank, trick
06 parody, satire, send-up
07 lampoon, leg-pull, mockery, take-off
09 burlesque, deception

spooky
05 eerie, scary, weird
06 creepy
07 ghostly, uncanny
09 unearthly
11 frightening, hair-raising
13 spine-chilling

spoon-feed
04 baby
05 spoil
06 cosset, pamper
07 indulge
10 featherbed
11 mollycoddle, overindulge

sporadic
06 random
07 erratic
09 irregular, spasmodic
10 infrequent, occasional
12 intermittent

sport
03 fun

04 game, play, wear
06 banter, humour, joking
07 display, exhibit, jesting, mockery, pastime, show off
08 activity, exercise, pleasure, ridicule, sneering
09 amusement, diversion
10 recreation
13 entertainment

➤ *Sports include*:
04 golf, judo, polo, pool
05 bowls, darts, fives, Rugby
06 boules, boxing, diving, hockey, karate, kung fu, quoits, rowing, skiing, soccer, squash, tennis
07 angling, archery, cricket, croquet, curling, fencing, fishing, gliding, hunting, jogging, jujitsu, keep-fit, netball, sailing, snooker, surfing, walking
08 aerobics, baseball, canoeing, climbing, football, handball, lacrosse, pétanque, ping-pong, rounders, shooting, swimming, yachting
09 athletics, badminton, billiards, bobsleigh, ice-hockey, pot-holing, sky-diving, tae kwon do, water polo, wrestling
10 basketball, drag-racing, gymnastics, ice-skating, volleyball
11 horse-racing, motor racing, show-jumping, table-tennis, water-skiing, windsurfing
12 orienteering, pitch and putt, rock-climbing, trampolining
13 roller-skating, tenpin bowling, weightlifting
14 mountaineering, stock-car racing
15 greyhound-racing

➤ See also **athletic**;
    gymnastic; **race**; **stadium**

➤ *Names of miscellaneous sportspeople*:
04 **Bird** (Larry), **Dean** (Christopher), **Khan** (Jahangir), **Witt** (Katerina)
05 **Curry** (John), **Davis** (Fred), **Davis** (Joe), **Davis** (Sharon), **Davis** (Steve), **Ender** (Kornelia), **Kelly** (Sean), **Spitz** (Mark), **White** (Jimmy)
06 **Fraser** (Dawn), **Hendry** (Stephen), **Jordan** (Michael), **Merckx** (Eddy),

    O'Neill (Shaquille), **Wilson** (Jocky)
07 **Bristow** (Eric), **Cousins** (Robin), **Gretzky** (Wayne), **Higgins** (Alex 'Hurricane'), **Hinault** (Bernard), **Johnson** (Earvin 'Magic'), **Reardon** (Ray), **Rodnina** (Irina), **Torvill** (Jayne)
08 **Boardman** (Chris), **Indurain** (Miguel), **Kerrigan** (Nancy), **Redgrave** (Stephen)
09 **Hazelwood** (Mike)
10 **Barrington** (Jonah)
11 **Chamberlain** (Wilt 'the Stilt'), **Weissmuller** (Johnny)

➤ See also **athlete**; **baseball**;
    boxer; **chess**; **cricket**;
    football; **golf**;
    gymnastics; **horse**;
    motor; **mountaineer**;
    rugby; **skier**; **tennis**

sporting
04 fair, just
10 honourable, reasonable
11 considerate, gentlemanly, respectable
13 sportsmanlike

sportive
06 frisky, jaunty, lively
07 coltish, playful
08 skittish
10 frolicsome, rollicking

sporty
05 natty, showy
06 casual, jaunty, snazzy, trendy
07 outdoor, stylish
08 athletic, informal

spot
03 bit, dot, fix, jam, see
04 area, bite, blot, boil, daub, espy, flaw, hole, mark, mess, pock, site, slot, soil, some
05 fleck, local, place, point, scene, speck, stain, taint
06 blotch, descry, detect, little, morsel, notice, papula, papule, pimple, plight, scrape, smudge, splash
07 blemish, discern, make out, observe, pustule, setting, speckle, splodge, splotch, trouble
08 identify, locality, location, position, quandary
09 blackhead, programme, recognize, situation
10 difficulty

11 predicament, small amount
12 catch sight of

spotless
04 pure
05 clean, white
07 shining
08 gleaming, innocent, unmarked, virginal
09 unstained, unsullied, untainted
10 immaculate
11 unblemished

spotlight
06 stress
07 feature, focus on, point up
08 emphasis
09 attention, emphasize, highlight, limelight, public eye, underline
10 accentuate, illuminate
15 draw attention to

spotted
04 pied
06 dotted, spotty
07 dappled, flecked, guttate, macular, mottled, piebald
08 brindled, polka-dot

spotty
04 pied
06 dotted, pimply
07 piebald, pimpled
08 speckled
12 inconsistent

spouse
04 mate, wife
05 hubby
06 missus
07 consort, husband, partner
09 companion, other half
10 better half

spout
03 jet
04 emit, flow, go on, gush, pour, rant, rose, spew
05 orate, shoot, spurt
06 geyser, nozzle, outlet, witter
08 fountain, gargoyle, rabbit on
09 discharge, expatiate, hold forth, sermonize
11 pontificate

sprawl
04 flop, loll
05 slump, trail
06 lounge, slouch, spread
07 recline, stretch

spray
03 jet, wet
04 foam, gush, mist, posy
05 froth, spout, sprig, spume

06 branch, shower, wreath
07 aerosol, bouquet, corsage, scatter, spatter
08 atomizer, sprinkle
09 spindrift, sprinkler, vaporizer

spread
03 lay, set
04 coat, grow, open, span
05 apply, cover, feast, layer, order, party, put on, reach, smear, strew, widen
06 dilate, expand, extend, extent, fan out, sprawl, unfold, unfurl, unroll
07 advance, arrange, banquet, broaden, diffuse, enlarge, expanse, open out, radiate, scatter, stretch
08 escalate, get round, transmit
09 advertise, broadcast, circulate, diffusion, expansion, large meal, make known, propagate, publicize, spill over
10 dispersion, distribute, escalation, grow bigger, make public, promulgate
11 communicate, development, dinner party, disseminate, proliferate
12 broadcasting, distribution, transmission
13 communication, dissemination, proliferation

spree
04 bout, orgy
05 binge, fling, revel
07 carouse, debauch, splurge

sprig
04 stem, twig
05 bough, shoot, spray
06 branch

sprightly
04 airy, spry
06 active, jaunty, lively, nimble
09 energetic, vivacious
10 frolicsome

spring
03 spa
04 grow, leap, root, well
05 arise, bound, issue, start
06 appear, bounce, derive, emerge, geyser, origin, source, spirit
07 develop, emanate, proceed, rebound
08 buoyancy, wellhead
09 briskness, originate
10 elasticity, resilience

11 flexibility
12 fountainhead

❑ **spring up**
04 grow
07 develop, shoot up
08 mushroom, sprout up
13 come into being

springy
06 bouncy, spongy
07 buoyant, elastic, rubbery, tensile
08 flexible, stretchy
09 resilient

sprinkle
04 dust
05 spray, strew
06 pepper, powder, shower
07 scatter, spatter, trickle

sprinkling
04 dash
05 touch, trace
07 dusting, handful
10 scattering, smattering

sprint
03 fly, run, zip
04 belt, dart, dash, race, tear
05 scoot, shoot

sprite
03 elf, imp
04 puck
05 dryad, fairy, naiad, nymph, pixie, pouke, sylph
06 goblin, kelpie, spirit
07 brownie
10 apparition, leprechaun

sprout
03 bud
05 shoot
06 come up
07 develop
08 put forth, spring up
09 germinate

spruce
04 chic, cool, neat, trim
05 natty, sleek, smart
06 dapper, snazzy
07 elegant
11 well-dressed, well-groomed
13 well-turned-out

❑ **spruce up**
05 groom, preen, primp
06 neaten, tidy up
08 titivate
09 smarten up

spry
05 agile, brisk
06 active, nimble, supple
09 energetic, sprightly

spume
04 fizz, foam, head, suds
05 froth
06 lather
07 bubbles
13 effervescence

spunk
04 grit, guts
05 heart, nerve, pluck
06 bottle, mettle, spirit
07 courage

spur
04 goad, poke, prod, urge
05 drive, impel, prick
06 fillip, incite, induce, motive, prompt, propel
07 impetus
08 stimulus
09 incentive, stimulant, stimulate
10 incitement, motivation

□on the spur of the moment
09 impromptu, on impulse
13 spontaneously, thoughtlessly
15 without planning

spurious
04 fake, mock, sham
05 bogus, false
06 phoney
10 artificial

spurn
04 snub
05 scorn
06 rebuff, reject
07 repulse, say no to
08 turn away, turn down
09 disregard, repudiate

spurt
03 jet
04 gush, pour, rush
05 burst, erupt, issue, shoot, spate, spray, surge
06 squirt, stream
08 eruption, increase

spy
03 see
04 espy, mole, spot
06 descry, notice
07 glimpse, observe, snooper
08 discover
10 enemy agent
11 double agent, secret agent
12 catch sight of, foreign agent
14 fifth columnist
15 undercover agent

► *Names of spies*:
04 **Hale** (Nathan), **Hiss** (Alger)

05 **Blake** (George), **Blunt** (Anthony Frederick), **Fuchs** (Klaus Emil Julius), **Wynne** (Greville)
06 **Howell** (James), **Philby** (Kim), **Tubman** (Harriet)
07 **Burgess** (Guy Francis de Moncy), **Maclean** (Donald)
08 **Lonsdale** (Gordon Arnold), **Mata Hari**
09 **Carstares** (William), **Rosenberg** (Ethel), **Rosenberg** (Julius)

□spy on
05 watch
07 observe
10 keep tabs on
11 keep an eye on

squabble
03 row
04 spat, tiff
05 argue, clash, set to, set-to
06 barney, bicker
07 dispute, quarrel, wrangle
08 argument
09 have words

squad
04 band, crew, gang, team, unit
05 force, group, troop
07 brigade, company, platoon

squalid
03 low
04 foul, mean, vile
05 dingy, dirty, grimy, mucky, nasty, seedy
06 filthy, grotty, grubby, sleazy, sordid, untidy
07 obscene, run-down, unclean, unkempt
08 slovenly, wretched
09 offensive, repulsive
10 broken-down, ramshackle, uncared-for

squall
04 blow, gale, gust, howl, moan, wail, wind, yell, yowl
05 groan, storm

squally
05 blowy, gusty, rough, windy
06 stormy
08 blustery

squalor
04 dirt
05 decay, filth, grime
07 neglect

squander
04 blow
05 spend, waste
07 consume, scatter, splurge

08 misspend
09 dissipate, throw away
11 fritter away

square
03 fit
04 even, fair, just, quad, true
05 adapt, agree, align, fogey, level, match, plaza, tally
06 accord, honest, settle
07 balance, conform, diehard
08 old fogey, put right, regulate, set right, settle up, straight
09 conformer, equitable, harmonize, reconcile
10 conformist, correspond, fuddy-duddy, on the level, quadrangle, straighten
11 rectangular, right-angled, strait-laced
12 conservative, old-fashioned
13 perpendicular, quadrilateral
14 traditionalist

squash
03 jam
04 mash, pack, pulp, snub
05 crowd, crush, grind, pound, press, quash, quell, smash, stamp
07 distort, flatten, put down, silence, squeeze, squelch, trample
08 compress, macerate, suppress
09 humiliate, pulverize

squashy
05 mushy, pappy, pulpy
06 spongy
07 squishy
08 squelchy, yielding

squat
03 sit
04 bend
05 dumpy, hunch, short
06 chunky, crouch, stocky, stubby
08 thickset

squawk
03 cry
04 crow, hoot, yelp
05 croak
06 cackle, scream, shriek
07 screech

squeak
04 peep, pipe
05 cheep, creak, whine
06 squeal

squeal
03 cry, rat
04 howl, shop, tell, wail, yelp

05 grass, shout, sneak, split
06 betray, inform, scream,
shriek, snitch, squawk
07 screech
09 tell tales

squeamish
06 queasy
08 delicate, nauseous
09 nauseated
10 fastidious, particular

squeeze
03 hug, jam, nip, ram
04 cram, grip, hold, mash, milk,
pack, pulp, push
05 bleed, crowd, crush, force,
pinch, press, shove, stuff,
wedge, wrest, wring
06 clutch, cuddle, extort, lean
on, squash
07 embrace, extract, tighten
08 compress, pressure
10 congestion, pressurize
14 put the screws on

squint
04 awry
05 askew
07 crooked, oblique
08 cock-eyed, indirect
09 off-centre, skew-whiff
10 strabismic, strabismus

squirm
05 shift, twist
06 fidget, wiggle, writhe
07 agonize, wriggle
08 flounder, squiggle

squirt
03 jet
04 emit, gush, pour, spew, well
05 eject, expel, issue, shoot,
spout, spray, spurt, surge
06 stream
07 spew out
09 discharge, ejaculate

stab
03 cut, jab, try
04 bash, gash, gore, pain, shot
05 crack, knife, prick, slash,
spear, stick, whirl, wound
06 pierce, skewer, thrust,
twinge
07 attempt, bayonet, venture
08 incision, puncture, transfix

◻**stab in the back**
06 betray
07 deceive, sell out, slander
08 inform on
11 double-cross

stabbing
08 piercing, shooting, stinging

stability
08 firmness, solidity
09 constancy, soundness
10 durability, regularity, uniformity
11 reliability

stable
04 fast, firm, sure
05 fixed, solid, sound
06 secure, static, steady, strong,
sturdy
07 abiding, durable, lasting,
regular, uniform
08 balanced, enduring
09 permanent
10 dependable, invariable,
unchanging
11 established, long-lasting,
well-founded

stack
04 heap, load, many, mass, pile,
save, tons
05 amass, heaps, hoard, loads,
mound, piles, stock, store
06 gather, masses, oodles
09 stockpile
10 accumulate, collection
12 accumulation

stadium
04 bowl, ring
05 arena, field, pitch, track
11 sports field
12 sports ground

➤ *Sporting stadia and venues
include:*
05 Ascot, Epsom, Ibrox, Imola,
Lords, Monza, Troon
06 Henley, Le Mans
07 Aintree, Anfield, Daytona,
Olympia, San Siro, The Oval
08 Highbury, Sandwich
09 Cresta Run, Edgbaston,
Muirfield, Newmarket, St
Andrews, Villa Park,
Wimbledon
10 Brooklands, Carnoustie,
Celtic Park, Cheltenham,
Headingley, Meadowbank,
Monte Carlo, Twickenham
11 Belmont Park, Brands
Hatch, Hampden Park,
Murrayfield, Old Trafford,
Royal Lytham, Sandown
Park, Silverstone, The
Crucible, The Rose Bowl,
Trent Bridge, Windsor Park
12 Goodison Park, Wembley
Arena
13 Caesar's Palace, Crystal
Palace, Heysel Stadium,
Royal Birkdale, The Albert
Hall, White Hart Lane

14 Anaheim Stadium, Stamford
Bridge, Wembley Stadium
15 Cardiff Arms Park,
Flushing Meadows,
Maracana Stadium

staff
03 man, rod
04 cane, crew, prop, team,
wand
05 baton, crook, equip, stick
06 crutch, occupy, supply
07 crosier, workers
08 officers, teachers
09 employees, personnel,
workforce

stage
03 lap, leg
04 dais, give, step, time
05 apron, arena, field, floor, lay
on, level, mount, phase,
point, put on, scene, stand
06 direct, length, period,
podium, sphere
07 arrange, perform, produce,
rostrum, setting, soapbox
08 backdrop, division,
engineer, juncture, platform
10 background
11 orchestrate

◻**the stage**
03 rep
05 drama
07 the play, theatre
09 dramatics, the boards,
theatrics
11 Thespian art
13 the footlights

stagger
04 reel, rock, roll, stun, sway
05 amaze, lurch, pitch, waver
06 falter, teeter, totter, wobble
07 astound, nonplus, stupefy
08 astonish, bowl over,
confound, hesitate, surprise
09 dumbfound, overwhelm
11 flabbergast

staggering
07 amazing
10 astounding, stupefying,
surprising
11 astonishing
12 mind-boggling

stagnant
04 dull, foul, slow
05 dirty, quiet, stale, still
06 filthy, smelly, torpid
08 brackish, inactive, sluggish,
standing
10 motionless

stagnate
04 idle
05 decay
07 decline, putrefy
08 languish, vegetate
09 do nothing
1 deteriorate

staid
04 calm, prim
05 grave, quiet, sober, stiff
06 proper, sedate, solemn, sombre, steady
07 serious, starchy
08 composed, decorous

stain
3 dye
04 blot, mark, slur, spot, tint
05 smear, sully, taint, tinge
06 blotch, colour, damage, injure, injury, smudge
07 blacken, blemish, tarnish
08 besmirch, disgrace
09 discolour, dishonour
3 discoloration

stake
3 bet, rod, tie
04 ante, hold, pale, pole, post, prop, race, risk
05 brace, claim, prize, put in, share, spike, state, stick, tie up, wager
06 chance, demand, fasten, gamble, hazard, hold up, paling, picket, pierce, pledge, secure
07 concern, contest, declare, support, venture
08 interest, standard, winnings
09 establish
0 investment, lay claim to
1 competition, involvement, requisition

stake out
05 watch
07 mark out, reserve
09 demarcate
11 keep an eye on

stale
3 dry, old
04 flat, hard, sour
05 jaded, stock, tired, trite
06 mouldy
07 clichéd, worn-out
09 hackneyed
11 commonplace, stereotyped

stalemate
3 tie
04 draw, halt
07 impasse
08 deadlock, stand-off

stalk
04 hunt, stem, tail, twig, walk
05 haunt, march, track, trail
06 branch, pursue, shadow
07 petiole
08 peduncle

stall
03 pen
04 coop
05 booth, defer, delay, hedge, kiosk, place, stand, table
06 hold up, put off
07 counter, cubicle, surface
08 obstruct, platform, postpone, put on ice
09 enclosure, stonewall, temporize
10 equivocate
11 compartment, play for time
12 drag your feet

stalwart
05 burly, hardy, loyal, stout
06 brawny, robust, rugged, strong, sturdy, trusty
07 devoted, staunch, valiant
08 faithful, muscular, reliable
09 steadfast, strapping
10 dependable, determined
11 indomitable

stamina
04 grit
05 force, power
06 energy, vigour
09 endurance, fortitude
10 resilience, resistance
12 staying power

stammer
04 lisp
06 falter
07 stumble, stutter
08 hesitate
12 speech defect

stamp
03 cut, fix, tag
04 beat, cast, form, kind, mark, mash, pulp, seal, sort, type
05 brand, breed, crush, label, mould, pound, print, tread
06 emboss, squash
07 engrave, impress, imprint, quality, trample, variety
08 hallmark, identify, inscribe
09 character, signature
10 categorize, impression
11 attestation, description
12 characterize
13 authorization

stamp out
05 crush, quash, quell
06 quench, scotch

07 destroy, put down
08 suppress
09 eliminate, eradicate, extirpate

stampede
03 fly, run
04 dash, flee, rout, rush
05 shoot
06 charge, flight, gallop, onrush, sprint

stance
04 line
05 angle, slant, stand
06 policy
07 bearing, opinion, posture
08 attitude, carriage, position
09 viewpoint
10 deportment, standpoint
11 point of view

stanch
04 halt, plug, stay, stem, stop
05 block, check

stand
04 base, bear, case, dais, hold, line, rack, rise
05 abide, allow, angle, booth, brook, erect, exist, frame, get up, place, shelf, slant, stage, stall, table, up-end
06 endure, locate, obtain, policy, remain, stance, suffer
07 be erect, be valid, counter, opinion, prevail, stand up, station, stomach, support, undergo, weather
08 attitude, cope with, pedestal, platform, position, tolerate
09 put up with, viewpoint, withstand
11 point of view

stand by
04 back
06 defend, hold to, uphold
07 stick by, support
08 adhere to, side with
10 stand up for, stick up for

stand down
04 quit
06 give up, resign, retire
08 step down, withdraw

stand for
04 bear, mean
05 allow, brook
06 denote, endure
07 betoken, signify, stomach
08 indicate, tolerate
09 put up with, represent, symbolize

□ stand in for
07 replace
08 cover for
10 understudy
11 deputize for
13 substitute for

□ stand out
06 extend, jut out
07 poke out, project
08 stick out
09 be obvious
11 catch the eye
12 be noticeable
13 be conspicuous, stick out a mile

□ stand up
04 rise
05 get up
06 cohere, hold up
09 hold water
13 get to your feet
14 rise to your feet

□ stand up for
06 adhere, defend, uphold
07 protect, stand by, support
08 champion, fight for
10 stick up for

□ stand up to
04 defy, face
05 brave
06 endure, oppose, resist
08 confront, face up to
09 challenge, withstand

standard
03 set
04 code, flag, norm, rule, type
05 ethic, gauge, grade, quality, level, moral, stock, usual
06 banner, normal, staple
07 average, colours, example, pattern, popular, quality, regular, scruple, typical
08 exemplar, gonfalon, ordinary, orthodox, paradigm
09 archetype, benchmark, criterion, customary, guideline, principle, yardstick
10 recognized, touchstone
11 established, requirement
12 conventional
13 authoritative, specification

standard-bearer
06 cornet, ensign
08 standard
11 gonfalonier

standardize
09 normalize
10 homogenize, regularize
11 systematize

stand-in
05 locum, proxy
06 deputy, second
08 delegate
09 surrogate
10 substitute, understudy
14 representative

standing
04 rank
05 erect, fixed
06 repute, status
07 footing, lasting, regular, station, up-ended, upright
08 duration, eminence, position, vertical
09 existence, permanent, perpetual, seniority
10 on your feet, reputation
13 perpendicular

stand-off
07 impasse
08 blockade, deadlock

standoffish
04 cold, cool
05 aloof
06 remote
07 distant
09 withdrawn
10 unfriendly, unsociable
14 unapproachable

standpoint
05 angle, slant
06 stance
07 station
08 position
11 perspective, point of view

standstill
04 halt, lull, rest, stop
06 hold-up, log-jam
07 impasse
08 dead stop, deadlock, stoppage
09 cessation, stalemate

staple
03 key
04 main
05 basic, chief, major
08 foremost, standard
09 essential, important, necessary

star
03 orb, sun
04 idol, lead
06 famous, planet
07 big name, big shot, leading
08 asteroid, luminary
09 brilliant, celebrity, paramount, principal, satellite, superstar

10 celebrated, leading man, pre-eminent
11 illustrious, leading lady
12 heavenly body, leading light
13 celestial body

► *Names and types of star and comet*:
04 Mira, nova, Vega
05 comet, Deneb, Merak, Spica
06 meteor, Pollux, pulsar, quasar, Sirius
07 Antares, Canopus, Capella, Dog Star, Polaris
08 Arcturus, Pole Star, red dwarf, red giant
09 Aldebaran, Fomalhaut, North Star, supernova
10 Betelgeuse, brown dwarf, supergiant, white dwarf
11 falling-star, neutron star
12 Barnard's star, shooting-star, Halley's comet
13 Alpha Centauri
15 Proxima Centauri
➤ See also **constellation**

starchy
04 prim
05 stiff
06 formal, stuffy
11 strait-laced

stare
04 gape, gawk, gawp, gaze, look
05 glare, watch
06 goggle

□ be staring you in the face
13 stick out a mile

stark
04 bald, bare, grim, pure
05 bleak, blunt, harsh, plain, quite, sheer, total, utter
06 arrant, barren, dreary, gloomy, severe, wholly
07 austere, totally, utterly
08 absolute, complete, desolate, entirely, flagrant, forsaken, thorough
09 downright, out-and-out, unadorned
10 absolutely, completely, consummate, depressing
11 unmitigated
13 unembellished

stark-naked
04 nude
05 naked
08 in the raw, starkers, stripped

09 in the buff, in the nude
15 in the altogether

start
04 dawn, jerk, jump, leap, open
05 arise, begin, birth, break, found, issue, leave, onset, set up, spasm, wince
06 create, flinch, launch, origin, outset, set off, set out, shrink, turn on, twitch
07 kick off, opening, trigger
08 activate, commence, embark on, fire away, get going, initiate
09 beginning, emergence, establish, inception, instigate, institute, introduce, originate
10 embark upon, inaugurate, initiation, trigger off
11 get cracking, get under way, institution, origination
12 commencement, inauguration, introduction
13 come into being
14 bring into being
15 get things moving

startle
05 alarm, amaze, scare, upset
07 astound
08 astonish, frighten, surprise

startling
08 alarming, dramatic
10 astounding, surprising, unexpected
11 astonishing

starvation
05 death
06 famine, hunger
07 fasting
12 malnutrition

starve
03 die
04 deny, diet, fast
06 hunger, perish
07 deprive

starving
05 dying
06 hungry
08 famished, ravenous, underfed

stash
04 fund, heap, hide, pile, stow
05 cache, hoard, lay up, store
07 conceal, reserve, secrete
08 salt away
09 reservoir, stockpile
12 accumulation

state
03 put, say
04 aver, flap, land, tell
05 glory, panic, realm, shape, tizzy, utter, voice
06 affirm, assert, bother, formal, nation, plight, public, report, reveal, set out
07 council, country, declare, divulge, express, kingdom, majesty, present, specify
08 announce, disclose, national, official, position, proclaim, republic
09 condition, make known, situation, territory
10 articulate, federation, government, promulgate
11 authorities, communicate, predicament
12 governmental
13 circumstances
➤ See also **borough**; **county**; **province**

─ *States in Australia*
08 Tasmania, Victoria
10 Queensland
13 New South Wales
14 South Australia
16 Western Australia
17 Northern Territory

─ *States in India*
03 Goa
05 Assam, Behar, Bihar
06 Kerala, Orissa, Punjab, Sikkim
07 Gujarat, Manipur, Tripura
08 Nagaland
09 Karnataka, Rajasthan, Tamil Nadu
10 West Bengal
11 Maharashtra
12 Jammu-Kashmir, Uttar Pradesh
13 Andhra Pradesh, Madhya Pradesh

─ *States in the USA*
04 Iowa, Ohio, Utah
05 Idaho, Maine, Texas
06 Alaska, Hawaii, Kansas, Nevada, Oregon
07 Alabama, Arizona, Florida, Georgia, Indiana, Montana, New York, Vermont, Wyoming
08 Arkansas, Colorado, Delaware, Illinois,
Kentucky, Maryland, Michigan, Missouri, Nebraska, Oklahoma, Virginia
09 Louisiana, Minnesota, New Jersey, New Mexico, Tennessee, Wisconsin
10 California, Washington
11 Connecticut, Mississippi, North Dakota, Rhode Island, South Dakota
12 New Hampshire, Pennsylvania, West Virginia
13 Massachusetts, North Carolina, South Carolina
18 District of Columbia

❑**in a state**
05 het up, upset
07 anxious, in a stew, ruffled
08 agitated, in a tizzy, worked up
09 flustered
10 distressed
13 panic-stricken

stately
05 grand, noble, regal, royal
06 august, solemn
08 imperial, imposing, majestic, measured, splendid
10 ceremonial, deliberate
11 ceremonious, magnificent

statement
06 report
07 account
09 assertion, testimony, utterance
10 disclosure, revelation
11 affirmation, declaration
12 announcement, proclamation
13 communication

state of affairs
04 case
09 condition, situation
12 lie of the land
13 circumstances

statesman, stateswoman
06 leader
08 diplomat
10 politician
11 grand old man

static
05 fixed, inert, still
07 resting
08 immobile, unmoving
10 motionless, stationary
13 at a standstill

station
03 set
04 base, halt, post, rank, send, site, stop
05 class, depot, grade, level, place
06 assign, locate, office, status
08 exchange, garrison, location, position, standing, terminus
09 establish, fare-stage

stationary
05 fixed, inert, still
06 moored, parked, static
08 constant, immobile, standing
10 motionless
13 at a standstill

statue
04 bust, head, idol
05 image
06 bronze, effigy, figure
07 carving
08 figurine
09 sculpture, statuette

statuesque
07 stately
08 handsome, imposing, majestic

stature
04 fame, rank, size
06 height, renown
08 attitude, eminence, prestige, standing, tallness

status
04 rank
05 class, grade, level, state
06 degree, weight
07 station
08 eminence, position, prestige, standing
09 condition
10 importance, reputation
11 consequence, distinction

statute
03 act, law
05 edict, ukase
09 enactment, ordinance

staunch
04 firm, halt, plug, stay, stem, stop, sure, true
05 block, check, loyal, stout
06 arrest, trusty
08 constant, faithful, reliable
09 steadfast
10 dependable
11 trustworthy

stave

◻stave off
04 foil
05 avert, avoid, parry, repel

07 deflect, fend off, repulse, ward off
09 keep at bay, turn aside

stay
04 curb, halt, keep, last, live, prop, rest, stop, wait
05 abide, block, board, brace, check, delay, lodge, pause, tarry, visit
06 arrest, endure, hinder, linger, put off, remain, reside, settle
07 adjourn, control, persist, prevent, sojourn, support, suspend
08 obstruct, postpone, prorogue, reprieve, restrain, stopover
09 deferment, remission, stanchion
10 suspension
12 postponement

staying power
04 grit
07 stamina
08 strength
09 endurance, fortitude
10 resilience, resistance

steadfast
06 stable, steady
07 staunch
08 constant, faithful, reliable
09 dedicated
11 unfaltering, unflinching

steady
04 calm, even, firm
05 brace, check, fixed, sober, still
06 poised, secure, stable
07 balance, compose, control, regular, serious, settled, support, uniform
08 balanced, constant, habitual, reliable, restrain
09 immovable, stabilize, steadfast, unvarying
10 consistent, dependable, motionless, unchanging, unvariable, unwavering
12 well-balanced
13 imperturbable

steal
04 lift, nick, slip, snip, take
05 creep, filch, heist, pinch, poach, slide, slink, sneak, swipe
06 abduct, kidnap, nobble, pilfer, pocket, rip off, snatch, thieve, tiptoe
07 bargain, good buy, purloin, snaffle

08 discount, embezzle, giveaway, knock off, peculate, shoplift
09 reduction
10 plagiarize
11 appropriate, make off with
12 make away with, special offer

stealing
05 theft
06 piracy
07 larceny, nicking, robbery
08 burglary, filching, pinching, poaching, thievery, thieving
09 pilferage, pilfering
10 peculation, plagiarism, purloining
11 shoplifting
12 embezzlement
13 appropriation

stealth
07 secrecy, slyness
10 covertness, sneakiness
11 furtiveness

stealthy
03 sly
06 covert, secret, sneaky
07 cunning, furtive
09 secretive, underhand
11 unobtrusive

steam
04 haze, mist
06 energy, vapour, vigour
07 stamina
08 dampness, moisture
10 enthusiasm
12 condensation

◻get steamed up
08 get angry, get het up
10 get annoyed, get excited
12 fly into a rage, get flustered

◻steam up
05 fog up
06 mist up

◻under your own steam
05 alone
10 by yourself
11 without help
13 independently

steamboat
06 packet
09 vaporetto
10 packet-boat, paddle-boat
13 paddle-steamer

steamy
03 hot
04 blue, damp, hazy, sexy
05 close, humid, misty, muggy
06 erotic, sticky, sultry, sweaty

07 amorous, gaseous, lustful, raunchy, sensual, vapoury
08 vaporous
10 passionate, sweltering

steed
03 nag
04 hack, jade
05 horse, mount
07 charger

steel
05 brace, nerve
06 harden
07 fortify, prepare, toughen

steely
04 firm, grey, hard
05 harsh
08 blue-grey, pitiless, resolute
09 merciless, steel-blue
10 determined, inflexible

steep
04 damp, dear, fill, high, soak
05 brine, imbue, sharp, sheer, souse, stiff
06 abrupt, costly, drench, imbrue, infuse, pickle, seethe, sudden
07 extreme, immerse, moisten, pervade, suffuse
08 headlong, macerate, marinate, permeate, saturate, submerge, vertical
09 excessive, expensive
10 exorbitant, inordinate, over the top, overpriced
11 acclivitous, declivitous, precipitous
12 extortionate, unreasonable

steeple
05 spire, tower
06 beltry, turret

steer
03 cox
05 guide, pilot, usher
06 direct
07 conduct, control
08 navigate

□**steer clear of**
04 shun
05 avoid, dodge, evade, skirt
06 bypass, escape, eschew
10 circumvent

stem
03 dam
04 come, curb, flow, halt, stop
05 arise, block, check, issue, shoot, stalk, stock, trunk
06 arrest, branch, derive, resist, spring, stanch

07 contain, develop, emanate, staunch
09 originate

stench
04 niff, pong, reek
05 odour, smell, stink, whiff
06 miasma

stentorian
06 strong
07 booming, ringing, vibrant
08 resonant, sonorous, strident
10 thunderous

step
03 act
04 deed, gait, move, pace, rank, rung, walk
05 grade, level, phase, point, print, stage, stair, stamp, trace, track, tramp, tread
06 action, degree, effort, stride
07 advance, measure, process
08 footstep, progress
09 expedient, footprint, manoeuvre, procedure
14 course of action

□**in step**
08 in unison, together
11 in agreement

□**out of step**
06 at odds

□**step by step**
06 slowly
08 bit by bit, gradatim
09 gradually

□**step down**
04 quit
05 leave
06 resign, retire
08 abdicate, withdraw

□**step in**
09 intercede, interfere, intervene

□**step up**
05 boost, raise
07 augment, build up, speed up
08 escalate, increase
09 intensify

□**watch your step**
07 look out
08 take care, watch out
09 be careful
12 mind how you go

stereotype
03 tag
05 label, model, mould
06 cliché
07 formula, pattern

08 typecast
10 categorize, pigeonhole

stereotyped
05 banal, corny, stale, stock, tired, trite
07 clichéd
08 overused, standard
09 hackneyed
12 cliché-ridden, standardized

sterile
04 arid, bare, pure, vain
05 clean
06 barren, futile
07 aseptic, useless
08 abortive, germ-free, germless, infecund
09 fruitless, infertile, pointless
10 antiseptic, sterilized
11 disinfected, ineffectual
12 unproductive, unprofitable

sterility
06 atocia, purity
07 asepsis
08 futility
09 cleanness, impotence
10 barrenness, inefficacy
11 infertility
13 fruitlessness, pointlessness
14 unfruitfulness
15 ineffectiveness

sterilize
04 geld, spay
06 doctor, neuter, purify
08 castrate, fumigate
09 disinfect

sterling
04 pure, real, true
07 genuine
08 standard
09 authentic, excellent
10 first-class

stern
04 back, grim, poop, rear, tail
05 cruel, harsh, rigid, stark, tough
06 severe, sombre, strict
07 austere, tail end
08 exacting, rigorous
09 demanding, draconian, stringent, unsparing
10 forbidding, inflexible, relentless, tyrannical, unyielding
11 unrelenting
13 authoritarian

stew
04 boil, cook, fret, fuss, hash
05 daube, sweat, tizzy, worry

06 bother, braise, pother, ragout, simmer
07 agonize, chowder, goulash
08 pot-au-feu
09 agitation, casserole

steward
06 butler, factor, waiter
07 marshal
09 attendant
15 flight attendant

stick
03 fix, gum, jab, jam, lay, pin, put, set
04 bear, bind, bond, clog, drop, flak, fuse, glue, grip, hold, join, last, poke, push, rest, site, stab, stay, stop, tack, tape, trap, twig, weld
05 abide, abuse, affix, blame, cling, dwell, paste, place, prick, spear, stand
06 adhere, attach, branch, cement, endure, fasten, impale, insert, linger, locate, pierce, remain, secure, solder, switch, thrust
07 carry on, deposit, install, persist, reproof, stomach
08 continue, position, puncture, tolerate, transfix
09 criticism, hostility, put up with
10 punishment

► *Types of stick*:
03 lug, rod
04 cane, club, cosh, pike, pole, post, wand, whip
05 baton, birch, crook, lathi, staff, stake
06 crutch, cudgel
07 sceptre
08 bludgeon
09 truncheon
10 shillelagh
11 hockey stick
12 walking stick

❏**stick at**
04 balk
05 demur, doubt, pause
06 keep at, recoil, stop at
07 persist, scruple
08 continue, hesitate, plug away
09 persevere

❏**stick by**
06 defend, hold to, uphold
07 stand by, support
08 adhere to, champion
10 stand up for

❏**stick it out**
07 persist
08 continue, keep at it, plug away
09 persevere
11 hang in there

❏**stick out**
06 extend, jut out
07 poke out, project
08 protrude
13 be conspicuous

❏**stick up for**
06 defend, uphold
07 protect, stand by, support
08 champion, fight for
13 take the part of, take the side of

❏**the sticks**
04 bush
07 boonies, hickdom, outback
09 backwoods, boondocks
15 middle of nowhere

stickiness
03 goo
09 glueyness, gooeyness, viscidity

stick-in-the-mud
05 fogey
06 fossil, square
08 old fogey
10 fuddy-duddy
13 unadventurous

stickler
06 maniac, pedant, purist
07 fanatic, fusspot
13 perfectionist

sticky
05 close, gluey, gooey, gummy, humid, muggy, tacky
06 clammy, sultry, tricky
07 awkward, viscoid, viscous
08 adhesive, delicate, ticklish
09 difficult, glutinous, sensitive
10 oppressive, sweltering

stiff
04 cold, firm, hard, prim, taut
05 brisk, fresh, harsh, large, rigid, solid, tense, tight, tough, windy
06 aching, chilly, formal, severe, strict, strong, tiring
07 arduous, austere, awkward, drastic, extreme, pompous
08 decorous, exacting, forceful, hardened, priggish, reserved, rigorous, strigent,
09 arthritic, demanding, difficult, inelastic, laborious, rheumatic, unbending

10 inflexible, unyielding
11 ceremonious, challenging, rheumaticky, stand-offish
12 intoxicating

stiffen
03 set
04 jell
05 brace, steel, tense
06 harden, starch
07 congeal, fortify, tense up, thicken, tighten
08 solidify
09 coagulate, reinforce
10 strengthen

stiff-necked
05 proud
07 haughty
08 arrogant, stubborn
09 obstinate
11 opinionated
12 contumacious
14 uncompromising

stifle
05 choke, crush
06 dampen, muffle
07 repress, silence, smother
08 hold back, restrain, suppress
09 suffocate
10 asphyxiate, extinguish

stigma
04 blot, mark, slur, spot
05 brand, shame, stain, taint
07 blemish

stigmatize
04 mark
05 brand, label, shame, stain
06 vilify
07 blemish, condemn
08 denounce, disgrace

still
03 but, yet
04 calm, hush
05 abate, allay, inert, peace, quiet
06 even so, hushed, pacify, serene, settle, silent, smooth, soothe, static, subdue, though
07 appease, assuage, however, quieten, restful, silence
08 although, immobile, inactive, lifeless, moderate, peaceful, restrain, serenity, stagnant, tranquil, unmoving, until now
09 noiseless, quietness, sedentary, unruffled
10 for all that, motionless, stationary, stock-still
11 nonetheless, undisturbed

12 nevertheless, peacefulness, tranquillity, tranquillize
15 notwithstanding

stilted
05 stiff
06 forced, wooden
08 laboured
09 unnatural
10 artificial

stimulant
05 tonic
07 pep pill, reviver
08 pick-me-up
11 restorative

stimulate
03 fan
04 fire, goad, spur, urge
05 impel, rouse
06 arouse, incite, induce, kindle, whip up
07 inspire, provoke, trigger
09 encourage, instigate
10 trigger off

stimulating
07 rousing
08 galvanic, stirring
09 inspiring, provoking
10 intriguing
11 provocative
12 exhilarating

stimulus
04 goad, jolt, prod, push, spur
06 fillip
07 impetus
10 incitement, inducement
11 provocation
12 shot in the arm

sting
03 con, nip
04 bite, burn, edge, hurt, pain
05 annoy, cheat, prick, smart, spite, trick, upset, wound
06 fiddle, fleece, grieve, injure, injury, malice, needle, nettle, offend, rip off, tingle
07 defraud, provoke, sarcasm, swindle
08 distress, irritate, pungency
12 incisiveness, take for a ride

stinging
07 burning, hurtful
08 aculeate, smarting, tingling, urticant, wounding
09 aculeated, offensive

stingy
04 mean
07 miserly
11 tight-fisted

12 cheeseparing, parsimonious
13 penny-pinching

stink
03 hum, row
04 flap, fuss, niff, pong, reek, stir
05 be bad, odour, smell
06 bother, furore, hassle, stench
08 bad smell, malodour
09 commotion, foul smell
12 song and dance

stinker
03 cad, cur, rat
05 creep, swine
06 horror, plight, rotter
07 bounder, dastard, problem, shocker
09 scoundrel
10 difficulty, impediment
11 predicament

stinking
03 bad
04 foul, vile
05 awful, nasty
06 rotten

stint
03 bit
04 save, time, turn
05 pinch, quota, share, shift, spell
06 period, scrimp
07 skimp on, stretch
08 begrudge, withhold
09 economize

stipulate
06 demand
07 lay down, require, set down, specify
08 insist on

stipulation
06 demand
07 proviso
11 requirement
12 precondition, prerequisite
13 specification

stir
04 beat, flap, fuss, move, whip
05 blend, budge, rouse, shake, shift, tizzy, touch
06 affect, bustle, excite, flurry, quiver, rustle, thrill, tumult, twitch, uproar
07 agitate, disturb, ferment, flutter, inspire, tremble
08 activity, disorder, movement
09 agitation, commotion
10 excitement
11 disturbance

❑**stir up**
04 fire, spur

05 drive, impel, rouse, waken
06 arouse, awaken, excite, incite, kindle, prompt
07 agitate, animate, inflame, inspire, provoke, quicken
08 motivate
09 galvanize, stimulate

stirring
05 heady
07 emotive, rousing
08 dramatic, exciting, spirited
09 inspiring, thrilling
12 exhilarating, intoxicating

stitch
03 hem, sew
04 darn, mend, seam, tack
09 embroider

stock
04 cows, fund, heap, keep, line, pigs, pile, race, sell
05 banal, basic, blood, bonds, breed, cache, carry, equip, funds, goods, herds, hoard, money, range, sheep, store, tired, trite, usual, wares
06 assets, cattle, deal in, flocks, handle, horses, market, shares, strain, supply
07 animals, capital, clichéd, descent, holding, lineage, regular, reserve, routine, species, variety, worn-out
08 ancestry, equities, ordinary, overused, pedigree, quantity, standard
09 essential, genealogy, hackneyed, inventory, livestock, parentage, relatives, reservoir, selection, stockpile
10 background, collection, extraction, investment, repertoire, securities
11 commodities, farm animals, merchandise, stereotyped
12 accumulation, conventional, run-of-the-mill

❑**in stock**
09 available

❑**stock up**
04 fill, heap, load, save
05 amass, buy up, hoard, lay in, store
09 provision, replenish, stockpile
10 accumulate

❑**take stock**
06 assess, review
07 weigh up
08 appraise, evaluate, reassess

09 re-examine
10 re-evaluate

stockpile
04 fund, heap, keep
05 amass, cache, hoard, store
10 accumulate

stock-still
05 inert, still
06 static
08 immobile
10 motionless, stationary

stocky
05 broad, dumpy, short, solid, squat
06 chunky, stubby, stumpy, sturdy
08 thickset

stodgy
04 dull
05 heavy, solid, staid
06 boring, formal, leaden, solemn, stuffy, turgid
07 filling, starchy, tedious
10 fuddy-duddy, spiritless

stoical
07 patient
08 resigned
09 accepting, impassive
10 forbearing, phlegmatic
13 long-suffering, uncomplaining

stoicism
07 ataraxy
08 ataraxia, fatalism, patience
11 forbearance, resignation
13 long-suffering

stolid
04 dull, slow
05 heavy
06 bovine, solemn, wooden
07 lumpish
09 apathetic, impassive
10 phlegmatic
11 unemotional

stomach
03 gut
04 bear, guts, take, zest
05 abide, belly, brook, stand, taste, tummy
06 desire, endure, hunger, liking, paunch, relish, suffer
07 abdomen, courage, insides, passion
08 appetite, pot-belly, submit to, tolerate
09 approve of, put up with
11 bread basket, corporation, inclination
13 determination

stone
03 gem, pip, pit, set
04 rock, seed, sett, slab
05 jewel, lapis
06 cobble, kernel, pebble
07 boulder
08 endocarp, gemstone
09 flagstone, headstone, tombstone
10 concretion, gravestone

stony
03 icy
04 cold, hard
05 blank, rocky, stern
06 chilly, frigid, frosty, gritty, pebbly, severe, steely
07 adamant, callous, deadpan, hostile, shingly
08 gravelly, pitiless
09 heartless, merciless
10 inexorable, poker-faced
11 indifferent, unforgiving
14 expressionless

stooge
04 butt, dupe, foil, pawn
06 lackey, puppet
07 cat's paw, fall guy

stoop
03 bow, sag
04 bend, duck, lean, sink
05 deign, droop, hunch, kneel, lower, slump, squat
06 crouch, resort, slouch
07 bending, descend, ducking, incline
09 go so far as, go so low as, vouchsafe
10 condescend
13 lower yourself

stop
03 bar, end
04 bung, halt, kick, live, plug, quit, rest, seal, stay, stem
05 block, board, break, cease, check, close, cover, dwell, lodge, pause, put up, stage, stall, visit
06 arrest, desist, finish, hinder, impede, pack in, reside, settle, stanch, thwart
07 abandon, bus stop, prevent, refrain, sojourn, station, staunch, suspend
08 conclude, give over, knock off, leave off, obstruct, terminus
09 cessation, fare stage, frustrate, intercept, interrupt, terminate
10 conclusion, standstill

11 come to an end, destination, discontinue, termination
12 bring to an end
14 discontinuance
15 discontinuation

stopgap
06 resort
09 expedient, makeshift, temporary
10 improvised, substitute
12 expediential
13 improvisation

stopover
04 rest, stop
05 break, visit
07 sojourn
13 overnight stay

stoppage
04 halt, stop
05 check, sit-in
06 arrest, strike
07 closure, removal, walk-out
08 blockage, shutdown
09 cessation, deduction, occlusion
10 standstill
11 obstruction, termination

stopper
04 bung, cork, plug, seal
06 spigot

store
04 bank, fund, heap, keep, load, mine, save, shop
05 cache, hoard, lay by, lay in, lay up, stash, stock
06 esteem, gather, larder, plenty, supply
07 buttery, collect, deposit, lay down, put down, reserve
08 put aside, quantity, salt away
09 abundance, reservoir, stockpile, warehouse
10 accumulate, chain store, corner shop, depository, repository, storehouse
11 hypermarket, supermarket
12 accumulation, retail outlet

❑ **lay store by, set store by**
05 value
06 admire
13 think highly of

storehouse
04 barn, fund, hold, silo
05 depot, vault
06 cellar, garner, larder, wealth
07 armoury, arsenal, granary
08 entrepot, treasury
09 repertory, warehouse
10 depository, repository

storey
04 deck, tier
05 floor, level, stage
06 flight

storm
03 row
04 fume, rage, rant, rave, roar, rush, stir, tear, to-do
05 shout, stamp
06 assail, attack, charge, furore, seethe, tumult, uproar
07 assault, clamour, explode, flounce, thunder, turmoil
08 brouhaha, outburst
09 commotion, kerfuffle, offensive, onslaught

Types of storm:
04 gale
05 buran
06 squall
07 cyclone, monsoon, tempest, tornado, typhoon
08 blizzard, downpour
09 dust-devil, dust-storm, hailstorm, hurricane, rainstorm, sand storm, snow storm, whirlwind
10 cloudburst
12 thunderstorm
15 electrical storm
➤ See also **wind**

stormy
04 foul, wild
05 gusty, rainy, rough, windy
06 choppy, raging
09 turbulent
11 tempestuous

story
03 lie, rib
04 item, plot, tale
06 record, report
07 account, article, episode, feature, fiction, history, recital, untruth
08 anecdote
09 chronicle, falsehood, narrative

storyteller
04 bard
08 narrator, novelist, tell-tale
09 raconteur
10 anecdotist, chronicler, raconteuse

stout
04 bold
05 beefy, brave, bulky, burly, gutsy, hardy, heavy, obese, plump, solid, thick, tough, tubby
06 brawny, fleshy, heroic, plucky, portly, robust, stocky, strong, sturdy
07 durable, hulking, valiant
08 fearless, forceful, muscular, resolute, valorous, vigorous
09 corpulent, dauntless
10 courageous, determined, overweight
11 substantial

stove
04 kiln, oven
05 grill, range
06 cooker, heater
07 furnace

stow
04 cram, load, pack
05 place, stash, store, stuff
07 deposit, put away

straggle
03 lag
04 roam, rove
05 amble, drift, range, stray, trail
07 scatter
09 string out
10 dilly-dally

straggly
06 random, untidy
08 drifting, rambling, straying
09 irregular, strung out

straight
04 even, fair, flat, just, neat, pure, tidy, true
05 blunt, frank, level, right
06 candid, decent, direct, honest, unbent
07 aligned, bluntly, clearly, frankly, in order, orderly, plainly, sincere, upright
08 arranged, candidly, directly, faithful, honestly, promptly, reliable, unbroken, vertical
09 on the trot, organized, outspoken, shipshape, unbending, undiluted
10 continuous, forthright, honourable, horizontal, law-abiding, point-blank, successive, unswerving
11 consecutive, immediately, respectable, trustworthy
12 continuously, conventional, forthrightly, successively
13 consecutively, unadulterated, uninterrupted
14 as the crow flies
15 straightforward

◻**straight away**
03 now

06 at once, pronto
08 directly
09 instantly, right away
11 immediately
12 there and then, without delay

straighten
04 tidy
05 align, order
06 adjust, neaten, tidy up
07 arrange
10 put in order

◻**straighten out**
06 settle, tidy up
07 clear up, correct, realign, rectify, resolve, sort out
08 put right
10 put in order, regularize
11 disentangle

◻**straighten up**
10 stand erect
12 stand upright

straightforward
04 easy, open
05 clear, frank
06 candid, direct, honest, simple
07 genuine, sincere
08 truthful
09 outspoken
10 child's play, elementary, forthright, unexacting
11 undemanding
12 a piece of cake
13 plain-speaking, uncomplicated

strain
03 air, tax, try, tug, way
04 kind, sift, song, sort, tear, tune, type, vein
05 blood, breed, drain, drive, exert, force, heave, sieve, stock, theme, trace, trait, twist, worry, wrick, wring
06 burden, demand, duress, effort, extend, family, filter, injure, injury, melody, screen, sprain, streak, stress, strive, tauten, weaken, wrench
07 descent, express, fatigue, lineage, overtax, quality, squeeze, stretch, tension, tighten, variety
08 ancestry, exertion, go all out, pedigree, pressure, separate, tendency
09 endeavour, weariness
10 exhaustion, suggestion
12 do your utmost

14 characteristic
15 make every effort

strained
05 false, stiff, tense
06 forced, uneasy, wooden
07 awkward
08 laboured
09 unnatural
11 constrained, embarrassed
13 uncomfortable

strainer
05 sieve
06 filter, riddle, screen, sifter
08 colander

strait
04 hole, kyle, mess
05 inlet, sound
06 crisis, pickle, plight
07 channel, dilemma, narrows, poverty
08 distress, hardship
09 emergency, extremity
10 difficulty, perplexity
11 predicament

straitened
04 poor
07 limited, reduced
09 difficult
10 distressed, restricted
12 impoverished

strait-laced
04 prim
06 narrow, proper, strict, stuffy
07 prudish, starchy

strand
04 sand, wire
05 beach, fibre, sands, shore
06 factor, length, string, thread
07 element, feature
08 filament, seashore
09 component, foreshore
10 ingredient, waterfront

stranded
07 aground, beached, wrecked
08 forsaken, marooned
10 high and dry
11 shipwrecked
14 left in the lurch

strange
03 new, odd
05 alien, funny, kinky, novel, queer, wacky, weird
06 exotic, freaky, unreal
07 bizarre, curious, foreign, oddball, offbeat, surreal, uncanny, unknown, unusual
08 abnormal, peculiar, singular, uncommon

09 eccentric, fantastic, irregular, unheard-of
10 unexpected, unfamiliar
11 unexplained
12 inexplicable
13 extraordinary

strangeness
06 oddity
07 oddness
09 queerness
10 exoticness
11 abnormality, peculiarity, singularity
12 eccentricity, irregularity

stranger
05 alien, guest
07 incomer, visitor
08 newcomer, outsider
09 foreigner, non-member

❑**a stranger to**
10 unversed in
14 unaccustomed to, unfamiliar with

strangle
03 gag
05 check, choke
06 keep in, stifle
07 inhibit, repress, smother
08 hold back, restrain, suppress, throttle
09 suffocate
10 asphyxiate

strap
03 tie
04 band, beat, belt, bind, cord, flog, lash, whip
05 leash, thong, truss
06 fasten, secure
07 bandage, scourge

strapping
03 big
05 beefy, burly, hunky, husky
06 brawny, sturdy
07 hulking
09 well-built

stratagem
04 plan, plot, ploy, ruse, wile
05 dodge, trick
05 device, scheme, tactic
08 artifice, intrigue
09 deception, manoeuvre
11 machination

strategic
03 key
05 vital
07 crucial, planned, politic
08 critical, decisive, tactical
09 essential, important
10 calculated, deliberate

strategy
04 game, plan
06 design, policy, scheme
07 tactics
08 approach, planning, schedule
09 blueprint, procedure, programme
12 plan of action

stratum
03 bed
04 lode, rank, seam, tier, vein
05 caste, class, grade, group, layer, level, table
07 bracket, station
14 stratification

stray
03 err, odd
04 lost, roam, rove
05 amble, drift, freak, range
06 chance, ramble, random, wander
07 deviate, digress, diverge, get lost, meander, roaming
08 go astray, homeless, straggle
09 abandoned, wander off
10 accidental, occasional
15 go off at a tangent

streak
04 band, dart, dash, race, rush, tear, vein, zoom
05 flash, fleck, smear, speed, spell, touch, trace
06 hurtle, period, sprint, strain, stripe, stroke
07 element, stretch, striate

streaked
05 lined
06 banded, barred
07 brinded, brindle, flecked, streaky, striate
08 brindled

stream
03 fly, jet, run
04 beck, burn, flap, flow, gush, pour, rill, rush, tide
05 brook, burst, creek, crowd, drift, float, flood, issue, river, spill, spout, surge, trail
06 deluge, efflux, rillet
07 cascade, rivulet, torrent
09 tributary
10 outpouring

streamer
04 flag
06 banner, ensign, pennon
07 pennant
08 gonfalon, standard, vexillum

streamlined
05 sleek, slick
06 smooth
07 well-run
09 efficient, organized
10 modernized, time-saving
11 aerodynamic

street

❑ **man in the street**
09 Joe Bloggs, Mr Average
10 Mrs Average
13 average person, average punter
14 ordinary person
15 ordinary citizen

strength
04 bent, gift, guts
05 asset, brawn, clout, force, forte, power, sinew
06 ardour, energy, muscle, métier, talent, vigour, weight
07 bravery, courage, fitness, passion, potency, stamina
08 aptitude, fervency, firmness, pungency, solidity
09 advantage, fortitude, hardiness, intensity, vehemence
10 durability, resilience, resistance, resolution, robustness, speciality
11 persistence, strong point
12 forcefulness
13 determination, effectiveness
14 impregnability, persuasiveness

❑ **on the strength of**
09 because of
10 by virtue of
11 on account of
12 on the basis of

strengthen
05 brace, rally, steel
06 back up, beef up, harden, prop up
07 bolster, build up, confirm, fortify, hearten, nourish, refresh, restore, shore up, stiffen, support, toughen
08 buttress, heighten, increase
09 encourage, intensify, reinforce
10 invigorate
11 consolidate, corroborate
12 substantiate

strenuous
04 bold, hard, keen
05 eager, heavy, tough
06 active, taxing, tiring, uphill
07 arduous, earnest, weighty

08 forceful, resolute, spirited, tireless, vigorous
09 demanding, difficult, energetic, gruelling, laborious, tenacious
10 determined, exhausting
13 indefatigable

stress
04 beat
05 force, ictus, value, worry
06 accent, hassle, strain, trauma, weight
07 anxiety, point up, tension, trouble
08 distress, emphasis, pressure
09 emphasize, highlight, spotlight, underline
10 accentuate, exaggerate, importance, underscore
12 accentuation, significance

stretch
03 run, tax, try
04 area, last, pull, push, term, test, time
05 offer, range, reach, space, spell, stint, sweep, tract, widen
06 expand, extend, extent, go up to, period, spread, strain, tauten, unfold, unroll
07 broaden, draw out, expanse, project, prolong
08 continue, distance, elongate, lengthen, protract, reach out
09 challenge, go as far as
10 straighten
11 become wider
12 become longer

❑ **stretch out**
05 reach, relax
06 extend, put out, sprawl
07 hold out, lie down, recline

❑ **stretch your legs**
05 stroll
08 exercise
09 move about, promenade, take a walk
10 go for a walk, take the air

strew
04 toss
06 litter, spread
07 bestrew, scatter
08 bespread, disperse, sprinkle
10 besprinkle

stricken
03 hit
06 struck
07 injured, smitten, wounded

08 affected
09 afflicted

strict
04 firm, hard, true
05 clear, close, exact, harsh, rigid, stern, total, tough, utter
06 narrow, severe
07 austere, literal, precise
08 absolute, accurate, clear-cut, complete, faithful, orthodox, rigorous
09 religious, stringent
10 inflexible, meticulous, no-nonsense, particular, scrupulous
13 authoritarian, conscientious, thoroughgoing
14 disciplinarian, uncompromising

strictness
06 rigour
08 accuracy, rigidity, severity
09 austerity, precision
10 stringency

stricture
04 flak
05 blame, bound, limit
06 rebuke
07 censure, confine, control, reproof
09 criticism, restraint, tightness
10 constraint
11 restriction
13 animadversion

stride
04 pace, step, walk
05 tread
07 advance
08 movement, progress
11 progression

strident
04 loud
05 harsh, rough
07 grating, jarring, raucous
08 clashing, jangling
09 clamorous, unmusical
10 discordant, screeching, stridulant, vociferous

strife
06 battle, combat
07 discord, dispute, ill-will, quarrel, rivalry, warfare
08 argument, conflict, fighting, friction, struggle
09 animosity, bickering, hostility, wrangling
10 contention, ill-feeling
11 controversy
12 disagreement

strike
03 aid, box, hit, rap
04 bang, beat, belt, biff, blow, cuff, feel, find, look, raid, rush, seem, slap, sock, trap
05 adopt, clout, knock, pound, punch, reach, sit-in, smack, sound, storm, swipe, thump, touch, whack
06 affect, ambush, appear, assail, assume, attack, batter, buffet, charge, clinch, come to, dawn on, go-slow, hammer, mutiny, revolt, stroke, take on, thrash, thwack, wallop
07 achieve, agree on, assault, clobber, embrace, impress, occur to, protest, uncover, unearth, walk out, walk-out
08 arrive at, come upon, discover, look like, pounce on, register, set about, settle on, stoppage, stop work
09 down tools, encounter
10 chance upon, come to mind, happen upon, work to rule
11 collide with

❑**strike back**
07 hit back
09 fight back, retaliate
11 get even with
14 get your own back, pay someone back

❑**strike down**
04 kill, ruin, slay
05 smite
06 murder
07 afflict, destroy
11 assassinate

❑**strike out**
05 erase
06 delete, remove, rub out
08 cross out

❑**strike up**
05 begin, start
07 kick off
08 commence, initiate
09 establish, instigate

striking
06 pretty
07 evident, obvious, salient, visible
08 dazzling, distinct, gorgeous, stunning
09 arresting, beautiful, glamorous, memorable
10 attractive, impressive, noticeable, remarkable
11 astonishing, conspicuous, good-looking, outstanding
13 extraordinary

string
03 row
04 cord, file, hang, line, link, loop, rope, yarn
05 cable, chain, fibre, queue, sling, tie up, train, twine
06 column, fasten, series, strand, stream, thread
07 catches, connect, festoon
08 provisos, sequence
10 conditions, succession
11 limitations
12 restrictions
13 prerequisites

❑**string along**
04 dupe, fool, hoax
05 bluff
06 humbug
07 deceive
12 take for a ride

❑**string out**
06 extend, fan out, wander
08 disperse, lengthen, protract, space out, straggle
09 spread out
10 stretch out

❑**string up**
03 top
04 hang, kill
05 lynch

stringent
04 firm, hard
05 harsh, rigid, tight, tough
06 severe, strict
08 exacting, rigorous
09 demanding
10 inflexible

stringy
04 ropy, wiry
05 chewy, tough
06 sinewy
07 fibrous, gristly
08 leathery

strip
03 bar, bit, gut
04 band, belt, flay, lath, loot, peel, sash, skin, slat, slip
05 clear, empty, piece, shred, strap, thong
06 denude, divest, expose, ribbon, stripe, swathe
07 deprive, disrobe, lay bare, ransack, uncover, undress
08 clean out, unclothe
09 dismantle, excoriate, pull apart, take apart

10 dispossess
12 take to pieces

stripe
03 bar
04 band, belt, line
05 flash, fleck, strip
06 streak

striped
06 banded, barred, stripy
07 streaky, vittate
08 striated

stripling
03 boy, lad
05 youth
08 teenager
09 fledgling, youngster
10 adolescent

strive
03 try, vie
04 toil, work
05 fight
06 battle, combat, engage, labour, strain
07 attempt, compete, contend, contest, try hard
08 campaign, struggle
09 endeavour
12 do your utmost

stroke
03 hit, pat, pet, rub
04 belt, biff, blow, coup, line, move, slap
05 knock, shock, smack, spasm, sweep, swipe, thump, touch, whack
06 action, attack, caress, fondle, thwack, wallop
07 clobber, massage, seizure
08 flourish, movement
10 thrombosis
14 accomplishment

stroll
04 turn, walk
05 amble
06 dawdle, ramble, wander
07 meander, saunter
10 go for a walk
14 constitutional
15 stretch your legs

stroller
06 walker
07 dawdler, rambler
08 wanderer
09 saunterer

strong
03 fit, hot
04 deep, firm, keen, well
05 beefy, brave, burly, clear, eager, great, gutsy, hardy,

heady, lusty, sharp, solid, sound, spicy, stout, tough, valid, vivid
06 active, ardent, biting, brawny, fierce, marked, mighty, potent, robust, rugged, severe, sinewy, sturdy, urgent
07 devoted, durable, fervent, graphic, healthy, intense, obvious, piquant, pungent, telling, violent, weighty
08 athletic, clear-cut, decisive, forceful, muscular, positive, powerful, profound, resolute, stalwart, vehement, vigorous
09 assertive, committed, confident, effective, heavy-duty, resilient, strapping, undiluted, well-built
10 aggressive, compelling, convincing, courageous, determined, formidable, passionate, persistent, persuasive, pronounced, reinforced, remarkable
11 hard-wearing, long-lasting
12 concentrated, enthusiastic, single-minded, strong-minded, strong-willed
13 well-protected
14 highly-seasoned

strongarm
08 bullying, coercive, forceful, physical, thuggish
11 threatening
12 intimidatory

stronghold
04 fort, keep
07 bastion, citadel
08 fortress

strong-minded
04 firm
08 resolute
09 tenacious, unbending
10 determined, iron-willed, unwavering
14 uncompromising

strong point
04 bent, gift
05 asset, forte, thing
06 métier, talent
08 strength

strong-willed
06 wilful
08 obdurate, stubborn
09 obstinate
10 inflexible, self-willed

11 intractable
12 intransigent, recalcitrant

stroppy
07 awkward
10 refractory
11 quarrelsome
12 cantankerous, obstreperous

structural
08 tectonic
11 formational
14 constructional

structure
04 form
05 build, frame, set-up, shape
06 design, fabric, make-up
07 arrange, edifice
08 assemble, building, erection, organize
09 construct, formation, framework
11 arrangement, composition
12 conformation, constitution, construction, organization
13 configuration

struggle
03 vie
04 toil, work
05 brawl, clash, fight
06 battle, combat, effort, labour, strain, strife, strive
07 contend, contest, grapple, scuffle, wrestle
08 conflict, exertion, skirmish
10 difficult
11 competition, hostilities
13 exert yourself

strut
05 swank
06 parade, prance
07 peacock, swagger

stub
04 butt
05 stump
06 dog-end, fag end
11 counterfoil

stubborn
05 rigid
06 dogged, mulish, wilful
08 obdurate
09 obstinate, pig-headed
10 headstrong, inflexible, unyielding
11 intractable, stiff-necked
12 intransigent, recalcitrant

stubby
05 dumpy, short, squat
06 chunky, stumpy
08 thickset

stuck
04 fast, firm
05 fixed, glued
06 beaten, jammed, rooted
07 at a loss, baffled, stumped
08 cemented, embedded, fastened, immobile
09 perplexed, unmovable
10 bogged down, nonplussed

▫**get stuck into**
06 tackle
07 set about
09 get down to

▫**stuck on**
05 mad on
06 fond of, keen on, nuts on
09 wild about
10 crazy about, dotty about

stuck-up
05 proud
06 snooty, uppish
07 haughty
08 arrogant, snobbish
10 hoity-toity
11 patronizing, toffee-nosed
13 high and mighty

studded
06 dotted
07 flecked, spotted

student
05 pupil
07 fresher, learner, scholar, trainee
08 disciple
09 schoolboy
10 apprentice, schoolgirl
12 postgraduate
13 undergraduate

studied
08 affected
09 conscious, contrived, unnatural
10 artificial, calculated, deliberate, purposeful
11 intentional

studio
06 school
07 atelier
08 workroom, workshop

studious
07 bookish, serious
08 academic, diligent, sedulous, thorough
09 assiduous, scholarly
10 meticulous, thoughtful
12 intellectual

study
03 den
04 cram, read, scan, swot

05 learn, mug up
06 bone up, peruse, ponder, read up, revise, thesis
07 analyse, examine, inquiry, library, major in, reading, thought
08 analysis, consider, critique, homework, learning, pore over, research, revision, scrutiny, workroom
09 attention, monograph
10 deliberate, inspection, scrutinize
11 contemplate, examination, investigate, preparation, scholarship
13 contemplation, investigation

stuff
03 jam, kit, pad, ram
04 cram, fill, gear, load, pack, push, sate, stow
05 block, crowd, force, goods, gorge, items, press, shove
06 bung up, fabric, gobble, guzzle, matter, pig out, tackle, things, thrust
07 clobber, essence, luggage, objects, satiate, squeeze
08 articles, compress, gross out, material, obstruct
09 equipment, materials, substance
10 belongings, gormandize
11 overindulge, possessions
13 paraphernalia

stuffing
05 farce, kapok
07 filling, packing, padding, wadding
08 quilting
09 forcemeat

stuffy
04 dull, prim
05 close, fuggy, heavy, muggy, musty, staid, stale, stiff
06 stodgy, sultry
07 airless, pompous, starchy
08 stifling
10 fuddy-duddy, oppressive
11 strait-laced, suffocating
12 unventilated

stultify
04 dull, numb
05 blunt
07 nullify, smother, stupefy

stumble
04 fall, reel, slip, trip
05 lurch
06 falter

07 blunder, stagger, stammer, stutter
08 flounder, hesitate
15 lose your balance

❑**stumble on**
04 find
08 discover
09 encounter
10 chance upon, happen upon

stumbling-block
04 snag
08 obstacle
09 hindrance
10 difficulty, impediment
11 obstruction

stump
04 butt, foil, stub
06 baffle, defeat, dog-end, fag end, outwit, puzzle
07 confuse, flummox, mystify, nonplus, perplex
08 bewilder, confound
09 bamboozle, dumbfound

❑**stump up**
05 pay up
06 chip in, donate, pay out
07 cough up, fork out
08 hand over, shell out
10 contribute

stumped
05 stuck
07 baffled, floored, stymied
09 flummoxed, perplexed
10 bamboozled, nonplussed

stumpy
05 dumpy, squat, thick
06 chunky, stocky, stubby
08 thickset

stun
04 daze
05 amaze, shock
07 astound, confuse, stagger, stupefy
08 astonish, bewilder, bowl over, confound, knock out
09 dumbfound, overpower
11 flabbergast, knock for six

stunned
04 numb
05 dazed
06 amazed
07 floored, shocked
09 astounded, staggered, stupefied

stunner
03 wow
05 peach, siren
06 beauty, looker, lovely
07 charmer, dazzler, smasher

08 knock-out
09 sensation
10 good-looker

stunning
07 amazing
08 dazzling, smashing, striking
09 ravishing, wonderful
10 marvellous, staggering
11 sensational, spectacular

stunt
03 act
04 curb, deed, feat, slow, stop, turn
05 check, dwarf, trick
06 action, arrest, hamper, hinder, impede, retard, wheeze
07 exploit
08 restrict

stunted
04 tiny
05 small
06 little
07 dwarfed
10 diminutive, undersized

stupefaction
04 daze
06 wonder
08 blackout, numbness
09 amazement
10 bafflement
12 bewilderment

stupefy
04 daze, dull, numb, stun
05 amaze, shock
07 astound, stagger
08 bowl over, knock out
09 devastate, dumbfound

stupendous
06 superb
07 amazing, immense
08 colossal, stunning
10 prodigious, tremendous
12 breathtaking, overwhelming

stupid
03 dim, mad
04 dull, dumb, rash, slow
05 crass, dazed, dense, dopey, inane, silly, thick
06 absurd, futile, groggy
07 fatuous, foolish, idiotic, lunatic, moronic, puerile, stunned
08 gormless, mindless, sluggish
09 brainless, foolhardy, imbecilic, ludicrous, senseless, stupefied
10 dull-witted, half-witted

11 meaningless, nonsensical, not all there
12 feeble-minded, simple-minded
13 thick as a plank

stupidity
05 folly
06 idiocy, lunacy
07 fatuity, inanity, naïvety
08 futility
09 absurdity, asininity, puerility
10 imbecility, ineptitude

stupor
04 coma, daze
06 torpor, trance
07 inertia
08 blackout, oblivion
12 state of shock, stupefaction
13 insensibility

sturdy
05 hardy, solid, stout
06 hearty, robust, strong
08 durable, staunch
08 muscular, powerful, resolute, stalwart, vigorous
09 steadfast, well-built
10 determined

stutter
06 falter, mumble
07 stammer, stumble
08 hesitate, splutter

style
03 cut, dub, tag, way
04 call, chic, dash, form, kind, make, mode, name, sort, term, tone, type
05 adapt, flair, genre, label, shape, taste, tenor, title, trend, vogue
06 custom, design, luxury, manner, method, polish, tailor, wealth
07 fashion, panache, pattern, produce, variety, wording
08 approach, category, elegance, grandeur, language, phrasing, urbanity
09 affluence, designate, technique
10 appearance, denominate, expression, refinement
11 methodology

stylish
04 chic
05 natty, ritzy, smart
06 classy, dressy, modish, snappy, snazzy, trendy, urbane
07 à la mode, elegant, in vogue, refined, voguish

08 polished
11 fashionable
13 sophisticated

stylus
03 pen
04 hand
05 index, probe, style
06 needle
07 pointer

stymie
04 balk, foil
05 stump
06 baffle, defeat, hinder, puzzle, thwart
07 flummox, mystify, nonplus, snooker
08 confound
09 bamboozle, frustrate

suave
04 glib
05 bland, civil
06 polite, smooth, urbane
07 affable, refined, worldly
08 charming, debonair, polished, unctuous
09 agreeable, civilized, courteous
13 sophisticated

suavity
05 charm
08 civility, courtesy, urbanity
10 refinement
14 sophistication

subaquatic
08 demersal, undersea
09 submarine, submersed
10 subaqueous, underwater

subconscious
02 id
03 ego
04 deep
05 inner
06 hidden, latent, psyche
08 super-ego
09 innermost, intuitive, repressed
10 subliminal, suppressed, underlying
11 instinctive, unconscious

subdue
04 damp, tame
05 check, crush, quash, quell
06 defeat, humble, master, mellow, reduce, soften, stifle
07 conquer, control, overrun, quieten, repress, subject
08 moderate, overcome, restrain, suppress, vanquish
09 overpower, subjugate
10 discipline

subdued
03 dim, sad
04 soft
05 grave, muted, quiet, sober, still
06 hushed, low-key, pastel, shaded, silent, solemn, sombre, subtle
08 dejected, delicate, downcast, lifeless, softened
09 depressed, toned down
10 restrained
11 crestfallen, unobtrusive
14 down in the dumps

subject
03 apt
05 bound, field, issue, point, prone, theme, topic
06 affair, aspect, client, expose, liable, likely, matter, subdue, submit, vassal, victim
07 captive, exposed, lay open
08 inferior, liegeman, national, question
09 dependant, dependent, subjugate, underling
10 answerable, contingent, discipline, subjugated, submissive, vulnerable
11 conditional, constrained, participant, subordinate, subservient, susceptible

subjection
06 chains, defeat
07 bondage, mastery, slavery
08 shackles
09 captivity
10 domination, oppression
11 enslavement, subjugation

subjective
06 biased
08 personal
09 emotional, intuitive
10 individual, prejudiced
11 instinctive
13 idiosyncratic

subjugate
04 tame
05 crush, quell
06 defeat, master, subdue, thrall
07 conquer, enslave, oppress
08 overcome, vanquish
09 overpower, overthrow
14 get the better of
15 gain mastery over

sublimate
06 divert, purify, refine
07 channel, elevate

08 heighten, redirect, transfer
09 transmute

sublime
04 high
05 grand, lofty, utter
07 exalted, supreme
08 elevated, glorious
09 spiritual
12 transcendent

submerge
03 dip
04 bury, duck, dunk, sink
05 drown, flood, swamp
06 deluge, engulf, go down, plunge
07 immerse, plummet
08 inundate, submerse
09 overwhelm
12 go under water
13 put under water

submerged
04 sunk
06 hidden, sunken, unseen
07 drowned, swamped
08 immersed
09 concealed, inundated, submersed
10 underwater

submission
05 entry
06 assent, tender
07 tabling
08 meekness, offering, proposal
09 assertion, deference, obedience, passivity, statement, surrender
10 compliance, suggestion
11 resignation
12 acquiescence, capitulation, introduction, presentation
14 submissiveness

submissive
04 meek, weak
06 docile, humble, supine
07 passive, servile
08 biddable, obedient, yielding
09 compliant, malleable
10 weak-willed
11 acquiescent, deferential, subservient, unresisting
12 ingratiating, self-effacing
13 accommodating, uncomplaining

submit
03 bow
04 aver, bend, move
05 argue, claim, offer, state, table, yield

06 accede, comply, give in, tender
07 give way, present, proffer, propose, succumb, suggest
09 acquiesce, introduce, surrender
10 capitulate, put forward
12 knuckle under
15 lay down your arms

subnormal
03 low
04 slow
08 backward, inferior, retarded
12 feeble-minded

subordinate
04 aide
05 lower, lowly, minor
06 deputy, junior, lesser, menial, second, skivvy, vassal
08 dogsbody, inferior, sidekick
09 ancillary, assistant, attendant, auxiliary, dependant, dependent, secondary, underling
10 subsidiary
12 second fiddle

subordination
09 servitude
10 dependence, subjection, submission
11 inferiority
12 subservience

subscribe
04 back, fork, give
05 agree
06 accede, donate, pledge
07 approve, consent, endorse, support
08 advocate, shell out
10 contribute, underwrite
13 take regularly
15 pay for regularly

subscription
04 dues, gift
07 payment
08 donation, offering
12 contribution
13 membership fee

subsequent
04 next
05 later
06 future
07 ensuing
09 following, resulting
10 consequent, succeeding

subsequently
05 after, later
10 afterwards
12 consequently

subservient
05 lower, minor
06 junior, lesser, useful
07 fawning, servile
08 inferior, toadying, unctuous
09 ancillary, auxiliary, secondary
10 obsequious, subsidiary
11 deferential, subordinate
12 ingratiating, instrumental

subside
03 ebb
04 drop, ease, fall, sink, wane
05 abate, let up, lower
06 cave in, lessen, recede, settle
07 decline, descend, dwindle, quieten, slacken
08 collapse, decrease, diminish, get lower, moderate

subsidence
07 decline, descent, sinking
08 decrease, settling
10 settlement, slackening
12 detumescence

subsidiary
05 minor
08 division, offshoot
09 ancillary, assistant, auxiliary
10 additional, supporting
11 subordinate, subservient

subsidize
03 aid
04 back, fund
07 endorse, finance, promote, sponsor, support
08 invest in
10 underwrite

subsidy
03 aid
04 help
05 grant
07 backing, finance, funding, support
10 subvention
11 endorsement, sponsorship
12 contribution, underwriting

subsist
04 live
05 exist
06 endure
07 survive

subsistence
06 living
07 aliment, support
08 survival
10 livelihood, sustenance
11 maintenance

substance
04 body, gist, mass, pith, text
05 basis, force, means, money, power, theme, topic
06 assets, burden, fabric, ground, import, matter, riches, wealth, weight
07 essence, meaning, reality, subject
08 material, solidity, validity
09 affluence, resources
10 foundation
11 materiality, tangibility
12 corporeality, significance
13 subject matter

substandard
04 poor
06 shoddy
08 below par, inferior
09 imperfect
10 inadequate, second-rate
14 not up to scratch

substantial
04 main, real, rich
05 basic, solid, sound, stout, tough
06 actual, strong, sturdy
07 durable, sizable, wealthy, weighty
08 concrete, inherent, material, powerful, tangible, valuable
09 corporeal, essential, intrinsic, well-built
10 prosperous, successful
11 fundamental, significant
12 considerable

substantially
07 largely
10 materially
11 essentially
12 considerably
13 fundamentally, significantly
14 to a great extent

substantiate
05 prove
06 back up, uphold, verify
07 bear out, confirm, support
08 validate
11 corroborate

substitute
04 swap, temp
05 agent, cover, locum, proxy
06 acting, change, deputy, fill in, relief, supply, switch
07 relieve, replace, reserve, stand-by, stand-in, stopgap
08 deputize, exchange
09 surrogate
10 understudy
11 locum tenens, replacement

substitution
04 swap
06 change, switch
08 exchange
11 interchange, replacement

subterfuge
04 ploy, ruse, wile
05 dodge, trick
06 excuse, scheme
07 evasion, pretext
08 artifice, intrigue, pretence
09 deception, duplicity, manoeuvre, stratagem
11 deviousness, machination

subtle
03 sly
04 deep, fine, mild, nice, wily
06 astute, crafty, low-key, shrewd, slight
07 complex, cunning, devious, elusive, implied, tactful
08 delicate, discreet, indirect
09 intricate, toned down
11 understated
14 discriminating

subtlety
05 guile, skill
06 acumen, nicety, nuance
07 cunning, finesse, slyness
08 delicacy, sagacity, wiliness
09 intricacy, mutedness
10 refinement
11 discernment
14 discrimination, sophistication

subtract
04 dock
05 debit
06 deduct, remove
08 take away, withdraw

suburb
08 purlieus, suburbia
09 outskirts
12 commuter belt
13 dormitory town

suburban
04 dull
06 narrow
07 insular
08 commuter
09 bourgeois, parochial
11 middle-class, residential
12 conventional

subversive
07 riotous, traitor
08 quisling
09 dissident, seditious, terrorist
10 disruptive, incendiary, traitorous, treasonous
11 seditionist, treacherous
12 inflammatory
13 revolutionary
14 fifth columnist, freedom fighter

subvert
04 ruin
05 upset, wreck
06 debase
07 corrupt, disrupt
08 sabotage
09 undermine

subway
04 tube
05 metro
06 tunnel
09 underpass
11 underground

succeed
04 work
05 ensue, get on
06 attain, do well, follow, fulfil, manage
07 achieve, prosper, pull off, realize, replace, work out
08 flourish, go places, make good
09 come after, win the day
10 accomplish, get results
14 fall on your feet, land on your feet, take the place of

□ succeed to
06 accede, assume
07 inherit, replace
08 come into, take over
09 enter upon, supersede

succeeding
04 next
05 later
06 coming, to come
07 ensuing
09 following
10 subsequent, successive

success
03 hit, VIP, wow
04 fame, luck, star
07 fortune, triumph, victory
08 eminence, somebody
09 celebrity, sensation
10 attainment, bestseller, fulfilment, prosperity
11 achievement, realization
14 accomplishment

successful
07 booming, popular, wealthy
08 affluent, fruitful, thriving
09 fortunate, lucrative, rewarding, well-known
10 prosperous, triumphant, victorious

11   bestselling, flourishing, moneymaking

successfully
04   fine, well
05   great
08   famously
10   swimmingly
11   beautifully
12   victoriously

succession
03   run
04   flow, line
05   chain, cycle, order, train
06   course, series, string
08   sequence
09   accession
10   assumption, procession
11   inheritance, progression
12   continuation

□**in succession**
07   running
09   on the trot
12   sequentially
13   consecutively

successive
06   serial
07   running
09   following
10   sequential, succeeding
11   consecutive

successively
07   running
09   on the trot
12   sequentially
13   consecutively

successor
04   heir
06   relief
09   inheritor
10   descendant, next in line, substitute
11   beneficiary, replacement

succinct
05   brief, crisp, pithy, short, terse
07   compact, concise, in a word
09   condensed
10   to the point

succour
03   aid
04   help
06   assist, foster, relief
07   comfort, relieve, support
10   assistance, minister to

succulent
04   lush, rich
05   juicy, moist
06   fleshy, mellow
08   luscious
13   mouthwatering

succumb
04   fall
05   catch, die of, yield
06   give in, pick up, submit
07   give way
08   collapse, contract
09   surrender
10   capitulate, go down with
12   knuckle under

suck
04   draw
05   drain
06   absorb, blot up, draw in, imbibe, soak up
07   extract

□**suck up to**
04   fawn
05   toady
07   flatter, truckle
10   ingratiate
11   curry favour

sucker
03   mug, sap
04   butt, dupe, fool
06   stooge, victim
07   cat's-paw
08   pushover

suckle
04   feed
05   nurse
10   breastfeed

sudden
04   fast, rash, snap
05   hasty, quick, rapid, sharp, swift
06   abrupt, prompt, speedy
07   hurried
09   immediate, impetuous, impulsive
13   instantaneous, unanticipated
15   spur-of-the-moment

suddenly
07   quickly, sharply
08   abruptly
11   immediately
12   all of a sudden, out of the blue
14   without warning
15   instantaneously

suddenness
05   haste
09   hastiness
10   abruptness
13   impulsiveness

suds
05   froth
06   lather
07   bubbles

sue
03   beg
05   plead
06   appeal, charge, indict, summon
07   beseech, solicit
08   petition
09   prosecute
11   take to court

suffer
04   ache, bear, feel, hurt
05   abide, stand
06   endure, grieve, sorrow
07   agonize, support, sustain, undergo
08   tolerate
09   go through, put up with
10   experience

suffering
04   hurt, pain
05   agony
06   misery, ordeal, plight
07   anguish, hurting, torment, torture
08   distress, hardship
09   adversity
10   affliction, discomfort
12   wretchedness

suffice
02   do
05   serve
06   answer
07   content, satisfy
10   be adequate, fit the bill
11   fill the bill

sufficiency
06   enough, plenty
08   adequacy
12   adequateness

sufficient
05   ample
06   decent, enough, plenty
08   adequate
09   effective
12   satisfactory

suffocate
05   choke
06   stifle
07   smother
08   strangle, throttle
10   asphyxiate

suffrage
09   franchise
11   right to vote
15   enfranchisement

suffuse
05   bathe, flood, imbue, steep
06   infuse, redden, spread

07 pervade
08 permeate

sugary
05 corny, gushy, mushy, soppy
06 sickly, sloppy, slushy
07 gushing, maudlin, mawkish
09 emotional, schmaltzy
10 lovey-dovey
11 sentimental

suggest
04 hint, move
05 evoke, float, imply, table
06 advise, submit
07 counsel, propose
08 advocate, indicate, intimate
09 insinuate, recommend
10 put forward
11 bring to mind

suggestion
04 hint, idea, plan
05 touch, trace
07 pointer
08 innuendo, proposal
09 suspicion
10 indication, intimation
11 implication, insinuation, proposition
14 recommendation

suggestive
04 blue, lewd
05 bawdy, dirty
06 ribald, risqué, sexual, smutty
08 immodest, improper, indecent, redolent
09 evocative, off-colour
10 expressive, indelicate, indicative
11 provocative, reminiscent, titillating

suicide
06 suttee
08 felo de se, hara-kiri
11 ending it all
15 killing yourself, self-destruction, topping yourself

suit
03 fit
04 case
05 befit, cause, dress, match, trial
06 action, answer, become, outfit, please
07 contest, costume, dispute, flatter, gratify, lawsuit, process, qualify, satisfy, suffice
08 argument, clothing, ensemble
09 agree with, tally with

10 complement, fit the bill, litigation
11 fill the bill, proceedings, prosecution

suitability
07 aptness, fitness
11 convenience, fittingness
12 appositeness
15 appropriateness

suitable
03 apt, due, fit
05 right
06 proper, seemly, suited
07 fitting
08 adequate, apposite, becoming, relevant
09 befitting, in keeping, opportune, pertinent
10 acceptable, applicable, compatible, convenient
11 appropriate, well-matched
12 satisfactory

suitably
05 fitly, quite
08 properly
09 fittingly
10 acceptably
11 accordingly
13 appropriately

suitcase
03 bag
04 case
05 trunk
06 valise
07 holdall
09 flight bag, travel bag
10 vanity-case
11 attaché case, hand-luggage, portmanteau
12 overnight-bag

suite
03 set
05 rooms, train
06 escort, series
07 retinue
08 sequence, servants
09 apartment, entourage, followers, furniture, household, retainers
10 attendants, collection

suitor
04 beau
05 lover, swain, wooer
07 admirer
08 follower, young man
09 boyfriend

sulk
04 huff, miff, mood, mope, pout

05 brood, grump, pique
06 grouse, temper

sulky
05 cross, huffy, moody, ratty
06 grumpy, miffed, put out, sullen
08 brooding, grudging
09 resentful
10 out of sorts

sullen
04 dark, dull, glum, sour
05 heavy, moody, sulky, surly
06 dismal, gloomy, leaden, morose, silent, sombre
08 churlish, perverse, stubborn
09 resentful

sullenness
08 brooding, glumness
09 glowering, moodiness, sulkiness, surliness

sully
03 mar
04 soil, spot
05 dirty, spoil, stain, taint
06 befoul, damage, defile
07 blemish, pollute, tarnish
08 besmirch, disgrace
11 contaminate

sultry
04 sexy
05 close, humid, muggy
06 sticky, stuffy
07 airless, sensual
08 alluring, stifling, tempting
09 seductive
10 oppressive, sweltering, voluptuous
11 provocative, suffocating

sum
05 score, tally, total, whole
06 amount, number, result
07 summary
08 entirety, quantity, sum total
09 aggregate, reckoning

❑**sum up**
06 embody, review
09 epitomize, exemplify, summarize
11 encapsulate
14 put in a nutshell

summarily
07 hastily, swiftly
08 abruptly, promptly, speedily
09 forthwith
11 arbitrarily, immediately
12 peremptorily, without delay

summarize
05 recap, sum up
06 précis, review, sketch

07 abridge, outline, shorten
08 condense
09 epitomize
10 abbreviate
11 encapsulate

summary
05 brief, hasty, short, swift
06 digest, prompt, précis, review, résumé, speedy
07 cursory, instant, outline, rundown
08 abstract, succinct, synopsis
09 arbitrary, immediate
10 main points, peremptory
11 abridgement
12 without delay

summerhouse
06 gazebo
08 pavilion
09 belvedere

summit
03 top
04 acme, apex, head, peak
05 crest, crown, point
06 apogee, climax, height, vertex, zenith
08 pinnacle
11 culmination

summon
05 order, rally, rouse
06 arouse, beckon, demand, gather, invite, muster
07 convene, convoke, send for
08 assemble, mobilize

❑**summon up**
05 evoke, rally, rouse
06 arouse, gather, muster
10 call to mind

summons
04 call, writ
05 order
08 citation, subpoena
10 injunction

sumptuous
05 grand, plush
06 costly, de luxe, lavish, superb
07 opulent
08 gorgeous, splendid
09 expensive, luxurious
11 extravagant, magnificent

sun
03 tan
04 bake, bask, star
05 brown, light
08 daylight, insolate, sunbathe, sunlight, sunshine

sunbathe
03 sun, tan

04 bake, bask
08 insolate

sunburnt
03 red
05 brown, burnt
06 tanned
07 bronzed, peeling
09 blistered, sun-tanned
13 weather-beaten

sunder
04 chop, part
05 sever, split
06 cleave, divide
08 dissever, separate

sundry
04 a few, some
07 diverse, several, various
08 assorted
09 different
13 miscellaneous

sunk
06 doomed, failed, in a fix, in a jam, ruined
07 done for
08 finished
10 up the creek, up the spout

sunken
05 drawn, lower
06 buried, hollow
07 concave, haggard, lowered
08 recessed
09 depressed, submerged

sunless
04 dark, grey, hazy
06 cloudy, dismal, dreary, gloomy, sombre
08 overcast
10 depressing

sunny
05 clear, happy, merry
06 blithe, bright, joyful, sunlit
07 beaming, radiant, smiling, summery
09 brilliant, cloudless
10 optimistic
12 light-hearted

sunrise
04 dawn
05 sun-up
06 aurora
08 cock-crow, daybreak, daylight
10 break of day, first light
11 crack of dawn

sunset
04 dusk
07 evening, sundown
08 gloaming, twilight
09 nightfall
10 close of day

super
03 ace
04 cool, mega, neat
05 brill, great
06 superb, wicked
08 glorious, peerless, smashing, terrific, top-notch
09 excellent, matchless, wonderful
10 marvellous
11 magnificent, outstanding, sensational
12 incomparable

superannuated
04 aged
07 elderly, retired
08 decrepit, obsolete
10 antiquated
12 pensioned off

superb
06 choice, lavish
08 fabulous, smashing, splendid, terrific
09 brilliant, excellent, exquisite, first-rate, wonderful
10 first-class
11 outstanding, superlative

supercilious
05 lofty, proud
06 lordly, snooty, snotty, uppity
07 haughty, stuck-up
08 arrogant, jumped up, scornful
09 imperious
10 disdainful
11 overbearing, patronizing
13 condescending

superficial
05 outer
06 casual, facile, slight
07 cursory, hurried, seeming, shallow, surface
08 cosmetic, external, skin-deep, slapdash
11 lightweight, perfunctory

superficially
08 casually
09 hurriedly, seemingly
10 externally, ostensibly
12 on the surface

superfluity
04 glut
06 excess
07 surfeit, surplus
08 pleonasm, plethora
10 exuberance, redundancy
14 superabundance

superfluous
05 extra, spare

06 excess
07 surplus
08 unneeded
09 excessive, redundant,
   remaining
10 gratuitous
11 uncalled-for, unnecessary,
   unwarranted
13 supernumerary

superhuman
06 divine, heroic
09 herculean
10 phenomenal, prodigious
12 supernatural
13 preternatural

superintend
06 direct, handle, manage
07 control, inspect, oversee
09 supervise
10 administer
12 be in charge of
13 be in control of

superintendence
06 charge
07 control, running
09 direction
10 management
11 supervision
12 surveillance

superintendent
07 curator
08 director, governor, overseer
09 conductor, inspector
10 controller, supervisor

superior
04 boss, fine
05 chief, lofty, prime, prize
06 better, choice, de luxe,
   higher, lordly, select,
   senior, snooty, uppish,
   uppity
07 foreman, greater, haughty,
   manager, quality, stuck-up
08 director, jumped up,
   snobbish, top-notch
09 admirable, excellent,
   exclusive, first-rate, high-
   class, preferred, principal,
   top-flight
10 disdainful, first-class,
   supervisor, unrivalled
11 exceptional, high-quality,
   patronizing, pretentious,
   toffee-nosed
12 higher in rank, supercilious
13 condescending

superiority
08 eminence
09 supremacy
10 ascendancy

11 pre-eminence
12 predominance

superlative
07 highest, supreme
08 greatest, peerless
09 excellent, first-rate, matchless
10 first-class, unrivalled
11 outstanding, unsurpassed
12 transcendent, unparalleled

supernatural
05 eerie, magic, weird
06 hidden, mystic, occult
07 ghostly, magical, phantom,
   psychic
08 mystical
09 spiritual, unnatural
10 paranormal
12 metaphysical, otherworldly
13 preternatural

supernumerary
05 extra, spare
06 excess
07 surplus
09 excessive, redundant
11 superfluous

supersede
05 usurp
07 replace, succeed
08 displace, supplant

superstition
04 myth
05 magic
12 old wives' tale

superstitious
08 mythical
10 groundless, irrational

supervise
05 watch
06 direct
07 conduct, control, inspect,
   oversee
09 look after, watch over
11 keep an eye on, preside over,
   superintend

supervision
06 charge
07 control
09 direction, oversight
10 inspection
12 surveillance
15 superintendence

supervisor
07 foreman, manager, steward
08 director, overseer
09 forewoman, inspector
14 superintendent

supervisory
10 overseeing

11 directorial
14 superintendent

supine
04 flat, idle
07 languid, passive
08 inactive
09 prostrate, recumbent
10 horizontal

supper
03 tea
05 snack
06 dinner
11 evening meal

supplant
04 oust
05 usurp
06 remove, topple, unseat
07 replace
08 displace
09 overthrow, supersede

supple
05 lithe
06 limber, pliant, supple
07 bending, elastic, plastic,
   pliable
08 flexible
11 loose-limbed
13 double-jointed

supplement
05 add to, add-on, boost, extra,
   rider, top up
06 eke out, extend, fill up,
   insert, sequel
07 augment, codicil, pull-out
08 addendum, addition,
   additive, appendix, increase
10 complement, postscript

supplementary
05 added, extra
09 auxiliary, secondary
10 additional
13 complementary

suppliant
07 begging, craving
09 imploring
10 beseeching, entreating
11 importunate
12 supplicating

supplicant
06 suitor
07 pleader
09 applicant, postulant,
   suppliant
10 petitioner

supplicate
04 pray
05 plead
06 appeal, invoke

07 beseech, entreat, request, solicit
08 petition

supplication
04 plea, suit
06 appeal, orison, prayer
07 request
08 entreaty, petition, pleading, rogation
10 invocation
11 imploration
12 solicitation

supplicatory
07 begging
09 imploring, precative
10 beseeching
11 imprecatory, petitioning
12 supplicating

supplier
06 dealer, seller, vendor
08 provider, retailer
10 wholesaler

supply
04 fill, food, fund, give, heap, mass, pile, sell
05 cache, endow, endue, equip, grant, hoard, stock, store, yield
06 amount, donate, fit out, outfit, source, stores
07 furnish, produce, proffer, provide, rations, reserve
08 quantity
09 equipment, materials, reservoir, stockpile
10 contribute, provisions

support
03 aid
04 back, base, bear, care, feed, food, fund, help, keep, post, prop, stay
05 brace, carry, grant
06 assist, back up, be with, crutch, defend, foster, hold up, pillar, prop up, ratify, relief, second, verify
07 backing, bear out, bolster, care for, comfort, confirm, endorse, finance, funding, loyalty, nourish, promote, run with, shore up, sponsor, subsidy, sustain, trestle
08 advocate, approval, be behind, buttress, champion, donation, maintain, skeleton, strength, sympathy, underpin, validate
09 bolster up, encourage, look after, patronage, provision, reinforce, subsidize

10 allegiance, foundation, protection, provide for, rally round, strengthen, sustenance, take care of, underwrite
11 corroborate, foundations, maintenance, sponsorship, subsistence
12 be in favour of, contribute to, contribution, substantiate, substructure, underpinning
15 take the weight of

supporter
03 fan
04 ally
05 donor, voter
06 friend, helper, patron
07 partner, sponsor
08 adherent, advocate, champion, co-worker, defender, follower, promoter, seconder
09 apologist

supportive
06 caring
07 helpful
10 comforting, reassuring
11 encouraging, sympathetic

suppose
05 fancy, guess, imply, infer, judge, posit, think
06 assume, expect, reckon
07 believe, imagine, presume, require, surmise
08 conclude, consider
09 postulate
10 conjecture, presuppose
11 hypothesize
14 take for granted

supposed
07 alleged, assumed, reputed
08 believed, imagined, presumed, putative, reported, rumoured, so-called
12 hypothetical

❏**supposed to**
07 meant to
09 obliged to
10 intended to, required to

supposition
04 idea
05 guess
06 notion, theory
07 surmise
10 assumption, conjecture, hypothesis
11 postulation, presumption, speculation
14 presupposition

suppress
05 check, crush, quash, quell
06 censor, squash, stifle, subdue
07 inhibit, repress, silence, smother
08 restrain, strangle, vanquish, withhold
10 put an end to
11 clamp down on, crack down on

suppression
07 cover-up
08 crushing, quashing, quelling
09 clampdown, crackdown
10 censorship, smothering

suppurate
04 ooze, weep
06 fester, gather
08 maturate
09 discharge

suppuration
03 pus
09 diapyesis, festering

supremacy
04 rule, sway
05 power
07 control, mastery, primacy
08 dominion, hegemony
10 ascendancy, domination
11 paramountcy, pre-eminence, sovereignty
12 predominance

supreme
03 top
04 best, head
05 chief, first, prime
06 utmost
07 extreme, highest, leading
08 crowning, foremost, greatest, peerless, ultimate
09 first-rate, matchless, principal, sovereign
10 first-class, pre-eminent
11 predominant, superlative
12 second-to-none, world-beating

sure
04 fast, firm, safe
05 bound, clear, loyal, solid
06 secure, stable, steady, tested
07 assured, certain, decided, precise
08 accurate, faithful, positive, reliable, sure-fire, unerring
09 confident, convinced, effective, foolproof, steadfast, undoubted, unfailing

10 dependable, guaranteed, home and dry, inevitable, infallible, sure-footed, undeniable, unwavering
11 trustworthy, unfaltering
12 indisputable, never-failing, safe as houses, unmistakable
14 unquestionable

surely
06 firmly
09 assuredly, certainly
10 definitely, inevitably
11 confidently, doubtlessly, indubitably, undoubtedly
12 without doubt
14 unquestionably

surety
04 bail, bond
06 pledge, safety
07 deposit, hostage, warrant
08 bondsman, security, warranty
09 certainty, guarantee, guarantor, indemnity, insurance, mortgagor

surface
03 top
04 face, rise, side, skin
05 arise, outer, plane
06 appear, come up, emerge, façade, veneer
07 outside, outward
08 covering, exterior, external
11 come to light, materialize, superficial

❏ **on the surface**
13 superficially

surfeit
04 cram, fill, glut
05 gorge, stuff
06 excess
07 satiate, satiety, surplus
08 bellyful, overfeed, overfill, plethora
14 superabundance

surge
04 eddy, flow, gush, pour, rise, roll, rush, wave
05 sweep, swell, swirl, waves
06 efflux, seethe, stream
07 pouring, upsurge, upswing

surgeon
➤ *Names of surgeons*:
04 **Bell** (Sir Charles), **Mayo** (Charles Horace), **Reed** (Walter)
05 **Broca** (Paul Pierre), **Paget** (Sir James)

06 **Carrel** (Alexis), **Cooper** (Sir Astley), **Hunter** (John), **Lister** (Joseph, Lord), **Treves** (Sir Frederick)
07 **Barnard** (Christian Neethling), **Burkitt** (Denis Parsons), **Cushing** (Harvey Williams)
08 **Beaumont** (William), **Billroth** (Theodor), **Charnley** (Sir John)
➤ See also **doctor**

surly
05 gruff
06 crusty, sullen
07 brusque, uncivil
08 churlish
10 ill-natured, ungracious

surmise
04 idea
05 fancy, guess, infer, opine
06 assume, deduce, notion
07 imagine, opinion, presume, suppose, suspect, thought
08 conclude, consider
09 deduction, inference, speculate, suspicion
10 assumption, conclusion, conjecture, hypothesis
11 possibility, presumption, speculation, supposition

surmount
06 exceed, master
07 conquer, get over, surpass
08 overcome, vanquish

surpass
04 beat
05 excel, outdo
06 better, exceed
07 eclipse
08 outclass, outshine, outstrip
09 transcend
10 overshadow, tower above

surpassing
09 matchless
10 inimitable, unrivalled
11 outstanding, unsurpassed
12 incomparable, transcendent

surplus
04 glut
05 extra, spare
06 excess, unused
07 balance, residue, surfeit
08 left over
09 leftovers, redundant, remainder, remaining

surprise
03 wow
04 stun

05 amaze
06 wonder
07 astound, startle
08 astonish, bewilder, bowl over
09 amazement, bombshell, burst in on, take aback
11 flabbergast, incredulity, knock for six
12 astonishment, bewilderment
13 catch in the act, catch unawares
14 catch red-handed
15 bolt from the blue

surprised
06 amazed
08 startled
10 astonished
11 open-mouthed

surprising
07 amazing
09 wonderful
10 astounding, incredible, remarkable, unexpected, unforeseen
11 astonishing, unlooked-for

surrender
04 cede
05 waive, yield
06 resign, submit
07 abandon, cession, concede, let go of, succumb, waiving
08 abdicate, renounce, yielding
10 abdication, relinquish
11 abandonment, leave behind, resignation
12 renunciation
14 relinquishment

surreptitious
03 sly
06 covert, sneaky
07 furtive
08 stealthy
09 underhand
11 clandestine

surrogate
05 proxy
07 stand-in
10 substitute
11 replacement

surround
04 gird, ring
05 beset, hem in
06 encase, girdle
07 confine, enclose, envelop, environ, fence in
08 encircle
09 encompass

surrounding
06 nearby
08 adjacent
09 adjoining, bordering
10 encircling
12 neighbouring

surroundings
05 scene
06 milieu
07 element, habitat, setting
08 ambience, environs, locality, vicinity
10 background
11 environment
13 neighbourhood

surveillance
05 watch
08 scrutiny
10 inspection, monitoring
11 observation, supervision
15 superintendence

survey
03 map
04 plan, plot, poll, scan, view
05 chart, probe, recce, study
06 assess, look at, review
07 examine, inspect, measure
08 appraise, consider, estimate, evaluate, look over, overview, research, scrutiny
09 appraisal, valuation
10 assessment, inspection
11 examination, opinion poll, reconnoitre
13 consideration, questionnaire
14 market research

surveyor
08 assessor, examiner
09 geodesist, inspector

survive
04 cope, last, live, stay
05 exist, rally
06 endure, live on, make it, manage, remain
07 hold out, outlast, outlive, persist, recover, weather
08 be extant, continue
09 withstand
11 pull through

susceptibility
08 tendency, weakness
09 liability, proneness
10 proclivity, propensity
11 gullibility, sensitivity
13 vulnerability
14 predisposition, suggestibility

susceptible
05 given, prone

06 liable, tender
07 subject
08 disposed, gullible, inclined
09 credulous, easily led, receptive, sensitive
10 responsive, vulnerable
11 defenceless, suggestible
14 impressionable

suspect
04 feel, iffy
05 dodgy, doubt, fancy, fishy, guess, infer
07 believe, dubious, suppose, surmise
08 be wary of, conclude, consider, distrust, doubtful, misdoubt, mistrust
09 debatable, smell a rat, speculate
10 conjecture, have a hunch, suspicious, unreliable
12 questionable
13 be uneasy about
15 have doubts about, have qualms about

suspend
04 hang
05 cease, defer, delay, swing
06 arrest, dangle, shelve
07 adjourn, exclude, keep out, shut out, unfrock
08 postpone, prorogue, put on ice
09 interrupt
11 discontinue
13 put in abeyance

suspended
07 hanging, pendent, pending
08 deferred, put on ice
09 postponed

suspense
07 anxiety, tension
10 expectancy
11 expectation, nervousness, uncertainty
12 anticipation, apprehension

suspension
04 stay
05 break, delay
07 respite
08 abeyance, deferral
09 cessation, deferment, exclusion, remission
10 moratorium, unfrocking
12 intermission, interruption, postponement

suspicion
04 hint, idea
05 hunch, shade, tinge, touch
06 notion, shadow

07 glimmer, soupçon
08 distrust, mistrust, wariness
09 chariness, misgiving, scintilla
10 scepticism, suggestion
12 apprehension, funny feeling

suspicious
03 odd
04 iffy, wary
05 chary, dodgy, fishy, shady
06 guilty, shifty, uneasy, unsure
07 dubious, strange, suspect
08 doubtful, peculiar
09 dishonest, sceptical
10 suspecting
11 distrustful, mistrustful
12 disbelieving, questionable

sustain
04 bear, feed, help, hold
06 assist, endure, foster, keep up, suffer, uphold
07 comfort, nourish, nurture, prolong, support, undergo
08 continue, happen to, maintain, protract
09 encourage, go through, keep going
10 experience, provide for
14 give strength to

sustained
06 steady
08 constant
09 perpetual, prolonged
10 continuous, protracted
11 unremitting
12 long-drawn-out

sustenance
04 fare, food, grub, nosh
06 viands
07 aliment, support
08 victuals
09 provender, refection
10 livelihood, provisions
11 comestibles, nourishment

svelte
04 slim
05 lithe
06 lissom, urbane
07 elegant, shapely, slender, willowy
08 graceful, polished
09 sylphlike
13 sophisticated

swagger
04 brag, crow, show
05 boast, strut, swank
06 parade, prance
07 bluster, show off
08 parading, prancing
09 arrogance
11 ostentation

swallow

03 buy, eat
04 bear, down, gulp, swig, take
05 abide, drink, quaff, scoff, stand, trust
06 accept, devour, endure, guzzle, ingest, stifle
07 believe, consume, contain, fall for, repress, smother, stomach
08 gobble up, hold back, suppress, tolerate
09 knock back, polish off, put up with

□ swallow up

06 absorb, enfold, engulf
07 envelop, overrun
09 overwhelm

swamp

03 bog, fen, mud
04 mire, quag, sink
05 beset, flood, marsh
06 deluge, drench, engulf, morass, slough
07 besiege, wash out
08 inundate, overload, quagmire, saturate, submerge, waterlog
09 overwhelm, weigh down

swampy

04 miry
05 boggy, fenny, soggy
06 marshy, quaggy
07 paludal
08 squelchy
11 waterlogged

swank

04 brag, show
05 boast, strut
07 conceit, show off, swagger
09 vainglory
10 showing-off
11 ostentation
15 pretentiousness

swanky

04 posh, rich
05 fancy, flash, grand, plush, ritzy, showy, smart, swish
06 de luxe, flashy, lavish, plushy
12 ostentatious

swap, swop

05 bandy, trade
06 barter, switch
08 exchange
09 transpose
10 substitute

swarm

03 mob
04 army, herd, host, mass, pack
05 crowd, drove, flock, flood, horde, shoal, surge
06 myriad, stream, throng
10 congregate

□ be swarming with

08 abound in
13 be crowded with, be overrun with, be teeming with
14 be crawling with

swarthy

05 black, brown, dusky
06 tanned
11 dark-skinned

swashbuckling

07 dashing, gallant
09 dare-devil
10 flamboyant

swathe

03 lap
04 bind, fold, furl, wind, wrap
05 cloak, drape
06 enwrap, shroud
07 bandage, envelop, sheathe, swaddle
08 enshroud

sway

04 bend, lean, reel, roll, rock, rule, veer, wave
05 clout, lurch, power, swing
06 affect, direct, divert, govern, induce, swerve, wobble
07 command, control, convert, incline, stagger, win over
08 convince, dominate, dominion, hegemony, overrule, persuade
09 authority, influence
10 ascendancy, bring round, government, leadership
11 prevail upon, sovereignty
12 jurisdiction, predominance

swear

03 eff, vow
04 aver, avow, cuss
05 blind, curse
06 abjure, affirm, assert, attest, insist, pledge
07 declare, promise, testify
08 maledict
09 blaspheme, imprecate
10 asseverate, take an oath
11 eff and blind, take the oath
14 pledge yourself, turn the air blue, use bad language

□ swear by

07 trust in
08 depend on
09 believe in
11 have faith in

swearing

07 cursing, cussing
09 blasphemy, profanity
10 coprolalia, expletives
12 imprecations, maledictions

swear-word

04 oath
05 curse
09 blasphemy, expletive, obscenity, profanity
11 bad language, imprecation
12 foul language
14 four-letter word

sweat

04 drip, flap, fuss, toil
05 chore, exude, panic, sudor, tizzy, worry
06 dither, effort, labour, sudate
07 anxiety, fluster, secrete, swelter
08 drudgery, hidrosis, moisture, perspire
09 agitation
10 stickiness
11 diaphoresis
12 perspiration

sweaty

04 damp
05 moist
06 clammy, sticky
10 perspiring

sweep

03 arc, fly
04 bend, drag, dust, move, pass, poke, push, race, sail, scud, skim, span, tear, whip
05 brush, clean, clear, curve, drive, elbow, force, glide, range, scope, shove, swing, vista, whisk
06 action, extent, remove, stroke, thrust
07 clean up, clear up, compass, expanse, gesture, stretch
08 movement, vastness
09 curvature, immensity

sweeping

04 wide
05 broad
06 global
07 blanket, general, radical
09 extensive, wholesale
11 far-reaching, wide-ranging
12 all-embracing, all-inclusive
13 comprehensive
14 across-the-board, indiscriminate

sweepstake

04 draw
05 sweep

07 lottery
08 gambling

sweet
04 cute, dear, kind, pure, ripe, soft
05 balmy, candy, clean, clear, fresh, glacé
06 afters, bonbon, dulcet, kindly, lovely, mellow, pretty, sickly, sugary, syrupy, tender
07 amiable, candied, darling, dessert, honeyed, lovable, musical, odorous, pudding, tuneful, winning, winsome
08 adorable, aromatic, charming, engaging, fragrant, likeable, luscious, perfumed, pleasant, pleasing, precious, redolent
09 agreeable, ambrosial, appealing, beautiful, cherished, delicious, melodious, treasured, wholesome
10 attractive, confection, delightful, euphonious, harmonious, saccharine
11 mellifluous, odoriferous
12 affectionate
13 confectionery

➤ *Sweets include*:
04 rock
05 fudge, halva
06 bonbon, confit, humbug, nougat, toffee
07 caramel, fondant, gumdrop, praline, truffle
08 acid drop, bull's eye, lollipop, marzipan, pear drop
09 chocolate, jelly baby, jelly bean, liquorice
10 gobstopper, peppermint
11 barley sugar, marshmallow, toffee apple
12 butterscotch, dolly mixture
13 fruit pastille
14 Turkish delight
➤ See also **food**

❑ **sweet on**
06 fond of, keen on
08 mad about
10 crazy about
14 infatuated with

sweeten
05 honey, sugar
06 mellow, soften, soothe, temper
07 appease, mollify, relieve
08 mitigate
09 alleviate

sweetheart
04 dear, love
05 flame, lover, Romeo, swain
06 steady, suitor
07 admirer, beloved, darling
09 betrothed, boyfriend, inamorata, inamorato, valentine
10 girlfriend

sweetness
07 euphony, harmony
09 dulcitude, fragrance
10 succulence, sugariness

sweet-smelling
07 odorous
08 aromatic, fragrant, perfumed, redolent
11 odoriferous

swell
04 beau, grow, posh, rise, wave
05 bloat, bulge, dandy, grand, great, mount, ritzy, smart, surge
06 bigwig, billow, blow up, de luxe, dilate, expand, extend, fatten, flashy, puff up, step up, swanky
07 augment, balloon, distend, enlarge, inflate, stylish
08 escalate, heighten, increase, mushroom, snowball
09 cockscomb, exclusive, intensify, skyrocket
10 accelerate, undulation

swelling
04 boil, bump, lump
05 bulge
07 blister
09 puffiness
10 distension, tumescence
12 protuberance

sweltering
03 hot
05 humid, muggy
06 baking, clammy, steamy, sticky, sultry, torrid
07 airless, boiling
08 roasting, sizzling, stifling
10 oppressive
11 suffocating

swerve
04 bend, skew, turn, veer
05 sheer, shift, swing, twist
07 deflect, deviate, diverge

swift
04 fast
05 agile, brief, brisk, fleet, hasty, nippy, quick, rapid

06 abrupt, flying, lively, nimble, prompt, speedy, sudden
07 express, hurried
11 expeditious

swiftly
07 express, hotfoot
09 instantly, posthaste
11 double-quick

swiftness
05 speed
08 alacrity, celerity, dispatch, velocity

swill
04 gulp, swig
05 drain, drink, quaff, slops, waste
06 guzzle, imbibe, refuse
07 consume, hogwash, swallow, toss off
08 pigswill
09 knock back, scourings

❑ **swill out**
05 clean, flush, rinse
06 drench, sluice
07 cleanse, wash out

swim
03 bob
05 bathe, float
07 snorkel
08 take a dip

➤ *Swimming strokes*:
05 crawl
09 butterfly, freestyle
10 backstroke, sidestroke
11 doggy-paddle
12 breaststroke

swimming-pool
04 lido, pond
11 leisure pool

swimsuit
06 bikini, trunks
11 bathing suit
14 bathing costume
15 swimming costume

swindle
03 con
04 dupe, rook, scam
05 cheat, fraud, sting, trick
06 diddle, fiddle, fleece, racket, rip off, rip-off
07 deceive, defraud, exploit
10 overcharge
12 put one over on
13 double-dealing, sharp practice

swindler
04 hood, rook
05 cheat, fraud, rogue, shark

06 con man
07 fiddler, hoodlum, hustler

swine
03 hog, pig
04 boar, boor
05 beast, brute, rogue

swing
04 bend, hang, lean, make,
   move, rock, spin, sway, turn,
   vary, veer, wave, wind
05 curve, fix up, pivot, set up,
   shift, twist
06 change, dangle, rhythm,
   rotate, stroke, swerve
07 achieve, arrange, incline
08 movement, organize
09 fluctuate, oscillate,
   pendulate
11 fluctuation, oscillation

swingeing
05 harsh, heavy
06 severe
07 drastic, serious
09 draconian, excessive,
   punishing, stringent
10 exorbitant, oppressive
12 extortionate

swinging
03 hip
06 lively, modern, trendy, with it
07 dynamic, stylish
10 jet-setting
11 fashionable

swipe
03 hit
04 biff, blow, lift, nick, slap,
   sock, whip
05 clout, filch, lunge, pinch,
   smack, steal, whack
06 pilfer, strike, stroke, wallop

swirl
04 curl, eddy, spin
05 twirl, twist, wheel, whirl
07 agitate, revolve
09 circulate

swish
04 flog, lash, posh, wave, whip
05 flash, grand, plush, ritzy,
   smart, swell, swing, swirl,
   twirl, whirl, whisk
06 de luxe, rustle, swanky,
   swoosh, thrash, whoosh
07 elegant, stylish, whistle
08 brandish, flourish
09 exclusive, sumptuous
11 fashionable

switch
03 rod
04 cane, swap, twig, veer, whip

05 birch, shift, trade, whisk
06 branch, divert, twitch
07 deflect, deviate, replace
08 exchange, reversal
09 about-turn, transpose
10 substitute
12 substitution
13 chop and change

swivel
04 spin, turn
05 pivot, twirl, wheel
06 gyrate, rotate
07 revolve

swollen
05 puffy, tumid
07 bloated, bulbous, bulging
08 inflated, puffed up
09 distended, tumescent

swoop
04 dive, drop, fall, rush
05 lunge, stoop
06 attack, plunge, pounce

swop see swap

sword
04 foil, épée
05 blade, sabre, steel
06 katana, rapier
08 scimitar

◻ cross swords
05 argue, fight
07 contend, contest, dispute,
   quarrel, wrangle

sworn
07 devoted, eternal
08 attested
09 confirmed
10 implacable

swot
04 cram, work
05 learn, mug up, study
06 bone up, revise
08 memorize

sybarite
07 epicure, playboy
08 hedonist, parasite
09 bon vivant, epicurean
10 sensualist, voluptuary
14 pleasure-seeker

sybaritic
07 sensual
09 epicurean, luxurious
10 hedonistic, voluptuous
14 pleasure-loving
15 pleasure-seeking

sycophancy
07 fawning
08 cringing, flattery, toadyism

09 adulation, kowtowing,
   servility, truckling
10 grovelling
11 bootlicking, slavishness
14 obsequiousness

sycophant
05 slave, toady
06 fawner, yes-man
07 cringer, sponger
08 hanger-on, parasite, truckler
09 flatterer, groveller,
   toad-eater
10 bootlicker

sycophantic
05 slimy
06 smarmy
07 fawning, servile, slavish
08 cringing, toadying, unctuous
09 truckling
10 flattering, grovelling,
   obsequious, toad-eating
11 bootlicking, time-serving
12 ingratiating

syllabus
04 plan
06 course
07 outline
08 schedule
09 programme
10 curriculum

syllogism
08 argument
09 deduction
11 epicheirema, proposition

sylph-like
04 slim
05 lithe
06 slight, svelte
07 elegant, slender, willowy

symbiotic
07 epizoan, epizoic
09 commensal, epizootic
10 endophytic, synergetic
11 co-operative, interactive
14 interdependent

symbol
04 logo, mark, sign, type
05 badge, image, token
06 emblem, figure
09 character, ideograph
14 representation

symbolic
05 token
07 typical
10 emblematic, figurative,
   meaningful, symbolical
11 allegorical, significant
12 illustrative, metaphorical
14 representative

symbolize

06 denote, typify
07 betoken, signify
08 stand for
09 epitomize, exemplify, personify, represent

symmetrical

04 even
07 regular, uniform
08 balanced, parallel
10 consistent, harmonious
12 proportional
13 corresponding

symmetry

07 balance, harmony
08 evenness
09 agreement, congruity
10 regularity, uniformity
11 consistency, parallelism, proportions
14 correspondence

sympathetic

04 kind, warm
06 caring, kindly, tender
07 pitying
08 likeable, pleasant, sociable
09 agreeable, concerned, congenial, consoling
10 comforting, compatible, interested, like-minded, solicitous, supportive
11 considerate, kind-hearted
12 appreciative, well-disposed
13 compassionate, understanding

sympathetically

09 feelingly
11 sensitively
12 responsively
14 appreciatively
15 understandingly

sympathize

04 pity
07 care for, console, feel for
09 empathize, respond to
10 appreciate, understand
11 commiserate
12 feel sorry for, identify with

sympathizer

03 fan
06 backer
08 adherent, condoler, partisan
09 supporter

sympathy

04 pity
06 accord, solace, warmth
07 comfort, empathy, harmony, rapport, support
08 affinity, approval, kindness
10 compassion, tenderness
11 condolences, consolation
13 commiseration, consideration, fellow-feeling, understanding
14 correspondence, thoughtfulness
15 warm-heartedness

symptom

04 mark, note, sign
05 token
06 signal
07 feature
08 evidence, prodrome
10 expression, indication
13 demonstration, manifestation
14 characteristic

symptomatic

07 typical
10 indicative, suggestive
14 characteristic

syndicate

04 bloc, ring
05 group
06 cartel
08 alliance
11 association

synonymous

07 similar, the same
09 identical
10 comparable, equivalent, tantamount
13 substitutable
15 interchangeable

synopsis

06 digest, précis, review, résumé
07 outline, summary
08 abstract
11 abridgement

synthesis

05 alloy, blend
07 amalgam
08 compound
09 composite

11 coalescence, combination, integration
12 amalgamation

synthesize

05 alloy, blend, merge
07 combine
08 coalesce, compound
09 integrate
10 amalgamate

synthetic

04 fake, mock, sham
06 ersatz, pseudo
07 man-made
09 imitation, simulated
10 artificial
12 manufactured

syrupy

05 mushy, soppy, sweet
06 sickly, slushy, sugary
07 honeyed, maudlin, mawkish
09 schmaltzy
10 lovey-dovey, saccharine
11 sentimental, sickly sweet

system

03 way
04 mode, plan, rule
05 logic, means, set-up
06 method, scheme
07 network, process, routine
08 approach, practice
09 mechanism, procedure, structure, technique
11 arrangement, methodology
12 co-ordination, organization
13 modus operandi
14 classification

systematic

07 logical, orderly, planned
09 efficient, organized
10 methodical, scientific, structured
11 well-ordered, well-planned
12 standardized
13 well-organized

systematize

04 plan
05 order
08 classify, organize, regiment, regulate, tabulate
09 structure
10 schematize
11 rationalize, standardize

tab
03 tag
04 flap
05 label
06 marker, ticket
07 sticker

□keep tabs on
07 observe
11 keep an eye on
12 watch closely

tabby
04 wavy
06 banded, stripy
07 mottled, striped
08 brindled, streaked

table
03 bar
04 desk, fare, food, grub, list, menu, move, plan, slab, tuck
05 board, chart, graph, index
06 figure, record, submit
07 propose, suggest, worktop
08 register, schedule
09 programme, timetable
10 put forward, tabulation

tableau
05 scene
08 vignette
09 portrayal, spectacle
13 tableau vivant

tablet
04 ball, pill
05 bolus
06 pellet
07 capsule, lozenge

taboo
05 curse
06 banned, vetoed
08 anathema, ruled out
09 forbidden
10 prohibited, proscribed
11 prohibition, restriction
12 interdiction, proscription
13 unmentionable

tabulate
04 list, sort
05 chart, index, order, range
06 codify
08 classify

09 catalogue
10 categorize, tabularize

tacit
06 silent
07 implied
08 implicit, inferred, unspoken, unvoiced, wordless
10 understood

taciturn
05 aloof, quiet
06 silent
08 detached, reserved, reticent
09 withdrawn
11 tight-lipped
12 close-mouthed
13 unforthcoming
15 uncommunicative

tack
03 add, fix, pin, sew, way
04 line, nail, path, plan
05 affix, annex, baste
06 append, attach, course, policy, staple, stitch
07 bearing, heading, process
08 approach, strategy
09 direction, thumbtack
10 drawing-pin
12 line of action

tackle
03 rig, try
04 gear, grab, halt, stop, take
05 begin, block, catch, grasp, seize, stuff, tools
06 attack, handle, things
07 attempt, go about, harness
08 confront, deal with, face up to, obstruct, set about
09 apparatus, equipment, intercept, trappings
12 interception, intervention
13 accoutrements, paraphernalia
15 apply yourself to

tacky
04 naff
05 gaudy, gluey, gooey, messy
06 flashy, shoddy, sticky, tawdry
07 kitschy, scruffy
09 tasteless

tact
08 delicacy, prudence, subtlety
09 diplomacy, judgement
10 adroitness, discretion
11 discernment, savoir-faire, sensitivity, tactfulness
13 consideration, understanding
14 thoughtfulness

tactful
06 adroit, polite, subtle
07 careful, politic, prudent
08 delicate, discreet
09 judicious, sensitive
10 diplomatic, thoughtful
11 considerate

tactic
04 move, plan, ploy, ruse
05 means, moves, shift, trick
06 device, method, scheme
08 approach, strategy
09 expedient, manoeuvre, procedure, stratagem
12 line of attack
14 course of action

tactical
05 smart
06 adroit, artful, clever, shrewd
07 planned, politic, prudent
09 judicious, strategic
10 calculated

tactician
05 brain
07 planner
10 mastermind, strategist

tactless
04 rude
05 rough
06 clumsy, gauche, unkind
07 awkward, hurtful
08 careless, impolite, unsubtle
09 impolitic, maladroit
10 blundering, indiscreet
11 insensitive, thoughtless
12 discourteous, undiplomatic

tactlessness
08 rudeness
09 bad timing, gaucherie
10 clumsiness, indelicacy
11 boorishness, discourtesy

12 impoliteness, indiscretion
13 insensitivity, maladroitness
15 thoughtlessness

tag
03 add, dub, tab
04 call, mark, name, tack, term
05 affix, annex, badge, label, motto, quote, style, title
06 append, attach, fasten, phrase, saying, ticket
07 epithet, proverb, sticker
08 allusion, christen, identify
11 description, stock phrase
14 identification

◻tag along
05 trail
06 follow, shadow
09 accompany

tail
03 dog, end
04 back, rear, rump
05 stalk, track, trail
06 behind, bottom, caudal, cercal, follow, pursue, shadow, shamus, sleuth
08 backside
09 appendage, posterior
10 conclusion, private eye
12 investigator

◻tail off
03 die
04 drop, fade, wane
07 decline, drop off, dwindle
08 decrease, peter out

◻ turn tail
04 bolt, flee
06 beat it, decamp, escape
07 abscond, run away, scarper
09 skedaddle

tailor
03 cut, fit
04 suit, trim
05 adapt, alter, shape, style
06 adjust, modify
07 convert, fashion, modiste
08 clothier, costumer, seamster
09 costumier, couturier, outfitter
10 dressmaker, seamstress
11 accommodate

tailor-made
05 ideal, right
06 fitted, suited
07 bespoke, perfect
11 custom-built
13 made-to-measure

taint
04 blot, flaw, harm, ruin, soil

05 dirty, fault, muddy, shame, smear, spoil, stain, sully
06 befoul, blight, damage, defile, infect, injure, stigma
07 blacken, blemish, corrupt, deprave, pollute, tarnish
09 contagion, dishonour, infection, pollution
10 adulterate, corruption
11 contaminate
13 contamination

take
03 bag, buy, eat, get, use, win
04 bear, deem, draw, gain, grab, haul, hire, hold, last, lead, lift, nick, rent, view
05 adopt, bring, carry, catch, drink, drive, ferry, fetch, filch, grasp, guide, learn, lease, pinch, seize, steal, study, think, use up, usher
06 abduct, accept, assume, choose, clutch, convey, deduct, demand, derive, devour, endure, escort, fathom, follow, gather, guzzle, imbibe, income, kidnap, obtain, occupy, pay for, profit, pursue, reckon, remove, return, select, snatch, suffer
07 achieve, acquire, believe, call for, capture, conduct, conquer, consume, contain, deliver, examine, major in, measure, presume, procure, profits, purloin, receive, require, returns, revenue, stomach, suppose, swallow
08 carry off, consider, cotton on, deal with, proceeds, purchase, receipts, settle on, shepherd, subtract, tolerate, vanquish
09 accompany, apprehend, eliminate, fathom out, gate-money, get hold of, put up with, respond to, transport, undertake, withstand
10 comprehend, confiscate, experience, understand
11 accommodate, appropriate, have room for, necessitate
12 have space for
15 have a capacity of

◻take aback
04 stun
05 shock, upset
06 dismay
07 astound, stagger, startle

08 astonish, bewilder, surprise
10 disconcert

◻take after
04 echo
06 be like, favour, mirror
08 look like

◻take against
07 despise, dislike
08 object to
12 disapprove of

◻take apart
07 analyse
08 separate
09 dismantle
11 disassemble

◻take back
04 deny
06 recant, regain, return
07 reclaim, restore, retract
08 disclaim, renounce, withdraw
09 repossess, repudiate
12 eat one's words

◻take down
04 note, raze
05 level, lower
06 record
08 demolish
10 put on paper, transcribe
11 disassemble, make a note of

◻take in
03 con
04 dupe, fool
05 cheat, cover, grasp, trick
06 absorb, digest
07 deceive, embrace, include, mislead, realize, receive, shelter, swindle, welcome
08 comprise, hoodwink
09 bamboozle, encompass
10 appreciate, assimilate, comprehend, understand
11 accommodate, incorporate

◻take off
04 doff, drop, flee, mock, rise
05 climb, leave, mimic, strip
06 decamp, deduct, depart, detach, divest, do well, parody, remove, send up
07 abscond, bunk off, catch on, discard, imitate, lift off, prosper, pull off, run away, scarper, succeed, tear off
08 discount, flourish, go places, satirize, subtract, throw off
09 do a runner, skedaddle
13 become popular
14 become airborne

◻take on
04 face, hire

05 enrol, fight
06 accept, assume, employ, engage, enlist, oppose, retain, tackle
07 acquire, recruit, vie with
09 undertake
11 compete with, contend with

❑**take out**
05 set up
06 borrow, cut out, detach, escort, excise, remove
07 arrange, extract, pull out
08 organize, settle on
09 accompany, go out with

❑**take over**
06 buy out
12 take charge of
13 gain control of

❑**take to**
04 like
05 begin, start
08 commence, set about
12 become keen on

❑**take up**
04 fill, lift
05 adopt, begin, raise, start
06 absorb, accept, assume, engage, occupy, pick up, pursue, resume
07 agree to, carry on, engross
08 commence, continue, embark on

take-off
05 spoof
06 ascent, flight, parody, send-up
07 lift-off, mimicry
08 climbing, travesty
09 departure, imitation
10 caricature
13 impersonation

takeover
04 coup
06 buyout, merger
09 coalition
12 amalgamation
13 incorporation

taking
04 gain, gate
05 yield
06 income
07 profits, returns, revenue
08 charming, earnings, engaging, fetching, pickings, proceeds, receipts
09 appealing, beguiling
10 attractive, compelling, delightful, enchanting
11 captivating, fascinating
13 prepossessing

tale
03 fib, lie
04 epic, myth, saga, yarn
05 fable, porky, spiel, story
06 legend, report, rumour
07 account, parable, untruth
08 allegory, anecdote
09 narrative, tall story
11 fabrication

talent
04 bent, feel, gift
05 flair, forte, knack, skill
06 genius
07 ability, aptness, faculty
08 aptitude, capacity, facility, strength

talented
04 able, deft
05 adept
06 adroit, clever, gifted
07 capable, skilful
09 brilliant, versatile
11 well-endowed
12 accomplished

talisman
04 idol, ju-ju
05 charm, totem
06 amulet, fetish, mascot
07 abraxas, periapt
10 phylactery

talk
03 jaw, say
04 blab, cant, chat, tell
05 grass, lingo, orate, slang, speak, spiel, voice, words
06 babble, confab, confer, debate, gossip, jargon, natter, rabbit, rumour, sermon, speech, squeal
07 address, chatter, chinwag, confess, dialect, discuss, express, lecture, meeting, oration, prattle, seminar
08 converse, dialogue, idiolect, inform on, language
09 discourse, interview, negotiate, symposium, tell tales, tête-à-tête, utterance
10 articulate, bargaining, conference, discussion
11 communicate, negotiation
12 consultation, conversation, disquisition, tittle-tattle
13 rabbit and pork, spill the beans, spread rumours
15 give the game away

❑**talk back**
06 retort
07 riposte

09 retaliate
10 answer back, be cheeky to

❑**talk big**
04 brag, crow
05 boast, swank, vaunt
07 bluster, show off
10 exaggerate

❑**talk down to**
09 patronize
10 look down on

❑**talk into**
04 coax, sway
07 win over
08 convince, persuade
10 bring round

❑**talk out of**
04 stop
05 deter
06 put off
07 prevent
08 dissuade
10 discourage

talkative
05 gabby, gassy, vocal, wordy
06 chatty, mouthy
07 gossipy, verbose, voluble
09 expansive, garrulous
10 longwinded, loquacious
11 forthcoming
13 communicative

talker
07 speaker
08 lecturer
10 chatterbox
11 speech-maker

talking-to
06 rebuke
07 lecture, reproof
08 reproach, scolding
09 carpeting, reprimand
10 telling-off, ticking-off
12 dressing-down

tall
03 big
04 hard, high
05 giant, great, lanky, lofty
07 dubious, sky-high, soaring
08 elevated, exacting, gigantic, towering, unlikely
09 demanding, difficult
10 far-fetched, improbable
11 challenging, implausible
12 preposterous, unbelievable

tallness
06 height
07 stature
08 altitude
09 loftiness

tally
03 add, fit, sum, tab, tag
05 add up, agree, count, match, score, tie in, total
06 accord, concur, reckon, record, square, ticket
09 duplicate, harmonize, reckoning
10 correspond
11 enumeration

tame
04 calm, curb, dull, flat, meek
05 bland, quell, train, vapid
06 boring, bridle, docile, feeble, gentle, master, pacify, soften, subdue
07 break in, insipid, subdued, tedious, trained
08 broken in, lifeless
09 subjugate, tractable
10 discipline, house-train, spiritless, unexciting
11 bring to heel, disciplined, domesticate
12 domesticated
13 unadventurous, uninteresting
14 unenterprising

tamper
03 fix, rig
06 meddle, monkey, tinker
09 interfere, mess about
10 manipulate
12 put your oar in
14 poke your nose in
15 stick your nose in

tan
04 beat, belt, cane, flog, lash
05 brown, clout, spank, strap
06 bronze, thrash, wallop
07 go brown, sunburn

tang
03 pep
04 bite, edge, hint, kick
05 punch, smack, smell, spice, taste, tinge, touch, trace
06 savour
07 flavour
08 piquancy, pungency
09 sharpness

tangible
04 hard, real
05 solid
06 actual
07 evident, tactile, visible
08 concrete, definite, material, palpable, physical, positive
09 touchable

11 discernible, perceptible, substantial, well-defined
12 unmistakable

tangle
03 mat, web
04 coil, knot, maze, mesh, mess
05 catch, mix-up, snarl, twist
06 enmesh, entrap, muddle
07 embroil, ensnare, involve
08 convolve, entangle
09 confusion, imbroglio, implicate, interlace
10 intertwine, intertwist
11 convolution, embroilment
12 complication, entanglement

tangled
05 messy
06 knotty, matted
07 complex, knotted, mixed up, muddled, snarled, twisted
08 confused, involved, tortuous
10 convoluted
11 complicated, dishevelled

tangy
04 acid, tart
05 fresh, sharp, spicy
06 biting, strong
07 piquant, pungent

tank
03 vat
05 basin
06 panzer
07 cistern
08 aquarium
09 container, reservoir
15 armoured vehicle

tantalize
04 bait, balk
05 taunt, tease, tempt
06 allure, entice, lead on, thwart
07 provoke, torment, torture
09 frustrate, titillate

tantamount
05 equal
08 as good as
09 the same as
10 equivalent, synonymous
12 commensurate

tantrum
03 fit, pet
04 fury, rage
05 paddy, scene, storm
07 flare-up
08 outburst, paroxysm
11 fit of temper

tap
03 bug, hit, pat, rap, use
04 beat, drum, milk, mine

05 bleed, drain, knock, spout, touch, valve
06 faucet, quarry, siphon, spigot, strike
07 exploit, stopper, utilize
08 receiver, stopcock
15 listening device

❏**on tap**
05 handy, ready
06 at hand, on hand
09 available
10 accessible

tape
03 tie
04 band, bind, seal
05 stick, strip, video
06 fasten, record, ribbon
07 binding
08 cassette
09 audiotape, recording, Sellotape®, videotape
10 sticky tape, tape-record
11 masking tape, video-record
12 adhesive tape, magnetic tape
13 tape-recording, videocassette
14 video recording

taper
04 fade, slim, thin, wane, wick
05 spill
06 candle, die off, narrow
07 die away, dwindle, tail off
08 decrease, diminish
09 attenuate

tardily
04 late
06 slowly
09 belatedly
10 sluggishly
12 late in the day, unpunctually
15 at the last minute

tardiness
08 dawdling, lateness, slowness
11 belatedness
12 dilatoriness, sluggishness
13 unpunctuality

tardy
04 late, slow
05 slack
07 belated, delayed, overdue
08 dawdling, dilatory, sluggish
10 last-minute, unpunctual

target
03 aim, end
04 butt, game, goal, mark, prey
06 object, quarry, victim
07 purpose
08 ambition, bull's eye
09 intention, objective

tariff
03 tax
04 duty, levy, menu, rate, toll
06 excise
07 charges, customs
09 price list
10 bill of fare

tarnish
03 dim, mar
04 blot, dull, film, rust, spot
05 spoil, stain, sully, taint
07 blacken, blemish, corrode
08 besmirch
09 discolour
13 discoloration

tarry
03 lag
04 bide, rest, stay, stop, wait
05 abide, dally, delay, pause
06 dawdle, linger, loiter, remain

tart
03 pie
04 acid, drab, flan, slut, sour
05 sharp, tangy, tramp, whore
06 biting, bitter, hooker, pastry
07 acerbic, caustic, cutting, piquant, pungent, trollop
08 call girl, incisive, sardonic, scathing, scrubber
09 sarcastic, trenchant
10 astringent, prostitute
11 fallen woman, fille de joie
12 street-walker

❑**tart up**
06 doll up
07 smarten
08 decorate, renovate
09 embellish, smarten up

task
03 job
04 duty, toil, work
05 chore
06 burden, charge, errand
07 mission
08 activity, business, exercise
10 assignment, commission, employment, engagement, enterprise, occupation
11 piece of work, undertaking

❑**take to task**
05 blame, scold
06 rebuke
07 censure, lecture, reprove, tell off, tick off, upbraid
08 reproach
09 criticize, reprimand

taste
03 bit, sip, try
04 dash, drop, feel, tang, test
05 grace, piece, smack, style

06 liking, morsel, nibble, relish, sample, savour, titbit
07 culture, finesse, flavour, leaning, soupçon, undergo
08 appetite, breeding, elegance, fondness, mouthful, penchant
09 encounter, etiquette, gustative, gustatory, judgement, propriety
10 preference, refinement
11 cultivation, discernment, inclination, stylishness
12 predilection, tastefulness
14 discrimination

tasteful
05 smart
07 elegant, refined, stylish
08 artistic, charming, cultured, delicate, graceful, pleasing
09 aesthetic, judicious
10 cultivated, harmonious, restrained, well-judged
14 discriminating

tasteless
04 dull, flat, loud, mild, naff, rude, thin, weak
05 bland, cheap, crass, crude, gaudy, showy, stale, tacky
06 flashy, kitsch, tawdry, vulgar
07 insipid, uncouth
08 improper, tactless, unseemly
09 inelegant, unfitting
11 flavourless, watered-down
13 uninteresting

tasting
05 assay, trial
07 testing
08 sampling
09 gustation

tasty
05 spicy, sweet, tangy, yummy
07 piquant, savoury
08 luscious
09 delicious, palatable
10 appetizing, delectable
11 flavoursome, scrumptious
13 mouth-watering

tatter

❑**in tatters**
06 broken, in rags, ruined
07 wrecked
08 in pieces, in shreds
09 destroyed, in ribbons

tattered
04 torn
05 tatty
06 frayed, ragged, ripped
07 scruffy

tattler
06 gossip
08 busybody, tell-tale
10 newsmonger, tale-teller
13 scandalmonger

taunt
03 dig, rib
04 bait, barb, gibe, jeer, mock
05 sneer, tease
06 deride, insult, revile
07 catcall, mockery, provoke, sarcasm, teasing, torment
08 derision, ridicule, taunting
09 make fun of, poke fun at

taut
05 rigid, stiff, tense, tight
06 tensed
08 strained
09 stretched, tightened
10 contracted

tautological
07 verbose
09 redundant
10 pleonastic, repetitive
11 superfluous

tautology
08 pleonasm
10 redundancy, repetition
11 duplication, perissology, superfluity
14 repetitiveness

tavern
03 bar, inn, pub
05 joint, local
06 boozer
08 alehouse, hostelry, tap-house
09 roadhouse
11 public house

tawdry
05 fancy, gaudy, showy, tacky
06 flashy, garish, vulgar
09 tasteless

tawny
03 tan
05 khaki, sandy
06 fulvid, golden, yellow
07 fulvous
08 xanthous

tax
03 sap, try
04 duty, levy, load, rate, test, tire
05 drain, exact, weary, weigh
06 charge, fiscal, strain, stress, tariff, weaken
07 exhaust, imposte, stretch
08 encumber, enervate, overload, pressure

09 weigh down
13 make demands on

taxi
03 cab
06 fiacre
07 minicab, taxicab
09 hansom-cab
12 hackney coach

taxing
04 hard
05 heavy, tough
06 tiring, trying
07 onerous, wearing
08 draining, exacting, wearying
09 demanding, punishing, stressful, wearisome
10 enervating, exhausting

teach
04 show
05 coach, drill, train, tutor
06 advise, direct, ground, impart, inform, school
07 counsel, educate, lecture
08 instruct
09 brainwash, condition, enlighten, inculcate
10 discipline
11 demonstrate, give lessons
12 indoctrinate

teacher
03 don
04 dean, guru
05 coach, guide, tutor
06 doctor, duenna, fellow, master, mentor, pundit
07 adviser, crammer, trainer
08 educator, lecturer, mistress
09 governess, maharishi, pedagogue, preceptor, principal, professor
10 head of year, headmaster, instructor, school-ma'am
11 form teacher, headteacher, housemaster, preceptress
12 demonstrator, headmistress, private tutor, schoolmaster
13 housemistress, supply teacher
14 schoolmistress

teaching
05 dogma, tenet
07 precept, tuition
08 doctrine, pedagogy
09 doctrinal, education
11 instruction

team
03 set
04 band, crew, gang, side
05 bunch, group, shift, squad

06 line-up, stable, troupe
07 company

☐ team up
04 join, yoke
05 match, unite
07 combine
09 co-operate
11 collaborate
12 work together

teamwork
10 fellowship, team spirit
11 co-operation, joint effort
12 co-ordination
13 collaboration, esprit de corps

tear
03 fly, nip, rip, run, zap, zip
04 belt, bolt, claw, dart, dash, gash, grab, hole, pull, race, rend, rent, rush, zoom
05 hurry, pluck, seize, sever, shoot, shred, slash, speed, split, whizz, wound, wrest
06 career, charge, divide, gallop, ladder, mangle, snatch, sprint, sunder
07 rupture, scratch
09 pull apart
10 break apart, laceration

☐ in tears
05 upset, weepy
06 crying
07 sobbing, wailing, weeping
09 emotional, sorrowful
10 blubbering

tearaway
05 rough, rowdy, tough
06 madcap, rascal
07 hoodlum, hothead, ruffian
09 daredevil, roughneck
10 delinquent
14 good-for-nothing

tearful
03 sad
05 upset, weepy
06 crying
07 doleful, sobbing, weeping
08 mournful
09 emotional, sorrowful
10 blubbering, distressed, lachrymose, whimpering

tease
03 kid, rag, rib, vex
04 bait, gibe, goad, mock
05 annoy, taunt, worry
06 badger, banter, needle
07 provoke, torment
08 irritate, ridicule
09 aggravate, tantalize

technical
06 expert
07 applied
09 practical
10 electronic, mechanical, scientific, specialist
11 specialized
13 technological

technique
03 art, way
05 craft, knack, means, style
06 manner, method, system
07 ability, fashion, know-how
08 approach, artistry, facility
09 dexterity, execution, expertise, procedure
11 proficiency, skilfulness
13 craftsmanship, modus operandi

tedious
04 drab, dull, flat
05 banal, samey
06 boring, dreary, tiring
07 humdrum, prosaic, routine
08 lifeless, tiresome, unvaried
09 laborious, wearisome
10 long-winded, monotonous,

tedium
05 ennui
07 boredom, routine
08 banality, drabness, dullness, monotony, sameness
10 dreariness

teem
04 bear, brim
05 burst, crawl, swarm
06 abound
07 bristle, produce
08 increase, multiply, overflow
09 pullulate
11 proliferate

teeming
04 full
05 alive, thick
06 packed
08 abundant, brimming, bursting, crawling, fruitful, numerous, swarming
09 bristling, chock-full
11 chock-a-block, overflowing, pullulating

teenage
08 immature, juvenile, teenaged, youthful
10 adolescent

teenager
03 boy
04 girl
05 minor, youth

08 juvenile
10 adolescent, young adult
11 young person

teeny
03 wee
04 tiny
06 minute, titchy
09 miniature, minuscule
10 diminutive, teeny-weeny
11 microscopic
12 teensy-weensy

teeter
04 reel, rock, roll, sway
05 pitch, pivot, shake, waver
06 seesaw, totter, wobble
07 balance, stagger, tremble

teetotal
09 abstinent, temperate
10 abstemious, on the
   wagon

teetotaller
09 abstainer, nephalist,
   Rechabite
10 non-drinker

telegram
04 wire
05 cable, telex
09 telegraph
11 Telemessage®

telegraph
04 send, wire
05 cable, telex
08 telegram, transmit
11 teleprinter
14 radiotelegraph

telepathy
03 ESP
10 sixth sense
11 mind-reading
12 clairvoyance

telephone
04 buzz, call, dial, ring
06 blower, call up, ring up
08 receiver
09 give a bell, give a buzz
11 give a tinkle

telescope
06 reduce, shrink, squash
07 abridge, compact, curtail,
   shorten, squeeze
08 compress, condense,
   contract, truncate
10 abbreviate, concertina

televise
03 air
04 beam, show
05 cable, put on, relay
06 screen

08 transmit
09 broadcast

television
02 TV
03 set
05 telly
06 the box
07 the tube
08 boob tube, idiot box
09 goggle-box
11 small screen

tell
03 bid, rat, say, see
04 blab, shop, show, talk
05 alter, brief, drain, grass,
   order, speak, state, utter
06 advise, betray, charge,
   decree, direct, impart,
   inform, notify, recite, relate,
   report, reveal, sketch, squeal
07 apprise, command, confess,
   declare, dictate, discern,
   divulge, exhaust, let know,
   make out, mention, narrate,
   portray, recount, require
08 acquaint, announce,
   denounce, disclose, identify,
   inform on, instruct
09 broadcast, delineate, make
   known, recognize
10 comprehend, understand
11 communicate, distinguish
12 discriminate
13 differentiate, spill the beans,
   take its toll of
14 give the low-down, have an
   effect on
15 give the game away

◻**tell off**
05 chide, scold
06 berate, rebuke
07 censure, lecture, reprove,
   tick off, upbraid
08 reproach
09 dress down, reprimand
14 give a talking-to

teller
05 clerk
06 banker
07 cashier
09 bank clerk, treasurer

telling
06 cogent, marked
09 effective, revealing
10 impressive, persuasive
11 significant

telling-off
06 rebuke
07 chiding, lecture, reproof
08 reproach, scolding

09 reprimand
10 ticking-off, upbraiding
12 dressing-down

tell-tale
03 spy
05 clype, grass, sneak
06 snitch
08 give-away, informer,
   snitcher, squealer
09 revealing
10 meaningful, noticeable
11 perceptible, secret agent
15 snake in the grass

temerity
04 gall
05 cheek, nerve
06 daring
08 audacity, boldness, rashness
09 impudence
12 impertinence, recklessness

temper
04 calm, cool, fury, mood, rage
05 allay, anger, paddy, storm
06 anneal, harden, humour,
   lessen, modify, nature,
   reduce, soften, weaken
07 assuage, flare-up, fortify,
   passion, tantrum, toughen
08 calmness, mitigate,
   moderate, palliate, tone
   down
09 alleviate, character,
   composure, ill-humour
10 resentment, strengthen
11 disposition, fit of temper,
   frame of mind,
   temperament
12 constitution, irritability

◻**lose your temper**
05 go mad
06 lose it, see red
07 explode
08 boil over, get angry
09 blow a fuse, do your nut
10 hit the roof
11 blow a gasket, blow your
   top, flip your lid, go up a wall,
   lose your rag
12 fly into a rage, lose your cool,
   throw a wobbly
13 get aggravated, hit the
   ceiling, throw a tantrum
14 foam at the mouth
15 fly off the handle, go off the
   deep end

temperament
04 bent, mood, soul
06 humour, make-up, nature
09 characte
10 complexion, volatility

11   disposition, frame of mind, personality, state of mind
12   constitution, excitability

temperamental
05   fiery, moody
06   inborn, innate, touchy
08   inherent, neurotic, volatile
09   emotional, excitable, explosive, hot-headed, impatient, ingrained, irritable, mercurial, sensitive
10   capricious, congenital, hot-blooded, passionate
12   highly-strung
13   over-emotional, unpredictable

temperance
08   sobriety
09   austerity, restraint
10   abstinence, continence, moderation, self-denial
11   prohibition, self-control, teetotalism
13   self-restraint
14   abstemiousness, self-discipline

temperate
04   calm, fair, mild
05   balmy, sober
06   gentle, stable
07   clement, equable
08   balanced, composed, moderate, pleasant, sensible, teetotal
09   abstinent, agreeable
10   abstemious, controlled, reasonable, restrained
12   even-tempered
14   self-controlled, self-restrained

tempest
04   gale
05   storm
06   furore, squall, tumult, uproar
07   cyclone, tornado, typhoon
09   commotion, hurricane

tempestuous
04   wild
05   gusty, rough, windy
06   fierce, raging, stormy
07   furious, squally, violent
09   turbulent
10   passionate, tumultuous
11   impassioned
12   uncontrolled

temple
06   church, mosque, pagoda
09   sanctuary
10   tabernacle
14   place of worship

tempo
04   beat, pace, rate, time
05   metre, pulse, speed, throb
07   cadence, measure
08   velocity

temporal
06   carnal, mortal
07   earthly, fleshly, profane, secular, worldly
08   material
11   terrestrial

temporarily
06   pro tem
07   briefly
10   fleetingly
11   momentarily, transiently
12   in the interim, transitorily
15   for the time being

temporary
05   brief
06   fill-in, pro tem
07   interim, passing, stopgap
08   fleeting, temporal
09   ephemeral, fugacious, makeshift, momentary, short-term, transient
10   evanescent, short-lived
11   impermanent, provisional

temporize
05   delay, pause, stall
09   hum and haw
10   equivocate
11   play for time
12   tergiversate

tempt
04   bait, coax, draw, lure
06   allure, cajole, entice, incite
07   attract, provoke
08   inveigle, persuade
09   tantalize

temptation
04   bait, draw, lure, pull
06   allure, appeal, urging
08   cajolery
09   influence, seduction
10   attraction, enticement, invitation, persuasion

tempting
08   alluring, enticing, inviting
09   seductive
10   appetizing, attractive
11   tantalizing
13   mouthwatering

temptress
04   vamp
05   flirt, siren
07   Delilah
08   coquette

10   seductress
11   enchantress, femme fatale

tenable
06   viable
08   credible, feasible, rational
09   plausible
10   believable, defendable
11   justifiable, supportable

tenacious
04   fast, firm
06   dogged, secure, sticky
07   adamant
08   adhesive, clinging, stubborn
09   obstinate, steadfast
10   determined, persistent, relentless, unswerving
11   unshakeable
12   intransigent, single-minded

tenacity
05   force, power
07   resolve
08   firmness, obduracy, strength
09   obstinacy, toughness
10   doggedness, resolution
11   application, persistence
12   perseverance, stubbornness
13   determination, steadfastness
14   indomitability

tenancy
05   lease
06   tenure
09   leasehold, occupancy
10   occupation, possession

tenant
08   occupant, occupier, resident
10   inhabitant, landholder
11   leaseholder

tend
04   bear, bend, keep, lead, lean
05   nurse, point, see to, watch
06   attend, manage, wait on
07   care for, incline, nurture
08   attend to, maintain
09   cultivate, look after
10   minister to, take care of

tendency
04   bent, bias
05   drift, trend
07   bearing, heading, leaning
09   direction, proneness
10   partiality, proclivity
11   disposition, inclination
14   predisposition

tender
03   bid, new, raw, red
04   fond, give, kind, soft, sore
05   early, frail, green, juicy, money, offer, price, young

06 aching, callow, caring, dainty, extend, fleshy, gentle, kindly, loving, submit
07 advance, amorous, bruised, proffer, propose, suggest
08 currency, delicate, estimate, immature, proposal, romantic, youthful
09 evocative, sensitive, succulent, volunteer
10 submission, suggestion
11 considerate, sentimental, soft-hearted, sympathetic
12 affectionate
13 compassionate, inexperienced

tender-hearted
04 fond, kind, mild, warm
06 benign, caring, gentle, humane, kindly, loving
09 sensitive
10 benevolent, responsive
11 considerate, kind-hearted, sentimental, soft-hearted, sympathetic, warm-hearted
12 affectionate
13 compassionate

tenderness
04 ache, care, love, pain, pity
06 aching, liking, warmth
08 bruising, devotion, fondness, humanity, kindness, softness, soreness, sympathy, weakness
09 affection, greenness
10 attachment, callowness, compassion, gentleness, humaneness, immaturity
11 amorousness, benevolence, painfulness, sensitivity
12 inexperience, inflammation
13 consideration, sensitiveness, vulnerability
15 soft-heartedness, warm-heartedness

tenet
04 rule, view
05 canon, credo, creed, dogma, maxim
06 belief, thesis
07 opinion, precept
08 doctrine, teaching
09 principle
10 conviction
11 presumption
14 article of faith

tennis
➤ *Names of tennis players*:
04 **Ashe** (Arthur), **Borg** (Bjorn), **Cash** (Pat), **Graf**
(Steffi), **Hoad** (Lewis Alan), **King** (Billie Jean), **Ryan** (Elizabeth), **Wade** (Virginia)
05 **Budge** (Donald), **Bueno** (Maria), **Court** (Margaret), **Evert** (Chris), **Laver** (Rod), **Lendl** (Ivan), **Lloyd** (Chris), **Perry** (Fred), **Seles** (Monica), **Wills** (Helen)
06 **Agassi** (Andre), **Barker** (Sue), **Becker** (Boris), **Cawley** (Yvonne), **Edberg** (Stefan), **Gibson** (Althea), **Henman** (Tim), **Hingis** (Martina)
07 **Brookes** (Sir Norman Everard), **Connors** (Jimmy), **Godfree** (Kitty), **LaCoste** (Rene), **Lenglen** (Suzanne), **Maskell** (Dan), **McEnroe** (John), **Nastase** (Ilie), **Novotna** (Jana), **Renshaw** (Willie), **Sampras** (Pete)
08 **Connolly** (Maureen Catherine), **Gonzales** (Pancho), **Rusedski** (Greg), **Sabatini** (Gabriela), **Williams** (Serena), **Williams** (Venus)
09 **Davenport** (Lindsay), **Goolagong** (Yvonne)
11 **Navratilova** (Martina)
➤ See also **sport**

tenor
04 gist, path
05 drift, point, sense, theme
06 burden, course, intent, spirit
07 essence, meaning, purpose
09 direction, substance

tense
04 edgy, taut, work
05 brace, jumpy, rigid, stiff, tight
06 strain, uneasy
07 anxious, charged, fidgety, fraught, jittery, keyed up, nervous, stiffen, stretch, tighten, uptight, worried
08 contract, exciting, strained
09 screwed up, stressful
10 distraught, nail-biting
11 overwrought, stressed out
12 apprehensive, nerve-racking

tension
05 clash, worry
06 nerves, strain, stress, unrest
07 anxiety, discord, dispute
08 conflict, disquiet, distress, edginess, friction, pressure, rigidity, suspense, tautness
09 agitation, antipathy, hostility, stiffness, straining, tightness
10 antagonism, contention, dissension, opposition,
11 nervousness
12 apprehension

tent
➤ *Types of tent. We have omitted the word **tent** from names given in the following list but you may need to include this word as part of the solution to some crossword clues.*
03 box, mat
04 bell, dome, kata
05 bivvy, black, frame, lodge, ridge, tepee, tupik
06 big top, canopy, canvas, tunnel, wigwam
07 marquee, trailer, yaranga
10 single hoop, tabernacle
11 hooped bivvy
13 barrel-vaulted

tentative
04 test
05 pilot, timid, trial
06 unsure
08 cautious, doubtful, hesitant
09 faltering, uncertain
11 conjectural, exploratory, provisional, speculative
12 experimental

tenterhooks
❑ **on tenterhooks**
07 anxious, excited, nervous, waiting
09 impatient
10 in suspense
15 with bated breath

tenuous
04 fine, hazy, slim, thin, weak
05 shaky, vague
06 flimsy, slight
07 dubious, fragile, slender
08 delicate, doubtful
12 questionable
13 insubstantial

tenure
04 term, time
07 holding, tenancy
09 occupancy, residence
10 habitation, incumbency, occupation, possession

tepid
04 cool
07 warmish
08 lukewarm
09 apathetic

11 half-hearted, indifferent
14 unenthusiastic

term
03 dub, end, tag
04 call, name, span, time, word
05 costs, label, limit, rates, space, spell, style, title
06 course, finish, period, phrase, points, prices, season, tariff
07 clauses, charges, details, entitle, epithet, footing, session, stretch
08 duration, fruition, interval, locution, position, provisos, semester, standing, terminus
10 conclusion, condition, expression, provisions
11 appellation, culmination, designation, particulars
12 relationship, stipulations
14 qualifications, specifications

▶ *Names of terms and sessions*:
04 Lent
06 Easter, Hilary
07 Trinity
10 Michaelmas

❑**come to terms**
06 accept, submit
14 resign yourself

❑**in terms of**
09 as regards
10 in regard to
12 in relation to, with regard to
13 with respect to

terminal
03 end, VDU
04 last
05 depot, dying, fatal, final
06 deadly, lethal, mortal
07 console, extreme, monitor
08 keyboard, terminus
09 extremity, incurable
10 concluding
11 termination

terminate
03 end
04 stop
05 abort, cease, close, lapse
06 cut off, expire, finish, result, run out, wind up
08 complete, conclude
10 put an end to
11 come to an end, discontinue
12 bring to an end

termination
03 end
05 close, finis, issue

06 demise, effect, ending, expiry, finale, finish, result
08 abortion
09 cessation
10 completion, conclusion
15 discontinuation

terminology
05 terms, words
06 jargon
08 language
10 vocabulary
11 expressions, phraseology
12 nomenclature

terminus
03 end
04 goal
05 close, depot, limit
06 garage, target
07 station
08 boundary, terminal
11 destination, termination

terrain
04 land
06 ground
07 country
09 landscape, territory
10 topography
11 countryside

terrestrial
06 global
07 earthly, mundane, worldly

terrible
04 foul, grim, poor, vile
05 awful, grave, great, nasty
06 horrid, severe
07 extreme, hateful, hideous, intense, serious
08 dreadful, gruesome, horrible, horrific, shocking
09 abhorrent, appalling, desperate, frightful, harrowing, obnoxious, offensive, repulsive, revolting
10 disgusting, outrageous
11 exceptional, unspeakable
12 incorrigible

terribly
04 much, very
07 awfully, greatly
09 decidedly, extremely, seriously
10 thoroughly
11 desperately, exceedingly, frightfully

terrific
03 ace
04 cool, huge, mega, neat
05 brill, crack, great, super

06 superb, wicked
07 amazing, awesome, intense
08 enormous, fabulous, gigantic, smashing
09 brilliant, excellent, fantastic, wonderful
10 marvellous, remarkable, stupendous, tremendous
11 magnificent, outstanding, sensational
12 breathtaking
13 extraordinary

terrified
04 awed
06 scared
07 alarmed
08 appalled, dismayed
09 horrified, petrified
10 frightened
11 intimidated, scared stiff
12 horror-struck
13 having kittens, panic-stricken, scared to death

terrify
05 appal, panic, scare, shock
07 horrify, petrify
08 frighten, paralyse
09 terrorize
10 intimidate, scare stiff

territorial
04 area
05 zonal
08 district, domainal, regional
09 localized, sectional
11 topographic
12 geographical

territory
04 area, land, zone
05 field, state, tract
06 domain, region, sector
07 terrain
08 district, preserve, province
10 dependency
12 jurisdiction

terror
04 fear
05 alarm, demon, devil, dread, fiend, panic, rogue, shock
06 dismay, fright, horror, rascal
07 monster
09 terrorism
12 intimidation

terrorize
05 alarm, bully, scare, shock
06 coerce, menace
07 horrify, oppress, terrify
08 browbeat, frighten, threaten
09 strongarm
10 intimidate

terse
04 curt
05 blunt, brief, crisp, pithy, short
06 abrupt, gnomic, snappy
07 brusque, concise, laconic
08 incisive, succinct
09 condensed
10 elliptical, to the point
12 epigrammatic

test
03 sap, try
05 assay, check, probe, proof,
prove, study, trial, weary
06 assess, ordeal, sample,
screen, try out, verify
07 analyse, check-up, examine,
exhaust, inspect, stretch,
wear out
08 analysis, appraise, audition,
enervate, evaluate
09 probation, questions
10 assessment, evaluation,
experiment, inspection,
pilot study, scrutinize
11 examination
13 questionnaire
14 scrutinization

testament
04 will
05 proof
07 earnest, tribute, witness
08 evidence
09 testimony
11 attestation
15 exemplification

testicles
04 nuts
05 balls, rocks
07 goolies

testify
04 avow, show
05 state, swear, vouch
06 affirm, assert, attest, verify
07 certify, confirm, declare,
endorse, support
11 bear witness, corroborate
12 give evidence, substantiate

testimonial
07 tribute
09 character, reference
10 credential
11 certificate, endorsement
12 commendation

testimony
05 proof
07 support, witness
08 evidence
09 affidavit, statement
10 profession, submission
11 affirmation, attestation

12 confirmation, verification
13 corroboration

testy
05 cross, ratty
06 crusty, grumpy, shirty,
snappy, sullen, tetchy, touchy
07 crabbed, peevish, waspish
08 captious, petulant, snappish
09 crotchety, impatient,
irascible, irritable, splenetic
11 bad-tempered, quarrelsome
12 cantankerous
13 quick-tempered

tetchy
05 ratty
06 crusty, grumpy, touchy
07 peevish
09 crotchety, irascible, irritable
11 bad-tempered

tête-à-tête
04 chat, talk
06 confab, natter
12 conversation, heart-to-heart

tether
03 tie
04 bind, bond, lead, line, rope
05 chain, leash
06 fasten, fetter, secure
09 fastening, restraint

text
05 theme, topic, verse, words
06 matter, source
07 chapter, content, passage,
set book, subject, wording
08 sentence, textbook

texture
04 feel
05 grain, touch, weave
06 fabric, finish, tissue
07 quality, surface
10 appearance
11 composition, consistency

thank
06 credit
09 recognize
10 appreciate, be grateful
11 acknowledge, say thank you

thankful
07 obliged, pleased
08 beholden, grateful,
indebted, relieved
12 appreciative

thankless
10 unrequited, unrewarded
11 unrewarding
12 unprofitable, unrecognized
13 unappreciated
14 unacknowledged

thanks
02 ta
06 cheers, credit
08 bless you
09 gratitude
11 much obliged, recognition
12 appreciation, gratefulness,
thanksgiving
15 acknowledgement

▢thanks to
05 due to
07 owing to, through
09 because of
11 as a result of, on account of

thaw
04 melt, warm
05 de-ice, relax
07 defrost, liquefy
08 defreeze, loosen up

theatre
03 rep
05 drama, odeon
06 lyceum
08 the stage
09 dramatics, playhouse, the
boards, theatrics
10 auditorium, opera house
11 Thespian art
12 amphitheatre
13 the footlights
➤ See also **director**

■ *Parts of a theatre:*
03 box, pit, set
04 flat, grid, loge
05 apron, flies, spots, stage,
wings
06 border, bridge, circle, floats,
floods, lights, loggia, scruto,
stalls
07 balcony, catwalk, gallery,
rostrum, the gods, upstage
08 coulisse, trapdoor
09 backstage, cyclorama,
downstage, forestage, green
room, mezzanine,
tormentor
10 auditorium, footlights,
fourth wall, prompt side,
proscenium
11 upper circle
12 orchestra pit
13 safety curtain
14 opposite prompt,
proscenium arch, revolving
stage

➤ *Names of theatres. We have*
omitted the word **theatre** *from*
names given in the following list
but you may need to include this
word as part of the solution to
some crossword clues.
05 Abbey, Globe, Lyric, Savoy
06 Apollo, Donmar, Lyceum,
   Old Vic
07 Adelphi, Aldwych,
   Almeida, Garrick,
   Gielgud, Mermaid,
   Olivier, Phoenix
08 Coliseum, Dominion,
   National, Young Vic
09 Cottesloe, Drury Lane,
   Lyttelton, Playhouse
10 Royal Court
11 Comedy Store, Her
   Majesty's, Shaftesbury
12 Covent Garden, Sadler's
   Wells, Theatre Royal
15 London Palladium

theatrical
05 showy
08 affected, dramatic,
   mannered, thespian
09 emotional
10 artificial, histrionic
11 exaggerated, extravagant
12 melodramatic, ostentatious

➤ *Theatrical forms include:*
04 mime, play
05 farce, opera, revue
06 ballet, circus, comedy,
   kabuki, masque
07 cabaret, mummery, musical,
   pageant, tableau, tragedy
08 operetta
09 burlesque, melodrama,
   monologue, music hall,
   pantomime
11 black comedy, kitchen-sink,
   miracle play, mystery play
12 Grand Guignol, Punch and
   Judy, morality play
13 fringe theatre, musical
   comedy, puppet theatre,
   street theatre
15 comedy of manners

theft
05 fraud
07 larceny, lifting, nicking,
   robbery, swiping
08 burglary, nobbling,
   pinching, stealing, thieving
09 pilfering, swindling
10 purloining
11 kleptomania, shoplifting
12 embezzlement

thematic
08 notional
10 conceptual

theme
04 gist, idea, text, tune
05 essay, motif, paper, topic
06 melody, thesis, thread
07 essence, keynote, subject
09 leitmotif
13 subject matter

then
04 also, next, soon, thus
05 after
07 besides, further, so and so
08 moreover
09 as a result, therefore
10 at that time, in addition
11 accordingly, at that point,
   furthermore, in those days
12 additionally, at a later date,
   consequently, subsequently

theologian

➤ *Names of theologians:*
03 **Eck** (Johann Mayer von)
04 **Bede** (St), **Otto** (Rudolf),
   Paul (St)
05 **Arius**, **Barth** (Karl),
   Buber (Martin), **Cyril**
   (of Alexandria, St),
   Paley (William), **Pusey**
   (Edward Bouverie),
   Young (Thomas)
06 **Alcuin**, **Anselm** (St),
   Calvin (John), **Hooker**
   (Richard), **Jansen**
   (Cornelius), **Jerome** (St),
   Mather (Increase),
   Newman (John Henry,
   Cardinal), **Origen**, **Pascal**
   (Blaise)
07 **Abelard** (Peter), **Aquinas**
   (St Thomas), **Bernard** (of
   Clairvaux, St), **Clement** (of
   Alexandria), **Cyprian** (St),
   Eckhart (Johannes),
   Gregory (of Nazianzus, St),
   Gregory (of Nyssa),
   Grotius (Hugo), **Lombard**
   (Peter), **Sankara**, **Spinoza**
   (Baruch), **Tillich** (Paul
   Johannes), **William** (of
   Ockham)
08 **Berengar** (of Tours),
   Bultmann (Rudolf Karl),
   Eusebius, **Ignatius** (of
   Loyola, St), **Irenaeus** (St),
   Sprenger (Jacob)
09 **Augustine** (St), **Nagarjuna**
10 **Bellarmine** (St Robert),
   Bonhoeffer (Dietrich),
   Duns Scotus (John),

   Schweitzer (Albert),
   Swedenborg (Emanuel),
   Tertullian
12 **Justin Martyr** (St)
➤ See also **religion**

theological
06 divine
09 doctrinal, religious
10 scriptural
12 hierological
14 ecclesiastical

theorem
04 rule
06 dictum
07 formula
09 postulate, principle
10 hypothesis
11 proposition

theoretical
04 pure
05 ideal
07 on paper
08 abstract, academic,
   notional
10 conceptual
11 conjectural, speculative
12 hypothetical

theorize
05 guess
08 propound
09 formulate, postulate
10 conjecture
11 hypothesize

theory
06 notion, scheme, thesis
07 opinion, surmise
08 proposal
10 conjecture, hypothesis
11 postulation, presumption,
   speculation, supposition

therapeutic
04 good
05 tonic
06 curing
07 healing
08 curative, remedial,
   salutary
10 beneficial, corrective
11 restorative
12 advantageous,
   ameliorative

therapy
04 cure
05 tonic
06 remedy
07 healing
09 treatment

➤ *Types of therapy. The word*
therapy *has been omitted from*
items in this list but you may
need to include this word as part
of the solution to some
crossword clues.
03 art, sex
04 play
05 drama, group, music
06 beauty, family, speech
07 Gestalt, Rolfing, shiatsu
08 aversion
09 herbalism
10 homeopathy, osteopathy,
   regression, ultrasound
11 acupressure, acupuncture,
   biofeedback, moxibustion,
   naturopathy, reflexology
12 aromatherapy,
   chemotherapy, chiropractic,
   faith healing, hydrotherapy,
   hypnotherapy, occupational,
   radiotherapy
13 physiotherapy,
   psychotherapy

thereabouts
05 about
07 roughly
13 approximately

thereafter
04 next
09 after that
10 afterwards
12 subsequently

therefore
04 ergo, then, thus
09 as a result
11 accordingly

thesaurus
07 lexicon
08 treasury, wordbook
10 dictionary, repository,
   storehouse, vocabulary
12 encyclopedia

thesis
04 idea, view
05 essay, paper, theme, topic
06 theory
07 opinion, premise, subject
08 argument, proposal, treatise
10 contention, hypothesis
11 composition, proposition
12 disquisition, dissertation

thick
03 big, fat, hub
04 deep, dull, dumb, full, slow
05 broad, bulky, close, dense,
   dopey, husky, midst, murky,
   solid, stiff, stout

06 centre, chunky, croaky,
   filled, middle, packed,
   simple, strong, stupid
07 clotted, compact, crowded,
   foolish, rasping, teeming,
   throaty, unclear, viscous
08 abundant, brimming,
   bursting, crawling, croaking,
   gormless, gravelly, guttural,
   numerous, swarming
09 abounding, brainless,
   condensed, dim-witted
10 coagulated, indistinct,
   noticeable, pronounced
11 overflowing, substantial
12 concentrated, impenetrable

thicken
03 gel, set
04 cake, clot, jell
07 congeal, stiffen
08 condense, solidify
09 coagulate

thicket
04 wood
05 copse, grove
06 maquis
07 coppice, spinney

thickhead
04 clot, dope, fool, twit
05 chump, dummy, dunce,
   idiot, moron
06 dimwit, nitwit
07 fathead, pinhead
08 imbecile, numskull
09 blockhead

thick-headed
04 slow
05 dense, dopey, thick
06 obtuse, stupid
07 asinine, doltish, moronic
08 gormless
09 dim-witted, imbecilic
10 dull-witted, slow-witted
11 blockheaded

thickness
03 bed, ply
04 body, bulk, film,
05 layer, sheet, width
07 breadth, density, stratum
08 diameter
09 bulkiness, closeness,
   solidness, viscosity
11 consistency

thickset
05 beefy, bulky, burly, solid
06 brawny, stocky, sturdy
08 muscular, powerful
09 well-built

thick-skinned
07 callous
08 hardened
09 hard-nosed, unfeeling
10 hard-boiled
11 insensitive
15 tough as old boots

thief
06 bandit, mugger, robber
07 brigand, burglar, filcher,
   nobbler, poacher, stealer
08 pilferer, swindler
09 embezzler, plunderer
10 pickpocket, shoplifter
12 house-breaker,
   kleptomaniac

thieve
03 rob
04 lift, nick
05 cheat, filch, heist, pinch,
   poach, steal, swipe
06 nobble, pilfer, rip off
07 plunder, purloin, snaffle
08 embezzle, knock off
14 misappropriate

thieving
05 theft
06 piracy
07 larceny, lifting, mugging,
   nicking, robbery
08 banditry, burglary, filching,
   stealing, thievery
09 pilferage, pilfering
10 peculation, ripping off
11 knocking off, shoplifting
12 embezzlement

thievish
09 dishonest, furacious,
   larcenous, rapacious
10 fraudulent
13 light-fingered
14 sticky-fingered

thin
04 bony, fine, lame, lean, poor,
   slim, soft, trim, weak
05 faint, filmy, gaunt, gauzy,
   lanky, light, quiet, runny,
   scant, sheer, spare, wispy
06 dilute, feeble, flimsy, lessen,
   meagre, narrow, paltry,
   rarefy, reduce, refine, scarce,
   skimpy, skinny, slight, sparse,
   wasted, watery
07 diluted, scraggy, scrawny,
   slender, spindly, weed out
08 anorexic, decrease, delicate,
   diminish, gossamer,
   shrunken, skeletal, straggly

09 attenuate, defective, deficient, emaciated, paper-thin, scattered, untenable
10 attenuated, diaphanous, see-through, wishy-washy
11 high-pitched, implausible, transparent, underweight
14 undernourished

□ on thin ice
06 at risk, unsafe
10 in jeopardy, precarious, vulnerable

thing
04 body, deed, fact, feat, idea, item, love, task, togs, tool
05 chore, fancy, gismo, goods, point, stuff, tools, trait
06 action, affair, aspect, attire, desire, detail, device, doodah, entity, factor, fetish, gadget, hang-up, horror, liking, matter, notion, object, phobia, tackle, thingy
07 apparel, article, baggage, clobber, clothes, concept, dislike, effects, exploit, feature, leaning, luggage, problem, thought, whatsit
08 affinity, aversion, clothing, creature, fixation, fondness, garments, idée fixe, incident, penchant, property, soft spot, thingamy, weakness
09 affection, apparatus, attribute, condition, equipment, happening, implement, mechanism, obsession, proneness, substance, thingummy
10 belongings, instrument, partiality, particular, phenomenon, preference, proceeding, propensity
11 contrivance, eventuality, inclination, possessions
12 predilection, thingummybob, thingummyjig, what's-its-name
13 paraphernalia, preoccupation
14 characteristic, responsibility, what-d'you-call-it

□ the thing
03 hip
04 cool
06 modish, latest
07 current, in vogue, popular
09 the latest
10 all the rage
11 fashionable

think
04 deem, hold, muse
05 brood, guess, judge, opine
06 expect, figure, ponder, reason, reckon, regard
07 believe, imagine, presume, reflect, suppose, surmise
08 chew over, cogitate, conceive, conclude, consider, estimate, meditate, mull over, ruminate
09 calculate, cerebrate, determine, visualize
10 cogitation, conjecture, deliberate, evaluation, meditation, reflection
11 concentrate, contemplate
12 deliberation
13 consideration, contemplation

□ think better of
06 revise
07 rethink
10 reconsider, think again, think twice
11 get cold feet

□ think much of
04 rate
05 prize, value
06 admire, esteem
07 respect
10 set store by
13 think highly of

□ think nothing of
13 consider usual
14 consider normal

□ think over
06 ponder
07 weigh up
08 consider, meditate, mull over, ruminate
11 contemplate, reflect upon

□ think up
06 create, design, devise, invent
07 concoct, dream up, imagine
08 conceive, contrive
09 visualize

thinkable
06 likely
08 feasible, possible
10 imaginable, reasonable
11 conceivable

thinker
04 sage
05 brain
07 scholar
08 theorist
09 intellect
10 ideologist, mastermind
11 philosopher

thinking
04 idea, view
07 logical, outlook, thought
08 rational, sensible, thoughts
09 appraisal, reasoning
10 analytical, assessment, conclusion, evaluation, meditative, philosophy, reflective, thoughtful
11 conclusions, intelligent
12 intellectual
13 contemplative, philosophical, sophisticated

thin-skinned
06 snappy, tender, touchy
09 irritable, sensitive
11 easily upset, susceptible
14 hypersensitive

third-rate
03 bad
04 naff, poor, ropy
06 shoddy
08 inferior, low-grade, mediocre, slipshod
10 low-quality

thirst
03 yen
04 long, lust
05 crave, yearn
06 desire, hanker, hunger
07 aridity, craving, drought, dryness, longing, passion
09 eagerness, hankering
11 drouthiness, parchedness

thirsty
03 dry
04 arid, avid, keen
07 burning, craving, gasping, itching, longing, parched
08 desirous, yearning
10 dehydrated

thong
04 band, belt, cord, lash
05 strap, strip

thorn
04 barb
05 point, spike, spine
06 needle
07 bristle, prickle

thorny
05 sharp, spiky, spiny, vexed
06 barbed, knotty, tricky, trying
07 awkward, bristly, complex, irksome, pointed, prickly, spinose, spinous
09 acanthous, difficult
10 convoluted
11 problematic, troublesome

thorough

04 deep, full, pure
05 sheer, total, utter
06 entire
07 careful, in-depth, perfect
08 absolute, complete
09 efficient, extensive, intensive, out-and-out
10 exhaustive, meticulous, scrupulous, widespread
11 painstaking, unqualified
12 all-embracing, all-inclusive
13 comprehensive

thoroughbred

08 pedigree
09 pedigreed, pure-blood
11 full-blooded, pure-blooded

thoroughfare

03 way
04 road
06 access, avenue, street
07 highway, passage, roadway
08 motorway, turnpike
10 passageway

thoroughly

05 fully, quite
07 totally, utterly
08 entirely
09 carefully, downright, every inch, inside out, perfectly
10 absolutely, completely
12 exhaustively, scrupulously
13 root and branch
15 comprehensively

though

03 but, yet
05 still, while
06 even if, even so
07 granted, however
08 allowing, although
10 all the same, for all that
11 nonetheless
12 nevertheless
15 notwithstanding

thought

04 care, heed, hope, idea, plan
05 dream, study, touch
06 belief, musing, notion, reason, regard, theory
07 concept, concern, feeling, gesture, opinion, purpose
08 prospect, sympathy, thinking
09 attention, intention, pondering, reasoning
10 cogitation, conception, conclusion, conviction, estimation, meditation, reflection, rumination
11 cerebration, expectation

12 anticipation, deliberation
13 consideration, contemplation, introspection

thoughtful

04 deep, kind, wary
05 quiet
06 caring, dreamy
07 careful, heedful, helpful, mindful, pensive, serious
08 profound, studious, thinking
09 attentive, unselfish
10 reflective, solicitous
11 considerate, sympathetic
13 contemplative, in a brown study, lost in thought

thoughtless

05 hasty, silly
06 remiss, stupid, unwise
07 foolish, selfish
08 careless, heedless, impolite, mindless, reckless, tactless
09 imprudent, negligent
10 ill-advised, indiscreet
11 insensitive, precipitate
12 absent-minded
13 ill-considered, inconsiderate

thrall

05 power
07 bondage, serfdom, slavery
08 thraldom
09 servitude, vassalage
10 subjection
11 enslavement, subjugation

thrash

03 hit, tan
04 beat, belt, cane, drub, flog, lash, lick, rout, toss, whip
05 crush, flail, spank, whack
06 defeat, hammer, punish
07 clobber, scourge, trounce
08 vanquish
09 overwhelm, slaughter

▢thrash out

07 discuss, resolve
09 hammer out, negotiate

thrashing

04 rout
06 caning, defeat, hiding
07 beating, belting, lamming, lashing, licking, pasting
08 crushing, drubbing
09 hammering, trouncing
10 clobbering, punishment

thread

04 ease, inch, line, move, pass, plot, push, wind, yarn
05 fibre, strip, theme, weave
06 course, strand, streak, string
08 filament

09 direction, storyline
14 train of thought

threadbare

03 old
04 worn
05 stale, tatty, tired
06 frayed, ragged, shabby
07 scruffy, worn-out
08 overused, well-worn
09 hackneyed, moth-eaten
12 cliché-ridden

threat

04 omen, risk
05 peril
06 danger, hazard, menace
07 portent, presage, warning
09 ultimatum
11 commination

threaten

04 loom, warn
05 augur, bully
06 extort, lean on, menace
07 imperil, portend, presage
08 endanger, forebode
09 blackmail, comminate, terrorize
10 be imminent, foreshadow, intimidate, jeopardize, pressurize, push around
14 put the screws on

threatening

07 looming, ominous, warning
08 menacing, minatory, sinister
09 impending, minacious
10 cautionary, foreboding
12 inauspicious, intimidatory

threesome

04 trio
05 triad
06 triple, triune, troika
07 trilogy, trinity, triplet
08 triptych
11 triumvirate

threshold

04 dawn, door, sill
05 brink, entry, start, verge
07 doorway, opening
08 doorstep, entrance
09 beginning, inception

thrift

06 saving
07 economy
09 frugality, husbandry, parsimony
11 carefulness
12 conservation

thriftless

08 prodigal, wasteful
09 imprudent, unthrifty

10 profligate
11 dissipative, extravagant, improvident, spendthrift

thrifty
06 frugal, saving
07 careful, prudent, sparing
10 conserving, economical
12 parsimonious .

thrill
04 buzz, glow, kick, move, stir
05 flush, rouse, shake, throb
06 arouse, charge, excite, quiver, shiver, tingle, tremor
07 delight, feeling, flutter, frisson, shudder, tremble
08 pleasure
09 adventure, sensation, stimulate, vibration
10 excitement, exhilarate
11 give a buzz to, give a kick to

thrilling
07 quaking, rousing, shaking
08 exciting, gripping, stirring
09 shivering, trembling
11 hair-raising, sensational
12 electrifying, soul-stirring

thrive
04 boom, gain, grow
05 bloom
06 do well, profit
07 advance, blossom, burgeon, develop, prosper, succeed
08 flourish, increase

thriving
07 booming, healthy, wealthy
08 affluent, blooming
10 blossoming, burgeoning, prosperous, successful
11 comfortable, flourishing

throat
04 craw
05 gorge, halse
06 fauces, gullet
07 jugular, weasand
08 guttural, thrapple, thropple, throttle, windpipe
10 oesophagus, the Red Lane

throaty
03 low
04 deep
05 gruff, husky, thick
06 hoarse
07 rasping, raucous
08 guttural

throb
04 beat, drum
05 pound, pulse, thump
07 pulsate, vibrate
08 pounding, thumping

09 palpitate, vibration
11 palpitation

throe
03 fit
04 pain, pang, stab
05 agony, spasm
07 anguish, seizure, travail
08 distress, paroxysm
10 convulsion

throng
03 jam, mob
04 bevy, cram, fill, host, mass
05 bunch, crowd, crush, horde
09 multitude
10 congregate, mill around
12 congregation

throttle
05 check, choke
06 keep in, stifle
07 inhibit, silence, smother
08 restrain, strangle, suppress
09 suffocate
10 asphyxiate
11 strangulate

through
02 by, in
03 via
04 done
05 due to, ended, using
06 across, direct, during
07 between, by way of, express, non-stop, owing to
08 finished, thanks to
09 because of, by means of, completed
10 by virtue of, terminated, throughout, to the end of
11 as a result of, on account of

□**through and through**
05 fully
06 wholly
07 totally, utterly
08 entirely
09 to the core
10 altogether, completely
12 unreservedly
15 from top to bottom

throughout
06 during, widely
07 all over
08 all round
10 all through, completely, everywhere, in all parts
11 extensively, in every part

throw
03 lob, put, shy
04 cast, emit, fell, give, hurl, send, shed, toss, turn, work
05 chuck, fling, floor, heave, pitch, sling, upset

06 baffle, propel, put out, unseat
07 confuse, disturb, perplex, project, radiate, unhorse
08 astonish, catapult, confound, dislodge, organize, overturn, surprise, switch on, unsaddle
09 bring down, discomfit, dumbfound, prostrate
10 disconcert

□**throw away**
04 blow, dump, lose
05 ditch, scrap, waste
07 discard
08 chuck out, get rid of, jettison
09 chuck away, dispose of
11 fritter away

□**throw off**
04 drop, shed
05 elude
07 abandon, cast off, discard
08 get rid of, jettison, shake off

□**throw out**
05 ditch, eject, evict, expel
07 diffuse, discard, dismiss, emanate, give off, produce, radiate, turf out, turn out
08 jettison, point out
12 dispense with

□**throw over**
04 drop, jilt, quit
05 chuck, leave
06 desert, reject
07 abandon, discard, forsake
10 finish with

□**throw up**
03 gag
04 puke, quit, spew
05 heave, leave, retch, vomit
06 jack in, pack in, resign
07 abandon, chuck in
08 disgorge, renounce
11 regurgitate

throwaway
05 cheap
06 casual
07 offhand, passing
08 careless
10 disposable, expendable
13 biodegradable

thrust
03 jab, jam, ram
04 butt, gist, push, stab, urge
05 drift, drive, foist, force, impel, lunge, point, power, shove, tenor, theme, wedge
06 burden, impose, pierce, plunge, propel, saddle
07 essence, impetus, inflict

thud
08 encumber, momentum
09 substance

thud
04 bang, bash, wham
05 clonk, clump, clunk, crash, knock, smack, thump
06 wallop

thug
05 rough, tough
06 killer, mugger, robber
07 hoodlum, ruffian, villain
08 assassin, gangster, hooligan
09 cut-throat, roughneck

thumb
□**thumb through**
08 glance at
11 flip through, leaf through
12 flick through
13 browse through

thumbnail
05 brief, pithy, quick, short
07 compact, concise
08 succinct
09 miniature

thumbs-down
02 no
06 rebuff
07 refusal
08 negation, turn-down
09 rejection
11 disapproval

thumbs-up
02 OK
03 yes
07 go-ahead
08 approval, sanction
10 acceptance, green light
11 affirmation

thump
03 box, hit, rap
04 bang, beat, blow, slap, thud
05 clout, crash, knock, pound, punch, smack, throb, whack
06 batter, hammer, strike, thrash, thwack, wallop
09 palpitate

thumping
04 huge, very
06 really, severe
07 extreme, greatly, immense, mammoth, massive, titanic
08 colossal, enormous, gigantic, severely, terrific
09 excessive, extremely
10 impressive, monumental, thundering, tremendous

thunder
04 bang, clap, peal, roar, roll
05 blast, crack, crash
06 bellow, rumble
07 resound
11 reverberate
13 reverberation

thundering
04 very
05 great
06 really
08 enormous, severely
09 excessive, extremely, intensely, unusually
10 monumental, remarkable, tremendous

thunderous
04 loud
07 booming, roaring
08 rumbling
09 deafening
10 resounding, tumultuous
12 ear-splitting

thunderstruck
05 agape, dazed
06 aghast, amazed
07 floored, shocked, stunned
09 astounded, flummoxed, paralysed, staggered
10 bowled over, nonplussed
11 dumbfounded, open-mouthed
13 flabbergasted, knocked for six

thus
02 so
04 ergo, then
05 hence
08 like this
09 as follows, in this way, therefore
11 accordingly
12 consequently

thwack
03 hit
04 bash, beat, blow, flog, slap
05 clout, smack, thump, whack
06 buffet, wallop

thwart
04 balk, foil, stop
05 block, check, cross
06 defeat, hamper, hinder, impede, oppose, stymie
07 prevent
08 obstruct
09 frustrate

tic
05 spasm
06 twitch
13 tic douloureux

tick
03 sec, tap
04 beat, line, mark
05 check, click, flash, jiffy, trice
06 minute, moment, second
08 indicate, tick-tock
09 twinkling

□**tick off**
04 mark
05 check, chide, scold
06 rebuke
07 reprove, tell off, upbraid
08 check off, indicate, reproach
09 reprimand
13 tear off a strip

ticket
03 tag
04 card, pass, slip, stub
05 label, token
06 coupon, docket
07 sticker, voucher

tickle
05 amuse, touch
06 divert, please, stroke, thrill
07 delight, gratify

ticklish
05 dodgy, risky
06 knotty, thorny, touchy, tricky
07 awkward
09 difficult, sensitive
11 problematic

tide
03 ebb, run
04 flow, flux
05 drift, tenor, trend
06 course, stream
07 current
08 movement, tendency

□**tide over**
03 aid
06 assist
07 help out
09 keep going
11 help through

tidings
03 gen
04 dope, news, word
06 advice, report
07 message
09 greetings
11 information

tidy
04 fair, good, neat, trim
05 ample, groom, order, smart
06 neaten, spruce
07 arrange, clean up, clear up, ordered, orderly, smarten
08 sizeable, spruce up
09 efficient, organized, shipshape

10 immaculate, methodical,
straighten, systematic
11 uncluttered, well-ordered
12 considerable,
spick-and-span

tie
03 fix
04 band, bind, bond, clip, curb,
draw, duty, join, knot, lash,
link, moor, rope, tape
05 chain, limit, strap, unite
06 attach, be even, couple,
fasten, hamper, hinder,
ribbon, secure, tether
07 be equal, confine, connect,
kinship, liaison, shackle
08 dead heat, restrain
09 constrain, fastening,
hindrance, restraint
10 allegiance, commitment,
connection, constraint,
friendship, limitation,
obligation
11 be all square, restriction
12 relationship

□**tie down**
06 hamper, hinder
07 confine
08 restrain, restrict
09 constrain

□**tie up**
04 bind, do up, lash, moor, rope
05 chain, truss
06 attach, engage, fasten,
occupy, secure, settle,
tether, wind up, wrap up
08 finalize, keep busy

tie-in
04 link
05 tie-up
06 hook-up
07 liaison
08 relation
10 connection
11 affiliation, association
12 co-ordination, relationship

tier
03 row
04 band, bank, belt, line, rank
05 floor, layer, level, stage
07 echelon, stratum

tiff
03 pet, row
04 huff, spat, sulk
05 scrap, set-to, words
07 dispute, quarrel, tantrum
08 squabble
10 difference, falling-out
12 disagreement

tight
04 fast, firm, mean, snug, taut
05 close, drunk, fixed, merry,
rigid, tense, tipsy, tough
06 pissed, scarce, sealed,
secure, severe, stingy,
stoned, strict, tiddly, tricky
07 compact, cramped, legless,
limited, miserly, sloshed,
smashed, sozzled
08 airtight, clenched, hermetic,
rigorous, strained, tanked up
09 niggardly, plastered,
skin-tight, stretched,
stringent, well-oiled
10 compressed, inadequate,
inflexible, restricted,
sound-proof, watertight
11 constricted, intoxicated,
neck and neck, tight-fisted,
12 close-fitting, parsimonious
13 figure-hugging,
penny-pinching

tighten
05 close, cramp, crush, tense
06 fasten, narrow, secure
07 squeeze, stiffen, stretch
09 constrict, pull tight
10 constringe

tight-fisted
04 mean
05 mingy, tight
06 stingy
07 miserly, sparing
08 grasping
09 niggardly
12 parsimonious
13 penny-pinching

tight-lipped
03 mum
04 mute
05 quiet
06 silent
09 secretive
12 close-mouthed
13 unforthcoming
15 uncommunicative

till
02 to
03 dig
04 farm, up to, work
05 until
06 plough
07 through
09 cultivate

tilt
03 tip
04 cant, duel, lean, list, spar
05 angle, clash, fight, joust,
pitch, slant, slope

06 attack, charge, combat
07 contend, contest, incline
10 tournament
11 inclination

□**at full tilt**
06 all out
07 flat out
08 very fast
10 at full pelt, at top speed
11 at full speed, very quickly

timber
03 log
04 beam, lath, pole, spar,
wood
05 board, plank, trees
06 forest, lumber

timbre
04 ring, tone
06 colour
07 quality
09 resonance
12 voice quality

time
03 age, era, fix, set
04 date, life, peak, span, term
05 clock, count, epoch, meter,
metre, point, space, spell,
stage, tempo, while
06 adjust, heyday, moment,
period, rhythm, season
07 arrange, control, instant,
measure, session, stretch
08 duration, instance, interval,
juncture, lifespan, lifetime,
occasion, temporal
09 calculate, programme

□**all the time**
06 always
07 forever
10 constantly
11 continually, incessantly,
perpetually

□**at one time**
04 once
07 long ago
08 formerly
10 at one point, previously
11 in times past

□**at the same time**
06 anyway, even so
07 however
11 all together, nonetheless
12 concurrently, nevertheless
14 simultaneously

□**at times**
09 sometimes
10 now and then
12 every so often

11 now and again,
on occasions
14 from time to time

behind the times
05 dated
06 old hat
09 out of date
10 fuddy-duddy
12 old-fashioned,
out of fashion
13 unfashionable

behind time
04 late
07 delayed, overdue
14 behind schedule

for the time being
06 for now, pro tem
08 meantime, right now
09 at present, meanwhile
11 at the moment, temporarily
12 for the moment
13 for the present

from time to time
07 at times
09 sometimes
10 now and then, on occasion
11 now and again
12 occasionally, once in a while,
periodically, sporadically
13 spasmodically
14 intermittently

in good time
05 early
11 ahead of time
15 ahead of schedule

in time
06 on time
10 not too late, punctually

on time
05 sharp
06 bang on, dead on, spot on
07 exactly
08 on the dot, promptly
09 precisely
10 punctually

play for time
05 delay, stall
08 hang fire, hesitate
10 filibuster
13 procrastinate

time after time
05 often
09 many times
10 frequently, repeatedly
12 time and again
13 again and again

time-honoured
03 old
05 fixed, usual

06 age-old
07 ancient
08 historic
09 customary, venerable
10 accustomed
11 established, traditional
12 conventional

timeless
07 abiding, eternal, lasting
08 immortal, unending
09 immutable, permanent
10 changeless, unchanging

timely
06 prompt
08 punctual, suitable
09 opportune, well-timed
10 convenient, felicitous
11 appropriate

timetable
04 list, rota
05 diary
06 agenda, roster
07 arrange, diarize, listing
08 calendar, schedule
09 programme
10 curriculum

time-worn
03 old
04 aged, worn
05 dated, hoary, lined, passé,
stale, stock, tired, trite
06 ragged, ruined, shabby
07 clichéd, run-down
08 bromidic, decrepit, dog-
eared, well-worn, wrinkled
09 hackneyed, weathered

timid
03 shy
06 afraid, scared, yellow
07 bashful, chicken, fearful,
gutless, nervous, wimpish
08 cowardly, retiring, timorous
09 shrinking, spineless
10 frightened, irresolute
12 apprehensive, faint-hearted

timorous
03 coy, shy
05 mousy, timid
06 afraid, modest, scared
07 bashful, fearful, nervous
08 cowardly, retiring
09 diffident, shrinking,
tentative, trembling
10 frightened, irresolute
12 apprehensive, faint-hearted
13 pusillanimous

tincture
03 dye, hue
04 dash, hint, tint

05 imbue, scent, shade, smack,
stain, tinge, touch, trace
06 colour, infuse, season
07 flavour, suffuse
10 suggestion

tinge
03 bit, dye
04 dash, drop, hint, tint, wash
05 imbue, shade, touch, trace
06 colour
08 tincture
10 smattering, suggestion

tingle
06 shiver, thrill, tickle, tremor
07 prickle, tremble, vibrate
08 stinging, tickling
09 prickling
10 gooseflesh
12 goose-pimples
14 pins and needles

tinker
03 toy
04 play
05 fixer, Gypsy
06 dabble, fiddle, meddle,
mender, potter, tamper, trifle
09 itinerant, mess about
10 fool around, mess around

tinkle
04 buzz, call, ding, peal, ring
05 chime, chink, clink
06 jangle, jingle
09 phone call

tinsel
07 display, glitter, spangle
08 frippery, gimcrack, specious
09 gaudiness
10 garishness, triviality
11 flamboyance, ostentation
13 artificiality, worthlessness

tint
03 dye, hue
04 cast, tone, wash
05 rinse, shade, taint, tinge
06 affect, colour, streak
08 tincture

tiny
03 wee
04 mini
05 small, teeny
06 little, midget, minute, petite,
pocket, slight
09 itsy-bitsy, miniature,
minuscule, pint-sized
10 diminutive, negligible
11 Lilliputian, microscopic
13 infinitesimal, insignificant

tip
03 cap, end, nib, top

04 acme, apex, cant, clue, dump, gift, head, hint, lean, list, peak, perk, pour, tell, tilt
05 bonus, point, slant, spill
06 advice, midden, reward, summit, topple, unload
07 incline, pointer, pour out, present, suggest, warning
08 forecast, forewarn, gratuity, pinnacle, slag heap
09 baksheesh, extremity, pourboire
10 perquisite, refuse-heap, suggestion, topple over
11 information, rubbish-heap
14 recommendation

tip-off
04 clue, hint
07 pointer, warning
11 information

tipple
04 swig
05 booze, drink, quaff, usual
06 imbibe, liquor, poison
07 alcohol, indulge

tippler
03 sot
04 lush, soak, wino
05 dipso, drunk, toper
06 bibber, boozer, sponge
07 drinker, wine-bag
08 drunkard
09 inebriate
11 dipsomaniac, hard drinker

tipsy
05 drunk, happy, merry, tight
06 mellow, squiff, tiddly
07 squiffy

tirade
05 abuse
08 diatribe, harangue, outburst
09 invective, philippic
11 fulmination

tire
04 bore, drop, flag
05 drain, weary
07 exhaust, fatigue, tire out
08 enervate

tired
05 all in, bored, corny, fed up, jaded, stale, trite, weary
06 bushed, drowsy, sleepy
07 clichéd, whacked, worn out
08 dead-beat, dog-tired, fatigued, flagging
09 enervated, exhausted, fagged out, hackneyed, knackered, shattered
11 ready to drop

tireless
08 diligent, resolute, untiring
09 energetic, unwearied
10 determined, unflagging
13 indefatigable

tiresome
04 dull
06 boring, tiring, trying
07 humdrum, irksome, tedious
08 annoying
09 fatiguing, laborious, vexatious, wearisome
10 irritating, monotonous
12 exasperating

tiring
04 hard
05 tough
06 taxing
07 arduous
08 draining, exacting, wearying
09 fatiguing, laborious, strenuous, wearisome
10 enervating, exhausting

tiro, tyro
05 pupil
06 novice
07 learner, student, trainee
08 beginner, freshman, initiate, neophyte
09 greenhorn, novitiate
10 apprentice, catechumen, tenderfoot

tissue
03 web
04 mesh
05 flesh, gauze, stuff
07 Kleenex®, network, texture
08 gossamer, material
11 toilet paper

tit for tat
07 revenge
08 requital
10 quid pro quo
11 blow for blow, lex talionis, like for like, retaliation
13 countercharge

titan
05 Atlas, giant
08 colossus, Hercules, superman
09 leviathan

titanic
04 huge, vast
05 giant, jumbo
06 mighty
07 immense, massive
08 colossal, enormous, gigantic, towering

09 cyclopean, herculean
10 monumental, prodigious
11 mountainous

titbit
05 scrap, snack, treat
06 dainty, morsel
11 bonne-bouche

tithe
03 pay, tax
04 duty, give, levy, rate, rent, to
05 tenth
06 charge, impost, tariff

titillate
05 tease
06 arouse, excite, thrill, tickle
08 interest, intrigue
09 stimulate, tantalize

titillating
04 lewd, sexy
06 erotic
07 teasing
08 arousing, exciting
09 seductive, thrilling
10 intriguing, suggestive
11 provocative, stimulating

titivate
05 preen, primp, prink
06 doll up, make up, tart up

title
03 dub, tag
04 call, game, name, rank, term
05 claim, crown, deeds, label, match, prize, right, style
06 credit, handle, legend, office, stakes, status, trophy
07 contest, credits, heading, moniker, titular
08 headline, position
09 designate, sobriquet
11 appellation, designation
12 championship
13 form of address

titter
04 mock
05 laugh
06 cackle, giggle
07 chuckle, snicker, snigger

tittle-tattle
03 jaw, yak
04 chat, yack
06 gossip, rumour
07 blather, blether, chatter, hearsay, prattle, twaddle
08 chitchat
09 tell tales
10 yackety-yak

titular
05 token
07 nominal

08 official, so-called

toadstool see **mushroom**

toady
04 fawn
05 crawl, creep
06 cringe, fawner, grovel, jackal, kowtow, lackey, minion, suck up, yes-man
07 crawler, flatter, flunkey
08 bootlick, butter up, hanger-on, parasite, truckler
09 flatterer, groveller, sycophant
10 arse-licker, bootlicker
11 curry favour, kiss the feet

toast
04 bake, heat, warm
05 brown, crisp, drink, grill
06 health, heat up, honour, pledge, salute, warm up
07 drink to, tribute
10 salutation
11 compliments

today
03 now
07 just now, this day
08 nowadays, right now
09 these days
11 this evening, this morning, this very day
12 at this moment
13 this afternoon
14 the present time

toddle
04 reel, rock, sway
05 lurch, shake, waver
06 falter, teeter, totter, waddle
07 stagger, stumble
14 walk unsteadily

to-do
04 flap, fuss, stew, stir
05 hoo-ha
06 bother, bustle, flurry, furore, rumpus, tumult, uproar
07 quarrel, ruction, turmoil
08 brouhaha
09 agitation, commotion
10 excitement
11 disturbance, performance

together
04 calm, cool
06 in a row, stable, united
07 as a team, jointly
08 composed, in unison
09 all at once, at one time, in concert, organized
10 hand in hand, side by side
11 down-to-earth, level-headed

12 collectively, concurrently, continuously, in succession, successively, well-adjusted, well-balanced
13 at the same time, consecutively, in conjunction
14 simultaneously
15 in collaboration

toil
04 slog, work
05 graft, grind, slave, sweat
06 drudge, effort, labour, strive
08 drudgery, exertion, hard work, industry, struggle
10 donkey-work
11 application, elbow grease
15 work like a Trojan

toiler
05 navvy, slave
06 drudge, menial, worker
07 grafter, slogger
08 labourer
10 workaholic

toilet
02 WC
03 bog, loo
04 john, kazi
06 urinal
07 latrine
08 bathroom, lavatory, rest room, the gents, washroom
09 cloakroom, the ladies
10 powder room
11 convenience

toilsome
04 hard
05 tough
06 severe, taxing, uphill
07 arduous, painful, tedious
09 difficult, fatiguing, herculean, laborious, strenuous, wearisome
12 backbreaking

token
04 clue, disc, mark, sign
06 coupon, emblem, symbol
07 counter, memento, minimal, nominal, voucher, warning
08 evidence, keepsake, memorial, reminder, souvenir, symbolic
10 emblematic, indication
11 perfunctory, recognition
12 demonstration
14 representation

tolerable
02 OK
04 fair, so-so
06 not bad

07 average
08 adequate, all right, bearable, mediocre, middling, ordinary, passable
10 acceptable, reasonable
13 no great shakes, unexceptional

tolerance
06 lenity
07 laxness, stamina
08 leniency, patience
09 allowance, clearance, endurance, fortitude, toughness, variation
10 indulgence, liberalism, toleration
11 forbearance
13 understanding
14 open-mindedness, permissiveness
15 broad-mindedness

tolerant
03 lax
04 fair, soft
07 lenient, liberal, patient
08 catholic
09 compliant, easy-going, forgiving, indulgent
10 charitable, forbearing, open-minded, permissive
11 broad-minded, kind-hearted, magnanimous, sympathetic
12 unprejudiced
13 understanding

tolerate
04 bear, take
05 abide, admit, allow, stand
06 accept, endure, permit
07 condone, indulge, receive
08 sanction
09 put up with
11 countenance

toleration
06 lenity
07 laxness, stamina
08 leniency, sympathy
09 allowance, endurance, fortitude, toughness
10 acceptance, indulgence, liberalism, resilience, resistance, sufferance
11 forbearance, magnanimity
14 open-mindedness, permissiveness
15 broad-mindedness

toll
03 fee, tax
04 call, cost, duty, levy, loss, peal, rate, ring, warn

05 chime, clang, knell, sound
06 charge, damage, herald, injury, signal, strike, tariff
07 payment, penalty
08 announce

tomb
05 crypt, grave, vault
08 catacomb, cenotaph
09 mausoleum, sepulchre
11 burial-place

tombstone
05 stone
08 memorial, monument
09 headstone
10 gravestone

tome
04 book, opus, work
06 volume

tomfoolery
05 hooey, larks
06 idiocy
07 inanity
08 clowning, mischief
09 horseplay, silliness
10 buffoonery, skylarking
11 foolishness, shenanigans
12 childishness, larking about

tone
03 air, hue
04 feel, mood, note, tint, vein
05 pitch, shade, sound, style, tenor, tinge, tonal
06 accent, colour, effect, go with, humour, manner, timbre
07 quality
08 attitude, tincture, tonality
10 co-ordinate, expression, go well with, inflection, intonation, modulation

◻**tone down**
06 dampen, soften, temper
08 mitigate, moderate, play down, restrain
09 alleviate, soft-pedal

◻**tone up**
04 trim
07 freshen, shape up, touch up
10 invigorate

tongue
04 cant, talk
05 argot, idiom, lingo, slang
06 jargon, patois, speech
07 dialect, glottic, lingual
08 language, parlance
10 vernacular

tongue-tied
04 dumb, mute
06 silent
10 dumbstruck, speechless

12 inarticulate, lost for words

tonic
06 bracer, fillip
08 pick-me-up
09 analeptic, refresher, stimulant
11 restorative
12 shot in the arm

too
04 also, over, very
06 as well, overly, unduly
07 besides
08 likewise, moreover
09 extremely
10 in addition
11 excessively, furthermore
12 inordinately

tool
04 dupe, pawn, work
05 agent, chase, gismo, means
06 agency, device, gadget, medium, puppet, stooge
07 cat's paw, fashion, flunkey, machine, utensil, vehicle
08 artefact, decorate, hireling
09 apparatus, implement
10 instrument
11 contraption, contrivance

➤ *Types of tool*:
03 awl, axe, hod, hoe, saw
04 adze, file, fork, jack, pick, rake, rasp, rule, vice
05 auger, bevel, clamp, dolly, drill, level, plane, punch, snips, spade, tongs
06 bodkin, chisel, dibber, gimlet, hammer, jig-saw, mallet, mortar, needle, pestle, pliers, plough, sander, scythe, shears, shovel, sickle, trowel, wrench
07 bradawl, chopper, cleaver, crowbar, forceps, fretsaw, hacksaw, handsaw, hay fork, mattock, pick-axe, pincers, scalpel, scriber, stapler, T-square
08 billhook, chainsaw, dividers, penknife, scissors, spraygun, tenon-saw, thresher, tweezers
09 grass-rake, pitchfork, plumb-line, secateurs, set-square
10 jackhammer, paper-knife, protractor
11 brace and bit, crochet hook, pocket-knife, screwdriver, spirit level
12 pruning-knife, sledgehammer,

socket-wrench
13 pinking-shears, pruning-shears, soldering-iron
➤ See also **saw**

tooth
04 fang, tush, tusk
05 molar, prong
06 dentil
07 incisor
08 denticle
10 masticator

➤ *Types of teeth. We have omitted the word* **tooth** *from names given in the following list but you may need to include this word as part of the solution to some crossword clues.*
03 cap, eye
04 baby, back, fang, gold, milk, tush, tusk
05 crown, false, first, molar, plate
06 bridge, canine, wisdom
07 denture, grinder, incisor
08 bicuspid, dentures, dog-tooth, premolar
09 bucktooth
10 carnassial
12 snaggletooth
14 central incisor, lateral incisor

toothsome
04 nice
05 sweet, tasty, yummy
08 luscious, tempting
09 delicious, palatable
10 appetizing, delectable
11 flavoursome, scrumptious
13 mouth-watering

top
03 cap, lid, tip
04 acme, apex, beat, best, head, lead, main, peak, rule
05 chief, crest, crown, first, outdo, prime, shirt, upper
06 apogee, better, blouse, climax, exceed, finest, jersey, jumper, summit, T-shirt, vertex, zenith
07 garnish, highest, leading, maximum, stopper, supreme, surpass, sweater, topmost
08 decorate, dominant, foremost, greatest, outstrip, pinnacle, pullover, surmount, tee shirt
09 finish off, paramount, principal, uppermost
10 pre-eminent, sweatshirt
11 culminating, culmination

on top of the world

05 happy
06 elated
08 ecstatic, exultant, thrilled
09 overjoyed
11 exhilarated, on cloud nine, over the moon

over the top

07 extreme, too much
09 excessive
10 exorbitant, immoderate
11 extravagant, uncalled-for
12 unreasonable

top up

05 add to, boost
06 refill, reload
07 augment
08 increase, recharge
09 replenish
10 supplement

topic

05 issue, point, theme
06 matter, thesis
07 subject
08 argument, question

topical

06 recent
07 current, popular
08 familiar, relevant, up-to-date
12 contemporary

topmost

03 top
05 first, upper
06 apical
07 highest, leading, supreme
08 dominant, foremost, loftiest
09 principal, uppermost

top-notch

02 A1
03 ace, top
04 cool, fine, mega
05 crack, prime, super
07 leading, premier, supreme
08 peerless, splendid, superior
09 admirable, excellent, first rate, matchless, top-flight
10 first-class
11 exceptional, outstanding
12 second-to-none

topple

04 fall, oust
05 upset
06 totter, tumble, unseat
08 collapse, dethrone, displace
09 bring down, overthrow
11 overbalance

topsy-turvy

07 chaotic, jumbled, mixed-up
08 confused
09 inside out
10 disorderly, upside down
11 disarranged, in confusion

torch

05 brand, light
07 cresset
08 flambeau
10 flashlight

torment

03 vex
04 bane, pain, pest
05 agony, annoy, tease, worry
06 badger, harrow, misery, ordeal, pester, plague
07 afflict, anguish, bedevil, scourge, torture, trouble
08 distress, vexation
09 persecute, suffering
10 affliction, harassment
11 persecution, provocation
15 thorn in the flesh

torn

03 cut
04 rent, slit
05 split
06 ragged, ripped, unsure
07 divided
08 wavering
09 dithering, lacerated, uncertain, undecided
10 irresolute
11 vacillating

tornado

04 gale
05 storm
06 squall
07 cyclone, monsoon, tempest, twister, typhoon
09 hurricane, whirlwind

torpid

04 dead, dull, lazy, numb, slow
05 inert
06 drowsy, sleepy, supine
07 passive
08 inactive, indolent, lifeless, listless, sluggish
09 apathetic, lethargic, nerveless, somnolent

torpor

05 sloth
06 apathy
07 inertia, languor
08 dullness, hebetude, laziness, lethargy, numbness
09 indolence, inertness, passivity, torpidity
10 drowsiness, inactivity, sleepiness, somnolence
12 listlessness, sluggishness

torrent

04 gush, rush
05 flood, spate, storm
06 deluge, stream, volley
07 barrage, cascade
08 downpour, outburst
10 inundation

torrid

03 hot
04 arid, sexy
06 desert, erotic, steamy
07 amorous, blazing, parched
08 scorched, sizzling, stifling
09 scorching, waterless
10 passionate, sweltering

tortuous

06 zigzag
07 curving, sinuous, winding
08 indirect, involved, twisting
10 circuitous, convoluted, roundabout, serpentine
11 complicated

torture

04 pain, rack
05 abuse, agony, worry
06 harrow, plague, punish
07 afflict, crucify, torment
09 persecute, suffering
10 affliction, excruciate
11 persecution

toss

03 lob, shy
04 cast, flip, jolt, rock, roll,
05 chuck, fling, heave, lurch, pitch, shake, sling, throw

tot

03 nip
04 baby, dram, mite, shot, slug
05 bairn, child
06 finger, infant
07 measure, toddler

tot up

03 add, sum
05 add up, count, tally, total
06 reckon
07 compute, count up
09 calculate

total

03 add, all, lot, sum, tot
04 full, make, mass, rank
05 add up, count, reach, sheer, sum up, tot up, utter, whole
06 all-out, come to, entire
07 count up, perfect
08 absolute, amount to, complete, entirety, outright, thorough, totality
09 aggregate, downright
11 unmitigated, unqualified
13 comprehensive

totalitarian
08 despotic, one-party
09 tyrannous
10 monolithic, oppressive
11 dictatorial
12 undemocratic
13 authoritarian

totality
03 all, sum
05 total, whole
06 cosmos
07 pleroma
08 entirety, fullness, universe
09 aggregate, wholeness
12 completeness

totally
05 fully, quite
06 wholly
07 utterly
08 entirely
10 absolutely, completely
12 consummately
14 wholeheartedly
15 unconditionally

totter
04 reel, rock, roll, sway
05 lurch, shake, waver
06 falter, teeter, wobble
07 be shaky, stagger, stumble
10 be unstable, be unsteady

touch
03 bit, eat, hit, jot, pat, pet, tap
04 abut, dash, feel, hint, hold, meet, move, skim, stir
05 brush, cover, drink, equal, flair, knack, match, pinch, reach, rival, skill, speck, style, taste, tinge, trace, upset, weave, whiff
06 adjoin, affect, aspect, attain, better, border, broach, caress, come to, detail, devour, finger, finish, fondle, handle, haptic, manner, method, nicety, regard, sadden, strike, stroke, tickle
07 concern, contact, disturb, impinge, impress, inspire, involve, mention, soupçon, surface, refer to, speak of, tactile, texture
08 addition, allude to, approach, come near
09 dexterity, direction, tactility, technique
10 connection, suggestion
13 hold a candle to
14 be contiguous to, have an effect on, have an impact on
15 come into contact

◻touch off
04 fire
05 begin, cause, light
06 foment, ignite, set off
07 actuate, provoke, trigger
08 initiate, spark off
10 trigger off

◻touch up
06 revamp
07 brush up, enhance, improve, patch up, perfect, retouch
08 polish up, renovate

touch-and-go
04 dire, near
05 close, dodgy, hairy, risky
06 sticky, tricky
08 critical, perilous
09 dangerous, uncertain

touched
03 mad
04 daft
05 barmy, batty, crazy, dotty, loopy, moved, nutty, upset
06 insane
07 bonkers, stirred
08 affected, deranged, inspired
09 disturbed, impressed
10 influenced, unbalanced

touchiness
09 bad temper, testiness
10 grumpiness, tetchiness
11 crabbedness, grouchiness
12 captiousness, irascibility, irritability

touching
06 moving, tender
07 piteous, pitiful
08 pathetic, pitiable, poignant
09 affecting, emotional

touchstone
04 norm, test
05 gauge, guide, model, proof
07 measure, pattern
08 standard, template
09 benchmark, yardstick

touchy
04 edgy
05 cross
06 grumpy
07 crabbed, grouchy, prickly
08 captious
09 irascible, irritable
11 bad-tempered, thin-skinned
13 over-sensitive

tough
03 fit, yob
04 firm, grim, hard, lout, thug

05 brute, bully, burly, chewy, hardy, harsh, rigid, rough, rowdy, solid, stern, stiff
06 knotty, robust, severe, strict, strong, sturdy, uphill
07 adamant, arduous, callous, durable, fibrous, gristly, rubbery, unlucky, violent
08 baffling, exacting, hardened, hooligan, leathery, muscular
09 difficult, laborious, obstinate, resilient, resistant, strenuous, well-built
10 determined, perplexing
11 distressing, unfortunate
14 tough as leather, uncompromising

toughen
05 brace
06 harden
07 fortify, stiffen
09 reinforce
10 strengthen

toughness
04 grit
08 firmness, obduracy, strength, tenacity
09 hardiness
10 resilience, resistance
13 determination, inflexibility

tour
04 ride, trip
05 drive, jaunt, round, visit
06 course, outing
07 circuit, go round
08 sightsee
09 excursion, walkabout
10 expedition, inspection
13 peregrination

tourist
07 tripper, visitor, voyager
09 sightseer, sojourner, traveller
10 day-tripper, rubberneck
12 holidaymaker

tournament
04 meet
05 event, joust, match
06 series
07 contest, meeting
11 competition
12 championship

tousled
07 ruffled, rumpled, tangled
11 disarranged, dishevelled

tout
03 ask
04 hawk, plug, push, sell
05 trade

06 appeal, market, peddle
07 promote, solicit
09 advertise

tow
03 lug, tug
04 drag, draw, haul, pull
05 trail

◻**in tow**
08 in convoy
12 accompanying

towards
02 to
03 for
06 almost, nearly
07 close to, nearing
10 concerning, on the way to

tower
03 cap, top
04 loom, rear, rise, soar
05 excel, mount
06 ascend, exceed
08 dominate, overlook
10 overshadow

▬ *Types of tower. We have
omitted the word* **tower** *from
names given in the following list
but you may need to include this
word as part of the solution to
some crossword clues.*
04 bell, fort, keep
05 minar, spire, water
06 belfry, castle, church,
   column, donjon, Eiffel,
   pagoda, turret
07 bastion, citadel, lookout,
   minaret, mirador, steeple
08 barbican, bastille, fortress,
   hill-fort, martello
09 belvedere, campanile,
   gate-tower, peel-tower
10 skyscraper, stronghold,
   tower block, watchtower
13 fortification, Tower of
   London

towering
04 high, tall
05 great, lofty
07 extreme, soaring
08 gigantic, imposing
10 impressive, monumental
11 magnificent, outstanding
12 overpowering

town
04 city
05 burgh, urban
06 pueblo
07 borough, new town,
   suburbs, village
08 township

10 county town, market town,
   metropolis, settlement
11 conurbation
12 municipality
➤ See also **city**

town-dweller
05 towny
07 burgher, citizen, oppidan
08 townsman, urbanite
10 townswoman

toxic
06 deadly, lethal
07 baneful, harmful, noxious
09 dangerous, poisonous

toy
04 play
05 dally, flirt, sport
06 bauble, fiddle, tinker, trifle
07 trinket
09 mess about, plaything

trace
03 bit, dog, jot, map
04 copy, dash, draw, find, hint,
   hunt, mark, seek, sign, spot
05 chart, draft, pinch, scent,
   smack, spoor, stalk, tinge,
   touch, track, trail
06 depict, detect, follow,
   pursue, shadow, sketch
07 mark out, outline, remains,
   remnant, soupçon, uncover,
   unearth, vestige
08 discover, evidence
09 suspicion, track down
10 indication, suggestion

track
03 dog, way
04 hunt, path, rail, tail, wake
05 chase, orbit, route, scent,
   spoor, stalk, trace, trail
06 course, groove, pursue
08 footmark, footstep
09 footprint
10 trajectory

◻**keep track of**
05 check, watch
06 follow, record
07 monitor, observe
11 keep an eye on

◻**make tracks**
02 go
04 dash
05 leave, scram
06 beat it, depart
10 hit the road

◻**track down**
04 find
05 catch, dig up, trace
06 expose, turn up

07 capture, nose out, run
   down, uncover, unearth
08 hunt down, sniff out
09 ferret out
10 run to earth

tract
03 lot
04 area, plot, zone
05 essay
06 homily, region, sermon
07 booklet, expanse, stretch
08 pamphlet, treatise
09 discourse, monograph
12 disquisition, dissertation

tractable
04 tame
06 docile, pliant
07 pliable, willing
08 amenable, biddable,
   obedient, yielding
09 compliant, malleable
10 governable, manageable
12 controllable

traction
04 drag, grip, pull
07 draught, haulage, pulling
08 adhesion, friction

trade
03 buy, job, run
04 deal, line, sell, swap, work
05 craft, skill
06 barter, buying, custom,
   market, peddle, switch
07 dealing, selling, traffic
08 business, commerce,
   exchange, transact
09 marketing
10 do business, line of work,
   occupation, profession
11 merchandise, trafficking
12 transactions

trademark
04 logo, mark, name, sign
05 badge, brand, label, stamp
06 emblem, symbol
08 hallmark, insignia
09 brand name, tradename
10 speciality
11 peculiarity
12 idiosyncrasy
14 characteristic

trader
05 buyer
06 broker, dealer, seller, vendor
07 peddler
08 merchant, retailer, supplier
09 marketeer, tradesman
10 shopkeeper, trafficker
11 tradeswoman

tradesman, tradeswoman
05 buyer
06 dealer, seller, vendor, worker
08 merchant, retailer
09 craftsman
10 journeyman, shopkeeper
11 craftswoman

tradition
03 way
04 rite
05 habit, usage
06 belief, custom, praxis, ritual
08 ceremony, folklore, practice
10 convention, observance
11 institution

traditional
03 old, set
04 folk, oral
05 fixed, usual
06 age-old
08 habitual, historic
09 customary, unwritten
11 established
12 conventional,
    time-honoured

traduce
04 slag
05 abuse, decry, knock, smear
06 defame, insult, malign,
    revile, vilify
07 blacken, run down, slander
09 denigrate, deprecate,
    disparage
10 calumniate, depreciate
12 misrepresent

traducer
06 abuser
07 defamer, knocker, smearer
08 asperser, vilifier
09 detractor, slanderer
10 denigrator, deprecator,
    disparager, mud-slinger

traffic
03 buy
04 cars, deal, sell
05 trade
06 barter, peddle
07 dealing, freight, trading
08 business, commerce,
    peddling, shipping, vehicles
09 relations, transport
10 do business, passengers
14 transportation

trafficker
06 broker, dealer, trader
07 peddler
08 merchant

tragedy
04 blow

08 calamity, disaster
10 affliction, misfortune
11 catastrophe, unhappiness

tragic
03 sad
04 dire
05 awful, fatal
07 unhappy, unlucky
08 dreadful, ill-fated, pitiable,
    shocking, terrible, wretched
09 appalling, miserable
10 deplorable, disastrous
11 unfortunate
12 catastrophic

trail
03 dog, lag, tow, way
04 drag, draw, hang, haul, hunt,
    path, pull, road, tail, wake
05 chase, route, scent, spoor,
    stalk, sweep, trace, track
06 dangle, dawdle, follow,
    pursue, shadow, stream
08 footpath, straggle
09 footmarks
10 footprints

▢ trail away
04 fade, sink
06 lessen, shrink, weaken
07 die away, dwindle, tail off
08 decrease, diminish, fade
    away, fall away, melt away,
    peter out, taper off, trail off
09 disappear

train
03 aim, set
04 file, line, path
05 coach, drill, focus, groom,
    learn, point, study, suite,
    teach, trail, tutor
06 column, convoy, ground,
    series, stream, string
07 caravan, cortège, educate,
    prepare, retinue, work out
08 exercise, instruct, practise,
    rehearse, sequence
09 entourage, followers,
    household, inculcate
10 attendants, discipline,
    procession, succession
13 concatenation

trainer
05 coach, tutor
07 handler, teacher
08 educator
10 instructor

training
05 drill
07 lessons, tuition, workout
08 coaching, exercise, learning,
    practice, teaching, tutoring

09 education, grounding,
    schooling
10 discipline, working-out
11 instruction, preparation
14 apprenticeship

traipse
04 plod, slog, trek
05 trail, tramp
06 slouch, trudge

trait
07 feature, quality
09 attribute
11 peculiarity
12 idiosyncrasy
14 characteristic

traitor
05 Judas
08 betrayer, deceiver, defector,
    deserter, informer, quisling,
    renegade, turncoat
12 collaborator, double-dealer
13 double-crosser
14 fifth columnist

traitorous
05 false
06 untrue
08 apostate, disloyal, renegade
09 faithless, seditious
10 perfidious, unfaithful
11 treacherous, treasonable
13 double-dealing
14 double-crossing

trajectory
04 line, path
05 orbit, route, track, trail
06 course, flight
10 flight path

trammel
03 bar, net, tie
04 bond, clog, curb, rein
05 block, catch, chain, check
06 enmesh, entrap, fetter,
    hamper, hinder, impede
07 ensnare, inhibit, shackle
08 handicap, restrain, restrict
09 hindrance
10 impediment

tramp
03 bum
04 hike, hobo, plod, roam, rove,
    slut, tart, trek, walk
05 march, stamp, stomp, stump,
    trail, tread, wench, whore
06 dosser, ramble, trudge
07 traipse, trollop, vagrant
08 scrubber, vagabond
10 down-and-out, loose
    woman, prostitute

trample
05 crush, stamp, tread
06 squash
07 flatten

trance
05 dream, spell
06 stupor
07 ecstasy, rapture, reverie
09 catalepsy

tranquil
04 calm, cool
05 quiet, still
06 hushed, placid, serene
07 relaxed, restful
08 laid-back, peaceful
12 even-tempered
13 imperturbable

tranquillity
04 calm, hush, rest
05 peace, quiet
06 repose
08 ataraxia, calmness,
   coolness, quietude, serenity
09 quietness, stillness
10 equanimity, sedateness
11 restfulness
12 peacefulness

tranquillize
04 calm, lull
05 quell, quiet, relax
06 pacify, sedate
09 narcotize

tranquillizer
06 downer, opiate
08 narcotic, sedative
09 calmative
11 barbiturate
12 sleeping pill

transact
06 handle, manage, settle
07 conduct, execute, perform
08 carry out, conclude
09 discharge, negotiate
10 accomplish

transaction
04 deal, deed
06 action, affair, annals, doings
07 affairs, bargain, minutes
08 business, handling
09 agreement, enactment
10 enterprise, proceeding
11 negotiation, proceedings

transcend
04 beat
05 excel, outdo
06 exceed
07 eclipse, surpass
08 go beyond, outshine
09 rise above

transcendence
09 sublimity, supremacy
10 ascendancy, excellence
11 pre-eminence, superiority
12 predominance
13 transcendency
15 incomparability

transcendent
07 sublime, supreme
08 numinous, peerless
09 excellent, excelling,
   ineffable, matchless, spiritual
10 superhuman, surpassing
11 magnificent, superlative
12 unparalleled
13 unsurpassable

transcendental
08 mystical
09 spiritual
10 mysterious
12 metaphysical, otherworldly,
   supernatural
13 preternatural

transcribe
04 note
06 copy up, record, render
07 copy out, rewrite, write up
08 take down, write out
09 reproduce, translate
13 transliterate

transcript
04 copy, note
06 record
10 manuscript
11 translation
13 transcription
15 transliteration

transfer
04 move, take
05 carry, grant, shift
06 change, convey, remove
07 consign, removal
08 relocate, transmit
09 transport, transpose
10 assignment, conveyance,
   relocation, transplant
12 displacement, transference,
   transmission
13 transposition

transfigure
05 alter, exalt
06 change
07 convert, glorify
09 transform, transmute
11 apotheosize
12 metamorphose

transfix
04 hold, stun
05 rivet, spear, spike, stick

06 impale, pierce, skewer
07 engross, petrify
08 paralyse
09 mesmerize, spellbind

transform
05 adapt, alter, renew
06 change
07 convert, rebuilt, remodel
11 reconstruct, transfigure
12 metamorphose,
   transmogrify

transformation
06 change
08 mutation
09 sea change
10 alteration, metastasis
13 metamorphosis
15 transfiguration

transfuse
06 instil
07 pervade, suffuse
08 permeate, transfer

transgress
03 err, sin
05 break, lapse
06 breach, exceed, offend
07 disobey, violate
08 infringe, overstep, trespass
09 misbehave

transgression
03 sin
04 debt
05 crime, fault, lapse, wrong
06 breach
07 misdeed, offence
08 iniquity, trespass
09 violation
10 infraction, peccadillo
12 infringement, misbehaviour,
   misdemeanour

transgressor
05 felon
06 debtor, sinner
07 culprit, villain
08 criminal, evil-doer, offender
09 miscreant, wrongdoer
10 lawbreaker, trespasser

transience
07 brevity
08 caducity, fugacity
09 briefness, shortness
11 evanescence
12 ephemerality, fleetingness
14 transitoriness

transient
05 brief, short
06 flying
07 passing
08 fleeting

09 ephemeral, fugacious,
   momentary, temporary
10 short-lived, transitory

transit
06 travel
07 haulage, journey, passage
08 carriage, crossing,
   shipment, transfer
10 conveyance, journeying
14 transportation

◻**in transit**
05 by air, by sea
06 by rail, by road
07 en route
08 on the way
10 travelling

transition
04 flux, move
06 change, switch
07 passage, passing
08 movement, progress
10 change-over, conversion
11 development, progression
13 metamorphosis,
   transmutation
14 transformation

transitional
07 passing
08 changing
09 temporary, unsettled
11 provisional
12 evolutionary, intermediate
13 developmental

transitory
05 brief, short
07 passing
08 fleeting
09 ephemeral, fugacious,
   temporary, transient

translate
04 move
05 alter, shift
06 change, decode, render
08 construe, decipher, transfer
09 interpret, transmute
10 paraphrase, transcribe
12 transmogrify

translation
04 crib, move
05 gloss, shift
06 change
09 rendering, rendition
10 alteration, conversion
11 explanation, metaphrasis
13 metamorphosis,
   transcription, transmutation
14 interpretation,
   transformation

translator
07 exegete, glosser
08 dragoman, linguist, polyglot
09 exegetist, glossator
10 metaphrast, paraphrast
11 interpreter, paraphraser

translucent
05 clear
06 limpid
08 pellucid
10 diaphanous, see-through
11 transparent

transmigration
13 reincarnation
14 metempsychosis,
   Pythagoreanism,
   transformation

transmission
04 show
06 signal, spread
07 episode, sending
08 relaying, shipment, transfer
09 broadcast, diffusion,
   programme, transport
10 conveyance, production
12 broadcasting, transference
13 communication, dissemination

transmit
04 bear, send
05 carry, radio, relay, remit
06 convey, pass on, spread
07 diffuse, forward, network
08 dispatch, transfer
09 broadcast, transport
11 communicate, disseminate

transmute
05 alter
06 change, remake
07 convert
09 transform, translate
11 transfigure
12 metamorphose,
   transmogrify

transparency
05 photo, slide, water
07 clarity, picture
09 filminess, frankness,
   gauziness, limpidity
10 candidness, directness,
   limpidness, photograph
12 apparentness, explicitness,
   pellucidness, translucence
13 translucidity

transparent
04 open
05 clear, filmy, gauzy, sheer
06 candid, direct, patent
07 evident, obvious, visible
08 distinct, explicit, pellucid

10 diaphanous, see-through
11 discernible, perceptible,
   translucent, undisguised
12 unmistakable

transpire
05 arise, ensue, occur, prove
06 appear, befall, happen
07 come out, turn out
09 come about, take place
10 come to pass
11 become known, be
   disclosed, come to light

transplant
04 move
05 graft, repot, shift
06 remove, uproot
07 replant
08 displace, relocate, resettle

transport
04 bear, haul, move, ship, take
05 bliss, bring, carry, exile
06 convey, deport, remove
07 delight, ecstasy, elation,
   freight, haulage, rapture,
   removal, transit, vehicle
08 carriage, euphoria,
   shipping, transfer
09 captivate, carry away,
   electrify, spellbind
10 conveyance
13 seventh heaven

transportation
07 freight, haulage, transit
08 carriage, shipment,
   shipping, transfer
10 conveyance

transpose
04 move, swap
05 alter, shift
06 change, invert, switch
07 convert, reorder
08 exchange, transfer
10 substitute

transverse
05 cross
07 oblique
08 diagonal
09 crossways, crosswise

trap
03 gin, net
04 dupe, lure, mesh, wile
05 catch, noose, snare, trick
06 ambush, corner, device,
   enmesh, entrap
07 beguile, confine, deceive,
   ensnare, pitfall, springe
08 artifice, inveigle, trickery
09 booby-trap, stratagem
10 subterfuge

trapped
05 duped, stuck
06 caught, netted, snared
08 ambushed, cornered, deceived, ensnared
09 inveigled
10 surrounded

trapper
06 hunter
08 huntsman, voyageur
12 backwoodsman, frontiersman

trappings
04 gear
05 dress
06 finery, livery, things
07 clothes, panoply, raiment
08 fittings, fixtures, housings
09 equipment, trimmings
10 adornments, fripperies
11 decorations, furnishings
13 accoutrements, paraphernalia

trash
03 rot
04 bull, bunk, junk, scum
05 dregs, tripe, waste
06 drivel, litter, rabble, refuse
07 garbage, rubbish
10 balderdash
12 gobbledygook

trashy
04 naff
05 cheap
06 flimsy, grotty, shabby, shoddy, tawdry, tinsel
08 inferior, rubbishy
09 third-rate, worthless

trauma
04 hurt, jolt, pain
05 agony, shock, upset, wound
06 damage, injury, lesion
07 anguish, torture
09 suffering

traumatic
07 harmful, hurtful, painful
08 shocking, wounding
09 stressful, upsetting
11 distressing, frightening

travail
04 slog, toil
05 grind, sweat, tears
06 effort, labour, strain, stress
08 distress, exertion, hardship
09 suffering
10 birth-pangs, childbirth
11 labour pains, tribulation

travel
04 move, roam, rove, tour

05 cover, cross
06 ramble, voyage, wander
07 explore, journey, passage, proceed, touring, tourism
08 progress, traverse
09 excursion, make a trip
10 expedition, go overseas, journeying, wanderings
11 see the world, sightseeing
13 globetrotting

traveller
03 rep
05 Gypsy, hiker, nomad, tramp
06 tinker, tourer
07 drifter, migrant, tripper, tourist, vagrant, voyager
08 commuter, explorer, wanderer, wayfarer
09 itinerant, passenger
12 globetrotter, holidaymaker

travelling
06 mobile, moving, roving
07 migrant, nomadic, vagrant
09 itinerant, migrating, migratory, wayfaring
11 peripatetic

travel-worn
07 waygone, wayworn
08 footsore
10 saddle-sore
11 travel-weary

traverse
03 ply
04 ford, roam, span
05 cross, range
06 bridge, wander
08 go across, pass over
09 go through, negotiate
12 travel across

travesty
04 sham
05 farce, spoof
06 parody, send-up, wind-up
07 apology, mockery, take-off
09 burlesque, tall story
10 caricature, perversion

treacherous
03 icy
05 false, risky
06 unsafe, untrue
08 disloyal, perilous, slippery
09 dangerous, deceitful, hazardous, two-timing
10 perfidious, traitorous, unfaithful, unreliable
11 duplicitous
12 back-stabbing
14 double-crossing

treacherously
07 falsely
10 disloyally
11 deceitfully, faithlessly
12 perfidiously

treachery
07 treason
08 betrayal, sabotage
09 duplicity, falseness, perfidy
10 disloyalty, infidelity
13 deceitfulness, double-dealing, faithlessness
14 double-crossing

tread
04 gait, pace, plod, step, trek
05 crush, march, press, stamp
06 squash, stride, trudge
07 flatten, trample
08 footfall, footmark, footstep
09 footprint, press down

❑**tread on someone's toes**
03 irk, vex
05 annoy, upset
06 bruise, injure, offend
07 affront
08 infringe

treason
06 mutiny
07 perfidy
08 sedition
09 duplicity, rebellion, treachery
10 disloyalty, subversion
11 lese-majesty

treasonable
08 disloyal, mutinous
09 faithless, seditious
10 perfidious, rebellious, subversive, traitorous

treasure
04 cash, gems, gold, love
05 adore, cache, guard, hoard, money, prize, value
06 jewels, riches, wealth
07 cherish, fortune, worship

treasurer
06 bursar, purser
07 cashier

treasury
04 bank
05 cache, hoard, store, vault
06 assets, corpus
07 capital, coffers
09 exchequer, thesaurus
10 repository, storehouse

treat
03 buy, fun, rub, use
04 cure, give, heal, tend, view

05 amuse, apply, lay on, nurse, put on, smear, stand
06 handle, manage, pay for, regale, regard, review, thrill
07 discuss, present, take out
08 attend to, consider, deal with, medicate, surprise
09 excursion, look after
10 indulgence, minister to
13 behave towards

treatise
05 essay, paper, study, tract
06 thesis
08 pamphlet, prodrome
09 discourse, monograph
10 exposition
12 disquisition, dissertation

treatment
04 care, cure
05 usage
06 action, remedy
07 conduct, dealing, healing, nursing, surgery, therapy
08 coverage, dealings, handling
09 behaviour
10 medicament, medication
12 manipulation, therapeutics

treaty
04 bond, deal, pact
07 bargain, compact
08 alliance, contract, covenant
09 agreement, concordat

➤ *Names of treaties and agreements*:
04 Rome (Treaty of)
05 Dover (Treaty of), Ghent (Treaty of), Paris (Treaties of)
06 Amiens (Treaty of), Poland (Partitions of), Tilsit (Treaties of)
07 Utrecht (Peace of)
09 Bucharest (Treaties of), Pressburg (Treaty of)
10 Magna Carta, Paris Pacts, Versailles (Treaty of), Warsaw Pact, Westphalia (Peace of)
11 Locarno Pact, Westminster (Treaty of)
12 Brest-Litovsk (Treaty of)
13 Social Chapter, Triple Entente
14 Hague Agreement, Hoare-Laval Pact
15 Entente Cordiale, Munich Agreement

treble
04 high
06 piping, shrill, triple

09 threefold
11 high-pitched

tree
04 bush
05 shrub
08 arboreal

➤ *Trees include*:
03 ash, bay, box, elm, fig, fir, gum, oak, yew
04 acer, lime, palm, pear, pine, plum, teak
05 alder, apple, aspen, balsa, beech, birch, cedar, elder, fruit, hazel, larch, maple, plane, rowan, yucca
06 acacia, almond, bonsai, cherry, laurel, linden, poplar, spruce, walnut, willow
07 conifer, cypress, dogwood, hickory, redwood, sequoia
08 chestnut, date palm, Dutch elm, hardwood, hawthorn, hornbeam, mahogany, softwood, sycamore, tamarisk
09 deciduous, evergreen, jacaranda, whitebeam
10 blackthorn, cottonwood, eucalyptus, rubber tree, witch hazel
11 coconut palm, mountain ash, pussy willow, silver birch
12 monkey puzzle
13 horse chestnut, weeping willow

➤ See also **plant**

trek
04 hike, plod, slog, trip, walk
05 march, tramp
06 ramble, safari, trudge
07 journey, odyssey, traipse
10 expedition

trellis
03 net
04 grid, mesh
05 grate
06 grille
07 grating, lattice, network
09 framework
12 reticulation

tremble
04 rock
05 quake, shake
06 judder, quiver, shiver, tremor
07 shudder, vibrate

trembling
06 shakes
07 quaking, rocking, shaking

09 quavering, quivering, shivering, vibration
11 oscillation

tremendous
04 huge, vast
05 great
06 wicked
07 amazing, immense, massive
08 colossal, enormous, gigantic, smashing, terrific
09 wonderful
10 impressive, incredible, marvellous, remarkable
11 exceptional, sensational
13 extraordinary

tremor
05 quake, shake, shock
06 quaver, quiver, wobble
07 tremble
09 trembling, vibration
10 earthquake

tremulous
05 jumpy, timid
06 afraid, scared
07 anxious, excited, fearful, jittery, nervous, shaking
08 agitated, unsteady, wavering
09 shivering, trembling
10 frightened

trench
03 cut, pit, sap
04 rill
05 ditch, drain, fosse
06 furrow, gutter, trough
07 channel
08 waterway
09 earthwork
10 excavation
12 entrenchment

trenchant
05 acute, blunt, sharp, terse
06 astute, biting
07 acerbic, caustic, mordant
08 clear-cut, emphatic, forceful, incisive, scathing
09 effective
10 forthright, perceptive
11 penetrating, unequivocal
13 perspicacious

trend
03 fad
05 craze, drift, style, vogue
06 course, latest
07 current, fashion, leaning
08 tendency
09 direction

trendy
02 in
03 hip

04 cool
05 funky, natty
06 groovy, modish, with it
07 stylish, voguish
10 all the rage
11 fashionable
13 up to the minute

trepidation
04 fear
05 alarm, dread, worry
06 dismay, fright, nerves, qualms, tremor, unease
07 anxiety, emotion, jitters
09 cold sweat, trembling
10 misgivings, uneasiness
11 butterflies, nervousness
12 apprehension, perturbation

trespass
03 sin
06 invade, offend
07 impinge, intrude, violate
08 encroach, infringe, invasion
09 intrusion, violation
10 transgress, wrongdoing
12 encroachment, infringement
13 contravention, transgression

trespasser
06 sinner
07 poacher
08 criminal, intruder, offender
12 transgressor

tress
04 curl, hair, lock, tail
05 braid, bunch, plait
07 pigtail, ringlet

trial
04 bane, case, pest, test
05 assay, dummy, grief, pilot
06 burden, dry run, hassle, misery, ordeal, try-out
07 hearing, inquiry, lawsuit, retrial, testing, trouble
08 audition, distress, dummy run, hardship, nuisance, practice, tribunal, vexation
09 adversity, probation, rehearsal, suffering
10 affliction, experiment
11 cross to bear, exploratory, provisional, tribulation
12 experimental, probationary

triangle
► *Triangles include*:
07 scalene
09 congruent, isosceles
11 acute-angled, equilateral, right-angled
12 obtuse-angled

triangular
08 trigonal, trigonic
09 trigonous
10 three-sided, trilateral
13 three-cornered
14 triangle-shaped

tribal
05 class, group
06 ethnic, family, native
10 indigenous

tribe
04 clan, race, sept
05 blood, caste, house, stock
06 family, nation, people
07 dynasty
11 ethnic group

tribulation
03 woe
04 blow, care, pain
05 curse, grief, trial, worry
06 misery, ordeal, sorrow
07 reverse, travail, trouble
08 distress, hardship, vexation
09 adversity, suffering
10 affliction, misfortune
11 unhappiness

tribunal
03 bar
05 bench, court, trial
07 hearing

tribute
03 tax
04 duty, gift, levy
05 paean, proof
06 charge, credit, eulogy, homage, honour, praise
07 payment, present, respect
08 accolade, applause, enconium, offering
09 gratitude, panegyric
10 compliment
11 recognition, testimonial
12 commendation

trice
03 sec
04 tick
05 flash, jiffy, shake
06 minute, moment, second
07 instant

trick
03 art, con, gag, kid
04 dupe, fake, fool, gift, hang, hoax, jape, joke, mock, ploy, ruse, scam, trap
05 antic, bluff, bogus, cheat, dodge, false, flair, fraud, knack, prank, skill, stunt

06 deceit, delude, diddle, ersatz, forged, have on, mirage, outwit, take in
07 ability, beguile, deceive, defraud, fast one, feigned, frame-up, know-how, mislead, swindle
08 artifice, capacity, facility, hoodwink, illusion
09 deception, imitation
10 apparition, artificial, capability, subterfuge
11 counterfeit, legerdemain
12 take for a ride, trick of light
13 practical joke
14 pull a fast one on

□**trick out**
04 do up
05 adorn, array
06 attire, bedeck, tart up
07 dress up
08 decorate, ornament

trickery
05 fraud, guile
06 deceit
07 cunning
08 artifice, cheating, illusion, pretence, wiliness
09 chicanery, deception, duplicity, swindling
10 dishonesty, subterfuge
11 shenanigans, skulduggery
13 double-dealing, funny business, jiggery-pokery, sleight of hand
14 monkey business

trickle
04 drip, drop, leak, ooze, seep
06 filter
07 dribble, seepage
09 percolate

trickster
05 cheat, fraud, joker
06 con man, hoaxer
07 cozener, diddler, tricker
08 deceiver, impostor, swindler
09 pretender, tregetour

tricky
03 sly
04 foxy, wily
05 dodgy
06 artful, crafty, subtle, thorny
07 awkward, cunning, devious
08 delicate, scheming, slippery
09 deceitful, difficult, sensitive

tried
06 proved, tested
08 reliable
10 dependable
11 established, trustworthy

trifle
03 bit, toy
04 dash, drop, fool, play, spot
05 dally, flirt, sport, touch, trace
06 bauble, dabble, trivia
07 nothing, trinket
09 mess about, plaything
10 knick-knack, triviality

trifling
05 minor, petty, silly, small
06 paltry, slight
07 foolish, shallow, trivial
09 frivolous, worthless
10 negligible
11 superficial, unimportant
13 insignificant
15 inconsequential

trigger
04 spur
05 catch, cause, lever, start
06 elicit, prompt, set off, switch
07 produce, provoke
08 activate, generate, initiate, spark off, stimulus
11 set in motion

trim
03 cut, fit
04 chop, clip, crop, dock, edge, neat, pare, slim, snip, tidy
05 adorn, array, braid, dress, frill, natty, order, prune, shape, shave, shear, smart, state
06 adjust, border, dapper, edging, fettle, fringe, health, neaten, reduce, snazzy, spruce, svelte, tidy up
07 arrange, compact, curtail, cut down, festoon, fitness, garnish, orderly, slender
08 contract, decorate, decrease, diminish, ornament, trimming
09 condition, cut back on, embellish, shipshape
11 in good order, presentable
12 spick-and-span
13 well-turned-out

trimming
05 braid, extra, frill
06 border, edging, fringe, paring, piping
07 cutting, falbala, garnish
08 clipping, frou-frou, furbelow
09 accessory, adornment
10 decoration
11 fimbriation
13 embellishment, ornamentation

trinket
05 jewel

trip
06 bauble, gewgaw, trifle
08 gimcrack, ornament
09 bagatelle
10 knick-knack

trio
05 triad
06 triune, troika
07 trilogy, trinity, triplet
08 triunity
09 threesome
10 triplicity
11 triumvirate

trip
03 hop, run
04 fall, ride, skip, slip, tour
05 caper, dance, dream, drive, error, foray, gaffe, jaunt, slide
06 gambol, outing, spring, tiptoe, tumble, voyage
07 fantasy, faux pas, journey, mistake, stagger, stumble
09 excursion, false step
10 apparition, expedition
13 hallucination
15 lose your footing

❑**trip up**
04 trap
05 catch, snare, trick
06 ambush, outwit, waylay
07 ensnare
08 catch out, outsmart, surprise

tripe
03 rot
04 blah, bosh, guff, tosh
05 balls, trash
06 bunkum, drivel
07 garbage, hogwash, inanity, rubbish, twaddle
08 bullshit, claptrap, nonsense
09 poppycock
10 balderdash

triple
04 trio
05 triad
06 treble, triune, troika
07 trilogy, trinity, triplet
08 three-ply, three-way, triunity
09 threefold, threesome
10 three times, tripartite, triplicate, triplicity
11 triumvirate

tripper
07 grockle, tourist, voyager
09 sightseer, traveller
12 excursionist, holidaymaker

trite
04 dull, worn
05 banal, corny, stale, stock
06 common
07 clichéd, routine, worn-out

08 clichéd, ordinary
09 hackneyed
10 threadbare, unoriginal
11 commonplace, stereotyped
12 run-of-the-mill
13 platitudinous

triumph
03 hit, joy, win
04 beat, coup, crow, feat
05 exult, gloat, glory, revel
06 defeat
07 conquer, elation, mastery, prevail, prosper, rejoice, succeed, success, victory
08 conquest, overcome, vanquish, walk-over
09 overwhelm, win the day
10 exultation, jubilation
11 achievement, celebration

triumphant
05 proud
06 elated, joyful
07 winning
08 exultant, glorious, jubilant
09 cock-a-hoop, rejoicing
10 conquering, successful, swaggering, victorious
12 prize-winning

trivia
03 pap
07 details, trifles
08 minutiae
12 trivialities
13 irrelevancies

trivial
05 banal, minor, petty, small
06 flimsy, little, measly, paltry
08 everyday, piddling, trifling
09 frivolous, worthless
11 meaningless, unimportant
13 insignificant, no great shakes
15 inconsequential

triviality
06 detail, trifle
09 frivolity, pettiness, smallness
11 foolishness
13 worthlessness
14 insignificance

trivialize
07 devalue, scoff at
08 belittle, minimize, play down
09 underplay

troop
03 mob
04 army, band, body, crew, gang, herd, pack, team, unit
05 crowd, group, horde, march
06 parade, stream, trudge
07 company, traipse

08 division, military, soldiers
10 contingent, servicemen
11 armed forces
12 servicewomen

trophy
03 cup
05 award, prize
06 spoils
07 laurels, memento
08 souvenir

tropical
03 hot
05 humid
06 steamy, sultry, torrid
07 boiling
08 stifling
10 sweltering

trot
03 jog, run
06 bustle, canter, scurry

◻**trot out**
06 adduce, recite, repeat
07 bring up, exhibit
08 bring out, rehearse
09 reiterate

troubadour
04 poet
06 singer
08 jongleur, minstrel, trouveur, trouvère
09 balladeer, cantabank
11 Minnesinger

trouble
03 ado, fix, jam, vex, woe
04 care, fuss, mess, pain
05 annoy, pains, upset, worry
06 bother, burden, effort, harass, hassle, pickle, put out, sadden, scrape, unease, unrest
07 afflict, ailment, concern, disturb, illness, perplex, perturb, problem
08 disorder, disquiet, distress, exertion, fighting, hardship, hot water, irritate, nuisance, problems, struggle, upheaval, vexation
09 adversity, annoyance, breakdown, commotion, complaint, heartache, suffering, tight spot, weigh down
10 affliction, difficulty, disability, disconcert, irritation, misfortune
11 malfunction, tribulation
13 inconvenience, make the effort
14 thoughtfulness

troublemaker
07 inciter, stirrer
08 agitator
10 incendiary, instigator, ringleader
12 rabble-rouser
13 mischief-maker

troublesome
05 rowdy
06 taxing, thorny, tricky, trying
07 awkward, irksome
08 annoying, tiresome
09 demanding, difficult, laborious, worrisome
10 bothersome, disturbing, irritating, rebellious

trough
04 crib, duct
05 ditch, drain, flame, gully
06 feeder, furrow, gutter, hollow, manger, trench
07 channel, conduit
10 depression

trounce
04 beat, best, drub, lick, rout
05 crush, paste
06 defeat, hammer, punish, thrash, wallop
07 clobber
09 overwhelm, slaughter

troupe
03 set
04 band, cast
05 group, troop
07 company

trouper
05 actor
06 player
07 artiste, old hand, veteran
08 thespian
09 performer
10 theatrical
11 entertainer

trousers
05 jeans, Levis®, pants
06 denims, shorts, slacks
08 breeches, flannels
09 dungarees

truancy
07 absence, skiving
08 shirking
11 absenteeism, French leave, malingering

truant
05 dodge, idler, shirk, skive
06 absent, dodger, skiver
07 missing, runaway, shirker
08 absentee, deserter, malinger, skive off

09 play hooky
10 malingerer, play truant

truce
04 lull, rest, stay
05 break, let-up, peace
09 armistice, cease-fire, cessation
10 moratorium, suspension

truck
03 HGV, van
05 float, lorry, trade, wagon
07 contact, traffic
08 business, commerce, dealings, exchange
09 relations
11 intercourse
13 communication

truculent
04 rude
05 cross
06 fierce, savage, sullen
07 defiant, hostile, violent
09 bellicose, combative
10 aggressive, pugnacious
11 bad-tempered, belligerent, ill-tempered, quarrelsome
12 antagonistic, discourteous, obstreperous
13 argumentative, disrespectful

trudge
04 haul, hike, plod, slog, toil, trek, walk
05 clump, march, stump, tramp
07 shuffle, traipse

true
04 fast, firm, real
05 close, exact, loyal, right
06 actual, honest, proper, trusty
07 correct, devoted, exactly, factual, genuine, precise, rightly, sincere, staunch
08 accurate, constant, faithful, honestly, properly, reliable, rightful, truthful, unerring
09 authentic, correctly, precisely, steadfast, veracious, veritable
10 accurately, dependable, faithfully, honourable, legitimate, truthfully
11 trustworthy, veraciously

true-blue
05 loyal
06 trusty
07 devoted, staunch
08 constant, faithful, orthodox
09 committed, dedicated

10 unwavering
12 card-carrying
13 dyed-in-the-wool
14 uncompromising

truism
05 axiom, truth
06 cliché

truly
04 very
06 in fact, indeed, really, surely
07 exactly, greatly, rightly
08 actually, honestly, properly
09 certainly, correctly,
   extremely, genuinely, in
   reality, precisely, sincerely
10 constantly, definitely,
   truthfully, undeniably
11 indubitably, undoubtedly

trump

□**trump up**
04 fake
06 cook up, create, devise,
   invent, make up
07 concoct
08 contrive
09 fabricate

trumped-up
04 fake
05 faked, false
06 made-up, phoney, untrue
08 cooked-up, invented,
   spurious
09 concocted, contrived,
   falsified
10 fabricated

trumpery
05 cheap, nasty, showy
06 flashy, grotty, shabby,
   shoddy, tawdry, trashy
07 useless
08 rubbishy, trifling
09 valueless, worthless
12 meretricious

trumpet
03 bay, cry
04 call, horn, roar
05 blare, blast, bugle, shout
06 bellow, herald
07 clarion
08 announce, proclaim

truncate
03 cut, lop
04 clip, crop, dock, pare, trim
05 prune
07 curtail, shorten
10 abbreviate

truncheon
04 club, cosh
05 baton, staff, stick

06 cudgel
10 knobkerrie, shillelagh

trunk
04 body, case, nose, stem
05 chest, crate, snout, torso
06 coffer
08 suitcase
09 proboscis
11 portmanteau

truss
03 pad, tie
04 bind, pack, prop, stay, wrap
05 brace, joist, strap, strut
06 bundle, fasten, pinion,
   secure, tether
07 bandage, binding, support
08 buttress

trust
04 care, duty, give, hope
05 faith
06 bank on, belief, charge,
   credit, expect, rely on
07 believe, confide, count on,
   custody, entrust, imagine
08 be sure of, credence,
   depend on, reliance
09 assurance, certainty
10 confidence, conviction
11 safekeeping, trusteeship
12 guardianship
14 responsibility

trustee
05 agent
06 keeper
08 executor, guardian
09 custodian, executrix,
   fiduciary
13 administrator

trusting
05 naïve
06 unwary
08 gullible, innocent, trustful
09 credulous, ingenuous
12 unsuspecting

trustworthy
04 true
05 loyal
06 honest, stable
07 devoted, ethical, upright
08 faithful, reliable, sensible
09 committed, steadfast
10 dependable, honourable
11 level headed, responsible

trusty
04 firm, true
05 loyal, solid
06 honest, steady, strong
07 staunch, upright
08 faithful, reliable

10 dependable, supportive
11 responsible, trustworthy

truth
04 fact
05 axiom, facts, maxim
06 honour, truism
07 candour, honesty, loyalty,
   realism, reality
08 accuracy, fidelity, veracity
09 actuality, exactness,
   frankness, home truth,
   integrity, precision
11 correctness, genuineness
12 authenticity, faithfulness,
   truthfulness
14 the gospel truth

truthful
04 open, true
05 exact, frank, right, valid
06 candid, honest
07 correct, factual, sincere
08 accurate, faithful, straight
09 realistic, veracious, veritable
11 trustworthy

truthfulness
07 candour, honesty
08 openness, veracity
09 frankness, sincerity
12 straightness
13 righteousness

try
02 go
03 aim, sap, tax
04 bash, shot, stab, test, tire
05 assay, crack, drain, judge,
   taste, trial, whirl
06 effort, sample, strain, stress,
   strive, try out, weaken
07 attempt, examine, exhaust,
   have a go, stretch, venture
08 appraise, evaluate
09 endeavour, have a bash,
   have a shot, have a stab
10 experiment, have a crack
11 investigate

□**try out**
04 test
05 taste, try on
06 sample
07 inspect
08 check out, evaluate

trying
04 hard
05 tough
06 taxing
07 arduous, testing
08 annoying, tiresome
09 demanding, difficult,
   vexatious, wearisome
10 bothersome, irritating

11 aggravating, troublesome
12 exasperating

tub
03 keg, tun, vat
04 bath, butt, cask
05 basin
06 barrel
07 bathtub
08 hogshead

tubby
03 fat
05 buxom, obese, plump, podgy, pudgy, stout
06 chubby, portly, rotund
08 roly-poly
09 corpulent
10 overweight
15 well-upholstered

tube
04 duct, hose, pipe
05 inlet, shaft, spout
06 outlet
07 channel, conduit
08 cylinder

tubular
06 tubate
08 pipelike, tubelike, tubiform, tubulate, tubulous, vasiform

tuck
04 cram, ease, eats, fold, food, grub, nosh, push
05 pleat, scoff, snack, stuff
06 crease, gather, insert, pucker, ruffle, snacks, thrust

❑tuck away
04 hide, save
05 hoard, store
06 save up
07 conceal
09 stash away

❑tuck in, tuck into
03 eat
05 eat up, feast, gorge, scoff
06 devour, gobble
08 wolf down

❑tuck in, tuck up
06 fold in, wrap up
07 cover up
08 make snug, put to bed

tuft
04 knot, wisp
05 beard, clump, crest, truss
06 tassel
09 flocculus

tug
03 lug, tow
04 drag, draw, haul, jerk, pull, yank

05 heave, pluck
06 wrench

tuition
07 lessons
08 coaching, guidance, teaching, training
09 education, schooling
11 instruction

tumble
04 dive, drop, fall, flop, roll, trip
05 heave, lurch, pitch, slide
06 plunge, topple, trip up
07 decline, plummet, stumble
08 collapse, decrease
09 knock down, overthrow
12 fall headlong

❑tumble to
04 twig
05 grasp
07 realize
08 perceive
10 cotton on to, understand

tumbledown
05 shaky
06 ruined, unsafe
07 crumbly, rickety, ruinous
08 decrepit, unstable, unsteady
09 crumbling, tottering
10 broken-down, ramshackle
11 dilapidated

tumbler
03 cup, mug
05 glass
06 beaker, goblet
07 acrobat, gymnast

tumid
07 bloated, bulbous, bulging, flowery, fulsome, pompous, stilted, swollen
08 affected, enlarged, inflated, puffed up
09 bombastic, distended, grandiose, high-flown, overblown, tumescent
10 euphuistic
11 pretentious, protuberant

tumour
04 lump
06 cancer, growth
07 myeloma, sarcoma
08 lymphoma, melanoma, neoplasm, swelling
09 carcinoma

tumult
03 din, row
04 riot, stir
05 babel, brawl, chaos, noise
06 bedlam, fracas, hubbub, racket, rumpus, uproar

07 clamour, turmoil
08 disarray, disorder, shouting
09 agitation, commotion, confusion
10 hullabaloo
11 disturbance, pandemonium

tumultuous
04 loud, wild
05 noisy, rowdy
06 fierce, hectic, raging, stormy
07 fervent, riotous, violent
08 frenzied, troubled
09 clamorous, deafening, disturbed, turbulent
12 uncontrolled

tune
03 air, set
04 song
05 adapt, motif, pitch, theme
06 adjust, attune, melody, strain, temper
08 regulate
09 harmonize

❑change your tune
14 change your mind

❑in tune with
12 agreeing with, in accord with
13 in harmony with
14 in sympathy with
15 in agreement with

tuneful
06 catchy, mellow
07 melodic, musical
08 pleasant, sonorous
09 agreeable, melodious
10 euphonious, harmonious
11 mellifluous

tuneless
05 harsh
06 atonal
08 clashing
09 dissonant, unmelodic, unmusical
10 discordant, unpleasant
11 cacophonous, horrisonant, unmelodious

tunnel
03 dig, sap
04 bore, hole, mine
05 shaft
06 burrow, subway
07 chimney, gallery, passage
08 excavate
09 undermine, underpass

turbid
03 dim
04 foul, hazy

05 dense, foggy, fuzzy, muddy, murky, thick
06 cloudy, impure, opaque
07 clouded, muddled, unclear
08 confused, feculent
09 turbulent, unsettled
10 disordered, incoherent

turbulence
05 chaos, storm
06 tumult, unrest
07 boiling, turmoil
09 agitation, commotion, confusion, roughness
11 instability, pandemonium

turbulent
04 wild
05 rough, rowdy
06 choppy, raging, stormy
07 furious, riotous, violent
08 agitated, blustery, mutinous
09 in turmoil, unsettled
10 boisterous, disorderly, rebellious, tumultuous
11 tempestuous

turf
03 sod
04 clod, lawn
05 divot, glebe, grass, sward

❑**turf out**
04 fire, oust, sack
05 eject, elbow, evict, expel
06 banish
07 dismiss, kick out, turn out
08 chuck out, throw out
10 dispossess

turgid
07 flowery, fulsome, pompous
08 affected, inflated
09 bombastic, grandiose, high-flown, overblown
11 extravagant, pretentious
12 magniloquent, ostentatious

turmoil
03 din, row
05 chaos, noise
06 bedlam, bustle, flurry, hubbub, tumult, uproar
07 ferment, trouble
08 disarray, disquiet, upheaval
09 agitation, commotion
10 turbulence
11 disturbance, pandemonium

turn
03 aim, fit
04 bend, cast, form, grow, make, move, pass, reel, roll, sour, spin, veer, wind
05 adapt, alter, apply, go bad, go off, hinge, mould, pivot,

point, shape, shift, spoil, swing, twirl, twist, whirl
06 adjust, appeal, become, change, circle, curdle, direct, divert, gyrate, invert, modify, mutate, resort, rotate, spiral, swerve, swivel
07 convert, fashion, go round, remodel, reverse, revolve
09 transform, transmute
12 metamorphose

❑**to a turn**
07 exactly
09 correctly, perfectly, precisely
12 to prefection

❑**turn against**
08 distrust
12 disapprove of

❑**turn aside**
05 avert, parry
06 depart
07 deflect, deviate, diverge

❑**turn away**
05 avert
06 depart, reject
07 deflect, deviate
08 move away
12 cold shoulder

❑**turn down**
04 mute, veto
05 lower, spurn
06 lessen, muffle, rebuff, reduce, refuse, reject, soften
07 decline, quieten
08 decrease

❑**turn in**
06 give in, give up, hand in, retire, return, submit, tender
07 deliver, go to bed
08 give back, hand over
09 hit the hay, surrender
10 hit the sack

❑**turn of events**
06 affair, result
07 outcome
08 incident
09 happening

❑**turn off**
04 bore, quit, stop
06 divert, offend, put off, sicken
07 deviate, disgust, turn out
08 nauseate, shut down
09 branch off, switch off
10 depart from, disconnect, discourage, disenchant

❑**turn of phrase**
05 idiom, style
06 saying
07 diction

08 locution, metaphor
10 expression
11 phraseology

❑**turn on**
05 start
06 arouse, attack, excite, fall on, please, plug in, rest on, thrill
07 attract, connect, hinge on, lay into, round on, set upon
08 activate, switch on
09 stimulate

❑**turn out**
02 go
04 come, fire, make, sack
05 clear, dress, empty, end up, ensue, evict, expel
06 appear, arrive, attend, banish, become, clothe, deport, emerge, happen, pan out, result, show up, turn up, unplug
07 develop, dismiss, drum out, kick out, present, turn off
08 assemble, chuck out, churn out, clean out, clear out
09 be present, come about, discharge, fabricate, switch off, transpire
10 disconnect
11 manufacture

❑**turn over**
05 upend, upset
06 assign, invert, ponder
07 capsize, consign, deliver, examine, reverse
08 consider, hand over, keel over, mull over, overturn, ruminate, transfer
09 reflect on, surrender
10 deliberate, turn turtle
11 contemplate

❑**turn over a new leaf**
05 amend, begin
06 change, reform
07 improve
10 begin again
12 mend your ways
14 change your ways
15 pull yours socks up

❑**turn up**
03 act
04 bash, bend, bias, come, find, loop, show, spin, stab, time
05 crack, curve, cycle, dig up, drift, raise, round, scare, shift, shock, spell, stint, trend, twirl, twist, whirl
06 appear, arrive, attend, change, expose, period, reveal, show up

07 amplify, leaning, turn out,
uncover, unearth
08 disclose, discover, increase,
reversal, rotation, tendency
09 be present, deviation,
direction, intensify,
performer, variation
10 alteration, difference,
divergence, make louder,
propensity, revolution
11 inclination, nervousness,
opportunity, performance
12 bring to light

turncoat
03 rat
04 fink, scab
07 seceder, traitor
08 apostate, blackleg,
defector, deserter,
renegade
10 backslider
13 tergiversator

turning
04 bend, fork, turn
05 curve
07 turn-off
08 junction

turning-point
04 crux
06 crisis
09 watershed
10 crossroads
13 moment of truth

turnout
04 gate, gear, togs
05 array, crowd, dress, get-up
06 attire, number, outfit
07 clobber, clothes
08 assembly, audience
09 gathering
10 assemblage, attendance
12 congregation

turnover
04 flow
05 yield
06 change, income, output
07 outturn, profits
08 business, movement
10 production
12 productivity

turpitude
04 evil
07 badness
08 baseness, foulness, iniquity,
vileness, villainy
09 depravity
10 corruption, degeneracy,
immorality, sinfulness,
wickedness
11 corruptness, viciousness

13 nefariousness
14 flagitiousness

tussle
03 vie
04 bout, fray
05 brawl, fight, melee, scrap,
scrum, set-to
06 battle, dust-up, fracas
07 contest, grapple, punch-up,
scuffle, wrestle
08 conflict, scramble, struggle
09 scrimmage

tutelage
03 eye
04 care
05 aegis
06 charge
07 custody, tuition
08 guidance, teaching
09 education, patronage,
schooling, vigilance
11 instruction, preparation
12 guardianship

tutor
04 guru
05 coach, drill, teach, train
06 direct, mentor, school
07 educate, lecture, teacher
08 guardian, instruct, lecturer
09 supervise
10 instructor, supervisor

tutorial
05 class
06 lesson
07 guiding, seminar, teach-in
08 coaching, didactic, teaching
09 educative, educatory
13 instructional

TV
03 set
05 telly
06 the box
07 the tube
08 boob tube, idiot box,
receiver
09 goggle-box
10 television
11 small screen

twaddle
03 rot
04 bunk, guff, tosh
05 balls, stuff, trash
06 bunkum, drivel, gabble,
hot air, piffle, waffle
07 blather, blether, garbage,
hogwash, inanity, rubbish
08 claptrap, nonsense
09 poppycock
10 balderdash
12 gobbledygook

tweak
03 nip, tug
04 jerk, pull
05 pinch, twist
06 twitch

twee
04 cute
05 sweet
06 dainty, pretty, quaint
08 affected, precious
11 sentimental

twiddle
04 turn
05 twirl, twist
06 adjust, fiddle, finger, swivel

twig
03 get, see
05 grasp, stick, withe, withy
06 branch, rumble, wattle
07 catch on, ramulus
08 cotton on, tumble to
10 comprehend, understand

twilight
03 dim, ebb
04 dusk, last
05 dying, final, gloom
06 ebbing, sunset
07 decline, dimness, evening
08 gloaming
09 darkening, declining,
half-light
10 crepuscule
11 crepuscular

twin
04 dual, join, mate, pair, yoke
05 clone, match
06 couple, double, ringer
07 matched, twofold
08 likeness, matching, parallel
09 corollary, duplicate,
identical, look-alike
10 complement, equivalent
11 counterpart, symmetrical
13 corresponding

twine
04 bend, coil, cord, curl, knit,
loop, wind, wrap, yarn
05 braid, plait, twist, weave
06 spiral, string, tangle, thread
07 entwine, wreathe

twinge
04 ache, pain, pang, stab
05 cramp, pinch, prick, spasm,
throb, three
06 stitch

twinkle
04 wink
05 flash, gleam, glint, light,
shine

07 flicker, glimmer, glisten,
glitter, shining, sparkle
09 coruscate
11 coruscation, scintillate

twinkling
02 mo
03 sec
04 jiff, tick
05 flash, jiffy, nitid, shake, trice
06 bright, moment, second
07 instant, shining, winking
08 flashing, gleaming
09 sparkling
10 flickering, glimmering,
glistening, glittering
11 coruscating

twirl
04 coil, curl, spin, turn, wind
05 pivot, twist, wheel, whirl
06 gyrate, rotate, spiral, swivel
07 revolve
08 gyration, rotation
09 pirouette

twirling
05 gyral
07 pivotal
08 gyratory, pivoting, rotating,
rotatory, spinning, whirling
09 revolving
11 pirouetting

twist
04 bend, coil, curl, flaw, kink,
loop, rick, roll, skew, spin,
turn, warp, whim, wind
05 alter, braid, break, curve,
freak, plait, quirk, screw,
twine, twirl, weave, wring
06 change, defect, deform,
foible, garble, oddity, rotate,
spiral, sprain, squirm, strain,
swivel, tangle, wrench,
wrench, writhe, zigzag
07 contort, distort, entwine,
falsify, pervert, revolve,
wreathe, wriggle
08 entangle, misquote,
misshape, squiggle, surprise
09 misreport, turnabout
10 aberration, contortion,
distortion, intertwine,
perversion
11 convolution, peculiarity
12 idiosyncrasy, misrepresent

◻**twist someone's arm**
05 bully, force
06 coerce, lean on
07 dragoon
08 bulldoze, persuade
10 intimidate, pressurize
14 put the screws on

twisted
03 odd
06 warped
07 deviant, sinuous, winding
09 perverted, unnatural

twister
05 cheat, crook, fraud, rogue
06 con man, phoney
08 deceiver, swindler
09 scoundrel, trickster
10 blackguard

twit
03 ass
04 clot, dope, fool
05 chump, clown, idiot, ninny,
twerp
06 nitwit
07 halfwit
09 blockhead, simpleton
10 nincompoop

twitch
03 tic, tug
04 jerk, jump, pull
05 blink, pluck, shake, spasm
06 quiver, shiver, snatch, tremor

twitter
03 cry
04 sing, song
05 cheep, chirp, tweet
06 gabble, gossip, warble,
witter
07 blather, blether, chatter,
chirrup, prattle, whistle
08 chirping, tweeting
10 chirruping

two-faced
05 false, lying
07 devious
09 deceitful, insincere
10 Janus-faced, perfidious
11 dissembling, duplicitous,
treacherous
12 hypocritical
13 double-dealing,
untrustworthy

tycoon
05 baron, mogul
06 fat cat
07 magnate, supremo
08 big noise
09 big cheese, financier
10 capitalist
12 entrepreneur
13 industrialist

type
04 face, font, form, kind, make,
mark, sort
05 brand, breed, class,
fount, genre, genus,

group, model, order,
print, stamp, style
06 letter, number, strain, symbol
07 letters, numbers,
pattern, species,
symbols, variety
08 category, exemplar,
original, printing,
specimen, standard
09 archetype, character,
lettering, prototype
11 description, designation
14 classification

typhoon
05 storm
06 squall
07 cyclone, tornado,
twister
09 hurricane, whirlwind

typical
05 model, stock, usual
06 normal
07 average, classic
08 ordinary, standard
10 archetypal, stereotype
12 conventional, illustrative
14 characteristic, quintessential

typically
07 as a rule, usually
08 normally
09 routinely
10 habitually, ordinarily

typify
06 embody
09 epitomize, exemplify,
represent, symbolize
11 encapsulate
12 characterize

tyrannical
05 cruel, harsh
06 severe, strict, unjust
08 despotic, ruthless
09 arbitrary, imperious
10 autocratic, high-handed,
oppressive, repressive
11 dictatorial, domineering,
magisterial, overbearing
12 overpowering, totalitarian
13 authoritarian

tyrannize
05 bully, crush
07 enslave, oppress,
repress
08 browbeat, domineer,
suppress
09 subjugate, terrorize
10 intimidate, lord it over

tyranny
07 cruelty

08 severity
09 autocracy, despotism,
   harshness, injustice
10 absolutism, oppression
12 dictatorship, ruthlessness
13 imperiousness

tyrant
05 bully
06 despot
08 autocrat, dictator,
   martinet
09 oppressor

11 slave-driver
13 authoritarian

tyro see **tiro**

U

ubiquitous
06 common, global
09 pervasive, universal
10 everywhere
11 ever-present, omnipresent

ubiquity
09 frequency
10 popularity, prevalence
12 omnipresence, universality

ugliness
04 evil
06 danger, horror, menace
08 enormity, vileness
09 deformity
11 monstrosity

ugly
04 evil, foul, vile
05 grave, nasty, plain
06 homely, horrid
07 hideous, hostile
08 deformed, shocking, sinister, terrible, unlovely
09 dangerous, grotesque, loathsome, misshapen, monstrous, obnoxious, offensive, repulsive, revolting, unsightly
10 disgusting, unpleasant
11 ill-favoured, threatening
12 disagreeable, unattractive
13 objectionable
15 unprepossessing

ulcer
04 boil, noma, sore
06 canker, fester
07 abscess
08 open sore
09 impostume

ulterior
06 covert, hidden, secret
07 private, selfish
09 concealed, secondary

ultimate
03 end
04 best, last, peak
05 basic, final
06 height, summit, utmost
07 epitome, highest, maximum, primary, supreme, topmost
08 eventual, furthest, greatest, last word, remotest, terminal
09 elemental
10 perfection
11 culmination, fundamental, superlative
14 daddy of them all

ultimately
06 at last
07 finally
08 after all, in the end
09 basically, primarily
10 eventually
13 fundamentally, sooner or later

ultra-
05 extra
09 extremely, unusually
10 especially, remarkably
11 excessively
13 exceptionally
15 extraordinarily

ululate
04 howl, keen, wail
05 mourn
06 holler, lament, scream

umbrage
□**take umbrage**
11 take offence
13 take exception
14 take personally

umbrella
04 gamp
05 aegis, cover
06 agency, brolly
07 parasol
08 sunshade
10 protection

umpire
03 ref
05 judge
07 arbiter, mediate, referee
08 linesman, mediator, moderate
09 arbitrate, moderator
10 arbitrator

umpteen
08 millions, numerous, very many

09 a good many, countless, thousands
11 innumerable

unabashed
04 bold
06 brazen
07 blatant
09 unashamed, undaunted

unable
05 unfit
08 impotent
09 incapable, powerless
10 unequipped
11 ineffectual, unqualified

unabridged
05 uncut, whole
06 entire
08 complete
10 full-length
11 uncondensed, unshortened

unacceptable
09 obnoxious, offensive
10 unpleasant, unsuitable
11 intolerable, undesirable
12 inadmissible
14 unsatisfactory

unaccommodating
05 rigid
09 unbending
10 inflexible, unyielding
11 disobliging
12 intransigent
13 unco-operative

unaccompanied
04 lone, solo
05 alone
06 single
09 on your own
10 by yourself, unattended, unescorted
12 single-handed

unaccountable
07 bizarre, curious
08 baffling, peculiar, puzzling
10 mysterious
11 astonishing
12 impenetrable, inexplicable, unfathomable

13 not answerable, unexplainable

unaccustomed
06 unused
07 strange, unusual
08 uncommon, unwonted
10 unexpected, unfamiliar
11 unpractised
12 unacquainted
13 unprecedented

unacquainted
06 unused
07 strange
08 ignorant
10 unfamiliar
12 unaccustomed
13 inexperienced

unadorned
05 plain, stark
06 severe, simple
11 undecorated, unvarnished
12 unornamented
13 unembellished
15 straightforward

unaffected
05 naïve, plain
06 candid, honest, simple
07 artless, genuine, natural, sincere, unmoved
08 unspoilt
09 guileless, ingenuous, unaltered, unchanged
10 unassuming
11 indifferent, unconcerned
13 unpretentious
15 straightforward

unafraid
05 brave
06 daring
08 fearless, intrepid
09 dauntless
10 courageous
13 imperturbable

unalterable
05 final, fixed, rigid
09 immutable, permanent
10 inflexible, invariable, unchanging, unyielding
12 unchangeable

unanimity
05 unity
06 accord, unison
07 concert, concord, harmony
09 agreement, consensus
10 congruence
11 concurrence, consistency
14 like-mindedness

unanimous
05 as one, joint

06 common, united
08 in accord
09 concerted
10 concordant, consistent, harmonious, like-minded
11 in agreement

unanimously
05 as one
06 nem con
09 in concert, of one mind, unopposed
10 conjointly
12 with one voice
15 by common consent

unanswerable
10 unarguable, undeniable
11 irrefutable
12 indisputable, irrefragable
13 incontestable

unappetizing
09 tasteless, unsavoury
10 uninviting, unpleasant
11 unappealing, unpalatable
12 disagreeable, unattractive

unapproachable
04 cold, cool
05 aloof
06 remote
07 distant
08 reserved
09 withdrawn
10 forbidding, unfriendly
11 standoffish
12 inaccessible, unresponsive

unapt
05 inapt, unfit
08 unfitted, unsuited
10 inapposite, malapropos, unsuitable
13 inappropriate

unarmed
07 exposed
08 helpless
10 vulnerable
11 defenceless, unprotected

unashamed
04 open
07 blatant
09 shameless, unabashed
10 impenitent
11 undisguised, unrepentant

unasked
08 unbidden, unsought
09 uninvited, voluntary
11 spontaneous, unannounced, unsolicited

unassailable
06 proven, secure
08 absolute, positive

10 conclusive, invincible, inviolable, undeniable
11 impregnable, irrefutable
12 indisputable, invulnerable
13 incontestable

unassertive
04 meek
05 mousy, quiet, timid
08 backward, retiring, timorous
09 diffident
10 unassuming

unassuming
04 meek
05 quiet
06 demure, humble, modest, simple
07 natural
08 reticent, retiring
10 restrained
13 unpretentious

unattached
04 free
06 single
09 available, fancy-free, footloose, unmarried
10 by yourself
11 independent, uncommitted
12 unaffiliated

unattended
05 alone
08 forsaken
09 neglected, unguarded
12 unsupervised
13 unaccompanied

unattractive
04 ugly
05 plain
06 homely
09 offensive, repellent, unsavoury, unsightly
10 off-putting, uninviting, unpleasant
11 distasteful, ill-favoured, unappealing, undesirable, unpalatable
12 disagreeable, unappetizing
15 unprepossessing

unauthorized
07 illegal, illicit
09 forbidden, irregular
10 prohibited, unofficial
12 illegitimate, unsanctioned

unavailing
04 vain
06 beaten, failed, futile, losing
07 unlucky, useless
08 abortive, defeated, luckless
09 fruitless
10 frustrated

11 ineffective, unfortunate
12 unprofitable, unsuccessful

unavoidable
08 destined, required
09 mandatory, necessary
10 compulsory, inevitable, inexorable, obligatory
11 ineluctable, inescapable, predestined

unaware
08 heedless, ignorant
09 in the dark, oblivious, unknowing, unmindful
10 insentient
11 unconscious
12 unsuspecting

unawares
08 off guard, on the hop
10 by surprise, mistakenly, unprepared
12 accidentally, unthinkingly
13 inadvertently
15 unintentionally

unbalanced
03 mad
05 barmy, crazy
06 biased, insane, uneven, unfair, unjust
07 lunatic, unequal, unsound
08 crackers, demented, deranged, lopsided, one-sided, partisan, unstable, unsteady
09 disturbed
10 irrational, prejudiced
11 inequitable, mentally ill
12 asymmetrical, round the bend
13 round the twist

unbearable
08 the limit
11 intolerable, unendurable
12 excruciating, insufferable, the last straw, unacceptable
13 insupportable

unbeatable
04 best
07 supreme
09 excellent, matchless
10 invincible
11 indomitable, unstoppable
13 unconquerable

unbeaten
07 supreme, unbowed
10 triumphant, undefeated, victorious
11 unconquered, unsurpassed

unbecoming
08 unseemly

09 unsightly
10 indecorous, indelicate, unladylike, unsuitable
11 unbefitting
12 unattractive
13 ungentlemanly

unbelief
05 doubt
07 atheism
10 scepticism
11 agnosticism, incredulity

unbelievable
07 amazing
10 far-fetched, impossible, improbable, incredible, outlandish, staggering
11 implausible, unthinkable
12 unconvincing, unimaginable
13 extraordinary, inconceivable

unbeliever
07 atheist, infidel, sceptic
08 agnostic
11 nullifidian

unbelieving
07 dubious
08 doubtful, doubting
09 sceptical
11 incredulous, nullifidian, unconvinced, unpersuaded

unbend
04 thaw
05 relax
06 uncoil, uncurl
08 loosen up, unbutton
10 straighten

unbending
04 firm
05 aloof, rigid, stern, stiff, tough
06 formal, severe, strict
08 hard-line, resolute, stubborn
10 inflexible, unyielding
12 intransigent

unbiased
04 fair, just
07 neutral
09 impartial, objective
10 even-handed, fair-minded, open-minded, uncoloured
12 unprejudiced
13 disinterested, dispassionate

unbidden
07 unasked
08 unforced, unwanted
09 uninvited, unwelcome, voluntary
10 unprompted
11 spontaneous, unsolicited

unbind
04 free, undo

05 loose, untie
06 loosen
07 release, unchain, unloose
08 unfasten, unfetter

unblemished
04 pure
05 clear
07 perfect
08 flawless, spotless, unflawed
09 unspotted, unstained
11 untarnished

unblinking
04 calm, cool
06 steady
07 assured
08 composed, fearless, unafraid
09 impassive
11 emotionless, unemotional, unflinching
13 imperturbable

unblushing
06 brazen
07 blatant
08 immodest
09 shameless

unborn
06 coming, future, to-come
07 awaited, in utero
08 expected
09 embryonic
10 subsequent, succeeding

unbosom
04 bare, tell
05 admit
06 let out, reveal
07 confess, confide, divulge, lay bare, pour out, tell all
08 disclose, unburden

unbounded
04 vast
07 endless
08 infinite
09 boundless, limitless, unchecked, unlimited
12 unrestrained, unrestricted

unbreakable
09 resistant, toughened
11 infrangible
12 shatterproof
14 indestructible

unbridled
07 rampant, riotous
08 uncurbed
09 excessive, unchecked
10 licentious, profligate
11 intemperate
12 uncontrolled, unrestrained
13 unconstrained

unbroken
05 solid, whole
06 entire, intact
07 endless, non-stop
08 complete, constant
09 perpetual, unceasing
10 continuous, successive
13 uninterrupted

unburden
04 bare, tell
06 let out, reveal
07 confess, confide, divulge, lay bare, offload, pour out, tell all, uncover
08 disclose

uncalled-for
07 unasked
08 needless, unsought
09 unwelcome
10 gratuitous, undeserved
11 unjustified, unwarranted

uncanny
03 odd
05 eerie, queer, weird
06 creepy, spooky
07 bizarre, strange
08 eldritch
09 unearthly
10 incredible, mysterious
12 supernatural
13 preternatural, unaccountable

uncaring
04 cold
07 callous, unmoved
09 unfeeling
11 indifferent, unconcerned
13 unsympathetic

unceasing
07 endless, non-stop
08 constant, unending
09 ceaseless, continual, incessant, perpetual
10 continuous, relentless
11 never-ending, unrelenting, unremitting

unceremonious
04 rude
06 abrupt, casual, sudden
08 impolite, informal, laid-back
09 easy-going
11 undignified
12 discourteous
13 disrespectful

uncertain
04 iffy, open
05 risky, shaky, vague
06 unsure
07 dubious, erratic

08 doubtful, hesitant, insecure, wavering
09 undecided, unsettled
10 ambivalent, changeable, inconstant, in two minds, indefinite, touch and go, unresolved, up in the air
11 speculative, unconfirmed, unconvinced, vacillating
12 equivocating, in the balance, undetermined
13 unforeseeable, unpredictable

uncertainty
05 doubt, qualm
06 qualms
07 dilemma
09 ambiguity, confusion
10 hesitation, insecurity, perplexity, puzzlement, scepticism, uneasiness
11 ambivalence
12 bewilderment, irresolution

unchallengeable
10 conclusive
11 irrefutable
12 indisputable
13 incontestable

unchangeable
09 immutable, permanent
10 changeless, invariable
12 irreversible

unchanging
07 abiding, eternal, lasting
08 constant, enduring
09 permanent, perpetual, steadfast, unvarying
10 changeless, invariable

uncharitable
04 hard, mean
05 cruel, harsh, stern
06 severe, unkind
07 callous
09 unfeeling
10 ungenerous
11 hard-hearted, insensitive, unforgiving

uncharted
06 virgin
07 foreign, strange, unknown
10 unexplored, unfamiliar

unchaste
04 lewd
05 loose
06 fallen, impure, wanton
08 depraved, immodest
10 licentious
11 promiscuous

uncivil
04 curt, rude
05 gruff, surly
06 abrupt
07 bearish, boorish, brusque, ill-bred, uncouth
08 churlish, impolite
10 ungracious, unmannerly
11 bad-mannered, ill-mannered
12 discourteous

uncivilized
04 wild
05 rough
06 savage
07 boorish, brutish, untamed
08 barbaric
09 barbarian, primitive
10 antisocial, uncultured

unclassifiable
07 elusive
10 ill-defined, indefinite, indistinct
11 indefinable, undefinable
13 indescribable, indeterminate
14 unidentifiable

unclean
03 bad
04 evil, foul
05 dirty, grimy
06 filthy, grubby, impure, soiled,
07 defiled, sullied, tainted
08 polluted
10 unhygienic
11 adulterated, unwholesome
12 contaminated

unclear
03 dim
04 hazy, iffy
05 foggy, vague
06 unsure
07 dubious, obscure
08 doubtful
09 uncertain, unsettled
10 indefinite, indistinct

unclothed
04 bare, nude
05 naked
08 disrobed, starkers, stripped
09 in the buff, undressed
10 stark naked
15 in the altogether

uncomfortable
04 cold, hard
05 tense
06 on edge, uneasy
07 anxious, awkward, nervous, painful, worried
08 troubled

09 disturbed
10 ill-fitting, irritating
11 discomfited, embarrassed
13 self-conscious

uncommitted
07 neutral
08 floating
09 fancy-free, undecided
10 non-aligned, uninvolved
11 non-partisan

uncommon
03 odd
04 rare
05 queer
06 scarce
07 strange, unusual
08 abnormal, atypical, peculiar, singular, striking
10 infrequent, unfamiliar
11 distinctive, outstanding
12 like gold dust
15 thin on the ground

uncommonly
09 extremely, strangely, unusually
10 abnormally, peculiarly, remarkably, singularly
12 particularly
13 exceptionally, outstandingly

uncommunicative
08 reserved, reticent, retiring, taciturn
09 diffident, withdrawn
11 tight-lipped
12 unresponsive
13 unforthcoming

uncomplicated
06 direct, simple
10 uninvolved
11 undemanding
15 straightforward

uncompromising
05 rigid
07 die-hard
08 obdurate, stubborn
09 immovable, obstinate, unbending
10 inexorable, inflexible, unyielding
12 intransigent

unconcealable
05 clear, plain
07 obvious
08 manifest
13 irrepressible

unconcealed
04 open
05 frank, overt
06 patent

07 blatant, evident, obvious, visible
08 apparent, manifest
10 noticeable
11 conspicuous

unconcern
06 apathy
10 detachment, remoteness
11 callousness, insouciance, nonchalance
12 indifference

unconcerned
04 cool
05 aloof
06 casual, remote
07 distant, unmoved
08 detached, uncaring
09 apathetic, oblivious
10 complacent, insouciant, nonchalant, uninvolved
11 indifferent, unperturbed
12 uninterested
13 dispassionate

unconditional
04 full
05 total, utter
08 absolute, complete, outright, positive
09 downright, out-and-out, unlimited
10 conclusive, unreserved
11 unequivocal, unqualified
12 unrestricted, whole-hearted
13 thoroughgoing

unconfirmed
08 unproved, unproven
10 unratified, unverified
14 uncorroborated
15 unauthenticated, unsubstantiated

unconformity
12 irregularity
13 disconformity, discontinuity

uncongenial
08 unsuited
10 discordant, unfriendly, uninviting, unpleasant
12 antipathetic, incompatible, unattractive

unconnected
08 detached, separate
09 illogical, unrelated
10 disjointed, incoherent, irrational, unattached
11 independent, off the point

unconquerable
10 inveterate, invincible, unbeatable, unyielding
11 indomitable, insuperable

12 overpowering, undefeatable
13 irrepressible
14 insurmountable

unconscionable
06 amoral
08 criminal
09 excessive, unethical
10 immoderate, outrageous
12 preposterous, unprincipled, unreasonable, unscrupulous

unconscious
03 out
05 blind, dazed
06 asleep, innate, latent, reflex, zonked
07 drugged, fainted, in a coma, out cold, stunned, unaware
08 comatose, heedless, ignorant
09 automatic, impulsive, oblivious, senseless, unmindful, unwitting
10 blacked out, insensible, knocked out, subliminal, suppressed, unthinking
11 inadvertent, incognizant, instinctive, involuntary
13 unintentional
14 dead to the world, out for the count

unconstraint
07 abandon, freedom
10 liberality
12 laissez-faire

uncontrollable
03 mad
04 wild
06 strong, unruly
07 furious, violent
11 intractable
12 out of control, ungovernable, unmanageable

uncontrolled
04 wild
06 unruly
07 rampant, riotous, violent
09 unbridled, unchecked
10 boisterous, unhindered
12 unrestrained
13 undisciplined

unconventional
03 odd
04 rare, zany
05 wacky
06 freaky, fringe, way-out
07 bizarre, oddball, offbeat
08 abnormal, bohemian, original, uncommon

09 different, eccentric, irregular
10 individual, unorthodox
11 alternative, uncustomary
13 idiosyncratic

unconvincing
04 lame, weak
06 feeble, flimsy
07 dubious, suspect
08 doubtful, unlikely
10 improbable
11 implausible
12 questionable

unco-ordinated
05 inept
06 clumsy
07 awkward
08 bumbling, bungling,
   ungainly
09 maladroit

uncouth
04 rude
05 crude, rough
06 clumsy, coarse, vulgar
07 awkward, boorish, loutish
08 impolite, unseemly
09 graceless, unrefined
10 uncultured
11 bad-mannered, ill-
   mannered, uncivilized
15 unsophisticated

uncover
04 bare, leak, open, peel, show
05 dig up, strip
06 detect, exhume, expose,
   reveal, unmask, unveil
07 divulge, lay bare, unearth
08 disclose, discover
09 make known
12 bring to light

uncritical
12 undiscerning
13 unquestioning
14 non-judgemental

unctuous
04 glib, oily
05 slick, suave
06 creamy, greasy, smarmy,
   smooth
07 fawning, gushing, servile
09 insincere, pietistic, plausible
10 obsequious
11 sycophantic
12 ingratiating

uncultivated
04 wild
06 fallow
07 natural

uncultured
09 unrefined

12 uncultivated
15 unsophisticated

undaunted
07 unbowed
08 fearless, intrepid, resolute
09 dauntless, steadfast
10 undeterred, undismayed
11 indomitable

undecided
04 moot, open
07 dubious, unknown
08 doubtful, hesitant, wavering
09 debatable, dithering,
   uncertain, unsettled
10 ambivalent, in two minds,
   irresolute, unresolved, up in
   the air
12 equivocating

undecorated
05 plain, stark
06 severe, simple
07 austere
08 inornate
09 classical, unadorned
10 functional
13 unembellished

undefeated
07 supreme, winning
08 unbeaten
10 triumphant, victorious
11 unconquered, unsurpassed
12 unvanquished

undefended
07 exposed, unarmed
09 pregnable, unguarded
10 vulnerable
11 defenceless, unfortified,
   unprotected

undefiled
04 pure
05 clean, clear
06 chaste, intact
08 spotless, unsoiled, virginal
09 inviolate, unsullied
10 immaculate

undefined
04 hazy
05 vague
06 woolly
07 inexact, tenuous, unclear
08 formless, nebulous
09 imprecise
10 indefinite, indistinct
11 unexplained, unspecified
13 indeterminate

undemonstrative
04 cold, cool
05 aloof, stiff
06 formal, remote

07 distant
08 reserved, reticent
10 phlegmatic, restrained
11 unemotional

undeniable
04 sure
06 patent, proven
07 certain, evident, obvious
08 definite, manifest, positive
11 beyond doubt, indubitable,
   irrefutable
12 indisputable, unmistakable
14 beyond question,
   unquestionable

undependable
07 erratic
08 unstable, variable
09 mercurial, uncertain
10 inconstant, unreliable
11 fair-weather, treacherous
12 inconsistent
13 irresponsible, unpredictable

under
04 down, less
05 below, lower
07 beneath
08 junior to, less than
09 lower than
10 inferior to, underneath
11 secondary to
13 subordinate to, subservient
   to

underclothes
06 smalls, undies
08 frillies, lingerie
09 underwear
13 underclothing,
   undergarments
14 unmentionables

undercover
06 covert, hidden, secret
07 furtive, private
08 hush-hush, stealthy
11 clandestine, underground
12 confidential, intelligence
13 surreptitious

undercurrent
04 aura, hint
05 drift, sense, tinge, trend
07 feeling, flavour
08 tendency, undertow
09 underflow, undertone
10 atmosphere, suggestion

undercut
08 excavate, gouge out, scoop
   out, underbid
09 hollow out, undermine
10 underprice

underestimate
08 misjudge, play down
09 underrate
10 look down on, trivialize, undervalue

undergo
04 bear
05 stand
06 endure, suffer
07 sustain, weather
08 submit to, tolerate
09 go through, put up with, withstand
10 experience

underground
04 tube
05 metro
06 covert, secret, subway
07 furtive, illegal
10 subversive, undercover, unofficial
11 alternative, below ground, clandestine
12 subterranean
13 revolutionary
15 below the surface

undergrowth
05 brush, scrub
06 bushes
07 thicket
09 brushwood
10 vegetation
11 ground cover

underhand
03 sly
05 shady
06 crafty, secret, sneaky
07 devious, furtive, immoral
08 improper, stealthy
09 deceitful, deceptive, dishonest, unethical
11 clandestine
12 unscrupulous

underline
06 stress
07 point up
09 emphasize, highlight
10 accentuate, underscore
15 draw attention to

underling
06 lackey, menial, minion
07 flunkey, servant
08 hireling, inferior
11 subordinate

underlying
04 root
05 basal, basic
06 hidden, latent, veiled
09 essential, intrinsic

10 elementary
11 fundamental

undermine
05 erode
06 damage, impair, injure, tunnel, weaken
07 destroy, subvert, vitiate
08 excavate, sabotage, wear away

underprivileged
04 poor
05 needy
06 in need, in want
08 deprived
09 destitute, oppressed
13 disadvantaged

underrate
08 belittle
09 sell short
10 depreciate, look down on, undervalue
13 underestimate

undersell
06 reduce
08 play down, undercut
09 disparage, sell short
10 depreciate, understate

undersized
04 pint-, puny, tiny
05 dwarf, pygmy, small
06 little, minute
07 runtish, stunted
09 miniature, pint-sized
11 underweight
14 underdeveloped
15 achondroplastic

understand
03 get, see
04 hear, know, twig
05 click, grasp, learn, savvy, think
06 accept, assume, fathom, gather, rumble, take in
07 believe, discern, make out, presume, realize, suppose
08 conclude, cotton on, perceive, tumble to
09 apprehend, empathize, figure out, recognize
10 appreciate, comprehend, sympathize
11 commiserate
12 get the hang of, identify with
13 get the message, get the picture

understanding
04 idea, kind, pact, view
05 grasp, sense, trust

06 accord, belief, loving, notion, tender, wisdom
07 bargain, comfort, compact, empathy, entente, feeling, harmony, insight, lenient, opinion, patient, support
08 sympathy, tolerant
09 agreement, awareness, intellect, judgement, knowledge, sensitive
10 compassion, forbearing, impression, perception, supportive, thoughtful
11 considerate, consolation, discernment, sympathetic
12 appreciation, apprehension, intelligence
13 compassionate, comprehension
14 interpretation

understate
08 belittle, minimize, play down
09 soft-pedal, underplay
11 make light of

understatement
07 litotes, meiosis
09 restraint
12 minimization, underplaying

understood
05 tacit
07 assumed, implied
08 accepted, implicit, inferred, presumed, unspoken, unstated
09 unwritten

understudy
05 locum
06 deputy, double, fill in, relief
07 reserve, stand-in
10 substitute
11 replacement

undertake
05 agree, begin
06 accept, assume, pledge, tackle, take on
07 attempt, promise
08 commence, contract, embark on, set about
09 endeavour, guarantee

undertaker
09 mortician
15 funeral director

undertaking
03 job, vow
04 task, word
06 affair, effort, pledge, scheme
07 promise, venture, warrant
08 business

09 assurance, guarantee
10 commitment, enterprise

undertone
04 aura, hint
05 tinge, touch, trace
06 murmur
07 feeling, flavour, whisper
10 intimation, suggestion
12 undercurrent

undervalue
09 disparage, sell short, underrate
10 depreciate, look down on
13 underestimate

underwater
06 sunken
08 immersed, undersea
09 submarine, submerged
10 subaquatic, subaqueous

underwear
06 smalls, undies
08 frillies, lingerie
12 underclothes
13 undergarments
14 unmentionables

underweight
04 thin
08 underfed
10 undersized
11 half-starved
14 undernourished

underworld
04 hell
05 Hades
06 the mob
08 gangland
10 the Inferno
13 criminal world
14 organized crime

underwrite
04 back, fund, sign
06 insure
07 approve, confirm, endorse, finance, support
09 authorize, guarantee

undesirable
04 foul
05 nasty
09 obnoxious, offensive, repugnant, unwelcome
13 objectionable

undeveloped
07 dwarfed, stunted
08 immature, inchoate, unformed
09 embryonic, potential
10 developing, Third World

undignified
08 improper, ungainly, unseemly
09 inelegant
10 indecorous

undisciplined
04 wild
06 unruly, wilful
07 wayward
11 disobedient
12 disorganized, obstreperous, uncontrolled, unrestrained

undisguised
04 open
05 frank, naked, overt, stark
06 patent
07 blatant, evident, obvious
08 explicit, manifest, outright
09 unadorned
11 transparent, unconcealed

undisguisedly
06 openly
07 frankly, overtly
08 outright, patently
09 blatantly, obviously
13 transparently

undisputed
04 sure
07 certain
08 accepted
09 undoubted
10 conclusive, recognized, undeniable
11 irrefutable, uncontested
12 indisputable, unchallenged, unquestioned

undistinguished
05 banal
06 common
08 inferior, mediocre, ordinary
10 not much cop, pedestrian
11 indifferent, not up to much
12 unremarkable
13 no great shakes, unexceptional

undisturbed
04 calm, even
05 quiet
06 placid, serene
07 equable
08 composed, tranquil
09 unruffled, untouched
10 unaffected, untroubled
11 unconcerned, unperturbed
13 uninterrupted

undivided
04 full
05 solid, total, whole
06 entire, intact, united

08 complete, unbroken
09 dedicated, exclusive, unanimous
12 concentrated, wholehearted

undo
05 loose, quash, spoil, untie, unzip, wreck
06 defeat, loosen, repeal, revoke, unhook, unlock
07 nullify, release, reverse
08 overturn, unbuckle, unbutton, unfasten

undoing
04 ruin
05 shame
06 defeat
08 collapse, disgrace, downfall
09 overthrow, ruination
11 destruction

undomesticated
04 wild
05 feral
06 savage
07 natural, untamed

undone
05 loose
06 ruined, untied
07 ignored, omitted, unlaced
08 betrayed, unlocked
09 destroyed
10 passed over, unbuttoned, unfastened, unfinished
11 outstanding, uncompleted, unfulfilled

undoubted
04 sure
07 certain
08 definite
10 undisputed
11 indubitable, irrefutable, uncontested
12 indisputable, unchallenged
14 unquestionable

undoubtedly
06 surely
07 no doubt
08 of course
09 assuredly, certainly
10 definitely, undeniably
11 beyond doubt, indubitably
12 unmistakably, without doubt
14 unquestionably

undreamed-of
08 undreamt
09 unheard-of
10 incredible, miraculous, unexpected, unforeseen, unhoped-for, unimagined
11 astonishing, unsuspected

undress
05 strip
06 divest, nudity, remove
07 disrobe, peel off, take off
08 unclothe
10 dishabille, déshabillé

undressed
04 bare, nude
05 naked
08 disrobed, stripped
09 unclothed
10 stark naked

undue
07 extreme
08 improper, needless
09 excessive
10 inordinate, undeserved
11 uncalled-for, unjustified, unnecessary, unwarranted
13 inappropriate

undulate
04 roll, wave
05 heave, surge, swell
06 billow, ripple
11 rise and fall

undulating
04 wavy
06 undate
07 rolling, sinuous
08 flexuose, flexuous, rippling
09 billowing

unduly
03 too
04 over
11 excessively
12 immoderately, inordinately
13 unjustifiably, unnecessarily

undutiful
05 slack
06 remiss
08 careless, disloyal, unfilial
09 negligent
10 neglectful

undying
07 abiding, eternal, lasting
08 constant, immortal, infinite, unending, unfading
09 deathless, perpetual
11 everlasting, sempiternal
12 imperishable
14 indestructible

unearth
05 dig up
06 exhume, expose, reveal
07 uncover
08 discover, disinter, excavate
12 bring to light

unearthly
05 eerie, weird
06 creepy
07 ghostly, phantom, strange, uncanny, ungodly
08 eldritch
12 other-worldly, supernatural
13 preternatural, spine-chilling

uneasiness
05 alarm, doubt, worry
06 qualms, unease
07 anxiety, dis-ease
08 disquiet
09 misgiving
10 inquietude
11 nervousness
12 apprehension, perturbation

uneasy
04 edgy
05 nervy, shaky, tense, upset
06 on edge, unsure
07 alarmed, anxious, jittery, keyed up, nervous, twitchy, worried, wound up
08 agitated, insecure, restless, strained, troubled, worrying
09 disturbed, perturbed, unnerving, unsettled
10 disturbing, perturbing
12 apprehensive
13 uncomfortable

uneconomic
10 loss-making
12 uncommercial, unprofitable

uneducated
06 unread
08 ignorant, untaught
09 benighted
10 illiterate, philistine, uncultured, unschooled

unemotional
04 cold, cool
08 detached, reserved
09 apathetic, impassive, objective, unfeeling
10 phlegmatic
11 indifferent
13 dispassionate

unemphatic
10 played-down
11 underplayed, understated

unemployed
04 idle
07 jobless, laid off, unwaged
09 on the dole, out of work, redundant

unending
07 endless, eternal, undying
09 ceaseless, continual, incessant, unceasing
11 everlasting, never-ending, unremitting
12 interminable

unendurable
10 unbearable
11 intolerable
12 insufferable, overwhelming
13 insupportable

unenthusiastic
04 cool
05 blasé, bored
07 neutral, unmoved
08 lukewarm
09 apathetic, Laodicean
10 nonchalant
11 half-hearted, unimpressed
12 uninterested, unresponsive

unenviable
09 difficult, thankless
11 uncongenial, undesirable
12 disagreeable

unequal
06 biased, uneven, unfair, unjust, unlike
07 not up to, varying
08 lopsided, unfitted, unsuited
09 incapable, unmatched
10 unbalanced
11 incompetent, inequitable, unqualified
12 asymmetrical, not cut out for
14 discriminatory

unequalled
08 peerless
09 matchless, nonpareil, paramount, unmatched
10 inimitable, unrivalled
11 unsurpassed
12 incomparable, unparalleled

unequivocal
05 clear, plain
06 direct
07 evident, express
08 absolute, definite, explicit, positive, straight
11 categorical, unambiguous
12 unmistakable
15 straightforward

unerring
04 dead, sure
05 exact
07 certain, perfect, uncanny
08 accurate
09 faultless, unfailing
10 impeccable, infallible

unerringly
04 bang, dead
10 accurately, infallibly
11 unfailingly

unethical
05 shady, wrong
07 illegal, illicit, immoral
08 improper
12 disreputable, unprincipled, unscrupulous
13 dishonourable

uneven
03 odd
05 bumpy, lumpy, rough
06 coarse, fitful, patchy, unfair
07 crooked, erratic, unequal
08 lopsided, one-sided, unsteady, variable
09 irregular, spasmodic
10 ill-matched, unbalanced
11 fluctuating, inequitable
12 asymmetrical, inconsistent, intermittent

uneventful
04 dull
05 quiet
06 boring
07 humdrum, routine, tedious
10 monotonous, unexciting

unexampled
05 novel
06 unique
09 unheard-of, unmatched
10 unequalled
12 incomparable, unparalleled
13 unprecedented

unexceptional
06 common, normal
07 average, typical
08 mediocre, ordinary
11 indifferent
12 run-of-the-mill, unimpressive, unremarkable
15 undistinguished

unexcitable
04 calm, cool
06 serene
08 composed, laid-back
09 easy-going
10 phlegmatic
13 imperturbable, self-possessed

unexpected
06 chance
10 accidental, fortuitous, unforeseen
11 unlooked-for
13 unanticipated, unpredictable

unexpectedly
08 by chance
12 fortuitously, out of the blue

13 unpredictably
14 without warning

unexpressive
06 vacant
07 dead-pan
09 impassive
11 emotionless, inscrutable
14 expressionless

unfading
07 abiding, durable, lasting
08 enduring
09 evergreen

unfailing
04 sure, true
06 steady
07 certain, staunch, undying
08 constant, faithful, reliable
09 steadfast
10 dependable, infallible

unfair
06 biased, unjust
07 bigoted, crooked, partial, slanted
08 one-sided, partisan
09 arbitrary, unmerited
10 prejudiced, unbalanced, undeserved
11 inequitable, uncalled-for, unwarranted
12 below the belt

unfairness
04 bias
07 bigotry
08 inequity
09 injustice, prejudice
10 partiality
12 one-sidedness, partisanship
14 discrimination

unfaithful
05 false
06 fickle, untrue
08 cheating, disloyal
09 deceitful, dishonest, faithless, two-timing
10 adulterous, inconstant, perfidious, unreliable
11 duplicitous, treacherous
13 untrustworthy

unfaltering
04 firm
06 steady
08 constant, resolute, tireless, untiring
09 steadfast, unfailing
10 unflagging, unswerving, unwavering, unyielding
11 unflinching
12 pertinacious
13 indefatigable

unfamiliar
05 alien
07 foreign, strange, unknown
09 uncharted
10 unexplored
12 unaccustomed

unfashionable
03 out
05 dated, passé
06 démodé, old hat, square
08 obsolete, outmoded
10 out of date, unpopular
12 old-fashioned

unfasten
04 open, undo
05 untie
06 detach, loosen, unlock
08 separate, uncouple
10 disconnect

unfathomable
04 deep
06 hidden
08 abstruse, baffling, esoteric, profound
09 unplumbed, unsounded
10 bottomless, fathomless, mysterious, unknowable
11 inscrutable
12 immeasurable, impenetrable, inexplicable
14 indecipherable

unfavourable
03 bad
04 poor
07 adverse, hostile, ominous
08 critical, inimical, negative
11 inopportune, threatening
12 discouraging, inauspicious
15 disadvantageous, uncomplimentary

unfeeling
04 cold, hard
05 cruel, harsh, stony
07 callous, inhuman
08 pitiless, uncaring
09 apathetic, heartless
11 hard-hearted, insensitive
13 unsympathetic

unfeigned
04 pure, real
07 genuine, natural, sincere
08 unforced
09 heartfelt
10 unaffected
12 wholehearted

unfettered
04 free
09 unbridled, unchecked
10 unhindered

11　uninhibited
12　unrestrained, untrammelled
13　unconstrained

unfinished
05　crude, rough
07　sketchy
10　incomplete
11　uncompleted, unfulfilled
14　unaccomplished

unfit
05　inapt
06　feeble, flabby, unable
07　unequal, useless
08　decrepit, unsuited
09　incapable, unhealthy, untrained
10　inadequate, unsuitable
11　debilitated, incompetent, ineffective, unqualified
13　inappropriate
14　out of condition

unflagging
06　steady
07　staunch
08　constant, tireless, untiring
09　unceasing, unfailing
10　persistent, unswerving
11　persevering, unfaltering
12　never-failing
13　indefatigable

unflappable
04　calm, cool
07　equable
08　composed
09　collected, unruffled
10　phlegmatic
11　level-headed
13　imperturbable, self-possessed

unflattering
06　candid, honest
08　critical
09　outspoken
10　unbecoming
12　unfavourable
15　uncomplimentary

unflinching
06　steady
07　staunch
08　resolute, stalwart, unshaken
09　steadfast
10　unblinking, unswerving
11　unfaltering

unfold
04　grow, open, show, tell
06　emerge, evolve, relate, result, reveal, spread
07　develop, explain, open out, present, work out

08　disclose
09　elaborate, spread out
10　straighten, stretch out

unforeseen
10　unexpected
11　unlooked-for, unpredicted
13　unanticipated, unpredictable

unforgettable
07　notable, special
08　historic, striking
09　memorable, momentous
10　noteworthy, remarkable
11　distinctive, exceptional, significant

unforgivable
08　shameful
10　deplorable, outrageous
11　disgraceful, inexcusable, intolerable
12　indefensible, unpardonable
13　reprehensible, unjustifiable

unforgiven
10　unabsolved, unredeemed

unfortunate
07　adverse, hapless, ruinous, unhappy, unlucky
08　hopeless, ill-fated, ill-timed, luckless, untimely, untoward
10　calamitous, deplorable, disastrous, ill-advised, lamentable, unsuitable
11　injudicious, inopportune, regrettable
12　unfavourable, unsuccessful
13　inappropriate
15　disadvantageous

unfortunately
04　alas
05　sadly
09　unhappily, unluckily, worse luck
11　regrettably

unfounded
08　baseless, spurious, unproven
10　groundless
11　conjectural, unjustified, unsupported
14　uncorroborated
15　unsubstantiated

unfrequented
06　remote
08　desolate, isolated, secluded
09　unvisited

unfriendly
04　cold, cool, sour
05　aloof, surly
06　chilly, frosty, unkind

07　distant, hostile
08　inimical, strained
10　aggressive, unsociable
11　ill-disposed, quarrelsome, standoffish, unwelcoming
12　antagonistic, inhospitable

unfrock
06　demote, depose
07　degrade, dismiss, suspend

unfruitful
06　barren
07　sterile
08　infecund
09　fruitless, infertile
11　infructuous, unrewarding
12　unproductive, unprofitable

ungainly
05　gawky
06　clumsy, gauche
07　awkward, loutish, uncouth
08　gangling, unwieldy
09　inelegant, lumbering, maladroit

ungodly
06　sinful, wicked
07　corrupt, godless, immoral, impious, profane
09　unearthly
10　iniquitous, outrageous
11　blasphemous, irreligious
12　preposterous, unreasonable

ungovernable
04　wild
06　unruly
10　rebellious, refractory
12　unmanageable
14　uncontrollable

ungracious
04　rude
07　boorish, ill-bred, uncivil
08　churlish, impolite
09　graceless
10　unmannerly
11　bad-mannered
12　discourteous
13　disrespectful

ungrateful
07　selfish, uncivil
08　heedless, impolite
09　thankless
10　ungracious, unthankful
14　unappreciative

unguarded
04　rash
06　unwary
08　careless, heedless, off guard
09　foolhardy, imprudent
10　incautious, indiscreet, unthinking, undefended

11 defenceless, inattentive, thoughtless, unprotected
13 ill-considered

unhappily
04 alas
05 sadly
08 sad to say
09 unluckily, worse luck
11 regrettably, sad to relate
13 unfortunately

unhappy
03 low, sad
04 blue, down, glum
05 fed up, inapt
06 clumsy, gloomy
07 awkward, hapless, unlucky
08 dejected, downcast, ill-fated, mournful, tactless
09 depressed, long-faced, miserable, sorrowful, woebegone
10 despondent, dispirited, ill-advised, ill-starred, melancholy, unsuitable
11 crestfallen, injudicious, unfortunate
12 disconsolate
13 inappropriate
14 down in the dumps

unharmed
04 safe
05 sound, whole
06 intact, unhurt
09 undamaged, uninjured, unscathed, untouched

unhealthy
03 ill
04 sick, weak
06 ailing, feeble, infirm, poorly, sickly, unwell
07 invalid, noxious, unsound
09 injurious, unnatural
10 insanitary, unhygienic
11 unwholesome
12 insalubrious

unheard-of
06 unsung
07 obscure, unknown, unusual
10 outrageous, unfamiliar
11 undreamed-of
12 unacceptable, unbelievable, undiscovered, unimaginable
13 inconceivable

unheeded
07 ignored, unnoted
09 disobeyed, unnoticed
10 overlooked, unobserved
11 disregarded

unheralded
10 unexpected, unforeseen
11 unannounced
12 unpublicized

unhesitating
06 prompt
07 instant
09 automatic, immediate
10 unwavering
11 spontaneous, unfaltering
12 wholehearted
13 instantaneous, unquestioning

unhinge
05 craze, upset
06 madden
07 confuse, derange, unnerve
08 disorder, distract, drive mad
09 unbalance

unholy
06 sinful, wicked
07 corrupt, godless, immoral, impious, ungodly
09 unearthly
10 iniquitous
11 blasphemous, irreligious

unhoped-for
10 unexpected, unforeseen
11 undreamed-of, unlooked-for
13 unanticipated

unhurried
04 calm, easy, slow
06 sedate
07 relaxed
08 laid-back
09 easy-going, leisurely
10 deliberate

unhurt
04 safe
05 sound, whole
06 intact
08 unharmed
09 uninjured, unscathed, untouched

unhygienic
04 foul
05 dirty
06 filthy, impure
07 noisome, noxious, unclean
08 feculent, infected, polluted
09 unhealthy
10 insanitary
12 contaminated, insalubrious

unidentified
07 strange, unknown, unnamed
08 nameless, unmarked

09 anonymous, incognito
10 mysterious, unfamiliar

unification
05 union
06 enosis, fusion, merger
07 uniting
11 coalescence, combination

uniform
04 even, flat, garb, same, suit
05 alike, dress, equal, robes
06 livery, outfit, smooth, stable
07 costume, regalia, regular
08 constant, insignia, unbroken
09 identical, unvarying
10 consistent, unchanging
11 homogeneous, regimentals

uniformity
08 evenness, monotony, sameness
09 constancy
10 regularity
11 homogeneity
12 homomorphism

unify
03 mix
04 bind, fuse, join, weld
05 blend, merge, unite
07 combine
08 coalesce
09 integrate
10 amalgamate
11 consolidate
12 come together
13 bring together

unifying
07 henotic, uniting
11 combinatory, esemplastic
13 consolidative

unimaginable
07 amazing
09 fantastic, unheard-of
10 far-fetched, incredible, outlandish
11 implausible, unthinkable
12 mind-boggling, preposterous, unbelievable
13 extraordinary, inconceivable

unimaginative
05 banal, samey, stale
06 barren, boring
07 mundane, routine
09 hackneyed
10 pedestrian, uninspired
12 matter-of-fact

unimpeachable
07 perfect
09 faultless
10 immaculate, impeccable
11 unblemished

12 unassailable
14 irreproachable

unimpeded
04 free, open
05 clear
08 all-round
09 unblocked, unchecked
10 unhampered, unhindered
12 unrestrained, untrammelled

unimportant
05 minor, petty
06 slight
07 trivial
08 marginal, nugatory, trifling
09 no big deal, secondary
10 immaterial, incidental,
   irrelevant, negligible,
   peripheral
13 insignificant
15 inconsequential

unimpressive
08 mediocre, ordinary
11 commonplace, indifferent
12 unremarkable
13 unexceptional,
   uninteresting,
   unspectacular
15 undistinguished

uninhabited
05 empty
06 vacant
08 deserted, desolate
09 abandoned, unpeopled
10 unoccupied
11 unpopulated

uninhibited
04 free, open
09 abandoned, liberated,
   outspoken
10 unreserved
11 spontaneous
12 unrestrained
13 unconstrained
15 unselfconscious

uninspired
04 dull
05 stale, stock, trite
06 boring
07 humdrum, prosaic
08 ordinary
10 pedestrian, unexciting
11 uninspiring
13 unimaginative, uninteresting

unintelligent
04 dull, dumb, slow
05 dense, silly, thick
06 obtuse, stupid
08 gormless
09 brainless

10 half-witted, unthinking
11 empty-headed

unintelligible
07 complex, garbled, jumbled,
   muddled, obscure
08 involved, puzzling
09 illegible, scrambled
10 incoherent, mysterious,
   unreadable
11 complicated, double Dutch
12 impenetrable, inarticulate,
   unfathomable
14 indecipherable

unintentional
09 unplanned, unwitting
10 accidental, fortuitous,
   unintended
11 inadvertent, involuntary
14 unpremeditated

uninterested
05 blasé, bored
09 apathetic, impassive
11 indifferent, unconcerned
14 unenthusiastic

uninteresting
03 dry
04 drab, dull, flat, tame
05 stale
06 boring, dreary
07 humdrum, prosaic, tedious
10 pedestrian, unexciting
11 uninspiring

uninterrupted
07 endless, non-stop
08 constant, unbroken
09 ceaseless, unceasing
10 continuous
11 undisturbed, unremitting

uninvited
07 unasked
08 unsought, unwanted
09 unwelcome
11 unsolicited

uninviting
09 offensive, repellent,
   repulsive, unsavoury
10 off-putting, unpleasant
11 distasteful, unappealing
12 unappetizing, unattractive

uninvolved
04 free
09 fancy-free, footloose
10 unattached, unhampered,
   unhindered
11 independent, uncommitted
12 untrammelled

union
04 club
05 blend, unity

06 fusion, merger
07 harmony, joining, mixture,
   wedding, wedlock
08 alliance, juncture, marriage,
   nuptials
09 agreement, coalition,
   matrimony, synthesis,
   unanimity
10 consortium, federation,
   trade union
11 combination, confederacy,
   unification

unique
04 lone, only, sole
06 one-off, single
08 peerless, solitary
09 matchless, nonpareil
10 inimitable, one and only, one
   of a kind, sui generis,
   unequalled, unrivalled
12 incomparable, unparalleled

unison
05 unity
06 accord
07 concert, concord
09 unanimity

unit
03 one
04 item, part
05 piece, whole
06 entity, module, system
07 element, section, segment
09 component

unite
04 ally, band, fuse, join, link,
   pool, weld
05 blend, marry, merge, unify
06 couple
07 combine, connect
08 coalesce, federate
09 associate, co-operate
10 amalgamate, join forces
11 confederate, consolidate
12 pull together

united
03 one
06 agreed, allied, pooled
07 unified
08 combined, in accord
09 concerted, unanimous
10 collective
11 in agreement

unity
05 peace, union
06 accord
07 concert, harmony, oneness
09 agreement, consensus,
   unanimity, wholeness
10 solidarity
11 unification

universal
05 total, whole
06 common, cosmic, global
07 general
08 all-round
09 worldwide
10 ubiquitous
11 omnipresent
12 all-embracing, all-inclusive
13 comprehensive
14 across-the-board

universality
08 entirety, totality, ubiquity
10 commonness, generality, prevalence

universally
06 always
09 uniformly
10 everywhere, invariably
12 ubiquitously

universe
05 world
06 cosmos, nature
08 creation
09 firmament, macrocosm

university
07 academy, college, varsity
08 academia
09 institute

───────────────
➤ *Names of Ivy League universities*:
04 Yale
05 Brown
07 Cornell, Harvard
08 Columbia
09 Dartmouth, Princeton
12 Pennsylvania
➤ See also **college**

unjust
06 biased, unfair
07 partial
08 one-sided, partisan
10 prejudiced, undeserved
11 inequitable, unjustified
12 unreasonable

unjustifiable
09 excessive
10 immoderate, outrageous
11 inexcusable, unwarranted
12 indefensible, unacceptable, unreasonable

unkempt
05 messy
06 shabby, sloppy, untidy
07 rumpled, scruffy, tousled
08 slobbish, slovenly, uncombed
09 shambolic, ungroomed
10 disordered
11 dishevelled

unkind
04 mean
05 cruel, harsh, nasty, snide
07 callous, inhuman, vicious
08 inhumane, pitiless, uncaring
09 heartless, malicious
10 malevolent, unfriendly
11 cold-hearted, hard-hearted
12 uncharitable

unkindness
05 spite
07 cruelty
08 meanness
09 harshness
15 hard-heartedness

unknowable
08 infinite
12 incalculable, unfathomable, unimaginable

unknown
05 alien
06 hidden, secret, untold
07 foreign, strange, unnamed
08 nameless
09 anonymous, uncharted
10 mysterious, unexplored, unfamiliar
12 unidentified

unlawful
06 banned
07 illegal, illicit
08 criminal, outlawed
09 forbidden
10 prohibited, unlicensed
12 illegitimate
13 against the law

unleash
04 free
05 loose, untie
07 release, unloose
08 let loose, untether

unlettered
08 ignorant, untaught
09 unlearned, untutored
10 illiterate, uneducated

unlike
07 diverse, opposed, unequal
08 distinct, opposite
09 different, disparate, divergent, unrelated
10 contrasted, dissimilar
11 as opposed to
12 in contrast to, incompatible

unlikely
06 remote, slight
07 distant, dubious, suspect
08 doubtful
10 far-fetched, improbable, unexpected

11 implausible
12 unbelievable, unimaginable
13 inconceivable

unlimited
07 endless, immense
08 complete, infinite
09 boundless, countless, extensive, unbounded
10 indefinite, unhampered
12 immeasurable, unrestricted
13 unconditional, unconstrained
15 all-encompassing

unload
04 dump
05 empty
07 offload, relieve
08 unburden
09 discharge

unlock
04 free, open, undo
05 unbar
06 unbolt
07 release, unlatch
08 unfasten

unlooked-for
06 chance
08 surprise
10 fortuitous, unexpected, unforeseen
11 unthought-of
13 unanticipated

unloved
08 loveless, unwanted
09 neglected
10 uncared-for

unlucky
04 poor
06 cursed, doomed, jinxed
07 adverse, hapless, ominous
08 ill-fated, luckless, untoward, wretched
09 miserable
10 calamitous, disastrous, ill-starred, unpleasant
11 star-crossed, unfortunate, unpromising
12 catastrophic, inauspicious, unfavourable, unpropitious, unsuccessful
14 down on your luck
15 disadvantageous

unmanageable
06 unruly
07 awkward
08 unwieldy
10 cumbersome, disorderly, refractory

12 incommodious, inconvenient, ungovernable
14 uncontrollable

unmanly
04 soft, weak
05 sissy, weedy
06 craven, feeble, yellow
07 wimpish
08 cowardly
09 weak-kneed
10 effeminate, namby-pamby
14 chicken-hearted

unmannerly
04 rude
07 boorish, ill-bred, low-bred, uncivil, uncouth
08 impolite
09 graceless
10 ungracious
12 discourteous
13 disrespectful

unmarried
05 unwed
06 single
08 celibate
09 available
10 unattached

unmask
04 bare, show
06 expose, reveal, unveil
07 uncover
08 disclose, discover

unmatched
06 unique
07 supreme
08 peerless
09 matchless, nonpareil, paramount
10 consummate, unequalled, unexampled, unrivalled
11 unsurpassed
12 incomparable, unparalleled
13 beyond compare

unmentionable
05 taboo
08 immodest, indecent, shameful, shocking
10 abominable, scandalous, unpleasant
11 disgraceful, unspeakable, unutterable
12 embarrassing

unmerciful
05 cruel
07 callous
08 pitiless
09 heartless, merciless
10 implacable, relentless
11 remorseless, unrelenting

unmethodical
07 muddled
09 haphazard, illogical
11 unorganized
12 unsystematic

unmindful
07 unaware
08 careless, heedless
09 forgetful, negligent, oblivious, unheeding
10 neglectful, regardless
11 inattentive, indifferent, unconscious

unmistakable
05 clear, plain
06 patent
07 blatant, certain, evident, glaring, obvious
08 clear-cut, definite, distinct, explicit, manifest, striking
10 pronounced, undeniable
11 conspicuous, indubitable
12 indisputable
14 beyond question, unquestionable

unmitigated
04 grim, pure, rank
05 harsh, sheer, utter
06 arrant
07 intense, perfect
08 absolute, complete, outright, thorough
09 downright, out-and-out
10 consummate, unmodified, unrelieved
11 unrelenting, unremitting
12 unalleviated, undiminished
13 thoroughgoing

unmoved
04 cold, firm
06 steady
07 adamant, dry-eyed
08 resolute, resolved, unshaken
09 impassive, unbending, untouched
10 inflexible, unaffected
11 indifferent, unimpressed

unnatural
05 false, queer, stiff
06 forced, staged
07 stilted, strange, uncanny, unusual
08 abnormal, affected, freakish, laboured, peculiar, strained
09 contrived, insincere, perverted
10 artificial
13 unspontaneous

unnecessary
06 wasted

08 needless, unneeded, unwanted
09 redundant
10 expendable, gratuitous, unrequired
11 dispensable, inessential, superfluous, uncalled-for
12 non-essential, tautological

unnerve
05 alarm, daunt, scare, shake, unman, upset, worry
06 deject, dismay, put out, rattle
07 fluster, perturb
08 confound, disquiet, frighten, unsettle
10 disconcert, intimidate

unnoticed
06 unseen
08 unheeded
10 overlooked, unobserved, unremarked
12 unrecognized

unobtrusive
05 quiet
06 low-key, modest
07 subdued
08 retiring
10 restrained, unassuming
12 unnoticeable
13 inconspicuous

unobtrusively
07 quietly
08 modestly
10 on the quiet
15 inconspicuously, surreptitiously

unoccupied
04 free, idle
05 empty
06 vacant
08 deserted, inactive
10 unemployed
11 uninhabited

unofficial
07 illegal, private
08 informal, personal
10 undeclared
12 confidential, off-the-record, unauthorized

unoriginal
05 stale, trite
06 copied
07 cribbed, derived
09 hackneyed
10 derivative, uninspired

unorthodox
06 fringe
07 unusual
08 abnormal

09 eccentric, heterodox
11 alternative
13 nonconformist
14 unconventional

unpaid
03 due
05 owing
07 overdue, payable, pending, unwaged
09 unsettled, voluntary
10 unsalaried
11 outstanding, uncollected

unpalatable
08 inedible
09 repugnant, uneatable, unsavoury
11 distasteful
12 disagreeable, unappetizing

unparalleled
04 rare
07 supreme
08 peerless
09 matchless, unmatched
10 unequalled, unrivalled
11 unsurpassed
12 incomparable, without equal
13 beyond compare, unprecedented

unpardonable
08 shameful
10 deplorable, outrageous, scandalous
11 disgraceful, inexcusable
12 indefensible, unforgivable
14 unconscionable

unperturbed
04 calm, cool
06 placid, poised, serene
08 composed, tranquil
09 unexcited, unruffled, unworried
10 untroubled
11 unflustered

unpleasant
03 bad
04 foul, mean, rude
05 nasty, surly
08 impolite
09 offensive
10 ill-natured, unfriendly
11 distasteful, undesirable, unpalatable
12 disagreeable, unattractive

unpleasantness
05 upset
06 bother, furore
07 scandal, trouble
10 ill-feeling

unpolished
04 rude
05 crude, rough
06 coarse, vulgar
07 uncouth
09 unrefined
13 rough and ready
15 unsophisticated

unpopular
07 ignored, shunned, unloved
08 disliked, rejected, unwanted
10 friendless
13 unfashionable

unprecedented
03 new
07 unknown, unusual
08 abnormal, freakish, original, uncommon
09 unheard-of
10 remarkable, unequalled, unrivalled
11 exceptional
12 unparalleled
13 extraordinary, revolutionary

unpredictable
06 chance, fickle, random
07 erratic
08 unstable, variable, volatile
09 mercurial
10 capricious, changeable, inconstant, unreliable
13 unforeseeable

unprejudiced
04 fair, just
08 balanced, unbiased
09 impartial, objective
10 even-handed, uncoloured
11 enlightened, non-partisan

unpremeditated
09 extempore, impromptu, impulsive, unplanned
10 off-the-cuff, unprepared
11 spontaneous, unrehearsed
15 spur-of-the-moment

unprepared
05 ad-lib
07 unready
09 unplanned, unwilling
10 improvised, off-the-cuff
11 ill-equipped, spontaneous, unrehearsed
12 unsuspecting

unpretentious
05 plain
06 honest, humble, modest, simple
07 natural
08 ordinary
10 unaffected, unassuming

11 unobtrusive
14 unostentatious
15 straightforward

unprincipled
07 corrupt, crooked, devious, immoral
09 deceitful, dishonest, underhand, unethical
12 unscrupulous

unproductive
04 arid, idle, vain
06 barren, futile, otiose
07 sterile, useless
09 fruitless, infertile, worthless
10 unfruitful
11 ineffective, unrewarding
12 unprofitable

unprofessional
09 negligent, unethical
10 amateurish
11 incompetent, inefficient
13 inexperienced

unpromising
08 doubtful
12 discouraging, inauspicious, unfavourable, unpropitious

unprotected
05 naked
07 exposed, unarmed
08 helpless
09 uncovered, unguarded
10 unattended, undefended, unshielded, vulnerable
11 defenceless, unfortified, unsheltered

unprovable
12 unverifiable
14 indemonstrable, undemonstrable

unqualified
05 total, unfit, utter
07 amateur, perfect
08 absolute, complete, outright, positive, thorough
09 downright, incapable, out and out, untrained
10 ineligible, unlicensed, unprepared, unreserved
11 categorical, ill-equipped, unequivocal, unmitigated
12 unrestricted, wholehearted
13 unconditional

unquestionable
04 sure
06 patent
07 certain, obvious
08 absolute, definite, manifest
09 faultless
10 conclusive, undeniable

11 indubitable, irrefutable, self-evident, unequivocal
12 indisputable, unmistakable
13 incontestable
14 beyond question

unquestioning
11 unqualified
12 unhesitating, wholehearted
13 unconditional

unravel
04 free, undo
05 solve
06 unknot, unwind
07 clear up, explain, resolve, sort out, work out
08 separate, untangle
09 extricate, figure out, penetrate
11 disentangle
13 straighten out

unreadable
07 complex, garbled, jumbled, muddled, obscure
09 illegible, scrambled
10 incoherent, mysterious
11 complicated, double Dutch
12 impenetrable, inarticulate, unfathomable
14 indecipherable, unintelligible

unreal
04 fake, mock, sham
05 false
06 made-up
07 bizarre, pretend
08 fanciful, illusory, mythical, nebulous
09 fairy-tale, fantastic, imaginary, synthetic
10 artificial, chimerical, fictitious, immaterial
11 make-believe, non-existent
13 insubstantial

unrealistic
08 quixotic, romantic
10 idealistic, impossible, unworkable
11 impractical, theoretical
13 impracticable
14 over-optimistic

unreasonable
05 silly, steep, undue
06 absurd, biased, stupid, unfair, unjust
08 perverse
09 arbitrary, excessive, expensive, illogical, ludicrous, senseless
10 far-fetched, immoderate, irrational, outrageous

11 nonsensical, uncalled-for, unjustified, unwarranted
12 extortionate, inconsistent, preposterous, unacceptable

unrecognizable
07 altered, changed
09 disguised, incognito
10 unknowable

unrecognized
06 unseen
07 ignored
08 unheeded
10 overlooked, unobserved, unremarked
11 disregarded

unrefined
03 raw
05 crude
06 coarse, vulgar
10 uncultured, unfinished, unpolished
11 unprocessed
12 uncultivated
15 unsophisticated

unregenerate
06 sinful, wicked
08 obdurate, stubborn
09 obstinate, shameless
10 impenitent, unreformed
11 intractable, unrepentant
12 incorrigible, recalcitrant

unrelated
09 different, disparate
10 dissimilar, extraneous, irrelevant
11 independent, off the point, unconnected
12 unassociated
14 beside the point

unrelenting
05 cruel
06 steady
08 constant, pitiless, ruthless, unabated, unbroken
09 ceaseless, continual, incessant, merciless, unceasing, unsparing
10 continuous, inexorable, relentless, unmerciful
11 remorseless, unforgiving, unremitting
12 intransigent

unreliable
04 iffy
06 fickle
07 unsound
08 doubtful, slippery
09 deceptive
10 inaccurate

12 unconvincing, undependable
13 irresponsible, untrustworthy

unremitting
08 constant, unabated
09 ceaseless, continual, incessant, perpetual, unceasing
10 continuous, relentless
11 remorseless, unrelenting

unrepentant
08 hardened, obdurate
09 shameless, unashamed
10 impenitent
12 incorrigible, unapologetic

unreserved
04 free, full, open
05 frank, total
06 candid, direct, entire
08 absolute, complete, outgoing
09 outspoken
10 forthright
11 uninhibited, unqualified
12 unrestrained, wholehearted
13 demonstrative, unconditional

unreservedly
07 utterly
08 entirely, outright
10 completely
14 wholeheartedly

unresisting
04 meek
06 docile
07 passive
08 obedient
10 submissive

unresolved
04 moot
05 vague, vexed
08 doubtful, unsolved
09 undecided, unsettled
10 indefinite, up in the air
12 undetermined

unresponsive
07 unmoved
09 apathetic
11 indifferent
13 unsympathetic

unrest
06 unease
07 discord, protest, turmoil
08 disorder, disquiet
09 agitation, rebellion
10 dissension, uneasiness
12 perturbation, restlessness

unrestrained
04 free

09 abandoned, unbounded, unbridled, unchecked
10 boisterous, immoderate, unhindered, unreserved
11 intemperate, uninhibited
12 uncontrolled
13 unconstrained

unrestricted
04 free, open
05 clear
09 unbounded, unimpeded, unlimited, unopposed
10 free-for-all, unhindered
12 unobstructed

unripe
05 green
07 unready
08 immature
09 unripened

unrivalled
07 supreme
08 peerless
09 matchless, nonpareil
10 inimitable, unequalled
12 incomparable, unparalleled, without equal
13 beyond compare

unruffled
04 calm, cool, even
06 serene, smooth
08 composed, tranquil
10 untroubled
11 undisturbed, unperturbed

unruly
04 wild
05 rowdy
07 lawless, riotous, wayward
10 disorderly, headstrong, rebellious, refractory
11 disobedient, intractable
12 obstreperous, ungovernable
14 uncontrollable

unsafe
05 dicey, hairy, risky
06 chancy
07 unsound
08 insecure, perilous, unstable
09 dangerous, hazardous
10 precarious

unsaid
08 unspoken, unstated, unvoiced
09 unuttered
10 undeclared
11 unexpressed, unmentioned
12 unpronounced

unsatisfactory
04 poor
08 inferior, mediocre

09 defective, deficient
10 inadequate, unsuitable
11 displeasing, frustrating
12 unsatisfying
13 disappointing, dissatisfying

unsavoury
06 sordid
07 squalid
09 obnoxious, offensive, repellent, repugnant, repulsive, revolting
10 unpleasant
11 distasteful, unpalatable
12 disagreeable, unappetizing

unscathed
04 safe
05 sound, whole
06 intact, unhurt
08 unharmed
09 undamaged, uninjured

unscrupulous
07 corrupt, crooked, immoral
08 improper, ruthless
09 dishonest, unethical
12 unprincipled

unseasonable
08 ill-timed, untimely
10 malapropos, unsuitable
11 inopportune

unseasoned
05 green
08 unprimed
09 unmatured, untreated
10 unprepared, untempered

unseat
04 oust
05 throw
06 depose, remove, topple
07 dismiss, unhorse
08 displace, unsaddle

unseemly
08 improper
10 indecorous, indelicate, unbecoming, unsuitable
11 unbefitting, undignified
13 inappropriate

unseen
06 hidden, veiled
09 concealed, invisible, unnoticed
10 undetected, unobserved

unselfish
04 kind
08 generous, selfless
10 altruistic, charitable, open-handed
11 magnanimous, self-denying
13 disinterested, philanthropic
15 self-sacrificing

unsentimental
05 tough
09 practical, pragmatic, realistic, unfeeling
10 hard-headed, unromantic
11 level-headed, unemotional

unsettle
05 shake, throw, upset
06 bother, rattle, ruffle
07 agitate, confuse, disturb, fluster, perturb, trouble
09 discomfit, unbalance
10 discompose, disconcert
11 destabilize

unsettled
04 edgy, open
05 owing, shaky, tense, upset
06 on edge, shaken, uneasy, unpaid
07 anxious, fidgety, payable
08 agitated, confused, deserted, desolate, doubtful, insecure, troubled, unnerved, unstable, unsteady, variable
09 abandoned, disturbed, flustered, in arrears, uncertain, undecided
10 changeable, inconstant, unoccupied, unresolved, up in the air
11 outstanding, uninhabited, unpopulated
12 undetermined
13 unpredictable

unshakable
04 firm, sure
05 fixed
06 stable
07 staunch
08 constant, resolute
09 immovable, steadfast
10 determined, unswerving, unwavering
12 unassailable

unsightly
04 ugly
07 hideous
12 disagreeable, unattractive
15 unprepossessing

unskilful
05 inept
06 clumsy, gauche
07 awkward
08 bungling, fumbling, inexpert, untaught
09 maladroit, unskilled
10 amateurish, untalented

11 incompetent, unpractised, unqualified
14 unprofessional

unskilled
08 inexpert
09 untrained
11 incompetent, unpractised, unqualified
13 inexperienced
14 unprofessional

unsociable
04 cold, cool
05 aloof
07 distant, hostile
08 reserved, retiring, taciturn
09 reclusive, withdrawn
10 unfriendly
11 introverted, standoffish, uncongenial

unsolicited
07 unasked
08 unsought, unwanted
09 uninvited, unwelcome, voluntary
10 gratuitous, unasked-for
11 uncalled-for, unrequested

unsophisticated
05 basic, crude, naïve, plain
06 simple
07 artless, natural
08 innocent
09 guileless, ingenuous, unworldly
13 inexperienced, uncomplicated
15 straightforward

unsound
04 weak
05 false, frail, shaky
06 ailing, broken, faulty, flawed, unsafe, unwell, wobbly
07 invalid, rickety
08 delicate, deranged, insecure, unhinged, unstable
09 defective, erroneous, illogical, unfounded
10 fallacious, ill-founded, unbalanced, unreliable

unsparing
05 harsh, stern
06 lavish, severe
07 liberal, profuse
08 abundant, generous
09 bountiful, plenteous
10 implacable, munificent, open-handed, relentless, unstinting

unspeakable
08 dreadful, horrible, shocking, terrible
09 appalling, execrable, frightful, monstrous
11 unthinkable, unutterable
13 indescribable, inexpressible

unspectacular
04 dull
06 boring, common
07 average
08 ordinary, plodding
12 unimpressive, unremarkable

unspoilt
07 natural, perfect
08 unharmed
09 preserved, unchanged, undamaged, untouched
10 unaffected, unimpaired
11 unblemished
15 unsophisticated

unspoken
05 tacit
06 silent, unsaid
07 assumed, implied
08 implicit, inferred, unstated, wordless
09 unuttered, voiceless
10 undeclared, understood
11 unexpressed

unstable
03 mad
05 barmy, crazy, moody, risky, shaky
06 fitful, insane, unsafe, wobbly
07 erratic, rickety, unsound
08 crackers, deranged, insecure, unhinged, unsteady, variable, volatile, wavering
09 disturbed, mercurial, tottering
10 capricious, changeable, inconstant, precarious, unbalanced, unreliable
11 fluctuating, vacillating
12 inconsistent
13 unpredictable, untrustworthy

unsteady
05 shaky
06 unsafe, wobbly
07 doddery, rickety
08 insecure, unstable
09 irregular, tottering
10 flickering, inconstant, precarious, unreliable
11 treacherous

unstinting
06 lavish

07 liberal, profuse
08 abundant, generous, prodigal
09 abounding, bountiful, plentiful, unsparing
10 munificent, ungrudging

unsubstantiated
07 dubious
08 unproved, unproven
09 debatable
10 disputable, unattested, unverified
11 unconfirmed, unsupported
12 questionable
14 uncorroborated

unsuccessful
04 vain
06 beaten, failed, futile, losing
07 sterile, unlucky, useless
08 abortive, defeated, luckless, thwarted
09 fruitless
10 frustrated, unavailing
11 ineffective, ineffectual

unsuitable
05 inapt, unfit
08 improper, unseemly
10 inapposite, malapropos, out of place
11 incongruous
12 incompatible, infelicitous
13 inappropriate

unsullied
04 pure
05 clean
06 intact
07 perfect
08 pristine, spotless, unsoiled
09 stainless
10 immaculate

unsung
07 obscure, unknown
08 unhailed
09 anonymous
12 uncelebrated, unrecognized
14 unacknowledged

unsure
07 dubious, unknown
08 doubtful, hesitant, insecure, wavering
09 dithering, sceptical, tentative, uncertain, undecided
10 ambivalent, in two minds, indefinite, irresolute, suspicious
11 uncommitted, unconvinced
12 equivocating

unsurpassed
08 unbeaten
09 matchless
10 unexcelled
11 exceptional, superlative
12 incomparable

unsurprising
08 expected, forecast, foreseen
09 looked-for, predicted
10 forseeable
11 anticipated

unsuspecting
06 unwary
07 unaware
08 innocent, trustful, trusting
09 credulous, ingenuous
11 unconscious
12 unsuspicious

unswerving
04 firm, sure, true
05 fixed
06 direct, steady
07 devoted, staunch
08 constant, resolute, untiring
09 dedicated, steadfast
10 unwavering
11 undeviating, unfaltering

unsympathetic
04 cold, hard
05 cruel, harsh, stony
07 callous, hostile, unmoved
08 pitiless, soulless, uncaring
11 indifferent, insensitive
12 antagonistic, unresponsive

unsystematic
07 chaotic, jumbled, muddled
08 confused, slapdash
09 haphazard, shambolic, unplanned
10 disorderly
11 unorganized
12 disorganized, unmethodical
14 indiscriminate

untamed
04 wild
05 feral
06 fierce, savage
09 barbarous
14 undomesticated

untangle
04 undo
05 solve
07 resolve, unravel, work out
09 extricate
11 disentangle
13 straighten out

untarnished
04 pure

05 clean
06 bright, intact
07 glowing, shining
08 polished, pristine, spotless, unsoiled, unspoilt
09 stainless, unspotted, unstained, unsullied
10 immaculate, impeccable
11 unblemished
13 unimpeachable

untenable
05 rocky, shaky
06 flawed
07 unsound
09 illogical
10 fallacious
13 insupportable, unsustainable

unthinkable
08 unlikely
09 illogical, unheard-of
10 impossible, outrageous
11 implausible
12 preposterous, unbelievable, unimaginable, unreasonable
13 inconceivable

unthinking
04 rash, rude
06 unkind
08 careless, heedless, impolite, tactless
09 automatic, impulsive, negligent
10 indiscreet, mechanical
11 insensitive, instinctive, involuntary, thoughtless, unconscious
12 undiplomatic
13 inconsiderate

untidy
05 messy
06 sloppy
07 chaotic, haywire, jumbled, muddled, rumpled, scruffy, unkempt
08 slipshod, slovenly
09 cluttered, shambolic
10 disorderly, topsy-turvy
11 dishevelled
12 disorganized, unsystematic

untie
04 free, undo
05 loose
06 loosen, unbind, unknot, unwrap
07 release, unhitch
08 unfasten

untimely
08 ill-timed
09 premature

10 malapropos, unsuitable
11 inopportune, unfortunate
12 inauspicious, inconvenient, infelicitous, unseasonable
13 inappropriate

untiring
06 dogged, steady
07 devoted, staunch
08 constant, resolute, tireless
09 tenacious, unfailing
10 determined, persistent, unflagging
11 persevering, unfaltering
13 indefatigable

untold
08 infinite
09 boundless, countless, uncounted
10 unnumbered, unreckoned
11 innumerable, uncountable, undreamed-of
12 immeasurable, incalculable, unimaginable
13 inconceivable, inexpressible

untouched
06 intact, unhurt
09 unaltered, unchanged, undamaged, unscathed
10 unaffected, unimpaired
11 unimpressed

untoward
07 adverse, awkward, ominous, unlucky
08 annoying, contrary, ill-timed, improper, unseemly, untimely, worrying
10 indecorous, unbecoming, unexpected, unsuitable
11 inopportune, unfortunate
12 inauspicious, inconvenient, unfavourable, unpropitious
13 inappropriate

untrained
07 amateur
08 inexpert, untaught
09 unskilled
10 uneducated, unschooled
11 incompetent, unqualified
13 inexperienced
14 unprofessional

untried
03 new
05 novel
08 unproved, untested
10 innovative, innovatory
11 exploratory
12 experimental
13 unestablished

untroubled
04 calm, cool
06 placid, serene, steady
08 composed, peaceful, tranquil
09 impassive, unexcited, unruffled, unworried
11 unconcerned, undisturbed, unflustered, unperturbed

untrue
05 false, wrong
06 made-up
07 inexact
08 disloyal, mistaken, two-faced
09 deceitful, deceptive, dishonest, erroneous, incorrect, trumped-up
10 fabricated, fallacious, fraudulent, inaccurate, misleading, perfidious, unfaithful, untruthful
13 untrustworthy

untrustworthy
05 false
06 fickle, untrue
08 disloyal, two-faced, untrusty
09 deceitful, dishonest, faithless
10 capricious, fly-by-night, unreliable
11 duplicitous, treacherous

untruth
03 fib, lie
04 tale
05 lying, porky, story
06 deceit
07 fiction, perjury, whopper
09 falsehood, invention, tall story
11 fabrication, made-up story

untruthful
05 false, lying
06 untrue
08 invented, two-faced
09 deceitful, dishonest, fictional, insincere
10 fabricated, fallacious, mendacious

untwine
06 uncoil, unwind
07 unravel, untwist
10 disentwine

untwist
06 uncoil, unwind
07 unravel, untwine

untutored
06 simple
07 artless

08 ignorant, inexpert, unversed
09 unlearned, untrained
10 illiterate, uneducated
13 inexperienced

unused
03 new
04 idle
05 blank, clean, extra, fresh, spare
07 surplus
08 leftover, untapped
09 available, remaining, untouched
10 unemployed, unfamiliar
12 unaccustomed

unusual
03 odd
04 rare
05 queer, weird
07 bizarre, curious, offbeat, special, strange
08 abnormal, atypical, singular, uncommon
09 anomalous, different
10 phenomenal, remarkable, surprising, unexpected, unfamiliar, unorthodox
11 exceptional
13 extraordinary
14 unconventional

unutterable
09 egregious, ineffable
11 unspeakable
13 indescribable

unvarnished
04 bare, pure
05 frank, naked, plain, sheer, stark
06 candid, honest, simple
09 unadorned
11 undisguised
15 straightforward

unveil
04 bare
06 betray, expose, reveal, unmask
07 divulge, lay bare, lay open, uncover
08 disclose, discover
09 make known
12 bring to light
13 take the lid off

unwanted
06 otiose
07 outcast, surplus, useless
08 rejected, unneeded
09 redundant, undesired, uninvited, unwelcome
11 superfluous, unnecessary, unsolicited

unwarranted
06 unjust
10 gratuitous, groundless, undeserved, unprovoked
11 inexcusable, uncalled-for, unjustified, unnecessary
12 indefensible, unreasonable
13 unjustifiable

unwary
08 heedless, off guard
09 imprudent, unguarded
10 incautious, unthinking
11 thoughtless

unwavering
06 steady, sturdy
07 staunch
08 resolute, unshaken, untiring
09 dedicated, steadfast, tenacious
10 consistent, determined, unflagging, unswerving
11 undeviating, unfaltering
12 single-minded

unwelcome
08 excluded, rejected, unwanted, worrying
09 uninvited, unpopular
11 undesirable, unpalatable
12 disagreeable, unacceptable

unwell
03 ill
04 sick
06 ailing, groggy, poorly, sickly
09 off-colour, unhealthy
10 indisposed, out of sorts
11 debilitated
15 under the weather

unwholesome
03 bad, wan
04 evil, junk, pale
05 pasty
06 pallid, sickly, wicked
07 anaemic, harmful, immoral, noxious, tainted
09 degrading, depraving, poisonous, unhealthy
10 corrupting, insalutary, insanitary, perverting, unhygienic
12 insalubrious

unwieldy
05 bulky, hefty
06 clumsy
07 awkward, hulking, weighty
08 ungainly
09 ponderous
10 cumbersome
12 unmanageable

unwilling
05 loath
08 grudging, hesitant, loathful
09 reluctant, resistant
10 indisposed
11 disinclined

unwillingness
08 nolition, slowness
09 hesitancy
10 reluctance
12 backwardness, loathfulness
13 indisposition
14 disinclination

unwind
04 undo
05 relax
06 cool it, uncoil, unreel, unroll, unwrap
07 unravel, untwist
08 chill out, wind down
10 take it easy
11 disentangle
13 put your feet up
14 take things easy
15 let your hair down

unwise
04 rash
05 silly
06 stupid
07 foolish
09 foolhardy, ill-judged, impolitic, imprudent, senseless
10 ill-advised, indiscreet
11 injudicious, thoughtless
12 short-sighted
13 ill-considered, irresponsible

unwitting
07 unaware
09 unknowing, unplanned
10 accidental, unintended, unthinking
11 inadvertent, unconscious
12 unsuspecting
13 unintentional

unwonted
04 rare
07 strange, unusual
08 atypical, peculiar, singular, uncommon
09 unheard-of
10 unexpected, unfamiliar
11 exceptional
12 unaccustomed

unworldly
05 green, naïve
08 gullible, innocent
09 ingenuous, spiritual, visionary
10 idealistic

11 impractical
12 metaphysical, otherworldly
14 transcendental

unworried
09 unruffled
10 undismayed, untroubled
11 unperturbed

unworthy
04 base
07 ignoble
08 improper, inferior, shameful
09 unfitting
10 despicable, ineligible, unbecoming, unsuitable
11 disgraceful, incongruous, unbefitting, undeserving
12 contemptible, disreputable
13 discreditable, dishonourable, inappropriate
14 unprofessional

unwritten
05 tacit
08 accepted, implicit
10 recognized, understood
11 traditional, word-of-mouth

unyielding
04 firm
05 rigid, solid, tough
07 adamant, staunch
08 hard-line, obdurate, resolute, stubborn
09 immovable, obstinate, steadfast, unbending
10 determined, implacable, inexorable, inflexible, relentless, unwavering
11 intractable, unrelenting
12 intransigent
14 uncompromising

up-and-coming
09 go-getting, promising

upbeat
06 bright, cheery
07 bullish, buoyant, hopeful
08 cheerful, positive
10 optimistic
11 encouraging

upbraid
05 chide, scold
06 berate, rebuke
07 censure, reprove
08 admonish, reproach
09 castigate, criticize, reprimand

upbringing
07 nurture, raising, rearing
08 breeding, teaching, training
09 education, parenting
11 cultivation, instruction

update
05 amend, renew
06 revamp, revise
07 correct, upgrade
09 modernize

upgrade
05 raise
06 better
07 advance, elevate, enhance, improve, promote
09 modernize
10 ameliorate, make better

upheaval
05 chaos, upset
07 shake-up, turmoil
10 disruption, revolution

uphill
04 hard
05 tough
06 taxing, tiring
07 arduous, onerous
09 difficult, gruelling, laborious, strenuous, wearisome
10 burdensome, exhausting

uphold
04 back, keep
06 defend, hold to
07 confirm, endorse, fortify, justify, promote, stand by, support, sustain
08 advocate, champion, maintain
09 vindicate
10 strengthen

upkeep
07 oncosts, running, support
08 expenses
09 overheads
10 sustenance
11 expenditure, maintenance, subsistence
12 conservation, preservation, running costs
14 operating costs

uplift
04 lift
05 boost, edify, elate, exalt, heave, hoist, raise
06 better, refine
07 advance, elevate, improve, inspire, upgrade
08 civilize
09 cultivate, enlighten
10 ameliorate, betterment, enrichment, refinement
11 advancement, cultivation, edification, enhancement, improvement
13 enlightenment

upper
03 top
04 high
06 higher, senior
07 eminent, exalted, greater, loftier, topmost
08 elevated, superior
09 important, uppermost

❑**upper hand**
04 edge, sway
07 control, mastery
08 dominion
09 advantage, dominance, supremacy
10 ascendancy, domination

upper-class
05 elite, noble
06 swanky
08 high-born, well-born, well-bred
09 exclusive, high-class, patrician, top-drawer
11 blue-blooded
12 aristocratic

uppermost
03 top
05 chief, first, major
07 highest, leading, primary, supreme, topmost
08 dominant, foremost, greatest, loftiest
09 paramount, principal
10 pre-eminent
11 predominant

uppity
07 stuck-up
08 arrogant, snobbish
09 big-headed, bumptious, conceited
10 hoity-toity
11 impertinent, overweening, toffee-nosed
12 presumptuous, supercilious
13 self-important

upright
04 good
05 erect, moral, noble, sheer, steep
06 decent, honest, worthy
07 ethical
08 straight, vertical, virtuous
09 reputable, righteous
10 high-minded, honourable, principled, upstanding
11 respectable, trustworthy
13 incorruptible, perpendicular

uprising
06 mutiny, putsch, revolt, rising
09 coup d'état, rebellion

10 insurgence, revolution
12 insurrection

uproar
03 din
04 riot
05 noise
06 bedlam, fracas, furore, hubbub, mayhem, outcry, racket, rumpus, tumult
07 clamour, ruction, turmoil
08 brouhaha, disorder
09 commotion, confusion
10 hullabaloo, turbulence
11 pandemonium

uproarious
04 loud, wild
05 noisy, rowdy
07 riotous
09 clamorous, deafening, hilarious
10 boisterous, rip-roaring, rollicking

uproot
05 rip up
06 pull up, remove
07 destroy, weed out, wipe out
08 displace

upset
03 bug, tip
05 het up, shake, shock, spill
06 dismay, grieve, put out, ruffle, shaken, topple
07 agitate, annoyed, capsize, fluster, illness, perturb, reverse, shake-up, trouble, unnerve, uptight
08 agitated, bothered, confused, dismayed, disorder, distress, in a state, overturn, sickness, surprise, troubled, unsteady, upheaval, worked up
09 agitation, complaint, disturbed, flustered, knock over, overthrow, perturbed, unsettled
10 discompose, disconcert, disruption, distressed
11 destabilize, discomposed, disorganize, disturbance
12 disconcerted, perturbation

upshot
06 finish, pay-off, result
07 outcome
10 conclusion, dénouement
11 consequence, culmination

upside down
05 upset
07 chaotic, jumbled, muddled, up-ended

08 confused, inverted, messed up, upturned
10 disordered, overturned, topsy-turvy, wrong way up
11 wrong side up

upstanding
04 firm, good, true
05 erect, moral
07 ethical, upright
08 virtuous
10 honourable, principled

upstart
07 parvenu
08 parvenue
09 arriviste
12 nouveau riche
13 social climber

uptight
04 edgy
05 nervy, tense
06 hung-up, on edge, uneasy
07 anxious, prickly

up-to-date
02 in
03 new
04 cool
06 latest, modern, recent, trendy
07 current
09 in fashion, prevalent
10 all the rage, present-day
11 fashionable
12 contemporary
13 state-of-the-art

upturn
04 rise
05 boost
07 revival, upsurge, upswing
08 increase, recovery
11 improvement
12 amelioration

urban
04 city, town
05 civic
07 built-up, oppidan
09 inner-city, municipal
12 metropolitan

urbane
05 civil, suave
06 smooth
07 elegant, refined
08 cultured, debonair, mannerly, polished
09 civilized, courteous
10 cultivated
12 well-mannered
13 sophisticated

urbanity
06 polish

07 culture, suavity
08 civility, courtesy, elegance
10 refinement, smoothness
11 cultivation, worldliness
14 sophistication

urchin
04 brat, waif
05 gamin
10 ragamuffin, street Arab
11 guttersnipe

urge
03 beg, yen
04 goad, itch, need, prod, push, spur, wish
05 drive, egg on, fancy, force, impel, plead, press
06 advise, appeal, compel, desire, exhort, hasten, incite, induce
07 beseech, counsel, entreat, impetus, implore, impulse, longing
08 advocate, persuade
09 constrain, eagerness, encourage, instigate, recommend, stimulate
10 compulsion
11 inclination

urgency
05 haste, hurry
08 exigency, pressure, priority
09 extremity, necessity
10 importance
11 importunity, seriousness
14 imperativeness

urgent
05 eager, grave, vital
07 crucial, earnest, exigent, instant, serious
08 critical, pressing
09 essential, immediate, important, insistent
10 compelling, imperative, persistent, persuasive
11 top-priority

urinate
03 pee, wee
04 leak
06 piddle, tinkle
09 micturate, pass water
11 spend a penny
15 relieve yourself

usable
05 valid
07 current, working
09 available, practical
10 functional
11 exploitable, operational, serviceable

usage
03 use, way
04 form, mode, rule
05 habit
06 custom, method
07 control, routine, running
08 handling, practice
09 etiquette, operation, procedure, tradition, treatment
10 convention, employment, management, regulation
11 application

use
03 end, ply
04 call, good, help, milk, need, work
05 abuse, apply, avail, bleed, cause, enjoy, point, right, spend, treat, usage, value, waste, wield, worth
06 demand, draw on, employ, expend, handle, misuse, object, profit
07 ability, benefit, consume, exhaust, exploit, operate, purpose, service, utilize
08 deal with, exercise, impose on, occasion, practise, resort to
09 advantage, go through, make use of, manoeuvre, necessity, operation, privilege
10 employment, get through, manipulate, usefulness
11 application, utilization
12 exploitation, manipulation
13 bring into play
15 take advantage of

▫ **used to**
08 inured to
10 adjusted to, at home with
12 accustomed to, familiar with, in the habit of, no stranger to
14 acclimatized to

▫ **use up**
05 drain, waste
06 absorb, devour, finish
07 consume, deplete, exhaust

used
07 cast-off
09 nearly new
10 hand-me-down, second-hand

useful
04 able
05 handy, nifty
06 expert

07 helpful, skilful, skilled
08 fruitful, valuable
09 effective, practical, practised, rewarding
10 all-purpose, beneficial, convenient, functional, productive, proficient, profitable, worthwhile
11 experienced
12 advantageous

usefulness
05 avail, value, worth
07 benefit, service, utility
08 efficacy
10 efficiency
11 convenience
12 practicality
15 serviceableness

useless
04 idle, vain, weak
06 futile
08 hopeless, unusable
09 fruitless, incapable, pointless, to no avail, unhelpful, worthless
10 broken-down, clapped-out, unavailing, unworkable
11 impractical, incompetent, ineffective, ineffectual
12 unproductive, unprofitable
13 inefficacious

uselessness
08 futility, idleness
10 ineptitude
12 hopelessness, incompetence
14 impracticality, ineffectuality
15 ineffectiveness

usher
04 lead, show
05 guide, pilot, steer
06 direct, escort
07 conduct
09 accompany, attendant, usherette

▫ **usher in**
06 herald, launch, ring in
07 precede
08 announce, initiate
09 introduce
10 inaugurate
13 pave the way for

usual
05 stock
06 common, normal, wonted
07 average, general, regular, routine, typical
08 everyday, familiar, habitual, ordinary, standard
09 customary

10 accustomed, recognized
11 established, traditional
12 conventional
13 unexceptional

usually
06 mainly, mostly
07 as a rule, chiefly
08 commonly, normally
09 generally, in the main, routinely, typically
10 by and large, on the whole, ordinarily

usurer
07 Shylock
09 loan-shark
11 money-lender
12 extortionist

usurp
05 annex, seize, steal
08 arrogate, take over
10 commandeer
11 appropriate

usury
09 extortion
12 money-lending

utensil
04 tool
06 device, gadget
09 apparatus, appliance, implement
10 instrument
11 contrivance

▶ *Kitchen utensils include:*
03 wok
04 fork
05 corer, knife, ladle, sieve, spoon, tongs, whisk
06 grater, mincer, peeler, sifter, skewer, tureen, zester
07 blender, cleaver, cocotte, milk pan, ramekin, skillet, spatula, steamer, terrine
08 breadbin, colander, cruet set, egg-timer, grill pan, saucepan, stockpot, tea caddy, teaspoon, wine rack
09 bain-marie, brochette, can-opener, casserole, corkscrew, egg slicer, fish slice, fondue set, frying-pan, punch bowl, spice rack, toast rack
10 breadboard, butter dish, egg coddler, egg poacher, jelly mould, knife block,

liquidizer, mixing bowl, nutcracker, pepper mill, rolling-pin, tablespoon, tea infuser, wine cooler
11 baking sheet, cheese board, garlic press, pastry board, pastry brush, roasting pan, tea strainer, wooden spoon
12 bottle opener, butter curler, cheese slicer, deep-fat fryer, dessertspoon, flour dredger, measuring jug, nutmeg grater, pastry cutter, potato masher, pudding basin, salad spinner
13 chopping-board, food processor, kitchen scales, lemon squeezer
14 pressure cooker

utilitarian
05 lowly
06 useful
08 sensible
09 effective, efficient, practical, pragmatic
10 convenient, functional
11 down-to-earth, serviceable
13 unpretentious

utility
03 use
04 good, help
05 avail, value, worth
07 benefit, fitness, service
10 efficiency, usefulness
12 practicality
15 serviceableness

utilize
03 use
06 employ
07 exploit
08 put to use, resort to
09 make use of
13 turn to account

utmost
03 top
04 best, last, most, peak
05 final
07 extreme, hardest, highest, maximum, supreme
08 farthest, furthest, greatest, remotest, ultimate
09 outermost, paramount
11 furthermost

Utopia
04 Eden
05 bliss
06 heaven
07 Elysium
08 paradise
09 Shangri-la
12 Garden of Eden
13 heaven on earth

Utopian
05 dream, ideal
07 Elysian, perfect, wishful
08 fanciful, illusory, romantic
09 fantastic, visionary
10 chimerical, idealistic, unworkable
11 impractical

utter
03 say
04 tell
05 sheer, sound, speak, stark, state, total, voice
06 arrant, entire, reveal
07 declare, deliver, divulge, express, perfect
08 absolute, announce, complete, positive, proclaim, thorough vocalize
09 downright, enunciate, out-and-out, pronounce, verbalize
10 articulate, consummate
11 unqualified
13 thoroughgoing

utterance
04 word
06 remark, speech
09 statement
10 expression
11 declaration, enunciation
12 announcement, articulation
13 pronouncement

utterly
06 wholly
07 totally
08 entirely
09 downright, perfectly
10 absolutely, completely

U-turn
08 reversal
09 about-turn, volte-face

vacancy
03 job
04 post, room
05 place
07 opening
08 position
09 situation

vacant
04 free, void
05 blank, empty, inane
06 absent, dreamy, unused
07 deadpan, vacuous
08 deserted, not in use, unfilled
09 abandoned, available
10 unoccupied, unthinking
11 inattentive, uninhabited
12 absent-minded
14 expressionless

vacate
04 quit
05 leave
08 evacuate, withdraw

vacation
04 rest
05 break, leave
06 recess
07 holiday, time off
08 furlough

vacillate
04 sway
05 haver, waver
08 hesitate
09 fluctuate, oscillate,
   temporize
12 shilly-shally, tergiversate

vacillating
08 hesitant, wavering
09 uncertain
10 irresolute

vacillation
08 wavering
09 hesitancy
10 hesitation, indecision
11 fluctuation, inconstancy
12 irresolution
13 temporization
14 tergiversation

vacuity
04 void

05 space
06 apathy, vacuum
07 inanity
09 blankness, emptiness

vacuous
04 idle, void
05 blank, empty, inane
06 stupid, vacant
08 unfilled
09 apathetic, incurious

vacuum
04 void
05 chasm, space
06 lacuna
09 emptiness
11 nothingness

vagabond
03 bum
04 hobo
05 nomad, rover, tramp
06 beggar, rascal
07 migrant, outcast, vagrant
08 wanderer, wayfarer
09 itinerant
10 down-and-out

vagary
04 whim
05 fancy, prank, quirk
06 humour, notion,
   whimsy
07 caprice

vagrancy
08 nomadism
09 wandering
10 itinerancy, travelling
12 homelessness, rootlessness

vagrant
04 hobo
05 tramp
06 beggar, roving
07 drifter, gangrel, nomadic
08 homeless, rootless,
   vagabond
09 itinerant, shiftless,
   wandering
12 rolling stone

vague
03 dim, lax
04 hazy

05 faint, foggy, fuzzy, loose,
   misty, rough
06 unsure, woolly
07 blurred, evasive, inexact,
   obscure, shadowy, unclear
08 nebulous
09 ambiguous, amorphous,
   imprecise, uncertain,
   undefined, unfocused
10 ill-defined, indefinite,
   indistinct, out of focus
13 indeterminate

vaguely
05 dimly
07 faintly
08 slightly, vacantly
09 inexactly, obscurely
11 imprecisely
14 absent-mindedly

vagueness
07 dimness
08 haziness
09 ambiguity, faintness,
   fuzziness, obscurity
10 woolliness
11 imprecision, uncertainty

vain
04 idle
05 empty, proud
06 futile, hollow
07 haughty, stuck-up, useless
08 abortive, arrogant
09 big-headed, conceited,
   fruitless, pointless, worthless
10 groundless, swaggering
11 egotistical, pretentious
12 narcissistic, unproductive
13 high and mighty, self-
   important, swollen-headed

⬠in vain
09 to no avail, uselessly
11 fruitlessly
14 unsuccessfully

valediction
07 goodbye, send-off
08 farewell
11 leave-taking

valedictory
04 last
05 final

valet
07 parting
08 farewell

valet
03 man
10 manservant
14 valet de chambre

valetudinarian
05 frail
06 feeble, infirm, sickly, weakly
07 invalid
08 delicate, neurotic

valiant
04 bold
05 brave
06 heroic, plucky
07 gallant, staunch
08 fearless, intrepid, valorous
10 courageous

valid
04 good, just
05 legal, sound
06 cogent, lawful, proper
07 logical, weighty
08 bona fide, credible
09 authentic
10 legitimate, reasonable
11 justifiable, well-founded

validate
06 attest, ratify
07 certify, confirm, endorse
08 legalize
10 underwrite
12 authenticate, substantiate

validity
05 force, logic, point
07 cogency, grounds
08 legality
09 soundness, substance
10 lawfulness, legitimacy

valley
03 cwm
04 dale, dell, glen, vale
05 gulch, slade
06 hollow, strath

valorous
04 bold
05 brave
06 heroic, plucky
07 doughty, gallant, valiant
08 fearless, intrepid, stalwart
10 courageous, mettlesome

valour
06 mettle, spirit
07 bravery, courage, heroism
09 fortitude, gallantry
11 intrepidity

valuable
06 costly, prized, useful, worthy

07 helpful
08 fruitful, precious
09 expensive, important, priceless, treasured
10 beneficial, profitable, worthwhile
12 advantageous, constructive

valuation
06 survey
08 estimate
10 assessment, evaluation
12 appraisement

value
03 use
04 cost, gain, good, rate
05 merit, price, prize, worth
06 admire, assess, esteem, ethics, morals, profit, survey
07 benefit, cherish, utility
08 appraise, estimate, evaluate, hold dear, treasure
09 advantage, standards
10 appreciate, importance, principles, usefulness
12 desirability, significance
15 set great store by

valued
04 dear
05 loved
06 prized
07 beloved
08 esteemed
09 cherished, treasured
14 highly regarded

van
05 lorry, truck, wagon
07 trailer
08 carriage

vanguard
04 fore, lead
05 front
09 forefront, front line, spearhead

vanish
04 exit, fade
06 depart, die out
07 fade out
08 dissolve, evanesce, fade away, melt away
09 disappear, fizzle out

vanity
04 airs
05 pride
07 conceit, egotism
08 futility, idleness, self-love
09 arrogance
10 narcissism, pretension, triviality

11 affectation, ostentation, self-conceit

vanquish
04 beat, rout
05 crush, quell
06 defeat, master, subdue
07 conquer, repress
08 confound, overcome
09 overwhelm, subjugate

vapid
04 dull, flat, limp, weak
05 banal, bland, stale, trite
06 boring, jejune, watery
07 insipid, tedious, vacuous
08 lifeless
10 colourless, wishy-washy

vaporous
04 fumy, vain
05 foggy, misty
06 fumous, steamy
07 gaseous
10 chimerical
13 insubstantial

vapour
03 fog
04 damp, haze, mist
05 fumes, smoke, steam
06 breath

variable
06 factor, fickle, fitful, uneven
07 mutable, protean
08 flexible, shifting, wavering
09 parameter
10 changeable, inconstant
11 chameleonic, fluctuating
13 unpredictable

variance
04 odds
06 strife
07 discord, dissent
08 conflict, division
10 difference, disharmony, dissension, divergence
12 disagreement

variant
07 derived, deviant
08 modified
09 different, divergent
11 alternative

variation
06 change
07 novelty, variety
09 departure, deviation
10 alteration, difference, inflection, modulation
11 discrepancy, fluctuation

varied
05 mixed
06 motley, sundry

7 diverse, various
8 assorted
9 different
2 multifarious
3 heterogeneous, miscellaneous

ariegated
6 motley
7 dappled, marbled, mottled
8 speckled, streaked

ariety
4 kind, make, sort, type
5 brand, breed, class, range
6 medley, strain
7 mixture, species
8 category
9 diversity, pot-pourri, variation
0 assortment, collection, difference, miscellany
2 multiplicity
3 dissimilarity

arious
4 many
5 mixed
6 motley, unlike, varied
7 diverse, several, varying
8 assorted, distinct
9 different, differing, disparate
0 dissimilar, variegated
1 diversified
3 heterogeneous, miscellaneous

arnish
3 lac
5 glaze, gloss, japan, resin
6 enamel, polish, veneer
7 coating, lacquer, shellac

ary
5 alter, clash
6 change, depart, differ, modify
7 diverge, inflect, reorder
8 be at odds, disagree, modulate
9 alternate, diversify, fluctuate, permutate, transform
2 metamorphose

ase
3 jar, jug, urn
4 ewer
6 hydria, vessel
7 amphora, pitcher

assal
4 serf
5 liege, slave
6 thrall
7 bondman, subject, villein

08 bondsman
11 bondservant

vassalage
07 bondage, serfdom, slavery
08 thraldom
09 servitude
10 dependence, villeinage
11 subjugation

vast
04 huge
07 immense, massive
08 colossal, enormous, far-flung, gigantic
09 boundless, extensive, limitless, monstrous
10 monumental
12 immeasurable

vat
03 tub
04 kier, tank
05 keeve
06 barrel

vault
04 arch, jump, roof, span, tomb
05 bound, clear, crypt
06 cavern, cellar, hurdle
08 leap-frog
09 mausoleum
10 depository, repository, strongroom, wine-cellar

vaunt
04 brag, crow
05 boast, swank
06 flaunt, parade
07 exult in, show off, trumpet
15 blow your own horn

veer
04 tack, turn
05 sheer, shift, swing, wheel
06 change, swerve
07 deviate, diverge

vegetable
► *Vegetables include:*
03 pea, yam
04 bean, kale, leek, okra, spud
05 chard, choko, cress, gumbo, mooli, onion, swede
06 carrot, celery, endive, fennel, garlic, lentil, marrow, pepper, potato, radish, squash, turnip
07 cabbage, chicory, lettuce, parsnip, pumpkin, salsify, shallot, spinach
08 beetroot, broccoli, celeriac, cucumber, eggplant, kohlrabi, mushroom, soya bean, zucchini

09 artichoke, asparagus, aubergine, broad bean, calabrese, courgette, mange tout, red pepper, sweetcorn
10 butter bean, French bean, red cabbage, runner bean, watercress
11 cauliflower, green pepper, lady's finger, spring onion, sweet-potato
12 savoy cabbage
14 Brussels sprout, globe artichoke
➤ See also **food**

vegetate
07 moulder
08 go to seed, languish, stagnate
10 degenerate
11 deteriorate

vegetation
05 flora, trees
06 plants
07 flowers, herbage, verdure
08 greenery

vehemence
04 fire, heat, zeal
05 force, power, verve
06 ardour, energy, warmth
07 fervour, passion, urgency
08 emphasis, fervency, strength, violence
09 animation, intensity
10 enthusiasm

vehement
06 ardent, fervid, fierce, heated, strong, urgent
07 earnest, fervent, intense, violent, zealous
08 animated, forceful, forcible, powerful, spirited
10 passionate
11 impassioned
12 enthusiastic

vehicle
05 means, organ
06 agency, medium
07 channel
09 mechanism, transport
10 conveyance, instrument

► *Vehicles include:*
03 bus, car, gig, HGV, van
04 bike, boat, dray, ship, sled, tank, taxi, tram, trap, tube
05 coach, cycle, lorry, plane, train, truck, wagon
06 hansom, landau, litter, sledge, sleigh, surrey, tandem, troika

07 bicycle, caravan, dog-cart, minibus, omnibus, phaeton, Pullman, scooter, sleeper, tractor, trailer

08 barouche, brougham, rickshaw, toboggan, tricycle, wagon-lit

09 bobsleigh, charabanc, motor-bike

10 juggernaut, motor-cycle, post-chaise, sedan-chair, stagecoach

11 steam-roller

12 double-decker, pantechnicon

13 fork-lift truck, penny-farthing

15 hackney-carriage

➤ See also **aircraft**; **bicycle**; **boat**; **car**; **motor**; **ship**

◼ *International Vehicle Registrations:*

01 **A** (Austria), **B** (Belgium), **C** (Cuba), **D** (Germany), **E** (Spain), **F** (France), **H** (Hungary), **I** (Italy), **J** (Japan), **K** (Cambodia), **L** (Luxembourg), **M** (Malta), **N** (Norway), **P** (Portugal), **S** (Sweden), **T** (Thailand), **V** (Vatican City), **Z** (Zambia)

02 **AL** (Albania), **BD** (Bangladesh), **BG** (Bulgaria), **BH** (Belize), **BR** (Brazil), **BS** (The Bahamas), **CH** (Switzerland), **CI** (Côte d'Ivoire), **CL** (Sri Lanka), **CO** (Colombia), **CR** (Costa Rica), **CY** (Cyprus), **CZ** (Czech Republic), **DK** (Denmark), **DY** (Benin), **DZ** (Algeria), **EC** (Ecuador), **ES** (El Salvador), **ET** (Egypt), **FL** (Liechtenstein), **FR** (Faroe Islands), **GB** (Great Britain), **GE** (Georgia), **GH** (Ghana), **GR** (Greece), **HK** (Hong Kong), **HR** (Croatia), **IL** (Israel), **IR** (Iran), **IS** (Iceland), **JA** (Jamaica), **KS** (Kyrgyzstan), **KZ** (Kazakhzstan), **LB** (Liberia), **LS** (Lesotho), **LT** (Lithuania), **LV** (Latvia), **MA** (Morocco), **MC** (Monaco), **MK** (Macedonia), **MS** (Mauritius), **MW** (Malawi), **NA** (Netherlands Antilles), **NL** (Netherlands), **NZ** (New Zealand), **PA**

(Panama), **PE** (Peru), **PK** (Pakistan), **PL** (Poland), **PY** (Paraguay), **RA** (Argentina), **RB** (Botswana), **RC** (Taiwan), **RH** (Haiti), **RI** (Indonesia), **RL** (Lebanon), **RM** (Madagascar), **RN** (Niger), **RO** (Romania), **RP** (Philippines), **RU** (Burundi), **SD** (Swaziland), **SK** (Slovakia), **SN** (Senegal), **SU** (Belarus), **SY** (Seychelles), **TG** (Togo), **TJ** (Tajikistan), **TM** (Turkmenistan), **TN** (Tunisia), **TR** (Turkey), **TT** (Trinidad and Tobago), **UA** (Ukraine), **VN** (Vietnam), **WD** (Dominica), **WG** (Grenada), **WL** (St Lucia), **WS** (Samoa), **WV** (St Vincent and the Grenadines), **YU** (Yugoslavia), **YV** (Venezuela), **ZA** (South Africa), **ZW** (Zimbabwe)

03 **ADN** (Yemen), **AFG** (Afghanistan), **AND** (Andorra), **AUS** (Australia), **BDS** (Barbados), **BIH** (Bosnia-Herzegovina), **BRN** (Bahrain), **BRU** (Brunei), **BUR** (Myanmar), **CDN** (Canada), **DOM** (Dominican Republic), **EAK** (Kenya), **EAT** (Tanzania), **EAU** (Uganda), **EST** (Estonia), **ETH** (Ethiopia), **FIN** (Finland), **FJI** (Fiji), **GBA** (Alderney), **GBG** (Guernsey), **GBJ** (Jersey), **GBM** (Isle of Man), **GBZ** (Gibraltar), **GCA** (Guatemala), **GUY** (Guyana), **HKJ** (Jordan), **IND** (India), **IRL** (Ireland), **IRQ** (Iraq), **KWT** (Kuwait), **LAO** (Laos), **LAR** (Libya), **MAL** (Malaysia), **MEX** (Mexico), **NAM** (Namibia), **NIC** (Nicaragua), **PNG** (Papua New Guinea), **RCA** (Central African Republic), **RCB** (Congo), **RCH** (Chile), **RIM** (Mauritania), **RMM** (Mali), **ROK** (Korea), **ROU** (Uruguay), **RSM** (San Marino), **RUS** (Russia), **RWA** (Rwanda), **SGP** (Singapore), **SLO**

(Slovenia), **SME** (Suriname), **SYR** (Syria), **USA** (United States of America), **WAG** (The Gambia), **WAL** (Sierra Leone), **WAN** (Nigeria), **ZRE** (Democratic Republic of Congo)

veil

04 film, hide, mask

05 blind, cloak, cover, shade

06 canopy, mantle, purdah, screen, shadow, shroud

07 conceal, curtain, obscure

08 covering, disguise

10 camouflage

vein

04 lode, mode, mood, seam

05 style, tenor

06 humour, strain, streak

07 stratum

11 blood vessel, disposition, inclination

◼ *Veins and arteries include*

05 aorta, iliac, renal

06 portal, radial, tibial

07 carotid, femoral, gastric, hepatic, jugular, saphena

08 axillary, brachial, temporal

09 pulmonary

veined

05 jaspe

07 marbled

08 streaked

velocity

04 pace, rate

05 speed

venal

04 bent

07 buyable, corrupt

08 bribable, grafting

10 simoniacal

11 corruptible

vendetta

04 feud

06 enmity

07 quarrel, rivalry

08 bad blood

09 blood-feud

vendor

06 seller, trader

08 merchant, stockist, supplier

veneer

04 mask, show

05 front, gloss, guise, layer

06 façade, finish

07 coating, display, surface

08 covering, pretence

venerable
04 aged, wise
06 august
07 revered
08 esteemed, honoured
09 dignified, respected

venerate
05 adore
06 esteem, honour, revere
07 respect, worship

veneration
03 awe
06 esteem
07 respect, worship
08 devotion
09 adoration, reverence

vengeance
07 revenge
08 reprisal, requital
11 retaliation, retribution

with a vengeance
09 furiously, like crazy, violently
10 forcefully, powerfully,
vigorously
11 to the utmost
13 energetically

vengeful
08 avenging, punitive, spiteful
09 rancorous
10 revengeful, vindictive
11 retaliatory, retributive

venial
05 minor
06 slight
09 excusable
10 forgivable, pardonable

venom
04 hate
05 spite, toxin
06 enmity, malice, poison
07 ill-will, rancour
08 acrimony
09 animosity, hostility, virulence
11 malevolence

venomous
05 fatal, toxic
06 bitter, deadly, lethal
07 noxious, vicious
08 spiteful, virulent
09 malicious, malignant,
poisonous, rancorous
10 malevolent, vindictive

vent
03 air, gap
04 duct, emit, hole
05 utter, voice
06 let out, outlet
07 express, passage, release
08 aperture

ventilate
03 air
04 cool
06 aerate, debate
07 discuss, express, freshen

venture
04 dare, risk
05 fling, stake, wager
06 chance, gamble, hazard
07 advance, exploit, imperil,
presume, project, suggest
08 endanger, make bold
09 adventure, endeavour,
speculate, volunteer
10 enterprise, put forward
11 speculation, undertaking

venturesome
04 bold
06 daring, plucky
08 fearless, intrepid
09 audacious, daredevil, dauntless
11 adventurous
12 enterprising

veracious
04 true
06 honest
07 factual, genuine
08 accurate, credible, truthful
15 straightforward

veracity
05 truth
07 candour, honesty, probity
08 accuracy
09 frankness, rectitude
10 exactitude
12 truthfulness

verbal
04 oral, said
05 vocal
06 spoken
10 linguistic

verbatim
07 closely, exactly
09 literally, precisely
11 to the letter, word for word

verbiage
06 waffle
08 pleonasm
09 prolixity, verbosity
11 periphrasis
14 circumlocution

verbose
05 windy, wordy
06 prolix
09 garrulous
10 long-winded, loquacious,
pleonastic
12 periphrastic
14 circumlocutory

verbosity
08 verbiage
09 garrulity, loquacity, prolixity,
windiness, wordiness
10 logorrhoea, multiloquy
14 long-windedness

verdant
04 lush
05 fresh, green, leafy, virid
11 viridescent

verdict
06 ruling
07 finding, opinion
08 decision, sentence
09 judgement
10 assessment, conclusion
12 adjudication

verdure
05 grass
07 foliage, herbage, pasture
08 greenery, verdancy, viridity
09 greenness
12 viridescence

verge
03 rim
04 brim, edge
05 brink, limit
06 border, edging, margin
08 boundary
09 threshold

verge on
08 approach, border on
11 come close to, tend towards

verification
05 proof
10 validation
11 attestation
12 confirmation
13 corroboration
14 authentication,
substantiation

verify
05 prove
06 attest
07 bear out, confirm
08 accredit, validate
11 corroborate
12 authenticate, substantiate

verisimilitude
09 semblance
10 likeliness
11 credibility, ring of truth
12 authenticity, plausibility

verity
05 truth
08 validity, veracity
09 actuality, soundness
12 authenticity, truthfulness

vernacular
05 idiom, lingo, local
06 common, jargon, native, speech, tongue, vulgar
07 dialect, popular
08 informal, language, parlance
10 colloquial, indigenous

versatile
08 all-round, flexible, variable
09 adaptable, many-sided
10 adjustable, all-purpose
12 multifaceted, multipurpose

verse
05 metre, rhyme
06 jingle, poetry, stanza
07 strophe
08 doggerel

versed
04 read
07 learned, skilled
08 familiar, seasoned
09 competent, practised
10 conversant, proficient
11 experienced
13 knowledgeable

versifier
04 poet
06 rhymer, verser
07 poetess, rhymist
09 poetaster, rhymester

version
04 form, kind, type
05 model, style
06 design, report
07 account, reading, variant
09 rendering
10 adaptation, paraphrase
14 interpretation

vertex
04 acme, apex, peak
06 apogee, height, summit, zenith
08 pinnacle
12 highest point

vertical
05 erect, on end, sheer
07 upright
10 straight up, upstanding
13 perpendicular

vertigo
09 dizziness, giddiness
15 light-headedness

verve
03 zip
04 brio, dash, life, élan
05 force, gusto
06 energy, relish, spirit, vigour
07 fervour, pizzazz, sparkle
08 vitality, vivacity

09 animation
10 enthusiasm, liveliness

very
04 bare, mere, pure, true
05 exact, sheer, truly, utter
06 actual, really, simple
07 acutely, genuine, perfect
08 selfsame, suitable
09 exceeding, extremely, identical
10 remarkably, uncommonly
11 appropriate, exceedingly
12 particularly
13 exceptionally

vessel
03 jar, jug, pot
04 boat, bowl, ship
05 craft
06 barque, holder
09 container
10 receptacle

vest
05 endow, grant
06 bestow, confer, supply
07 empower
08 sanction

vestibule
04 hall
05 foyer, lobby, porch
07 portico
08 anteroom, entrance
12 entrance hall

vestige
04 hint, mark, sign
05 print, scrap, token, touch, trace, track, whiff
06 relics
07 glimmer, inkling, remains, remnant, residue
09 remainder, suspicion
10 impression, indication

vestigial
07 reduced
09 remaining, surviving
10 incomplete
11 rudimentary, undeveloped

vestment
➤ *Types of clerical vestment:*
03 alb
04 cope, cowl, hood
05 cotta, ephod, frock, habit, mitre, scarf, stole
06 mantle, rochet, tippet, wimple
07 biretta, cassock, pallium, soutane, tunicle
08 chasuble, dalmatic, scapular, skullcap, surplice, yarmulka
09 dog-collar

10 Geneva gown
11 Geneva bands
14 clerical collar
➤ See also **religion**

vet
05 audit, check
06 review, survey
07 examine, inspect
08 appraise, check out
10 scrutinize
11 investigate

veteran
03 old, pro
07 old hand
08 old-timer, seasoned
09 old stager
10 past master
11 experienced, long-serving
13 battle-scarred

veto
03 ban
05 block
06 forbid, reject
07 embargo, rule out
08 disallow, prohibit, turn down
09 interdict, proscribe
11 prohibition
12 proscription

vex
04 fret
05 annoy, upset, worry
06 bother, harass, hassle, needle, pester, put out
07 agitate, disturb, perturb, provoke, torment, trouble
08 distress, irritate
09 aggravate
10 exasperate

vexation
04 bind, bore, pain
05 anger, pique, upset, worry
07 chagrin
08 headache, irritant, nuisance
09 annoyance
11 aggravation, frustration
12 exasperation
15 thorn in the flesh

vexatious
05 pesky
06 trying
07 irksome, nagging, teasing
08 annoying, worrying
09 provoking, worrisome
10 bothersome, irritating, tormenting
11 aggravating, infuriating, troublesome
12 exasperating

vexed

04 moot
05 irate, riled, upset
06 miffed, peeved, put out
07 annoyed, debated, hassled, nettled, ruffled, worried
08 agitated, bothered, disputed, harassed, provoked, troubled
09 contested, difficult, disturbed, flustered, in dispute, irritated, perplexed
10 aggravated, distressed
11 exasperated

viable

08 feasible, operable, possible, workable
10 achievable
11 practicable, sustainable

vibes

04 aura, feel
08 ambience, feelings
10 atmosphere, vibrations

vibrant

05 vivid
06 bright, lively
07 dynamic
08 animated, electric, spirited, striking, vigorous
09 brilliant, energetic, sparkling, vivacious
12 electrifying

vibrate

05 shake, swing, throb
06 quiver, shiver
07 pulsate, resound, tremble
08 resonate
11 reverberate

vibration

05 pulse, throb
06 judder, quiver, tremor
07 frisson, shaking
09 pulsation, resonance, throbbing, trembling
10 resounding
13 reverberation

vicar

06 parson, pastor, priest, rector
08 chaplain, minister
09 clergyman
11 clergywoman

vicarious

06 acting
08 indirect
09 surrogate
11 empathetic, second-hand
11 substituted

vice

03 sin

04 evil, flaw
05 fault
06 defect, foible
07 blemish, failing
08 bad habit, iniquity, weakness
09 depravity, evil-doing
10 degeneracy, immorality, wickedness, wrongdoing
12 besetting sin, imperfection
13 transgression

vice versa

09 inversely
10 oppositely
12 contrariwise

vicinity

08 district, environs, locality
12 surroundings
13 neighbourhood

vicious

04 mean, vile
05 catty, cruel, nasty
06 bitchy, brutal, fierce, savage
07 heinous, violent
08 depraved, spiteful, venomous, virulent
09 barbarous, ferocious, malicious
10 malevolent, vindictive

viciousness

05 spite, venom
06 malice
07 cruelty, rancour
08 ferocity, savagery
09 brutality, depravity, virulence
10 bitchiness
12 spitefulness

vicissitude

05 shift, twist
08 mutation
09 deviation, variation
10 alteration, revolution
11 alternation, fluctuation

victim

04 dupe, prey
06 martyr, quarry, sucker
07 fall guy
08 casualty, fatality, sufferer
09 sacrifice, scapegoat

victimize

05 bully, cheat, trick
06 pick on, prey on
09 persecute
15 take advantage of

victor

05 champ, first
06 top dog, winner
08 champion

09 conqueror
11 prize-winner
13 victor ludorum

victorious

05 first
07 winning
08 champion, unbeaten
10 conquering, successful
12 prize-winning

victory

03 win
07 mastery, success, triumph
08 conquest
11 subjugation, superiority

victuals

04 eats, food, grub, nosh, tuck
05 bread
06 stores, viands
07 aliment, edibles, rations
08 eatables, supplies
10 provisions, sustenance
11 comestibles

vie

05 fight, rival
06 strive
07 compete, contend, contest

view

03 see
04 idea, look, scan
05 angle, judge, scene, sight, study, vista, watch
06 belief, gaze at, look at, notion, regard, review, sketch, survey, vision
07 account, examine, feeling, glimpse, inspect, observe, opinion, outlook, picture, thought, witness
08 attitude, consider, panorama, perceive, portrait, prospect, scrutiny
09 judgement, landscape, portrayal, sentiment, spectacle
10 assessment, conviction, impression, inspection, perception, scrutinize
11 contemplate, examination, observation, perspective
13 contemplation, range of vision

◻in view of

11 considering
13 bearing in mind

viewer

07 watcher
08 observer, onlooker
09 spectator

viewpoint
05 angle, slant
06 stance
08 attitude, position
10 standpoint
11 perspective

vigil
05 watch
07 lookout
08 stake-out

vigilance
07 caution
09 alertness
11 observation, wakefulness
12 watchfulness
13 attentiveness

vigilant
05 alert, aware
08 cautious, watchful
09 observant, wide-awake
11 on your guard
12 on the lookout

vigorous
05 brisk, lusty, sound, stout, tough, vital
06 active, lively, robust, strong
07 dynamic, healthy, intense
08 animated, athletic, forceful, forcible, powerful, spirited
09 effective energetic, strenuous
11 flourishing, full-blooded

vigorously
07 briskly, eagerly, lustily
08 heartily, strongly
10 forcefully, powerfully
11 strenuously
13 energetically

vigour
03 pep, zip
04 brio, dash
05 force, gusto, might, oomph, power, verve
06 energy, health, spirit
07 potency, stamina
08 activity, dynamism, strength, vitality, vivacity

vile
03 bad, low
04 base, evil, foul, mean
05 nasty
06 impure, sinful, wicked
07 corrupt, debased, noxious, vicious
08 depraved, horrible, wretched
09 appalling, degrading, loathsome, miserable, obnoxious, offensive,

repugnant, repulsive, revolting, sickening
10 degenerate, despicable, disgusting, iniquitous, nauseating, unpleasant
11 disgraceful, distasteful
12 contemptible, disagreeable

vileness
04 evil
07 outrage
08 baseness, foulness, meanness, ugliness
09 depravity, profanity
10 corruption, degeneracy

vilification
05 abuse
07 calumny
09 aspersion, contumely, criticism, invective
10 defamation, scurrility
11 denigration, mud-slinging
12 calumniation, vituperation
13 disparagement

vilify
04 slam
05 abuse, decry, slate, smear
06 berate, debase, defame, malign, revile
07 asperse, slander, traduce
08 badmouth, denounce
09 denigrate, disparage
10 calumniate, stigmatize, vituperate

village
06 hamlet
09 community
10 settlement

villain
05 baddy, devil, knave, rogue
06 rascal, wretch
08 criminal, evildoer
09 miscreant, reprobate, scoundrel, wrongdoer
10 malefactor

villainous
03 bad
04 evil, vile
06 sinful, wicked
07 debased, heinous, vicious
08 criminal, fiendish
09 nefarious, notorious
10 degenerate, iniquitous
11 disgraceful, opprobrious

villainy
03 sin
04 vice
05 crime
07 badness, knavery, roguery
08 atrocity, baseness, iniquity

09 depravity, rascality, turpitude
10 wickedness
11 criminality, delinquency

vindicate
06 acquit, uphold, verify
07 absolve, justify, warrant
08 advocate, champion
09 exonerate
11 corroborate

vindication
07 apology, defence
11 exoneration, extenuation
13 justification
14 substantiation

vindictive
08 spiteful, vengeful, venomous
09 malicious, rancorous
10 revengeful
11 unforgiving

vintage
03 era, old
04 best, crop, fine, rare, ripe, time, year
05 epoch, prime
06 choice, mature, origin, period, select
07 classic, harvest, quality, supreme, veteran
08 enduring, superior
09 gathering, venerable
11 high-quality

violate
04 rape
05 break, flout, wreck
06 breach, defile, invade, molest, ravish
07 debauch, disobey, disrupt, infract, outrage, profane
08 infringe
09 desecrate
10 contravene, transgress
13 interfere with

violation
05 abuse
06 breach
07 offence, outrage
08 trespass
09 sacrilege
10 defilement, spoliation
11 desecration, profanation
12 infringement
13 contravention, transgression

violence
04 fury
05 force, might, power
06 frenzy, tumult
07 cruelty, passion

violent
08 ferocity, fighting, savagery, severity, strength, wildness
09 bloodshed, brutality, roughness, vehemence
10 aggression, fierceness, turbulence
11 hostilities

violent
04 wild
05 acute, cruel, fiery, great, harsh, rough, sharp
06 brutal, fierce, savage, strong
07 extreme, furious, intense, riotous, vicious
08 forceful, forcible, maddened, powerful, vehement
09 ferocious, hot-headed, impetuous, murderous, turbulent
10 aggressive, passionate, tumultuous
11 destructive, devastating
12 bloodthirsty, excruciating

VIP
04 star
07 big shot, magnate, notable
08 luminary
09 big cheese, celebrity, dignitary, personage

virago
04 fury
05 scold, shrew, vixen
06 dragon, gorgon, tartar
08 harridan
09 battle-axe, termagant, Xanthippe

virgin
03 new
04 girl, pure
05 fresh
06 chaste, intact, maiden, modest, vestal
08 celibate, maidenly, spotless, unspoilt, virginal
09 stainless, undefiled, untouched
10 immaculate

virginal
04 pure
05 fresh, snowy, white
06 chaste, vestal, virgin
08 maidenly, pristine, spotless
09 undefiled, untouched
10 immaculate
11 uncorrupted, undisturbed

virginity
06 purity, virtue
08 chastity
10 chasteness, maidenhood

virile
05 lusty, macho, manly
06 potent, strong
08 forceful, muscular, vigorous
09 masculine, strapping
10 red-blooded

virility
06 vigour
07 manhood, potency
08 machismo
09 manliness
11 masculinity

virtual
07 implied
08 implicit, in effect
09 effective, essential, potential, practical
11 prospective
12 in all but name

virtually
06 almost, nearly
08 as good as, in effect
09 in essence
10 more or less
11 effectively

virtue
04 plus
05 asset, merit, worth
06 credit, honour
07 benefit, honesty, justice, probity, quality
08 goodness, morality, strength
09 advantage, rectitude
10 excellence, worthiness
14 high-mindedness

▶ *The seven principal virtues:*
04 hope
05 faith
07 charity, justice
08 prudence
09 fortitude
10 temperance

▢**by virtue of**
07 by way of, owing to
08 by dint of, thanks to
09 because of, by means of
11 on account of

virtuosity
05 flair, skill, éclat
06 finish, polish
07 bravura, finesse, mastery
08 artistry, wizardry
09 expertise
10 brilliance

virtuoso
06 expert, genius, master
07 maestro, prodigy, skilful
08 dazzling, masterly
09 brilliant, excellent

virtuous
05 moral
06 decent, honest, worthy
07 angelic, ethical, upright
08 innocent
09 exemplary, righteous
10 honourable, upstanding
11 clean-living, respectable

virulence
05 spite, venom
06 hatred, malice, poison, spleen
07 rancour, vitriol
08 acrimony, toxicity
10 antagonism, malignancy, resentment
11 malevolence

virulent
05 fatal, toxic
06 bitter, deadly, lethal, severe
07 extreme, intense, vicious
08 spiteful, venomous
09 malicious, malignant, poisonous, vitriolic
10 malevolent, pernicious, vindictive

viscera
06 bowels, vitals
07 innards, insides
08 entrails, gralloch
10 intestines

viscous
05 gluey, gooey, gummy, tacky
06 mucous, sticky, viscid
07 treacly
09 glutinous
10 gelatinous
12 mucilaginous

visible
04 open
05 clear, overt, plain
06 patent
07 evident, exposed, obvious
08 apparent, manifest, palpable
10 noticeable, observable
11 conspicuous, discernible, perceivable, perceptible
15 distinguishable

vision
04 idea, view
05 dream, ghost, image, sight
06 mirage, seeing, wraith
07 chimera, fantasy, insight, phantom, picture, spectre
08 daydream, eyesight
09 foresight, intuition
10 apparition, conception, perception
11 imagination, mental image
13 hallucination, mental picture

14 far-sightedness
15 optical illusion

visionary
04 seer
06 dreamy, mystic, unreal
07 dreamer, prophet, utopian
08 fanciful, idealist, illusory, quixotic, romantic, theorist
09 fantasist, prophetic
10 daydreamer, Don Quixote, far-sighted, idealistic, ivory-tower, perceptive
11 impractical, unrealistic

visit
04 call, stay, stop
05 curse, pop in, smite
06 call in, call on, drop by, look in, plague, punish, stop by
07 afflict, sojourn, trouble
08 drop in on, go and see, go over to, stay with
09 excursion, go round to
13 spend time with

visitation
05 trial, visit
06 blight, ordeal
10 affliction, appearance, inspection, punishment
11 catastrophe, examination
13 manifestation

visitor
05 guest
06 caller
07 company, tourist
09 traveller
12 holidaymaker

vista
04 view
05 scene
07 outlook
08 panorama, prospect
11 perspective

visual
05 optic
06 ocular
07 optical, visible
10 observable
11 discernible, perceptible

visualize
03 see
07 imagine, picture
08 conceive, envisage

vital
03 key
05 alive, basic
06 lively, living, urgent
07 crucial, dynamic, vibrant
08 animated, critical, decisive, forceful, spirited, vigorous

09 energetic, essential, necessary, vivacious
10 imperative, life-giving, quickening
11 fundamental, significant
12 invigorating, life-and-death
13 indispensable

vitality
04 life, zest
05 oomph
06 energy, spirit, vigour
07 pizzazz, sparkle, stamina
08 strength, vivacity
09 animation
10 exuberance, get-up-and-go, liveliness

vitamin

▶ *Types of vitamins*:
01 A, B, C, D, E, G, H, K, P
06 biotin, citrin
07 retinol, thiamin
08 carotene, thiamine
09 folic acid, menadione
10 calciferol, pyridoxine, riboflavin, tocopherol
11 menaquinone
12 ascorbic acid
13 nicotinic acid

vitiate
03 mar
04 harm, ruin
05 spoil, sully, taint
06 blight, debase, defile, impair, injure, weaken
07 blemish, devalue, nullify
09 undermine
10 invalidate
11 contaminate

vitriolic
06 biting, bitter
07 abusive, acerbic, caustic, mordant, vicious
08 sardonic, scathing, venomous, virulent
09 malicious, trenchant
11 acrimonious, destructive
12 vituperative

vituperate
05 abuse, blame, slate
06 berate, revile, vilify
07 censure, slag off, upbraid
09 castigate

vituperation
05 abuse, blame, stick
07 censure, obloquy
08 diatribe
09 contumely, invective, philippic, reprimand
11 castigation, objurgation

vituperative
07 abusive
09 insulting, withering
10 censorious, derogatory
11 fulminatory, opprobrious
12 calumniatory, denunciatory

vivacious
06 bubbly, lively
08 animated, cheerful, spirited
09 ebullient, sparkling
12 effervescent, high-spirited, light-hearted

vivacity
04 brio, élan
06 energy, spirit
08 activity, dynamism, vitality
09 animation
10 ebullience, liveliness
13 effervescence

vivid
05 clear, lurid, sharp
06 bright, lively, strong
07 dynamic, glaring, glowing, graphic, intense, vibrant
08 animated, dazzling, distinct, dramatic, lifelike, powerful, spirited, striking, vigorous
09 brilliant, colourful, memorable, realistic

vividness
04 glow, life
07 clarity, realism
08 lucidity, radiance, strength
09 intensity
10 brilliancy, refulgence

vocabulary
05 idiom, lexis, words
07 lexicon
08 glossary, language, word-book
09 thesaurus
10 dictionary

vocal
04 oral, said
05 blunt, frank, noisy
06 shrill, spoken, voiced
07 uttered
08 eloquent, strident
09 expressed
10 articulate, vociferous

vocation
03 job
04 line, post, role, work
05 craft, trade
06 career, métier, office
07 calling, mission, pursuit
08 business
10 employment, occupation, profession

vociferous
04 loud
05 noisy, vocal
08 strident, vehement
09 clamorous, outspoken
10 forthright, thundering

vogue
03 fad
04 mode
05 craze, style, taste, trend
07 fashion, the rage
08 the thing
09 the latest
10 popularity

❑in vogue
02 in
06 modish, trendy, with it
07 popular, stylish
11 fashionable
13 up-to-the-minute

voice
03 air, say
04 tone, view, vote, will, wish
05 organ, sound, utter, words
06 airing, assert, convey, medium, speech, talk of
07 declare, divulge, express, mention, opinion, speak of
08 decision, disclose, language
09 enunciate, utterance, verbalize
10 articulate, inflection, intonation, mouthpiece
12 articulation

void
03 gap
04 emit, lack, vain, want
05 annul, blank, clear, empty, space
06 cancel, devoid, hollow, lacuna, vacant, vacuum
07 invalid, nullify, opening, useless, vacuity
08 defecate, evacuate
09 discharge, emptiness, nullified
10 invalidate, unoccupied

volatile
06 fickle, fitful, lively
07 erratic, flighty
08 unstable, unsteady, volcanic
09 explosive, mercurial, unsettled, up and down
10 capricious, changeable
13 temperamental, unpredictable

volcano
➤ *Names of volcanoes. We have omitted the word* mount *from names given in the following list but you may need to include this word as part of the solution to some crossword clues.*
03 Apo, Usu
04 Etna, Fuji, Taal
05 Hekla, Kenya, Mayon, Pelée, Thera, Thira
06 Hudson, Sangay
07 Kilauea, Rainier, Ruapehu, Vulcano
08 Cotopaxi, Krakatoa, Mauna Kea, Mauna Loa, Pinatubo, St Helens, Vesuvius
09 Paricutín, Pichincha, Santorini, Stromboli, Tongariro
10 Chimborazo, Tungurahua
12 Citlaltépetl, Popocatepetl
15 Haleakala Crater
➤ See also **mountain**

volition
04 will
06 choice, option
08 choosing, election, free will
10 preference, resolution
13 determination

volley
04 hail
05 blast, burst, salvo
06 shower
07 barrage
09 cannonade, discharge, fusillade

volte-face
05 U-turn
09 about-face, about-turn, turnabout

voluble
06 chatty, fluent
09 garrulous, talkative
10 articulate, loquacious

volume
04 book, bulk, mass, size
05 sound, space
06 amount
07 omnibus
08 capacity, loudness, quantity
09 aggregate, amplitude
10 dimensions

voluminous
04 full
05 ample, bulky, large, roomy
08 spacious
09 billowing, capacious

voluntarily
06 freely
08 by choice
09 purposely, willingly
15 of your own accord

voluntary
04 free
06 unpaid
08 honorary, optional
10 deliberate, purposeful
11 intentional

volunteer
05 offer
06 tender
07 proffer, propose, suggest
10 put forward
11 step forward

voluptuary
07 playboy
08 hedonist, sybarite
09 bon vivant, debauchee, epicurean, libertine
10 profligate, sensualist
14 pleasure-seeker

voluptuous
05 buxom
07 opulent, sensual, shapely
09 luxurious, seductive
10 hedonistic
11 full-figured
13 self-indulgent

vomit
04 barf, puke, spew
05 fetch, heave, retch
06 be sick
07 bring up, throw up
11 regurgitate

vomiting
06 emesis, puking
07 barfing, spewing
08 ejection, retching, sickness
10 chundering
13 regurgitation

voracious
04 avid
06 greedy, hungry
08 edacious, ravening
09 devouring, rapacious
10 gluttonous, prodigious

voracity
05 greed
06 hunger
07 avidity, edacity
08 rapacity
12 ravenousness

vortex
04 eddy

05 whirl
09 maelstrom, whirlpool,
   whirlwind

votary
06 addict
07 devotee
08 adherent, disciple,
   follower

vote
03 opt
04 poll
05 elect, put in
06 ballot, choose, return
07 declare, re-elect, suggest
08 election, plump for, suffrage
09 franchise
10 plebiscite, referendum
12 go to the polls
15 enfranchisement

vouch
□ **vouch for**
06 affirm, assert, verify
07 certify, confirm, endorse,
   support, swear to, warrant
08 attest to, speak for
09 answer for, guarantee
10 asseverate

voucher
05 paper, token
06 coupon, ticket
08 document

vouchsafe
04 cede, give
05 deign, grant, yield
06 bestow, confer, impart

vow
04 oath
05 swear
06 affirm, devote, pledge
07 profess, promise
08 dedicate
09 undertake
12 give your word

voyage
04 sail, tour, trip
06 cruise, safari, travel
07 journey, odyssey, passage,
   travels
08 crossing
10 expedition

vulgar
03 low
04 lewd, loud, rude
05 bawdy, crude, dirty, gaudy,
   rough, showy, tacky

06 coarse, common, filthy,
   flashy, garish, glitzy, kitsch,
   ribald, risqué, tawdry
07 boorish, general, ill-bred,
   obscene, popular, uncouth
08 impolite, improper,
   indecent, ordinary
09 off-colour, offensive,
   tasteless, unrefined
10 indelicate, suggestive,
   vernacular
11 distasteful, near the bone
12 ostentatious
13 cheap and nasty
15 unsophisticated

vulgarity
07 crudity
08 ribaldry
09 indecency
11 ostentation

vulnerable
07 exposed
08 helpless, wide open
09 powerless, sensitive
11 defenceless, susceptible,
   unprotected
12 open to attack

wacky
03 odd
04 daft, wild, zany
05 crazy, goofy, loony, loopy, nutty, silly
06 screwy
07 off beat
09 eccentric

wad
04 lump, mass, plug, roll
05 block, chunk, wodge
06 bundle

wadding
06 filler, lining
07 filling, packing, padding
08 stuffing
10 cottonwool

waddle
04 rock, sway
06 toddle, totter, wobble

wade
04 ford, loll, roll
05 cross, lurch
06 splash, wallow, welter
08 flounder, traverse

❑ wade in
05 set to
06 tear in
07 pitch in
08 launch in
10 get stuck in
12 trawl through
13 plough through

waffle
04 guff
06 babble, hot air, jabber
07 blather, padding, prattle
08 nonsense, witter on
09 verbosity, wordiness
12 gobbledygook

waft
04 blow, puff
05 carry, drift, float, glide, scent, whiff
06 breath, breeze
07 current, draught

wag
03 bob, nod, wit
04 fool, rock, wave

05 clown, comic, droll, joker, shake, swing
06 jester, quiver, waggle, wiggle, wobble
08 banterer, comedian, humorist

wage
03 fee, pay
06 reward, salary
07 carry on, conduct, payment
08 earnings, engage in, practise
09 allowance, emolument
12 remuneration

wager
03 bet
04 punt, risk
05 stake
06 gamble, hazard, pledge
07 flutter, lay odds, venture
09 speculate

waggish
05 droll, funny, merry, witty
07 comical, jesting, jocular, puckish, roguish
09 bantering, facetious

waggle
05 shake
06 jiggle, wiggle, wobble
09 oscillate

wagon
03 van
04 cart, dray
05 buggy, float, train, truck
08 carriage

waif
05 stray
06 orphan
09 foundling

wail
03 cry, sob
04 howl, keen, moan, yowl
06 lament
07 ululate, weeping
09 complaint, ululation

wait
04 halt, rest, stay
05 abide, delay, pause, tarry
06 hang on, linger, remain
08 hang fire, interval

10 hang around, hesitation
12 bide your time

❑ wait on
04 tend
05 serve
08 attend to
09 look after

waiter, waitress
04 host
06 butler, server
07 hostess, steward
09 attendant
10 stewardess

waive
05 defer, yield
06 forego, give up, resign
08 renounce, set aside
09 do without, surrender
10 relinquish

waiver
08 deferral
09 remission, surrender
10 abdication, disclaimer

wake
04 fire, goad, path, prod, rear, rise, stir, warn, wash, whet
05 arise, alert, awake, egg on, get up, rouse, track, trail, train, vigil, waken, watch
06 arouse, awaken, excite
07 animate, funeral
08 activate, backwash
09 aftermath, stimulate
10 death-watch

wakeful
04 wary
05 alert
08 vigilant, watchful
09 observant, sleepless
10 unsleeping

waken
04 fire, rise, stir, wake, whet
05 awake, get up, rouse
06 arouse, awaken, ignite, kindle
07 animate, enliven, quicken
08 activate
09 galvanize, stimulate

walk
03   pad, way
04   gait, hike, lane, pace, path, plod, roam, step, trek, trip
05   alley, amble, guide, march, mince, route, stalk, steal, stomp, strut, track, trail, tramp, tread
06   avenue, escort, hoof it, parade, patter, potter, ramble, stride, stroll, toddle, totter, trudge, wander
07   conduct, pathway, saunter, trample, walkway
08   carriage, footpath, pavement, shepherd
09   accompany, esplanade, promenade
10   shank's pony
11   perambulate
15   go by shanks's pony, stretch your legs

◻ walk away with, walk off with
04   lift, nick
05   pinch, steal
09   go off with
11   make off with

◻ walk of life
04   area, line
05   arena, field, trade
06   career, métier, sphere
07   calling, pursuit
08   activity, vocation
10   background, occupation

◻ walk out
06   mutiny, revolt, strike
09   down tools
10   go on strike

◻ walk out on
06   desert
07   abandon, forsake

walker
05   hiker
07   rambler
10   pedestrian

walk-out
06   revolt, strike
07   protest
08   stoppage

walk-over
05   cinch
06   doddle
08   pushover
10   child's play
11   piece of cake

walkway
04   lane, path
07   passage, pathway

08   footpath, pavement, sidewalk
09   esplanade, promenade

wall
03   dam
04   mani, mure
05   fence, gable
06   bailey, immure, parpen, puteal, vallum
07   barmkin, barrier, bulwark, fronton, parapet, parpend, perpent, trumeau
09   revetment
10   battlement, embankment

wallet
04   case
05   pouch, purse
06   folder, holder
08   bill-fold, notecase, pochette

wallop
03   hit
04   bash, beat, belt, blow, drub, kick, lick, rout, swat
05   clout, crush, paste, pound, punch, thump, whack
06   batter, buffet, defeat, strike, thrash, thwack
07   clobber, trounce

wallow
04   bask, loll, roll, wade
05   enjoy, glory, lurch, revel
06   relish, splash, welter
07   delight, indulge
08   flounder
09   luxuriate

wan
04   pale, weak
05   ashen, bleak, faint, pasty, waxen, weary, white
06   feeble, pallid, sickly
07   anaemic, ghastly
09   washed out, whey-faced
10   colourless

wand
03   rod
04   mace, twig
05   baton, sprig, staff, stick
07   sceptre

wander
04   rave, roam, rove, veer
05   amble, drift, range, stray
06   babble, depart, gibber, ramble, stroll
07   deviate, digress, diverge, meander, saunter
08   go astray, straggle
11   lose your way, peregrinate
12   talk nonsense

wanderer
05   Gypsy, nomad, rover, stray
07   drifter, rambler, vagrant
08   stroller, vagabond, wayfarer
09   itinerant, straggler, traveller
12   rolling stone

wandering
06   roving
07   journey, meander, nomadic, odyssey, travels, vagrant
08   drifting, homeless, rambling, rootless, vagabond
09   itinerant, migratory, strolling, walkabout, wayfaring
10   meandering, travelling
11   peripatetic
13   peregrination

wane
03   dim, ebb
04   drop, fade, fail, fall, sink
05   abate, decay, droop
06   lessen, shrink, weaken
07   decline, dwindle, subside
08   decrease, diminish, fade away, peter out

◻ on the wane
06   ebbing, fading
08   dropping, moribund
09   declining, dwindling, lessening, subsiding, weakening
11   on the way out
12   on the decline

wangle
03   fix
06   fiddle, manage, scheme
07   arrange, pull off
08   contrive, engineer

want
04   lack, like, lust, miss, need, wish
05   covet, crave, fancy
06   dearth, demand, desire, hunger, penury, pining, thirst
07   absence, call for, craving, hope for, long for, paucity, pine for, poverty, require
08   appetite, coveting, feel like, scarcity, shortage, yearn for, yearning
09   be without, hunger for, indigence, privation, thirst for
10   deficiency, inadequacy, scantiness
11   destitution, requirement
13   be deficient in, insufficiency

wanting
05   short
06   absent, faulty

07 lacking, missing
09 defective, deficient, imperfect
10 inadequate
11 substandard
12 insufficient, unacceptable
13 disappointing

wanton
04 lewd, rake, rash, roué, slut, tart, wild
05 whore
06 harlot, impure, lecher
07 Don Juan, immoral, trollop
08 Casanova, reckless
09 abandoned, debauchee, dissolute, pointless, shameless
10 dissipated, gratuitous, groundless, prostitute, unprovoked, voluptuary
11 extravagant, promiscuous
12 unrestrained
13 unjustifiable

war
05 clash, fight
06 battle, combat, enmity, strife, strive
08 campaign, conflict, fighting, skirmish, struggle
09 bloodshed
10 antagonism, take up arms
11 cross swords, hostilities

► *Types of war*:
05 blitz, jihad
06 ambush, attack, battle, hot war
07 assault, cold war, holy war
08 civil war, invasion, skirmish, struggle, total war, trade war, world war
10 blitzkrieg, engagement, manoeuvres, nuclear war, resistance
11 bombardment, germ warfare, war of nerves
12 state of siege
13 armed conflict, counter-attack, jungle warfare
14 war of attrition
15 chemical warfare

► *Names of wars*:
05 Roses (Wars of the)
07 Gulf War, Pacific (War of the), Zulu War
08 Boer Wars, Chaco War, Crusades, Religion (Wars of), Sikh Wars
09 Dutch Wars, Korean War, Maori Wars, Opium Wars, Punic Wars, Six-Day War, Trojan War, World War I

10 Afghan Wars, Balkan Wars, Crimean War, Gallic Wars, Indian Wars, Jenkins' Ear (War of), Mexican War, Vietnam War, World War II
11 Bishops' Wars, Football War, Iran-Iraq War, Peasants' War, Persian Wars
12 Black Hawk War, Falklands War, Independence (War of), Yom Kippur War
13 First World War, Peninsular War, Seven Years' War
14 Boxer Rebellion, Eighty Years' War, Indian Civil War, Indian Uprising, July Revolution, Napoleonic Wars, Second World War, Thirty Years' War
15 Easter Rebellion, Hundred Years' War, Russian Civil War, Spanish Civil War
➤ See also **battle**

warble
04 call, sing, song
05 chirp, trill, yodel
06 quaver
07 chirrup, twitter

war cry
06 slogan
09 battle cry, watchword
11 rallying-cry

ward
04 area, room, unit, zone
05 minor, pupil
06 charge
07 cubicle, protégé, quarter
08 district, division, precinct, protégée
09 apartment, dependant
11 compartment

□ **ward off**
05 avert, avoid, block, dodge, evade, parry, repel
07 beat off, deflect, fend off
08 stave off, turn away
09 drive back, turn aside

warden
06 keeper, ranger, warder
07 curator, janitor, steward
08 guardian, overseer, watchman
09 caretaker, custodian
10 supervisor
14 superintendent

warder
05 guard, screw
06 jailer, keeper, warden
08 wardress
09 custodian
13 prison officer

wardrobe
06 attire, closet, outfit
07 apparel, clothes
08 cupboard

warehouse
05 depot, store
08 entrepot
09 stockroom
10 depository, repository, storehouse

wares
05 goods, stock, stuff
07 produce
08 products
11 commodities, merchandise

warfare
04 arms
05 blows
06 battle, combat, strife
07 contest, discord
08 campaign, conflict, fighting
11 hostilities
13 passage of arms

warily
06 cagily
07 charily
08 gingerly, uneasily
09 carefully, guardedly
10 cautiously, hesitantly
12 suspiciously

wariness
04 care
06 unease
07 caution
08 caginess, distrust, prudence
09 alertness, attention, foresight, hesitancy, suspicion, vigilance
10 discretion
12 apprehension
14 circumspection

warlike
07 hawkish, hostile, martial
08 militant
09 bellicose, combative
10 aggressive, pugnacious
11 belligerent
12 antagonistic, bloodthirsty, militaristic, war-mongering

warlock
05 demon, witch
06 wizard
08 conjurer, magician, sorcerer
09 enchanter
11 necromancer

warm
04 fine, heat, melt, stir, thaw
05 balmy, eager, sunny, tepid

06 ardent, excite, hearty, heated, heat up, mellow, reheat
07 animate, cordial, enliven, fervent, intense, liven up, sincere
08 cheerful, friendly, lukewarm
09 heart-felt, temperate
15 put some life into

◻**warm up**
08 exercise, limber up, loosen up

warm-blooded
06 ardent, lively
07 earnest, fervent
08 spirited
09 excitable, vivacious
10 hot-blooded, passionate
12 enthusiastic

warm-hearted
04 kind
06 kindly, loving, tender
07 cordial
11 kind-hearted, sympathetic
12 affectionate
13 compassionate, tender-hearted

warmth
04 care, fire, heat, love, zeal
06 ardour
07 fervour, hotness, passion
08 sympathy
09 affection, intensity, vehemence
10 enthusiasm, kindliness, tenderness

warn
04 tell, urge
05 alert
06 advise, tip off
07 caution, counsel, reprove
08 admonish, forewarn
09 reprimand
10 give notice

warning
04 hint, omen, sign
05 alarm, alert
06 advice, augury, lesson, notice, signal, threat, tip-off
07 caution, counsel, ominous, portent, presage
10 admonition, admonitory, cautionary
11 information, premonition, premonitory, threatening
12 notification
13 advance notice

warp
04 bend, bent, bias, kink, turn
05 quirk, twist

06 defect, deform
07 contort, corrupt, pervert
08 misshape
10 contortion, distortion, perversion

warrant
04 back
05 allow, swear
06 affirm, avouch, permit, pledge, uphold
07 approve, call for, certify, consent, declare, empower, endorse, entitle, justify, licence, license, support, voucher
08 sanction, security, vouch for
09 answer for, authority, authorize, consent to, guarantee
10 commission, permission, underwrite, validation
11 necessitate
13 authorization

warrantable
05 legal, right
06 lawful, proper
09 allowable
10 defensible, reasonable
11 justifiable, permissible

warranty
04 bond
06 pledge
08 contract, covenant
09 assurance, guarantee

warring
07 hostile, opposed
08 fighting, opposing
09 combatant, embattled
11 belligerent, conflicting
14 at daggers drawn

warrior
07 fighter, soldier
08 champion, warhorse
09 combatant
11 fighting man

wart
04 lump
06 growth
07 verruca
12 protuberance

wary
05 alert, cagey, chary
07 careful, guarded
08 cautious, vigilant, watchful
09 attentive, wide-awake
10 on the alert, suspicious
11 circumspect, distrustful, on your guard
12 on the lookout

wash
03 mop
04 bath, flow, soak, wave, wipe
05 bathe, clean, rinse, scrub, surge, sweep, swill
06 douche, shower, splash, sponge, stream
07 cleanse, coating, launder, laundry, shampoo, stand up
08 cleaning, swab down
09 cleansing, freshen up
10 laundering, pass muster
11 carry weight
12 bear scrutiny
15 bear examination

◻**wash your hands of**
07 abandon
08 give up on

washed-out
03 wan
04 flat, pale
05 drawn, faded
06 pallid
07 drained, haggard
08 blanched, bleached
09 exhausted, knackered
10 colourless, lacklustre

washout
04 flop
06 fiasco
07 debacle, failure
08 disaster
11 lead balloon

waspish
05 cross, testy
06 bitchy, touchy
07 prickly
08 snappish
11 bad-tempered, ill-tempered

waste
04 bare, blow, loss, rape, raze, ruin, sack, wild
05 abuse, bleak, drain, dregs, dross, empty, erode, extra, scrap, slops, trash
06 barren, debris, litter, misuse, refuse, unused, wither
07 atrophy, consume, despoil, destroy, exhaust, garbage, neglect, pillage, rubbish, shrivel, splurge, useless
08 effluent, left-over, misspend, squander, unwanted
09 depredate, devastate, dissipate, leftovers
10 debilitate, devastated
11 dissipation, fritter away, offscouring, prodigality, squandering

12 extravagance, unproductive
13 supernumerary

wasted
04 high, weak
05 drunk, gaunt
07 smashed
08 shrunken, withered
09 atrophied, emaciated
10 shrivelled
11 intoxicated

wasteful
08 prodigal
10 profligate
11 extravagant, improvident, spendthrift
12 uneconomical

wasteland
04 void, wild
05 waste, wilds
06 desert
09 emptiness
10 barrenness, wilderness

wasting
08 marasmic
10 destroying, emaciating, enfeebling
11 devastating

wastrel
05 idler
06 loafer, skiver
07 lounger, shirker
10 ne'er-do-well, profligate
11 spendthrift

watch
04 heed, keep, mark, mind, note, scan, view
05 clock, guard, vigil
06 look on, regard, survey
07 inspect, look out, lookout, observe, protect, stare at
08 take care, take heed
09 alertness, attention, be careful, look after, timepiece, vigilance
10 keep tabs on, wristwatch
11 chronometer, contemplate, keep an eye on, observation, superintend, supervision
12 pay attention, surveillance

□**watch out**
06 notice
07 look out
10 be vigilant
12 keep a lookout

□**watch over**
04 mind
05 guard
07 protect

09 look after
11 keep an eye on
14 stand guard over

watchdog
07 monitor
08 guard dog, guardian
09 custodian, ombudsman, protector
10 scrutineer

watcher
03 spy
06 viewer
07 lookout, witness
08 audience, looker-on, observer, onlooker
09 spectator

watchful
04 wary
05 alert, chary
08 cautious, vigilant
09 attentive, observant, wide awake
11 on your guard
12 on the lookout, on the qui vive

watchfulness
07 caution
08 wariness
09 alertness, attention, suspicion, vigilance

watchman
05 guard
09 caretaker, custodian
13 security guard

watchword
05 maxim, motto
06 byword, signal, slogan
08 buzz word, password
09 battle-cry, catchword
10 shibboleth
11 catch phrase, rallying-cry

water
03 sea, wet
04 hose, lake, rain, soak
05 douse, flood, ocean, river, spray
06 dampen, drench, stream
07 current, moisten, torrent
08 flooding, irrigate, moisture, saturate, sprinkle

□**water down**
04 thin
06 dilute, soften, weaken
08 play down, tone down
10 adulterate

watercourse
04 wadi
05 canal, ditch, river
06 stream

07 channel
12 water-channel

waterfall
04 fall
05 chute, falls
07 cascade, torrent
08 cataract
► *Names of waterfalls. We have omitted the word* **falls** *from names given in the following list but you may need to include this word as part of the solution to some crossword clues.*
05 Angel, Pilao, Tysse
06 Ormeli, Ribbon
07 Niagara
08 Itatinga, Kaieteur, Victoria
09 Churchill, Multnomah
10 Cleve-Garth
13 Upper Yosemite

waterproof
07 proofed
09 damp-proof
10 impervious
14 water-repellent, water-resistant

watertight
05 sound
08 airtight, hermetic
09 foolproof
12 indisputable, unassailable

watery
04 damp, thin, weak
05 fluid, moist, runny, soggy
07 aqueous, diluted, hydrous, insipid
10 wishy-washy
11 flavourless

wave
04 flap, flow, foam, rash, rush, sign, stir, surf, sway, waft
05 drift, flood, froth, surge, sweep, swell, swing, trend
06 billow, comber, ripple, roller, signal, stream
07 breaker, current, flutter, gesture, upsurge, wavelet
08 brandish, flourish, undulate
10 undulation, white horse
11 gesticulate, ground swell

□**wave aside**
07 dismiss
09 disregard
10 brush aside

waver
04 rock, sway, vary
06 dither, falter, seesaw, teeter, totter, wobble
07 stagger, tremble

08 hesitate
09 fluctuate, hum and haw, oscillate, vacillate
10 equivocate

waverer
08 ditherer
14 shilly-shallier

wavering
08 doubtful, doubting, havering, hesitant
09 dithering
10 in two minds
15 shilly-shallying

wavy
05 curly, curvy
06 ridged, zigzag
07 curling, curving, rippled, sinuous, winding
10 undulating

wax
04 grow, rise
05 mount, swell, widen
06 become, expand
07 broaden, develop, enlarge, fill out, magnify
08 increase

waxen
03 wan
04 pale
05 ashen, livid, white
06 pallid
07 anaemic, ghastly, whitish
09 bloodless
10 colourless

waxy
04 soft
05 pasty, waxen
06 pallid
07 cereous
09 ceraceous

way
04 lane, mode, path, plan, road, tool, wont
05 habit, lines, means, route, style, track, trait, usage
06 access, avenue, course, custom, manner, method, street, system, temper
07 channel, conduct, fashion, highway, passage, pathway, process, roadway
08 approach, practice, strategy
09 behaviour, direction, mannerism, procedure, technique
11 disposition, peculiarity, personality, temperament
12 idiosyncrasy, thoroughfare

14 characteristic, course of action
15 instrumentality

□ **by the way**
09 en passant, in passing
12 incidentally
15 parenthetically

□ **give way**
05 break, yield
06 cave in, fall in, give in, submit
07 concede
08 collapse
10 capitulate

□ **under way**
05 afoot, begun, going
07 started
08 in motion
10 in progress
11 in operation

□ **way of life**
05 world
09 lifestyle, situation

□ **ways and means**
03 way
04 cash
05 funds, tools
07 capital, methods
08 capacity, reserves
09 procedure, resources
10 capability
11 wherewithal

wayfarer
05 Gypsy, nomad, rover
06 walker
07 trekker, voyager
08 wanderer
09 itinerant, journeyer, traveller

wayfaring
06 roving
07 nomadic, walking
08 drifting, rambling, voyaging
09 itinerant, wandering
10 journeying, travelling
11 peripatetic

waylay
05 catch, seize
06 accost, ambush, hold up
09 intercept

way-out
04 wild
05 crazy, weird
06 far-out, freaky
07 bizarre, off-beat, unusual
09 eccentric, fantastic
10 avant-garde, outlandish
11 progressive
12 experimental
14 unconventional

wayward
06 fickle, unruly, wilful
08 contrary, obdurate, perverse, stubborn
09 obstinate
10 capricious, rebellious, refractory, self-willed
11 disobedient, intractable

weak
03 dim, low
04 lame, poor, puny, soft
05 faint, frail, shaky, weedy
06 feeble, infirm, sickly, slight
07 diluted, exposed, fragile, insipid, lacking, stifled, unsound, worn out
08 cowardly, delicate, fatigued
09 defective, deficient, enervated, exhausted, imperfect, powerless, spineless, tasteless, unhealthy, untenable
10 inadequate, indecisive, irresolute, vulnerable
11 adulterated, debilitated, defenceless, ineffectual
12 inconclusive, unconvincing
13 imperceptible

weaken
03 sap
04 fade, fail, flag, thin, tire
05 abate, droop, lower
06 dilute, ease up, lessen, reduce, soften, temper
07 cripple, disable, exhaust
08 diminish, enervate, enfeeble, mitigate, moderate, soften up
09 undermine, water down
10 debilitate
12 incapacitate

weakening
06 easing, fading, waning
08 dilution, flagging, lowering
09 abatement, dwindling, lessening, reduction
10 moderation
12 diminishment

weakling
04 drip, weed, wimp
05 mouse, sissy, wally
06 coward

weak-minded
07 pliable
09 compliant, spineless
10 irresolute, submissive
11 complaisant, persuadable, persuasible
12 faint-hearted
13 pusillanimous**

weakness
04 flaw
05 fault
06 defect, foible, liking
07 failing, frailty, passion
08 debility, soft spot
09 impotence, infirmity
10 deficiency, enervation, feebleness, proclivity
11 inclination, shortcoming
12 Achilles' heel, predilection
13 powerlessness, vulnerability

weal
04 mark, scar, welt
05 ridge, wound
06 streak, stripe
08 cicatrix
09 cicatrice, contusion

wealth
04 cash, mass
05 funds, goods, means, money, store
06 assets, bounty, mammon, plenty, riches
07 capital, finance, fortune
08 opulence, property, treasure
09 abundance, affluence, plenitude, profusion, resources, substance
10 cornucopia, prosperity
11 copiousness, possessions

wealthy
04 rich
06 loaded
07 moneyed, opulent, well-off
08 affluent, well-to-do
10 prosperous, well-heeled
11 comfortable, made of money
12 stinking rich

weapon
➤ _Weapons include_:
03 gas, gun
04 bomb, Colt®, cosh, dirk, épée, foil, mine, pike, Scud
05 H-bomb, knife, lance, Luger®, rifle, sabre, sling, spear, sword
06 airgun, cannon, CS gas, cudgel, dagger, Exocet®, magnum, Mauser, mortar, musket, pistol, rapier, rocket, six-gun
07 assegai, bayonet, bazooka, Bren gun, carbine, halberd, harpoon, longbow, machete, pole-axe, poniard, shotgun, sten gun, torpedo

08 air rifle, atom bomb, blowpipe, catapult, claymore, crossbow, field gun, howitzer, land-mine, revolver, scimitar, stiletto, time-bomb, tomahawk, tommy-gun
09 battleaxe, boomerang, Mills bomb, truncheon
10 bowie knife, broadsword, flick-knife, gatling-gun, machine-gun, shillelagh, six-shooter
11 Agent Orange, blunderbuss, bow and arrow, cluster-bomb, depth-charge, elephant gun, hand grenade, kalashnikov
12 flame-thrower
13 Cruise missile, knuckleduster, submachine-gun
14 incendiary bomb
15 Winchester® rifle

wear
03 don, rub, use
04 bear, fray, have, show
05 carry, dress, erode, sport
06 abrade, attire, costume
07 clothes, corrode, display, dress in, erosion, exhibit
08 abrasion, clothing, friction
09 corrosion
10 durability, employment
11 be clothed in, deteriorate

☐ wear down
05 erode
06 abrade, lessen, reduce
07 consume, corrode, rub away
08 diminish, macerate
09 grind down, undermine
10 chip away at

☐ wear off
03 ebb
04 fade, wane
05 abate
06 lessen, weaken
07 dwindle, subside
08 decrease, diminish

☐ wear on
04 go by, go on, pass
06 elapse

☐ wear out
03 sap
04 fray, tire
05 drain, erode
06 impair, strain, stress
07 consume, exhaust, fatigue
08 enervate
11 deteriorate, wear through

weariness
05 ennui
07 fatigue, languor
09 lassitude, tiredness
10 enervation, exhaustion

wearing
06 taxing, tiring, trying
07 erosive, irksome
08 tiresome
09 fatiguing, wearisome
10 exhausting, oppressive

wearisome
04 dull
06 boring, dreary, trying
07 humdrum, irksome, tedious
08 annoying, tiresome
09 fatiguing, vexatious
10 bothersome, burdensome, exhausting, monotonous
11 troublesome
12 exasperating

weary
03 bug, fag, irk, sap, tax
04 bore, fade, fail, jade, tire
05 all in, drain, jaded, tired
06 burden, bushed, done in, drowsy, sicken, sleepy
07 drained, fatigue, tire out, whacked, worn out
08 dead beat, dog-tired, enervate, fatigued, irritate
09 exhausted, knackered
10 debilitate, exasperate
12 bored to tears, sick and tired

wearying
06 taxing, tiring, trying
07 wearing
08 draining
10 exhausting

weather
03 dry
05 brave, stand
06 endure, expose, harden, resist, season, suffer
07 climate, dryness, outlook, ride out, survive, toughen
08 humidity, overcome, stick out, surmount
09 rise above, withstand
10 cloudiness, conditions, get through
11 come through, pull through
➤ See also **storm**; **wind**

☐ under the weather
03 ill
04 sick
05 queer, seedy
06 ailing, groggy, poorly
08 below par, hung over
09 off-colour, squeamish

10 indisposed, out of sorts
15 the worse for wear

weave
04 fuse, knit, lace, spin, wind
05 braid, merge, plait, twist
06 create, make up, zigzag
07 compose, entwine
08 contrive
09 construct, fabricate
10 criss-cross, intertwine
11 put together

web
03 net
04 knot, mesh, trap, weft
06 tangle
07 complex, lattice, netting
08 lacework

wed
04 ally, fuse, join, link, yoke
05 marry, merge, unite
06 splice
07 combine, espouse
10 get hitched, tie the knot

wedded
06 joined, wifely
07 marital, married, nuptial
08 conjugal
09 connubial, husbandly
11 matrimonial

wedding
05 union
06 bridal
07 nuptial, wedlock
08 hymeneal, hymenean, marriage, nuptials
09 matrimony
11 epithalamic, matrimonial

wedge
03 fit, jam, ram
04 cram, lump, pack, push
05 block, chock, chunk, crowd, force, lodge, piece, wodge
06 thrust
08 triangle

wedlock
05 union
08 marriage
09 matrimony

wee
04 tiny
05 small, teeny, weeny
06 little, midget, minute
09 itsy-bitsy, miniature
10 diminutive, negligible
11 Lilliputian

weed
➤ *Weeds include*:
04 dock, moss

05 daisy, vetch
06 fat hen, oxalis, spurge, yarrow
07 bracken, ragweed, ribwort
08 bindweed, duckweed, knapweed, self-heal
09 chickweed, coltsfoot, dandelion, ground ivy, groundsel, horsetail, knotgrass, liverwort, pearlwort, snakeweed, speedwell, sun spurge
10 cinquefoil, couch grass, curled dock, deadnettle, sow thistle, thale cress
11 ground elder, meadow grass, white clover
12 rough hawkbit, sheep's sorrel
13 common burdock, field wood rush, pineapple weed
14 shepherd's purse
15 broad-leaved dock, lesser celandine
➤ See also **plant**

◻ **weed out**
06 remove
07 root out
08 get rid of
09 eliminate, eradicate

weedy
04 puny, thin, weak
06 feeble, skinny
07 insipid, scrawny, wimpish
08 gangling
10 undersized

weekly
09 every week, once a week
10 hebdomadal
12 hebdomadally

weep
03 cry, sob
04 bawl, blub, moan, wail
05 mourn, whine
06 grieve, lament, snivel
07 blubber, whimper
09 be in tears, shed tears

weepy
05 teary
06 crying, labile
07 sobbing, tearful, weeping
09 melodrama
10 lachrymose, tear-jerker

weigh
06 burden, ponder
07 afflict, examine, trouble
08 consider, evaluate
09 reflect on, think over
10 deliberate, meditate on
11 contemplate

◻ **weigh down**
04 load
06 burden
07 depress, get down, oppress
08 bear down, overload
09 press down

◻ **weigh up**
06 assess, ponder, size up
07 balance, compare, examine
08 chew over, consider, evaluate, mull over
09 think over
10 deliberate
11 contemplate

weight
04 duty, load, mass, onus, sway
05 angle, clout, force, power, slant, twist, value, worry
06 burden, impact, strain
07 ballast, gravity, oppress, tonnage, trouble
08 handicap, poundage, pressure, quantity
09 authority, influence, prejudice, substance, unbalance, weigh down
10 importance
11 avoirdupois, encumbrance
12 significance
14 responsibility

weightless
04 airy
05 light

weighty
05 bulky, grave, heavy, hefty
06 solemn, taxing
07 massive, serious
09 important, momentous
10 burdensome
11 significant, substantial
13 authoritative, consequential

weird
05 eerie, queer
06 creepy, spooky, way-out
07 bizarre, ghostly, uncanny
08 freakish
12 supernatural
13 preternatural

weirdo
03 nut
05 crank, freak, loony
06 nutter
07 nutcase, oddball
08 crackpot
09 eccentric, fruitcake, queer fish

welcome
04 hail, meet
05 greet

06 accept, salute
07 embrace, popular, receive
08 greeting, pleasant, pleasing
09 agreeable, approve of, desirable, reception, red carpet
10 acceptable, gratifying, refreshing, salutation
11 appreciated, hospitality

weld
04 bind, bond, fuse, join, link, seal, seam
05 joint, unite
06 cement, solder
07 connect

welfare
04 good
06 health, income, profit
07 benefit, comfort, payment, pension, sick pay, success
08 interest, security
09 advantage, allowance, happiness, well-being
10 prosperity

well
02 OK
03 far, fit, jet, run
04 ably, fine, flow, good, gush, ooze, pool, rise, rush, seep
05 flood, fount, fully, issue, lucky, right, sound, spout, spurt, surge, swell
06 proper, robust, source, spring, stream, strong
07 adeptly, happily, healthy, luckily, rightly, trickle
08 all right, brim over, expertly, fountain, genially, moreover, pleasing, probably, properly, suitably, thriving, well-head
09 agreeable, agreeably, carefully, correctly, fittingly, fortunate, reservoir, skilfully
10 able-bodied, completely, well-spring
11 approvingly, comfortably, competently, effectively, excellently, flourishing
12 considerably, in good health, proficiently, prosperously, satisfactory, successfully
13 hale and hearty, industriously, substantially
14 satisfactorily

❑**as well**
03 too, also
07 besides
08 moreover
10 in addition
11 furthermore
14 into the bargain

❑**as well as**
09 along with
12 in addition to, over and above, together with
14 to say nothing of

❑**well done**
05 bravo
06 encore, hurrah
15 congratulations

well-advised
04 wise
05 sound
06 shrewd
07 politic, prudent
09 judicious, sagacious

well-balanced
04 even, sane
05 sober, sound
06 stable
08 rational, sensible, together
10 harmonious, reasonable
11 level-headed, symmetrical
12 well-adjusted

well-behaved
04 good
08 obedient
10 good as gold, respectful
11 co-operative, considerate

well-being
04 good
07 comfort, welfare
09 happiness
10 good health

well-bred
05 civil
06 polite, urbane
07 gallant, genteel, refined
08 cultured, ladylike, mannerly
09 courteous
10 cultivated, upper-crust
11 blue-blooded, gentlemanly
12 aristocratic, well-mannered
13 well-brought-up

well-built
05 beefy, burly, stout
06 brawny, strong
08 muscular
09 strapping

well-deserved
04 just, meet
07 condign, merited
09 justified

well-disposed
08 amicable, friendly
09 agreeable, well-aimed
10 favourable
11 sympathetic

well-dressed
04 chic, neat, tidy, trim
05 natty, smart
06 dapper, spruce
07 elegant, stylish

well-founded
05 right, sound, valid
06 proper
08 sensible
09 plausible, warranted
10 reasonable
11 justifiable, sustainable

well-groomed
04 neat, tidy, trim
05 smart
06 dapper, spruce
11 well-dressed
13 well-turned-out

well-known
05 famed, noted, usual
06 common, famous
07 eminent, notable
08 renowned
10 celebrated
11 illustrious

well-nigh
06 all but, almost, nearly
09 just about, virtually
11 practically

well-off
04 rich
05 flush, lucky
07 moneyed, wealthy
08 affluent, thriving, well-to-do
10 prosperous
11 comfortable, rolling in it
12 stinking rich

well-read
08 cultured, educated, literate
12 well-informed
13 knowledgeable

well-spoken
05 clear
06 fluent
08 coherent, eloquent
10 articulate
13 well-expressed

well-thought-of
07 admired, revered
08 esteemed, honoured
09 respected, venerated
10 looked up to
14 highly regarded

well-to-do
04 rich
07 moneyed, wealthy
08 affluent
10 prosperous, well-heeled
11 comfortable, rolling in it

well-versed
06 au fait
10 conversant

well-wisher
03 fan
09 supporter
10 well-willer
11 sympathizer

well-worn
05 corny, stale, tired, trite
06 frayed, ragged, shabby
07 scruffy, worn out
08 overused, timeworn
09 hackneyed
10 threadbare, unoriginal
11 commonplace, stereotyped

welsh
05 cheat
06 diddle
07 defraud, swindle

welt
04 mark, scar, weal
05 ridge, wound
06 streak, stripe
08 cicatrix
09 cicatrice, contusion

welter
03 web
04 mess, roll, toss, wade
05 heave, lurch, pitch
06 jumble, muddle, wallow
08 flounder, mish-mash
09 confusion
10 hotchpotch

wend

□**wend your way**
02 go
04 hike, move, plod, walk
06 travel, trudge, wander
07 meander, proceed
08 progress

wet
03 dip
04 damp, dank, drip, fool, jerk, nerd, rain, soak, soft, wimp
05 douse, flood, humid, imbue, moist, rainy, soggy, spray, steep, swamp, water, weedy
06 clammy, dampen, drench, effete, feeble, liquid, soaked, sodden, splash, spongy
07 drizzle, milksop, moisten, pouring, raining, showery, soaking, sopping, wimpish
08 dampness, drenched, dripping, humidity, irrigate, moisture, pathetic, saturate, sprinkle, timorous, weakling
09 moistness, spineless

10 irresolute, namby-pamby
11 ineffectual, waterlogged

□**wet behind the ears**
03 new, raw
05 green, naïve
06 callow
08 immature, innocent
13 inexperienced

wetness
03 wet
04 damp
05 water
06 liquid
08 humidity, moisture
09 sogginess
12 condensation

whack
03 box, cut, hit, lot, rap
04 bang, bash, beat, belt, blow, cuff, part, slap, sock
05 clout, quota, share, thump
06 strike, stroke, thrash, wallop
07 clobber, portion, rake-off
09 allowance
10 allocation, proportion
14 slice of the cake

whale

➤ *Types of whale. We have omitted the word* **whale** *from names given in the following list but you may need to include this word as part of the solution to some crossword clues.*
03 fin
04 blue, grey
05 black, minke, pigmy, pilot, right, sperm, white
06 baleen, beaked, beluga, finner, killer
07 bowhead, dolphin, finback, grampus, Layard's, narwhal, rorqual, toothed
08 humpback, porpoise
09 Greenland, grindhval, razorback, whalebone
10 bottlenose, humpbacked
11 bottle-nosed
12 river dolphin
15 harbour porpoise
➤ See also **animal**

wharf
04 dock, pier, quay
05 jetty
08 dockyard, quayside
12 landing-stage

what's-its-name
06 doodah
09 thingummy

12 thingummybob, thingummyjig

wheedle
04 coax, draw
05 charm, court
06 cajole, entice, induce
07 beguile, flatter, win over
08 inveigle, persuade, talk into

wheel
04 roll, spin, turn
05 orbit, pivot, swing, whirl
06 circle, gyrate, rotate, swivel
07 go round, revolve
08 gyration, rotation
10 revolution

➤ *Types of wheel. We have omitted the word* **wheel** *from names given in the following list but you may need to include this word as part of the solution to some crossword clues.*
03 big
04 idle, mill, worm
05 wagon
06 castor, charka, escape, Ferris, paddle, prayer
07 potter's
08 cogwheel, flywheel, roulette, sprocket
09 cartwheel, Catherine, gearwheel
10 drive-wheel, water-wheel
12 ratchet-wheel
13 spinning-jenny, spinning-wheel, steering-wheel
14 wheel of fortune

□**at the wheel**
07 driving, turning
08 in charge, steering
09 at the helm, directing, in command, in control
11 responsible

wheeze
03 gag
04 gasp, hiss, idea, joke, pant, plan, ploy, rasp, ruse
05 cough, prank, stunt, trick
06 scheme
08 anecdote, chestnut
13 practical joke

whereabouts
08 location, position, vicinity

wherewithal
04 cash
05 funds, means, money
07 capital, readies
09 necessary, resources

whet
04 edge, file, hone, stir

05 grind, rouse
06 arouse, awaken, excite, incite, kindle
07 provoke, quicken, sharpen
09 stimulate, titillate

whiff
04 gust, hint, puff, reek
05 aroma, odour, scent, smell, sniff, stink, trace
06 breath, stench
10 suggestion

while
04 span, time
05 spell
06 period, season
08 interval

◻**while away**
04 pass
05 spend, use up
06 devote, occupy

whim
03 fad
04 idea, urge
05 craze, fancy, freak, quirk
06 humour, notion, vagary
07 caprice, conceit, impulse

whimper
03 cry, sob
04 mewl, moan, weep
05 groan, whine
06 snivel, whinge
07 grizzle, sniffle

whimsical
03 odd
05 droll, funny, queer, weird
06 quaint, quirky
07 curious, playful, unusual
08 fanciful, peculiar
09 eccentric, impulsive
10 capricious

whine
03 cry, sob
04 beef, carp, moan, wail
05 gripe, groan
06 grouch, grouse, whinge
07 grizzle, grumble, whimper
08 complain
09 belly-ache, complaint

whinge
04 beef, carp, moan
05 gripe, groan
06 grouse
07 grumble
08 complain
09 belly-ache, complaint

whip
03 fly, mix, tan
04 beat, belt, cane, crop, dart, dash, flit, flog, goad, jerk,

lash, prod, pull, push, rush, spur, stir, tear, urge, yank
05 birch, clout, drive, flash, rouse, strap, whack, whisk
06 jambok, punish, snatch, switch, thrash, wallop
07 agitate, scourge, sjambok
09 castigate, horsewhip
10 discipline, flagellate
10 riding-crop
13 cat-o'-nine-tails

◻**whip up**
06 arouse, excite, foment, incite, kindle, stir up
07 inflame, provoke, psych up
09 instigate

whippersnapper
06 nipper, rascal
09 scallywag
11 hobbledehoy

whipping
06 caning, hiding
07 beating, lashing, tanning
08 birching, flogging, spanking
09 thrashing, walloping
11 castigation
12 flagellation

whirl
04 daze, reel, roll, spin, turn
05 pivot, round, swirl, twirl, twist, wheel
06 bustle, circle, flurry, gyrate, hubbub, muddle, rotate, strive, swivel, tumult, uproar
07 revolve
08 gyration, rotation
09 agitation, commotion, confusion, giddiness, pirouette, turn round
10 hurly-burly, revolution
12 merry-go-round

◻**give something a whirl**
07 attempt, have a go, venture
09 endeavour, have a bash, have a shot, have a stab
10 have a crack

whirlpool
04 weel
06 vortex
09 maelstrom

whirlwind
05 hasty, quick, rapid, swift
06 speedy, vortex
07 cyclone, tornado
09 impetuous, impulsive, lightning

whisk
03 fly, mix

04 beat, bolt, dart, dash, dive, race, rush, stir, whip, wipe
05 brush, flick, hurry, shoot, speed, sweep, tears
06 beater, hasten, twitch
12 swizzle-stick

whisky
06 Scotch
07 bourbon, whiskey
10 usquebaugh

whisper
04 buzz, hint, hiss, sigh
05 sough, tinge, trace, whiff
06 breath, gossip, mumble, murmur, mutter, rumour
07 breathe, divulge, soupçon
08 innuendo, low voice
09 insinuate, suspicion, susurrate, undertone
10 suggestion
11 insinuation

whistle
04 call, pipe, sing, song
05 cheep, chirp, siren
06 hooter, warble

whit
03 bit, jot
04 atom, dash, hoot, iota, mite
05 crumb, grain, speck, trace
06 little
07 modicum
08 fragment, particle

white
03 wan
04 grey, pale, pure
05 ashen, hoary, ivory, light, milky, pasty, snowy, waxen
06 creamy, pallid, silver
09 stainless, undefiled
10 colourless, immaculate
12 light-skinned

white-collar
08 clerical, salaried
09 executive, non-manual
12 professional

whiten
04 fade, pale
06 blanch, bleach
08 etiolate

whitewash
04 beat, best, drub, hide, lick
05 crush, paste
06 hammer, thrash
07 conceal, cover up, trounce
08 suppress
09 deception, gloss over
10 camouflage
11 concealment, make light of

whittle
03 cut, hew, use
04 pare, trim
05 carve, shape, shave
06 reduce, scrape
07 consume, eat away
08 diminish, wear away
09 undermine

whole
03 all, fit, lot
04 full, mint, unit, well
05 piece, sound, total, uncut
06 entire, entity, intact, unhurt
07 healthy, perfect
08 complete, ensemble, entirety, totality
09 aggregate
10 everything, in one piece

❑ on the whole
06 mostly
07 as a rule
09 generally, in general, in the main
10 by and large
13 predominantly
14 for the most part

wholehearted
04 real, true, warm
07 devoted, earnest, genuine, sincere, zealous
08 complete, emphatic
09 committed, heartfelt
10 unreserved, unstinting
11 unqualified

wholesale
04 mass
05 broad, total
06 en bloc
07 massive, totally
08 outright, sweeping
09 extensive, massively
11 wide-ranging
12 all-inclusive
13 comprehensive
14 indiscriminate

wholesome
04 good, pure
05 clean, moral
06 decent, proper
07 bracing, ethical, healthy
08 edifying, salutary, virtuous
09 healthful, improving, righteous, uplifting
10 beneficial, honourable, nourishing, salubrious
11 respectable
12 invigorating

wholly
03 all
05 fully

06 purely
07 totally, utterly
08 entirely
09 perfectly
10 completely, thoroughly
11 exclusively
14 in every respect

whoop
04 hoop, hoot, roar, yell
05 cheer, shout
06 holler, hurrah, scream, shriek

whopper
03 lie
09 falsehood, tall story
11 fabrication

whopping
04 huge, vast
05 giant, great, large
07 immense, massive
08 enormous, gigantic
10 monumental, tremendous

whore
04 tart
06 harlot, hooker
07 hustler, trollop
08 call girl, strumpet
09 courtesan
10 prostitute
11 fallen woman, fille de joie
12 scarlet woman, street-walker

whorehouse
07 brothel
08 bordello, cat-house
10 bawdy-house

whorl
04 coil, turn
05 helix, twist
06 spiral, vortex
09 corkscrew
11 convolution

wicked
03 bad
04 cool, evil, foul, vile
05 awful, nasty
06 fierce, impish, severe, sinful
07 corrupt, debased, harmful, heinous, immoral, intense, ungodly, vicious
08 depraved, devilish, dreadful, rascally, shameful, terrible
09 admirable, atrocious, dissolute, egregious, excellent, nefarious, offensive, worthless
10 abominable, iniquitous, scandalous, villainous
11 troublesome, unrighteous
12 black-hearted, unprincipled

wickedness
03 sin
04 evil
08 atrocity, iniquity, vileness
09 amorality, depravity, reprobacy
10 corruption, immorality, sinfulness
11 abomination

wickerwork
06 wattle, wicker
10 basket-work, wattle-work

wide
04 full, vast
05 ample, baggy, broad, fully, great, loose, roomy
06 astray, remote
07 dilated, general, immense
08 expanded, spacious
09 all the way, extensive, off-course, off-target
10 completely, off the mark
11 far-reaching
13 comprehensive

wide-awake
04 keen, wary
05 alert, aware, sharp
06 astute, roused
07 heedful, wakened
08 vigilant, watchful
09 conscious, observant, on the ball
10 on your toes
11 quick-witted
12 on the qui vive

widely
07 broadly
11 extensively

widen
06 dilate, expand,, spread
07 broaden, distend, enlarge

wide-open
06 gaping, spread
07 exposed
10 vulnerable
11 defenceless, unprotected
12 outstretched

wide-ranging
05 broad
08 sweeping, thorough
09 extensive, important
10 widespread
11 far-reaching, significant
13 comprehensive

widespread
04 rife
05 broad
06 common
07 general

width

08 far-flung, sweeping
09 extensive, pervasive, prevalent, universal
11 far-reaching

width

04 beam, span
05 girth, range, reach, scope
06 extent
07 breadth, compass, measure
08 diameter, wideness
09 amplitude

wield

03 ply, use
04 have, hold, wave
05 exert, shake, swing
06 employ, handle, manage
07 command, control, possess
08 brandish, exercise, flourish
10 manipulate

wife

04 mate
05 bride
06 missus, spouse
07 partner
09 companion, other half
10 better half

wiggle

03 wag
05 shake, twist
06 jiggle, squirm, twitch, waggle, writhe
07 wriggle

wild

03 mad
04 daft, keen, nuts, rash
05 angry, crazy, feral
06 fierce, fuming, raging, savage, stormy, unruly
07 bananas, berserk, enraged, fervent, frantic, furious, lawless, natural, rampant, riotous, untamed, violent, wayward
08 demented, desolate, frenzied, incensed, reckless, unbroken, vehement
09 barbarous, ferocious, primitive, turbulent
10 boisterous, hopping mad, infuriated, passionate
11 extravagant, tempestuous
12 uncultivated, ungovernable, unmanageable
13 impracticable, undisciplined
14 undomesticated

wilderness

05 waste, wilds
06 desert, jungle
09 wasteland

wildlife

05 fauna
07 animals

wilds

07 outback
09 the sticks, wasteland
12 the boondocks
15 the back of beyond

wiles

04 ploy, ruse
05 dodge, fraud, guile, trick
06 deceit, device
07 cunning
08 cheating, trickery
09 chicanery, deception, manoeuvre, stratagem
10 artfulness, craftiness, subterfuge
11 contrivance

wilful

06 dogged, mulish
07 planned, wayward
08 contrary, obdurate, perverse, stubborn
09 obstinate, pig-headed
10 calculated, deliberate, determined, headstrong, inflexible, refractory, self-willed, unyielding
11 intentional, intractable
12 intransigent, premeditated
14 uncompromising

will

03 aim
04 mind, want, wish
05 fancy, leave, order
06 choice, compel, confer, decree, desire, intend, option, ordain, pass on
07 command, purpose, resolve
08 bequeath, decision, pass down, transfer, volition
09 dispose of, intention, willpower
10 discretion, resolution
11 disposition, inclination
13 determination

willing

04 game, glad, keen
05 eager, happy, ready
07 content, pleased
08 amenable, biddable, disposed, inclined, prepared, so-minded
09 agreeable, compliant
10 consenting, favourable
11 co-operative
12 enthusiastic, well-disposed

willingly

06 freely, gladly

07 eagerly, happily, readily
08 by choice
11 voluntarily

willingness

04 will, wish
06 desire, favour
08 volition
09 readiness
11 disposition, inclination

willowy

04 slim
06 lissom, supple
07 slender
08 graceful
09 lithesome, sylph-like

willpower

04 grit, will
07 resolve
10 doggedness, resolution
11 self-command, self-mastery
13 determination
14 self-discipline

willy-nilly

08 perforce
11 necessarily, of necessity

wilt

03 ebb, sag
04 fade, flag, sink, wane
05 droop, faint
06 lessen, weaken, wither
07 dwindle, shrivel

wily

03 fly, sly
04 foxy
06 artful, astute, crafty, shifty, shrewd, tricky
07 cunning
08 guileful, scheming
09 designing, underhand
10 intriguing

wimp

03 wet
04 clot, drip, fool, jerk, nerd
05 clown, softy, wally
07 milksop

win

03 get, net
04 earn, gain
06 attain, obtain, secure
07 achieve, acquire, collect, conquer, mastery, prevail, procure, receive, succeed, success, triumph, victory
08 conquest
10 accomplish, strike gold
12 come out on top, turn up trumps

❑**win over**

04 sway

05 charm
07 attract, convert
08 convince, persuade
09 influence, talk round
10 bring round

wince
04 jerk, jump
05 cower, quail, start
06 cringe, flinch, recoil, shrink

wind
03 air
04 bend, coil, curl, furl, gale,
   gust, loop, puff, reel, roll,
   turn, wrap
05 curve, snake, twine, twist
06 breath, breeze, spiral
07 bluster, current, draught,
   meander, tornado, wreathe
08 encircle
09 hurricane

➤ *Types of wind. We have
omitted the word* **wind** *from
names given in the following list
but you may need to include this
word as part of the solution to
some crossword clues.*
04 berg, bise, bora, east, föhn,
   helm
05 north, trade, zonda
06 El Niño, levant, samiel,
   simoom, zephyr
07 austral, chinook, cyclone,
   etesian, gregale, khamsin,
   meltemi, mistral, monsoon,
   pampero, sirocco
08 Favonian, libeccio, westerly,
   williwaw
09 harmattan, nor'wester,
   southerly
10 prevailing, tramontana,
   willy-willy
11 anticyclone
➤ See also **storm**

◻**in the wind**
06 likely
08 expected, probable
10 on the cards

◻**put the wind up**
05 alarm, daunt, panic, scare
07 agitate, startle, unnerve
08 frighten

◻**wind down**
05 relax
06 ease up, lessen, reduce
07 decline, dwindle, subside
08 calm down, slow down
11 come to an end, quieten
   down
12 bring to an end

◻**wind up**
03 end, kid
04 fool, stop
05 annoy, close, end up, trick
06 finish, settle
08 conclude, finish up
09 liquidate, make fun of
12 bring to an end
13 bring to a close
15 pull someone's leg

windbag
06 gasbag, gossip
07 blether, boaster
08 big-mouth, braggart

winded
06 puffed
09 out of puff, puffed out
10 breathless
11 out of breath

windfall
07 bonanza, godsend, jackpot
13 treasure-trove

winding
06 spiral
07 bending, crooked, curving,
   sinuate, sinuous, turning
08 flexuose, flexuous, sinuated,
   tortuous, twisting
10 convoluted, meandering,
   serpentine
11 anfractuous

window
04 pane
05 light

➤ *Types of window. We have
omitted the word* **window** *from
names given in the following list
but you may need to include this
word as part of the solution to
some crossword clues.*
03 bay, bow
04 rose, sash, shop
05 oriel
06 dormer, French, lancet,
   louvre, ticket
07 compass, lucarne
08 bull's eye, casement,
   fanlight, porthole, skylight
09 decorated, mullioned
10 windowpane, windscreen
11 oeil-de-boeuf
12 double-glazed, quarterlight,
   stained glass
13 double-glazing
14 Catherine wheel

windpipe
06 throat
07 pharynx, trachea, weasand

windy
05 blowy, gusty, nervy, wordy
06 breezy, on edge, prolix,
   scared, turgid, uneasy
07 nervous, squally, verbose
08 blustery, rambling
09 bombastic, garrulous
10 frightened, long-winded
11 tempestuous

wine
➤ *Types of wine:*
03 Dao, dry, sec
04 Asti, brut, Cava, fino, hock,
   port, rosé, Sekt
05 Douro, Fitou, Mâcon,
   Médoc, plonk, Rioja, Soave,
   sweet, Syrah
06 Alsace, Barolo, Beaune,
   claret, grappa, Graves,
   Malaga, Merlot, Muscat,
   sherry, Shiraz
07 Auslese, Chablis, Chianti,
   demi-sec, Madeira,
   Margaux, Marsala,
   moselle, oloroso,
   Orvieto, red wine,
   retsina, sangria, Vouvray
08 Bordeaux, Burgundy,
   Frascati, Grenache, house
   red, Malvasia, Muscadet,
   muscatel, New World,
   Pauillac, Pinotage, Riesling,
   ruby port, Sancerre,
   Sauterne, Sémillon,
   Spätlese, Spumante,
   Vermouth
09 blush wine, Bardolino,
   champagne, dry sherry,
   Frizzante, Hermitage, house
   wine, Lambrusco, Pinot
   Noir, Sauternes, sparkling,
   St-Émilion, table wine,
   tawny port, tonic wine,
   white port, white wine,
   Zinfandel
10 Beaujolais, Chambertin,
   Chardonnay, Constantia,
   house white, Manzanilla,
   Mateus Rosé, mulled wine,
   Pinot Blanc, vinho
   verde
11 alcohol-free, amontillado,
   Chenin Blanc, Niersteiner,
   sweet sherry, vintage port,
   vintage wine
12 Blanc de Noirs, Côtes du
   Rhône, medium sherry,
   Valpolicella
13 Blanc de Blancs, Château
   Lafite, fortified wine,
   Liebfraumilch

14 Lacrima Christi, Sauvignon
   Blanc
15 Gewürtztraminer
➤ See also **drink**

▶ *Wine-bottle sizes include*:
06 flagon, magnum
08 jeroboam, rehoboam
09 balthazar
10 methuselah, salmanazar
14 nebuchadnezzar
➤ See also **bottle**

wine glass
05 flute
06 goblet

wing
04 flit, race, soar, zoom
05 glide, group, hurry, speed
06 annexe, branch, hasten
07 faction, section, segment
09 extension

wink
05 blink, flash, gleam, glint
06 moment, second
07 flicker, flutter, glimmer,
   glitter, instant, nictate,
   sparkle, twinkle
10 glimmering
11 nictitation, split second

❑**wink at**
06 ignore
07 condone, neglect
08 overlook, pass over
09 disregard
15 turn a blind eye to

winkle
04 worm
05 prise
07 draw out, extract

winner
06 victor

winning
08 alluring, charming,
   engaging, fetching
09 beguiling, endearing
10 bewitching, conquering,
   successful, undefeated,
   victorious
11 captivating

winnings
05 booty, gains, prize
06 prizes, spoils
07 jackpot, profits

winnow
03 fan
04 sift, sort
06 divide
08 separate

winsome
05 sweet
06 comely, lovely, pretty
08 charming, fetching
09 beguiling, endearing
10 enchanting
11 captivating

wintry
03 icy, raw
04 cold, cool
05 bleak, harsh, snowy
06 arctic, biting, chilly, frosty,
   frozen, hiemal
07 glacial, hostile
08 freezing, hibernal
10 unfriendly

wipe
03 dry, mop, rub
04 dust, swab
05 brush, clean, clear, erase
06 remove, sponge
08 get rid of, take away

❑**wipe out**
05 erase
06 efface
07 blot out, destroy, expunge
08 demolish, massacre
09 eradicate, extirpate
10 annihilate, obliterate
11 exterminate

wire-pulling
05 clout
08 intrigue, plotting, scheming
09 influence
12 manipulation

wiry
04 lean, wavy
05 rough, tough
06 coarse, strong
08 muscular

wisdom
05 sense
06 reason, sinewy
07 insight
08 learning, prudence, sagacity,
   sapience
09 erudition, foresight,
   judgement, knowledge
11 common sense,
   discernment, penetration
12 intelligence
13 enlightenment,
   understanding
14 circumspection

wise
05 aware, sound
06 clever, shrewd
07 erudite, knowing, politic,
   prudent, sapient
08 rational, sensible

09 judicious, sagacious
10 discerning, far-sighted,
   perceptive, reasonable
11 circumspect, enlightened,
   experienced, well-advised
13 knowledgeable

❑**put wise**
04 tell, warn
06 clue in, fill in, inform, notify,
   tip off, wise up
07 apprise
15 put in the picture

wiseacre
09 smart alec
10 clever dick
11 smartypants

wisecrack
03 gag, pun
04 barb, gibe, jest, joke, quip
09 witticism

wish
03 ask, bid, yen
04 hope, long, lust, need, pine,
   urge, want, whim, will
05 crave, fancy, order, yearn
06 aspire, desire, direct, hanker,
   hunger, liking, prefer, thirst
07 bidding, command, craving,
   longing, request, require
08 fondness, instruct, yearning
09 hankering
10 aspiration, preference
11 inclination, instruction

wishy-washy
04 flat, thin, weak
05 bland, vapid
06 feeble, watery
07 insipid
09 tasteless
11 watered-down

wisp
04 lock
05 piece, shred, twist
06 strand, thread

wispy
04 fine, thin
05 faint, frail, light
06 flimsy
08 delicate, ethereal, gossamer
13 insubstantial

wistful
03 sad
06 dreamy, musing
07 forlorn, longing, pensive
08 dreaming, yearning
10 meditative, melancholy,
   reflective, thoughtful
13 contemplative

wit

03 wag
04 nous
05 comic, joker, sense
06 banter, brains, humour, levity, reason, wisdom
07 insight, marbles
08 badinage, comedian, gumption, humorist, repartee, sagacity, satirist
09 intellect, judgement
10 jocularity
11 common sense
12 intelligence
13 understanding

witch

03 hag, hex
08 magician
09 occultist, sorceress
11 enchantress, necromancer

witchcraft

05 magic, spell
06 voodoo
07 sorcery
08 wizardry
09 occultism, the occult
10 black magic, divination, necromancy
11 the black art

witch doctor

06 shaman
07 angekok
08 magician
11 medicine man
13 medicine woman

witch hunt

08 hounding
09 hue and cry
11 McCarthyism

with it

03 hip
04 cool
06 groovy, modish, trendy
08 up-to-date
13 up-to-the-minute

withdraw

06 recall, recant, recede, recoil, remove, retire, revoke
07 back out, drop out, extract, nullify, rescind, retract, retreat, scratch
08 disclaim, fall back, take away
14 absent yourself

withdrawal

04 exit
06 exodus, recall
07 removal, retreat
09 departure, secession
10 evacuation, extraction, retirement, revocation
11 falling back, recantation, repudiation

withdrawn

03 shy
05 aloof, quiet
06 hidden, remote, silent
07 distant, private
08 detached, isolated, reserved, retiring, secluded, solitary, taciturn
09 introvert, shrinking
10 unsociable
11 introverted, out-of-the-way
15 uncommunicative

wither

03 die, dry
04 fade, wane, wilt
05 decay, droop, dry up, waste
06 die off, shrink, weaken
07 decline, dwindle, shrivel
08 fade away, languish

withering

08 scathing, wounding
10 mortifying
11 humiliating
12 contemptuous

withhold

04 curb, hide
06 deduct, refuse, retain
07 conceal, control, decline, repress, reserve
08 hold back, keep back, restrain, suppress
11 keep in check

withstand

04 bear, defy, face
05 brave, fight, stand
06 endure, oppose, resist, take on, thwart
07 hold off, hold out, last out, survive, weather
08 confront, cope with, tolerate
09 put up with, stand fast, stand firm, stand up to

witless

04 daft, dull
05 crazy, inane, silly
06 stupid
07 foolish, idiotic, moronic
08 gormless, mindless
09 cretinous, imbecilic, senseless
11 empty-headed

witness

03 see
04 mark, note, sign, view
05 prove, watch
06 affirm, attest, depose, look on, notice, verify, viewer
07 bear out, confirm, endorse, observe, support, testify, watcher
08 deponent, looker-on, observer, onlooker, perceive
09 attestant, bystander, spectator, testifier
10 eye-witness
11 bear witness, corroborate, countersign

witticism

03 pun
04 quip
06 bon mot
07 epigram, riposte
08 one-liner, repartee
09 wisecrack
10 pleasantry

witty

05 comic, droll, funny
06 clever, lively
07 amusing, jocular, waggish
08 fanciful, humorous, original
09 whimsical

wizard

03 ace, fab
04 good, star, whiz
05 adept, great, super, witch
06 expert, genius, master, superb
07 hotshot, maestro, warlock
08 conjurer, magician, smashing, sorcerer, terrific, virtuoso
09 brilliant, enchanter, fantastic, occultist
10 marvellous, tremendous
11 necromancer, thaumaturge

wizened

07 dried up, gnarled
08 shrunken, withered, wrinkled
10 shrivelled

wobble

05 quake, shake, waver
06 teeter, totter
07 quaking, stagger, vibrate
09 fluctuate, oscillate, vibration
12 shilly-shally, unsteadiness

wobbly

05 shaky, wonky
07 doddery, rickety
08 unstable, unsteady
09 doddering, quavering, teetering, tottering
10 unbalanced

woe
04 pain
05 gloom, grief, tears, trial
06 burden, misery, sorrow
07 anguish, sadness, trouble
08 calamity, distress, hardship
09 adversity, dejection, heartache, suffering
10 affliction, heartbreak, melancholy, misfortune
11 tribulation

woebegone
03 sad
04 blue
06 gloomy
07 doleful, forlorn, tearful
08 dejected, downcast, mournful, wretched
09 miserable, sorrowful
10 dispirited, lugubrious
11 downhearted
12 disconsolate
14 down in the mouth

woeful
03 bad, sad
04 mean, poor
05 awful, cruel, lousy, sorry
06 feeble, gloomy, paltry, rotten, tragic
07 doleful, unhappy
08 dreadful, grieving, grievous, hopeless, mournful, pathetic, pitiable, shocking, terrible, wretched
09 miserable, sorrowful
10 calamitous, deplorable, disastrous, lamentable
11 disgraceful, distressing
12 catastrophic, disconsolate, heart-rending
13 heartbreaking

wolf
05 Romeo
06 lecher
07 Don Juan, seducer
08 Casanova
09 ladies' man, womanizer
10 lady-killer
11 philanderer

❏ wolf down
04 bolt, cram, gulp
05 gorge, scoff, stuff
06 devour, gobble

woman
04 girl, lady, maid
06 female, maiden

womanhood
05 woman
08 maturity

09 adulthood, womenfolk, womankind, womenkind

womanizer
04 wolf
05 Romeo
06 lecher
07 Don Juan, seducer
08 Casanova
09 ladies' man
10 lady-killer
11 philanderer

womanly
06 female
08 feminine, ladylike, motherly, womanish
10 effeminate

wonder
03 awe
05 doubt, query, sight, think
06 marvel, puzzle
07 miracle, prodigy, reflect
08 be amazed, question
09 amazement, curiosity, nonpareil, spectacle
10 admiration, conjecture, phenomenon, stand in awe
11 ask yourself, fascination
12 astonishment, be astonished, bewilderment

▶ *The seven wonders of the world*:
15 Pyramids of Egypt
16 Colossus of Rhodes
18 Pharos of Alexandria
21 Statue of Zeus at Olympia
23 Hanging Gardens of Babylon
24 Mausoleum of Halicarnassus, Temple of Artemis at Ephesus

wonderful
06 superb
07 amazing, awesome, strange
08 fabulous, smashing, terrific
09 admirable, brilliant, excellent, fantastic, startling
10 astounding, incredible, marvellous, phenomenal, stupendous, tremendous
11 astonishing, sensational
13 extraordinary
14 out of this world

wonky
05 amiss, askew, shaky, wrong
06 wobbly
08 unsteady
09 skew-whiff

wont
03 use, way
04 rule, used

06 custom
07 routine
08 inclined, practice
10 accustomed, habituated

wonted
05 usual
06 normal
08 habitual
09 customary

woo
04 seek
05 chase, court
06 pursue
07 attract, look for
09 cultivate, encourage
10 pay court to

wood
05 copse, grove, trees, woods
06 forest, lumber, planks, timber
07 coppice, spinney
08 woodland
10 plantation

▶ *Types of wood*:
03 ash, elm, oak
04 deal, lime, pine, sasa, teak
05 alder, balsa, beech, cedar, ebony, maple, plane, ramin, utile
06 cherry, linden, obeche, padauk, poplar, sapele, walnut, willow
07 barwood, boxwood, bubinga, camwood, hickory, plywood, redwood, sapwood
08 amaranth, basswood, chestnut, cocobolo, cordwood, firewood, hardwood, kindling, kingwood, mahogany, pinkwood, pulpwood, red lauan, rosewood, silky oak, softwood, sycamore
09 blackwood, brushwood, chipboard, green wood, hardboard, heartwood, matchwood, satinwood, tigerwood, tulipwood, whitewood, zebrawood
10 afrormosia, bitterwood, brazilwood, cottonwood, paper birch, sandalwood, wood veneer
11 black cherry, lignum vitae, purpleheart, tulip poplar, white walnut, yellow birch
12 seasoned wood
13 sweet chestnut

◻out of the wood, out of the woods
10 home and dry, in the clear
11 out of danger
12 safe and sound

wooded
05 woody
06 sylvan
08 forested, timbered

wooden
05 blank, empty, rigid, stiff
06 leaden, stodgy, timber
07 deadpan, stilted
08 lifeless
10 spiritless
12 unresponsive
14 expressionless

woodland
04 wood
05 copse, grove, trees, woods
06 forest
07 boscage, coppice, spinney

woody
05 bosky
06 sylvan, xyloid
08 forested, ligneous
11 tree-covered

wool
04 down, hair, yarn
06 fleece
07 floccus

◻pull the wool over someone's eyes
03 con
04 dupe, fool
06 delude, take in
07 deceive
08 hoodwink
09 bamboozle
12 put one over on
14 pull a fast one on

wool-gathering
11 day-dreaming, distraction, inattention
13 preoccupation

woolly
04 hazy
05 downy, foggy, fuzzy, hairy, vague
06 cloudy, fleecy, fluffy, frizzy, jersey, jumper, shaggy
07 muddled, sweater, unclear
08 cardigan, confused, nebulous, pullover
10 flocculent, ill-defined, indefinite, indistinct

woozy
05 dazed, dizzy, rocky, tipsy
06 wobbly

07 bemused, blurred, fuddled
08 confused, unsteady
09 befuddled, nauseated

word
03 gen, put, say, vow
04 book, chat, dope, info, name, news, oath, talk, term, text, will
05 couch, order, state, write
06 advice, decree, gossip, honour, lyrics, notice, phrase, pledge, remark, report, rumour, script, signal
07 account, comment, explain, express, go-ahead, hearsay, low-down, message, promise, tidings, vocable, warning, whisper
08 bulletin, dispatch, libretto, thumbs-up
09 assurance, dicky-bird, guarantee, statement, utterance
10 expression, green light
11 commandment, declaration, information, undertaking
12 conversation, intelligence
13 communication

◻have words
03 row
05 argue
06 bicker
07 dispute, quarrel
08 disagree, squabble

◻in a word
07 briefly, in brief, in short
09 concisely, to be brief
10 succinctly
11 in a nutshell

◻word for word
07 closely, exactly
08 verbatim
09 literally, precisely
10 accurately

wordiness
08 verbiage
10 logorrhoea
15 verbal diarrhoea

wording
05 style, words
07 diction, wordage
08 language, phrasing, verbiage
10 expression
11 phraseology, terminology
13 choice of words

word-perfect
05 exact
06 spot-on
08 accurate, faithful
13 letter-perfect

wordplay
03 wit
07 punning
08 repartee
10 witticisms

wordy
06 prolix
07 diffuse, verbose
08 rambling
10 discursive, long-winded, loquacious

work
03 art, dig, fix, job, run, use
04 acts, book, deed, duty, farm, form, guts, line, make, mill, move, opus, play, poem, shop, slog, task, till, toil
05 cause, chore, craft, drive, graft, guide, knead, model, mould, parts, piece, plant, shape, shift, skill, slave, trade
06 action, career, charge, create, doings, drudge, effect, effort, fiddle, go well, handle, labour, manage, métier, oeuvre, wangle
07 achieve, actions, arrange, calling, control, execute, factory, fashion, foundry, innards, mission, operate, peg away, perform, process, prosper, pull off, pursuit, succeed, travail, trouble, writing
08 business, contrive, creation, drudgery, engineer, exertion, function, have a job, industry, movement, painting, plug away, vocation
09 cultivate, mechanism
10 accomplish, assignment, be employed, bring about, commission, employment, livelihood, manipulate, occupation, production, profession
11 achievement, be effective, composition, elbow grease, undertaking, workmanship
12 be successful, working parts
13 exert yourself, installations
14 be satisfactory, earn your living, line of business
15 slog your guts out

◻work out
04 plan
05 drill, solve, total, train
06 come to, devise, evolve, go well, invent, pan out

07 add up to, arrange, clear up, come out, develop, keep fit, prosper, resolve, sort out, succeed, turn out
08 amount to, contrive, exercise, organize, practise
09 calculate, construct, figure out, formulate, puzzle out
10 understand
11 be effective, put together

◻ work up
05 rouse
06 arouse, incite, kindle, stir up
07 agitate, build up, inflame
08 generate
09 instigate, stimulate

workable
06 doable, viable
08 feasible, possible
09 practical, realistic
11 practicable

workaday
04 dull
06 common
07 humdrum, mundane, routine
08 everyday, familiar, ordinary
09 labouring, practical
11 commonplace
12 run-of-the-mill

worker
04 hand
07 artisan, workman
08 employee, labourer
09 craftsman, operative, tradesman, workhorse
10 wage-earner
11 craftswoman, proletarian
13 member of staff

workforce
05 staff
06 labour
08 manpower
09 employees, personnel
11 labour force

working
04 guts, mine
05 going, parts, shaft, works
06 action, active, manner, method, quarry, system
07 innards, process, routine, running
08 diggings, employed, movement
09 machinery, mechanism, operating, operative
11 excavations, functioning, operational
12 up and running

workman, workwoman
04 hand
05 navvy
06 worker
08 labourer

workmanlike
05 adept
06 expert
07 careful, skilful, skilled
10 proficient
12 professional, satisfactory

workmanship
03 art
05 craft, skill
06 finish
08 artistry
09 execution, handiwork
10 handicraft
13 craftsmanship

workmate
08 co-worker
09 associate, colleague

workout
05 drill
08 exercise, practice, training
10 gymnastics, isometrics

workshop
04 mill, shop
05 class, plant, works
06 garage, studio
07 atelier, factory, seminar
09 symposium
10 study group
15 discussion group

world
03 age, era, man
04 area, days, life, star
05 earth, epoch, field, globe, group, realm, times
06 cosmos, domain, nature, people, period, planet, sphere, system
07 kingdom, mankind, reality, section, society
08 creation, division, everyone, humanity, universe
09 everybody, existence, human race, humankind, situation, way of life
10 department, experience
12 heavenly body

▶ *World heritage sites include*:
03 Omo, Taï
04 Agra, San'a, Tyre
05 Aksum, Awash, Bosra, Copán, Delos, Galle, Hatra, Ohrid, Petra, Quito, Uluru
06 Abomey, Aleppo, Bassae, Byblos, Cyrene, Darién,

Göreme, Paphos, Potosí, Sangay, Sousse, Thebes, Treves
07 Abu Mena, Avebury, Baalbek, Djemila, Garamba, San Juan, Segovia, Virunga
08 Agra Fort, Alhambra, Altamira, Carthage, Chartres, Hattusas, Mount Tai, Palenque, Pyramids, Sabratha, Salvador, Shark Bay, Sigiriya, Stari Ras, Taj Mahal, Valletta
09 Abu Simbel, Auschwitz, Epidaurus, Gros Morne, Mesa Verde, Nemrut Dag, Parthenon, Serengeti
10 El Escorial, Everglades, Generalife, Hierapolis, Hildesheim, Ironbridge, Monte Albán, Monticello, Persepolis, Pont du Gard, Stonehenge, Versailles
11 Ajanta caves, Ellora caves, Gorée Island, Hagia Sophia, Leptis Magna, Machu Picchu, Madara Rider, Mohenjo-daro, Teotihuacán, Vatican City, Western Wall
12 Hadrian's Wall
13 Fontainebleau, Fontenay Abbey, Great Zimbabwe, Rila Monastery
14 Aldabra Islands, Blenheim Palace, Elephanta caves, Fountains Abbey, Giant's Causeway, Heraion of Samos, Imperial Palace
15 Aachen Cathedral, Mont-Saint-Michel, Speyer Cathedral, Statue of Liberty

◻ out of this world
08 fabulous
09 fantastic
10 incredible, marvellous, phenomenal, remarkable
13 indescribable

worldly
06 carnal, greedy, urbane
07 earthly, knowing, mundane, profane, secular
08 covetous, grasping, material, physical, temporal
09 ambitious, corporeal
10 avaricious, streetwise
11 experienced, terrestrial
12 cosmopolitan
13 materialistic, sophisticated

worldwide
06 global

07 general, mondial
08 catholic
09 universal

worm

Types of worm:
05 fluke, leech
07 eelworm, lugworm, pinworm, ragworm
08 flatworm, hookworm, sea mouse, tapeworm
09 earthworm, roundworm
10 blood fluke, liver fluke, ribbonworm, threadworm
11 annelid worm
➤ See also **animal**

worn

05 all in, drawn, jaded, spent, tatty, tired, weary
06 bushed, done in, frayed, ragged, shabby
07 haggard
08 careworn, dog-tired
09 exhausted, knackered
10 threadbare

❑ worn out

05 all in, tatty, weary
06 bushed, done in, shabby
08 decrepit, dog-tired, tired out
09 exhausted, knackered
10 threadbare
13 on its last legs

worried

05 tense, upset, wired
06 afraid, on edge, uneasy
07 anxious, nervous, uptight
08 agonized, bothered, dismayed, strained, troubled
09 concerned, disturbed, ill at ease, perturbed
10 disquieted, distracted, distraught, distressed, frightened
11 overwrought
12 apprehensive
14 hot and bothered

worrisome

06 uneasy, vexing
07 anxious, fretful, irksome, jittery
08 insecure, worrying
09 agonizing, upsetting
10 bothersome, disturbing, nail-biting, perturbing
11 disquieting, distressing, frightening, troublesome
12 apprehensive

worry

03 bug, nag, tiz, vex
04 bite, care, fear, fret, pest, stew
05 annoy, go for, harry, tease, tizzy, trial, upset
06 attack, bother, burden, hang-up, harass, hassle, misery, pester, plague, savage, strain, stress, unease
07 agitate, agonize, anguish, anxiety, concern, disturb, perturb, problem, tension, torment, trouble
08 disquiet, distress, irritate, nuisance, unsettle, vexation
09 aggravate, agitation, annoyance, misgiving
10 irritation, perplexity
11 disturbance, fearfulness
12 apprehension, perturbation
14 responsibility

worrying

06 trying, uneasy
07 anxious
08 niggling
09 harassing, upsetting
10 disturbing, nail-biting, perturbing, unsettling
11 disquieting, distressing, troublesome

worsen

04 sink, slip
06 weaken
07 decline, go to pot
08 heighten, increase
09 aggravate, intensify
10 degenerate, exacerbate, go downhill
11 deteriorate

worsening

05 decay
07 decline
10 pejoration
12 degeneration, exacerbation
13 deterioration, retrogression

worship

04 laud, love
05 adore, deify, exalt, glory
06 homage, praise, revere
07 adulate, glorify, idolize
08 devotion, idolatry, venerate
09 adoration, adulation, devotions
10 exaltation, veneration
11 deification
13 glorification

Places of worship include:
03 wat
04 fane, kirk, shul
05 abbey
06 bethel, church, mosque, pagoda, shrine, temple
07 chantry, minster
08 gurdwara
09 cathedral, synagogue
10 tabernacle
12 meeting-house
➤ See also **religion**

worst

04 beat, best, drub
05 crush
06 defeat, master, subdue
07 conquer
08 overcome, vanquish
09 overpower, overthrow, subjugate, whitewash
14 get the better of

worth

03 use
04 cost, gain, good, help, rate
05 avail, merit, price, value
06 credit, desert, profit, virtue
07 benefit, deserts, quality, service, utility
08 eminence
09 advantage
10 excellence, importance, usefulness, worthiness
12 significance

worthless

03 low
04 naff, poor, vile
05 cheap
06 futile, paltry, trashy
07 corrupt, trivial, useless
08 nugatory, rubbishy, trifling, unusable
09 pointless, valueless
10 despicable, unavailing
11 ineffectual, meaningless, unimportant
12 contemptible
13 insignificant
14 good-for-nothing

worthwhile

04 good
06 useful, worthy
07 gainful, helpful
08 valuable
10 beneficial, productive, profitable
11 justifiable
12 advantageous, constructive

worthy

03 fit
06 decent, honest
07 notable, upright
08 laudable, luminary, reliable, valuable, virtuous
09 admirable, big cheese, deserving, dignitary, excellent, personage, reputable, righteous

10 creditable, honourable, worthwhile
11 appropriate, commendable, meritorious, respectable

would-be
07 budding, hopeful
08 aspiring, striving

wound
03 cut, hit
04 ache, blow, gash, harm, hurt, pain, scar, stab, tear
05 graze, grief, shock, slash, upset
06 damage, grieve, injure, injury, insult, lesion, offend, pierce, slight, trauma
07 anguish, mortify, scratch, torment
08 distress, lacerate, puncture
10 heartbreak, laceration, traumatize

wraith
05 ghost, shade, spook
06 spirit
07 phantom, spectre
08 revenant
10 apparition

wrangle
03 row
04 spar, tiff
05 clash, fight, scrap, set-to
06 barney, bicker, tussle
07 contend, contest, dispute, fall out, quarrel
08 argument, squabble
09 altercate, argy-bargy
11 altercation, controversy

wrap
04 bind, cape, pack, robe, wind
05 cloak, cover, shawl, stole
06 cocoon, encase, enfold, mantle, muffle, parcel, roll up, shroud, swathe
07 enclose, envelop, immerse, package
08 bundle up, parcel up, surround

❑**wrap up**
03 end
06 pack up, parcel, wind up
07 package
08 complete, conclude, parcel up, round off
09 finish off, terminate
13 bring to a close, shut your mouth

wrapper
04 case
05 cover, paper
06 casing, jacket, sheath, sleeve

08 covering, envelope, Jiffy bag®, wrapping
09 packaging
10 dust jacket

wrapping
04 case, foil
05 paper
06 carton
07 tinfoil, wrapper
08 envelope, Jiffy bag®
09 packaging
10 bubble pack, Cellophane®
11 blister card, blister pack, silver paper

wrath
03 ire
04 fury, rage
05 anger
06 choler, spleen, temper

wrathful
05 angry, irate
06 bitter, ireful, raging
07 enraged, furious
08 furibund, in a paddy, incensed
12 on the warpath

wreak
04 vent
05 cause
06 bestow, create
07 execute, express, inflict, unleash
08 carry out, exercise
10 bring about, perpetrate

wreath
04 band, loop, ring
06 circle
07 chaplet, circlet, garland

wreathe
04 coil, wind, wrap
05 adorn, crown, twine, twist
06 enfold, enwrap, shroud
07 entwine, envelop, festoon
08 encircle, surround
10 intertwine, interweave

wreck
03 mar
04 loss, mess, ruin, sink
05 break, smash, spoil
06 debris, pieces, ravage, rubble
07 destroy, flotsam, remains, shatter, torpedo, undoing
08 breaking, demolish, derelict, disaster, smashing, write off
09 devastate, fragments, ruination, shipwreck
10 demolition, disruption, shattering

11 destruction, devastation
13 play havoc with

wreckage
06 debris, pieces, rubble
07 flotsam
08 detritus

wrench
03 rip, tug
04 ache, blow, jerk, pain, pang, pull, rick, tear, yank
05 force, twist, wrest, wring
06 sorrow, sprain, strain
07 distort, sadness
08 upheaval

wrest
03 win
04 pull, take
05 force, seize, twist, wring
06 strain, wrench
07 extract

wrestle
03 vie
05 fight
06 battle, combat, strive, tussle
07 contend, grapple, scuffle
08 struggle

wretch
03 rat
04 worm
05 devil, rogue, swine
06 rascal
07 outcast, ruffian, villain
08 vagabond
09 miscreant, scoundrel
14 good-for-nothing

wretched
03 bad, low, sad
04 base, mean, poor, vile
05 awful, sorry
06 gloomy, paltry
07 forlorn, hapless, piteous, pitiful, unhappy
08 dejected, downcast, dreadful, hopeless, horrible, inferior, pathetic, pitiable, shameful, shocking, terrible
09 appalling, atrocious, depressed, miserable, worthless
10 deplorable, despicable, distressed, melancholy, outrageous
11 crestfallen, unfortunate
12 contemptible, disconsolate
13 broken-hearted

wriggle
04 edge, jerk, turn, worm
05 crawl, dodge, sidle, slink, snake, twist

wring
06 jiggle, squirm, waggle, wiggle, writhe
08 squiggle
09 extricate, manoeuvre

wring
04 hurt, rack, rend, tear
05 exact, force, screw, twist, wound, wrest
06 coerce, extort, mangle, pierce, wrench
07 extract, squeeze, torture

wrinkle
06 crease, furrow, gather, pucker, rumple, wimple
07 crinkle, crumple, shrivel
09 corrugate
11 corrugation

wrinkled
06 ridged, rugate, rugose
07 creased, crinkly, rumpled
08 crinkled, crumpled, furrowed, puckered, rivelled

writ
06 decree
07 summons
08 subpoena
10 court order

write
03 pen
04 copy, note
05 draft, print
06 create, draw up, record, scrawl
07 compose, dash off, jot down, put down, set down
08 inscribe, note down, register, scribble, take down
10 correspond, transcribe
11 communicate

❑**write off**
05 annul, crash, smash, wreck
06 cancel, delete
07 nullify, smash up
08 cross out, demolish
09 disregard

writer
➤ *Writers include*:
04 bard, hack, poet
05 clerk
06 author, editor, pen-pal, rhymer, scribe
07 copyist, diarist
08 annalist, essayist, lyricist, novelist, reporter, satirist
09 columnist, dramatist, historian, pen-friend, penpusher, scribbler, sonneteer

10 biographer, chronicler, copywriter, journalist, librettist, playwright
11 contributor, ghost writer, storyteller
12 leader-writer, poet laureate, scriptwriter
13 calligraphist, correspondent, court reporter, fiction writer, lexicographer
14 autobiographer
➤ See also **biography**; **diary**; **essay**; **fable**; **history**; **journalist**; **lexicographer**; **novel**; **playwright**; **poet**; **satirist**

writhe
04 coil, jerk, toss
05 twist
06 squirm, thrash, wiggle
07 contort, wriggle
12 twist and turn

writing
04 hand, opus, text, work
05 print, words
06 scrawl, script, volume
08 document, scribble
10 penmanship
11 calligraphy, composition, handwriting, publication

written
07 drawn up, set down
08 recorded
10 documental, documented
11 documentary, transcribed

wrong
03 bad, sin
04 awry, back, evil, harm, hurt
05 amiss, crime, error, false
06 astray, faulty, injure, injury, inside, malign, sinful, unfair, unjust, wicked
07 crooked, illegal, illicit, immoral, in error, misdeed, offence, oppress, reverse, to blame, wrongly
08 contrary, criminal, faultily, ill-treat, improper, inequity, iniquity, inverted, maltreat, mistaken, trespass, unlawful
09 defective, discredit, dishonest, dishonour, erroneous, felonious, grievance, imprecise, incorrect, injustice, unethical, unfitting
10 fallacious, immorality, inaccurate, inapposite, malapropos, out of order, unsuitable, wickedness

11 blameworthy, unjustified
12 infringement, unlawfulness
13 dishonourable, inappropriate, transgression, wide of the mark

❑**go wrong**
04 fail
05 stray
08 collapse, go astray
09 break down
11 come to grief, malfunction
12 come a cropper
13 become unstuck

❑**in the wrong**
06 guilty
07 at fault, in error, to blame
08 mistaken

wrongdoer
05 felon
06 sinner
08 criminal
09 miscreant
10 law-breaker, trespasser
12 transgressor

wrongdoing
03 sin
04 evil
05 crime, error, fault
06 felony
07 misdeed, offence
08 iniquity, mischief
13 transgression

wrongful
04 evil
06 unfair, unjust, wicked
07 illegal, illicit, immoral
08 criminal, improper, unlawful
09 dishonest, unethical
11 unjustified, unwarranted
12 illegitimate
13 reprehensible

wrongly
05 badly
07 in error
10 mistakenly
11 erroneously, incorrectly
12 inaccurately

wrought
04 made
06 beaten, ornate, shaped
09 fashioned
10 ornamented

wry
03 dry
05 askew, droll, witty
06 ironic, uneven, warped
07 crooked, mocking, twisted
08 deformed, sardonic
09 contorted, distorted

xenophobia
06 racism
09 racialism, xenophoby
13 ethnocentrism

xenophobic
06 racist

09 parochial, racialist
13 ethnocentrist

xerox
04 copy
05 print
06 run off

09 duplicate, photocopy,
 Photostat®, reproduce

Xerox®

09 duplicate, facsimile,
 photocopy, Photostat®

yack
03 gab, jaw, yap
04 chat
06 confab, gossip, harp on, hot
 air, jabber, tattle
07 chatter, chinwag, prattle
08 witter on
11 yackety-yack

yank
03 tug
04 haul, jerk, pull
05 heave
06 snatch, wrench

yap
03 gab, jaw
04 bark, yelp
06 babble, jabber, yatter
07 chatter, prattle

yard
05 court
06 garden
09 courtyard
10 quadrangle

yardstick
05 gauge, scale
07 measure

09 benchmark, criterion,
 guideline

yarn
04 tale
05 fable, fibre, story
06 strand, thread
08 anecdote
09 tall story

yawning
04 huge, vast, wide
06 gaping
09 cavernous

yearly
08 annually, per annum
09 every year, once a year
11 perennially

yearn
04 ache, itch, long, pine, want
05 covet, crave, fancy
06 desire, hanker, hunger, thirst

yearning
03 yen
05 fancy
06 desire, hunger, pining, thirst
07 craving, longing
09 hankering

yell
04 bawl, howl, roar, yelp,
 yowl
05 shout, whoop
06 bellow, cry out, holler,
 scream, shriek, squeal
07 screech

yellow
04 buff, gold
05 lemon, tawny
06 canary, flaxen, golden
07 saffron
08 primrose

yelp
03 bay, cry, yap, yip
04 bark, yell, yowl

yen
04 itch, lust
06 desire, hunger
07 craving, longing, passion
08 yearning
09 hankering

yes
03 yep
04 yeah
05 quite, right

yes-man

06 agreed
11 affirmative

yes-man
05 toady
07 crawler
09 sycophant, toad-eater
10 arse-licker, bootlicker

yet
03 but, too
04 also, even
05 still
06 even so
07 already, besides, however
08 hitherto, moreover
10 all the same, for all that, heretofore, in addition
11 just the same, nonetheless
12 nevertheless
15 notwithstanding

yield
03 bow, net, pay
04 bear, cede, crop, earn
05 allow
06 accede, cave in, comply, give in, income, profit, return, supply
07 bring in, concede, consent, furnish, give way, harvest, produce, product, provide, revenue, succumb
08 earnings, generate, proceeds, renounce
09 acquiesce, surrender
10 capitulate, relinquish
15 throw in the towel

yielding
04 easy, soft

06 pliant, spongy, supple
07 elastic, pliable, springy
08 biddable, flexible
09 compliant, tractable
11 acquiescent, unresisting

yoke
04 bond, join, link
05 hitch, unite
06 burden, couple
07 bondage, harness
08 coupling
10 oppression

yokel
04 boor, hick
06 rustic
07 bucolic, peasant
09 hillbilly
10 clodhopper
13 country cousin
14 country bumpkin

young
03 kid, new
04 baby
05 brood, early, green, issue, small
06 babies, family, infant, junior, litter, little, recent
07 growing, progeny, teenage
08 childish, children, immature, juvenile, youthful
09 fledgling, offspring
10 adolescent, little ones

youngster
03 boy, kid, lad
04 girl, lass
05 child, youth
06 shaver

07 toddler
08 teenager
10 adolescent

youth
03 boy, kid, lad
05 teens
07 boyhood
08 girlhood, juvenile, teenager
09 childhood
10 adolescent, immaturity
11 adolescence
12 inexperience

youthful
05 fresh, young
06 active, boyish, lively
07 girlish
08 childish, immature, juvenile
09 sprightly
13 inexperienced

youthfulness
08 vivacity
09 freshness
10 juvenility, liveliness
13 sprightliness, vivaciousness

yowl
03 bay, cry
04 howl, wail, yell, yelp
09 caterwaul

yucky
05 dirty, messy, mucky
06 filthy, grotty, sickly
08 horrible
09 revolting
10 disgusting
11 sentimental

Zz

zany
05 crazy, kooky, loony, wacky
07 amusing, comical
09 eccentric
10 ridiculous

zap
03 hit

05 shoot
07 destroy, wipe out

zeal
04 fire, zest
05 gusto, verve
06 ardour, energy, spirit, vigour
07 fervour, passion

09 eagerness, intensity, vehemence
10 dedication, fanaticism

zealot
05 bigot
07 fanatic, radical
08 militant, partisan
09 extremist

zealous
05 eager, fiery
06 ardent, fervid
07 devoted, fervent, intense
09 dedicated, fanatical
10 passionate
11 impassioned

zenith
03 top
04 acme, apex, peak
06 apogee, height, summit
08 meridian, pinnacle
09 high point

zero
03 nil
04 duck, love
05 zilch
06 naught, nought
07 nothing

zero in on
05 fix on
07 focus on, level at, train on
08 home in on, pinpoint
13 concentrate on

zest
04 tang, zeal, zing
05 gusto, spice, taste
06 relish, savour, vigour
07 flavour
08 appetite, keenness, piquancy
09 eagerness, enjoyment
10 exuberance, liveliness
11 joie de vivre

zigzag
05 curve, snake
07 crooked, sinuous, winding
10 meandering, serpentine

zing
02 go
03 zip
04 brio, dash, life, zest, élan
05 oomph
06 energy, spirit, vigour
07 pizzazz, sparkle
08 vitality
09 animation
10 liveliness
11 joie de vivre

zip
02 go
03 fly, pep
04 dash, life, race, rush, tear, whiz, zest, zing, zoom, élan
05 drive, gusto, oomph, scoot, shoot, speed, verve
06 energy, spirit, vigour
07 pizzazz, sparkle
08 vitality
10 get-up-and-go, liveliness

zodiac
► *Signs of the Zodiac*:
03 Leo, Ram
04 Bull, Crab, Fish, Goat, Lion
05 Aries, Libra, Twins, Virgo
06 Archer, Cancer, Gemini, Pisces, Scales, Taurus, Virgin
07 Scorpio
08 Aquarius, Scorpion
09 Capricorn
11 Sagittarius, Water-bearer
12 Water-carrier

zone
04 area, belt
06 region, sector, sphere
07 section, stratum

08 district, province
09 territory

zoo
06 aviary
08 aquarium
09 menagerie
10 animal park, safari park

zoologist
► *Names of zoologists*:
04 **Beer** (Sir Gavin Rylands de), **Mayr** (Ernst Walter)
05 **Fabre** (Jean Henri), **Hubel** (David Hunter), **Kühne** (Wilhelm)
06 **Frisch** (Karl von), **Lorenz** (Konrad Zacharias), **Morris** (Desmond John), **Müller** (Johannes Peter), **Pavlov** (Ivan)
07 **Agassiz** (Louis), **Audubon** (John James), **Durrell** (Gerald), **Galvani** (Luigi), **Hodgkin** (Sir Alan Lloyd), **Mantell** (Gideon Algernon), **Medawar** (Sir Peter Brian)
09 **Aristotle**, **Tinbergen** (Nikolaas)
11 **Sherrington** (Sir Charles Scott)
► See also **scientist**

zoom
03 fly, zap, zip
04 buzz, dash, race, tear, whiz
05 flash, shoot, speed, vroom
06 hurtle, streak